THE HERITAGE OF WORLD CIVILIZATIONS

COMBINED EDITION

FIFTH EDITION

Albert M. Craig
Harvard University

William A. Graham
Harvard University

Donald Kagan
Yale University

Steven Ozment
Harvard University

Frank M. Turner
Yale University

Prentice Hall, Upper Saddle River, NJ 07458

Library of Congress Cataloging–in–Publication Data

The heritage of world civilizations/ Albert M. Craig…[et al.].—
    Combined 5th ed.
        p.   cm.
    Includes bibliographical references and index.
    ISBN 0-13-012459-1
    1. Civilization—History. I. Craig. Albert M.
    CB69.H45 2000   98-50129
    909—dc21   CIP

Editorial Director: *Charlyce Jones Owen*
Executive Editor: *Todd R. Armstrong*
Editor-in-Chief, Development: *Susanna Lesan*
Development Editor: *Roberta Meyer*
AVP, Director of Production and Manufacturing:
  Barbara Kittle
Project Manager: *Harriet Tellem*
Manufacturing Manager: *Nick Sklitsis*
Prepress and Manufacturing Buyer: *Lynn Pearlman*
Marketing Manager: *Sheryl Adams*
Creative Design Director: *Leslie Osher*
Art Director, Interior, and Cover Designer:
  Ximena P. Tamvakopoulos

Cover Art: The great mosque at Jenne, *Wolfgang*
  Kaehler/Wolfgang Kaehler Photography
Photo Research: *Barbara Salz*
Supervisor of Production Services: *John Jordan*
Electronic Page Layout: *Rosemary Ross*
Cartographers: *GEOSYSTEMS, Mirella*
  Signoretto
Line Art Coordinator: *Guy Ruggiero*
Copy Editor: *Sylvia Moore*
Editorial Assistant: *Holly Jo Brown*
Photo Permission Manager: *Kay Dellosa*
Photo Permission Specialist: *Michelina Viscusi*

This book was set in 10/12.5 Caslon 540 by the HSS in-house formatting and production services group and was printed and bound by RR Donnelley. The cover was printed by Phoenix Color Corp.

Printed in the United States of America
10 9 8 7 6 5 4 3 2 1

ISBN 0-13-012459-1

Pearson Education (UK) Limited, London
Prentice-Hall of Australia Pty. Limited, Sydney
Prentice-Hall Canada Inc., Toronto
Prentice-Hall Hispanoamericana, S.A., Mexico
Prentice-Hall of India Private Limited, New Delhi
Prentice-Hall of Japan, Inc. Tokyo
Pearson Education Pte. Ltd., Singapore
Editora Prentice-Hall do Brasil, Ltda., Rio de Janeiro

BRIEF CONTENTS

PART I — THE COMING OF CIVILIZATION   1

1   Birth of Civilization   2
    Technology and Civilizations: The Rise of Monumental Architecture   32
2   The Four Great Revolutions in Thought and Religion   36
    Religions of the World: Judaism   66

PART II — EMPIRES AND CULTURES OF THE ANCIENT WORLD   68

3   Greek and Hellenistic Civilization   72
4   Iran, India, and Inner Asia to 200 C.E.   112
    Religions of the World: Hinduism   132
5   Republican and Imperial Rome   134
6   Africa: Early History to 1000 C.E.   172
7   China's First Empire (221 B.C.E.–220 C.E.)   198
    Technology and Civilizations: Technology and Warfare in the Ancient World   216

PART III — CONSOLIDATION AND INTERACTION OF WORLD CIVILIZATIONS   220

8   Imperial China (589–1368)   224
9   Japan: Early History to 1467   250
     Religions of the World: Buddhism   276
10   Iran and India Before Islam   278
11   The Formation of Islamic Civilization (622–945)   294
12   The Early Middle Ages in the West to 1000: The Birth of Europe   314
13   The High Middle Ages (1000–1300)   338
     Technology and Civilizations: The Invention of Printing in China and Europe   370
14   The Islamic Heartlands and India (ca. 1000–1500)   374
15   Ancient Civilizations of the Americas   396

PART IV — THE WORLD IN TRANSITION   420

16   The Late Middle Ages and the Renaissance in the West (1300–1527)   424
17   The Age of Reformation and Religious Wars   448
     Technology and Civilizations: Navigating the Oceans: Antiquity to the Renaissance   488
     Religions of the World: Christianity   492
18   Africa (ca. 1000–1800)   494
19   Conquest and Exploitation: The Development of the Transatlantic Economy   518

20 East Asia in the Late Traditional Era 544

21 European State-Building and Worldwide Conflict 584

22 European Society Under the Old Regime 612

23 The Last Great Islamic Empires (1500–1800) 636

PART V — ENLIGHTENMENT AND REVOLUTION IN THE WEST 658

24 The Age of European Enlightenment 662
    Technology and Civilizations: The Shifting Balance of East and West 684

25 Revolutions in the Transatlantic World 688

26 Europe and North America 1815–1850: Political Reform, Economic Advance, and Social Unrest 718

PART VI — INTO THE MODERN WORLD 744

27 Political Consolidation in Europe and North America 748
    Technology and Civilizations: Technology and Imperialism 772

28 The Building of Northern Transatlantic Supremacy: Society and Politics to World War I 776

29 The Birth of Contemporary Western Thought 806

30 Latin America: From Independence to the 1940s 828

31 India, the Islamic Heartlands, and Africa: The Encounter with the Modern West (1800–1945) 852
    Religions of the World: Islam 878

32 Modern East Asia 880

PART VII — GLOBAL CONFLICT AND CHANGE 916

33 Imperialism and World War I 920

34 Depression, European Dictators, and the American New Deal 946

35 World War II 970

36 The West Since World War II 998

37 East Asia in the Late Twentieth Century 1032

38 The Emerging Nations of Africa, Asia, and Latin America Since 1945 1058

    Index I-1

CONTENTS

Preface   xxiii

PART I — THE COMING OF CIVILIZATION   1

1 Birth of Civilization   2

Early Human Beings and Their Culture   3
The Paleolithic Age   3
The Neolithic Age   4
The Emergence of Civilization   4
Early Civilizations in the Near East   4
Mesopotamian Civilization   5
Egyptian Civilization   10
Ancient Near Eastern Empires   13
The Hittites   13
The Assyrians   13
Early Indian Civilization   15
The Indus Civilization   16
The Vedic Aryan Civilization   18
Early Chinese Civilization   21
Neolithic Origins in the Yellow River Valley   21
Early Bronze Age: The Shang   22
Later Bronze Age: The Western Chou   24
Iron Age: The Eastern Chou   24
The Rise of Civilization in the Americas   27
Review Questions   30
Suggested Readings   30

*Technology and Civilizations: The Rise
of Monumental Architecture*   32

2 The Four Great Revolutions in Thought and Religion   36

Comparing the Four Great Revolutions   37
Philosophy in China   38
Confucianism   39
Taoism   42
Legalism   43
Religion in India   45
"Hindu" and "Indian"   45
Historical Background   45
The Upanishadic Worldview   46
Mahavira and the Jain Tradition   48
The Buddha's "Middle Path"   49
The Religion of the Israelites   51
From Hebrew Nomads to the Israelite Nation   52
The Monotheistic Revolution   53
Greek Philosophy   56
Reason and the Scientific Spirit   57
Political and Moral Philosophy   59
Review Questions   64
Suggested Readings   65

Religions of the World: Judaism   66

PART II — EMPIRES AND CULTURES OF THE ANCIENT WORLD   68

3 Greek and Hellenistic Civilization   72

Bronze Age on Crete and on the Mainland
to ca. 1150 B.C.E.   73
The Minoans   73
The Mycenaeans   75
Greek "Middle Age" to ca. 750 B.C.E.   76
Age of Homer   76
The Polis   77
Development of the Polis   78
The Hoplite Phalanx   78
Expansion of the Greek World   78
Greek Colonies   78
The Tyrants (ca. 700–500 B.C.E.)   80
Life in Archaic Greece   81
Society   81

Religion	83
Poetry	83
Major City-States	84
Sparta	84
Athens	86
The Persian Wars	88
Ionian Rebellion	88
The War in Greece	89
Classical Greece	90
The Delian League	90
The First Peloponnesian War	90
The Athenian Empire	92
Athenian Democracy	92
Women of Athens	94
The Great Peloponnesian War	96
Struggle for Greek Leadership	96
Culture of Classical Greece	98
Fifth Century B.C.E.	98
Fourth Century B.C.E.	99
Emergence of the Hellenistic World	100
Macedonian Conquest	100
Alexander the Great and His Successors	101
Hellenistic Culture	104
Philosophy	104
Literature	106
Architecture and Sculpture	106
Mathematics and Science	107
In World Perspective: The Achievement of Greek and Hellenistic Civilization	107
Review Questions	109
Suggested Readings	110

4 Iran, India, and Inner Asia to 200 C.E.   112

IRAN	113
Ancient Background	114
The Elamites	114
The Iranians	114
Ancient Iranian Religion	114
Zoroaster and the Zoroastrian Tradition	115
The First Iranian Empire (550–330 B.C.E.)	116
The Achaemenids	116
The Achaemenid State	117
The Achaemenid Economy	119
INDIA	120
The First Indian Empire (321–185 B.C.E.)	120
Political Background	120

The Mauryans	120
Consolidation of Indian Civilization (ca. 200 B.C.E.–300 C.E.)	124
The Economic Base	124
High Culture	124
Religion and Society	124
GREEK AND ASIAN DYNASTIES	126
Seleucids	126
Indo-Greeks	127
Steppe Peoples	127
Parthians	127
Sakas and Kushans	128
In World Perspective: Iran, India, and Inner Asia to the Third Century C.E.	129
Review Questions	130
Suggested Readings	130
Religions of the World: Hinduism	132

5 Republican and Imperial Rome   134

Prehistoric Italy	135
The Etruscans	135
Royal Rome	136
Government	136
Family	136
Clientage	137
Patricians and Plebeians	137
The Republic	137
Constitution	137
Conquest of Italy	139
Rome and Carthage	139
The Republic's Conquest of the Hellenistic World	141
Civilization in the Early Roman Republic: Greek Influence	143
Religion	143
Education	143
Roman Imperialism	145
Aftermath of Conquest	145
The Gracchi	146
Marius and Sulla	148
War Against the Italian Allies (90–88 B.C.E.)	148
Sulla's Dictatorship	148
Fall of the Republic	148
Pompey, Crassus, and Caesar	148
First Triumvirate	149
Dictatorship of Julius Caesar	149
Second Triumvirate and the Emergence of Octavian	149

The Augustan Principate 149
Administration 150
The Army and Defense 150
Religion and Morality 151
Civilization of the Ciceronian and Augustan Ages 151
The Late Republic 151
Age of Augustus 152
Peace and Prosperity: Imperial Rome
(14–180 C.E.) 152
Administration of the Empire 153
Culture of the Early Empire 155
Life in Imperial Rome: The Apartment House 157
Rise of Christianity 157
Jesus of Nazareth 158
Paul of Tarsus 158
Organization 159
Persecution of Christians 159
Emergence of Catholicism 160
Rome as a Center of the Early Church 160
The Crisis of the Third Century 161
Barbarian Invasions 161
Economic Difficulties 161
The Social Order 161
Civil Disorder 162
The Late Empire 162
*The Fourth Century and Imperial
Reorganization* 162
Triumph of Christianity 164
Arts and Letters in the Late Empire 167
Preservation of Classical Culture 167
Christian Writers 167
The Problem of the Decline and Fall
of the Empire in the West 168
In World Perspective: Republican
and Imperial Rome 168
Review Questions 169
Suggested Readings 169

6 Africa: Early History
to 1000 C.E. 172

Problems of Interpretation and Sources 173
The Question of "Civilization" 173
The Source Problem 173
Physical Description of the Continent 174
African Peoples 176
Africa and Early Human Culture 176
Diffusion of Languages and Peoples 176

Racial Distinctions 177
The Sahara and the Sudan to the Beginning
of the Christian Era 178
Early Saharan Cultures 178
Neolithic Sudanic Cultures 179
The Early Iron Age and the Nok Culture 180
Nilotic Africa and the Ethiopian Highlands 182
The Kingdom of Kush 182
The Napatan Empire 182
The Meroitic Empire 183
The Aksumite Empire 187
Isolation of Christian Ethiopia 188
The Western and Central Sudan 189
Agriculture, Trade, and the Rise of Urban Centers 189
*Formation of Sudanic Kingdoms in the First
Millennium* 191
Central, Southern, and East Africa 192
The Khoisan Peoples 192
Bantu Migrations and Diffusion 193
East Africa 193
In World Perspective: Africa to ca. 1000 C.E. 195
Review Questions 196
Suggested Readings 196

7 China's First Empire
(221 B.C.E.–220 C.E.) 198

Ch'in Unification of China 199
Former Han Dynasty (206 B.C.E.–8 C.E.) 201
The Dynastic Cycle 201
Early Years of the Former Han Dynasty 202
Han Wu Ti 202
Government During the Former Han 203
Decline and Usurpation 205
Later Han (25–220 C.E.) and Its Aftermath 206
First Century 206
Decline During the Second Century 206
Aftermath of Empire 207
Han Thought and Religion 208
Han Confucianism 209
History 209
Neo-Taoism 211
Buddhism 212
In World Perspective: China's First Empire 213
Review Questions 214
Suggested Readings 214

*Technology and Civilizations: Technology
and Warfare in the Ancient World* 216

8 Imperial China (589–1368)   224

Reestablishment of Empire: Sui (589–618) and
T'ang (618–907) Dynasties   225
The Sui Dynasty   225
The T'ang Dynasty   226
Transition to Late Imperial China: The Sung
Dynasty (960–1279)   234
*Agricultural Revolution of the Sung: From Serfs
   to Free Farmers*   235
Commercial Revolution of the Sung   236
Government: From Aristocracy to Autocracy   237
Sung Culture   238
China in the Mongol World Empire:
The Yuan Dynasty (1279–1368)   242
Rise of the Mongol Empire   242
Mongol Rule in China   243
Foreign Contacts and Chinese Culture   244
Last Years of the Yuan   246
In World Perspective: Imperial China   247
Review Questions   248
Suggested Readings   249

9 Japan: Early History to 1467   250

Japanese Origins   251
The Yayoi Revolution   251
Tomb Culture and the Yamato State   252
The Yamato Court and Korea   253
Religion in Early Japan   253
Nara and Heian Japan   254
Seventh Century   254
Nara and Early Heian Court Government   255
Land and Taxes   256
Rise of the Samurai   257
Late Heian Court Government   258
Aristocratic Culture and Buddhism in Nara
and Heian Japan   259
Chinese Tradition in Japan   260
Birth of Japanese Literature   260
Nara and Heian Buddhism   262
Japan's Early Feudal Age   264
Rise of Minamoto Yoritomo   264
The Question of Feudalism   266
Kamakura Rule After Yoritomo   267
Women in Warrior Society   268
The Ashikaga Era   268

Agriculture, Commerce, and Medieval Guilds   269
Buddhism and Medieval Culture   269
Japanese Pietism: Pure Land and Nichiren Buddhism   270
Zen Buddhism   272
Nō Plays   273
In World Perspective: Early Japanese History   274
Review Questions   275
Suggested Readings   275
Religions of the World: Buddhism   276

10 Iran and India Before Islam   278

IRAN   279
The Parthians   279
The Sasanid Empire (224–651 C.E.)   280
Society and Economy   281
Religion   281
Later Sasanid Developments   283
INDIA   283
Golden Age of the Guptas   283
Gupta Rule   283
Gupta Culture   284
The Development of "Classical" Traditions
in Indian Civilization (ca. 300–1000 C.E.)   286
Society   286
Religion   287
In World Perspective: Pre-Islamic Iran and India   291
Review Questions   292
Suggested Readings   292

11 The Formation of Islamic Civilization (622–945)   294

Origins and Early Development   295
The Setting   295
Muhammad and the Qur'an   296
Early Islamic Conquests   299
Course of Conquest   300
Factors of Success   301
The New Islamic Order   301
The Caliphate   302
The Ulama   303
The Umma   303
The High Caliphate   305
The Abbasid State   306

Society	306
Decline	307
The "Classical" Islamic Culture	307
Intellectual Traditions	307
Language and Literature	309
Art and Architecture	311
In World Perspective: The Formation of Islamic Civilization	311
Review Questions	312
Suggested Readings	312

12 The Early Middle Ages in the West to 1000: The Birth of Europe   314

The Decline of Roman Authority in the West	315
Germanic Migrations	315
Fall of the Western Roman Empire	316
The Byzantine Empire	317
The Reign of Justinian	317
Eastern Influences	318
The Impact of Islam on East and West	320
The Western Debt to Islam	320
The Developing Roman Church	322
Monastic Culture	322
The Doctrine of Papal Primacy	323
Division of Christendom	323
The Kingdom of the Franks	324
Merovingians and Carolingians: From Clovis to Charlemagne	324
Reign of Charlemagne (768–814)	327
Breakup of the Carolingian Kingdom	332
Feudal Society	333
Origins	334
Vassalage and the Fief	334
Fragmentation and Divided Loyalty	335
In World Perspective: The Early Middle Ages	335
Review Questions	336
Suggested Readings	336

13 The High Middle Ages (1000–1300)   338

Revival of Empire, Church, and Towns	340
Otto I and the Revival of the Empire	340
The Reviving Catholic Church	340
The First Crusades	342
Towns and Townspeople	344
Society	351
The Order of Life	351

Medieval Women	357
Medieval Children	358
Politics	360
England and France: Hastings (1066) to Bouvines (1214)	360
France in the Thirteenth Century: Reign of Louis IX	362
The Hohenstaufen Empire (1152–1272)	363
Medieval Russia	364
In World Perspective: The High Middle Ages	367
Review Questions	368
Suggested Readings	368
Technology and Civilizations: The Invention of Printing in China and Europe	370

14 The Islamic Heartlands and India (ca. 1000–1500)   374

THE ISLAMIC HEARTLANDS	375
Religion and Society	375
Consolidation of Sunni Orthopraxy	375
Sufi Piety and Organization	377
Consolidation of Shi'ite Traditions	378
Regional Developments	379
The Islamic West: Spain and North Africa	379
The Islamic West: Egypt and the Eastern Mediterranean World	380
The Islamic East: Before the Mongol Conquests	383
The Islamic East: The Mongol Age	384
The Spread of Islam Beyond the Heartlands	387
INDIA	387
The Spread of Islam to India	388
Muslim-Hindu Encounter	388
Islamic States and Dynasties	390
Religious and Cultural Accommodation	390
Hindu and Other Indian Traditions	393
In World Perspective: The Islamic Heartlands and India, 1000–1500	393
Review Questions	394
Suggested Readings	394

15 Ancient Civilizations of the Americas   396

Problems in Reconstructing the History of Native American Civilization	397
Mesoamerica	398
The Formative Period and the Emergence of Mesoamerican Civilization	399
The Olmec	399
The Valley of Oaxaca and the Rise of Monte Alban	400

The Classic Period in Mesoamerica 401
Teotihuacán 401
The Maya 403
The Post-Classic Period 406
The Toltecs 406
The Aztecs 406
Andean South America 411
The Preceramic and the Initial Period 412
Chavín de Huantar and the Early Horizon 412
The Early Intermediate Period 413
Nazca 413

Moche 413
The Middle Horizon Through the Late
Intermediate Period 414
Tiwanaku and Huari 414
The Chimu Empire 415
The Inca Empire 415
In World Perspective: Ancient Civilizations
of the Americas 418
Review Questions 418
Suggested Readings 418

PART IV — THE WORLD IN TRANSITION 420

16 The Late Middle Ages and the Renaissance in the West (1300–1527) 424

Political and Social Breakdown 425
*Hundred Years' War and Rise of National
Sentiment* 425
The Black Death 428
Ecclesiastical Breakdown and Revival:
The Late Medieval Church 431
Boniface VIII and Philip the Fair 431
*The Great Schism (1378–1417) and the Conciliar
Movement to 1449* 432
The Renaissance in Italy (1375–1527) 433
*The Italian City-State: Social Conflict
and Despotism* 433
Humanism 435
Renaissance Art 438
Slavery in the Renaissance 440
Italy's Political Decline: The French Invasions
(1494–1527) 441
Treaty of Lodi 441
Charles VIII's March Through Italy 441
Pope Alexander VI and the Borgia Family 441
Pope Julius II 442
Niccolò Machiavelli 443
Revival of Monarchy: Nation Building
in the Fifteenth Century 443
France 444
Spain 444
England 445
Review Questions 445
Suggested Readings 446

17 The Age of Reformation and Religious Wars 448

On the Eve of the Reformation 449
The Discovery of a New World 449
Religion and Society 452
The Northern Renaissance 453
The Reformation 454
Martin Luther and the German Reformation to 1525 454
Zwingli and the Swiss Reformation 458
Anabaptists and Radical Protestants 458
John Calvin and the Genevan Reformation 459
Political Consolidation of the Lutheran Reformation 461
The English Reformation to 1553 463
Catholic Reform and Counter-Reformation 464
The Social Significance of the Reformation
in Western Europe 465
The Revolution in Religious Practices and Institutions 465
The Reformation and the Changing Role of Women 466
Family Life in Early Modern Europe 467
Later Marriages 468
Arranged Marriages 468
Family Size 469
Birth Control 469
Wet Nursing 470
Loving Families? 470
The Wars of Religion 470
French Wars of Religion (1562–1598) 471
*Imperial Spain and the Reign of Philip II
(1556–1598)* 473
England and Spain (1558–1603) 475
The Thirty Years' War (1618–1648) 476
Superstition and Enlightenment:
The Battle Within 478

Witch Hunts and Panic	478
Writers and Philosophers	480
In World Perspective: The Renaissance and Reformation	484
Review Questions	485
Suggested Readings	486
Technology and Civilizations: Navigating the Oceans: Antiquity to the Renaissance	*488*
Religions of the World: Christianity	*492*

18 Africa (ca. 1000–1800) 494

North Africa and Egypt	495
The Spread of Islam South of the Sahara	496
Sahelian Empires of the Western and Central Sudan	497
Ghana	497
Mali	500
Songhai	501
Kanem and Kanem-Bornu	503
The Eastern Sudan	505
The Forestlands—Coastal West and Central Africa	505
West African Forest Kingdoms: The Example of Benin	505
European Arrivals on the Coastlands	506
Central Africa	507
East Africa	509
Swahili Culture and Commerce	509
The Portuguese and the Omanis of Zanzibar	512
Southern Africa	512
Southeastern Africa: "Great Zimbabwe"	512
The Portuguese in Southeastern Africa	514
South Africa: The Cape Colony	514
In World Perspective: Africa, 1000–1800	516
Review Questions	516
Suggested Readings	516

19 Conquest and Exploitation: The Development of the Transatlantic Economy 518

Periods of European Overseas Expansion	519
Mercantilist Theory of Economic Exploitation	520
Establishment of the Spanish Empire in America	522
Conquest of the Aztecs and the Incas	522
The Roman Catholic Church in Spanish America	523
Economies of Exploitation in the Spanish Empire	524
Varieties of Economic Activity	524
The Decline of the Native American Population	526
Commercial Regulation and the Flota System	526
Colonial Brazil and Slavery	528
French and British Colonies in North America	530
Slavery in the Americas	532
Establishment of Slavery	532
The Plantation Economy and Transatlantic Trade	534
Slavery on the Plantations	534
Africa and the Transatlantic Slave Trade	535
The Background of Slavery	536
Slavery and Slaving in Africa	536
The African Side of the Transatlantic Trade	537
The Extent of the Slave Trade	538
Consequences of the Slave Trade for Africa	539
In World Perspective: The Transatlantic Economy	541
Review Questions	542
Suggested Readings	542

20 East Asia in the Late Traditional Era 544

LATE IMPERIAL CHINA	546
Ming (1368–1644) and Ch'ing (1644–1911) Dynasties	546
Land and People	546
China's Third Commercial Revolution	546
Political System	549
Ming-Ch'ing Foreign Relations	553
Ming-Ch'ing Culture	556
JAPAN	558
Warring States Era (1467–1600)	559
War of All Against All	559
Foot Soldier Revolution	561
Foreign Relations and Trade	562
Tokugawa Era (1600–1868)	563
Political Engineering and Economic Growth During the Seventeenth Century	563
Eighteenth and Early Nineteenth Centuries	568
Tokugawa Culture	570
KOREA AND VIETNAM	575
Korea	575
Early History	575
The Choson Era: Late Traditional Korea	576

Vietnam 577
  Southeast Asia 577
  Early Vietnamese History 578
  Late Traditional Vietnam 579
In World Perspective: Late Traditional East Asia 580
Review Questions 581
Suggested Readings 582

21 European State-Building and Worldwide Conflict   **584**

Two Models of European Political Development 585
Constitutional Crisis and Settlement
in Stuart England 586
  James I 586
  Charles I 587
  The Long Parliament and Civil War 587
  Oliver Cromwell and the Puritan Republic 589
  Charles II and the Restoration of the Monarchy 589
  James II and Renewed Fears of a Catholic England 590
  The "Glorious Revolution" 590
  The Age of Walpole 591
Rise of Absolute Monarchy in France:
The World of Louis XIV 593
  Years of Personal Rule 593
  Versailles 593
  King by Divine Right 594
  Louis's Early Wars 595
  Revocation of the Edict of Nantes 595
  Louis's Later Wars 596
Russia Enters the European Political Arena 599
  Years of Turmoil 599
  Peter the Great 599
Central and Eastern Europe 601
  The Habsburg Empire and the Pragmatic Sanction 602
  Prussia and the Hohenzollerns 603
The First Worldwide Wars 605
  The Colonial Arena and the War of Jenkins's Ear 606
  The War of the Austrian Succession (1740–1748) 606
  The Seven Years' War (1756–1763) 606
In World Perspective: Eighteenth-Century
European States and Warfare 609
Review Questions 609
Suggested Readings 610

22 European Society Under the Old Regime   **612**

Major Features of Life in the Old Regime 613
  Maintenance of Tradition 614

  Hierarchy and Privilege 614
Aristocracy 614
  Great Britain 615
  France 615
  Eastern Europe 616
  Russia 616
The Land and Its Tillers 616
  Peasants and Serfs 616
Family Structures and the Family Economy 617
  Households 617
  The Family Economy 619
  Women and the Family Economy 621
  Children and the World of the Family Economy 621
Growth of Agriculture and Population 623
  The Revolution in Agriculture 623
  Population Expansion 626
The Eighteenth-Century Industrial
Revolution 626
  An Event in World History 626
  Industrial Leadership of Great Britain 627
Cities 629
  Patterns of Preindustrial Urbanization 629
  Urban Classes 630
The Jewish Population: Age of the Ghetto 632
In World Perspective: The European
Old Regime 633
Review Questions 634
Suggested Readings 634

23 The Last Great Islamic Empires (1500–1800)   **636**

ISLAMIC EMPIRES 637
The Ottoman Empire 637
  Origins and Development
    of the Ottoman State before 1600 637
  The "Classical" Ottoman Order 639
  After Süleyman: Challenges and Change 642
  The Decline of Ottoman Military
    and Political Power 644
The Safavid Shi'ite Empire 644
  Origins 644
  Shah Abbas I 645
  Safavid Decline 646
  Culture and Learning 647
The Empire of the Indian
Timurids, or "Mughals" 648
  Origins 648
  Akbar's Reign 649
  The Last Great Mughals 649

Sikhs and Marathas	650
Political Decline	650
Religious Developments	650
ISLAMIC ASIA	652
Central Asia: Islamization and Isolation	652
Uzbeks and Chaghatays	652
Consequences of the Shi'ite Rift	653

Power Shifts in the Southern Seas	654
Southern-Seas Trade	654
Control of the Southern Seas	654
The Indies: Acheh	655
In World Perspective: The Last Islamic Empires	655
Review Questions	656
Suggested Readings	657

PART V — ENLIGHTENMENT AND REVOLUTION IN THE WEST   658

24 The Age of European Enlightenment   662

The Scientific Revolution	663
Nicolaus Copernicus	664
Tycho Brahe and Johannes Kepler	665
Galileo Galilei	666
Francis Bacon	666
Isaac Newton	666
John Locke	667
The Enlightenment	668
Voltaire	668
The Encyclopedia	669
The Enlightenment and Religion	669
Deism	670
Toleration	671
The Enlightenment and Society	671
Adam Smith	671
Montesquieu and The Spirit of the Laws	672
Rousseau	673
Women in the Thought and Practice of the Enlightenment	674
Enlightened Absolutism	677
Joseph II of Austria	677
Catherine the Great of Russia	679
The Partition of Poland	681
In World Perspective: The Enlightenment Heritage	682
Review Questions	682
Suggested Readings	682
Technology and Civilizations: The Shifting Balance of East and West	684

25 Revolutions in the Transatlantic World   688

Revolution in the British Colonies in North America	689
Resistance to the Imperial Search for Revenue	689
American Political Ideas	689
Crisis and Independence	691
Revolution in France	692
Revolutions of 1789	692
Reconstruction of France	695
A Second Revolution	697
The Reign of Terror and Its Aftermath	699
The Napoleonic Era	702
The Congress of Vienna and the European Settlement	705
Wars of Independence in Latin America	708
Eighteenth-Century Developments	708
First Movements Toward Independence	709
San Martín in Río de la Plata	710
Simón Bolívar's Liberation of Venezuela	710
Independence in New Spain	710
Brazilian Independence	712
Toward the Abolition of Slavery in the Transatlantic Economy	713
In World Perspective: The Transatlantic Revolutions	715
Review Questions	716
Suggested Readings	716

26 Europe and North America 1815–1850: Political Reform, Economic Advance, and Social Unrest   718

The Challenges of Nationalism and Liberalism	719
The Emergence of Nationalism	719
Early-Nineteenth-Century Political Liberalism	721
Efforts to Liberalize Early-Nineteenth-Century Political Structures	723
Russia: The Decembrist Revolt of 1825 and the Autocracy of Nicholas I	723
Revolution in France (1830)	723
The Great Reform Bill in Britain (1832)	725
Testing the New American Republic	726
Toward Sectional Conflict	726

The Abolitionist Movement 729
Europe Moves Toward an Industrial Society 730
  Proletarianization of Factory Workers and Urban Artisans 731
  Family Structures and the Industrial Revolution 731
  Women in the Early Industrial Revolution 732
  Marxist Critique of the Industrial Order 736
1848: Year of Revolutions 739
  France: The Second Republic and Louis Napoleon 739

The Habsburg Empire: Nationalism Resisted 739
Italy: Republicanism Defeated 740
Germany: Liberalism Frustrated 740
In World Perspective: Early-Nineteenth-Century Europe and the United States 742
Review Questions 742
Suggested Readings 743

PART VI — INTO THE MODERN WORLD 744

27 Political Consolidation in Europe and North America 748

The Crimean War (1854–1856) 749
Italian Unification 750
German Unification 752
  Bismarck 752
  The Franco-Prussian War and the German Empire (1870–1871) 754
France: From Liberal Empire to the Third Republic 754
  Paris Commune 755
  The Third Republic 755
The Habsburg Empire: Formation of the Dual Monarchy 757
  Unrest of Nationalities 757
Russia: Emancipation and Revolutionary Stirrings 759
  Reforms of Alexander II 759
  Revolutionaries 760
Great Britain: Toward Democracy 761
  Gladstone and Disraeli 762
  The Irish Question 762
The United States: Civil War, Reconstruction, and Progressive Politics 764
  Dashed Hopes of Equality 766
  The Native American Experience 767
The Canadian Experience 768
  Road to Self-Government 769
  Keeping a Distinctive Culture 769
In World Perspective: European and North American Political Consolidation 770
Review Questions 770
Suggested Readings 770

Technology and Civilizations: Technology and Imperialism 772

28 The Building of Northern Transatlantic Supremacy: Society and Politics to World War I 776

EUROPE 778
The Middle Classes in Ascendancy 778
Jewish Emancipation 778
  Early Steps to Equal Citizenship 779
  Broadened Opportunities 779
Late-Nineteenth-Century Urban Life 780
  Redesign of Cities 780
  Urban Sanitation 781
  Housing Reform and Middle-Class Values 783
Late-Nineteenth-Century Women's Experience 783
  Social Disabilities Confronted by All Women 784
  New Employment Patterns for Women 785
  Working-Class Women 786
  Poverty and Prostitution 787
  Women of the Middle Class 788
  The Rise of Political Feminism 790
Labor, Socialism, and Politics to World War I 792
  The Working Classes 792
  Marx and the First International 793
  Germany: Social Democrats and Revisionism 793
  France: "Opportunism" Rejected 794
  Great Britain: The Labour Party and Fabianism 795
  Russia: Industrial Development and the Birth of Bolshevism 795
NORTH AMERICA 797
The New Industrial Economy 797
  European Immigration to the United States 798
  Unions: Organization of Labor 799
The Progressives 799
  Social Reform 800

The Progressive Presidency   801
In World Perspective: The Building
of Northern Transatlantic Supremacy   803
Review Questions   804
Suggested Readings   804

29 The Birth of Contemporary Western Thought   806

The Prestige of Science   807
  Darwin and Natural Selection   808
  Auguste Comte and Intellectual Development   809
  Herbert Spencer, Thomas Henry Huxley,
    and Social Darwinism   809
Christianity and the Church Under Siege   810
  The Intellectual Attack   810
  Conflict of Church and State   810
  Areas of Religious Revival   812
  The Missionary Effort   812
  The Roman Catholic Church and the Modern
    World   813
Toward a Twentieth-Century Frame of Mind   814
  Science: The Revolution in Physics   814
  Philosophy: Revolt Against Reason   816
  Birth of Psychoanalysis   817
Transformation in Social and Political Thought   818
  Retreat from Rationalism in Politics   818
  Racial Theory   819
  Antisemitism and the Birth of Zionism   819
  Late-Century Nationalism   820
Women and Modern Thought   821
  Antifeminism in Late-Century Thought   821
  New Directions in Feminism   822
In World Perspective: Intellectual Change   825
Review Questions   825
Suggested Readings   826

30 Latin America: From Independence to the 1940s   828

Independence Without Revolution   831
  Immediate Consequences
    of Latin American Independence   831
  Absence of Social Change   831
  Control of the Land   831
  Submissive Political Philosophies   832
Economy of Dependence   833
  New Exploitation of Resources   833
  Increased Foreign Ownership and Influence   835

Economic Crises and New Directions   835
Search for Political Stability   836
Three National Histories   836
  Argentina   836
  Mexico   840
  Brazil   845
In World Perspective: Latin American History   849
Review Questions   850
Suggested Readings   850

31 India, the Islamic Heartlands, and Africa: The Encounter with the Modern West (1800–1945)   852

THE INDIAN EXPERIENCE   854
British Dominance and Colonial Rule   854
  Building the Empire: The First Half
    of the Nineteenth Century   854
  British-Indian Relations   855
From British Crown Raj to Independence   858
  The Burden of Crown Rule   858
  Indian Resistance   858
  Hindu-Muslim Friction on the Road
    to Independence   860
THE ISLAMIC EXPERIENCE   861
Islamic Responses to Declining
Power and Independence   861
Western Political and Economic
Encroachment   862
The Western Impact   862
Islamic Responses to Foreign Encroachment   863
  Emulation of the West   863
  Integration of Western and Islamic Ideas   865
  Purification and Revival of Islam   866
  Nationalism   866
THE AFRICAN EXPERIENCE   866
New States and Power Centers   866
  Southern Africa   866
  East and Central Africa   867
  West Africa   868
Islamic Reform Movements   868
Increasing European Involvement   868
  Exploration   869
  Christian Missions   869
  The Colonial "Scramble for Africa"   870
African Resistance to Colonialism:
The Rise of Nationalism   871
In World Perspective: India, the Islamic
Heartlands, and Africa, 1800–1945   874
Review Questions   875

Suggested Readings 875
Religions of the World: Islam *878*

32 Modern East Asia 880

MODERN CHINA (1839–1949) 882
Close of Manchu Rule 882
The Opium War 882
Rebellions Against the Manchu 884
Self-Strengthening and Decline (1874–1895) 885
The Borderlands: The Northwest, Vietnam, and Korea 887
From Dynasty to Warlordism (1895–1926) 888
Cultural and Ideological Ferment:
The May Fourth Movement 890
Nationalist China 892
*Kuomintang Unification of China
and the Nanking Decade (1927–1937)* 892
War and Revolution (1937–1949) 894
MODERN JAPAN (1853–1945) 896

Overthrow of the Tokugawa *Bakufu*
(1853–1868) 896
Building the Meiji State (1868–1890) 898
Centralization of Power 898
Political Parties 899
The Constitution 899
Growth of a Modern Economy 900
First Phase: Model Industries 901
Second Phase: 1880s–1890s 901
Third Phase: 1905–1929 902
Fourth Phase: Depression and Recovery 904
The Politics of Imperial Japan (1890–1945) 904
From Confrontation to the Founding
of the Seiyūkai (1890–1900) 904
The Golden Years of Meiji 906
Rise of the Parties to Power 907
Militarism and War (1927–1945) 909
Japanese Militarism and German Nazism 912
In World Perspective: Modern East Asia 913
Review Questions 914
Suggested Readings 914

PART VII — GLOBAL CONFLICT AND CHANGE 916

33 Imperialism and World War I 920

Expansion of European Power
and the "New Imperialism" 921
The New Imperialism 923
*Motives for the New Imperialism:
Economic Interpretation* 923
*Cultural, Religious, and Social
Interpretations* 923
*Strategic and Political Interpretations:
The Scramble for Africa* 923
The Irrational Element 924
Emergence of the German Empire 925
Formation of the Triple Alliance (1873–1890) 925
Bismarck's Leadership (1873–1890) 925
Forging the Triple Entente (1890–1907) 928
World War I 929
The Road to War (1908–1914) 929
*Sarajevo and the Outbreak of War
(June–August 1914)* 931
Strategies and Stalemate (1914–1917) 932
The Russian Revolution 937
End of World War I 938
Military Resolution 938

Settlement at Paris 940
Evaluation of the Peace 943
In World Perspective: Imperialism
and World War I 944
Review Questions 945
Suggested Readings 945

34 Depression, European Dictators, and the American New Deal 946

After Versailles: Demands
for Revision and Enforcement 947
Toward the Great Depression in Europe 947
Financial Tailspin 947
Problems in Agricultural Commodities 948
Depression and Government Policy 949
The Soviet Experiment 949
War Communism 949
The New Economic Policy 950
Stalin Versus Trotsky 950
Decision for Rapid Industrialization 951
The Purges 953
The Fascist Experiment in Italy 954

Rise of Mussolini   954
The Fascists in Power   956
German Democracy and Dictatorship   957
The Weimar Republic   957
Depression and Political Deadlock   959
Hitler Comes to Power   960
Hitler's Consolidation of Power   961
The Police State   962
Women in Nazi Germany   963
The Great Depression and the New Deal
in the United States   964
Economic Collapse   966
New Role for Government   966
In World Perspective: The Economic
and Political Crisis   968
Review Questions   968
Suggested Readings   969

35 World War II   970

Again the Road to War (1933–1939)   971
Hitler's Goals   971
Destruction of Versailles   971
Italy Attacks Ethiopia   972
Remilitarization of the Rhineland   973
The Spanish Civil War   973
Austria and Czechoslovakia   973
Munich   976
The Nazi-Soviet Pact   977
World War II (1939–1945)   977
German Conquest of Europe   977
Battle of Britain   978
German Attack on Russia   978
Hitler's Europe   980
Racism and the Holocaust   980
The Road to Pearl Harbor   980
America's Entry into the War   982
The Tide Turns   983
Defeat of Nazi Germany   986
Fall of Japanese Empire   986
The Cost of War   988
The Domestic Fronts   988
Germany: From Apparent Victory to Defeat   988
France: Defeat, Collaboration, and Resistance   990
Great Britain: Organization for Victory   990
The Soviet Union: "The Great Patriotic War"   991
Preparations for Peace   992
The Atlantic Charter   992

Tehran   992
Yalta   993
Potsdam   994
In World Perspective: World War II   995
Review Questions   996
Suggested Readings   996

36 The West Since World War II   998

The Cold War Era   999
Initial Causes   999
Areas of Early Cold War Conflict   1000
NATO and the Warsaw Pact   1002
Crises of 1956   1003
The Cold War Intensified   1004
Detente and Afterward   1004
European Society in the Second Half
of the Twentieth Century   1006
Toward Western European Unification   1006
A Consumer Society   1007
Students and Popular Music   1007
The Movement of Peoples   1008
*New Patterns in the Work and Expectations
of Women*   1008
American Domestic Scene Since World
War II   1010
Truman and Eisenhower Administrations   1010
Civil Rights   1011
New Social Programs   1011
The Vietnam War and Domestic Turmoil   1011
Watergate Scandal   1012
The Triumph of Political Conservatism   1012
The Soviet Union to 1989   1013
The Khrushchev Years   1013
Brezhnev   1014
Communism and Solidarity in Poland   1015
Gorbachev Attempts to Redirect the Soviet Union   1015
1989: Year of Revolutions in Eastern Europe   1016
Solidarity Reemerges in Poland   1016
Hungary Moves Toward Independence   1016
*The Breach of the Berlin Wall
and German Reunification*   1017
The Velvet Revolution in Czechoslovakia   1017
Violent Revolution in Romania   1018
The Collapse of the Soviet Union   1018
*Renunciation of the Communist Political
Monopoly*   1018
The August 1991 Coup   1018

The Yeltsin Years 1019
The Collapse of Yugoslavia and Civil War 1021
Problems in the Wake of the Collapse
of Communism 1023
In World Perspective: The West Since 1945 1024
Review Questions 1024
Suggested Readings 1025

*Technology and Civilizations: Energy
and the Modern World* 1026

*Technology and Civilizations: The Coming
of the Computer* 1030

37 East Asia in the Late Twentieth Century 1032

Japan 1034
  The Occupation 1035
  Parliamentary Politics 1036
  Economic Growth 1038
  Society and Culture 1040
China 1042
  Soviet Period (1950–1960) 1042
  *The Great Proletarian Cultural
    Revolution (1965–1976)* 1043
  China After Mao 1044
Taiwan 1047
Korea 1049
  As Japanese Colony 1050
  North and South 1050
  Civil War and U.S. Involvement 1050
  Recent Developments 1051
Vietnam 1052
  The Colonial Backdrop 1052
  The Anticolonial War 1053
  The Vietnam War 1053
  War with Cambodia 1054
  Recent Developments 1055
In World Perspective: East Asia 1056
Review Questions 1057
Suggested Readings 1057

38 The Emerging Nations of Africa, Asia, and Latin America Since 1945 1058

The Postcolonial Era 1059
AFRICA, THE MIDDLE EAST, AND ASIA 1061
Postcolonial Africa 1062
  The Transition to Independence 1062
  The Nigerian Case 1063
  The South African Case 1064
  The African Future 1065
The Postcolonial Middle East and Central Asia 1066
  New Nations in the Middle East 1067
  The Arab-Israeli Conflict 1068
  Middle Eastern Oil 1071
  Islamism and Politics 1071
  Iran 1072
  Central Asia 1073
South and Southeast Asia 1074
  Pakistan and Bangladesh 1074
  India 1074
  Indonesia and Malaysia 1076
LATIN AMERICA SINCE 1945 1077
Revolutionary Challenges 1078
  The Cuban Revolution 1079
  Chile 1081
  The Sandinista Revolution in Nicaragua 1081
Pursuit of Stability
Under the Threat of Revolution 1082
  Argentina 1082
  Brazil 1082
  Mexico 1083
Continuity and Change
in Recent Latin American History 1084
In World Perspective: The Emerging Nations:
Opportunities and Frustrations
of Global Democratization: 1085
Review Questions 1087
Suggested Readings 1087

Index I-1

DOCUMENTS

CHAPTER 1

Hammurabi's Code on Women, Marriage,
   and Divorce in Babylonia   9
The "Israel Stele" of the Pharaoh Merenptah   13
Hymn to Indra   19
Human Sacrifice in Early China   26

CHAPTER 2

Confucius Defines the Gentleman   41
Taoism   43
Legalism   44
Discussions of *Brahman* and *Atman*
   from the Upanishads   47
The "Turning of the Wheel of the *Dharma*":
   Basic Teachings of the Buddha   50
God's Purpose with Israel   55
The Atomists' Account of the Origin
   of the World Order   59
The Sophists: From Rational Inquiry to Skepticism   60
Plato on the Role of Women in His Utopian
   Republic   62

CHAPTER 3

Hesiod's Farmer's Almanac   81
The Greek and Persian Ways of War—
   Autocracy versus Freedom under the Law   85
Athenian Democracy: An Unfriendly View   94
Medea Bemoans the Condition of Women   95
Plutarch Cites Archimedes and Hellenistic
   Science   107

CHAPTER 4

A Hymn of Zoroaster About the Two Spirits
   of Good and Evil   115
Inscription of Darius I: Building the Royal Palace
   at Susa   118
The Edicts of Ashoka   123

CHAPTER 5

A Women's Uprising in Republican Rome   142

The Ruin of the Roman Family Farm
   and the Gracchan Reforms   147
Daily Life in a Roman Provincial Town: Graffiti
   from Pompeii   155
The Bar-Kochba Rebellion: The Final Jewish
   Uprising Against Rome   157
Mark Describes the Resurrection of Jesus   160

CHAPTER 6

Kushite Conquest of Memphis   182
Herodotus on Carthaginian Trade and
   on the City of Meroe   185
Sixth-Century Account of Aksumite Trade   187
A Tenth-Century Arab Description of the East
   African Coast   194

CHAPTER 7

Chinese Women Among the Nomads   205
The Chao's Admonitions for Women   207
Ssu-ma Ch'ien on the Wealthy   210
The Peach Blossom Spring   211

CHAPTER 8

A Poem by Li Po   232
"Chaste Women" Shi   236
Su Tung-P'o Imagined on a Wet Day, Wearing
   a Rain Hat and Clogs   241
Marco Polo Describes the City of Hangchow   246

CHAPTER 9

Darkness and the Cave of High Heaven   255
Aristocratic Taste at the Fujiwara Court:
   Sei Shōnagon Records Her Likes
   and Dislikes   262
Hakuin's Enlightenment   272
The Arts and Zen Buddhism   273

CHAPTER 10

A Report of Mani's Words About His Mission   282

A Chinese Traveler's Report on the Gupta
   Realm   285
Devoting Oneself to Krishna   288
The Bodhisattva Ideal   291

CHAPTER 11

Imru l-Qais, the Wandering Poet-Hero   297
The Qur'an, or "Recitation," of God's Word   298
The Wit and Wisdom of al-Jahiz   308

CHAPTER 12

The Character and "Innovations" of Justinian
   and Theodora   318
Clovis Converts to Christianity   325
The Court Scholar Einhard Describes His
   Admired King, Charlemagne   329
The Carolingian Manor   331

CHAPTER 13

Pope Urban II (1088–1099) Preaches the First
   Crusade   343
Phillip II Augustus Orders Jews Out of France   349
The Services of a Serf   356
The English Nobility Imposes Restraints
   on King John   362

CHAPTER 14

Jalaluddin Rumi: Who is the Sufi?   378
A Muslim Biographer's Account of Maimonides   381
Quatrains (Ruba'iyat) from the Pen of Umar
   Khayyam (d. 1123)   384
The Mongol Catastrophe   385
How the Hindus Differ from the Muslims   391

CHAPTER 15

A Maya Myth of Creation   404
A Spaniard Describes the Glory of the Aztec
   Capital   407
Nezahualcoyotl of Texcoco Sings of the Giver
   of Life   411
The Incas Organize Their Empire   417

CHAPTER 16

Pico della Mirandola States the Renaissance
   Image of Man   436
Christine de Pisan Instructs Women on How
   to Handle Their Husbands   437

Machiavelli Discusses the Most Important Trait
   for a Ruler   443

CHAPTER 17

German Peasants Protest Rising Feudal
   Exactions   460
Rules Governing Genevan Moral Behavior   462
A German Mother Advises Her Fifteen-Year-Old
   Son, Who Is away from Home at School for the
   First Time (1578)   469

CHAPTER 18

Ghana and Its People in the Mid-Eleventh
   Century   498
Muslim Reform in Songhai   504
Affonso I of Kongo Writes to the King
   of Portugal   509
Visiting Mogadishu and Kilwa (1331)   511

CHAPTER 19

Buccaneers Prowl the High Seas   521
A Contemporary Describes Forced Indian Labor
   at Potosí   525
Visitors Describe the Portobello Fair   530
A Slave Trader Describes the Atlantic Passage   538

CHAPTER 20

The Thin Horse Market   548
The Seven Transformations of an Examination
   Candidate   551
Ch'ien Lung's Edict to King George III
   of England   557
A Star in Heaven   559
"On Husband-Sharing"   580

CHAPTER 21

Parliament Presents Charles I with the Petition
   of Right   588
Lady Mary Wortley Montague Advises Her
   Husband on Election to Parliament   591
Louis XIV Revokes the Edict of Nantes   596
The Great Elector Welcomes Protestant
   Refugees from France   604

CHAPTER 22

An English Traveler Describes Serfdom
   in Eighteenth-Century Russia   617

Priscilla Wakefield Demands More Occupations
  Be Opened to Women   620
An Edinburgh Physician Describes the Dangers
  of Childbirth   622
Turgot Describes French Landholding   624

CHAPTER 23

The Distinctiveness of Ottoman Identity
  and Culture   641
A Safavid Historian's Praise for Shah Abbas I   646
Some Reforms of Akbar   648
Guru Arjun's Faith   650

CHAPTER 24

Copernicus Ascribes Movement to the Earth   664
Rousseau Argues for Separate Spheres for Men
  and Women   675
Mary Wollstonecraft Criticizes Rousseau's View
  of Women   676
Maria Theresa and Joseph II of Austria Debate
  Toleration   678

CHAPTER 25

The Stamp Act Congress Addresses George III   690
The National Assembly Decrees Civic Equality
  in France   694
French Women Petition to Bear Arms   696
Napoleon Describes Conditions Leading
  to the Consulate   703
Bolívar Denounces Spanish Rule in Latin
  America   711

CHAPTER 26

Mazzini Defines Nationality   721
Daniel A. Payne Denounces American Slavery   730
Women Industrial Workers Explain Their
  Economic Situation   733
The Women of the Seneca Falls Convention
  Issue a Declaration of Female Independence   735
A Young Middle-Class French Woman Writes
  to Her Father About Marriage   736
The Pan-Slavic Congress Calls for the Liberation
  of Slavic Nationalities   741

CHAPTER 27

Walter Bagehot Analyzes the Power
  of Napoleon III   755
Lord Acton Condemns Nationalism   759

The People's Will Issues a Revolutionary
  Manifesto   761
William Gladstone Pleads for Irish Home Rule   764
Lincoln States the Ideals of American Liberty
  at Gettysburg   766

CHAPTER 28

A French Physician Describes a Working-Class
  Slum in Lille Before the Public Health
  Movement   782
The Virtues of a French Middle-Class Lady
  Praised   789
An English Feminist Defends the Cause
  of the Female Franchise   792
A Russian Social Investigator Describes
  the Condition of Children in the Moscow
  Tailoring Trade   796
Lenin Argues for the Necessity of a Secret
  and Elite Party of Professional Revolutionaries   798
Theodore Roosevelt States His Progressive Creed   802

CHAPTER 29

Darwin Defends a Mechanistic View of Nature   808
Leo XIII Considers the Social Question
  in European Politics   813
Herzl Calls for the Establishment of a Jewish
  State   820
Virginia Woolf Urges Women to Write   824

CHAPTER 30

Eva Perón Explains the Sources of Her Popularity   839
Emiliano Zapata Issues the Plan of Ayala   843
A Brazilian Liberal Denounces Slavery   846

CHAPTER 31

Macaulay Writes on Indian Education   856
Gandhi on Passive Resistance and Swarāj   860
A Middle Eastern Modernist Warns About
  Appeasing Religious Fanatics   864
Usman Dan Fodio on Evil and Good Government   869

CHAPTER 32

Commissioner Lin Urges Morality
  on Queen Victoria   883
Liang Ch'i-ch'ao Urges the Chinese
  to Reform (1896)   889
Ch'en Tu-hsiu's "Call to Youth" in 1915   891
On Wives and Concubines   901

A Japanese View on the Inventiveness
   of the West   903
Natsume Sōseki on the Costs of Rapid
   Modernization   905

CHAPTER 33

Carl Peters Demands Colonies for Germany   926
Lenin Establishes His Dictatorship   939

CHAPTER 34

A Communist Woman Demands a New Family
   Life   951
Mussolini Heaps Contempt on Political
   Liberalism   956
The Nazis Pass Their Racial Legislation   964
Hitler Rejects the Emancipation of Women   965

CHAPTER 35

Hitler Describes His Goals   972
Winston Churchill Warns of the Effects
   of the Munich Agreement   975
An Observer Describes the Mass Murder of Jews
   in Ukraine   982

CHAPTER 36

The Church and the Communist Party Clash
   over Education in Hungary   1001
Khrushchev Denounces the Crimes of Stalin:
   The Secret Speech   1014
Gorbachev Proposes the Soviet Communist Party
   Abandon Its Monopoly of Power   1019
Vaclav Havel Ponders the Future of Europe   1031

CHAPTER 37

The Occupation of Japan   1035
Two Views of the "Symbol Emperor"   1041
U.S. Foreign Policy: A Chinese View   1046
The Chinese Economy in Transition   1048

CHAPTER 38

Nelson Mandela's Vision: From His Inaugural
   Address   1066
A Modernist Muslim Poet's Eulogy for His Mother   1067
Jawaharlal Nehru Looks to the Future (1945)   1075
Castro Asserts the Necessary Marxist Character
   of Revolution   1080
Lourdes Arizpe Discusses the Silence of Peasant
   Women   1083

MAPS

1–1 The four great river valley civilizations to ca. 1000 B.C.E. — 5

1–2 The ancient Near East — 6

1–3 Indus and Vedic Aryan cultures — 15

1–4 Bronze Age China during the Shang dynasty, 1766–1050 B.C.E. — 22

1–5 Early Iron Age territorial states in China during the sixth century B.C.E. — 26

1–6 Civilization in Mesoamerica and the Andean region — 29

2–1 Ancient Palestine — 53

3–1 The Aegean area in the Bronze Age — 74

3–2 Phoenician and Greek colonization — 79

3–3 The Peloponnesus — 84

3–4 Attica and vicinity — 87

3–5 Classical Greece — 91

3–6 The Athenian Empire about 450 B.C.E. — 93

3–7 Alexander's campaigns — 102

3–8 The world according to Eratosthenes — 108

4–1 The Achaemenid Persian Empire — 117

4–2 Southwest Asia and India in Mauryan times — 121

5–1 Ancient Italy — 137

5–2 The western Mediterranean area during the rise of Rome — 140

5–3 Roman dominions of the Late Republic — 146

5–4 Provinces of the Roman Empire to 117 C.E. — 154

5–5 Divisions of the Roman Empire under Diocletian — 163

5–6 The Empire's neighbors — 164

5–7 The spread of Christianity — 166

6–1 Africa: Physical features and early sites — 175

6–2 Ancient African empires — 181

6–3 Africa: Early trade routes and early states of the western and central Sudan — 190

7–1 The unification of China by the Ch'in State — 200

7–2 The Han Empire 206 B.C.E.–220 C.E. — 204

7–3 The spread of Buddhism and Chinese states in 500 C.E. — 213

8–1 The T'ang Empire at its peak during the eighth century — 227

8–2 The Northern Sung and Liao Empires (top) and the Southern Sung and Chin Empires (bottom) — 235

8–3 The Mongol Empire in the late thirteenth century — 244

9–1 Yamato Japan and Korea (ca. 500 C.E.) — 254

9–2 Medieval Japan and the Mongol invasions — 265

10–1 International trade routes in Gupta and Sasanid times — 284

11–1 Muslim conquests and domination of the Mediterranean to about 750 C.E. — 300

11–2 The Abbasid Empire, ca. 900 C.E. — 306

12–1 Barbarian migrations into the west in the fourth and fifth centuries — 316

12–2 The Byzantine Empire at the death of Justinian — 319

12–3 The empire of Charlemagne to 814 — 327

12–4 The Treaty of Verdun (843) and the Treaty of Mersen (870) — 333

12–5 Viking, Muslim, and Magyar invasions to the eleventh century — 333

13–1 The early Crusades — 345

13–2 Medieval trade routes and regional products — 347

13–3 Germany and Italy in the Middle Ages — 365

14–1 The Islamic heartlands, 1000–1500 — 376

14–2 Islamic political sovereignty in 1500 — 388

14–3 The Indian subcontinent, 1000–1500 — 389

15–1 Pre-Aztec Mesoamerican sites discussed in this chapter — 399

15–2 The Aztec and Inca Empires on the eve of the Spanish conquest — 409

15–3 Pre-Inca sites discussed in this chapter — 413

16–1 The Hundred Years' War — 427

16–2 Spread of the Black Death — 429

16–3 Renaissance Italy   434

17–1 European voyages of discovery
and the colonial claims of Spain and Portugal
in the fifteenth and sixteenth centuries   450

17–2 The empire of Charles V   457

17–3 The Swiss confederation   459

17–4 The Netherlands during the Reformation   474

17–5 Religious division about 1600   476

17–6 The Holy Roman Empire about 1618   477

18–1 Africa ca. 900–1500   499

18–2 Africa ca. 1500–1800   502

19–1 Viceroyalties in Latin America in 1780   527

20–1 Ming Empire and the voyages of Cheng Ho   554

20–2 The Ch'ing Empire at its peak   555

20–3 Tokugawa Japan and the Korean peninsula   565

20–4 Vietnam and neighboring Southeast Asia   578

21–1 The early wars of Louis XIV   597

21–2 Europe in 1714   598

21–3 The Austrian Habsburg Empire, 1521–1772   602

21–4 Expansion of Brandenburg-Prussia   603

23–1 Sixteenth-century Islamic empires   638

24–1 Expansion of Russia, 1689–1796   680

24–2 Partitions of Poland, 1772, 1793, and 1795   681

25–1 North America in 1763   691

25–2 Napoleonic Europe in late 1812   706

25–3 Europe 1815, after the Congress of Vienna   707

25–4 The Independence Campaigns
of San Martín and Bolívar   710

26–1 Nineteenth-century North America   726

27–1 The unification of Italy   751

27–2 The unification of Germany   753

27–3 Nationalities within the Habsburg empire   758

30–1 Latin America in 1830   830

31–1 Imperial expansion in Africa up to 1880   872

31–2 Partition of Africa, 1880–1914   873

32–1 The Taiping, Nien, and Muslim rebellions   884

32–2 The northern expeditions
of the Kuomintang   894

32–3 Formation of the Japanese empire   906

33–1 Asia 1880–1914   922

33–2 The Balkans, 1912–1913   930

33–3 The Schlieffen Plan of 1905   934

33–4 World War I in Europe   935

33–5 The Western front, 1914–1918   937

33–6 World War I peace settlement in Europe
and the Middle East   942

35–1 The Spanish Civil War, 1936–1939   974

35–2 Partitions of Czechoslovakia and Poland,
1938–1939   976

35–3 Axis Europe 1941   979

35–4 The war in the Pacific   984

35–5 North African campaigns, 1942–1945   985

35–6 Defeat of the Axis in Europe, 1942–1945   987

35–7 Territorial changes after World War II   994

36–1 Major Cold War European alliance
systems   1003

36–2 The Commonwealth of independent
states   1020

36–3 The ethnic composition
in the former Yugoslavia   1022

37–1 Contemporary Asia   1034

37–2 An economist's map of the world   1048

37–3 Korea, 1950–1953   1051

37–4 Vietnam and its Southeast Asian
neighbors   1054

38–1 Decolonization since World War II   1060

38–2 The modern Middle East
and the distribution of major religious
communities   1068

38–3 Contemporary Central and South America   1077

PREFACE

The twenty-first century is upon us, and its arrival demands, as never before, an understanding of human history in a global context. The pressures of the present—of a new century and a new millennium—draw us to seek a more certain understanding of the past.

The idea of globalization was once just that, an idea. It is now a pressing reality in the life of nations, affecting the standard of living, the environment, and war and peace. Globalization is also a daily reality in the lives of ordinary people. Not only are global markets linked as never before, but the internet quickly delivers all manner of information to the readers of this book. People with different cultural heritages, religious beliefs, and economic and political expectations are being drawn into ever closer contact with one another. If that experience is to be one of peace and mutual respect, then understanding the historical experiences that have informed and shaped the world's cultures is essential. Globalization demands of world citizens greater historical knowledge than ever before. *The Heritage of World Civilizations* provides a path to such knowledge.

The Roots of Globalization

Globalization itself has resulted from two major historical developments: the closing of the European era of world history and the rise of technology. From approximately 1500 to the middle of the twentieth century, Europeans gradually came to dominate the world through colonization (most particularly in North and South America), political organization, economic productivity, and military power.

That era ended during the third quarter of the twentieth century after Europe had brought unprecedented destruction on itself during World War II and as the nations of Asia, the Near East, and Africa achieved new positions on the world scene. Their new political independence, their control over strategic natural resources, and the expansion of their economies (particularly those of the nations of the Pacific rim of Asia), and in some cases their access to nuclear weapons have changed the shape of world affairs.

The second historical development that continues to fuel the pace of globalization is technology, associated most importantly with transportation, military weapons, and electronic communication. The advances in transportation over the past two centuries including ships, railways, and airplanes made more parts of the world and its resources accessible to more people in ever shorter spans of time. Military weapons of increasingly destructive power over the past century and a half enabled Europeans to dominate other regions of the globe. Now, the spread of these weapons means that any nation with sophisticated military technology can threaten any other nation, no matter how far away. Most recently, the electronic revolution associated with computer technology in all its forms has sparked an unprecedented speed and complexity in global communications. It is astonishing to recall that personal computers have been generally available for less than twenty years and that rapid communication associated with them has existed for less than a decade.

Why not, then, focus only on new factors in the modern world, such as the impact of technology and the end of the European era? To do that would ignore the very deep roots that these developments have in the past. Modern technology and society were shaped by the values, ingenuity, and expectations of people centuries old. For that reason, *The Heritage of World Civilizations* continues to pay particular attention to the emergence of the major religious traditions. These link today's civilizations to their most ancient roots and continue to exert a powerful influence worldwide. We believe this emphasis on the great religious traditions recognizes not only a factor that has shaped the past but also one of the most dynamic, influential forces of today.

We also bring a comparative perspective to our survey, tracing the threads of interaction that have linked civilizations throughout history. In the end, students should emerge more culturally sensitive citizens of the global, twenty-first century.

Strengths of the Text

Balanced and Flexible Presentation In this edition, as in past editions, we have sought to present world history fairly, accurately, and in a way that does justice to its great variety. History has many facets, no one of which can account for the others. Any attempt to tell the story of civilization from a single perspective, no matter how timely, is bound to neglect or suppress some important part of that story.

Historians have recently brought a vast array of new tools and concepts to bear on the study of history. Our coverage introduces students to various aspects of social and intellectual history as well as to the more traditional political, diplomatic, and military coverage. We firmly believe that only through an appreciation of all pathways to understanding of the past can the real heritage of world civilizations be claimed.

The Heritage of World Civilizations, Fifth Edition, is designed to accommodate a variety of approaches to a course in world civilization, allowing teachers to stress what is most important to them. Some teachers will ask students to read all the chapters. Others will select among them to reinforce assigned readings and lectures.

Clarity and Accessibility   Good narrative history requires clear, vigorous prose. Our goal has been to make our presentation fully accessible to students without compromising on vocabulary or conceptual level. We hope this effort will benefit both teachers and students.

Recent Scholarship   As in previous editions, changes in this edition reflect our determination to incorporate the most recent developments in historical scholarship and the expanding concerns of professional historians.

Pedagogical Features   This edition retains the pedagogical features of the last edition, helping to make the text accessible to students, reinforcing key concepts, and providing a global, comparative perspective.

- *Chapter Topics* introduce each chapter.
- *Questions accompanying the source documents* direct students toward important, thought-provoking issues and help them relate the documents to the material in the text. They can be used to stimulate class discussion or as topics for essays and study groups.
- *Chapter review questions* help students focus on and interpret the broad themes of a chapter. These questions, too, can be used for class discussion and essay topics.
- *Part Essays* open each of the seven major sections of the book. These serve to preview the coverage in the subsequent chapters and highlight major trends and movements.

- *Part Timelines* show the major events in five regions—Europe, the Near East and India, East Asia, Africa, and the Americas—side by side. Appropriate photographs have been added to each timeline.
- *Chronologies* within each chapter help students organize a time sequence for key events.
- *Primary Source Documents*, including selections from sacred books, poems, philosophy, political manifestos, letters, and travel accounts, introduce students to the raw material of history, providing an intimate contact with the people of the past and their concerns.
- *In World Perspective* sections conclude most chapters. These brief essays place important developments in the chapter into a world context.
- *Comparative Perspectives* essays examine technology and civilizations from a cross-cultural perspective. (See below.)
- *Religions of the World* essays introduce students to the five major world religious traditions—Judaism, Hinduism, Buddhism, Christianity, and Islam.

New in the Fifth Edition

This edition of *The Heritage of World Civilizations* includes new pedagogical features, many content revisions, a new four-color design, and a new series of comparative essays on technology, described below.

Comparative Perspectives: Technology and Civilizations   We believe one of the clearest paths to thinking globally and comparatively about world history is through the history of technology. For that reason we have introduced a new series of essays relating to technology.

Each essay considers a particular technological advance from a comparative or global perspective. Topics include the rise of monumental architecture in the ancient world, ancient warfare and armaments, a comparison of the development of printing in China and western Europe, innovations in maritime transport, the shifting balance of technological advances and their broad impact on world history (located where students will have sufficient information to evaluate and criticize the presentation), technology and imperialism, the role of energy in world history, and the rise of the information age. Each essay is presented in its historical context, helping students to integrate its information and arguments with the other portions of the text.

Content and Organization   The many changes in content and organization in this edition of *The Heritage of World Civilizations* reflect our ongoing effort to present a truly global survey of world civilization that at the same time gives a rich picture of the history of individual regions.

In an effort to draw students into both a comparative and, in this case, transatlantic perspective, we have omitted the separate chapter on North America in the nineteenth century, transferring most of that material to chapters which deal with related topics in European history. Thus, for example, the Civil War in the United States appears in the chapter on nineteenth-century nation-state consolidation (Chapter 27). Similarly, the late nineteenth-century social development of the United States now appears with the contemporaneous developments in Europe (Chapter 28). We hope that such integration will enable students to understand the broad strands of the development of the United States in a broader context.

Revisions of specific chapters include the following:

- Chapter 17, "The Age of Reformation and Religious Wars" includes new sections on the social significance of the Reformation in Western Europe, the changing role of women, and family life in early modern Europe.
- Chapter 20, "East Asia in the Late Traditional Era" includes a considerable revision of the section on Vietnam. As a group, the chapters on East Asia include more documents relating to the position of women.
- Chapter 25, "Revolutions in the Transatlantic World" includes a new section on the crusade to abolish the slave trade in the transatlantic economy. The discussion integrates the themes of the eighteenth-century Enlightenment and Revolutions, developed in Chapter 24.
- Chapter 26, "Europe and North America 1815–1850: Political Reform, Economic Advance, and Social Unrest" now includes the topic, Testing the New American Republic, a discussion of sectional conflict and the rise of abolitionism in the North.
- Chapter 27, "Political Consolidation in Europe and North America" now includes a section on The United States: Civil War, Reconstruction, and Progressive Politics and another on The Canadian Experience.
- Chapter 28, "The Building of Northern Transatlantic Supremacy: Society and Politics to World War I" now includes discussions of The New Industrial Economy and The Progressives in a new section on North America.
- Our discussion of the "New Imperialism" in Europe has been moved to Chapter 33, "Imperialism and World War I."

- Chapter 37, "East Asia in the Late Twentieth Century" has been expanded to include more social history.

Maps and Illustrations   Probably the most striking change for readers familiar with previous editions of *The Heritage of World Civilizations* is the addition of relief to nearly one-half of the maps, making them both more accurate and useful pedagogically. New maps clarify the sites and spread of ancient African cultures. Modern Asia, drawn from an economic perspective, presents interesting, up-to-date comparisons. All maps have been carefully edited for accuracy. Sixty new color illustrations add to the beauty of the text.

A Note on Dates and Transliterations   We have used B.C.E. (before the common era) and C.E. (common era) instead of B.C. (before Christ) and A.D. (*anno domini*, the year of our Lord) to designate dates.

Until recently, most scholarship on China used the Wade-Giles system of romanization for Chinese names and terms. In order that students may move easily from the present text to the existing body of advanced scholarship on Chinese history, we have used the Wade-Giles system throughout. China today, however, uses another system known as *pinyin*. Virtually all Western newspapers have adopted it. Therefore, for Chinese history since 1949 we have included the *pinyin* spellings in parentheses after the Wade-Giles.

Also, we have followed the currently accepted English transliterations of Arabic words. For example, today *Koran* is being replaced by the more accurate *Qur'an;* similarly *Muhammad* is preferable to *Mohammed* and *Muslim* to *Moslem*. We have not tried to distinguish the letters *'ayn* and *hamza;* both are rendered by a simple apostrophe ('), as in *shi'ite*.

With regard to Sanskritic transliteration, we have not distinguished linguals and dentals, and both palatal and lingual *s* are rendered *sh*, as in *Shiva* and *Upanishad*.

Ancillary Instructional Materials

The Heritage of World Civilizations, Fifth Edition, comes with an extensive package of ancillary materials.

- *An Instructor's Manual* prepared by Perry Rogers, Ohio State University, provides summary and multiple choice questions for each part essay, as well as chapter summaries, outlines of key points and concepts, identification questions, and multiple choice and essay questions to be used for tests, and a suggested list of relevant films and videos for each chapter.

- A *Study Guide*, also prepared by Perry Rogers, includes chapter summaries, key concepts, identification questions, short-answer exercises, and essay questions.
- *Documents in World History* (Volumes 1 and 2) is a collection of additional primary source documents that underscore the themes in the text. Includes review questions for each document.
- A *Test Item File*, also prepared by Perry Rogers, provides more than 1,000 test questions.
- *Prentice Hall Custom Test*, Prentice Hall's new testing software program, permits instructors to edit any or all items in the Test Item File and add their own questions. Other special features of this program, which is available for DOS, Windows, and Macintosh, include random generation of an item set, creation of alternative versions of the same test, scrambling question sequence, and test preview before printing.
- *Color Transparencies* of maps, charts, and graphs from the text provide strong visual support for lectures.
- A *Map Workbook* helps students develop geographical knowledge. This workbook is free to students using new copies of this text.
- *Understanding and Answering Essay Questions*, prepared by Mary L. Kelley, San Antonio College. This brief guide suggests helpful study techniques as well as specific analytical tools for understanding different types of essay questions and provides precise guidelines for preparing well-crafted essay answers. The guide is available free to students when packaged with *The Heritage of World Civilizations*.
- *Reading Critically About History*, prepared by Rose Wassman and Lee Rinsky, both of DeAnza College. This brief guide provides students with helpful strategies for reading a history textbook. It is available free when packaged with *The Heritage of World Civilizations*.
- *Themes of the Times* is a newspaper supplement prepared jointly by Prentice Hall and the premier news publication, *The New York Times*. Issued twice a year, it contains recent articles pertinent to American history.  These articles connect the classroom to the world. For information about a reduced-rate subscription to *The New York Times*, call toll free: (800) 631-1222.

The ancillary package also includes an extensive list of multimedia supplements.

- *History on the Internet*, adapted by David A. Meier, Dickinson State University, is a brief guide that introduces students to the Internet and provides them with clear strategies for navigating the Internet and World Wide Web. Exercises within and at the end of chapters allow students to practice searching for the growing wealth of resources available on the Web to the student of history. This 48-page supplementary book is free to students using new copies of the text.
- *The Heritage of World Civilizations*, Interactive Edition, is a multimedia CD-ROM. It features self-playing multimedia presentations, historical photos with captions, more than 600 interactive study questions to strengthen the student's understanding of world history, the complete Webster's New World College Dictionary, Third Edition, and the complete text of *The Heritage of World Civilizations*, Fourth Edition. The past has never been so vibrant, so accessible, and so interesting.
- *The Heritage of World Civilizations*, Companion Website (http://www.prenhall.com/craig) works in tandem with the text to help students use the World Wide Web to enrich their understanding of world history. Featuring chapter objectives, study questions, new updates, labeling exercises, and much more, it links the text with related material available on the Internet.

Acknowledgments

We are grateful to the many scholars and teachers whose thoughtful and often detailed comments helped shape this as well as previous editions of *The Heritage of World Civilizations*:

Wayne Ackerson, *Salisbury State University*
Jack Martin Balcer, *Ohio State University*
Charmarie J. Blaisdell, *Northeastern University*
Deborah Buffton, *University of Wisconsin at La Crosse*
Loretta Burns, *Mankato State University*
Chun-shu Chang, *University of Michigan, Ann Arbor*
Mark Chavalas, *University of Wisconsin at La Crosse*
Anthony Cheeseboro, *Southern Illinois University at Edwardsville*
William J. Courteney, *University of Wisconsin*
Samuel Willard Crompton, *Holyoke Community College*
James B. Crowley, *Yale University*
Bruce Cummings, *The University of Chicago*
Stephen F. Dale, *Ohio State University, Columbus*
Raymond Van Dam, *University of Michigan, Ann Arbor*
Bill Donovan, *Loyola University of Maryland*
Suzanne Gay, *Oberlin College*
Robert Gerlich, *Loyola University*

Samuel Robert Goldberger, *Capital Community-Technical College*
Andrew Gow, *University of Alberta*
Katheryn L. Green, *University of Wisconsin, Madison*
David Griffiths, *University of North Carolina, Chapel Hill*
Louis Haas, *Duquesne University*
Joseph T. Hapak, *Moraine Valley Community College*
Hue-Tam Ho Tai, *Harvard University*
David Kieft, *University of Minnesota*
Frederick Krome, *Northern Kentucky University*
Lisa M. Lane, *Mira Costa College*
David Lelyveld, *Columbia University*
Jan Lewis, *Rutgers University, Newark*
James C. Livingston, *College of William and Mary*
Richard L. Moore Jr., *St. Augustine's College*
Beth Nachison, *Southern Connecticut State University*
Robin S. Oggins, *Binghamton University*
Louis A. Perez Jr., *University of South Florida*
Cora Ann Presley, *Tulane University*
Norman Ravitch, *University of California, Riverside*
Philip F. Riley, *James Madison University*
Thomas Robisheaux, *Duke University*

Dankwart A. Rustow, *The City University of New York*
James J. Sack, *University of Illinois at Chicago*
William Schella, *Murray State University*
Marvin Slind, *Washington State University*
Daniel Scavone, *University of Southern Indiana*
Charles C. Stewart, *University of Illinois*
Truong-buu Lam, *University of Hawaii*
Harry L. Watson, *Loyola College of Maryland*
Paul Varley, *Columbia University*

Finally, we would like to thank the dedicated people who helped produce this revision: our acquisitions editor, Todd Armstrong; our development editor, Roberta Meyer; our photo researchers, Barbara Salz and Francelle Carapetyan; Ximena Tamvakopoulos, who created the handsome new design for this edition; Harriet Tellem, our project manager; and Lynn Pearlman, our manufacturing buyer.

A.M.C.
W.A.G.
D.K.
S.O.
F.M.T.

ABOUT THE AUTHORS

Albert M. Craig is the Harvard-Yenching Professor of History at Harvard University, where he has taught since 1959. A graduate of Northwestern University, he took his Ph.D. at Harvard University. He has studied at Strasbourg University and at Kyoto, Keio, and Tokyo universities in Japan. He is the author of *Choshu in the Meiji Restoration* (1961), and, with others, of *East Asia, Tradition and Transformation* (1978). He is the editor of *Japan, A Comparative View* (1973) and co-editor of *Personality in Japanese History* (1970). At present he is engaged in research on the thought of Fukuzawa Yukichi. For eleven years (1976–1987) he was the director of the Harvard-Yenching Institute. He has also been a visiting professor at Kyoto and Tokyo Universities. He has received Guggenheim, Fulbright, and Japan Foundation Fellowships. In 1988 he was awarded the Order of the Rising Sun by the Japanese government.

William A. Graham is a Professor of the History of Religion and Islamic Studies, Chairman of the Near Eastern Languages and Civilizations, and Master of Currier House at Harvard University. From 1990–1996 he directed Harvard's Center for Middle Eastern Studies. He has taught for twenty-six years at Harvard, where he received the A.M. and Ph.D. degrees after graduating with an A.B. in comparative literature from the University of North Carolina at Chapel Hill. He also studied in Göttingen, Tübingen, and Lebanon. He is the author of *Divine Word and Prophetic Word in Early Islam* (1977); awarded the American Council of Learned Societies History of Religions book prize in 1978, and of *Beyond the Written Word: Oral Aspects of Scripture in the History of Religion* (1987). He has published a variety of articles in both Islamic studies and the general history of religion and is one of the editors of the forthcoming *Encyclopedia of the Qur'an*. He serves currently on the editorial board of several journals and has held John Simon Guggenheim and Alexander von Humboldt research fellowships.

Donald Kagan is Hillhouse Professor of History and Classics at Yale University, where he has taught since 1969. He received the A.B. degree in history from Brooklyn College, the M.A. in classics from Brown University, and the Ph.D. in history from Ohio State University. During 1958–1959 he studied at the American School of Classical Studies as a Fulbright Scholar. He has received four awards for undergraduate teaching at Cornell and Yale. He is the author of a history of Greek political thought, *The Great Dialogue* (1965); a four-volume history of the Peloponnesian War, *The Origins of the Peloponnesian War* (1969), *The Archidamian War* (1974), *The Peace of Nicias and the Sicilian Expedition* (1981), and *The Fall of the Athenian Empire* (1987); a biography of Pericles, *Pericles of Athens and the Birth of Democracy* (1991); and *On the Origins of War* (1995). With Brian Tierney and L. Pearce Williams, he is the editor of *Great Issues in Western Civilization*, a collection of readings.

Steven Ozment is McLean Professor of Ancient and Modern History at Harvard University. He has taught Western Civilization at Yale, Stanford, and Harvard. He is the author of nine books. *The Age of Reform, 1250–1550* (1980) won the Schaff Prize and was nominated for the 1981 National Book Award. Four of his books: *Magdalena and Balthasar: An Intimate Portrait of Life in Sixteenth Century Europe* (1986), *Three Behaim Boys: Growing Up in Early Modern Germany* (1990), *Protestants: The Birth of a Revolution* (1992), and *The Bürgermeister's Daughter: Scandal in a Sixteenth Century German Town* (1996) were selections of the History Book Club. His most recent book is *Flesh and Spirit: Private Life in Early Modern Germany* (1999).

Frank M. Turner is John Hay Whitney Professor of History at Yale University, where he served as University Provost from 1988 to 1992. He received his B.A. degree at the College of William and Mary and his Ph.D. from Yale. He has received the Yale College Award for Distinguished Undergraduate Teaching. He has directed a National Endowment for the Humanities Summer Institute. His scholarly research has received the support of fellowships from the National Endowment for the Humanities and the Guggenheim Foundation. He is the author of *Between Science and Religion: The Reaction to Scientific Naturalism in Late Victorian England* (1974), *The Greek Heritage in Victorian Britain* (1981), which received the British Council Prize of the Conference on British Studies and the Yale Press Governors Award, and *Contesting Cultural Authority: Essays in Victorian Intellectual Life* (1993). He has also contributed numerous articles to journals and has served on the editorial advisory boards of *The Journal of Modern History, Isis*, and *Victorian Studies*. He edited *John Henry Newman, The Idea of a University* (1996). Since 1996 he has served as a Trustee of Connecticut College.

Royal Standard of Ur, "Peace" side, 2750 B.C.E. [British Museum, London/The Bridgeman Art Library International]

THE COMING OF CIVILIZATION

The way of life of prehistoric cave dwellers differed immensely from that of today's civilized world. Yet the few millennia in which we have been civilized are but a tiny fraction of the long span of human existence. Especially during the recent millennia, changes in our culture have far outpaced changes in our bodies. We live a highly organized and often sedentary life, but still retain the emotional makeup and motor reflexes of primitive men and women.

Homo sapiens—Modern humans—first appeared about 100,000 years ago. Since then the pace of human control over the environment has constantly accelerated. It took us tens of thousands of years to domesticate animals and to master the rudiments of agriculture. It took us another 7,000–9,000 years to develop cities, systems of writing, then bronze and iron. Several hundred years later the great religious and philosophical revolutions of the ancient world occurred, followed by the empires of China, India, Iran, and Rome that straddled the B.C.E.–C.E. divide.

Now, 2,000 years later, humans have unlocked the power of the atom, walked on the moon, and broken the genetic code. The pace of new discoveries continues to quicken, but the earliest advances are no less impressive than more recent ones. The invention of writing late in the fourth millennium B.C.E., for example, may have been a less complex task than the breaking of the genetic code in the twentieth century C.E., but it was probably more difficult.

The timetable for the development of river-valley civilizations varied. The Near Eastern cultures began earlier, followed by India and China. But the parallelism in stages of development is remarkable. First came agriculture and pottery; then cities, writing, and bronze; and, finally, iron and empire. In the Americas the civilizations of Mesoamerica and the Andes followed a similar sequence from agriculture to urbanism to empire. Does the logic of nature dictate that once agriculture develops, cities will arise in alluvial river valleys favorable to intensive cultivation? Was it inevitable that the firing of clay to produce pots would reduce metallic oxides and lead to the discovery of smelting? Did the formation of the aristocratic and priestly classes, who controlled the resources of cities, automatically lead to record keeping and writing?

That is to say, did agriculture set in motion a train of similar events in widely separated regions? Or is diffusion a more likely cause? At least in Eurasia and Africa, if not between those continents and the Americas, is it not conceivable that contacts between the early civilizations were more numerous than we now imagine? The earliest written languages—the Sumerian cuneiform, the Egyptian hieroglyphs, and the Chinese ideographs—probably had independent origins. They are too dissimilar to be the result of diffusion. But what of seeds, bronze, and iron? Might not migrating peoples or wandering merchants have carried these items over long distances? Both hypotheses—diffusion and independent origins—are plausible. However, in the absence of evidence, a definitive answer cannot be given. Little remains even of the material culture of the men and women of these earliest civilizations. Understanding their lives is like reconstructing a dinosaur from a broken tooth and a fragment of jawbone.

In or near the same Eurasian and African river valleys that saw the birth of civilization occurred the religious and philosophical revolutions that permanently marked the world thereafter: monotheistic Judaism, from which would later develop the world religions of Christianity and Islam; Hinduism and Buddhism in southern Asia; and the philosophies of China and Greece. The simultaneity of their appearance was striking. The Hebrew prophets, Buddha, Confucius, and Socrates, if not all contemporaries, were grouped within a few hundred years of each other in the first millennium B.C.E. Most founders of the great religions based their teachings on intensely personal religious experiences, on experiences that cannot be analyzed in historical terms. Yet we can examine their historical contexts and note certain similarities.

The coming of the bronze and iron ages—and we speak of bronze and iron partly as a shorthand for many complex developments—led to a series of political and spiritual crises of the early civilizations across the world. The founders of the great religions and philosophies responded to these crises with new visions of humanity's place in the universe, and with new and more universal ethics. It is their greater universalism that distinguishes the world religions from those centered more narrowly on a particular tribe or people. Of course all religions spring from a common human impulse and treat the questions of how to live and what life means in the face of death. But Buddhism, Christianity, and Islam differed from the Shinto of Japan, the religions of the Egyptians or Mayas, or even the Zoroastrianism of ancient Iran in contending that their answers were true for all peoples and times. It was this universalism that made them missionary religions.

Similarly, the philosophies of China and Greece were more universal than previous systems of thought. Confucianism eventually spread to Korea, Japan, and Vietnam, countries whose customs were quite different from those of China. It became the basis for laws in these countries because its ethics transcended particular Chinese institutions.

Greek ideas played an equivalent role in the west. They joined Judaic concepts to form Christianity. The gospel according to Saint John starts: "In the beginning was the Word (*logos*), and the word was with God, and the Word was God." In Greek, *logos* means something like "universal principle" or "reason." Universal Greek conceptions also lay at the base of the Roman law code (*ius gentium*) used to govern provinces with different peoples and widely varying customs. This last example says something about the transition from the older civilizations to the empires of the ancient world. These empires, to be sure, were built by armies, not philosophies. But for their leaders to govern and their bureaucracies to function, they had to have philosophies and laws.

1 BIRTH OF CIVILIZATION

One of the hallmarks of the early river civilizations was the development of techniques to increase harvests. This statue from the Old Kingdom in Egypt (ca. 2700–2200 B.C.E.) shows a woman grinding wheat for bread. It is a rare picture of an ordinary person engaged in every day life in ancient Egypt. [Kenneth Garrettings/National Geographic Society]

CHAPTER TOPICS

♦ Early Human Beings and Their Culture   ♦ Ancient Near Eastern Empires   ♦ Early Chinese Civilization

♦ Early Civilizations in the Near East   ♦ Early Indian Civilization   ♦ The Rise of Civilization in the Americas

Scientists estimate that the earth may be as many as six billion years old and that the first humanlike creatures appeared perhaps three to five million years ago in Africa. Some one to two million years ago, erect and tool-using early humans spread over much of Africa, Europe, and Asia. Our own species, Homo sapiens, probably emerged some 200,000 years ago, and the earliest remains of fully modern humans date to about 100,000 years ago.

The earliest humans lived by hunting, fishing, and collecting wild plants. Only some ten thousand years ago did they learn to cultivate plants, herd animals, and make airtight pottery for storage. These discoveries transformed them from gatherers to producers and allowed them to grow in number and to lead a settled life. Beginning about five thousand years ago a far more complex way of life began to appear in some parts of the world. In these places humans learned how to increase harvests through irrigation and other methods, making possible much larger populations. They came together in towns, cities, and other centers, where they erected impressive structures and where industry and commerce flourished. They developed writing, enabling them to keep inventories of food and other resources. Specialized occupations emerged, complex religions took form, and social divisions increased. These changes marked the birth of civilization.

Early Human Beings and Their Culture

Humans, unlike other animals, are cultural beings. *Culture* may be defined as the ways of living built up by a group and passed on from one generation to another. It includes behavior such as courtship or child-rearing practices; it includes material things such as tools, clothing, and shelter; and it includes ideas, institutions, and beliefs. Language, apparently a uniquely human trait, lies behind our ability to create ideas and institutions and to transmit culture from one generation to another. Our flexible hands enable us to hold and make tools and so to create the material artifacts of culture. Because culture is learned and not inherited, it permits more rapid adaptation to changing conditions than biological evolution, making possible the spread of humanity to almost all the lands of the globe.

The Paleolithic Age

Anthropologists designate early human cultures by their tools. The earliest cultural period—the Paleolithic (from Greek, "old stone")—dates from the first use of stone tools some one or two million years ago to about 10,000 B.C.E. During this immensely long span, people were hunters, fishers, and gatherers—but not producers—of food. They learned to make and use increasingly sophisticated tools of stone and of perishable materials like wood; they learned to make and control fire; and they acquired language and the ability to use it to pass on what they had learned.

These early humans, dependent on nature for food and vulnerable to wild beasts and natural disasters, may have developed responses to the world rooted in fear of the unknown—of the uncertainties of human life or the overpowering forces of nature. Religious and magical beliefs and practices may have emerged in an effort to propitiate or coerce the superhuman forces thought to animate or direct the natural world. Evidence of religious faith and practice, as well as of magic, goes back nearly one hundred thousand years. Magnificent cave paintings and other art as well as evidence of ritual practices, such as burial, suggest the fear, awe, exultation, and empathy with which Paleolithic people approached the natural world. The sense that there is more to the world than meets the eye—in other words, the religious response to the world—seems to be as old as humankind.

During the Paleolithic Age, most likely relatively near its close, humans, probably pursuing game, crossed from Asia through the region of the Bering Sea, which was then dry land, into the American continent. This migration would ultimately separate their descendants from other human groups for

This Paleolithic cave painting of bulls and horses is found in the Dordogne valley of southern France. The animals, which were hunted by prehistoric humans, are depicted with remarkable realism. [Ancient Art and Architecture Collection/Ronald Sheridan's Photo Library]

many thousands of years. In their isolation, however, the inhabitants of the Americas experienced cultural changes parallel to those of Eurasia and Africa.

The style of life and the level of technology of the Paleolithic period could support only a sparsely settled society. If hunters were too numerous, game would not suffice. In Paleolithic times people were subject to the same natural and ecological constraints that today maintain a balance between wolves and deer in Alaska.

Paleolithic society was probably characterized by a division of labor by sex. Men most likely hunted, fished, and fought other families, clans, and tribes. Women, less mobile because of childbearing, most likely gathered nuts, berries, and wild grains, wove baskets, and made clothing. Women gathering food probably discovered how to plant and care for seeds, knowledge that eventually led to agriculture and the Neolithic revolution.

The Neolithic Age

Only a few Paleolithic societies made the initial revolutionary shift to agriculture, and anthropologists and archaeologists disagree as to why. However it happened, some ten thousand years ago parts of what we now call the Near East began to shift from a hunter-gatherer way of life to a settled agricultural one characteristic of the Neolithic ("new stone") Age. Neolithic people domesticated animals as well as plants. They invented pottery, allowing them to store surplus liquids, just as earlier people had learned to make baskets to store dry foods. They learned to weave cloth from flax and wool. And to give their crops the constant care they required from planting to harvest, Neolithic people built permanent buildings, usually in clusters near the best fields.

Throughout the Paleolithic Age, the human population had been small and relatively stable. The shift from food gathering to food production may not have been associated with an immediate change in population, but over time in the regions where agriculture and animal husbandry appeared, the number of human beings grew at an unprecedented rate. The Neolithic revolution was a major step in human control of nature, and it was a vital precondition for the emergence of civilization. The earliest Neolithic societies appeared in the Near East about 8000 B.C.E., in China about 4000 B.C.E., and in India about 5500 B.C.E. In the Americas, in Mesoamerica (modern Mexico and Central America) and in the Andean region of South America, settled agricultural societies were becoming prevalent by about 2500 B.C.E. The Neolithic revolution in the Near East and India was based on wheat; in China on millet and rice; and in the Americas on corn, beans, squash, and other crops.

The Emergence of Civilization

Neolithic agricultural villages and herding cultures gradually replaced Paleolithic culture in much of the world. Then, beginning between 4000 and 3000 B.C.E., another major shift occurred, the emergence of civilization. In the African-Eurasian landmass, civilization first appeared in the valley of the Tigris and Euphrates rivers in the region called Mesopotamia, later in the valley of the Nile River in Egypt, and somewhat later still in the Indus Valley in India and the Yellow River basin in China (see Map 1–1). It was marked by the appearance of urban centers, monumental architecture, complex hierarchical societies, and the invention of writing. The period in which these first Old World civilizations arose is known as the Bronze Age because it coincided with the discovery of the technique for smelting tin and copper to make bronze, a stronger and more useful metal. The civilizations of the Americas had somewhat different characteristics. Metallurgy came late to Mesoamerica, and in the Andean region, where the earliest monumental architecture dates to almost 3000 B.C.E., writing never developed (see Map 1–6).

Early Civilizations in the Near East

About 4000 B.C.E., people began to move in large numbers into the river-watered lowlands of Mesopotamia and Egypt. By about 3000 B.C.E., when the invention of writing gave birth to history, urban life and the organization of society into cen-

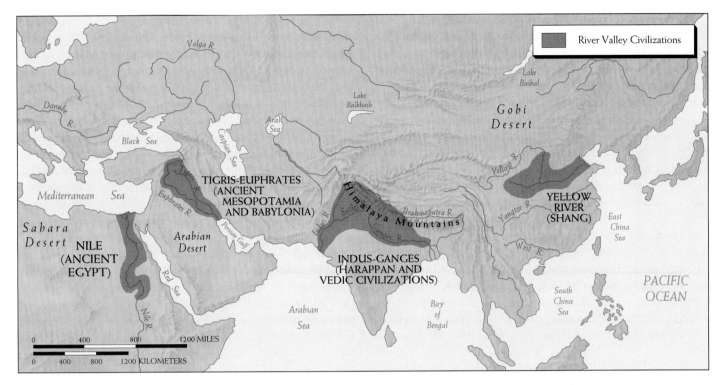

Map 1–1   The four great river valley civilizations to ca. 1000 B.C.E.   By ca. 2000 B.C.E. urban life was established along the Tigris and Euphrates rivers in Mesopotamia, the Nile River in Egypt, the Indus and Ganges rivers in India, and the Yellow River in China.

tralized states was established in the valleys of the Tigris and Euphrates rivers in Mesopotamia and the Nile River in Egypt.

The concentration of people in cities created something new. Unlike Neolithic villages, urban communities were not devoted simply to agriculture. Cities served as administrative, religious, manufacturing, entertainment, and commercial centers. To deal with the gods, great temples were built, and many priests worked in them. Commerce was important enough to support a merchant class. The earliest written records reflect this increasing complexity. Many texts deal with the care of animals, land management, and trade. In Mesopotamia, large temple complexes generated religious texts as well as records of the lands they owned, the offerings they received, the services they performed, and the people they employed. City governments, as they became larger and more complex, recorded their acts and laws as well as different kinds of literature. Because the need for record keeping was so great and the early writing so difficult and time consuming to master, a class of scribes emerged.

The logic of nature pointed in the direction of the unification of an entire river valley. Central control would put the river's water to the most efficient use, and the absence of central control would lead to warfare, chaos, and destruction. As a result, unified kingdoms appeared, ruled by powerful monarchs.

The typical king in a river valley civilization was regarded either as a god or the delegate of a god. Around him developed a rigid class structure. Beneath the monarch was a class of hereditary military aristocrats and a powerful priesthood; below them were several kinds of freemen, mostly peasants; and at the bottom were many slaves. People lived in peasant villages as well as the urban centers that were the locus of administration, commerce, religion, and military activity. Most of the land was owned or controlled by the king, the nobility, and the priests. These were traditional, conservative societies. Their cultural patterns formed early and changed only slowly and grudgingly.

Mesopotamian Civilization

The first civilization appears to have arisen in the valley of the Tigris and Euphrates rivers, an area the later Greeks and Romans called Mesopotamia. The region is naturally divided into two ecological zones, the south (Sumer), where irrigation is vital, and the north (Assyria), where agriculture depends on rainfall and wells. The oldest Mesopotamian cities seem to have been founded by a people called the Sumerians, around 3000 B.C.E. Sumerian civilization is generally associated with the southern part of the Tigris and Euphrates valleys, close to the head of the Persian Gulf, and the earliest city had long been thought to be Uruk, which lies in that region (see Map

1–2). Recent discoveries, however, have revealed Sumerian cities dating to the Uruk period in northern Syria, notably at Habuba Kabirah, suggesting that we still have much to learn about the earliest civilization of Mesopotamia.

From about 2800 to 2370 B.C.E., in what is called the early dynastic period, several Sumerian city-states, each controlling about 100 square miles, dotted the landscape of southern Mesopotamia. Among these cities are Ur, Uruk, Lagash, and Eridu. Quarrels over water rights and frontiers led to incessant fighting, and in time, stronger towns conquered weaker ones and expanded to form larger units, usually kingdoms.

The region immediately upstream from the principal Sumerian city-states was occupied mostly by people who probably originally came from North Syria and who, unlike the Sumerians, spoke a Semitic language (that is, a language in the same family as Arabic and Hebrew). These people absorbed Sumerian culture and established their own kingdom, with its capital at Akkad, near the site of a later city known to us as Babylon. Under their most famous king, Sargon, the Akkadians conquered the Sumerian cities and created an empire that extended in every direction. Sargon's name became legendary. He is said to have conquered the "cedar forests" of Lebanon, far to the west, near the coast of the Mediterranean Sea. He ruled from about 2370 B.C.E. and established a family, or dynasty, of Semitic kings that ruled Sumer and Akkad for two centuries.

External attack and internal weakness destroyed Akkad. About 2125 B.C.E. the Sumerian city of Ur rose to dominance, and the rulers of the Third Dynasty of Ur established a large empire. About 2000 B.C.E., however, it was swept aside by another invasion.

The fall of the Third Dynasty of Ur put an end to Sumerian rule and to the Sumerians as an identifiable group. The Sumerian language survived only in writing, as a kind of sacred language known only to priests and scribes, preserving the cultural heritage of Sumer. For about a century after the fall of Ur, dynastic chaos reigned. Then, about 1900 B.C.E. a

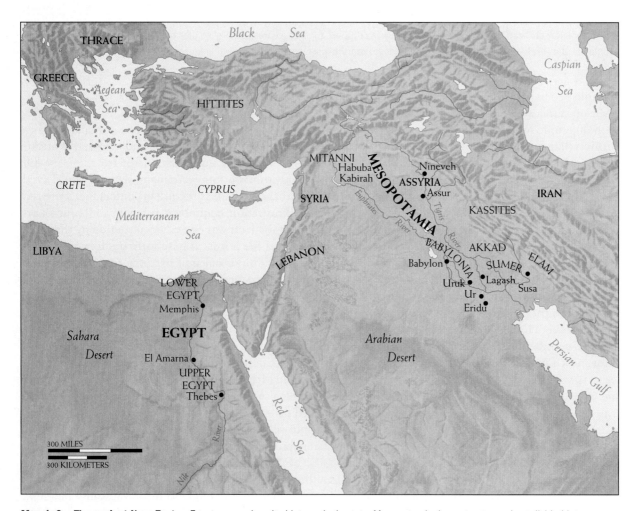

Map 1–2   The ancient Near East.   Egypt was early united into a single state. Mesopotamia, in contrast, was long divided into many city-states.

Sumerian statuettes from Tell Asmar. The group, dating from 3000–2500 B.C.E., was found buried beside the altar of a temple at a site near modern Baghdad. The tallest figure in this collection of gods, priests, and worshippers is the god Abu, the "lord of vegetation." [Courtesy of the Oriental Institute Museum, University of Chicago. Photo by Victor J. Boswell]

people called the Amorites gained control of the region, establishing their capital at Babylon.

The Amorite, or Old Babylonian, dynasty dominated Mesopotamia for about three hundred years. Its high point was the reign of its most famous king, Hammurabi (r. ca. 1792–1750 B.C.E.), best known for the law code that bears his name. Codes of law existed as early as the Sumerian period, and Hammurabi's plainly owed much to earlier models. His is the fullest and best-preserved legal code we have from ancient Mesopotamia, however. The Code of Hammurabi reveals a society strictly divided by class; there were nobles, commoners, and slaves, and the law did not treat them equally. In general, punishments were harsh, based literally on the principle of "an eye for an eye, a tooth for a tooth." The prologue to the code makes it clear that law and justice came from the gods through the king.

About 1600 B.C.E. the Babylonian kingdom fell apart under the impact of invasions from the north and east by the Hittites and the Kassites. The Hittites came only as raiders, plundering what they could and then withdrawing to their home in Asia Minor. The Kassites stayed and ruled Mesopotamia for five centuries.

Government   From the earliest historical records it is clear that the Sumerians were ruled by monarchs in some form. Some scholars have thought they could detect a "primitive democracy" in early Sumer, but the evidence, which is sketchy and hard to interpret, shows no more than a limited check on royal power even in early times. The first historical city-states had kings or priest-kings who led the army, administered the economy, and served as judges and as intermediaries between their people and the gods. At first the kings were thought of as favorites and representatives of the gods; later, on some occasions and for relatively short periods, they instituted cults and were worshiped as divine.

This union of Church and State (to use modern terminology) in the person of the king reflected the centralization of power typical of Mesopotamian life. The economy was managed from the center by the priests and the king and was planned very carefully. Each year the land was surveyed, fields were assigned to specific farmers, and the amount of seed to be used was designated. The government estimated the size of the crop and planned its distribution even before it was planted.

This process required a large and competent staff, the ability to observe and record natural phenomena, a good knowledge of mathematics, and, for all of this, a system of writing. The Sumerians invented the writing system known as *cuneiform* (from the Latin *cuneus*, "wedge") because of the wedge-shaped stylus with which they wrote on clay tablets.

The writing also came to be used in beautifully cut characters in stone. The Sumerians also began the development of a sophisticated system of mathematics. The calendar they invented had twelve lunar months. To make it agree with the solar year and to make possible accurate designation of the seasons, they introduced a thirteenth month about every three years.

Religion The Sumerians and their successors worshiped gods with human forms, each of whom was usually identified with some natural phenomenon. They were pictured as frivolous, quarrelsome, selfish, and often childish, differing from humans only in their greater power and their immortality. They each appear to have begun as local deities. The people of Mesopotamia had a vague and gloomy picture of the afterworld. Their religion dealt with problems of this world, and they used prayer, sacrifice, and magic to achieve their ends. Expert knowledge was required to reach the perfection in wisdom and ritual needed to influence the gods, and so the priesthood flourished. A high percentage of the cuneiform writing we now have is devoted to religious texts: prayers, incantations, curses, and omens.

The Babylonians, in an effort to discover the will and intentions of the gods, cultivated several methods of divination. Seeking evidence of divine action in the movements of the heavenly bodies, they gave birth to astrology. They also sought to discover the divine will by examining the entrails of sacrificial animals for abnormalities. All of this religious activity required armies of scribes to keep great quantities of records, as well as learned priests to interpret them.

Religion, in the form of myth, played a large part in the literature and art of Mesopotamia. In poetic language, the Babylonians told tales of the creation of the world, of a great flood that almost destroyed human life, of an island paradise from which the god Enki was expelled for eating forbidden plants, of a hero named Gilgamesh who performed great feats in his travels, and many more.

Religion was also the inspiration for the most interesting architectural achievement in Mesopotamia: the ziggurat. The ziggurat was an artificial stepped mound surmounted by a temple. Neighbors and successors of the Sumerians adopted the style, and the eroded remains of many of these monumental structures, some partly restored, still dot the Mesopotamian landscape.

Society Tens of thousands of texts from the mid-third millennium B.C.E. to the end of cuneiform writing give us a full and detailed picture of the way people in ancient Mesopotamia conducted their lives and of the social conditions in which they lived. The evidence from the time of the reign of Hammurabi—including more than fifty royal letters, many business contracts, and especially the Code of Ham-

murabi—is particularly good. It reveals a society that was legally divided into three classes: nobles, commoners, and slaves. Punishment for crimes committed against freemen was harsher than for those against slaves; likewise, crimes committed against nobles were held to be more serious than those against commoners.

Categorizing the Code of Hammurabi according to the aspects of life with which it deals reveals much about Babylonian society. The third largest category is commerce, and the many sections of the Code devoted to such issues as debts, rates of interest, security, and default indicate the importance and sophistication of Babylonian commercial life. Sections also deal with the regulation of builders, surgeons, and other professionals. The second largest category deals with land tenure, as is not surprising in a society based so heavily on agriculture. The largest category relates to the family and its maintenance and protection.

Marriages were arranged by the parents, and betrothal was followed by the signing of a marriage contract. The husband-to-be made a bridal payment, and the father of the bride-to-be agreed to a dowry for his daughter. A husband whose wife was childless or ill for a long time could take a second wife. Extramarital relations between the husband and concubines, female slaves, and prostitutes were common and accepted.

The wife did not have similar privileges, but she seems to have been treated as an individual with rights protected by the law. Divorce was relatively easy and not entirely inequitable. Women divorced by their husbands without good cause received their dowry back. A woman seeking divorce could also recover her dowry if her husband could not convict her of wrongdoing. On the other hand, a woman's place was thought to be in the home. One law states that if a wife "has made up her mind to leave in order to engage in business, thus neglecting her house and humiliating her husband, he may divorce her without compensation."

For most of Mesopotamian history slavery arose from debt. Parents could sell their children into slavery or pledge themselves and their entire family as surety for a loan. In

Key Events and People in Mesopotamian History	
ca. 3500 B.C.E.	Sumerians arrive
ca. 2800–2340 B.C.E.	Sumerian city-states: early dynastic period
ca. 2340 B.C.E.	Sargon establishes Semitic dynasty at Akkad
ca. 2125–2027 B.C.E.	Third Dynasty of Ur
ca. 1900 B.C.E.	Amorites at Babylon
ca. 1792–1750 B.C.E.	Reign of Hammurabi
ca. 1600 B.C.E.	Invasion by Hittites and Kassites

Hammurabi's Code on Women, Marriage, and Divorce in Babylonia

Hammurabi, of the Old Babylonian, or Amorite, Dynasty, was king of Babylonia from 1728 to 1686 B.C.E. His empire extended from the Mediterranean Sea to the Persian Gulf, with its capital at Babylon in what is now Iraq. His greatest legacy is his code of written law, derived and refined from a long tradition of law codes in ancient Mesopotamia. It is a uniquely valuable source for understanding the character of society at that time. The following laws from Hammurabi's law code focus on the place of women and marriage in that society.

What rights and protections did women have in Hammurabi's Babylonia? Under what conditions could a man divorce his wife? What might deter him from such a divorce? Was betrothal protected by law? How do the institutions of marriage and divorce in Babylonia compare with those in modern America? What do you think are some consequences of the differences?

If a seignior wishes to divorce his wife who did not bear him children, he shall give her money to the full amount of her marriage-price and he shall also make good to her the dowry which she brought from her father's house and then he may divorce her.

If there was no marriage-price, he shall give her one mina of silver as the divorce-settlement.

If he is a peasant, he shall give her one-third mina of silver.

If a seignior's wife, who was living in the house of the seignior, has made up her mind to leave in order that she may engage in business, thus neglecting her house (and) humiliating her husband, they shall prove it against her; and if her husband has then decided on her divorce, he may divorce her, with nothing to be given her as her divorce-settlement upon her departure. If her husband has not decided on her divorce, her husband may marry another woman, with the former woman living in the house of her husband like a maidservant.

If a woman so hated her husband that she has declared, "You may not have me," her record shall be investigated at her city council, and if she was careful and was not at fault, even though her husband has been going out and disparaging her greatly, that woman, without incurring any blame at all, may take her dowry and go off to her father's house.

If she was not careful, but was a gadabout, thus neglecting her house (and) humiliating her husband, they shall throw that woman into the water.

When a seignior married a woman and a fever has then seized her, if he has made up his mind to marry another, he may marry (her), without divorcing his wife whom the fever seized; she shall live in the house which he built and he shall continue to support her as long as she lives.

If that woman has refused to live in her husband's house, he shall make good her dowry to her which she brought from her father's house and then she may leave.

If a seignior, upon presenting a field, orchard, house, or goods to his wife, left a sealed document with her, her children may not enter a claim against her after (the death of) her husband, since the mother may give her inheritance to that son of hers whom she likes, (but) she may not give (it) to an outsider.

If a seignior, who had the betrothal-gift brought to the house of his (prospective) father-in-law (and) paid the marriage-price, has then fallen in love with another woman and has said to his (prospective) father-in-law, "I will not marry your daughter," the father of the daughter shall keep whatever was brought to him.

If a seignior, who had the betrothal-gift brought to the house of the (prospective) father-in-law (and) paid the marriage-price, has the daughter has then said, "I will not give my daughter to you," he shall pay back double the full amount that was brought to him.

If a seignior, who had the betrothal-gift brought to the house of his (prospective) father-in-law (and) paid the marriage-price, and then a friend of his has so maligned him that his (prospective) father-in-law has said to the (prospective) husband, "You may not marry my daughter," he shall pay back double the full amount that was brought to him, but his friend may not marry his (intended) wife.

From "The Code of Hammurabi," translated by Theophile J. Meek in James B. Pritchard, ed., *Ancient Near Eastern Texts*, Third Edition, © 1969, renewed 1978 by Princeton University Press, pp. 172–173. Reprinted by permission of Princeton University Press.

---

case of default, they would all become slaves of the creditor for a stated period of time. Although the practice of enslaving foreign war captives dates to early periods, and native Babylonians could be enslaved for certain crimes—kicking one's mother or striking an elder brother, for example—true chattel slavery did not become common until late in Mesopotamian history, in the Neo-Babylonian period (612–539 B.C.E.). Some slaves worked for the king and the state, others for the temple and the priests, and still others for private citizens. Their tasks varied accordingly. Most temple slaves appear to have been women, who were probably used to spin thread, weave cloth, and grind flour. Sometimes the royal slaves did the heavy work of building palaces, canals, and fortifications. Private owners used their slaves chiefly as domestic servants. Some female slaves were used as concubines.

Although laws against fugitive slaves or slaves who denied their masters were harsh, in some respects Mesopotamian slavery appears enlightened compared with other slave systems in history. Slaves could engage in business and, with certain restrictions, hold property. They could marry free men or women, and the resulting children would be free. A slave who acquired the necessary wealth could buy his or her freedom. Children of a slave by the master might be allowed to share his property after his death. Nevertheless, slaves were property, were subject to their master's will, and had little legal protection.

Egyptian Civilization

As Mesopotamian civilization arose in the valley of the Tigris and Euphrates, another great civilization emerged in Egypt. The center of Egyptian civilization was the Nile River. From its source in central Africa the Nile runs north some 4,000 miles to the Mediterranean, with long navigable stretches broken by several cataracts. Ancient Egypt included the 750 miles of the valley from the First Cataract to the sea and was shaped like a funnel with two distinct parts. Upper (southern) Egypt consisted of the narrow valley of the Nile. Lower (northern) Egypt consisted of the broad, triangular delta, which branches out about 150 miles along the Mediterranean coast (see Map 1–2).

The Nile alone made life possible in Egypt's almost rainless desert. Each year the river flooded and covered the land, and when it receded it left a fertile mud that could produce two crops a year. The construction and maintenance of irrigation ditches to preserve the river's water, along with careful planning and organization of planting and harvesting, produced agricultural prosperity unmatched in the ancient world.

The Nile also served as a highway connecting the long, narrow country and encouraging its unification. By 3100 B.C.E. Upper and Lower Egypt had been united into a single kingdom. Nature helped protect and isolate the ancient Egyptians from outsiders. The cataracts, the sea, and the desert made it difficult for foreigners to reach Egypt for either friendly or hostile purposes. Egypt knew far more peace

Seated Egyptian scribe, height 21″ (53 cm.) painted limestone, fifth dynasty, c. 2510–2460 B.C.E. One of the hallmarks of the early river valley civilizations was the development of writing. Ancient Egyptian scribes had to undergo rigorous training, but were rewarded with a position of respect and privilege.

[Musee du Louvre, Paris. © Giraudon/Art Resource, N.Y.]

and security than Mesopotamia. This security, along with the sunny, predictable climate, gave Egyptian civilization a more optimistic outlook than the civilizations of the Tigris and Euphrates, which were always in fear of assault from storm, flood, earthquake, and hostile neighbors.

Events in the more than three-thousand-year span of ancient Egyptian history are traditionally dated by reference to the reigns of thirty-one royal dynasties, which modern historians have clustered into eight periods (see the accompanying chronology). The First Dynasty was founded by Menes, the unifier of Upper and Lower Egypt, and the last by the Greek conqueror Alexander the Great in 332 B.C.E.

The Old Kingdom (2700–2200 B.C.E.) By the time of the Third Dynasty, Egypt's kings had achieved full supremacy. Ruling from their capital at Memphis, in Upper Egypt, just above the opening of the delta, they had the resources of a huge, prosperous nation at their disposal. Royal power was absolute. The king (the title *pharaoh*, meaning "great house" or "palace," was not used until later in Egyptian history) governed through his family, appointing and removing officials at his pleasure. Peasants were carefully regulated. Their movement was limited and they were taxed heavily, perhaps up to as much as one fifth of what they produced.

An Egyptian king was considered no mere representative of the gods, but a god himself, on whom the lives, safety, and prosperity of his people depended. The land was his own personal possession, and the people his servants. Because he was the direct source of law and justice, Egypt needed no law codes. Government was merely an aspect of religion, and religion dominated Egyptian life. The gods of Egypt took many forms: as animals, humans, and natural forces. In time, Re,

The great pyramids of Egypt, located at Giza, near Cairo, are the colossal tombs of three kings of the Fourth Dynasty (ca. 2620–2480 B.C.E.): Menkaure (left), Khafre (center), and Khufu (right). The smaller tombs in the foreground may have been those of the kings' wives and courtiers. [Pictor/Uniphoto Picture Agency]

the sun god, came to have a special and dominant place, but for centuries there was little order in the Egyptian pantheon.

Unlike the Mesopotamians, the Egyptians had a rather clear idea of an afterlife. They buried their dead according to elaborate conventions, supplying the grave with things the departed would need for a pleasant life after death. At first only kings were thought to achieve eternal life; then nobles, and finally all Egyptians—if properly embalmed and buried with the requisite spells—laid claim to immortality. Bodies were preserved as mummies. Tombs were beautifully decorated with paintings; offerings of food were regularly brought to the dead. Some royal tombs were provided with full-sized ships for the voyage to heaven.

Nothing better illustrates the extent of royal power than the three great pyramids built as tombs by the kings of the Fourth Dynasty. The largest, that of Khufu, was originally 481 feet high and 756 feet long on each side. It was built of 2.3 million stone blocks averaging 2.5 tons each. The Greek historian Herodotus claimed that 100,000 men spent twenty years building it. The pyramids are remarkable for the great technical skill they demonstrate, but even more for the concentration of resources they represent. They give evidence that the Egyptian kings controlled vast wealth, had the power to focus enormous human effort on a personal project, and possessed the confidence to undertake a project of such a long duration. There were pyramids built earlier and many built later, but those of the Fourth Dynasty were never surpassed.

The Egyptians developed a system of writing not much later than the Sumerians. Though the idea of writing may have come from Mesopotamia, Egyptian script developed independently. It began as picture writing and later combined pictographs with sound signs. The result was a difficult and complicated script that the Greeks later called *hieroglyph* ("sacred carvings"). Most Egyptian writing was done with pen and ink on a fine paper made from the papyrus reed found in the delta; much of what was preserved long enough to be available to us, however, is found on wall paintings and carvings. Egyptian literature consisted of hymns, myths, magical formulas, tales of travel, and "wisdom literature" (bits of advice to help one get on well in the world). But Egyptian society, happier and simpler than that of Mesopotamia, produced nothing as serious and probing as the Mesopotamian story of Gilgamesh.

The Middle Kingdom (2052–1786 B.C.E.) The power of the kings of the Old Kingdom waned as priests and nobles gained more independence and influence. The governors of the regions of Egypt, called *nomes*, established hereditary claims to their offices, and their families acquired large estates. About 2200 B.C.E. the Old Kingdom collapsed. After a period of confusion (the First Intermediate Period, ca. 2200–2052 B.C.E.), the nomarchs (governors) of Thebes in Upper Egypt eventually gained control of the country and established the Middle Kingdom in 2052 B.C.E.

The rulers of the Twelfth Dynasty restored the king's power over the whole of Egypt from their base at Thebes, but they could not completely control the nobles who ruled the nomes. Still, they brought order, peace, and prosperity after the troubles of the First Intermediate Period. They encouraged trade and extended Egyptian power and influence northward toward Palestine and southward toward Ethiopia. They eventually moved their capital from Thebes back to the more defensible site of Memphis, but continued to honor Amon, a god identified with Thebes. Amon eventually became identified with Re, emerging as Amon-Re, Egypt's chief god.

Tales of the Middle Kindgom stress the kings' interest in justice and in the welfare of their people. Statues often show them burdened with care.

The New Kingdom (Empire) (1575–1087 B.C.E.) and After

The resurgent power of the local nobility and the erosion of central authority in the Thirteenth Dynasty mark the end of the Middle Kingdom and the beginning of the Second Intermediate Period (1786–1575 B.C.E.). About 1700 B.C.E. a people called the Hyksos—apparently a collection of Semitic peoples from the eastern Mediterranean—conquered the Nile Delta. About 1575 B.C.E. a dynasty from Thebes drove out the Hyksos and reunited Egypt, marking the beginning of the New Kingdom, or Empire Period.

Contact with the Hyksos brought the Egyptians new military techniques and weapons. The kings of the New Kingdom built a powerful army and pushed out Egypt's frontiers to the south and east. The Eighteenth Dynasty—whose most prominent king, Thutmose III (r. 1490–1436 B.C.E.) was the first to refer to himself as "pharaoh"—forged an empire that extended across Palestine and Syria to the upper Euphrates. Egyptian expansion was finally checked by the powerful Hittite empire of Asia Minor. The struggle between these powers weakened both. Egypt survived, but by the end of the Twentieth Dynasty, the last dynasty of the New Kingdom, its period of glory had passed. Throughout the Post–Empire period (1087–30 B.C.E.) it fell victim repeatedly to foreign invasion and rule.

Toward the end of the Eighteenth Dynasty, after the New Kingdom empire had reached its greatest extent, Egypt witnessed an interesting religious struggle. One result of the successful imperial ventures was to increase the power of the priests of Amon, making them a threat to the position of the pharaoh. When young Amenhotep IV (r. 1367–1350 B.C.E.) came to the throne, he apparently determined to resist the priesthood of Amon. Supported by his family and advisers, he broke with the worship of Amon-Re, devoting himself instead to the worship of the god Aton, the physical disk of the sun. He changed his name to Akhnaton ("it pleases Aton") and moved his capital from Thebes, the center of Amon worship, to an entirely new city—Akhtaton—about three hundred miles to the north at a place now called El Amarna.

The new god was different from any that had come before him, for he was believed to be universal, not merely Egyptian. Unlike the other gods, he had no cult statue, but was represented in painting and relief sculpture as the sun disk. The new religion, however, was more remote than the old. Only the pharaoh and his family worshiped Aton directly; the people worshiped the pharaoh. Universal claims for Aton were matched by intolerance of the worshipers of the other gods. Their temples were shut down, and the name of Amon-Re was chiseled from monuments on which it was carved. The pharaoh selected new people, sometimes even foreigners, to serve him, depriving the old priests of their posts and privileges.

Akhnaton's interest in religious reform led him to ignore foreign affairs, which proved disastrous. The Asian possessions of Egypt fell away, and this imperial decline and its economic consequences probably increased hostility to the new religion. When the king died, a strong counterrevolution swept away his life's work.

His chosen successor was soon put aside and replaced by Tutankhamen (r. 1347–1339 B.C.E.), the young husband of one of the daughters of Akhnaton. The new pharaoh restored the old religion and wiped out as much as he could of the memory of the worship of Aton. He restored Amon to the center of the Egyptian pantheon, abandoned El Amarna, and returned the capital to Thebes. His magnificent tomb, remarkably, survived almost fully intact until its discovery in 1922.

The priests of Amon and the Egyptian military regained power on Akhnaton's death. A general named Horemhab became king (r. 1335–1308? B.C.E.) and recovered much of the lost empire. He referred to Akhnaton as "the criminal of Akhtaton" and erased his name from the records. Akhnaton's city and memory disappeared for over three thousand years, to be rediscovered only by chance about a century ago.

Following Akhnaton, Egypt returned to its traditional gods and culture, but its mood turned gloomy. *The Book of the Dead*, a product of this late period, was a collection of spells to help the dead reach the next world safely, avoiding destruction by a hideous monster. Egypt itself would soon be devoured by powerful empires no less menacing.

Periods in Ancient Egyptian History (dynasties in Roman numerals)

ca. 3100–2700 B.C.E.	Early Dynastic Period (I–II)
ca. 2700–2200 B.C.E.	Old Kingdom (III–VI)
ca. 2200–2052 B.C.E.	First Intermediate Period (VII–X)
ca. 2052–1786 B.C.E.	Middle Kingdom (XI–XII)
ca. 1786–1575 B.C.E.	Second Intermediate Period (XIII–XVII)
ca. 1700 B.C.E.	Hyksos invasion
ca. 1575–1087 B.C.E.	New Kingdom (or Empire) (XVIII–XX)
ca. 1087–30 B.C.E.	Post-Empire (XXI–XXXI)

The "Israel Stele" of the Pharaoh Merenptah

These lines from a black granite stele set up about 1220 B.C.E. by the Pharaoh Merenptah (r. ca. 1223–1211 B.C.E.), son of Ramses II of the Nineteenth Egyptian dynasty, commemorate his victories over various peoples in the region. Scholars have identified Tehenu with the Libyans, Hatti with the Hittites, and Hurru with the Hurrians of northern Mesopotamia. The reference to Israel is the first outside the Bible and is generally believed to confirm the story of the Israelites' exodus from Egypt and their flight to Canaan (see Chapter 2).

Who was responsible for taking on the trouble and expense to inscribe this document on stone? What purpose or purposes was it meant to serve? How reliable is it likely to be as an accurate account of what took place?

Great rejoicing has risen in Egypt,
   Jubilation has issued from the towns of To-meri;
They recount the victories
   Which Merenptah wrought in Tehenu:
"How beloved he is, the victorious ruler!
   How exalted is the king among the gods!
How fortunate he is, the master of command!

Ah, how pleasant it is to sit when one is engaged in
   chatter!"
One may walk freely on the road,
   Without any fear in the hearts of men.
Fortresses are left to themselves;
   Wells are open, accessible to messengers;
The ramparts of the encircling wall are secure in the
   sunlight
   Until their watchmen awake.
The Medjay are stretched out in sleep,
   The Tjukten hunt in the fields as they wish. . . .
The princes lie prostrate, saying, "Salaam"!
   Not one lifts his head among the Nine Bows.
Destruction for Tehenu! Hatti is pacified;
   Canaan is plundered with every evil;
Ashkelon is taken; Gezer is captured;
   Yanoam is made non-existent;
Israel lies desolate; its seed is no more;
   Hurru has become a widow for To-meri;
All the lands in their entirety are at peace,
   Everyone who was a nomad has been curbed by King
   Merenptah.

Trans. by R. J. Williams in *Documents from Old Testament Times*, lines 33–58, p. 139.

Ancient Near Eastern Empires

In the time of the Eighteenth Dynasty in Egypt, new groups of peoples established themselves in the Near East: the Kassites in Babylonia, the Hittites in Asia Minor, and the Mitanni in northern Mesopotamia (see Map 1–2). The Kassites and Mitanni were warrior peoples who ruled as a minority over more civilized folk and absorbed their culture without changing it. The Hittites established a kingdom of their own and forged an empire that lasted two hundred years.

The Hittites

The Hittites arrived in Asia Minor about 2000 B.C.E. By about 1500 B.C.E. they had established a strong, centralized kingdom with a capital at Hattusas (near Ankara, the capital of modern Turkey). Between 1400 and 1200 B.C.E. they contested Egypt's control of Palestine and Syria, and by 1265 B.C.E. they were strong enough to merit a dynastic marriage to the daughter of the powerful Nineteenth Dynasty Pharaoh Ramses II (r. 1292–1225 B.C.E.). By 1200 B.C.E. their kingdom was gone, swept away by new Indo-European migrants. Neo-Hittite centers, however, flourished in Asia Minor and Mesopotamia for a few centuries longer.

In most respects the Hittites reflected the influence of the dominant Mesopotamian culture of the region. Their government, however, was different. Their kings did not claim to be divine or even to be the chosen representatives of the gods. In the early period the king's power was checked by a council of nobles, and the assembled army had to ratify his succession to the throne. The Hittites appear to have been responsible for a great technological advance, the smelting of iron. They also played an important role in transmitting the ancient cultures of Mesopotamia and Egypt to the Greeks, who lived on their frontiers.

The Assyrians

The fall of the Hittites was followed by the rise of the Assyrians, who established the first of a succession of powerful empires in the Near East and extended the influence of the region's ancient civilizations to new areas. The homeland of the Assyrians was in the valleys and hills of northern

tine, and Egypt to its southern frontier. They succeeded thanks to a large, well-disciplined army and a society that powerfully valued military virtues. Fierce and cruel, they boasted of their own brutality, at least in part to terrorize real and potential enemies.

Unlike earlier empires, the Assyrian Empire systematically and profitably exploited the area it held. The Assyrians used various methods of control, ranging from the mere collection of tribute to the stationing of garrisons in conquered territory to the scattering of entire populations away from their homelands (a fate that befell the people of the kingdom of Israel). Because of their military and administrative skills, the Assyrians were able to hold vast areas even as they absorbed the teachings of the older cultures under their sway.

In addition to maintaining their empire, the Assyrians had to defend it against the incursions of barbarians on its frontiers. In the seventh century B.C.E. this task so drained the overextended empire that it was left vulnerable to internal rebellion. A new dynasty in Babylon threw off Assyrian rule, joined with the rising kingdom of Media to the east (in modern Iran), and defeated the Assyrians, destroying Nineveh in 612 B.C.E. The successor kingdoms, the Chaldean (or Neo-Babylonian) and the Median, did not last long. By 539 B.C.E., they were swallowed by yet another great eastern empire, that of the Persians (see Chapter 4).

Mesopotamia and the area east of the Tigris River. They had a series of capitals, of which the great city of Nineveh (modern Mosul, Iraq) is perhaps the best known. They spoke a Semitic language and, from early on, were culturally a part of Mesopotamia.

Akkadians, Sumerians, Amorites, and Mitanni had each in turn dominated Assyria. When the Hittites defeated the Mitanni in the fourteenth century B.C.E., they effectively liberated the Assyrians, allowing them to establish themselves as an independent state. After 1000 B.C.E. the Assyrians began a period of steady expansion, and by 665 B.C.E. they controlled all of Mesopotamia, much of Asia Minor, Syria, Pales-

A reconstruction drawing of Nimrud, one of the capitals of the Assyrian Empire. Some elements of this drawing may be fanciful, but it gives a sense of what an Assyrian city looked like. [Courtesy of the Trustees of the British Museum. © The British Museum.]

Early Indian Civilization

To the east of Mesopotamia, beyond the Iranian plateau and the mountains of Baluchistan, the Asian continent bends sharply southward below the Himalayan mountain barrier to form the Indian subcontinent (see Map 1–3). Several sizable rivers flow west and south out of the Himalaya in Kashmir and the Punjab (*Panjab*, "five rivers"), merging into the single stream of the Indus River in Sind before emptying into the Indian Ocean. The headwaters of South Asia's other great river system—the Ganges and its tributaries—are also in the Himalayas, but flow south and east to the Bay of Bengal on the opposite side of the subcontinent.

The earliest evidence of a settled, Neolithic way of life on the subcontinent comes from the foothills of Sind and Baluchistan and dates to about 5500 B.C.E. with evidence of barley and wheat cultivation, baked brick dwellings, and, a bit later, domestication of animals such as goats, sheep, and cows, and, after about 4000 B.C.E., metal working. The subcontinent's earliest literate, urban civilization arose in the valley of the Indus River sometime after 2600, and by about 2300 B.C.E. was trading with Mesopotamia. Known as the Indus-Valley Culture (or the Harappan civilization, after the archaeological site at which it was first recognized), it lasted only a few centuries and left many still unanswered questions about its history and culture. The region's second

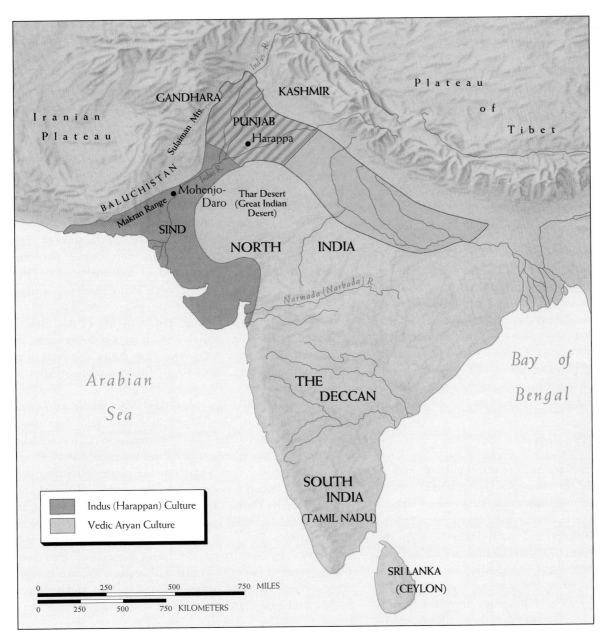

Map 1–3 Indus and Vedic Aryan cultures. Indus culture likely influenced the Vedic Aryans, even if the influence cannot be proved. Some scholars surmise, for example, that the fortified Aryan city of Hariyupiya, mentioned in later texts, may have been the same site as the older Indus city of Harappa.

Ancient Mohenjo-Daro, like most cities of the Indus Valley civilization, was built principally of mud brick. The structures are laid on straight lines; streets cross each other at right angles. The impression is one of order, prosperity, and civic discipline. [Borromeo/Art Resource, N.Y.]

identifiable civilization was of a very different character. Known as the Vedic Aryan civilization after the originally nomadic Indo-European (or "Aryan") immigrant people who founded it and their holy texts, or Vedas, it dates to about 1500 B.C.E. and endured for nearly a millenium without cities or writing, but with formidable religious and social traditions that commingled with older traditions in the subcontinent, notably that of the Indus culture, to form the Indian civilization as it has developed in the past two and a half millennia.

The Indus Civilization

No one knew of the existence of the Indus culture until archaeologists discovered it at the site of Harappa in the 1920s. Since then, some seventy cities, the largest being Harappa and Mohenjo-Daro, have been identified over a vast area from the Himalayan foothills west and south on the coasts of the Arabian Sea. This urban civilization had bronze tools, writing, covered drainage systems, and a diversified social and economic organization. Because it disappeared some time before 1500 B.C.E. and its writing is still undeciphered, it remains the least understood of the early river valley civilizations. Ar-

chaeological evidence and inferences from later Indian life, however, allow us to reconstruct something of its high and once thriving culture.

General Character The Indus culture covered an area many times larger than either Middle Kingdom Egypt or Third Dynasty Ur. Yet the archaeological finds show it to have been remarkably homogeneous. City layouts, building construction, highly developed weights and measures, seal inscriptions, fine patterned pottery and figurines, and even the burnt brick used for buildings and floodwalls are unusually uniform in all Indus towns, suggesting an integrated economic system and good internal communications.

Indus culture was also remarkably constant over time. Because the main cities and towns lay in river lowlands subject to periodic flooding, they were rebuilt often, each new level of construction closely following its precursor's pattern. Similarly, the Indus script, known from more than two thousand stamp seals and apparently using both pictographic and phonetic symbols, shows no evidence of change over time. This evidence of stability, regularity, and traditionalism has led some scholars to speculate that this far-flung society was controlled by a centralized government, perhaps a conservative (priestly) theocracy rather than a more unstable royal dynasty and court.

Cities Harappa and Mohenjo-Daro both apparently had populations of more than thirty-five thousand and were meticulously laid out on a similar plan. To the west of each stood a large, walled citadel on a raised rectangular platform about eight by fourteen hundred feet in size. East of this the town proper was laid out on a north-south, east-west grid of main avenues, some as much as thirty feet wide. The citadel apparently contained the main public buildings. An impressively large bath, with a brick-lined pool, a subterranean furnace, and columned porticoes, has been excavated at Mohenjo-Daro. Both sites have buildings tentatively identified as temples.

Each city boasted a large granary for food storage, with a cemetery laid out on the periphery of each. The town "blocks" formed by the main avenues were crisscrossed by small, less rigidly planned lanes, off which opened private houses of various sizes, sometimes of more than one story. The typical house was built around a central courtyard and presented only blank walls to the lanes or streets outside, an arrangement found in many Near Eastern and South Asian cities today.

Perhaps the most striking feature of these cities was a complex system of covered drains and sewers. Private houses were serviced by wells, bathrooms, and latrines, and the great bath at Mohenjo-Daro was filled from its own large well. The drainage system that served these facilities was an engineering feat unrivaled in the ancient world until the time of the Romans, nearly two thousand years later.

Economic Life   The economy of the Indus state or states was based on a thriving agriculture. The whole Indus region was apparently more densely vegetated and productive at that time than it is today. Wheat and barley were the main crops; rice, peas, lentils, sesame, dates, and cotton were also important. Cattle, dogs, cats, goats, sheep, and fowl were raised, and elephants and water buffalo were likely used as beasts of burden. The Indus Valley people wove cloth from cotton, made metal tools, and used the potter's wheel.

Evidence points to trade between the Indus culture and Mesopotamia. Indus stamp seals have been found in Mesopotamia, and Akkadian texts mention a "Melukka" region, perhaps the Indus basin, as a source of ivory, precious stones, and other wares. Excavations in the Persian Gulf indicate that the island of Bahrain may have been a staging point for Indus-Mesopotamian sea trade. Metals and semiprecious stones were apparently imported into the Indus region from present-day Iran and Afghanistan, as well as from Central Asia, from farther south on the Indian peninsula, and perhaps from Arabia. Similarities in artistic styles suggest that trade contacts resulted in cultural borrowings.

Material Culture   Among the most striking accomplishments of the Indus culture are a number of fine bronze and stone sculptures. Other evidence of the skill of Indus artisans can be seen in a variety of artifacts, including copper and bronze tools and vessels, black-on-red painted pottery, dressed stonework, stone and terra-cotta figurines and toys, silver vessels and ornaments, gold jewelry, and dyed woven fabric. Indus stamp seals, which provide the only examples of the still-undeciphered Indus script, also bear representations of animals, humans, and what are thought to be divine or semidivine beings. Similar figures are also found on painted pottery as well as in engravings on small copper tablets. From the surviving evidence, however, this art seems limited compared with that of Egypt or Mesopotamia. Except for some decorative brickwork, no monumental friezes, mosaics, or sculpture have been found.

Religion   The Indus remains give us somewhat more to speculate about in the religious realm, and until the Indus script is deciphered, speculation is necessary. The elaborate bath facilities suggest that ritual bathing and water purification rites were important, as they still are in India today. The stone images from the so-called "temples" of Mohenjo-Daro and the more common terra-cotta figurines from other sites also suggest links to later Indian religious practices and symbols. The many images of male animals such as the humped bull might be symbols of power and fertili-

Indus stone stamp seal. Note the familiar humped bull of India.
[© Scala/Art Resource, N.Y.]

ty or might indicate animal worship. Other animals depicted include tigers, snakes, and a unicornlike animal. A recurring image of a male figure with leafy headdress and horns, often seated in a posture associated later in India with yogic meditation, has been likened to the Vedic Aryan "Lord of All Creatures." He has features in common with the Hindu god Shiva, especially where he is depicted with three faces and an erect phallus. Also found in Indus artifacts are the pipal tree and the left-handed swastika, both symbols later important to Hindus.

Terra-cotta figurines of females, often pregnant or carrying a child, are suggestive of similar female images in several prehistoric cultures. As possible precursors of Shiva's consort (known as Devi, Durga, and other names), they too may represent an element of pre-Aryan religion that reemerged later to figure in "Hindu" culture. Yet other aspects of Indus religion—burial customs, for example—are not clearly related to later Indian practices. They remind us, however, that the Indus peoples, like all others, had their own ways of coming to terms ritually or aesthetically with the mysteries of birth, life, and death.

The Passing of Indus Civilization   Some time in the period from about 1800 to 1700 B.C.E., Indus civilization declined and disappeared. It is not clear whether or not its demise was related to the warlike Aryan invaders who may first have appeared in the upper Indus about 1800 B.C.E. and later used their horse-drawn chariots to subdue indigenous peoples and move in successive waves across the north Indian plains. Some scholars think it was destroyed by abnormal flooding (perhaps from careless damming of the Indus), changes in the course of the Indus, collapse of military power, or a long period of dessication even before the Aryans arrived. However that may be, the Indus culture disappeared by about 1700 and remains still too much in the shadows of pre-history for its proper influence to be gauged. Still, these predecessors of the Aryans likely made significant contributions to later life in the subcontinent in ways yet to be discovered.

The Vedic Aryan Civilization

By comparison with Indus civilization, we know more about the Aryan culture that effectively "refounded" Indian civilization around 1500 B.C.E. Yet unlike Indus civilization, it was not urban, leaving behind neither city ruins nor substantial artifacts beyond tools, weapons, and pottery. Virtually our only source of knowledge about ancient Aryan life is the "winged words" of the Vedas, the Aryan sacred texts—hence we know the culture as "Vedic." Although the latest Vedic texts date from perhaps 500 B.C.E., the earliest may go back to 1700 B.C.E. Transmitted orally through the centuries, no Vedas were written down until after the reintroduction of writing to India sometime after 700 B.C.E. (Indeed, until recently, writing down the Vedas at all was shunned in favor of an elaborate oral tradition of memorization and recitation among the Brahmans.) The Vedas are ritual, priestly, and speculative, not historical works. They tell us little about events but do offer insight into the religion, society, values, and thought of early Aryan India.

Veda, which means "knowledge," is the collective term for the texts still recognized today by most Indians as the holiest sources of their tradition. For Hindus, Veda is the eternal wisdom of primordial seers preserved for thousands of years in an unbroken tradition of oral transmission. We speak of "the Vedas" in the plural to refer to the four major compilations of Vedic ritual texts and the explanatory and speculative texts associated with each. The most significant of the four for the history of the early Aryans is the collection of 1,028 religious hymns known as the *Rig Veda*, which represent the oldest materials of the Vedas. The latest of these hymns date from ca. 1000 B.C.E., the oldest from perhaps 1700–1200 B.C.E., when the Aryans spread across the northern plains to the upper reaches of the Ganges.

"Aryan" is a different kind of term. The second-millennium invaders of northern India called themselves *Aryas* as opposed to the peoples that they conquered. Vedic Sanskrit, the language of the invaders, gave this word to later Sanskrit as a term for "noble" or "free-born" *(arya)*. The word is found also in old Iranian, or Persian, texts, and even the term *Iran* itself is derived from the Old Persian equivalent of arya. It was apparently the original name of peoples who migrated

out of the steppeland between Eastern Europe and Central Asia into Europe, Greece, Anatolia, the Iranian plateau, and India during the second and first millennia B.C.E. Those who came to India are thus more precisely designated *Indo-Aryans*, or *Vedic Aryans*.

In the nineteenth century, "Aryan" was the term applied to the widespread language group known more commonly today as *Indo-European*. To this widely distributed family belong Greek, Latin, the Romance and Germanic languages, the Slavic tongues, and the Indo-Iranian languages, including Persian and Sanskrit and their derivatives. The Nazi movement in twentieth-century Germany perversely misused "Aryan" to refer to a white "master race." Today *Aryan* is usually used only to identify the Indo-European speakers who invaded India and the Iranian plateau in the second millennium B.C.E., and in linguistics as a name for the Indo-Iranian languages.

"Aryanizing" of North India   The Vedic Aryans were seminomadic warriors who reached India through the mountain passes of the Hindu Kush. Theirs was probably a gradual migration of small tribal groups. They were horsemen and cattle herders rather than farmers and city builders. They left their mark not in material culture but in the changes that their conquests brought to the regions they overran: a new language, a new social organization, new techniques of warfare, and new religious forms and ideas.

Only the broad outlines of the early Aryans' gradual subjugation of northern India and their equally gradual shift from pastoral nomadism to settled agriculture and animal husbandry can be reconstructed. They penetrated first into the Punjab and the Indus Valley around 1800–1500 B.C.E., presumably in search of grazing lands for their cattle and other livestock. Their horses, chariots, and copper-bronze weapons likely gave them military superiority over the Indus peoples or their successors. Echos of early conflicts can be heard in some Rigvedic hymns. The god Indra, for example, is hailed as the warrior who smashes the fortifications of enemies (Indus citadels?) and slays the great serpent who had blocked the rivers (referring to the destruction of the dams that controlled the Indus waters?). The references to human rather than divine warriors in some later Rigvedic hymns may reflect actual historical events. One late hymn praises the king of the *Bharatas*, giving us the Indian name for modern India, *Bharat*, "land of the Bharatas."

During what is usually termed the *Rigvedic age* (ca. 1700–1000 B.C.E.) the newcomers settled in the Punjab and beyond, where they took up agriculture and stock breeding. The Thar desert blocked southward expansion, so their subsequent movement was to the east. How far they penetrated before 1000 B.C.E. is not clear, but their main locus remained the Punjab and the plains west of the Yamuna River. Then,

Hymn to Indra

This hymn celebrates the greatest deed ascribed to Indra, the slaying of the dragon Vritra to release the waters needed by people and livestock (which is also heralded at one point in the hymn as the act of creation itself). These waters are apparently those of the dammed-up rivers, but possibly also the rains as well. This victory also symbolizes the victory of the Aryans over the dark-skinned Dasas. *Note the sexual as well as water imagery. The* kadrukas *may be the bowls used for soma in the sacrifice. The* vajra *is Indra's thunderbolt; the name* Dasa *for the lord of the waters is also that used for the peoples defeated by the Aryans and for all enemies of Indra, of whom the* Pani *tribe is one.*

What are the main kinds of imagery used for Indra and his actions in the hymn? What divine acts does the hymn ascribe to Indra?

Indra's heroic deeds, indeed, will I proclaim, the first ones which the wielder of the vajra accomplished. He killed the dragon, released the waters, and split open the sides of the mountains.

He killed the dragon lying spread out on the mountain; for him Tvashtar fashioned the roaring vajra. Like bellowing cows, the waters, gliding, have gone down straightway to the ocean.

Showing off his virile power he chose soma; from the three *kadrukas* he drank of the extracted soma. The bounteous god took up the missile, the vajra; he killed the first-born among the dragons.

When you, O Indra, killed the first-born among the dragons and further overpowered the wily tricks *(maya)* of the tricksters, bringing forth, at that very moment, the sun, the heaven and the dawn—since then, indeed, have you not come across another enemy. Indra killed Vritra, the greater enemy, the shoulderless one, with his mighty and fatal weapon, the vajra. Like branches of a tree lopped off with an axe, the dragon lies prostrate upon the earth. . . .

Over him, who lay in that manner like a shattered reed flowed the waters for the sake of man. At the feet of the very waters, which Vritra had [once] enclosed with his might, the dragon [now] lay [prostrate]. . . .

With the Dasa as their lord and with the dragon as their warder, the waters remained imprisoned, like cows held by the Pani. Having killed Vritra, [Indra] threw open the cleft of waters which had been closed.

You became the hair of a horse's tail, O Indra, when he [Vritra] struck at your sharp-pointed vajra—the one god [eka deva] though you were. You won the cows, O brave one, you won soma; you released the seven rivers, so that they should flow. . . .

Indra, who wields the vajra in his hand, is the lord of what moves and what remains rested, of what is peaceful and what is horned. He alone rules over the tribes as their king; he encloses them as does a rim the spokes.

—*Rig Veda* 1.32

---

between about 1000 and 500 B.C.E., the *later Vedic age*, these Aryan Indians (they can no longer be considered a foreign people) spread across the plain between the Yamuna and the Ganges, and eastward. They cleared (probably by burning) the heavy forests that covered this region, and then settled there. They also moved farther northeast to the Himalayan foothills and southeast along the Ganges, in what was to be the cradle of subsequent Indian civilization. During this age the importance of the Punjab receded.

The Later Vedic period is also called the *Brahmanic age* because it was dominated by the priestly religion of the Brahman class, as evidenced in commentaries called the *Brahmanas* (ca. 1000–800 or 600 B.C.E.). It is also sometimes called the epic age because it provided the setting for India's two classical epics, the *Mahabharata* and the *Ramayana*. Both were composed much later, probably between 400 B.C.E. and 200 C.E., but contain older material and refer to older events. The *Mahabharata*, the world's longest epic poem, centers on

the rivalry of two Aryan clans in the region northwest of modern Delhi, perhaps around 900 B.C.E. The *Ramayana* tells of the legendary, dramatic adventures of King Rama, whose travels may at one level recall the movement of north Indian culture into southern India about the end of the Brahmanic period. Both epics reflect the complex cultural and social mixing of Aryan and other earlier subcontinent peoples.

By about 200 C.E., this mixing was to produce a distinctive new "Indian" civilization over most of the subcontinent. Its basis was clearly Aryan, but its language, society, and religion incorporated many non-Aryan elements. Harappan culture vanished, but both it and other regional cultures contributed to the formation of Indian culture as we know it.

Vedic Aryan Society Aryan society was apparently patrilineal—with succession and inheritance in the male line—and its gods were likewise predominantly male. Marriage appears to have been monogamous, and widows could remarry. Related families formed larger kin groups. The largest social grouping was the tribe, ruled by a chieftain or *raja* ("king" in Sanskrit), whose power was shared with a tribal council. In early Vedic days the ruler was chosen for his prowess; his chief responsibility was to lead in battle, and he had no priestly function or sacred authority. Beside him, a chief priest looked after the often elaborate sacrifices on which religious life centered. By the Brahmanic age the king, with the help of priests, had assumed the role of judge in legal matters. Whether he had this function earlier is not known. In this period the power of the priestly class increased, along with that of the king, who, with the sanction of the priestly establishment, became a hereditary ruler claiming divine qualities.

Although there were probably identifiable subgroups of warriors and priests, Aryan society seems originally to have had only two basic divisions: noble and common. The *Dasas*—the darker, conquered peoples—came to form a third group (together with those who intermarried with them) of the socially excluded. Over time, a more rigid scheme of four social classes (excluding the non-Aryan *Dasas*) evolved. By the late Rigvedic period, these four divisions, or *varnas*—the priestly *(Brahman)*, the warrior/noble *(Kshatriya)*, the peasant/tradesman *(Vaishya)*, and the servant *(Shudra)*—had become so basic as to be sanctioned explicitly in religious theory. Only the members of the three upper classes participated fully in social, political, and religious life. This scheme underlies the rigid caste system that later became fundamental to Indian society.

Material Culture   The early, seminomadic Aryans had little impressive material culture. They did not build cities or monuments as far as we know. A gray-painted pottery is one of the few physical remains of their culture. They lived simply in wood and thatch or, later, mud-walled dwellings. They measured wealth in cattle, and were accomplished at carpentry and bronze working (iron probably was not known in India before 1000 B.C.E.). They used gold for ornamentation and produced textiles from wool. In addition to animal husbandry, they cultivated some crops, especially grains. They were familiar with intoxicating drinks, including soma, used in religious rites, and a kind of mead.

References to singing, dancing, and various musical instruments suggest that music was a highly developed art and favored pastime in the Vedic period. Gambling appears to have been a popular and frequent vice. Betting on chariot racing may have attracted the more affluent, but it is dicing above all that we hear of in Vedic and epic texts. One of the few secular pieces among the Vedic hymns is a "Gambler's Lament," which closes with a plea to the dice: "Take pity on us. Do not bewitch us with your fierce magic. Let no one be trapped by the brown dice!"

The Brahmanic age is likewise poor in material remains. Urban culture remained undeveloped, although mud-brick towns appeared as new lands were cleared for cultivation. Established kingdoms with fixed capitals now existed. Trade was growing, especially along the Ganges, although there is no evidence of a coinage system. Later texts mention specialized groups of artisans, including goldsmiths, basketmakers, weavers, potters, and entertainers.

To judge from references to its common use by around 500 B.C.E., writing had been reintroduced to India some time earlier, perhaps about 700 B.C.E. Indian goods were again finding their way to Mesopotamia during this period, and writing may have returned to India from Mesopotamia along with traded goods. The prestige of oral transmission for the Vedas remained so high among the Brahman class, however, that, as noted before, writing continued to be scorned as an unworthy medium for truly sacred texts.

Religion   The main identifiable contributions of Vedic India to later history were religious. The Vedas reflect the broad development of Vedic-Brahmanic religion in the millenium after the coming of the first Aryans. They tell us primarily about the public cult and domestic rituals of the Aryan upper classes. Among the rest of the population, many Harappan and other non-Aryan practices and ideas likely continued to flourish. Apparently non-Aryan elements are visible occasionally even in the Vedic texts themselves, especially later ones such as the Upanishads (after ca. 800 B.C.E.), notably in their references to fertility and female deities, ritual pollution and ablutions, and the transmigration of the soul after death.

The central Vedic cult—controlled by priests serving a military aristocracy—remained dominant until the middle of the first millennium B.C.E. By that time other, perhaps older, religious forms were evidently asserting themselves among the populace. The increasing ritual formalism of Brahmanic religion provoked challenges both in popular practice and in religious thought that culminated in Buddhist, Jain, and Hindu traditions of piety and practice (see Chapter 2).

The earliest Indo-Aryans seem to have worshiped numerous gods, most of whom embodied or were associated with powers of nature. The Rigvedic hymns are addressed to anthropomorphic deities linked to natural phenomena such as the sky, the clouds, and the sun. These gods are comparable to those of ancient Greece (see Chapter 3) and are apparently distantly related to them through the Indo-European heritage the Greeks and Aryans shared. The name of the Aryan father-god *Dyaus*, for example, is linguistically related to the name of the Greek father-god, *Zeus*. In Vedic India, however, unlike Greece, the father-god had receded in importance before the developing cult of his children. Chief among them was Indra, god of war and the storm. A rowdy god not unlike the old Norse Thor, he led his heavenly warriors across the sky to slay dragons or other enemies with his thunderbolt in his hand.

Also of major importance was Varuna, who may have had connections with the later Iranian god Ahura Mazda (see Chapter 4) and the Greek god of the heavens, Uranos. Varuna was more remote from human affairs than Indra. Depicted as a regal figure seated on his heavenly throne, he guarded the cosmic order, *Rta*, which was both the law of nature and the universal moral law or truth. As the god who commanded particular awe and demanded righteous behavior, Varuna had characteristics of a supreme, omnipresent divinity.

Another prominent Vedic god was Agni, the god of fire (his name, which is the Sanskrit word for fire, is related to Latin *ignis*, "fire," and thus to English *ignite*). He had diverse roles. He mediated between heaven and earth through the fire sacrifice, and was thus the god of sacrifice and the priests. He was also god of the hearth, and thus of the home. Like flame itself, he was a mysterious deity about whose form and presence in all earthly fires there is much speculation in the Rig Veda.

Other Vedic gods include Soma, the god of the hallucinogenic soma plant and the drink made from it; Ushas, goddess of dawn (one of very few female deities); Yama, god of the dead; Rudra, the archer and storm god; Vishnu, a solar deity; and the sun god, Surya. The Vedic hymns praise each god they address as possessing almost all powers, including those associated with other gods.

Ritual sacrifice was the central focus of Vedic religion, its goal apparently to invoke the presence of the gods to whom an offering was made rather than to expiate sins or express thanksgiving. The drinking of soma juice, an intoxicant, was a prominent aspect of the sacrificial ritual. A recurring theme of the Vedic hymns that accompanied the rituals is the desire for the good things of this life: prosperity, health, and victory. Fire sacrifices, both public and domestic, were particularly important. There were also exclusively royal rituals, such as the elaborate, rarely performed horse sacrifice.

By Brahmanic times, a considerable body of mystical speculation had developed around the sacrificial ritual. The god, the offering, the sacrifice, and the sacrificer, for example, were all identified with one another. One Rigvedic hymn even describes the creation of the world as the sacrifice of a primordial being to himself by the lesser gods. The late Vedic texts also emphasize magical and cosmic aspects of ritual and sacrifice. Indeed, some of the *Brahmanas* maintain that only through exacting performance of the sacrifice is the world order maintained.

The word *Brahman*, originally used to designate the ritual utterance or word of power, came to refer also to the generalized divine power present in the sacrifice. In the Upanishads, some of the latest Vedic texts and the ones most concerned with speculation about the universe, *Brahman* was extended to refer to the Absolute, the transcendent principle of reality. As the guardian of ritual and the master of the sacred word, the priest was known throughout the Vedic Aryan

period by a related word, *Brahmana*, for which the English is *Brahman*. Echoes of these associations were to lend force in later Hindu tradition to the special status of the Brahman caste groups as the highest social class (see Chapter 4).

Early Chinese Civilization

Neolithic Origins in the Yellow River Valley

Agriculture began in China about 4000 B.C.E. in the basin of the southern bend of the Yellow River. This is the northernmost of East Asia's four great river systems. The others are the Yangtze in central China, the West River in southern China, and the Red River in what is today northern Vietnam (see Map 1–4). All drain eastward into the Pacific Ocean. In recent millennia, the Yellow River has flowed through a deforested plain, cold in winter and subject to periodic droughts. But in 4000 B.C.E., its climate was warmer, with forested highlands in the west and swampy marshes to the east. The bamboo rat that today can be found only in semitropical Southeast Asia lived along the Yellow River.

The chief crop of China's agricultural revolution was millet. A second agricultural development focusing on rice may have occurred on the Huai River between the Yellow River and the Yangtze near the coast. In time, wheat entered China from the west. The early Chinese cleared land and burned its cover to plant millet and cabbage and, later, rice and soybeans. When the soil became exhausted, fields were abandoned, and sometimes early villages were abandoned, too. Tools were of stone: axes, hoes, spades, and sickle-shaped knives. The early Chinese domesticated pigs, sheep, cattle, dogs, and chickens. Game was also plentiful, and hunting continued to be important to the village economy. In excavated village garbage heaps of ancient China are found the bones of deer, wild cattle,

Ancient India	
ca. 2250–1750 (2500–1500?) B.C.E.	Indus (Harappan) civilization (written script still undeciphered)
ca. 1800–1500 B.C.E.	Aryan peoples invade northwestern India
ca. 1500–1000 B.C.E.	Rigvedic period: composition of Rigvedic hymns; Punjab as center of Indo-Aryan civilization
ca. 1000–500 B.C.E.	Later Vedic period: Doab as center of Indo-Aryan civilization
ca. 1000–800/ 600 B.C.E.	Composition of *Brahmanas* and other Vedic texts
ca. 800–500 B.C.E.	Composition of major Upanishads
ca. 700–500 B.C.E.	Probable reintroduction of writing
ca. 400 B.C.E.–200 C.E.	Composition of great epics, the *Mahabharata* and *Ramayana*

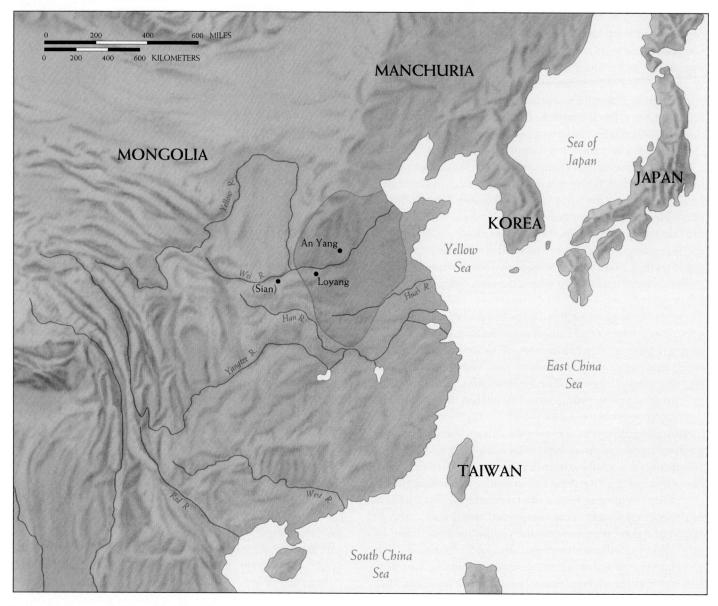

Map 1–4 Bronze Age China during the Shang dynasty, 1766–1050 B.C.E. An Yang was a late Shang dynasty capital. Sian and Loyang were the capitals of the Western and the Eastern Chou.

antelopes, rhinoceros, hares, and marmots. Grain was stored in pottery painted in bold, geometric designs of red and black. This pottery gave way to a harder, thin black pottery, made on a potter's wheel, whose use spread west along the Yellow River and south to the Yangtze. The tripodal shapes of Neolithic pots prefigure later Chinese bronzes.

The earliest cultivators lived in wattle-and-daub pit dwellings with wooden support posts and sunken, plastered floors. Their villages were located in isolated clearings along slopes of river valleys. Archaeological finds of weapons and remains of earthen walls suggest tribal warfare between villages. Of the religion of these people, little is known, although

some evidence indicates the worship of ancestral spirits. They practiced divination by applying heat to a hole drilled in the shoulder bone of a steer or the undershell of a tortoise, and then interpreting the resulting cracks in the bone. They buried their dead in cemeteries with jars of food. Tribal leaders wore rings and beads of jade.

Early Bronze Age: The Shang

The traditional history of China tells of three ancient dynasties: Hsia (2205–1766 B.C.E.), Shang (1766–1050 B.C.E.), and Chou (1050–256 B.C.E.). Until early in this century, modern historians saw the first two as legendary. Then, in the 1920s, archaeological excavations at "the wastes of Yin" near present-day An Yang uncovered the ruins of a walled city that had been a late Shang capital (see Map 1–4). Other Shang cities have been discovered more recently. The ruins contained the archives of the department of divination of the Shang court, with thousands on thousands of "oracle bones" incised with archaic Chinese writing. The names of kings on the bones fit almost perfectly those of the traditional historical record. The recognition that the Shang actually existed has led historians to suggest that the Hsia may also have been an actual dynasty. Perhaps the Hsia was a late Neolithic black-pottery kingdom; perhaps it already had bronze and was responsible for the earliest, still missing stage of Chinese writing.

The characteristic political institution of Bronze Age China was the city-state. The largest was the Shang capital, which, frequently moved, lacked the monumental architecture of Egypt or Mesopotamia. The walled city contained public buildings, altars, and the residences of the aristocracy; it was surrounded by a sea of Neolithic tribal villages. By late Shang times, several such cities were spotted across the north China plain. The Shang kings possessed political, economic, social, and religious authority. When they died, they were sometimes succeeded by younger brothers and sometimes by sons. The rulers of other city-states acknowledged their authority.

The military aristocracy went to war in chariots, supported by levies of foot soldiers. Their weapons were spears and powerful compound bows. Accounts tell of armies of three or four thousand troops and of a battle involving thirteen thousand. The Shang fought against barbarian tribes and, occasionally, against other city-states in rebellion against Shang rule. Captured prisoners were enslaved.

The three most notable features of Shang China were writing, bronzes, and the appearance of social classes. Scribes at the Shang court kept records on strips of bamboo, but these have not survived. What have survived are inscriptions on bronze artifacts and the oracle bones. Some bones contain the question put to the oracle, the answer, and the outcome of the matter. Representative questions were: Which ancestor is causing the king's earache? If the king goes hunting at Ch'i, will there be a disaster? Will the king's child be a son? If the king sends his army to attack an enemy, will the deity help him? Was a sacrifice acceptable to ancestral deities?

What we know of Shang religion is based on the bones. The Shang believed in a supreme "Deity Above," who had authority over the human world. There were also lesser natural deities—the sun, moon, earth, rain, wind, and the six clouds—who served at the court of the Deity Above. Even the Shang king sacrificed not to the Deity Above but to his ancestors, who interceded with the Deity Above on the king's behalf. Kings, while alive at least, were not considered divine but were the high priests of the state.

In Shang times, as later, religion in China was closely associated with cosmology. The Shang people observed the movements of the planets and stars and reported eclipses. Celestial happenings were seen as omens from the gods. The chief cosmologists also recorded events at the court. The Shang calendar had a month of 30 days and a year of 360 days. Adjustments were made periodically by adding an extra month. The calendar was used by the king to tell his people when to sow and when to reap.

Bronze appeared in China about 2000 B.C.E., a thousand years later than in Mesopotamia and five hundred years later than in India. The Shang likely developed bronze technology independently, however, because Shang methods of casting were more advanced than those of Mesopotamia, and because the designs on its bronzes emerged directly from those of the preceding black-pottery culture. Bronze was used for weapons, armor, and chariot fittings, and for a variety of ceremonial vessels of amazing fineness and beauty.

Among the Shang, as with all the early river-valley civilizations, the increasing control of nature through agriculture and metallurgy was accompanied by the emergence of a

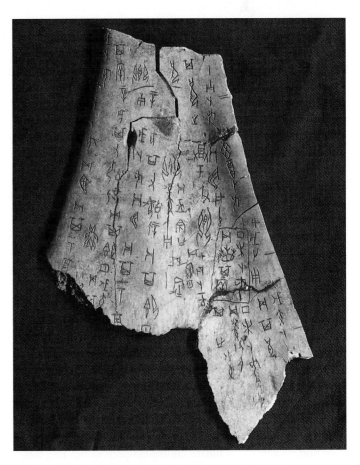

Inscribed oracle bone from the Shang Dynasty city of An Yang. [From the Collection of the C.V. Starr East Asian Library, Columbia University]

rigidly stratified society in which the many were compelled to serve the few. A monopoly of bronze weapons enabled aristocrats to exploit other groups. A hierarchy of class defined life in the Chinese city-state. The king and the officials of his court lived within the walled city. Their houses were spacious, built above the ground with roofs supported by rows of wooden pillars, resting on foundation stones. Their lifestyle was, for ancient times, opulent. They wore fine clothes, feasted at banquets, and drank wine from bronze vessels. In contrast, a far larger population of agricultural workers lived outside the city in cramped pit dwellings. Their life was meager and hard. Archaeological excavations of their underground hovels have uncovered only clay pots.

Nowhere was the gulf between the royal lineage and the baseborn more apparent than it was in the Shang institution of human sacrifice. One Shang tomb 39 feet long, 26 feet wide, and 26 feet deep contained the decapitated bodies of humans, horses, and dogs, as well as ornaments of bone, stone, and jade. When a king died, hundreds of slaves or prisoners of war, sometimes together with those who had served the king during his lifetime, might be buried with him. Sacrifices also were made when a palace or an altar was built.

Later Bronze Age: The Western Chou

To the west of the area of Shang rule, in the valley of the Wei River, a tributary of the Yellow River, lived the Chou people. Culturally closer to the Neolithic black-pottery people, they were less civilized and more warlike than the Shang. References to the Chou in the Shang oracle bones indicate that the Shang had relations with them—sometimes friendly, sometimes hostile. According to the traditional historical record, the last Shang kings were weak, cruel, and tyrannical. By 1050 B.C.E., they had been debilitated by campaigns against nomads in the north and rebellious tribes in the east. Taking advantage of this opportunity, the Chou made alliances with disaffected city-states and swept in, conquering the Shang.

In most respects, the Chou continued the Shang pattern of life and rule. The agrarian-based city-state continued to be the basic unit of society, and it is estimated that there were about two hundred of them in the eighth century B.C.E. The Chou social hierarchy was not unlike that of the Shang, with kings and lords at the top, officials and warriors below them, and peasants and slaves at the bottom. Slaves served primarily as

Bronze vessel of the Shang Dynasty. The little elephant on top forms the handle of the lid. Wine was poured through the spout formed by the big elephant's trunk. [The Freer Gallery of Art, Smithsonian Institution, Washington D.C.]

domestic servants. Themselves backward, the Chou assimilated Shang culture, continuing without interruption the development of China's ideographic writing. The Chou also maintained the practice of casting bronze ceremonial vessels, but their vessels lack the fineness that set the Shang above the rest of the Bronze Age world.

The Chou kept their capital in the west but set up a secondary capital at Loyang, along the southern bend of the Yellow River (see Map 1–4). They appointed their kinsmen or other aristocratic allies to rule in other city-states. Blood or lineage ties were essential to the Chou pattern of rule. The Chou king was the head of the senior branch of the family. He performed the sacrifices to the Deity Above for the entire family. The rankings of the lords of other princely states reflected their degree of closeness to the senior line of Chou kings.

One difference between the Shang and the Chou was in the nature of the political legitimacy each claimed. The Shang kings, descended from shamanistic (priestly) rulers, had an in-built religious authority and needed no theory to justify their rule. But the Chou, having conquered the Shang, needed a rationale for why they, and not the Shang, were now the rightful rulers. Their argument was that Heaven (the name for the supreme being that gradually replaced the Deity Above during the early Chou), appalled by the wickedness of the last Shang king, had withdrawn its mandate to rule from the Shang, awarding it instead to the Chou. This concept of the Mandate of Heaven was subsequently invoked by every dynasty in China down to the twentieth century. The ideograph for Heaven is related to that for man, and the concept initially had human, or anthropomorphic, attributes. In the later Chou, however, although it continued to be viewed as having a moral will, Heaven became less anthropomorphic and more of an abstract metaphysical force.

Iron Age: The Eastern Chou

In 771 B.C.E. the Wei valley capital of the Western Chou was overrun by barbarians. The explanation of the event in Chi-

Chinese Writing

The Chinese system of writing dates back at least to the Shang dynasty (1766–1050 B.C.E.), when animal bones and tortoise shells (the so-called oracle bones) were incised for the purpose of divination. About half of the three thousand characters used in Shang times have been deciphered. They evolved over the centuries into the fifty thousand characters found in the largest dictionaries. But even today only about three or four thousand are in common use. A scholar may know twice that number.

Characters developed from little pictures. Note the progressive stylization. By 200 B.C.E., the writing had become standardized and close to the modern form of the printed character.

	Shang (1400 B.C.E.)	Chou (600 B.C.E.)	Seal Script (200 B.C.E.)	Modern
Sun				
Moon				
Tree				
Bird				
Mouth				
Horse				

Other characters combined two pictures to express an idea. The following examples use modern characters:

Sun	日	+ moon	月	= bright	明
Mouth	口	+ bird	鳥	= to chirp	鳴
Woman	女	+ child	子	= good	好
Tree	木	+ sun	日	= east	東

It was a matter of convention that the sun behind a tree meant the rising sun in the east and not the setting sun in the west.

Characters were formed several other ways. In one, a sound element was combined with a meaning element. Chinese has many homonyms, or words with the same sound. The character 台, for example, is read *tai* and means "elevation" or "to raise up." But in spoken Chinese, there are other words with the same sound that mean "moss," "trample," "a nag," and "idle." Thus

Tai	台	+ grass	艹	= moss	苔
Tai	台	+ foot	足	= trample	跆
Tai	台	+ horse	馬	= a nag	駘
Tai	台	+ heart	心	= idle	怠

In each case the sound comes from the 台, and the meaning from the other element. Note that the 台 may be at the bottom, the top, or the right. This positioning, too, is a matter of convention.

Tables by A. Craig; calligraphy by Teruko Craig.

---

nese tradition calls to mind the story of "the boy who cried wolf." The last Western Chou king was so infatuated with a favorite concubine that he repeatedly lit bonfires signaling a barbarian attack. His concubine would clap her hands in delight at the sight of the army assembled in martial splendor. But the army tired of the charade, and when invaders actually came, the king's beacons were ignored. The king was killed and the Chou capital sacked. The heir to the throne, with some members of the court, escaped to the secondary capital at Loyang, two hundred miles to the east and just south of the bend in the Yellow River, beginning the Eastern Chou period.

The first phase of the Eastern Chou, sometimes called the Spring and Autumn period after a classic history by that name, lasted until 481 B.C.E. After their flight to Loyang, the Chou kings were never able to reestablish their old authority.

Loyang remained a center of culture and ritual observances, but by the early seventh century B.C.E., its political power was nominal. Kinship and religious ties to the Chou house had worn thin, and it no longer had the military strength to reimpose its rule. During the seventh and sixth centuries B.C.E. the political configuration was an equilibrium of many small principalities on the north-central plain surrounded by larger, wholly autonomous territorial states along the borders of the plain (see Map 1–5). The larger states consolidated the areas within their borders, absorbed tribal peoples, and expanded, conquering states on their periphery.

To defend themselves against the more aggressive territorial states, and in the absence of effective Chou authority, smaller states entered defensive alliances. The earliest alliance, of 681 B.C.E., was directed against the half-barbarian state of Ch'u, which straddled the Yangtze in the south.

Human Sacrifice in Early China

By the seventh century B.C.E., *human sacrifice was less frequent in China, but still happened. This poem was composed when Duke Mu of the state of Ch'in died in 631. (For want of better terms, Chinese titles are usually translated into roughly equivalent titles among the English nobility.) Were human feelings different, as Professor K. C. Chang has asked, a thousand years earlier during the Shang? The poem suggests that despite religious belief and the honor accorded the victims, they may not have gone gladly to the grave. Note the identification of Heaven with "that blue one," the sky.*

We believe today that it is honorable to die in war for one's nation. How is that different from dying to serve one's lord in the afterlife?

"Kio" sings the oriole
As it lights on the thorn-bush.
Who went with Duke Mu to the grave?
Yen-hsi of the clan Tsu-chu.
Now this Yen-hsi
Was the pick of all our men;

But as he drew near the tomb-hole
His limbs shook with dread.
That blue one, Heaven,
Takes all our good men.
Could we but ransom him
There are a hundred would give their lives.
"Kio" sings the oriole
As it lights on the mulberry-tree.
Who went with Duke Mu to the grave?
Chung-hang of the clan Tsu-chu.
Now this Chung-hang
Was the sturdiest of all our men;
But as he drew near the tomb-hole
His limbs shook with dread.
That blue one, Heaven,
Takes all our good men.
Could we but ransom him
There are a hundred would give their lives.

From *The Book of Songs*, trans. by Arthur Waley (New York: Grove Press, 1960), p. 311.

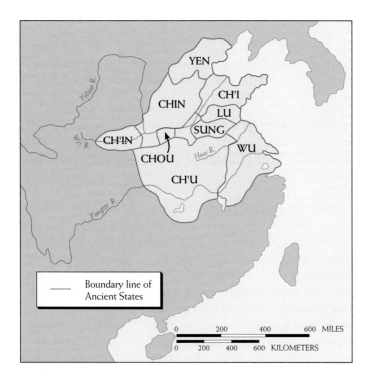

Map 1–5 Early Iron Age territorial states in China during the sixth century B.C.E. After the fall of the Western Chou in 771 B.C.E., large territorial states formed in China that became increasingly independent of the later Chou kings.

Princes and lords of smaller states elected as their *hegemon* (or military overlord) the lord of a northern territorial state and pledged him their support. At the formal ceremony that established the alliance, a bull was sacrificed. The hegemon and other lords smeared its blood on their mouths and before the gods swore oaths to uphold the alliance. That the oaths were not always upheld can be surmised from the Chinese expression "to break an oath while the blood is still wet on one's lips."

During the next two centuries, alliances shifted and hegemons changed. At best, alliances only slowed down the pace of military aggrandizement.

The second phase of the Eastern Chou is known as the Warring States period after a chronicle of the same name treating the years from 401 to 256 B.C.E. By the fifth century B.C.E., all defensive alliances had collapsed. Strong states swallowed their weaker neighbors. The border states grew in size and power. Interstate stability disappeared. By the fourth century B.C.E., only eight or nine great territorial states remained as contenders. The only question was which one would defeat the others and go on to unify China.

Three basic changes in Chinese society contributed to the rise of large territorial states. One was the expansion of population and agricultural lands. The walled cities of the Shang and Western Chou had been like oases in the wilds, bounded by plains, marshes, and forests. Game was plentiful; thus, hunting, along with sheep and cattle breeding, supplemented agriculture. But in the Eastern Chou, as population grew, wilds began to disappear, the economy became almost entirely agricultural, and hunting became an aristocratic pastime. Friction arose over boundaries as states began to abut. These changes accelerated in the late sixth century B.C.E. after the start of the Iron Age. With iron tools, farmers cleared new lands and plowed deeper, raising yields and increasing agricultural surpluses. Irrigation and drainage canals became important for the first time. Serfs gave way to independent farmers, who bought and sold land. By the third century B.C.E., China had about 20 million people, making it the most populous country in the world, a distinction it has never lost.

A second development was the rise of commerce. Roads built for war were used by merchants. Goods were transported by horses, oxcarts, riverboats, and the camel, which entered China in the third century B.C.E. The products of one region were traded for those of another. Copper coins joined bolts of silk and precious metals as media of exchange. Rich merchants rivaled in lifestyle the landowning lower nobility. New outer walls were added to cities to provide for expanded merchant quarters. Bronze bells and mirrors, clay figurines, lacquer boxes, and musical instruments found in late Chou tombs give ample evidence that the material and artistic culture of China leaped ahead during this period, despite its endemic wars.

A third change that doomed the city-state was the rise of a new kind of army. The war chariots of the old aristocracy, practical only on level terrain, gave way to cavalry armed with crossbows. Most of the fighting was done by conscript foot soldiers. Armies of the territorial states numbered in the hundreds of thousands. The old nobility gave way to professional commanders. The old aristocratic etiquette, which governed behavior even in battle, gave way to military tactics that were bloody and ruthless. Prisoners were often massacred.

Change also affected government. Lords of the new territorial states began to style themselves as kings, taking the title that previously only Chou royalty had enjoyed. At some courts, the hereditary nobility began to decline, supplanted by ministers appointed for their knowledge of statecraft. To survive, new states had to transform their agricultural and commercial wealth into military strength. To collect taxes and conscript soldiers, and to administer the affairs of state, required records and literate officials. Academies were established to fill the need. Beneath the ministers, a literate bureaucracy developed. Its members were referred to as *shih*, a term that had once meant "warrior" but gradually came to mean "scholar-bureaucrat." The *shih* were of mixed social origins, including petty nobility, literate members of the old warrior class, landlords, merchants, and rising commoners. From this class, as we will see in Chapter 2, came the philosophers who created the "one hundred schools" and transformed the culture of China.

The Rise of Civilization in the Americas

During the last ice age the Bering region between Siberia and Alaska was dry land. Sometime before twelve thousand years ago, and perhaps as early as thirty thousand years ago, humans crossed this land bridge, probably in several migrations. Over many centuries these Asian immigrants moved south and east until they eventually crossed the more than eleven thousand miles to the tip of South America and the more than four thousand miles to the eastern regions of North America. In light of the vast distances and imposing geographic barriers involved, these ancient migrations must have

Early China

4000 B.C.E.	Neolithic agricultural villages
1766 B.C.E.	Bronze Age city-states, aristocratic charioteers, pictographic writing
771 B.C.E.	Iron Age territorial states
500 B.C.E.	Age of philosophers
221 B.C.E.	China is unified

been as heroic as any in human history. From them a wide variety of original American cultures and many hundreds of languages arose.

The earliest immigrants to the Americas, like all other Paleolithic peoples, lived by hunting, fishing, and gathering. At the time of the initial migrations, herds of large game animals such as mammoths were plentiful. By the end of the ice age, however, mammoths and many other forms of game had become extinct in the Americas. Compared to Africa and Eurasia, many parts of North and South America were poor in animal resources and the rich source of protein they provide. Neither horses nor cattle populated the American continents. Where fishing or small game were not sufficiently plentiful, people had to rely on protein from vegetable sources. One result was that the original Americans participated in the Neolithic revolution in a quite remarkable manner. American production of plants providing protein far outpaced that of European agriculture. In this regard one of the most important early developments was the cultivation of maize. Wher-

Early Civilizations of Mesoamerica

1500–400 B.C.E.	The Olmec
200 C.E.–750 C.E.	The Classic period in Central Mexico. Dominance of Teotihuacán in the Valley of Mexico and Monte Alban in the Valley of Oaxaca
150 C.E.–900 C.E.	The Classic period of Maya civilization in the Yucatán and Guatemala

ever maize could be extensively grown, a major ingredient in the food supply was secured. The cultivation of maize appears to have been in place in Mexico by approximately 4000 B.C.E. and to have developed farther south somewhat later. Other important foods were potatoes (developed in the Andes), manioc, squash, beans, peppers, and tomatoes. Many of these foods entered the diet of Europeans, Asians, and other peoples after the European conquest of the Americas in the sixteenth century C.E.

Eventually four areas of relatively dense settlement emerged in the Americas. One of these, in the Pacific Northwest in the area around Puget Sound, depended on the region's extraordinary abundance of fish rather than on agriculture; this area did not develop urbanized states. Another was the Mississippi valley, where, based on maize agriculture, the inhabitants developed a high level of social and political integration that had collapsed several centuries before European contact. The other two, Mesoamerica and the Andean region of South America, saw the emergence of strong, long-lasting states. In other regions with maize agriculture and settled village life—notably the North American Southwest—food supplies might have been too insecure to support the development of states.

Chapter 15 examines Mesoamerican and Andean civilization in detail. Here we give only a brief overview of their development. Mesoamerica, which extends from the central part of modern Mexico into Central America, is a region of great geographical diversity, ranging from tropical rainforest to semiarid mountains (see Map 1–6). Archaeologists tradi-

Olmec Head. This colossal head, now in the Museo Nacional de Antropología in Mexico City, was excavated at San Lorenzo. Carved of basalt, it may be a portrait of an Olmec ruler. Olmec civilization thrived between 1500 and 800 B.C.E. [Josephius Daniels/Photo Researchers, Inc.]

Early Civilization of the Andes

c. 2750 B.C.E.	Monumental architecture at Aspero
800–200 B.C.E.	Chavín (Early) Horizon
200 B.C.E.–600 C.E.	Early Intermediate period (Moche on the northern coast of Peru, Nazca on the southern coast)

tionally divide its preconquest history into three broad periods: Preclassic or Formative (2000 B.C.E.–150 C.E.), Classic (150–900 C.E.), and Post-Classic (900–1521). The earliest Mesoamerican civilization, that of the Olmecs, arose during the Preclassic on the Gulf Coast beginning approximately 1500 B.C.E. The Olmec centers at San Lorenzo (c. 1200–c. 900 B.C.E.) and La Venta (c. 900–c. 400 B.C.E.) exhibit many of the characteristics of later Mesoamerican cities, including the symmetrical arrangement of large platforms, plazas, and other monumental structures along a central axis and possibly courts for the ritual ball game played throughout Mesoamerica at the time of the Spanish conquest. Writing developed in Mesoamerica during the late Formative period. As we will see in Chapter 15, succeeding civilizations—including the Classic period civilization of Teotihuacan, the Post-Classic civilizations of the Toltecs and Aztecs, and the Classic and Post-Classic civilization of the Mayas—created large cities, developed sophisticated calendar systems, and were organized in complex social and political structures.

The Andean region is one of dramatic contrasts. Along its western edge, the narrow coastal plain is one of the driest deserts in the world. The Andes rise abruptly from the coastal plain and then descend gradually into the Amazon basin to the east. Agriculture is possible on the coast only in the valleys of the many rivers that flow from the Andes into the Pacific. The earliest monumental architecture in the Andean region, built on the coast at the site of Aspero by people who depended on a combination of agriculture and the Pacific's rich marine resources, dates to about 2750 B.C.E., contemporary with the Great Pyramids of Egypt's Old Kingdom.

From 800 B.C.E. to 200 B.C.E. a civilization associated with the site of Chavín de Huantar in the highlands of Peru exerted great influence in the Andes. Artifacts in the distinctive Chavín style can be found over a large area dating to this period, which archaeologists call the Early Horizon. This was a time of technical innovation in many areas, including pottery, textiles, and metallurgy. Whether the spread of the Chavín style represents actual political integration or the influence of

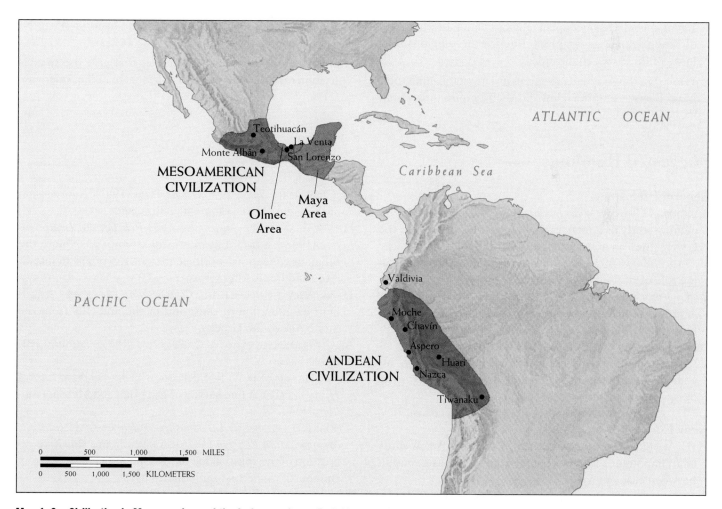

Map 1-6 Civilization in Mesoamerica and the Andean region. Both Mesoamerica and the Andean region of South America saw the development of a series of civilizations beginning between 1500 and 1000 B.C.E.

a strong religious center is not known. The period following the decline of Chavín, which archaeologists call the Early Intermediate period, saw the development of distinctive cultures in several regions. Notable among these are the Moche culture on the northern coast of Peru and the Nazca culture on the southern coast. A second period of transregional integration—called the Middle Horizon—occurred around 600 C.E., this time probably associated with empires centered on the highland sites of Huari and Tiahuanaco. The succeeding Late Intermediate period was dominated on the northern coast of Peru by the Chimu successors of the Moche state. This period ended with the founding of the vast, tightly controlled empire of the Incas in the fourteenth and fifteenth centuries C.E.

Review Questions

1. How was life during the Paleolithic Age different from that in the Neolithic Age? What advances in agriculture and human development had taken place by the end of the Neolithic era? Is it valid to speak of a "Neolithic Revolution"?

2. What defines civilization? What are the similarities and differences among the world's earliest civilizations?

3. What general conclusions can you draw about the differences in the political and intellectual outlooks of the civilizations of Egypt and Mesopotamia? Compare especially Egyptian and Mesopotamian religious views. In what ways did the regional geography influence the religious outlooks of these two civilizations?

4. Why were the Assyrians so successful in establishing their Near Eastern empire? How did their empire differ from that of the Hittites or Egyptians? In what ways did this empire benefit the civilized Middle East? Why did the Assyrian empire ultimately fail to survive?

5. How does the early history of Indian civilization differ from that of the river valley civilizations of China, Mesopotamia, and Egypt? What does the evidence available suggest were the social, economic, and political differences between the Indus civilization and the Vedic Aryan civilization?

6. What were the stages of early Chinese history? What led each to evolve toward the next?

7. What conclusions about the factors that give rise to civilization can you draw from its appearance in the Americas?

Suggested Readings

General Prehistory

V. GORDON CHILDE, *What Happened in History* (1946). A pioneering study of human prehistory and history before the Greeks from an anthropological point of view.

M. EHRENBERG, *Women in Prehistory* (1989). An account of the role of women in early times.

D. C. JOHNSON AND M. R. EDEY, *Lucy: The Beginning of Mankind* (1981). An account of the African origins of humans.

CHARLES L. REDMAN, *The Rise of Civilization* (1978). An attempt to use the evidence provided by anthropology, archaeology, and the physical sciences to illuminate the development of early urban society.

Near East

M. E. AUBER, *The Phoenicians and the West* (1996). A new study of an important sea-going people who served as a conduit between east and west.

BEN-TOR, ED., *The Archaeology of Ancient Israel* (1992). A useful and up-to-date survey.

H. CRAWFORD, *Sumer and the Sumerians* (1991). A discussion of the oldest Mesopotamian civilization.

HENRI FRANKFORT, *Ancient Egyptian Religion: An Interpretation* (1948). A brief but masterful attempt to explore the religious conceptual world of ancient Egyptians in intelligible and interesting terms.

HENRI FRANKFORT, ET AL., *Before Philosophy* (1949). A brilliant examination of the mind of the ancients from the Stone Age to the Greeks.

ALAN GARDINER, *Egypt of the Pharaohs* (1961). A sound narrative history.

W. W. HALLO AND W. K. SIMPSON, *The Ancient Near East: A History* (1971). A fine survey of Egyptian and Mesopotamian history.

THORKILD JACOBSEN, *The Treasures of Darkness: A History of Mesopotamian Religion* (1976). A superb and sensitive re-creation of the spiritual life of Mesopotamian peoples from the fourth to the first millennium B.C.E.

J. N. POSTGATE, *Early Mesopotamia* (1992). An excellent study of Mesopotamian economy and society from the earliest times to about 1500 B.C.E., helpfully illustrated with drawings, photos, and translated documents.

JAMES B. PRITCHARD, ED., *Ancient Near Eastern Texts Relating to the Old Testament* (1969). A good collection of documents in translation with useful introductory material.

D. B. REDFORD, *Akhenaten* (1987). A study of the controversial religious reformer.

W. F. SAGGS, *Everyday Life in Babylonia and Assyria,* rev. ed. (1987). A new edition of a classic work.

W. F. SAGGS, *The Might That Was Assyria* (1984). A history of the northern Mesopotamian empire and a worthy companion to the author's account of the Babylonian empire in the south.

B. G. TRIGGER ET AL., *Ancient Egypt: A Social History* (1982).

JOHN A. WILSON, *Culture of Ancient Egypt* (1956). A fascinating interpretation of the civilization of ancient Egypt.

India

D. P. AGRAWAL, *The Archaeology of India* (1982). A fine survey of the problems and data. Detailed, but with excellent summaries and brief discussions of major issues.

B. AND R. ALLCHIN, *The Birth of Indian Civilization: India and Pakistan Before 500 B.C.* (1968). A one-volume summary of prehistoric India from an archaeological perspective.

W. T. DE BARY ET AL., COMP., *Sources of Indian Tradition* (1958; 2nd rev. ed., 2 vols., New York, 1988). A fine anthology of original texts in translation from all periods of Indian civilization.

A. L. BASHAM, *The Wonder That Was India,* 2nd rev. ed. (1963). Chapters 1 and 2 provide a readable and carefully done introduction to ancient India through the Aryan culture. Still the classic survey.

E. C. L. DURING CASPERS, "Sumer, Coastal Arabia and the Indus Valley in Protoliterate and Early Dynastic Eras," *JESHO* 22, 2 (1979): 121–135.

C. CHAKRABORTY, *Common Life in the Rigveda and Atharvaveda—An Account of the Folklore in the Vedic Period* (1977). An interesting attempt to reconstruct everyday life in the Vedic period from the principal Vedic texts.

D. D. KOSAMBI, *Ancient India: A History of Its Culture and Civilization* (1965). The most readable survey history of India to the fourth century C.E. See Chapters 2–4 on prehistoric, Indus, and Aryan culture.

W. D. O'FLAHERTY, *The Rig Veda: An Anthology* (1981). An excellent selection of Vedic texts in prosaic but very careful translation, with helpful notes on the texts.

J. E. SCHWARTZBERG, ED., *A Historical Atlas of South Asia* (1978). The definitive reference work for historical geography. Includes chronological tables and substantive essays.

R. L. SINGH, ED., *India: A Regional Geography* (1971). An excellent reference source for each of the major regions of the subcontinent.

China

K. C. CHANG, *The Archeology of Ancient China,* 4th ed. (1986). The standard work on the subject.

K. C. CHANG, *Art, Myth, and Ritual, The Path to Political Authority in Ancient China* (1984). A study of the relation between shamans, gods, agricultural production, and political authority during the Shang and Chou dynasties.

K. C. CHANG, *Shang Civilization* (1980).

D. HAWKES, *Ch'u Tz'u, The Songs of the South* (1985). Chou poems from the southern state of Ch'u, superbly translated.

C. Y. HSU, *Ancient China in Transition: An Analysis of Social Mobility 722–222 B.C.* (1965). A study of the Eastern Chou dynasty.

C. Y. HSU, *Western Chou Civilization* (1988).

X. Q. LI, *Eastern Zhou and Qin Civilizations* (1986). This work includes fresh interpretations based on archaeological finds.

Americas

R. L. BURGER, *Chavín and the Origins of Andean Civilization* (1992). A lucid and detailed account of the rise of civilization in the Andes.

M. D. COE, *America's First Civilization* (1968). Examines the earliest civilizations of Mesoamerica.

L. S. CRESSMAN, *Prehistory of the Far West: Homes of Vanished Peoples* (1977). Examines the earliest history of native Americans in the Pacific Northwest.

V. W. FITZHUGH AND A. CROWELL, *Crossroads of Continents: Cultures of Siberia and Alaska* (1988). Covers the area where the immigration from Eurasia to the Americas began.

R. FORD, ED., *Prehistoric Food Production in North America* (1985). Examines the origins of agriculture in the Americas.

D. HEYDEN AND P. GENDREP, *Precolumbian Architecture of Mesoamerica* (1975). A discussion of the architecture of Mesoamerica.

P. D. HUNT, *Indian Agriculture in America: Prehistory to the Present* (1987). Includes a discussion of preconquest agriculture.

J. D. JENNINGS, ED., *Ancient South Americans* (1983). Articles on Andean prehistory.

S. MASUDA, I. SHIMADA, AND C. MORRIS, *Andean Ecology and Civilization* (1985). Includes coverage of the earliest civilizations in the Andes.

C. MORRIS AND A. VON HAGEN, *The Inka Empire and Its Andean Origins* (1993). An overview of Andean civilization with excellent illustrations.

M. MOSELEY, *The Incas and Their Ancestors: The Archaeology of Ancient Peru* (1992). An overview of Peruvian archaeology.

J. A. SABLOFF, *The New Archaeology and the Ancient Maya* (1990). A lively account of recent research in Maya archaeology.

COMPARATIVE PERSPECTIVES: TECHNOLOGY AND CIVILIZATIONS

The Rise of Monumental Architecture

In this technological age it seems natural to believe that great changes in society, let alone in society's artifacts, result from changes in technology. The record of the earliest civilizations shows that it was not always so. People in Egypt, Mesopotamia, the Andes, and the Indus Valley chose to start building monumental architecture, all for different reasons. They used varying techniques and technologies to build their structures, but in no case did a technological breakthrough spark or result from the creation of monuments that can still be seen today, almost 5,000 years later. On the contrary, religious, social, economic, and political reasons came together in various ways to convince people to try to build vast structures. They used the technologies and techniques already available, however arduous, to accomplish the tasks they had set themselves.

The pace of technological change was initially slow. The Paleolithic, or Old Stone, age, which was based on a technology of hunting, gathering, and fishing with tools of stone and bone, lasted for tens of thousands of years. Next came the Neolithic, or New Stone, age, with better stone tools, agriculture, domesticated animals, and pottery (see Chapter 1). The stone ages, in turn, were followed—in the valleys of the Nile, Tigris-Euphrates, Ganges, and Yellow rivers—by the Bronze and Iron ages. Each age takes its name from the material used for the construction of its tools. As technology advanced, human wealth increased, populations became more densely settled, cities appeared, systems of writing developed, and classes emerged, with powerful figures controlling the distribution of wealth for their own benefit.

Before cities arose the people of the fertile river valleys where civilization first emerged lived in small villages. The beginnings of sedentary agriculture in the Neolithic period gave rise to these villages. For the first time families were tied to the land they farmed. This type of settlement lasted for at least a thousand years before cities emerged. Although we might expect to see slowly evolving changes in human settlement leading to the gradual development of cities, archaeological evidence suggests that cities appeared suddenly and rapidly. Archaeologists recognize cities when they find

evidence of two things: an increase in population and in population density, and the presence of public buildings or monumental architecture.

The emergence of large public buildings tells us that the socioeconomic organization of a community has changed. Simple family dwellings and storage facilities, the earliest buildings in settled agricultural civilizations, fulfilled the community's needs for food and shelter. In this early subsistence level economy, all members of the community worked to produce or gather food. Monumental architecture indicates that the economy has passed the subsistence level, because surplus labor would have to be available for large construction projects. Public architecture also fulfills broad community needs. The first public buildings were often temples, indicating that the community shared organized religious rituals. The temples also show that the inhabitants of a community thought that their welfare—both physically and spiritually—depended on the welfare of the group as a whole. Monumental architecture also enhanced the status of a community in the eyes of its neighbors.

The magnificent and massive religious monuments such as the ziggurats of Mesopotamia, the temples of the Andes, and the pyramids of Egypt are all the more remarkable for their sudden appearance in the archaeological record. Did new developments in technology lead to the rapid rise of cities, permitting the types of construction that characterized the new settlements? Surprisingly, the answer is no. Although the earliest river-valley civilizations of Egypt, Mesopotamia, Peru, and the Indus Valley all produced monumental architecture for various reasons, they used building techniques and technologies that had been well established for centuries. In the earliest civilizations, technology was a tool, not the driving force for change.

Early Mesopotamia

The early builders of Southern Mesopotamia had neither stone nor timber. Instead, they made their houses from the reeds that grew in the marshy terrain. In the drier alluvial plain of Northern Mesopotamia, Neolithic settlers built their dwellings from pressed mud.

The earliest buildings emerged at the same time as settled agriculture. At all the northern Mesopotamian sites of this period the primary building material was pressed mud and the primary purpose was residential. At one early site, the small rooms surrounded a courtyard, which contained grain bins and ovens. Each dwelling shared walls with the next. At another site, inhabitants covered their walls with plaster and decorated them with paint or frescoes. The societies at Tell es-Sawwan and Choga Mami had more developed socioeconomic and religious institutions, reflected both in small finds, such as pottery and figurines, and in their architecture. Buildings at these sites were constructed from sun-dried bricks, which are more durable than simple mud-bricks. The stronger material permitted the construction of larger structures, which were further supported by buttresses at the outside corners. These two communities also surrounded their village with sophisticated defensive ditches and walls. Most agricultural villages in Mesopotamia in the Neolithic period probably resembled one of these sites. The villages seem to have remained at a fairly static level of social, economic, political, and religious organization for a long time. The changes that encouraged people to construct the first monumental buildings seem to have occurred suddenly.

The first monumental buildings in Mesopotamia were temples. The earliest temple known to us, Eridu (from the 'Ubaid period, 5300–3600 B.C.E.), was raised around a place that was already being used for religious purposes. Originally a square building containing an altar and an offering table, over time, the layout and construction of the temple became more complicated. The temple was built on raised platforms, and buttresses were regularly used to support thinner walls. For all its complexity and massiveness, the monumental temple at Eridu shows no new building technologies. All structures were mud brick, known to the first sedentary Northern Mesopotamian cultures. Even the more impressive temples and ziggurats of the Jemdet Nasr period (3200–2900 B.C.E.) still used mud brick.

These later shrines and precincts show more complex layouts, which would have required more elaborate design plan-

Ancient monumental building relied much more heavily on organizing large amounts of manual labor than on technological advances. The figures shown here, from Egypt, are making mud bricks. [The Bridgeman Art Library International]

ning. They also were more ornately decorated, both with geometric mosaic designs on the façade and with decorative (rather than supportive) half columns. But the greater architectural complexity of the early Mesopotamian temples does not reflect any improvement in materials technology. Nor is there archaeological evidence that new construction tools permitted the erection of larger and more complicated structures. Instead, monumental public buildings indicate that a change in the social and economic organization of Mesopotamian society had occurred. More than anything else, building temples required manpower to shape, place, and stack the bricks that formed the massive structures. Over time, as temples grew larger and more ornate, construction required architects to plan the structures and artists to decorate them, as well as a larger unskilled labor force. Probably, a temple elite recruited and organized such a labor force. The increasing monumentality of the buildings indicates that this elite was growing more powerful and could mobilize the population more effectively. The availability of this labor force implies that the population did not need to devote itself exclusively to agricultural production. These socioeconomic changes, then, rather than technological developments, facilitated the appearance of monumental architecture in Mesopotamia.

Ancient Coastal Peru

The first public buildings in the Andes were temples, just as their Mesopotamian counterparts, and date between 3000–2000 B.C.E. They also appear suddenly in the archaeological record, and they are not linked with significant technological changes. The thick, plaster-covered walls of the different temple units at El Paraíso, on the Peruvian coast, were formed from trimmed stones set in clay mortar. Small fiber bags preserved at the site helped people to carry stone fill, with which they filled rooms defined by these walls and thus raised the height of the structure. A similar structure at

Aspero, a coastal settlement to the north, was built from stone and clay, basaltic blocks set in mud mortar, and quarried stone fill. The fill is characteristic only of monumental architecture, and not of domestic structures, and so appears to be one of the few new architectural techniques that assisted in construction. Both of these sites have ritual remains, such as burnt clay and cloth offerings, indicating their religious function.

Monuments on the Peruvian coast are all the more remarkable because they predate settled agriculture. The first Andean peoples to build public structures gathered their food from the rivers and oceans nearby. Early monumental architecture in the Andes did not, therefore, result from socioeconomic changes such as specialization of labor, but from the desire of early peoples to worship the gods more effectively by building impressive facilities to house their worship. The ancient Peruvians may have believed the new temples would attract and please the gods. The centrality of the shared religion to the community as a whole, then, would have motivated people to devote energy to building projects.

Early Egypt

Nowhere is ancient monumental architecture more impressive than in Egypt, with its famous obelisks and legendary pyramids. In Egypt, as in Mesopotamia, social, economic, and political developments, rather than technological innovations, permitted the construction of pyramids. Unlike the temples of Mesopotamia and Peru, in which inhabitants might participate in ritual worship, the pyramids had no direct public function. Instead, they provided deceased Egyptian kings with a suitable dwelling on earth for their afterlife and a physical stairway to the gods, with whom they were supposed to spend time every day. The kings, then, were the ultimate organizers and beneficiaries of these structures. They provided the labor and the capital required for construction.

It is not surprising, therefore, that the pyramid builders used materials far different from those used to construct dwellings. Private homes in Egypt, as in Northern Mesopotamia, consisted of mud bricks, perhaps made stronger with straw. During the First and Second Dynasties (3100 to 2700 B.C.E.) even tombs and temples used this readily available material. By the First Dynasty, however, Egyptians were well acquainted with stone work and used it occasionally for lining and roofing parts of royal tombs. By the time of the pyramids the Egyptians had been building with stone for hundreds of years and had developed a high degree of sophistication in such construction. It was appropriate to build pyramids of stone, rather than mud brick, because stone provided the structural permanence that the Egyptian idea of an afterlife required, since the corpse had to remain undisturbed and uncorroded for all time.

The ability to quarry a vast quantity of stone, then, was a necessary prerequisite of pyramid building. Archaeologists disagree about precisely how this may have been done. The exterior layer of stonework in a pyramid consisted of limestone, which was relatively easy to quarry. Trenches could be cut in limestone in order to define a slab, which could then be released from the bottom by means of wooden wedges that were soaked with water to expand under the block. This technique, however, would not have worked with the harder granite that forms the interior of the pyramids. To cut the granite, quarriers may have used drills or other boring tools, chisels with bits made from gemstones, or abrasive powders made from emery, pumice, or ground quartz. These abrasive powders could have reinforced the cutting power of flint drill bits or stone chisel points, or could have sufficiently hardened copper saws to permit them to cut the hard stone. Copper itself, the only form of metal known to the early Egyptians, is too soft to cut granite on its own. Archaeological remains do show the existence of drills, and traces of abrasive powder appear in some drill holes.

These technological developments did not produce a sudden flurry of pyramid building, however. Egyptians were quarrying stone for approximately five hundred years before the construction of the first pyramid. Equally as important as these technological issues was the availability of a vast body of labor experienced at quarrying and a class of experts in the designing and building of stone structures. A master architect must have overseen the design and construction of the pyramid, and the name of the first such architect, Imhotep, has been preserved both in legend and in an inscription outside his creation. A sketch of a roof, drawn on limestone, has been found inside the step pyramid enclosure, complete with measurements in cubits; this was most likely an architectural plan. Indeed, the building of the later, true pyramids assumes a knowledge both of measurement and of some astronomy. The Great Pyramid was correctly oriented to true north, south, east, and west.

The first pyramid, the tomb of the Third Dynasty (which began in roughly 2700 B.C.E.) king Zoser, was 204 feet high, 411 feet from east to west, and 358 feet from north to south. It was not a true pyramid, but instead had stepped sides. The core of the monument was a 26-foot-high box, similar to a *mastaba*, the earlier type of royal tomb. A four-step pyramid was constructed around this mastaba. Eventually, this pyramid was enlarged along its north and west sides to create a larger, six-step structure. The pyramid had an extensive substructure, consisting of a deep shaft, ramps, corridors, and rooms where the dead would rest.

How did the Egyptians move and raise the stones that comprised such a massive and tall structure? They did not have effective pulleys or other lifting devices. Instead, the builders of the step pyramids constructed brick and earth ramps along each of the four faces of the structure. The steps of the pyramid helped to support the ramp, which was extended to reach the next tier when the one below was completed. Workmen dragged or pushed the quarried stones up the ramp to lay each level of the pyramid. After the pyramid was complete, the ramps were destroyed. True pyramids, which have no external steps to support ramps, required different, ramp-based, techniques—but archaeologists vehemently disagree about how and where these ramps were constructed.

The construction of pyramids was certainly an architectural triumph for ancient builders, but it neither sprung directly from nor gave rise to new technologies. It harnessed five hundred years of experimentation with quarrying stone, it eventually made use of (but did not require) independently developed sciences such as mathematics and astronomy, and it generated no mechanical devices for lifting. Instead, the construction of pyramids reflects the vision of a king and an architect about the best way for the former to dwell comfortably and eternally in his afterlife. Pyramids probably required the labor of 100,000 men every year to transport the quarried stone on sledges—wheels were unknown and unhelpful on the oily clay or sandy ground. Several thousand skilled men and unskilled laborers worked year round on construction for many years. The god-king of Egypt exerted extraordinarily powerful control of his subjects to compel them to contribute manpower and resources to such a project.

The Indus Valley

Public building in the early Indus River Valley had a different purpose from the monumental religious architecture found in early Mesopotamia and Egypt. The extent and function of such building is best illustrated by the well preserved site at Mohenjo-Daro (see page 16). Archaeologists have not been able to locate any shrine there, although further excavation may reveal that a few smaller buildings with monumental entrances are, in fact, temples. The remarkable Great

Evidence suggests that the Egyptians constructed step pyramids such as this one at Giza by hauling quarried stones up ramps that were destroyed after construction. [PhotoDisc, Inc.]

Bath may possibly have been used for ritual purification. Most major structures, however, clearly have civic purposes: a wall and citadel for defense, a large granary, an assembly hall, and the Great Bath for public use. The same materials comprised both the public and the typical domestic structures. Residences within the city were constructed of mud brick, but unlike the bricks used in Mesopotamia or Peru, these were baked in a hot oven, which improved their durability. Unbaked brick and mud plaster supplemented these materials. The citadel stood atop an artificial mound of mud brick or mud. Towers were supported by burnt brick foundations. Unlike the Mesopotamians and Egyptians, the inhabitants of Mohenjo-Daro had access to timber, beams of which further supported the brickwork of the towers. Unfortunately, although timber may support mud-bricks, when it decays it undermines the baked bricks, and so the towers had to be patched over time. The bath was also constructed of brick, although the floors were coated with bitumen to make them waterproof. As the evidence from Egypt and Mesopotamia has shown, the laying of mud bricks, fired or not, did not require technological breakthroughs, but manpower resources. The political organization of the Indus River Valley civilization is barely known. It would seem on the basis of the archaeological remains that it was less authoritarian than Egyptian civilization. It is certainly easier to imagine inhabitants willingly constructing fortifications, assembly places, and baths, all of which would benefit the inhabitants, than pyramids, which benefited only the royal family.

References

R. L. Burger, *Chavín and the Origins of Andean Civilization* (1992).
Maurice Daumas, ed. *A History of Technology and Invention*, Volume I, *The Origins of Technological Civilization* Eileen B. Hennessy, trans. (1969).
I. E. S. Edwards, *The Pyramids of Egypt*, rev. ed. (1993).
Seton Lloyd, *The Archaeology of Mesopotamia*, rev. ed. (1984).
A. Lucas, *Ancient Egyptian Materials and Industries*, third edition, revised (1948).
Charles L. Redman, *The Rise of Civilization* (1978).
Sir Mortimer Wheeler, *The Cambridge History of India*, Supplementary Volume, *The Indus Civilization*, second edition (1960).

2 THE FOUR GREAT REVOLUTIONS IN THOUGHT AND RELIGION

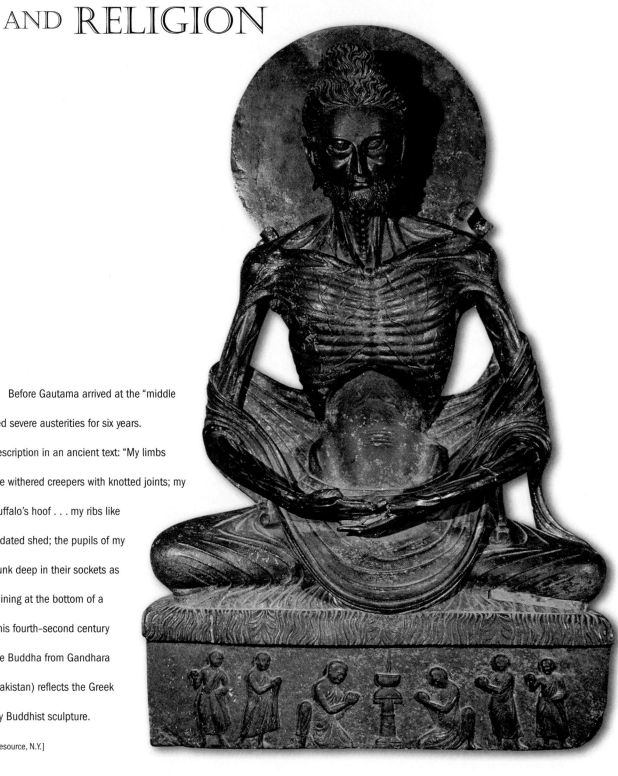

Fasting Buddha.   Before Gautama arrived at the "middle path," he practiced severe austerities for six years. According to a description in an ancient text: "My limbs became like some withered creepers with knotted joints; my buttocks like a buffalo's hoof . . . my ribs like rafters of a dilapidated shed; the pupils of my eyes appeared sunk deep in their sockets as water appears shining at the bottom of a deep well. . . ." This fourth–second century B.C.E. statue of the Buddha from Gandhara (in present-day Pakistan) reflects the Greek influence on early Buddhist sculpture.

[Borromeo, EPA/Art Resource, N.Y.]

◆ Comparing the Four Great Revolutions   ◆ Religion in India   ◆ Greek Philosophy
◆ Philosophy in China   ◆ The Religion of the Jews

Between 800 B.C.E. and 300 B.C.E., four philosophical or religious revolutions shaped the subsequent history of the world. The names of many involved in these revolutions—Socrates, Plato, Aristotle, the Buddha, Isaiah, and Confucius—are world famous. All the revolutions occurred in or near the four heartland areas in which the river valley civilizations (described in Chapter 1) had appeared one and a half or more millennia earlier. The transition from the early river-valley civilizations to the intellectual and spiritual breakthroughs of the middle of the first millennium B.C.E. is schematized in the chart on the following page.

Comparing the Four Great Revolutions

The most straightforward case is that of China. Both geographically and culturally, its philosophical breakthrough grew directly out of the earlier river-valley civilization. There was no such continuity anywhere else in the world. The natural barriers of the central Asian steppes, mountain ranges, and deserts allowed China to develop its own unique culture relatively undisturbed and uninfluenced by outside forces.

The sharpest contrast with China is the Indian subcontinent, which lacked geographic and cultural continuity. By the middle of the second millennium B.C.E., the Indus civilization had collapsed. It was replaced by the culture of the Indo-Aryan warriors who swept in from the northwest. Absorbing many particulars from the earlier tradition, they built a new civilization on the plains farther east along the mighty Ganges. The great tradition of Indian thought and religion emerged after 600 B.C.E. from this Ganges civilization.

In Southwest Asia and along the shores of the Mediterranean, the transition was more complex than that in either China or India. No direct line of development can be traced from the Nile civilization of ancient Egypt or the civilization of the Tigris-Euphrates river valley to Greek philosophy or Judaic monotheism. Rather, the ancient river-valley civilizations evolved into a complex amalgam that we call ancient Near Eastern civilization. This cosmopolitan culture included diverse older religious, mythical, and cosmological traditions, as well as newer mystery cults. The Greeks and the ancient Hebrews were two among many outside peoples who invaded this region, settled down, and both absorbed and contributed to the composite civilization.

Judaic monotheism and Greek philosophy—representing different outgrowths of this amalgam—were each important in their own right. They have continued as vital elements in Western and Near Eastern civilizations. But their greatest influence occurred centuries later when they helped shape first Christianity and then Islam. The major cultural zones in world history since the mid-first millennium C.E. are the Chinese, the Indian, the Western-Christian, and the Islamic. But the latter two were formed much later than the Chinese and the Indian. They represent a second-stage formation of which the first stage comprised the Judaic and the Greek.

Before considering each of the original breakthroughs that occurred between 800 and 300 B.C.E., we might ask whether they have anything in common. Five points are worth noting.

1. All the philosophical or religious revolutions occurred in or near the original river-valley civilizations. These areas contained the most advanced cultures of the ancient world. They had sophisticated agriculture, cities with many literate inhabitants, and specialized trades and professions. In short, they had the material preconditions for breakthroughs in religion and thought.

2. Each of the revolutions in thought and ethos was born of a crisis in the ancient world. The appearance of iron meant better tools and weapons and, by extension, greater riches and more powerful armies. Old societies began to change and then to disintegrate. Old aristocratic and priestly codes of behavior broke down, producing a demand for more universalized rules of behavior, that is to say, for ethics. The very relation of humans to nature or to the universe seemed to be changing.

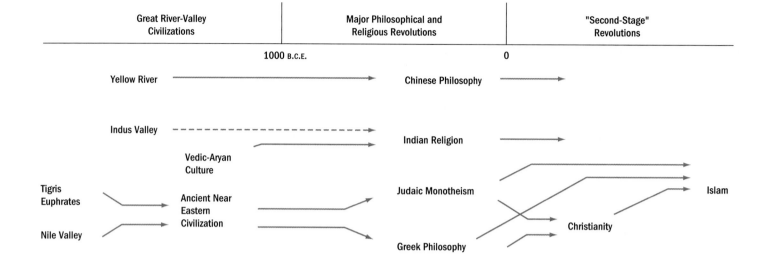

Great River-Valley Civilizations	Major Philosophical and Religious Revolutions	"Second-Stage" Revolutions

1000 B.C.E.   0

Yellow River — Chinese Philosophy

Indus Valley — Indian Religion

Vedic-Aryan Culture

Tigris Euphrates — Ancient Near Eastern Civilization — Judaic Monotheism — Islam

Nile Valley — Christianity

Greek Philosophy

This predicament led to new visions of social and political order. There is more than an accidental similarity between the Jewish Messiah, the Chinese sage-king, and Plato's philosopher-king. Each was a response to a crisis in a society of the ancient world. Each would reconnect ethics to history and restore order to a troubled society.

3. The number of philosophical and religious revolutions can be counted on the fingers of one hand. The reason is not that humans' creativity dried up after 300 B.C.E., but that subsequent breakthroughs and advances tended to occur within the original traditions, which, absorbing new energies, continued to evolve.

4. After the first- and second-stage transformations, much of the cultural history of the world involves the spread of cultures derived from these original heartlands to ever wider spheres. Christianity spread to northern and eastern Europe, the Americas, and parts of Asia and Africa; Buddhism to central, southeastern, and eastern Asia; Confucianism to Korea, Vietnam, and Japan; and Islam to Africa, southeastern Europe, and southern, central, and southeastern Asia. Sometimes the spread was the result of movements of people; other areas were like dry grasslands needing only the spark of the new ideas to be ignited. Typically, the process spread out over centuries.

5. Once a cultural pattern was set, it usually endured. Each major culture was resistant to the others and only rarely displaced. Even in modern times, although the culture of modern science, and the learning associated with it, has penetrated every cultural zone, it has reshaped—and is reshaping, not displacing—the major cultures. Only Confucianism, the most secular of the traditional cultures, crumbled at the touch of science, and even its

ethos remains a potent force in East Asian societies. These major cultures endured because they were not only responses to particular crises, but also attempts to answer universal questions concerning the human condition: What are human beings? What is our relation to the universe? How should we relate to others?

Philosophy in China

The beauty of Shang bronzes is breathtaking, but they also have an archaic strangeness. Like Olmec stone sculpture, they are products of a culture so far removed from our own as to be almost incomprehensible. By contrast, the humanism of the Confucian writings and the poetry of the Eastern Chou (771–256 B.C.E.) speaks to us directly. However much the philosophies of these centuries grew out of the earlier matrix of archaic culture, they mark a break with it and the beginning of what we think of today as the Chinese tradition.

The background of the philosophical revolution in China was the disintegration of the old Chou society (see Chapter 1 for details). New territorial states replaced the many Chou city-states. Ruthless, upstart, peasant armies, augmented by an early Iron Age cavalry armed with crossbows, began to replace the old nobility, who had gone to war in chariots. A rising merchant class disrupted the formerly stable agricultural economy. As the old etiquette crumbled—as old rituals lost their force—a search began for new principles by which to recreate a peaceful society and new rules by which to live.

Of the four great revolutions in thought of the first millennium B.C.E., the Chinese was more akin, perhaps, to the Greek than to the Indian religious transformations or to Judaic monotheism. Just as Greece had a gamut of philosophies, so in China there were the "one hundred schools." (When Mao Tse-tung said in 1956, "Let the one hundred flowers bloom"—encouraging a momentary easing of intellectual repression—he was referring to the creative era of Chou philosophy.) Whereas Greek thought was speculative and more concerned with the world of nature, Chinese thought was sociopolitical and more practical. Even the Taoist sages, who were inherently apolitical, found it necessary to offer a political philosophy. Chinese thought also had far greater staying power than Greek thought, which only a few centuries after the glory of Athens was submerged by Christianity. It became the handmaiden of theology and did not reemerge as an independent force until the Renaissance. In contrast, Chinese philosophy, although challenged by Buddhism, remained dominant until the early twentieth century. How were these early philosophies able to maintain such a grip on China when the cultures of every other part of the world fell under the sway of religions?

Part of the answer is that most Chinese philosophy had a religious dimension. But it was another kind of religion, with assumptions different from those derived from Judaic roots. In the Christian or Islamic worldview, there is a God who, however concerned with humankind, is not of this world. This worldview leads to dualism, the distinction between an otherworld, which is supernatural, and this world, which is natural.

In the Chinese worldview, the two spheres are not separate: The cosmos is single, continuous, and nondualistic. It includes heaven, earth, and man. Heaven is above. Earth is below. Man, ideally guided by a wise and virtuous ruler, stands in between and regulates or harmonizes the cosmological forces of heaven and earth by the power of his virtue and by performing the sacrifices. The forms that this cosmology took under the last Manchu dynasty (1644–1912) can be seen today in the city of Peking: The Temple of Heaven is in the south; the Temple of Earth is in the northeast; and the Imperial Palace is—symbolically, at least—in between. To say that the emperor's sacrifices at the Temple of Heaven were secular (and, therefore, not religious) or religious (and not secular) misses the point. It projects our own dualistic assumptions onto China. Similarly, when we speak of the Taoist sage becoming one with nature, it is not the nature of a twentieth-century natural scientist; it is a nature that contains metaphysical and cosmological forces that our worldview might label as religious.

Most of the one hundred schools—if, in fact, there were that many—are unknown today. Many works disappeared in the book burning of the Ch'in dynasty (256–221 B.C.E.). But apart from the three major schools of Confucianism, Taoism, and Legalism, enough other schools have survived to convey a sense of the range and vitality of Chou thought:

1. *Rhetoricians.* This school taught the arts of persuasion to be used in diplomatic negotiations. Its principal work instructed the rulers of territorial states by using historical anecdote. A practical work, it was popular for its humor and lively style.

2. *Logicians.* This school taught logic and relativity. For example, one proposition was "The south has no limit and has a limit." Another was "A white horse is not a horse": The concept of *horse* is not the same as the concept of *white horse*.

3. *Strategists.* *The Art of War* by Sun-tzu became the classic of military science in China and is studied today by guerrillas and in military academies around the world. It praises the general who wins victories without battles, but also talks of organizing states for war, of supply, of spies, and of propaganda.

4. *Cosmologists.* This school described the functions of the cosmos in terms of *yin* and *yang*, the complementary negative and positive forces of nature, and in terms of the five elements (metal, wood, earth, fire, and water). Its ideas were later absorbed by other schools.

5. *Mohists.* Mo-tzu (470–391 B.C.E.) was an early critic of Confucius. His goals were peace, wealth, and the increase of population. He taught an ethic of universal love—to overcome a selfish human nature. He preached discipline and austerity and was critical of whatever lacked utility, including music and the other arts, elaborate funerals, wasteful rites, and, above all, war. To achieve his goals, Mo-tzu argued for a strong state: Subjects must obey their rulers, who in turn must obey Heaven. Heaven would punish evil and reward good. To promote peace, Mo-tzu organized his followers into military units to aid states that were attacked.

Confucianism

Confucius was born in 551 B.C.E. in a minor state in northeastern China. Since he received an education in writing, music, and rituals, he probably belonged to the lower nobility or the knightly class. His father died when Confucius was young, so he may have known privation. He made his living by teaching. He traveled with his disciples from state to state, seeking a ruler who would put his ideas into practice. His ideas, however, were rejected as impractical, although he may once have held a minor position. He died in 479 B.C.E., honored as a teacher and scholar but having failed to find a ruler to advise. The name *Confucius* is the Latinized form of *K'ung Fu-tzu*, or *Master K'ung*, as he is known in China.

We know of Confucius only through the *Analects*, his sayings collected by his disciples, or perhaps by their disciples. They are mostly in the form of "The Master said," followed by his words. The picture that emerges is of a man of moderation,

Confucius, depicted wearing the robes of a scholar of a later age. [Collection of the National Palace Museum, Taiwan, Republic of China]

1. *The Book of Changes* (also known as the *Classic of Divination*). A handbook for diviners, this book was later seen as containing metaphysical truths about the universe.

2. *The Book of History.* This book contains documents and speeches from the early Chou, some authentic. Chinese tradition holds that it was edited by Confucius. It was interpreted as the record of sage-kings.

3. *The Book of Poetry.* This book contains some three hundred poems from the early Chou. Representing a sophisticated literary tradition, it includes love songs as well as poems of friendship, ritual, and politics. Many were given political and moral interpretations in later times.

4. *The Book of Rites.* This book includes both rituals and rules of etiquette. Rites were important to Confucians, both as a support for proper behavior and because they were seen as corresponding to the forces of nature.

5. *The Spring and Autumn Annals.* A brief record of the major occurrences from 722 to 481 B.C.E. in the state where Confucius was born, this book, according to Chinese tradition, was edited by Confucius and reflected his moral judgments on past historical figures.

Basing his teachings on these writings, Confucius proposed to resolve the turmoil of his own age by a return to the good old ways of the early Chou. When asked about government, he said, "Let the ruler be a ruler, the subject a subject, the father a father, the son a son." (The five Confucian relationships were ruler-subject, father-son, husband-wife, older brother-younger brother, and friend-friend.) If everyone fulfilled the duties of his or her status, then harmony would prevail. Confucius understood the fundamental truth that the well-being of a society depends on the morality of its members. His vision was of an unbroken social harmony extending from the individual family member to the monarch.

But a return to the early Chou was impossible. China was undergoing a dynamic transition from hundreds of small city-states to a few large territorial states. Specialized classes were appearing. Old rituals no longer worked. It was thus not enough to stress basic human relationships. The genius of Confucius was to transform the old aristocratic code into a new ethic that any educated Chinese could practice. His reinterpretation of the early Chou tradition can be seen in the concept of the *chun-tzu.* This term literally meant "the son of the ruler" (or the aristocrat). Confucius redefined it to mean one of noble behavior, a person with the inner virtues of humanity, integrity, righteousness, altruism, and loyalty, and an outward demeanor and propriety to match.

This redefinition was not unlike the change in the meaning of *gentleman* in England, from "one who is gentle-born" to "one who is gentle-behaved." But whereas *gentleman* re-

propriety, optimism, good sense, and wisdom. In an age of cruelty and superstition, he was humane, rational, and upright, demanding much of others and more of himself. Asked about death, he replied, "You do not understand even life. How can you understand death?"[1] Asked about how to serve the spirits and the gods, in which he did not disbelieve, he answered, "You are not able even to serve man. How can you serve the spirits?"

Confucius described himself as a transmitter and a conservator of tradition, not an innovator. He idealized the early Shang and Chou kings as paragons of virtue and particularly saw early Chou society as a golden age. He sought the secrets of this golden age in its writings. Some of these writings, along with later texts, became the Confucian classics, which through most of Chinese history had an authority not unlike Scripture in the West. Five of the thirteen classics were the following:

[1]This quotation and all quotations from Confucius in this passage are from Confucius, *The Analects,* trans. by D. C. Lau (Penguin Books, 1979).

Confucius Defines the Gentleman

For more than two thousand years in China, the cultural ideal was the gentleman, who combined knowledge of the ancient sages with an inner morality and outer propriety.

How does the injunction "to repay an injury with straightness" compare to the Christian injunction to turn the other cheek? Which do you think is more appropriate?

The Master said, "I never enlighten anyone who has not been driven to distraction by trying to understand a difficulty or who has not got into a frenzy trying to put his ideas into words.

"When I have pointed out one corner of a square to anyone and he does not come back with the other three, I will not point it out to him a second time."

The Master said, "Yu, shall I tell you what it is to know. To say you know when you know, and to say you do not when you do not, that is knowledge."

The Master said, "Is it not a pleasure, having learned something, to try it out at due intervals? Is it not a joy to have friends come from afar? Is it not gentlemanly not to take offence when others fail to appreciate your abilities?"

Someone said, "Repay an injury with a good turn. What do you think of this saying?" The Master said, "What, then, do you repay a good turn with? You repay an injury with straightness, but you repay a good turn with a good turn."

Lin Fang asked about the basis of the rites. The Master said, "A noble question indeed! With the rites, it is better to err on the side of frugality than on the side of extravagance; in mourning, it is better to err on the side of grief than on the side of formality."

The Master said, "I suppose I should give up hope. I have yet to meet the man who is as fond of virtue as he is of beauty in women."

The Master said, "The gentleman agrees with others without being an echo. The small man echoes without being in agreement."

The Master said, "The gentleman is at ease without being arrogant; the small man is arrogant without being at ease."

The Master said, "There is no point in seeking the views of a gentleman who, though he sets his heart on the Way, is ashamed of poor food and poor clothes."

Confucius, *The Analects*, trans. by D. C. Lau (New York: Penguin Classics, 1979), © D.C. Lau, 1979.

---

mained a fairly superficial category in the West, in China *chun-tzu* went deeper. Confucius saw ethics as grounded in nature. The true gentleman was in touch with his own basic nature, which in turn was a part of the cosmic order. Confucius expressed this saying: "Heaven is the author of the virtue that is in me." Confucius' description of his own passage through life goes far beyond good manners: "At fifteen I set my heart on learning; at thirty I took my stand; at forty I came to be free from doubts; at fifty I understood the Decree of Heaven; at sixty my ear was attuned; at seventy I followed my heart's desire without overstepping the line."

Confucius often contrasted the gentleman with the small or common person. The gentleman, educated in the classics and cultivating the Way, understands moral action. The common people, in contrast, "can be made to follow a path but not to understand it." Good government for Confucius depended on the appointment to office of good men, who would serve as examples for the multitude: "Just desire the good yourself and the common people will be good. The virtue of the gentleman is like wind; the virtue of the small man is like grass. Let the wind blow over the grass and it is sure to bend." Beyond the gentleman was the sage-king, who possessed an almost mystical virtue and power. For Confucius, the early Chou kings were clearly sages. But he wrote, "I have no hopes of meeting a sage. I would be content if I met someone who is a gentleman."

Confucianism was not adopted as the official philosophy of China until the second century B.C.E., during the Han dynasty (202 B.C.E.–9 C.E., see Chapter 7). But two other important Confucian philosophers had appeared in the meantime. Mencius (370–290 B.C.E.) represents the idealistic extension of Confucius' thought. His interpretation was accepted during most of history. He is famous for his argument that humans tend toward the good just as water runs downward. The role of education, therefore, is to uncover and cultivate that innate goodness. Moreover, just as humans tend toward the good, so does Heaven possess a moral will. The will of Heaven is that a government should see to the education and well-being of its people. The rebellion of people against a government is the primary evidence that Heaven has withdrawn its mandate. At times in Chinese history, only lip service was paid to a concern for the people. In fact, rebellions occurred more often against weak governments than against harsh ones. But the idea that government ought to care for the people became a permanent part of the Confucian tradition.

The other influential Confucian philosopher was Hsun-tzu (300–237 B.C.E.), who represents a tough-minded extension of Confucius' thought. Hsun-tzu felt Heaven was amoral, indifferent to whether China was ruled by a tyrant or a sage. He believed human nature was bad or at least that desires and emotions, if unchecked and unrefined, led to social conflict. So he emphasized etiquette and education as restraints on an unruly human nature, and good institutions, including punishments and rewards, as a means for shaping behavior. These ideas influenced the thinkers of the Legalist school.

Taoism

It is often said that the Chinese have been Confucian while in office and Taoist (pronounced "Dah-oh-ist") in their private lives. Taoism offered a refuge from the burden of social responsibilities. The classics of the school are the *Lao-tzu*, dating from the fourth century B.C.E., and the *Chuang-tzu*, dating from about a century later.

The central concept is the *Tao*, or way. It is mysterious, ineffable, and cannot be named. It is the creator of the universe, the sustainer of the universe, and the process or flux of the universe. The *Tao* functions on a cosmic, not a human, scale. As the *Lao-tzu* put it, "Heaven and Earth are ruthless, and treat the myriad creatures as straw dogs; the sage (in accord with the *Tao*) is ruthless, and treats the people as straw dogs."[2]

What does it mean to be a sage? How does a human join the rhythms of nature? The answer given by the *Lao-tzu* is by regaining or returning to an original simplicity. Various similes describe this state: "to return to the infinite," "to return to being a babe," or "to return to being the uncarved block." To attain this state, one must "learn to be without learning." Knowledge is bad because it creates distinctions, and because it leads to the succession of ideas and images that interfere with participation in the *Tao*. One must also learn to be without desires beyond the immediate and simple needs of nature: "The nameless uncarved block is but freedom from desire."

If the sage treats the people as straw dogs, it would appear that he is beyond good and evil. But elsewhere in the *Lao-tzu*, the sage is described as one who "excels in saving people." If not a contradiction, this is at least a paradox. The resolution is that the sage is clearly beyond morality but is not immoral or even amoral. On the contrary, by being in harmony with the *Tao*, the sage is impeccably moral—as one who clings to the forms of morality or makes morality a goal could never be. So in the *Lao-tzu* it is written, "Exterminate benevolence,

Lao-tzu, the founder of Taoism, as imagined by a later artist. [Courtesy of the Freer Gallery of Art, Smithsonian Institution, Washington D.C. (72.1)]

discard rectitude, and the people will again be filial; exterminate ingenuity, discard profit, and there will be no more thieves and bandits." In this formulation we also see the basis for the political philosophy of Taoism, which can be summed up as "not doing" (*wu wei*). This means something between "doing nothing" and "being, but not acting." In this concept, there is some overlap with Confucianism. The Confucian sage-king exerts a moral force by dint of his internal accord with nature. A perfect Confucian sage could rule without doing. Confucius said, "If there was a ruler who achieved order without taking any action, it was, perhaps, Shun [the sage emperor]. There was nothing for him to do but to hold himself in a respectful posture and to face due south." In Taoism, all true sages had this Shun-like power to rule without action: "The way never acts yet nothing is left undone. Should lords and princes be able to hold fast to it, the myriad creatures will be transformed of their own accord." Or, says the *Lao-tzu*, "I am free from desire and the people of themselves become simple like the uncarved block." The sage acts without acting, and "when his task is accomplished and his work is done, the people will say, 'It happened to us naturally.'"

Along with the basic Taoist prescription of becoming one with the Tao are two other assumptions or principles. One is that any action pushed to an extreme will initiate a countervailing reaction in the direction of the opposite extreme. The other is that too much government, even good government,

[2]All quotations from the *Lao-tzu* are from Lao-Tzu, *Tao Te Ching*, trans. by D. C. Lau (Penguin Books, 1963).

Taoism

Can inner, transformative, religious experience take people beyond everyday worldly concerns and imbue them with moral charisma or moral authority? What other religions might call "supernatural," Taoism sees as truly natural.

How does the "Way" in Taoism compare with Confucius' use of the same term?

Lao-Tzu Tells of the Way of the Sage

The way that can be spoken of
Is not the constant way;
The name that can be named
Is not the constant name.
The nameless was the beginning of heaven
    and earth;
The named was the mother of the myriad creatures.

The spirit of the valley never dies
This is called the mysterious female.
The gateway of the mysterious female
Is called the root of heaven and earth.
Dimly visible, it seems as if it were there,
Yet use will never drain it.

There is a thing confusedly formed,
Born before heaven and earth.
Silent and void
It stands alone and does not change,
Goes round and does not weary.
It is capable of being the mother of the world.
I know not its name
So I style it "the way."

When the way prevails in the empire, fleetfooted horses are relegated to ploughing the fields; when the way does not prevail in the empire, war-horses breed on the border.

One who knows does not speak; one who speaks does not know.
Therefore the sage puts his person last and it comes first,
Treats it as extraneous to himself and it is preserved.
Is it not because he is without thought of self that he is able to accomplish his private ends?

Chuang-tzu Compares Governmental Office to a Dead Rat

When Hui Tzu was prime minister of Liang, Chuang Tzu set off to visit him. Someone said to Hui Tzu, "Chuang Tzu is coming because he wants to replace you as prime minister!" With this Hui Tzu was filled with alarm and searched all over the state for three days and three nights trying to find Chuang Tzu. Chuang Tzu then came to see him and said, "In the south there is a bird called the Yuan-ch'u-I wonder if you've ever heard of it? The Yuan-ch'u rises up from the South Sea and flies to the North Sea, and it will rest on nothing but the Wu-t'ung tree, eat nothing but the fruit of the Lien, and drink only from springs of sweet water. Once there was an owl who had gotten hold of a half-rotten old rat, and as the Yuan-ch'u passed by, it raised its head, looked up at the Yuan-ch'u, and said, 'Shoo!' Now that you have this Liang state of yours, are you trying to shoo me?"

Lao-tzu selection from *Lao-tzu, Tao Te Ching*, trans. by D. C. Lau (New York: Penguin Classics, 1963). © D.C. Lau. Chuang-tzu selection from *The Complete Works of Chuang-tzu*, trans. by Burton Watson © 1968 by Columbia University Press. Reprinted by permission of the publisher.

---

can become oppressive by its very weight. As the *Lao-tzu* put it, "The people are hungry; it is because those in authority eat up too much in taxes that the people are hungry. The people are difficult to govern; it is because those in authority are too fond of action that the people are difficult to govern." Elsewhere, the same idea was expressed in even homelier terms: "Govern a large state as you would cook small fish," that is, without too much stirring.

Legalism

A third great current in classical Chinese thought, and by far the most influential in its own age, was Legalism. Like the philosophers of other schools, the Legalists were concerned to end the wars that plagued China. True peace, they felt, required a united country and thus a strong state. They favored conscription and considered war a means of extending state power.

The Legalists did not seek a model in the distant past. In ancient times, said one, there were fewer people and more food, so it was easier to rule; different conditions require new principles of government. Nor did the Legalists model their state on a heavenly order of values. Human nature is selfish, argued both of the leading Legalists, Han Fei-tzu (d. 233 B.C.E.) and Li Ssu (d. 208 B.C.E.). It is human to like rewards or pleasure and to dislike punishments or pain. If laws are

Legalism

According to Legalism, the state can only regulate behavior, it cannot affect the inner dimensions of human life. Rewards and punishments, furthermore, are far more efficient in controlling behavior than moral appeals.

Do the tenets of Legalism have any modern parallels? What do you think of Legalism as a philosophy of government? As an approach to the problem of crime? How does Legalism compare with other approaches to law, leadership, and government? [See, for example, "Hammurabi's Code on Women, Marriage, and Divorce in Babylonia" (Chapter 1), "Athenian Democracy: An Unfriendly View" (Chapter 3), "The Edicts of Ashoka" (Chapter 4), and "Machiavelli Discusses the Most Important Trait for a Ruler" (Chapter 16).]

Han Fei-Tzu Argues for the Efficacy of Punishments

Now take a young fellow who is a bad character. His parents may get angry at him, but he never makes any change. The villagers may reprove him, but he is not moved. His teachers and elders may admonish him but he never reforms. The love of his parents, the efforts of the villagers, and the wisdom of his teachers and elders—all the three excellent disciplines are applied to him, and yet not even a hair on his shins is altered. It is only after the district magistrate sends out his soldiers and in the name of the law searches for wicked individuals that the young man becomes afraid and changes his ways and alters his deeds. So while the love of parents is not sufficient to discipline the children, the severe penalties of the district magistrate are. This is because men became naturally spoiled by love, but are submissive to authority. . . .

That being so, rewards should be rich and certain so that the people will be attracted by them; punishments should be severe and definite so that the people will fear them; and laws should be uniform and steadfast so that the people will be familiar with them. Consequently, the sovereign should show no wavering in bestowing rewards and grant no pardon in administering punishments, and he should add honor to rewards and disgrace to punishments—when this is done, then both the worthy and the unworthy will want to exert themselves. . . .

Han Fei-Tzu Attacks Confucianism

There was once a man of Sung who tilled his field. In the midst of his field stood the stump of a tree, and one day a hare, running at full speed, bumped into the stump, broke its neck, and died. Thereupon the man left his plow and kept watch at the stump, hoping that he would get another hare. But he never caught another hare, and was only ridiculed by the people of Sung. Now those who try to rule the people of the present age with the conduct of government of the early kings are all doing exactly the same thing as that fellow who kept watch by the stump. . . .

Those who are ignorant about government insistently say: "Win the hearts of the people." If order could be procured by winning the hearts of the people, then even the wise ministers Yi Yin and Kuan Chung would be of no use. For all that the ruler would need to do would be just to listen to the people. Actually, the intelligence of the people is not to be relied upon any more than the mind of a baby. If the baby does not have his head shaved, his sores will recur; if he does not have his boil cut open, his illness will go from bad to worse. However, in order to shave his head or open the boil someone has to hold the baby while the affectionate mother is performing the work, and yet he keeps crying and yelling incessantly. The baby does not understand that suffering a small pain is the way to obtain a great benefit.

Now, the sovereign urges the tillage of land and the cultivation of pastures for the purpose of increasing production for the people, but they think the sovereign is cruel. The sovereign regulates penalties and increases punishments for the purpose of repressing the wicked, but the people think the sovereign is severe. Again he levies taxes in cash and in grain to fill up the granaries and treasuries in order to relieve famine and provide for the army, but they think the sovereign is greedy. Finally, he insists upon universal military training without personal favoritism, and urges his forces to fight hard in order to take the enemy captive, but the people think the sovereign is violent. These four measures are methods for attaining order and maintaining peace, but the people are too ignorant to appreciate them.

From *Sources of Chinese Tradition*, translated by William Theodore de Bary. © 1960 by Columbia University Press. Reprinted by permission of the publisher.

severe and impartial, if what strengthens the state is rewarded and what weakens the state is punished, then a strong state and a good society will ensue.

Laws, therefore, should contain incentives for loyalty and bravery in battle, and for obedience, diligence, and frugality in everyday life. The Legalists despised merchants as parasites and approved of productive farmers. They particularly despised purveyors of doctrines different from their own and were critical of rulers who honored philosophers while ignoring their philosophies.

Legalism was the philosophy of the state of Ch'in, which destroyed the Chou in 256 B.C.E. and unified China in 221

```
╔══════════════════════════════════════╗
  China

  551–479 B.C.E.        Confucius
  370–290 B.C.E.        Mencius
  Fourth century B.C.E. Lao-Tzu
  221 B.C.E.            Ch'in unifies China
╚══════════════════════════════════════╝
```

B.C.E. Because Ch'in laws were cruel and severe, and because Legalism put human laws above an ethic modeled on Heaven, later generations of Chinese have execrated its doctrines. They saw it, not without justification, as a philosophy that consumed its founders: Han Fei-tzu became an official of the Ch'in state but was eventually poisoned in a prison cell by Li Ssu, who was jealous of his growing influence. Li Ssu, although he became prime minister of Ch'in, was killed in 208 B.C.E. in a political struggle with a court eunuch. Yet for all the abuse heaped on Legalist doctrines, its legacy of administrative and criminal laws became a vital part of subsequent dynastic China. Even Confucian statesmen could not do without them.

Religion in India

By 400 B.C.E., new social and religious forms took shape in the Indian subcontinent. A tradition was created that drew both on the older traditions of the Aryan noble and priestly elites, and on non-Aryan ideas and practices. This tradition took its "classical" shape only later, in the early first millennium C.E. We can call it "Indian," as distinct from the earlier Vedic-Brahmanic culture (described in Chapter 1), in that its fundamental institutions and ideas came to prevail virtually throughout the subcontinent. Despite staggering internal diversity and divisions, and long periods of foreign rule, this Indian culture has survived for over two thousand years as a coherent tradition of cultural heritage, social organization, and religious worldview.

"Hindu" and "Indian"

Indian culture and tradition include more than is commonly implied by the word *Hindu* today. Earlier, "Hindu" simply meant "Indian." Taken from the Indo-Iranian name for the Indus, it was the term used by outsiders, like the Persians and the Greeks, for the people or land of the subcontinent. Later, first invading Muslims, then Europeans used Hindu to characterize the most prominent religious and social institutions of India as a whole. The concept of transmigration, the sacredness of the Vedas and of the cow, worship of Shiva and Vishnu, and caste distinctions head the list of such "Hindu" institutions. The vast majority, but by no means all Indians in the past 2500 years have accepted these institutions. Most obviously, Indian Buddhists, Jains, Muslims, Sikhs, and Christians have rejected some or all of them.

We cannot say exactly when the typical aspects of Hindu society and religious life as we know it today were "in place." Some argue that it was only after 200 (or even 400) C.E.; others argue for the latter half of the first millennium B.C.E. However we date the beginning of "Hindu" religion and culture, we must remember that such usage lumps together an immense diversity of social, racial, linguistic, and religious groups. It is totally inaccurate to think of *Hindu* as a term for any single or uniform religious community.

"Indian," on the other hand, commonly refers today to all native inhabitants of the subcontinent, including Muslims, Sikhs, and Christians (who belong to traditions considerably younger than the Buddhist, Jain, or Hindu). In this book we shall generally use the term *Indian* in this inclusive sense when referring to the subcontinent or to its peoples. However, for the period before the arrival of Muslim culture (ca. 1000 C.E.), *Indian* will be used to refer to the distinctively Indian tradition of thought and culture that began with the flowering of Upanishadic, Buddhist, and Jain thought around the middle of the first millennium B.C.E. This "Indian" tradition achieved its classical formulation in the Hindu society and religion of the first millennium C.E. However, the Jains of India and the Buddhists of wider Asia were also its legitimate heirs.

Historical Background

We saw in Chapter 1 how, in the later Vedic or Brahmanic period, a priest-centered cult dominated the upper classes of Aryanized northern Indian society. By the sixth century B.C.E., this cult had apparently grown so extreme in its basically magical approach to ritual and piety that it became an elite, esoteric cult to which most people had little or no access. Elaborate animal sacrifices on behalf of Aryan rulers were an economic burden on the peasants of the countryside, whose livestock provided the victims. Such sacrifices were also largely irrelevant to the religious concerns of peasant and town dweller alike. New, ascetic tendencies placed in question the basic values and practices of the older Aryan religion. Skepticism in religious matters accompanied social and political upheavals during the seventh and sixth centuries B.C.E.

The latest Vedic texts themselves reflected a reaction against excessive emphasis on the power of sacrifice and ritual formulas, accumulation of worldly wealth and power, and hope for an afterlife in some kind of paradise. The treatises of the *Brahmanas* (ca. 1000–800 B.C.E.) dealt with the ritual application of the old Vedic texts, the explanation of Vedic rites and mythology, and the theory of the sacrifice. Early on they focused on controlling the sacred power (*Brahman*) of the sacrificial ritual, but they gradually stressed acquiring this power through knowledge instead of ritual acts.

This tendency became central in the Upanishads (ca. 800–500 B.C.E.), which were extended meditations on the meaning of ritual and the nature of *Brahman*. These texts carried to new levels of subtlety older Vedic theories of the origin and nature of reality and the relation of thought and action to ultimate truth. As for the Jain and Buddhist traditions, they were but the most enduring of several sixth- and fifth-century-B.C.E. religious movements that explicitly rejected much of the Vedic-Brahmanic tradition of sacrificial ritualism and class distinction. The principal ideas that would guide all later Indian tradition are first clearly visible in the Upanishads, and together with the early Jain and Buddhist thinkers (fifth century B.C.E.), the Upanishadic thinkers rejected or transcended the Brahmanic tradition in many ways.

The Upanishadic sages and the early Jains and Buddhists shared certain revolutionary ideas and concerns. Their thinking and piety influenced not only all later Indian intellectual thought but, through the spread of the Buddhist tradition, much of the intellectual and religious life of East and Southeast Asia as well. Thus, the middle centuries of the first millennium B.C.E. in India began a religious and philosophical revolution that ranks alongside those of Chinese philosophy and religion, Judaic monotheism, and Greek philosophy as a turning point in the history of civilization.

The Upanishadic Worldview

In the Upanishads we see two new emphases: on knowledge over ritual and on immortality in terms not of an afterlife but of escape from existence itself. These were already evident in two sentences from the prayer of an early Upanishadic thinker who said, "From the unreal lead me to the Real. . . . From death lead me to immortality." The first sentence points to the Upanishadic focus on speculation about the nature of things, the quest for ultimate truth. Here ritual takes a back seat to meditation; knowledge, not the sacred word or act, has become the ultimate source of power. The second sentence reflects a new concern with life after death. The old Vedic ideal of living a full and upright life so as to attain an afterlife in a heaven of the fathers, among the gods, no longer appears an adequate ideal or goal. Immortality is now interpreted in terms of escape from existence in any earthly, heavenly, or other form. These two Upanishadic emphases gave birth to ideas that were to change the shape of Indian thought forever. They also provide the key to its basic worldview.

The Nature of Reality   The quest for knowledge by the Upanishadic sages focused on the nature of the individual self (*atman*) and its relation to ultimate reality (*Brahman*). The gods are now merely part of the total scheme of things,

subject to the laws of existence, and not to be put on the same plane with the transcendent Absolute. Prayer and sacrifice to particular gods for their help continue; but the higher goal is realization of *Brahman* through mental action alone, not ritual.

The culmination of Upanishadic speculation is the recognition that the way to the Absolute is through the self. Through contemplation, *Atman-Brahman* is recognized not as a deity, but as the very principle of reality itself: the unborn, unmade, unchanging infinite. Of this reality, all that can be said is that it is "neither this nor that," because the ultimate cannot be conceptualized or described in finite terms. Beneath the impermanence of ordinary reality is the changeless *Brahman*, to which every being's immortal self belongs. The difficulty is recognizing this self, and with it the Absolute, while one is enmeshed in mortal existence.

A second, related focus of Upanishadic inquiry was the nature of "normal" existence. The realm of life is seen to be ultimately impermanent, ever in change. What seem to be "solid" things—the physical world, our bodies and personalities, worldly success—are revealed in the Upanishads as finally insubstantial, impermanent, ephemeral. Even happiness is transient. Existence is neither satisfying nor lasting in any fundamental sense. Only *Brahman* is enduring, eternal, unchanging—the unmoved ground of existence. This perception already shows a marked tendency toward the eventual emphasis of the Buddhists on impermanence and suffering as the fundamental facts of existence as we know it.

Life After Death   The new understanding of immortality that emerges in the Upanishads is related to these basic perceptions about the self, the Absolute, and the world of existence. It runs, as we noted, counter to the Vedic-Aryan concept of an immortal existence either in heaven or in hell after this life is finished. The Upanishadic sages instead conceived of existence as a ceaseless cycle, a never-ending alternation between life and death. This idea proved not only of major importance for Indian speculative philosophy; it also became the basic assumption of all Indian thought and religious life.

The idea of the endless cycle of existence, or *samsara*, is only superficially similar to our idea of "transmigration" of souls. For Indians, it is the key to understanding reality. Furthermore, it is not liberating, but burdensome. In the Indian context, *samsara* refers to the terrifying prospect of endless "redeath" as the normal lot of all beings in this world, whether animals, plants, humans, or gods. This is the fundamental problem for all later Indian thought to which the great Indian thinkers of the mid-first millennium B.C.E., from the sages of the Upanishads to the Buddha, addressed themselves.

Karma   The key to resolving the dilemma of *samsara* lies in the concept of *karma*, which in Sanskrit literally

Discussions of *Brahman* and *Atman* from the Upanishads

Much of the Upanishads is couched in the form of teacher-student dialogue. The following two selections are responses of teachers to the questions of their disciples.

Is the intent of either of these passages to provide a guide to salvation? If so, why, and what is the suggested path to salvation? In what sense and degree are the passages concerned with ignorance and enlightenment?

A Report of the Sage Sandilya's Statement About the Identity of Atman and Brahman

"Verily, this whole world is Brahman. Tranquil, let one worship it as that from which he came forth, as that into which he will be dissolved, as that in which he breathes. Now, verily, a person consists of purpose. According to the purpose which a person has in this world, thus does he become on departing hence. So let him form for himself a purpose. He who consists of mind, whose body is life, whose form is light, whose conception is truth, whose soul [atman] is space, containing all odors, containing all tastes, encompassing this whole world, the unspeaking, the unconcerned—this Soul of mine within the heart is smaller than a grain of rice, or a barley-corn, or a mustard-seed, or a grain of millet; or the kernel of a grain of millet; this Soul of mine within the heart is greater than the earth, greater than the atmosphere, greater than the sky, greater than

these worlds. Containing all works, containing all desires, containing all odors, containing all tastes, encompassing this whole world, the unspeaking, the unconcerned—this Soul of mine within the heart, this is Brahman. Into him I shall enter on departing hence. If one would believe this, he would have no more doubt."—Thus used Sandilya to say. . . .

—Chandogya Upanishad 3.14

The Young Brahman, Shvetaketu, Is Instructed in the Identity of Atman and Brahman by His Father

"These rivers, my dear, flow, the eastern toward the east, the western toward the west. They go just from the ocean to the ocean. They become the ocean itself. As there they know not 'I am this one,' 'I am that one'—even so, indeed, my dear, all creatures here, though they have come forth from Being, know not 'We have come forth from Being.' Whatever they are in this world, whether tiger, or lion, or wolf, or boar, or worm, or fly, or gnat, or mosquito, that they become. That which is the finest essence—this whole world has that as its soul. That is Reality. That is Atman. That art thou, Shvetaketu."

—Chandogya Upanishad 6.10

---

means "work" or "action." At base, it is the concept that every action has its inevitable effects, sooner or later; as long as there is action of mind or body, there is continued effect, and hence continued existence. Good deeds bring good results, perhaps even rebirth in a heaven or as a god, and evil ones bring evil consequences, whether in this life or by rebirth in the next, whether in the everyday world or in the lower worlds of hell. Because of the fundamental impermanence of everything in existence (heavens and hells included), good as well as evil is temporary. The flux of existence knows only movement, change, endless cause and effect far transcending a mere human life span, or even a mere world eon.

Solutions   The Indian tradition developed two kinds of solutions to the problem of *samsara*. The first involves a strategy of maximizing good actions and minimizing bad actions to achieve the best possible rebirth in one's next round of existence. The second, and more radical, solution seeks "lib-

eration" (*moksha*) from existence: escaping all karmic effects by escaping action itself.

The first strategy has been followed by the great masses of Hindus, Buddhists, and Jains over the centuries. It has been characterized by Franklin Edgerton as the "ordinary norm," as opposed to the "extraordinary norm," the path of only the select elite, the greatest seekers of Upanishadic truth, Jain asceticism, or the Buddhist "middle path." Essentially, the ordinary norm aims at living according to a code of social and moral responsibility. The most significant such codes in Indian history are those of the masses of Hindus, Buddhists, and Jains over the centuries. On the other hand, the seekers of the extraordinary norm usually follow an ascetic discipline aimed at withdrawal from the karmic cycle altogether and the consequent release (*moksha*) from cause and effect, good and evil, birth and rebirth. These two characteristic Indian responses to the problem posed by *samsara* underlie the fundamental forms of Indian thought and piety that took shape in the mid- to late-first millennium B.C.E.

Social Responsibility: *Dharma* as Ideal

The "ordinary norm" of life in the various traditions of Indian religiousness can be summarized as life lived according to *dharma*. Although *dharma* has many meanings in Indian usage, its most common is similar to that of the Vedic-Aryan concept of *Rta* (see Chapter 1). In this sense, it means "the right (order of things)," "moral law," "right conduct," or even "duty." It includes the cosmic order (compare the Chinese *Tao*) as well as the right conduct of political, commercial, social, and religious affairs and individual moral responsibility. For most people—those we might call the laity, as distinguished from monks and ascetics—life according to *dharma* is the life of moral action that will lead to a better birth in the next round of existence.

Life according to *dharma* has several implications. First, it accepts action in the world of *samsara* as necessary and legitimate. Second, it demands acceptance of the responsibilities appropriate to one's sex, class and caste group, stage in life, and other circumstances. Third, it allows for legitimate self-interest: One's duty is to do things that acquire merit for one's eternal *atman* and to avoid those that bring evil consequences. Fourth, rebirth in heaven, in paradise, is the highest goal attainable through the life of *dharma*. However (fifth), all achievement in the world of *dharma* (which is also the world of *samsara*), even the attainment of heaven, is ultimately impermanent and is subject to change.

Ascetic Discipline: *Moksha* as Ideal

For those who have the mental and physical capacity to abandon the world of ordinary life to gain freedom from *samsara*, the implications for living are in direct contrast to those of the ordinary norm. First, any action, good or bad, is at least counterproductive, for action produces only more action, more *karma*, more rebirth. Second, nonaction is achieved only by withdrawal from "normal" existence. The person seeking release from *samsara* has to move beyond the usual responsibilities of family and society. Most often, this involves becoming a "renouncer" (*sannyasi*)—whether a Hindu hermit, yogi, or wanderer, or a Jain or Buddhist monk. Third, this renunciation of the world and its goals demands selflessness, absence of ego. One must give up the desires and attachments that the self normally needs to function in the world. Fourth, the highest goal is not rebirth in heaven at all, but liberation (*moksha*) from all rebirth and redeath. Finally, this *moksha* is lasting, permanent. Its realization means no more becoming, no more suffering in the realm of samsara. Permanence, eternity, transcendence, and freedom from suffering are its attributes.

Seekers of the Extraordinary Norm

The ideas that led individuals to seek the extraordinary norm appeared fully elaborated for the first time in the Upanishads. These ideas were particularly congenial to an increasing number of persons who abandoned both the ritualistic religious practices and the society of class distinctions and material concerns around them. Many of these seekers were of warrior-noble (*kshatriya*), not Brahmanic, birth. They took up the wandering or hermit existence of the ascetic, seeking spiritual powers in yogic meditation and self-denial or even self-torture. Such seekers wanted to transcend the body and bodily existence to realize the Absolute.

In the sixth century B.C.E., teachers of new ideas appeared, especially in the lower Ganges basin, in the area of Magadha (modern Bihar). Most of them rejected traditional religious practices as well as the authority of the Vedas in favor of ascetic discipline as the true spiritual path. The ideas and practices of two of these teachers became the foundations of new and lasting traditions of piety and faith, those of the Jains and the Buddhists.

Mahavira and the Jain Tradition

The Jains are an Indian community that traces its tradition to Vardhamana, known as Mahavira ("the great hero"), who is traditionally believed to have lived from about 540 to 468 B.C.E. Mahavira is hailed by the Jains as the final Jina ("victor" over *samsara*) or *Tirthankara* ("ford maker," one who finds a way across the waters of existence), in a line of twenty-four great teachers who have appeared in the latter, degenerative half of the present-world time cycle. The Jains (or *Jainas*, "adherents of the *Jina*") see in Mahavira not a god, but a human teacher who found and taught the way to extricate the self, or soul, from the bonds of the material world and its karmic accretions.

In the Jain view, there is no beginning or end to phenomenal existence, only innumerable, ceaseless cycles of generation and degeneration. The universe is alive from end to end with an infinite number of souls, all immortal, omniscient, and pure in their essence. But all are trapped in *samsara*, whether as animals, gods, humans, plants, or even inanimate stones or fire. *Karma* here takes on a quasi-material form: Any thought, word, or deed attracts karmic matter that clings to and encumbers the soul. The greatest amounts come from evil acts, especially those done out of hate, greed, or cruelty to any other being.

Mahavira's path to release focused on the elimination of evil thoughts and acts, especially those harmful to others. His radical ascetic practice aimed at destroying karmic defilements and, ultimately, all actions leading to further karmic bondage. At the age of thirty, Mahavira began practicing the radical self-denial of a wandering ascetic, eventually even giving up clothing altogether (the latter a practice still followed by one small sect of Jain mendicants). After twelve years of self-deprivation and yogic meditative discipline, he attained enlightenment. Then, for some thirty years, he went about teaching his discipline to others. At the age of seventy-two he chose to fast to death to burn out the last karmic residues, an action that has been emulated by some of the most advanced of Jain ascetics down to the present day.

It would, however, be wrong to think of the Jain tradition in terms only of the extreme ascetic practices of some Jain mendicants. (Such practices can involve the attempt to avoid hurting even the tiniest organisms by wearing cloth masks and drinking only strained water.) Jain Monks are bound basically by the five great vows they share with other monastic traditions like the Buddhist and the Christian: not to kill, steal, lie, engage in sexual activity, or own anything.

Most Jains are not monks. Today, as in earlier centuries, there is a thriving lay community of perhaps three million Jains, most in western India (Gujarat and Rajasthan). Laypersons of both sexes have close ties to the monks and nuns, whom they support with gifts and food. Many Jain laypersons spend some time during their lives in retreat with monks or nuns.

Jains tend to be merchants out of an aversion to farming and other occupations that involve harming plants or animals. They are vegetarians and regard *ahimsa* ("noninjury") to any being as paramount. In this they have had great influence on Indian values. For example, Mahatma Gandhi (1869–1948), who came from a Jain region, was likely influenced by them in his adoption of *ahimsa* as a central tenet of his thought. Jains are known for their hospitals—not only for humans, but also for animals. Compassion is the great virtue for them, as for Buddhists. The merit of serving the extraordinary-norm seekers who adopt the mendicant life and of living a life according to the high standards of the community provides a goal even for those who as laypersons are following the ordinary norm.

The Buddha's "Middle Path"

It can be argued that India's greatest contribution to world civilization was a religious tradition that ultimately faded out in India itself. The Buddhist tradition remains one of the great universalist forms of faith in the world today, but few people in India proper are Buddhists. Yet there it was born, there it developed its basic contours, and there it left its mark on Hindu and Jain religion and culture. Like the two other great universalist traditions, Christianity and Islam, it traces its origins to a single figure who has loomed larger than life in the community of the faithful for centuries.

This figure is Siddhartha Gautama, known as the "sage of the Shakya tribe (Shakyamuni)" and, above all, as the Buddha, or "enlightened/awakened one." A contemporary of Mahavira, Gautama was also born (ca. 566 B.C.E.) of a *Kshatriya* family in apparently comfortable—if not, as legend has it, royal—circumstances. His people lived near the modern

India	
ca. 800-500 B.C.E.	The Upanishads
540-ca. 468 B.C.E.	Mahavira, the Jina/Vardamana
ca. 566-ca. 486 B.C.E.	Siddhartha Gautama, the Buddha

Nepalese border in the Himalayan foothills. The traditional story of how Gautama came to teach the "middle path" to liberation from samsara begins with his sheltered life of ease as a young married prince.

At the age of twenty-nine, Gautama first perceived the reality of aging, sickness, and death as the human lot. Revolted at his previous delight in sensual pleasures and even his wife and child, he abandoned his home and family to seek an answer to the dilemma of the endless cycle of mortal existence. After this "Great Renunciation," he studied first with renowned teachers, then took up extreme ascetic disciplines of penance and self-mortification. Still unsatisfied, Gautama turned finally to intense yogic meditation under a pipal tree in the place near Varanasi (Banaras) known as Gaya. In one historic night, he moved through different levels of trance, during which he realized all of his past lives, the reality of the cycle of existence of all beings, and how to stop the karmic outflows that fuel suffering. Thus he became the Buddha; that is, he achieved full enlightenment—the omniscient consciousness of reality as it truly is. Having realized the truth of suffering existence, he pledged himself to achieving release for all beings.

From the time of the experience under the Bodh Tree, or "enlightenment tree," Gautama devoted the last of his earthly lives before his final release to teaching others his "middle path" between asceticism and indulgence. This path has been the core of Buddhist faith and practice ever since. It begins with realizing the "four noble truths": (1) all life is *dukkha*, or suffering; (2) the source of suffering is desiring; (3) the cessation of desiring is the way to end suffering; and (4) the path to this end is eightfold: right understanding, thought, speech, action, livelihood, effort, mindfulness, and concentration. The key idea of the Buddha's teaching, or *dharma*, is that everything in the world of existence is causally linked. The essential fact of existence is *dukkha*: All existing is suffering, for no pleasure—however great—is permanent (here we see the Buddhist variation on the central Indian theme of *samsara*). *Dukkha* comes from desire, from craving, from attachment to self.

Thus, Buddhist discipline focuses on the moral "eightfold path," and the cardinal virtue of compassion for all beings, as the way to eliminate the selfish desiring that is the root of samsara and its unavoidable suffering. The Buddha himself

The "Turning of the Wheel of the *Dharma*": Basic Teachings of the Buddha

The following are selections from the sermon said to have been the first preached by the Buddha. It was directed at five former companions with whom he had practiced extreme austerities. When he abandoned asceticism to meditate under the Bodh tree, they had left him. This sermon is said to have made them the first to follow him. Because it set in motion the Buddha's teaching, or dharma, *on earth, it is usually described as "setting in motion the wheel of* dharma." *The text is from the* Dhammacakkappavattanasutta.

What are the extremes that the "Middle Path" tries to avoid? What emotion drives the chain of suffering? How does the "knowledge" that brings salvation compare to the knowledge sought in the Hindu tradition?

Thus have I heard. The Blessed One was once living in the Deer Park at Isipatana (the Resort of Seers) near Baranasi (Benares). There he addressed the group of five bhikkhus.

"Bhikkhus, these two extremes ought not to be practiced by one who has gone forth from the household life. What are the two? There is devotion to the indulgence of sense-pleasures, which is low, common, the way of ordinary people, unworthy and unprofitable; and there is devotion to self-mortification, which is painful, unworthy and unprofitable.

"Avoiding both these extremes, the Tathagata has realized the Middle Path: it gives vision, it gives knowledge, and it leads to calm, to insight, to enlightenment, to Nibbana. And what is that Middle Path? It is simply the Noble Eightfold Path, namely, right view, right thought, right speech, right action, right livelihood, right effort, right mindfulness, right concentration. This is the Middle Path realized by the Tathagata, which gives vision, which gives knowledge, and which leads to calm, to insight, to enlightenment, to Nibbana. . . .

"The Noble Truth of suffering *(Dukkha)* is this: Birth is suffering; aging is suffering; sickness is suffering; death is suffering; sorrow and lamentation, pain, grief and despair are suffering; association with the unpleasant is suffering; dissociation from the pleasant is suffering; not to get what one wants is suffering—in brief, the five aggregates of attachment are suffering.

"The Noble Truth of the origin of suffering is this: It is this thirst (craving) which produces re-existence and re-becoming, bound up with passionate greed. It finds fresh delight now here and now there, namely, thirst for non-existence (self-annihilation).

"The Noble Truth of the Cessation of suffering is this: It is the complete cessation of that very thirst, giving it up, renouncing it, emancipating oneself from it, detaching oneself from it.

"The Noble Truth of the Path leading to the Cessation of suffering is this: It is simply the Noble Eightfold Path. . . .

" 'This is the Noble Truth of Suffering *(Dukkha)*': such was the vision, the knowledge, the wisdom, the science, the light, that arose in me with regard to things not heard before. 'This suffering, as a noble truth, should be fully understood.'

" 'This is the Noble Truth of the Cessation of suffering': such was the vision 'This Cessation of suffering, as a noble truth, should be realized.'

" 'This is the Noble Truth of the Path leading to the Cessation of suffering': such was the vision, 'This Path leading to the Cessation of suffering, as a noble truth, has been followed (cultivated).'

"As long as my vision of true knowledge was not fully clear regarding the Four Noble Truths, I did not claim to have realized the perfect Enlightenment that is supreme in the world with its gods, in this world with its recluses and brahmanas, with its princes and men. But when my vision of true knowledge was fully clear regarding the Four Noble Truths, then I claimed to have realized the perfect Enlightenment that is supreme in the world with its gods, in this world with its recluses and brahmanas, with its princes and men. And a vision of true knowledge arose in me thus: My heart's deliverance is unassailable. This is the last birth. Now there is no more rebecoming (rebirth)."

This the Blessed One said. The group of five bhikkhus was glad, and they rejoiced at his words.

—*Samyutta-nikaya*, LVI, II

---

had attained this goal; when he died (ca. 486 B.C.E.) after a life of teaching others how to master desiring, he passed from the round of existence forever. In Buddhist terminology, he attained nirvana, the extinguishing of karmic bondage. This attainment became the starting point for the growth and eventual spread of the Buddhist *Dharma*, which was to assume new and diverse forms in its long history.

The Buddhist movement, like the Jain, included not only those who were willing to renounce marriage and normal occupations to become part of the Buddha's communities of

An early carving showing the *chakra*, or wheel of *dharma*, the Buddha's teaching, adored by humans and gods. Above the wheel is an umbrella of Lordship. [Corbis-Bettmann]

monks or nuns, but also laypersons who would strive to live by the high moral standards of the tradition and support those willing and able to become mendicants in attaining full release. Buddhist tradition, again like that of the Jains, encompassed from the outset seekers of both the extraordinary and the ordinary norms in their present lives. This dual community has remained characteristic of all forms of Buddhism wherever it is practiced. Later we shall see how varied these forms have been historically. But however much the essentially a-theistic, a-ritualistic, and pragmatic tradition was later modified and expanded (so that popular Buddhism would cultivate even theistic devotion to a divinized Buddha and other enlightened beings), the fundamental vision persisted of a humanly attainable wisdom that leads to compassion and release.

The varying visions of Upanishadic, Jain, and Buddhist thought proved durable, albeit in different ways and degrees in India itself, as we have noted. The later emergence of "Hindu" tradition drew on all three of these revolutionary strands in Indian thought and integrated various of their fundamental ideas about the universe, human life, morality, and society into the cultic and mythic strands of both Brahmanic and popular Indian practice.

The Religion of the Israelites

The ancient Near East was a polytheistic world. Everywhere people worshiped local or regional gods and goddesses. Some of these deities were associated with natural phenomena such as mountains or animals, the sky or the earth. For example, Shamash in Mesopotamia and Re in Egypt were both sun gods. Others were tribal or local deities, such as Marduk in Babylonia or Atum, the patron god of the Egyptian city of On (Heliopolis). Still others represented elemental powers of this world or the next, as was the case with Baal, the fertility god of the Canaanites, and Ishtar, whom the Assyrians worshiped as goddess of love and of war. Furthermore, from our perspective, the gods were represented largely as capricious, amoral beings who were no more affected by the actions of humans than were the natural forces that some of them represented.

If the gods were many and diverse, so too were the religious traditions of the ancient Near Eastern world. Even the major traditions of religious thought in Egypt and Mesopotamia did not offer comprehensive interpretations of human life that linked history and human destiny to a transcendent or eternal realm of meaning beyond this world—or at least no one interpretation was able to predominate in this pluralistic, religiously fragmented region.

Out of this polytheistic and pluralistic world came the great tradition of monotheistic faith represented historically in the Jewish, Christian, and Islamic communities. This tradition traces its origin not to any of the great imperial cultures of the ancient world, but to the small nation of the Israelites, or Hebrews. Although they were only a tiny tribal people whose external fortunes were at the mercy of the ebb and flow of the great dynasties and empires of the second and first millennia B.C.E., their impact on world civilization was far greater than that of their giant neighbors. For all the glories of the major civilizations of the Fertile Crescent and Nile valley, it was the Israelites, not the Babylonians or Egyptians, who generated a tradition that significantly affected later history. This tradition was ethical monotheism.

Monotheism, faith in a single, all-powerful God as the sole creator, sustainer, and ruler of the universe, may be older than the Hebrews, but its first clear historical manifestation was with them. It was among the Hebrew tribes that emphasis on the moral demands and responsibilities that the one God placed on individual and community was first definitively linked to human history itself, and that history to a divine plan. This historically based ethical and monotheistic tradition culminated in the Jewish, Christian, and Islamic religions, but its direction was set among the ancient Hebrews.

The path from the appearance of the Hebrews as a nomadic people in the northern Arabian peninsula, sometime after 2000 B.C.E., to the full flowering of Judaic monotheism in the mid-first millennium B.C.E. was a long one. Before we turn to the monotheistic revolution itself, we need to look briefly at this history.

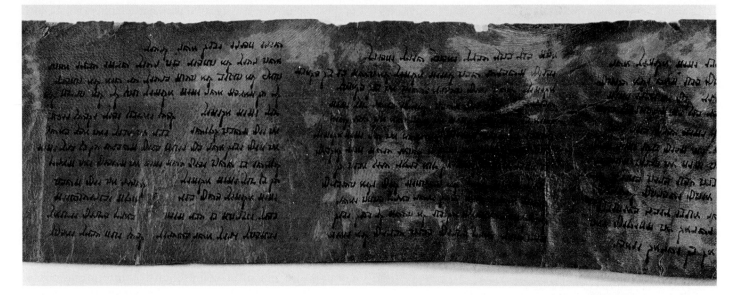

This is a photograph of part of one of the ancient scrolls found by Bedouins, beginning in 1947, in a remote cave at Khirbat near the Dead Sea in Jordan. The passage from the Hebrew Bible contains part of the Ten Commandments in the book of Deuteronomy. The scrolls were written some time between 200 B.C.E. and 68 C.E. They contain documents that suggest they belonged to a monastic sect of Jews called Essenes whose beliefs bear some similarity to those of John the Baptist and Jesus. [ASAP/David Harris Photography]

From Hebrew Nomads to the Israelite Nation

The history of the Hebrews, later known as Israelites, must be pieced together from various sources. They are mentioned only rarely in the records of their ancient Near Eastern neighbors, so we must rely on their own accounts as compiled in the Hebrew Bible (the "Old Testament" of Christian terminology). It was not intended as a history in our sense; rather, it is a complicated collection of historical narrative, wisdom literature, poetry, law, and religious witness. Scholars once tended to discard the Bible as a source for historians, but the trend today is to take it seriously while using it cautiously and critically. Although its earliest writings go back at most to the ninth century B.C.E. (it was fixed in its present form only in the second century C.E.), it contains much older oral materials that allow us at least some glimpses of the earliest history of the Hebrew people.

We need not reject the core reality of the tradition that the Hebrew Abraham came from Ur in southern Mesopotamia and wandered west with his Hebrew clan to tend his flocks in the land later known as Palestine. Such a movement would be in accord with what we know of a general westward migration of semi-nomadic tribes from Mesopotamia after about 1950 B.C.E. Any precise dating of the arrival of the Hebrews in Palestine is impossible, but it was likely between 1900 and 1600 B.C.E.

It is, however, with Moses, at about the beginning of the thirteenth century B.C.E., that the Hebrews tread clearly upon the stage of history. Some of Abraham's people had settled in the Palestinian region, but others apparently wandered farther, into Egypt, perhaps with the Hyksos invaders (see Chapter 1). By about 1400 B.C.E., as the biblical narrative tells it, they had become a settled but subjected, even enslaved, people there. Under Moses, part of the Egyptian Israelites fled Egypt to find a new homeland to the east, from which Abraham's descendants had come. They may then have wandered in the Sinai Desert and elsewhere for several decades before reaching Canaan, the province of Palestine that is described in the Bible as their promised homeland. The Bible presents this experience as the key event in Israel's history: the forging of the covenant, or mutual pact, between God, or *Yahweh*, and His people. We interpret this Exodus as the time when the Israelites emerged as a nation, a people with a sense of community and common faith.

By about 1200 B.C.E., they had displaced the Canaanite inhabitants of ancient Palestine. After perhaps two centuries of consolidation as a loose federation of tribes, the now-settled nation reached its peak as a kingdom under David (r. ca. 1000–961 B.C.E.) and Solomon (r. ca. 961–922 B.C.E.). But the kingdom split into two parts in the ninth century B.C.E.: Israel in the north and Judah, with its capital at Jerusalem, in the south (see Map 2–1).

The rise of great empires around them brought disaster to the Israelites. The northern kingdom fell to the Assyrians in 722 B.C.E.; its people were scattered and, according to tradition, lost forever—the so-called ten lost tribes. Only the kingdom of Judah, with its seat at Jerusalem, remained, and henceforward we may call the Israelites Jews. In 586 B.C.E., Judah was defeated by the Neo-Babylonian king Nebuchadnezzar II (d. 562 B.C.E.). He destroyed the Jewish cult center, the great temple built by Solomon, and carried off the cream of the Jewish nation as exiles to be resettled in Babylon. There, in the "Babylonian captivity" of the Exile, without a temple, the Jews clung to their traditions and faith. After the new Persian dynasty of the Achaemenids defeated the Babylonians in 539 B.C.E., the Jews were allowed to return and resettle in their homeland. Many, but not all, of the exiles did return, and by about 516 B.C.E., a second temple was erected in a restored Jerusalem.

The new Judaic state continued for centuries to be dominated by foreign peoples but was able to maintain its religious and national identity and occasionally to assert itself. However, it was again destroyed and its people dispersed after the Romans' destruction of Jerusalem, in 70 C.E. and again in 132 C.E. By this era, however, the Jews had developed a religious worldview that would long outlive any Judaic national state.

The Monotheistic Revolution

The fate of this small nation would be of little interest were it not for its unique religious achievement. It developed a tradition of faith that amounted to a revolution in ways of thinking about the human condition, the meaning of life and history, and the nature of the Divine. It was not the overt history of the Judaic state down to its catastrophic end in 132 C.E. that was to have lasting historical importance, but what the Jews made of that history—how they interpreted it and built upon it a lasting Jewish culture and identity. The revolutionary character of this interpretation lay in its uniquely moralistic understanding of human life and history and the uncompromising monotheism on which it was based.

At the root of this monotheistic tradition stands the figure of Abraham. Not only Jews but also Christians and Muslims look to him as the symbolic founder of their monotheistic faith. The Hebrews in Abraham's time were probably much like other primitive tribal peoples in their religious attitudes. For them, the world must have been alive with supernatural powers: ancestral spirits, personifications of the forces of nature, and deities of local places. Abraham probably conceived of his Lord simply as his chosen deity among the many divinities who might be worshiped. Yet for the strength of his faith in his God, the biblical account recognizes him as the "Father of the Faithful," the first of the Hebrew patriarchs to

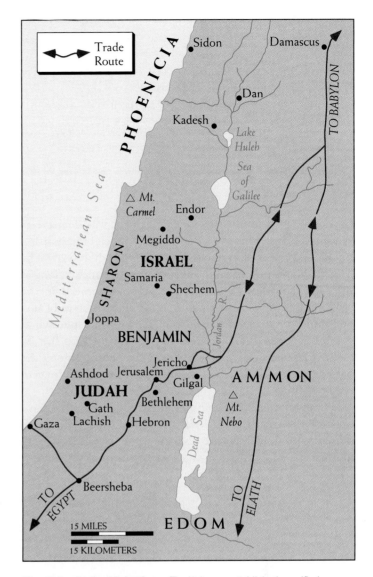

Map 2-1 Ancient Palestine. The Hebrews established a unified kingdom under Kings David and Solomon in the tenth century B.C.E. After Solomon the kingdom was divided into Israel in the north and Judah, with its capital, Jerusalem, in the south. North of Israel were the great commercial cities of Phoenicia.

make a covenant with the God who would become unique and supreme. In this, Abraham promised to serve only Him, and his God promised to bless his descendants and guide them as His special people.

After Abraham, the next major step came with Moses. As with Abraham's faith, it is difficult to say how much the Mosaic covenant at Sinai actually marked the achievement of an exclusively monotheistic faith. A notion of the supremacy of Yahweh is reflected in the biblical emphasis on the Israelites' rejection of all other gods after Sinai—and on their subsequent victory, through Yahweh's might, over the

Canaanites. Certainly, the covenant event was decisive in uniting the Israelites as a people with a special relationship to God. At Sinai, they received both God's holy Law (the Torah) and his promise of protection and guidance as long as they kept the law. This was the pivotal moment in the monotheistic revolution that came to full fruition only several hundred years later. But from the later perspective of the biblical redactors at least, from Sinai forward the Israelites saw themselves as God's chosen people among the nations and their history as the history of the mighty acts of the one God.

The monotheistic revolution might thus be said to have begun with Abraham or Moses. Historically, we can trace it primarily from the bipartite division of the Israelite kingdom in 922 B.C.E. After this, men and women known as the *prophets*

arose. These inspired messengers of God were sent to call their people back from worship of false gods to faith in the one true God, and from immorality to obedience to God's commandments.

The important point in the colorful history of the great and lesser prophets is that their activity was closely linked to the saga of Israelite national success, exile, and return in the mid-first millennium B.C.E. In the biblical interpretation of these events, we can see the progressive consolidation of Judaic religion. This consolidation, even amidst the political demise of the Israelite kingdom, was largely the work of the prophets. Their concern with purifying Jewish faith, and with morality, focused in particular on two ideas that proved central to Judaic monotheism.

The first was the significance of history in the divine plan. Calling on the Jews' awareness of the Sinai covenant, the prophets saw in Israel's past and present troubles God's punishment for failing in their covenant duties. Their prophecies of coming disaster from their enemies were based on the conviction that unless Israel changed its ways, more punishment would follow. But they were not only prophets of doom. When the predicted disasters arrived, their vision extended to seeing Israel as the "suffering servant" among the nations, the people who, by their trials, would purify other nations and bring them ultimately to God. Here the nationalistic, particularistic focus of previous Israelite religion gave way to a more complete, univer-

Exile of the Israelites. In 722 B.C.E. the northern part of Jewish Palestine, the kingdom of Israel, was conquered by the Assyrians. Its people were driven from their homeland and exiled all over the vast Assyrian Empire. This wall carving in low relief comes from the palace of the Assyrian king Sennacherib at Nineveh. It shows the Jews with their cattle and baggage going into exile. [Erich Lessing/Art Resource, N.Y.]

God's Purpose with Israel

The Ten Commandments that Moses received from God for the Israelites according to Jewish tradition are given in two different places with slightly different wording in the Torah. The Exodus passage is one of these; the other is in Deuteronomy 5, the chapter immediately followed by the second passage cited here, Deuteronomy 6:1–9. This latter passage contains the fundamental statement of Judaic faith (verses 4–5), known as the Shema *("Hear," the word that begins this divine command).*

How do these passages exemplify the moral consciousness and utter faith in God that Jewish monotheism is built upon?

And God spoke all these words, saying,

"I am the Lord your God, who brought you out of the land of Egypt, out of the house of bondage.

"You shall have no other gods before me.

"You shall not make for yourself a graven image, or any likeness of anything that is in heaven above, or that is in the earth beneath, or that is in the water under the earth; you shall not bow down to them or serve them; for I the Lord your God am a jealous God, visiting the iniquity of the fathers upon the children to the third and the fourth generation of those who hate me, but showing steadfast love to thousands of those who love me and keep my commandments.

"You shall not take the name of the Lord your God in vain; for the Lord will not hold him guiltless who takes his name in vain.

"Remember the sabbath day, to keep it holy. Six days you shall labor, and do all your work; but the seventh day is a sabbath to the Lord your God; in it you shall not do any work, you, or your son, or your daughter, your manservant, or your maidservant, or your cattle, or the sojourner who is within your gates; for in six days the Lord made heaven and earth, the sea, and all that is in them and rested the seventh day; therefore the Lord blessed the sabbath day and hallowed it.

"Honor your father and your mother, that your days may be long in the land which the Lord your God gives you.

"You shall not kill.

"You shall not commit adultery.

"You shall not steal.

"You shall not bear false witness against your neighbor.

"You shall not covet your neighbor's house; you shall not covet your neighbor's wife, or his manservant, or his maidservant, or his ox, or his ass, or anything that is your neighbor's."

Exodus 20:1–17

"Now this is the commandment, the statutes and the ordinances which the Lord your God commanded me to teach you, that you may do them in the land to which you are going over, to possess it; that you may fear the Lord your God, you and your son and your son's son, by keeping all his statutes and his commandments, which I command you, all the days of your life; and that your days may be prolonged. Hear therefore, O Israel, and be careful to do them; that it may go well with you, and that you may multiply greatly, as the Lord, the God of your fathers, has promised you, in a land flowing with milk and honey.

"Hear, O Israel: The Lord our God is one Lord, and you shall love the Lord your God with all your heart, and with all your soul, and with all your might. And these words which I command you this day shall be upon your heart; and you shall teach them diligently to your children, and shall talk of them when you sit in your house, and when you walk by the way, and when you lie down, and when you rise. And you shall bind them as a sign upon your hand, and they shall be as frontlets between your eyes. And you shall write them on the doorposts of your house and on your gates.

Deuteronomy 6:1–9

salist monotheism: Yahweh was now God of all, even the Babylonians or Assyrians.

The second idea centered on the nature of Yahweh. The prophets saw in Him the transcendent ideal of justice and goodness. From this view followed naturally the demand for justice and goodness, individually and collectively, among His worshipers. God was a righteous God who expected righteousness from human beings. No longer could He be only the object of a sacrificial cult: He was a moral God who demanded goodness, not blood offerings or empty prayers. A

corollary of God's goodness was His love for His people, as the prophet Hosea (late eighth century B.C.E.) emphasized. However much He might have to punish them for their sins, God would finally lead them back to His favor.

The crux of the breakthrough to ethical monotheism lay in linking the Lord of the Universe to history and morality. The Almighty Creator was seen as actively concerned with the actions and fates of His human creatures as exemplified in Israel. This concern was reflected in God's involvement in history, which thus took on transcendent meaning. God

The Temple Mount, seen from the west. The traditional site of the Jerusalem Temple (the Herodian western wailing wall is in the center), the Temple Mount is a holy site especially to Muslims, as well as to Jews and Christians. The dome at the left is the Muslim Dome of the Rock sanctuary (692 C.E.); at the far right is the Al-Aqsa mosque, built only a few years later. [David H. Wells, 1990]

had created humankind for an ultimately good purpose; they were called to be just and good like their Creator, for they were involved in the fulfillment of His divine purpose. This fulfillment would come in the restoration of Israel as a people purified of their sins: "I will put my law within them, and I will write it upon their hearts; and I will be their God, and they shall be my people" (Jeremiah 31:33).

However, even after the Exile, the realization of the prophesied days of peace and blessedness under God's rule clearly still had not come. Jews were scattered from Egypt to Babylonia, and their homeland was controlled by foreign powers. This context brought forth the late prophetic concept that history's culmination would come in a future Messianic age. Faith and morality were tied to human destiny, even without the still later Jewish idea that a day of judgment would cap the golden age of the Messiah. The significance of these ideas, some of which might have come from the Jews' encounter with Zoroastrian traditions during the Exile, did not stop with Judaic religion. They played a key role in similar Christian and Muslim ideas of a Messianic deliverer, resurrection of the body, and a life after death.

Alongside the prophets, the other key element in the monotheistic revolution of the Jews was the Law itself. The Law is embodied in the five books of Torah (the Pentateuch, or "five books": Genesis, Exodus, Leviticus, Numbers, and Deuteronomy). The central place of the Law in Jewish life was reestablished, after a period of decline, by King Josiah of Judah (c. 649–609 B.C.E.) shortly before the fall of Jerusalem and the Exile. Its presence and importance in Judaic faith enabled the Jews in exile to survive the loss of the Temple and its priestly cult, thereby fixing the Torah even

over Jerusalem as the ultimate earthly focus of faith in God. Its centrality for the Judaic nation was reaffirmed after the reestablishment of the Temple by the prophets Ezra and Nehemiah in the fifth century B.C.E.

In the second century B.C.E., the enduring role of Torah was ensured by its physical compilation, together with the books of the prophets and other writings, into the Holy Scriptures, or Bible (from Greek *bibloi*, "books"). In the Torah we have not only the Law itself, but also the record of the Jews' journey to the recognition of God's law for His people. A holy, authoritative, divinely revealed scripture as an element of Judaic monotheism had revolutionary consequences, not only for Jews, but also for Christians and Muslims. It put the seal on the monotheistic revolution that had made the sovereignty and righteousness of God the foci of faith.

In the evolution of Judaic monotheistic faith, we see the beginning of one of the major traditions of world religion. For the first time we find a nation defined not primarily by dynastic, linguistic, or geographic considerations, but by shared religious faith and practice. This was something new in human history. It was later to have still greater effects when not only Judaic but also Christian and Muslim tradition would change the face of much of the world.

Greek Philosophy

Greek thought offered different approaches and answers to many of the same concerns as those of the original monotheists. Calling attention to some of those differences will help to point up the distinctive outlook of the Greeks and of the later cultures of western civilization that have drawn heavily on it.

Greek ideas had much in common with those of earlier peoples. The Greek gods had most of the characteristics of the Mesopotamian deities; magic and incantations played a part in Greek lives; and their law was usually connected with divinity. Many, if not most, Greeks in the ancient world must have lived with notions similar to those held by other peoples. But surprisingly, some Greeks developed ideas that were strikingly different and, in so doing, set a part of humankind on an entirely new path. As early as the sixth century B.C.E., Greeks living in the Ionian cities of Asia Minor raised questions and suggested answers about nature that produced an intellectual revolution. In speculating about the nature of the world and its origin, they made guesses that were completely naturalistic and included no reference to supernatural powers. One historian of Greek thought, discussing the views of Thales (624–545 B.C.E.), the first Greek philosopher, put the case particularly well:

In one of the Babylonian legends it says: "All the lands were sea. Marduk bound a rush mat upon the face of the waters, he made dirt and piled it beside the rush mat." What Thales did was to leave Marduk out. He, too, said that everything was once water. But he thought that earth and everything else had been formed out of water by a natural process, like the silting up of the Delta of the Nile. It is an admirable beginning, the whole point of which is that it gathers together into a coherent picture a number of observed facts without letting Marduk in.[3]

By putting the question of the world's origin in a naturalistic form, Thales may have initiated the unreservedly rational investigation of the universe, and in so doing, initiated both western philosophy and western science.

The same relentlessly rational approach was applied even to the gods themselves. In the same century as Thales, Xenophanes of Colophon expressed the opinion that humans think of the gods as resembling themselves, that like themselves they were born, that they wear clothes like theirs, and that they have voices and bodies like theirs. If oxen, horses, and lions had hands and could paint like humans, Xenophanes argued, they would paint gods in their own image; the oxen would draw gods like oxen and the horses like horses. Thus Africans believed in flat-nosed, black-faced gods, and the Thracians in gods with blue eyes and red hair.[4] In the fifth century B.C.E. Protagoras of Abdera (c. 490–c. 420 B.C.E.) went so far in the direction of agnosticism as to say, "About the gods I can have no knowledge either that they are or that they are not or what is their nature."[5]

This rationalistic, skeptical way of thinking carried over into practical matters as well. The school of medicine led by Hippocrates of Cos (c. 400 B.C.E.) attempted to understand, diagnose, and cure disease without recourse to supernatural forces or beings. One of the Hippocratics wrote of the mysterious disease epilepsy:

It seems to me that the disease is no more divine than any other. It has a natural cause, just as other diseases have. Men think it divine merely because they do not understand it. But if they called everything divine which they do not understand, why, there would be no end of divine things.[6]

By the fifth century B.C.E., it was possible for the historian Thucydides (c. 460–c. 400 B.C.E.) to analyze and explain the behavior of humans in society completely in terms of human nature and chance, leaving no place for the gods or supernatural forces.

The relative unimportance of divine or supernatural forces also characterized Greek views of law and justice. Most Greeks, of course, liked to think that law came ultimately from the gods. In practice, however, and especially in the democratic states, they understood that laws were made by humans and should be obeyed because they represented the expressed consent of the citizens. Law, according to the fourth century B.C.E. statesman Demosthenes (384–322 B.C.E.), was "a general covenant of the whole State, in accordance with which all men in that State ought to regulate their lives."[7]

These ideas, so different from any that came before the Greek, opens the discussion of most of the issues that appear in the long history of civilization and that remain major concerns in the modern world: What is the nature of the universe and how can it be controlled? Are there divine powers, and if so, what is humanity's relationship to them? Are law and justice human, divine, or both? What is the place in human society of freedom, obedience, and reverence? These and many other problems were confronted and intensified by the Greeks.

Reason and the Scientific Spirit

The rational spirit characteristic of Greek culture blossomed in the sixth century B.C.E. into the intellectual examination of the physical world and the place of humankind in it that we

[3]Benjamin Farrington, *Greek Science* (London: Penguin Books, 1953), p. 37.
[4]Frankfort et al., *Before Philosophy* (1949), pp. 14–16.
[5]Hermann Diels, *Fragmente der Vorsokratiker*, 5th ed., by Walther Kranz (Berlin: Weidmann, 1934–1938), Frg. 4.
[6]Ibid., Frgs. 14–16.
[7]*Against Aristogeiton*, p. 16.

call *philosophy*. It is not surprising that the first steps along this path were taken in Ionia on the coast of Asia Minor, which was on the fringe of the Greek world and therefore in touch with foreign ideas and the learning of the East. The Ionians were among the first to recognize that the Greek account of how the world was created and maintained and of the place of humans in it was not universally accepted. Perhaps this realization helped spark the first attempts at disciplined philosophical inquiry.

We have already met Thales of Miletus. He believed that the earth floated on water and that water was the primary substance. This was not a new idea; what was new was the absence of any magical or mythical elements in the explanation. Thales observed, as any person can, that water has many forms: liquid, solid, and gaseous. He saw that it could "create" land by alluvial deposit and that it was necessary for all life. These observations he organized by reason into a single explanation that accounted for many phenomena without any need for the supernatural. The first philosopher thus set the tone for future investigations. Greek philosophers assumed that the world was knowable, rational, and simple.

The search for fundamental rational explanations of phenomena was carried forward by another Milesian, Anaximander (c. 611–546 B.C.E.). He imagined that the basic element was something undefined, "unlimited." The world emerged from this basic element as the result of an interaction of opposite forces—wet and dry, hot and cold. Anaximander pictured the universe in eternal motion, with all sensible things emerging from the "unlimited," then decaying and returning to it. He also argued that human beings originated in water and had evolved to the present state through several stages, including that of a fish.

Anaximenes, another Milesian who flourished about 546 B.C.E., believed air to be primary. It took different forms as a result of the purely physical processes of rarefaction and condensation.

Heraclitus of Ephesus, who lived near the end of the sixth century B.C.E., carried the dialogue further. His famous saying, "All is motion," raised important problems. If all is constantly in motion, nothing ever really exists. Yet Heraclitus believed that the world order was governed by a guiding principle, the *logos*, and that though phenomena changed, the *logos* did not. *Logos* has several meanings, among them "word," "language," "speech," and "reason." So when Heraclitus said that

the physical world was governed by Logos, he implied that it could be explained by reason. Speculations about the physical world, what we would call natural science, thus soon led the way toward even more difficult philosophical speculations about language, about the manner of human thought, and about knowledge itself.

In opposition to Heraclitus, the fifth-century B.C.E. philosopher Parmenides of Elea and his pupil Zeno argued that change was only an illusion of the senses. Reason and reflection showed that reality was fixed and unchanging because it seemed evident that nothing could be created out of nothingness. Such fundamental speculations were carried forward by Empedocles of Acragas (flourished c. 450 B.C.E.), who spoke of four basic elements: fire, water, earth, and air. Like Parmenides, he thought that reality was permanent but not immobile, for the four elements were moved by two primary forces, Love and Strife, or, as we might be inclined to say, attraction and repulsion.

This theory was clearly a step on the road to the atomic theory of Leucippus of Miletus (flourished fifth century B.C.E.) and Democritus of Abdera (c. 460–370 B.C.E.). They believed that the world consisted of innumerable tiny, solid particles (atoms) that could not be divided or modified and that moved about in the void. The size of the atoms and the arrangement in which they were joined with others produced the secondary qualities that the senses could perceive, such as color and shape. These qualities—unlike the atoms themselves, which were natural—were merely conventional. Anaxagoras of Clazomenae (c. 500–428 B.C.E.) had previously spoken of tiny fundamental particles called *seeds*, that were put together on a rational basis by a force called *nous*, or "mind." Thus, Anaxagoras suggested a distinction between matter and mind. The atomists, however, regarded "soul," or "mind," as material and believed that everything was guided by purely physical laws. In the arguments of Anaxagoras and the atomists, we have the beginning of the philosophical debate between materialism and idealism that has continued through the ages.

These discussions interested few; indeed, most Greeks were suspicious of such speculations. A far more influential

The Atomists' Account of the Origin of the World Order

Leucippus and Democritus were Greek thinkers of the fifth century B.C.E. who originated the theory that the world is entirely material, made up of atoms and the void, moving through space without external guidance. As these selections show, they provided a fundamental explanation of things that was purely natural, without divine or mythical intervention. Their view was passed on and later influenced such Renaissance scientists as Galileo.

Compare the Atomists' explanation of the origins of the world with that presented in the box titled "Hymn to the Lord of Creatures" in Chapter 1. How do these explanations of the nature of things and how they got that way differ from those offered by different civilizations and by the Greeks before the sixth century B.C.E.? What are the consequences and significance of this new way of looking at the universe?

1.

The world-orders arise in this way. Many bodies of all sorts of shapes "split off" from the infinite into a great void where, being gathered together, they give rise to a single vortex, in which, colliding and circling in all sorts of ways, they begin to separate apart, like to like. Being unable to circle in equilibrium any longer because of their congestion, the light bodies go off into the outer void like chaff, while the rest "remain together" and, becoming entangled, unite their motions and produce first a spherical structure. This stands apart like a "membrane," containing in itself all sorts of bodies; and, because of the resistance of the middle, as these revolve the surrounding membrane becomes thin as contiguous bodies continually flow together because of contact with the vortex. And in this way the earth arose, the bodies which were carried to the middle remaining together. Again, the surrounding membrane increases because of the acquisition of bodies from without; and as it moves with the vortex, whatever it touches it adds to itself. Certain of these, becoming entangled, form a structure at first very watery and muddy; but afterward they dry out, being carried about with the rotation of the whole, and ignite to form the substance of the heavenly bodies.

2.

Certainly the atoms did not arrange themselves in order by design or intelligence, nor did they propound what movements each should make. But rather myriad atoms, swept along through infinite time or myriad paths by blows and their own weight, have come together in every possible way and tried out every combination that they could possibly create. So it happens that, after roaming the world for aeons of time in making trial of every combination and movement, at length they come together—those atoms whose sudden coincidence often becomes the origin of mighty things: of earth and sea and sky and the species of living things.

The first selection is from Diogenes Laertius 9.31; the second is from Lucretius, *De Rerum Naturae* 5.419–431. Both selections from Robinson, John Mansley. *An Introduction to Early Greek Philosophy*. Copyright © 1968 by John Mansley Robinson. Used with permission of the author.

---

debate was begun by a group of professional teachers who emerged in the mid-fifth century B.C.E. Called *Sophists*, they traveled about and received pay for teaching practical techniques of persuasion, such as rhetoric, which were highly valued in democracies like Athens. Some claimed to teach wisdom and even virtue. They did not speculate about the physical universe but applied reasoned analysis to human beliefs and institutions. This human focus was characteristic of fifth-century-B.C.E. thought, as was the central problem that the Sophists considered: They discovered the tension and even the contradiction between nature and custom, or law. The more traditional among them argued that law itself was in accord with nature, and this view fortified the traditional beliefs about the *polis*, the Greek city-state (see Chapter 3).

Others argued, however, that laws were merely conventional and not in accord with nature. The law was not of divine origin but merely the result of an agreement among people. It could not pretend to be a positive moral force, but merely had the negative function of preventing people from harming each other. The most extreme Sophists argued that law was contrary to nature, a trick whereby the weak controlled the strong. Critias (c. 460–403 B.C.E.)went so far as to say that the gods themselves had been invented by some clever man to deter people from doing what they wished. Such ideas attacked the theoretical foundations of the *polis* and helped provoke the philosophical responses of Plato and Aristotle in the next century.

Political and Moral Philosophy

Like thinkers in other parts of the world around the middle of the first millennium B.C.E., some Greeks were vitally concerned with the formulation of moral principles for the governance of the state and the regulation of individual life, as well as with more abstract problems of the nature of existence and transcendence. Nowhere is the Greek concern with ethical,

The Sophists: From Rational Inquiry to Skepticism

The rational spirit inherent in Greek thought was carried to remarkable and dangerous extremes by the Sophists in the fifth century B.C.E. As these three selections suggest, they questioned even the nature, the existence, and the origin of the gods, subjecting these matters to rational analysis.

What was new in the thinking of the Sophists? How was it similar to the thought of the Atomists (Democritus and Leucippus)? How was it different? In what ways were Sophist ideas threatening to the Greek way of life?

1.

Concerning the gods, I do not know whether they exist or not. For many are the obstacles to knowledge: the obscurity of the subject and the brevity of human life.

2.

Prodicus says that the ancients worshiped as gods the sun, the moon, rivers, springs, and all things useful to human life, simply because of their usefulness—just as the Egyptians deify the Nile. For this reason bread is worshiped as Demeter, wine as Dionysus, water as Poseidon, fire as Hephaestus, and so on for each of the things that are useful to men.

3.

There was a time when the life of man was disorderly and bestial and subject to brute force; when there was no reward for the good and no punishment for the bad. At that time, I think, men enacted laws in order that justice might be absolute ruler and have arrogance as its slave; and if anyone did wrong he was punished. Then, when the laws prohibited them from doing deeds of violence, they began to do them secretly. Then, I think, some shrewd and wise man invented fear of the gods for mortals, so that there might be some deterrent to the wicked even if they did or said or thought something in secret. Therefore he introduced the divine, saying that there is a god, flourishing with immortal life, hearing and seeing with his mind, thinking of all things and watching over them and having a divine nature; who will hear everything that is said among mortals and will be able to see all that is done. And if you plan any evil in secret it will not escape the notice of the gods, for they are of surpassing intelligence. In speaking thus he introduced the prettiest of teachings, concealing the truth under a false account. And in order that he might better strike fear into the hearts of men he told them that the gods dwell in that place which he knew to be a source of fears to mortals—and of benefits too—namely, the upper periphery where they saw lightnings and heard the dreaded rumblings of thunder and saw the starry body of the heaven, the beauteous embroidery of that wise craftsman Time, where the bright glowing mass of the sun moves and whence dark rains descend to earth. With such fears did he surround men, and by means of them he established the deity securely in a place befitting his dignity, and quenched lawlessness. Thus, I think, did some man first persuade mortals to believe in a race of gods.

The first selection is from Diogenes Laertius 9.51; the next two are from Sextus Empiricus, *Against the Schoolmasters* 9.18, 9.54. From Robinson, John Mansley, *An Introduction to Early Greek Philosophy.* Copyright © 1968 by John Mansley Robinson. Used with permission of the author.

political, and religious issues clearer than in the philosophical tradition that began with Socrates in the latter half of the fifth century B.C.E. That tradition continued with Socrates' pupil Plato and with Plato's pupil Aristotle. Aristotle also had great interest in and made great contributions to the scientific understanding of the physical world, but he is perhaps more important for his impact on later western and Islamic metaphysics.

The starting point for all three of the philosophical giants of Hellenic political and moral philosophy was the social and political reality of the Greek city-state, or *polis*. The greatest crisis for the *polis* was the Great Peloponnesian War (435–404 B.C.E.), which is discussed in Chapter 3. Probably the most complicated response to this crisis may be found in the life and teachings of Socrates (469–399 B.C.E.). Because he wrote nothing, our knowledge of him comes chiefly from his disci-

ples Plato and Xenophon (c. 435–354 B.C.E.) and from later tradition. Although as a young man Socrates was interested in speculations about the physical world, he later turned to the investigation of ethics and morality. As the Roman writer and statesman Cicero (106–43 B.C.E.) put it, he brought philosophy down from the heavens.

Socrates was committed to the search for truth and for the knowledge about human affairs that he believed reason could reveal. His method was to go among men, particularly those reputed to know something, like craftsmen, poets, and politicians, to question and cross-examine them. The result was always the same: Those he questioned might have technical information and skills but seldom had any knowledge of the fundamental principles of human behavior. It is understandable that Athenians so exposed should become angry with their examiner, and it is not surprising that they thought Socrates was undermining the beliefs and values of the *polis*. Socrates' unconcealed contempt for democracy, which seemingly relied on ignorant amateurs to make important political decisions without any certain knowledge, created further hostility. Moreover, his insistence on the primacy of his own individualism and his determination to pursue philosophy even against the wishes of his fellow citizens reinforced this hostility and the prejudice that went with it.

But Socrates, unlike the Sophists, did not accept pay for his teaching; he professed ignorance and denied that he taught at all. His individualism, moreover, was unlike the worldly hedonism of some of the Sophists. It was not wealth or pleasure or power that he urged people to seek, but "the greatest improvement of the soul." He differed also from the more radical Sophists in denying that the *polis* and its laws were merely conventional. He thought, on the contrary, that they had a legitimate claim on the citizen, and he proved it in the most convincing fashion. In 399 B.C.E., he was condemned to death by an Athenian jury on the charges of bringing new gods into the city and of corrupting its youth. His dialectical inquiries had angered many important people, and his criticism of democracy must have been viewed with suspicion. He was given a chance to escape, but in Plato's *Crito* we are told of his refusal to do so because of his veneration of the laws.

Socrates' career set the stage for later responses to the travail of the *polis;* he recognized its difficulties and criticized its shortcomings. Although he turned away from an active political life, he did not abandon the idea of the *polis*. He fought as a soldier in its defense, obeyed its laws, and sought to use reason to put its values on a sound foundation.

The Cynics

One branch of Socratic thought—the concern with personal morality and one's own soul, the disdain for worldly pleasure and wealth, and the withdrawal from political life—was developed and then distorted almost beyond recognition by the Cynic school. Antisthenes (ca. 455–ca. 360 B.C.E.), a follower of Socrates, is said to have been its founder, but its most famous exemplar was Diogenes of Sinope (ca. 400–ca. 325 B.C.E.). Socrates disparaged wealth and worldly comfort, so Diogenes wore rags and lived in a tub. He performed shameful acts in public and made his living by begging to show his rejection of convention. He believed that happiness lay in satisfying natural needs in the simplest and most direct way. Because actions to this end, being natural, could not be indecent, they could and should be done publicly.

Socrates questioned the theoretical basis for popular religious beliefs; the Cynics ridiculed all religious observances. As Plato said, Diogenes was Socrates gone mad. Beyond that, the way of the Cynics contradicted important Socratic beliefs. Socrates believed that virtue was not a matter of birth but of knowledge, and that people did wrong only through ignorance of what is virtuous. The Cynics, on the contrary, believed that virtue was an affair of deeds and did not need a store of words and learning. Wisdom and happiness came from pursuing the proper style of life, not from philosophy. The Cynics moved even further from Socrates by abandoning the concept of the *polis* entirely. When Diogenes was asked about his citizenship, he answered that he was *kosmopolites*, a citizen of the world. The Cynics plainly had turned away from the past, and their views anticipated those of the Hellenistic Age (see Chapter 3).

Plato

Plato (429–347 B.C.E.) was the most important of Socrates' associates and is a perfect example of the pupil who becomes greater than his master. He was the first systematic philosopher and therefore the first to place political ideas in their full philosophical context. He was also a writer of genius, leaving us twenty-six philosophical discussions. Almost all are in the form of dialogues, which somehow make the examination of difficult and complicated philosophical problems seem dramatic and entertaining.

Born of a noble Athenian family, Plato looked forward to an active political career until he was discouraged by the excesses of Athenian politics and the execution of Socrates. Twice he went to Sicily in the hope of producing a model state at Syracuse under that city's rulers, but without success. In 386 B.C.E., Plato founded the Academy, a center of philosophical investigation and a school for training statesmen and citizens that had a powerful impact on Greek thought and endured until it was closed in the sixth century C.E.

Like Socrates, Plato firmly believed in the *polis* and its values. Its virtues were order, harmony, and justice, and one of its main objects was to produce good people. Like his master, and unlike the radical Sophists, Plato thought that the *polis* was in accord with nature. He accepted Socrates' doctrine of the identity of virtue and knowledge and made it plain what that knowledge was: *episteme*, science, a body of true and unchanging wisdom open to only a few philosophers whose training, character, and intellect allowed them to see reality. Only such people were qualified to rule; they themselves would prefer the life of pure contemplation but would accept their responsibility and take their turn as philosopher-kings. The training of such men required a specialization of function and a subordination of the individual to the community. This specialization would lead to Plato's definition of justice: that each man should do only that one thing to which his nature was best suited.

Plato understood that the *polis* of his day suffered from terrible internal stress, class struggle, and factional divisions. His solution, however, was not that of some Greeks—that is, conquest and resulting economic prosperity. For Plato the answer was in moral and political reform. The way to harmony

Plato on the Role of Women in His Utopian Republic

The Greek invention of reasoned intellectual analysis of all things led the philosopher Plato to consider the problem of justice, which is the subject of his most famous dialogue, the Republic. *This leads him to sketch out a utopian state in which justice may be found and where the most radical arrangements may be necessary. These include the equality of the sexes and the destruction of the family in favor of the practice of men having wives and children in common. In the following excerpts he argues for the fundamental equality of men and women and that women are no less appropriate as Guardians, leaders of the state, than men.*

What are Plato's reasons for treating men and women the same? What objections could be raised to that practice? Would that policy, even if appropriate in Plato's utopia, also be suitable to conditions in the real world of classical Athens? In the world of today?

"If, then, we use the women for the same things as the men, they must also be taught the same things."

"Yes."

"Now music and gymnastics were given to the men."

"Yes."

"Then these two arts, and what has to do with war, must be assigned to the women also, and they must be used in the same ways."

"On the basis of what you say," he said, "it's likely."

"Perhaps," I said, "compared to what is habitual, many of the things now being said would look ridiculous if they were to be done as is said."

"Indeed they would," he said.

"Well," I said, "since we've started to speak, we mustn't be afraid of all the jokes—of whatever kind—the wits might make if such a change took place in gymnastic, in music and, not the least, in the bearing of arms and the riding of horses."

"Then," I said, "if either the class of men or that of women shows its superiority in some art or other practice, then we'll say that that art must be assigned to it. But if they look as though they differ in this alone, that the female bears and the male mounts, we'll assert that it has not thereby yet been proved that a woman differs from a man with respect to what we're talking about; rather, we'll still suppose that our guardians and their women must practice the same things."

"And rightly," he said.

"Therefore, my friend, there is no practice of a city's governors which belongs to woman because she's woman, or to man because he's man; but the natures are scattered alike among both animals; and woman participates according to nature in all practices, and man in all, but in all of them woman is weaker than man."

"Certainly."

"So, shall we assign all of them to men and none to women?"

"How could we?"

"For I suppose there is, as we shall assert, one woman apt at medicine and another not, one woman apt at music and another unmusical by nature."

"Of course."

"And isn't there then also one apt at gymnastic and at war, and another unwarlike and no lover of gymnastic?"

"I suppose so."

"And what about this? Is there a lover of wisdom and a hater of wisdom? And one who is spirited and another without spirit?"

"Yes, there are these too."

"There is, therefore, one woman fit for guarding and another not. or wasn't it a nature of this sort we also selected for the men fit for guarding?"

"Certainly, that was it."

From *The Republic of Plato*, (2nd ed.) translated by Allan Bloom. Copyright © 1968 by Allan Bloom. Preface to paperback edition, © 1991 by Allan Bloom. pp. 130–134. Reprinted by permission of Basic Books, a member of Perseus Books, L.L.C.

was to destroy the causes of strife: private property, the family—anything, in short, that stood between the individual citizen and devotion to the *polis*.

The concern for the redemption of the *polis* was at the heart of Plato's system of philosophy. He began by asking the traditional questions: What is a good man, and how is he made? The goodness of a human being was a theme that belonged to moral philosophy, and when it became a function of the state, the question became part of political philosophy.

Because goodness depended on knowledge of the good, it required a theory of knowledge and an investigation of what the knowledge was that was required for goodness. The answer must be metaphysical and so required a full examination of metaphysics. Even when the philosopher knew the good, however, the question remained of how the state could bring its citizens to the necessary comprehension of that knowledge. The answer required a theory of education. Even purely logical and metaphysical questions, therefore, were

This is believed to be an ancient copy of an actual portrait of the philosopher Aristotle (384–322 B.C.E.). [Kunsthistorisches Museum, Vienna]

subordinate to the overriding political questions. Plato's need to find a satisfactory foundation for the beleaguered *polis* thus contributed to the birth of systematic philosophy.

Aristotle   Aristotle (384–322 B.C.E.) was a pupil of Plato who owed much to the thought of his master, but his different experience and cast of mind led him in new directions. He was born in northern Greece, the son of the court doctor of neighboring Macedon. As a young man, he came to study at the Academy, where he stayed until Plato's death. Then he joined a Platonic colony at Assos in Asia Minor, and from there, he moved to Mytilene. In both places, he carried on research in marine biology, and biological interests played a large part in all his thoughts. In 342 B.C.E., Philip, the king of Macedon, appointed him tutor to his son, the young Alexander (see Chapter 3). In 336 he returned to Athens, where he founded his own school, the Lyceum (or the Peripatos, as it was also called, based on the covered walk within it). In later years, its members were called *Peripatetics*. On the death of Alexander in 323 B.C.E., the Athenians rebelled against Macedonian rule, and Aristotle found it wise to leave Athens. He died the following year.

The Lyceum was different from the Academy. Its members took little interest in mathematics and were concerned with gathering, ordering, and analyzing all human knowledge. Aristotle wrote dialogues on the Platonic model, but none have survived. He and his students also prepared many collections of information to serve as the basis for scientific works, but of them only the *Constitution of the Athenians*, one of 158 constitutional treatises, remains. Almost all of what we possess of his work is in the form of philosophical and scientific studies, whose loose organization and style suggest that they were lecture notes. The range of treated subjects is astonishing, including logic, physics, astronomy, biology, ethics, rhetoric, literary criticism, and politics.

In each field, the method was the same. Aristotle began with observation of the empirical evidence, which in some cases was physical and in others was common opinion. To this body of information he applied reason and discovered inconsistencies or difficulties. To deal with these he introduced metaphysical principles to explain the problems or to reconcile the inconsistencies. His view on all subjects, like Plato's, was teleological; that is, he recognized purposes apart from and greater than the will of the individual human being. Plato's purposes, however, were contained in the Ideas, or Forms—transcendental concepts outside the experience of most people. For Aristotle, the purposes of most things were easily inferred by observing their behavior in the world.

Aristotle's most striking characteristics are his moderation and common sense. His epistemology finds room for both reason and experience; his metaphysics gives meaning and reality to both mind and body; his ethics aims at the good life, which is the contemplative life, but recognizes the necessity for moderate wealth, comfort, and pleasure.

All these qualities are evident in Aristotle's political thought. Like Plato, he opposed the Sophists' assertion that the *polis* was contrary to nature and the result of mere convention. His response was to apply the teleology that he saw in all nature to politics. In his view, matter existed to achieve an end, and it developed until it achieved its form, which was its end. There was constant development from matter to form, from potential to actual. Therefore, human primitive instincts could be seen as the matter out of which the human's potential as a political being could be realized. The *polis* made individuals self-sufficient and allowed the full

Major Greek Philosophers

469–399 B.C.E.	Socrates
429–347 B.C.E.	Plato
384–322 B.C.E.	Aristotle

realization of their potentiality. It was therefore natural. It was also the highest point in the evolution of the social institutions that serve the human need to continue the species: marriage, household, village, and finally, *polis*. For Aristotle, the purpose of the *polis* was neither economic nor military, but moral: "The end of the state is the good life," the life lived "for the sake of noble actions," a life of virtue and morality.[8]

Characteristically, Aristotle was less interested in the best state—the utopia that required philosophers to rule it—than in the best state practically possible, one that would combine justice with stability. The constitution for that state he called *politeia*, not the best constitution, but the next best, the one most suited to and most possible for most states. Its quality was moderation, and it naturally gave power to neither the rich nor the poor but to the middle class, which also had to be the most numerous. The middle class possessed many virtues: Because of its moderate wealth, it was free of the arrogance of the rich and the malice of the poor. For this reason, it was the most stable class. The stability of the constitution also came from being a mixed constitution, blending in some way the laws of democracy and those of oligarchy. Aristotle's scheme was unique because of its realism and the breadth of its vision.

All the political thinkers of the fourth century B.C.E. recognized that the *polis* was in danger and hoped to save it. All recognized the economic and social troubles that threatened it. Isocrates (436–338 B.C.E.), a contemporary of Plato and Aristotle, urged a program of imperial conquest as a cure for poverty and revolution. Plato saw the folly of solving a polit-

ical and moral problem by purely economic means and resorted to the creation of utopias. Aristotle combined the practical analysis of political and economic realities with the moral and political purposes of the traditional defenders of the *polis*. The result was a passionate confidence in the virtues of moderation and of the middle class, and the proposal of a constitution that would give it power. It is ironic that the ablest defense of the *polis* came soon before its demise.

The concern with an understanding of nature in a purely rational, scientific way remained strong through the fifth century B.C.E., culminating in the work of the formulators of the atomic theory, Democritus and Leucippus, and in that of the medical school founded by Hippocrates of Cos. In the mid-fifth century B.C.E., however, men like the Sophists and Socrates turned their attention to humankind and to ethical, political, and religious questions. This latter tradition of inquiry led, by way of Plato, Aristotle (in his metaphysical thought), and the Stoics, to Christianity; it had, as well, a substantial impact on Judaic and Islamic thought. The former tradition of thought, following a line from the natural philosophers, the Sophists, Aristotle (in his scientific thought), and the Epicureans, had to wait until the Renaissance in western Europe to exert an influence. Since the eighteenth century, this line of Greek thought has been the more influential force in western civilization. It may not be too much to say that since the Enlightenment of that century, the western world has been engaged in a debate between the two strands of the Greek intellectual tradition. As western influence has spread over the world in recent times, that debate has become of universal importance, for other societies have not separated the religious and philosophical from the scientific and physical realms as radically as has the modern West.

---

[8]Aristotle, *Politics*, 1280b, 1281a.

Review Questions

1. What do you think are the reasons for the emergence of so many revolutionary philosophical and religious ideas at about the same time in many different regions? Do these ideas share any fundamental concerns?

2. Is your outlook on life closer to Confucianism, Taoism, or Legalism? What makes you favor one over the others?

3. What fundamental assumptions about the world, the individual, and reality do the Jain, Hindu, and Buddhist traditions share? How do these assumptions compare with those that underlie Chinese philosophy, Jewish religious thought, and Greek philosophy?

4. How did the monotheism of the Hebrews differ from that of Egypt's Akhnaton (Chapter 1)? To what extent did their faith bind the Jews politically? Why was the concept of monotheism so radical for Near Eastern civilization?

5. In what ways did the ideas of the Greeks differ from those of other ancient peoples? How do Aristotle's political and ethical ideas compare with those of Confucius? What were Socrates' contributions to the development of philosophy?

Suggested Readings ———

China

H. G. Creel, *What Is Taoism? And Other Studies in Chinese Cultural History* (1970).

W. T. de Bary et al. *Sources of Chinese Tradition* (1960). A reader in China's philosophical and historical literature. It should be consulted for the later periods as well as for the Chou.

Y. L. Fung, *A Short History of Chinese Philosophy*, ed. D. Bodde (1948). A survey of Chinese philosophy from its origins down to recent times.

D. C. Lau, trans., *Lao-Tzu, Tao Te Ching* (1963).

D. C. Lau, trans., *Confucius, The Analects* (1979).

F. W. Mote, *Intellectual Foundations of China* (1971).

B. I. Schwartz, *The World of Thought in Ancient China* (1985).

A. Waley, *Three Ways of Thought in Ancient China* (1956). An easy yet sound introduction to Confucianism, Taoism, and Legalism.

A. Waley, *The Book of Songs* (1960).

B. Watson, trans., *Basic Writings of Mo Tzu, Hsun Tzu, and Han Fei Tzu* (1963).

B. Watson, trans., *The Complete Works of Chuang Tzu* (1968).

H. Welch, *Taoism, The Parting of the Way* (1967).

India

A. L. Basham, *The Wonder That Was India*, rev. ed. (1963). Still unsurpassed by more recent works. Chap. VII, "Religion," is a superb introduction to the Vedic-Aryan, Brahmanic, Hindu, Jain, and Buddhist traditions of thought.

W. N. Brown, *Man in the Universe: Some Continuities in Indian Thought* (1970). A penetrating yet brief reflective summary of major patterns in Indian thinking.

W. T. de Bary et al., *Sources of Indian Tradition* (1958). 2 vols. Vol. I, *From the Beginning to 1800*, ed. and rev. Ainslie T. Embree. (1988). Excellent selections from a variety of Indian texts, with good introductions to chapters and individual selections.

Peter Harvey, *An Introduction to Buddhism* (1990). Chs. 1–3 provide an excellent historical introduction.

T. J. Hopkins, *The Hindu Religious Tradition* (1971). A first-rate, thoughtful introduction to Hindu religious ideas and practice.

John M. Koller, *The Indian Way* (1982). A useful, wide-ranging handbook of Indian thought and religion.

W. Rahula, *What the Buddha Taught*, 2nd ed. (1974). A readable introduction to Buddhist thought from a Theravadin viewpoint, with primary-source selections.

R. H. Robinson and W. L. Johnson, *The Buddhist Religion*, 3rd ed. (1982). An excellent first text on the Buddhist tradition, its thought and development.

R. C. Zaehner, *Hinduism* (1966). One of the best general introductions to central Indian religious and philosophical ideas.

Israel

J. Bright, *A History of Israel* (1968), 2nd ed. (1972). One of the standard scholarly introductions to biblical history and literature.

W. D. Davies and L. Finkelstein, eds., *The Cambridge History of Judaism*. Vol. I, *Introduction: The Persian Period* (1984). Excellent essays on diverse aspects of the exilic period and later.

J. Neusner, *The Way of Torah: An Introduction to Judaism* (1979). A sensitive introduction to the Judaic tradition and faith.

L. W. Schwarz, ed., *Great Ages and Ideas of the Jewish People* (1956). Especially the first section, "The Biblical Age," by Yehezkel Kaufmann.

Greece

J. Burnet, *Early Greek Philosophy* (1963). Stresses the rational aspect of Greek thought and its sharp break with mythology.

F. M. Cornford, *From Religion to Philosophy* (1912). Emphasizes the elements of continuity between myth and religion on the one hand and Greek philosophy on the other.

B. Farrington, *Greek Science* (1953). A lively interpretation of the origins and character of Greek scientific thought.

G. B. Kerferd, *The Sophistic Movement* (1981). An excellent description and analysis.

J. Lear, *Aristotle: The Desire to Understand* (1988). A brilliant yet comprehensible introduction to the work of the philosopher.

J. M. Robinson, *An Introduction to Early Greek Philosophy* (1968). A valuable collection of the main fragments and ancient testimony to the works of the early philosophers, with excellent commentary.

G. Vlastos, *The Philosophy of Socrates* (1971). A splendid collection of essays illuminating the problems presented by this remarkable man.

G. Vlastos, *Platonic Studies*, 2nd ed. (1981). A similar collection on the philosophy of Plato.

G. Vlastos, *Socrates, Ironist and Moral Philosopher* (1991). The results of a lifetime of study by the leading interpreter of Socrates in our time.

RELIGIONS OF THE WORLD

Judaism

Monotheism, the belief in a unique God who is the creator of the universe and its all-powerful ruler, first became a central and lasting element in religion among the Hebrews, later called Israelites and also Jews. Their religion, more than the many forms of polytheistic worship that characterized the ancient world, demanded moral rectitude and placed ethical responsibilities both on individuals and on the community as a whole. Their God had a divine plan for human history; the behavior of his chosen people was linked to it. This vision of the exclusive worship of the true God, obedience to the laws governing the community that derive from Him, and a strong ethical responsibility was connected to humanity's historical experience in this world. Ultimately it gave rise to three great religions: Judaism, Christianity, and Islam.

At the beginning of this tradition stands Abraham, recognized as the founder of their faith by all three of its branches. According to the story recorded in the Torah (the first five books of the Hebrew Bible and the Christian Old Testament), this first of the Hebrew patriarchs entered into a covenant with God in which Abraham promised to worship only this God, who in turn promised to make Abraham's descendants his own chosen people—chosen to worship Him, to obey His laws, and to undertake a special set of moral responsibilities. The covenant was renewed with Moses at Mount Sinai. God freed the Israelites from bondage, promised them the land of Canaan (later

called Palestine and part of which is now Israel), and gave them the Law (the Torah), including the Ten Commandments, by which they were to guide their lives. As long as they lived by His law He would give them His guidance and protection.

In time the Israelites formed themselves into a kingdom which remained unified from about 1000 to 922 B.C.E. In the period after its division men and women called prophets emerged. These people, thought to be inspired by God, recalled the Israelites from their lapses into idolatry and immorality. Even as the kingdom was disintegrating and the Israelites falling under the control of alien empires, the prophets preached social reform and a return to more godly ways. At the center of their vision was their place in history, in the fulfillment of God's plan for mankind. The prophets saw Israel's misfortune as punishment for failing to keep the covenant in many ways and predicted disaster if the Israelites did not change their ways. When disasters came— the Jewish kingdoms captured, the people enslaved and exiled—the prophets interpreted Israel's status as a chosen people to mean that their sufferings were part of a process whereby they would become "a light unto the nations," leading other nations to the true worship of God. By this time, at the latest, the God of the Israelites was understood not only as the single God worshipped by the Jews but also as the universal God for all humanity.

It was also the prophets who gave full expression to the Jews' belief that God was righteous and demanded righteousness from his people. At the same time, he was also a God of love; although he might need to punish his

Jews in Fifteenth-Century Germany. These illuminations are on a page from a Hebrew manuscript in the State and University Library of Hamburg. [Staats- und Universitätsbibliothek, Hamburg]

Russian Persecution of the Jews. This 1900 painting, *After the Pogrom*, by the Polish painter Maurycy Minkowski, (oil on canvas laid on board, 98.8 x 148.8 cm) shows a group of women and children in the aftermath of a pogrom, an organized persecution of Jews that often became a massacre. Encouraged by the Russian government, pogroms were especially brutal in the late nineteenth and early twentieth centuries. [Gift of Mr. and Mrs. Lester Klein/Jewish Museum/Art Resource, N.Y.]

people for their sins, he would one day reward them with divine favor. Traditional Jewish belief expects that the Messiah, or "Anointed One," will someday come and establish God's kingdom on earth. He will be a descendant of King David who will restore the kingdom of Israel and rebuild the sanctuary in Jerusalem destroyed, finally, by the Romans. He will introduce an age of universal brotherhood in which all nations will acknowledge the true God and the righteous of past generations will be restored to life.

The Jews are very much "the people of the Book," and the foremost of their sacred writings is the Hebrew Bible, consisting of the Five Books of Moses (the Torah), the books of the prophets, and other writings. Its heart is the Torah, the source of law. Over the centuries new experiences required the interpretation of the law to fit new circumstances, which was accomplished by the oral Law, no less sacred than the written Law. Compilations of interpretation and commentary by wise and learned teachers were brought together to form the Talmud.

The destruction of their temple by the Romans in 70 C.E. hastened the scattering of the Jews throughout the empire. Thereafter almost all Jews lived in the Diaspora (dispersion), without a homeland, a political community, or a national or religious center until the establishment of the Jewish state of Israel in 1948. In the fifth and sixth centuries the decline of the Sasanid Empire in Iran and the collapse of the western Roman Empire undermined the institutions in which the Jews had found a stable way of life. In the seventh and eighth centuries the missionary zeal of the Christian church brought hard times for the Jews in western Europe and in the Byzantine East. In the West, their condition improved in the ninth century under Charlemagne and his successors.

Under Islam, Jews, like Christians, although required to pay a special tax, were tolerated as "people of the Book." Jewish settlements flourished throughout the Islamic world. After the Islamic conquest of Spain in 711, the Jews there enjoyed an almost 300-year-long "Golden Age." During this period of extraordinary intellectual and cultural accomplishment, Jews practiced their religion openly and flourished economically.

The beginning of the Crusades in the eleventh century brought renewed persecution of the Jews in both the Christian and Islamic worlds. In the wake of the Christian reconquest of Spain Jews were persecuted, killed, forced to convert, and finally expelled in 1492.

By the Middle Ages Jews had divided into two distinct families: those who lived in Christian Europe, called *Ashkenazim*, and those from the Muslim world, particularly Spain, called *Sephardim*. The Sephardim, with their greater opportunities, developed a more secular life. Their language, Ladino, combined Hebrew and Spanish elements. The Ashkenazim, scattered in tiny communities, were forced to turn inward. Centered in German lands, they developed Yiddish, a combination of Hebrew and a German dialect written in Hebrew characters. In time Yiddish became the language of most Jews in northern Europe.

Two of the dominant influences on modern Judaism have been Zionism—the effort to found a Jewish nation—and the death of some 6 million Jews in the Holocaust of World War II. Bolstered by the determination of Jews never again to find themselves victimized by the forces of antisemitism, the Zionist movement culminated in the founding of the state of Israel in 1948. Most Jews, however, live in other countries.

The adherents of Judaism are divided into several groups—reform, conservative, and orthodox, each holding significantly different views about the place of tradition and the traditional law in the modern world. Perhaps all of them, however, would give assent to the saying of Hillel, the great Talmudic teacher of the first century B.C.E.: "What is distasteful to you do not to your fellow man. This is the Law, all the rest is commentary. Now go and study."

"Imperial Procession" from the frieze of the *Ara Pacis*, Augustan Rome, 9 B.C.E. [Museum of the Ara Pacis, Rome/Nimatallah/Art Resource, N.Y.]

EMPIRES AND CULTURES OF THE ANCIENT WORLD

The last five hundred years before the beginning of the common era and the two centuries that followed saw the appearance of great empires in Iran, India, and China, and of the Roman Empire in the Mediterranean. Although each arose in response to local conditions, they had common features. Each replaced a confusion of local sovereign units, whether aristocratic family domains, smaller territorial states, tribal confederacies, or city-states, with vast centralized monarchies. Each had the large, efficient armies needed to conquer and control new lands. They all created well-organized bureaucracies to regulate their widespread empires and built extensive roads to ease communication and transportation. They all systematically imposed and collected taxes to pay for the armies and bureaucracies, for the construction of roads and defenses, and for the splendor of their imperial courts and palaces.

The military, political, and economic unification of vast territories produced considerable periods of relative peace and prosperity. There is evidence of communication and trade even between the Romans and the distant empires of India and China. Imperial unification also had cultural consequences. The imposition of a single rule over different peoples in a far-flung empire encouraged the use of a common tongue, at least as a second language, which assisted the formation of a common culture. The Greeks, the Romans, the Hindus, and the Chinese produced great works in a variety of literary genres, such as epic poetry, history, and philosophy, which set a stamp on their own societies and served as the bases for later cultural developments. In all four areas the wealth and patronage of the monarchs, the general prosperity of their empires, and the desire for splendor gave great impetus to such arts as painting, sculpture, and architecture.

The rise of these empires also brought important developments in religion. The Iranian conquests under the Achaemenid dynasty spread the religion of Zarathushtra (Zoroaster) throughout the Persian Empire, and the quasi-monotheistic faith had a powerful and broad influence before the tide of Islam swept over it in the seventh century C.E. In India in the third century B.C.E., under the Mauryan king Ashoka, Buddhism took on a missionary character and spread across Asia to the east and west. In the first century B.C.E., it came to China, where it competed not only with Confucianism but also with a new form of Taoism that had taken on a more mysterious and otherworldly character during the Later Han period. In Greece, as the city-states gave way to the great empires of Philip and Alexander of Macedon and their Hellenistic successors, a largely amoral paganism gave way to such quasi-religious philosophies as Stoicism. In the Roman Empire that succeeded the Hellenistic kingdoms, Christianity ultimately overcame all competitors to become the official religion by the end of the fourth century C.E. These religious movements stressed morality, and most of them were more otherworldly than their predecessors, placing greater emphasis on escape from the pain and troubles of this world and the search for personal immortality.

Such developments seem to have had some connection with the loss of prosperity; the increase of warfare, both internal and external; and the collapse of stability. None of the great empires could avoid a cycle of growth and decline. There was never enough wealth to sustain the cost of empire beyond a limited period of time. Taxes rose beyond the citizens' capacity to pay, and bureaucracies became bloated and ineffective. More and more depended on the central government, but talented leadership was not always available. The attractions of civilization drew the envy of vigorous barbarians outside the empires, at the same time as internal problems and diminished willingness to fight reduced the capacity of the empires to resist. The Achaemenids fell victim to Alexander the Great, but the rule of his Hellenistic successors was brief. The Parthians, who succeeded to the old Persian Empire, were never able to impose the same imperial and cultural unity. In India, the Mauryan Empire did not long survive the death of its remarkable king Ashoka, giving way to local uprisings and barbarian assaults from central Asia. Both China and Rome, weakened by internal struggles, gave way to barbarian assaults and saw the collapse of central authority. In both cases the conquering tribes were themselves conquered by the religions or philosophies of their victims, Buddhism and Confucianism in China and Christianity in Rome. In India, China, and Rome, moreover, the cultural achievements of the great empires would later serve as the bases for new advances in civilization.

3000 B.C.E.

ca. **2500–1100** Minoan civilization on Crete
ca. **1600–1100** Mycenaean civilization on Greek
　　　　mainland

ca. **3500–3000** Emergence of Sumerian city-states
ca. **3000** Emergence of civilization along the Nile
　　　　River
ca. **2300** Emergence of Harappan civilization
　　　　in Indus Valley
2276–2221 Sargon of Akkad creates the first
　　　　Mesopotamian Empire
ca. **2000** Epic of Gilgamesh
1750 Hammurabi's Code

1500 B.C.E.

Sixth century B.C.E. attic jar

ca. **1100–800** Greek "Dark Ages"
800 Etruscan civilization begins in Italy
ca. **750–550** Rise of the *polis*
594 Solon's legislation at Athens
509 Foundation of the Roman Republic
508 Democracy established in Athens

ca. **1500** Aryan peoples migrate into northwestern
　　　　India
960–933 Rule of Hebrew king Solomon
ca. **628–551** Traditional dates of Zarathushtra
ca. **537–486** Siddhartha Gautama
559–529 Cyrus the Great creates the Persian
　　　　Empire

500 B.C.E.

480–479 Persian invasion of Greece
478 Foundation of Delian League/Athenian Empire
431–404 Peloponnesian Wars
338 Battle of Chaeronia; Macedonian conquest
　　　　of Greece
336–323 Career of Alexander the Great

ca. **540–468** Vardhamana Mahavira, founder
　　　　of Jain tradition
334 Alexander begins conquest of the Near East;
　　　　invades India in 327
321–181 Mauryan Empire in India

300 B.C.E.

264 Rome rules all of Italy
146 Rome destroys Carthage; rules all of western
　　　　Mediterranean
44–31 Civil wars destroy Republic
31 Rome rules Mediterranean
31 B.C.E.– **14** C.E. Principate of Augustus

ca. **300** Foundation of Seleucid dynasty in Anatolia,
　　　　Syria, and Mesopotamia; Ptolemaic dynasty
　　　　in Egypt
269–232 Mauryan Emperor, Ashoka, patronizes
　　　　Buddhism
247 B.C.E.– **224** C.E. Parthian dynasty controls
　　　　Persia
180 B.C.E.– **320** C.E. India politically divided

1 C.E.

96–180 The Good Emperors rule Rome
180–284 Breakdown of the *Pax Romana*
306–337 Constantine reigns
313 Edict of Milan
325 Council of Nicaea
391 Theodosius makes Christianity the official
　　　　imperial religion
ca. **400–500** The Germanic invasions
426 *The City of God*, by Augustine
476 The last Western emperor is deposed

30 Crucifixion of Jesus
70 Romans destroy the Temple at Jerusalem
216–277 Mani
ca. **224** Fall of Parthians, rise of Sasanids, in Persia
ca. **320–500** Gupta Dynasty in India
ca. **400** Chandra Gupta (r. 375–415) conquers
　　　　western India; increases trade with Near East
　　　　and China
ca. **450** The Huns invade India

ca. 4000 Neolithic cultures in China
ca. 8000–300 Jōmon culture in Japan
ca. 1766–1050 Shang dynasty in China with city-states and writing

ca. 3000 Practice of agriculture spreads from Nile River Valley to the Sudan
ca. 2000 Ivory and gold trade between Kush (Nubia) and Egypt
ca. 1500 Practice of agriculture spreads from the Sudan to Abyssinia and the savannah region

ca. 4000 Maize already domesticated in Mexico

1027–771 Western Chou Dynasty, China
771–256 Eastern Chou dynasty in China
ca. 771 Iron Age territorial states in China
551–479 Confucius in China

750 Kushite king Kashta conquers Upper Egypt; founds 25th Egyptian dynasty
ca. 720 Kushite king Piankhy completes conquest of Egypt and reigns as king of Kush and Egypt
ca. 600 Meroitic period of Kushan civilization begins

ca. 1500–800 Olmec civilization in Mesoamerica
ca. 800–200 Chavín (Early) Horizon in Andean South America

Olmec monument, La Venta

ca. 500–200 Rise of Mohist, Taoist, and Legalist schools of thought in China
401–256 Period of the Warring States in China
ca. 300 Old Stone Age Jōmon culture in Japan replaced by Yayoi culture

ca. 500–200 Founding of Monte Alban

256–206 Ch'in dynasty in China
221 Ch'in emperor unites all of China
206 B.C.E.– 8 C.E. Former Han Dynasty in China
179–104 Han philosopher, Tung Chung-shu
145–90 Han historian, Ssu-ma Chien
141–187 Emperor Wu Ti of China reigns

25 Romans sack Kushite capital of Napata
100 B.C.E.– 1 C.E. Probable first Indonesian migrations to East African coast

Han dynasty sculpture

25–220 The Later Han Dynasty, China
ca. 220–590 Spread of Buddhism in China
220–589 Six Dynasties period in China
ca. 300–500 Barbarian invasions of China
ca. 300–680 Archaic Yamato state in Japan

ca. 200 Camel first used for trans-Saharan transport
ca. 200–900 Expansion of Bantu people
ca. 250 Aksum (Ethiopia) controls the Red Sea trade
ca. 300–400 Rise of kingdom of Ghana
ca. 350 Kush ceases to exist

ca. 200–600 Early Intermediate period in Andean South America; Moche and Nazca cultures
ca. 150–900 Classic period. Dominance of Teotihuacán in central Mexico, Tikal in southern Yucatán.

3 GREEK AND HELLENISTIC CIVILIZATION

This Attic wine cup depicts a famous scene from Homer's *Iliad*. It shows Priam, King of Troy, begging the Greek hero Achilles to return the body of the old man's son, Hector, the great Trojan warrior. The cup was painted about 490 B.C.E. [Kunsthistorisches Museum, Vienna Austria/Art Resource, N.Y.]

CHAPTER TOPICS

◆ **Bronze Age on Crete and on the Mainland to ca. 1150 B.C.E.**

◆ **Greek "Middle Age" to ca. 750 B.C.E.**

◆ **The Polis**

◆ **Expansion of the Greek World**

◆ **Life in Archaic Greece**

◆ **Major City-States**

◆ **The Persian Wars**

◆ **Classical Greece**

◆ **Culture of Classical Greece**

◆ **Emergence of the Hellenistic World**

◆ **Hellenistic Culture**

In World Perspective **The Achievement of Greek and Hellenistic Civilization**

About 2000 B.C.E., Greek-speaking peoples settled the lands surrounding the Aegean Sea at the eastern end of the Mediterranean, where they came in touch with the more advanced and earlier civilizations of the Near East, including the rich cultures of Egypt, Asia Minor, the Syria-Palestine region, and Mesopotamia. Adapting from these predecessors, the Greeks forged their own way of life, forming a set of ideas, values, and institutions that would spread far beyond their homeland. The foundation of this way of life was the independent city-state, or *polis* (plural *poleis*). In the eighth century B.C.E. the Greeks began to expand beyond the Aegean, establishing *poleis* on the shores of the Mediterranean Sea and, pushing on through the Dardanelles, placing many settlements on the coasts of the Black Sea in southern Russia and as far east as the approaches to the Caucasus Mountains. The center of Greek life, however, remained the Aegean Sea and the lands in and around it.

Early in the fifth century B.C.E., the great Persian Empire (see Chapter 4) threatened to extinguish Greek independence. The Greeks, however, led by the city-states of Sparta and Athens, won a remarkable victory over the Persians, securing for themselves a period of freedom and autonomy during which they realized their greatest political and cultural achievements. In Athens, especially, the victory produced a great sense of confidence and ambition. Sparta, however, withdrew from active leadership against the Persians, leaving the Delian league—an alliance of Greek cities led by Athens—to fill the vacuum. The Delian League soon turned into the Athenian Empire.

At the same time that it tightened its hold over the Greek cities in and around the Aegean Sea, Athens developed an extraordinarily democratic constitution at home. Fears and jealousies of this new kind of state and empire created a split in the Greek world that led to a series of major wars.

These wars impoverished Greece and left it vulnerable to conquest. In 338 B.C.E. Philip of Macedon conquered the Greek states, putting an end to the age of the *polis*. The conquests of Philip's son, Alexander, however, spread Greek culture far from its homeland, to Egypt and into Asia. Pre-served and adapted by the Romans, Greek culture powerfully influenced the society of western Europe in the Middle Ages and dominated the Byzantine Empire in the same period. The civilization emerging from the Greek and Roman experience spread across Europe and in time crossed the Atlantic to the Western Hemisphere.

Bronze Age on Crete and on the Mainland to ca. 1150 B.C.E.

One source of Greek civilization was the culture of the large island of Crete in the Mediterranean. With Greece to the north, Egypt to the south, and Asia to the east, Crete was a cultural bridge between the older civilizations and the new one of the Greeks.

The Minoans

In the third and second millennia B.C.E., a Bronze Age civilization arose on Crete that powerfully influenced the islands of the Aegean and the mainland of Greece (see Map 3–1). This civilization has been given the name *Minoan*, after Minos, the legendary king of Crete. Scholars have divided Minoan history into three major periods—Early, Middle, and Late Minoan—with some

Map 3-1 The Aegean area in the Bronze Age.   The Bronze Age in the Aegean area lasted from ca. 1900-ca. 1100 B.C.E. Its culture on Crete is called Minoan and was at its height about 1900-1400 B.C.E. Bronze Age Helladic culture on the mainland flourished from about 1600-1200 B.C.E.

subdivisions. Dates for Bronze Age settlements on the Greek mainland, for which the term *Helladic* is used, are derived from the same chronological scheme.

The civilization of the Middle and Late Minoan periods in eastern and central Crete centered around several great palaces, including those at Phaestus, Haghia Triada, and, most important, Cnossus. The distinctive and striking art and architecture of these palaces reflect the influence of Syria, Asia Minor, and Egypt, but have a uniquely Cretan style and quality. Minoan cities lacked strong defensive walls, suggesting that they were not built with defense in mind.

Along with palaces, paintings, pottery, jewelry, and other valuable objects, excavations at Minoan sites have revealed

A fresco showing acrobats leaping over a charging bull, from the east wing of the Minoan-period palace at Cnossus on the island of Crete. It is not known whether such acrobatic displays were for entertainment or were part of some religious ritual. [Scala/Art Resource, N.Y.]

clay writing tablets like those found in Mesopotamia. Tablets found at the royal palace at Cnossus, accidentally preserved when a great fire that destroyed the palace hardened them, have three distinct kinds of writing on them. One has proved to be an early form of Greek. The contents of the tablets, primarily inventories, reveal an organization centered on the palace and ruled by a king who was supported by an extensive bureaucracy that kept remarkably detailed records. This sort of organization is typical of early civilizations in the Near East but, as we shall see, is nothing like that of the Greeks after the Bronze Age. Yet some of the inventories were written in a form of Greek. Why should Minoans, who were not Greek, write in a language not their own? This question raises the larger one of what the relationship was between Crete and the Greek mainland during the Bronze Age, leading us to an examination of mainland, or Helladic, culture.

The Mycenaeans

In the third millennium B.C.E., most of the Greek mainland, including many of the sites of later Greek cities, was settled by people who used metal, built some impressive houses, and traded with Crete and the islands of the Aegean. The names they gave to places—names that were sometimes preserved by later invaders—make it clear that they were not Greeks and that they spoke a language that was not Indo-European (the language family to which Greek belongs).

Not long after 2000 B.C.E., many of the Early Helladic sites were destroyed by fire, some were abandoned, and still others appear to have yielded peacefully to an invading people. These signs of invasion, which mark the beginning of the Middle Helladic period, probably signal the arrival of the Greeks.

The shaft graves cut into the rock at the royal palace-fortress of Mycenae show that by the Late Helladic the conquerors had prospered and sometimes became very rich. At Mycenae the richest finds come from the period after 1600 B.C.E. The city's wealth and power reached their peak during this time, and the culture of the whole mainland during the Late Helladic period goes by the name *Mycenaean*. Greek invaders also established themselves in a still flourishing Crete, and there is good reason to believe that at the height of Mycenaean power (1400–1200 B.C.E.) Crete was part of the Mycenaean world.

Excavations at Mycenae, Pylos, and other Mycenaean sites reveal a culture influenced by, but very different from, Minoan culture. Mycenae and Pylos, like Cnossus, were built some distance from the sea. Defense against attack, however, was plainly foremost in the minds of the founders of the Mycenaean cities. Both were built on hills in positions commanding the neighboring territory. The Mycenaean people were warriors, as their art, architecture, and weapons reveal. All available evidence suggests that they were led by strong kings who, with their retainers, lived in palaces protected by defensive walls while most of the population lived outside the walls. Like the palaces of Crete, Mycenaean palaces were adorned with murals, but instead of the peaceful scenery and games depicted on the Cretan murals, the Mycenaean murals depicted scenes of war and boar hunting.

About 1500 B.C.E. *tholos* tombs—large, beehivelike chambers cut into hillsides—replaced the earlier, already impressive, shaft graves. The *tholos* tombs, built of enormous, well-cut, fitted stones, were approached through an unroofed passage cut horizontally into the side of the hill. The lintel block alone of one of these tombs weighs over a hundred tons. Only a strong king whose wealth was great, whose power was unquestioned, and who commanded the labor of many could undertake such a project. His wealth probably came from plundering raids, piracy, and trade. Some of this trade went westward to Italy and Sicily, but most of it was with the islands of the Aegean, the coastal towns of Asia Minor, and the cities of Syria, Egypt, and Crete. The Mycenaeans exchanged pottery, olive oil, and animal hides for jewels and other luxuries.

Further evidence that the Mycenaean world was made up of a number of independent, powerful, and well-organized monarchies comes from the many clay tablets with Mycenaean writing found throughout the mainland, and in particular from a large collection of tablets found at Pylos. These reveal a society similar to that of Cnossus on Crete. A king, whose title was *wanax*, held a royal domain, appointed officials, commanded servants, and kept a close record of what he owned and what was owed to him.

The Fall of Mycenaean Power   At the height of their power (1400–1200 B.C.E.) the Mycenaeans were prosperous and active. They enlarged their cities, expanded their trade, and even established commercial colonies in the east. They are mentioned in the archives of the Hittite kings of Asia Minor. They are named as marauders of the Nile Delta in Egyptian records. Sometime about 1250 B.C.E. they probably sacked Troy, on the coast of northwestern Asia Minor, giving rise to the epic poems of Homer, *The Iliad* and *The Odyssey* (see Map 3–1). Around the year 1200 B.C.E., however, the Mycenaean world showed signs of great trouble; by 1100 B.C.E. it was gone: Its palaces were destroyed; many of its cities abandoned; and its art, its pattern of life, its system of writing buried and forgotten.

The reasons for the collapse of Mycenaean civilization are not known for certain. Greek legends attribute it to a new wave of Greek invaders, the Dorians, into the Greek mainland from the north. The legends identify the Dorians as a rude people who spoke a different Greek dialect from that of the Mycenaean peoples. The legend of "The Return of the Heraclidae," for example, recounts how the Dorians joined one of the Greek tribes, the Heraclidae, in an attack on the southern Greek peninsula of Peloponnesus, which was repulsed. One hundred years later they returned and gained full control.

Greek "Middle Age" to ca. 750 B.C.E.

The immediate effects of the Mycenaean collapse were disastrous. Palaces were destroyed, the kings and bureaucrats who managed them were swept away, and the wealth and organization that had supported artists and merchants evaporated. Greece entered a dark "Middle Age" about which little is known. Many villages were abandoned and never resettled. Some of their inhabitants probably turned to a nomadic life, and many undoubtedly perished.

Another result of the turmoil surrounding the Mycenaean collapse was the spread of the Greek people eastward from the mainland to the Aegean islands and the coast of Asia Minor. The Dorians, after occupying most of the Peloponnesus, swept across the Aegean to occupy the southern islands and the southern part of the Anatolian coast. Another group, known as the Ionians, spread from Attica and Euboea to the Cyclades and the central Anatolian coast, which came to be called Ionia.

These migrations made the Aegean a Greek lake. Trade with the old civilizations of the Near East, however, was virtually ended by the fall of the advanced Minoan and Mycenaean civilizations; nor was there much internal trade among the different parts of Greece. The Greeks were forced to turn inward, and each community was left largely to its own devices. The Near East was also in disarray at this time, and no great power arose to impose its ways and its will on the helpless people who lived about the Aegean. The Greeks were allowed time to recover from their disaster and to create their unique style of life.

Age of Homer

For a picture of society in these "dark ages," the best source is Homer. His epic poems, *The Iliad* and *The Odyssey*, emerged from a tradition of oral poetry whose roots extend into the Mycenaean Age. Through the centuries bards had sung tales of the heroes who had fought at Troy, using verse arranged in rhythmic formulas to aid the memory. In this way some very old material was preserved into the eighth century B.C.E., when the poems attributed to Homer were finally written down. Although the poems tell of the deeds of Mycenaean heroes, the world they describe seems to be that of the tenth and ninth centuries B.C.E. rather than Mycenaean.

Homer's heroes are not buried in *tholos* tombs but are cremated; they worship gods in temples, whereas the Mycenaeans had no temples; and although they have chariots, like the Mycenaeans, they do not know their proper use in warfare.

Government   In the Homeric poems the power of the kings is much less than that of the Mycenaean rulers. Homeric kings were limited in their ability to make important decisions by the need to consult a council of nobles. The nobles felt free to discuss matters in vigorous language and in opposition to the king's wishes. In *The Iliad*, Achilles does not hesitate to address Agamemnon, the "most kingly" commander of the Trojan expedition, in these words: "you with a dog's face and a deer's heart." Such language may have been impolite, but it was not treasonous. The king could ignore the council's advice, but it was risky for him to do so.

The right to speak in council was limited to noblemen, but the common people could not be ignored. If a king planned a war or a major change of policy during a campaign, he would not fail to call the common soldiers to an assembly; they could listen and express their feelings by acclamation, though they could not take part in the debate. Homer shows that even in these early times the Greeks, unlike their predecessors and contemporaries, practiced some forms of limited constitutional government.

Society   Homeric society, nevertheless, was sharply divided into classes, the most important division being the one between nobles and everyone else. We do not know the origin of this distinction, but we cannot doubt that at this time Greek society was aristocratic. Birth determined noble status, and wealth usually accompanied it. Below the nobles were two other classes: *thetes* and slaves. We do not know whether the *thetes* owned outright the land they worked (and so were free to sell it) or worked a hereditary plot that belonged to their clan (and was therefore not theirs to dispose of as they chose).

Thetes who were landless laborers endured the worst condition in Homeric society. Slaves, at least, were attached to family households and so were protected and fed. In a world where membership in a settled group gave the only security, free laborers were desperately vulnerable. Slaves were few in number and were mostly women who served as maids and concubines. Some male slaves worked as shepherds. Few, if any, worked in agriculture, which depended chiefly on free labor throughout Greek history.

Homeric Values   The Homeric poems reflect an aristocratic code of values that powerfully influenced all future Greek thought. Homer was the schoolbook of the Greeks. They memorized his texts, settled diplomatic disputes by

The "Trojan Horse," depicted on a seventh-century-B.C.E. Greek vase. According to legend, the Greeks finally defeated Troy by pretending to abandon their siege of the city, leaving a giant wooden horse behind. Soldiers hidden in the horse opened the gates of the city to their compatriots after the Trojans had brought it within their walls. Note the wheels on the horse and the Greek soldiers who are hiding inside it holding weapons and armor. [Deutsches Archäologisches Institut, Athens]

citing passages in them, and emulated the behavior and cherished the values they found in them. Those values were physical prowess; courage; and fierce protection of one's family, friends, and property, and above all, one's personal honor and reputation. Speed of foot, strength, and, most of all, excellence at fighting make a man great, and all these attributes serve to promote personal honor. The great hero of *The Iliad*, Achilles, refuses to fight in battle, allowing his fellow Greeks to be slain and almost defeated, because Agamemnon has wounded his honor by taking away his battle prize. He returns to the army not out of a sense of duty but to avenge the death of his dear friend Patroclus. Odysseus, the hero of *The Odyssey*, returning home after his wanderings, ruthlessly kills the many suitors who had, in his long absence, sought to marry his wife, Penelope; they had dishonored him by consuming his wealth, wooing Penelope, and scorning his son.

The highest virtue in Homeric society was *arete*—manliness, courage in the most general sense, and the excellence proper to a hero. This quality was best revealed in a contest, or *agon*. Homeric battles are not primarily group combats, but a series of individual contests between great champions. One of the prime forms of entertainment is the athletic contest, and the funeral of Patroclus is celebrated by such a contest.

The central ethical idea in Homer can be found in the instructions that the father of Achilles gives to his son when he sends him off to fight at Troy: "Always be the best and distinguished above others." The father of another Homeric hero has given his son exactly the same orders and has added to them the injunction: "Do not bring shame on the family of your fathers who were by far the best in Ephyre and in wide Lycia." Here in a nutshell we have the chief values of the aristocrats of Homer's world: to vie for individual supremacy in *arete* and to defend and increase the honor of the family. These would remain prominent aristocratic values long after Homeric society was only a memory.

The Polis

The characteristic Greek institution was the *polis*. The common translation of that word as "city-state" is misleading, for it says both too much and too little. All Greek *poleis* began as little more than agricultural villages or towns, and many stayed that way, so the word "city" is inappropriate. All of them were states, in the sense of being independent political units, but they were much more than that. The *polis* was thought of as a community of relatives; all its citizens, who were theoretically descended from a common ancestor, belonged to subgroups such as fighting brotherhoods (*phratries*), clans, and tribes. They worshiped the gods in common ceremonies.

Aristotle (see Chapter 2) argued that the *polis* was a natural growth and that the human being is by nature "an animal who lives in a *polis*." Humans alone have the power of speech and from it derive the ability to distinguish good from bad and right from wrong, "and the sharing of these things is what makes a household and a *polis*." Therefore, humans who are incapable of sharing these things or who are so self-sufficient that they have no need of them are not humans at all, but either wild beasts or gods. Without law and justice humans are the worst and most dangerous of the animals. With them they can be the best, and justice exists only in the *polis*. These high claims were made in the fourth century B.C.E., hundreds of years after the *polis* came into existence, but they accurately reflect an attitude that was present from the first.

Development of the Polis

Originally the word *polis* referred only to a citadel, an elevated, defensible rock to which the farmers of the neighboring area could retreat in case of attack. The Acropolis in Athens and the hill called Acrocorinth in Corinth are examples. For some time such high places and the adjacent farms made up the *polis*. The towns grew gradually and without planning, as their narrow, winding, and disorderly streets show. For centuries they had no walls. Unlike the city-states of the Near East, they were not placed for commercial convenience on rivers or the sea. Nor did they grow up around a temple to serve the needs of priests and to benefit from the needs of worshipers. The availability of farmland and of a natural fortress determined their location. They were placed either well inland or far enough away from the sea to avoid piratical raids. Only later and gradually did the *agora*—a marketplace and civic center—appear within the *polis*. The agora was to become the heart of the Greeks' remarkable social life, distinguished by conversation and argument carried on in the open air.

Some *poleis* probably came into existence early in the eighth century B.C.E. The institution was certainly common by the middle of that century, for all the colonies that were established by the Greeks in the years after 750 B.C.E. took the form of the *polis*. Once the new institution had been fully established, true monarchy disappeared. Vestigial kings survived in some places, but they were almost always only ceremonial figures without power. The original form of the *polis* was an aristocratic republic dominated by the nobility through its council of nobles and its monopoly of the magistracies.

The Hoplite Phalanx

A new military strategy was crucial to the development of the *polis*. In earlier times the brunt of fighting had been carried on by small troops of cavalry and individual "champions" who first threw their spears and then came to close quarters with swords. Toward the end of the eighth century B.C.E., however, the hoplite phalanx came into being and remained the basis of Greek warfare thereafter.

The hoplite was a heavily armed infantryman who fought with a spear and a large shield. These soldiers were arrayed in close order, usually at least eight ranks deep, to form a phalanx. As long as the hoplites fought bravely and held their ground, there would be few casualties and no defeat, but if they gave way, the result was usually a rout. All depended on the discipline, strength, and courage of the individual soldier. At its best, the phalanx could withstand cavalry charges and defeat infantries not as well protected or disciplined. Until defeated by the Roman legion, it was the dominant military force in the eastern Mediterranean.

The usual hoplite battle in Greece was between the armies of two *poleis* quarreling over a piece of land. One army invaded the territory of the other when its crops were almost ready for harvest. The defending army had no choice but to protect the fields. If the defenders were beaten, the fields were captured or destroyed and the people of the *polis* might starve. This style of fighting produced a single decisive battle that reduced the time lost in fighting other kinds of warfare; it spared the houses, livestock, and other capital of the farmer-soldiers who made up the phalanx, and it minimized casualties. It perfectly suited the farmer-soldier-citizen who was the backbone of the *polis*, and, by keeping wars short and limiting their destructiveness and expense, it helped the *polis* prosper.

The phalanx and the *polis* arose together, and both heralded the decline of kings. The immediate beneficiaries of the royal decline were aristocrats, but because the phalanx, and with it the *polis*, depended on farmers working small holdings as well as aristocrats, the wishes of the small farmers could not for long be wholly ignored. The rise of the hoplite phalanx created a bond between aristocrats and family farmers who fought in it side by side, and this bond helps to explain why class conflicts were muted for some time in Greece. It also guaranteed, however, that the aristocrats, who dominated the *poleis* at first, would not always be unchallenged.

Expansion of the Greek World

From the middle of the eighth century B.C.E. until well into the sixth, the Greeks vastly expanded the territory they controlled, their wealth, and their contacts with other peoples. A burst of colonizing activity placed *poleis* from Spain to the Black Sea. A century earlier a few Greeks had established trading posts in Syria. There they had learned new techniques in art and crafts and much more from the older civilizations of the Near East. About 750 B.C.E. they borrowed a writing system from one of the Semitic scripts and added vowels to create the first true alphabet. The new Greek alphabet was easier to learn than any earlier writing system and made possible a widely literate society.

Greek Colonies

Syria and its neighboring territory were too strong to penetrate, so the Greeks settled the sparsely populated southern coast of Macedonia and the Chalcidic peninsula (see Map 3–2). Southern Italy and eastern Sicily were even more invit-

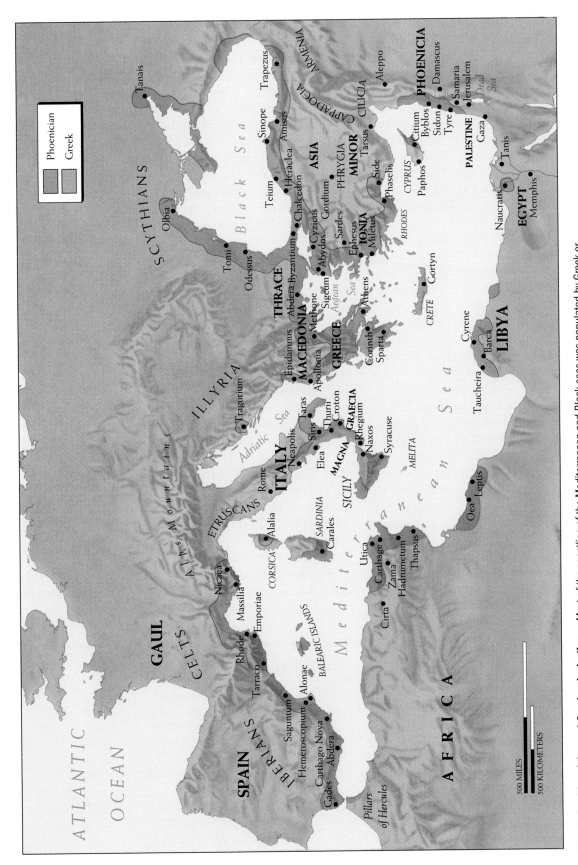

Map 3–2 Phoenician and Greek colonization. Most of the coastline of the Mediterranean and Black seas was populated by Greek or Phoenician colonies. The Phoenicians were a commercial people who planted their colonies in North Africa, Spain, Sicily, and Sardinia, chiefly in the ninth century B.C.E. The height of Greek colonization came later, between about 750 and 550 B.C.E.

ing areas. Before long, there were so many Greek colonies in Italy and Sicily that the Romans called the whole region *Magna Graecia* ("Great Greece"). The Greeks also put colonies in Spain and southern France. In the seventh century B.C.E. Greek colonists settled the coasts of the northeastern Mediterranean, the Black Sea, and the straits connecting them. At about the same time they established settlements on the eastern part of the north African coast. The Greeks now had outposts throughout the Mediterranean world. Most colonies, although independent, were friendly with their mother cities. Each might ask the other for aid in time of trouble and expect to receive a friendly hearing, although neither was obliged to help.

Colonization had a powerful influence on Greek life. By relieving the pressure and land hunger of a growing population, it provided a safety valve that allowed the *poleis* to escape civil wars. By confronting them with the differences between themselves and the new peoples they met, colonization gave the Greeks a sense of cultural identity and fostered a Panhellenic ("all-Greek") spirit that led to the establishment of a number of common religious festivals. The most important of these were at Olympia, Delphi, Corinth, and Nemea.

Colonization also encouraged trade and industry. The influx of new wealth from abroad and the increased demand for goods from the homeland stimulated a more intensive use of the land and an emphasis on crops for export, chiefly the olive and the wine grape. The manufacture of pottery, tools, weapons, and fine metalwork as well as perfumed oil, the soap of the ancient Mediterranean world, was likewise encouraged. New opportunities allowed some men, sometimes outside the nobility, to become wealthy and important. These newly enriched became a troublesome element in the aristocratic *poleis*, for, although increasingly important in the life of their states, they were barred from political power, religious privileges, and social acceptance by the ruling aristocrats. These conditions soon created a crisis in many states.

The Tyrants (ca. 700–500 B.C.E.)

In some cities, perhaps only a small percentage of the more than one thousand Greek *poleis*, the crisis produced by new economic and social conditions led to or intensified factional divisions within the ruling aristocracy. In the years between 700 and 500 B.C.E., the result was often the establishment of a tyranny.

The Rise of Tyranny A tyrant was a monarch who had gained power in an unorthodox but not necessarily wicked way and who exercised a strong one-man rule that might well be beneficent and popular.

The founding tyrant was usually a member of the ruling aristocracy who either had a personal grievance or led an unsuccessful faction. He often rose to power because of his military ability and support from the hoplites. He generally had the support of the politically powerless newly wealthy and of poor farmers. When he took power he often expelled many of his aristocratic opponents and divided at least some of their land among his supporters. He pleased his commercial and industrial supporters by destroying the privileges of the old aristocracy and by fostering trade and colonization.

The tyrants presided over a period of population growth that saw an increase especially in the number of city dwellers. They responded with a program of public works that included the improvement of drainage systems, care for the water supply, the construction and organization of marketplaces, the building and strengthening of city walls, and the erection of temples. They introduced new local festivals and elaborated the old ones. They were active in the patronage of the arts, supporting poets and artisans with gratifying results. All this activity contributed to the tyrant's popularity, to the prosperity of his city, and to his self-esteem.

In most cases the tyrant's rule was secured by a personal bodyguard and by mercenary soldiers. An armed citizenry, necessary for an aggressive foreign policy, would have been dangerous, so the tyrants usually pursued a program of peaceful alliances with other tyrants abroad and avoided war.

The End of the Tyrants By the end of the sixth century B.C.E. tyranny had disappeared from the Greek states and did not return in the same form or for the same reasons. The last tyrants were universally hated for their cruelty and repressiveness. They left bitter memories in their own states and became objects of fear and hatred everywhere.

Besides the outrages committed by individual tyrants, there was something about the very concept of tyranny that

Chronology of the Rise of Greece	
ca. 2900–1150 B.C.E.	Minoan period
ca. 1900 B.C.E.	Probable date of the arrival of the Greeks on the mainland
ca. 1600–1150 B.C.E.	Mycenaean period
ca. 1250 B.C.E.	Sack of Troy (?)
ca. 1200–1150 B.C.E.	Destruction of Mycenaean centers in Greece
ca. 1100–750 B.C.E.	Dark Ages
ca. 750–500 B.C.E.	Major period of Greek colonization
ca. 725 B.C.E.	Probable date of Homer
ca. 700 B.C.E.	Probable date of Hesiod
ca. 700–500 B.C.E.	Major period of Greek tyranny

Hesiod's Farmer's Almanac

Hesiod was a farmer and poet who lived in a village in Greece about 700 B.C.E. His poem Works and Days *contains wisdom on several subjects, but its final section amounts to a farmer's almanac, taking readers through the year and advising them on just when each activity is demanded. Hesiod painted a picture of a very hard life for Greek farmers. In the following passage he talks about one of the few times when the farmer is free from toil, during the hottest part of summer.*

What might be Hesiod's purposes in writing this poem? What can be learned from this passage about the character of Greek farming? How did it differ from other modes of agriculture? What are the major virtues Hesiod associates with farming? How do they compare with the virtues celebrated by Homer?

But when House-on-Back, the snail, crawls from the
    ground up
the plants, escaping the Pleiades, it's no longer time for
    vine-digging;
time rather to put an edge to your sickles, and rout out
    your helpers.
Keep away from sitting in the shade or lying in bed till
    the sun's up
in the time of the harvest, when the sunshine scorches
    your skin dry.
This is the season to push work and bring home your
    harvest;
get up with the first light so you'll have enough to live
    on.
Dawn takes away from work a third part of the work's
    measure.
Dawn sets a man well along on his journey, in his work
    also,

dawn, who when she shows, has numerous people going
    their ways; dawn who puts the yoke upon many oxen.
But when the artichoke is in flower, and the clamorous
    cricket
sitting in his tree lets go his vociferous singing, that
    issues
from the beating of his wings, in the exhausting season
    of summer,
then is when goats are at their fattest, when the wine
    tastes best,
women are most lascivious, but the men's strength fails
    them
most, for the star Seirios shrivels them, knees and heads
    alike,
and the skin is all dried out in the heat; then, at that
    season,
one might have the shadow under the rock, and the
    wine of Biblis,
a curd cake, and all the milk that the goats can give you,
the meat of a heifer, bred in the woods, who has never
    borne a calf,
and of baby kids also. Then, too, one can sit in the
    shadow
and drink the bright-shining wine, his heart satiated
    with eating
and face turned in the direction where Zephyros blows
    briskly,
make three libations of water from a spring that keeps
    running forever
and has no mud in it; and pour wine for the fourth
    libation.

Hesiod, *Works and Days*, trans. by Richmond Lattimore. Copyright © 1959, University of Michigan Press, Ann Arbor, MI. pp. 87, 89. Reprinted by permission.

was inimical to the idea of the *polis*. The notion of the *polis* as a community to which every member must be responsible, the connection of justice with that community, and the natural aristocratic hatred of monarchy all made tyranny seem alien and offensive. The rule of a tyrant, however beneficent, was arbitrary and unpredictable. Tyranny came into being in defiance of tradition and law, and the tyrant governed without either. He was not answerable in any way to his fellow citizens.

From a longer perspective, however, the tyrants made important contributions to the development of Greek civilization. They encouraged economic changes that helped secure the future prosperity of Greece. They increased communication with the rest of the Mediterranean world and cultivated the crafts and technology, as well as the arts and literature. Most important of all, they broke the grip of the aristocracy and put the productive powers of the most active and talented of its citizens fully at the service of the *polis*.

Life in Archaic Greece

Society

As the "dark ages" came to an end, the features that would distinguish Greek society thereafter took shape. The role of the artisan and the merchant grew more important as contact with the non-Greek world became easier, but the great majority of people continued to make their living from the land. Wealthy aristocrats with large estates, powerful households, families, and clans, however, led very different lives from those of the poorer peasants and the independent farmers who had smaller and less fertile fields.

Farmers Ordinary country people rarely leave a record of their thoughts or activities, and we have no such record from ancient Greece. The poet Hesiod (ca. 700 B.C.E.), however, was certainly no aristocrat. He presented himself as a small farmer, and his *Works and Days* gives some idea of the life of such a farmer. The crops included grain, chiefly barley but also wheat; grapes for the making of wine; olives for food, but mainly for oil, used for cooking, lighting, and washing; green vegetables, especially the bean; and some fruit. Sheep and goats provided milk and cheese. The Homeric heroes had great herds of cattle and ate lots of meat, but by Hesiod's time land fertile enough to provide fodder for cattle was needed to grow grain. He and small farmers like him tasted meat chiefly from sacrificial animals at festivals.

These farmers worked hard to make a living. Although Hesiod had the help of oxen and mules and one or two hired helpers for occasional labor, his life was one of continual toil. The hardest work came in October, at the start of the rainy season, the time for the first plowing. The plow was light and easily broken, and the work of forcing the iron tip into the earth was backbreaking, even with the help of a team of oxen. For the less fortunate farmer, the cry of the crane that announced the time of year to plow "bites the heart of the man without oxen." Autumn and winter were the time for cutting wood, building wagons, and making tools. Late winter was the time to tend to the vines, May the time to harvest the grain, July to winnow and store it. Only at the height of summer's heat did Hesiod allow for rest, but when September came it was time to harvest the grapes. No sooner was that task done than the cycle started again. The work went on under the burning sun and in the freezing cold.

Hesiod wrote nothing of pleasure or entertainment, but less austere farmers than he gathered at the blacksmith's shop for warmth and companionship in winter, and even he must have taken part in religious rites and festivals that were accompanied by some kind of entertainment. None-

This scene on an Attic jar from late in the sixth century B.C.E. shows how olives, one of Athens' most important crops, were harvested.

theless, the lives of ordinary farmers were certainly hard and their pleasures few.

Aristocrats Most aristocrats were rich enough to employ many hired laborers, sometimes sharecroppers and sometimes even slaves, to work their extensive lands and were therefore able to enjoy leisure for other activities. The center of aristocratic social life was the drinking party, or *symposion*. This activity was not a mere drinking bout, meant to remove inhibitions and produce oblivion. The Greeks, in fact, almost always mixed their wine with water, and one of the goals of the participants was to drink as much as the others without becoming drunk.

The *symposion* was a carefully organized occasion, with a "king" chosen to set the order of events and to determine that night's mixture of wine and water. Only men took part, and they ate and drank as they reclined on couches along the walls of the room. The sessions began with prayers and libations to the gods. Usually there were games, such as dice or *kottabos*, in which wine was flicked from the cups at different targets. Sometimes dancing girls or flute girls offered entertainment. Frequently the participants provided their own amusements with songs, poetry, or even philosophical disputes. Characteristically, these took the form of contests, with some kind of prize for the winner, for aristocratic values continued to emphasize competition and the need to excel, whatever the arena.

This aspect of aristocratic life appears in the athletic contests that became widespread early in the sixth century B.C.E. The games included running events; the long jump; the discus and javelin throws; the *pentathlon*, which included all of these; boxing; wrestling; and the chariot race. Only the rich could afford to raise, train, and race horses, so the chariot race was a special preserve of aristocracy. Wrestling, however, was also especially favored by the nobility, and the *palaestra* where they practiced became an important social center for the aristocracy. The contrast between the hard, drab life of the peasants and the leisured and lively one of the aristocrats could hardly be greater.

Religion

Like most ancient peoples, the Greeks were polytheists, and religion played an important part in their lives. A great part of Greek art and literature was closely connected with religion, as was the life of the *polis* in general.

The Greek pantheon consisted of the twelve gods who lived on Mount Olympus. These were

- Zeus, the father of the gods
- Hera, his wife
- Zeus's siblings:
  Poseidon, his brother, god of the seas and earthquakes
  Hestia, his sister, goddess of the hearth
  Demeter, his sister, goddess of agriculture and marriage
- Zeus's children:
  Aphrodite, goddess of love and beauty
  Apollo, god of the sun, music, poetry, and prophecy
  Ares, god of war
  Artemis, goddess of the moon and the hunt
  Athena, goddess of wisdom and the arts
  Hephaestus, god of fire and metallurgy
- Hermes, messenger of the gods, connected with commerce and cunning

The gods were seen as behaving very much as mortal humans behaved, with all the foibles of humans, except that they were superhuman in these as well as in their strength and immortality. On the other hand, Zeus, at least, was seen as a source of human justice, and even the Olympians were understood to be subordinate to the Fates. Each *polis* had one of the Olympians as its guardian deity and worshiped that god in its own special way, but all the gods were Panhellenic. In the eighth and seventh centuries B.C.E. common shrines were established at Olympia and at Nemea for the worship of Zeus, at Delphi for Apollo, and at the Isthmus of Corinth for Poseidon. Each held athletic contests in honor of its deity, to which all Greeks were invited and for which a sacred truce was declared.

The worship of these deities did not involve great emotion. Worshipers offered a god prayer, libations, and gifts in hopes of protection and favors. Greek religion offered no hope of immortality for the average human and little moral teaching. Most Greeks seem to have held to the commonsense notion that justice lay in paying one's debts. They thought that civic virtue consisted of worshiping the state deities in the traditional way, performing required public services, and fighting in defense of the state. To them, private morality meant to do good to one's friends and harm to one's enemies.

In the sixth century B.C.E., the influence of the cult of Apollo at Delphi and of his oracle there became very great. The oracle was the most important of several that helped satisfy human craving for a clue to the future. The priests of Apollo preached moderation; their advice was exemplified in the two famous sayings identified with Apollo: "Know thyself" and "Nothing in excess." Humans need self-control (*sophrosyne*). Its opposite is arrogance (*hubris*), which is brought on by excessive wealth or good fortune. *Hubris* leads to moral blindness and finally to divine vengeance. This theme of moderation and the dire consequences of its absence was central to Greek popular morality and appears frequently in Greek literature.

The somewhat cold religion of the Olympian gods and of the cult of Apollo did little to assuage human fears, hopes, and passions. For these needs, the Greeks turned to other deities and rites. Of them, the most popular was Dionysus, a god of nature and fertility, of the grapevine and drunkenness and sexual abandon. In some of his rites the god was followed by maenads, female devotees who cavorted by night, ate raw flesh, and were reputed to tear to pieces any creature they came across.

Poetry

The great changes sweeping through the Greek world were also reflected in the poetry of the sixth century B.C.E. The lyric style, whether sung by a chorus or sung by one singer, predominated. Sappho of Lesbos, Anacreon of Teos, and Simonides of Cous composed personal poetry, often speaking

The god Dionysus dances with two female followers.

The vase was painted in the sixth century B.C.E.

[Bibliothèque Nationale de France, Paris]

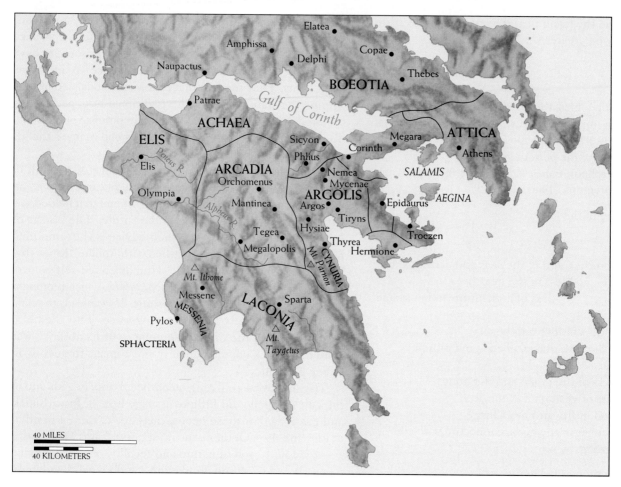

Map 3–3 The Peloponnesus. Sparta's region, Laconia, was in the Peloponnesus. Nearby states were members of the Peloponnesian League under Sparta's leadership.

of the pleasure and agony of love. Alcaeus of Mytilene, an aristocrat driven from his city by a tyrant, wrote bitter invective.

Perhaps the most interesting poet of the century from a political point of view was Theognis of Megara. An aristocrat who lived through a tyranny, an unusually chaotic and violent democracy, and an oligarchy that restored order but ended the rule of the old aristocracy, Theognis was the spokesman for the old, defeated aristocracy of birth. He divided everyone into two classes, the noble and the base; the former were good, the latter bad. Those nobly born must associate only with others like themselves if they were to preserve their virtue; if they mingled with the base, they became base. Those born base, on the other hand, could never become noble. Only nobles could aspire to virtue, and only nobles possessed the critical moral and intellectual qualities: respect (or honor) and judgment. These qualities could not be taught; they were innate. Even so, nobles had to guard themselves against corruption by wealth or by mingling with the base. Intermarriage between the noble and the base was especially condemned. These were the ideas of the unre-

constructed nobility, whose power had been destroyed or reduced in most Greek states by this time. They remained alive in aristocratic hearts throughout the next century and greatly influenced later thinkers, Plato among them.

Major City-States

Generalization about the *polis* becomes difficult not long after its appearance, for although the states had much in common, some of them developed in unique ways. Sparta and Athens, which became the two most powerful Greek states, had especially unusual histories.

Sparta

Sparta (see Map 3–3) began to assume its special character about 725 B.C.E., when population pressure and land hunger led the Spartans to conquer their western neighbor, Messenia, in the First Messenian War. The Spartans now had as much land as they would ever need, and because they re-

The Greek and Persian Ways of War—
Autocracy versus Freedom under the Law

The Greek historian Herodotus, who wrote his account of the wars between the Greeks and Persians more than half a century after they ended, was very interested in the differences between the ways of the Greeks and other peoples of the world. In the following passage he describes a conversation between Demaratus, an exiled king of Sparta, and Xerxes, the Great King of Persia. Demaratus had come to Xerxes' court after his exile. Xerxes received him kindly and made him a royal adviser.

On what does Xerxes rely for Persian military success? What is the source of Demaratus' confidence in the Spartans? Does the claim he makes hold for other Greeks as well as the Spartans? How is it possible to reconcile freedom with obedience to the laws?

'How is it possible that a thousand men, or ten thousand, or fifty thousand, should stand up to a army as big as mine, especially if they were not under a single master, but all perfectly free to do as they pleased? Suppose them to have five thousand men: in that case we should be more than a thousand to one! If, like ours, their troops were subject to the control of a single man, then possibly for fear of him, in spite of the disparity in numbers, they might show some sort of factitious courage, or let themselves be whipped into battle; but, as every man is free to follow his fancy, it is not conceivable that they should do either. Indeed, my own opinion is that even on equal terms the Greeks could hardly face the Persians alone. We, too, have this thing that you were speaking of—I do not say it is common, but it does exist; for instance, amongst the Persians in my bodyguard there are men who would willingly fight with three Greeks together. But you know nothing of such things, or you could not talk such nonsense.'

'My lord,' Demaratus answered, 'I knew before I began that if I spoke the truth you would not like it. But, as you demanded the plain truth and nothing less, I told you how things are with the Spartans. Yet you are well aware that I now feel but little affection for my countrymen, who robbed me of my hereditary power and privileges and made me a fugitive without a home—whereas your father welcomed me at his court and gave me the means of livelihood and somewhere to live. Surely it is unreasonable to reject kindness; any sensible man will cherish it. Personally I do not claim to be able to fight ten men—or two; indeed I should prefer not even to fight with one. But should it be necessary—should there be some great cause to urge me on—then nothing would give me more pleasure than to stand up to one of those men of yours who claim to be a match for three Greeks. So it is with the Spartans; fighting singly, they are as good as any, but fighting together they are the best soldiers in the world. They are free—yes—but not entirely free; for they have a master, and that master is Law, which they fear much more than your subjects fear you. Whatever this master commands they do; and his command never varies: it is never to retreat in battle, however great the odds, but always to stand firm, and to conquer or die. If, my lord, you think that what I have said is nonsense—very well; I am willing henceforward to hold my tongue. This time I spoke because you forced me to speak. In any case, I pray that all may turn out as you desire.'

Xerxes burst out laughing at Demaratus' answer, and goodhumouredly let him go.

From Herodotus, *The Histories*, trans. by Aubrey de Selincourt (Harmondsworth: Penguin Books, 1976), pp. 476–477.

---

duced the Messenians to serfs, or Helots, they no longer had to work this land themselves. When the Helots-assisted by Argos and some other Peloponnesian cities-rebelled in the Second Messenian War in about 650 B.C.E., the Spartans faced a turning point. The long and bitter war, which at one point threatened their city's existence, made it clear to the Spartans that they could not expect to keep down the Helots, who outnumbered them perhaps ten to one, and maintain the free-and-easy habits typical of most Greeks. They thus chose to introduce fundamental reforms that turned their city forever after into a military academy and camp.

Society   The new system, which emerged late in the sixth century B.C.E., exerted control over each Spartan from birth, when officials of the state decided which infants, male and female, were physically fit to survive. At age seven, the Spartan boy was taken from his mother and turned over to young instructors who trained him in athletics and the military arts and taught him to endure privation, to bear physical pain, and to live off the country, by theft if necessary. The Spartan youth was enrolled in the army at twenty and lived in barracks with his companions until he was thirty. He could marry, but could visit his wife only infrequently and by stealth. At thirty he became a full citizen, an "equal," and was allowed to live in his own house with his wife, although he took his meals at a public mess in the company of fifteen comrades. His food, a simple diet without much meat or wine, was provided by his own plot of land, which was worked by Helots.

Only when he reached sixty could the Spartan retire from military service to his home and family.

Spartan girls did not receive military training, but they were given gymnastic training and were permitted greater freedom than among other Greeks. Like boys, they too were indoctrinated with the idea of service to Sparta. The entire system was designed to change the natural feelings of devotion to family into a more powerful commitment to the *polis*. Privacy, luxury, and even comfort were sacrificed to the purpose of producing soldiers whose physical prowess, training, and discipline made them the best in the world. Nothing that might turn the mind away from duty was permitted. The very use of coins was forbidden for its potential to corrupt. Neither family nor money was allowed to interfere with the only ambition permitted to a Spartan male: to win glory and respect by bravery in war.

Government   In a mixture of monarchy, oligarchy, and democracy, Sparta was governed by two kings, a council of elders, and an assembly. The power of the kings was limited by law and by the rivalry that usually prevailed between them. The council of elders—twenty-eight men over sixty who were elected for life—had important judicial functions, sitting as a court in cases involving the kings. It was also consulted before any proposal was put before the assembly. In a traditional society like Sparta's, it must have had considerable influence. The assembly, which consisted of all males over thirty, was theoretically the final authority. In practice, however, it served only to ratify the decisions of magistrates, elders, and kings, or to decide between the positions of these leading figures.

Sparta also had another, unique, governmental institution, the board of ephors. This consisted of five men elected annually by the assembly. Apparently originally intended to check the power of the kings, the ephors gradually acquired other important functions. They controlled foreign policy, oversaw the generalship of the kings on campaign, presided at the assembly, and guarded against rebellion by the Helots.

Suppression of the Helots required all the effort and energy the Spartans had. They could not expand their borders, but at the same time they could not allow unruly independent neighbors to sow unrest among the Helots. Thus when the Spartans defeated Tegea, their northern neighbor, they imposed an unusual peace, allowing the Tegeans to keep their land and their freedom in exchange for following Sparta's lead in foreign affairs and supplying Sparta with a fixed number of troops on demand. As Sparta imposed this model on other neighbors, it emerged as the leader of an alliance—known to scholars today as the Peloponnesian League—that included every Peloponnesian state but Argos. This alliance provided the Spartans with the security they needed, and made Sparta the most powerful *polis* in Greece. Thanks to Sparta and the league, by 500 B.C.E. the Greeks had a force capable of facing mighty threats from abroad.

Athens

In the seventh century B.C.E. Athens and the region of Attica (see Map 3–4) constituted a typical aristocratic *polis*. Aristocrats held the most and best land and dominated religious and political life. There was no written law. The state was governed by the Areopagus, a council of nobles deriving its name from the hill where it held its sessions. Annually the council elected nine magistrates, called *archons*, who joined the Areopagus after their year in office. The Areopagus, however, not the archons, was the true master of the state. A broad-based citizens' assembly, which had little power, represented the four tribes into which Attica's inhabitants were traditionally divided.

Pressure for Change   In the seventh century B.C.E. quarrels within the nobility and the beginnings of an agrarian crisis disturbed the peaceful life of Athens. Many Athenians made their living from family farms, apparently planting wheat, the staple crop, year after year without rotating fields or using enough fertilizer. A shift to more intensive agricultural techniques and the cultivation of trees and vines, which required capital, forced some of the less successful farmers to borrow from wealthy neighbors. As their troubles grew, debtors pledged their wives, their children, and themselves as surety for new loans. Inevitably, many defaulted and were enslaved. Some were even sold abroad. Revolutionary pressures grew among the poor, who began to demand the abolition of debt and a redistribution of the land.

Reforms of Solon   In the year 594 B.C.E., as tradition has it, the Athenians elected Solon (c. 639–559 B.C.E.) as the only archon, with extraordinary powers to legislate and revise Athens' governing institutions. In a program called the "shaking off of burdens," Solon immediately canceled current debts and forbade future loans secured by the person of the borrower. He helped bring back many Athenians enslaved abroad and freed those in Athens enslaved for debt. Solon did not redistribute land and failed in the short run to end Athens' economic crisis. Some of his actions, however, were profoundly successful in the long run. He encouraged commerce and turned Athens in the direction that would lead it to great prosperity in the fifth century. He forbade the export of wheat, initially making wheat more available in Attica, but he also encouraged the export of olive oil and wine. As a result, by the fifth century B.C.E. much Athenian land was diverted from grain production to the cultivation of olive trees and vines as cash crops, making Athens dependent on

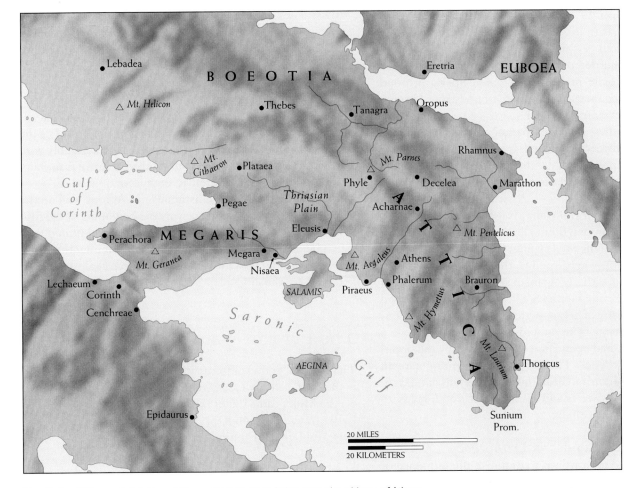

Map 3–4 Attica and vicinity. Citizens of all towns in Attica were also citizens of Athens.

imported wheat. Solon also encouraged industry by offering citizenship to foreign artisans, stimulating the development of outstanding pottery in Attica in the sixth century.

Solon also significantly changed the way Athens was governed. He expanded citizenship-previously limited to adult males whose fathers were citizens-to include immigrant artisans and merchants, and divided the citizenry into four classes on the basis of wealth. Only men of the wealthiest two classes could be archons and sit on the Areopagus. Men of the third class could serve as hoplites and on a council of four hundred chosen by the assembly of all male citizens. The fourth class, the *thetes*, voted in the assembly and also sat on a new court of appeal that would hear almost all cases in Athens by the fifth century B.C.E.

Pisistratus the Tyrant Despite Solon's reforms, Athens succumbed to factional strife that ended when the leader of one faction, Pisistratus (605?–527 B.C.E.), a nobleman and military hero, seized power firmly in 546 B.C.E. with the help of mercenary soldiers and made himself the city's first tyrant.

Pisistratus sought to increase the power of the central government at the expense of the nobles. To undermine their authority in the countryside, he sent out circuit judges to hear local cases. To fix attention on the capital, he engaged in great programs of public works, urban improvement, and religious piety. He built temples, expanded and improved religious centers, introduced new religious festivals, and increased the public appeal of traditional festivals. His reconstruction of Athens' Agora (marketplace) helped transform it into the center of public life. To add cultural luster to his court he supported poets and artists. Throughout his rule, Pisistratus made no formal change in the institutions of government. Assembly, councils, and courts met; magistrates and councils were elected; Pisistratus merely saw to it that his supporters filled key offices. The intended effect was to blunt the sharp edge of tyranny with the appearance of constitutional government, and it worked. The rule of Pisistratus was remembered as popular and mild. The unintended effect was to give the Athenians more experience in the procedures of self-government and a growing taste for it.

Invasion by Sparta Pisistratus was succeeded by his oldest son, Hippias (r. 527–510 B.C.E.), whose rule became increasingly nervous, suspicious, and harsh after his brother Hipparchus was murdered in 514 B.C.E. Hippias was deposed and driven into exile in 510 B.C.E. when Sparta invaded Athens with the cooperation of a noble family that Hippias had exiled. The tyranny was over.

After the withdrawal of the Spartan army, some factions in the Athenian aristocracy, led by Isagoras, tried to restore the aristocracy to the position of dominance it held before Solon. Isagoras purged the citizen lists, removing those who had been enfranchised by Solon or Pisistratus and any others thought to have a doubtful claim. Isagoras, however, faced competitors, chief among them Clisthenes, of a rival aristocratic clan. In a challenge to Isagoras, Clisthenes took an unprecedented action—he turned to the people for political support and won it with a program of great popular appeal. In response, Isagoras called in the Spartans again, who expelled Clisthenes and many of his supporters. But the fire of Athenian political consciousness, ignited by Solon and kept alive under Pisistratus, had been fanned into flames by the popular appeal of Clisthenes. The people refused to tolerate an aristocratic restoration and drove out the Spartans and Isagoras with them. Clisthenes and his allies returned, ready to put their program into effect.

Clisthenes, the Founder of Democracy A central aim of Clisthenes' reforms was to diminish the influence of traditional localities and regions in Athenian life, for they were an important source of power for the nobility and of factions in the state. Clisthenes immediately enrolled the disenfranchised who had supported him in the struggle with Isagoras. He also replaced Attica's traditional four tribes with ten new tribes organized to guarantee that no region would dominate any of them. Because members of a tribe had common religious activities and fought together in regimental units, the new organization increased devotion to the *polis*, weakening regional loyalties.

Clisthenes replaced Solon's council of four hundred with a new council of five hundred, but he vested final authority in all things in the assembly of all adult male Athenian citizens. Debate in the assembly was free and open; any Athenian could submit legislation, offer amendments, or argue the merits of any question. Although Clisthenes did not alter Solon's property qualifications for officeholders, his enlargement of the citizen rolls, his diminution of the power of the aristocrats, and his elevation of the role of the assembly with its effective and manageable council all give him a firm claim to the title of father of Athenian democracy.

Solon, Pisistratus, and Clisthenes put Athens well on the way to prosperity and democracy by the beginning of the fifth century B.C.E. It was much more centralized and united than it had been and was ready to take its place among the major states that would lead the defense of Greece against the dangers that lay ahead.

The Persian Wars

The Greeks' period of fortunate isolation and freedom ended in the sixth century B.C.E. when the Greek cities on the coast of Asia Minor came under the control first of King Croesus of Lydia (r. ca. 560–546 B.C.E.), and then in 546 B.C.E. of the powerful Persian Empire (see Chapter 4).

Ionian Rebellion

Initially the cities of Ionia (those on the central part of the west coast of Asia Minor and nearby islands) prospered under Persian rule and remained obedient. The private troubles of the ambitious tyrant of Miletus, Aristagoras, however, ended this calm and set in motion events that would threaten the independence of all the Greeks. Aristagoras had urged a Persian expedition against the island of Naxos; when it failed, he feared the consequences and organized a rebellion in Ionia in 499 B.C.E. To gain support, he overthrew the tyrannies the Persians had installed and proclaimed democratic constitutions. Next he turned to the mainland Greeks for help, first petitioning Sparta, which refused him, and then Athens. The Athenians, who were related to the Ionians and had close ties of religion and tradition with them, agreed to send a fleet of twenty ships to help the rebels. This expedition was strengthened by five ships from Eretria in Euboea.

In 498 B.C.E., the Athenians and their allies made a swift march and a surprise attack on Sardis, the old capital of Lydia and now the seat of the Persian governor, and burned it. The revolt spread throughout the Greek cities of Asia Minor outside Ionia, but the Athenians withdrew and the Persians gradually reimposed their will. In 495 B.C.E. they defeated the Ionian fleet at Lade, and in the next year they wiped out

Key Events in the Early History of Sparta and Athens	
ca. 725–710 B.C.E.	First Messenian War
ca. 650–625 B.C.E.	Second Messenian War; Solon institutes reforms at Athens
ca. 560–550 B.C.E.	Sparta defeats Tegea: beginning of Peloponnesian League
546–527 B.C.E.	Pisistratus reigns as tyrant at Athens (main period)
510 B.C.E.	Hippias, son of Pisistratus, deposed as tyrant of Athens
ca. 508–501 B.C.E.	Clisthenes institutes reforms at Athens

Miletus, killing many of the city's men, transporting others to the Persian Gulf, and enslaving its women and children. The Ionian rebellion was over.

The War in Greece

In 490 B.C.E. the Persian king, Darius (r. 521–486 B.C.E.), sent an expedition to punish Athens, to restore Hippias, and to gain control of the Aegean Sea. Miltiades (d. 489 B.C.E.), an Athenian who had fled from Persian service, led the city's army to a confrontation with the invaders at Marathon. A Persian victory at Marathon would have destroyed Athenian freedom and led to the conquest of all the mainland Greeks. The greatest achievements of Greek culture, most of which lay in the future, would never have occurred. But the Athenians won a decisive victory, instilling them with a sense of confidence and pride in their *polis*, their unique form of government, and themselves.

The Great Invasion For the Persians, Marathon was only a small and temporary defeat. In 481 B.C.E. Darius's successor, Xerxes (r. 486–465 B.C.E.), gathered an army of at least 150,000 men and a navy of more than 600 ships for the conquest of Greece. In Athens, Themistocles (c. 525–462 B.C.E.), who favored making Athens into a naval power, had become the leading politician. During his archonship in 493 B.C.E., Athens had already taken the first step in that direction by building a fortified port at Piraeus. A decade later the Athenians came upon a rich vein of silver in the state mines, and Themistocles persuaded them to use the profits to increase their fleet. By 480 B.C.E. Athens had more than 200 ships, the backbone of a navy that was to defeat the Persians.

Of the hundreds of Greek states, only thirty-one—led by Sparta, Athens, Corinth, and Aegina—were willing to fight as the Persian army gathered south of the Hellespont. In the spring of 480 B.C.E. Xerxes launched his invasion. The Persian strategy was to march into Greece, destroy Athens, defeat the Greek army, and add the Greeks to the number of Persian subjects. The huge Persian army needed to keep in touch with the fleet for supplies. If the Greeks could defeat the Persian navy, the army could not remain in Greece long. Themistocles knew that the Aegean was subject to sudden devastating storms. His strategy was to delay the Persian army and then to bring on the kind of naval battle he might hope to win.

The Greeks chose Sparta to lead them and first confronted the Persians at Thermopylae on land and off Artemisium at sea. The opening between the mountains and the sea at Thermopylae is so narrow that it might be held by a smaller army against a much larger one. Severe storms wrecked many Persian ships while the Greek fleet waited safely in a protected harbor. Then Xerxes attacked Thermopylae, and for two days the Greeks butchered his best troops without seri-

A Greek hoplite attacks a Persian soldier. The contrast between the Greek's metal body armor, large shield, and long spear, and the Persian's cloth and leather garments indicates one reason the Greeks won. This Attic vase was found on Rhodes and dates from ca. 475 B.C.E.
[The Metropolitan Museum of Art, Rogers Fund, 1906 (Acc. # 06.1021.117)]

ous loss to themselves. On the third day, however, a traitor showed the Persians a mountain trail that permitted them to come on the Greeks from behind. Many allies escaped, but Sparta's King Leonidas and the three hundred Spartans with him all died fighting. Although the naval battle at Artemisium was indecisive, the defeat at Thermopylae forced the Greek navy to withdraw. The Persian army then moved into Attica and burned Athens.

The fate of Greece was decided in a sea battle in the narrow straits to the east of the island of Salamis to which the Greek fleet withdrew after the battle of Artemisium. There the Greeks destroyed more than half the Persian fleet, forcing the rest to retreat to Asia with a good part of the Persian army.

The danger, however, was not over yet. The Persian general Mardonius spent the winter in central Greece, and in the spring he unsuccessfully tried to win the Athenians away from the Greek League. The Spartan regent, Pausanias (d. ca. 470 B.C.E.), then led the largest Greek army yet assembled to confront Mardonius in Boeotia. At Plataea, in the summer of 479 B.C.E., Mardonius died in battle, and his army fled toward home. Meanwhile, the Ionian Greeks urged King Leotychidas, the Spartan commander of the fleet, to fight the Persian fleet at Samos. At Mycale, on the nearby coast, Leotychidas destroyed the Persian camp and its fleet offshore. The Persians fled the Aegean and Ionia. For the moment, at least, the Persian threat was gone.

Classical Greece

The repulse of the Persians marks the beginning of the Classical Period in Greece, 150 years of intense cultural achievement that has rarely if ever been matched anywhere since (see Map 3–5). The Classical Period was also a time of destructive conflicts among the *poleis* that in the end left them weakened and vulnerable.

The Delian League

Greek unity, strained even during the life-and-death struggle with Persia, gave way within two years of the Persian retreat to division. Two spheres of influence emerged—one dominated by Sparta, the other by Athens. The reasons for the split lay in the Ionian Greeks' ongoing need for protection against the Persians and the desire of many Greeks for revenge and reparations. Sparta was ill suited to lead the Greeks under these conditions, which required a long-term commitment and continual naval action. It fell to Athens, the leading naval power in Greece, to lead the effort to drive the Persians from the Aegean and the Hellespont.

In the winter of 478–477 B.C.E. the islanders, the Greeks from the coast of Asia Minor, and some from other Greek cities on the Aegean met with the Athenians on the sacred island of Delos. Swearing themselves to a permanent alliance, they vowed to free Greeks under Persian rule, to protect all against a Persian return, and to obtain compensation from the Persians by attacking their lands and taking booty. Athens was clearly designated leader. Known as the Delian League, the alliance was remarkably successful, driving the Persians from Europe and the Hellespont and clearing the Aegean of pirates. A great Greek victory at the Eurymedon River in Asia Minor in 467 B.C.E. routed the Persians and added several cities to the league. Believing it necessary for their common safety, the members forced some states into the league and prevented others from leaving.

Leading Athens and the Delian League in this succession of victories was the statesman and soldier Cimon (d. 449 B.C.E.). Themistocles, the architect of the Greek victory in 480 B.C.E., was ostracized and driven from power soon after the Persian war by a coalition of his enemies, ironically ending his days at the court of the Persian king. Cimon dominated Athenian politics for almost two decades, pursuing a policy of aggressive attacks on Persia and friendly relations with Sparta. In domestic affairs, Cimon was conservative. He accepted the democratic constitution of Clisthenes, which appears to have become somewhat more limited when the aristocratic Areopagus usurped many powers from the council of five hundred, the assembly, and the popular courts after the Persian War.

The First Peloponnesian War

The Fall of Cimon In 465 B.C.E., the island of Thasos rebelled against the league. Cimon's suppression of this rebellion after a siege of more than two years marked the first time Athenian interests alone determined league policy and was thus a significant step in the evolution of the league into an Athenian empire. Despite his success, Cimon faced a challenge at home from a faction led by Ephialtes (d. 462 B.C.E.), whose chief supporter was Pericles (c. 495–429 B.C.E.), a member of a distinguished Athenian family. This faction wanted to reduce the power of the conservative Areopagus and increase the power of ordinary people in Athens, and abroad to break with Sparta and contest its claim to leadership.

When the Thasians began their rebellion they asked Sparta to invade Athens, and the Spartans agreed. An earthquake, however, accompanied by a rebellion of the Helots that threatened the survival of Sparta, prevented the invasion. The Spartans asked their allies, the Athenians among them, for help, and Cimon persuaded the Athenians, over the objections of Ephialtes, to send it. The results were disastrous for Cimon. While he was in the Peloponnesus helping the Spartans, Ephialtes stripped the Areopagus of almost all its power. The Spartans, meanwhile, fearing "the boldness and revolutionary spirit of the Athenians," ultimately sent them home. In 461 B.C.E. Cimon was exiled, and Athens made an alliance with Argos, Sparta's traditional enemy. Almost overnight, Cimon's domestic and foreign policies had been overturned.

Outbreak of War The policies of the confident and ambitious new regime at Athens helped bring on a conflict with Sparta known as The First Peloponnesian War. The war began after Megara, getting the worst of a border dispute with Corinth, withdrew from the Spartan-led Peloponnesian League and allied itself with Athens. Megara barred the way from the Peloponnesus to Athens, giving Athens a strategic advantage. The Athenians made great gains during the war's early years, conquering Aegina and gaining control of Boeo-

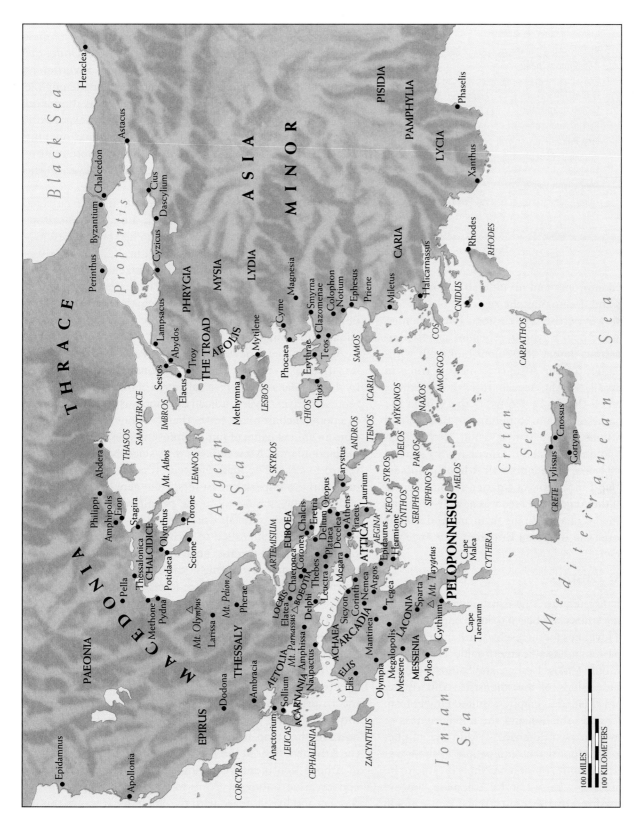

Map 3-5 Classical Greece. Greece in the classical period (ca. 480–338 B.C.E.) centered on the Aegean Sea. Although there were important Greek settlements in Italy, Sicily, and all around the Black Sea, the area shown in this general reference map embraced the vast majority of Greek states.

478–477 B.C.E.	Delian League founded
ca. 474–462 B.C.E.	Cimon leading politician
467 B.C.E.	Victory over Persians at Eurymedon River
465–463 B.C.E.	Rebellion of Thasos
462 B.C.E.	Ephialtes murdered; Pericles rises to leadership
461 B.C.E.	Cimon ostracized
461 B.C.E.	Reform of Areopagus
ca. 460 B.C.E.	First Peloponnesian War begins
454 B.C.E.	Athens defeated in Egypt; crisis in the Delian League
449 B.C.E.	Peace with Persia
445 B.C.E.	Thirty Years' Peace ends First Peloponnesian War

tia. They appeared supreme and invulnerable, controlling neighboring states and dominating the sea.

In 454 B.C.E., however, the tide turned. The Athenian fleet, dispatched to help an Egyptian rebellion against Persia, suffered a disastrous defeat. Rebellions broke out within the Delian League, forcing Athens to make a truce in Greece to subdue its allies in the Aegean. In 449 B.C.E. Athens ended the war against Persia. In 446 B.C.E. the war on the Greek mainland broke out again. Rebellions in Boeotia and Megara opened Athens to a Spartan invasion. Rather than fight, Pericles, the commander of the Athenian army, agreed to a peace of thirty years, abandoning all Athenian possessions on the mainland in return for Spartan recognition of Athenian control of the Aegean. Greece was now divided into two blocs: Sparta and its alliance on the mainland and Athens and what had become the Athenian Empire in the Aegean.

The Athenian Empire

After the Egyptian disaster, the Athenians moved the Delian League's treasury to Athens and began to keep one sixtieth of the league's annual revenues for themselves. Athens was clearly becoming the master and its allies mere subjects (see Map 3–6). By 445 B.C.E. only Chios, Lesbos, and Samos were autonomous and provided ships. All the other states paid tribute.

The change from alliance to empire resulted largely from the pressure of war and rebellion and the unwillingness of the allies to see to their own defenses. Within the subject states, many democratic politicians and people in the lower classes supported the empire, but it nevertheless came to be seen more and more as a tyranny. For the Athenians, however, the empire recognized by the Thirty Years' Peace of 445

B.C.E. had become the key to prosperity and security, and they were determined to defend it at any cost.

Athenian Democracy

Even as the Athenians were tightening their control over their empire, they were expanding democracy at home. Under the leadership of Pericles they evolved the freest government the world had yet seen. The hoplite class was made eligible for the archonship; in theory, no adult male was thereafter barred from that office on the basis of property class. Pericles proposed a law introducing pay for jury service, opening that important duty to the poor. Circuit judges were reintroduced, making swift impartial justice available even to the poorest residents in the countryside.

The benefits of this legislation were limited to citizens, and citizenship was sharply restricted. Pericles himself introduced a bill limiting it to those who had two citizen parents. In Greek terms this was quite natural. Democracy was the privilege of citizenship, making citizenship a valuable commodity. Limiting it would have increased its value and must have won a large majority. Participation in government in all the Greek states was also denied to slaves, resident aliens, and women.

Among citizens, however, the extent of the democracy was remarkable. Every decision of the state had to be approved by the popular assembly—a collection of the people, not their representatives. Every judicial decision was subject to appeal to a popular court of not fewer than fifty-one citizens, chosen from an annual panel of jurors representative of the Athenian male population. Most officials were selected by lot, without regard to class. The main elected officials, such as the generals and the imperial treasurers, were generally nobles and almost always rich men, but the people were free to choose others. All public officials were subject to scrutiny before taking office, could be called to account and removed from office during their tenure, and were held to a compulsory examination and accounting at the end of their terms. There was no standing army; no police force, open or secret; and no way to coerce the people.

Pericles was elected to the generalship (a military office with important political influence) fifteen years in a row and thirty times in all—not because he was a dictator but because he was a persuasive speaker, a skillful politician, a respected general, an acknowledged patriot, and patently incorruptible. When he lost the people's confidence, they did not hesitate to depose him from office. In 443 B.C.E., however, he stood at the height of his power. The defeat of the Athenian fleet in the Egyptian campaign and the failure of Athens' continental campaigns persuaded him to favor a conservative policy, seeking to retain the empire in the Aegean and live at peace with the Spartans. It was in this di-

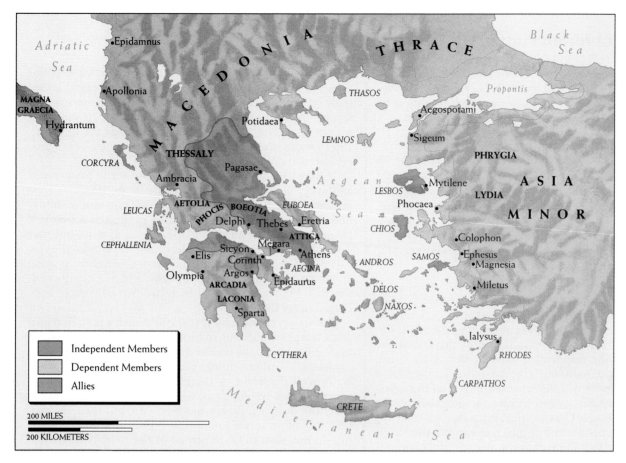

Map 3-6 The Athenian Empire about 450 B.C.E.   The empire at its fullest extent. We see Athens and the independent states that provided manned ships for the imperial fleet but paid no tribute, dependent states that paid tribute, and states allied to but not actually in the empire.

Independent Members
Dependent Members
Allies

200 MILES
200 KILOMETERS

The Acropolis was both the religious and civic center of Athens. In its final form it is the work of Pericles and his successors in the late fifth century B.C.E. This photograph shows the Parthenon and, to its left, the Erechtheum. [Meredith Pillon, Greek National Tourism Organization]

Athenian Democracy: An Unfriendly View

The following selection comes from an anonymous pamphlet thought to have been written in late fifth century B.C.E. The obviously anti-democratic views of its author were common among members of the upper classes in Athens late in the fifth century and thereafter.

What are the author's objections to democracy? Does he describe the workings of the Athenian democracy accurately? How would a defender of the Athenian constitution and way of life meet his complaints? Is there any merit in his criticisms? For other perspectives on law, leadership, and government, see "Hammurabi's Code on Women, Marriage, and Divorce in Babylon" (Chapter 1), "Legalism" (Chapter 2), "The Edicts of Ashoka" (Chapter 4), and "Machiavelli Discusses the Most Important Trait for a Ruler" (Chapter 16).

Now, in discussing the Athenian constitution, I cannot commend their present method of running the state, because in choosing it they preferred that the masses should do better than the respectable citizens; this, then, is my reason for not commending it. Since, however, they have made this choice, I will demonstrate how well they preserve their constitution and handle the other affairs for which the rest of the Greeks criticise them.

Again, some people are surprised at the fact that in all fields they give more power to the masses, the poor and the common people than they do to the respectable elements of society, but it will become clear that they preserve the democracy by doing precisely this. When the poor, the ordinary people and the lower classes flourish and increase in numbers, then the power of the democracy will be increased; if, however, the rich and the respectable flourish, the democrats increase the strength of their opponents. Throughout the world the aristocracy are opposed to democracy, for they are naturally least liable to loss of self control and injustice and most meticulous in their regard for what is respectable, whereas the masses display extreme ignorance, indiscipline and wickedness, for poverty gives them a tendency towards the ignoble, and in some cases lack of money leads to their being uneducated and ignorant.

It may be objected that they ought not to grant each and every man the right of speaking in the Ekklesia and serving on the Boule, but only the ablest and best of them; however, in this also they are acting in their own best interests by allowing the mob also a voice. If none but the respectable spoke in the Ekklesia and the Boule, the result would benefit that class and harm the masses; as it is, anyone who wishes rises and speaks, and as a member of the mob he discovers what is to his own advantage and that of those like him.

But someone may say: 'How could such a man find out what was advantageous to himself and the common people?' The Athenians realise that this man, despite his ignorance and badness, brings them more advantage because he is well disposed to them than the ill-disposed respectable man would, despite his virtue and wisdom. Such practices do not produce the best city, but they are the best way of preserving democracy. For the common people do not wish to be deprived of their rights in an admirably governed city, but to be free and to rule the city; they are not disturbed by inferior laws, for the common people get their strength and freedom from what you define as inferior laws.

From *Aristotle and Xenophon on Democracy and Oligarchy*, trans. with introductions and commentary by J. M. Moore, pp. 37–38. Copyright © 1975 J. M. Moore. Published by University of California Press. Reprinted by permission.

rection that he led Athens' imperial democracy in the years after the First Peloponnesian War.

Women of Athens

Greek society, like most societies all over the world throughout history, was dominated by men. This was true of the democratic Athens in the great days of Pericles in the fifth century B.C.E. no less than of other Greek cities. The actual position of women in classical Athens, however, has been the subject of much controversy.

Subjection   The bulk of the evidence, coming from the law, from philosophical and moral writings, and from information about the conditions of daily life and the organization of society, shows that women were excluded from most aspects of public life. Unlike Athenian men, they could not vote, take part in political assemblies, hold public office, or take any direct part at all in politics.

In private life, women were always under the control of a male guardian—a father, husband, or other appropriate male relative. Women married young, usually between the ages of twelve and eighteen, whereas their husbands were typically over thirty, making the relationship of a woman to her spouse similar to that of a daughter to her father. Marriages were arranged; the woman normally had no choice of husband, and her dowry was controlled by a male relative. Divorce was difficult for a woman to obtain, for she needed the approval of

Medea Bemoans the Condition of Women

In 431 B.C.E., Euripides (ca. 485–406 B.C.E.) presented his play Medea *at the Festival of Dionysus in Athens. The heroine is a foreign woman who has unusual powers. Her description of the condition of women in the speech that follows, however, appears to be an accurate representation of the condition of women in fifth-century-B.C.E. Athens.*

Apart from participation in politics, how did the lives of men and women differ in ancient Athens? How well or badly did that aspect of Athenian society suit the needs of the Athenian people and the state in the Classical Period? Since men had a dominant position in the state and the presentation of tragedies was managed and financed by the state, how do you explain the sympathetic account of the condition of women Euripides puts into the mouth of Medea?

Of all things which are living and can form a judgment
We women are the most unfortunate creatures.
Firstly, with an excess of wealth it is required
For us to buy a husband and take for our bodies
A master; for not to take one is even worse.
And now the question is serious whether we take
A good or bad one; for there is no easy escape
For a woman, nor can she say no to her marriage.
She arrives among new modes of behavior and manners,
And needs prophetic power, unless she has learned at home,
How best to manage him who shares the bed with her.
And if we work out all this well and carefully,
And the husband lives with us and lightly bears his yoke,
Then life is enviable. If not, I'd rather die.
A man, when he's tired of the company in his home,
Goes out of the house and puts an end to his boredom
And turns to a friend or companion of his own age.
But we are forced to keep our eyes on one alone.
What they say of us is that we have a peaceful time
Living at home, while they do the fighting in war.
How wrong they are! I would very much rather stand
Three times in the front of battle than bear one child.

From *Euripides, Medea, in Four Tragedies*, trans. by Rex Warner. Copyright © 1955 University of Chicago Press, Chicago, IL., pp. 66–67.

---

a male relative who had to be willing to serve as her guardian after the dissolution of the marriage. In case of divorce, the dowry returned with the woman but was controlled by her father or the appropriate male relative.

The main function and responsibility of a respectable Athenian woman of a citizen family was to produce male heirs for the household (*oikos*) of her husband. If, however, her father's *oikos* lacked a male heir, the daughter became an *epikleros*, the "heiress" to the family property. In that case she was required by law to marry a relative on her father's side in order to produce the desired male offspring. In the Athenian way of thinking, women were "lent" by one household to another for bearing and raising a male heir to continue the existence of the *oikos*.

Because the pure and legitimate lineage of the offspring was important, women were carefully segregated from men outside the family and were confined to the women's quarters in the house. Men might seek sexual gratification outside the house with prostitutes of high or low style, frequently recruited from abroad. Respectable women stayed home to raise the children, cook, weave cloth, and oversee the management of the household. The only public function of women—an important one—was in the various rituals and festivals of the state religion. Apart from these activities, Athenian women were expected to remain at home out of sight, quiet and unnoticed. Pericles told the widows and mothers of the Athenian men who died in the first year of the Peloponnesian War only this: "Your great glory is not to fall short of your natural character, and the greatest glory of women is to be least talked about by men, whether for good or bad."

Power Evidence from mythology, from pictorial art, and from the tragedies and comedies by the great Athenian dramatists portrays women in a different light. These often show women as central characters and powerful figures in both the public and the private spheres, suggesting that the role played by Athenian women may have been more complex than their legal status suggests. Clytemnestra in Aeschylus's tragedy *Agamemnon*, for example, arranges the murder of her royal husband and establishes the tyranny of her lover, whom she dominates.

As a famous speech in Euripides' tragedy *Medea* makes clear, we are left with an apparent contradiction. In this speech (see the accompanying document), Medea paints a bleak picture of the subjugation of women as dictated by their legal status. Yet Medea, as depicted by Euripides, is herself a powerful and terrifying figure who negotiates with kings. She is the central figure in a tragedy bearing her name, produced at state expense before most of the Athenian population, and written by one of Athens' greatest poets and dramatists. She is a cause of terror to the audience and, at the same time, an object of their pity and sympathy as a victim of injustice. She is certainly not "least talked about by men, whether for good or for bad."

The Great Peloponnesian War

The Thirty Years' Peace of 445 B.C.E. endured little more than ten years. About 435 B.C.E. a dispute flared in a remote and unimportant part of the Greek world that ensnared Athens and Sparta, plunging them back into conflict. This new war was long and disastrous, shaking the foundations of Greek civilization.

The Spartan strategy was traditional: to invade the enemy's country and threaten the crops, forcing the enemy to defend them in a hoplite battle. Such a battle the Spartans were sure to win, because they had the better army and they and their allies outnumbered the Athenians at least two to one. Any ordinary *polis* would have yielded or fought and lost, but Athens had an enormous navy, annual income from its empire, a vast reserve fund, and long walls that connected the fortified city with the fortified port of Piraeus.

The Athenian strategy was to allow the devastation of their own land to prove that Spartan invasions could not hurt Athens. At the same time, the Athenians launched seaborne raids on the Peloponnesian coast to show that Sparta's allies could be hurt. Pericles expected that within a year or two, three at most, the Peloponnesians would become discouraged and make peace. A conflict of longer than four or five years would strain Athenian resources.

The Athenian plan required restraint and the leadership only Pericles could provide, but Pericles died in 429 B.C.E. Ten years of war ended in stalemate. In 421 B.C.E. Athens and Sparta agreed to the Peace of Nicias, which was supposed to last for fifty years but proved far more tenuous. Neither

This red-figure kalyx crater, or wine bowl, was painted by the Dokimasia painter about 470–465 B.C.E. It shows the murder of King Agamemnon, on his return from the sack of Troy, by his wife Clytemnestra and her lover Aegisthus. In red-figure painting, the red color of the fired clay is used for the foreground (figure) and a black pigment for the background. [Museum of Fine Arts, Boston, William F. Warden Fund]

side carried out all the commitments of the peace, and several of Sparta's allies refused to ratify it.

In 415 B.C.E. Alcibiades (c. 450–404 B.C.E.), a young and ambitious leader, persuaded the Athenians to attack Sicily to bring it under their control. In 413 B.C.E., the entire expedition was destroyed. The Athenians lost some 200 ships, about 4,500 of their own men, and almost ten times as many allies. It was a disaster that shook Athenian prestige, reduced the power of Athens, provoked rebellions, and brought Persia into the war on Sparta's side.

It is remarkable that the Athenians were able to continue fighting in spite of the disaster. They survived a brief oligarchic coup in 411 B.C.E. and won several important victories at sea as the war shifted to the Aegean. As their allies rebelled, however, and were sustained by fleets paid for by Persia, the Athenians saw their financial resources shrink and finally disappear. When their fleet was caught napping and was destroyed at Aegospotami in 405 B.C.E., they could not build another. The Spartans, under Lysander (d. 395 B.C.E.), a clever and ambitious general who was responsible for obtaining Persian support, cut off the food supply to Athens, starving the city into submission. In 404 B.C.E. Athens surrendered unconditionally. Its walls were dismantled, its empire was gone, and it was forbidden from rebuilding its fleet. The Great Peloponnesian War was over.

Struggle for Greek Leadership

The Hegemony of Sparta The collapse of the Athenian empire created a vacuum of power in the Aegean and opened the way for Spartan leadership, or hegemony. Fulfilling the contract that had brought them the funds to win the

The Great Peloponnesian War

435 B.C.E.	Civil war at Epidamnus
432 B.C.E.	Sparta declares war on Athens
431 B.C.E.	Peloponnesian invasion of Athens
421 B.C.E.	Peace of Nicias
415–413 B.C.E.	Athenian invasion of Sicily
405 B.C.E.	Battle of Aegospotami
404 B.C.E.	Athens surrenders

war, the Spartans handed the Greek cities of Asia Minor back to Persia. Under the leadership of Lysander, the Spartans stepped into the imperial role Athens had lost. Making a mockery of the Spartan promise to free the Greeks, Lysander installed a board of ten local oligarchs loyal to him and supported by a Spartan garrison in most of the cities along the European coast and the islands of the Aegean. These tributaries brought Sparta almost as much revenue as the Athenians had collected.

Limited manpower, the Helot problem, and traditional conservatism all made Sparta less than an ideal state to rule a maritime empire. Some of Sparta's allies, especially Thebes and Corinth, were alienated by Sparta's increasingly arrogant policies. In 404 B.C.E. Lysander installed an oligarchic government in Athens whose outrageous behavior earned it the title "Thirty Tyrants." Democratic exiles took refuge in Thebes and Corinth and created an army to challenge the oligarchy. Sparta's conservative king, Pausanias, replaced Lysander, arranging a peaceful settlement and ultimately the restoration of democracy. Thereafter, Athenian foreign policy remained under Spartan control, but otherwise Athens was free.

In 405 B.C.E. Greek mercenaries recruited with Spartan help intervened in Persia on behalf of Cyrus the Younger, who was contesting the accession to the Persian throne of his brother Artaxerxes II (r. 404–358 B.C.E.) The Greeks marched inland to Mesopotamia, defeating the Persians at Cunaxa (see Map 3–7 on page 102) in 401 B.C.E. Cyrus was killed, however, and the Greeks marched back to the Black Sea and safety. Their success revealed the potential weakness of the Persian Empire.

The Greeks of Asia Minor had supported Cyrus and were now afraid of Artaxerxes' revenge. The Spartans accepted their request for aid and sent an army into Asia, attracted by the prospect of prestige, power, and money. In 396 B.C.E. the command of this army was given to Sparta's new king, Agesilaus (444–360 B.C.E.), whose aggressive policy was to dominate Sparta until his death.

The Persians responded to Agesilaus's plundering army by seeking assistance among Greek states disaffected with Spartan domination, offering them money and other support. Thebes forged an alliance with Argos, Corinth, and Athens and engaged Sparta in the Corinthian War (395–387 B.C.E.), ending Sparta's Asian adventure. In 394 B.C.E. the Persian fleet destroyed Sparta's maritime empire. Athens, meanwhile, had rebuilt its walls, resurrected its navy, and recovered some of its lost empire. The Persians, who dictated the terms of the peace that ended the Corinthian War to the exhausted Greeks, were alarmed by this Athenian recovery and turned the management of Greece over to Sparta.

Sparta's actions, however, grew increasingly arrogant and lawless. Agesilaus broke up all alliances except the Peloponnesian League and put friends in power in several Greek

Spartan and Theban Hegemonies	
404–403 B.C.E.	Thirty Tyrants rule at Athens
401 B.C.E.	Expedition of Cyrus, rebellious prince of Persia; Battle of Cunaxa
400–387 B.C.E.	Spartan War against Persia
398–360 B.C.E.	Reign of Agesilaus at Sparta
395–387 B.C.E.	Corinthian War
382 B.C.E.	Sparta seizes Thebes
378 B.C.E.	Second Athenian Confederation founded
371 B.C.E.	Thebans defeat Sparta at Leuctra; end of Spartan hegemony
362 B.C.E.	Battle of Mantinea; end of Theban hegemony

cities. In 382 B.C.E. Sparta seized Thebes during peacetime without warning or pretext. In 379 B.C.E. a Spartan army made a similar attempt on Athens. That action persuaded the Athenians to join with Thebes, which had rebelled from Sparta a few months earlier. In 371 B.C.E. the Thebans defeated the Spartans at Leuctra (see Map 3–5). They then encouraged the Arcadian cities of the central Peloponnesus to form a federal league and freed the Helots, helping them found a city of their own. Sparta's population had been shrinking so that it could field an army of fewer than two thousand men at Leuctra. Now, hemmed in by hostile neighbors, deprived of much of its farmland and of the slaves who had worked it, Sparta ceased to be a first-rank power. Its aggressive policies had led to ruin.

Theban Hegemony   Thebes's power after its victory lay in its democratic constitution, its control over Boeotia, and the two outstanding and popular generals—Pelopidas (d. 364 B.C.E.) and Epaminondas (d. 362 B.C.E.)—who led its forces at Leuctra. Under their leadership Thebes gained dominance over the Corinthian Gulf and all Greece north of Athens, challenging the reborn Athenian empire in the Aegean. This success provoked resistance, however, and by 362 B.C.E. Thebes faced a Peloponnesian coalition as well as Athens. Epaminondas, who was once again leading a Boeotian army into the Peloponnesus, confronted this coalition at Mantinea. His army was victorious, but Epaminondas was killed, ending Theban dominance.

The Second Athenian Empire   In 378 B.C.E. Athens organized a second confederation aimed at resisting Spartan aggression in the Aegean. Its constitution was careful to avoid the abuses of the Delian League, but the Athenians soon began to repeat them anyway. This time, however, they lacked the power to suppress resistance. When the collapse of Sparta and Thebes and the restraint of Persia removed any reason for voluntary membership, Athens' allies revolted. By 355 B.C.E. Athens had to abandon most of the empire. After two centuries of almost continual warfare, the Greeks returned to the chaotic disorganization that characterized the time before the founding of the Peloponnesian League.

Culture of Classical Greece

The term *classical* often suggests calm and serenity, but ironically the word that best describes the common element in Greek life, thought, art, and literature during the classical period is *tension*. Among the great achievements of this era, discussed in Chapter 2, were the philosophical works of Socrates (469–399 B.C.E.), Plato (427?–347 B.C.E.), and Aristotle (384–322 B.C.E.). The same concern with the nature, capacities, limits, and place in the universe of human beings that animated those works likewise animated all the arts of the time.

Fifth Century B.C.E.

Two sources of tension contributed to the artistic outpouring of fifth-century-B.C.E. Greece. One arose from the conflict between the Greeks' pride in their accomplishments and their concern that overreaching would bring retribution. The victory over the Persians brought a sense of exultation in the capacity of humans to accomplish great things, and a sense of confidence in the divine justice that had brought low the arrogant pride of Xerxes. But the Greeks recognized that the fate that had met Xerxes awaited all those who reached too far, creating a sense of unease. The second source of tension was the conflict between the soaring hopes and achievements of individuals and the claims and limits put on them by their fellow citizens in the *polis*. These tensions were felt throughout Greece. They had the most spectacular consequences, however, in Athens in its Golden Age, the time between the Persian and the Peloponnesian wars.

Attic Tragedy   Nothing reflects these concerns better than Attic (Athenian) tragedy, which emerged as a major form of Greek poetry in the fifth century B.C.E. The tragedies were selected in a contest and presented as part of public religious observations in honor of the god Dionysus.

Poets who wished to compete submitted their works to the archon. Each offered three tragedies, which might or might not have a common subject, and a satyr play (a comic choral dialogue with Dionysus) to close. The three best competitors were each awarded three actors and a chorus. The actors were paid by the state, and the chorus was provided by a wealthy citizen selected by the state to perform this service as *chorego*. Most of the tragedies were performed in the theater of Dionysus on the south side of the Acropolis, where as many as thirty thousand Athenians could attend. Prizes and honors were awarded to the author, the actor, and the *choregos* voted best by a jury of Athenians chosen by lot.

Attic tragedy served as a forum for poets to raise vital issues. Until late in the century the tragedies, drawing mostly on mythological subjects, dealt solemnly with difficult questions of religion, politics, ethics, or morality. The plays of the dramatists Aeschylus (525–456 B.C.E.) and Sophocles (c. 496–406 B.C.E.) follow this pattern. The plays of Euripides (c. 480–406 B.C.E.) are less solemn and more concerned with individual psychology.

Old Comedy   Comedy was introduced into the Dionysian festival early in the fifth century B.C.E. The great master of the genre called Old Comedy, Aristophanes (ca. 450–385 B.C.E.), the only one from whom we have complete plays,

The porch of the maidens is part of the Erechtheum on the Athenian Acropolis near the Parthenon. Built between 421 and 409 B.C.E., the Erechtheum housed the shrines of three different gods. In place of the usual fluted columns, the porch uses the statues of young girls taking part in a religious festival. [Meredith Pillon, Greek National Tourism Organization]

wrote political comedies filled with scathing invective and satire against such contemporary figures as Pericles, Socrates, and Euripides.

Architecture and Sculpture The great architectural achievements of Periclean Athens, like Athenian tragedy, reflect the tension generated by the union of individual genius with religious and civic responsibility. Beginning in 448 B.C.E. and continuing to the outbreak of the Great Peloponnesian War, Pericles undertook a great building program on the Acropolis with funds from the income of the empire. The new buildings included temples to honor the city's gods and a fitting gateway to the temples. They visually projected Athenian greatness, emphasizing the city's intellectual and artistic achievements rather than its military power and providing tangible proof of Pericles' claim that Athens was "the school of Hellas,"[1] the intellectual center of all Greece.

History The first prose history ever written was an account of the Persian War by Herodotus (484?–425? B.C.E.). "The father of history," as he has been deservedly called, was born shortly before the outbreak of the war. His account goes far beyond all previous chronicles, genealogies, and geographical studies, and attempts to explain human actions and to draw instruction from them.

Herodotus accepted the evidence of legends and oracles, although not uncritically, and often explained human events in terms of divine intervention. Yet his *History*, typical of its time, also celebrates the crucial influence of human intelligence on events, as exemplified by Miltiades at Marathon and Themistocles at Salamis. Herodotus also recognized the importance of institutions, pointing with pride to the way the Greek *polis* inspired discipline and a voluntary obedience to the law in its citizen soldiers, in contrast to the fear of punishment that motivated the Persians.

Thucydides, the historian of the Peloponnesian War, was born about 460 B.C.E. and died about 400, a few years after the end of the Great Peloponnesian War. His work, which was influenced by the secular, human-centered, skeptical rationalism of the Sophists (see Chapter 2), also reflects the scientific approach to medicine pioneered by his contemporary, Hippocrates of Cos (ca. 460–ca. 370 B.C.E.). The Hippocratic approach to the understanding, diagnosis, and treatment of disease combined careful observation with reason. Thucydides similarly took great pains to achieve factual accuracy and tried to use his evidence to discover meaningful patterns of human behavior. He believed that human nature was essentially unchanging, so that a wise person equipped with an

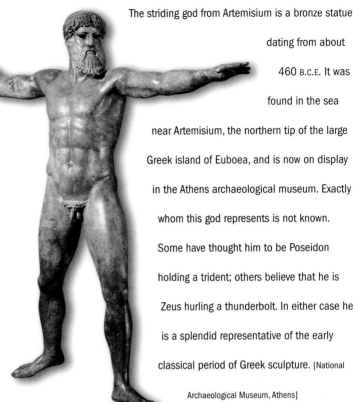

The striding god from Artemisium is a bronze statue dating from about 460 B.C.E. It was found in the sea near Artemisium, the northern tip of the large Greek island of Euboea, and is now on display in the Athens archaeological museum. Exactly whom this god represents is not known. Some have thought him to be Poseidon holding a trident; others believe that he is Zeus hurling a thunderbolt. In either case he is a splendid representative of the early classical period of Greek sculpture. [National Archaeological Museum, Athens]

understanding of history might accurately foresee events and help to guide them. He believed, however, that only a few were equipped to understand history and to put its lessons to good use, and that even the wisest could be foiled by the intervention of chance in human affairs. Thucydides focused on politics, and in that area his assumptions about human nature do not seem unwarranted.

Fourth Century B.C.E.

Historians often call the Great Peloponnesian War the "crisis of the *polis*" and the fourth century B.C.E. the period of its decline. But the Greeks of the fourth century B.C.E. did not know that their traditional way of life was on the verge of destruction. Some looked to the past for ways to shore up the weakened structure of the *polis*; others tended toward despair and looked for new solutions; and still others averted their gaze from the public arena altogether. All of these responses are apparent in the literature, philosophy, and art of the period.

Drama The tendency of some to turn away from the life of the *polis* and inward to everyday life, the family, and the self is apparent in the poetry of the fourth century B.C.E. A new genre, called Middle Comedy, replaced the political

[1]Thucydides, *The Peloponnesian War*, trans. by Richard Crawley (New York: Modern Library, 1982), p. 110.

subjects and personal invective of the Old Comedy with comic-realistic depictions of daily life, plots of intrigue, and mild domestic satire. Significantly, the role of the chorus, which in some ways represented the *polis*, was much diminished. These trends continued, resulting in New Comedy, whose leading exponent, Menander (342–291 B.C.E.), completely abandoned mythological subjects in favor of domestic tragicomedy. Menander's gentle satire of the foibles of ordinary people and his tales of lovers temporarily thwarted before a happy ending would be familiar to viewers of modern situation comedies.

Tragedy faded as a robust and original form in the fourth century B.C.E., but the great tragedies of the previous century were commonly revived. The plays of Euripides, which rarely won first prize when originally produced, became increasingly popular in the fourth century and after. Euripides was less interested in cosmic confrontations of conflicting principles than in the psychology and behavior of individual human beings. Some of his late plays, in fact, are less like the tragedies of Aeschylus and Sophocles than forerunners of later forms such as the New Comedy. Plays like *Helena*, *Andromeda*, and *Iphigenia in Tauris* are more like fairy tales, tales of adventure, or love stories than tragedies.

Sculpture Fourth-century sculpture reflects the same movement away from the grand, the ideal, and the general and toward the ordinary, the real, and the individual.

Emergence of the Hellenistic World

The term *Hellenistic* was coined in the nineteenth century to describe a period of three centuries during which Greek culture spread from its homeland to Egypt and far into Asia. The result was a new civilization that combined Greek and Asian elements. The Hellenistic world was larger than the world of classical Greece, and its major political units were much larger than the *poleis*, although these endured in modified forms. Hellenistic civilization had its roots in the rise to power of a dynasty in Macedonia whose armies conquered Greece and the Persian Empire in the space of two generations.

Macedonian Conquest

The kingdom of Macedon, north of Thessaly, had long served unknowingly as a buffer between the Greek states to the south and barbarian tribes farther to the north. The Macedonians were of the same stock as the Greeks and spoke a Greek dialect, and Macedonian nobles, at least, thought of themselves as Greeks. Macedon's kings, who claimed descent from Heracles and the royal house of Argos, sought to bring Greek culture into their court. By Greek standards,

however, Macedon, although allowed to participate in the Olympic games, was backward and semibarbaric. It had no *poleis* and was ruled loosely by a king in a rather Homeric fashion. The king was chosen partly on the basis of descent, but gained legitimacy only with the acclamation of the army gathered in assembly. Quarrels between pretenders to the throne and even murder to secure it were not uncommon. A council of nobles checked the royal power and could reject a weak or incompetent king. Plagued by constant war with the barbarians, internal strife, loose organization, and lack of money, Macedon played no great part in Greek affairs up to the fourth century B.C.E. Once unified under a strong king, however, it was destined to play a great part in Greek affairs.

Philip of Macedon That king was Philip II (r. 359–336 B.C.E.), who, while still under thirty, took advantage of his appointment as regent to overthrow his infant nephew and make himself king. Like many of his predecessors, he admired Greek culture. Between 367 and 364 B.C.E. he had been a hostage in Thebes, where he learned about Greek politics and warfare from Epaminondas. His natural talents for war and diplomacy and his boundless ambition made him the ablest king in Macedonian history. After first securing his hold on the throne and pacifying the tribes on his frontiers, he began to undermine Athenian control of the northern Aegean. Gaining control of a lucrative gold and silver mining region, he began to found new cities, to bribe foreign politicians, and to reorganize his army into the finest fighting force in the world.

Invasion of Greece So armed, Philip turned south toward central Greece, threatening the vital interest of Athens. Although it still had a formidable fleet of three hundred ships, the Athens of 350 B.C.E. was not the Athens of Pericles. It had neither imperial revenue nor allies to share the burden of war, and its population was smaller than it had been in the fifth century B.C.E. The Athenians, therefore, were reluctant to go on expeditions themselves or even to send out mercenary armies under Athenian generals, for mercenaries had to be paid from Athenian coffers.

The leading critic of this cautious policy was Demosthenes (384–322 B.C.E.), one of the greatest orators in Greek history. Convinced that Philip was a dangerous enemy, Demosthenes spent most of his career urging the Athenians to resist him. Demosthenes was right. Beginning in 349 B.C.E. Philip attacked several cities in northern and central Greece, firmly establishing Macedonian power in those regions. The king of "barbarian" Macedon was elected president of the Pythian Games at Delphi, and the Athenians were forced to concur in the election.

The years between 346 and 340 B.C.E. were spent in diplomatic maneuvering, each side trying to win strategically useful allies. In 340 B.C.E. Philip besieged Perinthus and Byzantium (see Map 3–5), the lifeline of Athenian commerce, and declared war. The Athenian fleet saved both cities, so in the following year Philip marched into Greece. Demosthenes rallied the Athenians and won Thebes over to the Athenian side. In 338 B.C.E., however, Philip defeated the allied forces at Chaeronea in Boeotia. The decisive blow in this great battle was a cavalry charge led by the eighteen-year-old son of Philip, Alexander.

Macedonian Government of Greece   Macedonian rule was not as harsh as many had feared, although in some cities Philip's supporters took power and killed or exiled their enemies. Demosthenes remained free to engage in politics. Athens was spared from attack on the condition that it give up what was left of its empire and follow the lead of Macedon. The rest of Greece was arranged in such a way as to remove all dangers to Philip's rule. To guarantee his security, Philip placed garrisons at Thebes, Chalcis, and Corinth.

In 338 B.C.E. Philip organized the Greek states into the Federal League of Corinth. The league's constitution provided its constituent states autonomy and freedom from tribute and garrisons, and called for the suppression of piracy and civil war. League delegates would make foreign policy, in theory without consulting their home governments or Philip. All this was a facade; not only was Philip of Macedon president of the league, he was its ruler. The defeat at Chaeronea ended Greek freedom and autonomy. Although it maintained its form and internal life for some time, the *polis* had lost control of its own affairs and the special conditions that had made it unique.

Philip's choice of Corinth as the seat of his new confederacy was deliberate. It was at Corinth that the Greeks had gathered to resist a Persian invasion almost 150 years earlier, and it was there in 337 B.C.E. that Philip announced his intention to invade Persia as leader of the new league. In the

spring of 336 B.C.E., however, as he prepared to begin the campaign, Philip was assassinated.

In 1977 excavations of a mound at the Macedonian village of Vergina revealed structures with extraordinarily rich associated artifacts that many scholars believe to be the royal tomb of Philip II. Philip certainly deserved so distinguished a resting place. He found Macedon a disunited kingdom of semibarbarians, despised and exploited by the Greeks. He left it a united kingdom, master and leader of the Greeks, rich, powerful, and ready to undertake the invasion of Asia.

Alexander the Great and His Successors

Philip's first son, Alexander III (356–323 B.C.E.), later called Alexander the Great, succeeded his father at the age of twenty. Along with his throne, the young king inherited his father's daring plans for the conquest of Persia.

The Conquest of Persia   The usurper Cyrus and his Greek mercenaries had shown the vast and wealthy Persian Empire to be vulnerable when they penetrated deep into its interior early in the fourth century B.C.E. In 334 B.C.E. Alexander crossed the Hellespont into Asia. His army consisted of about thirty thousand infantry and five thousand cavalry; he had no navy and little money. Consequently he sought quick and decisive battles to gain money and supplies from the conquered territory. To neutralize the Persian navy he moved along the coast, depriving it of ports.

Alexander met the Persian forces of Asia Minor at the Granicus River (see Map 3–7), where he won a smashing victory in characteristic style: He led a cavalry charge across the river into the teeth of the enemy on the opposite bank, almost losing his life in the process and winning the devotion of his soldiers. The coast of Asia Minor now open, Alexander captured the coastal cities, denying them to the Persian fleet.

In 333 B.C.E. Alexander marched inland to Syria, meeting the main Persian army under King Darius III (r. 336–330 B.C.E.) at Issus. Alexander himself led the cavalry charge that broke the Persian line and sent Darius fleeing to the east. He continued along the coast and captured previously impregnable Tyre after a long and ingenious siege, putting an end to the threat of the Persian navy. He took Egypt with little trouble and was greeted as liberator, pharaoh, and son of the Egyptian god Re. While Alexander was at Tyre, Darius offered him his daughter and his entire empire west of the Euphrates River in exchange for an alliance and an end to the invasion. But Alexander wanted the whole empire and probably whatever lay beyond that.

In the spring of 331 B.C.E. Alexander marched into Mesopotamia. At Gaugamela, near the ancient Assyrian city of Nineveh, he met Darius, ready for a last stand. Once again, Alexander's tactical genius and personal leadership carried

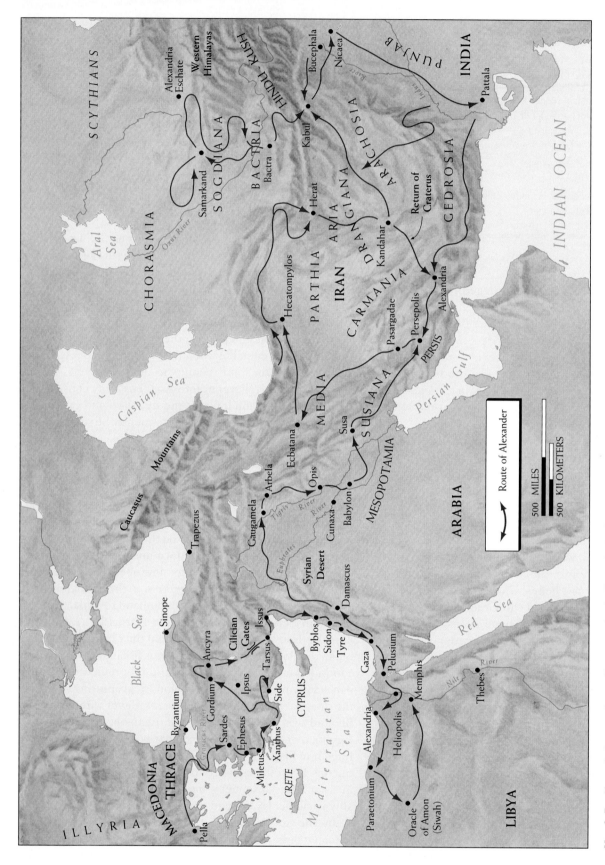

Map 3-7 Alexander's campaigns. The route taken by Alexander the Great in his conquest of the Persian Empire, 334–323 B.C.E. Starting from the Macedonian capital at Pella, he reached the Indus valley before being turned back by his own restive troops. He died of fever in Mesopotamia.

the day. The Persians were broken and Darius fled once more. Alexander entered Babylon, again hailed as liberator and king. In January of 330 B.C.E. he came to Persepolis, the Persian capital, which held splendid palaces and the royal treasury. This bonanza ended his financial troubles and put a vast sum of money into circulation, with economic consequences that lasted for centuries. After a stay of several months, Alexander burned Persepolis to dramatize the destruction of the native Persian dynasty and the completion of Hellenic revenge for the earlier Persian invasion of Greece.

Setting off after Darius, Alexander found him, dead, just south of the Caspian Sea. He had been murdered and replaced by his relative Bessus, with the support of the Persian nobility. Alexander soon captured Bessus, but this pursuit, and his own great curiosity and desire to see the most distant places, took him to the frontier of India.

Near Samarkand, in the land of the Scythians, he founded the city of Alexandria Eschate ("Furthest Alexandria"), one of the many cities bearing his name that he founded as he traveled. As a part of his grand scheme of amalgamation and conquest, he married the Bactrian princess Roxane and enrolled thirty thousand young Bactrians to be trained for his army.

In 327 B.C.E. Alexander took his army through the Khyber Pass to conquer the lands around the Indus River (modern Pakistan). Reducing the region's king, Porus, to vassalage, he pushed on in the hope of reaching the river called Ocean that the Greeks believed encircled the world. Finally his weary men refused to go on. By the spring of 324 B.C.E. the army was back at the Persian Gulf, celebrating Macedonian style with a wild spree of drinking.

Death of Alexander

Alexander was filled with plans for the future: for the consolidation and organization of his empire; for geographic exploration; for new cities, roads, and harbors; perhaps even for further conquests in the west. There is even some evidence that he asked to be deified and worshiped as a god, although we cannot be sure if he really did so or what he had in mind if he did. In June of 323 B.C.E. he was overcome by a fever and died in Babylon at the age of thirty-three. His memory has never faded, and he soon became the subject of myth, legend, and romance. Some have seen in him a man of vision who transcended Greek and Macedonian ethnocentrism and sought to forge human solidarity in a great world state. Others have seen him as a calculating despot, given to drunken brawls, brutality, and murder. The truth is probably in between. Alexander was one of the greatest generals the world has seen; he never lost a battle or failed in a siege, and with a modest army, he conquered a vast empire. He had rare organizational talents, and his plan for creating a multinational empire was the only intelligent way to consolidate his conquests. He established many new cities—seventy, according to tradition—mostly along trade routes. These cities promoted commerce and prosperity and introduced Hellenic civilization into new areas. It is hard to know if even Alexander could have held together the vast new empire he had created, but his death proved that only he had a chance to succeed.

Alexander's Successors

Alexander's sudden death left his enormous empire with no clear, strong heir. His able and loyal Macedonian generals, at first hoping to preserve the empire for the Macedonian royal house, appointed themselves governors of the various provinces of the empire. The conflicting ambitions of these strong-willed men, however, soon led to prolonged warfare among them in which three of the generals were killed and all of the direct members of the Macedonian royal house were either executed or murdered. The murder of Roxane and her son in 310 B.C.E. left the empire with no focus, and in 306 and 305 B.C.E. the surviving governors proclaimed themselves kings of their various holdings. Three of these generals founded dynasties of significance in the spread of Hellenistic culture:

- Ptolemy I, 367?–283 B.C.E.; founder of the thirty-first dynasty in Egypt, the Ptolemies, of whom Cleopatra, who died in 30 B.C.E., was the last
- Seleucus I, 358?–280 B.C.E.; founder of the Seleucid dynasty in Mesopotamia
- Antigonus I, 382–301 B.C.E.; founder of the Antigonid dynasty in Asia Minor and Macedon

For the first seventy-five years or so after the death of Alexander, the world ruled by his successors enjoyed considerable prosperity. The vast sums of money he and they had put into circulation greatly increased economic activity. Opportunities for service and profit in the east attracted many Greeks and relieved their native cities of some of the pressure of the poor. The opening of vast new territories to Greek trade, the increased demand for Greek products, and the new availability of things Greeks wanted, as well as the conscious policies of the Hellenistic kings, all helped stimulate commerce. The new prosperity, however, was not evenly distributed. The urban Greeks, the Macedonians, and the Hellenized natives who made up the upper and middle classes lived lives of comfort and even luxury, but native peasants did not.

Prosperity initially tempered these distinctions. After a while, however, war, inflation, and a gradual lessening of the positive effects of the introduction of Persian wealth led to economic crisis. The kings bore down heavily on the middle classes, who, however, were skilled in avoiding their responsibilities. The pressure on peasants and city laborers increased also, and they responded by slowing work and even by striking. In Greece, economic pressures brought clashes between rich and poor, demands for the abolition of debt and the redistribution of land, and even, on occasion, civil war.

Ongoing warfare and these internal divisions made the Hellenistic kingdoms vulnerable to outside attack, and by the middle of the second century B.C.E. the expanding empire of Rome had absorbed all but Egypt. The two centuries of Hellenistic rule, however, had great and lasting importance. They saw the entire eastern Mediterranean coast, Greece, Egypt, Mesopotamia, and the old Persian Empire formed into a single political, economic, and cultural unit.

Hellenistic Culture

Alexander's conquests and the establishment of the successor kingdoms, by ending the central role of the *polis* in Greek life and thought, marked a significant turning point in Greek literature, philosophy, religion, and art.

Deprived of control of their foreign affairs, their important internal arrangements determined by a foreign monarch, the postclassical cities lost the kind of political freedom that was basic to the old outlook. They were cities, perhaps—in a sense, even city-states—but not *poleis*. As time passed they lost their sovereignty, becoming municipalities within military empires. For the most part, the Greeks after Alexander turned inward, away from politics, to address their hopes and fears. The confident, sometimes arrogant, humanism of the fifth century B.C.E. gave way to a kind of resignation to fate, a recognition of helplessness before forces too great for humans to manage.

Philosophy

These developments are noticeable in the changes that overtook the established schools of philosophy as well as in the emergence of two new and influential groups of philosophers, the Epicureans and the Stoics.

Plato's Academy and Aristotle's Lyceum (see Chapter 2) continued to operate, reinforcing Athens' position as the center of philosophical studies. The Lyceum turned gradually away from Aristotle's universal investigations, even from his scientific interests, to become a center chiefly of literary and historical studies. The Academy turned even further from its founder's tradition, adopting the philosophical approach known as Skepticism, established by Pyrrho of Elis (c. 365–c. 275 B.C.E.). The Skeptics thought that nothing could be known and so consoled themselves and their followers by suggesting that nothing mattered. It was easy for them, therefore, to accept conventional morality and the world as it was. The Cynics continued to denounce convention and to advocate a crude life in accordance with nature, which some of them practiced publicly, to the shock and outrage of re-

spectable citizens. Neither of these views had much appeal to the middle-class city dweller of the third century B.C.E., who sought some basis for choosing a way of life now that the *polis* no longer provided one ready-made.

Epicureans Epicurus of Athens (342–271 B.C.E.), who founded a school in that city in 306 B.C.E., formulated a philosophy in keeping with the new mood. The goal of this philosophy was not knowledge but happiness, which Epicurus believed could be achieved through a life based on reason.

Accepting the description of the physical universe proposed by the atomists Democritus and Leucippus (see Chapter 2), the Epicureans took sense perception to be the basis of all human knowledge. According to Epicurus, atoms were continually falling through the void and giving off images in direct contact with the senses. These falling atoms could swerve in an arbitrary, unpredictable way to produce the combinations seen in the world. When a person died, the atoms that composed the body dispersed so that the person had no further existence or perception and therefore nothing to fear after death. The gods, according to Epicurus, took no interest in human affairs. This belief amounted to a practical atheism, and the Epicureans were often thought to be atheists.

The purpose of Epicurean physics was to liberate people from the fear of death, the gods, and the supernatural. Epicurean ethics were hedonistic, identifying happiness with pleasure. But *pleasure* for Epicurus was chiefly negative: the absence of pain and trouble. The goal of the Epicureans was *ataraxia*, the condition of being undisturbed, without trouble, pain, or responsibility. To achieve it, one should ideally have sufficient means to withdraw from worldly affairs; Epicurus even advised against marriage and children. He preached a life of genteel, restrained selfishness, which might appeal to intellectuals of means but was not calculated to be widely attractive.

Stoics The Stoic school, established by Zeno of Citium (335–263 B.C.E.) soon after Epicurus began teaching, took its name from the *Stoa Poikile*, or Painted Portico, in the Athenian Agora, where Zeno and his disciples met.

Like the Epicureans, the Stoics sought the happiness of the individual; but unlike Epicurean philosophy, Stoic philosophy was almost indistinguishable from religion. The Stoics believed that god and nature are the same and that humans must live in harmony within themselves and with nature. The guiding principle in nature is divine reason (*logos*), or fire. Every human has a spark of this divinity, and after death it returns to the eternal divine spirit. From time to time the world is destroyed by fire, from the ashes of which a new world arises.

Human happiness, according to the Stoics, lies in the virtuous life, lived in accordance with natural law, in which "all

This is a Roman copy of one of the masterpieces of Hellenistic sculpture, the Laocoön. According to legend, Laocoön was a priest who warned the Trojans hot to take the Greeks' wooden horse within their city. This sculpture depicts his punishment. Great serpents sent by the goddess Athena, who was on the side of the Greeks, devoured Laocoön and his sons before the horrified people of Troy. [Direzione Generale Musei Vaticani]

A page from *On Floating Bodies*. Archimedes' work was covered over by a tenth-century manuscript, but ultraviolet radiation reveals the original text and drawings underneath. [Christie's Images]

litical activity, and many Stoics were politically active, they believed the usual subjects of political argument to be indifferent. With their striving for inner harmony and a life lived in accordance with the divine will, their fatalistic attitude, and their goal a form of apathy, the Stoics fit the post-Alexandrian world well. The spread of Stoicism eased the creation of a new political system that relied on the docile not the active participation, submission of the governed.

Literature

The literary center of the Hellenistic world in the third and second centuries B.C.E. was Alexandria, Egypt. There, Egypt's Hellenistic rulers, the Ptolemies, had founded the museum—a great research institute where royal funds supported scientists and scholars—and a library with almost half a million books. The library housed much of the great body of past Greek literature, most of which has since been lost. Alexandrian scholars had what they judged to be the best works copied, editing and criticizing them from the point of view of language, form, and content, and writing biographies of the authors. It is to this work that we owe the preservation of most of what remains to us of ancient literature.

The scholarly atmosphere of Alexandria stimulated the study of history and its ancillary discipline, chronology. Eratosthenes (ca. 275–195 B.C.E.) developed a chronology of important events since the Trojan War, and others undertook similar tasks. Contemporaries of Alexander, such as Ptolemy I (d. 284 B.C.E.,) Aristobulus, and Nearchus, wrote apparently sober, factual accounts of his career. The fragments we have of the work of most Hellenistic historians suggest that they emphasized sensational and biographical detail over the rigorous, impersonal analysis characteristic of Thucydides.

Architecture and Sculpture

The Hellenistic monarchies greatly increased the opportunities open to architects and sculptors. Money was plentiful, rulers sought outlets for conspicuous display, new cities needed to be built and beautified, and the well-to-do created an increasing demand for objects of art. New cities were usually laid out on the grid plan introduced in the fifth century B.C.E. by Hippodamus of Miletus. Temples were built on the classical model, and the covered portico, or *stoa*, became a very popular addition to Hellenistic agoras.

Reflecting the cosmopolitan nature of the Hellenistic world, leading sculptors accepted commissions wherever they were attractive. The result was a certain uniformity, although Alexandria, Rhodes, and the kingdom of Pergamum in Asia Minor developed distinctive styles. In general, Hellenistic sculpture continued the trend that emerged in the fourth century B.C.E. toward the sentimental, emotional, and realistic

actions promote the harmony of the spirit dwelling in the individual man with the will of him who orders the universe."[2] Only the wise—who know what is good, what is evil, and what is "indifferent"—can live such a life. Good and evil are dispositions of the mind or soul. Thus prudence, justice, courage, and temperance are good, whereas folly, injustice, and cowardice are evil. Life, health, pleasure, beauty, strength, wealth, and so on are neutral—morally "indifferent." The source of misery is passion, a disease of the soul and an irrational mental contraction that arises from morally indifferent things. The goal of the wise is *apatheia*, or freedom from passion.

The Stoics viewed the world as a single large *polis* and all people as children of god. Although they did not forbid po-

[2]Diogenes Laertius, *Lives of Eminent Philosophers (Zeno)* (Cambridge, MA: Harvard University Press, 1931–1938).

Plutarch Cites Archimedes and Hellenistic Science

Archimedes (ca. 287–211 B.C.E.) was one of the great mathematicians and physicists of antiquity. He was a native of Syracuse in Sicily and a friend of its king. Plutarch discusses him in the following selection and reveals much about the ancient attitude toward applied science.

Archimedes, however, in writing to King Hiero, whose friend and near relation he was, had stated that given the force, any given weight might be moved, and even boasted, we are told, relying on the strength of demonstration, that if there were another earth, by going into it he could remove this. Hiero being struck with amazement at this, and entreating him to make good this problem by actual experiment, and show some great weight moved by a small engine, he fixed accordingly upon a ship of burden out of the king's arsenal, which could not be drawn out of the dock without great labour and many men; and, loading her with many passengers and a full freight, sitting himself the while far off, with no great endeavour, but only holding the head of the pulley in his hand and drawing the cords by degrees [he lifted the ship] . . . Yet Archimedes possessed so high a spirit, so profound a soul, and such treasures of scientific knowledge, that though these inventions had now obtained him the renown of more than human sagacity, he yet would not deign to leave behind him any commentary or writing on such subjects; but, repudiating as sordid and ignoble the whole trade of engineering, and every sort of art that lends itself to mere use and profit, he placed his whole affection and ambition in those purer speculations where there can be no reference to the vulgar needs of life. . . .

From Plutarch, "Marcellus," in *Lives of the Noble Grecians and Romans*, trans. by John Dryden, rev. by A. H. Clough (New York: Random House, n.d.), pp. 376–378.

and away from the balanced tension and idealism of the fifth century B.C.E. The characteristics of Hellenistic sculpture are readily apparent in the *Laocoön*, carved at Rhodes in the second century B.C.E.

Mathematics and Science

Among the most spectacular intellectual accomplishments of the Hellenistic age were those in mathematics and science. Indeed, Alexandrian scholars were responsible for most of the scientific knowledge available to the West until the scientific revolution of the sixteenth and seventeenth centuries C.E.

Euclid's Elements (written early in the third century B.C.E.) is still the foundation for courses in plane and solid geometry. Archimedes of Syracuse (ca. 287–212 B.C.E.), who also made advances in geometry, established the theory of the lever in mechanics and invented hydrostatics.

Advances in mathematics, when applied to Babylonian astronomical tables available to Hellenistic scholars, spurred great progress in astronomy. As early as the fourth century Heraclides of Pontus (ca. 390–310 B.C.E.) had argued that Mercury and Venus circulate around the sun and not the Earth. He appears to have made other suggestions leading in the direction of a heliocentric theory of the universe. It was Aristarchus of Samos (ca. 310–230 B.C.E.), however, who asserted that the sun, along with the other fixed stars, did not move and that the Earth revolved around the sun in a circular orbit and rotated on its axis while doing so. The helio-

centric theory, however, did not take hold. It ran contrary not only to the traditional view codified by Aristotle but to what seemed to be common sense. And, of course, planetary orbits are not circular. Hipparchus of Nicea (b. ca. 190 B.C.E.) constructed an ingenious and complicated geocentric model of the universe that did a good job of accounting for the movements of the sun, the moon, and the planets. Ptolemy of Alexandria (second century C.E.) adopted Hipparchus's system with a few improvements, and it remained dominant until the work of Copernicus, in the sixteenth century C.E.

Hellenistic scientists made progress in mapping the earth as well as the sky. Eratosthenes of Cyrene (ca. 275–195 B.C.E.) accurately calculated the circumference of the Earth and wrote a treatise on geography based on mathematical and physical reasoning and the reports of travelers. Eratosthenes' map (see Map 3–8) was in many ways more accurate than a later one, created by Ptolemy, that became standard during the Middle Ages.

IN WORLD PERSPECTIVE

The Achievement of Greek and Hellenistic Civilization

Hellenic civilization lies at the root of western civilization and has powerfully influenced the modern world. It emerged from the collapse of the Bronze Age Mycenaean civilization but differed in important ways from that predecessor. Mycenaean civilization and the Bronze Age civilization of Crete had more

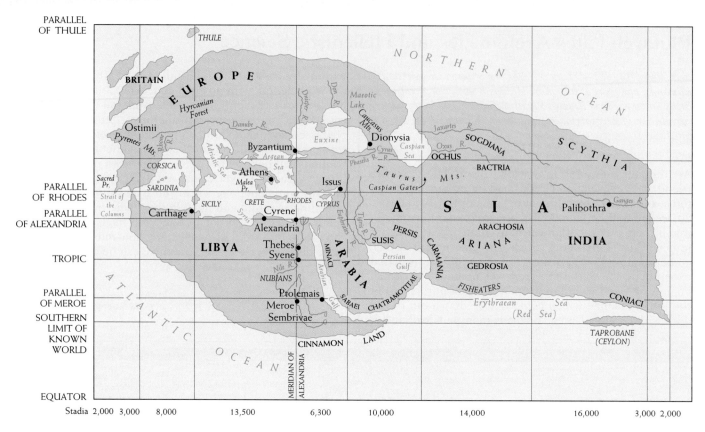

Map 3-8 The world according to Eratosthenes. Eratosthenes of Alexandria (ca. 275-195 B.C.E.) was a Hellenistic geographer. His map, reconstructed here, was remarkably accurate for its time. The world was divided by lines of "latitude" and "longitude," thus anticipating our global divisions.

in common with other early civilizations—in Egypt, Mesopotamia, Palestine-Syria, China, India, and elsewhere—than with Hellenic civilization. These civilizations were characterized by strong, centralized monarchical governments ruling through tightly organized, large bureaucracies; hierarchical social systems; professional standing armies; and a regular system of taxation to support it all. To varying degrees they all tended to cultural stability and uniformity. Hellenic civilization departed sharply from this pattern of development.

The crucial unit in the Greek way of life-forged in poverty and isolation following the Mycenaean collapse—was the *polis*, the Hellenic city-state. There were hundreds of them, ranging in size from a few thousand inhabitants to hundreds of thousands. Each evoked a kind of loyalty and attachment in its citizens that made it unthinkable for them to allow it to be part of a larger political unit. The result was a dynamic, many-faceted, competitive, sometimes chaotic society in which rivalry for excellence and victory had the highest value. This competitiveness led to almost constant warfare, but it also inspired the Greeks' extraordinary achievements in literature and art.

The *poleis* were republics. They were less marked by class distinctions than other civilizations, partly because the Greeks were so poor and the differences in wealth among them were relatively small. The introduction of the hoplite phalanx, which put the safety of the state in the hands of unpaid citizen-soldiers who returned to their farms after a campaign, further reduced class distinctions. As a result, a relatively large proportion of the population shared in political control, and participation in public life was highly valued.

The *poleis* had no kings and no bureaucracy. Most imposed no regular taxation. They had no priestly caste and little concern with life after death. This varied, dynamic, secular, and remarkably free context gave rise to a speculative natural philosophy based on observation and reason that lies at the root of modern natural science and philosophy.

Trade and colonization brought prosperity and increasing contact with new ideas to many Greek cities. Greek artists were powerfully influenced by Egyptian and Near Eastern models, adapting them in original ways. Social and economic unrest led to the overthrow of traditional aristocratic regimes by tyrants. These temporary regimes were usually replaced by oligarchies, but in Athens the destruction of the tyranny led to the world's first democracy.

The Classical Age, which followed in the wake of the Greeks' heroic defense of their homeland against the armies of the powerful Persian Empire in the early sixth century B.C.E., was a period of unparalleled achievement. While the rest of the world's civilizations remained monarchical, hierarchical, command societies, Athens, the seat of an Aegean empire, developed democratic government to an extent not seen again until modern times. Athenian citizenship—although limited to adult males of native parentage—granted full and active participation in every decision of the state without regard to wealth or class.

It was in this democratic imperial Athens that the greatest artistic, literary, and philosophical achievements of the Classical Period took place. Classical writers and thinkers created many still-vital literary genres and forms. Among their accomplishments are analytical, secular history; tragedy and comedy; the philosophical dialogue; systematic logic; and philosophical treatises on almost every conceivable subject. Greek artists developed a naturalistic style that has had an enduring impact on western art.

These accomplishments, diverging sharply from those of other civilizations, sprang largely from the unique political experience of the Greeks, which was based on the independent *polis* rather than on powerful monarchies and great, extended land empires. With the Macedonian conquest of Greece and the onset of the Hellenistic Period, however, the age of the *polis* came to an end.

The conquests of Alexander and the Hellenistic states that followed in their wake spread Greek culture over a remarkably wide area and made a significant and lasting impression on the conquered societies and their neighbors. The Seleucid dynasty ruled some parts of the old Persian Empire for almost two centuries, and its influence was felt in the region even longer. As we will see in Chapter 4, a group of Greeks who broke away from the Seleucids carried Hellenistic culture even farther east, to the Indus Valley in northwest India, creating the Indo-Greek Bactrian society. In art, Hellenistic influence reached even as far away as China. In the West, of course, the legacy of Hellenism was more substantial and enduring, powerfully shaping the culture of the Roman Empire that would ultimately dominate the entire Mediterranean world.

As it spread, Greek culture of the Hellenistic period adjusted to its new context, becoming simpler and more unified as it became more accessible to outsiders. The Attic tongue—the *koine*, or common language—supplanted other Greek dialects. Alexandrian scholars established canons of literary excellence and the scholarly tools with which to make the great treasures of Greek literature and art understandable to later generations. Shared over a wide area, Hellenistic culture helped widely differing peoples accommodate to one another. It powerfully impressed the conquering Romans who, although they captured the Hellenistic world, became, as the Roman poet Horace said, captives of its culture.

Review Questions ———

1. Describe the Minoan civilization of Crete. How did the later Bronze Age Mycenaean civilization differ from the Minoan civilization in political organization, art motifs, and military posture? How valuable are the Homeric epics as sources of early Greek history?

2. Define the concept of *polis*. What role did geography play in its development, and why did the Greeks consider it a unique and valuable institution?

3. Compare the fundamental political, social, and economic institutions of Athens and Sparta about 500 B.C.E. Why did Sparta develop its unique form of government? What were the main stages in the transformation of Athens from an aristocratic state to a democracy between 600 and 500 B.C.E.?

4. Why did the Greeks and Persians go to war in 490 and 480 B.C.E.? What benefit could the Persians have derived from conquering Greece? Why were the Greeks able to defeat the Persians, and how did they benefit from the victory?

5. How was the Delian League transformed into the Athenian empire during the fifth century B.C.E.? Did the empire offer any advantages to its subjects? Why was there such resistance to Athenian efforts to unify the Greek world in the fifth and fourth centuries B.C.E.?

6. Why did Athens and Sparta come to blows in the Great Peloponnesian War? What was each side's strategy for victory? Why did Sparta win the war?

7. Give examples from art, literature, and philosophy of the tension that characterized Greek life and thought in the Classical Period. How does Hellenistic art differ from that of the Classical Period?

8. Between 431 and 362 B.C.E. Athens, Sparta, and Thebes each tried to impose hegemony over the city-states of Greece, but none succeeded except for short periods of time. Why did each state fail? How was Philip II of Macedon able to conquer Greece? Where does more of the credit for Philip's success lie: in Macedon's strength, or in the

weakness of the Greek city-states? What does your analysis tell you about the components of successful rule?

9. What were the major consequences of Alexander's death?

Assess the achievement of Alexander. Was he a conscious promoter of Greek civilization, or just an egomaniac drunk with a lust for conquest?

Suggested Readings ———

The Rise of Greek Civilization

A. R. BURN, *Persia and the Greeks*, 2nd ed. (1984). A thorough narrative and analysis of the conflict between the Persians and the Greeks down to 479 B.C.E.

J. B. BURY AND R. MEIGSS, *A History of Greece*, 4th ed., (1975). A thorough and detailed one-volume narrative history.

P. CARTLEDGE, *Sparta and Lakonia* (1979).

J. CHADWICK, *The Mycenaean World* (1976). A readable account by a man who helped decipher Mycenaean writing.

R. DREWS, *The Coming of the Greeks* (1988). A fine discussion of the Greeks' arrival as part of the movements of the Indo-European peoples.

V. EHRENBERG, *The Greek State* (1964). A good handbook of constitutional history.

J. V. FINE, *The Ancient Greeks* (1983). An excellent survey that discusses historical problems and the evidence that gives rise to them.

M. I. FINLEY, *World of Odysseus*, REV. ED. (1965). A fascinating attempt to reconstruct Homeric society.

P. GREEN, *Xerxes at Salamis* (1970). A lively and stimulating history of the Persian War.

V. D. HANSON, *The Western Way of War* (1989). A brilliant and lively discussion of the rise and character of the hoplite phalanx and its influence on Greek society.

V. D. HANSON, *The Other Greeks* (1995). A revolutionary account of the Greek invention of the family farm and its centrality for the shaping of the *polis*.

S. HOOD, *The Minoans* (1971). A sketch of Bronze Age civilization on Crete.

D. KAGAN, *The Great Dialogue: A History of Greek Political Thought from Homer to Polybius* (1965). A discussion of the relationship between the Greek historical experience and political theory.

W. K. LACEY, *The Family in Ancient Greece* (1984).

J. F. LAZENBY, *The Defense of Greece, 490–479 B.C.* (1993). A new and valuable study of the Persian wars.

J. F. MCGLEW, *Tyranny and Political Culture in Ancient Greece* (1993). A recent account of political developments in the Archaic Age.

O. MURRAY, *Early Greece* (1980). A lively and imaginative account of the early history of Greece to the end of the Persian War.

C. ROEBUCK, *Economy and Society in the Early Greek World* (1984). A valuable study.

B. SNELL, *Discovery of the Mind* (1960). An important study of Greek intellectual development.

A. M. SNODGRASS, *The Dark Age of Greece* (1972). A good examination of the archaeological evidence.

C. G. STARR, *The Economic and Social Growth of Early Greece, 800–500 B.C.* (1977).

EMILY VERMEULE, *Greece in the Bronze Age* (1972). A study of the Mycenaean period.

A. G. WOODHEAD, *Greeks in the West* (1962). An account of the Greek settlements in Italy and Sicily.

W. J. WOODHOUSE, *Solon the Liberator* (1965). A discussion of the great Athenian reformer.

D. C. YOUNG, *The Olympic Myth of Greek Athletics* (1984). A lively challenge to the orthodox view that Greek athletes were amateurs.

Classical and Hellenistic Greece

M. AUSTIN AND P. VIDAL-NAQUET, *The Economic and Social History of Classical Greece* (1977). A combination of documents and explanation.

W. BURKERT, *Greek Religion* (1987). An excellent study by an outstanding student of the subject.

G. CAWKWELL, *Philip of Macedon* (1978). A brief but learned account of Philip's career.

J. K. DAVIES, *Democracy and Classical Greece* (1978). Emphasizes archeological evidence and social history.

J. R. LANE FOX, *Alexander the Great* (1973). An imaginative account that does more than the usual justice to the Persian side of the problem.

Y. GARLAN, *Slavery in Ancient Greece* (1988). An up-to-date survey.

PETER GREEN, *Alexander to Actium: The Historical Evolution of the Hellenistic Age* (1990). A remarkable synthesis of political and cultural history.

C. D. HAMILTON, *Agesilaus and the Failure of Spartan Hegemony* (1991). An excellent biography of the king who was the central figure in Sparta during its domination in the fourth century B.C.E.

N. G. L. HAMMOND, *Philip of Macedon* (1994). A new biography of the founder of the Macedonian Empire.

N. G. L. HAMMOND AND G. T. GRIFFITH, *A History of Macedonia*, Vol. 2, *550–336 b.c.* (1979). A thorough account of Macedonian history that focuses on the careers of Philip and Alexander.

R. JUST, *Women in Athenian Law and Life* (1988). An account of women's place in Athenian society.

D. KAGAN, *The Outbreak of the Peloponnesian War* (1969). A study of the period from the foundation of the Delian League to the coming of the Peloponnesian War that argues that war could have been avoided.

B. M. W. KNOX, *The Heroic Temper: Studies in Sophoclean Tragedy* (1964). A brilliant analysis of tragic heroism.

D. M. LEWIS, *Sparta and Persia* (1977). A valuable discussion of relations between Sparta and Persia in the fifth and fourth centuries B.C.E.

G. E. R. LLOYD, *Greek Science After Aristotle* (1974).

A. A. LONG, *Hellenistic Philosophy: Stoics, Epicureans, Sceptics* (1974). An account of Greek science in the Hellenistic and Roman periods.

R. MEIGGS, *The Athenian Empire* (1972). A fine study of the rise and fall of the empire, making excellent use of inscriptions.

H. W. PARKE, *Festivals of the Athenians* (1977). A fine discussion of the religious practices of the Athenians.

J. J. POLLITT, *Art and Experience in Classical Greece* (1972). A scholarly and entertaining study of the relationship between art and history in classical Greece, with excellent illustrations.

J. J. POLLITT, *Art in the Hellenistic Age* (1986). An extraordinary analysis that places the art in its historical and intellectual context.

M. I. ROSTOVTZEFF, *Social and Economic History of the Hellenistic World*, 3 vols. (1941). A masterpiece of synthesis by a great historian.

D. M. SCHAPS, *Economic Rights of Women in Ancient Greece* (1981).

B. S. STRAUSS, *Athens After the Peloponnesian War* (1987). An excellent discussion of Athens' recovery and of the nature of Athenian society and politics in the fourth century B.C.E.

B. S. STRAUSS, *Fathers and Sons in Athens* (1993). An unusual synthesis of social, political and intellectual history.

W. W. TARN, *Alexander the Great*, 2 vols. (1948). The first volume is a narrative account, the second a series of detailed studies.

W. W. TARN AND G. T. GRIFFITH, *Hellenistic Civilization* (1961). A survey of Hellenistic history and culture.

V. TCHERIKOVER, *Hellenistic Civilization and the Jews* (1970). A fine study of the impact of Hellenism on the Jews.

G. VLASTOS, *Socrates, Ironist and Moral Philosopher* (1991). The results of a lifetime of study by the leading interpreter of Socrates in our time.

F. W. WALBANK, *The Hellenistic World* (1981).

4 IRAN, INDIA, AND INNER ASIA TO 200 C.E.

Model gold chariot pulled by four gold horses. From the Oxus

Treasure, Achaemenid period, fifth to fourth century B.C.E.

[British Museum, London/SuperStock, Inc.]

CHAPTER TOPICS

IRAN

◆ Ancient Background

◆ The First Iranian Empire (550–330 B.C.E.)

INDIA

◆ The First Indian Empire (321–185 B.C.E.)

◆ Consolidation of Indian Civilization (ca. 200 B.C.E.–300 C.E.)

GREEK AND ASIAN DYNASTIES

◆ Seleucids

◆ Indo-Greeks

◆ Steppe Peoples

In World Perspective Iran, India, and Inner Asia to the Third Century C.E.

From the Mediterranean to China, the period from about 600 B.C.E. to 200 C.E. saw the rise of centralized empires on a new, unprecedented scale—a development in which Iran and India preceded both China and the Roman west. Well before the Ch'in unification (221–207 B.C.E.) or the Han dynasty (202 B.C.E.–9 C.E.) in China, and long before *imperium* replaced republic in Rome, imperial states flourished in Iran. First the Elamites, at various times in the third and the second millennia B.C.E., built regional empires centered on their homeland of Susa (modern Khuzistan) in lowland southwestern Iran. Then the Achaemenids (ca. 539–330 B.C.E.), an Aryan dynasty from the mountains of southwestern Iran, created an empire based in Babylonia and Iran that was the greatest yet seen anywhere. Two centuries later the Mauryans, a northeast Indian dynasty centered in the Ganges basin, founded the first great Indian empire (ca. 321–ca. 185 B.C.E.). Both of these empires, like their later Chinese and Roman counterparts, built sophisticated bureaucracies, professional armies, and strong communication systems.

They also contributed to new cultural, political, and religious developments in their domains.

Another characteristic of this period was increased and sustained contact among the major centers of culture from the Mediterranean to China. Large-scale empires created new markets for diverse goods, both material and human (such as slaves, soldiers, and artisans); new security along major trade routes; new impetus for both diplomacy and conquest; and a wider interest in the world at large.

Alexander the Great's conquest (334–323 B.C.E.) of the Persian Empire and the regions eastward to North India increased dramatically the growing contact among diverse cultures, races, and religious traditions. Although Alexander's empire did not long survive, his conquests ended the Achaemenid dynasty and, in the east, allowed the rising Mauryan power to extend its control across North India. The Hellenes and steppe peoples of northeastern Iran and Central (Inner) Asia, who ruled first post-Alexandrine Iran and then post-Mauryan India down to the third centu-

ry C.E., inherited a world with horizons irrevocably larger than those of their original homelands.

A third characteristic of this period was the rise, spread, and consolidation of major religious traditions that would substantially affect later history from Africa to China. The evolution of Judaism in the Second-Temple (rebuilt 520–515 B.C.E.) and early-Diaspora (second century C.E.) periods, and the rise and spread of Christianity and diverse Hellenistic cults had considerable impact on the history of the Mediterranean and western Asia (see Chapters 2, 3, and 5). This period saw in China the rise of Han Confucianism and classical Taoist thought (see Chapters 2 and 7); in Iran the growth of Zoroastrian tradition; in India, the emergence of an identifiable Hindu tradition and growth of the Buddhist movement; and in East Asia generally, the spread of Buddhist traditions, especially into Southeast Asia and China.

IRAN

"Iran" designates the vast expanse of southwest Asia bounded by the Caspian Sea and Jaxartes (Syr Darya) River to the north and northeast, the Indus Valley to the southeast, the Arabian Sea and Gulf to the south, the Tigris-Euphrates basin to the west, and Armenia and the Caucasus to the northwest. The heart of this region is the vast Iranian plateau, bounded on all sides by mighty mountain ranges, notably the Hindu Kush, the Sulaiman chain, the Zagros, and the Elburz. In its central reaches, the plateau contains two large, uninhabitable salt deserts whose desolation is an even more formidable barrier to travel than most of the great mountain ranges.

Early (and later) peoples in Iran clustered in the plains, lower mountain reaches, and fertile oases—wherever rainfall or ground water was plentiful and communication abroad easiest. The key areas were the slopes and lowlands between the Zagros Persis, Media, Hyrcania, and Parthia. The great Asian trade routes put Iran at the heart of east-west interchange. Their location, as well as the locations of the cities and towns that flourished because of them, were determined largely by mountain passes, river fords, and plateau crossings.

Ancient Background

The Elamites

The Elamites, a non-Semitic-speaking people, built a literate, flourishing civilization in the southwestern lowlands and adjacent highlands of Susa (Elam, later Ahwaz or Khuzistan) and the neighboring regions between the Zagros and the Gulf. Even though we have tablets, monumental inscriptions, and some brick imprints from Elamite remains at sites such as Persepolis and in the Susa region, scholars have not determined to which language group Elamite belongs. It did, however, long outlive the Elamite state, since it was still recognized as one of three official languages in the Persian empire of the Achaemenids. The Elamites typically used a federated system of governance relying on vassalage and a complicated system of succession. They were repeatedly at war with the great Mesopotamian dynasties of the Sumerians, Babylonians, and Assyrians from around 2700 B.C.E. until the end of the second millennium B.C.E. Their apogee came in the so-called "middle Elamite" period in the 12th century B.C.E. While we know of Elamite attempts to contest the

Assyrian power of the latter seventh and early sixth century, Assyrian armies set upon the Neo-Elamite rulers of the day from 692 until their complete destruction by Asshurbanipal's troops in 639, when their cities were ransacked and even their soil sown with salt.

The Iranians

The forefathers of the Iranian dynasts who would eventually build cities and palaces again at Susa as well in the Assyrian heartlands were Aryans. The oldest texts in ancient Persian dialects show that Aryan peoples settled on the Iranian plateau sometime around 1100 B.C.E. Like their Vedic or Indo-Aryan relations in North India, these peoples were evidently pastoralists—horse-breeders—from the Eurasian or Central Asian steppes. The most prominent of these ancient Iranians were the Medes and the Persians. By the eighth century B.C.E., they had spread around the deserts of the plateau to settle and control its western and southwestern reaches, to which they gave their names, Media and Persis (later Fars).

The Medes developed a tribal confederacy in western Iran. By 612 B.C.E., they and the Neo-Babylonians had defeated the mighty Assyrians and broken their hold on the Fertile Crescent. The rise of Persian power under the Achaemenid clan from the seventh century B.C.E. led to the end of Median supremacy on the Iranian plateau by the time of the Achaemenid ruler Cyrus the Great around 550 B.C.E. Many of the institutions that developed in the ensuing empire (such as the satrapy system of provincial administration) were apparently based on Median practices, which had in turn often been drawn from Babylonian and Assyrian models. Part of the genius of the Achaemenids' unparalleled imperial success lay in their ability to use existing institutions to build their own state and administer far-flung dominions well.

Ancient Iranian Religion

We know more about religious traditions of ancient Iran than about other

A fifth-century-B.C.E. Achaemenid amphora from southwestern Iran with double tube-handles. [Gisela Croon/Bildarchiv Preussischer Kulturbesitz]

A Hymn of Zoroaster About the Two Spirits of Good and Evil

The focus of Zoroaster's reform was the supremacy of Ahura Mazda (the "Wise Lord") over all the deities of the Iranian pantheon. He is pictured in the hymns, or Gathas, as the greatest of the ahuras, *the divinities associated with the good. The world is seen in terms of a moral dualism of good and evil, which is represented on the divine plane in the twin spirits created by Ahura Mazda, both of whom are given the freedom to choose the Truth or the Lie. The "Very Holy [Spirit]" chose truth ("Righteousness"), and the "evil [spirit]" (Angra Mainyu, or Ahriman), chose the evil of "the Lie." Similarly, humans can choose with which side—the good spirit and the* ahuras, *or the evil spirit and the* daevas *("the false gods")—they will ally themselves. This selection is from a gatha in Yasna ("Worship"), section 45 of the main Zoroastrian holy book, the* Avesta.

What lesson or values might the person who reads this be supposed to take from it? Is there a conflict between the seeming omnipotence ascribed to Ahura Mazda and the existence of Ahriman, the Evil Spirit? How does the sharp choice offered here compare to the Buddha's "middle path" (see "The 'Turning of the Wheel of Dharma': Basic Teachings of the Buddha," in Chapter 2)?

---

(1) Then shall I speak, now give ear and hearken, both you who seek from near and you from far. . . . (2) Then shall I speak of the two primal Spirits of existence, of whom the Very Holy thus spoke to the Evil One: 'Neither our thoughts nor teachings nor wills, neither our choices nor words nor acts, not our inner selves nor our souls agree.' (3) Then shall I speak of the foremost (doctrine) of this existence, which Mazda the Lord, He with knowledge, declared to me. Those of you who do not act upon this manthra, even as I shall think and speak it, for them there shall be woe at the end of life. (4) Then shall I speak of the best things of this existence. I know Mazda who created it in accord with truth to be the Father of active Good Purpose. And his daughter is Devotion of good action. The all-seeing Lord is not to be deceived. (5) Then shall I speak of what the Most Holy One told me, the word to be listened to as best for men. Those who shall give for me hearkening and heed to Him, shall attain wholeness and immortality. Mazda is Lord through acts of the Good Spirit. . . . (8) Him shall I seek to turn to us by praises of reverence, for truly I have now seen with my eyes (the House) of Good Purpose, and of good act and deed, having known through Truth Him who is Lord Mazda. Then let us lay up supplications to Him in the House of Song. (9) Him shall I seek to requite for us with good purpose, Him who left to our will (the choice between) holy and unholy. May Lord Mazda by His power make us active for prospering our cattle and men, through the fair affinity of good purpose with truth. (10) Him shall I seek to glorify for us with sacrifices of devotion, Him who is known in the soul as Lord Mazda; for He has promised by His truth and good purpose that there shall be wholeness and immortality within His kingdom (khshathra), strength and perpetuity within His house.

From Mary Boyce, ed. and trans., *Textual Sources for the Study of Zoroastrianism* (Manchester, U.K.: Manchester University Press, 1984), p. 36.

---

aspects of its culture because our only pre-Achaemenid texts are religious. They suggest that old Iranian culture and religion were similar to those of the Vedic Aryans. The importance of water, fire, sacrifice, and the cow, as well as the names and traits of major divine beings and religious concepts, all have counterparts in Vedic texts. The emphasis was on moral order, or the "Right"—that is, *asha* or *arta* (equivalent to the Vedic *rta*; see Chapter 1). The supreme heavenly deity was Ahura (the equivalent of the Vedic Varuna) Mazda, the "Wise Lord." However, Iranian religion in the early second millennium was far from monolithic. Cultural variations among the southeast (Sistan), northeast (Parthia, Herat, and Bactria), west (Media), and southwest (Persis) regions were substantial.

Zoroaster and the Zoroastrian Tradition

The first person who stands out in Iranian history was not Cyrus, the famous founder of the Achaemenid Empire, but the great prophet-reformer of Iranian religion, Zarathushtra, commonly known in the West by the Greek version of his name, Zoroaster. Until very recently, the consensus was that Zoroaster lived in northeastern Iran from 628 to 551 B.C.E., but today most scholars are accepting a revised dating for him of no later than 1000 B.C.E. Whatever his dates, it is clear from his hymns that, not unlike the Hebrew prophets, the Buddha, and Confucius, Zoroaster was an activist preacher who presented a message of moral reform in an age of materialism, political opportunism, and ethical indifference. While he is said to have gained the protection of an eastern Iranian tribal leader, it is unlikely that his preaching became any kind of official "state" creed during his lifetime.

Zoroaster was evidently trained as a priest in the old Iranian tradition, but his hymns, or *Gathas*, reflect the new religious vision he championed. In these hymns we glimpse the values of a peasant-pastoralist society that was growing up alongside early urban trade centers in northeastern Iran. These values—for example, the sacralization of cow and ox or honest dealings in trade—contrasted with those of the nomadic warrior peoples of the steppes. Zoroaster's personal experience of Ahura Mazda as the supreme deity led him to reinterpret the old sacrificial fire as Ahura's symbol. He called on people to abandon worship of and sacrifice to all lesser deities, or *daevas*, whom he identified as demons, not gods. He tried to reform his people's morality by exhorting them to turn from the "Lie" (*druj*) to the "Truth" (*asha*). He warned of a "final reckoning," when the good would be rewarded with "future glory" but the wicked with "long-lasting darkness, ill food, and wailing."

By the mid-fourth century B.C.E., the Zoroastrian reform had spread into western as well as eastern Iran. The quasi-monotheistic worship of Ahura Mazda, the Wise Lord, was rapidly accommodated to the veneration of older Iranian gods by the interpretation of these deities as secondary gods or even manifestations of the Wise Lord himself. What role the old Iranian priestly clan of the *Magi* played in these developments is not clear. They may have integrated Zoroastrian ideas and texts into their older, polytheistic tradition, becoming thereby architects of a reformed tradition. Certainly the name "magi" was later used for the priests of the tradition that we call "Zoroastrian."

Zoroastrianism probably influenced not only Jewish, Christian, and Muslim ideas of angels, devils, the messiah, the last judgment, and afterlife, but also some important Buddhist concepts as well. Zoroastrianism was wiped out as a major force in Iran by the spread of Islamic rule in the seventh and eighth centuries C.E. and later. However, its tradition continues in the faith and practice of the Parsis, a community today of perhaps one hundred thousand people, most of whom live in western India.

The First Iranian Empire (550–330 B.C.E.)

The Achaemenids

In October 1971 C.E., the Iranian monarch Muhammad Reza Shah (r. 1941–1979) hosted a lavish pageant amid the ruins of the ancient Persian capital of Persepolis. This extravagant celebration commemorated the 2500-year anniversary of the beginning, under Cyrus the Great, of "the imperial glory of Iran." The shah felt his modern secularist regime had recreated this traditional Iranian glory since the 1950s. Although the Iranian revolution of 1978 ended his heavy-handed attempts to kindle a secular Iranian nationalism, modern Iran does have an undeniably dual heritage: that of the rich Iranian Islamic culture and that of the far older, Indo-Iranian, Zoroastrian, and imperial culture of pre-Islamic Iran. The latter began with the Persian dynasty of the Achaemenids.

Achaemenid regional power in southwestern Iran (Persis) went back at least to Cyrus I (d. 600 B.C.E.), but the rise of Iran as a major civilization and empire is usually dated from the reign of his famous grandson, Cyrus the Great (559–530 B.C.E.). The empire the latter founded was anticipated in many ways by the large but loosely controlled empire of his predecessors, the Medes, in Anatolia (Asia Minor) and western Iran (and the Elamites to the southwest, in and beyond the Zagros). Cyrus defeated the last Median king about 550 B.C.E. He then moved swiftly westward, subduing northern Assyria, Cilicia, and the kingdom of Lydia, near the Aegean coast of Asia Minor. The Lydian capital, Sardis, became a provincial capital of the growing Persian state (and the base for diplomatic intrigue against the Hellenic *poleis*). Next, Cyrus turned to Babylon and, in less than three weeks, defeated the last Babylonian king.

This event, in 539 B.C.E., symbolically marks the beginning of the Achaemenid Empire, for it joined the Mesopotamian and Iranian spheres for the first time under one rule—a unity that would last for centuries (see Map 4–1). One of its results was the end of the Babylonian Exile of the Jews by Cyrus's decree that the Jews be allowed to return to their Holy Land and rebuild their temple in Jerusalem (see Chapter 2). Babylon became for a time Cyrus's capital, as did Susa, Ecbatana, and Pasargadae at later dates. Cyrus subsequently extended Achaemenid rule in the east before he was killed fighting steppe tribes there. Besides his ability to conquer, his readiness to rule through local elites and institutions rather than to impose new political superstructures was perhaps his most notable legacy to his heirs.

Early in his career, Cyrus had moved his capital from Susa to the old Median capital of Ecbatana (later Hamadan). He and his successors, in what was really a tribal confederation, adopted Median administrative practice, and many Medes were highly placed in the new state. Thus it is not surprising that the Achaemenid rulers are referred to in the Bible and other sources as the "Medes and Persians." What the Medes had set in motion, Cyrus and his heirs consolidated and expanded, so that the new Iranian Empire became the most extensive the world had ever seen.

Cyrus's successor, Cambyses (r. 529–522 B.C.E.) added Egypt to the Achaemenid dominions. His brief reign was followed by a succession struggle and civil war from Babylonia to the Hindu Kush. The winner, Darius I (521–486 B.C.E.), enjoyed a prosperous reign in which the Achaemenid empire reached its greatest extent—from Egypt northeast to southern Russia and Sogdiana (Transoxiana) and east to the Indus Valley. Susa and Persepolis were Darius's principal capitals.

The next five rulers (486–359 B.C.E.) fared less well, and after 478 B.C.E., the Persians found themselves militarily inferior to the Greeks. Although they kept the divided Greeks at bay by clever diplomacy, Greek cultural influence steadi-

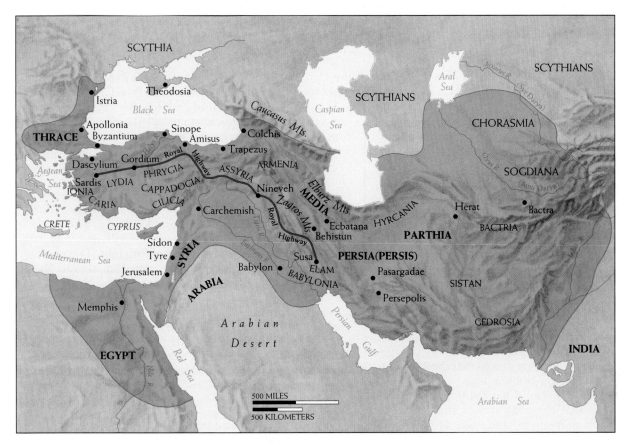

Map 4-1 The Achaemenid Persian Empire. The empire created by Cyrus had reached its fullest extent under Darius when Persia attacked Greece in 490 B.C.E. It extended from India to the Aegean, and even into Europe, including the lands formerly ruled by Egyptians, Hittites, Babylonians, and Assyrians.

ly grew in Asia Minor. Egyptian rebellions, succession struggles, renewed conflict with Scythian steppe tribes, and poor leadership now plagued Achaemenid rule. Much might have been recouped by the able, energetic Artaxerxes III (r. 359–338 B.C.E.), had he not been poisoned in a palace coup just as Philip of Macedon was unifying the Greeks. When Philip's son Alexander succeeded him, the days of Achaemenid rule were numbered.

The Achaemenid State

Perhaps the greatest achievement of the Achaemenids was the relative stability of their rule. To justify their sovereignty—and the title of *Shahanshah*, "king of kings"—they claimed that Ahura Mazda had entrusted them with universal sovereignty. An inscription of Darius reads: ". . . I am king by the will of Ahuramazda."[1] Other inscriptions reflect the

sense—underscored by elaborate court ceremony and impressive architectural monuments—that a ruler earned Ahura Mazda's trust through justice and uprightness. The ruler acted as priest and sacrificer in the court rituals; his role as cosmic ruler was symbolized by a special royal fire that burned throughout his reign. The talents and success of the early Achaemenids strengthened their claim to divinely sanctioned royal status.

The Achaemenids were, however, tolerant of other cultural and religious traditions in ways earlier empires had not been. In part, the sheer size of their realms demanded it, but the contrast to later Roman imperial practice here is striking. Even Darius's emphasis on Zoroastrian ritual and theology did not bring forced conformity or conversion to the "state cult," as his lenient treatment of the Jews vividly shows (see Chapter 2).

The Achaemenids built a powerful army, but were not simply military despots. Much of their success lay in their administrative abilities and willingness to learn and to borrow from predecessors like the Medes or Babylonians. Most of their leaders were adept at conciliation and worked to

[1]William W. Malandra, trans., *An Introduction to Ancient Iranian Religion* (Minneapolis: University of Minnesota Press, 1983), p. 50.

Inscription of Darius I: Building the Royal Palace at Susa

The Achaemenids, like other ancient rulers before them, used public inscriptions to underscore their victories and other accomplishments. These portions of an inscription of Darius were unearthed from the remains of Susa, the first of the two great palace-residences that he built (Persepolis being the second). They tell of his building accomplishments there and show also the extent of Achaemenid power and dominion in its heyday.

What were Darius's motivations for building the palace? For what does it appear he wants to be remembered? From how large an area did Darius draw the materials for his palace? What political purpose might he have had for using builders and artisans from the diverse nations and ethnic groups that made up his empire?

. . . This is the palace which I built at Susa. From afar its ornamentation was brought. Downward the earth was dug, until I reached rock in the earth. When the excavation has been made, then rubble was packed down. . . . On that rubble the palace was constructed. And that the earth was dug downward, and that the rubble was packed down, and that the sun dried brick was moulded, the Babylonian people, it did (these tasks). The cedar timber, this—a mountain by name Lebanon—from there was brought; the Assyrian people . . . brought it to Babylon; from Babylon the Carians and the Ionians brought it to Susa. The yak timber was brought from Gandara and from Carmania. The gold was brought from Sardis and from Bactria, which here was wrought. The precious stone lapis-lazuli and carnelian which was wrought here, this was brought from Sogdiana. The precious stone turquois, this was brought from Chorasmia, which was wrought here. The silver and the ebony were brought from Egypt. The ornamentation with which the wall was adorned, that from Ionia was brought. The ivory which was wrought here, was brought from Ethiopia and from Sind and from Arachosia. The stone columns which were here wrought—a village by name Abiradus, in Elam—from there were brought. The stone-cutters who wrought stone, these were Ionians and Sardians. The goldsmiths who wrought the gold, these were Medes and Egyptians. The men who wrought the wood, these were Sardians and Egyptians. The men who wrought the baked brick, these were Babylonians. The men who adorned the wall, these were Medes and Egyptians. Saith Darius the king: At Susa a very excellent [work] was [brought to completion]. Me may Ahuramazda protect, and Hystaspes, my father, and my country.

Reprinted from R. G. Kent, *Old Persian Grammar, Texts, Lexicon* © 1950. Reprinted by permission of the American Oriental Society, The University of Michigan, Ann Arbor, MI.

---

establish what has been termed a *pax Achaemenica*.[2] They were able to maintain continuity as their state evolved from a tribal confederation into a sophisticated monarchy. The state of Cyrus, with its largely Iranian troops and tribute system of revenue, was replaced by a monarchy supported by a noble class, professional armies (led by loyal Persian elite troops), an administrative system of provinces ruled by governors called *satraps*, and fixed-yield levies of revenue.

The excellence of Achaemenid administration can also be seen in their communication and propaganda systems. Couriers linked imperial outposts with the heartlands over a well-kept highway system, which also facilitated rapid troop deployment. Herodotus called the greatest of these highways, from Sardis to Susa, "the King's Road." A network of observers and royal inspectors kept the court abreast of activities outside the capital. An efficient chancery with large

The ruins of the famous royal complex at Persepolis, begun about 518 B.C.E. The foundation of the treasury is in the foreground; part of the recently restored women's quarters is visible on the left; and the tall pillars of the main audience hall stand in the rear. [Giraudon/Art Resource, N.Y.]

---

[2]Richard N. Frye, *The Heritage of Persia* (New York: New American Library, 1966), p. 110.

Darius I receiving tribute, from a relief on the treasury at Persepolis. Note the incense burners before the king and the noble tribute bringer's gesture of respect. The scepter and lotus blossom held by Darius symbolize his kingship; his son and heir, Xerxes, stands behind him (491–486 B.C.E.). [Corbis-Bettmann]

archives and numerous scribes served administrative needs. The bureaucratic adoption of Aramaic, which had become the common language of the Near East under the Assyrians, helped link east and west. Royal proclamations were rapidly and widely distributed, often in multilingual form. Little is known of the actual judicial system, but Achaemenid inscriptions reflect a strong emphasis on universal justice through the rule of law.

The choice of strategically located capitals in western Iran, such as Ekbatana and Susa, was important to central imperial control. For the most part, the Achaemenids moved the court as needed from one to another of their palaces, whether in Babylon or the Iranian highlands, and never had a single fixed capital. The satrapy divisions usually reflected the borders of former states incorporated into the empire. Satraps were powerful princes in their own right. Although some of them revolted on occasion, the centralized power of the "king of kings" held together the diverse provinces and tribute-paying states.

The Achaemenid Economy

Economic life from Greece to India received a substantial boost from Achaemenid success. Although a true coin-based monetary system had earlier been introduced in Lydia by Croesus (sixth century B.C.E.), the Achaemenids greatly expanded on this. Coinage was used to pay part of the workers' wages in the construction of Persepolis and gradually displaced in-kind payment altogether under Darius. Coinage stimulated banking operations, which had fallen off since the heyday of Mesopotamian rule in the previous millennium. Truly private banking houses grew up: deposits were taken, loans made available, checks accepted, leases sold, monopolies secured, and capital invested in property, shipping, canals, and commodities. The Achaemenids levied taxes on diverse sources of income—estates, livestock, mines, trade, and production. Wages were regulated and money-goods equivalences published (thus a sheep might be set at three shekels).

Agriculture remained the basic industry and normal occupation of free men. Serfs and slaves formed most of the labor force. Work animals were bred, bees colonized, and grapes, wheat, barley, and olives cultivated widely. Where water was scarce, the government dug both subterranean and surface canals for irrigation. Rulers such as Darius mandated the transfer of fruit trees and other plants to different parts of the empire; thus from the east pistachio cultivation came to Aleppo, rice to Mesopotamia, and sesame to Egypt.

Fishing, timbering, and mining flourished widely and were key elements in the economy. Some industries, such as those for production of clothing, shoes, and furniture, developed alongside the older luxury crafts directed at the wealthy. The unprecedented volume of trade in Achaemenid times included large quantities of everyday, household products that were now widely exchanged where earlier only luxury goods had been traded over long distances. Goods from India crossed paths with those of the Rhine valley; it was an era of prosperity, marked by expanding markets—into southern

ca. 2000–1000 B.C.E.	Indo-Iranian (Aryan) tribes move south into the Punjab of India and the Iranian Plateau
ca. 628–551 B.C.E. (or before 1000 B.C.E.?)	Traditional life of Zoroaster, probably in eastern/northeastern Iran (perhaps originally in Herat?)
559–530 B.C.E.	Reign of Cyrus the Great Persian Achaemenid ruler
539–330 B.C.E.	Achaemenid Empire
331–330 B.C.E.	Alexander (d. 323 B.C.E.) conquers Achaemenid empire
312–ca. 125 B.C.E.	Seleucid rule in part of Achaemenid realm
ca. 248 B.C.E.–224 C.E.	Parthian empire of the Arsacids in Iran, Babylonia

Europe especially—and increased foreign travel, exploration, and investment.

The empire's overall stability for over two centuries testifies to the quality of the *pax Achaemenica*. Within this stable environment the cosmopolitan basis for the coming Hellenization of western Asia in the wake of Alexander's conquests was laid.

INDIA

Large-scale imperial expansion came much later to the South Asian, or Indian, subcontinent than to Iran. A cultural and religious heritage going back to the Aryan invaders of North India left its mark on the subsequent history of the vast and diverse subcontinent, despite the many languages and regional traditions that have persisted there. Only rarely, however, has the subcontinent seen political unity among even a bare majority of its inhabitants. Today's division into India, Pakistan, and Bangladesh is just the most recent. Only on four occasions has a substantial part of the whole come under a single rule: in the Mauryan, Gupta, Mughal, and British imperial epochs. We look now at the first of these.

The First Indian Empire (321–185 B.C.E.)

The oriental campaigns of Alexander the Great achieved the conquest of the Achaemenids' northwest-Indian provinces of Gandhara and the Indus Valley in 327 B.C.E. The conquest had little or no impact on the Indian subcontinent except in Gandhara, where his passage opened the way for the increased Greek and Indian cultural interpenetration that developed under the Mauryan emperors of India. Only with the

Mauryans was much of North India incorporated into the first true Indian empire.

Political Background

The basis for empire in North India was the rise of regional states and commercial towns between the seventh and fourth centuries B.C.E. The most powerful of these were the monarchies of the Ganges plains. North and northwest of the plains, in the Himalayan foothills and in the Punjab and beyond, tribal republics were more common. The Buddha and Mahavira came from two of these republics (see Chapter 2), although both spent much of their lives in the two most powerful Gangetic monarchies, Kosala and Magadha. In their lifetimes, Magadha emerged as the strongest Indian state under King Bimbisara (d. 493 B.C.E.).

Bimbisara was, as far as we know, the first king to build (possibly on the Achaemenid model) a centralized state strong enough for imperial expansion. He emphasized good roads, able administrators, and fair agricultural taxes. His son annexed Kosala, giving Magadha control of the Ganges trade. Consequently, Magadha remained preeminent in the Ganges basin, even under some less competent successors. A new dynasty, the Nandas, replaced the last of these on the Magadhan throne in the mid-fourth century B.C.E.; their imperial hopes were soon dashed by the rise of the Mauryan clan.

The Mauryans

The first true Indian empire was established by Chandragupta Maurya (r. ca. 321–297 B.C.E.), an adventurer who seized Magadha and the Ganges basin in about 324 and made Pataliputra (modern Patna) his capital (see Map 4–2). He next marched westward into the vacuum created by Alexander's departure (326 B.C.E.) and brought the Indus region and much of west-central India under his control. A treaty with the invading Seleucus (ca. 358–280 B.C.E.), Alexander's successor in Bactria, added Gandhara and Arachosia to his empire. The Greek sources say the treaty (303 B.C.E.) included a marriage alliance, possibly of a Seleucid woman to Chandragupta. Whether or not such a marriage occurred, there was much Seleucid-Mauryan contact thereafter.

Chandragupta's fame as the first Indian empire builder is rivaled by that of his Brahman minister, Kautilya. Known as the "Indian Machiavelli," Kautilya may have joined with Chandragupta even before he defeated the last Nanda ruler of Magadha and been the actual architect of Mauryan rule. However, the most famous Indian treatise on the art of government, the *Arthashastra*, is probably wrongly ascribed to him.

Chandragupta's son and successor, Bindusara (r. ca. 297–272 B.C.E.), took up his father's imperial aspirations. He

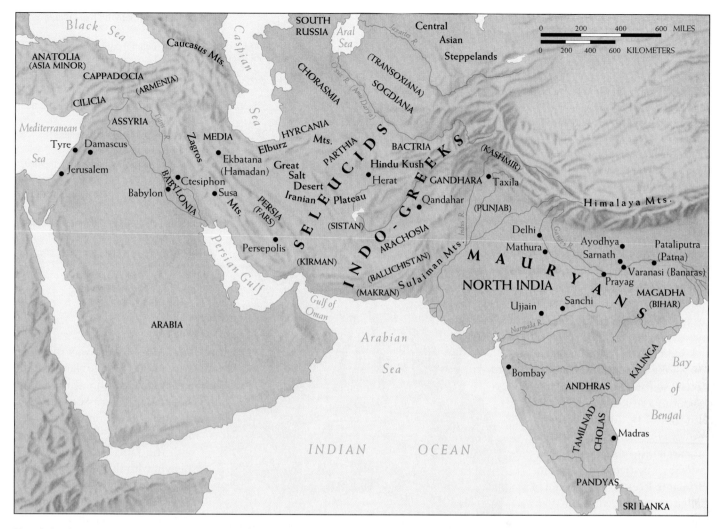

Map 4–2   Southwest Asia and India in Mauryan times.   This map shows not only the major cities and regions of greater Iran and the Indian subcontinent, but also the neighboring eastern Mediterranean world. Although the Mediterranean was closely tied to Iran from Achaemenid times onward, its contacts with India in the wake of the conquests of Alexander the Great were many and varied.

moved swiftly to conquer the Deccan, the great plateau that covers central India and divides the far south (Tamilnad) from North India. Like his father, he had substantial contact with the Seleucid Greeks, including Antiochus I (r. 297–261 B.C.E.) of Syria, from whom he is said to have requested wine, figs, and a court philosopher.

Ashoka   The third and greatest Mauryan, Ashoka (r. ca. 272–232 B.C.E.), left us numerous rock inscriptions—the first significant Indian written sources after the (still undeciphered) Indus seals. From Ashoka's edicts, we can piece together much of his reign and glimpse something of his character as well. In his first years as king, he continued the imperial tradition by conquering Kalinga, the last independent kingdom in North India and the Deccan. He thus extended Mauryan control over the whole subcontinent except the far south.

Apparently revolted by the bloody Kalinga war, Ashoka underwent a religious conversion. Thereafter he pursued the Buddhist "middle path" as his ideal of conduct in both personal and state relations. Accordingly, he forsook hunting and meat eating, championing nonviolence (*ahimsa*). He did not abandon all warfare, but he did eschew aggression in favor of the ideal of "conquest by righteousness" (*dharma*). He sought by moral example to win over others to humanitarian values. Within his realm he looked on all his subjects as, in the words of one edict, his "children." His edicts show that he pursued the laity's norm of the Buddhist *dharma*, striving to attain heaven by the merit of good actions. He was not exclusivist about his Buddhist faith, stressing tolerance for all traditions, but he did send envoys abroad to spread the Buddhist teaching. Among his efforts to raise standards of morality in his realm was the appointment of "*dharma* officials" to investigate public welfare problems and to foster just government at the local level.

Ashoka evidently did ease some burdens imposed on the populace by earlier governments, and he instituted many beneficial public works. However, by the end of his reign, the empire's size hampered effective administration, and under his successors, Mauryan rule fell apart. Neither Ashoka's Buddhism nor his rejection of aggression was, as some have suggested, the cause of decline; more likely factors were economic strains and increased bureaucratic corruption, as well as the inability of his heirs to claim the personal allegiances he had maintained. After his death local dynasties soon seized power in many areas.

Ashoka's enduring influence is hard to assess, but he did provide the model of the ideal king for later Hindu and Buddhist thought—the *chakravartin*, or universal monarch who rules with righteousness, justice, and wisdom. His name lives on as a symbol of enlightened rule with few if any equals in the history of East or West.

The Mauryan State

Mauryan bureaucracy was marked by centralization, standardization, and efficiency in long-distance communications, civil and military organization, tax collection, and information gathering (by a secret service). The fundamental unit of government, as before and ever after, was the village, with its headman and village council. Groups of villages formed districts within the larger provincial unit. The provinces were largely controlled through governors sent from the capital. Some local rulers were confirmed in these positions also, much as under the Achaemenids (who were probably a model for much of Mauryan imperialism).

The administration of the empire depended primarily on the king himself, who did, however, have an advisory coun-

The Lion Capital of Sarnath. This famous Ashokan column capital was taken by India as its state seal after independence in 1947. It reflects both Persian and Greek influences. Originally the capital stood atop a mighty pillar some fifty feet high; the lions supported a huge stone chakra, the Buddhist "Wheel of the Dharma," the symbol of universal law.

[Giraudon/Art Resource, N.Y.]

cil to assist him. Still, it was the king who commanded full allegiance of all subjects. Each of the three great Mauryan kings was associated with one of the "new" religious movements of the age: Chandragupta with the Jains (see Chapter 2), his son with the ascetic Ajivikas, and Ashoka with the Buddhists. Such links must have strengthened Mauryan claims to righteous leadership. The reputed ceremonialism of the Mauryan court must also have enhanced royal authority.

Revenues came primarily from taxing the produce of the land, which was regarded as the king's property. Urban trade and production were also taxed heavily. The Mauryan economic system also involved slavery, although most of it was domestic labor, often a kind of temporary indentured service.

The Mauryan Legacy

An imperial ideal, a strengthened Buddhist movement, and strong central administration were not the Mauryans' only gifts to Indian culture. They left behind new cosmopolitan traditions of external relations and internal communication that encouraged cultural development and discouraged provincialism. Their many contacts with the West reflect their

The Edicts of Ashoka

In the first of the two following excerpts from Ashokan edicts, we see the monarch's explanation of his change of heart and conversion to nonviolence after the Kalinga war and a statement of his determination to follow dharma. *"The Beloved of the Gods" was the common royal epithet used by Ashoka for himself. The second excerpt is from the end of Ashoka's reign and speaks of his efforts to better his and other people's lives by rule according to the dictates of* dharma.

What does Ashoka suggest is the role of the monarch? What is his concept of "conquest"? What does he think of those of other faiths and what does he want for them? What reforms does Ashoka propose, and why? Can you reconcile his expressed abhorrence of killing with his words to the forest tribes? How do these edicts compare to other approaches to law, leadership, and government? See, for example, "Hammurabi Creates a Code of Law in Mesopotamia" (Chapter 1), "Legalism" (Chapter 2), "Athenian Democracy: An Unfriendly View" (Chapter 3), and "Machiavelli on Why the Princes of Italy Lose Their States" (Chapter 16)."

From the Thirteenth Rock Edict

When the king, Beloved of the Gods and of Gracious Mien, had been consecrated eight years Kalinga was conquered, 150,000 people were deported, 100,000 were killed, and many times that number died. But after the conquest of Kalinga, the Beloved of the Gods began to follow Righteousness [*dharma*], to love Righteousness, and to give instruction in Righteousness. Now the Beloved of the Gods regrets the conquest of Kalinga, for when an independent country is conquered people are killed, they die, or are deported, and that the Beloved of the Gods finds very painful and grievous. . . . The Beloved of the Gods will forgive as far as he can, and he even conciliates the forest tribes of his dominions; but he warns them that there is power even in the remorse of the Beloved of the Gods, and he tells them to reform, lest they be killed.

For all beings the Beloved of the Gods desires security, self-control, calm of mind, and gentleness. The Beloved of the Gods considers that the greatest victory is the victory of Righteousness; and this he has won here [in India] and even five hundred leagues beyond his frontiers in the realm of the Greek king Antiochus, and beyond Antiochus among the four kings Ptolemy, Antigonus, Magas, and Alexander. Even where the envoys of the Beloved of the Gods have not been sent men hear of the way in which he follows and teaches Righteousness, and they too follow it and will follow it. Thus he achieves a universal conquest, and conquest always gives a feeling of pleasure; yet it is but a slight pleasure, for the Beloved of the Gods only looks on that which concerns the next life as of great importance. . . .

From the Seventh Pillar Edict

In the past kings sought to make the people progress in Righteousness, but they did not progress. . . . And I asked myself how I might uplift them through progress in Righteousness. . . . Thus I decided to have them instructed in Righteousness, and to issue ordinances of Righteousness, so that by hearing them the people might conform, advance in the progress of Righteousness, and themselves make great progress. . . . For that purpose many officials are employed among the people to instruct them in Righteousness and to explain it to them. . . .

Moreover I have had banyan trees planted on the roads to give shade to man and beast; I have planted mango groves, and I have had ponds dug and shelters erected along the roads at every eight kos. Everywhere I have had wells dug for the benefit of man and beast. But this benefit is but small, for in many ways the kings of olden time have worked for the welfare of the world; but what I have done has been done that men may conform to Righteousness. . . .

I have enforced the law against killing certain animals and many others, but the greatest progress of Righteousness among men comes from exhortation in favor of noninjury to life and abstention from killing living beings.

I have done this that it may endure as long as the moon and sun, and that my sons and my great-grandsons may support it; for by supporting it they will gain both this world and the next.

From *Sources of Indian Tradition* by William Theodore de Bary. Copyright © 1988 by Columbia University Press. Reprinted with permission of the publisher.

international perspective, as do the Ashokan edicts, which were executed in various languages and scripts. Writing and reading must have been common by this time (perhaps because of Buddhist monastic schooling?), or the edicts themselves would have had no purpose. The Mauryans' excellent road system facilitated internal and external contacts on an unprecedented scale, above all west to Herat and northwest to Bactria. These roads would later be the routes for Buddhism's spread to Central Asia and China, as well as corridors for successive invaders of the subcontinent moving in the opposite direction.

This era also saw the flourishing of cities across the empire: Pataliputra, Varanasi (Banaras), Ayodhya, Prayag (modern Allahabad), Ujjain, Taxila, and Qandahar. They were

India from the Sixth Century B.C.E. to the End of Mauryan Rule

ca. 600–400 B.C.E.	Late Upanishadic age: local/regional kingdoms and tribal republics along the Ganges and in Himalayan foothills, the Punjab, and northwestern India
ca. 540–ca. 468 B.C.E.	Vardhamana Mahavira, Jain founder
ca. 537–ca. 486 B.C.E.	Siddhartha Gautama, the Buddha
ca. 550–324 B.C.E.	Regional empire of Maghadan kings
330–325 B.C.E.	Alexander campaigns in Indus Valley, Soghdiana, Bactria, and Punjab
324–ca. 185 B.C.E.	Mauryan empire controls most of northern India and the Deccan
ca. 272–232 B.C.E.	Reign of the Mauryan emperor Ashoka

centers for arts, crafts, industry, literature, and education. The architecture of the Mauryan capital, Pataliputra, has not survived because of its wood-and-brick construction. But Greek travelers such as Megasthenes (who was active around 300 B.C.E.) reported that its glories surpassed those of the Achaemenid palaces. Certainly the stone buildings and sculpture of the Ashokan period reflect sophisticated aesthetics and technique, as well as strong Persian and Greek influence.

Consolidation of Indian Civilization (ca. 200 B.C.E.–300 C.E.)

In the post-Mauryan period, the history of North India was dominated by the influx of various foreign peoples whom we shall consider shortly. In the rest of the subcontinent, indigenous Indian dynasties held sway, often controlling substantial regional empires that became centers for developing Indian cultural styles. In this period a general pattern of regional and local political autonomy arose that would be broken only by the empire built much later by the Guptas (320 C.E.–ca. 550; see Chapter 10). However, religiously and culturally, the centuries between the Mauryans and Guptas still saw the consolidation of transregional patterns and styles that helped to shape Indian and, through the diffusion of Buddhism, Asian civilization ever after.

The Economic Base

Although agriculture remained the basis of the economy, commerce flourished amid the post-Mauryan political fragmentation. India's merchant classes prospered, as their patronage of Buddhist and Jain buildings shows. The fine Mauryan road

system facilitated trade throughout India. Chinese and Roman demand for Indian luxury goods—jewels, semiprecious stones, sandalwood, teak, spices, cotton and silk textiles, exotic animals, and slaves—made India a center of world trade. Considerable wealth flowed in, as archaeological finds of Roman gold-coin hoards and remains of Roman trading communities in the Tamil south show. Within India, guild organizations flourished and provided technical education in skilled crafts. Kings as well as the merchant classes invested in guilds. Coin minting increased greatly after Mauryan times, and banking flourished.[3]

High Culture

In the arts, the great achievements of this era were primarily Buddhist in inspiration. Northwestern India saw the rise of the Gandharan school of Buddhist art, named after the province that covered today's Pakistani Punjab and eastern Afghanistan. In Gandharan sculpture, Hellenistic naturalism of form joined with the more recent Indian tradition of Buddha images to produce relief and free-standing sculptural figures with flowing draped garments through which the muscular lines of the human body are readily discernible. In central India as early as the first century B.C.E., artists were producing stone-relief sculpture with the naturalistic, yet flowing, plastic human and animal forms that would become earmarks of the "classical" style of Indian art. The finest surviving examples are at the great Buddhist *stupas* (shrines) of Bharhut and Sanchi.

Language and literature during this period rested on the sophisticated Sanskrit grammar of Panini (ca. 300 B.C.E.?), which remains standard even today. Two masterpieces of Sanskrit culture, the epics of the *Mahabharata* and the *Ramayana*, probably took general shape by 200 C.E. The first is a composite work concerned largely with the nature of *dharma* (the moral and cosmic Law; see Chapter 2). Included in its earlier, narrative portions are systematic treatments of *dharma*, such as the Bhagavad Gita, or "Song of the Blessed Lord," the most influential of all Indian religious texts. Evidence of the rise of devotional cults is seen in the importance of Krishna in the *Mahabharata* (especially in the Gita) and Rama in the *Ramayana*. Both are major incarnations, or *avataras*, of the god Vishnu.

Religion and Society

The post-Mauryan period saw Buddhist monasticism and lay devotionalism thrive across the subcontinent. However,

---

[3]Romila Thapar, *A History of India*, vol. 1 (Harmondsworth, U. K.: Penguin Books, 1966), pp. 105–118.

The Great Stupa at Sanchi, an outstanding example of early Buddhist relic mounds. The mound, seated on an Ashokan foundation, was added to over the centuries. Magnificent carvings adorn its stone railings and gateways, one of which is shown in the left foreground. Sanchi is located in north-central India. [Dale Williams]

the Brahmans continued to dominate Vedic learning and ritual. It was also an era of diffusion of popular devotional cults of particular gods, above all Shiva and Vishnu. These traditions were to be the mainstays of all later "Hindu" religious life. The parallel development in Buddhist tradition was the rise, along with Mahayana thought (see Chapter 10), of a cult of the person of the Buddha. It focused on pilgrimages to sites where his relics were deposited or to places associated with his life. Toward the end of this age, Buddhism in its Mahayana form began to spread from India over the trade routes to Central Asia and eventually to China and Japan.

Hindu Tradition
What we now call Hinduism emerged in this era. The major developments shaping a Hindu tradition were (1) the consolidation of the caste system, Brahman ascendancy, and the "high" culture of Sanskrit learning; (2) the increasing dominance of theistic devotionalism (especially the cults of Vishnu and Shiva); and (3) the intellectual reconciliation of these developments with the older ascetic and speculative traditions deriving from the Upanishadic age.

These social and religious developments would continue and solidify in the Gupta era and beyond.

Buddhist Tradition
Indian Buddhist monastic communities prospered under mercantile and royal patronage, especially in or near urban centers—a trait they shared with the Jains. Merchants found both traditions attractive and strongly supported Jain and Buddhist monasteries, presumably for the merit to be gained.

Buddhist lay devotion figured prominently in Indian religious life, especially in the Ganges basin. It was, however, a different tradition from the Buddhism of the theological texts, which focuses on the quest for *nirvana* and the "extraordinary norm" (see Chapter 2). The Buddha and Buddhist saints were naturally identified with popular Indian deities, and Buddhist worship easily assimilated to common Indian patterns of theistic piety. Thus popular Buddhist practice was indistinguishable from countless other devotional cults that began to dominate the Indian scene. One reason that Buddhist tradition remained only one among many Indian religious paths was its absorption into the

Early Buddhist shrines cut into rock cliffs among the adjoining monasteries. Most of these rock-cut shrines are found in vertical cliffs not far from modern Bombay. [Dale Williams]

religious variety that then and now typifies the Hindu religious scene.

GREEK AND ASIAN DYNASTIES

Seleucids

We have seen that Alexander's successors in Achaemenid lands, the Greek general Seleucus and his heirs, soon lost Arachosia and Gandhara to the Mauryans. They did, however, rule most of the former Achaemenid realm from about 312 to 246 B.C.E. and lesser portions until about 125 B.C.E. Alexander's policies of Greco-Persian fusion—the appointment of Iranians and Greeks as satraps, as well as large-scale Greek and Persian intermarriage—helped make the Seleucid rule of many eastern areas viable. The new "cities"—more accurately, military colonies—that Alexander left behind provided bases for Seleucid control. As a foreign minority, the Seleucids had ultimately to maintain control with mercenary troops. It was, however, the leaders of their own troops and satrapies whose imperial aspirations gradually whittled away at Seleucid rule. Always at war, neither Seleucus (r. 311–281 B.C.E.; see Chapter 3) nor the greatest of his successors, Antiochus the Great (r. 223–187 B.C.E.), ever secured lasting dominion on the scale of the Achaemenids.

In the end, Alexander's policy of linking Hellenes with Iranians in political power, marriage, and culture bore fruit more lasting than empire. The Seleucid emphasis on the building of Greek-style cities stimulated the Hellenization process. During the second century B.C.E., Hellenistic culture and law became new ideals among the Seleucid elites. The Seleucids did not encourage cultural mixing as had Alexander, but they did welcome into the ruling classes those non-Hellenes willing to become hellenized. Aramaic, although declining in eastern Iran, remained the common tongue from Syria to the Hindu Kush. Local sociocultural forms were by no means displaced, but Greek culture did penetrate.

Zoroastrian religious tradition declined with the loss of its imperial-cult status. The many syncretic cults of the Mediterranean Hellenistic world made inroads even in the East in Seleucid and Parthian times. The later Parthians probably laid the groundwork for the subsequent revival of Zoroastrian tradition. Mystery and savior cults were becoming more popular in East and West. The new Hellenistic urban centers may have provided an environment in which the individual was less rooted in established traditions of culture and religious life. This would have enhanced the attractiveness of the focus on individual salvation common to many lesser Hellenistic cults and to emerging traditions like the Christian, Mahayana Buddhist, Manichaean, and Hindu devotionalist that came to dominate Eurasia over the next few centuries.

Indo-Greeks

The farthest reach of Hellenization in the East came not under the Seleucids but with another Alexandrine successor dynasty, the Indo-Greeks of Bactria.[4] About 246 B.C.E., Bactria's Greek satrap broke away from the Seleucids. His successor, Euthydemus (r. ca. 235–ca. 200 B.C.E.), extended his sway north and southwest and withstood a Seleucid attempt at reconquest by Antiochus the Great in 208 B.C.E. His son Demetrius exploited the growing Mauryan weakness and by 175 B.C.E. had crossed the Hindu Kush to conquer Arachosia. He then moved up the Indus Valley to take Gandhara. Demetrius and his successor, Menander, made Taxila their capital and were powerful enough to control other parts of northern India. Both were thoroughly "Indianized" in their orientation. Most of the Indo-Greeks were Indian in language, culture, and religion, as their coins and inscriptions show.

Before their demise at the hands of invading steppe peoples (ca. 130–100 B.C.E.), these Indo-Greeks left their mark on civilization in all the areas around their Bactrian center. Bactria was a major source of the later Greco-Buddhist art of Gandhara, one of history's remarkable examples of cross-cultural influence. The Indo-Greeks also probably helped spread Buddhism from India to Central Asia. The most famous of the Bactrian rulers, Menander, or Milinda (r. ca. 155–130 B.C.E.?), is depicted as a Buddhist convert in a later Buddhist text, *The Questions of King Milinda*.

Parthian marble head of a woman. [Trudy Kawamei]

Steppe Peoples

When we come to the Parthian Arsacid dynasty, which succeeded the Seleucids in Iran, and to the steppe dynasties that followed the Indo-Greeks in Bactria and North India, separation of Iranian from Indian history is misleading. The history of North India and the Iranian plateau was dominated from about 250 B.C.E. to 300 C.E. by incursions of Iranian tribal peoples originally from the Central Asian steppes. Although there is more tangible historical evidence for these incursions than for earlier Indo-Aryan migrations, they were neither the first nor the last such invasions from the steppe. Although commonly ignored, the nomadic steppe peoples have been a major force in Eurasian history.

Parthians

The Parni, said to be related to the Scythians, were probably the major group of Iranian steppe peoples who first settled the area south of the Aral Sea and Oxus. In late Achaemenid times, they moved south into Parthia and gradually adopted its dialect. Thenceforward we can call them Parthians. The independent control of Parthia by the dynastic family of the Arsacids dates from about 247 B.C.E. Shortly thereafter, the Parthians crossed the Elburz and began to extend their dominion onto the Iranian plateau. For decades only a regional power, they emerged under Mithradates I (ca. 171–138 B.C.E.) as a new Eurasian imperial force, the true Achaemenid successors.

Facing weak Seleucid and Indo-Greek opposition, Mithradates was able by ca. 140 B.C.E. to secure a sizable empire. It stretched across the Iranian plateau from Mesopotamia to Arachosia, and its center was Mithradates's new winter capital of Ctesiphon, on the Tigris. The Parthians' exact imperial borders and spheres of influence varied over time, but from their victory over the Romans at Carrhae in 53 B.C.E. (see Chapter 5) until their fall in 233 C.E., they were the major Eurasian power alongside Rome. Eventually the constant Roman wars of their last century and the pressure of the Kushan empire in the east

---

[4]In *The Indo-Greeks* (Oxford: Oxford University Press, 1957), A. K. Narian argues for "Indo-Greeks" as the appropriate term for these kings, who are usually called "Greco-Bactrians" or "Euthydemids."

weakened them sufficiently for a new Persian dynasty to replace them.

It is not easy to measure Parthian rule in Iran, despite its duration and successes, because of the scarcity and bias of available sources. For much of their long reign, the Parthians were under pressure on all fronts—in Armenia, in Mesopotamia, and along their Indian and Central Asian frontiers. Yet during their rule, trade in and around their domains apparently increased. In particular, there is evidence of vigorous commerce north over the Caucasus, on the "silk road" to China, and along the Indian Ocean coast (the ancient Arabs' "monsoon route," used for the spice trade with the Indies).

Culturally, the Parthians were oriented toward the Hellenistic world of their Seleucid predecessors until the mid-first century C.E., after which they seem to have experienced a kind of Iranian revival. They replaced Greek on their coins with Parthian and Aramaic, and their cities reverted to their older Iranian names. Their formerly Hellenic tastes in art turned to Iranian motifs like the hunt, battle, and feast. In late Parthian times, the Iranian national epic took its lasting shape. Similarly, the Magi preserved the worship of Ahura Mazda despite the success of other eastern and western cults and the common assimilation of Greek gods to Iranian ones. Still, the Parthians seem to have tolerated religious plurality. In their era, a huge variety of religious cults and cultural traditions rubbed shoulders with one another and vied for supremacy in different regions.

Sakas and Kushans

The successors of the Indo-Greeks were steppe peoples even closer to their nomadic past than the Parthians. These peoples are often ignored by modern historians because they impinge upon but do not figure centrally in Chinese, Iranian, or Indian history in our period. However, they played a major political and cultural role in Asia for several centuries, especially in the Indo-Iranian region. They reflect the cosmopolitan nature of the world of Central Asia, eastern Iran, and northwestern India at this time.

Beginning about 130 B.C.E., Scythian (Saka) tribes from beyond the Jaxartes (Syr Darya) overran northeastern Iran, taking Sogdiana's Hellenic cities and then Bactria. Thus ended the Indo-Greek heyday, although the last Greek petty ruler lasted in the upper Indus Valley until about 50 B.C.E. One group of Sakas soon extended their domain from Bactria into North India, as far as Mathura. Another went southwest into Herat and Sistan, where they encroached on the Parthians. In northwestern India the Sakas were in turn defeated by invading Iranians known as the Pahlavas, who went on to rule in northwestern India in the first cen-

Indo-Greek, Iranian, Indian, and Steppe Dynasties After Alexander	
312–ca. 125 B.C.E.	Seleucid rule in part of the old Achaemenid realm
ca. 248 B.C.E.–224 C.E.	Parthian empire of the Arsacids in Iran, Babylonia
246–ca. 50 B.C.E.	Indo-Greek ("Graeco-Bactrian," "Euthydemid") rulers of region from modern Afghanistan to Oxus
ca. 171–138 B.C.E.	Reign of Arsacid king Mithradates I
ca. 140 B.C.E.–ca. 100 C.E.	Movements west and south of Yüeh Chih (including Kushans) and Sythians (Sakas) into Sogdiana, then Bactria, then northwestern India
ca. C.E. 50–ca. 250	Height of Kushan power in Oxus to Ganges region
ca. 105 C.E.	Accession of King Kanishka to Kushan throne in Taxila (ruled about 28 years)

tury C.E.[5] Pahlava rule did not, however, wipe out the Sakas, for we find Saka dynasties ruling in parts of northwestern and western India through the fourth century C.E.

The Sakas had been displaced earlier in Sogdiana by another steppe people, known from Chinese sources as the Yüeh Chih. The building of the Great Wall (ca. 215 B.C.E.) or drought in the steppes may have driven them from western China. These peoples, led by the Kushan tribe, drove the Sakas out of Bactria in the mid-first century B.C.E. About a hundred years later, they swept over the mountains into northwestern India. Here they ended Pahlava rule and founded a long-lived Indian Kushan dynasty that controlled a relatively stable empire from the upper Oxus regions through Bactria, Gandhara, Arachosia, the Punjab, and over the Ganges plains as far as Varanasi (Banaras).

The Kushan kingdom of India was—along with Rome, China, and the weakened Parthian empire of Iran—one of four major centers of civilization in Eurasia around 100 C.E. Its greatest ruler, Kanishka, reigned either around 100 or possibly 150 C.E. He was the greatest patron of Buddhism since Ashoka. In their heyday (the first to third centuries C.E.), Kushan power in Central Asia facilitated the missionary activity that carried Buddhism across the steppes into China. A lasting Kushan contribution was the school of Greco-Buddhist art fostered in

[5]Tradition gives one of their rulers, Gondophares, the role of host to Saint Thomas, who is said to have brought Christianity to India. But because Gondophares probably ruled in the early to mid-first century C.E., it may be a confused report. Even if traditions of Thomas's mission to India are correct, some connect him instead with southern India.

The Buddha's Nirvana. This late second- or third-century-C.E. Gandharan-school relief has much in common with the style of contemporary Roman stone carvings. In this case the Indian-Buddhist concept does not mesh well with the realistic Roman style and craftsmanship. Note the emotions of the bystanders at their loss of the Lord Buddha; such depictions of emotion would not appear in native Indian style.
[Indian Musee, Giraudon/Art Resource, N.Y.]

Gandhara by Kanishka and his successors and supported by a later Kushan dynasty for another five hundred years.

IN WORLD PERSPECTIVE

Iran, India, and Inner Asia to the Third Century C.E.

By the second century C.E., we see in the Indo-Iranian world the development of imperial governments with power and influence far surpassing those of any before them. In and of themselves, such empires are not the measure of progress in what we call "civilization"—that is, citied, literate culture; technological sophistication; specialized division of labor; and complex social and political structures. Yet they are indices of the security and wealth requisite for progress in these areas. This was clearly the case in the empires of the Achaemenids and Mauryans. In this respect, developments in these regions paralleled those in the wider world, where Greek, Hellenistic, and Roman empires, like the Han empire of China, provided contexts in which civilization could flourish, grow, and spread.

In Asia this was also an era in which widely influential, lasting religious traditions came of age. Some of them—the Christian, Buddhist, Confucian, and even Judaic and Hindu traditions—spread to and took root in cultures outside their homelands. By contrast, the Zoroastrian tradition, like the Jain and the varied Hindu popular traditions in India, never had great appeal abroad, although much later its adherents were to carry it from Iran to western India, where they continue today as the small but influential community of Parsees.

In this period, another portentous development for the history of civilization was an increase in cross-cultural contact, epitomized by the Hellenizing conquests of Alexander. The Central Asian reaches of Iran and India especially provided the great meeting ground of Iranian, Indian, Greek, and steppe-people languages, customs, ideas, arts, and religious practices. In later centuries, the Iranian and Indian cultures continued to develop distinctive, largely independent forms, and Central Asia remained a fragmented but fertile cultural melting pot. Yet the developments of the age we have briefly surveyed here set in motion cross-cultural interchanges that would continue apace in later centuries. In this period we see in Rome, Iran, and India, if less so in China, increased contact with other cultures and increased influence from abroad. These contacts and influences were manifested in new peoples, governmental structures, technological innovations, specialized skills and arts, and ethico-religious ideas.

Review Questions

1. What were key factors in the success and long survival of the Achaemenid empire? What aspects of government control expanded the Achaemenid power base?
2. How was the Mauryan empire created? What role did Greeks play in its creation? What role did Ashoka play in the development of Mauryan power and prestige?
3. Referring to this chapter and Chapter 2, compare the major religious developments in Iran and India down to 200 C.E. How did the role of religion in the Achaemenid empire compare to its role in the Mauryan empire?
4. Compare the Achaemenid and Mauryan empires. What was their respective historical importance? How did each affect the world beyond its borders? How does each compare to the empires of Rome and China in the same centuries?
5. Compare the major features of the Hindu and Buddhist traditions. Why do you think Buddhism spread to southeast and east Asia whereas Hinduism did not?
6. In what ways did the Kushans, Sakas, and other inner Asian groups play important roles in world history?

Suggested Readings

Iran
M. BOYCE, *Zoroastrians: Their Religious Beliefs and Practices* (1979). The most recent survey, organized historically and based on extensive research.

M. BOYCE, ED. AND TRANS., *Textual Sources for the Study of Zoroastrianism* (1984). Well-translated selections from a broad range of ancient Iranian materials.

J. M. COOK, *The Persian Empire* (1983). Survey of the Achaemenid period.

JOHN CURTIS, *Ancient Persia* (1989). Excellent portfolio of photographs of artifacts and sites, with a clear historical survey of the arts and culture of ancient Iran.

W. D. DAVIES AND L. FINKELSTEIN, ED., *The Cambridge History of Judaism*, Vol. 1 (Introduction; The Persian Period). Good articles on Iran and Iranian religion as well as Judaism.

J. DUCHESNE-GUILLEMIN, TRANS., *The Hymns of Zarathushtra*, trans. M. Henning (1952, 1963). The best short introduction to the original texts of the Zoroastrian hymns.

R. N. FRYE, *The Heritage of Persia* (1963, 1966). A first-rate survey of Iranian history to Islamic times: readable but scholarly.

R. GHIRSHMAN, *Iran* (1954). Good material on culture, society, and economy as well as politics and history.

W. W. MALANDRA, TRANS. AND ED., *An Introduction to Ancient Iranian Religion: Readings from the Avesta and Achaemenid Inscriptions* (1983). Helpful especially for texts of inscriptions relevant to religion.

India
A. L. BASHAM, *The Wonder That Was India*, rev. ed. (1963). Excellent material on Mauryan religion, society, culture, and history.

A. L. BASHAM, ED., *A Cultural History of India* (1975). A fine collection of historical-survey essays by a variety of scholars. See Part I, "The Ancient Heritage" (Chapters 2–16).

N. N. BHATTACHARYYA, *Ancient Indian History and Civilization: Trends and Perspectives* (1988). Covers Mauryan and Gupta times as well as earlier periods, with chapters on political systems, cities and villages, ideology and religion, and art.

W. T. DE BARY ET AL., COMP., *Sources of Indian Tradition*, 2nd ed. (1958). Vol. I: *From the Beginning to 1800*, ed. and rev. Ainslie T. Embree (1988). Excellent selections from a wide variety of Indian texts, with good introductions to chapters and selections.

B. ROWLAND, *The Art and Architecture of India: Buddhist/Hindu/ Jain*, 3rd rev. ed. (1970). The standard work, lucid and easy to read. Note Part Three, "Romano-Indian Art in North-West India and Central Asia."

V. A. SMITH, ED., *The Oxford History of India*, 4th rev. ed. by Percival Spear et al. (1981), pp. 71–163. A dry, occasionally dated historical survey. Includes useful reference chronologies.

R. THAPAR, *Ashoka and the Decline of the Mauryans* (1973). The standard treatment of Ashoka's reign.

R. THAPAR, *A History of India, Part I* (1966), pp. 50–108. Three chapters that provide a basic survey of the period.

STANLEY WOLPERT, *A New History of India*, 2nd ed. (1982). A basic survey history. Chapters 5 and 6 cover the Mauryans, Guptas, and Kushans.

Greek and Asian Dynasties

A. K. NARAIN, *The Indo-Greeks* (1957. Reprinted with corrections, 1962). The most comprehensive account of the complex history of the various kings and kingdoms.

F. E. PETERS, *The Harvest of Hellenism* (1970), pp. 222–308. Helpful chapters on Greek rulers of the Eastern world from Seleucus to the last Indo-Greeks.

J. W. SEDLAR, *India and the Greek World: A Study in the Transmission of Culture* (1980). A basic work that provides a good overview.

D. SINOR, ED., *The Cambridge History of Early Inner Asia* (1990). See especially Chapters 6 and 7.

RELIGIONS OF THE WORLD

Hinduism

The term *Hinduism* is simply our modern word for the majority of the diverse religious traditions of India taken as a whole. Until the word was coined in the nineteenth century, it (like *Buddhism*) was not even a concept in the West, let alone in India itself. In contemporary usage, however, it has become a catchall term used for all the Indian religious communities that look upon the texts of the Vedas (see Chapter 1) as eternal, perfect truth.

The historical beginnings of the varied Hindu traditions can be traced to the ancient Aryan migrations into southern Asia in the second millenium before our common era. This was the age in which the Vedic hymns were composed. In them we find a pantheon of gods not unlike that found among the Greeks, the Romans, and other Indo-European peoples. Centered on a sacrificial cult of these gods, Vedic religion became more and more the preserve of the Brahman priestly class of early Indian society. The Brahmans gradually elaborated a cult characterized by complex rituals of sacrifice, involved purificatory rules, and increasingly fixed distinctions of birth on which India's later caste system was based. These developments are mirrored in the later Vedic, or Brahmanical, texts (ca. 1000–500 B.C.E.) that provide commentary on and instructions for ritual use of the Vedic hymns.

After about 700 B.C.E. new developments set in. North India produced a series of religious reformers, most of whom championed knowledge and ascetic discipline rather than purity and ritual action. Some of these reformers broke with the Vedic tradition. Of these, Siddhartha Gautama (the Buddha; b. ca. 563 B.C.E.) and Mahavira Vardhamana (founder of the Jain tradition; b. ca. 550 B.C.E.) were the two most famous. Other thinkers reinterpreted the older sacrifice as an inner activity and deepened its spiritual dimensions. They further tried to link or to identify Transcendence, or Ultimate Being (*Brahman*), with the inmost self (*atman*). Their thinking is represented especially in the Upanishads, which many Hindus consider the most sublime philosophical texts in the Indian tradition.

Developed so long ago, such notions have been part of the complex but logically compelling vision of existence that lies behind the myriad forms of religious life known to us as Hinduism. In this vision the immortal part of each human being, the *atman*, is enmeshed in existence, but not ultimately of it. The nature of existence is *samsara*—unending becoming and change, a ceaseless round of cause and effect determined by the inescapable consequences of *karma*, or "action." The doctrine of *karma* is a kind of moral as well as physical economy in which every act has unavoidable results; so long as mental or physical action occurs, becoming and life go on repeatedly. Birth determines one's place and duties in the traditional Indian caste system. Caste is the most visible and concrete reminder of the pervasiveness of the Hindu concept of absolute causality that keeps us enmeshed in existence. The final goal is to transcend at some point in this or another lifetime the endless round of rebirth, or *samsara*, in which we are all caught. Release, or *moksha*, is the only way out of this otherwise endless becoming and rebirth. *Moksha* may be gained through knowledge, action, or devotion.

Krishna Holding Up Govardhana. The beloved cycle of Krishna myths is popular not only among worshipers of Lord Krishna but also among most Indians. In this Bikaner painting from ca. 1690, Krishna uses the entire mountain of Govardhana as an umbrella to protect his homeland and sacred territory of Brindavan from the deluge sent down by the great god Indra. Indra appears on his elephant in the distance in the upper right of the painting. The women gathered around Lord Krishna are the cowherdesses, or gopis, famous from other tales of the Dark Lord. [British Museum, London, Great Britain/Sahibdin/Scala/Art Resource N.Y.]

On the popular level, the period after about 500 B.C.E. is most notable in Indian religious life for two developments. Both took place alongside the ever deeper entrenchment in society of caste distinctions and a supporting ethic of obligations and privileges. The first was the elaboration of ascetic traditions of inner quest and self-realization, such as that of yoga. The second was the rise of devotional worship of specific gods and goddesses who were seen by their worshipers as identical with the Ultimate—in other words, as supreme deities for those who served them. The latter development was of particular importance for popular religion in India. Evident in the famous and beloved Hindu devotional text, the Bhagavad Gita, it reached its highest level after 500 C.E. in the myriad movements of fervent, loving devotionalism, or *bhakti*, many of which remain important today. A striking aspect of Hindu piety has been its willingness to accommodate the focus on one "chosen deity" who is worshipped as supreme to a worldview that holds that the divine can and does take many forms. Thus most Hindus worship one deity, but they do so in the awareness that faith in other deities can also lead one to the Ultimate.

The period between about 500 B.C.E. and 1000 C.E. saw the rise of two gods, Vishnu and Shiva, to special prominence as the primary forms in which the supreme lord was worshipped. Along with the mother-goddess figure, who takes various names and forms (Kali and Durga, for example), Vishnu and Shiva have remained the most important manifestations of the divine in India. Their followers are known as Vaishnavas and Shaivas, respectively. Countless differing traditions of devotion are practiced among Vaishnavas and Shaivas, as well as other groups. However, a few recurring phenomena and ideas can suggest something of Indian religiousness in practice.

Hindu practice is characterized especially by temple worship (*puja*), in which offerings of flowers, food, and the like are brought by the worshipers. The temple images are especially sought out by the faithful for the blessing that the sight of these images brings. Recitation of sacred texts, many of which are vernacular hymns of praise to a particular deity, are another important part of Hindu devotionalism. *Mantras*, or special recitative texts from the Vedas, are also used by many Hindus in their original Sanskrit form. These texts are thought to have extraordinary power. Pilgrimage to sacred sites, especially rivers, mountains, and famous shrines, is a prominent part of Hindu religious life. India's entire landscape is filled with sacred sites and sacred pilgrim routes, both local and national in reputation. A prominent feature of Hindu life is preoccupation with purity and pollution, most evident in the food taboos associated with caste groupings.

The ascetic tendency in India is also highly developed. Although they are influential, only a tiny minority relative

Purification Rituals in the Waters of the Holy Ganges. Purification rituals are part of the obligatory daily rituals of all "twice-born" Hindus. The morning rituals performed by the women here in the Ganges include greeting the sun with recitation and prayer and purification by bathing. [Ian Berry/Magnum Photos, Inc.]

to the great masses of Indians take up a life of full renunciation. In this life the ascetic worshiper does not settle in one place, take on possessions, or perform regular worship. He or she rather wanders about in search of teachers and devotes himself or herself to meditation and self-realization. Even though the majority of Hindus have families and work at their salvation through merit gained by *puja* and moral living, the ascetic ideal has an important place in the overall Indian worldview. This ideal is seen as valid and worthy of respect; it stands as a constant reminder of the deeper reality beyond the everyday world and any individual life.

5 REPUBLICAN AND IMPERIAL ROME

This wall painting was found in a bedroom in a first century B.C.E. villa in Pompeii. It depicts a grand and fantastic

imaginary villa. [The Metropolitan Museum of Art, Rogers Fund, 1903 (Acc. # 03.14.13) © 1986 The Metropolitan Museum of Art]

CHAPTER TOPICS

- Prehistoric Italy
- The Etruscans
- Royal Rome
- The Republic
- Civilization in the Early Roman Republic: Greek Influence
- Roman Imperialism

- Fall of the Republic
- The Augustan Principate
- Civilization of the Ciceronian and Augustan Ages
- Peace and Prosperity: Imperial Rome (14–180 C.E.)
- Rise of Christianity

- The Crisis of the Third Century
- The Late Empire
- Arts and Letters in the Late Empire
- The Problem of the Decline and Fall of the Empire in the West

In World Perspective Republican and Imperial Rome

The ancient Romans were responsible for one of the most remarkable achievements in history. From their city in central Italy, which began as a small village, they conquered all of Italy, then the entire Mediterranean coastline, and finally most of the Near East and much of continental Europe. Their unifying government brought centuries of peace and prosperity to this vast region, which has never been unified again, and has only rarely since enjoyed prolonged peace and stability.

When it began its expansion, Rome had a nonmonarchical, republican government. Few nonmonarchical governments have lasted for more than a relatively short time, and the Roman republic, which endured for almost five hundred years and came to control a vast empire, has no parallel. The eventual fall of the republic and the imposition of an imperial monarchy under Augustus, Rome's first emperor, ended this unusual chapter in history. The transition was difficult. Romans continued to think in republican terms for

generations, and many longed for the republic's restoration. Augustus skillfully maintained the appearance of republican institutions, helping to mask the monarchical reality. The passage of time made such deception less necessary. Hard times and chaos in the third century C.E. revealed the military foundation of the emperors' increasingly autocratic rule. Beginning in the first century C.E. emperors were declared divine after death; by the second century they were worshiped as gods while alive, like the rulers of ancient Egypt and other early empires.

Rome's legacy was not just of military prowess and superb political organization. The Romans adopted and transformed the intellectual and cultural achievements of the Greeks, creating the Graeco-Roman tradition in literature, philosophy, and art. This tradition formed the core of learning during the Middle Ages and inspired the new intellectual paths taken during the Renaissance. It remains the heart of Western civilization.

Prehistoric Italy

About 1000 B.C.E. bands of warlike peoples speaking a set of closely related languages we call *Italic* began to infiltrate Italy. By 800 B.C.E. they had occupied the highland pastures of the Apennines and soon challenged the earlier settlers for control of the tempting western plains. The Romans would emerge from among the descendants of these tough mountain people. Others who shaped the future of Italy included the Etruscans, the Greeks who colonized Sicily and southern Italy, and the Celts, who established themselves in the north around 400 B.C.E.

The Etruscans

Etruscan civilization, which was to have a powerful influence on the Romans, arose about 800 B.C.E. (see Map 5–1). The Etruscans lived in self-governing, fortified city-states. They constituted a military ruling class, dominating the native people they had dispossessed and exploiting them to work their lands, and fight in their infantry. The Etruscan states were first ruled by kings and later by an agrarian aristocracy that governed through a council and annually elected magistrates. This

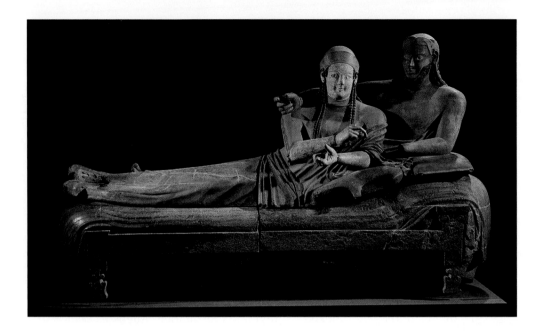

Much of what we know of the Etruscans comes from their funerary art. This sculpture of an Etruscan couple is part of a sarcophagus. [Erich Lessing/Art Resource, N.Y.]

aristocracy accumulated considerable wealth through agriculture, industry, piracy, and commerce with the Carthaginians of North Africa and the Greeks.

In the seventh and sixth centuries B.C.E. the Etruscans conquered Latium (which included Rome) and Campania, where they became neighbors of the Greeks of Naples. But after 500 B.C.E. Etruscan power rapidly declined. The Celts drove them from the Po Valley about 400 B.C.E., and soon thereafter they lost control of their Etrurian heartland to an expanding Rome.

Royal Rome

In the sixth century B.C.E. the town of Rome in Latium came under Etruscan control. Although it had been of little importance, it was a natural center for communication and trade. Led by Etruscan kings, the Roman army conquered most of Latium. Rome's effective political and social organization, which gave extraordinary power to its rulers, made this success possible.

Government

Roman kings had the awesome power of *imperium*, the right to issue commands and to enforce them by fines, arrests, and physical punishment, including execution. Although it tended to remain in families, kingship was elective. The Roman Senate approved the candidate for the office, and the Roman people, voting in assembly, formally granted the *imperium*. This procedure—the granting of great power to executive officers contingent on the approval of the Senate and ultimately

the people—would remain a basic characteristic of Roman government.

The king was the commander of the army, the chief priest, and the supreme judge. He conducted foreign affairs, commanded the army, and disciplined his troops, all by virtue of his *imperium*. In practice the royal power was much more limited.

The Senate, the second branch of the early Roman government, ostensibly had neither executive nor legislative power; it met only when summoned by the king and then only to advise him. In reality its authority was great, for the senators, like the king, served for life. The Senate, therefore, had continuity and experience, and it was composed of the most powerful men in the state. It could not be ignored lightly.

The third branch of government, the curiate assembly, was made up of all citizens as divided into thirty groups. The assembly also met only when summoned by the king. Usually, the assembly was called to listen and approve. Voting was not by head but by group; a majority within each group determined its vote, and the decisions were made by majority vote of the groups. Group voting would be typical of all future forms of Roman assembly.

Family

The center of Roman life was the family. At its head stood the father, whose power and authority resembled those of the king within the state. Over his children he held broad powers analogous to *imperium;* he could sell his children into slavery, and might even kill them. Over his wife he had less power; he could not sell or kill her. In practice his power to dispose of his children was limited by other family members, by public opinion, and, most of all, by tradition. A wife could be divorced only for

Map 5–1   Ancient Italy.   This map of ancient Italy and its neighbors before the expansion of Rome shows the major cities and towns as well as a number of geographical regions and the locations of some of the Italic and non-Italic peoples.

serious offenses, and only after she had been convicted by a court made up of her male blood relatives. The Roman woman had a respected position and the main responsibility for managing the household. The father was the chief priest of the family, leading it in daily prayers to the dead that reflected the ancestor worship central to the Roman family and state.

Clientage

Clientage was one of Rome's most important institutions. The client was "an inferior entrusted, by custom or by himself, to the protection of a stranger more powerful than he,

and rendering certain services and observances in return for this protection."[1] The client was said to be in the *fides*, or trust, of his patron, giving the relationship a moral dimension. The patron provided his client with physical and legal protection and economic support. In return the client would fight for his patron, work his land, and support him politically. These mutual obligations were enforced by public opinion and tradition. When early custom was codified in the mid-fifth century B.C.E., one of the twelve tablets of laws announced: "Let the patron who has defrauded his client be accursed."[2]

In early Rome patrons were rich and powerful, whereas clients were poor and weak, but in time, rich and powerful members of the upper classes increasingly became clients of even more powerful men. Because the client-patron relationship was hereditary and was sanctioned by religion and custom, it played an important part in the life of the Roman Republic.

Patricians and Plebeians

In the royal period Roman society was divided into two classes based on birth. The wealthy patrician upper class held a monopoly of power and influence. Its members alone could conduct state religious ceremonies, sit in the Senate, or hold office. They formed a closed caste by forbidding marriage outside their own group.

The plebeian lower class must have consisted originally of poor, dependent small farmers, laborers, and artisans, the clients of the nobility. As Rome grew, nonpatrician families acquired wealth. From early times, therefore, there were rich plebeians and patrician families that fell into poverty from incompetence or bad luck. The line between the classes and the monopoly of privileges nevertheless remained firm.

The Republic

According to Roman tradition, the outrageous behavior of the last kings provoked the noble families to revolt in 509 B.C.E., leading to the creation of the republic.

Constitution

The Roman constitution was an unwritten accumulation of laws and customs.

[1] E. Badian, *Foreign Clientelae (264–70 B.C.E.)* (Oxford: Oxford University Press, 1958), p. 1.
[2] *Roman Civilization: Selected Readings*, Vol. 1, ed. by Naphtali Lewis and Meyer Reinhold (New York: Columbia University Press, 1963).

Consuls   The Romans were never willing to deprive their chief magistrates of the great powers their kings had exercised. They elected two patricians to the office of consul and endowed them with *imperium*. Assisting the consuls were financial officials called *quaestors*. Like the kings, the consuls led the army, had religious duties, and served as judges. Consular power, however, was limited legally, institutionally, and by custom.

The power of the consulship was granted for a year only. Each consul could overrule the other, and they shared their religious powers with others. Even the *imperium* was limited. Although the consuls had full powers of life and death while leading an army, within the sacred boundary of the city of Rome, citizens could appeal to the popular assembly all cases involving capital punishment. Besides, after their year in office, the consuls would spend the rest of their lives as members of the Senate, so only a reckless consul would ignore its advice.

The many checks on consular action tended to prevent initiative, swift action, and change, but this was just what a conservative, traditional, aristocratic republic wanted. Only in military matters did these limitations create problems. In serious crises, the consuls could, with the advice of the Senate, appoint a *dictator*, who would have *imperium* not subject to appeal both inside and outside the city for six months. These devices sufficed in the early republic, when Rome's battles were near home, but longer wars and more sophisticated opponents required significant changes.

In 325 B.C.E. the Romans created the office of proconsul, which permitted a consul in the field to retain command during a long campaign. Another new office, that of *praetor*, was primarily judicial. But *praetors* also had *imperium* and served as generals. They too could have their one-year term of office extended for long campaigns. Eventually there were eight *praetors*.

After the middle of the fifth century B.C.E. the job of identifying citizens and classifying them according to age and property was delegated to a new office, that of *censor*. The Senate elected two censors every five years. They conducted a census and drew up the citizen rolls. Because the classification fixed taxation and status, the censors had to be men of reputation, former consuls. They soon acquired additional powers and by the fourth century B.C.E. had the authority to exclude senators from the Senate on moral as well as financial grounds. As the prestige of the office grew, it came to be considered the ultimate prize of a political career.

Senate and Assembly   The end of the monarchy increased the power of the Senate. Composed of leading patricians, often clan leaders and patrons with many clients, it became the only ongoing deliberative body in the Roman state and soon controlled finances and foreign policy.

Lictors, pictured here, attended the chief Roman magistrates when they appeared in public. The axe carried by one of the lictors and the bound bundle of staffs carried by the others symbolize both the power of Roman magistrates to inflict corporal punishment on Roman citizens and the limits on that power. The bound staffs symbolize the right of citizens within the city of Rome not to be punished without a trial. The axe symbolizes the power of the magistrates, as commanders of the army, to put anyone to death without a trial outside the city walls. [Alinari/Art Resource, N.Y.]

The *centuriate assemble*, the early republic's most important popular assembly, was, in a sense, the Roman army acting in a political capacity. Its basic unit was the century, theoretically one hundred fighting men who fought with the same kind of equipment. Because each man equipped himself, this organization divided the assembly into classes according to wealth.

Struggle of the Orders   Patricians monopolized power in the early republic. Plebeians were barred from all political and religious offices. In response, the plebeians launched the "struggle of the orders," a fight for political, legal, and social equality that lasted two hundred years.

Plebeians made up much of the Roman army, giving them great political leverage. They formed the plebeian tribal assembly, and elected *tribunes*, officials with the power to protect plebeians from abuse by patrician magistrates. In effect, a tribune could veto any action of a magistrate or any bill in a Roman assembly or the Senate.

In 450 B.C.E. the Twelve Tablets were published, the first attempt to codify Rome's harsh customs. In 445 B.C.E. plebeians won the right to marry patricians. It was not until 367

B.C.E. that one of the consuls was allowed to be of plebeian rank. Gradually other offices, including the dictatorship and the censorship, opened to them. In 300 B.C.E. they were admitted to the most important priesthoods. In 287 B.C.E. the plebeians secured the passage of a law making the decisions of the plebeian assembly binding on all Romans without the approval of the Senate.

The victory of the plebeians allowed wealthy plebeian families to enter politics and share the privileges of the patrician aristocracy. The *nobiles*—a relatively small group of wealthy and powerful families, both patrician and plebeian—dominated the increasingly powerful Senate and controlled the highest offices of the state.

The end of the struggle of the orders brought domestic peace under a republican constitution dominated by a capable, if narrow, senatorial aristocracy. Most Romans accepted this leadership, which secured them a growing empire and many benefits.

Conquest of Italy

Initial Expansion and Gallic Invasion   By the beginning of the fourth century B.C.E. the Romans were the chief power in central Italy, but in 387 B.C.E. the Gauls, marching south from the Po Valley, captured, looted, and burned Rome. Rome appeared finished, but by about 350 B.C.E. it had reclaimed the leadership of central Italy.

In 340 B.C.E. the city's Latin neighbors, the Latin League, sought to curtail Rome's expansion. In 338 B.C.E. the Romans defeated the league and dissolved it. The terms they imposed provided a model for the way they were to treat opponents as they incorporated the rest of Italy.

Roman Policy Toward the Conquered   The Romans did not destroy any of the Latin cities, nor did they treat them all alike. To some near Rome they granted full citizenship. To others farther away they granted municipal status, which included the right to local self-government and the right to trade and intermarry with Romans, but not to take part in Roman politics unless they moved to Rome and applied for citizenship. These states followed Rome's foreign policy and supplied soldiers for Rome's legions. Still other states became allies of Rome on the basis of treaties that differed from city to city. All the allies supplied troops to fight in auxiliary battalions under Roman officers, but they did not pay taxes to Rome.

The Romans established permanent colonies of veteran soldiers in conquered lands. The colonists remained Roman citizens and deterred rebellion. A network of durable roads—some still in use—connected the colonies to Rome, permitting troops to be moved swiftly to any trouble spot.

Rome divided its enemies and extended its influence through military force and diplomatic skill. Rebels were pun-ished harshly and swiftly. But Rome was also generous to those who submitted. The status of a newly conquered city was not permanent. Loyal allies could improve their prospects, even gaining full Roman citizenship. This policy gave allies a stake in Rome's future and a sense of being colleagues rather than subjects. As a result, most remained loyal even when put to the severest test.

Rome and Carthage

Late in the ninth century B.C.E. the Phoenician city of Tyre had planted a colony on the North African coast, calling it the New City, or Carthage (see Map 5–2). In the sixth century B.C.E. Carthage became independent and free to take advantage of its defensible position, excellent harbor, and rich countryside. The Carthaginians expanded along the coast of North Africa west beyond the Straits of Gibraltar and east into Libya. They also gained control of southern Spain, Sardinia, Corsica, Malta, the Balearic Islands, and western Sicily. The people of these territories became Carthaginian subjects, paying tribute and serving in the Carthaginian military. Carthage claimed an absolute monopoly on trade in the western Mediterranean.

First Punic War (264–241 B.C.E.)   Sicily was strategically important to both Carthage and Rome. It was there, in 264 B.C.E., that the two expanding powers first came to blows. Because the Romans called the Carthaginians *Poeni* or *Puni* (meaning "Phoenician"), the conflicts between them are called the Punic Wars.

Neither side made any progress against the other until the Romans built a fleet to blockade the Carthaginian ports at the western end of Sicily. Carthage capitulated in 241 B.C.E., giving up Sicily and the islands between Italy and Sicily and agreeing to pay a war indemnity, to keep its ships out of Italian waters, and not to recruit mercenaries in Italy. Neither side was to attack the allies of the other.

The terms of the peace were fair, but Rome broke them almost immediately, setting the stage for more conflict. In 238 B.C.E., while Carthage struggled to put down a revolt of unpaid mercenaries, Rome seized Sardinia and Corsica and demanded an additional indemnity. This cynical action provoked the Carthaginians without preventing them from recovering their strength to seek vengeance in the future.

Second Punic War (218–202 B.C.E.)   After 241 B.C.E., Carthage recovered strength by building a rich empire in Spain while Rome looked on with concern. In 221 B.C.E. Hannibal (247–182 B.C.E.) took command of Carthaginian forces in Spain. A few years earlier Rome had received an offer from the Spanish town of Saguntum to become the friends of Rome. The Romans accepted, thereby taking on the responsibilities of friendship with a foreign state. At first

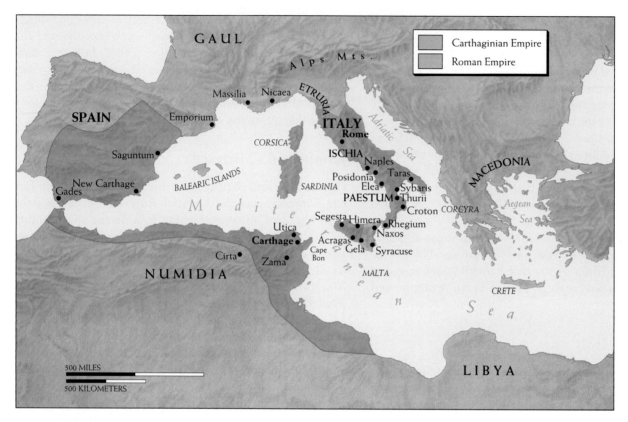

Map 5–2 The Western Mediterranean area during the rise of Rome. This map covers the theater of the conflict between the growing Roman dominions and those of Carthage in the third century B.C.E. The Carthaginian empire stretched westward from Carthage along the North African coast and into southern Spain.

Hannibal was careful to respect Saguntum, but the Saguntines, confident of Rome's protection, began to interfere with Spanish tribes allied with Hannibal. The Romans warned Hannibal to let Saguntum alone, but he ignored Rome's warning, besieged Saguntum, and captured it.

Rome declared war in 218 B.C.E. Starting in Spain, Hannibal launched a swift and daring invasion of Italy. By September of 218 B.C.E. he was across the Alps. His army was weary, bedraggled, and greatly reduced, but he was in Italy. Hannibal defeated the Romans in three consecutive battles, but his chances of prevailing would depend ultimately on Rome's ability to retain the loyalty of its allies.

In 216 B.C.E., at Cannae in Apulia, Hannibal destroyed a Roman army of some 80,000 men. It was the worst defeat in Roman history; Rome's prestige was shattered, and many of its allies went over to Hannibal. In 215 B.C.E. Philip V (r. 221–179 B.C.E.), king of Macedon, made an alliance with Hannibal and launched a war to recover his influence on the Adriatic. For more than a decade no Roman army would dare face Hannibal in the open field, and he was free to roam over all Italy and do as he pleased.

But crucial allies remained loyal to Rome, preventing Hannibal's victory. He had neither the numbers nor the supplies to besiege Rome or the cities of its major allies, nor did he

have the equipment to take them by assault. The Romans appointed Publius Cornelius Scipio (237–183 B.C.E.), later called Scipio Africanus, to the command in Spain with proconsular *imperium*. He was a general almost as talented as Hannibal. Within a few years Scipio had conquered all Spain and had deprived Hannibal of hope of help from that region.

In 204 B.C.E. Scipio landed in Africa and forced the Carthaginians to accept a peace whose main clause was the withdrawal of Hannibal and his army from Italy. Hannibal had won every battle but lost the war. His return inspired Carthage

The Punic Wars

264–241 B.C.E.	First Punic War
238 B.C.E.	Rome seizes Sardinia and Corsica
221 B.C.E.	Hannibal takes command of Punic army in Spain
218–202 B.C.E.	Second Punic War
216 B.C.E.	Battle of Cannae
202 B.C.E.	Battle of Zama
149–146 B.C.E.	Third Punic War
146 B.C.E.	Destruction of Carthage

A Roman warship. Rome became a naval power late in its history, in the course of the First Punic War. Roman sailors initially lacked the skill and experience in sea warfare of their Carthaginian opponents, who could maneuver their oared ships to ram the enemy. To compensate for this disadvantage, the Romans sought to make a sea battle more like an encounter on land by devising ways to grapple enemy ships and board them with armed troops. In time they also mastered the skillful use of the ram. This picture shows a Roman ship, propelled by oars, with both ram and soldiers, ready for either kind of fight. [Direzione Generale Musei Vaticani]

to risk all in battle. In 202 B.C.E. Scipio and Hannibal faced each other at Zama. Rome won and the new peace terms reduced Carthage to the status of a dependent ally of Rome. Carthage was no longer a great power. Rome ruled the seas and the entire Mediterranean coast from Italy westward.

The New Imperial System The Roman conquest of overseas territory presented a new problem. Instead of following the policy they had pursued in Italy, the Romans made Sicily, Sardinia, and Corsica provinces. It became common to extend the term of the governors of these provinces beyond a year. The governors were unchecked by colleagues and exercised full *imperium*. New magistracies, in effect, were thus created free of the limits put on the power of officials in Rome. The new populations were subjects who paid tribute instead of serving in the army. The old practice of extending citizenship and with it loyalty to Rome stopped at the borders of Italy. Rome collected the new taxes by "farming them out" at auction to the highest bidder. The tax collectors became powerful and wealthy by squeezing the provincials hard. These innovations were the basis for Rome's imperial organization; in time they so strained the constitution and traditions of Rome that the existence of the republic was threatened.

The Republic's Conquest of the Hellenistic World

The East By the middle of the third century B.C.E. the eastern Mediterranean had reached a stable balance of power. That equilibrium was threatened by two aggressive monarchs, Philip V of Macedon and the Seleucid Antiochus III (223–187 B.C.E.). Philip and Antiochus moved swiftly, the latter against Syria and Palestine, the former against Greek cities.

The threat that a more powerful Macedon might pose to Rome's friends and, perhaps, even to Italy persuaded the Romans to intervene. In 200 B.C.E. the Romans ordered Philip not to attack any Greek city and to pay reparations to the kingdom of Pergamum in Asia Minor. Philip refused. Two years later the Romans demanded that Philip withdraw from Greece entirely. In 197 B.C.E., with Greek support, they defeated Philip in Thessaly. The Greek cities taken from Philip were made autonomous and the freedom of the Greeks was proclaimed.

Soon after, the Romans came into conflict with Antiochus. On the pretext of freeing the Greeks from Roman domination, he landed an army on the Greek mainland. The Romans quickly drove him from Greece, and in 189 B.C.E. they crushed his army at Magnesia in Asia Minor. The peace of Apamia in the next year deprived Antiochus of his elephants and his navy and imposed a huge indemnity on him. Once again the Romans took no territory for themselves and left Greek cities in Asia free. They continued to regard Greece, and now Asia Minor, as a kind of protectorate in which they could intervene as they chose.

In 179 B.C.E. Perseus (r. 179–168 B.C.E.) succeeded Philip V as king of Macedon. He tried to gain popularity in Greece by favoring the democratic and revolutionary forces in the cities. The Romans, troubled by this threat to stability, defeated him in 168 B.C.E. and divided Macedon into four separate republics whose citizens were forbidden to intermarry or even to do business across the new national boundaries.

The new policy reflected the stern and businesslike approach favored by the conservative censor Cato (234–149 B.C.E.). The new harshness was applied to allies and bystanders as well as to defeated opponents. Leaders of anti-Roman factions in the Greek cities were punished severely.

A Women's Uprising in Republican Rome

In 195 B.C.E. Roman women staged a rare public political protest when they demanded the repeal of a law passed two decades earlier during the Second Punic War that they judged to limit their rights unfairly. Livy (59 B.C.E.–17 C.E.) describes the affair and the response of the traditionalist Marcus Porcius Cato (234–149 B.C.E.).

Of what did the women complain? How did they try to achieve their goals? Which of Cato's objections to their behavior do you think were most important? Since women did not vote or sit in assemblies, how can the outcome of the affair be explained?

Amid the anxieties of great wars, either scarce finished or soon to come, an incident occurred, trivial to relate, but which, by reason of the passions it aroused, developed into a violent contention. Marcus Fundanius and Lucius Valerius, tribunes of the people, proposed to the assembly the abrogation of the Oppian law. The tribune Gaius Oppius had carried this law in the heat of the Punic War, in the consulship of Quintus Fabius and Tiberius Sempronius, that no woman should possess more than half an ounce of gold or wear a parti-coloured garment or ride in a carriage in the City or in a town within a mile thereof, except on the occasion of a religious festival. The tribunes Marcus and Publius Iunius Brutus were supporting the Oppian law, and averred that they would not permit its repeal; many distinguished men came forward to speak for and against it; the Capitoline was filled with crowds of supporters and opponents of the bill. The matrons could not be kept at home by advice or modesty or their husbands' orders, but blocked all the streets and approaches to the Forum, begging the men as they came down to the Forum that, in the prosperous condition of the state, when the private fortunes of all men were daily increasing, they should allow the woman too to have their former distinctions restored. The crowd of women grew larger day by day; for they were now coming in from the towns and rural districts. Soon they dared even to approach and appeal to the consuls, the praetors, and the other officials, but one consul, at least, they found adamant, Marcus Porcius Cato, who spoke thus in favour of the law whose repeal was being urged.

"If each of us, citizens, had determined to assert his rights and dignity as a husband with respect to his own spouse, we should have less trouble with the sex as a

---

In 146 B.C.E., for instance, the ancient and wealthy commercial city of Corinth was completely destroyed.

The public treasury benefited to such a degree from these wars that the direct property tax on Roman citizens was abolished. Part of the booty went to the victorious general and part to their soldiers. New motives were thereby introduced into Roman foreign policy, or, perhaps, old motives were given new prominence. Foreign campaigns could bring profit to the state, rewards to the army, and wealth, fame, honor, and political power to the general.

The West

Harsh as the Romans had become toward the Greeks, they treated the Spaniards, whom they considered barbarians, even worse. The Romans committed dreadful atrocities; they lied, cheated, and broke treaties in their effort to exploit and pacify the natives, who fought back fiercely in guerrilla style. From 154 to 133 B.C.E. the fighting waxed, and it became hard to recruit Roman soldiers for the increasingly ugly war. At last, in 134 B.C.E., Scipio Aemilianus (185–129 B.C.E.) took the key city of Numantia by siege and put an end to the war in Spain.

Roman treatment of Carthage was no better. Although Carthage posed no threat, some Romans refused to abandon their hatred and fear of the traditional enemy. Cato is said to have ended all his speeches in the Senate with the same sentence, *"Ceterum censeo delendam esse Carthaginem"* ("Besides, I think that Carthage must be destroyed"). At last the Romans took advantage of a technical breach of the peace to destroy Carthage. In 146 B.C.E. Scipio Aemilianus took the city, plowed up its land, and put salt in the furrows as a symbol of the permanent abandonment of the site. The Romans incorporated Carthage as the province of Africa.

Roman Overseas Engagements

215–205 B.C.E.	First Macedonian War
200–197 B.C.E.	Second Macedonian War
196 B.C.E.	Proclamation of Greek Freedom
189 B.C.E.	Battle of Magnesia; Antiochus defeated in Asia Minor
172–168 B.C.E.	Third Macedonian War
168 B.C.E.	Battle of Pydna
154–133 B.C.E.	Roman wars in Spain
134 B.C.E.	Numantia taken

whole; as it is, our liberty, destroyed at home by female violence, even here in the Forum is crushed and trodden underfoot, and because we have not kept them individually under control, we dread them collectively. . . . But from no class is there not the greatest danger if you permit them meetings and gatherings and secret consultations. . . .

"I should have said, 'What sort of practice is this, of running out into the streets and blocking the roads and speaking to other women's husbands? Could you not have made the same requests, each of your own husband, at home? Or are you more attractive outside and to other women's husbands than to your own? And yet, not even at home, if modesty would keep matrons within the limits of their proper rights, did it become you to concern yourselves with the question of what laws should be adopted in this place or repealed.' Our ancestors permitted no woman to conduct even personal business without a guardian to intervene in her behalf; they wished them to be under the control of fathers, brothers, husbands; we (Heaven help us!) allow them now even to interfere in public affairs, yes, and to visit the Forum and our informal and formal sessions. What else are they doing now on the streets and at the corners except urging the bill of the tribunes and voting for the repeal of the law? Give loose rein to their uncontrollable nature and to this untamed creature and expect that they will themselves set bounds to their licence; unless you act, this is the least of the things enjoined upon women by custom or law and to which they submit with a feeling of injustice. It is complete liberty or, rather, if we wish to speak the truth, complete licence that they desire.

"If they win in this, what will they not attempt? Review all the laws with which your forefathers restrained their licence and made them subject to their husbands; even with all these bonds you can scarcely control them. What of this? If you suffer them to seize these bonds one by one and wrench themselves free and finally to be placed on a parity with their husbands, do you think that you will be able to endure them? The moment they begin to be your equals, they will be your superiors. . . . "

The next day an even greater crowd of women appeared in public, and all of them in a body beset the doors of those tribunes, who were vetoing their colleagues' proposal, and they did not desist until the threat of veto was withdrawn by the tribunes. After that there was no question that all the tribes would vote to repeal the law. The law was repealed twenty years after it was passed.

From *Livy*, trans. by Evan T. Stage (Cambridge, Mass.: Harvard University Press, 1935), XXXIV, i–iii; viii, pp. 413–419, 439.

Civilization in the Early Roman Republic: Greek Influence

Among the most important changes wrought by Roman expansion overseas were those in the Roman style of life and thought brought about by close and continued association with the Greeks of the Hellenistic world. Attitudes toward the Greeks themselves ranged from admiration for their culture and history to contempt for their constant squabbling, their commercial practices, and their weakness. Such Roman aristocrats as the Scipios surrounded themselves with Greek intellectuals, like the historian Polybius (ca. 203–ca. 123 B.C.E.) and the philosopher Panaetius (ca. 185–ca. 110 B.C.E.). Conservatives, such as Cato, might speak contemptuously of the Greeks as "Greeklings" (*Graeculi*), but even he learned Greek and absorbed Greek culture.

Religion

Roman religion was influenced by the Greeks almost from the beginning; the Romans identified their own gods with Greek equivalents and incorporated Greek mythology into their own. For the most part, however, Roman religious practice remained simple and Italian, until the third century B.C.E. brought important new influences from the east. In 205 B.C.E. the Senate approved the public worship of Cybele, the Great Mother goddess from Asia Minor. Hers was a fertility cult accompanied by ecstatic, frenzied, and sensual rites that so shocked and outraged conservative Romans that they soon banned the cult to Romans. Similarly, the Senate banned the worship of Dionysus, or Bacchus, in 186 B.C.E. In the second century B.C.E. interest in Babylonian astrology also grew, and the Senate's attempt in 139 B.C.E. to expel the "Chaldaeans," as the astrologers were called, did not prevent the continued influence of their superstition.

Education

Education was entirely the responsibility of the Roman family, the fathers teaching their own sons at home. It is not clear whether girls received any education in early Rome, although they certainly did later on. The boys learned to read, write, and calculate, as well as how to farm. They memorized the Twelve Tables, Rome's earliest code of law; learned how to perform religious rites; heard stories of the great deeds of early Roman history and particularly those of their ancestors; and engaged in the physical training appropriate for potential soldiers. This course of study was practical, vocational, and

This carved relief from the second century C.E. shows a schoolmaster and his pupils. The one at the right is arriving late. [Rheinisches Landesmuseum, Trien, Germany/Alinari/Art Resource, N.Y.]

moral. It aimed at making the boys moral, pious, patriotic, law-abiding, and respectful of tradition.

Contact with the Greeks of southern Italy produced momentous changes. Greek teachers came to Rome and introduced the study of language, literature, and philosophy, as well as the idea of a liberal education, or what the Romans called *humanitas*, the root of our concept of the humanities. This education emphasized broad intellectual training, critical thinking, an interest in ideas, and the development of a well-rounded person.

The first need was to learn Greek, for Rome did not yet have a literature of its own. Schools were established in which the teacher, called a *grammaticus*, taught his students the Greek language and its literature, particularly the works of Homer. Thereafter, educated Romans were expected to be bilingual. Roman boys of the upper classes then studied rhetoric—the art of speaking and writing well—with Greeks who were expert in it. The Greeks considered rhetoric less important than philosophy. But the more practical Romans took to it avidly, for it was of great use in legal disputes and was becoming ever more valuable in political life.

Some Romans, however, felt that the new learning would weaken Roman moral fiber. They were able to pass laws expelling philosophers and teachers of rhetoric. But these reactionary attempts failed. The new education suited the needs of the Romans of the second century B.C.E., who found themselves changing from a rural to an urban society and who were being thrust into the sophisticated world of the Hellenistic Greeks.

By the last century of the Roman republic the new Hellenized education had become dominant. Latin literature had come into being along with Latin translations of Greek poets, which formed part of the course of study. The Greek language and literature were still central to the curriculum. Many schools were established, and the number of educated people grew, extending beyond the senatorial class and outside Rome to the cities of Italy.

Girls of the upper classes were educated similarly to boys, at least through the earlier stages. They were probably taught by tutors at home rather than going to school. Young women did not study with philosophers and rhetoricians, for they were usually married by the age when the men were pursuing their higher education. Still, some women found ways to continue their education. Some became prose writers or poets. By the first century C.E. there were apparently enough learned women to provoke the complaints of a crotchety and conservative satirist:

Still more exasperating is the woman who begs as soon as she sits down to dinner, to discourse on poets and poetry, comparing Virgil with Homer; professors, critics, lawyers, auctioneers—even another woman—can't get a word in. She rattles on at such a rate that you'd think that all the pots and pans in the kitchen were crashing to the floor or that every bell in town was clanging. All by herself she makes as much noise as some primitive tribe chasing away an eclipse. She should learn the philosopher's lesson: "moderation is necessary even for intellectuals." And, if she still wants to appear educated and eloquent, let her dress as a man, sacrifice to men's gods and bathe in the men's baths. Wives shouldn't try to be public speakers; they shouldn't use rhetorical devices; they shouldn't read all the classics—there should be some things women don't understand. I myself cannot understand a woman who can quote the rules of grammar and never make a mistake and cites obscure, long-forgotten poets—as if men cared about such things. If she has to correct somebody let her correct her girl friends and leave her husband alone.[3]

[3]Juvenal, *Satires* 6.434–456, trans. by Roger Killian, Richard Lynch, Robert J. Rowland, and John Sims, cited by Sarah B. Pomeroy in *Goddesses, Whores, Wives, and Slaves* (New York: Schocken, 1975), p. 172.

A rich and ambitious Roman could support a Greek philosopher in his own home, so that his son could acquire through conversation the learning and polished thought necessary for the fully cultured gentleman. Some, like the great orator Cicero (106–43 B.C.E.), traveled to Greece to study with great teachers of rhetoric and philosophy. This style of education broadened the Romans' understanding and made them a part of the older and wider culture of the Hellenistic world, a world they had come to dominate and needed to understand.

Roman Imperialism

Rome's expansion in Italy and overseas was accomplished without a grand general plan. The new territories were acquired as a result of wars that the Romans believed were either defensive or preventive. Their foreign policy was aimed at providing security for Rome on Rome's terms, but these terms were often unacceptable to other nations and led to continued conflict. Whether intended or not, Rome's expansion brought the Romans an empire, and with it, power, wealth, and responsibilities (see Map 5–3).

Aftermath of Conquest

War and expansion changed the economic, social, and political life of Italy. Before the Punic Wars most Italians owned their own farms, which provided most of the family's needs. The Second Punic War did terrible damage to Italian farmland. Many veterans found it impossible or unprofitable to go back to their farms. Some moved to Rome to work as occasional laborers, but most stayed in the country as tenant farmers or hired hands. No longer landowners, they were also no longer eligible for the army. Often the land they abandoned was acquired by the wealthy who converted these farms, later called *latifundia*, into large plantations for growing cash crops—grain, olives, and grapes for wine—or into cattle ranches.

The upper classes had plenty of capital to stock and operate these estates as a result of profits from the war and from exploiting the provinces. Land was cheap, and slaves conquered in war provided cheap labor. By fair means and foul, large landholders obtained sizable quantities of public land and forced small farmers off it. These changes separated the people of Rome and Italy more sharply into rich and poor, landed and landless, privileged and deprived. The result was

This wall painting from the first century B.C.E. comes from the villa of Publius Fannius Synistor at Pompeii and shows a woman playing a cithera. [The Metropolitan Museum of Art, Rogers Fund, 1903 (Acc. # 03.14.5) © 1986 The Metropolitan Museum of Art]

political, social, and ultimately constitutional conflict that threatened the republic.

The Gracchi

By the middle of the second century B.C.E. the problems caused by Rome's rapid expansion troubled perceptive Roman nobles. The fall in status of the peasant farmers made it harder to recruit soldiers and came to present a political threat as well. The patron's traditional control over his clients was weakened by their flight from their land. Even those former landowners who worked on the land of their patrons as tenants or hired hands were less reliable. The introduction of the secret ballot in the 130s B.C.E. made them even more independent.

Tiberius Gracchus (168–133 B.C.E.) tried to solve these problems. He became tribune in 133 B.C.E. on a program of land reform. The program aroused great hostility. When Tiberius put it before the tribal assembly, another tribune interposed his veto. Unwilling to give up, Tiberius put his bill before the tribal assembly again. Again it was vetoed, so Tiberius, strongly supported by the people, had the offending tribune removed from office, thereby violating the constitution.

Tiberius then proposed a second bill, harsher than the first and more appealing to the people, for he had despaired of conciliating the Senate. There could be no compromise: Either Tiberius or the Roman constitution must go under.

Tiberius understood the danger he would face if he stepped down from the tribunate, so he announced his candidacy for a second successive term, another blow at tradition. At the elections a riot broke out, and a mob of senators and their clients killed Tiberius and some 300 of his followers and threw their bodies into the Tiber River. The Senate had put down the threat to its rule, but at the price of the first internal bloodshed in Roman political history.

The tribunate of Tiberius Gracchus permanently changed Roman politics. Heretofore, politics had generally involved struggles for honor and reputation between great families or coalitions of such families. Fundamental issues were rarely at stake. The revolutionary proposals of Tiberius, however, and the senatorial resort to bloodshed created a new situation.

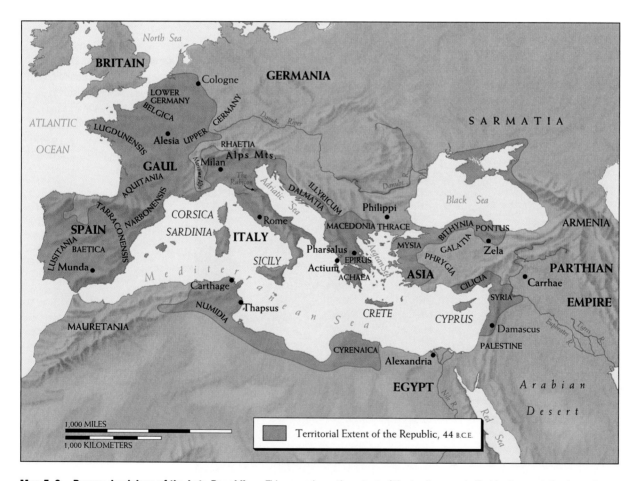

Map 5–3   Roman dominions of the Late Republic.   This map shows the extent of the territory controlled by Rome at the time of Caesar's death in 44 B.C.E.

The Ruin of the Roman Family Farm and the Gracchan Reforms

The independent family farm was the backbone of the early Roman Republic. Rome's conquests, the long wars that kept the citizen-soldier away from his farm, and the availability of numerous slaves at a low price, however, badly undercut the traditional way of farming and with it the foundations of republican society. In the following passage Plutarch describes the process of agricultural change and the response to it of the reformer Tiberius Gracchus, tribune in 133 B.C.E.

What were the causes of the troubles faced by Roman farmers? What were the social and political consequences of the changes in agricultural life? What solution did Tiberius Gracchus propose? Can you think of any reasons, besides selfishness and greed, that people might oppose his plan?

Of the territory which the Romans won in war from their neighbours, a part they sold, and a part they made common land, and assigned it for occupation to the poor and indigent among the citizens, on payment of a small rent into the public treasury. And when the rich began to offer larger rents and drove out the poor, a law was enacted forbidding the holding by one person of more than five hundred acres of land. For a short time this enactment gave a check to the rapacity of the rich, and was of assistance to the poor, who remained in their places on the land which they had rented and occupied the allotment which each had held from the outset. But later on the neighbouring rich men, by means of fictitious personages, transferred these rentals to themselves, and finally held most of the land openly in their own names. Then the poor, who had been ejected from their land, no longer showed themselves eager for military service, and neglected the bringing up of children, so that soon all Italy was conscious of a dearth of freemen, and was filled with gangs of foreign slaves, by whose aid the rich cultivated their estates, from which they had driven away the free citizens. . . .

And it is thought that a law dealing with injustice and rapacity so great was never drawn up in milder and gentler terms. For men who ought to have been punished for their disobedience and to have surrendered with payment of a fine the land which they were illegally enjoying, these men it merely ordered to abandon their injust acquisitions upon being paid their value, and to admit into ownership of them such citizens as needed assistance. But although the rectification of the wrong was so considerate, the people were satisfied to let bygones be bygones if they could be secure from such wrong in the future; the men of wealth and substance, however, were led by their greed to hate the law, and by their wrath and contentiousness to hate the lawgiver, and tried to dissuade the people by alleging that Tiberius was introducing a re-distribution of land for the confusion of the body politic, and was stirring up a general revolution.

From Plutarch, "Tiberius Gracchus," in *Lives 8–9*, vol. 10, trans. by Bernadotte Perrin and William Heinemann (London: G. P. Putnam's Sons, New York, 1921), pp. 159–167.

From then on Romans could pursue a political career that was not based solely on influence within the aristocracy; pressure from the people might be an effective substitute. In the last century of the republic such politicians were called *populares*, whereas those who supported the traditional role of the Senate were called *optimates* ("the best men").

The tribunate of Gaius Gracchus (c. 159–121 B.C.E.) brother of Tiberius, was much more dangerous to the Senate than that of Tiberius because all the tribunes of 123 B.C.E. were Gaius's supporters. There could be no veto, and tribunes could now be reelected. Gaius appealed to a variety of groups. He proposed to establish new colonies for landless veterans: two in Italy and one on the old site of Carthage. Among other popular acts, he put through a law stabilizing the price of grain in Rome.

Gaius also appealed to the equestrian order in his struggle against the Senate. The equestrians were rich men who could qualify to serve in the Roman cavalry, the most expensive form of military service. Many supplied goods and services to the Roman state and collected its taxes in the provinces. These wealthy men usually had the same outlook as the Senate; generally they used their profits to purchase land and to try to reach senatorial rank themselves. Still, they had a special interest in Roman expansion and in the exploitation of the provinces. When Pergamum became the Roman province of Asia in 129 B.C.E. Gaius gave them the right to collect taxes there.

Gaius easily won reelection as tribune for 122 B.C.E. He aimed at giving citizenship to the Italians, both to resolve their dissatisfaction and to add them to his political coalition. But the common people did not want to share the advantages of Roman citizenship, and the Senate seized on this proposal to drive a wedge between Gaius and his supporters.

The Romans did not reelect Gaius in 121 B.C.E., and a hostile consul provoked an incident that led to violence. The Senate established martial law. Gaius was hunted down and killed, and some 3,000 of his followers were put to death without trial.

Marius and Sulla

Before long the senatorial oligarchy faced more serious dangers arising from troubles abroad. Jugurtha (d. 104 B.C.E.) became king of Numidia, a client kingdom of Rome near Carthage, and his massacre of Roman and Italian businessmen in Numidia gained Roman attention. Pressure from the equestrians and the people forced the declaration of what became known as the Jugurthine War in 111 B.C.E.

The war dragged on until the people elected Gaius Marius (157–86 B.C.E.) to the consulship for 107 B.C.E., and the assembly, usurping the role of the Senate, assigned him to the province of Numidia. Marius was a *novus homo*, a "new man"—that is, the first in the history of his family to reach the consulship. He was outside the closed circle of the old Roman aristocracy and a political maverick.

Marius quickly defeated Jugurtha, but Jugurtha escaped and guerrilla warfare continued. Finally, Marius's subordinate, Lucius Cornelius Sulla (138–78 B.C.E.), trapped Jugurtha and brought the war to an end. Marius celebrated the victory, but Sulla, an ambitious but impoverished descendant of an old Roman family, resented being cheated of the credit. The seeds were planted for a personal rivalry that would last until Marius's death.

While the Romans were fighting Jugurtha, a far greater danger from barbarians threatened Rome from the north. To meet the danger, the Romans elected Marius to his second consulship when these tribes threatened again. He served five consecutive terms from 104 B.C.E. until 100 B.C.E.

Marius made important changes in the army. He began using volunteers, mostly the dispossessed farmers and rural proletarians whose problems had not been solved by the Gracchi. They enlisted for a long term of service and looked on the army as an opportunity and a career. They became semiprofessional clients of their general and sought guaranteed food, clothing, shelter, and booty from victories. They came to expect land as a form of mustering-out pay or veteran's bonus when they retired. Volunteers were most likely to join a man who was a capable soldier and influential enough to obtain what they wanted. They looked to him rather than to the state for their rewards. He, on the other hand, had to obtain grants from the Senate if he was to maintain his power and reputation.

Marius's innovation created both the opportunity and the necessity for military leaders to gain enough power to challenge civilian authority. The promise of rewards won these leaders the personal loyalty of their troops that allowed them to frighten the Senate into granting their demands.

War Against the Italian Allies (90–88 B.C.E.)

For a decade Rome ignored Italian discontent. In frustration, the Italians revolted and established a separate confederation with its own capital and its own coinage.

Employing the traditional device of divide and conquer, the Romans immediately offered citizenship to those cities that remained loyal and soon made the same offer to the rebels if they laid down their arms. By 88 B.C.E. the war against the allies was over. All the Italians became Roman citizens with the protections that citizenship offered, but they retained local self-government and a dedication to their own municipalities that made Italy flourish. The passage of time blurred the distinction between Romans and Italians and forged them into a single nation.

Sulla's Dictatorship

Sulla had performed well during the war against the allies, and he was elected consul for 88 B.C.E. A champion of senatorial control, he won a civil war against Marius and his friends. He now held all power and had himself appointed dictator to reconstitute the state. He had enough power to make himself the permanent ruler of Rome. Yet he was traditional enough to want to restore senatorial government, reformed to prevent the misfortunes of the past.

Sulla retired to a life of ease and luxury in 79 B.C.E. He could not, however, undo the effect of his own example: a general using the loyalty of his own troops to take power and massacre his opponents, as well as innocent people. These actions proved to be far more significant than his constitutional arrangements.

Fall of the Republic

Pompey, Crassus, and Caesar

Within a year of Sulla's death, his constitution came under assault. Marcus Licinius Crassus (115–53 B.C.E.) and Cnaeus Pompey (106–48 B.C.E.) were ambitious men whom the Senate feared. Both demanded special honors and election to the consulship for the year 70 B.C.E. They both won election and repealed most of Sulla's constitution. This led to further attacks on senatorial control and to collaboration between ambitious generals and demagogic tribunes.

In 67 B.C.E. a special law gave Pompey *imperium* for three years over the entire Mediterranean and fifty miles in from the coast. He also was given the power to raise great quantities of troops and money to rid the area of pirates. His power was then extended to fight a war that had broken out in Asia Minor. When he returned to Rome in 62 B.C.E. he had more power, prestige, and popular support than any Roman in history. The Senate and his personal enemies feared that he might emulate Sulla and establish his own rule.

Crassus had the most reason to fear Pompey's return. Although rich and influential, he did not have the confidence of the Senate, a firm political base of his own, or the kind of military glory needed to rival Pompey. During the 60s B.C.E., therefore, he allied himself with various popular leaders. The ablest of these men was Gaius Julius Caesar (100–44 B.C.E.), a descendant of an old but politically obscure patrician family.

First Triumvirate

To general surprise, Pompey disbanded his army, celebrated a great triumph, and returned to private life. He had achieved amazing things for Rome and simply wanted the Senate to approve his excellent arrangements in the east and to give land to his veterans. But the jealous and fearful Senate refused. Pompey was thus driven to an alliance with his natural enemies, Crassus and Caesar. So was born the First Triumvirate, an informal agreement among three Roman politicians, each seeking his private goals, that further undermined the future of the Republic.

Dictatorship of Julius Caesar

Caesar was rewarded with election to the consulship for 59 B.C.E. The Triumvirate's program was quickly enacted, and Caesar got the extraordinary command that would give him a chance to earn the glory and power with which to rival Pompey: the governorship of Illyricum and Gaul for five years.

Caesar was now free in Gaul to seek the military success he craved. By the time he was ready to return, after conquering the province and consolidating his gains, the Triumvirate had dissolved and a crisis was at hand. At Carrhae in 53 B.C.E. Crassus died trying to conquer the Parthians. Pompey joined the Senate in opposing Caesar.

Early in January of 49 B.C.E. the more extreme faction in the Senate ordered Pompey to defend the state and Caesar to lay down his command. For Caesar this meant exile or death, so he ordered his legions to cross the Rubicon River, the boundary of his province. This action was the first act of a civil war that ended in 45 B.C.E. when Caesar defeated the last of the enemy forces under Pompey's sons at Munda in Spain. As dictator Caesar, in Shakespeare's words, bestrode "the narrow world like a Colossus."

Caesar's innovations generally sought to make rational and orderly what was traditional and chaotic. His reforms also tended to elevate Italians and even provincials at the expense of the old Roman families, most of whom were his political enemies.

Caesar made few changes in the government of Rome, but his monopoly of military power made the whole structure a sham. He treated the Senate as his creature, sometimes with disdain. His enemies were quick to accuse him of aiming at monarchy and conspired against him. On March 15, 44 B.C.E., Caesar was stabbed to death in the Senate. The assassins regarded themselves as heroic "tyrannicides" and had no clear plan of action. No doubt they simply expected the republic

Fall of the Roman Republic	
133 B.C.E.	Tribunate of Tiberius Gracchus
123–122 B.C.E.	Tribunate of Gaius Gracchus
111–105 B.C.E.	Jugurthine War
104–100 B.C.E.	Consecutive consulships of Marius
90–88 B.C.E.	War against the Italian allies
70 B.C.E.	Consulship of Crassus and Pompey
60 B.C.E.	Formation of First Triumvirate
58–50 B.C.E.	Caesar in Gaul
53 B.C.E.	Crassus killed in Battle of Carrhae
49 B.C.E.	Caesar crosses Rubicon; civil war begins
46–44 B.C.E.	Caesar's dictatorship
45 B.C.E.	End of civil war
43 B.C.E.	Formation of Second Triumvirate
42 B.C.E.	Battle of Philippi
31 B.C.E.	Octavian defeats Antony at Actium

to be restored in the old way, but things had gone too far for that. Instead thirteen years more of civil war ensued, at the end of which the republic received its final burial.

Second Triumvirate and the Emergence of Octavian

Caesar's heir was his grandnephew, Octavian (63 B.C.E.–14 C.E.), a youth of eighteen. He joined Marcus Antonius (Mark Antony) (ca. 83–30 B.C.E.) and Lepidus (d. 13 B.C.E.), two of Caesar's officers, in the Second Triumvirate to fight the assassins. The new triumvirs defeated the enemy at Philippi in 42 B.C.E., but they soon quarreled among themselves. Octavian gained control of the western part of the empire. Antonius, together with Cleopatra (r. 51–30 B.C.E.), queen of Egypt, ruled the east. In 31 B.C.E. the forces of Octavian crushed the fleet and army of Antony and Cleopatra at Actium, resolving the conflict.

The civil wars were over, and at the age of thirty-two Octavian was absolute master of the Mediterranean world. His power was enormous, but so was the task before him. He had to restore peace, prosperity, and confidence, all of which required a constitution that would reflect the new realities without offending unduly the traditional republican prejudices that still had so firm a grip on Rome and Italy.

The Augustan Principate

If the problems facing Octavian after the Battle of Actium were great, so too were his resources for addressing them. He was the master of a vast military force, the only one in the

This statue of Emperor Augustus (r. 27 B.C.E.–14 C.E.), now in the Vatican, stood in the villa of Augustus's wife Livia. The figures on the elaborate breastplate are all of symbolic significance. At the top, for example, Dawn in her chariot brings in a new day under the protective mantle of the sky god; in the center, Tiberius, Augustus's successor, accepts the return of captured Roman army standards from a barbarian prince; and at the bottom, Mother Earth offers a horn of plenty. [Charitable Foundation, Leonard von Matt]

Roman world, and he had loyal and capable assistants. Yet the memory of Julius Caesar's fate was still clear in Octavian's mind; it was dangerous to flaunt unprecedented powers and to disregard all republican traditions.

Octavian's constitutional solution proved to be successful and lasting, subtle and effective. Behind the republican trappings and the apparent sharing of authority with the Senate, the government of Octavian, like that of his successors, was a monarchy. All real power—both civil and military—lay with the ruler, whether he was called by the unofficial title of "first citizen" (*princeps*) like Octavian, who was the founder of the regime, or "emperor" (*imperator*) like those who followed.

On January 13, 27 B.C.E., he put forward a new plan in dramatic style, coming before the Senate to give up all his powers and provinces. In what was surely a rehearsed response, the Senate begged him to reconsider, and at last he agreed to accept the provinces of Spain, Gaul, and Syria with proconsular power for military command and to retain the consulship in Rome. The Senate would govern the other provinces as before. Because his provinces contained twenty of the twenty-six legions, his true power was undiminished, but the Senate responded with almost hysterical gratitude, voting him many honors. Among them was the semireligious title "Augustus," which connoted veneration, majesty, and holiness. Historians thus speak of Rome's first emperor as Augustus and of his regime as the Principate. This would have pleased him, for it helps conceal the novel, unrepublican nature of the regime and the naked power on which it rested.

Administration

Augustus made important changes in the government of Rome, Italy, and the provinces, intending to reduce inefficiency and corruption, eliminate the threat to peace and order by ambitious individuals, and reduce the distinction between Romans and Italians, senators and equestrians. Augustus controlled the elections and saw to it that promising young men, whatever their origin, served the state as administrators and provincial governors. Thus, many equestrians and Italians who had no connection with the Roman aristocracy entered the Senate, which Augustus was always careful to treat with respect and honor.

The Augustan period was one of great prosperity, based on the wealth that Augustus had brought in by the conquest of Egypt, on the great increase in commerce and industry made possible by general peace and a vast program of public works, and on a revival of successful small farming by Augustus's resettled veterans.

The union of political and military power in the hands of the princeps enabled him to install rational, efficient, and stable government in the provinces for the first time.

The Army and Defense

Under Augustus, members of the armed forces became true professionals. Enlistment, chiefly by Italians, was for twenty years, but the pay was relatively good, and there were occasional bonuses and the promise of a pension on retirement in the form of money or land. Together with the auxiliaries from the provinces, these forces formed a frontier army of about 300,000 men. This was barely enough to hold the line. The Roman army permanently based in the provinces brought Roman culture to the natives. The soldiers spread their language and customs, often marrying local women and settling down there. They attracted merchants, who often became the nuclei of new towns and cities that became centers of Roman civilization. As time passed, the provincials on the frontiers became Roman citizens and helped strengthen Rome's defenses against the barbarians outside.

Religion and Morality

A century of political strife and civil war had undermined the foundations of traditional Roman society. Augustus undertook to preserve and restore the traditional values of the family and religion in Rome and Italy. He curbed adultery and divorce and encouraged early marriage and the procreation of legitimate children.

Augustus also worked to restore the dignity of formal Roman religion, building many temples, reviving old cults, and reorganizing and invigorating the priestly colleges; he also banned the worship of newly introduced foreign gods. During his lifetime he did not accept divine honors, although he was deified after his death; as with Julius Caesar, a state cult was dedicated to his worship.

Civilization of the Ciceronian and Augustan Ages

The high point of Roman culture came in the last century of the republic and during the Principate of Augustus. While Greek rhetoric, philosophy, and literature served as the mod-els for Roman writers and artists, the art and writing of both periods show uniquely Roman qualities in spirit and sometimes in form.

The Late Republic

Cicero (106–43 B.C.E.) The towering literary figure of the late republic was Cicero. He is most famous for his orations delivered in the law courts and the Senate. Together with many of his private letters, the speeches give us a clearer and fuller insight into his mind than the works of any other figure in antiquity. We see the political life of his period largely through his eyes. He also wrote treatises on rhetoric, ethics, and politics that put Greek philosophical ideas into Latin terminology and also changed them to suit Roman conditions and values.

Cicero believed in a world governed by divine and natural law that human reason could perceive and human institutions reflect. He looked to law, custom, and tradition to produce both stability and liberty. His literary style, as well as his values and ideas, was an important legacy for the Middle Ages and, reinterpreted, for the Renaissance.

Law The period from the Gracchi to the fall of the Republic was important in the development of Roman law. Before that time Roman law was essentially national and had developed chiefly by means of juridical decisions, case by case, but contact with foreign peoples and the influence of Greek ideas forced a change. From the last century of the republic on, the edicts of the *praetors*, which interpreted and even changed and added to existing law, had increasing importance in developing the Roman legal code. Quite early the edicts of the magistrates who dealt with foreigners developed the idea of the *jus gentium*, or "law of peoples," as opposed to that arising strictly from the experience of the Romans. In the first century B.C.E. the influence of Greek thought made the idea of *jus gentium* identical to that of the *jus naturale*, or "natural law," taught by the Stoics. It was this view of a world ruled by divine reason that Cicero enshrined in his treatise on the laws, *De Legibus*.

Poetry This was also the period of two of Rome's greatest poets, Lucretius and Catullus, each representing a different aspect of Rome's poetic tradition. The Hellenistic poets and literary theorists saw two functions for the poet, as entertainer and as teacher. They thought the best poet combined both roles, and the Romans adopted the same view. Lucretius (ca. 99–ca. 55 B.C.E.) pursued this path in his epic poem *De Rerum Natura (On the Nature of Things)*. In it, he set forth the scientific and philosophical ideas of Epicurus and Democritus with the zeal of a missionary trying to save society from fear and superstition. He knew that his doctrine might be bitter medicine to the reader: "That is why I have tried to administer it to you in the dulcet strains of poesy, coated with the sweet honey of the Muses."[4]

Catullus (ca. 84–ca. 54 B.C.E.) was thoroughly different. His poems were personal, even autobiographical. He wrote of the joys and pains of love, he hurled invective at important contemporaries like Julius Caesar, and he amused himself in witty poetic exchanges. He offered no moral lessons and was not interested in Rome's glorious history and in contemporary politics. In a sense, he is an example of the proud, independent, pleasure-seeking nobleman who characterized part of the aristocracy at the end of the republic.

Age of Augustus

The spirit of the Augustan Age, the Golden Age of Roman literature, reflected the new conditions of society. The old aristocratic order, with its system of independent nobles following their own particular interests, was gone. So was the world of poets of the lower orders, receiving patronage from individual aristocrats. Augustus replaced the complexity of republican patronage with a simple scheme in which all patronage flowed from the *princeps*, usually through his chief cultural adviser, Maecenas (d. 8 B.C.E.).

Two of the major poets of this time, Virgil and Horace, had lost their property during the civil wars. The patronage of the *princeps* allowed them the leisure and the security to write poetry and also made them dependent on him and limited their freedom of expression. They wrote on subjects that were useful for his policies and that glorified him and his family, but they were not mere propagandists. For the most part, they were persuaded of the virtues of Augustus and his reign and sincerely sang its praises. Because they were poets of genius, they were also able to maintain some independence in their work.

Virgil   Virgil (70–19 B.C.E.) was the most important of the Augustan poets. His greatest work is the *Aeneid,* a long national epic that placed the history of Rome in the great tradition of the Greeks and the Trojan War. Its hero, the Trojan Aeneas, personifies the ideal Roman qualities of duty, responsibility, serious purpose, and patriotism. As the Romans' equivalent to Homer, Virgil glorified not the personal honor and excellence of the Greek epic heroes, but the civic greatness represented by Augustus and the peace and prosperity that he and the Julian family had given to imperial Rome.

Horace   Horace (65–8 B.C.E.) was won over to the Augustan cause by the patronage of Maecenas and by the attractions of the Augustan reforms. His great skills as a lyric poet

are best revealed in his *Odes,* which are ingenious in their adaptation of Greek meters to the requirements of Latin verse. Two of the *Odes* are directly in praise of Augustus, and many of them glorify the new Augustan order, the imperial family, and the empire.

Ovid   The darker side of Augustan influence on the arts is revealed by the career of Ovid (43 B.C.E.–18 C.E.). He wrote light and entertaining love elegies that reveal the sophistication and the loose sexual code of a notorious sector of the Roman aristocracy. Their values and way of life were contrary to the seriousness and family-centered life that Augustus was trying to foster. Ovid's *Ars Amatoria,* a poetic textbook on the art of seduction, angered Augustus and was partly responsible for the poet's exile in 8 C.E. His most popular work is *Metamorphoses,* a kind of mythological epic that turns Greek myths into charming stories in a graceful and lively style. Ovid's fate was an effective warning to later poets.

History   The most important and influential prose writer of the time was Livy (59 B.C.E.–17 C.E.). His *History of Rome* treated the period from the legendary origins of Rome until 9 B.C.E. Only one fourth of his work survives; of the rest we have only pitifully brief summaries. He based his history on earlier accounts, and made no effort at original research. His great achievement was to tell the story of Rome in a continuous and impressive narrative. Its purpose was moral—setting up historical models as examples of good and bad behavior—and, above all, patriotic. He glorified Rome's greatness and connected it with Rome's past, just as Augustus tried to do.

Architecture and Sculpture   Augustus was the great patron of the visual arts, as he was of literature. He embarked on a building program that beautified Rome, glorified his reign, and contributed to the general prosperity and his own popularity. Most of the building was influenced by the Greek classical style, which aimed at serenity and the ideal type. The greatest monument of the age is the Altar of Peace (*Ara Pacis*), dedicated in 9 B.C.E. Its walls show a procession in which Augustus and his family appear to move forward, followed by the magistrates, the Senate, and the people of Rome. There is no better symbol of the new order.

Peace and Prosperity: Imperial Rome (14–180 C.E.)

Augustus tried to cloak the monarchical nature of his government, but his successors soon abandoned all pretense. The rulers came to be called *imperator*—from which comes our word *emperor*—as well as *Caesar.* The latter title signified

---

[4]Lucretius, *De Rerum Natura,* lines 931 ff. (New York: Oxford University Press, 1922).

A panel from the Ara Pacis (Altar of Peace). The altar was dedicated in 9 B.C.E. It was part of a propaganda campaign—involving poetry, architecture, myth, and history—that Augustus undertook to promote himself as the savior of Rome and the restorer of peace. This panel shows the goddess Earth and her children with cattle, sheep, and other symbols of agricultural wealth. [Nimatallah/Art Resource, N.Y.]

connection with the imperial house, and the former indicated the military power on which their authority was based. Because Augustus was ostensibly only the "first citizen" of a restored republic and his powers were theoretically voted him by the Senate and the people, he could not legally name his successor. In fact, he plainly designated his heirs by favors lavished on them and by giving them a share in the imperial power and responsibility (see Map 5–4).

Tiberius (emperor 14–37 C.E.), his immediate successor, was at first embarrassed by the ambiguity of his new role, but soon the monarchical and hereditary nature of the regime became patent. Gaius (Caligula, 37–41 C.E.), Claudius (41–54 C.E.), and Nero (54–68 C.E.) were all descended from Augustus's family. The year 69, however, saw four different emperors assume power in quick succession as different Roman armies took turns placing their commanders on the throne.

Vespasian (69–79 C.E.) emerged victorious from the chaos, and his sons, Titus (79–81 C.E.) and Domitian (81–96 C.E.), carried forward his line, the Flavian dynasty. Vespasian was the first emperor who did not come from the old Roman nobility.

The Flavian dynasty ended with the assassination of Domitian. Because Domitian had no close relative who had been designated as successor, the Senate put Nerva (96–98 C.E.) on the throne to avoid chaos. He was the first of the five "good emperors," who included Trajan (98–117 C.E.), Hadrian (117–138 C.E.), Antoninus Pius (138–161 C.E.), and Marcus Aurelius (161–180 C.E.). Until Marcus Aurelius, none of these emperors had sons, so they each followed the example set by Nerva of adopting an able senator and establishing him as successor. The result was almost a century of peaceful succession and competent rule, which ended when Marcus Au-

relius allowed his incompetent son, Commodus (180–192 C.E.), to succeed him, with unfortunate results.

There was, of course, opposition to imperial rule. Plots and the suspicion of plots led to repression, the use of spies and paid informers, book burning, and executions. The opposition consisted chiefly of senators who looked back to republican liberty for their class. Plots and repression were most common under Nero and Domitian. From Nerva to Marcus Aurelius, however, the emperors, without yielding any power, enlisted the cooperation of the upper class by courteous and modest deportment.

Administration of the Empire

From an administrative and cultural standpoint, the empire was a collection of cities and towns. Roman policy during the Principate was to raise urban centers to the status of Roman municipalities with the rights and privileges attached to them. The Romans enlisted the upper classes of the provinces in their own government, spread Roman law and culture, and won the loyalty of the influential people.

As the bureaucracy became more efficient, so did the number and scope of its functions and therefore its size. The importance and autonomy of the municipalities shrank as the central administration took a greater part in local affairs. The price paid for the increased efficiency offered by centralized control was the loss of the vitality of the cities throughout the empire.

Augustus's successors accepted his conservative and defensive foreign policy. Trajan was the first emperor to take the offensive in a sustained way. Between 101 and 106 C.E. he established the new province of Dacia between the Danube

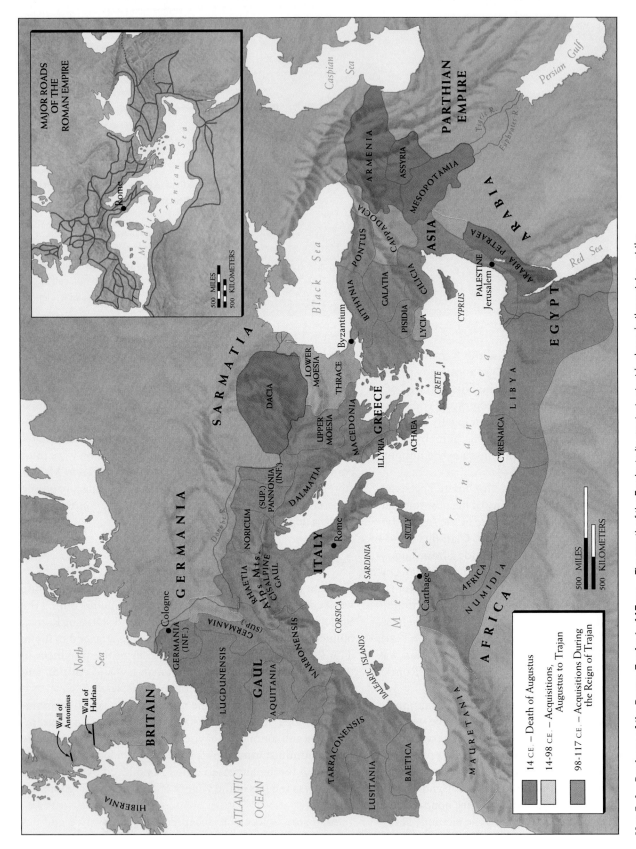

Map 5–4 Provinces of the Roman Empire to 117 C.E. The growth of the Empire to its greatest extent is shown in three states—at the death of Augustus in 14 B.C.E., at the death of Nerva in 98 C.E., and at the death of Trajan in 117 C.E. The division into provinces is also indicated. The inset outlines the main roads that tied the far-flung empire together.

Daily Life in a Roman Provincial Town: Graffiti from Pompeii

On the walls of the houses of Pompeii, buried and preserved by the eruption of Mount Vesuvius in 79 C.E., are many scribblings that give us an idea of what the life of ordinary people was like.

How do these graffiti differ from those one sees in a modern American city? What do they reveal about the similarities and differences between the ordinary people of ancient Rome and the people of today? How would you account for the differences?

I

Twenty pairs of gladiators of Decimus Lucretius Satrius Valens, lifetime flamen of Nero son of Caesar Augustus, and ten pairs of gladiators of Decimus Lucretius Valens, his son, will fight at Pompeii on April 8, 9, 10, 11, 12. There will be a full card of wild beast combats, and awnings [for the spectators]. Aemilius Celer [painted this sign], all alone in the moonlight.

II

Market days: Saturday in Pompeii, Sunday in Nuceria, Monday in Atella, Tuesday in Nola, Wednesday in Cumae, Thursday in Puteoli, Friday in Rome.

III

Pleasure says: "You can get a drink here for an as [a few cents], a better drink for two, Falernian for four."

IV

A copper pot is missing from this shop. 65 sesterces reward if anybody brings it back, 20 sesterces if he reveals the thief so we can get our property back.

V

The weaver Successus loves the innkeeper's slave girl, Iris by name. She doesn't care for him, but he begs her to take pity on him. Written by his rival. So long.

[Answer by the rival:] Just because you're bursting with envy, don't pick on a handsomer man, a lady-killer and a gallant.

[Answer by the first writer:] There's nothing more to say or write. You love Iris, who doesn't care for you.

VI

Take your lewd looks and flirting eyes off another man's wife, and show some decency on your face!

VII

Anybody in love, come here. I want to break Venus' ribs with a club and cripple the goddess' loins. If she can pierce my tender breast, why can't I break her head with a club?

VIII

I write at Love's dictation and Cupid's instruction;
But damn it! I don't want to be a god without you.

IX

[A prostitute's sign:] I am yours for 2 asses cash.

From *Roman Civilization*, edited by Naphtali Lewis and Meyer Reinhold. Copyright © 1955 by Columbia University Press. Reprinted with permission of the publisher.

and the Carpathian Mountains. He was tempted, no doubt, by its important gold mines, but he probably was also pursuing a new general strategy: to defend the empire more aggressively by driving wedges into enemy territory. The same strategy dictated the invasion of the Parthian Empire in the east (113–117 C.E.). Trajan's early success there was astonishing, but his lines were overextended. Rebellions sprang up, and the campaign crumbled. Trajan was forced to retreat and died before returning to Rome.

Hadrian kept Dacia but abandoned Trajan's eastern conquests. Under Hadrian the Roman defense became rigid, and initiative passed to the barbarians. Marcus Aurelius spent most of his reign resisting dangerous attacks in the east and on the Danube frontier, and these attacks put enormous pressure on the empire's resources.

Culture of the Early Empire

Literature In Latin literature, the years between the death of Augustus and the time of Marcus Aurelius are known as the Silver Age; as the name implies, work of high quality—although probably inferior to that of the Augustan era—was produced. The writers of the Silver Age were gloomy, negative, and pessimistic. Criticism and satire lurk everywhere in their work. Some of the most important writers of the Silver Age in the first century C.E. reflected the Stoic opposition's hostility to the growing power and personal excesses of the emperors.

The writers of the second century C.E. appear to have turned away from contemporary affairs and even recent history. Historical writing was about remote periods, so there

Spoils from the temple in Jerusalem were carried in triumphal procession by Roman troops. This relief from Titus's arch of victory in the Roman Forum celebrates his capture of Jerusalem after a two-year siege. The Jews found it difficult to reconcile their religion with Roman rule and frequently rebelled.

[Scala/Art Resource, N.Y.]

was less danger of irritating imperial sensibilities. Scholarship was encouraged, but we hear little of poetry, especially about any dealing with dangerous subjects.

During the third century C.E. romances written in Greek became popular as an escape from contemporary realities.

Architecture

The prosperity and relative stability of the first two centuries of imperial Rome allowed the full development of Roman architecture. To the fundamental styles of buildings developed by the Greeks, the Romans added little; the great public bath and a new, free-standing amphitheater were their main innovations.

The main contribution of the Romans lay in the size of the structures they could build and in the advances in engineering that made these large structures possible. To the basic post-and-lintel construction used by the Greeks, the Romans added the semicircular arch, borrowed from the Etruscans. They also made good use of concrete, a building material first used by the Hellenistic Greeks and fully developed by the Romans. The arch combined with the post and lintel produced the great Colosseum built by the Flavian emperors. When used internally in the form of vaults and domes, the arch permitted great buildings like the baths.

One of Rome's most famous buildings, the Pantheon, begun by Augustus's friend Agrippa (63–12 B.C.E.) and rebuilt by Hadrian, combines all these elements. Its portico of Corinthian columns is of Greek origin, but its rotunda of brick-faced concrete with its domed ceiling and relieving arches is thoroughly Roman. The new engineering also made possible the construction of more mundane but more useful structures like bridges and aqueducts.

Society

Seen from the harsh perspective of human history, the first two centuries of the Roman Empire deserve their reputation as a Golden Age, but by the second century C.E. troubles had arisen—troubles that foreshadowed the difficult times ahead. The literary efforts of the time reveal a flight from the present and from reality and the public realm to the past, to romance, and to private pursuits. Some of the same aspects may be seen in the more prosaic world of everyday life, especially in the decline of vitality in local government.

In the first century C.E. the upper classes vied for election to municipal office and for the honor of serving their communities. By the second century much of their zeal had disappeared, and the emperors had to correct abuses in local affairs and even force unwilling members of the ruling classes to accept public office. The reluctance to serve was caused largely by the imperial practice of holding magistrates and councilmen personally and collectively responsible for revenues that were due. Some magistrates even fled to avoid their office, a practice that eventually became widespread.

All of these difficulties reflected more basic problems. The prosperity brought by the end of civil war and the influx of wealth from the east, especially Egypt, could not sustain itself beyond the first half of the second century C.E. For reasons that remain mysterious the population also seems to have declined. The cost of government kept rising as the emperors were required to maintain an expensive standing army, to keep the people in Rome happy with "bread and circuses," to pay for an increasingly large bureaucracy, and to defend the frontiers against dangerous and determined enemies.

The Bar-Kochba *Rebellion: The Final Jewish Uprising Against Rome*

Unlike most conquered peoples the Jews found accommodation to Roman rule difficult. Their first rebellion was crushed by Vespasian's son, the future emperor Titus, in 70 C.E. At that time the Temple in Jerusalem was destroyed. A second revolt was put down in 117 C.E. Finally, when Hadrian ordered a Roman colony placed on the site of Jerusalem, Simon, who was called Bar Kochba, *or "Son of the Star," led a last uprising from 132 to 135. Dio Cassius describes the brutality of its suppression.*

Did the Romans treat the Jews differently from other people under their control? What special problems did the Roman conquest pose to the Jews? What problems did the Jews present to the Romans?

At Jerusalem Hadrian founded a city in place of the one which had been razed to the ground, naming it Aelia Capitolina, and on the site of the temple of the god he raised a new temple to Jupiter. This brought on a war of no slight importance nor of brief duration, for the Jews deemed it intolerable that foreign peoples should be settled in their city and foreign rites planted there. . . .

At first the Romans took no account of them. Soon, however, all Judea had been stirred up, and the Jews everywhere were showing signs of disturbance, were gathering together, and giving evidence of great hostility to the Romans, partly by secret and partly by overt acts; many outside peoples, too, were joining them through eagerness for gain, and the whole world, one might almost say, was being stirred up over the matter. Then, indeed, Hadrian sent his best generals against them. Foremost among these was Julius Sererus, who was dispatched against the Jews from Britain, where he was governor. . . . [In Judaea] he was able, rather slowly . . . but with comparatively little danger, to crush, exhaust, and exterminate them. Very few of them in fact survived. Fifty of their most important strongholds and 985 of their most famous villages were razed to the ground; 580,000 men were slain in the various raids and battles, and the number of those that perished by famine, disease, and fire was past finding out.

From Dio Cassius, *Roman History 59.* 12–14, trans, by Ernest Cary, London: Loeb Classical Library and William Heinemann, 1916.

The ever-increasing need for money compelled the emperors to raise taxes, to press hard on their subjects, and to cause inflation by debasing the coinage. These elements were to bring on the desperate crises that ultimately destroyed the empire.

Life in Imperial Rome: The Apartment House

The civilization of the Roman Empire depended on the vitality of its cities. While the typical city had about 20,000 inhabitants, Rome had more than 500,000, and some scholars think it may have had more than a million. Newcomers found Rome overwhelming and were either thrilled or horrified by its size, bustle, and noise.

The mass of its inhabitants were squeezed into increasingly tall multiple dwellings. Most Romans during the imperial period lived in apartment buildings called *insulae* ("islands") that rose to five or six stories and sometimes even more. The apartments were cramped and uncomfortable, hot in summer, cold in winter, and stuffy and smoky when the stoves were lit. These buildings were also dangerous. They were lightly built of concrete and brick, far too high for their foundations, and so they often collapsed. Even more serious was the threat of fire. The floors were supported by wooden beams, and the rooms were lit by torches, candles, and oil lamps and heated by braziers. Fires broke out easily but, without running water, were not easily put out; once started, they usually led to disaster.

When we compare these apartments to the attractive public places in the city, we can easily understand why the people of Rome spent most of their time outdoors.

Rise of Christianity

The story of how Christianity emerged, spread, survived, and ultimately conquered the Roman Empire is one of the most remarkable in history. Its origin among poor people from an unimportant and remote province of the empire gave little promise of what was to come. Christianity faced the hostility of the established religious institutions of its native Judea and had to compete not only against the official cults of Rome and the highly sophisticated philosophies of the educated classes, but also against "mystery" religions like the cults of Mithra, Isis, and Osiris. The Christians also faced the opposition of the imperial government and suffered formal persecution, yet Christianity finally became the official religion of the empire.

This is a reconstruction of a typical Roman apartment house found at Ostia, Rome's port. The ground floor contained shops, and the stories above it held many apartments. [Museo della Civilta Romana, Rome, Italy/Scala/Art Resource, N.Y.]

Jesus of Nazareth

An attempt to understand this amazing outcome must begin with a discussion of Jesus of Nazareth. The most important evidence of his life and teachings is in the Gospel accounts. Their authors believed that Jesus was the son of God and that he came into the world to redeem humanity and to bring immortality to those who believed in him and followed his way; to the Gospel writers, Jesus' resurrection was striking proof of his teachings. The Gospels also regard Jesus as a figure in history, and they recount events in his life as well as his sayings.

There is no reason to doubt that Jesus was born in the province of Judaea in the time of Augustus and that He was a most effective teacher in the tradition of the Jewish prophets. This tradition promised the coming of a Messiah (in Greek, *christos*—so *Jesus Christ* means "Jesus the Messiah"), the redeemer who would make Israel triumph over its enemies and establish the kingdom of God on earth. In fact, Jesus seems to have insisted that the Messiah would not establish an earthly kingdom but, at the Day of Judgment, would bring an end to the world as human beings knew it. On that day God would reward the righteous and condemn the wicked. Until that day, which his followers believed would come soon, Jesus taught the faithful to abandon sin and worldly concerns; to follow the moral code described in the Sermon on the Mount, which preached love, charity, and humility; and to believe in him and his divine mission.

Jesus won a considerable following, especially among the poor. This success caused great suspicion among the upper classes and provoked the hostility of the religious establishment in Jerusalem. They convinced the Roman governor that Jesus and his followers might be dangerous revolutionaries. He was put to death in Jerusalem by the cruel and degrading device of crucifixion, probably in 30 C.E. His followers believed that he was resurrected on the third day after his death, and that belief became a critical element in their religion.

Although the new belief spread quickly to the Jewish communities of Syria and Asia Minor, without the conversion and career of Saint Paul it might have had only a short life as a despised Jewish heresy.

Paul of Tarsus

Paul (?5–67 C.E.) was born Saul, a citizen of the city of Tarsus in Asia Minor. Even though he was trained in Hellenistic culture and was a Roman citizen, he was a zealous member of the Jewish sect known as the Pharisees, who were the strictest adherents of the Jewish law. He took a vigorous part in the persecution of the early Christians until his own conversion outside Damascus about 35 C.E. The great problem facing the early Christians was their relationship to Judaism. If the new faith was a version of Judaism, then it must adhere to the Jewish law and seek converts only among Jews. James, called the brother of Jesus, held that view, whereas Hellenist Jews tended to see Christianity as a new and universal religion.

Paul, converted and with his new name, supported the position of the Hellenists and soon won many converts among the gentiles. Paul believed it important that the followers of Jesus be evangelists ("messengers"), to spread the gospel ("good news") of God's gracious gift. He taught that Jesus would soon return for the Day of Judgment, and that all should believe in him and accept his way. Faith in Jesus as the

Christ was necessary but not sufficient for salvation, nor could good deeds alone achieve it. That final blessing of salvation was a gift of God's grace.

Organization

The new religion spread throughout the Roman Empire and even beyond its borders. It had its greatest success in the cities and among the poor and uneducated. The rites of the early communities appear to have been simple and few. Baptism by water removed original sin and permitted participation in the community and its activities. The central ritual was a common meal called the *agape* ("love feast"), followed by the ceremony of the *eucharist* ("thanksgiving"), a celebration of the Lord's Supper in which unleavened bread was eaten and unfermented wine drunk. There were also prayers, hymns, and readings from the Gospels.

At first the churches had little formal organization. Soon, it appears, affairs were placed in the hands of boards of *presbyters* ("elders") and *deacons* ("those who serve"). By the second century C.E., as their numbers grew, the Christians of each city tended to accept the authority and leadership of bishops (*episkopoi* or "overseers"), who were elected by the congregation. As time passed, bishops extended their authority over the Christian communities in outlying towns and the countryside. The power and almost monarchical authority of the bishops were soon enhanced by the doctrine of Apostolic Succession, which asserted that the powers Jesus had given his original disciples were passed on from bishop to bishop by the rite of ordination.

The bishops kept in touch with one another, maintained communications between different Christian communities, and prevented doctrinal and sectarian splintering, which would have destroyed Christian unity. They kept internal discipline and dealt with the civil authorities. In time they began coming together in councils to settle difficult questions, to establish orthodox opinion, and even to expel as heretics those who would not accept it. Christianity could probably not have survived without such strong internal organization and government.

Persecution of Christians

The new faith soon incurred the distrust of the pagan world and of the imperial government. The Christians' refusal to worship the emperor was considered treason. The privacy and secrecy of Christian life and worship ran counter to a traditional Roman dislike of any private association, especially any of a religious nature, and the Christians thus earned the reputation of being "haters of humanity." By the end of the first century "the name alone"—that is, simple membership in the Christian community—was a crime.

Most persecutions during this period, however, were instituted not by the government but by mobs. But even this adversity had its benefits. It weeded out the weaklings among the Christians, brought greater unity to those who remained

This early Christian art shows Christ arrested by soldiers on the night before his crucifixion. Note that Christ is portrayed clean-shaven and dressed in the toga of a Roman aristocrat. [Hirmer Fotoarchiv, Munich]

Mark Describes the Resurrection of Jesus

Belief that Jesus rose from the dead after his Crucifixion (about 30 C.E.) was and is central to traditional Christian doctrine. The record of the Resurrection in the Gospel of Mark, written a generation later (toward 70 C.E.), is the earliest we have. The significance to most Christian groups revolves about the assurance given them that death and the grave are not final and that, instead, salvation for a future life is possible. The appeal of these views was to be nearly universal in the West during the Middle Ages. The church was commonly thought to be the means of implementing the promise of salvation; hence the enormous importance of the church's sacramental system, its rules, and its clergy.

Why are the stories of miracles such as the one described here important for the growth of Christianity? What is special and important about this miracle? Why is it important in the story that days passed between the death of Jesus and the opening of the tomb? Why might the early Christians believe this story? Why was belief in the resurrection important for Christianity in the centuries immediately after the life of Jesus? Is it still important today?

And when evening had come, since it was the day of Preparation, that is, the day before the sabbath, Joseph of Arimathea, a respected member of the council, who was also himself looking for the kingdom of God, took courage and went to Pilate, and asked for the body of Jesus. And Pilate wondered if he were already dead; and summoning the centurion, he asked him whether he was already dead. And when he learned from the centurion that he was dead, he granted the body to Joseph. And he bought a linen shroud, and taking him down, wrapped him in the linen shroud, and laid him in a tomb which had been hewn out of the rock; and he rolled a stone against the door of the tomb. Mary Magdalene and Mary the mother of Jesus saw where he was laid.

And when the sabbath was past, Mary Magdalene, and Mary the mother of James, and Salome, bought spices, so that they might go and anoint him. And very early on the first day of the week they went to the tomb when the sun had risen. And they were saying to one another, "Who will roll away the stone for us from the door of the tomb?" And looking up, they saw that the stone was rolled back; for it was very large. And entering the tomb, they saw a young man sitting on the right side, dressed in a white robe; and they were amazed. And he said to them, "Do not be amazed; you seek Jesus of Nazareth, who was crucified. He has risen, he is not here, see the place where they laid him. But go, tell his disciples and Peter that he is going before you to Galilee; there you will see him, as he told you." And they went out and fled from the tomb; for trembling and astonishment had come upon them; and they said nothing to any one, for they were afraid.

From Gospel of Mark 15:42–47; 16:1–8, Revised Standard Version of the Bible (New York: Thomas Nelson and Sons, 1946, 1952).

faithful, and provided martyrs who inspired still greater devotion and dedication.

Emergence of Catholicism

Most Christians held to what even then were traditional, simple, conservative beliefs. This body of majority opinion and the church that enshrined it came to be called *Catholic*, which means "universal." Its doctrines were deemed orthodox; those holding contrary opinions were heretics.

The need to combat heretics, however, compelled the orthodox to formulate their own views more clearly and firmly. By the end of the second century an orthodox canon had been shaped that included the Old Testament, the Gospels, and the Epistles of Paul, among other writings. The process was not completed for at least two more centuries, but a vitally important start had been made. The orthodox declared the church itself to be the depository of Christian teaching and the bishops to be its receivers. They also drew up creeds, brief statements of faith to which true Christians should adhere. In the first century all that was required of one to be a Christian was to be baptized, to partake of the eucharist, and to call Jesus the Lord. By the end of the second century an orthodox Christian—that is, a member of the Catholic church—had to accept its creed, its canon of holy writings, and the authority of the bishops. The loose structure of the apostolic church had given way to an organized body with recognized leaders able to define its faith and to exclude those who did not accept it.

Rome as a Center of the Early Church

During this same period the church in the city of Rome came to have special prominence. Besides having the largest single congregation of Christians, Rome also benefited from the tradition that both Jesus' apostles Peter and Paul were martyred there. Peter, moreover, was thought to be the first bishop of Rome, and the Gospel of Matthew (16:18) reported Jesus' statement to Peter: "Thou art Peter [in Greek, *Petros*] and upon this rock [in Greek, *petra*] I will build my church." As a result, later bishops of Rome were to claim supremacy in the Catholic church.

The Crisis of the Third Century

The pressure on Rome's frontiers reached massive proportions in the third century C.E. In the east, by 224 C.E. a new Iranian dynasty, the Sassanids, reinvigorated Persia (see Chapter 10). They soon recovered Mesopotamia and raided deep into Roman territory.

Barbarian Invasions

On the western and northern frontiers the threat came from German tribes. The most aggressive in the third century C.E. were the Goths. In the 220s and 230s they began to put pressure on the Danube frontier, and by about 250 C.E. they overran the Balkan provinces. The need to meet these threats made the Romans weaken their western frontiers, and other Germanic peoples broke through there. There was a considerable danger that Rome would be unable to meet this challenge.

Septimius Severus (emperor 193–211 C.E.) and his successors transformed the character of the Roman army. Septimius was a military usurper who owed everything to the support of his soldiers. He was prepared to make Rome into an undisguised military monarchy. Septimius drew recruits for the army increasingly from peasants of the less civilized provinces, and the result was a barbarization of Rome's military forces.

Economic Difficulties

Inflation had forced Commodus (r. 180–192 C.E.) to raise the soldiers' pay, but the Severan emperors had to double it to keep up with prices, which increased the imperial budget by as much as 25 percent. The emperors invented new taxes, debased the coinage, and even sold the palace furniture to raise money. Even then it was hard to recruit troops, and the new style of military life introduced by Septimius—with its laxer discipline, more pleasant duties, and greater opportunity for advancement, not only in the army but also in Roman society—was needed to attract men into the army. The policy proved effective for a short time but could not prevent the chaos of the late third century.

The same forces that caused problems for the army hurt society at large. The shortage of workers reduced agricultural production. As external threats distracted the emperors, they were less able to preserve domestic peace. Piracy, brigandage, and the neglect of roads and harbors hampered trade. So, too, did the debasement of the coinage and the resulting inflation. Imperial exactions and confiscations of the property of the rich removed badly needed capital from productive use.

The government now had to demand services that had once been gladly volunteered. Because the empire lived on a hand-to-mouth basis, with no significant reserve fund and no system of credit financing, the emperors had to compel the people to provide food, supplies, money, and labor. The upper classes in the cities were made to serve as administrators without pay and to meet deficits in revenue out of their own pockets. There were provincial rebellions, and peasants and even town administrators fled to escape their burdens. These difficulties weakened Rome's economic strength when it was most needed.

The Social Order

The new conditions caused important changes in the social order. The Senate and the traditional ruling class were decimated by direct attacks from hostile emperors and by economic losses. Their ranks were filled by military men. The whole state began to take on an increasingly military appearance. Distinctions among the classes by dress had been traditional since the republic, but in the third and fourth centuries C.E. people's everyday clothing became a kind of uniform that precisely revealed their status. Titles were assigned to ranks in society as to ranks in the army. The most important distinction was the one formally established by Septimius Severus, which drew a sharp line between the *honestiores* (senators, equestrians, the municipal

Reigns of Selected Late Empire Rulers (all dates are C.E.)	
180-192	Commodus
193-211	Septimius Severus
249-251	Decius
253-260	Valerian
270-275	Aurelian
284-305	Diocletian
306-337	Constantine
324-337	Constantine sole emperor
337-361	Constantius II
361-363	Julian the Apostate
364-375	Valentinian
364-378	Valens
379-395	Theodosius

aristocracy, and the soldiers) and the lower classes, or *humiliores*. Septimius gave the *honestiores* a privileged position before the law. They were given lighter punishments, could not be tortured, and alone had the right of appeal to the emperor.

It became more difficult to move from the lower order to the higher, another example of the growing rigidity of the late Roman Empire. Farmers were tied to their lands, artisans to their crafts, soldiers to the army, merchants and shipowners to the needs of the state, and citizens of the municipal upper class to the collection and payment of increasingly burdensome taxes. Freedom and private initiative yielded to the needs of the state and its ever expanding control of its citizens.

Civil Disorder

By the mid-third century the empire seemed on the point of collapse, but two able soldiers, Claudius II Gothicus (r. 268–270 C.E.) and Aurelian (r. 270–275 C.E.), drove back the barbarians and stamped out disorder. The emperors who followed Aurelian on the throne were good fighters and changed Rome's system of defense. They built walls around Rome and other cities to resist barbarian attack. They drew back their best troops from the frontiers, relying chiefly on a newly organized heavy cavalry and a mobile army near the emperor's own residence. Hereafter, the army was composed largely of Germanic mercenaries whose officers gave personal loyalty to the emperor rather than to the empire. These officers became a foreign, hereditary caste of aristocrats that increasingly supplied high administrators and even emperors. In effect, the Roman people hired an army of mercenaries, only technically Roman, to protect them.

The Late Empire

The Fourth Century and Imperial Reorganization

The period from Diocletian (r. 284–305 C.E.) to Constantine (r. 306–337 C.E.) was one of reconstruction and reorganization.

Diocletian   The emperor Diocletian was a man of undistinguished birth who rose to the throne through the army. He knew that he was not a great general and that the job of defending and governing the entire empire was too great for one man. He therefore decreed the introduction of the tetrarchy, the rule of the empire by four men with power divided on a territorial basis (see Map 5–5). This system seemed to promise orderly, peaceful transitions instead of assassinations, chaos, and civil war.

Constantine   In 305 Diocletian retired and compelled his co-emperor to do the same. But his plan for a smooth succession failed completely. In 310 there were five competing emperors. Out of this chaos Constantine produced order. In 324 he defeated his last opponent and made himself sole emperor, uniting the empire once again; he reigned until 337.

The emperor had now become a remote figure surrounded by carefully chosen high officials. He lived in a great palace and was almost unapproachable. Those admitted to his presence had to prostrate themselves before him and kiss the hem of his robe, which was purple and had golden threads going through it. The emperor was addressed as *dominus* ("lord"), and his right to rule was not derived from the Roman people but from God. This remoteness and ceremony enhanced the dignity of the emperor and safeguarded him against assassination.

Constantine erected the new city of Constantinople on the site of ancient Byzantium on the Bosphorus, which leads to both the Aegean and the Black seas, and made it the new capital of the empire. Its strategic location was excellent for protecting the eastern and Danubian frontiers, and, surrounded on three sides by water, it was easily defended.

Administration and Finance   The autocratic rule of the emperors was carried out by a civilian bureaucracy, which was carefully separated from the military service to reduce the chances of rebellion. The entire system was supervised by a network of spies and secret police, without whom the increasingly rigid authoritarian organization could not be trusted to perform. Despite these efforts, the system was corrupt and inefficient.

The cost of maintaining a 400,000-man army as well as the vast civilian bureaucracy, the expensive imperial court, and the imperial taste for splendid buildings strained an already weak economy. Diocletian's attempts to establish a uniform and reliable currency merely increased inflation. To deal with it he resorted to price control with his Edict of Maximum Prices in 301. For each product and each kind of labor a maximum price was set, and violations were punishable by death. The edict failed, despite its harsh provisions.

Peasants unable to pay their taxes and officials unable to collect them tried to escape, and Diocletian resorted to stern regimentation to keep all in their places and at the service of the government. The terror of the third century had turned many peasants into tenant farmers who fled for protection to the country estates of powerful landowners. They were tied to the land, as were their descendants, as the caste system hardened.

Division of the Empire   The peace and unity established by Constantine did not last. His death was followed

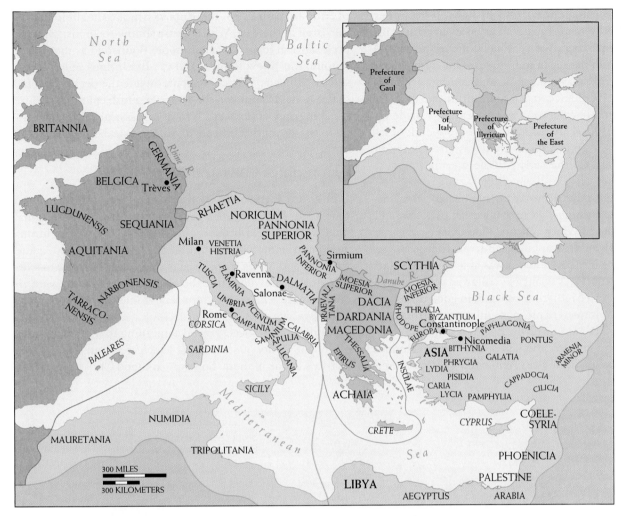

Map 5–5 Divisions of the Roman Empire under Diocletian. Diocletian divided the sprawling empire into four prefectures for more effective government and defense. The inset map shows their boundaries and the large map gives some details of regions and provinces. The major division between east and west was along the line running from north to south between Pannonia and Moesia.

by a struggle for succession that was won by Constantius II (r. 337–361). His death left the empire to his young cousin Julian (r. 361–363), called by the Christians "the Apostate" as a result of his attempt to restore paganism. Julian was killed in a campaign against the Persians. His death ended the pagan revival.

The Germans in the west attacked along the Rhine, but even greater trouble was brewing along the Danube (see Map 5–6) where the Visigoths had been driven from their home in the Ukraine by the fierce Huns, a nomadic people from central Asia. The Emperor Valentinian (r. 364–375) saw that he could not defend the empire alone and appointed his brother Valens (r. 364–378) as co-ruler. Valentinian made his own headquarters at Milan and spent the rest of his life fighting barbarians in the west. Valens was given control of the east. The empire was once again divided in two. The two emperors maintained their own courts, and the two halves of the

empire became increasingly separate and different. Latin was the language of the west and Greek of the east.

In 376 the hard-pressed Visigoths received permission to enter the empire to escape the Huns. When the Goths began to plunder the Balkan provinces, Valens attacked them and died, along with most of his army, at Adrianople in Thrace in 378. Theodosius (r. 379–395), an able and experienced general, was named co-ruler in the east. He tried to unify the empire again, but his death in 395 left it divided and weak.

Thereafter, the two parts of the empire went their separate and different ways. The west became increasingly rural as barbarian invasions grew. The villa, a fortified country estate, became the basic unit of life. There, *coloni* (tenant farmers) gave their services to the local magnate in return for economic assistance and protection from both barbarians and imperial officials. Many cities shrank to tiny walled fortresses ruled by military commanders and bishops. The upper classes moved to the country and asserted ever greater independence of imperial authority. The failure of the central authority to maintain the roads and the constant danger from robber bands sharply curtailed trade and communications, forcing greater self-reliance and a more primitive style of life. By the fifth century the west was increasingly made up of isolated units of rural aristocrats and their dependent laborers. The only unifying institution was the Christian church. The pattern for the early Middle Ages in the west was already formed.

The east was different. Constantinople became the center of a vital and flourishing culture that we call *Byzantine* and that lasted until the fifteenth century. Due to its defensible location, the skill of its emperors, and the firmness and strength of its base in Asia Minor, it was able to deflect and repulse barbarian attacks. A strong navy allowed commerce to flourish in the eastern Mediterranean and, in good times, far beyond it. Cities continued to prosper, and the emperors controlled the nobility. Byzantine civilization was a unique combination of classical culture, the Christian religion, Roman law, and eastern artistic influences. While the west was being overrun by barbarians, the Roman Empire, in altered form, persisted in the east. While Rome shrank to an insignificant ecclesiastical town, Constantinople flourished as the seat of empire, the "New Rome," and the Byzantines called themselves "Romans." When we contemplate the decline and fall of the Roman Empire in the fourth and fifth centuries, we are speaking only of the west. A form of classical culture persisted in the Byzantine east for another thousand years.

Triumph of Christianity

Religious Currents in the Empire   In the troubled fourth and fifth centuries people sought powerful, personal deities who would bring them safety and prosperity in this world and immortality in the next. Paganism was open and tolerant, and it was by no means unusual for people to worship new deities alongside the old and even to intertwine elements of several gods to form a new amalgam by the device called *syncretism*.

Christianity's success owed something to the same causes of the popularity of other cults, which are often spoken of as its rivals. None of them, however, attained Christianity's uni-

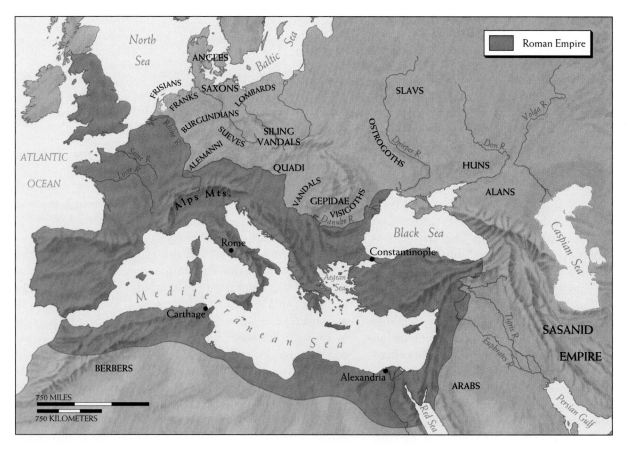

Map 5–6   The Empire's neighbors.   In the fourth century the Roman Empire was nearly surrounded by ever more threatening neighbors. The map shows who these so-called barbarians were and where they lived before their armed contact with the Romans.

versality, and none appears to have given the early Christians and their leaders as much competition as the ancient philosophies or the state religion (see Map 5–7).

Imperial Persecution   By the third century Christianity had taken firm hold in the eastern provinces and Italy. As times became bad and the Christians became more numerous and visible, popular opinion blamed disasters, natural and military, on the Christians. About 250 the Emperor Decius (r. 249–251) required that all citizens worship the state gods publicly. True Christians could not obey, and Decius instituted a major persecution. Valerian (r. 253–260) resumed the persecutions, partly to confiscate the wealth of rich Christians. His successors, however, let persecution lapse until the end of the century.

In 303 Diocletian launched the most serious persecution inflicted on the Christians in the Roman Empire. Because the martyrs often aroused pity and sympathy and because large ancient states were unable to carry out a program of terror with the thoroughness of modern totalitarian governments, the Christians and their church survived to enjoy what they must have considered a miraculous change of fortune. In 311 Galerius (r. 305–311), who had been one of the most vigorous persecutors, was influenced, perhaps by his Christian wife, to issue an edict of toleration permitting Christian worship.

This ivory relief, carved a little after 395 C.E., shows a Vandal warrior, Stilicho, who rose to prominence in the Roman army. From the third century onward the Roman army was composed increasingly of foreign mercenaries. [Alinari/Art Resource, N.Y.]

The victory of Constantine and his emergence as sole ruler of the empire transformed Christianity from a precariously tolerated sect to the religion favored by the emperor. In 394 Theodosius forbade the celebration of pagan cults and abolished the pagan religious calendar. At his death Christianity was the official religion of the Roman Empire.

The favored position of the church attracted opportunistic converts and diluted the moral excellence and spiritual fervor of its adherents. The relationship between church and state presented the possibility that religion would become subordinate to the state, as it traditionally had been. In the east, that largely happened. In the west, the weakness of the emperors permitted church leaders to exercise remarkable independence. In 390 Ambrose (ca. 339–397), bishop of Milan, excommunicated Emperor Theodosius, and the emperor did humble penance. This act provided an important precedent for future assertions of the church's autonomy and authority, but it did not stop secular interference and influence in the church by any means.

Arianism and the Council of Nicea   Internal divisions within the church proved to be even more troubling as new heresies emerged. The most important and the most threatening was Arianism, founded by a priest named Arius of Alexandria (ca. 280–336) in the fourth century. Arius's view that Jesus was not co-equal and co-eternal with God the Father did away with the mysterious concept of the Trinity, the difficult doctrine that holds that God is three persons (the Father, the Son, and the Holy Spirit) but also one in substance and essence.

Athanasius (ca. 293–373), later bishop of Alexandria, saw the Arian view as an impediment to salvation. Only if Jesus were both fully human and fully God could the transformation of humanity to divinity have taken place in Him and be transmitted by Him to his disciples. "Christ was made man," he said, "that we might be made divine."

To deal with the growing controversy, Constantine called a council of Christian bishops at Nicea, not far from Constantinople, in 325. For the emperor, the question was essentially political, but for the disputants, salvation was at stake. At Nicea the view expounded by Athanasius won out, became orthodox, and was embodied in the Nicene Creed. The Christian emperors hoped to unify their increasingly decentralized realms by imposing a single religion, and it did prove to be a unifying force, but it also introduced new divisions where none had previously existed.

Map 5-7 The spread of Christianity.   Christianity grew swiftly in the third, fourth, fifth, and sixth centuries—especially after the conversion of the emperors in the fourth century. By 600, on the eve of the birth of the new religion of Islam, Christianity was dominant throughout the Mediterranean world and most of western Europe.

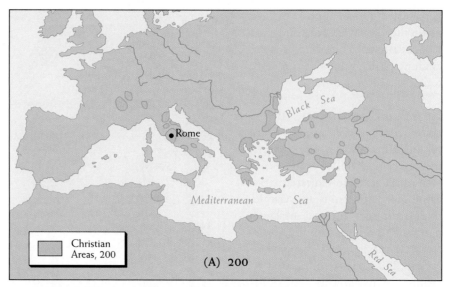

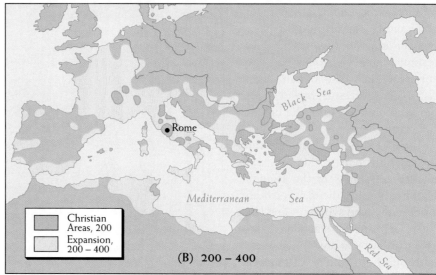

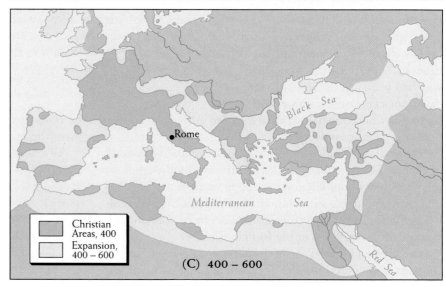

Arts and Letters in the Late Empire

The art and literature of the late empire reflect both the confluence of pagan and Christian ideas and traditions and the conflict between them. Much of the literature is polemical, and much of the art is propaganda.

The empire was saved from the chaos of the third century by a military revolution based on and led by provincials of lower-class origins. They brought with them the fresh winds of cultural change, which blew out not only the dust of classical culture but much of its substance as well. Yet the new ruling class thought of itself as effecting a great restoration rather than a revolution and sought to restore classical culture and absorb it. The confusion and uncertainty of the times were tempered in part, of course, by the comfort of Christianity, but the new aristocracy sought order and stability—ethical, literary, and artistic—in the classical tradition as well.

Preservation of Classical Culture

One of the main needs and accomplishments of this period was to preserve classical culture and make it available and useful to the new elite. The great classical authors were reproduced in many copies, and their works were transferred from perishable and inconvenient papyrus rolls to sturdier codices, bound volumes that were as easy to use as modern books. Scholars also digested long works like Livy's *History of Rome* into shorter versions and wrote learned commentaries and compiled grammars. Original works by pagan writers of the late empire were neither numerous nor especially distinguished.

Christian Writers

Of Christian writings, on the other hand, the late empire saw a great outpouring: Christian apologetics in poetry and prose, as well as sermons, hymns, and biblical commentaries. Christianity could also boast important scholars. Jerome (348–420), thoroughly trained in classical Latin literature and rhetoric, produced a revised version of the Bible in Latin, commonly called the Vulgate, which became the Bible used by the Catholic church.

Probably the most important eastern scholar was Eusebius of Caesarea (ca. 260–ca. 340). He wrote apologetics, an idealized biography of Constantine, and a valuable historical chronology. His most important contribution, however, was his *Ecclesiastical History*, an attempt to set forth the Christian view of history. He saw history as the working out of God's will. All of history, therefore, had a purpose and a direction, and Constantine's victory and the subsequent unity of empire and church were its culmination.

The closeness and complexity of the relationship between classical pagan culture and the Christianity of the late empire are nowhere better displayed than in the career and writings of Augustine (354–430), bishop of Hippo in North Africa. He was born at Carthage and was trained as a teacher of rhetoric. He passed through a number of intellectual way stations before his conversion to Christianity. His skill in pagan rhetoric and philosophy made him peerless among his contemporaries as a defender of Christianity and a theologian. His greatest works are his *Confessions*, an autobiography describing the road to his conversion, and *The City of God*. The latter was a response to the pagan charge that Rome's sack by the Goths in 410 was caused by the abandonment of the old gods and the advent of Christianity. The optimistic view held by some Christians that God's will worked its way in history and was easily comprehensible needed further support in the face of this disaster.

Augustine sought to separate the fate of Christianity from that of the Roman Empire. He contrasted the secular world—the city of Man—with the spiritual—the City of God. The former was selfish, the latter unselfish; the former evil, the latter good. Augustine argued that history was moving forward, in the spiritual sense, to the Day of Judgment, but that there was no reason to expect improvement before then in the secular sphere. The fall of Rome was neither surprising nor important, for all states, even a Christian Rome, were part of the City of Man and therefore corrupt and mortal. Only the

The Arch of Constantine, built in 315 C.E., represents a transition between classical and medieval, pagan and Christian. Many of the sculptures incorporated in it were taken from earlier works dating to the first and second centuries. Others, contemporary with the arch, reflect a new, less refined style. [Scala/Art Resource, N.Y.]

City of God was immortal, and it, consisting of all the saints on earth and in heaven, was untouched by earthly calamities.

Augustine believed that faith is essential and primary—a thoroughly Christian view—but that it is not a substitute for reason, the foundation of classical thought. Instead, faith is the starting point for the liberation of human reason, which continues to be the means by which people can understand what is revealed by faith. His writings constantly reveal the presence of both Christian faith and pagan reason, and the tension between them, a legacy he left to the Middle Ages.

The Problem of the Decline and Fall of the Empire in the West

Whether important to Augustine or not, the massive barbarian invasions of the fifth century ended effective imperial government in the West. For centuries people have speculated about why the ancient world collapsed. Every kind of reason has been put forward, and some seem to have nothing to do with reason at all. Soil exhaustion, plague, climatic change, and even poisoning from lead water pipes have been suggested as reasons for Rome's decline in population, vigor, and the capacity to defend itself. Some blame slavery and the failure to make advances in science and technology that they believe resulted from it. Others blame excessive government interference in the economic life of the empire; others, the destruction of the urban middle class, the carrier of classical culture.

Perhaps a more simple and obvious explanation can be found. The growth of so mighty an empire as Rome's was by no means inevitable. Rome's greatness had come from conquests that provided the Romans with the means to expand still further, until there were not enough Romans to conquer and govern any more peoples and territory. When pressure from outsiders grew, the Romans lacked the resources to advance and defeat the enemy as in the past. Still the tenacity and success of their resistance were remarkable. Without new conquests to provide the immense wealth needed to defend and maintain internal prosperity, the Romans finally yielded to unprecedented onslaughts by fierce and numerous attackers.

To blame the ancients and slavery for the failure to produce an industrial and economic revolution like that of the later Western world, one capable of producing wealth without taking it from another, is to stand the problem on its head. No one yet has a satisfactory explanation for those revolutions, so it is improper to blame any institution or society for not achieving what has been achieved only once in human history, in what are still mysterious circumstances.

We may do well to think of the decline of Rome as the historian Edward Gibbon did:

The decline of Rome was the natural and inevitable effect of immoderate greatness. Prosperity ripened the principle of decay; the cause of the destruction multiplied with the extent of conquest; and, as soon as time or accident had removed the artificial supports, the stupendous fabric yielded to the pressure of its own weight. The story of the ruin is simple and obvious; and instead of inquiring why the Roman Empire was destroyed, we should rather be surprised that it had subsisted so long.[5]

This explanation allows us to see the Roman Empire as one among several great empires around the world that had similar experiences.

IN WORLD PERSPECTIVE
Republican and Imperial Rome

The history of the Roman republic reflects almost as sharp a departure from the common experience of ancient civilizations as that of the Greek city-states. Rome abandoned the institution of monarchy and established an aristocratic republic somewhat like the *poleis* of the Greek dark ages. The Roman republic from the first found itself engaged in almost continual warfare. Wars were waged either in defense of its own territory, in fights over disputed territory, or in defense of other cities or states that were friends and allies of Rome. The force of Roman arms, the high quality of Roman roads and bridges, and the pragmatic character of Roman law helped create something unique: an empire ruled by a republic. Rome achieved its greatness with an army of citizens and allies, without a monarchy or a regular bureaucracy.

The temptations and responsibilities of governing a vast and rich empire, however, finally proved too much for the republican constitution. Ambitious military leaders fought among themselves for glory and political advantage. The result was civil war and the destruction of the republic.

Out of the civil wars and chaos that brought down the republic, Augustus brought unity, peace, order, and prosperity. As a result, he was regarded with almost religious awe and attained more military and political power than any Roman before him. He ruled firmly but with moderation. He tried to limit military adventures and expenses. He supported public works that encouraged trade and communication. He tried to invigorate the old civic pride, in which he had considerable success, and private morality based on family values, in which he was less successful. He patronized the arts to beautify

---

[5]Edward Gibbon, *Decline and Fall of the Roman Empire*, ed. by J. B. Bury, 2nd ed., Vol. 4 (London: J. Murray, 1909), pp. 173–174.

Rome and glorify his reign. On his death, he passed on the regime to his family, the Julio-Claudians.

For almost 200 years the empire was generally prosperous, peaceful, and well run, but problems developed. Management of the many responsibilities assumed by the government required the growth of a large bureaucracy, which placed a heavy and increasing burden on the treasury, required higher taxes, and stifled both civic spirit and private enterprise. Pressure from barbarian tribes on the frontiers required a large standing army, which was also costly and led to further rises in taxation.

In the late empire, Rome's rulers resorted to many devices for dealing with their problems, including putting down internal military rebellions led by generals from different parts of the empire. More and more, the emperors' rule and their safety depended on the loyalty of the army, so they courted the soldiers' favor with gifts. This only increased the burden of taxes; the rich and powerful avoided their obligations, making the load on everyone else all the heavier. The government's control over the lives of its people became ever greater and the society more rigid as people tried to escape the crushing load of taxes. Many measures were tried: inflating the currency, fixing farmers to the soil as serfs, building walls to keep the barbarians out, and bribing barbarian tribes to fight for Rome against other barbarians; but ultimately they all failed.

The conquest of a vast empire had moved the Romans away from their unusual historical traditions toward the more familiar path of empire trodden by rulers in Egypt, Mesopotamia, China, India, and Iran. It is especially instructive to look at Rome from the perspective of the historians who discern a "dynastic cycle" in China (see Chapter 7). The development of the Roman Empire, although by no means the same as the Chinese, fits the same pattern fairly well. Like the Former Han Dynasty in China, the Roman Empire in the West fell, leaving disunity, insecurity, disorder, and poverty. Like similar empires in the ancient world, it had been unable to sustain its "immoderate greatness."

Review Questions

1. How did the institutions of family and clientage and the establishment of patrician and plebeian classes contribute to the stability of the early Roman republic? How important was education to the success of the republic?

2. Discuss Rome's expansion to 265 B.C.E. How was Rome able to conquer and control Italy? In their relations with Greece and Asia Minor in the second century B.C.E., were the Romans looking for security? Wealth? Power? Fame?

3. Explain the clash between the Romans and the Carthaginians in the First and Second Punic wars. Could the wars have been avoided? How did Rome benefit from its victory over Carthage? What problems were created by this victory?

4. What were the problems that plagued the Roman republic in the last century? What caused these problems and how did the Romans try to solve them? To what extent was the republic destroyed by ambitious generals who loved power more than Rome itself?

5. Discuss the Augustan constitution and government. What solutions did Augustus provide for the problems that had plagued the Roman republic? Why was the Roman population willing to accept Augustus as head of the state?

6. Despite unpromising beginnings, Christianity was enormously popular by the fourth century C.E. Why were Christians persecuted by Roman authorities? What were the more important reasons for Christianity's success?

7. Discuss three theories that scholars have advanced to explain the decline and fall of the Roman Empire. What are the difficulties involved in explaining the fall? What explanation would you give?

Suggested Readings

From Republic to Empire

F. E. ADCOCK, *The Roman Art of War Under the Republic* (1940). An analysis of Roman military procedures.

E. BADIAN, *Foreign Clientelae* (1958). A brilliant study of the Roman idea of a client-patron relationship extended to foreign affairs.

E. BADIAN, *Roman Imperialism in the Late Republic*, 2nd ed. (1968).

A. H. BERNSTEIN, *Tiberius Sempronius Gracchus: Tradition and Apostacy* (1978). A new interpretation of Tiberius's place in Roman politics.

J. BOARDMAN, J. GRIFFIN, AND O. MURRAY, *The Oxford History of the Roman World* (1990). An encyclopedic approach to the varieties of the Roman experience.

P. A. BRUNT, *Social Conflicts in the Roman Republic* (1971).

T. J. CORNELL, *The Beginnings of Rome. Italy and Rome from the Bronze Age to the Punic Wars, c. 1000–264 B.C.* (1995). A consideration of the royal and early republican periods of Roman history.

T. CORNELL AND J. MATTHEWS, *Atlas of the Roman World* (1982). Much more than the title indicates, this book presents a comprehensive view of the Roman world in its physical and cultural setting.

S. DIXON, *The Roman Mother* (1988). Describes the place of women within the Roman family.

D. C. EARL, *The Moral and Political Tradition of Rome* (1967).

R. M. ERRINGTON, *The Dawn of Empire: Rome's Rise to Power* (1972). An account of Rome's conquest of the Mediterranean.

M. GELZER, *Caesar: Politician and Statesman*, trans. by P. Needham (1968). The best biography of Caesar.

E. S. GRUEN, *The Last Generation of the Roman Republic* (1973). An interesting but controversial interpretation of the fall of the republic.

E. S. GRUEN, *The Hellenistic World and the Coming of Rome* (1984). A new interpretation of Rome's conquest of the eastern Mediterranean.

W. V. HARRIS, *War and Imperialism in Republican Rome, 327–70 B.C.* (1975). An analysis of Roman attitudes and intentions concerning imperial expansion and war.

A. KEAVENEY, *Rome and the Unification of Italy* (1988). The story of how Rome organized her defeated opponents.

A. KEAVENEY, *Lucullus: A Life* (1992). A biography of the famous Roman epicure.

J. F. LAZENBY, *Hannibal's War: A Military History of the Second Punic War* (1978). A careful and thorough account.

F. B. MARSH, *A History of the Roman World from 146 to 30 B.C.*, 3rd ed., rev. by H. H. Scullard (1963). An excellent narrative account.

C. NICOLET, *The World of the Citizen in Republican Rome* (1980).

M. PALLOTTINO, *The Etruscans*, 6th ed. (1974). Makes especially good use of archaeological evidence.

R. T. RIDLEY, *The History of Rome* (1989). A solid general history.

E. T. SALMON, *Roman Colonization Under the Republic* (1970).

E. T. SALMON, *The Making of Roman Italy* (1982). The story of Roman expansion on the Italian peninsula.

H. H. SCULLARD, *A History of the Roman World 753–146 B.C.*, 4th ed. (1980). An unusually fine narrative history with useful critical notes.

H. H. SCULLARD, *From the Gracchi to Nero*, 5th ed. (1982). A work of the same character and quality.

A. N. SHERWIN-WHITE, *Roman Citizenship* (1939). A useful study of the Roman franchise and its extension to other peoples.

D. STOCKTON, *Cicero: A Political Biography* (1971). A readable and interesting study.

D. STOCKTON, *The Gracchi* (1979). An interesting analytic narrative.

L. R. TAYLOR, *Party Politics in the Age of Caesar* (1949). A fascinating analysis of Roman political practices.

B. H. WARMINGTON, *Carthage* (1960). A good survey.

G. WILLIAMS, *The Nature of Roman Poetry* (1970). An unusually graceful and perceptive literary study.

Imperial Rome

J. P. V. D. BALSDON, *Roman Women* (1962).

T. BARNES, *The New Empire of Diocletian and Constantine* (1982).

K. R. BRADLEY, *Slavery and Society at Rome* (1994). A study of the role of slaves in Roman life.

P. BROWN, *Augustine of Hippo* (1967). A splendid biography.

P. BROWN, *The World of Late Antiquity, A.D. 150–750* (1971). A brilliant and readable essay.

J. BURCKHARDT, *The Age of Constantine the Great* (1956). A classic work by the Swiss cultural historian.

E. R. DODDS, *Pagan and Christian in an Age of Anxiety* (1965). An original and perceptive study.

A. FERRILL, *The Fall of the Roman Empire, The Military Explanation* (1986). An interpretation that emphasizes the decline in the quality of the Roman army.

A. FERRILL, *Caligula: Emperor of Rome* (1991). A biography of the monstrous young emperor.

E. GIBBON, *The History of the Decline and Fall of the Roman Empire*, 2nd ed., 7 vols., ed. by J. B. Bury (1909–1914). One of the masterworks of the English language.

M. GRANT, *The Fall of the Roman Empire* (1990). A lively, well-written account.

N. HANNESTAD, *Roman Art and Imperial Policy* (1988). An analysis of how the emperors used the arts to further their own and imperial interests.

A. H. M. JONES, *The Later Roman Empire*, 3 vols. (1964). A comprehensive study of the period.

D. KAGAN, ED., *The End of the Roman Empire: Decline or Transformation?* 3rd ed. (1992). A collection of essays discussing the problem of the decline and fall of the Roman Empire.

J. LEBRETON AND J. ZEILLER, *History of the Primitive Church*, 3 vols. (1962). From the Catholic viewpoint.

J. E. LENDON, *Empire of Honor, The Art of Government in the Roman World* (1997). An original and path-breaking interpretation.

H. LIETZMANN, *History of the Early Church*, 2 vols. (1961). From the Protestant viewpoint.

F. LOT, *The End of the Ancient World and the Beginnings of the Middle Ages* (1961). A study that emphasizes gradual transition rather than abrupt change.

E. N. LUTTWAK, *The Grand Strategy of the Roman Empire* (1976). An original and fascinating analysis by a keen student of modern strategy.

R. MacMullen, *Paganism in the Roman Empire* (1981).

R. MacMullen, *Roman Social Relations, 50 B.C. to A.D. 284* (1981).

R. MacMullen, *Corruption and the Decline of Rome* (1988). A study that examines the importance of changes in ethical ideas and behavior.

R. W. Mathison, *Roman Aristocrats in Barbarian Gaul: Strategies for Survival* (1993). An unusual slant on the late empire.

W. A. Meeks, *The Origins of Christian Morality. The First Two Centuries.* An account of the shaping of Christianity in the Roman Empire.

F. G. B. Millar, *The Emperor in the Roman World, 31 B.C.–A.D. 337* (1977). A study of Roman imperial government.

F. Millar, *The Roman Empire and Its Neighbors*, 2nd ed. (1981).

A. Momigliano, ed., *The Conflict Between Paganism and Christianity* (1963). A valuable collection of essays.

H. M. D. Parker, *A History of the Roman World from A.D. 138 to 337* (1969). A good survey.

M. I. Rostovtzeff, *Social and Economic History of the Roman Empire*, 2nd ed. (1957). A masterpiece whose main thesis has been much disputed.

V. Rudich, *Political Dissidence Under Nero, The Price of Dissimulation* (1993). A brilliant exposition of the lives and thoughts of political dissidents in the early empire.

E. T. Salmon, *A History of the Roman World, 30 B.C. to A.D. 138* (1968). A good survey.

R. Syme, *The Roman Revolution* (1960). A brilliant study of Augustus, his supporters, and their rise to power.

R. Syme, *The Augustan Aristocracy* (1985). An examination of the new ruling class shaped by Augustus.

L. A. Thompson, *Romans and Blacks* (1989).

6 AFRICA: EARLY HISTORY TO 1000 C.E.

West African terra-cotta sculpture (36 cms high) from the Nok culture, which flourished in the Western Sudan from about 900 B.C.E. to about 200 C.E. The style of terra-cotta castings like this one suggests that they may have had wooden prototypes. [Werner Forman Archive, Art Resource, N.Y./National Museum, Lagos, Nigeria]

CHAPTER TOPICS

◆ Problems of Interpretation and Sources

◆ Physical Description of the Continent

◆ African Peoples

◆ The Sahara and the Sudan to the Beginning of the Christian Era

◆ Nilotic Africa and the Ethiopian Highlands

◆ The Western and Central Sudan

◆ Central, Southern, and East Africa

In World Perspective Africa to ca. 1000 C.E.

We now shift our focus from the ancient societies that emerged north and east of the Mediterranean—the Persian, Greek, Hellenistic, and Roman worlds—to the story of the world's second-largest continent, Africa, beginning with the earliest archaeological record. Africa forms the southern frontier of the Mediterranean world and connects to Asia through the Arabian peninsula and the Indian Ocean. The evidence suggests that the first humans emerged from eastern Africa to populate the rest of the world, and the continent's subsequent history is one of ongoing interaction, both internally across its many natural boundaries and externally with the rest of the world.

Problems of Interpretation and Sources

The Question of "Civilization"

In Chapter 1 we defined "civilization" in terms of a cluster of attributes—among them writing, urban life, and metallurgy—that relate to social complexity and technological development. Thus understood, the term usefully identifies some common characteristics of the ancient states that emerged in the Nile valley, Mesopotamia, the Indus and Ganges valleys, and China, and also of the larger, more complex societies developed since those ancient states. The term civilization, however, has also a broader sense, associated with the sophistication of a people's intellectual, cultural, and artistic traditions. Frequent confusion of the two meanings, however, leads often to the unfortunate assumption that societies that lack "civilization" in the narrow sense—being without writing, cities, or a state bureaucracy—are therefore "uncivilized" in the broader sense. Once we move outside the Nile valley and the Ethiopian highlands, most African societies down to recent times—indeed, most societies in the world for most of its history—may not have been civilizations in the narrow sense, but they were hardly uncivilized in the broader sense. African history reveals important states with writing, cities, and technology, but also many societies with rich, varied traditions that did not happen to be organized as bureaucratic states with literate, urban populations and new technologies.

The Source Problem

African history has flourished in recent decades, and scholars have given us glimpses of many formerly unknown or little-known African societies. Still, there is much we do not know. A major reason for this is the paucity of sources available to historians for many regions and periods. This second problem is especially acute for the small, local societies without writing, centralized governmental bureaucracies, or large urban centers that characterize much of sub-Saharan African history. As late as 1880, for example, 25 percent of all West Africans probably belonged to such "stateless" societies.

Stateless societies leave few historical records. Local oral traditions provide one valuable source of information about them. But even when combined with reports of outside observers, oral traditions can give us reliable access only to relatively recent history—no more than a few centuries. Another source for the history and prehistory of both Africa's states and its stateless societies is archaeological research. The tropical climate that prevails in much of sub-Saharan Africa unfortunately destroys many types of artifacts that survive in drier regions. Nonetheless, recent archaeological scholarship has brought to light many formerly unknown or little-known cultures. Some of this work indicates that ancient Africa may have had large and advanced societies and states that are still unknown or little understood. The Nok and Zimbabwean cultures, for example, left impressive but hard-to-decipher remains.

A third important source consists of the reports of outside observers. It is only after about 950 C.E., however, that we get—from writings of Islamic historians, geographers, and travelers, and still later, Europeans—real descriptions of life and peoples in the vast reaches of Africa beyond Egypt, Ethiopia, and the North African coast. Before this time, only a few brief Greek and Roman accounts are available. These outside written records, examples of which are given in this chapter, are of mixed value. Greek and Roman observers and, later, Islamic and European writers brought strong biases to their assessments of Africa and Africans, particularly sub-Saharan Africa; their commentaries did much to form the preconceived notions and stereotypes with which many outsiders still view this vast, diverse continent.

Because relatively little is known about small African communities that left no written documents, monuments, or other decipherable artifacts, surveys tend to focus on the larger societies, with known rulers, fighting forces, and towns or cities, which left their own records or were documented by outsiders. We shall try nonetheless to balance presentation of larger societies and states, for which we have more adequate evidence, with discussion of areas where smaller societies prevailed or where what may have been large states or societies have left us little in the way of source materials.

Physical Description of the Continent

Africa makes up over one fifth of the Earth's land mass (see Map 6–1). It is three and one-half times the size of the continental United States and second only to Asia in total area. It is geologically massive, with unusually high relief over virtually its entire expanse: The average elevation is 660 meters. The result is a dearth of natural harbors and islands and generally steep escarpments surmounting narrow coasts. This has made access to, as well as egress from, its interior difficult. All of Africa's major rivers (the Niger, Kongo [Zaïre], Nile, Zambezi, and Orange) lie largely in plateau basins and are navigable in their inland reaches. They are not, however, navigable across the cataracts they traverse before they reach the coastlands. (Only the Nile has a relatively long navigable reach below its cataracts in upper Egypt.) The vast size and sharp physical variations, from high mountains to swamplands, tropical forest, and deserts, have also made rapid long-distance communication and movement difficult and channeled both along certain corridors (such as the Rift valley of East Africa, the coastal reaches of East or North Africa, the Niger or Zambezi river valley, or the Sahelian savannah lands bordering the great equatorial forest).

The special character of various regions is due in considerable part to Africa's position astride the equator. As a whole, its climate is unusually hot. North and south of the equator, dense rain forests dominate a west-east band of tropical woodland territory from the southern coasts of West Africa across the Kongo, or Zaïre, basin nearly to the Kenyan high-

lands. (Note, however, that tropical rain forests cover only about 5 percent of the continent.) North and south of this band (and in the Kenyan highlands), the lush rain forests give way to the *savannah*—open woodlands and grassy plains. This in turn passes into steppe and semidesert known as the Sahel, and finally into true desert as one moves farther from the equator. Despite high rainfall and humidity in its equatorial regions (except in the eastern highlands) and along its Indian Ocean coast, Africa contains two of the world's greatest and driest deserts. The Sahara ("the Desert": Arabic *al-Sahra'*) is the world's largest desert and has been historically the major factor hindering contact between the Mediterranean world and sub-Saharan Africa. The Kalahari is its smaller but still vast counterpart in southwestern Africa. It partially cuts off the southern plateau and coastal regions from central Africa.

Other natural factors are of importance to Africa's history. The soils of Africa are typically tropical in character, which means they are devoid of much humus, or vegetable mold, and generally easily leached of mineral and nutrient content. Thus they are rapidly exhausted and not highly productive for extended periods. Water shortage is also a perennial problem for agriculture in most of Africa and a potent factor in its history. Crop pests and insects such as the tsetse fly, mosquito, and locust have also been enemies of both farming and pastoralism in Africa; the tsetse fly specifically has blocked the spread of domesticated cattle and horses to the forest regions of the continent. Still, abundant animal life has made hunting and fishing important means of survival in Africa, from early times down to the present in most regions.

Africa's great mineral wealth has shaped human activity throughout the continent. Salt was a crucial trading commodity for centuries. For example, it was an important focus of the trans-Saharan trade between the western Sudan and North Africa from as early as the first millennium C.E. Even earlier, iron was a major good traded between forest and savannah. Copper, mined in only limited areas, was also much sought after and much traded; it influenced the early development of an advanced civilization in Egypt. For centuries gold was a significant internal trading commodity as well as an export. The ancient Egyptians sought the gold of Nubia; later, gold from West and central Africa was in demand in North Africa, the Mediterranean world, and the Indian Ocean.

Finally, we should note that by convention Africa is often discussed in terms of several major regions, which we shall use on occasion, arbitrary and inexact though they be: *North Africa*—all the Mediterranean coastal regions from modern Morocco through modern Libya and the northern Sahara, including the Sahel that marks the transition from mountains to true desert; *Nilotic Africa* (i.e., the lands of the Nile), rough-

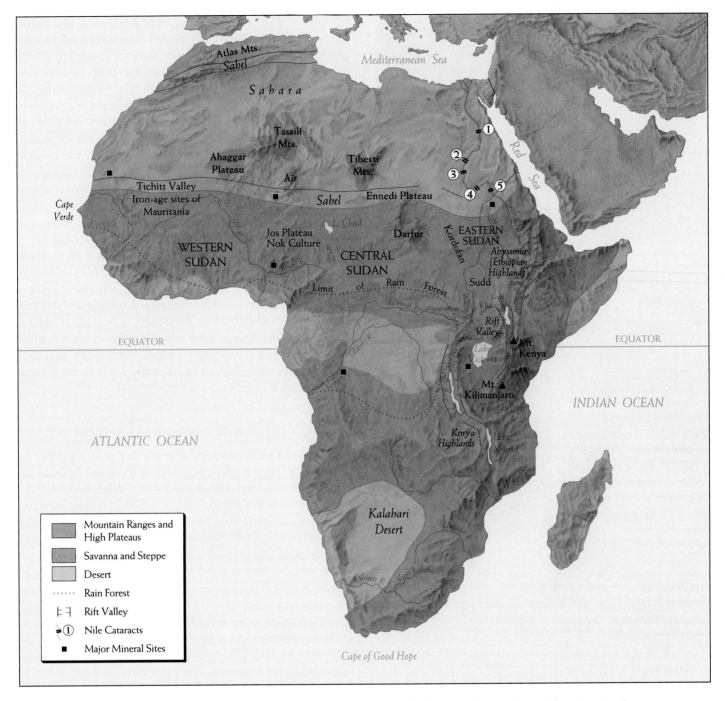

Map 6-1 Africa: Physical features and early sites. This map shows the major physical features of the continent and Iron Age sites of the western and central Sudan.

ly the area of the modern states of Egypt and Sudan; *the Sudan,* the broad belt of Sahel and savannah below the Sahara, stretching from the Atlantic east across the entire continent; *West Africa,* including the woodland coastal regions from Cape Verde to Cameroon and the desert, Sahel, and savannah of the western Sudan as far east as the Lake Chad basin; *East Africa,* from the Ethiopian highlands (a high, fertile plateau cut off by steppe, Sahel, and desert to its north and south) south over modern Kenya and Tanzania, an area split north to south by the Great Rift valley; *central Africa,* the region north of the Kalahari, from the Chad basin across the Zaïre basin and southeast to Lake Tanganyika and south to

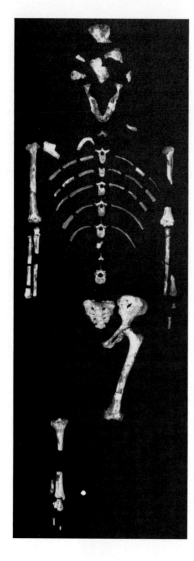

"Lucy," one of the most famous fossils found in the north end of the Great Rift valley, an area rich in fossils of species ancestral to humans. Lucy represents one of the earliest species to walk upright. [Cleveland Museum of Natural History]

Europeans distorts reality. Although its interior and southern reaches were isolated from direct contact with Eurasia until relatively recent centuries, African goods circulated for centuries through Indian Ocean as well as Mediterranean trade. Archaeological research is documenting the existence and substantial internal movements of peoples—and hence languages, cultures, and technologies—both north-south and east-west within the continent in ancient times. Commercial links between Africa and the outside date to earliest classical antiquity. Nilotic Egypt was always oriented to the Mediterranean and the easily accessible neighboring lands across the Red Sea. Well before the Christian era, the peoples of the upper Nile, the Ethiopian highlands, and the coastal areas of East Africa below the Horn maintained contacts with Egypt, south Arabia, and probably India and Indonesia, via the Indian Ocean. Like Egypt, the North African coast was engaged in Mediterranean trade throughout antiquity. Africa's Mediterranean littoral in particular was a place where Berber speakers mixed with other Mediterraneans such as the Phoenicians. Here the powerful Carthagenian Punic state arose in the mid-first millennium, only to fall prey to Rome (see Chapter 5).

Diffusion of Languages and Peoples

Cultural and linguistic diffusion shows that, despite the continent's natural barriers, Africans have not been as internally compartmentalized as was once thought. Language is a particularly interesting phenomenon in Africa. Between one thousand and three thousand languages can be found there, depending on how one distinguishes languages from dialects. As a whole, they can be roughly divided into four major groups, plus two late colonial arrivals, the Indo-European family from western Europe and the Malayo-Polynesian group (spoken only on Madagascar), which came with Southeast Asian colonists still earlier.

The four major groupings are the Afro-Asiatic, the Nilo-Saharan, the Niger-Kongo, and the "Khoisan." The first originated either in southwestern Asia and Arabia or in Africa, but in any case near the Red Sea. It is represented in the Semitic languages (which include Arabic, Hebrew, Aramaic, and Syriac) of southwestern Asia, as well as the ancient Egyptian, Berber, Chadic, Kushitic, and Omotic languages, all of which belong basically to North and northeastern Africa. The Nilo-Saharan family is spread over an area generally southwest of the Afro-Asiatic group, from the upper Nile across the central Sahara into the Rift highlands of Morocco. Niger-Kongo languages are found to the west and south of the Nilo-Saharan group, originally from the savannah and woodlands west of the Niger bend south and southeast to central and southern Africa. Finally,

the Zambezi (or, sometimes, the Limpopo) River; and *southern Africa*, from the Kalahari desert and Zambezi (or Limpopo) south to the Cape of Good Hope.

African Peoples

Africa and Early Human Culture

Archaeological research of recent decades indicates that our hominid ancestors evolved in the Great Rift region of highland East Africa at least 1.5 to 1.8 million years ago. It was probably also here that, sometime before 100,000 B.C.E., modern humans—the species *homo sapiens* (*sapiens*)—appeared and moved out to populate the rest of Africa and the world. In this sense, we are all African by descent.

The once popular view of sub-Saharan Africa as a vast region isolated from civilization until its "discovery" by

Khoisan is a collection of loosely related languages found today in southern Africa.[1]

Based on recent linguistic and archaeological investigations, the Africanist R. Oliver has attempted a plausible reconstruction of the diffusion of these language groups. He links the development of language families with a population growth that brought larger communities and extended movements of peoples. According to his interpretation, by near the end of the Stone Age, after about 8000 B.C.E., Afro-Asiatic languages from the Jordan and Nile valleys had spread to Arabia and across North Africa. Two southward extensions of these languages, from North Africa across the Sahara to the Chad basin, and from Egypt into the Ethiopian highlands and the Horn, likely occurred after 4000 B.C.E., possibly through the movement of pastoralists who brought sheep and cattle herding to these regions.

The Nilo-Saharan languages may have originated among fishing and cereal-growing societies in the Nubian region of the Nile and spread before ca. 5000 B.C.E. west into the Sahara. They were later largely displaced there by the southward extension of Afro-Asiatic languages into the Sahara with their pastoralist carriers. Isolated Nilo-Saharan tongues such as Zaghawa in the Tibesti, or Songhay above the Niger River, survived this influx. Nilo-Saharan languages must also have spread southeast with fishermen-farmers as far as the lakes region of the Great Rift valley, where at a later time they were partially displaced by Kushitic-speaking pastoralists or farmers.

The Niger-Kongo family had its homeland in the woodland savannah and equatorial forests of West and central Africa, perhaps near the Niger and Senegal headwaters west of the great bend of the Niger. Spoken by fisherfolk who may have turned to farming also, this group spread to the Atlantic coast from the Senegal River to the Cameroon mountains. Its largest subgroup, the Bantu speakers, later spread southward into the equatorial forestlands (largely as agriculturalists) and around the rain forests of central Africa (as herders as well as cultivators) until they entered finally the eastern and southern savannahs.

The fourth language family, nowadays called Khoisan, apparently covered most of the southern half of the African continent by late Neolithic times but was largely displaced by the migration of Niger-Kongo Bantu speakers. The varied peoples who were the ancestors of today's Khoisan speakers were likely still primarily hunter-gatherers at this time. Eventually, most of these peoples adopted the languages of the immigrant Bantu-speaking agriculturalists and pastoralists, making Bantu tongues the most widely dispersed African languages and confining the diverse Khoisan tongues to smaller areas than they had once covered.

The development of the complex language map of present-day Africa can thus be seen in terms of ancient developments in food production and movement of peoples and ways of life within the continent. We shall have occasion to return to several of these developments later in this chapter.

Racial Distinctions

Some interpreters have linked changes in African food production, development of local settled cultures, and even larger patterns of civilization to the apparent differences in appearance of African populations. In more recent historical times, lighter-skinned, Caucasoid African peoples have predominated in the Sahara, North Africa, and Egypt, whereas darker-skinned, Negroid peoples have been the majority in the rest of Africa.[2] (The Greeks called all the black peoples they were aware of in Africa *Ethiopians*, "those with burnt skins." The Arabs termed all of Africa south of the Sahara and Egypt *Bilad al-Sudan*, "the Land of the Blacks," and from this we get the term *Sudan*.) Other, yellowish-brown peoples occur in smaller numbers in sub-Saharan, especially southern, Africa, largely as herding or hunter-gatherer groups. These peoples are known as the Khoikhoi and San—the "Hottentots" and "Bushmen" of unfortunate traditional European usage—or today, collectively, the Khoisan; their greatest numbers are in the Kalahari and adjacent areas of southern Africa.

Some theories have attempted to relate color or racial differences to the development and spread of everything from language, agriculture, or cattle herding to iron working or state building in Africa. However, none of these theories is tenable, if only because the concept of race itself is problematic. As many scholars have noted, long periods of relative isolation of regional human populations in prehistory led to regionally differing common gene pools. Yet always, increasingly in more recent history, the mixing of gene pools produced constant change. In Africa, the various populations were so mixed that most Africans might best be considered to belong to one large race (or none), regardless of color or other physical attributes.[3] Thus one should not make too much out of the obvious color differences in Africa. These differences have resulted from differing gene pools and, perhaps, some climatic adaptation. We do not know at what

---

[1] For the entire discussion of language here and later in the chapter, we rely on the summary and analysis of R. Oliver, *The African Experience* (1991), pp. 38–50.

[2] Note, however, that actual distribution of skin color in the past is very hard to determine; there is even sharp disagreement as to whether the ancient Egyptians were more "white" or more "black." See the discussions in G. Mokhtar, ed., *Ancient Civilizations of Africa*, Vol. 2 of *UNESCO General History of Africa* (London: Heinemann, 1981), pp. 27–83; and W. MacGaffey, "Who Owns Ancient Egypt?" *Journal of African History* 32 (1991): 515–519.

[3] See Philip Curtin et al., *African History* (London, 1978), pp. 14–16.

prehistoric moment such factors led to differentiation among the Caucasoid peoples of North Africa, the Negroid peoples of the Sudan and south, and the "brown" peoples of the southern areas. All these types are found in an infinite variety of mixtures in most areas of Africa today, and categorizing them does not advance a reconstruction of the history of the continent.

The Sahara and the Sudan to the Beginning of the Christian Era

Early Saharan Cultures

One of the most striking and imposing physical features of the African continent is the Sahara. Since the second millennium B.C.E., this vast arid wilderness has separated the North African and Egyptian worlds from the wide expanse of the

Sudan and, farther south, West and central Africa. Still, this desert barrier never fully blocked north-south contact and exchange. The Nile Valley and the Great Rift plateau provided one corridor for movement of ideas and peoples south to north and vice versa. Similarly, the Red Sea, the Atlantic and Indian Ocean coasts, and a few routes through the Sahara itself allowed numbers of people and goods, not to mention ideas, to breach the great Saharan barrier as far back as our evidence takes us.

What is hard for us to imagine, however, is that until about 2500 B.C.E. the Sahara was arable land with lakes and rivers, trees, grasses, and a reasonable climate. We now know that during the so-called Wet Holocene period in Africa, from ca. 7500–2500 B.C.E., especially the southern half of the Sahara was positively well watered. In the earlier half of this period Lake Chad was a sea larger than the Caspian today. The swamplands of the upper White Nile region received water from not only Uganda but the Kenya rift as well, where in some lakes the water level was as much as five hundred feet above today's. The increased animal, fowl, reptile, and fish

A Stone Age Saharan rock painting, the Fresco of Tassili n'Ajjer, Algeria. One scholar believes this strikingly beautiful painting represents women gathering grain (represented by the dots, presumably). If so, it would have likely been wild grain unless cereal crops were cultivated very early here—something for which we have no evidence. Whether gathering grain or engaged in graceful dance, the figures here remind us of the ancient human presence in the once-green Saharan regions. [Henri Lhote Collection. Musee de l'Homme, Paris France/Erich Lessing/Art Resource, N.Y.]

Evidence of prehistoric Saharan contact with the Sudan. The discovery of cave paintings such as this from the Tassili mountains in the western Sahara gives credence to Herodotus' report (ca. 450 B.C.E.) of a people called Garamantes (probably Berber), who lived in the desert oases and used horse chariots. Such drawings have been found from the Sahara south almost to the Niger River. [Werner Forman Archive/Art Resource, N.Y.]

populations in these periods would have allowed riparian (river- and lakeside) communities of considerable size to live with ease off the land, and excavations near Khartoum in the Sudan support this likelihood. Here pottery was developed and used widely, as other excavations in the Aïr region of the Sahara have shown. Pastoralism and hunting as well as some domestication of food plants apparently developed in these regions.

Then, from ca. 2500 B.C.E. climatic changes caused the Sahara to undergo a relatively rapid dessication, and the riparian communities of this vast territory gradually disappeared. The pastoralist and hunting culture that, as we can see from cave paintings in the central Sahara, had developed in these regions was forced farther south into the Sudanic regions, or, in some cases, possibly north toward the Mediterranean.[4]

By 1000 B.C.E., the dessication process progressed enough to make the Sahara an immense east-west expanse of largely uninhabitable desert separating in substantial ways the greater part of the African continent from the Mediterranean coastal rim and the Near Eastern centers of early civilization. Even then, however, regular contacts in ancient times between sub-Saharan Africa and the Mediterranean continued. We know, for example, that various north-south routes across the western and central Sahara were traversed by horses and

carts or chariots and, most important, by migrating peoples long before the coming of the camel.

Neolithic Sudanic Cultures

Most interesting to speculate about are the repercussions of the Saharan dessication for later settled communities, especially those to the south in the Sahel and savannah of the Sudan. From the first millennium B.C.E., preliterate but complex agricultural communities of Neolithic and early Iron Age culture dotted the central and western reaches of the great belt of the sub-Saharan Sudan. We may surmise that these peoples, presumably speakers of Niger-Kongo languages, had once been spread farther north, in the then-arable Saharan lands they would have shared with ancestors of the Berber-speaking peoples of contemporary west-Saharan and North Africa.

This hypothesis has been bolstered by the excavation of town cultures from a more arable age in the Saharan regions of Mali, north of modern Timbuktu, and in the southwestern Sahara. These settlements date from the mid-fifth millennium B.C.E., when the Wet Holocene produced savannah conditions in this area (3,000–4,000 years later than in the central Sahara). Ancient settlements in Mali and Mauritania also date from this era. In inland Mauritania, remains of an ancient but later agricultural civilization with as many as two hundred towns have also been found. These reflect the transition from a hunting and fishing to a herding and rudimentary agricultural

[4]Oliver, pp. 31–37.

society. One theory proposes that the progressive dessication of the second millennium B.C.E. forced these peoples farther south. Pottery found in the first-millennium settlements in places such as Jenne (in Mali) are clearly "offshoots of a Saharan pottery tradition."[5] These migrants carried with them both languages and techniques of settled agriculture, especially those based on cereal grains, as well as techniques of animal husbandry, because they kept to the savannah lands below the desert and Sahel. They also domesticated new crops using their old techniques. Assisted ultimately by knowledge of iron working (probably passed on from North Africa or the Nilotic kingdom of Kush), they were able to effect an agricultural revolution. This meant considerable population growth in the more fertile Sudanic regions, especially near the great river basins of the Niger and Senegal, and the Lake Chad basin. (A similar spread of agricultural techniques and cattle and sheep raising seems to have occurred down the Rift valley of the East African highlands.) This agricultural revolution, completed during the first millennium B.C.E., paved the way for the growth of new cultural centers in the sub-Saharan regions thereafter.

Whatever their earlier history, we know that in the first millennium B.C.E. the Sudanic peoples developed and refined techniques of settled agriculture. They must have carried these together with their languages eastward through the savannahs and southward, largely along the rivers, into the tropical rain forests of central and West Africa. The result changed the face of sub-Saharan Africa, where before small groups of hunter-gatherers had predominated. With the advent of iron smelting, these settled peoples were able to develop larger and more complex societies than their predecessors.

The Early Iron Age and the Nok Culture

The common features of the oldest iron-smelting furnaces found in widely scattered sites across Africa over a span of

A terra-cotta head (20 cm high) from the Iron Age Nok culture, which occupied what is today northeastern Nigeria from about 900 B.C.E. to about 200 C.E. [Werner Forman Archive/Art Resource, N.Y./Jos Museum, Nigeria]

nearly a millennium—from the seventh century B.C.E. to the fourth century C.E.—suggest that smelting in Africa was invented within the continent. The earliest sites with evidence of smelting suggest that the process originated in the north—probably in Egypt and Nubia, or possibly in the central Saharan highlands of the Tibesti, Ahaggar, and Aïr. Thence it likely spread southward into western, central, and eastern parts of the continent. The western route lay between copper- and iron-rich southern Mauritania and both the great bend of the Niger River and the middle Senegal River farther west. The central route, to which we shall return, was from the Saharan mountains into northern Nigeria. In a route more to the east, iron appears to have spread indirectly from Meroe in Nubia (discussed below) through the Darfur or Ennedi highlands between the Chad basin and the Nile to the Bantu peoples in the northern Kongo basin, and thence to the lakelands of the East African Rift. The easternmost transmission route likely paralleled the East African coast from the Ethiopian highlands and Nubia south to the Zambezi and Limpopo.[6]

Some of the most significant Iron Age sites have been found in what is today northeastern Nigeria, on the Jos plateau. Here, near the village of Jos, archaeological digs have yielded evidence of an Iron Age people labeled the Nok culture (see Map 6–2). Excavations at Nok sites have yielded stone tools, iron implements, and highly artistic terra cotta sculptures. The sites date between 900 B.C.E. and 200 C.E. Excavations at Taruga have recently isolated layers with iron tools from lower strata without iron, allowing scholars to date the introduction of iron smelting to about the sixth century B.C.E. The Nok people cleared substantial woodlands from the plateau, and combined agriculture as their mainstay with some cattleherding.

The Nok culture is significant for two reasons. The first is that the Nok people, who mastered the relatively difficult art

[5]S. J. and R. J. McIntosh, *Prehistoric Investigations at Jenne, Mali* (Oxford, U.K.: B.A.R., 1980), p. 436.

[6]Oliver, pp. 64–76.

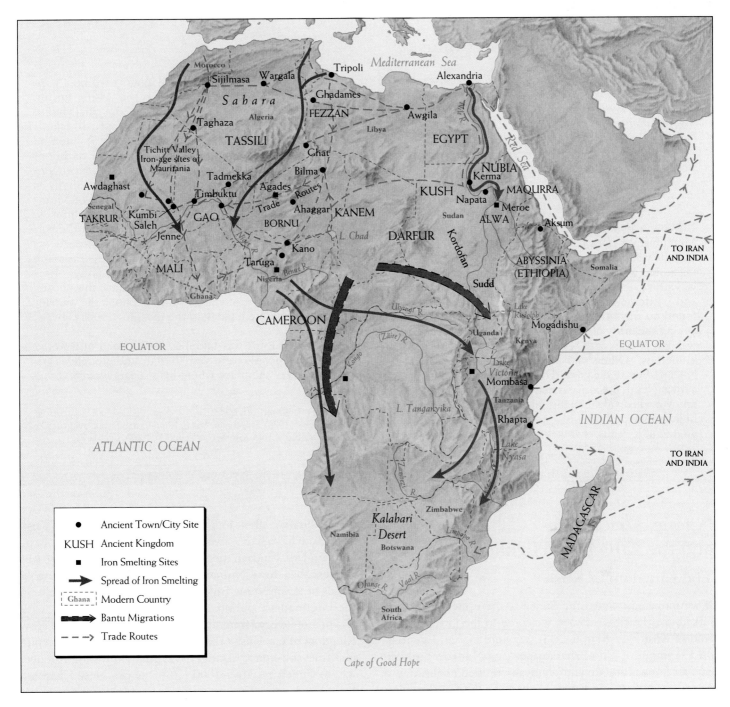

Map 6–2   Ancient African empires.

of smelting by at least 500 B.C.E., had the earliest Iron Age culture of West Africa. That they likely acquired this art by way of the Aïr mountains to the north is further evidence of early contact among African cultures. The second important aspect of Nok culture is its extraordinary sculptural art, most vividly evident in magnificent burial or ritual masks. The apparent continuities of Nok sculptural traditions with those of other, later West African cultures to the south suggest that this culture had an important impact on later West and central African life. These continuities indicate that ancient communities of considerable sophistication laid a basis on which later, better-known Sudanic civilizations must have built.

Kushite Conquest of Memphis

The following text is taken from a granite pillar, a victory stele that the Kushite king Piankhi had erected near Napata to commemorate his conquest of Egypt in the decade before 750 B.C.E. It describes the siege and capture of Memphis.

What elements in the description would you think might be slight exaggerations or hyperbole rather than sober chronicling?

When day broke, at early morning, his majesty reached Memphis. When he had landed on the north of it, he found that the water had approached to the walls, the ships mooring at (the walls of) Memphis. Then his majesty saw that it was strong, and that the wall was raised by a new rampart, and battlements manned with mighty men. There was found no way of attacking it. Every man told his opinion among the army of his majesty, according to every rule of war. Every man said: "Let us besiege it—; lo, its troops are numerous." Others said: "Let a causeway be made against it; let us elevate the ground to its walls. Let us bind together a tower; let us erect masts and make the spars into a bridge to it. We will divide it on this (plan) on every side of it, on the high ground and on the north of it, in order to elevate the ground at its walls, that we may find a way for our feet."

Then his majesty was enraged against it like a panther; he said: "I swear, as Re loves me, as my father, Amon (who fashioned me), favors me, this shall befall it, according to the command of Amon . . . I will take it like a flood of water. I have commanded . . . " Then he sent forth his fleet and his army to assault the harbor of Memphis; they brought to him every ferryboat, every (cargo) boat, every (transport), and the ships, as many as there were, which had moored in the harbor of Memphis, with the bow-rope fastened among its houses. (There was not) a citizen who wept, among all the soldiers of his majesty.

His majesty himself came to line up the ships, as many as there were. His majesty commanded his army: "Forward against it! Mount the walls! Penetrate the houses over the river. If one of you gets through upon the wall, let him not halt before it (so that) the (hostile) troops may not repulse you . . . ."

Then Memphis was taken as (by) a flood of water, a multitude of people were slain therein, and brought as living captives to the place where his majesty was.

From J. H. Breasted, *Ancient Records of Egypt* (Chicago: University of Chicago Press, 1906), Vol. 4, pars. 861 ff. Reprinted in Basil Davidson, *The African Past* (New York: Grosset and Dunlap, 1967), pp. 51–52.

Nilotic Africa and the Ethiopian Highlands

The Kingdom of Kush

If we move east across the Sudan to the upper Nile basin, just above the first cataract, we come to the lower Nubian land of Kush (see Map 6–2). It was here that an Egyptianized segment of Nilo-Saharan-speaking Nubians built the earliest known literate and politically unified civilization in Africa after Pharaonic Egypt. As early as the fourth millennium B.C.E., the Old Kingdom pharaohs had subjugated and colonized Nubia. In the early second millennium B.C.E., however, an independent kingdom arose in Kush in the broad floodplain just above the third cataract of the Nile. As early as 2000 B.C.E., its capital, Kerma, had been a major trading outpost for Middle Kingdom Egypt from which (and from neighboring settlements) a stream of building materials, ivory, slaves, mercenaries, and gold flowed north down the Nile.

The early Kushite kingdom reached its zenith in the period between the Middle and New kingdoms of Egypt, or about 1700–1500 B.C.E. The large tombs of eight rulers of this period survive, albeit long since plundered, at Kerma. Kush appears to have been a wealthy and prosperous kingdom by any standard. Finds in the palace fortress ruins and the tombs suggest that these Nubian kings may have taken the gold mines of lower Nubia from the weakened Egyptian state in the intermediate period. After the Hyksos invasions, with Egypt's recovery (from about 1500 B.C.E.) under the New Kingdom rulers, Kush came once more under Egyptian colonial rule and hence stronger Egyptian cultural influence. Then, sometime after 1000 B.C.E., as the New Kingdom floundered, a new Kushite state reasserted itself and by about 900 B.C.E. conquered lower as well as upper Nubia, regaining independence and the wealth from the Nubian gold mines.

The Napatan Empire

This new Kushite empire, centered first at Napata, just below the fourth Nile cataract, and then farther up the Nile at Meroe, proved a strong and lasting one (see Map 6–2). It survived from the tenth century B.C.E. until the fourth century C.E., when the Ethiopian Aksumites replaced Kush as the dominant power in northeastern Africa.

Kerma remained an important trading center after Kush regained its independence in the tenth century B.C.E. The leaders of the reestablished state, however, chose for their capital a site farther up the Nile than Kerma. This town, Napata, was to become the center of a new Nubian state and culture that flourished for three centuries as the true successor to pharaonic Egypt. The royal line that ruled at Napata was culturally heavily Egyptianized and saw themselves as Egyptian. They practiced the Pharaonic custom of marrying their own sisters, a practice known to many kingship institutions around the world. They buried their royalty embalmed in pyramids in traditional Egyptian style. They used Egyptian protocol and titles. In the eighth century B.C.E., they conquered Egypt and ruled it for about a century as the twenty-fifth Pharaonic dynasty. This Kushite dynasty was driven out of Egypt proper only by the iron-equipped military might of Assyria around the middle of the seventh century B.C.E.

The Meroitic Empire

Forced back above the lower cataracts of the Nile by the Assyrians and kept there by the Persians, the Napatan kingdom became increasingly isolated from Egypt and the Mediterranean and developed in its own distinctive ways. Napata itself was sacked by an Egyptian army in 591 B.C.E. This led to relocation of the capital farther south in the prosperous city of Meroe, bringing the seat of rule closer to the geographic center of the Kushite domains. By this time the Kushite kings had extended their sway westward into Kordofan, south above the confluence of the Blue and the White Nile, and southeast to the edges of the Abyssinian plateau. Meroe now became the kingdom's densely populated political and cultural capital. In the sixth century B.C.E. it was the center of a flourishing iron industry, from which iron smelting may first have spread west and south to the sub-Saharan world. Certainly the Kushites traded widely to the west across the Sudan as well as with the Hellenistic world and beyond. The Meroitic state was built on a staggeringly wide network of internal African as well as external, intercontinental commercial relations. It enjoyed a long and prosperous life before decline set in, apparently after about 100 C.E. The empire lasted, however, until it was defeated and divided in the fourth century by Nuba peoples from west of the upper Nile and replaced as the dominant regional power by the rival trading state of Aksum on the Abyssinian plateau.

Culture and Economy The heyday of Meroitic culture was from the mid-third century B.C.E. to the first century C.E. The kingdom was "middleman" for varied African goods in demand in the Mediterranean and Near East: animal skins, ebony and ivory, gold, oils and perfumes, and slaves. The Kushites traded with the Hellenistic-Roman

Ruins of the Great Amon Temple at Gebel (Mount) Barkal at the site of Napata, near Karima, Sudan. The Napatan kings were said to have been selected here by an oracle of the Egyptian god Amon, who was believed to reside inside the mountain. [Tim Kendall]

world, southern Arabia, and India, and in this regard were fully engaged in the larger international world. They shipped quality iron to Aksum and the Red Sea, and the Kushite lands between the Nile and the Red Sea were a major source of gold for Egypt and the Mediterranean world. Cattle breeding and other animal husbandry were their economic mainstays along with agriculture along the Nile, and more widely afield by irrigation. Cotton cultivation in Kush preceded that of Egypt and may have been an early export of the kingdom.

This was an era of prosperity. Many monuments were built, including royal pyramids and the storied palace and walls of the capital. Fine pottery and jewelry were produced. Meroitic culture is especially renowned for its two kinds of pottery: The first, turned on wheels, was the product of an all-male industry attuned apparently to market demands; the second, made exclusively by hand by women, was largely for domestic use. This latter pottery seems to have come from an older tradition of African pottery craft found well outside the region of Kush—an indication of ancient traditions shared in varied regions of Africa and of the antiquity of African internal trade.

Rule and Administration   The political system of the Meroitic empire, like the Pharaonic, was evidently stable over many centuries. There were several features that distinguished it from its Egyptian models. The king seems to have ruled strictly by customary law, presumably as interpreted by whatever priests or other clerics served the state's needs. According to Greek accounts, his actions were limited by firm taboos, and violation of those taboos could mean enforced royal suicide. There was also a royal election system. The priests presented several outstanding candidates for king, and from this group the god would choose the new sacred king (how, we are not told). The priests apparently considered the king a living god, an idea found in both ancient Egypt and many other African societies.

A Kushite inscription tells us that King Aspelta (r. 593–568 B.C.E.) was elected to succeed his brother from among his other royal brothers by twenty-four high officials and military

Meroitic culture produced many examples of fine pottery. This fired clay jar is decorated with giraffes and serpents. [University of Pennsylvania Museum]

Herodotus on Carthaginian Trade and on the City of Meroe

Herodotus reports (in about 430 B.C.E.) in the first passage below on what he has heard of the trading practices along the western or northwestern (Atlantic) coast of Africa ("Libya") as gleaned from the Carthaginian traders who passed beyond the Strait of Gibraltar ("Pillars of Hercules"). In the second passage he describes what he knows of the country, known to him as the land of the Ethiopians, above Elephantine [Aswan] on the Nile.

What can we infer from the two passages about trade and interregional contacts in the fifth century B.C.E.?

The Carthaginians also tell us that they trade with a race of men who live in a part of Libya beyond the Pillars of Hercules. On reaching this country, they unload their goods, arrange them tidily along the beach, and then, returning to their boats, raise a smoke. Seeing the smoke, the natives come down to the beach, place on the ground a certain quantity of gold in exchange for the goods, and go off again to a distance. The Carthaginians then come ashore and take a look at the gold; and if they think it represents a fair price for their wares, they collect it and go away; if, on the other hand, it seems too little, they go back aboard and wait, and the natives come and add to the gold until they are satisfied. There is perfect honesty on both sides; the Carthaginians never touch the gold until it equals in value what they have offered for sale, and the natives never touch the goods until the gold has been taken.

I went as far as Elephantine to see what I could with my own eyes, but for the country still further south I had to be content with what I was told in answer to my questions.

The most I could learn was that beyond Elephantine the country rises steeply; and in that part of the river boats have to be hauled along by the ropes—one rope on each side—much as one drags an ox. If the rope parts, the boat is gone in a moment, carried away by the force of the stream. These conditions last over a four days' journey, the river all the time winding greatly, like the Maeander, and the distance to be covered amounting to twelve *schoeni*. After this one reaches a level plain, where the river is divided by an island named Tachompso.

South of Elephantine the country is inhabited by Ethiopians who also possess half of Tachompso, the other half being occupied by Egyptians. Beyond the island is a great lake, and round its shores live nomadic tribes of Ethiopians. After crossing the lake one comes again to the stream of the Nile, which flows into it. At this point one must land and travel along the bank of the river for forty days, because sharp rocks, some showing above the water and many just awash, make the river impracticable for boats. After the forty days' journey on land one takes another boat and in twelve days reaches a big city named Meroë, said to be the capital city of the Ethiopians. The inhabitants worship Zeus and Dionysus alone of the Gods, holding them in great honor. There is an oracle of Zeus there, and they make war according to its pronouncements, taking from it both the occasion and the object of their various expeditions.

From the translation of *The Histories of Herodotus* by Aubrey de Selincourt Revised by A. R. Burn (New York: Penguin Classics, 1954, revised 1972), Copyright © The estate of Aubrey de Selincourt, 1954, © A. R. Burn, 1972.

A view of the ruins at Meroe. [Superstock, Inc.]

The Lion Temple and Kiosk at Naga in the Butana Desert, about sixty miles northeast of Khartoum. Naga, founded in the early first century C.E., was a Meroitic caravanserai on the Red Sea trade routes. Initially, Kushite religion appears to have followed Egyptian tradition. By the third century B.C.E., however, gods who were unknown to Egypt rose in importance. Judging by the presence of many temples like this, the lion-headed god Apedemak was one of the most important of these gods. [Tim Kendall]

leaders. Thus royal succession was not from father to son, but it was within the royal family. Other inscriptions tell us that the succession was often through the maternal rather than the paternal line, which would be in line with the evidence here and elsewhere of matrilineal succession as a widespread norm in ancient Africa. The role of the queen mother in the election appears to have been crucial—another parallel, if not a direct link, to African practices elsewhere. Indeed, the queen mother seems to have adopted formally her son's wife upon his succession. By the second century B.C.E. a woman had become sole monarch, initiating a long line of queens, or "Candaces" (*Kandake*, from the Meroitic word for "queen mother").

We know very little of Meroitic administration. The empire seems to have been under the autocratic rule of the royal sovereign, perhaps on the Egyptian model. He or she presided over a central administration run by numerous high officials: chiefs of the treasury, seal bearers, granary chiefs, army commanders, and chiefs of scribes and archives. The various provinces were delegated to princes who must have functioned with considerable autonomy, given the likely slow communication over the vast and difficult terrain of the upper Nile and eastern Sudanic region.

Society and Religion   Because of the limited sources for Kushite history, we have to speculate about the social structure outside the palace circle—the ruling class of monarch and relatives, priests, courtiers, and provincial nobility. We do find mention of slaves, most commonly female domestics, but also male laborers drawn largely from prisoners of war. We can presume that cattle breeders, farmers, traders, artisans, and minor government functionaries formed an intermediate class or classes between the slaves and the rulers.

In religious matters we have no direct records of actual Kushite practices, but it is clear that they closely followed Egyptian traditions for centuries. To judge from the great temples dedicated to him, Amon was the highest god for the earlier kings, and his priests had considerable influence. By the third century B.C.E., however, gods unknown to Egypt rose in importance alongside Amon and other Egyptian gods. Most notable was Apedemak, a warrior god with a lion's head. The many lion temples associated with him (as many as forty-six have been identified) reflect the great importance of this Kushite god. Such gods likely represented local deities who gradually rose to take their places alongside the

Early African Civilizations

ca. 7500–2500 B.C.E.	"Wet Holocene" period
ca. 2500 B.C.E.	Rapid dessication of Saharan region begins
ca. 2000–1000 B.C.E.	Increasing Egyptian influence in Nubia
ca. 1000–900 B.C.E.	Kushite kingdom with capital at Napata becomes independent of Egypt
751–663 B.C.E.	Kushite kings Piankhi and Taharqa rule all Egypt
ca. 600–500 B.C.E.	Meroe becomes new Kushite capital
ca. 500 B.C.E.–330 C.E.	Meroitic kingdom of Kush (height of Meroitic Kushite power ca. 250 B.C.E.–50 C.E.)
ca. 500 B.C.E.–500 C.E.?	Nok culture flourishes on Jos plateau in western Sudan (modern central Nigeria)
First century C.E.	Rise of Aksum as trading power on Ethiopian (Abyssinian) plateau
ca. 330 C.E.	Aksumite conquest of Kush

Sixth-Century Account of Aksumite Trade

The following document is taken from a description of a trading voyage to Sri Lanka in 625 C.E. by a Greek-speaking monk and former merchant from Alexandria, known as Cosmas Indicopleustes. In the excerpt he describes what he had heard of the Aksum area and its products and resources.

What might be inferred from the passage below about ancient contact of northern East Africa with Arabia and beyond?

The region which produces frankincense is situated at the projecting parts of Ethiopia, and lies inland, but is washed by the ocean on the other side. Hence the inhabitants of Barbaria, being near at hand, go up into the interior and, engaging in traffic with the natives, bring back from them any kinds of spices, frankincense, cassia, calamus, and many other articles of merchandise, which they afterwards send by sea to Adule, to the country of the Homerites, to Further India, and to Persia. This very fact you will find mentioned in the Book of Kings, where it is recorded that the Queen of Sheba, that is, of the Homerite country, whom afterwards our Lord in the Gospels calls the Queen of the South, brought to Solomon spices from this very Barbaria, which lay near Sheba on the other side of the sea, together with bars of ebony, and apes and gold from Ethiopia, which, though separated from Sheba by the Arabian Gulf, lay in its vicinity. We can see again from the words of the Lord that he calls these places the ends of the earth, saying: *The Queen of the South shall rise up in judgment with this generation and shall condemn it, for she came from the ends of the earth to hear the wisdom of Solomon,* Matt. xii. 42. For the Homerites are not far distant from Barbaria, as the sea which lies between them can be crossed in a couple of days, and then beyond Barbaria is the ocean, which is there called Zingion. The country known as that of Sasu is itself near the ocean, just as the ocean is near the frankincense country, in which there are many gold mines. . . .

From J. W. McCrindle, trans., *The Christian Topography of Cosmas, an Egyptian Monk* (London, 1897), as cited in G. S. P. Freeman-Grenville, ed., The East African Coast, 2nd ed. (London: Rex Collings, 1975), pp. 6–7.

---

highest Egyptian gods. However, some scholars have speculated about Iranian or Indian influences (via the Indian Ocean trading network) in the non-Egyptian elements of the Kushite cult.

The Aksumite Empire

A highland people who had developed their own commercially powerful trading state to the south of Kush delivered the *coup de grâce* to the weakened Kushite empire, apparently about 330 C.E. This was the newly Christianized state of Aksum, which centered in the northern Ethiopian, or Abyssinian, highlands where the Blue Nile rises. With the ascendancy of Aksum, our sources lapse into relative silence concerning the Nubian regions of the Nile. Not until the rise of new Christian Nubian states in the mid-sixth century can we again find clear evidence of the inheritors of the land of Kush.

The new conquerors, the peoples of Aksum, were the product of a linguistic, cultural, and genetic mixing of African Kushitic speakers with Semitic speakers from Yemenite southern Arabia. This mixing occurred after southern Arabians infiltrated and settled on the Ethiopian plateau around 500 B.C.E., giving Aksum, and later Ethiopia, Semitic speech and script closely related to South Arabian. Greek and Roman sources attest to the existence of an Aksumite kingdom from at least the first century C.E. By this time the kingdom, through its chief port of Adulis, had already become the major ivory and elephant market of northeastern Africa. Adulis had been important in Ptolemaic times, when it was captured by Egypt and used as a conduit for Egyptian influence in the highlands. After Egypt fell to the Romans, Aksum and its major port became an important cosmopolitan commercial center.

In the first two centuries C.E., their Red Sea location gave the Aksumites a strategic seat astride the increasingly important Indian Ocean trade routes. These trade routes linked India and the East Indies, Iran, Arabia, and the East African coast with the Roman Mediterranean. A further basis of Aksum's power was its key location for controlling trade between the African interior and the extra-African world, from Rome to Southeast Asia—notably exports of ivory, but also of elephants, obsidian, slaves, gold dust, and other inland products.

By the third century C.E., Aksum was one of the most impressive states of its age in the African or western Asian world, as the remains of the imposing stone buildings and monuments of its major cities—Aksum, Adulis, and Matara—attest. A work attributed to the prophet Mani, ca. 216–277 C.E., describes Aksum as one of the four greatest empires in the world. From the late second century onward, the Aksumites often held tributary territories across the Red Sea in southern Arabia. They also gained control of northern Ethiopia and conquered Meroitic Kush. Thus by the third and fourth centuries they controlled some of the most fertile cultivated regions of the ancient world: their own plateau, the rich

A giant stela at Aksum. Dating probably from the first century c.e., this giant carved monolith is the only one remaining of seven giant stelae—the tallest of which reached a height of 33 meters—that once stood in Aksum amidst numerous smaller monoliths. Although the exact purpose of the stelae is not known, the generally accepted explanation is that they were commemorative funerary monuments. Erecting them required engineering of great sophistication. [Werner Former Archive/Art Resource, N.Y.]

gold, silver, and copper (it was the first tropical African state to do so) was an index and symbol of both its political and economic power. The Aksumites enjoyed a long-lived economic prosperity. Goods of the Roman-Byzantine world and India and Sri Lanka, as well as of neighboring Meroe, flowed into Aksum. In addition to trade, vast herds and good agricultural produce gave a firm base to Aksumite prosperity.

In religion, the pre-Christian paganism of Aksum resembled the pre-Islamic paganism of southern Arabia, with various gods and goddesses closely tied to natural phenomena such as the sun, moon, and stars and worshiped or propitiated with animal sacrifices. There is also evidence of Jewish, Meroitic, and even Buddhist minorities living in the major cities of Aksum—an index of the cosmopolitanism of the society and its involvement with the larger Indian Ocean, western Asian, and South Asian worlds beyond the Red Sea.

In an inscription of the powerful fourth-century ruler King Ezana, we read of his conversion to Christianity, which led to the Christianizing of the kingdom as a whole. The conversion of Ezana and his realm was the work of Frumentius, a Syrian bishop of Aksum who served as secretary and treasurer to the king. Subsequently, under Alexandrian influence, the Ethiopian church became Monophysite in doctrine (that is, it adhered to the dogma of the single, unitary nature of Christ). Yet this did not end Aksumite trade with Byzantium, however much Constantinople persecuted Monophysites at home. In the fifth century C.E., the native Semitic language, Ge'ez, began to replace Greek in the liturgy, which proved a major step in the unique development of the Ethiopic or Abyssinian Christian church over the succeeding centuries.

Isolation of Christian Ethiopia

Aksumite trade continued to thrive through the sixth century, despite the decay of Rome. Strong enough at times to ex-

Yemenite highlands of southern Arabia, and much of the eastern Sudan across the upper Nile as far as the Sahara.

The resulting empire was ruled by a king of kings in Aksum through tribute-paying vassal kings in the other subject states. By the sixth century the Aksumite king was even appointing southern Arabian kings himself. Aksum's minting of coinage in

tend to the Yemen, Aksumite power was eclipsed in the end by the rise of Arab Islamic power. Nevertheless, the Aksumite state continued to exist long after its power had diminished. Having sheltered a refugee group of Muhammad's earliest Meccan converts, the Aksumites enjoyed relatively cordial relations with the new Islamic domains across the Red Sea and to the north in Egypt. But Aksum ceased to be a center of foreign trade and became increasingly isolated. Its center of gravity shifted south from the coast to the more rugged parts of the plateau. Here a Monophysite Christian, Ge'ez-speaking culture emerged in the region of modern Ethiopia and lasted in relative isolation until modern times, surrounded largely by Muslim peoples and states.

Ethiopia's northern neighbors, the Christian states of Maqurra and Alwa, also survived for centuries in the former Meroitic lands of the Nilotic Sudan under treaty relations with Muslim Egypt. However, incursions of the Muslim Mamluk rulers of Egypt in the fourteenth and fifteenth centuries and Arab migration from about 1300 led ultimately to the Islamization of the whole Nubian region. Ethiopia was left as the sole predominantly Christian state in Africa.

The Western and Central Sudan

Agriculture, Trade, and the Rise of Urban Centers

Earlier we noted the presumed movements of Neolithic peoples southward from the Saharan regions into the western and central Sudan and ultimately into the forests of the equatorial regions. The rain forests were inhospitable to cows and horses, largely because of the animals' inability to survive the sleeping sickness (*trypanosomiasis*) carried by the tsetse fly. But the agriculturalists who brought their cereal grains and stone tools south found particularly good conditions in the savannah just north of the West African forests. By the first or second century C.E., settled agriculture, augmented by the use of iron tools, had become the way of life of most inhabitants of the western Sudan; it had even made considerable progress in the forest regions farther south. The savannah areas seem to have experienced a substantial population explosion in the first few centuries C.E., especially around major water sources: along the Senegal River, around the great northern bend in the Niger River, and in the Lake Chad basin. Villages, and some chiefdoms consisting of several villages, remained normally the largest political units. As time went on, their growth provided the basis (and need) for the development of larger towns and political units in these areas of the western Sudan.

Trade was another element that promoted or at least accompanied the eventual rise of larger political entities in the western and central Sudan. Regional and interregional trade networks in the western and central Sudan date to ancient times; as we saw earlier, contacts between the Sudanic regions and the Mediterranean were maintained throughout the first millennium B.C.E. over trans-Saharan trading routes. Extensive east-west trade flourished in the Sahel, connecting the western Sahel to Egypt and the Nilotic Sudan. From the western Sahel this trade connected to Saharan routes and sites to the north (see Map 6–3).

By the latter half of the first millennium B.C.E., substantial urban settlements—such as Gao, Kumbi (or Kumbi Saleh), and Jenne—emerged in the western Sahel. Excavations at Jenne, in the upper Niger (the so-called Inland Delta) indicate that it dates from 250 B.C.E. and that its population reached more than ten thousand by the late first millennium C.E.[7]

We have already noted even earlier evidence of urbanism farther west and north, in the southern Mauritanian desert, where the remains of stone-walled towns of several thousand people have been dated to the second millennium B.C.E., when the area was a lakeland not yet dessicated by climatic changes. In addition, to the east, south of Lake Chad, in the lower reaches of the Chari and Lagone rivers that flow north to the great lake, as many as six hundred densely populated towns of the Sao, a Chadic-speaking people, can be dated with some confidence to the early first millennium C.E.

All of these early urbanized areas were characterized by an economy based on a mix of farming with fishing and hunting, and all developed in oasis or river regions rich enough to support dense populations and local and regional trade. The existence of relatively autonomous settlements made possible rather loose confederations or even widely dispersed imperial networks as time went on (and much earlier than scholars used to think).

The introduction of the domesticated camel (the one-humped Arabian camel, or dromedary) from the east around the beginning of the Christian era greatly increased the viability of trans-Saharan trade. By the early Christian centuries the West African settled communities had developed trading centers of considerable importance on their northern peripheries, in the Sahel near the edge of the true desert. The salt of the desert, so badly needed in the settled savannah, and the gold of West Africa, coveted in the north, were the prime commodities exchanged. However, many other items were also traded, including cola nuts, slaves, dates, and gum from West Africa, and horses, cattle, millet, leather, cloth, and weapons from the north.

---

[7]S. K. and R. J. McIntosh, pp. 41–59, 434–461; and R. Oliver, p. 90. The ensuing discussion of West African urban settlement is also taken primarily from Oliver's excellent summary of current knowledge about this subject, id., pp. 90–101.

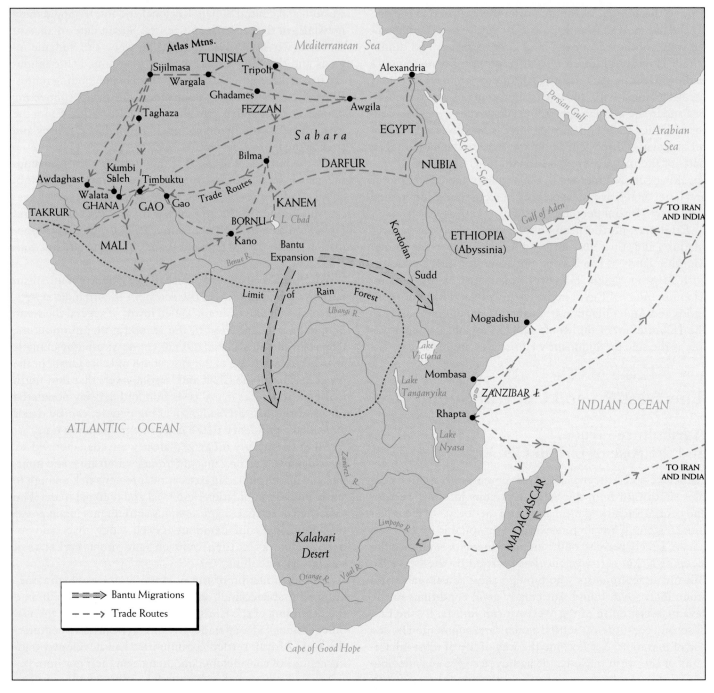

Map 6–3 Africa: Early trade routes and early states of the western and central Sudan. This map shows some of the major routes of north-south trans-Saharan caravan trade and their links with Egypt and with sudanic and forest West Africa.

Towns such as Awdaghast, Walata, Timbuktu, Gao, Tadmekka, and Agades were the most famous southern terminals for this trade over the centuries. These centers allowed the largely Berber middlemen who plied the desert routes to cross the ever-dangerous Sahara via oasis stations en route to the North African coasts or even Egypt. Some of the main routes ran as follows: (1) from Awdaghast, Walata, and Timbuktu to the major desert salt-producing center of Taghaza and thence to Morocco; (2) from Timbuktu or Gao over the desert direct to Morocco; and (3) from Tadmekka and Agades to the desert market town of Ghat in the north-central Sahara and on to the coasts of Libyan North Africa.

Other lines went north from the region of Lake Chad; one route stretched as far east as Egypt itself, passing through the mountain massifs of the central Sahara such as that of the Tassili and Ahaggar. Since a typical crossing could take two to three months, this was not an easy means of transporting goods.

Formation of Sudanic Kingdoms in the First Millennium

The first millennium C.E. saw the growth of settled agricultural populations and the expansion of trans-Saharan and other internal trade. These developments coincided with the

Excavations at Jenne-jeno (ancient Jenne), an early urban settlement in the western Sahel. Note the layer-cake stratification. This photograph shows work progressing in levels dating to the first centuries B.C.E. and the founding of the site by agriculturalists who came from the Saharan north. [R. J. Macintosh]

The Western and Central Sudan: Probable Dates for Founding of Regional Kingdoms	
ca. 400 C.E.	Takrur (Senegal River valley) or earlier
400–600 C.E.	Ghana (in Sahel between great northern bends of the Senegal and Niger rivers)
ca. 700–800 C.E.	Gao (on the Niger River or before southeast of great bend)
ca. 700–900 C.E.	Kanem (northeast of Lake Chad)

rise of several sizable states in the western and central Sudan, significantly in the Sahel and savannah border region near the great water sources below the Sahara. The most important states were located in Takrur on the Senegal River, from perhaps the fifth century, if not earlier; Ghana, between the northern bends of the Senegal and the Niger, from the fifth or sixth century; Gao, on the Niger southeast of the great bend, from before the eighth century; and Kanem, northeast of Lake Chad, from the eighth or ninth century. Although the origins and even the full extent of the major states in these areas are shrouded in obscurity, each represents only the first of a series of large political entities in its region. All continued to figure prominently in subsequent West African history (see Chapter 18).

The states developed by the Fulbe people of Takrur and the Soninke people of Ghana depended on their ability to draw gold for the Saharan trade with Morocco from the savannah region west of the upper Senegal. Of all the sub-Saharan kingdoms of the late first millennium, Ghana was the most famous outside of the region, largely owing to its substantial control of the gold trade. Its people built a large regional empire centered at its capital of Kumbi (or Kumbi Saleh). Inheriting his throne by matrilineal descent, the ruler was treated as a semidivine personage whose interaction with his subjects was mediated by a hierarchy of government ministers. He is described in an eleventh-century Arabic chronicle as commanding a sizable army, including horsemen and archers, and being buried with his retainers under a dome of earth and wood. In contrast to the Soninke of Ghana, the Songhai rulers of Gao had no gold trade until the fourteenth century. Unlike its western neighbors, Gao was oriented in its forest trade toward the lower, not the upper, Niger basin and in its Saharan trade toward eastern Algeria, not Morocco.

All of these states were based on agriculture and settled populations. By contrast, the power of Kanem, on the northwestern side of Lake Chad, originated in the borderlands of the central Sudan and southern Sahara with a nomadic federation of black tribal peoples that persisted long enough for the separate tribes to merge and form a single people, the

The introduction of the camel to the Saharan regions sometime around the beginning of the Christian era greatly increased the efficiency of trans-Saharan trade and contributed to the growth of major trading centers. [Super-Stock, Inc.]

Kanuri. They then moved south to take over the sedentary societies of Kanem proper, just east of Lake Chad, and later, Bornu, west of Lake Chad. By the thirteenth century the Kanuri had themselves become sedentary. Their kingdom controlled the southern terminus of perhaps the best trans-Saharan route-that running north via good watering stations to the oasis region of Fezzan in modern central Libya and thence to the Mediterranean. We shall return to Kanem and the western Sudanic states and their later development in Chapter 18.

Central, Southern, and East Africa

The African subcontinent is that part of central, southern, and East Africa that lies south of a line from roughly the Niger delta and Cameroon across to southern Somalia on the east coast. Paucity of sources makes it difficult to reconstruct in any detail the history of this region before 1000 C.E. Some relatively certain facts and reasonable hypotheses have, however, emerged from linguistic, archaeological, and other research.

The Khoisan Peoples

In southern Africa, as already noted, we find alongside the Bantu-speaking majority a minority who speak Khoi or San languages, collectively referred to as "Khoisan." The main two peoples that constitute the Khoisan speakers are the San and the Khoikhoi (the "Bushmen" and "Hottentots," respectively, in archaic Western usage). Current thinking has it that these are two interrelated, nonhomogeneous groups whose members can be distinguished linguistically, but not physically, from neighboring Bantu-speaking groups and other language groups of Africa.[8]

According to the conventional view, the Khoikhoi and San could be distinguished from each other largely by their livelihood. The Khoikhoi have generally been tagged as herdsmen and the San as hunter-gatherers, but recent research has challenged this. Both groups have also typically been seen

[8]On the vexing problem of distinguishing San and Khoikhoi, see Richard Elphick, *Kraal and Castle: Khoikhoi and the Founding of White South Africa* (New Haven: Yale University Press, 1977), pp. xxi–xxii, 3–42; on the "construction" of their respective identities and for a summary of recent research on their antiquity and history, see E. N. Wilmsen, *Land Filled with Flies* (Chicago: University of Chicago Press, 1989).

as surviving representatives of a "primitive" stage of cultural evolution, a view now rejected by many anthropologists and historians. These scholars argue that much of the common wisdom about these peoples, who do have low social and economic status in the Namibia-Botswana-Zimbabwe-South Africa areas where their small communities still can be found, is the result of colonialist and postcolonialist prejudice against them.

The San are likely the descendants of the Neolithic and early Iron Age peoples—originally hunter-gatherers and later also pastoralists—who created the striking prehistoric rock paintings of southern Africa. They do not form a single cultural group, but have developed linguistically and culturally diverse subgroups in different locales across southern Africa. Today they survive most prominently in the Kalahari region. The more homogeneous Khoikhoi were generally sheep- and cattle-herding pastoralists scattered across the south, yet speaking closely related Khoisan tongues. Their ancestors probably originated in northern Botswana. They were hunters who relatively late—likely between 700 and 1000 C.E.—adopted animal herding from their Bantu-speaking southern African neighbors. Thus they became primarily pastoralists and soon expanded over the best pasturelands of western southern Africa, as far south as the Cape of Good Hope. Here they flourished as pastoralist clans, sometimes united loosely as a tribe under a particularly strong chief, until their tragic encounter with the invading Dutch colonists in the mid-seventeenth century, which resulted in their demise as a distinct people.

Bantu Migrations and Diffusion

In the southern subcontinent, most people speak one of more than four hundred languages that belong to a single language group known as *Bantu*. All of these languages are as closely related as are the Germanic or Romance tongues of Europe. Although the place of origin and routes of diffusion of Bantu tongues have long been debated, there is increasing consensus that the location of the proto-Bantu language must have been in the region south of the Benue River, in eastern Nigeria and modern Cameroon. Thence, during the later centuries B.C.E. and the first millennium C.E., migrations of Bantu-speaking peoples must have carried their languages in two basic directions: (1) south into the lower Zaïre (Kongo) basin and ultimately to the southern edge of the equatorial forest in present-day northern Katanga; and (2) east around the equatorial forests into the lakes of highland East Africa.

In all these regions, Bantu tongues developed and multiplied in contact with other languages. Likewise, Bantu speakers intermixed and adapted in diverse ways, as the wide variety of physical types among Bantu peoples today demon-

strates. Further migrations, some as early as the fourth century C.E. and others as late as the twelfth or thirteenth century, dispersed Bantu peoples even more widely, into south-central Africa, coastal East Africa, and southern Africa. One result of this dispersion was the early civilization of "Great Zimbabwe" and Mapungubwe in the upper Limpopo region (treated in Chapter 18). The notion, however, that the Bantu and Khoikhoi arrived in southern Africa at about the same time as the first European settlers was a fabrication used to justify Apartheid (see Chapter 38).

How the Bantu peoples managed to impose their languages on the earlier cultures of these regions remains unexplained. The theory that they brought knowledge of iron smelting with them and used it to dominate other peoples is not borne out by linguistic or other studies. The proto-Bantu had apparently been fishermen and hunters who also cultivated yams, date palms, and some cereals. They raised goats and possibly sheep and cattle, but they did not bring cattle with them in their migrations. Most of the migrating Bantus seem to have been mainly cereal or grain farmers whose basic political and social unit was the village. Perhaps they had unusually strong social cohesion, which allowed them to absorb other peoples; there is no evidence that they were military conquerors. Possibly they simply had sufficient numbers to become dominant, or they may have brought diseases with them against which the aboriginals of the forests and southern savannah had no immunities, much as the European newcomers to the Cape later brought the ravages of smallpox to the susceptible Khoikhoi.

In any case, Bantu cultures became in time so fully interwoven with those of the peoples among whom they settled that these questions may never be answered. For example, Bantu-Arab mixing on the eastern coasts produced the Swahili culture, which we shall treat in Chapter 18. We find Bantu-speaking peoples as slash-and-burn farmers in the Zaïre River savannah, as cattle herders in the East African high plains, as perennial floodplain cultivators on the Zambezi River, and as terracing and irrigating farmers among the highland Kikuyu and Chagga peoples.

East Africa

The history of East Africa along the coast before Islam differed from that of the inland highlands. Long-distance travel was easy and common along the seashore but less so inland. The coast had had maritime contact with India, Arabia, and the Mediterranean via the Indian Ocean and Red Sea trade routes from at least as early as the second century B.C.E. By contrast, we know little about the long-distance contacts of inland regions with the coastal areas until after 1000 C.E. Nonetheless, both regional inland and coastal trade

A Tenth-Century Arab Description of the East African Coast

This selection is from the famous Baghdadi scholar, al-Mas'udi, who died in Cairo about 956 C.E. It treats the country of the Zanj, by which he means the coastal region of East Africa from the Horn down to Mozambique, a region that he himself visited on a voyage from Oman.

In what ways does this Muslim observer seem to be critical, and in what ways laudatory, of the East Africans?

The sea of the Zanj reaches down to the country of Sofala and of the Wak-Wak which produces gold in abundance and other marvels; its climate is warm and its soil fertile. It is there that the Zanj built their capital; then they elected a king whom they called *Waklimi.* . . .

The *Waklimi* has under him all the other Zanj kings, and commands three hundred thousand men. The Zanj use the ox as a beast of burden, for their country has no horses or mules or camels and they do not even know these animals. Snow and hail are unknown to them as to all the Abyssinians. Some of their tribes have sharpened teeth and are cannibals. The territory of the Zanj begins at the canal which flows from the Upper Nile and goes down as far as the country of Sofala and the Wak-Wak. Their settlements extend over an area of about seven hundred parasangs in length and in breadth; this country is divided by valleys, mountains and stony deserts; it abounds in wild elephants but there is not so much as a single tame elephant. . . .

Although constantly employed in hunting elephants and gathering ivory, the Zanj make no use of ivory for their own domestic purposes. They wear iron instead of gold and silver. . . .

. . . *Waklimi.* . . means supreme lord; they give this title to their sovereign because he has been chosen to govern them with equity. But once he becomes tyrannical and departs from the rules of justice, they cause him to die and exclude his posterity from succession to the throne, for they claim that in thus conducting himself he ceases to be the son of the Master, that to say of the king of heaven and earth. They call God by the name of Maklandjalu, which means supreme Master. . . .

The Zanj speak elegantly, and they have orators in their own language. . . . These peoples have no code of religion; their kings follow custom, and conform in their government to a few political rules. . . . Each worships what he pleases, a plant, an animal, a mineral.

They possess a great number of islands where the coconut grows, a fruit that is eaten by all the peoples of the Zanj. One of these islands, placed one or two days' journey from the coast, has a Muslim population who provide the royal family. . . .

Translated from the French version of de Meynard and de Courteille (1864) by Basil Davidson, *The African Past* (New York: Grosset and Dunlap, 1967), pp. 108–109.

---

must also be ancient. Both coastal and oversea trade remained important and interdependent over the centuries, because the Indian Ocean trade depended on the monsoon winds and could use only the northernmost coastal trading harbors of East Africa for round-trip voyages in the same year. The monsoon winds blow from the northeast from December to March and thus can carry sailing ships south from Iran, Arabia, and India only during those months; they blow from the southwest from April to August, so ships can sail from Africa northeast during those months. Local coastal shipping thus had to haul cargoes from south of Zanzibar and then transfer them to other ships for the annual round-trip voyages to Arabia and beyond.

Long-distance trade came into its own in Islamic times—about the ninth century—as an Arab monopoly. However, long before the coming of Islam, trade was apparently largely in the hands of Arabs, many of whom had settled in the East African coastal towns and in Iran and India to handle this international commerce. We have documentation of Greco-Roman contact with these East African centers of Red Sea and Indian Ocean trade from as early as the first century C.E. Most of the coastal trading towns apparently were independent, although Rhapta, the one town mentioned in the earliest Greek source, *The Periplus* (c. 89 C.E.), was a dependency of a southern Arabian state.

The overseas trade was, however, evidently even more international than the earliest sources indicate. Today, Malagasy, the imported Malayo-Polynesian language of Madagascar, points graphically to the antiquity of substantial contact with the East Indies via the coastal trading routes of Asia's ancient southern rim. Evidence of an Indonesian migration even before the beginning of our era is seen in the fact that bananas, coconut palms, and other food crops indigenous to Southeast Asia spread across the entire African continent as staple foods. Further, as a result of the early regular commercial ties to distant lands of Asia, extra-African ethnic and

Movement and Contact of Peoples in Central, Southern, and East Africa

ca. 1300–1000 B.C.E.	Kushitic-speaking peoples migrate from Ethiopian plateau south along Rift valley
ca. 400 B.C.E.–1000 C.E.	Probable era of major Bantu migrations into central, East, and southeastern Africa
200–100 B.C.E.	East African coast or earlier becomes involved in Indian Ocean trade
ca. 100 B.C.E.	Probable time of first Indonesian immigration to East African coast
ca. 100–1500 C.E.	Nilotic-speaking peoples spread over upper Nile valley; Nilotic peoples spread over Rift valley region

cultural mixing has long been the rule for the East African coast; even today, its linguistic and cultural traditions are rich and varied (see Chapter 18).

Other African imports included such items as Persian Gulf pottery, Chinese porcelain, and cotton cloth. The major African export good around which the east coast trade revolved was ivory, which was in perennial demand from Greece to India and, from the tenth century, even China. The slave trade was another major business. Slaves were procured, often inland, in East Africa and exported to the Arab and Persian world, as well as to India or China. Gold became important in external trade only in Islamic times, from about the tenth century onward, as we shall see in Chapter 18. Wood and cereals must also have been shipped abroad.

The history of inland East Africa south of Ethiopia is much more difficult to trace than that of the coast, again because of the absence of written sources and the immense difficulty of access until relatively recent times. We can, however, use linguistic clues and other evidence to note some key developments in the eastern highlands. These regions had seen an early diffusion of peoples from the north, and changing conditions of subsistence over the centuries continued to propel movements of small groups into new areas. Of the early migrants from the north, first came peoples speaking Kushitic languages of the Afro-Asiatic family, likely cattle herders and grain cultivators. Perhaps as early as 2000 B.C.E., they pushed from their homeland on the Ethiopian plateau south down the Rift valley as far as the southern end of Lake Tanganyika. They apparently displaced Neolithic hunter-gatherers who may have been related to the Khoisan minorities of modern East and southern Africa. Although Kushitic languages are spoken from east of Lake Rudolph northward in abundance, farther south only isolated remnants of Kushitic speakers remain today, largely in the Rift valley in Tanzania.

Later, Nilotic-Saharan speakers moved from the southwestern side of the Ethiopian plateau west over the upper Nile valley by about 1000 C.E. Then they pushed east and south, following older Kushite paths, to spread over the Rift valley area by the fifteenth century and subsequently much of the East African highlands of modern-day Uganda, Kenya, and Tanzania. Here they all but completely supplanted their Kushite predecessors. Two of these Nilotic peoples were the Lwo and Maasai. The Lwo spread over a nine-hundred-mile-long swath of modern Uganda and parts of southern Sudan and western Kenya. They did so over a long period of time and mixed readily with various other peoples, absorbing new cultural elements and adapting to new situations wherever they went. The Maasai, on the other hand, were and still are cattle pastoralists fiercely proud of their separate language, way of life, and cultural traditions. These features have distinguished them sharply from the farming or hunting peoples whose settlements abutted their pasturages at the top of the southern Rift valley in modern Kenya and Tanzania. Here, southwest and west of both Mount Kenya and Mount Kilimanjaro, the Maasai have concentrated and remained.

These migrations from the north and those of the Bantu peoples, who also entered the eastern highlands over many centuries from the west, have made the highlands a melting pot of Kushitic, Nilotic, Bantu, and Khoisan groups. Their characteristics are visible in today's populations, possessing an immense diversity of languages and cultures. Here, as well as anywhere, we can see the radical diversity of peoples and cultures of the entire African continent mirrored in a single region.

IN WORLD PERSPECTIVE

Africa to ca. 1000 C.E.

Pre-Islamic Africa is often viewed as a relatively isolated land mass that contributed little to political, cultural, and religious developments in the ancient world and was little engaged on the world scene. This view cannot withstand close scrutiny. To begin with, the human species probably originated in Africa. Pharaonic Egypt most notably, but also the Kushite kingdoms of Napata and Meroe and the Ethiopian state of Aksum, were all major political-military powers with highly developed cultures in regular interchange with other lands of the ancient world, from Rome to India and beyond.

Africa also made important contributions to other cultures. Nilotic cultures had a strong influence on the Hellenistic world. The Greek biblical translation known as the Septuagint was produced by Jewish scholars in Egyptian Alexandria. Muhammad's fledgling community of Muslims was in part sustained by sanctuary offered by Christian Abyssinia. Augustine of Hippo was an African. Even Christian monasticism began in Egypt.

Thus, from a world perspective, Africa was engaged with lands far and near from at least the first millennium B.C.E.—in trading, in conflict and cooperation, in religious life, and in cultural life. An active internal trade brought goods from the interior of the continent to the centers of external exchange. In Africa, however, as in much of Eurasia, the imminent coming of the last major world religious and cultural tradition—that of Islam—would affect, redefine, or even eliminate the overt presence of many previous centers of civilization.

Review Questions ——

1. How has the term "civilization" been interpreted to imply that Africa societies early and late lacked true "civilization"? What is your opinion on this?

2. What are the primary sources for study of Africa to 1000 C.E.? What are their advantages and drawbacks as reliable sources for early African history?

3. Do you find it a problem to think of Africa as a "dark" continent until European voyages of discovery and interior expeditions "discovered" it? Why? Discuss.

4. Discuss the diffusion of peoples and languages in African history. What does it tell us about early African history?

5. How was the political system of the Meroitic empire similar to and different from that of Egyptian rule?

6. How did Aksum become a Christian state? What effect did it have on relations with Byzantium?

7. What were the most important goods for African internal trade? Which products were traded abroad? What can we learn from these trade patterns?

8. In what ways did geography "control" early African history? What about the specific case of Ghana? Of North Africa? Of the East African littoral? Of southern Africa?

Suggested Readings ——

P. BOHANNAN AND P. CURTIN, *Africa and Africans*, rev. ed. (1971). An enjoyable and enlightening discussion of African history and prehistory and of major African institutions (e.g., arts, family life, religion).

P. CURTIN, S. FEIERMANN, L. THOMPSON, AND J. VANSINA, *African History* (1978). Probably the best survey history. The relevant portions are chaps. 1, 2, 4, 8, and 9.

T. R. H. DAVENPORT, *South Africa: A Modern History*, 3rd rev. ed. (1987). Chapter 1 gives excellent summary coverage of prehistoric southern Africa, the Khoisan peoples, and the Bantu migrations.

B. DAVIDSON, *The African Past* (1967). A combination of primary-source selections and brief secondary discussions trace sympathetically the history of the diverse parts of Africa.

J. D. FAGE, *A History of Africa* (1978). A fine general history. The relevant segment here is Part I, "The Internal Development of African Society" (chaps. 1–5).

P. GARLAKE, *The Kingdoms of Africa* (1978). A lavishly illustrated set of photographic essays that provide a helpful introduction to the various historically important areas of precolonial Africa.

R. W. JULY, *Precolonial Africa: An Economic and Social History* (1975). A very readable, topically arranged study. See especially "The Savannah Farmer," "The Bantu," "Cattlemen," and "The Traders" chapters.

R. W. JULY, *A History of the African People*, 3rd ed. (1980). Part I, "Ancient Africa" covers the precolonial centuries and offers a very readable historical introduction to African civilization.

J. KI-ZERBO, *Methodology and African Prehistory*. Vol. I of *UNESCO General History of Africa* (1981). Useful summary and interpretive articles (but of very uneven quality) treat diverse topics, including sources, languages, geography, and prehistory.

H. LOTH, *Woman in Ancient Africa*. Trans. S. Marnie (1987). An interesting survey of legal, familial, cultural, and other aspects of women's roles.

G. MOKHTAR, *Ancient Civilizations of Africa*. Vol. II of *UNESCO General History of Africa* (1981). As in other volumes, the quality of articles varies greatly. Relevant chaps. are 8–16 on Nubia, Meroe, and Aksum; 17–20 on the Saharan region in ancient times; and 22–29 on the early history of sub-Saharan Africa.

R. OLIVER, *The African Experience* (1991). A masterly, balanced, and engaging sweep through African history. The chapters on prehistory and early history are outstanding summaries of the results and implications of recent research.

I. VAN SERTIMA, *Black Women in Antiquity* (1984, 1988). Studies of queens, goddesses, matriarchy, and other aspects of the role and status of women in Egyptian, Ethiopian, and other African societies of the past.

7 CHINA'S FIRST EMPIRE (221 B.C.E.–220 C.E.)

Cast bronze horses and warriors excavated in 1969 from the vaulted brick and earth mounded tomb (circa 186–219 C.E.) of a general of the Later Han dynasty. The general may have served on China's Western frontier since the tomb was at Lei T'ai in Kansu province. The tomb also contained coins, silver seals, model chariots, and inscribed figures of male and female slaves. The beauty and energy of these bronzes suggests a continuity between Han art and that of the T'ang dynasty several centuries later. [National Museum, Beijing, China]

◆ Ch'in Unification of China

◆ Former Han Dynasty (206 B.C.E.–8 C.E.)

◆ Later Han (25–220 C.E.) and Its Aftermath

◆ Han Thought and Religion

In World Perspective China's First Empire

One hallmark of Chinese history is its striking continuity of culture, language, and geography. The Shang and Chou dynasties were centered in north China along the Yellow River or its tributary, the Wei. The capitals of China's first empire were in exactly the same areas, and north China would remain China's political center through history to the present. If Western civilization had experienced similar continuity, it would have progressed from Thebes in the valley of the Nile to Athens on the Nile; Rome on the Nile; and then, in time, to Paris, London, and Berlin on the Nile; and each of these centers of civilization would have spoken Egyptian and written in Egyptian hieroglyphics.

The many continuities in its history, however, did not mean that China was unchanging. One key turning point came in the third century B.C.E. when the old, quasi-feudal, multistate Chou system gave way to a centralized bureaucratic government. The new centralized state built an empire stretching from the steppe in the north to Vietnam in the south.

The history of the first empire is composed of three segments: The Ch'in dynasty, the Former Han dynasty, and the Later Han dynasty. The English word China is derived from the name of the first dynasty. The Ch'in overthrew the previous Chou dynasty in 256 B.C.E. and went on to unify China in 221 B.C.E. In reshaping China, the Ch'in developed such momentum that it became overextended and collapsed a single generation after the unification. The succeeding Han dynasties each lasted about two hundred years, the Early Han from 206 B.C.E. to 8 C.E., the Later Han (founded by a descendant of the Former Han) from 25 to 220 C.E. Historians usually treat each of the Han dynasties as a separate period of rule, although they occurred almost back to back and shared many institutions and cultural traits. So deep was the impression left by these two dynasties on the Chinese that even today they call themselves—in contrast to Mongols, Manchus, Tibetans, and other minorities—the "Han people," and their ideographs, "Han writing."

Ch'in Unification of China

Of the territorial states of the late Chou era, none was more innovative and ruthless than Ch'in. Its location on the Wei River in northwest China—the same area from which the Chou had launched their expansion a millennium earlier—gave it strategic advantages: It controlled the passes leading out onto the Yellow River plain and so was easy to defend and was a secure base from which to attack other states. From the late fourth century B.C.E., the Ch'in conquered a part of Szechwan and thus controlled two of the most fertile regions of ancient China. It welcomed Legalist administrators, who developed policies for enriching the country and strengthening its military. Despite its harsh laws, farmers moved to Ch'in from other areas, attracted by the order and stability of its society. Its armies had been forged by centuries of warfare against the nomadic raiders by whose lands it was half encircled. To counter these raiders, Ch'in armies adopted nomadic skills, developing cavalry in the fourth century. Other states regarded the Ch'in as tough, crude, and brutal, but recognized their formidable strengths.

In 246 B.C.E. the man who would unify China succeeded to the Ch'in throne at the age of thirteen. He grew to be vigorous, ambitious, intelligent, and decisive. He is famous as a Legalist autocrat; but he was also well liked by his ministers, whose advice he usually followed. (See Chapter 2 for a description of Legalism.) In 232 B.C.E., at the age of twenty-seven, he began the campaigns that destroyed the six remaining territorial states. On completing his conquests in 221 B.C.E., he adopted the glorious title we translate as "emperor"—a combination of

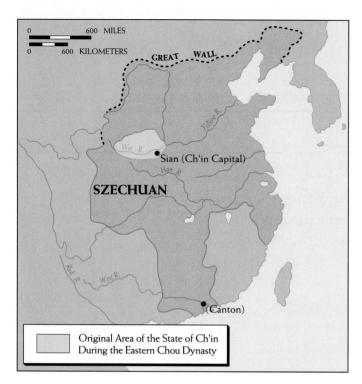

Map 7–1   The unification of China by the Ch'in State.   Between 221 and 206 B.C.E. the Ch'in state expanded and unified China.

ideographs hitherto used only for gods or mythic heroes—to raise himself above the kings of the former territorial states. Then, aided by officials of great talent, this First Ch'in Emperor set about applying to all of China the reforms that had been tried and found effective in his own realm. His accomplishments in the eleven years before his death in 210 B.C.E. were stupendous.

Having conquered the civilized world of north China and the Yangtze River basin, the First Emperor sent his armies to conquer new lands. They reached the northern edge of the Red River basin in what is now Vietnam. They occupied China's southeastern coast and the area about the present-day city of Canton (see Map 7–1). In the north and the northwest, the emperor's armies fought against the Hsiung Nu, Altaic-speaking Hunnish nomads. During the late Chou, northern border states had built long walls to protect settled lands from incursions by horse-riding raiders. The Ch'in emperor had them joined into a single Great Wall that extended fourteen hundred miles from the Pacific Ocean into central Asia. (By comparison, Hadrian's Wall in England was seventy-three miles long.) Construction of the Great Wall cost the lives of vast numbers of conscripted laborers—by some accounts, one hundred thousand; by others, as many as one million.

The most significant Ch'in reform, carried out by the Legalist minister, Li Ssu, extended the Ch'in system of bu-

reaucratic government to the entire empire. Li Ssu divided China into forty prefectures, which were further subdivided into counties. The county heads were responsible to prefects, who, in turn, were responsible to the central government. Officials were chosen by ability. Bureaucratic administration was impersonal, based on laws to which all were subject. No one, for example, escaped Ch'in taxation. This kind of bureaucratic centralism broke sharply with the old Chou pattern of establishing dependent principalities for members of a ruler's family. Furthermore, to ensure the smooth functioning of local government offices, former aristocrats of the territorial states were removed from their lands and resettled in the Ch'in capital, near present-day Sian. They were housed in mansions on one side of the river, from which they could gaze across at the enormous palace of the First Emperor.

Other reforms further unified the First Emperor's vast domain. Roads were built radiating out from the capital city. The emperor decreed a system of uniform weights and measures. He unified the Chinese writing system, establishing standard ideographs to replace the great variety that had hitherto prevailed. He established uniform axle lengths for carts. Even ideas did not escape the drive toward uniformity. Following the precepts of Legalism, the emperor and his advisers launched a campaign for which they subsequently have been execrated throughout Chinese history. They collected and burned the books of Confucianism and other schools, and were said to have buried alive several hundred scholars opposed to the Legalist philosophy. Only useful books on agriculture, medicine, or Legalist teachings were spared.

But the Ch'in had changed too much too quickly. To pay for the roads, canals, and the Great Wall, burdensome taxes were levied on the people. Commoners hated conscription and labor service, and nobles resented their loss of status. Merchants were exploited; scholars, except for Legalists, were oppressed. A Chinese historian wrote afterward: "The condemned were an innumerable multitude; those who had been tortured and mutilated formed a long procession on the roads. From the princes and ministers down to the humblest people everyone was terrified and in fear of their lives."[1] After the first Emperor died in 210 B.C.E., intrigues broke out at court and rebellions arose in the land. At the end, the Ch'in was destroyed by the domino effect of its own legal codes. When the generals sent to quell a rebellion were defeated, they joined the rebellion rather than return to the capital and incur the severe punishment decreed for failure. The dynasty collapsed in 206 B.C.E.

In 1974 a farmer near Sian discovered the army of eight thousand life-sized terra-cotta horses and soldiers that guarded the tomb of the First Emperor. The historical record tells

[1]C. P. Fitzgerald, *China, A Short Cultural History* (New York: Praeger, 1935), p. 147.

The Great Wall of China was originally built during the Ch'in dynasty (256-206 B.C.E.), but what we see today is the wall as it was completely rebuilt during the Ming dynasty (1368-1644 C.E.). [Paolo Koch/Photo Researchers, Inc.]

us that in the tomb itself, under a mountain of earth, are a replica of his capital; a relief model of the Chinese world with quicksilver rivers; other warriors with chariots of bronze; and the remains of horses, noblemen, and criminals sacrificed to accompany in death the emperor whose dynasty was to have lasted for ten thousand generations.

Former Han Dynasty (206 B.C.E.–8 C.E.)

The Dynastic Cycle

Confucian historians of China have seen a pattern in every dynasty of long duration. They call it the *dynastic cycle*. The stages of the cycle are interpreted in terms of the "mandate of heaven." The cycle begins with internal wars that even-

tually led to the military unification of China. Unification is proof that heaven has given the unifier the mandate to rule. Strong and vigorous, the first ruler, in the process of consolidating his political power, restores peace and order to China. Economic growth follows, almost automatically. The peak of the cycle is marked by public works, further energetic reforms, and aggressive military expansion. During this phase, China appears invincible. But then the cycle turns downward. The costs of expansion, coupled with an increasing opulence at the court, place a heavy burden on tax revenues just as they are beginning to decline. The vigor of the monarchs wanes. Intrigues develop at court. Central controls loosen, and provincial governors and military commanders gain autonomy. Finally, public works fall into disrepair, floods and pestilence occur, rebellions break out, and the dynasty collapses. For Confucian historians, the last emperors in a cycle are not only politically weak but morally culpable.

The army of life-size terra-cotta soldiers found in the tomb of the first emperor of the Ch'in dynasty (256–206 B.C.E.). [Erich Lessing/Art Resource, N.Y.]

Early Years of the Former Han Dynasty

The first sixty years of the Han may be thought of as the early phase of its dynastic cycle. After the collapse of the Ch'in, one rebel general gained control of the Wei basin and went on to unify China. He became the first emperor of the Han dynasty and is known by his posthumous title of Kao Tsu (r. 206–195 B.C.E.). He rose from plebeian origins to become emperor, which would happen only once again in Chinese history. Kao Tsu built his capital at Ch'ang-an, not far from the former capitals of the Western Chou and the Ch'in. It took Kao Tsu and his immediate successors many years to consolidate their power because they consciously avoided actions that would remind the populace of the hated Ch'in despotism. They made punishments less severe and reduced taxes. Good government prevailed, the economy rebounded, granaries were filled, and vast cash reserves were accumulated. Later historians often singled out the early Han rulers as model sage emperors.

Han Wu Ti

The second phase of the dynastic cycle began with the rule of Wu Ti (the "martial emperor"), who came to the throne in 141 B.C.E. at the age of sixteen and remained there for fifty-four years (141–87 B.C.E.). Wu Ti was daring, vigorous, and intelligent but also superstitious, suspicious, and vengeful. He wielded tremendous personal authority.

Building on the prosperity achieved by his predecessors, Wu Ti initiated new economic policies. A canal was built from the Yellow River to the capital in northwest China, linking the two major economic regions of north China. "Ever-level granaries" were established throughout the country so that the surplus from bumper crops could be bought and then resold in time of scarcity. To increase revenues, taxes were levied on merchants, the currency was debased, and some offices were sold. Wu Ti also moved against merchants who had built fortunes in untaxed commodities by reestablishing government monopolies—a practice of the Ch'in—on copper coins, salt, iron, and liquor. For fear of Wu Ti, no one spoke out against the monopolies, but a few years after his death, a famous debate was held at the court.

Known after the title of the chronicle as the "Salt and Iron Debate," it was frequently cited thereafter in China, and in Japan and Korea as well. On one side, quasi-Legalist officials argued that the state should enjoy the profits from the sale of salt and iron. On the other side, Confucians argued that these resources should be left in private hands, for the moral purity of officials would be sullied by dealings with merchants.

The Confucian scholars who compiled the chronicle made themselves the winner in the debate; but state monopolies became a regular part of Chinese government finance.

Wu Ti also aggressively expanded Chinese borders—a policy that would characterize every strong dynasty. His armies swept south into what is today northern Vietnam and northeast across Manchuria to establish a military outpost in northern Korea that would last until 313 C.E.

The principal threat to the Han was from the Hsiung Nu empire to the north. Their mounted archers could raid China and flee before an army could be sent against them. To combat them, Wu Ti employed the entire repertoire of policies that would become standard thereafter. When possible he "used the barbarian to control the barbarian," making allies of border nomads against those more distant. Allies were permitted to trade with Chinese merchants; they were awarded titles and honors; and their kings were sent Chinese princesses as brides. When this method did not work, he used force. Between 129 and 119 B.C.E. Wu Ti sent several armies of over one hundred thousand troops into the steppe, destroying Hsiung Nu power south of the Gobi Desert in southern Mongolia. To establish a strategic line of defense aimed at the heart of the Hsiung Nu empire further to the west, Wu Ti then sent seven hundred thousand Chinese colonists to the arid Kansu panhandle and extended the Great Wall to the Jade Gate outpost at the eastern end of the Tarim Basin. From this outpost, Chinese influence was extended over the rim oases of Central Asia, establishing the Silk Road that linked Ch'ang-an with Rome (see Map 7–2).

Government During the Former Han

To demonstrate their difference from the Ch'in emperor, the early Han emperors set up some Chou-like principalities: small, semiautonomous states with independent lords. This arrangement was, however, a token gesture. The principalities were closely superintended and then curtailed after several generations. Basically, despite its repudiation of the Ch'in and all its works, the Han continued the Ch'in form of centralized bureaucratic administration. Officials were organized by grades and were paid salaries in grain, plus cash or silk. They were recruited by sponsorship or recommendation: Provincial officials had the duty of recommending promising candidates. A school established at Ch'ang-an was said to have thirty thousand students by the Later Han. The bureaucracy grew until, by the first century B.C.E., there were more than one hundred thirty thousand officials—perhaps not too many for a population that, by that time, had reached sixty million.

Under the Han dynasty, this "Legalist" structure of government became partially Confucianized. It did not happen overnight. The first Han emperor, Kao Tsu, despised Confucians as bookish pedants— he once urinated in the hat of a scholar. But Confucian ideas proved useful. The mandate of heaven provided an ethical justification for dynastic rule. A respect for old records and the written word fit in well with the vast bookkeeping the empire entailed. The Confucian classics gradually were accepted as the standard for education. Confucianism was seen as shaping moral men who would be upright officials, even in the absence of external constraints. For Confucius had taught the transformation of self through ethical cultivation and had presented a vision of benevolent government by men who were virtuous as well as talented. No one attempted to replace laws with a code of etiquette, but increasingly laws were interpreted and applied by men with a Confucian education.

The court during the Han dynasty exhibited features that would appear in later dynasties as well. All authority centered on the emperor, who was the all-powerful "son of heaven." The will of a strong adult emperor was paramount. When the

Tomb figure of standing attendant from the Former Han dynasty, second century B.C.E. [The Asia Society, N.Y.: Mr. and Mrs. John D. Rockefeller 3rd Collection]

emperor was weak, however, or ascended to the throne when still a child, others competed to rule in his name. Four contenders for this surrogate role appeared and reappeared through Chinese history: court officials, the empress dowager, court eunuchs, and military commanders.

Court officials were selected for their ability to govern: They staffed the apparatus of government and advised the emperor directly. Apart from the emperor himself, they were usually the most powerful men in China. Yet their position was often precarious. Few officials escaped being removed from office or banished once or twice during their careers. Of the seven prime ministers who served Wu Ti, five were executed by his order.

Of the emperor's many wives, the empress dowager was the one whose child had been named as the heir to the throne. Her influence sometimes continued even after her child became an adult emperor. But she was most powerful as a regent for a child emperor. On Kao Tsu's death in 195 B.C.E., for example, the empress Lu became the regent for her child, the new emperor. Aided by her relatives, she seized control of the court and murdered a rival, and when her son was about to come of age, she had him killed and a younger son made the heir to continue her rule as regent. When she died in 180 B.C.E., loyal adherents of the imperial family who had opposed her rule massacred her relatives.

Court eunuchs came mostly from families of low social status. They were brought to the court as boys, castrated, and assigned to work as servants in the emperor's harem. They were thus in contact with the future emperor from the day he was born, they became his childhood confidants, and they often continued to advise him after he had gained the throne. Emperors found eunuchs useful as counterweights to officials. But to the scholars who wrote China's history, the eunuchs were greedy half men, given to evil intrigues.

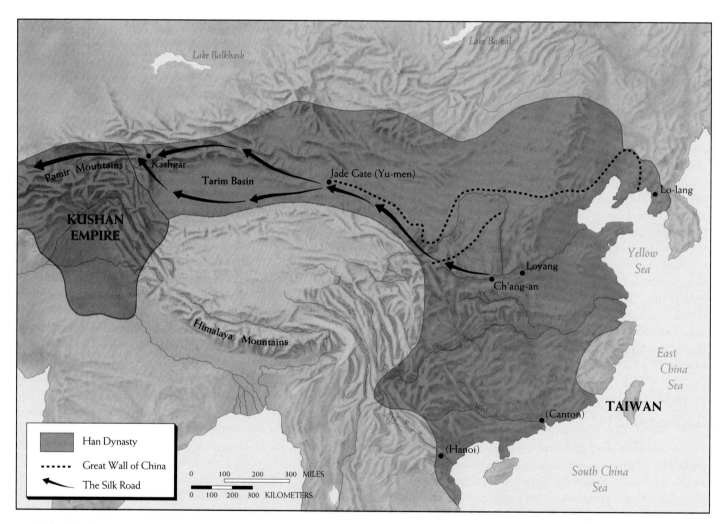

Map 7-2   The Han Empire 206 B.C.E.–220 C.E.   At the peak of the Han expansion, the Han armies advanced far out into the steppe north of the Great Wall and west into Central Asia. The silk road to Rome passed through the Tarim Basin and the Kushan Empire.

Chinese Women Among the Nomads

The first of these selections is the lament of Hsi-chun, a Chinese lady sent by Wu Ti in about 105 B.C.E. to be the wife of a nomad king of the Wu-sun people of central Asia. When she got there, she found her husband to be old and decrepit. He saw her only once or twice a year, when they drank a cup of wine together. They could not converse, as they had no language in common. The second selection, written centuries later, is by the T'ang poet Tu Fu, who visited the village of another woman sent to be the wife of a nomad king.

What does the fate of the women in these poems suggest about the foreign policy of the rulers of ancient China?

1.

My people have married me
In a far corner of Earth;
Sent me away to a strange land,
To the king of the Wu-sun.
A tent is my house,
Of felt are my walls;
Raw flesh my food
With mare's milk to drink.
Always thinking of my own country,
My heart sad within.
Would I were a yellow stork
And could fly to my old home!

2.

Ten thousand ranges and valleys approach the Ching
    Gate
And the village in which the Lady of Light was born and
    bred.
She went out from the purple palace into the desert-land;
She has now become a green grave in the yellow dusk.
Her face!—Can you picture a wind of the spring?
Her spirit by moonlight returns with a tinkling
Telling her eternal sorrow.

1. From *Chinese Poems* by Arthur Waley. Copyright © 1946 by George Allen and Unwin Ltd., an imprint of HarperCollins Publishers Ltd. Reprinted by permission of the Arthur Waley Estate.
2. From *The Jade Mountain: A Chinese Anthology* by Witter Bynner, trans. Copyright © 1929 and renewed 1957 by Alfred A. Knopf Inc. Reprinted by permission of the publishers.

Military leaders, whether generals or rebels, were the usual founders of dynasties. In the later phase of most dynasties, regional military commanders often became semi-independent rulers. A few even usurped the throne. Yet they were less powerful at the Chinese court than they were, for example, in imperial Rome, partly because the military constituted a separate category, lower in prestige than the better-educated civil officials. It was also partly because the court took great pains to prevent its generals from establishing a base of personal power. An appointment to command a Han army was given only for a specific campaign, and commanders were appointed in pairs so that each would check the other.

Another characteristic of government during the Han and subsequent dynasties was that its functions were limited. It collected taxes, maintained military forces, administered laws, supported the imperial household, and carried out public works that were beyond the powers of local jurisdictions. But government in a district that remained orderly and paid its taxes was left largely in the hands of local notables and large landowners. This pattern was not, to be sure, unique to China. Most premodern governments, even those that were bureaucratic, floated on top of local society and were not able to reach down and interfere in the everyday lives of their subjects.

Decline and Usurpation

During the last decade of Wu Ti's rule in the early first century C.E., military expenses ran ahead of revenues. His successor cut back on military costs, eased economic controls, and reduced taxes. But over the next several generations, large landowners began to use their growing influence in provincial politics to avoid paying taxes. State revenues declined. The tax burden on smaller landowners and free peasants grew heavier. In 22 B.C.E., rebellions broke out in several parts of the empire. At the court, too, a decline set in. There was a succession of weak emperors. Intrigues, nepotism, and factional struggles grew apace. Even officials began to sense that the dynasty no longer had the approval of heaven. The dynastic cycle approached its end.

Many at the court urged Wang Mang, the regent for the infant emperor and the nephew of an empress, to become the emperor and begin a new dynasty. Wang Mang refused several times—to demonstrate his lack of eagerness—and then accepted in 8 C.E. He drew up a program of sweeping reforms based on ancient texts. He was a Confucian, yet relied on new institutional arrangements rather than moral reform to improve society. He revived ancient titles, expanded state monopolies, abolished private slavery (about 1 percent of the population), made loans to poor peasants, and then moved to confiscate large private estates.

These reforms, however, alienated many. Merchants disliked the monopolies. Large landowners resisted the expropriation of their lands. Nature also conspired to bring down Wang Mang: The Yellow River overflowed its banks and changed its course, destroying the northern Chinese irrigation system. Several years of poor harvests produced famines. The Hsiung Nu overran China's northern borders. In 18 C.E., a

A green glazed pottery model of a Later Han dynasty watchtower (87.6 × 35.6 × 38.1 cm). Note the resemblance to later Chinese Buddhist pagodas.

The Dynastic History of China's First Empire	
256–206 B.C.E.	Ch'in dynasty
206 B.C.E.–8 C.E.	Former Han dynasty
25–220 C.E.	Later Han dynasty

peasant secret society rose in rebellion. In 23 C.E., rebels attacked Ch'ang-an, and Wang Mang was killed and eaten by rebel troops. He had tried to found a new dynasty from within a decrepit court without an independent military base. The attempt was futile. Internal wars continued in China for two more years until a large landowner, who had become the leader of a rebel army, emerged triumphant in 25 C.E. Because he was from a branch line of the imperial family, his new dynasty was viewed as a restoration of the Han.

Later Han (25–220 C.E.) and Its Aftermath

First Century

The founder of the Later Han moved his capital east to Loyang. Under the first emperor and his two successors, there was a return to strong central government and a laissez-faire economy. Agriculture and population recovered. By the end of the first century C.E., China was as prosperous as it had been during the good years of the Former Han. The shift from pacification and recuperation to military expansion came earlier than it had during the previous dynasty. Even during the reign of the first emperor, south China and Vietnam were retaken. Dissension among the Hsiung Nu enabled the Chinese to secure an alliance with some of the southern tribes in 50 C.E., and in 89 C.E. Chinese armies crossed the Gobi Desert and defeated the northern Hsiung Nu. This defeat sparked the migrations, some historians say, that brought the Hsiung Nu to the southern Russian steppes and then, in the fifth century C.E., to Europe, where they were known as the Huns of Attila. In 97 C.E. a Chinese general led an army to the shores of the Caspian Sea. The Chinese expansion in inner Asia, coupled with more lenient government policies toward merchants, facilitated the camel caravans that carried Chinese silk across the Tarim Basin to Iran, Palestine, and Rome.

Decline During the Second Century

Until 88 C.E. the emperors of the Later Han were vigorous; afterward they were ineffective and short lived. Empresses

Pan Chao's Admonitions for Women

Pan Chao (45–116) was the sister of the famous historian Pan Ku. Her guide to mortality, Admonitions for Woman, *was widely used during the Han Dynasty. Humility is one of the seven womanly virtues about which she wrote; the others are resignation, subservience, self-abasement, obedience, cleanliness, and industry.*

Given the range of female personalities in Chinese society, what are some of the likely responses to this sort of moral education? Are self-control and self-discipline more likely to be associated with weakness or with strength of character?

Humility

In ancient times, on the third day after a girl was born, people placed her at the base of the bed, gave her a pot shard to play with, and made a sacrifice to announce her birth. She was put below the bed to show that she was lowly and weak and should concentrate on humbling herself before others. Playing with a shard showed that she should get accustomed to hard work and concentrate on being diligent. Announcing her birth to the ancestors showed that she should focus on continuing the sacrifices. These three customs convey the unchanging path for women and the ritual traditions.

Humility means yielding and acting respectful, putting others first and oneself last, never mentioning one's own good deeds or denying one's own faults, enduring insults and bearing with mistreatment, all with due trepidation. Industriousness means going to bed late, getting up early, never shirking work morning or night, never refusing to take on domestic work, and completing everything that needs to be done neatly and carefully. Continuing the sacrifices means serving one's husband-master with appropriate demeanor, keeping oneself clean and pure, never joking or laughing, and preparing pure wine and food to offer to the ancestors.

There has never been a woman who had these three traits and yet ruined her reputation or fell into disgrace. If a woman loses these three traits, she will have no name to preserve and will not be able to avoid shame.

Reprinted with the permission of The Free Press, A Division of Simon & Schuster, Inc. From *Chinese Civilizations: A Sourcebook* by Patricia Buckley Ebrey. © 1993 by Patricia Buckley Ebrey.

---

plotted to advance the fortunes of their families. Emperors turned for help to palace eunuchs, whose power at times surpassed that of officials. In 159 C.E. a conspiracy of eunuchs in the service of an emperor slaughtered the family of a scheming empress dowager and ruled at the court. When officials and students protested against the eunuch dictatorship, over a hundred were killed and over a thousand were tortured or imprisoned. In another incident in 190 C.E., a general deposed one emperor, installed another, killed the empress dowager, and massacred most of the eunuchs at the court.

In the countryside, large landowners who had been powerful from the start of the dynasty grew more so. They harbored private armies. Farmers on the estates of the mighty were reduced to serfs. The landowners used their influence to avoid taxes. Great numbers of free farmers fled south for the same purpose. The remaining freeholders paid ever heavier taxes and labor services. Many peasants turned to neo-Taoist religious movements that provided the ideology and organization to channel their discontent into action. In 184 C.E. rebellions organized by members of the religious movements broke out against the government. Han generals suppressed the rebellions but stayed on to rule in the provinces they had pacified. In 220 C.E. they deposed the last Han emperor.

Aftermath of Empire

For more than three and a half centuries after the fall of the Han, China was disunited. For several generations it was divided into three kingdoms, whose heroic warriors and scheming statesmen were made famous by wandering storytellers. These figures later peopled the *Tales of the Three Kingdoms*, a great romantic epic of Chinese literature.

Chinese history during the post-Han centuries had two characteristics. The first was the dominant role played by the great aristocratic landowning families. With vast estates, huge numbers of serfs, fortified manor houses, and private armies, they were beyond the control of most governments. Because they took over many of the functions of local government, some historians describe post-Han China as having reverted to the quasi-feudalism of the Chou. The second characteristic of these centuries was that northern and southern China developed in quite different ways.

In the south, there followed a succession of ever weaker dynasties with capitals at Nanking. Although these six southern states were called dynasties—and the entire period of Chinese history from 220 C.E. to 589 C.E. is called the Six Dynasties era after them—they were in fact short-lived kingdoms, plagued by intrigues, usurpations, and coups d'état; frequently at war with northern states; and in constant fear of their own generals. The main developments in the south were (1) continuing economic growth and the emergence of Nanking as a thriving center of commerce; (2) the ongoing absorption of tribal peoples into Chinese society and culture; (3) large-scale immigrations of Chinese fleeing the north; and (4) the spread of Buddhism and its penetration to the heart of Chinese culture.

In the north, state formation depended on the interaction of nomads and Chinese. During the Han dynasty, Chinese invasions of the steppe had led to the incorporation of semi-Sinicized Hsiung Nu as the northernmost tier of the Chinese defense system—just as Germanic tribes had acted as the teeth and claws of the late Roman Empire. But as the Chinese state weakened, the highly mobile nomads broke loose, joined with other tribes, and began to invade China. The short-lived states that they formed are usually referred to as the "Sixteen Kingdoms." One kingdom was founded by invaders of Tibetan stock. Most spoke Altaic languages: the Hsien Pi (proto-Mongols), the Toba (proto-Turks), and the Juan Juan (who would later appear in eastern Europe as the Avars). But differences of language and stock were less important than these tribes' similarities:

1. All began as steppe nomads with a way of life different from that of agricultural China.

2. After forming states, all became at least partially Sinicized. Chinese from great families, which had preserved the Han traditions, served as their tutors and administrators.

3. All were involved in wars—among themselves, against southern dynasties, or against conservative steppe tribes that resisted Sinicization.

4. Buddhism was as powerful in the north as in the south. As a universal religion, it acted as a bridge between "barbarians" and Chinese-just as Christianity was a unifying force in post-Roman Europe. The barbarian rulers of the north were especially attracted to its magical side. Usually Buddhism was made the state religion. Of the northern states, the most durable was the Northern Wei (386–534 C.E.), famed for its Buddhist sculpture.

Han Thought and Religion

Poems describe the splendor of Ch'ang-an and Loyang: broad boulevards, tiled gateways, open courtyards, watchtowers, and imposing walls. Most splendid of all were the palaces of the emperors, with their audience halls, vast chambers, harem quarters, and parks containing artificial lakes and rare animals and birds. But today little remains of the grandeur of the Han. Whereas Roman ruins abound in Italy and circle the Mediterranean, in China nothing remains above ground.

Court figures painted on ceramic tile in a Han dynasty tomb (Gray earthenware; hollow tiles painted in ink and colors on a whitewashed ground 73.8 × 204.7 cm). [Denman Waldo Ross Collection and gift of C.T. Loo/Courtesy Museum of Fine Arts, Boston]

Only from the pottery, bronzes, musical instruments, gold and silver jewelry, lacquerware, and clay figurines that were buried in tombs do we gain an inkling of the rich material culture of the Han period. And only from paintings on the walls of tombs do we know of its art.

But a wealth of written records conveys the sophistication and depth of Han culture. Perhaps the two most important areas were philosophy and history.

Han Confucianism

A major accomplishment of the early Han was the recovery of texts that had been lost during the Ch'in persecution of scholars. Some were retrieved from the walls of houses where they had been hidden; others were reproduced from memory by scholars. Debate arose regarding the relative authenticity of the old and new texts—a controversy that has continued until modern times. In 51 B.C.E. and again in 79 C.E. councils were held to determine the true meaning of the Confucian classics. In 175 C.E. an approved, official version of the texts was inscribed on stone tablets.

In about 100 C.E. the first dictionary was compiled. Containing about nine thousand characters, it helped promote a uniform system of writing. In Han times, as today, Chinese from the north could not converse with Chinese from the southeastern coast. But a common written language bridged differences of pronunciation, contributing to Chinese unity.

It was also in Han times that scholars began writing commentaries on the classics, a major scholarly activity throughout Chinese history. Scholars learned the classics by heart and used classical allusions in their writing.

Han philosophers also extended Chou Confucianism by adding to it the teachings of cosmological naturalism. Chou Confucianists had assumed that the moral force of a virtuous emperor would not only order society but also harmonize nature. Han Confucianists explained why. Tung Chung-shu (ca. 179–104 B.C.E.), for example, held that all nature was a single, interrelated system. Just as summer always follows spring, so does one color, one virtue, one planet, one element, one number, and one officer of the court always take precedence over another. All reflect the systematic workings of yang and yin and the five elements. And just as one dresses appropriately to the season, so was it important for the emperor to choose policies appropriate to the sequences inherent in nature. If he was moral, if he acted in accord with Heaven's natural system, then all would go well. But if he acted inappropriately, then Heaven would send a portent as a warning—a blue dog, a rat holding its tail in its mouth, an eclipse, or a comet. If the portent was not heeded, wonders and then misfortunes would follow. It was the Confucian scholars, of course, who claimed to understand nature's messages and advised the emperor.

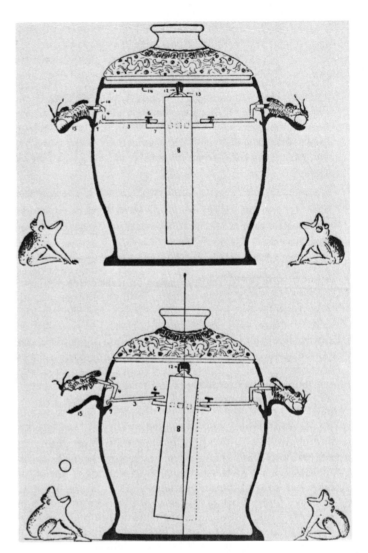

A Chinese seismograph. The suspended weight swings in the direction of the earthquake. This moves a lever and a dragon drops a ball into the mouth of one of the four waiting ceramic frogs. [New York Public Library at Lincoln Center]

It is easy to criticize Han philosophy as a pseudo-scientific or mechanistic view of nature. But it represented a new effort by the Chinese to encompass and comprehend the interrelationships of the natural world. This effort led to inventions like the seismograph and to advances in astronomy, music, and medicine. It was also during the Han that the Chinese invented paper, the wheelbarrow, the stern-post rudder, and the compass (known as the "south-pointing chariot").

History

The Chinese were the greatest historians of the premodern world. They wrote more history than anyone else, and what they wrote was usually more accurate. Apart from the *Spring*

Ssu-ma Ch'ien on the Wealthy

More than half of the chapters in Ssu-ma Ch'ien's Historical Records *(early first century B.C.E.) were biographies of extraordinary men and women. He wrote of scholars, wandering knights, diviners, harsh officials and reasonable officials, wits and humorists, doctors, and moneymakers. The following is his description of the vibrant economic life of Han cities and his judgments regarding the wealthy.*

What economic "principles" can you derive from this passage? Can you detect an echo of Ssu-ma Ch'ien's claims in current debates on economic policy?

Anyone who in the market towns or great cities manages in the course of a year to sell the following items: a thousand brewings of liquor; a thousand jars of pickles and sauces; a thousand jars of sirups; a thousand slaughtered cattle, sheep, and swine; a thousand chung of grain; a thousand cartloads or a thousand boat-lengths of firewood and stubble for fuel; a thousand logs of timber; ten thousand bamboo poles; a hundred horse carriages; a thousand two-wheeled ox carts; a thousand lacquered wooden vessels; brass utensils weighing thirty thousand catties; a thousand piculs of plain wooden vessels, iron vessels, or gardenia and madder dyes; two hundred horses; five hundred cattle; two thousand sheep or swine; a hundred male or female slaves; a thousand catties of tendons, horns, or cinnabar; thirty thousand catties of silken fabric, raw silk, or other fine fabrics; a thousand rolls of embroidered or patterned silk; a thousand piculs of fabrics made of vegetable fiber or raw or tanned hides; a thousand pecks of lacquer; a thousand jars of leaven or salted bean relish; a thousand catties of globefish or mullet; a thousand piculs of dried fish; thirty thousand catties of salted fish; three thousand piculs of jujubes or chestnuts; a thousand skins of fox or sable; a thousand piculs of lamb or sheep skins; a thousand felt mats; or a thousand chung of fruits or vegetables—such a man may live as well as the master of an estate of a thousand chariots. The same applies for anyone who has a thousand strings of cash [i.e., a million in cash] to lend out on interest. Such loans are made through a moneylender, but a greedy merchant who is too anxious for a quick return will only manage to revolve his working capital three times while a less avaricious merchant has revolved his five times. These are the principal ways of making money. There are various other occupations which bring in less than twenty percent profit, but they are not what I would call sources of wealth.

Thrift and hard work are without doubt the proper way to gain a livelihood. And yet it will be found that rich men have invariably employed some unusual scheme or method to get to the top. Plowing the fields is a rather crude way to make a living, and yet Ch'in Yang did so well at it that he became the richest man in his province. Robbing graves is a criminal offense, but T'ien Shu got his start by doing it. Gambling is a wicked pastime, but Huan Fa used it to acquire a fortune. Most fine young men would despise the thought of traveling around peddling goods, yet Yung Lo-ch'eng got rich that way. Many people would consider trading in fats a disgraceful line of business, but Yung Po made a thousand catties of gold at it. Vending sirups is a petty occupation, but the Chang family acquired ten million cash that way. It takes little skill to sharpen knives, but because the Chih family didn't mind doing it, they could eat the best of everything. Dealing in dried sheep stomachs seems like an insignificant enough trade, but thanks to it the Cho family went around with a mounted retinue. The calling of a horse doctor is a rather ignominious profession, but it enabled Chang Li to own a house so large that he had to strike a bell to summon the servants. All of these men got where they did because of their devotion and singleness of purpose.

From this we may see that there is no fixed road to wealth, and money has no permanent master. It finds its way to the man of ability like the spokes of a wheel converging upon the hub, and from the hands of the worthless it falls like shattered tiles. A family with a thousand catties of gold may stand side by side with the lord of a city; the man with a hundred million cash may enjoy the pleasures of a king. Rich men such as these deserve to be called the "untitled nobility," do they not?

From *Records of the Grand Historian of China* trans. by Burton Watson. Copyright © 1961 by Columbia University Press. Reprinted by permission of the publisher.

and Autumn Annals and the scholarship of Confucius himself, history writing in China began during the Han dynasty. Why the Chinese were so history-minded has been variously explained: because the Chinese tradition is this-worldly; because Confucianists were scholarly and their veneration for the classics carried over to the written word; because history was seen as a lesson book (the Chinese called it a mirror) for statesmen, and thus a necessity for the literate men who operated the centralized Chinese state.

The practice of using actual documents and firsthand accounts of events began with Ssu-ma Ch'ien (d. 85 B.C.E.), who set out to write a history of the known world from the

The Peach Blossom Spring

The poet Ta'o Ch'ien wrote in 380 C.E. of a lost village without taxes and untouched by the barbarian invasions and wars of the post-Han era. The simplicity and naturalness of his utopian vision were in accord, perhaps, with certain strains of Neo-Taoist thought. It struck a chord in the hearts of Chinese, and then Koreans and Japanese, inspiring a spate of paintings, poetry, and essays.

Utopias are often based on religion, but this one is not. What does this suggest regarding the Chinese view of human nature?

During the T'ai-yuan period of the Ch'in dynasty a fisherman of Wuling once rowed upstream, unmindful of the distance he had gone, when he suddenly came to a grove of peach trees in bloom. For several hundred paces on both banks of the stream there was no other kind of tree. The wild flowers growing under them were fresh and lovely, and fallen petals covered the ground—it made a great impression on the fisherman. He went on for a way with the idea of finding out how far the grove extended. It came to an end at the foot of a mountain whence issued the spring that supplied the stream. There was a small opening in the mountain and it seemed as though light was coming through it. The fisherman left his boat and entered the cave, which at first was extremely narrow, barely admitting his body; after a few dozen steps it suddenly opened out onto a broad and level plain where well-built houses were surrounded by rich fields and pretty ponds. Mulberry, bamboo and other trees and plants grew there, and criss-cross paths skirted the fields. The sounds of cocks crowing and dogs barking could be heard from one courtyard to the next. Men and women were coming and going about their work in the fields. The clothes they wore were like those of ordinary people. Old men and boys were carefree and happy.

When they caught sight of the fisherman, they asked in surprise how he had got there. The fisherman told the whole story, and was invited to go to their house, where he was served wine while they killed a chicken for a feast. When the other villagers heard about the fisherman's arrival they all came to pay him a visit. They told him that their ancestors had fled the disorders of Ch'in times and, having taken refuge here with wives and children and neighbors, had never ventured out again; consequently they had lost all contact with the outside world. They asked what the present ruling dynasty was, for they had never heard of the Han, let alone the Wei and the Chin. They sighed unhappily as the fisherman enumerated the dynasties one by one and recounted the vicissitudes of each. The visitors all asked him to come to their houses in turn, and at every house he had wine and food. He stayed several days. As he was about to go away, the people said, "There's no need to mention our existence to outsiders." After the fisherman had gone out and recovered his boat, he carefully marked the route. On reaching the city, he reported what he had found to the magistrate, who at once sent a man to follow him back to the place. They proceeded according to the marks he had made, but went astray and were unable to find the cave again.

From *The Poetry of Ta'o Ch'ien* by J. R. Hightower. Copyright © 1970 Clarendon Press. pp. 254–255. Reprinted by permission of Oxford University Press.

---

most ancient times down to the age of the emperor Wu Ti. His *Historical Records* consisted of 130 substantial chapters (with a total of over seven hundred thousand characters) divided into "Basic Annals"; "Chronological Tables"; "Treatises" on rites, music, astronomy, the calendar, and so on; "Hereditary Houses"; and seventy chapters of "Biographies," including descriptions of foreign peoples. A second great work, *The Book of the Han*, was written by Pan Ku (d. 92 C.E.). It applied the analytical schema of Ssu-ma Ch'ien to a single dynasty, the Former Han, and established the pattern by which each dynasty wrote the history of its predecessor.

Neo-Taoism

As the Han dynasty waned, the effort to realize the Confucian ethic in the sociopolitical order became increasingly difficult.

Some scholars abandoned Confucianism altogether in favor of Neo-Taoism, or "mysterious learning," as it was called. A few wrote commentaries on the classical Taoist texts that had been handed down from the Chou. The *Chuang Tzu* was especially popular. Other scholars, defining the natural as the pleasurable, withdrew from society to engage in witty "pure conversations." They discussed poetry and philosophy, played the lute, and drank wine. The most famous were the Seven Sages of the Bamboo Grove of the third century C.E. One sage was always accompanied by a servant carrying a jug of wine and a spade—the one for his pleasure, the other to dig his grave should he die. Another wore no clothes at home. When criticized, he replied that the cosmos was his home, and his house his clothes. "Why are you in my pants?" he asked a discomfited visitor. Still another took a boat to visit a friend on a snowy night, but on arriving at his friend's door, turned around and went home. When pressed for an explanation, he said that it had been his pleasure to go, and that when the impulse died, it was his pleasure to return. This story reveals a scorn for convention coupled with an admiration for an inner spontaneity, however eccentric.

Another concern of what is called Neo-Taoism was immortality. Some sought it in dietary restrictions and Yoga-like meditation, some in sexual abstinence or orgies. Others, seeking elixirs to prolong life, dabbled in alchemy, and although no magical elixir was ever found, the schools of alchemy to which the search gave rise are credited with the discovery of medicines, dyes, glazes, and gunpowder.

Meanwhile, among the common people, there arose popular religious cults that, because they included the Taoist classics among their sacred texts, are also called Neo-Taoist. Like most folk religions, they contained an amalgam of beliefs, practices, and superstitions. They had a pantheon of gods and immortals and taught that the good or evil done in this life would be recompensed in the innumerable heavens or hells of an afterlife. These cults had priests, shamans who practiced faith healing, seers, and sorceresses. For a time, they also had hierarchical church organizations, but these were smashed at the end of the second century C.E. Local Taoist temples and monasteries, however, continued until modern times. With many Buddhist accretions, they furnished the religious beliefs of the bulk of the Chinese population. Even today, these sects continue in Taiwan and in Chinese communities in Southeast Asia.

Buddhism

Central Asian missionaries, following the trade routes east, brought Buddhism to China in the first century C.E. It was at first viewed as a new Taoist sect, which is not surprising because early translators used Taoist terms to render Buddhist concepts. *Nirvana*, for example, was translated as "not doing" (*wu-wei*). In the second century B.C.E., confusion about the two religions led to the very Chinese view that Lao-tzu had gone to India, where the Buddha had become his disciple, and that Buddhism was the Indian form of Taoism.

Then, as the Han sociopolitical order collapsed in the third century C.E., Buddhism spread rapidly. We are reminded of the spread of Christianity at the end of the Roman Empire. Although an alien religion in China, Buddhism had some advantages over Taoism:

1. It was a doctrine of personal salvation, offering several routes to that goal.

2. It contained high standards of personal ethics.

3. It had systematic philosophies, and during its early centuries in China, it continued to receive inspiration from India.

4. It drew on the Indian tradition of meditative practices and psychologies, which were the most sophisticated in the world.

By the fifth century C.E. Buddhism had spread over all of China (see Map 7–3). Occasionally it was persecuted by Taoist emperors—in the north between 446 C.E. and 452 C.E., and again between 574 C.E. and 578 C.E. But most courts supported Buddhism. The "Bodhisattva Emperor" Wu of the southern Liang dynasty three times gave himself to a monastery and had to be ransomed back by his disgusted courtiers. Temples and monasteries abounded in both the north and the south. There were communities of women as well as of men. Chinese artists produced Buddhist painting and sculpture of surpassing beauty, and thousands of monk-scholars labored to translate sutras and philosophical treatises. Chinese monks went on pilgrimages to India. The record left by Fa Hsien, who traveled to India overland and back by sea between 399 and 413 C.E., became a prime source of Indian history. The T'ang monk Hsuan Tsang went to India from 629 until 645. Several centuries later, his pilgrimage was novelized as *Journey to the West*. The novel joins faith, magic, and adventure.

A comparison of Indian and Chinese Buddhism highlights some distinctive features of its spread. Buddhism in India had begun as a reform movement. Forget speculative philosophies and elaborate metaphysics, taught the Buddha, and concentrate on simple truths: Life is suffering, the cause of suffering is desire, death does not stop the endless cycle of birth and rebirth; only the attainment of *nirvana* releases one from the "wheel of *karma*." Thus, in this most otherworldly of the world's religions, all of the cosmic drama of salvation was compressed into the single figure of the Buddha meditating under the Bodhi tree. Over the centuries, however, Indian Buddhism developed contending philosophies and conflicting sects and, having become virtually indistinguishable from Hinduism, was reabsorbed after 1000 C.E.

In China, there were a number of sects with different doctrinal positions. But the Chinese genius was more syncretic. It took in the sutras and meditative practices of early Buddhism. It took in the Mahayana philosophies that depicted a succession of Buddhas, cosmic and historical, past and future, all embodying a single ultimate reality. It also took in the sutras and practices of Buddhist devotional sects. Finally, in the T'ien-t'ai sect, the Chinese joined together these various elements as different levels of a single truth. Thus the monastic routine of a T'ien-tai monk would include reading sutras, sitting in meditation, and also practicing devotional exercises.

Socially, too, Buddhism adapted to China. Ancestor worship demanded heirs to perform the sacrifices. Without progeny, ancestors might become "hungry ghosts." Hence, the

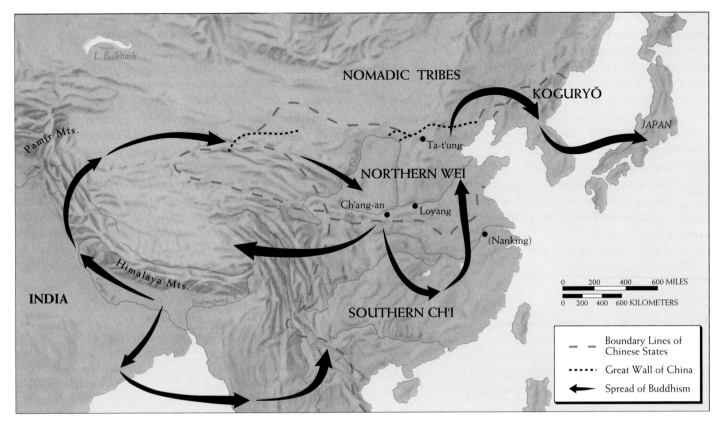

Map 7–3 The spread of Buddhism and Chinese states in 500 C.E.   Buddhism originated in a Himalayan state in northwest India. It spread in one wave south in India and on to Southeast Asia as far as Java. But it also spread into northwest India, Afghanistan, Central Asia, and then to China, Korea, and Japan.

first son would be expected to marry and have children, whereas the second son, if he were so inclined, might become a monk. The practice also arose of holding Buddhist masses for dead ancestors. Still another difference between China and India was the more extensive regulation of Buddhism by the state in China. Just as Buddhism was not to injure the family, so Buddhism was not to reduce the taxes paid on land. As a result, limits were placed on the number of monasteries, nunneries, and monastic lands, and the state had to give its permission before men or women abandoned the world to enter a religious establishment. The regulations, to be sure, were not always enforced.

IN WORLD PERSPECTIVE

China's First Empire

Were there world-historical forces that produced at roughly the same time great empires in China, India, and the Mediterranean? Certainly there were similar features in these

empires. All three came after revolutions in thought. The Han built on Chou thought (it would be hard to imagine the Han bureaucratic state without Legalism and Confucianism), just as Rome used Greek thought, and the Mauryan empire Buddhist thought. In each case, the conception of universal political authority sustaining the empire derived from earlier philosophies. All three were Iron Age empires, joining their respective technologies with new organizational techniques to create superb military forces.

The differences between the empires are also instructive. Contrast China and Rome. In China the pervasive culture—the only higher culture in the area—was Chinese, even before the first empire arose. This culture had been slowly spreading for centuries and in places outran the polity. Even the culture of the Ch'u peoples south of the Yangtze, although viewed as "semibarbarian" by northern Chinese, was only a variation of the higher culture. Thus cultural unity had paved the way for political unity.

In contrast, the polyglot empire of Rome encompassed quite different peoples, including older civilizations. The genius of Rome, in fact, was to fashion a government and a set of laws that could contain its cultural diversity. Geographically, however, Rome had an easier time of it, for the Mediterranean offered direct access to most parts of the empire and was a thoroughfare for commerce. China, in contrast, was largely landlocked. It was composed of several regional economic units, each of which, located in a segment of a river basin separated from the others by natural barriers, looked inward. It was the genius of Chinese administration, overcoming physical and spatial barriers, to integrate the country politically.

A second difference was that government in Han China was more orderly, more complex, and more competent than that of Rome. For example, civil officials controlled the Chinese military almost until the end, whereas in later Roman times, emperor after emperor was set on the throne by the army or the Praetorian Guard. The Roman empire was not a Chinese-type, single-family dynasty.

A third salient difference was in the military dynamics of the two empires. Roman power was built over centuries. Its history is the story of one state growing in power by steady increments, imposing its will on others, and gradually piecing together an empire. Not until the early centuries C.E. was the whole empire in place. China, in contrast, remained a multistate system right up to 232 B.C.E. and then, in a sudden surge, was unified by one state in eleven years. The greater dynamism of China during the first empire can be explained, perhaps, by the greater military challenge it faced across its northern border: an immense Hunnish nomadic empire. Because the threat was more serious than that posed to Rome by any European barbarian enemy, the Chinese response was correspondingly massive.

Review Questions ——

1. How did legalism help the Ch'in unify China? What other factors played a part? What were the main features of Ch'in administration? Why did the Ch'in collapse?

2. What was the "dynastic cycle"? In what sense was it a Confucian moral rationalization? Was a cycle of administrative and military decline especially true of Chinese government, or can we see the same pattern elsewhere?

3. Who were the players who sought power at the Han court? Did the means they used reflect the difference in their positions?

4. Did Buddhism "triumph" in China in the same sense in which Christianity triumphed in the Roman world? Compare China to the Roman Empire. What problems did both empires face and how did they try to resolve them?

Suggested Readings ——

D. BODDE, *China's First Unifier* (1938). A study of the Ch'in unification of China, viewed through the Legalist philosopher and statesman Li Ssu.

T. T. CH'U, *Law and Society in Traditional China* (1961). Treats the sweep of Chinese history from 202 B.C.E. to 1911 C.E.

T. T. CH'U, *Han Social Structure* (1972).

A. COTTERELL, *The First Emperor of China* (1981).

R. COULBORN, *Feudalism in History* (1965). One chapter interestingly compares the quasi-feudalism of the Chou with that of the Six Dynasties period.

J. K. FAIRBANK, E. O. REISCHAUER, AND A. M. CRAIG, *East Asia: Tradition and Transformation* (1989). A widely read single-volume history covering China, Japan, and other countries in East Asia from antiquity to recent times.

J. GERNET, *A History of Chinese Civilization* (1982). An excellent survey of Chinese history.

C. Y. HSU, *Ancient China in Transition* (1965). On social mobility during the Eastern Chou era.

C. Y. HSU, *Han Agriculture* (1980). A study of the agrarian economy of China during the Han dynasty.

J. LEVI, *The Chinese Emperor* (1987). A novel about the First Ch'in Emperor based on scholarly sources.

M. LOEWE, *Everyday Life in Early Imperial China* (1968). A social history of the Han dynasty.

J. NEEDHAM, *The Shorter Science and Civilization in China* (1978). An abridgment of the multivolume work on the same subject with the same title—minus Shorter—by the same author.

C. SCHIROKAUER, *A Brief History of Chinese and Japanese Civilizations* (1978). A standard text, especially good on literature and art.

M. SULLIVAN, *The Arts of China* (1967). An excellent survey history of Chinese art.

D. Twitchett and M. Loewe eds., *The Ch'in and Han Empires, 221 b.c.–a.d. 220* (1986). (Vol. 1 of *The Cambridge History of China*.)

Z. S. Wang, *Han Civilization* (1982).

B. Watson, *Ssu-ma Ch'ien, Grand Historian of China* (1958). A study of China's premier historian.

B. Watson, *Records of the Grand Historian of China*, Vols. 1 and 2 (1961). Selections from the Shih-chi by Ssu-ma Ch'ien.

B. Watson, *The Columbia Book of Chinese Poetry* (1986).

A. Wright, *Buddhism in Chinese History* (1959).

Y. S. Yu, *Trade and Expansion in Han China* (1967). A study of economic relations between the Chinese and their neighbors.

COMPARATIVE PERSPECTIVES: TECHNOLOGY AND CIVILIZATIONS

Technology and Warfare in the Ancient World

There may be evidence of organized warfare as early as the late Paleolithic Age, but there can be no doubt that by the Neolithic Age, organized warfare was a significant human activity. Weapons and other necessities of war are the product of technological development, and war and technology have had a mutually stimulating effect from the earliest times as new technologies have helped shape the character of war and the needs of armies have provoked technological advance.

Fortress Walls

Jericho, built about 7000 B.C.E. in the Neolithic Age, the earliest town yet discovered, already reveals the importance of warfare and the development of technology to deal with it. Jericho is surrounded by a stone wall 700 yards around, ten feet thick and thirteen feet high, protected by a moat ten feet deep and thirty feet wide. This made the town a powerful fortress that could be defeated only by an enemy who could besiege it successfully long enough to starve it out. Nobody would have undertaken the expense and effort to build such a structure unless war was a relatively common danger. The technological innovations needed to fortify Jericho, of course, were then available for peacetime uses.

Not too many years after the rise of civilization in Mesopotamia (ca. 3000 B.C.E.) fortified Sumerian cities appeared in the south. A thousand years later, the pharaohs of the Twelfth Dynasty had devised a strategic defense system of fortresses on their southern frontier with Nubia. In early China the towns had no walls because their plains lacked both trees and stones. During the Shang dynasty (ca. 1766–1050 B.C.E.), however, towns with walls made of beaten earth appeared. Once the techniques needed to build fortresses strong enough to withstand attack were mastered, kingdoms could expand into empires that could defend their conquered lands.

The history of warfare and of military technology is a story of continued change caused by a permanent competition between defense and offense. The construction of fortified strongholds in time provoked new devices and techniques for besieging them. Excavations in Egypt and Mesopotamia have uncovered scaling ladders, battering rams, siege towers, some of them mobile, and mines burrowing under fortress walls. Catapults capable of hurling stones against an enemy's walls appear in Greece in the fourth century B.C.E.; this weapon was brought to greater perfection and power by the Romans centuries later. Alexander the Great and some of his Hellenistic successors became skillful in storming fortified cities with the aid of such technology, but throughout ancient history success against a fortified place usually came as a result of starvation and surrender after a long siege. Not until the invention of gunpowder and powerful cannons did offensive technology overcome the defensive strength of fortification.

Army Against Army

A different kind of warfare, of army against army in the open field, appeared as early as the Stone Age. Scholars disagree as to whether it came in the Paleolithic Age or emerged in Neolithic times, but we know that warriors used such weapons as wooden or stone clubs, spears and axes with sharpened stone heads, and simple bows with stone-tipped arrows. The discovery of metallurgy brought the Bronze Age to Mesopotamia, perhaps as early as 3500 B.C.E., providing armies with weapons that were sharper and sturdier than stone and with body armor and helmets that brought greater safety to warriors. The Mesopotamian rulers already had wealth, a sizable population, civilized organization and substantial fortress walls. Now, with bronze weapons, they could expand their empires far beyond their early frontiers. When, not much later, the Bronze Age came to Egypt, its rulers too, used the new technology to expand and defend their wealthy kingdom.

The Chariot and the Bow

The great next revolution in military technology came with the inventions of the chariot and the composite bow. When these came together by about 1800 B.C.E. their users swept all before them, conquering both Egypt and Mesopotamia. The chariot was a light vehicle, a platform on two wheels pulled by a team of two or four horses that could move swiftly on a battlefield, strong enough to hold two men—a driver and a warrior—as it sped along on an open field. The wheels were wooden, not solid but with spokes and a hub attached to an axle; building them required great skill and experience. The warrior on the chariot wielded a new weapon, the composite

This carving in low relief from the seventh century B.C.E. shows an Assyrian war-chariot and its charioteer. It comes from the palace of King Ashurbanipal at Nineveh, the capital of the mighty Assyrian Empire that dominated the Near East in his time. [Erich Lessing/Art Resource, N.Y.]

bow, more powerful by far than anything that had come before it. Made of thin strips of wood glued together and fastened with animal tendons and horn, the bow was short and easy to use from a moving chariot. It would shoot a light arrow accurately for 300 yards and penetrate the armor of the day at about 100. A man on a chariot on a flat enough field, using a composite bow, with a quiver full of light arrows, could devastate an army of foot soldiers. "Circling at a distance of 100 or 200 yards from the herds of unarmoured foot soldiers, a chariot crew—one to drive, one to shoot—might have transfixed six men a minute. Ten minutes' work by ten chariots would cause 500 casualties or more. . . ."[1]

For several centuries, beginning about 1800 B.C.E., peoples from the north using such weapons smashed into Mesopotamia and conquered the kingdoms they attacked. The Hurrians and Hittites came down as raiders from Asia Minor and then turned north. The Kassites stayed to rule for centuries. In India the Aryans, who also spoke an Indo-European language, smashed the indigenous Indus civilization. In Egypt the Hyksos, speakers of a Semitic language, conquered the northern kingdom. In China the chariot-riding Shang dynasty established an aristocratic rule based on the new weapons. In Europe the Mycenaean Greeks used chariots, although it is not clear whether they had the composite bow and used the tactics that had brought such great success elsewhere.

The most sophisticated users of ancient military technology before Alexander the Great were the Assyrians. They had a wide range of devices for siege warfare, taking them along on all their campaigns. As always, new weapons made of new materials with new techniques do not in themselves constitute a revolution in military affairs. To use them effec-

tively armies require organizations that can devise appropriate operational plans and train soldiers in the needed skills and discipline. The Assyrians annals suggest that by the eighth century B.C.E. their kings had turned their chariot forces into:

a weapon of shock and terror, manipulated by the driver to charge at breakneck speed behind a team of perfectly schooled horses and used by the archer as a platform from which to launch a hail of arrows; squadrons of chariots, their drivers trained to act in mutual support, might have clashed much as armoured vehicles have done in our time, success going to the side that could disable the larger opposing number, while the footmen unlucky or foolhardy enough to stand in their way would have been scattered like chaff.[2]

Mounted Cavalry

The great Assyrian empire fell in 612 B.C.E. before a coalition of opponents, but they had already been weakened by enemies who commanded a new military technique: mounted cavalry. Ironically, the Assyrians themselves may have been the first to develop the critical skills of riding astride a horse while keeping both hands free to shoot with a bow. The first peoples to use the new cavalry technology to great effect were nomads from the steppes of northern Eurasia. About 690 B.C.E. a people whom the Greeks called Cimmerians flooded into Asia Minor on their warhorses, shaking the established order. Later in that century they were followed by another group of steppe-nomads called the Scythians, who came from the Altai

[1]John Keegan, *A History of Warfare* (New York: Vintage Books, 1993), p. 166.

[2]Ibid., pp. 176–177.

mountains in central Asia. They overthrew the Cimmerians and then joined with more settled peoples in the battles that destroyed the Assyrian empire. This was the beginning of a series of attacks by horse-riding nomads from the steppes against the settled lands to their south that lasted for two millennia. In China there is no clear evidence for such attacks before the fourth century B.C.E., but it is possible that attacks from Mongolia and nearby areas may have brought down the western Chou dynasty in 77 B.C.E.

In the Middle East the Babylonian Empire had succeeded the Assyrian, but was soon replaced by the Persian Empire. The Persians had no other way of preventing the nomads' devastating raids than to pay other nomads to defend their frontiers, and the Chinese emperors did the same. The Chinese also developed a cavalry that carried the crossbow, more powerful than the composite bow. Another device for defending against the invaders was the Great Wall of China, built during the Ch'in dynasty (256–206 B.C.E.) designed to keep the ravaging horsemen out. But this, too, proved ineffective: "Despite endless perturbations of the political and military relationships between grassland and plowland, peoples of the steppe enjoyed a consistent advantage because of their superior mobility and the cheapness of their military equipment. This produced a pattern of recurrent nomad conquests of civilized lands."[3]

Iron-Wielding Warriors

Even as the chariot and the warhorse were having so great an impact on the nature of ancient warfare a far more fundamental revolution in military affairs was under way. Bronze is an alloy of copper and tin, the latter being a rather rare metal, so it was expensive. Horses were costly to keep. So warfare that depended on bronze weapons and horses was necessarily limited to a relatively small number of men. About 1400 B.C.E., in Asia Minor, someone discovered the technique of working iron to give it an edge so hard and durable as to make tools and weapons clearly superior to bronze. Iron, moreover, is far more abundant than the components of bronze and easier to work, therefore much cheaper. For the first time it became possible for common people to own and use metal. Now a much larger part of the population could own arms and armor. "Ordinary farmers and herdsmen thereby achieved a new formidability in battle, and the narrowly aristocratic structure of society characteristic of the chariot age altered abruptly. A more democratic era dawned as iron-wielding invaders overthrew ruling elites that had based their power on a monopoly of chariotry."[4]

[3]William H. McNeill, *The Pursuit of Power* (University of Chicago Press, 1982), p. 16.
[4]Ibid., p. 12.

Within two centuries the new technology spread all over the Middle East and into Europe. A new round of invasions by iron-wielding warriors swept away kingdoms and empires and brought new peoples into power. The Assyrians, combining the bureaucratic organizational skills of Mesopotamian civilization with a warrior spirit and an ability to assimilate new techniques, achieved control of their own region with the aid of iron weapons, but many indigenous rulers of civilized lands were subdued or swept away. In Europe a Greek-speaking people we call the Myceneans had ruled the Greek peninsula and the Aegean Sea with a Bronze Age civilization similar to those of the Middle East. Between 1200 and 1100, however, the Myceneans were overthrown by a new wave of Greeks with iron weapons who obliterated the old civilization and brought into the world a new form of culture based on new ways of fighting.

The Shield and the Phalanx

The heart of this new Greek civilization, which is called "Hellenic," was the city state, or *polis,* hundreds of which came into being toward the end of the eighth century B.C.E. Their armies consisted of independent yeoman farmers who produced enough wealth to supply their own weapons and body armor, made cheap enough by the revolution in metallurgy. But again, these would have been of little value without organizational change. Now, a new way of warfare made infantry the dominant fighting force on land for centuries, permitting an alliance of poor Greek states to defeat the mighty and wealthy Persian Empire. The soldiers—wearing helmets, body armor, and a heavy, large round shield for protection—carried short iron swords but used iron-tipped wooden pikes as their chief weapon. Arrayed in compact blocks called phalanxes, usually eight men deep, these free men, or hoplites, well-disciplined and highly motivated, defeated lesser infantries, archers, and cavalry (see photo p. 89). Adapted by the Macedonians under King Philip II and his son Alexander the Great, the hoplite phalanx remained the dominant infantry force until defeated by the Roman legion in the second century B.C.E.

Trireme Warfare

The Greeks also achieved supremacy at sea by improving an existing technological innovation and providing it with an effective operational plan. Oared galleys are known at Cyprus as early as about 1000 B.C.E., and the Phoenicians improved their speed and maneuverability by superimposing a second and then a third bank of rowers over the first to produce a ship that the Greeks called a *trireme.* The Greeks added outriggers for the top rowers, and it is possible that this permitted their rowers to use the full power of their strongest leg muscles by sliding back and forth as they rowed. At first the main mode of trireme warfare was for one ship to come alongside another, grapple it, and send marines to board the enemy ship. In time, however, the Greeks placed a strong ram at the prow of each ship and learned how to row with great bursts of speed and to make sharp turns that allowed them to ram and disable their opponents by striking them in the side or rear. With such ships and tactics the Greek triremes repeatedly sank fleets of the Egyptians and Phoenicians who rowed for the Persian Empire, gaining complete naval mastery.

The Macedonians came to dominate the Greek world, to conquer the Persian Empire and rule its successor states in the Hellenistic Period (323–31 B.C.E.), but technological innovation in military affairs played only a small part in their success. They introduced the sarissa, a longer-two-handed pike for the phalanx, but their success came chiefly from the quality of their leaders; the number, spirit, and discipline of their troops; and the ability to combine infantry, cavalry, and light-armed troops to win battles. Alexander's engineers also brought unprecedented skill to the use of siege weapons.

Roman Legions and the Iron Javelin

The armies of the Roman Republic defeated Macedon in a series of wars in the third and second centuries B.C.E. and brought the entire Mediterranean world under their sway by the end of the second century. This conquest was achieved almost entirely by the power of their infantry. In time they moved from the phalanx formation to a looser, more open order of battle based on the legion, which was divided into smaller, self-sufficient units. They abandoned the pike as the chief infantry weapon, using instead the pilum, a heavy iron javelin that was thrown to cause disarray in the enemy line

and permit the Romans to use their short, double-edged swords at close quarters. In the Imperial period, beginning especially in the third century of our era, nomadic barbarian tribes began applying the severe pressure on Rome's frontiers that would ultimately bring down its empire. Like the Chinese, the Romans built walls in some places to ease the burden of defending their extensive borders. In the Empire's last years the Romans began to use heavy armored horses ridden by knights in heavy armor, carrying lances, capable of charging an enemy with great force and effect. These armored cavalrymen, called "cataphracts" in Greek, would in time develop into a major new system of fighting in the Western Middle Ages, but they were too few to take a significant role in the final futile defense of the empire.

The Crossbow in China

Although the new breed of large, powerful horses was introduced in China by the first century B.C.E., they never gained importance because Chinese technology had already developed a weapon that cancelled their effectiveness. At least since the Han dynasty (beginning 206 B.C.E.) the crossbow had been the chief weapon of Chinese armies. The crossbow was easy to use, accurate and deadly at 100 yards. With a few hours practice an ordinary man could learn to use it to good effect. What made the weapon so easy to use, the trigger, was itself the product of difficult and expert technological skill. It required highly advanced metallurgy and skilled and experienced artisans to produce, but it gave the Chinese armies that wielded the cross bow an enormous advantage against their enemies and helped the emperors to gain and maintain control of the vast Chinese Empire while other ancient empires crumbled.

A brick from a tomb structure with a design of a warrior shooting his bow while appearing to retreat on his galloping horse. This is believed to be the earliest known depiction of this method of fighting. From the Han dynasty c. 200 B.C.E.–200 C.E. [Werner Forman Archive]

Iranian explains chess to Hindu envoy. From *Shah-nameh*, Ferdowski, early 14th century. [Metropolitan Museum of Art]

CONSOLIDATION AND INTERACTION OF WORLD CIVILIZATIONS

Between 500 and 1500, the major civilizations of the world shaped themselves politically and culturally in new and lasting ways. China survived barbarian conquests and three centuries of political fragmentation to reestablish in 589 a united empire, the likes of which would never be known in Europe. In achieving this empire, the Chinese were aided by a universal philosophical system, Confucianism, which supported secular political power, and by a common written language and the technology to print it, which ensured cultural unity across China's vast regions. Even its dense population, close to 50 million in the year 750, encouraged unity and provided a base for communication, trade, and a stable empire. Chinese government evolved in this period from an imperial bureaucracy based on aristocratic families toward one based on a civil-service examination elite. In the transition, the emperor, at the head of the bureaucracy, became more powerful, more absolute. Chinese culture became increasingly conservative and inward looking.

In Japan regional tribal aristocracies gave way during the fifth and sixth centuries to the archaic Yamato kings. In Yamato society Shinto, the indigenous religion, was part and parcel of daily life, family status, and political authority. From the seventh century, these early kings adopted the Chinese model of centralized government. During the Nara and Heian periods—roughly the eighth to twelfth centuries—court life was reshaped by Chinese culture and the Buddhist tradition that was also imported from China. Yet the Japanese preserved a separate identity. During the early ninth century, *samurai* ("those who serve") warriors developed in local areas. Like knights in feudal Europe, they were responsible for maintaining the local order. During the Kamakura and Ashikaga periods—roughly the thirteenth to fifteenth centuries—confederations of samurai swept aside the Chinese-type court and established a distinctively Japanese form of government: military rule by feudal warriors under the shōgun, their military overlord. These same centuries were Japan's age of faith, centering on Pure Land and Zen Buddhism.

In the seventh century the new faith and culture of Islam emerged in Arabia. Muhammad, the proclaimed last in a line of monotheistic prophets, preached a fervent opposition to idolatry, immorality, and injustice in his homeland of western Arabia. Bound by a new supratribal allegiance, his Arab successors carried his crusade abroad, sweeping over most of the Byzantine realms, all of the Persian Empire, and into Spain, Central Asia, and the Indus Valley within a century. Muslim traders and mystical ("Sufi") brotherhoods spread Muslim faith and culture beyond the political boundaries of Islam. Turkish and Mongol peoples in later centuries expanded the political and military presence of Islam still further. Although split into factions, the Islamic community never experienced the regional and sectarian fragmentation that Christendom suffered. Only the Mongol invasions of the thirteenth and fourteenth centuries disrupted the political order in the Islamic heartlands.

In Africa this period witnessed the rise of regional empires. Outside of Islamic North Africa and Egypt, the most prominent were those in the western and central Sudan. Most notable was ancient Ghana, whose heyday was the late tenth and most of the eleventh centuries. However, the Kushite empire of Aksum, in the Ethiopian highlands, remained a major power even through the sixth century C.E.; it survived right through this age as the proud, culturally and religiously distinctive Christian state of Abyssinia, or Ethiopia. The remarkable regional culture of Great Zimbabwe, a southeastern African kingdom, held sway in the Zambezi-Limpopo area between about 1000 and 1500. In central and southern Africa Bantu-speaking peoples spread gradually from northwestern central Africa over most of the subcontinent. In western and northern Africa the centuries-old trans-Saharan trade routes saw increased commercial traffic, as well as new interchanges in people and ideas.

After 1000, Islam gradually penetrated across the Sahara into the Sudanic regions. In the same era, east Africa was undergoing even more pronounced Islamization in the development of Swahili civilization. It was also entering ever more prominently into the international trade network that reached across the Indian Ocean all the way to Indonesia and China. By 1500 much of Africa was firmly caught up in the larger global community.

In Iran, a state religion of Zoroastrian orthodoxy and official use of the Middle Persian dialect assisted political centralization during the reign of the Sasanid kings (224–651). The Sasanids further strengthened their rule by international trade and government monopolies on industries like silk and glass. However, their centuries-long conflict with their chief rival, the Byzantine Empire, and the growth of regional nobles' strength so weakened the Sasanids that they proved easy prey to the Arab armies of Islam. The Persian language and culture developed and nourished under the Sasanids persisted, however, and ultimately greatly enriched Islamic civilization.

In India the incursions of Hun peoples in the first half of the sixth century ended the great classical era of Gupta culture and empire. The next millennium saw the caste system solidify, establishing hierarchical divisions within Indian society based on rules regulating the groups with whom one could eat, marry, and work. Hindu tradition gained the general shape it has today. The end of the Gupta empire led to the ascendancy of regional kingdoms. The arrival of Muslim Turks and Afghans after 1000 in northern India brought an Islamic political and cultural presence on a scale previously unknown. By 1500 Islam was an important part of the Indian scene, putting its architectural as well as its religious and political marks on Indian society.

Western Europe survived barbarian and Muslim invasions to create a Christian empire under Charlemagne (768–814). Toward the end of this period, western Europe became through the Crusades an aggressor itself in Byzantium and the Near East. In the West the Christian Church never became the docile friend of kings and emperors that some Asian and Near Eastern religions were, and orthodox Christianity inclined also to be in the Byzantine Empire. In the West, emperor and pope struggled with each other repeatedly, occasionally to the death. During the twelfth and thirteenth centuries, "national" monarchies emerged in northern Europe, which henceforth developed as a collection of nation-states that remained politically and culturally diverse and highly competitive.

500 C.E.–800

511 Death of Clovis, Frankish ruler of Gaul
529 Benedict of Nursia founds Benedictine Order
590–604 Pontificate of Gregory I, "the Great"
768–814 Charles the Great (Charlemagne)

527–565 Justinian's reign
531–579 Reign of Chosroes Anosharvian in Iran
ca. 570–632 Muhammad
622 The Hijra
616–657 Reign of Harsha; neo-Gupta revival
    in India
651 Death of last Sasanid ruler
ca. 710 First Muslim invasion of India
661–750 Umayyad dynasty
680 Death of Al-Husayn at Karbala; second civil
    war begins
750–1258 Abbasid dynasty
786–809 Caliph Harun Al-Rashid reigns

Crown of the
Holy Roman Emperor

800–1100

ca. 800–1000 Invasions of England and the
    Carolingian Empire (Vikings, Magyars,
    and Muslims)
843 Treaty of Verdun divides Carolingian Empire
910 Cluny Monastery founded
1019–1054 Yaroslav the wise reigns; peak
    of Kievan Russia
1054 Schism between Latin and Greek churches
1066 Norman conquest of England
1073–1085 Investiture controversy
1096–1270 The Crusades

800–1200 Period of "feudal" overlordship in India
900–1100 Golden Age of Muslim learning
909–1171 Fatimids in North Africa and Egypt
945–1055 Buyid rule in Baghdad
994–1186 Ghaznavid rule in northwestern India,
    Afghanistan, and Iran
1055–1194 Seljuk rule in Baghdad
1071 Seljuk Turks capture Jerusalem
1081–1118 Byzantine emperor Alexius Comnenus
    reigns
ca. 1000–1300 Turko-Afghan raids into India

1100–1300

1154–1158 Frederick Barbarosa invades Italy
1182–1226 St. Francis of Assisi
1198–1216 Pontificate of Innocent III
ca. 1100–1300 Growth of trade and towns
1215 Magna Carta granted
ca. 1225–1274 St. Thomas Aquinas
1265–1321 Dante Alighieri

1174–1193 Saladin reigns
1192 Muslim conquerors end Buddhism in India
1206–1526 Delhi Sultanate in India; Indian culture
    divided into Hindu and Muslim
ca. 1220 Mongol invasions of Iran, Iraq, Syria, India
1258 Hulagu Khan, Mongol leader, conquers
    Baghdad
1260–1335 Il-Khans rule Iran

1300–1500

1337 Hundred Years' War begins
ca. 1340–1400 Geoffrey Chaucer
1347–1349 The Black Death
1375–1527 The Italian Renaissance
1485 Battle of Bosworth Field; accession of Henry
    Tudor to the throne of England
1492 Columbus's first voyage to the New World

1250–1517 Mamluk rule in Egypt
1366–1405 Timur (Tamerlane) reigns
1405–1494 Timurids rule in Transoxiana and Iran
1453 Byzantine Empire falls to the Ottoman Turks,
    with capture of Constantinople

589–618 Sui dynasty reunifies China
607 Japan begins embassies to China
618–907 T'ang dynasty in China
701–762 Li Po, T'ang poet
710–784 Nara court, Japan's first permanent capital
712 *Records of Ancient Matters*, in Japan
713–756 Emperor Hsuan Tsung reigns in China
755 An Lu-shan rebellion in China
794–1185 Heian (Kyoto) court in Japan

ca. 500 States of Takrur and Ghana founded
ca. 500–700 Political and commercial ascendancy of Aksum (Ethiopia)
ca. 600–1500 Extensive slave trade from sub-Saharan Africa to Mediterranean
ca. 700–800 Ghanians begin to supply gold to Mediterranean
ca. 700–900 States of Gao and Kanem
ca. 800 Appearance of the Kanuri people around Lake Chad

ca. 150–900 Classic period. Dominance of Teotihuacán in central Mexico, Tikal in southern Yucatán

Stela at Aksum

856–1086 Fujiwara dominate Heian court
960–1279 Sung dynasty in China
ca. 1000 *Pillow Book* by Shohōnagon and *Tale of Genji* by Murasaki Shikibu
1037–1101 Su Tung-p'o, Sung poet

ca. 800–900 Decline of Aksum
ca. 900–1100 Kingdom of Ghana; capital city, Kumbi Saleh
ca. 1000–1100 Islam penetrates sub-Saharan Africa
1000–1500 "Great Zimbabwe" center of Bantu Kingdom in southeastern Africa

ca. 600–1000 Middle (Huari/Tiwanaku) Horizon in Andean South America

1130–1200 Chu Hsi, Sung philosopher
1167–1227 Genghis Khan, founder of Mongol Empire
1185–1333 Kamakura shogunate in Japan
1274, 1281 Mongol invasions of Japan
1279–1368 Mongol (Yuan) dynasty in China

ca. 1100–1897 Kingdom of Benin in tropical rain forest region
1194–1221 Kanem Empire achieves greatest expansion
1203 Kingdom of Ghana falls to Sosso people
ca. 1230–1450 Kingdom of Mali
1230–1255 King Sundiata, first ruler of Mali Empire; Walata and Timbuktu become centers of trade and culture

ca. 800–1400 Chimu Empire on north coast of Peru

Genghis Khan

1336–1467 Ashikaga shogunate in Kyoto
1368–1644 Ming dynasty in China
1405–1433 Voyages of Cheng Ho to India and Africa
1467–1568 Warring States era in Japan
1472–1529 Wang Yang-ming, Ming philosopher

1307–1332 Mansa Musa, greatest king of Mali
1490s Europeans establish trading posts on western African coast
mid-1400s Decline of Mali Empire; creation of Songhai Empire
1468 Sonni Ali captures Timbuktu
1476–1507 Reign of King Mai Ali of Bornu in central Sudan
1493–1528 Songhai ruler Askia Muhammed reigns; consolidates Songhai Empire

1325 Founding of Aztec capital of Tenochtitlán
1428–1519 Period of Aztec expansion
1492 European encounter with America
1519 Cortes conquers Aztec Empire
ca. 1350–1533 Inca Empire in Peru
1533 Pizarro executes Inca ruler Atahualpa

8 IMPERIAL CHINA (589–1368)

A painting of irrigation methods on a farm of the Yangtze. A farmer and his wife use their legs and feet to work the square-pallet chain pump. At left a boy drives a large water buffalo to turn a larger water-pumping device. The boy in the background fishes. [Photograph by Wan-go Weng/Collection of H. C. Weng]

◆ Reestablishment of Empire: Sui (589–618) and T'ang (618–907) Dynasties

◆ Transition to Late Imperial China: The Sung Dynasty (960–1279)

◆ China in the Mongol World Empire: The Yuan Dynasty (1279–1368)

In World Perspective Imperial China

If Chinese dynasties from the late sixth to the mid-fourteenth centuries were given numbers like those of ancient Egypt, the Sui and T'ang dynasties would be called the Second Empire; the Sung, the Third; and the Yuan, the Fourth. Numbers, however, would not convey the distinct personalities of these dynasties. The T'ang (618–907) is everyone's favorite dynasty: open, cosmopolitan, expansionist, exuberant, and creative. It was the example of T'ang China that decisively influenced the formation of states and high cultures in Japan, Korea, and Vietnam. Poetry during the T'ang attained a peak that has not been equaled since. The Sung (960–1279) rivaled the T'ang in the arts; it was China's great age of painting and the most significant period for philosophy since the Chou, when Chinese philosophy began. Although not militarily strong, the Sung dynasty also witnessed an important commercial revolution. The Yuan (1279–1368) was a short-lived dynasty of rule by Mongols during which China became the most important unit in the largest empire the world has yet seen.

Reestablishment of Empire: Sui (589–618) and T'ang (618–907) Dynasties

In the period corresponding to the European early Middle Ages, the most notable feature of Chinese history was the reunification of China, the recreation of a centralized bureaucratic empire consciously modeled on the earlier Han dynasty (206 B.C.E.–220 C.E.). Reunification, as usual, began in the north. The first steps were taken by the Northern Wei (386–534), the most enduring of the northern Sino-Turkic states. It moved its court south to Loyang, made Chinese the language of the court, and adopted Chinese dress and surnames. It also used the leverage of its nomadic cavalry to impose a new land tax, mobilizing resources for state use. The Northern Wei was followed by several short-lived kingdoms. Because the emperors, officials, and military commanders of these kingdoms came from the same aristocratic stratum, the social distance between them was small, and the throne was often usurped.

The Sui Dynasty

The general of mixed Chinese-Turkic ancestry, Sui Wen-ti (d. 605), who came to power in 581 and began the Sui dynasty (589–618), was no exception to this rule. But he displayed great talent, unified the north, restored the tax base, reestablished a centralized bureaucratic government, and went on to conquer southern China and unify the country. During his reign, all went well. Huge palaces arose in his Wei valley capital. The Great Wall was rebuilt. The Grand Canal was constructed, linking the Yellow and Yangtze rivers. This canal enabled the northern conquerors to tap the wealth of central and southern China. Peace was maintained with the Turkic tribes along China's northern borders. Eastern Turkic khans (chiefs) were sent Chinese princesses as brides.

The early years of the Second Sui emperor were also constructive, but then, Chinese attempts to meddle in steppe politics led to hostilities and wars. The hardships and casualties in campaigns against Korea and along China's northern border produced rising discontent. Natural disasters occurred. The court became bankrupt and demoralized. Rebellions broke out, and once again, there was a free-for-all among the armies of aristocratic military commanders. The winner, and the founder of the T'ang dynasty, was a relative of the Sui empress and a Sino-barbarian aristocrat of the same social background as those who had ruled before him.

Chinese historians often compare the short-lived Sui dynasty with that of the Ch'in (256–206 B.C.E.). Each brought all of China under a single government after centuries of disunity. Each did too much, fell, and was replaced by a long-lasting dynasty. The T'ang built on the foundations that had been laid by the Sui, just as the Han had built on those of the Ch'in.

The T'ang Dynasty

The first T'ang emperor took over the Sui capital, re-named it Ch'ang-an, and made it his own. Within a decade or so the T'ang had extended its authority over all of China; tax revenues were adequate to government needs; and Chinese armies had begun the campaigns that would push Chinese borders out further than ever (see Map 8–1). Confucian scholars were em-ployed at the court, Buddhist temples and monas-teries flourished, and peace and order prevailed in the land. The years from 624 to 755 were the good years of the dynasty.

Government The first T'ang emperor had been a provincial governor before he became a rebel gen-eral. Many of those whom he appointed to posts in the new T'ang administration were former Sui officials who had served with him. In building the new admin-istration, he and his successors had to reconcile two conflicting sets of interests. On the one hand, the emperor wanted a bureaucratic government in which au-thority was centralized in his own person. On the other hand, he had to make concessions to the aristocrats—the dominant elements in Chinese society since the late Han—who staffed his government and continued to dominate early T'ang society.

The degree to which political authority was centralized was apparent in the formal organization of the bureaucracy (see chart on page 228). At the highest level were three or-gans: Military Affairs, the Censorate, and the Council of State. Military Affairs supervised the T'ang armies, with the em-peror, in effect, the commander-in-chief. The Censorate had watchdog functions: It reported instances of misgovernment directly to the emperor and could also remonstrate with the

During the T'ang dynasty (618–907), well-to-do families placed glazed pottery figurines in the tombs of their dead. Perhaps they were intended to accompany and amuse the dead in the afterlife. Note the fancy chignon hairstyle of this female flutist, one figure in a musical ensemble. Today these figurines are sought by collectors around the world. [Art Resource, N.Y.]

emperor when it considered his behavior improper. The Council of State was the most important body. It met daily with the emperor and was made up of the heads of the Secretariat, which drafted policies; the Chancellery, which re-viewed them; and State Af-fairs, which carried them out. Beneath State Affairs were the Six Ministries, which continued as the core of the central government down to the twentieth century; beneath them were the several levels of local administration.

Concessions to the interests of the aristocratic families were embodied in the tax system. All land was declared to be the property of the emperor and was then redistributed to able-bodied cultivators, who paid taxes in labor and grain. Because all able-bodied adult males received an equal allot-ment of land (women got less), the land-tax system was called the "equal field system." But the system was not egalitarian. Aristocrats enjoyed special exemptions and grants of "rank" and "office" lands that, in effect, confirmed their estate holdings.

Aristocrats were also favored in the recruiting of officials. Most officials either were recommended for posts or received posts because their fathers had been high officials. They were drawn almost exclusively from the aristocracy. Only a tiny percentage were recruited by examinations. Those who passed the examinations had the highest prestige and were more likely to have brilliant careers. But as only well-to-do families could afford the years of study needed to master the Confucian classics and pass the rigorous examinations, even the examination bureaucrats were usually the able among the

Imperial China

589–618	Sui Dynasty
618–907	T'ang Dynasty
960–1279	Sung Dynasty
1279–1368	Yuan (Mongol) Dynasty

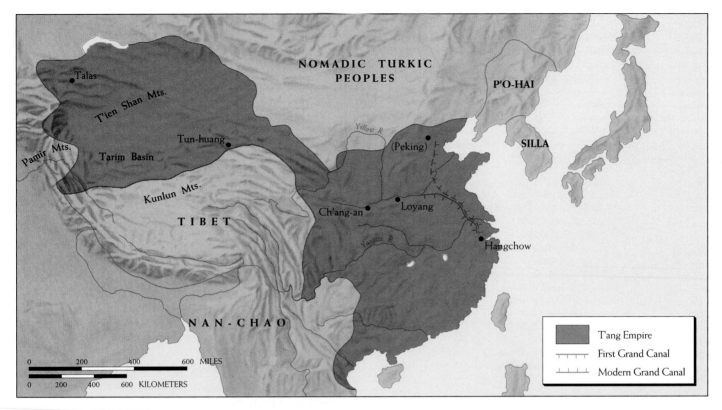

Map 8–1   The T'ang Empire at its peak during the eighth century.   The T'ang expansion into Central Asia reopened trade routes to the Middle East and Europe. Students from P'o-Hai, Silla (Korea), and Japan studied in the T'ang capital of Ch'ang-an, and then returned, carrying with them T'ang books and technology.

noble. Entrance to government schools at Ch'ang-an and the secondary capital at Loyang was restricted to the sons of nobles and officials.

The Empress Wu   Women of the inner court continued to play a role in government. For example, Wu Chao (626–ca. 706), a young concubine of the strong second emperor, had so entranced his weak heir by her charms that when he succeeded to the throne, she was recalled from the nunnery to which all the former wives of deceased emperors were routinely consigned and installed at the court. She poisoned or otherwise removed her rivals and became his empress. She also murdered or exiled the statesmen who opposed her. When the emperor suffered a stroke in 660, she completely dominated the court. After his death in 683 she ruled for seven years as regent and then, deposing her son, became emperor herself, the only woman in Chinese history to hold the title. She moved the court to Loyang in her native area and proclaimed a new dynasty. A fervent Buddhist with an interest in magic, she saw herself as the incarnation of the Buddha Maitreya and built temples throughout the land. She patronized the White Horse Monastery, appointing one of

her favorites as its abbot. Her sexual appetites were said to have been prodigious. She ruled China until 705, when at the age of eighty she was deposed.

After Empress Wu, no woman would ever become emperor again; yet her machinations did not seriously weaken the court. So highly centralized was power during these early years of the dynasty that the ill effects of her intrigues could be absorbed without provinces breaking away or military commanders becoming autonomous. In fact, her struggle for power may have strengthened the central government, for, to overcome the old northwestern Chinese aristocrats, she turned not to members of her family but to the products of the examination system and to a group known as the Scholars of the North Gate. This policy broadened the base of government by bringing in aristocrats from other regions of China. The dynamism of a young dynasty may also explain why her rule coincided with the maximal geographical expansion of T'ang military power.

The Ch'ang-an of Emperor Hsuan-tsung   Only a few years after Empress Wu was deposed—years filled with tawdry intrigues—Hsuan-tsung came to the throne. In

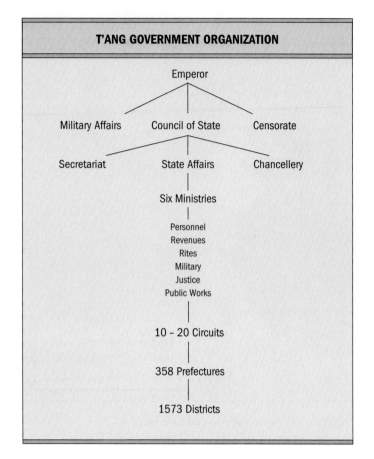

T'ANG GOVERNMENT ORGANIZATION

Emperor

Military Affairs — Council of State — Censorate

Secretariat — State Affairs — Chancellery

Six Ministries

Personnel
Revenues
Rites
Military
Justice
Public Works

10 – 20 Circuits

358 Prefectures

1573 Districts

reaction to Empress Wu, he appointed government commissions headed by distinguished aristocrats to reform government finances. Examination bureaucrats lost ground during his reign. The Grand Canal was repaired and extended. A new census extended the tax rolls. Wealth and prosperity returned to the court. Hsuan-tsung's reign (713–756) was also the most brilliant culturally. Years later, while in exile, the great poet Li Po (701–762) wrote a verse in which memories of youthful exhilaration merged with the glory of the capital of Hsuan-tsung:

Long ago, among the flowers and willows,
We sat drinking together at Ch'ang-an.
The Five Barons and Seven Grandees were of our
    company,
But when some wild stroke was afoot
It was we who led it, yet boisterous though we were
In the arts and graces of life we could hold our own
With any dandy in the town—
In the days when there was youth in your cheeks
And I was still not old.
We galloped to the brothels, cracking our gilded whips,
We sent in our writings to the palace of the Unicorn,
Girls sang to us and danced hour by hour on tortoise-
    shell mats.
We thought, you and I, that it would be always like this.

Pottery figures of court ladies playing polo, seventh century, T'ang dynasty. For over a millennium after the T'ang, participation in athletic contests was considered unfeminine. [The Nelson-Atkins Museum of Art, Kansas City, Missouri (Purchase: acquired through the generosity of Katherine Harvey) Copyright The Nelson Gallery Foundation. All Reproduction Rights Reserved.]

How should we know the grasses would stir and dust
    rise on the wind?
Suddenly foreign horsemen were at the Hsien-ku Pass
Just when the blossom at the palace of Ch'in was
    opening on the sunny boughs.[1]

Ch'ang-an was an imperial city, an administrative city that lived on taxes. It was designed to exhibit the power of the emperor and the majesty of his court. At the far north of the city, the palace faced south. The placement was traditional: Confucius, speaking of Shun, said he had only "to hold himself in a respectful posture and to face due south." In front of the palace was a complex of government offices from which an imposing five-hundred-feet-wide avenue led to the main southern gate. The city was laid out on a north-south, east-west grid, which one T'ang poet compared to a chessboard. Each block of the city was administered as a ward with interior streets and gates that were locked at night. Enclosed by great walls, the city covered thirty square miles. Its population was over a million: half within the walls, the other half in suburbs—the largest city in the world. (The population of China in the year 750 was about fifty million—less than 5 percent of the country's present-day population.) Ch'ang-an was also a trade center from which caravans set out across Central Asia. Merchants from India, Iran, Syria, and Arabia hawked the wares of the Near East and all of Asia in its two government-controlled markets.

The T'ang Empire A Chinese dynasty is like an accordion, first expanding into the territories of its barbarian neighbors and then contracting back to its original, densely populated core area. The principal threats to the T'ang state were from Tibetans in the west, Turks in the northwest and north, and Khitan Mongols in Manchuria.

To protect their border, the T'ang employed a four-tier policy. When nothing else would work, the T'ang sent armies. But armies were expensive, and using them against nomads was like sweeping back the waves with a broom. A victory might dissolve a tribal confederation, but a decade or two later it would reappear under a new leader. For example, in 630 T'ang armies defeated the eastern Turks; in 648 they took the Tarim Basin, opening trade routes to western Asia for almost a century; and in 657 they defeated the western Turks and extended Chinese influence across the Pamir Mountains to petty states near Samarkand. By 698, however, the Turks were back invading northeastern China, and between 711 and 736 they were in control of the steppe from the Oxus River to China's northern frontier.

Chinese efforts against Tibet were much the same. From 670 Tibet expanded and threatened China. In 679 it was defeated. In 714 it rose again; wars were fought from 727 to 729; and a settlement was reached in 730. But wars broke out anew. In 752 Tibet entered an alliance with the state of Nan Chao in Yunnan. In 763 Tibetan forces captured and looted Ch'ang-an. They were driven out, but the point is that even during the good years of the T'ang, no final victory was possible.

The human costs of sending armies far afield was detailed in a poem by Li Po:

Last year we were fighting at the source of the
    Sang-kan;
This year we are fighting on the Onion River road.
We have washed our swords in the surf of Parthian seas;
We have pastured our horses among the snows of the
    T'ien Shan,
The King's armies have grown grey and old
Fighting ten thousand leagues away from home.
The Huns have no trade but battle and carnage;
They have no fields or ploughlands,
But only wastes where white bones lie among yellow
    sands.
Where the House of Ch'in built the great wall that was
    to keep away the Tartars.
There, in its turn, the House of Han lit beacons of war.
The beacons are always alight, fighting and marching
    never stop.
Men die in the field, slashing sword to sword;
The horses of the conquered neigh piteously to Heaven.
Crows and hawks peck for human guts,
Carry them in their beaks and hang them on the
    branches of withered trees.
Captains and soldiers are smeared on the bushes and
    grass;
General schemed in vain.
Know therefore that the sword is a cursed thing
Which the wise man uses only if he must.[2]

The second tier of Chinese defenses was to use nomads against other nomads. The critical development for the T'ang was the rise to power of the Uighur Turks. From 744 to 840 the Uighurs controlled Central Asia and were staunch allies of the T'ang. Without their support, the T'ang dynasty would have ended sooner.

A third tier was the defense along China's borders, including the Great Wall. At mid-dynasty, whole frontier provinces in the north and the northwest were put under

[1]Arthur Waley, *The Poetry and Career of Li Po* © 1950, George Allen & Unwin Ltd, and imprint of Harper Collins Publishers, Ltd.

[2]Waley, pp. 34–35.

A bearded "barbarian" groom tends the charger of the second T'ang emperor (r. 626–649). This stone relief was found on the emperor's tomb. Note the stirrup, a Chinese invention of the fourth century C.E. [University of Pennsylvania Museum, Philadelphia (NEG.#S8–62840)]

military commanders, who in time came to control the provinces' civil governments as well. The bulk of the T'ang military was in such frontier commands. At times their autonomy and potential as rebels were as much a threat to the T'ang court as to the nomadic enemy.

Diplomacy is always cheaper than war. The fourth line of defense was to bring the potential enemy into the empire as a tributary. The T'ang defined the position of "tributary" with great elasticity. It included principalities truly dependent on China; Central Asian states conquered by China; enemy states, such as Tibet or the Thai state of Nan Chao in Yunnan, when they were not actually at war with China; the Korean state Silla, which had unified the peninsula with T'ang aid but had then fought T'ang armies to a standstill when they attempted to impose Chinese hegemony; and wholly independent states, such as Japan. All sent embassies

bearing gifts to the T'ang court, which housed and fed them and sent back costly gifts in return.

For some countries these embassies had a special significance. As the only "developed nation" in eastern Asia, China was a model for countries still in the throes of forming a state. An embassy gained access to the entire range of T'ang culture and technology: its philosophy and writing; governmental and land systems; Buddhism; and the arts, architecture, and medicine. In 640 there were eight thousand Koreans, mostly students, in Ch'ang-an. Never again would China exert such an influence, for never again would its neighbors be at that formative stage of development.

Rebellion and Decline From the mid-eighth century, signs of decline began to appear. China's frontiers started to contract. Tribes in Manchuria became unruly. Tibetans threatened China's western border. In 751 an overextended T'ang army led by a Korean general was defeated by Arabs near Samarkand in western Asia, shutting down China's caravan trade with the West for more than five centuries. Furthermore, in 755 a Sogdian general, An Lu-shan, who commanded three Chinese provinces on the northeastern frontier, led his 160,000 troops in a rebellion that swept across northern China, capturing Loyang and then Ch'ang-an. The emperor fled to Szechwan.

The event contained an element of romance. Ten years earlier the emperor Hsuan-tsung had taken a young woman, Yang Kuei Fei, from the harem of his son (he gave his son another in exchange). So infatuated was he that he neglected not only the other "three thousand beauties of his inner chambers" but the business of government as well. For a while his neglect did not matter because he had an able chief minister, but when the minister died Hsuan-tsung appointed his concubine's second cousin to the post, initiating a train of events that resulted in rebellion. En route to Szechwan, his soldiers, blaming Yang Kuei Fei for their plight, strangled her. The event was later immortalized in a poem that described her "snow-white skin," "flowery face," and "moth eyebrows," as well as the "eternal sorrow" of the emperor, who, in fact, was seventy-two at the time.

After a decade of wars and much devastation, a new emperor restored the dynasty with the help of the Uighur Turks, who looted Ch'ang-an as part of their reward. The recovery and the century of relative peace and prosperity that followed illustrate the resilience of T'ang institutions. China was smaller, but military governors maintained the diminished frontiers. Provincial governors were more autonomous, but taxes were still sent to the capital. Occasional rebellions were suppressed by imperial armies, sometimes led by eunuchs. Most of the emperors were weak, but three strong emperors appeared and reforms were carried out. Edwin O. Reischauer, after translating the diary of a Japanese monk who studied in China during the early ninth century, commented that the "picture of government in operation" that emerges "is amazing for the ninth century, even in China":

> The remarkable degree of centralized control still existing, the meticulous attention to written instructions from higher authorities, and the tremendous amount of paper work involved in even the smallest matters of administration are all the more striking just because this was a period of dynastic decline.[3]

Of the reforms of this era, none was more important than that of the land system. The official census, on which land allotments and taxes were based, showed a drop in population

from 53 million before the An Lu-shan rebellion to 17 million afterward. Unable to put people back on the registers, the government replaced the equal field system with a tax collected twice a year. The new system, begun in 780, lasted until the sixteenth century. Under it, a fixed quota of taxes was levied on each province. After the An Lu-shan rebellion, government revenues from salt and iron surpassed those from land.

During the second half of the ninth century the government weakened further. Most provinces were autonomous, often under military commanders, and resisted central control. Wars were fought with the state of Nan Chao in the southwest. Bandits appeared. Droughts led to peasant uprisings. By the 880s warlords had carved all of China into independent kingdoms, and in 907 the T'ang dynasty fell. But within half a century a new dynasty arose. The fall of the T'ang did not lead to the centuries of division that had followed the Han. Something had changed within China.

T'ang Culture The creativity of the T'ang period arose from the juxtaposition and interaction of cosmopolitan, medieval Buddhist, and secular elements. The rise of each of these cultural spheres was rooted in the wealth and the social order of the recreated empire.

T'ang culture was cosmopolitan not just because of its broad contacts with other cultures and peoples but also because of its

Stone sculpture of bodhisattva reflecting the full-bodied, almost voluptuous, T'ang ideal of beauty. [Corbis-Bettmann]

[3]E. O. Reischauer, *Ennin's Travels in T'ang China* (New York: Ronald Press, 1955), p. 7.

A Poem by Li Po

The great T'ang poet Li Po reputedly wrote twenty thousand poems, of which eighteen hundred have survived.

It has been said that concreteness of imagery is the genius of Chinese poetry. How does this example support that contention?

The River Merchant's Wife: A Letter

While my hair was still cut straight across my forehead
I played about the front gate, pulling flowers.
You came by on bamboo stilts, playing horse,
You walked about my seat, playing with blue plums.
And we went on living in the village of Chokan:
Two small people, without dislike or suspicion.

At fourteen I married My Lord you.
I never laughed, being bashful.
Lowering my head, I looked at the wall.
Called to, a thousand times, I never looked back.

At fifteen I stopped scowling,
I desired my dust to be mingled with yours
Forever and forever and forever.
Why should I climb the look out?

At sixteen you departed,
You went into far Ku-to-yen, by the river of swirling
   eddies,
And you have been gone five months.
The monkeys make sorrowful noise overhead.

You dragged your feet when you went out.
By the gate now, the moss is grown, the different
   mosses,
Too deep to clear them away!
The leaves fall early this autumn, in wind.
The paired butterflies are already yellow with August
Over the grass in the West garden;
They hurt me. I grow older.
If you are coming down through the narrows of the river
   Kiang,
Please let me know beforehand,
And I will come out to meet you,
As far as Cho-fu-Sa.

"The River Merchant's Wife: A Letter" by Ezra Pound, from *Personae.* Copyright ©1926 by Ezra Pound. Reprinted by permission of New Directions Publishing Corp.

---

openness to them. Buddhist pilgrims to India and a flow of Indian art and philosophies to China were a part of it. The voluptuousness of Indian painting and sculpture, for example, helped shape the T'ang representation of the *bodhisattva.* Commercial contacts were widespread. Foreign goods were vended in Ch'ang-an marketplaces. Communities of central and western Asians were established in the capital, and Arab and Iranian quarters grew up in the seaports of southeastern China. Merchants brought their religions with them. Nestorian Christianity, Zoroastrianism, Manichaeism, Judaism, and Islam entered China at this time. Most would be swept away in the persecutions of the ninth century, but Islam and small pockets of Judaism survived until the twentieth century.

Central Asian music and musical instruments became so popular as almost to displace the native tradition. T'ang ladies adopted foreign hairstyles. Foreign dramas and acrobatic performances by western Asians could be seen in the streets of the capital. Even among the pottery figurines customarily placed in tombs there were representations of western Asian traders and central Asian grooms, along with those of horses, camels, and court ladies that today are avidly sought by collectors and museums around the world. In T'ang poetry, too, what was foreign was not shunned but judged on its own merits or even presented as exotically attractive. Of a gallant of Ch'ang-an, Li Po wrote:

A young man of Five Barrows suburb east of the Golden
   Market,
Silver saddle and white horse cross through wind of spring.
When fallen flowers are trampled all under, where is it
   he will roam?
With a laugh he enters the tavern of a lovely Turkish
   wench.[4]

Later in the dynasty, another poet, Li Ho, wrote of service on the frontier:

A Tartar horn tugs at the north wind,
Thistle Gate shines whiter than the stream.
The sky swallows the road to Kokonor.
On the Great Wall, a thousand miles of moonlight.[5]

[4]S. Owen, *The Great Age of Chinese Poetry: The High T'ang.* © 1980, New Haven, CT: Yale University Press, p. 130. Reprinted by permission
[5]A. C. Graham, *Poems of the Late T'ang* trans. by A. C. Graham (Penguin Classics, 1965). Copyright © 1965, A. C. Graham.

The T'ang dynasty, although slightly less an age of faith than the preceding Six Dynasties, was the golden age of Buddhism in China nonetheless. Patronized by emperors and aristocrats, the Buddhist establishment acquired vast land-holdings and great wealth. Temples and monasteries were constructed throughout China. To gain even an inkling of the beauty and sophistication of the temple architecture, the wooden sculpture, or the paintings on the temple walls, one must see Hōryūji or the ancient temples of Nara in Japan, for little of note has survived in China. The single exception is the Caves of the Thousand Buddhas at Tunhuang in China's far northwest, which were sealed during the eleventh century for protection from Tibetan raiders and not rediscovered until the twentieth century. They were found to contain stone sculptures, Buddhist frescoes, and thousands of manuscripts in Chinese and Central Asian languages.

Only during the T'ang did China have a "church" establishment that was at all comparable to that of medieval Europe, and even then it was subservient to the far stronger T'ang state. Buddhist wealth and learning brought with them secular functions. T'ang temples served as schools, inns, or even bathhouses. They lent money. Priests performed funerals and dispensed medicines. Occasionally the state moved to recapture the revenues monopolized by temples. The severest persecution, which marked a turn in the fortunes of Buddhism in China, occurred from 841 to 845, when an ardent Taoist emperor confiscated millions of acres of tax-exempt lands, put back on the tax registers 260,000 monks and nuns, and destroyed 4,600 monasteries and 40,000 shrines.

During the early T'ang, the principal Buddhist sect was the T'ien-t'ai, but after the mid-ninth-century suppression, other sects came to the fore:

1. One devotional sect focused on Maitreya, a Buddha of the future, who will appear and create a paradise on earth. Maitreya (Mi Lo in Chinese and Miroku in Japanese) was a cosmic messiah, not a human figure. The messianic teachings of the sect often furnished the ideology for popular uprisings and rebellions like the White Lotus, which claimed that it was renewing the world in anticipation of Maitreya's coming.

2. Another devotional or faith sect worshiped the Amitabha (A Mi T'o in Chinese, Amida in Japanese) Buddha, the Lord of the Western Paradise or Pure Land. This sect taught that in the early centuries after the death of the historical Buddha, his teachings had been transmitted properly and people could obtain enlightenment by their own efforts, but that at present the Buddha's teachings had become so distorted that only by reliance on Amitabha could humans obtain salvation. All who called on Amitabha with a pure heart and perfect faith would be saved.

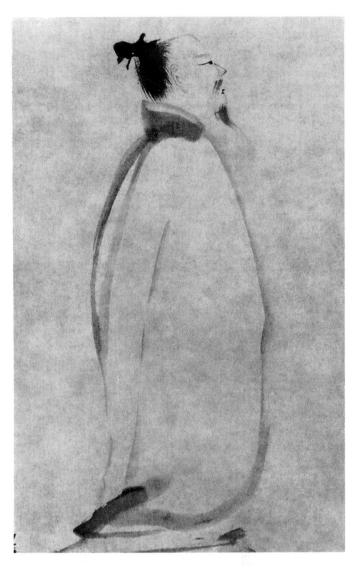

The T'ang poet Li Po, as imagined by the great Sung artist Liang K'ai.
[Tokyo National Museum]

Developing a congregational form of worship, this sect became the largest in China and deeply influenced Chinese popular religion.

3. A third sect, and the most influential among the Chinese elites, was known in China, where it began, as Ch'an and is better known in the West by its Japanese name, Zen. Zen had no cosmic Buddhas. It taught that the historical Buddha was only a man and exhorted each person to attain enlightenment by his or her own efforts. Although its monks were often the most learned in China, Zen was anti-intellectual in its emphasis on direct intuition into one's own Buddha-nature. Enlightenment was to be obtained by a regimen of physical labor and meditation. To jolt the monk into enlightenment—after he had been readied by long hours of meditation—some Zen sects used little problems not answerable by normal

ratiocination: "What was your face before you were conceived?" "If all things return to the One, what does the One return to?" "From the top of a hundred-foot pole, how do you step forward?" The psychological state of the adept attempting to deal with these problems is compared to that of "a rat pursued into a blocked pipe" or "a mosquito biting an iron ball." The discipline of meditation, combined with a Zen view of nature, profoundly influenced the arts in China and subsequently in Korea and Japan as well.

A third characteristic of T'ang culture was the reappearance of secular scholarship and letters. The reestablishment of centralized bureaucratic government stimulated the tradition of learning that had been partially interrupted after the fall of the Han dynasty in the third century C.E. A scholarly-bureaucratic complex emerged. Most men of letters were also officials, and most high-ranking officials painted or wrote poems. An anthology of T'ang poetry compiled during the Ming period (1368–1644) contained 48,900 poems by almost 2,300 authors. This secular stream of T'ang culture was not ideologically anti-Buddhist. Officials were often privately sympathetic to Buddhism. But as men involved themselves in the affairs of government, their values became increasingly this-worldly.

Court historians of the T'ang revived the Han practice of writing an official history of the previous dynasty. For the first time scholars wrote comprehensive institutional histories and regional and local gazetteers. They compiled dictionaries and wrote commentaries on the Confucian classics. Other scholars wrote ghost stories or tales of adventure, using the literary language. (Buddhist sermons, in contrast, were often written in the vernacular.) More paintings were Buddhist than secular, but Chinese landscape painting had its origins during the T'ang. Nowhere, however, was the growth of a secular culture more evident than in poetry, the greatest achievement of T'ang letters.

Whether Li Po (701–762) can be called wholly secular is questionable. He might better be called Taoist. But he clearly was not Buddhist. Born in Szechwan, he was exceptional among T'ang poets in never having sat for the civil service examinations, although he briefly held an official post at Ch'ang-an, given in recognition of his poetry. Large and muscular, he was a swordsman and a carouser. Of the 20,000 poems he is said to have composed, 1,800 have survived, and a fair number have titles like "Bring on the Wine" or "Drinking Alone in the Moonlight." According to legend, he drowned while drunkenly attempting to embrace the reflection of the moon in a lake. His poetry is clear, powerful, passionate, and always sensitive to beauty. It also contains a sense of fantasy, as when he climbed a mountain and saw a star-goddess, "stepping in emptiness, pacing pure ether, her rain-

bow robes trailed broad sashes." Li Po, nearer to heaven than to earth, looked down below where

> Far and wide Tartar troops were speeding,
> And flowing blood mired the wild grasses
> Where wolves and jackals all wore officials' caps.[6]

According to Li Po, life is brief and the universe is large, but this view did not lead him to renounce the world. His Taoism was not of the quietistic strain close to Buddhism. Rather, he exulted, identifying with the primal flux of yin and yang:

> I'll wrap this Mighty Mudball of a world all up in a bag
> And be wild and free like Chaos itself![7]

Tu Fu (712–770), an equally famous T'ang poet, was from a literary family. He failed the metropolitan examination at the age of twenty-three and spent years in wandering and poverty. At thirty-nine he received an official appointment after presenting his poetry to the court. Four years later he was appointed to a military post. He fell into rebel hands during the An Lu-shan rebellion, escaped, and was reappointed to a civil post. But he was then dismissed and suffered further hardships. His poetry is less lyrical and more allusive than Li Po's. It also reflects more compassion for human suffering: for the mother whose sons have been conscripted and sent to war; for brothers scattered by war; for his own family, to whom he returned after having been given up for dead. Like Li Po, he felt that humans are short-lived and that nature endures. Visiting the ruins of the palace of the second T'ang emperor, he saw "Grey rats scuttling over ancient tiles" and "in its shadowed chambers ghost fires green." "Its lovely ladies are the brown soil" and only "tomb horses of stone remain." But his response to this sad scene was to

> Sing wildly, let the tears cover your open hands.
> Then go ever onward and on the road of your travels,
> Meet none who prolong their fated years.[8]

His response was unlike that of Li Po. It was close to Stoicism but equally un-Buddhist.

Transition to Late Imperial China: The Sung Dynasty (960–1279)

Most traditional Chinese history was written in terms of the dynastic cycle, and for good reason: The pattern of rise and fall, of expansion and contraction, within each dynasty cannot be denied. Certainly the Sung can be viewed from this perspective. It reunified China in 960, establishing its capi-

[6]Owen, p. 134.
[7]Owen, p. 125.
[8]Owen, pp. 223–224.

tal at Kaifeng on the Yellow River (see Map 8–2). Mobilizing its resources effectively, it ruled for 170 years; this period is called the Northern Sung. Then it weakened. In 1127 it lost the north but for another 150 years continued to rule the south from a new capital at Hangchow in east-central China. The Southern Sung fell before the Mongol onslaught in 1279.

But there is more to Chinese history than the inner logic of the dynastic cycle. Longer term changes that cut across dynastic lines were ultimately more important. One such set of changes began during the late T'ang period and continued on into the Sung period, affecting its economy, society, state, and culture. Taken together, these changes help to explain why China after the T'ang did not relapse into centuries of disunity as it had after the Han, and why China would never again experience more than brief intervals of disunity. In this section we will skip over emperors and empresses, eunuchs and generals, and focus instead on more fundamental transformations.

Agricultural Revolution of the Sung: From Serfs to Free Farmers

Landed aristocrats had dominated local society in China during the Sui and the T'ang periods. The tillers of their lands were little more than serfs. Labor service was the heaviest tax, and whether performed on the office or rank lands of aristocrats or on other government lands, it created conditions of social subordination.

The aristocracy weakened, however, under the T'ang and after its fall. Estates were divided among male children at each change of generation. Drawn to the capital, the aristocracy became less a landed, and more a metropolitan, elite. After the fall of the T'ang, the aristocratic estates were often seized by warlords. As the aristocracy declined, the claims of those who worked the soil grew stronger, aided by changes in the land and tax systems. With the collapse of the equal field system (described earlier), farmers could buy and sell land. The ownership of land as private property gave the cultivators greater independence. They could now move about as they pleased. Taxes paid in grain gave way during the Sung to taxes in money. The commutation of the labor tax to a money tax gave the farmers more control over their own time. Conscription, the cruelest and heaviest labor tax of all, disappeared as the conscript armies of the early and middle T'ang gave way to professional armies.

Changes in technology also benefited the cultivator. New strains of an early-ripening rice permitted double cropping. In the Yangtze region, extensive water-control projects were carried out, and more fertilizers were used. New commercial crops were developed. Tea, which had been introduced during the Six Dynasties as a medicine and had been drunk by

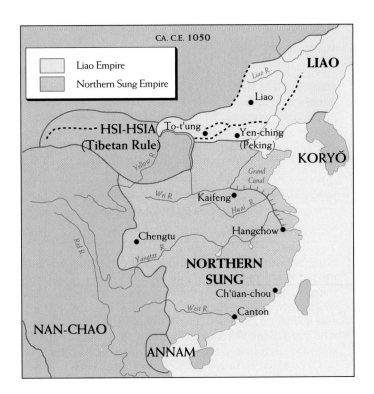

Map 8–2   The Northern Sung and Liao Empires (top) and the Southern Sung and Chin Empires (bottom).   During the Northern Sung, the Mongol Liao dynasty ruled only the extreme northern edge of China. During the Southern Sung, in contrast, the Manchurian Chin dynasty ruled half of China.

"Chaste Woman" Shi

Hung Mai (1123–1202 C.E.) was a collector of stories—fantastic, folkloric, and factual. Unlike the usual Confucian homilies on the proper virtues of women, his stories, and those told by other Sung storytellers, contained broader perspectives. They reflected the actual diversity of Chinese society. In this story the Chinese belief in ghosts enables the wronged Ning to have a hand in the villain's downfall.

Is the moral of this tale simply that justice ultimately prevails? Can a more complex interpretation be made? What does it say about the dynamics of Sung society?

Ning Six of South Meadow village, in the southern suburbs of Jianchang, was a simple-minded man who concentrated on his farming. His younger brother's wife, Miss Shi, was a little sleeker than her peers. She was also ruthless and licentious, and had an adulterous affair with a youth who lived there. Whenever Ning looked askance at her she would scold him and there was not much he could do.

Once Miss Shi took a chicken, wanting to cook it. When Ning learned of it, he went into her room, demanded that she give it to him, then left with it. Miss Shi quickly cut her arm with a knife, then went to the neighbors screaming, "Because my husband is not home, brother-in-law offered me a chicken and tried to force me to have sex with him. I resisted, threatening to kill myself with the knife I was holding, and so just managed to escape."

Ning at that time had no wife, so the neighbors thought she might be telling the truth. They took them to the village headman, then the county jail. The clerks at the jail reviewed the evidence and demanded 10,000 cash to set things right. Ning was poor and stingy, and moreover, knew himself to be in the right, so stubbornly refused. The clerks sent up the dossier to the prefect Dai Qi. Dai was unable to examine it but noted that it involved an ordinary village wife who was able to protect her virtue and her body and not be violated. The administrative supervisor, Zhao Shiqing, concurred with Qi, and they sent up the case making Ning look guilty. Ning received the death penalty and Miss Shi was granted 100,000 cash, regular visits from the local officials, and a banner honoring her for her chastity. From this, she acquired a reputation as a chaste wife. The local people all realized Ning had been wronged and resented how overboard she had gone.

In the end Miss Shi had an affair with a monk at the nearby Lintian temple. Charges were brought and she received a beating and soon became ill. She saw Ning as a vengeful demon and then died. The date was the sixth month of 1177.

From *Chinese Civilization, Sourcebook* Patricia Buckley Ebrey. Copyright © 1993 by Patricia Buckley Ebrey. Reprinted with permission of The Free Press, A Division of Simon & Schuster, Inc.

---

monks during the T'ang, became widely cultivated; cotton also became a common crop. Because taxes paid in money tended to become fixed, much of the increased productivity accrued to the cultivator. Of course, not all benefited equally; there were landlords and landless tenants as well as independent small farmers.

The disappearance of the aristocrats also increased the authority of the district magistrate, who no longer had to contend with their interference in local affairs. The Sung magistrate became the sole representative of imperial authority in local society. But there were too many villages in his district for him to be involved regularly in their internal governance. As long as taxes were paid and order maintained, affairs were left in the hands of the village elites. So the Sung farmer enjoyed not only a rising income and more freedom, but also substantial self-government.

One other development that began during the Sung—and became vastly more important later—was the appearance of a scholar-gentry class. The typical gentry family contained at least one member who had passed the provincial civil-service examination and lived in the district seats or market towns. Socially and culturally, these gentry were closer to magistrates than to villagers. But they usually owned land in the villages and thus shared some interests with the local landholders. Although much less powerful than the former aristocrats, they took a hand in local affairs and at times functioned as a buffer between the village and the magistrate's office.

Commercial Revolution of the Sung

Stimulated by changes in the countryside, and contributing to them as well, were demographic shifts, innovative technologies, the growth of cities, the spread of money, and rising trade. These developments varied by region, but overall the Sung economy reached new prosperity.

Emergence of the Yangtze Basin   Until late in the T'ang, northern China had been the most populous and productive region. But from the late ninth century the center of gravity of China's population, agricultural production, and culture shifted to the lower and eastern Yangtze region. Between 800 and 1100 the population of the region tripled as China's total population increased to about 100 million. Its rice paddies yielded more per acre than the wheat or millet fields of the north, making rice the tax base of the empire. Its wealth led to the establishment of so many schools that regional quotas for the examination system were set by the government to prevent the Yangtze region from dominating all of China. The Northern Sung capital itself was kept in the north for strategic reasons, but it was situated at Kaifeng, further east than Loyang, at the point where the Grand Canal, which carried tax rice from the south, joined the Yellow River.

New Technology   During the Northern Sung a coal and iron-smelting industry developed in north China that provided China with better tools and weapons. Using coke and bellows to heat furnaces to the temperatures required for carbonized steel, it was the most advanced in the world.

Printing began in China with the use of carved seals. The earliest woodblock texts, mostly on Buddhist subjects, appeared in the seventh century. By the tenth century a complete edition of the classics had been published, and by the mid-Sung books printed with movable type were fairly common.

Other advances during the Sung were the abacus, the use of gunpowder in grenades and projectiles, and improvements in textiles and porcelains.

Rise of a Money Economy   Exchange during the T'ang had been based on silk. Coins had been issued, but their circulation was limited. During the Northern Sung large amounts of copper cash were coined, but the demand rose more rapidly than the supply. Coins were made with holes in the center, and one thousand on a string constituted the usual unit for large transactions. Beginning in the Southern Sung, silver was minted to complement copper cash, ten times as much silver in the late twelfth century as in the early eleventh century. Letters of credit were used by merchants, and various kinds of paper money also were issued. The penetration of money into the village economy was such that by 1065 tax receipts paid in money had risen to 38 million strings of cash—in comparison with a mere 2 million in mid-T'ang.

Trade   The growth of trade spurred the demand for money. One may distinguish among trade within economic regions, trade between regions, and foreign trade. During the T'ang most cities had been administrative, supported by taxes from the countryside. Official salaries and government expenditures created a demand for services and commercial products, making the cities into islands of commerce in a noncommercial hinterland. In most of China's seven or eight economic regions this pattern continued during the Sung, but in the capital, and especially in the economically advanced regions along the Yangtze, cities became the hubs of regional commercial networks, with district seats or market towns serving as secondary centers for the local markets beneath them.

As this transition occurred, cities with more than 100,000 households almost quadrupled in number. The Northern Sung capital at Kaifeng is recorded as having had 260,000 households—probably more than one million inhabitants—and the Southern Sung capital at Hangchow had 391,000 households. Compare these capitals to those of backward Europe: London during the Northern Sung had a population of about 18,000; Rome during the Southern Sung had 35,000; and Paris even a century later had fewer than 60,000.

Furthermore, these Sung capitals, unlike Ch'ang-an with its walled wards that closed at night, were open within and spread beyond their outer walls. As in present-day Chinese cities, their main avenues were lined with shops. Merchant guilds replaced government officials as the managers of marketplaces. Growing wealth also led to a taste for luxury and an increasingly secular lifestyle. Restaurants, theaters, wine shops, and brothels abounded. Entertainment quarters with fortunetellers, jugglers, chess masters, acrobats, and puppeteers sprang up. Such activity had not been absent from Ch'ang-an, but the numbers increased, and now they catered to traders and rich merchants as well as to officials.

Trade between regions during the Sung was limited mainly to luxury goods like silk, lacquerware, medicinal herbs, and porcelains. Only where transport was cheap—along rivers, canals, or the coast—was interregional trade in bulk commodities economical, and even then it was usually carried on only to make up for specific shortages.

Foreign trade also reached new heights during the Sung. In the north, Chinese traders bought horses from Tibetan, Turkic, and Mongol border states, and sold silks and tea. Along the coast, Chinese merchants took over the port trade that during the T'ang had been in the hands of Korean, Arab, and Irani merchants. The new hegemony of Chinese merchants was based on improved ships using both sail and oars and equipped with watertight compartments and better rudders. Chinese captains, navigating with the aid of the compass, came to dominate the sea routes from Japan in the north to Sumatra in the south. The content of the overseas trade reflected China's advanced economy: It imported raw materials and exported finished goods. Porcelains were sent to Southeast Asia and then were carried by Arab ships to medieval trading centers on the Persian Gulf and down the coast of East Africa as far south as Zanzibar.

Government: From Aristocracy to Autocracy

The millennium of late imperial China after the T'ang is often spoken of as the age of autocracy or as China's age of absolute monarchy. Earlier emperors, as we have noted, were often personally powerful, but beginning with the Sung, changes occurred that made it easier for emperors to be autocrats.

One change was that Sung emperors had direct personal control over more offices than their T'ang predecessors. For example, the Board of Academicians, an advisory office, presented the emperor with policy options separate from those presented by the Secretariat-Chancellery. The emperor could thus use the one against the other and prevent bureaucrats in the Secretariat-Chancellery from dominating the government.

A second change was that the central government was better funded than it had been previously. Revenues in 1100 were three times the peak revenues of the T'ang, partly because of the growth of population and agricultural wealth, and partly because of the establishment of government monopolies on salt, wine, and tea and various duties, fees, and taxes levied on domestic and foreign trade. During the Northern Sung these commercial revenues rivaled the land tax; during the Southern Sung they surpassed it. Confucian officials would continue to stress the primacy of land, but throughout late imperial China, commerce became a vital source of revenues.

A third change that strengthened the emperors was the disappearance of the aristocracy. During the T'ang the emperor had come from the same Sino-Turkic aristocracy of northwestern China as most of his principal ministers, and he was, essentially, the organ of a state that ruled on behalf of this aristocracy. Aristocrats monopolized the high posts of government. They married among themselves and with the imperial family. They called the emperor the Son of Heaven, but they knew he was one of them. During the Sung, in contrast, government officials were commoners, mostly products of the examination system. They were separated from the emperor by an enormous social gulf and saw him as a person apart.

The Sung examination system was larger than that of the T'ang, if smaller than under later dynasties. Whereas only 10 percent of officials had been recruited by examination during the T'ang, the Sung figure rose to over 50 percent and included the most important officials. The first examination was given at regional centers. The applicant took the examination in a walled cubicle under close supervision. To ensure impartiality, his answers were recopied by clerks and his name was replaced by a number before his examination was sent to the officials who would grade it. Of those who sat for the examination, only a tiny percentage passed. The second hurdle was the metropolitan examination at the national capital, where the precautions were equally elaborate. Only one in five, or about two hundred a year, passed. The average successful applicant was in his mid-thirties. The final hurdle was the palace examination, which rejected a few and assigned a ranking to the others.

To pass the examinations, the candidate had to memorize the Confucian classics, interpret selected passages, write in the literary style, compose poems on themes given by the examiners, and propose solutions to contemporary problems in terms of Confucian philosophy. The quality of the officials produced by the Sung system was impressive. A parallel might be drawn with nineteenth-century Britain, where students in the classics at Oxford and Cambridge went on to become generalist bureaucrats. The Chinese examination system that flourished during the Sung continued, with some interruptions, into the twentieth century. The continuity of Chinese government during this millennium rested on the examination elite, with its common culture and values.

The social base for this examination meritocracy was triangular, consisting of land, education, and office. Landed wealth paid the costs of education. A poor peasant or city dweller could not afford the years of study needed to pass the examinations. Without passing the examinations, official position was out of reach. And without office, family wealth could not be preserved. The Chinese pattern of inheritance, as noted earlier, led to the division of property at each change of generation. Some families passed the civil service examinations for several generations running. More often, the sons of well-to-do officials did not study as hard as those with bare means. The adage "shirt sleeves to shirt sleeves in three generations" is not inappropriate to the Sung and later dynasties. As China had an extended-family or clan system, a wealthy official often provided education for the bright children of poor relations.

How the merchants related to this system is less clear. They had wealth but were despised by scholar-officials as grubby profit seekers and were barred from taking the examinations. Some merchants avoided the system altogether—a thorough education in the Confucian classics did little to fit a merchant's son for a career in commerce. Others bought land for status and security, and their sons or grandsons became eligible to take the exams. Similarly, a small peasant might build up his holdings, become a landlord, and educate a son or grandson. The system was steeply hierarchical, but it was not closed nor did it produce a new, self-perpetuating aristocracy.

Sung Culture

As society and government changed during the T'ang-Sung transition, so too did culture. Sung culture retained some of the energy of the T'ang while becoming more intensely and perhaps more narrowly Chinese. The preconditions for the rich Sung culture were a rising economy, an increase in the number of schools and higher literacy, and the spread of printing. Sung culture was less aristocratic, less cosmopolitan, and more closely associated with the officials and the scholar-gen-

An elegant Sung dynasty wine pot with green celadon glaze (24.8 cm. high).
[© Gift of The Asian Art Museum of San Francisco, The Avery Brundage Collection, B66P12]

try, who were both its practitioners and its patrons. It also was less Buddhist than the T'ang had been. Only the Zen (Ch'an) sect kept its vitality, and many Confucians were outspokenly anti-Buddhist and anti-Taoist. In sum, the secular culture of officials that had been a sidestream in the T'ang broadened and became the mainstream during the Sung.

Chinese consider the Sung dynasty as the peak of their traditional culture. It was, for example, China's greatest age of pottery and porcelains. High-firing techniques were developed, and kilns were established in every area. There was a rich variety of beautiful glazes. The shapes were restrained and harmonious. Sung pottery, like nothing produced in the world before it, made ceramics a major art form in East Asia. It was also an age of great historians. Ssu-ma Kuang (1019–1086) wrote *A Comprehensive Mirror for Aid in Government*, which treated not a single dynasty but all Chinese history. His work was more sophisticated than previous histories in that it included a discussion of documentary sources and an

explanation of why he chose to rely on one source rather than another. The greatest achievements of the Sung, however, were in philosophy, poetry, and painting.

Philosophy The Sung was second only to the Chou as a creative age in philosophy. A series of original thinkers culminated in the towering figure of Chu Hsi (1130–1200). Chu Hsi studied Taoism and Buddhism in his youth, along with Confucianism. A brilliant student, he passed the metropolitan examination at the age of eighteen. During his thirties he focused his attention on Confucianism, deepening and making more systematic its social and political ethics by joining to it certain Buddhist and native metaphysical elements. As a consequence, the new Confucianism became a viable alternative to Buddhism for Chinese intellectuals. Chu Hsi became famous as a teacher at the White Deer Grotto Academy, and his writings were widely distributed. Before the end of the Sung, his Confucianism had become the standard interpretation used in the civil service examinations, and it remained so until the twentieth century.

If we search for comparable figures in other traditions, we might pick Saint Thomas Aquinas (1224–1274) of medieval Europe or the Islamic theologian al-Ghazali (1058–1111), each of whom produced a new synthesis or worldview that lasted for centuries. Aquinas combined Aristotle and Latin theology just as Chu Hsi combined Confucian philosophy and metaphysical notions from other sources. Because Chu Hsi used terms such as the "great ultimate" and because he emphasized a Zenlike meditation called "quiet sitting," some contemporary critics said his Neo-Confucian philosophy was a Buddhist wolf in the clothing of a Confucian sheep. This was unfair. Whereas Aquinas would make philosophy serve religion, Chu Hsi made religion or metaphysics serve philosophy. In his hands, the great ultimate (also known as "principle" or *li*) lost its otherworldly character and became a constituent of all things in the universe. Perhaps the Chu Hsi philosophy may be characterized as innerworldly.

Later critics often argued that Chu Hsi's teachings encouraged metaphysical speculation at the expense of practical ethics. Chu Hsi's followers replied that, on the contrary, his teachings gave practical ethics a systematic underpinning and positively contributed to individual moral responsibility. What was discovered within by Neo-Confucian quiet sitting was just those positive ethical truths enunciated by Confucius over a thousand years earlier. The new metaphysics did not change the Confucian social philosophy.

Chu Hsi himself advocated the selection of scholar-officials through schools, rather than by examinations. It is ironic that his teachings became a new orthodoxy that was maintained by the channelizing effect of the civil-service examinations. Historians argue, probably correctly, that Chu

The Sung dynasty philosopher Chu Hsi (1130–1200), whose Neo-Confucian ideas remained central down to the twentieth century. [Collection of the National Palace Museum, Taiwan, R.O.C.]

Hsi's teachings were one source of stability in late imperial China. Like the examination system, the imperial institution, the scholar-gentry class, and the land system, his interpretation of Confucianism contributed to continuity and impeded change. Some historians go further and say that the emergence of the Chu Hsi orthodoxy stifled intellectual creativity during later dynasties, which probably is an overstatement. There were always contending schools.

Poetry   Sung poets were in awe of those of the T'ang, yet Sung poets were also among China's best. A Japanese authority on Chinese literature wrote

> T'ang poetry could be likened to wine, and Sung poetry to tea. Wine has great power to stimulate, but one cannot drink it constantly. Tea is less stimulating, bringing to the drinker a quieter pleasure, but one which can be enjoyed more continuously.[9]

The most famous poet of the Northern Sung was Su Tung-p'o (1037–1101), a man who participated in the full range of the culture of his age: He was a painter and calligrapher, particularly knowledgeable about inks; he practiced Zen and wrote commentaries on the Confucian classics; he superintended engineering projects; and he was a connoisseur of cooking and wine. His life was shaped by politics. He was a conservative, believing in a limited role for government and social control through morality. (The other faction in the Sung bureaucracy was the reformers, who stressed law and an expanded governmental role.)

Passing the metropolitan examination, Su rose through a succession of posts to become the governor of a province—a position of immense power. While considering death sentences, which could not be carried over into the new year, he wrote

> New Year's Eve—you'd think I could go home early
> But official business keeps me.
> I hold the brush and face them with tears:
> Pitiful convicts in chains,
> Little men who tried to fill their bellies,
> Fell into the law's net, don't understand disgrace.
> And I? In love with a meager stipend
> I hold on to my job and miss the chance to retire.
> Do not ask who is foolish or wise;
> All of us alike scheme for a meal.
> The ancients would have freed them a while at New
>   Year's—
> Would I dare do likewise? I am silent with shame.[10]

Eight years later, when the reformers came to power, Su himself was arrested and spent one hundred days in prison, awaiting execution on a charge of slandering the emperor. Instead, he was released and exiled. He wrote, "Out the gate, I do a dance, wind blows in my face; our galloping horses race along as magpies cheer."[11] Arriving at his place of exile, he reflected

> Between heaven and earth I live,
> One ant on a giant grindstone,
> Trying in my petty way to walk to the right
> While the turning of the mill wheel takes me endlessly
>   left.
> Though I go the way of benevolence and duty,
> I can't escape from hunger and cold.[12]

But exile was soon turned to art. He farmed a plot of land at the "eastern slope" from which he took his literary name, Tung-p'o. Of his work there, he wrote

[9]Kojiro Yoshikawa, *An Introduction to Sung Poetry,* trans. by Burton Watson (Cambridge: Harvard University Press, Harvard-Yenching Institute Monograph Series, 1967), p. 37.

[10]Yoshikawa, p. 119.
[11]Yoshikawa, p. 117.
[12]Yoshikawa, p. 105.

Su Tung-P'o Imagined on a Wet Day, Wearing a Rain Hat and Clogs

After Su's death, a disciple wrote these lines.

How does the sentiment in this poem relate to the Confucian humanism encountered in the document in Chapter 2?

When with tall hat and firm baton he stood in
    council,
The crowds were awed at the dignity of the statesman
    in him.
But when in cloth cap he strolled with cane and
    sandals,
He greeted little children with gentle smiles.

Reprinted by permission of the publisher. From *An Introduction to Sung Poetry*, by Kojiro Yoshikawa, trans. by Burton Watson, Cambridge, MA: Harvard University Press, Copyright ©1967 by the Harvard-Yenching Institute. Monograph Series, poem, p. 122, illustration located on un-numbered page opposite p. 65.

A good farmer hates to wear out the land;
I'm lucky this plot was ten years fallow.
It's too soon to count on mulberries;
My best bet is a crop of wheat.
I planted seed and within the month
Dirt on the rows was showing green.
An old farmer warned me,
Don't let seedlings shoot up too fast!
If you want plenty of dumpling flour
Turn a cow or sheep in here to graze.
Good advice—I bowed my thanks;
I won't forget you when my belly's full.[13]

After 1086 the conservatives regained control of the government, and Su resumed his official career. In 1094 another shift occurred, and Su was again exiled to the distant southern island of Hainan. After still another shift, Su was on his way back to the capital when he died in 1101.

Painting   In the West, penmanship and painting are quite separate, one merely a skill and the other esteemed as an art. In China, calligraphy and painting were equally appreciated and were seen as related. A scholar spent his life with brush in hand. The same qualities of line, balance, and strength needed for calligraphy carried over to painting. Chinese calligraphy is immensely pleasing even to the untutored Western eye, and it is not difficult to distinguish between the elegant strokes of Hui-neng, the last emperor of the Northern Sung, and the powerful brushwork of the Zen monk Chang Chi-chih.

Sung painting was varied—of birds or flowers; of fish or insects; of horses, monkeys, or water buffalo; of scholars, emperors, Buddhas, or Taoist immortals. But its crowning achievement was landscapes. Sung landscapes are different from those of the West. Each stroke of the brush on silk or paper was final. Mistakes could not be covered up. Each element of a painting was presented in its most pleasing aspect; the painting was not constrained by single-point perspective. Paintings had no single source of illumination with light and shadow, but contained an overall diffusion of light. Space was an integral part of the painting. A typical painting might have craggy rocks or twisted pine trees in the foreground, then mist or clouds or rain to create distance, and in the background the outlines of mountains or cliffs fading into space. If the painting contained human figures at all, they were small in a natural universe that was very large. Chinese painting thus reflected the same worldview as Chinese philosophy or poetry. The painter sought to grasp the inner reality of the scene and not to be bound up in surface details.

[13]Yoshikawa, pp. 119–120.

Is the enlightened man depicted in this painting meditating or dozing? Zen paintings often have a touch of humorous ambiguity. Note the broad calligraphic brushwork in this Southern Sung or Yuan dynasty painting done in the style of the Zen monk Shih K'o. [Tokyo National Museum]

In paintings by monks or masters of the Zen school, the presentation of an intuitive vision of an inner reality became even more pronounced. Paintings of Bodhidharma, the legendary founder of the Zen sect, are often dominated by a single powerful downstroke of the brush, defining the edge of his robe. Paintings of patriarchs tearing up sutras or sweeping dust with a broom from the mirror of the mind are almost as calligraphic as paintings of bamboo. A Yuan dynasty painting in the style of Shih K'o shows the figure of a monk or sage who is dozing or meditating. A Zen "broken ink" landscape might contain rocks, water, mountains, and clouds, each represented by a few explosive strokes of the brush.

China in the Mongol World Empire: The Yuan Dynasty (1279–1368)

The Mongols created the greatest empire in the history of the world. It extended from the Caspian Sea to the Pacific Ocean; from Russia, Siberia, and Korea in the north to Persia and Burma in the south. Invasion fleets were even sent to Java and Japan, although without success. Mongol rule in China is one chapter of this larger story.

Rise of the Mongol Empire

The Mongols, a nomadic people, lived to the north of China on grasslands where they raised horses and herded sheep. They lived in felt tents called yurts—they sometimes called themselves "the people of the felt tents." Women performed much of the work and were freer and more easygoing than women in China. Families belonged to clans, and related clans to tribes. Tribes would gather during the annual migration from the summer plains to winter pasturage. Chiefs were elected, most often from noble lineages, for their courage, military prowess, judgment, and leadership. Like Manchu or Turkic, the Mongol tongue was Altaic.

The Mongols believed in nature deities and in the sky god above all others. Sky blue was their sacred color. They communicated with their gods through religious specialists called *shamans*. Politically divided, they traded and warred among themselves and with settled peoples on the borders of their vast grassland domains.

The founder of the Mongol Empire, Temujin, was born in 1167, the son of a tribal chief. While Temujin was still a child, his father was poisoned. He fled and after wandering for some years, returned to the tribe, avenged his father, and in time became chief himself. Through his shrewd policy of alliances and remarkable survival qualities, by the time he was forty, he had united all Mongol tribes and had been elected their great khan, or ruler. It is by the title *Genghis* (also spelled *Jenghiz* or *Chinggis*) *Khan* that he is known to history. Genghis possessed an extraordinary charisma, and his sons and grandsons also became wise and talented leaders. Why the Mongol tribes, almost untouched by the higher civilizations of the world, should have produced such leaders at this point in history is difficult to explain.

A second conundrum is how the Mongols, who numbered only about a million and a half, created the army that conquered vastly denser populations. Part of the answer is institutional. Genghis organized his armies into "myriads" of ten thousand troops, with decimal subdivisions of one thousand, one hundred, and ten. Elaborate signals were devised so that in battle, even large units could be manipulated like the fingers of a hand. Mongol tactics were superb: Units would retreat, turn, flank, and destroy their enemies. The historical record makes amply clear that Genghis's nomadic cavalry had a paralytic effect on the peoples they encountered. Peerless horsemen, the Mongols' most dreaded weapon was the compound bow, short enough to be used from the saddle yet more powerful than the English longbow.

They were astonishingly mobile. Each man carried his own supplies. Trailing remounts, they covered vast distances quickly. In 1241, for example, a Mongol army had reached Hungary, Poland, and the shore of the Adriatic, and was poised for a further advance into western Europe. But when word arrived of the death of the great khan, the army turned and galloped back to Mongolia to help choose his successor.

When this army encountered walled cities, it learned the use of siege weapons from the enemies it had conquered. Chinese engineers were used in campaigns in Persia. The

Mongols also used terror as a weapon. Inhabitants of cities that refused to surrender in the Near East and China were put to the sword. Large areas in north China and Szechwan were devastated and depopulated. Descriptions of the Mongols by those whom they conquered dwell on their physical toughness and pitiless cruelty.

But the Mongols had strengths that went beyond the strictly military. Genghis opened his armies to recruits from the Uighur Turks, the Manchus, and other nomadic peoples. As long as they complied with the military discipline demanded of his forces, they could participate in his triumphs. In 1206 Genghis promulgated laws designed to prevent the normal wrangling and warring between tribes that would undermine his empire. Genghis also obtained thousands of pledges of personal loyalty from his followers, and he appointed these "vassals" to command his armies and staff his government. This policy gave to his forces an inner coherence that countered the divisive effect of tribal loyalties.

The Mongol conquests were all the more impressive in that, unlike the earlier Arab expansion, they lacked the unifying force of religious zeal. To be sure, at an assembly of chiefs in 1206, an influential shaman revealed that it was the sky god's will that Genghis conquer the world. Yet other unabashedly frank words attributed to Genghis may reveal a truer image of what lay behind the Mongol drive to conquest: "Man's highest joy is in victory: to conquer one's enemies, to pursue them, to deprive them of their possessions, to make their beloved weep, to ride on their horses, and to embrace their wives and daughters."[14]

Genghis divided his far-flung empire among his four sons. Trade and communications were maintained between the parts, but over several generations, each of the four khanates became independent. The khanate of Chagatai was in central Asia and remained purely nomadic. A second khanate of the Golden Horde ruled Russia from the lower Volga. The third was in Persia, and the fourth, led by those who succeeded Genghis as great khans, centered first in Mongolia and then in China (see Map 8–3).

Mongol Rule in China

The standard theory used in explaining Chinese history is the dynastic cycle. A second theory explains Chinese history in terms of the interaction between the settled people of China and the nomads of the steppe. When strong states emerged in China, their wealth and population enabled them to expand militarily onto the steppe. But when China was weak, as was more often the case, the steppe peoples overran China. To review briefly:

1. During the Han dynasty (206 B.C.E.–220 C.E.), the most pressing problem in foreign relations was the Hsiung Nu empire to the north.

2. During the centuries that followed the Han, various nomadic peoples invaded and ruled northern China.

3. The energy and institutions of these Sino-Turkic rulers of the northern dynasties shaped China's reunification during the Sui (589–618) and T'ang (618–907) dynasties. The Uighur Turks also played a major role in T'ang defense policy.

4. Northern border states became even more important during the Sung. The Northern Sung (960–1126) bought peace with payments of gold and silver to the Liao. The Southern Sung (1126–1279), for all its cultural brilliance, was little more than a tributary state of the Chin dynasty, which had expanded into northern China.

From the start of the Mongol pursuit of world hegemony, the riches of China were a target. But Genghis proceeded cautiously, determined to leave no enemy at his back. He first disposed of the Tibetan state to the northwest of China and then the Manchu state of Chin that ruled north China. Mongol forces took Peking in 1227, the year Genghis died. They went on to take Loyang and the southern reaches of the Yellow River in 1234, and all of north China by 1241. During this time, the Mongols were interested mainly in loot. Only later did Chinese advisers persuade them that more wealth could be obtained by taxation.

Kublai, a grandson of Genghis, was chosen as the great khan in 1260. In 1264 he moved his capital from Karakorum in Mongolia to Peking. It was only in 1271 that he adopted a Chinese dynastic name, the Yuan, and, as a Chinese dynasty, went to war with the Southern Sung. Once the decision was made, the Mongols swept across southern China. The last Sung stronghold fell in 1279.

Kublai Khan's rule in Peking reflected the mixture of cultural elements in Mongol China. From Peking, Kublai could rule as a Chinese emperor, which would not have been possible in Karakorum. He adopted the Chinese custom of hereditary succession. He rebuilt Peking as a walled city in the Chinese style. But Peking was far to the north of any previous Chinese capital, away from centers of wealth and population; to provision it, the Grand Canal had to be extended. From Peking, Kublai could look out onto Manchuria and Mongolia and maintain ties with the other khanates. The city proper was for the Mongols. It was known to the West as Cambulac, "the city (baliq) of the khan." Chinese were segregated in an adjoining walled city. The palace of the khan was designed by an Arab architect; its rooms were Central Asian in style. Kublai also maintained a summer palace at Shangtu (the "Xanadu" of Samuel Taylor Coleridge's poem)

---

[14] J. K. Fairbank, E. O. Reischauer, and A. M. Craig, *East Asia, Tradition and Transformation* (Boston: Houghton Mifflin, 1973), p. 164.

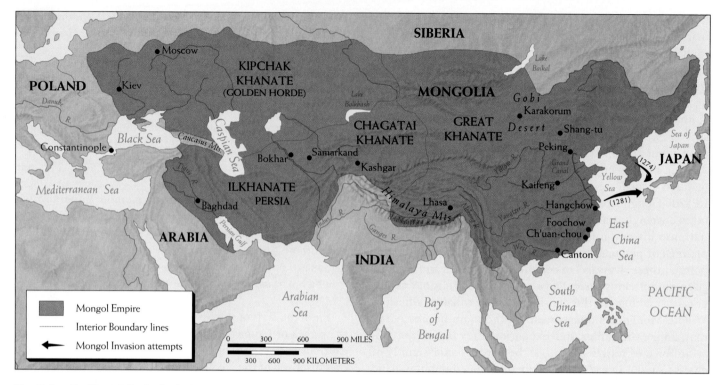

Map 8–3   The Mongol Empire in the late thirteenth century.   Note the four khanates: the Golden Horde in Russia, the Ilkhanate in Persia, Chagadai in Central Asia, and the Great Khanate extending from Mongolia to southern China.

in Inner Mongolia, where he could hawk and ride and hunt in Mongol style.

Early Mongol rule in northern China was rapacious and exploitative, but it later shifted toward Chinese forms of government and taxation, especially in the south and at the local level. Because it was a foreign military occupation, civil administration was highly centralized. Under the emperor was a Central Secretariat, and beneath it were ten "Moving Secretariats," which became the provinces of later dynasties. These highly centralized institutions and the arbitrary style of Mongol decision making accelerated the trend toward absolutism that had started during the previous dynasty.

About four hundred thousand Mongols lived in China during the Yuan period. For such a tiny minority to control the Chinese majority, it had to stay separate. One measure was to make military service a monopoly of Mongols and their nomadic allies. Garrisons were established throughout China, with a strategic reserve on the steppe. Military officers were always regarded as more important than civil officials. A second measure was to use ethnic classifications in appointing civil officials. The highest category was the Mongols, who held the top civil and military posts. The second category included Persians, Turks, and other non-Chinese, who were given high civil posts. The third category was the northern Chinese, including Manchus and other border peoples, and the fourth was the southern Chinese. Even when the exam-

ination system was sporadically revived after 1315, the Mongols and their allies took an easier examination; their quota was as large as that for Chinese, and they were appointed to higher offices.

The net result was an uneasy symbiosis. Chinese officials directly governed the Chinese populace, collecting taxes, settling disputes, and maintaining the local order. Only a small number of these officials ever learned to speak Mongolian, yet without their positive cooperation, Mongol rule in China would have been impossible. The Mongols, concentrated in Peking, large cities, and in garrisons, spoke Mongolian among themselves and usually did not bother to learn Chinese. A few exceptions wrote poetry in Chinese and painted in the Chinese style. Communication was through interpreters. When a Chinese district magistrate sent a query to the court, the ruling was made in Mongolian. (The Mongols had borrowed the alphabet of the Uighurs to transcribe their tongue.) A word-for-word translation in Chinese was written below the Mongolian and passed back down to the magistrate. As the two languages are syntactically very different, the resulting Chinese was grotesque.

Foreign Contacts and Chinese Culture

Diplomacy and trade within the greater Mongol Empire brought China into contact with other higher civilizations for the first time since the T'ang period. Persia and the Arab world were especially important. Merchants, missionaries, and diplomats voyaged from the Persian Gulf and across the Indian Ocean to seaports in southeastern China. The Arab communities in Canton and other ports were larger than they had been during the Sung. Camel caravans carrying silks and ceramics left Peking to pass through the central Asian oases and on to Baghdad. Although the Mongols did not favor Chinese merchants and most trade was in other hands, Chinese trade also expanded. Chinese communities became established in Tabriz, the center of trading in western Asia, and in Moscow and Novgorod. It was during this period that knowledge of printing, gunpowder, and Chinese medicine spread to western Asia. Chinese ceramics influenced those of Persia as Chinese painting influenced Persian miniatures.

In Europe, knowledge of China was transmitted by the Venetian trader Marco Polo, who said he had served Kublai as an official between 1275 and 1292. His book, *A Description of the World*, was translated into most European languages. Many readers doubted that a land of such wealth and culture could exist so far from Europe, but the book excited an interest in geography. When Christopher Columbus set sail in 1492, his goal was to reach Polo's Zipangu (Japan).

Other cultural contacts were fostered by the Mongol toleration or encouragement of religion. Nestorian Christianity, spreading from Persia to Central Asia, reentered China during the Mongol era. Churches were built in main cities. The mother of Kublai Khan was a Nestorian Christian. Also, several papal missions were sent from Rome to the Mongol court. An archbishopric was established in Peking; a church was built, sermons were preached in Turkish or Mongolian, and choirboys sang hymns. Kublai sent Marco Polo's father and uncle with a letter to the pope asking for a hundred intelligent men acquainted with the seven arts.

Tibetan Buddhism with its magical doctrines and elaborate rites was the religion most favored by the Mongols. But Chinese Buddhism also flourished. Priests and monks of all religions were given tax exemptions. It is estimated that half a million Chinese became Buddhist monks during the Mongol century. The foreign religion that made the greatest gains was Islam, which became permanently established in Central Asia and western China. Mosques were built in the Islamic areas, in Peking, and in southeastern port cities. Even Confucianism was regarded as a religion by the Mongols, and its teachers were exempted from taxes. But as the scholar-gentry rarely obtained important offices, they saw the Mongol era as a time of hardship.

Despite these wide contacts with other peoples and religions, the high culture of China appears to have been influenced almost not at all—partly because China had little to learn from other areas, and partly because the centers of Chinese culture were in the south, the last area to be conquered

Kublai Khan, wearing ermine coat, with Mongol warriors at the hunt. Note the camel caravan in the hills at rear. [National Palace Museum, Taiwan, R.O.C.]

and the area least affected by Mongol rule. Also, in reaction to the Mongol conquest, Chinese culture became conservative and turned in on itself. Scholars wrote poetry in the style of the Sung. New schools of painting developed, but the developments were from within the Chinese tradition, and the greatest Yuan paintings continued the style of the Sung. Yuan historians wrote the official history of the dynasties that preceded it. The head of the court bureau of historiography was a Mongol, but the histories produced by his Chinese staff were in the traditional mold. As the dynasty waned, unemployed scholars wrote essays expressing loyalty toward the Sung and satirizing the Mongols. Their writings were not censored: The Mongols either could not read them, did not read them, or did not care.

The major contribution to Chinese arts during the Yuan was by dramatists, who combined poetic arias with vaudeville theater to produce a new operatic drama. Performed by traveling troupes, the operas used few stage props. They relied for effect on makeup, costumes, pantomime, and stylized

Marco Polo Describes the City of Hangchow

Marco Polo was a Venetian. In 1300 Venice had a population of more than one hundred thousand and was one of the wealthiest Mediterranean city-states. But Polo was nonetheless unprepared for what he saw in China. Commenting on Hangchow, China's capital during the Southern Sung, he first noted its size (ten or twelve times larger than Venice), then its many canals and bridges, its streets "paved with stones and bricks," and its location between "a lake of fresh and very clear water" and "a river of great magnitude." He spoke of "the prodigious concourse of people" frequenting its ten great marketplaces and of its "capacious warehouses built of stone for the accommodation of merchants who arrive from India and other parts." He then described the life of its people.

Europeans who read Marco Polo's account of China thought it was too good to be true. Would you agree?

Each of the ten market-squares is surrounded with high dwelling-houses, in the lower part of which are shops, where every kind of manufacture is carried on, and every article of trade is sold; such, amongst others, as spices, drugs, trinkets, and pearls. In certain shops nothing is vended but the wine of the country, which they are continually brewing, and serve out fresh to their customers at a moderate price. The streets connected with the market-squares are numerous, and in some of them are many cold baths, attended by servants of both sexes, to perform the offices of ablution for the men and women who frequent them, and who from their childhood have been accustomed at all times to wash in cold water, which they reckon highly conducive to health. At these bathing places, however, they have apartments provided with warm water, for the use of strangers, who from not being habituated to it, cannot bear the shock of the cold. All are in the daily practice of washing their persons, and especially before their meals.

In other streets are the habitations of the courtesans, who are here in such numbers as I dare not venture to report; and not only near the squares, which is the situation usually appropriated for their residence, but in every part of the city they are to be found, adorned with much finery, highly perfumed, occupying well-furnished houses, and attended by many female domestics. These women are accomplished, and are perfect in the arts of blandishment

---

gestures. The women's roles were usually played by men. Except for the arias—the highlights of the performance—the dramas used vernacular Chinese, appealing to a popular audience. The unemployed scholars who wrote the scripts drew on the entire repertoire of the Sung storyteller. Among the stock figures in the operas were a Robin Hood-like bandit; a famous detective-judge; the T'ang monk who traveled to India; warriors and statesmen of the Three Kingdoms; and romantic heroes, villains, and ghosts. Justice always triumphed, and the dramas usually ended happily. In several famous plays the hero gets the girl, despite objections by her parents and seemingly insurmountable obstacles, by passing the civil-service examinations in first place. As the examinations were not in effect during most of the Yuan, this resolution of the hero's predicament is one that looked back to the Sung pattern of government. Yuan drama continued almost unchanged in later dynasties, and during the nineteenth century it merged with a form of southern Chinese theater to become today's Peking Opera.

Last Years of the Yuan

Despite the Mongol military domination of China and the highly centralized institutions of the Mongol court, the Yuan was the shortest of China's major dynasties. Little more than a century elapsed between Kublai's move to Peking in 1264 and the dynasty's collapse in 1368. The rule of Kublai and his successor had been effective, but thereafter a decline set in. By then, the Mongol Empire as a whole no longer lent strength to its parts. The khanates became separated by religion and culture as well as by distance. Even tribesmen in Mongolia rebelled now and then against the great khans in Peking, who, in their eyes, had become too Chinese. The court at Peking, too, had never really gained legitimacy. Some Chinese officials served it loyally to the end, but most Chinese saw the government as carpetbaggers and saw Mongol rule as a military occupation. When succession disputes, bureaucratic factionalism, and pitched battles between Mongol generals broke out, Chinese showed little inclination to rally in support of the dynasty.

Problems also arose in the countryside. Taxes were heavy, and some local officials were corrupt. The government issued excessive paper money and then refused to accept it in payment for taxes. The Yellow River changed its course, flooding the canals that carried grain to the capital. At great cost and suffering, a labor force of 150,000 workers and 20,000 soldiers rerouted the river to the south of the Shantung peninsula. Further natural disasters during the 1350s led to popular

and dalliance, which they accompany with expressions adapted to every description of person, insomuch that strangers who have once become so enchanted by their meretricious arts, that they can never divest themselves of the impression. Thus intoxicated with sensual pleasures, when they return to their homes they report that they have been in Kin-sai [Hangchow], or the celestial city, and pant for the time when they may be enabled to revisit paradise.

The inhabitants of the city are idolaters, and they use paper money as currency. The men as well as the women have fair complexions, and are handsome. The greater part of them are always clothed in silk, in consequence of the vast quantity of that material produced in the territory of Kin-sai, exclusively of what the merchants import from other provinces. Amongst the handicraft trades exercised in the place, there are twelve considered to be superior to the rest, as being more generally useful; for each of which there are a thousand workshops, and each shop furnishes employment for ten, fifteen, or twenty workmen, and in a few instances as many as forty, under their respective masters. The natural disposition of the native inhabitants of Kin-sai is pacific, and by the example of their former kings, who were themselves unwarlike, they have been accustomed to habits of tranquility. The management of arms is unknown to them, nor do they keep any in their houses. Contentious broils are never heard among them. They conduct their mercantile and manufacturing concerns with perfect candour and probity. They are friendly towards each other, and persons who inhabit the same street, both men and women, from the mere circumstance of neighbourhood, appear like one family. In their domestic manners they are free from jealousy or suspicion of their wives, to whom great respect is shown, and any man would be accounted infamous who should presume to use indecent expressions to a married woman. To strangers also, who visit their city in the way of commerce, they give proofs of cordiality, inviting them freely to their houses, showing them hospitable attention, and furnishing them with the best advice and assistance in their mercantile transactions. On the other hand, they dislike the sight of soldiery, not excepting the guards of the grand khan, as they preserve the recollection that by them they were deprived of the government of their native kings and rulers.

Excerpt from *The Travels of Marco Polo*, 1908, from Everyman's Library. Reprinted by permission of David Campbell Publishers, London, pp. 290–301.

uprisings. The White Lotus sect preached the coming of Maitreya. Regional military commanders, suppressing the rebellions, became independent of central control. Warlords arose. The warlord who ruled Szechwan was infamous for his cruelty. Important economic regions were devastated and in part depopulated by rebellions. At the end, a rebel army threatened Peking, and the last Mongol emperor and his court fled on horses to Shangtu. When that fell, they fled still deeper into the plains of Mongolia.

IN WORLD PERSPECTIVE

Imperial China

Rough parallels between China and Europe persisted until the sixth century C.E. Both saw the rise and fall of great empires. At first glance, the three-and-one-half centuries that followed the Han dynasty appear remarkably similar to the comparable period after the collapse of the Roman Empire: Central authority broke down, private armies arose, and aristocratic estates were established. Barbarian tribes, once allied to the empires, invaded and pillaged large areas. Otherworldly religions entered to challenge earlier official worldviews. In China, Neo-Taoism and then Buddhism challenged Confucianism, just as Christianity challenged Roman conceptions of the sociopolitical order.

But from the late sixth century C.E., a fundamental divergence occurred. Europe tailed off into centuries of feudal disunity and backwardness. A ghost of empire lingered in the European memory. But the reality, even after centuries had passed, was that tiny areas like France (one seventeenth the size of China), Italy (one thirty-second), or Germany (one twenty-seventh) found it difficult to establish an internal unity, much less recreate a pan-European or pan-Mediterranean empire. This pattern of separate little states has persisted in Europe until today. In contrast, China, which is about the size of Europe and geographically no more natural a political unit, put a unified empire back together again, attaining new wealth, power, and culture, and unified rule that has continued until the present. What is the explanation?

One reason the empire was reconstituted in China was that the victory of Buddhism in China was less complete than that of Christianity in Europe. Confucianism survived within the aristocratic families and at the courts of the Six Dynasties, and the idea of a united empire was integral to it. It is difficult even to think of Confucianism apart from the idea of a universal ruler, aided by men of virtue and ability, ruling "all under Heaven" according to Heaven's Mandate. In contrast, the Roman concept of political order was not maintained as an independent doctrine. Moreover, empire was not a vital element in Christian thought—except perhaps in Byzantium, where the empire lasted longer than it did in western Europe. The notion of a "Christian king" did appear in the West, but basically, the kingdom sought by Jesus was not of this world.

A second consideration was China's greater cultural homogeneity. It had a common written language that was fairly close to all varieties of spoken Chinese. Minority peoples and even barbarian conquerors—apart from the Mongols—were rapidly Sinicized. In contrast, after Rome, the Mediterranean fell apart into its component cultures. Latin became the universal language of the western church, but for most Christians it was a foreign language, a part of the mystery of the mass, and even in Italy it became an artificial language, separate from the living tongue. The European languages and cultures were divisive forces.

A third factor was the combination in the post-Han northern Chinese states of economic strength based on Chinese agriculture with the military striking force of a nomadic cavalry. There was nothing like it in Europe. Such a northern state reunified China in C.E. 589.

A fourth and perhaps critical factor was China's greater population density. The province (called a circuit at the time) of Hopei had a registered population of 10,559,728 during the eighth century C.E. Hopei was about one third the size of France, which in the eleventh century had a population of about two million. That is to say, even comparing China with France three centuries later, China's population density was fifteen times as great. (This comparison, it should be noted, is with a nonrice-producing area of China. Rice paddy areas were even more densely populated.) The far higher population density resulted in a different kind of history.

Population density explains why the Chinese could absorb barbarian conquerors so much more quickly than could Europe. More cultivators provided a larger agricultural surplus to the northern kingdoms than that enjoyed by comparable

kingdoms in Europe. Greater numbers of people also meant better communications and a better base for commerce. To be sure, the centuries that followed the Han saw a decline in commerce and cities. In some areas money was replaced by barter or the use of silk as currency. But the economic level remained higher than in early medieval Europe.

Several of the factors that explain the Sui-T'ang regeneration of a unified empire apply equally well or better to the Sung and subsequent dynasties. As schools were established and literacy rose, Confucianism and the ideal of a unified China became more widely accepted. Chinese culture was more homogeneous and less open to outside influences in the tenth century than it had been four centuries earlier. The population had also grown, with the Yangtze basin emerging as a new center of gravity.

The cyclic regeneration of centralized bureaucratic government—even under outside conquerors—can also be analyzed in terms of the interests it served. For the military figure who established the dynasty, the bureaucratic state was a huge tax machine that supported his armies and bestowed on him revenues beyond the imaginings of contemporary European monarchs. Government by civilian officials also offered some promise for the security of his progeny by acting as a counterweight against other military figures. For the scholar-gentry class, service to the state was the means to maintain family wealth, power, and status. Nothing was better. For merchants, a strong state was not an unmixed blessing. It might tax their profits or establish monopolies on the commodities they traded, but it also provided order and stability. More often than not, commerce expanded during such periods. For farmers, the picture was also unclear. Taxation was often exploitative, but orderly exploitation was usually preferable to rapacious warlords, bandits, or marauding armies.

Comparisons across continents are difficult, but it seems likely that T'ang and Sung China had longer stretches of good government than any other part of the contemporary world. Not until the nineteenth century would comparable bureaucracies of talent and virtue appear in the West.

Review Questions ———

1. Why could China recreate its empire—just 400 years after the fall of the Han—but Rome could not? Are there similarities between the Ch'in-Han transition and that of the Sui-T'ang? Between Han and T'ang expansion and contraction?

2. How did the Chinese economy change from the T'ang to the Northern Sung to the Southern Sung? The polity? China's relationships to surrounding states?

3. What do Chinese poetry and art tell us about Chinese society? About women? What position did poets occupy in Chinese society?

4. What drove the Mongols to conquer most of the known world? How could their military accomplish the task? Once they conquered China, how did they rule it? What was the Chinese response to Mongol rule?

Suggested Readings ———

General

J. CAHILL, *Chinese Painting* (1960). An excellent survey.

J. K. FAIRBANK, *China: A New History* (1992). The summation of a lifetime engagement with Chinese history.

F. A. KIERMAN, JR., AND J. K. FAIRBANK, EDS., *Chinese Ways in Warfare* (1974). Chapters by different authors on the Chinese military experience from the Chou to the Ming.

Sui and T'ang

P. B. EBREY, *The Aristocratic Families of Early Imperial China* (1978).

S. OWEN, *The Great Age of Chinese Poetry: The High T'ang* (1980).

E. G. PULLEYBLANK, *The Background of the Rebellion of An Lushan* (1955). A study of the 755 rebellion that weakened the central authority of the T'ang dynasty.

E. O. REISCHAUER, *Ennin's Travels in T'ang China* (1955). China as seen through the eyes of a ninth-century Japanese Marco Polo.

E. H. SCHAFER, *The Golden Peaches of Samarkand* (1963). A study of T'ang imagery.

D. TWITCHETT, ED., *Sui and T'ang China, 589–906, Part 1* (1984). (Part 2, also in *The Cambridge History of China*, is forthcoming.)

G. W. WANG, *The Structure of Power in North China During the Five Dynasties* (1963). A study of the interim period between the T'ang and the Sung dynasties.

A. F. WRIGHT, *The Sui Dynasty* (1978).

Sung

C. S. CHANG AND J. SMYTHE, *South China in the Twelfth Century* (1981). China as seen through the eyes of a twelfth-century Chinese poet, historian, and statesman.

J. GERNET, *Daily Life in China on the Eve of the Mongol Invasion* (1962).

J. W. HAEGER, ED., *Crisis and Prosperity in Sung China* (1975).

R. HYMES, *Statesmen and Gentlemen* (1987). On the transformation of officials into a local gentry elite during the twelfth and thirteenth centuries.

J. T. C. LIU AND P. J. GOLAS, EDS., *Change in Sung China: Innovation or Renovation?* (1969).

M. ROSSABI, *China Among Equals* (1983). A study of the Liao, Ch'in, and Sung empires and their relations.

W. M. TU, *Confucian Thought, Selfhood as Creative Transformation* (1985).

K. YOSHIKAWA, *An Introduction to Sung Poetry*, trans. by B. Watson (1967).

Yuan

T. T. ALLSEN, *Mongol Imperialism* (1987).

J. W. DARDESS, *Conquerors and Confucians: Aspects of Political Change in Late Yuan China* (1973).

H. FRANKE AND D. TWITCHETT, EDS., *Alien Regimes and Border States, 710–1368* (to appear soon as Vol. 6 of *The Cambridge History of China*).

J. D. LANGLOIS, *China Under Mongol Rule* (1981).

R. LATHAM, TRANS., *Travels of Marco Polo* (1958).

H. D. MARTIN, *The Rise of Chingis Khan and His Conquest of North China* (1981).

D. MORGAN, *The Mongols* (1986).

9 JAPAN: EARLY HISTORY TO 1467

In 1972, Japanese archeologists found this painting on the interior wall of a megalithic burial chamber at Takamatsuzuka in Nara Prefecture. The tomb dates to the 300–680 era and was covered with a mound of earth. The most sophisticated tomb painting found in Japan, it resembles paintings found in Korean and Chinese tombs. [Bildarchiv Preussischer Kulturbesitz]

CHAPTER TOPICS

◆ Japanese Origins
◆ The Yayoi Revolution
◆ Nara and Heian Japan

◆ Aristocratic Culture and Buddhism in Nara and Heian Japan
◆ Japan's Early Feudal Age

◆ Buddhism and Medieval Culture

In World Perspective Early Japanese History

Japanese history has three main turning points, each marked by a major influx of an outside culture and each followed by a massive restructuring of Japanese institutions. The first turning point was in the third century B.C.E., when an Old Stone Age Japan became an agricultural, metal-working society, similar to those on the Korean peninsula or in northeastern Asia. This era lasted until 600 C.E. The second turning point came during the seventh century, when whole complexes of Chinese culture entered Japan directly. Absorbing these, archaic Japan made the leap to a higher historical civilization, associated with the writing system, technologies, and philosophies of China, and with Chinese forms of Buddhism. Japan would remain a part of this civilization until the third turning point, in the nineteenth century, when it encountered the West.

Japanese Origins

The antiquity of humans in Japan is hotly debated there today. A new archaeological find makes the front page of newspapers throughout Japan. Bookstores have rows of books, most of them popular works, asking: Who are we and where did we come from?

During the ice ages, Japan was connected by land bridges to Asia. Woolly mammoths entered the northern island of Hokkaido, and elephants, sabre-toothed tigers, giant elks, and other continental fauna entered the lower islands. Did humans enter as well? Because Japan's acidic volcanic soil eats up bones, there are no early skeletal remains. The earliest evidence of human habitation is finely shaped stone tools dating from about 30,000 B.C.E. Then, from about 10,000 B.C.E., there is Jōmon or "cord-pattern" pottery, the oldest in the world.

Archaeologists are baffled by its appearance in an Old Stone Age hunting, gathering, and fishing society—when in all other early societies pottery developed along with agriculture as an aspect of New Stone Age culture.

The Yayoi Revolution

After eight thousand years of Jōmon culture, the second phase of Japanese prehistory began about 300 B.C.E. It is called the Yayoi culture, after a place in Tokyo where its distinctive hard, pale orange pottery was first unearthed. There is no greater break in the entire Japanese record than that between the Jōmon and the Yayoi. For at the beginning of the third century B.C.E. the agricultural revolution, the bronze revolution, and the iron revolution—which in the Near East, India, and China had been separated by thousands of years, and each of which singly had wrought profound transformations—burst into Japan simultaneously.

The new technologies were brought to Japan by peoples moving across the Tsushima Straits from the Korean peninsula. It is uncertain whether these immigrants came as a trickle and were absorbed—the predominant view in Japan—or whether they came in sufficient numbers to push back the indigenous Jōmon people. Physical anthropologists say that skulls from early Yayoi sites are different from those of the Jōmon. The early Yayoi migrants, using the same seacraft by which they had crossed from Korea, spread along the coasts of northern Kyushu and western Honshu. Yayoi culture rapidly replaced Jōmon culture as far east in Japan as the present-day city of Nagoya. After that the Yayoi culture diffused overland into eastern Japan more slowly and with greater difficulty. Conditions were less favorable for agriculture, and a mixed agricultural-hunting economy lasted longer.

The early "frontier settlements" of the Yayoi people were located next to their fields. Their agriculture was primitive. By the first century C.E., the Yayoi population had so expanded that wars were fought for the best land. Excavations reveal extensive stone-axe industries, and several skulls pierced by bronze and iron arrowheads have been found. An early Chinese chronicle describes Japan as made up of "more than one hundred countries" with wars and conflicts raging on all sides. During these wars, villages were relocated to

Along with the cord-patterned pots, the hunting and gathering Jōmon people produced mysterious figurines. Is this a female deity? Why are the eyes slitted like snow goggles? Earthenware with traces of pigment (Kamegoaka type); 24.8 cm high.

[Asia Society, N.Y.: Mr. and Mrs. John D. Rockefeller 3rd Collection]

defensible positions on low hills away from the fields. From these wars emerged a more peaceful order of regional states and a ruling class of aristocratic warriors. Late Yayoi excavations reveal villages once again alongside fields and far fewer stone axes.

During the third century C.E. a temporary hegemony was achieved over a number of such regional states—or, more accurately, regional tribal confederations—by a queen named Pimiko. In the Chinese chronicle Pimiko is described as a shaman who "occupied herself with magic and sorcery, bewitching the people." She was mature but unmarried. "After she became the ruler, there were few who saw her. She had one thousand women as attendants, but only one man. He served her food and drink and acted as a medium of communication. She resided in a palace surrounded by towers and stockades with armed guards in a state of constant vigilance."[1]

After Pimiko, references to Japan disappeared from the Chinese dynastic histories for a century and a half.

Tomb Culture and the Yamato State

Emerging directly from the Yayoi culture was a period, 300–600 C.E., characterized by giant tomb mounds, which even today dot the landscape of the Nara-Osaka region. The early tombs—patterned on those in Korea—were circular mounds of earth built atop megalithic burial chambers. Later tombs were sometimes keyhole-shaped. The tombs were surrounded by moats and adorned with clay cylinders and statues of warriors, scribes, musicians, houses, boats, and the like. Early tombs, like the Yayoi graves that preceded them, contained mirrors, jewels, and other ceremonial objects. From the fifth century C.E. these objects were replaced by armor, swords, spears, and military trappings. The change reflected a new wave of continental influences. The flow of people and culture from the Korean peninsula into Japan that began with Yayoi was continuous into historical times.

Japan reappeared in the Chinese chronicles in the fifth century C.E. This period was also covered in the earliest Japanese accounts of their own history, the *Records of Ancient Matters (Kojiki)* and the *Records of Japan (Nihongi)*, compiled in 712 and 720. These records dovetail with the evidence of the tombs. The picture that emerges is of regional aristocracies under the loose hegemony of the Yamato "great kings." Historians use the geographic label "Yamato" because the courts of the great kings were located on the Yamato plain, near present-day Osaka, the richest agricultural region of ancient Japan. The Yamato rulers also held lands and granaries throughout Japan. The tomb of the great king Nintoku is 486 meters long and 36 meters high, with twice the volume of the Great Pyramid of Egypt. By the fifth century C.E. the great kings possessed sufficient authority to commandeer laborers for such a project.

The great kings awarded Korean-type titles to court and regional aristocrats, titles that implied a national hierarchy centering on the Yamato court. That regional rulers had the same kind of political authority over their populations can be seen in the spread of tomb mounds throughout Japan.

The basic social unit of Yamato aristocratic society was the extended family *(uji)*, closer in size to a Scottish clan than to a modern household. Attached to these aristocratic families

---

[1]L. C. Goodrich, ed., and R. Tsunoda, trans., *Japan in the Chinese Dynastic Histories* (South Pasadena, CA: Perkins Asiatic Monographs, 1951), p. 13.

Chronology of Early Japanese History

8000–300 B.C.E.	Jōmon culture
Early Continental Influences	
300 B.C.E.–300 C.E.	Yayoi culture
300–680 C.E.	Tomb culture and the Yamato state
680–850 C.E.	Chinese T'ang pattern in Nara and Early Heian Japan

were groups of specialist workers called *be*. This word was of Korean origin and was originally used to designate potters, scribes, or others with special skills who had immigrated from Korea. It was then extended to include similar groups of indigenous workers and groups of peasants. Yamato society had a small class of slaves, possibly captured in wars. Many peasants were neither slaves nor members of aristocratic clans or specialized workers' groups.

What little is known of Yamato politics suggests that the court was the scene of incessant struggles for power between aristocratic families. There were also continuing efforts by the court to control outlying regions. Although marriage alliances were established and titles awarded, rebellions were not infrequent during the fifth and sixth centuries. Finally, there were constant wars with "barbarian tribes" in southern Kyushu and eastern Honshu on the frontiers of "civilized" Japan.

The Yamato Court and Korea

Under the Yamato court, a three-cornered military balance had emerged on the Korean peninsula between the states of Paekche in the southwest, Silla in the east, and Koguryo in the north (see Map 9–1). Japan was an ally of Paekche, and maintained extensive trade and military relations with the weak southern federation known as the Kaya States.

The Paekche connection enabled the Yamato court to expand its power within Japan. Imports of iron weapons and tools gave it military strength. The migration to Japan of Korean potters, weavers, scribes, metal workers, and other artisans increased its wealth and influence. The great cultural significance of the immigrants from Korea can be gauged by the fact that many became established as noble families. Paekche also served as a conduit for elements of Chinese culture. Chinese writing was adopted for the transcription of Japanese names during the fifth or sixth century. Confucianism entered in 513, when Paekche sent a "scholar of the Five Classics." Buddhism arrived in 538 when a Paekche king sent a Buddha image, sutras, and possibly a priest.

Eventually the political balance on the peninsula led to a break with Japan. In 532 Paekche turned against Japan and joined Silla in attacking the Kaya States, and by 562 the Kaya federation had been gobbled up. But the rupture of ties with Korea was less of a loss than it would have been earlier, for by this time Japan had established direct relations with China.

Religion in Early Japan

The indigenous religion of Yamato Japan was an animistic worship of the forces of nature, later given the name of *Shinto*, or "the way of the gods," to distinguish it from Buddhism. Shinto probably entered Japan from the continent as part of Yayoi culture. The underlying forces of nature might be embodied in a waterfall, a twisted tree, a strangely shaped boulder, a mountain, or in a great leader who would be worshiped as a deity after his death. Mount Fuji was holy not as the abode of a god but because the mountain itself was an upwelling of a vital natural force. Even today in Japan, a gnarled tree trunk may be circled with a straw rope and set aside as an object of veneration. The sensitivity to nature and natural beauty that pervades Japanese art and poetry owes much to Shinto.

Throughout Japan's premodern history most villages had shamans, religious specialists who, by entering a trance, could contact directly the inner forces of nature and gain the power to foretell the future or heal sickness. The queen Pimiko was such a shaman. The sorceress is a stock figure in tales of ancient or medieval Japan. More often than not, women, receiving the command of a god, have founded the "new" religions in this tradition, even into the nineteenth and twentieth centuries.

A second aspect of early Shinto was its connection with the state and the ruling post-tribal aristocracy. The more potent forces of nature such as the sea, the sun, the moon, the wind, and thunder and lightning became personified as deities. Each clan, or extended family, had its own myth centering on a nature deity *(kami)* that it claimed as its original ancestor. Aristocratic families possessed genealogies tracing their descent from the deity. A genealogy was a patent of nobility and a claim to political authority. The head of a clan was also its chief priest, who made sacrifices to its deity. When Japan was unified by the Yamato court, the myths of several clans apparently were joined into a composite national myth. The deity of the Yamato great kings was the sun goddess, so she became the chief deity, while other gods assumed lesser positions appropriate to the status of their clan. Had another clan won the struggle, its deity would have become paramount—perhaps a thunder god as in ancient Greece.

The *Records of Ancient Matters and Records of Japan* tell of the creation of Japan, of the

A clay statue of a warrior in armor from an ancient tomb.

[Tokyo National Museum]

deeds and misdeeds of gods on the "plain of high heaven," and of their occasional adventures on earth or in the underworld. In mid-volume, the stories of the gods, interspersed with the genealogies of noble families, give way to stories of early emperors and early Japanese history. The Japanese emperors, today the oldest royal family in the world, were viewed as the lineal descendants of the sun goddess and as "living gods." The Great Shrine of the sun goddess at Ise has always been the most important in Japan.

Nara and Heian Japan

The second major turning point in Japanese history was its adoption of the higher civilization of China. This is a prime example of the worldwide process (described in Chapter 2) by which the heartland civilizations spread into outlying areas. In Japan the process occurred between the seventh and twelfth centuries and can best be understood in terms of

three stages. The first stage was learning about China. The second stage, mostly during the eighth and ninth centuries, saw the implantation in Japan of Chinese T'ang-type institutions. The third involved the further transformation of these institutions to better fit them to conditions in Japan. By the eleventh century the creative reworking of Chinese elements had led to a distinctive Japanese culture, quite unlike that of China, yet equally different from that of the earlier Yamato court.

Seventh Century

The official embassies to China that began in 607 C.E. included traders, students, and Buddhist monks as well as representatives of the Yamato great kings. Like Third World students who study abroad today, Japanese who studied in China played key roles in their own government when they returned home. They brought back with them a quickening flow of technology, art, Buddhism, and knowledge of T'ang

Map 9–1 Yamato Japan and Korea (ca. 500 C.E.). Paekche was Japan's ally on the Korean peninsula. Silla, Japan's enemy, was the state that would eventually unify Korea. (Note: Nara was founded in 710; Heian in 794.)

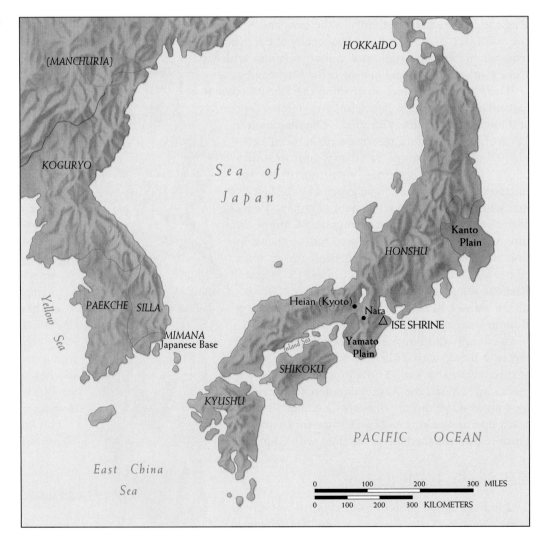

Darkness and the Cave of High Heaven

The younger brother of the sun goddess was a mischief maker. Eventually the gods drove him out of heaven. On one occasion, he knocked a hole in the roof of a weaving hall and dropped in a dappled pony that he had skinned alive. One weaving maiden was so startled that she struck her genitals with the shuttle she was using and died.

What does this myth suggest regarding the social relations of the Shinto gods? Entering a cave and then reemerging signifies death and rebirth in the religions of many peoples. Compare this passage to "Mark Describes the Resurrection of Jesus" in Chapter 5.

The Sun Goddess, terrified at the sight, opened the door of the heavenly rock cave, and hid herself inside. Then the Plain of High Heaven was shrouded in darkness, as was the Central Land of Reed Plains [Japan]. An endless night prevailed. The cries of the myriad gods were like the buzzing of summer flies, and myriad calamities arose.

The eight hundred myriad gods assembled in the bed of the Quiet River of Heaven. They asked one god to think of a plan. They assembled the long-singing birds of eternal night and made them sing. They took hard rocks from the bed of the river and iron from the Heavenly Metal Mountain and called in a smith to make a mirror. They asked the Jewel Ancestor God to make a string of 500 curved jewels eight feet long. They asked other gods to remove the shoulder blade of a male deer and to obtain cherry wood from Mount Kagu, and to perform a divination. They uprooted a sacred tree, attaching the string of curved jewels to its upper branches, hanging the large mirror from its middle branches, and suspending offerings of white and blue cloth from its lower branches.

One god held these objects as grand offerings and another intoned sacred words. The Heavenly Hand-Strong-Male God stood hidden beside the door. A goddess bound up her sleeves with clubmoss from Mount Kagu, made a herb band from the spindle-tree, and bound together leaves of bamboo-grass to hold in her hands. Then she placed a wooden box facedown before the rock cave, stamped on it until it resounded, and, as if possessed, she exposed her breasts and pushed her shirt-band down to her genitals. The Plain of High Heaven shook as the myriad gods broke into laughter.

The Sun Goddess, thinking this strange, opened slightly the rock-cave door and said from within: "Since I have hidden myself I thought that the Plain of Heaven and the Central Land of the Reed Plains would all be in darkness. Why is it that the goddess makes merry and the myriad gods all laugh?"

The goddess replied: "We rejoice and are glad because there is here a god greater than you." While she spoke two other gods brought out the mirror and held it up before the Sun Goddess.

The Sun Goddess, thinking this stranger and stranger, came out the door and peered into the mirror. Then the Hand-Strong-Male God seized her hand and pulled her out. Another god drew a rope behind her and said: "You may not go back further than this."

So when the Sun Goddess had come forth, the Plain of High Heaven and the Central Land of the Reed Plains once again naturally shone in brightness.

From the *Records of Ancient Matters (Kojiki)*, translated by Albert Craig, with appreciation to Basil Hall Chamberlain and Donald L. Phillippi.

---

legal and governmental systems. But the difficulties of mastering Chinese and comprehending China's philosophical culture were enormous for the Yamato Japanese. Large-scale institutional changes using the T'ang model actually began in the 680s with the Emperor Temmu and his successor, the Empress Jitō (r. 686–697).

Temmu's life illustrates the interplay between court politics and the adoption of Chinese institutions. He came to the throne by leading an alliance of eastern clans in rebellion against the previous great king, his nephew. The *Records of Japan* describe Temmu as "walking like a tiger through the eastern lands." He then used Chinese systems to consolidate his power. He promulgated a Chinese-type law code that greatly augmented the powers of the ruler. He styled himself as the "heavenly emperor" *(tennō)*, which thereafter re-

placed the earlier title of "great king." He rewarded his supporters with new court ranks and with positions in a new court government, both derived from the T'ang example. He extended the authority of the court and increased its revenues by a survey of agricultural lands and a census of their population. In short, although the admiration for Chinese things must have been enormous, much of the borrowing was dictated by specific, immediate, and practical Japanese concerns.

Nara and Early Heian Court Government

Until the eighth century the capital was usually moved each time an emperor died. Then, in 710 a new capital, intended to be permanent, was established at Nara. It was laid out on a checkerboard grid like the Chinese capital at Ch'ang-an.

Prince Shōtoku (574–622) and two of his sons. Prince Shōtoku was a Buddhist and a reformer who began sending regular embassies to China in 607. [Corbis-Bettmann]

But then it was moved again—some say to escape the meddling in politics of powerful Buddhist temples. A final move occurred in 794 to Heian (later Kyoto) on the plain north of Nara. This site remained the capital until the move to Tokyo in 1869. Even today, Kyoto's regular geometry reflects Chinese city planning.

The superimposition of a Chinese-type capital on a still backward Japan produced as stark a contrast as any in history. In the villages, peasants—who worshiped the forces in mountains and trees—lived in pit dwellings and either planted in crude paddy fields or used slash-and-burn techniques of dry-land farming. In the capital stood pillared palaces in which dwelt the emperor and nobles, descended from the gods on high. They drank wine, wore silk, and enjoyed the paintings, perfumes, and pottery of the T'ang. Clustered about the capital were Buddhist temples, more numerous than in Nara, with soaring pagodas and sweeping tile roofs.

With what awe must a peasant have viewed the city and its inhabitants!

The emperors at the Nara and Heian courts were both Confucian rulers with the majesty accorded by Chinese law and Shinto rulers descended from the sun goddess. Protected by an aura of the sacred, their lineage was never usurped. All Japanese history constitutes a single dynasty, although not a few emperors were killed and replaced by other family members.

Beneath the emperor, the same modified Chinese pattern prevailed. Like the T'ang, Japan had a Council of State, but it was more powerful than that of China. It was the office from which leading clans manipulated the authority of an emperor, who usually reigned but did not rule. Beneath this council were eight ministries—two more than in China. One was a Secretariat and the other the Imperial Household Ministry. Size affected function: Where T'ang China had a population of 60 million, Nara Japan had only 4 or 5 million. There were fewer people to govern in Japan; there were no significant external enemies; and much of local rule, in the Yamato tradition, was in mostly the hands of local clans. Consequently, more of the business of court government was with the court itself. Of the 6,000 persons in the central ministries, more than 4,000 were concerned in one way or another with the care of the imperial house. The Imperial Household Ministry, for example, had an official staff of 1,296, whereas the Treasury had 305 and Military Affairs only 198.

Under the central court government were sixty-odd provinces, which were further subdivided into districts and villages. In pre-Nara times the regions had been governed by largely autonomous regional clans; but under the new system provincial governors were sent out from the capital. This change reduced the old regional aristocrats to the lesser posts of district magistrates. The new system substantially increased the power of the central aristocracy.

In other respects, Japanese court government was unlike that of China. There were no eunuchs. There was little tension between the emperor and the bureaucracy—the main struggles were between clans. The T'ang movement from aristocracy toward meritocracy also was absent in Japan. Apart from clerks and monastics, only aristocrats were educated, and only they were appointed to important official posts. Family counted for more than grades. A feeble attempt to establish an examination meritocracy on the Chinese model failed completely.

Land and Taxes

The last Japanese embassy to China was in 839. By that time the frenetic borrowing of Chinese culture had already slowed. The Japanese had taken in all they needed—or, perhaps, all they could handle—and were sufficiently self-confident to use Chinese ideas in innovative and flexible ways. The 350 years that followed until the end of the twelfth century were a time of assimilation and evolutionary change. Nowhere was this more evident than in the system of taxation.

The land system of Nara and early Heian Japan was the equal field system of the early T'ang. All land belonged to the emperor; it was redistributed every six years, and taxes were levied on people, not land. Those receiving land were liable for three taxes: a light tax in grain; a light tax on local products, such as cloth or fish; and a heavy labor tax. The system was complex, requiring land surveys, the redrawing of boundaries, and elaborate land and population registers. Even in China, despite its sophisticated bureaucracy, this system broke down. In Japan the marvel is that it could be carried out at all. Old registers and recent aerial photographs suggest that it was, at least in western Japan. Its implementation speaks of the immense energy and ability of the early Japanese, who so quickly absorbed much of Chinese administrative techniques.

Of course the system was even less equal than in China. Imperial princes and high nobles received thousands or hundreds of units of rank lands, office lands, and merit lands, along with the labor to work them; local officials got less, and the cultivators did the work.

Whenever changes in a society are legislated or imposed from above, the results tend to be uniform. But when changes occur willy-nilly within a social system, the results are usually messy and difficult to comprehend. The evolution of the land system and taxation in late Heian Japan was of the second type.

One big change was from the equal field system to one of tax quotas payable in grain. First, the redistribution of land broke down, and land holdings became hereditary. Officials discovered that peasants would not care for land they did not own, for land that would be redistributed every six years. Second, the main tax of labor service was converted to a grain tax. Officials found it more efficient to pay hired workers in grain than to use the labor of peasants who had no incentive to work. Third, the taxes levied on provinces and districts were made over into fixed quotas. Court officials, unable to maintain the elaborate records needed for the equal field system, gave each governor a quota; the governor in turn gave one to each district magistrate. The governors kept any amount collected over the quota. The district magistrates, other local notables, and the military families associated with them gradually used their part of the surplus to transform themselves into a new local ruling class.

Another big change, one that affected about half the land in late Heian Japan, was the conversion of tax-paying lands to tax-free estates. Nobles and powerful temples in Kyoto did not want to pay taxes, so they used their influence at court to obtain immunities—exemptions from taxation for their lands. From the ninth century many cultivators began to commend their small holdings to such nobles, judging that they would be better off as serfs on tax-free estates than as free farmers subject to taxation. As a result of the random pattern of commendation, the typical estate in Japan was of scattered parcels of land, unlike the unified estates of Europe. The Japanese estates were managed by stewards, appointed from among local notables. They took a share of the surplus grain for themselves, and forwarded the rest to the noble owner in Kyoto. The stewards thus were from the same stratum of local society as those who collected the tax quotas. Like district magistrates, they had a vital interest in upholding the local order.

Rise of the Samurai

During the Nara period, Japan experimented with a military system based on conscription. One third of all able-bodied men between the ages of twenty-one and sixty were taken. Conscript armies, however, proved inefficient, so in 792 the court abolished conscription and began a new system relying on local mounted warriors. Some were stationed in the capital and some in the provinces. They were official troops whose taxes were remitted in exchange for military service. The Japanese verb "to serve" is *samurau*, so those who served became *samurai*—the noun form of the verb. Then, from the mid-Heian period, the officially recruited local warriors were replaced by nonofficial private bands of local warriors. They constituted the military of Japan for the next half millennium or so, until the foot-soldier revolution of the fifteenth and sixteenth centuries.

Being a samurai was expensive. Horses, armor, and weapons were costly, and their use required long training. The primary weapon was the bow and arrow, used from the saddle. Most samurai were from well-to-do local families, such as those of district magistrates or notables, or from military families supported by the local elites or by temples or shrines. Their initial function was to preserve local order and, possibly, to help with tax collection. But from the beginning they contributed at times to disorder. From the second half of the ninth century there are accounts of district magistrates leading local forces against provincial governors, doubtless in connection with tax disputes.

From the early tenth century regional military coalitions or confederations began to form. They first broke into history in 935–940, when a regional military leader, a descendant of an emperor, became involved in a tax dispute. He captured several provinces, called himself the new emperor, and appointed a government of civil and military officials. The Kyoto court responded by recruiting another military band as its champion. The rebellion was quelled, and the rebel leader died in battle. That the Kyoto court could summon a military band points up the connections that enabled it to manipulate local military leaders and maintain its political control of Japan.

This rebellion was the first of a number of conflicts between regional military bands. Many wars were fought in eastern Japan—the "wild east" of those days. The east was more militarized because it was the headquarters for the periodic campaigns against the tribal peoples to the north. By the middle of the twelfth century there were local and regional military bands in every part of Japan.

Late Heian Court Government

Even during the Nara period much of the elaborate apparatus of Chinese government was of little use. By the early Heian period the actual functions of government were taken over by three new offices outside the Chinese system:

1. *Audit officers*. A newly appointed provincial governor had to report on the accounts of his predecessor. Agreement was rare. So from the end of the Nara period audit officers were sent to examine the books. By early Heian times these auditors had come to superintend the collection of taxes and most other capital-province relationships. They tried to halt the erosion of tax revenues. But as the quota and estate systems developed, this office had less and less to do.

2. *Bureau of archivists*. This bureau was established in 810 to record and preserve imperial decrees. Eventually it took over the executive function at the Heian court, drafting imperial decrees and attending to all aspects of the emperor's life.

3. *Police commissioners*. Established in the second decade of the ninth century to enforce laws and prosecute criminals, the commissioners eventually became responsible for all law and order in the capital. They absorbed military functions as well as those of the Ministry of Justice and the Bureau of Impeachment.

While new institutions were evolving, there also occurred shifts in the control of the court. The key figure remained the emperor, who had the power of appointments. Until the early Heian—say, the mid-ninth century—some emperors actually ruled or, more often, shared power with nobles of leading clans. From 856 the northern branch of the Fujiwara clan became preeminent, and from 986 to 1086 its stranglehold on the court was absolute. The administrative offices of the Fujiwara house were almost more powerful than those of the central government, and the Fujiwara family monopolized all key government posts. They controlled the court by marrying their daughters to the emperor, forcing the emperor to retire after a son was born, and then ruling as regents in place of the new infant emperor. At times they even ruled as regents for adult emperors. Fujiwara Michinaga's words were no empty boast when he said, "As for this world, I think it is mine, nor is there a flaw in the full moon."

Fujiwara rule gave way, during the second half of the eleventh century, to rule by retired emperors. The imperial family and lesser noble houses had long resented Fujiwara domination. Disputes within the Fujiwara house itself enabled an emperor to regain control. Imperial control of government was reasserted by Emperor Shirakawa, who reigned from 1072 to 1086 and, abdicating at the age of thirty-three, ruled for forty-three years as retired emperor. After his death another retired emperor continued in the same pattern until 1156.

Ex-Emperor Shirakawa set up offices in his quarters not unlike the administrative offices of the Fujiwara family. He employed talented nobles of lesser families and sought to reduce the number of tax-free estates by confiscating those of the Fujiwara. He failed in this and instead garnered huge estates for the imperial family. He developed strong ties to regional military leaders. His sense of his own power was reflected in his words—more a lament than a boast: "The only things that do not submit to my will are the waters of the Kamo River, the roll of the dice, and the soldier-monks [of the Tendai temple on Mount Hiei to the northeast of Kyoto]." But Shirakawa's powers were exercised in a capital city that was increasingly isolated from the changes in outlying regions, and even the city itself was plagued by fires, banditry, and a sense of impending catastrophe.

A momentous change occurred in 1156. The death of the ruling retired emperor precipitated a struggle for power between another retired emperor and the reigning emperor. Each called on a Fujiwara and a local military force for backing. The force led by Taira Kiyomori defeated that led by a Minamoto, though it was challenged again in the Heiji War of 1159–1160. Taira Kiyomori had come to Kyoto to uphold an emperor, but finding himself in charge, he stayed to rule. His pattern of rule was quite Japanese: Court nobles kept their Chinese court offices; the reigning emperor, who had been supported by Kiyomori, retired and took control of the offices of the retired emperor and of the estates of the impe-

Who Was in Charge at the Nara and Heian Courts	
710–856	Emperors or combinations of nobles
856–1086	Fujiwara nobles
1086–1160	Retired emperors
1160–1180	Military house of Taira

In the Heiji War of 1159–1160, regional samurai bands became involved in Kyoto court politics. This is a scroll painting of the burning of the Sanjō Palace. Handscroll; ink and colors on paper, 41.3 X 699.7 cm. [Museum of Fine Arts, Boston. Fenollosa-Weld Collection]

rial family; the head of the Fujiwara family kept the post of regent, while Taira Kiyomori married his daughter to the new emperor, and when a son was born Kiyomori forced the emperor to retire and ruled as the maternal grandfather of the infant emperor. That is to say, the Taira ruled as a new stratum atop the old court hierarchy.

Aristocratic Culture and Buddhism in Nara and Heian Japan

If the parts of a culture could be put on a scale and weighed like sugar or flour, we would conclude that the culture of Nara and early Heian Japan was overwhelmingly one of Shinto religious practices and village folkways, an extension of the culture of the late Yamato period. The aristocracy was small and was encapsulated in the routine of court life, just as the Buddhist monks were contained within the rounds of their monastic life. The early Heian aristocracy comprised one tenth of one percent of Japan's population. Most of the court culture had only recently been imported from China. There had not been time for the commoners to ape their betters or for the powerful force of the indigenous culture to reshape that of the elite.

The resulting cultural gap helps to explain why the aristocrats, insofar as we can tell from literature, found commoners to be odd, incomprehensible, and, indeed, hardly human. The writings of courtiers reflect little sympathy for the suffering and hardships of the people—except in Chinese-style poetry, where such feelings were expected. When the fictional Prince Genji stoops to an affair with an impoverished woman, she is inevitably a princess. Sei Shōnagon was not atypical as a writer: She was offended by the vulgarity of mendicant nuns; laughed at an illiterate old man whose house had burned down; and found lacking in charm the eating habits of carpenters, who wolfed down their food a bowl at a time.

Heian high culture resembled a hothouse plant. It was protected by the political influence of the court. It was nourished by the flow of tax revenues and income from estates. Under these conditions, the aristocrats of the never-never land of Prince Genji indulged in a unique way of life and created canons of elegance and taste that are striking even today. The speed with which T'ang culture was assimilated and reworked was amazing. A few centuries after Mediterranean culture had been introduced into northern Europe, there appeared nothing even remotely comparable to the *Tale of Genji* or the *Pillow Book*.

Chinese Tradition in Japan

Education at the Nara and Heian courts was largely a matter of reading Chinese books and acquiring the skills needed to compose poetry and prose in Chinese. These were enormous tasks, not only because there was no prior tradition of scholarship in Japan but also because the two languages were so dissimilar. To master written Chinese and use it for everyday written communications was as daunting a challenge for the Nara Japanese as it would have been for any European of the same century, but the challenge was met. From the Nara period until the nineteenth century, most philosophical and legal writings, as well as most of the histories, essays, and religious texts in Japan, were written in Chinese. From a Chinese perspective the writings may leave something to be desired. It would be astonishing if this were not the case, for the soul of language is the music of the spoken tongue. But the Japanese writers were competent, and the feelings and ideas they expressed were authentic—when not copybook exercises in the style of a Chinese master. In 883, when Sugawara Michizane wrote a poem on the death of his son, he quite naturally wrote it in Chinese. The poem began

> Since Amaro died I cannot sleep at night;
> if I do, I meet him in dreams and tears come coursing
>   down.
> Last summer he was over three feet tall;
> this year he would have been seven years old.
> He was diligent and wanted to know how to be a good
>   son,
> read his books and recited by heart the "Poem on the
>   Capital."[2]

The capital was Ch'ang-an; the poem was one "used in Japan as a text for little boys learning to read Chinese."

Not only were Japanese writings in Chinese a vital part of the Japanese cultural tradition, but the original Chinese works themselves also became a part of the same tradition. The late T'ang poet Po Chu-i was early appreciated and widely read; later, Tu Fu and Li Po were also read and admired. As in China itself, Chinese history was read, and its stock figures were among the heroes and villains of the Japanese historical consciousness. Chinese history became the mirror in which Japan saw itself, despite the differences between the two societies. Buddhist stories and the books of Confucianism also became Japanese classics, continually accessible and consulted over the centuries for their wisdom and philosophy. The parallel might be the acceptance of "foreign books" such as the Bible and works of Plato and Aristotle in medieval and Renaissance England.

[2]From *The Country of Eight Islands* by Hiroaki Sato and Burton Watson. Copyright © 1981 by Hiroaki Sato and Burton Watson. Used by permission of Doubleday, a division of Random House, Inc.

Birth of Japanese Literature

Stimulated by Chinese models, the Japanese began to compose poetry in their native tongue. The first major anthology was the *Collection of Ten Thousand Leaves (Man'yōshū)*, compiled in about 760. It contained 4,516 poems. The sentiments in the poems are fresh, sometimes simple and straightforward, but often sophisticated. They reveal a deep sensitivity to nature and strong human relationships between husband and wife, parents and children. They also display a love for the land of Japan and links to a Shinto past.

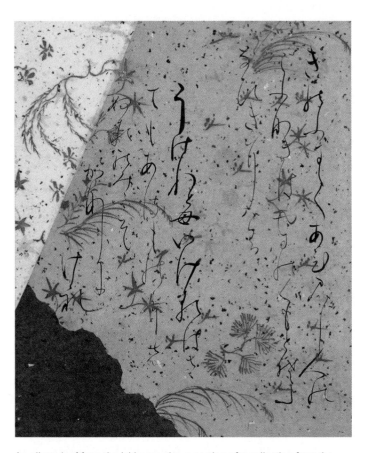

An album leaf from the Ishiyama-gire, a section of a collection from the works of 36 poets compiled in the early 12th century. The poem is by Ki no Tsurayuki (868?-945?), who in the Preface to another anthology wrote: "The poetry of Japan has its roots in the human heart and flourishes in the countless leaves of words . . . Hearing the warbler sing among the blossoms and the frog in his fresh waters—is there any living being not given to song? It is poetry which, without exertion, moves heaven and earth, stirs the feelings of gods and spirits invisible to the eye, softens the relations between men and women, calms the hearts of fierce warriors." The calligraphy is by Fujiwara no Sadanobu (1088-1154). The poem is written on layered rice paper with gold and silver and foliage designs. Even to the untutored eye, the effect is elegant. [Freer Gallery of Art, Smithsonian Institution, Washington, D.C.]

Development of Japanese Writing

No two languages could be more different than Chinese and Japanese. Chinese is nonsyllabic, uninflected, and tonal. Japanese is polysyllabic, highly inflected, and atonal. To adopt Chinese writing for use in Japanese was thus no easy task. What the Japanese did at first—when they were not simply learning to write in Chinese—was to use certain Chinese ideographs as a phonetic script. For example, in the *Man'yōshū* the eighth-century poetic anthology, *shira-nami* (white wave) was written with 之 for *shi*, 良 for *ra*, 奈 for *na*, and 美 for *mi*. Over several centuries, these phonetic ideographs evolved into a unique Japanese phonetic script:

	Original Chinese Ideograph	Simplified Ideograph	Phonetic Script (kana)
shi	之		し
ra	良		ら
na	奈		な
mi	美		み

It is apparent in the above examples how the original ideograph was first simplified according to the rules of calligraphy and was then further simplified into a phonetic script. In modern Japanese, unmodified Chinese ideographs are used for nouns, verb stems, and adjectives, and the phonetic script is used for inflections and particles.

学生 は 図書館 へ 行きました

Students/as for/library/to/went.
(The students went to the library.)

In the above sentence, the Chinese ideographs are the forms with many strokes, and the phonetic script is shown in the simpler, cursive forms.

An early obstacle to the development of a Japanese poetic tradition was the difficulty of transcribing Japanese sounds. In the *Ten Thousand Leaves*, Chinese characters were used as phonetic symbols. But there was no standardization, and the work soon became unintelligible. In 951, when an empress wished to read it, a committee of poets deciphered the work and put it into *kana*, the new syllabic script or alphabet that had developed during the ninth century. A second major anthology was the *Collection of Ancient and Modern Times*, compiled in 905. It was written entirely in *kana*.

The invention of *kana* opened the gate to the most brilliant developments of the Heian period. Most of the new works and certainly the greatest were by women, as most men were busy writing Chinese. One genre of writing was the diary or travel diary. An outstanding example of this genre was the *Izumi Shikibu Diary*, in which Izumi Shikibu reveals her tempestuous loves through a record of poetic exchanges.

The greatest works of the Heian period were by Sei Daimyo and Murasaki Shikibu. Both were daughters of provincial officials serving at the Heian court. The *Pillow Book* of Sei Shōnagon contains sharp, satirical, amusing essays and literary jottings that reveal the demanding aristocratic taste of the early-eleventh-century Heian court, for which, as Sir George Sansom said, "religion became an art and art a religion."[3]

The *Tale of Genji*, written by Murasaki Shikibu in about 1010, was the world's first novel. Emerging out of a short tradition of lesser works in which prose was a setting for poetry, *Genji* is a work of sensitivity, originality, and precise psychological delineation of character, for which there was no Chinese model. It tells of the life, loves, and sorrows of Prince Genji, the son of an imperial concubine, and, after his death, of his son Kaoru. The novel spans three-quarters of a century and is historical in nature, although the court society it describes is more emperor-centered than it was during the Fujiwara age in which Murasaki lived. The book may be seen as having had a "definite and serious purpose." In one passage Genji twits a court lady whom he finds reading an extravagant romance. She is "hardly able to lift her eyes from the book in front of her." But then Genji relents and says

I think far better of this art than I have led you to suppose. Even its practical value is immense.

[3]G. Sansom, *Japan, A Short Cultural History* (New York: Appleton-Century-Crofts, 1962), p. 239.

Aristocratic Taste at the Fujiwara Court: Sei Shōnagon Records Her Likes and Dislikes

Here are some passages from the Pillow Book *of Sei Shōnagon, one of the masterpieces of Heian Japan.*

In what sense can a literary work such as this also be considered a historical document? What kind of information can it provide about court life?

Elegant Things

A white coat worn over a violet waistcoat.

Duck eggs.

Shaved ice mixed with liana syrup and put in a new silver bowl.

A rosary of rock crystal.

Snow on wistaria or plum blossoms.

A pretty child eating strawberries.

Features That I Particularly Like

Someone has torn up a letter and thrown it away. Picking up the pieces, one finds that many of them can be fitted together.

A person in whose company one feels awkward asks one to supply the opening or closing line of a poem. If one happens to recall it, one is very pleased. Yet often on such occasions one completely forgets something that one would normally know.

Entering the Empress's room and finding that ladies-in-waiting are crowded round her in a tight group, I go next to a pillar which is some distance from where she is sitting. What a delight it is when Her Majesty summons me to her side so that all the others have to make way!

Hateful Things

A lover who is leaving at dawn announces that he has to find his fan and his paper. "I know I put them somewhere last night," he says. Since it is pitch dark, he gropes about the room, bumping into the furniture and muttering, "Strange! Where on earth can they be?" Finally he discovers the objects. He thrusts the paper into the breast of his robe with a great rustling sound; then he snaps open his fan and busily fans away with it. Only now is he ready to take his leave. What charmless behavior! "Hateful" is an understatement.

A good lover will behave as elegantly at dawn as at any other time. He drags himself out of bed with a look of dismay on his face. The lady urges him on: "Come,

---

Without it what should we know of how people lived in the past, from the Age of the Gods down to the present day? For history books such as the *Chronicles of Japan* show us only one small corner of life; whereas these diaries and romances, which I see piled around you contain, I am sure, the most minute information about all sorts of people's private affairs.[4]

Nara and Heian Buddhism

The Six Sects of the Nara period each represented a separate philosophical doctrine within Mahayana Buddhism. Their monks trained as religious specialists in monastic communities set apart from the larger society. They studied, read sutras, copied texts, meditated, and joined in rituals. The typical monastery was a self-contained community with a Golden Hall for worship, a pagoda that housed a relic or sutra,

a belfry that rang the hours of the monastic regimen, a lecture hall, a refectory, and dormitories with monks' cells.

As in China, monasteries and temples were involved with the state. Tax revenues were assigned for their support. In 741 temples were established in every province to protect the state by reading sutras. Monks prayed for the health of the emperor and for rain in time of drought. The Temple of the Healing Buddha (Yakushiji) was built by an emperor when his consort fell ill. In China, to protect tax revenues and the family, laws were enacted to limit the number of monks and nuns. In Nara Japan, where Buddhism spread only slowly outside the capital area, the same laws took on a prescriptive force. The figure that had been a limit in China became a goal in Japan. Thus the involvement of the state was patterned on that of China, but its role was far more supportive.

Japan in the seventh and eighth centuries was also much less culturally developed than China. The Japanese came to Buddhism not from the philosophical perspectives of Confucianism or Taoism but from the magic and mystery of Shinto. The appeal of Buddhism to the early Japanese was, consequently, in its colorful and elaborate rituals; in the gods,

[4]R. Tsunoda, W. T. deBary, and D. Keene, eds., *Sources of the Japanese Tradition* (New York: Columbia University Press, 1958), p. 181.

my friend, it's getting light. You don't want anyone to find you here." He gives a deep sigh, as if to say that the night has not been nearly long enough and that it is agony to leave. Once up, he does not instantly pull on his trousers. Instead he comes close to the lady and whispers whatever was left unsaid during the night. Even when he is dressed, he still lingers, vaguely pretending to be fastening his sash.

Presently he raises the lattice, and the two lovers stand together by the side door while he tells her how he dreads the coming day, which will keep them apart; then he slips away. The lady watches him go, and this moment of parting will remain among her most charming memories.

In Spring It Is the Dawn

In spring it is the dawn that is most beautiful. As the light creeps over the hills, their outlines are dyed a faint red and wisps of purplish cloud trail over them.

In summer the nights. Not only when the moon shines, but on dark nights too, as the fireflies flit to and fro, and even when it rains, how beautiful it is!

In autumn the evenings, when the glittering sun sinks close to the edge of the hills and the crows fly back to their nests in threes and fours and twos; more charming still is a file of wild geese, like specks in the distant sky. When the sun has set, one's heart is moved by the sound of the wind and the hum of the insects.

In winter the early mornings. It is beautiful indeed when snow has fallen during the night, but splendid too when the ground is white with frost; or even when there is no snow or frost, but it is simply very cold and the attendants hurry from room to room stirring up the fires and bringing charcoal, how well this fits the season's mood! But as noon approaches and the cold wears off, no one bothers to keep the braziers alight, and soon nothing remains but piles of white ashes.

Things That Have Lost Their Power

A large tree that has been blown down in a gale and lies on its side with its roots in the air.

The retreating figure of a sumo wrestler who has been defeated in a match.

A woman, who is angry with her husband about some trifling matter, leaves home and goes somewhere to hide. She is certain that he will rush about looking for her; but he does nothing of the kind and shows the most infuriating indifference. Since she cannot stay away for ever, she swallows her pride and returns.

From *The Pillow Book of Sei Shōnagon*, trans. by Ivan Morris. Copyright © 1991 by Columbia University Press. Reprinted with permission of the publisher.

---

demons, and angels of the Mahayana pantheon; and, above all, in the beauty of Buddhist art. The philosophy took longer to establish itself. The speed with which the Japanese mastered the construction of temples with elaborate wooden brackets and gracefully arching tile roofs, as well as the loveliness of Nara Buddhist sculpture, wall paintings, and lacquer temple altars, was no less an achievement than their establishment of a political system based on the T'ang codes.

Japan's cultural identity was also different. In China, Buddhism was always viewed as Indian and alien. Its earliest Buddha statues, like those of northwestern India, looked Greek. That Buddhism was part of a non-Chinese culture was one factor leading to the Chinese persecution of Buddhists during the ninth century. In contrast, Japan's cultural identity or cultural self-consciousness took shape only during the Nara and early Heian periods. One element in that identity was the imperial cult derived from Shinto. But as a religion, Shinto was no match for Buddhism. The Japanese were aware that Buddhism was foreign, but it was no more so than Confucianism and all the rest of the T'ang culture that had largely helped reshape the Japanese identity, so there was no particular bias against it. Consequently, Buddhism entered deeply into Japanese culture and retained its vitality longer. Not until the seventeenth or eighteenth centuries did Japanese elites became so Confucian as to be anti-Buddhist.

In 794 the court moved to Heian. Buddhist temples soon became as entrenched in the new capital as they had been in Nara. The two great new Buddhist sects of the Heian era were Tendai and Shingon.

Saichō (767–822) had founded a temple on Mount Hiei to the northwest of Kyoto in 785. He went to China as a student monk in 804 and returned the following year with the teachings of the Tendai sect (*T'ien T'ai* in Chinese). He spread in Japan the doctrine that salvation was not solely for monastic specialists but could be attained by all who led a life of contemplation and moral purity. He instituted strict monastic rules and a twelve-year training curriculum for novice monks at his mountain monastery. Over the next few centuries the sect grew until thousands of temples had been built on Mount Hiei, which remained a center of Japanese Buddhism until it was destroyed in the wars of the sixteenth century. Many later Japanese sects emerged from within the Tendai fold, stressing one or another doctrine of its syncretic teachings.

The Hōryūji Temple, built by Prince Shōtoku in 607, contains the oldest wooden buildings in the world. They are the best surviving examples of Chinese Buddhist architecture. Note the groups of visiting students in the foreground. [Susumu Takahashi/Reuters/ Corbis-Bettmann]

The Shingon sect was begun by Kūkai (774–835). He studied Confucianism, Taoism, and Buddhism at the court university. Deciding that Buddhism was superior, he became a monk at the age of eighteen. In 804 he went to China with Saichō. He returned two years later bearing the Shingon doctrines and founded a monastery on Mount Koya to the south of the Nara plain and far from the new capital. Kūkai was an extraordinary figure. He was a bridge builder, a poet, an artist, and one of the three great calligraphers of his age. He is sometimes credited with inventing the *kana* syllabary and with introducing tea into Japan. Shingon doctrines center on an eternal and cosmic Buddha, of whom all other Buddhas are manifestations. *Shingon* means "true word" or "mantra," a verbal formula with mystical powers. It is sometimes called *esoteric Buddhism* because it had secret teachings that were passed from master to disciple. In China, Shingon died out as a sect in the persecutions of the mid-ninth century, but it was tremendously successful in Japan. Its doctrines even spread to the Tendai center on Mount Hiei. Part of the appeal was in its air of mystery and its complex rituals involving signs, the manipulation of religious objects, and mandalas—maps of the cosmic Buddhist universe.

During the later Heian period, Buddhism began to be assimilated. At the village level, the folk religion of Shinto took in many Buddhist elements. In the high culture of the capital, Shinto was almost absorbed by Buddhism. Shinto deities came to be seen as the local manifestations of universal Bud-

dhas. The cosmic or "Great Sun Buddha" of the Shingon sect, for example, was easily identified with the sun goddess. Often, great Buddhist temples had smaller Shinto shrines on their grounds. The Buddha watched over Japan; the shrine deity guarded the temple itself. Not until the mid-nineteenth century was Shinto disentangled from Buddhism, and then for political ends.

Japan's Early Feudal Age

The year 1185, or 1160 if we include Taira rule in Kyoto, marked another major turning point in Japanese history. It began the shift from centuries of rule by a civil aristocracy to centuries of rule by one that was military. It saw the formation of the *bakufu* (tent government), a completely non-Chinese type of government. It saw the emergence of the *shōgun* as the *de facto* ruler of Japan, although in theory he was a military official of the emperor. It marked the beginning of new cultural forms and initiated changes in family and social organization.

Rise of Minamoto Yoritomo

Taira Kiyomori's seizure of Kyoto in 1160 fell far short of being a national military hegemony, for other bands still flourished elsewhere in Japan. After Kiyomori's victory, the Taira embraced the elegant lifestyle of the Kyoto court while ties to their base area along the Inland Sea weakened. They assumed that their tutelage over the court would be as enduring as had been that of the Fujiwara. In the meantime, the Minamoto were rebuilding their strength in eastern Japan. In 1180 Minamoto Yoritomo (1147–1199) responded to a call to arms by a disaffected prince, seized control of eastern Japan (the rich Kanto plain), and began the war that ended in 1185 with the downfall of the Taira.

Yoritomo's victory in 1185 was national, for his armies had ranged over most of Japan. After his victory, warriors from every area vied to become his vassals. Wary of the blandishments of Kyoto that had weakened the Taira forces, Yoritomo set up his headquarters at Kamakura, thirty miles south of present-day Tokyo, at the edge of his base of power in eastern Japan (see Map 9–2). He called his government the *bakufu* in contrast to the civil government in Kyoto. Like the house government of the Fujiwara or the "cloister government" of the retired emperors, the offices he established were few and practical: one to deal with his samurai retainers, one to administer and execute his policies, and one to hear legal suits. Each office was staffed by vassals. The decisions of these offices, built up into a body of customary law, were codified in 1232 as the Jōei Code. Yoritomo also appointed military governors in each province and military stewards on the former estates of the Taira and others who had fought against him. These appointments carried the right to some income from the land. The rest of the income, as earlier, went to Kyoto as taxes or as revenues to the noble owners of the estates.

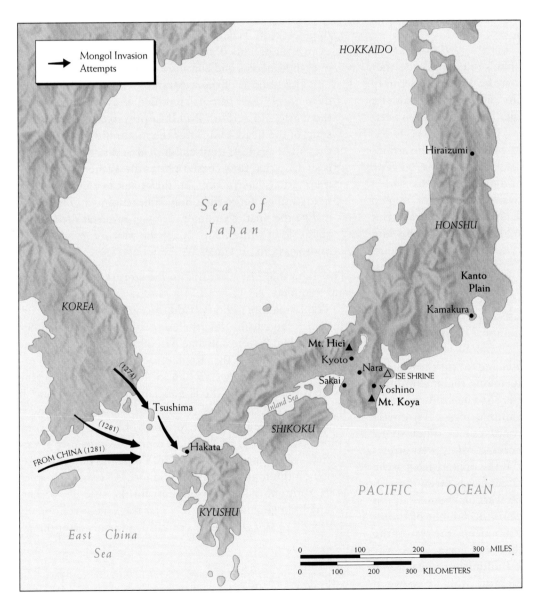

Map 9–2 Medieval Japan and the Mongol invasions. Kamakura and Kyoto were the two centers of power during the Kamakura period, 1185–1333. The *bakufu* was one and the court the other. After 1336 the Ashikaga *bakufu* was established in Kyoto, absorbing the powers of the court.

Government by Military Houses

1160–1180	Taira rule in Kyoto
1185–1333	Kamakura *bakufu*
1185	Founded by Minamoto Yoritomo
1219	Usurped by Hōjō
1221	Armed uprising by Kyoto court
1232	Formation of Jōei Code
1274 and 1281	Invasion by Mongols
1336–1467	Ashikaga *bakufu*
1336	Begun by Ashikaga Takauji
1392	End of Southern Court
1467	Start of warring states period

The Question of Feudalism

Scholars often contend that Yoritomo's rule marks the start of feudalism in Japan. Feudalism may be defined in terms of three criteria: lord-vassal relationships, fiefs given in return for military service, and a warrior ethic. Do these apply to Kamakura Japan?

Certainly, the mounted warriors who made up the armies of Yoritomo were predominantly his vassals, not his kin. The Minamoto and Taira houses had originally been extended families, very much like the Fujiwara or the earlier Yamato nobility. Yoritomo's brothers were among his generals. But after he came to power, he favored his vassals over his kin, and the lateral blood ties gave way to the vertical and political lord-vassal bond. As for fiefs, the answer is ambiguous. Kamakura vassals received rights to income from land in exchange for military service. But the income was usually a slice of the surplus from the estates of Kyoto nonmilitary aristocrats. Fiefs, as such, did not appear until the late fifteenth century.

However, there is no ambiguity regarding the warrior ethic, which had been developing among regional military bands for several centuries before 1185. The samurai prized martial qualities such as bravery, cunning, physical strength, and endurance. They gave their swords names. Their sports were hunting, hawking, and archery—loosing their arrows at the target while riding at full tilt. If the military tales of the period are to be believed, their combat was often individual, and before engaging in battle warriors would call out their pedigrees. That is to say, warriors thought of themselves as a military aristocracy that practiced "the way of the bow and arrow," "the way of the bow and horse," "the way of the warriors," and so on. In the Buddhism-tinged *Tale of Heike*, a military romance recounting the struggle between the Taira and the Minamoto, a Taira general asks a vassal from eastern Japan

"Sanemori, in the eight eastern provinces are there many men who are as mighty archers as you are?"

"Do you then consider me a mighty archer?" asked Sanemori with a scornful smile. "I can only draw an arrow thirteen handbreadths long. In the eastern provinces there are any number of warriors who can do so. There is one famed archer who never draws a shaft less than fifteen handbreadths long. So mighty is his bow that four or five ordinary men must pull together to bend it. When he shoots, his arrow can easily pierce two or three suits of armor at once. Even a warrior from a small estate has at least five hundred soldiers. They are bold horsemen who never fall, nor do they let their horses stumble on the roughest road. When they fight, they do not care if even their parents or children are killed; they ride on over their bodies and continue the battle.

"The warriors of the western province are quite different. If their parents are killed, they retire from the battle and perform Buddhist rites to console the souls of the dead. Only after the mourning is over will they fight again. If their children are slain, their grief is so deep that they cease fighting altogether. When their rations have given out, they plant rice in the fields and go out to fight only after reaping it. They dislike the heat of summer. They grumble at the severe cold of winter. This is not the way of the soldiers of the eastern provinces."[5]

The Taira soldiers, according to the story, "heard his words and trembled."

The Kamakura military band thus pretty well fits our definition of feudalism. Nonetheless, qualifications are in order, as warrior bands were only one part of the whole society. One large qualification is that Kamakura Japan still had two political centers. The *bakufu* had military authority, but the Kyoto court continued the late Heian pattern of civil rule. It appointed civil governors; it received tax revenues; and it controlled the region about Kyoto. Noble families, retired emperors, and the great Buddhist temples—in control of vast estates—also contributed to Kyoto's ongoing power. It also remained the fount of rank and honors. After his victory in 1185, Yoritomo asked the emperor for the title of "barbarian-quelling generalissimo" (*Sei i tai shōgun*, conventionally shortened to *shōgun*). He was refused, and only after the re-

[5]H. Kitagawa and B. Tsuchida, trans., *The Tale of Heike* (Tokyo: Tokyo University Press, 1975), p. 330.

tired emperor died in 1192 did Yoritomo get the title to match his power. Even then, the award of the title was justified because Yoritomo was a Minamoto offshoot of the imperial line.

The small size of Yoritomo's vassal band is an even more telling argument against viewing Japan as fully feudal at this time. Numbering about two thousand before 1221 and three thousand thereafter, most of the band were concentrated in eastern Japan. But even if as many as half were distributed about the rest of the country as military governors and stewards, there would have been only one hundred in a region the size of Massachusetts, because Japan in 1180 was about fifteen times larger than that state. Given the difficulties of transportation and communications, how could so few control such a large area? The answer is that they did not have to.

The local social order of the late Heian era continued into the Kamakura period. The Kyoto court, governors, district magistrates, and local notables—including many warriors who were not members of Yoritomo's band—functioned more or less as they had earlier. To influence the local scene, the newly appointed Kamakura vassals had to win the cooperation of the existing local power-holders. In short, even if the Kamakura vassals themselves could be called feudal, they were only a thin skim on the surface of a society constructed according to older principles.

Kamakura Rule After Yoritomo

As soon as Yoritomo died in 1199, his widow and her Hōjō kinsmen moved to usurp the power of the Minamoto house. The widow, having taken holy orders after her husband's death, was known as the Nun Shōgun. One of her sons was pushed aside. The other became shōgun but was murdered in 1219. After that, the Hōjō ruled as regents for a puppet shōgun, just as the Fujiwara had been regents for figurehead emperors. The Kyoto court, trying to use the Hōjō usurpation, led an armed uprising against Kamakura in 1221, but it was quickly suppressed. New military stewards were then placed on the lands of those who had joined in the uprising. Any society based on personal bonds faces the problem of how to transfer loyalty from one generation to another. That the Kamakura vassals fought for the Hōjō in 1221, despite the Hōjō usurpation of the Minamoto rule, suggests that loyalty had become institutional. They were loyal to the *bakufu*, which guaranteed their income from land. Their personal loyalty to the Minamoto had ended with the death of Yoritomo.

In 1266 Kublai Khan (see Chapter 8) sent envoys demanding that Japan submit to his rule. He had subjugated Korea in 1258, and his army looked outward across the Tsushima Straits. The Kyoto court was terrified, but the Hōjō at Kamakura refused. The first Mongol invasion fleet arrived with 30,000 troops in 1274, but retired after initial victories. The Mongols again sent envoys; this time, they were beheaded. A second invasion force arrived in 1281, two years after Kublai had completed his conquest of southern China. Carrying 140,000 troops, it was an amphibious operation on a scale new to world history. With gunpowder bombs and phalanxes of archers protected by a forward wall of soldiers carrying overlapping shields, the Mongol forces were formidable.

The Japanese tactics of fierce individual combat were not appropriate to their foe. But a wall of stone had been erected along the curved shoreline of Hakata Bay in northwestern Kyushu, and the Mongols were held off for two months until again *kamikaze*, or "divine winds," sank a portion of their

Mongol invaders battling with an intrepid samurai horseman. Note the bomb bursting in the air at the upper right of this late thirteenth-century Japanese scroll painting. [© Museum of Imperial Collections—Sannomaru Shozo Kan, Courtesy of the International Society for Educational Information, Inc.]

fleet and forced the rest to withdraw. Preparations for a third expedition ended with Kublai's death in 1294.

The burden of repelling the Mongols fell on Kamakura's vassals in Kyushu. Non-Kamakura warriors of Kyushu also were mobilized to fight under the command of military governors. But as no land was taken, unlike in 1221, there were few rewards for those who had fought, and dissatisfaction was rife. Even temples and shrines demanded rewards, claiming that their prayers had brought about the divine winds.

Women in Warrior Society

The Nun Shōgun was one of a long line of important women in Japan. Although historians no longer speak of an early matriarchal age, there is no denying that the central figure of Japanese mythology was the sun goddess, who ruled the Plain of High Heaven. In the late Yayoi age, the shaman ruler Pimiko was probably not an exceptional figure; she was followed by the empresses of the Yamato and Nara courts, and they in turn by the great women writers of the Heian period. Under the Kamakura *bakufu*, there was only one Nun Shōgun, but the daughters of warrior families, as well as the sons, often trained in archery and other military arts. Women also occasionally inherited the position of military steward. As long as society was stable, women fared relatively well. But as fighting became more common in the fourteenth century, their position began to decline; as warfare became endemic in the fifteenth, their status plummeted. To protect the integrity of the military fief—the warrior's reward for serving his lord in battle and the lord's guarantee that his warriors would continue their service—multigeniture, in which daughters as well as sons inherited property, gave way from this time to unigeniture, inheritance by the most able son.

The Ashikaga Era

At times, formal political institutions seem rocklike in their stability, and history unfolds within the framework they provide. Then, almost as if a kaleidoscope had been shaken, the old institutions collapse and are swept away. In their place appear new institutions and new patterns of personal relations that, often enough, had begun to take shape within the confines of the old. It is not easy to explain the timing of such upheavals, but they are easy to recognize. One occurred in Japan between 1331 and 1336.

Various tensions had developed within late Kamakura society. The patrimony of a warrior was divided among his children. Over several generations vassals became poorer, often falling into debt. High-ranking vassals of Kamakura were dissatisfied with the Hōjō monopolization of key *bakufu* posts. In the meantime, the ties of vassals to Kamakura were weakening, while the ties to other warriors within their region were growing stronger. New regional bands were ready to emerge. The precipitating event was a revolt in 1331 by an emperor who thought emperors should actually rule. Kamakura sent Ashikaga Takauji (1305–1358), the head of a branch family of the Minamoto line, to put down the revolt. Instead he joined it, giving a clear signal to other regional lords, who threw off Kamakura's control and destroyed the Hōjō *bakufu* in Kamakura.

What emerged from the dust and confusion of the period from 1331 to 1336 was a regional multistate system centering on Kyoto. Each region was based on a warrior band about the size of the band that had brought Yorimoto to power a century and a half earlier. In the central Kyoto region, Ashikaga Takauji established his *bakufu*. Its offices were simple and functional: a samurai office for police and military matters, an administrative office for financial matters, a documents office for land records, and a judicial board to settle disputes. The offices were staffed by Takauji's vassals, with the most trusted vassals holding the highest posts. They were lords (now called daimyo) in their own right who also usually held appointments as military governors in the provinces surrounding Kyoto. The *bakufu* also appointed vassals to watch over its interests in the far north, in eastern Japan, and in Kyushu.

Government in the outlying regions was more diverse. Some lords held several provinces, some only one. Some had integrated most of the warriors in their areas into their bands. Others had several unassimilated military bands in their territories, forcing them to rely more on the authority of Kyoto. Formally, all regional lords or *daimyo* were the vassals of the shogun. But the relationship was often nominal. Sometimes the regional lords lived on their lands; sometimes they lived in Kyoto.

The relationship between the Kyoto *bakufu* and the regional lords fluctuated from 1336 to 1467. At times, able lords made their regions into virtually independent states. At other times, the Kyoto *bakufu* became stronger. The third shōgun, for example, tightened his grip on the Kyoto court. He even relinquished the military post of shōgun—giving it to his son in 1394—in order to take the highest civil post of grand minister of state. He improved relations with the great Buddhist temples and Shinto shrines and established ties with Ming China. Most significant were his military campaigns, which dented the autonomy of regional lords outside of the inner Kyoto circle.

But even the third shōgun had to rely on his vassals. To strengthen them for his campaigns, he gave them the authority to levy taxes; to unify in their own hands all judicial, administrative, and military authority in their regions; and to take on unaffiliated warriors as their direct vassals. But in doing so, he left problems for his successors. As ties of personal loyalty wore thin, new local warrior bands began to form in the interstices of the Ashikaga regional states.

Agriculture, Commerce, and Medieval Guilds

Population figures for medieval Japan are rough estimates at best, but recent scholarship suggests six million for the year 1200 and twelve million for 1600. Much of the increase occurred during the late Kamakura and Ashikaga periods, when the country was fairly peaceful. The increase was brought about by land reclamation and improvements in agricultural technology. Iron-edged tools became available to all. New strains of rice were developed. Irrigation and diking improved. Double cropping began with vegetables planted during the fall and winter in dry fields, which were flooded and planted in rice during the spring and summer.

In the Nara and early Heian periods, the economy was almost exclusively agricultural. Japan had no money, no commerce, and no cities—apart from Nara, which developed into a temple town living on assigned revenues, and Kyoto, where taxes were consumed. Following the example of China, the government had established a mint, but little money actually circulated. Taxes were paid in grain and labor. Commercial transactions were largely barter, with silk or grain as the medium of exchange. Artisans produced for the noble households or temples to which they were attached. Peasants were economically self-sufficient.

From the late Heian period, partly as a side effect of fixed tax quotas, more of the growing agricultural surplus stayed in local hands. This trend accelerated during the Kamakura and Ashikaga periods, when there was a transfer of income from the court aristocrats to the warrior class. As this transfer occurred, artisans detached themselves from noble households and began to produce for the market. Military equipment was an early staple of commerce, but gradually *sake*, lumber, paper, vegetable oils, salt, and products of the sea also became commercialized. A demand for copper coins appeared, and as they were no longer minted in Japan, they were imported in increasingly huge quantities from China.

During the Kamakura period, independent merchants appeared to handle the products of artisans. Some trade networks spread over all Japan. More often, artisan and merchant guilds, not unlike those of medieval Europe, paid a fee in exchange for monopoly rights in a given area. Early Kyoto guilds paid fees to powerful nobles or temples, and later to the Ashikaga *bakufu*. In outlying areas guild privileges were obtained from the regional feudal lords. From the Kamakura period onward, markets were held periodically in many parts of Japan, by a river or at a crossroads. Some place names in Japan today reveal such an origin. Yokkaichi, today an industrial city, means "fourth-day market." It began as a place where markets were held on the fourth, fourteenth, and twenty-fourth days of each month. During the fourteenth and fifteenth centuries such markets were held with increasing frequency until, eventually, permanent towns were established.

The mid-Heian monk Kūya (903-972) preached Pure Land doctrines in Kyoto and throughout Japan. Little Buddhas emerge from his mouth.

[PPS/Sunset]

Buddhism and Medieval Culture

The Nara and Heian periods are often referred to as Japan's classical age. The period that followed—say, from 1200 to 1600—is often called medieval. It was medieval in the root sense of the word in that it lay between the other two major spans of premodern Japanese history. It was also medieval in that it shared some characteristics that we label medieval in

Europe and China. However, there is an important difference. Medieval Japan was a direct outgrowth of classical Japan; one can even say that there was some overlap during the early Kamakura. In contrast, Europe was torn by barbarian invasions, and a millennium separated the classical culture of Rome from high medieval culture. Even to have a Charlemagne, Europe had to wait for half a millennium. In China, too, the era of political disunity and barbarian invasions lasted four hundred years, and it was during these years that its medieval Buddhist culture blossomed.

The results of the historical continuity in Japan are visible in every branch of its culture. The earlier poetic tradition continued with great vigor. In 1205 the compilation of the *New Collection from Ancient and Modern Times (Shinko-kinshū)*, was ordered by the same emperor who began the 1221 rebellion against Kamakura. The flat *Yamato-e* style of painting that had reached a peak in the *Genji Scrolls* continued into the medieval era with scrolls on historical and religious themes or fairy-tale adventures. Artisanal production continued without a break. The same techniques of lacquerwork with inlaid mother-of-pearl that had been employed, say, to make a cosmetic box for a Heian court lady were now applied to produce saddles for Kamakura warriors. In short, just as Heian estates continued into the Kamakura era, and just as the authority of the court continued, so did Heian culture extend into medieval Japan. Nonetheless, medieval Japanese culture had some distinctly new characteristics. First, as the leadership of society shifted from court aristocrats to military aristocrats, new forms of literature appeared. The medieval military tales were as different from the *Tale of Genji* as the armor of the mounted warrior was from the no less colorful silken robes of the court

nobility. Second, a new wave of culture entered from China. If the Nara and Heian had been shaped by T'ang culture, medieval Japan—although not its institutions-was shaped by Sung culture. This link is immediately apparent in the ink paintings of medieval Japan. Third, and most important, the medieval centuries were Japan's age of Buddhist faith. A religious revolution occurred during the Kamakura period and deepened during the Ashikaga. It fundamentally influenced the arts of Japan.

Japanese Pietism: Pure Land and Nichiren Buddhism

Among the doctrines of the Heian Tendai sect was the belief that the true teachings of the historical Buddha had been lost and that salvation could be had only by calling on the name of Amida, the Buddha who ruled over the Western Paradise (or Pure Land). During the tenth and eleventh centuries, itinerant preachers began to spread Pure Land doctrines and practices beyond the narrow circles of Kyoto. Kūya (903–972), the "saint of the marketplace," for example, preached not only in Kyoto and throughout the provinces, but even to the aboriginal Ainu in northernmost Japan. The doctrine that the world had fallen on evil times and that only faith would suffice was given credence by earthquakes, epidemics, fires, and banditry in the capital, as well as wars throughout the land. The deepening Buddhist coloration of the age can be read in the opening lines of the thirteenth-century *Tale of Heiki*, written just two centuries after the *Tale of Genji* and the *Pillow Book*:

The sound of the bell of Jetavana echoes the impermanence of all things. The hue of the flowers of the

A twelfth century japanese fan superimposed on a painting of a gorgeously clad nobleman and his lady in a palace setting are verses in Chinese from a Buddhist sutra. The aesthetic pairing of sacred and secular was a feature of life at the Heian court. The fan might have been used by a figure in Sei Shōnagon's *Pillow Book*. [Tokyo National Museum]

An austere fifteenth-century Zen garden of rocks suggesting mountain peaks that rise from ocean waves of raked white sand. This garden is part of the Ryōanji temple in northwest Kyoto along the mountains' fringe.

[Japan National Tourist Office]

teak-tree declares that they who flourish must be brought low. Yea, the proud ones are but for a moment, like an evening dream in springtime. The mighty are destroyed at the last, they are but as the dust before the wind.[6]

In the early Kamakura era, two figures stand out as religious geniuses who experienced the truth of Pure Land Buddhism within themselves. Hōnen (1133–1212) was perhaps the first to say that the invocation of the name of Amida alone was enough for salvation and that only faith rather than works or rituals counted. These claims brought Hōnen into conflict with the older Buddhist establishment and marked the emergence of Pure Land as a separate sect. Hōnen was followed by Shinran (1173–1262), who taught that even a single invocation in praise of Amida, if done with perfect faith, was sufficient for salvation. But perfect faith was not the result of human effort: It was a gift from Amida. Shinran taught that pride was an obstacle to purity of heart. One of his most famous sayings is "If even a good man can be reborn in the Pure Land, how much more so a wicked man."[7] Shinran is saying that the evil man is less inclined to assume that he is the source of his own salvation and therefore more inclined to place his complete trust in Amida.

Shinran's emphasis on faith alone led him to break many of the monastic rules of earlier Buddhism: He ate meat; he

married a nun, and thereafter the Pure Land sect had a married clergy; and he taught that all occupations were equally "heavenly" if performed with a pure heart. Exiled from Kyoto, he traveled about Japan establishing "True Pure Land" congregations. (When the Jesuits arrived in Japan in the sixteenth century, they called this sect "the devil's Christianity.")

As a result of a line of distinguished teachers after Shinran, its doctrinal simplicity, and its reliance on the practice of piety, Pure Land Buddhism became the dominant form of Buddhism in Japan and remains so today. It was also the only sect in medieval Japan—apart from the Tendai sect on Mount Hiei—to develop political and military power. As a religion of faith, it developed a strong church as a protection for the saved while they were still in this world. As peasants became militarized during the fifteenth century, some Pure Land village congregations created self-defense forces. At times they rebelled against feudal lords. In one instance, Pure Land armies ruled the province of Kaga for over a century. These congregations were smashed during the late sixteenth century, and the sect was depoliticized.

A second devotional sect was founded by Nichiren (1222–1282), who believed that the Lotus Sutra perfectly embodied the teachings of the Buddha. He instructed his adherents to chant, over and over, "Praise to the Lotus Sutra of the Wondrous Law," usually to the accompaniment of rapid drumbeats. Like the repetition of "Praise to the Amida Buddha" in the Pure Land sect or comparable verbal formulas in other religions around the world, the chanting optimally induced a state of religious rapture. The concern with an in-

[6]A. L. Sadler, trans., *The Tenfoot Square Hut and Tales of the Heike* (Rutland, VT, and Tokyo: Charles E. Tuttle, 1972), p. 22.
[7]Tsunoda, deBary, and Keene, p. 217.

Hakuin's Enlightenment

Hakuin (1686–1769) was a poet, a painter, and a Zen master. He wrote in colloquial Japanese as well as in Chinese. He illustrated the continuing power of the Zen tradition in postmedieval times. The following passages are from an autobiographical account of his spiritual quest. The first follows a recounting of his disappointments and failures and tells of his initial enlightenment. His teacher did not accept this as adequate, however. The second passage tells of his experience eight years later.

Compare these passages to "The Bodhisattva Ideal" in Chapter 10.

1.

In the spring of my twenty-fourth year, I was painfully struggling at the Eiganji in the province of Echigo. I slept neither day nor night, forgetting either to eat or sleep. A great doubt suddenly possessed me, and I felt as if frozen to death in the midst of an icy field extending thousands of *li*. A sense of an extraordinary purity permeated my bosom. I could not move. I was virtually senseless. What remained was only *"Mu."* Although I heard the master's lectures in the Lecture Hall, it was as though I were listening to his disclosure from some sixty or seventy steps outside the Hall, or as if I were floating in the air. This condition lasted for several days until one night I heard the striking of a temple bell. All at once a transformation came over me, as though a layer of ice were smashed or a tower of jade pulled down. Instantly I came to my senses. Former doubts were completely dissolved, like ice which had melted away. "How marvelous! How marvelous!" I cried out aloud. There was no cycle of birth and death from which I had to escape, no enlightenment for which I had to seek.

2.

At the age of thirty-two I settled in this dilapidated temple [Shoinji]. In a dream one night my mother handed me a purple silk robe. When I lifted it I felt great weights in both sleeves. Examining it, I found in each sleeve an old mirror about five or six inches in diameter. The reflection of the right-hand mirror penetrated deep into my heart. My own mind, as well as mountains and rivers, the entire earth, became serene and bottomless. The left-hand mirror had no luster on its entire surface. Its face was like that of a new iron pan not yet touched by fire. Suddenly I became aware that the luster on the left-hand mirror surpassed that of the right by a million times. After this incident, the vision of all things was like looking at my own face. For the first time I realized the meaning of the words, "The eyes of the Tatha-gata behold the Buddha-nature."

From *The Buddhist Tradition in India, China, and Japan* by William Theodore de Bary. Copyright © 1969 by William Theodore de Bary. Reprinted by permission of Modern Library, a division of Random House Inc.

---

ternal spiritual transformation was common to both the devotional and the meditative sects of Buddhism. Nichiren was remarkable for a Buddhist in being both intolerant and nationalistic. He blamed the ills of his age on rival sects and asserted that only his sect could protect Japan. He predicted the Mongol invasions, and his sect claimed credit for the "divine winds" that sank the Mongol fleets. Even his adopted Buddhist name, the Sun Lotus, combined the term for the rising sun of Japan with that of the flower that had become the symbol of Buddhism.

Zen Buddhism

Meditation had long been a part of Japanese monastic practice. Zen meditation and doctrines were introduced by monks returning from study in Sung China. Eisai (1141–1215) transposed to Japan the Rinzai sect in 1191 and Dōgen (1200–1253) the Sōtō sect in 1227. Eisai's sect was patronized by the Hōjō rulers in Kamakura and the Ashikaga in Kyoto. Dōgen established his sect on Japan's western coast, far from centers of political power.

Zen in Japan was a religion of paradox. Its monks were learned, yet it stressed a return to ignorance, to the uncluttered "original mind," attained in a flash of intuitive understanding. Zen was punctiliously traditional, the most Chinese of Japanese medieval sects. The authority of the Zen master over his pupil-monks was absolute. Yet Zen was also iconoclastic. Its sages were depicted in paintings as tearing up sutras to make the point that it is religious experience and not words that count. Within a rigidly structured monastic regimen, a vital give-and-take occurred as monks tested their understanding, gained through long hours of meditation, in encounters with their master. Buddhism stressed compassion for all sentient beings, yet in Japan the Zen sect included many samurai whose duty it was to fight and kill. A few military leaders encouraged the practice of Zen among their retainers in the hope of instilling a single-minded attention to duty; a handful of Hōjō and Ashikaga rulers even went so far as to practice Zen themselves.

The most remarkable aspect of Zen was its influence on the arts of medieval Japan. The most beautiful gardens, for

The Arts and Zen Buddhism

Zen Buddhism in Japan developed a theory of art that influenced every department of high medieval culture. Put simply, the theory is that intuitive action is better than conscious, purposive action. The best painter is one so skilled that he no longer needs to think of technique but paints as a natural act. Substitute a sword for a brush, and the same theory applies: A warrior who has to stop to consider his next move is at a disadvantage in battle. To this concern with direct, intuitive action is added the Zen distinction between the deluded mind and the "original mind." The latter is also referred to as the "no mind," or the mind in the enlightened state. The highest intuitive action proceeds from such a state of being. This theory was applied, in time, to the performance of the actor, to the skill of the potter, to archery, to flower arrangement, and to the tea ceremony. Compare the following two passages, one by Seami (1363–1443), the author of many Nō plays, and the other by Takuan Sōhō (1573–1645), a famous Zen master of the early Tokugawa era (see Chapter 20).

Could the same theory be applied to baseball? If it were, would baseball change?

Sometimes spectators of the Nō say, "The moments of 'no-action' are the most enjoyable." This is an art which the actor keeps secret. Dancing and singing, movements and the different types of miming are all acts performed by the body. Moments of "no-action" occur in between. When we examine why such moments without actions are enjoyable, we find that it is due to the underlying spiritual strength of the actor which unremittingly holds the attention. He does not relax the tension when the dancing or singing come to an end or at intervals between the dialogue and the different types of miming, but maintains an unwavering inner strength. This feeling of inner strength will faintly reveal itself and bring enjoyment. However, it is undesirable for the actor to permit this inner strength to become obvious to the audience. If it is obvious, it becomes an act, and is no longer "no-action." The actions before and after an interval of "no-action" must be linked by entering the state of mindlessness in which one conceals even from oneself one's intent. This, then, is the faculty of moving audiences, by linking all the artistic powers with one mind.

Where should a swordsman fix his mind? If he puts his mind on the physical movement of his opponent, it will be seized by the movement; if he places it on the sword of his opponent, it will be arrested by the sword; if he focuses his mind on the thought of striking his opponent, it will be carried away by the very thought; if the mind stays on his own sword, it will be captured by his sword; if he centers it on the thought of not being killed by his opponent, his mind will be overtaken by this very thought; if he keeps his mind firmly on his own or on his opponent's posture, likewise, it will be blocked by them. Thus the mind should not be fixed anywhere.

1. From *Sources of Japanese Tradition*, trans. by William Theodore de Bary. Copyright © 1958 by Columbia University. Reprinted with permission of the publisher. 2. From *The Buddhist Tradition* by William Theodore de Bary. Copyright © 1969 by William Theodore de Bary. Reprinted by permission of Random House Inc.

---

example, were in Zen temples. Many were designed by Zen masters. The most famous, at Ryōanji, consists of fifteen rocks set in white sand. Others only slightly less austere contain moss, shrubs, trees, ponds, and streams. With these elements and within a small compass, rocks become cliffs, raked sand becomes rivers or the sea, and a little world of nature emerges. If a garden may be said to possess philosophic stillness, the Zen gardens of Daitokuji and other Kyoto temples have it.

Zen monks, such as Josetsu, Shūbun (ca. 1415), and Sesshū (1420–1506) certainly number among the masters of ink painting in East Asia. One painting by Josetsu shows a man trying to catch a catfish with a gourd. Like the sound of one hand clapping, the impossibility of catching a catfish with a gourd presents as art the kind of logical conundrum used to expound Zen teachings. Sesshū painted in both the broken-ink style, in which splashlike brush strokes represent an entire mountain landscape, and a more usual calligraphic style. Because the artist's creativity itself was seen as grounded in his experience of meditation, a painting of a waterfall or a crow on a leafless branch in winter was viewed as no less religious than a painting of the mythic Zen founder Bodhidharma.

Nō Plays

Another fascinating product of Ashikaga culture was the Nō play, a kind of mystery drama without parallels elsewhere in East Asia. The play was performed on an almost square, bare wooden stage (often outdoors) by male actors wearing robes of great beauty and carved, painted masks of enigmatic expressions. Many such masks and robes number among Japan's national treasures. The chorus was chanted to the accompaniment of flute and drums. The language was poetic. The action was slow and highly stylized: Circling about the stage could represent a journey, and a motion of the hand, the reading of a letter. At a critical juncture in most plays, the protagonist was possessed by the spirit of another and performed a dance. Spirit possession was a commonplace in Japanese folk religion and also occurred in the *Tale of Genji*. Several plays were shown in a single performance; comic skits called "Crazy Words" were usually interspersed between them to break the tension.

Nō plays reveal a medley of themes present in medieval Japanese culture. Some pivot on incidents in the struggle between the Taira and the Minamoto. Some are religious: A cormorant fisher is saved from the king of hell for having given lodging to a priest. Some plays pick up incidents from the *Tale of Genji* or the Heian court: The famous Heian beauty and poet Ono no Komachi is possessed by the spirit of a lover she has spurned; their conflict is left to be resolved in a Buddhist afterlife. The Buddhist idea of impermanence, of this world as a place of suffering, and of the need to relinquish worldly attachments are found in many plays. Some plays are close to fairy tales: A fisherman takes the feather robe of an angel, but when she begins to sicken and grow wan, he returns the robe and she dances for him a dance that is performed only in heaven. Some plays are based on stories from China: A traveler dreams an entire lifetime on a magical pillow while waiting for a bowl of millet to cook. Another play reflects the constant Japanese ambivalence toward Chinese culture from which Japan had borrowed so much: Po Chu-i, the T'ang poet most famous in Japan, rows a boat over the seas and comes to the shores of Japan, where he is met by fishermen who turn him back in the name of Japanese poetry. One fisherman speaks:

> You in China make your poems and odes out of the Scriptures of India; and we have made our "uta" out of the poems and odes of China. Since then our poetry is a blend of three lands, we have named it Yamato, the great blend, and all our songs "Yamato uta."[8]

At the end, the fisherman is transformed into the Shinto god of Japanese poetry and performs the "Sea Green Dance."

IN WORLD PERSPECTIVE

Early Japanese History

During the first millennium C.E., the major development in world history was the spread of the civilizations that had risen

[8]A. Waley, trans., *The Nō Plays of Japan* (New York: Grove Press, 1957), p. 252.

out of the earlier philosophical and religious revolutions. In the West the process began with the spread of civilization from Greece to Rome, continued with the rise of Christianity and its diffusion within the late Roman Empire, and entered a third phase when the countries of northern Europe became civilized by borrowing Mediterranean culture. The spread was slow because Rome was no longer a vital center. By contrast, in East Asia the spread of civilization from its Chinese heartland was more rapid because in the early seventh century the T'ang empire had been reestablished—more vital, more exuberant, and more powerful than ever before. Within the East Asian culture zone, and apart from post-T'ang China itself, there were three major developing areas: Vietnam, Korea, and Japan.

All three used Chinese writing for most of their history, combined indigenous and Chinese elements to create distinctive cultures and national identities, and in premodern times built independent states. The contrast between these countries and other areas around China is interesting. Vietnam, Korea, and Japan were more Chinese in their culture than Tibet, Mongolia, or Manchuria. Yet during the modern era the latter areas have been swallowed up by China, whereas Korea, Vietnam, and Japan have preserved their independence. These three nations used Chinese culture to forge self-identities that could resist Chinese domination, just as present-day Third World nations borrow Western systems and ideas to build states that are politically anti-Western.

For all their political independence and unique social institutions, Vietnam and Korea would absorb increasingly large amounts of Chinese culture as the centuries passed. By the eighteenth century Korea, some say, was more Confucian than China itself, although this is open to question. Vietnamese law codes in the same era were essentially Chinese codes with a few minor variations. Japan, too, was powerfully influenced by successive waves of Chinese culture; but because it was bigger, more populous, and more distant, it became the major variant to the Chinese pattern within East Asian civilization. It reflected, often brilliantly, the potentials of East Asian culture in a non-Chinese milieu.

Of particular interest to Western students are the striking parallels that developed between Japan and northwestern Europe. Both had centuries of feudalism: peasant-farmers on the estates or manors of nobles; castles and mounted warriors who wore armor and fought in the service of their lords, cultures in which the glorification of valor and military prowess conflicted with the gentler virtues of their religions; merchant guilds and decentralized political economies. These parallels should not be surprising because both Japan and northwestern Europe began as backward tribal or post-tribal societies onto which heartland cultures were grafted during the first millennium C.E.

Review Questions ━━━

1. Discuss the sense in which Yayoi society was defined by its eastern frontier. What changes in this early frontier society led to the building of tombs and the emergence of the Yamato great kings?

2. Discuss Japan's cultural ties with China during the Nara and Heian periods? How did Chinese culture affect Japan in government and religion? How did the Japanese change what they borrowed?

3. How did the Buddhism of the Nara and Heian periods differ from that of the early medieval era?

4. Trace the rise in Japan of a society dominated by military lords and their vassals. Do the late Heian, the Kamakura, and the Ashikaga represent different stages in the development of Japanese feudalism?

5. Contrast the Heian court culture with the "feudal" culture of the Kamakura and Ashikaga eras. Was the one not as aristocratic as the other? How did the role of women change over time?

Suggested Readings ━━━

C. BLACKER, *The Catalpa Bow* (1975). A fascinating study of folk Shinto.

R. BORGEN, *Sugawara no Michizane and the Early Heian Court* (1986). A study of a famous courtier and poet.

D. BROWN AND E. ISHIDA, EDS., *The Future and the Past* (1979). A translation of a history of Japan written in 1219.

M. COLLCUTT, *Five Mountains* (1980). A study of the monastic organization of medieval Zen.

P. DUUS, *Feudalism in Japan* (1969). An easy survey of the subject.

W. W. FARRIS, *Population, Disease, and Land in Early Japan, 645–900* (1985). An innovative reinterpretation of early history.

W. W. FARRIS, *Heavenly Warriors: The Evolution of Japan's Military, 500–1300* (1992).

K. F. FRIDAY, *Hired Swords: The Rise of Private Warrior Power in Early Japan* (1991). The interpretation in this book may be compared to that in Farris's Heavenly Warriors.

J. W. HALL, *Government and Local Power in Japan, 500–1700: A Study Based on Bizen Province* (1966). The best book on Japanese history to 1700.

J. W. HALL AND J. P. MASS, EDS., *Medieval Japan* (1974). A collection of topical essays on medieval history.

J. W. HALL AND T. TOYODA, *Japan in the Muromachi Age* (1977). Another collection of essays.

D. KEENE, ED., *Anthology of Japanese Literature from the Earliest Era to the Mid-Nineteenth Century* (1955).

D. KEENE, ED., *Twenty Plays of the Nō Theatre* (1970).

J. M. KITAGAWA, *Religion in Japanese History* (1966). A survey of religion in premodern Japan.

I. H. LEVY, *The Ten Thousand Leaves* (1981). A fine translation of Japan's earliest collection of poetry.

J. P. MASS, *The Development of Kamakura Rule, 1180–1250* (1979).

J. P. MASS AND W. HAUSER, EDS., *The Bakufu in Japanese History* (1985). Topics in *bakufu* history from the twelfth to the nineteenth centuries.

I. MORRIS, *The World of the Shining Prince: Court Life in Ancient Japan* (1964). A study of the court during the age in which *The Tale of Genji* was written.

I. MORRIS, TRANS., *The Pillow Book of Sei Shōnagonō* (1967). Observations about the Heian court life by the Jane Austen of ancient Japan.

S. MURASAKI, *The Tale of Genji*, trans. by A. Waley (1952). A comparison of this translation with that of Seidensticker is instructive.

S. MURASAKI, *The Tale of Genji*, trans. by E. G. Seidensticker (1976). The world's first novel and the greatest work of Japanese fiction.

R. J. PEARSON ET AL., EDS., *Windows on the Japanese Past: Studies in Archaeology and Prehistory* (1986).

D. L. PHILIPPI, TRANS., *Kojiki* (1968). Japan's ancient myths.

E. O. REISCHAUER AND A. M. CRAIG, *Japan: Tradition and Transformation* (1989). A widely used text covering the total sweep of Japanese history from the early beginnings to the present day.

D. T. SUZUKI, *Zen and Japanese Culture* (1959).

R. TSUNODA, W. T. DEBARY, AND D. KEENE, COMPS., *Sources of the Japanese Tradition* (1958). A collection of original religious, political, and philosophical writings from each period of Japanese history. The best reader.

H. P. VARLEY, *Imperial Restoration in Medieval Japan* (1971). A study of the 1331 attempt by an emperor to restore imperial power.

A. WALEY, TRANS., *The Nō Plays of Japan* (1957). Medieval dramas.

K. YAMAMURA, ED., *Medieval Japan* (1990), Vol. 5 of the *Cambridge History of Japan*.

RELIGIONS OF THE WORLD

Buddhism

Buddhism, Jainism, and Upanishadic Hinduism all arose out of the spiritual ferment of Vedic India after 700 B.C.E. Buddhism shares a kinship with these other religions much like the relationship among Judaism, Christianity, and Islam.

Siddhartha Gautama was born about 563 B.C.E., a prince in a petty kingdom near what is now the border of India and Nepal. He was reared amid luxury and comforts, married at sixteen, and had a child. According to legend, at age twenty-nine he saw an old man, decrepit and as bent as a roof gable; a sick man, suffering and fallen in his own excreta; and a corpse. He suddenly realized that all humans would suffer the same fate. Gautama renounced his wealth and family and entered the life of a wandering ascetic. He visited famous teachers, for almost six years practiced extremes of ascetic self-deprivation, and finally discovered the "middle path" between self-indulgence and self-mortification. At the age of thirty-five he attained *nirvana*, becoming the *Buddha*, or the "enlightened one." The rest of his eighty years the Buddha spent teaching others the truths he had learned.

Basic to the Buddha's understanding of the human condition were the "Four Noble Truths": (1) All life is suffering—an endless karmic chain of births and rebirths. (2) The cause of the suffering is desire—it is desire that binds humans to the wheel of *karma*. (3) Escape from suffering and the endless rebirths can only come by the cessation of desire and the attainment of *nirvana*. (4) The path to nirvana is eightfold, requiring right views, thought, speech, actions, living, efforts, mindfulness, and meditation. Buddhists say that nirvana cannot be described: It is the ground of all existence, ineffable, and beyond time and space—an ultimate reality that may be experienced, but not grasped intellectually.

The Buddha was a religious teacher, not a social reformer, yet it is of interest to note the ethical conclusions he reached on the basis of his religious understanding. He condemned the caste system that flourished in the India of his day. He denounced war, slavery, and the taking of life. He opposed appeals to miracles. He did not demand a blind faith in his doctrines: He told his followers to accept his teachings only after they had tested them against their own experience. He

Two seated Buddhas. This fifth-to-sixth-century painting adorns a wall of a cave in Ajanta, India. [Borromeo, EPA/Art Resource, N.Y.]

held that poverty was a cause of immorality, and that it was futile to attempt to suppress crime with punishments. He identified with all humanity, saying, "He who attends on the sick attends on me."

Because the goal of Buddhism is for all humans to become Buddhas, some have called Buddhism the most contemplative and otherworldly of the great world religions. Even for the historical Buddha the way was not easy, and one lifetime was not enough. For others less spiritually prepared, the way was hard. Monks and nuns might practice the eightfold path, meditate for months and years, and experience an inner spiritual awakening. But only a few would gain the release from the trammels of karmic causation known as enlightenment. Most could only hope for a rebirth in a higher spiritual state—to begin again closer, as it were, to the goal. For lay people outside of the communities of monks and nuns, the emphasis of Buddhism was on ethical living in human society—as a preparation for a more dedicated religous quest in a future life.

Buddhism spread rapidly along the Ganges River and through northern India. In the time of King Ashoka (272–232 B.C.E.) of the Mauryas, it spread to southern India, Ceylon, and beyond. This was its great missionary age. As it spread throughout India its influence on religious practice at the village level was enormous, and its meditative techniques helped reshape Hindu yogic exercises. Eventually, however, Buddhism in India was re–Hinduized. It developed competing schools of metaphysics, a pantheon of gods and cosmic Buddhas, and devotional sects focusing on one or another of these cosmic figures. Its original character as a reform movement of Hinduism was lost, and between 500 and 1500 C.E. it was largely reabsorbed into Hinduism.

India apart, two major currents of Buddhism spread out over Asia. One, known as the "Way of the Elders" (*Theravada*), swept through continental Southeast Asia and the islands that are today Indonesia. The Theravada teaching was close to early Indian Buddhism and, as it spread, it carried with it other strands of Indian culture as well. Scenes from the great Indian epic, the *Mahabharata*, adorn the inner walls of Thai temples in Bangkok today. Buddhism remains the predominant religion of Burma, Thailand, Cambodia, and Laos, although it must contend with more recent secular ideologies. In Thailand it remains the state religion: Thai kings rule as Buddhist monarchs; Thai boys spend short periods as Buddhist monks; and Thai temples (*wats*) continue as one center of village life. Before the spread of Islam, Buddhism also once flourished in Malaya, Sumatra, and Java.

The second major current, known to its adherents as the "Greater Vehicle" (*Mahayana*), spread through northwest India to Afghanistan and Central Asia, and then to China, Tibet and Mongolia, Vietnam, Korea, and Japan. In each region the pattern that unfolded was different. In what is today Pakistan, Afghanistan, and central Asia, Buddhism was overtaken and replaced by Islam. Mahayana doctrines entered Tibet during the sixth century C.E. and became firmly established several centuries later. Tibetan Buddhism also absorbed Tantric (secret) doctrines from India and elements of the indigenous "Bon" religion. Today Tibetan Buddhism is the predominant religion of Tibet and Mongolia—though severely curtailed by Chinese authorities—and of Nepal, Sikkim, and Bhutan. In China, and then spreading from China to Korea, Vietnam, and Japan, Mahayana Buddhism saw its fullest development. One key doctrine in this current was the ideal of the *bodhisattva*, a being who had gone all the way to nirvana, but held off in order to help others attain salvation. One such *bodhisattva*, who became elevated to the status of a cosmic Buddha ruling over the Western Paradise (or Pure Land), was Amitabha (or Amida). Devotion to this Buddha, or to others, was the key feature of some important East Asian Buddhist sects. Another Mahayana doctrine, that of the Ch'an (in China) or Zen (in Japan) sect, stressed meditation and perhaps was closer to the teachings of the historical Buddha.

In China, the T'ang dynasty (618–907) was the great Buddhist age, a time of unparalleled creativity in religious art, sculpture, and music. After that, though Buddhism continued to flourish at the village level, the governing scholar-gentry class shifted to the more worldly doctrines of Neo-Confucianism. In Vietnam, Korea, and Japan the overall pattern replicated that of China, but the shift occurred later and with tremendous local variations.

During the modern century the struggle, as in other parts of the world, has been between religion and the secular doctrines engendered by the scientific and industrial revolutions. What the outcome will be is unclear, except that it will be powerfully affected by the ongoing transformations of Asian societies.

Buddhist Stupa in Ladakh. A stupa contains a relic of the Buddha or a sutra containing his teachings. In Ladakh, Nepal, and Tibet, the stupa takes this form. In China, Korea, and Japan, it takes the form of a pagoda.

10 IRAN AND INDIA BEFORE ISLAM

The Bodhisattva Avalokiteshvara, detail of a Buddhist wall painting from the cave shrines at Ajanta (Maharashtra, India), Gupta

period, ca. 475 C.E. Avalokiteshvara (known in China as Kwan-yin and in Japan as Kannon) is the supreme figure of infinite mercy.

Note how this figure conveys both a serene majesty and a sense of compassion through the inclined head and tranquil face.

[Art Resource, N.Y.]

IRAN

◆ The Parthians

◆ The Sasanid Empire (224–651 C.E.)

INDIA

◆ Golden Age of the Guptas (ca. 320–450 C.E.)

◆ The Development of "Classical" Traditions in Indian Civilization (ca. 300–1000 C.E.)

In World Perspective Pre-Islamic Iran and India

In this chapter we look at southwest and south Asia before the spread of Muslim faith and Islamic rule changed both regions.

In Iran, the period from the breakdown of Parthian rule in the early third century C.E. to the coming of Islam in the seventh was one of relative political stability under one long-lived dynasty of Persian imperial rulers, the Sasanids. Although Zoroastrian traditions regained their vitality in this period, the social and political system came to be dominated by a small ruling nobility, and foreign policy focused on constant competition with the Byzantine empire. This competition finally exhausted Sasanid resources, much as it did those of Byzantium. Both empires were ripe for defeat at the hands of the Arabs, whose armies, flying the banner of Islam, moved out of the Arabian peninsula in the mid-seventh century.

India experienced a similarly spectacular imperial revival under the Gupta kings, who presided also over a cultural efflorescence of unprecedented magnificence. Then incursions of new waves of steppe peoples from about 500 C.E. led to political fragmentation. Nevertheless, regional empires emerged

that lasted until the thirteenth century, when Islamic power under the Delhi sultans began to forge new patterns of power and culture north and south.

The coming of Islamic civilization—with Muslim conquerors or, much more often, with Muslim traders and religious brotherhoods—took place at different times and with differing consequences in each of these two major cultural areas.

In Iran, Islamic presence was a prominent factor in government and public life from the early years of the Arab conquests in the mid-seventh century, although religious conversion of the populace in the regions of the traditional Iranian cultural sphere took considerably longer.

In northwestern India, Arab armies penetrated the Indus region as early as 711, and Muslim rulers of Central Asian extraction controlled the Panjab from around 1000. The establishment of the so-called Delhi Sultanate in 1205 marked the entrenchment of Muslim ruling dynasties in the Indian heartlands. Similarly, Sufi brotherhoods made significant converts in India from about the thirteenth century onward. Even earlier, in trading communities on the coasts

of Gujarat and South India, Muslim settlers and converts had already provided the nuclei of smaller, often scattered Muslim communities that grew up within the larger Hindu society.

IRAN

The Parthians

Parthian Arsacid rule (ca. 247 B.C.E.–223 C.E.) began in the eastern Iranian province of Parthia in Seleucid times, soon extended to the southeastern shores of the Caspian, and eventually dominated the Iranian heartlands of the Achaemenids (see Chapter 4). The Parthian dynasty even managed by 129 B.C.E. to extinguish Seleucid power east of the Euphrates. They also continued the Iranian imperial and cultural traditions of the Achaemenids. The relative Parthian tolerance of religious diversity was paralleled by the growth of regionalism in political and cultural affairs. A growing nobility built strong local power bases and became the backbone of the military power of the realm. Aramaic, the common language of the empire, gradually lost ground to regional Iranian tongues after the second century B.C.E. The Parthian dialect and Greek were widely influential but could not replace Aramaic.

Despite their general religious tolerance, the Parthians still upheld such Zoroastrian traditions as maintenance of a royal sacred fire at a shrine in their Parthian homeland and inclusion of priestly advisers on the emperor's council. The last century or so of their rule saw increased emphasis on Iranian as opposed to foreign traditions in religious and cultural affairs. This emphasis was perhaps in reaction to the almost constant warfare with the Romans on their west flank and the Greco-Bactrian Kushan threat to the east. By this time Christianity and Buddhism were making sufficient converts in western and eastern border areas to threaten Zoroastrian tradition directly for the first time. These threats may have stimulated Parthian attempts to collect the largely oral Zoroastrian textual heritage. In such ways, Parthian rule laid the groundwork for the nationalistic emphases of subsequent centuries, despite later Sasanid efforts to portray this era as one of decline in native Iranian traditions.

The Sasanid Empire (224–651 C.E.)

The Sasanids, like the earlier Achaemenids, were a Persian dynasty. Claiming to be the rightful Achaemenid heirs, they championed Iranian legitimacy and tried to brand the Parthi-

ans as outside invaders from the northeast who followed Greek and other foreign ways. Much of the bad reputation of the Parthians stems from their being known only through hostile Sasanid or Roman sources.

The first Sasanid king, Ardashir (reigned 224 C.E.–ca. 239), was a Persian warrior noble of priestly family background. The Sasanid name came from his grandfather, Sasan. Ardashir and his son, Shapur I (r. ca. 239–272), built a strong internal administration in Persia (Fars) and extended their sway to Ctesiphon and abroad. While still his father's field general, Shapur took Bactria from the Kushans, thereby greatly expanding the Sasanid domain. Under his long rule, the empire grew significantly in the east and also beyond the Caucasus in the north and into Syria, Armenia, and parts of Anatolia in the west. Shapur inflicted humiliating defeats on three Roman emperors, even capturing one of them, Valerian (r. 253–260). Thus he could justifiably claim to be a restorer of Iranian glory and a "king of kings," or *shahanshah*. He also centralized and rationalized taxation, the civil ministries, and the military, although neither he nor his successors could fully contain the growing power of the nobility.

The palace of the Sasanid Shahanshahs at Ctesiphon. Built by Shapur I in the capital that the Sasanids inherited from the Arsacids, the imperial palace is only partly preserved. The gigantic four-story structure is said to have greatly impressed the Arab invaders in the seventh century. The massive open-vaulted hall or bay was a feature of Persian architecture that would be used later in Iranian mosques.

[Corbis-Bettmann]

With the shift of the Roman Empire east to Byzantium in the early fourth century C.E., the stage of imperial conflict was set for the next 350 years: Byzantium (Constantinople) on the Bosporus and Ctesiphon on the Tigris were home to the two mightiest thrones of Eurasia until the coming of the Arabs. From time to time, each won victories over the other, and each championed a different religious orthodoxy, but neither could ever completely conquer the other. In the sixth century each produced its greatest emperor: the Byzantine Justinian (r. 527–565) and the Sasanid Chosroes Anosharvan ("Chosroes of the Immortal Soul," r. 531–579). Yet less than a century after their deaths, the new Arab power reduced one empire dramatically and destroyed the other. Byzantium survived with the loss of most of its territory for another eight hundred years, but the Sasanid imperial order was swept away in 651. Memory of the Sasanids did not, however, entirely die. Chosroes, for example, became a legendary model of greatness for Persians and a symbol of imperial splendor among the Arabs.

Society and Economy

Sasanid society was largely like that of earlier times. At all levels, the extended family was the basic social unit. Zoroastrian orthodoxy recognized four classes: priests, warriors, scribes, and peasants. However, a great divide separated the royal house, the priesthood, and the warrior nobility from the common people of the cities (artisans, traders, and so on) and the rural peasantry.

The basis of the economy remained agriculture. There was a long-term trend toward concentration of land ownership among an ever-richer minority of the royalty, nobility, and priesthood. The growth of great estates was similar to that in Roman domains and similarly responsible for a growing imbalance between the rich few and the impoverished many. Increasingly, small farmers were reduced to serfdom. The burden of land taxation, like that of conscript labor work and army duty, hit hardest those least able to afford it. All this was not without eventual popular reaction, as the Mazdakite movement, discussed below, shows.

The Sasanids also closely oversaw and heavily taxed the lucrative caravan trade that traversed their territory, as well as export and import trade by sea. Silk and glass production increased under government monopoly, and the state also controlled mining. The empire's many urban centers and its foreign trade relied on a money system. It was from Jewish bankers in Babylonia and their Persian counterparts that Europe and the rest of the world got the use of bills of exchange (the term *check* comes from a Pahlavi word).[1]

---

[1] R. Girshman, *Iran* (Harmondsworth, U.K.: Penguin Books, 1954), pp. 341–346. "Pahlavi" is the name of the middle Persian language that gradually replaced Aramaic as the Iranian *lingua franca* in Sasanid times.

Sasanid aristocratic culture drew on diverse traditions, from Roman, Hellenistic, and Bactrian-Indian to Achaemenid and other native Iranian ones. Its heyday was the reign of Chosroes. Iranian legendary history and courtly literature were popular, as were translations of Indian narrative literature. Indian influences—not only religious ones, as in the case of Buddhist ideas, but also artistic and scientific ones—were especially strong. Indian medicine and mathematics were notably in demand. Hellenistic culture was also revived in the academy at Jundishapur in Khuzistan, where refugee scholars from Byzantium came to teach medicine and philosophy after Justinian closed the Greek academies in the West.

Religion

Zoroastrian Revival Religion played a significant role in Sasanid life not only at the popular level but even in affairs of state. The Sasanids institutionalized Zoroastrian ritual and theology as state orthodoxy. Although they were simply continuing the Arsacid patronage of Zoroastrian worship, the Sasanids claimed to be restoring the true faith after centuries of neglect. The initial architect of this propaganda and the Zoroastrian revival was the first chief priest (Mobad) of the empire, Tosar (or Tansar). Under Ardashir, Tosar instituted a state church and began the fixation of an authoritative, written canon of the Avesta, the scriptural texts that include the hymns of Zarathushtra (see Chapter 4). He may also have instituted a calendar reform and banned all images in the temples of the land, replacing them with the sacred altar fires of Zoroastrian tradition.

The most influential figure in Sasanid religious history was Tosar's successor, Kartir (or Kirdir), who served as chief priest to Shapur I and three successors (ca. 239–293). Although his zealotry was initially restrained by the religiously tolerant and eclectic Shapur, Kirdir gained greater power and influence after Shapur's death. He is the one figure other than a Sasanid king for whom we have personal inscriptions in the dynasty's rock reliefs. He seems to have tried to convert not only pagans, but also Christians, Buddhists, and others. His chief opponents were the Manichaeans, whom he considered Zoroastrian heretics, much as Christian groups saw them as Christian heretics.

Manichaeism Mani (216–277 C.E.) was born of a noble Parthian family but raised in Babylonia. A cosmopolitan who spoke Aramaic, Persian, and Greek and traveled to India, Mani preached a message similar to, but at crucial points sharply divergent from, its Zoroastrian, Judaic, and Christian forerunners. It centered on a radically dualistic and moralistic view of reality in which good and evil, spirit and matter, always warred. His preaching was avowedly missionary, presenting itself as the culmination and restoration

A Report of Mani's Words About His Mission

The following excerpt is from The Cologne Mani Codex, a Greek biographical work on Mani's early life that was unknown until its recent discovery in a damaged but largely intact manuscript codex. The tiny parchment "pocketbook" on which it was written dates from around 400 C.E., within 150 years of Mani's death. In it, the Manichaean author cites one of Mani's "gospels."

What does Mani's proclamation suggest he shared with other Near Eastern traditions? What rank and role does he claim for himself? What seems to be his idea of scripture?

He wrote [thus again and] said in the Gospel of his most holy hope: "I, Mani, an apostle of Jesus Christ through the will of God, the Father of Truth, from whom I also was born, who lives and abides forever, existing before all and also abiding after all. All things which are and will be subsist through his power. For from this very one I was begotten; and I am from his will. From him all that is true was revealed to me; and I am from [his] truth. [The truth of ages which he revealed] I have seen, and [that] truth I have disclosed to my fellow travelers; peace I have announced to the children of peace, hope I have proclaimed to the immortal race. The Elect I have chosen and a path to the height I have shown to those who ascend according to this truth. Hope I have proclaimed and this revelation I have revealed. This immortal Gospel I have written, including in it these eminent mysteries, and disclosing in it the greatest works, the greatest and most august forms of the most eminently powerful works. These things which he [revealed], I have shown [to those who live from] the truest vision, which I have beheld, and the most glorious revelation revealed to me."

From *The Cologne Mani Codex*, trans. from the Greek by Ron Cameron and A. J. Dewey Reprinted by Permission: Copyright © 1979, Scholars Press, p. 53. Reprinted by permission.

---

of the original unity of Zoroastrian, Christian, and Buddhist teachings. Mani may have been the first person in history consciously to "found" a new religious tradition or to seek to create a "scripture" for his followers. He called his new system "Justice," although it has been known to outsiders as *Manichaeism*. Mani's movement proved attractive; its popularity probably contributed to Kirdir's and later attempts to establish a Zoroastrian "orthodoxy" and scriptural canon.[2]

Kirdir eventually had Mani executed as a heretic in 277, but Mani's movement was destined to have great consequences. It spread westward to challenge the young Christian church (Saint Augustine was once a Manichaean) and eastward along the silk route to coexist in Central Asia with Nestorian Christian and Mahayana Buddhist communities as a third major universalistic tradition until after the coming of Islam. Its ideas figured even centuries later in both Christian and Islamic heresies against the mainstream theologies of both. Its adherents probably carried the Western planetary calendar to China, where in some areas it was used for centuries.

Zoroastrian Orthodoxy   Kartir had firmly grounded Zoroastrian orthodoxy despite the persistence of challenges to it, such as that of Mani. This orthodoxy became the back-

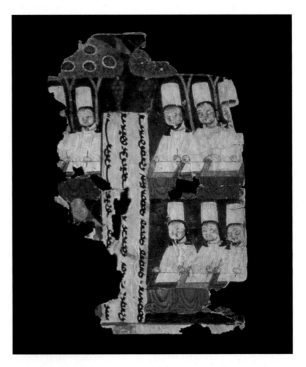

This leaf from a Manichaean book (ca. eighth-ninth century C.E.) shows priests in white robes and tall hats kneeling in front of low desks. Each has a sheet of white paper and some hold pens. Works such as this are an important source for our knowledge of Manichaean communities. [Museum fur Indische Kunst, Staatliche Museen Preussischer Kulturbesitz, Berlin]

---

[2]W. C. Smith, *The Meaning and End of Religion* (New York: Harper & Row, 1962), pp. 92–98.

bone of Sasanid culture. Soon the Sasanids' Persian dialect, *Pahlavi*, became the official imperial language, displacing Parthian (although many Parthian words entered the later Persian language). Eventually the Zoroastrian sacred texts were set down in Pahlavi. In later Sasanid times the priests produced many new writings, ranging from commentaries to myth, theology, and wisdom literature. Throughout Sasanid times, the priesthood increased its power as the jurists and legal interpreters as well as the liturgists and scholars of the land. With increasing endowments of new fire temples, the church establishment also eventually controlled much of Iran's wealth.

Later Sasanid Developments

Despite the high Zoroastrian moral intent of many of their rulers, the Sasanid ideal of justice did not include equal distribution of the empire's bounty. The radical inequalities between the aristocracy and the masses erupted at least once in conflict with the Mazdakite movement at the end of the fifth century. Its leader, Mazdak, preached asceticism, pessimism about the evil state of the material world, and the virtues of vegetarianism, tolerance, and brotherly love—all ideas apparently drawn ultimately from Manichaeism. Mazdak's egalitarian preaching included a demand for a more equal distribution of society's goods. This was attractive especially to the oppressed classes, although even one Sasanid ruler, Kavad I (r. 488–531), was sympathetic for a time to Mazdak's ideas of social justice. However, in 528 Kavad's third son, the later Chosroes Anosharvan, massacred Mazdak and his most important followers. Although this finished the Mazdakites, the name was still used later, in Islamic times, for various Iranian popular revolts.

Sasanid Iran	
223-224 C.E.	Ardashir (r. 224–ca. 239) defeats the last Arsacid ruler, becomes *shahanshah* of Iran
ca. 225–ca. 239	Tosar chief priest (Mobad) of realm
239-272	Reign of Shapur I; expansion of the empire east and west
ca. 239-293	Kirdir chief priest (Mobad) of the realm
216-277	Mani
ca. 307-379	Reign of Shapur II
488-531	Reign of Kavad I; height of Mazdakite movement
528	Mazdak and many of his followers massacred
531-579	Reign of Chosroes Anosharvan at Ctesiphon
651	Death of last Sasanid; Arabs conquer Persian empire

INDIA

Golden Age of the Guptas

Indians have always considered the Gupta era a high point of their civilization. Historians have seen in it the source of "classical" norms for Hindu religion and Indian culture—the symbolic equivalent of Periclean Athens, Augustan Rome, or Han China. The Guptas ruled when the various facets of Indian life took on the recognizable patterns of a single civilization that, however diverse its many cultural-linguistic units, extended its influence over the whole subcontinent. A major factor in this development was the relative peace and stability that marked most of the Guptas' reign.

Gupta Rule

The first Gupta king was Chandragupta (r. 320–ca. 330 C.E.). He ruled first in Magadha and then became prominent in the whole Ganges basin after he married princess Kumaradevi, daughter of a powerful tribal leader north of the Ganges. Although their reign inaugurated Gupta power, it was their son, Samudragupta (r. ca. 330–375), and especially their grandson, Chandragupta II (r. ca. 375–415), who turned kingdom into empire and presided over the Gupta "golden age."

The Gupta realm became the greatest in the subcontinent, extending from the Panjab and Kashmir south to the Narbada River in the western Deccan and east to modern Assam (see Map 10–1). The Gupta sphere of influence was still larger, including some of the Kushan and Saka kingdoms of the northwest as well as much of the eastern coast of India and possibly Ceylon (Sri Lanka). Unlike the Mauryans, the Guptas were usually ready to accept a defeated ruler as a vassal prince rather than to place his kingdom under direct rule. Seated at the old Mauryan capital, Pataliputra, Gupta splendor and power had no rival. Under Chandragupta II, India was arguably the most civilized and peaceful country in the world.

Two further Gupta kings sustained this prosperity for another half century, despite invasions by a new wave of steppe nomads, the Huns, after about 440. By about 500 the Huns had overrun western India. The Guptas were by then too weak to survive, and their empire collapsed about 550. Harsha, a descendant of the Guptas through his grandmother, did revive a semblance of former Gupta splendor between 616 and 657. His loosely held dominions again spanned North India, but when he died without heirs the empire broke up again, and the final echo of Gupta grandeur was gone.

The succeeding centuries before the arrival of Muslim invaders about 1000 C.E. saw several dynasties in North India share power, but no unified rule of any duration. Outside the north, several long-lived dynasties built regional empires in

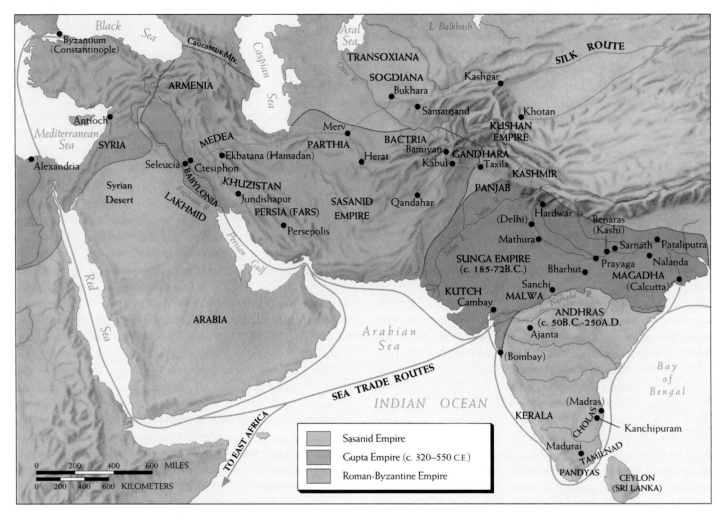

Map 10-1 International trade routes in Gupta and Sasanid times. This map shows the Gupta and Sasanid empires and the trade routes that linked them to each other and to other areas of the world.

the western Deccan and Tamilnad (the extreme south) after Gupta times, and in this period the main centers of Indian civilization shifted to the Deccan and the south.

Gupta Culture

With the decline of Rome in the West, Indian culture experienced little new outside influence from Gupta until Muslim times. India's chief contacts were now with Southeast Asia and China, and most of the cultural transmission was from India eastward, not vice versa.

The Gupta period and later centuries saw great artistic and literary productivity, of which only a few outstanding examples can be mentioned. The claim of the Gupta era to being India's golden age of culture could be sustained solely on the basis of its magnificent architecture and sculpture, the wall paintings of the Ajanta caves, and Kalidasa's match-

India from the Gupta Age to ca. 1000 C.E.

320 C.E.–ca. 467	Gupta period
320–330	Reign of Chandragupta, first Gupta king
376–454	Reigns of Chandragupta II and Kumaragupta: Kalidasa flourishes; heyday of Gupta culture
ca. 440	Beginning of Hun invasions from Central Asia
399–414	Chinese Buddhist monk, Fa-Hsien, travels in India
616–657	Reign of Harsha; revival of Gupta splendor and power
820	Death of Vedantin philosopher-theologian, Shankara
550–ca. 1000	Regional Indian kingdoms in north and south; major Puranas composed; age of first great Vaishnava and Shaivite devotional poets in southern India

A Chinese Traveler's Report on the Gupta Realm

Fa-Hsien, a Chinese Buddhist monk, was the first of several Chinese known for traveling to India to study and bring back Buddhist scriptures from the intellectual centers of Buddhist thought there. He, like later travelers of whom we know, wrote an account of his travels, first through Central Asia, then all over India, then through Ceylon and Indonesia again to China (399–414 C.E.).

What things about India seem most to surprise Fa-Hsien? Is his image of Indian rule a positive one? What do his remarks say about the prestige of the Buddhist tradition and its monks in the Indian state? What kinds of information does he give us about the society he is describing?

On the sides of the river, both right and left, are twenty *saṅ ghârâmas* [monasteries], with perhaps 3000 priests. The law of the Buddha is progressing and flourishing. Beyond the deserts are the countries of Western India. The kings of these countries are all firm believers in the law of Buddha. They remove their caps of state when they make offerings to the priests. The members of the royal household and the chief ministers personally direct the food-giving; when the distribution of food is over, they spread a carpet on the ground opposite the chief seat (the president's seat) and sit down before it. They dare not sit on couches in the presence of the priests. The rules relating to the almsgiving of kings have been handed down from the time of Buddha till now. Southward from this is the so-called middle-country (Mâdhyadeśa). The climate of this country is warm and equable, without frost or snow. The people are very well off, without poll tax or official restrictions. Only those who till the royal lands return a portion of profit of the land. If they desire to go, they go; if they like to stop, they stop. The kings govern without corporal punishment; criminals are fined, according to circumstances, lightly or heavily. Even in cases of repeated rebellion they only cut off the right hand. The king's personal attendants, who guard him on the right and left, have fixed salaries. Throughout the country the people kill no living thing nor drink wine, nor do they eat garlic or onions, with the exception of Chandâlas [outcasts] only. The Chandâlas are named "evil men" and dwell apart from others; if they enter a town or market, they sound a piece of wood in order to separate themselves; then men, knowing who they are, avoid coming in contact with them. In this country they do not keep swine nor fowls, and do not deal in cattle; they have no shambles or wine-shops in their market-places. In selling they use cowrie shells. The Chandâlas only hunt and sell flesh. Down from the time of Buddha's Nirvâna, the kings of these countries, the chief men and householders, have raised vihâras [monasteries] for the priests, and provided for their support by bestowing on them fields, houses, and gardens, with men and oxen. Engraved title-deeds were prepared and handed down from one reign to another; no one has ventured to withdraw them, so that till now there has been no interruption. All the resident priests having chambers (in these vihâras) have their beds, mats, food, drink, and clothes provided without stint; in all places this is the case. The priests ever engage themselves in doing meritorious works for the purpose of religious advancement (karma—building up their religious character), or in reciting the scriptures, or in meditation.

From "Buddhist Country Records," in Si-Yu-Ki: *Buddhist Records of the Western World*, trans. Samuel Beal (London, 1884: Reprint, Delhi: Oriental Books Reprint Corporation, 1969), pp. xxxvii–xxxviii. Reprinted by permission of Motilal Banarsidass Publishers Pvt. Ltd., Delhi, India.

---

less drama and verse. The "Shakespeare" of Sanskrit letters, Kalidasa, flourished in the time of Chandragupta II and his successor. Poetry, painting, sculpture, dance, drama, and music were popularly practiced as well as patronized by the aristocrats of the cities that defined the cultural standards in each region.

The depth of Gupta culture can be seen in the strong emphasis on education, whether in Jain and Buddhist monasteries or in Brahmanical schools. In addition to religious texts, typical subjects included rhetoric, prose and poetic composition, grammar, logic, medicine, and metaphysics. Using an older Indian number system that was transmitted later by the Arabs to the West as "Arabic numerals," Gupta scholars cultivated mathematics for theoretical as well as practical purposes.

In sculpture, the monastic complex at Sarnath was a great center of activity. The superb technique and expressive serenity of Gupta style grew out of native Mathura and Greco-Roman schools. Hindu, Jain, and Buddhist works all shared the same style and conventions. Even in handwork and luxury crafts, Gupta products achieved new levels of quality and were in great demand abroad: silks, muslin, linen, ivory and other carvings, bronze metalwork, gold and silver work, and cut stones, among others. In architecture, Gupta splendor is less evident, except in the culmination of cave-shrine (Chaitya-hall) development at Ajanta and in the earliest surviving free-standing temples in India. The Hindu temple underwent its important development in post-Gupta times, beginning in the eighth century.

Fifth century C.E. statue of Lokanatha from Sarnath, which despite damage, shows the fine sculptural work of the important school of Gupta artists at Sarnath and the influence on them of both Greco-Roman antecedents and native Indian traditions and conventions. [Scala/Art Resource, N.Y.]

The Development of "Classical" Traditions in Indian Civilization (ca. 300–1000 C.E.)

The Guptas' support of Brahmanic traditions and Vaishnava[3] devotionalism reflected the waning of Buddhist traditions in the mainstream of Indian religious life. In Gupta times and subsequently, down to the advent of Muslim rule, Indian civilization assumed its classical shape, its enduring "Hindu" forms of social, religious, and cultural life.

Society

In these centuries, the fundamentally hierarchical character of Hindu/Indian society solidified in practice and theory. The oldest manual of legal and ethical theory, the *Dharmashastra* of Manu, dates from about 200 C.E. Based on Vedic tradition, it treats the dharma appropriate to one's class and stage of life, rules for rites and study of the Veda, pollution and purification measures, dietary restrictions, royal duties and prerogatives, and other legal and moral questions.

In it we find the classic statement of the four-class theory of social hierarchy. This ideal construct rests on the basic principle that every person is born into a particular station in life (as a result of *karma* from earlier lives), and every station has its particular *dharma*, or appropriate duties and responsibilities, from the lowest servant to the highest prince or Brahman. The Brahmans' ancient division of Aryans into the four *varnas*, or classes, of *Brahman* (priest), *Kshatriya* (noble/warrior), *Vaishya* (tradesperson), and *Shudra* (servant) provides a schematic structure. These divisions reflect an attempt to fix the status and power of the upper three groups, especially the Brahmans, at the expense of the Shudras and the "fifth estate" of non-Aryan "outcasts," who performed the most polluting jobs in society. Although class distinctions had already hardened before 500 B.C.E., the classes were, in practice, somewhat fluid. If the traditional occupation of a varna was closed to a member, he could often take up another, all theory to the contrary. When Brahmans, Vaishyas, or even Shudras gained political power as rulers (as was evidently the case with the Mauryas, for example), their family gradually became recognized as *Kshatriyas*, the appropriate class for princes.

Although the four classes, or *varnas*, are the theoretical basis for caste relations, much smaller and far more numerous subgroups, or *jatis*, are the units to which our English term caste best refers, if only rather clumsily. (*Caste* comes from *casta*, the word the Portuguese used for *jati*.) These basic and lasting divisions (most representing occupational groups) were already the primary units of social distinction in Gupta times. *Jati* groupings are hereditarily determined and distinguished essentially on principles of purity and pollution, which are expressed in three kinds of regulation: (1) commensality (one may take food only from or with persons of the same or a higher group); (2) endogamy (one may marry only within the group); and (3) trade or craft limitation (one must practice only the trade of one's group).[4]

As much as the caste system has been criticized, it has been the basis of Indian social organization for at least two millennia. It enabled Hindus to accommodate foreign cul-

---

[3]*Vaishnava* or *Vaishnavite* means "related to Vishnu"; similarly, *Shaiva* or *Shaivite* refers to Shiva worship (compare with *Jaina/Jain* for devotees of the way of the *Jinas* such as Mahavira).

[4]A. L. Basham, *The Wonder That Was India* (New York: 1963), pp. 148–149.

The Vishnu Temple at Deogarh, Uttar Prdesh, India. This temple dates from ca. 530 C.E. Unfortunately, its shikara, or spire, has collapsed. Made of massive cut stones, the temple is an image of a sacred or cosmic mountain. Its single interior hall is like a sacred "womb" or cavern in which the deity's image is enshrined. The raised platform on which the temple building itself sits is characteristic of almost all later Indian architecture. [Archive Jean-Louis Nou, Paris]

tural, racial, and religious communities within Indian society by treating them simply as new caste groups. It enabled everyone to tell by dress and other marks how to relate to a given person or group, thus giving great stability and security to the individual and to society. It represented also the logical extension of the doctrine of karma into society—whether as justification, result, or partial cause of the system itself (see Chapter 2).

Religion

Hindu Religious Life   Gupta and later times saw the growth of devotional cults of deities, preeminently Vishnu and Shiva, who were unknown or unimportant in Vedic religion. The temple worship of a particular deity has ever since been a basic form of Hindu piety. After Vishnu (especially in his form as the hero-savior Krishna) and Shiva (originally a fertility god identified with the Vedic deity Rudra), the chief focus of devotion came to be the Goddess in one of her many forms, such as Parvati, Shakti, Durga, or Kali. Vishnu and Shiva, like Parvati, have many forms and names and have always been easily identified with other deities, who are then worshiped as one form of the Supreme Lord or Goddess. Animal or nature deities were presumably part of popular piety from Indus Valley days forward. Indian reverence for all forms of life and stress on *ahimsa*, or "noninjury" to living beings (see Chapter 2), is most vivid in the sacredness of the cow,

which has always been both symbolically and economically a mainstay of life in India.

In the development of Hindu piety and practice, a major strand was the tradition of ardent theism known as *bhakti*, or "loving devotion." *Bhakti* was already evident, at the latest by 200 C.E., in the Bhagavad Gita's treatment of Krishna. Gupta and later times saw the rise, especially in the Tamil-speaking south, of schools of bhakti poetry and worship. The central bhakti strand in Hindu life derives in good part from Tamil and other vernacular poets who first sang the praises of Shiva or Vishnu as Supreme Lord. Here, pre-Aryan religious sensibilities apparently reasserted themselves through the non-Aryan Dravidian peoples of the south. The great theologian of devotional Hinduism, Ramanuja (d. ca. 1137), would later come from this same Dravidian tradition. Of major importance also to devotional piety was the development in this era of the Puranas—epic, mythological, and devotional texts. They are still today the functional sacred scriptures of grassroots Hindu religious life (the Vedic texts remaining the special preserve of the Brahmans).

Whatever god or goddess a Hindu worships, it is usual to pay homage on proper occasions also to other appropriate deities. Most Hindus view one deity as Supreme Lord but see others as manifestations of the Ultimate at lower levels. Hindu polytheism is not "idolatry" but a vivid affirmation of the infinite forms that transcendence takes in this world. The

Devoting Oneself to Krishna

The Bhagavad Gita is the most widely revered and often quoted of all Hindu religious texts. In these verses (Bhagavad Gita 9:22–34), Krishna (Vishnu) tells his friend and disciple, the young warrior Arjuna, of the highest path to salvation, which involves both renouncing one's attachment to the objects ("fruits") of one's actions and devoting oneself in pure faith to the Supreme Lord Krishna.

How is the understanding of older Indian religious practices and ideals (about sacrifice, for example) transformed here? How does the Lord Krishna present himself in relation to other deities? Does the passage present a sharp dichotomy between faith and works? What are the social implications of the message here?

God and the Devotee

Those persons who, meditating on Me without any thought of another god, worship Me—to them, who constantly apply themselves [to that worship], I bring attainment [of what they do not have] and preservation [of what they have attained].

Even the devotees of other divinities, who worship them, being endowed with faith—they, too, O son of Kunti [actually] worship Me alone, though not according to the prescribed rites.

For I am the enjoyer, as also the lord of all sacrifices. But those people do not comprehend Me in My true nature and hence they fall.

Worshipers of the gods go to the gods; worshipers of the manes go to the manes; those who sacrifice to the spirits go to the spirits; and those who worship Me, come to Me.

A leaf, a flower, a fruit, or water, whoever offers to Me with devotion—that same, proffered in devotion by one whose soul is pure, I accept.

Whatever you do, whatever you eat, whatever you offer in sacrifice, whatever you give away, whatever penance you practice—that, O son of Kunti, do you dedicate to Me.

Thus will you be freed from the good or evil fruits which constitute the bondage of actions. With your mind firmly set on the way of renunciation [of fruits], you will, becoming free, come to Me.

Even-minded am I to all beings; none is hateful nor dear to Me. Those, however, who worship Me with devotion, they abide in Me, and I also in them.

Even if a person of extremely vile conduct worships Me being devoted to none else, he is to be reckoned as righteous, for he has engaged himself in action in the right spirit.

Quickly does he become of righteous soul and obtain eternal peace. O son of Kunti, know for certain that My devotee perishes not.

For those, O son of Pritha, who take refuge in Me, even though they be lowly born, women, vaishyas, as also shūdras—even they attain to the highest goal.

How much more, then, pious brāhmans, as also devout royal sages? Having come to this impermanent, blissless world, worship Me.

On Me fix your mind; become My devotee, My worshiper; render homage unto Me. Thus having attached yourself to Me, with Me as your goal, you shall come to Me. . . .

From *Sources of Indian Tradition* by William Theodore de Bary. Copyright ©1988 by Columbia University Press. Reprinted with permission of the publisher.

---

sense of the presence of the divine everywhere is evident at the popular level in the immense importance attached to sacred places in India. It is the land of religious pilgrimage *par excellence*. Sacred mountains, rivers, trees, and groves are all *tirthas*, or "river fords" to the divine.

The intellectual articulation of Hindu polytheism and relativism found its finest expression in post-Gupta formulations of Vedanta ("the end of the Veda"). This is one of six major Hindu systems of thought based on Vedic texts, especially the Upanishads. The major Vedantin thinker was Shankara (d. 820). He stressed a strict "nonduality" of the Ultimate, teaching that Brahman was the only Reality behind the "illusion" *(maya)* of the world of sense experience. Yet he accepted the worship of a lesser deity as appropriate

for those who could not follow his extraordinary norm—the intellectual realization of the formless Absolute beyond all "name and form."

Buddhist Religious Life   The major developments of these centuries were (1) the solidification of the two main strands of Buddhist tradition, the Mahayana and the Theravada, and (2) the spread of Buddhism abroad from its Indian homeland. The Mahayana ("Great Vehicle [of salvation]") arose in the first century B.C.E., although Mahayana ideas had been foreshadowed in some schools of Buddhist thought as early as the fourth century B.C.E. Its proponents differentiated it sharply from the older, more conservative traditions of monk-oriented piety and thought, which they labeled the

The Buddha preaching his first sermon. This seated, high-relief figure of the Buddha, found in the ruins of Sarnath, is one of the finest pieces of Gupta sculpture. Both the hand gesture, which signifies the setting in motion of the eternal dharma, and the etherealized body and head suggest the new concept of the Buddha that emerged with the Mahayana. In Gupta times Sarnath was a thriving monastic center as well as one of the major schools for the best sculpture of the day.
[The Granger Collection]

Hinayana ("Little Vehicle"). Mahayana speculation developed in the style of Upanishadic monism: Buddhas were seen as manifestations of a single principle of "Ultimate" Reality, and Sidhartha Gautama was held to be but one Buddha among many. In the Mahayana, the model of the Buddha's infinite compassion for all beings was paramount. The highest goal was not a *nirvana* of "selfish" extinction but the status of a *bodhisattva*, or "Buddha-to-be." The latter postpones his own nirvana and vows to remain in the round of existence until he has helped all other beings become enlightened.

The *bodhisattva* is capable of offering this aid because of infinite merit gained through his long career of self-sacrifice.

Salvation becomes possible not only through individual effort, but also through devotion to the Buddhas and *bodhisattvas*. At the popular level, this idea translated into devotional cults of transcendent Buddhas and *bodhisattvas* conceived of as cosmic beings. Of such cults, one of the most important was that of the Buddha Amitabha, who personifies infinite compassion. Amitabha presides over a Western Paradise, or Pure Land, to which (through his infinite compassion) all who have faith in him have access. (See Chapter 9 for a discussion of Pure Land Buddhism in Japan.)

The older, more conservative "way of the elders" (Theravada) was never the totally selfish elite tradition of the few that its Mahayana critics claimed it to be. Its focus was always

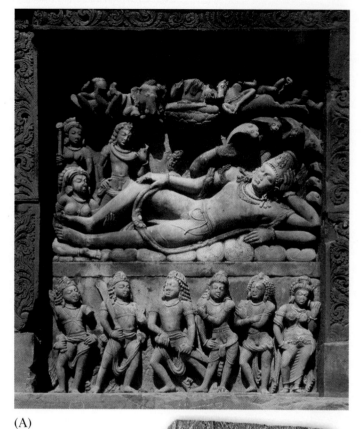

(A)

(B)

(C)

Images of three of India's most important Hindu deities, seventh to thirteenth centuries c.e. Figure A shows Vishnu reclining upon the cosmic waters at the beginning of creation, cushioned by the serpent infinity (Ananta) and dreaming the universe into existence (ca. 8th century; 150 cm high). Figure B shows the goddess Durga standing on a defeated bull-headed demon. Her six arms hold weapons lent to her by Shiva and Vishnu for the battle (ca. 8th century; 150 cm high). Figure C is a magnificent South Indian bronze of Shiva. The fluid, balanced image depicts the so-called "dancing Shiva" engaged in his dance of simultaneous destruction and creation of the universe, an artistic-mythical rendering of the eternal flux of all worldly existence (13th century; bronze; 33.5 X 24.8 cm).

The Bodhisattva Ideal

The following passages from two "perfection of wisdom" texts highlight the Mahayana doctrine of the Bodhisattva, who becomes a divine saviour as well as an example for others. The Mahayana tradition sees all who enter the Buddhist path as bodhisattvas in the making, beings bound to become Buddhas. It sees its bodhisattva ideal as a higher one than that of the older ideal of the enlightened being (arahant), or the pratyeka, or "private," Buddha of the Theravada tradition whose goal is to achieve nirvana for himself.

The ideal of compassion for all beings is held up as the central one in the Mahayana. How is this developed in the first passage? How is it used in the second to polemicize against the ideals of the Theravada? What might be the appeal of the bodhisattva ideal as opposed to the older Buddhist ideal of the self-perfected enlightened one, the Arahant?

---

1. The bodhisattva is endowed with wisdom of a kind whereby he looks on all beings as though victims going to the slaughter. And immense compassion grips him. His divine eye sees ... innumerable beings, and he is filled with great distress at what he sees, for many bear the burden of past deeds which will be punished in purgatory, others will have unfortunate rebirths which will divide them from the Buddha and his teachings, others must soon be slain, others are caught in the net of false doctrine, others cannot find the path [of salvation], while others have gained a favorable rebirth only to lose it again.

So he pours out his love and compassion upon all those beings, and attends to them, thinking, "I shall become the savior of all beings, and set them free from their sufferings."

2. "What do you think, Shāriputra? Do any of the disciples and Private Buddhas ever think, 'After we have gained full enlightenment we will bring innumerable beings ... to complete Nirvāna'?"

"Certainly not, Lord!"

"But," said the Lord, "the bodhisattva (has this resolve). . . . A firefly ... doesn't imagine that its glow will light up all India or shine all over it, and so the disciples and Private Buddhas don't think that they should lead all beings to Nirvāna ... after they have gained full enlightenment. But the disc of the sun, when it has risen, lights up all India and shines all over it. Similarly the bodhisattva, ... when he has gained full enlightenment, brings countless beings to Nirvāna."

From *Sources of Indian Tradition* by William Theodore de Bary. Copyright © 1988 by Columbia University Press. Reprinted with permission of the publisher.

---

the monastic community, but lay devotees were needed to support this community; moreover, their service and gifts to the monks were a major source of merit for the laity. The emphasis on gaining merit for a better rebirth through high standards of conduct was strong for monks and laity alike. Popular lay devotion to the Buddha and pilgrimage to his relics at various *stupas* also became prominent in Theravada practice. Conversely, the Mahayana also held up monastic life as the ideal, but some of its greatest attractions were its strong devotionalism and virtually polytheistic delight in divine Buddhas and *bodhisattvas* to whom the average person could pray for mercy, help, and rebirth in paradise. The basis of Theravada piety and practice was the scriptural collection of the traditional teachings ascribed to the Buddha, as reported by his disciples. Theravadins rejected the Mahayana claim that later texts (e.g., the Lotus Sutra) contained the highest teachings of the Buddha.

The Theravada was the form of Buddhism that India gave to Ceylon, Burma, and parts of Southeast Asia. The Mahayana was the dominant form carried into Central Asia and China, where it became the major form of religious practice. Tantric Buddhism, an esoteric Mahayana tradition heavily influenced by Hindu Tantric speculation and ritual, entered Tibet from North India in the seventh century and became the dominant tradition there. From China, Mahayana teachings spread in the fifth to eighth centuries to fertile new fields in Korea and Japan.

IN WORLD PERSPECTIVE

Pre-Islamic Iran and India

From a Western perspective, the center of the world in the early centuries of the Christian era is typically seen as having been the Roman-Byzantine world of late antiquity in the Mediterranean basin. Such a view fails to recognize that in global perspective the loci of major political power, cultural creativity, and religious vitality throughout most of the early centuries C.E. included, alongside the Roman world, Iran, India, and China.

Even in the Roman "West," Africa and southwestern Asia were prominent both politically and culturally. Roman imperial strength rapidly shifted east to Byzantium; Alexandria was the center of Hellenism for several centuries; and the major Christian doctrinal councils were held in Asia and Africa. Our perspective necessarily changes when we give proper recognition to historical realities still farther east before the seventh-century rise of Islam: the Sasanid imperial culture of Iran, the Zoroastrian revival, the Manichaean movement, the compilation of the Babylonian and Palestinian Tamuds, the completion of the *Mahabharata* and *Ramayana*, Gupta imperial power, Gupta art and literature, Indian religious thought, and the spread of the Mahayana across Central Asia to China and thence to Japan.

Portions of Asia and Africa were thus the settings for impressive, often momentous developments. Consequently, simplistic notions of a progressive "rise of the West" from classical antiquity to modern times do not hold for the first millennium C.E., especially when we take into account the coming of Islam in its last third. To any impartial observer, the Western world in these centuries did not hold much promise as a future global center of political or cultural life. Instead, progressiveness and culture seemed best embodied either in

Sasanid and Gupta culture in southwest and south Asia, or in China under the Han, Sui, and T'ang dynasties and Japan in Nara and Heian times.

A revised perspective would thus identify important centers of cultural, religious, and political traditions around the globe, both in the Asian kingdoms and also in the Mediterranean empire of Byzantium and in Aksumite Ethiopia. Hindu tradition and Indian culture were undergoing important developments, while Buddhism was waning in its Indian homeland even as it found new and rich fields for conversion in Central Asia, China, and Japan, as well as Southeast Asia. Zoroastrian Iran appeared well on its way into a second millennium of imperial splendor under the Sasanids.

Yet with the imminent rise of the last major world religious and cultural tradition, Islam, Iran would soon face cataclysmic changes—changes that would later overtake much of India and other parts of South Asia. Who could have suspected in the time of Chosroes Anoshirvan how radically Persian culture would be shaken, recast, and given new life in Islamic forms within three or four centuries?

Review Questions

1. What are the key elements of Manichaean religion? How might it be said to be an offspring of Christian and Zoroastrian traditions?

2. How did the Sasanid empire develop after the fall of the Parthians? What were the principal economic bases of the Sasanid state?

3. What were the major religious issues in the Sasanid empire? What role did Zoroastrian "orthodoxy" play in Sasanid affairs? What changes did Zoroastrianism undergo? Who were the main opponents of Zoroastrian tradition?

4. What might have been the importance of the Silk Route in bringing new religious ideas to Central Asia in these centuries?

5. In what ways can the high Gupta period (ca. 320–450) be considered a "golden age"? What was the extent of the empire in these years? Why did it collapse? Where did the locus of Indian culture move after the fifth century and why?

6. Consider Persia and India in the seventh century, just before the coming of Arab invaders. What factors might have made the subsequent conquests in both areas possible for the new forces from the west?

7. What major affinities do you see between the classical Buddhist and Hindu traditions that crystallized in the first half of the first millennium C.E.? What major differences? Discuss some of the main tenets and ideas of each.

Suggested Readings

Iran

M. BOYCE, *Zoroastrians: Their Religious Beliefs and Practices* (1979). A detailed survey by the current authority on Zoroastrian religious history. See Chapters 7–9.

M. BOYCE, ED. AND TRANS., *Textual Sources for the Study of Zoroastrianism* (1984). A valuable anthology with an important introduction that includes Boyce's arguments for a revision of the dates of Zoroaster's life (to between 1400 and 1200 B.C.E.).

R. N. FRYE, *The Heritage of Persia* (1963). Still one of the best surveys. Chapter 6 deals with the Sasanid era.

R. GHIRSHMAN, *Iran* (1954 [orig. ed. 1951]). An introductory survey of similar extent to Frye, but with differing material also.

R. GHIRSHMAN, *Persian Art: The Parthian and Sasanid Dynasties* (1962). Superb photographs, and a very helpful glossary of places and names. The text is minimal.

Geo Widengran, *Mani and Manichaeism* (1965). Still the standard introduction to Mani's life and the later spread and development of Manichaeism.

India

A. L. Basham, *The Wonder That Was India* (1963). The best survey of classical Indian religion, society, literature, art, and politics.

W. T. de Bary et al., comp. *Sources of Indian Tradition*, 2nd ed. (1958). Vol. I, *From the Beginning to 1800*, ed. and rev. by Ainslie T. Embree (1988). Excellent selections from a wide variety of Indian texts, with good introductions to the text selections.

S. Dutt, *Buddhist Monks and Monasteries of India* (1962). The standard work. See especially Chapters 3 ("Bhakti") and 4 ("Monasteries Under the Gupta Kings").

D. G. Mandelbaum, *Society in India* (1972). 2 vols. The first two chapters in Volume I of this study of caste, family, and village relations are a good introduction to the caste system.

B. Rowland, *The Art and Architecture of India: Buddhist/Hindu/Jain*, 3rd rev. ed. (1970). See the excellent chapters on Sungan, Andhran, and other early Buddhist art (6–8, 14), the Gupta period (15), and the Hindu Renaissance (17–19).

V. A. Smith, *The Oxford History of India*, 4th rev. ed. (1981). See especially pages 164–229 (the Gupta period and following era to the Muslim invasions).

R. Thapar, *A History of India, Part I* (1966), pp. 109–193. Three chapters covering the rise of mercantilism, the Gupta "classical pattern," and the southern dynasties to ca. C.E. 900.

P. Younger, *Introduction to Indian Religious Thought* (1972). A sensitive attempt to delineate classical concerns of Indian religious thought and culture.

11 THE FORMATION OF ISLAMIC CIVILIZATION (622–945)

The dome over the bay in front of the mihrab in the Great Mosque at Cordoba, Spain. The mihrab marks the direction of Mecca.

[Werner Forman Archive/Art Resource, N.Y.]

CHAPTER TOPICS

◆ Origins and Early Development

◆ Early Islamic Conquests

◆ The New Islamic Order

◆ The High Caliphate

◆ The "Classical" Islamic Culture

In World Perspective Formation of Islamic Civilization

Islamic civilization has been the last great world civilization to appear to date, if one excepts the post-Enlightenment modern West. On the one hand, its rise is the story of the creation and elaboration of distinctive Islamic religious, social, and political institutions within an initially Arab-dominated empire. On the other, it is the story of how, in older cultural environments, Islamic ideas and institutions evolved from their Arabian beginnings into a cosmopolitan array of cultures. Each was a new creation of a particular place and particular circumstances, yet each was part of a larger, international Islamic civilization.

The basic ideas and ideals of the Islamic worldview derived from a single, prophetic-revelatory event, Muhammad's proclamation of the Qur'an.[1] This event galvanized the Arabs into a new kind of unity—that of the community of Muslims, or "submitters" to God. This community subsequently spread far beyond Arabia, and Persians, Indians, and others raised it to new

heights. If Arab military prowess and cultural pride joined with a new religious orientation to effect one of the most permanent revolutions in history, it was the peoples of the older cultural heartlands who sustained it and built a new civilization upon it. Their acceptance of a new vision of society (and also of reality) as more compelling than any older vision—Jewish, Greek, Iranian, Christian, Buddhist—allowed an Islamic civilization to come into being.

Origins and Early Development

The Setting

By 600 C.E., the dominant Eurasian political powers, Christian Byzantium and Zoroastrian, Sasanid Iran, or Persia, had confronted one another for over four centuries. This rivalry did not, however, continue much longer. In the wake of one final, mutually exhausting conflict (608–627), a new Arab power broke in from the southern deserts to humble the one and destroy the other.

Pre-Islamic Arabia was not just a land of desert camel nomads. In the Fertile Crescent, Byzantium and Iran had managed to keep the nomads of the Syrian and northern Arabian steppe at bay by enlisting small Arab client kingdoms on the edge of the desert as

buffer states. One of the biggest of these was Christian in faith. There had long been settled Arab kingdoms in the agriculturally rich highlands of southern Arabia, which had direct access to the international trade that moved by land and sea along its coasts (see Chapter 4). Some of these kingdoms, including a Jewish one in the sixth century, had been independent; others had been under Persian or Abyssinian control. In the western Arabian highland of the Hijaz, astride its major trade route, the town of Mecca was a center of the caravan trade. It was also a pilgrimage center because of its famous sanctuary, the Ka'ba (or Kaaba), where many pagan Arab tribes had gods enshrined. The settled Arabs of Mecca ran a merchant republic in which older tribal values were breaking down under the strains of urban and commercial life. But neither the Meccans nor other settled Arabs were wholly cut off from the nomads, who lived on herding and sporadic raids on settlements and caravans.

The Arabic language, a Semitic tongue of the Afro-Asiatic family (see Chapter 4), defined and linked the Arab peoples, however divided they were by religion, blood feuds, rivalry, and conflict. From the Yemen north to Syria-Palestine and the Euphrates, the major element of culture that the Arabs shared was their highly developed poetic idiom. Traditionally, every tribe had a poet to exhort its warriors and insult its enemies before battle. Poetry contests were also held, often in conjunction

---

[1]The common English transliteration of this Arabic word, *Koran*, is today being replaced by the more accurate *Qur'an*; similarly, *Muhammad* is preferable to *Mohammed*, *Muslim* to *Moslem*, *amir* to *emir*, and *ulama* to *ulema*.

The Ka'ba in Mecca. The Ka'ba is viewed in Muslim tradition as the site of the first "house of God" built by Abraham and his son Ishmael at God's command. It is held to have fallen later into idolatrous use until Muhammad's victory over the Meccans and his cleansing of the holy cubical structure (*Ka'ba* means "cube"). The Ka'ba is the geographical point toward which all Muslims face when performing ritual prayer. It and the plain of Arafat outside Mecca are the two foci of the pilgrimage of Hajj that each Muslim aspires to make at least once in a lifetime. [Mehmet Biber/Photo Researchers, Inc.]

with the annual trade fairs that brought diverse tribes together under a general truce.

The popular notion of Islam as a "religion of the desert" is largely untrue. Islam began in a commercial center and first flourished in an agricultural oasis. Its first converts were settled Meccan townsfolk and date farmers of Yathrib (Medina). Before becoming Muslims, most of these Arabs were pagans, but some were Jews or Christians, or influenced by Jews or Christians. Caravans passed north and south through Mecca, and no merchant involved in this traffic, as Muhammad himself was, could have been ignorant of diverse cultures. Early Muslim leaders used the Arabs as warriors and looked to Arab culture for roots long after the locus of Islamic power had left Arabia. But the empire and civilization they built were centered in the heartlands of Eurasian urban culture and based on settled communal existence rather than desert tribal anarchy.

Muhammad and the Qur'an

Muhammad (ca. 570–632) was raised an orphan in one of the less well-to-do commercial families of the old Meccan tribe of Quraysh. Later, in the midst of a successful business career made possible by his marriage to Khadija (d. ca. 619), a wealthy Meccan widow and entrepreneur, he grew troubled by the idolatry, worldliness, and lack of social conscience around him. These traits would have equally offended sensitive Jewish or Christian morality, about which he certainly

knew something. Yet Muhammad did not find his answers in these traditions; they remained somehow foreign to the majority of Arabs, even though some Arab tribes were Jewish or Christian.

Muhammad's discontent with the moral status quo and older religious solutions paved the way for a sudden religious experience that changed his life when he was about forty years old. He felt himself called by the one true God to "rise and warn" his fellow Arabs about their frivolous disregard for morality and the worship due their creator. On repeated occasions revelation came to him through a figure who was gradually identified as God's messenger angel, Gabriel. It took the form of a "reciting" *(qur'an)* of God's word—now rendered in "clear Arabic" for the Arabs, just as it had been given to previous prophets in Hebrew or other languages for their peoples.

The message of the Qur'an was clear: The Prophet is to warn his people against worship of false gods and all immorality, especially injustice to the unfortunate or weak—the poor, orphans, widows, and women in general. At the end of time, on judgment day, every person will be bodily resurrected to face eternal punishment in hellfire or eternal joy in paradise, according to how he or she has lived. The way to paradise lies in gratitude to God for the bounties of creation, His prophetic and revelatory guidance, and His readiness to forgive the penitent. Social justice and obedient worship of the one Lord are required of every person. Each is to recognize his or her creatureliness and God's transcen-

Imru l-Qais, the Wandering Poet-Hero

Having little written or visual artistic tradition, the ancient Arabs focused on the perfection of the oral word. The great early Arab poets reinforced the cultural ideals that sprang from the life of the camel nomads of the desert: generosity and hospitality to a fault, family pride and honor, fearless audacity in love and battle, and delight in the animals and natural beauty of the marginal desert world. In this excerpt from a famous poem of Imru l-Qais (d. ca. 540?), we see a standard beginning of the Arabic lyric ode, or qasida: The sight of an abandoned camp recalls a past event to the poet. There follow boastful memories of amorous adventure and a brief segment from late in the poem about the poet's hardship (which began after his father, ruler of a northern desert kingdom, banished him because he refused to give up poetry—an occupation his father deemed improper for a prince).

What does this poem suggest were some of the sensibilities and values of the desert nomadic life? What do you see as the aesthetic strengths of the passages cited?

Here halt, and weep, for one long-remembered love, for an old
Camp at the edge of the sands that stretch from the
Brakes to Floodhead,
From Clearward to the Heights. The marks are not gone yet,
For all that's blown and blown back over them, northward, southward.
Look at the white-deer's droppings scattered in the old yards
And penfolds of the place, like black pepperseeds. . . .

I suffered so for love, so fast the tears ran down
Over my breast, the sword-belt there was soaked with weeping.
And yet-the happy days I had of them, of women. . . .

One day on a sandhill back she would not do my will,
And swore an oath, and swore she meant to keep her oath. . . .

That night I passed the wardens who watched their tents, the men
Who would have welcomed me, for the glory of murdering me,
In an hour when Pleiades glittered in the night-heaven
Like a jewelled girdle, gem and pearl and gem;
In such an hour I came; she was all doffed for sleep
But for a shift; close by the screen of the tent she lay.
God's oath on me! she whispered, but thou hast no excuse!
And now I know that thou wilt be wild for ever.
Forth we went together; I led; she trailed behind us
A robe's embroidered hem, that tracks might tell no tales.
When we were past the fenced folkyards, then we made straight
For the heart of the waste, the waves and tumbled hillocks of sand.
I pulled her head to mine by the lovelocks, and she pressed
Against me, slender, but soft even at the ankle.
Thin-waisted she was, and white, sweetly moulded about the belly,
And the skin above her breasts shone like a polished mirror,
Or a pearl of the first water, whiteness a little gilded,
Fed of a pure pool unstirred by the feet of men. . . .

And taking a water-skin from the house, I would strap it close
Over my shoulder—how often!—and meek to such a saddle
Crossing some hollow place like the flats of Starverib Waste
Have I heard the wolf, like a spendthrift who's gambled his darlings away,
Howl! He would howl. I would answer: It's a poor trade we follow
For profit, if thou hast kept as little as I have kept;
Whatever we get, thou and I, we bolt it; and it's gone.
A man will never be fat who thrives as we two thrive.

From *Muhammad's People*, Eric Schroeder, trans., (Portland, ME: Bond Wheelwright, 1955), pp. 3–5.

dence. The proper response is "submission" (*islam*) to God's will, becoming *muslim* ("submissive" or "surrendering") in one's worship and morality. All of creation praises and serves God by nature except humans, who can choose to obey or to reject Him.

In this Qur'anic message, the ethical monotheism of Judaic and Christian tradition (probably reinforced by Zoroastrian and Manichaean ideas) reached its logical conclusion in a radically theocentric vision; it demanded absolute obedience to the one Lord of the Universe. The Qur'anic revelations explicitly state

The Qur'an, or "Recitation," of God's Word

The Qur'an has many themes, from moral admonition, social justice, eternal punishment for the ungodly, and exemplary stories of past peoples and their prophets, to God's majesty and uniqueness, His bountiful natural world and compassion for humankind, and the joys of paradise.

Can you identify at least four major Qur'anic themes in the selections below? To what end are the bounties of creation cited? What is the image of God conveyed in these selections? What can you infer about the Qur'anic conception of prophethood? Of the Judgment Day?

The revelation of the Book is from God who is mighty and wise. There are signs for men of faith, in the heavens and in the earth, in your being created and in God's scattered throng of creatures—signs for people with a grasp of truth.

There are signs, too—for those with a mind to understand—in the alternation of night and day, and in the gracious rain God sends from heaven to renew the face of the parched earth, and in the veering of the winds.

These are the signs of God which truly We recite to you. Having God and His signs, in what else after that will you believe as a message?

—Sura 45:1–6

Were you set to count up the mercies of God you would not be able to number them. God is truly forgiving and merciful.

—Sura 16:18

Such is God your Lord. There is no god but He, creator of all things. Then worship Him who is guardian over all there is. No human perception comprehends Him, while He comprehends all perception. He is beyond all conceiving, the One who is infinitely aware.

—Sura 6:102–103

To God belong the east and the west, and wheresoever you turn there is the face of God. Truly God is all-pervading, all-knowing.

—Sura 2:115

You people of the Book, why are you so argumentative about Abraham, seeing that the Torah and the Gospel were only sent down after his time? Will you not use your reason? You are people much given to disputing about things within your comprehension: why insist on disputing about things of which you have no knowledge? Knowledge belongs to God and you lack it!

Abraham was not a Jew, nor was he a Christian. He was a man of pure worship (a hanif) and a Muslim: he was not one of those pagan idolaters. . . .

–Sura 3.65–67

Yet you [people] deny the reality of the judgement. There are guardians keeping watch over you, noble beings keeping record, who know your every deed. The righteous will dwell in bliss. The evil-doers will be in *Jahīm*, in the burning on judgement Day, and there will be no absconding for them.

What can make you realize the Day of judgement as it is? . . . the Day when there is no soul that can avail another soul. For the authority on that Day is God's alone.

–Sura 82.1–5, 9, 19

Excerpt from *Readings in the Qur'an* by Kenneth Cragg. Copyright © 1988 by Kenneth Cragg. Reprinted by permission of HarperCollins, Inc.

---

that Muhammad is only the last in a long line of prophets chosen to bring God's word: Noah, Abraham, Moses, Jesus, and nonbiblical Arabian figures like Salih had been sent before on similar missions. Because the communities of these earlier prophets had strayed from their scriptures' teachings or altered them, Muhammad was given one final iteration of God's message. Jews and Christians, like pagans, were summoned to respond to the moral imperatives of the Qur'an.

The Prophet's preaching fell largely on deaf ears in the first years after his calling. However, a few did follow the lead of his wife, Khadija, in recognizing him as a divinely chosen reformer of individual and communal life. Some prominent Meccans joined him, but the merchant aristocracy as a whole resisted. His preaching against their traditional gods and goddesses threatened both their ancestral ways and also the Meccan pilgrimage shrine and the lucrative trade it attracted. The Meccans began to persecute Muhammad's followers. After the deaths of Khadija and Muhammad's uncle and protector, Abu Talib, the situation worsened, and the Prophet even had to send a small band of Muslims to seek temporary refuge in Abyssinia. Then, as a result of his growing reputation as a moral and holy man, Muhammad was called to Yathrib (an agricultural oasis about 240 miles north of Mecca) as a neutral arbitrator among its five quarrelsome tribes, three of which were Jewish. Having sent his Meccan followers ahead, Muhammad fled Mecca in July 622 for Yathrib, afterward to be known as Medina (al-Madina, "the City [of the Prophet]"). Some dozen years later, this "emigration," or Hegira, became

Page from an eighth- or ninth-century Qur'an in Kufic script (23.8 x 35.5 cm). In part because of the Muslim aversion to images, calligraphy early became a major Islamic art form. The Arabic script developed primarily to render the Qur'anic text as exactly as possible, and the calligraphic art developed along with it. The horizontally elongated Kufic script was the earliest and dominated Qur'anic calligraphy for three centuries. [Courtesy of Freer Gallery of Art, Smithsonian Institution Washington, D.C.]

the starting point for the Islamic calendar, the event marking the creation of a distinctive Islamic community, or *Umma*.[2]

Muhammad quickly cemented ties between the Meccan emigrants and the Medinans, many of whom became converts. Raids on his Meccan enemies' caravans established his leadership. They reflect the economic dimension of the Medinan-Meccan struggle. The Arab Jews of Medina largely rejected his religious message and authority. They even made contact with his Meccan enemies, moving Muhammad to turn on them, kill or enslave some, banish others, and take their lands. Many of the continuing revelations of the Qur'an from this period pertain to communal order or to the Jews and Christians who rejected Islam.

The basic Muslim norms took shape in Medina: allegiance to the *Umma;* honesty in public and personal affairs; modesty in personal habits; abstention from alcohol and pork; fair division of inheritances; improved treatment of women, especially as to property and other rights in marriage; careful regulation of marriage and divorce; ritual ablution before any act of worship, be it Qur'an reciting or prayer; three (later five) daily rites of worship, facing the Meccan shrine of the Ka'ba; payment of a kind of tithe to support less fortunate Muslims; daytime fasting for one month each year; and, eventually, pilgrimage to Mecca (*Hajj*) at least once in a lifetime, if one is able.

[2]The twelve-month Muslim lunar year is shorter than the Christian solar year by about eleven days, giving a difference of about three years per century. Muslim dates are reckoned from the month in 622 in which Muhammad began his Hegira (Arabic: *Hijra*). Thus Muslims celebrated the start of their lunar year 1401 in November 1980 (1979–1980 C.E. = A.H. [Anno Hegirae] 1400), whereas it was only 1,358 solar years from 622 to 1980.

Acceptance of Islamic political authority brought a kind of tolerance. A Jewish oasis yielded to Muhammad's authority and was allowed, unlike the resistant Medinan Jews, to keep its lands, practice its faith, and receive protection in return for the payment of a head tax. This practice was followed ever after for Jews, Christians, and other "people of Scripture" who accepted Islamic rule. After long conflict, the Meccans surrendered to Muhammad, and his generosity in accepting them into the *Umma* set the pattern for the later Islamic conquests. Following an age-old practice, Muhammad cemented many of his alliances with marriage (although as long as Khadija was alive, he did not take a second wife). In the last years of the Prophet's life, the once tiny band of Muslims became the heart of a pan-Arabian tribal confederation, bound together by personal allegiance to Muhammad, submission (*islam*) to God, and membership in the *Umma* of "submitters."

Early Islamic Conquests

In 632 Muhammad died, leaving neither a son nor a designated successor. The new *Umma* faced its first major crisis. A political struggle between Meccan and Medinan factions ended in a pledge of allegiance to Abu Bakr, the most senior of the early Meccan converts. Following old Arabian patterns, many tribes renounced their allegiance to the Prophet at his death. Nevertheless, Abu Bakr's rule (632–634) as Muhammad's successor, or "caliph" (Arabic: *khalifa*), reestablished Medinan hegemony and at least nominal religious conformity for all Arabia. The Arabs were forced to recognize in the

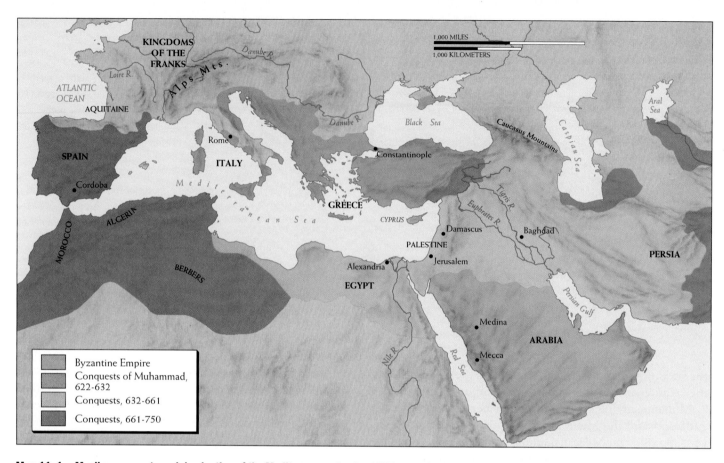

Map 11-1   Muslim conquests and domination of the Mediterranean to about 750 C.E.   The rapid spread of Islam (both religion and political-military power) is shown here. Within 125 years of Muhammad's rise Muslims came to dominate Spain and all areas south and east of the Mediterranean.

Umma a new kind of supratribal community that demanded more than allegiance to a particular leader.

Course of Conquest

Under the next two caliphs, Umar (634–644) and Uthman (644–656), Arab armies burst out of the peninsula, intent on more than traditional bedouin booty raids. In one of history's most astonishing sequences of military operations, by 643 they had conquered the Byzantine and Sasanid territories of the Fertile Crescent, Egypt, and most of Iran. For the first time in centuries the lands from Egypt to Iran came under one rule. Finally, Arab armies swept west over the Byzantine-controlled Libyan coast and, in the east, pushed to the Oxus, defeating the last Sasanid ruler by 651.

An interlude of civil war followed during the contested caliphate of Ali (656–661). Then the fifth caliph, Mu'awiya (661–680), directed further expansion and consolidated the new empire. In the Mediterranean, an Islamic fleet conquered Cyprus, plundered Sicily and Rhodes, and crippled Byzantine sea power. By 680 control of greater Iran was so-

lidified by permanent Arab garrisoning of Khorasan, much of Anatolia was raided, Constantinople was besieged (but not taken), and Armenia was under Islamic rule.

Succeeding decades saw the eastern Berbers of Libyan North Africa defeated and converted to Islam in substantial numbers, if often superficially or nominally. With their help, "the West" (*al-Maghrib*, modern Morocco and Algeria), fell quickly. In 711 raids into Spain began (the name of the Berber Muslim leader of the first invaders, Tariq, lives on in *Gibraltar*, a corruption of *Jabal Tariq*, "Mount Tariq"). By 716 the disunited Spanish Visigoth kingdoms had fallen, and much of Iberia was under Islamic control. Pushing north into France, the Arabs were finally checked by a defeat at the hands of Charles Martel south of Tours (732). At the opposite end of the empire, buoyed by large-scale Arab immigration, Islamic forces consolidated their holdings as far as the Oxus River basin. In 710 Arab armies reached the Indus region. Muslim leaders now ruled the former Sasanid Empire and beyond. The Byzantine realm was reduced by half and Islamic power was supreme from the Atlantic to central Asia (see Map 11–1).

Factors of Success

A combination of factors underlay this rapid expansion. The basic one was the weakened military and economic condition of the Byzantines and Sasanids—the result of their chronic warfare with one another over many decades. Also basic was the capacity of the new Islamic vision of society and life to unite the Arabs and to attract others as well. Its corollary was the commitment among the Islamic leadership to extend "the abode of submission" (*Dar al-Islam*) abroad. However, too much has been made of Muslim zeal for martyrdom. Assurance of paradise for those engaged in *jihad,* or "struggle (in the path of God)," is less likely to have motivated the average Arab tribesman—who, at least at the beginning, was usually only nominally a Muslim—as much as promise of the booty of war. The marginal life in the peninsula was such that the hope of greater prosperity must have been compelling.

Still, religious zeal cannot be wholly discounted, especially as time went on. The early policy of sending Qur'an reciters among the Arab armies to teach essentials of Muslim faith and practice had its effects. Another major factor was certainly the leadership of the first caliphs and field generals. This combined with Byzantine and Iranian economic and military exhaustion to give Arab armies a distinct advantage. Also important was the readiness of many subject populations to accept, even to welcome, Islamic rule as a relief from Byzantine or Persian oppression. Crucial here was the Muslim willingness to allow Christian, Jewish, and even Zoroastrian groups to continue as minorities (with their own legal systems and no military obligations) under protection of Islamic rule. In return, they had to recognize Islamic political authority, pay a non-Muslim head tax (*jizya*), and refrain from proselytizing or interfering with Muslim religious practice. (Ironically, as time went on, the economic and social realities of the head tax and other strictures on non-Muslims encouraged many Christians and Jews to convert.)

Finally, what gave the conquests overall permanence, besides the vitality of the new faith, were the astute policies of the early leaders: relatively little bloodshed, destruction, or disruption in conquest; adoption of existing administrative systems (and personnel) with minimal changes; adjustment of unequal taxation; appointment of capable governors; and strategic siting of new garrison towns like Basra, Kufa, and Fustat (later Cairo).

The New Islamic Order

Although they were quick to adopt and adapt existing traditions in the lands they conquered, the Muslims brought with them a new worldview that demanded a new political, social, and cultural reality, however long it might take to effect it. Beyond military and administrative problems loomed the ultimately more important question of the nature of Islamic society. Under the Prophet the new community of the *Umma*

The Dome of the Rock, in Jerusalem. An early example of Islamic architecture (but not a mosque), it dates from the seventh century and the first wave of Arab expansion. It is built on the rock from which Muslims believe Muhammad ascended into heaven and on which Jews believe Abraham prepared to sacrifice Isaac. The Dome of the Rock has special symbolic significance for Moslems because the site is associated with life and story of the prophet. For a few years of Muhammad's time in Madina, Muslims faced Jerusalem when they prayed, before a new Qur'anic revelation changed the direction to Mecca. [Scala/Art Resource, N.Y.]

Early Islamic coins. The development of early Islamic coinage reflects the evolution of Muslim self-awareness. The earliest Arabic kingdom had no coinage of its own. The first Islamic caliphs and governors took over the Byzantine and Sasanid coinage (Figure A: a Sasanid silver dirham with the head of the emperor), adding brief Arabic inscriptions (Figure B), and then slightly altering previous imagery on the coins (Figure C: "standing caliph" with sword and Arab headdress rather than Byzantine crown). It was only under Abd al-Malik, caliph from 685 to 705, that reform of the coinage led to the abandonment of all imagery depicting the human form in favor of Arabic inscriptions proclaiming the basic Muslim faith (Figure D: The inscription reads "There is no god but God, One, without partner"). [American Numismatic Society of New York]

(A)

(B)

(C)

(D)

had replaced, at least in theory and basic organization, the tribal, blood-based sociopolitical order in Arabia. Yet once the Arabs (most of whom became Muslims) had to rule non-Arabs and non-Muslims, new problems tested the ideal of an Islamic polity. Chief among these were leadership and membership qualifications, social order, and religious and cultural identity.

The Caliphate

Allegiance to Muhammad had rested on his authority as a divine spokesperson and gifted leader. His first successors were chosen much as were Arab *shaykhs* ("sheiks"), or tribal chieftains: by agreement of the leaders, or elders, of the new religious "tribe" of Muslims, on the basis of superior personal qualities. Added to these qualities was now the precedence in faith conferred by piety and association with the Prophet. Their titles were "successor" (*khalifa*, or caliph), "leader" (*imam*—literally, the one who stands in front to lead the ritual prayer), and "commander (*amir*) of the faithful." These names underscored religious and political authority, both of which most Muslims were willing to recognize in the caliphs

Abu Bakr and Umar, and potentially in Uthman and Ali. Unfortunately, by the time of Uthman and Ali, various dissensions led to internal strife, then civil war. Yet the first four caliphs had all been close to Muhammad, and this closeness gave their reigns a nostalgic aura of pristine purity, especially as the later caliphal institution was based largely on sheer power legitimized by hereditary succession.

The nature of Islamic leadership became an issue with the first civil war (656–661) and the recognition of Mu'awiya, a kinsman of Uthman, as caliph. He founded the first dynastic caliphate, that of his Meccan clan of Umayya (661–750). Umayyad descendants held power until they were ousted in 750 by the Abbasid clan, which based its legitimacy on descent from Abbas, an uncle of the Prophet. The Umayyads had the prestige of the office held by the first four, "rightly guided" caliphs. But they were also judged by many to be worldly kings in comparison to the first four, who were seen as true Muslim successors to Muhammad.

The Abbasids won the caliphate by open rebellion in 750, aided by exploitation of pious dissatisfaction with Umayyad worldliness, non-Arab Muslim resentment of Arab preference (primarily in Iran), and ongoing dissension among Arab tribal factions in the garrison towns. For all their stress on the Muslim character of their caliphate, they were scarcely less worldly and continued the hereditary rule begun by the Umayyads. This they did well enough to retain control of most of the far-flung Islamic territories until 945. Thereafter, although their line continued until 1258, the caliphate was primarily a titular office representing an Islamic unity that existed politically in name only.

The *Ulama*

Although the caliph could exert his power, as the Abbasids did occasionally, to influence religious matters, he was never "emperor and pope combined," as Western writers have claimed. Religious leadership in the *Umma* devolved instead on another group. The functional successors of the Prophet in society at large were those Muslims recognized for piety and learning and sought as informal or even formal (as with state-appointed judges) authorities. Initially, they were the "Companions" (male and female) of Muhammad with greatest stature in the old Medinan *Umma*—including the first four caliphs. This generation was replaced by those younger followers most concerned with preserving, interpreting, and applying the Qur'an, and with maintaining the norms of the Prophet's original *Umma*. Because the Qur'an contained few actual legal prescriptions, they had to draw on precedents from Meccan and Medinan practice, as well as on oral traditions from and about the Prophet and Companions. They also had to develop and standardize grammatical rules for a common Arabic language based on the Qur'an and pre-Islamic poetry. Furthermore, they had to improve the phonetic, cursive Arabic script, a task done so well that the script was gradually applied as the standard written medium for languages wherever Islamic religion and culture became dominant: among Iranians, Turks, Indians, Indonesians, Malays, East Africans, and others. Along with these and other religious, intellectual, and cultural achievements, they developed an enduring pattern of education based on study under those persons highest in the unbroken temporal chain of trustworthy Muslims linking the current age with that of the earliest *Umma*.

As an unofficial but generally recognized infrastructure in Islamic society, these scholars came to be known as *ulama* ("persons of right knowledge," the Anglicized Arabic plural of *'alim*). Some of the most pious *ulama* refused to be judges for the Umayyads. However, their personal legal opinions and collective discussions of issues, from theological doctrine to criminal punishments, established a basis for religious and social order. By the ninth century they had largely defined the understanding of the divine Law, or *Shari'a*, that Muslims ever after have held to be definitive for legal, social, commercial, political, ritual, and moral concerns. This understanding and the methods by which it was derived together form the Muslim science of jurisprudence, the core discipline of Islamic learning.

The centers of *ulama* activity were Medina, Mecca, and especially Iraq (primarily Basra and Kufa, later Baghdad), then Khorasan, Syria, North Africa, Spain, and Egypt. In Umayyad times, the *ulama* had already become the guardians of the Muslim conscience, often criticizing caliphal rule when it strayed too far from Muslim norms. In time they became a new elite, one eventually identified with the upper class of each regional society under Islamic rule. Caliphs and their governors regularly sought their advice, but often only for moral or legal (the two are, in Muslim view, the same) sanction of a contemplated (or accomplished) action. Some *ulama* gave dubious sanctions and compromised themselves. Yet incorruptible *ulama* were seldom persecuted for their opinions (except when they supported sectarian rebellions), mostly because of their status and influence among rank-and-file Muslims.

Thus, without building a formal clergy, Muslims developed a workable moral-legal system based on a formally trained if informally organized scholarly elite and a tradition of concern with religious ideals in matters of public affairs and social order. If the caliphs and their deputies were seldom paragons of piety and were often ruthless, they had at least to act with some circumspection and give compensating support for pious standards in public. Thus the *ulama* shared the de facto leadership in Muslim societies with the rulers, even if unequally—a pattern that has endured in Islamic states.

The *Umma*

A prime strength of the Qur'anic message was its universalism. Although Muhammad may have conceived of his community first as an Arab one, the logical extension of the Qur'anic preaching was the acceptance into the *Umma* of anyone, of any race or ethnicity, who would submit to God and follow Muslim precepts. By the time of the first conquests, the new state was already so rooted in Muslim ideals that non-Arab converts had to be accepted, even if it meant loss of tax revenue. The social and political status of new converts was, however, clearly second to that of Arabs. Umar had organized the army register, or *diwan*, according to tribal precedence in conversion to, or (in the unique case of Christian Arab tribes) fighting for, Islam. The *diwan* served as the basis for distribution and taxation of the new wealth, which perpetuated Arab precedence. The new garrisons, which rapidly became urban centers of Islamic culture, kept the Arabs enough apart that they were not simply absorbed into the cultural patterns or traditions of the new lands. The dominance of the Arabic language was ensured by the centrality of the Qur'an in Muslim life and the notion of its perfect Arabic

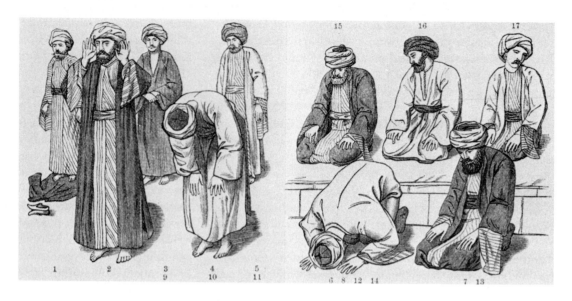

The ritual worship, or prayer. These illustrations show the sequence of movement prescribed for the ritual prayers that each Muslim should perform five times a day. Various words of praise, prayer, and recitation from the Qur'an accompany each position and movement. The ritual symbolizes the Muslim's complete obedience to God and recognition of God as the one, eternal, omnipotent Lord of the universe. [Library of Congress]

form, together with the increasing administrative use of Arabic to replace Aramaic, Greek, Middle Persian, or Coptic.

Non-Arab converts routinely attached themselves to Arab tribes as "clients," which assured protection and a place in the *diwan*. Still, this attachment also meant acceptance of a permanent second-class citizenship alongside the Arabs. Although many non-Arabs, especially Persians, mastered Arabic and prospered, dissatisfaction among client Muslims was widespread and led to uprisings against caliphal authority. Persian-Arab tensions were especially strong in Umayyad and early Abbasid times. Nevertheless, a Persian cultural renaissance eventually raised the Islamicized modern Persian language to high status in Islamic culture. Consequently, it profoundly affected religion, art, and literature in much of the Islamic world.

Caliphal administration joined with the evolution of legal theory and practice and the consolidation of religious norms to give stability to the emerging Islamic society. So powerful was the Muslim vision of society that, upon the demise of a caliph, or even a dynasty such as the Umayyads, the *Umma* and the caliphal office continued. There were, however, conflicting notions of that vision. In the first three Islamic centuries, two major interpretations crystallized that reflected idealistic interpretations of the *Umma*, its leadership and membership. When neither proved viable in the practical world of society and politics, they became minority visions that continued to fire the imaginations of some but failed to win broad-based support. A third, "centrist," vision found favor with the majority because it spoke to a wide spectrum and accommodated inevitable compromises in the higher cause of Islamic unity.

The Kharijites The most radical idealists traced their political origin to the first civil war (656–661). They were the

Kharijites, or "seceders" from Ali's camp because, in their view, he compromised with his enemies. The Kharijites' position was that the Muslim polity must be based on strict Qur'anic principles. They espoused total equality of the faithful and held that the leader of the *Umma* should be the best Muslim, whoever that might be. They took a moralistic, rigorist view of membership in the *Umma:* Anyone who committed a major sin was no longer a Muslim. Extreme Kharijites called on true Muslims to join them in rebellion against the morally compromised authority of the reigning caliph. The extremist groups were constant rallying points for opposition to the Umayyads and, to a lesser degree, the Abbasids.

More moderate Kharijites tempered their aversion to tolerating less-than-pious Muslims and the rule of less-than-ideal caliphs, yet they retained a strong sense of the moral imperatives of Muslim personal and collective duty. Their ideals proved attractive and influenced wider Muslim pietism in the long run. Although the movement declined in Abbasid times, even today moderate Kharijite groups survive in Oman and North Africa.

The Shi'a A second position was defined largely in terms of leadership of the *Umma*. Muhammad had no surviving sons, and his son-in-law and cousin Ali claimed the caliphate in 656, partly on the basis of his blood tie to the Prophet. His claim was contested by Mu'awiya in the first Islamic civil war. When Mu'awiya took over by default after a Kharijite murdered Ali in 661, many of Ali's followers felt that Islamic affairs had gone awry. Although it is difficult to date the crystallization of the developed ideology of the "partisans of Ali" (*Shi'at Ali*, or simply the *Shi'a*, or *Shi'ites*), their roots go back to Ali's murder and especially to that of his son Husayn at Karbala, in Iraq, at the hands of Umayyad troops (680).

Whereas all Muslims esteem Ali for his closeness to Muhammad, Shi'ites believe him to be the Prophet's appointed successor. Ali's blood tie with Muhammad was augmented in Shi'ite thinking by belief in the Prophet's designation of him as the true *imam*, or Muslim leader, after him. Numerous rebellions in Umayyad times rallied around persons claiming to be such a true successor, whether as an Alid or merely a member of Muhammad's clan of Hashim. Even the Abbasids based their right to the caliphate on their Hashimite ancestry. The major Shi'ite pretenders who emerged in the ninth and tenth centuries based their claims on both the Prophet's designation and their descent from Ali and Fatima, Muhammad's daughter. They also stressed the idea of a divinely inspired knowledge passed on by Muhammad to his designated heirs. Thus the true Muslim was the faithful follower of the *imams*, who carried Muhammad's blood and spiritual authority.

When Shi'ites failed to place a true *imam* at the head of the imperial state, they interpreted this failure theologically. They saw Ali's assassination by a Kharijite, and especially the brutal massacre of Husayn and his family, as proofs of the evil nature of this world's rulers, and as rallying points for true Muslims. The martyrdom of Ali and Husayn was extended to a line of Alid *imams* that varied among different groups of Shi'ites. True Muslims, like their *imams*, must suffer. But they would be vindicated in the end by an expected *mahdi*, or "guided one," who would usher in a messianic age and a judgment day that would see the faithful rewarded. (In the Sunni tradition, which we discuss next, similar "mahdist" movements arose throughout Islamic history.)

On several occasions in later history Shi'ite rulers did head some Islamic states. But only after 1500, in Iran, did Shi'ism prevail as the majority faith in a major Muslim state. The Shi'ite vision of the true *Umma* has been a powerful one, but not one that has been able to muster sufficient consensus to dominate the larger Islamic world.

The Centrists Kharijite and Shi'ite causes were repeatedly espoused by disaffected groups in the early and later Islamic empire. But it was a third, less sharply defined position on the nature of leadership and membership in the *Umma* that most Muslims ultimately accepted. In some ways a compromise, it proved acceptable not only to lukewarm Muslims or simple pragmatists, but also to persons of piety as intense as that of any Kharijite or Shi'ite. We may term the proponents of this position *centrists*. To emphasize the correctness of their views, they eventually called themselves *Sunnis*—followers of the tradition (*sunna*) established by the Prophet and the Qur'an. Neither they, nor the Shi'ites, nor the Kharijites, have ever been a single sect or group, but have always encompassed a wide range of reconcilable, if not always truly compatible, ideas and groups. They have made up the broad middle spectrum of Muslims who tend to put communal solidarity and maintenance of the Islamic polity above purist adherence to particular theological tenets. They have been inclusivist rather than exclusivist, a trait that has typified the Islamic (unlike the Jewish or Christian) community through most of its history.

The centrist position was simply the most workable general framework for the new Islamic state. Its basic ideas were: (1) The *Umma* is a theocratic entity, a state under divine authority; this translates into a nomocracy, or *Umma* under the authority of God's law, the Shari'a. The sources of guidance are, first, the Qur'an; second, Muhammad's precedent; and, third and fourth, the interpretive efforts and consensus of the Muslims (in practice, the *ulama*). (2) The caliph is the absolute temporal ruler, charged with administering and defending the Abode of Islam and protecting Muslim norms and practice; he possesses no greater authority than other Muslims in matters of faith. (3) A person who professes to be Muslim by witnessing that "There is no god but God, and Muhammad is His Messenger" should be considered a Muslim (because "only God knows what is in the heart"), and not even a mortal sin excludes such a person automatically from the *Umma*.

Under increasingly influential *ulama* leadership, these and other basic premises of Muslim community came to serve as the theological underpinnings of both the caliphal state and the emerging international Islamic social order.

The High Caliphate

The consolidation of the caliphal institution began with the victory of the Umayyad caliph Abd al-Malik in 692, in the second civil war. The ensuing century and a half mark the era of

---

Origins and Early Development of Islam

ca. 570	Birth of Muhammad
622	The Hijra ("emigration") of Muslims to Yathrib (henceforward *al-Madina*, "The City [of the Prophet]"); beginning of Muslim calendar
632	Death of Muhammad; Abu Bakr becomes first "successor" (*Khalifa*, caliph) to leadership, reigns 632-634
634-644	Caliphate of Umar; rapid conquests in Egypt and Iran
644-656	Caliphate of Uthman (member of Umayyad clan); more conquests; Qur'an text established; growth of sea power
656-661	Contested Caliphate of Ali; first civil war
661-680	Caliphate of Mu'awiya; founding of Umayyad dynasty (661-750); capital moved to Damascus; more expansion
680	Second civil war (680-692) begins with death of al-Husayn at Karbala

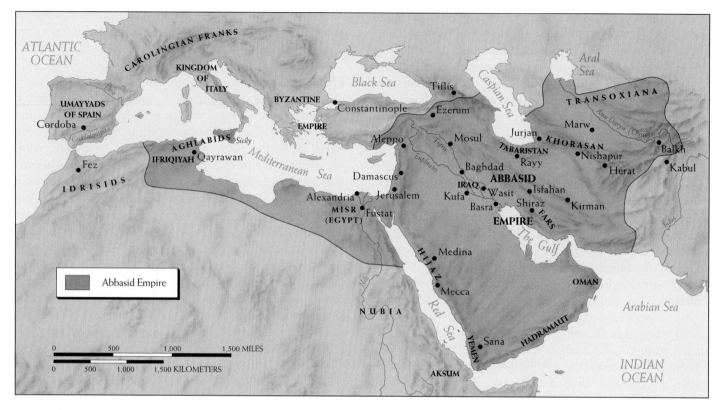

Map 11-2   The Abbasid Empire, ca. 900 C.E.

the "high caliphate," the politically strong, culturally vibrant, wealthy, and centralized institution that flourished first under the Umayyads in Damascus and then in the Abbasid capital of Baghdad.[3] The height of caliphal power and splendor came only after the Umayyad decline, in the first century of Abbasid rule, largely during the caliphates of the fabled Harun al-Rashid (786–809) and his third son, al-Ma'mun (813–833).

The Abbasid State

The Abbasids' revolution was based on non-Arab disaffection, Khorasanian regionalism, and Shi'ite religio-political hopes. Their victory effectively ended Arab dominance as well as Umayyad ascendancy (except in Spain). The shift of the imperial capital from Damascus to the new "city of peace" built at Baghdad on the Tigris (762–766) symbolized the eastward shift in cultural and political orientation under the new regime. In line with this shift, more and more Persians (albeit linguistically arabicized Persians) entered the bureaucracy. In the Abbasid heyday under Harun, the highest caliphal advisory office, that of the vizier (Arabic: *wazir*), was dominated by the Kho-

rasanian family of the Barmakids. Religiously, the Abbasids' disavowal of Shi'ite hopes for a divinely inspired imamate reflected their determination to gain the support of a broad spectrum of Muslims, even if they still stressed their descent from al-Abbas (ca. 565–653), uncle of both Muhammad and Ali.

Whereas the Umayyads had relied on Syrian Arab forces, the Abbasids used Khorasanian Arabs and Iranians and, in the provinces, regional mercenaries for their main troops. Beginning in the ninth century, however, they enlisted slave soldiers (*mamluks*), mostly Turks from the northern steppes, as their personal troops. The officers of these forces, themselves *mamluks*, soon seized the positions of power in the central and provincial bureaucracies and the army. Eventually the caliphs were dominated by their *mamluk* officers. This domination led to increasing alienation of the Muslim populace from their own rulers. This was evident in Iraq itself, where unrest with his overbearing Turkish guard led the Abbasid caliph to remove the government from Baghdad to the new city of Samarra sixty miles up the Tigris, where it remained from 836 to 892. (See Map 11–2.)

Society

The deep division between rulers and populace—the functionally secular state and its subjects—was ever after typical

---

[3]This periodization of early Islamic government follows that of M. G. S. Hodgson, *The Venture of Islam*, Vol. 1 (Chicago: University of Chicago Press, 1984), pp. 217–236.

Early Period of the High Caliphate	
680–694	Second civil war
685–705	Caliphate of Abd al-Malik; consolidation, arabization of administration
705–715	Caliphate of al-Walid; Morocco conquered, Spain invaded; Arab armies reach the Indus
ca. 750	Introduction of paper manufacture from China through Samarqand to Islamic world
750	Abbasids seize Caliphate from Umayyads, begin new dynasty (750–1258)
756	Some Umayyads escape to Spain, found new dynasty (756–1030)
762–766	New Abbasid capital built at Baghdad

of most Islamic societies. However, even while the independence of ever more provincial rulers reduced Abbasid central power after the mid-ninth century, such rulers generally chose to recognize caliphal authority at least nominally. This gave them legitimacy and underscored their role as guardians of the Islamic socio-religious order, which meanwhile found its real cohesiveness in the Muslim ideals being standardized and propagated by the *ulama*.

We must remember, however, that full conversion of the diverse populace of the Islamic Empire lagged far behind centralization of political power and development of Islamic socio-religious institutions. It appears that Iraq and Iran (especially Khorasan, which had substantial early Arab Muslim immigration) saw the fullest Islamization of local elites before the mid-twelfth century. They were followed by Spain, North Africa, and Syria. Conversion and fuller Islamization, when they came, meant the development of a self-confident Muslim polity no longer threatened by other religious communities or political forces and a correspondingly diminished need for centralized caliphal power.[4]

Decline

The eclipse of the caliphal empire was foreshadowed at the outset of Abbasid rule, when one of the last Umayyads fled west to Spain. Supported by Syrian, Yemenite, and Berber tribes, he founded a Spanish Islamic state (756–1030) that produced the spectacular Moorish culture of Spain. The Spanish Umayyads even claimed the title of caliph in 929, so strong were they and so weak the Abbasids by this time. In all the Abbasid provinces, regional governments were always potential bases for independent states. Besides small Khari-

jite states among the Berbers, the earliest separate state in North Africa was set up in 801 by Harun al-Rashid's governor in the area of modern Tunisia. A later North African dynasty, the Fatimids, even conquered Egypt and set up Shi'ite rule in 969 that claimed to be the only true caliphate.

In the East, Iran grew ever harder for Baghdad to control. Beginning in 821 in Khorasan, Abbasid governors or rebel groups started independent dynasties repeatedly for two centuries. As a result of weakness, the caliph had usually to recognize their de facto sway over various parts of the Iranian plateau. Among the longest-lived of these Iranian dynasties were the Samanids of Khorasan and Transoxiana, who ruled at Bukhara as nominal Abbasid vassals from 875 until 999. They gave northeastern Iran a long period of economic and political security from Turkish steppe invaders. Under their aegis, Persian poetry and Arabic scientific studies began what was to become in subsequent centuries a Persian Islamic cultural renaissance and a highly influential scientific tradition.

Of greatest consequence for the Abbasid caliphate, however, was the rise in the mountains south of the Caspian of a Shi'ite clan, the Buyids, who took over Abbasid rule in 945. Although they kept the caliph himself "in office," he and his descendants were henceforth largely puppets in the hands of a Buyid "commander" (*amirs* or *emirs;* later, *sultans*). In 1055 the Buyids were replaced by the more famous Seljuk *sultans.* Thus, the caliphal state broke up, even though Abbasid caliphs continued as figureheads of Muslim unity until Mongol invaders killed the last of them in 1258.

The "Classical" Islamic Culture

The pomp and splendor of the Abbasid court were grand enough to become the stuff of Islamic legends, such as those preserved much later in the popular tales of *The Thousand and One Nights.* Their rich cultural legacy similarly outlived the Abbasids themselves. Their achievements were made possible by a strong army and central government and vigorous internal and external trade. The latter may have been stimulated by the prosperous T'ang Empire of China, with which the Islamic world had much overland and sea contact. Material factors, such as the introduction of paper manufacture (introduced from China through Samarkand about 750) or the flight of Byzantine scholars east to new Abbasid centers of learning, contributed also to making the early Abbasid era special.

Intellectual Traditions

The Abbasid heyday was marked by sophisticated tastes and an insatiable thirst for knowledge—not simply religious

[4]Richard W. Bulliet, *Conversion to Islam in the Medieval Period* (Cambridge, MA: Harvard University Press, 1979), especially pp. 7–15, 128–138.

The Wit and Wisdom of al-Jahiz

One of the great masters of Arabic prose and adab writing, al-Jahiz (d. 869) left a number of works behind, among them his Book of Proof. *The following excerpts from this book of essays and clever sayings reflect his talent for the succinct and vivid.*

What are some of the values and personal qualities that these anecdotes seem to favor? What might be inferred about the author's attitude toward women? Toward wealth? Toward religious zealotry?

Ghailan son of Kharasha said to Ahnaf, "What will preserve the Arabs from decline?" He replied, "All will go well if they keep their swords on their shoulders and their turbans on their heads and ride horseback and do not fall a prey to the fools' sense of honour." "And what is the fools' sense of honour?" "That they regard forgiving one another as a wrong."

'Umar said, "Turbans are the crowns of the Arabs."

An Arab of the desert was asked why he did not lay aside his turban. "Surely," said he, "a thing which contains the hearing and the sight ought to be prized."

'Ali said—God be well pleased with him!—"The elegance of a man is in his bonnet, and the elegance of a woman is her boots." And Ahnaf said, "Let your shoes be fine, for shoes are to men what anklets are to women."

"Abdullah son of Ja'far said to his daughter, "O little daughter, beware of jealousy, for it is the key of divorce; and beware of chiding, for it breeds hate. Always adorn and perfume thyself, and know that the most becoming adornment is antimony and the sweetest perfume is water."

'Abdullah son of Ja'far bestowed largesse of every kind on Nusaib Abu'l-Hajina, who had made an ode in praise of him. "Why," they asked, "do you treat a fellow like this so handsomely—a negro and a slave?" "By God," he answered, "if his skin is black, yet his praise is white and his poem is truly Arabian. He deserves for it a greater reward than he has gotten. All he received was only some lean saddle-camels and clothes which wear out and money which is soon spent, whereas he gave an ode fresh and brilliant and praise that will never die."

Mu'awiyah held an assembly at Kufa to receive the oath of allegiance as Caliph. Those who swore loyalty to him were required to abjure allegiance to [the House of] 'Ali son of Abu Talib—may God honour him! A man of the Banu Tamim came to Mu'awiyah, who demanded that he should repudiate 'Ali. "O Prince of the Faithful," he replied, "we will obey those of you that are living, but we will not renounce those of you that are dead." Mu'awiyah turned to Mughia and said, "Now, this is a man! Look after him well!" ...

"Auf said on the authority of Hasan: "The feet of a son of Adam will not stir [from the place of judgment] until he be asked of three things—his youth, how he wore it away; his life, how he passed it; and his wealth, whence he got it and on what he spent it."

Yunus son of 'Ubaid said: "I heard three sayings more wonderful than any I have ever heard. The first is the saying of Hassan son of Abu Sinan—'Nothing is easier than abstinence from things unlawful: if aught make thee doubt, leave it alone.' The second is the saying of Ibn Sirin—'I have never envied any one any thing.' The third is the saying of Muwarrik al-'Ijli—'Forty years ago I asked of God a boon which He has not granted, and I have not despaired of obtaining it.' They said to Muwarrik, 'What is it?' He replied, 'Not to meddle with that which does not concern me.'"

knowledge, but *any* knowledge. An Arab historian called Baghdad "the market to which the wares of the sciences and arts were brought, where wisdom was sought as a man seeks after his stray camels, and whose judgment of values was accepted by the whole world."[5] Contacts (primarily among intellectuals) between Muslims and Christian, Jewish, Zoroastrian, and other "protected" religious communities contributed to the cosmopolitanism of the age. Some older intellectual traditions experienced a revival in early Abbasid times, as in the case of Hellenistic learning. Philosophy, astronomy, mathematics, medicine, and other natural sciences enjoyed strong interest and patronage. In Islamic usage, philosophy and the sciences were subsumed under *falsafa* (from Greek *philosophia*). Islamic culture took over the tradition of rational inquiry from the Hellenistic world and developed as well as preserved it at a time when Europe was by comparison a cultural wasteland.

Arabic translations of Greek and Sanskrit works stimulated progress in astronomy and medicine. Translation reached its peak in al-Ma'mun's new academy headed by a Nestorian Christian, Hunayn ibn Ishaq (d. 873), noted for his med-

[5]See Oleg Grabar, *The Formation of Islamic Art* (New Haven, CT: Yale University Press, 1973), especially pp. 1–103, 206–213.

A glazed ceramic bowl decorated with a gazelle or antelope, a symbolic figure of beauty and grace. From North Africa, tunisian area, Fatimid (10th-12th centuries). [Art Resource, N.Y.]

ical and Greek learning. Before, during, and after his time there were Arabic translations of everything from the Greek authors Galen, Ptolemy, Euclid, Aristotle, Plato, and the Neo-Platonists to the Indian fables that had been translated into Middle Persian under the Sasanids from Sanskrit originals. Such translations stimulated not only Arabic learning, but later also that of the less advanced European world, especially in the twelfth and thirteenth centuries.

"Classical" Period of the High Caliphate

786–809	Caliphate of Harun al-Rashid; apogee of caliphal power
813–833	Caliphate of al-Ma'mun; strong patronage of translations of Greek, Sanskrit, and other works into Arabic; first heavy reliance on slave soldiers (mamluks)
875	Rise of Samanid power at Bukhara; patronage of Persian poetry paves way for Persian literary renaissance
909	Rise of Shi'ite Fatimid dynasty in North Africa
945–1055	Buyid amirs rule the eastern empire at Baghdad; the Abbasid caliphs continue largely as figureheads
1055	Buyid amirs replaced by Seljuk sultans as effective rulers at Baghdad and custodians of the caliphate

Language and Literature

Arabic language and literature developed greatly in the expanded cultural sphere of the new empire. In *belles lettres* there developed, largely among the secretarial class of the Abbasid bureaucracy, a significant genre of Arabic writing known as *adab*, or "manners" literature. It included essays and didactic literature influenced by earlier Persian letters. At the same time, as translations of different literary genres increased the range of the original bedouin idiom, poetry flourished by building on the sophisticated tradition of the Arabic ode, or *qasida*. Grammar was central to the interpretation of the Qur'an that occupied the ulama and undergirded an emerging curriculum of Muslim learning. Historical and biographical writings became major genres of Arabic writing. They owed much to the ancient bedouin accounts of "the battle days of the Arabs" but arose primarily to record, first, the lives and times of the Prophet and earliest Companions, then those of subsequent generations of Muslims. This information was crucial to judging the reliability of the "chains" of transmitters included with each traditional report, or *hadith*. A *hadith* reports words or actions ascribed to Muhammad and the Companions; it became the chief source of Muslim legal and religious norms alongside the Qur'an, as well as the basic unit

(A)

The congregational mosque. Two examples of the finest great mosques of the classical Islamic world. Such buildings were designed not only for worship; their large courtyards and pillared halls were intended to hold the population of a given city and could be used for governmental purposes or for mustering troops in time of war. Their splendor also announced the power and wealth of Islamic rule. Figure A is the great mosque at Qayrawan in modern Tunisia, built between the eighth and ninth centuries. Figure B shows the Spanish Umayyad mosque in Cordoba, built and added to from the eighth to the tenth centuries, in a series of roofed extensions—unlike that in Qayrawan, which has only covered colonnades and one great hall (behind the photographer in this picture).

[(A) Werner Forman Archive, Art Resource, N.Y.; (B) Adam Lubroth, Art Resource, N.Y.]

(B)

of most prose genres, from history to Qur'an exegesis. Collections of the *hadith* formed also a separate genre that was mined by preachers and by the developing schools of legal interpretation, whose crowning glory was the work of al-Shafi'i (d. 820) on legal reasoning.

Art and Architecture

In art and architecture the Abbasid era saw the crystallization of a "classical" Islamic style by about 1000 C.E. Except for ceramics and Arabic calligraphy, there was nothing radically new about the discrete elements of Islamic art and architecture; most had clear antecedents in Greco-Roman, Byzantine, or Iranian art. What was new was the use of older forms and motifs for new purposes and in new combinations, and also the spread of such elements to new locales, generally in a movement from east (especially the Fertile Crescent) to west (Syria, Egypt, North Africa, and Spain). Sasanid stucco decoration techniques and designs turned up, for example, in Egypt and North Africa. Chronologically, urban Iraq developed an Islamic art first, then made its influence felt east and west, whether in Bukhara or in Syria and North Africa. Also new was the combination and elaboration of discrete forms, as in the case of the colonnade (or hypostyle) mosque or complex arabesque designs.

The Muslims had good reason to be self-confident about their faith and culture and to want to distinguish them from others. Most monuments of the age express the distinctiveness they felt. Particular formal items, such as calligraphic motifs and inscriptions on buildings, came to characterize Islamic architecture and define its functions. Most striking in many ways was the avoidance of pictures or icons in public art. This was, of course, in line with the strong Muslim aversion both to any hint of idolatry and to the strongly iconic Byzantine Christian art. Although this iconoclasm later diminished in several strands of Islamic culture, it was a telling expression of the general thrust of Muslim faith and the culture it animated. Overall, the Muslims' artistic achievements before the year 1000 impress us with an identifiable quality that is both distinctively and "classically" Islamic, whatever the details of a particular example.[6]

IN WORLD PERSPECTIVE

The Formation of Islamic Civilization

The rise of Islam as both an international religious tradition and an international civilization is by any standard one of the great pivotal moments in world history. The new traditions

[6]Ibid.

forged first in the Arabian peninsula and then in Syria, Iraq, North Africa, Iran, and beyond were to change much of Asia and Africa and parts of Europe in major ways. Religiously, the Islamic movement was destined to become, along with the Buddhist and Christian movements, one of the three major universalist, missionary traditions of world religious history. Politically and socially, the Islamic order for society spread and developed in new environments to an extent far beyond the imagination of Muhammad and his companions.

The Islamic polity was in its first three centuries the most dynamic and expansive imperial state of its day. During the same time Chinese emperors of the T'ang were rebuilding and improving on the previous Han imperium; Charlemagne and the Carolingians were struggling to hammer out a much smaller, more homogeneous empire and a cultural renaissance in the relatively backward world of western Europe; Byzantium was fighting to survive against Islamic arms and turning inward to conserve its traditions; and post-Gupta India was divided into diverse regional kingdoms and still vulnerable to new forces (including those of Islam) moving into northwestern India.

As different as the two were, only China compared favorably with or surpassed the Islamic world during this period in terms of political and military power as well as cultural unity, creativity, and self-consciousness. The T'ang and the Abbasids wielded commensurate power in their heydays, although over time the Chinese held together as a centralized state much better than the Islamic empire. Certainly they were the two greatest political and cultural units in the world in their age. They each had one cultural language, although Chinese was spoken by a greater percentage of Chinese than was Arabic by Islamic subjects. They also shared the military primacy of nomadic cavalry as well as the adaptive ability to incorporate new peoples into their larger culture—although Islamic cultures proved more flexible on this count. Indeed, the great elasticity and adaptability of Islam as a religious tradition and as a social order were striking in ways that clearly belie its present-day reputation in the West as an inherently inflexible system of values and practices.

Nevertheless, the bases of Islamic rule were clearly different, spread as the empire was over vastly more culturally heterogeneous and widely dispersed geographical areas than that of China. Conquest initially fueled the economy of the new Islamic state, but in the long run, trade and urban commercial centers were the backbone of Islamic prosperity, as well as the prime means of dissemination of Muslim faith to new lands. The Islamic empire was agrarian-based, yet the overall climate, soil, and water conditions for food production were not as good as those in China or western Europe. The key element that most Islamic lands lacked was abundant water; therefore, supporting dense populations well was difficult. This hindrance did not stop the development of impressive Islamic states, societies, and cultures, but it did set limits to it.

The Islamic achievement was different from any other in this period primarily in that it resulted from an effort to build something new rather than to recapture old traditions, whether religious, social, or political. In later centuries the early Arab impress of Islamic culture and religion was tempered and changed by the vast numbers of Persian- and Turkish-speaking Muslims and also the many regional groups, from Swahili-speakers in East Africa to the Malays and Indonesians of Southeast Asia. Nevertheless, Arabic went abroad with the holy Qur'an as the sacred medium of God's final revelation. Since Islam's emergence from the Arabian peninsula, indi-

vidual Muslims worldwide have learned little or much, but always something, of Arabic and the sacred Book.

This achievement was a new historical phenomenon, at least in its scale. Although Muslim faith can be seen as largely a reformation of Semitic monotheism, it was more fundamentally an effort to do something new—not merely to reform, but to subsume older traditions of Jews or Christians in a more comprehensive vision of God's plan on earth. This is not to say that Muslims did not build on previous traditions; they adopted and adapted the traditions of the many older Afro-Eurasian cultures. Yet as both a civilization and a religious tradition, Islam developed its own distinctive stamp that persisted wherever Muslims extended the *Umma*.

Review Questions ———

1. What was Arabian society like before the coming of Islam? What were the prime targets of the Qur'anic message in that society?

2. What are the main features of the Islamic worldview? How do Islamic ideas about history, salvation, law, social justice, and other key issues compare to those of Christianity and Judaism?

3. What were the primary kinds of leadership in the early Islamic polities? To what extent were political and religious leadership separated in different offices and functions?

4. Discuss the conversion of subject populations in the early centuries of Islamic empire. What were incentives and obstacles to conversion?

5. What explains the initial rapid conquests of the Arab armies? The decline of the imperial caliphal state? What were some of the lasting accomplishments of the Umayyad and Abbasid empires?

6. Discuss the "classical" culture of the high caliphate. What role did foreign traditions play in it? What were some of its prominent achievements in various fields?

Suggested Readings ———

J. ASHTIANI, T. M. JOHNSTONE, J. D. LATHAM, R. B. SERGEANT, AND G. R. SMITH, EDS., *Abbasid Belles Lettres* (1990). A wide-ranging survey of Arabic letters between 750 and 1258 C.E., arranged by genres and major writers.

A. F. L. BEESTON, T. M. JOHNSTONE, R. B. SERGEANT, AND G. R. SMITH, EDS., *Arabic Literature to the End of the Umayyad Period* (1983). The most comprehensive survey of the early Arabic historical, religious, poetic, and other literary sources.

K. CRAGG AND R. MARSTON SPEIGHT, EDS., *Islam from Within: Anthology of a Religion* (1980). One of the best and most sensitive collections of selections from Islamic primary sources.

F. M. DONNER, *The Early Islamic Conquests* (1981). The introduction and first chapter are especially good for an introduction to many important issues in the origin and spread of Islam.

H. A. R. GIBB, *Studies on the Civilization of Islam*, ed. by S. J. Shaw and W. R. Polk (1962). This volume of selected es-

says by Gibb has some very helpful general studies on Islamic political order and religion.

H. A. R. GIBB, *Mohammedanism: An Historical Survey* (1970). Despite the offensive title, still the best brief introduction to Islam as a religious tradition.

O. GRABAR, *The Formation of Islamic Art* (1973). A critical and creative interpretation of major themes in the development of distinctively Islamic forms of art and architecture.

G. E. VON GRUNEBAUM, *Classical Islam: A History 600–1258*, trans. by K. Watson (1970), pp. 1–140. A competent, culturally oriented introductory survey of formative developments.

M. G. S. HODGSON, *The Classical Age of Islam* (1974). 3 vols. Vol. I, *The Venture of Islam*. The most thoughtful and comprehensive attempt to deal with classical Islamic civilization as a whole and in relation to contemporaneous non-Islamic cultures.

A. HOURANI, *A History of the Arab Peoples* (1991). A masterly survey of the Arabs down through the centuries and a clear picture of many aspects of Islamic history and culture that extend beyond the Arab world.

B. LEWIS, ED., *Islam and the Arab World* (1976). A large-format, heavily illustrated volume with many excellent articles on diverse aspects of Islamic (not simply Arab, as the misleading title suggests) civilization through the premodern period.

F. RAHMAN, *Major Themes of the Qur'an* (1980). The best introduction to the basic ideas of the Qur'an and Islam, seen through the eyes of a perceptive Muslim modernist scholar.

M. A. SHABAN, *Islamic History: A New Interpretation (1971–76)*. 2 vols. An influential reassessment of the course of Islamic history to 1055 C.E.

D. SOURDEL, *Medieval Islam* (1979). Eng. trans. by W. M. Watt (1983). A brief but excellent survey of the world of medieval Islam with emphasis on social, religious, and political institutions.

12 THE EARLY MIDDLE AGES IN THE WEST TO 1000: THE BIRTH OF EUROPE

A crown of the emperor of the Holy Roman Empire from the early tenth century with a depiction of the Biblical King Solomon on the front section. The back sections of the crown bear depictions of King David and the prophet Isaiah.

[Kunsthistorisches Museum, Vienna.]

CHAPTER TOPICS

◆ The Decline of Roman Authority in the West

◆ The Byzantine Empire

◆ The Impact of Islam on East and West

◆ The Developing Roman Church

◆ The Kingdom of the Franks

◆ Feudal Society

In World Perspective The Early Middle Ages

The early Middle Ages (or early medieval period) marks the birth of Europe. This period of recovery from the collapse of Roman civilization was also a time of forced experimentation with new ideas and institutions. Within what had been the northern and western provinces of the Roman Empire, Greco-Roman culture combined with Germanic culture and an evolving Christianity to create distinctive political and cultural forms. In government, religion, and language, as well as geography, these regions grew separate from the eastern Byzantine world and the Islamic Arab world that extended across North Africa from Spain to the eastern Mediterranean.

German tribes had been settling peacefully around the Roman Empire since the first century B.C.E., but in the fourth century C.E. they began to migrate directly into it from the north and east. During the fifth century they turned fiercely against their hosts, largely because the Romans, who regarded them as uncultured barbarians, treated them so cruelly. To the south, Arab dominance transformed the Mediterranean into an often inhospitable "Islamic lake," greatly reducing western trade with the east. Surrounded and assailed from north, east, and south, western Europe became insular and even stagnant, its people losing touch with classical, especially Greek, learning and science. But forced to manage by themselves, they learned to develop their native resources. The reign of Charlemagne saw a modest renaissance of antiquity. And the peculiar social and political forms that emerged during this period—manorialism and feudalism—not only were successful at coping with unprecedented chaos on local levels, but also proved to be fertile seedbeds for the growth of distinctive western institutions.

The Decline of Roman Authority in the West

By the late third century the Roman Empire faced growing disarray. To strengthen it, the Emperor Diocletian (r. 284–305) divided it between himself and a co-emperor named Maximian. The result was a dual empire with its own emperor in the east and the west, and, eventually, independent imperial bureaucracies. A critical shift of the empire's resources and orientation to the east also accompanied these changes. In 284 Diocletian, emperor in the east, moved to Nicomedia (in modern Turkey), where he remained until the last two years of his reign. As imperial rule weakened in the west and strengthened in the east, it became increasingly autocratic.

In an attempt to end the factional strife that followed Diocletian's reign and to position himself more effectively against the empire's new eastern enemies, Emperor Constantine I (r. 306–337) briefly reunited the empire by conquest and ruled as sole emperor after 324. In 330 he dedicated a new imperial capital, Constantinople, built on the site of the ancient city of Byzantium at the mouth of the Black Sea and a major commercial crossroads. Now the new administrative center of the empire, Constantinople gradually became a "new Rome" as the "old" Rome, suffering from political division and geographically distant from the new military fronts in Syria and along the Danube River, declined in importance. Already in 286 the imperial residence in the west had moved from Rome to Milan, and would be moved again to Ravenna in 402. When the barbarian migrations began in the late fourth century, the west was in serious political disarray, imperial power, prestige, and focus having shifted decisively to Constantinople and the east.

Germanic Migrations

The German tribes did not burst on the west all of a sudden. They were at first a token and benign presence on the fringes of the empire and even within it. Roman and Germanic cultures had commingled peacefully for centuries. The Romans "imported" barbarians as domestics, slaves, and soldiers, and some of the latter rose to positions of leadership and even fame in Roman legions.

A great influx of Visigoths (west Goths) into the empire beginning in 376 ended this peaceful coexistence. The Visigoths, who were accomplished horsemen and fierce warriors, had themselves been pushed into the empire by the Huns, a particularly violent people whose original homeland was the region of modern Mongolia in Asia. Visigoths ultimately settled as far west as southern Gaul and Spain. In exchange for their services as *foederati*, or special allies, on the eastern frontier, the eastern emperor Valens (r. 364–378) promised them material assistance and the right to settle within the empire. The promise proved hollow, however, and the Romans treated their new allies harshly. The Visigoths, who entered the empire an impoverished people fleeing the Huns, ended up trading their own children to the Romans for dogs to eat, one child per dog. After repeated conflicts, they rebelled and handily defeated Roman armies under Valens at the Battle of Adrianople in 378.

After Adrianople, the Romans passively permitted the settlement of barbarians within the very heart of the western empire. Although the largest of the tribes numbered at most 100,000 people, the invaders were successful because they entered a badly overextended western empire divided politically by ambitious military commanders and physically weakened by decades of famine, disease, and overtaxation. By the second half of the fourth century, the Romans could no longer manage their frontiers in the west. Efforts to strengthen frontier defenses by "barbarizing" the Roman army—that is, by recruiting peasants and making the Germanic tribes key Roman allies—only weakened them further. The eastern empire retained enough wealth and vitality to field new armies or to buy off invaders. The western empire, in contrast, succumbed to a combination of military rivalry, political mismanagement, disease, and sheer poverty, not to mention the moral decay and materialism of its ruling elite.

Fall of the Western Roman Empire

In the early fifth century, Italy and the "eternal city" of Rome suffered a series of devastating blows. In 410 the Visigoths, under Alaric (ca. 370–410), revolted and sacked Rome. In 452 the Huns, led by Attila—known to contemporaries as the "scourge of God"—invaded Italy. And in 455 Rome was overrun yet again, this time by the Vandals.

By the mid-fifth century, power in western Europe had passed decisively from the hands of the Roman emperors to those of barbarian chieftains. In 476, the traditional date given for the fall of the Roman Empire, the barbarian Odovacer (ca. 434–493) deposed and replaced the western emperor Romulus Augustulus. The eastern emperor Zeno (r. 474–491) recognized Odovacer's authority in the west, and Odovacer acknowledged Zeno as sole emperor, contenting himself to serve as Zeno's western viceroy. By the end of the fifth century the barbarians had thoroughly overrun the western empire. The Ostrogoths settled in Italy, the Franks in northern Gaul, the Burgundians in Provence, the Visigoths in southern Gaul and Spain, the Vandals in Africa and the western Mediterranean, and the Angles and Saxons in England (see Map 12–1).

Map 12–1 Barbarian migrations into the west in the fourth and fifth centuries. The forceful intrusion of Germanic and non-Germanic tribes into the empire from the last quarter of the fourth century through the fifth century made for a constantly changing pattern of movement and relations. The map shows the major routes taken by the usually unwelcome newcomers and the areas most deeply affected by the main groups.

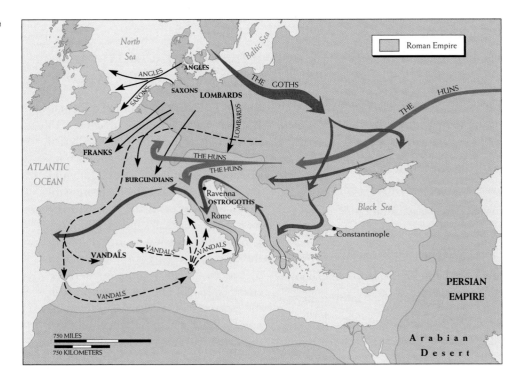

The barbarian military victories, however, did not result in a great defeat of Roman culture; western Europe's new masters were willing to learn from the people they had conquered. They admired Roman culture and had no desire to destroy it. Except in Britain and northern Gaul, Roman law, Roman government, and Latin, the Roman language, coexisted with the new Germanic institutions. In Italy under Theodoric, tribal custom gradually gave way to Roman law. Only the Vandals and the Anglo-Saxons—and, after 466, the Visigoths—refused to profess at least titular obedience to the emperor in Constantinople.

The Visigoths, the Ostrogoths, and the Vandals entered the west as Christians, which helped them accommodate to Roman culture. They were, however, followers of the Arian creed, which had been condemned at the Council of Nicea in 325 and was considered heretical in the west. Later, around 500, the Franks, who had settled in Gaul, would convert to the orthodox, or "Catholic," form of Christianity supported by the bishops of Rome. As we will see, the Franks ultimately dominated most of western Europe, helping convert the Goths and other barbarians to Roman Christianity.

All things considered, rapprochement and a gradual interpenetration of two strong cultures—a creative tension—marked the period of the Germanic migrations. The stronger culture was the Roman, and it became dominant in a later fusion. Despite western military defeat, the Goths and the Franks became far more romanized than the Romans were germanized. Latin language, Nicene Christianity, and eventually Roman law and government were to triumph in the west during the Middle Ages.

A sixth-century ivory panel depicting the Byzantine emperor Justinian as the champion of the Christian faith. From 500 to 1100, the Byzantine Empire was the center of Christian civilization. [Giraudon/Art Resource, N.Y.]

The Byzantine Empire

As western Europe succumbed to the Germanic invasions, imperial power shifted to the eastern part of the Roman Empire—known as the Byzantine Empire—and its capital, Constantinople. The Byzantine Empire would endure until 1453, passing from an early golden age of expansion and splendor to a time of contraction and splintering, and finally to catastrophic defeat by the Ottoman Turks.

The Reign of Justinian

In terms of territory, political power, and culture, the first period of Byzantine history (324–632) was by far its greatest. At the height of this period, Emperor Justinian (r. 527–565) ruled with the assistance of his brilliant wife, Empress Theodora. The daughter of a circus bear trainer and—if the controversial *Secret History* of Justinian's court historian, Procopius, is to be believed—perhaps at one time a prostitute, Theodora rose from lowly origins to become an influential counselor and a major figure in imperial government. When in 532 Jus-

tinian contemplated abdication following riots that left much of Constantinople in ruins and thousands dead, Theodora stiffened his resolve and saved his rule.

The imperial goal in the east—as reflected in the policy "one God, one empire, one religion"—was to centralize government and impose legal and doctrinal conformity throughout the empire. To this end Justinian collated and revised Roman law. This codification had become a pressing matter because of the accumulation of an enormous number of often contradictory legal decrees. Justinian's *Corpus Juris Civilis* (body of civil law) was a fourfold compilation undertaken by a learned committee of lawyers. These works had little immediate effect on medieval common law, but beginning with the Renaissance, they provided the foundation for most subsequent European law down to the nineteenth century, and they were especially helpful to rulers who aspired to centralize their states.

Religion also served imperial centralization. Since the fifth century the patriarch of Constantinople had crowned emperors in Constantinople. This practice reflected the close

The Character and "Innovations" of Justinian and Theodora

According to their court historian and biographer, Procopius, the emperor and his wife were tyrants, pure and simple. His Secret History *(sixth century), which some historians distrust as a source, had only criticism and condemnation for the two rulers. Procopius especially resented Theodora, and he did not believe that the rule of law was respected at the royal court.*

Is Procopius being fair to Justinian and Theodora? Is the *Secret History* an ancient tabloid? How does one know when a source is biased and self-serving and when it is telling the truth? What does Procopius most dislike about the queen? Was Theodora the last woman ruler to receive such criticism?

Formerly, when the senate approached the Emperor, it paid homage in the following manner. Every patrician kissed him on the right breast; the Emperor [then] kissed the patrician on the head, and he was dismissed. Then the rest bent their right knee to the Emperor and withdrew. It was not customary to pay homage to the Queen.

But those who were admitted [in]to the presence of Justinian and Theodora, whether they were patricians or otherwise, fell on their faces on the floor, stretching their hands and feet out wide, kissed first one foot and then the other of the Augustus [i.e., the emperor], and then retired. Nor did Theodora refuse this honor; and she even received the ambassadors of the Persians and other barbarians and gave them presents, as if she were in command of the Roman Empire: a thing that had never happened in all previous time.

And formerly intimates of the Emperor called him Emperor and the Empress, Empress. . . . But if anybody addressed either of these two as Emperor or Empress without adding "Your Majesty" or "Your Highness," or forgot to call himself their slave, he was considered either ignorant or insolent, and was dismissed in disgrace as if he had done some awful crime or committed some unpardonable sin.

And [whereas] before, only a few were sometimes admitted to the palace . . . when these two came to power, the magistrates and everybody else had no trouble in fairly living in the palace. This was because the magistrates of old had administered justice and the laws according to their conscience . . . but these two, taking control of everything to the misfortune of their subjects, forced everyone to come to them and beg like slaves. And almost any day one could see the law courts nearly deserted, while in the hall of the Emperor there was a jostling and pushing crowd that resembled nothing so much as a mob of slaves.

From *Procopius, Secret History*, in *The Early Middle Ages 500–1000*, ed. by Robert Brentano (New York: Free Press, 1964), pp. 70–71.

---

ties between rulers and the church. In 380 Christianity became the official religion of the eastern empire. The patriarchs of Constantinople, Alexandria, Antioch, and Jerusalem became very rich and powerful between the fourth and sixth centuries. As clerical ranks grew, the church in turn served the state as a welfare agency for the poor and needy.

During Justinian's reign the empire's strength was its more than fifteen hundred cities. Of these, the largest, with perhaps 350,000 inhabitants, was the imperial capital, Constantinople, the cultural crossroads of Asian and European civilizations (see Map 12–2). The large provincial cities had populations of 50,000. During the fourth and fifth centuries, councils composed of wealthy landowners known as *decurions* governed these cities. Decurions were the economic and intellectual elite of the empire. They were also heavily taxed and for this reason were not the emperor's most loyal servants. In the sixth century Justinian replaced the decurion councils with special governors and bishops on whom he could better rely.

The empire was also home, although at times a less than hospitable one, to large numbers of Jews. Under Roman law Jews had legal protection so long as they did not proselytize among Christians, build new synagogues, or try to enter sensitive public offices or professions. Justinian (the emperor most intent on religious conformity within the empire) adopted a policy of encouraging Jews to convert voluntarily. Later emperors ordered all Jews to be baptized and granted tax relief to those who voluntarily complied. But neither persuasion nor coercion succeeded in converting the empire's Jews.

Eastern Influences

During the reign of Heraclius (r. 610–641), the empire took an eastern, as opposed to a Roman, direction. Heraclius spoke Greek, not Latin. He spent his entire reign resisting Persian and Islamic invasions, which began in earnest in the seventh century. Islamic armies proved initially invincible; after 632, they progressively overran the empire and directly attacked Constantinople for the first time in 677. Not until the reign of Leo III (r. 717–741) were they repulsed and most of Asia Minor (modern Turkey) regained by the empire.

The empress Theodora and her attendants, Church of San Vitale, Ravenna, Italy, c. 547. The scene symbolizes the union of political and spiritual authority in the person of the empress. Like the Magi bearing gifts to the Virgin and the infant Jesus shown on the hem of her mantle, Theodora offers a jewel-studded chalice to Christ and the church. [Scala/Art Resource, N.Y.]

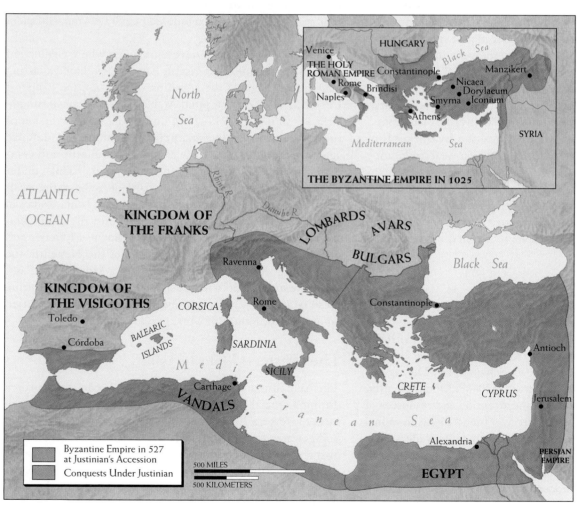

Map 12–2   The Byzantine Empire at the death of Justinian.   The inset shows the empire in 1025, before its losses to the Seljuq Turks.

Leo, however, offended western Christians when he forbade the use of images in eastern churches and tried to enforce the ban in the west. His efforts insulted the western church, which had carefully nurtured the adoration of Jesus, Mary, and the saints in images and icons. Historians have speculated that Leo and his immediate successors pursued this unfortunate policy under the influence of Islam, which condemned image veneration, perhaps hoping to placate the Muslims by joining them on this point of doctrine. Be that as it may, the banning of images reflected a degree of royal involvement in church affairs, routine in the east, which the western church greatly resisted. In addition to creating a new division within Christendom, the ban on images led to the destruction of much religious art until it was reversed in the late eighth century.

In 1071 the Byzantine Empire suffered a major defeat at the hands of the Muslim Seljuq Turks. Successful over Byzantine armies at Manzikert, the Turks rapidly overran the eastern provinces of the empire. This defeat marked the beginning of the end of the empire, although the actual end—at the hands of the Seljuqs' cousins, the Ottoman Turks—still lay centuries ahead. After two decades of steady Turkish advance, the eastern emperor asked for western aid in 1092. Three years later the west launched the first of the Crusades (see Chapter 13). A century later (1204) the Crusaders would inflict more damage on Constantinople and eastern Christendom than all previous non-Christian invaders had done.

Throughout the early Middle Ages, the Byzantine Empire remained a protective barrier between western Europe and hostile Persian, Arab, and Turkish armies. The Byzantines were also a major conduit of classical learning and science into the west until the Renaissance. While western Europeans were fumbling to create a culture of their own, the cities of the Byzantine Empire provided them a model of a civilized society.

The Impact of Islam on East and West

A new drama began to unfold in the sixth century with the rise of a rival far more dangerous to the west than the German tribes: the new faith of Islam (see Chapter 11). During the lifetime of the prophet Muhammad (570–632) and thereafter, invading Arab armies claimed the attention and resources of the emperors in Constantinople, who found themselves in a life-and-death struggle. Unlike the Germanic invaders, who absorbed and adopted the culture and religion of Rome, the Arabs, although generally tolerant of Christian and Jewish minorities, ultimately imposed their own culture and religion on the lands they conquered.

By the middle of the eighth century Arabs had conquered the southern and eastern Mediterranean coastline (territories currently held, for the most part, by Islamic states) and occupied parts of Spain, which they controlled or strongly influenced until the fifteenth century. In addition, their armies pushed north and east through Mesopotamia and Persia and beyond. The inhabitants of much of this territory, although Christian, were, like the Arabs, Semitic. Any religious unity they felt with the Byzantine Greeks may have been offset by hatred of the Byzantine Greek army of occupation. The Christian community was in any case badly divided. The Byzantine Emperor Heraclius had tried to impose Greek "orthodox" beliefs on the churches of Egypt and Syria, creating enmity between Greek and Semitic Christians. As a result, many Egyptian and Syrian Christians, hoping for deliverance from Byzantine oppression, may have welcomed the Islamic conquerors.

The Muslim conquerors tolerated Christians and Jews, provided they paid taxes, kept their distance, and made no efforts to proselytize Muslim communities. Always anxious to maintain the purity of their religion and culture, the Arabs forbade mixed marriages and any conscious cultural interchange. Special taxes on conquered peoples encouraged them to convert to Islam.

Assaulted from east and west and everywhere challenged in the Mediterranean, Christian Europe developed a lasting fear and suspicion of the Muslims. The Byzantine Emperor Leo III (r. 717–740) stopped Arab armies at Constantinople after a year's siege (717–718); during the next several centuries Byzantine rulers maintained a successful defense against the Arabs, for a time expanding militarily and commercially into Muslim lands. In the west, the Franks under Charles Martel defeated a raiding party of Arabs on the western frontier of the Frankish kingdom near Tours (today in central France) in 732, ending the possibility of Arab expansion into the rest of Europe by way of Spain. From the end of the seventh century to the middle of the eleventh, the Mediterranean remained something of a Muslim lake, and while western trade with East Asia was not cut off during these centuries, it was significantly diminished and carried on in keen awareness of Muslim dominance.

The Western Debt to Islam

The Arab invasions and presence in the Mediterranean area during a crucial part of the early Middle Ages helped give birth to western Europe as a distinctive cultural entity. Arab belligerence forced western Europeans to fall back on their own resources and to develop their own peculiar Germanic and Greco-Roman heritage into a unique culture. By diverting the attention and energies of the Byzantine Empire, the Arabs prevented it from expanding into western Europe, allowing two Germanic groups, the Franks and the Lombards (a group that invaded Italy in the sixth century and

(A) The great church of Hagia Sophia (Holy Wisdom). Built in Constantinople (now Istanbul, Turkey) by the emperor Justinian between 532 and 537, this church was one of the most influential achievements of Byzantine art and architecture. This interior view shows part of the great dome of the church (107 feet in diameter) and its rich decoration of marbles and mosaics. [Giraudon/Art Resource, N.Y.]

(A)

(B) The exterior of Hagia Sophia is plain and ordinary compared with the interior—a reflection of the priority the Byzantines attached to the inner life. The four towering minarets were among additions made by the Turkish Muslims after they conquered Constantinople in 1453 and transformed the building into a mosque. Since 1935 it has been a national museum.

[Giraudon/Art Resource, N.Y.]

(B)

settled in the Po Valley), to gain ascendancy. By controlling the Mediterranean, they also reduced western access to eastern trade and cultural influence.

Despite the hostility of the Christian west to the Islamic world during the early Middle Ages, there was much creative interchange between these two very different cultures. The more advanced Arab civilizations were then enjoying their golden age and taught western farmers how to irrigate fields and western artisans how to tan leather and refine silk. The west also gained from its contacts with Islamic scholars. Thanks to Arabic translators, major Greek works in astronomy, mathematics, and medicine became available to scholars in much of the west for the first time in Latin translation. And down to the sixteenth century, after the works of the famous ancient physicians Hippocrates and Galen, the basic gynecological and child-care manuals followed by western midwives and physicians were compilations by the famed Baghdad physician Al-Razi (Rhazes), the philosopher and physician ibn-Sina (Avicenna) (980–1037), and Averröes (1126–1198), Islam's greatest authority on Aristotle. Jewish scholars also thrived amid the intellectual culture Islamic scholars created. The famed Spanish-Jewish scholar Moses Maimonides (1135–1204) wrote in Arabic as well as Hebrew.

The Developing Roman Church

Throughout the period of imperial decline, Germanic invasions, and Islamic expansion, one western institution remained firmly entrenched and gained in strength: the Christian church. The church sought to organize itself according to the centralized, hierarchical administrative structure of the empire, with strategically placed "viceroys" (bishops) in European cities who looked for spiritual direction to their leader, the bishop of Rome (later pope). As the western empire crumbled, local bishops and cathedral chapters (ruling bodies of clergy) filled the resulting vacuum of authority. The local cathedral became the center of urban life and the local bishop the highest authority for those who remained in the cities. In Rome, on a larger and more fateful scale, the pope took control of the city as the western emperors gradually departed and died out. Left to its own devices, western Europe soon discovered that the Christian church was its best repository of Roman administrative skills and classical culture.

The Christian church had been graced with special privileges, great lands, and wealth by Emperor Constantine and his successors. In 313 Constantine issued the Edict of Milan, giving Christians legal standing and a favored status within the empire. In 391 Emperor Theodosius I (r. ca. 379–395) raised Christianity to the official religion of the empire. Both Theodosius and his predecessors acted as much for political

effect as out of religious conviction; in 313 Christians composed about one fifth of the population of the empire, making Christianity the strongest among the empire's competing religions. Mithraism, a religion popular among army officers and restricted to males, was its main rival.

Challenged by Rome's decline to become a major political force, the church survived the period of Germanic and Arab invasions as a somewhat spiritually weakened and compromised institution. Yet it remained a potent civilizing and unifying force. It had a religious message of providential purpose and individual worth that could give solace and meaning to life at its worst. It had a ritual of baptism and a creedal confession that united people beyond the traditional barriers of social class, education, and gender. And alone in the west, the church retained an effective hierarchical administration, scattered throughout the old empire, staffed by the best-educated minds in Europe and centered in emperorless Rome.

Monastic Culture

The church also enjoyed the services of growing numbers of monks, who were not only loyal to its mission but also objects of great popular respect. Monastic culture proved again and again to be the peculiar strength of the church during the Middle Ages.

The first monks were hermits who withdrew from society to pursue a more perfect way of life. They were inspired by the Christian ideal of a life of complete self-denial in imitation of Christ. The popularity of monasticism began to grow as Roman persecution of Christians waned and Christianity became the favored religion of the empire during the fourth century. Embracing the biblical "counsels of perfection" (chastity, poverty, and obedience), the monastic life became the purest form of religious practice.

Anthony of Egypt (ca. 251–356), the father of hermit monasticism, was inspired by Jesus' command to the rich young man: "If you will be perfect, sell all that you have, give it to the poor, and follow me" (Matthew 19:21). Anthony went into the desert to pray and work, setting an example followed by hundreds in Egypt, Syria, and Palestine in the fourth and fifth centuries. This hermit monasticism was soon joined by the development of communal monasticism. In the first quarter of the fourth century, Pachomius (ca. 286–346) organized monks in southern Egypt into a highly regimented community. Such monastic communities grew to contain a thousand or more inhabitants. They were little "cities of God," trying to separate themselves from the collapsing Roman and the nominal Christian world. Basil the Great (329–379) popularized communal monasticism throughout the East, providing a rule that lessened the asceticism of Pachomius and directed monks beyond their segregated enclaves of perfection into such social services as

The rule of St. Benedict, followed by most medieval monasteries, required monks to spend a third of their day in manual labor. This served to make the monastery self-sufficient and self-contained. Here monks are shown doing a variety of agricultural tasks. [Vincent Varga Archives]

caring for orphans, widows, and the infirm in surrounding communities.

Athanasius (ca. 293–373) and Martin of Tours (ca. 315–ca. 397) introduced monasticism into the west, where the teaching of John Cassian (ca. 360–435) and Jerome (ca. 340–420) helped shape its basic values and practices. The great organizer of western monasticism was Benedict of Nursia (ca. 480–547). In 529 he established a monastery at Monte Cassino, in Italy, founding the form of monasticism—Benedictine—that bears his name and that quickly came to dominate in the west. Benedict also wrote a sophisticated *Rule for Monasteries*, a comprehensive plan that both regimented and enriched monastic life. Following the *Rule*, Benedictine monasteries were hierarchically organized and directed by an abbot, whose command was beyond question. Periods of study and religious devotion (about four hours each day of prayers and liturgical activities) alternated with manual labor—a program that permitted not a moment's idleness and carefully promoted the religious, intellectual, and physical well-being of the monks. During the early Middle Ages Benedictine missionaries Christianized both England and Germany. Their disciplined organization and devotion to hard work made the Benedictines an economic and political power as well as a spiritual force wherever they settled.

The Doctrine of Papal Primacy

Constantine and his successors, especially the eastern emperors, ruled religious life with an iron hand and consistent-

ly looked on the church as little more than a department of the state. The bishops of Rome, however, never accepted such royal intervention and opposed it in every way they could. Taking advantage of imperial weakness and distraction, they developed for their own defense the doctrine of "papal primacy." This doctrine raised the Roman pontiff to an unassailable supremacy within the church when it came to defining church doctrine and maintaining clerical allegiance. It also put him in a position to make important secular claims, leading to repeated conflicts between Church and State, pope and emperor, throughout the Middle Ages.

Pope Damasus I (366–384) took the first step toward establishing the doctrine when he declared Rome's "apostolic" primacy. Pointing to Jesus' words to Peter in the Gospel of Matthew (16:18) ("Thou art Peter, and upon this rock I will build my church"), he claimed himself and all other popes to be Peter's direct successors as the unique "rock" on which the Christian church was built. Pope Leo I (440–461) took still another step by assuming the title *pontifex maximus*—"supreme priest." He further proclaimed himself to be endowed with a "plenitude of power," thereby establishing the supremacy of the bishop of Rome over all other bishops in the church. During Leo's reign an imperial decree recognized his exclusive jurisdiction over the western church. At the end of the fifth century Pope Gelasius I (492–496) proclaimed the authority of the clergy to be "more weighty" than the power of kings because priests had charge of divine affairs and the means of salvation.

Division of Christendom

As these events suggest, the division of Christendom into eastern (Byzantine) and western (Roman Catholic) churches has its roots in the early Middle Ages. The division was due

Major Political and Religious Developments of the Early Middle Ages

313	Emperor Constantine issues the Edict of Milan
325	Council of Nicea defines Christian doctrine
410	Rome invaded by Visigoths under Alaric
413–426	St. Augustine writes *The City of God*
451–453	Europe invaded by the Huns under Attila
476	Barbarian Odovacer deposes western emperor and rules as king of the Romans
488	Theodoric establishes kingdom of Ostrogoths in Italy
529	St. Benedict founds monastery at Monte Cassino
533	Justinian codifies Roman law
732	Charles Martel defeats Arabs at Tours
754	Pope Stephen II and Pepin III ally

in part to linguistic and cultural differences between the Greek east and the Roman west. As in the west, eastern church organization closely followed that of the secular state. A "patriarch" ruled over "metropolitans" and "archbishops" in the cities and provinces, and they, in turn, ruled over bishops, who stood as authorities over the local clergy. A novel combination of Greek, Roman, and Asian elements, however, shaped Byzantine culture, giving eastern Christianity more of a mystical orientation and a greater preoccupation with the hereafter than western Christianity. This difference in outlook may have predisposed eastern patriarchs to submit more passively than western popes ever could to royal intervention in their affairs.

Contrary to the evolving western tradition of universal clerical celibacy, which western monastic culture encouraged, the eastern church permitted the marriage of parish priests (but not monks), while strictly forbidding bishops to marry. The eastern church also used leavened bread in the Eucharist, contrary to the western custom of using unleavened bread. The Roman church also objected to the tendency of the eastern church to compromise with the politically powerful Arian Christians and the followers of another nonorthodox group, the Monophysite Christians. Finally, the Eastern and Western churches both laid claim to jurisdiction over newly converted areas in the northern Balkans.

Beyond these issues, three major factors lay behind the religious break between east and west. The first revolved around questions of doctrinal authority. The eastern church put more stress on the authority of the Bible and the ecumenical councils of the church in the definition of Christian doctrine than on the counsel and decrees of the bishop of Rome. The claims of Roman popes to a special primacy of authority on the basis of the Apostle Peter's commission from Jesus in the Gospel of Matthew were unacceptable to the east, where the independence and autonomy of regional churches held sway. This basic issue of authority in matters of faith lay behind the mutual excommunication of Pope Nicholas I and Patriarch Photius in the ninth century and that of Pope Leo IX (through his ambassador to Constantinople, Cardinal Humbert) and Patriarch Michael Cerularius in 1054.

A second major issue in the separation of the two churches was the western addition of the *filioque* clause to the Nicene-Constantinopolitan Creed. According to this anti-Arian clause, the Holy Spirit proceeds "also from the Son" *(filioque)* as well as from the Father, making clear the western belief that Christ was fully one essence with God the Father and not a lesser being.

The third factor dividing the eastern and western churches was the iconoclastic controversy of the first half of the eighth century. As noted earlier, after 725 the Byzantine Emperor Leo III (r. 717–741) attempted to force western popes to abolish the use of images in their churches. This stand met fierce official and popular resistance in the west, where images were greatly cherished, and in the east as well. To punish the West Leo confiscated valuable papal lands. This direct challenge to the papacy coincided with a threat to Rome and the western church from the Lombards of northern Italy. Assailed on two fronts, the Roman papacy seemed doomed. But there has not been a more resilient and enterprising institution in Western history than the papacy. Since the pontificate of Gregory the Great (590–604), who 150 years earlier had negotiated a treaty with the Lombards, popes had recognized the Franks of northern Gaul as Europe's ascendant power and seen in them their surest protectors. In 754 Pope Stephen II (752–757), initiating the most fruitful political alliance of the Middle Ages, enlisted the Franks and their ruler, Pepin III, to defend the church against the Lombards and as a western counterweight to the eastern emperor. This marriage of religion and politics created a new western church and empire; it also determined much of the course of western history into our time.

The Kingdom of the Franks

Merovingians and Carolingians: From Clovis to Charlemagne

Clovis (ca. 466–511), a warrior chieftain who converted to orthodox Christianity under the influence of his Christian wife around 496, founded the first Frankish dynasty, the Merovingians, named for Merovich, an early leader of one branch of the Franks. Clovis and his successors subdued the pagan Burgundians and the Arian Visigoths and established the kingdom of the Franks within ancient Gaul, making the Franks and the Merovingian kings a significant force in western Europe. The Franks themselves occupied a broad belt of territory that extended throughout modern France, Belgium, the Netherlands, and western Germany, and their loyalties remained strictly tribal and local. In attempting to govern their sprawling kingdom, the Merovingians encountered what proved to be the most persistent problem of medieval political history—the competing claims of the "one" and the "many," with the king (the "one") struggling to impose centralized government and transregional loyalty on powerful local magnates (the "many"), who sought to preserve their regional autonomy and traditions.

The Merovingian kings addressed this problem by making pacts with the landed nobility and by creating the royal office of count. The counts were men without possessions to whom the king gave great lands in the expectation that they would be, as the landed aristocrats often were not, loyal officers of the kingdom. But like local aristocrats, the Merovin-

Clovis Converts to Christianity

One of the attractions of Christianity in the late ancient and early medieval world was its belief in a God providentially active in history who assisted those loyal to him against their enemies. In the following account of Clovis's conversion, provided by the Christian church historian Gregory of Tours, the Frankish king is said to have turned Christian because he believed that the Christian God had given him victory over a rival German tribe, the Alemanni.

Why might an early medieval chieftain marry a confessing Christian in the sixth century? What did Clovis and Clotilde think being a Christian meant? Does the arrival of Remigius, bishop of Rheims, provide clues to Christianity's success among the German tribes?

Clovis took to wife Clotilde, daughter of the king of the Burgundians and a Christian. The queen unceasingly urged the king to acknowledge the true God, and forsake idols. But he could not in any wise be brought to believe until a war broke out with the Alemanni.... The two armies were in battle and there was great slaughter. Clovis' army was near to utter destruction. He saw the danger ... and raised his eyes to heaven, saying: Jesus Christ, whom Clotilde declares to be the son of the living God, who it is said givest aid to the oppressed and victory to those who put their hope in thee, I beseech thy ... aid. If thou shalt grant me victory over these I will believe in thee and be baptized in thy name. For I have called upon my gods, but ... they are far removed from my aid. So I believe that they have no power, for they do not succor those who serve them. Now I call upon thee, and I long to believe in thee.... When he had said these things, the Alemanni turned their backs and began to flee. When they saw that their king was killed, they submitted to the sway of Clovis, saying ... Now we are thine.

After Clovis had forbidden further war and praised his soldiers, he told the queen how he had won the victory by calling on the name of Christ. Then the queen sent for the blessed Remigius, bishop of the city of Rheims, praying him to bring the gospel of salvation to the king. The priest, little by little and secretly, led him to believe in the true God ... and to forsake idols, which could not help him nor anybody else.

From James Harvey Robinson (Ed.), *Readings in European History*, Vol. I (Boston: Athenaeum, 1904).

---

gian counts also let their immediate self-interests gain the upper hand. Once established in office for a period of time, they too became territorial rulers in their own right, with the result that the Frankish kingdom progressively fragmented into independent regions and tiny principalities. This centrifugal tendency was aggravated by the Frankish custom of dividing the kingdom equally among the king's legitimate male heirs.

Rather than purchasing allegiance and unity within the kingdom, the Merovingian largess simply occasioned the rise of competing magnates and petty tyrants, who became laws unto themselves within their regions. By the seventh century, the Frankish king was king in title only and had no effective executive power. Real power came to be concentrated in the office of the mayor of the palace, who was the spokesman at the king's court for the great landowners of the three regions into which the Frankish kingdom was divided: Neustria (roughly western France), Austrasia (roughly central Germany), and Burgundy. Through this office, the Carolingian dynasty rose to power.

The Carolingians (named for the dynasty's greatest ruler, Carolus, later known as Charlemagne, or Charles the Great) controlled the office of the mayor of the palace from the ascent to that post of Pepin I of Austrasia (d. 639) until 751, when, with the enterprising connivance of the pope, they simply expropriated the Frankish crown. Pepin II (d. 714) ruled in fact if not in title over the Frankish kingdom. His illegitimate son, Charles Martel ("the Hammer," d. 741), created a great cavalry by bestowing lands known as *benefices* or *fiefs* on powerful nobles, who, in return, agreed to be ready to serve as the king's army. It was such an army that checked the Arab probings at Tours in 732.

The fiefs so generously bestowed by Charles Martel to create his army came in large part from landed property that he usurped from the church. His alliance with the landed aristocracy in this grand manner permitted the Carolingians to have some measure of political success where the Merovingians had failed. The Carolingians created counts almost entirely out of the landed nobility from which the Carolingians themselves had risen. The Merovingians, in contrast, had tried to compete directly with these great aristocrats by raising the landless to power. By playing to strength rather than challenging it, the Carolingians strengthened themselves, at least for the short term. The church, by this time dependent on the protection of the Franks against the eastern emperor and the Lombards, had no choice but to tolerate the seizure of its lands. Later, although they never returned the lands, the Franks partially compensated the church for them.

Frankish Church The church played a large and enterprising role in the Frankish government. By Carolingian times, monasteries were a dominant force. Their intellectual achievements made them respected repositories of culture. Their religious teaching and example imposed order on surrounding populations. Their relics and rituals made them magical shrines to which pilgrims came in great numbers. Thanks to their donated lands and serf labor, many had become very profitable farms and landed estates, their abbots rich and powerful magnates. By Merovingian times, the higher clergy were already employed in tandem with counts as royal agents. It was the policy of the Carolingians, perfected by Charles Martel and his successor, Pepin III ("the Short"; d. 768), to use the church to pacify conquered neighboring tribes—Frisians, Thuringians, Bavarians, and especially the Franks' archenemies, the Saxons.

Conversion to Nicene Christianity became an integral part of the successful annexation of conquered lands and people; the cavalry broke bodies, while the clergy won hearts and minds. The Anglo-Saxon missionary Saint Boniface (born Wynfrith; ca. 680–754) was the most important of the German clergy who served Carolingian kings in this way. Christian bishops in missionary districts and elsewhere became lords, appointed by and subject to the king—an ominous integration of secular and religious policy in which lay the seeds of the later Investiture Controversy of the eleventh and twelfth centuries (see Chapter 13).

The church helped the Carolingians with more than territorial expansion. Pope Zacharias (741–752) also sanctioned Pepin the Short's termination of the vestigial Merovingian dynasty and the Carolingian accession to outright kingship of the Franks. With the pope's public blessing, Pepin was proclaimed king by the nobility in council in 751, and the last of the Merovingians, the puppet king Childeric III, was hus-

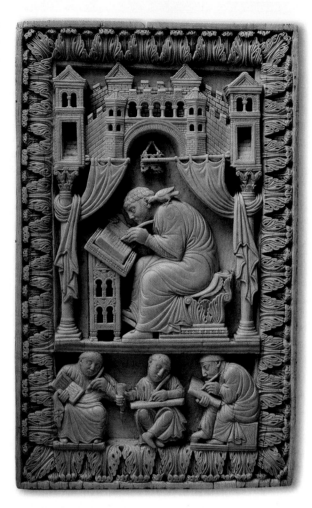

During the Carolingian Renaissance scholars made editions of the works of Gregory the Great, shown here in a monastic scriptorium (an area devoted to copying and preserving books) receiving the divine word from a dove perched on his shoulder. Below St. Gregory three monks are shown writing. Note the inkwell held by the middle monk. Before the invention of the printing press in about 1450, manuscripts could only be duplicated by laborious hand copying. Much of this painstaking work was done by monks. [Kunsthistorisches Museum, Vienna]

tled off to a monastery and dynastic oblivion. According to legend, Saint Boniface anointed Pepin, thereby investing Frankish rule from the very start with a certain sacral character.

Zacharias's successor, Pope Stephen II (752–757), did not let Pepin forget the favor of his predecessor. Driven from Rome in 753 by the Lombards, Pope Stephen appealed directly to Pepin to cast out the invaders and to guarantee papal claims to central Italy, which was dominated at this time by the eastern emperor. In 754 the Franks and the Church formed an alliance against the Lombards and the eastern emperor. Carolingian kings became the protectors of the Catholic church and thereby "kings by the grace of God." Pepin gained the title *patricius Romanorum*, "father-protector of the Romans," a title heretofore borne only by the representative of the eastern emperor. In 755 the Franks defeated the Lombards and gave the pope the lands surrounding Rome, creating what came to be known as the Papal States. In this period a fraudulent document appeared—the *Donation of Constantine* (written between 750 and 800)—that was enterprisingly designed to remind the Franks of the church's importance as the heir of Rome. Many believed it to be genuine until it was exposed as a forgery in the fifteenth century.

The papacy had looked to the Franks for an ally strong enough to protect it from the eastern emperors. It is an irony of history that the church found in the Carolingian dynasty a western imperial government that drew almost as slight a boundary between State and Church, secular and religious policy, as did eastern emperors. Although eminently preferable for the popes to eastern domination, Carolingian patronage of the church proved in its own way to be no less constraining.

Map 12-3 The empire of Charlemagne to 814.   Building on the successes of his predecessors, Charlemagne greatly increased the Frankish domains. Such traditional enemies as the Saxons and the Lombards fell under his sway.

Reign of Charlemagne (768–814)

Charlemagne, the son of Pepin the Short, continued the role of his father as papal protector in Italy and his policy of territorial conquest in the north. After King Desiderius and the Lombards of northern Italy were decisively defeated in 774, Charlemagne took the title "King of the Lombards" in Pavia. He widened the frontiers of his kingdom further by subjugating surrounding pagan tribes, foremost among them the Saxons, whom the Franks brutally Christianized and dispersed in small groups throughout Frankish lands. The Danu-

bian plains were brought into the Frankish orbit by the virtual annihilation of the Avars, a tribe related to the Huns. The Arabs were chased beyond the Pyrenees. By the time of his death on January 28, 814, Charlemagne's kingdom embraced modern France, Belgium, Holland, Switzerland, almost the whole of Germany, much of Italy, a portion of Spain, and the island of Corsica (see Map 12–3).

The New Empire   Encouraged by his ambitious advisers, Charlemagne came to harbor imperial designs. He desired to be not only king of all the Franks but a universal emperor as well. He had his sacred palace city, Aachen (in French, Aix-la-Chapelle), constructed in conscious imitation of the courts of the ancient Roman and of the contemporary eastern emperors. Although he permitted the church its independence, he looked after it with a paternalism almost as great as that of any eastern emperor. He used the church above all to promote social stability and hierarchical order throughout the kingdom—as an aid in the creation of a great Frankish Christian empire. Frankish Christians were ceremoniously baptized, professed the Nicene Creed (with the filioque clause), and learned in church to revere Charlemagne.

Charlemagne realized his imperial pretensions on Christmas Day, 800, when Pope Leo III (795–816) crowned him emperor. This event created what would later be called the Holy Roman Empire, a revival, based after 870 in Germany, of the old Roman Empire in the west. If the coronation benefited the church, as it certainly did, it also served Charlemagne's designs. Before his coronation, Charlemagne had been a minor western potentate in the eyes of eastern emperors. After the coronation, eastern emperors reluctantly recognized his new imperial dignity, and Charlemagne even found it necessary to disclaim ambitions to rule as emperor over the east.

The New Emperor

Charlemagne stood six feet, three-and-one-half inches tall—a fact confirmed when his tomb was opened and exact measurements of his remains were taken in 1861. He was restless, ever ready for a hunt. Informal and gregarious, he insisted on the presence of friends even when he bathed and was widely known for his practical jokes, lusty good humor, and warm hospitality. Aachen was a festive palace city to which people and gifts came from all over the world. In 802 Charlemagne even received from the caliph of Baghdad, Harun-al-Rashid, a white elephant, the transport of which across the Alps was as great a wonder as the creature itself.

Charlemagne had five official wives in succession, and many mistresses and concubines, and he sired numerous children. This connubial variety created problems. His oldest son by his first marriage, Pepin, jealous of the attention shown by his father to the sons of his second wife and fearing the loss of paternal favor, joined with noble enemies in a conspiracy against his father. He spent the rest of his life in confinement in a monastery after the plot was exposed.

An equestrian figure of Charlemagne (or possibly one of his sons) from the early ninth century. [Giraudon/Art Resource, N.Y.]

Problems of Government

Charlemagne governed his kingdom through counts, of whom there were perhaps as many as 250, strategically located within the administrative districts into which the kingdom was divided. In Carolingian practice, the count tended to be a local magnate, one who already had an armed following and the self-interest to enforce the will of a generous king. He had three main duties: to maintain a local army loyal to the king, to collect tribute and dues, and to administer justice throughout his district.

This last responsibility he undertook through a district law court known as the mallus, which heard testimony from the parties involved in a dispute or crime, passed judgment, and assessed a monetary compensation to be paid to the injured party. In very difficult cases, where guilt or innocence was unclear, recourse was often taken to judicial duels or "divine" tests and ordeals. Among these was the length of time a defendant's hand took to heal after immersion in boiling water. In another, the ordeal by water, a defendant was thrown with his hands and feet bound into a river or pond that a priest had blessed. If he floated, he was pronounced guilty, because the pure water had obviously rejected him; if, however, the water received him and he sank, he was deemed innocent.

As in Merovingian times, many counts used their official position and new judicial powers to their own advantage, becoming little despots within their districts. As they grew stronger and more independent, they came to regard the land grants with which they were paid as hereditary positions rather than generous royal donations. This development signaled the impending fragmentation of Charlemagne's kingdom. Charlemagne tried to supervise his overseers and improve local justice by creating special royal envoys known as *missi dominici*, lay and clerical agents (counts and archbishops and bishops) who made annual visits to districts other than their own. But their impact was marginal. In still another attempt to manage the counts and

The Court Scholar Einhard Describes His Admired King, Charlemagne

What are the distinguishing marks of leadership in this account? Which of Charlemagne's features, habits, and aspirations would appeal to his simple subjects, which to intellectuals like Einhard? Does Einhard's account have the ring of authenticity, or is this royal propaganda?

Charles was large and robust, of commanding stature and excellent proportions. . . . He took constant exercise in riding and hunting, which was natural for a Frank, since scarcely any nation can be found to equal them in these pursuits. He also delighted in the natural warm baths, frequently exercising himself by swimming, in which he was very skillful, no one being able to outstrip him. It was on account of the warm baths at Aix-la-Chapelle that he built his palace there and lived there constantly during the last years of his life and until his death. . . .

He wore the dress of his native country, that is, the Frankish. . . . He thoroughly disliked the dress of foreigners, however fine; and he never put it on except at Rome. . . .

In his eating and drinking he was temperate; more particularly so in his drinking, for he had the greatest abhorrence of drunkenness in anybody, but more especially in himself and his companions. . . . While he was dining he listened to music or reading. History and the deeds of men of old were most often read. He derived much pleasure from the works of St. Augustine, especially from his book called *The City of God*.

He was ready and fluent in speaking, and able to express himself with great clearness. He did not confine himself to his native tongue, but took pains to learn foreign languages, acquiring such knowledge of Latin that he could make an address in that language as well as in his own. Greek he could better understand than speak. Indeed, he was so polished in speech that he might have passed for a learned man.

He was an ardent admirer of the liberal arts, and greatly revered their professors, whom he promoted to high honors. In order to learn grammar, he attended the lectures of the aged Peter of Pisa, a deacon; and for other branches of knowledge, he chose as his preceptor Alcuin, also a deacon, a Saxon by race, from Britain, the most learned man of the day, with whom the king spent much time in learning rhetoric and logic, and more especially astronomy. He learned the art of determining the dates upon which the movable festivals of the Church fall, and with deep thought and skill most carefully calculated the courses of the planets.

Charles also tried to learn to write, and used to keep his tablets and writing book under the pillow of his couch, that when he had leisure he might practice his hand in forming letters; but he made little progress in this task, too long deferred and begun too late in life.

From James Harvey Robinson (ed.), *Readings in European History*, Vol 1 (Boston: Athenaeum, 1904), pp. 126–128.

organize the outlying regions of his realm, the king appointed permanent provincial governors with titles like prefect, duke, or margrave. But as these governors became established in their areas, they proved no less corruptible than the others.

Charlemagne never solved the problem of creating a loyal bureaucracy. Ecclesiastical agents proved no better than secular ones in this regard. Landowning bishops had not only the same responsibilities but also the same secular lifestyles and aspirations as the royal counts. Except for their attendance to the liturgy and to church prayers, they were largely indistinguishable from the lay nobility. Capitularies, or royal decrees, discouraged the more outrageous behavior of the clergy. But Charlemagne also sensed—rightly, as the Gregorian reform of the eleventh century would prove—that the emergence of a distinctive and reform-minded class of ecclesiastical landowners would be a danger to royal government. Charlemagne purposefully treated his bishops as

he treated his counts, that is, as vassals who served at the king's pleasure.

Alcuin and the Carolingian Renaissance   Charlemagne used much of the great wealth his conquests brought him to attract Europe's best scholars to Aachen, where they developed court culture and education. By making scholarship materially as well as intellectually rewarding, Charlemagne attracted such scholars as Theodulf of Orleans (d. 821), Angilbert (d. 814), his own biographer Einhard (ca. 770–840), and the renowned Anglo-Saxon master Alcuin of York (735–804), who at almost fifty became director of the king's palace school in 782. Alcuin brought classical and Christian learning to Aachen and was handsomely rewarded for his efforts with several monastic estates, including that of Saint Martin of Tours, the wealthiest in the kingdom.

Although Charlemagne also appreciated learning for its own sake, his grand palace school was not created simply for love

In this eleventh-century manuscript, peasants harvest vines and plow fields behind yoked oxen. The moldboard plow shown here came into use in Carolingian times. It had a heavier blade than the earlier "scratch" plow and could cut deep furrows in the soil, greatly improving crop yields. [Ardos Studio Fotografia]

of antiquity. Charlemagne intended it to upgrade the administrative skills of the clerics and officials who staffed the royal bureaucracy. By preparing the sons of nobles to run the religious and secular offices of the realm, court scholarship served kingdom building. With its special concentration on grammar, logic, rhetoric, and basic mathematics, the school provided training in the basic tools of bureaucracy: reading, writing, speaking, sound reasoning, and counting. Charlemagne's scholars also created a new, clear style of handwriting—Carolingian minuscule—and fostered the use of accurate Latin in official documents, developments that helped increase lay literacy. Through personal correspondence and visitations, Alcuin created a genuine, if limited, community of scholars and clerics at court and did much to infuse the highest administrative levels with a sense of comradeship and common purpose.

A modest renaissance, or rebirth, of antiquity occurred in the palace school as scholars collected and preserved ancient manuscripts for a more curious posterity. Alcuin worked on a correct text of the Bible and made editions of the works of Gregory the Great and the monastic Rule of Saint Benedict. These scholarly activities aimed at concrete reforms and served official efforts to bring uniformity to Church law and liturgy, to educate the clergy, and to improve moral life within the monasteries.

The Manor and Serfdom   The agrarian economy of the Middle Ages was organized and controlled through village farms known as manors. Here peasants labored as farmers in subordination to a lord, that is, a more powerful landowner who gave them land and a dwelling in exchange for their services and a portion of their crops. That part of the land farmed by the peasants for the lord was the demesne, on average about one quarter to one third of the arable land. All crops grown there were harvested for the lord.

Peasants were treated according to their social status and the size of their land holdings. A freeman—that is, a peasant with his own modest allodial, or hereditary, property (property free from the claims of an overlord)—became a serf by surrendering his property to a greater landowner—a lord—in exchange for protection and assistance. The freeman received his land back from the lord with a clear definition of his economic and legal rights. Although the land was no longer his property, he had full possession and use of it and the number of services and amount of goods he was to supply to the lord were carefully spelled out. Peasants who entered the service of a lord with little real property to bargain with (perhaps only a few farm implements and animals) ended up as unfree serfs and were much more vulnerable to the lord's demands, often spending up to three days a week working the lord's fields. Truly impoverished peasants who lived and worked on the manor as serfs had the lowest status and were the least protected.

Serfs were subject to so-called dues in kind: firewood for cutting the lord's wood, sheep for grazing their sheep on the lord's land, and the like. Thus the lord, who for his part furnished shacks and small plots of land from his vast domain, had at his disposal an army of servants who provided him with everything from eggs to boots. That many serfs were discontented is reflected in the high number of recorded escapes. An astrological calendar from the period marks the days most favorable for escaping. Escaped serfs roamed the land as beggars and vagabonds, searching for new and better masters.

By the time of Charlemagne, the moldboard plow, which was especially needed in northern Europe where the soil was heavy, and the three-field system of land cultivation were coming into use. These developments greatly improved agricultural productivity. Unlike the older "scratch" plow, which crisscrossed the field with only slight penetration, the moldboard cut deep into the soil and turned it to form a ridge, providing a natural drainage system for the field as well as permitting the deep planting of seeds. Unlike the earlier two-field system of crop rotation, which simply alternated fallow with planted fields each year, the three-field system increased the amount of cultivated land by leaving only one third fallow in a given year.

Religion and the Clergy   As owners of the churches on their lands, the lords had the right to raise chosen serfs to the

The Carolingian Manor

A capitulary (or ordinance) from the reign of Charlemagne (known as "De Villis") itemizes what the king received from his royal manors or village estates. It is a testimony to Carolingian administrative ability and domination over the countryside.

What gave a lord the right to absolutely everything? (Has anything been overlooked?) How did the stewards and workers share in manorial life? Was the arrangement a good deal for them as well as for the lord?

That each steward shall make an annual statement of all our income: an account of our lands cultivated by the oxen which our ploughmen drive and of our lands which the tenants of farms ought to plough; an account of the pigs, of the rents [a payment for the right to keep pigs in the woods], of the obligations and fines; of the game taken in our forests without our permission; of the various compositions; of the mills, of the forest, of the fields, of the bridges, and ships; of the free-men and the hundreds who are under obligations to our treasury; of markets, vineyards, and those who owe wine to us; of the hay, fire-wood, torches, planks, and other kinds of lumber; of the waste-lands; of the vegetables, millet, panic; of the wool, flax, and hemp; of the fruits of the trees, of the nut trees, larger and smaller; of the grafted trees of all kinds; of the gardens; of the turnips; of the fish-ponds; of the hides, skins, and horns; of the honey, wax; of the fat, tallow and soap; of the mulberry wine, cooked wine, mead, vinegar, beer, wine new and old; of the new grain and the old; of the hens and eggs; of the geese; the number of fishermen, smiths [workers in metal], sword-makers, and shoe-makers; of the bins and boxes; of the turners and saddlers; of the forges and mines, that is iron and other mines; of the lead mines; of the tributaries; of the colts and fillies; they shall make all these known to us, set forth separately and in order, at Christmas, in order that we may know what and how much of each thing we have.

In each of our estates our stewards are to have as many cow-houses, piggeries, sheepfolds, stable for goats, as possible, and they ought never to be without these.

They must provide with the greatest care that whatever is prepared or made with the hands, that is, lard, smoked meat, salt meat, partially salted meat, wine, vinegar, mulberry wine, cooked wine, garns [a kind of fermented liquor], mustard, cheese, butter, malt, beer, mead, honey, wax, flour, all should be prepared and made with the greatest cleanliness.

That each steward on each of our domains shall always have, for the sake of ornament, swans, peacocks, pheasants, ducks, pigeons, partridges, turtle-doves.

For our women's work they are to give at the proper time, as has been ordered, the materials, that is the linen, wool, woad [blue dye], vermillion, madder [red dye], wool-combs, teasels [plant used to create a soft, fuzzy surface on fabrics or leather], soap, grease, vessels and the other objects which are necessary.

Of the food-products other than meat, two-thirds shall be sent each year for our own use, that is of the vegetables, fish, cheese, butter, honey, mustard, vinegar, millet, panic, dried and green herbs, radishes, and in addition of the wax, soap and other small products.

That each steward shall have in his district good workmen, namely, blacksmiths, gold-smiths, silver-smiths, shoemakers, turners [lathe workers], carpenters, sword-makers, fishermen, foilers [sword-makers], soap-makers, men who know how to make beer, cider, berry, and all the other kinds of beverages, bakers to make pastry for our table, net-makers who know how to make nets for hunting, fishing and fowling, and the other who are too numerous to be designated.

Translations and reprints from the *Original Sources of European History*, Vol. 3 (Philadelphia: Department of History, University of Pennsylvania, 1909), pp. 2–4.

---

post of parish priest, placing them in charge of the churches on the lords' estates. Church law directed the lord to set a serf free before he entered the clergy, but lords were reluctant to do this and risk thereby a possible later challenge to their jurisdiction over the ecclesiastical property with which the serf, as priest, was invested. Lords preferred a "serf priest," one who not only said the mass on Sundays and holidays but also continued to serve his lord during the week, waiting on the lord's table and tending his steeds. Like Charlemagne with his bishops, Frankish lords cultivated a docile parish clergy.

The ordinary people baptized themselves and their children, confessed the Creed mass, tried to learn the Lord's Prayer, and received last rites from the priest when death approached. Local priests on the manors were no better educated than their congregations, and instruction in the meaning of Christian doctrine and practice remained at a bare minimum. People understandably became particularly attached in this period to the more tangible veneration of relics and saints.

Charlemagne shared many of the religious beliefs of his ordinary subjects. He collected and venerated relics, made pilgrimages to Rome, frequented the church of Saint Mary in Aachen several times a day, and directed in his last will and testament that all but a fraction of his great treasure be spent to endow masses and prayers for his departed soul.

Breakup of the Carolingian Kingdom

In the last years of his life, an ailing Charlemagne knew that his empire was ungovernable. The seeds of dissolution lay in regionalism, that is, the determination of each locality, no matter how small, to look first—and often only—to its own self-interest. In medieval society, a direct relationship existed between physical proximity to authority and loyalty to authority. Local people obeyed local lords more readily than they obeyed a glorious but distant king. Charlemagne had been forced to recognize and even to enhance the power of regional magnates in order to win needed financial and military support.

Louis the Pious   The Carolingian kings did not give up easily, however. Charlemagne's only surviving son and successor, Louis the Pious (r. 814–840) had three sons by his first wife; according to Salic or Germanic law, a ruler partitioned his kingdom equally among his surviving sons. Louis recognized that a tripartite kingdom would hardly be an empire and acted early in his reign to break this legal tradition. This he did by making his eldest son, Lothar (d. 855), coregent and sole imperial heir in 817. To Lothar's brothers he gave im-

portant but much lesser appanages, or assigned hereditary lands: Pepin (d. 838) became king of Aquitaine; Louis "the German" (d. 876) became king of Bavaria, over the eastern Franks.

In 823 Louis's second wife, Judith of Bavaria, bore him still a fourth son, Charles (d. 877). Determined that her son should receive more than just a nominal inheritance, the queen incited the brothers Pepin and Louis to war against Lothar, and persuaded Louis to divide the kingdom equally among his four living sons. As the bestower of crowns upon emperors, the pope had an important stake in the preservation of the revived western empire and the imperial title, both of which Louis's belated agreement to an equal partition of his kingdom threatened to undo. The pope condemned Louis and restored Lothar to his original magnificent inheritance. But Lothar's regained imperial dignity only stirred anew the resentments of his brothers, including his halfbrother, Charles, who joined in renewed war against him.

The Treaty of Verdun and Its Aftermath   In 843, with the treaty of Verdun, peace finally came to Louis's surviving heirs (Pepin had died in 838). The great Carolingian empire was partitioned into three equal parts. Lothar received a middle section, which came to be known as Lotharingia and embraced roughly modern Holland, Belgium, Switzerland, Alsace-Lorraine, and Italy. Charles the Bald received the western part of the kingdom, or roughly modern France. And Louis the German came into the eastern part, or roughly modern Germany (see Map 12–4). Although Lothar retained the imperial title, the universal empire of Charlemagne and Louis the Pious now ceased to exist. Not until the sixteenth century, with the election in 1519 of Charles I of Spain as the Holy Roman Emperor Charles V, would the western world again see a kingdom as vast as Charlemagne's.

The Treaty of Verdun proved to be only the beginning of Carolingian fragmentation. When Lothar died in 855 his kingdom was divided equally among his three surviving sons, leaving it much smaller and weaker than the kingdoms of Louis the German and Charles the Bald. Henceforth, western Europe would be divided into an eastern and a western Frankish kingdom—roughly Germany and France—at war over the fractionalized middle kingdom, a contest that has continued into modern times.

The political breakdown of the Carolingian Empire coincided with new external threats. In the late ninth and tenth centuries, successive waves of Normans (North men), better known as Vikings, swept into Europe from Scandinavia. Magyars, or Hungarians, who were great horsemen, likewise swept in from the eastern plains, while Muslims made incursions across the Mediterranean from North Africa (see Map 12–5). The Franks built fortified towns and castles in strategic lo-

The Oseberg Ship. Viking, ca. 850 c.e. Around sixty feet long and able to transport at least fifty fully armed men, and powered by both sail and oars. Viking long ships menaced towns along coastal areas and rivers from the Baltic and the English Channel in the north to the Mediterranean and Black Sea in the south, while also sailing to Iceland and farther west. [Werner Foreman/Art Resource, N.Y.]

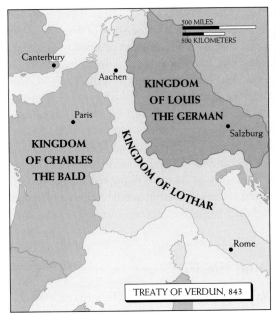

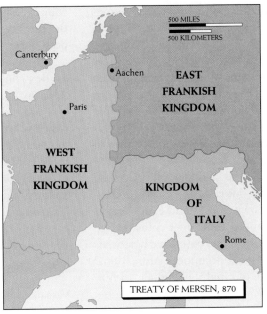

Map 12–4 The Treaty of Verdun (843) and the Treaty of Mersen (870). The Treaty of Verdun divided the kingdom of Louis the Pious among his three feuding children: Charles the Bald, Lothar, and Louis the German. After Lothar's death in 855 the middle kingdom was so weakened by division among his three sons that Charles the Bald and Louis the German divided it between themselves in the Treaty of Mersen.

cations as refuges. When they could, they bought off the invaders with outright grants of land and payments of silver. In the resulting turmoil, local populations became more dependent than ever on local strongmen for life, limb, and livelihood, creating the essential precondition for the maturation of feudal society.

Feudal Society

The Middle Ages were characterized by a chronic absence of effective central government and the constant threat of famine, disease, and foreign invasion. In this state of affairs the weaker sought the protection of the stronger, and the true

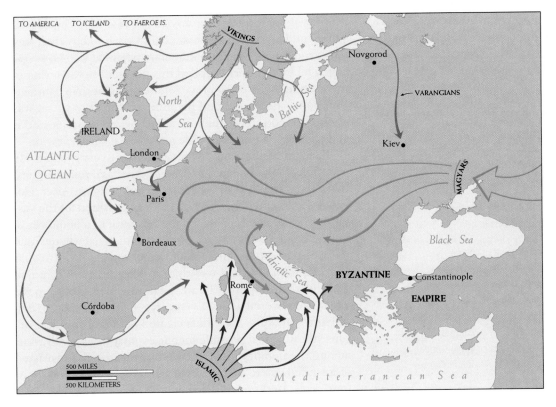

Map 12–5 Viking, Muslim, and Magyar invasions to the eleventh century. Western Europe was sorely beset by new waves of outsiders from the ninth to the eleventh century. From north, east, and south a stream of invading Vikings, Magyars, and Muslims brought the west at times to near collapse and of course gravely affected institutions within Europe.

lords and masters became those who could guarantee immediate protection from rapine and starvation. The term *feudal society* refers to the social, political, military, and economic system that emerged from these conditions.

A feudal society is a social order in which a regional prince or a local lord is dominant, and the highest virtues are those of mutual trust and fidelity. In a feudal society, what people require most is the firm assurance that others can be depended on in time of dire need. It is above all a system of mutual rights and responsibilities.

During the early Middle Ages, the landed nobility became great lords who ruled over their domains as miniature kingdoms. They maintained their own armies and courts, regulated local tolls, and even minted their own coins. Large groups of warrior vassals were created by extensive bestowals of land, and these developed into a prominent professional military class with its own code of knightly conduct. In feudal society, most serfs docilely worked the land, the clergy prayed and gave counsel, and lords and knights maintained law and order.

Origins

The origins of feudal government can be found in the divisions and conflicts of Merovingian society. In the sixth and seventh centuries, individual freemen began placing themselves under the protection of more powerful freemen. In this way, the latter built up armies and became local magnates, and the former solved the problem of simple survival. Freemen who so entrusted themselves to others were known as *ingenui in obsequio* (freemen in a contractual relation of dependence). Those who so gave themselves to the king were called *antrustiones*. All men of this type came to be described collectively as *vassi* ("those who serve"), from which evolved the term *vassalage*, meaning the placement of oneself in the personal service of another who promises protection in return.

Landed nobles, like kings, tried to acquire as many vassals as they could, because military strength in the early Middle Ages lay in numbers. Because it proved impossible to maintain these growing armies within the lord's own household, which was the original custom, or to support them by special monetary payments, the practice evolved of simply granting them land as a "tenement." Such land came to be known as a *benefice*, or a *fief*, and vassals were expected to dwell on it and maintain their horses and other accouterments of war in good order. Originally vassals, therefore, were little more than gangs-in-waiting.

Vassalage and the Fief

Vassalage involved "fealty" to the lord. To swear fealty was to promise to refrain from any action that might in any way threaten the lord's well-being and to perform personal services for him on his request. Chief among the expected services was military duty as a mounted knight. This could involve a variety of activities: a short or long military expedition, escort duty, standing castle guard, or the placement of one's own fortress at the lord's disposal, if the vassal was of such stature as to have one. Continuous bargaining and bickering occurred over the terms of service.

Limitations were placed on the number of days a lord could require services from a vassal. In France in the eleventh century, about forty days of service per year were considered sufficient. It also became possible for vassals to buy their way out of military service by a monetary payment known as *scutage*. The lord, in turn, applied this payment to the hiring of mercenaries, who often proved more efficient than contract-conscious vassals. Beyond his military duty, the vassal was also expected to give the lord advice when he requested it and to sit as a member of his court when it was in session.

The lord's obligations to his vassals were very specific. He was, first of all, obligated to protect the vassal from physical harm and to stand as his advocate in public court. After fealty was sworn and homage paid, the lord provided for the vassal's physical maintenance by the bestowal of a benefice, or fief. The fief was simply the physical or material wherewithal to meet the vassal's military and other obligations. It could take the form of liquid wealth as well as the more common grant of real property. There were so-called money fiefs, which empowered a vassal to receive regular payments from the lord's treasury. Such fiefs created potential conflicts because they made it possible for one country to acquire vassals among the nobility of another. Normally, the fief consisted of a landed estate of anywhere from a few to several thousand acres. But it could also take the form of a castle.

Carolingian Dynasty (751–987)

751	Pepin III "the Short" becomes king of the Franks
755	Franks drive Lombards out of central Italy; creation of Papal States
768–814	Charlemagne rules as king of the Franks
774	Charlemagne defeats Lombards in northern Italy
750–800	Fraudulent *Donation of Constantine* created in an effort to counter Frankish domination of church
800	Pope Leo III crowns Charlemagne
814–840	Louis the Pious succeeds Charlemagne as "Emperor"
843	Treaty of Verdun partitions the Carolingian Empire
870	Treaty of Mersen further divides Carolingian Empire
875–950	Invasions by Vikings, Muslims, and Magyars
962	Ottonian dynasty succeeds Carolingian in Germany
987	Capetian dynasty succeeds Carolingian in France

In Carolingian times, a benefice, or fief, varied in size from one or more small villas to several *mansi*, which were agricultural holdings of twenty-five to forty-eight acres. The king's vassals are known to have received benefices of at least thirty and as many as two hundred such mansi, truly a vast estate. Royal vassalage with a benefice understandably came to be widely sought by the highest classes of Carolingian society. As a royal policy, however, it proved deadly to the king in the long run. Although Carolingian kings jealously guarded their rights over property granted in benefice to vassals, resident vassals were still free to dispose of their benefices as they pleased. Vassals of the king, strengthened by his donations, in turn created their own vassals. These vassals, in turn, created still further vassals of their own—vassals of vassals of vassals—in a reverse pyramiding effect that had fragmented land and authority from the highest to the lowest levels by the late ninth century.

Beginning with the reign of Louis the Pious (r. 814–840), bishops and abbots swore fealty and received their offices from the king as a benefice. The king formally invested these clerics in their offices during a special ceremony in which he presented them with a ring and a staff, the symbols of high spiritual office. This presumptuous practice of lay investiture, like the Carolingian confiscation of church land mentioned earlier, was a sore point for the church. In the eleventh and twelfth centuries it would provoke a great confrontation between Church and State as reform-minded clergy rebelled against what they believed to be involuntary clerical vassalage.

Fragmentation and Divided Loyalty

In addition to the fragmentation brought about by the multiplication of vassalage, effective occupation of the land led gradually to claims of hereditary possession. Hereditary possession became a legally recognized principle in the ninth century and laid the basis for claims to real ownership. Fiefs given as royal donations became hereditary possessions and, with the passage of time, in some instances even the real property of the possessor. Further, vassal engagements came to be multiplied in still another way as enterprising freemen sought to accumulate as much land as possible. One man could become a vassal to several different lords. This development led in the ninth century to the concept of a "liege lord"—one master whom the vassal must obey even to the harm of the others, should a direct conflict among them arise.

The problem of loyalty was reflected not only in the literature of the period, with its praise of the virtues of honor and fidelity, but also in the ceremonial development of the very act of "commendation" by which a freeman became a vassal. In the mid-eighth century, an "oath of fealty" highlighted the ceremony. A vassal reinforced his promise of fidelity to the lord by swearing a special oath with his hand on a sacred relic or the Bible. In the tenth and eleventh centuries, paying homage to the lord involved not only the swearing of such an oath but also the placement of the vassal's hands between the lord's and the sealing of the ceremony with a kiss.

Despite their problems, feudal arrangements nonetheless provided stability throughout the early Middle Ages and aided the difficult process of political centralization during the High Middle Ages. The genius of feudal government lay in its adaptability. Contracts of different kinds could be made with almost anybody, as circumstances required. The process embraced a wide spectrum of people, from the king at the top to the lowliest vassal in the remotest part of the kingdom. The foundations of the modern nation-state would emerge in France and England from the fine-tuning of essentially feudal arrangements as kings sought to adapt their goal of centralized government to the reality of local power and control.

IN WORLD PERSPECTIVE

The Early Middle Ages

In western Europe, the centuries between 400 and 1000 witnessed both the decline of classical civilization and the birth of a new European civilization. Beginning with the fifth century, the barbarian invasions separated western Europe culturally from its classical age. No other world culture experienced such a prolonged separation. Although some important works and concepts survived from antiquity due largely to the Christian church, western civilization would for centuries be recovering its rich classical past in "renaissances" stretching into the sixteenth century. Out of the mixture of barbarian and surviving (or recovered) classical culture, western civilization, as we know it today, was born. Aided and abetted by the Christian church, the Carolingians created a new imperial tradition. But western society remained highly fragmented during the early Middle Ages. Two distinctive institutions arose during this period: manorialism and feudalism. Manorialism helped assure that all were fed and cared for, and feudalism provided for a region's defense. It was not a time of great cultural ambition.

In China, particularly in the seventh and eighth centuries, the T'ang dynasty rulers were also searching for ways to secure their borders against foreign expansion, in this case from Turkey and Tibet. As in western Europe, religion and philosophy served and did not compete with the state (although this would change in the West after the twelfth century). China at this time was, however, far more cosmopolitan and politically unified than western Europe, as well as being centuries ahead in technology. Printing with movable type appeared there by the tenth century, an invention the West would not see until the fifteenth century. The effective authority of Chinese rulers extended far beyond their immediate centers of government. The T'ang dynasty held sway over their empire in a way Carolingian rulers could only imagine.

In Japan, the Yamato court (300–680), much like those of the Merovingians and Carolingians, struggled to unify and control the countryside. It was also aided by a religion friendly to royalty, Shinto. As in the West, a Japanese identity evolved through struggle and accommodation with outside cultures, especially with the Chinese, the dominant influence on Japan between the seventh and twelfth centuries. But foreign cultural influence, again as in the West, never managed to eradicate the indigenous culture. By the ninth century a distinctive Sino-Japanese culture existed. But Japan, again like western Europe, remained a fragmented land during these centuries, despite a certain allegiance and willingness to pay taxes to an imperial court. Throughout Japan, as in western Europe, the basic unit of political control consisted of highly self-conscious and specially devoted armed retainers. A system of lordship and vassalage evolved around bands of local mounted warriors who were known as samurai. Through this system, local order was maintained in Japan until the fifteenth century. Like the

Merovingian and Carolingian courts, the Japanese court had to tolerate strong and independent regional rulers.

While western Europe struggled for political and social order in the fourth and fifth centuries, Indian civilization was enjoying a golden age under the reign of the Guptas (320–467). In this era of peace and stability, when a vocationally and socially limiting caste system neatly imposed order on Indian society from Brahmans to outcasts, culture, religion, and politics flourished.

In the seventh century, Islamic armies emerged from the Arabian peninsula, conquering from India to Spain by 710 and giving birth to a powerful new international civilization. Cosmopolitan and culturally vibrant, this civilization flourished despite the breakdown of Islamic political unity beginning in the ninth and tenth centuries, overshadowing the modest cultural Renaissance in the West under Charlemagne.

All things considered, one may say that most of the world's great civilizations were reaching a peak when that of the West was just coming to life. This may be because the other world civilizations never experienced cultural disruptions of the magnitude that foreign invaders created in the West during the early Middle Ages.

Review Questions ——

1. Trace the history of Christianity to the reign of the emperor Charlemagne. How did the church become a political power in the western Roman Empire?

2. How did the Franks become the dominant force in western Europe? What were the characteristics of Charlemagne's rule? Why did his empire break apart?

3. How and why was the history of the eastern or Byzantine half of the Roman Empire so different from the western half? What were the major political and religious

differences? How would you compare Justinian to Charlemagne?

4. What were the tenets of Islam? How were the Muslims able to build an empire so suddenly? Compare and contrast the teaching of Islam, Roman Catholicism, and Byzantine or Orthodox Christianity. Are they irreconcilable?

5. What were the defining features of feudalism? Is a feudal society a "backward" society?

Suggested Readings ——

R. BARTLETT, *Trial by Fire and Water: The Medieval Judicial Ordeal* (1986). Makes sense of these seemingly bizarre ways of letting God decide guilt or innocence.

R. BARTLETT, *The Making of Europe, 950–1350* (1992). A study of the way immigration and colonial conquest shaped the Europe we know.

M. BLOCH, *Feudal Society*, Vols. 1 and 2, trans. by L. A. Manyon (1971). A classic on the topic and as an example of historical study.

P. BROWN, *Augustine of Hippo: A Biography* (1967). Late antiquity seen through the biography of its greatest Christian thinker.

P. BROWN, *The Body and Society* (1988). Understanding late antiquity through people's attitudes toward the physical body.

J. H. BURNS, *The Cambridge History of Medieval Political Thought c. 350–c. 1450* (1991).

H. CHADWICK, *The Early Church* (1967). Among the best treatments of early Christianity.

B. CUNLIFFE, *Greeks, Romans and Barbarians* (1988). A quantitative account.

R. H. C. DAVIS, *A History of Medieval Europe: From Constantine to St. Louis* (1972). Unsurpassed in clarity.

K. F. DREW, ED., *The Barbarian Invasions: Catalyst of a New Order* (1970). Collection of essays that focus the issues.

G. DUBY, *The Early Growth of the European Economy: Warriors and Peasants from the Seventh to the Twelfth Century* (1974). Readable, authoritative account of rural society.

F. DVORNIK, *Byzantium and the Roman Primacy* (1966).

H. FICHTENAU, *The Carolingian Empire: The Age of Charlemagne*, trans. by Peter Munz (1964). Strongest on the political history of the era.

JOHN V. A. FINE, *The Early Medieval Balkans: Sixth–Twelfth Centuries* (1983). The formation of multiculturalism in the region.

F. L. GANSHOF, *Feudalism*, trans. by Philip Grierson (1964). A profound brief analysis of the subject.

P. GEARY, *Before France and Germany* (1988). The medieval evolution of these territories.

A. F. HAVIGHURST, ED., *The Pirenne Thesis: Analysis, Criticism, and Revision* (1958). Excerpts from the scholarly debate over the extent of western trade in the East during the early Middle Ages.

RICHARD HODGES ET AL., *Mohammed, Charlemagne, and the Origins of Europe* (1982). Good on the society and economy of early medieval Europe.

GEORGE HOLMES, ED., *The Oxford History of Medieval Europe* (1992). Overviews of Roman and northern Europe during the "Dark Ages."

A. HOURANI, *A History of the Arab Peoples* (1991). A comprehensive text that includes an excellent overview of the origins and early history of Islam.

D. KNOWLES, *Christian Monasticism* (1969). Sweeping survey with helpful photographs.

R. KRAUTHEIMER, *Early Christian and Byzantine Architecture* (1965). Makes the developments clear and interesting.

M. L. W. LAISTNER, *Thought and Letters in Western Europe, 500 to 900* (1957). Among the best surveys of early medieval intellectual history.

C. H. LAWRENCE, *Medieval Monasticism* (1989). Comprehensive survey.

J. LECLERCQ, *The Love of Learning and the Desire for God: A Study of Monastic Culture*, trans. by Catherine Misrahi (1962). Lucid, delightful, absorbing account of the ideals of monks.

J. LECLERCQ, F. VANDENBROUCKE, AND L. BOUYER, *The Spirituality of the Middle Ages* (1968). Perhaps the best survey of medieval Christianity, East and West, to the eve of the Protestant Reformation.

C. MANGO, *Byzantium: The Empire of New Rome* (1980).

JANET MARTIN, *Medieval Russia 980–1584* (1995). A concise narrative history.

M. McCORMICK, "Byzantium and the West, A.D. 700–900," in *The New Cambridge Medieval History*, Vol. 2: *The Early Medieval West 700–900* (1993). Up-to-date framing of events and political developments.

R. McKITTERNICK, *The Frankish Kingdoms Under the Carolingians, 751–987* (1983).

P. MUNZ, *The Age of Charlemagne* (1971). Penetrating social history of the period.

T. NOBLE, *The Republic of St. Peter* (1988). How the church became an empire.

H. PIRENNE, *A History of Europe, I: From the End of the Roman World in the West to the Beginnings of the Western States*, trans. by Bernhard Maill (1958). Comprehensive survey, with now-controversial views on the demise of western trade and cities in the early Middle Ages.

S. RUNCIMAN, *Byzantine Civilization* (1970). Succinct, comprehensive account by a master.

P. SAWYER, *The Age of the Vikings* (1962). The best account.

R. W. SOUTHERN, *The Making of the Middle Ages* (1973). Originally published in 1953, but still a fresh account by an imaginative historian.

C. STEPHENSON, *Medieval Feudalism* (1969). Excellent short summary and introduction.

A. A. VASILIEV, *History of the Byzantine Empire 324–1453* (1952). The most comprehensive treatment in English.

S. F. WEMPLE, *Women in Frankish Society: Marriage and the Cloister 500–900* (1981). The impact of Christian marriage customs on the Franks.

L. WHITE, JR., *Medieval Technology and Social Change* (1962). Often fascinating account of how primitive technology changed life.

13 THE HIGH MIDDLE AGES (1000–1300)

The Crusaders capture the city of

Antioch in 1098 during the First

Crusade. From Le Miroir Historical

(fifteenth century) by Vincent de

Beavais. [Museum Conde Chantilly/E. T.

Archive, London]

- ◆ Revival of Empire, Church, and Towns
- ◆ Society
- ◆ Politics

In World Perspective The High Middle Ages

The High Middle Ages were a period of both political expansion and consolidation and intellectual flowering and synthesis, an age that saw "the full development of all the potentialities of medieval civilization."[1] Some argue that it was a more creative time for the development of major western institutions than the Italian Renaissance or the German Reformation.

During the High Middle Ages the borders of western Europe were to a large degree secure from foreign invaders. Although Muslim aggression continued well into the sixteenth century, fear of assault from without greatly diminished. A striking change occurred in the late eleventh and twelfth centuries, when Western Europe, long the prey of foreign powers, became through the Crusades and booming foreign trade an aggressor in both the Byzantine and Arab worlds.

During the High Middle Ages the Latin, or western, church established itself in concept and law as a spiritual authority independent of secular monarchy, a development that sowed the seeds of the later western separa-tion of church and state. During the investiture controversy, a confrontation between popes and emperors, beginning in the late eleventh century and lasting through the twelfth, a reformed papacy overcame its previous long subservience to Carolingian and Ottonian kings. Under Pope Gregory VII (r. 1073–1085) and his successors, the papacy ended the authority of rulers to designate bishops and abbots at will and to invest them with the sacred symbols of church authority. It did so, however, by becoming itself something of a monarchy among the world's emerging secular dynasties, setting the stage for far more dangerous confrontations between popes and emperors in the later Middle Ages. Some later religious reformers saw in the papacy of Pope Gregory not only a declaration of the Church's independence from secular power, but also the beginning of the fall of the church from its spiritual mission.

During the High Middle Ages, powerful, self-aggrandizing monarchies emerged in France, England, and, regionally, Germany. Parliaments and popular assemblies accompanied their rise, seeking to protect local rights and customs and secure the interests of the local nobility, the clergy, and towns-people against dynastic and other foreign aggression. The foundations of modern representative institutions can be found in the development of these parliaments and assemblies. The Holy Roman Empire proved the great exception to this general trend on the part of higher powers to incorporate lower ones and create large dynastic states.

Despite a revival of the empire under the Ottonian rulers, named after Otto I (r. 936–972), the most powerful member of the new Saxon imperial dynasty, the events of these centuries rather left Germany a weak and fragmented territory until modern times.

The High Middle Ages saw a revolution in agriculture that increased food supplies and populations. Trade and commerce revived, towns expanded, protomodern forms of banking and credit developed, and a "new rich" merchant class, the ancestors of modern capitalists, became politically and economically ascendant in Europe's cities. Universities came into being at this time, and lasting vernacular and Romance literature was written. New trade with the Arab world, particularly by way of Spain, led to contacts with Muslim intellectuals and the beginning of the recovery of the writings of the

[1] *Western History in the Middle Ages—A Short History* (New York: Appleton: Century-Crofts, 1955), pp. 9, 127.

ancient Greek philosophers, which would in turn stimulate the great expansion of western education and culture during the late Middle Ages and the Renaissance. Unlike the Carolingian dabbling in antiquity, the twelfth century enjoyed a true renaissance of classical learning.

Revival of Empire, Church, and Towns

Otto I and the Revival of the Empire

The fortunes of both the old empire and the papacy began to revive when the Saxon Henry I ("the Fowler"; d. 936), the strongest of the German dukes, became the first non-Frankish king of Germany in 918. Henry rebuilt royal power by forcibly consolidating the duchies of Swabia, Bavaria, Saxony, Franconia, and Lotharingia. He secured imperial borders by checking the invasions of the Hungarians and the Danes. Although much smaller than Charlemagne's empire, Henry's German kingdom still placed his son and successor Otto I (r. 936–973) in a strong territorial position.

Otto I presents the Magdeburg Cathedral to Christ, as the pope (holding the keys to the kingdom of heaven) watches, a testimony to Otto's guardianship of the church. [Metropolitan Museum of Art, bequest of George Blumenthal, 1941 (41.100.157). Photograph © 1986 The Metropolitan Museum of Art.]

Otto maneuvered his own kin into power in Bavaria, Swabia, and Franconia. He refused to treat each duchy as an independent hereditary dukedom, as was the trend among the nobility, but dealt with each as a subordinate member of a unified kingdom. In a truly imperial gesture in 951, Otto invaded Italy and proclaimed himself its king. In 955 he won his most magnificent victory when he defeated the Hungarians at Lechfeld, a feat comparable to Charles Martel's victory over the Saracens near Tours in 732. Lechfeld secured German borders against new barbarian attack, further unified the German duchies, and earned Otto the well-deserved title "the Great."

As part of a careful rebuilding program, Otto, following the example of his predecessors, enlisted the church. Bishops and abbots, men who possessed a sense of universal empire yet did not marry and found competitive dynasties, were made royal princes and agents of the king. Because these clergy, as royal bureaucrats, received great landholdings and immunity from local counts and dukes, they also found such vassalage to the king attractive.

In 961 Otto, who had long aspired to the imperial crown, responded to a call for help from Pope John XII (955–964), in return for which John crowned him emperor on February 2, 962. Otto for his part recognized the existence of the Papal States and proclaimed himself their special protector. The Church was now more than ever under royal control. Its bishops and abbots were Otto's appointees and bureaucrats, and the pope reigned in Rome only by the power of the emperor's sword. Belatedly recognizing the royal web in which the church had become entangled, Pope John joined the Italian opposition to the new emperor. Otto's revenge was swift. An ecclesiastical synod over which the emperor personally presided deposed John and proclaimed that henceforth no pope could take office without first swearing allegiance to the emperor. Under Otto I popes ruled at the emperor's pleasure.

Otto thus shifted the royal focus from Germany to Italy. His successors became so preoccupied with Italy that their German base began to disintegrate, sacrificed to imperial dreams. They might have learned from the contemporary Capetian kings, the successor dynasty to the Carolingians in France, who concentrated their limited resources on securing a tight grip on their immediate royal domain, which was never neglected for foreign adventure. As the revived empire began to crumble in the eleventh century, the church, long unhappy with imperial domination, prepared to declare its independence and exact its own vengeance.

The Reviving Catholic Church

During the late ninth and early tenth centuries, the clergy had become tools of kings and magnates, and the papacy something of a toy of Italian nobles. The Ottonians made bishops their servile princes, and popes also served at their pleasure. A new day dawned for the church, however, thanks not only to the failing fortunes of the empire but also to a new force for reform within the church itself.

Cluny Reform Movement

In a great monastery at Cluny in east-central France, a reform movement was born. The reformers of Cluny were aided in their efforts by popular respect for the church that found expression in both religious fervor among laypersons and generous baronial patronage of religious houses. People admired clerics and monks because the church was medieval society's most democratic institution as far as lay participation was concerned. In the Middle Ages any man could theoretically become pope, since the pope was supposed to be elected by the people and the clergy of Rome. All people were candidates for the church's grace and salvation. The church promised a better life to come to the great mass of ordinary people, who found their present existence brutish and without hope.

The tenth and eleventh centuries saw an unprecedented boom in the construction of monasteries. William the Pious, duke of Aquitaine, founded Cluny in 910. It was a Benedictine monastery devoted to the strictest observance of Saint Benedict's *Rule for Monasteries* with a special emphasis on liturgical purity. Although the Cluniac reformers were loosely organized and their demands not always consistent, they were determined to maintain a spiritual church. They rejected the subservience of the clergy, especially that of the German bishops, to royal authority. They taught that the pope in Rome was sole ruler over all the clergy.

No local secular ruler, the Cluniacs asserted, could control their monasteries. They further denounced the transgression of ascetic piety by "secular" parish clergy, who maintained concubines in a relationship akin to marriage.

The Cluny reformers resolved to free the clergy from both kings and "wives," to create an independent and chaste clergy. The church alone was to be the clergy's lord and spouse. The distinctive western separation of Church and State and the celibacy of the Catholic clergy had their definitive origins in the Cluny reform movement.

From Cluny, reformers were dispatched throughout France and Italy. In time almost fifteen hundred dependent cloisters were devoted to monastic and church reform. In the later eleventh century, the Cluny reformers reached the summit when the papacy embraced their reforms.

Popes devoted to reforms like those urged by Cluny came to power during the reign of Emperor Henry III (r. 1039–1056). Pope Leo IX (r. 1049–1054) promoted regional synods to combat simony (that is, the selling of spiritual things, such as church offices) and clerical concubinage. He also placed Cluniacs in key administrative posts in Rome. In the second half of the eleventh century, reform popes asserted themselves more openly. Pope Stephen IX (r. 1057–1058) reigned without imperial ratification, contrary to the earlier declaration of Otto I. Pope Nicholas II (r. 1059–1061) established a College of Cardinals in 1059, and henceforth this body alone elected the pope.

Investiture Struggle: Gregory VII and Henry IV

Pope Gregory VII (1073–1085), a fierce advocate of church reform, put the church's declaration of independence to the test. Cluniacs had repeatedly inveighed against simony. In 1075 Pope Gregory condemned under penalty of excommunication the lay investiture of clergy at any level. He had primarily in mind the emperor's well-established custom of installing bishops by presenting them with the ring and staff that symbolized episcopal office. After Gregory's ruling, emperors were no more able to install bishops than they were to install popes. As popes were elected by the College of Cardinals and were not raised up by kings or nobles, so bishops would henceforth be installed by high clerics acting for the pope.

Gregory's prohibition came as a jolt to royal authority. Since the days of Otto I, emperors had routinely passed out bishoprics to favored clergy. Bishops, who received royal estates, were the emperors' appointees and servants of the state. Henry IV's predecessors had carefully nurtured the theocratic character of the empire in both concept and administrative bureaucracy. The church and religion were integral parts of government. Henry considered Gregory's action a direct challenge to his authority. The territorial princes, on the other hand, eager to see the emperor weakened, were quick to see the advantages of Gregory's ruling: if the emperor did not have a bishop's ear, then a territorial prince might. In the hope of gaining an advantage over both the emperor and the clergy in their territory, the princes fully supported Gregory's edict.

The lines of battle were quickly drawn. Henry assembled his loyal German bishops at Worms in January 1076 and had them proclaim their independence from Gregory. Gregory promptly responded with the church's heavy artillery; he excommunicated Henry and absolved all Henry's subjects from loyalty to him. The German princes were delighted, and Henry found himself facing a general revolt led by the duchy of Saxony. He had to come to terms with Gregory. In a famous scene, Henry prostrated himself outside Gregory's castle retreat at Canossa in northern Italy on January 25, 1077. There he reportedly stood barefoot in the snow off and on for three days before the pope absolved him. Papal power had, at this moment, reached a pinnacle, the first of several in the High Middle Ages. But Gregory's grandeur, as he must have known when he pardoned Henry and restored him to power, was soon to fade. In 1084 Henry

A twelfth-century German manuscript portrays the struggle between Emperor Henry IV and Pope Gregory VII. In the top panel, Henry installs the puppet pope Clement III and drives Gregory from Rome. Below, Gregory dies in exile. The artist was a monk; his sympathies were with Gregory, not Henry. [Thuringer Universitäts and Landesbibliothek, Jena]

forced Gregory into exile and installed his own anti-pope—Clement III—in his place.

The investiture controversy was finally settled in 1122 with the Concordat of Worms. Emperor Henry V (r. 1106–1125) formally renounced his power to invest bishops with ring and staff. In exchange, Pope Calixtus II (r. 1119–1124) recognized the emperor's right to be present and to invest bishops with fiefs before or after their investment with ring and staff by the church. The emperor also effectively retained the right to nominate or veto a candidate. The old church-state "back scratching" thus continued, but on different terms. The clergy received their offices and attendant religious powers solely from ecclesiastical authority and no longer from kings and emperors. Rulers continued to bestow lands and worldly goods on high clergy in the hope of influencing them; the Concordat of Worms made the clergy more independent but not necessarily less worldly.

The Gregorian party secured the independence of the clergy, but at the price of encouraging the divisiveness of the political forces within the empire. The pope had made himself strong by making imperial authority weak. In the end, the local princes profited most from the investiture controversy.

The new Gregorian fence between temporal and spiritual power did not prevent kings and popes from being good neighbors if each was willing. Succeeding centuries, however, proved that the aspirations of kings too often conflicted with those of popes for peaceful coexistence to endure. The most bitter clash between church and state occurred during the late thirteenth and early fourteenth centuries in the confrontation between Pope Boniface VIII and King Philip IV of France (see Chapter 16).

The First Crusades

If an index of popular piety and support for the pope in the High Middle Ages is needed, the Crusades amply provide it. What the Cluny reform was to the clergy, the first Crusades

Pope Urban II (1088–1099) Preaches the First Crusade

When Pope Urban II summoned the First Crusade in a sermon at the Council of Clermont on November 26, 1095, he painted a savage picture of the Muslims who controlled Jerusalem. Urban also promised the Crusaders, who responded by the tens of thousands, remission of their unrepented sins and assurance of heaven. Robert the Monk is one of four witnesses who has left us a summary of the sermon.

Is the pope engaging in a propaganda and smear campaign? What are the images he creates of the enemy and how accurate and fair are they? Did the Christian church have a greater claim to Jerusalem than the people then living there? Does a religious connection with the past entitle one group to confiscate the land of another?

From the confines of Jerusalem and the city of Constantinople a horrible tale has gone forth and very frequently has been brought to our ears, namely, that a race from the kingdom of the Persians [that is, the Seljuk Turks], an accursed race, a race utterly alienated from God, a generation forsooth which has not directed its heart and has not entrusted its spirit to God, has invaded the lands of those Christians and has depopulated them by the sword, pillage and fire; it has led away a part of the captives into its own country, and a part it has destroyed by cruel tortures; it has either entirely destroyed the churches of God or appropriated them for the rites of its own religion. They destroy the altars, after having defiled them with their uncleanness. They circumcise the Christians, and the blood of the circumcision they either spread upon the altars or pour into the vases of the baptismal font. When they wish to torture people by a base death, they perforate their navels, and dragging forth the extremity of the intestines, bind it to a stake; then with flogging they lead the victim around until the viscera having gushed forth the victim falls prostrate upon the ground. Others they bind to a post and pierce with arrows. Others they compel to extend their necks and then, attacking them with naked swords, attempt to cut through the neck with a single blow. What shall I say of the abominable rape of the women? The kingdom of the Greeks is now dismembered by them and deprived of territory so vast in extent that it can not be traversed in a march of two months. On whom therefore is the labor of avenging these wrongs and of recovering this territory incumbent, if not upon you? . . .

Jerusalem is the navel of the world; the land is fruitful above others, like another paradise of delights. This the Redeemer of the human race has made illustrious by His advent, has beautified by residence, has consecrated by suffering, has redeemed by death, has glorified by burial. This royal city, therefore, situated at the centre of the world, is now held captive by His enemies, and is in subjection to those who do not know God, to the worship of the heathens. She seeks therefore and desires to be liberated, and does not cease to implore you to come to her aid. From you especially she asks succor, because, as we have already said, God has conferred upon you above all nations great glory in arms. Accordingly undertake this journey for the remission of your sins, with the assurance of the imperishable glory of the kingdom of heaven.

From the *Original Sources of European History*, Vol. 1 (Philadelphia: Dept. of History, University of Pennsylvania) pp. 5–7.

---

to the Holy Land were to the laity: an outlet for the heightened religious zeal of the late eleventh and the twelfth centuries, Europe's most religious period before the Protestant Reformation.

Late in the eleventh century, the Byzantine Empire was under severe pressure from the Seljuk Turks, and Emperor Alexius I Comnenus (r. 1081–1118) appealed for western aid. At the Council of Clermont in 1095, Pope Urban II (r. 1088–1099) responded by launching the First Crusade. This has puzzled some historians, because the First Crusade was a risky venture. But the pope, the nobility, and western society at large had much to gain by sending large numbers of nobility temporarily away from Europe. Too many idle, restless noble youths were spending their lives feuding with each other and raiding other people's land. The pope recognized that peace and tranquility might be gained at home by sending factious aristocrats abroad with their accouterments of war (one hundred thousand went with the First Crusade). And the nobility recognized there were fortunes to be made in foreign wars. This was especially true of the younger sons

The Crusades

1095	Pope Urban II launches the First Crusade
1099	The crusaders take Jerusalem
1147-1149	The Second Crusade
1187	Jerusalem retaken by the Muslims
1189-1192	Third Crusade
1202-1204	Fourth Crusade

of noblemen, who, in an age of growing population and shrinking landed wealth, saw the Crusades as an opportunity to become landowners. Pope Urban may also have envisioned the Crusade leading to a reconciliation and possible reunion with the eastern church.

Religion was not the only motive inspiring the Crusaders; hot blood and greed were equally influential. But unlike the later Crusades, undertaken for patently mercenary reasons, the early Crusades were inspired by genuine religious piety and were carefully orchestrated by the revived papacy. Popes promised participants in the First Crusade a plenary indulgence should they die in battle—that is, a complete remission of any outstanding temporal punishment for their unrepented mortal sins and hence release from suffering for them in purgatory. In addition to this direct spiritual reward, the Crusaders were also impelled by their enthusiasm for a Holy War against the hated infidel and by the romance of a pilgrimage to the Holy Land. All these elements combined to make the First Crusade a rousing success (at least from the Christian point of view). Crusading zeal also sparked anti-Jewish riots and massacres in Europe, an expression of intolerance to Jews that became an enduring feature of militant Christianity.

Three great armies—tens of thousands of Crusaders—gathered in France, Germany, and Italy. Following different routes, they reassembled in Constantinople in 1097 (see Map 13–1). The convergence of these spirited soldiers on the eastern capital was a cultural shock that only deepened eastern antipathy toward the west. Alexis I suspected their motives, and the common people, who were forced to accommodate them, hardly considered them Christian brothers in a common cause—especially since Rome and Constantinople had separated in 1054. Nonetheless, these fanatical Crusaders accomplished what no eastern army had ever been able to do. They soundly defeated one Seljuk army after another in a steady advance toward Jerusalem, which fell to them on July 15, 1099. They divided the conquered territory into the "states" of Jerusalem, Edessa, Tripoli, and Antioch, which they held as alleged fiefs from the pope.

The Crusader states, however, were only small islands within a great sea of Muslims, who considered the western invaders savages. After only forty-odd years in the mid-eleventh century, the Latin presence in the east began to crumble. A Second Crusade, preached by Saint Bernard of Clairvaux (1091–1153), Christendom's most powerful monastic leader, was a dismal failure. In October 1187 Jerusalem itself was reconquered by Saladin (r. 1138–1193), king of Egypt and Syria. Save for a brief interlude in the thirteenth century, it remained in Islamic hands until the twentieth century.

A Third Crusade in the twelfth century (1189–1192) attempted yet another rescue, enlisting as its leaders the most powerful western rulers: Emperor Frederick Barbarossa (r. 1152–1190); Richard the Lion-Hearted, king of England (r. 1189–1199); and Philip Augustus, king of France (r. 1179–1223). But it became a tragicomic commentary on the passing of the original crusading spirit. Frederick Barbarossa drowned while en route to the Holy Land. Richard the Lion-Hearted and Philip Augustus reached the outskirts of Jerusalem, but their intense personal rivalry shattered the Crusaders' unity and chances of victory. Philip Augustus returned to France and invaded Richard's continental territories, and Richard fell captive to the Emperor Henry VI (r. 1165–1197) as he was returning to England, forcing the English to pay a handsome ransom for his release. Popular resentment of taxes for this ransom became part of the background of the revolt against the English monarchy that led to the royal recognition of the Magna Carta in 1215.

The long-term achievement of the first three Crusades had little to do with their original purpose. Politically and religiously, they were a failure, and the Holy Land remained as firmly Muslim as ever. However, the Crusades did provide a safety valve for violence-prone Europeans and stimulated western trade and cultural interaction with the east. The merchants of Venice, Pisa, and Genoa followed the Crusaders' cross to lucrative new markets. The need to resupply the new Christian settlements in the Near East not only reopened old trade routes that had long been closed by Arab domination of the Mediterranean, but also opened new ones. It is a commentary on both the degeneration of the original intent of the Crusades and their true historical importance that the Fourth Crusade (1202–1204) was reduced to an enterprising commercial venture manipulated by the Venetians.

Towns and Townspeople

In the eleventh and twelfth centuries, towns held only about 5 percent of western Europe's population. By modern comparison they were small. Of Germany's 3,000 towns, for example, 2,800 had populations under 1,000. The largest European towns were in Italy; Florence approached 100,000 inhabitants and Milan was not far behind. Despite their comparatively small size, the whole of medieval society, and especially its most creative segments, could be found in the towns.

The Chartering of Towns Towns were originally dominated by feudal lords, both lay and clerical. The lords created the towns by granting charters to those who would agree to live and work within them. The charters guaranteed the towns' safety and gave their inhabitants a degree of independence unknown to peasants who worked the land. The purpose was originally to concentrate skilled laborers who

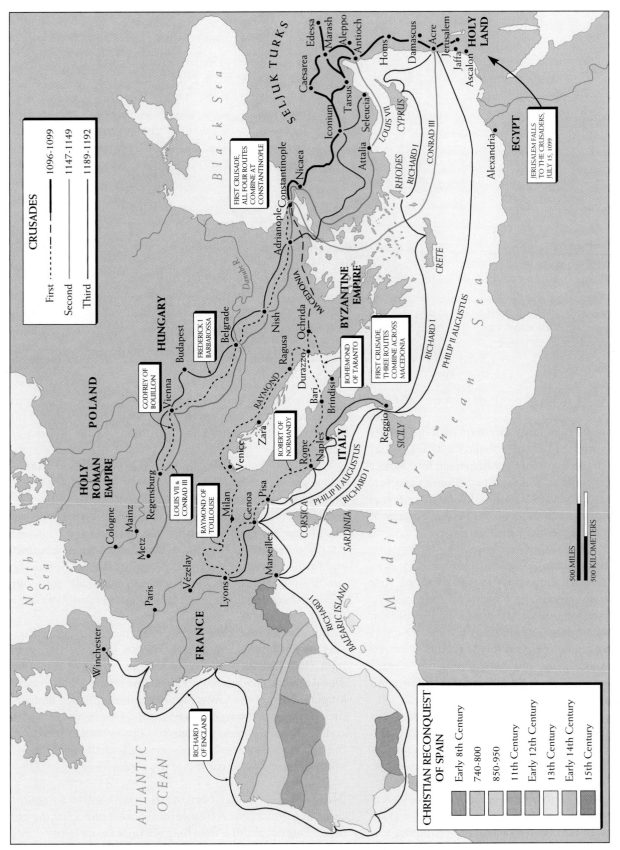

Map 13-1 **The early Crusades.** Routes and several leaders of the Crusades during the first century of the movement are shown. The names on this map do not exhaust the list of great nobles who went on the First Crusade. The even showier array of monarchs of the Second and Third still left the Crusades, on balance, ineffective in achieving their goals.

Skilled workers were an integral component of the commerce of medieval towns. This scene shows the manufacture of cannons in a foundry in Florence.
[Scala/Art Resource, N.Y.]

could manufacture the finished goods desired by lords and bishops.

As towns grew and beckoned, many serfs took their skills to the new urban centers. There they found the freedom and profits that could lift an industrious craftsperson into higher social ranks. As this migration of serfs to the towns accelerated, the lords in the countryside offered serfs more favorable terms of tenure to keep them on the land. The growth of towns thus improved the lot of serfs generally.

The Rise of Merchants   Rural society not only gave the towns their craftspeople and day laborers, but the first merchants themselves may also have been enterprising serfs. Certainly, some of the long-distance traders were people who had nothing to lose and everything to gain from the enormous risks of foreign trade. They traveled together in armed caravans and convoys, buying goods and products as cheaply as possible at the source, and selling them for all they could get in western ports (see Map 13–2).

At first the merchants were disliked because they were outside the traditional social groups of nobility, clergy, and peasantry. Over time, however, the powerful grew to respect the merchants, and the weak always tried to imitate them, because the merchants left a trail of wealth behind them.

As the traders established themselves in towns, they grew in wealth and numbers, formed their own protective associations, and soon found themselves able to challenge traditional seigneurial authority. Merchants especially wanted to end the arbitrary tolls and tariffs regional magnates im-

posed over the surrounding countryside. Such regulations hampered the flow of commerce on which both merchant and craftsman in the growing urban export industries depended.

Townspeople needed simple and uniform laws and a government sympathetic to their new forms of business activity, not the fortress mentality of the lords of the countryside. The result was often a struggle with the old nobility within and outside the towns. This conflict led towns in the High and later Middle Ages to form their own independent communes and to ally themselves with kings against the nobility in the countryside, a development that would eventually rearrange the centers of power in medieval Europe and dissolve classic feudal government.

Because the merchants were the engine of the urban economy, small shopkeepers and artisans identified far more with them than with aloof lords and bishops, who had been medieval society's traditional masters. The lesser nobility (small knights) outside the towns also recognized the new mercantile economy as the wave of the future. During the eleventh and twelfth centuries, the burgher upper classes increased their economic strength and successfully challenged the old noble urban lords for control of the towns.

New Models of Government   With urban autonomy came new models of self-government. Around 1100 the old urban nobility and the new burgher upper class merged into an urban patriciate. It was a marriage between those wealthy by birth (inherited property) and those who made their for-

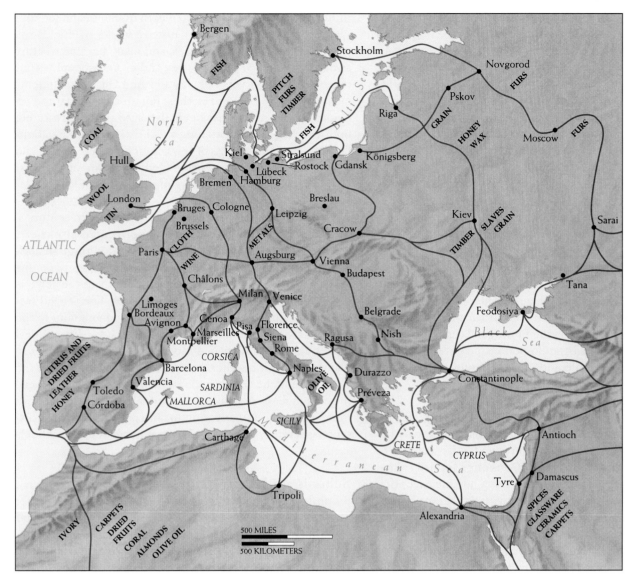

Map 13–2 Medieval trade routes and regional products. Trade in the west varied in intensity and geographical extent in different periods during the Middle Ages. The map shows some of the channels that came to be used in interregional commerce. Labels tell part of what was carried in that commerce.

tunes in long-distance trade. From this new ruling class was born the aristocratic town council, which henceforth governed towns.

Enriching and complicating the situation, small artisans and craftspeople also slowly developed their own protective associations or guilds and began to gain a voice in government. The towns' opportunities for the "little person" had created the slogan "Town air brings freedom." In the countryside the air one breathed still belonged to the lord of the land, but town residents were treated as freemen. Within town walls people thought of themselves as citizens with basic rights, not subjects liable to their masters' whim. Economic hardship certainly continued among the lower urban

groups despite their basic legal and political freedoms. But social mobility was at least a possibility in the towns.

Traditional measures of success had great appeal within the towns. Successful merchants wanted coats of arms, castles, country estates, and to lead the life of a gentleman and a lady on a great manor. When they became rich enough, merchants took their fortunes to the countryside.

A need to be socially distinguished and distinct pervaded urban society. The merchants were just the tip of the iceberg. Towns tried to control this need by defining grades of luxury in dress and residence for the various social groups and vocations. Overly conspicuous consumption was a kind of indecent exposure punishable by law. Such sumptuary laws restricted the types and amount of clothing a person could wear (the length and width of fur pieces, for example) and how dwellings might be decorated architecturally. People thus were forced to dress and live according to their station in life. Such laws sought to maintain social order and dampen conflict by keeping everyone clearly and peacefully in their place.

Over time, the formation of artisan guilds gave workers in the trades a direct voice in government. Ironically, this gain eventually limited the social mobility of the poorest artisans. The guilds gained representation on city councils, where, to discourage imports, they enforced quality standards and fair prices on local businesses. These actions created tight restrictions on guild membership, squeezing out poorer artisans and tradespeople. As a result, lesser merchants and artisans found their opportunities progressively limited. The dominant guilds became so rigid and exclusive that they often stifled their own creativity and inflamed the journeypeople whom they excluded from their ranks. Unrepresented artisans and craftspeople constituted a true urban proletariat prevented by law from forming their own guilds or entering existing ones. The efforts by guild-dominated governments to protect local craftspeople and industries tended to narrow trade and depress the economy for everyone.

Towns and Kings By providing kings with the resources they needed to curb factious noblemen, towns became a major force in the transition from feudal societies to national governments. Kings and towns often formally allied against the traditional lords of the land. A notable exception is England, where the towns joined with the barons against the oppressive monarchy of King John (1199–1216), becoming part of the parliamentary opposition to the crown. But by the fifteenth century, kings and towns had also joined forces in England, so much so that by century's end Henry VII, the first Tudor monarch (1485–1509) was known as the "burgher king."

Towns attracted monarchs for obvious reasons. They were a ready source of educated bureaucrats and lawyers who knew Roman law, the tool for running the state. Money was also to be found in the towns in great quantity, enabling kings to hire their own armies and free themselves from dependence on the nobility. Towns had the human, financial, and technological resources to empower kings. By such alliances, towns in turn won royal political recognition and had their constitutions guaranteed. In France, towns became integrated early into royal government. In Germany, they fell under ever-tighter control by the princes. In Italy, uniquely, towns expanded to dominate the surrounding countryside, becoming genuine city-states during the Renaissance.

Jews in Christian Society Towns also attracted Jews. It was in the major urban centers, particularly in France and Germany, that Jews gathered between the late twelfth and thirteenth centuries. They did so both by choice and for safety in the increasingly hostile Christian world. In cities, Jews plied trades in small businesses, and many became wealthy as moneylenders to kings, popes, and businesspeople. After the creation of universities, Jews loaned Christian students everything from books to clothes. Jewish intellectual and religious culture had always been elaborate and sophisticated, both dazzling and threatening to Christians. These various factors—the separateness of Jews, their economic power, and their cultural strength—encouraged suspicion and distrust among Christians, whose religious teaching held Jews responsible for the death of Christ.

Between the late twelfth and early fourteenth centuries, Jews were exiled from France and persecuted elsewhere. Two factors were behind this unprecedented surge in anti-Jewish sentiment. The first was a desire by kings to confiscate Jewish wealth and property and eliminate the Jews as economic competitors with the monarchy. The second factor was the church's increasing political vulnerability to the new dynastic monarchies. Faced with the loss of its political power, the church became more determined than ever to maintain its spiritual hegemony. With the beginning of the Crusades and the creation of new mendicant religious orders, the church reasserted claims to spiritual sovereignty over Europe and beyond, instigating major campaigns against dissenters, heretics, witches, and Jews at home as well as infidels abroad.

Schools and Universities In the twelfth century, Byzantine and Spanish Islamic scholars made it possible for the philosophical works of Aristotle, the writings of Euclid and Ptolemy, the texts of Greek physicians and Arab mathematicians, and the corpus of Roman law to circulate among western scholars. Islamic scholars especially preserved these works, writing extensive, thought-provoking commentaries on Greek texts that were translated into Latin and made available to western scholars and students. The result of this renaissance of ancient knowledge was an intellectual ferment that gave rise to western universities.

The first important western university was established in Bologna by Emperor Frederick Barbarossa in 1158. There we find the first formal organizations of students and masters and the first degree programs—the institutional foundations of the modern university. Originally the term university meant simply a corporation of individuals (students and masters) who joined for their mutual protection from overarching episcopal authority (the local bishop oversaw the university) and from the local townspeople. Because townspeople considered students foreigners without civil rights, such protective unions were necessary.

Bolognese students also "unionized" to guarantee fair rents and prices from their often reluctant hosts. And students demanded regular, high-quality teaching from their masters.

Philip II Augustus Orders Jews Out of France

Long the objects of Christian polemic, hated as moneylenders by ordinary people, and feared by the clergy as successful competitors with Christianity, Jews became easy scapegoats for rulers who wished to exploit fear and prejudice. In 1182, Philip II Augustus, eyeing the wealthy Jews of Paris, ordered all nonconverting Jews out of France and confiscated their property and possessions.

What is the king's argument for exiling Jews? Did Jewish moneylenders threaten the well-being of Christians? Are economic motives apparent in the king's actions? Why were religious pluralism and toleration so difficult for people then?

[When Philip became king] a great multitude of Jews had been dwelling in France for a long time. . . . [In Paris] they grew so rich that they claimed as their own almost half of the whole city, and they had Christians in their houses as menservants and maidservants, who were backsliders from the faith of Jesus Christ and judaized with the Jews. . . .

And whereas the Lord had said . . . in Deuteronomy (23:19–20): "Thou shall not lend upon usury to thy brother, but to the stranger," the Jews . . . understood by "stranger" every Christian, and they took from the Christians their money at usury. And so heavily burdened in this wise were citizens and soldiers and peasants . . . that many of them were constrained to part with their posses-sions. Others were bound under oath in houses of the Jews in Paris, held as if captives in prison.

The most Christian King Philip hearing of these things . . . released all Christians of his kingdom from their debts to the Jews, and kept a fifth part of the whole amount for himself. . . . [Then in] 1182, in the month of April . . . an edict went forth from . . . the king . . . that all the Jews of his kingdom should be prepared to go forth by the coming feast of St. John the Baptist. And the king gave them leave to sell each his movable goods before the time fixed.

When faithless Jews heard this edict some of them . . . converted to the Lord [Jesus Christ, and] to them the king, out of regard for the Christian religion, restored all their possessions . . . and gave them perpetual liberty. Others were blinded by their ancient error and persisted in their perfidy. . . . The infidel Jews . . . astonished and stupefied by the strength of mind of Philip the King and his constancy in the Lord . . . prepared to sell all their household goods. The time was now at hand when the king ordered them to leave France. . . . Then did the Jews sell all their movable possessions in great haste, while their landed property reverted to the crown. Thus the Jews, having sold their goods and taken the price for the expenses of their journey, departed with their wives and children and all their households in the . . . year of the Lord 1182.

From James Harvey Robinson, ed., *Readings in European History*, Vol. 2 (Boston: Athenaeum, 1906), pp. 426–428.

In Italy students actually hired their own teachers, set pay scales, and drew up desired lecture topics. Masters who did not keep their promises or live up to student expectations were boycotted. Price gouging by townspeople was met with the threat to move the university to another town. This could be done because the university did not have a fixed physical plant. Students and masters moved freely from town to town as they chose. Such mobility gave them a unique independence from their surroundings. Masters also formed their own protective associations and established procedures and standards for certification to teach within their ranks.

Bologna was famous for the revival of Roman law. From the seventh to the eleventh centuries, only the most rudimentary manuals of Roman law had survived. With the growth of trade and towns in the late eleventh century, western scholars had come into contact with the larger and more important parts of Justinian's compilation of civil law. The study and dissemination of this recovered material were undertaken in Bologna under the direction of a scholar named Irnerius, who flourished in the early twelfth century. He and his students thereby expanded legal knowledge. Around 1140 a monk named Gratian, also a resident of Bologna, created the standard legal text in church—or canon—law, the *Concordance of Discordant Canons*, known simply as Gratian's *Decretum*.

As Bologna was the model for the universities of Spain, Italy, and southern France and for the study of law, so Paris became the model for northern European universities and the study of theology. Oxford, Cambridge, and (much later) Heidelberg were among its imitators. All these universities required a foundation in the liberal arts for advanced study in the higher sciences of medicine, theology, and law. The arts program consisted of the trivium (grammar, rhetoric, and logic) and the quadrivium (arithmetic, geometry, astronomy, and music) or, more simply, the language arts and the mathematical arts.

Cathedral Schools   Before the emergence of universities, the liberal arts had been taught in cathedral and monastery schools. The purpose of these schools was to train the clergy, and their curricula tended to be narrowly restricted

The University of Bologna in central Italy was distinguished as the center for the revival of Roman law. This carving on the tomb of a Bolognese professor of law shows students attending one of his lectures. [Scala/Art Resource, N.Y.]

to this goal. By the late eleventh and twelfth centuries, cathedral schools also began to provide lectures for nonclerical students and to include training for purely secular vocations. In 1179 a papal decree obliged cathedrals to provide teachers for free to laity who wanted to learn.

After 1200 increasing numbers of future notaries and merchants who had no particular interest in becoming priests, but who needed Latin and related intellectual disciplines to fill their secular positions, studied alongside aspiring priests in cathedral and monastery schools. By the thirteenth century the demand for secretaries and notaries in the growing urban and territorial governments and for literate personnel in the expanding merchant firms gave rise to special schools for strictly secular vocational preparation. With the appearance of these schools, the church began to lose its monopoly on higher education.

The University of Paris, chartered in 1200 by King Philip Augustus and Pope Innocent III (r. 1198–1216), grew institutionally out of the cathedral school of Notre Dame, among others. At Paris the college, or house system, originated. At first a college was just a hospice providing room and board for poor students who could not afford to rent rooms in town. But the educational life of the university quickly expanded into fixed structures and began to thrive on their sure endowments. University-run colleges made the overseeing and protection of students easier and gave the university a new prominence as a permanent urban institution.

In Paris, the most famous college was the Sorbonne, founded around 1257 by Robert de Sorbon, chaplain to the king, to house theology students. In Oxford and Cambridge, the colleges became the basic unit of student life and were indistinguishable from the university proper. By the end of the Middle Ages, such colleges had tied universities to physical plants and fixed foundations. Their mobility was forevermore restricted; hence, their earlier autonomy and freedom were restricted as well.

As a group, students at Paris had power and prestige. They enjoyed royal protections and privileges denied ordinary citizens. Many Parisian students were well-to-do, and not a few were spoiled and petulant. They did not endear themselves to the townspeople, whom they considered their inferiors. That townspeople sometimes let their resentments lead to violence against students is clear from the city's ordinances. City law forbade the beating of students. Only those students who had clearly committed serious crimes could be imprisoned. Only in self-defense might a citizen strike a student. All citizens were obligated to testify against anyone seen abusing a student. University laws also required all teachers to be carefully examined before being licensed to teach Parisian students. The law thus recognized students as both a valuable and a vulnerable resource.

The Curriculum   In the High Middle Ages the learning process was basic. People assumed that truth was already known; one did not have to go out and find it. Truth only needed to be properly organized, elucidated, and defended. Students wrote commentaries on authoritative texts, especially those of Aristotle and the church fathers. Teachers did not encourage students to strive independently for undiscovered truth. Students rather learned to organize and harmonize the accepted truths of tradition, which were drilled into them.

This method of study, based on logic and dialectic, was known as scholasticism. It reigned supreme in law and medicine as well as in philosophy and theology. Students read the traditional authorities in their field, summarized their teaching, disputed them with their peers by elaborating traditional arguments pro and con, and then drew conclusions. Logic and dialectic were the tools that could discipline knowledge and thought. Dialectic is the art of discovering a truth by finding the contradictions in arguments against it. Astonishingly, medical students did no practical medical work; they studied and debated the authoritative texts in their field just as the law and theology students did in theirs.

Few books existed for students, and because printing with movable type did not yet exist, those available were expensive hand-copied works. So students could not leisurely master a subject in the quiet of their studies; they had to learn it through discussion, lecture, and debate. There was a lot of memorizing, and the ability to think on one's feet was stressed. Rhetoric, or persuasive argument, was the ultimate goal—that is, the ability to make an eloquent defense of the knowledge one had clarified by logic and dialectic. Successful students became virtual walking encyclopedias; their education filled their heads with knowledge and enabled them to recite it impressively.

University study normally began between the ages of twelve and fifteen. Students coming to university were expected to have a good knowledge of Latin gained in local schools or from a private tutor. Once there, students spent four years perfecting their Latin (particularly in the study of the trivium) before attaining the bachelor of arts degree. A master's degree thereafter might take three or four more years, during which time students studied classical texts in mathematics, natural science, and philosophy. A degree in theology at Paris could take more than twenty years of study from beginning to end.

The Summa   The twelfth century saw the rise of the summa, the authoritative summary of all that was allegedly known about a particular subject. The summa's main goal was to conciliate traditional authorities and present a body of clarified truth. In canon law there was Gratian's *Concordance of Discordant Canons* (around 1142), whose very title embodies the scholastic method. In theology, there was Peter Lombard's (ca. 1100–1164) *Four Books of Sentences* (1155–1157). Embracing traditional teaching on God, the Creation, Christ, and the sacraments, it remained the standard theological textbook until the Protestant reformers declared it unbiblical. It had evolved from Peter Abelard's (1079–1142) *Sic et Non* (around 1122), a much smaller work that juxtaposed seemingly contradictory statements on the same subject by revered authorities. Out of this same tradition came Saint Thomas Aquinas's (1225–1274) magnificent *Summa Theologiae*

(begun in 1265), to many the last word on theology, which the medieval summa was always intended to be.

Society

The Order of Life

In the art and literature of the Middle Ages, three basic social groups were represented: those who fought as mounted knights (the landed nobility), those who prayed (the clergy), and those who labored in fields and shops (the peasantry and village artisans). After the revival of towns in the eleventh century, a fourth social group emerged: the long-distance traders and merchants.

Nobles   As a distinctive social group, not all nobles were originally great men with large hereditary lands. Many rose from the ranks of feudal vassals or warrior knights. The successful vassal attained a special social and legal status based on his landed wealth (accumulated fiefs), his exercise of authority over others, and his distinctive social customs—all of which set him apart in medieval society. By the late Middle Ages, a distinguishable higher and lower nobility had evolved, living in both town and country. The higher were the great landowners and territorial magnates, long the dominant powers in their regions, the lower were petty landlords, the descendants of minor knights, newly rich merchants who could buy country estates, or wealthy farmers patiently risen from ancestral serfdom.

The nobility lived off the labor of others. Basically lords of manors, the nobility of the early and High Middle Ages neither tilled the soil like the peasantry nor engaged in the commerce of merchants—activities they considered beneath their dignity. The nobleman resided in a country mansion or, if he were particularly wealthy, a castle.

Arms were the nobleman's profession; waging war was his sole occupation and reason for living. In the eighth century the adoption of stirrups made mounted warriors, or cavalry, the key ingredient of a successful army. Good horses and the armor and weaponry of horse warfare were expensive. The nobleman's fief provided the means to acquire the expensive military equipment that his rank required. He maintained his enviable position as he had gained it, by fighting for his chief.

The nobility accordingly celebrated the physical strength, courage, and constant activity of warfare. Warring gave them both new riches and an opportunity to gain honor and glory. Knights were paid a share in the plunder of victory, and in time of war, everything became fair game. Peace meant economic stagnation and boredom. Whereas the peasants and the townspeople regarded peace as essential for their occupational success, the nobility despised it as unnatural to their profession.

The nobleman nurtured his sense of distinctiveness within medieval society by the chivalric ritual of dubbing to knighthood. This ceremonial entrance into the noble class became almost a religious sacrament. The ceremony was preceded by a bath of purification, confession, communion, and a prayer vigil. Thereafter, the priest blessed the knight's standard, lance, and sword. As prayers were chanted, the priest girded the knight with his sword and presented him his shield, enlisting him as much in the defense of the church as in the service of his lord. Dubbing raised the nobleman to a state as sacred in his sphere as clerical ordination made the priest in his. The comparison is legitimate. The clergy and the nobility were medieval society's privileged estates. The appointment of noblemen to high ecclesiastical office and their eager participation in the church's Crusades had strong ideological and social underpinnings as well as economic and political motives.

In the twelfth century knighthood was legally restricted to men of high birth. This circumscription of noble ranks came in reaction to the growing wealth, political power, and successful social climbing of newly rich townspeople (mostly merchants), who formed a new urban patriciate that was increasingly competitive with the lower nobility. Kings remained free, however, to raise up knights at will and did not shrink from increasing royal revenues by selling noble titles to wealthy merchants. But the law was building fences—fortunately not without gates—between town and countryside in the High Middle Ages.

In peacetime the nobility had two favorite amusements: hunting and tournaments. Where they could, noblemen monopolized the rights to game, forbidding the commoners from hunting in the "lords'" forests. This practice built resentment among common people to the level of revolt. Free game, fishing, and access to wood were basic demands in the petitions of grievance and the revolts of the peasantry throughout the High and later Middle Ages.

Tournaments also sowed seeds of social disruption, but more within the ranks of the nobility itself. Tournaments were designed not only to keep men fit for war, but also to provide the excitement of war without the useless maiming and killing of prized vassals. But as regions competed fiercely with one another for victory and glory, even mock battles with blunted weapons proved to be deadly. Often, tournaments got out of hand, ending in bloodshed and animosity among the combatants. (The intense emotions and occasional violence that accompany interregional soccer in Europe today may be seen as a survival of this kind of rivalry.) The church came to oppose tournaments as occasions of pagan revelry and senseless violence. Kings and princes also turned against them as sources of division within their realms. Henry II of England (r. 1154–1189) proscribed them in the twelfth century. They did not end in France until the mid-sixteenth century, after King Henry II (1547–1559) was mortally wounded by a shaft through his visor during a tournament celebrating his daughter's marriage.

From the repeated assemblies in the courts of barons and kings, set codes of social conduct, or courtesy, developed in noble circles. With the French leading the way, mannered behavior and court etiquette became almost as important as battlefield expertise. Knights became literate gentlemen, and lyric poets sang and moralized at court. The cultivation of a code of behavior and a special literature to eulogize it was not unrelated to problems within the social life of the nobility. Noblemen were notorious philanderers; their illegitimate children mingled openly with their legitimate offspring in their houses. The advent of courtesy was in part an effort to reform this situation.

Noblewomen watch a tournament. These mock battles were designed to provide the excitement of war without its mayhem. However, they tended to get out of hand, resulting in bloodshed and even death. [University of Heidelberg]

Dominicans (left) and Franciscans (right). Unlike the other religious orders, the Dominicans and Franciscans did not live in cloisters, but wandered about preaching and combating heresy. They depended for support on their own labor and the kindness of the laity. [Bibliothèque Nationale, Paris]

Although the poetry of courtly love was sprinkled with frank eroticism, and the beloved in these epics were married women pursued by those to whom they were not married, the love recommended by the poet was usually love at a distance, unconsummated by sexual intercourse. It was love without touching, a kind of sex without physical sex, and only as such was it considered ennobling. Court poets depicted those who succumbed to illicit carnal love as reaping at least as much suffering as joy from it.

No medieval social group was absolutely uniform—not the nobility, the clergy, the townspeople, not even the peasantry. Not only was the nobility a class apart, it also had strong social divisions within its own ranks. Noblemen formed a broad spectrum—from minor vassals without subordinate vassals to mighty barons, the principal vassals of a king or prince, who had many vassals of their own. Dignity and status within the nobility were directly related to the exercise of authority over others; a chief with many vassals obviously far excelled the small country nobleman who served another and was lord over none but himself.

By the late Middle Ages, several factors forced the landed nobility into a steep economic and political decline from which it never recovered. Climatic changes and agricultural failures created large famines, while the great plague (see Chapter 16) brought about unprecedented population losses. Changing military tactics occasioned by the use of infantry and heavy artillery during the Hundred Years War made the noble cavalry nearly obsolete. And the alliance of wealthy towns with the king weakened the nobility within their own domains. One can speak of a waning of the landed nobility after the fourteenth century. Thereafter, land and wealth counted for far more than lineage as qualification for entrance into the highest social class.

Clergy   Unlike the nobility and the peasantry, the clergy was an open estate. Although the clerical hierarchy reflected the social classes from which the clergy came, one was still a cleric by religious training and ordination, not because of birth or military prowess.

There were two basic types of clerical vocation: regular and secular. The regular clergy comprised the orders of monks who lived according to a special ascetic rule *(regula)* in cloisters separated from the world. The Gregorian reform led to the creation of new such orders aspiring to a life of poverty and self-sacrifice in imitation of Christ and the first apostles. Founded in 1098, the Cistercians (from Citeaux in Burgundy) were a reform wing of the Benedictines and were known as the "white monks," a reference to their all-white attire, symbolic of apostolic purity. They hoped to avoid the materialistic influences of urban society and maintain uncorrupted the original Rule of Saint Benedict, which their leaders believed Cluny was compromising. The Cistercians accordingly stressed anew the inner life and spiritual goals of monasticism. They located their houses in remote areas and denied themselves worldly comforts and distractions. Remarkably successful, the order could count three hundred chapter houses within a century of its founding, and many others imitated its austere spirituality.

In the thirteenth century, two new orders—the Franciscans and the Dominicans—gained the sanction of the church. The members of these mendicant orders, known as friars, did not confine themselves to the cloister. They went out into the world to preach the church's mission and to combat heresy, begging or working to support themselves (hence the term mendicant). The regular clergy were the spiritual elite among the clergy, and theirs was not a way of life lightly undertaken. Canon law required that one be at least twenty-one years of age before making a final profession of the monastic vows of poverty, chastity, and obedience. The monks' personal sacrifices and high religious ideals earned them great respect. This popularity was a major factor in the success of the Cluny reform movement and of the Crusades of the eleventh and twelfth centuries. The Crusades allowed laypeople to participate in the admired life of asceticism and prayer; in these holy pilgrimages they could imitate the suffering and perhaps even the death of Jesus, as the monks imitated his suffering and death by retreat from the world and severe self-denial.

The regular clergy, however, as a whole were never completely cut off from the secular world. They maintained frequent contact with the laity through charitable activities, teaching, and special pastoral commissions from the pope, and as supplemental preachers and confessors in parish churches during Lent and other peak religious seasons. The Dominican and Franciscan friars lived a common life according to a special rule, and still practiced a ministry in the world. Some monks, because of their learning and rhetorical skills, even became secretaries and private confessors to kings and queens.

The secular clergy, those who lived and worked directly among the laity in the world (saeculum), formed a vast hierarchy. At the top were the high prelates—the wealthy cardinals, archbishops, and bishops, who were drawn almost exclusively from the nobility—and below them the urban priests, the cathedral canons, and the court clerks. Finally, there was the great mass of poor parish priests, who were neither financially nor intellectually much above the common people they served (the basic educational requirement was an ability to say the mass). Until the Gregorian reform in the eleventh century, parish priests lived with women in a relationship akin to marriage, and their concubines and children were accepted within the communities they served. Because of their relative poverty, priests often moonlighted as teachers, artisans, or farmers. Their parishioners accepted and even admired this practice.

The monasteries and nunneries of the established orders recruited candidates from among the wealthiest social groups. Crowding in the convents and the absence of patronage gave rise in the thirteenth century to lay satellite convents known as beguine houses. These housed religiously earnest unmarried women from the upper and middle social strata. The city of Cologne established one hundred such houses between 1250 and 1350, each containing eight to twelve women. Several of these convents, in Cologne and elsewhere, fell prey to heresy. Among the responsibilities of the new religious orders of Dominicans and Franciscans was the "regularization" of such convents.

The clergy constituted a far greater proportion of medieval society than modern society. Estimates suggest that 1.5 percent of fourteenth-century Europe was in clerical garb. The clergy were concentrated in urban areas, especially in towns with universities and cathedrals. In late-fourteenth-century England, there was one cleric for every seventy laypeople, and in counties with a cathedral or a university, the proportion rose to one cleric for every fifty laypeople. In large university towns the clergy could exceed 10 percent of the population.

Despite the moonlighting of poorer parish priests, the clergy as a whole, like the nobility, lived on the labor of others. Their income came from the regular collection of tithes and church taxes according to an elaborate system that evolved in the High and later Middle Ages. The church was, of course, a major landowner and regularly collected rents and fees. Monastic communities and high prelates amassed great fortunes; there was a popular saying that the granaries were always full in the monasteries. The immense secular power attached to high clerical posts can be seen in the intensity of the investiture struggle. The loss of the right to present chosen clergy with the ring and staff of episcopal office threatened the emperor's control of his realm. The bishops had become royal agents and were endowed to that purpose with royal lands that the emperor could ill afford to have slip from his control.

During most of the Middle Ages, the clergy were the "first estate," and theology was the queen of the sciences. How did the clergy attain such prominence? A lot of it was self-proclaimed. However, there was also popular respect and reverence for the clergy's role as mediator between God and humanity. The priest brought the Son of God down to earth when he celebrated the sacrament of the Eucharist; his absolution released penitents from punishment for sin. It was declared improper for mere laypeople to sit in judgment on such a priest.

Theologians elaborated the distinction between the clergy and the laity to the clergy's benefit. The belief in the superior status of the clergy underlay the evolution of clerical privileges and immunities in both person and property. As holy persons, the clergy were not supposed to be taxed by secular rulers without special permission from the proper ecclesiastical authorities. Clerical crimes were under the jurisdiction of special ecclesiastical courts, not the secular courts. Because churches and monasteries were deemed holy places, they, too, were free from secular taxation and legal jurisdiction. Hunted criminals, lay and clerical, regularly sought asylum within them, disrupting the normal processes of law and order. When city officials violated this privilege of asylum, ecclesiastical authorities threatened excommunication and interdict. People feared this suspension of the church's sacraments, including Christian burial, almost as much as they feared the criminals to whom the church gave asylum.

By the late Middle Ages, townspeople came increasingly to resent the special immunities of the clergy. Although the separation of church and state and the distinction between clergy and laity have persisted into modern times, after the fifteenth century the clergy ceased to be the superior class they had been for much of the Middle Ages. In both Protestant and Catholic lands, governments progressively subjected them to the basic responsibilities of citizenship.

Peasants The largest and lowest social group in medieval society was one on whose labor the welfare of all others depended: the agrarian peasantry. Many peasants lived and worked on the manors of the nobility, the vital cells of rural social life. All peasants were dependent on their lords and considered their property. In Frankish times the manor was a plot of land within a village ranging from twelve to seventy-five acres and assigned by the leaders of a settled tribe or clan to favored members. This member and his family became lords of the land, and those who dwelt there formed a smaller, self-sufficient community within a larger village community. In the early Middle Ages, such manors consisted of the dwellings of the lord and his family, the cottages of the peasant workers, agricultural sheds, and fields.

The landowner or lord of the manor required a certain amount of produce (grain, eggs, and the like) and services from the peasant families that came to dwell on and farm his land. The tenants were free to divide the labor as they wished; and they owned whatever remained after the lord's levies were met. A powerful lord might own many such manors. Kings later based their military and tax assessments on the number of manors owned by a vassal landlord. No set rules governed the size of manors. There were manors of a hundred acres or less and some of several thousand or more.

There were both servile and free manors. The tenants of the latter had originally been freemen known as *coloni*. Original inhabitants and petty landowners, they swapped their small possessions for a guarantee of security from a more powerful lord, who thus came to possess their land. Unlike the pure serfdom of the servile manors, whose tenants had no original claim to a part of the land, the tenancy obligations on free manors tended to be limited and the tenants' rights more carefully defined. It was a milder serfdom. Tenants of servile manors were by comparison far more vulnerable to the whims of their landlords. These two types of manor tended, however, to merge. In most manors tenants of greater and lesser degrees of servitude dwelt together, their services to

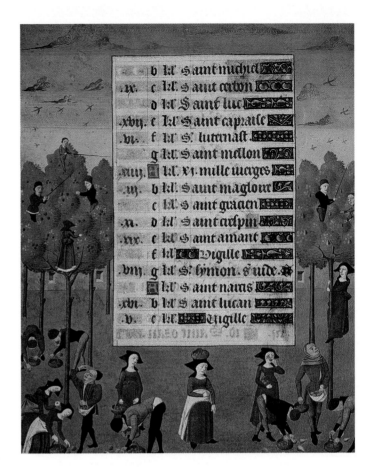

Men and women harvesting pears. From a Book of Hours (fifteenth century).
[Lauros-Giraudon/Art Resource, N.Y.]

the lord defined by their personal status and local custom. In many regions free, self-governing peasant communities existed without any overlords and tenancy obligations.

The lord held both judicial and police powers. He owned and operated the machines that processed crops into food and drink. A modern authority on manorial society has vividly depicted the duties of tenancy:

> On certain days the tenant brings the lord's steward perhaps a few small silver coins or, more often, sheaves of grain harvested on his fields, chickens from his farmyard, cakes of wax from his beehives or from the swarms of the neighboring forest. At other times he works on the arable or the meadows of the demesne [the lord's plot of land in the manorial fields, between one third and one half of that available]. Or else we find him carting casks of wine or sacks of grain on behalf of the master to distant residences. His is the labour which repairs the walls or moats of the castle. If the master has guests the peasant strips his own bed to provide the necessary extra bed-clothes. When the hunting season comes round

The Services of a Serf

By the fourteenth century, serfs were paid for their labor. This contract, from a manor in Sussex, England, describes the services required of one serf, John of Cayworth, stipulating the number of days he must devote to each and the pay he is to receive in return. Deductions for meals, which varied in price with the particular service performed, are factored into the serf's take-home pay.

Do the chores and the number of days the serf must work appear excessive? Was it worthwhile for the serf, given what he received in exchange? Would modern renters of land and lodging consider these payments reasonable today?

John of Cayworth holds a house and 30 acres of land, and owes yearly 2 s[shillings] at Easter and Michaelmas [in rent to his lord]; and he owes a cock and two hens at Christmas [also in rent] of the value of 4 d[enarii].

And he ought to harrow for 2 days at the Lenten sowing with one man and his own horse and his own harrow, the value of the work being 4d.; and he is to receive from the lord on each day 3 meals, of the value of 5d., and then the lord will be at a loss of 1d. . . .

And he ought to carry the manure of the lord for 2 days with one cart, with his own 2 oxen, the value of the work being 8d.; and he is to receive from the lord each day 3 meals at the value as above. . . .

And he shall find one man for 2 days, for mowing the meadow of the lord, who can mow, by estimation, 1 acre and a half, the value of the mowing of an acre being 6d.; the sum is there 9d. And he is to receive each day 3 meals of the value given above. . . .

And he ought to carry the hay of the lord for 1 day with a cart and 3 animals of his own, the price of the work being 6d. And he shall have from the lord 3 meals of the value of 2 1/2d. . . .

And he ought to carry in autumn beans or oats for 2 days with a cart and 3 animals of his own, the value of the work being 12d. And he shall receive from the lord each day 3 meals of the value given above. . . .

And he ought to carry wood from the woods of the lord as far as the manor, for two days in summer, with a cart and 3 animals of his own, the value of the work being 9d. And he shall receive from the lord each day 3 meals of the price given above. . . .

The totals of the rents with the value of the hens, is 2s. 4d.

From James Harvey Robinson, ed., *Readings in European History*, Vol. 1 (Boston: Athenaeum, 1906), pp. 400–402.

---

he feeds the pack. If war breaks out he does duty as a footsoldier or orderly, under the leadership of the reeve of the village.[2]

The lord also had the right to subject his tenants to exactions known as *banalities*. He could, for example, force them to breed their cows with his bull, and to pay for the privilege; to grind their bread grains in his mill; to bake their bread in his oven; to make their wine in his wine press; to buy their beer from his brewery; and even to surrender to him the tongues or other choice parts of all animals slaughtered on his lands. The lord also collected as an inheritance tax a serf's best animal. Without the lord's permission, a serf could neither travel nor marry outside the manor in which he served.

As exploited as the serfs may appear to have been from a modern point of view, their status was not chattel slavery. It was to a lord's advantage to keep his serfs healthy and happy; his welfare, like theirs, depended on a successful harvest. Serfs had their own dwellings and modest strips of land, and

they lived off the produce of their own labor and organization. They could also market for their own profit any surpluses that remained after the harvest. They were free to marry within the local village, although the lord's permission was required if a wife or husband was chosen from another village. And serfs could pass their property (their dwellings and field strips) on to their children, along with their worldly goods.

Two basic changes occurred in the evolution of the manor from the early to the later Middle Ages. The first was the fragmentation of the manor and the predominance of the single-family holding. This development was aided by such technological advances as the collar harness (ca. 800), the horseshoe (ca. 900), and the three-field system of crop rotation, which made it easier for smaller familial units to support themselves. As the lords parceled out their land (the demesne) to new tenants, their own plots became progressively smaller. The increase in tenants and the decrease in the lord's fields brought about a corresponding reduction in the labor services exacted from the tenants. Also, the bringing of new fields into production increased individual holdings and modified labor services. In France, by the reign of

[2] *Feudal Society*, trans. by L. A. Manyon (Chicago: University of Chicago Press, 1968), p. 250.

Louis IX (1226–1270), only a few days a year were required, whereas under Charlemagne (768–814) peasants had worked the lords' fields several days a week.

As the single-family unit replaced the clan as the basic nuclear group, assessments of goods and services fell on individual fields and households, no longer on manors as a whole. Family farms replaced manorial units. The peasants' carefully nurtured communal life enabled a family to retain its land and dwelling after the death of the head of the household. Land and property thus remained in the possession of a single family from generation to generation.

The second change in the evolution of the manor was the conversion of the serf's dues into money payments, a change made possible by the revival of trade and the rise of the towns. This development, completed by the thirteenth century, permitted serfs to hold their land as rent-paying tenants and to overcome their servile status. Although tenants thereby gained greater freedom, they were not necessarily better off materially. Whereas servile workers could have counted on the benevolent assistance of their landlords in hard times, rent-paying workers were left, by and large, to their own devices. Their independence caused some landlords to treat them with indifference and even resentment.

Lands and properties that had been occupied by generations of peasants and were recognized as their own were always under the threat of the lord's claim to a prior right of inheritance and even outright usurpation. As their demesnes declined, the lords were increasingly tempted to encroach on such traditionally common lands. The peasantry fiercely resisted such efforts, instinctively clinging to the little they had.

In many regions they successfully organized to gain a voice in the choice of petty rural officials.

By the mid-fourteenth century, a declining nobility in England and France, faced with the ravages of the great plague and the Hundred Years' War, tried to turn back the historical clock by increasing taxes on the peasantry and restricting their migration to the cities. The response was armed revolt. The revolts of the agrarian peasantry, like those of the urban proletariat, were brutally crushed. They stand out at the end of the Middle Ages as violent testimony to the breakup of medieval society. As growing national sentiment would break its political unity and heretical movements end its nominal religious unity, the peasantry's revolts revealed the absence of medieval social unity.

Medieval Women

The image and the reality of medieval women are two different things. The former was strongly influenced by the views of male Christian clergy, whose ideal was a celibate life of chastity, poverty, and obedience. Drawing on classical medical, philosophical, and legal traditions that predated Christianity, as well as on ancient biblical teaching, Christian theologians often depicted women as the physical, mental, and moral inferiors of men.

The clergy generally considered marriage a debased state by comparison with the religious life, and praised virgins and celibate widows over wives. In marriage the role of a wife was above all to love and obey her husband, and her husband had reciprocal duties of love, protection, and discipline. This

A fifteenth-century rendering of an eleventh- or twelfth-century marketplace. Medieval women were active in all trades, but especially in the food and clothing industries. [Scala/Art Resource, N.Y.]

image has suggested that a medieval woman had only two options in life: either a subjugated housewife or a cloistered nun. In reality, most medieval women were neither.

Image and Status   Both within and outside Christianity, real-life experience contradicted this image. In chivalric romances and courtly love literature of the twelfth and thirteenth centuries, as also in the contemporaneous cult of the Virgin Mary, women are praised and admired, even put on pedestals and treated as superior to men. If the church shared traditional condescending and occasional misogynistic sentiments, it also condemned them, as happened in the case of the *The Romance of the Rose* (late thirteenth century) and popular bawdy literature, demeaning to women in its eyes.

The learned churchman Peter Lombard (1100–1164) sanctioned an image of women that didactic Christian literature often invoked. Why, Lombard asked, was Eve created from Adam's rib and not instead taken from his head or his feet? The answer: God wanted woman neither to rule over man nor to be enslaved to him, but rather to stand squarely at his side as his companion and partner in mutual aid and trust. By so insisting on the spiritual equality of men and women and their shared responsibility to one another within marriage, the church also helped to raise the dignity of women by contemporary standards.

Under Germanic law women had basic rights that prevented them from being treated as chattel slaves. There was also far greater equality between the sexes in Germanic than in Roman law. Unlike Roman women, who as teens married much older men, German women married adults of similar age to themselves. Another practice unknown to the Romans was the groom's required conveyance of a dowry to his bride, which remained her own in the event of widowhood. All the major Germanic law codes recognized the right of women to inherit, administer, dispose of, and confer family property and wealth on their children. They could also press charges in court against men for bodily injury and rape. Depending on the country in question, punishments for rape ranged from fines, flogging, and banishment to blinding, castration, and death. In disputed cases, one fourteenth century law code permitted a woman to challenge an alleged rapist to a duel, the accused man forced to fight standing in a pit up to his waist to make the contest more even (few women, however, appear to have chosen such a course of action).

The nunnery was an option open to only a few unmarried women from the higher social classes. Entrance required a dowry *(dos)* and could be almost as expensive as a wedding, although it usually cost less. A nun could become abbess or mother superior and exercise an organizational and administrative authority denied her in much of the secular world. However, the nunneries of established religious orders were also under male supervision, and even mothers superior had to answer to higher male authority and receive the church's sacraments from male hands.

Nunneries also provided women an escape from the debilitating effects of multiple pregnancies. In the ninth century, under the influence of Christianity, the Carolingians made monogamous marriage their official policy. Heretofore, they had practiced polygyny and concubinage and also permitted divorce. The result of the new policy was both a boon and a burden to women. On one hand, the selection of a wife now became a special event, and wives gained greater dignity and legal security. On the other hand, a woman's labor as household manager and bearer of children greatly increased.

Most medieval women were neither aristocratic housewives nor nuns, but workers in fields, trades, and businesses. Much evidence suggests that they were respected and loved by their husbands, perhaps because they worked shoulder to shoulder and hour by hour with them. Between the ages of ten and fifteen, girls were apprenticed in a trade, much like boys, and they learned a marketable skill. If they married, they might continue their particular trade, operating their bakeshops or cloth shops next to their husbands' businesses, or become assistants and partners in their husbands shops. Women appeared in virtually every "blue-collar" trade, from butcher to goldsmith, although they were especially prominent in the food and clothing industries. Women belonged to guilds, just like men, and they could become craftmasters. In the later Middle Ages, it became increasingly common for townswomen to go to school and gain vernacular literacy.

Women were excluded by reason of gender from the professions of scholarship, law, and medicine. However, the vocational destinies of most men were no less fixed; socially inferior, propertyless men also could not enter these high professions. As is still true today in most of the world, women disproportionately filled the ranks of domestic servants and the clothing (sewing, weaving), food, and helping (midwifery, nursing) trades. In certain professions their freedom of movement was more circumscribed than that of male coworkers. Still, women remained a prominent and creative part of the medieval work force.

Medieval Children

The image and reality of medieval children are also contradictory. Until recently many historians had believed that medieval parents were emotionally bankrupt and treated their children as little adults. Evidence of low esteem for children has been conjured from a variety of sources.

Some historians maintain that children were rarely portrayed as being different from adults in medieval art and sculpture. There is also evidence of high infant and child mortality, which, it is argued, discouraged parents from making deep emotional commitments to their children. Why should a parent become attached to a child who had a 30–50 percent chance of dying before age five? During the Middle Ages children also assumed adult responsibilities much earlier in life than children do today. Peasant children labored in the fields alongside their parents as soon as they could physically manage the work. Urban artisans and burghers sent their children out of their homes into apprenticeships around the age of ten. That children were expected to grow up fast is also indicated by the canonical ages for marriage: twelve for girls and fourteen for boys. Very few actually married at such young ages, and when they did, it was usually a matter of royal dynasties and powerful noble families making long-range political plans. Such unions were more like engagements that became consummated, cohabiting marriages at later ages.

The practice of infanticide has been cited as an even more striking indication of low esteem for children in ancient and early medieval times. According to Tacitus, the Romans exposed unwanted children, especially girls, at birth—that is, abandoned them to die, as a way to control family size and gender. Surviving, or chosen, children, however, appear to have been given plenty of attention and affection. The Germanic tribes of medieval Europe, by contrast, had large families, but tended to neglect their children by comparison to the Romans. Infanticide, particularly of girls, continued to be practiced in the early Middle Ages, as shown by its condemnation in penance books and by the decrees of church synods. The church also forbade parents from sleeping with infants and small children as a way to prevent alleged accidental suffocations.

Among the German tribes, one paid a much lower *wergild*, or compensatory fine, for injury to a child than for injury to an adult, only one-fifth of that for injuring an adult. The *wergild* paid for injury to a female child under fifteen was one half that for injury to a male child—a strong indication that female children were the least esteemed members of German tribal society. Mothers appear also to have nursed boys longer than they did girls, which favored boys' health and survival. However, a woman's *wergild* increased a full eightfold between infancy and her childbearing years, at which time she had obviously become highly prized.[3]

Despite such varied evidence of parental distance and neglect, the evidence for parental love and responsibility is even stronger. Since the early Middle Ages, physicians and theologians portrayed childhood as a distinct and special stage of life. According to the medical authorities, infancy proper extended from birth to anywhere between six months

Depicted are two children's pastimes: catching butterflies with a net (center child) and spinning tops (lower left). The third child is using a walker, despite his appearance of being too old to need it. All three indicate contemporary recognition of children and the stages of life they go through despite the artist's crude workmanship. [The Bridgeman Art Library International]

and two years and covered the period of speechlessness and suckling. The period thereafter, until age seven, was considered a higher level of infancy, marked by weaning and the beginning of a child's ability to speak. At age seven, when a child could think, act decisively, and speak clearly, childhood proper was seen to begin. After this point, a child could be reasoned with, profit from regular discipline, and begin to train for a lifelong vocation. At seven a child was ready for schooling, private tutoring, or apprenticeship in a chosen craft or trade. Until physical growth was completed, however—and that could extend to twenty-one years of age—a child or youth was legally under the guardianship of parents or a surrogate authority.

There is evidence that high infant and child mortality, rather than distancing parents from children, actually made parents look on their children as all the more precious. The medical authorities of the Middle Ages—Hippocrates, Galen, and Soranus of Ephesus—dealt at length with postnatal care and childhood diseases. Both sensible and fanciful cures can be found for the leading killers of children (diarrhea, worms, pneumonia, and fever). When infants and children died, medieval parents grieved as pitiably as modern parents do. In the art and literature of the Middle Ages, we find mothers baptizing dead infants and children, or carrying them to pilgrim shrines hoping to revive them. There

[3]David Herlihy, "Medieval Children," in *Essays on Medieval Civilization*, ed. by B. K. Lackner and K. R. Philp (Austin: University of Texas Press, 1978), pp. 109–131.

are also examples of mental illness and suicide brought on by the death of a child.[4]

Clear evidence of special attention being paid to children is also evident in the great variety of children's toys, as well as devices like walkers and potty chairs that existed in the Middle Ages. The medieval authorities on child rearing widely condemned child abuse and advocated moderation in the disciplining of children. In church art and drama, parents were urged to love their children as Mary loved Jesus. Early apprenticeships may also be interpreted as an expression of parental love and concern rather than indifference and low esteem, for in the Middle Ages, no parental responsibility was thought greater than that of equipping a child for useful and gainful work.

Politics

England and France: Hastings (1066) to Bouvines (1214)

William the Conqueror   The most important change in English political life was occasioned in 1066 by the death of the childless Anglo-Saxon ruler Edward the Confessor (r. 1042–1066), so named because of his reputation of piety. Edward's mother was a Norman princess, which gave Duke William of Normandy (d. 1087) a hereditary claim to the English throne. The Anglo-Saxon assembly, however, customarily bestowed royal power, and it had a mind of its own. It chose instead Harold Godwinsson (ca. 1022–1066). That defiant action brought the swift conquest of England by the powerful Normans. William's forces defeated Harold's army at Hastings on October 14, 1066, and William was crowned king of England in Westminster Abbey within weeks of the invasion.

Thereafter William organized his new English state shrewdly, establishing a strong monarchy whose power was not fragmented by independent territorial princes. He first embarked on a twenty-year conquest that eventually made every landholder, both large and small, his vassal. He kept the Anglo-Saxon tax system and the practice of court writs (legal warnings) as a flexible form of central control over localities. And he took care not to destroy the Anglo-Saxon quasi-democratic tradition of frequent *parleying*—that is, the holding of conferences between the king and lesser powers who had vested interests in royal decisions. The result was a balancing of monarchical and parliamentary elements that remains true of English government today.

For administration and taxation, William commissioned a county-by-county survey of his new realm, known as the

[4]Klaus Arnold, *Kind and Gesellschaft im Mittelalter und Renaissance* (Paderborn, 1980), pp. 31, 37.

Domesday Book (1080–1086). The title of the book reflects the thoroughness of the survey: just as none would escape the doomsday judgment of God, so none was overlooked by William's assessors.

Henry II and Eleanor of Aquitaine   William's son, Henry I (r. 1100–1135), died without a male heir, throwing England into virtual anarchy until Henry II (r. 1154–1189) became king as head of the new Plantagenet dynasty. Henry brought to the throne greatly expanded French holdings, partly by inheritance from his father (Maine, Touraine, and Anjou) and partly by his marriage to Eleanor of Aquitaine (1122–1204), a union that created the so-called Angevin or English-French empire. Eleanor married Henry while he was still the count of Anjou and not yet king of England. The marriage occurred only eight weeks after the annulment of Eleanor's fifteen-year marriage to the ascetic French king Louis VII (r. 1137–1180) in March 1152. Although the annulment was granted on grounds of consanguinity (blood relationship), the true reason for the dissolution of the marriage was Louis's suspicion of Eleanor's infidelity. The annulment was costly to Louis, who lost Aquitaine together with his wife.

Eleanor of Aquitaine was a powerful influence on both court politics and culture in twelfth-century France and England. She had accompanied Louis VII on the Second Crusade, becoming an example for women of lesser stature, who were venturing in increasing numbers into war and business and other areas previously considered the province of men. Eleanor spent the years 1154 to 1170 as Henry's queen in England. She separated from Henry in 1170, partly because of his public philandering and cruel treatment, later (1173) taking revenge by helping provoke a rebellion against him by their three sons, who were unhappy with the terms of their inheritance.

After separating from Henry, Eleanor lived in Poitiers with her daughter Marie, the countess of Champagne, and the two made the court of Poitiers a famous center for the literature of courtly love. The most enduring example of the latter is the work of Chrétien de Troyes (d. 1183), whose tales of King Arthur and the Knights of the Round Table told the tragic story of Sir Lancelot's secret and illicit love for Arthur's wife, Guinevere.

Eleanor and Henry reunited in 1179, but he kept her under mild house arrest until his death in 1189.

Popular Rebellion and Magna Carta   As Henry II acquired new lands abroad, he became more autocratic at home. He forced his will on the clergy in the Constitutions of Clarendon (1164). These measures limited judicial appeals to Rome, subjected the clergy to the civil courts, and gave the king control over the election of bishops. The result was strong political resistance from both the nobility and the cler-

William the Conqueror on horseback urging his troops into combat with the English at the Battle of Hastings (October 14, 1066). From the Bayeux Tapestry, about 1073–1083. [Giraudon/Art Resource, N.Y.]

gy. The archbishop of Canterbury, Thomas à Becket (1118?–1170), once Henry's compliant chancellor, broke openly with the king. Becket's subsequent assassination in 1170 and his canonization by Pope Alexander III (r. 1159–1181) in 1172 helped focus popular resentment against the king's heavy-handed tactics.

Under Henry's successors, the brothers Richard the Lion-Hearted (r. 1189–1199) and John (r. 1199–1216), burdensome taxation in support of foreign Crusades and a failing war with France turned resistance into outright rebellion. In 1209 Pope Innocent III (r. 1198–1216), in a dispute with King John over the pope's choice for archbishop of Canterbury, excommunicated the king and placed England under interdict, which forbade church services. To extricate himself and keep his throne, John made humiliating concessions, even declaring England a fief of the pope. The last straw for the English came with the defeat of the king's forces by the French at Bouvines in 1214. With the full support of the clergy and the townspeople, English barons turned against John in a popular rebellion that ended with the king's grudging recognition of Magna Carta ("Great Charter") in 1215.

This famous cornerstone of modern English law put limits on autocratic behavior of the kind exhibited by Norman kings and their successors, and it secured the rights of the privileged to be represented at the highest levels of government in important matters like taxation.

Although political accident had more to do with its creation than political genius, the Great Charter enabled the English to avoid both a dissolution of the monarchy by the nobility and the abridgment of the rights of the nobility by the monarchy.

Philip II Augustus During the century and a half between the Norman Conquest (1066) and the Magna Carta

(1215), a strong monarchy was never in question in England. The English struggle in the High Middle Ages was to secure the rights of the many, not the authority of the king. The French faced the reverse problem during this period. Powerful feudal princes dominated France from the beginning of the Capetian dynasty (987) until the reign of Philip II Augustus (1180–1223). During this period the Capetian kings wisely concentrated their limited resources on securing the royal domain, their uncontested territory surrounding Paris known as the Île-de-France. They did not rashly challenge the more powerful nobility. Aggressively exercising their feudal rights in this area, they secured absolute obedience and a solid power base. By the time of Philip II, Paris had become the center of French government and culture, and the Capetian dynasty a secure hereditary monarchy. Thereafter, the kings of France were able to impose their will on the French nobles, who were always in law—if not in political fact—the king's sworn vassals.

The Norman conquest of England helped stir France to unity and enabled the Capetian kings to establish a truly national monarchy. The duke of Normandy, who after 1066 was master of England, was also among the vassals of the French king in Paris. Capetian kings understandably watched with alarm as the power of their Norman vassal grew.

Philip Augustus faced both an internal and an international struggle, and he succeeded at both. His armies occupied all the English territories on the French coast, except for Aquitaine. However, the Holy Roman Emperor Otto IV (r. 1198–1215) entered the fray on the side of the English, and the French found themselves assailed from both east and west. Still, when the international armies finally clashed at Bouvines on July 27, 1214, the French won handily over the English and the Germans. The victory unified France around the monarchy and thereby laid the foundation for French ascendancy in

The English Nobility Imposes Restraints on King John

The gradual building of a sound English constitutional monarchy in the Middle Ages required the king's willingness to share power. He had to be strong but could not act as a despot or rule by fiat. The danger of despotism became acute in England under the rule of King John. In 1215 the English nobility forced him to recognize Magna Carta, which reaffirmed traditional rights and personal liberties that are still enshrined in English law.

Are the rights protected by Magna Carta basic ones or special privileges? Do they suggest there was a sense of "fairness" in the past? Does the granting of such rights in any way weaken the king?

A free man shall not be fined for a small offense, except in proportion to the gravity of the offense; and for a great offense he shall be fined in proportion to the magnitude of the offense, saving his freehold [property]; and a merchant in the same way, saving his merchandise; and the villein [a free serf, bound only to his lord] shall be fined in the same way, saving his wainage [wagon], if he shall be at [the king's] mercy. And none of the above fines shall be imposed except by the oaths of honest men of the neighborhood. . . .

No constable or other bailiff of [the king] shall take anyone's grain or other chattels without immediately paying for them in money, unless he is able to obtain a postponement at the good will of the seller.

No constable shall require any knight to give money in place of his ward of a castle [i.e., standing guard], if he is willing to furnish that ward in his own person, or through another honest man, if he himself is not able to do it for a reasonable cause; and if we shall lead or send him into the army, he shall be free from ward in proportion to the amount of time which he has been in the army through us.

No sheriff or bailiff of [the king], or any one else, shall take horses or wagons of any free man, for carrying purposes, except on the permission of that free man.

Neither we nor our bailiffs will take the wood of another man for castles, or for anything else which we are doing, except by the permission of him to whom the wood belongs. . . .

No free man shall be taken, or imprisoned, or dispossessed, or outlawed, or banished, or in any way injured, nor will we go upon him, nor send upon him, except by the legal judgment of his peers, or by the law of the land.

To no one will we sell, to no one will we deny or delay, right or justice.

James Harvey Robinson, ed., *Readings in European History*, Vol. 1 (Boston: Athenaeum, 1904), pp. 400–402.

---

the later Middle Ages. Philip Augustus also gained control of the lucrative urban industries of Flanders. The defeat so weakened Otto IV that he fell from power in Germany.

France in the Thirteenth Century: Reign of Louis IX

If Innocent III realized the fondest ambitions of medieval popes, Louis IX (r. 1226–1270), the grandson of Philip Augustus, embodied the medieval view of the perfect ruler. Coming to power in the wake of the French victory at Bouvines (1214), Louis inherited a unified and secure kingdom. Although his moral character far excelled that of his royal and papal contemporaries, he was also at times prey to naiveté. Not beset by the problems of sheer survival, and a reformer at heart, Louis found himself free to concentrate on what medieval people believed to be the business of civilization.

Magnanimity in politics is not always a sign of strength, and Louis could be very magnanimous. Although in a position to drive the English from their French possessions during negotiations for the Treaty of Paris (1259), he refused to take such advantage. Had he done so and ruthlessly confiscated English territories on the French coast, he might have lessened, if not averted altogether, the Hundred Years War (ca. 1337–1453). He instead surrendered territory to the English. Although he occasionally chastised popes for their crude ambitions, Louis remained neutral during the long struggle between Emperor Frederick II and the papacy, and his neutrality redounded to the pope's advantage. For their assistance, both by action and by inaction, the Capetian kings of the thirteenth century received many papal favors.

Louis's greatest achievements lay at home. The efficient French bureaucracy, which his predecessors had used to exploit their subjects, became under Louis an instrument of order and fair play in local government. He sent forth royal commissioners *(enqueteurs)*, reminiscent of Charlemagne's far less successful royal governors *(missi dominici)*, to monitor the royal officials responsible for local governmental administration and ensure justice. These royal ambassadors were received as genuine tribunes of the people. Louis further abolished private wars and serfdom within his own royal domain, gave his subjects the right of appeal from local to higher courts, and made the tax system, by medieval standards, more equitable. The French people came to associate their king with justice; and national feeling, the glue of nationhood, grew strong during his reign.

Respected by the kings of Europe, Louis became an arbiter among the world's powers, having far greater moral authority than the pope. During his reign, French society and culture became an example to all of Europe, a pattern that would continue into the modern period. Northern France became the showcase of monastic reform, chivalry, and Gothic art and architecture. Louis's reign also coincided with the golden age of scholasticism, which saw the convergence of Europe's greatest thinkers on Paris, among them Saint Thomas Aquinas and Saint Bonaventure.

Louis's perfection remained, however, that of a medieval king. Like his father, Louis VIII (r. 1223–1226), Louis was something of a religious fanatic. He sponsored the French Inquisition. He led two disastrous Crusades against the Arabs. During the first (1248–1254), he was captured and had to be ransomed out of Egypt. He died of a fever during the second in 1270. It was especially for this selfless (although useless) service that the church, pressured by the ruthless king Philip the Fair (r. 1285–1314), honored the French state by bestowing sainthood on Louis IX.

The Hohenstaufen Empire (1152–1272)

During the twelfth and thirteenth centuries, stable governments developed in both England and France. The Holy Roman Empire, which embraced Germany, Burgundy, and northern Italy by the mid-thirteenth century, was a different story (see Map 13–3). There, primarily because of the efforts of the Hohenstaufen dynasty to extend imperial power into southern Italy, two centuries of disunity and blood feuding fragmented Germany until modern times.

Frederick I Barbarossa   With the accession to the throne of Frederick I Barbarossa (1152–1190), the first of the Hohenstaufens, a new day seemed to dawn for imperial power. The Hohenstaufens not only reestablished imperial authority but also initiated a new phase in the contest between popes and emperors, one that was to prove even more deadly than the investiture struggle had been. Never have rulers and popes despised and persecuted one another more than they did during the Hohenstaufen dynasty.

As Frederick I surveyed his empire, he saw powerful feudal princes in Germany and Lombardy and a pope in Rome who believed that the emperor should obey his command. There existed, however, widespread disaffection with the incessant warring among the princes and the theocratic pre-

The portal of Reims Cathedral, where the kings of France were crowned. This cathedral was built in the Gothic style—emblematic of the High and late Middle Ages—that originated in France in the mid-twelfth century. The earlier Romanesque (Roman-like) style from which it evolved is characterized by fortresslike buildings with thick stone walls, rounded arches and vaults, and few windows. The Gothic style, in contrast, is characterized by soaring structures, their interiors flooded with colored light from vast expanses of stained glass. Distinctive features of the style include ribbed, crisscrossing vaulting; pointed rather than rounded arches; and prominent exterior flying buttresses. The vaulting and the flying buttresses made possible the great height of Gothic buildings. By shifting structural weight from the walls, the buttresses also made possible the large, stained-glass-filled windows. The windows were used much as mosaics had been earlier, to show stories from the Bible, saints' lives, and local events.
[Scala/Art Resource, N.Y.]

tensions of the papacy. Popular opinion was on the emperor's side, and Frederick shrewdly took advantage of it. Making Switzerland his base of operation, he attempted to hold the empire together by stressing feudal bonds.

Frederick's reign ended, however, with stalemate in Germany and defeat in Italy. Before his death in 1190, an opportunity had opened to form a new territorial base of power for future emperors by an alliance with Sicily. Sealed in 1186 by the marriage of his son—the future Henry VI (r. 1190–1197)—and Constance, heiress to the kingdom of Sicily, the alliance became a fatal distraction for the Hohenstaufens. Equally ominous, this union of the empire with Sicily left Rome encircled, thereby ensuring the undying hostility of a papacy already thoroughly distrustful of the emperor.

When Henry VI died in September 1197, chaos followed. Germany was thrown into anarchy and civil war. England gave financial support to anti-Hohenstaufen factions, and helped Otto of Brunswick of the rival Welf dynasty to become Emperor Otto IV in 1198. With England supporting Otto, the French backed the Hohenstaufens—the beginning of periodic French fishing in troubled German waters. Meanwhile, Henry VI's four-year-old son, Frederick, who had a direct hereditary claim to the imperial crown, had for his own safety been made—fatefully, it would prove—a ward of Pope Innocent III.

Pope Innocent III (1198–1215)

Innocent III was a papal monarch in the Gregorian tradition of papal independence from secular domination. He proclaimed and practiced as none before him the doctrine of the plenitude of papal power. In a famous statement he likened the relationship of the pope to the emperor—or the church to the state—to that of the sun to the moon. As the moon received its light from the sun, so the emperor received his brilliance (that is, his crown) from the hand of the pope—an allusion to the famous precedent set on Christmas Day, 800, when Pope Leo III crowned Charlemagne.

Although this pretentious theory greatly exceeded his ability to practice it, Innocent and his successors did not hesitate to act on their ambitions. When Philip II tried unlawfully to annul his marriage, Innocent placed France under interdict, suspending all church services save baptism and the last rites; the same punishment befell England when King John presumed to appoint an unworthy archbishop of Canterbury. Innocent had both the will and the means to challenge the Hohenstaufens.

Frederick II

Hohenstaufen support had meanwhile remained alive in Germany despite the dynasty's fall, and Otto IV reigned over a divided kingdom. In October 1209 Pope Innocent crowned him emperor, but then quickly became a mortal enemy when, after his coronation, Otto proceeded to reconquer Sicily and to pursue again an imperial policy that left Rome encircled. Within four months of his papal coronation, Otto received a papal excommunication.

Casting about for a counterweight to the treacherous Otto, Pope Innocent joined the French, who had remained loyal to the Hohenstaufens against the English-Welf alliance. His new ally, Philip Augustus, suggested to the pope that a solution to their problems with Otto IV lay near at hand in Innocent's ward, Frederick of Sicily, son of the late Hohen-staufen Emperor Henry VI, who was now of age. In December 1212 young Frederick, with papal, French, and German support, became Emperor Frederick II. Within a year and a half, Philip Augustus ended the Welf interregnum of Otto IV on the battlefield of Bouvines. After the victory he sent Frederick II Otto's fallen flag taken from the battlefield, a bold gesture that suggests the extent to which Frederick's ascent to the throne was intended to create a French-papal puppet.

Frederick soon disappointed any such hopes. He was Sicilian and dreaded travel beyond the Alps. Only nine of his thirty-eight years as emperor were spent in Germany. Frederick desired only one thing from the German princes, the imperial title for himself and his sons, and he gave them what they wanted to secure it. His eager compliance with their demands laid the foundation for six centuries of German division. In 1220 he recognized the jurisdictional claims of the ecclesiastical princes of Germany, and in 1232 he extended the same recognition to the secular princes. The German princes thus became undisputed lords over their territories. Frederick's concessions have been characterized as a German equivalent to the Magna Carta in the sense that they secured the rights of the German nobility. Unlike the Great Charter, however, they failed to secure the rights of the monarchy. The Great Charter placed the king and the English nobility (parliament) in a creative tension; the reign of Frederick II simply made the German nobility petty kings.

Frederick had an equally disastrous relationship with the papacy, which excommunicated him four times. Pope Innocent IV (1243–1254) organized and led the newly empowered German princes against Frederick, launching the church into European politics on a massive scale. This transformation of the papacy into a formidable political and military power soon made the church highly vulnerable to the criticism of religious reformers and royal apologists alike.

When Frederick died in 1250, the German monarchy died with him. The princes established an informal electoral college in 1257 to pick the emperor, which thereafter reigned supreme (it was formally recognized by the emperor in 1356). The "king of the Romans" became their puppet, this time with firmly attached strings; he was elected and did not rule by hereditary right. Between 1250 and 1272 the Hohenstaufen dynasty slowly faded into oblivion.

Medieval Russia

In the late tenth century Prince Vladimir of Kiev (r. 972–1015), then Russia's dominant city, received delegations of Muslims, Roman Catholics, Jews, and Greek Orthodox Christians, each group hoping to win the Russians to its religion. Prince Vladimir chose Greek Orthodoxy, which became the religion of Russia, adding a new cultural bond to

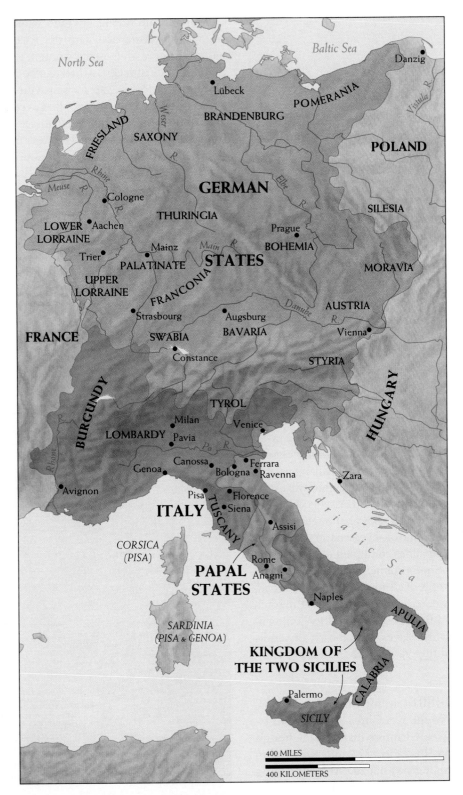

Map 13–3 Germany and Italy in the Middle Ages. Medieval Germany and Italy were divided lands. The Holy Roman Empire (Germany) embraced hundreds of independent territories that the emperor ruled only in name. The papacy controlled the Rome area and tried to enforce its will in the Romagna. Under the Hohenstaufens (mid-twelfth to mid-thirteenth centuries), internal German divisions and papal conflict reached new heights; German rulers sought to extend their power to southern Italy and Sicily.

Church and Empire	
910	Monastary of Cluny founded
918	Henry I becomes King of Germany
951	Otto I invades Italy
955	Otto I defeats the Hungarians at Lechfeld
962	Otto I crowned emperor by Pope John XII
1077	Gregory VII pardons Henry IV at Canossa
1122	Concordat of Worms settles the investiture controversy
1152–1190	Reign of Frederick Barbarossa
1198–1215	Reign of Innocent III
1214	Collapse of the claims of Otto IV
1220	Frederick II crowned emperor
1232	Frederick II devolves authority to the German princes
1257	The German monarchy becomes elective

the long-standing commercial ties the Russians had with the Byzantine Empire.

Politics and Society

Vladimir's successor, Yaroslav the Wise (r. 1016–1054), developed Kiev into a magnificent political and cultural center, with architecture rivaling that of Constantinople. He also sought contacts with the west in an unsuccessful effort to counter the strong political influence of the Byzantine emperors. After his death, rivalry among princes slowly split Russians into three cultural groups: the Great Russians, the White Russians, and the Little Russians (Ukrainians). Autonomous principalities also challenged Kiev's dominance, and it became just one of several national centers.

Government in the principalities combined monarchy (the prince), aristocracy (the prince's council of noblemen), and democracy (a popular assembly of all adult males). The broadest social division was between freemen and slaves. Freemen included the clergy, army officers, boyars (wealthy landowners), townsmen, and peasants. Slaves were mostly prisoners of war. Debtors working off their debts made up a large, semi-free, intermediate group.

Mongol Rule (1243–1480)

In the thirteenth century, Mongol (or Tatar) armies swept over China, much of the Islamic world, and Russia (see Chapters 8 and 14). Ghengis Khan (1155–1227) invaded Russia in 1223, and Kiev fell to Batu Khan in 1240. Russian cities became tribute-paying principalities of the segment of the Mongol Empire called the *Golden Horde* (a phrase derived from the Tatar words for the color of Batu Khan's tent), which had its capital at Sarai, on the lower Volga. The Golden Horde stationed officials in Russian towns to oversee taxation and the conscription of soldiers into Tatar armies.

Mongol rule further divided Russia from the west. The Mongols intermarried with the Russians and also created harems filled with Russian women. Russian women—under the influence of Islam, which had become the religion of the Golden Horde—began to wear veils and to lead more secluded lives. The Mongols, however, left Russian political institutions and religion largely intact and, thanks to their far-flung trade, brought most Russians greater peace and prosperity than they had enjoyed before.

Russian Liberation

The princes of Moscow cooperated with their overlords in the collection of tribute and grew wealthy under the Mongols. As Mongol rule weakened, the princes took control of the territory surrounding the city. In a process that has come to be known as "the gathering of the Russian land," they then gradually expanded the principality of Moscow through land purchases, colonization, and conquest.

In 1380 Grand Duke Dimitri of Moscow (1350–1389) defeated Tatar forces at Kulikov Meadow in a victory that marked the beginning of the decline of Mongolian hegemony. Another century would pass before Ivan III, called Ivan

The Cathedral of St. Basil in Moscow. Built between 1544 and 1560 during the reign of Ivan the Terrible, it reflects the enduring Byzantine influence on Russian architecture. [Sovfoto/Eastfoto]

the Great (d. 1505), would bring all of northern Russia under Moscow's control and end Mongol rule in 1480. By the last quarter of the fourteenth century, Moscow had replaced Kiev as the political and religious center of Russia. In Russian eyes it was destined to become the "third Rome" after the fall of Constantinople to the Turks in 1453.

IN WORLD PERSPECTIVE
The High Middle Ages

With its borders finally secured, western Europe concentrated during the High Middle Ages on its political institutions and cultural development, something denied it during the early Middle Ages. In England and France, modern western nations can be seen in formation. Within the empire, imperial rule both revived (under Otto I) and totally collapsed (during the Hohenstaufen dynasty). Everywhere, society successfully organized itself from noble to serf. With the flourishing of trade and the expansion of towns, a new wealthy class patronized education. Western Europe's first universities appeared, and a movement called scholasticism brought a new, and often forbidding, order to knowledge. The major disruption of the period, however, was an unprecedented conflict between former allies. The Roman Catholic Church had become a monarchy in its own right, able to compete with secular states and even to dethrone (by excommunication and interdict) kings and princes. The foundation was thereby laid both for perpetual conflict between popes and rulers, which lasted well into early modern times, and for the creation of the peculiar western separation of church and state.

Growth of National Monarchies	
987	Prince Vladimir of Kiev adopts Greek Orthodoxy
987	Beginning of the Capetian dynasty in France
1066	Battle of Hastings: William of Normandy conquers England
1152	Henry of Anjou (Henry II of England) marries Eleanor of Aquitane
1164	Constitutions of Clarendon give the English crown control over the church
1170	Assassination of Thomas à Becket
1180–1223	Reign of Philip II Augustus in France
1193–1194	Heavy English taxation to ransom Richard I
1215	Battle of Bouvines
1226–1270	Reign of Louis IX
1240	Mongols sack Kiev
1380	Dimitri of Moscow defeats the Mongols at Kulikov Meadow

For western Europe, the High Middle Ages were a period of clearer self-definition during which individual lands gained much of the geographic shape we recognize today. Other world civilizations had by this time become well-established and had even begun to depart their "classical" or "golden" periods. For the West, the best still lay ahead.

Under the Sung dynasty (960–1279), before Mongol rule, China continued its technological advance. In addition to the printing press, the Chinese invented the abacus and gunpowder. They also enjoyed a money economy unknown in the west. But culturally, these centuries between 1000 and 1300 were closed and narrow by comparison with those of the T'ang dynasty. Politically, the Sung was far more autocratic. In China (as in western European lands like England and France, although not in Italy and the empire), regional aristocracies ceased to be serious obstacles to a strong centralized government.

Chinese women generally held a lower status and had fewer vocational options than western women, as the practice of foot binding dramatically attests. As in the west, a higher degree of freedom and self-government developed in the countryside, especially by the fourteenth century, as peasants gained the right to buy and sell land and to fulfill traditional labor obligations by money payments. Intellectually, China, like the west, had a scholastic movement within its dominant philosophy; Confucianism made religious and philosophical thought more elaborate, systematic, and orthodox. Whereas western scholasticism made Christianity aloof, elitist, and ridiculed by its lay critics, Confucianism remained a philosophy highly adaptable and popular among laypeople.

In the late twelfth century Japan shifted from civilian to military rule; the Kamakura *bakufu* governed by mounted warriors who were paid with rights to income from land in exchange for their military services. This rise of a military aristocracy marked the beginning of Japan's "medieval," as distinct from its "classical," period. Three Mongol invasions in the thirteenth century also fostered a strong military to resist them. With a civilian court also in existence, Japan actually had a dual government (that is, two emperors and two courts) until the fourteenth century. However, this situation differed greatly from the deep and permanent national divisions developing at this time among the emerging states and autonomous principalities of western Europe.

Japanese women, more like those in western Europe than in China, traditionally played a prominent role in royal government and court culture. Nun Shogun, for example, succeeded her husband for a brief period of Kamakura rule in the late twelfth century. But the prominence of women in government would also change in Japan by the fourteenth century.

Within the many developing autonomous Islamic lands at this time, the teaching of Muhammad created an international culture. The regular practice of religious fundamentals enabled Muslims to transcend their new and often very deep regional divisions. Similarly, Christianity allowed Englishmen, Frenchmen, Germans, and Italians to think of themselves as one people and to unite in Crusades to the Holy Land. As these Crusades began in the late eleventh century, Islam too was on the march, penetrating Anatolia and Afghanistan, and impinging upon India, where it met a new challenge in Hinduism.

Review Questions

1. How did Otto I earn the title "the Great"?

2. How do you account for the success of the Cluny reform movement? Can major features of the modern Catholic Church be found in the Cluny's reforms?

3. Was the investiture controversy a political or a religious conflict? Summarize the respective arguments of Gregory VII and Henry IV. Is the conflict a precedent for the modern doctrine of the separation of church and state?

4. The eighteenth-century French intellectual Voltaire said the Holy Roman Empire was neither holy nor Roman. Do you agree?

5. What were the motives behind the Crusades to the Holy Land? Did they have any positive consequences for either western Europe or the Holy Land? If you had lived at this time and could have been a Crusader, which Crusade would you most liked to have joined?

6. Why did Germany remain divided while France and England began to coalesce into reasonably strong states during the High Middle Ages?

7. How did the responsibilities of the nobility differ from those of the clergy and the peasantry during the High Middle Ages? How did each social class contribute to the stability of society?

8. What gave rise to towns, and how did they change traditional medieval society?

9. How did the first universities differ from universities as we know them today?

10. Were the Middle Ages a time of rampant misogyny and child abuse? What were the opportunities of women and the protections for children?

Suggested Readings

EMILIE AMT, ED., *Women's Lives in Medieval Europe: A Sourcebook* (1992). Outstanding collection of sources.

P. ARIES, *Centuries of Childhood: A Social History of Family Life*, trans. by Robert Baldick (1962). Profound and controversial pioneer effort on the subject.

J. W. BALDWIN, *The Scholastic Culture of the Middle Ages: 1000–1300* (1971). Best brief synthesis available.

J. W. BALDWIN, *The Government of Philip Augustus* (1986). A scholarly feat.

M. W. BALDWIN, ED., *History of the Crusades, I: The First Hundred Years* (1955). Basic historical narrative.

G. BARRACLOUGH, *The Origins of Modern Germany* (1963). Penetrating political narrative.

G. BARRACLOUGH, *The Medieval Papacy* (1968). Brief, comprehensive survey, with pictures.

R. BARTLETT, *Trial by Fire and Water: The Medieval Judicial Ordeal* (1986).

R. BARTLETT, *The Making of Medieval Europe* (1992). Sees the interaction of different cultures as the decisive factor in the creation of West European civilization.

M. BLOCH, *French Rural Society*, trans. by J. Sondheimer (1966). A classic by a great modern historian.

J. BONY, *French Gothic Architecture of the Twelfth and Thirteenth Centuries* (1983).

J. BRUNDAGE, *Law, Sex, and Christian Society in Medieval Europe* (1987). Everything about the topic of sex in all its scholastic subtlety.

C. BYNAM, *Holy Feast, Holy Fast: The Religious Significance of Food to Medieval Women* (1987). An analysis of the mindset of cloistered women through their attitudes toward food.

A. CAPELLANUS, *The Art of Courtly Love*, trans. by J. J. Parry (1941). Translation of this classic along with other documents from the court of Marie de Champagne.

M. CLAGETT, G. POST, AND R. REYNOLDS, EDS., *Twelfth-Century Europe and the Foundations of Modern Society* (1966). Demanding but stimulating collection of essays.

F. COPLESTON, *A History of Philosophy, III/1: Ockham to the Speculative Mystics* (1963). The best introduction to Ockham and his movement.

F. C. COPLESTON, *Aquinas* (1965). Best introduction to Aquinas's philosophy.

R. H. C. DAVIS, *A History of Medieval Europe: From Constantine to St. Louis, Part 2* (1972).

G. DUBY, *Rural Economy and Country Life in the Medieval West* (1968). Slice-of-life analysis.

G. DUBY, *The Three Orders: Feudal Society Imagined*, trans. by Arthur Goldhammer (1981). Large, comprehensive, and authoritative.

R. AND J. GIES, *Marriage and Family in the Middle Ages* (1983).

E. GILSON, *Heloise and Abelard* (1968). An analysis and defense of medieval scholarly values.

J. GOODY, *The Development of the Family and Marriage in Europe* (1983). Bold interpretation of the church's marital legislation, ascribing unflattering, materialistic motives to the church.

ELIZABETH M. HALAM, *Capetian France 987–1328* (1980). Especially good on politics and heretics.

B. HANAWALT, *The Ties That Bound: Peasant Families in Medieval England* (1986). Analysis of family structure and relationships.

C. H. HASKINS, *The Renaissance of the Twelfth Century* (1927). Still the standard account.

C. H. HASKINS, *The Rise of Universities* (1972). A short, minor classic.

D. HERLIHY, *Medieval Households* (1985). Sweeping survey of Middle Ages that defends the medieval family against modern caricatures.

D. HERLIHY, *Opera Muliebria* (1990). Brief, pioneer effort to describe the many vocational and employment opportunities of medieval women.

J. C. HOLT, *Magna Carta*, 2nd ed. (1992). The famous document and its interpretation by succeeding generations.

E. H. KANTOROWICZ, *The King's Two Bodies* (1957). Controversial analysis of political concepts in the High Middle Ages.

G. LEFF, *Paris and Oxford Universities in the Thirteenth and Fourteenth Centuries: An Institutional and Intellectual History* (1968). Very good on debates on Scholasticism.

J. LE GOFF, *The Birth of Purgatory* (1981).

K. LEYSER, *Rule and Conflict in Early Medieval Society: Ottonian Saxony* (1979). Basic and authoritative.

K. LEYSER, *Medieval Germany and Its Neighbors, 900–1250* (1982). Basic and authoritative.

R. S. LOOMIS, ED., *The Development of Arthurian Romance* (1963). A basic study.

R. S. LOPEZ AND I. W. RAYMOND, EDS., *Medieval Trade in the Mediterranean World* (1955). An illuminating collection of sources, concentrated on southern Europe.

E. MÂLE, *The Gothic Image: Religious Art in France in the Thirteenth Century* (1913). A classic.

P. MANDONNET, *St. Dominic and His Work* (1944). The origins of the Dominican Order.

H. E. MAYER, *The Crusades*, trans. by John Gilligham (1972). Extremely detailed, and the best one-volume account.

R. I. MOORE, *The Formation of a Persecuting Society: Power and Deviance in Western Europe, 950–1250* (1987). A sympathetic look at heresy and dissent.

J. MOORMAN, *A History of the Franciscan Order* (1968). The best survey.

J. B. MORRALL, *Political Thought in Medieval Times* (1962). A readable and illuminating account.

J. T. NOONAN, *Contraception: A History of Its Treatment by the Catholic Theologians and Canonists* (1967). A fascinating account of medieval theological attitudes toward sexuality and sex-related problems.

E. PANOFSKY, *Gothic Architecture and Scholasticism* (1951). A controversial classic.

C. PETIT-DUTAILLIS, *The Feudal Monarchy in France and England from the Tenth to the Thirteenth Century*, trans. by E. D. Hunt (1964). A political narrative.

H. PIRENNE, *Medieval Cities: Their Origins and the Revival of Trade*, trans. by Frank D. Halsey (1970). A minor classic.

J. M. POWELL, *Innocent III: Vicar of Christ or Lord of the World* (1963). Excerpts from the scholarly debate over Innocent's reign.

F. W. POWICKE, *The Thirteenth Century* (1962). An outstanding treatment of English political history.

H. RASHDALL, *The Universities of Europe in the Middle Ages*, Vols. 1–3 (1936). Dated but still a standard comprehensive work.

J. RILEY-SMITH, *The Crusades: A Short History* (1987). Up-to-date, lucid, and readable.

F. RORIG, *The Medieval Town*, trans. by D. J. A. Matthew (1971). Excellent on northern Europe.

S. SHAHAR, *The Fourth Estate: A History of Women in the Middle Ages* (1983). Readable survey.

O. VON SIMSON, *The Gothic Cathedral* (1956).

R. W. SOUTHERN, *Medieval Humanism and Other Studies* (1970). Provocative and far-ranging essays on topics in the intellectual history of the High Middle Ages.

B. TIERNEY, *The Crisis of Church and State 1050–1300* (1964). A very useful collection of primary sources on key Church-State conflicts.

W. L. WAKEFIELD AND A. P. EVANS, EDS., *Heresies of the High Middle Ages* (1969). A major document collection.

J. WEISHEIPL, *Friar Thomas* (1980). Biography of Thomas Aquinas that attempts to do justice to the human side of the story as well as to the theological.

S. WILLIAMS, ED., *The Gregorian Epoch: Reformation, Revolution, Reaction* (1964). Variety of scholarly opinion on the significance of Pope Gregory's reign presented in debate form.

R. L. WOLFF AND H. W. HAZARD, EDS., *History of the Crusades 1189–1311* (1962).

COMPARATIVE PERSPECTIVES: TECHNOLOGY AND CIVILIZATIONS

The Invention of Printing in China and Europe

The ability to put information and ideas on paper and to circulate them widely in multiple identical copies has been credited in the West with the rise of Humanism, the Protestant Reformation, the modern state, and the Scientific Revolution. In truth, the message preceded the machinery: It was a preexisting desire to rule more effectively, to shape and control the world around one, that brought the printing press into existence in both China and Europe. Before there was printing, there were rulers, religious leaders, and merchants eager to disperse their laws, scriptures, and wares more widely and efficiently among their subjects, followers, and customers.

To create the needed skilled agents and bureaucrats, leaders of state, church, and business cooperated in the sponsorship of schools and education, which spurred the growth of reading and writing among the middle and upper urban classes. Literacy in turn fueled the desire for easily accessible and reliable information. Literacy came more slowly to the lower social classes, as authorities feared too much knowledge in the hands of the uneducated or poorly educated would only fan the fires of discontent. To the many who remained illiterate after the invention of printing, information was conveyed carefully in oral and pictorial form. Printed official statements were designed to be read to as well as read by people, and religious leaders put images and pictures in the hands of simple folk, hoping to content them with saints and charms.

Resources and Technology: Paper and Ink

Among the indispensable materials of the print revolution were sizable supplies of durable, inexpensive paper and a reliable ink. As early as the Shang period (1766–1122 B.C.E.) a water-based soot and gum ink was used across Asia. (Europe would not have such an ink until the early Middle Ages.) Also in the Shang period, official seals and stamps used to authenticate documents were made by carving bronze, jade, ivory, gold, and stone in a reverse direction (that is, in a mir-

ror form, to prevent the print from appearing backwards). Similar seals appeared in ancient Mesopotamia and Egypt, but only for religious use, not for the affairs of daily secular life. Later, more easily carved clay or wax seals reproduced characters on silk or bamboo surfaces.

Silk in the East and parchment in the West had been early, but very expensive, print media. Bamboo and wood were cheaper, but neither was suited to large scale printing.

A step forward occurred in the second century B.C.E., when the Chinese invented a crude paper from hemp fibers, which was used only for wrappings. Three centuries later (105 C.E.), an imperial eunuch named Ts`ia Lun combined tree bark, hemp, rags, and old fish nets into a superior paper on which one could reliably write. A better blend of mulberry bark, fish nets, and natural fibers became the standard paper mixture. By the Tang period (618–907), high-quality paper manufacturing had become a major industry.

In the eighth century the improved Chinese recipe began to make its way west, after Chinese prisoners taught their Arab captors how to make paper. By the ninth century Samarkand in Russian Turkestan had become the leading supplier of paper in the East. A century later Baghdad and Damascus shipped fine paper to Egypt and Europe. Italy became a major Western manufacturer in the thirteenth century followed by Nuremberg, Germany, in the late fourteenth.

Early Printing Techniques

By the seventh century C.E., multiple copies of the Confucian Scriptures were made by taking paper rubbings from stone and metal engravings, a direct prelude to block printing. At this time in the West, the arts of engraving, and particularly of coin-casting (by hammering hot alloy on an anvil that bore a carved design), took the first steps toward printing with movable type.

The invention of printing occurred much earlier in the East than in the West. The Chinese invented "block printing" (that is, printing with carved wooden blocks) in the eighth century, almost six hundred years before the technique appeared in Europe (1395). The Chinese also far outpaced the West in printing with "movable type" (that is, with individual characters or letters that could be arranged by hand to make a page)—a technique invented by Pi Scheng in the 1040s, four hundred years before Johann Gutenberg set up the first Western press in Mainz, Germany (around 1450).

The Diamond Sutra. This Chinese translation of a Sanskrit Buddhist work was printed in 868 and found at Tunhuang. It is the earliest dated piece of block printing yet discovered. [The Granger Collection]

Block printing used hard wood (preferably from pear or jujube trees), whose surface was glazed with a filler (glue, wax, or clay). A paper copy of what one wanted to duplicate (be it a drawn image, a written sentence, or both) was placed face down on a wet glaze covering the block and the characters cut into it. The process accommodated any artistic style, while allowing text and illustration to coexist harmoniously on a page. Once carved, the block was inked and mild pressure applied, allowing a great many copies to be made before it wore out.

The first movable type was ceramic. The printer set each character or piece in an iron form and arranged them on an iron backing plate filled with heated resin and wax, which, when cooled, created a tight page. After the print run was finished, the plate was heated again to melt the wax and free the type for new settings. Ceramic and later metal type were fragile and left uneven impressions, and metal type was expensive as well and did not hold water-based Chinese inks.

Carved wooden type did not have these problems and therefore became the preferred tool. Set in a wooden frame and tightened with wooden wedges, the readied page was inked face up and an impression made, just as in printing with carved wooden blocks. Cutting a complete set of type or font required much time and effort because of the complexity and enormity of Chinese script. To do the latter justice, a busy press required 10,000 individual characters, and that number could increase several-fold, depending on the project.

Printing Comes of Age

In 952, after a quarter century of preparation, a standardized Chinese text, unblemished by any scribal errors, was printed for the first time on a large scale. That text, the Confucian Classics, was an epochal event in the history of printing. The main reading of the elite, these famous scrolls became the basis of the entry exam for a government office. In awakening people to the power of printing, the Confucian Classics may be compared to the publication of Gutenberg's Latin Bible.

The Sung period (960–1278) saw the first sustained flowering of block printing. Still today among the Chinese the phrase "Sung style" connotes high quality. Three monumental publications stand out: the Standard Histories of previous Chinese dynasties, serially appearing between 994 and 1063; the Buddhist Scriptures in scrolls up to sixty feet and longer, requiring 130,000 carved wooden blocks (971–983); and the Taoist Scriptures (early eleventh century). For the literate, but not necessarily highly educated, numerous how-to books on medical, botanical, and agricultural topics became available. Printed paper money also appeared for the first time in copper-poor Szechwan during the Sung.

There is no certain evidence that printing was a complete gift of the Far East to the West. Although some scholars believe that Chinese block printing accompanied playing cards through the Islamic world and into Europe, the actual connecting links have not yet been demonstrated. So while there was a definite "paper trail" from East to West, Europe appears to have developed its own inks and invented its own block and movable type printing presses independently.[1]

Indeed in East and West, different writing systems would favor distinct forms of printing: In China, carved wood blocks suited an ideographic script that required a seemingly boundless number of characters. Each ideograph, or character, expressed a complete concept. In contrast, European writing was based on a very small phonetic alphabet. Each letter could express meaning only when connected to other letters, forming words. For such a system, movable metal type worked far better than carved wood blocks. So while China mastered movable type printing earlier than the West, the enormous number of characters required by the Chinese language made movable type impractical.

Ironically, the simpler machinery of block printing did greater justice to China's more intricate and complex script, while Europe's far simpler script required the more complex

A European Printshop. This 1568 woodcut by Hans Sachs shows typesetting (rear) and printing (front) underway in an early printshop. Printing made it possible to reproduce exactly and in quantity both text and illustrations, leading to the distribution of scientific and technical information on a scale unimaginable in the pre-print world. [Houghton Library, Harvard University]

machinery of movable type. Today, the Chinese still face the problem of storing and retrieving their rich language in digitized form, "the space-age equivalent of movable type." In telecommunications, they prefer faxes, "the modern-day equivalent of the block print."[2]

Society and Printing

In neither East nor West do the availability of essential material resources (wood, ink, and paper) and the development of new technologies sufficiently explain the advent of printing. Cultural and emotional factors played an equally large role. In China, the religious and moral demands of Buddhists, Taoists, and Confucians lay behind the invention of block printing. For Buddhists, copying and disseminating their sacred writings had always been a traditional path to salvation. Taoists wanted to hang protective charms or seals around their necks, printed sacred messages blessed by their priests that were up to four inches wide. These were apparently the first block prints. Confucianists, too, lobbied for standardized printed copies of their texts, which they had for centuries duplicated by crude rubbings from stone-carved originals.

In Europe, the major religious orders (Augustinians, Dominicans, and Franciscans) and popular lay religious movements (Waldensians, Lollards, and Hussites) joined with Humanists to promote the printing of standardized, orthodox editions of the Bible and other religious writings. As the numbers of literate laity steadily grew, the demand for cheap, practical reading material (calendars, newssheets, and how-to pamphlets) also rapidly increased. By 1500, fifty years after Gutenberg's invention, two hundred printing presses operated throughout Europe, sixty of them in German cities. And

---

[1]Carter, *The Invention of Printing in China and Its Spread Westward*, pp. 143, 150, 182. (See note 3.)

[2]Twitchett, *Printing and Publishing in Medieval China*, p. 86.

just as in China, the large print runs of the new presses tended to be religious or moral subjects in the early years: Latin Bibles and religious books, indulgences and Protestant pamphlets, along with decorated playing cards often bearing moral messages.

With the printing press came the first copyright laws. Knowledge had previously been considered to be "free." The great majority of medieval scholars and writers were clergy, who lived by church or other patronage and whose knowledge was deemed a gift of God to be shared freely with all. After the printing press, however, a new sense of intellectual property emerged. In Europe, primitive protective laws took the form of a ruler's "privilege," by which a ruler pledged to punish the pirating of a particular work within his or her realm over a limited period of time. Such measures had clear limits: More than half of the books published during the first century of print in the West were pirated editions, a situation that would not change significantly until the eighteenth century.

Government censorship laws also ran apace with the growth of printing. The clergy of Cologne, Germany, issued the first prohibition of heretical books in 1479. In 1485 the Church banned the works of the heretics John Wycliffe and John Huss Europe-wide, and two years later the pope promulgated the first bull against any and all books "harmful to the faith." In 1521 Emperor Charles V banned Martin Luther's works throughout the Holy Roman Empire, along with their author. In 1527 the first publisher was hanged for printing a banned book of Luther's. And in 1559 the pope established the Index of Forbidden Books, which still exists.

Printing stimulated numerous new ancillary trades. In addition to the proliferation of bookstores and the rise of traveling booksellers, who carried flyers from town to town promoting particular works, there were new speciality stationery shops, ink and inkstone stores, bookshelf and reading-table makers, and businesses manufacturing brushes and other printing tools. The new print industry also brought social and economic upheaval to city and countryside when, like modern corporations relocating factories to underdeveloped countries, it went in search of cheaper labor by moving presses out of guild-dominated cities and into the freer marketplace of the countryside.

For society's authorities, the new numbers of literate citizens and subjects made changes and reforms both easier and more difficult. As a tool of propaganda, the printing press remained a two-edged sword. On the one hand, it gave authorities the means to propagandize more effectively than ever. On the other hand, the new literate public found itself in an unprecedented position to recognize deceit, challenge tradition, and expose injustice.

References

Thomas F. Carter, *The Invention of Printing in China and Its Spread Westward* (1925).

Elisabeth L. Eisenstein, *The Printing Press as an Agent of Change*, I–II (1979).

Rudolf Hirsch, *Printing, Selling and Reading 1450–1550* (1967).

Constance R. Miller, *Technical and Cultural Prerequisites for the Invention of Printing in China and the West* (1983).

Denis Twitchett, *Printing and Publishing in Medieval China* (1983).

14 THE ISLAMIC HEARTLANDS AND INDIA (CA. 1000–1500)

A miniature painting of the Army of Tamerlane storming the walls of the Rajput city of Bhatnair in the year 1398. Bhatnair was one of the many north Indian cities and fortresses that fell to the relentless onslaught of Tamerlane's armies. From a Persian manuscript on the history of the Mongols and their Asian Muslim successors. [Bildarchiv Preussischer Kulturbesitz]

CHAPTER TOPICS

THE ISLAMIC HEARTLANDS

◆ Religion and Society

◆ Regional Developments

◆ The Spread of Islam Beyond the Heartlands

INDIA

◆ The Spread of Islam to India

◆ Muslim-Hindu Encounter

◆ Islamic States and Dynasties

◆ Religious and Cultural Accommodation

◆ Hindu and Other Indian Traditions

In World Perspective The Islamic Heartlands and India, 1000–1500

Centralized caliphal power in the Islamic world had broken down by the mid-tenth century. Regional Islamic states with distinctive political and cultural identities now dominated—a pattern that would endure to modern times (see Map 14–1). Yet the diverse Islamic lands remained part of a larger civilization. Muslims from Córdoba in Spain could (and did) travel to Bukhara in Transoxiana or Zanzibar on the East African coast and feel much at home. Both regionalism and cosmopolitanism, diversity and unity, have characterized Islamic civilization ever since.

Socially and religiously, the next five hundred years saw the growth of a truly international Islamic community, united by shared norms of communal order represented and maintained by the Muslim religious scholars (*ulama*). Sufism, that strand of Islam stressing piety and allegiance to a spiritual master, gained widespread popularity, especially after 1200, through the growth of Sufi affiliations or brotherhoods. These popular organizations deeply influenced Muslim life everywhere, often countering the more limiting aspects of *ulama* conformity. Shi'ite ideas also offered an alternative vision of society for many. Movements loyal to Ali and his heirs repeatedly challenged but ultimately failed to reverse centrist, Sunni predominance in most of the Islamic world, even though Shi'ite dynasties ruled much of the Islamic heartlands in the tenth and eleventh centuries, from Iran to Egypt and North Africa.

Culturally, the rise of the New Persian language in the tenth century resulted in a rich new Islamic literature. A cultural renaissance fueled the spread of Persian as the major language of Islam alongside (or, in the Islamic East, even above) Arabic. The Persian-dominated Iranian and Indian Islamic world became more and more distinct from the western Islamic lands.

Two Asian steppe peoples, the Mongols and the Turks, came to rule much of the Islamic world in these centuries, but with different results. The spread of the Turks added a substantial Turkish element, especially where they became rulers, as happened with the Saljuqs in Iran and Anatolia, the Mamluks in Egypt, and the "slave-kings" in Delhi. The Mongols conquered much of the Islamic heartlands in the thirteenth century. Nevertheless, their culture and religion, although not without considerable influence (chiefly in the ongoing impact of their legal code, the Yasa), did not become dominant in the Islamic lands any more than in their Chinese or Slavic Christian conquests. Islam impinged more and more in this age on the Indian subcontinent, Southeast Asia, and sub-Saharan Africa. Although Muslims remained a minority in these regions, Islam became the major new influence in all of them.

THE ISLAMIC HEARTLANDS

Religion and Society

The notable developments in this period for the shape of Islamic society were the consolidation and institutionalization of Sunni legal and religious norms, Sufi traditions and personal piety, and Shi'ite legal and religious norms.

Consolidation of Sunni Orthopraxy

The *ulama* (both Sunni and Shi'ite) gradually became entrenched religious,

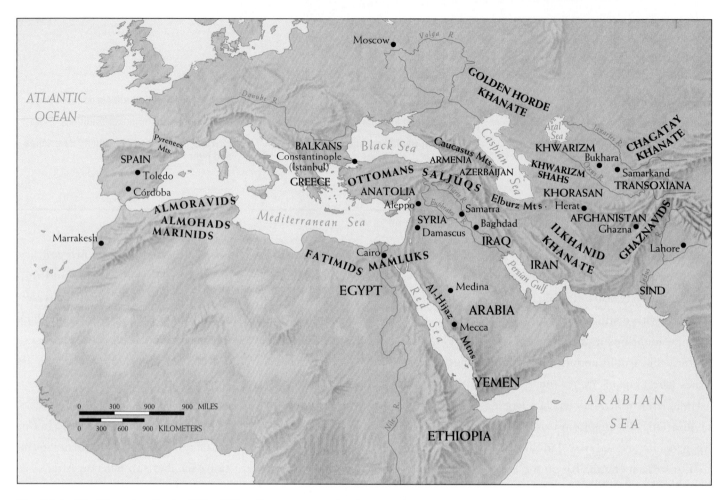

Map 14–1 The Islamic heartlands, 1000–1500. Shown are the major ruling dynasties.

social, and political elites throughout the Islamic world, especially after the breakdown of centralized power in the tenth century. Their integration into local merchant, landowning, and bureaucratic classes led to stronger identification of these groups with Islam.

From the eleventh century onward the *ulama's* power and fixity as a class were expressed in the institution of the *madrasa*, or college of higher learning. On the one hand, the *madrasa* had grown up naturally as individual experts frequented a given mosque or private house and attracted students seeking to learn the Qur'an, the *Hadith* ("Tradition"), jurisprudence, Arabic grammar, and the like. On the other hand, the *madrasa's* formal fixation through endowment of buildings, scholarships, and salaried chairs was a device employed by rulers for their own as well as for pious ends. It gave them some control over the *ulama* through their influence on teachers' appointments and hence on the bias of the curriculum. In theory, such control might combat unwelcome sectarianism. In contrast to the university, with its corporate organization and institutional degrees, the *madrasa* was a sup-

port institution for individual teachers, who personally certified students' mastery of particular subjects. It gave an institutional base (often providing not only teaching space but stipends and student living quarters) to Islam's long-developed system of students seeking out the best teachers and studying texts with them until they received the teachers' formal certification, or "permission" to transmit and teach those same texts themselves.

Largely outside *ulama* control, popular "unofficial" piety flourished in local pilgrimages to saints' tombs, in folk celebrations of Muhammad's birthday, in veneration of him in poetry, and in ecstatic chant and dance among some Sufi groups. But the shared traditions that directed family and civil law, the daily worship rituals, fasting in the month of Ramadan, and the yearly Meccan pilgrimage remained the public bond uniting almost all Muslims, even most Kharijites or Shi'ites. In the Christian world, theological dogmas determined sectarian identity. In contrast, the tendency among Muslims, for all their theological disputes and schools of opinion, was to define Islam in terms of what Muslims do—namely by orthopraxy (practice) rather than by orthodoxy (beliefs). The chief arbiters of "normative" Sunni and Shi'i Islam among the *ulama* were the *faqihs*, or legal scholars, not the theologians.

A basic Sunni orthopraxy, discouraging religious or social innovation, was well established by the year 1000 as the dominant tradition, even though Shi'ite aspirations often made themselves felt either politically or theologically. The emergence of a conservative theological orientation tied to one of the four main Sunni legal schools, the Hanbalites (after Ibn Hanbal, d. 969), narrowed the scope for creative doctrinal change. The Hanbalites stressed reliance only on the Qur'an and the *Hadith* and a literalist reading of both. Here a certain orthodoxy was joined with orthopraxy, although there was no "church" to enforce either. Further, a growing social conservatism among the *ulama* reflected their integration in regional social aristocracies. The *ulama* were often committed to the status quo, as were the rulers.

Sufi Piety and Organization

Sufi piety stresses the spiritual and mystical dimensions of Islam. The term *Sufi* apparently came from the Arabic *suf* ("wool"), based on the old ascetic practice of wearing only a coarse woolen garment. Sufi simplicity and humility had roots with the Prophet and the Companions but developed as a distinctive tendency when, after about 700 C.E., male and female pietists emphasized a godly life over and above mere observance of Muslim duties. Some stressed ascetic avoidance of temptations, others loving devotion to God. Psychologically, Sufi piety bridged the abyss between the human and the divine that is implied in the exalted Muslim concept of the omnipotent God of creation. Socially, Sufi piety merged with folk piety in such popular practices as saint veneration, shrine pilgrimage, ecstatic worship, and seasonal festivals. Sufi writers collected stories of saints, wrote treatises on the Sufi path, and composed some of the world's finest mystical poetry.

Some Sufis were revered as spiritual masters and saints. Their disciples formed brotherhoods that, from about the eleventh century on, became both regional and international organizations. Each had its distinctive mystical teaching, Qur'anic interpretation, and devotional practice. These fraternal orders became the chief instruments of the spread of Muslim faith, as well as a locus of popular piety in almost all Islamic societies. Organized Sufism has always attracted

The Sultan Hasan Madrasa and Tomb-Mosque. This imposing Mamluk building (1356–1363) was built to house teachers and students studying all four of the major traditions or "schools" of Islamic law. Living and teaching spaces are combined here in a building with a mosque and the Sultan's tomb enclosure. [SuperStock, Inc.]

Jalaluddin Rumi: Who Is the Sufi?

Rumi (d. 1273) was one of the greatest and most influential mystics of Islamic history. Originally from Khorasan, his family moved westward just before the Mongol invasion of Iran to settle finally in Seljuq Konya, in central Anatolia. Rumi succeeded his father as a madrasa professor and studied in Syria. The Mevlevi sufi brotherhood considers him its founder. The following two selections come from Rumi's two longest works of mystical poetry.

What qualities or attributes does the sufi seem to have, or to seek to develop? What seems to be the sufi's goal according to the witness of these selections? What might be the aim of the remarks about the "patched mantle" (a common mark of sufi initiation) and "lust perverse"? What does "Beauty" seem to refer to in the first poem?

What makes the sufi? Purity of heart;
Not the patched mantle and the lust perverse
Of those vile earth-bound men who steal his name.
He in all dregs discerns the essence pure:
In hardship ease, in tribulation joy.
The phantom sentries, who with batons drawn
Guard Beauty's palace gate and curtained bower,
Give way before him, unafraid he passes,
And showing the King's arrow, enters in.

Mathnawi, p. 54

What to do, Muslims? For I do not recognize myself;
   not a Christian I nor Jew, Zoroastrian nor
   Muslim. . . .
Not of India am I nor China, not Bulgar-land nor
   Turkistan;
   not the Kingdom of Both Iraqs nor the Land of
   Khurasan.
Not of this World am I nor the next, not of heaven or
   hell;
   not of Adam nor of Eve, not of Paradise nor
   Ridwan.
My place is no place, my trace has no trace;
   not body nor soul, for I belong to the soul of Love.
Duality have I put aside, I have seen both worlds as one.
   One I seek, One I know, One I see, One I call.
He is the first, He the last; he the Outward, He the
   inward.

Diwan-i Shams-i Tabriz

The first poem is from *Rumi: Poet and Mystic* by R. A. Nicholson. Copyright © 1950 by George Allen and Unwin Ltd., an imprint of HarperCollins Publishers Limited. The second poem translated from the Arabic by John Alden Williams, reprinted from *The World of Islam* edited by John Alden Williams, Copyright © 1994. By permission of the author and the University of Texas Press.

---

members from the populace at large (in this, it differs from monasticism), as well as those dedicated to poverty or other radical disciplines. Indeed, Sufi orders became in this age one of the typical social institutions of everyday Muslim life. Whether Sunni or Shi'ite, casually or seriously pious, many Muslims have ever since identified in some degree with one or another Sufi order.

Consolidation of Shi'ite Traditions

Shi'ite traditions crystallized between the tenth and twelfth centuries. Numerous states now came under Shi'ite rulers, some even before the Shi'ite Buyids took Baghdad in 945 (see Chapter 11). Yet the differences separating the diverse Shi'ite groups precluded a unified Shi'ism. Only the strongest Shi'ite state, that of the North African Fatimids in Egypt, established an important empire. A substantial Shi'ite populace developed only in Iran, Iraq, and the lower Indus (Sind).

Two Shi'ite groups emerged as the most influential. The first were the "Seveners," or "Isma'ilis," who recognized Isma'il (d. ca. 760), first son of the sixth Alid *imam*, as the seventh *imam* (rather than his brother). The Isma'ilis were often referred to as "Batinis" ("esoterics"). Their thought drew on Gnostic and Neo-Platonic philosophy, knowledge of which they reserved for a spiritual elite. Isma'ili groups were often revolutionary, and three of them founded states that had substantial impact on the Islamic world. One Isma'ili group, the Qarmatians of eastern Arabia, ruled or disrupted Iraq, Syria, and Arabia through much of the tenth century.

By the eleventh century, however, most Shi'ites accepted a line of twelve *imams* (through another son of the sixth *imam*), the last of whom is said to have disappeared in Samarra (Iraq) in 873 into a cosmic concealment from which he will eventually emerge as the Mahdi, or "Guided One," to usher in the messianic age and final judgment. The "Twelvers," the Shi'ite majority, still focus on the martyrdom of the twelve *imams* and look for their intercession on the Day of Judgment. They have flourished best in Iran, the home of most Shi'ite thought, whatever the sect. The Buyids who took control of the Abbasid caliphate in 945 were Twelvers. So were the Safavids of Iran, who made Twelver doctrine the "state religion" in the sixteenth century (see Chapter 23).

Regional Developments

The western half of the Islamic world after the tenth century developed two regional foci: (1) Spain, Moroccan North Africa, and to a lesser extent, west Africa; and (2) Egypt, Syria-Palestine, Anatolia, along with Arabia and Libyan North Africa. The history of the eastern half of the Islamic world in the period between 1000 and 1500 was most significantly marked by the violent incursion of the Mongols in the thirteenth century.

The Islamic West: Spain and North Africa

The grandeur of Spanish Islamic ("Moorish") culture is visible still in Córdoba's great mosque and the remnants of the legendary Alhambra castle. In European tradition, the *Chanson de Roland* preserves the echo of Charlemagne's retreat through the Pyrenees Mountains after failing to check the first Spanish Umayyad's growing power. That ruler, Abd al-Rahman I (r. 756–788), is less well known in the West, but he was the founder of the cosmopolitan tradition of Umayyad Spanish culture at Córdoba, which was the cultural center of the western world for the next two centuries. Renowned for its medicine, science, literature, intellectual life, commercial activity, public baths and gardens, and courtly elegance, Córdoba reached its zenith under Abd al-Rahman III (r. 912–961). He took the title of caliph in 929, and his absolutist but benevolent rule saw a largely unified, peaceful Islamic Spain. The mosque-university of Córdoba that he founded was the earliest of its kind, attracting students from Europe as well as the Islamic world.

A sad irony of this cosmopolitan world was recurring religious exclusivism among both Muslims and Christians, which from time to time sparked conflict between them—conflict stimulated perhaps by the daily proximity and social-status disparities of the two communities. Abroad, Abd al-Rahman

The Alhambra, Muqarnas dome in the Hall of the Abencerrahes, Palace of the Lions. Built largely in the fourteenth century by the Nasrid dynasty, the magnificent, sprawling palace buildings of the Alhambra marked the twilight of Islamic culture in Spain. [Art Resource, N.Y.]

Banner of Las Navas de Tolosa, made of silk tapestry with gold parchment (3.3 x 2.2 m) in southern Spain in the early thirteenth century, reflects the emphasis on architectural designs that emerged at this time among Spanish weavers. The central section of the banner, bordered with Qur'anic inscriptions, resembles a Spanish courtyard garden. The banner was captured in battle by Christians not long after it was made. [Arxiu Mas/Museo de Telas Medievales, Monasterio de Santa María la Real de Las Huelgas, Burgos, Spain, Patrimonio Nacional.]

III checked both the new Fatimid power in North Africa and the Christian kingdoms in northern Spain, making possible a golden era of Moorish power and culture. But after his death fragmentation into warring Muslim principalities allowed a resurgence of Spain's Christian states between about 1000 and 1085, when the city of Toledo fell permanently into Christian hands.

Brief Islamic revivals in Spain and North Africa came under the African reform movements of the Almoravids and Almohads. The Almoravids originated as a religious-warrior brotherhood among Berber nomads in West Africa. Having subdued virtually all of northwestern Africa, in 1086 they carried their zealotry from their new capital of Marrakesh into

Spain and reunited its Islamic kingdoms. Under their rule, arabized Christians (Mozarabs) were persecuted and many driven out, as were some Moorish Jews. The subsequent wars began the last major phase of the Spanish "Reconquest" (*Reconquista*). These conflicts, in which Christian rulers sought to regain and Christianize the peninsula, are best known in the West for the exploits of El Cid (d. 1099), the adventurer and mercenary who became the Spanish national hero.

The Almohads ended Almoravid rule in Morocco in 1147 and then conquered much of southern Spain. Before their demise (1225 in Spain; 1275 in Africa), they stimulated a brilliant revival of Moorish culture. During this era, paper manufacture reached Spain and then the rest of western Europe. The long westward odyssey of Indian fable literature through Iran and the Arab world ended with Spanish and Latin translations in thirteenth-century Spain. The greatest lights of this Spanish Islamic intellectual world were the major philosopher and physician, Ibn Rushd (Averroës, d. 1198); the great Muslim mystical thinker, Ibn al-Arabi (d. 1240); and the famous Arab-Jewish philosopher, Ibn Maymun, or Maimonides (d. 1204), who spent much of his life as an exile in Egypt.

The Islamic West: Egypt and the Eastern Mediterranean World

The Fatimids   The major Islamic presence in the Mediterranean from the tenth to the twelfth century was that of the Shi'ite Fatimids. They took their name from their claim to descent from Muhammad's daughter, Fatima. They began as a Tunisian dynasty, then conquered Morocco, Sicily, and Egypt (969). In Egypt they built their new capital, Cairo (*al-Qahira*, "the Victorious"), near the original garrison town of the earliest Arab conquest. Their rule as Shi'ite caliphs meant that, for a time, there were three "caliphates"—in Baghdad, Córdoba, and Cairo. The Fatimids were Isma'ilis (see above). Content to rule a Sunni majority in Egypt, they sought recognition as true imams by other Isma'ili groups. They won the allegiance of a Yemeni Shi'ite state and were able, for a time, to take western Arabia and most of Syria from the Buyid "guardians" of the Abbasid caliphate (see Chapter 11).

Fatimid rule spawned two splinter groups that have played visible, if minor, roles in history. The Druze of modern Lebanon and Syria originated around 1020 with a few members of the Fatimid court who professed belief in the divinity of one of the Fatimid caliphs. The tradition they founded is too far from Islam to be considered a Muslim sect. The Isma'ili Assassins, on the other hand, were a radical Muslim movement founded by a Fatimid defector in the Elburz mountains of Iran around 1100. The name "Assassins" comes not from the political assassinations that made them infamous but from a European corruption of the Arabic *Hashishiyyin*

A Muslim Biographer's Account of Maimonides

The following are excerpts from the entry on Maimonides (Arabic: Musa ibn Maymun) in the biographical dictionary of learned men by Ibn al-Qifti (d. 1248). In one section (omitted here), Ibn al-Qifti describes how this most famous Spanish Jewish savant at first feigned conversion to Islam when a new Berber ruler demanded the expulsion of Christians and Jews from Spain in about 1133. He tells how Maimonides moved his family to the more tolerant Islamic world of Cairo, where he eventually became the court physician. (It was not unusual for Jews or Christians to hold high office under Muslim rulers.) Other omitted material includes treatment of his famous books and his marriage, his death, and his other accomplishments.

Can you identify the probable Islamic dynasty whose rule forced Maimonides to leave Spain for Cairo? Why were the Fatimids in Cairo tolerant of Christians and Jews when their Berber co-religionists were not? From the Muslim biographer's treatment of his subject, what might you infer about Islamic societies and the intellectual atmosphere of the time?

Reading the Torah in a Spanish synagogue. A picture from a Hebrew Haggada, Spain, fourteenth century. Until their expulsion by Christian rulers at the end of the fifteenth century, Jews formed a significant minority in Spain. [By permission of The British Library]

. . . This man was one of the people of Andalus, a Jew by religion. He studied philosophy in Andalus, was expert in mathematics, and devoted attention to some of the logical sciences. He studied medicine there and excelled in it. . . .

. . . After assembling his possessions in the time that was needed for this, he left Andalus and went to Egypt, accompanied by his family. He settled in the town of Fustāt [part of greater Cairo], among its Jews, and practiced his religion openly. He lived in a district called al-Masīsa and made a living by trading in jewels and suchlike. Some people studied philosophy under him. . . .

He married in Cairo the sister of a Jewish scribe called Abu'l-Ma'ālī, the secretary of the mother of Nūr al-Dīn 'Alī, known as al-Afdal, the son of Salāh al-Dīn Yūsuf ibn Ayyūb, and he had a son by her who today is a physician in Cairo after his father. . . .

Mūsā ibn Maymūn died in Cairo in the year 605 [1208–9].[1] He ordered his heirs to carry his body, when the smell had ceased, to Lake Tiberias and bury him there, seeking to be among the graves of the ancient Israelites and their great jurists, which are there. This was done.

He was learned in the law and secrets of the Jews and compiled a commentary on the Talmud, which is a commentary and explanation of the Torah; some of the Jews approve of it. Philosophic doctrines overcame him, and he compiled a treatise denying the canonical resurrection. The leaders of the Jews held this against him, so he concealed it except from those who shared his opinion in this. . . .

In the latter part of his life he was troubled by a man from Andalus, a jurist called Abu'l-'Arab ibn Ma'īsha, who came to Fustāt and met him. He charged him with having been a Muslim in Andalus, accused him [of apostasy] and wanted to have him punished.[2] 'Abd al-Rahīm ibn 'Alī al-Fādil prevented this, and said to him, "If a man is converted by force, his Islam is not legally valid."

[1]In fact, he died in 1204.
[2]The penalty for apostasy was death.

Excerpt from *Islam from the Prophet Muhammad to the Capture of Constantinople,* Vol. 2 by Bernard Lewis, ed. and trans. Copyright © 1974 by Bernard Lewis. Reprinted by permission of HarperCollins Publishers, Inc.

("users of hashish"). A local Syrian name, it was possibly connected with the story that their assassins were manipulated with drugs to undertake their usually suicidal missions. The Assassins were defeated and their mountain fortress destroyed by the Mongols in the thirteenth century.

The Fatimids built the Azhar mosque in Cairo as a center of learning, a role it maintains today, although for Sunni, not (as then) Shi'ite, scholarship. Fatimid rulers treated Egypt's Coptic Christians generally as well as they did their Sunni majority. Many Copts held high offices, even that of vizier. Jews, like Copts, usually fared well under the Fatimids, except for the persecution of Jews and Christians under the apparently deranged caliph al-Hakim (d. 1021).

After 1100 the Fatimids weakened, falling in 1171 to Salah al-Din (Saladin, 1137–1193), a field general and administrator under the Turkish ruler of Syria, Nur al-Din (1118–1174). Saladin, a Sunni Kurd with immense leadership talent, is well known in the West for his battles (including the retaking of Jerusalem in 1187) and eventual compromise truce with the invading Crusaders. After Nur al-Din's death, Saladin added Syria-Palestine and Mesopotamia to his Egyptian dominions. In so doing, he founded the Ayyubid dynasty that, under his successors, controlled all three areas until Egypt fell to the Mamluks in 1250 and most of Syria and Mesopotamia to the Mongols by 1260.

Like Nur al-Din, and on the model of the Saljuqs (see Chapter 11), Saladin founded *madrasas* to teach and promote Sunni law. His and his Ayyubid successors' reigns in Egypt saw the entrenchment of a self-conscious Sunnism under a program of mutual recognition and teaching of all four Sunni schools of law. Henceforward Shi'ite Islam disappeared from Egypt.

The Mamluks   The heirs of the Fatimids and Saladin in the eastern Mediterranean were the redoubtable sultans ("[those with] authority") of the Mamluk dynasty. As rulers of Egypt, they styled themselves after the Saljuqs. The Mamluks were the only Islamic dynasty to withstand the Mongol invasions that closely followed their accession. Their victory at Ain Jalut in Palestine in 1260 marked the end of the Mongols' westward movement. The first Mamluk sultan, Aybak (r. 1250–1257), and his successors were elite Turkish and Mongol slave officers, mostly Kipchak Turks, drawn originally from the bodyguard of Saladin's dynasty. Whereas the early Mamluks were often succeeded by sons or brothers, succession after the 1390s was more often a survival of the fittest; no sultan reigned more than a few years. The Mamluk state was based on a military fief system and total control by the slave-officer elite.

The Mamluk sultan Baybars (r. 1260–1277), who took the last Crusader fortresses, is a larger-than-life figure in Arab legend. To legitimize his rule he revived the Abbasid caliphate at least in name after its demise in the fall of Baghdad (1258; discussed later) by installing an uncle of Baghdad's last Abbasid as Caliph at Cairo. He made treaties with Constantinople and European sovereigns, as well as with the newly converted Muslim ruler, or *khan*, of the Golden Horde—the Mongol Tatars of southern Russia. He was the first Egyptian sultan to appoint judges from all four law schools to administer justice, and his public works in Cairo were numerous. He extended Mamluk rule south to Nubia and west among the Berbers.

As trade relations with the Mongol domains improved gradually after 1300, the Mamluks enjoyed substantial prosperity. At their zenith, they commanded an empire worthy of the early Abbasids or the later Ottomans. The prosperity and peace of the reign of Ibn Qala'un (1310–1340) marked the last of the true heydays of Mamluk rule. The Black Death epidemic of 1347–1348 in the Arab Middle East hurt the Mamluk and other regional states badly. Still the Mamluks effectively survived even the Ottoman conquest of Egypt in 1517, since Mamluks continued to rule there as Ottoman governors into the nineteenth century.

Architecture, especially that of the reigns of Baybars and al-Nasir (r. 1293–1340), much of which still graces Cairo, remains the most magnificent Mamluk bequest to posterity. In addition, mosaics, calligraphy, and metalwork were among the arts and crafts of special note. The Mamluks were great patrons of scholars who excelled in history, biography, astronomy, mathematics, and medicine. The most important of these was Ibn Khal-

This elegant glass bottle was made in Mamluk workshops in Syria in the mid-fourteenth century for the rulers of the Yemen in southern Arabia. [John Tsantes/Courtesy of the Freer Gallery of Art, Smithsonian Institution, Washington, D.C.]

Western Islamic Lands	
756–1021	Spanish Umayyad dynasty
912–961	Rule of Abd al-Rahman III; height of Umayyad power and civilization
969–1171	Fatimid Shi'ite dynasty in Egypt
ca. 1020	Origin of Druze community (Egypt/Syria)
1171	Fatimids fall to Salah al-Din (Saladin), Ayyubid lieutenant of the ruler of Aleppo
1056–1275	Almoravid and Almohad dynasties in North Africa, West Africa, and Spain
1096–1291	Major European Christian crusades into Islamic lands; some European presence in Syria-Palestine
1189	Death of Ibn Rushd (Averroës), philosopher
1204	Death of Musa ibn Maymun (Maimonides), philosopher and Jewish savant
1240	Death of Ibn al-Arabi, theosophical mystic
1250–1517	Mamluk sultanate in Egypt and (from late 1200s) Syria; claim laid to Abbasid Caliphate
1260	Mamluk victory at Ain Jalut halts Mongol advance into Syria
1406	Death of Ibn Khaldun, historian and social philosopher
ca. 1300	Rise of Ottoman state in western Anatolia

dun (d. 1406). Born of a Spanish Muslim family in Tunis, he settled in Cairo as an adult. He is still recognized as the greatest social historian and philosopher.

The Islamic East: Before the Mongol Conquests

We noted in Chapter 11 that the Iranian dynasties of the Samanids at Bukhara (875–999) and the Buyids at Baghdad (945–1055) were the major usurpers of eastern Abbasid dominions. Their successes epitomized the rise of regional states that had begun to undermine the caliphate by the ninth century. Similarly, their demises reflected a second emerging pattern: the ascendancy of Turkish slave-rulers (like the Mamluks in the west) and of Oghuz Turkish peoples, known as Turkomans. With the Saljuq successors of the Buyids, the process begun with use of Turkish slave troops in ninth-century Baghdad ended in the permanent presence in the Islamic world of Turkish ruling dynasties. As late converts, they became typically the most zealous of Sunni Muslims.

The Ghaznavids   The rule of the Samanids in Transoxiana was finally ended by a Turkoman group in 999. But they had already lost all of eastern Iran south of the Oxus in 994 to one of their own slave governors, Subuktigin (r. 976–997). He set up his own state in modern Afghanistan, at Ghazna, whence he and his son and successor, Mahmud of Ghazna

(r. 998–1030), launched successful campaigns against his former masters. The Ghaznavids are notable for their patronage of Persian literature and culture and for their conquests in northwestern India, which began a lasting Muslim presence in India. Mahmud was their greatest ruler. He is still remembered for his booty raids and destruction of temples in western India. At its peak, his empire stretched from western Iran to the Oxus and to the Indus.

Mahmud attracted to Ghazna numerous scholars and artists, notably the great scientist and mathematician al-Biruni (d. 1048) and the epic poet Firdawsi (d. ca. 1020). Firdawsi's *Shahnama* ("The Book of Kings") is the masterpiece of Persian literature, an epic of sixty thousand verses that helped fix the New Persian language and revive the pre-Islamic Iranian cultural tradition. After Mahmud the empire began to break up, although Ghaznavids ruled at Lahore until 1186.

The Saljuqs   The Saljuqs were the first major Turkish dynasty of Islam. They were a steppe clan who settled in Transoxiana, became avid Sunnis, and extended their sway over Khorasan in the 1030s. In 1055 they took Baghdad, where the nominal Abbasid caliph greeted them as his deliverers from the Shi'ite Buyids. As the new guardian of the caliphate and master of an Islamic empire, the Saljuq leader Tughril Beg (r. 1037–1063) took the title of *sultan* (authority) to signify his temporal power and control. He was accordingly invested by the caliph as "king of east and west." He and his early successors made various Iranian cities their capitals instead of Baghdad.

As new Turkish tribes joined their ranks, the Saljuqs extended Islamic rule for the first time into the central Anatolian plateau at Byzantine expense, even capturing the Byzantine emperor in a victory in Armenia in 1071. They also conquered much of Syria and wrested Mecca and Medina from the Shi'ite Fatimids. The first Turkish rule in Anatolia dates from 1077, when the Saljuq governor there formed a separate sultanate. Known as the Saljuqs of Rum ("Rome," i.e., Byzantium), these latter Saljuqs were only displaced after 1300 by the Ottomans, another Turkish dynasty, who would eventually conquer all of Anatolia and southeastern Europe (see Chapter 23).

The most notable figure of Saljuq rule was the vizier Nizam al-Mulk, the real power behind two sultans from 1063 to 1092. In his time new roads and inns (caravanserais) for trade and pilgrimage were built, canals were dug, mosques and other public buildings were founded (including the first great Sunni *madrasas*, the personal projects of Nizam al-Mulk), and science and culture were patronized. He supported an extremely accurate calendar reform and authored a major work on the art of governing, the *Siyasatnamah*. Before his murder by an Isma'ili Assassin in 1092, he appointed as professor in his Baghdad *madrasa* Muhammad al-Ghazzali (d. 1111), probably the greatest Muslim religious thinker ever. He also patronized the mathematician and astronomer Umar Khayyam (d. 1123), whose Western fame rests on the poetry of his "Quatrains," or *Ruba'iyat*.

After declining fortunes in the early twelfth century, Iranian Saljuq rule crumbled and by 1194 was wholly wiped away by another Turkish slave dynasty from Khwarizm in the lower Oxus basin. By 1200 these Khwarizm Shahs had built a large if shaky empire and sphere of influence covering Iran and Transoxiana. In the same era the Abbasid caliph at Baghdad, al-Nasir (r. 1180–1225), established an independent caliphal state in Iraq. But neither his heirs nor the Khwarizm Shahs were long to survive in the face of events already unfolding on the Asian steppes.

The Islamic East: The Mongol Age

Mongols and Ilkhanids   The building of a vast Mongol empire spanning Asia from China to Poland in the thirteenth century proved momentous not only for Eastern Europe and China (see Chapter 8), but also for Islamic Eurasia and India. A Khwarizm Shah massacre of Mongol ambassadors brought down the full wrath of the Great Khan, Genghis (ca. 1162–1227), on the Islamic east. He plundered mercilessly (1219–1222) from Transoxiana and Khorasan to the Indus, razing entire cities. After his death, a division of his empire into four khanates under his four sons gave the Islamic world some respite. Then in 1255 Hulagu Khan (r. 1256–1265), a grandson of Genghis, led a massive army again across the

Genghis Khan holding an audience. This Persian miniature shows the great conqueror and founder of the Mongol empire with members of his army and entourage as well as an apparent supplicant (right, center). [E.T. Archive]

The Mongol Catastrophe

For the Muslim east, the sudden eruption of the Mongol hordes was an indescribable calamity. Something of the shock and despair of Muslim reaction can be seen in the history of the contemporary historian Ibn al-Athir (d. 1233). He writes here about the year 1220–1221, when the Mongols ("Tartars") burst in on the eastern lands.

Is this a positive, negative, or neutral description of the Mongols? Why might the Mongols be compared to Alexander rather than, say, the Huns (see Chapter 5)?

I say, therefore, that this thing involves the description of the greatest catastrophe and the most dire calamity (of the like of which days and nights are innocent) which befell all men generally, and the Muslims in particular; so that, should one say that the world, since God Almighty created Adam until now, hath not been afflicted with the like thereof, he would but speak the truth. For indeed history doth not contain aught which approaches or comes nigh unto it. . . .

Now this is a thing the like of which ear hath not heard; for Alexander, concerning whom historians agree that he conquered the world, did not do so with such swiftness, but only in the space of about ten years; neither did he slay, but was satisfied that men should be subject to him. But these Tartars conquered most of the habitable globe

and the best, the most flourishing and most populous part thereof, and that whereof the inhabitants were the most advanced in character and conduct, in about [a] year; nor did any country escape their devastations which did not fearfully expect them and dread their arrival.

Moreover they need no commissariat, nor the conveyance of supplies, for they have with them sheep, cows, horses, and the like quadrupeds, the flesh of which they eat, [needing] naught else. As for their beasts which they ride, these dig into the earth with their hoofs and eat the roots of plants, knowing naught of barley. And so, when they alight anywhere, they have need of nothing from without. As for their religion, they worship the sun when it arises, and regard nothing as unlawful, for they eat all beasts, even dogs, pigs, and the like; nor do they recognise the marriage-tie, for several men are in marital relations with one woman, and if a child is born, it knows not who is its father.

Therefore Islâm and the Muslims have been afflicted during this period with calamities wherewith no people hath been visited. These Tartars (may God confound them!) came from the East, and wrought deeds which horrify all who hear of them, and which thou shalt, please God, see set forth in full detail in their proper connection. . . .

From Edward C. Sachau, *Alberuni's Indian*, Vol. I (London: Kegan Paul, Trench, Truebner, 1910). pp. 17, 19, 20.

Oxus. Adding Turkish troops to his forces as he went (Mongol armies typically included many Turks), he went from victory to victory, destroying the Assassins of northwestern Iran along with every other Iranian state. In 1258, when the Abbasid caliph foolishly refused to surrender, Hulagu's troops smashed Baghdad's defenses and plundered the city, killing at least eighty thousand inhabitants, including the caliph and his sons.

Under the influence of his wife and many Nestorian Christians and Buddhists in his inner circle, Hulagu spared the Christians of Baghdad. He followed this policy in his other conquests, including the later sack of Aleppo—which, like Baghdad, resisted. When Damascus surrendered, Western Christians had what proved to be a vain hope of the impending fall of Mamluk Cairo and a consequent collapse of Islamic power. But Hulagu's drive west was slowed by rivalry with his kinsman Berke. A Muslim convert, Berke ruled the khanate of the Golden Horde, the Mongol state centered in southern Russia north of the Caucasus. He was in contact

with the Mamluks, and some of his Mongol troops even fought with them in their major victory over Hulagu in Palestine (1260), which prevented a Mongol advance into Egypt. A treaty in 1261 between the Mamluk sultan and Berke established a formal alliance that confirmed the breakup of Mongol unity and the autonomy of the four khanates: in China (the Yuan dynasty), in Iran (the Ilkhans), in Russia (the Golden Horde), and in Transoxiana (the Chagatays).

For his part, Hulagu gave allegiance to the new Great Khan of China. He and his heirs ruled the old Persian Empire from Azerbaijan for some seventy-five years as the Great Khan's viceroys (*Il-Khans;* from which Hulagu's line is named *Ilkhanid*). Here, as elsewhere, the rule of the Mongols did not eradicate the society they inherited. Unlike the Arabs before them, they did not convert Muslim subject populations to their own faith. Instead, both their native paganism and their Buddhist and Christian leanings yielded to Muslim faith and practice, although religious tolerance remained the norm under their rule. After 1335 Ilkhanid rule fell prey to the

The Gur-i-mir, the tomb of Timur in Samarkand. Built from 1490 to 1501 by Timur's grandson, this tile-covered structure houses the tombs of Shahrukh, Ulug Beg, and other Timurid heirs, as well as that of Timur himself. [Giraudon, Art Resource, N.Y.]

merce and punisher of the injustices of regional petty tyrants and populist—often Shi'ite—extremist groups alike. Still, whatever his ends, his means were singularly brutal. In successive campaigns he swept everything before him in a wave of devastation: eastern Iran (1379–1385); western Iran, Armenia, the Caucasus, and upper Mesopotamia (1385–1387); southwestern Iran, Mesopotamia, and Syria (1391–1393); Central Asia from Transoxiana to the Volga and as far as Moscow (1391–1395); North India (1398); and northern Syria and Anatolia (1400–1402). Timur's sole positive contributions seem to have been the buildings he sponsored at Samarkand, his capital. He left behind him ruins, death, disease, and political chaos across the entire eastern Islamic world, which did not soon recover. His was, however, the last great steppe invasion, for firearms soon removed the steppe horsemen's advantage forever.

Timur's sons ruled after him with varying results in Transoxiana and Iran (1405–1494). The most successful Timurid was Shahrukh (r. 1405–1447), who ruled a united Iran for a time. His capital, Herat, became an important center of Persian Islamic culture and Sunni piety. He patronized the famous Herat school of miniature painting as well as Persian literature and philosophy. The Timurids had to share Iran itself with Turkoman dynasties in western Iran, once even losing Herat to one of them. They and the Turkomans were the last Sunnis to

Eastern Islamic Lands	
875-999	Samanid dynasty, centered at Bukhara
945-1055	Buyid Shi'ite dynasty in Baghdad, controls caliphs
994-1186	Ghaznavid dynasty in Ghazna (modern Afghanistan) and Lahore (modern Pakistan), founded by Subuktigin (r. 976-997) and his son, Mahmud of Ghazna (r. 998-1030)
1020	Death of Firdawsi, compiler of *Shahnama*
ca. 1050	Death of al-Biruni, scientist and polyglot
1055-1194	Saljuq rule in Baghdad
1063-1092	Viziership of Nizam al-Mulk
1111	Death of al-Ghazzali, theologian and scholar
1219-1222	Genghis Khan plunders eastern Iran to Indus region
1258	Hulegu Khan conquers Baghdad
1261	Mamluk-Mongol treaty halts westward Mongol movement
1260-1335	Hulegu and his Il-Khanid successors rule Iran
1379-1405	Campaigns of Timur-i Lang (Tamerlane) devastate entire Islamic East
1405-1494	Timurids, successors of Tamerlane, rule in Transoxiana and Iran
1405-1447	Shahrukh, Timurid ruler at Herat; great patronage of the arts and philosophy

familiar pattern of a gradual breaking away of provinces, and for fifty years, Iran was again fragmented.

Timurids and Turkomans This situation prepared the way for a new Turko-Mongol conquest from Transoxiana, under Timur-i Lang ("Timur the Lame," or "Tamerlane," 1336–1405). Even Genghis Khan's invasions could not match Timur's savage campaigns between 1379 and his death in 1405. These raids were not aimed at building a new empire but at sheer conquest. Timur was a Muslim convert evidently possessed of a strong sense of his role as protector of com-

Building the castle of Khawarnaq, ca. 1494. This is one of the magnificent illustrations of the Khamsa, or "Fire Poems" of Nizami, painted by the head of the great art academy of Herat, Bihzad (died ca. 1515). It was Shahrukh's patronage that led to this flourishing school of painting. [By permission of The British Library]

rule Iran. Both were eclipsed at the end of the fifteenth century by the militant Shi'ite dynasty of the Safavids, who ushered in a new, Shi'ite era in the Iranian world (see Chapter 23).

The Spread of Islam Beyond the Heartlands

The period from roughly 1000 to 1500 saw the spread of Islam as a lasting religious, cultural, and political force into new areas (see Map 14–2). Not only Eurasia from the Caspian and Black Seas north to Moscow (under the Golden Horde), but also Greece and the Balkans, through the Ottoman Turks, came under the control of Islamic rulers (see Chapter 23). India, Malaysia, Indonesia, inland West Africa, and coastal East Africa all became major spheres of Islamic political or commercial power. In all these regions Sufi orders were most often responsible for converting people and spreading Islamic cultural influences. Merchants, too, were major agents of Islamization in these regions.

Conquest was a third (but demographically less important) means of the eventual conversion to Islam of significant numbers in these regions. Sometimes only ruling elites, sometimes wider circles, became Muslim, but in India, Southeast Asia, and sub-Saharan Africa large numbers, often the majority, of the populace retained their inherited religious traditions. Therefore, if we treat the most important of these regions, India, from the standpoint of the coming of Islam, it is not because Islam was the only, or even the major, element in Indian civilization during this period. It is rather that the coming of Islam signaled epochal changes in the history of South Asia.

INDIA

Islamic civilization in India (like earlier Indian civilization) was formed by creative interaction between invading

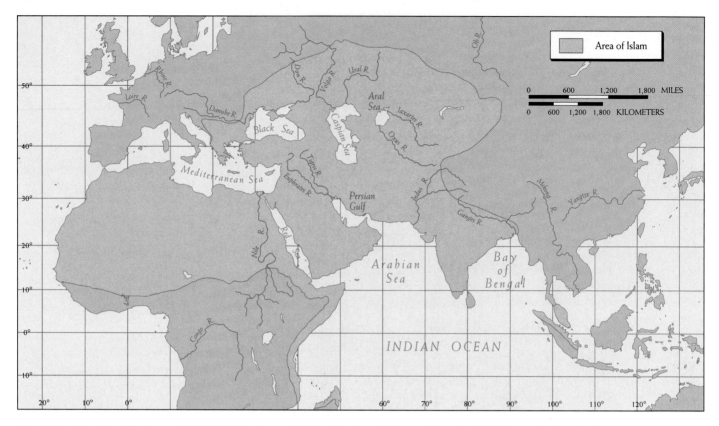

Map 14–2 Islamic political sovereignty in 1500. Areas with either Islamic political control or majority Muslim populations. Southern Spain had been under Islamic control until 1492.

foreigners and indigenous peoples. The early Arab and Turkish invaders were a foreign Muslim minority; their heirs were truly "Indian" as well as Muslim, adding a new dimension both to Indian and to Islamic civilization. From then on, Indian civilization would both include and enrich Islamic traditions.

The Spread of Islam to India

Well before the Ghaznavids came to the Punjab, Muslims were to be found even outside the original Arab conquest areas in Sind (see Map 14–3). Muslim merchants had settled in the port cities of Gujarat and southern India to profit from internal Indian trade as well as from trade with the Indies and China. Wherever Muslim traders went, converts to Islam were attracted by business advantages as well as by the straightforward ideology and practice of Islam and its officially egalitarian, "classless" ethic. Sufi orders had also gained a foothold in the south, giving today's South Indian Muslims very old roots. Sufi piety also drew converts in the north, especially when the Mongol devastation of Iran in the thir-

teenth century sent refugees streaming over the mountains into North India. Many of these Muslim refugees strengthened Islamic armies and administration as well as Muslim cultural and religious life in the subcontinent.

Muslim-Hindu Encounter

From the outset Muslim leaders faced the problem of ruling a country dominated by utterly different cultural and religious traditions. Much as early Muslim rulers in Iran had given Zoroastrians legal status as "People of Scripture" (like Christians and Jews; see Chapter 11), the first Arab conquerors in Sind (711) had treated Hindus similarly not as pagans but as "protected peoples" under Muslim sovereignty. These precedents gave the Ghaznavids and later Indian Muslim rulers a legal basis for coexistence with their Hindu subjects. They did not, of course, remove Hindu resistance to Muslim rule.

The chief obstacle to Islamic expansion in India was the military prowess of the Hindu warrior class that emerged after the Hun and other Asian invasions of the fifth and sixth

How the Hindus Differ from the Muslims

Al-Biruni (d. ca. 1050), the greatest scholar-scientist of medieval Islam, was born in northeastern Iran. Much of his later life was spent at the court of Mahmud of Ghazna, whom he accompanied on expeditions into northwestern India. Alongside his scientific work, he learned Sanskrit, studied India and the Hindus, and wrote a "History of India." The following selections from the beginning of this work show something of the reach and sophistication of his mind.

How does the emphasis on purity and the impurity of foreigners that Biruni imputes to the Hindus compare with the attitudes of Islam and other religions? Does this passage suggest any possible answers to why the Hindu tradition has remained largely an Indian one, while Islam became an international religion? At what might Biruni's comments about the relative absence of religous controversy among Hindus be aimed?

. . . The barriers which separate Muslims and Hindus rest on different causes.

First, they differ from us in everything which other nations have in common. And here we first mention the language, although the difference of language also exists between other nations. If you want to conquer this difficulty (i.e., to learn Sanskrit), you will not find it easy, because the language is of an enormous range, both in words and inflections, something like the Arabic, calling one and the same thing by various names, both original and derived, and using one and the same word for a variety of subjects, which, in order to be properly understood, must be distinguished from each other by various qualifying epithets. . . .

Secondly, they totally differ from us in religion, as we believe in nothing in which they believe, and vice versá.

On the whole, there is very little disputing about theological topics among themselves; at the utmost, they fight with words, but they will never stake their soul or body or their property on religious controversy. On the contrary, all their fanaticism is directed against those who do not belong to them—against all foreigners. They call them *mleecha*, i.e., impure, and forbid having any connection with them, be it by intermarriage or any other kind of relationship, or by sitting, eating, and drinking with them, because thereby, they think, they would be polluted. They consider as impure anything which touches the fire and the water of a foreigner; and no household can exist without these two elements. Besides, they never desire that a thing which once has been polluted should be purified and thus recovered, as, under ordinary circumstances, if anybody or anything has become unclean, he or it would strive to regain the state of purity. They are not allowed to receive anybody who does not belong to them, even if he wished it, or was inclined to their religion. This, too, renders any connection with them quite impossible, and constitutes the widest gulf between us and them.

In the third place, in all manners and usages they differ from us to such a degree as to frighten their children with us, with our dress, and our ways and customs, and as to declare us to be devil's breed, and our doings as the very opposite of all that is good and proper. By the by, we must confess, in order to be just, that a similar depreciation of foreigners not only prevails among us and the Hindus, but is common to all nations towards each other.

From Edward C. Sachau, *Alberuni's India*, Vol. 1 (London: Kegan Paul, Trench, Truebner, 1910), pp. 17, 19, 20.

---

status as literary and administrative languages, and Persian became the language of intellectual and cultural life for the ruling elites of North India into the mid-nineteenth century. However, the coming of substantial numbers of Muslims to the subcontinent led to the emergence of a new language with both Perso-Arabic and indigenous Indian elements. This language, Urdu-Hindi, would ultimately gain wide use and influence in the subcontinent by modern times. A derivative of the Sanskrit-related Prakrit dialects of the Punjab and Uttar Pradesh, it began to take shape not long after the initial Muslim influx in the eleventh century (its first literary use goes back to the fourteenth century) and developed in response to the increasing need of Hindus and Muslims for a shared medium of communication. It became the spoken idiom of the Delhi region and developed into a literary language of North Indian and Deccan Muslims in the seventeenth and eighteenth centuries. Indo-European in grammar, it used Perso-Arabic vocabulary and script and was at first called *Hindi* ("Indian") or *Dakani* ("southern"), then in British times *Hindustani*. The name *Urdu* came into use also about the end of the seventeenth century and, during the nineteenth century, with growing Hindu-Muslim communal tensions, came to serve as the name for one of two versions of the language. Urdu designated the Muslim version that continued to draw on its Perso-Arabic heritage, whereas Hindi was used for the version associated with Hindu culture and oriented in its further development toward its Hindu and Sanskritic heritage. Each would later become an official national language: Urdu for modern Pakistan and Hindi for modern India.

Indian Muslims—Arabs, Turks, Iranians, Mongols, Afghans, indigenous converts, or whatever-were always susceptible to Hindu influence (in language, marriage customs, and caste

South Indian bronze figure of Krishna dancing on the head of the serpent Kaliya, from Vijayana-gar, ca. fifteenth century. Kaliya, according to a legend, was infesting the waters of the Jumna River until Krishna leaped in and emerged dancing on the vanquished snake. [Asian Art Museum of San Francisco, The Avery Brundage Collection B65B72]

consciousness). However, unlike earlier invaders, they were never utterly absorbed into the varied but identifiable Hindu culture that predominated in the subcontinent. Their religious commitment and their identification of themselves culturally as Muslims ensured that they remained in some measure a group apart, conscious of their uniqueness in the Hindu world and proud to be distinct. The Muslim ruling classes saw themselves as the protectors and propagators of Islam in India. It is a measure of their sense of belonging to a larger community, the Muslim *Umma* (see Chapter 11), that despite their independence of the rest of the Islamic world, most of the sultans of Delhi sought formal recognition for their rule in India from the nominal Abbasid caliphs in Baghdad or, in Mamluk times, in Cairo.

Nevertheless, reciprocal influence of Muslims and Hindus was inevitable, especially in popular piety. Sufi devotion had an appeal similar to that of Hindu devotional, or *bhakti* movements (see Chapter 10), and each at times influenced the other. Some of India's most revered Sufi and *bhakti* saints date from the fourteenth and fifteenth centuries. During this period, various theistic mystics strove to transcend the mutual antagonism and exclusivism of the more legalistic and communalist Muslims and Hindus. They typically preached devotion to a God who saves His worshipers without regard either to Hindu caste obligations or to legalistic observance of Muslim orthopraxy. The poet-saints Ramananda (d. after 1400) and Kabir (d. ca. 1518) were the two most famous such reformers.

Hindu and Other Indian Traditions

The history of India from 1000 to 1500 was also important for the other religious and cultural communities of India that as a whole vastly outnumbered the Muslims. The Jain tradition continued to flourish, notably in Gujarat, Rajputana, and Karnataka. In the north the Muslim conquests effectively ended by the eleventh century the Indian Buddhist monastic and lay traditions. The role of the Muslim destruction of temples and monasteries in the virtual disappearance of Buddhism during this period has, however, been overemphasized. Buddhism was already waning in the seventh century as a major factor in Indian culture, long before Islam came to India. On the other hand, Islam's attraction for the merchant classes, traditional supporters of Buddhism, may have been underestimated until now by modern scholars. In sum, the coming of Islam either dealt the *coup de grâce* to Buddhism in India or coincided with the final stage of its reduction to small-minority status.

Hindu religion and culture continued to flourish, even under Muslim control, as the continuing social and religious importance of the Brahmans and the popularity of *bhakti*

movements throughout India attest. This was an age of Brahmanic scholasticism that produced many commentaries and manuals but few seminal works. *Bhakti* creativity was much greater. The great Hindu Vaishnava Brahman, Ramanuja (d. 1137), provided a theological basis for *bhakti*, reconciling its ideas with the classical Upanishadic Hindu worldview in the Vedantin tradition. Important examples of *bhakti* movements are the Shaivite and Vaishnavite traditions associated, respectively, with the *bhakti* poets of the *nayanars* and *alvars* in Tamilnad. *Bhakti* piety underlies the masterpiece of Hindu mystical love poetry, Jayadeva's *Gita Govinda* (twelfth century), which is devoted to Krishna, the most important of Vishnu's incarnations.

The south continued to be the center of Hindu cultural, political, and religious activity. Of several important dynastic states in the south during this age, the foremost was that of the Cholas which flourished from about 900–1300. Aside from their military exploits and long political ascendancy, this dynasty can claim lasting fame purely for the school of bronze sculpture that they patronized at their capital of Tanjore. Their mightiest successor, the kingdom of Vijayanagar (1336–1565), subjugated the entire south in the fourteenth century and resisted its Muslim foes longer than any other kingdom. Vijayanagar itself was one of India's most lavishly developed cities and a center of the cult of Shiva before its destruction by the Bahmanid sultan of the Deccan.

IN WORLD PERSPECTIVE

The Islamic Heartlands and India, 1000–1500

This period in both Islamic and other Asian territories is difficult to characterize simply. The spread of Islam to new peoples or their ruling elites has been taken as a theme of this chapter. However, we have also seen that the history of Islam in India is hardly the history of India as a whole. The vast conquests and movements of the Mongols and Central Asian Turks across inner Asia were among the most striking developments in world history in this period; they often had cataclysmic effects, whether on Chinese, south Asian, west Asian, or eastern European societies. These conquests and migrations did not build lasting major states or civilizations, but they did wipe out existing orders and force the further migration of many who fled their advance. They contributed, even if unintentionally, new and often significant human resources to existing civilizations like those of China and the Islamic heartlands.

In this age Islam became a truly international tradition of religious, political, and social values and institutions. It did so by being highly adaptable and open to "indigenization" in the seemingly hostile contexts of polytheistic Hindu and African societies. Also in this period, distinct traditions of art, language, and literature, for all their local or regional diversity, became identifiably part of a larger whole defined by a Muslim identity. Islamic civilization had none of the territorial contiguity or linguistic and cultural homogeneity of either Chinese or Japanese civilization. Nevertheless, the Islamic world was an international reality in which a Muslim could travel and meet other Muslims of radically diverse backgrounds with much common ground for understanding.

Indian traditional culture was not bound up with an expanding missionary religious tradition like that of Islam. Yet in this age Hindu kingdoms flourished in Indonesia. Buddhism was expanding across much of Central and eastern Asia, thereby solidifying its place as an international missionary tradition.

Christianity, by contrast, was not rapidly expanding in Africa, Asia, or Europe; but by 1500 its western European branch was poised on the brink of internal revolution in religion and culture and international proselytism following upon the recently launched, fateful "voyages of discovery." In the year 1000 Europe was almost a backwater of culture and power by comparison with major Islamic or Hindu states, let alone that of China. By 1500, however, European civilization was riding the crest of a cultural renaissance, enjoying economic and political growth, and starting the global exploration that would turn into a flood of imperial expansion and affect most of the rest of the globe. Neither Islamic, Indian, African, Chinese, nor Japanese culture and society were so radically changed or changing in their basic ideas and institutions as were those of western Europe over these five hundred years.

Review Questions ———

1. In the period 1000–1500, no Muslim leader was able to build a large-scale Islamic empire of the extent of the early Abbasids. What might be some of the reasons for this?

2. Discuss the role of the *ulama* in Muslim society. How were they educated? What was their relationship to political leadership? What social roles did they play?

3. What was the role and impact of religious sectarianism in this period? Of the institutionalization of sufi piety and thought?

4. Discuss the cultural developments in Spain before 1500. Why was Córdoba considered to be such a model of civilized culture?

5. Why might Islam have been able to survive the successive invasions by steppe peoples (Turks and Mongols) from 945 on? What were the lasting results of these "invasions" for the Islamic world?

6. What were the primary obstacles to stable rule for India's Muslim invaders and immigrants? How did they deal with them?

Suggested Readings ———

The Islamic Heartlands

C. E. BOSWORTH, *The Islamic Dynasties: A Chronological and Genealogical Handbook* (1967). A handy reference work for dynasties and families important to Islamic history in all periods and places.

J. A. BOYLE, ED., *The Cambridge History of Iran*, Vol. 5, *The Saljuq and Mongol Periods* (1968). Useful and reasonably detailed articles on political, social, religious, and cultural developments.

P. K. HITTI, *History of the Arabs*, 8th ed. (1964). Still a useful English resource, largely for factual detail. See especially Part IV, "The Arabs in Europe: Spain and Sicily."

M. G. S. HODGSON, *The Expansion of Islam in the Middle Periods*, Vol. 2 of *The Venture of Islam*. 3 vols. (1964). The strongest of Hodgson's monumental three-volume survey of Islamic civilization and the only English work of its kind to give the period 945–1500 such broad and unified coverage.

A. HOURANI, *A History of the Arab Peoples* (1991). The newest survey history and the best, at least for the Arab Islamic world.

S. K. JAYYUSI, ED., *The Legacy of Muslim Spain*, 2 vols. (1994). A comprehensive survey of the arts, politics, literature, and society by experts in various fields.

B. LEWIS, ED., *Islam and the Arab World* (1976). A large-format, heavily illustrated volume with many excellent articles on diverse aspects of Islamic (not simply Arab, as the misleading title indicates) civilization through the premodern period.

D. MORGAN, *The Mongols* (1986). A recent and readable survey history.

J. J. SAUNDERS, *A History of Medieval Islam* (1965). A brief and simple, if sketchy, introductory survey of Islamic history to the Mongol invasions.

D. SOURDEL, *Medieval Islam*, trans. by W. M. Watt (1983). The synthetic, interpretive chapters on Islam and the political and social orders (4, 5) and on towns and art (6) are especially helpful.

B. SPULER, *The Muslim World: A Historical Survey*, trans. by F. R. C. Bagley (1960). 3 vols. Volumes I and II are handy references offering a highly condensed chronicle of Islamic history from Muhammad through the fifteenth century.

B. SPULER, *The Mongols in History*, trans. by Geoffrey Wheeler (1971). A short introductory survey of Mongol history, of which Chapters 2–5 are most relevant.

India

W. T. DE BARY ET AL., COMP., *Sources of Indian Tradition*, 2nd ed. (1958). Vol. I, *From the Beginning to 1800*, ed. and rev. by Ainslie T. Embree (1988). Excellent selections from a wide variety of Indian texts, with good introductions to chapters and individual selections.

S. M. IKRAM, *Muslim Civilization in India* (1964). The best short survey history, covering the period 711 to 1857.

R. C. MAJUMDAR, GEN. ED., *The History and Culture of the Indian People*, Vol. VI, *The Delhi Sultanate*, 3rd ed. (1980). A comprehensive political and cultural account of the period in India.

M. MUJEEB, *The Indian Muslims* (1967). The best cultural study of Islamic civilization in India as a whole, from its origins onward.

F. ROBINSON, ED., *The Cambridge History of India, Pakistan, Bangladesh, Sri Lanka, Nepal, Bhutan, and the Maldives* (1989). A recent and very helpful quick reference source with brief but well-done survey essays on a wide range of topics relevant to South Asian history down to the present.

A. WINK, *Al-Hind: The Making of the Indo-Islamic World*, Vol. 1 (1991). The first of five promising volumes to be devoted to the Indo-Islamic world's history. This volume treats the seventh to eleventh centuries.

15 ANCIENT CIVILIZATIONS OF THE AMERICAS

This

magnificent

ear spool of

gold, turquoise,

quartz, and shell was

found in the tomb of the

warrior priest in the Moche site of

Sipan, Peru, ca. 300 C.E. [Courtesy of UCLA

Fowler Museum of Cultural History/Susan Einstein]

CHAPTER TOPICS

- Problems in Reconstructing the History of Native American Civilization
- Mesoamerica
- The Formative Period and the Emergence of Mesoamerican Civilization
- The Classic Period in Mesoamerica

- The Post-Classic Period
- Andean South America
- The Preceramic and the Initial Period
- Chavín de Huantar and the Early Horizon

- The Early Intermediate Period
- The Middle Horizon Through the Late Intermediate Period
- The Inca Empire

In World Perspective Ancient Civilizations of the Americas

Humans first settled the American continents between 12,000 and 40,000 years ago. At that time glaciers locked up much of the world's water, lowering the sea level and opening a bridge of dry land between Siberia and Alaska. The earliest undisputed evidence of humans in Tierra del Fuego, at the southern tip of South America, dates to 11,000 years ago, indicating that at least by then the immigrants and their descendants had spread over all of both North and South America. When the glaciers receded the oceans rose, flooding the Bering Straits and severing Asia from America. Despite some continued contact in the Arctic and perhaps sporadic contacts elsewhere, the inhabitants of the Americas were now isolated from the inhabitants of Africa and Eurasia, and would remain so until overwhelmed by European invaders after 1492.

Although isolated from one another, the peoples of the Americas and the peoples of Africa and Eurasia experienced similar cultural changes at the end of the Paleolithic. In the Americ-

as, as in the eastern hemisphere, people in some regions gradually shifted from hunting and gathering to a settled, agricultural way of life. And in some places civilization emerged as society grew increasingly stratified, villages coalesced into urban centers, monumental architecture appeared, and craft specialists developed sophisticated artistic traditions.

The two most prominent centers of civilization—and the focus of this chapter—were Mesoamerica, in what is today Mexico and Central America, and the Andean region of South America. Both regions have a long, rich history of civilization that reaches back thousands of years. At the time of the European conquest of the Americas in the sixteenth century both regions were dominated by powerful expansionist empires—the Aztecs, or Mexica, in Mesoamerica and the Inca in the Andes. In both regions Spanish conquerors obliterated the native empires and nearly succeeded in obliterating native culture. But in both, native American traditions have endured, overlaid and combined in com-

plex ways with Hispanic culture, to provide clues to the prehispanic past.

Problems in Reconstructing the History of Native American Civilization

Several difficulties confront scholars trying to understand the ancient civilizations of the Americas. One is simply the nature of the evidence. Andean civilizations never developed writing, and in Mesoamerica much of the written record was destroyed by time and conquest, and what remained was until recently undeciphered. The primary source of information has thus been archaeology, the study of the physical remains left by past cultures. Archaeologists have been successful at teasing out many details of the American past. Turning from the study of monumental remains in great urban centers to the study of the remains left by ordinary people in their everyday lives, they have been able to create an increasingly rich picture of the economic and social organization of ancient American civilizations. But archaeology alone cannot produce the kind of narrative history that thousands of years of written records have made possible for Eurasian civilization. For at least one ancient Mesoamerican people, however—the Maya—this situation is changing. Scholars have recently been able to decipher their writing and attach specific names, dates, and events to heretofore silent ruins.

We also have accounts of the history and culture of the Aztecs and Inca, the last great native American civilizations, that were related to Spanish missionaries and officials in the wake of the conquest. Although these accounts are invaluable sources of information, it is almost impossible to know how much they are colored by the conquest and the needs and expectations of the conquerors. This dilemma raises another. The long physical separation of the peoples of the Americas from the peoples of Asia and Europe created a great cultural separation as well. Since the conquest, however, European culture has predominated. Both the Spanish conquerors seeking to make sense of the wonders they encountered and later scholars seeking to understand preconquest Native American civilization and reconstruct its history have had to rely on the language and categories of European thought to describe and analyze peoples and cultural experiences that had nothing to do with Europe. Cultural blinders and arrogance—the Spaniards, for example, sought to eradicate Native American religion and replace it with Christianity—have exacerbated this gap.

Again and again, European words, categories, and values have been used to describe the experience of America before it was America. Columbus and other early explorers (see Chapter 17), believing they had reached the East Indies, called the people they met in the Caribbean "Indians." This misnomer stuck, extending to all Native American peoples who, of course, have other names for themselves. The name "America" itself is European, taken from Amerigo Vespucci (1451–1512), a Florentine who explored the coast of Brazil in 1501 and 1502.

Mesoamerica

Mesoamerica, which means "middle America," extends from central Mexico into Central America. This is a region of great physical diversity, ranging from lowland tropical rain forests to temperate highlands with fertile basins and valleys. Lowland

Major Periods in Ancient Mesoamerican Civilization	
Archaic	8000–2000 B.C.E.
Formative (or Pre-Classic)	2000 B.C.E.–150 C.E.
Classic	150–900 C.E.
Post-Classic	900–1521 C.E.

regions include the Yucatan peninsula and the Gulf and Pacific coasts. Highland regions include Mexico's central plateau, with the Valley of Mexico and the Oaxaca region, and the mountainous areas of Guatemala. Most of Mesoamerica's mineral resources are found in the highlands. The lowlands were the source of many important trading goods, including hardwoods, plant dyes, and the prized feathers of exotic birds.

Mesoamerica also designates a distinctive and enduring cultural tradition that emerged in this region between 1000 and 2000 B.C.E., manifested itself in a succession of impressive and powerful states until the coming of European conquerors in the sixteenth century, and continues to express itself in the lives of the region's Native American peoples. This is not to say that Mesoamerica was or is culturally homogeneous. The peoples of Mesoamerica were and are ethnically and linguistically diverse. There was no single Mesoamerican civilization, nor was there a single linear development of civilization in the region. Nonetheless, Mesoamerican civilizations shared many traits, including writing, a sophisticated calendrical system, many gods and religious ideas, a ritual ball game, and urban centers with religious and administrative buildings symmetrically arranged around large plazas.

Throughout its history the peoples of the region were linked by long-distance trade. Unlike the Andean region, where sophisticated metallurgy developed early, metallurgy came late to Mesoamerica. When it did come, it was used primarily for ceremonial objects rather than for weapons and tools. Instead, Mesoamericans made weapons and other tools from obsidian, a volcanic glass capable of holding a razor-sharp edge, and for that reason a valued trade commodity.

Mesoamerican history before the Spanish conquest is conventionally divided into four major periods: The term "Classic," with its associations to ancient Greece and its connotations of "best" or "highest," derives from European historical frameworks. It reflects the view of many early Mesoamericanists that the Classic period, which corresponds more or less to the time during which the Maya civilizations of the southern Yucatan erected dated stone monuments, was the high point of Mesoamerican civilization. That view is no longer so prevalent, but the terminology has endured. The chronology continues to provide a useful framework for understanding Mesoamerican history.

The transition from hunting and gathering to settled village life occurred gradually in Mesoamerica during the Archaic period. The cornerstone of the process was the domestication of maize (corn) and other staple crops, including beans and squash. Other plants native to the Americas that were domesticated in this period include tomatoes, chili peppers, and avocado. Maize and beans were particularly important because together they provide a rich source of protein compared to the grains that were the basis of the Neolithic revolution in the

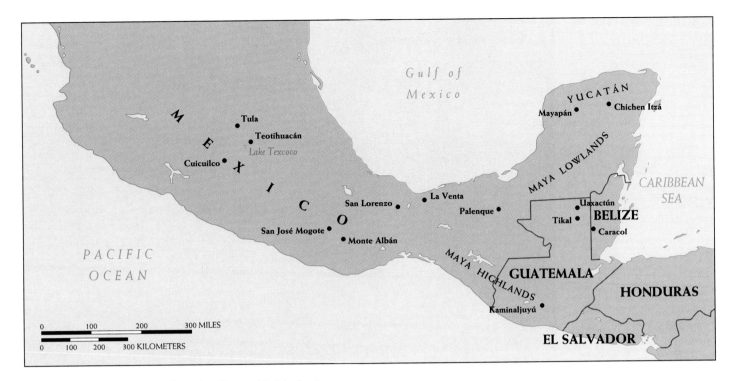

Map 15-1 Pre-Aztec Mesoamerican sites discussed in this chapter.

Ancient Near East and China. In those regions domesticated animals supplied the protein settled agriculturalists needed in their diet. Mesoamerica, however, was poor in sources of animal protein. It had only a few domesticated animals—among them dogs and turkeys—and no large herd animals like the cattle, sheep, and goats of the Old World.

The domestication of maize, beans, and other plants secured the people of Mesoamerica an adequate and dependable diet. Over time they devised myriad ways to prepare and store these staples. Maize has also been one of Mesoamerica's major contributions to the world. Since the conquest, maize cultivation has spread to many other parts of the world. Corn is now one of North America's most important crops, and it is used to feed livestock in both North and South America.

Probably because they had no large draft animals—no horses or oxen—the people of the Americas, including Mesoamerica, never developed the wheel, although they made wheeled toys. In Mesoamerica humans did all the carrying. And because there were no horses and chariots, warfare in Mesoamerica (and in Andean South America) was always between armies of foot soldiers.

Between 5000 and 2500 B.C.E. villages began to appear in both highland and lowland regions of Mesoamerica. By about 2000 B.C.E. settled agricultural life had taken hold in much of the region. As in the Old World when this happened, people began to make fired clay vessels, and ceramic technology appeared. Nomadic hunter-gatherers have little need of storage, but farmers do, and clay vessels filled that need. Pottery

is also a medium for artistic expression, and it played a role in religion and ritual observance throughout Mesoamerican history.

The Formative Period and the Emergence of Mesoamerican Civilization

By about 1500 B.C.E. Mesoamerica's agricultural villages were beginning to coalesce into more complicated societies, with towns and monumental architecture, the division of society into elite and commoner classes, long-distance trade among regions, and the emergence of sophisticated artistic traditions.

The Olmec

The most prominent of the early Formative period cultures is that of the Olmec, centered on the lowlands of Mexico's Gulf Coast. This is a densely vegetated region with slow, meandering streams bordered by areas of rich, alluvial soil. The Olmec were once thought of as Mesoamerica's "mother culture," but evidence is accumulating that similarly complex societies were emerging at about the same time throughout Mesoamerica.

Most of what is known about the Olmecs comes from the archaeological sites of San Lorenzo and La Venta (see Map 15-1). Other Olmec centers have not been as intensively

A large carved monument from the Olmec site of La Venta with a naturalistically rendered human figure. [Robert and Linda Mitchell Photography]

studied. San Lorenzo was first occupied about 1500 B.C.E. and had developed into a prominent center by about 1200 B.C.E. It included public buildings, a drainage system linked to artificial ponds, and what was probably the earliest court for the Mesoamerican ballgame. The center flourished until about 900 B.C.E. but then went into decline and had been abandoned by about 400 B.C.E. As San Lorenzo declined, La Venta rose to prominence, flourishing from about 900 to 400 B.C.E. La Venta's most conspicuous feature is a 110-foot, scalloped pyramid, known as the Great Pyramid, which stands at one end of a group of platforms and plazas aligned along a north-south axis. Archaeologists have recovered many caches of carved jade, serpentine, and granite artifacts that had been buried along the center line of this axis. Like San Lorenzo, La Venta also had an elaborate drainage system.

Probably the best-known Olmec works of art are the massive stone heads, some weighing more than twenty tons, that have been found at both San Lorenzo and La Venta. Thought to be portraits of Olmec rulers, these were carved from basalt from quarries as much as 65 miles distant and transported, probably by raft, to the centers. The Olmec also carved other large basalt monuments, including altars and seated figures.

The population of San Lorenzo and La Venta was never great, probably less than 1,000 people. The monumental architecture and sculpture at these sites nonetheless suggests that Olmec society was dominated by an elite class of ruler-priests able to command the labor of the rest of the population. The elite probably lived in the centers, supported by farmers who lived in villages of pole-and-thatch houses.

Among the most pervasive images in Olmec art is that of the were-jaguar, a half-human, half-feline creature. The were-jaguar may have been a divine ancestor figure, perhaps providing the elite with the justification for their authority. Similarities between the were-jaguar iconography and that of later Mesoamerican deities suggests some of the underlying continuities linking Mesoamerican societies over time.

The raw material for many Olmec artifacts, such as jade and obsidian, comes from other regions of Mesoamerica. Likewise, Olmec goods and Olmec iconography like the were-jaguar are found in other regions, all suggesting that from an early time the parts of Mesoamerica were linked in a web of trade. These contacts would have fostered the spread of ideas, contributing to the formation of common Mesoamerican traditions. Control of trade in high-status materials like jade and obsidian by the Olmec elite would also have contributed to their prestige and authority.

The Valley of Oaxaca and the Rise of Monte Alban

Olmec civilization faded after about 400 B.C.E. and had disappeared by about 200 B.C.E. Other regions, however, were rising to prominence. Some of the most significant developments in the Late Formative period occurred in the Valley of Oaxaca. The site of San José Mogote, located in one branch of the valley, had arisen at about the same time as San Lorenzo. By about 600 B.C.E. San José Mogote was a thriving center of perhaps 1,000 people. Around 500 B.C.E. a new center,

Monte Alban, was built on a hill where three branches of the valley meet. Monte Alban's population soon grew to about 5,000, and it emerged as the capital of a state that dominated the Oaxaca region. Carved images of bound prisoners at Monte Alban suggest that warfare played a role in establishing its authority. They also suggest an early origin for the practice of ritual human sacrifice that characterized most Mesoamerican cultures. Monte Alban retained its authority in Oaxaca into the Classic period, maintaining its independence against the growing power of the greatest Classic Period city, Teotihuacán.

The Emergence of Writing and the Mesoamerican Calendar The earliest evidence of writing and the Mesoamerican calendar have been found in the Valley of Oaxaca at San José Mogote and Monte Alban. The Mesoamerican calendar is based on two interlocking cycles, each with its own day and month names. One cycle, tied to the solar year, was of 365 days; the other was of 260 days. Combining the two cycles produced a "century" of 52 years, the amount of time required before a particular combination of days in each cycle would repeat itself. The hieroglyphs found in Oaxaca relate to the 260-day cycle.

At the time of the Spanish conquest, all the peoples of Mesoamerica used this 52-year calendrical system. As we will see, only the Maya developed a calendar based on a longer time period, anchored—like the Jewish, Christian, or Muslim calendars—to a fixed starting point in the past.

The Classic Period in Mesoamerica

The Classic Period was a time of cultural florescence in Mesoamerica. In Central Mexico, it saw the rise of Teotihuacán, a great city that rivaled the largest cities of the world at the time. The Maya, who built densely populated cities in the seemingly inhospitable rain forests of the southern Yucatán, developed a sophisticated system of mathematics and Mesoamerica's most advanced hieroglyphic writing. Indeed, Classic Period urban life in Mesoamerica was richer and on a larger scale than in Europe north of the Alps at the same time.

Archaeologists and art historians have recently made enormous strides in understanding Classic Period civilization. Progress in deciphering Maya hieroglyphics has opened a window on the politics and statecraft of the Maya elite. Archaeological studies have broadened our understanding of Teotihuacán and Maya cities, revealing their extent and structure and providing clues to the lives of the people who lived in them.

Classic Period cities, with their many temples, plazas, and administrative buildings, were religious and administrative centers whose rulers combined secular and religious author-

ity. It was once thought that Classic Period society was composed of peaceful theocracies, without the chronic warfare characterizing Mesoamerica at the time of the Spanish conquest. It is now clear, however, that warfare was common during the Classic Period and that Classic Period rulers did not hesitate to use force to expand their influence and maintain their authority. The ritual sacrifice of captive enemies was also a feature of Classic Period societies.

Teotihuacán

In the late Formative Period two centers competed for dominance over the rapidly growing population of the Valley of Mexico. One of these, Cuicuilco, was located at the southern end of the valley. The other, Teotihuacán, was located about thirty miles northeast of Mexico City. When a volcano destroyed Cuicuilco in the first century C.E. Teotihuacán was left unopposed and grew explosively into a great city, perhaps Mesoamerica's first true city-state, dominating central Mexico for many centuries and strongly influencing the rest of Mesoamerica.

Several natural advantages contributed to Teotihuacán's rise. The original source of its prestige may have been a network of caves recently discovered under its most prominent monument, the Pyramid of the Sun (the name by which the Aztecs knew it). These caves may have been considered an entrance to the underworld. Recent studies indicate that stone quarried from them was used to construct the city, creating a direct symbolic link between the city's buildings and its sacred origins. Teotihuacán is also located near an important source of obsidian, straddling a trade route to the Gulf Coast and southern Mesoamerica. The quarrying of obsidian and the manufacture and trade of obsidian goods were apparently a major source of the city's wealth and influence. Finally, Teotihuacán is surrounded by fertile farmland susceptible to intensive cultivation with terracing and irrigation.

At its height in about 500 C.E. this remarkable city extended over almost nine square miles and had a population of more than 150,000, making it one of the largest cities in the world at the time. Its size and organization suggest that it was ruled by a powerful, centralized authority. It is laid out on a rigid grid plan dominated by a broad, three-mile-long thoroughfare known as the Avenue of the Dead. Religious and administrative structures and a market occupy the center of the city. At one end of the Avenue of the Dead is the so-called Pyramid of the Moon, and near it, to one side, is the 210-foot-high Pyramid of the Sun. More than 2,000 residential structures surround the city center. The most lavish of these, the homes of the city's elite, lie nearest the center. Most of the city's residents lived in walled apartment compounds farther from the center. These compounds were also centers of craft manufacture, with neighborhoods devoted to

The Pyramid of the Sun stands near the southern end of Teotihuacán's great central thoroughfare, the Avenue of the Dead. [Kal Muller/Woodfin Camp & Associates]

pottery, obsidian work, and other specialties. Some parts of the city were reserved for foreign traders. One neighborhood, for example, was home to people from Monte Alban and the Oaxaca region. Paintings and murals adorned the interiors of many buildings, including those of the common people as well as the elite. The humble dwellings of poor farmers occupied the city's periphery. As the city grew, local farmers had apparently been forced to abandon their villages and move to Teotihuacán, another indication of the power of the city's rulers.

Teotihuacán's influence extended throughout Mesoamerica. In the central highlands, dispersed settlements were consolidated into larger centers laid out similarly to Teotihuacán, suggesting conquest and direct control—a Teotihuacán empire. The city's influence in other, more distant regions may have reflected close trading ties rather than conquest. Buildings in Teotihuacán's distinctive architectural style at the site of Kaminaljuyu in the highlands of modern Guatemala, for example, may have been residences for Teotihuacano merchants. The city's obsidian and pottery were exchanged widely for items like the green feathers of the quetzal bird and jaguar skins, valued for ritual garments.

Many of the buildings in Teotihuacán were decorated with striking, skillfully made sculptures and murals of the city's gods and ritual practices. Among the deities of Teotihuacán are a storm god and his goddess counterpart, whose representation suggests a link to the Aztec's rain god, Tlaloc, and his consort, Chalchiuhtlicue. The people of Teotihuacán also worshipped a feathered serpent who is recognizably antecedent to the god the Aztecs worshipped as Quetzalcoatl and the Maya as Kukulcan. Murals also suggest that the Teotihuacán elite, like the Maya and later Mesoamerican peoples, drew their own blood as a form of sacrifice to the gods. A mass burial under one of the city's principal temples indicates that they also practiced human sacrifice.

After 500 C.E. Teotihuacán's influence began to wane, and some time in the eighth century, for reasons that are still poorly understood, its authority collapsed. A fire swept through the city, destroying the ritual center and the residences of the elite and hinting at an internal revolt. Although a substantial population lived on in the city, it never regained its former status. It retained its hold on the imagination of succeeding generations of Mesoamericans, however, much like the ruins of ancient Greece and Rome on the imaginations of later Europeans. The name by which we know it, Teotihuacán, is an Aztec word meaning "City of the Gods," and it was still a revered pilgrimage site at the time of the Spanish conquest.

The Maya

Maya civilization arose in southern Mesoamerica, which includes modern Guatemala, the Yucatan peninsula, Belize, and parts of Honduras and El Salvador. Village life established itself in this region during the first millennium B.C.E., and thereafter the population began to rise steadily. The earliest distinctively Maya urban sites date to around 300 B.C.E. in the late Formative period. During the Classic Period, Maya civilization experienced a remarkable florescence in the lowland jungles of the southern Yucatan.

All the pre-Spanish societies of Mesoamerica were literate, recording historical and religious information on scrolled or screenfold books made with deerhide or bark paper. Only a handful of these books, four of them Mayan, have survived the ravages of time and the Spanish conquest. (Spanish priests, who viewed native religious texts as idolatrous, burned almost all of them.) The Maya of the Classic Period, who developed Mesoamerica's most advanced writing system, were unique in the extent to which they inscribed writing and calendrical symbols in stone, pottery, and other imperishable materials.

Thanks to rapid advances in the decipherment of Maya writing and to intensive archaeological work at Maya cities, our understanding of the nature of Classic Period Maya civilization has changed radically in recent decades. According to earlier views, Maya cities were not really cities but empty ceremonial centers inhabited by scholar-priests. The inscriptions were thought to be concerned entirely with astronomical and calendrical observations tied to Maya ritual. Scattered farming communities were thought to have surrounded the centers, supporting the priestly elite. Relations between centers were thought to be peaceful. Contributing to this view was the belief that intensive agriculture capable of supporting dense populations was impossible in the tropical forests of the southern Yucatan where Classic Period Maya civilization developed.

Archaeologists have shown that Maya centers were indeed cities, and that the largest of them, Tikal, probably had a population of between 50,000 and 70,000 at its height. They have also found evidence of terracing, irrigation systems, and other agricultural technologies that would have increased yields enough to support dense populations. Powerful ruling families and their elite retainers dominated these cities, supported by a far larger class of farmer-commoners. The inscriptions are almost entirely devoted to recounting important events in the lives of these rulers. Cities competed for dominance, and warfare between them was chronic. As murals and sculptures show, captured prisoners were sacrificed to appease the gods and glorify the victorious ruler.

This reproduction of one of the remarkable murals found at the Maya site of Bonampak shows the presentation of captives to the city's ruler, Chan Muan. [Copyright © President and Fellows of Harvard College 1998. All rights reserved Peabody Museum, Harvard University. Photograph by Hillel Burger.]

Religion deeply informed the social and political realm of the Maya. They believed that the world had gone through several cycles of creation before the present one. They recognized no clear distinction between a natural and a supernatural world. As was probably true also of Teotihuacán, rulers and the elite combined religious and political authority, mediating between humans and gods through elaborate rituals in the temples and plazas of their cities. Rulers claimed association with the gods to justify their authority. They wore special regalia that symbolized their power, and they performed rituals to sustain the gods and the cosmic order. These rituals included bloodletting ceremonies, the sacrifice of captives, and ballgames.

The significance of sacrifice and the ballgame in Maya ideology is reflected in a Maya creation myth recorded in the *Popol Vuh*, a Maya book transcribed into European script by a Maya noble in the sixteenth century. Imagery in Classic Period Maya art has been linked to this myth, which tells how the Hero Twins defeated the gods of the underworld in the ballgame and returned to life after being sacrificed. One became the sun and the other Venus, and in their regular rising and setting reenact their descent into the underworld and their subsequent rebirth. All Maya cities had ball courts. The games played there were a symbolic reenactment of the confrontation between the Hero Twins and the lords of the underworld, and the losing team was sometimes sacrificed.[1]

---

[1] Robert J. Sharer, *The Ancient Maya*, 5th ed., (Stanford: Stanford University Press 1994), p. 522.

A Maya Myth of Creation

This segment of the Maya creation myth is from the Popol Vuh, *a compendium of Maya mythology and history transcribed into European script by a Quiche Maya noble in the sixteenth century.*

How does this myth describe the world before creation? Who are the beings that exist before creation and decide how it is to be carried out? What did they do to create the earth?

There was not yet one person, one animal, bird, fish, crab, tree, rock, hollow, canyon, meadow, forest, Only the sky alone is there; the face of the earth is not clear. Only the sea alone is pooled under all the sky; there is nothing whatever gathered together. It is at rest; not a single thing stirs. It is held back; kept at rest under the sky.

Whatever might be is simply not there: only murmurs, ripples, in the dark, in the night. Only the Maker, Modeler alone, Sovereign Plumed Serpent, the Bearers, Begetters are in the water, a glittering light. . . .

So there were three of them, as Heart of Sky, who came to the Sovereign Plumed Serpent, when the dawn of life was conceived:

"How should it be sown, how should it dawn? Who is to be the provider, nurturer?"

"Let it be this way, think about it: this water should be removed, emptied out for the formation of the earth's own plate and platform, then comes the sowing, the dawning of the sky-earth. But there will be no high days and no bright praise for our work, our design, until the rise of the human work, the human design," they said.

And then the earth rose because of them; it was simply their word that brought it forth. For the forming of the earth, they said, "Earth." It arose suddenly, just like a cloud, like a mist, now forming, unfolding. Then the mountains were separated from the water, all at once the great mountains came forth. By their genius alone, by their cutting edge alone they carried out the conception of the mountain-plain, whose face grew instant groves of cypress and pine.

The Classic Period Maya developed a sophisticated mathematics and were among the first peoples in the world to invent the concept of zero. In addition to the 52-year calendar round based on interlocking 260- and 365-day cycles they shared with other Mesoamerican societies, the Maya developed an absolute calendar, known as the Long Count, tied to a fixed point in the past. The calendar had great religious as well as practical significance for the Maya. They viewed the movements of the celestial bodies to which the calendar was tied—including the sun, moon, and Venus—as deities. The complexity and accuracy of their calendar reflect Maya skills in astronomical observation. They adjusted their lunar calendar for the actual length of the lunar cycle (29.53 days) and may have had provisions like our leap years for the actual length of the solar year. They also made accurate observations of Venus and recognized before other peoples that it is both the morning and the evening star. The importance of the calendar, its association with divine forces, and the esoteric knowledge required to master it must have been an important source of prestige and power for its elite guardians.

Scholars have been able to correlate the Long Count calendar with the European calendar, and so can date Maya monuments with a precision unknown for other ancient Mesoamerican societies. The commemorative monuments erected by Classic Maya rulers to record their accomplishments almost always have Long Count dates. As a result, it is now possible to reconstruct the dynastic histories of many Maya cities in detail, keeping in mind, of course, that Maya rulers—like rulers everywhere throughout history—may have exaggerated their accomplishments to put themselves in a favorable light.

During the Classic Period no single center dominated the Maya region. Rather, many independent units, each composed of a capital city and smaller subject towns and villages, alternately vied and cooperated with each other, rising and falling in relative prominence. Tikal, at its height the largest Classic Maya city, is also one of the most thoroughly studied. The residential center covers more than fourteen square miles and has more than 3,000 structures. The city follows the uneven terrain of the rain forest and is not, like Teotihuacán, laid out on a grid. Monumental causeways link the major structures of the site.

Tikal emerged as an important center in the Late Formative, benefiting from its strategic position. The city is located near a source of flint, valued as a raw material for stone tools. It is also located near swamps that, with modification, might have been agriculturally productive. And it has access to river systems that lead both to the Gulf and the Caribbean coasts, giving it control of the trade between those regions.

A single dynasty of thirty-nine rulers reigned in Tikal from the Early Classic until the eighth century. The early rulers in this Jaguar Paw line were buried in a structure known as the North Acropolis, and the inscriptions associated with their tombs provide us with details about them, including in many cases their names, the dates of their rule, and the dates of major military victories. Monuments associated with the ruler Great Jaguar Paw, for example, suggests that in 378 C.E. he conquered the city of Uaxactún and installed a relative on its throne.

Late in the fourth century links developed between Tikal and Teotihuacán. One ruler, Curl Nose, who ascended to the throne in 379, may have married into the ruling family from the Teotihuacán-dominated city of Kaminaljuyu in the southern highlands.

For about 100 years beginning in the mid-sixth century, Tikal and most other lowland Maya sites experienced a hiatus during which there was little new construction. The city lost much of its influence and may have suffered a serious defeat at the hands of the city of Caracol. Then in 682 the ruler Ah Cacau (r. 682–723?) ascended the throne and initiated a new period of vigor and prosperity for Tikal, again expanding its influence through conquest and strategic marriage alliances. He and his two immediate successors, Yax Kin (r. 734–?) and Chitam (r. 769–?), began an ambitious building program, creating most of the Tikal's surviving monumental structures, including the dramatic, soaring temples that dominate the site. Chitam was the last ruler in the Jaguar Paw dynasty. After he died Tikal again declined and, like other sites in the southern lowlands, it never recovered.

Similar dynastic histories have been emerging from research at other Classic Maya sites. Inscriptions in the shrine above the tomb of Lord Pacal (r. 615–683), the greatest ruler of the city of Palenque, located in the west of the Maya region in hills overlooking the Gulf Coast plain, record the city's entire dynastic history back to mythic ancestors. Two of the rulers in this genealogy were women, one of them Pacal's mother, Lady Zac Kuk (r. 612–640), and another predecessor, Lady Kanal Ikal (r. 583–604). Palenque is also remarkable for its architectural innovations, which permitted its architects to build structures with thinner walls and larger rooms than at other Classic Period sites.

Between 800 and 900 C.E. Classic Period civilization collapsed in the southern lowlands. The ruling dynasties all came to an end, the construction of monumental architecture and sculpture with Long Count dates ceased, and the great cities were virtually abandoned. The cause of the collapse has long been a subject of intense speculation, and is still not known for sure. The factors that may have contributed to it, however, are becoming clearer. Among them are intensifying warfare, population growth, increased population concentration, and attempts to increase agricultural production that ultimately backfired. As the urban areas around the ceremonial centers grew, so did the demand for food. Ambitious building projects continued in the centers right up to the collapse, and some scholars believe that as a growing proportion of the population was employed in these projects, fewer were left to produce food. Overfarming may then have led to soil exhaustion. Some archaeologists also believe a major drought may have occurred. Clearly the

Ruins of Tikal. The structure on the right, towering above the jungle canopy, is known as Temple I or the Temple of the Giant Jaguar. It housed the tomb of Ah Cacao, who ruled Tikal from 682 to about 723. [Robert Frerk/Odyssey Productions]

Maya exceeded the capacities of their resources, but exactly why and how remain unknown.

After the abandonment of the Classic sites in the southern lowlands, the focus of Maya civilization shifted to the northern Yucatan. There the site of Chichén Itzá, located next to a sacred well, flourished from the ninth to the thirteenth centuries. Stylistic resemblances between Chichén Itzá and Tula, the capital of the Post-Classic Toltec Empire in central Mexico (see the next section) suggest ties between the two cities, but archaeologists are uncertain of their nature. Chichén Itzá had the largest ball court in the Maya area. After Chichén Itzá's fall, Mayapan became the main Maya center. By the time of the Spanish conquest it too had lost sway, and the Maya had divided into small, competing centers.

The Post-Classic Period

No new strong, centralized power arose immediately to replace Teotihuacán in the wake of its collapse in the eighth century. Warfare increased, and several smaller, militaristic states emerged, many centered around fortified hilltop cities. At the same time interregional trade and market systems became increasingly important, and secular and religious authority, closely linked during the Classic period, began to diverge.

The Toltecs

About 900 C.E. a people known as the Toltecs rose to prominence. Their capital, Tula, is located near the northern periphery of Mesoamerica. Like Teotihuacán, it lay close to an important source of obsidian. The Toltecs themselves were apparently descendants of one of many "barbarian" northern peoples (like the later Aztecs) who began migrating into Mesoamerica during the Late Classic.

Aztec mythology glorified the Toltecs, seeing them as the fount of civilization and attributing to them a vast and powerful empire to which the Aztecs were the legitimate heirs. Other Mesoamerican peoples at the time of the conquest also attributed legendary status to the Toltecs. The archaeological evidence for a Toltec empire, however, is ambiguous. Although a substantial city with a population of between 35,000 and 60,000 people, Tula was never as large or as organized as Teotihuacán. Toltec influence reached many regions of Mesoamerica—as already noted, there were many stylistic affinities between Tula and the Maya city of Chichén Itzá—but archaeologists are uncertain whether that influence translated into political control.

Toltec iconography, which stresses human sacrifice, death, blood, and military symbolism, supports their warlike reputation. Their deities are clearly antecedent to those worshipped by the Aztecs, including the feathered serpent Quetzalcoatl and the warlike trickster Tezcatlipoca.

Whatever the reality of Toltec power, it was short-lived. By about 1100 Tula was in decline and its influence gone.

The Aztecs

The people commonly known as the Aztecs referred to themselves as the *Mexica*, a name that lives on as *Mexico*. At the time of the arrival of the Spanish in 1519 the Aztecs controlled a powerful empire that dominated much of Mesoamerica. Their capital city, Tenochtitlán, was the most populous yet seen in Mesoamerica. Built on islands and landfill in the southern part of Lake Texcoco in the Valley of Mexico, it was home to some 200,000 to 300,000 people. Its great temples and palaces gleamed in the sun. Bearing tribute to its rulers and goods to its great markets, canoes crowded the city's canals and people on foot thronged its streets and the great causeways linking it to the mainland. The city's traders brought precious goods from distant regions; vast wealth flowed in constantly from subject territories. Yet the people responsible for these accomplishments were relative newcomers, the foundation of their power being less than 200 years old.

Because of the dramatic clash with Spanish adventurers that brought their empire to an end, we have more direct information about the Aztecs than any other pre-conquest Mesoamerican people. Many of the conquistadors recorded their experiences, and post-conquest administrators and missionaries collected valuable information about their new subjects while at the same time seeking to extirpate their religion and culture. Although filtered through the bitterness of defeat for the Aztecs and the biases of the conquerors, these records nevertheless provide detailed information about Aztec society and Aztec history.

According to their own legends, the Aztecs were originally a nomadic people inhabiting the shores of a mythical Lake Aztlán somewhere to the northwest of the Valley of Mexico. At the urging of their patron god Huitzilopochtli, they began to migrate, arriving in the Valley of Mexico early in the thirteenth century. Scorned by the people of the cities and states already there, but prized and feared as mercenaries, they ended up in the marshy land on the shores of Lake Texcoco. They finally settled on the island that became Tenochtitlán in 1325 after seeing an eagle perched there on a prickly pear cactus, an omen Huitzilopochtli had said would identify the end of their wandering.

The Aztecs accepted a position as tributaries and mercenaries for Azcazpotzalco, then the most powerful state in the valley, but soon became trusted allies with their own tribute-paying territories. They further consolidated their position with marriage alliances to the ruling families of other cities. These alliances gave their own rulers claim to descent from the Toltecs. In 1428, under their fourth ruler, Itzcoatl (r. 1427–1440), the Aztecs formed a triple alliance with Texcoco and

A Spaniard Describes the Glory of the Aztec Capital

On November 8, 1519, a group of approximately 400 Spaniards under the command of Hernán Cortés entered the Aztec capital of Tenochtitlán. One of them was Bernal Díaz del Castillo (b. 1492) who later wrote The Conquest of New Spain, *a chronicle of his experience. This gives some sense of the magnificence of the Aztec capital.*

What elements of Aztec life especially astonished Díaz? What can one conclude about the social and political life of the Aztec elite from the manner in which Montezuma was attended? What forms of wealth were most apparent?

Early next day we left Iztapalapa [where Cortés' forces had been camped] with a large escort of these great Caciques [Aztec nobles], and followed the causeway, which is eight yards wide and goes so straight to the city of Mexico [Tenochtitlán] that I do not think it curves at all. Wide though it was, it was so crowded with people that there was hardly room for them all. Some were going to Mexico and others coming away, besides those who had come out to see us, and we could hardly get through the crowds that were there. For the towers and the cues [temples] were full, and they came in canoes from all parts of the lake. No wonder, since they had never seen horses or men like us before.

With such wonderful sights to gaze on we did not know what to say, or if this was real that we saw before our eyes. On the land side there were great cities, and on the lake many more. The lake was crowded with canoes. At intervals along the causeway there were many bridges, and before us was the great city of Mexico. . . .

We marched along our causeway to a point where another small causeway branches off to another city . . . and there, beside some towerlike buildings, which were their shrines, we were met by many more Caciques and dignitaries in very rich cloaks. The different chieftains wore different brilliant liveries, and the causeways were full of them. . . .

. . . When we came near to Mexico, at the place where there were some other small towers, the great Montezuma descended from his litter, and these other great Caciques supported him beneath a marvelously rich canopy of green feathers, decorated with gold work, silver, pearls . . . which hung from a sort of border. It was a marvelous sight. The great Montezuma was magnificently clad, in their fashion and wore sandals . . . the soles of which are of gold and the upper parts ornamented with precious stones. And the four lords who supported him were richly clad also in garments that seem to have been kept ready for them on the road so they could accompany their master . . . and many more lords . . . walked before the great Montezuma, sweeping the ground on which he was to tread, and laying down cloaks so that his feet should not touch the earth. Not one of these chieftains dared to look him in the face. All kept their eyes lowered most reverently except those four lords, his nephews, who were supporting him.

. . . Who could now count the multitude of men, women, and boys in the streets, on the roof-tops and in canoes on the waterways, who had come out to see us? . . .

They led us to our quarters, which were in some large houses capable of accommodating us all and had formerly belonged to the great Montezuma's father. . . . Here Montezuma now kept the great shrines of his gods, and a secret chamber containing gold bars and jewels. This was the treasure he had inherited from his father, which he never touched.

From *The Conquest of New Spain,* by Bernal Díaz, J. M. Cohen, trans. (New York: Penguin Books, 1963), copyright © J. M. Cohen, 1963, pp. 216–218.

Tlacopan, turned against Azcazpotzalco, and became the dominant power in the Valley of Mexico. It was at this time, less than 100 years before the arrival of Cortés, that the Aztecs, as head of the Triple Alliance, began the aggressive expansion that brought them their vast tribute-paying empire (see Map 15–2).

Itzcoatl also laid the foundation of Aztec imperial ideology. He ordered the burning of all the ancient books in the valley, expunging any history that conflicted with Aztec pretensions, and restructured Aztec religion and ritual to support and justify Aztec preeminence. The Aztecs now presented themselves as the divinely ordained successors to the ancient Toltecs, and with each new conquest and the growing splendor of Tenochtitlán, they seemed to ratify that claim.

Aztec conquests ultimately included almost all of central Mexico. To the west, however, they were unable to conquer the rival Tarascan empire with its capital of Tzintzuntzan. And within the Aztec realm several pockets, most prominently Tlaxcala, remained unsubdued but nonetheless locked into a pattern of ritual warfare with the Aztecs.

The Aztec Extractive Empire   The Aztec empire was extractive. After a conquest, the Aztecs usually left the local elite intact and in power, imposing their rule indirectly. But they demanded heavy tribute in goods and labor. Tribute included goods of all kinds, including agricultural products, fine craft goods, gold and jade, textiles, and precious feathers. Tribute lists in Tenochtitlán, which the Spanish preserved because they, too, wished to exploit the empire they had conquered, indicate the immense quantity of goods that flowed into Tenochtitlán's coffers as a result. In a given year, for example, tribute included as much as 7,000 tons of maize and 2,000,000 cotton cloaks. One nearby province alone was responsible for "12,800 cloaks . . . , 1600 loin cloths, 1600 women's tunics, 8 warriors' costumes . . . , 32,000 bundles of paper, 8000 bowls, and 4 bins of maize and beans."[2] It was this wealth that underwrote the grandeur of Tenochtitlán, making it, as one commentator has described it, "a beautiful parasite, feeding on the lives and labour of other peoples and casting its shadow over all their arrangements."[3]

Aztec Religion and Human Sacrifice

Aztec imperial exploitation did not end with food, cotton, and valued craft goods. Human sacrifice on a prodigious scale was central to Aztec ideology. The Aztecs believed that Huitzilopochtli, as sun god, required human blood to sustain him as he battled the moon and stars each night to rise again each day, and that it was their responsibility to provide the victims. The prime candidates for sacrifice were war captives, and the Aztecs often engaged in "flowery wars" with traditional enemies like Tlaxcala just to obtain captives. On major festivals, thousands of victims might perish. Led up the steps of the temple of Huitzilopochtli, a victim was thrown backward over a stone, his arms and legs pinned, while a priest cut out his heart. He would then be rolled down the steps of the temple, his head placed on a skull rack, and his limbs butchered and distributed to be eaten. Small children were sacrificed to the rain god Tlaloc, who, it was believed, was pleased by their tears.

Victims were also selected as god impersonators, stand-ins for particular gods who were sacrificed after a series of rituals. The rituals involved in the festivals honoring the powerful god Tezcatlipoca were particularly elaborate. A beautiful male youth was chosen to represent the god for an entire year, during which he was treated with reverence. He wandered through the city dressed as the god and playing the flute. A month before the end of his reign he was given four young women as wives. Twenty days before his death he was

dressed as a warrior and for a few days he was virtually ruler of the city. Then he and his guardians left the city for an island in the lake. As he ascended the steps of the temple, there to be sacrificed, the new Tezcatlipoca began playing his flutes in Tenochtitlán.

As we have seen, human sacrifice had long been characteristic of Mesoamerican societies, but no other Mesoamerican people practiced it on the scale of the Aztecs. Whatever other reasons for it there might have been, one effect must certainly have been to intimidate subject peoples. It may also have had the effect of reducing the population of fighting-age men from conquered provinces, and with it the possibility of rebellion. Together with the heavy burden of tribute, human sacrifice may also have fed resentment and fear, explaining why so many subject peoples were willing to throw in their lot with Cortés when he challenged the Aztecs.

Tenochtitlán Three great causeways linked Tenochtitlán to the mainland. These met at the ceremonial core of the city, dominated by a double temple dedicated to Huitzilopochtli and the rain god Tlaloc. It was here that most of the Aztec's sacrificial victims met their fate. The palaces of the ruler and high nobles lay just outside the central precinct. The ruler's palace was the empire's administrative center, with government officials, artisans and laborers, gardens, and a zoo of exotic animals. The rest of the city was divided into four quarters, and these further divided into numerous wards (*calpulli*). Some *calpulli* were specialized, reserved for merchants (*pochteca*) or artisans. The city was laid out on a grid formed of streets and canals. Agricultural plots of great fertility known as *chinampas* bordered the canal and the lake shores. Aqueducts carried fresh water from springs on the lake shore into the city. A massive dike kept the briny water of the northern part of Lake Texcoco from contaminating the waters around Tenochtitlán. The neighboring city of Tlatelolco was noted for its great marketplace.

Society Aztec society was hierarchical, authoritarian, and militaristic. It was divided into two broad classes, noble and commoner, with merchants and certain artisans forming an intermediate category. The nobility enjoyed great wealth and luxury. Laws and regulations relating to dress reinforced social divisions. Elaborate and brilliantly colored regalia distinguished nobles from commoners and rank within the nobility. Commoners were required to wear rough, simple garments.

The Aztecs were morally austere. They valued obedience, respectfulness, discipline, and moderation. Laws were strict and punishment severe. Standards for the nobility were higher than for commoners, and punishments for sexual and social offenses were more strictly enforced the higher one stood

[2]Frances F. Berdan, *The Aztecs of Central Mexico: An Imperial Society,* New York Holt, Rinehart and Winston, 1982, p. 36.
[3]Inga Clendinnen, *Aztecs: An Interpretation,* (Cambridge: Cambridge University Press, 1991), p. 8.

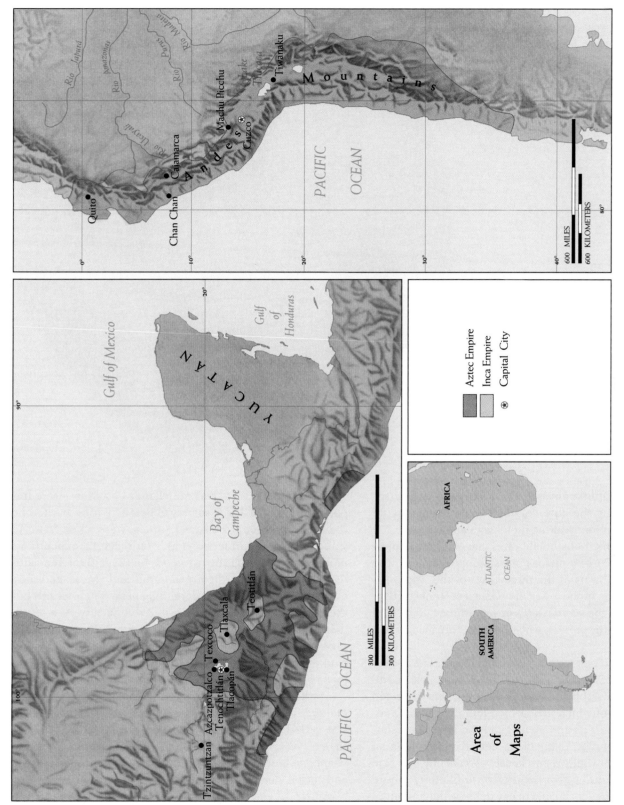

Map 15-2   The Aztec and Inca empires on the eve of the Spanish conquest.

A disc with relief carving showing the dismembered body of the Aztec moon goddess Coyolxauhqui, Huitzilopochtli's sister. She and the stars tried to prevent Huitzilopochtli's birth, but he emerged fully armed from his mother and killed her. This disc lay at the foot of the temple of Huitzilopochtli in Tenochtitlán (Stone 3.5 m diameter). [Barbara and Justin Kerr Studio]

in the hierarchy. Drunkenness was frowned upon and harshly punished among the elite. Parents would even execute their own children for breaking moral laws and customs.

The highest rank in the nobility was that of *Tlatoani* (plural *tlatoque*), or ruler of a major political unit. Of these, the highest were the rulers of the three cities of the Triple Alliance; of them, the highest was the *tlatoani* of Tenochtitlán. Below them were the *tetcutin*, lords of subordinate units. And below them were the *pipiltin*, who filled the bureaucracy and the priesthood.

The bulk of the population were commoners. It was they who farmed the *chinampas*, harvested fish from the lake, and provided labor for public projects. All commoners belonged to a *calpulli*, each of which had its own temple. Children received training in ritual and ideology in the song houses attached to these temples. Young men received military training in the *telpochcalli*, or young men's house. *Calpulli* officials were responsible for assuring that the *calpulli* fulfilled its tribute obligations. Commoners unable to pay debts or their required tribute might become slaves. They might also become slaves for some criminal offenses. A class of serfs worked the estates of noblemen.

Professional traders and merchants—*pochteca*—were important figures in Aztec society. Their activities, backed by the threat of force from Aztec armies, were a key factor in spreading Aztec influence. Their far-reaching expeditions brought back precious luxury goods for the lords of Tenochtitlán. They organized their own guilds and established their own laws and customs for doing business. Their wealth put them in an ambiguous position in Aztec society. As a result, they tended to be self-effacing and avoided ostentatious display. Artisans of luxury goods—including lapidaries, feather workers, and goldsmiths—also had their own *calpulli* and enjoyed a special status.

Markets were central to Aztec economic life. The great market at Tlatelolco impressed the Spaniards for its great size, orderliness, and the variety of goods traded there. More than 60,000 people went there daily. Market administrators, women as well as men, regulated transactions. Cacao beans and cotton cloaks served as mediums of exchange.

Above all else, Aztec society was organized for war. Although there was no standing army as such, the entire society stood on a war footing. All young men received military training, nobles in special schools reserved for them, commoners in their *calpulli* schools. Battles were fought to capture

Nezahualcoyotl of Texcoco Sings of the Giver of Life

Nezahualcoyotl, ruler of Texcoco, lived from 1402 to 1472 and was admired as a philosopher-king. In this poem he sings of the presence of the Giver of Life who invents Himself and of the ability of human beings to invoke this divinity, but at the same time he emphasizes the impossibility of achieving any close relationship with the divinity.

In what ways does this song remind you of the thought and religious traditions of the early civilizations of China, India, Egypt, and Greece? What are the characteristics of "He Who invents Himself"? What kind of relationship can human beings achieve with this being? Why does the singer compare seeking the Giver of Life with seeking someone among flowers?

In no place can be the house of He Who invents
    Himself.
But in all places He is invoked,
in all places He is venerated,
His glory, His fame are sought on the earth.
It is He Who invents everything
He is Who invents Himself: God.
In all places He is invoked,
in all places He is venerated,
His glory, His fame are sought on the earth.
No one here is able,
no one is able to be intimate
with the Giver of Life;

only He is invoked, at His side,
near to Him,
one can live on the earth.
He who finds Him,
knows only one thing; He is invoked,
at His side, near to Him,
one can live on the earth.
In truth no one is intimate with You,
O Giver of Life!
Only as among the flowers,
we might seek someone,
thus we seek You,
we who live on the earth,
while we are at Your side.
Our hearts will be troubled,
only for a short time,
we will be near You and at Your side.
The Giver of Life enrages us,
He intoxicates us here.
No one can be perhaps at His side,
be famous, rule on the earth.
Only You change things
as our hearts know it:
No one can be perhaps at His side,
be famous, rule on the earth.

From *Fifteen Poets of the Aztec World* by Miguel León-Portilla. Copyright © 1992 University of Oklahoma Press, pp. 86–86. Reprinted by permission.

---

new territory, punish rebellious or recalcitrant tributaries, protect trading expeditions, and secure access to important natural resources. Some battles—the flowery wars—were fought just to secure sacrificial victims. Combat was a matter of individual contests, not the confrontation of massed infantry. A warrior's goal was to subdue and capture prisoners for sacrifice. Prowess in battle, as measured by the number of prisoners a warrior captured, was key to social advancement and rewards for both commoners and nobles. Failure in battle brought social disgrace.

Women in Aztec society could inherit and own property. They traded in the marketplace and served as market officials. With their craft work they could provide their families with extra income. Girls and boys alike were educated in the song houses, and women had access to priestly roles, although they were barred from high religious positions. In general, however, the Aztec emphasis on warfare left women in a subordinate position, tending hearth and home and excluded from positions of high authority. As a man's primary role was to be a warrior, a woman's was to bear children, and childbirth was compared to battle. Death in childbirth, like death in battle, guaranteed rewards in the afterlife.

Andean South America

The Andean region of South America—primarily modern Peru and Bolivia—had, like Mesoamerica, a long history of indigenous civilization when Spanish conquerors arrived in the sixteenth century. This is a region of dramatic contrasts. From near the equator south, a narrow strip of desert, one of the driest in the world, lines the Pacific Coast. Beyond this strip the Andes mountains rise abruptly. Small river valleys descend the western face of the mountains, cutting the desert plain to create a series of oases from north to south. The cold waters of the Humboldt current sweep north along the coast from the Antarctic, carrying rich nutrients that support abundant sea life. Within the Andes are regions of high peaks and steep terrain, regions of grassland (*puna*), and deep, warm, fertile intermontane valleys. The eastern slopes of the

The Periods of Andean Civilization	
Preceramic	ca. 3000–ca. 2000 B.C.E.
Initial Period	ca. 2000–ca. 800 B.C.E.
Early Horizon	ca. 800–ca. 200 B.C.E.
Early Intermediate Period	ca. 200 B.C.E.–ca. 600 C.E.
Middle Horizon	ca. 600 B.C.E.–ca. 800/1000 C.E.
Late Intermediate Period	ca. 800/1000–ca. 1475
Late Horizon (Inca Empire)	ca. 1475–1532

mountains, covered with dense vegetation, descend into the great tropical rain forest of the Amazon basin.

From ancient times, the people of the coast lived by exploiting the marine resources of the Pacific and by cultivating maize, beans, squash, and cotton. They also engaged in long-distance trade by sea along the Pacific Coast.

The people of the highlands domesticated several plants native to the Andean region, including the potato, other tubers, and a grain called quinoa. They cultivated (and still cultivate) these crops on the high slopes of the Andes. In the intermontane valleys they cultivated maize. And in the *puna* grasslands they kept herds of llamas and alpacas—the Andean camelids—using them for their fur, their meat, and as beasts of burden. Highland communities since ancient times have maintained access to the different resources available in different altitude zones, with holdings in each zone that can be far distant from each other. They share this adaptation, which anthropologists sometimes call *verticality*, with people in other mountainous regions, such as the Alps and the Himalayas.[4]

Andean civilization is conventionally divided into seven periods: The Early, Middle, and Late Horizons are periods in which a homogeneous art style spread over a wide area. The intermediate periods are characterized by regional stylistic diversity.

The Preceramic and the Initial Period

The earliest monumental architecture in Peru dates to the early third millenium B.C.E., roughly contemporary with the Great Pyramids of Egypt. Located on the coast mostly near the shore, these earliest centers consist of ceremonial mounds and plazas and predate the introduction of pottery to Peru.

[4]Michael Mosley, *The Incas and Their Ancestors*, (New York and London: Thames and Hudson, 1992), p. 42.

Coastal people at this time subsisted primarily on the bounties of the sea, supplementing their diets with squash, beans, and chili peppers cultivated in the floodplains of the coastal rivers. They also cultivated gourds—for use as containers and utensils—and cotton. The cotton fishing nets and other textiles of this period represent the beginning of the sophisticated Andean textile tradition.

The earliest public buildings in the highlands date to before 2500 B.C.E. These are typically stone-walled structures enclosing a sunken fire pit used to burn ritual offerings. The distribution of these structures, first identified at the site of Kotosh, suggests that highland people shared a set of religious beliefs that archaeologists have called the *Kotosh religious tradition*. Highland people were more dependent on agriculture than coastal people during the late Preceramic, cultivating maize as well as potatoes and other highland tubers. Llamas and alpacas were fully domesticated by about 2500 B.C.E.

There is little evidence of social stratification for the late Preceramic. The public structures of both the coast and the highlands appear to have been centers of community ritual for relatively egalitarian societies.

The introduction of pottery to Peru around 2000 B.C.E. marks the beginning of the Initial period and corresponds to a major shift in settlement and subsistence patterns on the coast. People became increasingly dependent on agriculture as well as on maritime resources. They moved their settlements inland, built irrigation systems, began cultivating maize, and built large and impressive ceremonial centers. The form of these centers varied by region. On the central coast, for example, they consisted primarily of large U-shaped structures that faced inland, toward the mountains and the source of the water that nourished the coastal crops. On the north coast they consisted of large circular sunken courts and large platform structures. Centers were adorned with stone and adobe sculpture, and their facades were brightly painted. Population grew and society became gradually but increasingly stratified. Incised carvings of bodies with severed heads at Cerro Sechín and Sechín Alto in the Casma suggest growing conflict. Centers apparently remained independent of one another, however, with little evidence to suggest larger political groupings.

Chavín de Huantar and the Early Horizon

The large coastal centers of the Initial period declined early in the first millenium B.C.E. At about the same time, beginning around 800 B.C.E., a site in the highlands, Chavín de Huantar, was growing in influence (see Map 15–3). Located on a trade route between the coast and the lowland tropical

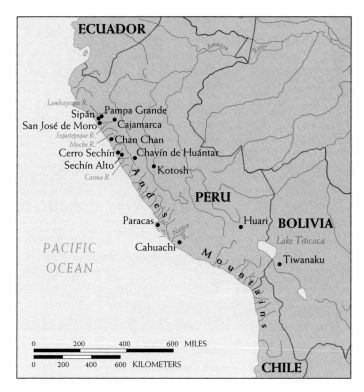

Map 15-3 Pre-Inca sites discussed in this chapter.

mains at Chavín, for example, suggests that people who lived closer to the ceremonial center ate better than people living on the margins of the site.

The Early Intermediate Period

Signs of increasing warfare accompany the collapse of the Chavín culture and the ideological unity it had brought to the Andes. The subsequent Early Intermediate Period saw increasing regional diversity combined with increasing political centralization and the emergence of what were probably the first territorial states in the Andes. We will discuss briefly here only the two best-known cultures of this period, that of Nazca on the south coast of Peru, and of Moche on the north coast.

Nazca

The Nazca culture, which flourished from about 100 B.C.E. to about 700 C.E. was centered in the Ica and Nazca valleys. The people of the Nazca Valley built underground aqueducts to tap ground water in the middle of the valley and divert it into irrigation canals. Cahuachi, the largest Nazca site, was once thought to be a large, permanently occupied urban center. Recent research, however, indicates that it was empty most of the year, filling periodically with pilgrims during religious festivals. It may have been the capital of a Nazca confederation, with each of its many temple platforms representing a member unit.

The earlier Paracas culture on the south coast produced some of the world's finest and most intricate textiles. The Nazca too are renowned for their textiles as well as their fine polychrome pottery, elaborately decorated with images of Andean plants and animals. They may be most famous, however, for their colossal earthworks, or geoglyphs, the so-called Nazca lines. These were created by brushing away the dark gravel of the desert to reveal a lighter-colored surface. Some geoglyphs depict figures like hummingbirds, spiders, and killer whales that appear on Nazca pottery. These are usually located on hillsides visible to passers-by. Others, usually consisting of radiating lines and geometric forms, are drawn on the Nazca pampa flats and are only visible from the air.

Moche

The Moche culture flourished from about 200 to 700 C.E. on the north coast of Peru. At its height it dominated all the coastal river valleys from Piura in the north to Huarmey in the south, a distance of some 370 miles. The culture takes its name from the Moche Valley, the location of its largest center next to Cerro Blanco. Two huge structures, the Pyramid of

rain forest, Chavín was the center of a powerful religious cult with a population of perhaps 3,000 at its height. The architecture of its central temple complex, which includes U-shaped structures and a sunken circular courtyard, reflects coastal influence. Its artistic iconography draws on many tropical forest animals, including monkeys, serpents, and jaguars. The structure known as the Old Temple is honeycombed with passageways and drains. Archaeologists think that water could be deliberately channeled through these drains to produce a roaring sound. At the end of the central passageway is an imposing stela in the shape of a knife with the blade in the floor and the handle in the ceiling. Known as the Lanzon, this stela is carved in the image of a fanged deity that combines human and feline features. A small hole in the ceiling above the Lanzon suggests that it may have been an oracle whose "voice" was that of a priest in the gallery above.

Between about 400 and 200 B.C.E. Chavín influence spread widely throughout Peru, from the Nazca Valley in the south to beyond Cajamarca in the north. This spread is seen in both the distribution of goods made at Chavín and in the incorporation of Chavín iconography into local traditions. Archaeologists believe Chavín influence reflects the prestige of its cult, not political or military expansion. The florescence of Chavín was also marked by important technological innovations in ceramics, weaving, and metallurgy.

Excavations at Chavín and other Early Horizon sites point to increasing social stratification. Examination of skeletal re-

"Embroidered Mantle with Bird Impersonators." Fine textiles were a source of prestige and wealth in ancient Peruvian societies. This mantle was made by the people of the Paracas culture on the south coast of Peru around 50–100 C.E. (Plain weave w/stem stitch embroidery, camelid fiber). [Gift of Denman W. Ross, Courtesy of Museum of Fine Arts, Boston. ©1996. All Rights Reserved]

the Sun and the Pyramid of the Moon, overlook this site. The cross-shaped Pyramid of the Sun, the largest adobe structure in the Americas, was some 1,200 feet long by 500 feet wide and rose in steps to a height of 60 feet. It was made with more than 143 million adobe bricks, each of which had a mark that probably identified the group that made it. Archaeologists think the marks enabled Moche lords to be sure that subject groups fulfilled their tribute obligations.

It was once thought that Cerro Blanco was the capital of a unified Moche empire. It appears now, however, that the Moche may not have been so centralized. Instead the Moche area may have been divided into northern and southern realms, and each valley ruled by Moche lords from its own center. Pampa Grande, a Moche site in the Lambayeque Valley, was almost as large as Cerro Blanco.

The Moche were skilled potters, producing molded and painted vessels that reveal much about Moche life, religion, and warfare. Realistic portrait vessels may depict actual people. Other vessels provide evidence about the appearance of Moche architecture and the kind of regalia worn by the elite. The discovery in the late 1980s of the undisturbed tombs of Moche rulers at the site of Sipan in the Lambayeque Valley and San José de Moro in the Jequetepeque Valley suggests that a central theme in Moche iconography—the sacrifice ceremony—was an actual Moche ritual. Depictions of the sacrifice ceremony show elaborately dressed figures drinking the blood of sacrificed prisoners. Archaeologists have labeled one of the central figures the Warrior Priest and another the Priest-

ess. The Moche lord in one of the tombs at Sipan was buried in the regalia of the Warrior Priest, and the occupant of one of the tombs at San José de Moro was buried in the regalia of the Priestess. (See page 396 for an example of Mochean art.)

The Moche were also the most sophisticated smiths in the Andes. They developed innovative alloys, cast weapons and agricultural tools, and used the lost-wax process to create small, intricate works.

The Middle Horizon Through the Late Intermediate Period

Tiwanaku and Huari

In the fifth century C.E., when the Germanic invasions were leading to the disintegration of the Roman Empire and as Teotihuacán was reaching its height in Mesoamerica, the first expansionist empires were emerging in the Andean highlands. One of these was centered at Tiwanaku in the Bolivian altiplano near the south shore of Lake Titicaca, and the other at Huari, in the south-central highlands of Peru. Although they differ in many ways, both are associated with productive new agricultural technologies, and both show evidence of a form of statecraft that reflects Andean verticality—the practice of sending out settlements to exploit the region's varied ecological zones—and that foreshadows the administrative practices of the later Inca empire. The artistic symbolism of both also shares many features, suggesting a shared religious ideology. Archaeologists still do not have a firm grip on the chronology of Tiwanaku and Huari or the relationship between them.

Tiwanaku lies at more than 12,600 feet above sea level, making it the highest capital in the ancient world. Construction apparently began at the site about 200 C.E. It began its expansionist phase about 500–600 C.E., and collapsed some 500 years later in the eleventh century. The city occupied one to two square miles, and may have had a population of some 20,000–40,000 people at its height. Laid out on a grid, it is dominated by several large and impressive public structures and ceremonial gateways. The effort expended in transporting the stone for these monuments was enormous, and indicates the power of the Tiwanaku's rulers over the labor of their subjects.

A system of raised-field agriculture on the shores of Lake Titicaca provided Tiwanaku with its economic base. This system involved farming on artificial platforms capped with rich topsoil and separated by basins of water. Experimental reconstructions have shown it to be extremely productive.

Tiwanaku dominated the Titicaca basin and neighboring regions. It probably exerted its influence through its religious prestige and by establishing colonies and religious-administrative structures in distant territories.

The Huari empire flourished from about 600 to 800 C.E., dominating the highlands from near Cuzco in the south to Cajamarca in the north. For a brief period it also extended a fortified colony into Tiwanaku territory. The capital, Huari, covers about 1.5 square miles. It consists of a sprawl of large, high-walled stone enclosures, and had a population of 20,000–30,000 people.

Huari is located in an intermontane valley and its rise is associated with the development of techniques for terracing and irrigating the slopes of the valley to increase their productivity. The spread of this beneficial technology may have facilitated the expansion of the Huari empire, explaining its acceptance in most places without signs of overt military domination. Huari administrative centers were undefended and built in accessible places. Many archaeologists think they may have functioned like later Inca administrative centers, housing a small Huari elite that organized local labor for state projects. Again like the Inca, Huari administrators used *quipu* record-keeping devices made of string. Inca *quipu*, however, used knots, whereas Huari *quipu* used different-colored string.

The Chimu Empire

Although there is evidence of Huari influence on the Peruvian north coast, it is unlikely to have taken the form of direct political control. After the demise of Moche authority,

two new states emerged on the north coast. One, named for the site of Sican, was centered in the Lambayeque Valley. The central figure in Sican iconography, the Sican Lord, may have been a representation of a mythical founder figure named Nyamlap, mentioned in post-conquest Spanish chronicles. Like their Moche predecessors in the Lambayeque Valley, the Sican people were skilled smiths who produced sumptuous gold objects.

The other new north coast state, known as Chimu, was centered in the Moche Valley. In two waves of expansion the Chimu built an empire that incorporated the Lambayeque Valley and stretched for 800 miles along the coast, from the border of Ecuador in the north to the Chillon Valley in the south. The administrative capital of this empire, Chan Chan, in the Moche Valley, was a vast city. Its walls enclosed eight square miles and its central core covered over two square miles. The focus of the city are some ten immense adobe-walled enclosures known as *ciudadelas*. With their large open plazas, their administrative and storage facilities, and their large burial mounds, these probably housed the empire's ruling elite. Surrounding them were smaller compounds that probably housed the lesser nobility. And surrounding these were the homes and workshops of the artisans and workers who served the elite. Two areas were apparently transport centers, where llama caravans brought raw materials to the capital from the empire's territories. The total population of the city was between 30,000 and 40,000.

In about 1470, only sixty years before the arrival of the Spaniards, the Chimu empire was swept away by a powerful new state from the southern highlands of Peru, the Inca empire.

The Inca Empire

In 1532, when Francisco Pizarro and his companions happened on it, the Inca empire was one of the largest states in the world, rivaling China and the Ottoman empire in size. Its domains encompassed the area between the Pacific Coast and the Amazon basin for some 2,600 miles, from Ecuador to northern Chile (see Map 15–2). Its ethnically and linguistically diverse population numbered in the millions.

The Inca themselves called their domain *Tawantinsuyu*, the Land of the Four Quarters. Their capital, Cuzco, lay at the intersection of these divisions. Home to the ruler (Inca) and the ruling elite, it was a city of great splendor and magnificence. Its principal temples, dedicated to the sun and moon, gleamed with gold and silver.

The origins of the Inca are obscure. According to their own traditions, Inca expansion began only in the fifteenth century in the wake of a revolt of the Chanca people that nearly destroyed Cuzco. Inca Yupanqui, son of the city's aging ruler, led a heroic resistance and crushed the revolt. Assuming the name Pachacuti, he laid the foundations of Inca statecraft; he and his successors expanded their domains to bring the blessings of civilization to the rest of the Andean world. There is clearly an element of imperial propaganda in this legend. The Inca did expand dramatically in the fifteenth century, but archaeological evidence suggests that they had been expanding their influence for decades and perhaps centuries before the Chanca revolt.

The Inca enlarged their empire through a combination of alliance and intimidation as well as conquest. They organized their realm into a hierarchical administrative structure and imposed a version of their language, Quechua, as the administrative language of the empire. As a result, Quechua is still widely spoken in the Peruvian Andes.

Unlike the Aztecs, who extracted tribute from their subject peoples, the Inca relied on various forms of labor taxation. They divided agricultural lands into several categories, allowing local populations to retain some for their own support and reserving others for the state and the gods. In a system known as the *mita*, local people worked for the state on a regular basis, receiving in return gifts and lavish state-sponsored ritual entertainments. Men also served in the army and on public works projects, building cities and roads, for example, and terracing hillsides. In a policy that reflects the Andean practice of colonizing ecologically varied regions, the Inca also designated entire communities as *Mitimaqs*, moving them about, sometimes great distances, to best exploit the resources of their empire. They sometimes settled loyal people in hostile regions and moved hostile people to loyal regions.

The Inca employed several groups of people in what amounted to full-time state service. One of these, the *mamakuna*, consisted of women who lived privileged but celibate and carefully regulated lives in cities and towns throughout the empire. *Mamakuna* might also be given in marriage by Inca rulers to cement alliances. These so-called "Virgins of the Sun" played an important economic as well as religious role, weaving and brewing the maize beer known as *chicha* for the Inca elite. Textiles were highly prized in Andean society, and cloth was a form of wealth among the Incas. Chicha had great ritual importance and was consumed at state religious festivals. Another group of full-time state workers, the *yanakuna*, were men whose duties included tending the royal llama herds.

Cloth and clothing was not only a principal source of wealth and prestige in Inca society. It was also a means of

The Inca city of Machu Picchu perches on a saddle between two peaks on the eastern slopes of the Andes. [Robert Frerk/Odyssey Productions]

The Incas Organize Their Empire

The Incas were remarkable for their ability to organize a vast and diverse empire. One of their chief devices of government was the movement of large groups of people to new, unfamiliar provinces. The Incas were also very sensitive to the power of religion and religious rituals. Once they had moved a population, they required that the chief object of worship belonging to that people be moved to the Inca capital of Cuzco where it was attended by representatives of its original worshippers. This latter group was changed from time to time, allowing portions of the transferred population to become familiar with the language and customs of the court city of Cuzco. These processes of government are described in the following passage by Bernabé Cobo (1582–1657), a Jesuit, whose account is regarded as among the most complete and accurate discussions of Inca culture.

To what extent did the Incas appear to be following a classic mode of rule by dividing and conquering? How did the Incas use one group to balance the threat to their rule from another group? How did they use religion and language to strengthen their authority?

The first thing that these kings did after conquering a province was to remove six or seven thousand families . . . and to transfer these families to the quiet, peaceful provinces, assigning them to different towns. In their stead they introduced the same number of people, taken from the places to which the former families had been sent or from such other places as seemed convenient. . . . In these transfers of population they saw to it that the migrants, both the newly conquered persons and the others, were moved to lands whose climate and conditions were the same as, or similar to, those which they had left behind them. . . .

The Incas introduced these changes of domicile in order to maintain their rule with greater ease, quiet, and security. . . . [T]hey ordered the majority of the *mitimaes* [the groups transferred] whom they sent to the recently conquered towns to make their homes in the provincial capitals, where they served as garrisons. . . . As soldiers they received certain privileges to make them appear of nobler rank, and they were ordered always to obey the slightest commands of their captains and governors. Under this plan, it the natives revolted, the *mitimaes*, being devoted to the governors, soon reduced them to obedience to the Inca; and if the *mitimaes* rioted they were repressed and punished by the natives; thus, through this scheme of domiciling the majority of the people of some province in other parts, the king was made secure against revolts in his dominions. . . . The Incas required everyone to absorb their language, laws, and religion with all the beliefs about these matter that were established at Cuzco. . . . In order to introduce and establish these things more effectively, . . . they would remove the principal idol from a conquered province and set it up in Cuzco with the same attendance and worship that it had formerly had; all this was seen to by persons who had come from that province . . . For this reasons Indians from every province of the kingdom were at all times in residence in the capital and court, occupied in guarding and ministering to their own idols. Thus they learned the usages and customs of the court; and when they were replaced by others . . . they taught their people what they had seen and learned in the court.

From *Historia del Nuevo Mundo* Bernabé Cobe (Seville, 1890–1893), 3: 222–225; Benjamin Keen, trans., as reprinted in Benjamin Keen, ed., *Readings in Latin American Civilization 1492 to the Present* (Boston: Houghton Mifflin Company, 1955), pp. 29–30.

communication. Complex textile patterns served as insignia of social status, indicating a person's rank and ethnic affiliation. Textile production was among the forms of labor service required by the state, and Inca warehouses were filled with textiles as well as with food and other craft goods.

The Incas made their presence felt in their empire through regional administrative centers and warehouses linked by a remarkable system of roads. The centers served to organize, house, and feed people engaged in *mita* labor service and to impress upon them the power and beneficence of the state with feasting and ritual. The wealth of the empire, collected in storehouses, sustained the *mita* laborers, fed and clothed the army, and enriched the Inca elite. Although the Inca lacked writing, they kept detailed administrative records on string accounting devices called *quipu*.

To move their armies, administer their domains, and distribute the wealth of their empire efficiently, the Inca built more than 14,000 miles of road. These ranged from narrow paths to wide thoroughfares. Rope suspension bridges crossed gorges and rivers, and stairways eased the ascent of steep slopes. A system of relay runners sped messages to Cuzco from the reaches of the empire.

Over their long history the people of the Andes developed an adaptation to their challenging environment that allowed them to prosper and grow, bringing more land under cultivation than today. Building on ancient Andean traditions, the

Inca appear to have engineered a productive economy that brought its people a measure of well-being that would not survive the destruction of the empire by Spanish invaders.

IN WORLD PERSPECTIVE

Ancient Civilizations of the Americas

Civilization in the Americas before 1492 developed independently of civilization in the Old World. As the kings of Egypt were erecting their pyramid tombs, the people of the desert coast of Peru were erecting temple platforms. While King Solomon ruled in Jerusalem, the Olmec were creating their monumental stone heads. As Rome reached its apogee and then declined, so did the great city of Teotihuacán in the Valley of Mexico. As Islam spread from its heartland, the rulers of Tikal brought their city to its greatest splendor before its abrupt collapse. Maya mathematics and astronomy rivaled that of any other peoples of the ancient world. And as the aggressive nation-states of Europe were emerging from their feudal past, the Aztecs and Incas were consolidating their great empires.

The encounter between Old World and New, however, would prove devastating for American civilization. The technology that allowed Europeans to embark on the voyages of discovery and fight destructive wars among themselves caught the great native empires unprepared. Uncertain how to respond to these aggressive foreigners, they succumbed.

Review Questions

1. Describe the rise of civilization in Mesoamerica and Andean South America. What does it have in common with the rise of civilization in Africa and Eurasia? In what ways was it different?

2. The appearance of monumental architecture in the ancient world was often associated with hierarchical agricultural societies. Was this the case for the Peruvian coast?

3. What were some of the accomplishments of the Classic Period civilizations of Mesoamerica? How do they compare with contemporary civilizations elsewhere in the world?

4. How was the Aztec empire organized? The Inca empire? How do they compare to the early empires of the ancient world in the Near East, Europe, and Asia?

5. Both the Aztec and Inca empires fell in the early sixteenth century when confronted with Spanish forces of a few hundred men. What do you think might have been some of the reasons for their defeat?

Suggested Readings

B. S. BAUER, *The Development of the Inca State* (1992). An important new work that emphasizes archaeological evidence over the Spanish chronicles in accounting for the emergence of the Inca empire.

F. F. BERDAN, *The Aztecs of Central Mexico: An Imperial Society* (1982). An excellent introduction to the Aztecs.

R. E. BLANTON, S. A. KOWALEWSKI, G. FEINMAN, AND J. APPEL, *Ancient Mesoamerica: A Comparison of Change in Three Regions* (1981). Concentrates on ancient Mexico.

K. O. BRUHNS, *Ancient South America* (1994). A clear discussion of the archaeology and civilization of the region with emphasis on the Andes.

R. L. BURGER, *Chavín and the Origins of Andean Civilization.* (1992). A detailed study of early Andean prehistory by one of the leading authorities on Chavín.

R. M. CARMACK, J. GASCO, AND G. H. GOSSEN, *The Legacy of Mesoamerica: History and Culture of a Native American Civilization* (1996). A survey of Mesoamerica from its origins to the present.

I. CLENDINNEN, *Aztecs: An Interpretation* (1995). A fascinating attempt to reconstruct the Aztec world.

M. D. COE, *Breaking the Maya Code* (1992). The story of the remarkable achievement of deciphering the ancient Maya language.

M. D. COE, *The Maya* (1993). The best introduction.

M. D. COE, *Mexico from the Olmecs to the Aztecs* (1994). A wide-ranging introductory discussion.

G. CONRAD AND A. A. DEMAREST, *Religion and Empire: The Dynamics of Aztec and Inca Expansionism* (1984). An interesting comparative study.

S. D. GILLESPIE, *The Aztec Kings* (1989).

R. HASSIG, *Aztec Warfare.*

J. HYSLOP, *Inka Settlement Planning* (1990). A detailed study.

M. LEÓN-PORTILLA, *Fifteen Poets of the Aztec World* (1992). An anthology of translations of Aztec poetry.

M. E. MILLER, *The Art of Mesoamerica from Olmec to Aztec* (1986). A well-illustrated introduction.

C. MORRIS AND A. VON HAGEN, *The Inka Empire and Its Andean Origins* (1993). A clear overview of Andean prehistory by a leading authority. Beautifully illustrated.

M. E. MOSELY, *The Incas and Their Ancestors: The Archaeology of Peru* (1992). Readable and thorough.

J. A. SABLOFF, *The Cities of Ancient Mexico* (1989). Capsule summaries of ancient Mesoamerican cultures.

J. A. SABLOFF, *Archaeology and the Maya* (1990). A look at changing views of the ancient Maya.

L. SCHELE and M. E. MILLER, *The Blood of Kings* (1986). A rich and beautifully illustrated study of ancient Maya art and society.

R. S. SHARER, *The Ancient Maya*, 5th ed. (1994). A classic. Readable, authoritative, and thorough.

M. P. WEAVER, *The Aztecs, Maya, and Their Predecessor.* A classic textbook.

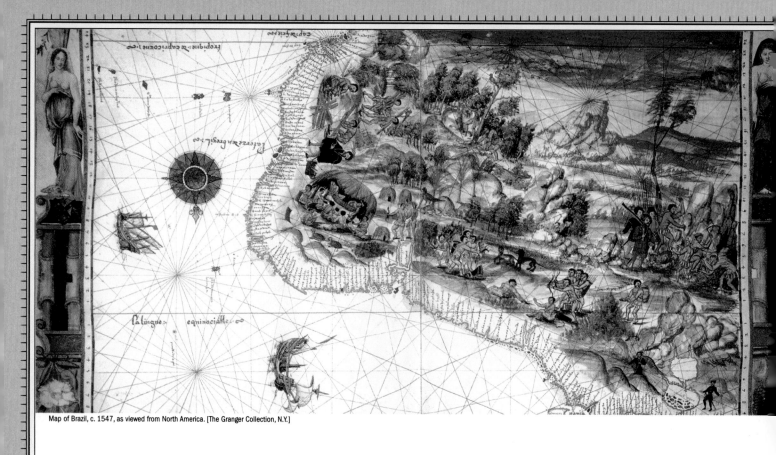

Map of Brazil, c. 1547, as viewed from North America. [The Granger Collection, N.Y.]

THE WORLD
IN TRANSITION

Between 1500 and 1800, the major centers of world civilization achieved political organization and stability that in some cases endured to the end of the 20th century. This period also witnessed a shift in the balance of world political and economic power toward Europe. That shift was anything but inevitable. It was the result of paths taken by Europeans and not taken by the peoples and governments of other areas of the world.

Sixteenth-century Japan was torn by feudal wars among its various small states and regions. This civil conflict eroded the manorial social structure. The adoption of the spear and then the musket in place of the sword allowed the development of foot-soldier armies that displaced the mounted samurai. By approximately 1600, however, a new political regime was estab-lishing itself on the basis of a "feudal" society involving complex vassal-lord relationships in many, although not all, ways similar to those in medieval Europe. Tokugawa Ieyasu established his government in Edo (now Tokyo). Through a series of land transfers and confiscations, he surrounded himself with unquestionably loyal retainers and placed those of less certain loyalty at far geographical locations removed from his capital. He and his successors required their vassals to send their families to live as virtual hostages near the court in Edo. Finally, Tokugawa Japan adopted a policy of isolation from the rest of the world. Although stable and relatively prosperous, Japan remained separated from the larger world from the 1630s until the middle of the nineteenth century.

Spared comparable civil strife, China entered on an epoch of remarkable strength, expansion, and cultural achievement. The Ming and Ch'ing dynasties ruled for more than five centuries, and only a short period of strife accompanied the transfer of power from one to the other in 1644. The emperors of both dynasties governed in an absolute manner. The bureaucracy—referred to as *mandarins* by the Jesuits, who came to China in the sixteenth century—was chosen meritocratically through a complex series of examinations, and it governed efficiently. The population of China expanded steadily. China experienced a third commercial revolution. Chinese shipping expanded. Although a truly national economy did not emerge, China possessed several regional economies, each as large as that of a major European national state. A banking system spread through the country to foster commerce. What did not occur in China, for all its commercial enterprise, was the development of industrialism. Nonetheless, at the end of this era China appeared to be a very strong, stable nation. As in Japan, Confucian teachings had become ever more influential.

In 1550, over a century of continued political and military strength lay before the Islamic world. The Ottoman Empire was at the time perhaps the most powerful military state in the world. The Safavids securely governed Iran as would the Mughals in India a few years later. However, by the middle of the seventeenth century the power of all three empires was on the wane even as their cultural vitality was still immense. The growing military and naval strength of Europe defeated the Ottoman Turks at the sea battle of Lepanto in 1571 and in numerous land engagements during the seventeenth century. The final Turkish siege of Vienna failed in 1683. In Iran the intense religiosity of the Shi'ite Safavids led to the neglect of political and military structures and, consequently, to difficulty in halting aggression from the Turks. At the same time, a distinctive mode of Shi'ite pietism arose among the populace in Iran. The Mughal Empire in India experienced a slow but steady decline after the late seventeenth century. By the battle of Plassey in 1757 the British East India Company had established a position of strength from which, within less than a century, Britain would come to govern the entire Indian subcontinent.

Early in the sixteenth century western Europe began to be divided between Protestantism and Roman Catholicism. The sectarian splintering that has resulted in hundreds of modern Protestant denominations also began at this time. Even within Catholicism, deep divisions developed between Catholics who favored traditional practices and those who championed the reforms of the Counter-Reformation and the Jesuits. A century and a half of religious war and theological conflict followed.

Rulers made the most of these divisions to consolidate their territories politically. Confessionalization (that is, strict enforcement of a particular "orthodox" religious belief and practice) went hand in hand with the creation of modern Western states.

Four factors account largely for this momentous shift in the cultural balance of the Western world. First, the new monarchies that had arisen in the late Middle Ages, particularly in France, England, and Spain, now successfully unified their realms. Between 1500 and the middle of the eighteenth century those monarchs learned to tame their aristocracies, to collect taxes efficiently, and to build effective armies and navies. Second, in league with the commercial sectors of their national economies, the monarchs and their bureaucrats encouraged voyages of commercial expansion and discovery. Through those voyages Europeans penetrated markets across the globe. They also conquered and colonized the American continents and thereby Europeanized two vast, rich land masses much larger than Europe itself.

Third, during the seventeenth century European thinkers carried out new intellectual explorations that culminated in the Scientific Revolution. The new knowledge and methods of rational investigation of physical nature permitted them to develop their technological skills more fully. As a consequence, the fourth factor came into play as Europeans, and most particularly the British, achieved an early foundation of industrial manufacturing that would permit further domination of world markets with inexpensive consumer goods.

1500–1600

1517–1555 Protestant Reformation
1533–1584 Ivan the Terrible of Russia reigns
1540 Jesuit Order founded by Ignatius Loyola
1543–1727 Scientific Revolution
1556–1598 Philip II of Spain reigns
1558–1603 Elizabeth I of England reigns
1562–1598 French wars of religion
1581 The Netherlands declares its independence from the Spanish Habsburgs
1588 Defeat of the Spanish Armada
1589–1610 Henry IV, Navarre, founds Bourbon dynasty of France

1500–1722 Safavid Shi'ite rule in Iran
1512–1520 Ottoman ruler Selim I
1520–1566 Ottoman ruler Suleiman the Magnificent
1525–1527 Babur founds Mughal dynasty in India
1540 Hungary under Ottoman rule
1556–1605 Akbar the Great of India reigns
1571 Battle of Lepanto; Ottomans defeated
ca. 1571–1640 Safavid philosopher-writer Mullah Sadra
1588–1629 Shah Abbas I of Iran reigns

Queen Elizabeth I

1600–1700

1618–1648 Thirty Years' War
1640–1688 Frederick William, the Great Elector, reigns in Brandenburg-Prussia
1642–1646 Puritan Revolution in England
1643–1715 Louis XIV of France reigns
1682–1725 Peter the Great of Russia reigns
1688 Glorious Revolution in England
1690 "Second Treatise of Civil Government," by John Locke

1628–1657 Shah Jahan reigns; builds Taj Mahal as mausoleum for his beloved wife
1646 Founding of Maratha empire
1648 Delhi becomes capital of Mughal Empire
1658–1707 Shah Aurangzeb, the "World Conqueror," reigns in India; end of religious toleration toward Hindus; beginning Mughal decline
1669–1683 Last military expansion by Ottomans: 1669, seize Crete; 1670s, the Ukraine; 1683, Vienna

1700–1800

1701 Act of Settlement provides for Protestant succession to English throne
1702–1713 War of Spanish Succession
1740–1748 War of Austrian Succession
1756–1763 Seven Years' War
ca. 1750 Industrial Revolution begins in England
1772 First partition of Poland
1789 First French Revolution
1793 and 1795 Last two partitions of Poland

1700 Sikhs and Marathas bring down Mughal Imperial Power
1708 British East India Company and New East India Company merge
1722 Last Safavid ruler forced to abdicate
1724 Rise in the Deccan of the Islamic state of Hyderabad
1725 Nadir Shah of Afghanistan becomes ruler of Persia
1739 Persian invasion of northern India, by Nadir Shah
1748–1761 Ahmad Shah Durrani of Afghanistan invades India
1757 British victory at Plassey, in Bengal

1500–1800 Commercial revolution in Ming-Ch'ing China; trade with Europe; flourishing of the novel

1543 Portuguese arrive in Japan

1568–1600 Era of unification follows end of Warring States Era in Japan

1587 Spanish arrive in Japan

1588 Hideyoshi's sword hunt in Japan

1592–1598 Ming troops battle Hideyoshi's army in Korea

1506 East coast of Africa under Portuguese domination

1507 Mozambique founded by Portuguese

1517 Spanish crown authorizes slave trade to its South American colonies; rapid increase in importation of slaves to the New World

1554–1659 Sa'did Sultanate in Morocco

1575 Union of Bornu and Kanem by Idris Alawma (r. 1575–1610); Kanem-Bornu state the most fully Islamic in West Africa

1591 Moroccan army defeats Songhai army; Songhai Empire collapses

1519 Conquest of the Aztecs by Cortes; Aztec ruler, Montezuma (r. 1502–1519) killed; Tenochtitlán destroyed

1529 Mexico City becomes capital of the Viceroyalty of New Spain

1533 Pizarro begins his conquest of the Incas

1536 Spanish under Mendoza arrive in Argentina

1544 Lima becomes capital of the Viceroyalty of Peru

1584 Sir Walter Raleigh sends expedition to Roanoke Island (North Carolina)

Algonquin village of Secoton

1600 Tokugawa Ieyasu wins battle of Sekigahara, completes unification of Japan

1600–1868 Tokugawa shogunate in Edo

1630s Seclusion adopted as national policy in Japan

1644–1694 Bashō, Japanese poet

1644–1911 Ch'ing (Manchu) dynasty in China

1661–1722 K'ang Hsi reign in China

1673–1681 Revolt of southern generals in China

1699 British East India Company arrives in China

1600s English, Dutch, and French enter the slave trade; slaves imported to sugar plantations in the Caribbean

1619 First African slaves in North America land in Virginia

1652 First Cape Colony settlement of Dutch East India Company

1660–1856 Omani domination of East Africa; Omani state centered in Zanzibar; 1698, takes Mozambique from Portuguese

1607 The London Company establishes Jamestown Colony (Virginia)

1608 Champlain founds Quebec

1619 Slave labor introduced at Jamestown (Virginia)

African captives, eighteenth century print

1701 Forty-seven rōnin incident in Japan

1716–1733 Reforms of Tokugawa Yoshimune in Japan

1737–1795 Reign of Ch'ien Lung in China

1742 Christianity banned in China

1784 American traders arrive in China

1787–1793 Matsudaira Sadanobu's reforms in Japan

1798 White Lotus Rebellion in China

1702 Asiento Guinea Trade Company founded for slave trade between Africa and the Americas

1700s Transatlantic slave trade at its height

1741–1856 United Sultanate of Oman and Zanzibar

1754–1817 Usman Dan Fodio, founder of sultanate in northern and central Nigeria; the Fulani become the ruling class in the region

1762 End of Funj Sultanate in eastern Sudanic region

1733 Georgia founded as last English colony in North America

1739–1763 Era of trade wars in Americas between Great Britain and the French and Spanish

1763 Peace of Paris establishes British government in Canada

1776–1781 American Revolution

1783–1830 Simón Bolívar, Latin American soldier, statesman

1789 U.S. Constitution

1791 Negro slave revolt in French Santo Domingo

1791 Canada Constitution Act divides the country into Upper and Lower Canada

16 THE LATE MIDDLE AGES AND THE RENAISSANCE IN THE WEST (1300–1527)

This work by Donatello shows a youthful, sexy David standing awkwardly and seemingly puzzled on the head of the slain Goliath. Created in 1440, it is the first free-standing nude sculpted in the west since Roman times.

[Erich Lessing/Art Resource, N.Y.]

◆ Political and Social Breakdown

◆ Ecclesiastical Breakdown and Revival:
  The Late Medieval Church

◆ The Renaissance in Italy (1375–1527)

◆ Italy's Political Decline:
  The French Invasions (1494–1527)

◆ Revival of Monarchy: Nation Building
  in the Fifteenth Century

The late Middle Ages and the Renaissance were a time of unprecedented calamity and of bold new beginnings in Europe. France and England grappled with each other in a bitter conflict known as the Hundred Years' War (1337–1453), an exercise in seemingly willful self-destruction made even more terrible in its later stages by the introduction of gunpowder and the invention of heavy artillery. Bubonic plague, known to contemporaries as the Black Death, swept over almost all of Europe, killing as much as one third of the population in many regions between 1348 and 1350 and transforming many pious Christians into believers in the omnipotence of death. A schism emerged within the church that lasted thirty-nine years (1378–1417) and led, by 1409, to the election of no fewer than three competing popes and colleges of cardinals. In 1453 the Turks captured Constantinople and threatened the west. As their political and religious institutions buckled; as disease, bandits, and wolves attacked their cities in the wake of war; and as Islamic armies assailed their southwestern borders, Europeans beheld what seemed to be the imminent total collapse of western civilization.

But despite the unprecedented chaos, the late Middle Ages also witnessed a rebirth that would continue into the seventeenth century. Two modern Dutch scholars have employed the same word (*Herfsttij*, "harvesttide") with different connotations to describe the period, one interpreting the word as a "waning" or "decline" (Johan Huizinga), the other as a true "harvest" (Heiko Oberman). If something was dying, ripe fruit and seed grain were also being gathered.

During this period scholars criticized medieval assumptions about the nature of God, humankind, and society, and kings worked through parliaments and clergy church councils to limit the pope's temporal power. The principle that sovereigns are accountable to the bodies they head was established. The fifteenth century also saw an unprecedented scholarly renaissance. Italian and northern humanists made a full recovery of classical knowledge and languages and began educational reforms and cultural changes that would spread throughout Europe by the sixteenth century. The Italian humanists virtually invented critical historical scholarship and exploited a new fifteenth-century invention, the "divine art" of printing with movable type. The vernacular, the local language, began to take its place alongside Latin, the international language, both in literature and political discourse. The independent nation-states of Europe progressively superseded the universal church as the community of highest allegiance, as patriotism and incipient nationalism became a major force.

Political and Social Breakdown

Hundred Years' War and Rise of National Sentiment

Medieval governments were by no means all-powerful and secure. Petty lords kept localities in turmoil; dynastic rivalries could plunge entire lands into war, especially when power was being transferred to a new ruler, and woe to the dynasty that failed to produce a male heir.

To field their armies and collect their revenues, late medieval rulers depended on carefully negotiated alliances among a wide range of lesser powers. Like earlier rulers, they practiced the art of feudal government, but on a grander and more sophisticated scale. To maintain the order they required, the Norman kings of England and the Capetian kings of France fine-tuned traditional feudal relationships, stressing the duties of lesser to higher power and the unquestioning loyalty noble vassals owed the king. The result was an unprecedented degree of centralized royal power and a nascent "national" consciousness that equipped both France and England for international warfare.

The Causes of the War

The conflict that came to be known as the Hundred Years' War began in May 1337 and lasted until October 1453. The English king Edward III (r. 1327–1377), the grandson of Philip the Fair of France (r. 1285–1314), claimed the French throne when the French king Charles IV (r. 1322–1328), the last of Philip the Fair's surviving sons, died without a male heir. The French barons had no intention of placing the then fifteen-year-old Edward on the French throne, choosing instead the first cousin of Charles IV, Philip VI of Valois (r. 1328–1350), the first of a new French dynasty that ruled into the sixteenth century.

But the war was more than a dynastic quarrel. England and France were emergent territorial powers in too close proximity to one another. Edward was actually a vassal of Philip's, holding several sizable French territories as fiefs from the king of France. England and France also quarreled over control of Flanders, which, although a French fief, was subject to political influence from England because its principal industry, the manufacture of cloth, depended on imported English wool. Compounding these frictions was a long history of prejudice and animosity between the French and English. These factors made the Hundred Years' War a struggle for national identity as well as for control of territory.

French Weakness

France had three times the population of England, was far wealthier, and fought on its own soil. Yet for most of the conflict, until after 1415, most of the major battles were stunning English victories (see Map 16–1). The primary reason for these French failures was internal disunity caused by endemic social conflicts. Unlike England, France was still struggling to make the transition from a fragmented feudal society to a centralized modern state.

Desperate to raise money for the war, French kings resorted to financial policies that aggravated internal conflicts. In 1355, in a bid to secure funds, the king convened a representative council of townsmen and noblemen that came to be known as the *Estates General*. Although it levied taxes at the king's request, its members also used the king's plight to enhance their own regional rights and privileges, thereby deepening territorial divisions.

France's defeats also resulted from incompetent leadership and English military superiority. The English infantry was more disciplined than the French, and English archers carried a formidable weapon, the longbow. With it they could fire six arrows a minute with enough force to pierce an inch of wood or the armor of a knight at two hundred yards.

The Treaty of Troyes to the Reign of Edward III

The war had three major stages, each ending with a seemingly decisive victory by one or the other side. In the first stage, Edward embargoed English wool to Flanders, sparking urban rebellions there by merchants and the trade guilds. The Flemish cities revolted against the French, thereafter allying with England and acknowledging Edward to be the king of France. In the first great battle of the war, Edward defeated the French fleet in the Bay of Sluys, but his subsequent effort to invade France by way of Flanders failed.

In 1346 Edward defeated the French at Crécy and seized Calais. Exhaustion of both sides and the onset of the Black Death forced a truce in late 1347. In 1356, near Poitiers, the English won their greatest victory, and political order in France collapsed. Power now suddenly lay with the Estates General, which took advantage of royal weakness, demanding and receiving rights similar to those granted the English privileged classes in Magna Carta. Unlike the English Parliament, however, the French Estates General remained too divided to become an instrument for effective government.

To secure their rights, the French privileged classes forced the peasantry to pay more taxes and to repair without compensation the war-damaged properties of the nobility, inciting a series of bloody rebellions in 1358 known as the *Jacquerie* (after the peasant revolutionary popularly known as "Jacques Bonhomme" or Simple Jack).

Another milestone of the war was reached in 1360, when England forced the Peace of Bretigny on the French; Edward renounced his claim to the French throne in return for full sovereignty over his lands in France.

After Edward's death in 1377, the English war effort lessened, partly because of domestic problems within England. During the reign of Richard II (r. 1377–1399), England had its own version of the *Jacquerie*. In June 1381 long-oppressed peasants and artisans revolted under the leadership of John Ball, a secular priest, and Wat Tyler, a journeyman. As in France, the revolt was brutally crushed within the year; it left England divided for decades.

In the second stage, Henry V (r. 1413–1422) took advantage of the turmoil created in France by the rise of the duchy of Burgundy. Burgundian power caused such division and disruption that France now became Henry V's for the taking—at least in the short run. In 1420 the Treaty of Troyes disinherited the French heir and proclaimed Henry V the successor to the French throne. When Henry and the French king Charles VI both died in 1422, the infant Henry VI (r. 1422–1461) of England was proclaimed in Paris to be king of both France and England. The dream of Edward III that had set the war in motion—to make the ruler of England also the ruler of France—for the moment had been realized.

Joan of Arc and the War's Conclusion

The son of Charles VI had retreated to Bourges, where, on the death of

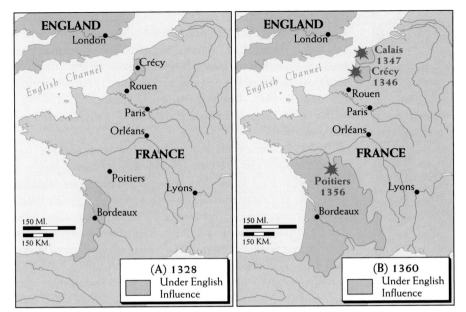

(A) 1328
Under English Influence

(B) 1360
Under English Influence

Map 16-1 The Hundred Years' War. The Hundred Years' War went on intermittently from the late 1330s to 1453. These maps show the remarkable English territorial gains up to the sudden and decisive turning of the tide of battle in favor of the French by the forces of Joan of Arc in 1429.

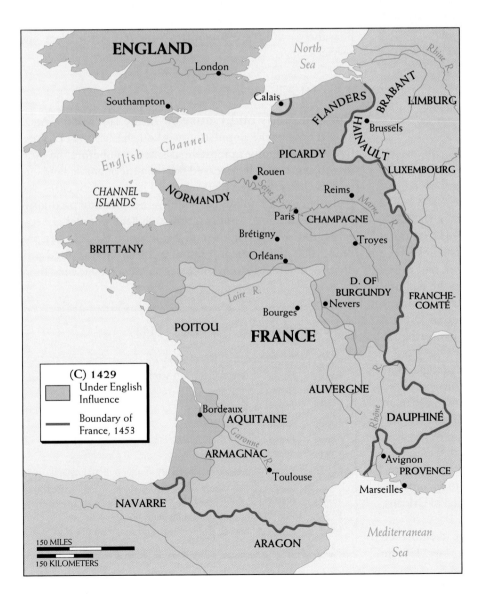

(C) 1429
Under English Influence
Boundary of France, 1453

A contemporary portrait of Joan of Arc (1412–1431) in the National Archives of Paris. [Archives Nationales, Paris, France/Giraudon/Art Resource, N.Y.]

could have secured her release but did not. The Burgundians and the English wanted her publicly discredited, believing this would demoralize French resistance. She was turned over to the Inquisition in English-held Rouen, where, after ten weeks of interrogation, she was executed as a relapsed heretic on May 30, 1431. The war continued, however, until 1453, when all that remained to the English was their coastal enclave of Calais.

In 1456 Charles VII reopened Joan's trial, and she was found innocent. In 1920 the Church declared her a saint.

The Hundred Years' War, with sixty-eight years of nominal peace and forty-four of hot war, had lasting political and social consequences. It devastated France, but it also awakened French nationalism and hastened the country's transition from a feudal monarchy to a centralized state. It saw Burgundy become a major European political power. And it encouraged the English, in response to the seesawing allegiance of the Netherlands during the conflict, to develop their own clothing industry and foreign markets. In both France and England the burden of the war fell most heavily on the peasantry, who were forced to support it with taxes and services.

The Black Death

Preconditions and Causes   In the late Middle Ages, nine tenths of the population worked the land. The three-field system, in use in most areas since well before the fourteenth century, had increased the amount of arable land and thereby increased the food supply. The growth of cities and trade had also stimulated agricultural science and productivity. But as the food supply grew, so did the population. It is estimated that Europe's population doubled between the years 1000 and 1300, and then began to outstrip food production. There were now more people than food to feed them

his father, he became Charles VII (1422–1461) to most of the French people, who simply ignored the Treaty of Troyes. Displaying unprecedented national feeling, they soon rallied to his cause in an ultimately victorious coalition, thanks to the inspiring leadership of Joan of Arc (1412–1431). A peasant from Lorraine, Joan presented herself to Charles VII in March 1429, declaring that the King of Heaven had called her to deliver the besieged city of Orléans from the English. The king was skeptical, but he was willing to try anything to reverse French fortunes. And the deliverance of Orléans would be a godsend. Charles's desperation overcame his skepticism, and he gave Joan his leave.

Circumstances worked perfectly to her advantage. The English force was already exhausted by an unsuccessful six-month siege and at the point of withdrawing when Joan arrived with fresh French troops. After repulsing the English from Orléans, the French enjoyed a succession of victories they attributed to Joan. She deserved much of that credit not because she was a military genius, but because she gave the French inspiration and a sense of national identity and self-confidence. Within a few months of the liberation of Orléans, Charles VII was crowned in Rheims.

Charles forgot his liberator as quickly as he had embraced her. When the Burgundians captured Joan in May 1430, he

The Hundred Years' War (1337–1443)	
1340	English victory at Bay of Sluys
1346	English victory at Crécy and seizure of Calais
1347	Black Death strikes
1356	English victory at Poitiers
1358	*Jacquerie* disrupts France
1360	Peace of Bretigny recognizes English holdings in France
1381	English Peasants Revolt
1422	Treaty of Troyes proclaims Henry VI ruler of both England and France
1429	Joan of Arc leads French to victory at Orléans
1431	Joan of Arc executed as a heretic
1453	War ends; English retain only the coastal town of Calais

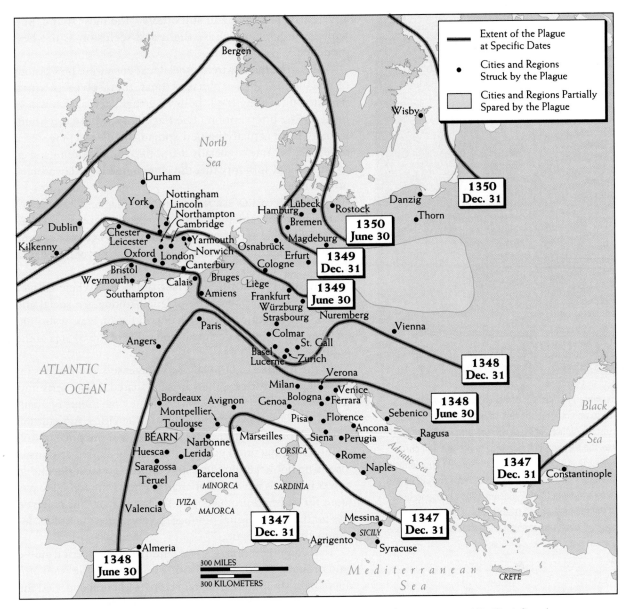

Map 16–2 Spread of the Black Death.   Apparently introduced by sea-borne rats from areas around the Black Sea where plague-infested rodents have long been known, the Black Death had great human, social, and economic consequences. According to one of the lower estimates, it killed 25 million in Europe. The map charts the spread of the plague in the mid-fourteenth century. Generally following trade routes, it reached Scandinavia by 1350, and some believe it then went on to Iceland and even Greenland. Areas off the main trade routes were largely spared.

or jobs to employ them, and the average European faced the probability of famine at least once during his or her expected thirty-five-year life span.

Between 1315 and 1317 crop failures produced the greatest famine of the Middle Ages. Densely populated urban areas like the industrial towns of the Netherlands suffered greatly. Decades of overpopulation, economic depression, famine, and bad health made Europe's population highly vulnerable to a virulent bubonic plague that struck with full force in 1348.

This Black Death, so called because it discolored the body, followed the trade routes from Asia into Europe. Appearing in Sicily in late 1347, it entered Europe through Venice, Genoa, and Pisa in 1348, and from there it swept rapidly through Spain and southern France and into northern Europe. Areas that lay outside the major trade routes, like Bohemia, appear to have remained virtually unaffected. Bubonic plague reappeared in succeeding decades. By the early fifteenth century, it may have killed two fifths of western Europe's population (see Map 16–2).

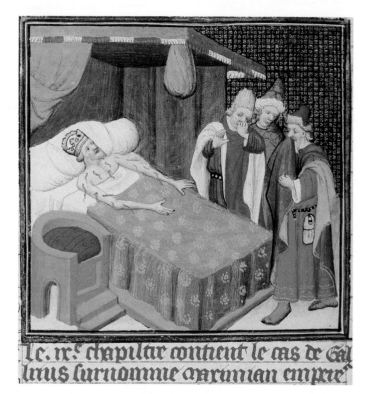

In this scene from an illustrated manuscript of Boccaccio's *Decameron*, physicians apply leeches to an emperor. The text says he suffered from a disease that caused a terrible stench, which is why the physicians are holding their noses. Bleeding was the agreed-upon best way to prevent and cure illness and was practiced as late as the nineteenth century. Its popularity was rooted in the belief that a build-up of foul matter in the body caused illness by disrupting the body's four humors (blood, phlegm, yellow bile, and black bile). Bleeding released the foul matter and restored equilibrium among the humors, thus preserving good health by strengthening resistance to disease.

[Jean-Loup Charmet/Science Photo Library/Photo Researchers Inc.]

Popular Remedies

The plague, transmitted by rat- or human-borne fleas, often reached a victim's lungs, from which it could be spread from person to person by sneezing and wheezing. Physicians had no understanding of these processes, and thus lacked even the most rudimentary prophylaxis against the disease. To contemporaries the Black Death was a catastrophe with no apparent explanation and against which there was no defense. Throughout much of western Europe, it inspired an obsession with death and dying and a deep and enduring pessimism.

Popular wisdom held that a corruption in the atmosphere caused the disease. Some blamed poisonous fumes released by earthquakes. Many adopted aromatic amulets as a remedy. According to the contemporary observations of Giovanni Boccaccio (1313–1375), some sought a remedy in moderation and a temperate life; others gave themselves over entirely to their passions (sexual promiscuity within the stricken areas

apparently ran high); and still others, "the most sound, perhaps, in judgment," chose flight and seclusion as the best medicine.[1]

Among the most extreme social reactions were processions of flagellants. These fanatics beat themselves in ritual penance until they bled, believing that such action would bring divine intervention. The flagellants, whose dirty bodies may have actually helped spread the disease, created a terror that became so socially disruptive and threatening even to established authority that the church finally outlawed such processions.

Jews were cast as scapegoats for the plague. Centuries of Christian propaganda had bred hatred toward them, as had their willing role as society's moneylenders. Pogroms occurred in several cities, sometimes incited by the arrival of flagellants.

Social and Economic Consequences

Whole villages vanished in the wake of the plague. Among the social and economic consequences of this depopulation were a shrunken labor supply and a decline in the value of the estates of the nobility.

As the number of farm laborers decreased, their wages increased, and those of skilled artisans soared. Many serfs now replaced their labor services with money payments or abandoned the farm altogether for jobs in the cities. Agricultural prices fell because of lowered demand, and the price of luxury and manufactured goods—the work of skilled artisans—rose. The noble landholders suffered the greatest decline in power from this new state of affairs. They were forced to pay more for finished products and for farm labor, but received less for their agricultural produce. Everywhere their rents declined after the plague.

To recoup their losses, some landowners converted arable land to sheep pasture, substituting more profitable wool production for labor-intensive grain crops. Others abandoned the effort to farm and leased their land. Landowners also sought simply to reverse their misfortune—to close off the new economic opportunities opened for the peasantry by the demographic crisis—through repressive legislation that forced peasants to stay on their farms and froze their wages at low levels. In France the direct tax on the peasantry, the *taille*, was increased, and opposition to it was a prominent cause of the *Jacquerie*. In 1351 the English Parliament passed a Statute of Laborers, which limited wages to preplague levels and restricted the ability of peasants to leave the land of their traditional masters. Opposition to such legislation also helped spark the English Peasants Revolt of 1381.

Although the plague hit urban populations especially hard, the cities and their skilled industries eventually prospered from

[1]*The Decameron of Giovanni Boccaccio*, trans. by J. M. Rigg (New York: Dutton, 1930), p. 5.

its effects. Cities had always protected their interests by regulating competition and immigration from rural areas. After the plague the reach of such laws was extended beyond the cities.

The omnipresence of death whetted the appetite for goods that only skilled urban industries could produce. Expensive cloths, jewelry, furs, and silks were in great demand. Faced with life at its worst, people insisted on having the best. Initially this new demand could not be met, as the first wave of plague transformed the already restricted supply of skilled artisans into a shortage almost overnight. As a result, the prices of manufactured and luxury items soared to new heights, but this in turn encouraged workers to migrate to the city to become artisans. Townspeople in effect profited coming and going from the forces that impoverished the landed nobility. As wealth poured into the cities and per capita income rose, urban dwellers paid less for agricultural products from the countryside.

There was also gain as well as loss for the church. Although it suffered losses as a great landholder and was politically weakened, it had received new revenues from the vastly increased demand for religious services for the dead and the dying and from the multiplication of gifts and bequests.

New Conflicts and Opportunities By increasing the importance of skilled artisans, the plague contributed to new conflicts within the cities. The economic and political power of local artisans and trade guilds grew steadily in the late Middle Ages along with the demand for their goods and services. The merchant and patrician classes only grudgingly gave guild masters a voice in city government. As the guilds won political power, they encouraged restrictive legislation to protect local industries. These restrictions in turn brought confrontations between master artisans, who wanted to keep their numbers low and expand their industries at a snail's pace, and the many journeypeople, who were eager to become masters. To the long-existing conflict between the guilds and the urban patriciate was now added a conflict within the guilds themselves.

After 1350, and largely as a consequence of the plague, the two traditional "containers" of monarchy—the landed nobility and the church—were politically on the defensive. Kings used the new situation to centralize their governments and economies. As already

noted, the plague reduced the economic power of the landed nobility, while the battles of the Hundred Years' War demonstrated the military superiority of paid professional armies over the traditional noble cavalry. The plague also killed many of the clergy—perhaps one third of the German clergy fell victim to it as they dutifully ministered to the sick and dying. The reduction in clerical ranks occurred in the same century in which the residence of the pope in Avignon (1309–1377) and the Schism (1378–1415) undermined much of the church's popular support.

Ecclesiastical Breakdown and Revival: The Late Medieval Church

During the reign of Pope Innocent III (1198–1216), papal power had reached its height. Innocent elaborated the doctrine of papal plenitude of power and on that authority declared saints, disposed of benefices, and created a centralized papal monarchy with a clear political as well as spiritual mission. And what Innocent began, his successors perfected. The thirteenth-century papacy became a powerful political institution governed by its own law and courts, serviced by an efficient international bureaucracy, and preoccupied with secular goals.

Boniface VIII and Philip the Fair

By the fourteenth century popes faced rulers far more powerful than the papacy. Boniface VIII (r. 1294–1303) became pope when England and France were maturing as nation-states and would not be intimidated by the papacy. In England, a long tradition of consultation between the king and powerful members of English society evolved into formal "parliaments" during the reigns of Henry III (1216–1272) and Edward I (1272–1307), and these parliaments helped to

Pope Boniface VIII (1294–1303), who opposed the taxation of the clergy by the kings of France and England and issued one of the strongest declarations of papal authority, the bull *Unam Sanctam*. This statue is in the Museo Civico, Bologna, Italy. [Scala/Art Resource, N.Y.]

create a unified kingdom. During the reign of the French king Philip IV the Fair (1285–1314) France was an efficient, centralized monarchy. Boniface had the further misfortune of bringing to the papal throne memories of the way earlier popes had brought kings and emperors to their knees.

France and England were on the brink of war in 1294. Both countries used the pretext of preparing for a crusade to tax the clergy heavily. Viewing this as an assault on traditional clerical rights, Boniface issued a bull, *Clericis Laicos,* which forbade lay taxation of the clergy without prior papal approval.

In England, Edward I retaliated by denying the clergy the right to be heard in the royal court, in effect removing his protection from them. But it was Philip the Fair who struck back with a vengeance. In August 1296 he forbade the exportation of money from France to Rome, thereby denying the papacy revenues without which it could not operate. Boniface had no choice but to concede Philip the right to tax the French clergy "during an emergency."

In the year 1300, Boniface's fortunes appeared to revive. Tens of thousands of pilgrims flocked to Rome for the Jubilee celebration. Heady with this display of popular religiosity, Boniface reinserted himself into international politics. When in 1301 Philip arrested the pope's Parisian legate, Boniface pointedly informed him that "God has set popes over kings and kingdoms" and demanded his legate's unconditional release.

Philip unleashed a ruthless antipapal campaign. Boniface made a last-ditch stand against state control of national churches on November 18, 1302, when he issued the bull *Unam Sanctam.* This famous statement of papal power declared that temporal authority was "subject" to the spiritual power of the church.

After *Unam Sanctam,* the French moved against Boniface with force. Philip's troops surprised the pope in mid-August 1303 at his retreat in Anagni, beat him up badly, and might even have executed him had not an aroused populace liberated the pope and returned him safely to Rome.

There was, however, to be no papal retaliation. The weakened papacy under Pope Clement V (r. 1305–1314) declared that *Unam Sanctam* did not intend to diminish royal authority. He subsequently moved the papal court to Avignon (1309), on the southeastern border of France where it remained until 1377.

Despite continuing papal excommunications and political intrigue, no pope after Boniface VIII ever again so seriously threatened kings and emperors. Future relations between Church and State would henceforth tilt toward state control of religion within particular monarchies.

The Great Schism (1378–1417) and the Conciliar Movement to 1449

Pope Gregory XI (r. 1370–1378) reestablished the papacy in Rome in January 1377, ending what had come to be known as the "Babylonian Captivity" of the church in Avignon, the ref-

erence being to the biblical bondage of the Israelites. The return to Rome proved to be short-lived, however. On Gregory's death on March 27, 1378, the cardinals, in Rome, elected an Italian as Pope Urban VI (r. 1378–1389), who immediately proclaimed his intention to reform the Curia. This announcement alarmed the cardinals, most of whom were French, and made them amenable to royal pressures to return the papacy to Avignon. Not wanting to surrender the benefits of a papacy under French influence, the French king, Charles V (r. 1364–1380), supported a schism in the church.

Five months after Urban's election, on September 20, 1378, thirteen cardinals, all but one of whom was French, elected a cousin of the French king as Pope Clement VII (r. 1378–1397). Thereafter the papacy became a "two-headed thing" and a scandal to Christendom. Allegiance to the two papal courts divided along political lines: England and its allies (the Holy Roman Empire, Hungary, Bohemia, and Poland) acknowledged Urban VI, whereas France and its orbit (Naples, Scotland, Castile, and Aragon) supported Clement VII. Only the Roman line of popes, however, is recognized as official by the church.

The Council of Constance (1414–1417) In 1409 a council was convened in Pisa that deposed both the Roman and the Avignon popes and elected its own new pope. But to the council's consternation, neither Rome nor Avignon accepted its action, so after 1409 there were three contending popes. This intolerable situation ended when the emperor Sigismund (r. 1410–1437) prevailed on the Pisan pope to summon a legal council of the church in Constance in 1414, a council also recognized by the reigning Roman pope Gregory XII (r. 1406–1415). Gregory, however, soon resigned his office, raising grave doubts forevermore about whether the council was truly convened with Rome's blessing and hence valid. In a famous declaration entitled *Haec Sancta,* the council fathers asserted their supremacy and proceeded to conduct the business of the church.

They also made their new powers clear by executing the Bohemian reformer Jan Hus (1369–1415). Hus, the rector of the University of Prague, had advocated communion for laity with both wine and bread (traditionally only the priest had received both, an indication of the clergy's spiritual superiority), denied the dogma of transubstantiation (that wine and bread become the true body and blood of Christ by priestly consecration), and questioned the validity of sacraments performed by priests who led immoral lives. After the three contending popes had either resigned or been deposed, the council elected a new pope, Martin V (r. 1417–1431), in November 1417, reuniting the church.

The Council of Basel (1431–1449) Conciliar government of the church both peaked and declined during the Council of Basel. The council not only curtailed papal powers of appointment and taxation, but negotiated peace with the Hussites of Bohemia, conceding their demands for communion with cup as well as bread, free preaching by their ordained clergy, and more equal punishment of clergy and laity for the same mortal sins. The council also recognized the right of the Bohemian church to govern its own internal affairs, much as the church in France and England had been doing.

Under Pope Eugenius IV (r. 1431–1447), the papacy successfully challenged the Council of Basel, again regaining much of its prestige and authority. The notion of conciliar superiority over popes died when the council collapsed in 1449. A decade later the papal bull *Execrabilis* (1460) condemned all appeals to councils as "erroneous and abominable" and "completely null and void." But the conciliar movement was not a total failure. It had planted deep within the conscience of all western peoples the conviction that the leader of an institution must be responsive to its members and not act against their best interests.

The Renaissance in Italy (1375–1527)

In his famous study, *Civilization of the Renaissance in Italy* (1867), Jacob Burckhardt described the Renaissance as the prototype of the modern world. He believed that it was in fourteenth- and fifteenth-century Italy, through the revival of ancient learning, that new secular and scientific values first began to supplant traditional religious beliefs. People began to adopt a rational, objective, and statistical approach to reality and to rediscover the importance of the individual. The result, in Burckhardt's words, was a release of the "full, whole nature of man."

Other scholars have found Burckhardt's description too modernizing an interpretation and have accused him of overlooking the continuity between the Renaissance and the Middle Ages. His critics especially stress the strongly Christian character of Humanism and the fact that earlier "renaissances" also revived the ancient classics, professed interest in Latin and in Greek science, and appreciated the worth and creativity of individuals.

Most scholars nonetheless agree that the Renaissance was a real transition from the medieval to the modern world. Medieval Europe, especially before the twelfth century, had been a fragmented feudal society with an agricultural economy, its thought and culture dominated by the church. Renaissance Europe, especially after the fourteenth century, was characterized by growing national consciousness and political centralization, an urban economy based on organized commerce and capitalism, and ever greater lay and secular control of thought and culture.

The distinctive features and achievements of the Renaissance are most strikingly revealed in Italy from roughly 1375 to 1527, the year of the infamous sack of Rome by imperial soldiers. What was achieved in Italy during these centuries also deeply influenced northern Europe.

The Italian City-State: Social Conflict and Despotism

Renaissance society took distinctive shape within the cities of late medieval Italy. Italy had always had a cultural advantage over the rest of Europe because it was the natural gateway between East and West. Venice, Genoa, and Pisa traded uninterruptedly with the Near East throughout the Middle Ages, and maintained vibrant urban societies. During the thirteenth and fourteenth centuries, the trade-rich Italian cities became powerful city-states, dominating the political and economic life of the surrounding countryside. By the fifteenth century, the great Italian cities had become the bankers for much of Europe.

The growth of Italian cities and urban culture was also assisted by the endemic warfare between the emperor and the pope. Either might have successfully challenged the cities. They chose instead to weaken one another; thus they strengthened the urban oligarchies. Where northern European cities tended to be dominated by kings and princes, Italian cities were free to expand into states. They absorbed the surrounding countryside and assimilated the local nobility in a unique urban meld of old and new rich. There were five such major, competitive states in Italy: the duchy of Milan, the republics of Florence and Venice, the Papal States, and the kingdom of Naples (see Map 16–3).

Social strife and competition for political power were so intense within the cities that for survival's sake, most had evolved into despotisms by the fifteenth century. Venice, ruled by a successful merchant oligarchy, was the notable exception. Elsewhere, the new social classes and divisions within society produced by rapid urban growth fueled chronic, near-anarchic conflict.

Florence was the most striking example. There were four distinguishable social groups within the city. The first was the old rich, or *grandi*, the nobles and merchants who had traditionally ruled the city. The second group was the emergent new-rich merchant class, capitalists and bankers known as the *popolo grasso*, or "fat people." They began to challenge the old rich for political power in the late thirteenth and early fourteenth centuries. Then there were the middle-burgher ranks of guild masters, shopkeepers, and professionals, those small businesspeople who, in Florence as elsewhere, tended to side with the new rich against the conservative policies of the old rich. Finally, there were the omnipresent *popolo minuto*, the "little people" who made up the lower economic classes. In 1457 one third of the

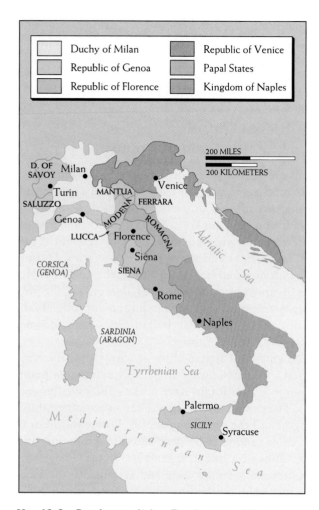

Map 16–3 Renaissance Italy. The city-states of Renaissance Italy were self-contained principalities whose internal strife was monitored by their despots and whose external aggression was long successfully controlled by treaty.

and order. He held executive, military, and judicial authority, and his mandate was simple: to protect, by whatever means required, the normal flow of business. Because these despots could not depend on the divided populace, they operated through mercenary armies.

Political turbulence and warfare gave birth to diplomacy, through which the various city-states stayed abreast of foreign military developments and, if shrewd enough, gained power and advantage without actually going to war. Most city-states established resident embassies during the fifteenth century. Their ambassadors not only represented them in ceremonies and as negotiators but also became their watchful eyes and ears at rival courts.

Whether within the comparatively tranquil republic of Venice, the strong-arm democracy of Florence, or the undisguised despotism of Milan, thought and culture flourished. Renaissance culture was promoted as vigorously by despots as by republicans and by popes as enthusiastically as by the secularized ones.

Cosimo de' Medici (1389–1464), Florentine banker and statesman, in his lifetime the city's wealthiest man and most successful politician. This portrait is by Jacopo da Pontormo (1494–1556). [Erich Lessing/Art Resource, N.Y.]

population of Florence, about thirty thousand people, were officially listed as paupers.

These social divisions produced conflict at every level of society. In 1378 a great revolt by the poor, known as the Ciompi Revolt, established a chaotic four-year reign of power by the lower Florentine classes. True stability did not return to Florence until the ascent to power in 1434 of Cosimo de' Medici (1389–1464). The wealthiest Florentine and a most astute statesman, Cosimo controlled the city internally from behind the scenes, skillfully manipulating the constitution and influencing elections. His grandson Lorenzo the Magnificent (1449–1492, r. 1478–1492), ruled Florence in almost totalitarian fashion.

Despotism was less subtle elsewhere in Italy. To prevent internal social conflict and foreign intrigue from paralyzing their cities, the dominant groups in many cities cooperated to install a hired strongman, known as a *podesta*, to maintain law

Florentine women doing needlework, spinning, and weaving. These activities took up much of a woman's time and contributed to the elegance of dress for which both Florentine men and women were famed. [Alinari/Art Resource, N.Y.]

Humanism

Some scholars describe humanism as an unchristian philosophy that stressed the dignity of humankind and championed individualism and secular values. Others argue that the humanists were true champions of authentic Catholic Christianity. Still others see humanism as a form of scholarship consciously designed to promote a sense of civic responsibility and political liberty. One commentator, Paul O. Kristeller, has accused all these views of dealing more with the secondary effects of humanism than with its essence, which he believes was simply an educational program that concentrated on rhetoric and sound scholarship for their own sake.

There is truth in each of these definitions. Humanism was the scholarly study of the Latin and Greek classics and the ancient Church Fathers both for their own sake and to promote a rebirth of ancient norms and values. Humanists advocated the *studia humanitatis*, a liberal arts program that embraced grammar, rhetoric, poetry, history, politics, and moral philosophy. The Florentine Leonardo Bruni (1374–1444) first gave this learning the name humanitas ("humanity"). Bruni was a student of Manuel Chrysoloras (ca. 1355–1415), a Byzantine scholar who opened the world of Greek scholarship to a generation of young Italian humanists when he taught at Florence between 1397 and 1403.

The first humanists were orators and poets. They wrote original literature in both the classical and vernacular languages, inspired by the newly discovered works of the ancients, and they taught rhetoric within the universities. Their talents were sought as secretaries, speech writers, and diplomats in princely and papal courts.

Classical and Christian antiquity had been studied before the Italian Renaissance—during the Carolingian renaissance of the ninth century, for example. However, the Italian Renaissance of the late Middle Ages was more secular and lay dominated, had broader interests, recovered more manuscripts, and possessed far superior technical skills than earlier rebirths of antiquity.

Unlike their scholastic rivals, humanists were not content only to summarize and compare the views of recognized authorities on a question, but instead went directly to the original source and drew their own conclusions. Avidly searching out manuscript collections, Italian humanists made the full sources of Greek and Latin antiquity available to scholars during the fourteenth and fifteenth centuries. Mastery of Latin and Greek was their surgeon's tool. There is a kernel of truth—but only a kernel—in the arrogant boast of the humanists that the period between themselves and classical civilization was a "dark middle age."

Petrarch, Dante, and Boccaccio   Francesco Petrarch (1304–1374) was the father of humanism. He left the legal profession to pursue his love of letters and poetry. Petrarch celebrated ancient Rome in his writings and tirelessly

Pico della Mirandola States the Renaissance Image of Man

One of the most eloquent Renaissance descriptions of the abilities of humankind comes from the Italian humanist Pico della Mirandola (1463–1494). In his famed Oration on the Dignity of Man *(ca. 1486), Pico described humans as free to become whatever they choose.*

In what does the dignity of humankind consist? Does Pico reject the biblical description of Adam and Eve's fall? Does he exaggerate a person's ability to choose freely to be whatever he or she wishes? What inspired such seeming hubris during the Renaissance?

The best of artisans [God] ordained that that creature (man) to whom He [God] had been able to give nothing proper to himself should have joint possession of whatever had been peculiar to each of the different kinds of being. He therefore took man as a creature of indeterminate nature and, assigning him a place in the middle of the world, addressed him thus: "Neither a fixed abode nor a form that is thine alone or any function peculiar to thyself have we given thee, Adam, to the end that according to thy longing and according to thy judgment thou mayest have and possess what abode, what form, and what functions thou thyself shalt desire. The nature of all other beings is limited and constrained within the bounds of laws prescribed by Us. Thou, constrained by no limits, in accordance with thine own free will, in whose hand We have placed thee, shalt ordain for thyself the limits of thy nature. We have set thee at the world's center that thou mayest from thence more easily observe whatever is in the world. We have made thee neither of heaven nor of earth, neither mortal nor immortal, so that with freedom of choice and with honor, as though the maker and molder of thyself, thou mayest fashion thyself in whatever shape thou shalt prefer. Thou shalt have the power to degenerate into the lower forms of life, which are brutish. Thou shalt have the power, out of thy soul's judgment, to be reborn into the higher forms, which are divine." O supreme generosity of God the Father, O highest and most marvelous felicity of man! To him it is granted to have whatever he chooses, to be whatever he wills.

From Giovanni Pico della Mirandola, *Oration on the Dignity of Man*, in *The Renaissance Philosophy of Man*, ed. by E. Cassirer et al. Phoenix Books, 1961, pp. 224–225. Reprinted by permissin of The University of Chicago Press.

---

collected ancient manuscripts; among his finds were letters by Cicero. His critical textual studies, elitism, and contempt for the allegedly useless learning of the scholastics were shared by many later humanists. Petrarch's most famous contemporary work was a collection of highly introspective love sonnets to Laura, a married woman whom he admired from a safe distance. Medieval Christian values can be seen in his imagined dialogues with Saint Augustine and in his defense of the personal immortality of the soul.

Petrarch was, however, far more secular in orientation than Dante Alighieri (1265–1321), whose *Vita Nuova* and *Divine Comedy* form, with Petrarch's sonnets, the cornerstones of Italian vernacular literature. Petrarch's student and friend Giovanni Boccaccio (1313–1375), author of the *Decameron*, one hundred bawdy tales told by three men and seven women in a country retreat from the plague that ravaged Florence in 1348, also pioneered humanist studies. An avid collector of manuscripts, Boccaccio assembled an encyclopedia of Greek and Roman mythology.

Educational Reforms and Goals   Pietro Paolo Vergerio (1349–1420) wrote the following summary of the humanist concept of a liberal education:

We call those studies liberal which are worthy of a free man; those studies by which we attain and practice virtue and wisdom; that education which calls forth, trains, and develops those highest gifts of body and mind ennoble men and are rightly judged to rank next in dignity to virtue only [and], for to a vulgar temper, gain and pleasure are the one aim in existence, to a lofty nature, moral worth and fame.[2]

This classical ideal of a useful education that produces well-rounded people inspired far-reaching reforms in traditional education. The most influential Italian Renaissance tract on education, Vergerio's *On the Morals that Befit a Free Man*, was written directly from classical models. Vittorino da Feltre (d. 1446) directed his students to a highly disciplined reading of ancient authors, together with vigorous physical exercise and games with intellectual pursuits. Another educator, Guarino da Verona (d. 1460), rector of the new University of Ferrara, streamlined and systematized the study of classical languages. Baldassare Castiglione (1478–1529) wrote the *Book of the Courtier*, a how-to book for the cultured nobil-

[2]Cited by De Lamar Jensen, *Renaissance Europe: Age of Recovery and Reconciliation* (Lexington, MA: D. C. Heath, 1981), p. 111.

Christine de Pisan Instructs Women on How to Handle Their Husbands

Renowned Renaissance noblewoman Christine de Pisan has the modern reputation of being perhaps the first feminist, and her book The Treasure of the City of Ladies *(also known as* The Book of Three Virtues*) has been described as the Renaissance woman's survival manual. Here she gives advice to the wives of artisans.*

How does Christine de Pisan's image of husband and wife compare with other medieval views? Would the church take issue with her advice? As a noblewoman commenting on the married life of artisans, does her high social standing influence her advice? Would she give similar advice to women of her own social class?

All wives of artisans should be very painstaking and diligent if they wish to have the necessities of life. They should encourage their husbands or their workmen to get to work early in the morning and work until late. . . . [And] the wife herself should [also] be involved in the work to the extent that she knows all about it, so that she may know how to oversee his workers if her husband is absent, and to reprove them if they do not do well. . . . And when customers come to her husband and try to drive a hard bargain, she ought to warn him solicitously to take care that he does not make a bad deal. She should advise him to be chary of giving too much credit if he does not know precisely where and to whom it is going, for in this way many come to poverty. . . . In addition, she ought to keep her husband's love as much as she can, to this end: that he will stay at home more willingly and that he may not have any reason to join the foolish crowds of other young men in taverns and indulge in unnecessary and extravagant expense, as many tradesmen do, especially in Paris. By treating him kindly she should protect him as well as she can from this. It is said that three things drive a man from his home: a quarrelsome wife, a smoking fireplace, and a leaking roof. She too ought to stay at home gladly and not go off every day traipsing hither and yon gossiping with the neighbours and visiting her chums to find out what everyone is doing. That is done by slovenly housewives roaming about the town in groups. Nor should she go off on these pilgrimages got up for no good reason and involving a lot of needless expense.

From Christine de Pisan, *The Treasure of the City of Ladies or The Book of the Three Virtues*, trans. by Sarah Lawson (Penguin Classics, 1985), pp. 167–168. The translation © Sarah Lawson, 1985.

---

ity at the court of Urbino. It stressed the importance of integrating the knowledge of language and history with athletic, military, and musical skills, and crowning them all with good manners and moral character.

Educated and cultured noblewomen also had a prominent place at Renaissance courts, among them Christine de Pisan (1363?–1434). The Italian-born daughter of French king Charles V's physician and astrologer, she received as fine an education as any man at the French court. An expert in classical, French, and Italian languages and literature, she had married early (at fifteen) and by twenty-seven was the widowed mother of three children. She wrote lyric poetry to support herself, becoming a well-known woman of letters in the courts of Europe. Her most famous work, *The City of Ladies*, describes the accomplishments of the great women of history.

The Florentine "Academy" and Revival of Platonism
Of all the important recoveries of the past made during the Italian Renaissance, the revival of Greek studies, especially the works of Plato in fifteenth-century Florence, stands out. Many factors combined to bring about this revival. An important foundation had been laid in 1397 when the city invited Manuel Chrysoloras to come from Constantinople and promote Greek learning. A half century later (1439), the ecumenical Council of Ferrara-Florence, convened by the church to negotiate the reunion of the eastern and western churches, enabled many Greek scholars and manuscripts to enter the west. After the fall of Constantinople to the Turks (1453), several important Greek scholars took refuge in Florence. This was the background against which the study of Plato developed under the patronage of Cosimo de' Medici and the supervision of Marsilio Ficino (1433–1499) and Pico della Mirandola (1463–1494).

Although every variety of ancient wisdom interested the thinkers of the Renaissance, they were especially attracted to Platonism and those Church Fathers who had tried to synthesize Plato's philosophy with Christian teaching. In private residences, Florentine humanists met to discuss the works of Plato and the Neoplatonists. This was the so-called "Florentine Academy," not in fact a formal school but a highly productive informal gatherings of scholars.

The appeal of Platonism lay in its flattering view of human nature. Platonism sharply distinguished between an eternal sphere of being and the perishable world in which humans now lived. Human reason was believed to belong properly only to the former— having preexisted in the pristine world of being and continuing still to commune with it, as Plato and his followers believed the innate knowledge of mathematical and moral truths attested.

Critical Work of the Humanists: Lorenzo Valla

Guided by a scholarly ideal of philological accuracy and historical truthfulness, the humanists could become critics of tradition even when that was not their intention. The pursuit of dispassionate critical scholarship shook long-standing foundations, including those of the medieval church.

The work of Lorenzo Valla (1406–1457), author of the standard Renaissance text on Latin philology, *The Elegance of the Latin Language* (1444), reveals the explosive character of the new learning. Although a good Catholic, Valla became a hero to later Protestants by virtue of his defense of predestination against free will and his exposé of the *Donation of Constantine* as a forgery (see Chapter 12). Valla did not intend for the latter to be so devastating. He believed he had only demonstrated in a careful, scholarly way what others had long suspected. Using the most rudimentary textual analysis and historical logic, he proved beyond reasonable doubt that the document contained anachronistic terms (such as *fief*) and made references to people and places that would have been meaningless in the fourth century. In the same dispassionate way, he also pointed out errors in the Latin Vulgate, the authorized version of the Bible for the Roman Catholic Church.

Such discoveries did not make Valla any less loyal to the church, nor did they prevent him from serving as apostolic secretary under Pope Nicholas V (r. 1447–1455). Nonetheless, historical criticism of this type served those less loyal to the medieval church well, and it was no accident that young humanists formed the first identifiable group of Martin Luther's supporters (see Chapter 17).

Renaissance Art

In Renaissance Italy, as later in Reformation Europe, the values and interests of the laity were less subordinated to those of the clergy. In education, culture, and religion, the laity now assumed a greater leading role and even established models for the clergy to imitate. This resulted in part from the church's loss of its international power during the great crises of the late Middle Ages. But it was also encouraged by the rise of national sentiment, the creation of competent national bureaucracies staffed by laity rather than clerics, and the accelerating growth of lay education during the fourteenth and fifteenth centuries. Medieval Christian values were adjusting to a more this-worldly spirit. Men and women began again to appreciate and even to glorify the secular world, secular learning, and purely human pursuits as ends in themselves.

This perspective on life is especially prominent in the painting and sculpture of the High Renaissance (late fifteenth and early sixteenth centuries), when Renaissance art reached its full maturity. In imitation of Greek and Roman art, painters and sculptors attempted to create harmonious, symmetrical, and properly proportioned figures, portraying the human form with a glorified realism. Whereas Byzantine and Gothic art had been religious and idealized in the extreme, Renaissance art, especially in the fifteenth century, realistically reproduced nature and human beings as a part of nature.

Giotto's portrayal of the funeral of Saint Francis of Assisi. The saint is surrounded by his admiring brothers and a knight of Assisi (first on the right). Giotto's (1266–1336) work signals the evolution toward Renaissance art. The damaged areas on this fresco resulted from the removal of nineteenth-century restorations. [Scala/Art Resource, N.Y.]

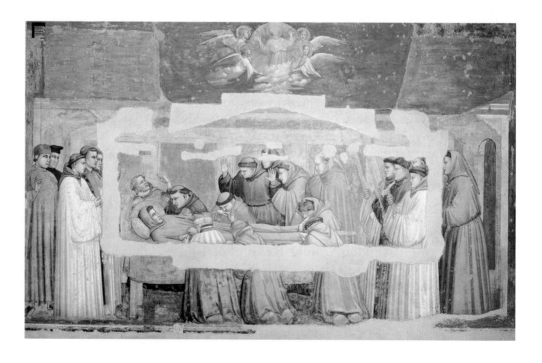

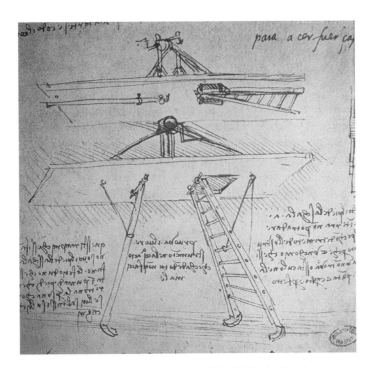

Aviation drawings by Leonardo da Vinci (1452–1519), who imagined a possible flying machine with a retractable ladder for boarding. [David Forbert/SuperStock, Inc.]

Renaissance artists took advantage of new technical skills and materials developed during the fifteenth century: the use of oil paints, using shading to enhance realism (chiaroscuro), and adjusting the size of figures to give the viewer a feeling of continuity with the painting (linear perspective). Compared with their flat Byzantine and Gothic counterparts, Renaissance paintings seem filled with energy and life and stand out from the canvas in three dimensions.

The emergence of Renaissance art was anticipated in the work of Giotto (1266–1336). An admirer of Saint Francis of Assisi, whose love of nature he shared, Giotto depicted the world in a less abstract and unnatural way than his Byzantine and Gothic predecessors. The characteristics of Italian Renaissance art proper can be seen in the work of the painter Masaccio (1401–1428) and the sculptor Donatello (1386–1466). The great masters of the High Renaissance included Leonardo da Vinci (1452–1519), Raphael (1483–1520), and Michelangelo Buonarroti (1475–1564).

Leonardo da Vinci Leonardo personified the Renaissance ideal of the universal person, one who is not only a jack-of-all-trades but also a master of many. A military engineer and advocate of scientific experimentation, he dissected corpses to learn anatomy and was a self-taught botanist. He foresaw such modern machines as airplanes and submarines. The variety of his interests tended to shorten his attention span, so that he constantly moved from one activity to another. As a painter, his great skill lay in conveying inner moods through complex facial features, such as that seen in the most famous of his paintings, the *Mona Lisa*.

Raphael Raphael, an unusually sensitive man who died young (thirty-seven), was apparently loved by contemporaries as much for his person as for his work. He is famous for his tender madonnas, the best known of which graces the monastery of San Sisto in Piacenza. Art historians praise his fresco *The School of Athens*, which depicts Plato and Aristotle surrounded by philosophy and science, as one of the most perfect examples of Renaissance artistic theory and technique.

Michelangelo This melancholy genius also excelled in a variety of arts and crafts. His eighteen-foot godlike sculpture

Raphael's portrait (ca. 1515) of Baldassare Castiglione (1478–1529), now in the Louvre. Castiglione, author of the *Book of the Courtier*, was Raphael's close friend. The self-restraint and inner calm that he considered the chief qualities of the gentleman are also qualities of Raphael's art, reflected in the portrait's perfect balance and harmony. This painting greatly influenced Rembrandt, who later tried unsuccessfully to buy it. [Cliche des Musées Nationaux, Paris]

Michelangelo's Pietà (made between 1498 and 1500), St. Peter's, Rome. This work of the artist's youth, sculpted between his twenty-third and twenty-fifth years, portrays a Mary who is younger than her son. Unsurpassed in delicacy, realism, and emotional impact, it exemplifies the creativity of the Italian Renaissance. [Scala/Art Resource, N.Y.]

David is a perfect example of the Renaissance artist's devotion to harmony, symmetry, and proportion, as well as his extreme glorification of the human form. Four different popes commissioned works by Michelangelo, the best known of which are the frescoes for the Sistine Chapel, painted for Pope Julius II (1503–1513), with whom Michelangelo often quarreled about art, and who set Michelangelo to work as well on the pope's own magnificent tomb. The Sistine frescoes originally covered ten thousand square feet and involved 343 figures, over half of which exceeded ten feet in height. This labor of love and piety, much of it painted while Michelangelo lay on his back or was stooping, took four years to complete.

His later works mark, artistically and philosophically, the passing of High Renaissance painting and the advent of a new, experimental style known as *mannerism*, which reached its peak in the late sixteenth and early seventeenth centuries. A reaction against the simplicity and symmetry of High Renaissance art, which also found expression in music and literature, mannerism made room for the strange and even the abnormal and gave freer rein to the subjectivity of the artist. It derived its name from the fact that it permitted the artist to express his own individual perceptions and feelings, to paint, compose, or write in a "mannered" or "affected" way.

Tintoretto (d. 1594) and especially El Greco (d. 1614) became its supreme representatives.

Slavery in the Renaissance

Slavery flourished in Renaissance Italy almost as extravagantly as art and culture. A Mediterranean slave market had existed since the twelfth century, when the Spanish sold Muslim slaves captured in raids and war to wealthy Italians and other interested buyers. After the Black Death (1348–1350) had reduced the supply of laborers everywhere in western Europe, the demand for slaves soared. They now began to be imported from Africa, the eastern Mediterranean, and the lands around the Black Sea. At this time slavery was multicultural; slaves were taken randomly from conquered people and represented many different races: whites and Asians as well as Africans, Tartars, Circassians, Greeks, Russians, Georgians, and Iranians. "By the end of the fourteenth century," a contemporary writes, "there was hardly a well-to-do household in Tuscany without at least one slave: brides brought them [to their marriages] as part of their dowry, doctors accepted them from their patients in lieu of fees—and it was not unusual to find them even in the service of a priest."[3]

In addition to such household or domestic slavery, plantation slavery following East Asian models had developed in the east Mediterranean world. In the savannas of Sudan and on Venetian estates on Cyprus and Crete, sugar cane plantations were worked by gangs of slaves—an anticipation of later New World slavery.

Owners had complete dominion over their slaves; in Italian law, this meant the "[power] to have, hold, sell, alienate, exchange, enjoy, rent or unrent, dispose of in [their] will[s], judge soul and body, and do with in perpetuity whatsoever may please [them] and [their] heirs and no man may gainsay [them]."[4]

A strong, young, healthy slave cost the equivalent of the wages paid a free servant over several years. But taking into account a lifetime of free service thereafter, such slaves were good bargains. The Tartars and Africans appear to have been the worst treated. But as in ancient Greece and Rome, slaves at this time were generally accepted as family members and integrated into households. Not a few women slaves bore their masters' children, and there is plenty of evidence that wives resisted their husbands' acquisition of young female slaves. Many children of such unions were adopted and raised as legitimate heirs of their fathers. It was also in the interest of their owners to keep slaves healthy and happy; otherwise they would be of little use and could even become a threat.

[3]Iris Origo, *The Merchant of Prato: Francesco di Marco Datini 1335–1410* (New York: Godine, 1957), pp. 90–91.
[4]Ibid., p. 209.

This portrait of Katharina, by Albrecht Dürer, provides evidence of African slavery in Europe during the sixteenth century. Katharina was in the service of one João Bradao, a Portuguese economic minister living in Antwerp, then the financial center of Europe. Dürer became friends with Bradao during his stay in the Low Countries in the winter of 1520-1521. [Bildarchiv Foto Marburg/Art Resource, N.Y.]

Still, slaves remained a foreign and suspected presence in Italian society; they were, as all knew, uprooted and resentful people.

Italy's Political Decline: The French Invasions (1494–1527)

Treaty of Lodi

Autonomous city-states of Italy had always preserved their peace and safety from foreign invasion, especially from invasion by the Turks, by cooperation with each other. Such cooperation had been maintained during the last half of the fifteenth century, thanks to an alliance known as the Treaty of Lodi (1454–1455). The treaty brought Milan and Naples, traditional enemies, into alliance with Florence. These three stood together for decades against Venice, which was frequently joined by the Papal States, to create an internal balance of power that also made possible a unified front against Italy's external enemies.

However, in 1494 Naples, supported by Florence and the Borgia pope Alexander VI (1492–1503), prepared to attack Milan. At this point, the Milanese despot Ludovico il Moro (r. 1476–1499) made a fatal miscalculation. Breaking a wise Italian rule, he invited the French to revive their dynastic claim to Naples. But France also had dynastic claims to Milan, and the French appetite for new territory became insatiable once French armies had crossed the Alps and reestablished themselves in Italy.

Charles VIII's March Through Italy

The French king Louis XI (r. 1461–1483) had resisted the temptation to invade Italy, while nonetheless maintaining French dynastic claims there. His successor, Charles VIII (r. 1483–1498), an eager youth in his twenties, responded rapidly to Ludovico's call. Within five months he had crossed the Alps (August 1495) and raced as conqueror through Florence and the Papal States into Naples.

Charles's lightning march through Italy also alarmed non-Italians. Ferdinand of Aragon (r. 1479–1516), who was also king of Sicily, now became vulnerable to a French-Italian axis, and helped to create a counteralliance: the League of Venice. This set the stage for a conflict between France and Spain that would not end until 1559.

Ludovico il Moro meanwhile recognized that he had sown the wind; having desired a French invasion only so long as it weakened his enemies, he now saw Milan threatened by the whirlwind of events that he had himself created. In reaction, he joined the League of Venice, and this alliance was able to force Charles to retreat.

Pope Alexander VI and the Borgia Family

The French returned to Italy under Charles's successor, Louis XII (r. 1498–1515), this time assisted by a new Italian ally who also acted against Italy's best interests, the Borgia pope Alexander VI (1492–1503). Alexander, probably the most corrupt pope who ever sat on the papal throne, openly promoted the political careers of the children he had had before he became pope, Cesare and Lucrezia. Papal policy sought to secure a political base in Romagna, officially part of the Papal States, for Cesare.

In Romagna, several principalities had arisen during the Avignon papacy, and Venice, the pope's ally within the League of Venice, continued to contest the Papal States for their loyalty. Seeing that a French alliance could allow him to reestablish control over the region, Alexander agreed to abandon the League of Venice, a withdrawal of support that made the league too weak to resist a French reconquest of Milan. In exchange for this betrayal, Cesare Borgia got the hand of the sister of the king of Navarre, land grants from Louis XII, and a promise of French military aid in Romagna. Such cunning and determination later made him the model for Machiavelli's *The Prince*.

It was a scandalous trade-off, but one that enabled both the French king and the pope to realize their ambitions within Italy. Louis successfully invaded Milan in August 1499. In 1500 he and Ferdinand of Aragon divided Naples between themselves, while the pope and Cesare Borgia conquered the cities of Romagna without opposition.

Pope Julius II

Cardinal Giuliano della Rovere, a strong opponent of the Borgias, became Pope Julius II (1503–1513). He suppressed the

Major Political Events of the Italian Renaissance (1375–1527)	
1378–1382	Ciompi revolt in Florence
1434	Medici rule in Florence established by Cosimo de' Medici
1454–1455	Treaty of Lodi allies Milan, Naples, and Florence (in effect until 1494)
1494	Charles VIII of France invades Italy
1495	League of Venice unites Venice, Milan, the Papal States, the Holy Roman Empire, and Spain against France
1499	Louis XII invades Milan (the second French invasion of Italy)
1500	The Borgias conquer Romagna
1512–1513	The Holy League (Pope Julius II, Ferdinand of Aragon, Emperor Maximilian I, and Venice) defeat the French
1513	Machiavelli writes *The Prince*
1515	Francis I leads the third French invasion of Italy
1516	Concordat of Bologna between France and the papacy
1527	Sack of Rome by imperial soldiers

Santi di Tito's portrait of Machiavelli, perhaps the most famous Italian political theorist, who advised Renaissance princes to practice artful deception and inspire fear in their subjects if they wished to succeed.
[Scala/Art Resource, N.Y.]

Borgias and placed their newly conquered lands in Romagna under papal jurisdiction. Julius came to be known as the "warrior pope" because he brought the Renaissance papacy to a peak of military prowess and diplomatic intrigue.

Assisted by the French, Pope Julius drove the Venetians out of the rest of Romagna in 1509, thereby ending Venetian claims in the region and fully securing the Papal States. Having realized this long-sought papal goal, Julius turned to the second major undertaking of his pontificate: ridding Italy of his former ally, the French invaders. Julius, Ferdinand of Aragon, and Venice formed a second Holy League in October 1511, and soon Emperor Maximilian I (r. 1493–1519) and the Swiss joined them. By 1512 the French were in full retreat and were beaten by the Swiss in 1513 at Novara.

The French invaded Italy again under Louis's successor, Francis I (r. 1515–1547). French armies massacred Swiss soldiers of the Holy League at Marignano in September 1515, revenging the earlier defeat at Novara. That victory won from the Medici pope Leo X (r. 1513–1521) an agreement known as the Concordat of Bologna (August 1516), which gave the French king control over the French clergy and the right to collect taxes from them, in exchange for French recognition of the pope's superiority over church councils. This was an important compromise that would help to keep France Catholic after the outbreak of the Protestant Reformation. But the new French entry into Italy also led to the first of four major wars with Spain in the first half of the six-

Machiavelli Discusses the Most Important Trait for a Ruler

Does Machiavelli share Pico della Mirandola's image of humankind? (See p. 436.)

Why is the ability to inspire fear more important for a ruler than the ability to inspire love? Are there any limitations on a ruler?

Here the question arises; whether it is better to be loved than feared or feared than loved. The answer is that it would be desirable to be both but, since that is difficult, it is much safer to be feared than to be loved, if one must choose. For on men in general this observation may be made: they are ungrateful, fickle, and deceitful, eager to avoid dangers, and avid for gain, and while you are useful to them they are all with you, offering you their blood, their property, their lives, and their sons so long as danger is remote . . . but when it approaches they turn on you. Any prince, trusting only in their words and having no other preparations made, will fall to his ruin, for friendships that are bought at a price and not by greatness and nobility of soul are paid for indeed, but they are not owned and cannot be called upon in time of need. Men have less hesitation in offending a man who is loved than one who is feared, for love is held by a bond of obligation which, as men are wicked, is broken whenever personal advantage suggests it, but fear is accompanied by the dread of punishment which never relaxes.

From Niccolò Machiavelli, *The Prince* (1513), trans. and ed. by Thomas G. Bergin (New York: Appleton-Century-Crofts, 1947), p. 48.

---

teenth century: the Habsburg-Valois wars, none of which France won.

Niccolò Machiavelli

The foreign invasions made a shambles of Italy. The same period that saw Italy's cultural peak in the work of Leonardo, Raphael, and Michelangelo also witnessed Italy's political tragedy. One who watched as French, Spanish, and German armies wreaked havoc on his country was Niccolò Machiavelli (1469–1527). The more he saw, the more convinced he became that Italian political unity and independence were ends that justified any means. A humanist and a careful student of ancient Rome, Machiavelli admired the heroic acts of ancient Roman rulers, what Renaissance people called their *Virtu*. Romanticizing the old Roman citizenry, he lamented the absence of heroism among his compatriots. Such a perspective caused his interpretation of both ancient and contemporary history to be exaggerated.

The juxtaposition of what Machiavelli believed the ancient Romans had been with the failure of contemporary Romans to realize such high ideals made him the famous cynic we know in the popular epithet *Machiavellian*. Only an unscrupulous strongman, he concluded, using duplicity and terror, could impose order on so divided and selfish a people.

It has been suggested that Machiavelli wrote *The Prince* in 1513 as a cynical satire, not as a serious recommendation of unprincipled despotic rule. To take his advocacy of tyranny literally, it is argued, contradicts both his earlier works and his own strong family tradition of republican service. But Machiavelli seems to have been in earnest when he advised rulers to discover the advantages of fraud and brutality. He apparently hoped to see a strong ruler emerge from the Medici family. The Medicis, however, were not destined to be Italy's deliverers. The second Medici pope, Clement VII (1523–1534), watched helplessly as Rome was sacked by the army of Emperor Charles V (r. 1519–1556) in 1527, the year of Machiavelli's death.[5]

Revival of Monarchy: Nation Building in the Fifteenth Century

With the emergence of sovereign rulers after 1450, unified national monarchies progressively replaced fragmented and divisive feudal governance. The dynastic and chivalric ideals of feudalism did not however disappear. Minor territorial princes continued to exist, and representative assemblies persisted and even grew in influence in some regions. But by the late fifteenth and early sixteenth centuries, the old problem of the one and the many was being decided clearly in favor of monarchy.

In the feudal monarchy of the High Middle Ages the basic powers of government were divided between the king and his semiautonomous vassals. The nobility and the towns acted with varying degrees of unity and success through such

---

[5]To place the western Renaissance in world perspective, see the conclusion of Chapter 17, where the Renaissance and the Reformation are discussed together.

evolving representative bodies as the English Parliament, the French Estates General, and the Spanish Cortes to thwart the centralization of royal power. However, as a result of the Hundred Years' War and the schism in the church, the landed nobility and the clergy were in decline in the late Middle Ages. The increasingly important towns now began to ally with the king. Loyal, business-wise townspeople, not the nobility and the clergy, staffed the royal offices, becoming the king's lawyers, bookkeepers, military tacticians, and diplomats. This new alliance between king and town would slowly break the bonds of feudal society and made possible the rise of the modern sovereign state.

In a sovereign state, the powers of taxation, war making, and law enforcement are no longer the local right of semi-autonomous vassals, but are concentrated in the monarch and exercised by his chosen agents. Taxes, wars, and laws become national rather than merely regional matters. Only as monarchs were able to act independently of the nobility and the representative assemblies could they overcome the decentralization that had been the basic obstacle to nation building.

Monarchies also began to create standing national armies in the fifteenth century. As the noble cavalry receded and the infantry and the artillery became the backbone of armies, mercenary soldiers were recruited from Switzerland and Germany to form the mainstay of the "king's army."

The growing cost of warfare increased the need to develop new national sources of royal income. The expansion of royal revenues was especially hampered by the stubborn belief among the highest classes that they were immune from government taxation. The nobility guarded their properties and traditional rights and despised taxation as an insult and a humiliation. Royal revenues accordingly grew at the expense of those least able to resist and least able to pay. Monarchs had several options. As feudal lords they could collect rents from their royal domain. They might also levy national taxes on basic food and clothing, such as the *gabelle* or salt tax in France and the *alcabala* or 10 percent sales tax on commercial transactions in Spain. Kings could also levy direct taxes on the peasantry and on commercial transactions in towns under royal protection. This they did through agreeable representative assemblies of the privileged classes in which the peasantry did not sit. The French *taille* was such a tax. Sale of public offices and the issuance of high-interest government bonds appeared in the fifteenth century as innovative fund-raising devices. But kings did not levy taxes on the powerful nobility. They turned to rich nobles, as they did to the great bankers of Italy and Germany, for loans, bargaining with the privileged classes, who often remained as much the kings" creditors and competitors as their subjects.

France

There were two cornerstones of French nation building in the fifteenth century. The first was the collapse of the English holdings in France following the Hundred Years' War. The second was the defeat of Charles the Bold (r. 1467–1477) and the duchy of Burgundy. Perhaps Europe's strongest political power in the mid-fifteenth century, Burgundy aspired to lead a dominant middle kingdom between France and the Holy Roman Empire. It might have succeeded had not the continental powers joined together in opposition. When Charles the Bold was killed at Nancy in 1477, the dream of Burgundian empire died with him.

The dissolution of Burgundy ended its constant intrigue against the French king and left Louis XI (r. 1461–1483) free to secure the monarchy. The newly acquired Burgundian lands and his own Angevin inheritance permitted the king to double the size of his kingdom. Louis successfully harnessed the nobility, expanded trade and industry, created a national postal system, and even established a lucrative silk industry at Lyons (later transferred to Tours).

A strong nation is a two-edged sword. It was because Louis's successors inherited such a secure and efficient government that France was able to pursue Italian conquests in the 1490s and to fight a long series of losing wars with the Habsburgs in the first half of the sixteenth century. By the mid-sixteenth century France was again a defeated nation and almost as divided internally as it had been during the Hundred Years' War.

Spain

Spain, too, became a strong country in the late fifteenth century. Both Castile and Aragon had been poorly ruled, divided kingdoms in the mid-fifteenth century. The marriage of Isabella of Castile (r. 1474–1504) and Ferdinand of Aragon (r. 1479–1516) changed that situation. The two future sovereigns married in 1469, despite strong protests from neighboring Portugal and France, both of which foresaw the formidable European power such a union would create. Castile was by far the richer and more populous of the two, having an estimated five million inhabitants to Aragon's population of under one million. Castile was also distinguished by its lucrative sheep-farming industry, which was run by a government-backed organization called the *Mesta*, another example of developing centralized economic planning. Although the two kingdoms were dynastically united by the marriage of Ferdinand and Isabella in 1469, each retained its own government agencies—separate laws, armies, coinage, and taxation—and cultural traditions.

Ferdinand and Isabella could do together what neither was able to accomplish alone: subdue their realms, secure their borders, and venture abroad militarily. Townspeople allied themselves with the crown and progressively replaced the nobility within the royal administration. The crown also extended its authority over the wealthy chivalric orders, a further circumscription of the power of the nobility.

Spain had long been remarkable as a place where three religions—Islam, Judaism, and Christianity—coexisted with a certain degree of toleration. This toleration ended dramatically under Ferdinand and Isabella, who made Spain the prime example of state-controlled religion. Ferdinand and Isabella exercised almost total control over the Spanish church as they placed religion in the service of national unity. They appointed the higher clergy and the officers of the Inquisition. The Inquisition, run by Tomás de Torquemada (d. 1498), Isabella's confessor, was a key national agency established in 1479 to monitor the activity of converted Jews (conversos) and Muslims (Moriscos) in Spain. In 1492 the Jews were exiled and their properties were confiscated. In 1502 nonconverting Moors in Granada were driven into exile. Spanish spiritual life remained largely uniform and regimented, a major reason for Spain's remaining a loyal Catholic country throughout the sixteenth century and providing a base of operation for the European Counter-Reformation.

Ferdinand and Isabella had wide horizons. They contracted anti-French marriage alliances that came to determine much of European history in the sixteenth century. In 1496 their eldest daughter, Joanna, later known as "the Mad" (1479–1555), married Archduke Philip (1478–1506), the son of Emperor Maximilian I (1493–1519). Their son, Charles I, the first ruler over a united Spain, came by his inheritance and election as Emperor Charles V in 1519 to rule over a European kingdom almost equal in size to that of Charlemagne. A second daughter, Catherine of Aragon (1485–1536), married King Henry VIII of England. The failure of this latter marriage became the key factor in the emergence of the Anglican Church and the English Reformation.

The new Spanish power was also evident in Ferdinand and Isabella's promotion of overseas exploration. Their patronage of the Genoese adventurer Christopher Columbus (1451–1506), who discovered the islands of the Caribbean while sailing west in search of a shorter route to the spice markets of the Far East, led to the creation of the Spanish empire in Mexico and Peru, whose gold and silver mines helped to make Spain Europe's dominant power in the sixteenth century.

England

The last half of the fifteenth century was a period of especially difficult political trial for the English. Following the Hundred Years' War, a defeated England was subjected to internal warfare between two rival branches of the royal family, the House of York and the House of Lancaster. This conflict, known to us today as the Wars of the Roses (as York's symbol, according to legend, was a white rose, and Lancaster's a red rose), kept England in turmoil from 1455 to 1485.

The Lancastrian monarchy of Henry VI (r. 1422–1461) was consistently challenged by the duke of York and his supporters in the prosperous southern towns. In 1461 Edward IV (r. 1461–1483), son of the duke of York, seized power and, assisted by loyal and able ministers, effectively bent Parliament to his will. His brother and successor was Richard III (r. 1483–1485), whose reign saw the growth of support for the exiled Lancastrian Henry Tudor. Henry returned to England to defeat Richard on Bosworth Field in August 1485.

Henry Tudor ruled as Henry VII (r. 1485–1509), the first of the new Tudor dynasty that would endure until 1603. To bring the rival royal families together and to make the hereditary claim of his offspring to the throne uncontestable, Henry married Edward IV's daughter, Elizabeth of York. He succeeded in disciplining the English nobility through a special and much-feared instrument of the royal will known as the Court of Star Chamber. Henry shrewdly construed legal precedents to the advantage of the crown, using English law to further his own ends. He confiscated so much noble land and fortunes that he governed without dependence on Parliament for royal funds, always a cornerstone of strong monarchy. Henry thus began to shape a monarchy that became one of early modern Europe's most exemplary governments during the reign of his granddaughter, Elizabeth I (r. 1558–1603).

Review Questions

1. How did the Hundred Years' War, the Black Death, and the great schism in the church affect the course of history? Which had the most lasting effects on the institutions it touched?

2. Was the church an aggressor or a victim in the late Middle Ages and Renaissance? How successful was it in its confrontations with Europe's emerging dynastic states?

3. What was "reborn" in the Renaissance? Were the humanists the forerunners of modern secular education and culture, or eloquent defenders of a still-medieval Christian view of the world against the church's secular and pagan critics?

4. Historians find features of modern states developing in west European lands during the late Middle Ages and Renaissance. What modern features can you identify in the governments of the Italian city-states and the northern monarchies?

Suggested Readings ——

L. B. ALBERTI, *The Family in Renaissance Florence*, trans. by R. N. Watkins (1962). A contemporary humanist, who never married, explains how a family should behave.

M. ASTON, *The Fifteenth Century: The Prospect of Europe* (1968). Crisp social history, with pictures.

H. BARON, *The Crisis of the Early Italian Renaissance*, Vols. 1 and 2 (1966). A major work, setting forth the civic dimension of Italian humanism.

B. BERENSON, *Italian Painters of the Renaissance* (1901). Still incisive.

G. BRUCKER, *Renaissance Florence* (1983). Considered the best introduction to the subject.

G. BRUCKER, *Giovanna and Lusanna: Love and Marriage in Renaissance Florence* (1986). A tale of unhappy marriage and extramarital love, more in the spirit of Bergman than of Fellini, and apparently typical of much of Renaissance Italy.

J. BURCKHARDT, *The Civilization of the Renaissance in Italy* (1867). The old classic that still has as many defenders as detractors.

C. CIPOLLA, *Before the Industrial Revolution: European Society and Economy, 1000–1700* (1976). Readable, sweeping account.

W. K. FERGUSON, *The Renaissance* (1940). A brief, stimulating summary of the Renaissance in both Italy and northern Europe.

W. K. FERGUSON, *Europe in Transition 1300–1520* (1962). A major survey that deals with the transition from medieval to Renaissance society.

F. GILBERT, *Machiavelli and Guicciardini* (1984). The two great Renaissance historians compared.

M. GILMORE, *The World of Humanism 1453–1517* (1952). A comprehensive survey, especially strong in intellectual and cultural history.

J. R. HALE, *Europe in the Renaissance* (1994). New, learned survey focusing on social and cultural history.

D. HAY, *The Italian Renaissance* (1977). For those who want the subject in a nutshell.

D. HERLIHY, *The Family in Renaissance Italy* (1974). Excellent on family structure and general features.

D. HERLIHY AND C. KLAPISCH-ZUBER, *Tuscans and Their Families* (1985). Important work based on unique demographic data that gives the reader an appreciation of quantitative history.

A. HUDSON, *The Premature Reformation: Wycliffite Texts and Lollard History* (1988). The teaching of John Wycliffe and the movement it stimulated.

J. HUIZINGA, *The Waning of the Middle Ages: A Study of the Forms of Life, Thought, and Art in France and The Netherlands in the Dawn of the Renaissance* (1924). A classic study of "mentality" at the end of the Middle Ages.

G. HUPPERT, *After the Black Death* (1986). A social historian's perspective on the transition from the Renaissance to modern times.

D. JENSEN, *Renaissance Europe: Age of Recovery and Reconciliation* (1981). Up-to-date textbook.

R. KELSO, *Doctrine of the Lady of the Renaissance* (1978). Noblewomen in the Renaissance.

R. KIECKHEFER, *Unquiet Souls* (1984). Penetrating and sympathetic study of fourteenth-century religious life.

C. KLAPISCH-ZUBER, *Women, Family, and Ritual in Renaissance Italy* (1985). Sober essays, stressing the negative status of women and unfairness of male treatment of them.

R. J. KNECHT, *Francis I* (1982). Up-to-date biography of the French king.

P. O. KRISTELLER, *Renaissance Thought: The Classic, Scholastic, and Humanist Strains* (1961). A master shows the many sides of Renaissance thought.

I. MACLEAN, *The Renaissance Notion of Women* (1980). A study of largely unflattering theories about women found in learned tracts on theology, philosophy, law, and medicine.

W. H. McNEILL, *Plagues and Peoples* (1976). The Black Death in a broader context.

L. MARTINES, *Power and Imagination: City States in Renaissance Italy* (1980). Stimulating account of cultural and political history.

H. A. MISKIMIN, *The Economy of Early Renaissance Europe 1300–1460* (1969). Shows the interaction of social, political, and economic change.

E. MUIR, *Civic Ritual in Renaissance Venice* (1981). A study of the use of pageantry for political purposes.

F. OAKLEY, *The Western Church in the Later Middle Ages* (1979). Vigorous defense of the integrity of late medieval religion.

E. PERROY, *The Hundred Years' War,* trans. by W. B. Wells (1965). The most comprehensive one-volume account.

Q. SKINNER, *The Foundations of Modern Political Thought I: The Renaissance* (1978). A broad survey, very comprehensive.

M. SPINKA, *John Hus's Concept of the Church* (1966). Intellectual history with documents.

J. W. THOMPSON, *Economic and Social History of Europe in the Later Middle Ages 1300–1530* (1958). A bread-and-butter account.

B. TIERNEY, *The Crisis of Church and State 1050–1300* (1964). Part 4 provides the major documents in the clash between Boniface VIII and Philip the Fair.

W. ULLMANN, *Origins of the Great Schism* (1948). A basic study by a controversial interpreter of medieval political thought.

P. ZIEGLER, *The Black Death* (1969). A highly readable journalistic account.

17 THE AGE OF REFORMATION AND RELIGIOUS WARS

Lutherans made Jesus's blessing of infants and small children (Mark 10:13) a new theme in art and a forceful polemic against Catholics, who believed good works to be a condition of salvation, and Anabaptists, who rejected infant baptism. Lucas Cranach the Elder (1472–1553) painted over twenty versions of this scene, which served as a polemical summary of Protestant teaching. Here he portrays Jesus directly accessible to those with simple childlike faith, who do no special good works and have nothing to recommend them except God's grace. The painting also expressed the Protestant affirmation of marriage and family and rejection of celibacy and of clerical polemics against woman and sex. [Elke Walford/Hamburger Kunsthalle]

◆ On the Eve of the Reformation

◆ The Reformation

◆ The Social Significance
of the Reformation in Western Europe

◆ Family Life in Early Modern Europe

◆ The Wars of Religion

◆ Superstition and Enlightenment:
The Battle Within

In World Perspective The Renaissance
and Reformation

In the second decade of the sixteenth century, a powerful religious movement began in Saxony in Germany and rapidly spread throughout northern Europe, deeply affecting society and politics as well as the spiritual lives of men and women. Attacking what they believed to be burdensome superstitions that robbed people of both their money and their peace of mind, Protestant reformers led a revolt against the medieval church. In a short time, hundreds of thousands of people from all social classes set aside the beliefs of centuries and adopted a more simplified religious practice.

The Protestant Reformation challenged aspects of the Renaissance, especially its tendency to follow classical sources in glorifying human nature and its loyalty to traditional religion. Protestants were more impressed by the human potential for evil than by the inclination to do good; they encouraged parents, teachers, and magistrates to be firm disciplinarians. On the other hand, Protestants also embraced many Renaissance values, especially in educational reform and in learning ancient languages, for here they found the tools to master Scripture and challenge the papacy.

Protestantism was not the only reform movement to grow out of the religious grievances and reforms of the late Middle Ages. Within the church itself a reform was emerging that would give birth to new religious orders, rebut Protestantism, and win back a great many of its converts.

As different groups identified their political and social goals with either Protestantism or Catholicism, a hundred years of bloody opposition between Protestants and Catholics darkened the second half of the sixteenth century and the first half of the seventeenth. In the second half of the sixteenth century the political conflict that had previously been confined to central Europe and a struggle for Lutheran rights and freedoms shifted to western Europe—to France, the Netherlands, England, and Scotland—and became a struggle for Calvinist recognition. In France Calvinists fought Catholic rulers for the right to form their own communities, to practice their chosen religion openly, and to exclude from their lands those they deemed heretical. During the Thirty Years' War (1618–1648), international armies of varying religious persuasions clashed in central and northern Europe. By 1649 English Puritans had overthrown the Stuart monarchy and the Anglican Church.

For Europe the late fifteenth and sixteenth centuries were also a period of unprecedented territorial expansion. Permanent colonies were established within the Americas, and the exploitation of the New World's human and mineral resources began. Imported American gold and silver spurred scientific invention and a new weapons industry. The new bullion also helped create an international traffic in African slaves as rival tribes sold their captives to the Portuguese. These slaves were brought in ever-increasing numbers to work the mines and the plantations of the New World as replacements for faltering American natives.

On the Eve of the Reformation

The Discovery of a New World

The discovery of the Americas dramatically expanded the geographical and intellectual horizons of Europeans. Knowledge of the New World's inhabitants and exploitation of its vast wealth

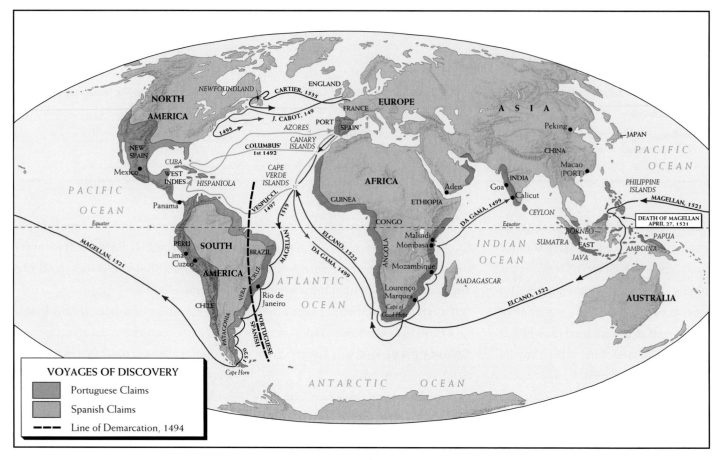

Map 17-1 European voyages of discovery and the colonial claims of Spain and Portugal in the fifteenth and sixteenth centuries.
The map dramatizes Europe's global expansion in the fifteenth and sixteenth centuries.

set new cultural and economic forces in motion throughout western Europe. Beginning with the successful voyages of Christopher Columbus (1451–1506) in the late fifteenth century, commercial supremacy started to shift from the Mediterranean and the Baltic to the Atlantic seaboard, and western Europe's global expansion began in earnest (see Map 17–1).

Gold and Spices
Mercenary motives, reinforced by traditional missionary ideals, had earlier inspired Prince Henry the Navigator (1394–1460) to sponsor Portuguese exploration of the African coast. His main object was the gold trade, which Muslims had monopolized for centuries. By the late fifteenth century gold from Guinea was entering Europe on Portuguese ships calling at the port cities of Lisbon and Antwerp, rather than via the traditional Arab overland routes. Antwerp became the financial center of Europe, a commercial crossroads where enterprise and daring could find capital funds.

The rush for gold quickly expanded into a rush for the spice markets of India as well. In the fifteenth century most Europeans ate a dull combination of bread and gruel, cabbage, turnips, peas, lentils, and onions, together with what

meat became available during seasonal periods of slaughter. Spices, especially pepper and cloves, were in great demand both as preservatives and to enhance the taste of food.

Bartholomew Dias (d. 1500) opened the Portuguese empire in the East when he rounded the Cape of Good Hope at the tip of Africa in 1487. A decade later, in 1498, Vasco da Gama (d. 1524) stood on the shores of India. When he returned to Portugal, his cargo was worth sixty times the cost of the voyage. Later, the Portuguese established themselves firmly on the Malabar Coast with colonies in Goa and Calcutta and successfully challenged the Arabs and the Venetians for control of the European spice trade.

While the Portuguese concentrated on the Indian Ocean, the Spanish set sail across the Atlantic, hoping to establish a shorter route to the rich spice markets of the East Indies. Rather than beating the Portuguese at their own game, however, Columbus discovered the Americas instead.

The Voyages of Columbus
On October 12, 1492, after a thirty-three-day voyage from the Canary Islands, Columbus landed in San Salvador (Watlings Island) in the eastern Bahamas. Having undertaken his journey in the belief that

Japan would be the first land mass he would reach as he sailed west, he thought San Salvador was an outer island of Japan. That belief was based on Marco Polo's account of his years in China during the thirteenth century and the global map of Martin Behaim, which showed only ocean between the west coast of Europe and the east coast of Asia.

Naked and extremely friendly natives met Columbus and his crew on the beaches of the New World. They were Taino Indians, who spoke a variant of a language known as Arawak. Mistaking the island for the East Indies, Columbus called the native people Indians, a name that stuck even after it became known that he had discovered a continent, unknown to Europeans, the Far East. The natives' generosity amazed Columbus. They freely gave his men all the corn and yams they desired, along with many sexual favors as well. "They never say no," Columbus marveled. At the same time he observed how easily they could be enslaved.

On the heels of Columbus, Amerigo Vespucci (1451–1512), after whom America is named, and Ferdinand Magellan (1480–1521) carefully explored the coastline of South America. Their travels documented that the new lands discovered by Columbus were not the outermost territory of the Far East, but a new continent that opened on the still greater Pacific Ocean. Magellan, in search of a westward route to the East Indies, sailed to the Philippines, where he died.

Impact on Europe and America   Columbus's voyage of 1492 marked, unknowingly to those who undertook and

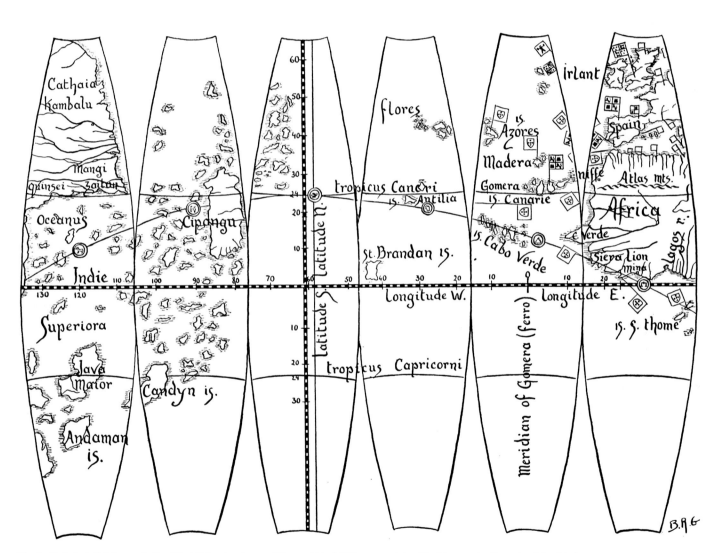

Martin Behaim's "globe apple."   What Columbus knew of the world in 1492 was contained in this map by Nuremberg geographer Martin Behaim (1440-1507), creator of the first spherical globe of the earth. The ocean section of Behaim's globe is reproduced here. Departing the Canary Islands (in the second section from the right), Columbus expected his first major landfall to be Japan, or what he calls Cipangu (in the second section from the left). When he landed at San Salvador, he thought he was on an outer island of Japan; after reaching Cuba, he believed it to be Japan. Only slowly did it dawn on him that these new lands had never before been seen by Europeans.

[Samuel Eliot Morison, *Admiral of the Ocean Sea.* Copyright 1942 © renewed 1970 by Samuel Eliot Morison. By permission of Little, Brown and Company, Boston, MA.]

financed it, the beginning of more than three centuries of Spanish conquest, exploitation, and administration of a vast American empire. What had begun as voyages of discovery soon became expeditions of conquest that resembled the warfare of Christian Aragon and Castile against the Islamic Moors. Those wars had just ended in 1492, and they imbued the early Spanish explorers with a zeal for conquering and converting non-Christian peoples.

The voyages to the New World had important consequences for the cultures of both Europe and America. For Spain the venture created the largest and longest surviving European trading bloc, while spurring other European countries to undertake their own colonial ventures. The great wealth from its American possessions financed Spain's commanding role in the age's religious and political conflicts. It also ignited a gradual, Europe-wide inflation during the sixteenth century.

For the native peoples of America, the voyages triggered a long period of conquest that virtually destroyed their civilizations, as warfare, new diseases, and exploitation of labor and resources devastated their populations. In both South and North America, Spanish rule set an imprint of Roman Catholicism, economic dependency, and hierarchical social structure that is still highly visible today.

Religion and Society

The Protestant Reformation occurred at a time of sharp conflict between the emerging nation-states of Europe, bent on conformity and centralization within their realms, and the self-governing small towns and regions, long accustomed to running their own affairs. Since the fourteenth century the king's law and custom had progressively overridden local law

and custom almost everywhere. Many towns and territories were keenly sensitive to the loss of traditional rights and freedoms. Many townspeople and villagers saw the religious revolt as part of their struggle to remain politically free and independent. The Reformation came to be closely identified in the minds of its supporters with what we today might call states' rights or local control.

Social and Political Conflict   The Reformation broke out first in the free imperial cities of Germany and Switzerland. There were about sixty-five such cities, and each was in a certain sense a little kingdom unto itself. Most had Protestant movements, but with mixed success and duration. Some quickly turned Protestant and remained so. Some were Protestant only for a short time. Others developed mixed confessions, frowning on sectarianism and aggressive proselytizing, and letting Catholics and Protestants coexist.

What seemed a life-and-death struggle with higher princely or royal authority was not the only conflict cities were experiencing. They also suffered deep internal social and political divisions. Certain groups favored the Reformation more than others. In many places, guilds like that of the printers, whose members were economically prospering and socially rising, and who had a history of conflict with local governmental authority, were often in the forefront of the Reformation. There is evidence to suggest that it was people who felt pushed around and bullied by either local or distant authority—a guild by an autocratic local government; an entire city or region by a powerful prince or king—who perceived in the Protestant movement an ally, at least initially.

Social and political experience thus coalesced with the larger religious issues in both town and countryside. When

The Reformation broke out against a background of deep social and political divisions that bred resentment against authority. This early sixteenth-century woodcut by Georg Pencz presents a warning against tyranny. It shows a world turned upside down, with the hunted becoming the hunters. The rabbits capture the hunters and their dogs and subject them to the same brutal treatment (skinning, butchering, and cooking) that the hunters and dogs routinely inflict on rabbits. The message: tyranny begets tyranny. [Hacker Art Books, 1974. Used by permission of Hacker Art Books]

Martin Luther and his comrades wrote, preached, and sang about a priesthood of all believers, scorned the authority of ecclesiastical landlords, and ridiculed papal laws as arbitrary human inventions, they touched political as well as religious nerves in German and Swiss cities. This was also true in the villages, for the peasants on the land also heard in the Protestant sermon and pamphlet a promise of political liberation and even a degree of social betterment.

Popular Movements and Criticism of the Church

The Protestant Reformation could also not have occurred without the monumental crises of the late medieval church and the Renaissance papacy. For many people, the church had ceased to provide a viable foundation for religious piety. Laity and clerics alike began to seek a more heartfelt, idealistic, and often—in the eyes of the pope—increasingly heretical religious piety. The late Middle Ages were marked by independent lay and clerical efforts to reform local religious practice and by widespread experimentation with new religious forms that shared a common goal of religious simplicity in imitation of Jesus.

A variety of factors contributed to the growth of lay criticism of the church. The laity in the cities were becoming increasingly knowledgeable about the world and those who controlled their lives. They traveled widely—as soldiers, pilgrims, explorers, and traders. New postal systems and the printing press increased the information at their disposal. The new age of books and libraries raised literacy and heightened curiosity. Laypeople were increasingly able to take the initiative in shaping the cultural life of their communities.

The Modern Devotion   One of the most constructive lay religious movements in northern Europe on the eve of the Reformation was that of the Brothers of the Common Life, or what came to be known as the *Modern Devotion*. The brothers fostered religious life outside formal ecclesiastical offices and apart from formal religious vows. Established by Gerard Groote (1340–1384), the Modern Devotion was centered at Zwolle and Deventer in the Netherlands. The brother and (less numerous) sister houses of the Modern Devotion, however, spread rapidly throughout northern Europe and influenced parts of southern Europe as well. In these houses clerics and laity shared a common life, stressing individual piety and practical religion. Their practices clearly met a need for a more personal piety and a better-informed religious life.

Secular Control over Religious Life   On the eve of the Reformation, Rome's international network of church offices began to fall apart in many areas, hurried along by a growing sense of regional identity—incipient nationalism—and local secular administrative competence. The late medieval church had permitted important ecclesiastical posts ("benefices") to be sold to the highest bidders and had not enforced residency requirements in parishes. Rare was the late medieval German town that did not have complaints about the maladministration, concubinage, or fiscalism of its clergy, especially the higher clergy (bishops, abbots, and prelates).

City governments also sought to restrict the growth of ecclesiastical properties and clerical privileges and to improve local religious life by bringing the clergy under the local tax code and by endowing new clerical positions for well-trained and conscientious preachers.

The Northern Renaissance

The scholarly works of northern humanists created a climate favorable to religious and educational reforms. Northern humanism was initially stimulated by the importation of Italian learning through such varied intermediaries as students who had studied in Italy, merchants, and the Brothers of the Common Life. The northern humanists tended to come from more diverse social backgrounds and to be more devoted to religious reforms than were their Italian counterparts. They were also more willing to write for lay audiences.

The growth of schools and lay education combined with the invention of cheap paper to create a mass audience for printed books. In response, Johann Gutenberg (d. 1468) invented printing with movable type in the German city of Mainz around 1450. Thereafter, books were rapidly and handsomely produced on topics both profound and practical. By 1500, printing presses operated in at least sixty German cities and in more than 200 throughout Europe. A new medium now existed for politicians, humanists, and reformers alike. (See Comparative Perspectives: "The Invention of Printing in China and Europe.")

The most famous of the northern humanists was Desiderius Erasmus (1466–1536), the "prince of the humanists." Idealistic and pacifistic, Erasmus gained fame as both an educational and a religious reformer. He aspired to unite the classical ideals of humanity and civic virtue with the Christian ideals of love and piety. He believed that disciplined study of the classics and the Bible, if begun early enough, was the best way to reform both individuals and society. He summarized his own beliefs with the phrase *philosophia Christi*, a simple, ethical piety in imitation of Christ. He set this ideal against what he believed to be the dogmatic, ceremonial, and factious religious practice of the later Middle Ages. To promote his own religious beliefs, Erasmus edited the works of the Church Fathers and made a Greek edition of the New Testament (1516), which became the basis for a new, more accurate Latin translation (1519). Martin Luther later used both these works as the basis for his famous German translation.

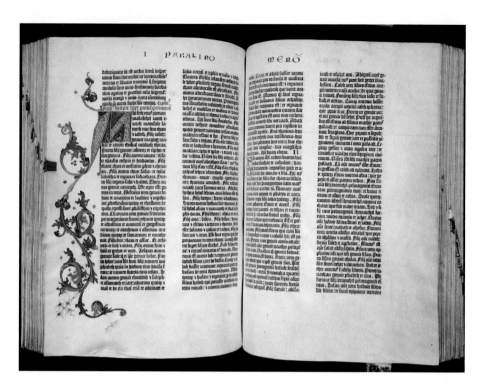

The printing press made possible the diffusion of Renaissance learning. But no book stimulated thought more at this time than did the Bible. With Gutenberg's publication of a printed Bible in 1454, scholars gained access to a dependable, standardized text, so that Scripture could be discussed and debated as never before. [Huntington Library]

Both Catholic and Lutheran authorities turned against Erasmus's middle-of-the-road theology and piety. Catholic authorities viewed him as a crypto-Lutheran, whose scholarly works and satires of church abuses aided and abetted the Reformation. Erasmus once satirized the great Renaissance Pope Julius II as a man turned away from the gates of heaven by St. Peter, who could not find in him any qualities of a godly man. At mid-century all of Erasmus's works were temporarily placed on the *Index of Forbidden Books*. Lutherans initially accused Erasmus of hypocrisy and cowardice, when he continued to remain a loyal Catholic after having so boldly criticized the papacy. For his part, Erasmus dismissed the new teaching of Luther, particularly his views on human sinfulness and bondage to the devil, as harshly as he did the corruption of the papacy. Yet despite his alienation from both camps, Erasmus's religious writings and educational reforms inspired Catholic and Protestant reformers alike.

The best known of early English humanists was Sir Thomas More (1478–1535), a close friend of Erasmus. It was while visiting More that Erasmus wrote his most famous work, *The Praise of Folly* (1511), an amusing and profound exposé of human self-deception that was quickly translated from the original Latin into many vernacular languages. More's *Utopia* (1516), a criticism of contemporary society, depicts an imaginary society based on reason and tolerance that requires everyone to work and has rid itself of all social and political injustice. Although More would remain staunchly Catholic, humanism in England, as in Germany, paved the way for the English Reformation. A circle of English humanists, under the direction of Henry VIII's minister Thomas Cromwell, translated and disseminated late medieval criticisms of the papacy and many of Erasmus's satirical writings as well.

Whereas in Germany, England, and France, humanism helped the Protestants, in Spain it entered the service of the Catholic Church. Here the key figure was Francisco Jiménez de Cisneros (1437–1517), a confessor to Queen Isabella, and after 1508 Grand Inquisitor—a position from which he was able to enforce the strictest religious orthodoxy. Jiménez was a conduit for humanist scholarship and learning. He founded the University of Alcalá near Madrid in 1509, printed a Greek edition of the New Testament, and translated many religious tracts that aided clerical reform and control of lay religious life. His greatest achievement, taking fifteen years to complete, was the *Complutensian Polyglot Bible*, a six-volume work that placed the Hebrew, Greek, and Latin versions of the Bible in parallel columns. Such scholarly projects and internal church reforms joined with the repressive measures of Ferdinand and Isabella to keep Spain strictly Catholic.

The Reformation

Martin Luther and the German Reformation to 1525

Late medieval Germany lacked the political unity to enforce "national" religious reforms during the late Middle Ages.

Thomas More (1478-1535), painted by Hans Holbein the Younger in 1527. The English statesman and author was beheaded by Henry VIII for his refusal to recognize the king's sovereignty over the English church. [The Frick Collection]

Ordained in 1507, he pursued a traditional course of theological study in the Bible and the *Sentences* of Peter Lombard, the basic theological text of the later Middle Ages. In 1510 he journeyed to Rome on the business of his order, finding there justification for the many criticisms of the church he had heard in Germany. In 1511 he was transferred to the Augustinian monastery in Wittenberg, where he earned his doctorate in theology (1512), thereafter to become a leader within the monastery, the new university, and the spiritual life of the city.

The Attack on Indulgences Reformation theology grew out of a problem common to many clergy and laity at this time: the failure of traditional medieval religion to provide full personal or intellectual satisfaction. Luther was especially plagued by the disproportion between his own sense of sinfulness and the perfect righteousness that medieval theology taught that God required for salvation. Traditional church teaching and the sacrament of penance were no consolation. Luther wrote that he came to despise the phrase "righteousness of God," for it seemed to demand of him a perfection he knew neither he nor any other human being could ever achieve. His insight into the meaning of "justification by faith alone" was a gradual process that extended over several years, between 1513 and 1518. The righteousness God demands, he concluded, was not one that came from many religious works and ceremonies but was present in full measure in those who simply believed and trusted in the work of Jesus Christ, who alone was the perfect righteousness satisfying to God. To believe in Christ was to stand before God clothed in Christ's sure righteousness.

This new theology made indulgences unacceptable. An indulgence was a remission of the temporal penalty imposed by the priest on penitents as a "work of satisfaction" for their sins. According to medieval theology, after the priest had absolved penitents of guilt for their sins, God still imposed on them a temporal penalty, a manageable "work of satisfaction" that the penitent could perform here and now (for example, through prayers, fasting, almsgiving, retreats, and pilgrimages). Penitents who defaulted on such prescribed works of satisfaction could expect to suffer for their sins in purgatory.

At this point, indulgences came into play as an aid to a laity made genuinely anxious by the belief in a future suffering in purgatory for neglected penances or unrepented sins. Originally, indulgences had been given only for the true self-sacrifice of going on a crusade to the Holy Land. By Luther's time, they were regularly dispensed for small cash payments (modest sums that were regarded as almsgiving) and were presented to the laity as remitting not only their own future punishments, but also those of their dead relatives presumed to be suffering in purgatory.

In 1517 a Jubilee indulgence, proclaimed under Pope Julius II (1503–1513) to raise funds for the rebuilding of Saint

What happened on a unified national level in England and France occurred only locally and piecemeal in Germany. As popular resentment of clerical immunities and ecclesiastical abuses, especially regarding the selling of indulgences, spread among German cities and towns, an unorganized "national" opposition to Rome formed. German humanists had long given voice to such criticism, and by 1517 it provided a solid foundation for Martin Luther's reform.

Luther (1483–1546), the son of a successful Thuringian miner, received his early education in the Saxon towns of Mansfeld, Magdeburg (where the Brothers of the Common Life were his teachers), and Eisenach. Between 1501 and 1505 he attended the University of Erfurt, taking a master of arts' degree in 1505. He registered with the Law Faculty in accordance with his parents' wishes, but he never began that course of study. To the shock and disappointment of his parents, he instead entered the Order of the Hermits of Saint Augustine in Erfurt on July 17, 1505, a decision that had apparently been building in him for some time.

Johannes Tezelius Dominicaner Münch/mit seinen Römischen Ablaßkram/welchen er im Jahr Christi 1517. in Deutschen landen zu marckt gebracht/wie er in der Kirchen zu Pirn in seinem Vaterland abgemahlet ist.

O ihr deutschen mercket mich recht/
Des heiligen Vaters Papstes Knecht/
Bin ich/vnd br in euch jst allein/
Zehn tausent vnd neun hundert carein/
Gnad vnd Ablaß von einer Sünd/
Vor euch/ewer Eltern/Weib vnd Kind/
Sol ein jeder gewehret sein
So viel ihr legt ins Kästelein/
So bald der Gülden im Becken klingt/
Im huy die Seel im Himel springt/

A contemporary caricature depicts John Tetzel, the famous indulgence preacher. The last lines of the jingle read: "As soon as gold in the basin rings, right then the soul to heaven springs." It was Tetzel's preaching that spurred Luther to publish his ninety-five theses. [Courtesy Lutherhalle, Wittenberg]

Peter's in Rome, was revived and preached on the borders of Saxony in the territories of Archbishop Albrecht of Mainz, who had large debts. The selling of the indulgence was a joint venture by Albrecht, the Augsburg banking house of Fugger, and Pope Leo X (1513–1521), half the proceeds going to the pope and half to Albrecht and his creditors. The famous indulgence preacher John Tetzel (d. 1519) was enlisted to preach the indulgence in Albrecht's territories because he was a seasoned professional who knew how to stir ordinary people to action. As he exhorted on one occasion:

> Don't you hear the voices of your dead parents and other relatives crying out, "Have mercy on us, for we suffer great punishment and pain. From this you could release us with a few alms. . . . We have created you, fed you, cared for you, and left you our temporal goods. Why do you treat us so cruelly and leave us to suffer in the flames, when it takes only a little to save us?"[1]

When on October 31, 1517, Luther posted his ninety-five theses against indulgences, according to tradition, on the door

[1]*Die Reformation in Augenzeugen Berichten*, ed. by Helmar Junghans (Dusseldorf: Karl Rauch Verlag, 1967), p. 44.

of Castle Church in Wittenberg, he protested especially against the impression created by Tetzel that indulgences actually remitted sins and released the dead from punishment in purgatory—claims he believed went far beyond the traditional practice and seemed to make salvation something that could be bought and sold.

Election of Charles V and the Diet of Worms

Humanists and other proponents of reform embraced the ninety-five theses. They made Luther famous overnight and prompted official proceedings against him. As sanctions were being prepared against Luther, Emperor Maximilian I died (January 12, 1519), which diverted attention from heresy in Saxony to the contest for a new emperor.

The pope backed the French king, Francis I. However, Charles I of Spain, a youth of nineteen, succeeded his grandfather and became Emperor Charles V (1519–1556) (see Map 17–2). Charles was assisted by both a long tradition of Habsburg imperial rule and a massive Fugger campaign chest, which secured the votes of the seven electors.

During the same month in which Charles was elected emperor, Luther entered a debate in Leipzig (June 27, 1519) with the Ingolstadt professor John Eck (1486–1543). During this contest Luther challenged the infallibility of the pope and the inerrancy of church councils, appealing for the first time to the sovereign authority of Scripture alone. All his bridges to the old church were burned when he further defended certain teachings of Jan Hus that had been condemned by the Council of Constance. In 1520 Luther signaled his new direction with three famous pamphlets: the *Address to the Christian Nobility of the German Nation*, which urged the German princes to force reforms on the Roman Church, especially to curtail its political and economic power in Germany; the *Babylonian Captivity of the Church*, which attacked the traditional seven sacraments, arguing that only two were proper, and which exalted the authority of Scripture, church councils, and secular princes over that of the pope; and the eloquent *Freedom of a Christian*, which summarized the new teaching of salvation by faith alone. On June 15, 1520, the papal bull *Exsurge Domine* condemned Luther for heresy and gave him sixty days to retract. The final bull of excommunication, *Decet Pontificem Romanum*, was issued on January 3, 1521.

In April 1521 Luther presented his views before a diet of the empire in Worms, over which Charles V presided. Ordered to recant, Luther declared that to do so would be to act against Scripture, reason, and his own conscience. On May 26, 1521, he was placed under the imperial ban and thereafter became an "outlaw" to secular as well as to religious authority. Friends hid him in Wartburg Castle, where he spent almost a year in seclusion, from April 1521 to March 1522. During his stay he translated the New Testament into

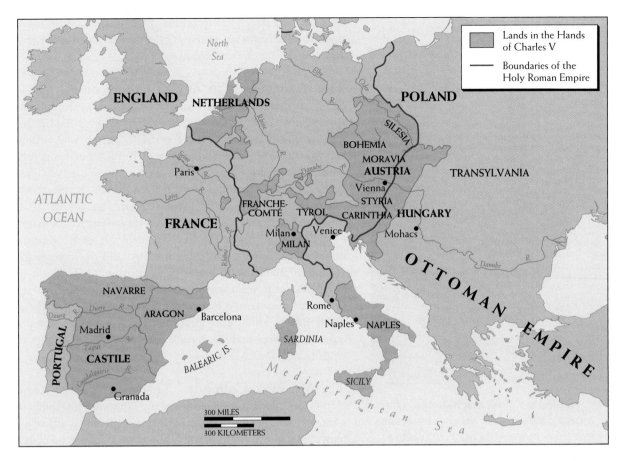

Map 17–2 The empire of Charles V. Dynastic marriages and good luck concentrated into Charles's hands rule over the lands shown here, plus Spain's overseas possessions. Crowns and titles rained down on him; election in 1519 as emperor gave him new burdens and responsibilities.

German, using Erasmus's new Greek text, and he attempted by correspondence to oversee the first stages of the Reformation in Wittenberg.

The Reformation was greatly assisted in these early years by the emperor's war with France and the advance of the Ottoman Turks into eastern Europe. Against both adversaries Charles V, who also remained a Spanish king with dynastic responsibilities outside the empire, needed German troops; to that end, he promoted friendly relations with the German princes. Between 1521 and 1559, Spain (the Habsburg dynasty) and France (the Valois dynasty) fought four major wars. In 1526 the Turks overran Hungary at the Battle of Mohacs, while in western Europe the French-led League of Cognac formed against Charles for the second Habsburg-Valois war. Thus preoccupied, the emperor agreed through his representatives at the German Diet of Speyer in 1526 that each German territory was free to enforce the Edict of Worms (1521) against Luther "so as to be able to answer in good conscience to God and the emperor." That concession, in effect, gave the German princes territorial sov-

ereignty in religious matters and the Reformation time to put down deep roots.

The Peasants' Revolt In its first decade, the Protestant movement suffered more from internal division than from imperial interference. By 1525 Luther had become as much an object of protest within Germany as was the pope. Original allies, sympathizers, and fellow travelers declared their independence from him.

Like the German humanists, the German peasantry also had at first believed Luther to be an ally. The peasantry had been organized since the late fifteenth century against efforts by territorial princes to override their traditional laws and customs and to subject them to new regulations and taxes. Peasant leaders, several of whom were convinced Lutherans, saw in Luther's teaching about Christian freedom and his criticism of monastic landowners a point of view close to their own, and they openly solicited Luther's support of their political and economic rights, including their revolutionary request for release from serfdom. Luther and his

The punishment of a peasant leader in a village near Heilbronn. After the defeat of rebellious peasants in and around the city of Heilbronn, Jacob Rorbach, a well-to-do peasant leader from a nearby village, was tied to a stake and slowly roasted to death. [Badische Landesbibliothek]

followers sympathized with the peasants, but the Lutherans were not social revolutionaries. When the peasants revolted in 1524–1525, Luther condemned them in the strongest possible terms as "unchristian" and urged the princes to crush their revolt without mercy. Tens of thousands of peasants (estimates run between seventy thousand and one hundred thousand) had died by the time the revolt was put down.

For Luther, the freedom of the Christian was an inner release from guilt and anxiety, not a right to restructure society by violent revolution. Had Luther supported the Peasants' Revolt, he would have not only contradicted his own teaching and belief but also ended any chance that his reform would survive beyond the 1520s.

Zwingli and the Swiss Reformation

Although Luther's was the first, Switzerland and France had their own independent reform movements almost simultaneously with Germany's. From them developed churches as prominent and lasting as the Lutheran.

Switzerland was a loose confederacy of thirteen autonomous cantons or states and allied areas (see Map 17–3). Some became Protestant, some remained Catholic, and a few

managed to effect a compromise. The two preconditions of the Swiss Reformation were the growth of national sentiment and a desire for church reform.

The Reformation in Zurich   Ulrich Zwingli (1484–1531), the leader of the Swiss Reformation, was strongly influenced by Erasmus, whom he credited with having set him on the path to reform. By 1518 Zwingli was widely known for opposition to the sale of indulgences and religious superstition.

In 1519 he became people's priest in Zurich, the base from which he engineered the Swiss Reformation. Zwingli's reform guideline was very simple and very effective: Whatever lacked literal support in Scripture was to be neither believed nor practiced. A disputation held on January 29, 1523, concluded with the city government's sanction of Zwingli's Scripture test. Thereafter Zurich became, to all intents and purposes, a Protestant city and the center of the Swiss Reformation. The new Protestant regime imposed a harsh discipline, making Zurich one of the first examples of a puritanical Protestant city.

The Marburg Colloquy   Landgrave Philip of Hesse (1504–1567) sought to unite Swiss and German Protestants in a mutual defense pact, a potentially significant political alliance. His efforts were spoiled, however, by theological disagreements between Luther and Zwingli over the nature of Christ's presence in the Eucharist. Zwingli maintained a symbolic interpretation of Christ's words, "This is my body"; Christ, he argued, was only spiritually, not bodily, present in the bread and wine of the Eucharist. Luther, to the contrary, insisted that Christ's human nature could share the properties of His divine nature; hence, where Christ was spiritually present, He could also be bodily present, for His was a special nature.

Philip of Hesse brought the two Protestant leaders together in his castle in Marburg in early October 1529, but they were unable to work out their differences on this issue. Luther left thinking Zwingli a dangerous fanatic. The disagreement splintered the Protestant movement theologically and politically.

Anabaptists and Radical Protestants

The moderate pace and seemingly small ethical results of the Lutheran and Zwinglian reformations discontented many people, among them some of the original co-workers of Luther and Zwingli. Many desired a more rapid and thorough implementation of primitive Christianity and accused the major reformers of going only halfway. The most important of these radical groups were the Anabaptists, the sixteenth-century ancestors of the modern Mennonites and

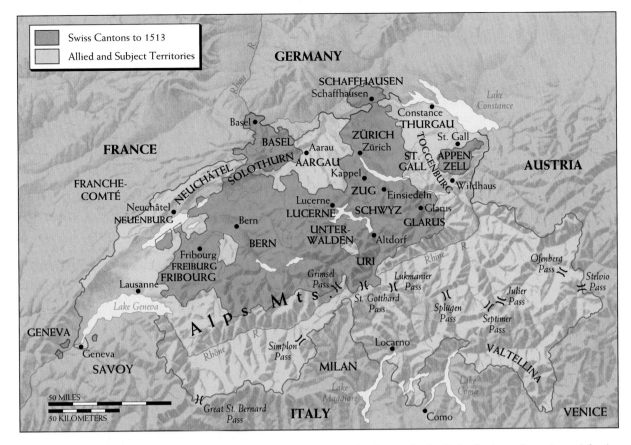

Map 17–3 The Swiss confederation. While nominally still a part of the Holy Roman Empire, Switzerland grew from a loose defensive union of the central "forest cantons" in the thirteenth century to a fiercely independent association of regions with different languages, histories, and, finally, religions.

Amish. The Anabaptists were especially distinguished by their rejection of infant baptism and their insistence on only adult baptism (*anabaptism* derives from the Greek word meaning "to rebaptize"), believing that baptism as a consenting adult conformed to Scripture and was more respectful of human freedom.

Anabaptists physically separated from society to form a more perfect community in imitation of what they believed to be the example of the first Christians. Due to the close connection between religious and civic life in this period, the political authorities viewed such separatism as a threat to basic social bonds.

At first Anabaptism drew its adherents from all social classes. But as Lutherans and Zwinglians joined with Catholics in opposition to it, a more rural, agrarian class came to make up the great majority of Anabaptists. In 1529 rebaptism became a capital offense throughout the Holy Roman Empire. It has been estimated that between 1525 and 1618 at least one thousand and perhaps as many as five thousand men and women were executed for rebaptizing themselves as adults.

John Calvin and the Genevan Reformation

Calvinism was the religious ideology that inspired or accompanied massive political resistance in France, the Netherlands, and Scotland. Believing strongly in both divine predestination and the individual's responsibility to reorder society according to God's plan, Calvinists became zealous reformers determined to transform society according to their religious beliefs. In a famous and controversial study, *The Protestant Ethic and the Spirit of Capitalism* (1904), the German sociologist Max Weber argued that this peculiar combination of religious confidence and self-disciplined activism produced an ethic that stimulated and reinforced emergent capitalism, bringing Calvinism and later Puritanism into close association with the development of modern capitalist societies.

Political Revolt and Religious Reform in Geneva

Whereas in Saxony religious reform paved the way for a political revolution against the emperor, in Geneva a political revolution against the local prince-bishop laid the foundation

German Peasants Protest Rising Feudal Exactions

In the late fifteenth and early sixteenth centuries, German feudal lords, both secular and ecclesiastical, tried to increase the earnings from their lands by raising demands on their peasant tenants. As the traditional freedoms and property rights of peasants were restricted, massive revolts occurred in southern Germany in 1525. The following, representative statement of peasant grievances, summarized in twelve articles, came from the town of Memmingen.

Are the peasants more interested in material than in spiritual freedom? Which of their demands are the most revolutionary, and which are the least problematic for their lords to grant? Why do some centuries exhibit greater social and political equality that others?

---

1. It is our humble petition and desire that in the future each community should choose and appoint a pastor, and that we should have the right to depose him should he conduct himself improperly....

2. We are ready and willing to pay the fair tithe of grain.... The small tithes [of cattle], whether [to] ecclesiastical or lay lords, we will not pay at all, for the Lord God created cattle for the free use of man....

3. We ... take it for granted that you will release us from serfdom as true Christians, unless it should be shown us from the Gospel that we are serfs.

4. It has been the custom heretofore that no poor man should be allowed to catch venison or wildfowl or fish in flowing water, which seems to us quite unseemly and unbrotherly as well as selfish and not agreeable to the Word of God....

5. We are aggrieved in the matter of woodcutting, for the noblemen have appropriated all the woods to themselves....

6. In regard to the excessive services demanded of us which are increased from day to day, we ask that this matter be properly looked into so that we shall not continue to be oppressed in this way....

7. We will not hereafter allow ourselves to be further oppressed by our lords, but will let them demand only what is just and proper according to the word of the agreement between the lord and the peasant. The lord should no longer try to force more services or other dues from the peasant without payment....

8. We are greatly burdened because our holdings cannot support the rent exacted from them.... We ask that the lords may appoint persons of honor to inspect these holdings and fix a rent in accordance with justice....

9. We are burdened with a great evil in the constant making of new laws.... In our opinion we should be judged according to the old written law....

10. We are aggrieved by the appropriation ... of meadows and fields which at one time belonged to a community as a whole. These we will take again into our own hands....

11. We will entirely abolish the due called Todfall [that is, *heriot* or *death tax*, by which the lord received the best horse, cow, or garment of a family upon the death of a serf] and will no longer endure it, nor allow widows and orphans to be thus shamefully robbed against God's will, and in violation of justice and right....

12. It is our conclusion and final resolution, that if any one or more of the articles here set forth should not be in agreement with the Word of God, as we think they are, such article we will willingly retract.

Translations and Reprints from the *Original Sources of European History*, Vol. 2 (Philadelphia: Department of History, University of Pennsylvania, 1897).

---

for religious change. Genevans successfully revolted against the ruling House of Savoy and their resident prince-bishop in the late 1520s. In late 1533 Bern dispatched Protestant reformers to Geneva. In the summer of 1535, after much internal turmoil, the Protestants triumphed, and the traditional mass and other religious practices were abolished. On May 21, 1536, the city voted officially to adopt the Reformation: "to live according to the Gospel and the Word of God ... without ... any more masses, statues, idols, or other papal abuses."

John Calvin (1509–1564), a reform-minded humanist and lawyer, arrived in Geneva after these events, in July 1536. Guillaume Farel (1489–1565), the local Protestant reformer, persuaded him to stay and assist the Reformation. Before a year had passed, Calvin had drawn up articles for the governance of the new church, as well as a catechism to guide and discipline the people, both of which were presented for approval to the city councils in early 1537. As a result of the strong measures proposed to govern Geneva's moral life, many suspected the reformers of desiring to create a "new papacy." Both within and outside Geneva, Calvin and Farel were perceived as going too far too fast, and in February 1538 they were exiled from the city.

Calvin went to Strasbourg, a model Protestant city, where he became pastor to the French exiles there. During his two years in Strasbourg he wrote biblical commentaries and a second edition of his masterful *Institutes of the Christian Religion*, which many consider the definitive theological statement of the Protestant faith. He also married and participated in the ecumenical discussions urged on Protestants and Catholics by Charles V. Most important, he learned from the Strasbourg reformer Martin Bucer (1491–1551) how to implement the Protestant Reformation successfully.

Calvin's Geneva In 1540 Geneva elected officials who were favorable to Calvin and invited him to return. This he did in September 1540, never to leave the city again. Within months of his arrival, new ecclesiastical ordinances were implemented that provided for cooperation between the magistrates and the clergy in matters of internal discipline.

Calvin and his followers were motivated above all by a desire to transform society morally. Faith, Calvin taught, did not sit idly in the mind but conformed one's every action to God's law. The "elect" should live in a manifestly God-pleasing way, if they were truly God's elect. The majesty of God

demanded nothing less. To realize this goal, Calvin spared no effort. The consistory (a judicial body composed of clergy and laity) became his instrument of power. This body was composed of elders and pastors of the church and was presided over by one of the city's four civil magistrates. It enforced the strictest moral discipline, meting out punishments for a broad range of moral and religious transgressions—from missing church services (a fine of three sous) to fornication (six days on bread and water and a fine of sixty sous) and, as time passed, increasingly for criticism of Calvin.

After 1555 the city's magistrates were all devout Calvinists, and Geneva became home to thousands of exiled Protestants who had been driven out of France, England, and Scotland. Refugees (more than five thousand), most of them utterly loyal to Calvin, came to make up over one third of the population of Geneva. From this time until his death in 1564, Calvin's position in the city was greatly strengthened and the magistrates were very cooperative.

Political Consolidation of the Lutheran Reformation

By 1530 the Reformation was in Europe to stay. It would, however, take several decades and major attempts to eradicate it before all would recognize this fact. With the political

This seventeenth-century Calvinist church in the Palatinate has no interior decoration to distract the worshipper from the Word of God. The intent was to create an atmosphere of quiet introspection and reflection on one's spiritual life and God's Word. [German National Museum, Nuremberg]

Rules Governing Genevan Moral Behavior

During Calvin's lifetime, Geneva gained the reputation of being a model evangelical city. Persecuted Protestants in the outside world considered it Europe's freest and most godly city. Strict moral enforcement conformed faith and practice. It also gave the city and the new church the order they needed to survive against their enemies. The following selections are from ordinances governing the village churches around Geneva.

Are Calvin's rules designed primarily to protect the Reformation? What do these rules suggest that he fears most? Are the penalties heavy or slaps on the wrist? Is it a sign of the failure of his reform that the Genevan people never stopped doing these things?

Concerning the Time of Assembling at Church

That the temples be closed for the rest of the time [when religious services are not being held] in order that no one shall enter therein out of hours, impelled thereto by superstition; and if any one be found engaged in any special act of devotion therein or near by he shall be admonished for it: if it be found to be of a superstitious nature for which simple correction is inadequate, then he shall be chastised.

Blasphemy

Whoever shall have blasphemed, swearing by the body or by the blood of our Lord, or in similar manner, he shall be made to kiss the earth for the first offence; for the second to pay 5 sous, and for the third 6 sous, and for the last offence be put in the pillory for one hour.

Drunkenness

1. That no one shall invite another to drink under penalty of 3 sous.

2. That taverns shall be closed during the sermon, under penalty that the tavern-keeper shall pay 3 sous, and whoever may be found therein shall pay the same amount.

3. If any one be found intoxicated he shall pay for the first offence 3 sous and shall be remanded to the consistory; for the second offence he shall be held to pay the sum of 6 sous, and for the third 10 sous and be put in prison.

4. That no one shall make roiaumes [great feasts] under penalty of 10 sous.

Songs and Dances

If any one sing immoral, dissolute or outrageous songs, or dance the virollet or other dance, he shall be put in prison for three days and then sent to the Consistory.

Usury

That no one shall take upon interest or profit more than five per cent upon penalty of confiscation of the principal and of being condemned to make restitution as the case may demand.

Games

That no one shall play at any dissolute game or at any game whatsoever it may be, neither for gold nor silver nor for any excessive stake, upon penalty of 5 sous and forfeiture of stake played for.

Translations and Reprints from the *Original Sources of European History*, Vol. 3 (Philadelphia: Department of History, University of Pennsylvania, 1909), pp. 10–11.

---

triumph of Lutheranism in the empire by the 1550s, Protestant movements elsewhere gained a new lease on life.

Diet of Augsburg   Charles V returned to the empire in 1530 to direct the Diet of Augsburg, a meeting of Protestant and Catholic representatives assembled to resolve religious divisions. With its terms dictated by the Catholic emperor, the diet adjourned with a blunt order to all Lutherans to revert to Catholicism. The Reformation was too firmly established for that to occur, and in February 1531 the Lutherans formed their own defensive alliance, the Schmalkaldic League, which achieved a stalemate with the emperor, who was again distracted by renewed war with France and the Turks.

Expansion of the Reformation   In the 1530s German Lutherans formed regional consistories, which oversaw and administered the new Protestant churches. These consistories replaced the old Catholic episcopates. Under the leadership of Philip Melanchthon (1497–1560), Luther's most admired colleague, educational reforms were enacted that provided for compulsory primary education, schools for girls, a humanist revision of the traditional curriculum, and catechetical instruction of the laity in the new religion.

The Reformation also dug in elsewhere. Introduced into Denmark by Christian II (r. 1513–1523), Lutheranism became the state religion under Christian III (r. 1536–1559). In Sweden, Gustavus Vasa (r. 1523–1560), supported by a nobility greedy for church lands, confiscated church property and subjected the clergy to royal authority at the Diet of Vesteras (1527).

In politically splintered Poland, Lutherans, Calvinists, and others found room to practice their beliefs. The absence of a central political authority made Poland a model of religious pluralism and toleration in the second half of the sixteenth century.

Reaction Against Protestants: The "Interim"

Charles V made abortive efforts in 1540–1541 to enforce a compromise agreement between Protestants and Catholics. As these and other conciliar efforts failed, he turned to a military solution. In 1547 imperial armies crushed the Protestant Schmalkaldic League.

The emperor established puppet rulers in Saxony and Hesse and issued as imperial law the Augsburg Interim, a new order that Protestants everywhere must readopt Catholic beliefs and practices. But the Reformation was too entrenched by 1547 to be ended even by brute force. Confronted by fierce Protestant resistance and weary from three decades of war, the emperor was forced to relent.

The Peace of Augsburg in September 1555 made the division of Christendom permanent. This agreement recognized in law what had already been well established in practice: *cuius regio, eius religio,* meaning that the ruler of a land would determine the religion of the land. Lutherans were permitted to retain all church lands forcibly seized before 1552. Those discontented with the religion of their region were permitted to migrate to another.

Calvinism was not recognized as a legal form of Christian belief and practice by the Peace of Augsburg. Calvinists remained determined not only to secure the right to worship publicly as they pleased, but also to shape society according to their own religious convictions. They organized to lead national revolutions throughout northern Europe.

The English Reformation to 1553

Late medieval England had a well-earned reputation for maintaining the rights of the crown against the pope. Edward I (r. 1272–1307) had rejected efforts to exempt the clergy from secular taxation. Parliament curtailed payments and judicial appeals to Rome and limited the pope's power to make appointments in England. Humanism and widespread anticlerical sentiment (sometimes referred to derisively by clerical authorities as *Lollardy*) prepared the way religiously and intellectually for Protestant ideas, which sprouted in England in the early sixteenth century. It was, however, the unhappy marriage of King Henry VIII (r. 1509–1547) that ensured the success of those ideas.

The King's Affair

Henry had married Catherine of Aragon (d. 1536), a daughter of Ferdinand and Isabella of Spain, and the aunt of Emperor Charles V. By 1527 the union had produced only one surviving child, a daughter, Mary Tudor. Henry was justifiably concerned about the political

Progress of Protestant Reformation on the Continent	
1517	Luther posts ninety-five theses against indulgences
1519	Charles I of Spain elected Holy Roman Emperor (as Charles V)
1519	Luther challenges infallibility of pope and inerrancy of church councils at Leipzig Debate
1521	Papal bull excommunicates Luther for heresy
1521	Diet of Worms condemns Luther
1521–1522	Luther translates the New Testament into German
1524–1525	Peasants Revolt in Germany
1529	Marburg Colloquy between Luther and Zwingli
1530	Diet of Augsburg fails to settle religious differences
1531	Formation of Protestant Schmalkaldic League
1536	Calvin arrives in Geneva
1540	Jesuits, founded by Ignatius of Loyola, recognized as order by pope
1546	Luther dies
1547	Armies of Charles V crush Schmalkaldic League
1555	Peace of Augsburg recognizes rights of Lutherans to worship as they please
1545–1563	Council of Trent institutes reforms and responds to the Reformation

consequences of leaving only a female heir. People in this period believed it unnatural for women to rule over men. At best, a woman ruler meant a contested reign; at worst, turmoil and revolution. Henry even came to believe that his union with Catherine, who had had numerous miscarriages and stillbirths, had been cursed by God, because before their marriage Catherine had briefly been the wife of his late brother, Arthur.

By 1527 Henry, thoroughly enamored of Anne Boleyn (c. 1504–1536), one of Catherine's ladies in waiting, decided to put Catherine aside and marry Anne. This he could not do in Catholic England without papal annulment of the marriage to Catherine. And therein lay a problem. In 1527 the reigning pope, Clement VII (1523–1534), was a prisoner of Charles V, Catherine's nephew. Even if this had not been the case, it would have been virtually impossible for the pope to grant an annulment of the marriage. Not only had it survived for eighteen years, but it had been made possible in the first place by a special papal dispensation required because Queen Catherine had previously been the wife of Henry's brother, Arthur.

After Cardinal Wolsey (1475–1530), Lord Chancellor of England since 1515, failed to secure the annulment, Thomas Cranmer (1489–1556) and Thomas Cromwell (1485–1540), both of whom harbored Lutheran sympathies, became the king's closest advisers. Finding the way to a papal annulment closed, Henry's new advisers struck a different course: Why not simply declare the king supreme in English spiritual affairs as he was in English temporal affairs? Then the king could settle his own affair.

Reformation Parliament
In 1529 Parliament convened for what would be a seven-year session that earned it the title of "Reformation Parliament." It passed a flood of legislation that harassed and finally placed royal reins on the clergy. In January 1531 the clergy publicly recognized Henry as head of the church in England "as far as the law of Christ allows." In 1533 Parliament passed the Submission of the Clergy, effectively placing canon law under royal control and thereby the clergy under royal jurisdiction.

In January 1533 Henry wed the pregnant Anne Boleyn, with Thomas Cranmer officiating. In 1534 Parliament ended all payments by the English clergy and laity to Rome and gave Henry sole jurisdiction over high ecclesiastical appointments. The Act of Succession in the same year made Anne Boleyn's children legitimate heirs to the throne, and the Act of Supremacy declared Henry "the only supreme head in earth of the church of England."

The Protestant Reformation Under Edward VI
Despite his political break with Rome, Henry remained decidedly conservative in his religious beliefs, and Catholic doctrine remained prominent in a country seething with Protestant sentiment. Henry forbade the English clergy to marry and threatened to execute clergy caught twice in concubinage. The Six Articles of 1539 reaffirmed transubstantiation, denied the Eucharistic cup to the laity, declared celibate vows inviolable, provided for private masses, and ordered the continuation of auricular confession.

Edward VI (r. 1547–1553), Henry's son by his third wife, Jane Seymour, became king when he was only ten years old. Under Edward, England fully enacted the Protestant Reformation. Henry's Six Articles and laws against heresy were repealed, and clerical marriage and communion with cup were sanctioned. An Act of Uniformity imposed Thomas Cranmer's *Book of Common Prayer* on all English churches, which were stripped of their images and altars. A forty-two-article confession of faith, also written by Cranmer, was adopted, setting forth a moderate Protestant doctrine.

These changes were short-lived, however. In 1553 Catherine of Aragon's daughter, Mary Tudor (d. 1558), succeeded to the throne and proceeded to restore Catholic doctrine and practice with a single-mindedness that rivaled that of her father. It was not until the reign of Anne Boleyn's daughter, Elizabeth I (r. 1558–1603), that a lasting religious settlement was worked out in England.

Catholic Reform and Counter-Reformation

The Protestant Reformation did not take the medieval church completely by surprise. There were many internal criticisms and efforts at reform before there was a Counter-Reformation in reaction to Protestant successes.

Sources of Catholic Reform
Before the Reformation began, ambitious proposals had been made for church reform. But sixteenth-century popes, mindful of how the councils of Constance and Basel had stripped the pope of his traditional powers, quickly squelched such efforts to bring about basic changes in the laws and institutions of the church. Despite such papal foot-dragging, the church was not without its reformers. Many new religious orders sprang up in the sixteenth century to lead a broad revival of piety within the church.

Ignatius of Loyola and the Society of Jesus
Of the various reform groups, none was more instrumental in the success of the Counter-Reformation than the Society of Jesus, the new order of Jesuits. Organized by Ignatius of Loyola in the 1530s, it was officially recognized by the church in 1540. Within a century the society had more than 15,000 members scattered throughout the world, with thriving missions in India, Japan, and the Americas.

Ignatius of Loyola (1491–1556) was a heroic figure. A dashing courtier and caballero in his youth, he began his spiritual pilgrimage in 1521 after he had been seriously wounded in the legs during a battle with the French. During a lengthy and painful convalescence, he read Christian classics. So impressed

---

Main Events of the English Reformation

1529	Reformation Parliament convenes
1532	Parliament passes the Submission of the Clergy, an act placing canon law and the English clergy under royal jurisdiction
1533	Henry VIII weds Anne Boleyn
1534	Act of Succession makes Anne Boleyn's children legitimate heirs to the English throne
1534	Act of Supremacy declares Henry VIII the only supreme head of the church of England
1535	Thomas More executed for opposition to Acts of Succession and Supremacy
1535	Publication of Coverdale Bible
1539	Henry VIII imposes the Six Articles, condemning Protestantism and reasserting traditional doctrine
1547	Edward VI succeeds to the throne
1549	First Act of Uniformity imposes *Book of Common Prayer* on English churches
1553–1558	Mary Tudor restores Catholic doctrine
1558–1603	Elizabeth I fashions an Anglican religious settlement

was he with the heroic self-sacrifice of the church's saints and their methods of overcoming mental anguish and pain that he underwent a profound religious conversion. Henceforth, he, too, would serve the church as a soldier of Christ.

After recuperating, Ignatius applied the lessons he had learned during his convalescence to a program of religious and moral self-discipline that came to be embodied in the *Spiritual Exercises*. This psychologically perceptive devotional guide contained mental and emotional exercises designed to teach one absolute spiritual self-mastery. A person could shape his or her own behavior, even create a new religious self, through disciplined study and regular practice.

Whereas in Jesuit eyes Protestants had distinguished themselves by disobedience to church authority and by religious innovation, the exercises of Ignatius were intended to teach good Catholics to submit without question to higher church authority and spiritual direction. Perfect discipline and self-control were the essential conditions of such obedience. To these were added the enthusiasm of traditional spirituality and mysticism and uncompromising loyalty to the church's cause above all else. This potent combination helped counter the Reformation and win many Protestants back to the Catholic fold, especially in Austria and Germany.

The Council of Trent (1545–1563)   The broad success of the Reformation and the insistence of the Emperor Charles V forced Pope Paul III (r. 1534–1549) to call a general council of the church to reassert church doctrine. The pope also appointed a reform commission, whose report, presented in February 1537, bluntly criticized the fiscality and simony[2] of the papal Curia (court) as the primary source of the church's loss of esteem. The report was so critical that Paul attempted unsuccessfully to suppress its publication, and Protestants reprinted and circulated it to justify their criticism.

The long-delayed council met in 1545 in the imperial city of Trent in northern Italy. There were three sessions, spread over eighteen years, with long interruptions due to war, plague, and politics. Unlike the general councils of the fifteenth century, Trent was strictly under the pope's control, with high Italian prelates prominent in the proceedings.

The council's most important reforms concerned internal church discipline. The selling of church offices and other religious goods was forbidden. Trent strengthened the authority of local bishops so they could effectively discipline popular religious practice. Bishops who resided in Rome were forced to move to their appointed seats of authority. They had to preach regularly and conduct annual visitations. Parish priests were required to be neatly dressed, better educated, strictly celibate, and active among their parishioners. To train better

priests, Trent also called for the establishment of a seminary in every diocese.

Not a single doctrinal concession was made to the Protestants, however. In the face of Protestant criticism, the council of Trent reaffirmed the traditional scholastic education of the clergy; the role of good works in salvation; the authority of tradition; the seven sacraments; transubstantiation; the withholding of the Eucharistic cup from the laity; clerical celibacy; the reality of purgatory; the veneration of saints, relics, and sacred images; and the granting of letters of indulgence.

Rulers initially resisted Trent's reform decrees, fearing a revival of papal political power within their lands. But in time the new legislation took hold, and parish life revived under the guidance of a devout and better-trained clergy.

The Social Significance of the Reformation in Western Europe

It was a common trait of the Lutheran, Zwinglian, and Calvinist reformers to work within the framework of reigning political power. Luther, Zwingli, and Calvin saw themselves and their followers as subject to definite civic responsibilities and obligations. Their conservatism in this regard has led scholars to characterize them as "magisterial reformers," meaning not only that they were the leaders of the major Protestant movements but also that they succeeded by the force of the magistrate's sword. Some have argued that this willingness to resort to coercion led the reformers to compromise their principles. They themselves, however, never contemplated reform outside or against the societies of which they were members. They wanted it to take shape within the laws and institutions of the sixteenth century. To that end, they remained highly sensitive to what was politically and socially possible in their age. Some scholars believe that the reformers were too conscious of the historically possible, that their reforms went forward with such caution that they changed late medieval society very little and actually encouraged acceptance of the sociopolitical status quo.

The Revolution in Religious Practices and Institutions

The Reformation may have been politically conservative, but by the end of the sixteenth century it had brought about radical changes in traditional religious practices and institutions in those lands where it succeeded.

Religion in Fifteenth-Century Life   In the fifteenth century, on the streets of the great cities of central Europe that later turned Protestant (for example, Zurich, Strasbourg,

---

[2]The sin of selling of sacred or spiritual things, in this instance church offices.

Nuremberg, or Geneva), the clergy and the religious were everywhere. They made up 6 to 8 percent of the total urban population, and they exercised considerable political as well as spiritual power. They legislated and taxed; they tried cases in special Church courts; and they enforced their laws with threats of excommunication.

The Church calendar regulated daily life. About one-third of the year was given over to some kind of religious observance or celebration. There were frequent periods of fasting. On almost a hundred days out of the year a pious Christian could not, without special dispensation, eat eggs, butter, fat, or meat.

Monasteries and especially nunneries were prominent and influential institutions. The children of society's most powerful citizens resided there. Local aristocrats were closely identified with particular churches and chapels, whose walls recorded their lineage and proclaimed their generosity. On the streets, friars from near and far begged alms from passersby. In the churches the Mass and liturgy were read entirely in Latin. Images of saints were regularly displayed, and on certain holidays their relics were paraded about and venerated.

There was a booming business at local religious shrines. Pilgrims gathered there by the hundreds, even thousands, many sick and dying, all in search of a cure or a miracle, but also for diversion and entertainment. Several times during the year special preachers arrived in the city to sell letters of indulgence.

Many clergy walked the streets with concubines and children, although they were sworn to celibacy and forbidden marriage. The Church tolerated such relationships upon payment of penitential fines.

People everywhere could be heard complaining about the clergy's exemption from taxation and, in many instances, also from the civil criminal code. People also grumbled about having to support Church offices whose occupants actually lived and worked elsewhere. Townspeople also expressed concern that the Church had too much influence over education and culture.

Religion in Sixteenth-Century Life   In these same cities after the Reformation had firmly established itself, few changes in politics and society were evident. The same aristocratic families governed as before, and the rich generally got richer and the poor poorer. But overall numbers of clergy fell by two-thirds and religious holidays shrunk by one-third. Monasteries and nunneries were nearly absent. Many were transformed into hospices for the sick and poor or into educational institutions, their endowments also turned over to these new purposes. A few cloisters remained for very devout old monks and nuns, who could not be pensioned off or who lacked families and friends to care for them. But these remaining cloisters died out with their inhabitants.

In the churches, which had also been reduced in number by at least one-third, worship was conducted almost completely in the vernacular. In some, particularly those in Zwinglian cities, the walls were stripped bare and whitewashed to make sure the congregation meditated only on God's word. The laity observed no obligatory fasts. Indulgence preachers no longer appeared. Local shrines were closed down, and anyone found openly venerating saints, relics, and images was subject to fine and punishment.

Copies of Luther's translation of the New Testament or, more often excerpts from it, could be found in private homes, and meditation on them was encouraged by the new clergy. The clergy could marry, and most did. They paid taxes and were punished for their crimes in civil courts. Domestic moral life was regulated by committees composed of roughly equal numbers of laity and clergy, over whose decisions secular magistrates had the last word.

Not all Protestant clergy remained enthusiastic about this new lay authority in religion. And the laity themselves were also ambivalent about certain aspects of the Reformation. Over half of the original converts returned to the Catholic fold before the end of the sixteenth century. Whereas one-half of Europe could be counted in the Protestant camp in the mid-sixteenth century, only one-fifth would be there by the mid-seventeenth century.[3]

The Reformation and the Changing Role of Women

The Protestant reformers took a positive stand on clerical marriage and strongly opposed monasticism and the celibate life. From this position they challenged the medieval tendency alternately to degrade women as temptresses (following the model of Eve) and to exalt them as virgins (following the model of Mary). Protestants opposed the popular antiwoman and antimarriage literature of the Middle Ages. They praised woman in her own right, but especially in her biblical vocation as mother and housewife. Although from a modern perspective, women remained subject to men, new marriage laws gave them greater security and protection.

Relief of sexual frustration and a remedy of fornication were prominent in Protestant arguments for marriage. But the reformers also viewed their wives as indispensable companions in their work, and this not solely because they took domestic cares off their husbands' minds. Luther, who married in 1525 at the age of forty-two, wrote of women:

[3]Geoffrey Parker, *Europe in Crisis, 1598–1648* (Ithaca, N.Y.: Cornell University Press, 1979), p. 50.

Imagine what it would be like without women. The home, cities, economic life, and government would virtually disappear. Men cannot do without women. Even if it were possible for men to beget and bear children, they still could not do without women.[4]

John Calvin wrote at the death of his wife:

> I have been bereaved of the best companion of my life, of one who, had it been so ordered, would not only have been the willing sharer of my indigence, but even of my death. During her life she was the faithful helper of my ministry.[5]

Such tributes were intended in part to overcome Catholic criticism that marriage distracted the cleric from his ministry. They were primarily the expression of a new value placed on the estate of marriage and family life. In opposition to the celibate ideal of the Middle Ages, Protestants stressed as no religious movement before them the sacredness of home and family. This attitude contributed to a more respectful and sharing relationship between husbands and wives and between parents and children.

The ideal of the companionate marriage—that is, of husband and wife as coworkers in a special God-ordained community of the family, sharing authority equally within the household—led to an important expansion of the grounds for divorce in Protestant cities as early as the 1520s. Women now had an equal right with men to divorce and remarry in good conscience—unlike in Catholicism, where only a separation from bed and table, not divorce and remarriage, was permitted a couple in a failed marriage. The reformers were actually more willing to permit divorce and remarriage on grounds of adultery and abandonment than were secular magistrates, who feared liberal divorce laws would lead to social upheaval.

Protestant doctrines were as attractive to women as they were to men. Renegade nuns wrote exposés of the nunnery in the name of Christian freedom and justification by faith, declaring that the nunnery was no special woman's place at all and that supervisory male clergy (who alone could hear the nuns' confessions and administer sacraments to them) made their lives as unpleasant and burdensome as any abusive husband. Women in the higher classes, who enjoyed new social and political freedoms during the Renaissance, found in Protestant theology a religious complement to their greater independence in other walks of life. Some cloistered noblewomen, however, protested the closing of nunneries. They

Albrecht Dürer's portrait of a young girl (1515). The Protestant movement encouraged girls to be literate in their native languages.
[Kupferstichkabinett Staatliche Museen, Preussischer Kulturbesitz, Berlin]

believed the cloister provided them a more interesting and independent way of life than they would have known in the secular world.

Because they wanted women to become pious housewives, Protestants also encouraged the education of girls to literacy in the vernacular, expecting them thereafter to model their lives on the Bible. During their studies, however, women found biblical passages that suggested they were equal to men in the presence of God. Education also gave some women a role as independent authors in the Reformation. From a modern perspective, these may seem like small advances, but they were significant, if indirect, steps in the direction of the emancipation of women.

Family Life in Early Modern Europe

Changes in the timing and duration of marriage, in family size, and in infant and child care suggest that family life was under a variety of social and economic pressures in the sixteenth and

---

[4] *Luther's Works*, Vol. 54: *Table Talk*, ed. and trans. by Theodore G. Tappert (Philadelphia: Fortress Press, 1967), p. 161.
[5] *Letters of John Calvin*, Vol. 2, trans. by J. Bonnet (Edinburgh: T. Constable, 1858), p. 216.

seventeenth centuries. The Reformation was a factor in these changes, but not the only or even the major one.

A family has a certain force and logic of its own, regardless of the time and place in which it exists. The routine of family life conspires with basic instincts to establish characteristic patterns of behavior, reinforcing natural feelings and building expectations among family members. Time, place, and culture, however, are important. A person raised in a twelfth-century family would be different from one raised in a twentieth-century family, and growing up in Europe is not the same as growing up in China. But the differences do not lie in the ability of husbands and wives to love one another or of parents to make sacrifices for their children. They lie, rather, in the ways different cultures and religions infuse family life with values and influence the behavior of family members.

Later Marriages

Between 1500 and 1800 men and women in western Europe and England married at later ages than they had in previous centuries. Men tended to be in their mid- to late twenties rather than in their late teens and early twenties, and women in their early to mid-twenties rather than in their teens. The canonical, or church-sanctioned, age for marriage remained fourteen for men and twelve for women, and engagements might occur at these young ages, especially among royalty and nobility. As it had done throughout the high and later Middle Ages, the church also recognized as valid free, private exchange of vows between a man and a woman at these minimal ages. However, after the Reformation, which condemned such clandestine unions, the church increasingly required both parental agreement and public vows in church before a marriage could be recognized as fully licit—procedures it had always actually preferred.

Late marriage in the West reflected the difficulty couples had supporting themselves independently. The difficulty arose because of the population growth that occurred during the late fifteenth and early sixteenth centuries, when western Europe recovered much of the population loss incurred during the Great Plague. Larger families meant more heirs and hence a greater division of resources. In Germanic and Scandinavian countries, the custom of a fair sharing of inheritance among all male children worked to delay marriages, for divided inheritances often meant small incomes for the recipients. It simply took the average couple a longer time than previously to prepare themselves materially for marriage. In the sixteenth century one in five women never married, and these, combined with the estimated 15 percent who were unmarried widows, constituted a sizable unmarried female population.

A later marriage meant a marriage of shorter duration, since couples who married in their thirties would not spend as

A young couple in love (ca. 1480) by an anonymous artist.
[Bildarchiv Preussischer Kulturbesitz]

much time together as couples who married in their twenties. Such marriages also contributed to more frequent remarriage for men because women who bore children for the first time at advanced ages had higher mortality rates than younger mothers. Moreover, as growing church condemnation and the rapid growth of orphanages and foundling homes between 1600 and 1800 confirm, delayed marriage increased premarital sex and raised the number of illegitimate children.

Arranged Marriages

Marriage tended to be "arranged" in the sense that the parents customarily met and discussed the terms of the marriage before the prospective bride and bridegroom became party to the discussions. But the wealth and social standing of the bride and the bridegroom were not the only things considered when parents arranged a marriage. By the fifteenth century it was not unusual for the two involved people to have known each other in advance and even to have had some prior relationship. Also, emotional feeling for one another was increasingly respected by parents. Parents did not force total strangers to live together, and children had a legal right to

A German Mother Advises Her Fifteen-Year-Old Son, Who Is away from Home at School for the First Time (1578)

Although only fourteen miles away from his Nuremberg home, Friedrich Behaim was fifteen and on his own for the first time at the Altdorf Academy, where he would spend the next three years of his life. As there was daily traffic back and forth, mother and son could correspond regularly and Frau Behaim could give her son needed advice and articles of clothing.

What is the mother most concerned about? What do her concerns suggest about life in the sixteenth century? Does she appear to be more strict and demanding of her son than a modern mother would be? Is the son clueless, or adroitly manipulating the mother?

Dear son Friederich . . . You write that you have been unable to get by on the money [I gave you]. I will let it pass this quarter, but see that you manage on it in the future. Enclosed is another gulden.

As for your clothes, I do not have Martin [a servant] here with me now (we are quarreling), but he has begun to work on your clothes. He has made stockings for your leather holiday trousers, which I am sending you with this letter. Since your everyday trousers are so bad, wear these for now until a new pair of woolen ones can be made and sent to you, which I will do as soon as I can. Send me your old trousers in the sack I sent you the pitcher in. As for the smock that you think should be lined [for the winter], I worry that the skirt may be too short and will not keep you warm. You can certainly wear it for another summer if it is not too small for you then and the weather not too warm. Just keep it clean and brushed. I will have a new coat made for you at the earliest.

You also write about [unhappiness with] your food. You must be patient for a while. You may not at the outset lodge a complaint against [your master], and especially while you are sitting at his table. [Only] he may speak out who eats his food and is also an authority in the house. So it would be better if the Inspector, who is there for a reason, reports it to him.

Will you once tell me who your table companions are! Also, let me know by All Saints what you have spent on beer and what you owe the tailor, so I may know how much to send you for the quarter.

As for your [sore] throat, there is nothing you can take for it but warm mead. Gargle often with it and keep your head warm. Put a muffler or scarf around your neck and wear your night coat when you are in your room. Avoid cold drinks and sit perhaps for a while by the fire. And do not forget to be bled on time [people then bled themselves once or twice a year as a health measure] . . . When you need paper, let me know . . .

I am sending some cleaning flakes for your leather pants. After you have worn them three times, put some on the knees . . . I will have your old coat patched and send it to you with the next carter [so that you can wear it] until the new one is made. Send me the two sacks with the next carter. You will find the [aforementioned] gulden in the trouser foot tied with a string.

Nothing more for now. God bless. 14 October, 1578.

Mrs. Paul Behaim

From *Three Behaim Boys: Growing Up in Early Modern Germany: A Chronicle of Their Lives,* ed. and trans. by Steven Ozment, pp. 107–108. Copyright © 1990 Yale University Press. Reprinted by permission of Yale University Press.

---

protest and resist an unwanted marriage. A forced marriage was by definition invalid, and parents understood that unwanted marriages could fail. The best marriage was one desired by both parties and supported by their families.

Family Size

The western European family was conjugal, or nuclear; that is, it consisted of a father and a mother and two to four children who survived into adulthood. This nuclear family lived with a larger household, consisting of in-laws, servants, laborers, and boarders. The average husband and wife had seven or eight children—a birth about every two years. Of these, however, an estimated one third died by age five, and

one half by their teens. Rare is the family, at any social level, that did not experience infant mortality and child death.

Birth Control

Artificial birth control has existed since antiquity. The ancient Egyptians used alligator dung and other acidic sperm killers, and sponges were also popular. In the West, the church's condemnation of *coitus interruptus* (male withdrawal before ejaculation) during the thirteenth and fourteenth centuries suggests that a contraceptive mentality—that is, a conscious and regular effort at birth control—may have been developing at this time. But early birth control measures, when applied, were not very effective, and for both historical and moral reasons the church firmly opposed them. During the eleventh century it suppressed an extreme ascetic sect, the Cathars, whom it accused of practicing birth control. The church also opposed (and still opposes) contraception on moral grounds. According to Saint Thomas Aquinas, a moral act must always aid and abet, never frustrate, the natural end of the being or thing in question, and he believed that the natural end of sex could be only the birth of children and their godly rearing within the bounds of holy matrimony and the community of the church.

Wet Nursing

The church allied with the physicians of early modern Europe on another intimate family matter: the condemnation of women who hired nurses to suckle their newborn children, sometimes for as long as a year and a half. The practice was popular among upper-class women, who looked on it as a symbol of their high rank. Wet nurses were women who had recently had a baby or were suckling a child of their own, and who, for a fee, agreed also to suckle another child. The practice appears to have increased the risk of infant mortality, exposing infants to a strange and shared milk supply from women who were usually not as healthy as the infants' own mothers and who often lived under less sanitary conditions. But nursing an infant was a chore some upper-class women found distasteful, and their husbands also preferred that they not do it. Among women, vanity and convenience appear to have been motives for turning to wet nurses. For husbands, more was at stake in the practice. Because the church forbade sexual intercourse while a women was lactating, and sexual intercourse was also believed to spoil a lactating woman's milk (pregnancy, of course, eventually ended her milk supply), a nursing wife often became a reluctant lover. In addition, nursing had a contraceptive effect (about 75 percent effective). Some women prolonged nursing their children precisely to delay a new pregnancy, and some husbands understood and cooperated in this form of family planning. For other husbands, however, especially noblemen and royalty who desired an abundance of male heirs, nursing seemed to rob them of offspring and to jeopardize the patrimony; hence, their support of wet nursing.

Loving Families?

The traditional western European family had features that may seem cold and unloving. When children were between the ages of eight and thirteen, parents routinely sent them out of their homes into apprenticeships, off to school, or into employment in the homes and businesses of relatives, friends, and even strangers. In addition, the emotional ties between spouses seem to have been as tenuous as those between parents and children. Widowers and widows often married again within a few months of their spouses' deaths, and marriages with extreme disparity in age between partners also suggest limited affection.

In response to modern-day criticism, an early modern parent would surely have asked, "What greater love can parents have for their children than to equip them to make their way vocationally in the world?" An apprenticed child was a self-supporting child, and hence a child with a future. Considering primitive living conditions, contemporaries could also appreciate the purely utilitarian and humane side of marriage and understand when widowers and widows quickly married again. On the other hand, marriages with extreme disparity in age were no more the norm in early modern Europe than the practice of wet nursing, and they received just as much criticism and ridicule.

The Wars of Religion

After the Council of Trent adjourned in 1563, Catholics began a Jesuit-led counteroffensive against Protestants. At the time of John Calvin's death in 1564, Geneva had become both a refuge for Europe's persecuted Protestants and an international school for Protestant resistance, producing leaders fully equal to the new Catholic challenge.

Genevan Calvinism and the reformed Catholicism of the Council of Trent were two equally dogmatic, aggressive, and irreconcilable church systems. Calvinists may have looked like "new papists" to critics when they dominated cities like Geneva, but when, as minorities, they found their civil and religious rights denied in the empire and elsewhere, they became true firebrands and revolutionaries.

Calvinism adopted a presbyterian organization that magnified regional and local religious authority. Boards of presbyters, or elders, representing the many individual congregations of Calvinists, directly shaped the policy of the church at large. By contrast, the Counter-Reformation sponsored a centralized episcopal church system, hierarchically arranged from pope to parish priest and stressing absolute obedience to the person at the top. The high clergy—the pope and his bishops—not the synods of local churches, ruled supreme. Calvinism proved attractive to proponents of political decentralization who opposed totalitarian rulers, whereas Catholicism remained congenial to proponents of absolute monarchy determined to maintain "one king, one church, one law."

The wars of religion were both internal national conflicts and truly international wars. Catholic and Protestant subjects struggled to control France, the Netherlands, and England.

The Catholic governments of France and Spain conspired and finally sent armies against Protestant regimes in England and the Netherlands. The outbreak of the Thirty Years' War in 1618 made the international dimensions of the religious conflict especially clear; before it ended in 1648, the war drew every major European nation directly or indirectly into its deadly net.

French Wars of Religion (1562–1598)

When Henry II (r. 1547–1559) died accidentally during a tournament in 1559, his sickly fifteen-year-old son, Francis II (d. 1560), came to the throne under the regency of the queen mother, Catherine de Médicis (1519–1589). With the monarchy so weakened, three powerful families began to compete to control France. They were the Bourbons, whose power lay in the south and west; the Montmorency-Châtillons, who controlled the center of France; and the Guises, who were dominant in eastern France. The Guises were by far the strongest, and the name of Guise was interchangeable with militant, ultra-Catholicism. The Bourbon and Montmorency-Châtillon families, in contrast, developed strong Huguenot sympathies, largely for political reasons. (French Protestants were called Huguenots after Besançon Hughes, the leader of Geneva's political revolt against the Savoyards in the late 1520s.) The Bourbon Louis I, prince of Condé (d. 1569), and the Montmorency-Châtillon Admiral Gaspard de Coligny (1519–1572) became the political leaders of the French Protestant resistance.

Often for quite different reasons, ambitious aristocrats and discontented townspeople joined Calvinist churches in opposition to the Guise-dominated French monarchy. In 1561 over two thousand Huguenot congregations existed throughout France. Although they made up only about one fifteenth of the population, Huguenots held important geographic areas and represented the more powerful segments of French society. Over two fifths of the French aristocracy became Huguenots. Many apparently hoped to establish within France a principle of territorial sovereignty akin to that secured within the Holy Roman Empire by the Peace of Augsburg (1555). Calvinism thus indirectly served the forces of political decentralization.

Catherine de Médicis and the Guises   Following Francis II's death in 1560, Catherine de Médicis continued as regent for her second son, Charles IX (r. 1560–1574). Fearing the Guises, Catherine, whose first concern was always to preserve the monarchy, sought allies among the Protestants. Early in 1562 she granted Protestants freedom to worship publicly outside towns—although only privately within them—and to hold synods or church assemblies. In March

of the same year this royal toleration ended when the duke of Guise surprised a Protestant congregation worshipping illegally at Vassy in Champagne and proceeded to massacre several score—an event that marked the beginning of the French wars of religion. Perpetually caught between fanatical Huguenot and Guise extremes, Queen Catherine always sought to play the one side against the other. She wanted a Catholic France but not a Guise-dominated monarchy.

On August 22, 1572, four days after the Huguenot Henry of Navarre had married Charles IX's sister—another sign of growing Protestant power in the queen mother's eye—the Huguenot leader Coligny, who increasingly had the king's ear, was wounded by an assassin's bullet. Catherine had apparently been a part of this Guise plot to eliminate Coligny. After its failure, she feared both the king's reaction to her complicity and the Huguenot response under a recovered Coligny. Catherine convinced Charles that a Huguenot coup was afoot, inspired by Coligny, and that only the swift execution of Protestant leaders could save the crown from a Protestant attack on Paris. On the eve of Saint Bartholomew's Day, August 24, 1572, Coligny and three thousand fellow Huguenots were butchered in Paris. Within three days an estimated twenty thousand Huguenots were executed in coordinated attacks throughout France.

This event changed the nature of the struggle between Protestants and Catholics both within and beyond the borders of France. It was thereafter no longer an internal contest between Guise and Bourbon factions for French political influence, nor was it simply a Huguenot campaign to win basic religious freedoms. Henceforth, in Protestant eyes, it became an international struggle to the death for sheer survival against an adversary whose cruelty justified any means of resistance.

Rise to Power of Henry of Navarre   Henry III (r. 1574–1589), who was Henry II's third son and the last Valois king, found the monarchy wedged between a radical Catholic League, formed in 1576 by Henry of Guise, and vengeful Huguenots. Like the queen mother, Henry III sought to steer a middle course, and in this effort he received support from a growing body of neutral Catholics and Huguenots who put the political survival of France above its religious unity. Such *politiques*, as they were called, were prepared to compromise religious creeds to save the nation.

In the mid–1580s the Catholic League, supported by the Spanish, became completely dominant in Paris. Henry III failed to rout the league with a surprise attack in 1588 and had to flee Paris. Forced by his weakened position into guerrilla tactics, the king had both the duke and the cardinal of Guise assassinated. The Catholic League reacted with a fury that matched the earlier Huguenot response to the Massacre of Saint Bartholomew's Day. The king was now forced to

The St. Bartholemew's Day Massacre, as depicted by the contemporary Protestant painter François Dubois. In this notorious event, 3,000 Protestants were slaughtered in Paris and an estimated 20,000 others died throughout France. The massacre transformed the religious struggle in France from a contest for political power into an all-out war between Protestants and Catholics. [Musée Cantonal des Beaux Arts, Palais de Rumine, Lausanne]

strike an alliance with his Protestant cousin and heir, Henry of Navarre, in April 1589.

As the two Henrys prepared to attack Paris, however, a fanatical Dominican friar murdered Henry III. Thereupon the Bourbon Huguenot Henry of Navarre became Henry IV of France (r. 1589–1610).

Henry IV came to the throne as a *politique*, weary of religious strife and prepared to place political peace above absolute religious unity. He believed that a royal policy of tolerant Catholicism would be the best way to achieve such peace. On July 25, 1593, he publicly abjured the Protestant faith and embraced the traditional and majority reli-

gion of his country. "Paris is worth a Mass," he is reported to have said.

The Edict of Nantes   Five years later, on April 13, 1598, Henry IV's famous Edict of Nantes proclaimed a formal religious settlement. In 1591 he had already assured the Huguenots of at least qualified religious freedoms. The Edict of Nantes made good that promise. It recognized and sanctioned minority religious rights within what was to remain an officially Catholic country. This religious truce—and it was never more than that—granted the Huguenots, who by this time numbered well over one million, freedom of public wor-

The Milch Cow, a sixteenth-century satirical painting depicting the Netherlands as a land all the great powers of Europe wish to exploit. Elizabeth of England is feeding her (England had long-standing commercial ties with Flanders); Philip II of Spain is attempting to ride her (Spain was trying to reassert its control over the entire region); William of Orange is trying to milk her (he was the leader of the anti-Spanish rebellion); and the king of France holds her tail (France hoped to profit from the rebellion at Spain's expense). [Rijksmuseum, Amsterdam]

ship, the right of assembly, admission to public offices and universities, and permission to maintain fortified towns. Most of the new freedoms, however, were to be exercised within their own localities. Concession of the right to fortify towns reveals the continuing distrust between French Protestants and Catholics. The edict only transformed a long hot war between irreconcilable enemies into a long cold war. To its critics, it created a state within a state.

A Catholic fanatic assassinated Henry IV in May 1610. Although he is best remembered for the Edict of Nantes, the political and economic policies Henry IV put in place were equally important. They laid the foundations for the transformation of France into the absolutist state it would become in the seventeenth century. Ironically, in pursuit of the political and religious unity that had escaped Henry IV, his grandson Louis XIV (r. 1643–1715), calling for "one king, one church, one law," would later revoke the Edict of Nantes in 1685 (see Chapter 21). This action would force France and Europe to learn again by bitter experience the hard lessons of the wars of religion. Rare is the politician who learns from the lessons of history rather than repeating its mistakes.

Imperial Spain and the Reign of Philip II (1556–1598)

Until the English defeated his mighty Armada in 1588, no one person stood larger in the second half of the sixteenth century than Philip II of Spain. During the first half of his reign, attention focused on the Mediterranean and Turkish expansion. On October 7, 1571, a Holy League of Spain,

Venice, and the pope defeated the Turks at Lepanto in the largest naval battle of the sixteenth century. Before the engagement ended, thirty thousand Turks had died and over one third of the Turkish fleet was sunk or captured.

Revolt in the Netherlands The spectacular Spanish military success in southern Europe was not repeated in northern Europe when Philip attempted to impose his will within the Netherlands and on England and France. The resistance of the Netherlands especially proved the undoing of Spanish dreams of world empire.

The Netherlands were the richest area in Europe (see Map 17–4). The merchant towns of the Netherlands were however, Europe's most independent; many, like magnificent Antwerp, were also Calvinist strongholds. A stubborn opposition to the Spanish overlords formed under William of Nassau, the Prince of Orange (r. 1533–1584). Like other successful rulers in this period, William of Orange was a *politique* who placed the Netherlands' political autonomy and well-being above religious creeds. He personally passed through successive Catholic, Lutheran, and Calvinist stages.

The year 1564 saw the first fusion of political and religious opposition to Spanish rule, the result of Philip II's unwise insistence that the decrees of the Council of Trent be enforced throughout the Netherlands. A national covenant was drawn up called the *Compromise*, a solemn pledge to resist the decrees of Trent and the Inquisition.

Philip dispatched the duke of Alba (1508–1582) to suppress the revolt. His army of ten thousand men marched northward from Milan in 1567 in a show of combined Spanish

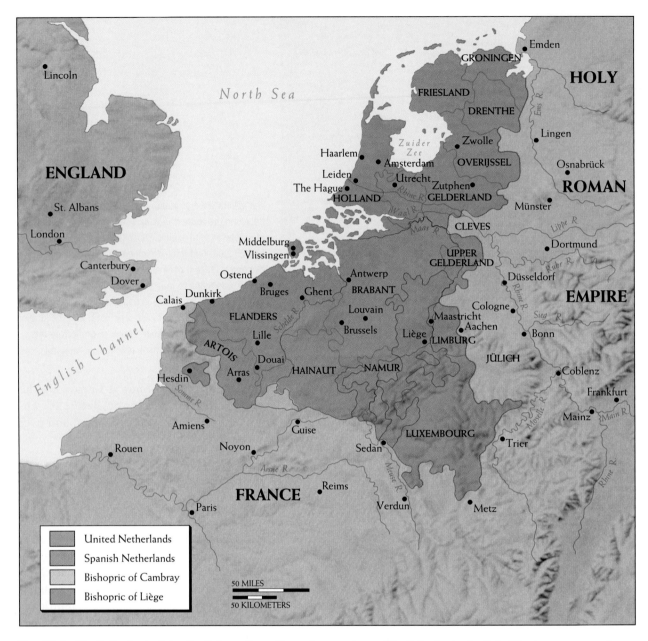

Map 17–4   The Netherlands during the Reformation.   The northern provinces of the Netherlands—the United Provinces—were mostly Protestant in the second half of the sixteenth century. The southern provinces—the Spanish Netherlands—made peace with Spain and remained largely Catholic.

and papal might. A special tribunal, known to the Spanish as the Council of Troubles and among the Netherlanders as the Council of Blood, reigned over the land. Several thousand suspected heretics were publicly executed before Alba's reign of terror ended.

William of Orange had been an exile in Germany during these turbulent years. He now emerged as the leader of a broad movement for the Netherlands' independence from Spain.

After a decade of persecution and warfare, the ten largely Catholic southern provinces (what is roughly modern Bel-

gium) came together in 1576 with the seven largely Protestant northern provinces (what is roughly the modern Netherlands) in unified opposition to Spain. This union, known as the Pacification of Ghent, declared internal regional sovereignty in matters of religion. It was a Netherlands version of the Peace of Augsburg.

After more fighting, in January 1579 the southern provinces formed the Union of Arras and made peace with Spain. The northern provinces responded with the formation of the Union of Utrecht. Spanish preoccupation

Map 17–6 The Holy Roman Empire about 1618. On the eve of the Thirty Years' War the Empire was politically and religiously fragmented, as this somewhat simplified map reveals. Lutherans dominated the north and Catholics the south, while Calvinists controlled the United Provinces and the Palatinate and also had an important presence in Switzerland and Brandenburg.

not a unified nation like Spain, England, or even strife-torn France.

Religious Division Religious conflict accentuated the international and internal political divisions (see Map 17–5). The Holy Roman Empire was about equally divided between Catholics and Protestants, the latter having perhaps a slight numerical edge by 1600 (see Map 17–6). The terms of the Peace of Augsburg (1555) had attempted to freeze the terri-

torial holdings of the Lutherans and the Catholics. In the intervening years, however, the Lutherans had gained political control in some Catholic areas, as had the Catholics in a few previously Lutheran areas. There was also religious strife between liberal and conservative Lutherans and between Lutherans and the growing numbers of Calvinists.

As elsewhere in Europe, Calvinism was the political and religious leaven within the Holy Roman Empire. Unrecognized as a legal religion by the Peace of Augsburg, Calvinism established a strong foothold within the empire when Elector Frederick III (r. 1559–1576), a devout convert to Calvinism, made it the official religion within the Palatinate in 1559. By 1609 Palatine Calvinists headed a Protestant defensive alliance supported by Spain's sixteenth-century enemies: England, France, and the Netherlands.

If the Calvinists were active within the Holy Roman Empire, so also were their Catholic counterparts, the Jesuits. Staunchly Catholic Bavaria, supported by Spain, became militarily and ideologically for the Counter-Reformation what the Palatinate was for Protestantism. From Bavaria, the Jesuits launched successful missions throughout the empire. In 1609 Maximilian, duke of Bavaria (1573–1651), organized a Catholic League to counter a new Protestant alliance that had been formed by the Calvinist Elector Palatine, Frederick IV (r. 1583–1610). When the league fielded a great army under the command of Count Johann von Tilly (1559–1632), the stage was set, both internally and internationally, for the Thirty Years' War, the worst European catastrophe since the Black Death of the fourteenth century.

The Treaty of Westphalia　In 1648 all hostilities within the Holy Roman Empire were brought to an end by the Treaty of Westphalia. It firmly reasserted the major feature of the religious settlement of the Peace of Augsburg (1555), as rulers were again permitted to determine the religion of their lands. The treaty also gave the Calvinists their long-sought legal recognition. The independence of the Swiss Confederacy and the United Provinces of Holland, long recognized in fact, now became law.

By confirming the territorial sovereignty of Germany's many political entities, the Treaty of Westphalia perpetuated German division and political weakness into the modern period. Only two German states attained any international significance during the seventeenth century: Austria and Brandenburg-Prussia. The petty regionalism within the empire also reflected on a small scale the drift of larger European politics. During the seventeenth century distinctive nation-states, each with its own political, cultural, and religious identity, reached maturity and firmly established the competitive nationalism of the modern world.

Superstition and Enlightenment: The Battle Within

Religious reform and warfare permanently changed religious institutions in major European lands. They also moved intellectuals to rethink human nature and society. One side of that reconsideration was dark and cynical, perhaps because the peak years of religious warfare had also been those of the great European witch hunts. Another side, however, was brilliantly skeptical and constructive, reflecting the growing scientific movement of the years between 1500 and 1700.

Witch Hunts and Panic

Nowhere is the dark side of the period better seen than in the witch hunts and panics that erupted in almost every western land. Between 1400 and 1700, courts sentenced an estimated seventy thousand to one hundred thousand people to death for harmful magic (*malificium*) and diabolical witchcraft. In addition to inflicting harm on their neighbors, these witches were said to attend mass meetings known as *sabbats*, to which they were believed to fly. They were also accused of indulging in sexual orgies with the Devil, who appeared in animal form, most often as a he-goat. Still other charges against them were cannibalism (they were alleged to be especially fond of small Christian children) and a variety of ritual acts and practices designed to insult every Christian belief and value.

Where did such beliefs come from, and how could seemingly enlightened people believe them? Their roots were in society-at-large, in both popular and elite cultures, especially the clergy.

Village Origins　In village societies, so-called cunning folk played a positive role in helping people cope with calamity. People turned to them for help in the face of natural disasters or physical disabilities. The cunning folk provided consolation and gave people hope that such calamities might be averted or reversed by magical means. They thus provided an important service and kept village life moving forward.

Possession of magical powers, for good or ill, made one an important person within village society. Not surprisingly, claims to such powers most often were made by the people most in need of security and influence—namely, the old and the impoverished, especially single or widowed women. Witch beliefs in village society may also have been a way of defying urban Christian society's attempts to impose its laws and institutions on the countryside. From this perspective, village Satanism became a fanciful substitute for an impossible social revolt, a way of spurning the values of one's new masters. It is also possible, although unlikely, that witch beliefs in rural society had a foundation in local fertility cults, whose semipagan practices, designed to ensure good harvests, may have acquired the features of diabolical witchcraft under church persecution.

Influence of the Clergy　Popular belief in magic was the essential foundation of the great witch hunts of the sixteenth and seventeenth centuries. Yet the contribution of learned society was equally great. The Christian clergy also

Three witches suspected of practicing harmful magic are burned alive on a pyre in Baden. On the left, two of them are shown feasting and cavorting with demons at a sabbat. [Bildarchiv Preussischer Kulturbesitz]

practiced magic, that of the holy sacraments, and the exorcism of demons was one of their traditional functions within society. Fear of demons and the Devil, which the clergy actively encouraged, allowed them to assert their moral authority and enforce religious conformity.

In the late thirteenth century the church declared that only its priests possessed legitimate magical power. Since such power was not human, theologians reasoned, it had to come either from God or from the Devil. If it came from God, then it was properly confined to and exercised only by the church. Those who practiced magic outside the church evidently derived their power from the Devil. From such reasoning grew accusations of "pacts" between non-Christian magicians and Satan.

The church based its intolerance of magic outside its walls on sincere belief in and fear of the Devil. But attacking witch-es was also a way for established Christian society to extend its power and influence into new areas. To accuse, try, and execute witches was also a declaration of moral and political authority over a village or territory. As the cunning folk were local spiritual authorities, revered and feared by people, their removal became a major step in establishing a Christian beachhead in village society.

Why Women? A good 80 percent of the victims of witch hunts were women, most single and between forty-five and sixty years of age. This has suggested to some that misogyny fueled the witch hunts. Based on male hatred and sexual fear of women, and occurring at a time when women threatened to break out from under male control, witch hunts, it is argued, were simply woman hunts. Older single women may, however, have been vulnerable for more basic social reasons.

They were a largely dependent social group in need of public assistance and natural targets for the peculiar "social engineering" of the witch hunts. Some accused witches were women who sought to protect and empower themselves within their communities by claiming supernatural powers.

However, gender may have played a largely circumstantial role. Because of their economic straits, more women than men laid claim to the supernatural powers that made them influential in village society. They thus found themselves on the front lines in disproportionate numbers when the church declared war against all who practiced magic without its blessing. Also, the involvement of many of these women in midwifery associated them with the deaths of beloved wives and infants and thus made them targets of local resentment and accusations. Both the church and their neighbors were prepared to think and say the worst about these women. It was a deadly combination.

Witch Panics   Political self-aggrandizement also played a role. As governments expanded and attempted to control their realms, they, like the church, wanted to eliminate all competition for the loyalty of their subjects. Secular rulers as well as the pope could pronounce their competitors "devilish."

Some also argue that the Reformation was responsible for the witch panics. Having weakened the traditional religious protections against demons and the Devil, while still portraying them as powerful, the Reformation is said to have forced people to protect themselves by executing perceived witches.

End of the Witch Hunts   Many factors helped end the witch hunts. The emergence of a new, more scientific worldview made it difficult to believe in the powers of witches. When in the seventeenth century mind and matter came to be viewed as two independent realities, words and thoughts lost the ability to affect things. A witch's curse was merely words. With advances in medicine and the beginning of insurance companies, people learned to rely on themselves when faced with natural calamity and physical affliction; they no longer searched for supernatural causes and solutions. Witch hunts also tended to get out of hand. Accused witches sometimes alleged that important townspeople had also attended sabbats; even the judges could be so accused. At this point the trials ceased to serve the purposes of those who were conducting them. They not only became dysfunctional but threatened anarchy as well.

Although Protestants, like Catholics, hunted witches, the Reformation may also have contributed to an attitude of mind that put the Devil in a more manageable perspective. Protestants ridiculed the sacramental magic of the old church as superstition and directed their faith to a sovereign God absolutely supreme over time and eternity. Even the Devil was believed to serve God's purposes and acted only with His permission. Ultimately God was the only significant spiritual force in the universe. This belief made the Devil a less fearsome creature. "One little word can slay him," Luther wrote of the Devil in the great hymn of the Reformation.

Writers and Philosophers

By the end of the sixteenth century, many could no longer embrace either old Catholic or new Protestant absolutes. Intellectually as well as politically, the seventeenth century would be a period of transition, one already well prepared by the humanists and scientists of the Renaissance and post-Renaissance (see Chapter 24), who reacted strongly against medieval intellectual traditions.

The writers and philosophers of the late sixteenth and seventeenth centuries were aware that they lived in a period of transition. Some embraced the emerging new science wholeheartedly (Hobbes and Locke), some tried to straddle the two ages (Cervantes and Shakespeare), and still others ignored or opposed the new developments that seemed mortally to threaten traditional values (Pascal).

Miguel de Cervantes Saavedra (1547–1616)   Spanish literature of the sixteenth and seventeenth centuries was influenced by the peculiar religious and political history of Spain in this period. Spain was dominated by the Catholic church, whose piety was strongly promoted by the state. The intertwining of Catholic piety and Spanish political power underlay literary preoccupation with medieval chivalric virtues—in particular, honor and loyalty.

Generally acknowledged to be the greatest Spanish writer of all time, Cervantes was preoccupied in his work with the strengths and weaknesses of religious idealism. He was the son of a nomadic physician. Having received only a smattering of formal education, he educated himself by insatiable reading in vernacular literature and immersion in the school of life. As a young man, he worked in Rome for a Spanish cardinal. In 1570 he became a soldier and was decorated for gallantry at Lepanto (1571). He conceived and began to write his most famous work, *Don Quixote*, in 1603, while languishing in prison after conviction for theft.

The first part of *Don Quixote* appeared in 1605, and a second part in 1615. If, as many argue, the intent of this work was to satirize the chivalric romances so popular in Spain, Cervantes failed to conceal his deep affection for the character he had created as an object of ridicule, Don Quixote. Don Quixote, a none-too-stable middle-aged man, is driven mad by reading too many chivalric romances. He comes to believe that he is an aspirant to knighthood and must prove his wor-

A view of London indicating the Swan Theatre, where many of Shakespeare's plays were performed. [Folger Shakespeare Library]

thiness. To this end, he acquires a rusty suit of armor, mounts an aged horse, and chooses for his inspiration a quite unworthy peasant girl whom he fancies to be a noble lady to whom he can, with honor, dedicate his life.

Don Quixote's foil in the story—Sancho Panza, a clever, worldly-wise peasant who serves as his squire—watches with bemused skepticism, but also with genuine sympathy, as his lord does battle with a windmill (which he mistakes for a dragon) and repeatedly makes a fool of himself as he gallops across the countryside. The story ends tragically with Don Quixote's humiliating defeat by a well-meaning friend, who, disguised as a knight, bests Don Quixote in combat and forces him to renounce his quest for knighthood. The humiliated Don Quixote does not, however, come to his senses as a result. He returns sadly to his village to die a shamed and broken-hearted old man.

Throughout *Don Quixote*, Cervantes juxtaposed the down-to-earth realism of Sancho Panza with the old-fashioned religious idealism of Don Quixote. Cervantes admired the one as much as the other. He wanted his readers to remember

that to be truly happy, men and women need dreams, even impossible ones, just as much as a sense of reality.

William Shakespeare   There is much less factual knowledge about William Shakespeare (1564–1616), the greatest playwright in the English language, than one would expect of such an important figure. He apparently worked as a schoolteacher for a time and in this capacity acquired his broad knowledge of Renaissance learning and literature. His work shows none of the Puritan distress over worldliness. He took the new commercialism and the bawdy pleasures of the Elizabethan Age in stride and with amusement. In politics and religion, he was a man of his time and not inclined to offend his queen.

That Shakespeare was interested in politics is apparent from his history plays and the references to contemporary political events that fill all his plays. He seems to have viewed government simply, however, through the character of the individual ruler, whether Richard III or Elizabeth Tudor, not in terms of ideal systems or social goals. By modern standards he was a political conservative, accepting the social rankings and the power structure of his day and demonstrating unquestioned patriotism.

Shakespeare knew the theater as one who participated in every phase of its life. A member and principal dramatist of a famous company of actors known as the King's Men, he was a playwright, actor, and part owner of a theater. His work brought together in an original synthesis the best past and current achievements in the dramatic arts. He particularly mastered the psychology of human motivation and passion and had a unique talent for psychological penetration.

Shakespeare wrote histories, comedies, and tragedies. The tragedies are considered his unique achievement. Four of these were written within a three-year period: *Hamlet* (1603), *Othello* (1604), *King Lear* (1605), and *Macbeth* (1606). The most original of the tragedies, *Romeo and Juliet* (1597), transformed an old popular story into a moving drama of "star-cross'd lovers."

In his lifetime and ever since, Shakespeare has been immensely popular with both audiences and readers. As Ben Jonson (1572–1637), a contemporary classical dramatist who created his own school of poets, put it in a tribute affixed to the First Folio edition of Shakespeare's plays (1623): "He was not of an age, but for all time."

Blaise Pascal   Pascal (1623–1662) was a French mathematician and a physical scientist widely acclaimed by his contemporaries. Torn between the continuing dogmatism and the new skepticism of the seventeenth century, he aspired to write a work that would refute both the Jesuits, whose casuistry (i.e., confessional tactics designed to minimize and even excuse sinful acts) he considered a distortion of Christian teaching, and the skeptics, who either denied religion altogether (atheists) or accepted it only as it conformed to reason (deists). Pascal never realized such a definitive work, and his views on these matters exist only in piecemeal form. He wrote against the Jesuits in his *Provincial Letters* (1656–1657), and he left behind a provocative collection of reflections on humankind and religion that was published posthumously under the title *Pensées*.

Pascal was early influenced by the Jansenists, seventeenth-century Catholic opponents of the Jesuits. Although good Catholics, the Jansenists shared with the Calvinists St. Augustine's belief in the total sinfulness of human beings, their eternal predestination by God, and their complete dependence on faith and grace for knowledge of God and salvation.

Pascal believed that reason and science, although attesting to human dignity, remained of no avail in religion. Here only the reasons of the heart and a "leap of faith" could prevail. Pascal saw two essential truths in the Christian religion: that a loving God, worthy of human attainment, exists; and that

human beings, because they are corrupted in nature, are utterly unworthy of God. Pascal believed that the atheists and deists of the age had spurned the lesson of reason. For him, rational analysis of the human condition attested to humankind's utter mortality and corruption and exposed the weakness of reason itself in resolving the problems of human nature and destiny. Reason should rather drive those who truly heed it to faith and dependence on divine grace.

Pascal made a famous wager with the skeptics. It is a better bet, he argued, to believe that God exists and to stake everything on his promised mercy than not to do so; if God does exist, everything will be gained by the believer, whereas the loss incurred by having believed in God should He prove not to exist is, by comparison, very slight.

Pascal was convinced that belief in God measurably improved earthly life psychologically and disciplined it morally, regardless of whether God proved in the end to exist. He thought that great danger lay in the surrender of traditional religious values. Pascal urged his contemporaries to seek self-understanding by "learned ignorance" and to discover humankind's greatness by recognizing its misery. Thereby he hoped to counter what he believed to be the false optimism of the new rationalism and science.

Baruch Spinoza   The most controversial thinker of the seventeenth century was Baruch Spinoza (1632–1677), the son of a Jewish merchant of Amsterdam. Spinoza's philosophy caused his excommunication by his own synagogue in 1656. In 1670 he published his *Treatise on Religious and Political Philosophy*, a work that criticized the dogmatism of Dutch Calvinists and championed freedom of thought. During his lifetime, both Jews and Protestants attacked him as an atheist.

Spinoza's most influential writing, *Ethics*, appeared after his death in 1677. Religious leaders universally condemned it for its apparent espousal of pantheism. God and nature were so closely identified by Spinoza that little room seemed left either for divine revelation in Scripture or for the personal immortality of the soul, denials equally repugnant to Jews and to Christians.

The most controversial part of *Ethics* deals with the nature of substance and of God. According to Spinoza there is only one substance, which is self-caused, free, and infinite, and God is that substance. From this definition, it follows that everything that exists is in God and cannot even be conceived of apart from Him. Such a doctrine is not literally pantheistic, because God is still seen to be more than the created world that He, as primal substance, embraces. Nonetheless, in Spinoza's view, statements about the natural world are also statements about divine nature. Mind and matter are seen to be extensions of the infinite substance of God; what transpires in the world of humankind and nature is a necessary outpouring of the divine.

Such teaching clearly ran the danger of portraying the world as eternal and human actions as unfree and inevitable, the expression of a divine fatalism. Such points of view had been considered heresies by Jews and Christians because these views deny the creation of the world by God and destroy any voluntary basis for personal reward and punishment.

Thomas Hobbes Thomas Hobbes (1588–1679) was the most original political philosopher of the seventeenth century. Although he never broke with the Church of England, he came to share basic Calvinist beliefs, especially the low view of human nature and the ideal of a commonwealth based on a covenant, both of which find eloquent expression in his political philosophy.

Hobbes was an urbane and much-traveled man and one of the most enthusiastic supporters of the new scientific movement. During the 1630s he visited Paris, where he came to know Descartes; after the outbreak of the Puritan Revolution (see Chapter 21) in 1640, he lived as an exile in Paris until 1651. Hobbes also spent time with Galileo (see Chapter 24) in Italy and took a special interest in the works of William Harvey. Harvey was a physiologist famed for the discovery of how blood circulated through the body; his scientific writings influenced Hobbes's own tracts on bodily motions.

Hobbes was driven to the vocation of political philosophy by the English Civil War (see Chapter 21). In 1651 his *Leviathan* appeared. Its subject was the political consequences of human passions, and its originality lay in (1) its making natural law, rather than common law (i.e., custom or precedent), the basis of all positive law, and (2) its defense of a representative theory of absolute authority against the theory of the divine right of kings. Hobbes maintained that statute law found its justification only as an expression of the law of nature and that rulers derived their authority from the consent of the people.

Hobbes viewed humankind and society in a thoroughly materialistic and mechanical way. Human beings are defined as a collection of material particles in motion. All their psychological processes begin with and are derived from bare sensation, and all their motivations are egotistical, intended to increase pleasure and minimize pain.

Despite this seemingly low estimate of human beings, Hobbes believed much could be accomplished by the reasoned use of science. All was contingent, however, on the correct use of that greatest of all human powers, one compounded of the powers of most people: the commonwealth, in which people are united by their consent in one all-powerful person.

The key to Hobbes's political philosophy is a brilliant myth of the original state of humankind. According to this myth, human beings in the natural state are generally inclined to a "perpetual and restless desire of power after power that

Thomas Hobbes (1588–1679), whose political treatise, *Leviathan,* portrayed rulers as absolute lords over their lands, incorporating in their persons the individual wills of all their people. [Bildarchiv Preussischer Kulturbesitz]

ceases only in death."[6] As all people desire—and in the state of nature have a natural right to—everything, their equality breeds enmity, competition, and diffidence, and the desire for glory begets perpetual quarreling—"a war of every man against every man."[7]

Whereas earlier and later philosophers saw the original human state as a paradise from which humankind had fallen, Hobbes saw it as a corruption from which only society had delivered people. Contrary to the views of Aristotle and of Christian thinkers like Thomas Aquinas, Hobbes saw human beings not as sociable, political animals, but as self-centered beasts, laws unto themselves, utterly without a master unless one is imposed by force.

According to Hobbes, people escape the impossible state of nature only by entering a social contract that creates a

[6]*Leviathan* Parts I and II, ed. by H. W. Schneider (Indianapolis: Bobbs-Merrill, 1958), p. 86.
[7]Ibid., p. 106.

commonwealth tightly ruled by law and order. The social contract obliges every person, for the sake of peace and self-defense, to agree to set aside personal rights to all things. We should impose restrictions on the liberty of others only to the degree that we would allow others to restrict our own.

Because words and promises are insufficient to guarantee this state, the social contract also establishes the coercive force necessary to compel compliance with the covenant. Hobbes believed that the dangers of anarchy were far greater than those of tyranny, and he conceived of the ruler's power as absolute and unlimited. There is no room in Hobbes's political philosophy for political protest in the name of individual conscience, nor for resistance to legitimate authority by private individuals—features of *Leviathan* criticized by his contemporary Catholics and Puritans alike.

John Locke

Locke (1632–1704) has proved to be the most influential political thinker of the seventeenth century.[8] His political philosophy came to be embodied in the so-called Glorious Revolution of 1688–1689 (Chapter 21). Although he was not as original as Hobbes, his political writings were a major source of the later Enlightenment criticism of absolutism, and they gave inspiration to both the American and French revolutions.

Locke's two most famous works are the *Essay Concerning Human Understanding* (1690) (discussed in Chapter 24) and *Two Treatises of Government* (1690). Locke wrote *Two Treatises of Government* against the argument that rulers were absolute in their power. Rulers, Locke argued, remain bound to the law of nature, which is the voice of reason, teaching that "all mankind [are] equal and independent, [and] no one ought to harm another in his life, health, liberty, or possessions,"[9] inasmuch as all human beings are the images and property of God. According to Locke, people enter social contracts, empowering legislatures and monarchs to "umpire" their disputes, precisely to preserve their natural rights, and not to give rulers an absolute power over them.

"Whenever that end [namely, the preservation of life, liberty, and property for which power is given to rulers by a commonwealth] is manifestly neglected or opposed, the trust must necessarily be forfeited and the power devolved into the hands of those that gave it, who may place it anew where they think best for their safety and security."[10] From Locke's point of view, absolute monarchy was "inconsistent" with civil society and could be "no form of civil government at all."[11]

[8]Locke's scientific writings are discussed in Chapter 24.
[9]*The Second Treatise of Government*, ed. by T. P. Peardon (Indianapolis: Bobbs-Merrill, 1952), chap. 2, sects. 4–6, pp. 4–6.
[10]Ibid., chap. 13, sect. 149, p. 84.
[11]Ibid.

Locke's main differences with Hobbes stemmed from the latter's views on the state of nature. Locke believed that the natural human state was one of perfect freedom and equality in which the natural rights of life, liberty, and property were enjoyed, in unregulated fashion, by all. The only thing lacking was a single authority to adjudicate disputes. Contrary to the view of Hobbes, human beings in their natural state were not creatures of monomaniacal passion, but were possessed of extreme goodwill and rationality. They did not surrender their natural rights unconditionally when they entered the social contract; rather, they established a means whereby these rights could be better preserved. The warfare that Hobbes believed characterized the state of nature emerged for Locke only when rulers failed in their responsibility to preserve the freedoms of the state of nature and attempted to enslave people by absolute rule, that is, to remove them from their "natural" condition. Only then were the peace, goodwill, mutual assistance, and preservation, in which human beings naturally live and socially ought to live, undermined, and a state of war was created.

IN WORLD PERSPECTIVE

The Renaissance and Reformation

During the Renaissance, western Europe rediscovered its classical cultural heritage, from which it had been separated for almost eight centuries. No previous world civilization had experienced such alienation from its cultural past. The west owed the recovery of its heritage to the work of Byzantine and Islamic scholars. During the Renaissance, western European lands bound up the wounds of internal warfare and established permanent centralized states and regional governments. Even the great population losses of the fourteenth century were largely recovered by 1500. In the late fifteenth and sixteenth centuries, Europeans sailed far from their own shores, reaching Africa, southern and eastern Asia, and the new world of the Americas. From Japan to Peru, they now directly confronted for the first time the civilizations of the world.

Western history between 1500 and 1650 was also powerfully shaped by an unprecedented schism in Christianity, as Protestant groups broke ranks with Rome. The religious divisions contributed to new national and international warfare, which by the seventeenth century had devastated the Holy Roman Empire on a scale unseen since the Black Death.

The other world civilizations moved less dynamically during these centuries, maintaining greater social and political unity and exhibiting a greater tolerance of religious differences. Under Mongol rule (1279–1368), China recognized all indigenous religions as well as Islam and Eastern Christianity. No crises on the scale of those that rocked the west struck China, although plagues between 1586 and 1589 and between 1639 to 1644 killed between a quarter and a third of the inhabitants in populous regions. China moved steadily from Mongol to Ming (1368–1644) to Ching (1644–1911) rule without any major social and political upheavals. Compared to the west, its society was socially stable and its rulers in sure, if despotic, control. While the west also had highly centralized and authoritarian governments between 1350 and 1650, the interests of citizens and subjects were arguably contested more vigorously and accommodated more successfully. That was particularly true in regional and urban governments, where parliaments, estates general, and city councils represented the interests of powerful noblemen, patricians, and well-to-do burghers. But lesser political bodies, too, representing the rights of the middling and lower classes, also had recognized platforms for the expression of their grievances.

Although parallels may be drawn between the court culture of the Forbidden Palace in Peking and that of King Louis XIV in seventeenth-century France, the Chinese government and its official religious philosophy of Confucianism remained more unified and patriarchal than their counterparts in the west. In China, there was never the same degree of political dissent and readiness to fragment society in the name of religion that existed in western societies, even during the west's "Age of Absolutism." On the other hand, the Chinese readily tolerated other religions, as their warm embrace of Jesuit missionaries attests. There is no similar western demonstration of tolerance for Asian religious philosophy.

Voyages of exploration also set forth from Ming China, especially between 1405 and 1433, reaching India, the Arabian Gulf, and East Africa. These voyages did not, however, prove to be commercially profitable as those of the west would be, nor did they spark any notable commercial development in China. It is an open question whether this was because the Chinese were less greedy, curious, or belligerent than the Portuguese and Spanish.

Like the west in the later Middle Ages, Japan experienced its own political and social breakdown after 1467, when the *bakufu* government began to collapse. Japan's old manorial society progressively fell apart, and a new military class of vassalized foot soldiers, armed with spears and muskets, re-placed the mounted samurai as the new military force. In 1590 Hideyoshi (r. 1536–1598) disarmed the peasantry and froze the social classes, thereby laying the foundation for a new social and political order in Japan. Building on this achievement, Tokugawa rule (1600–1850) managed to stabilize and centralize the government by 1650. Much as western kings had to "domesticate" their powerful noblemen to succeed, Japanese rulers learned to integrate the many regional daimyo lords into government. Like Louis XIV, Tokugawa shōguns required these lords to live for long periods at court, where their wives and children also remained. As in most western countries, the shōguns of Japan thus avoided both fragmented and absolutist government.

Like the Chinese, the Japanese were also admirers of the Jesuits, who arrived in Japan with the Portuguese in 1543. The admiration was mutual, leading to three hundred thousand Christian converts by 1600. As in China, the Jesuits treated native religion as a handmaiden and prelude to superior Christian teaching. But the tolerance of Christianity did not last as long in Japan as in China. Christianity was banned in the late sixteenth century as part of Hideyoshi's internal unification program. With the ascent of more-tolerant Confucianism over Buddhism among the Japanese ruling classes, Christianity and western culture would again be welcomed in the nineteenth century.

During the age of Reformation in the west, absolutist Islamic military regimes formed in the Ottoman empire, among the Safavids in Iran, and among the Mughals in India. In all three cultures religion became tightly integrated into government, so that they never knew the divisiveness and political challenge periodically prompted in the west by Christianity. In opposition to the expansive Ottomans, Shah Abbas I (r. 1588–1629) allied with the Europeans and welcomed Dutch and English traders. Embracing Shi'ite religion and the Persian language (the rest of the Islamic world was mostly Sunni and spoke Arabic or different regional languages), Iran progressively isolated itself. Unlike the west, the Timurid empire of the Indian Mughals, particularly under Akbar the Great (r. 1556–1605), and extending into the late seventeenth century, encouraged religious toleration even to the point of holding discussions among different faiths at the royal court. Like China and Japan, India too was prepared to live with and learn from the west.

Review Questions

1. What were the main problems of the church that contributed to the Protestant Reformation? Why was the church unable to suppress dissent as it had earlier?

2. How did the theologies of Luther, Zwingli, and Calvin differ? Were their differences only religious, or did they have harmful political consequences for the Reformation as well?

3. Why did the Reformation begin in Germany and not in France, Italy, England, or Spain?

4. What was the Catholic reformation? Did the Council of Trent alter the character of traditional Catholicism?

5. Why did Henry VIII break with the Catholic church? Was the "new" religion he established really Protestant?

6. Were the wars of religion really over religion?

7. Henry of Navarre (later Henry IV of France), Elizabeth I, and William of Orange have been called *politiques*. What does that term mean, and how might it apply to each?

8. Why was England more successful than other lands in resolving its internal political and religious divisions peacefully during the sixteenth and seventeenth centuries?

9. "The Thirty Years' War is the outstanding example in European history of meaningless conflict." Evaluate this statement and provide specific reasons.

Suggested Readings ——

R. ASHCRAFT, *Revolutionary Politics and Locke's Two Treatises of Government* (1986). The most important study of Locke to appear in recent years.

R. H. BAINTON, *Here I Stand: A Life of Martin Luther* (1957). The most readable and positive biography of the reformer.

R. H. BAINTON, *Erasmus of Christendom* (1960). Charming, readable presentation.

W. BOUWSMA, *John Calvin. A Sixteenth Century Portrait* (1988). Interpretation of Calvin against background of Renaissance intellectual history.

C. BOXER, *Four Centuries of Portuguese Expansion 1415–1825* (1961). A comprehensive survey by a leading authority.

F. BRAUDEL, *The Mediterranean and the Mediterranean World in the Age of Philip the Second*, Vols. 1 and 2 (1976). A widely acclaimed work by a French master.

K. C. BROWN, *Hobbes Studies* (1965). A collection of important essays.

E. CAMERON, *The European Reformation* (1990). Large synthesis of recent studies, with most attention given to the German Reformation.

O. CHADWICK, *The Reformation* (1964). Among the best short histories; especially strong on theological and ecclesiastical issues.

J. DELUMEAU, *Catholicism Between Luther and Voltaire: A New View of the Counter Reformation* (1977). Programmatic essay for a new social history of the Counter Reformation.

A. G. DICKENS, *The Counter Reformation* (1969). A brief narrative with pictures.

A. G. DICKENS, *The English Reformation* (1974). The best one-volume account.

B. DIEFENDORF, *Beneath the Cross: Catholics and Huguenots in Sixteenth Century Paris* (1991). Stresses the primary forces of popular religion in the French wars of religion.

G. DONALDSON, *The Scottish Reformation* (1960). A dependable, comprehensive narrative.

R. DUNN, *The Age of Religious Wars 1559–1689* (1979). An excellent brief survey of every major conflict.

M. DURAN, *Cervantes* (1974). Detailed biography.

J. H. ELLIOTT, *Europe Divided 1559–1598* (1968). A direct, lucid narrative account.

G. R. ELTON, *England Under the Tudors* (1955). A masterly account.

G. R. ELTON, *Reformation Europe 1517–1559* (1966). Among the best short treatments, especially strong on political issues.

H. O. EVENNETT, *The Spirit of the Counter Reformation* (1968). An essay on the continuity of Catholic reform and its independence from the Protestant Reformation.

J. H. FRANKLIN, ED. AND TRANS., *Constitutionalism and Resistance in the Sixteenth Century: Three Treatises by Hotman, Beza, and Mornay* (1969). Three defenders of the right of people to resist tyranny.

HANS-JÜRGEN GOERTZ, *The Anabaptists* (1996). Best treatment of minority protestants.

P. GEYL, *The Revolt of The Netherlands, 1555–1609* (1958). The authoritative survey.

M. GREENGRASS, *The French Reformation* (1987). Summary account, pulling everything together succinctly.

C. HAIGH, *The English Reformation Revised* (1988). Argues that the English Reformation was less revolutionary than historians have traditionally argued.

R. HSIA, *The German People and the Reformation* (1989). Collection illustrative of the new social history of the German Reformation.

H. JEDIN, *A History of the Council of Trent*, Vols. 1 and 2 (1957–1961). Comprehensive, detailed, and authoritative.

D. JENSEN, *Reformation Europe, Age of Reform and Revolution* (1981). An excellent, up-to-date survey.

T. F. JESSOP, *Thomas Hobbes* (1960). A brief biographical sketch.

W. K. JORDAN, *Edward VI: The Young King* (1968). The basic biography.

R. KIECKHEFER, *European Witch Trials: Their Foundations in Popular and Learned Culture 1300–1500* (1976). One of the best treatments of the subject.

R. J. KNECHT, *The French Wars of Religion, 1559–1598* (1989).

A. KORS AND E. PETERS, EDS., *European Witchcraft, 1100–1700* (1972).

P. LASLETT, *Locke's Two Treatises of Government*, 2nd ed. (1970). Definitive texts with very important introductions.

CARTER LINDBERG, *The European Reformations* (1996). New survey with traditional strengths and clarity.

A. MACFARLANE, *The Family Life of Ralph Josselin: A Seventeenth Century Clergyman* (1970). Exemplary family history.

J. MCNEILL, *The History and Character of Calvinism* (1954). The most comprehensive account, very readable.

G. MATTINGLY, *The Armada* (1959). A masterpiece, novellike in style.

H.C. ERIK MIDELFORT, *The Mad Princes of Renaissance Germany* (1996).

K. MOXLEY, *Peasants, Warriors, and Wives* (1989). The English Reformation through popular art.

CHARLES G. NAUERT, JR., *Humanism and the Culture of Renaissance Europe* (1995). Lucid up-to-date overview.

J. NEALE, *Queen Elizabeth I* (1934). A superb biography.

J. E. NEALE, *The Age of Catherine de Medici* (1962). A short, concise summary.

D. NUGENT, *Ecumenism in the Age of Reformation: The Colloquy of Poissy* (1974). A study of the last ecumenical council of the sixteenth century.

J. W. O'MALLEY, *The First Jesuits* (1993). Extremely detailed account of the creation of the Society of Jesus and its original purposes.

S. OZMENT, *The Age of Reform 1250–1550: An Intellectual and Religious History of Late Medieval and Reformation Europe* (1980). Broad, lucid survey.

S. OZMENT, *When Fathers Ruled: Family Life in Reformation Europe* (1983). Effort to portray the constructive side of Protestant thinking about family relationships.

S. OZMENT, *Protestants: The Birth of a Revolution* (1992). Original synthesis of the German Reformation with critical analysis of reigning scholarly views.

S. OZMENT, *Three Behaim Boys: Growing Up in Early Modern Germany* (1990). Teenagers and young adults in their own words.

S. OZMENT, *The Bürgermeister's Daughter: Scandal in a Sixteenth Century German Town* (1996). A woman's struggle for justice.

GEOFFREY PARKER, *The Thirty Years' War* (1984). Large, lucid survey.

J. H. PARRY, *The Age of Reconnaissance* (1964). A comprehensive account of explorations from 1450 to 1650.

E. F. RICE, JR., *The Foundations of Early Modern Europe 1460–1559* (1970). A broad, succinct narrative.

J. H. M. SALMON, ED., *The French Wars of Religion: How Important Were the Religious Factors?* (1967). Scholarly debate over the relation between politics and religion.

J. J. SCARISBRICK, *Henry VIII* (1968). The best account of Henry's reign.

A. SOMAN, ED., *The Massacre of St. Bartholomew's Day: Reappraisals and Documents* (1974). The results of an international symposium on the anniversary of the massacre.

L. SPITZ, *The Religious Renaissance of the German Humanists* (1963). Comprehensive and entertaining.

G. STRAUSS, *Luther's House of Learning: The Indoctrination of the Young in the German Reformation* (1978). Account of Protestant efforts to rear children in the new faith, stressing the authoritarian elements.

G. STRAUSS, ED. AND TRANS., *Manifestations of Discontent in Germany on the Eve of the Reformation* (1971). A rich collection of sources for both rural and urban scenes.

R. H. TAWNEY, *Religion and the Rise of Capitalism* (1947). Advances beyond Weber's arguments relating Protestantism and capitalist economic behavior.

K. THOMAS, *Religion and the Decline of Magic* (1971). Something of a classic on the subject.

E. TROELTSCH, *The Social Teaching of the Christian Churches*, Vols. 1 and 2, trans. by Olive Wyon (1960).

M. WEBER, *The Protestant Ethic and the Spirit of Capitalism*, trans. by Talcott Parsons (1958). First appeared in 1904–1905; it has continued to stimulate debate over the relationship between religion and society.

C. V. WEDGWOOD, *The Thirty Years' War* (1939). The authoritative account.

C. V. WEDGWOOD, *William the Silent* (1944). An excellent political biography.

F. WENDEL, *Calvin: The Origins and Development of His Religious Thought*, trans. by Philip Mairet (1963). The best treatment of Calvin's theology.

MERRY WIESNER, *Working Women in Renaissance Germany* (1986). Sketch of women's opportunities in six German cities.

G. H. WILLIAMS, *The Radical Reformation* (1962). A broad survey of the varieties of dissent within Protestantism.

HEIDE WUNDER, *He Is the Sun, She Is the Moon: Women in Early Modern Germany* (1998). The best book in any language on the subject to date.

COMPARATIVE PERSPECTIVES: TECHNOLOGY AND CIVILIZATIONS

Navigating the Oceans: Antiquity to the Renaissance

While curiosity, courage and discipline have played their parts in command of the high seas, technical skill and the ability to translate scholarly theories into practical applications have been fundamental to the development of modern nautical science. Indeed, the desire to master water-borne travel for conquest and trade appears in some of the world's earliest recorded history. The Phoenicians sailed westward to Carthage in the ninth century B.C.E., Herodotus, the Greek historian, recounted Egyptian voyages around 600 B.C.E., and the Greeks moved westward to the end of the Mediterranean and eastward along the coastline of the Black Sea from about 800 to 500 B.C.E. The early mariners faced numerous challenges. Wind patterns, ocean currents, and powerful waters—not to mention the fear of the unknown—limited the travels of the first seafarers. Given the hazards of sea travel, charting a course hundreds of miles from land, sailing through unnavigated waters, and returning to the exact port of departure demanded technical developments in both nautical science and ship construction.

To master the high seas, generations of maritime experience and discovery had to be fused with the classical knowledge of geography, mathematics, and astronomy. Sailors and scholars had to combine their expertise to build ships, chart maps, determine nautical distances, and navigate currents and winds. Such undertakings in nautical progress did not, however, occur independently from political, mercantile, and religious activities. In fact, like the history of many other technological developments, the history of maritime innovation is intimately related to the demands and ambitions of rulers, merchants, and religious leaders. As civilizations and dynasties rose, so too did the quest to dominate water-borne travel. Ultimately, the Portuguese Empire of the fifteenth century, with great assistance from both earlier maritime innovations and the contemporaneous seafarers of the Indian Ocean basin, revolutionized the skill of high-seas navigation. In so doing, they provided the know-how for westward expansion to the New World and laid the foundations of modern, nautical science.

Early Chinese, Arab, and African Maritime Innovations

Thousands of years of coastline travel in seas such as the Mediterranean provided important knowledge for the cultivation of maritime technology. Ancient sailors relied on the moon, stars, and sun to determine direction and keep time. Accumulated knowledge was passed from sailor to sailor, and with it rudimentary charts and maps were produced. The first developments that made maritime travel a more exact science can be traced to as early as the eleventh century. Fueled by their own desires for exploration and by the demands from merchants and rulers alike, the mariners of Europe began to move beyond the utilitarian skills of navigation. They looked to the revival of earlier Greek writings on mathematics and astronomy, which in turn led to the development of the first astrolabe. This device, which allowed for more accurate celestial observation and navigation, would continue to be refined by scholars and seamen throughout the centuries.

Equally important was the use of the magnetic needle. The ancients recognized that an iron needle floating in water would turn to the direction of a magnet. They also observed that when a magnetized needle was left without a magnet to attract it, it would continue to point North. This, of course, had profound implications for sea-borne travel. European mariners first used the rudimentary compass for navigation in the early twelfth century. What is less clear, however, is whether they independently invented this device, or whether they received the knowledge from the East. Evidence strongly points to the mariner's compass being invented in China in the eleventh century and then transmitted to the West by Arab sailors during the time of the Crusades. Indeed, while maritime technology was advancing in Europe, it was also evolving rapidly in China and throughout the Arab-dominated Indian Ocean basin. (For an interesting perspective on Chinese maritime technology, see the essay entitled Technology and Imperialism.)

Arab and Chinese seamen were aided not only by the early invention of the mariner's compass, but also by celestial navigation, the knowledge of seasonal trade winds, and innovative ship and sail construction. Sea-borne trade throughout the Indian Ocean basin was well underway by the tenth century. The Chinese and Arab seamen, together with the Swahili mariners from the East Coast of Africa,

Shared knowledge of the sun, moon, and stars was all that ancient sailors had to guide them on long sea voyages. By the eleventh century, merchants, rulers, and explorers all had a need for more scientific navigating instruments. Those desires fueled the development of maritime instruments, beginning with the astrolabe. Shown here is a collection of European and Arab copper astrolabes from the fourteenth to the sixteenth centuries. [Bridgeman Art Library International]

combined their early nautical ingenuity to forge trading routes that continue even today. Their greatest contribution to maritime progress was an understanding of the seasonal monsoons and the Arab development of the lateen sail and a distinctively effective ship design. The regularity of the trade winds—which blew from the northeast from November to March, and from the southwest from June to September—made it possible to sail great distances upon a prearranged course. These monsoons enabled vessels laden with spices, silks, and other luxury goods to travel the 2,200 miles from the Persian Gulf and India to East Africa in as few as twenty-five days. Similarly, the vessels could return from Africa with ivory, gold, and slaves in the same amount of time. In effect, nature provided a reliable means for long-distance oceanic travel and trade. However, without the Arab invention of the lateen sail, nature's gift would have been lost. Woven from the leaves of the coconut or palm tree, the lateen sail was a triangular fore-and-aft sail that was very tall and high-peaked. Unlike the square sail used universally in the West at the time, the lateen sail was easily maneuvered. This innovation allowed the mariners to take advantage of the seasonal monsoons since they could sail very close to the wind and tack back and forth with ease. During the fourteenth and fifteenth centuries, these sails were attached to

ships that had several distinctively Arab features. The hulls of these handy vessels were very stout, they were constructed exclusively from Indian teak, and their planks were sewn edge to edge. Continued refinements in nautical innovation allowed the Arabs to master travel in the Indian Ocean, extending their trade routes throughout the region. By the fifteenth century, when the Portuguese turned to honing their maritime skills and mastering the high seas, they found they had much to learn from their contemporaries in the East.

The "Age of Discovery"

Historians still disagree on the precise reasons why, at the beginning of the fifteenth century, the Portuguese embarked on an unprecedented period of maritime innovation and overseas expansion. Certainly, powerful motives must have spurred such a rapid and extensive advance in technology. In fact, four main impulses can be attributed to forging what is known as the "Age of Discovery." These motives were economic, religious, strategic, and political in nature. More specifically, the desire to exploit the extensive trading network of luxury goods, slaves, spices, ivory, and jewels that was established throughout the Indian Ocean basin; the

Sailing on the Indian Ocean in a square-rigged ship, a seaman navigates with the help of an astrolabe as his boat-mate adjusts the sail. This illustration comes from the *Livre des Merveilles (The Book of Wonders)* partly compiled by the Benedictine Jean Le Long in 1351. [Bridgeman Art Library International]

crusading zeal against the Muslims; and the search for Guinea gold all came together to propel the Portuguese headlong into modernizing nautical science and maritime skills. Of practical importance too were Portugal's ideal positioning with a long ocean seaboard and its strong tradition of commercial shipping and sea travel.

Perhaps the greatest catalyst of Portuguese maritime advance was the Infante Dom Henry, a man more commonly known as Prince Henry the Navigator. A self-interested friend of merchants and seamen and a patron of learned institutions, Prince Henry spearheaded his country's maritime endeavors by bringing together the seafaring and learned worlds of Europe and the East. Under his leadership, the naval arsenal and school of navigation were founded in the town of Sagres. It was there that the Portuguese both refined existing nautical innovations and gave new practical applications to classical knowledge.

Two areas of technical advancement proved to be of the greatest importance. First was the study of astronomy and geography and its relevance to solving the problems of navigation. Here the Portuguese relied upon the academic knowledge of the Ancients in mathematics and cosmography, particularly Ptolemy's work on astronomy, commonly known by its Arabic title, the *Almagest*. In fact, earlier Arab cosmographers had made great use of Ptolemy's writings. Together, Ptolemy's work and the subsequent Arab advances in astrology and latitude calculations using the Pole Star provided the Portuguese with important precedents. By distill-

ing and improving upon these earlier theories and practices, the Portuguese of the fifteenth century could calculate with increasing accuracy their position at sea by a combination of dead-reckoning—whereby a seaman would lay down a compass course and estimate his distance each day—and observed latitude. Moreover, their navigation was further sharpened by refining and developing the principal nautical instruments, the astrolabe and later the first rudimentary quadrant. With such continued innovations, celestial navigation became more and more precise. The Portuguese also refined the mariner's compass, and with help from the work of earlier Italian and Catalan hydrographers, they created maritime charts for the still unnavigated oceans. By the later fifteenth century the Portuguese were creating sophisticated charts that mapped their new voyages of discovery down the coast of Africa, around the continent's tip, and into the Indian Ocean. Importantly, these early voyages around Africa brought newfound wealth in slaves, ivory, gold, and Malaguette pepper that both helped to fund the maritime work at Sagres and heightened the desire to participate in the Indian Ocean trade.

Just as the Portuguese adapted many of the navigational techniques of their predecessors and contemporaries, they vastly improved upon ship and sail designs of their counterparts in the East. Indeed, the second important technical advance of the Portuguese was in the realm of shipbuilding and vessel maneuvering. Before the fifteenth century maritime innovations, the square-rigged sailing ships of Western Europe, though larger were clumsy and impractical for deep-sea voyages. Unlike the agile Arab vessels with lateen sails, Europe's ships were completely unsuited for exploring new coastlines and navigating strange winds and currents. Again, the Portuguese looked to the maritime ingenuity of their neighbors to the East. Arab nautical designs had already been transferred to the West during the Crusades. Now the Portuguese developed a new alternative—the Arab-inspired lateen caravel. With this vessel, the Portuguese made their way around Africa and into the Indian Ocean. There they encountered the Arab shipmasters who dominated the region and from whom they learned about the monsoon winds, ocean currents, and variations on sail and ship design.

The sailors from Portugal made steady improvements in sail and ship construction, and by the end of the fifteenth century, the Portuguese combined into one vessel all of the advantages of the earlier European square-rigged vessels with the sophistication of the Arab lateen-rigged ships. This wholly new creation was called the *caravela redonda*, or the square-rigged caravel. This was a design of major importance in maritime innovation. Indeed, it was with this ship that most of the voyages of discovery of the late fifteenth and sixteenth centuries were made.

Maritime Innovation and New World Discovery

While the Portuguese inaugurated many of the nautical improvements of the fifteenth century, they were not the only European country interested in voyages of exploration. Of all the competition they faced from the West, the Spaniards were by far the most formidable. In fact, disputes over new territorial possessions and overseas trade increasingly punctuated relations between Portugal and Spain from the fifteenth cen-

tury onwards. As the competition grew, so too did westward expansion and maritime expertise. It was, in fact, the constant development and refinement of maritime skill and ship design that enabled Christopher Columbus to embark upon his first voyage of New World discovery in 1492. Aware of the nautical innovations of his time, Columbus presented his plan for a westward journey to the Portuguese Crown. Rejected, Columbus turned for support to Spain, where Queen Isabella defied her husband's advisers and funded Columbus' expedition. Her patronage included the outfitting of two square-rigged caravels, the *Niña* and the *Pinta*, and the larger cargo vessel, the *Santa Maria*. In fact, Columbus' fleet, though smaller in number, was much like those of the later voyages of the fifteenth and sixteenth centuries. Caravels and ships, together, comprised the great fleets of discovery.

The lighter and swifter caravels were essential for reconnaissance and escort for the larger, cargo-carrying boats, but Columbus also needed the navigational skills that sailors and scholars had honed during the 1400s. The explorer had sailed on both Portuguese and Genoese ships for many years and was trained in the use of contemporary navigational techniques and instruments. On his first voyage, Columbus used his knowledge of the stars, the quadrant, and a variety of compass needles, together with the requisite magnetizing lodestone. Of all his maritime abilities, however, it was Columbus' skill of dead-reckoning for which he is most noted. Used together, these maritime devices allowed him to sail his first fleet westward into a vast and uncharted ocean, and return to Spain with the claim of a new-found passage to the East. Indeed, such a western route would have to wait for the travels of Ferdinand Magellan and Sebastián del Cano, but the early voyages of Columbus represent the first applications of fifteenth century maritime innovation to European exploration of the New World.

RELIGIONS OF THE WORLD

Christianity

The teaching of Jesus gave birth to Christianity. His simple message of faith in God and self-sacrificial love of one's neighbor attracted many people whose religious needs were not adequately met by the philosophies and religions of the ancient world. After Jesus' crucifixion, his devout followers proclaimed his resurrection and expected him to return in glory, defeat sin and evil, and take them away with him to heaven—a radical vision of judgment and immortality that also heightened Christianity's initial appeal. In the writings of St. Paul and the teachings of the early church, Jesus became the Christ, the son of God, the long-awaited Messiah of Jewish prophecy. According to John's gospel, Jesus was also the *logos*, the eternal principle of all being, after which the thinkers of antiquity had quested. Christianity thus offered people something more than philosophy, law, and ritual.

Christianity proclaimed the very incarnation of God in a man, the visible presence of eternity in time. According to early Christian teaching, the power of God's incarnation in Jesus lived on in the preaching and sacraments of the church under the guidance of the Holy Spirit. Christian thinkers here borrowed from the popular Asian cults of the Roman world, which had also offered their followers a sacramental participation in deity and spiritual redemption from sin. But Christianity went beyond them all when it declared the source of all being to be no longer transcendent and proclaimed the Messiah to have arrived. The Christian message was that, in Jesus, eternity had made itself accessible to every person here and now and forevermore.

The first Christians were drawn from among the rich and poor alike. People flocked to the new religion for both materialistic and deeply religious reasons. For some believers Christianity promised a better material life. But its appeal also lay in its unique ability to impart to people a sense of spiritual self-worth regardless of their place or prospects in society. The gospel of Jesus appealed to the hopelessly poor and powerless as readily as to the socially rising and well-to-do.

In the late second century the Romans began persecuting Christians both as "heretics" (because of their rejection of the traditional Roman gods) and as social revolutionaries. At

The Annunciation. This scene, painted in 1430 by Fra Angelico, illustrates a passage from the Gospel of Luke (1:26 ff.): "The angel Gabriel was sent from God" to Mary "and said unto her, the Holy Ghost shall come upon thee, and the power of the Highest shall overshadow thee: therefore also that holy thing which shall be born of thee shall be called the Son of God." The impending redemption of humanity through Mary, the new Eve, and Christ, the new Adam, is juxtaposed with the fall of Adam and Eve and their expulsion from paradise (shown on the left). The beam of light represents the Holy Spirit. The small panels at the bottom illustrate scenes from the life of Mary. [Joseph Martin/Bildarchiv Preussischer Kulturbesitz]

the same time dissenting Christians, particularly sects claiming a direct spiritual knowledge of God apart from Scripture, brought new internal divisions to the young church by advocating Christian heresies of their own. Such challenges had to be met, and by the fourth century effective weapons against both state terrorism and Christian heresy were in place: an ordained official clergy; a hierarchical church organization; orthodox creeds; and a biblical canon, the New Testament. Christianity not only gained legal status within the Roman Empire, but, by the fourth century, was the favored religion of the emperor as well.

Women are entering the ministry and priesthood of many Christian denominations. The first woman bishop of the Episcopal Church of North America is here shown consecrating the Eucharist. The Church of England has also voted to admit women to the priesthood. [Ira Wyman/Sygma]

The fortune of Christianity after the fall of the Western Roman Empire in the fifth century C.E. is one of history's great success stories. Aided by the enterprise of its popes and the example of its monks, the church cultivated an appealing lay piety centered on the Lord's Prayer, the Apostles' Creed, veneration of the Virgin, and the sacrament of the Eucharist. Clergy became both royal teachers and bureaucrats within the kingdom of the Franks. Despite a growing schism between the Eastern (Byzantine) and Western churches, and a final split in 1054, by 1000 the church held real economic and political power. In the eleventh century reform-minded prelates ended secular interference in its spiritual affairs; the traditional lay practice of investing clergy in their offices was condemned under penalty of excommunication. For several centuries thereafter the church would remain a formidable international force, successfully challenging kings and emperors and inspiring crusades against the non-Christian world.

By the fifteenth century the new states of Europe had stripped the church of much of this political power. It would henceforth be progressively confined to its present role of spiritual and moral authority. Christianity's greatest struggles ever since have been not with kings and emperors over political power, but with materialistic philosophies and worldly ideologies, over spiritual and moral hegemony within an increasingly pluralistic and secular world. Since the sixteenth century a succession of Humanists, Skeptics, Deists, Rationalists, Marxists, Freudians, Darwinians, and atheists have attempted to explain away some of traditional Christianity's most basic teachings. In addition, the church has endured major internal upheaval. After the Protestant Re-

formation (1517–1555) made the Bible widely available to the laity, the possibilities for internal criticism of Christianity multiplied geometrically. Beginning with the split between Lutherans and Zwinglians in the 1520s, Protestant Christians have fragmented themselves into hundreds of sects, each claiming the true interpretation of Scripture. The Roman Catholic church, by contrast, has maintained its unity through these perilous times. However, present-day discontent with papal authority threatens the modern Catholic church almost as seriously as the Protestant Reformation once did.

But Christianity is nothing if not resilient. It continues to possess the simple, almost magically appealing gospel of Jesus. It finds itself within a world whose religious needs and passions still remain deep and basic, and like other religions, it has experienced a remarkable revival in recent decades. The Roman Catholic church, although troubled by conflicts over papal authority, has become far more pluralistic than in earlier periods. The pope has become a world figure, traveling to all continents to represent the church and advance its position on public issues. A major ecumenical movement emerging in the 1960s has promoted unprecedented cooperation among all Christian denominations. In the United States, many Protestant denominations have been politically active. Black ministers took the lead in the civil-rights struggle of the 1960s and continue to lend their voice and moral authority to issues of concern to the African-American community. White fundamentalist clergy have frequently promoted conservative political agendas, turning to television to spread their messages. Catholics and Protestants alike have struggled with the role of women in the church.

18 AFRICA (CA. 1000–1800)

A bronze plaque showing three warriors from Benin, West Africa. The famous Benin bronze sculptures are among the finest artistic works of all African cultures. Note that the two small figures in the background apparently depict Portuguese or other European soldiers.

CHAPTER TOPICS

◆ North Africa and Egypt

◆ The Spread of Islam
   South of the Sahara

◆ Sahelian Empires of the Western
   and Central Sudan

◆ The Eastern Sudan

◆ The Forestlands—Coastal West
   and Central Africa

◆ East Africa

◆ Southern Africa

In World Perspective Africa, 1000–1800

The history of Africa in the first half of the second millennium C.E. reveals widely diverse experiences for different parts of this vast continent. For example, while North Africa and Egypt were involved in the major power struggles of the Islamic heartlands, sub-Saharan Africa developed more according to internal African dynamics and non-Islamic external influences. Similarly, by 1500, although many African regions were little influenced by outsiders or their affairs, others were strongly affected by new developments in Europe and the Islamic world and the changing power balance between them.

In this chapter we explore, region by region, some salient developments in Africa from 1000 to 1800. The major phenomenon that affected almost all of Africa between the fifteenth and nineteenth centuries, the Atlantic slave trade, is treated in Chapter 19. However, its importance in disrupting and reconfiguring African economies, social organization, and political life must be kept in mind as we treat the period's other developments. We begin with Africa above the equator, where the influence of Islam increased and where substantial empires and kingdoms developed and flourished. Then we discuss west, east, central, and southern Africa and the effects of first Arab-Islamic and then European influence in both regions.

North Africa and Egypt

As we saw in Chapter 14, Egypt and other North African societies played a central role in Islamic and Mediterranean history after 1000 C.E. From Tunisia to Egypt, Sunni religious and political leaders and their Shi'ite, especially Isma'ili, counterparts struggled for the minds of the masses. By the thirteenth century, however, the Shi'ites had become a small minority of the Muslim population of Mediterranean Africa. In Egypt a Sunni revival confirmed the Sunni character of Egyptian religiosity and legal interpretation.

In politics, this period witnessed the influential dynasties of the Fatimids (909–969 in Tunisia; 969–1171 in Egypt), the Almoravids (1056–1147 in Senegal and the western Sudan; 1062–1118 in Marrakesh and western North Africa; 1086–1147 in Spain), the Almohads (1130–1269 in western North Africa; 1145–1212 in Spain), the Ayyubids (1169–1250 in Egypt), the Mamluks (1250–1517 in Egypt and the eastern Mediterranean); and the Ottomans (from the fourteenth century) across most of mediterranean Africa. In general, a feisty regionalism characterized states, city-states, and tribal groups north of the Sahara and along the lower Nile, especially vis-à-vis external power centers, such as Baghdad and Spain. No single power controlled them for long. Regionalism persisted even after 1500, when most of North Africa came under the influence—and often direct control—of the Ottoman Empire centered in Istanbul and felt the pressure of Ottoman-European naval rivalry in the Mediterranean.

By 1800 the nominally Ottoman domains from Egypt to Algeria were effectively independent principalities. In Egypt the Ottomans had established direct rule after their defeat of the Mamluks in 1517, but by the seventeenth and eighteenth centuries power had already passed to Egyptian governors descended from the former ruling Mamluks. Even though greatly weakened by 1700, these Mamluk governors survived until the rise of Muhammad Ali in the wake of the French invasion of 1800 (see Chapter 31). The Mediterranean coastlands between Egypt and Morocco were officially Ottoman provinces, or regencies, whether under local governors or Ottoman deputies drawn from Janissary ranks (see Chapter 23). By the eighteenth century, however, the Regency of Algiers to the east of Morocco was a separate, locally run principality with an economy based on piracy. The Regency of Tripoli (in

Feluccas on the Nile. These lateen-rigged sailing vessels are the traditional river boats of Egypt and are still in use today.

[Photograph by Eliot Elisofon, Courtesy of the Freer Gallery of Art, Smithsonian Institution, Washington, D.C.]

modern Libya) was ruled by a family of hereditary, effectively independent rulers. In Tunisia a Janissary state operated virtually independent of its nominal Ottoman overlords.

Morocco, ruled by a succession of *Sharifs* (leaders claiming descent from the family of the prophet Muhammad), was the only North African sultanate to remain fully independent after 1700. The most important *Sharifian* dynasty was that of the Sa'dis (1554–1659). One major reason for Morocco's independence was that its Arab and Berber populations united after 1500 to oppose the Portuguese and Spaniards.

The Spread of Islam South of the Sahara

Islamic influence in sub-Saharan Africa began as early as the eighth century and by 1800 affected most of the Sudanic belt and the coast of East Africa as far south as modern Zimbabwe. All in all, the process was peaceful, gradual, and partial. Typically, Islam never penetrated beyond the ruling or commercial classes of a region and tended to coexist or blend with indigenous ideas and practices. Nevertheless, Islam and its carriers strongly affected these regions. Agents of Islam brought commercial and political changes as well as the Qur'an, new religious practices, and literate culture. West and east, the arrival of literate culture proved as important for subsequent history as any other development. Many innovations, from architecture and technology to intellectual life and administrative practice, depended on writing and literacy, two major bases for developing large-scale societies and cultures.

Comparison of the spread of Islam in West and central Africa with that in East Africa is instructive. In East Africa,

Muslim traders moving down the coastline with the ancient monsoon trade routes had begun the "Islamization" of port towns and coastal regions even before 800 C.E. From the thirteenth century on, the growth of not only Islamic trading communities but also Islamic city-states along the coast from Mogadishu to Kilwa became a major factor in the region.

By contrast, in the western and central parts of the continent, Islam penetrated south of the Sahara into the Sudan not by sea, but by overland routes, primarily from North Africa and the Nile valley. Yet as in East Africa, wherever Islamization occurred, its agents were traders, chiefly Berbers who plied the desert routes (see Chapter 6) to trading towns such as Awdaghast on the edge of the Sahel, as early as the eighth century. From there Islam spread south to centers such as Kumbi and beyond, southeast across the Niger, and west into Senegambia. Another source for the gradual spread of Islam into the central and western Sudan was Egypt and the Nilotic Sudan. Its agents were sometimes traders, but primarily emigrants from the east seeking new land; migrating Arab tribal groups in particular came west to settle in the central sub-Saharan Sahel. Although many more Arab migrants moving west followed the Mediterranean coast from Egypt to North Africa, substantial numbers sifted westward to Lake Chad and the Niger regions from the ninth to the sixteenth centuries and later.

Some Muslim conversion in the western and central Sudan came early, again virtually always through the agency of Muslim traders. The year 985 marks the first time a West Africa royal court—that of the kingdom of Gao, east of the Niger bend—officially became Muslim (see Chapter 6 and below). The Gao rulers did not, however, try to convert their subjects. By contrast, as we shall see later in the chapter, the rulers of the later kingdom of Ghana long maintained their in-

The Djinguereber mosque in Timbuktu. This mud and wood building is typical of western Sudanese mosques. The distinctive tower of the mosque was a symbol of the presence of Islam, which came to places like Timbuktu in central and West Africa by way of overland trade routes. [Photograph by Eliot Elisofon, National Museum of African Art, Eliot Elisofon Archives, Smithsonian Institution, Washington, D.C.]

digenous traditions even though they traded with Muslims and used them for advisers.

From the 1030s zealous militants known as Almoravids (Arabic *al-Murabitun*, after their fortified retreat centers, or *ribats*; see Chapter 14) began an overt conversion campaign that extended to the western Sahel and Sahara. This movement eventually swept into Ghana's territory, taking first Awdaghast and finally Kumbi in 1076. Thereafter, the forcibly converted Soninke ruling group of Ghana spread Islam among their own populace and farther south in the savannah. Here they converted Mande-speaking traders, who brought Islam south into the forests. Farther west, the Fulbe rulers of Takrur along the Senegal became Muslim in the 1030s and propagated their new faith among their subjects. The Fulbe, or Fulani, remained important carriers of Islam over the next eight centuries as they migrated gradually into new regions as far east as Lake Chad, where some rulers were Muslim as early as 1100.

Major groups in West Africa, especially in the sub-Niger region, strongly resisted Islamization. Notable among them were the Mossi kingdoms founded in the Volta region at Wagadugu around 1050 and Yatenga about 1170.

Sahelian Empires of the Western and Central Sudan

It is not the case, as was once believed, that urbanization and state formation in sub-Saharan Africa occurred only in response to trans-Saharan trade with the Islamic world (the fabled "golden trade of the Moors"), which dates largely from the end of the first millennium.[1] As we noted in Chapter 6, substantial states had risen in the first millennium C.E. in the Sahel regions just south of the Sahara proper. From about 1000 to 1600, four of these developed into notable and relatively long-lived empires: Ghana, Mali, and Songhai in the western Sudan, and Kanem-Bornu in the central Sudan.

Ghana

Ghana established the model for later empires of the sahel region of the western Sudan, even though those that succeeded it were larger. A regional empire noted and esteemed even by distant Arab Islamic writers, Ghana was located well north of modern Ghana (and unrelated to it except by name) in the region between and north of the inland Niger delta and the upper Senegal. A Ghanaian kingdom originated as early as 400–600 C.E., but Ghana emerged as a regional power only near the end of the first millennium and flourished for about two centuries. Its capital, Kumbi (or Kumbi Saleh), on the desert's edge, was well sited for the Saharan and Sahelian trade networks. Ghana's major population group were the Soninke. *Ghana*, the Soninke term for "ruler," was used by Berbers and Arabs to name the region and hence is the name passed on in our earliest written sources.

The Ghanaian rulers were matrilineally descended (through the previous king's sister). They ruled through a council of ministers. The reports we have, especially from the eleventh-century Muslim writer al-Bakri (see the box on p. 498), indicate that the king was supreme judge and held court regularly to hear grievances. The royal ceremonies reported to have been held in Kumbi Saleh were embellished with the full trappings of regal wealth and power appropriate to a king held to be divinely blessed if not semidivine himself.

Ghana's power rested on a solid economic base. Tribute from the empire's many chieftaincies and taxes on royal lands

[1]S. K. and R. J. McIntosh, *Prehistoric Investigations at Jenne, Mali* (1980), pp. 41–59, 434–461; R. Oliver, *The African Experience* (New York: Harper-Collins, 1991), pp. 90–101.

Ghana and Its People in the Mid-Eleventh Century

The following excerpt is from the geographical work of the Spanish Muslim geographer al-Bakri (d. 1094). In it he describes with great precision some customs of the ruler and the people of the capital of Ghana as he carefully gleaned them from other Arabic sources and travelers (he never visited West Africa himself, it seems).

How did the ruler of Ghana deal with the differing religious groups in his capital?

Ghana is a title given to their kings; the name of the region is Awkar, and their king today, namely in the year 460 [1067–8], is Tanka Manin. . . . This Tanka Manin is powerful, rules an enormous kingdom, and possesses great authority.

The city of Ghana consists of two towns situated on a plain. One of these towns, which is inhabited by Muslims, is large and possesses twelve mosques, in one of which they assemble for the Friday prayer. There are salaried imams and muezzins, as well as jurists and scholars. In the environs are wells with sweet water, from which they drink and with which they grow vegetables. The king's town is six miles distant from this one and bears the name of Al-Ghaba. Between these two towns there are continuous habitations. The houses of the inhabitants are of stone and acacia (*sunt*) wood. The king has a palace and a number of domed dwellings all surrounded with an enclosure like a city wall (*sur*). In the king's town, and not far from his court of justice, is a mosque where the Muslims who arrive at his court . . . pray. Around the king's town are domed buildings and groves and thickets where the sorcerers of these people, men in charge of the religious cult, live. In them too are their idols and the tombs of their kings. . . .

All of them shave their beards, and women shave their heads. The king adorns himself like a woman [wearing necklaces] round his neck and [bracelets] on his forearms, and he puts on a high cap (*tartur*) decorated with gold and wrapped in a turban of fine cotton. He sits in audience or to hear grievances against officials (*mazalim*) in a domed pavilion around which stand ten horses covered with gold-embroidered materials. Behind the king stand ten pages holding shields and swords decorated with gold, and on his right are the sons of the [vassal] kings of his country wearing splendid garments and their hair plaited with gold. The governor of the city sits on the ground before the king and around him are ministers seated likewise. . . . When the people who profess the same religion as the king approach him they fall on their knees and sprinkle dust on their heads, for this is their way of greeting him. As for the Muslims, they greet him only by clapping their hands.

Their religion is paganism and the worship of idols (*dakakir*). When their king dies they construct over the place where his tomb will be an enormous dome of saj wood. Then they bring him on a bed covered with a few carpets and cushions and place him beside the dome. At his side they place his ornaments, his weapons, and the vessels from which he used to eat and drink, filled with various kinds of food and beverages.

From J. F. P. Hopkins, trans.; N. Levtzion and J. F. P. Hopkins, eds., *Corpus of Early Arabic Sources for West African History.* Reprinted with permission of Cambridge University Press, pp. 79–80.

---

and crops (primarily grown near the Niger and Senegal Rivers) supplemented the major source of income: duties levied on all incoming and outgoing trade. This trade, both north-south between the Sahara and the savannah and especially east-west through the Sahel between Senegambia and more easterly trading towns like Gao on the Niger Bend, involved a variety of goods—notably imported salt, cloth, and metal goods such as copper—probably in exchange for gold and perhaps kola nuts from the south. The regime apparently also controlled the gold (and, presumably, the slave) trade that originated in the savannah to the south and west, in the tributary regions of the Bambuk and Galam regions of the middle Senegal and its southern tributary, the Faleme, and in the Boure region of the upper Niger and its tributaries.

Although the king and court of Ghana did not convert to Islam, they made elaborate arrangements to accommodate Muslim traders and government servants in their own settlement a few miles from the royal preserve in Kumbi Saleh. Muslim traders were prominent in the court, literate Muslims administered the government, and Muslim legists advised the ruler. In Ghana's hierarchical society, slaves were at the bottom; farmers and draftsmen above them; merchants above them; and the king, his court, and the nobility on top.

A huge, well-trained army secured royal control and enabled the kings to extend their sway in the late tenth century to the Atlantic shore and to the south as well (see Map 18–1). Ghanaian troops captured Awdaghast, the important southern terminus of the trans-Saharan trade route to Morocco, from the Berbers in 992. The empire was, however, vulnerable to attack from the desert fringe, as Almoravid Berber forces proved in 1054 when they took Awdaghast in a single raid.

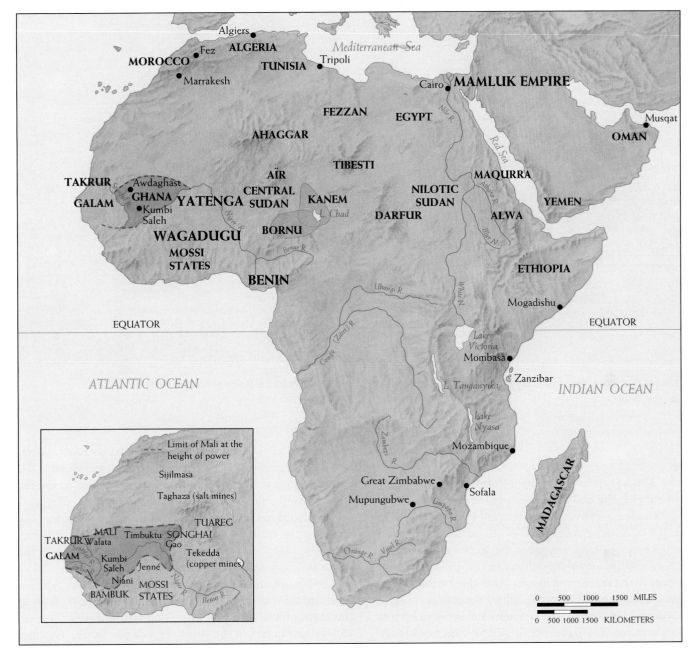

Map 18-1 Africa ca. 900–1500. Shown are major cities and states referred to in the text. The main map shows the region of West Africa occupied by the empire of Ghana from ca. 990 to ca. 1180. The inset shows the region occupied by Mali between 1230 and 1450.

Some traditions suggest that further Berber raids toppled the Ghanaian state in 1076, but this has recently been questioned. There are reports of Ghanaian involvement in trade even in the late twelfth century. Still more, there are indications that Ghana's rulers may have converted to Islam soon after 1100 and that throughout the twelfth century they cooperated with the Almoravids in proselytizing for Islam and in military and economic matters. Ghana's empire was probably destroyed in the late twelfth century by the actively anti-Muslim Soso people from the mountains southeast of Kumbi Saleh, a Malinke clan who had long been part of the Ghanaian empire. Their brief ascendancy between 1180 and 1230 apparently spelled the end of the once great transregional power centered at Kumbi.[2]

[2]D. Conrad and H. Fisher, "The Conquest That Never Was: Ghana and the Almoravids, 1076," *History in Africa 9* (1982): 1–59; 10 (1983): 53–78.

The great mosque at Jenne, one of the important commercial centers controlled by the empire of Mali in the thirteenth and fourteenth centuries. [Ann Stalcup]

Mali

After the Almoravids brought their reform movement to the western Sahel at the end of the eleventh century, their proselytizing zeal led to conversion of many of the region's ruling classes. It was, however, over a half-century after the breakup of Ghana's empire before anyone in the western Sahel, Muslim or non-Muslim, could reestablish an empire of comparable extent. With Ghana's collapse and the Almoravids' failure to build a new empire below the Sahara (largely because of their focus on North Africa), the western Sudan broke up into smaller kingdoms. The former Ghanaian provinces of Mande and Takrur were already independent before 1076, and in the early twelfth century Takrur's control of the Senegal valley and the gold-producing region of Galam made it briefly the strongest state in the western Sudan. Like Ghana, however, it was soon eclipsed by developments to the east, along the upper Niger—first the brief Soso ascendancy and then the rise of Mali.

In the mid-thirteenth century the Keita ruling clan of a Ghanaian successor kingdom, Mali, forged a new and lasting empire. This empire seems to have been built on the same economic base as that of Ghana and Takrur earlier: monopolization of the lucrative north-south gold trade. The Keita kings dominated enough of the Sahel to control the flow of West African gold from the Senegal regions and the forest-lands south of the Niger to the trans-Saharan trade routes, and the influx of copper and especially salt in exchange. Because they were farther south, in the fertile land along the Niger, than their Ghanaian predecessors had been, they were better placed to control all trade on the upper Niger and to add to it the Gambia and Senegal trade to the west. They were also able to use war captives for plantation labor in the Niger inland delta to produce surplus food for trade.

Agriculture and cattle farming were the primary occupations of Mali's population and, together with the gold trade, the mainstays of the economy. Rice was grown in the river valleys and millet in the drier parts of the Sahel. Together with beans, yams, and other agricultural products, this made for a plentiful food supply. Fishing flourished along the Niger and elsewhere. Animal husbandry was strongest among pastoralists of the Sahel, such as the Fulani (or Fulbe), but cattle, sheep, and goats were also plentiful in the Niger valley by the fourteenth century. Many of the Fulani seem to have been attracted by excellent pasturages to the riverine regions. The chief craft specialties were metalworking (iron and gold) and weaving of cotton grown within the empire.

The Malinke, a southern Mande-speaking people of the upper Niger region, formed the core population of the new state. They apparently lived in walled urban settlements typical of the western savannah region. Each walled town was surrounded by its own agricultural land, held perhaps one thousand to fifteen thousand people, and presumably had enough arable land within its walls to deal with an emergency siege. Each was linked to its neighboring cities by trade and possibly intermarriage.

The Keita dynasty had converted early to Islam (ca. 1100) and even claimed descent from Muhammad's famous muezzin (the person who calls the faithful to worship) Bilal, a former black slave from Abyssinia whose son was said to have settled in the Mande-speaking region. During Mali's heyday in the thirteenth and fourteenth centuries, its kings often made the pilgrimage to Mecca. From their travel in the central Islamic lands, they brought back with them not only military aids, such as large Barbary war horses, but also new ideas about political and military organization. Through Muslim traders' networks, Islam also connected Mali to other areas of Africa, especially those to the east, from Kano and Hausaland in the Sahel south to the forests.

Mali's imperial power was built largely by one leader, the Keita King Sundiata (or Sunjaata; r. 1230–1255). Sundiata and his successors, aided by significant population growth in the western savannah, exploited their agricultural resources and Malinke commercial skills to build an empire even more powerful than its Ghanaian predecessor. Sundiata extended his control well beyond the former domains of Ghana, west to the Atlantic coast and east beyond Timbuktu. By controlling the commercial entrepôts of Gao, Walata, and Jenne, he was able to dominate the Saharan as well as the Niger trade. He built his capital, Niani, into a major city. Niani was located on a tributary of the Niger in the savannah at the edge of the forest in a gold and iron-rich region, well away from the lands of the Sahel nomads and well south of Ghana's capital, Kumbi. It had access to the forest trade products of gold, kola nuts, and palm oil; it was easily defended by virtue of its surrounding small hills; and it was easily reached by river.

The empire that Sundiata and his successors built ultimately encompassed three major regions and language groups of Sudanic West Africa: (1) the Senegal region (including Takrur), occupied by speakers of the West Atlantic Niger-Kongo language group (including Fulbe, Tukulor, Wolof, Serer); (2) the central Mande states between Senegal and Niger, occupied by the Niger-Kongo-speaking Soninke and Mandinke peoples; and (3) the peoples of the Niger in the Gao region who spoke Songhai, the only Nilo-Saharan language west of the Lake Chad basin. Mali was less a centralized bureaucratic state than the center of a vast sphere of influence that included provinces and tribute-paying kingdoms. Many individual chieftaincies retained much of their independence but recognized the sovereignty of the supreme, sacred *mansa*, or "emperor," of the Malian realms.

The greatest Keita king proved to be Mansa Musa (r. 1312–1337), whose pilgrimage through Mamluk Cairo to Mecca in 1324 became famous in Egypt and elsewhere abroad. He paid out or gave away so much gold in Cairo alone that he started massive inflation lasting over a decade. He returned with many Muslim scholars, artists, and architects to grace his court. At home, he consolidated Mali's power, securing peace for most of his reign throughout his vast dominions. Musa's devoutness as a Muslim fostered the further spread of Islam in the empire and beyond. Under his rule, Timbuktu became known far and wide for its *madrasas* and libraries, and for its poets, scientists, and architects, making the city the leading intellectual center of sub-Saharan Islam as well as a major trading city of the Sahel-roles it retained long after Mali's imperial dominance ended.

Mali's dominance waned after Musa's time, most sharply in the fifteenth century, evidently as the result of destructive rivalries for succession to the *mansa's* throne. As time went on, more and more subject dependencies became independent, and the empire withered. In the 1430s Berber Tuaregs took over much of Mali's Sahelian dominions, including Timbuktu and Walata. The non-Muslim Mossi kingdom in the savannah and tropical forestlands to the south made large inroads on Malian territory in the middle of the century, and after 1450 a new Songhai power in Gao to the east ended Mali's imperial authority.

Songhai

Evidence suggests that as early as the eleventh or twelfth century there was a Songhai kingdom in the region of Gao, on the eastern arc of the Great Bend of the Niger. In 1325 Mansa Musa brought this kingdom and the Gao region under the control of Mali and the Malinke. Mali's domination ended with the rise of a dynasty in Gao known as the Sunni or Sonni around 1375. For the next century the kingdom flourished, but not until the reign of the greatest Sunni ruler, Sonni Ali (1464–1492), did it become an imperial power. Sonni Ali made the Songhai empire so powerful in the entire upper Niger region and beyond that it dominated the political history of the western Sudan for more than a century and was arguably the most powerful state in Africa (see Map 18–2). With a strong military built around a riverboat flotilla and cavalry of great mobility, Sonni Ali took Jenne and Timbuktu. He pushed the Tuareg Berbers back into the northern Sahel and Sahara—extending his control as far as Taghaza and Walata—and stifled any threats from the southern forestland.

After Sonni Ali's accidental death in 1492, rule passed to the Askia, an Islamic Soninke dynasty. Askia Muhammad al-Turi (r. 1493–1528) continued Sonni Ali's expansionist policies. Between them, Sonni Ali and Askia Muhammad built an empire that stretched west nearly to the Atlantic, northwest into the Sahara, and east into the central Sudan. Taking advantage of their control of access to the gold and other desirable commodities of West Africa, they emulated their

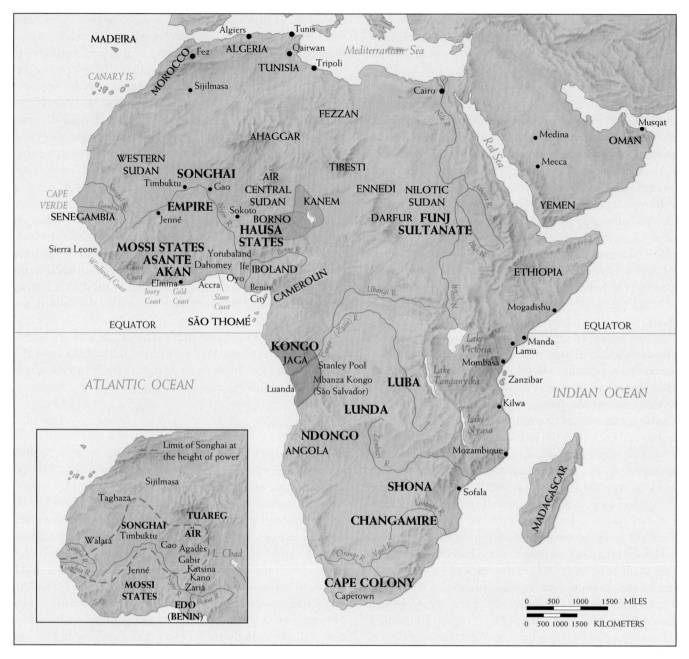

Map 18-2 Africa ca. 1500–1800.   Important towns, regions, peoples, and states. The inset shows the empire of Songhai at its greatest extent in the early sixteenth century.

Ghanaian predecessors in cultivating and expanding the ancient caravan trade across the Sahara to the North African coasts of Libya and Tunisia. This provided their major source of wealth.

Sonni Ali, who held to the traditional African religious faith of his people, was never a good Muslim and remained at odds with the *ulama* of Timbuktu throughout his reign. Muhammad al-Turi, in contrast, was an enthusiastic Muslim. He built up the Songhai state after the model of the Islamic empire of

Mali. In his reign, Muslim scholars came in substantial numbers to the Songhai cities of Gao, Timbuktu, and Jenne. He appointed Muslim judges (*qadis*) in towns throughout the empire and made Timbuktu a major intellectual and legal training center for the whole Sudan. He also replaced native Songhais with Arab Muslim immigrants as government officials to strengthen his centralized power. Taking Islam seriously, Muhammad made a triumphal pilgrimage to Mecca much like Mansa Musa before him. At Mecca he was hailed

A mosque tomb in Gao reputed to have been built for the Askia rulers of Songhai. [John O. Hunwick]

as "Caliph of the western Sahara." From his vast royal treasury he supported the poor and the sufi leaders, or *marabouts*, as well as the construction of mosques throughout the realm. Nevertheless, his reforms failed in the end to Islamize the empire or to ensure a strong central state under his less able successors.

The last powerful Askia leader was Askia Dawud (r. 1549–1583), under whom Songhai economic prosperity and intellectual life achieved its apogee. The trans-Saharan trade reached new heights, and royal patronage of the arts rose correspondingly to new levels. Still, difficulties mounted. The Askia battled the Mossi to the south and Berber forces from as far away as the Moroccan Sultanate in the north (Taghaza was taken by the Moroccans just after Dawud's death). Civil war broke out over succession to the throne in 1586, and the empire was divided thereafter. In a battle in 1591 a military force sent by the Sa'dis of Morocco used superior gunpowder weapons and the aid of disaffected Songhai princes to defeat the last Askia of Gao at Tondibi. This battle was as much a measure of the empire's weakness as of Moroccan power, but it proved decisive for the collapse of the Gao empire. The once great state was reduced to its original holdings in the Niger valley and became only one among many regional competitors in the western Sudan.

Kanem and Kanem-Bornu

A fourth sizable Sahelian empire—this one in the central Sudan—arose after 1100. Called Kanem, it began in the region of the same name that stretches over the Sahel into the Sahara northeast of Lake Chad. Roughly contemporaneous with the Malian empire to the west, Kanem began as a south-

ern Saharan confederation of the black nomadic tribes known as Zaghawah. These tribes were spread over much of the south-central and southeastern Sahara. By the twelfth century a Zaghawah group known as the Kanuri had apparently settled in Kanem, and from there they began a campaign of military expansion during the thirteenth century. Their key leader in this, Mai Dunama Dibbalemi (r. ca. 1221–1259), was a contemporary of Sundiata in Mali. Like Sundiata, Dibbalemi was a Muslim-probably the first Kanuri leader to embrace Islam, although there are traditions recalling a Muslim ruler in the Kanem region as early as 1085. In any case, Islam appears to have entrenched itself among the Kanuri ruling class during

Sahelian Empires of the Western Sudan

ca. 990–ca. 1180?	Empire of Ghana
1076	Ghana loses Awdaghast to Almoravids
1180–1230	Soso clan briefly controls the old Ghanaian territories
ca. 1230–1450	Empire of Mali, founded by Sundiata
1230–1255	Reign of Sundiata
1312–1337	Reign of Mansa Musa
1374	Independent Songhai state emerges in Gao after throwing off Malian rule
ca. 1450–1600	Songhai empire at Gao
1464–1591	Askia dynasty
1464–1492	Reign of Sonni Ali
1493–1528	Reign of Askia Muhammad al-Turi
1549–1583	Reign of Askia Dawud
1590s	Collapse of the Songhai empire

Muslim Reform in Songhai

Around 1500 Askia Muhammad al-Turi, the first Muslim among the rulers of Songhai, wrote to the North African Muslim theologian Muhammad al-Maghili (d. 1504) with a series of questions about proper Muslim practices. These excerpts are from the seventh question of al-Turi and the answers given by al-Maghili. Here one sees something of the zeal of the new convert to conform to traditional religious norms, as well as the rather strict and puritanical "official line" of the conservative Maliki ulama on "pagan" mores. Also evident is the king's desire for bettering social order and his concern for justice in the market and elsewhere. However, also manifest is that many of the more strongly Shari`a-minded ulama did not want to compromise at all, let alone allow syncretism to emerge among formerly pagan, newly converted groups.

What are the problems and corresponding solutions listed in the letter? Which problem did al-Maghili find most serious? Why? Which do you think would have been most serious? Why?

From Al-Turi's Seventh Question

Among the people [of the Songhay Empire said Askia Muhammad], there are some who claim knowledge of the supernatural through sand divining and the like, or through the disposition of the stars . . . [while] some assert that they can write (talismans) to bring good fortune . . . or to ward off bad fortune. . . . Some defraud in weights and measures. . . .

One of their evil practices [continued Askia Muhammad] is the free mixing of men and women in the markets and streets and the failure of women to veil themselves . . . [while] among the people of Djenné [Jenne] it is an established custom for a girl not to cover any part of her body as long as she remains a virgin . . . and all the most beautiful girls walk about naked among people. . . .

So give us legal ruling concerning these people and their ilk, and may God Most High reward you!

From Al-Maghili's Answer

The answer-and God it is who directs to the right course—is that everything you have mentioned concerning people's behavior in some parts of this country is gross error. It is the bounden duty of the commander of the Muslims and all other believers who have the power [replied al-Maghili] to change every one of these evil practices.

As for any who claims knowledge of the supernatural in the ways you have mentioned . . . he is a liar and an unbeliever. . . . Such people must be forced to renounce it by the sword. Then whoever renounces such deeds should be left in peace, but whoever persists should be killed with the sword as an unbeliever; his body should not be washed or shrouded, and he should not be buried in a Muslim graveyard. . . .

As for defrauding in weights and measures [continued al-Maghili] it is forbidden (*haram*) according to the Qur'an, the Sunna and the consensus of opinion of the learned men of the Muslim community. It is the bounden duty of the commander of the Muslims to appoint a trustworthy man in charge of the markets, and to safeguard people's means of subsistence. He should standardize all the scales in each province. . . . Similarly, all measures both large and small must be rectified so that they conform to a uniform standard. . . .

Now, what you mentioned about the free mixing of men and women and leaving the pudenda uncovered is one of the greatest abominations. The commander of the Muslims must exert himself to prevent all these things. . . . He should appoint trustworthy men to watch over this by day and night, in secret and in the open. This is not to be considered as spying on the Muslims; it is only a way of caring for them and curbing evildoers, especially when corruption becomes widespread in the land as it has done in Timbuktu and Djenné [Jenne] and so on.

From *The African Past*, trans. by J. O. Hunwick, reprinted in Basil Davidson (Grosset and Dunlap, The Universal Library), pp. 86–88. Reprinted by permission of Curtis Brown Ltd. Copyright © 1964 by Basil Davidson.

Dibbalemi's reign. Dibbalemi used it to sanction his rule, which otherwise had the familiar African trappings of sacred kingship. It also provided a rationale for expansion through *jihad*, or holy "struggle" against polytheists.

Dibbalemi and his successors expanded Kanuri power north into the desert to include the Fezzan in modern Libya and northeast along the Sahel-Sahara fringe toward Nilotic Africa. In both directions they controlled important trade routes—north to Libya and east to the Nile and Egypt. The next two centuries saw the mixing of Kanuri and local Kanembu peoples, primarily those known as the So. There was a corresponding transformation of the Kanuri leader from a nomadic *shaykh* to a Sudanic king and a shift of Kanem from a nomadic to a largely sedentary kingdom with quasi-feudal institutions. Like Mali to the west, Kanem's dominion was of two kinds: direct rule over and taxation of core territories and groups, and indirect control over and collection of tribute from a wider region of vassal chieftaincies. Linguistic and (Muslim) religious acculturation progressed most rapidly in the core territories under direct rule.

Civil strife, largely over the royal succession, weakened the Kanuri state in the later fourteenth and especially the fifteenth centuries. Kanuri control of Kanem weakened, and after 1400 the locus of power shifted from Kanem proper westward, to the land of Bornu, southwest of Lake Chad. Here, at the end of the fifteenth century, a new Kanuri empire arose almost simultaneously with the collapse of the Askia dynasty of the Songhai empire at Gao. Near the end of the sixteenth century firearms and Turkish military instructors enabled the Kanuri leader Idris Alawma (r. ca. 1575–1610) to unify Kanem and Bornu. He set up an avowedly Islamic state and extended his rule even into Hausaland, between Bornu and the Niger River. The center of trading activity as well as political power and security now shifted from the Niger Bend east to the territory under Kanuri control.

Deriving its prosperity from the trans-Saharan trade, Idris Alawma's regional empire survived for nearly a century. It was finally broken up by a long famine, repeated Tuareg attacks, lack of strong leadership, and loss of control over trade to smaller, better-organized Hausa states. The ruling dynasty held out until 1846, but by 1700 its power had been sharply reduced by the growing Hausa states to the west. These states, in what is now northern Nigeria, had first become important in the late fifteenth century. Their real power was to come only in the nineteenth century with their unification under the Fulani sultanate of Sokoto (see Chapter 31).

The Eastern Sudan

The Christian states of Maqurra and Alwa in the Nilotic Sudan, or Nubia, lasted for more than six hundred years from their early seventh-century beginnings. Often thought of as isolated, Christian Nubia in fact maintained political, religious, and commercial contact with Egypt, the Red Sea world, and the east-central and even central Sudan. Architectural influence in the form of Nubian red brick construction has been traced as far west as Chadic Bornu and even northeastern Nigeria.

After 1000 C.E. Maqurra and Alwa continued treaty relations with their more powerful northern Egyptian neighbors, first the Fatimids and then the Ayyubids and Mamluks who succeeded them. Mamluk times strained the old relations, however. The Mamluks intervened repeatedly in their Nubian neighbors' affairs, and Arab nomads constantly threatened not only the Mamluks but even more the Nubian states. From late Fatimid times onward, both Maqurra and Alwa were increasingly subject to immigrating Arab Muslim tribesmen as well as the influence of Arab Muslim traders (especially in the coastal towns on the Red Sea) and growing Muslim minorities. The result was a long-term intermingling

Central Sudanic Empires	
ca. 1100–1500	Kanuri empire of Kanem
ca. 1220s–1400	Height of empire of Kanem
1221–1259	Reign of Mai Dunama Dibbalemi
1575–1846	Kanuri empire of Kanem-Bornu
1575–1619	Reign of Idris Alawma, major architect of the state

of Arabic and Nubian cultures and the creation of a new Nilotic Sudanese people and culture.

Islam spread slowly with Arab immigration into the upper Nile region. A significant factor in the gradual disappearance of Christianity in Nubia was the apparently elite character of Christianity there to begin with and its association with the northern and foreign Egyptian world of Coptic Christianity. Maqurra became officially Muslim at the beginning of the fourteenth century after a change in rulers orchestrated by the Mamluks; although Christianity survived until late in the same century, its days were numbered. The Islamization of Alwa came somewhat later, most effectively through Muslim religious teachers, often trained in Cairo, who combined Sufi teachings with the legal training and expertise of the *ulama*. Their work was most successful under the long-lived Funj sultanate that replaced the Alwa state.

The Funj state flourished between the Blue and White Niles and to the north along the main Nile from just after 1500 until 1762. The Funj were originally cattle nomads who apparently adopted Islam soon after setting up their kingdom. During the late sixteenth and the seventeenth centuries, with the influx of Arabic-speaking Nubians from the north, the Funj developed an Islamic society whose Arabized character was unique in sub-Saharan Africa. A much-reduced Funj state held out until an Ottoman-Egyptian invasion in 1821.

The Forestlands— Coastal West and Central Africa

West African Forest Kingdoms: The Example of Benin

We have little or no written evidence before the sixteenth century of the many states and smaller societies that flourished in the southern forests of the Sudanic savannahs and the forestlands to their south. However, other kinds of evidence reveal that many states, some with distinct political, religious, and cultural traditions, had developed in the southern and coastal regions of West Africa several centuries before the first Portuguese reports in 1485. Even those states like Asante or the Yoruba kingdoms of Oyo and Ife, which reached their height only after 1500, had much earlier origins. Benin, the best known of these forest kingdoms, reflects, especially in its art, the sophistication of West African culture before 1500.

Benin State and Society   According to linguistic evidence, the Edo speakers of Benin have occupied the southern Nigerian region between Yorubaland and the Ibo peoples east of the lower Niger for millennia. Traditional Edo society is organized according to a patrilineal lineage system emphasizing primogeniture. The village is the fundamental political unit, and authority is built around the organization of males into age-grade units.[3]

According to archaeological evidence, the local traditions of the Edo culture of Benin were closely linked to those of Ife, one of the most prominent Yoruba states northwest of Benin. Some kind of distinct kingdom of Benin likely existed as early as the twelfth century, and traditional accounts of both Ife and Edo agree that an Ife prince was sent to rule in Benin around 1300. There are indications that the power of the king, or *oba*, at this time was sharply limited by the Edo leaders who invited the foreign ruler. These leaders were known as the *uzama*, an order of hereditary indigenous chiefs. According to tradition, the fourth *oba* managed to wrest more control from these chiefs and instituted something of the ceremonial of absolute monarchy. However, only in the fifteenth century, with King Ewuare, did Benin become a royal autocracy and a large state of major regional importance.

Ewuare rebuilt the capital—known today as Benin City—and named it and his kingdom Edo. He apparently established a government in which he had sweeping authority, although he exercised it in light of the deliberations of a royal council. Ewuare formed this council not only from the palace *uzama* but also from the townspeople. He gave each chief specific administrative responsibilities and rank in the government hierarchy. Ewuare and his successors developed a tradition of military kingship and engaged in major wars of expansion, both into Yorubaland to the west and Ibo country east across the Niger River. They also claimed for the office of *oba* an increasing ritual authority that presaged more radical developments in the king's role.

In the seventeenth century the *oba* virtually withdrew into the palace; becoming much less active, he was transformed from a military leader into a religious figure with supernatural powers. Human sacrifice, specifically of slaves, seems to have accompanied the cult of deceased kings and became even more frequent later, in the nineteenth century. The succession by primogeniture that Ewuare established was discontinued, and new *obas* were chosen by the *uzama* from any branch of the royal family.

Benin	
ca. 1100–1897	Benin state
ca. 1300	First Ife king of Benin state
1440–1475	Reign of Ewuare

tinued, and new *obas* were chosen by the *uzama* from any branch of the royal family.

Benin Art   The lasting significance of Benin, however, lies not in its political history but in its court art, especially its famous brass sculptures. An ancient tradition suggests that the Benin ruler brought in an Ife craftsman to teach the brass- and bronze-casting techniques developed first in Ife. Certainly the splendid terra-cotta, ivory, and brass statuary sculpture of Ife-Benin are among the glories of human creativity. These magnificent sculptures, initially realistic or naturalistic and later sometimes highly stylized, seem to be wholly indigenous African products. Their artistic and technical lineage is today often traced by scholars to the sculptures of the Nok culture of ancient West Africa (see Chapter 6), although this linkage is not yet proven.

The best sculptures before the sixteenth century and the coming of the Portuguese (who themselves figure in later representations) are cast bronze plaques depicting legendary and historical scenes. These were mounted on the walls and columns of the royal palace in Benin City (cf. p. 494). There are also brass heads, apparently of royalty, that resemble the many life-size terra-cotta and brass heads found at Ife. The heads at Ife are held to represent the Oni, or religious chief of ancient Ife, or particular ancestors, who are thereby reverently remembered by their descendants.

These artistic traditions were not limited only to Ife and Benin; similar sculptures have been found both well to the north and in the Niger delta. Most spectacularly, recent excavations east of the Niger at Igbo-Ukwu have unearthed stunning terra cottas and bronzes that, although distinct, belong to the same general artistic culture, which is dated as early as the ninth century. These artifacts testify to the high cultural level attained in traditional African societies that had little or no contact with the extra-African world.

European Arrivals on the Coastlands

Along the coasts of West and central Africa, many changes portentous for African history as a whole occurred between 1500 and 1800. Those wrought by the burgeoning Atlantic slave trade are the most famous (see Chapter 19). Of comparable importance are changes connected with trade in West

[3]A. F. C. Ryder, *Benin and the Europeans, 1485–1897* (New York: Longman, 1969), p. 1. Ryder's work is a basic reference for the following brief summary about Benin.

African gold and other commodities and the effects associated with the importation and spread in West and central Africa of food crops, such as maize, peanuts, squash, sweet potatoes, cocoa, and cassava (manioc) from the Americas. The gradual involvement of Africa in the emerging global economic system paved the way for eventual colonial domination of the continent, especially its coastal regions, by the Europeans. The European names for segments of the coastline—the Grain (or Pepper) Coast, the Ivory Coast, the Gold Coast, and the Slave Coast—identify the main exports that could be extracted by ship and vividly indicate the nature of the emerging relationship.

Senegambia   In West Africa, Senegambia—which takes its name from the Senegal and Gambia rivers—was one of the earliest regions affected by European trade. Its interior had long been involved in both trans-Saharan trade and east-west trade in the Sahel and savannah, especially in the heydays of the empires of Ghana, Mali, and Songhai. Senegambia's maritime trade with European powers, like the older overland trade, was primarily in gold and products such as salt, cotton goods, hides, and copper. For roughly a century Senegambian states also provided slaves to the coast for European purchase; indeed, perhaps a third of all African slaves exported during the sixteenth century came from Senegambia. Thereafter, however, the focus of the slave trade shifted south and east along the coast, and although the number of slaves taken from Senegambia remained steady, the importance of slaving relative to other forms of trade declined (see Chapter 19). Over time, Portuguese-African mulattos and the British came to control the Gambia River trade, while the French won the Senegal River markets. These developments presaged the long-term division of the region into spheres of influence among European powers, particularly the British and French, in colonial times.

The Gold Coast   The Gold Coast, like Senegambia, was one of the West African coastal districts most affected by the arrival of international maritime trade. The name derives from

This naturalistic brass head (29 cm high), which dates to the thirteenth century, conveys the remarkable power of Ife art. [© Frank Willet]

the region's importance after 1500 as the outlet for the more southern of West Africa's gold fields in the forestland of Akan. Here, beginning with the Portuguese at Elmina in 1481, but primarily after 1600, European states and companies built numerous coastal forts to protect their trade from each other's predations and from pirates' raids and to serve as depots for inland goods. The trade in gold, kola nuts, and other commodities seems to have encouraged the growth of larger states in the region—like the Akan forest states near the coast and the Gonja state just north of the forest—perhaps because they could better handle and control the overland commerce.

The intensive contact of the Gold Coast with Europeans also led to the importation and spread of American crops, notably maize and cassava, into the tropical forests of this region. The success of these crops here as elsewhere in West and central Africa likely contributed to substantial population growth in the sixteenth and seventeenth centuries, especially in the Akan region.

The Gold Coast escaped the ravages of the slave trade for some decades; it was even an importer of slaves until long after 1500. Slaves, however, became big business here in the late seventeenth century, especially in the Accra region. The economy was so disrupted by the slave trade that gold mining declined sharply. Eventually more gold came into the Gold Coast from the sale of slaves than went out from its mines (see Chapter 19).

Central Africa

The vast center of the subcontinent is bounded by swamps in the north, coastal rain forests to the west, highlands to the east, and deserts in the south. Before 1500 these natural barriers impeded international contact and trade with the interior. They also shaped the two-pronged route by which Bantu peoples and languages moved, over many centuries, from western and west-central Africa south into the Zaire basin and east around the equatorial forest into the lakes of highland East Africa. In the tropical central area, regional interaction in movements of peoples and in trade and culture had always been the norm. Here as elsewhere in Africa, however, large as well as small political, economic, and social units could be found. Peoples such as the Lunda and Luba, for example, on the southern savannah below the rain forest, carved out sizable kingdoms by the fifteenth century and expanded their control over neighboring areas into the eighteenth century.

The coming of the Portuguese and their maritime trade to the western coastal regions broke down the regional isolation of the central African lands, albeit slowly. The Portuguese came looking for a new source of gold and silver but found none. Instead, they exported such goods as ivory and palm cloth. Ultimately, their main export was human beings for foreign slavery. These slaves were taken first for gang labor to the Portuguese sugar plantations on Sao Thomé island in the Gulf of Guinea. Then, in vast numbers, people were sent as slaves to perform similar plantation labor in Brazil. In the 1640s the Dutch briefly succeeded the Portuguese as the major suppliers of African slaves to English and French plantations in the Caribbean. Until then, however, the Portuguese were the European presence in central Africa.

The Kongo Kingdom

Kongo was the major state with which the Portuguese dealt after coming to central Africa in 1483. Dating from probably the fourteenth century, the Kongo kingdom was located on a fertile, well-watered plateau south of the lower Zaïre River valley, between the coast and the Kwango River in the east. Here, astride the border between forest and grassland, the Kongo kings had built a central government based on a pyramid structure of tax or tribute collection balanced by rewards for those faithful in paying their taxes. Kongo society was dominated by the king, whose authority was tied to acceptance of him as a kind of spiritual spokesman of the gods or ancestors. By 1600 Kongo was half the size of England and alongside farming boasted a high state of specialization in weaving and pottery, salt production, fishing, and metalworking.

The Portuguese brought Mediterranean goods, preeminently luxury textiles from North Africa, to use in the Kongo tribute-reward system and to trade for African goods. Amidst the rather hard agrarian life of most of the Kongo peoples, such luxuries augmented the prestige and wealth of the ruler and his elites. However, because the greatest central African resource turned out to be its peoples, rather than gold or minerals, slaves became the primary export that could be used for obtaining foreign luxury goods. Meanwhile, imports such as fine clothing, tobacco, and alcohol did nothing to replace the labor pool lost to slavery.

At first the Portuguese put time and effort into education and Christian proselytizing, but the need for more slaves brought a focus on exploiting the human resources of central Africa. Regional rulers sought to procure slaves from neighboring kingdoms, as did Portuguese traders who went inland themselves. As the demand grew, local rulers increasingly attacked neighbors to garner slaves for Portuguese traders (see Chapter 19).

The Kongo ruler Affonso I (r. ca. 1506–1543), a Christian convert, began by welcoming Jesuit missionaries and supporting conversion. But in time he broke with the Jesuits and encouraged traditional practices, even though he himself remained a Christian. Affonso consolidated the government, but he had constant difficulty curbing the more exploitative slaving practices as well as the more independent-minded provincial governors. The latter often dealt directly with the Portuguese, undermining royal authority. Affonso's successor moved finally to restrict Portuguese activity to Mpinda harbor and the Kongo capital of Mbanza Kongo (São Salvador). A few years later, Portuguese attempts to name the Kongo royal successor caused a bloody uprising against them that led in turn to a Portuguese boycott on trade with the kingdom.

Thereafter, disastrous internal wars waged by rebellious warriors known as the Jaga shattered the Kongo state. Slavery apparently contributed significantly to the provincial factionalism and unrest that fueled the Jaga wars. Their aftermath saw an increase in independent Portuguese traders and adventurers, who soon did their business outside of government channels and tried to manipulate the Kongo kings. A period of renewed strong royal leadership after the 1570s could not halt the fragmentation that split the kingdom a century later.

Kongo, however, enjoyed renewed vigor in the seventeenth century. The Kongo kings, all descended from Affonso, ruled as divine-right monarchs at the apex of a complex sociopolitical pyramid that rose from district headmen through provincial governors to the court nobility and king. Royal power came to depend on a guard of musket-armed

Central Africa	
1300s	Kongo kingdom founded
1483	Portuguese come to central African coast
ca. 1506–1543	Reign of Affonso I as king of Kongo
1571	Angola becomes Portuguese proprietary colony

Affonso I of Kongo Writes to the King of Portugal

Affonso, the Christian African king of Kongo, wrote a number of letters to the Portuguese monarch about the Portuguese presence in his dominions. The one reproduced here was written in 1526. It complains ostensibly of the effects of slaving on the Kongo people and economy, but behind this masterly diplomatic lament lies the real issue: that the Portuguese were circumventing his own royal monopoly on the inland slave trade. One of the insidious effects of the massive demand of the Atlantic trade for slaves was the ever increasing engagement of African monarchs and chieftains as well as merchants in one or another aspect of slaving.

How had the introduction of Portuguese merchants and European goods upset the social and political situation in Kongo? How had these goods tempted Affonso's subjects into the slave trade? How did Affonso wish to change the relationship of his people to Portugal? Do you think the king was more worried about human rights or his economic losses?

Sir, Your Highness [of Portugal] should know how our Kingdom is being lost in so many ways that it is convenient to provide for the necessary remedy, since this is caused by the excessive freedom given by your factors and officials to the men and merchants who are allowed to come to this Kingdom to set up shops with goods and many things which have been prohibited by us, and which they spread throughout our Kingdoms and Domains in such an abundance that many of our vassals, whom we had in obedience, do not comply because they have the things in greater abundance than we ourselves; and it was with these things that we had them content and subjected under our vassalage and jurisdiction, so it is doing a great harm not only to the service of God, but the security and peace of our Kingdoms and State as well.

And we cannot reckon how great the damage is, since the mentioned merchants are taking every day our natives, sons of the land and the sons of our noblemen and vassals and our relatives, because the thieves and men of bad conscience grab them wishing to have the things and wares of this Kingdom which they are ambitious of; they grab them and get them to be sold; and so great, Sir, is the corruption and licentiousness that our country is being completely depopulated, and Your Highness should not agree with this nor accept it as in your service. And to avoid it we need from those [your] Kingdoms no more than some priests and a few people to teach in schools, and no other goods except wine and flour for the holy sacrament. That is why we beg of Your Highness to help and assist us in this matter, commanding your factors that they should not send here either merchants or wares, because it is *our will that in these Kingdoms there should not be any trade of slaves nor outlet for them.** Concerning what is referred above, again we beg of Your Highness to agree with it, since otherwise we cannot ... remedy such an obvious damage. Pray Our Lord in His mercy to have Your Highness under His guard and let you do for ever the things of His service. I kiss your hands many times. . . .

*Emphasis in the original.

From *The African Past*, trans. by J. O. Hunwick, reprinted in Basil Davidson (Grosset and Dunlap, The Universal Library), pp. 191–193. Reprinted by permission of Curtis Brown Ltd. Copyright © 1964 by Basil Davidson.

---

hired soldiers from tribes of the Stanley Pool area. The financial base of the kingdom rested on tribute from officials holding positions at the king's pleasure and on taxes and tolls on commerce. Christianity, the state religion, was accommodated to the traditional ancestor cult, talismanic magic, and sorcery. Kongo sculpture, iron and copper technology, and dance and music flourished.

Angola To the south, in Portuguese Angola, the experience was even worse than in Kongo. The Ndongo kingdom flourished among the Mbundu people during the sixteenth century. In 1571 a Portuguese decision to make Angola a proprietary colony (the first white colonial enterprise in black Africa) set in motion colonizing and "civilizing" efforts that ended in failure. By the end of the century Angola was exporting thousands of slaves yearly through the port of Luanda. In less than a century the hinterland had been plundered and depopulated. New internal trade in salt and the eventual spread of American food crops such as maize and cassava (which became part of the staple diet of the populace) did produce some positive changes in the interior, but in the coastal region among the western Mbundu, the Portuguese arrival brought economic and social catastrophe.

East Africa

Swahili Culture and Commerce

The participation of East African port towns in the lucrative southern-seas trade was ancient. Arabs, Indonesians, and even some Indians had trafficked there for centuries. Many had been absorbed into what had become, sometime during the first millennium C.E., from Somalia south, a predominantly

The Friday mosque at Shela on the southeastern coast of Lamu Island, Kenya. This fine example of late Swahili architecture dates to the early nineteenth century. It is the only surviving pre-twentieth-century mosque in the region with a minaret. Swahili settlements on Lamu Island date to about the fifteenth century and enjoyed a period of substantial wealth that reached its zenith in the nineteenth century. [Peter Greenberg]

Bantu-speaking population. From the eighth century onward Islam traveled with Arab and Persian sailors and merchants to these southerly trading centers of what the Arabs called the land of the *Zanj*, or "Blacks" (hence "Zanzibar"). Conversion to Islam, however, went on slowly and only along the coast. In the thirteenth century Muslim traders from Arabia and Iran began to come in increased numbers and to dominate the coastal cities. Henceforward, Islamic faith and culture were influential and often predominant along the seacoast, from Mogadishu to Kilwa. By 1331 the traveler Ibn Battuta writes of Mogadishu as a thoroughly Islamic port and of the ruler and inhabitants of Kilwa as Muslims. He also notes that there were now mosques for the faithful in these towns.[4]

[4]*Travels in Asia and Africa, 1325–1354*, trans. and selected by H. A. R. Gibb (New York: Robert M. McBride, 1929), pp. 110–113.

By this time a common language had developed from the interaction of Bantu and Arabic speakers along the coast. This tongue is called *Swahili*, or *Kiswahili*, from the Arabic *sawahil*, "coastlands," a word used from ancient times for the East African coast. Its structure is Bantu, and its vocabulary has a strong admixture of Arabic. It is written in Arabic script, like Persian, Ottoman Turkish, Urdu, and many other languages of Islamic peoples that are totally unrelated to the Semitic language family.

The hybrid nature of the Swahili language mirrors the hybrid character of Swahili culture, with its distinctive combination of African and Islamic features. Current theory suggests that, like the language, Swahili culture is originally basically African with a large contribution by Arab, Persian, and other extra-African elements. This admixture created a new consciousness and identity. Today, the many coastal peoples who share Swahili language and culture are of mixed ethnic character, joining African to Persian, Indian, Arab, and other ancestry, and older Swahili families take pride in claiming illustrious Persian or Arab lineages.

Swahili language and culture probably developed first in the northern towns of Manda, Lamu, and Mombasa, then farther south along the coast to Kilwa. They remained localized largely along the coast until recently. Likewise, the spread of Islam was largely limited to the coastal civilization and did not reach inland—with the possible exception of the Zambezi valley, where Muslim traders penetrated upriver. This contrasts with lands farther north, in the Horn of Africa, where Islamic kingdoms developed in the Somali hinterland as well as on the coast.

Swahili civilization reached its apogee in the fourteenth and fifteenth centuries. The harbor trading towns were the administrative centers of the local Swahili states, and most of them were sited on coastal islands or easily defended peninsulas. To these ports came merchants from abroad and from the African hinterlands, some to settle and stay. These towns were impressive. Beginning in the twelfth century we can trace the development of stone-building techniques (using coral blocks on first red clay, later lime mortar). These techniques were used for mosques, fortress-palaces, harbor fortifications, fancy residences, and commercial buildings alike; all have their own distinctive cast, which bespeaks a creative joining of African and Arabo-Persian elements.

Today historians are recognizing that the Swahili states' ruling dynasties were probably African in origin, with an admixture of Arab or Persian immigrant blood. Swahili coastal centers boasted an advanced, cosmopolitan level of culture; by comparison, most of the populace in the small villages lived in mud and sometimes stone houses and earned their living by farming or fishing, the two basic coastal occupations besides trade. Society seems to have consisted of three prin-

Visiting Mogadishu and Kilwa (1331)

Ibn Battuta (d. 1369 or 1377), a native of Tangier, became one of history's most famous travelers through his voluminous and entertaining writings about his long years of relentless journeying from West and East Africa to India and China. In the following two excerpts from his description of his trip down the East African coast in 1331, he describes first the daily proceedings at the grievance and petitions court presided over by the Sultan of Mogadishu, then the generosity of the Sultan of Kilwa. The East Africans referred to their Sultan as "Shaikh" (a term used also for any religiously learned man). A qadi *is a judge; a* faqih, *a jurisconsult or legal scholar; a* wazir, *a government minister; an* amir, *a military commander; and a* sharif, *a descendant of the Prophet Muhammad (which carries special social status).*

What Muslim values and practices seem to be represented in the activities and traits described in the two reports? Does Ibn Battuta as a Muslim, but also an Arab outsider to the African Muslim societies he is visiting, seem to approve or disapprove of what he reports?

Mogadishu

When it is Saturday, the people come to the door of the shaikh (the local term for the Sultan), and they sit in covered halls outside the house. The *qadi,* the *faqihs,* the *sharifs,* the men of piety, the shaikhs and the men who have performed the pilgrimage enter the second council room. They sit on wooden platforms prepared for the purpose. The *qadi* is on a platform by himself and each group on a platform reserved for them which nobody shares with them. Then the shaikh sits in his council and sends for the *qadi* who sits on his left. Then enter the *faqihs* and their leaders sit in front of him while the rest of them salute and go away. Then the *sharifs* enter, their leaders sit before him, the rest of them salute and go away. If they are guests, they sit on his right. Then enter the shaikhs and those who have performed the pilgrimage, and their great ones sit and the rest salute and go away. Then enter the *wazirs* and *amirs;* the heads of the soldiers, rank upon rank, they salute and go. Food is brought and the *qadi,* the

sharifs and whoever is sitting in that session eat with the shaikh and the shaikh eats with them. If he wishes to honour one of the leaders of his *amirs,* he sends for him that he should eat with them. The rest of the people eat in the dining hall and their eating is according to precedence in the manner of their entrance before the shaikh. Then the shaikh goes into his house and the *qadi,* the *wazirs,* the private secretary, and four of the leading *amirs* sit for hearing litigation between the members of the public and hearing the cases of people with complaints. In a matter connected with the rules of the *shari'a* [religious law] the *qadi* passes judgement; in a matter other than that, the members of the council pass judgement, that is, the ministers and the *amirs.* In a matter where there is need of consultation with the sultan, they write about it to him and he sends out the reply to them immediately on the back of the note in accordance with his view. And such is always their custom.

The Sultan of Kilwa

When I arrived, the Sultan was Abu al-Muzaffar Hasan surnamed Abu al-Mawahib [the Father of Gifts] on account of his numerous charitable gifts. He frequently makes raids into the Zanj country, attacks them and carries off booty, of which he reserves a fifth, using it in the manner prescribed by the Koran. That reserved for the kinsfolk of the Prophet is kept separate in the Treasury, and, when sharifs come to visit him, he gives it them. They come to him from Iraq, the Hijaz, and other countries. I found several sharifs from the Hijaz at his court, among them Muhammad ibn Jammaz, Mansur ibn Labida ibn Abi Nami and Muhamma ibn Shumaila ibn Abi Nami. At Mogadishu I saw Tabl ibn Kubaish ibn Jammaz, who also wished to visit him. This Sultan is very humble: he sits and eats with beggars, and venerates holy men and descendants of the Prophet.

From Said Hamdun and Noèl King, ed. and trans., *Ibn Battuta in Black Africa,* (Princeton, NJ: Markus Wiener, rev. ed., 1994), pp. 20–21. Reprinted by permission of Markus Wiener Publishers, Inc.

cipal groups: the local nobility, the commoners, and resident foreigners engaged in local commerce. Slaves constituted a fourth class of people, although their local extent (as opposed to their sale) is disputed.

The flourishing trade of the coastal centers was fed mainly by export of inland ivory. Other exports included gold, slaves, turtle shells, ambergris, leopard skins, pearls, fish, sandalwood, ebony, and local cotton cloth. The chief imports were cloth, porcelain, glassware, china, glass beads, and glazed pottery. Certain exports tended to dominate particular ports: cloth, sandalwood, ebony, and ivory at Mogadishu; ivory at Manda; and gold at Kilwa (brought up the coast from Sofala, still farther south). Cowrie shells were a common currency in the inland trade, but coins minted at Mogadishu and Kilwa from the fourteenth century on were increasingly used in the major trading centers. The gold trade itself apparently became important only in the fifteenth century.

The Portuguese and the Omanis of Zanzibar

The decline of the original Swahili civilization in the sixteenth century can be attributed primarily to the waning of the trade that had originally made everything possible. This in turn stemmed evidently from the arrival of the Portuguese and their subsequent destruction of both the old oceanic trade (in particular, the Islamic commercial monopoly) and of the main Islamic city-states along the eastern coast. However, some scholars believe that decreases in rainfall or invasions of Zimba peoples from inland regions also contributed to the decline.

Nevertheless, the Portuguese undoubtedly intended to gain control of the southern-seas trade for their own purposes (see Chapter 19). In Africa, as everywhere, they saw the "Moors" as their implacable enemies. Many Portuguese viewed the struggle to wrest the commerce and the seaport commercial centers of Africa and Asia from Islamic control not only in commercial and nationalist terms but also as a Christian crusade.

The initial Portuguese victories along the African coast led to the submission of many small Islamic coastal ports and states. Still, there was no concerted effort to spread Christianity beyond the fortified settlements established in places like Sofala, Zanzibar, Mozambique, and Mombasa. Thus the long-term cultural and religious consequences of the Portuguese presence were slight.

The Portuguese did, however, cause widespread economic decline on the east coast. When the inland Africans refused to cooperate with them, the formerly heavy gold trade up the Zambezi from Sofala dried up. The militant Portuguese presence also sharply reduced Muslim coastal shipping from India and Arabia. Ottoman efforts in the late sixteenth century failed to defeat the Portuguese, but after 1660 the strong eastern Arabian state of Oman raided the African coast with impunity. In 1698 the Omanis took Mombasa and ejected the Portuguese everywhere north of Mozambique.

The Omanis soon shifted their home base to Zanzibar, which became a new and major power center in East Africa. Their control of the coastal ivory and slave trade seems to have fueled a substantial recovery of prosperity by the later eighteenth century. Zanzibar itself benefited from the introduction of clove cultivation from Mauritius in the 1830s; cloves became its staple export thereafter. (The clove plantations became also the chief market for a new, devastating internal slave trade, which flourished in East Africa into the late nineteenth century even as the external trade in slaves

was crushed.) The domination of the east coast by Omani African sultans, descendants of the earlier invaders, continued with some lapses until 1856. Thereafter, Zanzibar and its coastal holdings became independent under a branch of the same family that ruled in Oman. Zanzibar passed eventually to the British when they, the Germans, and the Italians divided East Africa in the late 1880s. Still, the Islamic imprint on the whole coast survives today.

Southern Africa

Southeastern Africa: "Great Zimbabwe"

At about the same time that the east-coast trading centers were beginning to flourish, a different kind of civilization was enjoying its heyday inland and farther south, in the rocky, savannah-woodland watershed between the Limpopo and Zambezi rivers, in modern southern Zimbabwe. This civilization was a purely African one sited far enough inland never to have felt the impact of Islam. It was founded in the tenth or eleventh century by Bantu-speaking Shona people, who still inhabit the same general area today. It seems to have become a large and prosperous state between the late thirteenth and the late fifteenth centuries. We know it only through the archaeological remains of an estimated 150 settlements in the Zambezi-Limpopo region.

The most impressive of these ruins, and the apparent capital of this ancient Shona state, is known today as "Great Zimbabwe"—a huge, sixty-odd-acre site encompassing two major building complexes. One—the so-called acropolis—is a series of stone enclosures on a high hill. It overlooks another, much larger enclosure that contains many ruins and a circular tower, all surrounded by a massive wall some thirty-two feet high and up to seventeen feet thick. The acropolis complex may have contained a shrine, whereas the larger enclosure was apparently the royal palace and fort. The stonework reflects a wealthy and sophisticated society. Artifacts from the site include gold and copper ornaments, soapstone carvings, and imported beads, as well as china, glass, and porcelain of Chinese, Syrian, and Persian origins.

The state itself seems to have had partial control of the increasing gold trade between inland areas and the east-coast port of Sofala. Its territory lay east and south of substantial gold-mining enterprises that tapped both the alluvial gold of the Zambezi tributaries and the gold-ore deposits that stretched southwest in a broad band below the middle Zambezi. We can speculate that this large settlement was the capital city of a prosperous empire and the residence of a ruling elite. Its wider domain was made up mostly of smaller settlements whose inhabitants lived by subsistence agriculture

which is treated only in passing in this text, is note-worthy.

R. W. JULY, *Precolonial Africa: An Economic and Social History* (1975). Chapter 10 gives an interesting overall picture of slaving in African history.

R. W. JULY, *A History of the African People*, 3rd ed. (1980). Chapters 3–6 treat Africa before about 1800 area by area; chapter 7 deals with "The Coming of Europe."

I. M. LEWIS, ED., *Islam in Tropical Africa* (1966), pp. 4–96. Lewis's introduction is one of the best brief summaries of the role of Islam in West Africa and the Sudan.

D. T. NIANI, ED. *Africa from the Twelfth to the Sixteenth Century, UNESCO General History of Africa*, Vol. IV (1984). Many survey articles cover the various regions and major states of Africa in the centuries noted in the title.

R. OLIVER, *The African Experience* (1991). A masterly, balanced, and engaging survey, with outstanding syntheses and summaries of recent research.

J. A. RAWLEY, *The Transatlantic Slave Trade: A History* (1981). Impressively documented, detailed, and well-presented survey history of the Atlantic trade; little focus on African dimensions.

A. F. C. RYDER, *Benin and the Europeans: 1485–1897* (1969). A basic study.

JOHN K. THORNTON, *The Kingdom of Kongo: Civil War and Transition, 1641–1718* (1983). A detailed and perceptive analysis for those who wish to delve into Kongo state and society in the seventeenth century.

M. WILSON AND L. THOMPSON, EDS., *The Oxford History of South Africa*, Vol. I., *South Africa to 1870* (1969). Relatively detailed, if occasionally dated, treatment.

19 CONQUEST AND EXPLOITATION: THE DEVELOPMENT OF THE TRANSATLANTIC ECONOMY

During the seventeenth and eighteenth centuries European maritime nations established overseas empires, and set up trading monopolies within them, in an effort to magnify their economic strength. As this painting of the Old Custom House Quay in London suggests, trade from these empires and the tariffs imposed on it were expected to generate revenue for the home country. But behind many of the goods carried in the great sailing ships in the harbor and landed on these docks lay the labor of African slaves working on the plantations of North and South America. [Michael Holford/Samuel Scott "Old Custom House Quay" Collection/By Courtesy of the Trustees of the Victoria and Albert Museum]

CHAPTER TOPICS

◆ Periods of European Overseas Expansion
◆ Mercantilist Theory of Economic Exploitation
◆ Establishment of the Spanish Empire in America
◆ Economies of Exploitation in the Spanish Empire
◆ Colonial Brazil and Slavery
◆ French and British Colonies in North America
◆ Slavery in the Americas
◆ Africa and the Transatlantic Slave Trade

In World Perspective The Transatlantic Economy

The late fifteenth-century European encounter with the American continents changed the world. The more than two and a half centuries of European domination and government that followed the encounter made the Americas a region where European languages, legal and political institutions, trade, and religion prevail. These developments in the Americas gave Europe more influence over other world cultures and civilizations than it would otherwise have achieved.

Within decades of the European voyages of discovery, Native Americans, Europeans, and Africans began to interact in a manner unprecedented in human history. The Native Americans of North and South America encountered bands of European conquerors and European Roman Catholic missionaries. Technological and military superiority as well as political divisions among the Native Americans allowed the Europeans to realize their material and religious ambitions. By the middle of the sixteenth century Europeans had begun to import black Africans into the American continents as chattel slaves,

converting them to Christianity in the process. Consequently, by the close of the sixteenth century Europe, the Americas, and Africa had become linked in a vast transatlantic economy that extracted material and agricultural wealth from the American continents largely on the basis of the nonfree labor of impressed Native Americans and imported African slaves.

The next century would see English and French colonists settling in North America and the Caribbean, introducing different political values and, through the English, Protestantism. These North American colonists would also become part of the transatlantic economy, and many would become economically involved directly or indirectly with African slavery. They too would interact with the Native Americans of North America, sometimes destroying their cultures, sometimes converting them to Christianity, and always drawing them into the transatlantic economy as they exploited the American wilderness.

Beginning in the sixteenth century the importation of African slaves and

the use of slave labor were fundamental to the plantation economy that eventually extended from Maryland to Brazil. The slave trade intimately connected the economy of certain sections of Africa to the transatlantic economy. The slave trade had a devastating effect on the African people and cultures involved in it, but it also enriched the Americas with African culture and religion.

Periods of European Overseas Expansion

It may be useful to see the establishment of this vast new transatlantic economy in the larger context of European overseas expansion. That expansion loosed the forces that created the transatlantic economy.

Since the late fifteenth century European contacts with the rest of the world have gone through four distinct stages. The first was that of the European discovery, exploration, initial conquest, and settlement of the Americas and commercial expansion elsewhere in the world. By the close of the seventeenth century Spain governed South America, except for Portuguese-ruled Brazil. French and British colonies had been established in North America.

The Dutch established a major trading base at Batavia in the East Indies. The city they called Batavia is now Djakarta, Indonesia. [Bildarchiv Preussischer Kulturbesitz]

France, Britain, the Netherlands, and Spain controlled various islands in the Caribbean. The French, British, and Dutch held outposts in Asia.

The second era was one of colonial trade rivalry among Spain, France, and Great Britain. The Anglo-French side of the contest has often been compared to a second Hundred Years War. During this second period both the British colonies of the North American seaboard and the Spanish colonies of Mexico and Central and South America emancipated themselves from European control. This era may be said to have closed during the 1820s. (See Chapter 25.)

The third stage of European contact with the non-European world occurred in the nineteenth century when European governments carved new formal empires in Africa and Asia. Those nineteenth-century empires also included new areas of European settlement such as Australia, New Zealand, and South Africa. The bases of these empires were trade, national honor, racial theories, religious expansion, and military superiority. (See Chapter 27.)

The last period of European empire occurred during the mid-twentieth century with the decolonization of peoples who had previously been under European colonial rule. (See Chapters 37 and 38.)

During the four and a half centuries before decolonization, Europeans exerted political dominance over much of the rest of the world that was out of all proportion to Europe's size or population. Europeans frequently treated other peoples as social, intellectual, and economic inferiors. They ravaged existing cultures because of greed, religious zeal, or political ambition. These actions significantly affect the contemporary relationship between Europe and its former colonies. What allowed the Europeans to exert such influ-ence and domination for so long over so much of the world was not any innate cultural superiority but a technological supremacy related to naval power and gunpowder. Ships and guns allowed the Europeans to exercise their will almost wherever they chose.

Mercantilist Theory of Economic Exploitation

The early modern European empires of the sixteenth through the eighteenth centuries—empires based on commerce—existed primarily to enrich trade. Extensive trade rivalries sprang up around the world. The protection of these empires required naval power. Spain dominated the largest of these empires and constructed elaborate naval, commercial, and political structures to exploit and govern it. Finally, these empires depended largely on slave labor. Indeed, the Atlantic slave trade was a major way in which European merchants enriched themselves. That trade in turn forcibly brought the peoples of Africa into the life and culture of the New World.

To the extent that any formal economic theory lay behind the conduct of these empires, it was mercantilism, that practical creed of hard-headed business people. The terms *mercantilism* and *mercantile system* (coined by later opponents) designate a system in which governments heavily regulate trade and commerce in hope of increasing individual national wealth. Economic writers of the time believed that a nation had to gain a favorable trade balance of gold and silver bullion. A nation was truly wealthy only if it amassed more bullion than its rivals.

From beginning to end, the economic well-being of the home country was the primary concern of mercantilist writ-

Buccaneers Prowl the High Seas

Piracy was a major problem for transatlantic trade. There was often a fine line between freewheeling, buccaneering pirates operating for their own gain and privateers who in effect worked for various European governments who wanted to penetrate the commercial monoploy of the Spanish Empire. Alexander Exquemelin was a ship's surgeon who for a time plied his trade on board a pirate ship and then later settled in Holland. He wrote an account of those days in which he emphasizes the careful code of conduct among the pirates themselves and the harshness of their behavior to both wealthy ships they captured and poor farmers and fishermen whom they robbed and virtually enslaved.

How did the restrictive commercial policy of the Spanish Empire encourage piracy and privateering? Was there a code of honor among the pirates? What kinds of people may have suffered most from piracy? To what extent did pirates have any respect for individual freedom? How romantic was the real world of pirates?

When a buccaneer is going to sea he sends word to all who wish to sail with him. When all are ready, they go on board, each bringing what he needs in the way of weapons, powder and shot.

On the ship, they first discuss where to go and get food supplies. . . . The meat is either [salted] pork or turtle . . . Sometimes they go and plunder the Spaniards' *corrales*, which are pens where they keep perhaps a thousand head of tame hogs. The rovers . . . find the house of the farmer . . . [whom] unless he gives them as many hogs as they demand, they hang . . . without mercy. . . .

When a ship has been captured, the men decide whether the captain should keep it or not: if the prize is better than their own vessel, they take it and set fire to the other. When a ship is robbed, nobody must plunder and keep the loot to himself. Everything taken . . . must be shared . . . , without any man enjoying a penny more than his faire share. To prevent deceit, before the booty is distributed everyone has to swear an oath on the Bible that he has not kept for himself so much as the value of sixpence . . . And should any man be found to have made a false oath, he would be banished from the rovers, and never be allowed in their company. . . .

When they have captured a ship, the buccaneers set the prisoners on shore as soon as possible, apart from two or three whom they keep to do the cooking and other work they themselves do not care for, releasing these men after two or three years.

The rovers frequently put in for fresh supplies at some island or other, often . . . lying off the south coast of Cuba. . . . Everyone goes ashore and sets up his tent, and they takes turns to go on marauding expedition in their canoes. They take prisoner . . . poor men who catch and set turtles for a living, to provide for their wives and children. Once captured, these men have to catch turtle for the rovers as long as they remain on the island. Should the rovers intend to cruise along a coast where turtle is abound, they take the fishermen along with them. The poor fellows may be compelled to stay away from their wives and families four or five years, with no news whether they are alive or dead.

From John Exquemeling, *The Bucaneers of America*, Alexis Brown, trans. Penguin Books © 1969. pp. 70–72..

---

ers. Colonies existed to provide markets and natural resources for the industries of the home country. In turn, the home country furnished military security and political administration for the colonies. For decades both sides assumed that the colonies were the inferior partner in the relationship. The mercantilist statesmen and traders regarded the world as an arena of scarce resources and economic limitation. They assumed that one national economy could grow only at the expense of others. The home country and its colonies were to trade exclusively with each other. To that end, they tried to forge trade-tight systems of national commerce through navigation laws, tariffs, bounties to encourage production, and prohibitions against trading with the subjects of other monarchs. National monopoly was the ruling principle.

Mercantilist ideas were always neater on paper than in practice. By the early eighteenth century mercantilist assumptions were far removed from the economic realities of the colonies. The colonial and home markets simply did not mesh. Spain could not produce enough goods for South America. Economic production in the British North American colonies challenged English manufacturing and led to British attempts to limit certain colonial industries, such as iron and hat making.

Colonists of different countries wished to trade with each other. English colonists could buy sugar more cheaply from the French West Indies than from English suppliers. The traders and merchants of one nation always hoped to break the monopoly of another. For all these reasons, the eighteenth century became the "golden age of smugglers."[1] The

---

[1] Walter Dorn, *Competition for Empire, 1740–1763* (New York: Harper, 1940), p. 266.

A sixteenth-century Aztec drawing depicts a battle in the Spanish conquest of Mexico. [Corbis-Bettmann]

governments could not control the activities of all their subjects. Clashes among colonists could and did lead to war between governments. Consequently, the problems associated with the European mercantile empires led to conflicts around the world.

This brief overview of the periods of the European empire and of mercantile theory should provide a clearer context for understanding the character of the conquest of America and the establishment of the transatlantic economy.

Establishment of the Spanish Empire in America

Conquest of the Aztecs and the Incas

Within twenty years of the arrival of Columbus (1451–1506), Spanish explorers in search of gold had claimed the major islands of the Caribbean and brutally suppressed the native peoples. These actions presaged what was to occur on the continent. The Caribbean islands became the staging areas for the further exploration and conquest of other parts of the Americas.

In 1519 Hernan Cortés (1485–1547) landed in Mexico with about five hundred men and a few horses. He opened communication with nearby communities and then with Moctezu-

ma II (1466–1520), the Aztec emperor. Moctezuma may initially have believed Cortés to be the god Quetzalcoatl, who, according to legend, had been driven away centuries earlier but had promised to return. Whatever the reason, Moctezuma hesitated to confront Cortés, attempting at first to appease him with gifts of gold that only whetted Spanish appetites. Cortés succeeded in forging alliances with some subject peoples and, most importantly, with Tlaxcala, an independent state and traditional enemy of the Aztecs. His forces then marched on the Aztec capital of Tenochtitlán (modern Mexico City), where Moctezuma welcomed him. Cortés soon seized Moctezuma, making him a prisoner in his own capital. Moctezuma died in unexplained circumstances, and the Aztec's wary acceptance of the Spaniards turned to open hostility. The Spaniards were driven from Tenochtitlán and nearly wiped out, but they ultimately returned and laid siege to the city. The Aztecs, under their last ruler, Cuauhtemoc (c. 1495–1525), resisted fiercely but were finally defeated in late 1521. Cortés razed Tenochtitlán, building his own capital over its ruins, and proclaimed the Aztec Empire to be New Spain.

In 1532, largely inspired by Cortés's example in Mexico, Francisco Pizarro (c. 1478–1541) landed on the western coast of South America to take on the Inca Empire, about which he knew almost nothing. His force included about two hundred men armed with guns, swords, and horses, the military power of which the Incas did not understand. Pizarro lured the Inca ruler Atahualpa (c. 1500–1533) into a conference, then seized him. The imprisoned Atahualpa tried to ransom himself with a hoard of gold, but instead of releasing him Pizarro treacherously had him garroted in 1533. The Spaniards fought their way to Cuzco, the Inca capital, and captured it, effectively ending the Inca Empire. The Spanish faced insurrections, however, and fought among themselves for decades. Effective royal control was not established until the late 1560s.

The conquests of Mexico and Peru are among the most dramatic and brutal events in modern world history. Small military forces armed with advanced weapons subdued, in a remarkably brief time, two advanced, powerful peoples. The spread of European diseases, especially smallpox, among the Native Americans also aided the conquest. The native populations had long lived in isolation, and many of them succumbed to the new diseases. But beyond the drama and bloodshed, these conquests, as well as those of other Native American peoples, marked a fundamental turning point. Whole civilizations with long histories and a record of enormous social, architectural, and technological achievement were effectively destroyed. Native American cultures endured, accommodating to European dominance, but there was never any doubt about which culture had the upper hand.

The Roman Catholic Church in Spanish America

The Spanish conquest of the West Indies, Mexico, and the South American continent opened that vast region to the Roman Catholic faith. Roman Catholic priests followed in the steps of the explorers and conquerors. As it had in the Castilian reconquest of the Iberian peninsula from the Moors, religion played a central role in the conquest of the New World. In this respect the crusade against Islamic civilization in Spain and the crusade against the indigenous religions of the Americas were closely related. In both cases the Castilian monarchy received approval from church authorities for a policy of military conquest on the grounds of converting non-Christians to the Christian faith and eradicating their indigenous religious practices. The mission of conversion justified military conquest and the extension of political control and dominance. As a consequence of this policy, the Roman Catholic church in the New World was always a conservative force working to protect the political power and prestige of the conquerors and the interests of the Spanish authorities.

The relationship between political authority and the propagation of religious doctrine was even closer in the New World than on the Iberian peninsula. The papacy recognized that it could not from its own resources support so extensive a missionary effort, the full requirements for which became clear only after the conquests of Mexico and Peru. The papacy therefore turned over much of the control of the church in the New World directly to the Spanish monarchy. There was thus always a close relationship between the political and economic goals of the monarchy and the role of the church. The zeal of both increased early in the sixteenth century as the papacy and the Habsburg monarchy fought the new enemy of Protestantism, which they were determined should have no foothold in America. As a consequence, the Roman Catholicism that spread throughout the Spanish domains of America took the form of the increasingly zealous faith associated with the Counter-Reformation.

During the sixteenth century the Roman Catholic church, represented more often than not by the mendicant orders such as the Franciscans and Dominicans, and later by the newly formed Jesuits, sought to convert the Native Americans. In the early decades these conversions often occurred shortly before the Spanish exterminated Native Americans or after they had conquered them. The conversion effort also involved attempts to eradicate surviving Indian religious practices. The Roman Catholic authorities tended to tolerate some residual Indian ceremonies in the sixteenth century, but worked to prohibit them during the seventeenth century. Thus religious conversion represented, among other things, an attempt to destroy still another part of the Native American culture. Furthermore, conversion did not bring acceptance; even until late in the eighteenth century, there were few Native American Christian priests.

Real tension, however, existed between the early Spanish conquerors and the mendicant friars who sought to minister to the Native Americans. Without conquest the church could not convert the Native Americans, but the priests often deplored the harsh conditions imposed on the native peoples. By far the most effective and outspoken clerical critic of the Spanish conquerors was Bartolomé de Las Casas (1474–1566), a Dominican. He contended that conquest was not necessary for conversion. One result of his campaign was new royal regulations after 1550.

Another result of Las Casas's criticism was the emergence of the "Black Legend," according to which all Spanish treatment of the Native Americans was unprincipled and inhumane. Those who created this view of Spanish behavior drew heavily on Las Casas's writings. Although substantially true, the "Black Legend" nonetheless exaggerated the case against Spain. Certainly the rulers of the native empires—as the Aztec demands for sacrificial victims attest—had often themselves been exceedingly cruel to their subject peoples.

By the end of the sixteenth century the church in Spanish America had become largely an institution upholding the colonial status quo. Although individual priests did defend the communal rights of Indian tribes, the colonial church

Bartolomé de Las Casas (1474–1566) was the most outspoken and effective defender of the Native Americans against Spanish exploitation. [Bildarchiv Preussischer Kulturbesitz]

prospered as the Spanish elite prospered through its exploitation of the resources and peoples of the New World. The church became a great landowner through crown grants and through bequests from Catholics who died in the New World. The monasteries took on an economic as well as a spiritual life of their own. Whatever its concern for the spiritual welfare of the Native Americans, the church remained one of the indications that Spanish America was a conquered world. Those who spoke for the church did not challenge Spanish domination or any but the most extreme modes of Spanish economic exploitation. The church at best only modestly moderated the forces exploiting human labor and material wealth. By the end of the colonial era in the late eighteenth century, the Roman Catholic church had become one of the single most conservative forces in Latin America and would continue to be so for at least the next century and a half.

Economies of Exploitation in the Spanish Empire

The colonial economy of Spanish America was an economy of exploitation in two senses. First, the organization of labor within the Spanish empire in one situation after another involved structures of highly dependent servitude or slavery. Second, the resources of the continent were exploited in mercantilist fashion for the economic advantage of Spain.

Varieties of Economic Activity

The early *conquistadores* ("conquerors") had been interested primarily in gold, but by the middle of the sixteenth century silver mining provided the chief source of metallic wealth. The great silver mining centers were Potosí in present-day Bolivia and smaller sites in northern Mexico. The Spanish crown was particularly interested in mining because it received one fifth (the *quinto*) of all mining revenues. The crown thus maintained a monopoly over the production and sale of mercury, which was required for separating silver from the other impurities in the ore. Silver mining was a flourishing source of wealth for the Spanish until the early seventeenth century, when the industry underwent a recession because of lack of new investment and the increasing costs involved in deeper mines. Nonetheless, silver predominated during the colonial era and experienced a major boom, especially in Mexico, during the eighteenth century. Its production for the benefit of Spaniards and the Spanish crown epitomized the wholly extractive economy on which Latin American colonial life was based.

The activities associated with this extractive economy—mining the ore, smelting it, harvesting wood to feed the smelters' fires—required labor. From the initial contact with America, there were too few Spanish colonists to provide the needed labor. Furthermore, the social status and expectations of those colonists who did come to the Americas made them unlikely to provide wage labor. Consequently, the Spaniards looked first to the native Indian population and then to black African slaves. Indian labor dominated on the continent and African labor in the Caribbean.

Encomienda The Spanish devised a series of institutions to exploit Native American labor. The first was the *encomienda*, a formal grant by the crown of the right to the labor of a specific number of Native Americans for a particular time.

A Contemporary Describes Forced Indian Labor at Potosí

The Potosí range in Bolivia was the site of the great silver-mining industry in the Spanish Empire. The vast wealth of the region became legendary almost as soon as mining commenced there in the 1540s. Native Americans, most of whom were forced laborers working under the mita *system of conscription, did virtually all of the work underground. This description, written by a Spanish friar in the early seventeenth century, portrays both the large size of the enterprise and the harsh conditions that the Native Americans endured. At any one time only one third of the 13,300 conscripted Native Americans were employed. The labor force was changed every four months.*

How efficient does the description suggest the mines were? What would have been the likely effects of working so long underground surrounded by burning candles?

According to His Majesty's warrant, the mine owners on this massive range have a right to the *mita* [conscripted labor] of 13,300 Indians in the working and exploitation of the mines, both those which have been discovered, those now discovered, and those which shall be discovered. It is the duty of the Corregidor [municipal governor] of Potos' to have them rounded up and to see that they come in from all the provinces between Cuzco over the whole of El Collao and as far as the frontiers of Tarija and Tomina. . . .

The *mita* Indians go up every Monday morning to the locality of Guayna Potosí which is at the foot of the range; the Corregidor arrives with all the provincial captains or chiefs who have charge of the Indians assigned them, and he there checks off and reports to each mine and smelter owner the number of Indians assigned him for his mine or smelter; that keeps him busy till 1 P.M., by which time the Indians are already turned over to these mine and smelter owners.

After each has eaten his ration, they climb up the hill, each to his mine, and go in, staying there from that hour until Saturday evening without coming out of the mine; their wives bring them food, but they stay constantly underground, excavating and carrying out the ore from which they get the silver. They all have tallow candles, lighted day and night; that is the light they work with, for as they are underground, they have need of it all the time. . . .

These Indians have different functions in the handling of the silver ore; some break it up with bar or pick, and dig down in, following the vein in the mine; others bring it up; others up above keep separating the good and the poor in piles; others are occupied in taking it down from the range to the mills on herds of llamas; every day they bring up more than 8,000 of these native beasts of burden for this task. These teamsters who carry the metal do not belong to the *mita*, but are mingados–hired.

From Antonio Vázquez de Espinosa, *Compendium and Description of the Indies* (ca. 1620), trans. by Charles Upson Clark (Washington, DC: Smithsonian Institution Press, 1968), p. 62, quoted in Helen Delpar, ed., *The Borzoi Reader in Latin American History* (New York: Alfred A. Knopf, 1972), pp. 92–93.

An *encomienda* usually involved a few hundred Native Americans, but might grant the right to the labor of several thousand. The *encomienda* was first used on Hispaniola, but spread to the continent as the conquest took place. *Encomienda* as an institution persisted in some parts of Latin America well into the eighteenth century, but had generally declined by the middle of the sixteenth. Some Native Americans substituted payments in kind or cash for labor.

The Spanish crown disliked the *encomienda* system. The monarchy was distressed by reports from concerned clergy that the Native Americans were being mistreated under the system and feared that *encomienda* holders were attempting to transform themselves into a powerful independent nobility in the New World.

Repartimiento   The passing of the *encomienda* led to another arrangement of labor servitude, the *repartimiento*, which was largely copied from the draft labor practices of the Incas. *Repartimiento*, in an adaptation of the Incan *mita*, required adult male Native Americans to devote a set number of days of labor annually to Spanish economic enterprises. In the mines of Potosí, the *repartimiento* was known as the *mita*. The time limitation on *repartimiento* led some Spanish managers to use their workers in an extremely harsh manner, under the assumption that more fresh workers would soon be appearing on the scene. Native Americans sometimes did not survive their days of labor rotation.

The Hacienda   Outside the mines, the major institution using dependent labor in the Spanish colonies was the *hacienda*. This institution, which dominated rural and agricultural life in Spanish colonies on the continent, developed when the crown, partly to counter the extension of the *encomienda*, made available grants of land. These grants led to the establishment of large landed estates owned by *peninsulares*, whites born in Spain, or creoles, whites born in America. The crown thus continued to use the resources of the New World for patronage without directly impinging on the Native

POTOSI

The silver mines of Potosí, worked by conscripted Indian laborers under extremely harsh conditions, provided Spain with a vast treasure in silver.
[Hulton/Corbis-Bettmann]

Americans because the grazing that occurred on the *haciendas* required far less labor than did the mines. The establishment of *haciendas* represented the transfer of the principle of the large unit of privately owned land, which was characteristic of Europe and especially of Spain, to the New World. Such estates would become one of the most important features of Latin American life. Laborers on the *hacienda* usually stood in some relation of formal servitude to the owner. Furthermore, they were usually required to buy goods for everyday living on credit from the owner. They were rarely able to repay the resulting debts and thus could not move to work for new landowners. This system was known as *debt peonage*. There were two major products of the *hacienda* economy: foodstuffs for mining areas and urban centers, and leather goods used in vast quantities on mining machinery. Both farming and ranching were thus subordinate to the mine economy.

The Decline of the Native American Population

The conquest and the economy of exploitation and forced labor (and the introduction of European diseases) produced extraordinary demographic consequences for the Indian population. Beginning in the sixteenth century Native Americans had begun to die off in huge numbers. The pre-Columbian population of America is a matter of great controversy, but conservative estimates put the Indian population at the time of Columbus's discovery at well over 50 million. In New Spain (Mexico) alone, the population probably declined from ap-

proximately 25 million to fewer than 2 million within the first century after the conquest. Similar depopulation of native peoples appears to have occurred elsewhere in Spanish America during approximately the same period. Thereafter the Indian population began to expand slowly. Whatever the exact figures, the precipitous drop eliminated the *conquistadores'* easy supply of exploitable labor.

Commercial Regulation and the Flota System

Because Queen Isabella of Castile (r. 1474–1504) had commissioned Columbus, the technical legal link between the New World and Spain was the crown of Castile. Its powers both at home and in America were subject to few limitations. Government of America was assigned to the Council of the Indies, which, in conjunction with the monarch, nominated the viceroys of New Spain and Peru. These viceroys were the chief executives in the New World and carried out the laws promulgated by the Council of the Indies. Each of the viceroyalties included subordinate judicial councils known as *audiencias*. There were also a variety of local officers, the most important of which were the *corregidores*, who presided over municipal councils. These offices provided the monarchy with a vast array of opportunities for patronage, usually bestowed on persons born in Spain. Virtually all political power flowed from the top of this political structure downward; in effect, there was little or no local initiative or self-government (see Map 19–1).

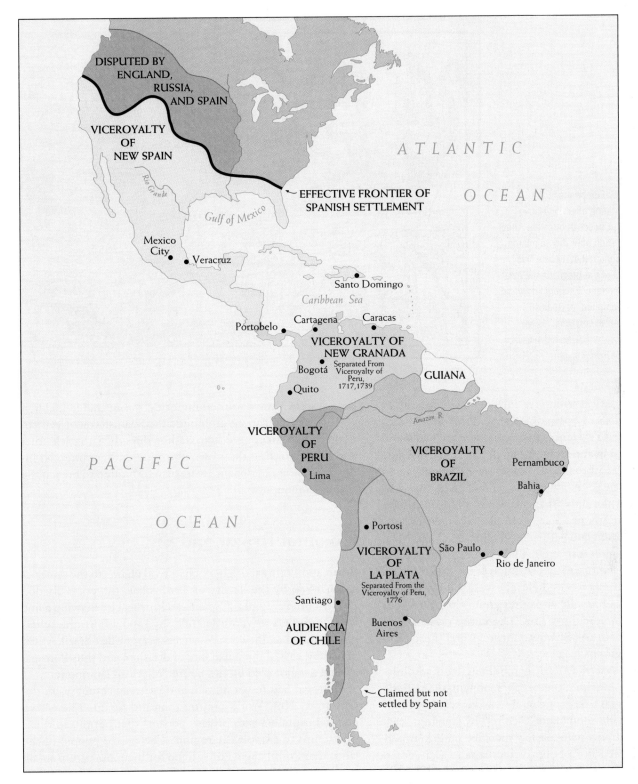

Map 19-1 Viceroyalties in Latin America in 1780. Spain organized its vast holdings in the New World into viceroyalties, each of which had its own governor and other administrative officials.

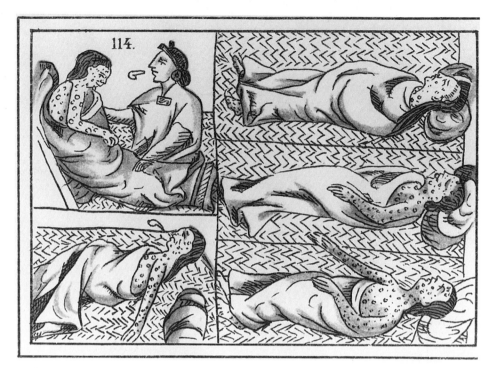

Smallpox, introduced by Europeans to the Americas, had a devastating effect on Native American populations. It swept through the Aztec capital of Tenochtitlán soon after the Spaniards arrived, contributing to the fall of the city. This illustration of the effect of the plague in the Aztec capital is from a post-conquest history known as the Florentine Codex compiled for Spanish Church authorities by Aztec survivors. [Courtesy President and Fellows of Harvard College, Peabody Museum, Harvard University, Photograph by Hillel Burger]

The colonial political structures existed largely to support the commercial goals of Spain. Spanish control of its American empire involved a system of monopolistic trade regulation that was more rigid in appearance than in practice. The trade monopoly was often breached. The Casa de Contratación (House of Trade) in Seville regulated all trade with the New World. Cádiz was the only Spanish port to be used for the American trade. In America there were similarly specific ports for trade both to Spain and with non-Spanish merchants. The latter trade was highly restricted. The Casa de Contratación was the single most influential institution of the Spanish Empire, and its members worked closely with the Consulado (Merchant Guild) of Seville and other groups involved with the American commerce in Cádiz. The entire organization was geared to benefit the Spanish monarchy and these privileged merchant groups.

A complicated system of trade and bullion fleets administered from Seville provided the key for maintaining the trade monopoly. Each year a fleet of commercial vessels (the *flota*) controlled by Seville merchants, escorted by warships, carried merchandise from Spain to a few specified ports in America. These included Portobello, Veracruz, and Cartagena. There were no authorized ports on the Pacific Coast. Areas far to the south, such as Buenos Aires, received goods only after the shipments had been unloaded at one of the authorized ports. After selling their wares, the ships were loaded with silver and gold bullion, usually wintered in heavily fortified Caribbean ports, and then sailed back to Spain. The flota system always worked imperfectly, but trade outside it was illegal. Regulations prohibited the Spanish colonists within the American empire from trading directly with each other and from building their own shipping and commercial industry. Foreign merchants were also forbidden to breach the Spanish monopoly.

Colonial Brazil and Slavery

Spain and Portugal originally had rival claims to the Americas. In 1494, by the Treaty of Tordesillas, the pope divided the seaborne empires of Spain and Portugal by drawing a line west of the Cape Verde Islands. In 1500 a Portuguese explorer landed on the coast of what is present-day Brazil, which extended east of the papal line of division, and thus Portugal gained a major hold on the South American continent.

Portugal had fewer human and material resources to devote to its New World empire than did Spain. The crown granted captaincies to private persons that permitted them to attempt to exploit the region. The native people in the lands that Portugal governed lived for the most part in small, nomadic groups. In this they differed from the native peoples of Spanish America, with their centralized empires, cities, and organized political structures. As a result, labor practices in the two regions were also different. The Portuguese imported Africans as slaves rather than using the native Indian population, as did the Spanish in most areas.

By the mid-sixteenth century, sugar production had gained preeminence in the Brazilian economy, although some minerals were discovered and some cattle raised. Because sugar cane was grown on large estates (*fazendas*) with African slave labor, the dominance of sugar meant also the dominance of slavery.

Toward the close of the seventeenth century, sugar prices declined and the economy suffered. In the early eighteenth century, however, significant deposits of gold were discovered in southern Brazil. Immigrants from Portugal joined the ensuing gold rush, and economic activity moved suddenly toward the south. This shift, however, did not reduce Brazil's reliance on slave labor. In fact, the expansion of gold mining also led to the increased importation of African slaves. Nowhere, except perhaps in the West Indies, was slavery so important as it was in Brazil, where it persisted until 1888.

The taxation and administration associated with gold mining brought new, unexpected wealth to the eighteenth-century Portuguese monarchy, allowing it to rule without recourse to the Cortés or traditional parliament for taxation. Through transatlantic trade the new wealth generated from Brazilian gold also filtered into all the major trading nations, which could sell their goods to Portugal as well as profit from the slave trade.

As in the Spanish empire, the Portuguese crown attempted to establish a strong network of regulation around Brazilian trade. Brazil, however, required less direct control by the Portuguese than the Spanish Empire required from Spain, and as a result, Brazil's colonial settlers may have felt less resentment toward the Portuguese government than the settlers of the Spanish Empire felt toward the Spanish administrators. In Brazil, where the basic unit of production was the plantation, there were fewer large cities than in Spanish America. The Crown's determination in Spanish America to have precious metals sent to Spain required a vast colonial administration. The sugar plantations of Brazil, in contrast, did not require such direct administration. Consequently, the Portuguese were willing to allow more local autonomy than was Spain. More local officials were allowed to serve in the government in Brazil than in Spanish America, where the administration was dominated by officials born in Spain. In Spanish America the use of Indian labor, which was important to the colonial economy, required government supervision. Brazil, less dependent on Indian labor, felt no such constraints. Indeed, the Portuguese government condoned policies whereby Indian tribes were driven into the back country or exterminated. Throughout the eighteenth century the

The fortress of El Morro in the harbor of San Juan, Puerto Rico. This massive citadel protected the Spanish treasure fleets that carried gold and silver each year to Spain from the mines of Mexico and Peru. [Comstock]

Visitors Describe the Portobello Fair

The Spanish tried to restrict all trade within their Latin American empire to a few designated ports. Each year a fair was held in certain of these ports. The most famous of these was Portobello on the Isthmus of Panama. In the 1730s two visitors saw the event and described it. This fair was the chief means of facilitating trade between the western coast of South America and Spain.

What products were sold at this fair? How might the actual sale of gold bullion at this fair have led to attitudes such as were seen in the earlier document by Thomas Mun? How does this passage illustrate the inefficiency of monopoly trade in the Spanish empire and the many chances for smuggling?

The town of Portobello, so thinly inhabited, by reason of its noxious air, the scarcity of provisions, and the soil, becomes, at the time of the [Spanish] galleons one of the most populous places in all South America. . . .

The ships are no sooner moored in the harbour, than the first work is, to erect, in the square, a tent made of the ship's sails, for receiving its cargo; at which the proprietors of the goods are present, in order to find their bales, by the marks which distinguish them. These bales are drawn on sledges, to their respective places by the crew of every ship, and the money given them is proportionally divided.

Whilst the seamen and European traders are thus employed, the land is covered with droves of mules from Panama, each drove consisting of above an hundred, loaded with chests of gold and silver, on account of the merchants of Peru. Some unload them at the exchange, others in the middle of the square; yet, amidst the hurry and confusion of such crowds, no theft, loss, or disturbance, is ever known. He who has seen this place during the tiempo muerto, or dead time, solitary, poor, and a perpetual silence reigning everywhere; the harbour quite empty, and every place wearing a melancholy aspect; must be filled with astonishment at the sudden change, to see the bustling multitudes, every house crowded, the square and streets encumbered with bales and chests of gold and silver of all kinds; the harbour full of ships and vessels, some bringing by the way of Rio de Chape the goods of Peru, such as cacao, quinquina, or Jesuit's bark, Vicuña wool, and bezoar stones; others coming from Carthagena, loaded with provisions; and thus a spot, at all times detested for its deleterious qualities, becomes the staple of the riches of the old and new world, and the scene of one of the most considerable branches of commerce in the whole earth.

The ships being unloaded, and the merchants of Peru, together with the president of Panama, arrived, the fair comes under deliberation. And for this purpose the deputies of the several parties repair on board the commodore of the galleons, where, in the presence of the commodore, and the president of Panama, . . . the prices of the several kinds of merchandizes are settled. . . . The purchases and sales, as likewise the exchanges of money, are transacted by brokers, both from Spain and Peru. After this, every one begins to dispose of his goods; the Spanish brokers embarking their chests of money, and those of Peru sending away the goods they have purchased, in vessels called chatas and bongos, up the river Chagres. And thus the fair of Portobello ends.

From George Juan and Antonio de Ulloa, *A Voyage to South America*, Vol. 1 (London, 1772), pp. 103–110, as quoted in Benjamin Keen, ed., *Readings in Latin-American Civilization 1492 to the Present* (New York: Houghton Mifflin, 1955), pp. 107–108.

Portuguese government also favored the continued importation of slaves.

French and British Colonies in North America

French explorers had pressed down the St. Lawrence River valley in Canada during the seventeenth century. French fur traders and Roman Catholic Jesuit missionaries had followed in their wake, with the French government supporting the missionary effort. By the end of the seventeenth century a significant but sparsely populated French presence existed in Canada. Trade rather than extensive settlements character-ized the French effort. The largest settlement was Quebec, founded in 1608. Some French settlers married Native American women; the absence of a drive to permanently claim land reduced conflict between the French and Native Americans. It was primarily through the fur trade that French Canada functioned as part of the early transatlantic economy.

For most readers of this volume, the story of the founding of the English-speaking colonies along the Atlantic seaboard is relatively familiar, but it needs to be set in the larger world context. Beginning with the first successful settlement in Jamestown, Virginia, in 1607 and ending with the establishment of Georgia in 1733, the eastern seaboard of the United States became populated by a series of English colonies. Other nations, including the Dutch and Swedes, had found-

The sugar plantations of Brazil and the West Indies were a major source of the demand for slave labor. Slaves are here shown grinding sugar cane and refining sugar, which was then exported to the consumer markets in Europe. [Hulton/Corbis-Bettmann]

ed settlements, but all of them were eventually taken over during the seventeenth century by the English.

A wide variety of reasons led to the founding of the English colonies. Settlement for enrichment from farming and trade accounted for some settlements, such as Virginia and New Amsterdam (after 1664, New York). Others, such as the Carolinas, were developed by royal favorites who were given vast land tracts. James Oglethorpe founded Georgia as a refuge for English debtors. But the pursuit of religious liberty constituted the major driving force of the Pilgrim and Puritan founders of Massachusetts, the Baptist Roger Williams in Rhode Island, the Quaker William Penn in Pennsylvania, and the Roman Catholic Lord Baltimore in Maryland.

With the exception of Maryland, these colonies were Protestant. The Church of England dominated the southern colonies. In New England, varieties of Protestantism associated with or derived from Calvinism were in the ascendancy. In their religious affiliations, the English-speaking colonies manifested two important traits derived from the English experience. First, much of their religious life was organized around self-governing congregations. Second, their religious outlook derived from those forms of Protestantism that were suspicious of central political authority and especially of po-

tentially despotic monarchs. In this regard, their cultural and political outlook differed sharply from the cultural and political outlook associated with the Roman Catholicism of the Spanish empire. In a sense the values of the extreme Reformation and Counter-Reformation confronted each other on the two American continents.

The English colonists had complex interactions with the Native American populations. Unlike the Spanish to the south or the French to the north, they had only modest interest in missionary enterprise. As in South America, new diseases imported from Europe took a high death toll among the native population. Unlike Mexico and Peru, however, North America had no large Native American cities. The Native American populations were far more dispersed, and intertribal animosity was intense. The English often encountered well-organized resistance, as from the Powhatan conspiracy in Virginia and the Pequots in New England. The most powerful of the Native American groups was the Iroquois Nation, organized in the early eighteenth century in New York. The Iroquois battled successfully against other tribes and long negotiated successfully with both the Dutch and the English. The English also often used one tribe against another, and the Native Americans also tried to use the English or the French in their own conflicts. The outcome of these struggles between the English settlers and the Native Americans was rarely full victory for either side, but rather mutual exhaustion, with the Native Americans temporarily retreating beyond the reach of English settlements and the English temporarily restraining their initial claims. From the late seventeenth century through the American Revolution, however, the Native Americans of North America were drawn into the Anglo-French Wars that were fought in North America as well as Europe. Indeed, Native American alliances became important for the Anglo-French conflict on the continent, which was intimately related to their rivalry over transatlantic trade. (See Chapter 21.)

The largest economic activity throughout the English-speaking colonies was agriculture. From New England through the Middle Atlantic states there were mostly small farms tilled by free white labor; from Virginia southward it was the plantation economy, dependent on slavery. During the early eighteenth century the chief products raised on these plantations were tobacco, indigo, rice, and sugar. Although slavery was a dominant institution in the South, all of the colonies included slaves. The principal port cities along the seaboard—Boston, Newport, New York, Philadelphia, Baltimore, and Charleston—resembled small provincial English cities. They were primarily trading centers through which goods moved back and forth between the colonies and England and the West Indies. The commercial economies of these cities were all related to the transatlantic slave trade.

Until the 1760s the political values of the Americans resembled those of their English counterparts. The colonials were thoroughly familiar with events in England. They sent many of their children there to be educated. They were

monarchists but, like their English counterparts, suspicious of monarchical power. Their politics involved vast amounts of patronage and individual favors. Their society was clearly hierarchical, with an elite that functioned like a colonial aristocracy and many ordinary people who were dependent on that aristocracy. Throughout the colonies during the eighteenth century, the Anglican church grew in influence and membership. The prosperity of the colonies might eventually have led them to separate from England, but in 1750 few people thought that would occur.

Both England and France had important sugar islands in the Caribbean. England held Jamaica and Barbados, and France held Saint Domingue (Haiti), Guadeloupe, and Martinique. The plantations on these islands were worked by African slaves, and the trade and commerce of the northern British colonies were closely related to meeting the needs of these islands.

Slavery in the Americas

Black slavery was the final mode of forced or subservient labor in the New World. Unlike the labor exploitation of Native Americans discussed earlier in this chapter, black slavery extended throughout not only the Spanish empire but also Portuguese Brazil and the English-speaking colonies of North America.

Establishment of Slavery

As the numbers of Native Americans in South America declined due to disease and exploitation, the Spanish and the Portuguese turned to the labor of imported African slaves.

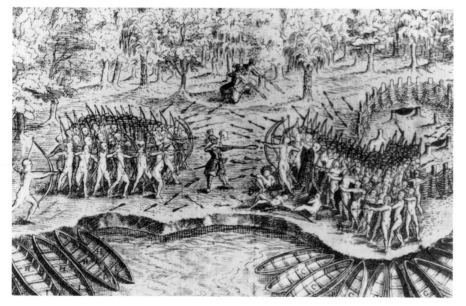

Native Americans in the Saint Lawrence region of North America were drawn into the transatlantic economy through interaction with French fur traders in the early seventeenth century. This illustration shows Samuel de Champlain, the founder of New France, assisting his Huron allies in an attack on the Iroquois in part of an ongoing struggle for control of valuable fur grounds. The palm trees in the background suggest that the artist was unfamiliar with the region. [New York Public Library, Rare Book Division]

er, in Brazil and in the Caribbean. Later, starting with the importation of slaves to Jamestown in 1619, slavery spread into the British North American colonies and became a fundamental institution there.

One of the forces that led to the spread of slavery in Brazil and the West Indies was the cultivation of sugar. Sugar cane required a large investment in land and equipment, and only slave labor could provide enough workers for the extremely profitable sugar plantations. As the production of sugar expanded, so did the demand for slaves, and more slaves were imported.

By the close of the seventeenth century the Caribbean Islands were the world center for sugar production. As the European appetite for sugar continued to grow, the slave population continued to expand. By 1725 black slaves may have constituted almost 90 percent of the population of Jamaica. The situation was similar throughout the West Indies. There and elsewhere, in Brazil and the southern British colonies, prosperity and slavery went hand in hand. The wealthiest and most prized of the colonies were those that raised consumer staples, such as sugar, rice, tobacco, or cotton, by slave labor.

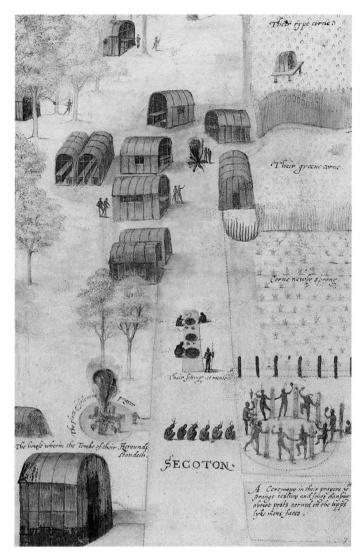

The first successful English colonies in North America in the seventeenth century were preceded by two failed efforts on Roanoke Island in what is now North Carolina in the late sixteenth century. John White accompanied both attempts, the second as governor. White was a perceptive and sensitive observer whose watercolor paintings provide invaluable information about Native American life in the coastal Carolina region at the time of contact. This painting shows the Algonquian village of Secoton. The houses were bark covered. In the lower left is a mortuary temple. The dancers in the lower right are performing a fertility ceremony. The man sitting in the platform in the upper right is keeping birds away from the corn crop. [The Bridgeman Art Library International]

By the late sixteenth century, in the islands of the West Indies and the major cities of South America, black slaves equalled or surpassed the white European population.

On much of the South American continent dominated by Spain, the number of slaves declined during the late seventeenth century, and the institution became less fundamental there than elsewhere. Slavery continued to prosper, howev-

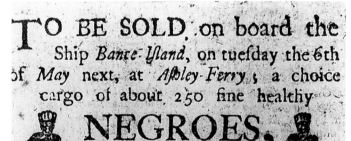

Africans who survived the voyage across the Atlantic were immediately sold into slavery in the Americas. This slave-auction notice relates to a group of slaves whose ship had stopped at Charleston, South Carolina, and then landed elsewhere in the region to auction its human cargo. Notice the concern to assure potential buyers that the slaves were healthy. [Corbis-Bettmann]

The Plantation Economy and Transatlantic Trade

The plantations that stretched from Maryland through the West Indies and into Brazil formed a vast corridor of slave societies in which social and economic subordination was based on both involuntary servitude and race. This kind of society, in its total dependence on slave labor and racial differences, was something novel in world history; it had not existed before the European discovery and exploitation of the Americas. The social and economic influence of plantation slavery touched not only the plantation societies themselves but also West Africa, Western Europe, and New England. It persisted from the sixteenth century through the second half of the nineteenth century, ending with the British effort to outlaw the slave trade during the first half of the nineteenth century, the Latin American Wars of Independence, the Emancipation Proclamation of 1862 in the United States, and the Brazilian emancipation of 1888. Every society in which it existed still contends with its long-term effects.

The slave trade was part of the larger system of transatlantic trade that linked Europe, Africa, and the European colonies in South America, the Caribbean, and North America. In this system the Americas supplied labor-intensive raw materials like tobacco, sugar, coffee, precious metals, cotton, and indigo. Europe supplied manufactured goods like textiles, liquor, guns, metal wares, and beads, not to mention various forms of cash, including even gold. And Africa supplied gold, ivory, wood, palm oil, gum, and other products, as well as the slaves who provided the labor to create the American products. By the eighteenth century slaves were the predominant African export.

Slavery on the Plantations

The plantations in the Americas to which the African slaves eventually arrived were always in a fairly isolated rural setting. Their products, however, were agricultural goods produced for an external overseas market that was part of a larger integrated transatlantic economy. The plantation might raise food for its owners and their slaves, but the main production—whether sugar, tobacco, or, later, cotton and coffee—was intended for export. In turn, plantation owners imported from other parts of the world virtually all the finished or manufactured goods they used or consumed.

The life conditions of plantation slaves differed from colony to colony. Most owners possessed relatively few slaves, and vast slave holdings were the exception. Black slaves living in Portuguese areas had the fewest legal protections. In the Spanish colonies the church attempted to provide some small protection for black slaves, but devoted much more ef-

In the American South, the islands of the Caribbean, and in Brazil, the slaves labored on sugar plantations under the authority of overseers. [The Granger Collection]

fort toward protecting the Native Americans. Slave codes were developed in the British and the French colonies during the seventeenth century, but they provided only the most limited protection. Virtually all slaveowners feared a slave revolt; slave-related legislation and other regulations were intended to prevent such an event. Slave laws favored the master rather than the slave. Masters were permitted to punish slaves by whipping and other harsh corporal punishment. Furthermore, slaves were often forbidden to gather in large groups lest they plan a revolt. In most slave-owning societies, the marriages of slaves were not recognized by law. The children of slaves continued to be slaves and were owned by the owner of the parents. Slave families could be separated by the owner or after the owner's death.

The daily life of most slaves during these centuries was one of hard agricultural labor, poor diet and clothing, and inadequate housing. The death rate among slaves was high.

Their welfare and their lives were sacrificed to the ongoing expansion of the plantations that made their owners wealthy and that produced goods demanded by consumers in Europe. Scholars have argued that slaves in one area or another had a better existence than others, but it is generally accepted that slaves in all plantation societies suffered under difficult conditions. The specifics of those conditions may have varied, but they were not significantly better in one place than another.

The African slaves who were transported to the Americas were, like the Native Americans, converted to Christianity: in the Spanish domains to Roman Catholicism, and in the English colonies to various forms of Protestantism. In both cases, they became largely separated from African religious outlooks. Although some African practices survived in muted forms, and slaves did manage to mix Christianity with African religion, the conversion of Africans to Christianity nonetheless represented another example of the crushing of a set of non-European cultural values in the context of the New World economies and social structures.

The European settlers in the Americas and the slave traders were also prejudiced against black Africans. Many Europeans thought Africans were savage or less than civilized. Others looked down on them simply because they were slaves. These attitudes had been shared by both Christians and Muslims in the Mediterranean world, where slavery had long existed. Furthermore, many European languages and European cultures attached negative connotations to the idea and image of blackness. In virtually all plantation societies, race was an important element in keeping black slaves subservient. Although racial thinking in regard to slavery became more important in the nineteenth century, the fact that slaves were differentiated from the rest of the population by race as well as by their status as chattel property was fundamental to the system.

Africa and the Transatlantic Slave Trade

It was the establishment of plantations demanding the use of slave labor that drew Africa and its peoples into the heart of the transatlantic economy. As Native American peoples were decimated by conquest and European diseases or proved unsatisfactory as plantation laborers, colonial entrepreneurs began to look elsewhere for peoples to work their plantations. First the Portuguese, and then the Spanish, Dutch, French, and English (others would follow, including Americans) turned to west, central, and, to a lesser degree, southeastern Africa for an ample supply of slaves. Thus the Atlantic slave trade was not overtly the result of racist principles, but of the economic needs of the colonial powers and their willingness to exploit weaker peoples to satisfy them. However, this willingness was based on the tacit racist assumption that non-European, non-white tribal peoples were sub-human and could be enslaved for European purposes.

The Portuguese, who were the principal carriers throughout most of the history of the trade, had a virtual monopoly until the Dutch broke it in the 1640s and briefly became the chief carriers. The French and English came into the trade only in the late seventeenth century; yet during the eighteenth century, which saw the greatest shipments, they carried

Slave dealing in the streets of Zanzibar. Slaving was a part of East African trade for centuries. [Corbis-Bettmann]

almost half the total traffic. Americans, too, were latecomers but avid slavers who managed to make considerable profits before and even after Britain and the United States outlawed slaving in 1807.

If gold and the search for a sea route to Asia brought the first European ships to Africa, slaves were the main commodity for which they returned for a long time. Slaving was an important part of the massive new overseas trade that financed much European and American economic development that so dramatically changed the west during the nineteenth century. The success of this trade, bought at the price of immense human suffering, helped propel Europe and some of its colonial offshoots in the Americas into world dominance.

The Background of Slavery

Slavery seems to have been one of the tragic facts of human societies as far back as we can trace its history. Although linked to warfare and the age-old practice of taking captives, it cannot be fully explained by military or economic necessity.

Virtually every premodern state around the globe depended on slavery to some extent. The Mediterranean and African worlds were no exception, in both the pre-Islamic and the Islamic periods. Slave institutions in sub-Saharan Africa were ancient and included traffic with the Mediterranean world. The Islamic states of southwestern Asia and North Africa continued and even increased this traffic, importing slaves from both the Sudan and Horn of Africa as well as the East African coast, although they took fewer slaves from Africa than from Eastern Europe and central Asia. Central Asia, for example, was the source of most of the (largely Turkish) slave-soldier dynasties that came to rule many Islamic states from India to North Africa. (Hence it is not surprising that the word *slave* is derived ultimately from *Slav.*) Both Mediterranean-Christian and Islamic peoples were using slaves—mostly Greeks, Bulgarians, Turkish prisoners of war, and Black Sea Tartars, but also Africans—well before the voyages of discovery opened sub-Saharan sources of slaves for the new European colonies overseas.

Not all forms of slavery were as dehumanizing as the chattel slavery that came to predominate (with the sanction of Christian authorities) during the colonization of the Americas. Islamic law, for example, although permitting slavery, also ameliorated it. All slavery, however, involved the forceful exploitation and degradation of some human beings for the profit of others, the denial of basic freedoms, and sometimes the sundering, often violently, of even the closest family ties.

Africa suffered immense social devastation when it was the chief supplier of slaves to the world. The societies that were built to a great extent on the exploitation of African slavery also suffered enduring consequences, not the least of which, many believe, is racism.

Slavery and Slaving in Africa

The trade that long before the fifteenth century supplied African slaves to the Islamic lands of the Mediterranean and to southwestern and southern Asia has conventionally been termed the "oriental" slave trade. The savannahs of the Sudan and the Horn of Africa were the two prime sources of slaves for this trade. The trade managed by Europeans, conventionally called the "occidental" slave trade, can be traced at least to the thirteenth century, when Europeans established sugar cane plantations on Cyprus soon after Muslim forces had driven them out of the Holy Land. In Cypress, as later in Brazil and the Caribbean islands, slaves proved an especially profitable work force for the labor-intensive process of sugar production. This industry subsequently spread westward to Crete and Sicily and, in the fifteenth century, to the Portuguese Atlantic islands of Madeira and São Thomé.

The Portuguese in particular developed the plantation system of slave labor as they began their expansion into the Atlantic and beyond. Although the savannah and Horn regions were the earliest sources for this trade, voyages beginning in the fifteenth century by first the Portuguese and then other Europeans opened the western coasts of Africa as far south as Angola, making them the prime slaving areas. A third but less important source region for both occidental and oriental trades was the eastern coast of Africa below the Horn.

Before the full development of the transatlantic slave trade by about 1650, slavery and slave trading had been no more significant in Africa than anywhere else in the world.[2] Indigenous African slavery resembled that of other premodern societies. It was apparently most common, if still limited, in the areas of the savannah and Horn, presumably because these areas were involved in external slave trading. In the western and central Sudan, slavery came largely to be regulated by Islamic norms, but in the Horn, specifically in Ethiopia, slavery was practiced in both Christian and Muslim communities. Estimates suggest that about ten thousand slaves per year, most of them female, were taken from sub-Saharan Africa through the oriental trade.

By about 1650 the newer occidental slave trade of the Europeans had become as large as the oriental trade and for the ensuing two centuries far surpassed it. It affected adversely all of Africa, disrupting especially western and central African

---

[2]The summary follows closely that of P. Manning, *Slavery and African Life: Occidental, Oriental, and African Slave Trades* (Cambridge: Cambridge University Press, 1990), pp. 127–140.

society. As a result of the demand for young male slaves on the plantations of the Americas, West Africa experienced a sharp drain on its productive male population. Between 1640 and 1690, although the price of a slave at the coast remained constant, the number of slaves sold to European carriers doubled, indicating the increasing participation of Africans in the expanding trade. With the growing demand for slaves came an increase in internal warfare in western and central Africa. Moreover, as the external trade destroyed the regional male-female population balance, an internal market for female slaves in particular arose.

These developments accelerated during the eighteenth century—at the height of the occidental trade. It was also during this period that African states and slave traders were most heavily involved as regulators and suppliers of the trade. Slave prices at times accelerated accordingly. Owing to population depletion and regional migrations, however, the actual number of sold slaves declined in some areas. The population declined sharply in the coastal and inland areas hardest hit by the ravages of the trade in the later eighteenth century and continued to decline in places even until 1850.

As European nations, followed by nations in the Americas, slowly began to outlaw slaving and slavery in the nineteenth century, occidental demand slowed and prices for slaves sank. The result was that the oriental and internal trades increased. Slave exports from East Africa and the Sudan and Horn increased significantly after about 1780, and indigenous African slavery, predominantly of women, also expanded. Indeed, by about l850 the internal African trade surpassed the combined oriental and (now outlawed and decreasing) occidental trade. This traffic was dominated by the same figures—merchants, warlords, and rulers—who had previously profited from external trade.

Indigenous African slavery began a real decline only at the end of the nineteenth century, in part because of the dominance of European colonial regimes and in part because of internal changes. The formal end of African indigenous slavery occurred over a long period, beginning in 1874 in the Gold Coast and ending only in 1928 in Sierra Leone.

The African Side of the Transatlantic Trade

Africans were actively involved in the transatlantic slave trade. Except for the Portuguese in central Africa, European slave traders generally obtained their human cargoes from private or government-sponsored African middlemen at coastal forts or simply at anchorages along the coast. A system of forts built by Europeans mostly between 1640 and 1750, for example, dominated the Gold Coast. This situation was the result of both the desire and ability of Africans to control inland trade and the vulnerability of Europeans to tropical disease (a new European arrival stood a less than 50 percent chance of surviving a year on the tropical African coast). Thus it was largely African middlemen who undertook the actual capture or procurement of slaves and the difficult, dangerous task of marching them to the coast. These middlemen were generally either wealthy merchants who could mount slaving expeditions inland or the agents of African chieftaincies or kingdoms that sought to profit from the trade.

The media of exchange were varied. At first they usually involved mixed barter for goods that ranged from gold dust or firearms to beads and alcohol. As time went on they came increasingly to involve some form of monetary payment. This exchange drained productive resources (human beings) in return for nonproductive wealth.

The chief West and central African slaving regions provided different numbers of slaves at different times, and the total number of exported slaves varied sharply between periods. When one area was unable to produce sufficient numbers to meet demand (whether as a result of depopulation of choice areas, local warfare, or changing state

This eighteenth-century print shows bound African captives being forced to a slaving port. It was largely African middlemen who captured slaves in the interior and marched them to the coast. [North Wind Picture Archives]

A Slave Trader Describes the Atlantic Passage

During 1693 and 1694 Captain Thomas Phillips carried slaves from Africa to Barbados on the ship Hannibal. *The financial backer of the voyage was the Royal African Company of London, which held an English crown monopoly on slave trading. Phillips sailed to the west coast of Africa, where he purchased the Africans who were sold into slavery by an African king. Then he set sail westward.*

Who are the various people described in this document who in one way or another were involved in or profited from the slave trade? What dangers did the Africans face on the voyage? What contemporary attitudes could have led this ship captain to treat and think of his human cargo simply as goods to be transported? What are the grounds of his self-pity for the difficulties he met?

Having bought my complement of 700 slaves, 480 men and 220 women, and finish'd all my business at Whidaw [on the Gold Coast of Africa], I took my leave of the old king and his cappasheirs [attendants], and parted, with many affectionate expressions on both sides, being forced to promise him that I would return again the next year, with several things he desired me to bring from England. . . . I set sail the 27th of July in the morning, accompany'd with the East-India Merchant, who had bought 650 slaves, for the Island of St. Thomas . . . from which we took our departure on August 25th and set sail for Barbadoes.

We spent in our passage from St. Thomas to Barbadoes two months eleven days, from the 25th of August to the 4th of November following: in which time there happened such sickness and mortality among my poor men and Negroes. Of the first we buried 14, and of the last 320, which was a great detriment to our voyage, the Royal African Company losing ten pounds by every slave that died, and the owners of the ship ten pounds ten shillings, being the freight agreed on to be paid by the charter-party for every Negro delivered alive ashore to the African Company's agents at Barbadoes. . . . The loss in all amounted to near 6500 pounds sterling.

The distemper which my men as well as the blacks mostly died of was the white flux, which was so violent and inveterate that no medicine would in the least check it, so that when any of our men were seized with it, we esteemed him a dead man, as he generally proved. . . .

The Negroes are so incident to the small-pox that few ships that carry them escape without it, and sometimes it makes vast havock and destruction among them. But tho' we had 100 at a time sick of it, and that it went thro' the ship, yet we lost not above a dozen by it. All the assistance we gave the diseased was only as much water as they desir'd to drink, and some palm-oil to annoint their sores, and they would generally recover without any other helps but what kind nature gave them. . . .

But what the small pox spar'd, the flux swept off, to our great regret, after all our pains and care to give them their messes in due order and season, keeping their lodgings as clean and sweet as possible, and enduring so much misery and stench so long among a parcel of creatures nastier than swine, and after all our expectations to be defeated by their mortality. . . .

No gold-finders can endure so much noisome slavery as they do who carry Negroes; for those have some respite and satisfaction, but we endure twice the misery; and yet by their mortality our voyages are ruin'd, and we pine and fret ourselves to death, and take so much pains to so little purpose.

From Thomas Phillips, *"Journal," A Collection of Voyages and Travels*, Vol. VI, ed. by Awnsham and John Churchill (London, 1746), as quoted in Thomas Howard, ed., *Black Voyage: Eyewitness Accounts of the Atlantic Slave Trade* (Boston: Little, Brown and Company, 1971), pp. 85–87.

---

policies), the European traders shifted their buying to other points. Thus, between 1526 and 1550 the major sources of the slaves for the Atlantic trade were the Kongo-Angola region (34 percent), the Guinea coast of Cape Verde (25.6 percent), and Senegambia (23.5 percent).[3] By contrast, between 1761 and 1810 the French drew some 52 percent of their slaves from Angola and 24 percent from the Bight of Benin, but only 4.8 percent from Senegambia, whereas the British relied most heavily on the Bight of Biafra and central Africa.[4] Traders naturally went where population density and the presence of active African merchant or state suppliers promised the best numbers and prices, although prices do not seem to have varied radically in a given period.

The Extent of the Slave Trade

The slave trade varied sharply in extent from period to period. Only about 3 percent of the total occidental trade occurred

---

[3]Philip Curtin, *The Atlantic Slave Trade: A Census* (Madison: University of Wisconsin Press, 1969), p. 101.

[4]Curtin, pp. 101, 129; James A. Rawley, *The Transatlantic Slave Trade: A History* (New York: W. W. Norton, 1981), p. 129.

before 1600, and only about 14 percent between 1600 and 1700. The period of greatest activity, 1701–1810, accounted for over 60 percent of the total, and even the final half-century of slaving until 1870 accounted for over 20 percent of the total. Despite moves by European nations to abolish slaving in the early 1800s, the Portuguese still transported more than a million slaves to Brazil between 1811 and 1870. In fact, more slaves landed in the Americas in these final years of the trade than during the entire seventeenth century.[5] We would do well to remember how long it actually took the "modern" occidental world to abolish the trade in African slaves.

The overall number of African slaves exported during the occidental trade—effectively, between 1451 and 1870—is still debated and must be seen in the larger context of all types of slaving in Africa in the same period. A major unknown—for both the occidental and the oriental trades—is the number of slaves who died under the brutal conditions to which they were subjected when captured and transported overland and by sea. The most reliable estimates pertain only to those slaves who actually landed abroad, and these estimates are more reliable for the occidental trade than for the older, smaller, and more dispersed oriental trade. As Table 19–1 shows, just those who actually reached an American or Old World destination in the occidental trade totaled more than eleven million souls.

Recent scholarship estimates that at a minimum Africa lost some thirteen million people to the Atlantic trade alone during its four centuries of existence. Another five million or more were lost to the oriental trade. Finally, the occidental trade spurred an apparently huge increase in internal slavery, and according to the estimate of one expert, an additional fifteen million people were enslaved within African societies themselves.[6]

Consequences of the Slave Trade for Africa

The statistics in the previous section hint at the massive impact slave trading had on African life and history. Still, the question of the actual effects remains difficult and disputed. Modern scholarship has tended to emphasize the importance for African history of the coming of the maritime European powers in general and the Atlantic slave trade in particular. Regarding the slave trade, it is safe to say that the impact was considerable, however much that general conclusion must be qualified in the light of particular cases. Consider some examples.

We do not know for certain if the Atlantic trade brought net population loss or gain to specific areas of West Africa. The wide and rapid spread of maize and cassava cultivation

Estimated Slave Imports into the Americas and Old World by Region, 1451–1870	
British North America	523,000
Spanish America	1,687,000
British Caribbean	2,443,000
French Caribbean	1,655,000
Dutch Caribbean	500,000
Danish Caribbean	50,000
Brazil (Portuguese)	4,190,000
Old World	297,000
Total	**11,345,000**

Figures as calculated by James A. Rawley, *The Transatlantic Slave Trade: A History* (New York: W. W. Norton, 1981), p. 428, based on his and other more recent revisions of the careful but older estimates of Philip D. Curtin, *The Atlantic Slave Trade: A Census* (Madison: University of Wisconsin Press, 1969), especially pp. 266, 268.

in forest regions after these plants had been imported from the Americas may have fueled African population increases that offset regional human loss through slaving. We know, however, that slaving took away many of the strongest young men in many areas and, in the oriental-trade zones, most of the young women.

Similarly, we do not know if more slaves were captured as byproducts of local wars or from pure slave raiding, but we do know they were captured and removed from their societies.

Nor do we know if slaving always inhibited development of trade or perhaps sometimes stimulated it because commerce in a range of African products—from ivory to wood and hides—often accompanied that in slaves. Still, we do know that in general, the exchange of productive human beings for money or goods that were generally not used to build a productive economy was a great loss for African society as a whole.

Finally, because we do not yet have accurate estimates of the total population of Africa at different times over the four centuries of the Atlantic slave trade, we cannot determine with certainty its demographic impact. We can, however, make some educated guesses. If, for example, tropical Africa had possibly fifty million inhabitants in 1600, it would then have had 30 percent of the combined population of the Americas, the Middle East, Europe, and Africa. If in 1900, after the depredations of the slave trade, it had seventy million inhabitants, its population would have dropped to only slightly more than 10 percent of the combined population of the same world regions. Accordingly, current best estimates indicate that overall African population growth suffered significantly as a result of the devastating numbers of people lost to enslavement or to the increased warfare and decreased birth-rate tied to the slave trade. Figures like these also give some idea of slavery's probable impact on

[5]Rawley, p. 429; Curtin, p. 268.
[6]Manning, pp. 37, 170–171.

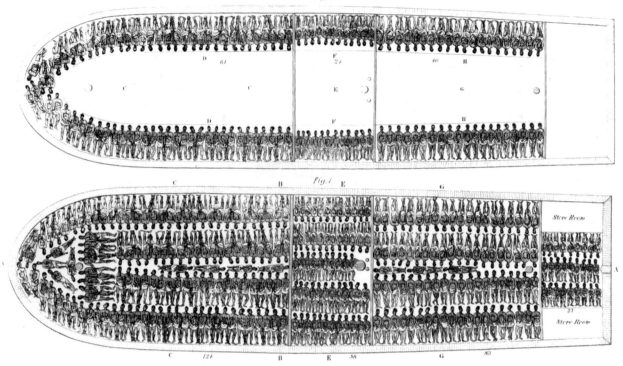

Loading plan for the main decks of the 320-ton slave ship Brookes. The Brookes was only 25 feet wide and 100 feet long, but as many as 609 slaves were crammed on board for the nightmarish passage to the Americas. The average space allowed each person was only about 78 inches by 16 inches. [Photographs and Prints Division, Schomburg Center for Research in Black Culture, The New York Public Library, Astor, Lenox, and Tilder Foundations]

Africa's ability to keep up with the modern industrializing world.[7]

It is important to remember that even in West and central Africa, which bore the brunt of the Atlantic trade, its impact and the response to it were so varied in different places and times that even accurate overall statistics could be misleading for particular cases. In a few cases, kingdoms such as Dahomey (the present Republic of Benin) seem to have sought and derived immense economic profit for a time by making slaving a state monopoly. Other kingdoms, such as Benin, sought to stay almost completely out of slaving and derived no gain from it. In many instances, including the rise of Asante power or the fall of the Yoruba Oyo empire, it now appears that increased slaving was in part a result as well as a cause of regional instability and change. Increased warfare meant increased prisoners to be enslaved and a surplus to be sold off; however, whether slaving gave good cause for war is still a major question in each regional context.

Similarly, if one can establish, as seems evident, a major increase in indigenous slavery as a result of the external trade

to occident and orient during the centuries in question, we have to assume major social consequences for African society as a whole, but the specific consequences would differ according to the specifics of regional situations. For example, in West Africa relatively more men were taken as slaves than women, whereas in the Sahelian Sudanic regions relatively more women than men were taken. In the west the loss of so many men increased the pressures for polygamy and possibly the regional use of women slaves as well, whereas in the Sahelian Sudanic regions the loss of women may have stimulated polyandry and reduced the birthrate significantly.

Even though slavery existed previously in Africa, the scale of the Atlantic trade was unprecedented and hence had an unprecedented impact on indigenous social, political, and economic realities. In general, the slave trade measurably changed patterns of life and balances of power in the main affected areas, whether by stimulating trade or warfare (or at least raiding for new supplies), by disrupting previous market and political structures, by substantially increasing slavery inside Africa, or by disturbing the male-female ratio (and hence the work-force balance and birthrate patterns) and consequently the basic social institution of monogamous marriage.

[7]On all of the preceding points regarding probable impact of the trade, see Manning, pp. 126–148, 168–176.

If the overseas slave trade did not substantially and irrevocably change every region it touched, at the least it siphoned indigenous energy into ultimately counterproductive or destructive directions. This, in turn, meant the inhibition of true economic development, especially in central and coastal West Africa. The Atlantic slave trade must by any standard be described as one of the most tragic aspects of European involvement in Africa.

IN WORLD PERSPECTIVE

The Transatlantic Economy

The contact between the native peoples of the American continents and the European explorers of the fifteenth and sixteenth centuries transformed world history. In the Americas, the native peoples—whose ancestors had migrated from Asia millennia before—had established a wide variety of civilizations. Some of their most remarkable architectural monuments and cities were constructed during the very centuries when European civilizations were reeling from the collapse of Roman power. Until the European explorations, the civilizations of the Americas and the civilizations of Eurasia and Africa had had no significant contact with each other.

Within half a century of the landing of Columbus, millions of America's native peoples in Florida, the Caribbean islands, Mesoamerica, and South America had encountered Europeans intent on conquest, exploitation, and religious conversion. Because of their advanced weapons, navies, and the new diseases they brought with them, as well as internal divisions among the Native Americans, the Europeans were able to achieve a rapid conquest. Thereafter, Spain and Portugal dominated Latin America, and England, France, and Holland set out to settle North America.

In both North and South America economies of exploitation were established. The Europeans were generally determined to do little labor themselves. In Latin America various institutions were developed to extract native labor. From the mid-Atlantic English colonies through the Caribbean and into Brazil a long corridor of slave-labor plantation systems was established. The slaves were forcibly imported from Africa and sold in America to plantation owners. The economies and peoples of Europe, Africa, and the Americas were thus drawn into a vast worldwide web of production based on slave labor.

The impact of slavery in the Americas was not limited to the life of the black slaves. Whites in the New World numbered about twelve million in 1820, compared to some six million blacks. However, up to that time only about two million whites had migrated there, compared to some eleven million or more Africans forcibly imported as slaves. Such numbers reveal the effects of brutal slave work conditions and the high mortality and sharply reduced birthrates of slave populations relative to those of the white free populations.

None of these statistics, however, enables us to assess adequately the role that slavery has played in the Americas or, in particular, the United States. The United States actually received only a bit more than a quarter as many slaves as did Brazil alone or the British and French Caribbean regions together, yet the consequences of the forced migration of just over a half-million Africans have been and remain massive. Consider just the American Civil War and the endurance of societal racism and inequality or, more positively, the African contribution to American industrial development, language, music, literature, and artistic culture. The Atlantic slave trade's impact has been and continues to be felt at both ends of the original "trade."

Review Questions ———

1. How were small groups of Spaniards able to conquer the Aztec and Inca empires?

2. What was the basis of the mercantilist theory of economics? What was the relationship between the colonial economies and those of the homelands?

3. Describe the economies of Spanish America and Brazil. What were the similarities and differences between them and the British and French colonies in the Caribbean and North America? What role did the various colonies play in the transatlantic economy?

4. Why did forced labor and slavery develop in tropical colonies? How was slavery in the Americas different from slavery in earlier societies?

5. What was the effect of the transatlantic slave trade on West African societies? On east Africa? What role did Africans themselves play in the slave trade?

Suggested Readings ———

P. BAKEWELL, *A History of Latin America* (1997). A recent accessible survey.

L. BETHWELL, *The Cambridge History of Latin America*, Vols. 1 and 2 (1984). Excellent essays by leading scholars.

B. COBO, *History of the Inca Empire* (1979). A major discussion.

G. A. COLLIER, R. I. ROSALDO, AND J. D. WIRTH, *The Inca and Aztec States 1400–1800* (1982). An important collection of advanced essays.

M. CRATON, ED., *Roots and Branches: Current Directions in Slave Studies* (1979). Diverse articles by scholars such as Curtin and Lovejoy; note especially those on the European plantation system by S.M. Greenfield.

P. D. CURTIN, *The Atlantic Slave Trade: A Census* (1969). Still a basic work, and useful for an overview of the trade, even though figures in many areas have since been refined or amended by other work.

P. D. CURTIN, *Economic Change in Precolonial Africa: Senegambia on the Eve of the Slave Trade.* (1975) The chapter on slave trading is an illuminating treatment of the topic with respect to one area of Africa.

D. B. DAVIS, *The Problem of Slavery in Western Culture* (1966). A brilliant and far-ranging discussion.

H. A. GEMERY AND J. S. HOGENDORN, EDS., *The Uncommon Market: Essays in the Economic History of the Atlantic Slave Trade* (1979). Useful statistics on trans-Saharan and particular African regions of the Atlantic slave trade.

C. GIBSON, *The Aztecs Under Spanish Rule: A History of the Native Americans of the Valley of Mexico* (1964). An exceedingly interesting book.

C. GIBSON, *Spain in America* (1966). A splendidly clear and balanced discussion.

S. GRUZINSKI, *The Conquest of Mexico: The Incorporation of Indian Societies into the Western World, 16th–18th Centuries* (1993). Interprets the experience of native Americans, from their own point of view, during the time of the Spanish conquest.

L. HANKE, *Bartolomé de Las Casas: An Interpretation of His Life and Writings* (1951). A classic work.

J. HEMMING, *The Conquest of the Incas,* (1970). A lucid account of the conquest of the Inca Empire and its aftermath.

J. HEMMING, *Red Gold: The Conquest of the Brazilian Native Americans, 1500–1760 (1978).* A careful account with excellent bibliography.

M. LEON-PORTILLA, ED., *The Broken Spears: The Aztec Account of the Conquest of Mexico* (1961). A collection of documents recounting the experience of the Aztecs from their own point of view.

J. LOCKHARDT AND S. B. SCHWARTZ, *Early Latin America: A History of Colonial Spanish America and Brazil* (1983). The new standard work.

J. R. MCNEIL, *Atlantic Empires of France and Spain: Louisbourg and Havana, 1700–1763* (1985). An examination of imperial policies in terms of two key overseas outposts.

P. MANNING, *Slavery and African Life: Occidental, Oriental, and African Slave Trades* (1990). An admirably concise yet probing and careful economic-historical synthesis of the evidence, with multiple tables and statistics to supplement the magisterial analysis. An indispensible attempt at presenting the "big picture" of African slavery.

S. W. MINTZ, *Sweetness and Power: The Place of Sugar in Modern History* (1985). Traces the role of sugar in the world economy and sugar's impact on world culture.

A. PAGDEN, *Lords of All the World: Ideologies of Empire in Spain, Britain, and France c. 1500–c. 1800* (1955). An effort to explain the imperial thinking of the major European powers.

R. PARES, *War and Trade in the West Indies* (1936). Relates the West Indies to Britain's larger commercial and naval concerns.

J. H. PARRY, *Trade and Dominion: The European Overseas Empires in the Eighteenth Century* (1971). A comprehensive account with attention to the European impact on the rest of the world.

J. A. Rawley, *The Transatlatic Slave Trade: A History* (1981). Impressively documented, detailed, and well-presented survey history of the Atlantic trade; little focus on African dimensions.

C. D. Rice, *The Rise and Fall of Black Slavery* (1975). An excellent survey of the subject with careful attention to the numerous historiographical controversies.

S. B. Schwartz, *Sugar Plantations in the Formation of Brazilian Society: Bahia, 1550–1835* (1985). A broad-ranging study of the emergence of the plantation economy.

I. K. Steele, *The English Atlantic, 1675–1740s: An Exploration of Communication and Community* (1986). An exploration of culture and commerce in the transatlantic world.

R. L. Stein, *The French Sugar Business in the Eighteenth Century* (1988). A study that covers all aspects of the French sugar trade.

S. J. Stein, *Peru's Indian Peoples and the Challenge of Spanish Conquest: Huamanga to 1640* (1933). A work that examines the impact of the conquest of the Inca empire over the scope of a century.

H. Thomas, *Conquest: Montezuma, Cortés, and the Fall of Old Mexico* (1993). A splendid modern narrative of the event with careful attention to the character of the participants.

J. Thornton, *Africa and Africans in the Making of the Atlantic World, 1400–1680* (1992). A discussion of the role of Africans in the emergence of the transatlantic economy.

N. Wachtel, *The Vision of the Vanquished: The Spanish Conquest of Peru Through Indian Eyes, 1530–1570* (1977). A presentation of Incan experience of conquest.

20 EAST ASIA IN THE LATE TRADITIONAL ERA

Detail of Ming ceramic. In East Asia ceramics are a major art form like painting, calligraphy, and poetry. Connoisseurs see the Sung dynasty as the peak of ceramic art, but relatively few pots of that age have survived and they are mostly in museum collections. Collectors usually focus on Ming and Ch'ing products. Their volume and variety was great and the quality still high. Some pots were a chaste blue and white. Some others, which were imitated by the nascent ceramic industry in Europe, were decorated with flowers and colorful scenes. The detail from the pot shown here is unusually vigorous and bright. [Museum of Oriental Ceramics, Osaka]

CHAPTER TOPICS

LATE IMPERIAL CHINA

◆ Ming (1368–1644) and Ch'ing (1644–1911) Dynasties

JAPAN

◆ Warring States Era (1467–1600)

◆ Tokugawa Era (1600–1868)

KOREA AND VIETNAM

◆ Korea

◆ Vietnam

In World Perspective Late Traditional East Asia

One difficulty in comparing East Asian countries is that although they shared many cultural elements, they were so different in their institutions and history. Their cultural affinity is immediately apparent if we look at Chinese, Japanese, Korean, and Vietnamese paintings side by side. Less visible, but no less basic, was a range of social values shared at least by their elites. To the extent that it was based on Confucianism, the similarity may have been greatest in the mid-nineteenth century, when Japan, Korea, and Vietnam had become more Confucian than ever before.

But when we compare their histories and institutions, the similarities diminish. China and Japan were furthest apart. Each had gone its own way. Korea and Vietnam, even while forging an identity in reaction to China, were more directly influenced by China in their history and closer to China in their culture and institutions.

For China, the Ming (1368–1644) dynasties and the Ch'ing (1644–1911) were just two more centralized bureaucratic regimes of a kind that had been

in place for centuries. In the T'ang (618–907) the Chinese had forged a pattern of government so efficient and so closely geared to the deeper familial and educational constitution of the society that, thereafter, they rebuilt it after each dynastic breakdown. This pattern continued during the Ming and the Ch'ing, giving their histories a recognizable cyclical cast, even though they are also replete with historical trends that cut across dynastic lines.

Japanese political history, in contrast, is not cyclical. Each period of Japanese history reflects a new and different configuration. The centralized governments of the Nara and early Heian gave way to a manorial social order in which a powerful, local warrior class emerged. From this "feudal" class arose first the Kamakura *bakufu*, and then the Ashikaga. These in turn were followed by an era of warring states and then a lengthy period of centralized "feudalism." Superficially at least, Japan's history was more like that of Europe than of China. Neither Europe nor Japan ever found a pattern of rule that worked so well, was so satisfactory to the rulers,

and was so deeply embedded in the institutions of the society that it was recreated over and over again. In fact, from a Japanese or European point of view, that is not how history works.

This chapter underlines the dynamism of both China and Japan during these late centuries. "Late traditional society" does not mean "late static society." In both countries the society became more integrated and the apparatus of government became more sophisticated than ever before. These advances shaped Chinese and Japanese responses to the West during the nineteenth century. Even Korea and Vietnam did not lack dynamism. But we must also note that during these centuries the West was transformed. In fact, Greece and Rome apart, most of what seems important in Western history—the Renaissance, the Reformation, the scientific revolution, the formation of nation-states, the industrial revolution, the Enlightenment, and the democratic revolution—happened while the Ming and the Ch'ing dynasties were reigning in China. As we view East Asia from the perspective of Europe, it appears to have been caught in a tar pit of slow motion. But it was actually the West that had accelerated.

LATE IMPERIAL CHINA

Ming (1368–1644) and Ch'ing (1644–1911) Dynasties

The Ming and the Ch'ing were China's last dynasties. The first was Chinese, the second a dynasty of conquest in which the ruling house and an important segment of the military were foreign (Manchus). They were nevertheless remarkably similar in their institutions and pattern of rule, so much so that historians sometimes speak of "Ming-Ch'ing despotism" as if it were a single system. The two dynasties are also coupled as a result of certain demographic and economic trends that began during the Ming and continued through the Ch'ing.

Land and People

China's population doubled from about 60 million in 1368 at the start of the Ming dynasty to about 125 million in 1644 at its end. The population then tripled during the early and middle Ch'ing dynasty, reaching about 410 million people several decades into the mid-nineteenth century. This population density stimulated the growth of commerce and also gave new prominence to the scholar-gentry class.

Population growth was paralleled by an increase in the food supply. During the Ming, the spread of Sung agricultural technology and new strains of rice accounted for 40 percent of the higher yields, and newly cultivated lands accounted for the rest. During the Ch'ing, half the increased food supply was due to new lands and the other half to better seeds, fertilizers, and irrigation. New crops introduced from America during the late Ming, such as maize, sweet potatoes, and peanuts (which could be planted on dry sandy uplands and were not competitive with rice), also bolstered the food supply. By the nineteenth century maize was grown in all parts of China.

In north China the population had declined from 32 million to 11 million during the Mongol conquests. The Ming government repopulated its open lands, resettling villages, building water control systems, and reopening the Grand Canal in 1415. The movement of people to the north continued until the nineteenth century. In the north, most farmers owned the land they worked and at times used hired labor. The land consisted mainly of irrigated dry fields, and the chief crops were millet, sorghum, and wheat.

South and southwest China also saw an influx of migrants from the densely populated lower Yangtze region, many set-tling in hilly or mountainous border areas that were agriculturally marginal. The White Lotus Rebellion of 1796–1804 occurred in such a recently settled area far from centers of governmental authority. The Miao Wars of the late eighteenth century also were precipitated by the movement of Chinese settlers into southwestern uplands previously left to the slash-and-burn agriculture of the Miao tribes. Other Chinese crossed over to Taiwan or emigrated overseas. During the Ch'ing dynasty, large Chinese mercantile communities became established in Southeast Asia.

The Yangtze basin, meanwhile, became even more densely populated. The Lower Yangtze region and the delta, well supplied with waterways, had long been the rice basket of China, but from the late Ming agricultural cash crops, such as silk and cotton, predominated. Cotton was so widely grown in the delta that food had to be brought in from other areas by the early nineteenth century. In the lower Yangtze absentee landlords owned almost half of the land. A typical landlord's holdings were subdivided among tenants, who paid fixed rents in kind. South China also had extensive absentee landlordism, but far more land was owned collectively by clans, which managed the land and distributed rents among their members.

There are many unanswered questions regarding the population growth during these six centuries. Was there a decline in the death rate and, if so, why? Or was it simply that new lands and technology enabled more mouths to be fed? Did the population oblige by promptly increasing? Certainly the Ming-Ch'ing era was the longest continuous period of good government in Chinese history. The good years of Ming rule were longer than such periods in earlier dynasties, and the transition to Ch'ing rule was quicker and less destructive. How much did these long periods of good government contribute to the population growth? Epidemic disease was not absent. In the great plagues from 1586 to 1589 and from 1639 to 1644, as many as 20 to 30 percent of the people died in the most populous regions of China, and in specific counties and villages the figure was often higher. Another epidemic occurred in 1756 and a cholera epidemic from 1820 to 1822. The growth of China's population more than overcame such losses. Because of the growth in agriculture and population, most accounts view the eighteenth century as the most prosperous in Chinese history. But by the early nineteenth century the Chinese standard of living may have begun to decline. Ever increasing numbers of people were no blessing.

China's Third Commercial Revolution

Commerce in China flourished between 300 B.C.E. and 220 C.E. (the late Chou through the Han dynasties), only to decline in the centuries of disunity that followed. In Chapter 7 we read Ssu-ma Ch'ien's description of wealthy Han mer-

"Fishermen on Autumn River," a Ming dynasty scroll painting by Tai Ch'in (1390–1460). [Courtesy of Freer Gallery of Art, Smithsonian Institution, Washington, D.C.]

chants. Between 850 and 1250 (Late T'ang through Sung) commerce again surged, only to contract during the Mongol conquest. At the end of the Mongol dynasty, warlords confiscated merchant wealth. Early Ming emperors, isolationist and agrarian in orientation, restricted the use of foreign goods, required licenses for junks, and attempted to encase foreign trade within the constraints of the tribute system. The early Ming also operated government monopolies that stifled enterprise and depressed the southeastern coastal region by their restrictions on maritime trade and shipping. In the mid-sixteenth century commerce started to grow again, buoyed by the surge of population and agriculture and aided by a relaxation of government controls. If the growth during the Han and Sung dynasties may be called China's first and second commercial revolutions, respectively, then the expansion between 1500 and 1800 was the third. This revolution was partly the extension to other parts of China of changes begun earlier in the Yangtze area, but it had new features as well. By the early nineteenth century China was the most highly commercialized nonindustrial society in the world.

One stimulus to commerce was imported silver, which played the role in the Ming-Ch'ing economy that copper cash had played in the Sung dynasty. The Chinese balance of trade was favorable. Beginning in the mid-sixteenth century silver from mines in western Japan entered China, and from the 1570s Spanish galleons sailing from Acapulco to China via Manila brought in Mexican and Peruvian silver. In exchange, Chinese silks and porcelains were vended in the shops of Mexico City. The late Ming court also opened silver mines in Kweichow and Yunnan provinces. In the eighteenth century copper mines were opened in South China. Also, private

"Shensi banks" opened branches throughout China to facilitate the transfer of funds from one area to another and extended credit for trade. Eventually they opened offices in Singapore, Japan, and Russia, as well.

As in Europe, so in China, the influx of silver and the overall increase in liquidity led to inflation and commercial growth. The price of land rose steadily. During the sixteenth century the thirty or forty early Ming taxes on land that were payable in grain, labor service, and cash were consolidated into one tax payable in silver, the so-called Single Whip Reform. To obtain the silver, farmers sold their grain in the market, and some switched from grain to cash crops. Moreover, by the early nineteenth century there were six times as many farm families as in the mid-fourteenth century.

Urban growth between 1500 and 1800, responding to flourishing local markets, was mainly at the level of intermediate market towns. These towns grew more rapidly than the population as a whole and provided the link between the local markets and the larger provincial capitals and cities, such as Peking, Hangchow, or Canton. The commercial integration of local, intermediate, and large cities was not entirely new, having occurred during the Sung dynasty in the lower Yangtze region. But now it spread over all of China. Interregional trade also gained. Where Sung trade between regions was mainly in luxury goods such as silk, lacquerware, porcelains, medicines, and paintings, early Ch'ing traders also dealt in staples, such as grain, timber, salt, iron, and cotton. Not that China developed a national economy. Seven or eight regional economies, each the size of a large European nation, were still the focus for most economic activity. But a new level of trade developed among them, especially where water

The Thin Horse Market[1]

In China, ancestors without descendants to perform the rites ran the danger of becoming hungry ghosts or wandering spirits. Consequently, having a son who would continue the family line was an act of filial piety. If a wife failed to produce an heir, an official, merchant, or wealthy landowner might take a concubine and try again. Or he might do so simply because he was able to, because it gave him pleasure, and because it was socially acceptable. For a poor peasant household, after a bad harvest and faced with high taxes, the sale of a comely daughter often seemed preferable to the sale of ancestral land.

Concubines usually had no choice in the matter. But neither did many brides in premodern China. Was a woman better off as the wife of a poor peasant, experiencing hardship, hunger, and want, or as the concubine in a wealthy household with servants, good food, and the likelihood that her children would receive an education? What does the following passage tell us about attitudes toward women in premodern China?

Upwards of a hundred people in Yangzhou earn a living in the "thin horse" business. If someone shows an interest in taking a concubine, a team of a broker, a drudge, and a scout stick to him like flies. Early in the morning, the teams gather to wait outside the doors of potential customers, who usually give their business to the first team to arrive. Any teams coming late have to wait for the next opportunity. The winning team then leads their customer to the broker's house. The customer is then served tea and seated to wait for the women. The broker leads out each of them, who do what the matchmaker tells them to do. After each of her short commands, the woman bows to the customer, walks forward, turns toward the light so the customer can see her face clearly, draws back her sleeves to show him her hands, glances shyly at him to show her eyes, says her age so he can hear her voice, and finally lifts her skirt to reveal whether her feet are bound. An experienced customer could figure out the size of her feet by listening to the noise she made as she entered the room. If her skirt made noise when she walked in, she had to have a pair of big feet under her skirt. As one woman finishes, another comes out, each house having at least five or six. If the customer finds a woman to his liking, he puts a gold hairpin in her hair at the temple, a procedure called "inserting the ornament." If no one satisfies him, he gives a few hundred cash to the broker or the servants.

If the first broker gets tired, others will willingly take his place. Even if a customer has the stamina to keep looking for four or five days, he cannot finish visiting all the houses. Nevertheless, after seeing fifty to sixty white-faced, red-dressed women, they all begin to look alike and he cannot decide which are pretty or ugly. It is like the difficulty of recognizing a character after writing it hundreds or thousands of times. Therefore, the customer usually chooses someone once his mind and eyes can no longer discriminate. The owner of the woman brings out a piece of red paper on which are listed the "betrothal presents," including gold jewelry and cloth. Once he agrees to the deal, he is sent home. Before he even arrives back at his lodgings, a band and a load of food and wine are already waiting there. Before long, presents he was to send are prepared and sent back with the band. Then a sedan chair and all the trimmings—colorful lanterns, happy candles, attendants, sacrificial foods—wait outside for the customer's arrangement. The cooks and the entertainer for the wedding celebration also arrive together with foods, wine, candy, tables, chairs, and tableware. Without the customer's order, the colorful sedan chair for the girl and the small sedan chair for her companion are dispatched to get the girl. The new concubine performs the bowing ceremony with music and singing and considerable clamor. The next morning before noon the laborers ask for rewards from the man, then leave to prepare another wedding for another customer in the same manner.

[1]A horse market is for the sale of horses. A "thin horse" market is the market for concubines. The name implies a measure of criticism.

transport made such trade economical. A final feature of eighteenth-century Chinese economic life was the so-called "putting out" system in textiles, under which merchant capitalists organized and financed each stage of production from fiber to dyed cloth.

Women and the Commercial Revolution   The Confucian family ideal changed little during the Ming and Ch'ing dynasties. A woman was expected first to obey her parents, then her husband, and finally her son—when he became the new family head. Physically, women became more restricted. Footbinding, which had begun among the elite during the Sung dynasty, spread through the upper classes during the Ming and to some commoners during the mid to late Ch'ing. Most girls were subjected to this cruel and deformative procedure. Even in villages, women with big—that is to say, normal feet—were sometimes considered unmarriageable. One exception to the rule was the Hakka people of south China. Hakka women with unbound feet worked in the fields alongside their male kinsmen. Another exception was the Manchus. One Manchu (Ch'ing) emperor even issued an edict banning footbinding, but it was ignored by the Chinese.

As population grew and the size of the average landholding shrunk, growing numbers of women worked at home, spinning, weaving, and making other products for the burgeoning commercial markets. As the woman's contribution to the household income grew, her voice in household decisions often became larger than Confucian doctrines would suggest. But the same commercial revolution also increased the number of rich townsmen who could afford concubines and patronize tea houses, restaurants, and brothels.

Political System

One might expect these massive demographic and economic changes to have produced, if not a bourgeois revolution, at least some profound change in the political superstructure of China. They did not. Government during the Ming and Ch'ing was much like that of the Sung or Yuan, only improved and made stronger. Historians sometimes describe it as the "perfected" late imperial system. This system, they argue, was able to contain and use the new economic energies that destroyed the weaker late-feudal polities of Europe. The sources of strength of the perfected Ming-Ch'ing system were the spread of education, the use of Confucianism as an ideology, a stronger emperor, better government finances, more competent officials, and a larger gentry class with an expanded role in local society.

Role of Confucianism   Confucian teachings were more widespread in late imperial China than ever before. There were more schools in villages and towns. Academies preparing candidates for the civil service examinations multiplied. Publishing flourished, bookstores abounded, and literacy outpaced population. The Confucian view of society was patriarchal. The family, headed by the father, was the basic unit. The emperor, the son of heaven and the ruler-father of the empire, stood at its apex. In between were the district magistrates, the "father-mother officials." The idea of the state as the family writ large was not just a matter of metaphor but carried with it duties and obligations that were binding at every level.

The sociopolitical worldview of Confucianism was also buttressed by Neo-Confucian metaphysics, which gave a unitary character to Ming and Ch'ing culture. This is not, of course, to deny the existence of different schools of Confucian thought. The vitality of late Ming thinkers was especially notable. Still, in comparison to Europe, where religious philosophies were less involved with the state and where a revolution in science was reshaping both religious and political doctrines, the greater unity and integration of the Chinese worldview cannot be denied.

Emperor   In Ming-Ch'ing times the emperor was stronger than ever. The Secretariat of high officials that had coordinated government affairs during the Sung and the Yuan was abolished by the first Ming emperor, who himself made all important and many unimportant decisions. His successors, often aided by Grand Secretaries, continued this pattern of direct, personal rule. During the late fourteenth and fifteenth centuries the emperor was the bottleneck official, without whose active participation the business of government would bog down.

Then, during the sixteenth and early seventeenth centuries, a series of emperors appeared who were not interested in government. One spent his days on wine, women, and sports; another on Taoist rites; and still another emperor, who never learned to write, passed his days making furniture. During this era the emperor's authority was exercised either by Grand Secretaries or by eunuchs. But the Ch'ing reestablished the pattern of personal government by emperors.

Emperors wielded despotic powers at their courts. They had personal secret police and prisons where those who gave even minor offense might be cruelly tortured. Even high officials might suffer the humiliating, and sometimes fatal, punishment of having their bared buttocks beaten with bamboo rods at court—a practice inherited from the Mongols. The dedication and loyalty even of officials who were cruelly mistreated attest to the depth of their Confucian ethical formation. One censor who had served three emperors ran afoul of a powerful eunuch. The eunuch obtained an imperial order and had the official tortured to death in 1625. In his deathbed notes to his sons, the official blamed the villain for his agonies but wrote that he welcomed death because his body belonged to his "ruler-father." An earlier mid-sixteenth century incident involved Hai Jui, the most famous censor of the Ming period:

> Hai presented himself at the palace gate to submit a memorial denouncing some of the emperor's notorious idiosyncrasies. The emperor flew into a rage and ordered that Hai not be permitted to escape. "Never fear, sire," the eunuch go-between told the emperor. "He has said goodbye to his family, has brought his coffin with him, and waits at the gate!" Shih-tsung [the emperor] was so taken aback by this news that he forgave Hai for his impertinence.[1]

[1]C. O. Hucker, *China's Imperial Past* (Stanford: Stanford University Press, 1975), p. 206.

During the Ch'ing the life-and-death authority of emperors did not diminish, but officials were generally better treated. As foreign rulers, the Manchu emperors took care not to alienate Chinese officials.

The Forbidden Palace in Peking, rebuilt when the third Ming emperor moved the capital from Nanking to Peking, was an icon of the emperor's majesty. Unlike the Kremlin, which consists of an assortment of buildings inside a wall, the entire palace complex in Peking focused on the single figure of the ruler. Designed geometrically, its massive outer and inner walls and vast courtyards progress stage by stage to the raised area of the audience hall. During the T'ang, emperors had sat together with their grand councilors while discussing matters of government. In the Sung, officials stood in his presence. By the Ming, the emperor sat on an elevated dais above the officials, who knelt before him. Behind the audience hall were the emperor's private chambers and his harem. In 1425 the palace had 6,300 cooks serving 10,000 persons daily. These numbers later increased. By the seventeenth century there were 9,000 palace ladies and perhaps 70,000 eunuchs. The glory of the emperor extended to his family, whose members were awarded vast estates in North China.

Bureaucracy A second component of the Ming-Ch'ing system was the government itself. The formal organization of offices was little different from that in the T'ang or the Sung. At the top were the military, the censorate, and the administrative branch, and beneath the administration were the six ministries and the web of provincial, prefectural, and district offices. But government was better financed than under earlier dynasties. The productivity of China became steadily greater, whereas the apparatus of government grew only slowly. Government finances had ups and downs, but as late as the 1580s huge surpluses were still accumulated at both the central and the provincial levels. These surpluses probably braked the process of dynastic decline. Only during the last fifty years of the Ming did soaring military expenses bankrupt government finances.

Then, in the second half of the seventeenth century the Manchus reestablished a strong central government and restored the flow of taxes to levels close to those of the Ming. In fact, revenues were so ample that early in the eighteenth century the emperors were able to freeze taxes on agriculture at the 1711 level and fix quotas for each province.

This contributed to the general prosperity of the eighteenth century but led to problems during the nineteenth century. Because agricultural productivity continued to rise, even though local officials collected some of the surplus, fixed quotas meant a declining share of the product. Both cultivators and gentry probably benefited from the new wealth, with the latter obtaining the larger share.

If the Ming-Ch'ing system can be spoken of as perfected, the good government it brought to China was largely a product of the ethical commitment and the exceptional ability of its officials. No officials in the world today approach in power or prestige those of the Ming and the Ch'ing. When the Portuguese arrived early in the sixteenth century, they called these officials "mandarins." (This term began as a Sanskrit word for "counselor" that became Hindi, entered Malay, and was then picked up by the Portuguese and adopted by other Europeans.) As in the Sung, the rewards of an official career were so great that the competition to enter it was intense. As population grew and schools increased, entrance became even more competitive.

After being screened at the district office, a candidate first took the county examination. If he passed he became a mem-

The dilapidated remains of the examination stalls at Nanking. Doors to individual cubicles can be seen to the right and left of the three-story gate. Thousands of such cubicles made up the old examination stalls. Those who passed the exams governed China. [The Bettmann Archive]

The Seven Transformations of an Examination Candidate

The Chinese civil-service examination was a grueling ordeal. Like a chess tournament, it required physical strength. Chinese critics said, "To pass the provincial examination a man needed the spiritual strength of a dragon-horse, the physique of a donkey, the insensitivity of a wood louse, and the endurance of a camel." The following selection is by a seventeenth-century writer who never succeeded in passing.

Is the style of this passage overdone or effective? What is distinctively Chinese about it?

When he first enters the examination compound and walks along, panting under his heavy load of luggage, he is just like a beggar. Next, while undergoing the personal body search and being scolded by the clerks and shouted at by the soldiers, he is just like a prisoner. When he finally enters his cell and, along with the other candidates, stretches his neck to peer out, he is just like the larva of a bee.

When the examination is finished at last and he leaves, his mind in a haze and his legs tottering, he is just like a sick bird that has been released from a cage. While he is wondering when the results will be announced and waiting to learn whether he passed or failed, so nervous that he is startled even by the rustling of the trees and the grass and is unable to sit or stand still, his restlessness is like that of a monkey on a leash. When at last the results are announced and he has definitely failed, he loses his vitality like one dead, rolls over on his side, and lies there without moving, like a poisoned fly. Then, when he pulls himself together and stands up, he is provoked by every sight and sound, gradually flings away everything within his reach, and complains of the illiteracy of the examiners. When he calms down at last, he finds everything in the room broken. At this time he is like a pigeon smashing its own precious eggs. These are the seven transformations of a candidate.

From I. Miyazaki, *China's Examination Hell*, trans. by C. Schirokauer. Copyright © 1976 Weatherhill, pp. 57–58.

---

ber of the gentry. He gained the cap and sash of the scholar and exemption from state labor service. Even this examination required years of arduous study. About half a million passed each year. The second hurdle was the provincial examination held every third year. Only one in a hundred or more was successful. The final hurdle was the metropolitan examination, also held triennially. During the Ming fewer than ninety passed each year. As in earlier dynasties, regional quotas were set to prevent the Yangtze region from dominating the officialdom.

Gentry   A final component in the Ming-Ch'ing system—if not new, at least vastly more significant than in earlier dynasties—was the gentry class. It was an intermediate layer between the elite bureaucracy above and the village below. The lowest level of bureaucratic government was the office of the district magistrate. Although the population increased six-fold during the Ming and the Ch'ing, the number of district magistrates increased only from 1,171 to 1,470. Thus the average district, which had had a population of 50,000 in the early Ming and 100,000 in the late Ming, had two or three times that number by the early nineteenth century. The district magistrate came to his district as an outsider. The "law of avoidance," designed to prevent conflicts of interest, prevented him from serving in his home province. His office compound had a large staff of secretaries, advisers, specialists, clerks, and runners; but even then, he could not govern such a large population directly. To govern effectively, the magistrate had to obtain the cooperation of the local literati or gentry.

By *gentry* we do not mean a rural elite, like English squires. The Chinese gentry was largely urban, living in market towns or district seats. Socially and educationally, its members were of the same class as the magistrate—a world apart from clerks, runners, or village headmen. They usually owned land, which enabled them to avoid manual labor and to send their children to private academies. As absentee landlords whose lands were worked by sharecroppers, they were often exploitative; rebels at the end of the Ming attacked landlords as they did governmental offices. But the gentry were also local leaders. They represented community interests, which they interpreted conservatively, vis-à-vis the bureaucracy. They also performed quasi-official functions on behalf of their communities: maintaining schools and Confucian temples; repairing roads, bridges, canals, and dikes; and writing local histories.

The gentry class was the matrix from which officials arose; it was the local upholder of Confucian values. During the mid-nineteenth century, at a time of crisis, it would become the sustainer of the dynasty.

Pattern of Manchu Rule   The collapse of the Ming dynasty in 1644 and the establishment of Manchu rule was less of a break than might be imagined. First, the transition was short. Second, the Manchus, unlike the Mongols, were already partially Sinicized at the time of the conquest. They had been vassals of the Chinese state during the Ming, organized by tribal units into commanderies. Even before entering China, they had had the experience of ruling over Chinese who had settled in Manchuria to the north of the Great Wall.

In the late sixteenth century an extremely able leader unified the Manchurian tribes and proclaimed a new dynasty. While still based in Mukden, the dynasty established a Confucian government with six ministries, a censorate, and other Chinese institutions. When the Ming collapsed and rebel forces took over China, the Manchus presented themselves as the conservative upholders of the Confucian order. The Chinese gentry preferred the Manchus to Chinese rebel leaders, whom they regarded as bandits. After the Manchu conquest, a few scholars and officials became famous as Ming loyalists. Most, however, shifted their loyalty and served the new dynasty. The Ch'ing as a Chinese dynasty dates from 1644, when the capital was moved from Mukden to Peking. All of South China was taken by 1659, with the aid of Ming generals who switched their allegiance to the new regime.

As a tiny fraction of the Chinese population, the Manchus adopted institutions to maintain themselves as an ethnically separate elite group. One was their military organization. The basic unit was the banner—the unit took the name of its flag. There were eight Manchu banners, eight Mongol, and eight Chinese. There were more companies (of 300 men each) in the Manchu banners than in either of the other two; together with their steppe allies, the Mongols, the Manchus outnumbered the Chinese by more than two to one. Furthermore, the Chinese banners were mainly of Manchurian Chinese, who had been a part of the regime from its inception. Manchu garrison forces were segregated and were not under the jurisdiction of Chinese officials. They were given stipends and lands to cultivate. They were not permitted to marry Chinese, their children had to study Manchu, and they were not permitted to bind the feet of their daughters. In 1668 northern and central Manchuria were cordoned off by a willow palisade as a Manchu strategic tribal territory and closed to Chinese immigrants.

In addition to the Manchu banners, there were also Chinese constabulary forces known as "armies of the green standard." At first the distinction between the banners and the Chinese military was critical. Later, as the dynasty became Sinicized and accepted, the ethnic basis of its military strength became less important.

The second particular feature of Manchu government was what has been termed "dyarchy": the appointment of two persons, one Chinese and one Manchu, to each key post in the central government. Early in the dynasty the Chinese appointments were often bannermen or bondservants who were personally loyal to the Manchus. At the provincial level Chi-

The great Manchu emperor Ch'ien Lung (r. 1736–1795). [© Metropolitan Museum of Art, Rogers Fund, 1942 (42.141.8)]

nese governors were overseen by Manchu governor-generals. Beneath the governors most officials and virtually all district magistrates were Chinese.

Another strength of the Manchu dynasty was the long reigns of two extremely able emperors, K'ang Hsi (1661–1722) and Ch'ien Lung (1736–1795). K'ang Hsi was born in 1654, ten years after the start of the dynasty. He ascended the throne at the age of seven, began to rule at thirteen, and held sway until his death in 1722. He was a man of great vigor.

He rose at dawn to read memorials (official documents) before beginning his daily routine of audiences with officials. He sired thirty-six sons and twenty daughters by thirty consorts. He presided over palace examinations. Well versed in the Confucian classics, he won the support of scholars by his patronage of the *Ming History,* a new dictionary, and a 5,000-volume encyclopedia.

K'ang Hsi also displayed an interest in European science, which he studied with Jesuit court astronomers whom the Ch'ing had inherited from the Ming. He opened four ports to foreign trade and carried out public works, improving the dikes on the Huai and Yellow rivers and dredging the Grand Canal. During his reign he made six tours of China's southern provinces. K'ang Hsi, in short, was a model emperor. But he was also responsible for the various policies that sought to preserve a separate Manchu identity. Like Kublai Khan (r. 1271–1294) before him, he built a summer palace on the plains of Manchuria, where he hunted, hawked, and rode horseback with the freedom of a steppe lord.

Ch'ien Lung began his reign in 1736, fourteen years after the death of his grandfather K'ang Hsi, and ruled until 1795. During his reign the Ch'ing dynasty attained its highest level of prosperity and power. Like K'ang Hsi, he was strong, wise, conscientious, careful, and hard-working. He visited South China on inspection tours. He patronized scholars on a grand scale: His *Four Treasures* of the classics, history, letters, and philosophy put 15,000 copyists to work for almost fifteen years. (But he also carried out a literary inquisition against works critical of Manchu rule.)

Only in his last years did Ch'ien Lung lose his grip and permit a court favorite to practice corruption on an almost unprecedented scale. In 1796 the White Lotus Rebellion broke out. Ch'ien Lung's successor put down the rebellion and permitted the corrupt court favorite to take his own life. The ample financial reserves that had existed throughout the eighteenth century were never reestablished. China nevertheless entered the nineteenth century with its government intact and with a peaceful and stable society. There were few visible signs of what was soon to come.

Ming–Ch'ing Foreign Relations

Ming Some scholars have contended that post-Sung China was not an aggressive or imperialist state. They cite its inability to resist foreign conquest; the civility, self-restraint, and gentlemanliness of its officials; and the Sung adage that good men should not be used to make soldiers just as good iron is not used to make nails. The early Ming convincingly disproves this contention. The first Ming emperor (r. 1368–1398) oversaw the vigorous expansion of China's borders. At his death, China controlled the northern steppe from Hami at the gateway of Central Asia to the Sungari River in Manchuria and had regained control of the southern tier of Chinese provinces as well. The Mongols were expelled from Yunnan in 1382 (see Map 20–1).

During the reign of the third Ming emperor (1402–1424) China became even more aggressive. The emperor sent troops into northern Vietnam, which became a Chinese province for two decades. He also personally led five expeditions into the Gobi Desert in pursuit of Mongol troops.

Whenever possible, the third emperor and his successors "managed" China's frontiers with the tribute system. In this system the ambassadors of vassal kings acted out their political subordination to the universal ruler of the celestial kingdom. An ambassador approached the emperor respectfully, performed the kowtow (kneeling three times and bowing his head to the floor nine times), and presented his gifts. In return, the vassal kings were sent seals confirming their status, given permission to use the Chinese calendar and year-period names, and appointed to the Ming nobility.

The system conferred notable benefits on those willing to participate. While in Peking the ambassadors were housed and fed in a style appropriate to their status. The gifts they received were far more valuable than those they gave. In addition, they were permitted to trade private goods in the markets of the city. So attractive were these perquisites that some Central Asian merchants invented imaginary kingdoms of which they appointed themselves the emissaries. Eventually China had to set limits on the size, frequency, and cargos of these missions.

The most far-ranging ventures of the third Ming emperor were the maritime expeditions that sailed to Southeast Asia, India, the Arabian Gulf, and East Africa between 1405 and 1433. They were commanded by the eunuch Cheng Ho, a Muslim from Yunnan (see Map 20–1). The first of these armadas had sixty-two major ships and hundreds of smaller vessels and carried 28,000 sailors, soldiers, and merchants. Navigating by compass, the expeditions followed the sea routes of the Arab traders. Trade was not the primary purpose of the expeditions, although some eunuchs used the opportunity to make fortunes, and records show that giraffes, zebras, and other exotic items were presented at the Chinese court. Probably the expeditions were intended to make China's glory known to distant kingdoms and to enroll them in the tribute system. Cheng Ho's soldiers installed a new king in Java. They captured and brought back to China hostile kings from Borneo and Ceylon, and they signed up nineteen other states as Chinese tributaries.

The expeditions ended as suddenly as they had begun. They were costly and offered little return at a time when the dynasty was fighting in Mongolia and building the new capital at Peking. What was remarkable about these expeditions was not that they came a half-century earlier than the Portuguese voyages of discovery, but that China had the necessary

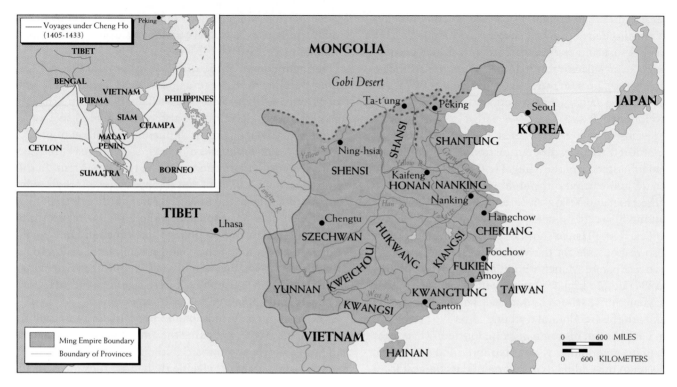

Voyages under Cheng Ho
(1405-1433)

Map 20-1 Ming Empire and the voyages of Cheng Ho. The ships of Cheng Ho, venturing beyond Southeast Asia and India, reached the coast of East Africa.

maritime technology and yet decided not to use it. China lacked the combination of restlessness, greed, faith, and curiosity that would motivate the Portuguese.

The chief threat to the Ming dynasty was the Mongols. In disarray after the collapse of their rule in China, the Mongols had broken into eastern, western, and southern tribes. The Chinese, "using the barbarian to control the barbarian," made allies of the southern tribes (those settled just north of the Great Wall) against the more fearsome grassland Mongols. This policy worked most of the time, but twice the Mongols formed confederations—pale imitations of the war machine of Genghis—strong enough to defeat Chinese armies: In the 1430s they captured the emperor, and in 1550 they overran Peking. The Mongol forces involved in the latter attack were defeated by a Chinese army in the 1560s and signed a peace treaty in 1571.

A second foreign threat to the Ming dynasty was the Japanese and the Chinese pirates associated with them. Warriorlords of decentralized Japan had begun raids on Korea and the northeastern Chinese coast during the thirteenth and early fourteenth centuries; they extended their activities down the coast to southeastern China and beyond during the fifteenth and sixteenth centuries. Hitherto, the coast had been China's most secure frontier. China built defenses and used a scorched-earth policy to make raiding less profitable, but mostly had to put up with the depredations. The most se-

rious threat from Japan was its invasions of Korea in 1592 and 1597–1598. Korea resisted with some initial success. China sent troops only after Japanese armies had occupied the entire Korean peninsula. Eventually the Japanese armies withdrew, but the strain on Ming finances had severely weakened the dynasty.

Ch'ing The final foreign threat to the Ming was the Manchus, who, as we have seen, were the mouse that swallowed the elephant. After coming to power in 1644, the Manchu court spent decades consolidating its rule within China. The last Ming prince was pursued into Burma and killed in 1662. But then the three Chinese generals who had helped the Manchus conquer the south revolted and were supported by a Sino-Japanese pirate state on Taiwan. The emperor K'ang Hsi suppressed the revolts by 1681; most Chinese troops in the Manchu armies remained loyal. In 1683 he took Taiwan, which became a part of China for the first time (see Map 20–2).

As always, the principal foreign threats to China, even to the Manchu dynasty, which had itself come from the north, came from the north and northwest. Russia had begun expanding east across Siberia and south against the remnants of the Golden Horde during the reign of Ivan the Terrible (1533–1584). By the 1660s Russian traders, trappers, and adventurers had reached northern Manchuria, where they built forts and traded with the eastern Mongols. One is reminded of the French penetration of Canada during the same decades. To prevent a rapprochement between the Russians and Mongols, K'ang Hsi set up military colonies in Manchuria during the 1680s and drove the Russians from the lower Amur River. This victory during the early years of the reign of Peter the Great (1682–1725) led to the 1689 Treaty of Nerchinsk. Negotiated with the assistance of Jesuit translators, this treaty excluded Russia from northern Manchuria while permitting its caravans to visit Peking.

In the west the situation was more complex, with a three-corner relationship among Russia, the western Mongols, and Tibet. K'ang Hsi, and then Ch'ien Lung, campaigned against the Mongols, invaded Tibet, and in 1727 signed a new treaty with Russia. During the campaigns the Chinese temporarily came to control millions of square miles of new territories. It is a telling comment on the Chinese concept of empire that ever since that time, even after China's borders contracted during the nineteenth century, the Chinese have insisted that the Manchu conquests of non-Chinese peoples define their legitimate borders. The roots of the present-day contention over borders between China and the countries of the former Soviet Union go back to these events during the eighteenth century, as does the Chinese claim to Tibet.

Contacts with the West   Europeans had made their way to China during the T'ang and the Yuan dynasties. But only with Europe's oceanic expansion in the sixteenth century did they arrive in large numbers. Some came as missionaries, of whom the most calculating, disciplined, enterprising, and successful were the Jesuits. On first arriving in Ming China, they put on the robes of the Buddhist monk; on learning something of the country they switched to the gowns of the Confucian scholar. They studied Chinese and the Confucian classics and engaged in conversations with scholars. They used their knowledge of astronomy, geography, engraving, and firearms to win entry to the court at Peking and appointments in the bureau of astronomy.

When the Manchus came to power in 1644 the Jesuits kept their position. They appealed to the curiosity of the court

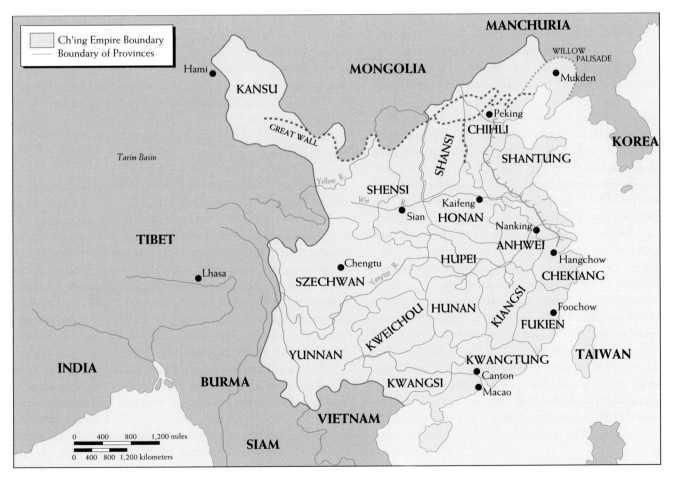

Map 20-2   The Ch'ing Empire at its peak.   The Willow Palisade was the line of demarcation between the Manchurian homeland of the Ch'ing rulers and China. Chinese were excluded from Manchuria.

Late Imperial China

Ming Dynasty 1368-1644

1368–1398	Reign of first Ming emperor; Chinese armies invade Manchuria, Mongolia, and eastern Central Asia
1402–1424	Reign of third Ming emperor; Chinese armies invade Vietnam and Mongolia
1405–1433	Voyage of Cheng Ho to India and Africa
1415	Grand Canal reopened
1472–1529	Wang Yang-ming, philosopher
1592–1598	Chinese army battles Japanese army in Korea

Ch'ing (Manchu) Dynasty 1644–1911

1668	Manchuria closed to Chinese immigrants (by Willow Palisade)
1661–1722	Reign of K'ang Hsi
1681	Suppression of revolts by Chinese generals
1683	Taiwan captured
1689	China and Russia sign Treaty of Nerchinsk
1736–1795	Reign of Ch'ien Lung
1793	Macartney mission

with instruments such as telescopes, clocks, and clavichords. They tried to propagate Christianity. They attacked Taoism and Buddhism as superstitions but argued that Confucianism as a rational philosophy complemented Christianity, just as Aristotle's teaching complemented Christian theology in Europe. They handled the problem of the Confucian rites of ancestor worship by interpreting them as secular and nonantagonistic to Christianity. A few high court officials were converted. K'ang Hsi was sympathetic to the scholarly personalities of the Jesuits and appreciated the cannon they cast but was unsympathetic to their religion: "I had asked [the Jesuit] Verbiest why God had not forgiven his son without making him die, but though he had tried to answer I had not understood him."[2]

Meanwhile, their Franciscan and Dominican rivals had reported to Rome that the Jesuits condoned the Confucian rites. The ensuing debate was long and complex, but in the end, papal bulls issued in 1715 and 1742 decided against the Jesuits and forbade Chinese Christians to participate in the family rites of ancestor worship. Thereupon the emperor banned Christianity in China, churches were seized, missionaries were forced to flee, and congregations declined.

Other Europeans came to China to trade. The Portuguese came first in the early sixteenth century but behaved badly and were expelled. They returned in mid-century and were permitted to trade on a tiny peninsula at Macao that was walled off from China. They were followed by Dutch from the East Indies (Indonesia), by the British East India Company in 1699, and by Americans in 1784.

At first the Westerners mingled with ships from Southeast Asia in a fairly open multiport pattern of trade. Then, during the early eighteenth century, the more restrictive "Canton system" evolved. Westerners could trade only at Canton. They were barred from entering the city proper but were assigned land outside its walls along the river. They could not bring their wives to China. They were subject to the harsh dispositions of Chinese law. They were under the control of official merchant guilds. Nevertheless, the trade was profitable to both sides.

The British East India Company developed a triangular commerce among China, India, and Britain that enabled the English to drink tea and wear silk. Private fortunes were built. For China this trade produced an influx of specie, and the Chinese officials in charge grew immensely wealthy. Chafing under the various restrictions, the British government in 1793 sent the Macartney mission to China to negotiate the opening of other ports, fixed tariffs, representation at Peking, and so on. The emperor Ch'ien Lung graciously permitted Lord Macartney (1736–1806) to present his gifts—which the Chinese described as tribute, even though Macartney refused to perform the kowtow—but he turned down Macartney's requests. Western trade remained encapsulated at Canton, distant from Peking and little noted elsewhere in China.

Ming-Ch'ing Culture

One thing that can be said of Ming-Ch'ing culture, like population or agricultural productivity, is that there was more of it. Whether considering gentry, scholar officials, or a professionalized class of literati, their numbers and works were far greater than in previous dynasties. Even local literary figures or philosophers were likely to publish their collected works or have them published by admiring disciples. Bookstores came of age in the Ming, selling the Confucian classics; commentaries on them; collections of T'ang and Sung poetry; and also colored prints, novels, erotica, and model answers for the civil-service examinations.

Chinese culture had begun to turn inward during the Sung in reaction to Buddhism. This tendency was accelerated by the Chinese antipathy to Mongol rule and continued into the Ming and Ch'ing, when Chinese culture became virtually impervious to outside influences. Even works on mathematics and science translated into Chinese by the Jesuits left few traces in Chinese scholarly writings. Chinese cultural self-sufficiency, of course, reflected a tradition and a social order that had stood the test of time, but it also indicated a closed

[2]J. D. Spence, *Emperor of China: Self-Portrait of K'ang-Hsi* (New York: Alfred A. Knopf, 1974), p. 84.

Ch'ien Lung's Edict to King George III of England

The Chinese emperor rejected the requests of the 1793 Macartney mission for change in the restrictive Canton system. His edict reflects the Chinese sense of their superiority to other peoples and their belief that China was the "central kingdom" of the world.

What philosophical principles underlie the emperor's sense of superiority?

You, O King, are so inclined toward our civilization that you have sent a special envoy across the seas to bring to our Court your memorial of congratulations on the occasion of my birthday and to present your native products as an expression of your thoughtfulness. On perusing your memorial, so simply worded and sincerely conceived, I am impressed by your genuine respectfulness and friendliness and greatly pleased. . . .

The Celestial Court has pacified and possessed the territory within the four seas. Its sole aim is to do its utmost to achieve good government and to manage political affairs, attaching no value to strange jewels and precious objects. The various articles presented by you, O King, this time are accepted by my special order to the office in charge of such functions in consideration of the offerings having come from a long distance with sincere good wishes. As a matter of fact, the virtue and prestige of the Celestial Dynasty having spread far and wide, the kings of the myriad nations come by land and sea with all sorts of precious things. Consequently there is nothing we lack, as your principal envoy and others have themselves observed. We have never set much store on strange or ingenious objects, nor do we need any more of your country's manufactures. . . .

Reprinted by permission of the publisher from *China's Response to the West* by Ssu-yu Teng and John K. Fairbank, Cambridge, MA: Harvard University Press. Copyright © 1954, 1979 by the President and Fellows of Harvard College. Reprinted by permission of Harvard University Press.

---

system of ideas with weaknesses that would become apparent in the nineteenth century. Orthodox thought during these five centuries was Chu Hsi Neo-Confucianism. From the mid- to the late Ming, some perturbations were caused by the Zenlike teachings of the philosopher Wang Yang-ming (1472–1529), whose activism caused him to be jailed, beaten, and exiled at one point in an otherwise illustrious official career.

Several other original thinkers' refusal to accept bureaucratic posts under the Ch'ing won them plaudits during the anti-Manchu nationalism of the early twentieth century, but they had only a limited influence on their own times. The most interesting was Ku Yen-wu, who wrote on both philology and statecraft. He used philology and historical phonetics to get at the original meanings of the classics and contrasted their practical ethics with the "empty words" of Wang Yang-ming. Ku's successors extended his philological studies, developing empirical methods for textual studies, but lost sight of their implications for politics. The Manchus clamped down on unorthodox thought, and the seventeenth-century burst of creativity guttered out into a narrow, bookish, conservative scholasticism. Not until the end of the nineteenth century did thinkers draw from these studies the kind of radical inferences that philological studies of the Bible had produced in Europe.

Ming and Ch'ing Chinese esteemed most highly, and not without reason, the traditional categories of high culture: painting, calligraphy, poetry, and philosophy. Porcelains of great beauty were also produced. In the early Ming the blue-on-white glazes predominated. During the later Ming and Ch'ing more decorative wares with enamel painted over the glaze became widespread. The pottery industry of Europe was begun during the sixteenth century to imitate these wares, and Chinese and Japanese influences have dominated Western ceramics down to the present. Chinese today, however, look back and see the novel as the characteristic cultural achievement of the Ming and Ch'ing.

The novel in China grew out of plot-books used by earlier storytellers. Like the stories, Chinese novels consisted of episodes strung together, and chapters in early novels often ended with an admonition to the reader not to miss the next exciting development. Ming and Ch'ing novels were usually written by scholars who had failed the examinations, which may account for their caustic comments on officials. As most novels were written in colloquial Chinese, which was not quite respectable in the society of scholars, their authors wrote under pseudonyms.

Two collections of lively short stories are available in English: *Stories from a Ming Collection* and *The Courtesan's Jewel Box.* Many other stories were pornographic. In fact, the Ming may have invented the humorous pornographic novel. One example available in English is *The Carnal Prayer Mat.* This genre was suppressed in China during the Ch'ing and rediscovered in Japanese collections in the twentieth century.

Ming dynasty ink painting by Wu Wei (1479-1508). The seated human figure is a part of the tranquility of nature. Nature, densely concentrated at the left and lower portions of the painting, stretches off into space in the middle and upper right portion. [© 1996. All rights reserved. Courtesy of Museum of Fine Arts, Boston]

Short descriptions of several major novels may convey something of their flavor:

1. *The Romance of the Three Kingdoms* was published in 1522. It tells of the political and military struggles in China in the aftermath of the Han dynasty. Like Shakespeare, the author, whose identity is uncertain, used a historical setting to create a dramatic world in which human character determines the outcome of events. More than twenty editions had appeared by the end of the Ming, and the novel was also extremely popular in Japan and Korea.

2. *All Men Are Brothers* (also translated as *The Water Margin*) tells of 108 bandit heroes who flee government repression during the late northern Sung, establish a hideout on a mountain amid marshes, and like Robin Hood, avenge the wrongs perpetrated by corrupt officials. Separate episodes tell why each had to leave society and of their many daring and funny adventures. Of all Chinese novels, this was the most popular. It was officially banned as subversive during the Ch'ing but was widely read nonetheless.

3. *The Golden Lotus* is a pornographic novel about the sexual adventures of an urban merchant. It gives vivid descriptions of individual women and satirical descriptions of venal officials and greedy monks. In the end the hero dies of his excesses and his family—all six wives and their children—disintegrates. The early English translation of this novel had long passages in Latin to protect those whose minds were not disciplined by the study of that language. Despite its literary merits, the book, like all of its genre, is proscribed in China today. Copies in universities are kept under lock and key.

4. *The Dream of the Red Chamber* (also translated as *The Story of the Stone*) is generally considered China's greatest novel. It tells the story of a youth growing up in a wealthy but declining family during the early Ch'ing. Critics praise its subtlety and psychological insight. Anthropologists mine the novel for information on the Chinese extended family and for its depiction of social relations. Like other Ming and Ch'ing novels, it was recognized as a respectable work of art only during the twentieth century, after Western novels entered China.

5. *The Scholars* is a social satire of the early Ch'ing that pokes fun at scholars and officials.

JAPAN

The two segments of late traditional Japan could not be more different. The Warring States era (1467–1600), really the last phase of Japan's medieval history, saw the unleashing of internal wars and anarchy that scourged the old society from the bottom up. Within a century all vestiges of the old manorial or estate system had been scrapped and almost all of the Ashikaga lords had been overthrown. The Tokugawa era (1600–1868) that followed saw Japan reunited and stable, with a stronger government than ever. During the Tokugawa era Japanese culture was brilliantly transformed, preparing it for the challenge it would face during the mid-nineteenth century.

A Star in Heaven

Among the officials whose stories are told in The Scholars *is Fan Chin, thin and sallow with a grizzled beard and threadbare linen gown, who finally passes the county examination at the age of fifty-four. On his return home, he is given a feast and advice by his domineering father-in-law, Butcher Hu. But when Fan Chin asks Hu for money to travel to the provincial examination, he gets the following reaction.*

Why did a satire such as *The Scholars* not undermine the premises on which Ch'ing society rested?

Butcher Hu spat in his face and let loose a stream of abuse. "Don't forget who you are!" he bellowed. "Just passing one examination and you become like a toad thinking to dine on the flesh of a swan. I hear you passed the examination not because of your essay, but because the examiner took pity on your old age. Now, like a fool, you aspire to be an official. Don't you know that those who have passed the higher examination are all stars in heaven! Haven't you seen the Changs in the city? Those officials all have tons of money and generously proportioned faces and ears. Now look at you with your protruding mouth and monkey chin. Piss on the ground and take a good look at yourself in the puddle! A miserable creature like you can't even hope to swallow a swan's fart! Forget it!

[Fan Chin takes the examination anyway. When he returns home, he discovers that his family has been hungry for two days. Fan goes to the market to sell a chicken. In the meantime, heralds on horseback arrive to proclaim he has passed the provincial examination. Returning home, Fan sees the posted announcement and falls into a dead faint. When revived, he begins ranting incoherently. A herald suggests that Butcher Hu, whom Fan fears, bring him to his senses with a slap. Butcher Hu demurs.]

"He may be my son-in-law," he said, "but now he has become a member of the gentry, a star in heaven. How can I hit a star in heaven? I've heard from Buddhist priests that whoever strikes a star in heaven will be carried away by the King of Hell, struck one hundred times with an iron rod, consigned to the eighteenth hell, and never return to human form again. I wouldn't dare do it."

[Eventually Butcher Hu slaps him, and Fan recovers in time to receive a visit from a member of the local gentry, who is wearing "an official's gauze cap, sunflower-coloured gown, gilt belt and black shoes." "Sir," he says to Fan, "although we live in the same district, I regret that we have never become acquainted." After paying his respects, the visitor presents Fan with fifty taels of silver and a more appropriate house. Soon others give him land, goods, money, rice, and servants. The chapter ends with the maids cleaning up under the supervision of Fan Chin's wife after several days of feasting. Fan Chin's mother enters the courtyard.]

"You must be very careful," the old lady warned her daughter-in-law and the maids. "These things all belong to someone else, so don't break them."

The maids replied:"How can you say they belong to others, madam?They all belong to you."

"Oh no! How could our house have such things?" she said with a smile. "How can you talk of their belonging to others?" the maids replied in unison. "And not only these things, but all of us and the house, too, belong to you."

When the old lady heard this, she picked up the bowls and dishes of fine porcelain and the cups and chopsticks inlaid with silver and examined them one by one. She burbled:" These things are all mine."Laughing wildly, she fell over backward, choked on phlegm, and lost consciousness.

If you want to know what became of the old lady, please read the next chapter.

Translation by Shang Wei.

Warring States Era (1467–1600)

War is the universal solvent of old institutions. Nowhere in history was this clearer than in Japan between 1467 and 1600. In 1467 a dispute arose over who would be the next Ashikaga shōgun . The dispute led to war between two territorial lords who were important supporters of the *bakufu*. Other lords used the opportunity to gain territory at the expense of weaker neighbors, and wars raged throughout Japan for eleven years. Most of Kyoto was destroyed in the fighting, and the authority of the Ashikaga *bakufu* came to an end. This first war ended in 1477, but the fighting resumed and continued for more than a century.

War of All Against All

Even before 1467 the Ashikaga equilibrium had been precarious. The regional daimyo lords had relied on their relationship to the *bakufu* to hold their stronger vassals in check,

Construction of the "White Heron" castle in Himeji, was begun during the Warring States era and was completed shortly after 1600. During the Tokugawa peace, it remained as a monument to the glory of the daimyo. Today it can be seen from the "bullet train." [Japan Airlines/Photo by Morris Simoncelli]

while relying on these vassals to preserve their independence against strong neighbors. The collapse of *bakufu* authority after 1467 pulled the linchpin from the system. It left the regional lords standing alone, removing the last barrier to wars among them.

The regional lords, however, were too weak to stand alone. A region was a hodgepodge of competing jurisdictions. Lands might be "public," or in estates, and some were starting to look like private fiefs. Revenues might be paid to nobles in Kyoto, to regional lords, or to samurai vassals. Most regions contained military bands that were not the vassals of the daimyo. Several daimyo had lands in the territories of other lords. Occasionally vassals were militarily more powerful than their daimyo lords. Some local vassals commanded bands of village warriors. Once the regional daimyo were forced to stand alone, they became prey to the stronger among their vassals as well as to neighboring states.

By the end of the sixteenth century all Ashikaga daimyo had fallen, with one exception in remote southern Kyushu. In their place emerged hundreds of little "Warring States daimyo," each with his own warrior band. In one prefecture along the Inland Sea, the remains of 200 hillside castles of such daimyo have been identified. The constant wars among these men were not unlike those of the early feudal era in Europe.

A Japanese term for "survival of the fittest"—"the strong eat and the weak become the meat"—is often applied to this century of warfare. Of the daimyo bands, the most efficient in revamping their domain for military ends survived. The less ruthless, who tried to preserve old ways, were defeated and absorbed. It was an age, as one Warring States general put it, "when only muscle counts." Another said, "The warrior doesn't care if he's called a dog or beast, the main thing is winning."[3]

Early in this period, when there were hundreds of small states, castles were built on a bluff above a river or on a mountainside with natural defenses against a surprise attack. Inuyama Castle, today a thirty-minute streetcar ride from Nagoya, is the most impressive surviving example.

[3]G. Elison and B. L. Smith, eds., *Warlords, Artists, and Commoners* (Honolulu: Hawaii University Press, 1981), p. 57.

As fighting continued, hundreds of local states gave way to tens of regional states. The castles of such regional states were often located on plains, and as castle towns grew up around them, merchants flocked to supply the needs of their growing soldiery. Eventually, alliances of these regional states fought it out, until in the late sixteenth century all of Japan was brought under the hegemony of a single lord. Oda Nobunaga (1534–1582) completed the initial unification of central Honshu and would have finished the job had he not been assassinated by a treacherous vassal in 1582. Toyotomi Hideyoshi (1536–1598), who had begun life as a lowly foot soldier, completed the unification in 1590. After his death his vassal generals once again went to war, and it was only with the victory of Tokugawa Ieyasu (1542–1616) at the Battle of Sekigahara in 1600 that true unification was finally achieved. Ieyasu's unification of 1600 superficially resembled that of the Minamoto in 1185 but was in fact based on a sweeping transformation of Japan's society.

Foot Soldier Revolution

During the Warring States period, the foot soldier replaced the aristocratic mounted warrior as the backbone of the military in Japan. Soldiers were still called *samurai*. They were still the vassals of daimyo or, sometimes, the vassals of vassals of daimyo. But their numbers, social status, and techniques of warfare changed dramatically. As a result, Japanese society changed from what it had been only a century earlier.

The changes began on the land. Ashikaga daimyo had diverted more and more land revenues for their own use, but Warring States daimyo took them all. Public lands and estates, including those of the imperial house, were seized and converted into fiefs. Soldiers were paid stipends from the revenues of the daimyo's lands, and important vassals, usually the officers or commanders of the daimyo's army, were awarded fiefs of their own. The governance of fiefs was essentially private, in the hands of the fief holder.

Inheritance patterns changed to fit the new circumstances. Multigeniture—the division of a warrior's rights to revenues from land among his children—was not appropriate to a society with a hereditary military class. It had impoverished the Kamakura vassals. To protect the integrity of the warrior's household economy, multigeniture had begun to give way to single inheritance during the Ashikaga period. After 1467 single inheritance became universal. As the fief was often passed to the most able son and not necessarily to the eldest, the pattern is usually called *unigeniture* rather than *primogeniture*.

With larger revenues, Warring States daimyo built larger armies. They recruited mainly from the peasantry. Some of the new soldiers moved to the castle town of the daimyo. Others lived on the land or even remained in their villages, farming in peace and fighting in war. The growth of the military class had begun earlier. Accounts of twelfth-century battles tell of fighting by tens of hundreds of warriors, sometimes more. Scroll paintings of the Heiji wars corroborate these figures. By the fourteenth century battles involved thousands or tens of thousands of troops. By the late sixteenth century hundreds of thousands were deployed in major campaigns. Screen paintings show massed troops in fixed emplacements with officers riding about on horseback. Of course, special cavalry strike forces were still used.

In the mid-fourteenth century a new weapon was developed: a thrusting spear with a thick shaft and a heavy chisel-like blade. Held in both hands, it could penetrate medieval armor as a sword could not. It could also be swung about like a quarterstaff. It was used by soldiers positioned at intervals of three feet, in a pincushion tactic to impale charging cavalry. The weapon spelled the end of the aristocratic warrior in Japan, just as the pikes used by Swiss soldiers ended knighthood in northern Europe during the fifteenth century. After 1467 this spear became the principal weapon of Warring States Japan. Not surprisingly, its spread coincided with the recruitment of peasant soldiers, for it required only short training. By the early sixteenth century it was every warrior's dream to be the "number one spearsman" of his lord. Even generals trained in its use. One famous general wrote that "one hundred spearsmen are more effective than ten thousand swords."

A second change in military technology was the introduction of the musket by the Portuguese in the mid-sixteenth century. It was quickly adopted by Warring States generals. Its superiority was proved in the Battle of Nagashino in 1575, in which Oda Nobunaga and Tokugawa Ieyasu used spear and musket platoons against the cavalry of a famous military tactician. Massing 3,000 muskets behind a bamboo barrier-fence and firing in volleys, Nobunaga decimated the forces of his enemy. As individual combat gave way to mass armies, warfare became pitiless, cruel, and bloody.

How, then, shall we characterize the society that emerged from the Warring States? Does the word *feudal* apply, with its suggestion of lords and vassals and manorial life on the fiefs of aristocratic warriors? In some respects, it does: By the late sixteenth century all warriors in Japan were part of a pyramid of vassals and lords headed by a single overlord; warriors of rank held fiefs and vassals of their own.

In other respects Japan was more like postfeudal Europe. First, most of the military class were soldiers, not aristocrats. Even though they were called samurai and were vassals, they were something new. They were not given fiefs but were paid with stipends of so many bales of rice. Second, unlike, say, feudal England, where the military class was about one quarter of 1 percent of the population, in mid-sixteenth-century Japan it may have reached 7 or 8 percent. It was more of a size with the mercenary armies of Europe during the fifteenth or

Warring States Japan (1467–1600)	
1543	Portuguese arrive in Japan
1575	Battle of Nagashino
1582	Oda Nobunaga is assassinated
1587	Spanish arrive in Japan
1588	Hideyoshi's sword hunt
1590	Hideyoshi unifies Japan
1592, 1597–1598	Hideyoshi sends armies to Korea; battles fought against Chinese troops
1597	Hideyoshi bans Christianity
1598	Hideyoshi dies
1600	Tokugawa victory in Battle of Sekigahara

sixteenth centuries. Third, the recruitment of village warriors added significantly to the power of Warring States daimyo but gave rise to problems as well. Taxes became harder to collect. Local samurai were often involved in uprisings. When organized by Pure Land Buddhist congregations, these uprisings sometimes involved whole provinces. Again, the parallels with postfeudal Europe seem closer. Fourth, even in a feudal society, not everything is feudal. The commercial growth of the Kamakura and Ashikaga periods continued through the dark decades of the Warring States era.

Foreign Relations and Trade

Japanese pirate-traders plied the seas of East Asia during the fifteenth and sixteenth centuries. To halt their depredations, the Ming emperor invited the third Ashikaga shōgun to trade with China. An agreement was reached in 1404. The shōgun as appointed the "King of Japan." During the next century and a half, periodic "tribute missions" were sent to China. The opening of official trade channels did not, however, end piracy. It stopped only after Japan was reunified at the close of the sixteenth century.

The content of the trade reflected the progress of Japanese crafts. Early Japanese exports to China were raw materials such as raw copper, sulphur, or silver, but by the sixteenth century manufactured goods were rising in importance and included swords, spears, wine bottles, folding fans, picture scrolls, screen paintings, ink slabs, and the like. In exchange, Japan received copper cash, porcelains, paintings, books, and medicines.

After establishing his hegemony over Japan, Hideyoshi permitted only ships with his vermilion seal to trade with China, a policy continued by the Tokugawa. Between 1604 and 1635 over 350 ships went to China in this "vermilion-seal trade." Then, in 1635, the imposition of seclusion ended Japan's foreign trade: No Japanese could leave Japan; the con-

struction of large ships was prohibited; trade with the continent was limited to a small community of Chinese merchants in Nagasaki, and to quiet trading with China through the Ryukyu Islands and with Korea through the Tsushima Islands.

Overlapping Japan's maritime expansion in the seas of East Asia was the arrival of European ships. Portuguese pirate-traders made their way to Goa in India, to Malacca, to Macao in China, and arrived in Japan in 1543. Spanish galleons came in 1587 via Mexico and the Philippines. These eastern and western waves of Iberian expansion were followed by the Dutch and the English after the turn of the century.

The Portuguese, from a tiny country with a population of 1.5 million, were motivated by a desire for booty and profits and by religious zeal. Their ships were superior. Taking advantage of the Chinese ban on maritime commerce, they became important as shippers. They carried Southeast Asian goods and Japanese silver to China and Chinese silk to Japan, and they used their profits to buy Southeast Asian spices for the European market. The Portuguese, initially at least, found it easier to trade with the daimyo of a disunited Japan than to deal with the authorities of a united China. A few Kyushu daimyo, thinking to attract Portuguese traders, even converted to Christianity.

Traders brought with them Jesuit missionaries. The Society of Jesus had been founded in 1540 to act as soldiers in the pope's campaign against the Reformation. Only nine years later Saint Francis Xavier (1506–1552) arrived in Japan. He soon wrote back that the Japanese were "the best [people] who have yet been discovered." Another Jesuit wrote that the Japanese "are all white, courteous, and highly civilized, so much so that they surpass all other known races of the world." The Japanese, for their part, also appeared to admire the Jesuits for their asceticism, devoutness, and learning.

As they had attempted to convert scholar-officials in China, so the Jesuits in Japan directed their efforts toward the samurai. Moving to Kyoto, they won the favor of Nobunaga, who was engaged in campaigns against warrior monks on Mount Hiei and against Pure Land strongholds in Osaka. Portuguese and Christian objects became fashionable. Painters produced "Southern Barbarian screens" that depicted the "black ships" of the Portuguese. Christian symbols were used on lacquer boxes and saddles. Nobunaga himself occasionally wore Portuguese clothes and a cross and said he might become a Christian if only the Jesuits would drop their insistence on monogamy. Christian converts increased from a few in the early years to 130,000 in 1579, and to about 300,000 in 1600. That is to say, in the late sixteenth century a higher percentage of Japanese were Christian than today.

It is difficult to explain why Christianity met with greater success in Japan than in other Asian lands. When introduced, it was seen as a new Buddhist sect. There seemed little difference to the Japanese between the cosmic Buddha of Shingon and the Christian God, between the paradise of Amida and the Christian heaven, or between prayers to Kannon—the female *bodhisattva* of mercy—and to the Virgin Mary. The Japanese also noted the theological similarity between the pietism of the Pure Land sect and that of Christianity. To Japanese ears, the passage in Romans 10:13, "whosoever shall call upon the name of the Lord shall be saved," was reminiscent of the Pure Land practice of invoking the name of Amida. The Jesuits, too, noted these parallels and felt that the devil had established these sects in Japan to test their faith. Xavier, who, despite his admirable personal characteristics, was narrow-minded, referred to the historical Buddha and Amida as "two demons." Although this intolerance gave rise to certain tensions and animosities, Christianity spread, and to no small measure as a result of the personal example of the Jesuits.

The fortunes of Christianity began to decline in 1597, when Hideyoshi banned Christianity and had six Spanish Franciscans and twenty Japanese converts crucified in Nagasaki. Hideyoshi was aware of Spanish colonialism in the Philippines, and it was said that a Spanish pilot had boasted that merchants and priests represented the first step toward the conquest of Japan. Sporadic persecutions continued until 1614, when Tokugawa Ieyasu began a serious movement to extirpate the foreign religion. Faced with torture, some Christians recanted. Over 3,000 others were martyred.

The last resistance was an uprising near Nagasaki in 1637 and 1638 in which 37,000 Christians died. After that, Christianity survived in Japan only as a hidden religion with secret rites and devotions to "Maria-Kannon," the mother of Jesus represented or disguised as the Buddhist goddess of mercy holding a child in her arms. A few of these "hidden Christians" reemerged in the later nineteenth century. Otherwise, apart from muskets and techniques of castle building, all that remained of the Portuguese influence were certain loan words that became a permanent part of the Japanese language: *pan* for bread, *birodo* for velvet, *kasutera* for sponge cake, *karuta* for playing cards, and *tempura* for that familiar Japanese dish.

Tokugawa Era (1600–1868)

Political Engineering and Economic Growth During the Seventeenth Century

From 1467 to 1590 Japan's energies were absorbed in ever bigger wars. But after the unifications of 1590 and 1600 Japan's leaders sought to create a peaceful, stable, orderly society. Like a great tanker that requires many times its own length to come about, Japan made this transition slowly. Many of the values and habits of mind of the Warring States era

"The Arrival of the Portuguese in Japan." Portuguese merchants arrived in Japan in 1543 from India and the East Indies. Their crews were multi-ethnic, and they brought Jesuit priests as well. [Giraudon/Art Resource, N.Y.]

continued into the seventeenth century. By the middle or late seventeenth century, however, its society and political system had been radically reengineered. Vigorous economic and demographic growth had also occurred. This combination of political and economic change made the seventeenth century a period of great dynamism.

Hideyoshi's Rule   One pressing problem faced by Japan's unifiers was how to cope with an armed peasantry. In war, village warriors fought for their lord: Their advantage to the lord was greater than their cost. In peace, only the cost remained: their resistance to taxation and the threat of local uprisings. Accordingly, in the summer of 1588 Hideyoshi ordered a "sword hunt" to disarm the peasants. Records of the collected weaponry exist for only one county of 3,400 households in Kaga, a domain on the Sea of Japan: 1,073 swords, 1,540 short swords, 700 daggers, 160 spears, 500 suits of armor, and other miscellaneous items. Once the hunt was completed, the 5 percent of the population who remained samurai used their monopoly on weapons to control the other 95 percent.

After the sword hunt, Hideyoshi attempted to freeze the social classes. Samurai were prohibited from quitting the service of their lord. Peasants were barred from abandoning their fields to become townspeople. This policy was continued by the Tokugawa after 1600, and by and large succeeded. Samurai, farmers, and townspeople tended to marry within their respective classes, and each class developed a unique cultural character. The authorities even attempted to dictate life styles, prescribing who could ride in palanquins, who could wear silk, and who was permitted to build fancy gates in front of their houses.

But to grasp the class structure of Tokugawa society, we must note the vast range of social gradations within each class. A farmer who was a landlord and a district official was a more important figure than most lower samurai and lived in a different social world from a landless "water-drinking" peasant too poor to buy tea. A townsman could be the head of a great wholesale house, or a humble street peddler or clog mender. A samurai could be an elder, a key decision maker of his domain, with an income of thousands of bushels of rice and several hundred vassals of his own, or an impecunious foot soldier who stood guard at the castle gate.

Once the peasantry was disarmed, Hideyoshi ordered cadastral surveys on his own lands and on those of his vassals. The surveys defined each parcel of land by location, size, soil quality, product, and cultivator's name. For the first time, an attempt was made to standardize the rods used to measure land and the boxes used to measure quantities of rice. These standards marked the beginning of the detailed record keeping that characterized the Tokugawa era. Hideyoshi's survey laid the foundations for a systematic land tax. Based on these surveys, domains and fiefs were henceforth ranked in terms of their assessed yield.

Establishment of Tokugawa Rule Bedazzled by his own power and military successes, and against all the evidence of Warring States political behavior, Hideyoshi assumed that his vassals would honor their sworn oaths of loyalty to his heir. Hideyoshi was especially trustful of his great ally Tokugawa Ieyasu, whose domains were larger than his own. His trust was misplaced. After his death in 1598, Hideyoshi's former vassals, paying little attention to his heir, broke apart into two opposing camps and fought a great battle in 1600 from which the alliance headed by Tokugawa Ieyasu emerged victorious. Ieyasu was wise, effective in maintaining alliances, and a master strategist, but above all patient. In comparing the three unifiers, the Japanese tell the story that when a cuckoo failed to sing, Nobunaga said, "I'll kill it if it doesn't sing"; Hideyoshi said, "I'll make it sing"; but Ieyasu sat down and said, "I'll wait until it sings."

Like the Minamoto of twelfth-century Kamakura, Ieyasu spurned the Kyoto court and established his headquarters in Edo (today's Tokyo), in the center of his military holdings in eastern Japan (see Map 20–3). He took the title of shōgun in 1603 and called his government the *bakufu*. In Edo he built a great castle, surrounded by massive fortifications of stone and concentric moats. The inner portion of these moats and stone walls remains today as the Imperial Palace. Ieyasu then used his military power to reorganize Japan.

Ieyasu's first move was to confiscate the lands of his defeated enemies and to reward his vassals and allies. During the first quarter of the seventeenth century the *bakufu* confiscated the domains of 150 daimyo, some of former enemies and some for infractions of the Tokugawa legal code, and transferred 229 daimyo from one domain to another. The transfers completed the work of Hideyoshi's sword hunt by severing long-standing ties between daimyo and their disarmed former village retainers. When a daimyo was transferred to a new fief, he took his samurai retainers with him. During the second quarter of the seventeenth century transfers and confiscations ended and the system settled down.

The reshuffling of domains had not been random. The configuration that emerged was, first, of a huge central Tokugawa domain. It contained the following: most of the domains of "house daimyo"—those who had been Tokugawa vassals before 1600; the fiefs of the 5,000 Tokugawa bannermen (upper samurai); and the lands that furnished the stipends of the other 17,000 Tokugawa direct retainers (middle and lower samurai). Then, strategically placed around the Tokugawa heartland were the domains of the "related daimyo." These domains had been founded by the second and third sons of early shōgun and furnished a successor to the main Tokugawa line when a shōgun had no heir. Beyond the related daimyo was a second tier of "outside daimyo" who had fought as allies of Tokugawa Ieyasu in 1600 but became his vassals only after the battle was over.

Finally, at the antipodes of the system were those outside daimyo who had been permitted to survive despite having fought against the Tokugawa in 1600. Their domains were drastically reduced. They remained the "enemies" within the system, although they had submitted and become Tokugawa vassals after 1600. Thus, the entire arrangement constituted a defensive system, with the staunchest Tokugawa supporters nearest to the center.

The Tokugawa also established other systemic controls. Legal codes regulated the imperial court, the temples and shrines, and the daimyo. Military houses were enjoined to use men of ability and to practice frugality. They were prohibited from engaging in drinking parties, wanton revelry, sexual indulgence, habitual gambling, or the ostentatious display of wealth. Only with *bakufu* consent could daimyo marry or repair their castles.

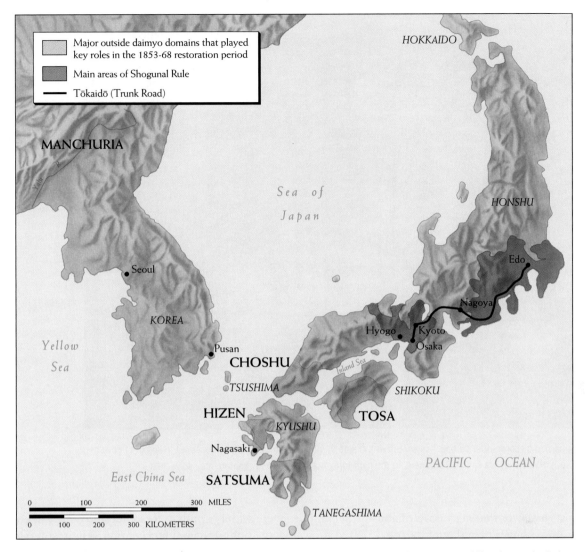

Map 20-3 Tokugawa Japan and the Korean peninsula. The area between Edo and Osaka in central Honshu was both the political base of the Tokugawa *bakufu* and its rice basket. The domains that would overthrow the Tokugawa *bakufu* in the late nineteenth century were mostly in outlying areas of southwestern Japan.

A second control was a hostage system, firmly established by 1642, that required the wives and children of daimyo to reside permanently in Edo and the daimyo themselves to spend every second year in Edo. Like the policy of Louis XIV (r. 1643–1715) at Versailles, this requirement transformed feudal lords into courtiers. The palatial Edo compounds of the daimyo contained hundreds or thousands of retainers and servants and occupied much of the city.

A third key control, established during the 1630s, was the national policy of seclusion. Seclusion was no barrier to cultural imports from China and Korea. But except for small Chinese and Dutch trading contingents at Nagasaki, no foreigners were permitted to enter Japan, and on pain of death, no Japanese were allowed to go abroad. Nor could oceangoing ships be built. This policy was strictly enforced until 1854. Like the case of a watch, seclusion enclosed the workings of the entire system. Cut off from substantial outside political contacts, for Japanese, Japan became the world.

An interesting parallel can be drawn between Europe and Tokugawa Japan. Between the fifteenth and eighteenth centuries France moved from a late feudal pattern toward ever greater centralization, whereas Germany moved toward a decentralized order of many independent states. In Japan these two tendencies were delicately balanced. On the one hand, representing the forces of centralization, was the *bakufu*, which governed its own domain and also administered the controls over the whole system. Its offices were staffed by its vassals—its highest councils by house daimyo and high-ranking

A daimyo seated in a palanquin carried by commoner porters. The screen at the side is rolled up so that he can observe the sights of Edo. Surrounding the palanquin are several dozen of his samurai retainers. In the right foreground are Edo townsmen. [Courtesy A. Craig]

bannermen, and lesser posts by lower-ranking vassals of ability. The pool of rank was always larger than that of the available posts.

On the other hand, representing decentralization were the domains of the 260 or so daimyo. Except for the house daimyo, they were excluded from service in the *bakufu*. Their domain governments, like miniature *bakufu*, were staffed by their samurai vassals. Each domain had its own autonomous military, finances, judiciary, schools, paper money, and so on. This balance between centralization and decentralization has led Japanese scholars to label the Tokugawa polity the "*bakufu*-domain system."

The Seventeenth-Century Economy The political dynamism of the period from Hideyoshi through the first century of Tokugawa rule was matched by economic growth. By the late sixteenth century there existed a backlog of agricultural techniques, the spread of which had been impeded by regionalism and wars: methods of water control and irrigation that made double-cropping easier, better tools, new seed strains, the use of bony fish or of night soil from cities as fertilizers, and so on. During the seventeenth century these

techniques were widely applied. Resources no longer needed for war were applied to land reclamation. The result was a doubling of agricultural production, as well as a doubling of population from about 12 million in 1600 to 24 million in 1700. The production of agricultural byproducts—cotton, silk, indigo, lumber, dyes, *sake*, and so on—also grew, especially in central Japan and along the shores of the Inland Sea.

Peace also sustained growth in commerce. The merchants in Warring States Japan, like geese who lay golden eggs, had always been at risk. They had to pay for security; they operated within cramped regional economies. On coming to power, Nobunaga and Hideyoshi knew that political unification alone was not enough. They recognized that prosperity would make their rule easier and, acknowledging the enterprise of the merchants, they abolished the medieval guilds and freed Japan's central markets from monopolistic restrictions. The result was a burgeoning of trade and the formation of a national market network atop the domain economies. As this network expanded during the seventeenth century, economic functions became more differentiated and more efficient. The economic chain that began with a local buyer might extend to a merchant house in a regional port, to coastal shippers, to warehousers in Osaka or Edo, and then to great wholesale houses.

Seclusion ended most foreign trade. One might expect the sharp decline in trade to have dampened Japan's domestic economy. Instead, commerce continued to grow for the remainder of the seventeenth century.

To explain this growth, we must look at the tax system and the pattern of consumption in the castle towns and Edo. Tokugawa tax policy was based on land, not commerce. Taxes took about one third of the peasant's production. It was a heavier tax rate than that in neighboring China and bespeaks the effective grasp of the military class had on Japanese society. Most taxes were paid in grain. Even as late as the mid-nineteenth century, only a third was collected in money payments. Thus, the 87 percent of the population who lived in the countryside paid almost one third of the country's agricultural wealth to the 5 percent in the military class. The remaining 8 percent of townspeople also lived off the tax flow by providing goods and services for samurai. This distribution of benefits was mirrored in the three-area city planning common to all castle towns: a large parklike area with castle, trees, stone walls, and moats for the daimyo and his government; an extensive samurai quarter; and a meaner townspeople's quarter.

Moreover, just as the castle towns were the consumption centers of the regional tax economies, so was Edo the national consumption center and a super-castle town. It had the same three-area layout, although on a far grander scale. When the great daimyo of Kaga, from a domain on the Japan Sea, was in attendance at Edo, he was served by 8,000 samurai. When he returned to his domain, 4,000 stayed on to manage the Kaga estates in Edo: 267 acres of houses and gardens, barracks, schools, warehouses, and so on. One of these estates, with its magnificent red gate still intact, is today the main campus of Tokyo University. Other daimyo had establishments proportional to their domains. By 1700 Edo had a population of about a million.

To support their Edo establishments, the daimyo sold tax rice in Osaka. Called the "kitchen of Japan," Osaka became the redistribution center from which competing fleets of coastal shippers brought to Edo food, clothing, lumber, oil, and other supplies. By 1700 Osaka's population was about 400,000. Kyoto, rebuilt after its destruction in the early Warring States period, was almost as big. It continued as a center of handicraft production. It also was the location of the "captive" imperial court, which, after suffering penury during the Warring States era, was given support lands equivalent in revenues to those of a small daimyo.

The system of alternate-year attendance at Edo also contributed to the development of overland transportation. The most traveled grand trunk road was the Tōkaidō Road between Edo and Kyoto. The artist Hiroshige (1797–1858) made a series of woodblock prints that depicted the scenery at its fifty-three post stations. The post stations had official inns for traveling daimyo and requisitioned supplies and

The commercial district of Osaka, the "kitchen" of Tokugawa Japan. Warehouses bear the crests of their merchant houses. Ships (upper right) loaded with rice, cotton goods, sake, and other goods are about to depart for Edo (Tokyo). Their captains vied with one another to arrive first and get the best price. [Courtesy A. Craig]

horses as a tax obligation from adjacent villages. These stations often grew into thriving local towns.

The growth and the national integration of the economy produced a richness and diversity in urban life. Townsmen governed their districts. Samurai city managers watched over the city as a whole. Official services were provided by schools, police, and companies of firefighters—a proverb of the time was "Fires are the flowers of Edo." But there were also servants, cooks, messengers, restaurant owners, priests, doctors, teachers, sword sharpeners, book lenders, instructors in the martial arts, prostitutes, and bathhouse attendants. In the world of popular arts there were woodblock printers and artists, book publishers, puppeteers, acrobatic troupes, storytellers, and Kabuki and Nō actors. Merchant establishments included money changers, pawnbrokers, peddlers, small shops, single-price retail establishments like the House of Mitsui, and great wholesale merchants. Merchant households furnished the raw materials for the personae of Edo fiction: the skinflint merchant who pinches every penny, the profligate son who runs through an inheritance to an inevitable bankruptcy, an erring wife, or the clerk involved in a hopeless affair with a prostitute.

Eighteenth and Early Nineteenth Centuries

By the late seventeenth century the political engineering of the Tokugawa state was complete. After that, few major new laws were enacted, and few important changes were made in governing institutions. In the economy, too, from the early eighteenth century, dynamic growth gave way to slower growth within a high-level equilibrium. In the words of some historians, the society had become "frozen," "unchanging," or "strangely preserved." Yet changes of a different kind were under way.

The Forty-Seven Rōnin   The eighteenth century began with high drama. In the spring of 1701 a daimyo on duty at Edo Castle drew his sword and slightly wounded a *bakufu* official who had insulted him. Even to unsheath a sword within the castle was punishable by death. On the same day the daimyo was ordered to commit *harakiri* (literally, to cut his stomach), and his domain was confiscated. Fearing an attempt at revenge, the *bakufu* police kept an eye on the daimyo's retainers—now *rōnin*, or "masterless samurai." The retainers dissembled, working at lowly jobs, staying at home with their families, or leading lives of drunkenness and debauchery.

Twenty-one months later, on a snowy night in January, forty-seven of the retainers gathered in Edo, attacked the residence of the *bakufu* official, took his head, and then surrendered to the authorities. Their act struck the imagination of the citizenry of Edo and was widely acclaimed. But the *bakufu* council, after deliberating for two months, ordered all forty-seven to commit *harakiri*. Embodying as it did the perennial theme of duty versus human feelings, the incident was quickly taken up by writers of Kabuki drama and puppet theater, and to this day has been reworked into novels, movies, and television scripts. Just as in Western theater there have been different Hamlets, so have there been many characterizations of Ōishi Kuranosuke, the leader of the band of forty-seven.

Viewed historically, three points may be noted about the incident. First, in a similar situation the more practical samurai of the Warring States period would have forgotten their former lord and rushed to find a new one. Loyalty was highly valued because disloyalty was a live option. But this was no longer true in the Tokugawa era. With the authority of the daimyo backed by that of the shōgun, there was no room for disloyalty. So loyalty became deeply internalized and was viewed almost as a religious obligation. It was also easier for Tokugawa samurai to be loyal unto death because, for the most part, there was so little likelihood in an era of peace that such a loyalty would be called for. In any case, in 1701 it was this Tokugawa species of absolute loyalty that moved the forty-seven rōnin.

Second, the incident tells something of the state in Tokugawa Japan. The 1615 "Laws for the Military Houses" contains the passage: "Law is the basis of the social order. Reason may be violated in the name of law, but law may not be violated in the name of reason. Those who break laws deserve heavy punishments."[4] One Tokugawa law forbade private vendettas. So, despite the moral purity of their act—which was recognized by all, even by those who condemned them to death—the forty-seven "virtuous warriors" had to die. The state was above ethics. Their death sentence was a bureaucratic necessity.

Third, loyalty and idealism were not a monopoly of the males. In the drama, at least, samurai wives and daughters displayed the same heroic spirit of self-sacrifice.

Cycles of Reform   Most political history of late Tokugawa Japan is written in terms of alternating cycles of laxity and reform. Even during the mid-seventeenth century the expenses of the *bakufu* and daimyo states were often greater than their income. In part, the reason was structural: Taxes were based on agriculture in an economy that was becoming commercial. In part, it was simple mathematics: After the samurai were paid their stipends, not enough was left for the expenses of domain government and the costs of the Edo establishments. In part, it was the toll of extraordinary costs, such as a *bakufu* levy, the wedding of a daimyo's daughter, or the rebuilding of a castle after a fire. And finally, in part, it was a taste for luxury among daimyo and retainers of rank.

---

[4]R. Tsunoda, W. T. de Bary, and D. Keene, eds., *Sources of the Japanese Tradition* (New York: Columbia University Press, 1958), p. 336.

The bridal procession of Yohime, the twenty-first daughter of the eleventh Tokugawa shōgun, approaches the Edo mansion of the Kaga daimyo. The red gate (upper right), built in 1827 for this occasion, is today an entrance to the main campus of Tokyo University. The eleventh shōgun had twenty-eight sons and twenty-seven daughters by his more than forty concubines. Of his children, thirteen sons and twelve daughters survived to maturity. This woodblock print by Kunisada is a "national treasure." [Courtesy A. Craig]

Over the years a familiar pattern emerged. To make ends meet, domains would borrow from merchants. Then, as finances became even more difficult, a reformist clique of officials would appear, take power, retrench the domain's finances, eliminate extravagance, and return the domain to a more frugal and austere way of life. Debts would be repaid or repudiated. A side effect of reform was the depression of the local merchant economy. But no one likes to practice frugality forever. So, after some of the goals of the reform had been achieved, a new clique would take over the government and a new round of spending would begin. The *bakufu* carried out three great reforms:

1787–1793	Tokugawa Yoshimune	17 years
1787–1793	Matsudaira Sadanobu	6 years
1841–1843	Mizuno Tadakuni	2 years

The first two were long and successful; the third was not. Its failure set the stage for the ineffective response of the *bakufu* to the West in the mid-nineteenth century. Reforms were also carried out by daimyo domains. Some were successful, enabling them to respond more effectively to the political crisis of the mid-nineteenth century.

Bureaucratization   The balance between centralization and decentralization lasted, surprisingly, until the end of the Tokugawa era. Not a single domain ever tried to overthrow the *bakufu* hegemony. Nor did the *bakufu* ever try to extend its control over the domains. But bureaucracy grew steadily both within the *bakufu* and within each domain. One development was the extension of public authority into areas that had been private. In 1600 most samurai fiefs were run by their samurai fief holders. They collected the taxes, often at a heavier rate than that set by the domain, and appointed fief stewards to oversee the fiefs. By 1850, however, all but the largest of samurai fiefs were administered by district officials. They collected the standard domain taxes and forwarded to the samurai their income. In periods of retrenchment, samurai were often paid only half the amount due.

A second development was the proliferation of administrative codes and government by paperwork. Surviving domain archives house room after room of records of every imaginable kind, mostly from the late eighteenth and early nineteenth centuries: records of births, adoptions, name changes, samurai ranks, fief registers, stipend registers, land and tax registers, records of court proceedings, historical records, and so on. Administrative codes for the *bakufu* exchequer, for example, grew from a single page during the seventeenth century to forty pages in the late Tokugawa. They define among other things an elaborate structure of offices and suboffices, their jurisdictional boundaries, and detailed instructions about how many copies of each document should be made and to which offices they should be forwarded.

Of course, there were limits to bureaucratization. Only samurai could aspire to official posts. They came to the office wearing their two swords. Decision-making posts were limited to upper-ranking samurai. In periods of financial crises—endemic in the late Tokugawa—a demand arose for men of ability, and middle- or lower-middle-ranking samurai joined domain decision-making by becoming staff assistants to bureaucrats of rank.

The Later Tokugawa Economy By 1700 the economy approached the limit of expansion within the available technology. The population, an important index, reached 26 million early in the eighteenth century and was at the same figure in the mid-nineteenth century, a period during which the population of China more than doubled. Within this constant figure were various smaller movements. Population declined during epidemics in the 1750s and the 1760s, and during famines in the 1780s. The northeast never fully recovered. Southwestern Japan along the Inland Sea gained in population. Central Japan stayed even; it was more urban, and like most premodern cities, Tokugawa cities had higher death rates.

After 1700 taxes became stabilized and land surveys were few. But evidence suggests little increase in grain production and only slow growth in agricultural byproducts. Some families made conscious efforts to limit their size in order to raise their standard of living. Contraception and abortion were commonplace, and infanticide (euphemistically called *mabiki*, the term for thinning out rice shoots in a paddy) was practiced in hard times. But periodic disease, shortages of food, and late marriages among the poor were more important. A study of one rural village showed the daughters of poor farmers marrying at twenty-two and having an average of 4.6 children, whereas for the daughters of rich farmers the figures were nineteen and 6.2. A study of another domain showed a decline in the size of the average farm household from 7 to 4.25 members.

During the Tokugawa some farmers remained independent small cultivators, but others became landlords or tenants. About a quarter of all cultivated lands were worked by tenants by the mid-nineteenth century. Most landlords were small, lived in their villages, and often were village leaders. They were not at all like the Chinese gentry. The misery of the lower stratum of rural society contributed to an increase in peasant uprisings during the late eighteenth and early nineteenth centuries. Authorities had no difficulty in quelling them, although some involved thousands of protestors and were locally destructive. No uprising in Japan even remotely approached those of late Manchu China.

Commerce grew slowly during the late Tokugawa. In the early eighteenth century it was reencased within guilds. Merchants paid set fees, usually not especially high, in return for monopoly privileges in central marketplaces. Guilds were also reestablished in the domains, and some domains established domain-run monopolies on products such as wax, paper, indigo, or sugar. The problem facing domain leaders was how to share in the profits without injuring the competitive standing of domain exports. Most late Tokugawa commercial growth was in countryside industries—*sake*, soy sauce, dyes, silks, or cotton—and was especially prominent in central and western Japan. Some were organized and financed by city merchants under the putting-out system. Others competed with city merchants, shipping directly to the end markets to circumvent monopoly controls. The expansion of labor in such rural industries may explain the population shrinkage in late Tokugawa cities.

The largest question about the Tokugawa economy concerns its relation to Japan's amazing industrialization, which began later in the nineteenth century. Some scholars have suggested that Japan had a "running start." Others have stressed Japanese backwardness in comparison with European late developers. The question is still unresolved.

Tokugawa Culture

If The *Tale of Genji* represents the classical culture of the aristocratic Heian court, and if Nō drama or an ink painting by Sesshū represents the austere samurai culture of medieval Japan, then a satire by Saikaku (1642–1693), a drama by Chikamatsu (1653–1724), or a woodblock print of a beauty by Utamaro (1753–1806) may be taken to represent the new urban culture of the Tokugawa era. In such works, one discerns a new secular consciousness, an exquisite taste put to plebeian ends, occasional vulgarities, and a sense of humor not often encountered in the earlier Japanese tradition.

But there was more to Tokugawa culture than the arts and literature of the townspeople. Two hundred and fifty years of peace and prosperity provided a base for a culture more complex than ever and for a broader popular participation in cultural life. In the villages Buddhism became more deeply rooted; new folk religions proliferated; and by the early nineteenth century most well-to-do farmers could read and write. The aristocratic culture of the ranking samurai houses also remained vigorous. Nō plays continued to be staged. The medieval tradition of black ink paintings was continued by the Kanō school and other artists.

The Ashikaga tradition of restraint, simplicity, and naturalness in architecture was extended. The imperial villa in Katsura outside of Kyoto has its roots in medieval architecture and to this day inspires Japanese architects. The gilded and colored screen paintings that had surged in popularity during Hideyoshi's rule developed further, culminating in the powerful works of Ogata Kōrin (1658–1716).

Zen Buddhism, having declined during the Warring States period, was revitalized by the monk Hakuin (1686–1769).

"Mother Bathing Her Son." Woodblock print (37.8 x 25.7 cm) by Kitagawa Utamaro (1753-1806). Note the cooper's craft seen in the barrel, the wooden clog, the simple yet elegant kimono design, and a second kimono hanging to dry at the upper right corner. [Photo: M. McLean The Nelson-Atkins Museum of Art, Kansas City, MO (Purchase: Nelson Trust). © The Nelson Gallery Foundation. All Reproduction Rights Reserved.]

One of the great cultural figures of the Tokugawa era, Hakuin was also a writer, a painter, a calligrapher, and a sculptor. His autobiographical writings have been translated as *The Embossed Tea Kettle*.

Some scholars have argued that Tokugawa urban culture had a double structure. On the one hand were the samurai, serious and high-minded, who produced a vast body of Chinese-style paintings, poetry, and philosophical treatises. On the other hand was the culture of the townspeople: lowbrow, irreverent, secular, satirical, and often scatological. The samurai esteemed Sung-style paintings of mountains or waterfalls, often adorned with quotations from the Confucian classics or T'ang poetry. The townspeople collected prints of pretty local beauties, actors, courtesans, and scenes from everyday life. Samurai moralists saw money as the root of evil. Merchants saw it as their goal in life; in Osaka, they even held an "abacus festival," at which their adding machines were consecrated to the gods of wealth and commerce.

In poetry, too, a double structure appeared. Bashō (1644–1694) was born a samurai but gave up his warrior status to live as a wandering poet. He is famous for his travel journal, *The Narrow Road of Oku*, and especially for his haiku, little word-picture poems:

> Such stillness—
> The cries of the cicadas
> Sink into the rocks.

> A crow perches
> On a leafless branch
> An autumn evening.

Or, on visiting a battlefield of the past, he wrote

> The summer grass
> All that is left
> Of a warrior's dream.[5]

Contrast Bashō's sense of the transience of life with the worldly humor of the townsman:

> From a mountain temple
> The snores of a monk and
> the voice of the cuckoo.

> Showing a love-letter
> to her mother
> From a man she doesn't love.

> Even the most virtuous woman
> will undo her sash
> For a flea.[6]

This is not to say, of course, that townspeople did not write proper haiku as well.

Literature and Drama   Is cultural creativity more likely during periods of economic growth and political change or during periods of stability? The greatest works of literature and philosophy of Tokugawa Japan were produced between 1650 and 1725, just as the initial political transformation was being completed, but the economy was still growing and the society not yet set in its ways.

One of the major literary figures and certainly the most entertaining was Ihara Saikaku (1642–1693), who is generally credited with having recreated the Japanese novel. Saikaku

[5]D. Keene, ed., *Anthology of Japanese Literature* edited by Donald Keene (New York: Grove Press, 1955), p. 371. Used by permission of Grove/Atlantic, Inc.
[6]R. H. Blyth, *Japanese Humor* (Tokyo: Japanese Travel Bureau, 1957), p. 141.

One of Edo's three Kabuki theaters during the 1790s. The male actors provide the drama—even female roles are played by men. The audience eats, drinks, and smokes while watching the action. Note the mix of social classes: Day laborers at center-left sit on boards while well-to-do merchants occupy more expensive seats in the right and left foreground. At bottom-center an artisan cadges a light for his pipe. Several boxes to his left, another pours a drink. A reprint of a three-panel woodblock print by Utagawa Toyokuni (1769–1825) from the late 1790s. [Musee Guimet, Paris, France/Giraudon/Art Resource, N.Y.]

was the heir to an Osaka merchant house. He was raised to be its master, but after his wife died he let the head clerk manage the business and devoted himself to poetry, the theater, and the pleasure quarters. At the age of forty he wrote and illustrated *The Life of an Amorous Man*, the story of a modern and bawdy Prince Genji who cuts a swath through bathhouse girls, shrine maidens, courtesans, and boy actors. The overnight success of the work led to a sequel, *The Life of an Amorous Woman*, the tale of a woman undone by passion and of her downward spiral through the minutely graded circles of the Osaka demimonde. Saikaku also wrote more than twenty other works, including *The Japanese Family Storehouse*, which humorously chronicles the contradictions between the pursuit of wealth and the pursuit of pleasure.

A second major figure of Osaka culture at the turn of the century was the dramatist Chikamatsu Monzaemon (1653–1724). Born a samurai in Echizen province, Chikamatsu entered the service of a court aristocrat in Kyoto and then, in 1705, moved to Osaka to write for both the Kabuki and the puppet theater. Kabuki had begun early in the seventeenth century as suggestive skits and erotic dances performed by troupes of actresses. In 1629 the *bakufu* forbade women to perform on the stage. By the 1660s Kabuki had evolved into a more serious drama with male actors playing both male and female roles. Actors entered the stage on a raised runway or "flower path" through the audience. Famous actors took great liberties in interpreting plays, to roars of approval from the audience. There was a ready market for woodblock prints of actors in their most famous roles—like posters of rock musicians today, but done with incomparably greater artistry.

The three main types of Kabuki plays were dance pieces, which were influenced by the tradition of the Nō; domestic dramas; and historical pieces. Chikamatsu wrote all three. In contrast to Saikaku's protagonists, the men and women in

Chikamatsu's dramas struggle to fulfill the duties and obligations of their stations in life. Only when their passions become uncontrollable, which is generally the case, do the plays end in tragedy. The emotional intensity of the ending is heightened by the restraint shown by the actors before they reach their breaking point. In some plays the hero and heroine leave duty behind and set out on a flight to death. Another favorite ending is the double suicide, in which the unfortunate lovers choose union in the next world. Indeed, this ending was banned by *bakufu* authorities when the excessive popularity of the drama led to its imitation in real life.

It is interesting to compare Kabuki and the Nō drama. Nō is like early Greek drama in that the chorus provides the narrative line. In Nō, the stylization of action is extreme. In Kabuki, as in Elizabethan drama, the actors declaim their lines in the dramatic realism demanded by the commoner theatergoers of seventeenth-century Japan. But to convey the illusion of realism required some deviation from it. As Chikamatsu himself noted about Kabuki: "Many things are said by the female characters which real women could not utter. . . . It is because they say what could not come from a real woman's lips that their true emotions are disclosed." For him, "Art is something that lies in the slender margin between the real and the unreal."[7] Yet, for all that Chikamatsu was concerned with the refinements of his craft and the balance between emotional expressiveness and unspoken restraints, he never talked of the mysterious "no mind" as the key to an actor's power. His dramas are a world removed from the religiosity of the medieval Nō.

In the early eighteenth century Kabuki was displaced in popularity by the puppet theater (Bunraku). Many of Chika-

---

[7]R. Tsunoda, p. 448.

matsu's plays were written for this genre. The word "puppet" does not do justice to the half-life-sized human figures, which rival Nō masks in their artistry. Manipulated by a team of three, a puppet does not only kneel and bow or engage in swordplay, but can also mimic brushing a tear from the eye with its kimono sleeve or threading a needle. In the late eighteenth century the puppet theater, in turn, declined, and as the center of culture shifted from Osaka to Edo, Kabuki again blossomed as Japan's premier form of drama.

Confucian Thought

The most important change in Tokugawa intellectual life was that the ruling elite abandoned the religious worldview of Buddhism in favor of the more secular worldview of Confucianism, opening many avenues for further changes. The reworking occurred slowly. During the seventeenth century samurai were enjoined never to forget the arts of war and to be ever ready to die for their lord. One samurai in his deathbed poem lamented dying on *tatami*—with his boots off, as it were. In this period, most samurai were illiterate. They saw book learning as unmanly. Nakae Tōju (1608–1648), a samurai and a Confucian scholar, recounted that as a youth he swaggered around with his friends during the day and studied secretly at night so as not to be thought a sissy. Schools, too, were slow to develop. One Japanese scholar has noted that in 1687 only four domains had schools; in 1715, only ten.

The great figures of Tokugawa Confucianism lived during the same years as Saikaku and Chikamatsu, in the late seventeenth and early eighteenth centuries. They are great because they succeeded in the difficult task of adapting Chinese Confucianism to fit Japanese society. One problem, for example, was that in Chinese Confucianism there was no place for a shōgun, whereas in the Japanese tradition of sun-line emperors, there was no room for the mandate of Heaven. Most Tokugawa thinkers handled this discrepancy by saying that Heaven gave the emperor its mandate and that the emperor then entrusted political authority to the shōgun. One philosopher suggested that the divine emperor acted for Heaven and gave the mandate to the shōgun. Neither solution was very comfortable, for, in fact, the emperor was as much a puppet as those in the Osaka theater.

Another problem was the difference between China's centralized bureaucratic government and Japan's "feudal" system of lord-vassal relationships. Samurai loyalty was clearly not that of a scholar-official to the Chinese emperor. Some Japanese Confucianists solved this problem rather ingeniously by saying that it was China that had deviated from the feudal society of the Chou sages, whereas in Japan, Tokugawa Ieyasu had recreated just such a society.

A third problem concerned the "central flowery kingdom" and the barbarians around it. No philosopher could quite bring himself to say that Japan was the real middle kingdom and China the barbarian, but some argued that centrality was relative, and still others suggested that China under barbarian Manchu rule had lost its claim to universality. These are just a few of a large range of problems related to Japanese political organization, Shinto, and with Japanese family practices. By the early eighteenth century these problems had been addressed, and a revised Confucianism acceptable for use in Japan had come into being.

Another point to note is the continuing intellectual vitality of Japanese thought—Confucian and otherwise—into the mid-nineteenth century. This vitality is partly explained by the disputes among different schools of Confucianism and partly, perhaps, by Japan's lack of an examination system. The best energies of its samurai youth were not channeled into writing the conventional and sterile "eight-legged essay" that was required for the Chinese examination system. Official preferment—within the constraints of Japan's hereditary system—was more likely to be obtained by writing a proposal for domain reforms, although this could sometimes lead to punishments as well.

The intellectual vitality was also a result of the rapid expansion of schools from the early eighteenth century. By the early nineteenth century every domain had its own official school on its Edo estate. Commoner schools *(terakoya)*, in which reading, writing, and the rudiments of Confucianism were taught, grew apace. In the first half of the nineteenth century private academies also appeared throughout the country. By the mid-nineteenth century about 40 to 50 percent of the male population and 15 to 20 percent of the female population was literate—a far higher rate than in most of the world, and on a par with some European late developers.

Other Developments in Thought

For Tokugawa scholars, the emotional problem of how to deal with China was vexing. Their response was usually ambivalent. They praised China as the teacher country and respected its creative tradition. They studied its history, philosophy, and literature, and began a tradition of scholarship on China that has remained powerful to this day. But they also sought to retain a separate Japanese identity. Most scholars dealt with this problem by adapting Confucianism to fit Japan. But two schools—never in the mainstream of Tokugawa thought, but growing in importance during the eighteenth and early nineteenth centuries—arrived at more radical positions. The schools of National Studies and Dutch Studies were diametrically opposed in most respects but alike in criticizing the Chinese influence on Japanese life and culture.

National Studies began as philological studies of ancient Japanese texts. One source of its inspiration was Shinto. Another was the Neo-Confucian School of Ancient Learning. Just as the School of Ancient Learning had sought to discover the original, true meanings of the Chinese classics before they were contaminated by Sung metaphysics, so the scholars in the National Studies tradition tried to find in the Japanese classics the original true character of Japan before it had been contaminated by Chinese ideas. On studying the *Record of Ancient Matters, The Collection of Myriad Leaves,* or *The Tale of Genji,* they found that the early Japanese spirit was free, spontaneous, clean, lofty, and honest, in contrast to the Chinese spirit, which they characterized as rigid, cramped, and artificial. Some writings of this school appear to borrow the anti-Confucian logic of Taoism.

A second characteristic of National Studies was its reaffirmation of Japan's emperor institution. Motoori Norinaga (1730–1801) wrote of Shinto creationism as the "Right Way":

Heaven and Earth, all the gods and all phenomena, were brought into existence by the creative spirits of two deities. . . . This . . . is a miraculously divine act the reason for which is beyond the comprehension of the human intellect.

But in foreign countries where the Right Way has not been transmitted, this act of divine creativity is not known. Men there have tried to explain the principle of Heaven and earth and all phenomena by such theories as in the yin and yang, the hexagrams of the Book of Changes, and the Five Elements. But all of these are fallacious theories stemming from the assumptions of the human intellect and they in no wise represent the true principle.

The "special dispensation of our Imperial Land" means that ours is the native land of the Heaven-Shining Goddess who casts her light over all countries in the four seas. Thus our country is the source and fountainhead of all other countries, and in all matters it excels all the others.[8]

National Studies became influential during the late Tokugawa era. It had a small but not unimportant influence on the Meiji Restoration. Its doctrines continued thereafter as one strain of modern Japanese ultranationalism. Its most enduring achievement was in Japanese linguistics. Even today, scholars admire Motoori's philology. Moreover, in an age when the prestige of things Chinese was overwhelming, Motoori helped redress the balance by appreciating and giving a name to the aesthetic sensibility found in the Japanese classics. The phrase he used was *mono no aware,* which means, literally, "the poignancy of things."

But National Studies had several weaknesses that prevented it from becoming the mainstream of Japanese thought. First, even the most refined sensibility is no substitute for philosophy. In its celebration of the primitive, National Studies ran headlong into the greater rationality of Confucian thought. Second, National Studies was chiefly literary, and apart from its enthusiasm for the divine emperor, it had little to offer politically in an age when political philosophy was central in both the domain and the *bakufu* schools.

A second development was Dutch Studies. After Christianity had been proscribed and the policy of seclusion adopted, all Western books were banned in Japan. Some knowledge of Dutch was maintained among the official interpreters who dealt with the Dutch at Nagasaki. The ban on Western books (except for those propagating Christianity) was ended in 1720 by the shōgun Tokugawa Yoshimune (r. 1716–1745), following the advice of a scholar whom he had appointed to reform the Japanese calendar.

During the remainder of the eighteenth century, a school of "Dutch medicine" became established in Japan. Japanese pioneers early recognized that Western anatomy texts were superior to Chinese. The first Japanese dissection of a corpse occurred in 1754. In 1774 a Dutch translation of a German anatomy text was translated into Japanese. By the mid-nineteenth century there were schools of Dutch Studies in the main cities of Japan, and instruction was available in some domains as well. Fukuzawa Yukichi (1835–1901), who studied Dutch and Dutch science during the mid-1850s at a school begun in 1838 in Osaka, wrote in his *Autobiography* of the hostility of his fellow students toward Chinese learning:

Though we often had discussions on many subjects, we seldom touched upon political subjects as most of us were students of medicine. Of course, we were all for free intercourse with Western countries, but there were few among us who took a serious interest in that problem. The only subject that bore our constant attack was Chinese medicine. And by hating Chinese medicine so thoroughly, we came to dislike everything that had any connection with Chinese culture. Our general opinion was that we should rid our country of the influences of the Chinese altogether. Whenever we met a young student of Chinese literature, we simply felt sorry for him. Particularly were the students of Chinese medicine the butt of our ridicule.[9]

Medicine was the primary occupation of those who studied Dutch. But some knowledge of Western astronomy, geography, botany, physics, chemistry, and arts also entered Japan. Works on science occasionally influenced other thinkers as well. Yamagata Bantō (1748–1821) was a rich and

---

[8]Tsunoda, pp. 521, 523.

[9]E. Kiyooka, trans., *The Autobiography of Fukuzawa Yukichi* (New York: Columbia University Press, 1966), p. 91.

Tokugawa Era (1600–1868)

1600	Tokugawa Ieyasu reunifies Japan
1615	"Laws of Military Houses" issued
1639	Seclusion policy adopted
1642	Edo hostage system in place
1644–1694	Bashō, poet
1653–1724	Chikamatsu Monzaemon, dramatist
1701	The forty-seven rōnin avenge their lord
1853, 1854	Commodore Matthew Perry visits Japan

scholarly Osaka merchant who produced a rationalistic philosophy based on a synthesis of Neo-Confucianism and Western science. After studying a work on astronomy, he wrote in 1820 that conditions on other planets "varied only according to their size and their proximity to the sun." Bantō also speculated that "grass and trees will appear, insects will develop; if there are insects, fish, shellfish, animals and birds will not be absent, and finally there will be people too." Bantō qualified his argument with the naturalistic supposition that Mercury and Venus would probably lack human life, "since these two planets are near to the sun and too hot." He contrasted his rational arguments regarding evolution with the "slap-dash" arguments of Buddhists and Shintoists.[10]

From the late eighteenth century the Japanese began to be aware of the West, and especially of Russia, as a threat to Japan. In 1791 a concerned Japanese wrote *A Discussion of the Military Problems of a Maritime Nation*, advocating a strong navy and coastal defenses. During the early nineteenth century such concerns mounted. A sudden expansion in Dutch Studies occurred after Commodore Matthew Perry's visits to Japan in 1853 and 1854. During the 1860s Dutch Studies became Western Studies, as English, French, German, and Russian were added to the languages studied at the *bakufu* Institute for the Investigation of Barbarian Books. In sum, Dutch Studies was not a major influence on Tokugawa thought. It cannot begin to compare with Neo-Confucianism. But it laid a foundation on which the Japanese built quickly when the need arose.

KOREA AND VIETNAM

A feature of world history, noted earlier, is the spread of heartland civilizations into their surrounding areas. In East Asia

the heartland civilization was that of China, the surrounding areas that were able to take in Chinese learning were Japan, Korea, and Vietnam. Like the Japanese, Koreans and Vietnamese learned to write using Chinese ideographs. They partially modeled their governments on those of China. They accepted Chinese Buddhism and Confucianism, and with them Chinese conceptions of the universe, state, and human relationships. The Confucian definitions of the relations between ruler and minister, father and son, and husband and wife were emphasized in Korea and Vietnam as they were in China. But at the same time, Koreans and Vietnamese spoke non-Chinese tongues, they saw themselves as separate peoples, and they gradually came to take pride in their independence. In Europe, Germany might be a parallel case: it became civilized by borrowing the heartland Greco-Christian culture of the Mediterranean area, but it kept its original tongue and elements from its earlier culture.

Korea

A range of mountains along its northern rim divides the Korean peninsula from Manchuria, making it a distinct geographical unit. Mountains continue south through the eastern third of Korea, while in the west and south are coastal plains and broad river valleys. The combination of mountains, rice paddies, and sea makes Korea a beautiful land. The traditional name for Korea may be translated as the "land of the morning calm." Two further geographical factors affected Korean history. One was that the northwestern corner of Korea was only three hundred miles from the northeastern corner of historical China: close enough for Korea to be vulnerable to invasions by its powerful neighbor but far enough away so that most of the time China found it easier to treat Korea as a tributary than to control it directly. The other factor was that the southern rim of Korea was just one hundred miles distant from the Japanese southern island of Kyushu across the Tsushima Straits.

Early History

During its old and new stone ages, Korea was peopled by Tungusic tribes moving south from northeast Asia. They spoke an Altaic tongue—distantly related to Japanese and to Manchurian, Mongolian, and Turkic. They lived by hunting, gathering, and fishing, and, like other early peoples of northeast Asia, made comb-patterned pottery and practiced an animistic religion. During the first millennium B.C.E. agriculture, bronze and iron were introduced, transforming their primitive society. But Koreans were still ruled by tribal chiefdoms in 108 B.C.E. when the Han Emperor Wu Ti sent an army into north Korea to menace the flank of the Hunnish (Hsiung Nu)

[10]M. Jansen, ed., *Changing Japanese Attitudes Toward Modernization* (Princeton: Princeton University Press, 1965), p. 144.

empire that spread across the steppe to the north of China. Wu Ti built a Chinese city—near the present-day capital of North Korea—which survived into the fourth century C.E., and established commanderies and prefectures to administer the land.

Between the fourth and seventh centuries three archaic states emerged from earlier tribal confederations. Silla, one of the three, together with armies from T'ang China, conquered the other two in the seventh century. The T'ang armies wanted to stay and rule Korea, but after battles with Silla troops they withdrew, and Silla was recognized by China in 675 as an autonomous tribute state. The period of Silla rule may be likened to Nara Japan: Korea borrowed Chinese writing, established some government offices on the Chinese model, sent annual embassies to the T'ang court, and took in Chinese Buddhism and Chinese arts and philosophies. Yet within the Silla government, birth mattered more than scholarship and rule by aristocrats continued, while in village Korea, the worship of nature deities was only lightly touched by the Buddhism that spread among the ruling elites.

Silla underwent a normal end-of-dynasty decline, and in 918 a warlord general founded a new dynasty, the Koryo. The English word "Korea" is derived from this dynastic name. This was a creative period. Korean scholars advanced in their mastery of Chinese principles of government. New genres of poetry and literature appeared. Korean potters made celadon vases rivaling those of China. The craft of history advanced: the earliest surviving history of Korea was compiled in 1145. Printing using moveable metallic type was invented during the thirteenth century. But most important of all was the growth of Buddhism. Temples, monasteries, and nunneries were built throughout the land, and Buddhist arts flourished. During the thirteenth century, Buddhist scholars produced in classical Chinese a printed edition of the Tripitaka, a huge compendium of sutras and other sacred writings.

Despite cultural advances, the Koryo state was weak. For one thing, the Koryo economy was undeveloped: trade was by barter, money did not circulate, and Chinese missions commented on the extravagance of officials in the capital and the squalor of commoners and slaves in Korea's villages. For another, the dynasty was aristocratic from the start, and as centuries passed, private estates and armies arose, and civil officials were replaced by military men. For still another, fre-

Celadon glazes spread from China to Korea during the Koryo period (918-1392). Pots such as this late 12th or early 13th century ewer are prized by collectors around the world for their graceful contours and detail.
[The Avery Brundage Collection/Asian Art Museum of San Francisco]

quent incursions from across Korea's northern border weakened the state. The cost of wars with the Mongols was particularly high. The Koryo court survived as long as it did by becoming in succession the tributary of the Sung, Liao, Chin, and Mongol dynasties.

The Choson Era: Late Traditional Korea

In 1392, a Koryo general, Yi Songgye, switched his allegiance from the Mongols to the rising Ming state, deposed the Koryo king, and founded a new dynasty. It lasted for 518 years until 1910; its amazing longevity was directly related to the stability of Ming-Ch'ing China.

After seizing power, Yi carried out an extensive land reform and strengthened his government by absorbing into his officialdom members of the great Koryo families. During the Yi or Choson period, these elite families, known as *yangban*, monopolized education, official posts, and land. Beneath them were the commoners known as "good people," tax-paying free subjects of the king. Beneath the commoners and constituting perhaps one-third of the population were government and private slaves. Korean scholars argue that they were not like slaves in other lands, since there were no slave auctions, and, following Confucian teachings, husbands were not separated from their wives. But Korean slaves were nonetheless property. They were often attached to land, they could be given as gifts, and their children were slaves to be used as their owners willed.

Early Choson culture showed many signs of vigor. Lyrical poetry and then prose reached new heights. In 1443, a group of scholars under King Sejong—who was regarded as a sage—invented a simple alphabet for the transcription of Korean without the burden of Chinese ideographs. Such was the prestige of Chinese writing that the simple alphabet was not used until modern times. The most important intellectual trend during the Choson era was the gradual movement of the *yangban* away from Buddhism and their acceptance of

Neo-Confucianism. By the late fifteenth century, Korean philosophers were making original contributions to the philosophy of this school, contributions that later became influential in Japan.

But at mid-dynasty, invasions dealt a severe blow to the well-being of Choson society. Hideyoshi, having brought all of Japan under his control, decided to conquer China; for him, the path to China was through Korea. His samurai armies devastated Korea twice, once in 1592 and again in 1596. The invasions ended with his death in 1598. On both occasions the Ming court sent troops to aid its tributary, but the rescuing Chinese armies, in turn, devastated the land almost as much as had the Japanese. A third disaster occurred in 1627 and 1637 when Manchu troops invaded pro-Ming Korea, laying waste to the northwest and to Seoul. The result of these multiple incursions was a drop in taxable land to about a quarter of its late-sixteenth-century level. Behind this statistic lay a grim reality of famine, death, and misery.

Had the late-sixteenth-century Choson government been stronger, it might have recovered. But from the end of the fifteenth century cliques of officials had begun to fight among themselves, and their partisan struggles intensified during the centuries that followed. On the surface, the struggles took the form of debates over issues relating to the king or queen. In actuality, they were bitter contests between the growing numbers of educated sons of *yangban* families over a limited number of official positions. Many in the losing factions were executed—at times dismembered—or imprisoned. As the struggles became more fierce, the effectiveness of government declined, except for a brief recovery during the early eighteenth century. High officials in Seoul used their power to garner private agricultural estates, and established local academies to prepare their own kinsmen for the official examinations.

From the mid-seventeenth century on, Korea offers a mixed picture. Literacy rose and a new popular fiction of fables, romances, and novels appeared. Women writers became important for the first time. Among some *yangban* there was a philosophic reaction against what was perceived as the emptiness of Neo-Confucianism. Calling for "practical learning" to effect a renewal of Korean society, scholars criticized the Confucian classics and outlined plans for administrative reforms and the encouragement of commerce. Unfortunately, their recommendations were not adopted, and the society continued its decline. More Koreans died in the famine of 1671 than during Hideyoshi's invasions. Overtaxation, drought, floods, pestilence, and famine became commonplace. Robberies occurred in daytime Seoul, and bandits plagued the countryside. Disgruntled officials led peasants in month-long revolts in 1811 and 1862. Because of the concentration of officials, wealth, and military power at Seoul

Korea	
108 B.C.E.–4th century C.E.	Chinese rule in northern Korea
4th century C.E.–675	Three archaic states
675–918	Silla
918–1392	Koryo
1392–1910	Choson
1592, 1596	Japanese invasions of Korea
1627, 1637	Manchu invasions of Korea
1671	Famine

and because of Manchu support for the ruling house, neither revolt succeeded in toppling the dynasty, but the revolts left Korea with neither the will nor the means to meet the challenges it would soon face.

Vietnam

Southeast Asia

The historical civilizations of Southeast Asia were shaped by three movements. One was the movement of peoples and languages from north to south. Ranges of mountains rising in Tibet and South China extend southward, dividing Southeast Asia into river valleys. The Mon and Burmese peoples had moved from the southeast slopes of the Tibetan plateau into the Upper Irrawaddy by 500 B.C.E., and continued south along the Irrawaddy and Salween Rivers, founding the kingdom of Pagan in 847 C.E.. Thai tribes moved south from China down the valley of the Chao Phraya River somewhat later, founding the kingdoms of Sukhothai (1238–1419) and Ayutthaya (1350–1767). Even today Thai-speaking tribes are still to be found in several south China provinces. The Vietnamese, too, arose in the north and moved into present-day central and south Vietnam only in recent historical times.

A second movement was the Indianization of southeast Asia. Between the first and fifteenth centuries Indian traders and missionaries crossed the Bay of Bengal and established outposts throughout southeast Asia. As Hinduism and Buddhism spread through the region, Indian-type states with god-kings were established, and Indian scripts, legal codes, literature, drama, art, and music were adopted by the indigenous peoples. Today, Burma, Thailand, and Cambodia retain an Indian-type of Buddhism; on the walls of Bangkok temples are painted scenes from the great Hindu epic, the *Mahabharata*.

A third movement of shorter duration but considerable dynamism was of Arab and Indian traders who sailed across

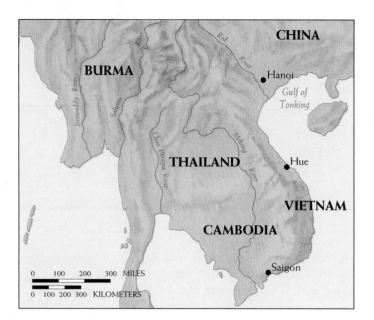

Map 20–4 Vietnam and neighboring Southeast Asia.

the Indian Ocean to dominate trade with the Spice Islands (the Moluccas of present-day Indonesia) between the thirteenth and fifteenth centuries. Settling on the coasts and islands of southeast Asia, they married into local ruling families and spread the teachings of Islam. Local rulers who converted became sultans. Today Malaysia and Indonesia are predominantly Muslim. The majestic Buddhist temple at Borobudur in central Java is a monument of an earlier age, submerged today in a sea of Islamic practice. Only the Hindu island of Bali to the east of Java retains the Indian religion that once covered the entire Indonesian archipelago.

Early Vietnamese History

Vietnam was the odd man out. While geographically defined as a part of southeast Asia, it was untouched by either Indian or Islamic culture. Instead, most of its higher culture came from China.

To comprehend Vietnamese history, one must immediately distinguish between the people and the land. Until the fifteenth century C.E., the Vietnamese people inhabited only a small portion of what is today Vietnam, only the basin of the Red River, which flows from west to east and empties into the gulf of Tongking. Central Vietnam and the southeastern coast was ruled by the state of Champa. Most of the Mekong River delta in the south was ruled by Cambodian empires.

The political history of the Vietnamese began in 208 B.C.E. when a renegade Han dynasty general formed the archaic state of Nan Yueh. It ruled over populations in southeastern China and the Red River basin from its capital, which was located near present-day Canton. In Vietnamese the Chinese ideograph "Yueh" is read "Viet." The name "Vietnam," literally "Viet to the south," is derived from the name of this early state. Nan Yueh lasted for less than a century. In 111 B.C.E. the armies of Han Wu Ti conquered it and brought it under Chinese rule.

For more than a millennium after 111 B.C.E., Vietnam was ruled by China. For the first seven centuries, it was ruled as a military commandery—like those established in Korea and other Chinese border regions for rule over non-Chinese "barbarian" populations. The administrative center was a fort with a Chinese governor and Chinese troops. The governor ruled indirectly through local Vietnamese chiefs or magnates, who were the heads of powerful local families. Then in 39 C.E., the Truong sisters led a revolt against Chinese rule—the husband of one sister had been executed by the Chinese. Thereafter more officials were sent from China and direct bureaucratic rule was instituted. Later Vietnamese historians made the two sisters into national heroes. A fifteenth century poet, for example, wrote:

> All the male heroes bowed their heads in submission;
> Only the two sisters proudly stood up to avenge the
> country.[11]

During these early centuries, change was slow. Buddhism was introduced into Vietnam from China. Chinese officials and immigrants married Vietnamese women, which led to the formation of a Sino-Vietnamese political elite. The influence of Chinese higher culture was largely confined to this elite.

The pace of change increased slightly during the T'ang dynasty (618–907). Vietnam was still treated as a border region, but Chinese administration became stronger. Elements of Chinese law and, possibly, the Chinese land and tax system were introduced at this time. Also, Vietnam was divided into provinces, which the Chinese referred to as *Annam*, the "pacified south." This old name was never lost: when the French came to Vietnam in the nineteenth century, they called its people the *Annamese*.

It was during the T'ang that Japan and Korea also reached out and took in Chinese learning. Was Vietnam's experience a parallel case? In some respects it was. In all three societies Buddhism entered, flourished in the capitals, and then gradually percolated into local areas, where it absorbed elements from earlier religious traditions. In all three, other aspects of China's higher culture affected mainly the elites of the society. In villages an older way of life continued. But the differences were also significant. Japanese and Korean rulers reached out for Chinese civilization, took it in, and used it

[11]K. W. Taylor, *The Birth of Vietnam* (1983), p. 334.

for their own ends. Japanese, in particular, were willing to transform what they had borrowed. During the ninth century they invented a syllabary for the transcription of their native language, which, by the year 1000, made possible works such as the *Tale of Genji* and the *Pillow Book*—representing a fusion of native and Chinese cultures. In Vietnam, because the rulers were Chinese, no such transformation occurred.

Late Traditional Vietnam

Ten major revolts occurred during the millennium of Chinese rule—a not unusual number for a Chinese border region with a non-Chinese population. The last revolt, in 939 when China was weak, led to the establishment of an independent Vietnamese government. Vietnam never again became a part of China.

Several approaches have been used in writing the history of Vietnam's second millennium. One sees it in terms of dynasties:

Ly	1009–1225
Tran	1225–1400
Le	1428–1787
Nguyen	1802–1880s

As in China, dynasties began with strong military figures, who established courts, extended their political control over the countryside, and collected taxes. Most founders of dynasties were members of the Sino-Vietnamese elite. Dynasties ended with the decentralization of power, the breakdown of taxation, and the rise of regional armies centering on powerful local figures. But the idea of a "dynastic cycle" of slow administrative decline fits Vietnam less well than China. For one thing, even early in a dynasty, administrations were weaker and less efficient than in China. Local magnates effectively contested central control for longer periods of time. For another, each new Chinese dynasty invaded Vietnam, feeling it proper to regain control over an area that had once been ruled by China. These invasions often reshaped dynasties. The Tran dynasty, for example, was extended for twenty extra years by Ming invasion forces. For still another, the dynastic name was sometimes kept even after its ruling house had lost its power. During the seventeenth and eighteenth centuries, for example, Vietnam was divided into two states, one ruling from Hanoi and the other from Hue. In short, though the "dynasty" may be a convenient unit for dividing the second millennium into large blocks of time, it is less useful for analysis.

Another approach is to see Vietnam in relation to the Chinese state and Chinese civilization. Although Chinese invasions of Vietnam were unsuccessful, Vietnamese rulers found it easier to "manage" China than to defy it altogether. So every Vietnamese dynasty became a "tributary" of China. Missions were sent to China bearing tribute. The head of the mission professed the Vietnamese ruler's submission to the Chinese emperor and performed the kowtow—prostrating himself before the emperor nine times with his head touching the floor. In correspondence with the Chinese "emperor," too, the Vietnamese rulers styled themselves as "kings," a title indicating their subordinate status. Yet this formal submission was little more than a ritual. Within Vietnam, Vietnamese rulers styled themselves as "emperors." They claimed their mandate to rule came directly from Heaven, separate but equal to the mandate received by the Chinese ruler. They denied the universality of the Chinese imperium by referring to China not as the Middle Kingdom but as the Northern Court —their own government being the Southern Court. In 1076, a Vietnamese general fighting Chinese troops wrote the following poem:

> The Southern emperor rules the Southern land
> Our destiny is writ in Heaven's Book
> How dare you bandits trespass on our soil
> You shall meet your undoing at our hands[12]

The poem, of course, was written in Chinese. Over the centuries the imprint of Chinese culture became more pronounced. One highpoint was the era of Le Thanh Tong (1442–1497), an early Le dynasty ruler and one of the strongest figures in all Vietnamese history. Le used Chinese culture and institutions as an advanced technology to strengthen his government. He established schools. He introduced Neo-Confucianism, institutionalized the recruitment of officials through an examination system, and promulgated in 1483 a legal code that remained in effect through the rest of the dynasty.

A third approach to Vietnamese history was the "march to the south" between the fifteenth and eighteenth centuries. Vietnam has been likened to two baskets on a carrying pole. One basket is the Red River delta centering on Hanoi in the north, the other the delta of the Mekong centering on Saigon in the south. The carrying pole is the narrow mountainous strip of central Vietnam. Until the fifteenth century, Vietnamese inhabited only the north. Central and southeastern Vietnam was Champa, the kingdom of the Chams, a sea-faring Malayan people who engaged in trade and piracy. The Chams had early been Hindu and later converted to Islam. They lived mainly on small, coastal river deltas that were separated by mountains running down to the sea. For centuries Vietnamese and Chams had waged intermittent wars. In 1357 when Tran rule was weak, a Cham army drove deep into Vietnam to pillage Hanoi. But under Le Thanh Tong Vietnam

[12]S. T. Huynh, *The Heritage of Vietnamese Poetry* (1979), p. 3. Reprinted by permission. Yale University Press.

went on the offensive, and by 1471 had destroyed Champa. Vietnam established colonies of soldier-peasants along the coast of the former Champa lands.

The destruction of Champa pulled the cork from the bottle. Landless settlers from the crowded Red River delta began to pour into the less densely settled south. Political authority followed the settlers. During the seventeenth century the once great Cambodian empire of Angkor was weak and unable to resist. By 1700 a southern Vietnamese state with a capital at Hue had pushed into the Mekong delta and conquered Saigon, and by 1757 its control extended west to the Gulf of Siam—occupying territories roughly corresponding to present-day southern Vietnam. This chain of events made south Vietnam quite different from the north. It was less Confucian and, as a frontier society, less educated. It was ethnically diverse with large minority populations of Muslim Chams and Cambodians, who practiced a southeast Asian form of Buddhism. Massive emigrations of Chinese into southeast Asia—a diaspora of sorts—also began during these centuries. Today about one million Chinese live in south Vietnam alone, and many play key roles in its economy. Such ethnic and religious diversity made the south far more difficult to govern than the more homogenous north.

During the last half of the eighteenth century Vietnam was wracked by further wars. In 1802, one warlord defeated opposing armies, unified the north and south, and established Vietnam's last dynasty, the Nguyen. It capital was at Hue. In coming to power the new emperor had been aided by French advisors and adventurers, and several were rewarded with high official posts. The Nguyen dynasty, nonetheless, became more Chinese than any previous dynasty. It adopted the law codes of Manchu China and established institutions such as the Six Boards, Hanlin Academy, Censorate, and a hierarchy of civil and military officials recruited by examina-

tions. The reasons for these initiatives were to placate Confucian scholars in the north, to strengthen the court, and to weaken the military figures who had helped the dynasty's rise. From the time of the second emperor it also became anti-French and strongly anti-Christian in its policies.

During the first half of the 19th century, Vietnam was probably governed better than at any previous time and better than any other southeast Asian state. By any traditional standard, it governed competently. But it had weaknesses. There were tensions between the north, which was overpopulated, well-schooled, and furnished most of the official class, and the south, which was ethnically diverse, educationally backward, and poorly represented in government. Trade and artisanal industries were less developed than in China and Japan, only small amounts of specie circulated, and periodic markets were more common than market towns. The government rested on a society composed largely of self-sufficient villages. In sum, Vietnam entered the second half of the nineteenth century even less prepared than China or Japan for the challenges it would soon face.

IN WORLD PERSPECTIVE

Late Traditional East Asia

The history of late traditional East Asia underlines the exceptional nature of the European development from commerce to industry. The arguments and counterarguments as to why this development did not occur in China and Japan are illuminating. One often-cited argument is that East Asia lacked the Protestant ethic that inspired Western capitalism. The counterargument is that all East Asian nations have strong family-centered ethics with an emphasis on frugality, hard work, and saving. Is that not a Protestant ethic of sorts? Moreover, if the problem is as deeply rooted as a religious ethic, why have parts of East Asia been able to achieve such explosive economic growth since the 1960s?

Another argument stresses the absence of a scientific revolution in premodern East Asia. The counterargument is that science made only a minimal contribution to England's early industrialization. Some scholars argue that in China merchant capital, instead of being put into industry, was invested in land, which was honorable and secure from rapacious officials. But this argument applies to the Ch'ing less well than the Ming and does not apply to Japan, where merchants could not buy land at all.

Still another argument stresses incentives and rewards. In England the self-educated technicians who invented the water loom and the steam engine reaped enormous rewards and honors. In China wealth and prestige were reserved largely for officials and gentry, who were literary or political in orientation and despised those who worked with their hands. No patent laws protected inventors. But other scholars ask whether the Ming and Ch'ing were so different from past dynasties during which the Chinese had been brilliantly inventive. Whatever the explanation, all agree that substantial commercial growth in both China and Japan did not lead to an indigenous breakthrough to machine industry.

Another comparison concerns bureaucracy. Bureaucracy does for administration what the assembly line does for manufacturing: It breaks complex tasks into simple ones to achieve huge gains in efficiency. In the West bureaucracies appeared only in recent centuries. They strengthened first monarchies and then nation-states against landed aristocrats. They are viewed as a sign of modernity, the triumph of ability over hereditary privilege. In some respects Chinese bureaucracy was similar: It was reasonably efficient, and it strengthened the central state. Would-be officials in nineteenth-century Britain studied the Greek and Roman classics, whereas those of China studied the Confucian classics.

But in other regards, Western historians of Chinese bureaucracy feel as if they have passed through Alice's looking glass: What was recent in the West had flourished for over a thousand years in China. Chinese officials themselves were a segment of a landed gentry class in a country from which hereditary aristocracies had long since disappeared. Moreover, although Chinese officials were certainly men of talent, they would become a major obstacle to modernity.

A final point to note is the difference between Chinese and Japanese attitudes toward outside civilizations. When the Jesuits tried to introduce science, the Chinese response was occasional curiosity and massive indifference. A few Jesuits were appointed as interpreters and court astronomers, or were used to cast cannon. The Chinese lack of interest in outside cultures may be explained by the coherence of China's core institutions of government—the emperor, bureaucracy, examination system, gentry, and Confucian schools—which had been in place for centuries. Having proved their worth, they were so deeply rooted and internalized as to approximate a closed system, impervious to outside influences. In contrast, the Tokugawa Japanese, despite a national policy of seclusion, reached out for Dutch science as they earlier had reached out for Chinese Neo-Confucianism. This difference would shape the respective responses of China and Japan to the West during the mid-nineteenth century.

For Korea and Vietnam, the problem is to explain why they were so much less developed in commerce—to say nothing of industry—than China and Japan. Were both the Korean *yangban* and the Vietnamese mandarins more aristocratic than Chinese gentry? Was the *yangban's* distaste for merchants greater than that of Chinese officials? Vietnam clearly lacked the long periods of peace—a necessary condition for commercial growth—enjoyed by China and Japan. Did the travails and social unrest during the last centuries of Choson rule in Korea also stifle the growth of commerce? These are questions for which scholars have not yet provided answers.

Review Questions

1. Why did the economy grow in late traditional China?

2. Did Manchu rule resemble Mongol rule, or was it different? In what regards were K'ang Hsi and Ch'ien Lung indistinguishable from Chinese emperors?

3. Ming-Ch'ing foreign relations set the stage for China's nineteenth-century encounter with the West. How would you describe the setting?

4. How did military technology in Japan change during the fifteenth and sixteenth centuries? Was unification the consequence or would it have happened anyway?

5. Contrast the dynamism of social engineering in seventeenth-century Japan with the high-level equilibrium of the eighteenth and early nineteenth centuries. How were these affected by changes in Japanese thought?

6. In what sense was Chinese culture a "technology" used by Japan, Korea, and Vietnam for state building? Why were the results in each country so different?

Suggested Readings ——

China

D. BODDE AND C. MORRIS, *Law in Imperial China* (1967). Focuses on the Ch'ing dynasty (1644–1911).

C. S. AND S. L. H. CHANG, *Crisis and Transformation in Seventeenth Century China: Society, Culture, and Modernity* (1992).

W. T. DE BARY, *Learning for One's Self: Essays on the Individual in Neo-Confucian Thought* (1991). A useful corrective to the view that Confucianism is simply a social ideology.

M. ELVIN, *The Pattern of the Chinese Past: A Social and Economic Interpretation* (1973). A controversial but stimulating interpretation of Chinese economic history in terms of technology. It brings in earlier periods as well as the Ming, Ch'ing, and modern China.

J. K. FAIRBANK, ED., *The Chinese World Order: Traditional China's Foreign Relations* (1968). An examination of the Chinese tribute system and its varying applications.

H. L. KAHN, *Monarchy in the Emperor's Eyes: Image and Reality in the Ch'ien-lung Reign* (1971). A study of the Chinese court during the mid-Ch'ing period.

LI YU, *The Carnal Prayer Mat*, trans. by P. Hanan (1990).

F. MOTE AND D. TWITCHETT, EDS., *The Ming Dynasty 1368–1644*, Part 1 of *The Cambridge History of China*, Vol. 7 (1987).

S. NAQUIN AND E. S. RAWSKI, *Chinese Society in the Eighteenth Century* (1987).

J. B. PARSONS, *The Peasant Rebellions of the Late Ming Dynasty* (1970).

P. C. PERDUE, *Exhausting the Earth, State and Peasant in Hunan, 1500–1850* (1987).

D. H. PERKINS, *Agricultural Development in China, 1368–1968* (1969).

M. RICCI, *China in the Sixteenth Century: The Journals of Matthew Ricci, 1583–1610* (1953).

W. ROWE, *Hankow* (1984). A study of a city in late imperial China.

G. W. SKINNER, *The City in Late Imperial China* (1977).

J. D. SPENCE, *Ts'ao Yin and the K'ang-hsi Emperor: Bondservant and Master* (1966). An excellent study of the early Ch'ing court.

J. D. SPENCE, *Emperor of China: A Self-Portrait of K'ang-hsi* (1974). The title of this readable book does not adequately convey the extent of the author's contribution to the study of the early Ch'ing emperor.

F. WAKEMAN, *The Great Enterprise* (1985). On the founding of the Manchu dynasty.

Japan

M. E. BERRY, *Hideyoshi* (1982). A study of the sixteenth-century unifier of Japan.

H. BOLITHO, *Treasures Among Men: The Fudai Daimyo in Tokugawa Japan* (1974). A study in depth.

C. R. BOXER, *The Christian Century in Japan, 1549–1650* (1951).

M. CHIKAMATSU, *Major Plays of Chikamatsu*, trans. by D. Keene (1961).

R. P. DORE, *Education in Tokugawa Japan* (1965).

C. J. *Dunn, Everyday Life in Traditional Japan* (1969). A descriptive study of Tokugawa society.

G. S. ELISON, *Deus Destroyed: The Image of Christianity in Early Modern Japan* (1973). A brilliant study of the persecutions of Christianity during the early Tokugawa period.

J. W. HALL, ED., *Early Modern Japan*, Vol. 4 of *The Cambridge History of Japan* (1991).

J. W. HALL AND M. JANSEN, EDS., *Studies in the Institutional History of Early Modern Japan* (1968). A collection of articles on Tokugawa institutions.

J. W. HALL, K. NAGAHARA, AND K. YAMAMURA, EDS., *Japan Before Tokugawa* (1981).

H. S. HIBBETT, *The Floating World in Japanese Fiction* (1959). An eminently readable study of early Tokugawa literature.

M. JANSEN, ED., *The Nineteenth Century*, Vol. 5 in *The Cambridge History of Japan* (1989).

D. KEENE, TRANS., *Chushingura, The Treasury of Loyal Retainers* (1971). The puppet play about the forty-seven rōnin who took revenge on the enemy of their former lord.

M. MARUYAMA, *Studies in the Intellectual History of Tokugawa Japan*, trans. by M. Hane (1974). A seminal work in this field by one of modern Japan's greatest scholars.

K. W. NAKAI, *Shogunal Politics* (1988). A brilliant study of Arai Hakuseki's conceptualization of Tokugawa government.

P. NOSCO, ED., *Confucianism and Tokugawa Culture* (1984). A lively collection of essays.

H. OOMS, *Tokugawa Ideology* (1985). A study of seventeenth-century Confucianism.

I. SAIKAKU, *The Japanese Family Storehouse*, trans. by G. W. Sargent (1959). A lively novel about merchant life in seventeenth-century Japan.

G. B. SANSOM, *The Western World and Japan* (1950).

C. D. SHELDON, *The Rise of the Merchant Class in Tokugawa Japan* (1958).

T. C. SMITH, *The Agrarian Origins of Modern Japan* (1959). On the evolution of farming and rural social organization in Tokugawa Japan.

R. P. TOBY, *State and Diplomacy in Early Modern Japan: Asia in the Development of the Tokugawa Bakufu* (1984).

C. TOTMAN, *Tokugawa Ieyasu: Shōgun* (1983).

C. TOTMAN, *Green Archipelago, Forestry in Preindustrial Japan* (1989).

H. P. VARLEY, *The Ōnin War: History of Its Origins and Background with a Selective Translation of the Chronicle of Ōnin* (1967).

K. YAMAMURA AND S. B. HANLEY, *Economic and Demographic Change in Preindustrial Japan, 1600–1868* (1977).

Korea

T. HATADA, *A History of Korea* (1969).

W. E. HENTHORN, *A History of Korea* (1971).

KI-BAIK LEE, *A New History of Korea* (1984).

PETER LEE, *Sourcebook of Korean Civilization*, Vol. I (1993).

Vietnam

J. BUTTINGER, *A Dragon Defiant, a Short History of Vietnam* (1972).

NGUYEN DU, *The Tale of Kieu* (1983).

N. TARLING, ED., *The Cambridge History of Southeast Asia* (1992).

K. TAYLOR, *The Birth of Vietnam* (1983).

A. B. WOODSIDE, *Vietnam and the Chinese Model* (1988).

Louis XIV of France (r. 1643–1715) was the dominant European monarch in the second half of the seventeenth century. The powerful centralized monarchy he created established the prototype for the mode of government later termed absolutism. [Giraudon/Art Resource, N.Y.]

CHAPTER TOPICS

◆ Two Models of European Political Development

◆ Constitutional Crisis and Settlement in Stuart England

◆ Rise of Absolute Monarchy in France: The World of Louis XIV

◆ Russia Enters the European Political Arena

◆ Central and Eastern Europe

◆ The First Worldwide Wars

In World Perspective Eighteenth-Century European States and Warfare

Between the early seventeenth and mid-twentieth century no region so dominated other parts of the world politically, militarily, and economically as Europe. Such had not been the situation before that date and would not be the situation after World War II. However, for approximately three and a half centuries northwestern Europe became the chief driving force in one world historical development after another. This era of European dominance, which appears quite temporary in the large scope of world history, also coincided with a shift in power within Europe itself from the Mediterranean, where Spain and Portugal had taken the lead in the conquest and early exploitation of America, to the states of the northwest and later north-central Europe. During the seventeenth and early eighteenth centuries certain states in northern Europe so organized themselves politically to dominate Europe and later to influence and even govern other large areas of the world through military might and economic strength. Even within the region of northern Europe there occurred a sorting out of influence among political states with

some successfully establishing long-term positions of dominance and others passing from the scene after relatively brief periods of either military or economic strength.

By the mid-eighteenth century five major states had come to dominate European politics and would continue to do so until at least World War I. They were Great Britain, France, Austria, Prussia, and Russia. Through their military strength, economic development, and in some cases colonial empires, they would affect virtually every other world civilization. Within Europe, these states established their dominance at the expense of Spain, Portugal, the United Provinces of the Netherlands, Poland, Sweden, and the Ottoman Empire. Equally essential to their rise was the weakness of the Holy Roman Empire after the Peace of Westphalia (1648).

By the middle of the eighteenth century the five successful states entered upon three quarters of a century of warfare among themselves. These wars were fought both in Europe and in the European colonial empires, making them the first extensive world wars aris-

ing from conflict in Europe. These conflicts represented the most extensive European impact on the non-European world since the early sixteenth century when the Spanish had conquered the civilizations of Mexico and Peru.

Two Models of European Political Development

In the second half of the sixteenth century changes in military organization, weapons, and tactics sharply increased the cost of warfare. Because traditional sources of income could not finance these growing costs, in addition to the costs of government, monarchs sought new revenues. Only monarchies that succeeded in building a secure financial base that was not deeply dependent on the support of noble estates, diets, or assemblies achieved absolute rule. The French monarchy succeeded in this effort, whereas the English monarchy failed. That success and failure led to the two models of government—absolutism in France and parliamentary monarchy in England—that shaped subsequent political development in Europe.

In their pursuit of adequate income, English monarchs of the seventeenth century threatened the local political interests and economic well-being of the nobility and landed and commercial elite. These groups invoked traditional English liberties to effectively resist the monarchs.

The experience of Louis XIV (r. 1643–1715), the French king, was different. After 1660 he made the French nobility dependent on his goodwill and patronage. In turn, he supported their local influence and their place in a firm social hierarchy. But even Louis's dominance had limits. He accepted the authority of the noble-dominated *Parlement* of Paris to register royal decrees before they officially became law, and he permitted regional parlements to exercise considerable authority over local administration and taxation. Funds from taxes levied by the monarchy found their way into many local pockets.

Religious factors also affected the political destinies of England and France. In England a strong Protestant religious movement known as Puritanism actively opposed the Stuart monarchy and eventually overturned it. Louis XIV, in contrast, crushed the Protestant communities of France. He was generally supported in these efforts by Roman Catholics, who benefited from the enforced religious uniformity.

There were also major institutional differences between the two countries. The English Parliament had long bargained with the monarch over political issues. In the early seventeenth century, to be sure, Parliament did not meet regularly and was not the strong institution it would become by the close of the century. Nor was there anything certain or inevitable about the transformation it underwent during the century. The institutional basis for it, however, was in place. Parliament existed and expected to be consulted. Its members—nobility and gentry—had experience organizing and speaking, writing legislation, and criticizing royal policies. Furthermore, the English had a legal and political tradition of liberty to which members of Parliament and their supporters could and did appeal against the monarchy.

France lacked a similarly strong tradition of broad liberties, representation, and bargaining between the monarchy and other national institutions. The Estates General had met from time to time to grant certain revenues to the monarch, but it played no role after 1614. Thereafter the monarchy found other sources of income, and the Estates General was not called again until the eve of the French Revolution in 1789. Consequently, opposition to the monarchy lacked both an institutional base and a forum in which the necessary political skills might have been developed.

Finally, personalities were important. During the first half of the century France profited from the guidance of two of its most able statesmen, Cardinals Richelieu and Mazarin. Mazarin trained Louis XIV to be a hard-working, if not always wise, monarch. Louis employed strong and capable ministers. The first four Stuart monarchs of England (r. 1603–1689), on the other hand, were distrusted. They did

not always keep their word. They acted on whim. Their judgment was often faulty. They rarely offered to compromise. They offended significant groups of their subjects unnecessarily. In a nation that saw itself as strongly Protestant, they were suspected, sometimes accurately, of Catholic sympathies. Many of their opponents in Parliament, of course, had flaws of their own, but attention and criticism were focused on the king.

In both England and France, the nobility and large landowners stood at the top of the social hierarchy and sought to protect their privileges and local interests. Important segments of the British nobility and landed classes came to believe that the Stuarts sought to undermine their local political control and social standing. Parliamentary government was the result of the efforts of these English landed classes to protect their interests and limit the power of the monarchy to interfere with life on the local level. The French nobility under Louis XIV, in contrast, eventually concluded that the best way to secure their own interests was to support the throne. Louis provided them with many forms of patronage, and he protected their tax exemptions, wealth, and local social standing.

Constitutional Crisis and Settlement in Stuart England

James I

In 1603 James VI of Scotland (r. 1603–1625), the son of Mary Stuart, Queen of Scots, without opposition or incident succeeded the childless Elizabeth I as James I of England. He also inherited a large royal debt and a fiercely divided church.

Parliament met only when the monarch summoned it, which James hoped to do rarely. In place of parliamentarily approved revenues, James developed other sources of income, largely by levying new custom duties known as impositions. Members of Parliament regarded this as an affront to their authority over the royal purse, but they did not seek a serious confrontation. Rather, throughout James's reign they wrangled and negotiated.

Puritans within the Church of England had hoped that James would favor their efforts to further reform the English church. But to their dismay, he firmly supported the Anglican episcopacy.

James's foreign policy also roused opposition. In 1604 he concluded a much-needed peace with Spain, England's longtime adversary. His subjects considered this a sign of pro-Catholic sentiment. James's unsuccessful attempt to relax penal laws against Catholics further increased their suspicions, as did his wise hesitancy in 1618 to rush English troops to the aid of German Protestants at the outbreak of the Thirty Years' War. His efforts to arrange a marriage between his son Charles and a Spanish princess and then Charles's marriage in 1625 to Henrietta Marie, daughter of Henry IV of France, further increased religious suspicions. In 1624, shortly before James's death, England again went to war against Spain largely in response to parliamentary pressures.

Charles I

Parliament had favored the war with Spain but would not adequately finance it because its members distrusted the monarchy. Unable to gain adequate funds from Parliament, Charles I (r. 1625–1649), like his father, resorted to extra-parliamentary measures. These included levying new tariffs and duties, attempting to collect discontinued taxes, and subjecting English property owners to a so-called forced loan (a tax theoretically to be repaid) and then imprisoning those who refused to pay. All these actions, as well as quartering troops in private homes, challenged local control of nobles and landowners.

When Parliament met in 1628 its members would grant new funds only if Charles recognized the Petition of Right. This required that henceforth there should be no forced loans or taxation without the consent of Parliament, that no freeman should be imprisoned without due cause, and that troops should not be billeted in private homes. It thus expressed resentment and resistance to the intrusion of the monarchy on the local level. Charles agreed to the petition, but whether he would keep his word was doubtful.

Charles I ruled for several years without calling Parliament, but once he began a war with Scotland, he needed revenues that only Parliament could supply. [Photographique de la Réunion des Musées Nationaux/Cliche des Musées Nationaux]

Years of Personal Rule   In January 1629 Parliament declared that religious innovations leading to "popery" and the levying of taxes without parliamentary consent were acts of treason. Charles promptly dissolved Parliament and did not recall it again until 1640.

To conserve his limited resources, Charles made peace with France in 1629 and Spain in 1630. This policy again roused fears that he was too friendly to Roman Catholic powers. To allow Charles to rule without renegotiating financial arrangements with Parliament, his chief minister, Thomas Wentworth (1593–1641; after 1640, earl of Strafford), instituted a policy known as *thorough*. This policy imposed strict efficiency and administrative centralization in government. Its goal was absolute royal control of England. Its success depended on the king's ability to operate independently of Parliament, which no law required him to summon. Charles's ministers exploited every legal fund-raising device, enforced previously neglected laws, and extended existing taxes into new areas.

Charles might have ruled indefinitely without Parliament had not his religious policies provoked war with Scotland. James I had allowed a wide variety of religious observances

in England, Scotland, and Ireland; by contrast, Charles hoped to impose religious conformity at least within England and Scotland. In 1637 Charles and Archbishop William Laud (1573–1645), against the opposition of both the English Puritans and the Presbyterian Scots, tried to impose on Scotland the English episcopal system and a prayer book almost identical to the Anglican *Book of Common Prayer*.

The Scots rebelled, and Charles, with insufficient resources for war, was forced to call Parliament. Parliament refused even to consider funds for war until the king agreed to redress a long list of political and religious grievances. The king, in response, immediately dissolved Parliament—hence its name, the Short Parliament (April–May 1640). When the Scots defeated an English army at the Battle of Newburn in the summer of 1640, Charles reconvened Parliament, this time on its terms, for a long and fateful duration.

The Long Parliament and Civil War

The landowners and the merchant classes represented in Parliament had long resented the king's financial measures and

Parliament Presents Charles I with the Petition of Right

After becoming monarch in 1625 Charles I (1625–1649) had imposed unparliamentary taxes, coerced freemen, and quartered troops in transit in private homes. These actions deeply offended Parliament, which in 1628 refused to grant him any funds until he rescinded those practices by recognizing the Petition of Right (June, 1628). The Petition constituted a general catalog of the offenses associated with the exercise of arbitrary royal authority.

What limits does the Petition attempt to place on royal taxation? How did the Petition criticize arbitrary arrest? Why was the quartering of soldiers in private homes so offensive?

[The Lords Spirit and Temporal, and commons in Parliament assembled] do humbly pray your Most Excellent Majesty, that no man hereafter be compelled to make or yield any gift, loan, benevolence, tax, or such like charge, without common consent by Act of parliament; and that none be called to make answer, to take such oath, or to give attendance, or be confined, or otherwise molested or disquieted concerning the same, or for refusal thereof; and that no freeman, in any such manner as in before-mentioned, be imprisoned or detained; and that your Majesty will be pleased to remove the said soldiers and mariners [who have been quartered in private homes], and that your people may not be so burdened in time to come; and that the foresaid commissions for proceeding by martial law, may be revoked and annulled; and that hereafter no commissions of like nature may issue forth to any person or persons whatsoever, to be executed as aforesaid, lest by colour of them any of your Majesty's subjects be destroyed or put to death, contrary to the laws and franchise of the land. All which they most humbly pray of your Most Excellent Majesty, as their rights and liberties according to the laws and statues of this realm.

The King's Reply: The King willeth that right be done according to the laws and customs of the realm; and that the statues be put in due execution, that his subjects may have no cause to complain of any wrong or oppressions, contrary to their just rights and liberties, to the preservation whereof he holds himself as well obliged as of his prerogative.

From *The Constitutional Documents of the Puritan Revolution*, ed. by Samuel R. Gardiner (Oxford: Clarendon Press, 1889), pp. 4–5.

---

paternalistic rule. The Puritans in Parliament resented his religious policies and deeply distrusted the influence of his Roman Catholic wife. The Long Parliament (1640–1660) thus acted with widespread support and general unanimity when it convened in November 1640.

The House of Commons impeached both Strafford and Laud. Both were executed—Strafford in 1641, Laud in 1645. Parliament abolished the courts that had enforced royal policy and had prohibited the levying of new taxes without its consent. Finally, Parliament resolved that no more than three years should elapse between its meetings and that it could not be dissolved without its own consent.

Parliament, however, was divided over religion. Both moderate Puritans (the Presbyterians) and more extreme Puritans (the Independents) wanted to abolish the episcopalcy and the *Book of Common Prayer*. The majority Presbyterians sought to reshape England religiously along Calvinist lines, with local congregations subject to higher representative governing bodies (presbyteries). Independents wanted every congregation to be its own final authority. Finally, many conservatives in both houses of Parliament were determined to preserve the English church in its current form. These divisions intensified in October 1641, when Parliament was asked to raise funds for an army to suppress a rebellion in Scotland. Charles's opponents argued that he could not be trusted with an army and that Parliament should become the commander-in-chief of English armed forces.

Civil War   On December 1, 1641, Parliament presented the king with the "Grand Remonstrance," a summary of popular and parliamentary grievances against the crown, containing more than two hundred articles. In January 1642 Charles invaded Parliament, intending to arrest certain of his opponents, but they managed to escape. The king then left London and began to raise an army. Shocked, a majority of the House of Commons passed the Militia Ordinance, which gave Parliament authority to raise an army of its own. The die was now cast. For the next four years (1642–1646), civil war engulfed England.

Charles's supporters, known as Cavaliers, were located in the northwestern half of England. The parliamentary opposition, known as Roundheads because of their close-cropped hair, had its stronghold in the southeastern half of the country. There were nobility, gentry, and townspeople on both sides. The chief factor distinguishing them was religion; the Puritans tended to favor Parliament.

Oliver Cromwell and the Puritan Republic

Two factors led finally to Parliament's victory. The first was an alliance with Scotland in 1643 that committed Parliament to a Presbyterian system of church government. The second was the reorganization of the parliamentary army under Oliver Cromwell (1599–1658), a country squire of iron discipline and strong independent religious sentiment. Cromwell and his "godly men" were willing to tolerate an established majority church, but only if it permitted Protestant dissenters to worship outside it.

Defeated by June 1645, Charles tried to take advantage of divisions within Parliament, but Cromwell and his army foiled him. Members who might have been sympathetic to the monarch were expelled from Parliament on January 30, 1649, after a trial by a special court. Charles was executed as a public criminal. Parliament then abolished the monarchy, the House of Lords, and the Anglican Church.

From 1649 to 1660 England became officially a Puritan republic, although it was dominated by Cromwell. His army conquered Ireland and Scotland, creating the single political entity of Great Britain. Cromwell, however, was no politician. When in 1653 the House of Commons wanted to disband his expensive army of fifty thousand, Cromwell disbanded Parliament. He ruled thereafter as Lord Protector.

Cromwell's military dictatorship, however, proved no more effective than Charles's rule and became just as harsh and hated. His great army and foreign adventures inflated the budget to three times what it was under Charles. Cromwell was as intolerant of Anglicans as Charles had been of Puritans. People deeply resented his Puritan prohibitions of drunkenness, theatergoing, and dancing. Political liberty vanished in the name of religious conformity. When Cromwell died in 1658, the English were ready to restore both the Anglican Church and the monarchy.

Oliver Cromwell's New Model Army defeated the royalists in the English Civil War. After the execution of Charles I in 1649, Cromwell dominated the short-lived English republic, conquered Ireland and Scotland, and ruled as Lord Protector from 1653 until his death in 1658. [Historical Pictures Collection/Stock Montage, Inc.]

Charles II and the Restoration of the Monarchy

After negotiations with the army Charles II (r. 1660–1685) returned to England amid great rejoicing. A man of considerable charm and political skill, Charles set a refreshing new tone after eleven years of somber Puritanism. England returned to the status quo of 1642, with a hereditary monarch, a Parliament that met only when the king summoned it, and the Anglican Church, with its bishops and prayer book, supreme in religion.

The king, however, had secret Catholic sympathies and favored religious toleration. He wanted to allow loyal Catholics and Puritans to worship freely. But in Parliament even the ultraroyalist Anglicans did not believe patriotism and religion could be separated. Between 1661 and 1665, through a series of laws known as the Clarendon Code, Parliament excluded Roman Catholics, Presbyterians, and Independents from the religious and political life of the nation.

In 1670 by the Treaty of Dover, England and France formally allied against the Dutch, their chief commercial competitor. In a secret portion of this treaty Charles pledged to announce his conversion to Catholicism as soon as conditions in England permitted. In return for this announcement (which was never made), Louis XIV promised to pay Charles a substantial subsidy. In an attempt to unite the English people behind the war with Holland, and as a sign of good faith to Louis XIV, Charles issued a Declaration of Indulgence in

William and Mary became the monarchs of England in 1689. Their accession brought England's economic and military resources into the balance against the France of Louis XIV. [Robert Harding Picture Library, London]

1672 suspending all laws against Roman Catholics and non-Anglican Protestants. But Parliament refused to fund the war until Charles rescinded the measure. After he did, Parliament passed the Test Act requiring all officials of the crown, civil and military, to swear an oath against the doctrine of transubstantiation—which no loyal Roman Catholic could honestly do. Parliament had aimed the Test Act largely at the king's brother, James, duke of York, heir to the throne and a recent, devout convert to Catholicism.

James II and Renewed Fears of a Catholic England

When James II (r. 1685–1688) became king in 1685, he immediately demanded the repeal of the Test Act. When Parliament balked, he dissolved it and proceeded openly to appoint known Catholics to high positions in both his court and the army. In 1687 he issued another Declaration of Indulgence suspending all religious tests and permitting free worship. Local candidates for Parliament who opposed the declaration were replaced by James's supporters. In June 1688 James imprisoned seven Anglican bishops who had refused to publicize his suspension of laws against Catholics. Each of these actions represented a direct royal attack on the local authority of nobles, landowners, the church, and other corporate bodies whose members believed they possessed particular legal privileges. Under the guise of a policy of enlightened toleration, James was actually seeking to subject all English institutions to the power of the monarchy.

The English had hoped that James would be succeeded by Mary (r. 1689–1694), his Protestant eldest daughter. She was the wife of William III of Orange (1650–1702), stadtholder of the Netherlands, great-grandson of William the Silent (1533–1584), and the leader of European opposition to Louis XIV. But on June 20 James II's Catholic second wife gave birth to a son. There was now a Catholic male heir to the throne. The Parliamentary opposition invited William to invade England to preserve its "traditional liberties," that is, the Anglican Church and parliamentary government.

The "Glorious Revolution"

William of Orange arrived with his army in November 1688 and was received without opposition by the English people. James fled to France, and Parliament in 1689 proclaimed William III and Mary II the new monarchs, thus completing the bloodless "Glorious Revolution." William and Mary, in turn, recognized a Bill of Rights that limited the powers of the monarchy and guaranteed the civil liberties of the English privileged classes. Henceforth, England's monarchs would be subject to law and would rule by the consent of Parliament, which was to be called into session every three years.

England	
1603	James VI of Scotland becomes James I of England
1625	Charles I becomes king of England
1628	Petition of Right
1629	Charles I dissolves Parliament and embarks on eleven years of personal rule
1640	April-May, Short Parliament; November, Long Parliament convenes
1641	Great Remonstrance
1642	Outbreak of the Civil War
1649	Charles I executed
1649-1660	Various attempts at a Puritan Commonwealth
1660	Charles II restored to the English throne
1670	Secret Treaty of Dover between France and England
1672	Parliament passes the Test Act
1685	James II becomes king of England
1688	Glorious Revolution
1689	William III and Mary II come to the throne of England
1701	Act of Settlement provides for Hanoverian Succession
1702-1714	Queen Anne, the last of the Stuarts
1714	George I of Hanover becomes king of England
1724-1742	Ascendancy of Sir Robert Walpole

Lady Mary Wortley Montague Advises Her Husband on Election to Parliament

In this letter of 1714, Lady Mary Wortley Montagu discussed how her husband might be elected to the House of Commons. Note her emphasis on knowing the right people and on having large amounts of money to spend on voters. Eventually her husband was elected in a borough that was controlled through government patronage.

What are the various ways in which candidates and their supporters used money to campaign? What role did friendships play in the campaigning? How important do the political ideas or positions of the candidates seem to be? Women could not vote in eighteenth-century parliamentary elections, but what kind of influence do they seem to exert?

You seem not to have received my letters, or not to have understood them: you had been chose undoubtedly at York, if you had declared in time; but there is not any gentleman or tradesman disengaged at this time; they are treating every night. Lord Carlisle and the Thompsons have given their interest to Mr. Jenkins. I agree with you of the necessity of your standing this Parliament, which, perhaps, may be more considerable than any that are to follow it; but, as you proceed, 'tis my opinion, you will spend your money and not be chose. I believe there is hardly a borough unengaged. I expect every letter should tell me you are sure of some place; and, as far as I can perceive you are sure of none. As it has been managed, perhaps it will be the best way to deposit a certain sum in some friend's hands, and buy some little Cornish borough: it would, undoubtedly, look better to be chose for a considerable town; but I take it to be now too late. If you have any thoughts of Newark, it will be absolutely necessary for you to enquire after Lord Lexington's interest; and your best way to apply yourself to Lord Holdernesse, who is both a Whig and an honest man. He is now in town, and you may enquire of him if Brigadier Sutton stands there; and if not, try to engage him for you. Lord Lexington is so ill at the Bath, that it is a doubt if he will live 'till the elections; and if he dies, one of his heiresses, and the whole interest of his estate, will probably fall on Lord Holdernesse.

'Tis a surprize to me, that you cannot make sure of some borough, when a number of your friends bring in so many Parliament-men without trouble or expense. 'Tis too late to mention it now, but you might have applied to Lady Winchester, as Sir Joseph Jekyl did last year, and by her interest the Duke of Bolton brought him in for nothing; I am sure she would be more zealous to serve me, than Lady Jekyl.

From Lord Wharncliffe, ed., Letters and Works of Lady Mary Wortley Montagu, 3rd ed., Vol. 1 (London, 1861), p. 211.

The Bill of Rights also prohibited Roman Catholics from occupying the English throne. The Toleration Act of 1689 permitted worship by all Protestants and outlawed only Roman Catholics and those who denied the Christian doctrine of the Trinity.

The measure closing this century of strife was the Act of Settlement in 1701. This bill provided for the English crown to go to the Protestant House of Hanover in Germany if Anne (r. 1702–1714), the second daughter of James II and the heir to the childless William III, died without issue. Thus, at Anne's death in 1714, the Elector of Hanover became King George I of England (r. 1714–1727), the third foreigner to occupy the English throne in just over a century.

The Age of Walpole

George I almost immediately confronted a challenge to his title. The Stuart pretender James Edward Stuart (1688–1766), the son of James II, landed in Scotland in December 1715 but met defeat less than two months later.

Despite the victory over the pretender, the political situation after 1715 remained in flux until Robert Walpole (1676–1745) took over the helm of government. George I gave Walpole his full confidence. For this reason Walpole has often been regarded as the first prime minister of Great Britain—although he never bore the title—and the originator of the cabinet system of government. Unlike a modern prime minister, he was not chosen by a majority of the House of Commons. His power largely depended on the goodwill of the king. Although Walpole generally demanded that all cabinet ministers agree on policy, he could not prevent frequent public differences among them.

The real source of his power was the combination of the support of the king, Walpole's ability to handle the House of Commons, and his iron-fisted control of government patronage. To oppose Walpole meant the almost certain loss of government patronage. Through the skillful use of patronage, Walpole bought support for himself and his policies from people who wanted jobs, appointments, favors, and government contracts. Such corruption cemented political loyalty.

This etching by Hogarth is part of a series satirizing the notoriously corrupt English electoral system. Hogarth shows voters being bribed and plied with free gin on their way to the polls. (Voting was then in public. The secret ballot was not introduced in England until 1872.)

[The Metropolitan Museum of Art, Harris Brisbane Dick Fund, 1932. Acc. #32.35 (212)]

The eighteenth-century British House of Commons was neither a democratic nor a representative body. Each county elected two members, but if the more powerful landed families agreed on the candidates, as often happened, there was no contest. Other members—many more than those elected from counties—were elected from units called *boroughs*. A few boroughs were large enough for elections to be relatively democratic. Most, however, had few electors. Proper management, which involved favors to the electors, could control the composition of the House of Commons.

The structure of Parliament and the manner in which the House of Commons was chosen resulted in the domination of the government of England by the owners of property and especially by wealthy nobles. They did not pretend to represent people and districts or to be responsive to what would later be called public opinion. They regarded themselves as representing various economic and social interests, such as the West Indian interest, the merchant interest, or the landed interest. These owners of property were suspicious of an

administrative bureaucracy controlled by the crown or its ministers. For this reason, they or their agents served as local government administrators, judges, militia commanders, and tax collectors. In this sense, the British nobility and other substantial landowners actually did govern the nation. Moreover, because they regarded Parliament as the political sovereign, there was no absence of central political authority and direction. The supremacy of Parliament consequently provided Britain with the unity that elsewhere in Europe was achieved through the institutions of absolutism.

British political life was freer than that on the Continent. Walpole's power had real limits. Parliament could not wholly ignore popular pressure. Even with the extensive use of patronage, many members of Parliament maintained independent views. Newspapers and public debate flourished. Free speech could be exercised, as could freedom of association. There was no large standing army. Walpole's enemies could and did openly oppose his policies, which would not have been possible on the Continent.

Walpole's ascendancy, which lasted from 1721 to 1742, brought the nation a stability that it had not enjoyed for over a century. He maintained peace abroad and promoted the status quo at home. Britain's foreign trade spread from New England to India. Agriculture became more productive. All forms of economic enterprise seemed to prosper. The navy became stronger. As a result of this political stability and economic growth, Great Britain became not only a European power of the first order but eventually a world power. Its government and economy during the next generation were models for all progressive Europeans.

As will be seen later in this chapter, the peaceful and prosperous Walpole era would come to an end in 1739 with a colonial war fought with Spain and then France. Thereafter, for over three quarters of a century, Britain and France would fight around the world for colonial domination. The France with which Britain engaged in that conflict had developed a system of government very different from the British.

Rise of Absolute Monarchy in France: The World of Louis XIV

Historians once portrayed Louis XIV's reign (r. 1643–1715) as a time when the French monarchy exerted far-reaching, direct control of the nation at all levels. A somewhat different picture is now emerging.

The groundwork for Louis's absolutism had been laid first by Cardinal Richelieu (1585–1642), the powerful chief minister for Louis XIII (r. 1610–1643), and then by Cardinal Mazarin (1602–1661). Both Richelieu and Mazarin had tried to impose direct royal administration on France. These efforts finally aroused a series of widespread rebellions among French nobles between 1649 and 1652 known as the Fronde (after the slingshot used by street boys).

These unsuccessful rebellions convinced Louis XIV and his advisors that heavy-handed policies could endanger the monarchy. Louis would concentrate unprecedented authority in the monarchy, but he would be more subtle than his predecessors. His genius was to make the monarchy the most important and powerful political institution in France while also assuring the nobles and other wealthy groups of their social standing and political and social influence on the local level. Rather than destroying existing local social and political institutions, Louis largely worked through them. Nevertheless, the king was clearly the senior partner in the relationship.

Years of Personal Rule

On the death of Mazarin in 1661 Louis XIV assumed personal control of the government at the age of twenty-three. He appointed no chief minister. Rebellious nobles would now be challenging the king directly; they could not claim to be resisting only a bad minister.

Louis ruled through powerful councils that controlled foreign affairs, the army, domestic administration, and economic regulations. Each day he spent hours with the chief ministers of these councils, whom he chose from families long in royal service or from among people just beginning to rise in the social structure. Unlike the more ancient noble families, they had no real or potential power bases in the provinces and depended solely on the king for their standing in both government and society.

Louis made sure, however, that the nobility and other major social groups would benefit from the growth of his own authority. Although he controlled foreign affairs and limited the influence of noble institutions on the monarchy, he never tried to abolish those institutions or limit their local authority. The crown, for example, usually conferred informally with regional parlements before making rulings that would affect them. Likewise, the crown would rarely enact economic regulations without consulting local opinion. Local parlements enjoyed considerable latitude in regional matters. Louis did clash with the Parlement of Paris, which had the right to register royal laws. In 1673 he curtailed its power. Many regional parlements and other regional authorities, however, had long resented the power of that body.

Versailles

Louis and his advisors became masters of propaganda and political image creation. Louis never missed an opportunity to impress the grandeur of his crown on the French people. When the dauphin (the heir to the French throne) was born in 1662, for example, Louis appeared for the celebration dressed as a Roman emperor.

The central element of the image of the monarchy, however, was the palace of Versailles. More than any other monarch of the day, Louis XIV used the physical setting of his court to exert political control. The palace at Versailles, built between 1676 and 1708 on the outskirts of Paris, became Louis's permanent residence after 1682. It was a temple to royalty, architecturally designed and artistically decorated to proclaim the glory of the Sun King, as Louis was known. A spectacular estate with magnificent fountains and gardens, it housed thousands of the more important nobles, royal officials, and servants. Although it consumed over half Louis's annual revenues, Versailles paid significant political dividends.

Because Louis ruled personally, he was the chief source of favors and patronage in France. To emphasize his prominence, he organized life at court around every aspect of his own daily routine. Elaborate court etiquette governed every detail of life at Versailles. Moments near the king were important to most court nobles because they were effectively excluded

Versailles, as painted in 1668 by Pierre Patel the Elder (1605–1676). The central building is the hunting lodge built for Louis XIII earlier in the century. The wings that appear here were some of Louis XIV's first expansions. [Giraudon/Art Resource, N.Y.]

from the real business of government. The king's rising and dressing were times of rare intimacy, when nobles could whisper their special requests in his ear. Fortunate nobles held his night candle as they accompanied him to his bed.

Some nobles, of course, avoided Versailles. They managed their estates and cultivated their local influence. Many others were simply too poor to cut a figure at court. All the nobility understood, however, that Louis, unlike Richelieu and Mazarin, would not threaten their local social standing. Louis supported France's traditional social structure and the social privileges of the nobility.

King by Divine Right

An important source for Louis's concept of royal authority was his devout tutor, the political theorist Bishop Jacques-Bénigne Bossuet (1627–1704). Bossuet defended what he called the "divine right of kings" and cited examples of Old Testament rulers divinely appointed by and answerable only to God. Medieval popes had insisted that only God could

judge a pope; so Bossuet argued that only God could judge the king. Although kings might be duty bound to reflect God's will in their rule, yet as God's regents on earth they could not be bound to the dictates of mere nobles and parliaments. Such assumptions lay behind Louis XIV's alleged declaration: *"L'état, c'est moi"* ("I am the state").

Despite these claims, Louis's rule did not exert the oppressive control over the daily lives of his subjects that police states would do in the nineteenth and twentieth centuries. His absolutism functioned primarily in the classic areas of European state action—the making of war and peace, the regulation of religion, and the oversight of economic activity. Even at the height of his power local institutions, some controlled by townspeople and others by nobles, retained their administrative authority. The king and his ministers supported the social and financial privileges of these local elites. But in contrast to the Stuart kings of England, Louis firmly prevented them from interfering with his authority on the national level. This system would endure until the French monarchy was demoralized by financial crisis at the end of the eighteenth century.

Throughout the age of the splendor at the court of Louis XIV millions of French peasants endured lives of poverty and hardship. [Erich Lessing/Art Resource, N.Y.]

Louis's Early Wars

By the late 1660s, however, France was superior to any other European nation in administrative bureaucracy, armed forces, and national unity. Louis could afford to raise and maintain a large and powerful army and was in a position to dominate Europe. He spent most of the rest of his reign attempting to do so, looking for opportunities to extend the borders of his domain and displace the power of the Habsburgs.

The early wars of Louis XIV included conflicts with Spain and the United Netherlands. The first was the War of the Devolution in which Louis supported the alleged right of his first wife, Marie Thérèse, to inherit the Spanish Netherlands.[1] He contended that through complex legal arrangements they should have "devolved" upon her, hence the name of the war. In 1667 Louis's armies invaded Flanders and the Franche-Comté. He was repulsed by the Triple Alliance of England, Sweden, and the United Provinces. By the Treaty of Aix-la-Chapelle (1668) he gained control of certain towns bordering the Spanish Netherlands (Map 21–1).

In 1670, with the Treaty of Dover, England and France became allies against the Dutch. Louis invaded the Netherlands again in 1672. The Dutch rallied around the leadership of the Prince of Orange, the future William III of England.

Orange forged an alliance with the Holy Roman Emperor, Spain, Lorraine, and Brandenburg against Louis, now regarded as a menace to the whole of western Europe, Catholic and Protestant alike. The war ended inconclusively with the Peace of Nijmwegen, signed with different parties in successive years (1678, 1679). France gained more territory, including the Franche-Comté.

Revocation of the Edict of Nantes

After the Edict of Nantes in 1598, relations between the great Catholic majority (nine tenths of the French population) and the Protestant minority had remained hostile. There were about 1.75 million Huguenots in France in the 1660s, but their numbers were declining. The French Catholic church had long supported their persecution as both pious and patriotic.

After the Peace of Nijmwegen, Louis launched a methodical campaign against the Huguenots in a determined effort to unify France religiously. He hounded them out of public life, banning them from government office and excluding them from such professions as printing and medicine. He used financial incentives to encourage them to convert to Catholicism. And in 1681 he bullied them by quartering his troops in their towns. Finally, Louis revoked the Edict of Nantes in October 1685. Protestant churches and schools were closed, Protestant ministers exiled, nonconverting laity forced to be galley slaves, and Protestant children ceremonially baptized by Catholic priests.

The revocation was a major blunder. Henceforth, Protestants considered Louis a fanatic who must be resisted at all costs. The revocation prompted the voluntary emigration of more than a quarter million people, who formed new

---

[1]The political divisions during the seventeenth and eighteenth centuries in what are today the Netherlands and Belgium were complex. The independence of the United Netherlands, a loosely federated union, was recognized at the Peace of Westphalia in 1764. Most of its population were Protestants. It was often referred to as "Holland," although Holland was simply the most important of its several provinces. Present-day Belgium, which included Flanders and Brabant, was governed by the Habsburgs, first Spanish, then Austrian—after 1714. Its population was overwhelmingly Roman Catholic. Both states enjoyed considerable commercial wealth and prosperity.

Louis XIV Revokes the Edict of Nantes

Believing that a country could not be under one king and one law unless it was also under one religious system, Louis XIV stunned much of Europe in October 1685 by revoking the Edict of Nantes, which had protected the religious freedoms and civil rights of French Protestants since 1598. Compare this document to the one later in the chapter in which the Elector of Brandenburg welcomes displaced French Protestants.

What specific actions does this declaration order against Protestants? Does it offer any incentives for Protestants to convert to Catholicism? How does this declaration compare with the English Test Act?

Art. 1. Know that we . . . with our certain knowledge, full power and royal authority, have by this present, perpetual and irrevocable edict, suppressed and revoked the edict of the aforesaid king our grandfather, given at Nantes in the month of April, 1598, in all its extent . . . together with all the concessions made by [this] and other edicts, declarations, and decrees, to the people of the so-called Reformed religion, of whatever nature they be . . . and in consequence we desire . . . that all the temples of the people of the aforesaid so-called Reformed religion situated in our kingdom . . . should be demolished forthwith.

Art. 2. We forbid our subjects of the so-called Reformed religion to assemble any more for public worship of the above-mentioned religion. . . .

Art. 3. We likewise forbid all lords, of whatever rank they may be, to carry out heretical services in houses and fiefs . . . the penalty for . . . the said worship being confiscation of their body and possessions.

Art. 4. We order all ministers of the aforesaid so-called Reformed religion who do not wish to be converted and to embrace the Catholic, Apostolic, and Roman religion, to depart from our kingdom and the lands subject to us within fifteen days from the publication of our present edict . . . on pain of the galleys.

Art. 5. We desire that those among the said [Reformed] ministers who shall be converted [to the Catholic religion] shall continue to enjoy during their life, and their wives shall enjoy after their death as long as they remain widows, the same exemptions from taxation and billeting of soldiers, which they enjoyed while they fulfilled the function of ministers. . . .

Art. 8. With regard to children who shall be born to those of the aforesaid so-called Reformed religion, we desire that they be baptized by their parish priests. We command the fathers and mothers to send them to the churches for that purpose, on penalty of a fine of 500 livres or more if they fail to do so; and afterwards, the children shall be brought up in the Catholic, Apostolic, and Roman religion. . . .

Art. 10. All our subjects of the so-called Reformed religion, with their wives and children, are to be strongly and repeatedly prohibited from leaving our aforesaid kingdom . . . or of taking out . . . their possessions and effects. . . .

The members of the so-called Reformed religion, while awaiting God's pleasure to enlighten them like the others, can live in the towns and districts of our kingdom . . . and continue their occupation there, and enjoy their possessions . . . on condition . . . that they do not make public profession of [their religion].

From S. Z. Ehler and John B. Morrall, ed. and trans., *Church and State Through the Centuries: A Collection of Historic Documents*. Copyright © 1967 Biblo and Tannen, pp. 209–213.

---

communities and joined the resistance to France in England, Germany, Holland, and the New World.

Louis's Later Wars

The League of Augsburg and the Nine Years' War
After the Treaty of Nijmwegen, Louis maintained his army at full strength and restlessly probed beyond his borders. In 1681 his forces occupied the free city of Strasbourg, prompting new defensive coalitions to form against him. One of these, the League of Augsburg, grew to include England, Spain, Sweden, the United Provinces, and the major German states. It also had the support of the Habsburg emperor Leopold I (r. 1658–1705). Between 1689 and 1697 the League and France battled each other in the Nine Years' War, while England and France struggled to control North America.

The Peace of Ryswick, signed in September 1697, secured Holland's borders and thwarted Louis's expansion into Germany.

War of the Spanish Succession
On November 1, 1700, Charles II of Spain (r. 1665–1700) died without direct heirs. Before his death negotiations had begun among the nations involved to partition his inheritance in a way that would preserve the existing balance of power. Charles II, however, left his entire inheritance to Louis's grandson Philip of Anjou, who became Philip V of Spain (r. 1700–1746).

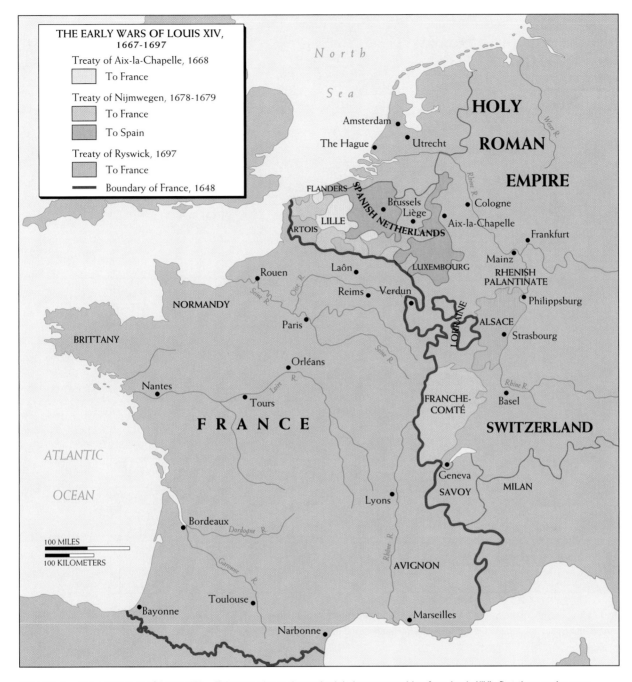

Map 21-1 The early wars of Louis XIV. This map shows the territorial changes resulting from Louis XIV's first three major wars (1667–1697).

THE EARLY WARS OF LOUIS XIV,
1667-1697

Treaty of Aix-la-Chapelle, 1668
☐ To France

Treaty of Nijmwegen, 1678-1679
☐ To France
☐ To Spain

Treaty of Ryswick, 1697
☐ To France
— Boundary of France, 1648

Spain and the trade with its American empire appeared to have fallen to France. In September 1701 England, Holland, and the Holy Roman Empire formed the Grand Alliance to preserve the balance of power by once and for all securing Flanders as a neutral barrier between Holland and France and by gaining for the emperor his fair share of the Spanish inheritance. Louis soon increased the political stakes by recognizing the Stuart claim to the English throne.

In 1701 the War of the Spanish Succession (1701–1714) began, and it soon enveloped western Europe. France for the first time went to war with inadequate finances, a poorly equipped army, and mediocre generals. The English, in contrast, had advanced weaponry (flintlock rifles, paper cartridges, and ring bayonets) and superior tactics (thin, maneuverable troop columns rather than the traditional deep ones). John Churchill, the duke of Marlborough (1650–1722)

Map 21–2   Europe in 1714. The War of the Spanish Succession ended a year before the death of Louis XIV. The Bourbons had secured the Spanish throne, but Spain had forfeited its possessions in Flanders and Italy.

bested Louis's soldiers in every major engagement, although French arms triumphed in Spain. After 1709 the war became a bloody stalemate.

France finally made peace with England at Utrecht in July 1713 and with Holland and the emperor at Rastatt in March 1714. Philip V remained king of Spain but England got Gibraltar, making it a Mediterranean power (see Map 21–2). Louis also recognized the right of the House of Hanover to accede to the English throne.

After Louis's death the authority of the monarchy weakened. France was economically exhausted. Louis XV (r. 1715–1744) was only five years old at his accession, and the regency allowed the *Parlement* of Paris greater authority. By 1726 the general political direction of the nation had come under the authority of Cardinal Fleury (1653–1743). He worked to maintain the authority of the monarchy while continuing to preserve the local interests of the French nobility. Like Walpole in Britain, he pursued economic prosperity at home and peace abroad. Again like Walpole, after 1740, Fleury could not prevent France from entering a worldwide colonial conflict, which will be discussed later in this chapter.

France

1649–1652	The Fronde, a revolt of nobility and townspeople against the crown
1661	Louis assumes personal rule
1667–1668	War of Devolution fought over Louis's claims to the Spanish Netherlands
1672	France invades the United Provinces
1678–1679	Peace of Nimwegen
1682	Louis establishes his court at Versailles
1685	Edict of Nantes revoked
1689–1697	Nine Years' War between France and the League of Augsburg
1697	Peace of Ryswick
1702–1714	War of the Spanish Succession
1713	Treaty of Utrecht between England and France
1714	Treaty of Rastadt between the Emperor and France
1726–1743	Ascendency of Cardinal Fleury

Russia Enters the European Political Arena

The emergence of Russia as an active European power constituted a wholly new factor in European politics. Previously Russia had been considered a part of Europe only by courtesy. Geographically and politically, it was peripheral. Hemmed in by Sweden on the Baltic and by the Ottoman Empire on the Black Sea, Russia had no warm-water ports. Its chief outlet to the west was Archangel on the White Sea, which was icebound much of the year. There was little trade. Russia did have vast, largely undeveloped natural and human resources.

Years of Turmoil

Ivan IV (r. 1533–1584), later known as Ivan the Terrible, came to the throne as a child. When he began his personal rule at the age of sixteen, he appointed able advisors, undertook sensible revisions of the law and local government, and reorganized the army. About 1560 he underwent a profound personality change and began to distrust virtually everyone around him. He then established a small group of advisors and a military force loyal to himself and loosed them against anyone he regarded as an enemy. He imprisoned, tortured, and executed *boyars* (the Russian term for noble) without cause or trial. He even killed his own son.

Ivan's reign was followed by a period of anarchy and civil war known as the Time of Troubles. In 1613, hoping to end the uncertainty, an assembly of nobles elected as tsar a sev-

enteen-year-old boy named Michael Romanov (r. 1613–1645). Thus began the dynasty that ruled Russia until 1917.

Michael Romanov and his two successors, Aleksei I (r. 1645–1676) and Theodore III (r. 1676–1682), brought stability and bureaucratic centralization to Russia. The country, however, remained weak and impoverished. The boyars largely controlled the bureaucracy. Furthermore, the government and the tsars faced the danger of mutiny from the *streltsy*, or guards of the Moscow garrison.

Peter the Great

In 1682 a ten-year-old boy ascended the fragile Russian throne as co-ruler with his half brother. His name was Peter (r. 1682–1725), and Russia would never be the same. He and his feeble half brother, Ivan V (d. 1696), had come to power on the shoulders of the *streltsy*, who expected rewards in return. Much violence and bloodshed had surrounded the disputed succession. Matters became even more confused when the boys' sister, Sophia (1657–1704), was named regent.

Peter the Great (r. 1682–1725), seeking to make Russia a major military power, reorganized the country's political and economic structures. His reign saw Russia enter fully into European power politics. [Corbis-Bettmann]

Peter's followers overthrew her in 1689; thereafter, Peter ruled personally. The dangers and turmoil of his youth convinced him that the power of the tsar must be made secure from the jealousy of the boyars and the greed of the streltsy and that Russian military power had to be increased.

Peter I, who came to be known as Peter the Great, was fascinated by western Europe, particularly its military resources. He was an imitator of the first order. The products and workers from the West who had filtered into Russia impressed and intrigued him. In 1697 he made a famous visit, supposedly in disguise, to western Europe. There he talked with the great and the powerful, who considered this almost-seven-foot-tall ruler both crude and rude. He inspected shipyards, docks, and the manufacture of military hardware and returned to Moscow determined to copy what he had seen abroad, for he knew that only warfare would make Russia a great power. The tsar's drive to modernize his nation, though unsystematic, had four general areas of concern: taming the boyars and the *streltsy*, achieving secular control of the church, reorganizing the internal administration, and developing the economy.

Peter pursued each of these goals with violence and ruthlessness. His successes strengthened his monarchy and allowed him to expand his military strength. By bringing the boyars, *streltsy*, and church under control, Peter curbed the power of the groups that might have opposed his expansion of the army and navy. Developing Russia's economy enabled him to finance his military ventures.

He made a sustained attack on the boyars. In 1698, immediately on his return from abroad, he personally shaved the long beards of the court boyars and sheared off the customary long, hand-covering sleeves of their shirts and coats, which had made them the butt of jokes throughout Europe. More important, he demanded they serve his state.

In 1722 Peter published a Table of Ranks, which henceforth equated a person's social position and privileges with his rank in the bureaucracy or the army rather than with his position in the nobility. However, the Russian nobility never became perfectly loyal to the state. It repeatedly sought to reassert its independence and control over the Russian imperial court.

The *streltsy* fared less well than the boyars. In 1698 they had rebelled while Peter was on his European tour. When he returned he retaliated brutally against both leaders and followers. There were private tortures and public executions, in which Peter's own ministers took part. Almost twelve hundred of the rebels were put to death, and their corpses long remained on public display to discourage future disloyalty.

Peter dealt with the potential political independence of the Russian Orthodox Church with similar ruthlessness. He wanted to avoid two kinds of difficulties with the Russian church. First, he sought to prevent the clergy from opposing change and westernization. Second, he sought to prevent the church hierarchy from making religious reforms that might provoke popular discontent, as had happened in the previous century. Consequently, in 1721 Peter replaced the posi-

Peter the Great built St. Petersburg on the Gulf of Finland to provide Russia with better contact with western Europe. He moved Russia's capital there from Moscow in 1703. This is an eighteenth-century view of the city. [The Granger Collection]

tion of patriarch of the Russian church with a synod headed by a layman to rule the church in accordance with the needs of the state.

In his reorganization of domestic administration, Peter looked to Swedish models, creating "colleges," or bureaus, composed of several officials rather than departments headed by a single minister. The colleges were to look after the collection of taxes, foreign affairs, war, and economic matters. This new organization was an attempt to breathe life into the country's stagnant and inefficient administration. In 1711 Peter created a senate of nine members to direct the central government when the tsar was away with the army. The purpose of these reforms was to establish a bureaucracy that could collect and spend tax revenues to support an efficient army.

Peter's economic policies were closely related to his military needs. He encouraged the establishment of an iron industry in the Ural Mountains, and by mid-century Russia had become the largest iron producer in Europe. He sent prominent young Russians abroad to acquire technical and organizational skills. He attempted to lure western European craftsmen to Russia. However, except for the striking growth of the iron industry, which later languished, these efforts had only marginal success.

These internal reforms and political departures supported a policy of warfare. Peter was determined to secure warm-water ports that would allow Russia to trade with the West and to intervene in European affairs. This led to wars with the Ottoman Empire and Sweden. Peter's armies captured Azov on the Black Sea in 1696, but he had to return it in 1711.

Peter had more success against Sweden, thanks to the inconsistency and irrationality of that country's king, Charles XII (r. 1697–1718). In 1700, in the opening of the Great Northern War, Russia moved against the Swedish territory on the Baltic but was defeated at the Battle of Narva. Charles's failure to follow up his victory allowed Peter to regroup his forces and hoard his resources. In 1709, when Charles XII returned to fight Russia again, Peter was ready and at the Battle of Poltava sealed the fate of Sweden. In 1721 the Peace of Nystad, which ended the Great Northern War, confirmed the Russian conquest of Estonia, Livonia, and part of Finland. Henceforth, Russia possessed warm-water ports and a permanent influence on European affairs.

At one point the domestic and foreign policies of Peter the Great literally intersected. This was at the spot on the Gulf of Finland where Peter founded his new capital city of Saint Petersburg (renamed Leningrad during much of the twentieth century). There he built government structures and compelled his boyars to construct town houses. In this fashion he imitated those western European monarchs who themselves had copied Louis XIV by constructing smaller versions of Versailles. The founding of Saint Petersburg, how-

Rise of Russian Power	
1533–1584	Reign of Ivan the Terrible
1584–1613	Time of Troubles
1613	Michael Romanov becomes tsar
1682	Peter the Great becomes tsar as a boy
1689	Peter assumes personal rule
1697	European tour of Peter the Great
1698	Peter suppresses the *streltsy*
1700	The Great Northern War opens between Russia and Sweden; Russia defeated at Narva by Charles XII
1703	Saint Petersburg founded
1709	Russia defeats Sweden at Poltava
1718	Death of Alexis, son of Peter the Great
1721	Peace of Nystad ends the Great Northern War
1721	Peter establishes control over the Russian church
1722	The Table of Ranks
1725	Peter dies, leaving an uncertain succession

ever, also symbolized a new orientation for Russia toward western Europe and indicated Peter's determination to keep the Baltic coast. He began the construction of the city and had moved the capital there in 1703, even before his victory over Sweden was assured.

Despite his success on the Baltic, Peter's reign ended with a great question mark. He had long quarreled with his only son, Alexis, the heir to the throne. Peter was jealous of the young man and fearful that he might undertake sedition. Alexis was imprisoned in 1718 and died mysteriously. Thereafter, Peter claimed the right to name a successor, but he could never bring himself to designate one either orally or in writing. Consequently, when Peter died in 1725 Russia had no firmer policy on succession than it had had when he acceded to the throne. For more than thirty years after his death, soldiers and nobles would once again determine who ruled Russia. Peter had laid the foundations of a modern Russia, but he had failed to lay the foundations of a stable state.

Central and Eastern Europe

As Russia became a major European power, the political contours of central Europe also changed. The Habsburgs realized they must expand their political base outside of Germany. Within Germany the Hohenzollerns over three generations forged Prussia into a major state. Thereafter, for over a century the Habsburg Empire and Prussia would duel for dominance in Germany. By the middle of the century that conflict would become united with the colonial conflict

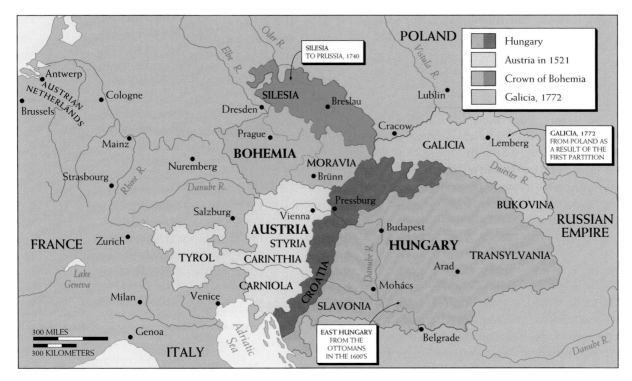

Map 21–3 The Austrian Habsburg Empire, 1521–1772. The Empire had three main units—Austria, Bohemia, and Hungary. Expansion was mainly eastward: Eastern Hungary from the Ottomans (seventeenth century) and Galicia from Poland (1772). Meantime, Silesia was lost, but the Habsburgs remained Holy Roman Emperors.

between Great Britain and France to create the first truly worldwide European war.

The Habsburg Empire and the Pragmatic Sanction

The close of the Thirty Years' War marked a fundamental turning point in the history of the Austrian Habsburgs. Previously, in alliance with their Spanish cousins, they had hoped to bring all of Germany under their control and back to the Catholic fold. In this they had failed, and the decline of Spanish power meant that the Austrian Habsburgs were on their own (see Map 21–3).

After 1648 the Habsburg family retained a firm hold on the title of Holy Roman Emperor, but the power of the emperor depended less on force of arms than on the cooperation he could elicit from the various political bodies in the empire. These included large German units (such as Saxony, Hanover, Bavaria, and Brandenburg) and scores of small German cities, bishoprics, principalities, and territories of independent knights. While establishing their new dominance among the German states, the Habsburgs also began to consolidate their power and influence within their hereditary possessions outside the Holy Roman Empire, which included the Crown of Saint Wenceslas, encompassing the kingdom of Bohemia (in modern Czechoslovakia) and the duchies of Moravia and Silesia; and the Crown of Saint Stephen, which ruled Hungary, Croatia, and Transylvania. Much of Hungary was only liberated from the Turks at the end of the seventeenth century (1699).

Through the Treaty of Rastadt in 1714 the Habsburgs further extended their domains, receiving the former Spanish (thereafter Austrian) Netherlands and Lombardy. Thereafter, the Habsburgs' power and influence would be based primarily on their territories outside Germany.

In each of their many territories the Habsburgs ruled by virtue of a different title and needed the cooperation of the local nobility, which was not always forthcoming. They repeatedly had to bargain with nobles in one part of Europe to maintain their position in another. Their domains were so geographically diverse and the people who occupied them of so many diverse languages and customs that almost no grounds existed on which to unify them politically. Even Roman Catholicism proved ineffective as a common bond, particularly in Hungary, the most recalcitrant province, where many Magyar nobles were Calvinist and seemed ever ready to rebel. Over the years Habsburg rulers established various central councils to chart common policies for their far-flung domains. Virtually all of these bodies, however, dealt with only a portion of the Habsburg holdings.

Despite these internal difficulties, Leopold I (r. 1658–1705) managed to resist the advances of the Turks into central Europe, which included a siege of Vienna in 1683, and to thwart the aggression of Louis XIV. He achieved Ottoman recognition of his sovereignty over Hungary in 1699 and extended his territorial holdings over much of the Balkan peninsula and western Romania. These southeastward extensions allowed the Habsburgs to hope to develop Mediterranean trade through the port of Trieste and helped compensate for their loss of domination over the Holy Roman Empire. Strength in the east gave them greater political leverage in Germany. Leopold was succeeded by Joseph I (r. 1705–1711), who continued his policies.

When Charles VI (r. 1711–1740) succeeded Joseph, a new problem was added to the chronic one of territorial diversity. He had no male heir, and there was only the weakest of precedents for a female ruler of the Habsburg domains. Charles feared that on his death the Austrian Habsburg lands might fall prey to the surrounding powers, as had those of the Spanish Habsburgs in 1700. He was determined to prevent that disaster and to provide his domains with the semblance of legal unity. To those ends, he devoted most of his reign to seeking the approval of his family, the estates of his realms, and the major foreign powers for a document called the *Pragmatic Sanction*.

This instrument provided the legal basis for a single line of inheritance within the Habsburg dynasty through Charles VI's daughter Maria Theresa (1740–1780). Other members of the Habsburg family recognized her as the rightful heir. After extracting various concessions from Charles, the nobles of the various Habsburg domains and the other European rulers did likewise. Consequently, when Charles VI died in October 1740, he believed that he had secured legal unity for the Habsburg Empire and a safe succession for his daughter. He had indeed established a permanent line of succession and the basis for future legal bonds within the Habsburg holdings. Despite the Pragmatic Sanction, however, his failure to provide his daughter with a strong army or a full treasury left her inheritance open to foreign aggression. Less than two months after his death, the fragility of the foreign agreements became apparent. In December 1740 Frederick II of Prussia invaded the Habsburg province of Silesia. Maria Theresa had to fight for her inheritance.

Prussia and the Hohenzollerns

The rise of Prussia occurred within the German power vacuum created by the Peace of Westphalia. It is the story of the extraordinary Hohenzollern family, which had ruled Brandenburg since 1417. Through inheritance the family had acquired Cleves and Mark and Ravensburg in 1614, East Prussia in 1618, and Pomerania in 1648 (see Map 21–4).

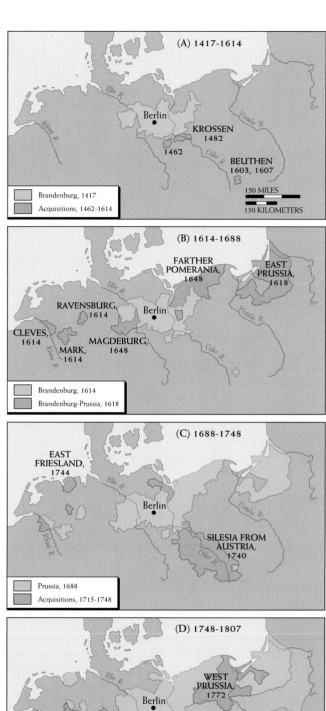

Map 21–4   Expansion of Brandenburg-Prussia.   In the seventeenth century Brandenburg-Prussia expanded mainly by acquiring dynastic titles in geographically separated lands. In the eighteenth century it expanded through aggression to the east, seizing Silesia in 1740 and various parts of Poland in 1772, 1793, and 1795.

The Great Elector Welcomes Protestant Refugees from France

The Hohenzollern dynasty of Brandenburg-Prussia pursued a policy of religious toleration. The family itself was Calvinist, whereas most of its subjects were Lutherans. When Louis XIV of France revoked the Edict of Nantes in 1685, Frederick William, the Great Elector, seized the opportunity to invite into his realms French Protestants. He wanted to attract persons with productive skills who could aid the economic development of his domains.

In reading this document, do you believe religious or economic concerns more nearly led the Elector of Brandenburg to welcome the French Protestants? What specific privileges did the Elector extend to them? To what extent were these privileges a welcoming measure and to what extent were they inducements to emigrate to Brandenburg? In what kind of economic activity does the Elector expect the French refugees to engage?

We, Friedrich Wilhelm, by Grace of God Margrave of Brandenburg. . . .

Do hereby proclaim and make known to all and sundry that since the cruel persecutions and rigorous ill-treatment in which Our co-religionists of the Evangelical-Reformed faith have for some time past been subjected in the Kingdom of France, have caused many families to remove themselves and to betake themselves out of the said Kingdom into other lands, We now . . . have been moved graciously to offer them through this Edict . . . a secure and free refuge in all Our Lands and Provinces. . . .

Since Our Lands are not only well and amply endowed with all things necessary to support life, but also very well suited to the reestablishment of all kinds of manufactures and trade and traffic by land and water, We permit, indeed, to those settling therein free choice to establish themselves where it is most convenient for their profession and way of living. . . .

The personal property which they bring with them, including merchandise and other wares, is to be totally exempt from any taxes, customs dues, licenses, or other imposts of any description, and not detained in any way. . . .

As soon as these Our French co-religionists of the Evangelical-Reformed faith have settled in any town or village, they shall be admitted to the domiciliary rights and craft freedoms customary there, gratis and without payments of any fee; and shall be entitled to the benefits, rights, and privileges enjoyed by Our other, native, subjects, residing there. . . .

Not only are those who wish to establish manufacture of cloth, stuffs, hats, or other objects in which they are skilled to enjoy all necessary freedoms, privileges and facilities, but also provision is to be made for them to be assisted and helped as far as possible with money and anything else which they need to realize their intention. . . .

Those who settle in the country and wish to maintain themselves by agriculture are to be given a certain plot of land to bring under cultivation and provided with whatever they need to establish themselves initially. . . .

From *The Habsburg and Hohenzollern Dynasties in the Seventeenth and Eighteenth Centuries*, C. A. Macartney, ed. Copyright © 1970, Walker and Company, pp. 270–273. Reprinted by permission.

Except for Pomerania, none of these lands was contiguous with Brandenburg. East Prussia lay inside Poland and outside the authority of the Holy Roman Emperor. All of the territories lacked good natural resources, and many of them were devastated during the Thirty Years' War. Still, by the late seventeenth century, the scattered Hohenzollern holdings represented a block of territory within the Holy Roman Empire second in size only to that of the Habsburgs.

The person who began to forge these areas into a modern state was Frederick William (r. 1640–1688), who became known as the Great Elector. He established himself and his successors as the central uniting power by breaking the medieval parliaments or estates, organizing a royal bureaucracy, and building a strong army.

Between 1655 and 1660 Sweden and Poland fought each other across the Great Elector's holdings in Pomerania and East Prussia. Frederick William had neither an adequate army nor the tax revenues to confront this foreign threat. In 1655 the Brandenburg estates refused to grant him new taxes; however, he proceeded to collect them by military force. In 1659 a different grant of taxes, originally made in 1653, elapsed; Frederick William continued to collect them as well as those he had imposed by his own authority. He used the money to build an army, which allowed him to continue to enforce his will without the approval of the nobility. Similar coercion took place against the nobles in his other territories.

There was, however, a political and social tradeoff between the Elector and his various nobles. These *Junkers*, or German noble landlords, were allowed almost complete control over the serfs on their estates. In exchange for their obedience to the Hohenzollerns, the *Junkers* received the right to demand obedience from their serfs. Frederick William also tended to choose as the local administrators of the tax structure men who would normally have been members of the noble branch of the old parliament. He thus co-opted potential opponents into his service. The taxes fell most heavily on the backs of the peasants and the urban classes. As the years passed, *Junkers* increasingly dominated the army officer corps, and this became even more pronounced during the eighteenth century. All officials and army officers took an oath of loyalty directly to the Elector. The army and the Elector thus came to embody the otherwise absent unity of the state. The army made Prussia a valuable potential ally.

Yet even with the considerable accomplishments of the Great Elector, the house of Hohenzollern did not possess a crown. The achievement of a royal title was one of the few state-building accomplishments of Frederick I (r. 1688–1713). This son of the Great Elector was the least "Prussian" of his family during these crucial years. He built palaces, founded Halle University (1694), patronized the arts, and lived luxuriously. In the War of the Spanish Succession he put his army at the disposal of the Habsburg Holy Roman Emperor Leopold I. In exchange, the emperor permitted Frederick to assume the title of "King in Prussia" in 1701.

His successor, Frederick William I (r. 1713–1740) was both the most eccentric monarch to rule the Hohenzollern domains and one of the most effective. He organized the bureaucracy along military lines. The discipline that he applied to the army was fanatical. The Prussian military grew from about thirty-nine thousand in 1713 to over eighty thousand in 1740, making it the third- or fourth-largest army in Europe. Prussia's population, in contrast, ranked thirteenth in size. Separate laws applied to the army and to civilians. Laws, customs, and royal attention made the officer corps the highest social class of the state. Military service thus attracted the sons of *Junkers*. In this fashion the army, the *Junker* nobility, and the monarchy became forged into a single political enti-

Maria Theresa of Austria provided the leadership that saved the Habsburg Empire from possible disintegration after the Prussian invasion of Silesia in 1740. [Kunsthistorisches Museum, Vienna]

ty. Military priorities and values dominated Prussian government, society, and daily life as in no other state in Europe. It has often been said that whereas other nations possessed armies, the Prussian army possessed its nation.

Although Frederick William I built the best army in Europe, he avoided conflict. His army was a symbol of Prussian power and unity, not an instrument for foreign adventures or aggression. At his death in 1740 he passed to his son Frederick II (r. 1740–1786; Frederick the Great) this superb military machine, but not the wisdom to refrain from using it. Almost immediately on coming to the throne, Frederick II upset the Pragmatic Sanction and invaded Silesia. He thus crystallized the Austrian-Prussian rivalry for the control of Germany that would dominate central European affairs for over a century.

The First Worldwide Wars

The War of the Spanish Succession had been fought mainly in Europe. The wars that Europe fought between 1739 and 1763 were worldwide in scope and impact. By the end of the conflicts the French had been driven out of North America,

Austria and Prussia

1640–1688	Reign of Frederick William, the Great Elector
1657–1705	Leopold I rules Austria and resists the Turks and Louis XIV
1683	Turkish siege of Vienna
1701	Frederick I becomes "King in Prussia"
1699	Peace between Turks and Habsburgs
1711–1740	Charles VI rules Austria and secures agreement to the Pragmatic Sanction
1713–1740	Frederick William I builds the military power of Prussia
1740	Maria Theresa succeeds to the Habsburg throne; Frederick II invades Silesia

and the British had established a domination in India that would last until 1947.

The Colonial Arena and the War of Jenkins's Ear

The Treaty of Utrecht established the boundaries of empire during the first half of the eighteenth century. Except for Brazil, which was governed by Portugal, Spain controlled all of mainland South America, as well as Florida, Mexico, and California in North America. Spain also ruled Cuba and half of Hispaniola. The British Empire consisted of the colonies along the North Atlantic seaboard, Nova Scotia, Newfoundland, Jamaica, and Barbados. Britain also possessed a few trading stations on the Indian subcontinent. The Dutch controlled Surinam, or Dutch Guiana, in South America; various trading stations in Ceylon and Bengal; and, most important, the trade with Java in what is today Indonesia.

The French had also established an empire in America and southern Asia. It covered the Saint Lawrence River valley; the Ohio and Mississippi River valleys; Saint Domingue (Haiti), Guadeloupe, and Martinique in the West Indies; and stations in India and West Africa. The economy of their West Indian islands resembled those of the Spanish and the British. Their holdings in Canada were sparsely populated, Quebec being the largest settlement, and the economy was based on agriculture and the fur trade. French and English settlers in North America clashed throughout the eighteenth century.

Each of the powers sought to make its imperial holdings into impenetrable trading areas. The Spanish Empire, however, especially stood on the defensive throughout the eighteenth century. The Spanish government lacked the capacity to maintain a commercial monopoly over its sprawling territory.

The Treaty of Utrecht gave the British a thirty-year *asiento*, or contract, to furnish slaves to the Spanish Empire and the right to send one ship each year to the trading fair at Portobello. Little but friction arose from these rights. Much to the chagrin of the British, the Spanish government under the Bourbons took its own alleged trading monopoly seriously and maintained coastal patrols, which searched English vessels for contraband.

In 1731, during one such search, there was a fight, and an English captain named Robert Jenkins had his ear cut off by the Spaniards. Thereafter, he preserved his ear in a jar of brandy. This incident was of little importance until 1738, when Jenkins appeared before the British Parliament, reportedly brandishing his ear as an example of Spanish atrocities to British merchants in the West Indies. British commercial interests put great pressure on Parliament to do something about Spanish interference in their trade. Robert Walpole could not resist these pressures, and in late 1739

Great Britain went to war with Spain. This might have been a relatively minor clash, but as a result of the Prussian invasion of Silesia, it became the opening encounter in a series of worldwide European wars that lasted off and on until 1815.

The War of the Austrian Succession (1740–1748)

In December 1740 the new king of Prussia, Frederick II, seized the Austrian province of Silesia. The invasion shattered the Pragmatic Sanction and upset the continental balance of power as established by the Treaty of Utrecht. In response to the Prussian aggression, the young Maria Theresa of Austria recognized Hungary as the most important of her crowns and promised the Magyars considerable local autonomy. She thus preserved the Habsburg state, but at great cost to the power of the central monarchy.

The war over the Austrian succession and the British-Spanish commercial conflict could have remained separate disputes. What united them was the role of France. A group of aggressive court aristocrats compelled the elderly Cardinal Fleury to support the Prussian aggression against Austria, the traditional enemy of France.

This proved to be one of the most fateful decisions in world history. French aid to Prussia helped to consolidate a new and powerful German state that could, and indeed later did, endanger France itself. The French move against Austria also brought Great Britain into the continental war against France and Prussia in an attempt to assure that Belgium remained in the friendly hands of Austria. In 1744 the British-French conflict expanded beyond the Continent when France decided to support Spain against Britain in the New World. The war ended in military stalemate in 1748 with the Treaty of Aix-la-Chapelle. Prussia retained Silesia, but the treaty was a truce rather than a permanent peace.

The Seven Years' War (1756–1763)

Before the rivalries again erupted into war, a dramatic shift of alliances took place. In 1756 Prussia and Great Britain signed the Convention of Westminster, a defensive alliance aimed at preventing the entry of foreign troops into the Germanies. Frederick feared invasions by both Russia and France. The convention meant that Great Britain, the ally of Austria since the wars of Louis XIV, had now joined forces with Austria's major eighteenth-century enemy. Later in 1756 Austria achieved a defensive alliance with France. Thus the traditional European alliances of the past century were reversed.

Conflict between France and Great Britain had continued unofficially on the colonial front. There were continual clashes between English and French settlers in the Ohio River valley and in upper New England. These skirmishes were

Though economically weak and with a small population, Prussia became an important state because it developed a large, well-trained army. Prussian troops were known for their discipline, the result of constant drill and harsh punishment. In this mid-eighteenth-century engraving one soldier is being whipped while another is about to run a gauntlet of other soldiers. [Bildarchiv Preussischer Kulturbesitz]

the prelude to what is known in American history as the French and Indian War. Once again, however, the factor that opened a general European war that extended into a colonial theater was the action of the king of Prussia.

In August 1756, what would become the Seven Years' War opened when Frederick II invaded Saxony. Frederick considered this a preemptive strike against a conspiracy by Saxony, Austria, and France to destroy Prussian power. In the spring of 1757 France and Austria made a new alliance dedicated to the destruction of Prussia. They were eventually joined by Sweden, Russia, and the smaller German states. Two factors, in addition to Frederick's strong leadership (it was after this war that he came to be called Frederick the Great), saved Prussia—British financial aid and the death in 1762 of Empress Elizabeth of Russia (r. 1741–1762). Her successor Tsar Peter III (d. 1762), a fervent admirer of Freder-

ick, immediately made peace with Prussia, thus allowing Frederick to hold off Austria and France. The Treaty of Hubertusburg of 1763 closed the continental conflict with no significant changes in prewar borders.

More impressive to the rest of Europe than the survival of Prussia were the victories of Great Britain in every theater of conflict. The architect of victory was William Pitt the Elder (1708–1778). Although Pitt had previously criticized British involvement with the Continent, once he was named secretary of state in charge of the war in 1757 he reversed himself and pumped huge financial subsidies to Frederick the Great. But North America was Pitt's real concern. Put simply, he wanted all of North America east of the Mississippi for Great Britain, and that was exactly what he won as he directed unprecedented resources into the overseas colonial conflict. The French government was unwilling and unable to direct

Benjamin West's (1738–1820) famous painting of the death of General Wolfe at the Battle of the Plains of Abraham in 1759. In this decisive battle, British forces under General Wolfe captured the city of Quebec from the French, ending French rule in Canada. [National Gallery, Ottawa, Ontario, Canada]

similar resources against the English in America. In September 1759 the British took Quebec City. Montreal fell the next year. The French empire in Canada was coming to an end.

Pitt's colonial vision, however, was global. The French West Indies fell to the British fleets. On the Indian subcontinent the British forces under Robert Clive (1725–1774) defeated the French in 1757 at the Battle of Plassey. This victory opened the way for the eventual conquest of all India by the British East India Company. Never had any other European power experienced such a complete worldwide military victory. Never had a European military victory affected so many non-Europeans.

The Treaty of Paris of 1763 was somewhat less triumphant. Pitt was no longer in office. George III (r. 1760–1820) had succeeded to the British throne and replaced Pitt with the Earl of Bute (1713–1792) in 1762. The new minister was responsible for the peace settlement, in which Britain received all of Canada, the Ohio River valley, and the eastern half of the Mississippi River valley. France retained footholds in India at Pondicherry and Chandernagore, and regained the West Indies sugar islands of Guadeloupe and Martinique.

The mid-century wars among European powers resulted in a new balance of power on the European continent and the high seas. Great Britain gained a world empire, and Prussia was recognized as a great continental power. With the surrender of Canada, France retreated from North America and thus opened the way for a continent largely dominated by the English language and Protestantism. By contrast, Latin America would be dominated by the Spanish and Portuguese languages and Roman Catholicism. For many years, West Africa would continue to furnish slaves to the economies of both Americas. On the subcontinent of Asia the foundations were laid for almost two centuries of British dominance. By 1760, therefore, a true world economy had been established

Mid-Eighteenth Century Conflicts	
1739	Outbreak of War of Jenkins's Ear between England and Spain
1740	War of the Austrian Succession commences
1748	Treaty of Aix-la-Chapelle
1756	Convention of Westminster between England and Prussia
1756	Seven Years' War opens
1757	Battle of Plassey
1759	British forces capture Quebec
1763	Treaty of Hubertusburg
1763	Treaty of Paris

in which political and economic developments in one region could directly and relatively quickly affect others.

IN WORLD PERSPECTIVE

Eighteenth-Century European States and Warfare

By the second quarter of the eighteenth century, the major European powers were not yet nation-states in which the citizens felt themselves united by a shared sense of community, culture, language, and history. They were still monarchies in which the personality of the ruler and the personal relationships of the great noble families considerably influenced public affairs.

These European states displayed certain problems that also characterized the governments of China and Japan during the same epochs. In particular, as in Japan, the problem of a balance between centralization and decentralization arose in virtually all the European states. In France, Russia, and Prussia the forces of centralization proved quite strong. In Austria the forces of decentralization were powerful. Eng-

land achieved a rather delicate balance. Furthermore, as in Tokugawa, Japan, European states of the eighteenth century generally saw an increase in legal codification and in the growth of bureaucracy. Only in Prussia did the military influence on society resemble that in Japan.

The role of the personality of the monarch in Europe bore some resemblance to that of certain Manchu emperors in China, such as K'ang Hsi (1662–1722) and Ch'ien Lung (r. 1736–1795). Louis XIV and Peter the Great had no less influence on their nations than did these great Manchu emperors. All of them built up military strength and fostered innovation. However, although European rulers developed state bureaucracies, none of them put together so brilliant a group of trained civil servants as those who administered China.

The global commercial empires of France, Spain, and England gave rise to fierce commercial rivalries. The drive for empire and commercial supremacy propelled these states into contact with Africa, Latin America, India, China, and Japan. Spain and Portugal had long exploited Latin America as their own monopoly, an arrangement that England challenged in the eighteenth century. Both France and England fought for commercial supremacy in India, and by the 1760s England had, in effect, conquered the subcontinent. The slave trade between Africa and the New World flourished throughout the eighteenth century. European merchants and navies also sought to penetrate East Asia. As a result of these developments, European commerce would dominate the world for the next two centuries. Europe and its colonists extracted labor and other natural resources from virtually all other continents of the world. The European military, especially naval dominance, made all this possible.

Consequently, by the mid-eighteenth century, the European states that just two centuries earlier had only started to settle the Americas and to engage in limited long-range trade had made their power and influence felt throughout the world. Beginning in the early eighteenth century, the political power of the European states became linked to a qualitatively different economic base than any seen elsewhere in the world. That political and economic combination allowed Europe to dominate the world from the 1750s to the Second World War.

Review Questions

1. By the end of the seventeenth century, England and France had different systems of government with different religious policies. What were the main differences? Similarities? Why did each nation develop as it did?

2. Why did the English king and Parliament come into conflict in the 1640s? What were the most important issues be-

hind the war between them, and who bears more responsibility for it? What was the Glorious Revolution, and why did it take place? What role did religion play in each event? How did England in 1700 differ from England in 1600?

3. Discuss the development of absolutism in France. What were the chief ways Louis XIV consolidated his monarchy?

What limits were there on his authority? What was Louis's religious policy? What were the goals of his foreign policy?

4. How was the Hohenzollern family able to forge a conglomerate of diverse land holdings into the state of Prussia? Who were the major personalities involved in this process and what were their individual contributions? Why was the military so important in Prussia? Compare and contrast the varying success with which the Hohenzollerns and Habsburgs each handled their problems. Which family was more successful and why?

5. How and why did Russia emerge as a great power? Discuss the character of Peter the Great. How were his domestic reforms related to his military ambitions? What were his methods of reform? To what extent did he succeed?

6. What were the main points of conflict between Britain and France in North America, the West Indies, and India? What were the results of these conflicts by 1763? Which countries emerged stronger from the Seven Years' War and why?

Suggested Readings ———

M. S. ANDERSON, *Europe in the Eighteenth Century, 1713–1783* (1988). A good one-volume introduction to the individual states.

T. M. BARKER, *Army, Aristocracy, Monarchy: Essays in War, Society and Government in Austria, 1618–1780* (1982). Examines the intricate power relationships among these major institutions.

W. BEIK, *Absolutism and Society in Seventeenth-Century France* (1985). An important study that questions the extent of royal power.

J. BLACK, *Eighteenth-Century Europe 1700–1789* (1990). An excellent survey.

R. BONNEY, *Political Change in France Under Richelieu and Mazarin 1624–1661* (1978). An important examination of the emergence of French absolutism.

J. BREWER, *The Sinews of Power: War, Money, and the English State, 1688–1783* (1989). A study that emphasizes the financial power behind British military success.

G. BURGESS, *Absolute Monarchy and the Stuart Constitution* (1996) A new study that challenges many of the traditional interpretative categories.

P. BURKE, *The Fabrication of Louis XIV* (1992). Examines the manner in which the public image of Louis XIV was forged in art.

F. L. CARSTEN, *The Origins of Prussia* (1954). Discusses the groundwork laid by the Great Elector in the seventeenth century.

J. C. D. CLARKE, *English Society: 1688–1832: Social Structure and Political Practice During the Ancien Régime* (1985). An important, controversial work that emphasizes the role of religion in English political life.

L. COLLEY, *Britons: Forging the Nation, 1707–1837* (1992) A major study of the making of British nationhood.

WALTER DORN, *Competition for Empire, 1740–1763* (1940). Still one of the best accounts of the mid-eighteenth-century struggle.

W. DOYLE, *The Old European Order, 1660–1800* (1992). The most thoughtful treatment of the subject.

P. DUKES, *The Making of Russian Absolutism: 1613–1801* (1982). An overview based on recent scholarship.

R. J. W. EVANS, *The Making of the Habsburg Monarchy, 1550–1700: An Interpretation* (1979). Places much emphasis on intellectual factors and the role of religion.

F. FORD, *Robe and Sword: The Regrouping of the French Aristocracy after Louis XIV* (1953). Remains an important book for political, social, and intellectual history.

P. GOUBERT, *Louis XIV and Twenty Million Frenchmen* (1966). A fine overview of seventeenth-century French social structure.

R. HATTEN, ED., *Louis XIV and Europe* (1976). Covers foreign policy.

D. HIRST, *Authority and Conflict: England 1603–1658* (1986). Scholarly survey integrating history and historiography.

J. M. HITTLE, *The Service City: State and Townsmen in Russia, 1600–1800* (1979). Examines the relationship of cities in Russia to the growing power of the central government.

L. HUGHES, *Russia in the Age of Peter the Great* (1998). A major new account.

H. C. JOHNSON, *Frederick the Great and His Officials* (1975). An excellent recent examination of the Prussian administration.

P. LANGFORD, *A Polite and Commercial People: England 1717–1783* (1989). An excellent survey of mid-eighteenth-century Britain based on the most recent scholarship covering social history as well as politics, the overseas wars, and the American revolution.

A. LOSSKY, *Louis XIV and the French Monarchy* (1994). The most recent major analysis.

R. K. MASSIE, *Peter the Great: His Life and His World* (1980). A good popular biography.

R. MIDDLETON, *The Bells of Victory: The Pitt-Newcastle Ministry and the Conduct of the Seven Years' War, 1757–1762* (1985). A careful study of the intricacies of eighteenth-century cabinet goverment that questions the centrality of Pitt's role in the British victory.

J. H. PLUMB, *Sir Robert Walpole*, 2 vols. (1956, 1961). A masterful biography ranging across the sweep of European politics.

J. H. PLUMB, *The Growth of Political Stability in England, 1675–1725* (1969). An important interpretive work.

J. G. A. POCOCK, ED., *Three British Revolutions: 1641, 1688, 1776* (1980). An important collection of essays.

N. V. RIASANOVSKY, *The Image of Peter the Great in Russian History and Thought* (1985). Examines the ongoing legacy of Peter in Russian history.

J. C. RILEY, *The Seven Years' War and the Old Regime in France: The Economic and Financial Toll* (1986). An analysis of pressures that would undermine the French monarchy.

H. ROSENBERG, *Bureaucracy, Aristocracy, and Autocracy: The Prussian Experience, 1660–1815* (1960). Emphasizes the organization of Prussian administration.

C. RUSSELL, *The Fall of the English Monarchies, 1637–1642* (1991). A major revisionist account, which should be read with Stone's book.

D. L. RUBIN, *The Sun King: The Ascendancy of French Culture During the Reign of Louis XIV* (1992). A collection of useful essay.

K. SHARPE, *The Personal Rule of Charles I* (1992). A major narrative work.

L. STONE, *The Causes of the English Revolution 1529–1642* (1972) Survey stressing social history and ruminating over historians and historical method.

G. TREASURE, *Mazarin: The Crisis of Absolutism in France* (1996). An examination not only of Mazarin, but also of the larger national and international background.

D. UNDERDOWN, *Fire from Heaven: Life in an English Town in the Seventeenth Century* (1992). A lively account of how a single English town experienced the religious and political turmoil of the century.

J. WEST, *Gunpower, Government, and War in the Mid-Eighteenth Century* (1991). A study of how warfare touched much government of the day.

J. B. WOLF, *Louis XIV* (1968). Authoritative and readable.

22 EUROPEAN SOCIETY UNDER THE OLD REGIME

During the eighteenth century, with their employment opportunities tightly restricted, many unmarried women and widows served as governesses to children of the aristocracy and other wealthier groups in Europe. At the other end of the spectrum, many children born out of wedlock or to very poor parents might be left at foundling hospitals where many of them died quite young.

[Chardin, Jean-Baptiste-Simeon: "The Governess" (#6432), National Gallery of Canada, Ottawa]

CHAPTER TOPICS

◆ Major Features of Life in the Old Regime
◆ Aristocracy
◆ The Land and Its Tillers

◆ Family Structures and the Family Economy
◆ Growth of Agriculture and Population
◆ The Eighteenth-Century Industrial Revolution

◆ Cities
◆ The Jewish Population: Age of the Ghetto
In World Perspective The European Old Regime

At the opening of the eighteenth century European merchants and traders dominated the transatlantic economy, and European states governed much of the American continents, though in North America only along the Atlantic seaboard. During the century the peoples living primarily in northwestern Europe undertook a series of economic advances that laid the foundation for the social and economic transformation of the world. Europeans began for the first time in their history to achieve a more or less stable food supply. For reasons still much debated the population of Europe commenced a major period of growth. New inventions in the manufacture of textiles transformed Europe's productive capacity, and the invention of the steam engine, powered by coal as a fuel, opened the way for moving manufacturing from the countryside to cities. Furthermore, the production of iron greatly expanded. These developments, known collectively as the Industrial Revolution, gave Europe a productive capacity unknown before in human history. For a time that state of economic advance provided Europeans with the tools to dominate much of the world both economically and militarily. At the same time, the industrial achievement of Europe became an example that for the next two centuries less economically advanced areas of the world would seek to imitate. All of this potential for change emerged in a society whose institutions had been in large measure designed to inhibit or even prevent major social and economic change.

During the turmoil of the French Revolution and its aftermath, it became customary to refer to the patterns of social, political, and economic relationships that had existed in France before 1789 as the *ancien régime*, or the "Old Regime." The term has come to be applied generally to the life and institutions of prerevolutionary continental Europe. Politically, it meant the rule of theoretically absolute monarchies with growing bureaucracies and aristocratically led armies. Economically, the Old Regime was characterized by food shortages, the predominance of agriculture, slow transport, a low level of iron production, comparatively unsophisticated financial institutions, and, in some cases, competitive commercial overseas empires. Socially, men and women saw themselves less as individuals than as members of distinct corporate bodies that possessed certain privileges or rights as a group.

Tradition, hierarchy, corporateness, and privilege were thus the chief social characteristics of the Old Regime. Yet change and innovation were fermenting in its midst as farming became more commercialized and the size of the population increased. The early Industrial Revolution expanded the quantity of consumer goods. The colonies in the Americas provided strong demand for European products and manufactures. Merchants in seaports and trading cities prospered. By preparing for war, European governments put new demands on their states' resources and economic organizations. The Old Regime itself thus fostered changes that eventually transformed it and later vast areas of the non-European world.

Major Features of Life in the Old Regime

Socially, prerevolutionary Europe was based on (1) aristocratic elites with many inherited legal privileges; (2) established churches intimately related to the state and the aristocracy; (3) an urban labor force usually organized into guilds; and (4) a rural peasantry subject to high taxes and feudal dues. Of course, the men and women of this period did not know it was the Old Regime. Most of them lived as their forebears had done for generations and as they expected their children to do after them.

Maintenance of Tradition

Few persons outside the political, commercial, and intellectual elite wanted change or innovation. This was especially true of social relationships. Both nobles and peasants repeatedly called for the restoration of traditional or customary rights. The nobles asserted what they considered their ancient rights against the intrusion of the expanding monarchical bureaucracies. The peasants, through petitions and revolts, called for the revival or the maintenance of the customary manorial rights that allowed them access to particular lands, courts, or grievance procedures.

Except for the early industrial development in Britain, the economy was also predominantly traditional. The quality and quantity of the grain harvest remained crucial for most of the population and the gravest concern for governments.

Hierarchy and Privilege

The medieval sense of hierarchy became more rigid during the century. Several cities retained sumptuary laws forbidding persons in one class or occupation from dressing like their social superiors. These laws were largely ineffective.

What really enforced the hierarchy was the corporate nature of social relationships.

Each state or society was considered a community composed of numerous smaller communities. Eighteenth-century Europeans did not enjoy what Americans regard as individual rights. Instead, persons enjoyed such rights and privileges as were guaranteed to whatever communities or groups of which they were a part. The "community" might include the village, the municipality, the nobility, the church, the guild, a university, or the parish. In turn, each of these bodies enjoyed certain privileges—some great, some small. The privileges might involve exemption from taxation or degrading punishment, the right to practice a trade or craft, the right of one's children to pursue a particular occupation, or, for the church, the right to collect the tithe.

Aristocracy

The eighteenth century was the great age of the aristocracy. The nobility constituted approximately 1 to 5 percent of the population of any given country. In every European state, it was the single wealthiest sector of the population; possessed the widest degree of social, political, and economic power; and dominated polite society. Land provided the aristocracy with its largest source of income, but the influence of aristocrats was felt in every area of life. Across the Continent, to be an aristocrat was a matter of birth and legal privilege, but in almost every other respect, they differed markedly from country to country.

The foundation of aristocratic life was the possession of land. English aristocrats and large landowners controlled local government as well as the English Parliament. This painting of Robert Andrews and his wife by Thomas Gainsborough (1728–1788) shows an aristocratic couple on their estate. The gun and the hunting dog in this portrait suggest the importance landowners assigned to the virtually exclusive hunting privileges they enjoyed on their land. [The National Gallery Publications Ltd., London]

Eighteenth-century France had some of the best roads in the world, but they were often built with forced labor. French peasants were required to work part of each year on such projects. This system, called the *corvée*, was not abolished until the French Revolution in 1789. [Claude Vernet "Construction of a Road." Louvre, Paris/Giraudon/Art Resource, N.Y.]

Great Britain

The smallest, wealthiest, best-defined, and most socially responsible aristocracy resided in Great Britain. It consisted of about four hundred families, whose eldest male members sat in the House of Lords. Through the corruptions of the electoral system, these families also controlled most seats in the House of Commons. Their estates ranged from a few thousand to fifty thousand acres, from which they received rents. The nobles owned approximately one fourth of all the arable land in Britain. Increasingly, their money was invested in commerce, canals, urban real estate, mines, and sometimes industrial ventures. Because only the eldest son inherited the title and the land, younger sons moved into commerce, the army, the professions, and the church. Most members of the House of Commons were also landowners. They paid taxes and had few significant legal privileges, but their control of local government gave them immense political power and social influence. Socially and politically, the aristocracy dominated the English counties.

France

In France, the nobility was theoretically divided between nobles of the sword and those of the robe. The former families' nobility derived from military service; the latter had either gained their titles by serving in the bureaucracy or by purchasing them. The two groups had frequently quarreled in the past but tended to cooperate during the eighteenth century to defend their common privileges.

The nobility who held office or favor with the royal court at Versailles reaped the immense wealth that came from holding high office. The noble hold on such offices intensified during the century. By the late 1780s appointments to the church, the army, and the bureaucracy tended to go to the court aristocracy. Whereas these well-connected aristocrats were quite rich, other nobles, known as *hobereaux*, lived in the provinces and were sometimes scarcely better off than well-to-do peasants.

Despite their differences, all French aristocrats enjoyed certain hereditary privileges. They were exempt from many taxes. For example, most did not pay the *taille*, the basic land tax of the old regime. They were technically liable to pay the *vingtième*, or the "twentieth," which resembled an income tax, but rarely had to pay it in full. Unlike peasants, nobles were not subject to the royal *corvées*, or labor donations. Moreover, the approximately four hundred thousand French nobles could collect feudal dues from their tenants and enjoyed exclusive hunting and fishing rights.

Eastern Europe

In eastern Europe, the character of the nobility became more complicated and repressive. In Poland, thousands of nobles were entirely exempt from taxes. Until 1768 they could legally execute their serfs. While most Polish aristocrats were relatively poor, a few very rich nobles dominated the fragile Polish state.

In Austria and Hungary, the nobility had broad judicial powers over the peasantry and enjoyed exemptions from taxation. The wealthiest of them, Prince Esterhazy of Hungary, owned ten million acres of land.

In Prussia, after the accession of Frederick the Great in 1740, the position of the *Junkers* became much stronger. Frederick's wars required the nobles' support. He drew his officers and increasingly his bureaucrats almost wholly from the *Junker* class. The Prussian nobles also enjoyed extensive authority over their serfs.

Russia

In Russia, a new, service nobility arose in the eighteenth century. Peter the Great linked noble status to state service through the Table of Ranks (1722). Resistance to compulsory state service created among Russian nobles a self-conscious class identity. In 1736 Empress Anna (r. 1730–1740) reduced such service to twenty-five years. In 1762 Peter III removed the liability for compulsory service entirely from the greatest nobles. In 1785, in the Charter of the Nobility, Catherine the Great granted an explicit legal definition of noble rights and privileges in exchange for assurances of voluntary state service from the nobility. The noble privileges included the right of transmitting noble status to one's wife and children, the judicial protection of noble rights and property, considerable power over the serfs, and exemption from personal taxes.

Throughout the century, in a European-wide *aristocratic resurgence*, the various nobilities sought to protect their social position and privileges against the expanding power of the monarchies and the growing wealth of commercial groups. First, all nobilities attempted to restrict entry into their ranks and institutions.

Second, they also attempted to monopolize appointments to the officer corps of the armies, the bureaucracies, the government ministries, and the church. The nobles thus hoped to control the power of the monarchies.

Third, the nobles attempted to use institutions they already controlled against the monarchies. These institutions included the British Parliament, the French *parlements*, local aristocratic estates, and provincial diets.

Fourth, the aristocracies pressed the peasantry for higher rents or long-forgotten feudal dues. This was part of an effort by the nobility to shore up its position by appealing to tradition and reasserting old privileges that had lapsed. To contemporaries, this aristocratic resurgence was one of the most fundamental political facts of the day.

The Land and Its Tillers

Land was the economic basis of eighteenth-century life. Well over three fourths of all Europeans lived on the land, and most never traveled more than a few miles from their birthplaces. With the exception of the nobility and the wealthier landowners, the dwellers on the land were poor, and by any modern standard, their lives were hard. They lived in various modes of economic and social dependency, exploitation, and vulnerability.

Peasants and Serfs

The major forms of rural social dependency related directly to the land. Those who worked the land were subject to immense influence and in some cases direct control by the landowners. This situation prevailed in different degrees for free peasants, such as English tenants and most French cultivators, and for the serfs of Germany, Austria, and Russia, who were legally bound to a particular plot of land and a particular lord. In all cases, the class that owned most of the land also controlled the local government and the courts.

Landlord power increased as one moved from west to east. Most French peasants owned some land, but a few were serfs. However, nearly all peasants were subject to certain feudal dues and to forced labor on the lord's estate for a certain number of days each year. Because French peasants rarely owned enough land to support their families, they were also subject to feudal dues attached to the plots of land they rented.

In Prussia and Austria, despite attempts by the monarchies late in the century to improve the lot of the serfs, the landlords continued to exercise almost complete control over them. Moreover, throughout continental Europe the burden of state taxation fell on the tillers of the soil. Many peasants, serfs, and other agricultural laborers were forced to undertake supplemental work to pay the tax collector. Through various legal privileges and the ability to demand further concessions from the monarchs, the landlords escaped the payment of numerous taxes. They also presided over the manorial courts.

The condition of the serfs was the worst in Russia. The Russian custom of reckoning one's wealth by the number of owned "souls" (that is, male serfs) rather than by the size of an estate reveals the contrast between Russia and Eastern Europe. The serfs were, in effect, regarded merely as economic commodities. Their services were attached to an individual lord rather than to a particular plot of land. Russian landlords could demand as many as six days a week of labor,

An English Traveler Describes Serfdom in Eighteenth-Century Russia

William Coxe was an Englishman who traveled widely in eastern Europe. His description of Russian serfdom portrays the brutality of the institution. It also illustrates his amazement at the absence in Russia of civil liberties such as he and more humble citizens enjoyed in England.

What are the examples of a Russian master not being restrained by law in his treatment of his serfs? What rights did the serfs have in regard to possessing property acquired through their own industry? How did Russian masters improve the skills of their serfs for their own economic benefit?

Peasants belonging to individuals are the private property of the landholders, as much as implements of agriculture, or herds of cattle; and the value of an estate is estimated, as in Poland, by the number of boors [serfs], and not by the number of acres. . . . If the Polish boor is oppressed, and he escapes to another master, the latter is liable to no pecuniary penalty for harboring him; but in Russia the person who receives another's vassal is subject to a heavy fine. With respect to his own demands upon his

peasants, the lord is restrained by no law, either in the exaction of any sum, or in the mode of employing them. He is absolute master of their time and labour: some he employs in agriculture: a few he makes his menial servants, and perhaps without wages; and from others he exacts an annual payment.

Each vassal, therefore, is rated according to the arbitrary will of his master. Some contribute four or five shillings a year; others, who are engaged in traffic or trade, are assessed proportion to their supposed profits. . . . With regard to any capital which they may have acquired by their industry, it may be seized, and there can be no redress. . . .

. . . . [S]ome of the Russian nobility send their vassals to Moscow or Petersburg for the purpose of learning various handcraft trades: they either employ them on their own estates; let them out for hire; sell them at an advanced price; or receive from them an annual compensation for the permission of exercising trade for their own advantage.

From William Coxe, *Travels into Poland, Russia, Sweden, and Denmark,* 4th ed., Vol. 3 (London: T. Cadell, 1972, first printed 1784), pp. 174–181.

---

and like Prussian and Austrian landlords, they could punish their serfs or even exile them to Siberia. Although serfs had little recourse against their lords, custom, tradition, and law did provide a few protections. For example, the marriages of serfs, unlike those of most slaves throughout the world, were legally recognized. The landlord could not disband the family of a serf.

The Russian monarchy itself contributed to the degradation of the serfs. Peter the Great (r. 1682–1725) gave whole villages to favored nobles. Catherine the Great (r. 1762–1796) confirmed the authority of the nobles over their serfs in exchange for the nobility's political cooperation. This situation led to considerable unrest. There were well over fifty peasant revolts between 1762 and 1769. They culminated between 1773 and 1774 in Pugachev's rebellion, during which all of southern Russia was in ferment. Emelyan Pugachev (1726–1775) promised the serfs land and freedom. The rebellion was brutally suppressed, and any thought of liberalizing the condition of the serfs was set aside for a generation.

Pugachev's was the largest peasant uprising of the eighteenth century. Smaller peasant revolts or disturbances occurred in Bohemia in 1775, in Transylvania in 1784, in Moravia in 1786, and in Austria in 1789. Western Europe was more tranquil, but England experienced numerous enclosure riots. Rural rebellions were violent, but the peasants and serfs normally

directed their wrath against property rather than persons. The rebels usually sought to reassert traditional or customary rights against practices they perceived as innovations. In this respect, the peasant revolts were conservative in nature.

Family Structures and the Family Economy

In preindustrial Europe, the household was the basic unit of production and consumption. That is to say, very few productive establishments employed more than a handful of people not belonging to the owner's family. These rare establishments were located in cities. But most Europeans lived in rural areas. There, as well as in small towns and cities, the household mode of organization predominated on farms, in artisans' workshops, and in small merchants' shops. With that mode of economic organization, there developed what is known as the *family economy*.

Households

What was a household under the Old Regime? There were two basic models, one characterizing northwestern Europe and the other eastern Europe.

Emelyan Pugachev (1726–1775) led the largest peasant revolt in Russian history. In this contemporary propaganda picture he is shown in chains. An inscription in Russian and German was printed below the picture decrying the evils of revolution and insurrection. [Bildarchiv Preussischer Kulturbesitz]

Northwestern Europe

Here, the household almost invariably consisted of a married couple, their children through their early teenage years, and their servants. Except for the wealthy few, households were small, rarely consisting of more than five or six members. Furthermore, high mortality and late marriage generally meant that grandparents rarely lived in the same household as their grandchildren. The family structure of northwestern Europe was thus nuclear rather than extended; that is to say, these families consisted of parents and children rather than of several generations under the same roof.

Children lived with their parents only until their early teens. Then they normally left home, usually to enter the work force of young servants who lived and worked away from home. A child of a skilled artisan might remain with his or her parents to acquire the valuable skill, but only rarely would more than one of the children do so because their labor would be more valuable elsewhere.

These young men and women who had left home would eventually marry and begin to form independent households of their own. This practice of moving away from home is

known as *neolocalism*. The effort to acquire the economic resources needed to establish a household meant the age of marriage would be relatively late. For men it was over twenty-six, and for women, over twenty-three. The couple usually quickly began a family. The marriage often occurred at the end of a long courtship when the woman was already pregnant. Family and community pressures seem more often than not to have compelled the man to marry the woman, but premarital sexual relations were not rare, although illegitimate births were uncommon. The new couple would soon employ a servant, and everyone, including the growing children, would help the household support itself.

Servant in this context does not refer to someone looking after the needs of wealthy people. Rather, in preindustrial Europe, a servant was a person—either male or female—who was hired, often under a clear contract, to work for the head of the household in exchange for room, board, and wages. The servant was usually young and by no means socially inferior to his or her employer. Normally, the servant was an integral part of the household and ate with the family. Young men and women became servants when their labor was no longer needed in their parents' household or when they could earn more money for their family outside it. Being a servant for several years—often as many as eight or ten—allowed young people to acquire productive skills and save enough money to begin their own households. This period of working as a servant between leaving home and beginning a new household largely explains the late age of marriage in northwestern Europe.

Eastern Europe

As one moved east, the structure of the household and the pattern of marriage changed. In Russia and elsewhere in eastern Europe, marrying involved not starting a new household but continuing in and expanding one already established. Consequently, marriage occurred early, before the age of twenty for both men and women. Children were born to parents of a much younger age than in western Europe. Often, especially among Russian serfs, wives were older than their husbands. Eastern European households tended to be larger than those in the west. The rural Russian household could have more than nine and possibly more than twenty members, with three or perhaps even four generations of the same family living together. Early marriage made this situation more likely.

The landholding pattern in eastern Europe accounted, at least in part, for these patterns of marriage and the family. The lords of the manor who owned land wanted to ensure that it would be cultivated so that they could receive their rents. To that end, for example, in Poland landlords might forbid marriage between their own serfs and those from another estate. They might also require widows and widowers to remarry so there would be adequate labor for a particular plot of land. Polish landlords also frowned on the hiring of free laborers—the equivalent of servants in the west—to help cultivate the land. The landlords preferred to use other serfs. This practice inhibited the possible formation of independent households. In Russia, landlords ordered the families of young people in their villages to arrange marriages within a short, set time. These lords discouraged single-generation family households because the death or serious illness of a person in such a household might mean that the land assigned to it would go out of cultivation.

The Family Economy

Throughout Europe the household was the fundamental unit of production and consumption. People thought and worked in terms of sustaining the economic life of the family, and family members saw themselves as working together in an interdependent rather than an independent or individualistic manner. The goal of the family household was to produce or secure through wages enough food to support its members. In the countryside, that effort virtually always involved farming. In cities and towns, artisan production or working for another person was the usual pattern. Almost everyone lived within a household because ordinary people could rarely support themselves independently. Indeed, except for members of religious orders, people living outside a household were viewed with great suspicion as potentially criminal or disruptive or, at least, potentially dependent on the charity of others.

Marriage and the family within this economy meant that everyone in the household had to work. On a farm, much of the effort went directly into raising food or producing other agricultural goods that could be exchanged for food. In western Europe, however, few people had enough land to support their households from farming alone. For this reason, one or more family members might work elsewhere and send wages home. For example, the father or older children might be migrant workers, perhaps many miles from home. The burden of the farm work would then fall on the wife and the younger children. This was not uncommon. Within this family economy, all of the goods and income produced went to the benefit of the household rather than to the individual family member. Depending on their ages and skills, everyone worked. The need to survive poor harvests or economic slumps meant that no one could be idle.

The family economy also dominated the life of skilled urban artisans. The father was usually the chief craftsman. He generally had one or more servants in his employ, but he would also expect his children to work in the enterprise. His

Painted by the English artist Francis Wheatley (1747-1801) near the close of the eighteenth century, this scene is part of a series illustrating a day in the life of an idealized farm family. Note the artist's assumptions about the division of labor by gender. Men work in the fields, women work in the home or look after the needs of men and children. As other illustrations in this chapter show, many eighteenth-century women in fact worked outside the home, but considerable social pressure was developing at this time to restrict them to domestic roles. This painting and the others in the series are thus more prescriptive than descriptive, intended in part to persuade their viewers that women belonged in their separate family sphere. Many, perhaps most, families living in the countryside could not maintain the closeness that these paintings extol. To survive, many had to send members to work on other farms or even to other regions.
[Francis Wheatley (RA)(1747-1801), "Evening," signed and dated 1799, oil on canvas, 17 x 21 in. (44.5 x 54.5 cm), Yale Center for British Art, Paul Mellon Collection, B1977.14.118]

Priscilla Wakefield Demands More Occupations Be Opened to Women

At the end of the eighteenth century, several English women writers began to demand a wider life for women. Priscilla Wakefield was among such authors. She was concerned that women found themselves able to pursue only occupations that paid poorly. Often they were excluded from work on the grounds of their alleged physical weakness. She also believed that women should receive equal wages for equal work. Many of the issues she raised have yet to be adequately addressed on behalf of women.

From reading this passage, what do you understand to have been the arguments at the end of the eighteenth century to limit the kinds of employment that women might enter? Why did women receive lower wages for work similar to or the same as that done by men? What occupations traditionally filled by men does Wakefield believe women might also pursue?

Another heavy discouragement to the industry of women, is the inequality of the reward of their labor, compared with that of men; an injustice which pervades every species of employment performed by both sexes.

In employments which depend on bodily strength, the distinction is just; for it cannot be pretended that the generality of women can earn as much as men, when the produce of their labor is the result of corporeal exertion; but it is a subject of great regret, that this inequality should prevail even where an equal share of skill and application is exerted. Male stay-makers, mantua-makers, and hair-dressers, are better paid than female artists of the same professions; but surely it will never be urged as an apology for this disproportion, that women are not as capable of making stays, gowns, dressing hair, and similar arts, as men; if they are not superior to them, it can only be accounted for upon this principle, that the prices they receive for their labor are not sufficient to repay them for the expense of qualifying themselves for their business; and that they sink under the mortification of being regarded as artisans of inferior estimation. . . .

Besides these employments which are commonly performed by women, and those already shown to be suitable for such persons as are above the condition of hard labor, there are some professions and trades customarily in the hands of men, which might be conveniently exercised by either sex.—Watchmaking requiring more ingenuity than strength, seems peculiarly adapted to women; as do many parts of the business of stationer, particularly, ruling account books or making pens. The compounding of medicines in an apothecary's shop, requires no other talents than care and exactness; and if opening a vein occasionally be a indispensable requisite, a woman may acquire the capacity of doing it, for those of her own sex at least, without any reasonable objection. . . . Pastry and confectionery appear particularly consonant to the habits of women, though generally performed by men; perhaps the heat of the ovens, and the strength requisite to fill and empty them, may render male assistants necessary; but certain women are most eligible to mix up the ingredients, and prepare the various kinds of cakes for baking.—Light turnery and toy-making depend more upon dexterity and invention than force, and are therefore suitable work for women and children. . . . .

Farming, as far as respects the theory, is commensurate with the powers of the female mind: nor is the practice of inspecting agricultural processes incompatible with the delicacy of their frames if their constitution be good.

From Priscilla Wakefield, *Reflections on the Present Condition of the Female Sex* (1798), (London, 1817), pp. 125–127, as quoted in Bridget Hill, ed., *Eighteenth-Century Women: An Anthology.* Copyright © 1984 George Allen & Unwin, pp. 227–228.

---

eldest child was usually trained in the trade. His wife often sold the wares, or had a small shop. The wife of a merchant also often ran the husband's business, especially when he traveled to purchase new goods. In any case, everyone in the family was involved. If business was poor, family members would look for employment elsewhere, not to support themselves but to help the family unit survive.

In western Europe, the death of a father could destroy the economy of the household. The family's economic life usually depended on his land or skills. The widow might take on the farm or the business, or her children might do so. She usually sought to remarry quickly to have the labor and skills of a male once more in the household and to prevent herself

from falling into a state of dependence. The high mortality rate of the time meant that many households were reconstituted second family groups with stepchildren. But some households simply dissolved. The widow and children became dependent on charity or relatives, or the children moved earlier than they would otherwise have done into the work force of servants. In desperate situations survivors resorted to crime or begging. The personal, emotional, and economic vulnerability of the family economy cannot be overemphasized.

In eastern Europe, the family economy existed in the context of serfdom and landlord domination. Peasants clearly thought in terms of their families and of expanding the land available for cultivation. The village structure may have mitigated the pressures of the family economy, as did the multigenerational family. Dependence on the available land was the chief fact of life, and there were many fewer artisan and merchant households and far less mobility than in western Europe.

Women and the Family Economy

The family economy established many of the chief constraints on the lives and the personal experiences of women in preindustrial society. Most of the historical research that has been undertaken on this subject relates to western Europe. There, a woman's life experience was largely the function of her capacity to establish and maintain a household. For women, marriage was an institution of economic necessity as well as one that fulfilled sexual and psychological needs. A woman outside a household was highly vulnerable. Unless she were an aristocrat or a member of a religious order, she probably could not support herself by her own efforts alone. Consequently, much of a woman's life was devoted first to aiding the maintenance of her parents' household and then to getting her own household to live in as an adult. In most cases, bearing and rearing children were subordinate to these goals.

As a child, certainly by the age of seven, a girl was expected to begin to contribute to the household work. On a farm, she might look after chickens or water animals or carry food to adult men and women working the land. In an urban artisan's household, she would do some form of light work, perhaps involving cleaning or carrying and later sewing or weaving. The girl would remain in her parents' home as long as either she made a real contribution to the family enterprise or her labor elsewhere was not more valuable to the family. An artisan's daughter might not leave home until marriage because she could learn increasingly valuable skills from her parents.

The labor of the much larger number of girls growing up on farms quickly became of little value to the family. These girls would then leave home, usually between the age of twelve and fourteen. They might go to another farm, but were more likely to migrate to a nearby town or city. They would rarely travel more than thirty miles from their parents' household and would then normally become servants in the household of an employer.

Having migrated from home, the young woman's chief goal was to accumulate a dowry. Her savings would allow her to make the necessary contribution to form a household with her husband. Marriage within the family economy was a joint economic undertaking, and the wife was expected to make an immediate contribution of capital for the establishment of the household. A young woman might well work for ten years or more to accumulate a dowry. This practice meant that marriage was usually postponed until a woman's mid- to late twenties.

Within the marriage, earning enough money or producing enough farm goods to ensure an adequate food supply was always the dominant concern. Domestic duties, childbearing, and child rearing were subordinate to economic survival. Consequently, couples would often practice birth control, usually through *coitus interruptus*, or withdrawal of the male before ejaculation. Young children were often placed with wet nurses so the mother could continue to contribute to the household economy. The wet nurse, in turn, was contributing to her own household. The child would be fully reintegrated into its family when it was weaned and would be expected to aid the family at an early age.

A married woman's work was in many ways a function of her husband's occupation. If the peasant household possessed enough land to support itself, the wife spent much of her time literally carrying things for her husband—water, food, seed, harvested grain, and the like. But few peasants had such adequate landholdings. If the husband had to do work other than farming, such as fishing or migrant labor, the wife might do the plowing, planting, and harvesting. In the city, the wife of an artisan or merchant often acted like a business manager. She might manage the household finances and participate in the trade or business. When her husband died, she might take over the business, perhaps hiring an artisan.

Finally, if economic disaster struck the family, more often than not it was the wife who organized what Olwen Hufton has called the "economy of expedients,"[1] within which family members might be sent off to find work elsewhere or even to beg in the streets.

In all phases of life within the family economy, women led active, often decisive roles. Industriousness rather than idleness was their lot in life. Finding a functional place in the household was essential to their well-being, but once that place had been found, their function was essential to the ongoing well-being of the household.

Children and the World of the Family Economy

Childbirth was a time of grave danger to both mother and infant, who were immediately exposed to the possible contraction of contagious diseases. Puerperal fever and other infections from unsterilized medical instruments were common. Not all midwives were skillful practitioners. Furthermore, the immense poverty and wretched housing conditions

---

[1]"Women and the Family Economy in Eighteenth-Century France," *French Historical Studies* 9 (1975): 19.

An Edinburgh Physician Describes the Dangers of Childbirth

Death in childbirth was a common occurrence throughout Europe until the twentieth century. This brief letter from an Edinburgh physician illustrates how devastating infectious diseases could be to women at the time of childbirth.

How does this passage illustrate a health danger that only women confronted? How might the likelihood of the death of oneself or a spouse in childbirth have affected one's attitudes toward children? How does this passage illustrate limitations on knowledge about disease in the eighteenth century?

We had puerperal fever in the infirmary last winter. It began about the end of February, when almost every woman, as soon as she was delivered, or perhaps about twenty-four hours after, was seized with it; and all of them died, though every method was tried to cure the disorder. What was singular, the women were in good health before they were brought to bed, though some of them had been long in the hospital before delivery. One woman had been dismissed from the ward before she was brought to bed; came into it some days after with her labor upon her; was easily delivered, and remained perfectly well for twenty-four hours, when she was seized with a shivering and the other symptoms of the fever. I caused her to be removed to another ward; yet notwithstanding all the care that was taken of her she died in the same manner as the others.

From a letter to Mr. White from a Dr. Young of Edinburgh, 21 November 1774, cited in C. White, *Treatise on the Management of Pregnant and Lying-In Women* (London, 1777), pp. 45–46, as quoted in Bridget Hill, ed., *Eighteenth-Century Women: An Anthology.* Copyright © 1984 George Allen & Unwin, p. 102.

---

of most Europeans endangered the lives of the newborn child and the mother.

However, the safe birth of a child was not always welcome. The child might be illegitimate or be another economic burden on an already hard-pressed household. Through at least the end of the seventeenth century, and to a lesser degree beyond it, various forms of infanticide were practiced, especially among the poor. Unwanted infants might be smothered or exposed to the elements. These practices were one result of both the ignorance and the prejudice surrounding contraception. Although many married couples seem to have succeeded in limiting their families, unmarried young men and women whose sexual relationships may have been the result of a fleeting acquaintance were less fortunate. Numerous young women, especially among servants, found themselves pregnant and without husbands. This situation and the consequent birth of illegitimate children seem to have become much more frequent during the eighteenth century. It probably arose from the more frequent migration of young people from their homes and the disturbance of traditional village life through enclosures (to be discussed later), the commercialization of agriculture, wars, and the late-century revolutions.

In the late seventeenth and the early eighteenth centuries, reflecting a new interest in preserving the lives of abandoned children, large foundling hospitals were established in all the major nations. (Earlier foundling hospitals had been fewer and smaller than these new institutions.) Two of the most famous, the Paris Foundling Hospital (1670) and the London Foundling Hospital (1739), cared for thousands of children. The demands on their resources vastly increased during the eighteenth century. For example, early in the century, an average of about 1,700 children were admitted to the Paris Foundling Hospital annually. But 7,676 were admitted in the peak year of 1772. Not all of those children came from Paris. Many had been taken to the city from the provinces, where local foundling homes and hospitals were also overburdened. The London Foundling Hospital lacked the income to deal with all of the children brought to it and, in the middle of the eighteenth century, found itself compelled to choose children for admission by a lottery system.

Sadness and tragedy were the lot of abandoned children. Most were illegitimate infants drawn from across the social spectrum, but many seem to have been left with the foundling hospitals because their parents could not support them. The numbers of abandoned children increased when food prices rose in Paris. Parents would sometimes leave personal tokens or saints' medals on the abandoned baby in the vain hope that they might eventually be able to reclaim the child. Few children were so reclaimed. Leaving a child at a foundling hospital did not guarantee its survival. In Paris, only about 10 percent of all abandoned children lived to the age of ten years.

Despite these perils, children did grow up and come of age across Europe. The world of the child may not have received the kind of attention it does today, but during the eighteenth century the seeds of that modern sensibility were sown. Particularly among the upper classes, new interest arose in the ed-

Few children in the eighteenth century were as privileged as these in this landed English family. Most began working to help support their families as soon as they were physically able. It was during the eighteenth century, however, that Europeans apparently began to view childhood as a distinct period in human development. Even though Arthur Devis has painted these children to look something like little adults, he has included various toys associated with childhood. [Arthur Devis (© 1711–1787), "Children in an Interior," © 1742–1743, oil on canvas, 39 x 49 in. (99.0 x 125.5 cm), Yale Center for British Art, Paul Mellon Collection, B1978.43.5]

ucation of children. As economic skills became more demanding, literacy became more valuable and more common during the century. However, most education remained firmly in the hands of the churches. Most Europeans remained illiterate. It was not until the late nineteenth century that the world of childhood and the process of education became inextricably linked. Then children would be reared to become members of a national citizenry. In the old regime, they were reared to make their contribution to the economy of their parents' family and then to set up their own households.

Growth of Agriculture and Population

Thus far this chapter has examined those groups who sought stability and generally resisted change. Other groups, however, wished to pursue significant new directions in social and economic life. The remainder of this chapter will consider those forces and developments that would during the next century transform first Europe and then much of the rest of the world. These developments first appeared in agriculture.

The Revolution in Agriculture

The main goal of traditional European peasant society was to ensure the stability of the local food supply. That supply was never certain and became more uncertain the farther east one traveled. A failed harvest meant not only hardship but death

from either outright starvation or protracted debility. Food was often harder to find in the country than in cities because city governments usually stored reserve supplies of grain.

Poor harvests also played havoc with prices. Smaller supplies or larger demand raised grain prices. Even small increases in the cost of food could squeeze peasant or artisan families. If prices increased sharply, many of those families fell back on poor relief from their local government or the church. What made the situation of food supply and prices so difficult was the peasants' sense of helplessness before the whims of nature and the marketplace. Despite differences in rural customs throughout Europe, peasants resisted changes that they felt might endanger the sure supply of food, which they generally believed traditional cultivation practices ensured.

During the century, historians now believe, bread prices slowly but steadily rose, spurred largely by population growth. This put pressure on all of the poor. The prices rose faster than urban wages and brought no appreciable advantage to the small peasant producer. On the other hand, the rise in grain prices benefited landowners and those wealthier peasants who had surplus grain to sell.

The increasing price of grain allowed landlords to improve their income and lifestyle. They began a series of innovations in farm production that are known as the *agricultural revolution*.

New Crops and New Methods This movement began during the sixteenth and seventeenth centuries in the Low Countries, where Dutch landlords and farmers devised better ways to build dykes and to drain land so that they could

Turgot Describes French Landholding

The economy of Europe until the nineteenth century was over-whelmingly rural. That meant that economic growth and political stability depend largely on agricultural production. During the eighteenth century, many observers became keenly aware that different kinds of landholding led to different attitudes toward work and to different levels of production. Robert Jacques Turgot (1727–1781), who later became finance minister of France, analyzed these differences in an effort to reform French agriculture. He was especially concerned with arrangements that encouraged long-term investment. The métayer *system, discussed by Turgot, was an arrangement whereby landowners arranged to have land farmed by peasants, who received part of the harvest as payment for their working the land. The peasant had no long-term interest in improving the land. Virtually all observers regarded the system as inefficient.*

Why does Turgot clearly favor those farmers who can make investments in the land they rent from a proprietor? What are the structures of the *métayer* system? Why did it necessarily lead to poor investments and lesser harvests? What is Turgot's attitude toward work and entrepreneurship?

---

1. What really distinguishes the area of large-scale farming from the areas of small-scale production is that in the former areas the proprietors find farmers who provide them with a permanent revenue from the land and who buy from them the right to cultivate it for a certain number of years. These farmers undertake all the expenses of cultivation, the ploughing, the sowing and the stocking of the farm with cattle, animals and tools. They are really agricultural entrepreneurs, who possess, like the entrepreneurs in all other branches of commerce, considerable funds, which they employ in the cultivation of land. . . .

They have not only the brawn but also the wealth to devote to agriculture. They have to work, but unlike workers they do not have to earn their living by the sweat of their brow, but by the lucrative employment of their capital, just as the shipowners of Nantes and Bordeaux employ theirs in maritime commerce.

2. *Métayer* System   The areas of small-scale farming, that is to say at least 4/7ths of the kingdom, are those where there are no agricultural entrepreneurs, where a proprietor who wishes to develop his land cannot find anyone to cultivate it except wretched peasants who have no resources other than their labor, where he is obliged to make, at his own expense, all the advances necessary for tillage, beasts, tools, sowing, even to the extent of advancing to his *métayer* the wherewithal to feed himself until the first harvest, where consequently a proprietor who did not have any property other than his estate would be obliged to allow it to lie fallow.

After having deducted the costs of sowing and feudal dues with which the property is burdened, the proprietor shares with the *métayer* what remains of the profits, in accordance with the agreement they have concluded. The proprietor runs all the risks of harvest failure and any loss of cattle: he is the real entrepreneur. The *métayer* is nothing more than a mere workman, a farm hand to whom the proprietor surrenders a share of his profits instead of paying wages. But in his work the proprietor enjoys none of the advantages of the farmer who, working on his own behalf, works carefully and diligently; the proprietor is obliged to entrust all his advances to a man who may be negligent or a scoundrel and is answerable for nothing.

This *métayer,* accustomed to the most miserable existence and without the hope and even the desire to obtain a better living for himself, cultivates badly and neglects to employ the land for valuable and profitable production; by preference he occupies himself in cultivating those things whose growth is less troublesome and which provide him with more foodstuffs, such as buck wheat and chestnuts which do not require any attention. He does not worry very much about his livelihood; he knows that if the harvest fails, his mater will be obliged to feed him in order not to see his land neglected.

A. M. R. Turgot, *Oeuvres, et documents le concernant,* ed. by F. Schelle, 5 vols. (Paris, 1914), Vol. II, pp. 448–450, as quoted and translated in S. Pollard and C. Holmes, eds., *Documents of European Economic History,* Vol. I (London: Edward Arnold, 1968), pp. 38–39. Reprinted by permission.

---

farm more extensive areas. They also experimented with new crops, such as clover and turnips, that would increase the supply of animal fodder and replenish the soil.

These methods were extensively adopted in England during the early eighteenth century. There, new methods of farming, new crops, and new modes of landholding eventually led to greater productivity. This advance in food production was necessary for an industrial society to develop. It ensured adequate food for the cities and freed surplus agricultural labor for industrial production. The changing modes of agriculture sponsored by the landlords undermined the assumptions of traditional peasant production. Farming now took place not only to provide the local food supply but also to earn the landlord a handsome profit.

Enclosure Replaces Open-Field Method   Many of the agricultural innovations, which were adopted only slowly, were incompatible with the existing organization of land

in Britain. Small cultivators who lived in village communities still farmed most of the soil. Each farmer tilled an assortment of unconnected strips. The two- or three-field systems of rotation left much land fallow and unproductive each year. Animals grazed on the common land in the summer and on the stubble of the harvest in the winter. Until at least the middle of the eighteenth century the decisions about what crops would be planted were made communally. The entire system discouraged improvement and favored the poorer farmers, who needed the common land and stubble fields for their animals. The village method made it almost impossible to increase pasture land and with it the size of herds and the production of manure for fertilizer. Traditional methods aimed to produce a steady but not a growing supply of food.

In 1700 approximately half the arable land in Britain was farmed by this open-field method. By the second half of the century the rising price of wheat encouraged landlords to consolidate or enclose their lands to increase production. The enclosures were intended to use land more rationally and to raise profits. The process involved the fencing of common lands, the reclamation of previously untilled waste, and the transformation of strips into block fields. These procedures disrupted the economic and social life of the countryside. Riots often ensued. Because many British farmers either owned their strips or rented them in a manner that amounted to ownership, the larger landlords had usually to resort to parliamentary acts to legalize the enclosure of the land, which they owned but rented to the farmers. Because the large landowners controlled Parliament, such measures passed easily. Between 1761 and 1792, almost 500,000 acres were enclosed through parliamentary act, as compared with 75,000 acres between 1727 and 1760. In 1801 a general enclosure act streamlined the process.

The enclosures have remained controversial. By permitting the extension of both farming and innovation, they increased food production on larger agricultural units. However, they also disrupted the small traditional communities. They forced off the land some independent farmers, who had needed the common pasturage, and very poor cottagers, who had lived on the reclaimed waste land. However, the enclosures did not depopulate the countryside. In some counties where the enclosures took place, the population increased. New soil had come into production, and services subsidiary to farming also expanded.

Limited Improvements in Eastern Europe   Improving agriculture tended to characterize farm production west of the Elbe. Dutch farming was efficient. In France, despite the efforts of the government to improve agriculture, enclosures were restricted. Yet there was much discussion about improving agricultural methods. These new procedures benefited the ruling classes because better agriculture increased their incomes and assured a larger food supply, which discouraged social unrest.

In Prussia, Austria, Poland, and Russia, agricultural improvement was minimal. Nothing in the relationship between serf and lord encouraged innovation. In eastern Europe, the chief method of increasing production was to farm previously untilled lands. By extending tillage the great landlords sought to squeeze more labor from their serfs rather than greater productivity from the soil. As in the west, the goal was increased profits for the landlords. But on the whole, eastern European landlords were much less ambitious and

Grain production lay at the heart of eighteenth-century farming. In this engraving farm workers can be seen threshing wheat, winnowing the grain, and finally putting the grain in bags so it can be carried to a mill and ground into flour. In many cases the mill would be owned by the local landlord, who would charge peasants for its use.

[Bildarchiv Preussischer Kulturbesitz]

successful. The only significant nutritional gain their efforts achieved was the introduction of maize and the potato. Livestock production did not increase significantly.

Population Expansion

Agricultural improvement was both a cause and a result of an immense expansion in the population of Europe. The current population explosion seems to have had its origins in the eighteenth century. Exact figures are lacking, but the best estimates suggest that in 1700 Europe's population, excluding the European provinces of the Ottoman Empire, was between 100 million and 120 million people. By 1800 the figure had risen to almost 190 million, and by 1850 to 260 million. The population of England and Wales rose from 6 million in 1750 to over 10 million in 1800. France grew from 18 million in 1715 to approximately 26 million in 1789. Russia's population increased from 19 million in 1722 to 29 million in 1766. Such extraordinary sustained growth put new demands on all resources and considerable pressure on existing social organization.

The population expansion occurred across the Continent in both the country and the cities. Only a limited consensus exists about the causes of this growth. There was a clear decline in the death rate. There were fewer wars and somewhat fewer epidemics in the eighteenth century. Hygiene and sanitation also improved. But changes in the food supply itself may have been the chief reason for sustained population growth. One contributing factor was improved and expanding grain production. Another, even more important, was the introduction in the eighteenth century of widespread cultivation of a New World tuber, the potato. Enough potatoes could be raised on a single acre to feed one peasant's family for an entire year. With this more certain food supply, more children could be reared, and more could survive.

The Eighteenth-Century Industrial Revolution

An Event in World History

In the second half of the eighteenth century the European economy began to industrialize. This development, more than any other single factor, distinguished Europe and eventually North America from the rest of the world for the next two centuries. The consumer products of the slowly industrializing businesses gave Europeans vast amounts of new goods to sell throughout the world and thus encouraged more international trade in which Western nations supplied the finished goods in exchange for raw materials. As a consequence, the prosperity of other areas of the globe became economically dependent on European and American demand. The wealth achieved through this uneven commerce allowed Europeans to dominate world markets for almost two centuries.

Furthermore, by the early nineteenth century iron and steel production and the new technologies of manufacture allowed European states and later the United States to build more powerful military forces, especially navies, than those of Africa, Latin America, or Asia. Both the economic and the military dominance of the West arose directly from the industrial achievement.

Much of the history of the non-Western world from the middle of the eighteenth century to the present can be understood in terms of how the nonindustrialized nations initially reacted to the penetration of their world by Europeans and Americans made wealthy and powerful through industrialized economies. Africa and Latin America became generally dependent economies. Japan, by the middle of the nineteenth century, decided it must imitate the European pattern and did so successfully. China did not make that decision and became indirectly ruled by Europeans. The Chinese revolutions of the twentieth century have largely represented efforts to achieve real self-direction. Southeast Asia and the Middle East became drawn into the network of resource supply to the West; they could achieve movement toward economic independence only through imitation or, like Arab nations in the early 1970s, by refusing to supply oil to the West. The process of industrialization that commenced in small factories in eighteenth-century Europe has changed the world more than any other single development in the last two centuries.

The European Industrial Revolution of the eighteenth century constituted the achievement of sustained economic growth. Previously, production had been limited. The economy of a province or a country might grow, but soon reached a plateau. However, since the late eighteenth century the economy of Europe has expanded relatively uninterruptedly. Depressions and recessions have been temporary, and even during such economic downturns the Western economy has continued to grow.

At considerable social cost and dislocation, industrialism produced more goods and services than ever before in human history. Industrialism in Europe eventually overcame the economy of scarcity. The new means of production demanded new kinds of skills, new discipline in work, and a large labor force. The produced goods met immediate consumer demand and created new demands. In the long run, industrialism clearly raised the standard of living; the poverty in which most Europeans had always lived was overcome. Industrialization provided human beings greater control over the forces of nature than they had ever known.

The wealth produced by industrialism upset the political and social structures of the old regime and led to reforms. The economic elite of the emerging industrial society would eventually challenge the political dominance of the aristocracy. Industrialization also undermined traditional communities and, along with the growth of cities, displaced many people. These processes repeated themselves virtually everywhere that industrialization occurred during the next two centuries.

Industrial Leadership of Great Britain

Great Britain was the home of the Industrial Revolution and, until the late nineteenth century, remained the industrial leader of Europe and the world. Several factors contributed to the early start of industrialization in Britain. Britain was the single largest free-trade area in Europe, with good roads and waterways without tolls or other internal trade barriers. There were rich deposits of coal and iron ore. The political structure was stable, and property was absolutely secure. A sound system of banking and public credit created a good investment climate. Taxation in Britain was heavy, but it received legal approval from Parliament. Taxes were efficiently and fairly collected, largely from indirect taxes with all regions and persons from all classes paying the same taxes. Besides satisfying domestic consumer demand, the British economy also benefited from the demand for goods from the North American colonies.

Finally, British society was relatively mobile. Persons who had money or could earn it could rise socially. The British aristocracy would accept people who had amassed large fortunes. No one of these factors preordained the British advance toward industrialism. The combination of them, however, plus the progressive state of British agriculture, provided the nation with a marginal advantage in the creation of a new mode of economic production. No less important, the wars and revolutions of the late eighteenth and early nineteenth centuries disrupted those parts of the Continent where an industrialized economy might also have begun to develop.

While this economic development was occurring, people did not call it a *revolution*. That term came to be applied to the British economic phenomena only after the French Revolution, when continental writers contended that what had taken place in Britain was the economic equivalent of the political events in France. From this comparison arose the concept of an *industrial* revolution. The process, however, was revolutionary less in its pace, which was on the whole rather slow, than in its implications for the future of European society.

New Methods of Textile Production   Although eighteenth-century society was devoted primarily to agriculture, manufacturing permeated the countryside. The same peasants who tilled the land in spring and summer often spun thread or wove textiles in winter. Under the *domestic* or *putting-out* system, agents of urban textile merchants took wool or

During the eighteenth century, most goods were produced in small workshops, such as this English blacksmith shop painted by Joseph Wright of Derby (1734–1797), or in the homes of artisans. Not until very late in the century, with the early stages of industrialization, did a few factories appear. [Joseph Wright of Derby, "The Blacksmith's Shop," signed and dated 1771, oil on canvas, 50 x 41 in. (128.3 x 104.0 cm). Yale Center for British Art, Paul Mellon Collection]

other unfinished fiber to the homes of peasants, who spun it into thread. The agent then transported the thread to other peasants, who wove it into the finished product. The merchant sold the wares. In literally thousands of peasant cottages from Ireland to Austria stood either a spinning wheel or a hand loom. Sometimes the spinners or weavers owned their own equipment, but more often than not, by the middle of the century, the merchant capitalist owned the machinery as well as the raw material.

What must be kept constantly in mind is that eighteenth-century industrial development took place within a rural setting. The peasant family living in a one- or two-room cottage, not the factory, was the basic unit of production. The family economy, rather than the industrial factory economy, characterized the century.

The domestic system of textile production was a basic feature of this family economy. However, by mid-century bottlenecks had developed within the domestic system. The demand for cotton textiles was growing more rapidly than production. This demand arose particularly in Great Britain,

The pithead of an eighteenth-century coal mine in England. The machinery on the left includes a steam engine that lifted coal and pumped water from the mine. Britain's rich veins of coal were one of the factors contributing to its early industrialization. ["British School—A Pithead." Board of Trustees of the National Museums and Galleries on Merseyside, Walker Art Gallery, Liverpool]

whose growing population wanted cotton textiles, as did its colonies in North America. The most famous inventions of the Industrial Revolution were devised in response to this consumer demand for cotton textiles.

Cotton textile weavers had the technical capacity to produce enough fabric to satisfy demand. However, the spinners could not produce as much thread as the weavers needed and could use. This imbalance had been created during the 1730s by James Kay's invention of the flying shuttle, which increased the productivity of the weavers. Thereafter, manufacturers and merchants offered prizes for the invention of a machine to eliminate this bottleneck. In about 1765 James Hargreaves (d. 1778) invented the spinning jenny. Initially this machine allowed sixteen spindles of thread to be spun, but by the close of the century it included as many as 120 spindles.

The spinning jenny broke the bottleneck between the productive capacity of the spinners and the weavers, but it was still a piece of machinery that was used in the cottage. The invention that took cotton textile manufacture from the home to the factory was Richard Arkwright's (1732–1792) water frame, patented in 1769. It was a water-powered device designed to permit the production of a purely cotton fabric rather than a cotton fabric containing linen fiber for durability. Eventually Arkwright lost his patent rights, and other manufacturers were able to use his invention freely. As a result, numerous factories sprang up in the countryside near streams that provided the necessary water power. From the 1780s onward the cotton industry could meet an ever-expanding demand. Between 1780 and 1800 cotton output increased by 800 percent. By 1815 cotton composed 40 percent of the value of British domestic exports, and by 1830 just over 50 percent.

The Steam Engine   The new technology in textile manufacture vastly increased cotton production and revolutionized a major consumer industry. But the invention that more than any other enabled industrialization to grow on itself and expand into one area of production after another was the steam engine. This machine provided for the first time in human history a steady and essentially unlimited source of inanimate power. Unlike engines powered by water or wind, the steam engine, driven by the burning of coal, was a portable source of industrial power that did not fail or falter as the seasons of the year changed. Unlike human or animal power, the steam engine depended on mineral energy that never tired. Finally, the steam engine could be applied to many industrial and, eventually, transportation uses.

The first practical engine using steam power was invented by Thomas Newcomen (1663–1729) in the early eighteenth century. It was large, inefficient in its use of energy, and practically untransportable. Nonetheless, English mine operators used it to pump water out of coal and tin mines. By the late eighteenth century almost a hundred Newcomen machines were operating in the mining districts of England.

During the 1760s James Watt (1736–1819) began to experiment with a model of a Newcomen machine at the University of Glasgow. He gradually understood that if the condenser were separated from the piston and the cylinder, much greater efficiency would result. In 1769 he patented his new invention, but his design required exceedingly precise metalwork. Watt soon found a partner in Matthew Boulton (1728–1809), a toy manufacturer in Birmingham, the city with the most skilled metalworkers in Britain. Watt and Boulton in turn consulted with John Wilkinson (1728–1808), a cannon manufacturer, to find ways to drill the precise metal cylinders required by Watt's design. In 1776 the Watt steam engine found its first commercial application pumping water from mines.

The use of the steam engine spread slowly because until 1800 Watt retained the exclusive patent rights and was reluctant to modify the engine. Boulton eventually persuaded him to adapt the engines for use in running cotton mills. By the early nineteenth century the steam engine had become the prime mover for all industry. With its application to ships and then to wagons on iron rails, it also revolutionized transportation.

Iron Production   The manufacture of high-quality iron has been basic to modern industrial development. It constitutes the chief element of all heavy industry and land or sea transport and is the material out of which most productive machinery itself has been manufactured. During the early eighteenth century British ironmakers produced less than 25,000 tons annually. Three factors held back the production of the metal. First, charcoal rather than coke was used to smelt the ore. Charcoal, which is derived from wood, was becoming scarce, and it did not burn at as high a temperature as coke, which is derived from coal. Second, until the perfection of the steam engine, insufficient blasts could be achieved in the furnaces. Finally, the demand for iron was limited. The elimination of the first two problems eliminated the third.

In the course of the century, British ironmakers began to use coke, and the steam engine provided new power for the blast furnaces. Coke was abundant because of Britain's large coal deposits. The steam engine both improved iron production and increased the demand for iron.

**Major Inventions
in the Textile-Manufacturing Revolution**

1733	James Kay's flying shuttle
1765	James Hargreaves's spinning jenny (patent 1770)
1769	James Watt's steam engine patent
1769	Richard Arkwright's waterframe patent
1787	Edmund Cartwright's power loom

In 1784 Henry Cort (1740–1800) introduced a new method for melting and stirring the molten ore. Cort's process produced a purer iron. He also developed a rolling mill that continually shaped the still-molten metal into bars, rails, or other forms. Previously, the metal had been pounded into these forms.

All of these innovations achieved a better, more versatile, and cheaper product. The demand for iron grew as its price went down. By the early nineteenth century annual British iron production amounted to over a million tons. The lower cost of iron in turn lowered the cost of steam engines and allowed them to be used more widely.

Cities

Patterns of Preindustrial Urbanization

Remarkable changes occurred in the pattern of city growth between 1500 and 1800. In 1500 there were approximately 156 cities within Europe (excluding Hungary and Russia) with a population greater than 10,000. Only four of those cities—Paris, Milan, Venice, and Naples—had more than 100,000 inhabitants. By 1800 approximately 363 cities had 10,000 or more inhabitants, and 17 of those had populations larger than 100,000. The percentage of the European population living in urban areas had risen from just over 5 percent to just over 9 percent. The urban concentration had also shifted from southern, Mediterranean Europe to the north.

These raw figures conceal significant changes that took place in the manner in which cities grew and the population distributed itself. Major urban development in the sixteenth century was followed in the seventeenth by leveling and even decline. New growth began in the early eighteenth century and accelerated thereafter.

Growth of Capitals and Ports   Capitals and ports were the urban areas that displayed the most growth and vigor between 1600 and 1750. This reflects the success of monarchical state building and the consequent burgeoning of bureaucracies, armies, courts, and other groups related to the process of government who lived in the capitals. The growth of port cities in turn reflects the expansion of European overseas trade and most especially that of the Atlantic routes. With the exception of Lyons, France, significant growth did not take place in industrial cities. Furthermore, between 1600 and 1750 cities with populations of fewer than 40,000 inhabitants declined. These cities included older landlocked trading centers, medieval industrial cities, and ecclesiastical centers. They contributed less to the new political regimes, and since rural labor was cheaper than urban

Until it was destroyed by Allied bombing in World War II, Dresden was regarded as one of the most beautiful cities in Europe. Here, as in many other cities in Germany, social and economic life centered on the royal court. Cities like Dresden were usually centers for the arts as well as for politics. [Bildarchiv Preussischer Kulturbesitz]

labor, cities with concentrations of labor declined as production sites were moved from urban workshops into the countryside.

Emergence of New Cities and Growth of Small Towns   After 1750 a new pattern emerged. Large cities grew more slowly. New cities arose, and older smaller cities began to grow. Several factors were at work in the process, which Jan De Vries has termed "an urban growth from below."[2] First, there was the general overall population increase. Second, the early stages of the Industrial Revolution, particularly in Britain, occurred in the countryside and tended to aid the growth of smaller towns and cities located near the factories. Factory organization itself fostered new concentrations of population. But cities also grew where there was little industrialization, probably because of the new prosperity of European agriculture. Greater agricultural production aided the growth of nearby market towns and other urban centers that served agriculture or allowed more prosperous farmers to have access to the consumer goods and recreation they wanted. This new pattern of urban growth—new cities

and the expansion of smaller existing cities—would continue into the nineteenth century.

Urban Classes

Social divisions were as marked in the cities of the eighteenth century as they were in the industrial centers of the nineteenth.

The Upper Classes   At the top of the urban social structure stood a generally small group of nobles, large merchants, bankers, financiers, clergy, and government officials. These men (and they were always men) controlled the political and economic affairs of the town. Normally they constituted a self-appointed and self-electing oligarchy who governed the city through its corporation or city council. These rights of self-government had generally been granted by a royal charter that gave the city corporation its authority and the power to select its own members. In a few cities on the Continent artisan guilds controlled the corporations, but most councils were under the influence of the local nobility and the commercial elite.

The Middle Class   The prosperous but not immensely wealthy merchants, tradesmen, bankers, and professional people were the most dynamic element of the urban popu-

[2]"Patterns of Urbanization in Pre-Industrial Europe, 1500–1800," in H. Schnal, ed., *Patterns of European Urbanization Since 1500* (London: Croom Helm, 1981), p. 103.

Consumption of all forms of consumer goods increased greatly in the eighteenth century. This engraving illustrates a shop, probably in Paris. Here women, working apparently for a woman manager, are making dresses and hats to meet the demands of the fashion trade.

[Bildarchiv Preussischer Kulturbesitz]

lation and constituted the group traditionally regarded as the middle class, or *bourgeoisie.* The middle class had less wealth than most nobles but more than urban artisans. Middle-class people lived in the cities and towns, and their sources of income had little or nothing to do with the land. The middle class normally supported reform, change, and economic growth. Middle-class businessmen and professionals often found their pursuit of profit and prestige blocked by aristocratic privilege and social exclusiveness. The bourgeoisie (and some progressive aristocrats) also wanted more rational regulations for trade and commerce.

During the eighteenth century the middle class and the aristocracy frequently collided. The former often imitated the lifestyle of the latter, and nobles increasingly embraced the commercial spirit of the middle class. The bourgeoisie was not rising to challenge the nobility; both were seeking to enhance their existing power and prestige. However, tradition and political connection gave the advantage to the nobility. Consequently, as the century passed, the middle class

increasingly resented the aristocracy. That resentment became more bitter as the bourgeoisie grew wealthier and more numerous, and the aristocratic control of political and ecclesiastical power tightened. The growing influence of the nobility seemed to mean that the middle class would continue to be excluded from the political decisions of the day.

On the other hand, the middle class tended to fear the lower urban classes as much as they resented the nobility. The lower orders constituted a potentially violent element in society; a potential threat to property; and, in their poverty, a drain on national resources. The lower orders, however, were much more varied than either the city aristocracy or the middle class cared to admit.

Artisans The segment of the urban population that suffered from both the grasping of the middle class and the local nobility was made up of shopkeepers, artisans, and wage earners. These people constituted the single largest group in any city. They included grocers, butchers, fishmongers, carpenters,

During the Old Regime, European Jews were separated from non-Jews, typically in districts known as ghettos. Relegated to the least desirable section of a city or to rural villages, most lived in poverty. This watercolor painting depicts a street in Kazimlesz, the Jewish quarter of Cracow, Poland. [Judaica Collection Max Berger, Vienna Austria/Erich Lessing/Art Resource, N.Y.]

cabinetmakers, smiths, printers, hand-loom weavers, and tailors, to give but a few examples. They had their own culture, values, and institutions. Like the peasants of the countryside, they were in many respects conservative. Their economic position was highly vulnerable. If a poor harvest raised the price of food, their own businesses suffered.

The entire life of these artisans and shopkeepers centered on their work. They usually lived near or at their place of employment. Most of them worked in shops with fewer than a half-dozen other craftsmen. Their primary institution had historically been the guild, but by the eighteenth century most guilds had lost influence.

Nevertheless, the guilds were not to be ignored. They played a conservative role. They did not seek economic growth or innovation. They attempted to preserve the jobs and the skills of their members. They still were able in many countries to determine who might and might not pursue a particular craft. They attempted to prevent too many people from learning a particular skill. The guilds also provided a framework for social and economic advancement. A young boy might become an apprentice to learn a craft or trade. After several years he would be made a journeyman. Still later, if successful, he might become a master. The artisan could also receive certain social benefits from the guilds, including aid for his family during sickness or the promise of admission into the guild for his son. The guilds constituted the chief protection for artisans against the operation of the commercial market. They were particularly strong in central Europe.

The Jewish Population: Age of the Ghetto

Although the small Jewish communities of Amsterdam and other western European cities became famous for their intellectual life and financial institutions, most European Jews lived in Eastern Europe. In the eighteenth century and thereafter, no fewer than three million Jews dwelled in Poland, Lithuania, and Ukraine. There were perhaps 150,000 in the Habsburg lands, primarily in Bohemia, around 1760. Fewer than 100,000 lived in Germany and approximately 40,000 in France. England and Holland had Jewish populations of fewer than 10,000. There were even smaller groups of Jews in Italy.

In 1762 Catherine the Great of Russia specifically excluded Jews from a manifesto that welcomed foreigners to settle in Russia. She relaxed the exclusion a few years later. After the first partition of Poland in 1772, to be discussed in Chapter 24, Russia had a large Jewish population. The partition also resulted in larger Jewish communities in Prussia and Austria.

Jews dwelled in most nations without enjoying the rights and privileges of other subjects of the monarchs, unless such rights were specifically granted to them. They were regarded as aliens whose status might well be changed at the whim of local rulers or the monarchical government.

No matter where they dwelled, the Jews of Europe under the Old Regime lived apart from non-Jews. In cities they usually lived in distinct districts known as *ghettos;* in the countryside, in primarily Jewish villages. Thus this period in

Jewish history, which may be said to have begun with the expulsion of the Jews from Spain in 1492, is known as the age of the ghetto, or separate community. Jews were also treated as a distinct people religiously and legally. In Poland for much of the century they were virtually self-governing. Elsewhere they lived under the burden of discriminatory legislation. Except in England, Jews could not mix in the mainstream of the societies in which they dwelled.

During the seventeenth century a few Jews helped finance the wars of major rulers. These financiers often grew close to the rulers and came to be known as "court Jews." They tended to marry among themselves. Perhaps the most famous was Samuel Oppenheimer (1630–1703), who helped the Habsburgs finance their struggle against the Turks, including the defense of Vienna. Their position at court and their financial abilities may have brought them privilege and fame, but court Jews, including Oppenheimer, often failed to have their loans repaid.

Unlike the court Jews, however, most European Jews lived in poverty. They occupied the most undesirable sections of cities or poor rural villages. A few were money lenders, but most worked at the lowest occupations. Their religious beliefs, rituals, and community set them apart. A wall of laws and social institutions—as well as the physical walls of the ghetto—kept them in positions of social inferiority.

Under the Old Regime, it is important to emphasize, this discrimination was based on religious separateness. Jews who converted to Christianity were welcomed, even if not always warmly, into the major political and social institutions of European society. But until the late eighteenth century those Jews who remained loyal to their faith were subject to various religious, civil, and social disabilities. They were not free to pursue the professions or often change residence, and they stood outside the political structures of the nations in which they lived. Jews could be expelled from the cities where they dwelled, and their property could be confiscated. They were regarded as socially and religiously inferior. They could be required to listen to sermons that insulted them and their religion. Their children could be taken away from them and given Christian instruction. And they knew their non-Jewish neighbors might suddenly turn violently against them. As will be seen in subsequent chapters, however, the end of the Old Regime brought major changes in the lives of Jews and in their relationship to the larger culture.

IN WORLD PERSPECTIVE

The European Old Regime

This chapter opened by describing eighteenth-century European society as traditional, hierarchical, corporate, and privileged. These features had characterized Europe and much of the rest of the world for centuries. Virtually every society on the globe at the opening of the eighteenth century was characterized by marked social dependence and discrepancies between great wealth and poverty. All societies also confronted the grave problems of scarce food supplies.

The eighteenth century witnessed important changes in all these societies. The population explosion was a global event not limited to Europe. Its exact causes still remain uncertain, but whether in Europe or China, an improved food supply resulting from expanded acreage and new crops helped support the larger population. In China, lands once thought to be marginal were settled. Agricultural techniques improved in Europe, but emigration to the New World also opened vast expanses of land. In contrast to Europe, the farmland of China continued to be cultivated by clans or communities. But in all cases, the vast, expanding population created pressures on the existing social structures.

Another striking similarity between China and Europe is apparent in the growth of commerce during the eighteenth century. In both cultures banking was improved and a more certain money supply established. Agriculture became more commercialized, with more money payments. As in Europe, Chinese cities expanded. During the eighteenth century Chinese trade grew within Asia as well as within a larger world market. However, only Europe experienced industrialization.

Eighteenth-century Japan stood, of course, in marked contrast to both Europe and China. Tokugawa rule had achieved remarkable stability, but Japan had chosen not to enter the world-trading network, except as a depot for Dutch and Chinese goods. The population grew less rapidly than that of Europe or China, and the general economy seems to have grown slowly. Like the situation in many European cities, guilds controlled manufacture. In all these respects, Japan in the eighteenth century sought to spurn innovation and preserve stable tradition.

Throughout the eighteenth century, Africa continued to supply slave labor to both North and South America. The slave trade drew Africa deeply into the transatlantic economy.

Latin America remained at least in theory the monopolized preserve of Spain and Portugal. But that monopoly could not survive the expansion of the British economy and the determination of Britain to enter the Latin American market. At the same time, British forces established a hegemony in mid-eighteenth-century India that would last almost two centuries.

Seen in this world context, European society stood on the brink of a new era in which the social, economic, and political relationships of centuries would be destroyed. The commercial spirit and the values of the marketplace clashed with the traditional values and practices of peasants and guilds. That commercial spirit proved to be a major vehicle of social change; by the early nineteenth century it led increasingly to a conception of human beings as individuals rather than as members of communities.

The expansion of the European population further stimulated change and challenge to tradition, hierarchy, and corporateness. The traditional economic and social organization had presupposed a stable or declining population. A larger population meant that new ways had to be devised to solve old problems. The social hierarchy had to accommodate itself to more people. Corporate groups, such as the guilds, had to confront an expanded labor force. New wealth meant that birth would eventually cease to determine social relationships, except in regard to the social roles assigned to the two sexes.

Finally, the conflicting political ambitions of the monarchies, the nobilities, and the middle class generated innovation. The monarchies wanted to make their nations rich enough to wage war. The nobilities wished to reassert their privileges. The middle class, in all of its diversity, was growing wealthier from trade, commerce, and the practice of the professions. Its members wanted social prestige and influence equal to their wealth.

All of these factors meant that the society of the late eighteenth century stood at the close of one era of European history and at the opening of another. However, as these social and economic changes became connected to the world economy, the transformation of Europe led to the transformation of much of the non-European world. For the first time in the history of the world, major changes in one region left virtually no corner of the globe politically or economically untouched. By the close of the eighteenth century a movement toward world interconnectedness and interdependence that had no real precedent in terms of depth and extent had begun, and it has not yet ended.

Review Questions ———

1. Describe the privileges of the various European nobilities. How did they differ as one moved west to east across the Continent? What was the economic basis of the life of the nobility? What authority did they have over other groups in their various societies?

2. How would you define the term *family economy*? What were some of the particular characteristics of the northwestern European household as opposed to that in eastern Europe? In what ways were the lives of women constrained by the family economy in preindustrial Europe?

3. What caused the Agricultural Revolution? How did technological innovations help change European agriculture? To what extent did the English aristocracy contribute to the Agricultural Revolution? What were some of the reasons for peasant revolts in Europe in the eighteenth century?

4. What factors explain the increase in Europe's population in the eighteenth century? What were the effects of the population explosion? How did population growth contribute to changes in consumption?

5. What caused the Industrial Revolution of the eighteenth century? What were some of the technological innovations and why were they important? Why did Great Britain take the lead in the Industrial Revolution? How did the consumer contribute to the Industrial Revolution?

6. Describe city life during the eighteenth century. Were all European cities of the same character? What changes had taken place in the distribution of population in cities and towns? Compare the lifestyle of the upper class with those of the middle and lower classes.

Suggested Readings ———

I. T. BEREND AND G. RANKI, *The European Periphery and Industrialization, 1780–1914* (1982). Examines the experience of eastern and Mediterranean Europe.

J. BLUM, *Lord and Peasant in Russia from the Ninth to the Nineteenth Century* (1961). A thorough and wide-ranging discussion.

J. BLUM, *The End of the Old Order in Rural Europe* (1978). The most comprehensive treatment of life in rural Europe, especially central and eastern, from the early eighteenth through the mid-nineteenth centuries.

F. BRAUDEL, *The Structures of Everyday Life: The Limits of the Possible*, trans. by M. Kochan (1982). A magisterial survey by the most important social historian of our time.

J. CANNON, *Aristocratic Century: The Peerage of Eighteenth-Century England* (1985). A useful treatment based on the most recent research.

G. CHAUSSINAND-NOGARET, *The French Nobility in the Eighteenth Century* (1985). Suggests that culture, not class, was the decisive element in late eighteenth-century French society.

P. DEANE, *The First Industrial Revolution*, 2nd ed. (1979). A well-balanced and systematic treatment.

J. DE VRIES, *The Economy of Europe in an Age of Crisis, 1600–1750* (1976). An excellent overview that sets forth the main issues.

J. DE VRIES, *European Urbanization 1500–1800* (1984). The most important and far-ranging of recent treatments of the subject.

W. DOYLE, *Venality: The Sale of Offices in Eighteenth-Century France* (1997). Examines the manner in which the phenomena characterized much of the society.

P. EARLE, *The Making of the English Middle Class: Business, Community, and Family Life in London, 1660–1730* (1989). The most careful study of the subject.

M. W. FLINN, *The European Demographic System, 1500–1820* (1981). A major summary.

F. FORD, *Robe and Sword: The Regrouping of the French Aristocracy after Louis XIV* (1953). An important treatment of the growing social tensions within the French nobility during the eighteenth century.

R. FORSTER AND O. RANUM, *Deviants and the Abandoned in French Society* (1978). This and the following volume contain important essays from the French journal *Annales*.

R. FORSTER AND O. RANUM, *Medicine and Society in France* (1980).

D. V. GLASS AND D. E. C. EVERSLEY, EDS., *Population in History: Essays in Historical Demography* (1965). Fundamental for an understanding of the eighteenth-century increase in population.

P. GOUBERT, *The Ancien Regime: French Society, 1600–1750*, trans. by Steve Cox (1974). A superb account of the peasant social order.

D. HAY ET AL., *Albion's Fatal Tree: Crime and Society in Eighteenth-Century England* (1976). Separate essays on a previously little-explored subject.

D. HAY AND N. ROGERS, *Eighteenth-Century English Society: Shuttles and Swords* (1997). Explores the social experience of the lower orders.

O. H. HUFTON, *The Poor of Eighteenth-Century France, 1750–1789* (1975). A brilliant study of poverty and the family economy.

C. JONES, *Charity and Bienfaisance: The Treatment of the Poor in the Montpellier Region, 1740–1815* (1982). An important local French study.

E. L. JONES, *Agriculture and Economic Growth in England, 1650–1815* (1968). A good introduction to an important subject.

A. KAHAN, *The Plow, the Hammer, and the Knout: An Economic History of Eighteenth-Century Russia* (1985). An extensive and detailed treatment.

H. KAMEN, *European Society, 1500–1700* (1985). A useful one-volume treatment.

P. LASLETT, *The World We Have Lost* (1984). Examination of English life and society before the coming of industrialism.

R. K. MCCLURE, *Coram's Children: The London Foundling Hospital in the Eighteenth Century* (1981). A moving work that deals with the plight of all concerned with the problem.

N. MCKENDERICK, ED., *The Birth of a Consumer Society: The Commercialization of Eighteenth-Century England* (1982). Deals with several aspects of the impact of commercialization.

F. E. MANUEL, *The Broken Staff: Judaism Through Christian Eyes* (1992). An important discussion of Christian interpretations of Judaism.

M. A. MEYER, *The Origins of the Modern Jew: Jewish Identity and European Culture in Germany, 1749–1824* (1967). A general introduction organized around individual case studies.

S. POLLARD, *The Genesis of Modern Management: A Study of the Industrial Revolution in Great Britain* (1965). Treats industrialization from the standpoint of factory owners.

S. POLLARD, *Peaceful Conquest: The Industrialization of Europe, 1760–1970* (1981). A useful survey.

A. RIBEIRO, *Dress in Eighteenth-Century Europe, 1715–1789* (1985). An interesting examination of the social implication of style in clothing.

G. RUDE, *The Crowd in History 1730–1848* (1964). A pioneering study.

G. RUDE, *Paris and London in the Eighteenth Century* (1973).

H. SCHMAL, ED., *Patterns of European Urbanization Since 1500* (1981). Major essays.

L. STONE, *An Open Elite?* (1985). Raises important questions about the traditional view of open access to social mobility in England.

T. TACKETT, *Priest and Parish in Eighteenth-Century France: A Social and Political Study of the Cures in a Diocese of Dauphine, 1750–1791* (1977). An important local study that displays the role of the church in the fabric of social life in the old regime.

L. A. TILLY AND J. W. SCOTT, *Women, Work, and Family* (1978). An excellent survey of the issues in western Europe.

D. VALENZE, *The First Industrial Woman* (1995). An elegant work exploring the manner in which industrialization transformed the work of women.

A. VICKERY, *The Gentleman's Daughter: Women's Lives in Georgian England* (1998). Argues that women experienced expanding social horizions in the eighteenth-century.

R. WALL, ED., *Family Forms in Historic Europe* (1983). Essays that cover the entire continent.

C. WILSON, *England's Apprenticeship, 1603–1763* (1984). A broad survey of English economic life on the eve of industrialism.

E. A. WRIGLEY, *Continuity, Chance and Change: The Character of the Industrial Revolution in England* (1988). A major conceptual reassessment.

E. A. WRIGLEY AND R. S. SCHOFIELD, *The Population History of England, 1541–1871: A Reconstruction* (1982). One of the most ambitious demographic studies ever undertaken.

One of the many superb paintings that grace the best examples of Persian manuscripts of the *Shah-namah*, the Iranian national epic by the poet Firdausi (c. 940–1020). The *Shah-namah* recounts the glories of Iran's past from the arrival of the Persians to the coming of the Arabs. In this scene the Iranian hero Zal slays the leader of an invading army. The painting is attributed to Abdul-Vahhab. [Metropolitan Museum of Art, gift of Arthur A. Houghton, Jr., 1970 (1970.301.15)]

ISLAMIC EMPIRES

♦ The Ottoman Empire

♦ The Safavid Shi'ite Empire

♦ The Empire of the Indian Timurids, or "Mughals"

ISLAMIC ASIA

♦ Central Asia: Islamization and Isolation

♦ Power Shifts in the Southern Seas

In World Perspective The Last Islamic Empires

Between 1450 and 1650 Islamic culture and statecraft blossomed. The creation of three powerful empires and several strong regional states was the culmination of long processes in Islamic history. During this time the ideal of a universal Muslim caliphate yielded to the reality of multiple secular, albeit distinctively "Islamic," sultanates.

The simultaneous growth of the Ottoman, Safavid, and Mughal empires marked the global apogee of Islamic culture and power. By about 1600 the Ottoman Turks controlled Asia Minor, the Fertile Crescent, the Balkans, Crimean Europe, the Islamic Mediterranean, and Arabia; the Persian Safavids ruled all of greater Iran; and descendants of Timur—the Timurid line known as the Mughals—governed Afghanistan and most of the Indian subcontinent. Around these were arrayed Muslim khanates of Central Asia and Russia, sultanates of Southeast Asia and East Africa, the Sharifian state of Morocco, and regional empires of the Sudan in which Islam played a significant role (see Map 23–1).

In 1600 Islamic civilization seemed as strong and vital as that of western Europe, China, or Japan. Yet hard on the heels of this Islamic prosperity and power came a sharp decline in Islamic military preeminence and gradually diminishing economic and political strength. By the late seventeenth century Islamic commercial, political, and military power was almost everywhere in retreat before the rising tide of western European military and economic imperialism, even though Islamic cultural life flourished and Muslim religion still spread significantly between 1500 and 1800.

In this chapter we focus first on the three major Islamic empires of the period and their varied political, social, and cultural histories. We then turn briefly to the important, but smaller, less widely influential Islamic political and cultural centers of Central Asia and the coastlands of southern Asia and the Indies. In the latter areas we note especially the impact of European power on what had been a virtual Muslim monopoly on maritime trade.

ISLAMIC EMPIRES

The Ottoman Empire

Origins and Development of the Ottoman State before 1600

The Ottomans were a Turkish dynasty that rose to prominence as one of various groups of western, or Oghuz, Turks from the steppes of Central Asia who came to Anatolia as settlers and, in some cases, as *ghazis*, or frontier warriors dedicated to extending Muslim rule by *jihad*, or "struggle" in God's cause.[1] The Ottomans reached Anatolia (Asia Minor) in the time of the Seljuqs of Rum (1098–1308), who were the first western Turks to have founded a lasting state there. By about 1300, the newcomers had built one of several small military states along the Byzantine-Seljuq frontier in western Anatolia. In the fourteenth century several vigorous leaders expanded their territories east into central Anatolia and west across the Dardanelles (in 1356) onto European soil, in the

---

[1]The Ottomans, sometimes called *Osmanlis*, are named after Osman (1259–1326), also rendered *Othman* or *Uthman*, a *ghazi* said to have founded the dynasty when he set up a border state about 1288 on the Byzantine frontier in northwestern Anatolia.

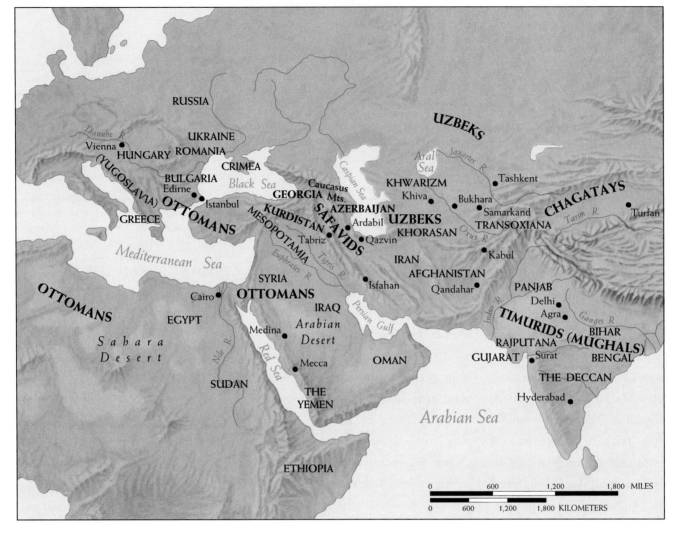

Map 23–1 Sixteenth-century Islamic empires. Major Islamic dynasties in the central Islamic lands, ca. 1600. Note that the Sharifian state of Morocco does not show on the far left of this map.

Byzantine lands of Macedonia and modern Bulgaria. Exchanging grants of revenue-producing conquered land (*timars*) for military service, the Ottomans built both a formidable fighting force and a loyal military aristocracy.

By 1402 the center of Ottoman rule had shifted northwest to Edirne on the Balkan peninsula itself. Ottoman control then extended northwest as far as the Danube and east across central Anatolia. Only the completely encircled tip of Balkan Europe, on which sat Constantinople, formed an alien pocket within these dominions.

The Byzantine capital had survived repeated Islamic sieges long before Ottoman times. However, the reasons for Ottoman interest in Constantinople were not simply ideological but economic—one being its potential for increasing profitable trade with Genoa. Strategically, the Ottomans needed the city also to secure their hold on their larger Balkan do-

mains. It finally fell in 1453 to Sultan Mehmed II, "the Conqueror" (r. 1451–1481). Constantinople now replaced Edirne as the Ottoman capital; it was formally renamed "Istanbul," a local dialect name of uncertain origin—although "Constantinople" continued in common usage. After hundreds of years proud Byzantium, the center of eastern Christendom, was no more, although the Ottomans allowed the Christian patriarch still to preside in Istanbul over the eastern church.

By 1512 Ottoman rule was secure in virtually all of southeastern Europe and north of the Black Sea in most of the Ukraine. Under Selim I (r. 1512–1520) and Süleyman, "the Lawgiver" (known in the West as "Süleyman the Magnificent"; r. 1520–1566), this sovereignty was greatly expanded and consolidated. Selim established the Ottoman state as a major Asian as well as European empire by subjugating the Egyptian Mamluks (1517) and annexing Syria-Palestine and

Egypt, as well as most of North Africa. The Yemen and western Arabia, including the sacred precincts of Mecca and Medina, also were brought under Ottoman rule. Selim nullified the Shi'ite threat from Iran in the east (see below). Süleyman extended Ottoman control over Kurdistan and Georgia (in the Caucasus), as well as Mesopotamia and Iraq. He also advanced Ottoman borders in eastern Europe. Having won much of Hungary and nearly taken Vienna by siege in 1526–1529, he was able by battle and treaty to bring virtually all of Hungary under direct Ottoman rule in the 1540s.

The Ottoman ruler could now claim to be the Abbasid heir and caliph for all Muslims. This claim was symbolized by the addition (begun by Selim I, after the Mamluk conquest in 1517) of the title "Protector of the Sacred Places [Mecca and Medina]" to that of emperor (*padishah*). At this point, Ottoman military might was unmatched by any state in the world, except possibly China.

The "Classical" Ottoman Order

Mehmed II was the true founder of the Ottoman order. He broke the power of tribal chieftains in Ottoman affairs and replaced them with loyal servants of the ruler; he initiated a tradition of formal governmental legislation with his *Qanunname* ("Lawbook"); and he organized the *ulama* into a hierarchy under a single "Sheikh of Islam." In the next century Süleyman earned his title "Lawgiver" by his legislation touching all aspects of life and all social ranks, his reconciliation of *Shari'a* and customary law, and his long-term effort to regularize both law and bureaucracy.

The entire Ottoman state was organized as one vast military institution. All members, whatever their function, held military ranks as the standing "army" of the state under the hereditary leadership of the Sultan. This centralized state was supported by the productivity of its Muslim and non-Muslim

The oldest known Ottoman illustration of the great city of Istanbul, by the Ottoman painter Matrakci Nasuh (c. 1537). The waters of the Golden Horn flow up (to the east) in the middle to the Bosphorus and divide the city into Galata on the left (with its main hill topped by the Galata Tower) and the Istanbul peninsula on the right (the Sea of Marmara lies off the page to the right). The huge Topkapi palace complex, with Hagia Sophia on its lower right, occupies the tip of the peninsula on the upper right of the Gold Horn. [Istanbul University Library, T. 56964, fols. 8b-9a/Photograph courtesy of Talat Halman]

Süleyman the Lawgiver (r. 1520–1566), giving advice to the Crown Prince, Mehmed Khan. From a contemporaneous Ottoman miniature. [Folio 79a of the *Talikizade Shenamesi*, Library of the Topkapi Palace Museum, A3592/Photograph courtesy of Talat Halman].

ing to assert himself and seize power, after which he was expected to execute all of his brothers to eliminate future competing claims to the throne.

By institutionalizing the religious institution, the Ottomans coopted the legal-religious and educational-intellectual roles of the religious scholars, or *ulama*, for the service of the state, making them an arm of the government under a single religious authority, the Grand Mufti or "Shaykh of Islam." This highly organized branch of the state was open only to Muslim men and included the entire system of courts and judges. It was based on a comprehensive network ranging from local mosque schools to the four elite madrasas built around the Süleymaniye mosque in Istanbul during Süleyman's reign. Scholars' ranks within the graded hierarchy of the *ulama* reflected the level of schooling and teaching they had attained.

While the *ulama* were thus under state control, the state itself was formally committed to maintaining the divinely ordained *Shari'a,* and the *ulama* enjoyed great esteem in Ottoman society. This may account for the fact that whereas the *ulama* in both Safavid Iran and Mughal India often differed with their rulers, the Ottoman *ulama* functioned more often tamely as part of the larger state apparatus.

Although the religious establishment upheld the supremacy of the *Shari'a* and the sultan recognized its authority, the functional law of the land was the state administrative law—the practical code, or *Qanun,* established by the ruler. This had been de facto characteristic of most Islamic states, but under the Ottomans, administrative law was unusually highly organized. The *Shari'a* as interpreted by the *ulama* theoretically governed the *Qanun,* and often the sultan formally applied traditional religious norms in his regulations. The conformity of these regulations to the *Shari'a* sometimes came from the genuine piety of a particular administrator or ruler and was sometimes only a pious fiction, something also true for Safavid Iran and Mughal India.

As for the military institution, the Ottoman rulers kept its loyalty by two means: checks on the power of the old landed aristocracy by careful registry and control of *timar* lands, and the use of slave soldiers with allegiance only to the sultan. The army was based originally on the provincial cavalry, whose officers were supported with *timar* land revenues in lieu of cash wages. The state held all conquered agricultural land as its direct property, granting peasants hereditary land use but not ownership. Careful records were kept of the revenue due on all lands, and as long as the state was strong, so too was its control over productive land and the cavalry-gentry whom *timar* revenues supported. But even as early as 1400 the Ottoman rulers tried to reduce the cavalry-gentry's preeminence by employing specialized infantry troops of well-trained and well-paid slave soldiers (equipped, unlike the cavalry, with firearms) whose loyalty was to the sultan alone.

subjects. The ruling class were all Muslims, shared the common Ottoman culture, and had to give utter allegiance to the sultan. The state organization included the palace and three further functional divisions: the administrative or ruling institution, the military institution, and the religious or learned institution. The palace included the sultan, his harem, his ministers, and those who served in the palace. The privy council, headed by the grand vizier, together with the chancery, the imperial treasury, and the remaining civil bureaucracy, formed the backbone of the ruling or administrative institution.

Several measures helped ensure the ongoing strength of the sultan at the apex of the ruling institution. Young Ottoman princes were given administrative and leadership training in the provinces, which kept them from being sheltered in the palace and gave them experience of life outside the capital. Stability of succession was traditionally guaranteed by the practice of fratricide in the ruling family, which, legalized formally in Mehmed II's *Qanun-name,* continued until the late sixteenth century. Thus the succession was theoretically left to God, the strongest aspirant to the sultanate hav-

The Distinctiveness of Ottoman Identity and Culture

Presiding over a pluralistic culture, the Ottoman Turks, themselves a people from the periphery of the central Islamic lands, developed a distinctive "Ottoman" identity and culture that was most evident in their ruling elite. The following selections from members of that elite describe some of the values and qualities they saw as important to Ottoman identity. In the first, Mustafa Ali (d. 1600), a major historian, intellectual, and official of the Ottoman state, lists the special divine favors granted the Ottoman rulers. In the second, another historian, Kinalizade Ali, adopts an ancient political saying attributed to Aristotle and others to describe the prerequisites for an ordered polity under the Shari'a.

Compare the two passages. What common themes emerge?

---

1. The Gifts of Divine Favor Given the Ottoman Dynasty

The first gift: They reside all by themselves in a palace like unique jewels in the depth of the oyster-shell, and totally sever all relations with relatives and dependents. The slave girls and slave pages that have access to their honored private quarters (*harem*), who are evidently at least three to four thousand individuals, are all strangers and the person of the monarch is like a single gem in their midst. . . .

The second gift: Their religious convictions being immaculate and their character like a shining mirror, it has never happened that a single member of that noble family ever swerved from the road of orthodoxy or that one valiant sultan befriended himself with an unseemly doctrine.

The third gift: The Lord, the Creator and Protector, has always hidden that great race under His protection and it has never been heard that the plague would have entered their flourishing palace or that an individual belonging to that blemishless progeny would have been struck by the horror of the pestilence and would have died of it.

The fourth gift: Whenever they conquered a province and, destroying and eradicating its castles and estates, were confronted with the necessity of appointing a magistrate and assigning a substantial force on their own authority

they considered it a sign of weakness, like Alexander the Great, to appoint again one of the great of that province and to assign him certain revenues; may [that province] be as far away as can be, they would opt to send one of the attendants of their Gate of Happiness [there] as *sanjaq begi*, and to Yemen and Ethiopia and to very remote places like Algeria a *begler-begi*. No such absolute power was given to the earlier sovereigns.

The fifth gift: The various special troops in their victory-oriented army and the various tools of war and battle use that are given to them were not available to the brawny fists of anyone of the countless armies [of previous times]. To their attacks going downward and going upward are the same, to their victory-imprinted military music low and high notes are of the same level and equal. In their eyes, as it were, the conquest of a castle is like destroying a spider's web, and in their God-assisted hands to beat the enemies is clearly like pulling out a hair from the beard of a decrepit old man.

The sixth gift: The coherence of the figures in the registers of their revenues and the order of the recordings in the ledgers of their expenses are so strict that they and their salaried classes are free of worries. Consequently, their income exceeds their necessary expenses, their gain is larger than [the expenses for] the important affairs of state.

2. The Need of Authority to Uphold the Shari'a

There can be no royal authority without the military
There can be no military without wealth
The subjects produce the wealth
Justice preserves the subjects' loyalty to the sovereign
Justice requires harmony in the world
The world is a garden, its walls are the state
The Holy Law [*Shari'a*] orders the state
There is no support for the Holy Law except through
    royal authority.

Selection 1 From Andreas Tietze, *Mustafa Ali's Counsel for Sultans of 1581*, Verlag Der Österreichischen Akademie Der Wissenshaften, Vienna, 1979, pp. 38–39. Selection 2 From Cornell H. Fleischer, *Bureaucrat and Intellectual in the Ottoman Empire: The Historian Mustafa Ali (1541–1600)*, Princeton University Press, 1986, p. 262.

To sustain the quality of these slave troops, the Ottomans developed as early as the late fourteenth century a unique institution: the provincial slave levy, or *devshirme*. This institution selected young Christian boys from the provincial peasantry to be raised as Muslims; most came from the Balkan peasantry. They were trained to serve in both army and bureaucracy at all levels, from provincial officer to grand vizier. How high slave soldiers could rise is exemplified by the famous imperial architect, Sinan (d. 1578), who as a *devshirme* recruit rose through the military organization by virtue of his excellence. The most famous slave corps was the Janissaries, the elite infantry troops of the empire. Muslim boys were not allowed into the slave corps, although some parents tried to buy them a place in what offered the most promising careers in the empire. Until 1572 marriage was forbidden to the slave soldiers, which further ensured loyalty and prevented hereditary claims on office.

The Süleyman mosque, named after its founder, Süleyman the Lawgiver, is one of the finest mosques in Istanbul. Completed in 1557 by the architect Sinan, who is buried in the mosque, it rises above the Golden Horn on Istanbul's third hill. Sinan was a slave-soldier recruit who rose through the ranks to his high position. [Chester Beatty Library and Gallery of Oriental Art, Dublin/The Bridgeman Art Library International]

After Süleyman: Challenges and Change

The reign of Süleyman is usually characterized as the "classical" period in Ottoman history. It marked the peak of Ottoman prestige and power. Further territorial gains were made in the seventeenth century, and the Ottoman state long remained a major force in European and Asian politics. However, beginning with the reign of Süleyman's weak son, Selim II (1566–1574), the empire faced repeated new challenges. It was plagued ever more by military corruption, governmental decentralization, and maritime setbacks. Economically there arose problems related to agricultural failures, commercial imbalances, and inflation that were hard to check. Yet culturally and intellectually, the seventeenth and eighteenth centuries were periods of impressive accomplishments and

lively activity. Overall, the ensuing two centuries witnessed a seesaw battle between forces of decline and vitality.

Political and Military Developments   The post-Süleyman era began on a sour political and military note with the loss of territory in the Caucasus and Mesopotamia to the Persian Safavids (1603). By this time the Ottoman military apparatus was already weakened, partly from fighting two-front wars with the Safavids and the Hapsburgs and partly because of European advances in military and naval technology. The Janissaries, once the backbone of Ottoman power, became ever more independent of imperial control and correspondingly disruptive. By 1600 these troops were increasingly based in the provinces, and during the ensuing century, they largely displaced the *timar* holders of the provincial cavalry as new warfare styles made cavalry ever more obsolete. By 1600 Muslims were allowed into the Janissary corps, marriage was possible, and the *devshirme* was declining in use (it ended just over a century later). During the seventeenth century, Janissaries engaged increasingly in public life, becoming involved

An Ottoman portrayal of the *Devshirme*. This miniature painting from about 1558 depicts the recruiting of young Christian children for the Sultan's elite Janissary corps. [Topkapi Sarayi Musesi, H. 1517, folio 31b, Topkapi Palace Museum. Photograph courtesy of Talat Halman]

with craft guilds and trade and taking over *timars;* financial considerations were a prime motive, prompted by growing debasement of coinage and general decrease in wages. Corruption grew rife in their ranks as the Janissaries tampered more and more with politics, trying to influence decision making and even dynastic succession. Finally, the increasing employment of mercenaries resulted in peacetime in the release of masses of unemployed armed men into the countryside, which led to the sacking of provincial towns and general banditry and contributed to political revolts. Such activities forced citizen migrations and generally disrupted the agrarian and urban social orders.

Murad IV (r. 1623–1640) introduced various reforms and ruled with an iron hand, but his death left again a weak central authority. The Köprülüs, father and son, two efficient and capable viziers (r. 1656–1676), briefly renewed strong administrative control and military success, but thereafter the central institutions decayed.

Economic Developments   Financing the Ottoman state grew ever more difficult. The threefold increase in the Janissary corps from 12,000 to 36,000 men between the early 1500s and 1600 drained state coffers. Already in the sixteenth century, fluctuations in silver caused damaging inflation. In contrast to the mercantilist and protectionist policies of European powers, the Ottomans discouraged exports and encouraged imports, since too many exports would have raised domestic prices. This damaged the Ottoman economy in the long run. The population doubled in the sixteenth century, which led to a reduction in size of the average unit of arable land per capita and to increased unemployment, a trend that grew after 1600. *Timar* lands began to be leased to tax farmers for short periods (and were even converted at times to lifetime leases) to meet the treasury's urgent cash needs (such as Janissary and mercenary pay), which increased dramatically in the seventeenth century. This increased decentralization and paved the way for the rise of provincial notables (*ayan*), most of whom became virtually independent in the eighteenth century. Tax farming also coincided with (and probably influenced) the rise of large private estates. Owners of these estates had full control of their land, and although these private estates constituted only a small percentage of arable lands, they contributed much to the commercialization of agriculture, especially through crop exports to European markets. A similar transformation took place in taxation from the late 1600s on. New taxes were imposed and old emergency levies regularized. Also new was the levy of taxes principally in cash rather than in kind and increasingly on a communal rather than an individual basis.

Culture and Society   The seventeenth and eighteenth centuries were an era of genuine vitality in poetry, prose, music, painting, historiography, astronomy, and other fields. The seventeenth century saw especially lively intellectual exchange, both religious and secular. It was also, however, the period in which the *ulama* became an aristocratic social elite and fell prey to significant corruption: Major religious posts were controlled by a handful of families that had produced prominent *ulama*. These became hereditary sinecures for sons and other relatives, and were often sold or leased.

In literature and the arts, the seventeenth and eighteenth centuries were highly productive. Katib Chelebi (d. 1657) was only the most illustrious of many polymaths who wrote histories, social commentary, geographies, and encyclopedic works. Other important writers were the great historian of the Ottomans, Na'ima (d. 1716), the tireless traveler and travel writer Evliya Chelebi (d. ca. 1685), and probably the greatest Ottoman poet, Nedim (d. 1730). Ottoman art had been highly eclectic in the first century after Mehmed II, but in the latter sixteenth century a more conservative turn produced distinctively Ottoman artistic and architectural forms. The greatest name here is that of the imperial master architect Sinan. The first half of the eighteenth century was the golden age of Ottoman poetry and art; it also saw the first Ottoman printing press introduced and the beginning of strong European influence in the arts, architecture, and manners. In the popular sphere, the now classical form of Turkish theater (in which two men play male and female parts) began as early as the sixteenth century, perhaps under Jewish immigrant influence.

Socially, the period saw the consolidation of Ottoman society as a multi-ethnic and multi-religious state. The empire encompassed a dizzying array of languages, religions, and ethnic identities. Considerable Jewish immigration into Ottoman societies following their expulsion from Spain (1492) had brought new craftsmen, physicians, bankers, scholars, and even entertainers. The first printing house for Jewish texts had opened in Istanbul in the late fifteenth century, for example. The large Christian population of the empire was generally well treated, but in the seventeenth century they began to suffer from increasing taxes and other discrimination, partly because of religious conservatism among the *ulama*, partly because of the waning of the *devshirme* (which had placed men in power from among the rural Christian population), and partly because of the ruthless administration of a class of Greek Christians who gained high Ottoman provincial offices in the Balkans in the late seventeenth and the eighteenth centuries. The long-term result of the deteriorating situation of the Christians was that they looked as never before to Christian Europe and Russia for liberation.

Overall, while the situation of non-Muslims did not radically change, the increased economic hardships of Ottoman subjects in the seventeenth century were certainly shared, perhaps disproportionately, by non-Muslims. Still, state policy encouraged just treatment of all subjects; for example, issuing "rescripts of justice" (mostly against the malpractices of tax collectors) was a prominent practice. Royal decrees stressed differences between Muslims and non-Muslims, with special privileges reserved for the former. However, such decrees had long been issued without significantly affecting mass behavior. In the eighteenth century strained relations between Muslims and non-Muslims increased, in part because of the remarkable rise in the economic and social status of non-Muslims—in particular the rich mercantile middle class. Non-Muslims virtually monopolized foreign trade, and in the eighteenth century European countries gave many of them citizenship, which allowed them the trade privileges granted to foreign governments by the sultan.

One of the major social institutions of later Ottoman society, the coffeehouse, flourished from the mid-sixteenth century on. Probably originally a sufi institution that came to the Mediterranean from the Yemen, the Ottoman coffeehouse spread with the adoption of the coffee habit and rapidly became a major common space for socializing. Here people gathered to drink coffee, play games, watch puppet shows, read books, discuss public affairs, and even engage in political agitation, which made these gathering places suspect among the governing elite. However, despite bans by the Sheikh of Islam because of the stimulant qualities of coffee, both the coffee habit and coffeehouses, like the similarly new imported habit of cigarette smoking, could not be suppressed. Different types of coffeehouse developed, each identified by its primary focus: music, theater, reading and recitation, poetry, Janissary or other professional affiliation (e.g., firefighting), among others. All in all, the coffeehouse stimulated the development of a common Ottoman urban culture among lower and middle classes.

The Decline of Ottoman Military and Political Power

After the failure in 1683 of a second siege of Vienna, the Ottomans were driven out of Hungary and Belgrade and never again seriously threatened Europe. The treaty of Karlowitz sealed the loss of Hungary to Austria as well as other European territory losses to Venice and Poland. A second major defeat came in 1718 at the hands of the Habsburgs. After several victories of Mahmud I (r. 1730–1754) at the expense of the divided European powers, a crushing third defeat by Russia cost the Ottomans the Crimea, which made the tsar the formal protector of the Orthodox Christians of the Islamic empire (1774). Henceforth, the Ottomans were prey to the West, never regaining their earlier power and influence before their final demise in 1918.

The Ottoman Empire	
ca. 1280	Foundation of early Ottoman principality in Anatolia
1356	Ottomans Cross Dardanelles into Europe
1451–1481	Rule of Sultan Mehmed II, "the Conqueror"
1453	Fall of Constantinople to Mehmed the Conqueror
1512–1520	Rule of Selim I
1517	Ottoman conquest of Egypt, assumption of claim to Abbasid caliphal succession from Mamluks
1520–1556	Rule of Süleyman, "the Lawgiver"
1526–1529	First Ottoman siege of Vienna
1578	Death of Ottoman master architect, Sinan
1656–1676	Governance of Koprülüs as viziers
1683	Second Ottoman siege of Vienna
1699	Treaty of Karlowitz, loss of Hungarian and other European territory
1774	Loss of Crimea to Russia; Tsar becomes formal protector of Ottoman Orthodox Christians
1918	End of empire

Outflanked by the rising power of Russia to their north and by growing European sea power to the south and west, the Ottomans found themselves blocked in the east by their implacable Shi'ite foes in Iran. They could not sustain the level of external trade needed to support their expensive wars. Ultimately, their dependence on an agrarian-age economy proved insufficient to face the rising commercial and industrial powers of Europe.

The Safavid Shi'ite Empire

Origins

As noted in Chapter 14, Iranian history changed under the Safavid dynasty after 1500. The Safavids had begun in the fourteenth century as hereditary Turkish spiritual leaders (*shaykhs*) of a Sunni Sufi order, or *tariqa*, in the northwestern Iranian province of Azerbaijan. (The tomb shrine of the founding head of the order, Shaykh Safi al-Din [d. 1334], still stands in Ardabil, in eastern Azerbaijan.) In the fifteenth century the Safavid order evolved a new and militant Shi'ite ideology, and by the 1480s its members were operating as *ghazis*, or border raiders, against Christians in the southern Caucasus. The Safavid spiritual masters (*shaykhs*, or *pirs*) of the order claimed descent from the seventh imam of the Twelver Shia (see Chapter 14), which made them (the *pirs*) the focus of Shi'ite religious allegiance. Many adherents were won to the order and to Shi'ism from among the Turkoman tribesmen of eastern Anatolia, northern Syria, and northwestern Iran.

These mounted warriors were called *Kizilbash* ("Red Heads") because of their distinctive red uniform hats, which signaled their allegiance to the twelve Shi'ite imams and their Safavid master.

The growing strength of the Safavids brought about conflict with the dominant Sunni Turkoman groups in the region around Tabriz. The Safavids emerged victorious in 1501 under the leadership of the young Safavid master-designate Isma'il. Recognized as a divinely appointed representative of the "hidden" imam (see Chapter 11), Isma'il extended his sovereignty over the southern Caucasus, Azerbaijan, the Tigris-Euphrates valley, and all of western Iran by 1506. In the east by 1512 the Safavids, in league with Babur, the Timurid ruler of Kabul, had taken all of eastern Iran from the Oxus River south to the Arabian Sea from the Uzbek Turks. The Uzbeks, however, became implacable foes of the Safavids and throughout the ensuing century often forced them to fight a debilitating two-front war, with Uzbeks in the east, and Ottomans in the west.

A strong central rule now united traditional Iranian lands for the first time since the heyday of the Abbasid caliphate. It was a regime based on the existing Persian bureaucratic institutions, which in turn were based on Seljuq institutions. Shah Isma'il ruthlessly enforced Shi'ite conformity on the Sunni majority of the Iranian lands, even importing Shi'ite *ulama* from Lebanon and Bahrain, and his efforts proved successful. Shi'ite conformity, which demanded at least the formal denunciation of the first three caliphs (as usurpers of Ali's

office), slowly took root across the realm—perhaps bolstered by a rising Persian self-consciousness in the face of the Sunni Ottomans, Arabs, Uzbeks, and Mughals who surrounded Iran.

In the west, however, Isma'il's aggressive efforts against the Ottomans proved futile. The better-armed army of Selim I soundly defeated the Kizilbash forces of the Safavids at Chaldiran, near Tabriz, in 1514, marking the beginning of an extended series of Ottoman-Safavid conflicts over the next two centuries. Chaldiran also marked the beginning of Kizilbash disaffection with Shah Isma'il and consequent efforts to take over power from the Safavids. Furthermore, this defeat gave the Ottomans control of the Fertile Crescent and forced the Safavids to move their capital and their focus eastward, out of the extreme western parts of Iran (Azerbaijan) where they had first come to power. First Qazwin, and then Isfahan, became the new Iranian capital instead of Tabriz.

Shah Abbas I

Isma'il's less able but often underestimated successor, Tahmasp I (r. 1524–1576), lost more territory to Süleyman's powerful Ottoman forces but managed to survive repeated attacks by both Ottomens and Uzbeks. In part, the strength of Shi'ite religious feeling and the allegiance of the Iranian bureaucracy enabled the regime to survive. A few years later, however, the greatest Safavid ruler, Shah Abbas I (r. 1588–1629), brought firm and able leadership to the Safavid domains. He regained provincial land for the state and used the revenue to

Shah Abbas I receiving a diplomatic embassy from the Turks in 1609. [Staatliche Museen zu Berlin/Bildarchiv Preussischer Kulturbesitz-Museum für Islamic Kunst]

A Safavid Historian Praises Shah Abbas I

The following passage presents a panegyric but interesting depiction of the great Safavid ruler by a contemporary chronicler of Abbas's reign (1587–1629).

What positive human values does the writer want to demonstrate that Shah Abbas embodies?

On Shah 'Abbas's Breadth of Vision, and His Knowledge of World Affairs and of the Classes of Society

After he has dealt with the affairs of state, Shah 'Abbas habitually relaxes. He has always been fond of conviviality and, since he is still a young man, he enjoys wine and the company of women. But this does not affect the scrupulous discharge of his duties, and he knows in minute detail what is going on in Iran and also in the world outside. He has a well-developed intelligence system, with the result that no one, even if he is sitting at home with his family, can express opinions which should not be expressed without running the risk of their being reported to the Shah. This has actually happened on numerous occasions.

As regards his knowledge of the outside world, he possesses information about the rulers (both Muslim and non-Muslim) of other countries, about the size and composition of their armies, about their religious faith and the organization of their kingdoms, about their highway systems, and about the prosperity or otherwise of their realms. He has cultivated diplomatic relations with most of the princes of the world, and the rulers of the most distant parts of Europe, Russia, and India are on friendly terms with him. Foreign ambassadors bearing gifts are never absent from his court, and the Shah's achievements in the field of foreign relations exceed those of his predecessors.

Shah 'Abbas mixes freely with all classes of society, and in most cases is able to converse with people in their own particular idiom. He is well versed in Persian poetry; he understands it well, indulges in poetic license, and sometimes utters verses himself. He is a skilled musician, an outstanding composer of rounds, rhapsodies, and part-songs; some of his compositions are famous. As a conversationalist, he is capable of elegant and witty speech.

From Eskandar Beg Monshi, *History of Shah 'Abbas the Great*, Volume I, translated by Roger M. Savory, (Westview Press, 1978), p. 533.

---

salary new troops from his Caucasian territories directly, thereby providing a counterweight to the sometimes unruly Qizilbash, who (like the old Ottoman cavalry) were supported by land-revenue assignments. Militarily, Shah Abbas not only pushed the Ottomans out of Azerbaijan and Iraq but also turned back new Uzbek invasions in Khorasan. He also sought alliances with the Ottomans' European enemies. This latter tactic, used by several Safavid rulers, reflects the deep division the new militant Persian Shi'ism had brought to the Islamic world. Abbas also broke the century-long Portuguese monopoly on trade along Persian shores and opened trade with the English and Dutch commercial companies. Although Abbas's European military ventures did not produce real results, his commercial enterprises did, and his reign brought considerable prosperity to Iran, symbolized by the magnificent capital he built at Isfahan.

Safavid Decline

After Shah Abbas, with the exception of the reigns of Abbas II (1642–1666) and, to a lesser degree, the last Safavid to exercise real control, Husayn I (1694–1722), the empire never again enjoyed truly able leadership. This led finally to its decline and collapse, the chief causes of which were (1) continued two-front pressure from Ottoman and Uzbek armies; (2) the growing concentration of wealth at the center of, and the corresponding economic decline in, the empire; and (3) the increasing power and religious bigotry of the more conservative Shi'ite *ulama*. The conservative *ulama* not only introduced a Shi'ite legalism but also emphasized their own authority as interpreters of the law over the authority of the Safavid monarch. They also persecuted religious minorities and encouraged hatred of Sunni Muslims.

One result of Shi'ite exclusivism was a series of tribal revolts among the Sunni Afghans. In the end, an Afghan leader took Qandahar (in modern Afghanistan) and then went on to capture Isfahan and force the abdication of Husayn I in 1722. Safavid princes managed to retake control of western Iran, but the powerful shahs were gone and the empire's greatness was past. A revived, but officially Sunni, monarchy under the talented Kizilbash tribal leader Nadir Shah (r. 1736–1747) and several successors restored much of Iran's lost territories. However, Nadir Shah's military ventures, which included an invasion of North India and the conquest of Delhi, sapped the empire's finances. After his autocratic and despotic reign, Iran could not regain stability for another half-century.

Culture and Learning

In the long run, the most impressive aspect of Safavid times, besides the conversion of Iran to Shi'ism, was the cultural and intellectual renaissance of the sixteenth and seventeenth centuries. The traditions of painting, with their origins in the powerful miniatures of the preceding century—most notably those from Herat after 1450, exemplified by the work of the painter Bihzad (1440–1514) in late Timurid times—were taken up, cultivated, and modified in Safavid times. Portraiture and scenes from everyday life become popular. Among the most developed crafts were ceramic tile, porcelain, and carpet design and production, which reached new heights in sophistication, technique, and execution. In architecture, the magnificently planned public squares, parks, palaces, hospitals, caravanserais, mosques, and other buildings of Isfahan constructed in Shah Abbas's time give breathtaking evidence of the developed sense of proportion, color, and design of Safavid taste. The marvelously embellished monumental architecture for which this period is famous marks a high point in the lavish use of ceramic tiles to decorate both the facades and, especially, the great domes of major buildings.

In intellectual life, the prominence of the *Ishraqi* or "illuminationist" school of theological-philosophical thought deserves special mention. In this school the mystical bent of Persian Islamic thought and the long Islamic traditions of Aristotelianism and Platonism came together in the form of Shi'ite religious speculation into the nature of divine truth and its accessibility to human reason and imagination. The illuminationists' two key ideas were the concept of transcendence and the notion of a "realm of images." They conceived of transcendence in terms of a divine light identified with the Light of Truth. This divine light was expressed most fully in Muhammad and the Shi'ite imams. The realm of images was a sphere of being in which true visions were possible for the attuned spirit. These ideas opened a way to reconceive human experience of the divine in a way that transcended logic and had to

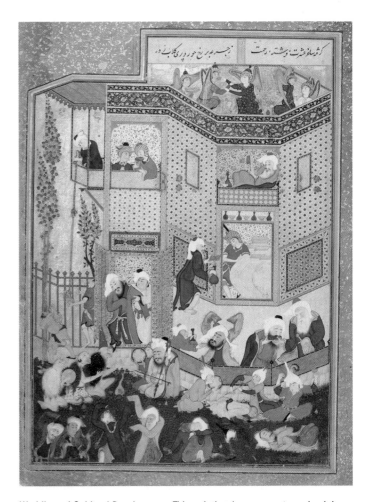

Worldly and Spiritual Drunkenness. This painting (opaque water color, ink and gold on paper, 28.9 x 21.6 cm) by the great sixteenth-century Safavid Iranian court painter, Sultan Muhammad, is from an illustrated copy of the *Diwan*, or collected works of the lyric and mystical poet Hafiz (1319–1389?). Hafiz appears himself as a drunken figure in the upper window. The entire picture plays the worldly drunkenness and debauchery of the characters in the center against the spiritual inebriation of the dancing Sufis in the garden and the angels on the roof. The angels, too, are shown drinking, a visual reference to the line of Hafiz at the top: "The angel of mercy took the cup of revelry." [Courtesy of the Metropolitan Museum of Art and Arthur M. Sackler Museum, Harvard University. Promised gift of Mr. and Mrs. Stuart Cary Welch, 1988; ©1989 Metropolitan Museum of Art]

be experienced individually. At stake were basic notions of the human psyche and the larger cosmos. The most prominent exponent of the *Ishraqi* school was Mulla Sadra (d. 1640).

The lasting legacies of Safavid rule were the firmly Shi'ite character of the whole Iranian region and the Persian culture that was elaborated largely under Safavid patronage in literature, theology, philosophy, painting, crafts (e.g., carpets), and architecture. The Safavid age also saw a distinctively Shi'ite piety develop. It focused on commemorating the suffering

The Safavid Empire	
1334	Death of Safi al-Din, founder of Safavid sufi order
ca. 1500	Rise of Safavids under Shah Isma'il
1501–1510	Safavid conquest of greater Iran; Shi'ite state founded
1588–1629	Rule of Shah Abbas I
1722	Forced abdication of last Safavid ruler
1736–1747	Rule of the Sunni Afghan leader, Nadir Shah; revival of Sunni monarchy in Iran
1739	Nadir Shah invades northern India, sacks Delhi

Some Reforms of Akbar

Akbar (r. 1556–1605) was certainly one of history's great rulers, but some of his fame is surely due to the laudatory quality of the voluminous Persian chronicle of his reign written by Abu'l-Fazl (d. 1602). The often exaggerated praise was, however, a convention of such Persian works. It would not have hidden from its readers Abu'l-Fazl's message about the statecraft and significant achievements of his ruler.

What does this excerpt suggest might have been some practical reasons for Akbar's reforms? How does this document compare to others concerned with law, leadership, and government? See for example: "Hammurabi's Code on Women, Marriage, and Divorce in Babylonia" (Chapter 1), "Legalism" (Chapter 2), "Athenian Democracy: An Unfriendly View" (Chapter 3), "The Edicts of Ashoka" (Chapter 4), and "Machiavelli Discusses the Most Important Trait for a Ruler" (Chapter 16).

One of the glorious boons by His Majesty the Shahinshah which shone forth in this auspicious year was the abolition of enslavement. The victorious troops which came into the wide territories of India used in their tyranny to make prisoners of the wives and children and other relatives of the people of India, and used to enjoy them or sell them. His Majesty the Shahinshah, out of his thorough recognition of and worship of God, and from his abundant foresight and right thinking gave orders that no soldier of the victorious armies should in any part of his dominions act in this manner. Although a number of savage natures who were ignorant of the world should make their fastnesses a subject of pride and come forth to do battle, and then be defeated by virtue of the emperor's daily increasing empire, still their families must be protected from the onset of the world-conquering armies. No soldier, high or low, was to enslave them, but was to permit them to go freely to their homes and relations. It was for excellent reasons that His Majesty gave his attention to this subject, for although the binding, killing or striking the haughty and the chastising the stiff-necked are part of the struggle for empire—and this is a point about which both sound jurists and innovators are agreed—yet it is outside of the canons of justice to regard the chastisement of women and innocent children as the chastisement of the contumacious. If the husbands have taken the path of insolence, how is it the fault of the wives, and if the fathers have chosen the road of opposition what fault have the children committed? Moreover the wives and innocent children of such factions are not munitions of war! In addition to these sound reasons there was the fact that many covetous and blindhearted persons from vain imaginings or unjust thoughts, or merely out of cupidity attacked villages and estates and plundered them, and when questioned about it said a thousand things and behaved with neglect and indifference. But when final orders were passed for the abolition of this practice, no tribe was afterwards oppressed by wicked persons on suspicion of sedition. As the purposes of the Shahinshah were entirely right and just, the blissful result ensued that the wild and rebellious inhabitants of portions of India placed the ring of devotion in the ear of obedience, and became the materials of world-empire. Both was religion set in order, for its essence is the distribution of justice, and things temporal were regulated, for their perfection lies in the obedience of mankind.

From Abul'l-Fazl ibn Mubarak, *The Akbarnama*, trans. by H. Beveridge (Calcutta: The Asiatic Society, 1905–1939); reprinted in W. H. McNeill and M. R. Waldman, *The Islamic World*. Copyright © 1973 Oxford University Press, pp. 360–361.

---

of the imams and loyalty to the Shi'ite *ulama*, who (through their knowledge of the Qur'an and the traditions from Muhammad and the Imams) alone provided guidance in the absence of the hidden imam (see Chapter 11).

The Empire of the Indian Timurids, or "Mughals"

Origins

Invaders from the northwest, in the age-old pattern of Indian history, began a new era in the subcontinent in the early sixteenth century: They ended the political fragmentation that by 1500 had reduced the Delhi sultanate to only one among many Indian states. These invaders were Chaghatay Turks descended from Timur (Tamerlane) and known to history, not entirely correctly, as the *Mughals* (a Persianate form of *Mongol*). They had come from beyond the Oxus and ruled in Kabul after being driven out of Transoxiana by Uzbek Turks. In 1525–1527 the founder of the Mughal dynasty, Babur, marched on India, replaced the last sultan of Delhi, and then defeated a Rajput confederacy. Before his death in 1530 he ruled an empire stretching from the Oxus to Bihar, and the Himalaya to the Deccan. Akbar "the Great" (r. 1556–1605), however, was the real founder of the Mughal Empire and the greatest Indian ruler since Ashoka (c. 264–223 B.C.E.). Indeed, he was as great a ruler as, if not greater than, his famous contemporaries, Elizabeth I (r. 1558–1603), Charles V (r. 1519–1556), and Süleyman.

Akbar's Reign

Akbar would be important if only for his conquests, which added North India and the northern Deccan to the Mughal dominions. Even more significant, however, were his governmental reforms, cultural patronage, and religious toleration. He completely reorganized the central and provincial governments and rationalized the tax system. His marriages with Rajput princesses and his appointment of Hindus to positions of power eased Muslim-Hindu tensions. So did his cancellation of the poll tax on non-Muslims (1564) and his efforts to reduce the power of the more literalist, "hard-line" *ulama*. Under his leadership the Mughal Empire became a truly Indian empire.

Akbar was a religious eclectic who showed not only tolerance of all faiths but also unusual interest in different religious traditions. He frequently brought together representatives of all faiths—Jain and Buddhist monks, Brahmans, *ulama*, Parsis (Zoroastrians), and Jesuits—to discuss religion. These debates took place in a special hall in Akbar's magnificent palace complex at Fatehpur Sikri outside the Mughal capital, Agra. Akbar tried to promulgate among his court intimates a new monotheistic creed that subsumed Muslim, Hindu, and other viewpoints. He did not, however, try to spread his ideas widely, and they died with him.

The Last Great Mughals

Akbar's three immediate successors were Jahangir (r. 1605–1627), Shah Jahan (r. 1628–1658), and Awrangzeb (r. 1658–1707). Although each left behind significant achievements, none matched Akbar in diversity of accomplishments. The problems of sustaining an Indian empire took their toll on Mughal power. The reigns of Jahangir and Shah Jahan were arguably the golden age of Mughal culture, notably in architecture and painting. But the burdens imposed by new building, by military campaigns, and by the erosion of Akbar's administrative and tax reforms led to progressive economic decline. Jahangir set a fateful precedent in permitting English merchants to establish a trading post, or "factory," at Surat on the western coast in Gujarat. Shah Jahan was able to bring the Deccan wholly under Mughal control. However, he lost Qandahar to Shah Abbas II in 1648. His unsuccessful efforts to regain it or the old Timurid homelands of the Oxus region further strained the Mughal economy. No less a burden on the treasury were his elaborate building projects, the most magnificent of which was the Taj Mahal (built 1632–1653), the unparalleled tomb that he built for his beloved consort, Mumtaz.

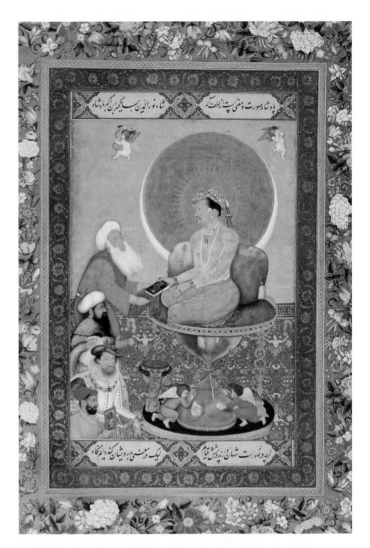

Jahangir showing preference to the Chishti Sufi *shaykh* and saint, Husain, over three temporal rulers: the Ottoman emperor, the King of England, and a Hindu prince. The Timurid emperor presents a book to Shaykh Husain, the descendant of the great Chishti saint, Mu'inuddin, while ignoring the temporal rulers in the lower left corner. The artist copied the likeness of King James I from an English portrait given to Jahangir by Sir Thomas Roe, the British ambassador from 1615 to 1619. The magnificent floral borders to the miniature (ca. 1615-1618) were added in 1727 by Muhammad Sadiq. (Opaque watercolor, gold and ink on paper, 25.3 x 18.1 cm) [Bichitr, *Jahangir Preferring a Sufi Shakikh to Kings*, ca. 1660-70, Album Page; Courtesy of the Freer Gallery of Art, Smithsonian Institution, Washington, D.C.]

With Shah Jahan, religious toleration retreated noticeably; under his son, Awrangzeb, a narrow religious fanaticism almost completely reversed Akbar's earlier policies. The resulting internal disorder and instability hastened the decline of Mughal power. Awrangzeb was an active, determined ruler with his own agenda. He persecuted non-Muslims, destroying Hindu temples, reimposing the poll tax (1679), and wholly alienating the Rajput leaders, whose forebears Akbar had

Guru Arjun's Faith

These lines are from the pen of the fifth guru of the Sikh community, Arjun (d. 1606). In them he repeated the teaching of Kabir, a fifteenth-century Indian saint whose teachings are included with those of Guru Nanak and other religious poets in the Sikh holy scripture, the Adi Granth. This teaching focuses on the error of clinging to a doctrinaire communalist faith, be it that of the Hindus or of the Muslims.

Why do think syncretic teachings, such as those of the Sikhs, might have been appealing in seventeenth-century India?

I practice not fasting, nor observe the [month of]
    Ramazan:
I serve Him who will preserve me at the last hour.
The one Lord of the earth is my God,
Who judgeth both Hindus and Muslims.

I go not on a pilgrimage to Mecca, nor worship at Hindu
    places of Pilgrimage.
I serve the one God and no other.
I neither worship as the Hindus, nor pray as the
    Muslims.
I take the Formless God into my heart, and there make
    obeisance unto Him.
I am neither a Hindu nor a Muslim.
The soul and the body belong to God whether He be
    called Allah or Ram.
Kabir hath delivered this lecture.
When I meet a true guru or pīr, I recognize my own
    Master.

From Max Arthur Macauliffe, *The Sikh Religion*, 6 vols. (Oxford: Clarendon Press, 1909), p. 422.

---

so carefully cultivated. His intransigent policies coincided with and perhaps contributed to the spread of the militant reformism of the Sikh movement throughout the Panjab and the rise of Hindu Maratha nationalism in western India.

Sikhs and Marathas

In the late sixteenth and early seventeenth centuries the Sikhs, who trace their origins to the irenic teachings of Guru Nanak (d. 1538), developed into a distinctive religious movement. Explicitly neither Muslim nor Hindu, they had their own scripture, ritual, and moralistic and reformist ideals. Angered by their rejection of Islam, Awrangzeb earned their lasting enmity by persecution that culminated in the martyrdom of their ninth leader, or guru, Teg Bahadur, in 1675. Thereafter, the tenth and last Sikh guru, Gobind Singh (d. 1708), developed the Sikhs into a formidable military force. Awrangzeb and his successors had to contend with repeated Sikh uprisings ever afterward.

The Hindu Marathas, led by the charismatic Shivaji (d. 1680), rose in religious and nationalistic fervor to found their own regional empire about 1646. On Shivaji's death, the Maratha state controlled the mountainous western coast, and its army was the most disciplined force in India. Despite Awrangzeb's subsequent defeat of the Marathas and his conquest of the entire south of India, the Marathas continued to fight him. After his death they brought about a confederation of almost all the Deccan States under their leadership. While formally acknowledging Mughal sovereignty, the

Marathas actually controlled far more of India after about 1740 than did the Mughals.

Political Decline

In addition to the Rajput, Sikh, and Maratha wars, other factors sealed the fate of the once great Mughal empire after Awrangzeb's death in 1707: the rise in the Deccan of the powerful Islamic state of Hyderabad in 1724; the Persian invasion of North India by Nadir Shah in 1739; the invasions (1748–1761) by the Afghan tribal leader Ahmad Shah Durrani (r. 1747–1773), "founder of modern Afghanistan"; and the British victories over Bengali forces at Plassey in Bengal (1757) and over the French on the southeastern coast (1740–1763). By 1819 the dominance of the British East India Company had utterly eclipsed Mughal as it did Maratha and almost all regional Indian power, even though the Mughal line came to an official end only in 1858.

Religious Developments

The period from about 1500 to 1650 was of major importance for Indian religious life. Akbar's eclecticism mirrored the atmosphere of the sixteenth century in India. A number of religious figures preached a spiritually or mystically oriented piety that transcended the legalism of both the *ulama* and the Brahmans and typically rejected all caste distinctions. In these ideas, we can see both Muslim Sufi and Hindu *bhakti* influences at work. We mentioned in Chapter 14 two forerunners of such reformers, Ramananda and Kabir. Guru Nanak, the spiritual father of the Sikh movement, took up Kabir's ideas and preached faith and devotion to one loving and merciful God. He opposed narrow allegiance to particular creeds or rites and excessive pride in external religious observance. Nanak's hymns of praise contain both Hindu and Muslim ideas and imagery. Dadu (d. 1603), the father of the modern Dadu Panth, preached a similar message. He was born a Muslim but, like Kabir and Nanak, strove to get people to go beyond either Muslim or Hindu allegiance to a more spiritual love and service of God.

On the Hindu side, there was an upsurge of *bhakti* devotionalism that amounted to a Hindu revival. It was epitomized by the Bengali Krishna devotee Chaitanya (d. ca. 1533), who stressed total devotion to Lord Krishna. The forebears of present-day Hare Krishna devotees, his followers spread widely his ecstatic public praise of God and his message of the equality of all in God's sight. The other major figure in Hindu devotionalism in this era was Tulasidas (d. 1623), whose Hindi retelling of the story of the Sanskrit *Ramayana* remains among the most popular works of Indian literature.

Tulasidas used the story of Rama's adventures to present *bhakti* ideas that remain as alive in current everyday Hindu life as do his verses.

Muslim eclectic tendencies came primarily from the Sufis. By 1500 numerous Sufi retreat centers had been established in India. The Chishtiya Sufi order especially had already won many converts to Islam. Many Sufis' enthusiastic forms of worship and their inclination to play down the externals of religion proved particularly congenial to Indian sensibilities. Such Sufis were, however, often decried and opposed by the more puritanical of the *ulama*, many of whom held powerful positions as royal advisers and judges responsible for upholding the religious law. To check puritan bigotry among the *ulama*, Akbar finally named himself the supreme spiritual authority in the empire, secured *ulama* approval, then ordered that toleration be the law of the land.

After Akbar's death the inevitable reaction set in. It was summed up in the work of the Indian leader of the central Asian Sufi order of the Naqshbandiya, Ahmad Sirhindi (d. 1624). He sought to purge Sufism of its extreme tendencies and of all popular practices not sanctioned by the

The Taj Mahal. Probably the most beautiful tomb in the world, the Taj was built from 1631 to 1653 by Shah Jahan for his beloved wife, Mumtaz Mahal. Located on the south bank of the Yamuna River at Agra, the Mughal capital, the Taj Mahal remains the jewel of Mughal architecture.
[Michael Gotin]

India: The Mughals and Contemporary Indian Powers	
1525–1527	Rule of Babur, founder of Indian Timurid state
1538	Death of Guru Nanak, founder of Siteh religious tradition
1556–1605	Rule of Akbar "the Great"
1605–1627	Rule of Jahangir
1628–1658	Rule of Shah Jahan, builder of the Taj Mahal
1646	Founding of Maratha Empire
1658–1707	Rule of Awrangzeb
1680	Death of Maratha leader, Shivaji
1708	Death of tenth and last Sikh guru, Gobind Singh
1724	Rise of Hyderabad state
1739	Iranian invasion of North India under Nadir Shah
1757	British East India Company victory over Bengali forces at Plassy

schools of law. He crusaded against any practices that smacked of Hindu influence and also against tolerant treatment of the Hindus themselves. Among Akbar's royal successors, Awrangzeb, as noted above, was known for his strictures against non-Muslims. However, his intolerance has often been unfairly exaggerated, as indicated by these excerpts from one of his royal commands to a governor concerning the wrongful persecution of some Hindus in Banaras (Varanasi):

> . . . In accordance with our Shari'a, we have decided that the ancient temples shall not be destroyed, but new ones shall not be built.
>
> . . . information has reached our noble and most holy court that certain persons interfere and harass the Hindu residents of the town of Banares and its neighborhood and the brahman keepers of the temples. . . .
>
> Therefore our royal command is that . . . in future, no person shall in unlawful way interfere or disturb the brahmans and other Hindu residents at these places, so that they may, as before, remain in their occupation and continue with peace of mind to offer prayers for the continuance of our God-gifted empire, so that it may last forever. Treat this order as urgent.[2]

Still, the more intolerant side of the spirit of Awrangzeb's time eventually won the day during and after his reign. The many possibilities for Hindu-Muslim rapprochement that had

[2]Cited in W. T. de Bary et al., comp., *Sources of Indian Tradition*, 2nd ed. (New York: Columbia University Press, 1958), Vol. I, *From the Beginning to 1800*, ed. and rev. by Ainslie T. Embree (1988), pp. 445–446.

emerged in Akbar's time waned, presaging the communal strife that has so marred southern Asian history in our own century.

ISLAMIC ASIA

Central Asia: Islamization and Isolation

The solid footing of Islam in Central Asia can be traced to the post-Timur era of the fifteenth century. Even in the preceding century, as the peoples of western Central Asia had begun to shift from nomadic to settled existence, the familiar pattern of Islamic diffusion from trading and urban centers to the countryside had set in. Islamization by Sunni Sufis, traders, and tribal rulers went on apace thereafter, even as far as western China and Mongolia. It was slowed only in the late sixteenth century by the conversion of the tribes of Mongolia proper to the Buddhism of the Tibetan lamas. Thus, after 1500 the Safavid Shi'ite realm was bounded by Sunni states in India, Afghanistan, Anatolia, Mesopotamia, Transoxiana, and western Turkestan (Khwarizm, the region between the Aral and Caspian seas). In these last two areas, the most important states were those founded by Uzbek and Chaghatay Turks, both of whom were ruled by Muslim descendants of Genghis Khan.

Uzbeks and Chaghatays

During the fifteenth century Timur's heirs had ruled Transoxiana and most of Iran (see Chapter 14). To the north, above the Jaxartes River (Syr Darya) and the Aral Sea, a new steppe khanate had been formed by the unification in 1428 of assorted clans of Turks and Mongols known as the Uzbeks. In time, an Uzbek leader who was descended from Genghis Khan, Muhammad Shaybani (d. 1510), invaded Transoxiana (1495– 1500). There he founded a new Uzbek (or Shaybanid) Islamic empire that replaced Timurid rule. Soon afterward he confirmed the Uzbek hold on the region by defeating the Chaghatay Timurid prince Babur when the latter tried to take Transoxiana for himself. (This defeat drove Babur south to rule in Kabul and thus led indirectly to his founding Timurid Mughal rule in Delhi, as described earlier.) Muhammad's line continued Uzbek rule in Transoxiana at Bukhara into the eighteenth century, while another Uzbek line broke away and ruled the independent khanate of Khiva in western Turkestan from 1512 to 1872.

Of the other Central Asian Islamic states after 1500, the most significant was that of the Chaghatay Turks in the Tarim basin area. The Chaghatays had been the successors of

The great central square of the Registan, in Samarkand, with the seventeenth-century Shir Dar Madrasa on the right and the fifteenth century Ulugh Beg madrasa on the left. Samarkand and other major Central Asian cities were centers of Islamic culture and learning as well as political power. [Michael Gotin]

Genghis Khan in the whole region from the Aral Sea and the Oxus River to Yuan China. After 1350 Timur's invasion broke up their khanate. From about 1514 a revived Chaghatay state flourished in eastern Turkestan—the Tarim basin and the territory north of it, between Tashkent in the west and the Turfan oasis in the east. Although the Chaghatay rulers lasted until 1678 in one part of the Tarim basin, their real power was lost after about 1555 to various Khoja princes. These princes were Sunni zealots who claimed to be *Sharifs* (descendants of the Prophet); they gained a substantial following in their efforts to spread Islam and Muslim rule. They were *ghazi* warriors much like the early Ottomans in Anatolia or the Almoravids of North Africa and Spain. Some of them were popularly ascribed miraculous powers and venerated posthumously as local saints.

Consequences of the Shi'ite Rift

On the face of it, the Ottoman, Mughal, Safavid, and Central Asian Islamic states had much in common. All were Muslim in faith and culture; all shared similar systems of taxation and law; in all four regions, the common language of cultured Muslims was Persian, and Turkish rulers were predominant.

Yet the deep religious division between the Shi'ite Safavids and all their Sunni neighbors proved stronger than their common bonds. The result was a serious geographic division that isolated Central Asian Muslims in particular.

Shi'ite-Sunni political competition was sharpened by Safavid militancy, to which the Sunni states responded in kind. Attempts to form alliances with non-Muslim states, previously unheard of in the Islamic world, became a commonplace of Shi'ite political strategy. The Sunnis also resorted to such tactics; the Ottomans, for example, made common cause with Protestants against their Catholic Habsburg enemies. Although trade went on despite the political situation, the international flow of Islamic commerce was hurt by the presence of a militant Shi'ite state astride the major overland trade routes of the larger Islamic world.

The Safavid Shi'ite schism also ruptured the shared cultural traditions of the "abode of Islam." This rupture was especially reflected in the fate of Persian literary culture. As a result of its ever stronger association with Shi'ite religious ideas after the rise of the Safavids, Persian made little further progress as a potential *lingua franca* alongside—let alone above—Arabic in Sunni lands. Outside Iran it was destined to remain a language only of high culture and bureaucracy.

In India, Urdu became the common Muslim idiom (see Chapter 14), and in Ottoman and Central Asian lands, one or another Turkic tongue was spoken in everyday life. The Persian classics continued to inspire Persian learning among educated Sunnis everywhere, but Safavid Persian literature was largely ignored.

Central Asia was ultimately the Islamic region most decisively affected by the Shi'ite presence in Iran. Combined with the growing pressure of Christian Russian power from the west, the militant Shi'ism of Iran isolated Central Asia from the rest of the Muslim world. Political and economic relations with other Islamic lands became increasingly difficult after 1500, as did religious and cultural interchange. However healthy Islam remained in this region, its contact with the original Islamic heartlands (and even with India) shrank. Contact came primarily through a few pilgrims, members of Sufi orders, *ulama,* and students. Occasionally traders traversed the Shi'ite empire or the other political and natural barriers that separated Central Asian Sunnis from Ottoman or Mughal Sunnis. Still, Central Asian Islam mostly developed in isolation, destined to be a large but peripheral area to the Islamic mainstream communities.

Power Shifts in the Southern Seas

Southern-Seas Trade

Along the southern rim of Asia, from the Red Sea and East Africa to Indonesia and the South China Sea, the first half of the second millennium witnessed the gradual spread of Islamic religion and culture into new regions and among new peoples of diverse backgrounds. In port cities in Java, Sumatra, the Malaysian peninsula, South India, Gujarat, East Africa, Madagascar, and Zanzibar, Islamic traders established thriving communities. Their enclaves in these cities often became the dominant presence. Initially the Muslims' economic stature attracted especially the socially and religiously mobile peoples of these cosmopolitan centers; many of them found the ideas and practices of Islam compelling as well. Typically this first stage of conversion was followed by Islam's transmission to surrounding areas and finally to inland centers of Hindu, Buddhist, or pagan culture and power. In this transmission, Sufi orders and their preachers and holy men played the main role. However, conquest by Muslim coastal states quickened the process later, at least in Indonesia and East Africa.

The international trade network that the Muslims inherited in the southern seas was ancient. Before 1200 much of the trade in these waters had been dominated by Hindu or Buddhist kingdoms on the Malay Peninsula or Sumatra; Arab traders had also been active at least in the Indian Ocean. Hindu culture had been carried, along with an Indonesian language, as far as Madagascar in the first millennium C.E. Hindus were the chief religious group the Muslims displaced. In the east, Islam never ousted the Indian Buddhist cultures of Burma, Thailand, and Indochina, although Muslim traders lived in their port cities. Islam did, however, gradually win most of Malaysia, Sumatra, Java, and the "Spice Islands" of the Moluccas—always the coastal areas first, then the inland regions. By the end of the fifteenth century Islam had also spread along the East African coast and become the identifying religio-cultural symbol of identity for most of the port cities from Mogadishu all the way south to Kilwa (as we saw in Chapter 18).

Control of the Southern Seas

The next newcomers to the eastern coastal settlements were the Portuguese. They reached the East African coast in 1498. In the following three centuries, the history of the lands along the trade routes of the southern Asian seas, from the shores of East Africa to Indonesia and Malaysia, was bound closely not only with Islamic religious, cultural, and commercial networks but also with the rising power of Christian western Europe. For all the outside peoples and powers who went there, the key attractions of these diverse lands were their commercial and strategic possibilities.

In the sixteenth century the Europeans began to compete with and to displace by armed force the Muslims who, by 1500, had come to dominate the maritime southern rim of Asia. European success was based on two key factors. One was that their naval and commercial ventures were backed by national support systems. The other, for a time at least, was their superior warships. Nowhere was the effectiveness of this combination more evident than along the west coast of India. Here the Portuguese managed to carve out a major power base in the early sixteenth century at the expense of the Muslim traders and sailors who dominated Indian maritime trade. They did so through superior naval power, cunning exploitation of indigenous rivalries, and terrorization of all who opposed them.

However, in the southern-seas trade centers, Islamization continued apace, even in the face of Christian proselytizing and growing European political and commercial presence. The Muslims, unlike most of the European Christians, never kept aloof from the native populations and were largely assimilated everywhere. They rarely abandoned their faith, which proved generally attractive to new peoples they encountered. The result was usually an Islamicized and racially mixed population.

The Southern Seas: Arrival of the Portuguese	
1498	The Portuguese come to the East African coast and to the west coast of India
1500-1512	The Portuguese establish bases on west Indian coast, replace Muslims as Indian Ocean power
early 1500s	Muslim sultanates replace Hindu states in Java, Sumatra
1524-1910	State of Acheh in northwestern Sumatra
1600s	Major increase in Islamization and connected spread of Malay language in the archipelago
1641	Dutch conquest of Malacca
ca. 1800	Dutch replace Muslim states as main archipelago power
1873-1910	War between Holland and Acheh

The upshot of these developments was that, on the one hand, European gunboat imperialism had considerable military and economic success, often at the expense of Islamic states. On the other, however, European culture and Christian missionary work made remarkably little headway where Islam had first gotten a foothold. From East Africa to the Pacific, all along the trade routes, only in the northern Philippines did a substantial population become largely Christian.

The Indies: Acheh

As we have seen, the history of the Indonesian archipelago has always revolved around the international demand for its spices, peppers, and other produce. By the fifteenth century the coastal Islamic states were centered on the trading ports of the Malaysian peninsula, the north shores of Sumatra and Java, and the Moluccas, or "Spice Islands." The last great Hindu kingdom of inland Java was defeated by an Islamic coalition of states in the early 1500s. Several substantial Islamic sultanates arose in the sixteenth and seventeenth centuries, even as Europeans were carving out their own economic empires in the region. The most powerful and extensive of these Islamic states was that of Acheh, in northwestern Sumatra (ca. 1524–1910).

In its early years Acheh provided the only counterweight to the Portuguese presence across the straits in Malacca (Malaysia). Although the Acheh sultans were unable to drive the better armed invaders out, neither could the Portuguese subdue them. In the fight with the Portuguese, Acheh called for and received at least token help from the Ottomans in the form of artillery and some logistical support, which reflected the Ottomans' awareness of the Portuguese (and European) threat in the southern seas. Despite Portuguese control of Indies commerce, Acheh managed to dominate the pepper trade of Sumatra and to thrive until the end of the sixteenth century. In the first half of the seventeenth century the sultanate controlled both coasts of Sumatra and substantial parts of the Malay peninsula. Meanwhile, also in the seventeenth century, the Dutch replaced the Portuguese in the business of milking the Indies of their wealth, and by the eighteenth century they were doing it just as ruthlessly and more efficiently. In the early twentieth century the Dutch finally won full control in the region, but only after nearly forty years of intermittent war with Acheh (1873–1910).

IN WORLD PERSPECTIVE

The Last Islamic Empires

The period from 1500 to 1800 in Islamic and South Asian lands and in the Afro-Asian southern seas can be characterized in various ways. Here we have focused on the striking cultural and political blossoming of Islamic societies and their ensuing sharp decline. We have also seen briefly the beginning of radically new kinds of European intrusion upon the societies of the Islamic heartlands and of Africa, India, and Southeast Asia. By contrast, in the sixteenth and seventeenth centuries Japan and China were not subject to much influence from either the powerful Islamic empires or the burgeoning commercial and political imperialism of western European nation-states.

The Islamic vitality in the first half of this period was exemplified in the three mighty empires and prosperous societies of the Ottomans, Safavids, and Mughals. All three built new and vast bureaucracies using Islamic ideology, but even more their own imperial vigor, to legitimize their rule. They built arguably the greatest cities in the world of their time and patronized the arts to stimulate important new traditions of Islamic literature, calligraphy, painting, and architecture. Yet for all this vitality, they were profoundly conservative societies. Economically they remained closely tied to agricultural production and taxation based on land. They did not undergo the kind of social or religio-political revolutions that rocked the Western world after 1500. Thus, much like the contemporaneous societies of China and Japan, they did not undergo the sort of generative changes in material and intellectual life that the Western world was experiencing during the same period, although their intellectual culture was vibrant and diverse. There was no compelling challenge to traditional Islamic ideals of societal organization and human responsibility, even though numerous Islamic movements of the eighteenth century did call for communal and personal reform through return to the essentials of the tradition.

As one historian has put it, the striking growth of Islamic societies and cultures in this age was "not one of *origination*, but rather one of *culmination* in a culture long already mature."[3] Even in their heydays, these empires produced much scientific work, but no scientific revolution; much art, architecture, and literature of high quality, but none that departed radically in concept or inspiration from previous traditions; political consolidation and also expansion, but no conquest of significant new markets or territories; commercial prosperity, but no beginnings of a real commercial or industrial revolution. Furthermore, by the latter half of this period, all were in economic, political, and military decline, even if intellectual and artistic vigor held on.

Thus it is not surprising that European expansionism impinged fatefully in these three centuries upon Africa, India, Indonesia, and the heartland cultures of the Islamic world, rather than the reverse. Neither the great imperial Islamic

states, the smaller Islamic sultanates and amirates, the diverse Hindu kingdoms, nor the varied African states (let alone the smaller societies of Africa, the Americas, and the South Pacific) fared well in their encounters with Europeans during this age. A keynote of the age was the growing European domination of the world's seas. This allowed Europeans to contain as well as to bypass the major Islamic lands in their quest for commercial empires.

Industrial development joined economic wealth and political stability by the late 1700s to give the West global military supremacy for the first time. Before 1800 the Europeans were able to bring only minor Islamic states under colonial administrations. However, the footholds they gained in Africa, India, and Southeast Asia laid the groundwork for rapid colonial expansion after 1800. The age of the last great Muslim empires was the beginning of the first great modern European empires. The colonialism of the nineteenth century accompanied the relentless advance of Western industrial, commercial, and military power that would hold sway globally until the mid-twentieth century.

[3]M. G. S. Hodgson, *The Venture of Islam* (Chicago: University of Chicago Press, 1974), Vol. 3, p. 15.

Review Questions ———

1. Why did the Ottoman Empire expand into Europe? What brought about this rapid expansion? Why did the empire fail to hold certain areas in Europe?

2. What were the most important reasons for the success of the Safavid empire in Iran? What role did Islamic religion have in this development? Who were the major foes of this empire?

3. What were the most important elements that united all Islamic states? Why was there a lack of unity between these states from 1500 to 1800? How and why were the European powers able to promote division among these various states?

4. The Mughal conquest of India was led by Akbar "the Great." What were his main policies toward the Hindu population? Why did he succeed and his followers fail in this area? What were his main governmental reforms?

5. Discuss the importance of the Sikhs to Indian politics. How and why did they develop into a formidable military

power? Why did they become separatist in their orientation to the larger Indian world?

6. What were some of the main tenets of the *Ishraqi* or "illumination" school of theological-philosophical thought? How would you define the concept of "transcendence" and the notion of a "realm of images"?

7. Why were outside powers attracted to the South Seas lands? Why were the European powers able to win out in the long struggle for control of this area?

8. How appropriate might it be to compare the Sunni-Shi'ite split within the Islamic world (1500–1800) with that of the Protestant-Catholic split within the Christian world during that same time period? For example, can we compare politics between England and Spain in the sixteenth century with politics between the Ottomans and the Safavids during the same period?

Suggested Readings ———

A. L. BASHAM, ED., *A Cultural History of India* (1975). Part II, "Age of Muslim Dominance," is of greatest relevance here.

S. S. BLAIR AND J. BLOOM, *The Art and Architecture of Islam, 1250–1800* (1994). A fine survey of the period for all parts of the Islamic world.

K. CHELEBI, *The Balance of Truth* (1957). A marvelous volume of essays and reflections by probably the major intellectual of Ottoman times.

M. A. COOK, ED., *A History of the Ottoman Empire to 1730* (1976). Articles from *The Cambridge History of Islam* and *The New Cambridge Modern History*, with a brief introduction by Cook.

W. T. DE BARY ET AL., COMP., *Sources of Indian Tradition*, 2nd ed. (1958). Vol. I, *From the Beginning to 1800*, ed. and rev. by Ainslie T. Embree (1988). Excellent selections from a wide variety of Indian texts, with good introductions to chapters and individual selections.

C. H. FLEISCHER, *Bureaucrat and Intellectual in the Ottoman Empire: the Historian Mustafa Ali (1541–1600)* (1986). A major study of Ottoman intellectual history.

G. HAMBLY, *Central Asia* (1966). Excellent survey chapters (9–13) on the Chagatay and Uzbek (Shaybanid) Turks.

R. S. HATTOX, *Coffee and Coffee-houses: The Origins of a Social Beverage in the Medieval Near East* (1985). A fascinating piece of social history.

M. G. S. HODGSON, *The Gunpowder Empires and Modern Times*, Vol. 3 of *The Venture of Islam*, 3 vols. (1974). Less ample than Vols. 1 and 2 of Hodgson's monumental history, but a thoughtful survey of the great post–1500 empires.

P. M. HOLT, ANN K. S. LAMBTON, AND BERNARD LEWIS, *The Cambridge History of Islam*, 2 vols. (1970). A traditional, somewhat compartmentalized history useful for reference. Vol. I has important surveys on the Ottoman empire and Safavid Iran. Vol. II includes chapters on post–1500 India, Southeast Asia, and Africa.

S. M. IKRAM, *Muslim Civilization in India* (1964). Still the best short survey history, covering the period from 711 to 1857.

H. INALCIK, *The Ottoman Empire: The Classical Age 1300–1600* (1973). An excellent, if dated, survey with solid treatment of Ottoman social, religious, and political institutions.

H. INALCIK, *An Economic and Social History of the Ottoman Empire, 1300–1914* (1994). A masterly survey by the dean of Ottoman studies today.

C. KAFADAR, *Between Two Worlds: The Construction of the Ottoman State* (1995). A readable analysis of theories of Ottoman origins and early development.

N. R. KEDDIE, ED., *Scholars, Saints, and Sufis: Muslim Religious Institutions in the Middle East Since 1500* (1972). A collection of interesting articles well worth reading.

R. C. MAJUMDAR, GEN. ED., *The History and Culture of the Indian People*, Vol. VII, *The Mughal Empire* (1974). A thorough and readable political and cultural history of the period in India.

M. MUJEEB, *The Indian Muslims* (1967). The best cultural study of Islamic civilization in India as a whole, from its origins onward.

G. NECIPOGLU, *Architecture, Ceremonial, and Power: the Topkapi Palace in the Fifteenth and Sixteenth Centuries* (1991). A superb analysis of the symbolism of Ottoman power and authority.

S. A. A. RIZVI, *The Wonder That Was India*, Vol. II (1987). A sequel to Basham's original *The Wonder That Was India*; treats Mughal life, culture, and history from 1200 to 1700.

F. ROBINSON, *Atlas of the Islamic World Since 1500* (1982). Brief, excellent historical essays, color illustrations with detailed accompanying text, and chronological tables, as well as precise maps, make this a refreshing general reference work.

R. SAVORY, *Iran Under the Safavids* (1980). A solid and readable survey.

S. J. SHAW, *Empire of the Gazis: The Rise and Decline of the Ottoman Empire, 1280–1808*, Vol. I of *History of the Ottoman Empire and Modern Turkey* (1976). A solid historical survey with excellent bibliographic essays for each chapter and a good index.

J. O. VOLL, *Islam: Continuity and Change in the Modern World* (1982). Chapter 3 provides an excellent overview of eighteenth-century revival and reform movements in diverse Islamic lands.

Ana Ipatescu leads Transylvanian revolutionaries against Russia, 1848. [E.T. Archives]

ENLIGHTENMENT AND REVOLUTION IN THE WEST

Between approximately 1750 and 1850 certain extraordinary changes occurred in Western civilization. Although of immediate significance primarily for the nations of Europe and the Americas, these developments produced in the long run an immense impact throughout the world. No other civilizations ultimately escaped the influence of the European intellectual ferment and political turmoil of these years. Most of the intel-

lectual, political, economic, and social characteristics associated with the *modern* world came into being during this era. Europe became the great exporter of ideas and technologies that in time transformed one area after another of the human experience.

Intellectually, the ideals of reform and of challenge to traditional cultural authority captured the imagination of numerous writers. That movement, known as the *Enlightenment*, drew con-

fidence from the scientific worldview that had emerged during the seventeenth century. Its exponents urged the application of the spirit of critical rationalism in one area of social and political life after another. They posed serious historical and moral questions to the Christian faith. They contended that laws of society and economics could be discovered and could then be used to improve the human condition. They embraced the idea of economic growth and development. They called for political reform and more efficient modes of government. They upheld the standard of rationality in order to cast doubt on traditional modes of thought and behavior that seemed to them less than rational. As a result of their labors in Europe and eventually throughout the world, the idea of change that has played so important a role in modern life came to have a generally positive value attached to it for the first time.

For many people, however, change seemed to come too rapidly and violently when revolution erupted in France in 1789. Commencing as an aristocratic revolt against the monarchy, the revolution rapidly spread to every corner of French political and social life. The rights of man and citizen displaced those of the monarchy, the aristocracy, and the church. By 1792 the revolution had become a genuinely popular movement and had established a French republic whose armies challenged the other major European monarchies. The reign of terror that saw the execution of the French king unloosed domestic violence unlike anything witnessed in Europe since the age of the religious wars. By the end of the 1790s, to restore order, French political leaders turned themselves over to the leadership of Napoleon. Thereafter, for more than a decade his armies overturned the institutions of the old regime across the continent. Only in 1815, after the battle of Waterloo, was the power of France and Napoleon finally contained.

The French Revolution in one way or another served as a model for virtually all later popular revolutions. It unleashed new forces and political creeds in one area of the world after another. The French Revolution, with its broad popular base, brought *the people* to the forefront of world political history. In the early revolutionary goals of establishing a legal framework of limited monarchical power, of securing citizen rights, and of making possible relatively free economic activity, the supporters of the revolution spawned the political creed of *liberalism*. The wars of the French Revolution and of Napoleon, stretching from 1792 to 1815, awakened the political force of *nationalism*, which has proved to be the single most powerful ideology of the modern world. Loyalty to the nation defined in terms of a common language, history, and culture replaced loyalty to dynasties. As a political ideology, nationalism could be used both to liberate a people from the domination of another nation and to justify wars of aggression. Nationalism was put to both uses in Europe and throughout the rest of the world in the two centuries following the revolution in France. Nationalism became a kind of secular religion that aroused a degree of loyalty and personal self-sacrifice previously called forth only by the great religious traditions.

Finally, between 1750 and 1850 Europe became an exporter not only of reform and revolution but also of manufactured commodities. The technology and the society associated with industrialism took root throughout the western portion of the continent. Europeans achieved a productive capacity that, in cooperation with their naval power, permitted them to dominate the markets of the world. Thereafter, to be strong, independent, and modern seemed to mean to become industrialized and to imitate the manufacturing techniques of Europe and later of the United States.

But industrialism and its society fostered immense social problems, dislocations, and injustices. The major intellectual and political response was *socialism*, several varieties of which emerged from the European social and economic turmoil of the 1830s and 1840s. History eventually proved the most important to be that espoused by Karl Marx, whose *Communist Manifesto* appeared in 1848.

Remarkable ironies are attached to the European achievements of the late eighteenth and the early nineteenth centuries. Enlightenment, revolution, and industrialism contributed to an awakening of European power that permitted the continent to dominate the world for a time at the end of the nineteenth century. Yet those same movements fostered various intellectual critiques, political ideas, and economic skills that twentieth-century non-European peoples would turn against their temporary European masters. It is for that reason that the age of enlightenment and revolution in the West was of such significance not simply in the history of Europe but in the history of the entire modern world.

1750–1800

1762–1796 Catherine II, "the Great" reigns
   in Russia
1763 Peace of Paris Seven Years' War
1772 First partition of Poland
1789 French Revolution begins
1793 and 1795 Last partitions of Poland

1757 British victory at Plassey, in Bengal
1761 English oust French from India
1772–1784 Warren Hastings' administration
   in India
1772–1833 Ram Mohan Roy, Hindu reformer
   in India
1794–1925 Qajar shahs in Iran
1805–1849 Muhammad Ali in Egypt

July 14, 1789, Bastille prison, Paris

1800–1850

1804–1814 Napoleon's empire
1814–1815 Congress of Vienna
1830–1848 Louis Philippe reigns in France
1832 First British Reform Act
1837–1901 Queen Victoria of England
1848 Revolutions across Europe

1835 Introduction of English education in India

British colonial rule in India (1880)

ca. 1839–1880 Tanzimat reforms, Ottoman Empire
1839–1897 Muslim intellectual, Jamal al-Din
   Al-Afghani
1845–1905 Muhammad Abduh

1753–1806 Kitagawa Utamaro, Tokugawa era artist

1787–1793 Matsudaira Sadanobu's reforms in Japan

1789 White Lotus Rebellion in China

1823–1901 Li Hung-chang, powerful Chinese governor-general

Utamaro woodblock print

1754–1817 Usman Dan Fodio, founder of Sultanate in northern and central Nigeria

1762 End of Funj sultanate in eastern Sudanic region

1759–1788 Spain reorganizes government of its American Empire

1776 American Declaration of Independence

1791 First ten amendments to U.S. Constitution (Bill of Rights) ratified

1791 Negro slave revolt in French Santo Domingo

1791 Canada Constitutional Act divides the country into Upper and Lower Canada

---

1835–1908 Empress Dowager Tz'u-hsi

1839–1842 Opium War; 1842, Treaty of Nanking grants Hong Kong to the British and allows them to trade in China

1844 Similar treaties made between China and France and the United States

1804 Fulani Jihad into Hausa lands

1806 British take Cape Colony from the Dutch

1817–1828 Zulu chief Shaka reigns

1830–1847 French invasion of Algeria

1830s Dutch settlers, the Boers, expand northward from Cape Colony

1848–1885 Sudanese Madhi, Muhammad Ahmad

1804 Haitian independence

1808–1824 Wars of independence in Latin America

1822 Brazilian Independence

1847 Mexican War

Simón Bolívar

24 THE AGE OF EUROPEAN ENLIGHTENMENT

The world of the Enlightenment has often been portrayed as entirely optimistic. Such was hardly the case. Some people feared that the expansion of knowledge might bring danger as well as liberation. In this famous painting of the bird in an air pump, Joseph Wright of Derby captures some of that uncertainty. The scene is suffused in light, a metaphor for scientific enlightenment, but the bird will probably die as a result of the experiment. The group gathered around it are clearly having varied reactions to what they are witnessing. [The National Gallery, London/The Bridgeman Art Library International]

CHAPTER TOPICS

◆ The Scientific Revolution
◆ The Enlightenment
◆ The Enlightenment and Religion

◆ The Enlightenment and Society
◆ Enlightened Absolutism

In World Perspective The Enlightenment Heritage

No single intellectual force during the past three centuries has so transformed every region of the world as western science and the technology that has flowed from its understanding of nature. Although throughout the world today there has arisen much interest in nontraditional methods of healing, the impact of science on every area of human life remains a dominant force. Furthermore, the attainment of scientific knowledge, often for the purposes of military advantage as well as medical and economic advance, has become a goal of most modern states. The emergence of science as this vast culturally transforming force began in Europe during the sixteenth century in a process of discovery and formation of theory known as the *Scientific Revolution*, which gained enormous momentum during the next two centuries. Then as now scientific knowledge and methods challenged other areas of intellectual and religious life, and then as now governments sought to use that knowledge to maximize their advantage against other states. Non-European states in the nineteenth and twentieth centuries often gained power and influence to the extent that science

as understood in the West came to dominate their intellectual life, health care systems, and military planning.

The impact of science could make itself felt first in Europe and then elsewhere only as the conviction came to spread that change and reform were both possible and desirable. This attitude is now commonplace, but it came into its own in Europe only after 1700. The capacity and even eagerness to embrace change, especially change as justified on the grounds of science, represents one of the primary intellectual inheritances from that age. The movement of people and ideas that fostered such thinking is called the *Enlightenment*. Its leading voices combined confidence in the human mind inspired by the Scientific Revolution and faith in the power of rational criticism to challenge the intellectual authority of tradition and revealed religion. Its writers believed that human beings could comprehend the operation of physical nature and mold it to the ends of material and moral improvement. The rationality of the physical universe became a standard against which the customs and traditions of society could be measured and criticized. Such criti-

cism penetrated every corner of contemporary society. As a result, the spirit of innovation and improvement came to characterize modern Western society. This outlook would become perhaps the most important European cultural export to the rest of the world.

The Scientific Revolution

The sixteenth and seventeenth centuries witnessed a sweeping change in the scientific view of the universe. From being considered the center of the universe, the earth was now seen as only another planet orbiting about the sun. The sun itself became one of millions of stars. This transformation led to a vast rethinking of moral and religious matters as well as of scientific theory. Science and the scientific method became so impressive and so influential that they set a new standard for evaluating knowledge in the Western world.

The process by which this new view of the universe and of scientific knowledge came to be established is normally termed the Scientific Revolution. However, care must be taken in the use of this metaphor. The word *revolution* normally denotes fairly rapid changes in the political world, involving many people. The Scientific Revolution was not rapid, nor did it involve more than a few hundred people. It was a complex

Copernicus Ascribes Movement to the Earth

Copernicus published De Revolutionibus Orbium Caelestium (On the Revolutions of the Heavenly Spheres) *in 1543. In his preface, addressed to Pope Paul III, he explained what had led him to think that the earth moved around the sun and what he thought were some of the scientific consequences of the new theory.*

How does Copernicus justify his argument to the pope? How important was historical precedent and tradition to the pope? Might Copernicus have thought that the pope would be especially susceptible to such argument, even though what Copernicus proposed (the movement of the earth) contradicted the Bible?

I may well presume, most Holy Father, that certain people, as soon as they hear that in this book about the Revolutions of the Spheres of the Universe I ascribe movement to the earthly globe, will cry out that, holding such views, I should at once be hissed off the stage. . . .

So I should like your Holiness to know that I was induced to think of a method of computing the motions of the spheres by nothing else than the knowledge that the Mathematicians [who had previously considered the problem] are inconsistent in these investigations.

For, first, the mathematicians are so unsure of the movements of the Sun and Moon that they cannot even explain or observe the constant length of the seasonal year. Secondly, in determining the motions of these and of the other five planets, they use neither the same principles and hypotheses nor the same demonstrations of the apparent motions and revolutions. . . . Nor have they been able thereby to discern or deduce the principal thing—namely the shape of the Universe and the unchangeable symmetry of its parts. . . .

I pondered long upon this uncertainty of mathematical tradition in establishing the motions of the system of the spheres. At last I began to chafe that philosophers could by no means agree on any one certain theory of the mechanism of the Universe, wrought for us by a supremely good and orderly Creator. . . . I therefore took pains to read again the works of all the philosophers on whom I could lay hand to seek out whether any of them had ever supposed that the motions of the spheres were other than those demanded by the [Ptolemaic] mathematical schools. I found first in Cicero that Hicetas [of Syracuse, fifth century B.C.] had realized that the Earth moved. Afterwards I found in Plutarch that certain others had held the like opinion. . . .

Thus assuming motions, which in my work I ascribe to the Earth, by long and frequent observations I have at last discovered that, if the motions of the rest of the planets be brought into relation with the circulation of the Earth and be reckoned in proportion to the circles of each planet, not only do their phenomena presently ensue, but the orders and magnitudes of all stars and spheres, nay the heavens themselves, become so bound together that nothing in any part thereof could be moved from its place without producing confusion of all the other parts of the Universe as a whole.

As quoted in Thomas S. Kuhn, *The Copernican Revolution: Planetary Astronomy in the Development of Western Thought* (New York: Vintage Books, 1959), pp. 137–139, 141–142.

---

movement with many false starts and many brilliant people with wrong as well as useful ideas. However, the ultimate result of this transformation of thought revolutionized how Europeans thought about physical nature and themselves. This new outlook would later be exported to every other major world civilization.

Nicolaus Copernicus

Copernicus (1473–1543) was a Polish astronomer who enjoyed a high reputation throughout his life. He had been educated in Italy and corresponded with astronomers throughout Europe. However, he had not been known for strikingly original or unorthodox thought. In 1543, the year of his death, Copernicus published *On the Revolutions of the Heavenly Spheres*. Because he died near the time of publication, the fortunes of his work are not the story of one person's crusade for progressive science. Copernicus's book was "a revolution-making rather than a revolutionary text."[1]

Before Copernicus, the standard explanation of the earth and the heavens was that associated with Ptolemy (c. 90–168) and his work, entitled the *Almagest* (150 C.E.). There were several versions of the Ptolemaic system but most of them assumed that the earth was the center of the universe. Above the earth lay a series of crystalline spheres, one of which contained the moon, another the sun, and still others the planets and the stars. At the outer regions of these spheres lay the realm of God and the angels. Aristotelian physics provided the intellectual underpinnings of the Ptolemaic systems. The earth had to be the center because of its heaviness.

---

[1]Thomas S. Kuhn, *The Copernican Revolution: Planetary Astronomy in the Development of Western Thought* (New York: Vintage, 1959), p. 135.

The stars and the other heavenly bodies had to be enclosed in the crystalline spheres so that they could move. Nothing could move unless something was moving it. The state of rest was natural; motion was the condition that required explanation.

Numerous problems were associated with this system, and they had long been recognized. The most important was the observed motions of the planets. Planets could be seen moving in noncircular patterns around the earth. At times the planets appeared to be going backward. The Ptolemaic systems explained that these strange motions occurred primarily through *epicycles*. The planets were said to make a second revolution in an orbit tangent to their primary orbit around the earth. The epicycle was compared to a jewel on a ring. Other intellectual but nonobservational difficulties related to the immense speed at which the spheres had to move around the earth. To say the least, the Ptolemaic systems were cluttered. However, they were effective explanations as long as one assumed Aristotelian physics and the Christian belief that the earth rested at the center of the created universe.

Copernicus's *On the Revolutions of the Heavenly Spheres* challenged this picture in the most conservative manner possible. It suggested that if the earth were assumed to move about the sun in a circle, many of the difficulties with the Ptolemaic systems would disappear or become simpler. The motive behind this shift away from an earth-centered universe was to find a solution to the problems of planetary motion. By allowing the earth to move around the sun, Copernicus was able to construct a more mathematically elegant basis for astronomy. He considered the traditional system mathematically clumsy and inconsistent. The primary appeal of his new system was its mathematical aesthetics: With the sun at the center of the universe, mathematical astronomy would make more sense. A change in the conception of the position of the earth meant that the planets were actually moving in circular orbits and only seemed to be doing otherwise as a result of the position of observers on earth.

Except for the modification in the position of the earth, most of Copernicus's book was Ptolemaic. The path of the planets remained circular. Genuine epicycles still existed in the heavens. His system was no more accurate than the existing ones for predicting the location of the planets. He had employed no new evidence. His work provided another way of confronting some of the difficulties inherent in Ptolemaic astronomy. It did not immediately replace the old astronomy, but it did allow those who were also discontented with the Ptolemaic systems to think in new directions.

Copernicus's concern about mathematics provided an example of the single most important factor in the developing new science. The key to the future development of the Copernican revolution lay in the fusion of mathematical astronomy with further empirical data and observation, and

mathematics became the model to which the new scientific thought would conform. The new empirical evidence helped to persuade the learned public.

Tycho Brahe and Johannes Kepler

The next major step toward the conception of a sun-centered system was taken by the Danish astronomer Tycho Brahe (1546–1601). He spent most of his life opposing Copernicus and advocating a different kind of earth-centered system. He suggested that the moon and the sun revolved around the earth and that the other planets revolved around the sun. However, in attacking Copernicus, he gave the latter's ideas more publicity. More important, his major weapon against Copernican astronomy was a series of new astronomical observations made with the naked eye. Brahe constructed the

Tycho Brahe in the Uranienburg observatory on the Danish island of Hven (1587). Brahe made the most important observations of the stars since antiquity. Kepler used his data to solve the problem of planetary motion in a way that supported Copernicus's sun-centered view of the universe. Ironically, Brahe himself had opposed Copernicus's view. [Bildarchiv Preussischer Kulturbesitz]

most accurate tables of observations that had been drawn up for centuries.

When Brahe died, these tables came into the possession of Johannes Kepler (1571–1630), a German astronomer. Kepler was a convinced Copernican, but for philosophical, not scientific, reasons. Kepler was deeply influenced by Renaissance Neoplatonists who, following upon Plato's (c. 428–c. 328 B.C.E.) association of knowledge with light, honored the sun. These Neoplatonists were also determined to discover mathematical harmonies that would support a sun-centered universe. After much work, Kepler discovered that to keep the sun at the center of things, he must abandon the Copernican concept of circular orbits. The mathematical relationships that emerged from a consideration of Brahe's observations suggested that the orbits of the planets were elliptical. Kepler published his findings in 1609 in a book entitled *On the Motion of Mars*. He had solved the problems of planetary orbits by using Copernicus's sun-centered universe and Brahe's empirical data.

Kepler had, however, also defined a new problem. None of the available theories could explain why the planetary orbits were elliptical. That solution awaited the work of Sir Isaac Newton.

Galileo Galilei

From Copernicus to Brahe to Kepler, there had been little new information about the heavens that might not have been known to Ptolemy. However, in 1609 an Italian scientist named Galileo Galilei (1564–1642) first turned a telescope on the heavens. He saw stars where none had been known to exist, mountains on the moon, spots moving across the sun, and moons orbiting Jupiter. The heavens were far more complex than anyone had formerly suspected. None of these discoveries proved that the earth orbited the sun, but they did suggest the complete inadequacy of the Ptolemaic system. It simply could not accommodate these new phenomena. Some of Galileo's colleagues at the University of Padua were so unnerved that they refused to look through the telescope, because it revealed the heavens to be different from the teachings of the church and from Ptolemaic theories.

Galileo publicized his findings and arguments for the Copernican system in numerous works, the most famous of which was his *Dialogues on the Two Chief Systems of the World* (1632). This book brought down on him the condemnation of the Roman Catholic Church. He was compelled to recant his opinions. However, he is reputed to have muttered after the recantation, *"E pur si muove"* ("It [the earth] still moves").

Galileo's most important achievement was to articulate the concept of a universe totally subject to mathematical laws. More than any other writer of the century, he argued that nature in its most minute details displayed mathematical regularity. Copernicus had thought that the heavens conformed to mathematical regularity; Galileo saw this regularity throughout all physical nature. He believed that the smallest atom behaved with the same mathematical precision as the largest heavenly sphere.

Galileo stood as one of the foremost champions of the application of mathematics to scientific investigation and of the goal of reducing phenomena to mathematical formulas. However, earlier in the century the English philosopher Francis Bacon had advocated a method based solely on empiricism. As the century passed, both empirical induction and mathematical analysis proved fundamental to scientific investigation.

Francis Bacon

Bacon (1561–1626) has been regarded as the father of empiricism and of experimentation in science. Much of this reputation is unearned. He was not a scientist, except in the most amateur fashion. What he did was set a tone and help create a climate in which other scientists worked. In books such as *The Advancement of Learning* (1605), the *Novum Organum* (1620), and the *New Atlantis* (1627), Bacon attacked the scholastic belief that most truth had already been discovered and only required explanation, as well as the scholastic reverence for intellectual authority in general. He believed that scholastic thinkers paid too much attention to tradition and to the work of the ancients. He urged contemporaries to strike out on their own in search of a new understanding of nature. He wanted seventeenth-century Europeans to have confidence in themselves and their own abilities rather than in the people and methods of the past.

Bacon was one of the first major European writers to champion innovation and change. Most people in Bacon's day, including the intellectuals, thought that the best era of human history lay in antiquity. Bacon dissented vigorously from that view. He looked to a future of material improvement achieved through the empirical examination of nature. His own theory of induction from empirical evidence was unsystematic, but his insistence on appeal to experience influenced others whose methods were more productive. His great achievement was persuading thinkers that scientific thought must conform to empirical experience.

Isaac Newton

Isaac Newton (1642–1727) drew on the work of his predecessors and his own brilliance to solve the major remaining problem of planetary motion and to establish a basis for physics that endured for more than two centuries. The question that continued to perplex seventeenth-century scientists who accepted the theories of Copernicus, Kepler, and Galileo was how the planets and other heavenly bodies moved in an orderly fashion. Numerous unsatisfactory theories had been set forth to deal with the question.

In 1687 Newton published *The Mathematical Principles of Natural Philosophy*, better known by its Latin title of *Principia Mathematica*. Much of the research and thinking for this great work had taken place more than fifteen years earlier. Newton was heavily indebted to the work of Galileo and particularly to the latter's view that inertia could exist in either a state of motion or a state of rest. Galileo's mathematical bias permeated Newton's thought. Newton reasoned that the planets and all other physical objects in the universe moved through mutual attraction. Every object in the universe affected every other object through gravity. The attraction of gravity explained why the planets moved in an orderly rather than a chaotic manner. He had found that "the force of gravity towards the whole planet did arise from and was compounded of the forces of gravity towards all its parts, and towards every one part was in the inverse proportion of the squares of the distances from the part."[2] Newton demonstrated this relationship mathematically. He made no attempt to explain the nature of gravity itself.

Newton was a mathematical genius, but he also upheld the importance of empirical data and observation. He believed, in good Baconian fashion, that one must observe phenomena before attempting to explain them. The final test of any theory or hypothesis for him was whether it described what could actually be observed.

With the work of Newton, the natural universe became a realm of law and regularity. Spirits and divinities were no longer necessary to explain its operation, a point of view that also contributed to skepticism about witchcraft and an end to witch hunts. Thus the Scientific Revolution liberated human beings from the fear of a chaotic or haphazard universe. Most of the scientists were devout people. They saw the new picture of physical nature as suggesting a new picture of God. The Creator of this rational, lawful nature must also be rational. To study nature was to better understand that Creator. Science and religious faith were not only compatible but mutually supporting.

This reconciliation of faith and science allowed the new physics and astronomy to spread rapidly. Just when Europeans were finally tiring of the wars of religion, the new science provided the basis for a view of God that might lead away from irrational disputes and wars over religious doctrine. Faith in a rational God encouraged faith in the rationality of human beings and in their capacity to improve their lot once liberated from the traditions of the past. The Scientific Rev-

Sir Isaac Newton discovered the mathematical and physical laws governing the force of gravity. Newton believed that religion and science were compatible and mutually supportive, and that the study of nature gave one a better understanding of the Creator. This portrait of Newton is by Sir Godfrey Kneller. [Bildarchiv Preussischer Kulturbesitz]

olution provided the model for the desirability of change and for criticizing inherited views.

John Locke

John Locke (1632–1704) attempted to achieve for philosophy a lawful picture of the human mind similar to that which Newton had presented of nature. Locke's three most famous works were the *Essay Concerning Human Understanding* (1690), *Two Treatises of Government*, and his *Letter Concerning Toleration* (1689). Each of them sounded philosophical themes that later writers of the Enlightenment found welcome. No other philosopher had so profound an impact on European and American thought during the eighteenth century.

In the *Essay Concerning Human Understanding*, Locke envisioned the human mind as being blank at the time of an individual's birth. In Locke's view, contrary to that of much medieval philosophy, there are no innate ideas (i.e., ideas people were born with); all knowledge is derived from actual

[2]Quoted in A. Rupert Hall, *From Galileo to Newton, 1630–1720* (London: Fontana, 1970), p. 300.

John Locke (1632-1704), defender of the rights of the people against rulers who think their power absolute. [By courtesy of the National Portrait Gallery, London]

sense experience. Each individual mind grows through experience as it confronts the world of sensation. Human ideas are either simple (that is, passive receptions from daily experience) or complex (that is, products of sustained mental exercise). What people know is not the external world in itself but the results of the interaction of their minds with the outside world. Locke's thinking thus represented an early form of behaviorism. Human nature is changeable and can be molded by modifying the surrounding physical and social environment. Locke also, in effect, rejected the Christian view that human beings were creatures permanently flawed by original sin. Human beings do not need to wait for the grace of God or other divine aid to better their lives. They can take charge of their own destiny.

Locke wrote *Two Treatises of Government* during the reign of Charles II (1660–1685). Locke argued that rulers are not absolute in their power. They remain bound to the law of nature. That law is the voice of reason, teaching that human

beings are equal and independent and that they should not harm one another or disturb one another's property because all persons are the images and property of God. According to Locke, people enter political contracts, empowering legislatures and monarchs to judge their disputes in order to preserve their natural rights (which include the possession of property) but not to give rulers an absolute power over them. Locke also contended that a monarch who violated the trust that had been placed in him could be overthrown. This argument reappeared in the American Declaration of Independence in 1776. But in eighteenth-century Europe it was Locke's argument against absolutism and in favor of limited government that was most influential. Like his philosophy, it opened a wider arena for individual action.

Locke's *Letter on Toleration* contended that each person was responsible for his own religious salvation. Governments existed to protect property and the civil order. Matters only became confused when governments undertook to legislate on religion and require conformity to a single church. Yet Locke himself drew the line in England against toleration of Roman Catholics and Unitarians. During the eighteenth century, however, the logic of his argument was extended to advocate toleration for those faiths as well.

The Enlightenment

The movement that came to be known as the Enlightenment included a number of writers living at different times in various countries. Its early exponents, known as the *philosophes*, popularized the rationalism and scientific ideas of the seventeenth century. They worked to expose contemporary social and political abuses and argued that reform was necessary and possible. The advancement of their cause and ideas was anything but steady. They confronted vested interests, political oppression, and religious condemnation. Yet by the mid-century they had brought enlightened ideas to the European public in a variety of formats.

By the second half of the century the *philosophes* were sufficiently safe from persecution to quarrel among themselves. They had stopped talking in generalities, and their major advocates were addressing themselves to specific abuses. Their books and articles had become more specialized and more practical. They were more concerned with politics than with religion. Having convinced Europeans that change was a good idea, they began to suggest exactly which changes were most desirable. They had become honored figures.

Voltaire

One of the earliest and by far the most influential of the *philosophes* was François Marie Arouet, known to posterity as

Voltaire (1694–1778). During the 1720s Voltaire had offended the French authorities by certain of his writings. He was arrested and briefly imprisoned. Later he went to England, visiting its best literary circles, observing its tolerant intellectual and religious climate, relishing the freedom he felt in its moderate political atmosphere, and admiring its science and economic prosperity. In 1733 he published *Letters on the English*, which appeared in French the next year. The book praised the virtues of the English and indirectly criticized the abuses of French society. In 1738 he published *Elements of the Philosophy of Newton*, which popularized the thought of the great scientist. Both works enhanced his reputation.

Thereafter, Voltaire lived part of the time in France and part near Geneva, just across the French border, where the royal authorities could not bother him. His essays, history, plays, stories, and letters made him the literary dictator of Europe. He turned the bitter venom of his satire and sarcasm against one evil after another in French and European life. His most famous satire is *Candide* (1759), in which he attacked war, religious persecution, and what he regarded as unwarranted optimism about the human condition. Like most *philosophes*, Voltaire believed that human society could and should be improved. But he was never certain that reform, if achieved, would be permanent. The optimism of the Enlightenment constituted a tempered hopefulness rather than a glib certainty. Pessimism was an undercurrent in most of the works of the period.

The Encyclopedia

The mid-century witnessed the publication of the *Encyclopedia*, one of the greatest monuments of the Enlightenment. Under the heroic leadership of Denis Diderot (1713–1784) and Jean le Rond d'Alembert (1717–1783), the first volume appeared in 1751. When completed in 1772, it numbered seventeen volumes of text and eleven of plates. The *Encyclopedia* was the product of the collective effort of more than one hundred authors, and its editors had solicited articles from all the major French *philosophes*. The project reached fruition only after numerous attempts to censor it and to halt its publication. The *Encyclopedia* set forth the most advanced critical ideas in religion, government, and philosophy. This criticism often had to be hidden in obscure articles or under the cover of irony. The articles represented a collective plea for freedom of expression. However, the large volumes also provided important information on manufacturing, canal building, ship construction, and improved agriculture.

Between 14,000 and 16,000 copies of various editions of the *Encyclopedia* were sold before 1789. The project had been designed to secularize learning and to undermine the intellectual assumptions remaining from the Middle Ages and the Reformation. The articles on politics, ethics, and society ig-

Philosopher, dramatist, poet, historian, and popularizer of scientific ideas, Voltaire (1694–1778) was the most famous and influential of the eighteenth-century philosophes. His sharp satire and criticism of religious institutions opened the way for a more general critique of the European political and social status quo. [Bildarchiv Preussischer Kulturbesitz]

nored concerns about divine law and concentrated on humanity and its immediate well-being. The encyclopedists looked to antiquity rather than to the Christian centuries for their intellectual and ethical models. The future welfare of humankind lay not in pleasing God or following divine commandments, but rather in harnessing the power of the earth and its resources and in living at peace with one's fellow human beings. The good life was to be achieved through the application of reason to human relationships.

With the publication of the *Encyclopedia*, enlightened thought became more fully diffused over the Continent. Enlightened ideas penetrated German and Russian intellectual and political circles.

The Enlightenment and Religion

Throughout the century, in the eyes of the *philosophes*, the chief enemy of the improvement of humankind and the enjoyment of happiness was the church. The hatred of the

Printing shops were the productive center for the book trade and newspaper publishing which spread the ideas of the Enlightenment. [The Granger Collection]

philosophes for the church and Christianity was summed up in Voltaire's cry of "Crush the Infamous Thing." Almost all varieties of Christianity, but especially Roman Catholicism, invited the criticism of the *philosophes*. Intellectually, the churches perpetuated a religious rather than a scientific view of humankind and physical nature. The clergy taught that human beings were basically sinful and that they required divine grace to become worthy creatures. The doctrine of original sin in either its Catholic or its Protestant formulation suggested that meaningful improvement in human nature was impossible. Religious concerns turned human interest away from this world to the world to come. For the *philosophes,* the concept of predestination suggested that the fate of the human soul after death bore little or no relationship to virtuous living. Through their disagreements over obscure doctrines, the various churches favored the politics of intolerance and bigotry that in the past had caused human suffering, torture, and war.

Deism

The *philosophes* believed that religion should be reasonable and lead to moral behavior. The Newtonian world view had convinced many writers that nature was rational. Therefore, the God who had created nature must also be rational, and the religion through which that God was worshiped should be rational. Moreover, Lockean philosophy, which limited human knowledge to empirical experience, cast doubt on whether divine revelation was possible. These considerations gave rise to a movement for enlightened religion known as *deism*.

The title of one of its earliest expositions, *Christianity Not Mysterious* (1696) by John Toland, indicates the general tenor of this religious outlook. Toland and later writers wished to

consider religion a natural and rational, rather than a supernatural and mystical, phenomenon. In this respect the deists differed from Newton and Locke, who had regarded themselves as distinctly Christian. Newton had believed that God might interfere with the natural order, whereas the deists regarded God as resembling a divine watchmaker who had set the mechanism of nature to work and then let them operate without intervention.

There were two major points in the deists' creed. The first was a belief in the existence of God, which they thought could be empirically deduced from the contemplation of nature.

Because nature provided evidence of a rational God, that deity must also favor rational morality. Consequently, the second point in the deists' creed was a belief in life after death, when rewards and punishments would be meted out according to the virtue of the life a person led on this earth.

Deism was empirical, tolerant, reasonable, and capable of encouraging virtuous living. It was the major positive religious component of the Enlightenment. Voltaire declared:

> The great name of Deist, which is not sufficiently revered, is the only name one ought to take. The only gospel one ought to read is the great book of Nature, written by the hand of God and sealed with his seal. The only religion that ought to be professed is the religion of worshiping God and being a good man.[3]

If such a faith became widely accepted, it would overcome the fanaticism and rivalry of the various Christian sects. Re-

[3]Quoted in J. H. Randall, *The Making of the Modern Mind*, rev. ed. (New York: Houghton Mifflin, 1940), p. 292.

ligious conflict and persecutions would end. There would also be little or no necessity for a priestly class to foment fanaticism, denominational hatred, and bigotry.

Toleration

A primary social condition for such a life was the establishment of religious toleration. Voltaire took the lead in championing this cause. In 1762 the political authorities in Toulouse ordered the execution of a Huguenot named Jean Calas (1698–1762). He stood accused of having murdered his son to prevent him from converting to Roman Catholicism. Calas had been viciously tortured and publicly strangled without ever having confessed his guilt. The confession would not have saved his life, but it would have given the Catholics good propaganda to use against Protestants.

Voltaire learned of the case only after Calas's death. He made the dead man's cause his own. In 1763 he published a *Treatise on Tolerance* and hounded the authorities for a new investigation. Finally, in 1765 the judicial decision against the unfortunate man was reversed. For Voltaire, the case illustrated the fruits of religious fanaticism and the need for rational reform of judicial processes. Somewhat later in the century the German playwright and critic Gotthold Lessing (1729–1781) wrote *Nathan the Wise* (1779) as a plea for toleration not only of different Christian sects but also of religious faiths other than Christianity. All of these calls for toleration stated, in effect, that human life should not be subordinated to religion. Secular values and considerations were more important than religious ones.

Major Publication Dates of the Enlightenment

1687	Newton's *Principia Mathematica*
1690	Locke's *Essay Concerning Human Understanding*
1696	Toland's *Christianity Not Mysterious*
1733	Voltaire's *Letters on the English*
1738	Voltaire's *Elements of the Philosophy of Newton*
1748	Montesquieu's *Spirit of the Laws*
1750	Rousseau's *Discourse on the Moral Effects of the Arts and Sciences*
1751	First volume of the *Encyclopedia* edited by Diderot and d'Alembert
1755	Rousseau's *Discourse on the Origin of Inequality*
1762	Rousseau's *Social Contract*
1763	Voltaire's *Treatise on Toleration*
1776	Smith's *Wealth of Nations*
1779	Lessing's *Nathan the Wise*
1792	Wollstonecraft's *A Vindication of the Rights of Woman*

The Enlightenment and Society

Although the *philosophes* wrote much about religion, humanity was the center of their interest. As one writer in the *Encyclopedia* observed, "Man is the unique point to which we must refer everything, if we wish to interest and please amongst considerations the most arid and details the most dry."[4] The *philosophes* believed that the application of human reason to society would reveal laws in human relationships similar to those found in physical nature. Although the term did not appear until later, the idea of social science originated with the Enlightenment. The purpose of discovering social laws was to remove the inhumanity that existed through ignorance of them.

Adam Smith

The most important Enlightenment exposition of economics was Adam Smith's (1723–1790) *An Inquiry into the Nature and Causes of the Wealth of Nations* (1776). Smith, who was for a time a professor at Glasgow, urged that the mercantile system of England—including the navigation acts, the bounties, most tariffs, special trading monopolies, and the domestic regulation of labor and manufacture—be abolished. Smith believed that these modes of economic regulation by the state interfered with the natural system of economic liberty. They were intended to preserve the wealth of the nation, to capture wealth from other nations, and to assure a maximum amount of work for the laborers of the country. However, Smith regarded such regulations as constricting the wealth and production of the country. He wanted to encourage economic growth and a consumer-oriented economy by unleashing individuals to pursue their own selfish economic interest. The free pursuit of economic self-interest would ensure economic expansion as each person sought enrichment by meeting the demands of the marketplace. Consumers would find their wants met as manufacturers and merchants sought their business.

Smith's book challenged the concept of scarce goods and resources that lay behind mercantilism and the policies of the guilds. Smith saw nature as a boundless expanse of water, air, soil, and minerals. The physical resources of the earth seemed to demand exploitation for the enrichment and comfort of humankind. In effect, Smith was saying that the nations and peoples of Europe need not be poor. The idea of the infinite use of nature's goods for the material benefit of humankind—a concept that has dominated western life until recent years—stemmed directly from the Enlightenment. When Smith

---

[4]Quoted in F. L. Baumer, *Main Currents of Western Thought*, 4th ed. (New Haven, CT: Yale University Press, 1978), p. 374.

wrote, the population of the world was smaller, its people were poorer, and the quantity of undeveloped resources per capita was much greater. For people of the eighteenth century, the true improvement of the human condition seemed to lie in the uninhibited exploitation of natural resources.

Smith is usually regarded as the founder of *laissez-faire* economic thought and policy, which has argued in favor of a limited role for the government in economic life and regulation. However, *The Wealth of Nations* was a complex book. Smith was no simple dogmatist. For example, he was not opposed to all government activity in the economy. The state should provide schools, armies, navies, and roads. It should also undertake certain commercial ventures, such as the opening of dangerous new trade routes that were economically desirable but too expensive or risky for private enterprise. His reasonable tone and recognition of the complexity of social and economic life displayed an important point about the *philosophes*. Most of them were much less rigid and doctrinaire than any brief summary of their thought may suggest. They recognized the passions of humanity as well as its reason. They adopted reason and nature as tools of criticism through which they might create a climate of opinion that would allow the fully developed human personality to flourish.

Montesquieu and *The Spirit of the Laws*

Charles Louis de Secondat, Baron de Montesquieu (1689–1755), was a French noble of the robe and a magistrate. His work, *The Spirit of the Laws* (1748), perhaps the single most influential book of the century, exhibits the internal tensions of the Enlightenment. Montesquieu pursued an empirical method, taking illustrative examples from the political experience of both ancient and modern nations. From them he concluded that no single set of political laws could apply to all peoples at all times and in all places. Rather, the good political life depended on the relationship of many political variables. Whether a monarchy or a republic was the best form of government depended on the size of the political unit and its population, its social and religious customs, economic structure, traditions, and climate. Only a careful examination and evaluation of these elements could reveal what mode of government would prove most beneficial to a particular people. A century later such speculations would have been classified as sociology.

So far as France was concerned, Montesquieu believed in a monarchy whose power was tempered and limited by various intermediary institutions, including the aristocracy, the towns, and the other corporate bodies that enjoyed particular liberties that the monarch must respect. These corporate bodies might be said to represent various segments of the general population and thus of public opinion. In France he regarded the *parlements*, judicial courts dominated by aristocrats like himself, as the major example of an intermediary as-

sociation. Their role was to limit the power of the monarchy and thus to preserve the liberty of the subjects. In championing these aristocratic bodies and the general role of the aristocracy, Montesquieu was a political conservative. He adopted that stance, however, in the hope of achieving reform, for he considered the oppressive and inefficient absolutism of the monarchy responsible for the degradation of French life.

One of Montesquieu's most influential ideas was that of division of power. He took Great Britain for his model of a government with power wisely separated among different branches. There he believed he had found a system in which executive power resided in the king, legislative power in the Parliament, and judicial power in the courts. He thought any two branches could check and balance the power of the other. His perception of the eighteenth-century British constitution was incorrect, because he failed to see how patronage and electoral corruption allowed a handful of aristocrats to dominate the government. Moreover, he was also unaware of the emerging cabinet system, which meant that the executive power was slowly becoming a creature of the Parlia-

Charles de Secondat, Baron de Montesquieu (1689-1755) was the author of *The Spirit of the Laws,* possibly the most influential work of political thought of the eighteenth century. [Hulton/UPI/Corbis-Bettmann]

ment. Nevertheless, the analysis illustrated Montesquieu's strong sense of the need to limit the exercise of power through a constitution and for legislatures, not monarchs, to make laws. Although Montesquieu set out to defend the political privileges of the French aristocracy, his ideas had a profound and enduring effect on the liberal democracies of the next two centuries.

Rousseau

Jean-Jacques Rousseau (1712–1778) held a different view of political power. Rousseau was a strange, isolated genius who never felt comfortable with the other *philosophes*. Yet perhaps more than any other writer of the mid-eighteenth century, he transcended the thought and values of his own time. Rousseau had a deep antipathy toward the world and the society in which he lived. It seemed impossible for human beings living according to contemporary commercial values to achieve moral, virtuous, or sincere lives. In 1750, in his *Discourse on the Moral Effects of the Arts and Sciences*, he contended that civilization and enlightenment had corrupted human nature. Human beings in the state of nature had been more dignified. In 1755, in a *Discourse on the Origin of Inequality*, Rousseau blamed much of the evil in the world on maldistribution of property.

In both works, Rousseau directly challenged the social fabric of the day. He questioned the concepts of material and intellectual progress and the morality of a society in which commerce and industry were regarded as the most important human activities. He felt that the real purpose of society was to nurture better people. Rousseau's vision of reform was much more radical than that of other contemporary writers.

Rousseau carried these same concerns into his political thought. His most extensive discussion of politics appeared in *The Social Contract* (1762). Compared to Montesquieu's *The Spirit of the Laws*, *The Social Contract* is an abstract book. It does not propose specific reforms but outlines the kind of political structure that Rousseau believed would overcome the evils of contemporary politics and society.

In the tradition of John Locke, most eighteenth-century political thinkers regarded society as a collection of independent individuals pursuing personal, selfish goals. These writers wished to liberate these individuals from the undue bonds of government. Rousseau picked up the stick from the other end. His book opens with the declaration, "All men are born free, but everywhere they are in chains."[5] The rest of the volume constitutes a defense of the chains of a properly organized society over its members. Rousseau suggested that society is more important than its individual

The writings of Jean-Jacques Rousseau (1712-1778) raised some of the most profound social and ethical questions of the Enlightenment. This portrait by Maurice Quentin was made around 1740. [Bildarchiv Preussischer Kulturbesitz]

members, because they are what they are only as a result of their relationship to the larger community. Independent human beings living alone can achieve little. Through their relationship to the larger community, they become moral creatures capable of significant action. The question then becomes what kind of community allows people to behave morally. Rousseau sought to project the vision of a society in which each person could maintain personal freedom while also behaving as a loyal member of the larger community. He drew on the traditions of Plato and Calvin to define freedom as obedience to law. In his case, the law to be obeyed was that created by the general will. This concept normally indicated the will of the majority of voting citizens who acted with adequate information and under the influence of virtuous customs and morals. Such democratic participation in decision making would bind the individual citizen to the community. Rousseau believed that the general will must always be right and that to obey the general will was to be

[5]Jean-Jacques Rousseau, *The Social Contract and Discourses*, trans. by G. D. H. Cole (New York: Dutton, 1950), p. 3.

The salon of Mme. Marie-Thérèse Geoffrin (1699–1777) was one of the most important gathering spots for Enlightenment writers during the middle of the eighteenth century. Well-connected women such as Mme. Geoffrin were instrumental in helping the philosophes they patronized to bring their ideas to the attention of influential people in French society and politics.

[Giraudon/Art Resource, N.Y.]

free. This argument led him to the notorious conclusion that some people must be forced to be free. His politics thus constituted a justification for radical direct democracy and for collective action against individual citizens.

Rousseau had, in effect, assaulted the eighteenth-century cult of the individual and the fruits of selfishness. He stood at odds with the commercial spirit that was transforming society. Adam Smith wanted people to be prosperous; Rousseau wanted them to be good even if it meant they might remain poor. He saw human beings not as independent individuals but as creatures enmeshed in necessary social relationships. He believed that loyalty to the community should be encouraged. As one device to that end, he suggested a civic religion based on deism. Such a shared tolerant religious faith would unify society. Rousseau's chief intellectual inspiration arose from his study of Plato and the ancient Greek *polis*. Especially in Sparta, he thought he had discovered human beings dwelling in a moral society inspired by a common purpose. He hoped that modern human beings might also create such a moral commonwealth in which virtuous living would not become subordinate to commercial profit.

Women in the Thought and Practice of the Enlightenment

Women, especially in France, helped significantly to promote the careers of the *philosophes*. In Paris the salons of women such as Marie-Thérèse Geoffrin (1699–1777), Julie de Lespinasse (1733–1776), and Claudine de Tencin (1689–1749) gave the *philosophes* access to useful social and political contacts and a receptive environment for their ideas. These women were well connected to major political figures who could help

protect the *philosophes* and secure them pensions. The marquise de Pompadour (1721–1764), the mistress of Louis XV, for example, played a key role in overcoming efforts to censor the *Encyclopedia*. She also helped block the circulation of works attacking the *philosophes*.

Nonetheless, the *philosophes* were on the whole not strong feminists. Although many criticized the education women received as overly religious and tended to reject ascetic views of sexual relations, the *philosophes* advocated no radical changes in the social condition of women.

Montesquieu, for example, maintained in general that the status of women in a society was the result of climate, the political regime, culture, and women's physiological nature. He believed women were not naturally inferior to men and should have a wider role in society. He was well aware of the personal, emotional, and sexual repression women endured in his day. Yet there were limits to his willingness to consider change in women's social role. He retained a traditional view of marriage and family and expected men to dominate those institutions. Furthermore, although he supported the right of women to divorce and opposed laws that directly oppressed them, he upheld the ideal of female chastity.

The views about women expressed in the *Encyclopedia* were less generous. The editors, Diderot and d'Alembert, recruited men almost exclusively as contributors and saw no need to include many articles by women. Most of the articles that dealt with women specifically or that discussed women in connection with other subjects often emphasized their physical weakness and inferiority, usually attributed to menstruation or childbearing. Contributors disagreed on the social equality of women. Some favored it, others opposed it, and still others were indifferent. The articles conveyed a general sense that women were reared to be frivolous and un-

Rousseau Argues for Separate Spheres for Men and Women

Rousseau published Émile, *a novel about education, in 1762. In it he made one of the strongest and most influential arguments of the eighteenth century for distinct social roles for men and women. Furthermore, he portrayed women as fundamentally subordinate to men. See page 676 for a contemporary rebuttal.*

How does Rousseau move from the physical differences between men and women to an argument for distinct social roles and social spheres? What would be the proper kinds of social activities for women in Rousseau's vision? What kind of education would he think appropriate for women?

There is no parity between the two sexes in regard to the consequences of sex. The male is male only at certain moments. The female is female her whole life or at least during her whole youth. Everything constantly recalls her sex to her; and, to fulfill its functions well, she needs a constitution which corresponds to it. She needs care during her pregnancy; she needs rest at the time of childbirth; she needs a soft and sedentary life to suckle her children; she needs patience and gentleness, a zeal and an affection that nothing can rebuff in order to raise her children. She serves as the link between them and their father; she alone makes him love them and gives him the confidence to call them his own. How much tenderness and care is required to maintain the union of the whole family! And, finally, all this must come not from virtues but from tastes, or else the human species would soon be extinguished.

The strictness of the relative duties of the two sexes is not and cannot be the same. When woman complains on this score about unjust man-made inequality, she is wrong. This inequality is not a human institution—or, at least, it is the work not of prejudice but of reason. It is up to the sex that nature has charged with the bearing of children to be responsible for them to the other sex. Doubtless it is not permitted to any one to violate his faith, and every unfaithful husband who deprives his wife of the only reward of the austere duties of her sex is an unjust and barbarous man. But the unfaithful woman does more; she dissolves the family and breaks all the bonds of nature....

Once it is demonstrated that man and woman are not and ought not be constituted in the same way in either character or temperament, it follows that they ought not to have the same education. In following nature's directions, man and woman ought to act in concert, but they ought not to do the same things. The goal of their labors is common, but their labors themselves are different, and consequently so are the tastes directing them....

The good constitution of children initially depends on that of their mothers. The first education of men depends on the care of women. Men's morals, their passions, their tastes, their pleasures, their very happiness also depend on women. Thus the whole education of women ought to relate to men. To please men, to be useful to them, to make herself loved and honored by them, to raise them when young, to care for them when grown, to counsel them, to console them, to make their lives agreeable and sweet—these are the duties of women at all times, and they ought to be taught from childhood. So long as one does not return to this principle, one will deviate from the goal, and all the precepts taught to women will be of no use for their happiness or for ours.

From Émile; or, On Education, by Jean-Jacques Rousseau, *by Allan Bloom, trans. Copyright © 1979 by Basic Books, a member of Perseus Books L.L.C.*

---

concerned with important issues. The encyclopedists discussed women primarily in a family context—as daughters, wives, and mothers—and considered motherhood their most important occupation. On sexual behavior, the encyclopedists upheld an unquestioned double standard.

In contrast to the articles, however, illustrations in the *Encyclopedia* showed women deeply involved in the economic activities of the day. The illustrations also showed the activities of lower- and working-class women, about whom the articles have little to say.

Rousseau urged a traditional role for women. In his novel *Émile* (1762) he declared that women should be educated for a position subordinate to men, emphasizing especially women's function in bearing and rearing children. He portrayed them as weaker and inferior to men in virtually all respects except perhaps for their capacity for feeling and giving love. He excluded them from political life. Women were assigned the domestic sphere alone. Many of these attitudes were not new—some have roots as ancient as Roman law—but Rousseau's powerful presentation and the influence of his other writings gave them new life, including in the legislation of the French Revolution.

Paradoxically, despite these views and his own ill treatment of the many women who bore his many children, Rousseau achieved a vast following among women in the eighteenth century. He is credited with persuading thousands of upper-class

Mary Wollstonecraft Criticizes Rousseau's View of Women

Mary Wollstonecraft published A Vindication of the Rights of Woman *in 1792, thirty years after Rousseau's* Émile *had appeared. She criticized and rejected Rousseau's argument for distinct and separate spheres for men and women as defending the continued bondage of women to men and as hindering the wider education of the entire human race.*

What specific criticisms does Wollstonecraft direct against Rousseau's views? Why does Wollstonecraft put so much emphasis on a new kind of education for women?

The most perfect education . . . is such an exercise of the understanding as is best calculated to strengthen the body and form the heart. Or, in other words, to enable the individual to attain such habits of virtue as will render it independent. In fact, it is a farce to call any being virtuous whose virtues do not result from the exercise of its own reason. This was Rousseau's opinion respecting men: I extend it to women. . . .

I may be accused of arrogance; still I must declare what I firmly believe, that all the writers who have written on the subject of female education and manners from Rousseau to Dr. Gregory [a Scottish physician], have contributed to render women more artificial, weak characters, than they would other wise have been; and, consequently, more useless members of society. . . .

. . . Strengthen the female mind by enlarging it, and there will be an end to blind obedience; but, as blind obedience is ever sought for by power, tyrants and sensualists are in the right when they endeavour to keep women in the dark, because the former only wants slaves, and the latter a play-thing. The sensualist, indeed, has been the most dangerous of tyrants, and women have been duped by their lovers, as princes by their ministers, whilst dreaming that they reigned over them.

. . . Rousseau declares that a woman should never, for a moment, feel herself independent, that she should be governed by fear to exercise her natural cunning, and made a coquettish slave in order to render her a more alluring object of desire, a sweeter companion to man, whenever he chooses to relax himself. He carries the arguments, which

he pretends to draw from the indications of nature, still further, and insinuates that truth and fortitude, the corner stones of all human virtue, should be cultivated with certain restrictions, because, with respect to the female character, obedience is the grand lesson which ought to be impressed with unrelenting rigour.

What nonsense! When will a great man arise with sufficient strength of mind to put away the fumes which pride and sensuality have thus spread over the subject! If women are by nature inferior to men, their virtues must be the same in quality, if not in degree, or virtue is a relative idea; consequently, their conduct should be founded on the same principles, and have the same aim.

Connected with man as daughters, wives, and mothers, their moral character may be estimated by their manner of fulfilling those simple duties; but the end, the grand end of their exertions should be to unfold their own faculties and acquire the dignity of conscious virtue. . . .

But avoiding . . . any direct comparison of the two sexes collectively, or frankly acknowledging the inferiority of women, according to the present appearance of things, I shall only insist that men have increased that inferiority till women are almost sunk below the standard of rational creatures. Let their faculties have room to unfold, and their virtues to gain strength, and then determine where the whole sex must stand in the intellectual scale. . . .

. . . I . . . will venture to assert, that till women are more rationally educated, the progress of human virtue and improvement in knowledge must receive continual checks. . . .

The mother, who wishes to give true dignity of character to her daughter, must, regardless of the sneers of ignorance, proceed on a plan diametrically opposite to that which Rousseau has recommended with all the deluding charms of eloquence and philosophical sophistry: for his eloquence renders absurdities plausible, and his dogmatic conclusions puzzle, without convincing, those who have not ability to refute them.

From Mary Wollstonecraft, *A Vindication of the Rights of Woman*, ed. by Carol H. Poston. Copyright © 1975 W. W. Norton & Co., Inc., pp. 21, 22, 24–26, 35, 40, 41.

---

women to breast-feed their own children rather than putting them out to wet nurses. One explanation for this influence is that his writings, although they did not advocate liberating women or expanding their social or economic roles, did stress the importance of their emotions and subjective feelings. He portrayed the domestic life and the role of wife and mother as a noble and fulfilling vocation, giving middle- and upper-class women a sense that their daily occupations had purpose. He assigned them a degree of influence in the domestic sphere that they could not have competing with men outside it.

In 1792 in *A Vindication of the Rights of Woman*, Mary Wollstonecraft (1759–1797) brought Rousseau before the judgment of the rational Enlightenment ideal of progressive knowledge. Wollstonecraft (who, like so many women of her day, died shortly after childbirth of puerperal fever) accused Rousseau and others after him who upheld traditional roles for women of attempting to narrow women's vision and limit their experience. She argued that to confine women to the separate domestic sphere because of their supposed physiological limitations was to make them the sensual slaves of men. Confined in this separate sphere, as the victims of male tyranny, they could never achieve their own moral or intellectual identity. Denying good education to women would impede the progress of all humanity. Wollstonecraft was demanding for women the kind of intellectual liberty that male writers of the Enlightenment had been championing for men for more than a century.

Enlightened Absolutism

During the last third of the century it seemed that several European rulers had embraced many of the reforms set forth by the *philosophes*. *Enlightened absolutism* is the term used to describe this phenomenon. The phrase indicates monarchical government dedicated to the rational strengthening of the central absolutist administration at the cost of lesser centers of political power. The monarchs most closely associated with it—Frederick II of Prussia, Joseph II of Austria, and Catherine II of Russia—often found that the political and social realities of their realms caused them to moderate both their enlightenment and their absolutism. Frederick II corresponded with the *philosophes*, invited Voltaire to his court, and even wrote history and political tracts. Catherine II, who was a master of what would later be called public relations, consciously sought to create the image of being enlightened. She read the works of the *philosophes*, became a friend of Diderot and Voltaire, and made frequent references to their ideas, all in the hope that her nation might seem more modern and Western. Joseph II continued numerous initiatives begun by his mother, Maria Theresa, and imposed a series of religious, legal, and social reforms that contemporaries believed he had derived from suggestions of the *philosophes*.

Despite such appearances, the relationship between these rulers and the writers of the Enlightenment was more complicated. The rulers did wish to see their subjects enjoy better health, more accessible education, a more rational political administration, and economic prosperity. In many of these policies, they were more advanced than the rulers of western Europe. However, the humanitarian and liberating zeal of the Enlightenment directed only part of their policies. Frederick II, Joseph II, and Catherine II were also determined to play major diplomatic and military roles in Europe. In no small measure they sought the rational economic and social integration of their realms, so they could achieve military strength. After the Seven Years' War all the states of Europe understood that they would require stronger armed forces, which meant they needed new revenues. The search for new revenues and for more political support for their rule led these monarchs to make "enlightened" reforms. Consequently, they and their advisers used rationality to pursue many goals admired by the *philosophes* but also to further what the *philosophes* considered irrational militarism.

Joseph II of Austria

No eighteenth-century ruler so embodied rational, impersonal force as the emperor Joseph II of Austria. He was the son of Maria Theresa (r. 1740–1780) and co-ruler with her from 1765 to 1780. During the next ten years he ruled alone. He has been aptly described as "an imperial puritan and a good deal of a prig."[6] He slept on straw and ate little but beef. He prided himself on a narrow, passionless rationality, which he sought to impose by his own will on the various Habsburg domains. Despite his eccentricities and cold personality, Joseph II genuinely and sincerely wished to improve the lot of his peoples. His well-intentioned efforts led to a series of aristocratic and peasant rebellions from Hungary to the Austrian Netherlands.

Of all the rising states of the eighteenth century, Austria was the most diverse in its people and problems. The Habsburgs never succeeded in creating either a unified administrative structure or a strong aristocratic loyalty. The price of preserving the monarchy during the War of the Austrian Succession (1740–1748) had been guarantees of considerable aristocratic independence, especially in Hungary.

During and after the conflict, however, Maria Theresa had strengthened her powers in Austria and Bohemia. Through major administrative reorganization she imposed a much more efficient system of tax collection that extracted funds even from the clergy and the nobles, and she established several central councils to deal with governmental problems. She was particularly concerned about bringing all educational institutions into the service of the crown so that she could have enough educated officials, and she expanded primary education on the local level.

Maria Theresa was also concerned about the welfare of the peasants and serfs. The extension of the authority of the royal bureaucracy over that of the local nobilities helped the peasants, as did the empress's decrees limiting the services that landowners could demand from them. This concern arose from her desire to assure a good military recruitment pool. In all these policies and in her general desire to stimulate prosperity and military strength by royal initiative, Maria Theresa anticipated the policies of her son.

[6]R. J. White, *Europe in the Eighteenth Century* (New York: St. Martin's, 1965), p. 214.

Maria Theresa and Joseph II of Austria Debate Toleration

In 1765 Joseph, the eldest son of the Empress Maria Theresa, had become co-regent with his mother. He began to believe that some measures of religious toleration should be introduced into the Habsburg realms. Maria Theresa, whose opinions on many political issues were quite advanced, adamantly refused to consider adopting a policy of toleration. This exchange of letters sets forth their sharply differing positions. The toleration of Protestants in dispute related only to Lutherans and Calvinists. Maria Theresa died in 1780; the next year Joseph issued an edict of toleration.

How does Joseph define toleration, and why does Maria Theresa believe it is the same as religious indifference? Why does Maria Theresa fear that toleration will bring about political as well as religious turmoil? Why does Maria Theresa think the belief in toleration has come from Joseph's acquaintance with wicked books? Compare the positions for and against religious toleration expressed in this correspondence to the actions of previous European rulers. See "Louis XIV Revokes the Edict of Nantes" and "The Great Elector Welcomes Protestant Refugees from France," both in Chapter 21.

Joseph to Maria Theresa, July 20, 1777

. . . [I]t is only the word "toleration" which has caused the misunderstanding. You have taken it in quite a different meaning [from mine expressed in an earlier letter]. God preserve me from thinking it a matter of indifference whether the citizens turn Protestant or remain Catholic, still less, whether they cleave to, or at least observe, the cult which they have inherited from their fathers! I would give all I possess if all the Protestants of your states would go over to Catholicism.

The word "toleration," as I understand it, means only that I would employ any persons, without distinction of religion, in purely temporal matters, allow them to own property, practice trades, be citizens, if they were qualified and if this would be of advantage to the State and its industry. Those who, unfortunately, adhere to a false faith, are far further from being converted if they remain in their own country than if they migrate into another, in which

they can hear and see the convincing truths of the Catholic faith. Similarly, the undisturbed practice of their religion makes them far better subjects and causes them to avoid irreligion, which is a far greater danger to our Catholics than if one lets them see others practice their religion unimpeded. . . .

Maria Theresa to Joseph, Late July, 1777

Without a dominant religion? Toleration, indifference are precisely the true means of undermining everything, taking away every foundation; we others will then be the greatest losers. . . . He is no friend of humanity, as the popular phrase is, who allows everyone his own thoughts. I am speaking only in the political sense, not as a Christian; nothing is so necessary and salutary as religion. Will you allow everyone to fashion his own religion as he pleases? No fixed cult, no subordination to the Church—what will then become of us? The result will not be quiet and contentment; its outcome will be the rule of the stronger and more unhappy times like those which we have already seen. A manifesto by you to this effect can produce the utmost distress and make you responsible for many thousands of souls. And what are my own sufferings, when I see you entangled in opinions so erroneous? What is at stake is not only the welfare of the State but your own salvation. . . . Turning your eyes and ears everywhere, mingling your spirit of contradiction with the simultaneous desire to create something, you are ruining yourself and dragging the Monarchy down with you into the abyss . . . . I only wish to live so long as I can hope to descend to my ancestors with the consolation that my son will be as great, as religious as his forebears, that he will return from his erroneous views, from those wicked books whose authors parade their cleverness at the expense of all that is most holy and most worthy of respect in the world, who want to introduce an imaginary freedom which can never exist and which degenerates into license and into complete revolution.

From *The Habsburg and Hohenzollern Dynasties in the Seventeenth and Eighteenth Centuries*, C. A. Macartney, ed., Copyright © 1980, Walker and Company, pp. 151–153. Reprinted by permission.

Joseph II, however, was more determined, and his projected reforms were more wide ranging than his mother's. He was ambitious to expand at the expense of Poland, Bavaria, and the Ottoman Empire. But his greatest ambition was to change the authority of the Habsburg emperor over his various realms. He sought to overcome the pluralism of the Habsburg holdings by increasing the power of the central monarchy in areas of political and social life that Maria There-

sa had wisely not disturbed. In particular, Joseph sought to lessen Hungarian autonomy. He refused to have himself crowned king of Hungary and even had the Crown of Saint Stephen sent to Vienna. He thus avoided having to guarantee existing or new Hungarian privileges in a coronation oath. He reorganized local government in Hungary to increase the authority of his own officials, and he required the use of the German language in all governmental matters. But the Magyar nobility resisted, and in 1790 Joseph had to rescind most of his centralizing measures.

Another target of Joseph's assertion of royal absolutism was religion. In October 1781 Joseph extended freedom of worship to Lutherans, Calvinists, and the Greek Orthodox. They were permitted to have their own churches, to sponsor schools, to enter skilled trades, and to hold academic appointments and positions in the public service. From 1781 through 1789 Joseph relieved the Jews of certain taxes and signs of personal degradation and gave them the right of private worship. Despite these benefits the Jews still did not enjoy general legal rights equal to those of other Habsburg subjects.

Above all, Joseph sought to bring the various institutions of the Roman Catholic church directly under his control. He forbade direct communication between the bishops of his realms and the pope. He regarded most orders of monks and nuns as unproductive. Consequently, he dissolved over six hundred monasteries and confiscated their lands, although he excepted certain orders that ran schools or hospitals. He also dissolved the traditional Roman Catholic seminaries, which he believed taught priests too great a loyalty to the papacy and too little concern for their future parishioners. In their place he sponsored eight general seminaries that emphasized parish duties. In effect, Joseph's policies made Roman Catholic priests the employees of the state and ended the influence of the church as an independent institution in Habsburg lands. In many respects, the ecclesiastical policies of Joseph II, known as *Josephinism*, prefigured those of the French Revolution.

Toward serfdom and the land, Joseph II again pursued policies initiated by Maria Theresa to more far-reaching ends. During his reign he introduced reforms that touched the heart of rural society. He abolished the legal status of serfdom defined in terms of servitude to another person. He gave peasants much more personal freedom. They could marry, engage in skilled work, or have their children trained in such skills without permission of the landlord. The procedures of the manorial courts were reformed, and avenues of appeal to royal officials were opened. Joseph also encouraged landlords to change land leases, so that it would be easier for peasants to inherit them or to transfer them to another peasant without bringing into doubt the landlord's title of ownership. Joseph believed that reducing traditional burdens would make the peasant tillers of the land more productive and industrious.

In 1789 Joseph proposed a new and daring system of land taxation. All proprietors were to be taxed, regardless of social status. No longer were the peasants alone to bear the burden of taxation. He commuted compulsory service into a monetary tax, split between the landlord and the state. The decree was drawn up, but resistance from the nobles delayed its implementation. Then in 1790 Joseph died, and the decree never went into effect. However, his measures had stirred up turmoil throughout the Habsburg realms. Peasants revolted

over disagreements about the interpretation of their newly granted rights. The nobles of the various realms protested the taxation scheme.

On Joseph's death, the crown went to his brother Leopold II (r. 1790–1792). Although sympathetic to Joseph's goals, Leopold had to repeal many of the most controversial decrees, such as that changing taxation.

Catherine the Great of Russia

Joseph II never grasped the practical necessity of cultivating political support for his policies. Catherine II (r. 1762–1796), who had been born a German princess, understood only too well the fragility of the Romanov dynasty's power base.

After the death of Peter the Great in 1725, the court nobles and the army had determined the Russian succession. As a result, the crown fell into the hands of people with little talent until 1741, when Peter's daughter Elizabeth came to the throne. At her death in 1762 Elizabeth was succeeded by Peter III, one of her nephews. He was a weak and possibly insane ruler who had been married in 1745 to a young German princess, the future Catherine the Great. Catherine had neither love nor loyalty for her demented husband. After a few months of rule Peter III was deposed and murdered with Catherine's approval, if not aid. On his deposition she was immediately proclaimed empress.

Catherine's familiarity with the Enlightenment and the general culture of western Europe convinced her that Russia must make major reforms if it were to remain a great power. Since she had come to the throne through a palace coup, she

Russia from Peter the Great Through Catherine the Great

1725	Death of Peter the Great
1741–1762	Elizabeth
1762	Peter III
1762	Catherine II (the Great) becomes empress
1767	Legislative Commission summoned
1768	War with Turkey
1771–1774	Pugachev's Rebellion
1772	First Partition of Poland
1774	Treaty of Kuchuk-Kainardji ends war with Turkey
1775	Reorganization of local government
1783	Russia annexes the Crimea
1785	Catherine issues the Charter of the Nobility
1793	Second Partition of Poland
1795	Third Partition of Poland
1796	Death of Catherine the Great

Catherine the Great, here portrayed as a young princess, ascended to the Russian throne after the murder of her husband. She tried initially to enact major reforms but she never intended to abandon absolutism. She assured the nobility of their rights and by the end of her reign had imposed press censorship. [Corbis-Bettmann]

problems brought to light by the Legislative Commission. She put most local offices into the hands of nobles rather than creating a royal bureaucracy. In 1785 Catherine issued the Charter of the Nobility, which guaranteed many noble rights and privileges. She issued a similar charter to the towns of her realms. In part, the empress had to favor the nobles. There were too few educated subjects in her realm to establish an independent bureaucracy, and the treasury could not afford an army strictly loyal to the crown. So Catherine wisely made a virtue of necessity. She strengthened the stability of her crown by a convenient alliance with her nobles and urban leaders.

Catherine continued the Russian drive for warm-water ports (see Map 24–1). This led to warfare with the Turks be-

Map 24–1   Expansion of Russia, 1689–1796.   The overriding territorial aim of the two most powerful Russian monarchs of the eighteenth century, Peter the Great (in the first quarter of the century) and Catherine the Great (in the last half of the century) was to secure navigable outlets to the sea in both the north and the south for Russia's vast empire; hence Peter's push to the Baltic Sea and Catherine's to the Black Sea. Catherine also managed to acquire much of Poland through the partitions of that country.

understood that any major reform must enjoy wide political and social support.

Consequently, in 1767 Catherine summoned a Legislative Commission to advise her on revising the law and government of Russia. There were over five hundred delegates drawn from all sectors of Russian life. Before the commission convened, Catherine wrote a set of *Instructions*, containing ideas drawn from the political writings of the *philosophes*. The revision of Russian law, however, did not occur for more than a half century. In 1768 Catherine dismissed the commission before several of its key committees had reported. Yet the commission had gathered a vast amount of information about the conditions of local administration and economic life throughout Russia. The inconclusive debates and the absence of programs from the delegates themselves suggested that most Russians saw no alternative to an autocratic monarchy. Catherine herself had no intention of departing from absolutism.

Catherine proceeded to carry out limited reforms on her own authority. She supported the rights and local power of the nobility. In 1775 she reorganized local government to solve

Map 24–2   Partitions of Poland, 1772, 1793, and 1795. The callous eradication of Poland from the map displayed eighteenth-century power politics at its most extreme. Poland, without a strong central government, fell victim to the strong absolute monarchies of central and eastern Europe.

pearances. After long, complicated, secret negotiations, the three powers agreed that Russia would abandon the Danubian provinces in return for a large chunk of Polish territory with almost 2 million inhabitants. As a reward for remaining neutral, Prussia annexed most of the Polish territory between East Prussia and Prussia proper, which allowed Frederick to unite two previously separate sections of his realm. Finally, Austria took Galicia, with its important salt mines, and other Polish territory with over 2.5 million inhabitants. The Polish state had lost approximately one third of its territory.

There were two additional partitions of Poland by Russia and Prussia, and one more by Austria. They occurred in 1793 and 1795 and removed Poland from the map of Europe until 1919. The great powers contended that they were saving themselves, and by implication the rest of Europe, from Polish anarchy. The argument was plausible to some contemporaries because of the fears spurred by the French Revolution. However, the truth was that the political weakness of Poland

This French engraving is a satirical comment on the first partition of Poland (1772) by Russia, Austria, and Prussia. The distressed monarch attempting to retain his crown is Stanislaus of Poland. Catherine of Russia, Joseph of Austria, and Frederick of Prussia point out their respective shares of the loot.
[Bildarchiv Preussischer Kulturbesitz]

tween 1768 and 1774, when the Treaty of Kuchuk-Kainardji gave Russia a direct outlet on the Black Sea, free navigation rights in its waters, and free access through the Bosphorus. Moreover, the Crimea became an independent state, which Catherine painlessly annexed in 1783.

The Partition of Poland

These Russian military successes made the other states of eastern Europe uneasy. Their anxieties were allayed by the First Partition of Poland (see Map 24–2). The Russian victories along the Danube River in what is today Romania were most unwelcome to Austria, which had its own ambitions there. At the same time, the Ottoman Empire was pressing Prussia for aid against Russia. Frederick the Great made a proposal to Russia and Austria that would give each something it wanted, prevent conflict among them, and save ap-

made the country and its resources a rich field for plunderous aggression.

IN WORLD PERSPECTIVE

The Enlightenment Heritage

No other movements of European thought have remained as influential as the Scientific Revolution and the Enlightenment. A direct line of intellectual descent exists from those movements to the science and social criticism of the present day. Wherever modern science and technology are pursued and their effects felt, the spirit of the Enlightenment persists. From the eighteenth century to the present the *philosophes* provided a pattern for intellectuals who wished to make their societies more rational, scientific, and secular.

The Enlightenment *philosophes* believed in the emotions and passions as well as reason. But they used reason as a weapon for reform and the basis for a more productive economic life. In the two centuries since the Enlightenment, such a use of critical reason has become a mark of reforming and progressive social and intellectual movements. The *philosophes* first used reason against Christianity, but reason came to be used against other world religions as well.

The heritage of the Enlightenment has been more complex than was its political impact in the eighteenth century. One strand of Enlightenment political thought contributed to constitutionalism and modes of government in which the power and authority of the central government stand sharply circumscribed. Montesquieu, for example, influenced the Constitution of the United States and the numerous constitutions that document itself later influenced.

Another strand of Enlightenment political thought, found in Voltaire, contributed to the growth of strong central governments, as was the case with enlightened absolutism. Advocates of this method of government believed that a monarch or strong central bureaucracy could formulate and impose rational solutions to political or social problems.

Still another strand of political thought, arising from Rousseau, led to the socialist concern with inequality of wealth. In the modern world, liberal, socialist, and authoritarian governments all partake of the Enlightenment heritage.

Review Questions ⎯⎯

1. Discuss the contributions of Copernicus, Brahe, Kepler, Galileo, and Newton to the Scientific Revolution. Which do you think made the most important contributions and why? How would you define the term *Scientific Revolution*? In what ways was it truly revolutionary? Which is more enduring, a political revolution or an intellectual one?

2. How did the Enlightenment change basic Western attitudes toward reform, faith, and reason? What were the major formative influences on the *philosophes*? How important were Voltaire and the *Encyclopedia* in the success of the Enlightenment?

3. Why did the *philosophes* consider organized religion to be their greatest enemy? Discuss the basic tenets of deism. What criticism might a deist direct at traditional Christianity, and how might he or she improve it?

4. What were the attitudes of the *philosophes* toward women? What was Rousseau's view of women? What were the separate spheres he imagined men and women occupying? What were Mary Wollstonecraft's criticisms of Rousseau's view?

5. Discuss the political views of Montesquieu and Rousseau. Was Montesquieu's view of England accurate? Was Rousseau a child of the Enlightenment or its enemy? Which did Rousseau value more, the individual or society? On what issues might Rousseau and Adam Smith have agreed and differed?

6. Were the enlightened monarchs true believers in the ideal of the *philosophes* or was their enlightenment a mere veneer? Were they really absolute in power? What motivated their reforms? What does the partition of Poland indicate about the spirit of enlightened absolutism?

Suggested Readings ⎯⎯

R. ASHCRAFT, *Revolutionary Politics and Locke's Two Treatises of Government* (1986). The most important study of Locke to appear in recent years.

R. P. BARTLETT, *Human Capital: The Settlement of Foreigners in Russia 1762–1804* (1979). Examines Catherine's policy of attracting farmers and skilled workers to Russia.

D. BEALES, *Joseph II: In the Shadow of Maria Theresa, 1741–1780* (1987). The best treatment in English of the early political life of Joseph II.

C. BECKER, *The Heavenly City of the Eighteenth Century Philosophers* (1932). An influential but very controversial discussion.

T. BESTERMANN, *Voltaire* (1969). A biography by the editor of Voltaire's letters.

M. BIAGIOLI, *Galileo Courtier: The Practice of Science in the Culture of Absolutism* (1993). A major revisionist work that emphasizes the role of the political setting on Galileo's career and thought.

D. D. BIEN, *The Calas Affair: Persecution, Toleration, and Heresy in Eighteenth-Century Toulouse* (1960). The standard treatment of the famous case.

R. CHARTIER, *The Cultural Origins of the French Revolution* (1991). A wide-ranging discussion of the emergence of the public sphere and the role of books and the book trade during the Englightenment.

H. CHISICK, *The Limits of Reform in the Enlightenment: Attitudes Toward the Education of the Lower Classes in Eighteenth-Century France* (1981). An attempt to examine the impact of the Enlightenment on nonelite classes.

I. B. COHEN, *Revolution in Science* (1985). A general consideration of the concept and of historical examples of change in scientific thought.

R. DARNTON, *The Literary Underground of the Old Regime* (1982). Essays on the world of printers, publishers, and booksellers.

I. DE MADARIAGA, *Catherine the Great: A Short History* (1990). A good brief biography.

J. DUNN, *The Political Thought of John Locke: An Historical Account of the "Two Treatises of Government"* (1969). An excellent introduction.

M. A. FINOCCHIARO, *The Galileo Affair: A Documentary History* (1989). A collection of all the relevant documents with an introductory commentary.

J. GAGLIARDO, *Enlightened Despotism* (1967). Remains a useful discussion.

P. GAY, *The Enlightenment: An Interpretation*, 2 vols. (1966, 1969). The most important and far-reaching treatment.

A. GOLDGAR, *Impolite Learning: Conduct and Community in the Republic of Letters, 1680–1750* (1995). A lively survey of the structure of the European intellectual community.

D. GOODMAN, *The Republic of Letters: A Cultural History of the French Enlightenment* (1994). Concentrates on the role of salons.

I. HARRIS, *The Mind of John Locke: A Study of Political Theory in Its Intellectual Setting* (1994) The most comprehensive recent treatment.

M. C. JACOB, *Living the Enlightenment: Freemasonry and Politics in Eighteenth-Century Europe* (1991). The best treatment in English of Freemasonry.

R. KREISER, *Miracles, Convulsions, and Ecclesiastical Politics in Early Eighteenth-Century Paris* (1978). An important study of the kind of religious life that the *philosophes* opposed.

T. S. KUHN, *The Copernican Revolution* (1957). Remains the most influential treatment.

D. LINDBERG AND R. L. NUMBERS, EDS., *Good and Nature: Historical Essays on the Encounter Between Christianity and Science* (1986). The best collection of essays on the subject.

C. A. MACARTNEY, *The Habsburg Empire, 1790–1918* (1971). Provides useful coverage of major mid-eighteenth-century developments.

F. MANUEL, *The Eighteenth Century Confronts the Gods* (1959). A broad examination of the *philosophes'* treatment of Christian and pagan religion.

R. R. PALMER, *Catholics and Unbelievers in Eighteenth-Century France* (1939). A discussion of the opponents of the *philosophes*.

G. RITTER, *Frederick the Great* (trans. 1968). A useful biography.

R. O. ROCKWOOD, ED., *Carl Becker's Heavenly City Revisited* (1958). Important essays qualifying Becker's thesis.

H. M. SCOTT, ED., *Enlightened Absolutism: Reform and Reformers in Later Eighteenth-Century Europe* (1990). A useful collection that incorporates recent scholarship.

S. SHAPIN, *The Scientific Revolution* (1996). An important revisionist survey emphasizing social factors.

J. N. SHKLAR, *Men and Citizens, a Study of Rousseau's Social Theory* (1969). A thoughtful and provocative overview of Rousseau's political thought.

D. SPADAFORA, *The Idea of Progress in Eighteenth Century Britain* (1990). A recent major study that covers many aspects of the Enlightenment in Britain.

L. STEINBRÜGGE, *The Moral Sex: Woman's Nature in the French Enlightenment* (1995). Emphasizes the conservative nature of Enlightenment thought on women.

L. STEWART, *The Rise of Public Science: Rhetoric, Technology, and Natural Philosophy in Newtonian Britain, 1660–1750* (1992). Examines how science became related to public life and economic development.

R. S. WESTFALL, *Never at Rest: A Biography of Isaac Newton* (1981). A very important major study.

A. M. WILSON, *Diderot* (1972). A splendid biography of the person behind the project for the *Encyclopedia* and other major Enlightenment publications.

L. WOLFF, *Inventing Eastern Europe: The Map of Civilization on the Mind of the Enlightenment* (1994). A remarkable study of the manner in which Englightenment writers recast the understanding of this part of the continent.

COMPARATIVE PERSPECTIVES: TECHNOLOGY AND CIVILIZATIONS

The Shifting Balance of East and West

The *philosophes* of the European enlightenment were fascinated by the history of the ancient cultures of the non-European world. They were convinced that the advance of technology so fully illustrated in the pages and prints of the *Encyclopedia* would raise the standard of living on their continent. During the eighteenth century, Europe began to achieve the technological superiority that allowed it to influence much of the rest of the world for the next two centuries. There had, however, been nothing inevitable about the development of Europe's technological strength. This situation becomes clear if we look at the emergence of technology from the ancient world onward.

Among the empires of the ancient Iron Age world, technology may have been equally distributed. If we compare the technological achievements of the Roman empire with those of the Han empire in China—the two empires about which we know the most—we find them to have been roughly equal, just as the two empires were roughly similar in duration, size, and commerce. Rome was clearly ahead in the construction of monumental public buildings and aqueducts and probably in road building, too, although the Han also built an extensive network of roads. In metallurgy China was ahead, having developed iron casting and piston bellows by the second century B.C.E. In 81 B.C.E., when Confucian scholars opposed the government monopolies on salt and iron, they pointed out that plows made by private enterprises were superior to those cast in government foundries. Iron casting did not appear in Europe until the thirteenth century. Both Rome and China had irrigation projects, but those of China were more extensive and equipped with canals and gates to control the level of rivers. The effectiveness of both Han armies and Roman legions was due more to military organization than to weapons, but the weapons of the Chinese included a crossbow with metal-edged triggers of a kind not seen in Europe until the thirteenth century.

Advanced Technology in China and the Abbasid Empire

After the collapse of these ancient empires, however, China grew more advanced technologically than the rest of the world. The Chinese invention of the breast strap in the second century B.C.E. and the padded collar in the fourth century C.E. enabled horses to be harnessed for farming. The Chinese developed porcelain between the third and seventh centuries, ships with waterproof compartments in the fifth century, and ships with sternpost rudders in the eighth century. In the ninth century they cast plows with concave curved moldboards and invented gunpowder. All these technologies did not appear in Europe until centuries later. It seems safe to say that until 1300, and perhaps even a century longer, China was the world leader in technology. One reason for the advance of Chinese technology was that the Chinese had succeeded in recreating a rich and stable empire during the sixth century C.E. after three centuries of barbarian invasions and fragmented rule. In Europe, in contrast, the barbarian invasions were more devastating, the land more sparsely settled, and the collapse into feudal disunity more complete.

During the same "medieval" period, the Islamic lands, although behind China, were also far ahead of Europe in technology. In the eighth century the Abbasid empire experienced an agricultural revolution, the rise of large cities, and an expansion of commerce and international trade. Its ships sailed to India and farther on to the East Indies. Chemistry was advanced, and was applied to the manufacture of soap, the distillation of liquors and perfumes, and metallurgy and medicines. Greek medical texts were translated into Arabic, and Arab doctors improved on the medical procedures they described. Progress was made in harnessing the power of both wind and water. The world's first windmills were invented in Iran during the eighth century, spread through the Islamic world to Spain, and entered France in 1180 and England in 1191. Arab lands, often dry, were watered by dams, aqueducts, and canals. Arab gardens were built around fountains and pools of water. But waterpower also sawed timbers, crushed ores, and drove triphammers in the paper mills of Samarkand. Even today the memory of medieval Islamic technology lingers in our vocabulary in words such as *cordovan (Cordoba) leather, muslin, damask,* and *Arabic numerals.* The numerals had reached Baghdad from India in 700 C.E., spread across North Africa, and arrived in Europe during the thirteenth century.

Technology, however, is not an independent variable. (Virtually all historical variables are interdependent.) No automatic process guarantees that the leading countries in the

In his watercolor *The Bowery at Night,* painted in 1895, W. Louis Sonntag Jr. shows a New York City scene transformed by electric light. Electricity transformed the city in other ways as well, as seen in the electric streetcars and elevated railroad. [Museum of the City of New York]

technology of one age will be confirmed as the leaders of the next. Rather, invention and the application of the techniques of production depend on the total configuration of a society. After 1300 or so, technological innovation seemed to dry up in China. One writer characterized the later Chinese economy as a case of "quantitative growth, qualitative standstill." Even more markedly, in the Muslim world, as empires waned and as science and philosophy became subordinated to religion, technology declined. And just as the other areas receded, Europe began to advance.

European Advances

By 1100 the awakening of Europe had only begun, by 1300 it was well underway—by then Europe had recovered most of the techniques of ancient Greece and Rome—and by 1500 it was pulling ahead of the rest of the world. It is easier to describe what happened in Europe than to explain why it hap-

pened there rather than elsewhere. Europe's initial advance came largely from borrowing. From Islamic countries it obtained both new technologies, as noted previously, and new crops such as rice, sugar, cotton, dates, and oranges. From China and India, by way of Byzantium, it borrowed a variety of technologies, a few of which have been documented. The stirrup, which was invented in Central Asia and used by Muslim cavalry in the seventh century, spread to western Europe in the eighth. Papermaking began in China in the second century C.E. (see the essay beginning on p. 370) and then spread to Samarkand (751), Baghdad (794), Cairo (810), and farther west to Spain (1150); from Spain it quickly entered France and the rest of Europe. Scholars debate whether other important medieval technologies such as the magnetic compass, gunpowder, and printing spread to Europe by diffusion or were invented independently

Europe continued to forge ahead between 1500 and 1750, becoming the world leader in technology. Although the family

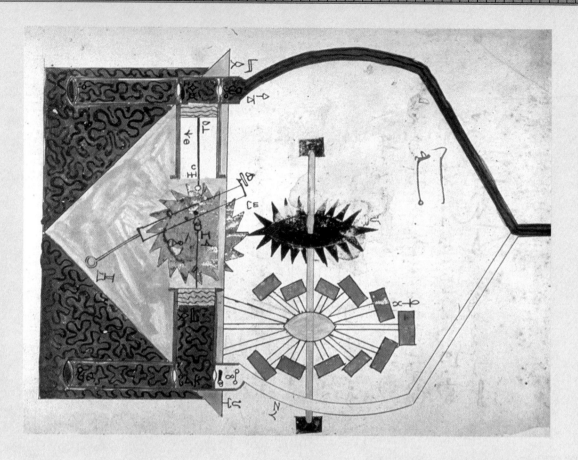

The Al-Jazari reciprocating water pump, with two cylinders, dates from approximately 1200. This drawing appeared in a mid-fourteenth century Arabic manuscript. [The Granger Collection]

remained the unit of production, the manufacture of woolen and cotton textiles became partly mechanized: Women spun and men wove. Coal replaced charcoal in the manufacture of glass, pottery, and bricks. In 1709 coke was first used in blast furnaces. In 1712 Thomas Newcomen invented the rocker-beam steam engine, which was used for pumping water out of mines. Commerce grew apace. European, and especially British, sailing ships became faster and more maneuverable and were armed with superior cast iron cannon. The early voyages of exploration were followed by the overseas expansion of naval power and the establishment of colonies. An incident in China in 1636 suggests how far the balance between East and West had tipped: When the late Ming court needed weapons for its campaigns against the Manchus, it called on Adam Schall, a Jesuit missionary, to set up a foundry and cast twenty cannon. That China had invented iron casting a millennium and a half earlier no longer mattered.

The Industrial Revolution Begins

Then, between 1750 and 1850 there occurred the very rapid economic growth that we call the Industrial Revolution. It began in England and quickly spread to Europe and North America. New sources of power were developed: Better windmills, better waterwheels—leading to the invention of the water turbine—and then in 1769 James Watt's steam engine. These machines underwent constant improvement during the century that followed. Spearheading the Industrial Revolution were cotton textiles and railroads. In the textile industry steam power drove power looms and carding, spinning, and printing machines. Steam power required a shift of production from rural families to urban factories. Cheaper and better cotton cloth enabled Britain to dominate world markets. George Stephenson's *Rocket*, the first commercially successful steam locomotive, inaugurated the age of the railroad in the 1820s and 1830s. Railroads made inland transport cheaper. The application of steam power to ships began in 1807 with Robert Fulton's *Clermont*, a paddle-steamer; by the 1840s transoceanic, screw-propelled steamships were in use. Comparable advances also occurred in metallurgy, machine tools, chemicals, agriculture, electrical devices (the telegraph, 1837), military ordnance, and printing. Advances in one area stimulated others. The quickening pace of change led to profound social and political upheavals.

Technology Joins Science

Until the nineteenth century science and technology were separate. Medieval and early modern technologies, like those of Greece, Rome, and the rest of the world, were in the hands of craftsmen who tinkered, improved, and passed on their skills to other craftsmen. They were separated by a social barrier from the natural philosophers, who were educated in the cumulative written tradition. In the sixteenth century Francis Bacon suggested that scholars study the techniques of artisans and that artisans study science, but few did. Even the new worldview of Galileo and Newton contributed only indirectly to the Industrial Revolution. The thinkers of the eighteenth century Enlightenment were the first to be keenly aware of technology. But it was not until the nineteenth century that technology became science-driven. Thomas Edison, the inventor of the electric light (1879), drew on the studies of electromagnetism of Michael Faraday and Joseph Henry and also established in Palo Alto the first laboratory for technological development. Alexander Graham Bell, inventor of the telephone (1876), drew on the research of Hermann Helmholtz, a professor of physics at the University of Berlin; Guglielmo Marconi, inventor of radio-telegraphy (1895), drew on the theory of electromagnetic waves propounded by Heinrich Hertz and James Maxwell. The first scientist to become a major figure in technology was Justus von Liebig, the inventor of artificial fertilizer and the father of agricultural science and organic chemistry.

The first Industrial Revolution is usually said to have ended about 1850. In fact, it was then just beginning its spread around the world, and in the West it was followed by new waves of revolutionary developments in organic chemistry, electronics, metallurgy, and, eventually, in atomic energy, computers, and biotechnology. The pace of development has continued to accelerate. Of all the scientists who ever lived, 90 percent are alive today. Government, corporate, and university laboratories systematically apply science to the solution of technological problems. To say that science-based technology shapes our world is so obvious as to need no commentary. But today it has also become clear that technology has destructive as well as beneficial consequences, an issue we explore further in "Technology and Imperialism," p. 772 and "Energy and the Modern World," p. 1026.

25 REVOLUTIONS IN THE TRANSATLANTIC WORLD

To symbolize the beginning of a new era in human history, French revolutionary legislators established a new calendar. The year 1793 became Year One in this new calendar and all the months of the year were given new names. This calendar for Year Two proclaims the indivisible unity of the revolution and the goals of Liberty, Equality, and Fraternity. [Bildarchiv Preussischer Kulturbesitz]

CHAPTER TOPICS

◆ **Revolution in the British Colonies in North America**

◆ **Revolution in France**

◆ **Wars of Independence in Latin America**

◆ **Toward the Abolition of Slavery in the Transatlantic Economy**

In World Perspective **The Transatlantic Revolutions**

Between 1776 and 1824 a world-transforming series of revolutions occurred in France and the Americas. In a half century the peoples of the two American continents established their independence of European political control. In Europe the French monarchy collapsed from the forces of aristocratic resistance and popular revolution. All the revolutionary leaders sought to establish new governments based largely, though never entirely, on Enlightenment principles.

From start to finish these revolutions were connected. The financial pressures from the Seven Years' War (1756–1763) had led Britain, Spain, and France to undertake a search for revenue that politically destabilized the Americas and France itself. Once the American Revolution began, France aided the colonists, thus exacerbating its own financial problem. In turn the French Revolution and the ensuing Napoleonic Wars created situations in Spain and Portugal to which the colonial elites in Latin America responded by seeking independence. Thus the transatlantic revolutions, despite their individual characters and developments, were interconnected events in world history. Furthermore, the era witnessed the commencement of a vast international crusade, first to abolish the slave trade and then to abolish slavery in the transatlantic world. The same ideas from the Enlightenment which inspired many of the revolutionaries also inspired the opponents of slavery as did religious convictions. The political and economic dislocations of the revolutionary era helped the antislavery forces achieve their goals. The political, social, and economic life of the transatlantic world would never be the same again.

Revolution in the British Colonies in North America

Resistance to the Imperial Search for Revenue

After the Treaty of Paris in 1763 ended the Seven Years' War, the British government faced two imperial problems (Map 25–1). The first was the sheer cost of empire, which the British felt they could no longer carry alone. The second was that the defeat of the French required the British to organize a vast expanse of new territory: all of North America east of the Mississippi, with its French settlers and, more important, its Indian possessors.

The British drive for revenue began in 1764 with the Sugar Act, which at-tempted to produce more revenue from imports into the colonies by the rigorous collection of what was actually a reduced tax on sugar. Smugglers were to be tried in admiralty courts without juries. The next year, Parliament passed the Stamp Act, which put a tax on legal documents and certain other items such as newspapers. The British considered these taxes legal and just because they had been approved by Parliament and because the revenue was to be spent in the colonies. The Americans responded that they alone through their assemblies had the right to tax themselves and that they were not represented in Parliament. Furthermore, the Americans feared that if colonial government were financed from Britain, they would cease to control it.

In October 1765 the Stamp Act Congress met in America and drew up a protest to the Crown. There was much disorder in the colonies, particularly in Massachusetts, led by groups known as the Sons of Liberty. The colonists agreed to boycott British goods. In 1766 Parliament repealed the Stamp Act but, through the Declaratory Act, claimed the power to legislate for the colonies.

American Political Ideas

The political ideas of the American colonists had largely arisen from the struggle of seventeenth-century English aristocrats and gentry against the absolutism of the Stuart monarchs. The American colonists believed that the English Revolution of 1688 had established many of their own fundamental

The Stamp Act Congress Addresses George III

In 1765 the Stamp Act Congress met to protest the British imposition of taxes on the colonies. American leaders believed Great Britain had no right to impose such taxation. Their argument was that they were not and could not be represented in Parliament and that they were subject to the taxation only of their own assemblies. Later clauses implied that the taxation would prevent the colonists from purchasing manufactured goods from Britain and demanded the repeal of the act.

Why does the Congress insist on the same rights for subjects born in the colonies as those born in England? On what grounds does the Congress declare that Parliament may not levy taxes in the colonies? Why is the Congress so concerned about what courts may try cases arising from the Stamp Act?

The Members of this Congress, sincerely devoted, with the warmest sentiments of affection and duty to His Majesty's person and government . . . and with minds deeply impressed by a sense of the present and impending misfortunes of the British colonies on this continent; having considered as maturely as time will permit, the circumstances of the said colonies, esteem it our indispensable duty to make the following declarations of our humble opinion, respecting the most essential rights and liberties of the colonists, and of the grievances under which they labor, by reason of several late acts of Parliament.

I. That His Majesty's subjects in these colonies, owe the same allegiance to the crown of Great Britain, that is owing from his subjects born within the realm, and all due subordination to that august body the Parliament of Great Britain.

II. That His Majesty's liege subjects in these colonies are entitled to all the inherent rights and liberties of his natural born subjects, within the kingdom of Great Britain.

III. That it is inseparably essential to the freedom of a people, and the undoubted right of Englishmen, that no taxes be imposed on them but with their own consent, given personally, or by their representatives.

IV. That the people of these colonies are not, and cannot, be represented in the House of Commons in Great Britain.

V. That the only representatives of the people of these colonies are persons chosen therein by themselves, and that no taxes ever have been, or can be constitutionally imposed on them, but by their respective legislatures.

VI. That all supplies to the crown being free gifts of the people, it is unreasonable and inconsistent with the principles and spirit of the British constitution, for the people of Great Britain to grant to His Majesty the property of the colonists.

VII. That trial by jury, is the inherent and invaluable right of every British subject in these colonies.

VIII. That the late act of Parliament entitled, *An act for granting and supplying certain stamp duties, and other duties, in the British colonies and plantations, in America, etc.* by imposing taxes on the inhabitants of these colonies, and the said act, and several other acts, by extending the jurisdiction of the courts of admiralty beyond its ancient limits, have a manifest tendency to subvert the rights and liberties of the colonists.

From *Journal of the First Congress of the American Colonies* . . . 1765 (New York, 1845), pp. 27–29, as quoted in Oscar Handlin, ed., *Readings in American History.* Copyright © 1957 Alfred A. Knopf, pp. 116–117.

political liberties. The colonists claimed that, through the measures imposed from 1763 to 1776, George III (r. 1760–1820) and the British Parliament were attacking those liberties and dissolving the bonds of moral and political allegiance that had formerly united the two peoples. Consequently, the colonists employed a theory that had originally been developed to justify an aristocratic rebellion in England to support their own popular revolution.

These Whig political ideas, largely derived from John Locke (1632–1704), were only a part of the English ideological heritage that affected the Americans. Throughout the eighteenth century they had become familiar with a series of British political writers called the *Commonwealthmen*. These writers held republican political ideas that had their intellectual roots in the most radical thought of the Puritan revolution. They had relentlessly criticized the government patronage and parliamentary management of Robert Walpole (1676–1745) and his successors. They argued that such government was corrupt and that it undermined liberty. They regarded much parliamentary taxation as simply a means of financing political corruption. They also attacked standing armies as instruments of tyranny. In Great Britain this re-

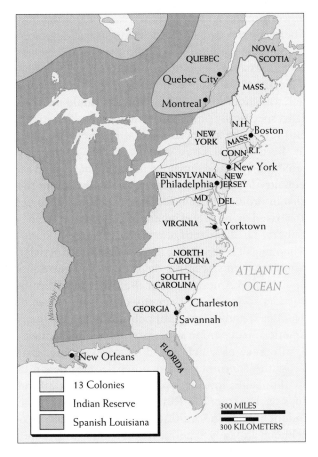

Map 25-1   North America in 1763.   In the year of the victory over France, the English colonies lay along the Atlantic seaboard. The difficulties of organizing authority over the previous French territory in Canada and west of the Appalachian Mountains would contribute to the coming of the American Revolution.

In May 1773 Parliament allowed the East India Company to import tea directly into the American colonies. Although the law lowered the price of tea, it retained the tax without the colonists' consent. In some cities the colonists refused to permit the tea to be unloaded; in Boston, a shipload of tea was thrown into the harbor, known since as the Boston Tea Party.

The British ministry of Lord North (1732–1792) was determined to assert the authority of Parliament over the resistant colonies. In 1774 Parliament passed a series of laws known in American history as the Intolerable Acts. These measures closed the port of Boston, reorganized the government of Massachusetts, allowed troops to be quartered in private homes, and removed the trials of royal customs officials to England. In the same year Parliament approved the Quebec Act, which extended the boundaries of Quebec to include the Ohio River valley. The Americans regarded the Quebec Act as an attempt to prevent the extension of their mode of self-government westward beyond the Appalachian Mountains.

During these years committees of correspondence, composed of citizens critical of Britain, had been established

This view of the "Boston Massacre" of March 5, 1770, by Paul Revere owes more to propaganda than fact. There was no order to fire and the innocent citizens portrayed here were really an angry, violent mob. [Collection of New York Historical Society/The Granger Collection, N.Y.]

publican political tradition had only a marginal impact. Most Britons regarded themselves as the freest people in the world. In the colonies, however, these radical books and pamphlets were read widely and were often accepted at face value. The policy of Great Britain toward America after the Treaty of Paris made many colonists believe that the worst fears of the Commonwealthmen were coming true.

Crisis and Independence

In 1767 Charles Townshend (1725–1767) led Parliament to regulate and tax colonial imports. The colonists again resisted. The ministry sent over its own customs agents to administer the laws. To protect these new officers, the British sent troops to Boston in 1768. The obvious tensions resulted, and in March 1770 British troops killed five citizens in the Boston Massacre. In that same year Parliament repealed the Townshend duties except for the one on tea.

The American Revolution

1760	George III becomes king
1763	Treaty of Paris concludes the Seven Years' War
1764	Sugar Act
1765	Stamp Act
1766	Sugar Act repealed and Declaratory Act passed
1767	Townshend Acts
1770	Lord North becomes George III's chief minister
1770	Boston Massacre
1773	Boston Tea Party
1774	Intolerable Acts
1774	First Continental Congress
1775	Second Continental Congress
1776	Declaration of Independence
1778	France enters the war on the side of America
1781	British forces surrender at Yorktown
1783	Treaty of Paris concludes War of the American Revolution

throughout the colonies. In September 1774 these committees organized the First Continental Congress in Philadelphia. This body hoped to persuade Parliament to restore self-government in the colonies and to abandon its attempt at direct supervision of colonial affairs. Conciliation, however, was not forthcoming. By April 1775 the battles of Lexington and Concord had been fought. In June the colonists were defeated at the Battle of Bunker Hill.

The Second Continental Congress gathered in May 1775. It still sought conciliation with Britain, but soon undertook the government of the colonies. By August 1775 George III had declared the colonies in rebellion. During the winter Thomas Paine's (1737–1809) pamphlet *Common Sense* galvanized public opinion in favor of separation from Great Britain. A colonial army and navy were organized. In April 1776 the Continental Congress opened American ports to the trade of all nations. Finally, on July 4, 1776, the Continental Congress adopted the Declaration of Independence. Thereafter, the War of the American Revolution continued until 1781, when the forces of George Washington (1732–1799) defeated those of Lord Cornwallis (1738–1805) at Yorktown. Early in 1778, however, the war had widened into a European conflict when Benjamin Franklin (1706–1790) persuaded the French government to support the rebellion. In 1779 the Spanish also came to the aid of the colonies. The 1783 Treaty of Paris concluded the conflict, and the thirteen American colonies had established their independence.

As the crisis with Britain unfolded during the 1760s and 1770s, the American colonists came to see themselves as first preserving traditional English liberties against a tyrannical

Crown and corrupt Parliament and then as developing a new sense of liberty. By the mid-1770s the colonists had embraced republican political ideals. They would govern themselves through elected assemblies without any monarchical authority. The Constitutional Convention met in 1787. After the constitution was adopted in 1788, Americans would insist on a bill of rights specifically protecting civil liberties. The Americans would reject the aristocratic social hierarchy that had existed in the colonies. They would embrace democratic ideals, even if the franchise remained limited. They would assert the equality of white male citizens not only before the law but also in ordinary social relations. They would reject social status based on birth and inheritance and assert the necessity of liberty for all citizens to improve their social standing and economic lot by engaging in free commercial activity. They did not free their slaves, nor did they address the rights of women or Native Americans, but the American Revolution produced a society freer than any the world had seen, one that would expand the circle of political and social liberty. The American Revolution was a genuinely radical movement, the influence of which would increase as Americans moved across the continent and as other peoples began to question traditional European government. The political and social values of the American Revolution would inspire the Wars of Independence in Latin America and, to a lesser extent, both liberal and radical political movements in Europe.

Revolution in France

The French monarchy emerged from the Seven Years' War both defeated and deeply in debt. The later French support for the American Revolution exacerbated the financial difficulties. Given the economic vitality of France, the government debt was neither overly large nor disproportionate to the debts of other European powers. The problem was the government's inability to collect sufficient taxes to service and repay the debt.

Between 1786 and 1788 Louis XVI (r. 1774–1792) appointed several different ministers to deal with the financial crisis. All failed to persuade the aristocracy and the church to pay more taxes. As these negotiations dragged on, the parlement of Paris declared that only the Estates General could institute new taxes. The Estates General had not met since 1614. Consequently, in July 1788, Louis XVI agreed to convene the Estates General the next year.

Revolutions of 1789

The Estates General Becomes the National Assembly The Estates General had three divisions: the First Estate of the clergy, the Second Estate of the nobility, and

On July 14, 1789, crowds stormed the Bastille, a prison in Paris. This event, whose only practical effect was to free a few prisoners, marked the first time the populace of Paris redirected the course of the revolution. [Musee de la Ville de Paris, Musee Carnavalet/Giraudon/Art Resource, N.Y.]

the Third Estate, representing everyone else in the kingdom. Before the Estates General met at Versailles in May 1789, there had been much public debate over its organization. The monarchy had agreed that the Third Estate should have twice as many members as either that of the nobility or the clergy. Then there arose the question of how voting should be organized. The nobility wanted all votes to be taken by Estate, which would have allowed the nobles and clergy to outvote the Third Estate. The Third Estate wanted each member to vote individually so that, with its larger membership, it would dominate.

From the beginning the Third Estate, composed largely of local officials, professional men, and lawyers, refused to sit as a separate order as the king desired. For several weeks there was a standoff. Then, on June 1 the Third Estate invited the clergy and the nobles to join it in organizing a new legislative body. A few of the lower clergy did so. On June 17 that body declared itself the National Assembly.

Three days later, finding themselves accidentally locked out of their usual meeting place, the National Assembly moved to a nearby tennis court, where its members took the famous Tennis Court Oath to continue to sit until they had given France a constitution. Louis XVI ordered the National Assembly to desist, but shortly afterward most of the clergy and many nobles joined the assembly. On June 27 the king capitulated and formally requested the First and Second Estates to meet with the National Assembly, where voting would occur by head rather than by order. Government by the privileged orders thus ended, and the National Assembly became the National Constituent Assembly.

Fall of the Bastille   Two new factors soon intruded. First, Louis XVI attempted to regain the initiative by mustering troops near Versailles and Paris. This was the beginning of a steady, and consistently poorly executed, royal attempt to halt the revolution. Most of the National Constituent

The National Assembly Decrees Civic Equality in France

These famous decrees of August 4, 1789, in effect created civic equality in France. The special privileges previously possessed or controlled by the nobility were removed.

What institutions and privileges are included in "the feudal regime"? How do these decrees recognize that the abolition of some privileges and former tax arrangements will require new kinds of taxes and government financing to support religious, educational, and other institutions?

---

1. The National Assembly completely abolishes the feudal regime. It decrees that, among the rights and dues . . . all those originating in real or personal serfdom, personal servitude, and those which represent them, are abolished without indemnification; all others are declared redeemable, and that the price and mode of redemption shall be fixed by the National Assembly. . . .
2. The exclusive right to maintain pigeon-houses and dove-cotes is abolished. . . .
3. The exclusive right to hunt and to maintain unenclosed warrens is likewise abolished. . . .
4. All manorial courts are suppressed without indemnification.

5. Tithes of every description and the dues which have been substituted for them . . . are abolished, on condition, however, that some other method be devised to provide for the expenses of divine worship, the support of the officiating clergy, the relief of the poor, repairs and rebuilding of churches and parsonages, and for all establishments, seminaries, schools, academies, asylums, communities, and other institutions, for the maintenance of which they are actually devoted. . . .

---

7. The sale of judicial and municipal offices shall be suppressed forthwith. . . .
8. Pecuniary privileges, personal or real, in the payment of taxes are abolished forever. . . .

---

11. All citizens, without distinction of birth, are eligible to any office or dignity, whether ecclesiastical, civil or military. . . .

Frank Maloy Anderson, ed. and trans., *The Constitutions and Other Select Documents Illustrative of the History of France, 1789–1907*, 2nd ed., rev. and enl. (Minneapolis: H. W. Wilson, 1908), pp. 11–13.

Assembly wished to create some form of constitutional monarchy, but from the start Louis's refusal to cooperate thwarted that effort.

The second new factor was the populace of Paris. The mustering of royal troops created anxiety in the city, where there had been several bread riots. By June the Parisians were organizing a citizen militia and collecting arms.

On July 14 around eight hundred people, mostly small shopkeepers, tradespeople, artisans, and wage earners, marched to the Bastille in search of weapons for the militia. This great fortress had once held political prisoners. Through miscalculations and ineptitude by the governor of the fortress, the troops in the Bastille fired into the crowd, killing ninety-eight people and wounding many others. The crowd then stormed the fortress, released its seven prisoners, none of whom was there for political reasons, and killed several soldiers and the governor. They found no weapons.

This was the first of many crucial *journées*, or days when the populace of Paris would redirect the course of the revolution. The fall of the Bastille signaled that the political future of the nation would not be decided solely by the National Constituent Assembly. As the news spread, similar disturbances took place in the provincial cities. A few days later Louis XVI, again bowing to events, came to Paris and recognized both the new elected government of the city and its National Guard. The citizens of Paris were, for the time being, satisfied.

The Great Fear and Surrender of Feudal Privileges

As popular urban disturbances erupted in various cities, a movement known as the *Great Fear* swept across much of the French countryside. Peasants were reclaiming rights and property that they had lost through the aristocratic resurgence of the last quarter century, as well as venting their anger against the injustices of rural life. The Great Fear, which was an intensification of peasant disturbances that had begun during the spring, witnessed the burning of châteaux, the destruction of records and documents, and the refusal by peasants to pay feudal dues.

On the night of August 4, 1789, aristocrats in the National Constituent Assembly attempted to halt the disorder in the countryside. By prearrangement, liberal nobles and churchmen rose in the assembly and surrendered hunting and fishing rights, judicial authority, tithes, and special exemptions. In a sense, these nobles gave up what they had already lost and what they could not have regained without

A Versaille a Versaille. du 5 Octobre 1789.

The women of Paris marched to Versailles on October 5, 1789. The following day the royal family was forced to return to Paris with them. Henceforth, the French government would function under the constant threat of mob violence. [Musee de la Ville de Paris, Musee Carnavalet/ Giraudon/Art Resource, N.Y.]

civil war. Later, many would also be compensated for their losses. Nonetheless, after August 4 all French citizens were subject to the same and equal laws.

Declaration of the Rights of Man and Citizen On August 27, 1789, the assembly issued the *Declaration of the Rights of Man and Citizen.* This declaration drew together much of the political language of the Enlightenment and was also influenced by the Declaration of Rights adopted by Virginia in America in June 1776. The French declaration proclaimed that all men were "born and remain free and equal in rights." Their natural rights were "liberty, property, security, and resistance to oppression." Governments existed to protect those rights. All political sovereignty resided in the nation and its representatives. All citizens were to be equal before the law and were to be "equally admissible to all public dignities, offices and employments, according to their capacity, and with no other distinction than that of their virtues and talents." There were to be due process of law and presumption of innocence until proof of guilt. Freedom of religion was affirmed. Taxation was to be apportioned equally according to capacity to pay. Property constituted "an inviolable and sacred right."[1]

Louis XVI stalled before ratifying both the declaration and the aristocratic renunciation of feudalism. His hesitations

[1]Quoted in Georges Lefebvre, *The Coming of the French Revolution,* trans. by R. R. Palmer (Princeton, NJ: Princeton University Press, 1967), pp. 221–223.

fanned suspicions that he might try to resort to force. Moreover, bread shortages continued. On October 5 several thousand Parisian women marched to Versailles, demanding more bread. This was one of several occasions when women played a major role in the actions of the Parisian crowd. On this day they milled about the palace, and many stayed the night. Under this pressure the king agreed to sanction the decrees of the assembly. The Parisians believed that the king had to be kept under the watchful eye of the people. Consequently they demanded that Louis and his family return to Paris. The monarch had no real choice. On October 6, 1789, his carriage followed the crowd into the city, where he and his family settled in the palace of the Tuileries. The National Constituent Assembly soon followed. Thereafter, both Paris and France remained relatively stable and peaceful until the summer of 1792.

Reconstruction of France

Once established in Paris, the National Constituent Assembly set about reorganizing France. Throughout its proceedings the Assembly was determined to protect property and to limit the impact on national life of small-property owners as well as of the unpropertied elements of the nation. While championing civic equality before the law, the Assembly spurned social equality and extensive democracy. The Assembly thus charted a general course that, to a greater or lesser degree, nineteenth-century liberals across Europe and in other areas of the world would follow.

French Women Petition to Bear Arms

The issue of women serving in the revolutionary French military appeared early in the revolution. In March 1791 Pauline Léon presented a petition to the National Assembly on behalf of more than 300 Parisian women asking the right to bear arms and train for military service for the revolution. Similar requests were made during the next two years. Some women did serve in the military, but in 1793 legislation specifically forbade it on the grounds that women belonged in the domestic sphere and that military service would lead them to abandon family duties.

Citoyenne is the feminine form of the French word for citizen. How does this petition seek to challenge the concept of citizenship in the *French Declaration of the Rights of Man and Citizen*? How do these petitioners relate their demand to bear arms to their role as women in French society? How do the petitioners relate their demands to the use of all national resources against the enemies of the revolution?

Patriotic women come before you to claim the right which any individual has to defend his life and liberty.

. . . We are *citoyennes* [female citizens], and we cannot be indifferent to the fate of the fatherland.

. . . Yes, Gentlemen, we need arms, and we come to ask your permission to procure them. May our weakness be no obstacle; courage and intrepidity will supplant it, and the love of the fatherland and hatred of tyrants will allow us to brave all dangers with ease. . . .

No, Gentlemen, We will [use arms] only to defend ourselves the same as you; you cannot refuse us, and society cannot deny the right nature gives us, unless you pretend the *Declaration of Rights* does not apply to women and that they should let their throats be cut like lambs, without the right to defend themselves. For can you believe the tyrants would spare us? . . . Why then not terrorize aristocracy and tyranny with all the resources of civic effort and the pure zeal, zeal which cold men can well call fanaticism and exaggeration, but which is only the natural result of a heart burning with love for the public weal? . . .

. . . If, for reasons we cannot guess, you refuse our just demands, these women you have raised to the ranks of *citoyennes* by granting that title to their husbands, these women who have sampled the promises of liberty, who have conceived the hope of placing free men in the world, and who have sworn to live free or die—such women, I say, will never consent to concede the day to slaves; they will die first. They will uphold their oath, and a dagger aimed at their breasts will deliver them from the misfortunes of slavery! They will die, regretting not life, but the uselessness of their death; regretting moreover, not having been able to drench their hands in the impure blood of the enemies of the fatherland and to avenge some of their own!

But, Gentlemen, let us cast our eyes away from these cruel extremes. Whatever the rages and plots of aristocrats, they will not succeed in vanquishing a whole people of united brothers armed to defend their rights. We also demand only the honor of sharing their exhaustion and glorious labors and of making tyrants see that women also have blood to shed for the service of the fatherland in danger.

Gentlemen, here is what we hope to obtain from your justice and equity:

1. Permission to procure pikes, pistols, and sabres (even muskets for those who are strong enough to use them), within police regulations.

2. Permission to assemble on festival days and Sundays on the Champ de la Fédération, or in other suitable places, to practice maneuvers with these arms.

3. Permission to name the former French Guards to command us, always in conformity with the rules which the mayor's wisdom prescribes for good order and public calm.

From "French Women Petition to Bear Arms" in *Women in Revolutionary Paris 1789–1795*, trans. by Darline Gay Levy, Harriet Branson Applewhite, and Mary Durham Johnson. © 1979 by the Board of Trustees of the University of Illinois. Used with permission of the authors and the University of Illinois Press.

Political Reorganization   The Constitution of 1791, the product of the National Constituent Assembly's deliberations, established a constitutional monarchy. There was a unicameral Legislative Assembly vested with powers of war and peace. The monarch could delay but not halt legislation. The system of voting was complex and restricted. Only about 50,000 citizens of the French nation of 26 million could actually elect or serve in the Legislative Assembly.

The exclusion of women from both voting and holding office did not pass unnoticed. In 1791 Olympe de Gouges (d. 1793), a butcher's daughter who became a major radical in Paris, composed a *Declaration of the Rights of Woman*, which she ironically addressed to Queen Marie Antoinette (1755–1793). Much of the document reprinted the *Declaration of the Rights of Man and Citizen*, adding the word *woman* to the various original clauses. That strategy demanded that women be regarded as citizens and not merely as daughters, sisters, wives, and mothers of citizens. Olympe de Gouges further outlined rights that would permit women to own property and require men to recognize the paternity of their children. She called for equality of the sexes in marriage and improved education for women. She declared, "Women, wake up; the tocsin of reason is being heard throughout the whole universe; discover your rights."[2] Her demands illustrated how the public listing of rights in the *Declaration of the Rights of Man and Citizen* created universal civic expectations even among those it did not cover.

The National Constituent Assembly abolished the ancient French Provinces, such as Burgundy, and replaced them with eighty-three departments *(départements)* of generally equal size named after rivers, mountains, and other geographical features. The ancient judicial courts, including the seigneurial courts and the *parlements*, were suppressed and replaced by established uniform courts with elected judges and prosecutors. Legal procedures were simplified, and the most degrading punishments abolished.

Economic Policy   In economic matters the National Constituent Assembly suppressed the guilds and liberated the grain trade. The assembly established the metric system to provide the nation with uniform weights and measures. These policies of economic freedom and uniformity disappointed both peasants and urban workers caught in the cycle of inflation. By the decrees of 1790 the Assembly placed the burden of proof on the peasants to rid themselves of the residual feudal dues for which compensation was to be paid. On June 14, 1791, the Assembly enacted the Chapelier Law forbidding worker associations, thereby crushing the attempts of urban workers to protect their wages. Peasants and workers were to be left to the mercy of the free marketplace.

The National Constituent Assembly decided to pay the troublesome royal debt by confiscating and then selling the lands of the Roman Catholic church in France. The Assembly then authorized the issuance of *assignats*, or government bonds, the value of which was guaranteed by the revenue to be generated from the sale of church property. When the *assignats* began to circulate as currency, the Assembly issued even larger quantities of them to liquidate the national debt. However, within a few months the value of *assignats* began to fall. Inflation increased and put new stress on the lives of the urban poor.

Civil Constitution of the Clergy   In July 1790 the National Constituent Assembly issued the Civil Constitution of the Clergy, which transformed the Roman Catholic church in France into a branch of the secular state. This measure reduced the number of bishoprics, made borders of dioceses conform to those of the new departments, and provided for the election of priests and bishops, who henceforth became salaried employees of the state. The Assembly consulted nei-

ther the pope nor the French clergy about these broad changes. The king approved the measure only with the greatest reluctance.

The Civil Constitution of the Clergy was the major blunder of the National Constituent Assembly. The measure roused immense opposition within the French church, even from bishops who had long championed Gallican liberties over papal domination. Faced with this resistance, the Assembly unwisely ruled that all clergy must take an oath to support the Civil Constitution. Only seven bishops and about half the clergy did so. In reprisal, the assembly designated the clergy who had not taken the oath as "refractory" and removed them from their clerical functions. Refractory priests immediately attempted to celebrate mass.

In February 1791 the pope condemned not only the Civil Constitution of the Clergy but also the *Declaration of the Rights of Man and Citizen*. That condemnation marked the opening of a Roman Catholic offensive against liberalism in Europe and revolution throughout the world that continued for over a century. Within France itself, the pope's action meant that religious devotion and revolutionary loyalty became incompatible for many people. French citizens quickly divided between those who supported the constitutional priests and those who resorted to the refractory clergy. Louis XVI and his family favored the latter.

Counterrevolutionary Activity   In the summer of 1791 the queen and some nobles who had already left the country persuaded Louis XVI also to flee. The escape failed when Louis, along with his family, was recognized and stopped in the town of Varennes. On June 24 soldiers escorted the royal family back to Paris. Thereafter, the leaders of the National Constituent Assembly knew that the chief counterrevolutionary sat on the French throne.

Two months later, on August 27, 1791, Emperor Leopold II of Austria (r. 1790–1792), who was the brother of Marie Antoinette, and Frederick William II (r. 1786–1797), the king of Prussia, issued the Declaration of Pillnitz. The two monarchs promised to intervene in France to protect the royal family and to preserve the monarchy if the other major European powers agreed. The latter provision rendered the statement meaningless because Great Britain would not have given its consent. In France, however, the revolutionaries felt surrounded by aristocratic and monarchical foes.

Near its close in September 1791 the National Constituent Assembly forbade any of its own members to sit in the Legislative Assembly then being elected. This new body met on October 1 to confront immense problems.

A Second Revolution

Since the earliest days of the revolution, various clubs of politically like-minded persons had organized themselves in

[2]Quoted in Sara E. Melzer and Leslie W. Rabine, eds., *Rebel Daughters: Women and the French Revolution* (New York: Oxford University Press, 1992), p. 88.

One of the key events of the French revolution was the unsuccessful attempt by Louis XVI and his family to escape the country in June, 1791. They were recognized and captured in the French city of Varennes and then returned to Paris under armed escort.
[Corbis-Bettmann]

Paris. The best organized were the *Jacobins,* whose name derived from the fact that the group met in a former Dominican (Jacobin) monastery located in the Rue St. Jacques. The Paris club was linked to other local clubs in the provinces. In the Legislative Assembly a group of Jacobins known as the *Girondists* (because many of them came from the department of the Gironde) assumed leadership.[3] They led the Legislative Assembly on April 20, 1792, to declare war on Austria, by this time governed by Francis II (r. 1792–1835) and allied to Prussia.

End of the Monarchy   The war radicalized the revolution and led to what is usually called the *second revolution,* which overthrew the constitutional monarchy and established a republic. The war initially went poorly, and the revolution seemed in danger. Late in July, under radical working-class pressure, the government of Paris passed from the elected council to a committee, or commune, of representatives from the sections (municipal wards) of Paris. On August 10, 1792, a large crowd invaded the Tuileries and forced Louis XVI and Marie Antoinette to take refuge in the Legislative Assembly itself. During the disturbance several hundred of the royal Swiss guards and many Parisians died. Thereafter, the royal family was imprisoned in comfortable quarters, but the king was suspended from his political functions.

The Convention and the Role of Sans-Culottes
During the first week of September, in what are known as the September Massacres, the Paris Commune summarily killed about twelve hundred people in the city jails. Many were aristocrats or priests, but most were simply common criminals. The crowd had assumed that the prisoners were all counterrevolutionaries. The Paris Commune then compelled the Legislative Assembly to call for the election, by universal manhood suffrage, of a new assembly to write a democratic constitution. That body, called the Convention after its American counterpart of 1787, met on September 21, 1792.

As its first act the Convention declared France a republic, that is, a nation governed by an elected assembly without a king. The second revolution had been the work of Jacobins more radical than the Girondists and of the people of Paris known as the *sans-culottes.* The name of the latter means "without breeches," and was derived from the long trousers that, as working people, they wore instead of aristocratic knee breeches. The *sans-culottes* were shopkeepers, artisans, wage earners, and a few factory workers. The politics of the old regime had ignored them, and the policies of the National Constituent Assembly had left them victims of unregulated economic liberty.

[3]The Girondists are also frequently called the *Brissotins* after Jacques-Pierre Brissot (1754–1793), who was their chief representative in early 1792.

The *sans-culottes,* whose labor and military service were needed for the war effort, generally knew what they wanted. They sought immediate price controls for relief from food shortages and rising prices. They believed that all people had a right to subsistence and profoundly resented most forms of social inequality. They felt intense hostility toward the aristocracy and the original leaders of the revolution, whom they believed simply wanted to take over the social privileges of the aristocracy. They did not demand the abolition of property, but advocated a community of relatively small property owners. They were antimonarchical, strongly republican, and suspicious even of representative government.

In contrast, the Jacobins were republicans who sought representative government. Their hatred of the aristocracy did not extend to a general suspicion of wealth. Basically, the Jacobins favored an unregulated economy. However, from Louis XVI's flight to Varennes onward, the more extreme Jacobins began to cooperate with leaders of the Parisian *sans-culottes* and the Paris Commune to overthrow the monarchy. Once the Convention began its deliberations, these advanced Jacobins, known as the Mountain because of their seats high in the assembly hall, worked with *sans-culottes* to carry the revolution forward and win the war.

In December 1792 Louis XVI was put on trial as mere "Citizen Capet." (Capet was the family name of medieval forebears of the royal family.) The Girondists sought to spare his life, but the Mountain defeated the effort. By a narrow majority, Louis was convicted of conspiring against the liberty of the people and the security of the state. Condemned to death, he was beheaded on January 21, 1793.

The next month, the Convention declared war on Great Britain, Holland, and Spain. France was now at war with virtually all Europe. Civil war soon followed. In March 1793 aristocratic officers and priests commenced a royalist revolt in the Vendée in western France and roused much local popular support. The Girondists had led the country into the war but had proved themselves incapable either of winning it or of suppressing the enemies of the revolution at home. The Mountain stood ready to take up the task.

The Reign of Terror and Its Aftermath

The Reign of Terror is the name given to the months of quasi-judicial executions and murders stretching from the autumn of 1793 to the midsummer of 1794. The Terror can be understood only in the context of the internal and external wars, on the one hand, and the revolutionary expectations of the Convention and the *sans-culottes,* on the other.

Committee of Public Safety   In April 1793 the Convention established a Committee of General Security and a Committee of Public Safety to perform the executive duties of the government. The latter committee eventually enjoyed almost dictatorial power. The committee conceived of their task as saving the revolution from mortal enemies at home and abroad. They generally enjoyed a working political relationship with the *sans-culottes* of Paris, but it was an alliance of expediency for the committee.

The major problem was to secure domestic support for the war. In early June 1793 the Parisian *sans-culottes* invaded the Convention and secured the expulsion of the Girondist members. That gave the Mountain complete control. On June 22 the Convention approved a fully democratic constitution but suspended its operation until after the war emergency. August 23 saw a *levée en masse,* or general military requisition of population, which conscripted males into the army and directed economic production for military purposes. On September 29 a maximum on prices was established in accord with *sans-culottes'* demands. During these same months the armies of the revolution also crushed many of the counterrevolutionary disturbances in the provinces.

The Society of Revolutionary Republican Women Revolutionary women established their own distinct institutions to fight the internal enemies of the revolution. In May 1793 Pauline Léon and Claire Lacombe founded the Society of Revolutionary Republican Women. Its members and other women filled the galleries of the Convention to hear the debates and cheer their favorite speakers. The Society became increasingly radical, however. Its members sought stricter controls on the price of food and other commodities, worked to ferret out food hoarders, and brawled with working market women thought to be insufficiently revolutionary. The women of the Society also demanded the right to wear the revolutionary cap or cockade usually worn only by male citizens. By October 1793 the Jacobins in the Convention had begun to fear the turmoil the Society was causing and banned all women's clubs and societies.

There were other examples of repression of women in 1793. Olympe de Gouges, author of the *Declaration of the Rights of Woman,* opposed the Terror and accused certain Jacobins of corruption. She was tried and guillotined in November 1793. In the same year women were formally excluded from the French army and from attending the galleries of the Convention.

The Republic of Virtue   The pressures of war made it relatively easy to dispense with legal due process. However, the people in the Convention and the Committee of Public Safety also believed they had made a new departure in world history. They had established a republic in which civic virtue rather than aristocratic and monarchical corruption might flourish.

On the way to her execution in 1793, Marie Antoinette was sketched from life by Jacques-Louis David as she passed his window. [Bibliotheque Nationale, Paris, France/Giraudon/Art Resource, N.Y.]

forcing priests to marry. This religious policy roused much opposition and deeply separated the French provinces from the revolutionary government in Paris.

Progress of the Terror   During late 1793 and early 1794 Maximilien Robespierre (1758–1794) emerged as the chief figure on the Committee of Public Safety. The Jacobin Club provided his primary forum and base of power. A shrewd and sensitive politician, he had opposed the war in 1792, believing it to be a measure that might aid the monarchy. He largely depended on the support of the *sans-culottes* of Paris, but continued to dress as he had before the revolution and opposed dechristianization as a political blunder. For him, the republic of virtue meant wholehearted support of republican government and the renunciation of selfish gains from political life. He once told the Convention:

> If the mainspring of popular government in peace-time is virtue, amid revolution it is at the same time virtue and terror: virtue, without which terror is fatal; terror, without which virtue is impotent. Terror is nothing but prompt, severe, inflexible justice; it is therefore an emanation of virtue."[5]

The Reign of Terror manifested itself through a series of revolutionary tribunals established by the Convention during the summer of 1793. The tribunals were to try the enemies of the republic, but the definition of enemy remained uncertain and shifted as the months passed. The first victims were Marie Antoinette, other members of the royal family, and aristocrats, who were executed in October 1793. They were followed by Girondist politicians who had been prominent in the Legislative Assembly.

By early 1794 the Terror had moved to the provinces, where the deputies-on-mission presided over the summary execution of thousands of people who had allegedly supported internal opposition to the revolution. In Paris during the late winter of 1794 Robespierre turned the Terror against republican political figures of the left and right. On March 24 he secured the execution of certain extreme *sans-culottes* leaders. Shortly thereafter he moved against more conservative republicans. Robespierre thus exterminated the leadership from both groups that might have threatened his own position. Finally, on June 10 he secured passage of a law that permitted the revolutionary tribunal to convict suspects without hearing substantial evidence.

In May 1794, at the height of his power, Robespierre, considering the worship of reason too abstract for most citizens, abolished it and established the Cult of the Supreme Being.

Dechristianization   The most dramatic departure of the republic of virtue was an attempt to dechristianize France. In October 1793 the Convention proclaimed a new calendar dating from the first day of the French Republic. There were twelve months of thirty days with names associated with the seasons and climate. Every tenth day, rather than every seventh, was a holiday. Many of the most important events of the next few years became known by their dates on the revolutionary calendar.[4]

In November 1793 the convention decreed the Cathedral of Notre Dame to be a Temple of Reason. The legislature then sent trusted members, known as deputies on mission, into the provinces to enforce dechristianization by closing churches, persecuting clergy and believers, and occasionally

---

[4]From summer to spring, the months on the revolutionary calendar were *Messidor, Thermidor, Fructidor, Vendémiaire, Brumaire, Frimaire, Nivose, Pluviose, Ventose, Germinal, Floréal,* and *Prairial.*

[5]Quoted in Richard T. Bienvenu, *The Ninth of Thermidor: The Fall of Robespierre* (New York: Oxford University Press, 1968), p. 38.

He did not long preside over this new religion. On June 26 he made an ill-tempered speech in the Convention, declaring the existence of a conspiracy among other leaders of the government against him and the revolution. Such accusations against unnamed persons had usually preceded his earlier attacks. On July 27 (the Ninth of Thermidor) members of the Convention, by prearrangement, shouted him down when he rose to speak. Robespierre was arrested that night and executed the next day.

The Reign of Terror soon ended, having claimed as many as forty thousand victims. Most were peasants and *sans-culottes* who had rebelled against the revolutionary government. By the late summer of 1794 those provincial uprisings had been crushed, and the war against foreign enemies was also going well. Those factors, combined with the feeling in Paris that the revolution had consumed enough of its own children, brought the Terror to an end.

The Thermidorian Reaction: End of the Terror and Establishment of the Directory

The tempering of the revolution, called the Thermidorian Reaction, began in July 1794. It destroyed the machinery of terror and set up a new constitutional regime. The influence of generally wealthy middle-class and professional people replaced that of the sans-culottes. Many of the people responsible for the Terror were removed from public life. The Paris Jacobin Club was closed, and provincial Jacobin clubs were forbidden to correspond with each other.

The Thermidorian Reaction also involved still further political reconstruction. In place of the fully democratic constitution of 1793, which had never gone into effect, the Convention issued the Constitution of the Year III. It was a conservative document that provided for a bicameral legislative government heavily favoring property owners. The executive body, consisting of a five-person Directory, was elected by the upper legislative house, known as the Council of Elders.

By the Treaty of Basel of March 1795, the Convention concluded peace with Prussia and Spain. With the war effort succeeding, the Convention severed its ties with the *sans-culottes*. True to their belief in an unregulated economy, the Thermidorians repealed the ceiling on prices. When food riots resulted during the winter of 1794–1795, the Convention put them down to prove that the era of the *sans-culottes journées* had ended. On October 5, 1795 (13 Vendémiaire) the sections (municipal units, each with their own assembly) of Paris rebelled against the Convention. For the first time in the history of the revolution, artillery was turned against the people of Paris. A general named Napoleon Bonaparte (1769–1821) commanded the cannon, and with what he termed a "whiff of grapeshot" dispersed the crowd. Other enemies of the Directory would be more difficult to disperse.

The French Revolution

1789

May 5	Estates General opens at Versailles
June 17	Third Estate declares itself the National Assembly
June 20	National Assembly takes the Tennis Court Oath
July 14	Fall of the Bastille
July	Great Fear spreads in the countryside
August 4	Nobles surrender their feudal rights in a meeting of the National Constituent Assembly
August 27	*Declaration of the Rights of Man and Citizen*
October 5–6	Parisian women march to Versailles and force Louis XVI and his family to return to Paris

1790

July 12	Civil Constitution of the Clergy adopted
July 14	New constitution accepted by the king

1791

June 20–24	Louis XVI and his family attempt to flee France and are stopped at Varennes
August 27	Declaration of Pillnitz
October 1	Legislative Assembly meets

1792

April 20	France declares war on Austria
August 10	Tuileries palace stormed, and Louis XVI takes refuge with the Legislative Assembly
September 2–7	September Massacres
September 21	Convention meets, and monarchy abolished

1793

January 21	Louis XVI executed
February 1	France declares war on Great Britain
March	Counterrevolution breaks out in the Vendée
April 6	Committee of Public Safety formed
June 22	Constitution of 1793 adopted but not put into operation
July	Robespierre enters Committee of Public Safety
August 23	*Levée en masse* proclaimed
September 29	Maximum prices set on food and other commodities
October 16	Queen Marie Antoinette executed
November 10	Cult of Reason proclaimed; revolutionary calendar beginning in September

1794

May 7	Cult of the Supreme Being proclaimed
June 8	Robespierre leads the celebration of Festival of the Supreme Being
July 27	Ninth of Thermidor and fall of Robespierre
July 28	Robespierre executed

1795

August 22	Constitution of the Year III adopted, establishing the Directory

The Napoleonic Era

Napoleon Bonaparte was born in 1769 to a poor family of lesser nobles in Corsica. Because France had annexed Corsica in 1768, he went to French schools, pursued a military career, and in 1785 obtained a commission as a French artillery officer. He strongly favored the revolution and was a fiery Jacobin. In 1793 he played a leading role in recovering the port of Toulon from the British. As a reward the government appointed him a brigadier general. His defense of the new regime on 13 Vendémiaire won him another promotion and a command in Italy. By October 1797 he had crushed the Austrian army in Italy and concluded on his own initiative the Treaty of Campo Formio which took Austria out of the war. Soon all of Italy and Switzerland lay under French domination.

In November 1797 the triumphant Bonaparte returned to Paris to be hailed as a hero and to confront France's only remaining enemy, Britain. Judging it impossible to cross the channel and invade England at that time, he chose to capture Egypt from the Ottoman Empire. He thus hoped to drive the British fleet from the Mediterranean, cut off British communication with India, damage British trade, and threaten the British Empire. But the invasion of Egypt was a failure. Admiral Horatio Nelson (1758–1805) destroyed the French fleet at Aboukir on August 1, 1798. The French army could then neither accomplish anything of importance in the Near East nor get home. The French invasion of Egypt had alarmed Russia, which had its own ambitions in the Near East. The Russians, the Austrians, and the Ottomans joined Britain to form the Second Coalition. In 1799 the Russian and Austrian armies defeated the French in Italy and Switzerland and threatened to invade France.

Having heard of these misfortunes, Napoleon abandoned his army in Egypt and returned to France in October 1799. On November 10, 1799 (19 Brumaire) his troops overthrew the Directory. Bonaparte issued the Constitution of the Year VII in December 1799, establishing himself as the First Consul. The constitution received overwhelming approval from the electorate in a largely rigged plebiscite. The establishment of the Consulate, in effect, closed the revolution in France.

The Consulate in France (1799–1804)

Bonaparte quickly justified the public's confidence by achieving peace with France's enemies. Russia had already left the Second Coalition. A campaign in Italy brought another victory over Austria at Marengo in 1800. The Treaty of Lunéville early in 1801 took Austria out of the war and confirmed the earlier settlement of Campo Formio. Britain was now alone and, in 1802, concluded the Treaty of Amiens, which temporarily brought peace to Europe.

Bonaparte also restored peace and order at home. Although he used generosity, flattery, and bribery to win over some of his enemies, issued a general amnesty, and employed persons from all political factions, Bonaparte was ruthless and efficient in suppressing political opposition. He established a highly centralized administration in which all departments were managed by prefects directly responsible to the central government in Paris. He employed secret police. He stamped out, once and for all, the royalist rebellion in the west and moved against other royalist plots.

Napoleon also alleviated the hostility of French Catholics. In 1801 he concluded a concordat with Pope Pius VII (r. 1800–1823), to the shock and dismay of his anticlerical supporters. The concordat declared that "Roman Catholicism is the religion of the great majority of French citizens." This was merely a statement of fact and fell far short of what the pope had wanted—religious dominance for the Roman Catholic church. Both refractory and constitutional clergy were forced to resign. Their replacements received their spiritual investiture from the pope, but the state named the bishops and paid their salaries and the salary of one priest in each parish. In return, the church gave up its claims to its confiscated property. The clergy had to swear an oath of loyalty to the state, and the Organic Articles of 1802, which were actually distinct from the concordat, established the supremacy of State over Church. Similar laws were applied to the Protestant and Jewish religious communities as well, reducing still further the privileged position of the Catholic church.

In 1802 another plebiscite appointed Napoleon consul for life, and he soon produced still another new constitution, which granted him what amounted to full power. He transformed the basic laws and institutions of France on the basis of both liberal principles derived from the Enlightenment and the early years of the revolution and conservative principles going back to the Old Regime, on the one hand, and the spirit that had triumphed at Thermidor, on the other. This was especially true of the Civil Code of 1804, usually called the Napoleonic Code. However, these laws stopped far short of the full equality advocated by liberal rationalists. Fathers were granted extensive control over their children and men over their wives. Labor unions were still forbidden, and the rights of workers were inferior to those of their employers.

In 1804 Bonaparte seized on a bomb attack on his life to make himself emperor. He argued that the establishment of a dynasty would make the new regime secure and make further attempts on his life useless. Still another new constitution, ratified by a plebiscite, was promulgated, designating Napoleon Emperor of the French instead of First Consul of the Republic. Napoleon summoned the pope to Notre Dame to take part in the coronation. But at the last minute the pope agreed that Napoleon should actually crown himself. The emperor had no intention of allowing anyone to think that

Napoleon Describes Conditions Leading to the Consulate

In late 1799 various political groups in France became convinced that the constitution that had established the Directory could not allow Frane to achieve military victory. They also feared domestic unrest and new outbreaks of the radicalism that had characterized the French Revolution during the mid-1790s. With the aid of such groups Napoleon Bonaparte seized power in Paris in November, 1799. Thereafter, under various political arrangements, he governed France until 1814. He later gave his own version of the situation that brought him to power.

What are the factors that Napoleon outlines as having created a situation in which the government of France required change? In his narration how does he justify the use of military force? How does he portray himself as a savior of political order and liberty?

On my return to Paris I found division among all authorities, and agreement upon only one point, namely, that the Constitution was half destroyed and was unable to save liberty.

All parties came to me, confided to me their designs, disclosed their secrets, and requested my support; I refused to be the man of a party.

The Council of Elders summoned me; I answered its appeal. A plan of general restoration had been devised by men whom the nation has been accustomed to regard as defenders of liberty, equality, and property; this plan required an examination, calm, free, exempt from all influence and all fear. Accordingly, the Council of Elders resolved upon the removal of the Legislative Body to Saint-Cloud; it gave me the responsibility of disposing the

force necessary for its independence. I believe it my duty to my fellow citizens, to the soldiers perishing in our armies, to the national glory acquired at the cost of their blood, to accept the command. . . .

I presented myself to the Council of Five Hundred, alone, unarmed, my head uncovered, just as the Elders had received and applauded me; I came to remind the majority of its wishes, and to assure it of its power.

The stilettos which menaced the deputies were instantly raised against their liberator; twenty assassins threw themselves upon me and aimed at my breast. The grenadiers of the Legislative Body whom I had left at the door of the hall ran forward, placed themselves between the assassins and myself. One of these brave grenadiers had his clothes pieced by a stiletto. They bore me out.

At the same moment cries of "Outlaw" were raised against the defender of the law. It was the fierce cry of assassins against the power destined to repress them.

They crowded around the president, uttering threats, arms in their hands; they commanded him to outlaw me. I was informed of this; I ordered him to be rescued from their fury, and six grenadiers of the Legislative Body secured him. Immediately afterwards some grenadiers of the Legislative Body charged into the hall and cleared it.

The factions, intimidated, dispersed and fled. . . .

Frenchmen, you will doubtless recognize in this conduct the zeal of a soldier of liberty, a citizen devoted to the Republic. Conservative, tutelary, and liberal ideas have been restored to their rights through the dispersal of the rebels who oppressed the Councils. . . .

From J. H. Stuart, *A Documentary Survey of the French Revolution* (New York: Macmillan, 1951), pp. 763–765.

---

his power and authority depended on the approval of the church. Henceforth he was called Napoleon I.

Napoleon's Empire (1804–1814)

Between his coronation as emperor and his final defeat at Waterloo (1815), Napoleon conquered most of Europe in military campaigns that astonished the world. France's victories changed the map of Europe, ended the old regime and its feudal trappings in western Europe, and forced the eastern European states to reorganize themselves to resist Napoleon's armies. Everywhere, Napoleon's advance unleashed the powerful force of nationalism.

The Treaty of Amiens with Britain (1802) could not last. Napoleon intervened militarily to extend French influence in Europe. The British issued an ultimatum. When Napo-

leon ignored it, Britain declared war in May 1803. William Pitt the Younger (1759–1806) returned to office as prime minister in 1804 and began to construct the Third Coalition. By August 1805 he had persuaded Russia and Austria to move once again against French aggression. On October 21, 1805, Lord Nelson destroyed the combined French and Spanish fleets at the Battle of Trafalgar just off the Spanish coast. Nelson was killed, but the British lost no ships. Trafalgar put an end to the French hope of invading Britain and guaranteed British control of the sea.

On land, however, the story was different. Between mid-October 1805 and July 1807 Napoleon had defeated the armies of Austria, Prussia, and Russia in stunning victories. The most famous of the victories was that of Austerlitz on December 2, 1805. Through these campaigns he forced

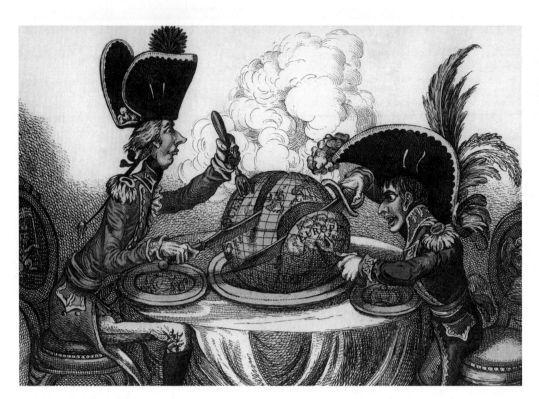

In this early-nineteenth-century cartoon England, personified by a caricature of William Pitt, and France, personified by a caricature of Napoleon, are carving out their areas of interest around the globe. [Cartoon by Gillray/Corbis-Bettmann]

Austria to withdraw from northern Italy, where Napoleon himself was recognized as king. He replaced the ancient Holy Roman Empire with the Confederation of the Rhine. On July 7, 1807, Napoleon and Emperor Alexander I (r. 1800–1825) of Russia concluded the Treaty of Tilsit, which confirmed France's gains in central and eastern Europe. Prussia and Russia became allies of Napoleon.

Napoleon knew that he could not be genuinely secure until he had defeated Britain. Unable to compete with the British navy, he adopted economic warfare to cut off all British trade with the European continent. He thus hoped to cripple British commercial and financial power, cause domestic unrest and revolution, and drive the British from the war. On November 21, 1806, he had issued the Berlin Decrees forbidding his allies to import British goods. The Milan Decree of 1807 attempted to halt neutral nations, such as the United States, from trading with Britain. Nonetheless, the British economy survived because of its access to the growing markets of North and South America and the eastern Mediterranean. Known as the Continental System, Napoleon's policies harmed the European economies and roused resentment against France.

The Wars of Liberation   In 1807, as part of the strategy of crippling the British economy, a French army invaded the Iberian Peninsula to force Portugal to abandon its traditional alliance with Britain. The army stayed in Spain to protect lines of supply and communication. When a revolt broke out in Madrid in 1808, Napoleon deposed the Bourbons and placed his brother Joseph (1768–1844) on the Spanish throne. Attacks on the privileges of the church increased public outrage.

In Spain Napoleon faced a kind of warfare not vulnerable to his usual tactics. Guerrilla bands cut communications, killed stragglers, destroyed isolated units, and then disappeared. The British landed an army under Sir Arthur Wellesley (1769–1852), later the duke of Wellington, to support the Spanish insurgents. Thus began the long peninsular campaign that would drain French strength and play a critical role in Napoleon's eventual defeat.

Encouraged by the French troubles in Spain, the Austrians renewed the war in 1809. The French army nonetheless marched swiftly into Austria and won the battle of Wagram. The resulting peace deprived Austria of much territory and 3.5 million subjects. Another spoil of victory was the Archduchess Marie Louise (1791–1847), Francis I's eighteen-year-old daughter, whom Napoleon married for dynastic purposes after divorcing his wife Josephine de Beauharnais (1763–1814), who had borne him no children.

The Franco-Russian alliance concluded at Tilsit was faltering. The Continental System had harmed the Russian economy. Napoleon's organization of a Polish state, the Grand Duchy of Warsaw, on the Russian doorstep and its enlargement in 1809 after the battle of Wagram angered Alexander I. Napoleon's annexation of Holland in violation of the Treaty of Tilsit, his recognition of the French Marshal Bernadotte as the future king of Sweden (r. 1818–1844), and his marriage to an Austrian princess further disturbed the tsar. At the end of

1810 Russia withdrew from the Continental System and began to prepare for war (see Map 25–2).

Determined to stifle the Russian military threat, Napoleon amassed an army of over 600,000 men, including over 400,000 non-French soldiers drawn from his empire and allies. He intended the usual short campaign crowned by a decisive battle, but the Russians retreated before his advance. His vast superiority in numbers—the Russians had only about 160,000 troops—made it foolish for them to risk a battle. Instead, they destroyed all food and supplies as they retreated. The so-called Grand Army of Napoleon could not live off the country, and Russia was too vast for supply lines. Terrible rains, fierce heat, shortages of food and water, and the courage of the Russian rear guard eroded the morale of Napoleon's army.

In September 1812 Russian public opinion forced the army to stand and fight. At Borodino, not far west of Moscow, the bloodiest battle of the Napoleonic era cost the French 30,000 casualties and the Russians almost twice as many. Yet the Russian army was not destroyed. Napoleon had won nothing substantial. By October, after occupying Moscow, the Grand Army was forced to retreat. By December Napoleon realized that the Russian fiasco would encourage plots against him at home. He returned to Paris, leaving the remnants of his army to struggle westward. Perhaps only as many as 100,000 lived to tell the tale of their terrible ordeal. Even as the news of the disaster reached the west, the total defeat of Napoleon was far from certain. He was able to suppress his opponents in Paris and raise another 350,000 men.

In 1813 patriotic pressure and national ambition brought together the last and most powerful coalition against Napoleon. Financed by the British, the Russians drove westward to be joined by Prussia and then Austria. From the west Wellington marched his peninsular army into France. Napoleon waged a skillful campaign in central Europe and defeated the allies at Dresden. In October, however, he met decisive defeat at Leipzig from the combined armies of his enemies, in what the Germans called the Battle of the Nations. At the end of March 1814 the allied army marched into Paris. Napoleon abdicated and went into exile on the island of Elba off the coast of northern Italy.

The Congress of Vienna and the European Settlement

Once Napoleon was removed, the allies began to pursue their own separate ambitions. The key person in achieving eventual agreement among the allies was Robert Stewart, Viscount Castlereagh (1769–1822), the British foreign secretary. Even before the victorious armies had entered Paris, he achieved the Treaty of Chaumont on March 9, 1814, providing for the restoration of the Bourbons to the French throne and the contraction of France to its 1792 frontiers. Even more important, Britain, Austria, Russia, and Prussia formed a Quadruple Alliance for twenty years to preserve whatever settlement they later agreed on. Remaining problems—and there were many—and final details were left for a conference to be held at Vienna.

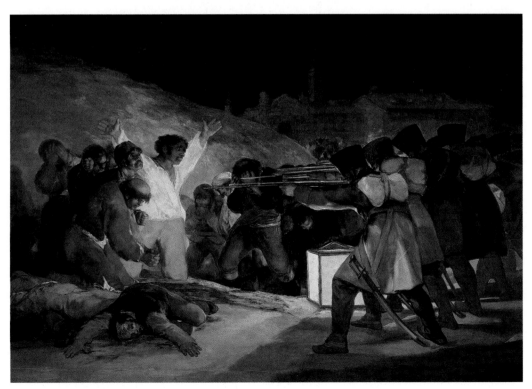

The Spanish artist Francisco Goya (1746-1828) was horrified by the atrocities perpetrated by both sides during the guerrilla warfare that followed Napoleon's occupation of Spain. This painting, entitled *The Third of May, 1808,* depicts French troops executing Spanish insurgents. Events like this roused popular resistance in Spain. The British soon began to assist the insurgency. [Erich Lessing/Art Resource, N.Y.]

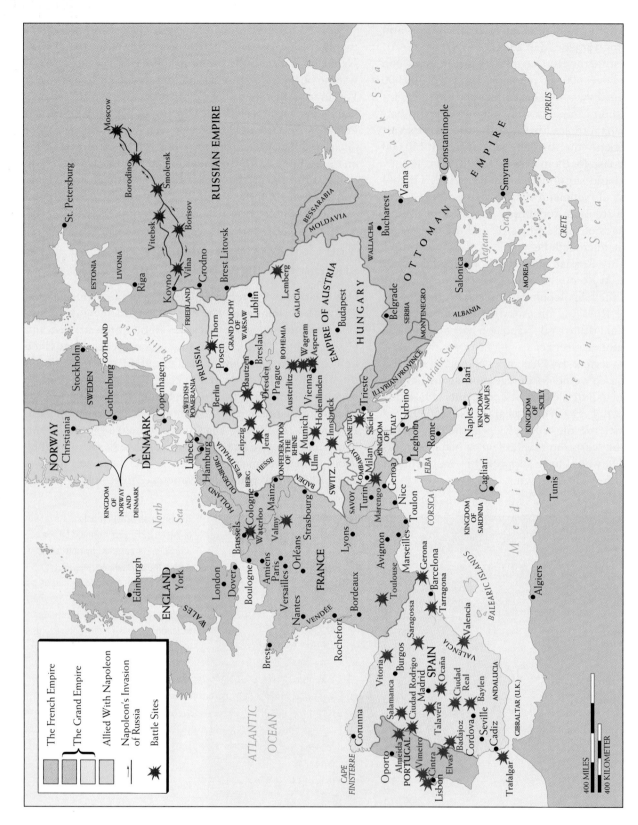

Map 25-2 Napoleonic Europe in late 1812. By mid-1812 the areas shown in peach were incorporated into France, and most of the rest of Europe was directly controlled by or allied with Napoleon. But Russia had withdrawn from the failing Continental System, and the decline of Napoleon was about to begin.

Legend:
- The French Empire
- The Grand Empire
- Allied With Napoleon
- Napoleon's Invasion of Russia
- Battle Sites

400 MILES
400 KILOMETER

Map 25–3 Europe 1815, after the Congress of Vienna. The Congress of Vienna achieved the post-Napoleonic territorial adjustments shown on the map. The most notable arrangements dealt with areas along France's borders (the Netherlands, Prussia, Switzerland, and Piedmont) and in Poland and northern Italy.

The Congress of Vienna assembled in September 1814 but did not conclude its work until November 1815. The four great powers conducted the important work of the conference. The victors agreed that no single state should be allowed to dominate Europe. They constructed a series of states to serve as barriers to any new French expansion (see Map 25–3). Thus, they established the kingdom of the Netherlands, including Belgium in the north, and added Genoa to Piedmont in the south. Prussia, whose power was increased by acquisitions in eastern Europe, was given important new territories in the west to deter French aggression along the Rhine River. Austria was given full control of northern Italy to prevent a repetition of Napoleon's con-

quests there. Most of Napoleon's arrangements in the rest of Germany were left untouched. The Holy Roman Empire was not revived. The Congress established the rule of legitimate monarchs and rejected any hint of the republican and democratic politics that had flowed from the French Revolution.

However, the settlement of eastern Europe sharply divided the victors. Alexander I wanted Russia to govern all of Poland. Prussia was willing if it received all of Saxony. Austria, however, refused to surrender its share of Poland or to see Prussian power grow and Russia penetrate deeper into central Europe. The Polish-Saxon question enabled France to rejoin the great powers. The French Foreign Minister

Talleyrand (1754–1838) suggested that the weight of France, added to that of Britain and Austria, might bring Alexander to his senses. When news of a secret treaty among the three leaked out, the tsar agreed to become ruler of a smaller Poland, and Frederick William III of Prussia (r. 1797–1840) agreed to settle for part of Saxony. Thereafter, France was included as a fifth great power in all deliberations.

Napoleon's escape from Elba on March 1, 1815, further restored unity among the victors. He promised a liberal constitution and a peaceful foreign policy, but the allies declared him an outlaw (a new device under international law) and sent their armies to crush him. Wellington, with the crucial help of the Prussians, defeated Napoleon at Waterloo in Belgium on June 18, 1815. Napoleon again abdicated and was exiled to Saint Helena, a tiny Atlantic island off the coast of Africa, where he died in 1821.

The Hundred Days, as the period of Napoleons' return is called, made the peace settlement somewhat harsher for France, but the other main outlines of the Vienna Settlement remained in place. The Quadruple Alliance between England, Austria, Prussia, and Russia was renewed on November 20, 1815. Henceforth, it was as much a coalition for the maintenance of peace as for the pursuit of victory over France. A coalition with such a purpose had not previously existed in European intentional relations. Its existence and later op-eration represented an important new departure in European affairs. Unlike the situation in the eighteenth century, certain European powers were determined to prevent the outbreak of future war. The statesmen at Vienna, unlike their eighteenth-century counterparts, had seen the armies of the French Revolution change major frontiers of the European states and overturn the political and social order of much of the continent. They had seen unprecedented military destruction. They were determined to prevent a recurrence of those upheavals. The shared purpose of the diplomats was to establish a framework for future stability, not to punish a defeated France. The great powers through the Vienna Settlement framed international relations in such a manner that the major powers would respect that settlement and not as in the eighteenth century use military force to change it.

The Congress of Vienna succeeded in preventing future French aggression and in arranging an acceptable settlement for Europe that produced a long-lasting peace. Its work has been criticized for failing to recognize and provide for the great forces that would stir the nineteenth century—nationalism and democracy—but such criticism is inappropriate. The settlement, like all such agreements, was aimed at solving past ills, and in that it succeeded. The Vienna settlement remained essentially intact for almost half a century and spared Europe a general war until 1914.

Napoleonic Europe	
1797	Napoleon concludes Treaty of Campo Formio
1798	Nelson defeats French navy at Abukir
1799	Consulate established
1801	Concordat between France and papacy
1802	Treaty of Amiens
1803	War renewed between France and Britain
1804	Execution of duke of Enghien; Napoleonic Civil Code issued; Napoleon crowned emperor
1805	Nelson defeats French fleet at Trafalgar (October 21); Austerlitz (December 2)
1806	Continental System established by Berlin Decrees
1807	Treaty of Tilsit
1808	Beginning of Spanish resistance to Napoleonic domination
1809	Wagram; Napoleon marries Archduchess Marie Louise of Austria
1812	Invasion of Russia
1813	Leipzig (Battle of the Nations)
1814	Treaty of Chaumont (March) establishes Quadruple Alliance; Congress of Vienna convenes (September)
1815	Napoleon returns from Elba (March 1); Waterloo (June 18); Holy Alliance formed (September 26); Quadruple Alliance renewed (November 20)
1821	Napoleon dies on Saint Helena

Wars of Independence in Latin America

The wars of the French Revolution, particularly those of Napoleon, sparked movements for independence throughout Latin America. Between 1804 and 1824 France was driven from Haiti, Portugal lost control of Brazil, and Spain was forced to withdraw from all of its American empire except for Cuba and Puerto Rico. Three centuries of Iberian colonial government over the South American continent ended.

Eighteenth-Century Developments

Spain was one of the defeated powers in 1763. Charles III (r. 1759–1788) and the government circles in Spain were convinced that the American colonial system had to be changed. After 1765 the monarch abolished the monopolies of Seville and Cádiz and permitted other Spanish commercial centers to trade with America. He also opened more South American and Caribbean ports to trade and authorized commerce between American ports. In 1776 he organized a fourth viceroyalty in the region of the Río de la Plata, which included much of present-day Argentina, Uruguay, Paraguay, and Bolivia. Charles III also attempted to make tax collection more efficient and to eliminate bureaucratic corruption. To achieve those ends, he introduced into the empire *intendents*, who were royal bureaucrats loyal only to the crown.

These reforms, which took place during the same years as the unsuccessful British effort to reorganize its authority in its North American colonies, largely succeeded in returning the empire to direct Spanish control. Many *peninsulares*, whites born in Spain, went to the New World to fill new posts at the expense of Creoles, whites born in America. Expanding trade likewise brought more Spanish merchants to Latin America. The economy retained its export orientation, and economic life continued to be organized for the benefit of Spain. There matters stood until the early nineteenth century.

First Movements Toward Independence

Haiti achieved independence from France in 1804, following a slave revolt that commenced in 1794 led by Toussaint L'Ouverture (1746–1803) and Jean-Jacques Dessalines (c. 1756–1806). Haiti's revolution involved the popular uprising of a repressed social group, which proved to be the great exception in the Latin American drive for liberty from European masters. Generally speaking, on the South American continent it was the Creole elite—merchants, landowners, and professional people—who led the movements against Spain and Portugal. Few Indians, blacks, mestizos, mulattos, or slaves became involved or benefited from the end of Iberian rule. Indeed, the Haitian slave revolt haunted the Creoles, as did an Indian revolt in the Andes in 1780 and 1781. The Creoles were determined that political independence from Spain and Portugal should not cause social disruption or the loss of their social and economic privileges. In this respect the Creole revolutionaries were not unlike American revolutionaries in the southern colonies who wanted to reject British rule but keep their slaves, or French revolutionaries who wanted to depose the king but not extend liberty to the French working class.

Creole complaints resembled those of the American colonists against Great Britain. Latin American merchants wanted to trade more freely within the region and with North American and European markets. They wanted commercial regulations that would benefit them rather than Spain.

Creoles also feared that Spanish imperial regulations might affect landholdings, access to commissions in the army, local government policy, and the treatment of slaves and Indians in ways that would harm their interests. They also deeply resented Spanish policies favoring *peninsulares* for political patronage, including appointments in the colonial government, church, and army. They believed the *peninsulares* improperly secured all the best positions. Seen in this light, the royal patronage system represented another device with which Spain extracted wealth and income from America for its own people rather than its colonial subjects.

Toussaint L'Ouverture (1743–1803) began the revolt that led to Haitian independence in 1804. [Historical Pictures Collection/Stock Montage, Inc.]

From the 1790s onward Spain suffered military reverses in the wars associated with the French Revolution and Napoleon, and the commercial situation turned sharply against the inhabitants of the Spanish empire. The military pressures led the Spanish monarchy into a desperate search for new revenues, including increased taxation and the confiscation of property in the American empire. The policies harmed the economic life of the Creole elite.

Creole leaders had read the Enlightenment *philosophes* and regarded their reforms as potentially beneficial to the region. They were also well aware of the events and the political philosophy of the American Revolution. But something more than reform programs and revolutionary example was required to transform Creole discontent into revolt against the Spanish government. That transforming event occurred in Europe when Napoleon toppled the Portuguese monarchy in 1807 and the Spanish government in 1808 and then placed his own brother on the thrones of both countries. The Portuguese royal family fled to Brazil and established its government there. But the Bourbon monarchy of Spain seemed wholly vanquished.

The Creole elite feared that a liberal Napoleonic monarchy in Spain would impose reforms in Latin America harmful to their economic and social interests and would drain the region of the wealth and resources needed for Napoleon's wars. To protect their interests, various Creole juntas, or political committees, between 1808 and 1810 claimed the right to govern different regions of Latin America. After the establishment of these local juntas, the Spanish would not again directly govern the continent and after ten years of politically and economically exhausting warfare were to recognize the permanence of Latin American independence.

San Martín in Río de la Plata

The first region to assert its independence was the Río de la Plata, or modern Argentina. As early as 1806 the citizens of Buenos Aires had fought off a British invasion and thus had learned that they could look to themselves rather than Spain for effective political and military action. In 1810 the junta in Buenos Aires not only thrust off Spanish authority but also sent liberation forces against Paraguay and Uruguay. The armies were defeated, but Spain nonetheless soon lost control in the two areas. Paraguay asserted its own independence. Uruguay was eventually absorbed by Brazil.

Undiscouraged by these early defeats, the Buenos Aires government remained determined to liberate Peru, the greatest stronghold of royalist power and loyalty on the continent. By 1814 José de San Martín (1778–1850), the leading general of the Río de la Plata forces, had organized and led a disciplined army in a daring march over the Andes Mountains. By early 1817 he had occupied Santiago in Chile, and established the Chilean independence leader Bernardo O'Higgins (1778–1842) as supreme dictator. San Martín then constructed a naval force that in 1820 transported his army to Peru. The next year, he drove royalist forces from Lima and assumed the title of Protector of Peru (Map 25–4).

Simón Bolívar's Liberation of Venezuela

While San Martín had been liberating the southern portion of the continent, Simón Bolívar (1783–1830) had been pursuing a similar task in the north. In 1810, as a firm advocate of both independence and republicanism, Bolívar had helped organize a liberating junta in Caracas, Venezuela. Between 1811 and 1814 civil war broke out throughout Venezuela as both royalists, on the one hand, and slaves and *llaneros* (Venezuelan cowboys), on the other, challenged the authority of the republican government. Bolívar had to go into exile. In 1816, with help from Haiti, he launched a new invasion against Venezuela. He first captured Bogotá, capital of New Granada (including modern Colombia, Bolivia, and Ecuador), as a base for attacking Venezuela. By the summer of 1821 his forces had captured Caracas, and he had been named president.

A year later, in July 1822, the armies of Bolívar and San Martín joined to liberate Quito. At a famous meeting in Guayaquil the two leaders sharply disagreed about the future political structure of Latin America. San Martín believed that monarchies were required; Bolívar maintained his republicanism. Not long thereafter San Martín quietly retired from public life and went into exile in Europe. Meanwhile, Bolívar purposefully allowed the political situation in Peru to fall into confusion, and in 1823 he sent troops to establish his control. On December 9, 1824, at the battle of Ayacucho, the Spanish royalist forces suffered a major defeat at the hands of the liberating army. The battle marked the conclusion of Spain's effort to retain its American empire.

Independence in New Spain

The drive for independence in New Spain, which included present-day Mexico as well as Texas, California, and the rest of the southwestern United States, clearly illustrates the socially conservative outcome of the Latin American colonial revolutions. As elsewhere, a local governing junta was orga-

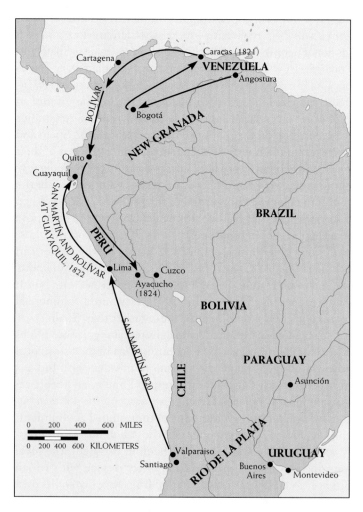

Map 25–4 The Independence Campaigns of San Martín and Bolívar.

Bolívar Denounces Spanish Rule in Latin America

In September 1815 Simón Bolívar published a long statement, often called The Jamaica Letter, in which he explained the political and economic difficulties under which the Creole elite of the Spanish Empire had lived. He defined Americans as referring to those persons in Latin America who were neither Indian nor European by birth. He also implicitly excluded black slaves. Consequently his attack on Spain was voiced on behalf of the white population of the South American continent who had been born there and who demanded rights of political participation and economic freedom.

Why does Bolívar describe the Creole elite as having lived in a permanent political infancy? What are the economic disadvantages that he describes, and why had those become more burdensome in the half century before he wrote this letter? How had Spanish economic regulation prevented the Creole elite from achieving positions of responsibility in Latin America? How does this document compare with others concerned with movements of independence and nationalism? See "The Stamp Act Congress Addresses George III" (earlier in this chapter), "Mazzini Defines Nationality" (Chapter 26), "The Pan-Slavic Congress Calls for the Liberation of Slavic Nationalities" (Chapter 26), "William Gladstone Pleads for Irish Home Rule" (Chapter 27), "Herzl Calls for the Establishment of a Jewish State" (Chapter 29), and "Gandhi on Passive Resistance and Swaraj" (Chapter 31).

The role of the inhabitants of the American hemisphere has for centuries been purely passive. Politically they were non-existent. We are still in a position lower than slavery, and therefore it is more difficult for us to rise to the enjoyment of freedom. . . . We have been harassed by a conduct which has not only deprived us of our rights but has kept us in a sort of permanent infancy with regard to public affairs. If we could at least have managed our domestic affairs and our internal administration, we could have acquainted ourselves with the processes and mechanics of public affairs. . . .

Americans today, and perhaps to a greater extent than ever before, who live within the Spanish system occupy a position in society no better than that of serfs destined for labor, or at best they have no more status than that of mere consumers. Yet even this status is surrounded with galling restrictions, such as being forbidden to grow European crops, or to store products which are royal monopolies, or to establish factories of a type the [Spanish] Peninsula itself does not possess. To this add the exclusive trading privileges, even in articles of prime necessity, and the barriers between American provinces, designed to prevent all exchange of trade, traffic, and understanding. In short, do you wish to know what our future held?—simply the cultivation of the fields of indigo, grain, coffee, sugar cane, cacao, and cotton; cattle raising on the broad plains; hunting wild game in the jungles; digging in the earth to mine its gold—but even these limitations could never satisfy the greed of Spain.

So negative was our existence that I can find nothing comparable in any other civilized society, examine as I may the entire history of time and the politics of all nations. Is it not an outrage and a violation of human rights to expect a land so splendidly endowed, so vast, rich, and populous, to remain merely passive?

As I have just explained, we were cut off and, as it were, removed from the world in relation to the science of government and administration of the state. We were never viceroys or governors, save in the rarest of instances; seldom archbishops and bishops; diplomats never; as military men, only subordinates; as nobles, without royal privileges. In brief, we were neither magistrates nor financiers and seldom merchants. . . .

From Harold A. Bierck, Jr., ed., *Selected Writings of Bolívar,* Vol. 1. Copyright © 1951 The Colonial Press, pp. 110–112.

---

nized. But before it had undertaken any significant measures, a Creole priest, Miguel Hidalgo y Costilla (1753–1811), issued a call for rebellion to the Indians in his parish. They and other repressed groups of black and mestizo urban and rural workers responded. Father Hidalgo set forth a program of social change, including hints of land reform. Soon he stood at the head of a rather unorganized group of 80,000 followers and marched on Mexico City. Both Hidalgo's forces and the royalist army that opposed them committed numerous atrocities. In July 1811 he was captured and executed. Leadership of his movement then fell to José María Morelos y Pavón (1765–1815), a mestizo priest. Far more radical than Hidalgo, he called for an end to forced labor and for substantial land reforms. He was executed in 1815, ending five years of popular uprising.

In 1820, however, the conservative political groups in Mexico, both Creole and Spanish, found their recently achieved security challenged from an unexpected source. A revolution in Spain had forced Ferdinand VII (r. 1813–1833) to accept a liberal constitution. Conservative Mexicans feared that the new liberal monarchy would attempt to impose liberal reforms on Mexico. Therefore, for the most conservative of reasons, they rallied to a former royalist general, Agustín de Iturbide (1783–1824), who in 1821 declared Mexico independent of Spain. Shortly thereafter, Iturbide was declared emperor. His own regime did not last long, but an independent Mexico,

Simón Bolívar was the liberator of much of Latin America. He inclined toward a policy of political liberalism. [Hulton/Corbis-Bettmann]

respects long overdue because Brazil was far larger and more prosperous than Portugal itself. Then in 1820 a revolution occurred in Portugal, and its leaders demanded Joao's return to Lisbon. They also demanded the return of Brazil to colonial status. Joao, who had become Joao VI in 1816, returned to Portugal but left his son Pedro (r. 1822–1831) as regent in Brazil, encouraging him to be sympathetic to the political aspirations of the Brazilians. In September 1822 Pedro embraced Brazilian independence against the recolonializing efforts of Portugal. By the end of the year he had become emperor of an independent Brazil, which remained a monarchy until 1889. Thus in contrast to virtually all other nations of Latin America, Brazil achieved independence in a way that left no real dispute as to where the center of political authority lay.

Another factor aided the peaceful transition to independence in Brazil. The political and social elite there were determined to preserve slavery against the forces (to be discussed in the next section) that were challenging that in-

governed by persons determined to resist any significant social reform, had been created.

Great Britain was highly sympathetic to the independence movements in the different regions of Latin America. By breaking the hold of the Spanish Empire the movement toward independence opened the markets of the continent to British trade and investment. Consequently in 1823 Great Britain supported the American Monroe Doctrine that prohibited further colonization and intervention by European powers in America. Britain soon recognized the Spanish colonies as independent states. Through the rest of the century, British commercial interests dominated Latin America.

Brazilian Independence

Brazilian independence, in contrast to that of Spanish Latin America, came relatively simply and peacefully. As already noted, the Portuguese royal family, along with several thousand government officials and members of the court, took refuge in Brazil in 1807. Their arrival immediately transformed Rio de Janeiro into a court city. The prince regent Joao (r. 1816–1826) addressed many of the local complaints, equivalent to those of the Spanish Creoles. In 1815 he made Brazil a kingdom, which meant that it was no longer to be regarded merely as a colony of Portugal. This transformation was in many

---

The Wars of Latin American Independence

1759–1788	Charles III of Spain carries out imperial reforms
1776	Organization of Viceroyalty of Río de la Plata
1780–1781	Revolt of Indians in the Andes
1794	Toussaint L'Ouverture leads slave revolt in Haiti
1804	Independence of Haiti
1807	Portuguese royal family flees to Brazil
1808	Spanish monarchy falls to Napoleon
1808–1810	Creole Committees organized to govern much of Latin America
1810	Buenos Aires junta sends forces to liberate Paraguay and Uruguay
1811	Miguel Hidalgo y Costilla leads rebellion in New Spain and is executed
1811–1815	José María Morelos y Pavón leads rebellion in New Spain and is executed
1814	San Martín organizes army
1815	Brazil declared a kingdom
1816	Bolívar invades Venezuela
1817	San Martín occupies Santiago, Chile
1820	Revolution in Spain
1821	
February 24	New Spain declares independence
June 29	Bolívar captures Caracas, Venezuela
July 28	San Martín liberates Peru
1822	
July 26–27	San Martín and Bolívar quarrel at Guayaquil; San Martín goes into exile in Europe
September 7	Dom Pedro declares Brazilian independence
1824	Battle of Ayacucho—final Spanish defeat

---

stitution. The Wars of Independence elsewhere had led to the abolition of slavery or moved the independent states closer to abolition. Any attempt to gain independence from Portugal through warfare might have caused social as well as political turmoil that would open the slavery question.

Toward the Abolition of Slavery in the Transatlantic Economy

In 1750 almost no one seriously questioned the institution of slavery; by 1888 slavery no longer existed in the transatlantic economy. This vast transformation of economic and social life occurred as the result of an international effort, first to abolish the slave trade and then to abolish the institution of slavery itself. At no previous time in world history had a society actually attempted to abolish slavery. Its eventual abolition in the transatlantic world stands as one of the most permanent achievements of the forces unleashed by the eighteenth-century Enlightenment and Revolutions.

The eighteenth-century crusade against slavery in the plantation economy that stretched from Maryland south to Brazil (See Chapter 19) originated among writers of the Enlightenment and religious critics of slavery. Although some authors associated with the Enlightenment, including John Locke, were reluctant to question slavery or even defended it, the general Enlightenment rhetoric of equality stood in sharp contrast to the radical inequality of slavery. Montesquieu satirized slavery in *The Spirit of the Laws*. Adam Smith's emphasis in *The Wealth of Nations* on free labor and the efficiency of free markets undermined economic defenses of slavery. Much eighteenth-century literature idealized primitive peoples living in cultures very different from those of Europe and portrayed them as embodying a lost human virtue. This literature allowed some Europeans to look upon African slaves in the Americas as having been betrayed and robbed of an original innocence. In such a climate, slavery, once considered the natural and deserved result of some deficiency in slaves themselves, grew to be regarded as undeserved and unacceptable. Other Enlightenment ethical thinking led reformers to believe that by working against slavery, for virtually the first time defined as an unmitigated evil, they would realize their own highest moral character.

The initial religious protest against slavery originated among English Quakers, a radical Protestant religious group founded by George Fox in the seventeenth century. By the early eighteenth century it had solidified itself into a small but relatively wealthy sect in England. Members of Quaker congregations at that time actually owned slaves in the West Indies and participated in the transatlantic slave trade. During the Seven Years' War (1756–1763), however, many Quakers experienced economic hardship. Furthermore, the war created other difficulties for the English population as a whole. Certain Quakers decided that the presence of the evil of slavery in the world explained these troubles. They then sought to remove this evil from their own lives and from the lives of their congregations by taking action against the whole system of slavery that characterized the transatlantic economy.

Just as the slave system was a transatlantic affair, so was the crusade against it. There were Quaker communities in America, and soon Quakers in both Philadelphia and England wrote and organized against the institution. By the earliest stages of the American Revolution small groups of reformers, usually spearheaded by Quakers, had established an antislavery network. The turmoil of the American Revolution and the founding of the American republic gave these groups the occasion for some of their earliest successes. Emancipation gradually, but nonetheless steadily, spread among the northern states. In 1787 the Continental Congress forbade slavery in the newly organized Northwest Territory north of the Ohio River.

Despite these American developments, Great Britain became and remained the center for the antislavery movement. In 1772 a decision by the chief justice affirmed that slaves brought into Great Britain could not forcibly be removed. During the early 1780s the antislavery reformers in Great Britain decided to work toward ending the slave trade rather than the institution of slavery itself. The horrors of the slave trade caught the public's attention in 1783 when the captain of the slave ship *Zong* threw more than 130 slaves overboard in order to collect insurance. Soon after, groups from the Church of England and the English Quakers formed the Society for the Abolition of the Slave Trade. The most famous of the new leaders was William Wilberforce, who, each year for the rest of his life, introduced a bill to end the slave trade.

For the reformers, attacking the trade rather than the institution appeared a less radical and more achievable reform. To many, the slave trade appeared a more obvious crime than the holding of slaves, which seemed a more passive act. Furthermore, attacking slavery itself involved serious issues of property rights, which might alienate potential supporters of the abolition of the slave trade. The antislavery groups also believed that if the trade were ended, planters would have to treat their remaining slaves more humanely.

While the British reformers worked for the abolition of the slave trade, slaves themselves in certain areas took matters into their own hands. Indeed, the largest emancipation of slaves to occur in the eighteenth century came on the island of Saint Domingue (Haiti), France's wealthiest colony, as a result of the slave revolt of 1794 led by Toussaint L'Ouverture and Jean-Jacques Dessalines (see p. 709). The revolt in Haiti and Haiti's eventual independence in 1804 stood as a warning

After 1807 the British Royal Navy patrolled the West African coast attempting to intercept slave-trading ships. In 1846 the British ship HMS *Albatross* captured a Spanish slave ship, the *Albanoz* and freed the slaves. A British officer depicted the appalling conditions in the slavehold in this watercolor. [The Granger Collection, N.Y.]

to slave owners throughout the West Indies. Other slave revolts occurred, such as those in Virginia led by Gabriel Prosser in 1800 and by Nat Turner in 1831, in South Carolina led by Denmark Vesey in 1822, in British-controlled Demarra in 1823 and 1824, and in Jamaica in 1831. Each of these was brutally suppressed.

For complicated economic reasons some British West Indies planters began to consider abolition of the slave trade useful to their interests. Within the West Indies themselves the planters were experiencing soil exhaustion and competition from newly tilled islands opened for sugar cultivation. Some older plantations were being abandoned while others operated with low profitability. With the new islands there was a glut of sugar on the market, and as a consequence the price was falling. Under these conditions some British West Indies planters, for reasons that had nothing to do with religion or enlightened humanitarianism, began to favor curtailing the slave trade. Without new slaves competing French planters would lack the labor they needed to exploit their islands.

Then, during the Napoleonic Wars, the British captured a number of the valuable French islands. In 1805 to protect the planters of the older British West Indies island, the British cabinet forbade the importation of slaves into the newly acquired French islands. By 1807 the abolition sentiment was strong enough for Parliament to pass Wilberforce's often proposed measure prohibiting slave trading from any British port.

Thereafter the suppression of this trade became one of the fundamental pillars of nineteenth-century British foreign policy. The British navy maintained a squadron of ships around the coast of West Africa to halt slave traders. Although the French and Americans also patrolled the West African coast, neither was deeply committed to ending the slave trade. Nonetheless, in 1824 the American Congress had made slave trading a capital offense.

Leaders of the Latin American wars of independence, disposed by Enlightenment ideas to disapprove of slavery, had sought the support of slaves by promises of emancipation. Once free of Spanish domination, the newly independent nations slowly freed their slave populations in order to maintain good relations with Great Britain from whom they needed economic support. Despite the gradual nature of this abolition, slavery would disappear from all nations of Latin America by the middle of the century, with the important exception of Brazil.

Having slowly recognized that the abolition of the slave trade had not actually improved the lot of slaves, British reformers in 1823 adopted as a new goal the gradual emancipation of slaves and founded the Abolition Society. The savagery with which West Indian planters put down slave revolts in 1823 and 1824 and again in 1831 strengthened the resolve of the antislavery reformers. By 1830 the reformers abandoned the goal of gradual abolition and demanded immediate complete abolition of slavery. In 1833, following the passage of the Reform Bill in Great Britain, they achieved that goal when Parliament abolished the right of British subjects to hold slaves. In the British West Indies, 750,000 slaves were freed within a few years.

The other old colonial powers in the New World tended to be much slower in their abolition of slavery. Portugal did little or nothing about slavery in Brazil, and when that nation became independent, its new government continued slavery. Portugal ended slavery elsewhere in its American possessions in 1836; the Swedes, in 1847; the Danes, in 1848, but the Dutch not until 1863. France had witnessed a significant antislavery movement throughout the first half of the century, but did not abolish slavery in its West Indian possessions until the revolutions of 1848.

Despite all of these considerable achievements of the antislavery movement, during the first thirty years of the nineteenth century the institution of slavery actually revived and achieved new footholds in the transatlantic world. These areas included the lower south of the United States for the cultivation of cotton, Brazil for the cultivation of coffee, and Cuba for the cultivation of sugar. World demand for those products made the slave system economically viable in those regions. Slavery would end in the United States only after American abolitionists brought it to the center of American politics in the 1850s and the Civil War was fought during the next decade. In Cuba it would persist until 1886, and full emancipation would occur in Brazil only in 1888. (See Chapters 26, 27, and 30.)

The emancipation crusade, like slave trading itself, drew Europeans into African affairs. In 1787 the British established a colony for poor free blacks from Britain in Sierra Leone, which actually succeeded only after the British navy began to settle Africans rescued from captured slave trading ships. The French established a smaller experiment at Libreville in Gabon. The most famous and lasting attempt to settle former black slaves in Africa was the establishment of Liberia through the efforts of the American Colonization Society after 1817. Liberia became an independent republic in 1847. All of these efforts to move former slaves back to Africa had only modest success, but they did affect the future of West Africa itself.

Other antislavery reformers were less interested in establishing outposts for settlement of former slaves than in transforming the African economy itself. These reformers attempted to spread both Christianity and free trade to Africa, hoping to exchange British manufactured goods, particularly textiles, for tropical goods produced by Africans. These commercial efforts of the antislavery movement marked the first serious intrusions of European powers well beyond the coast of West Africa into the heart of the continent.

After the American Civil War finally halted any large-scale demand for slaves from Africa, the antislavery reformers began to focus on ending the slave trade in East Africa and the Indian Ocean. This new drive against slavery and the slave trade in Africa itself became one of the rationales for European interference in Africa during the second half of the century and served as one of the foundations for the establishment of the late-century colonial empires.

IN WORLD PERSPECTIVE

The Transatlantic Revolutions

The revolutions and the crusade against slavery that occurred throughout the transatlantic world between 1776 and 1824 transformed the political, social, and economic life of three continents. In North America, in France and other parts of Europe, and in South America bold political experiments challenged government by both monarchy and aristocracy. The foundations of modern liberal democracy were laid. The largest republic since ancient times had been established in North America. In France, despite the ongoing political turmoil after 1789, written constitutions and elected legislatures remained essential parts of the government. In Latin America republicanism triumphed soon after independence everywhere except Brazil. Never again could government be undertaken in these regions without some form of participation by and consultation with the governed.

The expanding forms of political liberty found their counterparts in an economic life freed from the constraints of the old colonial empires and the slavery that marked their plantations. The new American republic constituted a vast free trade zone. Its commerce and ports were open to the whole world. And for the first time since the encounter with Europe, all of Latin America could trade freely among its own peoples and those of the rest of the world. In France and across much of Europe, where the Napoleonic armies had carried the doctrines of the rights of man, economic life had been rationalized and freed from the domination of local authorities and local weights and measures. National law formed the framework for economic activity. The movement to abolish slavery fostered a wage economy of free laborers. That kind of economy would generate its own set of problems and social dislocation, but it was nonetheless an economy of free human beings who were the chattel of no other human being.

Finally, the age of transatlantic revolutions saw the emergence of nationalism as a political force. All of the revolutions, because of their popular political base, had given power to the idea of nations defined by their own character and historical past rather than by dynastic rulers. The Americans saw themselves as forming a new kind of nation. The French had demonstrated the power of a nation fully mobilized for military purposes. In turn the aggression of France had aroused national sentiment, especially in Great Britain, Spain, and Germany. The new nations of Latin America also sought to define themselves by their heritage and historical experience rather than by their past in the Spanish and Portuguese empires.

These various revolutions, their political doctrines, and their social and economic departures provided examples to peoples elsewhere in the world. But even more important, the transformations of the transatlantic revolutions and eventual abolition of slavery meant that new political classes and newly organized independent nations would become actors on the world scene. Europeans would have to deal with a score of new nations in the Americas. The rest of the world confronted new nations freed from the direction and authority of European powers. In turn the political changes in Europe meant that those nations and their relationships with the rest of the world would be directed by a broader range of political groups and forces than in the past.

Review Questions

1. Discuss the American Revolution in the context of transatlantic history. To what extent were the colonists influenced by their position in the transatlantic economy? To what extent were they influenced by European ideas and political developments? How did their demands for liberty compare and contrast with the ideas of liberty championed during the French Revolution?

2. How was the Estates General transformed into the National Assembly? How does the *Declaration of the Rights of Man and Citizen* reflect the social and political values of the eighteenth-century Enlightenment? What were the chief ways in which France and its government were reorganized in the early years of the revolution? Why has the Civil Constitution of the Clergy been called the greatest blunder of the National Assembly?

3. Why were some political factions dissatisfied with the constitutional settlement of 1791 in France? What was the revolution of 1792 and why did it occur? What were the causes of the reign of Terror and what political coalitions made it possible?

4. How did Napoleon rise to power? What were his major domestic achievements? Did his rule more nearly fulfill or betray the ideals of the French Revolution? Why did Napoleon decide to invade Russia? Why did he fail? What were the major outlines of the peace settlement achieved by the Congress of Vienna?

5. What political changes took place in Latin America in the twenty years between 1804 and 1824? What were the main reasons for Creole discontent with Spanish rule? Who were some of the primary leaders of Latin American independence and why were they successful? How were the movements to Latin American independence influenced by the American and French Revolutions? What were the factors that made the Latin American Wars of Independence different from those two revolutions?

6. A motto of the French Revolution was "liberty, equality, and fraternity." How might one compare the American Revolution, the French Revolution, and the Latin American Wars of Independence in regard to the achievement of these goals? Which groups in each country or region benefitted from the revolution and which gained little or nothing from the changes?

7. What intellectual and religious factors contributed to the rise of the antislavery movement? To what extent did nonhumanitarian forces contribute to it? What opposition did it meet? Why did slavery receive a new lease on life during the same years that the antislavery movement emerged?

Suggested Readings

R. ANSTEY, *The Atlantic Slave Trade and British Abolition, 1760–1810* (1975). A standard overview that emphasizes the role of religious factors.

B. BAILYN, *The Ideological Origins of the American Revolution* (1967). An important work illustrating the role of English radical thought in the perceptions of the American colonists.

K. M. BAKER, *Inventing the French Revolution: Essays on French Political Culture in the Eighteenth Century* (1990). Important essays on political thought before and during the revolution.

K. M. BAKER AND C. LUCAS, EDS., *The French Revolution and the Creation of Modern Political Culture*, 3 vols. (1987). A splendid collection of important original articles on all aspects of politics during the revolution.

R. J. BARMAN, *Brazil: The Forging of a Nation, 1798–1852* (1988). The best coverage of this period.

C. BECKER, *The Declaration of Independence: A Study in the History of Political Ideas* (1922). Remains an important examination of the political and imperial theory of the Declaration.

J. F. BERNARD, *Talleyrand: A Biography* (1973). A useful account.

L. BETHELL, *The Cambridge History of Latin America*, Vol. 3 (1985). Contains an extensive treatment of independence.

R. BLACKBURN, *The Overthrow of Colonial Slavery, 1776–1848* (1988). A major discussion quite skeptical of the humanitarian interpretation.

T. C. W. BLANNING, ED., *The Rise and Fall of the French Revolution* (1996). A wide-ranging collection of essays illustrating the debates over the French Revolution.

J. BROOKE, *King George III* (1972). The best biography.

R. COBB, *The People's Armies* (1987). The major treatment in English of the revolutionary army.

O. CONNELLY, *Napoleon's Satellite Kingdoms* (1965). The rule of Napoleon and his family in Europe.

E. V. DA COSTA, *The Brazilian Empire* (1985). Excellent coverage of the entire nineteenth-century experience of Brazil.

D. B. DAVIS, *The Problem of Slavery in the Age of Revolution, 1770–1823* (1975). A transatlantic perspective on the issue.

F. FEHÉR, *The French Revolution and the Birth of Modernity* (1990). A wide-ranging collection of essays on political and cultural facets of the revolution.

A. FORREST, *The French Revolution and the Poor* (1981). A study that expands consideration of the revolution beyond the standard social boundaries.

M. GLOVER, *The Peninsular War, 1807–1814: A Concise Military History* (1974). An interesting account of the military campaign that so drained Napoleon's resources in western Europe.

J. GODECHOT, *The Counter-Revolution: Doctrine and Action, 1789–1804* (1971). An examination of opposition to the revolution.

A. GOODWIN, *The Friends of Liberty: The English Democratic Movement in the Age of the French Revolution* (1979). A major work that explores the impact of the French Revolution on English radicalism.

L. HUNT, *Politics, Culture, and Class in the French Revolution* (1986). A series of essays that focus on the modes of expression of the revolutionary values and political ideas.

W. W. KAUFMANN, *British Policy and the Independence of Latin America, 1802–1828* (1951). A standard discussion of an important relationship.

E. KENNEDY, *A Cultural History of the French Revolution* (1989). An important examination of the role of the arts, schools, clubs, and intellectual institutions.

M. KENNEDY, *The Jacobin Clubs in the French Revolution: The First Years* (1982). A careful scrutiny of the organizations chiefly responsible for the radicalizing of the revolution.

M. KENNEDY, *The Jacobin Clubs in the French Revolution: The Middle Years* (1988). A continuation of the previously listed study.

H. KISSINGER, *A World Restored: Metternich, Castlereagh and the Problems of Peace, 1812–1822* (1957). A provocative study by an author who became an American secretary of state.

G. LEFEBVRE, *The Coming of the French Revolution* (trans. 1947). A classic examination of the crisis of the French monarchy and the events of 1789.

G. LEFEBVRE, *Napoleon*, 2 vols., trans. by H. Stockhold (1969). The fullest and finest biography.

J. LYNCH, *The Spanish American Revolutions, 1808–1826* (1986). An excellent one-volume treatment.

G. MASUR, *Simón Bolívar* (1969). The standard biography in English.

P. MAIER, *American Scripture: Making the Declaration of Independence* (1997) Stands as a major revision of our understanding of the Declaration.

S. E. MELZER AND L. W. RABINE, EDS., *Rebel Daughters: Women and the French Revolution* (1992). A collection of essays exploring various aspects of the role and image of women in the French Revolution.

M. MORRIS, *The British Monarchy and the French Revolution* (1998) Explores the manner in which the British monarchy saved itself from possible revolution.

R. MUIR, *Tactics and the Experience of Battle in the Age of Napoleon* (1998). Examines the wars from the standpoint of the soldiers in combat.

H. NICOLSON, *The Congress of Vienna* (1946). A good, readable account.

T. O. OTT, *The Haitian Revolution, 1789–1804* (1973). An account that clearly relates the events in Haiti to those in France.

R. R. PALMER, *Twelve Who Ruled: The Committee of Public Safety During the Terror* (1941). A clear narrative and analysis of the policies and problems of the committee.

R. R. PALMER, *The Age of the Democratic Revolution: A Political History of Europe and America, 1760–1800*, 2 vols. (1959, 1964). An impressive survey of the political turmoil in the transatlantic world.

C. PROCTOR, *Women, Equality, and the French Revolution* (1990). An examination of how the ideas of the Enlightenment and the attitudes of revolutionaries affected the legal status of women.

A. J. RUSSELL-WOOD, ED., *From Colony to Nation: Essays on the Independence of Brazil* (1975). A series of important essays.

P. SCHROEDER, *The Transformation of European Politics, 1763–1848* (1994). A fundamental treatment of the diplomacy of the era.

T. E. SKIDMORE AND P. H. SMITH, *Modern Latin America*, 4th ed. (1997). A very useful survey.

A. SOBOUL, *The Parisian Sans-Culottes and the French Revolution, 1793–94* (1964). The best work on the subject.

A. SOBOUL, *The French Revolution* (trans. 1975). An important work by a Marxist scholar.

D. G. SUTHERLAND, *France, 1789–1825: Revolution and Counterrevolution* (1986). A major synthesis based on recent scholarship in social history.

T. TACKETT, *Religion, Revolution, and Regional Culture in Eighteenth-Century France: The Ecclesiastical Oath of 1791* (1986). The most important study of this topic.

T. TACKETT, *Becoming a Revolutionary: The Deputies of the French National Assembly and the Emergence of a Revolutionary Culture (1789–1790)* (1996). The best study of the early months of the revolution.

J. M. THOMPSON, *Robespierre*, 2 vols. (1935). The best biography.

D. K. VAN KEY, *The Religious Origins of the French Revolution: From Calvin to the Civil Constitution, 1560–1791* (1996). Examines the manner in which debates within French Catholicism influenced the coming of the revolution.

M. WALZER, ED., *Regicide and Revolution: Speeches at the Trial of Louis XVI* (1974). An important and exceedingly interesting collection of documents with a useful introduction.

I. WOLOCH, *The New Regime: Transformations of the French Civic Order, 1789–1820s* (1994). An important overview of just what had and had not changed in France after the quarter-century of revolution and war.

G. WOOD, *The Radicalism of the American Revolution* (1991). A major interpretation.

26 EUROPE AND NORTH AMERICA 1815–1850: POLITICAL REFORM, ECONOMIC ADVANCE, AND SOCIAL UNREST

Cities all across Europe grew during the first half of the nineteenth century. Some developed with little planning into bewildering places. Others—as this Berlin street scene suggests—developed in ways more congenial to their residents, with neighborhoods that continued to combine workshops, stores, and residences. [Photo: Jorg P. Anders/Staatliche Museen zu Berlin/Gemalde von Eduard Gaertner, 1831, "Die Parochialstraße"/Bildarchiv Preussischer Kulturbesitz]

C H A P T E R T O P I C S

◆ The Challenges of Nationalism and Liberalism

◆ Efforts to Liberalize Early-Nineteenth-Century European Political Structures

◆ Testing the New American Republic

◆ Europe Moves Toward an Industrial Society

◆ 1848: Year of Revolutions

In World Perspective Early-Nineteenth-Century Europe and the United States

The decades immediately after the Congress of Vienna ushered in political and social departures throughout the transatlantic world. In Europe, the defeat of Napoleon and the diplomatic settlement of the Congress of Vienna had restored a conservative political and social order. Legitimate monarchies, landed aristocracies, and established churches constituted the major pillars of conservatism. The institutions themselves were ancient, but the self-conscious alliance of throne, land, and altar was new. Throughout the eighteenth century these groups had clashed. Only the upheavals of the French Revolution and the Napoleonic era transformed them into natural, if sometimes reluctant, allies. They retained their former arrogance but not their former privileges or their old confidence. What worried the conservatives were the dual challenges of political liberalism, derived from Enlightenment ideals, and the concept of nationalism, a legacy of the Napoleonic Wars that were beginning to reshape Europe.

The conservatives regarded themselves as standing permanently on the defensive against the forces of liberal-

ism, nationalism, and popular sovereignty. These potential sources of unrest had to be confronted both at home and abroad, where new social forces were creating new sources of political discontent. In Europe the modest base for industrialization that existed in 1815 began to expand as people from the countryside crowded into cities, seeking work in newly built factories. The result was an era of considerable social tension. By 1848 those tensions, enhanced by nationalistic stirrings, erupted as revolutions spread across much of the continent.

In Latin America, as will be seen in Chapter 30, these years saw much turmoil as the newly independent states sought, often unsuccessfully, to organize stable political and economic structures. The developments in the United States were quieter but no less momentous. During these same years the republican experiment continued, while slavery also continued to drive the economy of the southern states. Americans began to move in large numbers across the Appalachian mountains forming new cities, towns, and thousands of family farms. From New England south to Delaware an industrialized economy began to

grow. At the same time the plantation economy moved west across the lower South, where cotton became king and black slaves provided the labor. The dispute over slavery in the United States coincided with the first conflicts over industrial labor in Europe. Thus by the 1850s the politics of both Europe and the United States stood sharply divided over the issues of labor and what it meant for laborers to be free.

The Challenges of Nationalism and Liberalism

The Emergence of Nationalism

Nationalism proved to be the single most powerful European political ideology of the nineteenth and early twentieth centuries. It has reasserted itself in present-day Europe following the collapse of Communist governments in eastern Europe and in the former Soviet Union. Furthermore, during the twentieth century peoples who were once subject to European colonial rule used the force and ideals of nationalism to establish their own independence from Europe.

Nationalism is based on the relatively modern concept that a nation is composed of people who are joined together by the bonds of common language, customs, culture, and history, and who, because of those bonds, should share the same government. That is to say, political and ethnic boundaries should coincide. This idea came into its own during the late eighteenth and the early nineteenth centuries.

Opposition to the Vienna Settlement

Early-nineteenth-century nationalists directly opposed the principle upheld at the Congress of Vienna that legitimate monarchies or dynasties, rather than ethnicity, should provide the basis for political unity. Nationalists naturally protested multinational states such as the Austrian or Russian empires. They also objected to peoples of the same ethnic group, such as Germans and Italians, dwelling in political units smaller than that of the ethnic nation. Consequently, nationalists challenged both the domestic and the international order of the Vienna settlement.

Creating Nations

Nationalists actually created nations in the nineteenth century. During the first half of the century a group of nationalistically minded writers using the printed word spread a nationalistic concept of the nation. They were frequently historians who chronicled a people's past or writers and literary scholars who established a national literature by collecting and publishing earlier writings in the people's language. In effect, they gave a people a sense of their past and a literature of their own. In time schoolteachers, by imparting a nation's official language and history, spread nationalistic ideas.

The language to be used in the schools and in government offices was always a point of contention for nationalists. In France and Italy official versions of the national language were imposed in the schools and replaced local dialects. In parts of Scandinavia and eastern Europe nationalists attempted to resurrect from earlier times what they regarded as purer versions of the national language. Often these resurrected languages were virtually invented by modern scholars or linguists. This process of establishing national languages led to far more linguistic uniformity within European nations than had existed before the nineteenth century. In most countries spoken and written proficiency in the official printed language became a path to social and political advancement and employment within government bureaucracies. The growth of a uniform language helped to persuade people who had not thought of themselves as constituting a nation that they were a nation. Yet even in 1850 perhaps less than half of the inhabitants of France spoke official French.

Meaning of Nationhood

Nationalists used a variety of arguments and metaphors to express what they meant by nationhood. Some argued that gathering, for example, Italians into a unified Italy or Germans into a unified Germany, thus eliminating the petty dynastic states that governed those regions, would promote economic and administrative efficiency. Some nationalists claimed that nations, like biological species in the natural world, were distinct creations of God. Other nationalists claimed a place for their nations in the divine order of things. Throughout the nineteenth century, for example, Polish nationalists portrayed Poland as the suffering Christ among nations, thus implicitly suggesting that Poland, like Christ, would experience resurrection and a new life.

A significant difficulty for nationalism was, and is, determining which ethnic groups could be considered nations, with claims to territory and political autonomy. In theory, any of them could, but in reality nationhood came to be associated with groups that were large enough to support a viable economy, that had a history of significant cultural association, that possessed a cultural elite that could nourish and spread the national language, and that could conquer other peoples to establish and protect their own independence. Throughout the century many smaller ethnic groups claimed to fulfill these criteria but could not effectively achieve either independence or recognition. They could and did, however, create domestic unrest within the political units they inhabited. Such was the situation in Europe. A similar situation, though in many ways quite different, prevailed for a time in the United States, where by the middle of the century leaders of many southern states began to make statements very much resembling those of nationalist leaders in Europe. One can view the defeat of the Confederate States of America, which will be discussed in Chapter 27, as an example of the military failure of a region to establish itself as a kind of nationality.

Regions of Nationalistic Pressure in Europe

During the nineteenth century nationalists challenged the political status quo in six major areas of Europe. England had brought Ireland under direct rule in 1800, allowing the Irish to elect members to the British Parliament in Westminster. Irish nationalists, however, wanted independence or at least self-government. The "Irish problem" would haunt British politics for the next two centuries. German nationalists sought political unity for all German-speaking peoples, challenging the multinational Austrian Empire and pitting Prussia and Austria against each other. Italian nationalists sought to unify the peninsula and drive out the Austrians. Polish nationalists struggled, primarily against Russia, to restore Poland as an independent nation. In eastern Europe a host of national groups, including Hungarians, Czechs, Slovenes, and others, sought either autonomy or formal recognition within the Austrian Empire. Finally, in the Balkans national groups, including Serbs, Greeks, Albanians, Romanians, and Bulgarians, sought independence from Ottoman and Russian control. Al-

Mazzini Defines Nationality

No political force in the nineteenth century was stronger than nationalism. It replaced dynastic political loyalty with loyalty based on ethnic considerations. In 1835 the Italian nationalist and patriot Giuseppe Mazzini (1805–1872) explained his understanding of the concept. Note how he combined a generally democratic view of politics with a religious concept of the divine destiny of nations.

What are the specific qualities of a people that Mazzini associates with nationalism? How and why does Mazzini relate nationalism to divine purposes? How does this view of nationality relate to the goals of liberal freedom? How does it compare to other perspectives on nationalism and independence movements, for example "William Gladstone Pleads for Irish Home Rule" (Chapter 27), "Herzl Calls for the Establishment of a Jewish State" (Chapter 29), and "Gandhi on Passive Resistance and Swarāj" (Chapter 31).

The essential characteristics of a nationality are common ideas, common principles and a common purpose. A nation is an association of those who are brought together by language, by given geographical conditions or by the role assigned them by history, who acknowledge the same principles and who march together to the conquest of a single definite goal under the rule of a uniform body of law.

The life of a nation consists in harmonious activity (that is, the employment of all individual abilities and energies comprised within the association) towards this single goal. . . .

But nationality means even more than this. Nationality also consists in the share of mankind's labors which God assigns to a people. This mission is the task which a people must perform to the end that the Divine Idea shall be realized in this world; it is the work which gives a people its rights as a member of Mankind; it is the baptismal rite which endows a people with its own character and its rank in the brotherhood of nations. . . .

Nationality depends for its very existence upon its sacredness within and beyond its borders.

If nationality is to be inviolable for all, friends and foes alike, it must be regarded inside a country as holy, like a religion, and outside a country as a grave mission. It is necessary too that the ideas arising within a country grow steadily, as part of the general law of Humanity which is the source of all nationality. It is necessary that these ideas be shown to other lands in their beauty and purity, free from any alien mixture, from any slavish fears, from any skeptical hesitancy, strong and active, embracing in their evolution every aspect and manifestation of the life of the nation. These ideas, a necessary component in the order of universal destiny, must retain their originality even as they enter harmoniously into mankind's general progress.

The people must be the basis of nationality; its logically derived and vigorously applied principles its means; the strength of all its strength; the improvement of the life of all and the happiness of the greatest possible number its results; and the accomplishment of the task assigned to it by God its goal. This is what we mean by nationality.

From *Absolutism to Revolution, 1648–1848*, 2nd ed., Herbert H. Rown, ed. Copyright © 1969. Reprinted by permission of Prentice-Hall, Inc., Upper Saddle River, N.J.

---

though there were never simultaneous disturbances in all six areas, any one of them could erupt into turmoil. In each area, nationalist activity ebbed and flowed. The dominant governments often thought they needed only to repress the activity or ride it out until stability returned. During the century, however, nationalists changed the political map and political culture of Europe in the manner in which the Confederate States of America failed to do in the mid-nineteenth-century United States.

Early-Nineteenth-Century Political Liberalism

In the present-day United States, the word *liberal* carries meanings and connotations that have little or nothing to do with its significance for nineteenth-century Europeans. European conservatives of the last century saw liberals as more radical than they actually were; present-day Americans often think of nineteenth-century liberals as more conservative than they were. In any case, the term *liberal* as used in present-day American political rhetoric has virtually no relationship to its nineteenth-century counterpart.

Politics European liberals derived their political ideas from the Enlightenment, the example of English liberties, and the so-called principles of 1789 as embodied in the French *Declaration of the Rights of Man and Citizen*. Liberal political figures sought to establish a framework of legal equality, religious toleration, and freedom of the press. They sought to limit the arbitrary power of the government against the persons and property of individual citizens. They generally believed that the legitimacy of government emanated from the freely given consent of the governed expressed through elected representative or parliamentary bodies. Most

Prince Klemens von Metternich (1773–1859) the Austrian foreign minister, epitomized nineteen-century conservatism. [The Royal Collection Enterprises, Ltd./Royal Library, Windsor Castle]

important, free government required that state or crown ministers be responsible to the representatives of the nation rather than to the monarch.

These goals were limited. Such responsible government, however, existed in none of the major European countries in 1815. Even in Great Britain the ministers were at least as responsible to the monarch as to the House of Commons. The people who espoused these changes in government tended to be those who were excluded from the existing political processes but whose wealth and education made them believe such exclusion was unjustified. Liberals were often academics, members of the learned professions, and people involved in the rapidly expanding commercial and manufacturing sectors. They believed in and were products of the career open to talent. The existing monarchical and aristocratic regimes often failed to recognize sufficiently their new status and to provide for their economic and professional interests.

Although European liberals wanted broader political participation, they were not democrats. Second only to their hostility to the privileged aristocracies was their general contempt for the lower, unpropertied classes. Liberals transformed the eighteenth-century concept of aristocratic liberty into a new concept of privilege based on wealth and property instead of

birth. By the mid-century this widely shared attitude meant that throughout Europe, liberals had separated themselves from both the rural and the urban working class. In the first half of the nineteenth century political liberals generally did not support the extension of political rights to women, but liberal political principles provided women with strong arguments to do so, as seen for example in the *Declaration of Female Independence* issued by the Seneca Falls convention in the United States in 1848.

Economics   The economic goals of the liberals also furthered their separation from the working class. Here, the Enlightenment and the economic thought deriving from Adam Smith set the pattern. The manufacturers of Great Britain, the landed and manufacturing middle class of France, and the commercial interests of Germany and Italy wanted to be able to manufacture and sell goods freely. They thus favored the removal of international tariffs as well as internal barriers to trade. To that end, liberals across the continent and those who imitated them outside of Europe favored the rapid construction of railways from the 1830s onward.

European economic liberals opposed the old paternalistic legislation that established wages and labor practices by government regulation or by guild privileges. Labor was simply one more commodity to be bought and sold freely. Liberals sought an economic structure in which people were free to use their talents and property to enrich themselves. The liberals contended that this would lead to more goods and services for everyone at lower prices. Economic liberty was to provide the basis for material progress.

The economic goals of European liberals found many followers outside Europe among groups who favored the expansion of free trade, new transport systems, and a free market in labor. In the United States people of this outlook often attacked slavery as an inefficient, paternalistic institution. In Latin America political liberals sought to remove paternalistic legislation that had protected Native Americans during the centuries of the Spanish Empire.

Relationship of Nationalism and Liberalism   Nationalism was not necessarily or logically linked to liberalism, and some conservative nationalists, for example, ignored the rights of national minorities. Liberalism and nationalism, however, were often complementary. Behind the concept of a people joined naturally together by the bonds of common language, customs, culture, and history lurked the idea of popular sovereignty. The idea of the career open to talent could be applied to suppressed national groups who were not permitted to realize their cultural or political potential. The efficient government and administration required by commerce and industry would mean replacing the small German and Italian states with larger political units. Moreover, nationalist groups in one country could gain the sympathy of liberals in other nations by espousing representative government and political liberty.

Efforts to Liberalize Early-Nineteenth-Century European Political Structures

Russia: The Decembrist Revolt of 1825 and the Autocracy of Nicholas I

In the process of driving Napoleon's army across Europe, and then occupying defeated France, many officers in the Russian army were introduced to the ideas of the French Revolution and the Enlightenment. They realized how economically backward and politically stifled Russia was. Under these conditions, groups within the officer corps formed secret societies. These societies were small and divided in their goals; they agreed only that there must be a change in the government of Russia. Sometime during 1825 they seem to have decided to carry out a coup d'état in 1826.

Other events intervened. In late November 1825 Tsar Alexander I suddenly and unexpectedly died. His death created two crises. The first was a dynastic one: Alexander had no direct heir. His brother Constantine stood next in line to the throne. However, Constantine, who was the commander

Tsar Nicholas I (r. 1825-1855) resisted all attempts to reform Russia and offered the use of Russian troops to other rulers threatened by revolution. [Historical Pictures Collection/Stock Montage, Inc.]

of Russian forces in Poland, had renounced any claim to be tsar. Through a series of secret instructions made public only after his death, Alexander had named his younger brother, Nicholas (r. 1825–1855), as the new tsar. Once Alexander was dead, the legality of these instructions became uncertain. Constantine acknowledged Nicholas as tsar, and Nicholas acknowledged Constantine.

This family muddle continued for about three weeks, during which Russia actually had no ruler, to the astonishment of Europe. Then, in early December, the army command reported to Nicholas the existence of a conspiracy among certain officers. Able to wait no longer, Nicholas had himself declared tsar.

The second crisis now unfolded—a plot by junior officers to rally the troops under their command to the cause of reform. On December 26, 1825, the army was to take the oath of allegiance to Nicholas, who was less popular than Constantine and was regarded as more conservative. Nearly all of the regiments did so. But the Moscow regiment, whose chief officers, surprisingly, were not secret society members, marched into the Senate Square in Saint Petersburg and refused to swear allegiance. Rather, they called for Constantine and a constitution. Attempts to settle the situation peacefully failed. Late in the afternoon Nicholas ordered the cavalry and the artillery to attack the insurgents. Five of the plotters were executed, and over 100 other officers were exiled to Siberia.

The immediate result of the revolt was the crushing of liberalism as even a moderate political influence in Russia. Nicholas I also manifested extreme conservatism in foreign affairs. Russia under Nicholas became the policeman of Europe, ever ready to provide troops to suppress liberal and nationalist movements.

Revolution in France (1830)

In 1824 Louis XVIII (r. 1814–1824), the Bourbon restored to the throne by the Congress of Vienna, died. He was succeeded by his brother, Charles X (r. 1824–1830). The new king considered himself a monarch by divine right.

Charles had the Chamber of Deputies in 1824 and 1825 indemnify those aristocrats who had lost their lands in the revolution. The existing land settlement was confirmed. By lowering the interest rates on government bonds, however, the Chamber created a fund from which the survivors of the *émigrés* who had forfeited land would be paid an annual sum of money. The middle-class bondholders, who lost income, resented this measure. Another measure restored the rule of primogeniture, whereby only the eldest son of an aristocrat inherited the family domains. Charles also supported the Roman Catholic church with a law punishing sacrilege with imprisonment or death. Liberals disapproved of these measures.

The French Bourbons were restored to the throne in 1815 but would rule only until 1830. This picture shows Louis XVIII, seated, second from left, and his brother, who would become Charles X, standing on the left. Notice the bust of Henry IV in the background, placed there to associate the restored rulers with their popular late-sixteenth, early-seventeenth-century forebear.
[Bildarchiv Preussischer Kulturbesitz]

The results of the elections of 1827 compelled Charles to appoint a less conservative ministry. Laws directed against the press and those allowing the government to dominate education were eased. Yet the liberals, who wanted a genuinely constitutional regime, remained unsatisfied. In 1829 the king decided that his policy of accommodation had failed. He dismissed his ministers and in their place appointed an ultraroyalist ministry.

In 1830 Charles X called for new elections, in which the liberals scored a stunning victory. Instead of attempting to accommodate the new Chamber of Deputies, the king and his ministers decided to undertake a royalist seizure of power. In June and July 1830 the ministry had sent a naval expedition against Algeria. On July 9 reports of its victory, and the consequent foundation of a French empire in North Africa, reached Paris. On July 25, 1830, under the euphoria of this foreign diversion, Charles X issued the Four Ordinances, which restricted freedom of the press, dissolved the recently elected Chamber of Deputies, and called for new elections under a franchise restricted to the wealthiest people in the country.

"Liberty Leading the People" by Eugene Delacroix is a famous evocation of the Revolution of 1830. [Giraudon/Art Resource, N.Y.]

Liberal newspapers immediately called on the nation to reject the monarch's actions. The laboring populace of Paris, burdened since 1827 by an economic downturn, took to the streets and erected barricades. The king called out troops, and over 1,800 people died during the ensuing battles in the city. On August 2 Charles X abdicated and left France for exile in England. The liberals in the Chamber of Deputies named a new ministry composed of constitutional monarchists. They proclaimed Louis Philippe (r. 1830–1848), the duke of Orléans, the head of the liberal branch of the royal family, the new monarch. Under what became known as the July Monarchy, Louis Philippe was called the king of the French rather than of France. The king had to cooperate with the Chamber of Deputies; he could not dispense with laws on his own authority. The revolutionary tricolor replaced the white flag of the Bourbons. The Charter, or constitution, was regarded as embodying the rights of the people rather than a concession granted by the monarch. Catholicism was recognized only as the religion of the majority of the people, not the official religion. Censorship was abolished. The franchise, though still restricted, was extended.

Socially, however, the Revolution of 1830 proved quite conservative. The landed oligarchy retained its economic, political, and social influence. Money became the path to power and influence in the government. There was much corruption. Most important, the liberal monarchy displayed scant sympathy for the lower and working classes.

The Great Reform Bill in Britain (1832)

The passage of the Great Reform Bill, which became law in 1832, was the result of events different from those that occurred on the Continent. In Britain the forces of conservatism and reform compromised with each other.

English determination to maintain the union with Ireland caused the first step in the reform process. England's relationship to Ireland was not unlike that of Russia's to Poland or Austria's to Hungary. After the Act of Union in 1800 between England and Ireland, only Protestant Irishmen could be elected to represent overwhelmingly Catholic Ireland.

During the 1820s, under the leadership of Daniel O'Connell (1775–1847), Irish nationalists organized the Catholic Association to agitate for Catholic emancipation, as the movement for legal rights for Roman Catholics was known. In 1828 O'Connell was elected to Parliament but could not legally take his seat. The British ministry of the duke of Wellington (1769–1852) realized that henceforth a predominantly Catholic delegation might be elected from Ireland. If they were not seated, civil war might erupt. Consequently, in 1829 Wellington and Robert Peel (1788–1850) steered the Catholic Emancipation Act through Parliament. Roman Catholics could now become members of Parliament.

Despite laws forbidding disrespect to the government, political cartoonists had a field day with Louis Philippe. Here, an artist emphasizes the king's resemblance to a pear and in the process attacks restraints on freedom of the press. [Corbis-Bettmann]

This measure, together with the repeal in 1828 of restrictions against Protestant nonconformists, ended the monopoly held by members of the Church of England on British political life.

Catholic emancipation was a liberal measure that was passed for the conservative purpose of preserving order in Ireland. It included a provision raising the franchise in Ireland, so that only the wealthier Irish could vote. Nonetheless, this measure alienated many of Wellington's Anglican Tory supporters. In the election of 1830 a large number of supporters of parliamentary reform were returned to Parliament. Even some Tories believed that parliamentary reform was necessary because they had concluded that Catholic emancipation could have been passed only by a corrupt House of Commons. The Wellington ministry soon fell. The Tories were badly divided, and King William IV (r. 1830–1837) turned to the Whigs under the leadership of Earl Grey (1764–1845) to form a government.

The Whig ministry soon presented the House of Commons with a major reform bill that had two broad goals. The first was to replace "rotten" boroughs, which had few voters, with representatives for the previously unrepresented manufacturing districts and cities. The second was to increase the number of voters in England and Wales. In 1831 the House of Commons narrowly defeated the bill. Grey called for a new election, in which a majority in favor of the bill was returned to the Commons. The House of Commons passed the reform

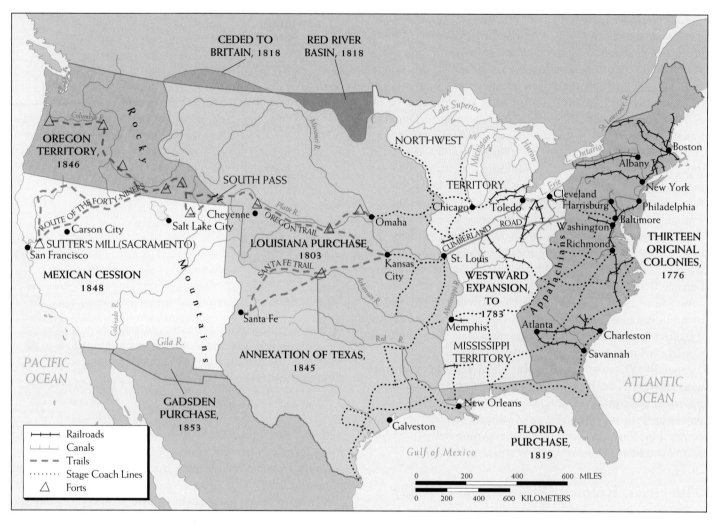

Map 26–1 **Nineteenth-century North America.** During the nineteenth century the United States expanded across the entire North American continent. The revolutionary settlement had provided most of the land east of the Mississippi. The single largest addition thereafter was the Louisiana Purchase of 1803. The annexation of Texas, and later the Mexican Cession following the Mexican War, added the major southwestern territories. The borders of the Oregon Territory were settled through long, difficult negotiations with Great Britain.

bill, but the House of Lords rejected it. Mass meetings were held throughout the country, and riots broke out in several cities. Finally, William IV agreed to create enough new peers to give a third reform bill a majority in the House of Lords. Under this pressure, the measure became law in 1832.

The Great Reform Bill expanded the size of the English electorate, but it was not a democratic measure. The electorate was increased by over 200,000 persons, or by almost 50 percent. The basis of voting, however, remained a property qualification. Some working-class voters actually lost the vote as a result of the abolition of old franchise rights. New urban boroughs gave the growing cities a voice in the House of Commons. Yet the passage of the reform act did not, as it was once thought, constitute the triumph of the middle-class interest in England. For every new urban electoral district, a

new rural district was also drawn. It was expected that the aristocracy would dominate the rural elections.

Testing the New American Republic

Toward Sectional Conflict

While the nations of Western Europe moved very slowly toward embracing political liberalism, the United States of America was continuing its bold republican political experiment. By the first quarter of the century, however, serious sectional tensions had arisen, the most important of which related to the presence of black slavery in the southern states. The westward expansion after the Louisiana Purchase of 1803 (see Map 26–1) would extend the country to the Rockies, thus allowing the possible expansion of slavery. This brought the issue of slavery to the forefront of American politics.

The Constitutional Convention of 1788 had debated the sectional difference relating to what proportion of the slave population would be counted toward representation in the House of Representatives. A compromise allowed the slaveholding states to count three fifths of their slaves when calculating their population for representation in Congress. The Constitution also forbade any federal attempt to prevent the importation of slaves before 1808. Between 1788 and 1808 thousands of slaves were imported into the United States.

The westward movement, however, meant that slavery could not be permanently ignored. The Ordinance of 1787, passed by Congress under the Articles of Confederation, had prohibited slavery in the Northwest Territory, which stretched from the Appalachians to the Mississippi northward. Territory south of the Ohio River and beyond the Mississippi was, however, open to slavery, and there it spread. By 1820 the number of slave and free states was evenly divided; this meant an equal number of senators from slave and free states. That year, Missouri was admitted as a slave state and Maine as a free one. It was also decided that in the future no slave states would be carved out of land north of the southern border of Missouri. For the time being, this compromise ended congressional debate over slavery. Nonetheless, the economies of the North and South were rapidly diverging.

Northern Economic Development Family farms, free labor, commerce, and early industrialization in textiles characterized the economy of the northern states. The northern farmers tended primarily to produce foodstuffs for their local communities. The farms were relatively small and worked by families. Farm laborers were free. Similarly, free laborers worked in the towns, on the ships, and in the factories of the North. The political spokesmen for the North tended to favor tariffs to protect their young industries from cheaper foreign competition. In this favoring of tariffs, many Americans whose political views otherwise often resembled European liberals differed from their European counterparts.

The North was the site of the earliest textile factories in the United States. Samuel Slater had established the first in Rhode Island in 1790. He had learned how to manufacture textiles in the new mills of industrializing Great Britain. His transfer of that technology to America provides an important example of how British and European advances were transported to the United States. Much of the early industrialization of the United States depended on such technological transfers. By the second decade of the nineteenth century there were hundreds of cotton factories in the North. These mills used cotton that was produced in the South, but most southern cotton sold overseas, mainly in England, where the textile industry was growing.

The most famous factory experiment in the United States occurred at a textile factory in Lowell, Massachusetts. The owners placed the entire process of textile manufacture—from the carding of the cotton or wool through the weaving of the final product—under one roof, resulting in the mass production of textiles. This Lowell system produced textiles more cheaply than could women working in their own homes. As had occurred in England, textile manufacture slowly moved from the home to the factory.

One of the most interesting and important features of the Lowell system was the way it employed young women. A shortage of labor meant that the United States was a land of high wages. However, American parents were loath to allow their daughters to leave home to work in the factories and to live alone. The owners of the Lowell mills established factory communities where the women could live and be carefully supervised. The company's boardinghouses were regarded as comfortable; they offered recreation, opportunities to pursue hobbies, and books to read. Some women published a magazine known as the *Lowell Offering*. Nonetheless, even at the Lowell mills, the workday was as long as thirteen hours.

The Lowell mills were not the norm. In New England and in cities throughout the North a labor force developed that was sharply divided along class lines. There were some early attempts at labor unions in crafts such as printing, hat making, and tailoring. In 1834 even the Lowell mills endured a major strike. Other strikes occurred as owners introduced more efficient machinery or lowered wages during economic downturns. Nonetheless, virtually all of these early labor

In New England, as in Europe, textile manufacturing was the first of the highly mechanized industries. American and European textile mills closely resembled each other because those in America had been copied from European and most particularly English technology. [The Granger Colleciton, N.Y.]

organizations collapsed during major recessions when workers sought scarce jobs despite low wages. American businessmen and factory owners, like their European counterparts, opposed these efforts at unionization.

During the second quarter of the century innovations in transportation led to the fuller integration of different parts of the northern economy. Canals were built to link the major rivers and the Great Lakes. The most famous was the Erie Canal, which connected the Hudson River to the Great Lakes. In turn, there were canals from the Great Lakes to the Ohio River. Major efforts were to be undertaken to make the Ohio, Mississippi, and Missouri rivers navigable, which allowed the use of steamboats to transport goods.

But by the late 1840s, in America as in Europe, the major transportation innovation was the railroad. Most of the railways linked the Northeast and the West. These rail lines fostered the commercial agriculture of the Midwest. Its products were sold in the Northeast and exported from northern ports. Hence, the development of east–west railways undermined the older river-based trade routes along the Ohio and down the Mississippi. Few major lines ran north and south, so former ties between the sections based on the rivers weakened. The building of the early railways also aided the development of the northern coal and iron industries. The further expansion of railways at mid-century caused new sectional tensions, as it became clear the railways could open for settlement vast territories, and thus could also open for national debate the future of slavery. That prospect sharpened the sectional debate and led to civil war.

The North also possessed vast farming resources. Rivers, canals, and railways allowed the upper Midwest to develop into a rich area for agriculture. Thousands of small farms raised corn, wheat, and livestock that could be shipped on the expanding transportation system. In this sense much of the northern economy was as rural and agricultural as the southern. What most distinguished the two regions was their differing labor systems. Free wage labor characterized the northern economy and its expansion. Slavery characterized the southern economy, which could expand only if slavery were allowed to expand as well.

The Southern Economy   The overwhelmingly rural economy of the American South was dependent on cotton and slavery. In those respects, the southern economy resembled the economies of many Latin American countries which were based on exporting a single crop or natural resource and on slave labor. The South had to export goods, primarily raw cotton, either to the North or to Europe, primarily to Great Britain, to maintain its standard of living.

Cotton was king. The invention of the cotton gin by Eli Whitney (1765–1825) in 1793 made cotton cultivation much more profitable. The industrial revolution in textiles kept cotton prices high, and the expansion in world population kept the demand for cotton cloth steady. The South profited from growing the cotton, New England from shipping it, and other parts of the North from supplying the manufacturing needs of the South. The South had virtually no incentive to diversify its agriculture.

Slavery   Slavery was abolished in the North by the early nineteenth century largely in response to the egalitarian values of the American Revolution. In any case it had never been fundamental to the northern economy. But in the South, the expansion of the cotton empire in the Mississippi Delta in the early nineteenth century gave slavery a new lease on life. Although most southern families never owned slaves and relatively few slave owners had possessed more than a few slaves, the institution of slavery survived for many reasons. For one, it was economically viable, and no one could devise a way politically or socially acceptable to white southerners to abolish it. No less important was the strong commitment to the protection of private property, which included slaves, throughout American society in both the North and the South. Perhaps the most basic reason for the endurance of slavery after the early nineteenth century, however, was racist thinking that saw blacks as fundamentally inferior to whites. Such thinking was not peculiar to the South, but it functioned there as one more argument against abolishing slavery.

What was the life of an American slave like? All American slaves were nonwhite, the descendants of Africans who had been forcibly captured and shipped in the most wretched of conditions to the United States (see Chapter 19). Despite much miscegenation among Africans and their white slaveowners and Native Americans, the various slave codes defined as black virtually anyone who had African antecedents. Slaves were regarded as chattel property; that is, they could be sold, given away, or even gambled away like any other piece of property. They had no recourse to law or constitutional protections and could be, and often were, treated badly by their masters. Whipping and beating were permitted. State laws protected slaves from extreme violence, but were laxly enforced; slaves lived with no serious protection from the law or legal authorities.

Their standard of living was generally poor. Although owners wanted to see their slave investments reproduce themselves, slaves suffered from diseases associated with poor nutrition, sanitation, and housing.

Slaves worked primarily in the fields, where they plowed, hoed, and harvested cotton, rice, tobacco, or corn. They were usually organized into work gangs supervised by white overseers. This work was, like all farming, seasonal; but during planting or harvest seasons, labor would persist from sunrise to sunset. Children would work in the fields as helpers. Older or more privileged slaves might work in the house, cleaning, cooking, or taking care of children.

Americans were prominent in the abolitionist movement. Harriet Tubman, standing on the far left, was an escaped slave who helped hundreds of other slaves escape to freedom. She is pictured here with some of those she helped to free. [Smith College, Sophia Smith Collection, Northampton, Massachusetts]

Recent scholarship has emphasized how the slave communities helped to preserve the family life and inner personalities of the slaves. Some elements of African culture persisted in the slave communities. African legends were passed on orally. Religion proved extraordinarily important. Slaves also adopted for their own cultural needs the Old Testament stories of the Jews' liberation from Egypt. They also often combined elements of African religion with evangelical Protestantism.

Yet despite these efforts to preserve a sense of community and even of family, marriages and family lives of slaves had no legal recognition. The integrity of the slave family could be violated at the master's whim or changing economic circumstances. White masters and their sons often sexually exploited black slave women. Because slaves were property, they could be sold for profit or transported when the owner moved to a different region. Consequently, families could be, and were, separated by sale or perhaps after an owner's death. Many young children were reared and cared for by other slaves to whom they were not related. In a world of white dominance, the institutions, customs, and religions of the slave community were the only means black slaves had to protect the autonomy of their own personalities.

The Abolitionist Movement

During the 1830s a militant antislavery movement emerged in the North. Its leaders and followers refused to accept what they regarded as the moral compromise of living in a nation that tolerated slavery. Abolitionists such as William Lloyd Garrison, editor of *The Liberator*, condemned the Union and the Constitution as structures that simply perpetuated slavery. Former slaves who had escaped slavery, such as Frederick Douglas and Sojouner Truth, and freeborn black Americans, such as Daniel A. Payne, also joined the cause. Abolitionism profited from the general climate of reform at the time. From the 1820s onward, movements for temperance reform, women's rights, education improvement, and the like attracted many supporters. These movements had learned how to organize supporters and publicize their cases. They also had persuaded many people that the moral, social, and economic life of the nation needed to be changed. Of the various evils that needed to be addressed, slavery came to loom large by the middle of the century, but for the moment abolitionism was only one of several moral reform movements.

The antislavery movement gained new adherents during the 1840s as the question of extending slavery into the new territories came to the fore in 1847 at the end of the Mexican War. That military victory added significant new territory in the Southwest and California, in addition to Texas, which had been annexed in 1845. The United States also acquired the vast Oregon territory in the Northwest.

Victory in the Mexican War opened debate on the extension of slavery into the huge new territory it created. Southerners feared that the changing climate of national debate

Daniel A. Payne Denounces American Slavery

Daniel A. Payne was an African American who became an ordained Lutheran minister. He delivered this speech in June 1839, on the occasion of his ordination. Though born in Charleston, South Carolina, he was the son of free African Americans. As a young man he had opened a school in that state to educate African-American children. He had to abandon this effort after the legislature passed a law imposing fines for the teaching of either free or enslaved African Americans to read and write. Later he became president of Wilberforce University in Xenia, Ohio, dedicated to the education of African Americans.

On what grounds does Payne condemn slavery? What are the examples of moral brutalization that Payne associates with slavery? How does Payne bring religious arguments against the evils of slavery?

. . . I am opposed to slavery, not because it enslaves the black man, but because it enslaves *man*. And were all the slaveholders in this land men of color, and the slaves white men, I would be as thorough and uncompromising an abolitionist as I now am; for whatever and whenever I may see a being in the form of a man, enslaved by his fellow man, without respect to his complexion, I shall lift up my voice to please his cause, against all the claims of his proud oppressor; and I shall do it not merely from the sympathy which man feels towards suffering man, but because *God, the living God,* whom I dare not disobey, has commanded me to open my mouth for the dumb, and to plead the cause of the oppressed.

Slavery brutalizes man. . . . This being God created but a little lower than the angels, and crowned him with glory and honor; but slavery hurls him down from his elevated position, to the level of brutes, strikes this crown of glory from his head and fastens upon his neck the galling yoke, and compels him to labor like an ox, through summer's sun and winter's snow, without remuneration. Does a man take the calf from the cow and sell it to the butcher? So slavery tears the child from the arms of the reluctant mother, and barters it to the soul trader for a young colt, or some

other commodity! Does the bird catcher tear away the dove from his mate? So slavery separates the groaning husband from the embraces of his distracted and weeping wife! . . . The very moment that a man conceives the diabolic design of enslaving his brother's body, that very moment does he also conceive the still more heinous design of fettering his will, for well does he know that in order to make his dominion supreme over the body, he must fetter the living spring of all its motions. Hence, the first lesson the slave is taught is to yield his will unreservedly and exclusively to the dictates of his master. And if a slave desire to educate himself or his children, in obedience to the dictates of reason or the laws of God, he does not, he cannot do it without the consent of his master. . . .

In view of the moral agency of man, God hath most wisely and graciously given him a code of laws, and certain positive percepts, to control and regulate moral actions. This code of laws, and these positive percepts, with the divine influence which they are naturally calculated to exert on the mind of man, constitutes his moral government. . . .

Now, slavery nullifies these laws and percepts—weakens and destroys their influence over the human mind, and hinders men from yielding universal and entire obedience to them; therefore slavery subverts the moral government of God. This is the climax of the sin of slavery. . . .

. . . Slavery never legislates for the religious instruction of slaves, but, on the contrary, legislates to perpetuate their ignorance; and there are laws this very moment in the statute books of South Carolina and other states, prohibiting the religious instruction of slaves. . . .

In a word, slavery tramples the laws of the living God under its unhallowed feet—weakens and destroys the influence which those laws are calculated to exert over the mind of man, and constrains the oppressed to blaspheme the name of the Almighty.

Speech originally printed in the *Lutheran Herald and Journal of the Fort Plain, N. Y., Franckean Synod,* Vol. 1, No 15 (August 1, 1839) as reprinted in Philip S. Foner, ed., *The Voice of Black America: Major Speeches by Negroes in the United States, 1797–1971.* Copyright © 1972, New York: Simon & Schuster, pp. 67–71.

and the opening of territories where slavery might be prohibited would give the South a minority status and thus eventually overturn its political and social culture. Northerners came to believe that a slave-power conspiracy exercised decisive control over the the federal government. The Compromise of 1850 temporarily restored political calm and stability, and reassured the South. But many northerners came to believe that the compromise only demonstrated the strength of the slave power conspiracy in Washington.

Europe Moves Toward an Industrial Society

As citizens of the United States and thousands of new immigrants moved across the North American continent and debated slavery, Europe headed toward a more fully industrial society. By 1830 only Great Britain had already attained that status, but new factories and railways were beginning to be constructed elsewhere in Europe. However, what characterized the second quarter of the century was less the triumph of industrialism than the final gasps of those economic groups that opposed it and were displaced by it. Intellectually, the period saw the formulation of the major creeds supporting and criticizing the new society.

Proletarianization of Factory Workers and Urban Artisans

In much of northern Europe both artisans and factory workers underwent a process of proletarianization. This term indicates the entry of workers into a wage economy and their gradual loss of significant ownership of the means of production, such as tools and equipment, and of control over the conduct of their own trades. The process occurred rapidly wherever the factory system arose. The factory owner provided the financial capital to construct the factory, purchase the machinery, and secure the raw materials. The factory workers contributed their labor for a wage. Those workers also submitted to factory discipline, which meant that work conditions became largely determined by the demands for smooth operation of the machines. Closing of factory gates to late workers, fines for lateness, dismissal for drunkenness, and public scolding of faulty laborers constituted attempts to enforce human regularity that would match the regularity of cables, wheels, and pistons. The factory workers had no direct say over the quality of the product or its price. It should be noted that for all their difficulties, factory conditions were often better than those of textile workers who resisted the factory mode of production. In particular, English hand-loom weavers, who continued to work in their homes, experienced decades of declining trade and growing poverty in their unsuccessful competition with power looms.

Urban artisans in the nineteenth century experienced proletarianization more slowly than factory workers, and machinery had little to do with the process. The emergence of factories in itself did not harm urban artisans. Many even prospered from the development. For example, the construction and maintenance of the new machines generated major demand for metalworkers, who consequently did well. The actual erection of factories and the expansion of cities benefited all craftsmen in the building trades, such as carpenters, roofers, joiners, and masons. The lower prices for machine-made textiles aided artisans involved in the making of clothing, such as tailors and hatters, by reducing the costs of their raw materials. Where the urban artisans encountered difficulty, and found their skills and livelihood threatened, was in the organization of production.

In the eighteenth century a European town or city workplace had usually consisted of a few artisans laboring for a master, first as apprentices and then as journeymen, according to established guild regulations and practices. The master owned

the workshop and the larger equipment, and the apprentices and journeymen owned their tools. The journeyman could expect to become a master. This guild system had allowed considerable worker control over labor recruitment and training, production pace, product quality, and price.

In the nineteenth century the situation of the urban artisan changed. It became increasingly difficult for artisans to continue to exercise corporate or guild direction and control over their trades. The French Revolution had outlawed such organizations in France. Across Europe, political and economic liberals disapproved of labor and guild organizations and attempted to make them illegal.

Other destructive forces were also at work. The masters often found themselves under increased competitive pressure from larger, more heavily capitalized establishments or from the possibility of the introduction of machine production into a previously craft-dominated industry. In many workshops masters began to follow a practice, known in France as *confection*, whereby goods such as shoes, clothing, and furniture were produced in standard sizes and styles rather than by special orders for individual customers. This practice increased the division of labor in the workshop. Each artisan produced a smaller part of the uniform final product. Consequently, less skill was required of each artisan, and the particular skills possessed by a worker became less valuable. Masters also attempted to increase production and reduce their costs for piecework. Those attempts often led to work stoppages or strikes. Migrants from the countryside or small towns into the cities created, in some cases, a surplus of relatively unskilled workers who were willing to work for lower wages or under less favorable and protected conditions than traditional artisans. The dilution of skills and lower wages, caused not by machinery but by changes in the organization of artisan production, made it much more difficult for urban journeymen ever to hope to become masters with their own workshops where they would be in charge. Increasingly, these artisans became lifetime wage laborers whose skills were simply bought and sold in the marketplace.

It is significant to note that in the United States defenders of slavery frequently compared what they claimed to be the protected situation of slaves living on plantations with the plight of factory workers in both Europe and the northern United States. They argued that a free market in wage labor left workers in a worst situation than that of slaves. But the situation in the European labor market as in the American North was much more complicated than the defenders of slavery contended.

Family Structures and the Industrial Revolution

It is more difficult to generalize about European family structure in the age of early industrialism than under the Old

Regime. Industrialism developed at different rates across the continent, and the impact of industrialism cannot be separated from that of migration and urbanization. Yet the process of factory expansion, proletarianization, and growth of commercial and service sectors related to industrialism did change the structures of much family life and the character of gender roles within families. Much more is known about the relationships of the new industry to the family in Great Britain than elsewhere. It would seem that many of the British developments foreshadowed those in other countries as the factory system spread.

The adoption of new machinery and factory production did not destroy the working-class family. Before the late-eighteenth-century revolution in textile production in England, the individual family involved in textiles was the chief unit of production. The earliest textile inventions, such as the spinning jenny, did not change that situation; the new machine was simply brought into the home. It was the mechanization of weaving that led to the major change. The father who became a machine weaver was employed in a factory. His work was thus separated from his home. The structure of early English factories, however, allowed him to preserve many of his traditional family roles as they had existed before the factory system.

In the domestic system of the family economy, the father and mother had worked with their children in textile production as a family unit. They had trained and disciplined the children within the home setting. Their home life and their economic life were largely the same. In the early factories the father was permitted to employ his wife and children as his assistants. The tasks of education and discipline were not removed from the workplace or from the institution of the family. Parental training and discipline were thus transferred from the home into the early factory. In some cases, in both Britain and France, whole families would move near a new factory so that the family as a unit could work there.

A major shift in this family and factory structure began in the mid-1820s in England and was more or less completed by the mid-1830s. As spinning and weaving were put under one roof, the size of factories and of the machinery became larger. These newer machines required fewer skilled operators but many relatively unskilled attendants. Machine tending became the work of unmarried women and children, who would accept lower wages and were less likely than adult men to attempt any form of worker or union organization. Factory wages for skilled adult males, however, became sufficiently high to allow some fathers to remove their children from the factory and to send them to school. The children who were now working in the factories as assistants were often the children of the economically depressed hand-loom weavers. The wives of the skilled operatives also tended no longer to work in the factories. Consequently, the original links of the family in the British textile factory that had existed for well over a quarter century largely disappeared.

At this point in the 1830s concern about the plight of child labor came to dominate workers' attention. The workers were concerned about the treatment of factory children because discipline was no longer being exercised by parents over their own children in the factories. The English Factory Act of 1833, passed to protect children by limiting their workday to eight hours and requiring two hours of education paid for by the factory owner, further divided work and home life. The workday for adult males remained twelve hours. Children often worked in relays of four or six hours. Consequently, the parental link was thoroughly broken. The education requirement began the process of removing nurturing and training from the home and family and setting them into a school, where a teacher rather than the parents was in charge of education.

After this act was passed many of the working-class demands for shorter workdays for adults related to the desire to reunite, in some manner, the workday of adults with that of their children, or at least to allow adults to spend more hours with their children. In 1847 Parliament mandated a ten-hour day. By present standards this was long, but it allowed parents and children more time together as a domestic unit because their relationship as a work or production unit had ceased wherever the factory system prevailed. By the middle of the 1840s, in the lives of industrial workers the roles of men as breadwinners, as fathers, and as husbands had become distinct in the British textile industry.

As the British example illustrates, with the spread of the factory system the European family became the chief unit of consumption rather then the chief unit of both production and consumption. This development did not mean the end of the family as an economic unit. Parents and children, however, now came to depend on sharing wages often derived from several sources rather than on sharing work in the home or factory.

Ultimately the wage economy did loosen family ties. Because wages could be sent over long distances to parents, children might move farther away from home, and the economic link was often broken. During the next generation, however, once settled in an industrial city, children might once again find wage employment in the same city and then continue to live at home until they had accumulated enough savings to marry and begin their own households. That situation meant that children often remained with their parents to a later age than they had in the past.

Women in the Early Industrial Revolution

The industrial economy ultimately produced an immense impact on the home and the family life of women. First, it took virtually all productive work out of the home and al-

Women Industrial Workers Explain Their Economic Situation

In 1832 there was much discussion in the British press about factory legislation. Most of that discussion was concerned with the employment of children, but The Examiner *newspaper made the suggestion that any factory laws should not only address the problem of child labor but also in time eliminate women from employment in factories. That article provoked the following remarkable letter to the editor, composed by or on behalf of women factory workers, which eloquently stated the real necessity of such employment for women and the unattractive alternatives.*

What are the reasons these women enumerate to prove the necessity of their holding manufacturing jobs? What changes in production methods have led women from the home to the factory? How does the situation of these women relate to the possibility of their marrying? Compare the plight of these English working-class women with that of the French middle-class woman in the next document.

Sir,

Living as we do, in the densely populated manufacturing districts of Lancashire, and most of us belonging to that class of females who earn their bread either directly or indirectly by manufactories, we have looked with no little anxiety for your opinion on the Factory Bill. . . . You are for doing away with our services in manufactories altogether. So much the better, if you had pointed out any other more eligible and practical employment for the surplus female labour, that will want other channels for a subsistence. If our competition were withdrawn, and short hours substituted, we have no doubt but the effects would be as you have stated, "not to lower wages, as the male branch of the family would be enabled to earn as much as the whole had done," but for the thousands of females who are employed in manufactories, who have no legiti-mate claim on any male relative for employment or support, and who have, through a variety of circumstance, been early thrown on their own resources for a livelihood, what is to become of them?

In this neighbourhood, hand-loom has been almost totally superseded by power-loom weaving, and no inconsiderable number of females, who must depend on their own exertions, or their parishes for support, have been forced, of necessity into the manufactories, from their total inability to earn a livelihood at home.

It is a lamentable fact, that, in these parts of the country, there is scarcely any other mode of employment for female industry, if we except servitude and dressmaking. Of the former of these, there is no chance of employment for one-twentieth of the candidates that would rush into the field, to say nothing of lowering the wages of our sisters of the same craft; and of the latter, galling as some of the hardships of manufactories are (of which the indelicacy of mixing with the men is not the least), yet there are few women who have been so employed, that would change conditions with the ill-used genteel little slaves, who have to lose sleep and health, in catering to the whims and frivolities of the butterflies of fashion.

We see no way of escape from starvation, but to accept the very tempting offers of the newspapers, held out as baits to us, fairly to ship ourselves off to Van Dieman's Land [Tasmania] on the very delicate errand of husband hunting, and having safely arrived at the "Land of Goshen," jump ashore, with a "Who wants me?" . . .

The Female Operatives of Todmorden

From *The Examiner,* February 26, 1832, as quoted in Ivy Pinchbeck, *Women Workers and the Industrial Revolution, 1750–1850* © 1969 Augustus M. Kelley, pp. 199–200.

---

lowed many families to live on the wages of the male spouse alone. That transformation prepared the way for a new concept of gender-determined roles in the home and in general domestic life. Women came to be associated with domestic duties such as housekeeping, food preparation, child rearing and nurturing, and household management. The man came to be associated almost exclusively with breadwinning. Children were reared to match these gender patterns. Previously, this domestic division of labor had prevailed only among the relatively small middle and gentry class. During the nineteenth century it came to characterize the working class as well. Second, industrialization created new modes of employment that allowed many young women to earn enough money to marry or, if necessary, to support themselves inde-pendently. Third, industrialism, although fostering more employment for women, lowered the skills required of them.

Because the early Industrial Revolution had begun in textile production, women and their labor were deeply involved from the start. While both spinning and weaving were still domestic industries, women usually worked in all stages of production. Hand spinning was virtually always a woman's task. When spinning was moved into factories and involved large machines, however, women tended to be displaced by men. The higher wages commanded by male cotton-factory workers allowed many women to stop working or to work only to supplement their husbands' wages.

With the next generation of machines in the 1820s unmarried women rapidly became employed in the factories.

As textile production became increasingly automated in the nineteenth century, textile factories required fewer skilled workers and more unskilled attendants. To fill these unskilled positions, factory owners turned increasingly to unmarried women and widows, who worked for lower wages than men and were less likely to form labor organizations. [Bildarchiv Preussischer Kulturbesitz]

However, their jobs tended to require less skill than most work done by men and than women had previously exercised in the home production of textiles. There was thus a certain paradox in the impact of the factory on women. Many new jobs opened to them, but those jobs were less skilled than what had been available to them before. Moreover, the women in the factories were almost always young and single or widows. At marriage or perhaps at the birth of the first child, a woman usually found that her husband earned enough money for her to leave the factory. Factory owners also disliked employing married women because of the likelihood of pregnancy, the influence of husbands, and the duties of child rearing.

In Britain and elsewhere by mid-century, industrial factory work accounted for less than half of all employment for women. The largest group of employed women in France continued to work on the land. In England they were domestic servants. Domestic industries, such as lace glove and garment making and other kinds of needlework, employed many women. Their conditions of labor were almost always harsh, whether they worked in their homes or in sweated workshops. Generally all work done by women commanded low wages and involved low skills. They had virtually no way

to protect themselves from exploitation. The charwoman was a common sight across the continent and symbolized the plight of working women.

One of the most serious problems facing working women was the uncertainty of employment. Because they virtually always found themselves in the least skilled jobs and trades, their employment was never secure. Much of their work was seasonal. This was one reason so many working-class women feared they might be compelled to turn to prostitution. On the other hand, cities and the more complex economy did allow a greater variety of jobs. Movement to cities and entrance into the wage economy also gave women wider opportunities for marriage. Cohabitation before marriage seems to have been common. Parents did not arrange marriages as frequently as in the past. Marriage also generally meant that a woman would leave the work force to live on her husband's earnings. If all went well, that arrangement might improve her situation, but if the husband became ill or died, or deserted her, she would have to reenter the market for unskilled labor at a much advanced age.

Nonetheless, many of the traditional practices associated with the family economy survived into the industrial era. As a young woman came of age, both family needs and her desire to marry still directed what she would do with her life. The most likely early occupation for a young woman was domestic service. A girl born in the country normally migrated to a nearby town or city for such employment, often living initially with a relative. As in the past, she would attempt to earn enough in wages to give herself a dowry so that she might marry and establish her own household. If she became a factory worker she would probably live in a supervised dormitory. Such dormitories were one of the ways factory owners attracted young women workers, by convincing parents that their daughters would be safe. The life of young women in the cities seems to have been more precarious than it had been earlier. There seem to have been fewer family and community ties. There were also perhaps more available young men. These men, who worked for wages rather than in the older apprenticeship structures, were more mobile, so relationships between men and women were often more fleeting. In any case, illegitimate births increased. That is to say, fewer women who became pregnant before marriage found the father willing to marry them.

Marriage in the wage industrial economy was also different. It still involved the starting of a separate household, but the structure of gender relationships within the household was different. Marriage was less an economic partnership: The husband might be able to support the entire family. The wage economy and the industrialization separating workplace and home made it difficult for women to combine domestic duties with work. When married women worked, it was

The Women of the Seneca Falls Convention Issue a Declaration of Female Independence

Although women during the French Revolution had called for equal rights, their demands had been ignored and their social and legal position actually made less secure by the legislation of the revolutionary era. The cause of women's independence thereafter received some of its strongest defence in the United States, with the European women's movement emerging somewhat later. The early women's rights movement in the United States was one of many reform efforts of the 1840s. In July 1848, while much of Europe was in the turmoil of the revolutions of that year, the first national women's rights convention gathered at Seneca Falls, New York, and issued a declaration that self-consciously imitated the U.S. Declaration of Independence. This declaration raised the issues of the political rights of women, their position in the family and under family law, and their economic opportunities. Society within both the United States and in Europe still has not confronted many of these issues.

Which of the absent rights listed here apply to the public political sphere and which to the home? What are the specific economic disabilities under which women are said to labor? How, according to the declaration, have the personal and cultural confidence of women been broken? What additions or qualifications might women from other parts of the world have made to this declaration in the 1840s and then later in the 1880s?

When, in the course of human events, it becomes necessary for one portion of the family of man to assume among the people of the earth a position different from that which they have hitherto occupied, but one to which the laws of nature and nature's God entitle them, a decent respect to the opinions of mankind requires that they should declare the causes that impel them to such a course. . . .

The history of mankind is a history of repeated injuries and unsurpations on the part of man toward woman, having in direct object the establishment of an absolute tyranny over her. To prove this, let facts be submitted to a candid world.

He has never permitted her to exercise her inalienable right to the elective franchise.

He has compelled her to submit to laws, in the formation of which she had no voice. . . .

Having deprived her of this first right of a citizen, the elective franchise, thereby leaving her without representation in the halls of legislation, he has oppressed her on all sides.

He has made her, if married, in the eye of the law, civilly dead.

He has taken from her all rights in property, even to the wages she earns.

He has made her, morally an irresponsible being, as she can commit many crimes with impunity, provided they be done in the presence of her husband. In the covenant of marriage, she is compelled to promise obedience to her husband, he becoming, to all intents and purposes, her master—the law giving him power to deprive her of her liberty, and to administer chastisement.

He has so framed the laws of divorce, as to what shall be the proper causes, and in case of separation, to whom the guardianship of the children shall be given, as to be wholly regardless of the happiness of women—the law, in all cases, going upon a false supposition of the supremacy of man, and given all power into his hands. . . .

He has monopolized nearly all the profitable employments, and from those she is permitted to follow, she receives but a scanty remuneration. He closes against her all the avenues to wealth and distinction which he considers most honorable to himself. As a teacher of theology, medicine or law, she is not known.

He has denied her the facilities for obtaining a thorough education, all colleges being closed against her. . . .

He has created false public sentiment by giving to the world a different code of morals for men and women. . . .

He has endeavored, in every way that he could, to destroy her confidence in her own powers, to lessen her self-respect, and to make her willing to lead a dependent and abject life.

Now, in view of this entire disfranchisement of one-half the people of this country . . . we insist that they have immediate admission to all the rights and privileges which belong to them as citizens of the United States.

In entering upon the great work before us, we anticipate no small amount of misconception, misrepresentation and ridicule; but we shall use every instrumentality within our power to effect our object.

From "Declaration of Sentiments of the Seneca Falls Convention" (July 19–20, 1848); quoted in E. C. Stanton, S. B. Anthony, and M. J. Gage, *History of Woman Suffrage* (Rochester, NY, 1887), Vol. I, pp. 70–71; as cited in Oscar Handlin, ed., *Readings in American History*. Copyright © 1957 Alfred A. Knopf, pp. 317–318.

A Young Middle-Class French Woman Writes to Her Father About Marriage

Stéphanie Jullien was a young middle-class woman whose father wished her to marry a man who was courting her. She had already rejected one suitor and was thus a great concern to her father. In this letter she explains to her father the matters that disturb her and make her wish to delay her decision. Ultimately, she did marry the man in question, and the marriage appears to have been happy.

How does Stéphanie Jullien distinguish between the vocational and social opportunities available to a woman and those to a man? What are her expectations of a relationship with a husband? What does the letter also tell you about her sense of her relationship to her father? Compare this letter with the preceding letter by English working-class women. What problems do the women share? How are their lives different? What does a comparison of the two letters tell you about the difference in class experience in the early nineteenth century?

You men have a thousand occupations to distract you: society, business, politics, and work absorb you, exhaust you, upset you. . . . As for us women who, as you have said to me from time to time, have only the roses in life, we feel more profoundly in our solitude and in our idleness the sufferings that you can slough off. I don't want to make a comparison here between the destiny of man and the destiny of woman: each sex has its own lot, its own troubles, its own pleasures. I only want to explain to you that excess of moroseness of which you complain and of which I am the first to suffer. . . . I am not able to do anything for myself and for those around me. I am depriving my brothers in order to have a dowry. I am not even able to live alone, being obliged to take from others, not only in order to live but also in order to be protected, since social convention does not allow me to have independence. And yet the world finds me guilty of being the only person that I am at liberty to be; not having useful or productive work to do, not having any calling except marriage, and not being able to look by myself for someone who will suit me, I am full of cares and anxieties. . . .

I am asking for more time [before responding to a marriage proposal]. It is not too much to want to see and know a man for ten months, even a year when it is a matter of passing one's life with him. There is no objection to make, you say. But the most serious and the most important presents itself: I do not love him. Don't think I am talking about a romantic and impossible passion or an ideal love, neither of which I ever hope to know. I am talking of a feeling that makes one want to see someone, that makes his absence painful and his return desirable, that makes one interested in what another is doing, that makes one want another's happiness almost in spite of oneself, that makes, finally, the duties of a woman toward her husband pleasures and not efforts. It is a feeling without which marriage would be hell, a feeling that cannot be born out of esteem, and which to me, however, seems to be the very basis of conjugal happiness. I can't feel these emotions immediately. . . . Let me have some time. I want to love, not out of any sense of duty, but for myself and for the happiness of the one to whom I attach my life, who will suffer if he only encounters coldness in me, when he brings me love and devotion.

From the Jullien Family Papers, 39 AP 4, Archives Nationales, Paris, trans. by Barbara Corrado Pope, as quoted in Erna Olafson Hellerstein, Leslie Parker Hume, and Karen M. Offen, eds., *Victorian Women: A Documentary Account of Women's Lives in Nineteenth-Century England, France, and the United States*. Copyright © 1981 Stanford University Press, pp. 247–248.

usually in the nonindustrial sector of the economy. More often than not children rather than the wife were sent to work, which may help explain the increase of fertility within marriages, since children in the wage economy tended to be an economic asset. Married women worked outside the home only when family needs or illness or the death of a spouse really required them to do so.

Within the home, the domestic duties of working-class women were an essential factor in the family wage economy. Homemaking came to the fore when a life at home had to be organized that was separate from the place of work. Wives were primarily concerned with food and cooking, but they often also were in charge of the family's finances. The role of the mother expanded when the children still living at home became wage earners. She was then providing home support for her entire wage-earning family. She created the environment to which the family members returned after work. The longer period of home life of working children may also have strengthened the affection between those children and their hard-working, homebound mothers.

Marxist Critique of the Industrial Order

The eighteen forties, in the thought of Karl Marx, produced the most influential of all critiques of the newly emerged industrial order. His analysis became so important because later in the century, as will be seen in Chapter 28, it was adopted by the leading socialist political party in Germany, which in turn influenced most other European socialist parties including a small group of exiled Russian socialists led by V. I. Lenin. Marx (1818–1883) was born in the Rhineland. His Jewish middle-class parents sent him to the University of Berlin, where he became deeply involved in radical politics. During 1842 and 1843 he edited the radical *Rhineland Gazette*. Soon the German authorities drove him into exile—first in Paris; then in Brussels; and finally, after 1849, in London.

In 1844 Marx met Friedrich Engels (1820–1895), another young middle-class German, whose father owned a textile factory in Manchester, England. The next year, Engels published *The Condition of the Working Class in England*, which presented a devastating picture of industrial life. The two men became fast friends. Late in 1847 they were asked to write a pamphlet for a newly organized and ultimately short-lived secret communist league. *The Communist Manifesto*, published in German, appeared early in 1848. Marx, Engels, and the league had adopted the name *communist* because the term was much more self-consciously radical than *socialist*. *Communism* implied the outright abolition of private property rather than some less extensive rearrangement of society. The *Manifesto* itself was a work of fewer than fifty pages. It would become the most influential political document of modern European history, but that development lay in the future. At the time it was simply one more political tract. Moreover, neither Marx nor his thought had any effect on the revolutionary events of 1848.

In *The Communist Manifesto* Marx and Engels contended that human history must be understood rationally and as a whole. According to their analysis, history is the record of humankind's coming to grips with physical nature to produce the goods necessary for survival. That basic productive process determines the structures, values, and ideas of a society. Historically, the organization of the means of production has always involved conflict between the classes who owned and controlled the means of production and those classes who worked for them. That necessary conflict has provided the engine for historical development; it is not an accidental by-product of mismanagement or bad intentions. Consequently, only a radical social transformation, not piecemeal reforms, can eliminate the social and economic evils inherent in the very structures of production. Such a revolution will occur as the inevitable outcome of the development of capitalism.

In Marx's and Engels's eyes, during the nineteenth century the class conflict that had characterized previous western history had become a struggle between the bourgeoisie and the proletariat, or between the middle class and the workers. The character of capitalism ensured the sharpening of the struggle. Capitalist production and competition would steadily increase the size of the unpropertied proletariat. Large-scale mechanical production crushed both traditional

Karl Marx's socialist philosophy eventually triumphed over most alternative versions of socialism in Europe, but his monumental work has been subject to varying interpretations, criticisms, and revisions that continue to this day. [Bildarchiv Preussischer Kulturbesitz]

and smaller industrial producers into the ranks of the proletariat. As the business structures grew larger and larger, smaller middle-class units would be squeezed out by the competitive pressures. Competition among the few remaining gigantic concerns would lead to more intense suffering by the proletariat. As the workers suffered increasingly from the competition among the ever-enlarging firms, they would foment revolution and finally overthrow the few remaining owners of the means of production. For a time the workers would organize the means of production through a dictatorship of the proletariat, which would eventually give way to a propertyless and classless communist society.

This proletarian revolution was inevitable, according to Marx and Engels. The structure of capitalism required competition and consolidation of enterprise. Although the class conflict involved in the contemporary process resembled that of the past, it differed in one major respect. The struggle between the capitalistic bourgeoisie and the industrial proletariat would culminate in a wholly new society that would be free of class conflict. The victorious proletariat, by its very nature, they contended, could not be a new oppressor class: "The proletarian movement is the self-conscious, independent movement of the immense majority, in the interest of

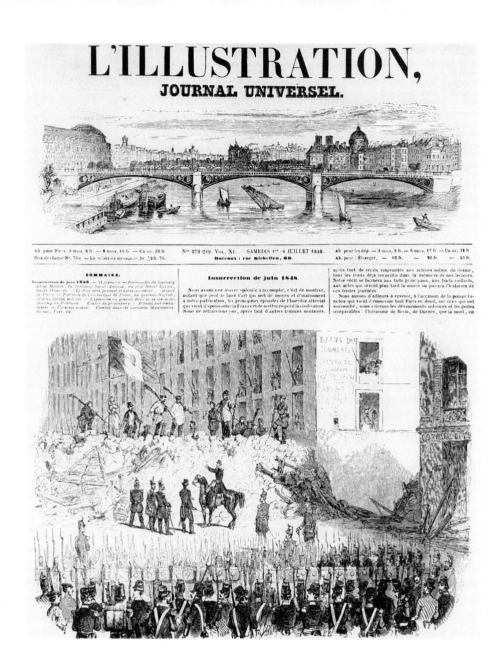

During June 1848 troops moved against the insurrection in Paris. This edition of a French journal is reporting those events and illustrates a moment before a clash between troops and revolutionaries. [Bildarchiv Preussischer Kulturbesitz]

the immense majority."[1] The result of the proletarian victory would be "an association, in which the free development of each is the condition for the free development of all."[2] The victory of the proletariat over the bourgeoisie represented the culmination of human history. For the first time, one group of people would not be oppressing another.

Marx's analysis was conditioned by his own economic environment. The 1840s had seen much unemployment and deprivation. Capitalism, however, did not collapse as he predicted, nor did the middle class during the rest of the centu-

ry or later become proletarianized. Rather, more and more people came to benefit from the industrial system. Nonetheless, within a generation Marxism had captured the imagination of many socialists and large segments of the working class. Its doctrines were allegedly based on the empirical evidence of hard economic fact. This much proclaimed scientific aspect of Marxism helped the ideology, as science became more influential during the second half of the century. Marx had made the ultimate victory of socialism seem certain. His works also suggested that the path to socialism lay with revolution rather than reform. As Marxist thought permeated the international socialist movement during the next seventy-five years, it would provide the ideological basis for some of the most momentous and ultimately repressive po-

[1]Robert C. Tucker, ed., *The Marx-Engels Reader* (New York: W. E. Norton, 1972), p. 353.
[2]Ibid.

litical movements in the history of virtually the entire modern world.

1848: Year of Revolutions

In 1848 a series of liberal and nationalistic revolutions and revolts spread across the Continent. No single factor caused this general revolutionary ground swell; rather, similar conditions existed in several countries. Severe food shortages had prevailed since 1846 due to poor harvests. The commercial and industrial economy was in recession, with widespread unemployment. However, the dynamic for change in 1848 originated not with the working classes but with the political liberals, who were generally drawn from the middle classes. Throughout the Continent liberals were pushing for more representative governments, civil liberty, and unregulated economic life.

To put additional pressure on their governments, the liberals began to appeal for the support of the urban working classes, even though the goals of the two groups were different. The working classes sought improved employment and better working conditions rather than political reform for its own sake. The liberals refused to follow political revolution with social reform and thus isolated themselves from their temporary working-class allies. Once separated from potential mass support, the liberal revolutions became an easy prey to the armies of reactionary governments. As a result, the revolutions of 1848 failed to establish genuinely liberal or national states.

France: The Second Republic and Louis Napoleon

Early in 1848 liberal political opponents of Louis Philippe had organized a series of political banquets to criticize the regime. On February 21, 1848, the government forbade further banquets. During the next several days crowds erected barricades in Paris, and fighting occurred between the citizenry and the municipal guards. On February 24, 1848, Louis Philippe abdicated and fled to England.

The liberal opposition organized a provisional government. It was soon confronted by working-class groups seeking social as well as political revolution. Under working-class pressure the provisional government organized national workshops to provide work and relief for thousands of unemployed workers. The election held on April 23 produced a National Assembly dominated by moderates and conservatives who had little sympathy for the expensive national workshops, which they considered socialistic. Throughout May government troops and the Parisian crowd of unemployed workers and artisans clashed. By late June barricades again appeared in Paris. On June 24 the government ordered

Louis Kossuth, a Magyar nationalist, seeking to raise troops to fight for Hungarian independence during the revolutionary disturbances of 1848.
[Bildarchiv Preussischer Kulturbesitz]

troops to destroy the barricades, and more than 3,000 people died in street fighting.

The so-called June Days confirmed the political predominance of conservative property owners in French life. Their search for social order led, in 1848, to the election to the presidency of Louis Napoleon Bonaparte (1808–1873), a nephew of the great emperor. This election of the "Little Napoleon" doomed the Second Republic. Louis Napoleon was the first of the modern dictators who, by playing on political instability and social insecurity, have so changed European life. For three years he quarreled with the National Assembly; then, on December 2, 1851, he seized power in a military coup. In a plebiscite of December 21, 1851, over 7.5 million voters supported his actions, with only 640,000 disapproving. A year later, in December 1852, another plebiscite made France an empire. Louis Napoleon became Emperor Napoleon III (r. 1852–1870) in deference to the first Napoleon's deceased young son.

The Habsburg Empire: Nationalism Resisted

The events of February 1848 in Paris immediately reverberated throughout the Habsburg domains, which were highly susceptible to revolutionary challenge. Their government rejected liberal institutions. Their geographical borders ignored the principle of nationalism. Their society perpetuated serfdom. In 1848 the regime confronted major rebellions in Vienna, Prague, Hungary, and northern Italy.

The Habsburg troubles commenced on March 3, 1848, when Louis Kossuth (1802–1894), a Magyar nationalist, attacked

The Revolutionary Crisis of 1848–1851

1848

February 22–24	Revolution in Paris forces the abdication of Louis Philippe
February 26	National workshops established in Paris
March 3	Kossuth attacks Habsburg domination of Hungary
March 13	Revolution in Vienna
March 15	Habsburg emperor accepts Hungarian March Laws
	Revolution in Berlin
March 18	Frederick William IV of Prussia promises a constitution
	Revolution in Milan
March 22	Piedmont declares war on Austria
April 23	Election of French National Assembly
May 17	Habsburg Emperor Ferdinand flees from Vienna to Innsbruck
May 18	Frankfurt Assembly gathers to prepare a German constitution
June 17	Czech revolution in Prague is suppressed
June 23–26	Workers' insurrection in Paris is suppressed
July 24	Austria defeats Piedmont
November 25	Pius IX flees Rome
December 2	Franz Joseph becomes emperor of Austria
December 10	Louis Napoleon elected president of the second French Republic

1849

January 5	Austrian troops occupy Budapest
February 2	Roman Republic is proclaimed
March 12	War resumes between Piedmont and Austria
March 23	Piedmond is defeated; Charles Albert abdicates the crown of Piedmont in favor of Victor Emmanuel II
April 21	Frederick William IV of Prussia rejects crown offered by Frankfurt Parliament
June 18	Remaining members of Frankfurt Parliament dispersed by troops
July 3	Collapse of Roman Republic after invasion by French troops

1851

December 2	Coup d'état of Louis Napoleon

Austrian domination of Hungary. Shortly thereafter student riots broke out in Vienna. After the army failed to restore order, Metternich fled the country. On May 17 Emperor Ferdinand (r. 1835–1848) fled Vienna for Innsbruck. In December he abdicated in favor of his nephew Franz Joseph (1848–1916).

Even more than urban disturbances, the Habsburg government feared an uprising of the serfs. Almost immediately after the Vienna riots, the imperial government emancipated the serfs in most of Austria. The Hungarian Diet also abolished serfdom in March 1848. These actions smothered the most serious potential threat to order in the empire.

In each section of the empire the Habsburg government confronted revolution by making concessions that it later repudiated. In Hungary the emperor had approved a series of liberal laws in March 1848. By January 1849, however, the army had occupied Budapest and restored its own mode of government. Similarly, in March 1848 Czech nationalists in Bohemia and Moravia organized a Pan-Slavic Congress that called for national equality of Slavs in the Habsburg Empire. But the Habsburg forces occupied Prague and suppressed the revolution there. In Italy nationalists drove the Austrians from Milan in March 1848. King Charles Albert of Piedmont (r. 1831–1849) supported them and went to war against Austria, but by July the Habsburg army had defeated Piedmont and suppressed the revolution. The Habsburg government had survived its gravest internal challenge as a result of the divisions among its enemies and its own willingness to use military force with a vengeance.

Italy: Republicanism Defeated

The defeat of Piedmont was a sharp disappointment to Italian nationalists who had hoped to unify the peninsula. Liberal and nationalist hopes then shifted to the pope. Pius IX (1846–1878) had a liberal reputation. He had reformed the administration of the Papal States. Nationalists believed that a united Italian state might emerge under his leadership.

In November 1848 political disturbances erupted in Rome, and Pius IX fled to Naples. In February 1849 the radicals proclaimed the Roman Republic. The next month radicals in Piedmont forced Charles Albert to renew the patriotic war against Austria. Piedmont was quickly defeated and Charles Albert abdicated in favor of his son Victor Emmanuel II (r. 1849–1878). In early June French troops attacked Rome, overthrew the republic, and restored the pope; these troops remained in Rome until 1870 to protect the pope. Pius IX renounced his previous liberalism. Leadership for Italian unification would have to come from another direction.

Germany: Liberalism Frustrated

In Germany the major revolution occurred in Prussia in March 1848. Frederick William IV (r. 1840–1861) had to call a constituent assembly to write a constitution and to appoint a moderately liberal cabinet. In time, the king and his advisers decided to ignore the assembly. In April 1849 Frederick William dissolved the assembly and proclaimed his own conservative constitution.

On May 18, 1848, representatives from all the German states gathered in Frankfurt to revise the the German Con-

The Pan-Slavic Congress Calls for the Liberation of Slavic Nationalities

The first Pan-Slavic Congress met in Prague in June 1848. In this "Manifesto" it called for the reorganization of the Austrian Empire and the political reorganization of most of the rest of eastern Europe. Its calls for changes in the national standing of the various Slavic peoples would have touched the Russian, Austrian, and Ottoman empires as well as some of the not yet united states of Germany. The national aspirations voiced in this document would affect Europe from that time to the present. It is also important to note that the authors recognize that the principle of nationality as adapted to the political life of Slavic peoples is relatively new in 1848.

How did the authors of this manifesto apply the individual freedoms associated with the French Revolution to the fate of individual nations? What are the specific areas of Europe that these demands would have changed? What potential national or ethnic differences among the Slavic peoples does this manifesto ignore or gloss over?

The Slavic Congress in Prague is something unheard-of, in Europe as well as among the Slavs themselves. For the first time since our appearance in history, we, the scattered members of a great race, have gathered in great numbers from distant lands in order to become reacquainted as brothers and to deliberate our affairs peacefully. We have understood one another not only through our beautiful language, spoken by eighty millions, but also through the consonance of our hearts and the similarity of our spiritual qualities. . . .

It is not only in behalf of the individual within the state that we raise our voices and make known our demands.

The nation, with all its intellectual merit, is as sacred to us as are the rights of an individual under natural law. . . .

In the belief that the powerful spiritual stream of today demands new political forms and that the state must be re-established upon altered principles, if not within new boundaries, we have suggested to the Austrian Emperor, under whose constitutional government we, the majority [of Slavic peoples] live, that he transform his imperial state into a union of equal nations. . . .

. . . We raise our voices vigorously in behalf of our unfortunate brothers, the Poles, who were robbed of their national identity by insidious force. We call upon the governments to rectify this curse and these old onerous and hereditary sins in their administrative policy, and we trust in the compassion of all Europe. . . . We demand that the Hungarian Ministry abolish without delay the use of inhuman and coercive means toward the Slavic races in Hungary, namely the Serbs, Croats, Slovaks, and Ruthenians, and that they promptly be completely assured of their national rights. Finally, we hope that the inconsiderate policies of the Porte will no longer hinder our Slavic brothers in Turkey from strongly claiming their nationality and developing it in a natural way. If, therefore, we formally express our opposition to such despicable deeds, we do so in the confidence that we are working for the good of freedom. Freedom makes the peoples who hitherto have ruled more just and makes them understand that injustice and arrogance bring disgrace not to those who must endure it but to those who act in such a manner.

From *Man, State, and Society in East European History*, Stephen Fisher-Galati, ed. © Copyright 1970, pp. 156–159. Reproduced with permission of Greenwood Publishing Group Inc., Westport, CT.

---

federation. The Frankfurt Parliament intended to write a moderately liberal constitution. However, it quickly lost the support of German workers and artisans by refusing to restore the economic protection once afforded by the guilds. In September 1848 the Frankfurt Parliament called in troops of the German Confederation to suppress a radical working-class insurrection in the city.

The Frankfurt Parliament also floundered on the issue of German unification. Members differed over whether to include Austria in a united Germany. Austria, however, rejected the whole notion of German unification, which raised too many other nationality problems within the Habsburg domains. Consequently, the Frankfurt Parliament looked to Prussian leadership. This tactic also failed because Frederick William IV refused to accept the crown of a united Germany

from the liberal parliament. On his refusal in the spring of 1849, the Frankfurt Parliament began to dissolve. Not long afterward troops dispersed the remaining members. In many respects German liberalism never recovered from the failures of the Frankfurt Parliament. One additional result of the collapse of German liberalism in 1848 and 1849 was the immigration of numerous Germans of liberal political inclination to the United States where during the 1850s they tended often to settle in the northern states and to become opponents of southern slavery.

The turmoil of 1848 through 1850 ended the era of liberal revolution that had begun in 1789. Liberals and nationalists had discovered that rational argument and small insurrections would not help them to achieve their goals. The working class also adopted new tactics and organization.

The era of the riot and urban insurrection was ending. In the future, workers would turn to trade unions and political parties to achieve their political and social goals. Finally, after the revolutions of 1848, the political initiative in Europe passed for a time to the conservative political groups.

IN WORLD PERSPECTIVE

Early-Nineteenth-Century Europe and the United States

The first half of the nineteenth century witnessed three major developments in Europe that would affect the entire world. First, the modern industrial economy permanently established itself in European life. This achievement gave Europeans for decades a disproportionate economic and military influence throughout the world. At the same time, Europe experienced social dislocation that foreshadowed the pressures on family and community that would arise elsewhere in the world when predominantly agricultural economies made the difficult transition to industrialized ones.

Second, during the first half of the century Europeans developed political ideologies that eventually spread over most of the globe, although in all cases adapted to local circumstances. The ideas associated with liberalism would come to

be used against traditional forms of government elsewhere in the world. In the non-European world nationalism would often most forcefully display itself in the twentieth century as an ideological weapon used against European colonial rule. Marxism, originating in a protest against European industrial conditions, would spread around the world during the twentieth century as various poor and relatively underdeveloped nations sought to reject the dominance of wealthy, industrialized ones.

Third, the defeat of liberal political forces in 1848 and the triumph of conservative powers influenced the modernization of Japan. Within a few years Japan would emerge from its long self-imposed isolation. After the Meiji Restoration the new leaders of Japan looked to European examples of successful modern nations. The nation they would most clearly copy was the conservative, militaristic Germany that emerged after the defeat of the liberals of 1848.

During this same era the United States continued to pursue the most politically advanced democratic experiment of any nation in the world. It saw itself as an arena where reform and progress could fully manifest themselves. Part of that drive to reform led to its debate over slavery, which would ultimately result in civil war. Its economy grew and prospered in a manner that sharply differed from its neighbors in Latin America. That prosperity, along with its democratic politics, attracted immigrants from much of Europe, an attraction that would grow all the stronger in the second half of the century.

Review Questions ——

1. Define nationalism. What were the goals of nationalists? What were the difficulties they confronted in realizing those goals? Why was nationalism a special threat to the Austrian Empire? What areas saw significant nationalist movements between 1815 and 1830? Which were successful and which unsuccessful?

2. What were the tenets of liberalism? Who were the liberals and how did liberalism affect the political developments of the early nineteenth century? What relationship does liberalism have to nationalism?

3. Discuss why France experienced political change by revolution in 1830 and why England achieved political change through parliamentary reform in 1832.

4. What economic differences between the American North and South gave rise to sectional conflict? Why was slavery the core issue in that conflict? How did the westward

movement contribute to making slavery so important an issue?

5. What changes did industrialism make in society? Why were the years covered in this chapter so difficult for artisans? What is meant by the expression "the proletarianization of workers"?

6. In what ways did the industrial economy change the working-class family? What roles and duties did various family members assume? Most specifically, how did the role of women change in the new industrial era?

7. What factors, old and new, led to the widespread outbreak of revolutions in 1848? Were the causes in the various countries essentially the same or did each have its own particular set of circumstances? Why did these revolutions fail throughout Europe? What roles did liberals and nationalists play in these revolutions? Why did they sometimes clash?

Suggested Readings ——

B. ANDERSON, *Imagined Communities*, rev. ed. (1991). A discussion of the forces that have fostered national identity.

R. M. BERDAHL, *The Politics of the Prussian Nobility: The Development of a Conservative Ideology, 1770–1848* (1988). A major examination of German conservative outlooks.

I. BERLIN, *Karl Marx: His Life and Environment*, 4th ed. (1996). A volume that remains an excellent introduction.

J. BLASSINGAME, *The Slave Community* (1975). Emphasizes the manner in which slaves shaped their own community.

S. G. CHECKLAND, *The Rise of Industrial Society in England, 1815–1885* (1964). Strong on economic institutions.

A. CLARKE, *The Struggle for the Breeches: Gender and the Making of the British Working Class* (1995). An examination of the manner in which industrialization made problematical the relationships between men and women.

W. COLEMAN, *Death Is a Social Disease: Public Health and Political Economy in Early Industrial France* (1982). One of the first works in English to study this problem.

I. DEAK, *The Lawful Revolution: Louis Kossuth and the Hungarians, 1848–1849* (1979). The most significant study of the topic in English.

M. DUBERMAN, ED., *The Anti-Slavery Vanguard* (1965) Important essays.

T. DUBLIN, *Women at Work: The Transformation of Work and Community in Lowell, Massachusetts, 1826–1860* (1979). The best work on this important setting of early American industrialization.

J. ELSTER, *An Introduction to Karl Marx* (1985). The best volume to provide a discussion of Marx's fundamental concepts.

E. GENOVESE, *Roll Jordan Roll* (1974). The best overview of American slavery.

L. GREENFIELD, *Nationalism: Five Roads to Modernity* (1992). A major comparative study.

T. HAMEROW, *Restoration, Revolution, and Reaction: Economics and Politics in Germany, 1815–1871* (1958). Traces the forces that worked toward the failure of revolution in Germany.

R. F. HAMILTON, *The Bourgeois Epoch: Marx and Engels on Britain, France, and Germany* (1991). Examines Marx's and Engels's observations against what is known to have been the situation in each nation.

G. HIMMELFARB, *The Idea of Poverty: England in the Early Industrial Age* (1984). A major work covering the subject from the time of Adam Smith through 1850.

E. J. HOBSBAWM, *The Age of Revolution, 1789–1848* (1962). A very comprehensive survey emphasizing the social ramifications of the liberal democratic and industrial revolutions.

E. J. HOBSBAWM, *Nations and Nationalism Since 1780: Programme, Myth, Reality*, rev. ed. (1992). The best recent introduction to the subject.

A. JARDIN AND A. J. TUDESQ, *Restoration and Reaction, 1815–1848* (1984). Surveys this period in France.

K. KOLAKOWSKI, *Main Currents of Marxism: Its Rise, Growth, and Dissolution*, 3 vols. (1978). A very important and comprehensive survey.

D. LANDES, *The Unbound Prometheus: Technological Change and Industrial Development in Western Europe from 1750 to the Present* (1969). The best one-volume treatment of technological development in a broad social and economic context.

W. L. LANGER, *Political and Social Upheaval, 1832–1852* (1969). A remarkably thorough survey strong in both social and intellectual history as well as political narrative.

R. MAGRAW, *A History of the French Working Class*, 2 vols. (1992). A major overview based on the most recent literature.

H. PERKIN, *The Origins of Modern English Society, 1780–1880* (1969). A provocative attempt to look at the society as a whole.

M. D. PETERSON, *The Great Triumvirate: Webster, Clay, and Calhoun* (1988). A splendid narrative of American politics from the 1820s through the 1850s.

D. H. PINKNEY, *Decisive Years in France, 1840–1847* (1986). A detailed and careful examination of the years leading up to the Revolution of 1848.

P. ROBERTSON, *An Experience of Women: Pattern and Change in Nineteenth-Century Europe* (1982). A useful survey.

W. H. SEWELL, JR., *Work and Revolution in France: The Language of Labor from the Old Regime to 1848* (1980). A very fine analysis of French artisans.

J. SHEEHAN, *German History, 1770–1866* (1989). A very long work that is now the best available survey of the subject.

N. SMELZER, *Social Change in the Industrial Revolution: An Application of Theory to the British Cotton Industry* (1959). Important sections on the working-class family.

P. STEARNS, *Eighteen Forty-Eight: The Tide of Revolution in Europe* (1974). A good discussion of the social background.

E. P. THOMPSON, *The Making of the English Working Class* (1964). An important, influential, and controversial work.

L. A. TILLY AND J. W. SCOTT, *Women, Work, and Family* (1978). A useful and sensitive survey.

A. B. ULAM, *Russia's Failed Revolutionaries* (1981). Contains a useful discussion of the Decembrists as a background for other nineteenth-century Russian revolutionary activity.

S. WILLENTZ, *Chants Democratic: New York City and the Rise of the American Working Class, 1788–1850* (1984). An important examination of labor and politics.

A. S. WOHL, *Endangered Lives: Public Health in Victorian Britain* (1983). An important and wide-ranging examination of the health problems created by urbanization and industrialization.

"Place de L'Europe on a Rainy Day," 1876. Gustave Caillebotte (1848–1894). [The Art Institute of Chicago]

INTO THE MODERN WORLD

Between approximately 1850 and 1945 the nations of Europe achieved an unprecedented measure of political, economic, and military power across the globe. The century may thus quite properly be regarded as the European era of world history. But no less impressive than the vast reach of European influence was its brevity. By 1945 much of Europe, from Britain to the Soviet Union, literally lay in ruins. Within a few years the United States and the Soviet Union would emerge as superpowers with whom no European state could compete. Furthermore, nations throughout Asia, Africa, and Latin America that had once experienced direct or indirect European rule thrust off their colonial status. Both the rise and the decline of European world dominance fostered violence, warfare, and human exploitation all over the world.

In 1850 the major European states were recovering from the shock of the revolutions of 1848. Neither Germany nor Italy was united. British imperial influence lay at a relatively low ebb. The United States stood on the brink of a great sectional crisis that would result in the American Civil War. Japan still stood isolated from the rest of the world. China had already encountered immense pressures from Western nations, in particular from Britain, but the Ch'ing dynasty still maintained its power. The British East India Company governed the Indian subcontinent. Except in the south, the African continent had not yet been seriously penetrated by Europeans. The Ottoman Empire continued to play its role as the "sick man" of Europe. The nations of Latin America had achieved independence, but they were neither politically stable nor economically prosperous.

The half century after 1850 witnessed momentous changes in this picture. Italy and Germany were united by the military forces and the skillful diplomats of the conservative monarchies of Piedmont and Prussia. As a major new political and economic power in central Europe, Germany loomed as a potential rival to Great Britain, France, and Russia. For a time, shrewd diplomacy and a series of complex alliances contained that rivalry. But while sorting out the new power relationships on the continent, the nations of Europe exported potential conflicts overseas. The result of this externalized rivalry was a period of imperialist ventures. By the turn of the century these ventures had resulted in the reduction of Latin America to the status of economic dependency; in the extensive penetration of China by European merchants, administrators, and missionaries; and in the outright partition of Africa into areas directly governed by Europeans. After the Indian mutiny in 1857, Britain directly administered India. European influence had reached its zenith. Following the Civil War, the United States began its rise to world economic dominance.

What permitted this unprecedented dominance of the globe by the peoples of one portion of it was the economic and technological base of late-nineteenth-century European civilization. Europeans and, by the close of the century, Americans possessed the productive capacity to dominate world markets. Their banks controlled or influenced vast amounts of capital throughout the world economy. Their military technology, especially their navies, allowed them to back up economic power with armed force. While this vast European power emerged, other centers of world civilization, for quite independent reasons, were left vulnerable by political decay and by the less advanced technology at their disposal.

The one great and important exception to the general vulnerability of the nations of the world to European domination was Japan. Beginning in the 1860s, the Japanese emerged from two centuries of self-imposed isolation as their leaders determined to retain national autonomy. To that end, they set out to imitate the technological and, to some extent, the political structures of Europe. The Japanese effort proved immensely successful. By 1905, they had defeated Russia in a war. Twenty years later, they stood as a major naval rival of the United States and Great Britain. By 1941, they directly, if ultimately unsuccessfully, challenged the United States in the Pacific after transforming themselves into an Asian colonial power.

There were, however, other paths to resistance to European dominance. In China a revolution overthrew the last Manchu emperor in 1911. China became a republic and entered a period of enormous turmoil that culminated in the Communist victory in 1949. In India after World War I under the leadership of Mohandas (Mahatma) Gandhi, the Congress Party commenced years of protest against British rule that galvanized world opinion against imperialism. Those efforts resulted in the British retreat from India in 1947. Within Latin America one nation after another attempted to find ways to establish economic independence. These efforts led to revolution in Mexico, Perónism in Argentina, and efforts to establish a new political and economic order in Brazil.

Two major developments emerged during the century of European dominance. First, the entire globe entered various modes of economic and political interdependence far greater and more intense than in the past. Second, peoples subject to the dominance of Europe and North America began to resist that dominance and change the distribution of political power and economic resources. The second development—resistance to European and North American dominance—was the direct result of the first: the binding of the non-European world fully into the orbit of European and American political and economic power.

In 1900 many European and American leaders regarded their position of world dominance as secure, permanent, and "normal," a view that shaped European and American attitudes toward the rest of the globe for much of this century. What these leaders did not grasp were the very special circumstances that had allowed them to achieve their power and the resentment that its exercise would foster. Furthermore, Europeans and Americans did not realize that as modern technology and the ideas of equality, democracy, and socialism penetrated the rest of the world, they would transform other parts of the world no less than they had Europe and America.

1850–1899

German Empire proclaimed

1852–1870 The Second French Empire, under Napoleon III
1854–1856 The Crimean War
1861 Italy unified
1861 Emancipation of Russian serfs
1866 Austro-Prussian War; creation of Dual Monarchy of Austria-Hungary in 1867
1870–1871 Franco-Prussian War; German Empire proclaimed in 1871
1873 Three Emperors League
1882 Triple Alliance
1890 Bismarck dismissed by Kaiser Wilhelm II

1857–1858 Sepoy Rebellion: India placed directly under the authority of the British government in 1858
1869 Suez Canal completed; 1875, British purchase controlling interest
1869–1948 Mohandas (Mahatma) Gandhi
1876–1949 Muhammad Ali Jinnah, "founder of Pakistan"
1882 English occupation of Egypt
1886 India National Congress formed
1889–1964 Jawaharlal Nehru
1899 Ottoman sultan Abdulhamid II grants concession to Kaiser Wilhelm II to extend railway to Baghdad ("Berlin-to-Badhdad" Railway)

1900–1914

1902 Entente Cordiale
1905 January 22, "Bloody Sunday"
1905 Revolution in Russia
1914 War begins in Europe

1908 "Young Turk" Revolt

1850–1873 Taiping and other rebellions

1853–1854 Commodore Perry "opens" Japan to the West, ending seclusion policy

1859 French seize Saigon

1860s Establishment of treaty ports in China

1864 French protectorate over Cambodia

1868 Meiji Restoration in Japan

1870s Civilization and Enlightenment movement in Japan

1870s–1890s Self-Strengthening movement in China

1889 Meiji Constitution in Japan

1894–1895 Sino-Japanese War; Japan gets Taiwan as colony

1898–1900 Boxer Rebellion in China

The empress dowager Tz'u-hsi, Manchu court

1856–1884 King Mutasa of Buganda reigns

1870 British protectorate in Zanzibar

1879–1880 Henry M. Stanley gains the Congo for Belgium

1880s Mahdist revival and uprising in Sudan

1880 French protectorate in Tunisia and the Ivory Coast

1884–1885 International Conference in Berlin to prepare rules for further acquisition of African territory; the Congo free State declared

1884 German Southwest Africa

1885 British control Nigeria and British East Africa

1894 French annex Dahomey

1899 German East Africa; British in Sudan

1899–1902 Boer War

1854 Kansas-Nebraska Act

1856 Dred Scott Decision

1859 Raid on Harper's Ferry

1860 Abraham Lincoln elected U.S. president

1861–1865 U.S. Civil War

1862–1867 French invasion of Mexico

1863 Emancipation Proclamation in United States

1865–1877 Reconstruction

1865–1870 Paraguayan War

1879–1880 Argentinian conquest of the desert

1880s Slavery eliminated in Cuba and Brazil

1898 Spanish-American War

Abraham Lincoln

1904–1905 Russo-Japanese War

1910 Japan annexes Korea

1911 Republican Revolution begins in China; Ch'ing dynasty overthrown

1900 Nigeria a British crown colony

1907 Orange Free State and the Transvaal join with Natal and Cape Colony to form the Union of South Africa

1911 Liberia becomes a virtual U.S. protectorate

1914 Ethiopia the only independent state in Africa

1901 Theodore Roosevelt elected U.S. president

1910–1917 Mexican Revolution

1912 Woodrow Wilson elected U.S. president

27 POLITICAL CONSOLIDATION IN EUROPE AND NORTH AMERICA

The proclamation of the German Empire in the Hall of Mirrors at Versailles, January 18, 1871, after the defeat of France in the Franco-

Prussian War. Kaiser Wilhelm I is standing at the top of the steps under the flags. Bismarck is in the center in a white uniform. [Bildarchiv

Preussicher Kulturbesitz/Original: Friedrichsruher Fassung, Bismarck-Museum]

CHAPTER TOPICS

◆ The Crimean War (1854–1856)

◆ Italian Unification

◆ German Unification

◆ France: From Liberal Empire to the Third Republic

◆ The Habsburg Empire: Formation of the Dual Monarchy

◆ Russia: Emancipation and Revolutionary Stirrings

◆ Great Britain: Toward Democracy

◆ The United States: Civil War, Reconstruction, and Progressive Politics

◆ The Canadian Experience

In World Perspective European and North American Political Consolidation

Between 1850 and 1875 both Europe and North America underwent extensive political consolidation which strengthened the authority and military power of central governments. In Europe the defeat of the revolutions of 1848 resulted in the entrenchment of conservative, authoritarian regimes except in Great Britain. Yet only twenty-five years later conservative governments had actually carried out many of the major goals of early-nineteenth-century liberals and nationalists. The Habsburg emperor had accepted constitutional government; the Magyars had attained recognition of their liberties. In Russia the serfs had been emancipated. France was again a republic. Great Britain adopted a second Reform Bill moving it toward democracy under the leadership of the Tory Party. Conservative political groups had moved either opportunistically to shore up support for themselves or defensively to gain broader political support for governments that had encountered foreign policy difficulties. At the end of this process Great Britain, France, Italy, and Germany had achieved considerable political stability. However, such was not really the case with the Habsburg Empire, where the discontent of various national groups challenged the central government, or with Russia, where social and political turmoil continued to challenge the Tzarist government.

The same quarter century witnessed similar political consolidation and centralization in North America. By 1861 the sectional conflict in the United States had erupted into a major and profoundly destructive civil war. That conflict transformed the character of the American union, leading to new authority for the federal government and to the abolition of slavery. During the same decade Canada made a peaceful transition to self-government, and in both North American nations, the westward movement continued.

The various nations of the North Atlantic region became the most powerful political units in the world. Their foreign policies would, as will be seen in other chapters, lead them to undertake a new imperialism whereby they came to dominate economically and militarily much of the rest of the world. They would also in the early twentieth century come into a worldwide conflict with each other. The policies of imperialism and the onset of war would draw the United States into a new world role.

The Crimean War (1854–1856)

As has so often been true in modern European history, war made change possible. In this case a conflict disrupted the international balance that had prevailed since 1815 and quickly unleashed forces that upset the political situation in several of the involved states. The war itself was in some respects less important than the political consequences that flowed from it during the next decade.

The Crimean War (1854–1856), named after the Black Sea peninsula on which it was largely fought, originated from a long-standing rivalry between Russia and the Ottoman Empire. Russia wanted to extend its influence over the Ottoman provinces of Moldavia and Walachia (now in Romania). In 1853 Russia went to war against the Ottomans on the pretext that the Empire had given Roman Catholic France, instead of Orthodox Russia, the right to protect Christians and Christian shrines in the Holy Land. The next year France and Great Britain supported the Ottoman Empire to protect their interests in the eastern Mediterranean, while Austria and Prussia remained

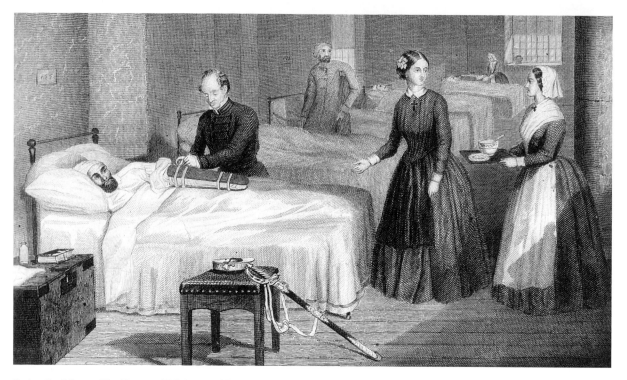

During the Crimean War, Florence Nightingale of Great Britain organized nursing care for the wounded. [Corbis-Bettmann Archive]

neutral. The war quickly bogged down. In March 1856 a peace conference in Paris concluded a treaty highly unfavorable to Russia.

The Crimean War shattered the image of an invincible Russia that had prevailed since the close of the Napoleonic wars. It also shattered the power of the Concert of Europe to deal with international relations on the Continent. As historian Gordon Craig has commented, "After 1856 there were more powers willing to fight to overthrow the existing order than there were to take up arms to defend it."[1]

The major European powers were no longer willing to cooperate to maintain the existing borders between themselves and their neighbors. For the next twenty-five years instability prevailed in European affairs, allowing a largely unchecked adventurism in foreign policy.

Italian Unification

Italian nationalists had long wanted to unite the small absolutist principalities of the peninsula into a single state, but could not agree on how to do it. Romantic republicans such as Giuseppe Mazzini (1805–1872) and Giuseppe Garibaldi (1807–1882), sought to drive out the Austrians by popular

[1]*The New Cambridge Modern History*, Vol. 10 (Cambridge, UK: Cambridge University Press, 1967), p. 273.

military force and then to establish a republic. They not only failed but also frightened more moderate Italians. The person who eventually achieved unification was Count Camillo Cavour (1810–1861), the prime minister of Piedmont.

Piedmont (officially styled the "Kingdom of Sardinia"), in northwestern Italy, was the most independent state on the peninsula (see Map 27–1). It had unsuccessfully fought against Austria in 1848 and 1849. Following the second defeat, Charles Albert (r. 1831–1849) abdicated in favor of his son, Victor Emmanuel II (r. 1849–1878). In 1852 the new monarch chose Cavour—a moderate liberal in economics and a strong monarchist who rejected republicanism—as his prime minister.

Cavour believed that if Italians proved themselves to be efficient and economically progressive, the great powers might decide that Italy could govern itself. He worked for free trade, railway construction, credit expansion, and agricultural improvement. He also fostered the Nationalist Society, which established chapters in other Italian states to press for unification under the leadership of Piedmont. Cavour furthermore believed that Italy could be unified only with the aid of France.

Cavour joined the French and British side in the Crimean War to be able to raise the question of Italian unification at the peace conference. There he gained no specific rewards, but did achieve the sympathy of Napoleon III (r. 1852–1870) of France. In 1858 Cavour and the French Emperor met and plotted to start a war with Austria.

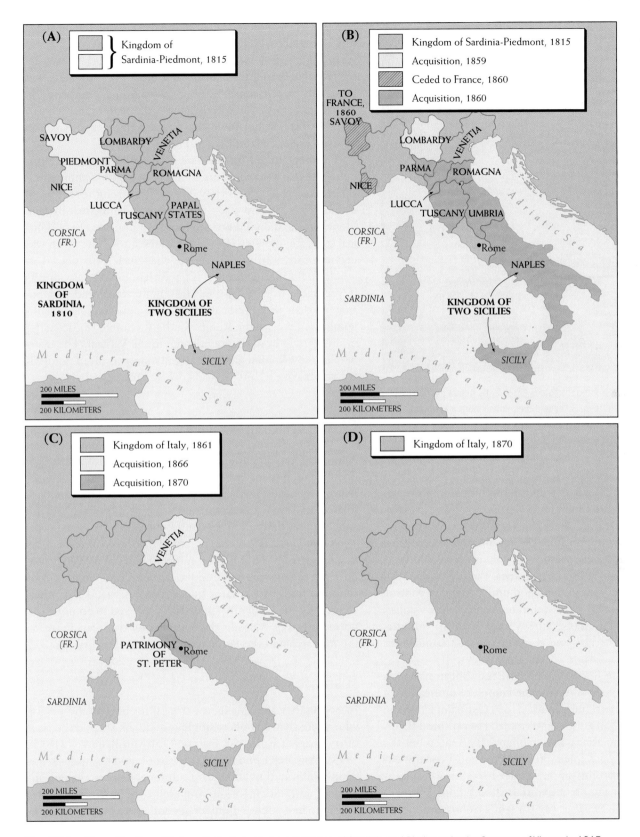

(A)

Kingdom of Sardinia-Piedmont, 1815

SAVOY
LOMBARDY
VENETIA
PIEDMONT
PARMA
NICE
ROMAGNA
LUCCA
TUSCANY
PAPAL STATES
CORSICA (FR.)
•Rome
NAPLES
KINGDOM OF SARDINIA, 1810
KINGDOM OF TWO SICILIES
SICILY
Adriatic Sea
Mediterranean Sea
200 MILES
200 KILOMETERS

(B)

Kingdom of Sardinia-Piedmont, 1815
Acquisition, 1859
Ceded to France, 1860
Acquisition, 1860

TO FRANCE, 1860 SAVOY
LOMBARDY
VENETIA
PARMA
ROMAGNA
NICE
LUCCA
TUSCANY
UMBRIA
CORSICA (FR.)
•Rome
SARDINIA
NAPLES
KINGDOM OF TWO SICILIES
SICILY
Adriatic Sea
Mediterranean Sea
200 MILES
200 KILOMETERS

(C)

Kingdom of Italy, 1861
Acquisition, 1866
Acquisition, 1870

VENETIA
CORSICA (FR.)
PATRIMONY OF ST. PETER
•Rome
SARDINIA
SICILY
Adriatic Sea
Mediterranean Sea
200 MILES
200 KILOMETERS

(D)

Kingdom of Italy, 1870

CORSICA (FR.)
•Rome
SARDINIA
SICILY
Adriatic Sea
Mediterranean Sea
200 MILES
200 KILOMETERS

Map 27–1   The unification of Italy.   Beginning with the association of Sardinia and Piedmont by the Congress of Vienna in 1815, unification was achieved through the expansion of Piedmont between 1859 and 1870. Both Cavour's statesmanship and the campaigns of ardent nationalists played large roles.

Giuseppe Garibaldi represented the forces of romantic Italian nationalism. The landing of his Redshirts on Sicily and their subsequent invasion of southern Italy in 1860 forced Cavour to unite the entire peninsula sooner than he had intended. [Bildarchiv Preussischer Kulturbesitz]

During the winter and spring of 1859 tension grew between Austria and Piedmont as the latter mobilized its army. In late April war erupted. On June 4 the Austrians were defeated at Magenta, and on June 24, at Solferino. Fearing too extensive a Piedmontese victory, Napoleon III concluded a separate peace on July 11 at Villafranca. Piedmont received Lombardy, but the Veneto remained under Austrian control. Cavour felt betrayed by France, but nonetheless the war had driven Austria from most of northern Italy. Later that summer Parma, Modena, Tuscany, and Romagna voted to unite with Piedmont.

At this point the forces of romantic republican nationalism compelled Cavour to pursue the complete unification of northern and southern Italy. In May 1860 Garibaldi landed in Sicily with more than a thousand troops. He captured Palermo and prepared to attack the mainland. By September the city and kingdom of Naples, probably the most corrupt example of Italian absolutism, lay under his control. To forestall a republican victory Cavour rushed troops south to confront Garibaldi. On the way Cavour's troops conquered the Papal States except for the area around Rome, which remained under the direct control of the pope.

Garibaldi's nationalism won out over his republicanism, and he unhappily accepted the Piedmontese domination. In late 1860 the southern Italian state voted to join the northern union forged by Piedmont.

In March 1861 Victor Emmanuel II was proclaimed king of Italy. Three months later Cavour died. The new state was governed by the conservative constitution promulgated in 1848 by Charles Albert. Italy gained the Veneto in 1866 as a result of the war between Austria and Prussia, and Rome in 1870 as a result of the Franco-Prussian War.

The new united Italian state confronted numerous difficulties that would continue to affect the nation throughout the twentieth century. Italy lacked the strong resources of France and Germany and the overseas trade of Great Britain. Hence unification did not produce economic power or political strength to match the great nation-states. The north was economically advanced, whereas the south remained overwhelmingly rural and poor. The parliamentary system was never stable, with ministries often more concerned with patronage than with national policy. The new state had an ongoing conflict with the Roman Catholic church, whose leader now regarded himself as a prisoner in the Vatican. The overwhelmingly Roman Catholic population was often culturally at odds with its anticlerical government.

German Unification

A united German nation was the single most important political development in Europe between 1848 and 1914. Germany was united by the conservative army and monarchy of Prussia and by Prussia's conservative prime minister, who sought to outflank the Prussian liberals.

William I (r. 1861–1888) regarded the Prussian army as his first concern. In 1860 his war minister and chief of staff proposed to enlarge the army and to increase the period of conscription from two to three years. The Prussian Parliament, created by the Constitution of 1850, refused to approve the necessary taxes. A deadlock continued for two years between the monarch and the Parliament dominated by liberals.

Bismarck

In September 1862 William I turned for help to the person who, more than any other single individual, shaped the next thirty years of European history: Otto von Bismarck (1815–1898). Bismarck came from *Junker* stock, and his outlook was deeply informed by the most traditional Prussian values, including admiration for the monarchy, the nobility, and the army. He had attended university and there displayed an interest in German unification. Then he retired to his father's estate. During the 1840s he was elected to the local provincial diet. In 1848 he was so reactionary as to disturb even the king and the leading state ministers. Yet he had made his mark. From 1851 to 1859 Bismarck was the Prussian representative at the Frankfurt Diet of the German Confederation. Later he served as Prussian ambassador to Saint Petersburg and then Paris.

After being appointed minister president and foreign minister in 1862, Bismarck immediately moved against the liberal Parliament. He contended that the Prussian constitution permitted the government to function on the basis of previously granted taxes. Therefore, taxes could be collected and spent, despite the parliamentary refusal to vote them. The army and most of the bureaucracy supported this interpretation of the constitution. However, in 1863 new elections sustained the liberal majority in the Parliament. Bismarck had to find some way to attract popular support away from the liberals and toward the monarchy and the army. To that end, he set about uniting Germany through the conservative institutions of Prussia. The tactic amounted to diverting public attention from domestic matters to foreign affairs. It also meant that Prussia now assumed a position of leadership in the effort to unify Germany.

Bismarck pursued a *kleindeutsch*, or small German, solution to unification. Austria was to be excluded from German affairs when an opportunity presented itself. To achieve that end, Bismarck undertook two brief wars.

In 1864 he went to war with Denmark over the question of the duchies of Schleswig and Holstein, German-speaking areas that had long been administered by the Danish monarchy (see Map 27–2). The Austrians joined in this war, helped defeat Denmark, and then with Prussia undertook the joint administration of the two duchies. Thereafter, Bismarck concluded various alliances with France and Italy to gain their support against Austria. War between Prussia and Austria broke out in the summer of 1866. This Seven Weeks' War led to the decisive defeat of Austria at Königgrätz. The Prussian victory and the consequent Treaty of Prague excluded the Habsburgs from German affairs. Prussia became the only major power among the German states.

In 1867 Hanover, Hesse, Nassau, and the city of Frankfurt, all of which had supported Austria during the war, were annexed by Prussia, and their rulers deposed. Prussia and these

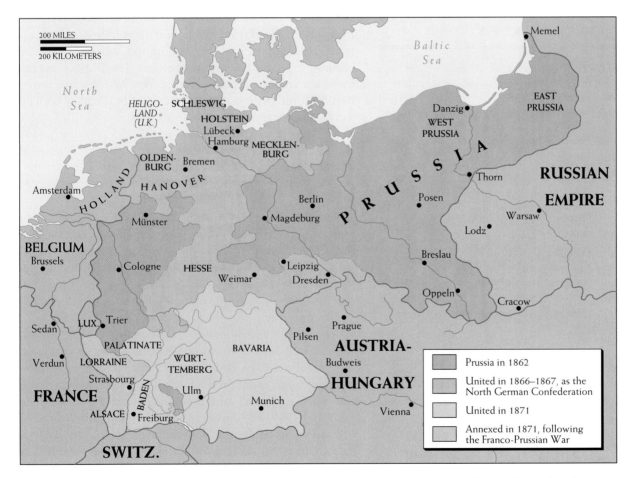

Map 27–2   The unification of Germany.   Under Bismarck's leadership, and with the strong support of its royal house, Prussia used diplomatic and military means, on both the German and international stages, to forcibly unify the German states into a strong national entity.

newly incorporated territories, plus Schleswig and Holstein and the rest of the German states north of the Main River, constituted the North German Confederation. Prussia was its undisputed leader. The constitution of the confederation, which after 1871 became the governing document of the German Empire, possessed the appearance but not the substance of liberalism. Bismarck provided for a lower legislative house, or Reichstag, to be chosen by universal manhood suffrage. He did not fear this broad franchise because he sensed that the peasants would tend to vote conservatively. The Reichstag had little real power, and its members knew that the army would always support the king and his ministers. Germany was, in effect, a military monarchy dominated by Prussia.

The Franco-Prussian War and the German Empire (1870–1871)

Bismarck now awaited an opportunity to complete unification by bringing the states of southern Germany into the confederation. The occasion arose as a result of complex

German and Italian Unification

1854	Crimean War opens
1855	Cavour leads Piedmont into war on side of France and England
1856	Treaty of Paris concludes Crimean War July 20
1858	Secret conference between Louis Napoleon and Cavour
1859	War of Piedmont and France against Austria
1860	Garibaldi lands his forces in Sicily and conquers southern Italy
1861	March 17, Proclamation of the Kingdom of Italy
	June 6, death of Cavour
1862	Bismarck becomes prime minister of Prussia
1864	Danish War
1866	Austro-Prussian War; Veneto ceded to Italy
1867	North German Confederation formed
1870	June 19–July 12, crisis over Hohenzollern candidacy for the Spanish throne
	July 13, Bismarck publishes edited press dispatch
	July 19, France declares war on Prussia
	September 1, France defeated at Sedan and Napoleon III captured
	September 4, French Republic proclaimed
	October 2, Italian state annexes Rome
1871	January 18, Proclamation of the German Empire at Versailles
	March 18–May 28, Paris Commune
	May 10, Treaty of Frankfurt between France and Germany

diplomacy surrounding the possibility of a cousin of William I of Prussia becoming king of Spain. France was, of course, opposed to the idea of a second state on its borders ruled by a Hohenzollern. Bismarck personally edited a press dispatch surrounding these negotiations to make it appear that William I had insulted the French ambassador, even though such had not been the case. Bismarck intended to goad France into war.

The French government quickly fell for Bismarck's bait, and on July 19 declared war. Napoleon III hoped that victory would give his regime a new and stronger popular base. Once the war began, the states of southern Germany supported Prussia. On September 1, at Sedan, the Germans not only defeated the French army but also captured Napoleon III. By late September, Paris was besieged. It finally capitulated on January 28, 1871. Ten days earlier, in the Hall of Mirrors at the Palace of Versailles, the German Empire had been proclaimed. The rulers of the states of South Germany had requested William I to accept the imperial title. They, in turn, retained their thrones.

The unification of Germany established a strong, coherent state in the middle of Europe. It had been forged by the Prussian army and would be dominated by Prussian institutions. Its center of power rested on the monarchy and the military. It possessed enormous economic resources and nationalistic ambitions. For the next eighty years Europe would have to come to grips with this new political reality both on the Continent and abroad.

France: From Liberal Empire to the Third Republic

The reign of Napoleon III (1851–1870) is traditionally divided into the years of the authoritarian empire and those of the liberal empire. After his coup in December 1851, Napoleon III kept a close rein on the legislature, strictly controlled the press, and harassed political dissidents. His support came from property owners, the French Catholic church, and businessmen.

From the late 1850s onward Napoleon III became less authoritarian, but all of his liberal concessions, such as the relaxation of the press laws, were attempts to compensate for an increasingly unsuccessful foreign policy. First he lost control of the diplomacy of Italian unification. Then, between 1861 and 1867, he supported a military expedition against Mexico led by Archduke Maximilian of Austria (1832–1867) (see Chapter 30) that ended in defeat and the execution of the archduke. The war of 1870 against Germany was simply Napoleon III's last and most disastrous attempt to shore up French foreign policy and secure domestic popularity.

Walter Bagehot Analyzes the Power of Napoleon III

Walter Bagehot (1826–1877) was an astute English observer of continental politics and an important journalist. This passage of 1863 explains the manner in which Napoleon III had to please various elements of French society in order to retain his power.

What did Bagehot mean by referring to Napoleon III as "the Crowned Democrat of Europe"? What did Bagehot see as the chief sources of Napoleon III's support? What accounted in each case for that support? Are there elements in Bagehot's analysis that would explain why Napoleon III would fall at the end of the decade once France had encountered military defeat?

The Emperor is the Crowned Democrat of Europe. The position is no doubt one of great elevation and of enormous power, but it is also one full of peril and full of exigencies. "The masses," though an effective and under many circumstances, an almost resistless servant make a capricious, exacting, and relentless master. Both at home and abroad Napoleon III has a contract with the agencies that have made him what he is and that sustain him where he is, the terms of which must be rigidly fulfilled. At home he rules over the middle classes, *in defiance* of the educat-

ed classes, and *by the support* of which the lower classes and the army. In ultimate resort he may be said to reign by the right of numbers and by the instrumentality of bayonets. It is true that he has done much—perhaps as much as lay in his power—to widen the basis of his throne, and to make all classes interested in maintaining him. He has tentatively and modestly allowed the intellectual classes to raise their heads; he has conciliated the *bourgeoisie* by the material prosperity which he has so sagaciously and indefatigably fostered; and he has canceled or moderated the hostility once felt towards him by the rich and great by convincing them that property was in habitual danger from the *Rouges* [Reds], and that he was the only hand that could avert that danger. So that beyond dispute the number of those who wish to overthrow him has largely diminished, and the number of those who desire to maintain him has largely increased, each year since 1852. Still it remains true that to retain his popularity and prestige with *FRANCE*, . . . he must be sedulous to please, or at all events careful not to offend, the populace, the peasantry, and the army.

Reprinted by permission of the publisher from *The Collected Works of Walter Bagehot*, Norman St. John-Stevas, ed. Cambridge, Mass.: Harvard University Press, Copyright © 1968 by the Economist.

Shortly after the news of Sedan reached Paris, a republic was proclaimed, and a Government of National Defense set up. Paris itself was soon under siege, during which the French government was transferred to Bordeaux. Paris finally surrendered in January 1871, but the rest of France had been ready to sue for peace before the capital surrendered.

Paris Commune

The division between the provinces and Paris deepened after the fighting stopped. Monarchists dominated the new National Assembly, which met at Versailles. Under the leadership of Adolphe Thiers (1797–1877), the assembly negotiated a peace settlement that required France to pay a large indemnity and surrender Alsace-Lorraine to Germany.

Paris resented this settlement. On March 26, 1871, the Parisians elected a new municipal government, called the Paris Commune. It intended to administer the city of Paris separately from the rest of France. Political radicals of all stripes participated in the Paris Commune. The National Assembly reacted rapidly. By early April its army had besieged Paris and broke through the city's defenses on May 21. Dur-

ing the next seven days the troops killed about 20,000 Parisians. Others were slain by the communards.

The Third Republic

The National Assembly had put down the Paris Commune, but it created a republic much against its will. Its monarchist majority was divided between adherents of the House of Bourbon and the House of Orléans. While they quarreled, events marched on. The monarchists elected as president Marshal MacMahon (1808–1893), whom they expected would restore the monarchy. In 1875, unable to agree on a candidate for the throne, the National Assembly adopted a law that provided for a chamber of deputies elected by universal manhood suffrage, a senate chosen indirectly, and a president elected by the two legislative houses. This relatively simple republican system had resulted from the bickering and frustration of the monarchists.

The Dreyfus Affair The greatest trauma of the new republic occurred over the Dreyfus affair. On December 22, 1894, a French military court found Captain Alfred Dreyfus

(1859–1935) guilty of spying for the German army. The flimsy evidence supporting his guilt was later revealed to have been forged. Someone in the officer corps had been passing documents to the Germans, and it suited the army investigators to accuse Dreyfus, who was Jewish. However, after Dreyfus had been sent to Devil's Island, secrets continued to flow to the German army. In 1896 a new head of French counter-intelligence reexamined the Dreyfus file and found evidence of forgery. A different officer was implicated, but a military court quickly acquitted him of all charges. The officer who had discovered the forgeries was transferred to a distant post.

By then the matter had provoked widespread and sometimes near-hysterical public debate. The army, the French Catholic church, political conservatives, and vehemently anti-Semitic newspapers repeatedly contended that Dreyfus was guilty. Such anti-Dreyfus opinion was quite powerful at the beginning of the affair. In 1898, however, the novelist Emile Zola (1840–1902) published a newspaper article entitled *"J'accuse"* ("I Accuse"), in which he contended that the army had consciously denied due process to Dreyfus and had plotted to suppress and forge evidence. Zola was convicted of libel and received a one-year prison sentence, which he avoided only by fleeing to England.

Numerous liberals, radicals, and socialists demanded a new trial for Dreyfus. They realized that his cause could aid their own public image. They portrayed the conservative institutions of the nation as having denied Dreyfus the rights belonging to any citizen of the republic. They also claimed, and properly so, that Dreyfus had been singled out to protect the guilty persons, who were still in the army. In August 1898 further evidence of forged material came to light. The officer responsible for those forgeries committed suicide in jail. In a new military trial, Dreyfus was again found guilty by officers who refused to admit the original mistake. The president of France immediately pardoned him, and in 1906 a civilian court set aside the results of both previous military trials.

The Dreyfus case divided France as no issue had done since the Paris Commune. By its conclusion, the conservatives stood on the defensive. They had allowed themselves to persecute an innocent person and to manufacture evidence against him to protect themselves from disclosure. They had also embraced a strongly anti-Semitic posture.

On the political left, radicals, republicans, and socialists developed an informal alliance that outlived the fight over the Dreyfus case itself. These groups realized that republican institutions must be preserved if they were to achieve their goals.

Mass graves were dug for thousands of Parisians killed or executed during the fighting that marked the suppression of the Paris Commune in 1871. [Bibliothèque Nationale, Paris, France/Snark/Art Resource, N.Y.]

The prosecution of Captain Alfred Dreyfus, shown here standing on the right at his military trial, provoked the most serious crisis of the Third Republic. [Corbis-Bettmann Archive]

Outside political circles, most French citizens understood that their rights and liberties were safer under a republic than under some alternative mode of conservative government. The divisions, suspicions, and hopes growing out of the Dreyfus affair would continue to mark and divide the Third Republic until its defeat by Germany in 1940. The anti-Semitism associated with the attack on Dreyfus would more fully manifest itself in the Vichy regime during World War II.

The Habsburg Empire: Formation of the Dual Monarchy

In the age of national states, liberal institutions, and industrialism, the Habsburg domains remained primarily dynastic, absolutist, and agrarian. The response to the revolts at the end of the 1840s had been the reassertion of absolutism (see Map 27–3).

During the 1850s Emperor Francis Joseph (r. 1848–1916) and his ministers attempted to impose a centralized administration on the multinational empire. The system amounted to a military and bureaucratic government dominated by German-speaking Austrians. In particular, it divided Hungary into military districts.

The defeats in 1859 and 1866 and the exclusion of Austria from Italy and from German affairs compelled Francis Joseph

to come to terms with the Hungarian nobility. The subsequent *Ausgleich*, or Compromise, of 1867 transformed the Habsburg Empire into a dual monarchy. Francis Joseph was crowned king of Hungary in Budapest. Except for the common monarch, foreign policy, and army, Austria and Hungary became almost separate states.

Many of the other national groups within the empire—including the Czechs, the Ruthenians, the Romanians, and the Serbo-Croatians—opposed the Compromise because it permitted the German-speaking Austrians and the Hungarian Magyars to dominate all other nationalities in their respective states. The Czechs of Bohemia were the most vocal group. For over twenty years they were conciliated by generous Austrian patronage and posts in the bureaucracy. By the turn of the century the Czechs had become more vocal. They and German-speaking groups in the Austrian Reichsrat disrupted parliament rather than permit a compromise on language issues. The emperor ruled thereafter by imperial decree with the support of the bureaucracy. Constitutionalism was dead in Austria. It flourished in Hungary only because the Magyars used it to dominate competing national groups.

Unrest of Nationalities

Nationalist unrest within the Habsburg empire not only caused internal political difficulties, but also constituted one

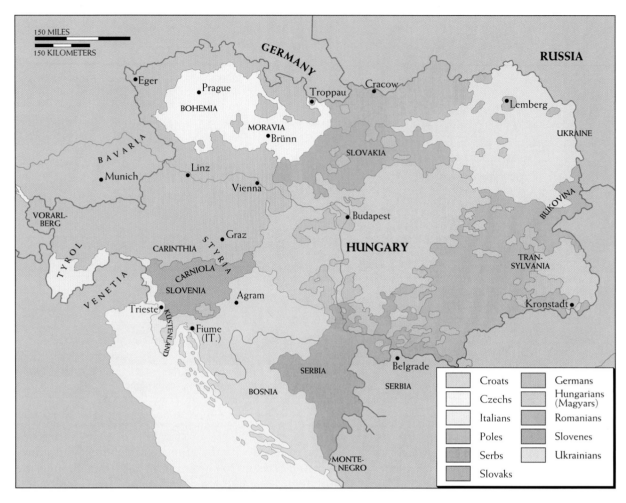

Map 27-3 Nationalities within the Habsburg empire. The patchwork appearance reflects the unusual problem of the numerous ethnic groups that the Habsburgs could not, of course, meld into a modern national state. Only the Magyars were recognized in 1867, leaving nationalist Czechs, Slovaks, and the others chronically dissatisfied.

of the major sources of political instability for all of central and eastern Europe. Virtually all the nationality problems had a foreign policy as well as a domestic political dimension. Both the Serbo-Croatians and the Poles believed they deserved a wholly independent state in union with their fellow nationals who lived outside the empire. Other national groups, such as Ukrainians, Romanians, and Bosnians, saw themselves as potentially linked to Russia, to Romania, to Serbia, or to a larger yet-to-be-established Slavic state. Many of these nationalities looked to Russia for protection. Out of these nationalistic tensions emerged much of the turmoil that would spark the First World War.

The dominant German population of Austria proper was generally loyal to the emperor. However, a significant segment of the Austrian German population was strongly nationalistic and yearned to be part of the united German state being established by Bismarck. These nationalistic Germans in the Austrian empire often hated the non-German national groups, particularly the Jews. Such attitudes would influence the youth and young adulthood of Adolph Hitler (1889–1945) and shape many of his political opinions.

Finally, nationality problems touched each of the three great central and eastern European empires—the German, the Russian, and the Austrian. All had Polish populations. Each shared at least two other major national groups. Each nationality regarded its own aspirations and discontents as more important than the larger good or even survival of the empire they inhabited. The stirrings of nationalism affected the fate of all three empires from the 1860s through the outbreak of World War I. The government of each would be overturned during the war, and the Austrian empire would disappear. These same unresolved problems of central and eastern European nationalism would then lead directly to World War II. During more recent years they have led to civil war in what was formerly Yugoslavia and to the breakup of what used to be jointly called Czechoslovakia.

Lord Acton Condemns Nationalism

Lord Acton (1834–1902) was a major nineteenth-century English historian and commentator on contemporary religious and political events. He was deeply concerned with the character and preservation of liberty. His was one of the earliest voices to point to the political dangers of nationalism.

Why does Acton see the principle of nationality as dangerous to liberty? Why does he see nationalism as a threat to minority groups? Why does he see nationalism as a threat to democracy?

The greatest adversary of the rights of nationality is the modern theory of nationality. By making the State and the nation commensurate with each other in theory, it reduces practically to a subject condition all other nationalities that may be within the boundary. It cannot admit them to an equality with the ruling nation which constitutes the State, because the State would then cease to be national, which would be a contradiction of the principle of its existence. According, therefore, to the degree of humanity and civilization in that dominant body which claims all the rights of the community, the inferior races are exterminated, or reduced to servitude, or outlawed, or put in a condition of dependence.

If we take the establishment of liberty for the realization of moral duties to be the end of civil society, we must conclude that those states are substantially the most perfect which, like the British and Austrian Empires, include various distinct nationalities without oppressing them. Those in which no mixture of races has occurred are imperfect; and those in which its effects have disappeared are decrepit. A State which is incompetent to satisfy different races condemns itself; a State which labors to neutralize, to absorb, or to expel them, destroys its own vitality; a State which does not include them is destitute of the chief basis of self-government. The theory of nationality, therefore, is a retrograde step in history. . . .

. . . [N]ationality does not aim either at liberty or prosperity, both of which it sacrifices to the imperative necessity of making the nation the mold and measure of the State. Its course will be marked with material as well as moral ruin, in order that a new invention may prevail over the works of God and the interests of mankind. There is no principle of change, no phrase of political speculation conceivable, more comprehensive, more subversive, or more arbitrary than this. It is a confutation of democracy, because it sets limits to the exercise of the popular will, and substitutes for it a higher principle.

From John Emerich Edward Dalberg-Acton, First Baron Acton, *Essays in the History of Liberty*, ed. by J. Rufus Fears. Copyright © 1985 Liberty Classics, pp. 431–433.

Russia: Emancipation and Revolutionary Stirrings

Reforms of Alexander II

Defeat in the Crimean War and the humiliation of the Treaty of Paris compelled the Russian government to reconsider its domestic situation. Nicholas I (r. 1825–1855) had died during the conflict. As a result of extensive travel in Russia and training in government procedures, Nicholas's son Alexander II (r. 1855–1881) was familiar with the chief difficulties facing Russia. The debacle of the war had made reform both necessary and possible. Alexander II took advantage of this to institute the most extensive restructuring of Russian society and administration since Peter the Great (r. 1682–1725). Like Peter, Alexander imposed his reforms from the top.

In March 1856, at the conclusion of the Crimean War, Alexander II announced his intention to abolish serfdom. He had decided that only abolition would permit Russia to organize its human and natural resources so as to remain a great power. Serfdom had become economically inefficient; there was always the threat of revolt; the serfs recruited into the army had performed poorly in the Crimean conflict; and moral opinion increasingly condemned serfdom. For more than five years government commissions wrestled over how to implement the tsar's desire. Finally, in February 1861, against much opposition from the landlords, Alexander II promulgated the long statute ending serfdom in Russia.

The procedures of emancipation were so complicated and the immediate benefits so limited that many serfs believed that real emancipation was still to come. They received the personal rights to marry without their landlord's permission as well as to purchase and sell property freely, to engage in court actions, and to pursue trades. But they did not receive free title to their frequently too-small allotments of land. Instead, they had to pay for the land over a period of forty-nine years. The redemption payments, which included interest to the government, led to endless difficulty and resentment. Facing widespread unrest following the defeat of Russia by Japan in 1905, the tsarist government grudgingly cancelled the remaining debts.

The abolition of serfdom required the reorganization of both local government and the judicial system. Village elders now settled family quarrels, imposed fines, and collected taxes. In 1864 nobles were authorized to form *zemstvos*, or councils, to oversee local matters, such as road or bridge repairs and education. Inadequate funding meant that the local governments never became vigorous. Also in 1864 Alexander II promulgated a new statute on the judiciary that for the first time introduced principles of western European legal systems into Russia. They included equality before the law, impartial hearings, uniform procedures, judicial independence, and trial by jury. The new system was far from perfect, but justice became more efficient and less corrupt.

Revolutionaries

The tsarist regime had long had its critics. One of the most prominent was Alexander Herzen (1812–1870), who lived in exile. From London, he published a newspaper called *The Bell*, in which he set forth reformist positions. The initial reforms of Alexander II had raised great hopes among Russian students and intellectuals, but they soon became discontented with the limited character of the restructuring. Drawing on the ideas of Herzen and other radicals, these students formed a revolutionary movement known as Populism. They sought a social revolution based on the communal life of the Russian peasants. The chief radical society was called Land and Freedom. In the early 1870s hundreds of young Russians, both men and women, took their revolutionary message into the countryside. They intended to live with the peasants, gain their trust, and teach them about the coming revolution. The bewildered and distrustful peasants turned most of the youths over to the police. In the winter of 1877–1878 almost two hundred students were tried. Most were acquitted or given light sentences, because they had been held for months in preventive detention and because the court believed that a display of mercy might lessen public sympathy for them. The tsar, however, let it become known that he favored heavy penalties for all involved in revolutionary activity.

In 1879, Land and Freedom split into two groups. One group, known as People's Will, was dedicated to the overthrow of the autocracy. Its members decided to assassinate the tsar himself. Several attempts failed, but on March 1, 1881, a bomb hurled by a member of People's Will killed Alexander II. Four men and two women were sentenced to death for the deed. All were willing to die for their cause. The emergence of such dedicated revolutionary opposition constituted as much a part of the reign of Alexander II as did

Life in Russian villages during the 1870s was very difficult. Tsar Alexander II abolished serfdom in 1861, but peasants were required to pay compensation to the government for 49 years, and living standards remained dismal. This painting shows peasants waiting patiently outside a government office while insensitive officials inside take their time over lunch. [Bildarchiv Preussischer Kulturbesitz]

The People's Will Issues a Revolutionary Manifesto

In the late 1870s a revolutionary movement appeared in Russia calling itself the People's Will. It called for the overthrow of the tsarist government and the election of an Organizing Assembly to form a government based on popular representation. It embraced terrorism as a path toward its goal of the Russian people governing themselves. Eventually members of this group assassinated Alexander II in 1881.

Which of the group's seven demands might be associated with liberalism and which go beyond liberalism in their radical intent? Why does the group believe it must engage in terrorism as well as propaganda? Would any reforms or steps toward reform by the Russian government have satisfied this group or dissuaded them from terrorist action?

Although we are ready to submit wholly to the popular will, we regard it as none the less our duty, as a party, to appear before the people with our program. . . . It is as follows:

1. Perpetual popular representation, . . . having full power to act in all national questions.

2. General local self-government, secured by the election of all officers, and the economic independence of the people.

3. The self-controlled village commune as the economic and administrative unit.

4. Ownership of the land by the people.

5. A system of measures having for their object the turning over to the laborers of all mining works and factories.

6. Complete freedom of conscience, speech, association, public meeting, and electioneering activity.

7. The substitution of a territorial militia for the army.

In view of the stated aim of the party its operations may be classified as follows:

1. *Propaganda and agitation.* Our propaganda has for its object the popularization, in all social classes, of the idea of a political and popular revolution as a means of social reform, as well as popularization of the party's own program. Its essential features are criticism of the existing order of things, and a statement and explanation of revolutionary methods. The aim of agitation should be to incite the people to protest as generally as possible against the present state of affairs, to demand such reforms as are in harmony with the party's purposes, and, especially, to demand the summoning of an Organizing Assembly. . . .

2. *Destructive and terroristic activity.* Terroristic activity consists in the destruction of the most harmful persons in the Government, the protection of the party from spies, and the punishment of official lawlessness and violence in all the more prominent and important cases in which such lawlessness and violence are manifested. The aim of such activity is to break down the prestige of Governmental power, to furnish continuous proof of the possibility of carrying on a contest with the Government, to raise in that way the revolutionary spirit of the people and inspire belief in the practicability of revolution, and, finally, to form a body suited and accustomed to warfare.

As quoted in George Kennan, *Siberia and the Exile System* (New York: The Century Co., 1891), Vol. 2: 495–499.

---

his reforms, for the limited character of those reforms convinced many that the autocracy could never truly redirect Russian society.

Alexander III, whose reign (1881–1894) further underscored that pessimistic conviction, possessed all the autocratic and repressive characteristics of his grandfather Nicholas I and none of the enlightened qualities of his father. Some attention was directed toward improving conditions in Russian factories, but Alexander III sought primarily to roll back his father's reforms. He favored centralized bureaucracy over the new limited modes of self-government. He strengthened the secret police and increased press censorship. In effect, he confirmed all the evils that the revolutionaries saw inher-

ent in autocratic government. His son, Nicholas II (r. 1894–1917), would discover that autocracy could not survive the pressures of the twentieth century.

Great Britain: Toward Democracy

Great Britain continued to symbolize the confident liberal state. A large body of ideas emphasizing competition and individualism was accepted by the members of all classes. Even the leaders of trade unions during these years asked only to receive some of the fruits of prosperity and to prove their own social respectability. Parliament itself continued to

Tsar Alexander II (r. 1855–1881) was assassinated on March 1, 1881. The assassins first threw a bomb that wounded several Imperial guards. When the Tsar stopped his carriage to see to the wounded, the assassins threw a second bomb, killing him. [Bildarchiv Preussischer Kulturbesitz]

provide an institution that permitted the absorption of new groups and interests into the existing political processes.

The most important example of the opening of parliamentary processes was the Second Reform Act passed by a Conservative government in 1867. It increased the number of voters from approximately 1,430,000 to 2,470,000. Britain had taken a major step toward democracy. Benjamin Disraeli (1804–1881), who led the Conservatives in the House of Commons, thought significant portions of the working class would eventually support Conservative candidates who were responsive to social issues. He also thought the growing suburban middle class would become more conservative.

Gladstone and Disraeli

The immediate election of 1868, however, dashed Disraeli's hopes. William Gladstone (1809–1898) became the new prime minister. His ministry of 1868–1874 witnessed the culmination of classical British liberalism. Gladstone introduced competitive examinations into the civil service, abolished the purchase of army officers' commissions, and introduced the secret ballot. He opened Oxford and Cambridge universities to students of all religious denominations and, by the Education Act of 1870, made the British government responsible for establishing and running elementary schools, which had been supported by the various churches.

The liberal policy of creating popular support for the nation by extending political liberty and reforming abuses had its conservative counterpart in concern about social reform. Disraeli succeeded Gladstone as prime minister in 1874. Whereas Gladstone looked to individualism, free trade, and competition to solve social problems, Disraeli believed the state should protect weaker citizens. In his view, paternalistic legislation would alleviate class antagonism. His most important measures were the Public Health Act of 1875, which consolidated and extended previous sanitary legislation, and the Artisans Dwelling Act of 1875, through which the government became actively involved in providing housing for the working class.

The Irish Question

The major issue of the 1880s was Ireland. From the late 1860s onward, Irish nationalists had sought to achieve home rule for Ireland, by which they meant more Irish control of local government. Their demands of the British government in that respect very much resembled the demands of the Czechs to-

A House of Commons debate: William Ewart Gladstone, standing on the right, is attacking Benjamin Disraeli, who sits with legs crossed and arms folded. Gladstone served in the British Parliament from the 1830s through the 1890s. Four times the Liberal Party Prime Minister, he was responsible for guiding major reforms through Parliament. Disraeli, regarded as the founder of modern British conservatism, served as Prime Minister from 1874 to 1880. [Mary Evans Picture Library]

ward the Habsburg government. The Irish, like the Czechs in the Habsburg Empire, proved a profoundly disruptive force in British politics.

The leader of the Irish movement for home rule was Charles Stewart Parnell (1846–1891). By 1885 Parnell had organized eighty-five Irish members of the House of Commons into a tightly disciplined party that often voted as a bloc. In the election of 1885 the Irish Party emerged holding the balance of power between the English Liberals and Conservatives. The Irish could decide which party would take office. In December 1885 Gladstone announced support for home rule for Ireland.

Parnell gave his votes to the formation of a Liberal ministry. However, the issue split the Liberal Party. In 1886 a group known as the Liberal Unionists joined with the Conservatives to defeat Gladstone's Home Rule Bill. Gladstone called for a new election, which the Liberals lost. They remained permanently divided. The new Conservative min-

istry of Lord Salisbury (1830–1903) attempted to reconcile the Irish to English government through public works and administrative reform. The policy had only marginal success.

In 1892 Gladstone returned to power and sponsored a second Home Rule Bill that passed the House of Commons but was defeated in the House of Lords. With the failure of this bill, further action on the Irish question was suspended until a Liberal ministry passed the third Home Rule Bill in the summer of 1914. However, the implementation of Home Rule was suspended for the duration of World War I.

The Irish question affected British politics in a manner not unlike that of the Austrian nationalities problem. Normal British domestic issues could not be adequately addressed because of the political divisions created by Ireland. The split of the Liberal Party hurt the cause of further social and political reform. The people who could agree about reforms could not agree on Ireland, and Ireland seemed more important. As the two traditional parties failed to deal with the

William Gladstone Pleads for Irish Home Rule

Since 1800 Ireland had been governed as part of Great Britain, sending representatives to the British Parliament in Westminster. Throughout the nineteenth century there had been tension and violent conflict between the Irish and their English governors. Agitation for Home Rule, whereby the Irish would directly control many of their own affairs, reached a peak in the 1880s. In 1886 William Gladstone introduced a Home Rule Bill into Parliament. The evening when Parliament voted on the measure Gladstone made a long speech, part of which is quoted here, asking Parliament to reject the traditions of the past and to grant Ireland this measure of independence. That night the Home Rule Bill of 1886 went down to defeat, but the problem remained to vex British politics from that time to the present.

Why did Gladstone support Irish home rule in 1886? How does he pose the issue as a matter of redeeming the reputation of England? Compare this document to others dealing with nationalism and independence movements, for example "Bolívar Denounces Spanish Rule in Latin America" (Chapter 25), "Mazzini Defines Nationality" (Chapter 26), "Herzl Calls for the Establishment of a Jewish State" (Chapter 29), and "Gandhi on Passive Resistance and Swaraj" (Chapter 31).

What is the case of Ireland at this moment? . . . Can anything stop a nation's demand, except its being proved to be immoderate and unsafe? But here are multitudes, and, I believe, millions upon millions, out-of-doors, who feel this demand to be neither immoderate nor unsafe. In our opinion, there is but one question before us about this demand. It is as to the time and circumstance of granting it. There is no question in our minds that it will be granted. . . .

Ireland stands at your bar expectant, hopeful, almost suppliant. Her words are the words of truth and soberness. She asks a blessed oblivion of the past, and in that oblivion our interest is deeper than even hers. My right honourable Friend the Member [of Parliament] for East Edinburgh asks us tonight to abide by the traditions of which we are the heirs. What traditions? By the Irish traditions? Go into the length and breadth of the world, ransack the literature of all countries, find, if you can, a single voice, a single book, find, I would almost say, as much as a single newspaper article, unless the product of the [present] day, in which the conduct of England towards Ireland is anywhere treated except with profound and bitter condemnation. Are these the traditions by which we are exhorted to stand? No; they are a sad exception to the glory of our country. They are a broad and black blot upon the pages of its history; and what we want to do is to stand by the traditions of which we are the heirs in all matters except our relations with Ireland, and to make our relations with Ireland to conform to the other traditions of our country. So we treat our traditions—so we hail the demand of Ireland for what I call a blessed oblivion of the past. She also asks a boon [a favor] for the future; and that boon for the future, unless we are much mistaken, will be a boon to us in respect of honour, no less than a boon to her in respect of happiness, prosperity, and peace. Such . . . is her prayer. Think, I beseech you, think well, think wisely, think, not for the moment, but for the years that are to come, before you reject this Bill.

As quoted in Hans Kohn, ed., *The Modern World: 1848 to the Present*, 2nd ed. (New York: The Macmillan Company; London:Collier-Macmillan Limited, 1968), pp. 116, 118. Reprinted by permission of the estate of Hans Kohn.

---

social questions, by the turn of the century a newly organized Labour Party began to fill the vacuum.

The United States: Civil War, Reconstruction, and Progressive Politics

While European nations consolidated and unified themselves, the United States reforged the character of its union and democracy through a civil war that ended with the abolition of slavery. The abolition of slavery in the United States occurred in the same decade as the abolition of serfdom in Russia. Both processes left the groups who were legally freed—Russian serfs and black American slaves—in very precarious social and political positions. The war also ended with the triumph of the central federal government over the authority of the individual states. The southern states' attempt to forge their own independent nation had failed and a wider nationalism succeeded. That victory, however, left a North-South economic and political problem in the United States similar to the North-South problem in Italy after Piedmont unified that nation under its monarchy.

As noted in Chapter 26, the acquisition of vast new territories by the United States at the end of the Mexican War in 1849 re-opened the American debate over slavery. During the 1850s that debate grew, with various political groups upholding more extreme positions. Northern abolitionists resented the enforcement of the federal Fugitive Slave Law, which required the return of escaped slaves to their owners without recourse to the courts. During the same years the South became more economically dependent on the manufactures and trading interests of the North. Southerners began to fear that the North was determined to dominate the South economically and politically.

In 1854 the introduction of the Kansas-Nebraska Bill renewed the formal national political debate over slavery and galvanized the antislavery forces. The principle of the bill, introduced by Stephen A. Douglas (1813–1861), was that of popular sovereignty. The people of each new territory would decide whether slavery was to be permitted within its borders. Douglas was thus willing to repeal the Missouri Compromise, which had prohibited slavery in the majority of the Louisiana Territory. Popular sovereignty meant that every newly organized territory became the site for a debate over slavery. In 1854 the new Republican Party was organized largely in opposition to the Kansas-Nebraska Bill. Not everyone, however, was willing just to argue. For example, John Brown went to Kansas, where armed conflict had already broken out, and carried out virtual guerrilla warfare against slaveholding settlers. During 1854 "Bleeding Kansas" was in a state of civil war.

In 1857, in the Dred Scott decision, the Supreme Court effectively repealed the Missouri Compromise by declaring that Congress could not prohibit slavery in the territories. The decision further declared that slaves did not become free by living in free states and that slaves did not have rights that others were bound to respect. For radical antislavery northerners, the decision raised the most serious questions about the morality of the Union itself, and it demonstrated again, a Southern conspiracy to protect slavery. Thereafter, slavery dominated national political debate.

In 1859 John Brown seized the federal arsenal at Harpers Ferry, West Virginia, as part of an effort to foment a possible slave rebellion. He was captured, tried, and hanged, further increasing sectional polarization. Radical southerners feared more than ever a northern conspiracy to attack the institution of slavery, while northern radicals feared that the South now controlled the federal government and would use it to protect slavery. Thus the politics of both sections became radicalized.

The Republican Party had become the party that opposed slavery, although it did not necessarily favor outright abolition. In 1858 Abraham Lincoln (1809–1865) ran against Stephen Douglas for the U.S. Senate in Illinois. Lincoln lost, but made a national reputation for himself in the debates leading up to the election. In 1860 Lincoln, the Republican candidate, was elected president. Neither he nor the Republican Party had campaigned for the abolition of slavery. Nonetheless, southerners perceived his election as the victory of a party and a president dedicated to the eradication of slavery. In December 1860 southern states began to secede and formed the Confederate States of America. Attempts at political compromise to maintain the Union failed, and when confederate forces fired on Fort Sumter in Charleston Harbor in April 1861, the most destructive war in U.S. history began.

The Civil War lasted almost exactly four years, and a different nation emerged from the violence. In 1863, two years after Alexander II ended Russian serfdom, Lincoln emancipated the slaves in the rebelling states. The Emancipation Proclamation transformed the northern cause from that of suppressing a southern rebellion into that of extending liberty. By the time the Confederacy was defeated in 1865, the South was occupied by northern armies, its farms were often fallow, its transportation network disrupted, and many of its cities in ruins. Southern political leaders had virtually no impact on the immediate postwar decisions. The Thirteenth, Fourteenth, and Fifteenth amendments largely recast the character of the Union. The Thirteenth abolished slavery; the Fourteenth granted citizenship to the former slaves; and the Fifteenth allowed them to vote. The Fourteenth amendment also prohibited much political activity by people who had taken up arms against the Union. These amendments resolved the issues of slavery and the relative roles of the state and federal governments.

The election of Lincoln in 1860 sparked the secession crisis that started the Civil War. This picture shows Lincoln as he was when elected, without the famous beard that he grew later. [Preston Butler/Library of Congress]

Lincoln States the Ideals of American Liberty at Gettysburg

The battle of Gettysburg in 1863 was the largest battle of the American Civil War and marked the farthest intrusion of Confederate forces into the North. The Union won the battle after great losses to both sides. A few months later President Lincoln journeyed to Gettysburg to participate in the dedication of a military cemetery. There he delivered one of his very few public speeches during the war. In it he set forth what he considered to be the ideals of democratic government that he had come to believe constituted the goals for which the Union stood and fought. Note that he traced American liberty to the Declaration of Independence rather than to the Constitution, which had had actually embraced slavery.

How did this speech transform the Union position in the American Civil War from an effort to suppress a rebellion into a war for human liberty? What would Lincoln have included in the unfinished work that the living must continue? What did he mean by "a new birth of freedom"?

Four score and seven years ago our fathers brought forth on this continent, a new nation, conceived in Liberty, and dedicated to the proposition that all men are created equal.

Now we are engaged in a great civil war, testing whether that nation or any nation so conceived and so dedicated, can long endure. We are met on a great battlefield of that war. We have come to dedicate a portion of that field, as a final resting place for those who here gave their lives that that nation might live. It is altogether fitting and proper that we should do this.

But, in a larger sense, we cannot dedicate—we cannot consecrate—we cannot hallow—this ground. The brave men, living and dead, who struggled here, have consecrated it, far above our poor power to add or detract. The world will little note, nor long remember what we say here, but it can never forget what they did here. It is for us the living, rather, to be dedicated here to the unfinished work which they who fought here have thus far so nobly advanced. It is rather for us to be here dedicated to the great task remaining before us—that from these honored dead we take increased devotion to that cause for which they gave the last full measure of devotion—that we here highly resolve that these dead shall not have died in vain—that this nation, under God, shall have a new birth of freedom—and that government of the people, by the people, for the people, shall not perish from the earth.

From Abraham Lincoln, *The Gettysburg Address, November 19, 1863*, as quoted in Henry Steele Commager, *Documents of American History*, 8th ed., Vol. 1. Copyright © 1968 Appleton-Century-Crofts, pp. 428–429.

The Civil War and the Reconstruction era that followed it overturned the antebellum social and political structures of the South. The slaves were freed and for a time participated broadly and actively in the politics of the southern states. For more than ten years federal troops occupied parts of the South. Many of the antebellum southern leaders left political life. Economically, the South remained generally rural and still dependent on cotton. For the first time since the earliest colonial days, it became an area of free labor. Many of the freed slaves and poor whites who tilled the land remained hopelessly in debt to wealthier landowners. Attempts to bring manufacturing into the South met with limited success. Rampant racism also blocked free economic development.

For the rest of the century the South remained in a semicolonial relationship to the North. More than ever, the goods and services the South needed had to be paid for by exporting raw materials or partially finished goods to the North, according to the economic rules set by northern manufacturers and financiers. Throughout the rural South, poverty was the norm. In this respect, there is a parallel between the fate of the American South after the Civil War and the fate of the Italian South after unification.

Within the context of world history, the American Civil War is important for several reasons. It was the greatest war that occurred anywhere in the world between the defeat of Napoleon in 1815 and the onset of World War I in 1914. It represented the triumph of the same kind of central or centralizing political authority that was also triumphing in Italy, Germany, and France in the 1860s. It resulted in the establishment of a continent-wide free labor market, even though freed blacks lived in great poverty and an economic dependence not unlike that of the rural classes of Latin America. The free labor market, purged of slavery, helped to open the entire North American continent to economic development. The war also allowed American political and economic interests to develop without the distraction of the debates over states rights and the morality of slavery. Thereafter, free labor would become the American norm, and the debates over the role of industrial labor in the United States resembled those in Europe.

Dashed Hopes of Equality

The single most visible result of the Civil War was the end of slavery in the South and the promise of equality. However, the fruits of liberty for blacks in the quarter century following the war proved ephemeral. During the same era the liberty of Native Americans was even more curtailed.

Emergence of Segregation of Black Americans

Throughout the era of Reconstruction (1865–1877) black Americans gained prominence in southern political life. Freedmen, as former slaves were called, voted, held office, and owned property. These years proved to be a false spring of political liberty for blacks.

In 1876 the Republican Rutherford B. Hayes (1822–1893) was elected only after a series of secret political compromises whereby Hayes promised to remove the last federal troops from the South and to build railways there. In return, conservative southern politicians promised to protect the freedmen. For the former slaves, it was a bad bargain. With the federal troops gone, promises were quickly ignored. Simultaneously, the North, concern for the fate of the freedmen diminished as both the economy and urban social stresses grew. Northerners who had wanted to end slavery retreated from the promise of extending full civil rights to free blacks.

Racism backed by legislation grew to dominate the political and social life of the south. Within the states of the old Confederacy, the border states, and, to a lesser extent, elsewhere, a system of legalized discrimination against blacks slowly arose in the form of segregation. Through laws passed by city councils and state legislatures, social life became divided into black and white spheres. Race defined nearly every institution and limited access to every public facility. Restaurants, hospitals, prisons, churches, trains, streetcars, beaches, drinking fountains, Bibles used in courtrooms, and even burial grounds were divided according to race. In 1896 the Supreme Court declared these arrangements to be constitutional in *Plessy v. Ferguson*. That decision remained in force until 1954.

Within this segregated world American blacks were subject to discrimination simply on the basis of the color of their skin. Furthermore, southern states legalized poll taxes and literacy tests, depriving blacks of their right to vote. American blacks were also subject to physical intimidation and terrorism. Well into the twentieth century, waves of lynchings spread across the South. Most victims were blacks.

In the late nineteenth century many black leaders, Booker T. Washington (1856–1915) being the most prominent, argued that their fellow blacks should wait for better times, submit to the discrimination, and practice economic virtues such as hard work and thrift that might lead them out of poverty. Drawing on the ideas of European economic liberalism that admonished against government action, they contended that by behaving in a careful, deferential manner blacks might eventually convince the dominant whites of

W. E. B. Dubois, a founder of the National Association for the Advancement of Colored People (NAACP), called for full equality of African Americans with white Americas. [Schomburg Center, New York Public Library]

their worthiness for inclusion in political activity. A generation later, different black voices made themselves heard.

After the turn of the century W. E. B. DuBois (1868–1963), who had been educated at Harvard and in Berlin, urged more direct claims to political rights and the establishment of a well-educated black leadership group. He understood that racism in the forms of riots, lynchings, and segregation was continuing to spread and had penetrated the North as well as the South. Deference had achieved nothing. In 1909 DuBois and others undertook to organize the National Association for the Advancement of Colored People. In time, that organization would spearhead much of the effort of black Americans toward greater equality, but almost half a century would pass before segregation was declared illegal.

The Native American Experience

During the second half of the nineteenth century, European powers gained vast military and administrative control over various peoples in Africa and Asia. The United States pursued somewhat similar policies toward Native Americans during the ongoing westward migration across the North American continent.

In the early nineteenth century the Native Americans who had originally lived east of the Mississippi—including the Cherokees, Creeks, and Seminoles—were pushed farther and

Because General George Custer and his entire army were destroyed at the Battle of the Little Big Horn in 1876, the only record of the event is that of a Native American artist illustrating Custer's defeat.

[The Granger Collection, N.Y.]

farther west. These forced removals by the federal government became known as the Trail of Tears. By the close of the Civil War there were more than 300,000 Native Americans, most of whom lived west of the Mississippi. Most of these people were indigenous to the region; others had been forced to migrate there.

The virtual end of the Native American way of life took place between 1865 and the 1890s; during these years Native Americans constantly clashed with the U.S. Army. While the transcontinental railways opened the West to white settlement, the buffalo and other food supplies of the Native Americans were destroyed. The army suppressed resistance. There were rare Native American victories, such as the Battle of the Little Big Horn of 1876, in which Major General George Custer and his force of over 200 soldiers were killed by the Sioux and Cheyenne. But such victories were ultimately futile, as the technologically better-armed troops of the U.S. Army suppressed opposition. In some cases, such as the infamous attack on Sioux Indians at Wounded Knee in 1890, the army massacred women and children.

The federal policy against Native Americans had much in common with that of the southern states against blacks. Both policies were fundamentally antidemocratic and calculated to make social and economic life safe and profitable for white Americans. Racist thinking played a major role in both instances. Blacks were segregated and excluded from political life and their labor extracted at low wages. Native Americans were, in effect, segregated from the rest of the nation and excluded from political life, in addition to having their lands appropriated. In 1867 the federal government began to place Native Americans on reservations. As the conquest of the

Great Plains continued, the reservation system spread. The land assigned to Native Americans was almost invariably of poor quality and far removed from areas that white Americans wished to develop.

The Canadian Experience

Under the Treaty of Paris of 1763, all of Canada came under the control of Great Britain. Canada then, as now, included both an English-speaking and a French-speaking population. The latter was concentrated primarily in Quebec. The Quebec Act of 1774, which had so disturbed the English colonists along the Atlantic seaboard, recognized the Roman Catholic church and made it the established church in Quebec. During the American Revolution approximately 30,000 English loyalists fled the colonies and settled in Canada. They thus established a larger English presence and were strongly loyal to the British crown.

The tension between the French and English populations led, in part, to the Constitutional Act of 1791, which divided the colony into Upper Canada (primarily English in ethnic composition) and Lower Canada (primarily French). Each section had its own legislature, and a governor-general presided over the two provinces on behalf of the British crown. Newfoundland, Nova Scotia, New Brunswick, Cape Breton Island, and Prince Edward Island remained separate colonies.

In the early nineteenth century relations with the United States were often tense. There were local disputes over the fur trade and fear that the United States would dominate

Canada. That apprehension, along with the Anglo-French ethnic divisions, came to constitute two of the major themes of Canadian history.

By the late 1830s the political situation in Canada was beginning to generate considerable internal pressure. Tension arose between long-established families with powerful economic interests in both Upper and Lower Canada and new settlers who hoped to achieve prosperity for themselves. There were quarrels over the influence of the British Crown in local affairs. In 1837 rebellions occurred in both Upper and Lower Canada. Although there were relatively few casualties, the British realized that some action had to be taken.

Road to Self-Government

The British government, operating in the more liberal political climate following the first Reform Act (1832), was determined to avoid another North American revolution. Consequently, it sent the Earl of Durham (1792–1840) to Canada with extensive powers to make reforms. In 1839 his *Report on the Affairs of British North America* advocated responsible government for Canada. Durham contended that both Canadian provinces should be united into one political unit. He thought that such political unification would eventually lead to a thoroughly English culture throughout Canada which would overwhelm the French influence in Quebec. He also believed that most Canadian affairs should be in the hands of a Canadian legislature and that only foreign policy and defense should remain under British control. In effect, Durham wanted Canadians generally to govern themselves, so that English culture would dominate. His policy was carried out in the Canada Act of 1840, which gave the nation a single legislature composed of two houses.

The Durham Report established the political pattern that the British government would, to a greater or lesser extent, follow with its other English-speaking colonies during the nineteenth century. Britain sought to foster responsible self-government in Australia, New Zealand, and South Africa. The Canadian experience thus had a considerable impact throughout the world. But, until well into the twentieth century, the British government, like other Western imperial powers, also generally believed that nonwhite peoples, such as those of India, required direct British colonial administration.

Keeping a Distinctive Culture

Canadians did learn to exercise self-government, but distinct English and French cultures continued to exist. Within the legislature there were almost always tradeoffs between the eastern and western sections of the nation. Furthermore, during the American Civil War, fears arose that the American re-public might seek to invade Canada or otherwise dominate it. One response to this fear was an attempt to unite the maritime provinces in 1862. Those discussions led to broader considerations of the desirability for a stronger federation among all the parts of Canada.

The result of those debates and discussions was the British North America Act of 1867, which created a Canadian federation. Canadians hoped to avoid what they regarded as flaws in the constitution of the United States. The Canadian system of government was to be federal, but with much less emphasis on states' rights than in the United States. Canadians established a parliamentary mode of government, but also chose to retain the presence of the British monarchy in the person of the governor-general as head of state. The person who was most responsible for establishing this new government and who led it for most of the period between 1867 and 1891 was John A. MacDonald (1815–1891).

Like settlers in the United States, Canadians during the nineteenth century pressed westward. The St. Lawrence River had determined the corridor of settlement in eastern Canada. Initially, the far western portions of Canada had been explored and exploited by fur traders and the Hudson Bay Company. The path for the later settlement of the western prairies and the Canadian Northwest was provided by the construction of the Canadian Pacific Railway, completed in 1885. The railroad crossed the continent as a kind of spine along which settlements grew. In turn, the Canadian economy became highly integrated with that of the United States. This situation, which has continued to the present day, created fears of being dominated economically by the powerful industrial economy of Canada's southern neighbor.

As Canadians established a nation that stretched across a continent and demonstrated their capacity for stable self-government, the domination of Britain diminished. The link with the British Crown remained; however, Canada established a largely independent foreign policy by the close of the century. The role of the governor-general became increasingly ceremonial as real political power came to reside in the Canadian political parties and parliamentary system. Canada supported Great Britain in the Boer War, World War I, and World War II—but as an ally, not a colony.

The Canadian transition from colony to self-governing nation was thus quite different from that of the United States. Throughout the process the British government and its representatives were actively involved. Furthermore, the presence of a strong and continuing French culture in which the Roman Catholic church played a major role led to real cultural differences between French- and English-speaking Canada. English-speaking Canadians dominated both political and economic life. French-speaking Canadians virtually always felt like second-class citizens.

IN WORLD PERSPECTIVE
European and North American Political Consolidation

The movement toward strong, centralized national states in Europe and North America during the nineteenth century had its counterparts elsewhere in the world. In Asia during this same period, Japan sought to imitate the military and economic power of the European states. Late nineteenth-century Latin America enjoyed one of its most successful and stable periods. Its governments established centralized regimes on the basis of relatively prosperous economies.

In the United States the Civil War established the power of the central federal government over that of the individual states. The role of the war in the forging of a single American nation was similar to the role that military force played in the unifications of Italy and Germany and the suppression of the Paris Commune.

In Italy and Germany many people regarded the triumph of nationalism as a positive achievement. However, the last half of the century also saw various national and ethnic groups use the power of a national state to repress or dominate other groups. Examples include the Hungarian treatment of smaller subject nationalities and the British treatment of the Irish.

Elsewhere around the globe, strong national governments similarly repressed weak groups. Native Americans failed to gain rights in Latin America. In the United States the westward movement brought warfare against Native Americans; legislation of the late century saw the segregation of American blacks. In Canada, English speakers fared better than French speakers. Throughout the world nationalism involved the extension of liberty to some peoples and its denial to others. In almost all cases the repression of some groups generated social and political problems that would haunt the twentieth century.

Finally, the emergence of strong European nation-states set the stage for the transfer of their rivalry from Europe to other areas of the globe. The militarily and economically strong states of Europe soon turned to foreign adventures that would subjugate vast areas of Africa and Asia. This imperialism led many of the colonialized peoples to become aware that only strong nationalistic movements of their own could eventually end subjugation by the militarily stronger Europeans. Consequently, during the first quarter of the twentieth century, the nationalistic principle that less than fifty years earlier had stirred European politics began to influence the politics of the peoples on whom Europeans had imposed their government and administration. In time the United States would be drawn into those worldwide conflicts.

Review Questions

1. Why was it so difficult to unify Italy? What were the contributions of Mazzini, Cavour, and Garibaldi to Italian unification?

2. Who was Otto von Bismarck and why did he try to unify Germany? What was Bismarck's method of unification and why did he succeed? What effect did the unification of Germany have on the rest of Europe?

3. Discuss the transformation of France from the Second Empire of Napoleon II to the establishment of the Third Republic.

4. Describe the government changes in Austria after 1848. What unique problems did Austria confront? Why was nationalism a more pressing problem for Austria than for any other nation?

5. What reforms were instituted by Tsar Alexander II in Russia? Were they effective in solving some of Russia's domestic problems? Can Alexander II be regarded as a "visionary" reformer? Why or why not?

6. How would you contrast the British Liberal and Conservative parties between 1860 and 1890? How did British politicians handle the Irish Question? What were the parallels between England's relationship with Ireland and the nationality problem of the Austrian Empire?

7. Compare and contrast the results of the American Civil War with Italian and German unification. Compare the situation of freed American slaves and freed Russian serfs.

Suggested Readings

M. BENTLEY, *Politics Without Democracy, 1815–1914* (1984). A well-informed survey of British development.

R. BLAKE, *Disraeli* (1967). The best biography.

J. BLUM, *Lord and Peasant in Russia from the Ninth to the Nineteenth Century* (1961). A clear discussion of emancipation in the later chapters.

M. Burns, *Rural Society and French Politics: Boulangism and the Dreyfus Affair, 1886–1900* (1984). An examination of the subject from the rural perspective.

G. Chapman, *The Dreyfus Affair: A Reassessment* (1955). A detached treatment of a subject that still provokes strong feelings.

D. G. Creighton, *John A. MacDonald* (1952, 1955). Major biography of the first Canadian prime minister.

G. Craig, *Germany, 1866–1945* (1978). An excellent survey.

D. Donald, *Lincoln* (1995). Now the standard biography.

S. Edwards, *The Paris Commune of 1871* (1971). A useful examination of a complex subject.

D. Fehrenbacher, *The Dred Scott Case* (1978). A brilliant study that goes far beyond the subject of the title.

D. K. Fieldhouse, *The Colonial Experience: A Comparative Study from the Eighteenth Century* (1966). An excellent study.

E. Hobsbawm, *The Age of Empire, 1875–1914* (1987). A stimulating survey that covers cultural as well as political developments.

I. V. Hull, *The Entourage of Kaiser Wilhelm II, 1888–1918* (1982). An important discussion of the scandals of the German court.

R. A. Kann, *The Multinational Empire*, 2 vols. (1950). The basic treatment of the nationality problem of Austria-Hungary.

G. Kitson Clark, *The Making of Victorian England* (1962). The best introduction.

W. L. Langer, *The Diplomacy of Imperialism* (1935). A major study of the diplomatic intricacies of late-century imperialism.

R. R. Locke, *French Legitimists and the Politics of Moral Order in the Early Third Republic* (1974). An excellent study of the social and intellectual roots of monarchist support.

P. Magnus, *Gladstone: A Biography* (1955). A readable biography.

A. J. May, *The Habsburg Monarchy, 1867–1914* (1951). Narrates in considerable detail and with much sympathy the fate of the dual monarchy.

M E. McGerr, *The Decline of Popular Politics: The American North, 1865–1928* (1986). A study of the decline in popular political participation.

F. McMillan, *Napoleon III* (1991). The best recent study.

J. M. McPherson, *The Battle Cry of Freedom: The Civil War Era* (1988). An excellent one-volume treatment.

W. N. Medlicott, *Bismarck and Modern Germany* (1965). An excellent brief biography.

W. J. Mommsen, *Theories of Imperialism* (1980). A study of the debate on the meaning of imperialism.

W. E. Mosse, *Alexander II and the Modernization of Russia* (1958). A brief biography.

N. M. Naimark, *Terrorists and Social Democrats: The Russian Revolutionary Movement Under Alexander III* (1983). Based on the most recent research.

M. E. Neely, Jr., *The Fate of Liberty: Abraham Lincoln and Civil Liberties* (1991). A major discussion of the issue.

C. C. O'Brien, *Parnell and His Party* (1957). An excellent treatment of the Irish question.

J. P. Parry, *The Rise and Fall of Liberal Government in Victorian Britain* (1994). An outstanding study.

O. Pflanze, *Bismarck and the Development of Germany*, 3 vols. (1990). Carries the story from the achievement of unification to the end of Bismarck's career.

A. Plessis, *The Rise and Fall of the Second Empire, 1852–1871* (1985). A useful survey of France under Napoleon III.

D. M. Potter, *The Impending Crisis, 1848–1861* (1976)

R. Shannon, *Gladstone: 1809–1865* (1982). Best coverage of his early career.

D. M. Smith, *Cavour* (1984). An excellent biography.

C. P. Stacey, *Canada and the Age of Conflict* (1977, 1981). A study of Canadian foreign relations.

A. J. P. Taylor, *The Habsburg Monarchy, 1809–1918* (1941). An opinionated but highly readable work.

R. Tombs, *The War Against Paris, 1871* (1981). Examines the role of the army in suppressing the Paris Commune.

A. B. Ulam, *Russia's Failed Revolutionaries* (1981). A recent study of revolutionary societies and activities before the Revolution of 1917.

R. M. Utley, *The Indian Frontier and the American West, 1846–1890* (1984). A broad survey of the pressures of white civilization againt Native Americans.

F. Venturi, *The Roots of Revolution* (trans. 1960). A major treatment of late-nineteenth-century revolutionary movements.

H. S. Watson, *The Russian Empire, 1801–1917* (1967). A far-ranging narrative.

H. U. Wehler, *The German Empire, 1871–1918* (1985). An important, controversial work.

C. B. Woodham-Smith, *The Reason Why* (1953). A lively account of the Crimean War and the charge of the Light Brigade.

C. V. Woodward, *The Strange History of Jim Crow* (1966). A clear discussion of the imposition of racial segregation in the United States.

T. Zeldin, *France: 1848–1945*, 2 vols. (1973, 1977). Emphasizes the social developments.

R. E. Zelnick, *Labor and Society in Tsarist Russia: The Factory Workers of St. Petersburg, 1855–1870* (1971). An important volume that considers the early stages of the Russian industrial labor force in the era of serf emancipation.

COMPARATIVE PERSPECTIVES: TECHNOLOGY AND CIVILIZATIONS

Technology and Imperialism

66 "Imperial," having to do with an empire or emperor, comes from the Latin *imperium*. Throughout most of history it was considered normal for stronger countries to conquer and rule their weaker neighbors. As soon as civilizations arose, empires arose: first in Egypt and Mesopotamia; then around the Mediterranean (the Roman empire), in India (Maurya), and in China (the Han Dynasty); and later on Byzantium, the Arab Caliphates, Persia, the Gupta in India, and the succeeding Chinese dynasties. All of these fit what might be called the premodern pattern of empire. They possessed military technologies adequate to dominate surrounding states and tax bases sufficient to field armies. But the chief limitation of early empires was that they were regional and landlocked. However much they claimed universality, however formidable they were in the eyes of their neighbors, communications and transportation placed limits on their ability to expand indefinitely, much less to expand across oceans.

Premodern Empires

Few comparative studies have been made of the military technologies of premodern empires. One almost insuperable problem is that military superiority was not simply a matter of technology in the narrow sense of the term. It is not enough to analyze the relative merits of, say, the English longbow and the Mongol compound bow. It is also a matter of training, organization, and command, and, perhaps most important, of the vitality of an empire's home government. Chinese dynasties, and the same is true of other empires as well, were powerful during their early decades but decrepit at the end, even though their weaponry remained much the same during the course of the dynasty.

Another difficulty in comparing the military might of premodern regional empires is that they only occasionally came in contact. To ask which would have triumphed in a war, the legions of the Roman Empire or those of the Han dynasty, is like the child's question about the lion and the tiger. But at times empires in the Middle East and elsewhere did exist side by side and occasionally do battle. In ancient times the Egyptian empire, for example, unable to defeat the Hittites

in northern Syria, agreed to coexist with them. In the second century B.C.E., the Han Dynasty coexisted with a nomadic Hunnish empire to the north. A Chinese writer of the day compared the military abilities of the two empires. The nomads, he wrote, had the edge in horses, in the fusion of riding and archery, and in their hardiness in the face of cold and hunger. But on a level field the Chinese light cavalry was better, their crossbows had a greater range and could penetrate the nomads' shields of leather and wood, and their infantry formations with sharp swords and long halberds were superior in close-quarter battle.

The most notable exception to the limited regional character of premodern empires was the Mongols, whose empire, expanding from the steppes of Mongolia, stretched from Hungary to Korea, from Siberia to Vietnam. Were nomadic empires different because of the striking power of their cavalry against settled populations, and their ability to communicate over great distances by courier and to live off the land? The Mongols might suggest that this was so. But most nomads lacked the organizational talent of the Mongols, and even the overland Mongol empire quickly dissolved into regional khanates.

If we look at world history prior to the year 1000, or even prior to 1400, China was the indisputable leader in technology. Without the knowledge of hindsight a contemporary observer might well have predicted that China would continue to lead in the centuries that followed. In the early fifteenth century a Chinese armada of sixty-eight ships sailed to southeast Asia, India, and Ceylon, a few ships even reaching the coast of east Africa. The expedition subdued local kings and established short-lived tributaries—a half century before the Portuguese began their voyages of exploration. The expedition, however, had no follow-up, partly because the Chinese court focused its attention, as always, on its vulnerable northern frontier, partly because the court decided that little of value could be gained from contacts with "southern barbarians." Prior to 1400, the Chinese had already invented the compass, clock, triangular sail, printing, iron casting, piston bellows, sternpost rudder, crossbow, gunpowder, rockets, and projectile artillery. But within the Chinese economy there was no sustained pattern of development leading from one set of inventions to another. By the Ming dynasty (1368–1644) and perhaps even earlier, the regards for an official career had become greater than those for a career in commerce, and commerce, in turn, was more rewarding than industry.

In the nineteenth century, Britain, the world's most powerful maritime nation, became the greatest imperial power. Here, the steamship "Great Britain" is launched in Bristol. [The Bridgeman Art Library International]

Early European Imperialism

After 1500, the most remarkable changes in relations between the civilizations of the world was the establishment of new empires across oceans by European nations. Until then, the West had been a relative backwater in world history. What made the difference was its mastery and application of new technologies and its subsequent development of the sciences. In the first phase of the new overseas imperialism, from the sixteenth through the eighteenth century, Portugal, Spain, Holland, France, and England established colonies in the New World, coastal Africa, coastal India, and the East Indies.

Two characteristics mark this early phase. One was mercantilism, that is, government backing for the armed merchantmen that became the agents of imperial expansion. For example, the East India Company was responsible for early British penetration of India, while the Dutch East India Company took Batavia (Java) and enjoyed a monopoly of trade with the Spice Islands in what is now Indonesia. The second characteristic is that during this early phase Europe's technological edge was slight: a better compass, improved sailing ships, and cast iron cannon. With this advantage European countries established colonies in sparsely inhabited lands or in coastal enclaves, but they were singularly unsuccessful against more highly organized states, such as China and Japan. European traders in eighteenth-century China were forced to live along the river outside the city walls of Canton. Their lives were encumbered by onerous regulations, and their trade was supervised by Chinese merchant guilds. In Japan only the Dutch were permitted to trade, and they lived as virtual prisoners on the tiny island of Deshima in Nagasaki harbor. During these early centuries of European expansion, it also should be noted that "traditional" empires continued to flourish and new ones were formed: the Moguls in India, the Ottomans in the Middle East, the Ming and Ch'ing dynasties in China, and the Austro-Hungarian empire in Europe itself.

The Industrial Revolution and Imperialism

In the second half of the eighteenth century the Industrial Revolution began in England and then spread to western Europe and North America. Industries developed rapidly and improvements in one fed those in others. Better steel, tools, chemicals, clocks, and instruments appeared. The invention of the steam engine transformed production and transportation. The locomotive and steamship developed during the early nineteenth century. The screw propeller was tested in 1839. The first iron-hulled transatlantic steamer appeared in 1843. The telegraph was invented in the 1830s, and crossed the English Channel in 1851 and the Atlantic Ocean in 1866.

These developments led to better warships and weapons. After 1750, for example, instead of casting, cannons were produced by boring a solid block of steel. This made for a stronger barrel that could take a larger charge and fire greater distances. It also made possible standardized weapons. Until then, each cast cannon had idiosyncrasies that had to be mastered by it gunner. The new lighter and more powerful cannons were used on warships. The same technology also made possible easily transported light artillery that revolutionized field warfare. By the mid-nineteenth century smoothbore muskets gave way to rifles. Jacketed ammunition and smokeless powder also contributed to the superiority of Western military forces. At the turn of the century the Englishman Hilaire Belloc could write a ditty about an invention by a man from Maine: "Whatever happened we have got, the Maxim gun and they have not." The Maxim automatic machine gun was merely one of a new array of weapons that grew more formidable with each passing decade.

In Perry's account of his 1853–1854 visits to Japan he described an incident in which an American sailor got the better of a Japanese *sumō* wrestler. This 1861 woodblock print portrays another incident with an opposite outcome. [Courtesy of A. Craig]

The industrial revolution transformed the dynamics of empire. Even well-organized traditional states could no longer withstand Western warships, however distant from their homelands. China was defeated by England in the Opium War in 1839–1842, and in 1854, under the threat of Commodore Perry's "black ships," Japan was forced to end its centuries of seclusion and sign a "Treaty of Friendship" with the United States. A letter sent by the shōgun to the Japanese emperor late in 1865 reflects the feelings of a nation confronting irresistible Western forces.

If we were recklessly to resort to arms, we should not have the least hope of victory. Even if we obtained a temporary success, our country, surrounded on all sides by sea, would be attacked night and day, from east and from west, from north and from south; and through ceaseless war our people would thenceforth be plunged in misery.

[Consequently], our most urgent immediate task is to follow the example of the foreigners in using the profits from trade to construct many ships and guns, adopting the strategy of using the barbarians to subdue the barbarians.

Although the shōgun was overthrown in 1868, by following this strategy Japan itself became an imperial power at the turn of the century.[1]

From the 1880s and 1890s, a race for new colonies broke out. Sub-Saharan Africa was divided up by the European powers; France took colonies in Southeast Asia and North Africa; the United States acquired the Philippines; while England, the most successful, consolidated its rule of India and

[1]W. G. Beasley, *Select Documents on Japanese Foreign Policy, 1853–1868* (1955), p. 288.

established colonies around the world. Pre-World War II maps with the British holdings colored in red made it clear why "the sun never set" on that nation's empire.

Various theories attempt to explain why the European nations colonized the world. All of the theories take for granted the technological superiority of the West and ask why this was used to subordinate other peoples. Hobson speculated that the Industrial Revolution produced surplus wealth that could not be invested profitably at home. The export of such capital and the need to protect it, he argued, led to imperialism. Lenin took up Hobson's idea in his influential work on imperialism, and tailoring it to fit the developmental economics of Marx, situated imperialism as the final stage of capitalism. Schumpeter, an ardent defender of capitalism, countered Lenin by arguing that imperialism runs against the principles of capitalism and can only be explained by the survival into modern times of the mindset of a precapitalist military aristocracy. Other writers, seeking to explain why free traders should have established colonies, have suggested that colonies were established "in a fit of absence of mind." That is to say, a situation arose in which the superior military technology of Western forces was called on to restore order, and, as an outcome, the Western power found itself in charge.

Needless to say, no such single-factor explanation is adequate. The economic reasons for taking colonies were many: a need for markets, raw materials, investment opportunities, and outlets for surplus population. Colonies were also seen as conferring glory on the home country, as strategically vital, and as potential missionary fields. A few were seized merely to forestall their being taken by someone else. Japan, the only non-Western imperial power, took Taiwan and Korea as colonies as a part of its drive to catch up with the advanced nations of the West and win recognition from them. Explanations apart, we might note that the world "imperialism" was coined in the early nineteenth century by French and British critics of their nation's expansionistic policies. From its inception the term was a pejorative.

Colonies fell into disfavor during and after World War I. Not only were there vigorous independence movements in the colonies, but colonies also came to be seen as impediments to free trade, and the subjugation of one people by another ran contrary to the rising tide of democratic sentiments in the West. It was during the war that President Wilson spoke out for self-determination. No country went so far as to give up its colonies, but there was a general agreement that new ones should not be taken. Consequently, when Japan invaded Manchuria in 1931 and Italy took over Abyssina (Ethiopia) in 1936, they were severely censured by the League of Nations. By the early decades after World War II, colonies became untenable. Some were given up peacefully, others only after protracted struggles. The modern history of empire-building lasted for four and a half centuries. Its most intense phase, from the late nineteenth century to the mid-twentieth, was remarkably short-lived. Even as imperialism drew to an end, the technology gap between advanced and backward nations continued to widen. Ultimately, ideas and political action, not technology, won the former colonies their independence.

28 THE BUILDING OF NORTHERN TRANSATLANTIC SUPREMACY:

SOCIETY AND POLITICS TO WORLD WAR I

Railways were an important part of late-nineteenth-century middle-class life. They helped promote the development of suburbs, allowing breadwinners to commute into the city to work, leaving their families at home. They also promoted travel to the vacation spots that were being developed across Europe during this era. [Photo: Alfredo Dagli Ori/Bildarchiv Preussischer Kulturbesitz]

CHAPTER TOPICS

EUROPE

◆ The Middle Classes in Ascendancy

◆ Jewish Emancipation

◆ Late-Nineteenth-Century Urban Life

◆ Late-Nineteenth-Century Women's Experience

◆ Labor, Socialism, and Politics to World War I

NORTH AMERICA

◆ The New Industrial Economy

◆ The Progressives

In World Perspective The Building of Northern Transatlantic Supremacy

---

Between 1860 and 1914 European and American political, economic, and social life assumed many characteristics of our present-day world. In Europe nation-states with large electorates, political parties, centralized bureaucracies, and universal military service emerged. In the United States the politics associated with the Progressive Movement brought the Presidency to the center of American political life. On both sides of the north Atlantic business adopted large-scale corporate structures, and the labor force organized itself into trade unions. The numbers of white-collar laborers grew as urban life became predominant throughout western Europe. But even as new vast cities arose in the United States, farming continued to spread across the central midwest and upper southwest. During this period, too, women began to assert new political awareness and to become politically active in both Europe and America. Socialism became a major ingredient in the political life of all European nations, but made virtually no inroads in the United States.

During this half century the extensive spread of industrialism created an unparalleled productive capacity in Europe and expanded in the north and upper midwest of the United States. The age of the automobile, the airplane, the bicycle, the refrigerated ship, the telephone, the radio, the typewriter, and the electric light bulb dawned. The world's economies, based on the gold standard, became increasingly interdependent. European goods flowed into markets across the globe.

Europe had quietly become dependent on the resources and markets of the rest of the world. Farms in the United States, Canada, Latin America, Australia, and New Zealand supplied food to much of the world. Consequently climate changes in Kansas, Argentina, or New Zealand might now affect the European economy. However, before World War I the dependence was concealed by Europe's industrial, military, and financial supremacy. At the time Europeans assumed their supremacy to be natural, but the twentieth century would reveal it to have been temporary. Nevertheless, while it prevailed, Euro-

peans dominated most of the other peoples of the earth and displayed extreme self-confidence. Toward the close of the century the United States, having achieved the status of a major industrial power as well as agricultural supplier, now entered the world stage as a military power, defeating Spain in the Spanish American War. With that victory, the United States also acquired its first colonial territories.

The Europe of this era became, for many decades, the model for economic, social, and political development for much of the rest of the world. Two things explained this situation: First, through imperialism, Europeans dominated much of the globe. Second, Europe appeared so powerful and wealthy that it often seemed that only by emulating at least parts of European life could non-European nations challenge Europe's imperial dominance. The socialist critique of late-nineteenth-century European society would in time be adopted by non-European political leaders to criticize the European domination of the rest of the world. Citizens of the United States often went to

Europe to educate themselves or to participate in its artistic communities, but the United States retained its own political direction, spurning socialism and other radical political alternatives. Its citizens, like those of other nations, looked to Europe for cultural and economic leadership but often regarded its politics with skepticism. Progressive politics sought to preserve capitalism while using government bodies to restrain capitalistic excess without redistribution of property.

EUROPE

The Middle Classes in Ascendancy

The sixty years before World War I were the age of the middle classes. The London Great Exhibition of 1851, held in the Crystal Palace, had displayed the products and the new material life they had forged. Thereafter, the middle classes be-

Electricity transformed industry and everyday life in Europe. This painting is of an early electric generating plant in France. [The Bridgeman Art Library International]

came the arbiter of consumer taste. After 1848 the middle classes ceased to be revolutionary. Large and small property owners across the Continent moved to protect what they possessed against demands from socialists and other working-class groups.

The middle classes, never perfectly homogeneous, grew increasingly diverse. Their most prosperous members—the owners and managers of great businesses and banks—lived in splendor that rivaled and sometimes exceeded that of the aristocracy. Some, such as W. H. Smith (1825–1891), the owner of railway newsstands in England, were made members of the House of Lords. The Krupp family of Germany were pillars of the state and received visits from the German emperor and his court.

Few families gained such wealth. Beneath them were the comfortable small entrepreneurs and professional people, whose incomes permitted private homes, large quantities of furniture, pianos, pictures, books, journals, education for their children, and vacations. Also in this group were the shopkeepers, schoolteachers, librarians, and others who had either a bit of property or a skill derived from education that provided respectable, nonmanual employment.

Finally, there was a wholly new element, white-collar workers, who formed the lower middle class or petite bourgeoisie. They included secretaries, retail clerks, and lower-level bureaucrats in business and government. They often had working-class origins and might even belong to unions, but they had middle-class aspirations and consciously sought to distance themselves from a lower-class lifestyle. They pursued educational opportunities and chances for even the slightest career advancement for themselves and especially their children. Many of them spent much of their disposable income on consumer goods, such as stylish clothing and furniture, that were distinctively middle class in appearance.

Significant tensions and social anxieties marked relations among the various middle-class groups. Small shopkeepers resented the power of the great capitalists, with their department stores and mail-order catalogs. The professions may have become overcrowded. People who had only recently attained a middle-class lifestyle feared losing it in bad economic times. Nonetheless, the decades immediately before the First World War saw the middle classes setting the values and goals for most of the society.

Jewish Emancipation

One of the most important social changes to occur throughout Europe during the nineteenth century was the emancipation of European Jews from the narrow life of the ghetto

The era of Jewish emancipation allowed more freedom to European Jews and a wider recognition of their faith and culture. This painting by G. E. Opitz portrays the dedication of a new synagogue in Alsace in 1820. [Jewish Museum, N.Y./Art Resource, N.Y.]

into a world of equal or nearly equal citizenship and social status. This transformation represented one of the major social impacts of political liberalism on European life.

Early Steps to Equal Citizenship

Emancipation, slow and never fully completed, began in the late eighteenth century and continued throughout the nineteenth. It moved at different paces in different countries. In 1782 Joseph II (r. 1765–1790), the Habsburg emperor, issued a decree that placed the Jews of his empire under more or less the same laws as Christians. In France the National Assembly recognized Jews as French citizens in 1789. During the Napoleonic wars Jewish communities in Italy and Germany were allowed to mix on a generally equal footing with the Christian population.

These various steps toward political emancipation were frequently limited or partially repealed with changes in rulers or governments. Even in countries that had advanced Jews political rights, they could not own land and could be subject to discriminatory taxes. Nonetheless, by the first half of the nineteenth century Jews in western Europe and to a much lesser extent in central and eastern Europe had begun to acquire equal or nearly equal citizenship.

In Russia, however, the traditional modes of prejudice and discrimination continued unabated until World War I. Jews were treated as aliens under Russian rule. The government undermined Jewish community life, limited publication of Jewish books, restricted areas where Jews might live, required internal passports from Jews, banned them from many forms of state service and from many institutions of higher education. The police and others were allowed to conduct pogroms—organized riots—against Jewish neighborhoods and villages.

Broadened Opportunities

After the Revolutions of 1848, and especially in western Europe, the situation of European Jews improved for several decades. Throughout Germany, Italy, the Low Countries, and Scandinavia, Jews were allowed full rights of citizenship. After 1858 Jews in Great Britain could sit in Parliament. In Austria-Hungary full legal rights were extended to Jews in 1867. From approximately 1850 to 1880 there was relatively little organized or overt prejudice toward Jews. They entered the professions and other occupations once closed to them. They participated fully in the literary and cultural life of their nations. They were active in the arts and music. They became leaders in science and education. Jews intermarried freely with non-Jews as legal prohibitions against such marriages were repealed during the last quarter of the century.

Outside of Russia, Jewish political figures served in the highest offices of the state. Politically they tended to be aligned with liberal parties because such groups had championed equal rights. Later in the century, especially in eastern Europe, many Jews became associated with the socialist parties.

The prejudice that had been associated with religious attitudes toward Jews seemed to have dissipated, although it still appeared in rural Russia and eastern Europe. From these regions hundreds of thousands of European Jews immigrated to the United States. Almost anywhere in Europe Jews might encounter prejudice on a personal level. But in western

Europe, including England, France, Italy, and Germany as well as the Low Countries, the Jewish populations seem to have felt relatively secure from the old dangers of legalized persecution and discrimination.

That began to change during the last two decades of the nineteenth century. In the 1870s antisemitic sentiments attributing the economic stagnation of that decade to Jewish bankers and financial interests began to be voiced. In the 1880s organized antisemitism erupted in Germany as it did in France at the time of the Dreyfus Affair (see Chapter 27). As will be seen in the next chapter, those developments gave birth to Zionism, the movement to establish a Jewish state in Palestine. However, Zionism was initially a minority movement within the Jewish community. Most Jewish leaders believed the attacks on Jewish life to be temporary recurrences of older prejudice; they felt that their communities would remain safe under the legal protections that had been extended during the century. That analysis would be proved disastrously wrong during the second quarter of the twentieth century.

Late-Nineteenth-Century Urban Life

After 1850 Europe became more urbanized than it ever had been. Migration within the Continent and Great Britain continued to move toward the cities. In France the percentage of the urban population within the whole population rose between 1850 and 1911 from approximately 25 to 44 percent, and in Germany the shift was from 30 to 60 percent. The rural migrants to the cities were largely uprooted from traditional social ties. They often confronted poor housing, social anonymity, and potential unemployment because they rarely possessed skills that would make them easily employable. The difficulties that peoples from different ethnic backgrounds had in mixing socially and the competition for too few jobs generated new varieties of political and social discontent, such as those experienced by the thousands of Russian Jews who migrated to western Europe. Much of the political antisemitism of the latter part of the century had its social roots in these problems of urban migration.

Redesign of Cities

The inward urban migration placed new social and economic demands on already strained city resources and gradually transformed the patterns of urban living. The central portions of many major European cities were redesigned during the second half of the century. Previously, the central areas of cities had been places where many people from all social classes both lived and worked. From the middle of the cen-

Growth of Major European Cities (in thousands)			
	1850	1880	1910
Berlin	419	1,122	2,071
Birmingham	233	437	840
Frankfurt	65	137	415
London	2,685	4,470	7,256
Madrid	281	398	600
Paris	1,053	2,269	2,888
Vienna	444	1,104	2,031

tury onward they became transformed into districts where relatively few people resided and where businesses, government offices, large retail stores, and theaters were located. Commerce, trade, government, and leisure activities now dominated central cities.

Development of Suburbs The commercial development of the central portions of cities, the clearing of slums, and the extension of railways into cities displaced many people who had previously lived in city centers. These developments also raised the price of centrally located urban land and of the rents charged on buildings located in the centers of cities. Consequently, both the middle classes and the working class began to seek housing elsewhere. The middle classes sought to avoid urban congestion, the working class to find affordable housing. As a result, outside the urban center proper, suburbs arose in virtually all countries to house the families whose breadwinner worked in the central city or in factories within the city limits.

The expansion of railways with cheap workday fares and the introduction of mechanical and, later, electric tramways allowed thousands of workers from all classes to move daily between the city and the outlying suburbs. For hundreds of thousands of Europeans, home and work became physically separated as never before.

The New Paris This remarkable social change and the values it reflected became embodied in the new designs of many European cities. The most famous and extensive transformation of a major city occurred in Paris. Like so many other European cities, Paris had expanded from the Middle Ages onward with little or no design or planning. Great public buildings and squalid hovels stood near each other. The Seine River was an open sewer. The streets were narrow, crooked, and crowded. It was impossible to cross easily from one part of Paris to another either on foot or by carriage. In 1850 a fully correct map of the city did not even exist. Of more concern to the government of Napoleon III (r. 1852–

1870), those streets had for sixty years provided the battle-ground for urban insurrections that had often, most recently in 1848, toppled French governments.

Napoleon III personally determined that Paris must be redesigned. He wished the city to be beautiful and to reflect the achievements of his regime and of modern technology. He put Georges Haussmann (1809–1891) in charge of the rebuilding program. As prefect of the Seine from 1853 to 1870, Haussmann oversaw a vast urban reconstruction program. Whole districts were destroyed to create the broad boulevards and streets that became the hallmark of modern Paris. Much, though by no means all, of the purpose of this street planning was political. The wide vistas not only were beautiful but also allowed troops to put down riots. The eradication of the many small streets and alleys removed areas where barricades could be and had been erected.

The project was political in another sense as well: Parks, such as the Bois de Boulogne, and major public buildings, such as the Paris Opera, were also constructed or completed. These projects, along with the demolition and street building, created public jobs for thousands of people. Many other laborers found employment in the private construction that paralleled the public action.

The Franco-Prussian War ended the Second Empire in 1870, and the Paris Commune destroyed parts of the city. Further rebuilding and redesign took place under the Third Republic. There was much private construction of department stores, office complexes, and largely middle class apartment buildings. By the late 1870s mechanical trams were operating in Paris. After long debate a subway system (the Métro) was begun in 1895, long after that of London (1863). New railway stations were also erected near the close of the century. This transport linked the refurbished central city to the suburbs. In 1889 the Eiffel Tower was built, originally as a temporary structure for an international trade exposition.

Not all the new structures of Paris bespoke the impact of middle-class commerce. Between 1873 and 1914 the French Roman Catholic church oversaw the construction of the Basilica of the Sacred Heart high atop Montmartre as an act of national penance. Those two landmarks—the Eiffel Tower and the Basilica of the Sacred Heart—symbolized the social and political divisions between liberals and conservatives in the Third Republic.

Urban Sanitation

The efforts of governments and of the increasingly conservative middle classes to maintain public order after 1848 led to a growing concern with the problems of public health and housing for the poor. A widespread feeling arose that the health of the middle classes and the stability of the political order depended on improving the health and housing of the working class.

Impact of Cholera   These concerns first manifested themselves as a result of the great cholera epidemics of the 1830s and 1840s, during which thousands of Europeans, especially those in cities, had died from this disease of Asian origin, previously unknown in Europe. Cholera, unlike many other common deadly diseases of the day that touched only the poor, struck persons from all classes and thus generated middle-class demand for a solution. Before the development of the bacterial theory of disease late in the century, physicians and sanitary reformers believed that cholera and other diseases were spread through infection from miasmas in the air. The miasmas, the presence of which was noted by their

The vast sewer systems constructed during the nineteenth century to remove waste from cities were among the genuine wonders of the period. They were a source of public fascination and even a tourist attraction. [Corbis-Bettmann]

A French Physician Describes a Working-Class Slum in Lille Before the Public Health Movement

It is difficult to conceive of the world before the sanitation movement. The work of medical doctors frequently carried them into working-class areas of industrial cities rarely visited by the middle class. Louis Villermé was such a French physician. He wrote extensive descriptions of the slums and the general living conditions of industrial workers. The passage here, published in 1840, describes a particularly notorious section of Lille, a major cotton-manufacturing town in northern France.

What does this physician find most disturbing about the scene he describes? How is his description possibly designed to evoke sympathy and concern from a middle-class reader? How might the conditions described have led the poor of France toward socialism or radical politics? How would addressing the problems described have led to a larger role for government?

The poorest live in the cellars and attics. These cellars . . . open onto the streets or courtyards, and one enters them by a stairway which is very often at once the door and the window. . . . Commonly the height of the ceiling is six or six and a half feet at the highest point, and they are only ten to fourteen or fifteen feet wide.

It is in these somber and sad dwellings that a large number of workers eat, sleep, and even work. The light of day comes an hour later for them than for others, and the night an hour earlier.

Their furnishings normally consist, along with the tools of their profession, of a sort of cupboard or a plank on which to deposit food, a stove . . . a few pots, a little table, two or three poor chairs, and a dirty pallet of which the only pieces are a straw mattress and scraps of a blanket. . . .

In their obscure cellars, in their rooms, which one would take for cellars, the air is never renewed, it is infected; the walls are plastered with garbage. . . . If a bed exists, it is a few dirty, greasy planks; it is damp and putrescent straw; it is a coarse cloth whose color and fabric are hidden by a layer of grime; it is a blanket that resembles a sieve. . . . The furniture is dislocated, worm-eaten, covered with filth. Utensils are thrown in disorder all over the dwelling. The windows, always closed, are covered by paper and glass, but so black, so smoke-encrusted, that the light is unable to penetrate . . . everywhere are piles of garbage, of ashes, of debris from vegetables picked up from the streets, of rotten straw; of animal nests of all sorts; thus, the air is unbreathable. One is exhausted, in these hovels, by a stale, nauseating, somewhat piquante odor, odor of filth, odor of garbage. . . .

And the poor themselves, what are they like in the middle of such a slum? Their clothing is in shreds, without substance, consumed, covered, no less than their hair, which knows no comb, with dust from the workshops. And their skin? . . . It is painted, it is hidden, if you wish, by indistinguishable deposits of diverse exudations.

From Louis René Villermé, *Tableau de l'état et de soie* (Paris, 1840), as quoted and trans. in William H. Sewell, Jr., *Work and Revolution in France: The Language of Labor from the Old Regime to 1848*. Copyright © 1980 Cambridge University Press, p. 224.

---

foul odors, were believed to arise from filth. The way to get rid of the dangerous, foul-smelling air was to clean up the cities.

New Water and Sewer Systems The proposed solution to the health hazard was cleanliness, to be achieved through new water and sewer systems. Construction of these new facilities proceeded slowly. They were usually first begun in capital cities and then much later in provincial cities. Some major urban areas lacked good water systems until after 1900. Nonetheless, the building of these systems constituted one of the major health and engineering achievements of the second half of the nineteenth century. The sewer system of Paris became one of the most famous parts of Haussmann's rebuilding program. In London, the construction of the Albert Embankment along the Thames involved not only large sewers discharging into the river but gas mains and water pipes as well, encased in thick walls of granite and concrete. Wherever these sanitary reforms were undertaken, the mortality rate decreased.

Expanded Government Involvement in Public Health This concern with public health led to an expansion of governmental power. In Britain, the Public Health Act of 1848; in France the Melun Act of 1851; and various laws in the still disunited German states, as well as later legislation, introduced new restraints on private life and enterprise. This legislation allowed medical officers and building inspectors to enter homes and other structures in the name of public health. Private property could be condemned for posing health hazards. Private land could be excavated to construct the sewers and water mains required to protect the public. New building regulations restrained the activities of private contractors.

When the bacterial theory of disease had become fully accepted at the close of the century, the necessity of cleanliness assumed an ever greater role in public life. The discoveries of Louis Pasteur (1822–1895) in France, Robert Koch (1843–1910) in Germany, and Joseph Lister (1827–1912) in Britain paved the way for the slow acceptance of the use of antiseptics in medicine and public health policy. Thereafter, throughout Europe, the maintenance of public health and the physical well-being of national populations repeatedly opened the way for government intervention in the lives of citizens and vastly expanded the social role of medical and scientific experts and governmental bureaucracies.

Housing Reform and Middle-Class Values

The information about working-class living conditions brought to light by the sanitary reformers also led to heated debates over the housing problem. The wretched dwellings of the poor were themselves a cause of poor sanitation and thus became one of the newly perceived health hazards. Furthermore, middle-class reformers and bureaucrats were shocked by the domestic arrangements of the poor, whose large families might live in a single room with no personal privacy. A single toilet facility might serve a whole block of tenements. After the revolutions of 1848, the overcrowding in housing and the social discontent that it generated also appeared to be politically dangerous.

Middle-class reformers thus turned to housing reform to solve the medical, moral, and political dangers posed by slums. They praised the home, as it was understood by the middle class, as a remedy for these dangers. Proper, decent housing would foster a good home life, which would in turn lead to a healthy, moral, and politically stable population. As A. V. Huber, one of the early German housing reformers, declared, "Certainly it would not be too much to say that the home is the communal embodiment of family life. Thus the purity of the dwelling is almost as important for the family as is the cleanliness of the body for the individual. Good or bad housing is a question of life and death if ever there was one."[1] Later advocates of housing reform, such as Jules Simon (1814–1896) in France, saw good housing as leading to good family life and then to strong national patriotism on the part of the well-housed family. It was also believed that the personal saving and investment required for owning a home would lead the working class to adopt the thrifty habits of the middle classes.

[1]Quoted in Nicholas Bullock and James Read, *The Movement for Housing Reform in Germany and France, 1840–1914* (Cambridge, UK: Cambridge University Press, 1985), p. 42.

The first attacks on the housing problem came from private philanthropy. Companies that operated on a low margin of profit or that loaned money for housing construction at low interest rates encouraged the building of housing for the poor. Some major industrial companies undertook similar housing programs. They tended to favor the construction of small individual houses or cottages that would ensure for the working class the kind of detached dwellings associated with the middle classes. Industrial firms, such as the German Krupp armament concern, constructed model housing projects and industrial communities in all the major European nations to ensure a contented, healthy, and stable work force. These early private efforts to address the housing problem reflected the usual liberal tendency to favor private rather than governmental enterprise.

By the mid-1880s, as a result of mass migration into the cities, the housing issue had become a major political question. Governmental action seemed inescapable. The actual policies differed markedly in each country, but all were hesitant. In England an 1885 act lowered interest rates for the construction of cheap housing. A few years later town councils, especially that of London, began to construct public housing. In Germany action came later in the century, primarily through the initiative of municipalities. In 1894 France made credit more available for housing the poor, and this legislation was expanded after 1900. No government had undertaken really large-scale housing experiments before World War I. Most legislation, though not all, only facilitated the construction of cheap housing by the private sector.

By 1914 the necessity for planning and action was fully recognized if not adequately addressed. The middle-class housing reformers had, moreover, defined the debate. The values and the character of the middle-class family house and home had become the ideal. The goal of housing reform across western Europe came to be that of a dwelling—whether a detached house or an affordable city apartment with several rooms, a private entrance, and separate toilet facilities—that would allow the working class to enjoy a family life along the lines of the middle classes.

Late-Nineteenth-Century Women's Experience

In this period European women, like European men, led lives that reflected their social rank. Yet within each rank, the experience of women was distinct from that of men. Women remained, generally speaking, economically dependent and legally inferior, whatever their social class. Their position thus resembled that of women around the world in that all women found their lives circumscribed by traditional social customs and expectations.

Social Disabilities Confronted by All Women

At mid-century virtually all European women faced social and legal disabilities in property rights, family law, and education. By the close of the century each area had shown improvement.

Women and Property   Until the last quarter of the century in most European countries no married women, whatever their social class, could own property in their own names. In effect, upon marriage women lost to their husbands' control any property they owned or that they might inherit or earn by their own labor. Their legal identities were subsumed into their husbands', and they had no independent standing before the law. The courts saw the theft of a woman's purse as a theft of her husband's property. Because European society was based on private property and wage earning, these disabilities put married women at a great disadvantage, limiting their freedom to work, save, and relocate.

Reform of women's property rights came slowly. By 1882 Great Britain allowed married women to own property in their own right. In France, however, a married woman could not even open a savings account in her own name until 1895, and not until 1907 were married women granted possession of their own wages. In 1900 Germany allowed women to take jobs without their husbands permission, but a German husband retained control of most of his wife's property except for her wages. Similar laws prevailed elsewhere in Europe.

Family Law   European family law also worked to the disadvantage of women. Legal codes required wives to obey their husbands. The Napoleonic Code and the remnants of Roman law made women legal minors throughout Europe. Divorce was difficult for most of the century. In England until 1857 divorce required an act of Parliament. Most nations did not permit divorce by mutual consent. French law forbade divorce between 1816 and 1884. Thereafter the chief recognized legal cause for divorce was cruelty and injury, which had to be proven in court. In Great Britain adultery was the usual cause for divorce, but a woman had to prove her husband's adultery plus other offenses, whereas a man only had to prove his wife's adultery. In Germany only adultery or serious maltreatment was recognized as grounds for divorce. Across Europe extramarital sexual relations of husbands were more tolerated than those of wives. Everywhere, divorce required legal hearings and proof, making the process expensive and all the more difficult for women who did not control their own property.

The authority of husbands also extended to children. A husband could take children away from their mother and give them to someone else to rear. Only the husband, in most countries, could permit his daughter to marry. In some countries he could virtually force his daughter to marry the man of his choice. In cases of divorce and separation, the husband normally assumed authority over children no matter how he had treated them previously.

The sexual and reproductive rights of women, which have been so widely debated recently, could hardly be discussed in the nineteenth century. Both contraception and abortion were illegal. The law on rape normally worked against women. Wherever they turned—whether to physicians or lawyers—women confronted an official or legal world populated and controlled by men.

Educational Barriers   Throughout the nineteenth century women had less access to education than men, and what was available to them was inferior. Not surprisingly, the percentage of illiterate women exceeded that of men. Most women were educated only enough for the domestic careers they were expected to follow.

University and professional education remained reserved for men until at least the third quarter of the century. The University of Zurich opened its doors to women in the 1860s. The University of London admitted women for degrees in 1878. Women were not awarded degrees at Oxford until 1920 or at Cambridge until 1921. They could not attend Sorbonne lectures until 1880. Just before the turn of the century universities and medical schools in the Austrian Empire allowed women to matriculate, but Prussian universities did not until after 1900. Russian women did not attend universities before 1914, but other institutions that awarded degrees were open to them. Italian universities were more open to both women students and women instructors than similar institutions elsewhere in Europe.

The absence of a system of private or public secondary education for women prevented most of them from gaining the qualifications they needed to enter a university whether or not the university prohibited them. Considerable evidence suggests that educated, professional men feared the competition of women. Women who attended universities and medical schools were sometimes labeled political radicals.

By 1900 men in the educated elites also feared the challenge educated women posed to traditional gender roles in the home and workplace. Restricting their access to secondary and university education helped bar women from social and economic advancement. Women would benefit only marginally from the expansion of professional employment that occurred during the late nineteenth and early twentieth centuries. Although a few women did enter the professions, especially medicine, most nations prevented women from becoming lawyers until after World War I.

Women only gradually gained access to secondary and university education during the second half of the nineteenth century and the early twentieth century. Young women on their way to school, the subject of this 1880 English painting, would thus have been a new sight when it was painted. [Sir George Clausen (RA) (1852-1944), *School Girls, Haverstock Hill*, signed and dated 1880, oil on canvas, 20 x 30 in. (52 x 77.2 cm), Yale Center for British Art, Paul Mellon Collection, B1985.10.1]

Schoolteaching at the elementary level, which was seen as a female job because of its association with the nurturing of children, became a professional haven for women. Trained at institutions that were equivalent to normal schools, women schoolteachers were regarded as educated, but not as university educated. Secondary education remained largely the province of men.

The few women who pioneered in the professions and on government commissions and school boards or who dispersed birth control information faced grave social obstacles, personal humiliation, and often outright bigotry. These women and their male supporters were challenging that clear separation of life into male and female spheres that had emerged in middle-class European society during the nineteenth century. Women themselves often hesitated to support feminist causes or expanded opportunities for themselves because they had been so thoroughly acculturated into the recently stereotyped roles. Many women saw a real conflict between family responsibilities and feminism.

New Employment Patterns for Women

During the late nineteenth century two major developments affected the economic lives of women. The first was an ex-

pansion in the variety of jobs available outside the better-paying learned professions. The second was a withdrawal of married women from the work force. These two seemingly contradictory developments require explanation.

Availability of New Jobs The expansion of governmental bureaucracies, the emergence of corporations and other large-scale businesses, and the expansion of retail stores opened many new employment opportunities for women. The need for elementary school teachers, usually women, grew with compulsory education laws. Technological inventions and innovations, such as the typewriter and eventually the telephone exchange, also fostered female employment. Women by the thousands became secretaries and clerks for governments and private businesses. More thousands became shop assistants.

Although these jobs did open new and often better employment opportunities for women, they nonetheless required low-level skills and involved minimal training. They were occupied primarily by unmarried women or widows. Few women had prominent positions.

Employers continued to pay women low wages because they assumed, often knowing better, that a woman did not need to support herself independently but could expect additional financial support from her father or husband. Consequently, a woman who did need to support herself independently could rarely find a job paying an adequate income or a position that paid as well as one held by a man who was supporting himself independently.

Withdrawal from the Labor Force Most of the women filling these new service positions were young and unmarried. After marriage, or certainly after the birth of her first child, a woman normally withdrew from the labor force. She either did not work or she worked at home. This pattern was not new, but it had become more common by the end of the nineteenth century. The industrial occupations that women had filled in the mid-nineteenth century, especially textile and garment making, were shrinking. Those industries thus offered fewer jobs for either married or unmarried women. Employers in offices and retail stores preferred young, unmarried women whose family responsibilities would not interfere with their work. The decline in the number of births also meant that fewer married women were needed to look after other women's children.

The real wages paid to male workers increased during this period, thus reducing families' need for a second income. Also, thanks to improving health conditions, men lived longer than before, and so wives were less likely to be thrust into the work force by an emergency. Smaller families also lowered the need for supplementary wages. Working children stayed longer at home and continued to contribute to the family's wage pool.

Finally, the cultural dominance of the middle class, with its generally idle wives, established a pattern of social expectations. The more prosperous a working-class family became, the less involved in employment its women were supposed to be. Indeed, the less income-producing work a wife did, the more prosperous and stable the family was considered.

Yet behind these generalities stands the enormous variety of social and economic experience late-nineteenth-century women actually encountered. As might be expected, social class largely determined these individual experiences.

Working-Class Women

Although less dominant than earlier in the century, the textile industry and garment making continued to employ many women. The German clothing-making trades illustrate the kind of vulnerable economic situation that women could encounter as a result of their limited skills and the organization of the trade. The manufacture of mass-made clothes in Germany was designed to require minimal capital investment by manufacturers and to protect them from significant risk. A major manufacturer would arrange to produce clothing through a putting-out system. He would purchase the mate-

Women working at a Telephone Exchange. The invention of the telephone opened new employment opportunities for women. [Mary Evans Picture Library]

Although new opportunities opened to them in the late nineteenth century, many working-class women, like these women ironing in a laundry, remained in traditional occupations. As the wine bottle suggests, alcoholism was a problem for women as well as men engaged in tedious work. The painting is by Edgar Degas (1834–1917). [Photo R.M.N./Service Photographique des Musées Nationaux, Paris]

rial and then put it out for tailoring. The clothing was made not in a factory but usually in independently owned, small sweatshops or by workers in their homes.

In Berlin in 1896 there were more than 80,000 garment workers, mostly women. When business was good, employment for these women was high. If business became poor, however, less and less work was put out, idling many of them. In effect, the workers who actually sewed the clothing carried much of the risk of the enterprise. Some women did work in factories, but they too were subject to layoffs. Furthermore, women in the clothing trade were nearly always in positions less skilled than those of the male tailors or the male middlemen who owned the workshops.

The expectation of separate social and economic spheres for men and women and the definition of women's chief work as pertaining to the home contributed mightily to the exploitation of women workers outside the home. Because their wages were regarded merely as supplementing their husbands', they became particularly vulnerable to the economic exploitation that characterized the German putting-out system for clothing production. Women were nearly always treated as casual workers in Europe.

Poverty and Prostitution

A major but little-recognized social fact of most nineteenth-century cities was the presence of a surplus of working women who did not fit the stereotype of wife or daughter supplementing a family's income. There were almost always many more women seeking employment than there were jobs. The economic vulnerability of women and the consequent poverty many of them faced were among the chief causes of prostitution. Any large late-nineteenth-century European city had thousands of prostitutes.

Prostitution was, of course, not new. It had always been one way for poor women to earn money. In the late nineteenth century, however, it was closely related to the difficulty poor women who were trying to make their way in an overcrowded female labor force encountered. On the Continent prostitution was generally subject to governmental and municipal regulations. Those regulations were, it should be noted, passed and enforced by male legislatures and councils and were enforced by male police and physicians. In Great Britain prostitution received only minimal regulation.

Many myths and misunderstandings have surrounded the subject of prostitution. The most recent studies of the subject in England emphasize that most prostitutes were active on the streets for a very few years, generally from their late teens to about age twenty-five. Certain cities—those with large army garrisons or naval ports or those, like London, with large transient populations—attracted many prostitutes. There were far fewer prostitutes in manufacturing towns, where there were more opportunities for steady employment and where community life was more stable.

Family was central to the middle-class conception of a stable and respectable social life. This portrait of the Bellelli family is by Degas. Notice that the husband and father sits at his desk, suggesting his association with business and the world outside the home, whereas the wife and mother stands with their children, suggesting her domestic role. [Giraudon/Art Resource, N.Y.]

Women who became prostitutes usually came from families of unskilled workers and had minimal skills and education themselves. Many had been servants. They also often were from broken homes or were orphaned. Contrary to many sensational late-century newspaper accounts, child prostitutes were rare. Furthermore, women were seldom seduced into prostitution by middle-class employers or middle-class clients, although working-class women were always potentially subject to such pressure. The customers of poor working-class prostitutes were primarily working-class men.

Women of the Middle Class

A vast social gap separated poor working-class women from their middle-class counterparts. As their fathers' and husbands' incomes permitted, middle-class women participated in the vast expansion of consumerism and domestic comfort that marked the late nineteenth and early twentieth cen-

turies. They filled their homes with manufactured items. They enjoyed all the improvements of sanitation and electricity. They could command the services of numerous domestic servants. They moved into the fashionable new houses being constructed in the suburbs.

The Cult of Domesticity   For the middle classes the distinction between work and family, defined by gender, had become complete and constituted the model for all other social groups. Middle-class women, if at all possible, did not work. More than any other women, they became limited to the roles of wife and mother. As a result, they might enjoy great domestic luxury and comfort, but their lives were markedly circumscribed.

Middle-class women largely became the product of a particular understanding of social life. The home was to be a private place of refuge from the life of business and the marketplace, a view set forth in women's journals across Europe.

The Virtues of a French Middle-Class Lady Praised

One of the chief social roles assigned to middle-class French women was that of charitable activity. This obituary of Mme Émile Delesalle from a Roman Catholic church paper of the late nineteenth century describes the work of this woman among the poor. It is a very revealing document because it clearly shows the class divisions that existed in the giving of charity. Also, through the kinds of virtues it praises, it gave instruction to its women readers. Note the emphasis on home life, spirituality, and instruction of children in charitable acts.

What assumptions about the character of women allowed writers to see charity as a particularly good occupation for women? What middle-class attitudes toward the poor are displayed in this passage? How did the assignment of charity work to women lead to their being excluded from other kinds of work and the learned professions?

The poor were the object of her affectionate interest, especially the shameful poor, the fallen people. She sought them out and helped them with perfect discretion which doubled the value of her benevolent interest. To those whom she could approach without fear of bruising their dignity, she brought, along with alms to assure their existence, consolation of the most serious sort—she raised their courage and their hopes. To others, each Sunday, she opened all the doors of her home, above all when her children were still young. In making them distribute these alms with her, she hoped to initiate them early into practices of charity.

In the last years of her life the St. Gabriel Orphanage gained her interest. Not only did she accomplish a great deal with her generosity, but she also took on the task of maintaining the clothes of her dear orphans in good order and in good repair. When she appeared in the courtyard of the establishment at recreation time, all her protégés surrounded her and lavished her with manifestations of their profound respect and affectionate gratitude.

From Bonnie G. Smith, *Ladies of the Leisure Class: The Bourgeois of Northern France in the Nineteenth Century.* Copyright © 1981 Princeton University Press, pp. 147–148. Reprinted by permission of Princeton University Press.

As studies of the lives of middle-class women in northern France have suggested, this image of the middle-class home and of the role of women in the home is different from the one that had existed earlier in the nineteenth century. During the first half of the century, the spouse of a middle-class husband might contribute directly to the business, handling accounts or correspondence. These women also frequently left child rearing to nurses and governesses. The reasons for the change during the century are not certain, but it appears that men began to insist on doing business with other men. Magazines and books directed toward women began to praise motherhood, domesticity, religion, and charity as the proper work of women in accordance with the concept of separate spheres.

For middle-class French women, as well as for middle-class women elsewhere, the home came to be seen as the center of virtue, children, and the proper life. Marriages were usually arranged for some kind of family economic benefit. Romantic marriage was viewed as a danger to social stability. Most middle-class women in northern France married by the age of twenty-one. Children were expected to follow soon after marriage, and the first child was often born within the first year. The rearing and nurturing of her children were a woman's chief task. She would receive no experience or training for any role other than that of dutiful daughter, wife, and mother.

Within the home a middle-class woman performed major roles. She was largely in charge of the household. She oversaw virtually all domestic management and child care. She was in charge of the home as a unit of consumption, which is why so much advertising was directed toward women. All this domestic activity, however, occurred within the limits of the approved middle-class lifestyle that strictly limited a woman's initiative. In her conspicuous idleness, a woman symbolized first her father's and then her husband's success.

Religious and Charitable Activities   The cult of domesticity in France and elsewhere assigned firm religious duties to women, which the Roman Catholic church strongly supported. Women were expected to attend mass frequently and assure the religious instruction of their children. They were charged with observing meatless Fridays and with participating in religious observances. Prayer was a major part of their lives and daily rituals. They internalized those portions of the Christian religion that stressed meekness and passivity. In other countries as well, religious activities became part of the expected work of women. For this reason, political liberals regarded women as especially susceptible to the influence of priests. This close association between religion and a strict domestic life for women led later to tension between feminism and religious authorities.

Another important role for middle-class women was the administration of charity. Women were judged especially qualified for this work because of their presumed innate spirituality and their capacity to instill domestic and personal discipline. Middle-class women were often in charge of clubs for poor youth, societies to protect poor young women, schools for infants, and societies for visiting the poor. Women were supposed to be particularly interested in the problems of poor women, their families, and their children. Charity from middle-class women often required the recipient to demonstrate good character. By the end of the century middle-class women seeking to expand their spheres of activity became social workers for the church, for private charities, or for the government. These vocations were a natural extension of the roles socially assigned to them.

Sexuality and Family Size   Diaries, letters, and even early medical and sociological sex surveys indicate that sexual enjoyment rather than sexual repression was fundamental to middle-class marriages. Much of the inhibition about sexuality stemmed from the dangers of childbirth rather than from any dislike or disapproval of sex itself.

One of the major changes in this regard during the second half of the century was the acceptance of small family size among the middle classes. The fertility rate in France dropped throughout the nineteenth century. It began to fall in England steadily from the 1870s onward. During the last decades of the century various new contraceptive devices became available, which middle-class couples used. One of the chief reasons for limiting family size was to maintain a relatively high level of material consumption. Children had become much more expensive to rear, and at the same time, more material comforts had become available. Fewer children probably meant more attention for each of them, possibly bringing mothers and their children emotionally closer.

The Rise of Political Feminism

As can be seen from the previous discussion, liberal society and its values neither automatically nor inevitably improved the lot of women. In particular, it did not give them the vote or access to political activity. Male liberals feared that granting the vote to women would benefit political conservatives, because women were thought to be unduly controlled by the clergy. Consequently, anticlerical liberals often had difficulty working with feminists.

Obstacles to Achieving Equality   But women also were often reluctant to support feminist causes. Political issues relating to gender were only one of several priorities for many women. Some were sensitive to their class and economic interests. Others subordinated feminist political issues to national unity and nationalistic patriotism. Still others would not support particular feminist organizations because of differences over tactics. The various social and tactical dif-

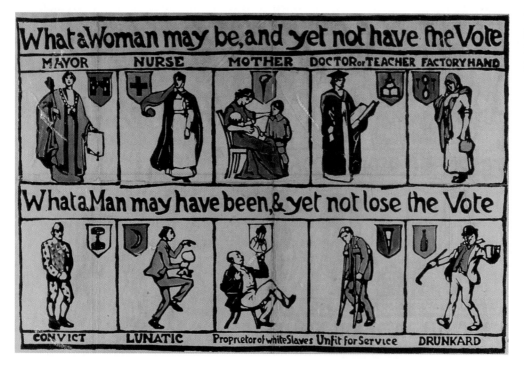

The creator of this poster cleverly reveals the hypocrisy and foolishness of denying the vote to women. [The Bridgeman Art Library International]

ferences among women often led to sharp divisions within the feminists' own ranks. Except in England, it was often difficult for working-class and middle-class women to cooperate. Roman Catholic feminists were uncomfortable with radical secularist feminists.

Although liberal society and law presented women with many obstacles, they also provided feminists with many of their intellectual and political tools. As early as 1792 in Britain, Mary Wollstonecraft (1759–1797), in *The Vindication of the Rights of Woman*, had applied the revolutionary doctrines of the rights of man to the predicament of the members of her own sex (see Chapter 24). John Stuart Mill (1806–1873), with his wife Harriet Taylor (1804–1858), had applied the logic of liberal freedom to the position of women in *The Subjection of Women* (1869). The arguments for utility and efficiency so dear to middle-class liberals could be used to expose the human and social waste implicit in the inferior role assigned to women.

Furthermore, the socialist criticism of capitalist society often, though by no means always, included a harsh indictment of the social and economic position to which women had been relegated. The earliest statements of feminism arose from critics of the existing order and were often associated with people who had unorthodox opinions about sexuality, family life, and property. This hardened resistance to the feminist message, especially on the Continent.

These difficulties prevented continental feminists from raising the kind of massive public support or mounting the large demonstrations that feminists in Great Britain and the United States could. Everywhere in Europe, however, including Britain, the feminist cause was badly divided over both goals and tactics.

Votes for Women in Britain

Europe's most advanced women's movement was in Great Britain. There Millicent Fawcett (1847–1929) led the moderate National Union of Women's Suffrage Societies. She believed Parliament would grant women the vote only when convinced that they would be respectable and responsible in their political activity. In 1908 this organization could rally almost half a million women in London. Fawcett was the wife of a former Liberal Party cabinet minister and economist. Her tactics were those of English liberals.

Emmeline Pankhurst (1858–1928) led a different and much more radical branch of British feminists. Pankhurst's husband had been active in both labor and Irish nationalist politics. Irish nationalists had developed numerous disruptive political tactics. Early labor politicians had also sometimes had confrontations with police over the right to hold meetings. In 1903 Pankhurst and her daughters founded the Women's Social and Political Union. For several years

they and their followers, known derisively as *suffragettes*, lobbied publicly and privately for women's suffrage. By 1910, having failed to move the government, they turned to the violent tactics of arson, window breaking, and sabotage of postal boxes. They marched en masse on Parliament. The Liberal government of Herbert Asquith (1852–1928) imprisoned many of the demonstrators and force-fed those who went on hunger strikes in jail. The government refused to extend the franchise. Only in 1918, and then as a result of their contribution to the war effort, did some British women receive the vote.

Political Feminism on the Continent

The contrast of France and Germany shows how advanced the British women's movement was. In France, when Hubertine Auclert (1848–1914) began campaigning for the vote in the 1880s, she stood virtually alone. During the 1890s several women's organizations emerged. In 1901 the National Council of French Women (CNFF) was organized among upper-middle-class women, but it did not support the vote for women for several years. French Roman Catholic feminists, such as Marie Mauguet (1844–1928), supported the franchise. Almost all French feminists, however, rejected violence. They also were never able to organize mass rallies. The leaders of French feminism believed that the vote could be achieved through careful legalism. In 1919 the French Chamber of Deputies granted the vote to women, but in 1922 the French Senate defeated the bill. French women did not receive the right to vote until after World War II.

In Germany feminist awareness and action were even more underdeveloped. German law actually forbade German women from political activity. Because no group in the German empire enjoyed extensive political rights, women were not certain that they would benefit from demanding them. Any such demand would be regarded as subversive of both the state and society.

In 1894 the Union of German Women's Organizations (BDFK) was founded. By 1902 it was calling for the right to vote. But it was largely concerned with improving women's social conditions, their access to education, and their right to other protections. The group also worked to see women admitted to political or civic activity on the municipal level. Their work usually included education, child welfare, charity, and public health. The German Social Democratic Party supported women's suffrage, but that socialist party was so disdained by the German authorities and German Roman Catholics that this support only made suffrage more suspect in their eyes. Women received the vote in Germany only in 1918 under the constitution of the Weimar Republic. Before World War I, only in Norway (1907) could women vote on national issues.

An English Feminist Defends the Cause of the Female Franchise

Frances Power Cobbe (1822–1904) wrote widely on many religious and social issues of the second half of the century. She had been a feminist since early adulthood. In this letter to a British feminist magazine in 1884, she explained why women should seek the vote.

What motives does Cobbe assign to the pursuit of the right to vote? Why does she emphasize the issue of "womanliness" as one that must not be allowed to undermine the cause of women? What is Cobbe's attitude toward violence? Why would later British advocates of votes for women turn to violent tactics?

If I may presume to offer an old woman's counsel to the younger workers in our cause, it would be that they should adopt the point of view—that it is before all things our duty to obtain the franchise. If we undertake the work in this spirit, and with the object of using the power it confers, whenever we gain it, for the promotion of justice and mercy and the kingdom of God upon earth, we shall carry on all our agitation in a corresponding manner, firmly and bravely, and also calmly and with generous good temper. And when our opponents come to understand that this is the motive underlying our efforts, they, on their part, will cease to feel bitterly and scornfully toward us, even when they think we are altogether mistaken. . . .

The idea that the possession of political rights will destroy "womanliness," absurd as it may seem to us, is very deeply rooted in the minds of men; and when they oppose our demands, it is only just to give them credit for doing so on grounds which we should recognize as valid, if their premises were true. It is not so much that our opponents (at least the better part of them) despise women, as that they really prize what women now are in the home and in society so highly that they cannot bear to risk losing it by any serious change in their condition. These fears are futile and faithless, but there is nothing in them to affront us. To remove them, we must not use violent words, for every such violent word confirms their fears; but, on the contrary, show the world that while the revolutions wrought by men have been full of bitterness and rancor and stormy passions, if not of bloodshed, we women will at least strive to accomplish our great emancipation calmly and by persuasion and reason.

From Letter to the *Woman's Tribune*, May 1, 1884, quoted in Frances Power Cobbe, *Life of Frances Power Cobbe by Herself*, Vol. 2. Copyright © 1894 Houghton Mifflin, pp. 532–533.

Labor, Socialism, and Politics to World War I

The Working Classes

The late-century industrial expansion wrought further changes in the life of the labor force. In all industrializing continental countries, the urban proletariat increased. Proportionally, there were many fewer artisans and highly skilled workers. For the first time, factory wage earners predominated. The increasingly mechanized factories often required less highly technical skills from their operatives. The unskilled work associated with shipping, transportation, and building also expanded. Work became more impersonal. Factories were located in cities, and most links between factory or day-labor employment and home life dissolved. Large corporate enterprise meant less personal contact between employers and their workers. During the late nineteenth century a few big businesses attempted to provide some security for their employees through company housing and pension plans. Although these efforts were sometimes pioneering, they were not adequate for the mass of the labor force.

Trade Unionism Workers still had to look to themselves to improve their situation. However, after 1848 European workers ceased taking to the streets to voice their grievances in the form of riots. They also stopped trying to revive the old paternalistic guilds. After mid-century the labor force accepted the fact of modern industrial production and its general downgrading of skills and attempted to receive more benefits from that system. Workers turned to new institutions and ideologies. Chief among them were trade unions, democratic political parties, and socialism.

Trade unionism came of age as legal protections were extended to unions throughout the second half of the century. Unions became fully legal in Great Britain in 1871 and were allowed to picket in 1875. In France the Third Republic fully legalized unions in 1884. After 1890 they could function in Germany with little disturbance. Initially, most trade unions were slow to enter political process directly. As long as the traditional governing classes looked after labor interests, members of the working class rarely sought office themselves.

The mid-century organizational efforts of the unions aimed to improve the wages and working conditions of skilled workers. By the close of the century large industrial unions for unskilled workers were also being organized. They confronted extensive opposition from employers, and were often recognized only after long strikes. In the decade before 1914 strikes were common throughout Europe as the unions attempted to raise wages to keep up with inflation. However, despite the advances of unions and the growth of their membership in 1910 to approximately 3 million in Britain, 2 million in Germany, and 977,000 in France, they never included a majority of the industrial labor force. The unions did represent a new collective fashion in which workers could associate to confront the economic difficulties of their lives and attain better security.

Democracy and Political Parties   The democratic franchise gave workers direct political influence, which meant they could no longer be ignored. Except for Russia, all the major European states adopted broad-based, if not perfectly democratic, electoral systems. Democracy brought new modes of popular pressure to bear on all governments. It meant that discontented groups could now voice their grievances and advocate their programs within government rather than from outside it.

The advent of democracy witnessed the formation for the first time in Europe of organized mass political parties, such as had existed throughout the nineteenth century in the United States. In the liberal European states with narrow electoral bases, most voters had been men of property who understood what they had at stake in politics. Organization had been minimal. The expansion of the electorate brought into the political processes many people whose level of political consciousness and interest was low. This electorate had to be organized and taught the nature of power and influence in the liberal democratic state. The organized political party—with its workers, newspapers, offices, social life, and discipline—was the vehicle that mobilized the new voters. The largest single group in these mass electorates was the working class. The democratization of politics presented the socialists with opportunities and required the traditional ruling class to vie with them for the support of the new voters.

Marx and the First International

Karl Marx (1818–1883) himself accommodated the new practical realities that developed during the third quarter of the century. He did not abandon the revolutionary doctrines of *The Communist Manifesto*, and in *Capital* (Vol. 1, 1867), he continued to predict the disintegration of capitalism. His private thoughts, as revealed in his letters, also remained revolutionary, but his practical, public political activity reflected a different approach.

In 1864 a group of British and French trade unionists founded the International Working Men's Association. Known as the First International, its membership encompassed a vast array of radicals, including socialists, anarchists, and Polish nationalists. The First International allowed Marx to write its inaugural address. In it, he urged radical social change and the economic emancipation of the working class, but he also approved efforts by workers and trade unions to reform the conditions of labor within the existing political and economic processes. He urged revolution but tempered the means. Privately, he often criticized such reformist activity, but those writings were not made public until after his death.

During the late 1860s the First International gathered statistics, kept labor groups informed of mutual problems, provided a forum for the debate of socialist doctrine, and extravagantly proclaimed its own size and influence. From these debates and activities, Marxism emerged as the most important strand of socialism. In 1872 Marx and his supporters drove the anarchists out of the First International. Marx was determined to preserve the role of the state against the anarchist attack on authority and large political organizations. German socialists became deeply impressed by Marx's thought. Because they became the most important socialist party in Europe, they were the chief channel for Marxist thought.

The First International was destroyed by the events surrounding the Paris Commune. Few socialists and only one real Marxist were involved in the Commune. However, Marx, in a major pamphlet, glorified it as a genuine proletarian uprising. British trade unionists, who in 1871 were finally receiving new legal protection, wanted no connection with the crimes of the Parisians. The French authorities used the uprising to suppress socialist activity. Throughout Europe the events in Paris cast a pall over socialism. The First International was dissolved in 1876. Thereafter, the fate of Marxism, socialism, and the labor movement depended largely on the economic and political conditions of the individual European countries.

Germany: Social Democrats and Revisionism

The organizational success of the German Social Democratic Party (SPD), more than any other single factor, kept Marxist socialism alive. Founded in 1875, the SPD suffered twelve years of persecution by Otto von Bismarck (1815–1898), who believed socialism would undermine German politics and society. In 1878 there was an attempt to assassinate William I (r. 1861–1888). Bismarck unfairly blamed the socialists and steered antisocialist laws through the *Reichstag*. These measures suppressed the organization, meetings, newspapers, and other public activities of the SPD. Nonetheless, the SPD steadily polled more votes in elections to the *Reichstag*.

Repression having failed, Bismarck enacted social welfare legislation to wean German workers from socialist loyalties. These measures provided health insurance, accident insurance, and old age and disability pensions. The German state itself thus organized a system of social security that did not change the system of property holding or politics.

In 1891, after forcing Bismarck's resignation, Emperor William II (r. 1888–1918) allowed the antisocialist legislation to expire. The SPD then had to decide how to operate as a legalized party. Their new direction was announced in the Erfurt Program of 1891. In good Marxist fashion, the program declared the imminent doom of capitalism and the necessity of socialist ownership of the means of production. However, these goals were to be achieved by legal political participation rather than by revolutionary activity. Since the revolution was inevitable, it was argued, the immediate task of socialists was to improve workers' lives. In theory, the SPD was vehemently hostile to the German empire, but in practice the party functioned within its institutions.

This situation of the SPD, however, generated the most important internal socialist challenge to the orthodox Marxist analysis of capitalism and the socialist revolution. Eduard Bernstein (1850–1932) wrote what was regarded as this socialist heresy. Bernstein, who was familiar with the British Fabians, questioned whether Marx and his later orthodox followers had been correct in their pessimistic appraisal of capitalism and the necessity of revolution. In *Evolutionary Socialism* (1899), Bernstein pointed to the rising standard of living in Europe, the ongoing power of the middle class, and the opening of the franchise to the working class. He argued that a humane socialist society required not revolution but more democracy and social reform. Bernstein's doctrines, known as *revisionism*, were widely debated among German socialists and were finally condemned as theory, although the party actually pursued a peaceful, reformist program. His critics argued that evolution toward social democracy might be possible in liberal, parliamentary Britain but not in authoritarian, militaristic Germany with its basically powerless *Reichstag*. Therefore, the German SPD continued to advocate revolution.

The German debate over revisionism became important for the later history of Marxist socialism. The German SPD was, as noted, the most successful prewar socialist party. Its rejection of an ideology of reform socialism in favor of revolutionary socialism influenced all socialists who looked to the German example. Most significant, Lenin adopted this position, as did the other leaders of the Russian revolution. Thereafter, wherever Soviet Marxism was influential, the goal of its efforts would be revolution rather than reform.

Jean Juarès was one of the great French socialist orators. In this contemporary print he is addressing a meeting being disrupted by the police. [Roger Viollet/The Gamma Liason Network]

France: "Opportunism" Rejected

French socialism gradually revived after the suppression of the Paris Commune. The major problem for French socialists was their own internal division rather than government opposition. There were no fewer than five separate parties, plus other independent socialists. They managed to elect approximately forty members to the Chamber of Deputies by the early 1890s.

At the turn of the century the two major factions of French socialism were led by Jean Jaurès (1859–1914) and Jules Guesde (1845–1922). Jaurès believed, like the revisionists in Germany, that socialists should cooperate with radical middle-class ministries to enact social legislation. Guesde argued that socialists could not support a bourgeois Cabinet that they were theoretically dedicated to overthrowing. The quarrel came to a head as a by-product of the Dreyfus Affair (see Chapter 27) in 1899, when Prime Minister René Waldeck-Rousseau (1846–1904) appointed the socialist Alexander Millerand (1859–1943) to the Cabinet.

By 1904 "opportunism," the term applied to such Cabinet participation by socialists, was debated at the Amsterdam Congress of the Second International. This organization had been founded in 1889 to unify the various national socialist parties and trade unions. The Congress condemned "opportunism" in France and ordered the French socialists to form a single party. Jaurès accepted the decision. French socialists began to work together, and by 1914 the recently united Socialist Party was the second largest group in the Chamber of Deputies. But Socialist Party members would not again serve in a French Cabinet until 1936.

Great Britain: The Labour Party and Fabianism

No form of socialism made significant progress in Great Britain, the most advanced industrial society of the day. The members of the growing trade unions normally supported Liberal Party candidates. The "new unionism" of the late 1880s and the 1890s organized the dock workers, the gas workers, and similar unskilled groups. Employer resistance to unions heightened class antagonism. In 1892 Keir Hardie (1856–1915) became the first independent worker elected to Parliament. In 1893 the socialist Independent Labour Party was founded, but it remained ineffective.

In 1901, however, a decision by the House of Lords (Britain's supreme court) removed the legal protection previously accorded union funds. The Trades Union Congress responded by launching the Labour Party, which sent twenty-nine members to Parliament in the election of 1906. Their goals did not yet encompass socialism. The British labor movement also became more militant. In scores of strikes, workers fought for wages to meet the rising cost of living. The government intervened to mediate these strikes, which in 1911 and 1912 involved the railways, the docks, and the mines.

British socialism itself remained primarily the preserve of intellectuals. The socialists who exerted the most influence were from the Fabian Society, founded in 1884. The society took its name from Q. Fabius Maximus (d. 203 B.C.E.), the Roman general who defeated Hannibal by waiting before attacking. Its name thus indicated a gradualist approach to social reform. Its leading members were Sydney (1859–1947) and Beatrice (1858–1943) Webb, H. G. Wells (1866–1946), and George Bernard Shaw (1856–1950). Many of the Fabians were civil servants who believed that the problems of industry, the expansion of ownership, and the state direction of production could be solved and achieved gradually, peacefully, and democratically. They sought to educate the country to the rational wisdom of socialism. They were particularly interested in collective ownership on the municipal level, or so-called gas-and-water socialism.

Russia: Industrial Development and the Birth of Bolshevism

In the late nineteenth century the tsarist government was determined to make Russia an industrial power. It favored the growth of heavy industries, such as railways, iron, and steel. A small but significant industrial proletariat arose. By 1900 Russia had approximately 3 million factory workers. Their working and living conditions were bad by any standard.

New political departures accompanied this economic development. In 1901 the Social Revolutionary Party was founded. It opposed industrialism and looked to the communal life of rural Russia as a model for the economic future. In 1903 the Constitutional Democratic Party, or Cadets, was formed. Liberal in outlook, they were drawn from people who participated in the *zemstvos* (local governments). They wanted a parliamentary regime with responsible ministries, civil liberties, and economic progress. The Cadets hoped to model themselves on the liberal parties of western Europe.

Lenin's Early Thought and Career   The situation for Russian socialists differed radically from that in other major European countries. Russia had no representative political institutions and only a small working class. The compromises and accommodations achieved elsewhere were meaningless in Russia, where socialism in both theory and practice had to be revolutionary. The Russian Social Democratic Party had been established in 1898. It was Marxist, and its members greatly admired the German SPD, but tsarist repression meant that it had to function in exile.

The leading late-nineteenth-century Russian Marxist was Georgii Plekhanov (1857–1918), based in Switzerland. His chief disciple was Vladimir Illich Ulyanov (1870–1924), who took the name of Lenin. The future leader of the Communist Revolution was the son of a high bureaucrat. His older brother had been executed in 1887 for participating in a plot against Alexander III (r. 1881–1894). In 1893 Lenin moved to Saint Petersburg, where he briefly practiced law. Soon he, too, was drawn to the revolutionary groups among the factory workers. In 1895 he was exiled to Siberia. After his release in 1900, Lenin spent most of the next seventeen years in Switzerland.

In Switzerland Lenin became deeply involved in the organizational and policy disputes of the exiled Russian Social Democrats. They all considered themselves Marxists, but quarreled about the proper nature of a Marxist revolution in primarily rural Russia and the structure of their own party.

A Russian Social Investigator Describes the Condition of Children in the Moscow Tailoring Trade

E. A. Oliunina was a young Russian woman who had been active among union organizers during the Revolution of 1905. Later, as a student at the Higher Women's Courses in Moscow, a school for women's postsecondary education, she began to investigate and to write about child garment workers. The clothes produced by these children might have ended up in Russian department stores.

Why might the parents of these children have allowed them to work in these sweatshops? Why was alcoholism so prevalent? Why does Oliunina regard schools as the solution to this problem?

Children begin their apprenticeship between the ages of twelve and thirteen, although one can find some ten- and eleven-year-olds working in the shops. . . .

Apprenticeship is generally very hard on children. At the beginning, they suffer enormously, particularly from the physical strain of having to do work well beyond the capacity of their years. They have to live in an environment where the level of morality is very low. Scenes of drunkenness and debauchery induce the boys to smoke and drink at an early age.

For example, in one subcontracting shop that made men's clothes, a fourteen-year-old boy worked together with twelve adults. When I visited there at four o'clock one Tuesday afternoon, the workers were half-drunk. Some were lying under the benches, others in the hallway. The boy was as drunk as the rest of them and lay there with a daredevil look on his face, dressed only in a pair of longjohns and a dirty, tattered shirt. He had been taught to drink at the age of twelve and could now keep up with the adults.

"Blue Monday" is a custom in most subcontracting shops that manufacture men's clothes. The whole workshop gets drunk, and work comes to a standstill. The apprentices do nothing but hang around. Many of the workers live in the workshop, so the boys are constantly exposed to all sorts of conversations and scenes. In one shop employing five workers and three boys, "Blue Monday" was a regular ritual. Even the owner himself is prone to alcoholic binges. In these kinds of situations, young girls are in danger of being abused by the owner or his sons. . . .

In Russia, there have been no measures taken to improve the working conditions of apprentices. As I have tried to show, the situation in workshops in no way provides apprentices with adequate training in their trade. The young workers are there only to be exploited. Merely limiting the number of apprentices would not better their position, nor would it eradicate the influx of cheap labor. An incomparably more effective solution would be to replace apprenticeship with a professional educational system and well-established safeguards for child workers. However, the only real solution to the exploitation of unpaid child labor is to introduce a minimum wage for minors.

From Victoria E. Bonnell, *The Russian Worker: Life and Labor Under the Tsarist Regime.* Copyright © 1983 The Regents of California. Published and reprinted by permission of the Univeristy of California Press. Excerpts from pp. 177, 180–181, 182–183.

The Social Democrats were modernizers who favored further industrial development. Most believed that Russia must develop a large proletariat before the revolution could come. This same majority hoped to mold a mass political party like the German SPD.

Lenin dissented from both positions. In *What Is to Be Done?* (1902), he condemned any accommodations. He also criticized a trade unionism that settled for short-term gains rather than true revolutionary change for the working class. Lenin further rejected the concept of a mass party composed of workers. Revolutionary consciousness would not arise spontaneously from the working class. It must be carried to them by a small, elite party, "people who make revolutionary activity their profession."[2] The guiding principle of that party should be "the strictest secrecy, the strictest selection of members, and the training of professional revolutionaries."[3]

Establishment of the Bolsheviks In 1903, at the London Congress of the Russian Social Democratic Party, Lenin split the party ranks. Although it lost most of the votes during the congress, near the close Lenin's group mustered a slim majority. Thereafter, his faction assumed the name *Bolsheviks,* meaning "majority," and the other, more moderate, democratic revolutionary faction became known as the *Mensheviks,* or "minority." There was, of course, a considerable public relations advantage to the name *Bolshevik.* (In 1912 the Bolsheviks organized separately from other Social Democrats.) In 1905 Lenin complemented his organizational

[2]Quoted in Albert Fried and Ronald Sanders, eds., *Socialist Thought: A Documentary History* (Garden City, NY: Anchor Doubleday, 1964), p. 459.

[3]Fried and Sanders, p. 468.

theory with a program for revolution in Russia: His *Two Tactics of Social Democracy in the Bourgeois-Democratic Revolution* urged that the socialist revolution unite the proletariat and the peasants. He grasped better than any other revolutionary the profound discontent in the Russian countryside. He knew that an alliance of workers and peasants in rebellion probably could not be suppressed. Lenin's two principles of an elite party and a dual social revolution allowed the Bolsheviks, in late 1917, to capture the leadership of the Russian Revolution and to transform the political face of the modern world.

The Revolution of 1905 and Its Aftermath
The quarrels among the Russian socialists had no immediate influence within Russia itself. In 1904 Russia went to war with Japan, but the result was defeat and political crisis. The Japanese captured Port Arthur, Russia's base on the eastern coast of China, early in 1905. A few days later, on January 22, a priest named Father Gapon (1870–1906) led thousands of workers to petition the tsar for improvements in industrial conditions. As the petitioners approached the Winter Palace in Saint Petersburg, troops opened fire. About 100 people were killed, and many more were wounded.

Revolutionary disturbances spread throughout Russia: Sailors mutinied, peasants revolted, and property was attacked. The uncle of Nicholas II was assassinated. Liberal Constitutional Democrat leaders from the *zemstvos* demanded political reform. University students went on strike. In early October 1905 strikes broke out in Saint Petersburg, and worker groups, called *soviets*, virtually controlled the city.

Nicholas II (r. 1894–1917) promised Russia constitutional government.

Early in 1906 the tsar announced the election of a parliament, the Duma, with two chambers. However, he reserved for himself ministerial appointments, financial policy, and military and foreign affairs. Nicholas named as his chief minister P. A. Stolypin (1862–1911). Neither the tsar nor his minister was sympathetic to the Duma. It would meet, disagreements would occur, and it would be dismissed. In 1906, however, the government canceled any redemptive payments the peasants still owed from the emancipation of the serfs in 1861. Thereafter Stolypin repressed rural discontent.

After Stolypin's assassination in 1911 by a Social Revolutionary, the tsarist government simply muddled along. But the imperial family became surrounded by scandal over the influence of Grigori Rasputin (1871?–1916), who seemed able to heal the tsar's hemophilic son, the heir to the throne. The undue influence of this strange and uncouth man, the continued social discontent, and the conservative resistance to liberal reforms rendered the position and policy of the tsar uncertain after 1911.

NORTH AMERICA

The New Industrial Economy

The full industrialization of the United States followed a pattern not unlike that of nineteenth-century Europe. The first industry to become thoroughly mechanized was textile

In this photograph taken in 1895, Lenin sits at the table among a group of other young Russian radicals from St. Petersburg. [Corbis-Bettmann]

Lenin Argues for the Necessity of a Secret and Elite Party of Professional Revolutionaries

Social democratic parties in western Europe had mass memberships and generally democratic structures of organization. In this passage from What Is to Be Done? *(1902), Lenin explained why the autocrtic political conditions of Russia demanded a different kind of organization for the Russian Social Democratic Party. Lenin's ideas became the guiding principle of Bolshevik organization.*

What does Lenin mean by "professional revolutionaries"? Why are such revolutionaries especially needed in Russia? How does he reconcile his antidemocratic views to the goal of aiding the working class?

I assert that it is far more difficult [for government police] to unearth a dozen wise men than a hundred fools. This position I will defend, no matter how much you instigate the masses against me for my "anti-democratic" views, etc. As I have stated repeatedly, by "wise men," in connection with organization, I mean *professional revolutionaries*, irrespective of whether they have developed from among students or working men. I assert: (1) that no revolutionary movement can endure without a stable organi-

zation of leaders maintaining continuity; (2) that the broader the popular mass drawn spontaenously into the struggle, which forms the basis of the movement and participates in it, the more urgent the need for such an organization, and the more solid this organization must be . . . ; (3) that such an organization must consist chiefly of people professionally engaged in revolutionary activity; (4) that in an autocratic state [such as Russia], the more we *confine* the membership of such an organization to people who are professional engaged in revolutionary activity and who have been professionally trained in the art of combating the political police, the more difficult will it be to unearth the organization; and (5) the *greater* will be the number of people from the working class and from other social classes who will be able to join the movement and perform active work in it. . . .

The only serious organization principle for the active workers of our movement should be the strictest secrecy, the strictest selection of members, and the training of professional revolutionaries.

From Albert Fried and Ronald Sanders, eds., *Socialist Thought: A Documentary History* (Garden City, N.Y.: Anchor Doubleday, 1964), pp. 460, 468.

---

manufacture, followed by growth in the iron and steel industries. There were certain significant differences, however. The United States industrialized considerably later than Great Britain. Its major expansion in iron and steel took place after the Civil War and was thus approximately contemporary to the economic rise of the newly united Germany. In the United States there had always been enormous social respect for entrepreneurial enterprise. American manufacturers and commercial developers thus encountered little of the prejudice against trade and commerce that existed among the European aristocracy. Wealthy American businessmen had considerable political influence. The United States possessed an immense internal market that functioned without trade restraints for the shipment of unprocessed goods to factories or of finished products to their markets. Much of the capital for American industrial expansion came from British bankers who saw the United States as an area of secure investment. Finally, the United States had a relative shortage of labor and consequently relatively high wages, the factors that attracted so many immigrants to the industrial sector during the second half of the century.

In America as in Europe, however, the railways spurred the most intense industrial growth. The number of railway

miles increased from approximately 50,000 in the mid-1860s to almost 200,000 by 1900. Much of the construction was made possible by vast European investments in the United States. The railways created enormous demand for iron, steel, coal, and lumber. They also stimulated settlement, vastly expanded markets , and helped to knit the country together.

European Immigration to the United States

The same conditions that made American life so difficult for blacks and Native Americans (see Chapter 27) turned the United States into a land of vast opportunity for white European immigrants. These immigrants faced religious and ethnic discrimination as well as frequent poverty in the United States; however, for many of them and their children, the social and economic structures of the United States allowed for assimilation and remarkable upward social mobility. This was especially true of those immigrants, mostly from northern and western Europe, who arrived between approximately 1840 and 1890—the great period of German, English, Welsh, Scottish, and Irish immigration. Among this group, the Irish undoubtedly encountered the most difficulties and resistance.

Toward the end of the century and well into the next—in what is sometimes known as the New Immigration—millions of people arrived from the Mediterranean, eastern Europe, and the Balkans. Most of these peoples left economically depressed areas, and financed their immigration themselves. However, some American companies did send ships to Italy for immigrants to work in American factories and mines.

These new immigrants, who generally came to work in the growing industrial cities, were perceived as fundamentally different from those who had come before them. They were seen and treated as of a lower class and inherently more difficult to assimilate than the earlier immigrants. Predominately Roman Catholic, Orthodox, and Jewish, they encountered much intolerance. The same kind of racial theory that spread through Europe during these years was present in the United States. These new immigrants were often regarded as being from less desirable racial stocks. As a result, turn-of-the-century immigrants often encountered serious prejudice and endured lives of enormous poverty. They also often settled into communities of people from their own ethnic background. What ultimately held them together were various private organizations, such as churches and synagogues, clubs, newspapers in their own languages, and social agencies they organized for themselves.

Although none of these immigrants faced the same legal discrimination as did American blacks, the Jews encountered restricted covenants on real estate, obstacles to joining private clubs, and quotas for admission to many schools and universities. Asian immigrants to the West Coast of the United States faced harsher prejudice.

Unions: Organization of Labor

The expansion of industrialism led to various attempts to organize labor unions. In America as in Europe, workers faced great resistance from employers and those who feared that labor unions might lead to socialism. Another difficulty arose from the social situation of the labor force itself. White laborers would not organize alongside blacks. Different ethnic minorities would not cooperate. The ongoing flood of immigration ensured a supply of workers willing to work for low wages. The owners of businesses more often than not could divide and conquer the sprawling, ethnically mixed labor force.

The first effort at labor organization occurred in the 1870s with the National Labor Union and railroad unions. In 1881 the American Federation of Labor (AFL) was founded. In contrast to earlier organizations and the advanced European socialist movement, such as that in Germany, it did not seek to transform the life of workers in a radical fashion but rather focused on higher wages and better working conditions. The AFL concentrated on organizing skilled workers; it did not seek to organize whole industries. Among its most effective leaders was Samuel Gompers (1850–1924). Other unions, such as the United Mine Workers and the Railway Brotherhoods, organized workers by industry.

The industrialization of the United States—again, like that of Europe—saw major periods of business crisis or downturn. Serious depressions occurred in both the 1870s and the 1890s. There was no government relief. What little relief there was came from local authorities and private charities. This pattern would continue until the Great Depression of the 1930s. The economic turmoil of the 1880s and 1890s spawned violent strikes. Perhaps the most famous of these incidents was the breaking of the Pullman strike in Chicago in 1894 by federal troops. The major goal of labor thereafter was to achieve the full legal right to organize. Although the Clayton Act of 1914 moved in that direction, the clear right to organize with the protection of the federal government was achieved only through the legislation of Franklin Roosevelt's (1882–1945) New Deal in the 1930s.

Socialism was a path not taken by American labor and one not allowed to be taken. The leaders of the conservative unions worked against them, and spokesmen for business did everything possible to block their influence. The federal and state governments actively sought to repress socialist activities wherever they appeared. After the Bolshevik Revolution of 1918 virtually all American socialists were persecuted as Bolshevists during the 1920s and beyond. The United States thus became the land where many social issues tended to be addressed by trade unions rather than by socialist parties. Furthermore, although many conservative American political and business leaders disliked them, unions were not legally attacked here as they were in Britain, which led to the founding of the British Labour Party after the turn of the century.

In many European countries, socialist parties, or ministers like Bismarck who attempted to outflank the socialists, had pressed their governments to pass legislation providing social security and other social services. As with so many other policies favorable to labor, no significant legislation of this kind was passed in the United States, at either the federal or state level, until the New Deal.

The Progressives

Much of the power in American politics in the decades after the Civil War, especially in cities, often lay in the hands of political bosses. This system depended on patronage at every level of government. In return for jobs, contracts, licenses, favors, and sometimes actual services, the boss expected and received political support. Government was a vehicle for distributing spoils. The point of boss politics was not merely venality; it was also a way, however crude and unattractive, of

In 1894 federal troops were called in to escort trains out of the Chicago stockyards during the Pullman strike.

[Corbis-Bettmann]

organizing the disorderly social and economic forces of the great cities. It was a way of managing cities that were growing as never before with highly diverse populations.

Toward the close of the century, reform-minded political figures began to emerge on the city and state levels. These reformers feared that people such as themselves from the white upper-middle classes might soon lose political and social influence. Deeply disturbed by the corruption of much of political life, these reformers found the urban environment with its slums an unacceptable picture of disorder. They wanted to see more efficient and less corrupt government. They also wanted the government to become a direct agent of change and reform. Pursuing these goals, they ushered in what has been called the progressive era, which lasted from approximately 1890 through 1914. Although the progressives were reformers, they were not always liberal by later standards. For example, progressives in the South often disenfranchised blacks and poor whites by imposing literacy tests and similar devices.

The progressives began their reform work on the local level, especially in the cities, before they launched into national politics. The disorder and extreme disparity of wealth and poverty in the cities disturbed them. Urban reformers believed that the politics of bosses and patronage robbed cities of the money needed to make them livable places. In place of patronage, they demanded social and municipal services to clean up the cities. They repeatedly attacked special interests who blocked reform. Progressive mayors called for lower utility rates and streetcar fares and also attacked police corruption.

Social Reform

Not only politicians joined the progressive crusade. Churches began to address the question of social reform. It was in this era that the "Social Gospel" was first preached, with its message that Christianity involved civic action. Young men and women began to work in settlement houses in the slums. The most famous was Chicago's Hull House, led by Jane Addams (1860–1935). Other young persons from the middle class became active in housing and health reform, education, and charities. They conducted extensive surveys of the poorest parts of the great cities. These people believed that the urban environment could be cleaned up and social order made to prevail. Their vision of such social order was that of the white middle class.

Beginning in the mid-nineties, progressivism began to affect state governments. There the impulse toward reform involved various attempts to protect whole classes of persons who were perceived as unable to protect themselves against exploitation, especially children and women working under unwholesome conditions for low wages. Other aspects of progressivism at the state level involved the civil-service requirements and the regulation of railways. Virtually all of these reformers partook of the cult of science that was so influential in the late nineteenth century. They believed that the problems of society were susceptible to scientific, rational management. The general public interest should replace special interests.

The Progressive Presidency

Roosevelt   Theodore Roosevelt became president in 1901 after the assassination of William McKinley (1843–1901). He had been police commissioner of New York City and later a reforming governor of New York State. Roosevelt, in effect, created the modern American presidency. By force of personality and intelligence, he began to make the presidency the most important and powerful branch of government. As president, he began to set the agenda for national affairs and to define the problems that the federal government was to address. He surrounded himself with strong advisers and cabinet members. He used his own knowledge of party patronage to beat the bosses at their own game.

In domestic policy, Roosevelt was determined to control the powerful business trusts. No centers of economic power should, through their organization, be stronger than the federal government. He successfully moved against some of the most powerful financiers in the country, such as J. P. Morgan and John D. Rockefeller. Through legislation associated with the term "Square Deal," Roosevelt attempted to assert the public interest over that of the various powerful special interests. He was not opposed to big business in itself, but he wanted it to operate according to rules established by the government for the public good.

In 1902 Roosevelt brought the moral power of the presidency to the aid of mine workers who were on strike. He appointed a commission to arbitrate the dispute. This was a major intrusion of the federal government into the economic system. It reversed the policies that had prevailed a decade earlier, when the government had used federal troops to break strikes. Roosevelt sought to make the presidency and the federal government the guarantor of fairness in economic relations. Thus he fostered the passage of the Pure Food and Drug Act and the Meat Packing Act in 1906, which protected the public against adulterated foodstuffs. Here again, the regulatory principle came to the fore. His conservation policies ensured that millions of acres of national forests came under the care of the federal government.

Roosevelt was associated with a vigorous, imperialistic foreign policy that had roots in the 1890s. In 1898 McKinley had led the nation into the Spanish-American War, and the United States had emerged as an imperial power with control of Cuba, Puerto Rico, Guam, and the Philippines. Roosevelt believed that the United States should be a major world power, and he sent a war fleet around the world. In Latin

This picture, taken in 1910, shows women working in a New England shoe factory. Women were also working in similar factory workshops in Europe. [The Granger Collection, N.Y.]

Theodore Roosevelt States His Progressive Creed

In 1912 Theodore Roosevelt ran unsuccessfully for the presidency on a third-party ticket challenging both traditional Republicans and Democrats. At the Progressive Party convention he delivered a remarkable speech in which he set forth his most important progressive convictions. The issues Roosevelt raised in this speech have continued to echo all through the rest of twentieth-century American politics.

Why does Roosevelt attack the idea of old established parties? What political reforms does he advocate? What social reforms? Why have some people seen Roosevelt as one of the first presidents to be concerned with the environment?

The Old parties are husks, with no real soul within either, divided on artificial lines, boss-ridden and privilege-controlled, each a jumble of incongruous elements, and neither daring to speak out wisely and fearlessly what should be said on the vital issues of the day. This new movement is a movement of truth, sincerity, and wisdom, a movement which proposes to put at the service of all our people the collective power of the people, through their governmental agencies. . . .

The first essential in the Progressive program is the right of the people to rule. . . . We should provide by a national law for presidential primaries. We should provide for the election of United States Senators by popular vote . . . there must be stringent and efficient corrupt-practices acts, applying to the primaries as well as the elections; and there should be publicity of campaign contributions during the campaign. . . .

We stand for a living wage. Wages are subnormal if they fail to provide a living for those who devote their time and energy to industrial occupations. The monetary equivalent of a living wage varies according to local conditions, but must include enough to secure the elements of a normal standard of living—a standard high enough to make morality possible, to provide for education and recreation, to care for immature members of the family, to maintain the family during periods of sickness, and to permit of reasonable saving for old age.

Hours are excessive if they fail to afford the worker sufficient time to recuperate and return to his work thoroughly refreshed. We hold that the night labor of women and children is abnormal and should be prohibited. We hold that the seven-day working week is abnormal, and we hold that one day of rest in seven should be provided by law. . . . Working women have the same need to combine for protection that working men have; the ballot is as necessary for one class as for the other . . . and therefore we favor woman suffrage.

I believe in a protective tariff, but I believe in it as a principle, approached from the standpoint of the interest of the whole people, and not as a bundle of preferences to be given to favored individuals. . . .

There can be no greater issue than that of conservation in this country. Just as we must conserve our men, women and children, so we must conserve the resources of the land on which they live. . . .

Our cause is based on the eternal principle of righteousness; and even though we who now lead may for the time fail, in the end the cause itself shall triumph. . . . I say in closing: We stand at Armageddon, and we battle for the Lord.

From Theodore Roosevelt's Confession of Faith Before the Progressive National Convention, August 6, 1912, as quoted in Oscar Handlin, ed., *Readings in American History*. Copyright © 1957 Alfred A. Knopf, pp. 477–480.

America naval intervention assured the success of the Panamanian revolt of 1903 against Colombia. A treaty with the new Panamanian government allowed the United States to construct and control a canal across the Isthmus of Panama. The United States was thus following the model of the European great powers, which had been intervening in Africa and Asia. Like the other great powers, the imperialist policies of the United States were built on a conviction of racial superiority.

Roosevelt was succeeded in 1909 by William Howard Taft (1857–1930), his hand-picked successor. Taft disappointed Roosevelt, and in 1912 the election was a three-way contest among Taft, Roosevelt (running as a third-party candidate), and Woodrow Wilson. The Democrat Wilson won and brought a different concept of progressivism to the White House.

Wilson Woodrow Wilson (1856–1924) was a former president of Princeton University and a reforming governor of New Jersey, where he had battled the bosses. While still an academic, he had criticized the weak presidency of the late nineteenth century. Wilson, like Roosevelt, accepted a modern industrialized nation. However, unlike Roosevelt, Wilson disliked big business almost in and of itself. He believed in economic competition in which the weak would receive protection from the government. Wilson termed his attitude and policy the New Freedom. Although he had pressed this idea during the campaign, in office he followed a policy of moderate regulation of business.

Wilson also had a different view of the presidency. He saw the office as responsible for leading Congress to legislative decisions. He deeply admired the British parliamentary system and British Prime Minister William Gladstone (1809–1898). Wilson was the first American president since 1800 to deliver the State of the Union address to Congress in person. He presented Congress with a vast agenda of legislation and then worked carefully with the Democratic leadership to see that it was passed. Although Wilson appeared to be an advanced reformer, he retained many beliefs that have disappointed his later admirers. For example, he reinstated racial segregation in the federal civil service and opposed female suffrage.

Wilson had long seen his real goals in terms of domestic reform. But war broke out in Europe in August 1914. Although Wilson was reelected in 1916 on the slogan "He Kept Us Out of War!" in April 1917 he led the nation into the European conflict. The expertise that he and other progressives had brought to the task of efficient domestic government was then turned to making the nation an effective military force. These two impulses—the first toward domestic reform, the second toward a strong international role—had long marked the progressive movement and would shape American history in the years after the war.

The American Progressives resembled political leaders of their generation in Great Britain. The Conservative Benjamin Disraeli (1804–1881) and liberals William Gladstone (1809–1898) and David Lloyd-George (1863–1945) had supported various measures of social reforms. Elsewhere in Europe political leaders in France and Germany had undertaken reforms in housing and urban life to forestall the advance of socialism and to address the problems of industrialization and urbanization. These leaders had favored unprecedented use of central government authority and the establishment of stronger governments.

IN WORLD PERSPECTIVE

The Building of Northern Transatlantic Supremacy

Between 1850 and 1914 Europe had more influence throughout the world than it had ever before or since. The United States was beginning to develop its industrial capacity. Together, Europe and North American were the most industrially advanced regions of the world. Nonetheless, the preponderance of economic power lay with Europe. Its in-

dustrial base was more advanced than that of any other region, including the still-developing United States. European banks exercised vast influence across the globe. Europeans financed the building of railways in Africa, Asia, and the Americas. Financial power brought political influence. The armaments industry gave European armies and navies predominant power over the peoples of Africa and Asia. The United States had begun to exercise such power as a result of the Spanish American War. These economic developments established a pattern that still persists. First European and later American banks, companies, and corporations penetrated the economies and societies of Asia, Africa, and Latin America. These nonpolitical groups often expected their own governments to protect their interests. Thus, what started as commercial contact often evolved into the exercise of direct political influence.

During these years European culture was also probably enjoying its greatest influence. Many capital cities in Latin America, especially Buenos Aires and Montevideo, adopted European-style architecture. Paris became synonymous with high fashion. Paris, London, and Vienna were world intellectual centers. The advanced industrial and urban civilization of Europe was regarded as a model. This was partly because more non-Europeans were visiting and studying in Europe than ever before. During this period many American artists and writers flocked to Europe to absorb its culture.

Another cultural feature of western Europe and the United States that would affect the rest of the world during the next century was the emerging role of women. In particular, the demand for the entrance of women into the political process and the professions would become a hallmark of the next century. On both sides of the Atlantic, women assumed leadership roles in social reform movements.

The nation that most clearly understood the nature of European power and sought to imitate it was Japan. Its administrators and intellectuals after the Meiji restoration (1868) came to Europe to study the new technology, political structures, and military organizations. The Japanese proved sufficiently successful to defeat Russia in 1905, providing the first example of a non-European nation using Western weapons, organizations, and economic power to defeat a European nation. In the twentieth century other non-European nations would find ways to import or manufacture technology that would allow them to challenge European and later American hegemony. Indeed, today the proliferation of weaponry usually developed in the United States or Europe has allowed regional powers to challenge Western dominance. This destabilizing trade began in the second half of the nineteenth century.

In contrast to Japan, China, India, the countries of the Middle East, and Africa were overwhelmed by the economic and military power of Europe. In time, however, the peoples of those lands who were dominated by the European powers embraced the ideologies of revolutionary protest, most particularly those of nationalism and socialism. As people from the colonial world came to work or study in Europe, they encountered ideas and criticisms that were most effective against European and Western culture. They adapted those ideas and then turned them against their colonial governors.

The Europeans eventually turned their military power against each other in 1914. World War I destroyed the late-nineteenth-century European self-confidence. At home, the Bolsheviks brought revolution to Russia. Abroad after the war, anticolonial movements began to grow, especially in India, in a manner that most Europeans in 1900 could not have imagined. In turn, those movements found many sympathetic supporters in Europe as a result of the spread of socialist ideas regarding social justice and public policy. Furthermore, because the political and economic systems of the world had become so interconnected during the second half of the nineteenth century, the influence and impact of the European conflict could not be limited to Europe. The United States would be drawn into World War I and would never again be able to avoid worldwide responsibilities.

Review Questions ———

1. What were the chief features of the late-nineteenth-century European middle-class society?

2. How did Jewish emancipation take place in the nineteenth century, and what were its chief features?

3. How would you describe living conditions in European cities during the late nineteenth century? Why were European cities redesigned during this period? Why were housing and health key issues for urban reform?

4. What were the major characteristics of Jewish emancipation in the nineteenth century? Why did women grow discontented with their lot? What factors led to change? To what extent had they improved their position by 1914? Was the emancipation of women inevitable? How did women approach their situation differently from country to country?

5. What was the status of the working class groups in the United States and Europe in 1860? What improvements if any had been achieved by 1914? What caused the emergence of trade unions and organized mass political parties in Europe? How did the American progressives, as reformers, differ from the various European socialists? Why were the debates of "opportunism" and "revisionism" important to the socialist parties?

6. Assess the value of industrialism for Russia. Were the tsars wise in attempting to modernize their country or would they have been better off leaving it as it was? How did Lenin's view of socialism differ from that of socialists in western Europe? Why did socialism not emerge as a major political force in the United States?

Suggested Readings ———

J. ALBISETTI, *Secondary School Reform in Imperial Germany* (1983). Examines the relationship between politics and education.

I. M. ARONSON, *Troubled Waters: The Origins of the 1881 Anti-Jewish Pogroms in Russia* (1990). The best discussion of this subject.

J. H. BATES, *St. Petersburg: Industrialization and Change* (1976). Impact of industrialization on the capital of imperial Russia.

G. BEHLMER, *Child Abuse and Moral Reform in England, 1870–1908* (1982). An important study of changes in the treatment of children.

L. R. BERLANSTEIN, *The Working People of Paris, 1871–1914* (1985). Interesting and comprehensive.

P. BRANCA, *Silent Sisterhood: Middle Class Women in the Victorian Home* (1975). A well-researched work.

N. BULLOCK AND J. READ, *The Movement for Housing Reform in Germany and France, 1840–1914* (1985). An important and wide-ranging study of the housing problem.

A. D. CHANDLER, JR., *The Visible Hand: Managerial Revolution in American Business* (1977). The best discussion of the innovative role of American business.

J. M. COOPER, JR., *The Warrior and the Priest: Woodrow Wilson and Theodore Roosevelt* (1983). An interesting dual biography.

W. CRONIN, *Nature's Metropolis: Chicago and the Great West, 1848–1893.* (1991) The best examination of any major American nineteenth-century city.

P. GAY, *The Dilemma of Democratic Socialism: Eduard Bernstein's Challenge to Marx* (1952). A clear presentation of the problems raised by Bernstein's revisionism.

D. F. GOOD, *The Economic Rise of the Habsburg Empire, 1750–1914* (1985). The best available study.

S. C. HAUSE, *Women's Suffrage and Social Politics in the French Third Republic* (1984). A wide-ranging examination of the question.

G. HIMMELFARB, *Poverty and Compassion: The Moral Imagination of the Late Victorians* (1991). The best examination of late Victorian social thought.

E. J. HOBSBAWM, *The Age of Capital* (1975). Explores the consolidation of middle-class life after 1850.

L. HOLCOMBE, *Wives and Property: Reform of the Married Women's Property Law in Nineteenth-Century England* (1983). The standard work on the subject.

S. KERN, *The Culture of Time and Space, 1880–1918* (1983). A lively discussion of the impact of the new technology.

S. KERN, *The Culture of Love: Victorians to Moderns* (1992) A major discussion of how Europeans have thought and behaved in regard to love, family, and sexuality.

L. KOLAKOWSKI, *Main Currents of Marxism: Its Rise, Growth, and Dissolution*, 3 vols. (1978). Especially good on the last years of the nineteenth century and the early years of the twentieth.

P. KRAUSE, *The Battle for Homestead, 1880–1892* (1992). Examines labor relations in the steel industry.

D. LANDES, *The Wealth and Poverty of Nations: Why Some Are So Rich and Some So Poor* (1998). A major international discussion of the subject.

A. H. MCBRIAR, *Fabian Socialism and English Politics, 1884–1918* (1962). The standard discussion.

A. MACLAREN, *Sexuality and Social Order: The Debate over the Fertility of Women and Workers in France, 1770–1920* (1983). Examines the debate over birth control in France.

G. L. MOSSE, *German Jews Beyond Judaism* (1985). Sensitive essays exploring the relationship of Jews to German culture in the nineteenth and early twentieth centuries.

R. A. NYE, *Crime, Madness, and Politics in Modern France: The Medical Concept of National Decline* (1984). Relevant to issues of family and women.

H. PELLING, *The Origins of the Labour Party, 1880–1900* (1965). Examines the sources of the party in the activities of British socialists and trade unionists.

D. H. PINKNEY, *Napoleon III and the Rebuilding of Paris* (1958). A classic study.

F. K. PROCHASKA, *Women and Philanthropy in Nineteenth-Century England* (1980). Studies the role of women in charity.

J. RENDALL, *The Origins of Modern Feminism: Women in Britain, France and the United States, 1780–1860* (1985). A well-informed introduction.

T. RICHARDS, *The Commodity Culture of Victorian England: Advertising and Spectacle, 1851–1914* (1990). A study of how consumers were persuaded of their need for new commodities.

H. ROGGER, *Russia in the Age of Modernization and Revolution, 1881–1917* (1983). The best synthesis of the period.

H. ROGGER, *Jewish Policies and Right-Wing Politics in Imperial Russia* (1986). A very learned examination of Russian antisemitism.

M. L. ROZENBLIT, *The Jews of Vienna, 1867–1914: Assimilation and Identity* (1983) Covers the cultural, economic, and political life of Viennese Jews.

C. E. SCHORSKE, *German Social Democracy, 1905–1917* (1955). Remains a brilliant study of the difficulties of the Social Democrats under the empire.

A. L. SHAPIRO, *Housing the Poor of Paris, 1850–1902* (1985). Examines what happened to working-class housing during the remodeling of Paris.

B. G. SMITH, *Ladies of the Leisure Class: The Bourgeoises of Northern France in the Nineteenth Century* (1981). Emphasizes the importance of the reproductive role of women.

R. A. SOLOWAY, *Birth Control and the Population Question in England, 1877–1930* (1982). An important book that should be read with MacLaren *(listed above).*

N. STONE, *Europe Transformed* (1984). A sweeping survey that emphasizes the difficulties of late-nineteenth-century liberalism.

S. TRACHTENBERG, *The Incorporation of America: Culture and Society in the Gilded Age* (1982). Studies the manner in which corporate organization affected various aspects of American life outside the realm of business.

A. B. ULAM, *The Bolsheviks: The Intellectual and Political History of the Triumph of Communism in Russia* (1965). Early chapters discuss prewar developments and the formation of Lenin's doctrines.

A. M. VERNER, *The Crisis of Russian Autocracy: Nicholas II and the 1905 Revolution* (1990). A major study of this crucial event.

J. R. WALKOWITZ, *Prostitution and Victorian Society: Women, Class, and the State* (1980). A work of great insight and sensitivity.

E. WEBER, *Peasants into Frenchmen: The Modernization of Rural France, 1870–1914* (1976). An important and fascinating work on the transformation of French peasants into self-conscious citizens of the nation-state.

M. J. WIENER, *English Culture and the Decline of the Industrial Spirit, 1850–1980* (1981). The best study of the problem.

29 THE BIRTH OF CONTEMPORARY WESTERN THOUGHT

In two works of seminal

importance, *The Origin of*

Species (1859) and *The*

Descent of Man (1871),

Charles Darwin enunciated

the theory of evolution by

natural selection and applied

that theory to human beings.

The result was a storm of

controversy that affected not

only biology but also religion,

philosophy, sociology, and

even politics.

[London, National Portrait

Gallery/Photo: Jochen Remmer/

Bildarchiv Preussischer Kulturbesitz]

CHAPTER TOPICS

◆ **The Prestige of Science**
◆ **Christianity and the Church Under Siege**

◆ **Toward a Twentieth-Century Frame of Mind**
◆ **Transformations in Political and Social Thought**

◆ **Women and Modern Thought**
In World Perspective **Intellectual Change**

The second half of the nineteenth century, when the modern nation-state developed and the industrial growth that laid the foundations for the modern material lifestyle occurred, was also the age in which the ideas and concepts that marked Western thought for much of the twentieth century took shape. Many of the traditional intellectual signposts disappeared. The death of God was proclaimed. Christianity suffered severe attack. The picture of the physical world that had dominated since Newton was transformed. Darwin and Freud challenged the special place that Western thinkers had assigned to humankind. The value long ascribed to rationality was questioned. The political and humanitarian ideals of liberalism and socialism yielded to new, aggressive nationalism. By 1900 European intellectuals were more daring, but also probably less certain and less optimistic than they had ever been. At the same time, however, though Christian institutions met severe challenges in Europe they displayed much strength in the United States. Missionaries from both Europe and the United States established small Christian communities in both Africa and Asia, which in several cases by the close of the twentieth century became major outposts for both Roman Catholic and Protestant Christianity.

The impact of the advanced ideas of the second half of the nineteenth century did not remain limited to Europe. They found a wide audience in the United States within the scientific community, within colleges and universities, and within the world of journalism. Furthermore, during the late nineteenth and early twentieth centuries numerous students from regions in Africa and Asia that were governed by European colonial administrations, as well as students from Latin America, came to study in European universities. They took home the ideas they had encountered, which they associated with modern society and politics, and often attempted to apply those ideas in their homelands. Consequently for much of the twentieth century people around the world who regarded themselves as educated, who wished their nations to become modern, and who wished to be politically active drew upon the new world of European ideas discussed in this chapter as well as the ideas of European socialism discussed in the previous chapter. They often saw the application of such ideas, most particularly scientific ideas and technology, as a path to power and wealth and as weapons that could be turned against their European colonial administrators. In both the Western and the non-Western worlds the ideas that emanated from Europe in the second half of the nineteenth century thus became powerful vehicles for challenging traditional modes of thought and society.

The Prestige of Science

In about 1850 the basic Newtonian picture of physical nature still prevailed. Nature was a vast machine that operated according to mechanical principles. During the first half of the century scientists extended mechanistic explanation into several important areas. John Dalton (1766–1844), for example, formulated the modern theory of chemical composition. However, at mid-century and for long thereafter, atoms and molecules were thought to resemble billiard balls. During the 1840s several independent researchers arrived at the concept of the conservation of energy, according to which energy is never lost in the universe but is simply transformed from one form to another. The principles of mechanism were extended to geology through the work of Charles Lyell (1797–1875), whose *Principles of Geology* (1830) postulated that changes in geological formation were the result of the mechanistic operation of natural causes over eons.

Darwin Defends a Mechanistic View of Nature

In the closing paragraphs of The Origin of Species *(1859), Charles Darwin contrasted the view of nature he championed with that of his opponents. He argued that an interpretation of organic nature based on mechanistic laws was actually nobler that an interpretation based on divine creation. In the second edition, however, Darwin, added the term* Creator *to these paragraphs.*

Why does Darwin believe a mechanistic creation suggests no less dignity than creation by God? How does the insertion of the term *Creator* change this passage? What is the grandeur that Darwin finds in his view of life?

Authors of the highest eminence seem to be fully satisfied with the view that each species has been independently created. To my mind it accords better with what we know of the laws impressed on matter by the Creator, that the production and extinction of the past and present inhabitants of the world should have been due to secondary causes, like those determining the birth and death of the individual. When I view all beings not as special creations, but as the lineal descendants of some few beings which lived long before the first bed of the Cambrian [geological] system was deposited, they seem to me to become ennobled. . . .

It is interesting to contemplate a tangled bank, clothed with many plants of many kinds, with birds singing on the bushes, with various insects flitting about, and with worms crawling through the damp earth, and to reflect that these elaborately constructed forms, so different from each other, and dependent upon each other in so complex a manner, have all been produced by laws acting around us. These laws, taken in the largest sense, being Growth with Reproduction; Inheritance which is almost implied by reproduction; Variability from the indirect and direct action of the conditions of life, and from use and disuse: a Ratio of Increase so high as to lead to a struggle for Life, and as a consequence to Natural Selection, entailing Divergence of Character and the Extinction of less-improved forms. Thus, from the war of nature, from famine and death, the most exalted object which we are capable of conceiving, namely the production of the higher animals, directly follows. There is grandeur in this view of life, with its several powers, having been originally breathed by the Creator into a few forms or into one; and that, whilst this planet has gone cycling on according to the fixed law of gravity, from so simple a beginning endless forms most beautiful and most wonderful have been, and are being evolved.

From Charles Darwin, *The Origin of Species and the Descent of Man* (New York: Modern Library, n.d.), pp. 373–374.

At mid-century the physical world was thus regarded as rational, mechanical, and dependable. Its laws could be ascertained objectively through experiment and observation. Scientific theory purportedly described physical nature as it really existed. Moreover, almost all scientists also believed, like Newton and the deists of the eighteenth century, that their knowledge of nature demonstrated the existence of a God or a supreme being.

Darwin and Natural Selection

In 1859 Charles Darwin (1809–1882) published *The Origin of Species*, which carried the mechanical interpretation of physical nature into the world of living things. The book proved to be one of the seminal works of Western thought and earned Darwin the honor of being regarded as the Newton of biology. Both Darwin and his book have been much misunderstood. He did not originate the concept of evolution, which had been discussed widely before he wrote. What he and Alfred Russel Wallace (1823–1913) did, working independently, was to formulate the principle of natural selection, which explained how species had changed or evolved over time. Earlier writers had believed that evolution might occur; Darwin and Wallace explained how it *could* occur.

Drawing on Malthus, the two scientists contended that seeds and living organisms come into existence in numbers greater than those able to survive in their environment. Those organisms possessing some marginal advantage in the struggle for existence live long enough to propagate. This principle of survival of the fittest Darwin called *natural selection*. The principle was naturalistic and mechanistic. Its operation required no guiding mind behind the development and change in organic nature. What neither Darwin nor anyone else in his day could explain was the origin of those chance variations that provided some members of a species with a marginally better chance for survival than others. Only when the work on heredity by the Austrian monk Gregor Mendel (1822–1884) received public attention after 1900 did the mystery of those variations begin to be unraveled.

Darwin's and Wallace's theory represented the triumph of naturalistic explanation, which removed the idea of purpose from organic nature. Eyes were not made for seeing according to the rational wisdom and purpose of God, but had developed mechanistically over time. Thus, the theory of evolution through natural selection not only contradicted the biblical Creation, but also undermined the deistic argument for the existence of God from the design of the universe. Moreover, Darwin's work undermined the whole concept of fixity in nature or the universe at large. The world was a realm of flux and change. The fact that physical and organic nature might be constantly changing allowed people in the late nineteenth century to believe that society, values, customs, and beliefs should also change.

In 1871 Darwin carried his work further. In *The Descent of Man* he applied the principle of evolution by natural selection to human beings. Darwin was hardly the first person to treat human beings as animals, but his arguments brought greater plausibility to that point of view. He contended that humankind's moral nature and religious sentiments, as well as its physical frame, had developed naturalistically in response largely to the requirements of survival. Within Darwin's thought neither the origin nor the character of humankind on earth required the existence of a God for its explanation.

Darwin's theory of evolution by natural selection encountered criticism from both the religious and the scientific communities. By 1900 evolution was widely accepted by scientists, but not yet Darwin's mechanism of natural selection. The acceptance of the latter within the scientific community really dates from the 1920s and 1930s, when Darwin's theory became combined with the insights of modern genetics. Yet the role of natural selection is still controversial within the scientific community.

Auguste Comte and Intellectual Development

The French philosopher Auguste Comte (1798–1857), a late child of the Enlightenment, developed a philosophy of human intellectual development that regarded science as its culmination. In *The Positive Philosophy* (1830–1842), Comte argued that human thought had gone through three stages of development. In the theological stage, physical nature was explained in terms of the action of divinities or spirits. In the metaphysical stage, abstract principles were regarded as the operative agencies of nature. In the final or positive stage, nature was explained by exact descriptions of phenomena, without recourse to an unobservable operative principle. Physical science had, in Comte's view, entered the positive stage, and similar thinking should penetrate other areas of analysis. In particular, Comte thought that positive laws of social behavior could be discovered in the same fashion as laws of physical nature. He is therefore generally regarded as the father of sociology. Works like Comte's helped to convince learned Europeans that genuine knowledge in any field must resemble scientific knowledge.

Comte exerted only modest influence within Europe itself except among small circles of intellectuals in France and England. His thinking, however, achieved a considerable impact in Latin America. For example, during the 1880s in Brazil persons influenced by Comte came to the fore in the universities and among the military. They hoped to use the ideas of science to challenge the continued presence of slavery in Brazil and what they saw as a backward economy dependent almost entirely on coffee. Comte's slogan of "Order and Progress" appears on the Brazilian flag. Similarly, in Mexico during the middle of the nineteenth century Comtean ideas were important in teacher training schools. At the turn of the century many people associated with business, technology, railway building, and the military saw themselves guided by Comtean ideas. Throughout Latin America those who opposed the widespread influence of the Church had often embraced such thought. What made Comteanism so attractive was the combination of advocating scientific, technological advance and of urging such advance in a generally non-democratic manner. Those who wanted their countries to become modern but feared disorder turned to Comte's thought.

Herbert Spencer, Thomas Henry Huxley, and Social Darwinism

Theories of ethics were modeled on science during the last half of the century. The concept of the struggle for survival was widely applied to human social relationships. The phrase "survival of the fittest" predated Darwin and reflected the competitive outlook of classical economies. Darwin's use of the phrase gave it the prestige associated with advanced science.

The most famous advocate of evolutionary ethics was Herbert Spencer (1820–1903), who believed that human society progressed through competition. If the weak received too much protection, the rest of humankind was the loser. In Spencer's work, struggle against one's fellow human beings became a kind of ethical imperative. The concept could be applied to justify not aiding the poor and the working class or dominating colonial peoples, or to urge aggressively competitive relationships among nations. Evolutionary ethics and similar concepts, all of which are usually termed *social Darwinism*, often came very close to saying "Might makes right." Spencer's ideas proved very attractive to business groups in the United States, Latin America, and Asia who saw themselves as particularly well-suited to guide their nations in the struggle for economic existence.

One of the chief opponents of such thinking was Thomas Henry Huxley (1825–1895), the great defender of Darwin. In 1893 Huxley declared that the physical cosmic process of evolution was at odds with the process of human ethical development. The struggle in nature held no ethical implications except to demonstrate how human beings should not behave.

Scientists and their admirers enjoyed a supreme confidence during the last half of the century. They genuinely believed that they had discovered all of the principles that might be discovered. In the future, science would extend these principles and refine measurement. However, in the twentieth century that confident, self-satisfied world vanished. Although, as will be seen later in this chapter, a much more complicated picture of nature developed, the pursuit of science and technology became associated with the military and economic dominance of Europe. By the late nineteenth century political leaders around the world who wished their nations to resist European inroads or who wished to see their peoples become more prosperous embraced what often amounted to a cult of science. Quite often their model was Germany. The most important example of such new departures were the events in late nineteenth century Japan that led to a vast reorganization of its society and government, resulting in an expanding economy and military establishment. By 1905 Japan thought this pursuit of technological power was able to defeat the navy of Russia.

Christianity and the Church Under Siege

The nineteenth century was one of the most difficult periods in the history of the organized Christian churches. Many European intellectuals left the faith. The secular, liberal nation-states attacked the political and social influence of the church. The expansion of population and the growth of cities challenged its organizational capacity. Yet the churches still made considerable headway at the popular level, and thousands of European and American missionaries labored in the non-Western world.

The Intellectual Attack

The intellectual attack on Christianity challenged its historical credibility, its scientific accuracy, and its pronounced morality. The *philosophes* of the Enlightenment had delighted in pointing out contradictions in the Bible. The historical scholarship of the nineteenth century brought new issues to the fore.

In 1835 David Friederich Strauss (1808–1874) published *Life of Jesus,* in which he questioned whether the Bible provided any genuine historical evidence about Jesus. Strauss contended that the story of Jesus was a myth that had arisen from the particular social and intellectual conditions of first-century Palestine. Jesus' character and life represented the aspirations of the people of that time and place rather than events that had occurred. Other skeptical "lives of Jesus" were written and published elsewhere. Doubts on the historical validity of the Bible caused more literate people to lose faith in Christianity than any other single cause.

Science also undermined Christianity. Many eighteenth-century writers had led Christians to believe that the scientific examination of nature buttressed their faith. But Charles Lyell (1797–1875) suggested that the earth was much older than the biblical records contended. By appealing to natural causes to explain floods, mountains, and valleys, Lyell removed the miraculous hand of God from the physical development of the earth. Darwin's theory cast doubt on the Creation. His ideas and those of other writers suggested that the moral nature of humankind could be explained without God. Finally, anthropologists, psychologists, and sociologists suggested that religion itself and religious sentiments were just natural phenomena.

Other intellectuals questioned the morality of Christianity. The old issue of immoral biblical stories was again raised. Much more important, the moral character of the Old Testament God came under fire. His cruelty and unpredictability did not fit well with the progressive, tolerant, rational values of liberals. They also wondered about the morality of the New Testament God, who would sacrifice for His own satisfaction the only perfect being ever to walk the earth. Many of the clergy began to ask themselves if they could honestly preach doctrines they felt to be immoral.

These widespread skeptical intellectual currents seem to have directly influenced only the upper levels of educated society. Yet they created a climate in which Christianity lost much of its intellectual respectability. Fewer educated people joined the clergy. More and more people found that they could lead their lives with little or no reference to Christianity. The secularism of everyday life proved as harmful to the faith as the direct attacks. This situation prevailed especially in the cities, which were growing faster than the churches' ability to meet the challenge. Whole generations of the urban poor grew up with little or no experience of the church as an institution or of Christianity as a religious faith. There was not even enough room in the existing urban churches for the potential worshipers to sit.

Conflict of Church and State

The secular state of the nineteenth century clashed with both the Protestant and the Roman Catholic churches. Liberals generally disliked the dogma and the political privileges of the established churches. National states were often suspicious of the supranational character of the Roman Catholic church. However, the primary area of conflict was education.

The conflict between Church and State disrupted German politics during the 1870s. In this contemporary cartoon Bismarck and Pope Pius IX seek to checkmate each other in a game of chess. [Bildarchiv Preussischer Kulturbesitz]

The churches feared that future generations would emerge from the schools without the rudiments of religious teaching. The advocates of secular education feared the production of future generations more loyal to religion or the churches than to the nation. From 1870 through the turn of the century, religious education was heatedly debated in every major European country.

Great Britain In Great Britain the Education Act of 1870 provided for the construction of state-supported school-board schools, whereas earlier the government had given small grants to religious schools. The new schools were to be built where the religious denominations failed to provide satisfactory education. There was rivalry not only between the Anglican Church and the state but also between the Anglican Church and the Nonconformist denominations, that is, those Christian denominations that were not part of the Church of England. There was intense local hostility among all these groups. The churches of all denominations had to oppose improvements in education because such changes would have increased the costs of their own schools. In the Education Act of 1902 the government decided to provide state support for both religious and nonreligious schools but imposed the same educational standards on each.

France The British conflict was relatively calm compared with that in France, where a dual system of Catholic and public schools existed. Under the Falloux Law of 1850 the local priest provided religious education in the public schools. The conservative French Catholic church and the Third French Republic detested each other. Between 1878 and 1886 the government passed a series of educational laws sponsored by Jules Ferry (1832–1893) that replaced religious instruction in the public schools with civic training. Members of religious orders were no longer permitted to teach in the public schools, the number of which was to be expanded. After the Dreyfus Affair (1894–1899), the French Catholic church again paid a price for its reactionary politics. The Radical government of René Waldeck-Rousseau (1846–1904), drawn from pro-Dreyfus groups, suppressed the religious orders. In 1905 the Napoleonic Concordat was terminated, and Church and State were totally separated.

Germany and the *Kulturkampf* The most extreme Church-State conflict occurred in Germany during the 1870s. At unification, the German Catholic hierarchy had wanted freedom for the churches guaranteed in the constitution. Bismarck left the matter to the discretion of each federal state, but he soon felt threatened by the activity of the Roman Catholic church and the Catholic Center Party. Through administrative orders in 1870 and 1871 Bismarck removed both Catholic and Protestant clergy from overseeing local education in Prussia and set education under state direction. The secularization of education was merely the beginning of a concerted attack on the independence of the Catholic church in Germany.

The "May Laws" of 1873, which applied only to Prussia, required priests to be educated in German schools and universities and to pass state-administered examinations. The state could veto the appointments of priests. The disciplinary power of the pope and the church over the clergy was transferred to the state. When the bishops and many of the clergy refused to obey these laws, Bismarck used force. In 1876 he had either arrested or driven from Prussia all the Catholic bishops. In the end Bismarck's *Kulturkampf* ("cultural struggle") against the Catholic church failed. Not for the first time, Christian martyrs aided resistance to persecution. By 1880 the chancellor had abandoned his attack. He had gained state control of education and civil laws governing marriage only at the price of lingering Catholic resentment against the German state. The *Kulturkampf* was probably Bismarcks greatest blunder.

Church-State Conflict Outside of Europe Although the conflict between the Church and the State is often seen as occurring only in Europe, it also constituted one of the chief elements in nineteenth-century Latin American politics as well. The Roman Catholic Church had played an enormous role in forging the civilization of Latin America from the time of the encounter onward. By the time of the Wars of Independence the Church had become a major landholder in much of Latin America and generally a force for social conservatism. Consequently, after the Wars of Independence liberal political movements tended to oppose the Church as they worked toward expanding education and reforming landholding. Much of this conflict had concluded by the turn of the century, but such conflict and often violent anticlericalism marked Latin American social and political life throughout the middle and late nineteenth century.

Areas of Religious Revival

The successful German Catholic resistance to the secular state illustrates the continuing vitality of Christianity. In Great Britain both the Anglican church and the Nonconformist denominations grew in membership. Vast sums of money were raised for new churches and schools. In Ireland the 1870s saw a widespread Catholic devotional revival. Priests in France after the defeat by Prussia organized special pilgrimages by train for thousands of penitents who believed that France had been defeated because of their sins. The cult of the miracle of Lourdes became popular during these years. Churches of all denominations tried to give more attention to the urban poor.

The Missionary Effort

The churches also attempted to spread the Christian faith around the world in an unprecedented fashion. The Spanish conquest of South America had led to a major effort to bring the newly discovered lands and their peoples under the sway of the Roman Catholic church. Catholic missionaries had also settled in China and attempted to penetrate Japan and India, but these efforts had enjoyed only modest success. Thereafter, churches in Europe and in America made little effort to spread their faith beyond those parts of the world where it was well established.

During the nineteenth century, however, Protestant denominations, especially in Great Britain and the United States, initiated the modern missionary movement. Considerable irony surrounds this effort. It occurred during the very decades when many intellectuals had begun to doubt the Christian faith. Nonetheless, throughout the century several thousand missionaries—often drawn from the more humble classes of Europeans and Americans—began to preach Christianity in Africa, Asia, and throughout the Pacific. Most of these missionaries were Protestant, but by 1900 the Roman Catholic church was also active.

The missionary societies at home that sponsored all this activity acted as political pressure groups. As a result, the home governments took considerable interest in the welfare of their missionaries, helping to give them an influence and impact beyond their numbers.

The English Baptist William Cary (1761–1834), among the most famous of missionaries, is regarded as the founder of modern missions. He began his work in India in 1793, after trying to persuade English Christians that missionary work was necessary. The Church of England founded the Church Missionary Society in 1799 and thereafter sent out many missionaries. The Scottish Presbyterian David Livingston (1813–1873)—perhaps the most famous of all nineteenth-century missionaries as well as a celebrated Western explorer of Africa—established a mission in Africa. In 1865 the China Inland Mission was founded, and in time spread its work across China. American Protestant denominations sent out hundreds of other missionaries during the century.

Roman Catholic missionary work was directed primarily by the clergy and hierarchy. The renewed effort was initially sponsored by Pope Gregory XVI (1831–1846), who sent out priests beyond the areas where the church had normally dominated and established new bishoprics in Africa and Asia. China was the scene of the most notable Roman Catholic successes. Charles Cardinal Lavigerie (1825–1892) of Algiers established the Society of Missionaries of Africa in 1868. The priests of this order, in addition to spreading Christian teaching, attacked the slave trade. They came to be known as the White Fathers because of their flowing white robes.

Christian missionaries were often among the first Western people to meet, describe, and interact with Africans and Asians. In turn Europeans and Americans frequently learned about non-Western peoples through their reports. Some missionaries were sympathetic to the peoples whom they hoped to convert. For others, spreading the Christian faith primarily meant spreading their own culture. There were long debates among missionaries about how much of local religious belief and practice to tolerate in the newly formed churches. There were also difficulties about allowing indigenous leadership to grow. By 1900 many people associated the mission-

Leo XIII Considers the Social Question in European Politics

In his 1891 encyclical Rerum Novarum, *Pope Leo III addressed the social question in European politics, providing the Catholic Church's answer to secular calls for social reforms. The pope denied the socialist claim that class conflict was the natural state of affairs. He urged employers to seek just and peaceful relations with workers.*

How does Leo XIII reject the concept of class conflict? What responsibilities does he assign to the rich and to the poor? Are these responsibilities equal? What kinds of social reform might emerge from these ideas?

The great mistake that is made in the matter now under consideration is to possess oneself of the idea that class is naturally hostile to class; that rich and poor are intended by Nature to live at war with one another. So irrational and so false is this view that the exact contrary is the truth. . . . Each requires the other; capital cannot do without labour, nor labour without capital. Mutual agreement results in pleasantness and good order; perpetual conflict necessarily produces confusion and outrage. Now, in preventing such strife as this, and in making it impossible, the efficacy of Christianity is marvelous and manifold. . . . Religion teaches the labouring man and the workman to carry out honestly and well all equitable agreements freely made; never to injure capital, or to outrage the person of an em-

ployer; never to employ violence in representing his own cause, or to engage in riot or disorder; and to have nothing to do with men of evil principles, who work upon the people with artful promises and raise hopes which usually end in disaster and in repentance when too late. Religion teaches the rich man and the employer that their work people are not their slaves; that they must respect in every man his dignity as a man and as a Christian; that labour is nothing to be ashamed of, if we listen to right reason and to Christian philosophy, but is an honourable employment, enabling a man to sustain his life in an upright and creditable way; and that it is shameful and inhuman to treat men like chattels to make money by, or to look upon them merely as so much muscle or physical power. Thus, again, Religion teaches that, as among the workman's concerns are Religion herself and things spiritual and mental, the employer is bound to see that he has time for the duties of piety; that he be not exposed to corrupting influences and dangerous occasions; and that he be not led away to neglect his home and family or to squander his wages. Then, again, the employer must never tax his work people beyond their strength, nor employ them in work unsuited to their sex or age. His great and principal obligation is to give every one that which is just.

As quoted in F. S. Nitti, *Catholic Socialism*, trans. by Mary Mackintosh. (London: S. Sonnenschein, 1895), p. 409.

---

ary effort with the general determination of Europeans and Americans to dominate the rest of the world with their culture, values, and economic interests.

By the eve of World War I, when it enjoyed popular support throughout Europe and America, the missionary movement of the nineteenth century had reached its crest. It has, however, had enduring consequences. For example, there are more members of the Church of England in Nigeria than in England itself. Korea has become a major Christian nation. And leaders of the Roman Catholic church at the end of the twentieth century came to see the world beyond Europe and America as its primary area for growth and expansion.

The Roman Catholic Church and the Modern World

Perhaps the most striking example of religious revival amidst intellectual skepticism and political hostility was the resilience of the papacy. The brief hope of liberals for a liber-

al pontificate from Pope Pius IX (1846–1878) vanished on the night in 1848 when he fled the turmoil in Rome. In the 1860s Pius IX, embittered by the effects of Italian unification, launched a counteroffensive against liberalism, in thought and deed. In 1864 he issued the *Syllabus of Errors*, which condemned the major tenets of political liberalism and modern thought. He set the Roman Catholic church squarely against contemporary science, philosophy, and politics. In 1869 the pope summoned the First Vatican Council. The next year, through the political manipulations of the pontiff and against much opposition from many bishops, the council promulgated the dogma of the infallibility of the pope when speaking officially on matters of faith and morals. No earlier pope had gone so far. The First Vatican Council ended in 1870 when Italian troops occupied Rome during the Franco-Prussian War.

Pius IX died in 1878 and was succeeded by Leo XIII (1878–1903). Leo sought to make accommodation with the modern age and to address the great social questions. He looked to the philosophical tradition of Thomas Aquinas (1225–1274) to reconcile faith and reason. His encyclicals of 1885 and 1890 permitted Catholics to participate in the politics of liberal states. Leo XIII's most important pronouncement on public issues was the encyclical *Rerum Novarum* (1891). In that document he defended private property, religious education, and religious control of the marriage laws, and he condemned socialism and Marxism. However, he also declared that employers should treat their employees justly, pay them proper wages, and permit them to organize labor unions. He supported laws and regulations to protect workers. The pope urged that modern society be organized in corporate groups, including people from various classes, that might cooperate according to Christian principles. The corporate society, derivative of medieval social organization, was to be an alternative to both socialism and competitive capitalism. On the basis of Leo XIII's pronouncements, democratic Catholic parties and Catholic trade unions were founded throughout Europe.

The emphasis of Pius X (r. 1903–1914), who has been proclaimed a saint, was to restore traditional devotional life. Between 1903 and 1907 he condemned Catholic Modernism, a movement of modern biblical criticism within the church, and in 1910 he required an anti-Modernist oath from all priests. By these actions, Pius X set the church against the intellectual currents of the day and in conflict with much of modern thought. Although Pius X did not strongly support the social policy of Leo XIII, he and his successors continued to permit Catholics to participate in social and political movements.

The post-World War II era has seen momentous changes in the church. These began in 1959 when Pope John XXIII (r. 1958–1963) summoned the twenty-first Ecumenical Council, which came to be called Vatican II. The Council finished its work in 1965 under John's successor, Pope Paul VI (r. 1963–1978). The Council ended the practice of celebrating the mass in Latin, requiring it instead to be said in the vernacular. It also permitted freer relations with other Christian denominations and gave more power to bishops. In recognition of the growing importance to the church of the world outside Europe and North America, Pope Paul also appointed cardinals from nations of the former colonial world, transforming the church into a truly world body. However, Paul and his successors have firmly upheld the celibacy of priests, maintained the church's prohibition on contraception, and opposed the ordination of women.

John Paul II (r. 1978–m), has pursued a three-pronged policy. First, he has maintained a traditional policy in doctrinal matters, stressing the authority of the papacy and attempting to limit doctrinal and liturgical experimentation. Second, he took a firm and important stand against Communism and directly contributed to the spirit of freedom in eastern Europe that destroyed the Communist regimes. Finally, he has en-

couraged the expansion of the church in the non-Western world, stressing the need for social justice while limiting the political activity of priests. He has been especially critical of the social activism of Roman Catholic priests in Latin America.

Toward a Twentieth-Century Frame of Mind

World War I is often regarded as the point of departure into the contemporary world. This view may be true of political and social developments, but not of intellectual history. The late nineteenth century and the early twentieth century constituted the crucible of contemporary Western and European thought. Philosophers, scientists, psychologists, and artists began to portray physical reality, human nature, and human society in ways different from those of the past. Their new concepts challenged the major presuppositions of mid-nineteenth-century science, rationalism, liberalism, and bourgeois morality.

Science: The Revolution in Physics

Modifications in the scientific worldview originated within the scientific community itself. By the late 1870s the excessive realism of mid-century science was being questioned. Critics suggested that the belief of many scientists—that their mechanistic models, solid atoms, and theories about absolute time and space actually described the real universe—was not well-founded. In 1883 Ernst Mach (1838–1916) published *The Science of Mechanics*, in which he urged that the concepts of science be considered descriptive not of the physical world but of the sensations experienced by the scientific observer. Science could describe only sensations, not the physical world that underlay the sensations. In line with Mach, the French scientist and mathematician Henri Poincaré (1854–1912) urged that the concepts and theories of scientists be regarded as hypothetical constructs of the human mind rather than as descriptions of the true state of nature. In 1911 Hans Vaihinger (1852–1933) suggested that the concepts of science be considered "as if" descriptions of the physical world. By World War I few scientists believed any longer that they could portray the "truth" about physical reality. Rather, they saw themselves as recording the observations of instruments and as setting forth useful hypothetical or symbolic models of nature.

New discoveries in the laboratory paralleled the philosophical challenge to nineteenth-century science. With those discoveries the comfortable world of supposedly "complete" nineteenth-century physics vanished forever. In December 1895 Wilhelm Roentgen (1845–1923) published a paper on

rather as a combined continuum. Moreover, the measurement of space and time depends on the observer as well as on the entities being measured. In 1927 Werner Heisenberg (1901–1976) set forth the uncertainty principle, according to which the behavior of subatomic particles is a matter of statistical probability rather than of exactly determinable cause and effect. Much that only fifty years earlier had seemed certain and unquestionable about the physical universe now once again became problematical.

Nineteenth-century popularizers of science had urged its importance as a path to rational living and decision making. By the early twentieth century the developments in the scientific world itself had dashed such optimistic hopes. The mathematical complexity of twentieth-century physics meant that despite valiant efforts, science would rarely again be successfully popularized. However, through applied technology and further research in physics and medicine, science also affected daily living more than ever before. Consequently, nonscientists in legal, business, and public life have been called on to make decisions involving technological matters that they rarely can or do understand in depth or detail and have

Marie (1869-1934) and Pierre Curie (1859-1906) were two of the most important figures in the advance of physics and chemistry. Marie was born in Poland but worked in France for most of her life. She is credited with the discovery of radium, for which she was awarded the Nobel Prize in Chemistry in 1911. [Bildarchiv Preussischer Kulturbesitz]

his discovery of X rays, a form of energy that penetrated various opaque materials. His paper was soon followed by major steps in the exploration of radioactivity. In 1896 Henri Becquerel (1852–1908), through experiments based on Roentgen's work, found that uranium emitted a similar form of energy. The next year J. J. Thomson (1856–1940) formulated the theory of the electron. The interior world of the atom had become a new area for human exploration. In 1902 Ernest Rutherford (1871–1937), who had been Thomson's assistant, explained the cause of radiation through the disintegration of the atoms of radioactive materials. Shortly thereafter he speculated on the immense store of energy present in the atom.

The discovery of radioactivity and discontent with the existing mechanical models led to revolutionary theories in physics. In 1900 Max Planck (1858–1947) pioneered the articulation of the quantum theory of energy, according to which energy is a series of discrete quantities or packets rather than a continuous stream. In 1905 Albert Einstein (1879–1955) published his first epoch-making papers on relativity. He contended that time and space exist not separately but

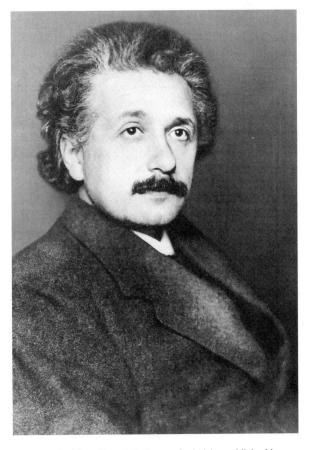

The physicist Albert Einstein's theory of relativity, published in 1905, revolutionized fundamental concepts in physics. [Bildarchiv Preussischer Kulturbesitz]

thus become increasingly dependent upon persons equipped with scientific expertise.

Philosophy: Revolt Against Reason

Philosophical circles were questioning whether rational thinking could adequately address the human situation.

Friedrich Nietzsche   No late-nineteenth-century writer better exemplified this new attitude than the German philosopher Friedrich Nietzsche (1844–1900). He was wholly at odds with the predominant values of the age. At one time or another he attacked Christianity, democracy, nationalism, rationality, science, and progress. He sought less to change values than to probe their sources in the human mind and character. He wanted not only to tear away the masks of respectable life but also to explore how human beings made such masks.

His first important work was *The Birth of Tragedy* (1872), in which he urged that the nonrational aspects of human nature were as important and noble as the rational characteristics. He insisted on the positive function of instinct and ecstasy in human life. To limit life to strictly rational behavior was to impoverish it. In Nietzsche's view, the strength for the heroic life and the highest artistic achievement arose from sources beyond rationality.

In later works, such as the prose poem *Thus Spake Zarathustra* (1883), Nietzsche criticized democracy and Christianity. Both would lead only to the mediocrity of sheepish masses. He announced the death of God and proclaimed the coming of the Overman *(Ubermensch)*, who would embody heroism and greatness. This term was frequently interpreted to refer to some mode of superman or superrace, but such was not Nietzsche's intention. He was highly critical of contemporary racism and antisemitism. What he sought was a return to the heroism that he associated with Greek life in the Homeric age. He thought that the values of Christianity and of bourgeois morality prevented humankind from achieving life on a heroic level. Those moralities forbade too much of human nature from fulfilling and expressing itself. Christianity demanded a useless and debilitating sacrifice of the flesh and spirit rather than full-

Friedrich Nietzsche (1844–1900) was the most influential German philosopher of the late nineteenth century. His books, which challenged existing morality and values, have exerted a powerful influence on twentieth-century literature and philosophy. Detail from portrait by Kurt Stoeving, 1904. [Staatliche Museen zu Berlin/Photograph: Klaus Goken/Bildarchiv Preussischer Kulturbesitz]

blooded heroic living and daring. He observed, "War and courage have accomplished more great things than love of neighbor."[1]

Nietzsche sought to discover not what is good and what is evil but the social and psychological sources of the judgment of good and evil. He declared, "There are no moral phenomena at all, but only a moral interpretation of phenomena."[2] He dared to raise the question of whether morality itself was valuable: "We need a critique of moral values; the value of these values themselves must first be called in question."[3] In Nietzsche's view morality was a human convention that had no independent existence apart from humankind. For Nietzsche this discovery did not condemn morality but liberated human beings to create life-affirming instead of life-denying values, values that would glorify pride, assertiveness, and strength rather than meekness, humility, and weakness.

Birth of Psychoanalysis

A determination to probe beneath surface or public appearances united the major figures of late-nineteenth-century science, art, and philosophy. They sought to discern the various undercurrents, tensions, and complexities that lay below the smooth, calm surfaces of hard atoms, respectable families, rationality, and social relationships. As a result of their theories and discoveries, articulate, educated Europeans could never again view the surface of life with smugness or complacency or even with much confidence. No single intellectual development more clearly and stunningly exemplified this trend than the emergence of psychoanalysis through the work of Sigmund Freud (1856–1939).

Freud was born into an Austrian Jewish family that settled in Vienna soon after his birth. In 1886 he opened his medical practice in Vienna, where he continued to live until driven out by the Nazis in 1938. All of Freud's research and writing were done from the base of his medical practice. His earliest medical interests had been psychic disorders, to which he sought to apply the critical method of science. In late 1885 he had studied for a few months in Paris with Jean-Martin Charcot (1825–1893), who used hypnosis to treat hysteria. In 1895 Freud and another Viennese physician, Josef Breuer (1842–1925) published *Studies in Hysteria*.

In the mid–1890s Freud changed his technique. He abandoned hypnosis and allowed his patients to talk freely and spontaneously about themselves. Repeatedly, he found that they associated their particular neurotic symptoms with experiences related to earlier experiences, going back to childhood. He also noticed that sexual matters were significant in his patients' problems. By 1897 he formulated a theory of infantile sexuality, according to which sexual drives and energy exist in infants and do not simply emerge at puberty. In Freud's view, human beings are creatures of sexuality from birth through adulthood. He thus radically questioned the concept of childhood innocence. He also portrayed the little-discussed or little-acknowledged matter of sex as one of the bases of mental order and disorder.

Freud also examined the psychic phenomena of dreams. Romantic writers had taken dreams seriously, but no one had examined them scientifically. As a good rationalist, Freud believed that the irrational content of dreams must have a reasonable, scientific explanation. His examination led him to reconsider the general nature of the human mind. He concluded that during dreams, unconscious wishes, desires, and drives that were excluded from everyday conscious life and experience enjoyed relatively free play in the mind. He argued, "The dream is the (disguised) fulfillment of a

Sigmund Freud forced a reconsideration of the role of rationality in human motivation. After Freud it was no longer possible to see reason as the sole determinant of behavior. [Bildarchiv Preussischer Kulturbesitz]

[1] Walter Kaufmann, ed. and trans., *The Portable Nietzsche* (New York: Viking, 1967), p. 159.
[2] Walter Kaufmann, ed. and trans., *The Basic Writings of Nietzsche* (New York: The Modern Library, 1968), p. 275.
[3] Kaufman, p. 456.

(suppressed, repressed) wish."[4] During the waking hours the mind repressed or censored those wishes, which were as important to one's psychological makeup as conscious thought. In fact, those unconscious drives and desires contributed to conscious behavior. Freud related these concepts to his idea of infantile sexuality in *The Interpretation of Dreams* (1900). It was his most important book.

In later books and essays, Freud continued to argue for the significance of the human unconscious. He developed a new model of the internal organization of the mind. According to this model, the mind is an arena for struggle and conflict among three entities: the id, the ego, and the superego. The id consists of amoral, irrational, driving instincts for sexual gratification, aggression, and general physical and sensual pleasures. The superego embodies the external moral imperatives and expectations imposed on the personality by society and culture. The ego is the mediator between the impulses of the id and the asceticism of the superego. The ego allows the personality to cope with the inner and outer demands of its existence. One's personality, as expressed in everyday behavior, reflects the result on the ego of the partial and unconscious repression of the impulses of the id to satisfy the demands of the external world embodied in the superego. Freud did not advocate thrusting off all repression. He believed that excessive repression could lead to mental disorder, but that some repression of sexuality and aggression was necessary for civilized living and the survival of humankind.

Freud was a son of the Enlightenment. Like the *philosophes*, he was a realist who wanted human beings to live free of fear and illusions by rationally understanding themselves and their world. He saw the personalities of human beings as determined by finite physical and mental forces in a finite world. He was hostile to religion and spoke of it as an illusion. Freud, like the writers of the eighteenth century, wished to see civilization and humane behavior prevail. However, more fully than those predecessors, he understood the immense sacrifice of instinctual drives required for civilized behavior. He understood how many previously unsuspected obstacles lay in the way of rationality. Freud believed that the sacrifice and struggle were worthwhile, but he was pessimistic about the future of civilization in the West.

Freud's work marked the beginning of the psychoanalytic movement. By 1910 he had gathered around him a small but highly able group of disciples. Several of his early followers soon developed theories of which the master disapproved. The most important of these dissenters was Carl Jung (1875–1961), a Swiss whom for many years Freud regarded as

his most distinguished and promising student. Before World War I, however, the two men had come to a parting of the ways. By the 1920s psychoanalysis had become even more fragmented as a movement. Nonetheless, in its several varieties it touched not only twentieth-century psychology but also sociology, anthropology, religious studies, and literary theory. However, despite its impact on European thought and upon thinking in the United States, psychoanalysis exerted at best modest influence elsewhere in the world. Toward the close of the century psychoanalysis came under much criticism, and the future of its influence in the next century remains to be determined.

Transformation in Political and Social Thought

Retreat from Rationalism in Politics

Both nineteenth-century liberals and nineteenth-century socialists agreed that society and politics could be guided according to rational principles and that rational analysis could identify and solve the problems of society. They generally felt that once given the vote, individuals would behave in their own rational political self-interest. Improvement of society and the human condition was possible through education. By 1900 these views were under attack in both theory and practice. Political scientists and sociologists painted politics as frequently irrational. Racial theorists questioned whether rationality and education could affect human society at all.

During this period, however, one major social theorist remained profoundly impressed by the role of reason in human society. The German sociologist Max Weber (1864–1920) regarded the emergence of rationalization throughout society as the major development of human history. According to this view, rationalization displayed itself in both the development of scientific knowledge and the rise of bureaucratic organization. Weber saw bureaucratization as the most fundamental feature of modern social life. He used this view to oppose Marx's concept of the development of capitalism as the driving force in modern society. Bureaucratization involved the extreme division of labor, requiring individuals to fit themselves into some particular small role in a much larger organization. Furthermore, Weber believed that in modern society people derived their own self-images and senses of personal worth from their positions in these organizations. Weber also contended, again in contrast to Marx, that noneconomic factors might account for major developments in human history. For example, in his most famous essay, *The Protestant Ethic and the Spirit of Capitalism* (1905), Weber traced much of the rational character of capitalist enterprise to the ascetic reli-

[4]*The Basic Writings of Sigmund Freud*, trans. by A. A. Brill (New York: The Modern Library, 1938), p. 235.

gious doctrines of Puritanism. The Puritans, in his opinion, had accumulated wealth and had worked for worldly success less for its own sake than to assure themselves that they stood among the elect of God.

In emphasizing the individual and the dominant role of rationality, Weber differed from many contemporary social scientists such as Gustave Le-Bon, Émile Durkheim, and Georges Sorel in France; and Graham Wallas in England. Le Bon (1841–1931) was a psychologist who explored the activity of crowds and mobs. He believed that crowds abandoned rational behavior. Sorel (1847–1922) argued in *Reflections on Violence* (1908) that people did not pursue rationally perceived goals but were led to action by collectively shared ideals. Durkheim (1858–1917) and Wallas (1858–1932) became deeply interested in the necessity of shared values and activities in a society. These elements, rather than a logical analysis of the social situation, bound human beings together. Instinct, habit, and affections instead of reason directed human social behavior. Besides playing down the function of reason in society, these theorists emphasized the role of collective groups in politics rather than the individual formerly championed by the liberals.

Racial Theory

The same tendencies to question or even to deny the constructive activity of reason in human affairs and to sacrifice the individual to the group manifested themselves in theories of race. Racial thinking had long existed in Europe. Renaissance explorers had displayed considerable prejudice against nonwhites. Since at least the eighteenth century, biologists and anthropologists had classified human beings according to the color of their skin, their language, and their stage of civilization. Late-eighteenth-century linguistic scholars had observed similarities between many of the European languages and Sanskrit. They then postulated the existence of an ancient race called the *Aryans*, who had spoken the original language from which the rest derived. During the Romantic period, writers had called the different cultures of Europe *races*. The debates over slavery in the European colonies and the United States had given further opportunity for the development of racial theory. However, in the late nineteenth century the concept of race emerged as a single dominant explanation of the history and the character of large groups of people.

Arthur de Gobineau (1816–1882), a reactionary French diplomat, enunciated the first important theory of race as the major determinant of human history. In his four-volume *Essay on the Inequality of the Human Races* (1853–1854) Gobineau portrayed the troubles of Western civilization as being the result of the long degeneration of the original white Aryan race. It had unwisely intermarried with the inferior yellow and black races, thus diluting the greatness and ability that originally existed in its blood. Gobineau saw no way to reverse this degeneration.

Gobineau's essay remained relatively obscure for years. In the meantime, a growing literature by anthropologists and explorers helped to spread racial thinking. In the wake of Darwin's theory, the concept of survival of the fittest was applied to races and nations. The recognition of the animal nature of humankind made the racial idea all the more persuasive. Houston Stewart Chamberlain (1855–1927), an Englishman who settled in Germany, drew together these strands of racial thought into the two volumes of his *Foundations of the Nineteenth Century* (1899). He championed the concept of biological determinism through race, but he was somewhat more optimistic than Gobineau. Chamberlain believed that through genetics, the human race could be improved and even that a superior race could be developed. Chamberlain added another element. He pointed to the Jews as the major enemy of European racial regeneration. Chamberlain's book and the lesser works on which it drew thus aided the spread of antisemitism. Other writings in Germany emphasized the supposed racial and cultural dangers posed by the Jews to traditional German national life.

Antisemitism and the Birth of Zionism

Political and racial antisemitism, which have cast such dark shadows across the twentieth century, emerged in part from this atmosphere of racial thought and the retreat from rationality in politics. Religious antisemitism dated from at least the Middle Ages. Since the French Revolution western European Jews had gradually gained entry into the civil life of Britain, France, and Germany. Popular antisemitism, which identified the Jewish community with money and banking interests, persisted. During the last third of the century, as finance capitalism changed the economic structure of Europe, people pressured by the changes became hostile toward the Jewish community. This was especially true of the socially and economically insecure middle class. In Vienna Mayor Karl Lueger (1844–1910) used this kind of antisemitism as a major attraction to his successful Christian Socialist Party. In Germany the ultraconservative Lutheran chaplain Adolf Stoecker (1835–1909) revived antisemitism. The Dreyfus Affair in France allowed a new flowering of hatred toward the Jews.

To this already ugly atmosphere, racial thought contributed the belief that no matter to what extent Jews assimilated themselves and their families into the culture of their country, their Jewishness—and thus their alleged danger to the society—would remain. The problem of race was not in the character but in the blood of the Jew. An important Jewish response to this new, rabid outbreak of antisemitism

Herzl Calls for the Establishment of a Jewish State

In 1896 Theodor Herzl published his pamphlet The Jewish State. Herzl had lived in France during the turmoil and antisemitism associated with the Dreyfus affair. He became convinced that only the establishment of a separate state for Jews would halt the various outbreaks of antisemitism that characterized late-nineteenth-century European political and cultural life. Following the publication of this pamphlet, Herzl began to organize the Zionist movement among Jews in both eastern and western Europe.

Why does Herzl define what he calls the Jewish Question as a national question? What objections does he anticipate to the founding of a Jewish state? Why does he believe the founding of a Jewish state will be an effective move against anti-Semitism?

The idea which I develop in this pamphlet is an age-old one: the establishment of a Jewish State.

The world resounds with outcries against the Jews, and this is what awakens the dormant idea. . . .

I believe I understand anti-Semitism, a highly complex movement. I view it from the standpoint of a Jew, but without hatred or fear. I think I can discern in it the elements of vulgar sport, of common economic rivalry, of inherited prejudice, of religious intolerance—but also of a supposed need for self-defense. To my mind, the Jewish Question is neither a social nor a religious one, even though it may assume these and other guises. It is a national question, and to solve it we must first of all establish it as an international political problem which will have to be settled by the civilized nations of the world in council.

We are a people, one people.

Everywhere we have sincerely endeavored to merge with the national communities surrounding us and to preserve only the faith of our fathers. We are not permitted to do so. . . .

And will some people say that the venture is hopeless, because even if we obtain the land and the sovereignty only the poor people will go along? They are the very ones we need first! Only desperate men make good conquerors.

Will anybody say, Oh yes, if it were possible it would have been done by now?

It was not possible before. It is possible now. As recently as a hundred, even fifty years ago it would have been a dream. Today it is all real. The rich, who have an epicurean acquaintance with all technical advance, know very well what can be done with money. And this is how it will be: Precisely the poor and plain people, who have no idea of the power that man already exercises over the forces of Nature, will have the greatest faith in the new message. For they have never lost their hope of the Promised Land. . . .

Now, all this may seem to be a long-drawn-out affair. Even in the most favorable circumstances it might be many years before the founding of the State is under way. In the meantime, Jews will be ridiculed, offended, abused, whipped, plundered, and slain in a thousand different localities. But no; just as soon as we begin to implement the plan, anti-Semitism will immediately grind to a halt everywhere. . . .

From Theodor Herzl, *The Jewish State*. Copyright © 1970 The Herzl Press, pp. 27, 33, 109, as quoted in William W. Hallo, David B. Ruderman, and Michael Stanislawski, eds., *Heritage: Civilization and the Jews Source Reader*. Copyright © 1984 Praeger, pp. 234–235.

---

was the launching in 1896 of the Zionist movement to found a separate Jewish state. Its founder was the Austro-Hungarian Theodor Herzl (1860–1904). The conviction in 1894 of Captain Dreyfus in France and Karl Lueger's election in 1895 as mayor of Vienna, as well as Herzl's personal experiences of discrimination, convinced him that liberal politics and the institutions of the liberal state could not protect the Jews in Europe or ensure that they would be treated justly. In 1896 Herzl published *The Jewish State*, in which he called for a separate state in which the Jews of the world might be assured of those rights and liberties that they should be enjoying in the liberal states of Europe. Furthermore, Herzl followed the tactics of late-century mass democratic politics by directing his appeal in particular to the economically poor Jews who lived in the ghettos of eastern Europe and the slums of western Europe. The original call to Zionism thus combined a rejection of the antisemitism of Europe with a desire to establish some of the ideals of both liberalism and socialism in a state outside Europe.

Late-Century Nationalism

Racial thinking and revived antisemitism were part of a wider late-century aggressive nationalism. Previously, nationalism had been a literary and liberal movement. Writers had sought to develop what they regarded as the historically distinct qualities of particular national or ethnic literatures. The liberal nationalists had hoped to redraw the map of Europe to re-

Theodor Herzl's visions of a Jewish state would eventually lead to the creation of Israel in 1948. [BBC Hulton/Corbis-Bettmann]

flect ethnic boundaries. The drive for the unification of Italy and Germany had been a major cause, as had the liberation of Poland from foreign domination. The various national groups of the Habsburg Empire had also sought emancipation from Austrian domination.

From the 1870s onward, however, nationalism became a movement with mass support, well-financed organizations, and political parties. Nationalists tended to redefine nationality in terms of race and blood. The new nationalism opposed the internationalism of both liberalism and socialism. The ideal of nationality was used to overcome the pluralism of class, religion, and geography. The nation and its duties replaced religion for many secularized people. It sometimes became a secular religion in the hands of state school teachers, who were replacing the clergy as the instructors of youth. This aggressive, racist nationalism would prove to be the most powerful ideology of the early twentieth century.

Women and Modern Thought

Despite the often radically new ideas about the world and society that shook European thought after 1850, views of women and their roles in society remained remarkably unchanged.

Antifeminism in Late-Century Thought

Much of the biological thought that challenged religious ideas and the received wisdom in science actually reinforced the traditional view of women as creatures weaker and less able than men. Darwin himself expressed such views in his scientific writings. Medical thought concurred. Whatever social changes were to be wrought through science, significant changes in the organization of the home and the relationship of men and women were not among them.

This conservative and hostile understanding of women manifested itself in several ways within the scientific community. In London in 1860 the Ethnological Society excluded women from its discussions on the grounds that the customs of primitive peoples were an unfit subject for women and that women were amateurs whose presence would lower the level of the discussion. T. H. Huxley, the great defender of Darwin, took the lead in this exclusion as he had in a previous exclusion of women from meetings of the Geological Society. Male scientists also believed women should not discuss reproduction or other sexual matters. Huxley, in public lectures, claimed to have found scientific evidence of the inferiority of women to men. Karl Vogt (1817–1895), a leading German anthropologist, held similar views. Darwin would repeat the ideas of both Huxley and Vogt in his *Descent of Man*. Late Victorian anthropologists tended likewise to assign women, as well as nonwhite races, an inferior place in the human family. Nonetheless, both Darwin and Huxley supported education for women.

The position of women in Freud's thought has always been controversial. Many of his earliest patients, upon whose histories he developed his theories, were women. Critics have claimed, nonetheless, that Freud portrayed women as incomplete human beings who might be inevitably destined to unhappy mental lives. He saw the natural destiny of women as motherhood, and their greatest fulfillment the rearing of sons. The first psychoanalysts were trained as medical doctors, and their views of women reflected contemporary medical education, which, like much of the rest of the scientific establishment, tended to portray women as inferior. Distinguished women psychoanalysts, such as Karen Horney (1885–1952) and Melanie Klein (1882–1960), would later sharply challenge Freud's views on women, and other writers would try to establish a psychoanalytic basis for feminism. Nonetheless, the psychoanalytic profession would remain dominated by men, as would nonpsychoanalytic academic psychology. Since psychology would increasingly influence child-rearing practices and domestic relations law in the twentieth century, it would, ironically, give men a large impact in the one area of social activity that women had dominated.

The social sciences of the era similarly reinforced traditional gender roles. Virtually all major theorists believed that women's role in reproduction and child rearing demanded a social position inferior to men. Auguste Comte, whose thought in this area owed much to Rousseau (1712–1778), portrayed women as biologically and intellectually inferior to men. Herbert Spencer thought women could never achieve genuine equality with men. Émile Durkheim portrayed women as essentially creatures of feeling and family rather than intellect. Max Weber favored improvements in the social condition of women but did not really support significant changes in their social roles or in their relationship to men. Virtually all of the early sociologists took a conservative view of marriage, the family, child rearing, and divorce.

New Directions in Feminism

The feminists of the turn of the century, more than any of their predecessors, demanded a rethinking of gender roles. They normally urged equal treatment of women under the law and the right to vote, but they also contended that the relationship of men and women within marriage and the family required rethinking. They set forth much of the feminist agenda for the twentieth century.

Sexual Morality and the Family   In various nations, middle-class women began to challenge the double standard of sexual morality and the traditional male-dominated family. Often this challenge took the form of action relating to prostitution.

Between 1864 and 1886 English prostitutes were subject to the Contagious Diseases Acts. The police in certain cities with naval or military bases could require any woman identified as or suspected of being a prostitute to undergo immediate internal medical examination for venereal disease. Those found to have a disease could without legal recourse be confined for months to lock hospitals (women's hospitals for the treatment of venereal diseases). The law took no action against their male customers. Indeed, the purpose of the laws were to protect men, presumably sailors and soldiers, not the women themselves, from infection.

These laws angered English middle-class women who believed that the working conditions and the poverty imposed on so many working-class women were the true causes of prostitution. They framed the issue in the context of their own efforts to prove that women were as human and rational as men and thus properly subject to equal treatment. They saw poor women being made victims of the same kind of discrimination that prevented themselves from entering the universities and professions. The Contagious Diseases Acts assumed that women were inferior to men and treated them as less than rational creatures. The laws literally took women's bodies from their own control and put them under the control of male customers, medical men, and the police. They denied to poor women the freedoms that all men enjoyed in English society.

By 1869 the Ladies' National Association for the Repeal of the Contagious Diseases Acts, a distinctly middle-class organization led by Josephine Butler (1828–1906), began actively to oppose these laws. The acts were suspended in 1883 and repealed in 1886. Government and police regulation of prostitution roused similar movements in other nations, which adopted the English movement as a model. In Vienna during the 1890s the General Austrian Women's Association, led by Auguste Ficke (1833–1916), combated the introduction of legally regulated prostitution, which would have put women under the control of police authorities. In Germany women's groups divided between those who would have penalized prostitutes and those who saw them as victims of male society. By 1900 the latter had come to dominate, although tensions between the groups persisted.

The Swedish feminist Ellen Key maintained that motherhood was so crucial to society that the support of mothers and children should be a government responsibility. [Hulton Getty Picture Collection/Tony Stone Images]

The feminist groups that demanded the abolition of laws that punished prostitutes without questioning the behavior of their customers were challenging the double standard and, by extension, the traditional relationship of men and women in marriage. In their view, marriage should be a free union of equals with men and women sharing responsibility for their children. In Germany, the Mothers' Protection League *(Bund für Mutterschutz)* contended that both married and unmarried mothers required the help of the state, including leaves for pregnancy and child care. This radical group emphasized the need to rethink all sexual morality. In Sweden, Ellen Key (1849–1926), in *The Century of the Child* (1900) and *The Renaissance of Motherhood* (1914), both widely read in Europe, maintained that motherhood was one of women's chief roles and was so crucial to society that the government, rather than husbands, should support mothers and their children.

Virtually all turn-of-the-century feminists in one way or another supported wider sexual freedom for women, often claiming that it would benefit society as well as improve women's lives. Many of the early advocates of contraception had also been influenced by social Darwinism. They hoped that limiting the number of children would allow more healthy and intelligent children to survive. Such was the outlook of Marie Stopes (1880–1958), an Englishwoman with a doctorate in geology who pioneered contraceptive clinics in the poor districts of London.

Women Defining Their Own Lives For Josephine Butler and Auguste Ficke, as well as other Continental feminists, achieving legal and social equality for women would be one step toward transforming Europe from a male-dominated society to one in which both men and women could control their own destinies. Ficke wrote, "Our final goal is therefore not the acknowledgement of rights, but the elevation of our intellectual and moral level, *the development of our personality*."[5] Increasingly, feminists would concentrate on freeing and developing women's personalities through better education and government financial support for women engaged in traditional social roles, whether or not they had gained the vote.

Some women also became active within socialist circles. There they argued that the socialist transformation of society should include major reforms for women. Socialist parties usually had all-male leadership. Most male socialist leaders, including Lenin and later Stalin, were intolerant of demands for changes in the family or greater sexual freedom for either men or women. Nonetheless, socialist writings began to include calls for improving the economic situation of women that were compatible with more advanced feminist ideals.

[5]Quoted in Harriet Anderson, *Utopian Feminism: Women's Movements in Fin-de-Siècle Vienna* (New Haven, CT: Yale University Press, 1992), p. 13.

Virginia Woolf charted the changing sentiments of a world with most of the nineteenth-century social and moral certainties removed. In *A Room of One's Own* she also challenged some of the received notions of feminist thought, asking whether women writers should bring to their work any separate qualities they possessed as women, and concluding that men and women writers should strive to share each other's sensibilities. [Hulton Getty Picture Collection/Tony Stone Images]

It was within literary circles, however, that feminist writers often most clearly articulated the problems that they now understood themselves to face. Distinguished women authors, such as Virginia Woolf (1882–1941), were actually doing, on a more or less equal footing, something that men had always done: leading some to wonder whether simple equality was the main issue. Woolf's *A Room of One's Own* (1929) became one of the fundamental texts of twentieth-century feminist literature. In it she discussed the difficulties that women of both brilliance and social standing encountered in being taken seriously as writers and intellectuals. She concluded that a woman who wished to write required both a room of her own, meaning a space not dominated by male institutions, and an adequate independent income. But Woolf was concerned with

Virginia Woolf Urges Women to Write

In 1928 Virginia Woolf, the English novelist, delivered two papers at women's colleges at Cambridge University. Those papers provided the basis for A Room of One's Own, *published a year later. In this essay Woolf discussed the difficulty a woman writer confronted in finding previous women authors as models. She also outlined many of the obstacles that women faced in achieving the education, the time, and the income that would allow them to write. At the close of her essay she urged women to begin to write so that future women authors would have models. She then set forth an image of Shakespeare's sister who, lacking such models, had not written anything, but who through the collective efforts of women might in the future emerge as a great writer because she would have the literary models of the women Woolf addressed to follow and to imitate.*

How does Woolf's fiction of Shakespeare's sister establish a benchmark for women writers? What does Woolf mean by the common life through which women will need to work to become independent writers? Why does she emphasize the need for women to have both income and space if they are to become independent writers?

A thousand pens are ready to suggest what you should do and what effect you will have. My own suggestion is a little fantastic, I admit; I prefer, therefore, to put it in the form of fiction.

I told you in the course of this paper that Shakespeare had a sister; but do not look for her in Sir Sidney Lee's life of the poet. She died young—alas, she never wrote a word. She lies buried where the omnibuses now stop, opposite the Elephant and Castle [a London intersection]. Now my belief is that this poet who never wrote a word and was buried at the crossroads still lives. She lives in you and in me, and in many other women who are not here tonight, for they are washing up the dishes and putting the children to bed. But she lives; for great poets do not die; they are continuing presences; they need only the opportunity to walk among us in the flesh. This opportunity, as I think, it is now coming within your power to give her. For my belief is that if we live another century or so—I am talking of the common life which is the real life and not of the little separate lives which we live as individuals—and have five hundred [pounds income] a year each of us and rooms of our own; if we have the habit of freedom and the courage to write exactly what we think; if we escape a little from the common sitting-room and see human beings not always in their relation to each other but in relation to reality; and the sky, too, and the trees or whatever it may be in themselves; . . . if we face the fact, for it is a fact, that there is no arm to cling to, but that we go alone and that our relation is to the world of reality and not only to the world of men and women, then the opportunity will come and the dead poet who was Shakespeare's sister will put on the body which she has so often laid down. Drawing her life from the lives of the unknown who were her forerunners, as her brother did before her, she will be born. As for her coming without that preparation, without that effort on our part, without that determination that when she is born again she shall find it possible to live and write her poetry, that we cannot expect, for that would be impossible. But I maintain that she would come if we worked for her, and that so to work, even in poverty and obscurity, is worth while.

From Virginia Woolf, *A Room of One's Own*. Copyright © 1974 The Hogarth Press, pp. 170–172.

---

more than asserting the right of women to participate in intellectual life. Establishing a new stance for feminist writers, she asked whether women as writers must imitate men or should bring to their endeavors separate intellectual and psychological qualities that they possessed as women. As she had challenged some of the literary conventions of the traditional novel in her fiction, in *A Room of One's Own* she challenged some of the received notions of feminist thought and concluded that male and female writers must be able to think as both men and women and share the sensibilities of each. She thus sought to open the whole question of gender definition.

By World War I feminism in Europe, fairly or not, had become associated in the popular imagination with challenges to traditional gender roles and sexual morality and with either socialism or political radicalism. So when extremely conservative political movements arose between the world wars, their leaders often emphasized traditional roles for women and traditional ideas about sexual morality.

Ideas associated with feminism encountered a mixed reception in the non-Western World. Feminist voices have appeared on every continent, but they have often encountered resistance. In some areas, such as India and Pakistan, women have achieved the highest political office and have entered the educated professions. The fundamentalist Islamic revival, by contrast, had asserted a much more traditional role for women. Worldwide, women still stand far behind their male counterparts in terms of education, economic advance, and healthcare coverage.

IN WORLD PERSPECTIVE

Intellectual Change

The remarkable scientific achievements of the European intellectual community during the second half of the nineteenth century were exported with mixed results. Racism and social Darwinism came to undergird much of the ideology of imperialism. Racial thinking allowed Europeans to believe that they were inherently superior to other peoples and cultures. The concept of survival of the fittest provided for many Europeans a pattern for their relations with the rest of the world. In both Europe and the United States nonwhites were regarded as inferior. State governments in the southern United States enacted segregation laws based in part on racial thinking. In the opinion of certain scientific writers, non-European peoples stood on a lower level of the evolutionary ladder. Consequently, when European states conquered and administered large portions of Africa and Asia, they justified their actions partly on the grounds that the native peoples were less fit than Europeans to govern themselves. Racial thinking of this kind informed the minds of virtually all colonial administrators.

The technology and scientific theories that had made the Second Industrial Revolution possible also provided the technological superiority that allowed Europe and the United States to dominate so much of the world between 1850 and 1945. That technological domination gave plausibility to the conclusions of racial thinking. However, science and technology could be copied and eventually turned against its originators. Japan after the Meiji restoration (1858) successfully set out to copy the science as well as the political administration associated with modern Western thought. In doing so, it succeeded in defending itself against the intrusions of the West and defeated a major Western power, Russia, in war.

China, at the same time, failed to embrace modern science and technology and fell victim to both the Western powers and Japan. However, after those humiliations, at the turn of the century China began to abandon its dedication to Confucian education. Reforming leaders embraced a vast spectrum of Western ideas, including social Darwinism and socialism. By the end of World War I a strong sense of nationalism also permeated China. The need to embrace science and a concern for social reform combined in China to contribute to the appeal of Marxism, which was viewed as a form of scientific socialism.

The emergence of a strong industrialized Japan and of a China stirred by nationalism and Marxist revolution thus illustrates the double influence of late-nineteenth-century Western ideas. Those scientific and political ideas first led to the degradation of those Asian peoples. In turn, other Western ideas, along with long-standing Asian ideas and values, provided the technological and ideological basis for national revivals leading those nations to challenge Western imperialism.

Review Questions

1. How would you account for the dominance of science in the thought of the second half of the nineteenth century? What were some of the major changes in scientific outlook between 1850 and 1914? Comment especially on advances in physics. How would you define positivism? Describe Darwin and Wallace's theory of natural selection. What effect did it have on theories of ethics, on Christianity, and on European views of human nature?

2. How and why did Christianity come under attack in the late nineteenth century? Discuss the politics of Pius IX, Leo XIII, and Pius X. Why was Leo XIII regarded as a liberal pope? How do you account for the resilience of the papacy during this period of attack on the church?

3. How did Nietzsche and Freud challenge traditional middle class and religious morality? Would you describe Freud more as a product of the Enlightenment or of Romanticism?

4. How do you account for the fear and hostility many late-nineteenth-century intellectuals displayed toward women? How did Freud view the position of women? What were some of the social and political issues affecting women in the late nineteenth and early twentieth centuries and how did reformers confront them? What new directions did feminism take?

5. What was the character of late-nineteenth-century racial theory? How did it become associated with antisemitism? What personal and contemporary political experiences led Herzl to develop the idea of Zionism?

Suggested Readings ———

R. ARON, *Main Currents in Sociological Thought*, 2 vols. (1965, 1967). An introduction to the founders of the science.

S. ASCHHEIM, *The Nietzsche Legacy in Germany* (1992). Important study of the influence of Nietzsche's thought.

S. AVINERI, *The Making of Modern Zionism: The Intellectual Origins of the Jewish State* (1981). An excellent introduction to the development of Zionist thought.

S. BARROWS, *Distorting Mirrors: Visions of the Crowd in Late Nineteenth-Century France* (1981). An important and imaginative examination of crowd psychology as it related to social tension in France.

M. D. BIDDIS, *Father of Racist Ideology: The Social and Political Thought of Count Gobineau* (1970). Sets the subject in the more general context of nineteenth-century thought.

D. BLACKBOURNE, *Marpingen: Apparitions of the Virgin Mary in Nineteenth-Century Germany* (1993). A major study of popular religious movments and the religious revival of the late century.

P. BOWLER, *The Eclipse of Darwinism: Anti-Darwinian Evolution Theories in the Decades Around 1900* (1983). A major study of the fate of Darwinian theory in the nineteenth-century scientific community.

P. BOWLER, *Evolution: The History of an Idea* (1989). An outstanding survey of the subject.

O. CHADWICK, *The Secularization of the European Mind in the Nineteenth Century* (1975). The best available treatment.

A. DANTO, *Nietzsche as Philosopher* (1965). A very helpful and well-organized introduction.

A. DESMOND AND J. MOORE, *Darwin* (1992). A brilliant biography.

J. EFRON, *Defenders of the Race: Jewish Doctors and Race Science in Fin-de-Siecle Europe* (1994). A study of the manner in which Jewish physicians responded to late-century antisemitic racial thought.

P. GAY, *Freud: A Life for Our Time* (1988). A major new biography.

C. C. GILLISPIE, *Genesis and Geology* (1951). A classic discussion of the impact of modern geological theory during the nearly nineteenth century.

R. HELMSTADTER, *Freedom and Religion in the Nineteenth Century* (1997). A series of important essays primarily on church-state relations.

H. S. HUGHES, *Consciousness and Society: The Reorientation of European Social Thought, 1890–1930* (1958). A wide-ranging discussion of the revolt against positivism.

W. IRVINE, *Apes, Angels, and Victorians* (1955). A lively and sound account of Darwin and Huxley.

C. JUNGNICKEL AND R. MCCORMMACH, *Intellectual Mastery of Nature: Theoretical Physics from Ohm to Einstein*, 2 vols. (1986). A demanding but powerful exploration of the creation of modern physics.

W. A. KAUFMANN, *Nietzsche: Philosopher, Psychologist, Antichrist*, rev. ed. (1968). An exposition of Neitzsche's thought and its sources.

J. T. KLOPPENBERG, *Uncertain Victory: Social Democracy and Progressivism in European and American Thought* (1986). An extremely important comparative study.

W. LACQUER, *A History of Zionism.* (1989). The most extensive one-volume treatment.

K. S. LATOURETTE, *A History of the Expansion of Christianity (1837–1945)* (1975). Remains the most extensive coverage of the missionary movement.

B. LIGHTMAN, *The Origins of Agnosticism: Victorian Unbelief and the Limits of Knowledge* (1987). The best study of the subject.

J. MORRELL AND A. THACKRAY, *Gentlemen of Science: Early Years of the British Association for the Advancement of Science* (1981). An important study that examines the role of science in early and mid-nineteenth-century Britain.

G. L. MOSSE, *Toward the Final Solution: A History of European Racism* (1978). A sound introduction.

S. NEIL, *A History of Christian Missions* (1986). A good introduction with excellent guides to further reading.

L. POLIAKOV, *The Aryan Myth: A History of Racist and Nationalist Ideas in Europe* (1971). The best introduction to the problem.

P. G. J. PULZER, *The Rise of Political Anti-Semitism in Germany and Austria* (revised, 1989). A sound discussion of antisemitism in the world of central European politics.

A. RABINBACH, *The Human Motor: Energy, Fatigue, and the Origins of Modernity* (1990). A broad study of the impact of metaphors of energy as related to the study of human nature.

C. E. SCHORSKE, *Fin de Siecle Vienna: Politics and Culture* (1980). Major essays on the explosively creative intellectual climate of Vienna.

W. SMITH, *Politics and the Sciences of Culture in Germany, 1840–1920* (1991). A major survey of the interaction between sciences and the various social sciences.

F. STERN, *The Politics of Cultural Despair: A Study in the Rise of the German Ideology* (1965). An important examination of antimodern and antisemitic thought in imperial Germany.

F. M. TURNER, *Contesting Cultural Authority: Essays in Victorian Intellectual Life* (1993). Essay dealing with the relationship of science and religion and the problem of faith for intellectuals.

J. P. VON ARX, *Progress and Pessimism: Religion, Politics, and History in Late Nineteenth Century Britain* (1985). A major study that casts much new light on the nineteenth-century view of progress.

C. WELCH, *Protestant Thought in the Nineteenth Century*, 2 vols. (1972, 1985). The most extensive recent study.

R. WOHL, *A Passion for Wings: Aviation and the Western Imagination, 1908–1918* (1994). An examination of the relationship of technology, art, and culture.

30 LATIN AMERICA: FROM INDEPENDENCE TO THE 1940S

Orgy—The Night of the Rich, a mural by the Mexican artist Diego Rivera (1886–1957). In this acerbic painting Rivera casts a scornful eye on the Europeanized decadence of Mexico's elite in the early twentieth century. (Mural, 2.05 x 1.54 m, Court of Fiestas, Level 3, North Wall. Secretaría de Educación Pública, Mexico City, Mexico) [Schalkwijk/Art Resource, NY © Estate of Diego Rivera]

CHAPTER TOPICS

◆ Independence Without Revolution   ◆ Search for Political Stability   *In World Perspective* Latin American History

◆ Economy of Dependence   ◆ Three National Histories

By the mid-1820s, Latin Americans had driven out their colonial rulers and broken the colonial trade monopolies (see Map 30–1). Although rich in natural resources, the region did not achieve widespread prosperity and long-lasting political stability for more than a century after independence. The Wars of Independence had not been popular, grass-roots movements. They had originated with the Creole elite, who were seeking to resist the imposition of European liberalism by Napoleon or, later, the Spanish liberals. In effect, the wars had been fought to break the colonial trade monopolies and to preserve the existing social structure. The military leaders of the wars held much of the political power in the new nations the wars had created.

The wars also destroyed much of the economic infrastructure of the region. Mines had been flooded, livestock depleted, and the work force disrupted. Whereas previously colonial Latin America had been dependent on Spain for its exports and financial credits, it now became dependent on Great Britain and later on the United States.

Latin America shares many cultural features with Europe and North America. Its languages are primarily European, although much of its population speaks Native American languages. Its primary religion is Roman Catholicism. Its nations have often adopted the constitutional traditions of Europe and the United States. Many of its elite have studied abroad. Despite these important similarities, however, the economic and political development of Latin America has been different from that of much of Europe or the United States.

The reasons for these differences have long puzzled historians. Why has Latin America been less stable and less prosperous than Europe and North America? The answers appear to lie in the role Latin America played in the integrated global economic system that began to develop in the nineteenth century, just when it achieved political independence. This system prevented Latin Americans from achieving economic independence. The region's leaders thought they could best satisfy the economic interests of their nations by providing raw materials to the world economy. Most Latin American nations consequently developed export economies devoted to raw materials or semi-finished goods. Unfortunately, this decision made their export products vulnerable to worldwide fluctuations in demand. They were also susceptible to undue influence from foreign business and banking interests and to political interference by the governments of the United States and Europe.

Latin America had much in common with other regions of the world—Africa and Asia, for example—during the nineteenth and early twentieth centuries. In all three regions, particular nations or areas would specialize in a particular niche in the increasingly integrated world economy. In Asia and Africa vast plantations produced products such as rubber; in Latin America plantations might produce sugar or coffee. In all three regions huge mining industries extracted resources such as copper, phosphates, gold, and diamonds. Virtually all such enterprises were dominated by Europeans or North Americans. Filling a particular niche by supplying a particular raw product might bring initial prosperity but provided too narrow an economic base for sustained economic well-being. In contrast, the economic advance of the United States and Europe was largely due to their ability to exploit niche economies around the globe.

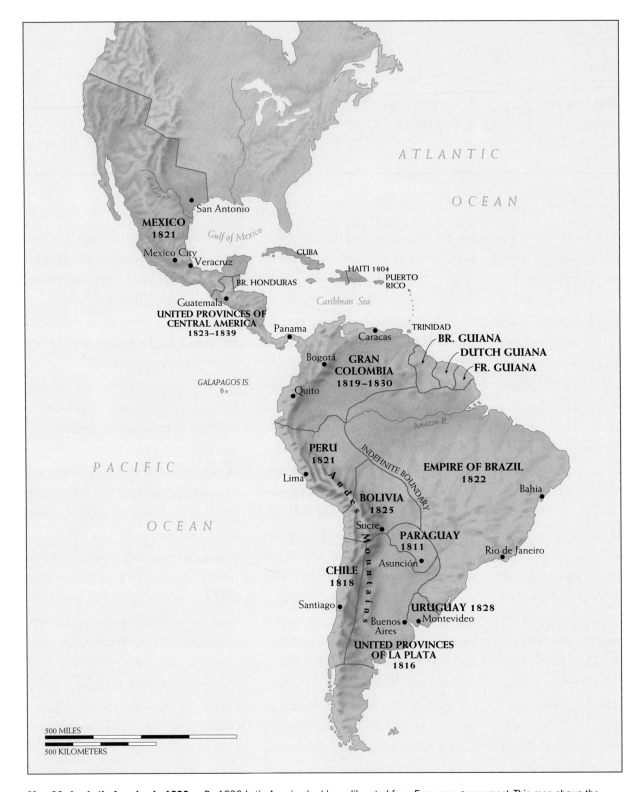

ATLANTIC

OCEAN

San Antonio

MEXICO
1821

Gulf of Mexico

Mexico City
Veracruz

CUBA

HAITI 1804

PUERTO
RICO

BR. HONDURAS

Guatemala

Caribbean Sea

TRINIDAD

UNITED PROVINCES OF
CENTRAL AMERICA
1823–1839

Panama

Caracas

BR. GUIANA

DUTCH GUIANA

FR. GUIANA

Bogotá

GRAN
COLOMBIA
1819–1830

GALAPAGOS IS.

Quito

Amazon R.

PERU
1821

Lima

A
n
d
e
s

INDEFINITE BOUNDARY

EMPIRE OF BRAZIL
1822

Bahia

PACIFIC

BOLIVIA
1825

Sucre

OCEAN

PARAGUAY
1811

Rio de Janeiro

M
o
u
n
t
a
i
n
s

Asunción

CHILE
1818

Santiago

URUGUAY 1828

Buenos
Aires

Montevideo

UNITED PROVINCES
OF LA PLATA
1816

500 MILES

500 KILOMETERS

Map 30–1   Latin America in 1830.   By 1830 Latin America had been liberated from European government. This map shows the initial borders of the states of the region with the dates of their independence. The United Provinces of La Plata formed the nucleus of what later became Argentina.

Independence Without Revolution

Immediate Consequences of Latin American Independence

The Wars of Independence left Latin America by the late 1820s liberated from direct European control but economically exhausted and politically unstable. Only Brazil tended to prosper immediately after independence. In contrast, the new republics of the former Spanish empire felt themselves weak and vulnerable. Because the Wars of Independence had been largely civil wars, the new governments knew that many of their populations might welcome their collapse. Economic life on the continent contracted, and in 1830 overall production was lower than it had been in 1800. Difficult terrain over vast distances made interregional trade difficult, and few institutions fostered it. The old patterns of overseas trade had been disrupted. There was an absence of funds for investment. Many wealthy *peninsulares* returned to Spain or departed for Cuba. Consequently, Latin American governments and businesses looked to Britain for protection, markets, and capital investment.

Independence itself also created several new sources of discontent. There was much disagreement about the character of the future government, even among those who had most wanted to oust the Spanish. Certain institutions, such as the Roman Catholic church, that had enjoyed a privileged status in the colonial period sought to maintain those privileges under new and often unfriendly governments. Indian communities, which had also been somewhat protected by paternalistic colonial policies, found themselves subject to new exploitation once Indians were made equal citizens under the law. Major disagreements arose between the Creole elites of different regions of the new nations. The agricultural hinterlands resented the predominance of the port cities, whose merchants set the terms of trade. Investors or merchants from one Latin American nation found themselves in conflict with those of others over transport tariffs on rivers or over mining regulations. Civilians often became rivals of the military for political authority.

Absence of Social Change

Yet no matter what the actual or potential conflict among various groups in the literate political and economic elites might be, they all opposed substantial social reform. The Creole victors in the Wars of Independence granted equal rights to all persons; and except for Brazil, the independent states had abolished slavery by 1855. However, the right to vote depended on a property qualification, and peasants remained dependent on and often subservient to their landlords. The racial codes of the colonial empires disappeared, but not the racial prejudice. Although mestizos, mulattos, and even Indians who achieved economic success were assimilated into the higher ranks of the social structure, persons of white or nearly white complexion tended to constitute the elite of Latin America. The Creole elite generally discriminated against the peoples of color in their midst. Most important, no major changes in landholding accompanied the Wars of Independence; the ruling classes of all the newly independent nations protected the interests of landholders.

Except for Mexico in 1910, no Latin American nation, from the Wars of Independence until the 1950s, experienced a fundamental revolution that overthrew the social and economic structures dating from the colonial period. The absence of such social revolution, which would necessarily have involved changes in landholding, is perhaps the single most important factor in Latin American history during the first century of independence. The rise and fall of political regimes represented quarrels among the elite and did not substantially change the structures or expectations of everyday life for most of the population. Throughout the social structure there was no mutually shared trust or allegiance to the political system.

Control of the Land

Most Latin Americans during the nineteenth century lived in the countryside. Agriculture continued to be dominated by large *haciendas*, or plantations. The landowners virtually ruled these estates as small domains. They were nearly a law unto themselves. The *latifundia* (the large rural estates) actually grew larger during the nineteenth century. Confiscated church lands and conquered Indian territories augmented existing estates or led to the establishment of new ones. These estates might include tens of thousands of acres yet be attended by a relatively sparse work force. Work was labor intensive because little machinery was available; virtually none was manufactured in Latin America. Herding and stock raising produced salted meat, leather, tallow, and wool for the export market. For some products—salted meats, for example—there was a limited manufacturing stage in Latin America. Other agricultural exports included cereal crops, tobacco, sugar, coffee, and cacao.

Landowners constituted a society of their own. Their families intermarried. They sometimes formed friendships or family alliances with members of the wealthy urban classes who were involved in export commerce or the law. Younger sons might enter the army or the church. The landowners served in the various postindependence national parliaments or congresses. Their wealth, literacy, and social connections

A Chilean cattle estate. The great landowners of Latin America ruled their huge estates as small domains. [Sergio Larrain/Magnum Photos Inc.]

The second half of the nineteenth century witnessed a remarkable growth in Latin American urban life. There was some movement from the countryside to the city and an influx of European immigrants as well as some from Asia. The Creole elite favored European immigration, which increased the size of the white population; Asian immigration was a source of inexpensive labor. Throughout this period there arose a political and social trade-off between the urban and rural elites. Each more or less permitted the other to pursue its economic self-interest, to profit from the commodity export economy through commerce or production, and to repress any discontent. Nonetheless, the growth of the urban centers shifted political influence from the countryside to the cities and gave rise to an urban working class and all the social discontents associated with vast numbers of relatively poor people working in difficult situations. Urban growth in Latin America created social and political difficulties not unlike those that arose in Europe and the United States at about the same time.

Submissive Political Philosophies

The political philosophies embraced by the educated and propertied Creole elites also discouraged any real challenge to the social order. The political ideas associated with European liberalism, which flourished in Latin America immediately after independence, supported republican government but also limited the franchise to property holders. Thus in Latin America, as in Europe, liberalism protected property and tended to ignore the social problems of the poor and propertyless. In addition, the Creole elite frequently exhibited racial prejudice toward the mulatto, mestizo, and Indian populations.

Economic liberalism and the need for British investment led to the championing of free trade. During the decades immediately after independence, Latin America actually exported less than it had under colonial rule. The region achieved a trade balance by exporting precious metals. Because these metals often came from stocks mined years earlier, this in effect amounted to a flight of capital. The general economic view was that Latin America would produce raw materials for export in exchange for manufactured goods imported from Europe, and especially from Britain.

For most of the nineteenth century the landed sector of the economy dominated because cheap imports from abroad and a shortage of local capital discouraged indigenous attempts at industrialism. Latin American liberals championed the extension of great landed estates and all the forms of social dependence associated with them. The produce of the new land could contribute raw materials or lightly processed goods for export to pay for the import of finished goods. Liberals thus favored confiscating land owned by the church and

made them the rulers of the countryside, and the army would protect them from any social uprising.

The landowners lived well and comfortably, although often on isolated estates. Most of the rural work force were socially and economically dependent on them. In Brazil slavery persisted until 1888. Although it was once argued that slavery in Roman Catholic Latin America was more paternalistic and less harsh than elsewhere, that view has long been abandoned among scholars who now believe Latin American slavery was as harsh as that in North America and perhaps more so. In other rural areas many people lived as virtual slaves. Debt peonage was widespread and often tied a peasant to the land like a European serf. A peon would become indebted to his landlord and could never repay the debt. Later in the nineteenth century the new lands that were opened were generally organized as large holdings with tenants rather than as small land holdings with independent farmers. This was markedly different from both the United States and Canada. Poor roads and limited railways made internal travel difficult and kept many people on the land. Little effort was made to provide even a primary education, leaving millions of Latin American peasants ignorant, lacking any significant technological skills, and incapable of improving their condition or of protesting or escaping their bondage to the land and its owners.

the Indian communities, because these groups did not exploit their lands in a progressive manner, according to the liberals.

During the second half of the century the political ideas stemming from the French positivist philosopher Auguste Comte (1798–1857) swept across Latin America. Comte and his followers, as explained in Chapter 29, had advocated the cult of science and technological progress. This highly undemocratic outlook suggested that either technocrats or dictatorial governments could best achieve modernization. It was especially popular among military officers and influenced the ongoing Latin American struggle between civilian and military elites. The great slogan of Latin American positivism, emblazoned on the flag of the Brazilian republic, was "Order and Progress." Social or political groups that created disorder or challenged the existing social order were by definition unprogressive.

Toward the close of the century the military forces in various countries—following the model of European armies, especially Germany's—became more professionalized. Their new training often made the officer corps the most important educated elite in a country. Their education and attachment to the armies they served gave them considerable influence, generally of a conservative character.

Finally, the late-nineteenth-century European theories of "scientific" racism were used to preserve the Latin American social status quo and the dominance of those of white or more nearly white complexions. Racial theory could attribute the economic backwardness of the region to its vast nonwhite or mixed blood population. This explanation, of course, shifted responsibility for the economic difficulties of Latin America away from the mostly white governing elites toward Indians, blacks, mestizos, and mulattos, who had long been exploited or repressed.

This conservative intellectual heritage continued to affect twentieth-century political thought. First, it can be seen in the ongoing tendency of military groups in Latin America to view themselves as the guarantors of order. These groups were ready to intervene in political affairs and seize control from civilians to protect the status quo or to thwart social change. Second, it can be seen in the way the political elites of Latin America naturally and actively opposed communism after the Russian Revolution. Although many Latin American nations had small organized Communist parties, governments used the fear of communism to resist virtually all political movements—Communist or not—that advocated social reform or questioned property arrangements. From the 1920s onward, in Latin America as in Europe, the fear of communism brought support to conservative governments, whether civilian or military. Communism would become an even more powerful issue throughout the region after the successful Cuban Revolution of 1957 installed an actual Soviet-dominated Communist state in Latin America.

Economy of Dependence

The Wars of Independence destroyed the Spanish and Portuguese colonial trade monopolies. Where previously only a few dozen ships called annually at any port, hundreds laden with goods from all over the world could now drop anchor. Consequently, Latin America had many new trading partners, but it remained heavily dependent on non-Latin American economies. Trade was free and the nations were politically independent, but other nations continued to shape Latin American economic life in the most fundamental manner.

One of the chief reasons for this dependence on foreign trading partners was the absence of large internal markets. Had such markets existed during the colonial period itself, the newly independent nations might have been able to trade with each other rather than primarily with nations outside the region. Trade after independence flowed in the same direction that trade had flowed before independence because Europe remained the source of imports of finished goods. Furthermore, then as now, geographical barriers hindered internal trade. The jungles of the Amazon and the Andes Mountains prevented any easy east–west trade. No road systems allowed goods to travel between countries or even easily within them, and there was little domestic investment in transport. European and American investments in railways generally facilitated exports rather than internal trade.

New Exploitation of Resources

As previously noted, the Wars of Independence sharply disrupted the Latin American economy. In both Mexico and Peru, mines were flooded; machinery was in disrepair; labor was dispersed. Agricultural production was also disrupted. Between 1825 and 1850 the new nations attempted to set their economic houses in order, but with mixed results. Capital financing to restore the mining industry and establish new industries was totally inadequate. Virtually no domestic industries existed to manufacture heavy equipment or build ships. Both to restore old industries, such as mining, and to have access to modern transport, such as steamships and railroads, Latin Americans had to turn to Europe and North America. For many decades Britain exercised the predominant economic influence over Latin America. Britain had sought to break the old colonial monopoly. Once it was gone, the British rapidly established their own economic dominance. This desire to pour manufactured goods into Latin America also led Britain and other nations to discourage the

Chapter 30 ∞ Latin America: From Independence to the 1940s **833**

Brazilian coffee being loaded onto a British ship. Most Latin American countries developed an export economy based on the exchange of agricultural products, raw materials, and semi-finished goods for finished goods and services from abroad. From the 1890s onward, the coffee industry dominated both the political and economic life of Brazil.

[Corbis-Bettmann]

development of manufacturing industries there. Europeans and Americans had no desire to see competitors emerge. Foreign investment did help revive the mining industry in Mexico, Peru, and Chile. But mining produces raw materials, not manufactured goods.

To pay for imports and foreign services, Latin American nations turned to the production of agricultural commodities for which there was great European demand. This shift meant that the rural areas of Latin America and the commercial centers serving agriculture became politically and economically more important than many of the old colonial urban centers. The production of wheat, beef, hides, hemp, coffee, cocoa, and other foodstuffs for the export market also raised the value of land and led governments to expand into previously unsettled territory and to confiscate the lands of the church. Because so much land was available, agricultural production was increased by putting more land under cultivation rather than by finding more efficient ways to farm areas already

under cultivation. So much wealth could be accumulated through land speculation and land development that little incentive existed for alternative investments in manufacturing. It would also have been difficult, if not impossible, for new Latin American industries to compete with the cheap goods imported from more established industrial economies abroad.

After 1850 the Latin American republics became, relatively speaking, more prosperous. Chile exported copper and nitrates as well as wheat. Peru exported guano to be used as fertilizer. Coffee was becoming king in Venezuela, Brazil, Colombia, and Central America. Sugar continued to be produced in the West Indies as well as in Cuba, which remained under Spanish control. Argentina supplied hides and tallow. But this limited prosperity and recovery were based on the export of agricultural commodities or extracted minerals or nonreplenishable resources, such as guano, and the importation of finished goods from abroad.

Yet the period from approximately 1870 through 1930 came to be seen as a kind of golden age for the Latin American economy. There was more prosperity than ever before, especially in Chile, Argentina, Brazil, and Mexico. The export economy seemed to foster genuine economic growth. The economies of the Latin American nations grew because industrial production in Europe and the United States created a demand for more exports. The Latin American export economy also allowed large quantities of new products to be imported from Europe and the United States. Both the exports and the imports drew Latin America more deeply than ever into the world economy.

There were three broad varieties of late-nineteenth-century Latin American exports. First were foodstuffs raised in Latin America that were more or less like those that could be raised in Europe, chiefly wheat and beef products, for which Argentina became the great exporter. Second were distinctly tropical products, such as bananas, sugar, and coffee. Third were natural resources, including metals, of which copper was the most important; minerals, such as nitrates; and, later, oil.

Both the trading patterns for these goods and the internal improvements in Latin American production deeply and inextricably linked the economy of the region to Europe and, after 1900, to the United States. Europeans and North Americans provided capital and the technological and managerial skills to build bridges, roads, railroads, steam lines, and new mines. Most of the transport system was constructed to service the existing export economy rather than to foster the development of alternative forms of domestic economic development. Furthermore, whenever the economy of Europe or the United States floundered, Latin America was hurt. The region could not control its own economic destiny. A decline in the prices of commodities and raw materials could, of course, force Latin America to reduce the amount of goods it imported, harming its European and North American trading partners. But the major economic difficulties almost always struck Latin America first and lasted there longest.

Increased Foreign Ownership and Influence

During the late nineteenth century the relative prosperity of the export sector increased the degree of dependence. The growing European demand generated by spreading industrialism gave Latin Americans a false sense of the long-term security of their export markets. The vast profits to be made through mining and agricultural exports discouraged investment in local industry, except as it served the export economy. Land still remained the most favored form of domestic investment. Foreigners saw no reason to capitalize local industry that might replace goods being imported. By late in the century the wealthy classes in Latin America had, in effect, lost control and even ownership of some of the most valuable sectors of their economy. For example, in 1901 British and other foreign investors owned approximately 80 percent of the Chilean nitrate industry. Foreigners also owned and operated most of the steamship lines and railroads.

The European and American economic penetration of Latin America was more subtle than that experienced by India or China, but it was no less real. Foreign ownership was not the only indication of economic dependence. Foreign powers used their political and military influence to protect their economic interests. Britain was the dominant power until the turn of the century. Its diplomats and military and naval officers were frequently involved directly or indirectly in the domestic political affairs of the Latin American nations. From the Spanish American War of 1898 onward the United States began to exercise more direct influence in the region. In 1903, to facilitate its plans to build a canal across the Isthmus of Panama, the United States participated in the rebellion that allowed Panama to separate from Colombia. There were numerous other instances of U.S. military intervention in the Caribbean and in Central America. By the 1920s U.S. investments had become dominant as a result of two decades of "Dollar Diplomacy." During that decade, largely as a result of economic dislocations arising from World War I, the United States generally replaced Great Britain as the dominant trading partner of Latin American nations. The role of the United States remains controversial, but from a structural standpoint it was just one more example of a dominant foreign power treating Latin America as a junior and dependent economic partner.

The United States interventions were one cost to Latin America of being a dependent economy. More significant costs, however, arose from fundamental shifts in world trade that were brought on by World War I and continued through the 1920s. First, the overall amount of trade carried on by European countries decreased, particularly during the war, when traditional trading partners divided into two warring camps. Second, during the 1920s world prices of agricultural commodities dropped steadily. Latin American nations had to produce more goods to pay for their imports, and no easy or rapid adjustment was possible. Third, various synthetic products manufactured in Europe or North America replaced the natural products long supplied by Latin American producers. Most important among these products were synthetic nitrates. Finally, petroleum began to replace other natural products as an absolute percentage of world trade. This shift meant that petroleum-exporting countries, such as Mexico, gained a greater share of export income.

U.S. influence and investments in Latin America grew rapidly after 1900 and surpassed those of Britain by the 1920s. As this cartoon illustrates, the U.S. tended to regard its southern neighbors as at best junior and dependent partners. [Corbis-Bettmann]

Economic Crises and New Directions

The Great Depression turned the difficult economic conditions of the 1920s into a genuine crisis. Commodity prices virtually collapsed. The economic decline in Europe and the United States also lessened the demand for Latin American products. The republics of Latin America could not repay their debts to foreign banks, and a number of them suspended interest payments. Those decisions in turn worsened the economic crisis in the more developed creditor nations. The Depression led eventually to the beginning of a new economic era in Latin America. The new era, which really began after the conclusion of World War II, was marked by strong economic nationalism and a determination to create sectors of the various national economies that were not wholly dependent on events and wealth outside Latin America. These various drives toward economic independence have had mixed success, but they date only from the turmoil of the Depression.

Where did industrialism fit into this general picture of a dependent economy, or what is sometimes termed a *neocolonial economy*? The brief answer is, almost always, on the periphery of the export sector. Until the 1940s major industrialization did not occur in Latin America. There were, however, significant earlier developments. Before World War I light manufacturing was done in connection with preparing exports, such as beef processing in Argentina. Light manufactured goods such as textiles were also produced. With the Depression, however, it became necessary to substitute domestically manufactured goods for those traditionally imported from abroad. Various nations pursued different policies of what was called *import substitution*, but all of these policies were undertaken because of the collapse of the export economy rather than because of any independent decision to industrialize. In that regard, the effort to industrialize was itself a result of being dependent.

By the mid-1940s there were three major varieties of manufacturing in Latin America. First, there were industries that, as in the past, transformed raw materials for export. They included sugar and other food processing, tin and copper mining, and petroleum refining. Second, there were industries addressing local demands, such as power plants, textiles, foundries, machine shops, and food companies. Third, there were industries depending generally on the transformation of imported materials. These industries were basically assembly plants whose owners could take advantage of inexpensive labor. None of this manufacturing was particularly sophisticated, and none of it involved heavy industry. Not until the 1950s would significant steel production, for example, occur in the region.

Search for Political Stability

The new states of independent Latin American, unlike the British colonies of North America, had little or no experience in self-government. The Spanish Empire had been ruled directly by the monarchy and by Spanish-born royal bureaucrats. Spain had persistently discriminated against the Creole elite as well as against mulattos, mestizos, and Indians. This monarchical or paternalistic heritage survived in two forms. First, many traditionalists and conservatives favored the establishment of monarchies in Latin America, including José de San Martín (1778–1850). Monarchy was briefly established

in Mexico. In Brazil, an emperor from the Portuguese royal family governed until 1889.

The second heritage of the colonial monarchy was the proclivity of the Latin American political elites to tolerate or actively to support strong executives. Few of the early republic constitutions endured or established a stable political life. They were frequently suspended or rewritten, so that a strong leader could consolidate his own power. Such figures, who appeared throughout Latin America during the nineteenth century, were called *caudillos*. They usually came from the army officer corps or enjoyed strong ties to the army. Whatever constitutional justification they provided for themselves, the real basis of their rule was force and repression. *Caudillos* might support conservative causes, such as protection of the church or strong central government, or they might pursue liberal policies, such as the confiscation of church land, the extension of landed estates, and the development of education.

Initially, such dictatorial government was accepted simply to ensure political stability when republican regimes floundered. In many countries the early years of independence saw internal conflicts among regions. In this situation, a national *caudillo* might reach a compromise with various regional *caudillos* that allowed them to retain substantial local control.

These strongmen also encountered little opposition because of their repressive policies. Later in the century the new relative prosperity of expanding economies quieted potential discontent. The dictators became more skilled at both repression and patronage. The political and social elites also rallied to their support when, around the turn of the century, the young labor movement called strikes.

Even when *caudillos* were forced from office and parliamentary government was more or less restored, the regimes that replaced them were neither genuinely liberal nor democratic. Parliamentary governments usually ruled by courtesy of the military and in the economic interest of the existing elites. No matter who ruled, the life of the overwhelming mass of the population changed little. Except for the Mexican Revolution of 1910, Latin American politics was run by and for the elite.

Three National Histories

Three Latin American nations possess over 50 percent of the land, people, and wealth of the region. They are Argentina, Mexico, and Brazil. Their national histories illustrate the more general themes of Latin American history.

Argentina

Argentine history from independence to World War II can be divided into three general eras. From the rebellion against

Spain in 1810 until mid-century, the question of which region of the nation would dominate political and economic life was foremost. From 1853 until 1916 Argentina experienced extraordinary economic expansion and large-scale immigration from Europe, which transformed its society and its position in the world. From 1916 to 1943 Argentines failed to establish a democratic state and struggled with the ramifications of an economy they did not really control.

Buenos Aires versus the Provinces

In 1810 the junta in Buenos Aires had overturned Spanish government in the viceroyalty of Río de la Plata. However, the other regions of the viceroyalty refused to accept the leadership of the province and city of Buenos Aires. Paraguay, Uruguay, and Upper Peru (Bolivia) went their separate ways. Conflicts between Buenos Aires and the remaining provinces dominated the first seventy years of Argentine history. It was the story of *porteños*, as the inhabitants of Buenos Aires were called, versus provincials. Eventually Buenos Aires established its primacy because of its capacity to dominate trade on the Río de la Plata and its control of the international customhouse, which assured revenue.

Between 1821 and 1827 Bernardino Rivadavia (1780–1845) worked to create a liberal political state but could not overcome the centrifugal forces of regionalism. His major accomplishment was a commercial treaty in 1823 that established Great Britain as a dominant trading partner. Thus began a deep intermeshing of trade and finance between the two nations that would continue for over a century. After Rivadavia's resignation in 1827 came the classical period of *caudillo* rule in Argentina. The strongman of the province of Buenos Aires was Juan Manuel de Rosas (1793–1877). In 1831 he negotiated the Pact of the Littoral, whereby Buenos Aires was put in charge of foreign relations, trade, and the customhouse, while the other provinces were left to run their own internal affairs. Within Buenos Aires, Rosas set up what amounted to dictatorial rule. He tolerated no dissent, no civil liberties, and no political power distinct from his own. One of his devices was the secret *Mazorca* (ear of corn) association, which terrorized his opponents. His major policies were expansion of trade and agriculture, suppression of the Indians, and nationalism. In Argentine history Rosas symbolized government by a single strong figure.

Expansion and Growth of the Republic

Rosas' success in strengthening Buenos Aires bred resentment in other provinces. In 1852 Justo José de Urquiza (1800–1870), the *caudillo* of the state of Entre Rios, overthrew Rosas. The next year a federal constitution was promulgated for the Argentine Republic. Buenos Aires remained aloof until the republic conquered the province in 1859. Disputes continued. In 1880 the city of Buenos Aires was made a distinct federal

Juan Manuel de Rosas (1793-1877), caudillo of Buenos Aires from 1827 to 1852. [Corbis-Bettmann]

province, separate from its rich hinterland. Provincials had hoped that this arrangement would lessen the influence of the city; however, the economic prosperity of the end of the century simply gave the capital new prominence.

The Argentine economy was overwhelmingly agricultural, the chief exports at mid-century being animal products. Internal transportation was poor and the country was sparsely populated. Technological advances changed this situation during the last quarter of the century. In 1876 the first refrigerator ship, *La Frigiorique*, steamed into Buenos Aires. Henceforth, it would be possible to transport large quantities of Argentine beef to Europe. Furthermore, at about the same time it became clear that wheat farming could be extended throughout the pampas. In 1879 and 1880 a government army under General (and later President) Julio Roca (president 1880–1886, 1898–1904) carried out a major campaign against the Indian population known as the *Conquest of the Desert*. The British soon began to construct and manage railways to carry wheat from the interior to the coast, where it would be loaded on British and other foreign steamships. Government policy made the purchase of land by wealthy Argentines simple and cheap. The owners, in turn, rented the land to tenants. The predominance both of large landowners and of foreign business interests thus continued

Eva Perón was as influential as her husband, Juan Perón, during his years in power in the late 1940s and early 1950s. She was especially effective in attracting popular support for his government. They are shown here in a reception line in 1951. [Corbis-Bettmann]

throughout the most significant economic transformation in Argentine history.

The development of the pampas and the vastly increased production of beef and wheat made Argentina one of the wealthiest nations of Latin America and a major agricultural rival of the United States. The opening of land, even if only for tenant farming and not ownership, encouraged hundreds of thousands of Europeans, particularly from Spain and Italy, to emigrate to Argentina. The immigrants also provided workers for the food-processing, service, and transportation industries in Buenos Aires. By 1900 the new economic life and the thousands of new citizens had drastically changed Argentina. It became much more urbanized and industrialized. More people had reason to be politically discontent. Moreover, the children of the nineteenth-century immigrants often became the strongest Argentine nationalists during the twentieth century.

The prosperity of economic expansion quieted most political opposition for some time. The conservative landed oligarchy continued to govern under presidents who sought to perpetuate a strong export economy. Like similar groups elsewhere, they ignored the social questions raised by urbanization and industrialization. However, they also ignored the political aspirations of the urban middle and professional classes, whose members wanted a greater share in political life and

an end to political corruption. In 1890 these groups founded the Radical Party, which for many years achieved few successes. However, in 1912 the conservative government expanded the franchise and provided for the secret ballot.

Four years later, Hipólito Irigoyen (1850–1933), leader of the Radical Party, was elected president (first term 1916–1922). Without significant support in the legislature, his presidency brought fewer changes than might have been expected. He remained neutral in World War I, so Argentina could trade with both sides. Nonetheless, the war put great pressure on the economy, and much labor agitation resulted. Although previously sympathetic toward labor, Irigoyen as president used troops against strikers. The most violent labor clash occurred in January 1919, when troops quelled a general strike in Buenos Aires during what became known as the *Semana Trágica*, or Tragic Week. Thereafter, the Radical Party attempted to consolidate support among conservatives and pursued policies that benefited landowners and urban business interests. This was possible because of the close relationship between agricultural producers and processors and because both the landed and the middle classes wanted to resist concessions to the working classes.

The Military in Ascendence   By the end of the 1920s the onetime reformist Radical Party had become corrupt and

Eva Perón Explains the Sources of Her Popularity

The Perónist movement in Argentina drew broad support from workers and the poor. The movement involved a cult of personality around both Perón and his wife Eva. In 1951 Eva Perón published a book entitled My Mission in Life (La razón de mi vida). *Here she explains how she sought to relate to her husband's political supporters.*

Why was Eva Perón's accepting the name "Evita" a political act? How did her use of this name separate her from the ruling elites of Argentina? What is the role she projects for herself in her relationship to various social groups in Argentina? Do you believe her discussion of herself to be sincere or politically opportunistic?

When I chose to be "Evita," I chose the path of my people. . . .

Only the people call me "Evita." Only the *descamisados* [the "unshirted," as Perón's working-class followers were termed] learned to call me so. . . .

I appeared to them thus the day I went to meet the humble of my land, telling them that I preferred being "Evita" to being the wife of the president, if that "Evita" could help to mitigate some grief, or dry a tear.

If a man of the government, a leader, a politician, an ambassador, who normally calls me "Señora," should call me "Evita," it would sound as strange and out of place to me as if a street-urchin, a workingman, or a humble person of the people should call me "Señora." . . .

Now, if you ask me which I prefer, my reply would be immediately that I prefer the name by which I am known to the people.

When a street-urchin calls me "Evita," I feel as though I were the mother of all urchins, and of all the weak and the humble of my land.

When a working man calls me "Evita," I feel glad to be the companion of all the workingmen of my country and even of the whole world.

When a woman of my country calls me "Evita," I imagine myself her sister, and that of all the women of humanity,

And so, almost without noticing it, I have classified in these three examples the principal activities of "Evita" relating to the humble, the workers, and women.

The truth is that, without any artificial effort, at no personal cost, as though I had been born for all this, I feel myself responsible for the humble as though I were the mother of all of them; I fight shoulder to shoulder with the workers as though I were another of their companions from the workshop or factory; in front of the women who trust in me, I consider myself something like an elder sister, responsible to a certain degree for the destiny of all of them who have placed their hopes in me.

And certainly I do not deem this an honor but a responsibility. . . .

Yes. I confess that I have an ambition, one single, great personal ambition: I would like the name of "Evita" to figure somewhere in the history of my country.

From *Women's Writing in Latin America: An Anthology* by Sara Castro-Klarén, Sylvia Malloy, and Beatriz Sarlo. Selection translated by Ethel Cherry. Copyright © 1991 by Westview Press. Reprinted by permission of Westview Press.

---

directionless. The worldwide commodity depression hurt exports. In 1930 the military staged a coup against the aged Irigoyen, who had returned to the presidency in 1928. The officers eventually returned power to conservative civilians, and Argentina remained heavily dependent on the British export market. U.S. interests also began to establish plants in Argentina, removing still more economic activity from Argentine control.

Throughout the 1930s a right-wing nationalistic movement, *nacionalismo*, arose among writers, political journalists, and a few active politicians. This movement resembled the fascist political movements then active in Europe. Its supporters were angered by British and American domination of the economy, equating their influence with imperialism. In politics the movement's supporters rejected liberalism and spread the fear of international communism. They also exhibited a strong antisemitic spirit and warmly supported the Roman Catholic church. *Nacionalismo* was associated with a relatively progressive social policy rooted in the social values of the late-nineteenth-century papacy of Leo XIII (see Chapter 29). It advocated social reforms that recognized the needs of workers and the poor, but that also sought to promote social harmony rather than Communist revolution or Socialist reconstruction of the economy. The various writers who set forth these ideas also looked back to Rosas as a role model for Argentine politics. In effect these groups were anti-imperialistic, socially concerned, authoritarian, and sympathetic to the rule of a modern *caudillo*. The pressures that came to the fore as a result of World War II gave these attitudes and their supporters influence that they had not previously enjoyed.

The war closed almost all of Europe to Argentine exports, creating a sudden economic crisis. The country's leadership seemed incapable of responding to the crisis, and in 1943 the military again seized control. Its leaders had lost patience with politicians more interested in patronage than in patriotism. Many of the officers were children of immigrants and were fiercely nationalistic. They regarded liberal politics as a system that permitted politicians to look after themselves. Some officers had become deeply impressed by the Fascist and Nazi movements and their rejection of European liberal politics. The officers also shared the Fascist and Nazi hostility to Britain. They contended that the government must address social questions, industrialize the country, and liberate it from foreign economic control. In all these respects, they echoed the *nacionalistas*.

Between 1943 and 1946 Juan Perón (1895–1974), one of the colonels involved in the 1943 coup, forged this social discontent and these authoritarian political attitudes into a remarkable political movement known as Perónism. It was authoritarian, initially militaristic, anti-Communist, and socially progressive. Perón understood better than his fellow officers that political power could be exerted by appeals to the Argentine working class, particularly in Buenos Aires. He gained the support of the trade unions that were opposed to Communism. In 1945 he had been arrested by other military leaders, but he was freed when it became clear that he alone could silence working-class discontent. In 1946 he made himself the voice of working-class democracy, even though after his election to the presidency he created an authoritarian regime that only marginally addressed industrial problems. He was greatly aided by his wife, the former actress Eva Duarte (1919–1952). She enjoyed charismatic support among trade-union members and the working class.

Perón became the most famous of the postwar Latin American dictators, but his power and appeal were rooted in the antiliberal attitudes that had been fostered by the corruption and aimlessness of Argentine politics during the Depression. He was the supreme twentieth-century embodiment of the *caudillo*. He was ousted in 1956, but long-term stability would elude Argentine politics after his departure.

Mexico

The heritage of Mexican independence was a combination of the thwarted social revolution led by Father Hidalgo and José María Morelos between 1811 and 1815 and the conservative political coup carried out in 1820 by the Creole elite against a potentially liberal Spanish crown. For the first century of independence conservative forces held sway, but in 1910 the Mexican people launched the most far-reaching revolution in Latin American history.

Turmoil Follows Independence   The years from 1820 to 1876 were a time of political turmoil, economic floundering, and national humiliation. Newly independent Mexico attempted no liberal political experiments. Its first ruler was Agustín de Iturbide (1783–1824), who ruled until 1823 as an emperor. After this unsuccessful effort to adopt monarchical rule, Mexico was governed by a succession of presidents, most of whom were *caudillos* from the army or depended on the army for support. The strongest of these figures was Antonio López de Santa Anna (1795–1863), a general and a political opportunist always willing to modify his principles and policies to attain or retain power. Usually he supported conservative political and social interests. He ruled in a thoroughly dictatorial manner. More than once he was driven from office, but inevitably returned until finally exiled in 1855.

The mid-century movement against Santa Anna's autocracy was called *La Reforma*. In theory, its supporters were liberal, but Mexican liberalism was associated primarily with anticlericalism, confiscation of church lands, and opposition to military influence on national life and politics. *La Reforma* aimed to produce political stability, civilian rule, and an economic policy that would attract foreign capital and immigrants. Having deposed Santa Anna, the leaders of the reform movement passed legislation to break up large landed estates, particularly those owned by the church, and to promote the establishment of small farms. However, the actual content of the laws permitted existing large landowners to purchase additional land cheaply and thus made great estates even larger. The legislative attack on privileges of the church led to further civil war between 1857 and 1860. In January 1861 Benito Juárez (1806–1872) entered Mexico City as the temporary victor.

Political instability was matched by economic stagnation. After 1820 many Spanish officials and merchants fled Mexico, taking with them large quantities of gold and silver. The mines that had produced Mexico's colonial wealth were in poor condition, and the country lacked the investment capital or technological knowledge to repair them. The inefficiencies of the *hacienda* system left farming in a backward condition. Cheap imports of manufactured goods spelled the end of domestic industries. Transportation was primitive. The

This twentieth-century portrait of Benito Juárez (oil on canvas, 1948, from Presidential Collection of Portraits of Mexican Presidents) emphasizes his major accomplishments. The foreground shows him drafting the Constitution of 1857. In the background to the left is the execution of Maximilian; to the right are scenes of road construction and farmers (who thanks to Juárez's reforms were given clear title to their lands) working their fields.

[Corbis-Bettmann]

government's remedy for these weaknesses was massive foreign borrowing; as a result, interest payments became one of the largest portions of the national budget.

Foreign Intervention

Political weakness and economic disarray invited foreign intervention. The territorial ambitions of the United States impinged on Mexico in two ways. In 1823 the Mexican government allowed Stephen F. Austin (1793–1836) to begin the colonization of Texas. During the next decade, the policies of Santa Anna stirred resentment among the Texas settlers, and in 1835 they rebelled. The next year Santa Anna destroyed the defenders of the Alamo but was decisively defeated at the battle of San Jacinto. Texas

became an independent republic that was annexed by the United States in 1845. Border clashes between Mexican and U.S. forces enabled President James Polk to launch a war against Mexico in 1846 that saw the United States army occupy Mexico City. Through the treaty of Guadalupe Hidalgo (1848), the United States gained a vast portion of Mexican territory, including what is now New Mexico, Arizona, and California.

Further foreign intervention occurred as a direct result of Juárez's liberal victory in 1861. Mexican conservatives and clerics invited the Austrian Habsburg Archduke Maximilian (1832–1867) to become the emperor of Mexico. Napoleon III (r. 1852–1870) of France, who portrayed himself as a defender of the Roman Catholic church, provided support for this imperial venture. In May 1862 French troops invaded Mexico, and two years later Maximilian became emperor. He disappointed his conservative supporters by accepting much of the former government's liberal policy toward the church but was unable to gain support from other segments of the population. By 1867 Juárez had organized strong resistance forces. He captured the unhappy emperor and executed him. The Mexicans had been victorious, but their vulnerability to foreign powers had again been exposed.

Díaz and Dictatorship

Once restored to office, the liberal leaders continued their measures against the church but failed to rally significant popular support. Consequently, in 1876 Porfirio Díaz (1830–1915), a liberal general, led a revolt on the grounds that he was restoring a true republic. Except for four years in the 1880s, when a surrogate held office, Díaz retained the presidency until 1911. He maintained what became one of the most successful dictatorships in Latin American history by giving almost every political sector something it wanted. He allowed landowners to purchase public land cheaply; he favored the army, whose support he required; and he made peace with the church by not enforcing anticlerical measures. Later, he freely used repression against opponents to diffuse their political activity and bribery to cement the loyalty of his supporters. Wealthy Mexicans grew even richer under Díaz, and Mexico became a respectable member of the international financial community. Unprecedented quantities of foreign capital flooded the nation. Foreign companies, especially from the United States, invested heavily in what, by 1900, appeared to be a thoroughly stable country.

Yet problems remained. The peasants wanted land and resented the ever-growing power of the landlords. Because food production actually declined during the Díaz regime, many Mexicans were malnourished. Labor unrest and strikes afflicted the textile and mining industries. Like other Latin American rulers, and governments in Europe and the United States, Díaz used military force against workers. Due to inflation, real wages for the working class declined in the first

Porfirio Díaz (1830-1915). From 1876 to 1911 Díaz ran one of the most successful dictatorships in Latin American history. [Brown Brothers]

decade of this century. The Panic of 1907 in the United States disrupted the Mexican economy. By 1910 the so-called *Pax Porfiriana* was unravelling.

Revolution   In 1908 the elderly Díaz announced that he would not seek reelection. Although he later changed his mind and was reelected in 1910, his first announcement spurred public discussion of Mexico's political and social future. In 1910 Díaz was opposed by Francisco Madero (d. 1913), a wealthy landowner and moderate liberal. Madero's campaign slogan was "Effective Suffrage—No Reelection," which ironically Díaz himself had coined two generations earlier. Díaz won, but Madero then led an insurrection that drove the dictator into European exile by May 1911.

Shortly thereafter, Madero was elected president. He recognized the right of trade unions to organize and to strike, but he was unwilling to undertake significant agrarian reform that might have changed the pattern of landholding. He ended by being distrusted both by conservatives, who wanted little or no change from the days of Díaz, and by reformist leaders, who thought the time had come for extensive social and political restructuring. Far more radical leaders emerged, calling for social change. Pancho Villa (1874–1923) in the north and Emiliano Zapata (1879–1919) in the south rallied mass followings of peasants who demanded fundamental structural changes in rural landholding. In late 1911 Zapata proclaimed his Plan of Ayala, which in effect set forth a program of large-scale peasant confiscation of land. Much of the struggle during the next ten years would be between supporters and opponents of such agrarian reform.

Madero found himself squeezed between the conservative supporters of the deposed Díaz and the radical peasant revolutionaries. No one trusted him, and in early 1913 he was overthrown by General Victoriano Huerta (1854–1916), who had the help of the United States, and was assassinated not long thereafter. Huerta, who was basically a dictator, failed to quash the peasant rebellion. His attacks against the forces of Zapata involved considerable loss of life. In the meantime, Venustiano Carranza (1859–1920), a wealthy landowner, joined Villa's cause. He soon put himself at the head of a large Constitutionalist Army—so called because it advocated the restoration of constitutional government in opposition to the political dictatorship of Huerta—that initially received the support of both Zapata and Villa. Huerta's government collapsed on August 15, 1914, when Constitutionalist forces entered Mexico City. Thereafter disputes erupted between Carranza and Villa and then between Carranza and Zapata. These conflicts arose both from simple political rivalry and from Carranza's refusal to embrace the kind of radical agrarian reform the two peasant leaders sought. Carranza eventually won out, thanks to his political skills and the effectiveness of his army.

Chronology of Mexico

1820-1823	Agustín de Iturbide rules unsuccessfully as emperor
1833-1855	Santa Anna dominates Mexican political scene
1846-1848	Mexico defeated by United States and loses considerable territory
1861	Victory of liberal forces under Juárez
1862-1867	French troops led by Archduke Maximilian of Austria unsuccessfully invade Mexico
1876-1911	Era of Porfirio Díaz
1911	Beginning of Mexican Revolution
1911	Zapata proclaims Plan of Ayal
1917	Forces of Carranza proclaim constitution
1929	Institutional Revolutionary Party organized

Emiliano Zapata Issues the Plan of Ayala

By November 1911 the Díaz regime had fallen in Mexico, and Francisco Madero was attempting to establish a moderately liberal government. He was confronted by a major popular peasant revolution led in the valley of Morelos by Emiliano Zapata. On November 28 the rebel leader set forth his opposition to Madero and announced sweeping goals of land reform. Zapata never took dominant control of the Mexican Revolution, but the radical economic demands of his Plan of Ayala would influence the course of Mexican social development for the next thirty years.

Why did Zapata place so much emphasis on collective ownership of natural resources? What is Zapata's vision of future economic life? Who would be the winners and losers from his proposed policies?

. . . be it known: that the lands, woods, and water usurped by the *hacendados* [great landowners] . . . henceforth belong to the towns or citizens in possession of the deeds concerning these properties of which they were despoiled through the devious action of our oppressors. The possession of said properties shall be kept at all costs, arms in hand. The usurpers who think they have right to said

goods may state their claims before special tribunals to be established upon the triumph of the Revolution.

. . . the immense majority of Mexico's villages and citizens own only the ground on which they stand. They suffer the horrors of poverty without being able to better their social status in any respect, or without being able to dedicate themselves to industry or agriculture due to the fact that the lands, woods, and water are monopolized by a few. For this reason, through prior compensation, one-third of such monopolies will be expropriated from their powerful owners in order that the villages and citizens of Mexico may obtain *ejidos* [agricultural communities], colonies, town sites, and rural properties for sowing or tilling, and in order that the welfare and prosperity of the Mexican people will be promoted in every way.

The property of those *hacendados* . . . who directly or indirectly oppose the present plan shall be nationalized, and two-thirds of their remaining property shall be designated for war indemnities—pensions for the widows and orphans of the victims that succumb in the struggle for this plan.

From James W. Wilkie and Albert L. Michaels, eds., *Revolution in Mexico: Years of Upheaval, 1910–1940*. Copyright © 1969 by Alfred A. Knopf, p. 46.

Carranza's political skills also helped him build a broad base and edge out both Villa and Zapata as the chief leader of the revolution. One particularly skillful move followed an attempt by President Woodrow Wilson (1856–1924) of the United States to support Carranza by sending U.S. Marines to Veracruz in April 1914. Carranza shrewdly denounced the United States for this action, thus casting himself in the role of patriot and nationalist, and the Marines departed. In another skillful move, he addressed himself to the concerns of urban industrial workers as well as the land hunger of rural peasants, successfully separating the two groups. This division ultimately doomed the effort to implement an agrarian revolution. Carranza made many promises, especially about agrarian reform, that he had little or no intention of carrying out.

Beginning in early 1915 Carranza's military forces began an ultimately successful campaign against Villa and Zapata. The peasant leaders still commanded regional support but could not win control of the nation. During 1916 Carranza confronted U.S. military intervention along the border that continued until early 1917, when the United States became involved in World War I in Europe. Throughout the turmoil in Mexico, the government of the United States attempted to protect American interests. These activities involved on-

going diplomatic initiatives with the various groups in Mexico as well as the threat of military action.

By 1917, after years of deadly and destructive civil war, Carranza's forces were sufficiently confident to write a constitution. The Constitution of 1917 set forth a program for ongoing social revolution—never pursued with any vigor—and political reform. Perhaps its two most famous provisions were Articles 27 and 123. Article 27 provided for the government, on behalf of the nation, to become the owner of water and mineral rights and other subsoil property rights. This article abrogated all prerevolutionary contracts with foreign companies in regard to oil and minerals. Together with other provisions, it meant that peasant villages could reclaim land they had lost over the past half century. Article 123 guaranteed certain rights for the organization of labor. Many years would pass before all the provisions of the constitution could be enforced, but from 1917 onward it provided the ongoing goals of the revolution and the ideals toward which Mexican governments were expected to strive.

Carranza and his immediate subordinates were much more conservative than either Villa or Zapata. They recognized the agrarian problem but were cautious about changing existing property arrangements.

The forces of Emiliano Zapata march on Xochimilco in 1914. Women fought alongside men and played other prominent roles during the Mexican Revolution. [UPI/Corbis-Bettmann]

Carranza and his chief supporters were associated with northwestern Mexico and admired the economic development they had seen in California. They were determined to modernize Mexican political life and attract capital investment; Mexican leaders would share these goals from that time onward. Thus despite all the radical rhetoric associated with the revolution and the vast upheaval among peasants that it involved, the Mexican revolution saw the victory of a more or less middle-class political and economic elite who would attempt to govern the country through enlightened paternalism. Although turmoil would persist for many years, with Carranza's victory the general direction of Mexican political life had been established.

The decade after 1917 witnessed both confusion and consolidation. In 1919 Zapata was lured into an ambush and killed. Carranza was assassinated in 1920. Three years later Villa was also assassinated. In this turmoil, Carranza's gener-

als provided stability. During the 1920s military leaders drawn from Carranza's revolutionary Constitutionalist Army served as presidents. They moved cautiously and hesitated to press land redistribution too quickly. They were opposed by the Roman Catholic church, which at one point suspended all services for more than two years. In 1929 Plutarco Elías Calles (1877–1945) organized the PRI, the Institutional Revolutionary Party, which quickly became the most important political force in the nation and remains so today. The Mexican political system became one dominated by a single party within which most political debate occurred, rather than a system dominated by a single strong leader. Despite external criticism and internal tensions, the PRI has overseen the longest period of political stability experienced by any Latin American nation in this century.

In 1934 Lázaro Cárdenas (1895–1970) was elected president. More than any of the other leaders to emerge after the revolution, he moved directly to fulfill the promises and programs of 1917. He turned tens of millions of acres of land over to peasant villages. In 1938, when Mexico was the third largest producer of petroleum, he expropriated the oil industry. His nationalization policy established PeMex, which remains the Mexican national oil company. Cárdenas left other mineral industries in private and generally foreign hands. His extensive reforms went through smoothly because he worked through bureaucratic and administrative means.

With the election of Manuel Ávila Camacho (1897–1955) in 1940, the era of revolutionary politics ended. Thereafter, the major issues in Mexico were those generally associated with postwar economic development. But unlike other Latin American nations, Mexico, because of its revolution, could confront those issues with a democratic perspective and a sense of collective social responsibility, no matter how imperfectly those goals might be realized.

Slavery lasted longer in Brazil than in any other nation on the American contient. Anti-slavery groups circulated prints such as this one published in France to illustrate the brutality of slave life in Brazil. [The Granger Collection, N.Y.]

Brazil

Postcolonial Brazil, the largest Latin American country, differed in several important respects from other newly independent nations in the region. Its language and colonial heritage were Portuguese rather than Spanish. For the first sixty-seven years of its independence it had a relatively stable monarchical government. And most distinctively, it retained the institution of slavery until 1888.

Brazil had moved directly from being part of the Portuguese monarchy to becoming an independent empire in 1822. The first emperor, Pedro I (r. 1822–1831), while serving as regent for his father, the king of Portugal, had put himself at the head of the independence movement. Although he granted Brazil a constitution in 1823, Pedro's high-handed rule and his patronage of Portuguese courtiers rather than Brazilians led to his forced abdication in 1831. Brazilians then took hold of their own destinies.

Afters a decade of political uncertainty under a regency, Pedro II (r. 1831–1889), the fifteen-year-old son of Pedro I, assumed direct power in 1840 and governed Brazil until 1889. Pedro II made wise and shrewd use of patronage. He established a reputation as a constitutional monarch by asking leaders of both the conservative and the liberal political parties to form ministries. Consequently, Brazil enjoyed remarkable political stability. However, the government took few initiatives to develop the economy.

The Slavery Issue The great divisive issue in Brazil's social and political life was slavery. Sugar production remained the mainstay of the economy until the middle of the nineteenth century. Most sugar plantations were located in the coastal provinces of the northeast. Their owners were conservative and resistant to changes in production. Soil exhaustion and inefficient farming methods made profits impossible without the cheap labor of slaves. From about 1850 coffee cultivation began to spread in the southern provinces, marking a key shift in Brazilian agriculture. Coffee would soon become the nation's most important product. Coffee producers also used slave labor and wanted to retain slavery, but their profits were much larger than those of the sugar producers, so a transition to free labor would have been easier for them. Coffee planters also tended to see themselves as being on the side of economic progress. Hence, people investing in coffee were more open to emancipation than those who had invested in sugar.

As early as 1826 the Brazilian government had made a treaty with Great Britain, agreeing to suppress the slave trade. For many years Brazil refused to honor these treaty provisions, but by 1850 had virtually ceased importing slaves, putting the sugar planters on the defensive and freeing the capital once spent on slaves for investments in coffee. The end of slave imports effectively doomed the institution of slavery because the birth rate among slaves was too low for the slave population to reproduce itself. It was nonetheless one thing to face this technical inevitability and another to abolish slavery.

The Paraguayan War of 1865–1870 postponed consideration of the slave question. This conflict, which pitted Brazil, Argentina, and Uruguay against Paraguay, originated in border disputes and in larger commercial conflicts about ongoing Paraguayan access to the ports on the lower Plate River, in particular Montevideo. The conflict became a long,

A Brazilian Liberal Denounces Slavery

Critics sharply attacked slavery in Brazil from the mid-nineteenth century onward. The first major attempt to emancipate slaves occurred in 1871. That law proposed gradual emancipation by liberating the children of slaves. The abolitionist movement continued to grow resulting in the final emancipation of slaves in Brazil in 1888. In 1883 Joaquim Nabuco, a major leader of the abolitionist movement, published O Abolicionismo *which stands as one of the chief examples of Brazilian anti-slavery literature. Although not quoted in the passage below, Nabuco drew extensive parallels between the slavery of Brazil and that which had existed in the United States before the Civil War. Here Nabuco seeks to demonstrate the manner in which the continuation of slavery prevents commercial economic development in Brazil and inhibits the country from embracing the progressive forces of the day. Note the manner in which Nabuco has absorbed the ideas of the eighteenth-century Enlightenment and nineteenth-century European liberalism.*

What are the values and outlooks that Nabuco associates with the expansion of commerce? Why does he see slavery as undermining those values? How and why does he see slavery inhibiting progressive social and intellectual forces? In this passage, what are possible arguments against slavery that Nabuco does not raise?

Slavery does not permit the existence of a true working class, nor is it compatible with the wage system and the personal dignity of the artisan. . . . [T]here can be no strong, respected, and intelligent working class where the employers of labor are accustomed to order slaves about. . . .

Slavery and industry are mutually exclusive terms, like slavery and colonization. The spirit of the former, spreading through a country, kills every one of the human faculties from which industry springs—initiative, inventiveness, individual energy, and every one of the elements that industry requires—the formation of capital, an abundance of labor, technical education of the workers, confidence in the future. . . .

. . . . [C]ommerce, in the absence of industry and free labor, can function only as an agent of slavery, buying whatever it offers and selling whatever its needs. This is why in Brazil commerce does not develop or open new perspectives for the country. . . . Slavery distrusts commerce, as its distrusts any agency of progress, whether it is a business man's office, a railroad station, or a primary school; yet slavery needs commerce. . . . But so long as slavery endures, commerce must always be the servant of a class, and not an independent national agent. . . .

Of the classes whose growth slavery artificially stimulates, none is more numerous than that of government employees. . . . Officeholding is . . . the asylum of the descendants of formerly rich and noble families that have squandered the fortunes made from slavery. . . . But officeholding is also our political olive tree, that shelters all those young men of brains and ambition but no money who form the great majority of our talented people. . . .

Among the forces of progress and change around which slavery has created a vacuum as hostile to its interests, the press is notable—and not only the newspaper but the book, and everything that concerns education. . . . The slave hut and the school are poles that repel each other. . . .

Among the forces whose emergence slavery has impeded is public opinion, the consciousness of a common destiny. Under slavery there cannot exist that powerful force called public opinion, that simultaneously balances and offers a point of support to the individuals who represented the most advanced thoughout of the country. Just as slavery is incompatible with spontaneous immigration, so will it prevent the influx of new ideas. Itself incapable of invention, it will have nothing to do with progress.

Joaquim Nabuco, *O Abolicionismo* (São Paulo, 1938), excerpted from Benjamin Keen, translator, as reprinted in Benjamin Keen, editor, *Readings in Latin-American Civilization 1492 to the Present* (Boston: Houghton Mifflin Company, 1955), pp. 339–343.

---

exceedingly destructive struggle because the dictator of Paraguay, Francisco Solano López (1827–1870) mobilized his entire country into a war of attrition and refused to surrender. His death in battle in 1870 finally ended the war, but only after more than half (and perhaps a larger portion) of the adult male population of Paraguay had been killed. The victorious powers installed a friendly government in Paraguay, which sold off state lands to foreign speculators.

The end of the war returned slavery to the forefront of Brazilian politics. Brazil and the Spanish colonies of Puerto Rico and Cuba were now the only slaveholding countries in the hemisphere. The emperor favored gradual emancipation. A law of 1871 set the stage for such emancipation by freeing slaves owned by the crown and by decreeing legal freedom for future children of slaves. The law actually had little effect because it required the children of slaves to work on plantations until the age of twenty-one. However, throughout the 1870s and 1880s the abolition movement grew in Brazil. Public figures from across the entire political spectrum called for an end to slavery. Abolitionists helped slaves to escape. The army, many of whose officers held political views associated with positivism, resented having to enforce laws protecting slavery. In 1888 Pedro II was in Europe for medical treatment, and his daughter was regent. She favored abolition rather than gradual emancipation. When Parliament in that year passed a law abolishing slavery without any compensation to the slave owners, she signed it, thus ending slavery in Brazil.

A Republic Replaces Monarchy   The abolition of slavery brought to a head other issues that in 1889 caused the collapse of the monarchy. Planters who received no financial compensation for their slaves were resentful. Roman Catholic clerics were disaffected by disputes with the emperor over education. Pedro II was unwell; his daughter, the heir to the throne, was unpopular and distrusted. The officer corps of the army had been dissatisfied with what it regarded as insufficient political influence since its victory in the Paraguayan War. In November 1889 the army sent Pedro II into exile in France.

The Brazilian republic lasted from 1891 to 1930. Like the monarchy, it was dominated by a small group of wealthy persons, the most dominant of whom were the coffee planters. The political arrangement that allowed the republic to function smoothly was an agreement among the state governors. The president was to be chosen alternately from the states of São Paulo and Minas Gerais. In turn, the other eighteen governors had considerable local political latitude. Fixed elections and patronage kept the system in operation. Literacy replaced property as the qualification for voting, leaving few people qualified to vote. There was consequently little organized opposition and, for that matter, little political life at all within the republic.

From the 1890s onward the coffee industry dominated both the political and the economic life of the nation. Around 1900 Brazil was producing over three fourths of the world's coffee. The crop's success led almost inevitably to overproduction. To meet this problem, the government devised policies for maintaining high prices that required large loans from foreign banks. High world coffee prices encouraged competition from other Latin American producers, which in turn required more price supports in Brazil. In addition to the international loans, maintaining the price of coffee required considerable payments to the government from all of the non-coffee-related sectors of the economy. These sectors in turn felt exploited by the coffee interests. As a result of these arrangements, throughout the life of the Republic Brazil remained essentially a country producing a single product for export and few goods for internal consumption.

Economic Problems and Military Coups   The end of slavery, the expansion of coffee production, and the be-

ginning of a slow growth of urban industry attracted foreign immigrants to Brazil. They tended to settle in the cities and constituted the core of the early industrial labor force. In Brazil, as elsewhere, World War I caused major economic disruption. Urban labor discontent appeared. There was a general strike in São Paulo in 1917, with the inevitable military action against the strikers. The failure to address urban and industrial social problems and the political corruption of the republic led to attempted military coups in 1922 and 1924. Both revolts failed to bring down the republic, but they indicated profound discontent with a political structure designed primarily to protect the producers of a single agricultural commodity. The revolts also demonstrated that certain segments of the military were determined to change the political system. They wanted a modern nation that was not dependent on a single exportable product and a political system that depended on more than corruption and recognized interests besides those of the coffee planters.

Coffee had ruled as the economic "king" of the Brazilian republic, and its collapse brought the republic down with it. In 1929 coffee prices hit record lows; currency exchange rates fell; and foreign loans were unavailable. Millions of bags of coffee lay in warehouses. Government reserves were depleted in an unsuccessful attempt to hold up the price of coffee and to pay for imports no longer being funded by coffee exports. The economic structure of the republic lay in shambles. In October 1930 a military coup installed Getulio Vargas (1883–1954) in the presidency. Vargas governed Brazil until 1945.

The Vargas years represent a major turning point in Brazilian history. Vargas was initially supported by the reform elements in the military, by professional middle-class groups, and by urban workers. In office, he moved first to the right and then to the left and then back again. He was an experimentalist and pragmatist who primarily wanted to hold on to power and to make Brazil a modern nation. Vargas was able to recognize the new social and economic groups shaping Brazilian political life. First with constitutionalism and then with dictatorship, he attempted to allow the government to act on behalf of those groups without allowing them to influence or direct the government in a genuinely democratic manner. However, despite the personal power that accrued to him, he did not form his own political party or movement as Perón would later do in Argentina or as the Mexican revolutionaries had done. Vargas rather attempted to function like a ringmaster directing the various forces in Brazilian life. His failure to establish a genuinely stable institutional political framework for a Brazil that included many interest groups besides the coffee planters has influenced Brazil to the present day.

Vargas and his supporters sought to lessen dependence on coffee by fostering industries that would produce domestically

goods that had previously been imported from abroad. They thus attempted to create internal suppliers for goods needed in the internal Brazilian economy. The policy succeeded, and by the mid-1930s domestic manufacturing was increasing. These years mark the real beginning of Brazilian manufacturing. In the constitution of 1934 Vargas established a legal framework for labor relations. The structures were paternalistic but included an eight-hour day and a minimum wage. The constitution also asserted government responsibility to protect mineral and water rights.

In the Brazilian context these measures appeared reformist, if not necessarily liberal, and marked a departure from government policy dominated by the coffee oligarchy and politics by patronage. However, in the late 1930s Vargas confronted major political opposition from both the Brazilian Communist Party (founded in 1922) and a new right-wing movement called *Integralism*. In 1937, facing these political opponents, Vargas assumed personal dictatorial power. His regime thereafter was repressive. He claimed to have established an *Estado Novo* ("new state"). He wrapped himself in the flag of nationalism and order and presented himself as the protector of national stability against factions that would foster instability and of the national interest against international opponents.

Like the European dictators of the same era, Vargas used censorship, secret police, and torture against his political opponents. He also used his newly assumed power to diversify and modernize the economy. In 1940 a five-year plan provided more state direction for the economy. His government favored the production of goods from heavy industry that would be used in Brazil itself. To maintain the support of workers and trade unions, the state also issued a progressive labor code. Siding with the Allies in World War II, Brazil built up large reserves of foreign currency through the export of foodstuffs. This economic activity and imposed political stability allowed the government to secure foreign loans for still further economic development. By the end of the war Brazil was becoming the major Latin American industrial power.

Participation in World War II on the side of the Allies had led many in Brazil to believe that they should not remain subject to a dictatorship. This attitude was widespread in the military, which had fought in Europe and established close contact with the United States. In 1945 Vargas promised that he would lead the nation toward democracy and hold presidential as well as congressional elections. His actions, however, suggested that he planned to manipulate the elections. In response, the military carried out a coup, and Vargas retired temporarily from political life.

The new regime, which was democratic, continued the general policy of economic development through foreign-financed industrialization. The state, however, assumed a much smaller role. When in 1950 Vargas was elected president, his return to office was anticlimactic. He was by then an elderly man, well past his prime. Yet in 1953 he established Petrobas, a state-owned petroleum exploration company. His presidency remained controversial. There was much criticism of him and of the corruption of his appointments. A member of his staff became involved in the assassination of a prominent civilian journalist. The military demanded that Vargas resign. Instead he took his own life in 1954, leaving a public testament in which he presented himself as the protector of the poor and of the broad national interest.

In the decade after Vargas's death, Brazil remained a democracy, although a highly unstable one. The government itself began to undertake vast projects such as the enormously costly construction of the new capital of Brasília, begun in 1957. Located far inland, Brasília required the creation of a vast road system. With Brasília underway, the government of Juscelino Kubitschek (1902–1976), who had supported the building of the new capital, fostered the establishment of a large automobile industry. The rapid growth of cities and the expansion of a working class radicalized political life. The political system could not readily accommodate itself to the concerns of workers and the urban poor. Widespread poverty and illiteracy continued to plague both the cities and the countryside. In a structural problem created by the constitution of 1946, the presidency was controlled by urban voters, whereas the congress was controlled by rural voters.

By the early 1960s, when President João Goulert (1918–1977) took office, Brazilian political life was in turmoil. Goulert's predecessors, including Vargas, had always attempted to balance interests or to move among various political forces without firmly favoring a single sector. After months of wavering, however, Goulert committed himself to a policy favored by the left. In 1964 he announced his support for land reform. Peasants had already tried to seize land and landowners had fought them. Political conservatives and moderates expected some favors to urban radicals, which they might have tolerated, but vigorously resisted any hint of significant political or land reform in the countryside. Goulert also questioned the authority of the military hierarchy. Moreover, Brazil faced economic problems: Both industrial and farm production had fallen from the levels achieved in 1960, fostering discontent. In March 1964 the military, claiming to protect Brazil from communism, seized control of the government, ending its post-World War II experiment with democracy.

IN WORLD PERSPECTIVE
Latin American History

Since the early nineteenth century, Spanish- and Portuguese-speaking America stretching from the Rio Grande to Cape Horn has posed a paradox. Languages, religion, economic ties, and many political institutions render the area part of the Western world. Yet the economics, politics, and social life of Latin America have developed differently from other parts of the West. A region exceedingly rich in natural resources, possessing gold, silver, nitrates, and oil, has been plagued with extreme poverty. As other Western nations have moved toward liberal democracy and social equality, the states of Latin America have had millions of citizens living in situations of marked inequality and social dependence. For over a century and a half, the political life of Latin America has been characterized by uncertain democracy, authoritarian regimes, and a general tendency toward instability. Three major explanations have been set forth to account for these difficulties, which have led to so much tragedy and human suffering.

The first and most widely accepted view contends that after the Wars of Independence the new states of Latin America remained economically and culturally dependent. In effect, it is argued, the colonial framework was never abolished. Under Spanish and Portuguese rule, Latin America's wealth was extracted and exported for the benefit of those powers. After independence, the Creole elite turned toward foreign investors, first British and then American, to finance economic development and to provide the technology for mining, transport, and industry. As a result, Latin America became dependent on wealthy foreign powers for investment and for markets.

A second explanation emphasizes the Iberian heritage. Its advocates contend that Latin America should be viewed as a region on the periphery of the Western world in the same manner that Spain, Portugal, and Italy lie on the Mediterranean periphery of Europe. All of these Latin nations, dominated by Roman Catholicism, have had similar unstable governments. They have often tended toward some version of dictatorship, uneven development, anticlericalism, and social cleavage between urban and rural areas and between wealthy middle-class or landed elites and poor peasant populations. Viewed in this Iberian-Mediterranean context, Latin America is less puzzling than when it is viewed in the context of northern Europe.

Chronology of Brazil	
1822	Brazil becomes an independent empire
1840	Pedro II assumes personal rule
1840s and 1850s	Spread of coffee cultivation
1865–1870	Paraguayan War
1871	First law curbing slavery
1888	Slavery abolished
1889	Fall of the monarchy
1917	General strike in São Paulo
1929	Collapse of coffee prices
1930–1945	Vargas Era
1957	Construction of Brasília begins
1964	Military takes control of the government

A third explanation emphasizes conscious political, economic, and cultural decisions taken by the Latin American Creole elite after independence. This explanation contends that the elite, including the army officers who won the wars, sought to enrich themselves and to maintain their positions at the cost of all other segments of the population. These officers, landowners, and urban middle-class leaders aligned their various national economies with the industrializing regions of Europe and North America. They also adopted the liberal political and economic ideologies of Europe to justify unlimited exploitation of economic resources on the basis of individualistic enterprise. They embraced European concepts of progress to dismiss the legitimacy of the culture and the communal values of the Indians or the peasants.

None of these interpretations actually excludes the others. To truly understand the region and its past, all three viewpoints seem necessary. And as noted at the beginning of this chapter, it also helps to view Latin America within a global perspective. Beginning in the nineteenth century much of the region, like much of Asia and Africa, was drawn into an integrated worldwide economic system dominated by Europe and North America. Many nations in Latin America and elsewhere developed narrow economies based on the export of one or a few raw materials or semi-finished products. They were vulnerable to fluctuations in worldwide demand for these products and to political and economic interference from Europe and North America. The result was often economic turbulence and political instability.

Review Questions ——

1. What was the condition of the Latin American economies after independence? What was their relation to Britain? Why were most Latin American states slow to develop an industrial base? What role did their economies play in the worldwide economy that developed in the nineteenth century?

2. Did the structure of Latin American societies change after independence? What role did the traditional elites play in the economic and political life of their nations? What was the condition of the mass of the population?

3. How did European and United States investment in Latin America affect the region economically? Politically?

4. Why did so many Latin American nations find it difficult to develop stable political regimes? What role did the military play?

5. What was the effect of increased European immigration on Argentina? How did the Argentine elite cope with growing urbanization and industrialization? Why was Juan Perón able to seize and hold power?

6. Did Mexico experience a real revolution in the early twentieth century? How does this experience distinguish Mexico from other Latin American countries? What caused the turmoil?

7. Why was the Brazilian experience of independence and early nationhood different from that of Spanish-speaking Latin America? What was the role of coffee in Brazil's economy? How did the Vargas regime change the Brazilian economy? Why did Brazilian democracy end in a military coup in 1964?

Suggested Readings ——

S. ARROM, *The Women of Mexico City, 1790–1857* (1985). A pioneering study.

E. BERMAN, ED., *Women, Culture, and Politics in Latin America* (1990). Useful essays.

L. BETHELL, ED., *The Cambridge History of Latin America*, 8 vols. (1992). The single most authoritative coverage, with extensive bibliographical essays.

V. BULMER-THOMAS, *The Economic History of Latin America Since Independence* (1994). A major study in every respect.

E. B. BURNS, *The Poverty of Progress: Latin America in the Nineteenth Century* (1980). Argues that the elites suppressed alternative modes of cultural and economic development.

E. B. BURNS, *A History of Brazil* (1993). The most useful one-volume treatment.

D. BUSHNELL AND N. MACAULAY, *The Emergence of Latin America in the Nineteenth Century* (1994). A survey that examines the internal development of Latin America during the period.

R. CONRAD, *The Destruction of Brazilian Slavery, 1850–1889* (1971). A good survey of the most important problem in Brazil in the second half of the nineteenth century.

R. CONRAD, *World of Sorrow: The African Slave Trade to Brazil* (1986). An excellent survey of the subject.

E. V. DA COSTA, *The Brazilian Empire: Myths and Histories* (1985). Essays that provide a thorough introduction to Brazil during the period of the empire.

H. S. FERNS, *Britain and Argentina in the Nineteenth Century* (1968). Explains clearly the intermeshing of the two economies.

M. FONT, *Coffee, Contention, and Change in the Making of Modern Brazil* (1990). Extensive discussion of the problems of a single-commodity economy.

R. GRAHAM, *Britain and the Onset of Modernization in Brazil* (1968). Another study of British economic dominance.

S. H. HABER, *Industry and Underdevelopment: The Industrialization of Mexico, 1890–1940* (1989). Examines the problem of industrialization before and after the revolution.

G. HAHNER, *Emancipating the Female Sex: The Struggle for Women's Rights in Brazil, 1850–1940* (1990). An extensive examination of a relatively understudied issue in Latin America.

C. H. HARING, *Empire in Brazil: A New World Experiment with Monarchy* (1958). Remains a useful overview.

J. HEMMING, *Amazon Frontier: The Defeat of the Brazilian Indians* (1987). A brilliant survey of the experience of Native Americans in modern Brazil.

R. A. HUMPHREYS, *Latin America and the Second World War*, 2 vols. (1981–1982). The standard work on the topic.

F. KATZ, ED., *Riot, Rebellion, and Revolution in Mexico: Social Base of Agrarian Violence, 1750–1940* (1988). Essays that put the violence of the revolution in a longer context.

A. KNIGHT, *The Mexican Revolution*, 2 vols. (1986). The best treatment of the subject.

S. MAINWARING, *The Catholic Church and Politics in Brazil, 1916–1985* (1986). An examination of a key institution in Brazilian life.

M. C. MEYER AND W. L. SHERMAN, *The Course of Mexican History* (1995). An excellent survey.

M. MORNER, *Adventurers and Proletarians: The Story of Migrants in Latin America* (1985). Examines immigration to Latin America and migration within it.

J. PAGE, *Perón: A Biography* (1983). The standard English treatment.

D. ROCK, *Politics in Argentina, 1890–1930: The Rise and Fall of Radicalism* (1975). The major discussion of the Argentine Radical Party.

D. ROCK, *Argentina, 1516–1987: From Spanish Colonization to Alfonsin* (1987). Now the standard survey.

D. ROCK, ED., *Latin America in the 1940s: War and Postwar Transitions* (1994). Essays examining a very difficult decade for the continent.

R. M. SCHNEIDER, *"Order and Progress": A Political History of Brazil* (1991). A straightforward narrative with helpful notes for further reading.

T. E. SKIDMORE, *Black into White: Race and Nationality in Brazilian Thought* (1993). Examines the role of racial theory in Brazil.

P. H. SMITH, *Argentina and the Failure of Democracy: Conflict among Political Elites, 1904–1955* (1974). An examination of the one the major political puzzles of Latin American history.

S. J. AND B. H. STEIN, *The Colonial Heritage of Latin America: Essays on Economic Dependence in Perspective* (1970). A major statement of the dependence interpretation.

D. TAMARIN, *The Argentine Labor Movement, 1930–1945: A Study in the Origins of Perónism* (1985). A useful introduction to a complex subject.

H. J. WIARDA, *Politics and Social Change in Latin America: The Distinct Tradition* (1974). Excellent essays that stress the ongoing role of Iberian traditions.

J. D. WIRTH, ED., *Latin American Oil Companies and the Politics of Energy* (1985). A series of case studies.

J. WOLFE, *Working Women, Working Men: São Paulo and the Rise of Brazil's Industrial Working Class, 1900–1955* (1993). Pays particular attention to the role of women.

J. WOMACK, *Zapata and the Mexican Revolution* (1968). A classic study.

31 INDIA, THE ISLAMIC HEARTLANDS, AND AFRICA: THE ENCOUNTER WITH THE MODERN WEST (1800–1945)

An Indian artist's painting of James Todd (c. 1880) riding in a ceremonial procession on

a royal elephant. [E. T. Archive/Victoria and Albert Museum]

CHAPTER TOPICS

THE INDIAN EXPERIENCE

◆ British Dominance and Colonial Rule

◆ From British Crown Raj to Independence

THE ISLAMIC EXPERIENCE

◆ Islamic Responses to Declining Power and Independence

◆ Western Political and Economic Encroachment

◆ The Western Impact

◆ Islamic Responses to Foreign Encroachment

THE AFRICAN EXPERIENCE

◆ New States and Power Centers

◆ Islamic Reform Movements

◆ Increasing European Involvement

◆ African Resistance to Colonialism: The Rise of Nationalism

In World Perspective India, the Islamic Heartlands, and Africa, 1800–1945

The encroachment of the European nations on the rest of the world from the late fifteenth century onward brought radical, often devastating changes. In the West itself, spiritual and material disruption accompanied the Renaissance, the Reformation, the Enlightenment, and the Industrial and Scientific revolutions. When Western expansion brought the ideas and innovations of these watershed European developments to the Indian, Asian, and African worlds, the effects on these societies were often much more radical than they had been in Europe. Certainly the challenges and changes that ensued came much more rapidly, in greater concentration, and with much less preparation than they had in the West.

To speak of these complex processes under the rubric of "modernization" still does not reflect the acute differences between the relatively lengthy and gradual processes of change in western Europe and the more rapid and more disruptive changes that European imperialism and colonialism brought to other parts of the world. Nor does it do justice to the degree to which the very concept of "modernity" has been appropriated by the West. Although every advanced society in any age has presumably viewed its culture as "modern," the dominance of the West in recent centuries has led it to a specific and novel notion of modernity: namely, as a special set of ideas and institutions that evolved in Europe between the Renaissance and the early twentieth century and was then gradually exported to, or imposed upon, other societies around the globe. The expression "the impact of modernity" refers to the way the introduction of social, economic, technological, scientific, and ideological forms of "modern" Western civilization affected traditional cultures.

The consequences of the spread of Western culture have been so massive that today non-Western peoples are seen all too often as merely its passive recipients. The American or European view of the world often reflects a simplistic dualism that enhances Western self-esteem by portraying the West as the active, creative, dominant force in recent history.[1] This view places the "modern" West on one side and the "backward" "Orient" on the other, as though all of the world outside Europe, North America, and their most westernized offshoots were some monolithic, archaic entity. Popular Western stereotypes of the Arab, the African, the Indian, the Chinese, and so on reinforce the Westerner's sense of being the true "modern" of recent history.

As parochial as such chauvinistic generalizations are—and as much as the processes of change in most non-Western cultures have their own internal dynamics—these generalizations may nonetheless have a certain grim historical core, as suggested by the crises experienced by many non-Western cultures under the material and spiritual impact of Western modernity and its agents. The impingement of the West has been a major element in the recent history of African, Asian, and Indian

---

[1]See the ground-breaking and important, if also polemical and flawed, book of Edward W. Said, *Orientalism* (New York: Pantheon, 1978).

civilizations. Not all non-Western societies have had equal success in either retaining or reasserting their precolonial independence and identity, nor in responding creatively to the ongoing challenges of Western-style modernity. The spectrum of postimperial or postcolonial experience ranges from the largely positive response of Japan or the mixed experience of China to the painful and often destructive experiences of most African societies, with India, Iran, and the Middle East somewhere in between.

Nevertheless, in all of these "Third World" areas, Western modernity entered cultures that had ancient and highly developed social, religious, and political traditions of their own. These traditions did not simply melt away on the arrival of the Westerners with their powerful new traditions. In the last 200 years—both during and after the onslaught of the West—Islamic, Hindu, and other regions of the Third World maintained considerable continuity with the past. Much of the history of the twentieth-century Asian and African societies hit hardest by the new "modernity" has been and continues to be shaped by their peoples' realization of the importance of their own traditions.

THE INDIAN EXPERIENCE

British Dominance and Colonial Rule

In the eighteenth century Britain became the dominant naval and commercial power in the Southern Seas, overshadowing Portugal and Holland, which had developed trade in the region in the sixteenth and seventeenth centuries. In India the British defeated the French and regional Indian powers for domination of the subcontinent (see Chapter 23). By the early nineteenth century they had built the largest European colonial empire in the Afro-Asian world. India, the greatest traditional civilization of Africa or Asia to come under direct European colonial rule, was the "jewel in the crown" of that empire.

Building the Empire: The First Half of the Nineteenth Century

As we saw in Chapter 23, as early as a half century before the British crown asserted direct rule over India in 1858, the British wielded effective imperial control through the East India Company. As the Company's pressure on smaller states to pay "subsidies" for military "protection" brought ever more of them to either collapse or rebellion, the British annexed more and more territory. Those areas not annexed were recognized as independent princely states. Ranging in size from less than a square mile to more than 80,000 square miles (Hyderabad), these independent states retained their status only so long as they remained faithfully allied to Britain and contributed money to their common "defense." Private Indian businessmen as well as disaffected revenue farmers and other members of Indian elites often colluded with the British against local or regional rulers. The state of Mysore, the Maratha confederation, and the Sikhs of the Panjab were overpowered between 1797 and 1853. The India that resulted was a polyglot mixture of diverse small and large tributary states and provinces that the British administered directly.

The economic impact of Company rule was extensive. To pay the debts incurred by their military actions, the Company's administrators organized and exploited Indian land revenues. The need for ever higher revenues crowded out considerations of economic expansion and equitable tax distribution. Squeezed by these demands, many peasants deserted their land; by the 1830s land revenues were in sharp decline. In addition, demand for Indian indigo, cotton, and opium in the China and British trade also slacked off in the 1830s, and famines brought widespread suffering. The economic and social reforms (1828–1836) of Governor General Lord William Bentinck (1774–1839) were not sufficient to turn things around substantially.

Company rule, especially in the early nineteenth century, also dramatically affected the physical face of India. Company policies encouraged widespread increase of settled agriculture and small commodity production at the expense of the nomadic and pastoralist cultures that had been a major presence across North and central India only a half century earlier. British "pacification" involved the clearing of land to deny natural cover to military enemies and the often forced settlement of peasants as pioneer farmers in new regions. Early in the nineteenth century the Company and European entrepreneurs also undertook massive commercial logging operations. These activities caused extensive deforestation throughout the subcontinent. The devastation included southern, western, and central forests (in Tanjore and Mysore, the Bombay presidency, and Hyderabad); the forests of the sub-Himalayan hills (as in Awadh); and, after 1840, the tracts leveled for tea and coffee plantations in Assam and the Bengal hills. This ecological destruction was a major by-product of the transformation of India into a more homogeneous peasant farming society that provided a better base for colonial administration.[2]

---

[2]C. A. Bayly, *Indian Society and the Making of the British Empire* (Cambridge, UK: Cambridge University Press, 1988), pp. 138–146.

A tea planter on his estate. One of the symbols of the *raj*, the great tea plantations of Sri Lanka and northeastern India—especially those of Assam—were major sources of wealth for the British overlords. They were also partly responsible for the deforestation of much of the subcontinent that occurred under British colonial rule in the nineteenth century. [Hulton/Corbis-Bettmann]

The Indians were by no means passive in the face of this misuse of their lands and peoples. The first half of the nineteenth century saw almost constant revolt in one place or another. Although often disjointed, the revolts occurred in virtually every corner of the subcontinent, particularly in North and central India. They included peasant movements of noncooperation, Muslim farm workers' attacks on British and Hindu estate owners, grain riots, the open warfare of tribal revolts, and other actions. They culminated in a watershed event, the Indian Revolt of 1857 (the so-called Sepoy Mutiny or Rebellion). Thus the commonly accepted image of this era as one of general tranquillity prior to a "mutiny" against British custodianship turns out to have been a product of British propaganda.

The immediate trigger of the Revolt of 1857 was the concern among Bengal troops that animal grease on newly issued rifles exposed them to ritual pollution. Behind this issue, however, lay a variety of grievances, including the recent addition of Sikhs, Gurkhas, and lower-caste soldiers to the army; the deteriorating economic conditions of many of the Hindu troops' higher-caste relatives back home; outrage at excessive tax rates, especially among troops from Meerut; and anger at the 1856 British annexation of the rich princely state of Awadh (home to many of the troops). One can also see in the revolt the desire, widespread at least in the northern districts along the great trunk road between Bengal and the Panjab, to recover and rebuild a pre-British political order in North India. The revolt was not an all-India affair. It centered on Delhi, where the last Mughal emperor joined in the rebel cause, and involved uprisings in other cities and towns from Chittagong in Bengal to Lahore and even Peshawar in the Panjab. Civil uprisings in the countryside around Delhi and Lucknow extended the base of the revolt to the rural peasantry.

The British were at first unable to respond effectively to the widespread risings, but because their real power bases in Bengal and the Panjab were not destroyed, nor their ability to communicate and move new troops impaired, they eventually won the day. With their forces augmented by Sikhs from the Panjab and Gurkhas from Bengal, they overcame the internally divided Indian opposition. Begun in the spring of 1857, the revolt was broken, often with great brutality, by autumn, and it was completely finished before the end of the year. In the next year the East India Company was dissolved, and India came under direct rule of the British Crown.

The "Mutiny" of 1857, although drawing on widespread disaffection, was not a nationalist revolution. It showed a unity of Indian feeling but not yet enough unity to oust the British. Still, it presaged the rise of an effective unified response and highlighted underlying resentment of the burdens of foreign domination that were to grow increasingly oppressive for Indians of all regions and religions over the ensuing ninety years of Crown rule.

British-Indian Relations

The overall impact of British presence on the Indian masses, under both Company and Crown rule, was brutal but

Macaulay Writes on Indian Education

The momentous decision in 1835 to introduce and encourage English-language study and the British school curriculum in Indian schools was hotly disputed by the English and Indians alike. In the end it bred a new generation of elite Indians prepared to act as advocates for their nation, as well as a class of bureaucrats for the British raj. *It also worked to the advantage of Hindus at the expense of the Muslims, because the Muslims tended to reject English schooling and lost ground in the long run. This famous position paper by Thomas Babington Macaulay expresses the thinking of the "Anglicists," who prevailed over the "Orientalists," and reveals British prejudices about the superiority of Western culture over Sanskrit (or any regional Indian) culture.*

When Macaulay writes "that English is better worth knowing than Sanscrit or Arabic," is he making an objective judgment or is he engaging in "cultural imperialism"? From your perspective, which are the laudable, and which the problematic, intentions and goals of the writer?

We now come to the gist of the matter. We have a fund to be employed as government shall direct for the intellectual improvement of the people of this country. The simple question is, what is the most useful way of employing it?

All parties seem to be agreed on one point, that the dialects commonly spoken among the natives of this part of India contain neither literary nor scientific information, and are, moreover, so poor and rude that, until they are enriched from some other quarter, it will not be easy to translate any valuable work into them. It seems to be admitted on all sides that the intellectual improvement of those classes of the people who have the means of pursuing higher studies can at present be affected only by means of some language not vernacular amongst them.

What then shall that language be? One-half of the committee maintain that it should be the English. The other half strongly recommend the Arabic and Sanscrit. The whole question seems to me to be, which language is the best worth knowing? . . .

To sum up what I have said, I think it clear that we are free to employ our funds as we choose; that we ought to employ them in teaching what is best worth knowing; that English is better worth knowing than Sanscrit or Arabic; that the natives are desirous to be taught English, and are not desirous to be taught Sanscrit or Arabic; that neither as the languages of law, nor as the languages of religion, have the Sanscrit and Arabic any peculiar claim to our engagement; that it is possible to make natives of this country thoroughly good English scholars; and that to this end our efforts ought to be directly. In one point I fully agree with the gentlemen to whose general views I am opposed. I feel with them, that it is impossible for us, with our limited means, to attempt to educate the body of the people. We must at present do our best to form a class who may be interpreters between us and the millions whom we govern; a class of persons, Indian in blood and color, but English in taste, in opinions, in morals, and in intellect. To that class we may leave it to refine the vernacular dialects of the country, to enrich those dialects with terms of science borrowed from the Western nomenclature, and to render them by degrees fit vehicles for conveying knowledge to the great mass of the population.

From *Sources of Indian Tradition* edited by William Theodore de Bary. Copyright © 1958 by Columbia University Press. Reprinted with permission of the publisher.

---

impersonal, in that it was largely economic. India was effectively integrated into Britain's economy, becoming a market for British goods, providing Britain with raw materials and other products, and consequently helping Britain maintain a healthy balance of trade. Britain's involvement in India's internal affairs included politics, education, the civil-service infrastructure, communications, and transportation, but the consequences of its domination and exploitation of India's labor and resources were especially far-reaching.

British cultural imperialism was never a major nor even an official policy of the East India Company. In fact, like Warren Hastings (1732–1818), Governor General of the Company from 1774 to 1785, many Britons expressed interest in and at least partial openness to Indians and their culture. A few mixed and even intermarried with Indians. The Company itself required many of its India officers to learn Persian and Sanskrit. Nor did it try to propagate Christianity or impose Western culture; indeed, it actively opposed Christian missionary activity in India until forced by British public pressure in the 1830s and 1840s to reverse its policy. Nonetheless the British-Indian relationship had a paternalistic and patronizing dimension, both before and after the events of 1857. Even with the improved access of Indians to English education and to civil-service positions of greater responsibility in the late nineteenth and early twentieth centuries, the fundamental imbalance between overlords and subjects remained and was frequently expressed in racial terms. The ethos of the British rulers included the understanding that they had the task of governing an inferior "race" that could not handle the job by itself. Even Indians whose university degrees or army training gave them qualifications that were impeccable by British standards were never accepted as true equals. From army to civil-service ranks, the upper echelon of command was British; the middle and lower echelons of administration were Indian.

Despite this unequal relationship, British ideas and ways of doing things significantly influenced a small but powerful Indian elite. It was felt in both their business and political life and their manners and customs. Conversion to Christianity was rare, but Christian and secular values associated with the European Enlightenment—the ideals of British liberalism, for example—influenced Hindu and Muslim educated classes.

In the nineteenth century, probably the most influential and controversial member of the Indian elite to engage the British on their own ground was Ram Mohan Roy (1772–1833). Roy, a Bengali Hindu, rose to the top of the native ranks of East India Company service and became a strong voice for reform, both of Hindu life and practice and of British colonial policy where it deviated from European and Christian ideals. The spiritual father of the Brahmo Samaj (1828), a Hindu reform movement opposed to "barbarous" practices that ranged from *sati* (immolation of widows on their husbands' funeral pyres) to "idol worship" and Brahmanic "ritualism," Roy was an avowed modernist who wanted to meld the best of European-Christian morality and thought with the best of Hindu piety and thought. He was quick to oppose autocratic and unfair British legal and commercial practices and campaigned in India and in England for reform of the Company's India policies. He studied the Christian scriptures and the great thinkers of European civilization and was

influenced by the values in them that he found of worth. He drew upon these sources also in his own Hindu reform efforts. His wide-ranging writings and his public campaigns for education, political involvement, and social progress and against the "backward" practices and ideas of many of his Hindu compatriots alienated most of the leading Hindu thinkers and activists of his age, but twentieth-century Indians have often seen him as a visionary.

The cultural relationship between Britain and India was not, of course, a one-way affair. During the Company era, and increasingly after 1858, Britons at home became aware of India and Indians. The image that came to them, however, was filtered through the experience of other Britons who had spent time in the subcontinent and were not always either sympathetic or objective interpreters. Even many of those officers of the Company who made India a career developed little interest in Indians beyond what they needed to know to extract economic gain from them. Others, however, devoted substantial time to learning about Indians and their cultures. They studied their languages and got to know at least some of the Indian elite as friends. However, after the implementation of direct crown rule in 1858, a stricter social segregation of white rulers from Indian subjects set in.

Despite the keen interest in Indian culture that many of them had, the British, much more than their Central Asian Mughal predecessors, treated Indians all too often as backward heathen in need of the "civilizing" influences of their own "enlightened" culture, law, political system, education, and religion. A vivid example of this dismissive attitude to Indian culture is evident in the argument of the nineteenth-century British historian and statesman Lord Macaulay (1800–1859) in favor of an English-language curriculum in Indian schools (see the box on page 856).

Faces of the *raj*. A tennis party at the Residency, Kapurkala, Panjab, ca. 1894. [Hulton/Corbis-Bettmann]

If many Indians sought to acquire British ways and join the British in regional business and administration, many more deeply resented their subordinate status. Current research shows that the anti-imperial and anticolonial sentiment that blossomed into the nationalist movement at the end of the nineteenth century was not, as was once argued, restricted to the elite. It extended, rather, to the grass-roots level—among tribal groups, peasant farmers, and home or small-industry workers—and expressed itself even in the first half of the century, as already mentioned, in the constant revolts that preceded the Rebellion of 1857. Whatever their status, the distrust and animosity most Indians—including some who had profited enormously from British rule—felt toward their foreign rulers erupted in rebellion in 1857. But these feelings were not new, and they continued to grow.[3]

From British Crown Raj to Independence

The Burden of Crown Rule

The Revolt of 1857 had numerous consequences beyond the transfer of the administration of India from the East India Company to the British Parliament. The bloody conflict had involved such atrocities on both sides that it exacerbated mutual fear and hatred. Before the revolt, the British had maintained a largely native army under British officers. After the revolt, feeling threatened by this system, they tried to maintain a ratio of at least one British to three Indian soldiers. As before, the army was financed by Indian, not British, revenues. This imposed a huge economic burden on India, diverting one third of its total annual revenues to pay for its own military occupation.

British economic policies and accelerating population growth put great strains on India's poor. Cheap British machine-produced goods were exchanged for Indian raw materials and the products of its home industries, harming or destroying Indian craft industries and forcing multitudes into poverty or onto the land. Industrialization, which might have provided work for India's unemployed masses, was avoided. During the Civil War in the United States (1861–1865), when Britain's source of cotton in the U.S. South was interrupted, there was a shift from food to cotton farming in India. This shift intensified the effects of a drought in the 1870s, leading to widespread famine. Finally, many peasants lost their hereditary lands because of other British agrarian policies, forcing thousands to emigrate to Britain's dominions in South Africa, where they worked as indentured servants.

Another effect of the Revolt of 1857 was to create a poisonous distrust of Indians within the British colonial administration. "Cantonments" segregating white masters from "untrustworthy" natives became the rule in Indian towns and cities. Despite the just intentions expressed in royal statements and the opening of the civil service, at least nominally, to Indian candidates, the raj discouraged equality between Indian and Britisher. One bright exception to this trend was the tenure (1880–1884) of the Marquess of Ripon (1827–1909) as viceroy of India. Ripon fought to erase legal racial discrimination by allowing Indian judges to try British as well as Indian citizens. His efforts earned him the hatred of most of his British compatriots in India, but he was an example to emerging Indian leaders of the best that British egalitarianism could produce. Although his British foes managed by agitation to dilute his measures, in doing so they unwittingly gave Indians a model for political agitation of their own.[4]

Indian Resistance

Indians soon took up political activism. Late in the nineteenth century they founded the institutions that over the ensuing decades would help overcome traditional regionalism, build national feeling, and ultimately end colonial rule. In 1885 Indian modernists formed The Indian National Congress to reform traditional Hindu and Muslim practices that were out of line with their liberal ideals and to change British Indian policies that were equally out of line with British democratic ideals. Other Indians, taking a harder line, agitated for the rejection of British rule altogether. The Muslim League developed as a counterbalance to the Hindu-dominated Congress. The League eventually made common cause with the Congress in the quest for home rule, but ultimately worked for, and gained, a separate independent Muslim state, Pakistan. Heavy-handed and erratic British policies in legal administration, political representation, and taxation strengthened the growing desire for nationhood and independence.

Besides the British themselves, Indian internal divisions were the major obstacle to independence. These divisions included the many language groups and the many tiny subject princely states of the subcontinent. These, however, were not the only divisions or even the most critical. For much of British rule, every Indian politician was first a representative

---

[3]See, for example, Bayly, pp. 169–199; David Arnold, "Rebellious Hillmen: The Gudem-Rampa Risings, 1839–1924," in Ranajit Guha, ed., *Subaltern Studies* (Delhi: Oxford University Press, 1982), pp. 88–142; Ranajit Guha, *Elementary Aspects of Peasant Insurgency in Colonial India* (New Delhi, 1984); cf. Eric Stokes, *The Peasant and the Raj: Studies in Agrarian Society and Peasant Rebellion in Colonial India* (Cambridge, UK: Cambridge University Press, 1978).

[4]Stanley Wolpert, *A New History of India*, 2nd ed. (New York: Oxford University Press, 1982), pp. 256–257.

of his own region or state and second an Indian nationalist. Furthermore, the educated Indian elite shared little common ground with the masses of farmers and laborers beyond an antagonism to foreign rule, making unified resistance or political action difficult. Communal mistrust and overt conflict among Hindus, Muslims, Sikhs, and Jains also impeded concerted political action.

Despite these obstacles, a nationalist movement with many sub-branches took root. There were three principal elements within the independence movement that led to the creation of India and Pakistan in 1947.

The first consisted of those in the National Congress organization who sought gradual reform and progress toward Indian self-governance, or *swarāj*. This position did not preclude outright opposition to or defiance of the British on many matters, but it did mean trying to deal with the colonial rulers to change the system from within wherever possible. Among the proponents of this approach were G. K. Gokhale (1866–1915), the champion of moderate, deliberate, peaceful work toward self-determination; the spiritual and political genius Mohandas K. Gandhi (1869–1948); and his follower Jawaharlal Nehru (1889–1964), who became the first prime minister of India. Gandhi was the principal Indian leader after World War I and directed the all-India drive that finally forced the British out. Himself an English-trained lawyer, Gandhi drew on not only his own native Hindu (and Jain and Buddhist) heritage, but also on the ideas of Western liberal and Christian thinkers like Henry David Thoreau (1817–1862) and Leo Tolstoy (1828–1910). In the end, Gandhi became a world figure as well as an Indian leader.

The second element consisted of the militant Hindu nationalists, whose leader, the extremist B. G. Tilak (1856–1920), stressed the use of Indian languages and a revival of Hindu culture and learning. Tilak also subscribed to an anti-Muslim, Hindu communalist vision of Indian "self-governance." Where earlier in the nineteenth century foreign ideas had stimulated a Hindu renaissance and various reform movements, the Hindu extremists now looked to a return to traditional Indian values and self-sufficiency. Although their movement dissipated in the common resistance effort after 1914, their religious and political ideas still influence Indian political life. The resurgence of Hindu extremist groups in recent years and the communal strife, especially with Muslims, they have provoked are unhappy testimony to that continuing influence.

Muslims made up the third element. This is not, however, to suggest that there was only one Muslim position. In fact, the subcontinent held many divergent regional and even sectarian Muslim constituencies. Generally their leaders could be brought to make common cause only by the fear among Muslims that as a minority they stood to lose what power they had in a Hindu-majority, all-India state. Muslims

The "Great Soul," "Mahatma" Mohandas K. Gandhi, father of the modern state of India. [UPI/Corbis-Corbis-Bettmann]

had been slower than the Hindus to take up British ideas and education and thus lagged behind the Hindu intelligentsia in numbers and influence with the British or other Indians. Because of the prominence of Muslims in the 1857 Revolt, the British were at first much less inclined to foster their advancement than that of Hindus. Nonetheless, the Muslims, distrusting the largely Hindu National Congress after its founding in 1885, sought rapprochement with the British at first, rather than risk being submerged in Hindu-led movements of opposition.

The man who did the most to win back respect and a voice for the Muslims in India under the Crown was Sayyid Ahmad Khan (1817–1898). A long-time supporter of modernist ideas and of cooperation with the British, he could also be sharply critical of their mistakes in India. His opposition to Muslim participation in the National Congress foreshadowed the trend toward tension and conflict in Hindu-Muslim relations. He was also the founder of the Muslim educational initiative that led to the creation of the Muhammadan Anglo-Oriental College at Aligarh. This college became the center for modernist Muslim attempts to integrate Muslim faith with

Gandhi on Passive Resistance and Swarāj

Gandhi's powerful thinking and prose were already evident in his Hind Swarāj, *or* Indian Home Rule *of 1909. This work was to remain his basic manifesto. The following excerpts reflect important points in his philosophy.* Swadeshī *refers to reliance only on what one produces at home (rather than on foreign goods).*

How does Gandhi relate the ideas of passive resistance and *swarāj* to his theory of Indian self-rule? What are the advantages and disadvantages of his strategy for effecting political and social change? How does this document compare with others concerned with movements of independence and nationalism? See "The Stamp Act Congress Addresses George III" (Chapter 25), "Mazzini Defines Nationality" (Chapter 26), "The Pan-Slavic Congress Call for the Liberation of Slavic Nationalities" (Chapter 26), "William Gladstone Pleads for Irish Home Rule" (Chapter 27), and "Herzl Calls for the Establishment of a Jewish State" (Chapter 29).

Passive resistance is a method of securing rights by personal suffering; it is the reverse of resistance by arms. When I refuse to do a thing that is repugnant to my conscience, I use soul-force. For instance, the government of the day has passed a law which is applicable to me. I do not like it. If by using violence I force the government to repeal the law, I am employing what may be termed body-force. If I do not obey the law and accept the penalty for its breach, I use soul-force. It involves sacrifice of self.

Everybody admits that sacrifice of self is infinitely superior to sacrifice of others. Moreover, if this kind of force is used in a cause that is unjust, only the person using it suffers. He does not make others suffer for his mistakes. . . .

. . . The real meaning of the statement that we are a law-abiding nation is that we are passive resisters. When we do not like certain laws, we do not break the heads of law-givers but we suffer and do not submit to the laws. . . .

If man will only realize that it is unmanly to obey laws that are unjust, no man's tyranny will enslave him. This is the key to self-rule or home-rule. . . .

Let each do his duty. If I do my duty, that is, serve myself, I shall be able to serve others. Before I leave you, I will take the liberty of repeating:

1. Real home-rule is self-rule or self-control.
2. The way to it is passive resistance: that is soul-force or love-force.
3. In order to exert this force, *Swadeshī* in every sense is necessary.
4. What we want to do should be done, not because we object to the English or because we want to retaliate, but because it is our duty to do so. Thus, supposing that the English remove the salt-tax, restore our money, give the highest posts to Indians, withdraw the English troops, we shall certainly not use their machine-made goods, nor use the English language, nor many of their industries. It is worth noting that these things are, in their nature, harmful; hence we do not want them. I bear no enmity towards the English but do towards their civilization.

In my opinion, we have used the term *Swarāj* without understanding its real significance. I have endeavored to explain it as I understand it, and my conscience testifies that my life henceforth is dedicated to its attainment.

From *Sources of Indian Tradition* edited by William Theodore de Bary. Copyright © 1958 by Columbia University Press. Reprinted with permission of the publisher.

modern Western thought and learning. It is still one of the major Muslim intellectual centers in the subcontinent today.

Hindu-Muslim Friction on the Road to Independence

In the twentieth century the rift between Muslims and Hindus in the subcontinent grew wider, despite periods of cooperation against the British. Arguments for coexistence with Hindus floundered, and Muslim fears of loss of communal identity and rights grew. In the end the great Indo-Muslim poet, thinker, and "spiritual father of Pakistan,"

Muhammad Iqbal (1873–1938), and the "founder of Pakistan," Muhammad Ali Jinnah (1876–1949), helped move Muslims to separatism.

The independence of India and Pakistan from Western domination was only achieved with suffering and violence. Blood was spilled in the long battle with the British, in communal violence among Indians themselves, in the violence between Hindus and Muslims that accompanied partition in 1947, and in the subsequent (and still festering) dispute over Kashmir between India and Pakistan. Still, the victory of 1947 gave the peoples of the subcontinent, Indians and Pakistanis, at last a sense of participation in the world of na-

India

1772-1784	Administration of Warren Hastings
1772-1833	Ram Mohan Roy, Hindu reformer
1817-1898	Sayyid Ahmed Khan, Muslim reformer
1835	Introduction of English education
1857-1858	Sepoy Revolt, or "Mutiny," followed by direct Crown rule as a British colony
1885	Indian National Congress formed
1869-1948	Mohandas K. Gandhi
1873-1938	Muhammad Iqbal
1876-1949	Muhammad Ali Jinnah
1889-1964	Jawaharlal Nehru
1947	Independence and partition

tions on their own terms instead of on those dictated by a foreign power. The British influence was in some ways a sad one but in other respects also a good one. The British left a legacy of administrative and political unity and egalitarian and democratic ideals that Indian nationalists turned to their own uses.

THE ISLAMIC EXPERIENCE

Islamic Responses to Declining Power and Independence

The eighteenth century saw the weakening of the great Muslim empires and the increasing ascendancy of the West in international trade, military-political power, imperialist expansion, industrial specialization and productivity, and technological progress. The diverse Islamic peoples and states were thrust from previous positions of global power into what became, by the nineteenth century, a pitched struggle for survival. Although, as in the Indian case, the decline of Islamic preeminence was partly due to the rise of the modern West, it was also the result of internal problems.

By the eighteenth century all of the largest Muslim empires—Mughal, Ottoman, Safavid, Moroccan, and Central Asian—had declined politically, militarily, and economically from their heydays in the sixteenth and seventeenth centuries. They had grown increasingly decentralized, were less stable economically and politically, and were increasingly dominated by entrenched hereditary elites, including those among the landed gentry, palace guards, military castes, local princes, urban craft guilds, and even religious leaders (the *ulama*) and the Sufi orders.

A conservative, legalistic temper held sway among the *ulama*. Especially in Sunni lands, they were now commonly state functionaries rather than the typically antigovernment voices of Muslim conscience they once had been. The Sufi orders, taking up the voice of conscience, sometimes protested *ulama* conformism and governmental neglect of Islam. Yet many of the Sufi orders had themselves become closely linked with particular interest groups (the Ottoman guilds and the Janissaries, for example). Sufism, furthermore, had become increasingly identified with popular piety and syncretic accommodation—that is, the integration of Islamic practices with local pre- or non-Islamic practices. Some Sufi orders had degenerated into institutions perpetuating rather crass cults of personality, esotericism, and authoritarian religious discipline centered on Sufi masters.

During the eighteenth century a variety of reform movements sought to revive Islam as a comprehensive guide for living and to purify it of the effects of many of the more stultifying developments in Islamic societies during the preceding centuries. Most of these movements combined an emphasis on inner piety with a puritanical stress on external practice.

The most famous of these movements was that of the Wahhabis, the followers of Ibn Abd al-Wahhab (1703–1792) in Arabia. It sought to combat excesses of popular and Sufi piety, such as saint worship, visitations to saints' tombs, and faith in the intercession of Sufi masters and saints. It also sought to break the stranglehold of the *ulama*'s conformist interpretations of legal and religious issues, favoring instead the exercise of independent judgment. The only authorities were to be the Qur'an and the traditions of the Prophet, not the scholastic edifices of the traditional schools of legal and theological interpretation. Allied with a local Arab prince, Sa'ud, the Wahhabi movement swept much of the Arabian peninsula. It was crushed in the early nineteenth century by Egyptian military forces acting for the Ottoman regime. Still, the movement did not die; it finally saw victory under a descendant of Sa'ud at the onset of this century and has been institutionalized as the guiding ideology of present-day Saudi Arabia.

Other Muslim reform movements reflected similar revivalist and even militantly pietist responses to Islamic decadence and decline. Examples include that of Usman Dan Fodio in Africa in the late eighteenth century (discussed later in this chapter) and in the present day that of the Muslim Brotherhood in modern Egypt (see Chapter 38). Such groups call for a pristine Islam divested of the authoritarianism of the medieval legal schools, *ulama* theological conformity, and degenerate Sufi orders, as well as the excesses of popular piety and Sufi esotericism. This call continues to rally various movements from Africa to Indonesia. In Islamic societies everywhere in recent times it has provided a response to the challenge posed by Western-style "modernity" and a model for cultural and religious life on both the individual and the collective levels.

Western Political and Economic Encroachment

Internal decline was only one source of ferment in Islamic societies. From the late 1700s until World War II the political fortunes of Arab, Turkish, Persian, Indian, Southeast Asian, and African Islamic states were increasingly dictated from outside by Western powers—including Britain, Russia, Germany, and France—and at the mercy of the commercial, political, and military rivalries among them.

Western governments extracted capitulations favorable to their own economic and political interests from indigenous governments in exchange for promises of military protection or other considerations. These capitulations took the form of treaty clauses granting commercial concessions, special protection, and "extraterritorial" legal status to various European merchant enclaves. Such concessions (the earliest had been granted in the sixteenth century) had originally been reciprocal and had served the commercial purposes of Muslim rulers and some merchants as well as Western traders. However, they eventually provided Western powers with pretexts for direct intervention in Ottoman as well as in Iranian, Indian, and African affairs. The Ottoman Empire, like the Mughal Empire, suffered from internal disunity; its provincial rulers, or *pashas*, were virtually independent. This, combined with the increasing economic problems facing all the agrarian societies of Asia and Africa, made it easy for the Western powers—with their rapidly industrializing economies and increasingly effective militaries—to take control almost at will. Repeated Ottoman diplomatic and military defeats made that once great imperial power "the sick man of Europe" after 1800; similar weakness allowed Westerners to control the destinies of Indian and Iranian states and principalities.

The event that marked symbolically the onset of European domination of the Islamic heartlands was Napoleon Bonaparte's (1769–1821) invasion of Egypt in 1798. This venture failed when the French were forced by Britain, Russia, and the Ottomans to evacuate Egypt in 1801. It nevertheless heralded a new era of European imperialism and, ultimately, colonialism in the region. By this date the British had already wrested control over India and the Persian Gulf from the French; they now became the preeminent European power in the eastern Mediterranean as well. The French were to continue to contest British ascendancy in the larger Middle Eastern area until the disastrous Franco-German war of 1870. It was, however, the Russians who presented the most serious nineteenth-century challenge to Britain's colonial empire.

Russia, which had already won control of the Black Sea from the Ottomans, sought to gain as much territory and influence in the Iranian and Central Asian regions as possible. Afghanistan, an independent kingdom established by Ahmad Shah Durrani (r. 1737–1773), acted as a buffer that effectively prevented Russia from penetrating southwestward into British India. In the Iranian and Ottoman regions, however, Russia and Britain—with French involvement—struggled directly with each other for supremacy. The Crimean War of 1854–1856 (see Chapter 27) was one result of this conflict.

The Western Impact

Beyond the overt political and commercial impact of the West, the effect of Western political ideology, culture, and technology proved a critical factor for change in Islamic societies. Outside of India, this effect was most strongly felt in Egypt, Lebanon, North Africa, and Anatolia (modern Turkey), as we shall see. Of all the Islamic states, including those in Africa and India, the ones least and last affected by Western "modernity" were Iran, Afghanistan, and the Central Asian khanates. The Iranian case deserves at least brief attention.

The rulers of Iran from 1794 to 1925 were the Qajar shahs, a Turkoman dynasty whose absolutist reign was not unlike that of the Safavids. However, the Qajars (themselves formerly among the "Red Hats" supporting the Safavids; see Chapter 23) did not make religious claims, as had the Safavids, to descent from the Shi'ite *imams*. Under Qajar rule, in marked contrast to Safavid rule, the *ulama* of the Shi'ite community became less and less strongly connected with the state apparatus, and eventually only a minority had formal, active government appointments. This period also saw the emergence of a Shi'i traditionalist doctrine that encouraged all Shi'ites, in the absence of a living *imam*, to choose a *mujtahid*—a qualified scholarly guide—from among the *ulama* and follow him in all matters requiring religious-legal interpretation. A result of these developments was that the *ulama* actually gained strength as an independent power in the state. As the guardians of law and faith, they were often the chief critics of the government (not least for its every attempt to admit foreign, Western influences) and exponents of the people's grievances against it.

A prime demonstration of *ulama* power occurred in the late nineteenth century. In 1890 the Qajar Shah granted a special concession—a fifty-year monopoly on tobacco sales—to a British corporation. In 1891 the leading authority in the *ulama* decreed a tobacco boycott to protest the concession. This popular action was also supported by modernist-nationalist opponents of the Qajar regime who had strong connections to Iran's commercial, or *bazaari*, middle classes. It forced the Shah to rescind the concession.

This kind of religious, commercial, and popular opposition to the Shahs was not an isolated occurrence. As early as 1872–1873, an *ulama-bazaari* alliance against Qajar efforts to strengthen central government and grant concessions to Europeans had also blocked a wide-ranging concession on all types of Iranian products to a British concern.

Subject as it was to the machinations of outsiders, such as Russia, Britain, and France, Iran inevitably felt the impact of Western ideas about education, science, law, and government. This occurred especially in the latter half of the century, when younger Iranian intellectuals began to warm to Western liberalism on economic, social, and political issues. As in other Islamic countries, the seeds of a new, secular nationalism were being sown where, previously, sectarian or communalist religious sentiments had held sway. It coincided with, and worked with, a growing desire among larger sectors of the populace for a voice in government. An uneasy alliance of Iranian modernists with conservative *ulama* proved, on occasion, an effective counterforce to Qajar absolutism, as in the tobacco boycott and in at least the early stages of the important effort to force the Qajars to accept a constitution in the years 1906–1911. Yet such alliances did not bridge the inherent ideological divisions of the two groups, as subsequent twentieth-century history would demonstrate all too clearly.

Islamic Responses to Foreign Encroachment

As the Iranian case shows, Western impingement on the Islamic world in the nineteenth and twentieth centuries elicited varied responses. Every people or state had a different experience, according to its particular circumstances and history. Yet we can point to at least three typical styles of reaction: (1) a tendency to emulate and to adopt Western ideas and institutions; (2) the integrative attempt to join Western innovations with traditional Islamic institutions; and (3) a traditionalist rejection of things Western in favor of either the status quo or return to a purified Islamic community, or *Umma*. We must remember that these are oversimplified "types" of reactions that rarely if ever could be isolated in "pure" form; instead they should be seen as indicators of the range of possible reactions. None was confined to one class or group in Islamic societies, and none was uniform within a country or across political, ethnic, and cultural boundaries.

Emulation of the West

Primary emphasis on a strategy of emulation is exemplified in the career of the virtually independent Ottoman viceroy

Muhammad Ali (1769–1849). The famous viceroy of Egypt is depicted as an equestrian in this portrait. [Hulton/Corbis-Bettmann]

Muhammad Ali (ca. 1769–1849), pasha of Egypt from 1805 to 1849. He set out to rejuvenate Egypt's failing agriculture, to introduce modern mechanized industry, to modernize the army with European help, and to introduce European education and culture in government schools. Although ultimately unsuccessful in bringing Egypt to a position of power alongside the European states of his day, Muhammad Ali did set his country on the path to becoming a distinct modern national state. Hence he is rightly called "the father of modern Egypt." Although his successors' financial and political catastrophes led the British to occupy Egypt (1882–1922), Muhammad Ali's policies set Egypt irrevocably on a path that would bring more westernizing attempts, (and inevitable countermovements) in the future.

Efforts to appropriate Western experience and success were made by several Ottoman sultans and viziers after the devastating defeat of the Turks by Russia in 1774, although all of these represent to some degree "integrative" programs of reform rather than purely "imitative" ones. Nevertheless the focus on employing European models in the Middle Eastern context was a signal earmark of these efforts. Most notable were the reforms of Selim III (r. 1762–1808), Mahmud II (r. 1808–1839), and the so-called Tanzimat, or beneficial "legislation" (literally, "[re-]ordering") era from about 1839 to 1880. Selim made serious efforts at economic as well as administrative and military reform. He brought European

A Middle Eastern Modernist Warns About Appeasing Religious Fanatics

The modernists came to dominate in the nineteenth-century Ottoman world of political discourse. Sémsettin Sami (d. 1910) was a prominent modernist thinker who was later influential for the Young Turk movement. In the passage below from the early 1880s he writes about fanaticism and modernist appeasers of reactionary fanatics in Islamic lands.

Why is Sami so opposed to attempts to reconcile Islam with western civilization and to employ Islam as a modernizing tool? What is his argument against those who want to stress "Islamic influence on European thought" or otherwise "appease" religious fanatics?

Some of our intellectuals, in order to avoid fanatical reactions, have attempted to make European culture more acceptable and so to insinuate modern culture into Islamic lands. They even claimed that European culture had Islamic origins. In newspapers, in their books, and in other writings, they have maintained that European science and technology derived from Muslim discoveries. This is a worthy effort. But although there is much truth in what they assert, there is also great exaggeration, and they have spawned new problems. However diligently we might renew our study of the medicine of Avicenna, the physics of Averroës, and the chemistry of Jahiz, translate their books, publish them, and found schools for these purposes, we must likewise obtain the best scientific works of our century. For just as we cannot cure malaria with the medicine of Avicenna, so we cannot build a railroad, a ship, or use the telegraph with the chemistry or physics of Jahiz. If we wish to modernize ourselves we must do so by borrowing from contemporary science and technology. . . . Even in Europe there appeared some intellectuals who tried to reconcile religious texts with modern science and to extinguish fanaticism by appeasing it. However, since fanaticism is not a monster that can be seduced through gentleness, it has brutally destroyed those who have attempted to appease it. Finally the intellectuals gathered together, hand in hand, and waged a war against fanaticism, using axes and powder to demolish it, and only then did progress in civilization begin. In our society, too, in order to achieve progress in civilization and save the Muslims from the ignorance that is precipitating their annihilation, a war must be declared against fanaticism to forcibly crush it and thus open the road to civilization.

officers in to train new military corps that were to supplant the conservative Janissaries. Mahmud's reforms were much like those of Muhammad Ali, his contemporary and sometime ally, sometime enemy. Most important were his destruction of the Janissary corps, his tax and bureaucratic reforms, and his encouragement of Western military and educational methods among the Ottoman elites. Like Selim and Muhammad Ali, he was less interested in promoting European enlightenment ideas about citizen rights and equity than in building a stronger, more modern central government.

The Tanzimat reforms, introduced by several liberal Ottoman ministers of state, continued the efforts of Selim and Mahmud. Aimed at legal, penal, tax, military, minority-rights, educational, and governmental issues, they were intended to bring the Ottoman state into line with ideals espoused by the European states. They were also intended to give European powers less cause for intervention in Ottoman affairs and to regenerate domestic confidence in the state.

The nineteenth-century Ottoman reforms failed to save the empire or truly to revive it as an economically sound, culturally vibrant, or militarily and politically powerful state. Nevertheless, they paved the way for the rise of Turkish nationalism, the "Young Turk" revolution of 1908, and ultimately the nationalist revolution of the 1920s that produced modern Turkey. (Ironically, this development simultaneously frustrated similar nationalist aspirations among old Ottoman minorities like the Greeks, the Armenians, and the Kurds.)

The creation of the Turkish republic out of the ashes of the Ottoman state after World War I is probably the most extreme example of an effort to modernize and nationalize an Islamic state on a Western model. This state was largely the child of Mustafa Kemal (1881–1938), known as "Atatürk" ("father of the Turks"), its founder and first president (1922–1938). Atatürk's major reforms ranged from the introduction of a European-style code of civil law to the abolition of the caliphate, Sufi orders, Arabic script, and the Arabic call to prayer. These changes constituted a truly radical attempt to secularize an Islamic state and to separate religious from political and social institutions decisively. Nothing quite like it had ever been tried, nor has it yet been repeated. Despite many intervening years of adjustments and even reversals of some of

Kemal Atatürk (right) giving instruction in the Latin alphabet. This 1928 photograph reflects the personal engagement of Mustafa Kemal in the many reform efforts he instituted. [Historical Pictures Collection/Stock Montage Inc.]

Atatürk's measures and programs, Turkey has successfully maintained its independence, reaffirmed its commitment to democratic government, and emerged with a unique but still distinctly Islamic identity.

Integration of Western and Islamic Ideas

The attempt to join modernization with traditional Islamic institutions and ideas is exemplified in the thought of famous Muslim intellectuals, such as Jamal al-Din al-Afghani (1839–1897), Muhammad Abduh (1845–1905), and Muhammad Iqbal (1873–1938). These thinkers argued to some degree for a progressive Islam rather than a materialist Western secularism as the best answer to life in the modern world.

Afghani is best known for his emphasis on the unity of the Islamic world, or "pan-Islamism," and on a populist, constitutionalist approach to political order. His ideas influenced political activist movements in Egypt, Iran, Ottoman Turkey, and elsewhere.

His Egyptian disciple, Muhammad Abduh, worked especially to modernize Muslim education. He argued that a firm, revealed Qur'anic base could be combined harmoniously with modern science and its open questioning of reality. Through his efforts as Grand Mufti and head of state education, he introduced substantial modernist reforms. These reforms af-

fected even the curriculum of the most venerable traditionalist institution of higher learning in the Islamic world, the great Azhar school in Cairo, where Abduh was ostracized by its more traditional leaders.

Muhammad Iqbal (1873–1938) was the most celebrated Indian Muslim thinker of the present century. He went even further in his emotional, sometimes contradictory, arguments for a modernist revival of Muslim faith focused on purifying and uplifting the individual self above enslavement either to reason or to traditionalist conformity. Often credited with the original idea of a separate Muslim state in the Indian subcontinent, Iqbal still felt that Islam was essentially nonexclusivist and supranationalist:

> The truth is that Islam is not a church. It is a state conceived as a contractual organism. . . . and animated by an ethical ideal which regards man not as an earth-rooted creature, defined by this or that portion of the earth, but as a spiritual being understood in terms of a social mechanism, and possessing rights and duties as a living factor in that mechanism[5]. . . .

[5]Quoted in K. Cragg and R. M. Speight, eds., *Islam from Within* (Belmont, CA: Wadsworth, 1980), p. 213.

Islamic Lands

1703–1792	Ibn Abd al-Wahhab
1737–1773	Rule of Ahmad Shah Durrani, founder of modern Afghanistan
1794–1925	Qajar shahs of Iran
1798	Invasion of Egypt by Napoleon Bonaparte
1805–1849	Rule of Muhammad Ali in Egypt
ca. 1839–1880	Era of the Tanzimat reforms of the Ottoman Empire
1839–1897	Jamal Al-Din Al-Afghani
1845–1905	Muhammad Abduh
1882–1922	British occupation of Egypt
1908	"Young Turk" revolution
1922–1938	Mustafa Kemal, "Atatürk" in power

Iqbal participated in major political discussions about the future of India. Although his poetry and essays excited Muslim fervor and dynamism, it is difficult to say how great his actual impact on Islamic political and social life really was.

Purification and Revival of Islam

A third kind of Muslim reaction to Western domination has focused on recourse to Islamic values and ideals to the exclusion of "outside" forces. This approach has involved either the kind of reformist revivalism already seen in Wahhabism or the kind of conservatism often associated with Sunni or Shi'ite "establishment" *ulama*, as in the case of Iran since 1979. The conservative spirit itself has often been the target of revivalist reformers who see in it the worst legacy of medieval Islam. Still, it has sometimes legitimized revivalist reforms once they have been effected. Both conservative and revivalist Muslim thinkers share at least the conviction that it is within, not outside, the Islamic tradition that answers to the questions facing Muslims in the modern world are to be found.

Traditionalist conservatism is much harder to pin down as the ethos of particular movements and organized groups than is reformist revivalism. Whereas Muslim revivalism (today commonly called "Islamism" [*Islamiyyah*]) usually focuses on Qur'an and Prophetic example as the sole authorities for Islamic life, Muslim conservatism commonly champions those forms of Islamic life and thought embodied in traditional law, theology, and sometimes even certain strands of Sufism. It is seen in the legalistic tendencies that have often resurfaced when Islamic norms have been threatened by the breakdown of traditional society and the rise of secularism. Although such conservatism has often been associated with the most reactionary forces in Islamic society, it has often also served to pre-serve basic Muslim values while allowing for gradual change in a way that reformist revivalism could not accept. Where conservatives have formed alliances with governments or simply been coopted by them, the credibility of the establishment *ulama* has often been destroyed. This is because the masses of Muslims—on issues ranging from personal piety through social conscience and action to political order—have been more and more attracted to Islamist agendas for change.

Nationalism

Nationalism is a product of modern history. Although not merely a response to Western encroachment, nationalist movements in the Islamic world have been either largely stimulated by Western models or produced in direct reaction to Western imperialist exploitation and colonial occupation. Indeed, the often arbitrary or artificial division of the colonial world by European administrators has frequently produced national units where none had existed—notably in Africa, but also in the Middle East (Syria, Jordan, Iraq, and so on) and Central Asia. As in India, nationalism has been an important aspect of the response to Western domination in the Islamic heartlands. In Turkey in the 1920s it took a secularist form; in Libya, Iran, and elsewhere since the 1970s and 1980s it has taken an Islamic-revivalist form. As an Afro-Asian phenomenon, it will reappear in the next section and in Chapter 38.

THE AFRICAN EXPERIENCE

The century and a half between 1800 and 1945 saw striking change in virtually every part of Africa, but nowhere more than in sub-Saharan Africa. North Africa and Egypt were more closely bound up in the politics of the Ottoman Empire and Europe throughout this period. With the important exception of South Africa below the Transvaal, tropical and southern Africa came under major influence and finally colonial control from outside only after 1880. Before then, internal developments—first, demographic and power shifts and then the rise of important Islamic reform movements—overshadowed the slowly increasing European presence in the continent.

New States and Power Centers

Southern Africa

In the south, below the Limpopo River, the first quarter of the nineteenth century saw devastating internal warfare, depopulation, and forced migrations of many Bantu peoples in

Mosheshwe, king and founder of Lesotho. Not all of the Bantu peoples followed the militaristic example of Shaka. Mosheshwe, prince of a subtribe of the Sotho Bantus, fought off Zulu attacks and led his people to a mountain stronghold in southern Africa, where, through diplomacy and determination, he founded a small nation that has endured to the present. The kingdom became the British protectorate of Basutoland in 1868. In 1966 it achieved independence as the kingdom of Lesotho under Mosheshwe's great-grandson, King Mosheshwe II. [Courtesy of the Library of Congress]

what is known as the *mfecane*, or "crushing" era. Likely brought on by a population explosion and perhaps fueled by increasing economic competition in the preceding decades, the *mfecane* was marked by the rapid rise of sizable military states among the northern Nguni-speaking Bantu. Its result was a lengthy period of perpetual warfare and chaos; widespread depopulation by death and emigration; and the creation of new, multitribal, multilingual Bantu states in the regions of modern Zimbabwe, Mozambique, Malawi, Zambia, and Tanzania.

The Nguni warrior-king Dingiswayo formed the first of the new military states between ca. 1800 and 1818. The second and most important state of all was formed by his successor, Shaka, leader of the Nguni-speaking Zulu nation and kingdom (ca. 1818–1828). Shaka's radical and brutal military tactics led to the Zulu conquest of a vast dominion in southeastern Africa and the virtual depopulation of some 15,000 square miles. Refugees from Shaka's "total war" zone fled north into Sotho-speaking Bantu territory or south to put in-

creasing pressure on the southern Nguni peoples. Virtual chaos ensued, both north and south of Zululand and even in the high veld above the Orange River, where severe depopulation also resulted from the troubles.

The net result, beyond widespread suffering and death, was the creation of many new diverse states. Some people tried to imitate the unique military state of Shaka; others fled to mountainous areas; others even went west into the Kalahari and built up new, largely defensive states. The most famous of these was Lesotho, the Sotho kingdom of King Mosheshwe, which survived as long as he lived (from the 1820s until 1870). Not only was Mosheshwe able to defend his people from the Zulu, but he was also able to hold off the Afrikaners, missionaries, and British. After his death these latter groups soon became Lesotho's chief predators.

The new state-building spawned by the *mfecane* was destined to be cut off and nullified by Boer expansion and British annexation of the Natal province (1843). These developments stemmed from the Great Trek of Boer *voortrekers*, which took place between 1835 and 1841. This migration brought about 6,000 Afrikaners from the eastern Cape Colony northeastward into the more fertile regions of southern Africa, Natal, and especially the high veld above the Orange River. It resulted in the creation after 1850 of the Afrikaner republics of the Orange Free State between the Orange and Vaal rivers and the South African Republic north of the Vaal.

East and Central Africa

Farther north in East and East Central Africa, increasing external trade was the basis for the formation of several strong regional states. In the Lakes region, peoples such as the Nyamwezi to the east of Lake Tanganyika and the Baganda west of Lake Victoria gained regional power from as early as

Southern Africa	
ca. 1800–1818	Dingiswayo, Nguni Zulu king, forms new military state
1800–1825	The *mfecane* among the Bantu of southeastern Africa
1806	British take Cape Colony from the Dutch
ca. 1818–1828	Shaka's reign as head of the Nguni state; major warfare, destruction, and expansion
ca. 1825–1870	Sotho kingdom of King Moshweshwe in Lesotho region
1836–1854	Great Trek of Boers into Natal and north onto the high veld beyond the Orange
1843	British annexation of Natal province
1852–1860	Creation of the Orange Free State and South African Republic

the late eighteenth century through trade with the Arab-Swahili eastern coast and the states of the eastern Congo to the west. The chief traffic in this east–west commerce across central Africa involved slaves; ivory; copper; and, from the outside, Indian cloth, firearms, and other manufactured goods.

West Africa

In West Africa the slave trade was only slowly curtailed. European demand for other products, however—notably palm oil and gum arabic—gained sharply in relative importance by the 1820s. In the first half of the century *jihad* (holy struggle) movements of the Fulbe (or Fulani) and others shattered the stability of the western savanna and forest regions from modern Senegal and Ghana through southern Nigeria. Protracted wars and dislocation resulted in the rise of regional kingdoms, such as those of Asante and Dahomey (modern Benin). These flourished for a time before succumbing to internal dissension and the colonial activities of Britain and France later in the century.

Islamic Reform Movements

The expansive vitality of Islam was one of the significant agents of change in sub-Saharan Africa before the European rush for colonies in the 1880s. It has remained a factor on the wider African scene ever since. In 1800 Islam was already a long-established tradition from West Africa across the Sudan to the Red Sea and along the East African coast, as well as over all of Arabic-speaking North Africa. It had long been widespread in the southern Sahara and northern Sahel and was common among merchant classes in various parts of West Africa. Islam was officially the law of the land in states such as the sultanate of Zanzibar on the eastern coast and the waning Funj sultanate on the Blue Nile in the eastern Sudan. Even so, in many "Islamic" states in Africa, the rural populace were still semipagan, if not wholly so; and often even the ruling and urban elites of the towns were only nominally Muslim.

The nineteenth century is notable for the number and strength of a series of militant Islamic revivalist and reform movements of *jihad*. Aimed at a more truly Muslim society and wider allegiance to Muslim values, these movements both fixed and spread Islam as a lasting part of the African scene. The West African *jihad* ("struggle") movements began in the seventeenth century in the southwestern Sahara to the north of Fuuta Tooro and the Wolof states of Senegal. They originated with the activities of militant, reformist Sufi brotherhoods that had penetrated West Africa from the north, especially through Mauritania. These movements eventually spread to other regions and flourished, especially in the eighteenth century among widely dispersed groups of people.

Central Sudan

1754–1817	Usman Dan Fodio, Fulbe leader of major Islamic *jihad*
1810	Dan Fodio founds Islamic sultanate in lands of former Hausa states of northern and central Nigeria
1817–1837	Reign at Sokoto of Muhammad Bello, son of Dan Fodio

The most important *jihad* movement came just at the beginning of the nineteenth century and was led by a Fulbe Muslim scholar from Hausa territory in the central Sahel. Usman Dan Fodio (1754–1817) was influenced by the reformist ideas that spread throughout the Muslim world in the eighteenth century, from India to Saudi Arabia and Africa. Shortly after 1804 he gathered an immense army of fervent supporters and conquered most of the Hausa lands of modern northern and central Nigeria, bringing an explicitly Islamic order to the area. Dan Fodio left behind an impressive sultanate centered on the new capital of Sokoto and governed by one of his sons, Muhammad Bello, until 1837. In his wake the Fulbe became the ruling class in the Hausa regions, and Islam spread into the countryside, where it still predominates.

Other nineteenth-century reform movements had similar success both in gaining at least ephemeral political power and in spreading a revivalist, reformist Islamic message among the masses. Most notable alongside several West African *jihads* were the Sanusi reform and missionary movement of Libya and the eastern Sahara (after about 1840) and the famous Mahdist uprising of the eastern Sudan (1880s and 1890s). The Libyan movement took such hold that it still could provide the focus for resistance to the Italian invasion of 1911. The Sudanese Muhammad Ahmad (1848–1885) condemned the widespread corruption of basic Muslim ideals and declared himself the awaited deliverer, or Mahdi, in 1881. He led the northern Sudan in rebellion against Ottoman-Egyptian control, defeating even the British forces from Egypt under Charles George Gordon (1833–1885) at Khartoum. His successor governed the Sudan until the British finally destroyed the young Islamic state in 1899.

Increasing European Involvement

Although Muslim reform movements helped to spread and entrench Islam in important parts of Africa, they were not the only important developments on the continent during the nineteenth century. Another was the growing involvement of Europe in African affairs, which led eventually to European domination of the continent's politics and economy. Before

Usman Dan Fodio on Evil and Good Government

Following in the tradition of the Wahhabis in Arabia and virtually all previous Islamic reform movements, Dan Fodio (1754–1817) stressed adherence to Muslim norms as expressed in the Shari`a, the divine law. In the two excerpts that follow, he enumerated some of the evils of the previous Hausa rulers and their "law," then listed five principles of proper Islamic government.

What does the first principle of good government, that "authority shall not be given to one who seeks it," mean? What abuses by government listed by Dan Fodio might be most appalling to the average Muslim? Why?

One of the ways of their government [that is, of the Hausa or Habe kings] is succession to the emirate by hereditary right and by force to the exclusion of consultation. And one of the ways of their government is the building of their sovereignty upon three things: the people's persons, their honour, and their possessions; and whomsoever they wish to kill or exile or violate his honour or devour his wealth they do so in pursuit of their lusts, without any right in the Shari`a. One of the ways of their government is their imposing on the people monies not laid down by the Shari`a, being those which they call janghali and kurdin ghari and kurdin salla. One of the ways of their governments is their intentionally eating whatever food they wish, whether it is religiously permitted or forbidden, and wearing whatever clothes they wish, whether religiously permitted or forbidden, and drinking what beverages [ta'am] they wish, whether religiously permitted or forbidden, and riding whatever riding beasts they wish, whether religiously permitted or forbidden, and taking what women they wish without marriage contract, and living in decorated palaces, whether religiously permitted or forbidden, and spreading soft (decorated) carpets as they wish, whether religiously permitted or forbidden. . . .

And I say—and help is with God—the foundations of government are five things: the first is that authority shall not be given to one who seeks it. The second is the necessity for consultation. The third is the abandoning of harshness. The fourth is justice. The fifth is good works. And as for its ministers, they are four. (The First) is a trustworthy wazir to wake the ruler if he sleeps, to make him see if he is blind, and to remind him if he forgets, and the greatest misfortune for the government and the subjects is that they should be denied honest wazirs. And among the conditions pertaining to the wazir is that he should be steadfast in compassion to the people, and merciful towards them. The second of the ministers of government is a judge whom the blame of a blamer cannot overtake concerning the affairs of God. The third is a chief of police who shall obtain justice for the weak from the strong. The fourth is a tax collector who shall discharge his duties and not oppress the subjects. . . .

From translation of Usman Dan Fodio's *Kitab al-Farq* by M. Hiskett, *Bulletin of the School of Oriental and African Studies*, London, 1960, Part 3, p. 558. Reprinted by permission of Oxford University Press, Oxford, Great Britain.

---

the mid-1800s the actual penetration of white outsiders had been limited largely to coastal areas, although their slave trade had had significant effects even further inland (see Chapter 19). This changed drastically as, first, trading companies, explorers, and missionaries and, finally, colonial troops and governments moved into Africa. Ironically, the gradual elimination of the slave trade (primarily through Britain's efforts) was accompanied by increased European exploration and increased Western Christian missionizing, which ushered in imperial and colonial ventures that were to have even more disastrous consequences than slaving for Africa's future.

Exploration

The nineteenth-century European explorers—mostly English, French, and German—gradually uncovered for Westerners the great "secrets" of Africa: the sources and courses of the Niger, Nile, Zambezi, and Congo rivers; natural wonders, such as Mount Kilimanjaro and Lake Tanganyika; and fabled places like Timbuktu, the once great Berber trading gateway and the center of Islamic learning in the western Sahara and the Sudan. The history of European exploration is one of fortune hunting, self-promotion, violence, and mistakes. But it is also one of patience and perseverance, bravery, and dedication.

The explorers' main importance for Africa lay in their stimulation of European interest and their opening of the way for traders, missionaries, and finally soldiers and governors from the Christian West. One of the greatest explorers was Dr. David Livingstone (1813–1873). Livingstone was a missionary in love with and dedicated to Africa and its peoples as were few other Westerners before or after him.

Christian Missions

The latter part of the nineteenth century saw a mounting influx of Christian missionaries, both Protestant and Catholic

A missionary visit to a Zulu Kraal. The nineteenth-century European-American enthusiasm for working toward "the evangelization of the world in our time" found one of its major outlets in missionary efforts in Africa. [Kyrkans Internationella AV-tjanst/Uppsala/Cooperative Creamery Association]

(by 1900, perhaps as many as 10,000 altogether). These vied—sometimes with one another, sometimes with Muslim traders and teachers—for the souls of Africans. Part of their motivation for coming to Africa was to eradicate the remaining slave trade, especially that in East Africa run by Arabs from Zanzibar.

The missionaries came to know the African peoples far better than did the explorers. Their accounts of Africa contained, to be sure, chauvinistic and misleading descriptions of the "degraded" state of African culture and religion, but they did bring real knowledge of and interest in Africa to Europe. Their translation work and mission schools also brought some alphabetic culture and literacy to the African tribal world. Although their settlements, often in remote areas, provided European governments with convenient pretexts for intervention in the affairs of African tribes and states, the missionaries themselves were more often idealists than opportunists. For many their work was fatal; as many as half of those who went into the tropical regions succumbed to indigenous diseases, such as malaria, yellow fever, and sleeping sickness. If they were often paternalistic and virtual instruments of the imperialism of their home countries, they also sought to provide Africans with medicine and education. Through the ideals of their faith, they provided Africans—sometimes intentionally, sometimes inadvertently—with a weapon of principle to use against their European exploiters. African Christian churches, for example, played a leading role in the resistance to apartheid in South Africa, despite white Christian oppression and collusion with racism in that country and elsewhere in Africa (see Chapter 38). As this discussion sug-

gests, the role of Africans in the European domination of Africa was not simple nor by any means wholly positive.

The Colonial "Scramble for Africa"

Before 1850 the only significant conflict between Europeans and Africans over European attempts to take African territory was in South Africa and Algeria. In South Africa, as we have noted, the Boers came into conflict with Bantu tribes after leaving the British-ruled Cape Colony on their Great Trek to find new lands. The French invaded Algeria in 1830, settled Europeans on choice farmlands, and waged war on native resistance fighters. Over most of the continent, however, the European presence was felt with real force only from the 1880s (see Map 31–1). Yet by World War I virtually all of Africa (Ethiopia and Liberia were the only exceptions) was divided rather arbitrarily into a patchwork of large territories ruled directly or indirectly by European colonial administrations (see Map 31–2).

This foreign takeover of Africa was supported by mounting European popular interest as well as commercial interest. Both factors were fueled by the publicity given African exploration and missionary work. The European desire for the industrial markets and natural resources of Africa, together with intra-European competition for power and prestige, pushed one European state after another to lay claim to whatever segments of Africa they could.

What made this wholesale takeover possible was the superior economic, technological, and military power the West commanded. In particular, European technical expertise did much to open up the interior of the continent in the last few decades before World War I. Except for the Nile and the Niger, all the great African rivers have impassible waterfalls only a short way inland from the sea, where the coastal plains rise sharply to the largely highland interior. Steamboats above the falls and railroads around them (or where no navigable rivers ran) provided access to the African interior and opened its riches to commercial and colonial exploitation.

Great Britain and France were the vanguard of the European nations that sought to include African lands in their imperial domains. The British had the largest involvement. On one axis, it ranged from their ever-increasing South African holdings (begun when they took the Cape Colony from the Dutch in 1795) to their effective protectorate in Egypt (from 1882). On another axis, it extended from trading interests in West Africa to colonies such as Sierra Leone and Gambia, set up in 1807, to protectorate rule, as in the Niger districts after 1885, and to a Zanzibar-based sphere of influence in East Africa in the 1870s (and finally a protectorate for Zanzibar in 1890).

The British long resisted African colonial involvement and then chose "indirect" as preferable to "direct" colonial administration. In the end their rule was only slightly more en-lightened than that of the French, who began early to carve out a colonial empire under their direct control. The French had long had government-supported trading outposts in Senegal and other parts of West Africa. After a long, bitter struggle (1830–1847) they conquered Algeria, creating the first major European colony in Africa. In addition, Tunisia and the Ivory Coast became French protectorates in the 1880s, Dahomey was bloodily annexed in 1894, and the colony of French Equatorial Africa was proclaimed in 1910.

Beginning in the mid-1880s the major European powers began to seek mutual agreement to their claims on particular segments of Africa. Leopold II of Belgium (r. 1865–1909) and Otto von Bismarck (1815–1898) in Germany established their own claims to parts of South, central, and East Africa. France and England set about consolidating their African interests. Italy, too, eventually tried to take African colonial territory in Eritrea, Somaliland, Ethiopia, and Libya. Only the Italian design on Ethiopia was thwarted, when Ethiopia used its newly modernized army to defeat an Italian invasion in 1896. This failure the Italians recouped only in 1935 by a second invasion. The "scramble for Africa" was largely over by the outbreak of World War I. In the aftermath of the war Germany lost its African possessions to other colonial powers. It was not until the changes in the worldwide balance of power and in attitudes toward colonial rule that followed World War II that Europe's colonies in Africa gained independence (see Chapters 36 and 38).

European colonial rule in Africa is one of the uglier chapters of modern history. If German, French, Belgian, Portuguese, and Boer rule was notoriously brutal and produced worse atrocities, Britain also had its share of misrule and exploitation. The paternalistic attitudes of late-nineteenth-century Europe and America amounted in the end to sheer racism when applied in Africa. The regions with large-scale white settlement produced the worst exploitation at the expense of vastly greater native populations. Everywhere, white minorities exercised disproportionate power over the lives of black or brown majorities. The worst legacy of the

European exploitation of Africa. Photograph of white foremen and black laborers in a gold-mining company of South Africa (undated). [Hulton/Corbis-Bettmann]

European presence was the white racist state of modern South Africa, which only ended in 1994. No Western nation has the right to a clear conscience about its involvement in Africa.

African Resistance to Colonialism: The Rise of Nationalism

African states were not, however, simply passive objects of European manipulation and conquest. Many astute native rulers sought, by diplomacy, trade leverage, and warfare, to use the European presence to their own advantage. Some, like the Bagandan king Mutesa in the 1870s (in what is today Uganda), were remarkably successful for some time. Direct armed resistance was in every case (even Ethiopia's) doomed because of European technological superiority. Nevertheless, such resistance was widespread—during the 1890s, for example, in the Hehe people's fight against German troops in Tanganyika and the Asante's battle against British forces; and it continued in the twentieth century in many places. In the end, however, it was less this resistance than other factors that brought an end to most foreign rule on African soil.

The most prominent of these factors was the rise of various kinds of nationalism across the African continent, especially after World War I. However little the colonial partition of Africa reflected native linguistic, racial, or cultural divisions,

Colonial Africa

1830	French invasion of Algeria
1870	British protectorate in Zanzibar
ca. 1880	French protectorate in Tunisia and Ivory Coast
1880s–1890s	Mahdist uprising in eastern Sudan
1882	British protectorate in Egypt
1894	French annexation of Dahomey
1910	French colony of Equatorial Africa

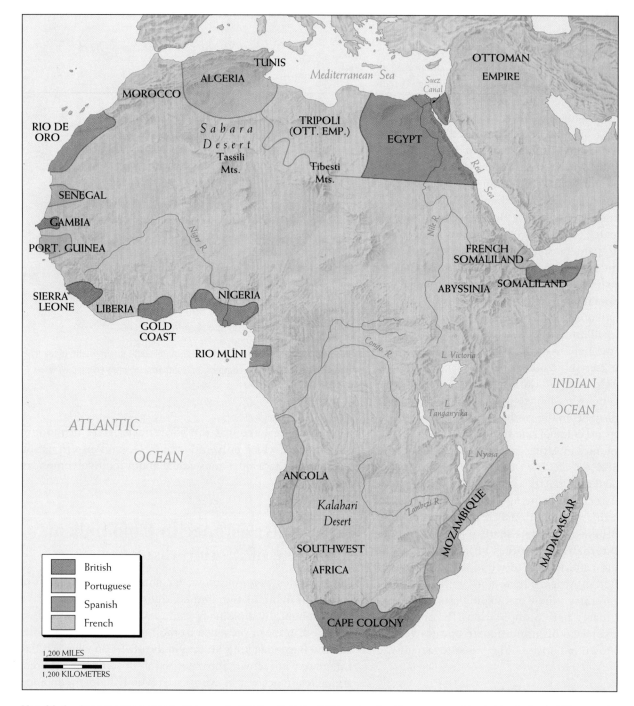

Map 31–1 Imperial Expansion in Africa up to 1880. Until the 1880s only a few European countries held colonies in Africa, mostly on the fringes of the continent. A comparison of this map with Map 31–2 shows how rapidly the situation changed.

it still had considerable influence on both nationalist movements and the eventual shape of African states. The "national" consciousness of the diverse peoples of a given colonial unit was fueled by common opposition to foreign rule. It was also fed by the use of a common European tongue and through the assimilation of European thought and culture by a growing educated native elite. These elites were typically educated in mission schools and sometimes foreign universities. Their ranks gradually increased in the early twentieth century. From them came the leaders of Africa's nationalist movements between the two world wars and of Africa's new independent nations after World War II.

The severest indigenous critiques of the Western treatment of Africa often drew on Western religious and political

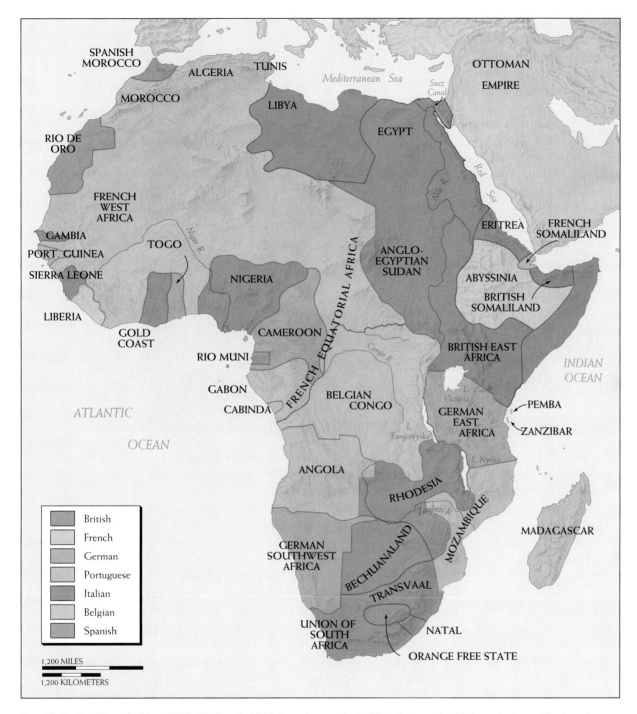

Map 31-2 Partition of Africa, 1880–1914. By 1914 the only countries in Africa that remained independent were Liberia and Abyssinia (Ethiopia). The occupying powers included most large European states.

ideals. The African leaders of the twentieth century learned well from the West and used their learning to help end Western domination. The process culminated in the creation of over forty self-governing African nations after 1945 (see Chapter 38). African independence movements were eventually based on modern nationalist models from Europe and America rather than ancient ones derived from native tradition. The nationalist and independence movements typically sought to eject the colonial intruders and not to return to an earlier status quo. Their aim was to take over and to run for themselves the Western institutions that had been introduced by colonialism. This legacy from the West is still visible today.

Mutesa of Buganda and his court. Noted for his cunning and diplomatic skill and for his autocratic and often cruel conduct, Mutesa was one of the few African rulers who was able to maintain a powerful and successful army and court, which enabled him to deal effectively with Egyptian and British efforts to encroach on his sphere of influence. [Brown Brothers]

IN WORLD PERSPECTIVE

India, the Islamic Heartlands, and Africa, 1800–1945

The century and a half following the French Revolution in Europe was a bleak one for the fortunes of the Indian subcontinent, Africa, and the Islamic societies of the Middle East and elsewhere. For centuries there had been a rough but long-term balance in advances and setbacks in material and intellectual culture, commercial development, and political stability among the major cultural regions of the world. Suddenly, over 150 years, the European sector of the global community came to dominate in crushing fashion not only the diverse parts of the Islamic heartlands, Africa, and India, but also the rest of the world, including even East Asia.

The Middle East, Africa, Iran, Central Asia, India, and Indonesia-Malaysia, along with Central and South America—what is today referred to as "the Third World" of "developing nations"—were the areas most drastically affected by European imperialism and colonialism. Regardless of indigenous

developments in these regions, the overarching and decisive development of this era was new and unprecedented domination of the world's economy, intellectual life, and political and military history by a single segment of the global community. Certainly the histories of the less "developed" nations of the world in this age have their own internal dynamics; in fact, numerous smaller African or South American societies were until recently not even directly affected by Western dominance. Still, the impact of Western dominance, sometimes positive, often sordid and ugly, was great. It was by no means synonymous with "progress," as Westerners have often liked to think. It has been, nevertheless, a hallmark of the "modern" age in most of Asia, Africa, and South America.

The vitality of so many of the cultures and traditions that bore the brunt of the Western onslaught has been striking. Arab, Iranian, Indian, African, and other encounters with Western material and intellectual domination were diverse and produced different responses and initiatives. These have borne full fruit in political, economic, and intellectual independence only since 1945; however, most began much earlier, some even well before 1800. For example, modern Islamic reform and resurgence began in the eighteenth century, although it has become a major global factor only in recent years. Indian national, as opposed to regional, consciousness developed from the late eighteenth century onward in response to British imperial and colonial domination, even though it led to national union and independence only after World War II.

Certainly one result of the imperial-colonial experience almost everywhere has been the sharpening in recent times of cultural self-consciousness and ultimately self-confidence among those peoples most negatively affected by Western dominance. The imperial-colonial experiences of the Third World nations may well prove to have been not only ones of misery and reversal, but also of transition to positive development and resurgence, despite the looming economic, educational, and demographic problems that plague many of these nations.

Review Questions

1. What does the "impact of modernity" mean to traditional cultures of the Afro-Asian-Indian world? What patterns of reaction can you discern? Why was the West so successful in imposing itself upon these other cultures?

2. Why was India called the "jewel in the crown" of the British Empire? How did the British gain control of the subcontinent? What kind of policies did they follow in government and economics?

3. What kinds of political activism against British rule can you cite from Indian history of the period after 1800? What kinds of success or failure did they have?

4. How was the Islamic world internally divided after 1800? How did those divisions influence the coming of European powers?

5. How did nationalism affect European control in south Asia, Africa, and the Middle East? How and when did its various manifestations arise? Were there any successful "national states" from these regions before 1945?

6. Discuss the new African states and power centers of sub-Saharan Africa before 1870. Why was there a failure to develop a modern state in the area? What role did Islam play in the development of new entities? What role did trade play?

7. What were the three main interests of Europeans in the "Dark Continent"? Why were native Africans unable to stop the "scramble for Africa" in their various regions?

8. What was the role of African nationalism in resisting foreign control?

Suggested Readings

India

A. AHMAD, *Islamic Modernism in India and Pakistan, 1857–1964* (1967). The standard survey of Muslim thinkers and movements in India during the period.

C. A. BAYLY, *Indian Society and the Making of the British Empire, The New Cambridge History of India*, II.1 (Cambridge, UK: Cambridge University Press, 1988). One of several major contributions of this author to the ongoing revision of our picture of modern Indian history since the eighteenth century.

R. GUHA, ED., *Subaltern Studies: Writings on South Asian History and Society* (1982). Essays on the colonial period that focus on the social, political, and economic history of "subaltern" groups and classes (hill tribes, peasants, etc.) rather than the elites of India only.

S. N. HAY, ED., "Modern India and Pakistan," Part VI of Wm. Theodore de Bary et al., eds., *Sources of Indian Tradition*, 2nd ed., (1988). A superb selection of primary-source documents with brief introductions and helpful notes.

D. KOPF, *British Orientalism and the Bengal Renaissance: The Dynamics of Indian Modernization, 1773–1835* (1969). An intriguing study of British-Indian interchange and mutual influence in the heyday of the East India Company.

F. ROBINSON, ED., *The Cambridge Encyclopedia of India, Pakistan, Bangladesh, Sri Lanka, Nepal, Bhutan, and the Maldives* (1989). A fine collection of survey articles by various scholars, organized into topical chapters ranging from "Economies" to "Cultures."

W. C. SMITH, *Modern Islam in India: A Social Analysis* (1943). A Marxist critique. Still the best survey and analysis of Indian Muslim thought from Sayyid Ahmad Khan to the early 1940s.

P. SPEAR, *The Oxford History of Modern India, 1740–1947* (1965). Still a helpful quick reference tool.

M. N. SRINIVAS, *Social Change in Modern India* (1966). An older but highly influential treatment of topics such as "sanskritization," "westernization," and "secularization."

E. STOKES, *The Peasant Armed: The Indian Revolt of 1857* (1986). The basic starting point for study of the revolt. A posthumously edited work on the battles and the involvement of rural districts of North India in what Stokes saw as a "peasant revolt."

S. WOLPERT, *A New History of India,* 2nd ed. (1982). Chapters 14–25. A solid survey and useful quick reference source.

Central Islamic Lands

K. CRAGG, *Counsels in Contemporary Islam* (1965). A brief survey of intellectual trends in the modern Islamic world in the nineteenth and twentieth centuries.

J. J. DONAHUE AND J. L. ESPOSITO, EDS., *Islam in Transition: Muslim Perspectives* (1982). An interesting selection of primary-source materials on Islamic thinking in this century.

D. F. EICKELMAN, *Knowledge and Power in Morocco: The Education of a Twentieth-Century Notable* (1985). A fascinating study of traditional Islamic education and society in the twentieth century through a social biography of a Moroccan religious scholar and judge.

M. G. S. HODGSON, *The Venture of Islam* (1974). Vol. 3, The Gunpowder Empires and Modern Times. Although less ample than his first two volumes, this volume still provides a solid interpretative introduction.

A. HOURANI, *Arabic Thought in the Liberal Age, 1798–1939* (1967). The standard work, by which all subsequent scholarship on the topic is to be judged.

N. R. KEDDI, *An Islamic Response to Imperialism* (1968). A brief study of al-Afghani, the great Muslim reformer, with translations of a number of his writings.

N. R. KEDDI, ED., *Religion and Politics in Iran* (1983). A collection of essays with a helpful historical introduction by the editor and varied articles on modern Iran.

M. H. KERR, *Islamic Reform: The Political and Legal Theories of Muhammad 'Abduh and Rashid Rida* (1966). A fine study of two major Muslim reformers in the colonial period in Egypt.

B. LEWIS, *The Emergence of Modern Turkey,* 2nd ed. (1968). A concise but thorough history of the creation of the Turkish state, including nineteenth-century background.

E. MORTIMER, *Faith and Power: The Politics of Islam* (1982). A fine survey of contemporary Islamic countries by a knowledgeable and thoughtful journalist.

F. RAHMAN, *Islam* (1966). Chapters 12 and 13. These two chapters from a fine introductory survey of Islam by a major modern Muslim historian and thinker deal with reform movements and other modern developments in the Islamic world.

J. C. B. RICHMOND, *Egypt, 1798–1952: Her Advance Towards a Modern Identity* (1977). A basic history, with focus on political change.

S. J. SHAW AND E. K. SHAW, *History of the Ottoman Empire and Modern Turkey* (1977). Vol. II, *Reform, Revolution, and Republic: The Rise of Modern Turkey, 1808–1975.* Detailed and careful analytic and survey history of the modern period.

W. C. SMITH, *Islam in Modern History* (1957). Dated, but still the most penetrating analysis of the dilemmas facing Muslim individuals and states in the twentieth century.

J. O. VOLL, *Islam: Continuity and Change in the Modern World* (1982). Chapters 1–6. An interpretive survey of the Islamic world since the eighteenth century. Its emphasis on eighteenth-century reform movements is especially noteworthy.

Africa

A. A. BOAHEN, *Africa Under Colonial Domination, 1880–1935* (1985). Vol. VII of the UNESCO *General History of Africa.* Excellent chapters on various regions of Africa in the period. Chapters 3–10 detail African resistance to European colonial intrusion in diverse regions.

W. CARTEY AND M. KILSON, EDS., *The Africa Reader: Colonial Africa* (1970). Original source materials give a vivid picture of African resistance to colonial powers, adaptation to foreign rule, and the emergence of the African masses as a political force.

P. CURTIN, S. FEIERMANN, L. THOMPSON, AND J. VANSINA, *African History* (1978). The relevant portions are chapters 10–20.

B. DAVIDSON, *The African Genius: An Introduction to African Social and Cultural History* (1969). A sensitive analysis of Africa from the standpoint of African rather than European thought and action. Especially interesting are African responses to imperial and colonial penetration.

J. D. FAGE, *A History of Africa* (1978). The relevant chapters, which give a particularly clear overview of the colonial period, are 12–16.

D. FODE AND P. M. KABERRY, EDS., *West African Kingdoms in the Nineteenth Century* (1967). Very useful treatments of the different West African states such as Benin, Asante, and Gonja.

B. FREUND, *The Making of Contemporary Africa: The Development of African Society Since 1800* (1984). A refreshingly direct synthetic discussion and survey that take an avowedly, but not reductive, materialist approach to interpretation.

R. HALLETT, *Africa Since 1875: A Modern History* (1974). Detailed survey of modern African history from the outset of the colonial period.

R. W. JULY, *A History of the African People,* 3rd ed. (1980). The strongest portions of the book are those on the nineteenth and twentieth centuries.

M. A. KLEIN, *Islam and Imperialism in Senegal: Sine-Saloum, 1847–1914* (1968). A first-rate study of the shift in the Serer states of Senegal from traditional authority to that of the colonial French.

B. A. OGOT AND J. A. KIERAN, EDS., *Zamani: A Survey of East African History*, 2nd rev. ed. (1974). Good material on the nineteenth century and colonial period in the various regions.

A. D. ROBERTS, ED., *The Colonial Moment in Africa: Essays on the Movement of Minds and Materials, 1900–1940* (1986). Chapters from *The Cambridge History of Africa* treating various aspects of the colonial period in Africa, including economics, politics, and religion.

RELIGIONS OF THE WORLD

Islam

The Islamic tradition is one of the youngest of the major traditions of world religion. Since its inception during the lifetime of the Prophet Muhammad (632 B.C.E.) it has grown, like the Christian and Buddhist traditions, into a worldwide community not limited by national boundaries or defined in racial or ethnic terms. It began among the Arabs, but spread widely. Islam's historical heartlands are those Arabic-, Turkic-, and Persian-speaking lands of the Near East between the Nile and the Oxus rivers. However, today more than half of its faithful live in Asia east of Karachi, Pakistan; and more Muslims live in sub-Saharan Africa than in all of the Arab lands. Muslims are also growing into significant religious minorities in the United States and Europe.

The central vision of Muslims is one of a human society built on the collective piety of individuals faithful to God. It focuses on a human community of worshipers who recognize the absolute sovereignty and oneness of God and strive to do His will. That divine will is held to be found first in His revealed word, the Qur'an; then as elaborated and specified in the actions and words of his final prophet, Muhammad; and finally as interpreted and extended in the scriptural exegesis and legal traditions of the Muslim community over the past thirteen and one-half centuries.

The Muslim vision thus centers on one god who has guided humankind throughout history by means of prophets or apostles and repeated revelations. God is the creator of all, and in the end all will return to God just as all came from Him. His majesty would seem to make Him a distant, threatening deity of absolute justice; there is such an element in the Muslim understanding of the wide chasm between the human and the divine. Still, there is an immanent as well as a transcendent side to the divine in the Muslim view. Indeed, Muslims have given us some of the greatest images of God's closeness to His faithful worshiper, images that have a special place in the thought of the Muslim mystics, who are known as *Sufis* (taken originally from *suf*, "wool," because of the early Muslim ascetics' use of simple wool dress).

Muhammad and Ali Cleanse the Ka'ba of Its Idols. This Iranian (Shirazi) miniature illustration (painted 1585–1595 c.e.) of The Garden of Purity by Mir Havand presents a Shi'ite perspective on a famous incident that followed Muhammad and the Medinan Muslims' taking of Mecca in 630 c.e. Here Ali, according to the Shi'is the rightful leader, or imam, of the Muslim community after Muhammad (and, according to Sunnis, the fourth "successor," or caliph, after Muhammad), joins the Prophet in smashing the idols that tradition says had been set up by the pagan Meccans in the holy house of God before Muhammad's lifetime. Note the veiling of both Muhammad's and Ali's faces—a pious expression of the concern about representation of God's holy persons too graphically being a presumptuous imitation of the divine prerogative of creation. [Bildarchiv Preussischer Kulturbesitz]

Muslims understand God's word in the Qur'an and the elaboration of that word by tradition to be a complete prescription for human life. Thus Islamic law is not law in the Western sense of civil, criminal, or international systems. Rather, it is a comprehensive set of standards for the moral, ritual, social, political, economic, aesthetic, and even hygienic and dietary dimensions of life. By being faithful to God's law the Muslim hopes to gain salvation on the Last Day, when human history shall end and all of God's creatures who have ever lived will be resurrected and called to account for their thoughts and actions during their lives on earth. Some will be saved, but others will be eternally damned.

Thus *Islam*, which means "submission [to God]," has been given as a name to the religiously defined system of life that Muslims have sought to institute wherever they have lived. Muslims have striven to organize their societies and political realities around the ideals represented in the traditional picture of the Prophet's community in Medina and Mecca. This approach necessitated compromise in which power was given to temporal rulers and accepted by Muslim religious leaders so long as those rulers protected God's law, the *Shari'ah.* The ideal of a single international Muslim community, or *Umma,* has never been fully realized politically, even in the heyday of the Umayyad or Abbasid empires. But it remains an ideal. Many movements of reform over the centuries have called for greater adherence to rigorous interpretations of Islamic law and greater dominance of piety and religious values in socio-political as well as individual life.

The major sectarian, or minority, groups among Muslims are those of the Shi'ites, who have held out for an ideal of a temporal ruler who is also the spiritual heir of Muhammad and God's designated deputy on earth. Most Shi'ites, notably those of Iran, hold that after eleven designated blood descendants of the prophets each had failed to be recognized by the majority of Muslims as the rightful leader or *Imam,* the

Friday Congregational Worship. Every Friday at the noon hour of daily worship, Muslims are enjoined to gather in as large a congregation as possible to worship together and listen to a weekly preaching in the major mosque in their town or city. Here at the Friday Mosque of Mopti, Mali, West African Muslims are seen in the midst of worship rites, prostrating themselves against the dramatic backdrop of the mud walls and minarets of the mosque. [George Gerster/Comstock Photography]

twelfth disappeared and remains to this day physically absent from the world, although not dead. He will come again at the end of time to vindicate his faithful followers and set things right. A smaller number of Shi'ites disagree with these "twelver" Shi'ites about the rightful successor to the sixth *imam;* known as "Seveners," they recognize a different line of succession beginning with the seventh *imam,* Isma'il. One of these Sevener, or "Isma'ili," groups recognizes in the contemporary Aga Khan the living *imam* of the present day and follows his guidance.

Muslim piety takes many forms. The common duties of Muslims are central for Muslims everywhere: faith in God and trust in His Prophet; regular performance of ritual worship *(Salat);* fasting during daylight hours for thirty days in Ramadan (the ninth month of the lunar year); giving of one's wealth to the needy *(zakat);* and at least once in a lifetime, if able, making the pilgrimage to Mecca and its environs *(Hajj).* Other more regional or popular, but ubiquitous, practices are also important. Celebration of the Prophet's birthday indicates the exalted popular status of Muhammad, even though any divine status for him is strongly rejected theologically. Recitation of the Qur'an permeates all Muslim practice, from daily worship to celebrations of all kinds. Visitation of saints' tombs is a prominent form of popular devotion. Sufi chanting or even ecstatic dancing are also practiced by Muslims around the world.

Muslims vary enormously in their physical environment, language, ethnic background, and cultural allegiances; yet all are united as part of, first, a great historical tradition of culture and religion and, second, a larger community of the faithful that transcends national and other boundaries. What binds them now as in the past are not political allegiances but religious affinities and a shared heritage of religious faith and culture. How these allegiances and sensibilities will fare in the face of the global challenges of the coming decades will be one of the important factors in shaping the world of the twenty-first century.

Japan's first foreign mission, headed by Prince Iwakura, Ambassador Extraordinary and Plenipotentiary, leaving Yokohama for the

U.S. and Europe on December 23, 1871. [Scala/Art Resource, N.Y.]

CHAPTER TOPICS

MODERN CHINA (1839–1949)

◆ Close of Manchu Rule

◆ From Dynasty to Warlordism (1895–1926)

◆ Cultural and Ideological Ferment: The May Fourth Movement

◆ Nationalist China

MODERN JAPAN (1853–1945)

◆ Overthrow of the Tokugawa *Bakufu* (1853–1868)

◆ Building the Meiji State (1868–1890)

◆ Growth of a Modern Economy

◆ The Politics of Imperial Japan (1890–1945)

◆ Japanese Militarism and German Nazism

In World Perspective Modern East Asia

From the mid-nineteenth century, the West was the expanding, aggressive, imperialistic force in world history. Its industrial goods and gunboats reached every part of the globe. It believed in free trade and had the military might to impose it on others. It was the trigger for change throughout the world. But the response to the Western impact depended on the internal array of forces in each country. In fact, the "response to the West" was only one small though vital part of the history of each country. Still, Japan and China were both relatively successful in their responses, for although each was subject to "unequal treaties," neither became a colony.

The two countries were also similar in that their governing elites were educated in Confucianism. Unlike the otherworldly religions of Buddhism, Islam, or Christianity, Confucianism was just secular enough to crumble in the face of the more powerful secularism of nineteenth-century science and the doctrines associated with it. In both Japan and China, although much more rapidly in Japan, the leading intellec-

tuals abandoned Confucianism in favor of Western secular doctrines. To be sure, many Confucian values, deeply embedded in the societies, survived the philosophies of which they had once been a part. In fact, one of the "breakdown products" of the Confucian sociopolitical identity was a strong new nationalism in both China and Japan.

But there the similarities end. In most other respects, modern Japan and China could hardly be more different. Perhaps the difference was only to be expected, given the pattern of recurrent dynasties in China's premodern history and of feudal evolution in Japan's.

The coming of Commodore Matthew Perry (1794–1858) in 1853–1854 precipitated a rapid political change in Japan. Within fifteen years the old Tokugawa regime had collapsed, and the Japanese were building a modern state. Economic growth followed. By 1900 Japan had defeated China and was about to defeat imperial Russia in war. Sustained economic growth continued during the early twentieth century.

After the Great Depression, Japan, like Italy and Germany, became an aggressive and militarized state and was eventually defeated in World War II. But after the war Japan reemerged more stable, more productive, and with a stronger parliamentary government than ever before.

The Chinese polity, in contrast, easily weathered the Opium War (1839–1842), an event of considerably greater magnitude than Perry's visit to Japan. The hold of tradition in China was remarkable, as was the effectiveness of traditional remedies in dealing with political ills. Only in its relations with the Western powers did traditional patterns not work. In one sense the strength of tradition was China's weakness, for it took seventy years after the Opium War to overthrow the dynasty. Only then was China willing to begin the modernization that Japan had started in 1868, and even then it was unsuccessful. Along with warlordism and the other problems that had accompanied the dissolution of past dynasties, new ills arose from the rending of the very fabric of the dynastic pattern. To these was added the unprecedented experience of being confronted by nations more powerful than itself. That China in some sense "failed" during this modern century is not a Western view imposed on China; it is the view held by Chinese themselves.

MODERN CHINA (1839–1949)

China's modern century was not the century in which it became modern as much as it was the century in which it encountered the modern West. Its first phase, from the Opium War to the fall of the Ch'ing or Manchu dynasty (1911), was remarkably little affected by Western impact. Indeed, it was only during the decade before 1911 that the Confucian tradition began to be discarded in favor of new ideas from the West. The second phase of China's modern history, from 1911 to the establishment of a Communist state in 1949, was a time of turmoil and suffering. The fighting incidental to the collapse of the dynasty gave way to decades of warlord rule; to partial military unification and continual military campaigns; to war with Japan; and then, while most countries were returning to peace, to four bitter years of civil war.

Close of Manchu Rule

The Opium War

The eighteenth-century three-country trade—British goods to India, Indian cotton to China, and Chinese tea to Britain—was in China's favor. The silver flowing into China spurred the monetization of Chinese markets. Then the British replaced cotton with Indian opium. By the 1820s the balance of trade was reversed, and silver began to flow out of China.

A crisis arose in the 1830s when the British East India Company lost its monopoly on British trade with China. The opium trade became wide open. To check the evil of opium and the outflow of specie, the Chinese government banned opium in 1836, closing the dens where it was smoked and executing Chinese dealers. In 1839 the government sent Imperial Commissioner Lin Tse-hsu (1785–1850) to Canton to superintend the ban. He continued the crackdown on Chinese dealers and destroyed over 20,000 chests—a six-month supply—of opium belonging to foreign merchants. This action led to a confrontation between the Chinese and British.

War broke out in November 1839 when Chinese war junks clashed with a British merchantman. The following June sixteen British warships arrived at Canton, and for the next two years the British bombarded forts, fought battles, seized cities, and attempted negotiations. The Chinese troops, with their antiquated weapons and old-style cannon, were ineffective. The war was finally ended in August 1842 by the Treaty of Nanking, the first of the "unequal treaties."

The treaty not only ended the "tribute system," but also provided Britain with a superb deep-water port at Hong Kong, a huge indemnity, and the opening of five ports: Canton, Shanghai, Amoy, Ningpo, and Foochow. British merchants and their families could reside in the ports and engage in trade; Britain could appoint a consul for each city; and British residents gained extraterritoriality, under which they were subject to British and not Chinese law. The treaty also contained a "most-favored-nation" clause, a provision that any further rights gained by any other nation would automatically accrue

The Opium War, 1840. Armed Chinese junks were no match for British warships. The war ended in 1842 with the Treaty of Nanking. [Corbis-Bettmann]

Commissioner Lin Urges Morality on Queen Victoria

In 1839 the British in China argued for free trade and protection for the legal rights of their citizens. The Chinese position was that behind such lofty arguments, the British were pushing opium.

What does this document suggest about the Ch'ing dynasty's view of China's place in the world in 1839? Does it still view China as a universal empire?

A communication: magnificently our great Emperor soothes and pacifies China and the foreign countries, regarding all with the same kindness. If there is profit, then he shares it with the peoples of the world; if there is harm, then he removes it on behalf of the world. This is because he takes the mind of heaven and earth as his mind.

The kings of your honorable country by a tradition handed down from generation to generation have always been noted for their politeness and submissiveness. We have read your successive tributary memorials saying, "In general our countrymen who go to trade in China have always received His Majesty the Emperor's gracious treatment and equal justice," and so on. Privately we are delighted with the way in which the honorable rulers of your country deeply understand the grand principles and are grateful for the Celestial grace. For this reason the Celestial Court in soothing those from afar has redoubled its polite and kind treatment. The profit from trade has been enjoyed by them continuously for two hundred years. This is the source from which your country has become known for its wealth. But after a long period of commercial intercourse, there appear among the crowd of barbarians both good persons and bad, unevenly. Consequently there are those who smuggle opium to seduce the Chinese people and so cause the spread of the poison to all provinces. Such persons who only care to profit themselves, and disregard their harm to others, are not tolerated by the laws of heaven and are unanimously hated by human beings. His Majesty the Emperor, upon hearing of this, is in a towering rage. . . .

We find that your country is sixty or seventy thousand *li* [three *li* make one mile, ordinarily] from China. Yet there are barbarian ships that strive to come here for trade for the purpose of making a great profit. The wealth of China is used to profit the barbarians. That is to say, the great profit made by barbarians is all taken from the rightful share of China. By what right do they then in return use the poisonous drug to injure the Chinese people? Even though the barbarians may not necessarily intend to do us harm, yet in coveting profit to an extreme, they have no regard for injuring others. Let us ask, where is your conscience? I have heard that the smoking of opium is very strictly forbidden by your country; that is because the harm caused by opium is clearly understood. Since it is not permitted to do harm to your own country, then even less should you let it be passed on to the harm of other countries—how much less to China!

Suppose there were people from another country who carried opium for sale to England and seduced your people into buying and smoking it; certainly your honorable ruler would deeply hate it and be bitterly aroused. We have heard heretofore that your honorable ruler is kind and benevolent. Naturally you would not wish to give unto others what you yourself do not want.

Now we have set up regulations governing the Chinese people. He who sells opium shall receive the death penalty and he who smokes it also the death penalty. Now consider this: if the barbarians do not bring opium, then how can the Chinese people resell it, and how can they smoke it? The fact is that the wicked barbarians beguile the Chinese people into a death trap. How then can we grant life only to those barbarians? He who takes the life of even one person still has to atone for it with his own life; yet is the harm done by opium limited to the taking of one life only? Therefore in the new regulations, in regard to those barbarians who bring opium to China, the penalty is fixed at decapitation or strangulation. This is what is called getting rid of a harmful thing on behalf of mankind.

[However] All those who within the period of the coming one year (from England) or six months (from India) bring opium to China by mistake, but who voluntarily confess and completely surrender their opium, shall be exempt from their punishment. This may be called the height of kindness and the perfection of justice.

to Britain as well. The treaty with Britain was followed in 1844 by similar treaties with the United States and France. The American treaty permitted churches in treaty ports, and the French treaty permitted the propagation of Catholicism.

After the signing of the British treaty, Chinese imports of opium rose from 30,000 chests to 87,000 in 1879. Thereafter, imports declined to 50,000 chests in 1906, and ended during World War I. But other kinds of trade did not grow as much as had been hoped, and Western merchants blamed the lack of growth on artificial restraints imposed by Chinese officials. They also complained that, despite the treaties, Canton remained closed to trade. The Chinese authorities, for their

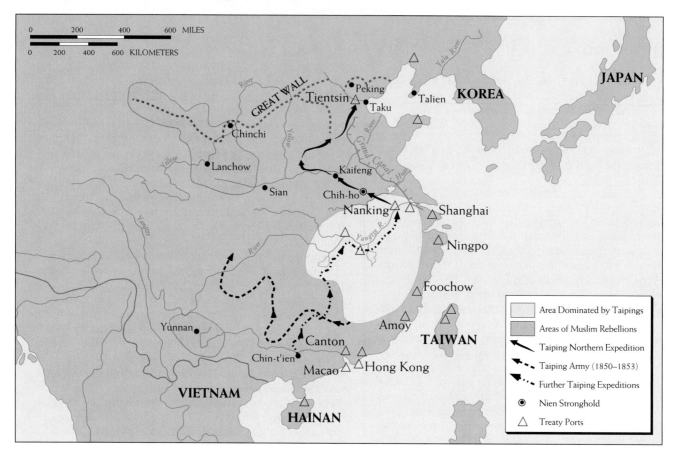

Map 32–1 The Taiping, Nien, and Muslim rebellions. Between 1850 and 1873 China was wracked by rebellions that almost ended the Manchu dynasty. The dynasty was saved by Chinese "gentry armies."

part, were incensed by the export of coolies to work under harsh conditions in Cuba and Peru. A second war broke out in 1856, which continued sporadically until Lord Elgin (1811–1863), the British commander, together with a French contingent, captured Peking in 1860. A new set of conventions and treaties provided for indemnities, the opening of eleven new ports, the stationing of foreign diplomats in Peking, the propagation of Christianity anywhere in China, and the legalization of the opium trade.

While the British fought China for trading rights, the Russians were encroaching on China's northern frontier. During the 1850s Russia established settlements along the Amur River. In 1858 China signed a treaty ceding the north bank of the Amur to Russia, and in 1860 China gave Russia the Maritime Province between the Ussuri River and the Pacific. These lands are claimed by China even today.

Rebellions Against the Manchu

Far more immediate a threat to Manchu rule than foreign gunboats and unequal treaties were the Taiping, Nien, and Muslim rebellions that convulsed China between 1850 and 1873 (see Map 32–1). The torment and suffering they caused were unparalleled in world history. Estimates of those killed during the twenty years of the Taiping Rebellion range from 20 to 30 million. If one adds in losses due to other rebellions, droughts, and floods, China's population dropped by 60 million and did not recover to prerebellion levels until almost the end of the dynasty in 1911.

The Taipings were begun by Hung Hsiu-ch'uan (1814–1864), a schoolteacher from a poor family in a minority Hakka group in the southern province of Kwangtung. Hung had four times failed to pass the civil-service examinations. He became ill and saw visions. Influenced by Protestant tracts he had picked up in Canton, Hung announced that he was the younger brother of Jesus and that God had told him to rid China of evil demons—including Manchus, Confucians, Taoists, and Buddhists. He formed an Association of God Worshipers. His followers cut off their queues as a sign of resistance to the Manchus, who called them "long-haired rebels." The Taipings began by attacking local Confucian temples, arousing the opposition of the gentry. The Taipings were soon joined by peasants, miners, and workers. Hung proclaimed the Heavenly Kingdom of Great Peace in 1851 and two years later took Nanking and made it his capital. The fighting spread until the Taipings controlled most of the Yangtze basin; their expeditions eventually entered sixteen of the eighteen Chinese provinces. By that time their army numbered almost a million.

The Taiping ideology joined Old Testament Christianity with an ancient text often used by reformers, the *Chou Rites*. The puritanical ethics of the Taipings came from the former, and the notion of sharing property equally came from the latter. The Taipings prohibited opium, tobacco, alcohol, gambling, adultery, prostitution, and footbinding. They upheld filial piety. They maintained that women were men's equals and appointed them to administrative and military posts. In short, like earlier rebels, the Taipings combined moral reform, religious fervor, and a vision of a transformed egalitarian society.

The weaknesses of the movement were several. Most Taiping leaders were too poorly educated to govern effectively, and the Taipings could not draw on the gentry. When the Taiping area was divided into kingdoms, dissension broke out. The Taipings failed to cultivate the secret societies, which were also anti-Manchu. They also failed to cultivate Westerners, who had been neutral before the 1860 treaty settlements and aided the Manchus thereafter. In addition, many Taiping ideals remained unfulfilled; for example, land was not redistributed, and, although Taiping teachings emphasized frugality and the sanctity of monogamous marriage, Hung lived with many concubines in the midst of luxury.

The other rebellions were of lesser note but longer duration. The Nien were located north of the Taipings along the Huai River. They began as bandits who lived in walled villages, were organized in secret societies, and lived by raiding the surrounding countryside. Eventually they built an army, collected taxes, and ruled 100,000 square miles. The Ch'ing court feared that the Nien would join forces with the Taipings. An even longer revolt was of Muslims against Chinese in the southwest and the northwest. One rebel set up an Islamic kingdom with himself as sultan. Like the Taiping Rebellion, these various rebellions took advantage of the weakened state of the dynasty. They occurred in areas that had few officials and no Ch'ing military units.

Against the rebellions, the Manchu Banners and the Chinese Army of the Green Standard proved helpless: The one was useful only for defense, the other only against civilians. The first effective step was taken against the rebellions when, in 1852, the court sent Tseng Kuo-fan (1811–1872) to Hunan Province in south-central China to organize a local army. Tseng was a product of the Confucian examination system and had served in Peking. He saw the Manchu government, of which he was an elite member, as the upholder of morali-ty and the social order, and Chinese rebels as would-be destroyers of that order. Arriving in Hunan, he recruited members of the gentry as officers. They were of the class that, since the late Ming, had been growing in importance and performing many local government functions, in some cases organizing local militia. Not only were they Confucian, but as landlords they had the most to lose from rebel rule. They recruited soldiers from their local areas. Tseng's "Hunan Braves" stopped the Taipings' advance.

Until 1860 the Ch'ing court was dominated by Manchu conservatives who limited Tseng's role and dragged their feet in upholding the treaties. In 1860 the conservatives lost their footing when the British and the French occupied Peking. A reform government replaced the conservatives, began internal changes, adopted a policy of cooperation with the Western powers, and put Tseng in charge of suppressing the rebellions. Tseng appointed other able officials to raise regional armies. Li Hung-chang (1823–1901), with his Anhwei Army, was especially effective. Foreigners and Shanghai merchants gave their support. Revenues from the customs service and foreign ships and weapons were essential to Tseng's armies. The Taipings collapsed when Nanking was captured in 1864 after protracted fighting. Tseng and Li suppressed the Nien by 1868, and the Muslim rebellion was put down five years later. Scholar-officials, relying on local gentry, had saved the dynasty.

Self-Strengthening and Decline (1874–1895)

The two decades after the suppression of the mid-century rebellions illustrate the dictum that there is no single "correct" view of history. In comparison, for example, with the late Sung or the late Ming, the last decades of the nineteenth century look good. In view of the dynasty's advanced stage of administrative decentralization, the Chinese resiliency and capacity to rebuild after unprecedented destruction were impressive. Even on its borders the Manchu state was able to maintain or regain some territories while losing others. But if we ask instead how effective China's response was to the West, or if we compare China's progress with that of Japan, then China during the same decades looks almost moribund. Historians often call these years the period of "self-strengthening," after a catch phrase in vogue at the time. This term is not inappropriate, as the list of new initiatives taken during the period is long. Yet, since the firepower of Western naval forces doubled each decade, the forces that China faced at the end of the century were vastly more formidable than those of the Opium War. Despite self-strengthening, China was relatively weaker at the end of the period than at the start.

In 1895 Li Hung-chang met with Itō Hirobumi (1838– 1909) of Japan to negotiate a peace treaty after China's defeat

The empress dowager Tz'u-hsi (1835–1908), who manipulated the levers of power at the Manchu court in Peking. [Hulton Picture Library/Corbis-Bettmann]

in the Sino-Japanese War. Itō asked with uncharacteristic bluntness: "Ten years ago when I was at Tientsin, I talked about reform with the Grand Secretary [Li]. Why is it that up to now not a single thing has been changed or reformed?" Li replied: "Affairs in my country have been so confined by tradition that I could not accomplish what I desired. . . . Now in the twinkling of an eye ten years have gone by, and everything is still the same. I am even more regretful. I am ashamed of having excessive wishes and lacking the power to fulfill them. . . ." Itō responded blandly: "The providence of heaven has no affection, except for the virtuous."[1] Considering that Li was the single most powerful figure in China during these decades, Itō's puzzlement was not surprising.

The Court at Peking   China's inability to act effectively is explained partly by the situation at the court. Prince Kung (1833–1898) and the empress dowager (1835–1908) were coregents for the young emperor. For a Manchu noble, Prince Kung was a man of ideas. After signing the treaties of

1860 he established in 1861 a new office directly under the Grand Council to handle the court's relations with foreign diplomats in Peking. The following year he established a school to train Chinese in foreign languages. Over time, however, his position at the court grew weaker. Outmaneuvered by the empress dowager, he was ousted in 1884.

The empress dowager was the daughter of a Manchu official. She had become an imperial concubine and had produced the only male child of the former emperor. She was educated, clever, petty, strong-willed, and narrow-minded. She did not oppose change, except by circumstance, nor did she favor it. She had no conception of how to reform China. Her single goal was to gather political power into her own hands. She acquired this by forging a political machine of conservative bureaucrats, military commanders, and eunuchs, and by maintaining a balance between the court and the regional strength of the powerful governor-generals. The result was a court just able to survive, too weak to govern effectively, and not inclined to do more than approve of initiatives taken at the provincial level.

Regional Governments   The most vital figures during these decades were a handful of governors-general whose names are legend: Tseng Kuo-fan, Li Hung-chang, Tso Tsung-t'ang (1812–1885), and Chang Chih-tung (1837–1909). Each had a staff of 200 or 300 and an army, and was in charge of two or three provinces. They were loyal to the dynasty that they had restored in the face of almost certain collapse, and in return for their allegiance they were allowed great autonomy.

Their first task was reconstruction. The rebellions in central China had destroyed the mulberry trees on which the silkworms fed and those in the northwest, the irrigation systems. Millions were hungry or homeless. The leaders' response to these ills was massive and effective. Just as they had mobilized the gentry to suppress the rebellions, now they obtained their cooperation in rebuilding. They set up refugee centers and soup kitchens, reduced taxes in the devastated Yangtze valley, reclaimed lands gone to waste, began water-control projects, and built granaries. By the early 1890s considerable well-being had been restored to China's late dynastic society.

Their second task was self-strengthening—the adoption of Western arms and technology. The governors-general were keenly aware of China's weakness. To strengthen China, they built arsenals and shipyards during the 1860s and 1870s, and during the 1870s and 1880s they began commercial ventures as well. The China Merchants Steam Navigation Company was established in 1872, the Kaiping Coal Mine in 1876, and then a telegraph company, short stretches of railways, and cotton mills. The formula applied in running these enterprises was "official supervision and merchant operation." The major decisions were made by scholar-officials like Tseng, but day-to-day operations were left to the merchants. This

[1]S. Y. Teng and J. K. Fairbank, *China's Response to the West* (Cambridge: Harvard University Press, 1954), p. 126.

division of labor led to contradictions. The Steam Navigation Company, for example, was funded partly by the government because private capital was inadequate.

Li Hung-chang awarded the company a monopoly on shipments of the rice paid in taxes and official cargos to Tientsin and won tariff concessions for the company as well. For a time these advantages enabled it to compete successfully with foreign lines. But Li also used company ships to transport his troops; he took company funds to reward his political followers; and he interfered in the company by hiring and firing managers. Under these conditions, both investors and managers took their profits quickly and did not reinvest in the line. Soon British lines once again dominated shipping in China's domestic waters.

Treaty Ports Conditions in the treaty ports, of which there were fourteen by the 1860s, were different from the rest of China. The ports were little islands of privilege where foreigners lived in mansions staffed with servants, raced horses at the track, participated in amateur theatricals, drank (in Shanghai, at the longest bar in the world), and went to church on Sunday. But the ports were also islands of security, under the rule of foreign consuls, where capital was safe from confiscation, trade was free, and "squeeze" (extortion by officials) was the exception and not the rule. Foreign companies naturally located in the ports. The Hong Kong and Shanghai Bank, for example, was funded in 1865 by British interests to finance international trade and to make loans to Chinese firms and banks. Chinese merchants were also attracted by these conditions and located their businesses on rented lands in the foreign concessions. Joint ventures, such as steamboats on the Yangtze, were also begun by Chinese and foreign merchants. Well into the twentieth century the foreign concessions (treaty-port lands leased in perpetuity by foreigners) remained the vital sector of China's modern economy.

The effects of the treaty ports and of Western imperialism on China were mainly negative. Under the low tariffs mandated by the treaties, Chinese industries had little protection from imports. Native cotton spinning was almost destroyed by imports of yarn—although the cloth woven from the yarn remained competitive with foreign cloth. Chinese tea lost ground to Indian tea and Chinese silk to Japanese silk, as these countries developed products of standard quality and China did not. China found few products to export: pig bristles, soybeans, and vegetable oils. The level of foreign trade stayed low, and China's interior markets were affected only slightly.

By the 1870s the foreign powers had reached an accommodation with China. They counted on the court to uphold the treaties; in return, they became a prop for the dynasty during its final decades. By 1900, for example, the court's revenues from customs fees were larger than those from any other source, including the land tax. The fees were collected by the Maritime Customs Service, a notably efficient and honest treaty-port institution headed by an Irishman, Sir Robert Hart (1835–1911), who saw himself as serving the Chinese government. In 1895 the Maritime Customs Service had 700 Western and 3,500 Chinese employees.

The Borderlands: The Northwest, Vietnam, and Korea

China's other foreign relations were with fringe lands inhabited by non-Chinese but which China claimed by right of past conquest or as tributaries. Often distant from the pressing concerns of Chinese government, the tributaries were nonetheless the mirrors in which China saw reflected its own self-image as a universal empire. During the late nineteenth century this image was strengthened in the northwest but dealt a fatal blow in Vietnam and Korea.

The Northwest In the northwest, China confronted imperial Russia. Both countries had been expanding onto the steppe since the seventeenth century. Both had firearms.

An American view of the "Open Door." The combination of high self-esteem and anti-foreignism at the turn of the century was not a Chinese monopoly.
[Corbis-Bettmann]

Caught in a pincers between them, the once proud, powerful, and independent nomadic tribes gradually were rendered impotent. Conservatives at the Manchu court ordered Tso Tsung-t'ang, who had suppressed Muslim rebels within China, to suppress a Muslim leader who had founded an independent state in Chinese Turkestan (the Tarim basin, the area of the old Silk Road). Tso led his army across 3,000 miles of deserts, and by 1878 had reconquered the area, which was subsequently renamed Sinkiang, or the "New Territories." A treaty signed with Russia in 1881 also restored most of the Ili region in western Mongolia to Chinese control. These victories strengthened court conservatives who wished to take a stronger stance toward the West.

Vietnam   To the south was Vietnam, which had retained its independence from China since 935. It saw itself as an independent and separate state, but it used the Chinese writing system, modeled its laws and government on those of China, and traded with China within the framework of the tribute system. China, more simply, saw Vietnam as a tributary that could be aided or punished as necessary.

During the 1840s the second emperor of the Nguyen dynasty, which had begun in 1802, moved to reduce French influences and suppress Christianity. Thousands were killed, including French and Vietnamese priests. The French responded by seizing Saigon and the three provinces of Cochin China in 1859, establishing a protectorate over Cambodia in 1864, and taking three more provinces in 1867 and Hanoi in 1882. China, flush with confidence after its victories in central Asia, in 1883 sent in troops to aid its tributary. The result was a two-year war in which French warships ranged the coast of China, attacking shore batteries and sinking ships. In 1885 China was forced to sign a treaty abandoning its claims to Vietnam. By 1893 France had brought together Vietnam, Cambodia, and Laos to form the Federation of Indochina, which remained a French colony until 1940.

Korea   A third area of contention was Korea. Unlike Vietnam, Korea saw itself as a tributary of China. Even at his own court the Korean ruler styled himself as a king and not an emperor. It was the only rim area of China that accepted the tribute system on Chinese terms.

During the last decades of the long (1392–1910) Choson dynasty, the Korean state was weak. It hung on to power, in part, by enforcing a policy of seclusion almost as total as that of Tokugawa Japan, which won it the name of the Hermit Kingdom. Its only foreign ties were its tribute relations with China and its trade and occasional diplomatic missions to Japan. In 1876 Japan "opened" Korea to international relations, using much the same tactics that Perry had used twenty-two years earlier against Japan. Japan then contended with China for influence in Korea's internal politics. Conservatives

and moderate reformers in Korea looked to China for support. Radical reformers, weaker and fewer in number, looked to Japan, arguing that only sweeping changes such as those that had occurred in Japan would enable Korea to survive. The radicals, however, were soon suppressed.

In 1893 a popular religious sect unleashed a rebellion against the weak and corrupt Seoul government. When the government requested Chinese help to suppress the rebellion, China sent troops, but Japan sent more, and in 1894 war broke out between China and Japan. China and the Western powers expected an easy Chinese victory, but they had not understood the changes occurring within Japan. Japan won handily. Neither the Chinese fleet nor the Chinese armies were a match for the discipline and the superior tactics of the Japanese units. It was after this war that Taiwan became Japan's first colony. The defeat by Japan convinced many throughout China that basic changes were inevitable.

From Dynasty to Warlordism (1895–1926)

China was ruled by officials who had mastered the Confucian classics and the historical and literary tradition that had developed along with them. This intellectual formation was highly resistant to change. For most officials living in China's interior, the foreign crises of the nineteenth century were "coastal phenomena" that, like bee stings, were painful for a time but then forgotten. Few officials realized the magnitude of the foreign threat.

China's defeat in 1895 by Japan, another Asian nation and one for which China had had little regard, came as a shock. The response within China was a new wave of reform proposals. The most influential thinker was K'ang Yu-wei (1858–1927), who described China as "enfeebled" and "soundly asleep atop a pile of kindling." For this state of affairs, K'ang blamed the "conservatives." They did not understand, K'ang argued, that Confucius himself had been a reformer and not simply a transmitter of past wisdom. Confucius had invented the idea of a golden age in the past in order to persuade the rulers of his own age to adopt his ideas. All of history, K'ang continued, was evolutionary—a march forward from absolute monarchy to constitutional monarchy to democracy. Actually, K'ang was not well versed in Western ideas; he equated the somewhat mystical Confucian virtue of humanity *(jen)* with electricity and ether. Nonetheless, his reinterpretation of the essentials of Confucianism removed a major barrier to the entry of Western ideas into China.

In 1898 the emperor himself became sympathetic to K'ang's ideas and, on June 11, launched "one hundred days of reform." He took as his models not past Chinese monarchs, but Peter the Great (r. 1682–1725) and the Japanese

Liang Ch'i-ch'ao Urges the Chinese to Reform (1896)

Next to K'ang Yu-wei, Liang Ch'i-ch'ao (1873–1929) was the most influential thinker of late Ch'ing China.

What kind of reform program do you imagine Liang advocating? Compare this response to the challenge of the West to that of a Japanese commentator in the document box entitled "A Japanese View of the Inventiveness of the West," later in this chapter.

On the *Harm of not Reforming.* Now here is a big mansion which has lasted a thousand years. The tiles and bricks are decayed and the beams and rafters are broken. It is still a magnificently big thing, but when wind and rain suddenly come up, its fall is foredoomed. Yet the people in the house are still happily playing or soundly sleeping and as indifferent as if they have seen or heard nothing. Even some who have noted the danger know only how to weep bitterly, folding their arms and waiting for death without thinking of any remedy. Sometimes there are people a little better off who try to repair the cracks, seal up the leaks, and patch up the ant holes in order to be able to go on living there in peace, even temporarily, in the hope that something better may turn up. These three types of people use their minds differently, but when a hurricane comes they will die together. . . . A nation is also like this. . . .

India is one of the oldest countries on the great earth. She followed tradition without change; she has been rendered a colony of England. Turkey's territory occupied three continents and had an established state for a thou-sand years; yet, because of observing the old ways without change, she has been dominated by six large countries, which have divided her territory. . . . The Moslems in central Asia have usually been well known for their bravery and skill in warfare, and yet they observe the old ways without changing. The Russians are swallowing them like a whale and nibbling them as silkworms eat mulberry leaves, almost in their entirety.

The age of China as a country is equal to that of India and the fertility of her land is superior to that of Turkey, but her conformity to the defective ways which have accumulated and her incapacity to stand up and reform make her also like a brother of these two countries. . . . Whenever there is a flood or drought, communications are severed, there is no way to transport famine relief, the dead are abandoned to fill the ditches or are disregarded, and nine out of ten houses are emptied. . . . The members of secret societies are scattered over the whole country, waiting for the chance to move. Industry is not developed, commerce is not discussed, the native goods daily become less salable. . . . "Leakage" [i.e., squeeze] becomes more serious day by day and our financial sources are almost dried up. Schools are not well-run and students, apart from the "eight-legged" essays, do not know how to do a thing. The good ones are working on small researches, flowery writing, and miscellaneous trifles. Tell them about the vast oceans, they open their eyes wide and disbelieve it.

Reprinted by permission of the publisher from *China's Response to the West* by Ssu-Yu Teng and John K. Fairbank, Cambridge, MA: Harvard University Press. Copyright © 1954, 1979 by the President and Fellows of Harvard College.

Meiji Emperor (r. 1867–1912). Edicts were issued for sweeping reforms of China's schools, railroads, police, laws, military services, bureaucracy, post offices, and examination system. But the orders were implemented in only one province; conservative resistance was nationwide. Even at the court, the empress dowager regained control and ended the reforms. K'ang and most of his associates fled to Japan. One reformer who remained behind was executed.

The response of the Western powers to China's 1895 defeat has been described as "carving up the melon." Each nation tried to define a sphere of interest, which usually consisted of a leasehold along with railway rights and special commercial privileges. Russia gained a leasehold at Port Arthur; Germany acquired one in Shantung. Britain got the New Territories adjoining Kowloon at Hong Kong. New ports and cities were opened to foreign trade. The United States, busy acquiring the Philippines and Guam, was in a weaker position in China. So it enunciated an "open-door" policy: equal commercial opportunities for all powers and the preservation of the territorial integrity of China.

There was in China at this time a religious society known as the Boxers. The Chinese name translates more literally as the "Righteous and Harmonious Fists." The Boxers had rituals, spells, and amulets which they believed made them impervious to bullets. They rebelled first in Shantung in 1898, and, gaining court support, entered Peking in 1900. The court declared war on the treaty powers, and there followed a two-month siege of the foreign legation quarter. Support for the rebellion was fueled by pent-up resentments against decades of foreign encroachments. Eventually an international force captured Peking, won a huge indemnity, and obtained the right to maintain permanent military forces in the capital. In the aftermath of the Boxer Rebellion, the Russians occupied Manchuria.

The defeat of the Boxers convinced even conservative Chinese leaders of the futility of clinging to old ways. A more powerful reform movement began, with the empress dowager herself in its vanguard. But as the movement gained momentum, the dynasty could not stay far enough in front and eventually was overrun.

Educational reforms began in 1901. Women, for the first time, were admitted as students to newly formed schools. In place of Confucianism, the instructors taught science, mathematics, geography, and an anti-imperialist version of Chinese history that fanned the flames of nationalism. Western doctrines, such as classical economics, liberalism, socialism, anarchism, and social Darwinism, were also introduced into China. Most entered via translations from Japanese, and in the process the modern vocabulary coined by Japanese scholars was implanted in China. By 1906 there were 8,000 Chinese students in Japan, which had become a hotbed of Chinese reformist and revolutionary societies.

Military reforms were begun by Yuan Shih-k'ai (1859–1916), whose New Army drew on Japanese and Western models. Young men from gentry families, spurred by patriotism, broke with the traditional Chinese animus against military careers and joined the New Army as officers. Their loyalty was to their commanders and to their country, not to the dynasty.

Political reforms began with a modification of the examination system to accommodate the learning at the new schools. Then in 1905 the examination system was abolished altogether. Henceforth, officials were to be recruited from the graduates of the schools and those who had studied abroad. Provincial assemblies were formed in 1909, and a consultative assembly with some elected members was established in Peking in 1910. These representative bodies were intended to gather the new gentry nationalism in support of the court, but they became forums for the expression of interests at odds with those of the dynasty.

In sum, during the first decade of the twentieth century the three vital components of the imperial system—Confucian education, the bureaucracy, and the gentry—had been discarded or changed in ways that even a few decades earlier would have been unimaginable.

These changes sparked the 1911 revolution. It began with an uprising in Szechwan province against a government plan to nationalize the main railways. The players were:

1. Gentry who stood to lose their investments in the railways.

2. Ch'ing military commanders, who broke with Peking, declaring their provinces independent.

3. Sun Yat-sen (1866–1925), a republican revolutionary. Born a peasant, he had learned English and became a

Sun Yat-sen (1866–1925), father of China's 1911 republican revolution. [Brown Brothers]

Christian in Hawaii; then studied medicine in Canton and Hong Kong. He organized the Revolutionary Alliance in Tokyo in 1905 and was associated with the Nationalist Party (Kuomintang) formed in 1912.

4. Yuan Shih-k'ai, who was called on by the court to preserve the dynasty. Instead, he arranged for the last child emperor to abdicate, for Sun to step aside, and for himself to become president of the new Republic of China.

The Nationalists won the election called in 1913. Yuan thereupon had their leader assassinated, crushed the military governors who supported them, and forced Sun Yat-sen and other revolutionaries to flee again to Japan. Yuan emerged as the uncontested ruler of China. Mistaking the temper of the times, he proclaimed a new dynasty with himself as emperor. The idea of another dynasty, however, met implacable opposition from all quarters, forcing Yuan to abandon the attempt. He died three months later in June 1916. After Yuan, China fell into the hands of warlord armies. The years until the late twenties were a time of agony, frustration, and travail for the Chinese people. Yet they also were a time of intense intellectual ferment.

Cultural and Ideological Ferment: The May Fourth Movement

In the century after the Opium War, China's leading thinkers responded to the challenge of the West in terms of four successive modes of thought:

Ch'en Tu-hsiu's "Call to Youth" in 1915

Struggle, natural selection, and organic process are the images of Ch'en Tu-hsiu. How different from those of Confucianism!

How does Ch'en's "Call to Youth" relate to the political conditions in China in 1915?

The Chinese compliment others by saying, "He acts like an old man although still young." Englishmen and Americans encourage one another by saying, "Keep young while growing old." Such is one respect in which the different ways of thought of the East and West are manifested. Youth is like early spring, like the rising sun, like trees and grass in bud, like a newly sharpened blade. It is the most valuable period of life. The function of youth in society is the same as that of a fresh and vital cell in a human body. In the processes of metabolism, the old and the rotten are incessantly eliminated to be replaced by the fresh and living. . . . According to this standard, then, is the society of our nation flourishing, or is it about to perish? I cannot bear to answer. As for those old and rotten elements, I shall leave them to the process of natural selection. . . . I only,

with tears, place my plea before the young and vital youth, in the hope that they will achieve self-awareness, and begin to struggle.

What is the struggle? It is to exert one's intellect, discard resolutely the old and the rotten, regard them as enemies and as the flood or savage beasts, keep away from their neighborhood and refuse to be contaminated by their poisonous germs. Alas! Do these words really fit the youth of our country? I have seen that, out of every ten youths who are young in age, five are old in physique; and out of every ten who are young in both age and physique, nine are old in mentality. Those with shining hair, smooth countenance, a straight back and a wide chest are indeed magnificent youths! Yet if you ask what thoughts and aims are entertained in their heads, then they all turn out to be the same as the old and rotten, like moles from the same hill. . . . It is the old and rotten air that fills society everywhere. One cannot even find a bit of fresh and vital air to comfort those of us who are suffocating in despair.

Reprinted by permission of the publisher from *China's Response to the West* by Ssu-Yu Teng and John K. Fairbank, Cambridge, MA: Harvard University Press. Copyright © 1954, 1979 by the President and Fellows of Harvard College.

---

1. During the 1840s and the 1850s, and into the 1860s, the key event in China was the Taiping Rebellion. The success of gentry Confucianism in putting down the rebellion and in reestablishing the social order afterward underlined for most Chinese the effectiveness, vitality, and validity of traditional doctrines.

2. From the 1860s to the 1890s, the dominant intellectual modality was *"ti-yung* reformism." The essence *(ti)* was to remain Chinese, but useful contrivances *(yung)* could be borrowed from the West. This formula enabled a restabilized China to borrow and reform in small ways and to build arsenals and a few railroads, while remaining Chinese at the core. It was the ideology of the "self-strengthening" movement.

3. Then, during the last decade of the Manchu dynasty, the *ti-yung* distinction came to be seen as inadequate. The *ti* itself was reinterpreted. The dominant view was that of K'ang Yu-wei, who argued that Confucius had been a reformer and that Confucianism, properly understood, was a philosophy of change. This kind of thought was behind the rash of reforms of 1900–1911.

4. The fourth stage was a period of freedom and vigorous experimentation with new doctrines that began in 1914

and extended into the 1920s. It is called the May Fourth Movement after an incident in Peking in 1919 in which thousands of students protested the settlement at Versailles that awarded former German possessions in Shantung to Japan. The powerful nationalism that led the students to demonstrate in the streets changed the complexion of Chinese thought. Instead of appealing to tradition, leading thinkers began to judge ideas in terms of their value in solving China's problems. It was also not accidental that this era of intellectual excitement corresponded almost exactly with the period of warlord rule—which afforded a breathing space between the ideological constraints of the old dynasty and those of the nationalist and Communist eras that would follow.

Scholars who returned from abroad during the last years of Manchu rule often located in the safety of the treaty ports. During the May Fourth era, however, the center of advanced thought was Peking. Ts'ai Yuan-p'ei (1867–1940), who had been minister of education under the republic, became the chancellor of Peking University, and Ch'en Tu-hsiu (1880–1939) became his dean of letters. Both men had had a classical education and had passed the traditional examinations. Ts'ai joined the party of Sun Yat-sen and went to study in Germany. After the fall of Yuan Shih-k'ai, he made Peking University into a haven for scholars who had returned from study in Japan or the West.

Ch'en Tu-hsiu had studied in Japan and France. In 1915 he launched *New Youth*, a magazine that played a role in the intellectual revolution of early twentieth-century China comparable to the *cahiers* in the French Revolution or the pamphlets of Thomas Paine in the American Revolution. In his magazine Ch'en placed the blame for Chinese ills on the teachings of Confucius. He called for a generation of progressive, cosmopolitan, and scientific youth who would uphold the values of liberty, equality, and fraternity.

The greatest modern Chinese writer was Lu Hsun (1881–1936). Like most other leading intellectuals of the period, he had been born in a scholar-official family. He went to Japan for eight years to study medicine but switched in midcourse to literature. His first work, *A Madman's Diary*, appeared in *New Youth* in 1918. Its protagonist is a pathetic figure whose madness takes the form of a belief that people eat people. Lu Hsun's message was that only the vision of a madman could truly comprehend an abnormal and inhumane society.

As the May Fourth Movement developed, ideas propounded in Peking quickly spread to the rest of China, especially to its urban centers. Protest demonstrations against imperialist privilege broke out in Shanghai, Wuhan, and Canton, as they had in the capital. Nationalism and anti-imperialist sentiment were stronger than liberalism, although few thinkers did not speak of democracy. Only members of an older generation of reformers, such as K'ang Yu-wei, came full circle and, appalled by the slaughter of World War I and what they saw as Western materialism, advocated a return to traditional Chinese philosophies.

At the onset of China's intellectual revolution, Marxism had small appeal. Marx's critique of capitalist society did not fit Chinese conditions. The anarchism of Peter Kropotkin (1842–1921), who taught that mutual aid was as much a part of evolution as the struggle for survival, was more popular. But after the Russian Revolution of 1917, Marxism-Leninism entered China. The Leninist definition of imperialism as the last crisis stage of capitalism had an immediate appeal, for it put the blame for China's ills on the West and offered "feudal" China the possibility of leapfrogging over capitalism to socialism. As early as 1919 an entire issue of *New Youth* was devoted to Marxism. Marxist study groups formed in Peking and other cities. In 1919 a student from Hunan, Mao Tsetung, who had worked in the Peking University library, returned to Changsha to form a study group. Ch'en Tu-hsiu was converted to Marxism in 1920. Instructed in organizational techniques by a Comintern agent, Ch'en and others formed the Chinese Communist Party in Shanghai in 1921; Chou En-lai (1898–1976) formed a similar group in Paris during the same year. The numbers involved were small but grew steadily.

Nationalist China

Kuomintang Unification of China and the Nanking Decade (1927–1937)

Sun Yat-sen had fled to Japan during the 1913–1916 rule by Yuan Shih-k'ai. He returned to Canton in 1916, but despite his immense personal attractiveness as a leader he was a poor organizer, and his Kuomintang (KMT)—or Nationalist Party—made little headway. For a time in 1922 he was driven out of Canton by a local warlord. From 1923 Sun began to receive Soviet advice and support. With the help of Comintern agents like Michael Borodin, he reorganized his party on the Leninist model, with an executive committee on top of a national party congress and, below this, provincial and county organizations and local party cells.

Since 1905 Sun had enunciated his "three principles of the people": nationality, livelihood, and rights. Sun's earlier nationalism had been directed against Manchu rule; it was now redirected against Western imperialism. The principle of

Chiang Kai-shek (1887–1975) as a young revolutionary officer.

people's livelihood was defined in terms of equalizing land holdings and nationalizing major industries. By "people's rights" Sun meant democracy, although he argued that full democracy must be preceded by a preparatory period of tutelage under a single party dictatorship. Sun sent his loyal lieutenant Chiang Kai-shek (1887–1975) to the Soviet Union for study. Chiang returned after four months with a cadre of Russian advisers and established a military academy at Whampoa to the south of Canton in 1924. The cadets of Whampoa were to form a "party army." Sun died in 1925. By 1926 the Whampoa Academy had graduated several thousand officers, and the KMT army numbered almost 100,000. The KMT had become the major political force in China, with 200,000 members; its leadership was divided between a left and a right wing.

The growth of the party was spurred by changes occurring within Chinese society. Industries arose in the cities. Labor unions were organized in tobacco and textile factories. New ventures were begun outside the treaty ports, and chambers of commerce were established even in medium-sized towns. Entrepreneurs, merchants, officials, journalists, and the employees of foreign firms formed a new and politically conscious middle class.

The quicksilver element in cities was the several million students at government, Catholic, and Protestant schools. In May 1925 students demonstrated against the treatment of workers in foreign-owned factories at Shanghai. Police in the international settlement fired on the demonstrators, killing thirteen and wounding fifty. The incident further inflamed national and anti-imperialist feelings. Strikes and boycotts of foreign goods were called throughout China. Those in Hong Kong lasted for fifteen months.

Under these conditions the Chinese Communist Party (CCP) also grew, and in 1926 it had about 20,000 members. The party was influential in student organizations, labor unions, and even within the KMT. By an earlier agreement Sun had permitted CCP members to join the KMT as individuals, but had enjoined them from organizing CCP cells within the KMT. Moscow approved of this policy. It felt that the CCP was too small to accomplish anything on its own, and that by working within the KMT its members could join in the "bourgeois, national, democratic struggle" against "imperialism and feudal warlordism." Chou En-lai, for example, became deputy head of the Political Education Department of the Whampoa Academy.

By 1926 the KMT had established a base in the area around Canton, and Chiang Kai-shek felt ready to march north against the warlord domains. He worried about the growing Communist strength, however, and before setting off he ousted the Soviet advisers and CCP members from the KMT offices in Canton. The march north began in July. By the spring of 1927 Chiang's army had reached the Yangtze, de-

feating, and often absorbing, warlord armies as it advanced (see Map 32–2).

After entering Shanghai in April 1927 Chiang carried out a sweeping purge of the CCP—against its members in the KMT, against its party organization, and against the labor unions that it had come to dominate. Many were killed. The CCP responded by trying to gain control of the KMT left wing, which had established a government at Wuhan, and by armed uprisings. Both attempts failed. The surviving CCP members fled to the mountainous border region of Hunan and Kiangsi to the southwest and established the "Kiangsi Soviet." The left wing of the KMT, disenchanted with the Communists, rejoined the right wing at Nanking, China's new capital. Chiang's army continued north, took Peking, and gained the nominal submission of most northern Chinese warlords during 1928. By this time most foreign powers had recognized the Nanking regime as the government of China.

Chiang Kai-shek was the key figure in the Nanking government. By training and temperament he believed in military force. He was unimaginative, strict, feared more than loved, and, in the midst of considerable corruption, incorruptible. Chiang venerated Sun Yat-sen and his three "people's principles." The grandeur of Sun's tomb in Nanking surpassed that of the Ming emperors. But where Sun, as a revolutionary, had looked back to the zeal of the Taiping rebels, Chiang, trying to consolidate his rule over provincial warlords, looked back to Tseng Kuo-fan, who had put down the rebels and restabilized China. Like Tseng, Chiang was conservative and, though a Methodist, often appealed to Confucian values. The New Life Movement begun by Chiang in 1934 was an attempt to revitalize these values.

Chiang's power rested on the army, the party, and the government bureaucracy. The army was dominated by the Whampoa clique, which was personally loyal to Chiang, and by officers trained in Japan. After 1927 Soviet military advisers were replaced by German advisers. They reorganized Chiang's army along German lines with a general staff system. The larger part of KMT revenues went to the military, which was expanded into a modernized force of 300,000. Whampoa graduates also controlled the secret military police and used it against Communists and any others who opposed the government. The KMT was a dictatorship under a central committee. Chiang became president of the party in 1938.

The densely populated central and lower Yangtze provinces were the area of KMT strength. The party, however, was unable to control the outlying areas occupied by warlords, Communists, and Japanese. Some gains were made during the Nanking decade: Chiang's armies defeated the northern warlords in 1930, put down a rebellion in Fukien in 1934, and extended their control over southern and southwestern China two years later. But warlords ruled some areas

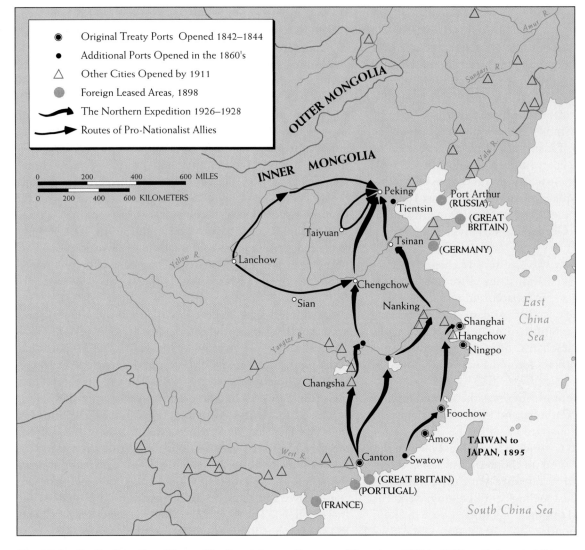

Map 32–2 The Northern Expeditions of the Kuomintang. These expeditions, from 1926 to 1928, unified most of China under the Nationalist (Kuomintang) government of Chiang Kai-shek, inaugurating the Nanking decade. Warlord armies continued to hold power on the periphery.

until 1949. In 1931 Chiang attacked the Kiangsi Soviet. In 1934 the Communists were forced to abandon their mountain base and flee to the southwest and then north to Shensi province in northwestern China. Of the 90,000 troops that set out on this epic "Long March" of 6,000 miles, only 20,000 survived. It was during this march that Mao Tse-tung wrested control of the CCP from the Moscow-trained, urban-oriented leaders and established his unorthodox view that a revolutionary Leninist party could base itself on the peasantry.

The Japanese had held special rights in Manchuria since the Russo-Japanese War of 1905. When Chiang's march north and the rise of Chinese nationalism threatened the Japanese position, field-grade officers of Japan's Kwantung Army engineered a military coup in 1931 and in 1932 proclaimed the independence of Manchukuo, their puppet state. In the years

that followed, Japanese forces moved south as far as the Great Wall. Chinese nationalism demanded that Chiang resist. Chiang, well aware of the disparity between his armies and those of Japan, said that the internal unification of China must take precedence over war against a foreign power. But on a visit to Sian in 1936 Chiang was imprisoned by a northern warlord until he agreed to join with the CCP in a united front against Japan. In the following year, however, a full-scale war with Japan broke out, and China's situation again changed.

War and Revolution (1937–1949)

In 1937 the KMT controlled most of China and was recognized as its government, whereas the CCP survivors of the Long March had just begun to rebuild their strength in arid

Modern China

1839–1842	Opium War
	Close of Manchu Rule
1850–1873	Taiping and other rebellions
1870s–1880s	Self-strengthening movement
1894–1895	Sino-Japanese War
1898	One hundred days of reform
1898–1900	Boxer Rebellion
1911	Republican revolution overthrows Ch'ing dynasty

Warlordism

1912–1916	Yuan Shih-k'ai president of Republic of China
1916–1928	Warlord era
1919	May Fourth incident

Nationalist China

1924	Founding of Whampoa Military Academy
1926–1928	March north and Kuomintang reunification of China
1928–1937	Nanking decade
1934–1935	Chinese Communists' Long March to Yenan
1937–1945	War with Japan
1945–1949	Civil war and the establishment of the People's Republic of China

densely populated Yangtze valley territories that had constituted the KMT base. The withdrawal to Chungking cut the KMT off from most of the Chinese population; programs for modernization ended; and the KMT's former tax revenues were lost. Inflation increased geometrically, reducing the real income of officials, teachers, and soldiers alike. By the end of World War II and during the early postwar years salaries were paid in large packages of almost worthless money, which was immediately spent for food or goods possessing real value. Inflation produced demoralization and exacerbated the already widespread corruption.

The United States sent advisers and military equipment to strengthen Chiang's forces after the start of the Pacific War. The advisers, however, were frustrated by Chiang, who wanted not to fight the Japanese but to husband his forces for the anticipated postwar confrontation with the Communists. Within his own army a gap appeared between officers and men. Conditions in the camps were primitive, food poor, and medical supplies inadequate. The young saw conscription almost as a sentence of death. Chiang's unwillingness to commit his troops against the Japanese also meant that the surge of anti-Japanese patriotism was not converted to popular support for the KMT.

For the Communists, the Japanese occupation was an opportunity. Headquartered at Yenan, they consolidated their base in Shensi province. They began campaigns to promote literacy and production drives to promote self-sufficiency. Soldiers farmed so as not to burden the peasants. The CCP abandoned its earlier policy of expropriating lands in favor of reductions in rents and interest. (This change led to the American view that the CCP were not Communists but agrarian reformers, despite their protests to the contrary.) They took only those provincial and county offices needed to ensure their control and shared the rest with the KMT and other parties. They expanded village councils to include tenants and other previously excluded strata. But while compromising with other political and social groups, they strengthened their party internally.

Party membership expanded from 40,000 in 1937 to 1.2 million in 1945. Schools were established in Yenan to train party cadres. Even as the party expanded, orthodoxy was maintained by a rectification campaign begun in 1942. Those tainted by liberalism, individualism, or other impure tendencies were criticized and made to confess their failings and repent at public meetings. Mao's thought was supreme. To the Chinese at large Mao represented himself as the successor to Sun Yat-sen, but within the Communist Party he presented himself as a theoretician in the line of Marx (1818–1883), Engels (1820–1895), Lenin (1870–1924), and Stalin (1879–1953).

Whereas the KMT ruled through officials and often in cooperation with local landlords, the Communists learned to

Shensi, an area too remote for Chiang's army to penetrate. But by 1949 CCP forces had conquered China, including border areas never under KMT rule, and Chiang and the KMT had been forced to flee to Taiwan. What happened?

The war with Japan was the key event. It began in July 1937 as an unplanned clash at Peking and then spread. Battlefield victories soon convinced the Japanese military leaders to abandon negotiations in favor of a knockout blow. Peking and Tientsin fell within a month, Shanghai was attacked in August, and Nanking fell in December. During the following year the Japanese took Canton and Wuhan and set up puppet regimes in Peking and Nanking. In 1940, frustrated by trying to work with Chiang, the leader of the left wing of the KMT and many of his associates joined the Japanese puppet government. Japan proclaimed its "New Order in East Asia," which was to replace the system of unequal treaties. It expected Chiang to recognize his situation as hopeless and to submit. Instead, in 1938 he relocated his capital to Chungking, far to the west behind the gorges of the Yangtze. He was joined by thousands of Chinese, students and professors, factory managers and workers, who moved from occupied to free China.

Chiang's stubborn resistance to the Japanese occupation won admiration from all sides. But the area occupied by the Japanese included just those eastern cities, railways, and

Mao Tse-tung (1893–1976) at his cave headquarters in Shensi province during World War II. He wears a padded winter jacket and writes with a Chinese brush. On his desk are the Collected Works of Lu Hsun. [FPG International LLC]

American military equipment left by the KMT forces, and by October 1948 the KMT forces had been driven from Manchuria. In January of 1949 Peking and Tientsin fell. By late spring CCP armies had crossed the Yangtze, taking Nanking and Shanghai. A few months later all of China was in Communist hands. Many Chinese fled with Chiang to Taiwan or escaped to Hong Kong; they included not only KMT officials and generals but entrepreneurs and academics as well. Not a few subsequently made their way to the United States.

In China apprehension was mixed with anticipation. The disciplined, well-behaved soldiers of the "Peoples' Liberation Army" were certainly a contrast to those of the KMT. As villages were liberated, lands were taken from landlords and given to the landless. In the cities crowds welcomed the CCP troops as liberators. The feeling was widespread that the future of China was once again in the hands of the Chinese.

MODERN JAPAN (1853–1945)

Overthrow of the Tokugawa *Bakufu* (1853–1868)

From the seventeenth century into the nineteenth, the natural isolation of the islands of Japan was augmented by its policy of seclusion, making Japan into a little world of its own. The 260-odd domains were the states of this world, the *bakufu* in Edo was its hegemon, and the imperial court in Kyoto provided a sacerdotal or religious sanction for the *bakufu*-domain system. Then at mid-century the American ships of Commodore Perry came and forced Japan to sign a Treaty of Friendship, opening it to foreign intercourse. Fourteen years later the entire *bakufu*-domain system collapsed, and a new group of unusually talented leaders seized power. Seclusion, like the case of a watch, had been necessary to preserve the Tokugawa political mechanism. With the case removed, the jolt of the foreign intrusion caused the inner workings to fly apart.

It was surprising how little changed during the first four years after Perry. The *bakufu* attended to its affairs and the domains to theirs. The daimyo continued to spend every other year living in Edo. Political action consisted mainly of daimyo cliques trying to influence *bakufu* policy. The break came in 1858 when the *bakufu*, ignoring the imperial court's disapproval, was persuaded to sign a commercial treaty with the United States. In reaction, some daimyo, who wanted a voice in national policy making, criticized the treaty as contravening the hallowed policy of seclusion. Younger samurai, frustrated by their exclusion from power, started a movement to "honor the emperor." The *bakufu*, in turn, responded with a

operate at the grass-roots level. They infiltrated Japanese-controlled areas and also penetrated some KMT organizations and military units. CCP armies were built up from 90,000 in 1937 to 900,000 in 1945. These armies were supplemented by a rural people's militia and by guerrilla forces in nineteen mountainous "base areas." By most accounts the Yenan leadership and its party, army, and mass organizations possessed a cohesion, determination, and high morale that were lacking in Chungking.

But the strength of the Chinese Communists as of 1945 should not be overstated. Most Chinese villagers were influenced by neither the CCP nor the KMT, and although intellectuals in free China had become disaffected with the KMT, most did not positively support the CCP. When the war in the Pacific ended in 1945, China's future was unclear. The Soviet Union allowed CCP cadres to enter Manchuria, which it had seized during the last few days of the war, and blocked the entry of KMT troops until the following year. But even the Soviet Union recognized the KMT as the government of China and expected it to win the postwar struggle. The Allies directed Japanese armies to surrender to the KMT forces in 1945. The United States flew Chiang's troops from Chungking to key eastern cities. His armies were by then three times the size of the Communists' and far better equipped.

A civil war broke out immediately. Both sides knew that the earlier united front had been a sham. Efforts by U.S. General George Marshall (1880–1959) to mediate were futile. Until the summer of 1947 KMT armies were victorious—even capturing Yenan. But the tide turned in July as CCP armies went on the offensive in north China. They captured

After delivering President Fillmore's letter in 1853, Commodore Perry confers with *bakufu* officials. [Historical Pictures Collection/Stock Montage Inc.]

purge: Dissident daimyo were forced into retirement, while samurai critics were executed or imprisoned. The purge was effective until 1860, when the head of the *bakufu* council was himself assassinated by extremist samurai. His successors lacked the nerve to continue his tough policies, thus opening the way for a new kind of politics between 1861 and 1868.

In 1861 two domains, Chōshū and Satsuma, emerged to mediate, to heal the breach that had opened between the *bakufu* and the court. The first to come forth was the domain of Chōshū: Its officials traveled between Kyoto and Edo, proposing a policy that favored the *bakufu* but made concessions to the court. Next Satsuma sallied forth with a policy that made further concessions and ousted Chōshū as "the friend of the court." In response, the moderate reformist government of Chōshū adopted the pro-emperor policy of its extremist faction and, in turn, ousted Satsuma. Beaten in the diplomatic game, Satsuma seized the court in 1863 in a military coup, and the Chōshū radicals returned disgruntled to their domain.

Several points may be noted about the 1861–1863 diplomatic phase of domain action: (1) Even after 250 years of *bakufu* rule, several domains were still viable, autonomous units that could act when the opportunity occurred. (2) The two domains that acted first and most of the others that followed were large domains with many samurai—Chōshū had 10,000 samurai families and substantial financial resources. (3) Both Satsuma and Chōshū had fought against the Tokugawa in 1600 and remembered an earlier independence. (4) By the 1861–1863 period, politics was no longer in the hands of daimyo and their high-ranking advisers. In both Satsuma and Chōshū, the new politics had opened decision-making to middle-ranking samurai officials in a way that would have been impossible before 1853.

The 1863 Satsuma coup at the Kyoto court initiated a military phase of politics in which war would determine every turning point. Events were complicated, for besides the court and the *bakufu*, there were more than 260 domains—somewhat like a circus with too many rings and sideshows. But most domains were too small to carry weight in national politics. Hereditary daimyo, for example, were influential mainly as *bakufu* officials. Of the larger domains, some were insolvent and others too closely associated with the *bakufu* to act independently. As long as Satsuma and Chōshū remained enemies, politics stalemated and the *bakufu* continued as hegemon. But when the two domains became allies in 1866, the *bakufu* was overthrown in less than two years.

One movement contributing to this process was for a "union of court and camp"; daimyo, who earlier had criticized the *bakufu*, campaigned for a new conciliar rule in which they would participate together with the emperor. The movement came to nothing, but it led daimyo to withdraw support that might otherwise have gone to the *bakufu*. A second feature of these years was a strong antiforeignism. Extremists assassinated foreigners as well as *bakufu* officials; one of their slogans was "expel the barbarians." Early on, Chōshū and Satsuma fired on foreign ships. But when Western gunboats bombarded those domains in retaliation, they immediately dropped their xenophobic slogan and set about buying rifles and gunboats.

A third aspect of the military phase of politics from 1863 to 1868 was the formation of new rifle units, commanded mostly by lower samurai. These units transformed political power in Japan. For example, Chōshū troops armed with Spencers and Minies—mostly surplus left over from the U.S. Civil War—defeated a traditionally armed but numerically superior *bakufu* army in mid-1866 with a numbing force.

A fourth development was a cultural shift in the way Japanese saw themselves. During the Tokugawa era the Japanese saw themselves as civilized Confucians and most of the rest of the world as barbarians. But in the face of Western gunboats, this view seemed hollow. In 1866 Fukuzawa Yukichi, a student of Western studies and a *bakufu* translator, introduced a Western theory of stages of history: The West, with its technology, science, and humane laws, was seen as "civilized and enlightened"; China, Japan, and countries like Turkey were seen as half civilized; and other areas were seen as barbarian. This theory stood the traditional view almost on its head. Fukuzawa argued, furthermore, that technology was not detachable but grew out of the Western legal, political, economic, and educational systems. James Watt (1736–1819) had invented the steam engine, Fukuzawa suggested, because inventions were protected by patents and inventors were rewarded with profits and honors. He argued that Western systems required political freedoms and a citizenry with a spirit of independence. Fukuzawa's writings became immensely influential after the Restoration, eventually sparking the "Civilization and Enlightenment Movement" of the 1870s.

Building the Meiji State (1868–1890)

Most attempts by non-Western nations to build modern states have occurred during the twentieth century. The idea of a "developing nation" did not exist in the mid-nineteenth century. Yet Japan after the 1868 Meiji Restoration was a developing nation. (The years from 1868 to 1912 are referred to as the Meiji period, after the name of the emperor.) It was committed to progress, by which it meant achieving wealth and power of the kind possessed by Western industrial nations. In retrospect, we are aware that Japan had important assets that contributed to the attainment of these goals. But it also had liabilities, and they loomed large in the eyes of the Meiji leaders. There was no blueprint for progress. The government faced tough decisions as it advanced by trial and error. It also demanded that the Japanese people make sacrifices for the sake of the future.

The announcement of the restoration of rule by an emperor was made on January 3, 1868. In the battles that followed, Chōshū and Satsuma troops defeated those of the *bakufu*. In May, Edo surrendered to the imperial forces. Within months Edo castle became the imperial palace and Edo was renamed Tokyo, the "eastern capital." A year later the last *bakufu* holdouts surrendered in Hokkaido. At the start the Meiji government was only a small group of samurai leaders from Chōshū, Satsuma, and a few other domains. These men controlled the youthful emperor through a handful of Kyoto nobles. They controlled their own domains through domain officials and the samurai commanders of the domain armies. They have been described, only half humorously, as twelve bureaucrats looking for a bureaucracy. But such a description belittles the vision with which they defined the goals of the new government.

Centralization of Power

Their immediate goal was to centralize political power. What this entailed, concretely, was using the leverage of the Chōshū and Satsuma domain armies to destroy the domains. This was a ticklish operation because many in these armies were loyal to their domain rather than to the young samurai leaders, who had left the domains to form the new central government. Nevertheless, by 1871 the young leaders had replaced the domains with prefectures controlled from Tokyo. To ensure a complete break with the past, each new prefectural governor was chosen from samurai of other regions. The first governor of the Chōshū area, for example, was a samurai of a former Tokugawa domain.

Having centralized political authority, in 1871 about half of the most important Meiji leaders went abroad for a year and a half—ostensibly to revise the unequal treaties but in fact to study the West. They traveled in the United States and Europe, visiting parliaments, schools, and factories. On their return to Japan in 1872 they discovered that the stay-at-home officials were planning war with Korea. They quickly quashed the plan, insisting that the highest priority be given to domestic development.

The second goal or task of the Meiji leaders was to stabilize government revenues that, because the land tax was collected mostly in grain, fluctuated with the price of rice. The government converted the grain tax to a money tax, shifting the burden of fluctuations onto the shoulders of the nation's farmers. But a third of the revenues still went to pay for samurai stipends, so in 1873 the government raised a conscript army and subsequently abolished the samurai class. The samurai were paid off in government bonds; but as the bonds fell during the inflation of the 1870s, most former samurai became impoverished. What had begun as a reform of government finance ended as a social revolution.

Some samurai rebelled. Those in the domains that had carried out the Restoration were particularly indignant at their treatment. The last and greatest uprising was in 1877 by Satsuma samurai led by Saigō Takamori (1827–1877), who had broken with the government over the issue of Korea. When the uprising was suppressed in 1878, the Meiji government became militarily secure.

Political Parties

Other samurai opposed the government by forming political parties and campaigning for popular rights, elections, and a constitution. They drew heavily on liberal Western models that had become widely known through "civilization-and-enlightenment" thought. National assemblies, they argued, were the means used by advanced societies to tap the energies of their peoples. Parties in a national assembly would unite the emperor and the people, thereby curbing the arbitrary actions of the Satsuma-Chōshū clique. Samurai were the mainstay of the early party movement, despite its doctrines proclaiming all classes to be equal. During the mid-1870s there was some movement between the parties and the rebellions. But as the rebellions ended, the people's rights movement became more stable.

Then, with the government's formation of prefectural assemblies in 1878, what had been, in fact, unofficial pressure groups became true political parties. Many farmers joined, wanting their taxes cut; the poor joined, hoping to improve their condition. The parties were given another boost after a political crisis in 1881, when the government promised a constitution and a national assembly within ten years. During the 1880s the parties had ups and downs. When poorer peasant members rebelled, the parties dissolved for a time to dissociate themselves from the uprisings. But as the date for national elections approached, the parties regained strength, and the ties between party notables and local men of influence grew closer.

The Constitution

The government viewed the party movement with distaste but was not sure how to counter it. Itō Hirobumi (1841–1909), originally from Chōshū, went abroad to shop for a constitution that would serve the needs of the Meiji government. He found principles to his liking in Germany, and brought home a German jurist to help adapt the conservative Prussian constitution of 1850 to Japanese uses. As promulgated in 1889, the Meiji Constitution was notable for the extensive powers granted to the emperor and for the severely limited powers it granted to the lower house in the Diet (the English term for Japan's bicameral national assembly).

The emperor was sovereign. According to the constitution, he was "sacred and inviolable," and in Itō's commentaries the sacredness was defined in Shinto terms. As in Prussia, the emperor was given direct command of the armed forces. Yamagata Aritomo (1838–1922) had set up a German-type general staff system in 1878. The emperor had the right to name the prime minister and to appoint the Cabinet. He could dissolve the lower house of the Diet and issue imperial ordinances when the Diet was not in session. The Imperial Household Ministry, which was outside the Cabinet, administered the great wealth given to the imperial family during the 1880s—so that the emperor would never have to ask the Diet for funds. In every case, it was intended and understood that the Meiji leaders would act for the emperor in all of these matters. Finally, the constitution itself was presented as a gift from the emperor to his subjects.

The lower house of the Diet, in contrast, was given the authority only to approve budgets and pass laws, and both of these powers were hedged. The constitution provided that the previous year's budget would remain in effect if a new budget was not approved. The appointive House of Peers, the upper house of the Diet, had to approve any bill to become law. Furthermore, to ensure that the parties themselves would represent the stable and responsible elements of Japanese society, the vote was given only to adult males paying fifteen yen or more in taxes. In 1890 this was about 5 percent of the adult male population. In sum, Itō's intention was to create not a parliamentary system, but a constitutional system that included a parliament as one of its parts.

During the 1880s the government also created institutions designed to limit the future influence of the political parties. In 1884 it created a new nobility, honorable and conservative, with which to stock the future House of Peers. The nobility was composed of ex-nobles and the Meiji leaders themselves. Itō, born a lowly foot soldier in Chōshū, began in the new nobility as a count and ended as a prince. In 1885 he established a cabinet system and became the first prime minister, followed by Kuroda Kiyotaka (1840–1900) of Satsuma, and then by Yamagata Aritomo of Chōshū. In 1887 Itō established a Privy Council, with himself as its head, to approve the constitution he had written. In 1888 laws were passed and civil-service examinations instituted to insulate the imperial bureaucracy from the tawdry concerns of

The issuance of the Meiji Constitution in 1889. The emperor standing under the canopy, was declared "sacred and inviolable." Seated on the throne, at the left, is the empress. [The Metropolitan Museum of Art, Gift of Lincoln Kirstein, 1959]

politicians. By this time the bureaucracy, which had begun as a loose collection of men of ability and of their protégés, had become highly systematized. Detailed administrative laws defined their functions and governed their behavior. They were well paid. In 1890 there were 24,000 officials; by 1908 there were 72,000.

Growth of a Modern Economy

The late Tokugawa economy was backward and not markedly different from the economies of other East Asian countries. Almost 80 percent of the population lived in the countryside at close to a subsistence level. Sophisticated but labor-intensive paddy-field techniques were used in farming. Taxes were high, as much as 35 percent of the product, and two thirds of the land tax was paid in kind. That is to say, money had only partially penetrated the rural economy. Japan had not developed factory production with machinery, steam power, or large accumulations of capital.

Early Meiji reforms unshackled the late Tokugawa economy. Occupations were freed, which meant that farmers could trade and samurai could farm. Barriers on roads were abolished, as were the monopolistic guilds that had restricted access to the central markets. The abolition of domains threw open regional economies that had been partially self-

enclosed. Most large merchant houses were too closely tied to daimyo finances and went bankrupt, but there rose a groundswell of new commercial ventures and of traditional agriculturally based industries.

Silk was the wonder crop. The government introduced mechanical reeling, enabling Japan to win markets previously held by the hand-reeled silk of China. About two thirds of Japanese silk production was exported, and not until the 1930s did cotton become more important. Silk production rose from 2.3 million pounds in the post-Restoration era to 93 million in 1929.

A parallel unshackling occurred on the land. The land tax reform of the 1870s, although initially lowering taxes only slightly, created a powerful incentive for growth by giving farmers a clear title to their land and by fixing the tax in money. The freedom to buy and sell land led to a rise in tenancy from perhaps 25 percent in 1868 to about 44 percent at the turn of the century. Progressive landlords bought fertilizer and farm equipment. Rice production rose from 149 million bushels a year during 1880–1884 to 316 million during 1935–1937. More food, combined with a drop in the death rate—the result of better hygiene—led to population growth: from about 30 million in 1868 to 45 million in 1900 to 73 million in 1940. Because the farm population remained constant, the extra hands were available for factory and other urban jobs.

On Wives and Concubines

During the 1870s and 1880s leading Japanese thinkers introduced a wide range of Western ideas into their country. Among them were freedom and equality as rights inherent in human nature. Debating the questions of equality in marriage and the rights of wives, intellectuals voiced a radical criticism of concubinage and prostitution. As a consequence of these debates, laws were passed during the eighties and nineties that strengthened the legal status of wives. Mori Arinori (1847–1889), a leading thinker who had studied in the United States and England, wrote the following passage in 1874. He later became a diplomat and, between 1885 and 1889, the minister of education.

Can you think of a comparable instance in American or European history where new ideas led to dramatic social change? How long did the changes last and how deeply rooted did they become?

The relation between man and wife is the fundamental of human morals. The moral path will be achieved by establishing this fundamental, and the country will only be firmly based if the moral path is realized. When people marry, rights and obligations emerge between them so that neither can take advantage of the other.

There have hitherto been a variety of marriage practices [in our country]. . . . Sometimes there may be one or even several concubines in addition to the wife, and sometimes a concubine may become the wife. Sometimes the wife and the concubines live in the same establishment.

Sometimes they are separated, and the concubine is the favored one while the wife is neglected. . . .

Taking a concubine is by arbitrary decision of the man and with acquiescence of the concubine's family. The arrangement, known as *ukedashi*, is made by paying money to the family of the concubine. This means, in other words, that concubines are bought with money. Since concubines are generally *geisha* and prostitutes patronized by rich men and nobles, many descendants in the rich and noble houses are the children of bought women. Even though the wife is superior to the concubine in households where they live together, there is commonly jealousy and hatred between them because the husband generally favors the concubine. Therefore, there are numerous instances when, the wife and the concubines being scattered in separate establishments, the husband repairs to the abode of the one with whom he is infatuated and wilfully resorts to scandalous conduct. . . .

Thus, I have here explained that our country has not yet established the fundamental of human morality, and I hope later to discuss how this situation injures our customs and obstructs enlightenment.

From *Journal of the Japanese Enlightenment* by Meiroku Zasshi, translated and with introduction by William Reynolds Braisted, assisted by Adachi Yasushi and Kikuchi Yūji (Cambridge, MA: Harvard University Press, 1976), pp. 104–105. © 1976 by the President and Fellows of Harvard College. Reprinted by permission of Harvard University Press.

First Phase: Model Industries

The modern sector of the economy was the government's greatest concern. It developed in four phases. The first was the era of model industries, which lasted until 1881. With military strength as one of its major goals, the Meiji government expanded the arsenals and the shipyards that it had inherited from the Tokugawa. It also built telegraph lines, made a start on railroads, developed coal and copper mines, and established factories for textiles, cement, glass, tools, and other products. Every new industry begun during the 1870s was the work of the government; many were initiated by the Ministry of Industry, which was set up in 1870 under Itō Hirobumi. The quantitative output of these early industries was insignificant, however. Essentially they were pilot-plant operations that doubled as "schools" for technologists and labor.

Just as important to economic development was a variety of other new institutions: banks, post offices, ports, roads, commercial laws, a system of primary and secondary schools, a government university, and so on. They were patterned after European and American examples, although the pattern was often altered to fit Japan's needs; for example, Tokyo Imperial University had a faculty of agriculture earlier than any university in Europe.

Second Phase: 1880s–1890s

More substantial growth in the modern sector took place during the 1880s and 1890s. It was marked by the appearance of what would later become the great industrial combines known as *zaibatsu*. Accumulating capital was the greatest problem for would-be entrepreneurs. Iwasaki Yatarō (1834–1885) used political connections. After the Restoration he gained control of the ships that he had managed as a samurai official for the Tosa domain. He then acquired government ships that had been used to transport troops during the 1874 Taiwan Expedition and the 1877 Satsuma Rebellion. From these beginnings he built a shipping line to compete with foreign companies, started a bank, and invested in the enterprises that later became the Mitsubishi combine.

Women textile workers at a turn-of-the-century silk-weaving mill in Japan. Their product, made from mechanically reeled silk thread, was superior. A company officer, at center, is visiting the shop floor. Behind him is a supervisor, wearing a Meiji-style mustache. Women constituted more than half of Japan's industrial labor force well into the twentieth century. They worked a span of years after leaving primary school and before marrying. Their hours were long, their dormitories crowded, and they often contracted tuberculosis. [Keystone Press Agency]

Shibusawa Eiichi (1840–1931) was another maverick entrepreneur. Born into a peasant family that produced indigo, he became a merchant, joined the pro-emperor movement, then switched sides and became a *bakufu* retainer. After 1868 he entered the Finance Ministry. In 1873 he made the so-called heavenly descent from government to private business. Founding the First Bank, he showed a talent for beginning new industries with other people's money. His initial success was the Osaka Cotton Spinning Mill, established as a joint stock company in 1882. The investors profited hugely, and money poured in to found new mills; by 1896 the production of yarn had reached 17 million pounds, and by 1913 it was over ten times that amount. After the turn of the century cotton cloth replaced yarn as the focus of growth: Production rose more than 100-fold, from 22 million square yards in 1900 to 2,710 million in 1936.

Another area of growth was railroads. Before railroads, most of Japan's commerce was carried on by coastal shipping. It cost as much during the early Meiji period to transport goods fifty miles overland as it did to ship them to Europe. Railroads gave Japan an internal circulatory system, opening up hitherto isolated regions. In 1872 Japan had 18 miles of track; in 1894, 2,100 miles; and by 1934, 14,500 miles.

Cotton textiles and railroads were followed during the 1890s by cement, bricks, matches, glass, beer, chemicals, and other private industries. One can only admire the foresight, vigor, and daring of the bold entrepreneurs who pioneered in these products. At the same time, the role of government in creating a favorable climate for growth should not be forgotten: The society and the polity were stable, the yen was sound, capital was safe, and taxes on industry were low. In every respect, the conditions enjoyed by Japan's budding entrepreneurs differed from those of China.

Third Phase: 1905–1929

Economic growth continued after the Russo-Japanese War in 1905 and spurted ahead during World War I. Light industries and textiles were central, but iron and steel, shipping, coal mining, electrical power, and chemicals also grew. An

A Japanese View of the Inventiveness of the West

Serious Japanese thinkers reacted to their country's weakness with proposals to adopt Western science and industry. But the "Civilization and Enlightenment Movement" of the 1870s had its lighter side as well. In 1871 the novelist Kanagaki Robun wrote a satire about a man with an umbrella, a watch, and eau de cologne on his hair, who was eating and drinking in a new beef restaurant. Before the Restoration, Buddhism had banned beef eating as a defilement. The comic hero, however, wonders, "Why we in Japan haven't eaten such a clean thing before." He then goes on to rhapsodize about Western inventions. See also "Liang Ch'i-ch'ao Urges the Chinese to Reform" earlier in this chapter.

What do pickled onions have to do with the marvels of Western technology?

In the West they're free of superstitions. There it's the custom to do everything scientifically, and that's why they've invented amazing things like the steamship and the steam engine. Did you know that they engrave the plates for printing newspapers with telegraphic needles? And that they bring down wind from the sky with balloons? Aren't they wonderful inventions! Of course, there are good reasons behind these inventions. If you look at a map of the world you'll see some countries marked "tropical," which means that's where the sun shines closest. The people in those countries are all burnt black by the sun. The king of that part of the world tried all kinds of schemes before he hit on what is called a balloon. That's a big round bag they fill with air high up in the sky. They bring the bag down and open it, causing the cooling air inside the bag to spread out all over the country. That's a great invention. On the other hand, in Russia, which is a cold country where the snow falls even in summer and the ice is so thick that people can't move, they invented the steam engine. You've got to admire them for it. I understand that they modeled the steam engine after the flaming chariot of hell, but anyway, what they do is to load a crowd of people on a wagon and light a fire in a pipe underneath. They keep feeding the fire inside the pipe with coal, so that the people riding on top can travel a great distance completely oblivious to the cold. Those people in the West can think up inventions like that, one after the other. . . . You say you must be going? Well, good-bye. Waitress! Another small bottle of sake. And some pickled onions to go with it!

From *Modern Japanese Literature*, D. Keene, ed. and trans. pp. 32–33. Copyright © 1956 Grove Press. Reprinted by permission of Grove/Atlantic, Inc.

---

economic slump followed the war, and the economy grew slowly during the twenties. One factor was renewed competition from a Europe at peace; another was the great earthquake that destroyed Tokyo in 1923. Tokyo was rebuilt with loans, but they led to inflation. Agricultural productivity also leveled off during the twenties: It became cheaper to import foodstuffs from the colonies than to invest in new agricultural technology at home.

By the twenties Japanese society, especially in the cities, was becoming modern. The Japanese ate better, were healthier, and lived longer. Personal savings rose with the standard of living. Even workers opened postal saving accounts, drank beer, went to movies, and read newspapers. In 1890 31 percent of girls and 64 percent of boys went to primary schools; by 1905 the figures were 90 and 96 percent; and in 1925 primary school education was universal. Japan had done what no other non-Western nation had even attempted: It had achieved universal literacy. During the twenties, the thirties, and the war years more and more primary-school graduates went on to middle and higher schools, or entered the new technical colleges. Nevertheless, an immense cultural and social gap remained between the majority who had only a primary school education and the 3 percent who attended university. This gap was a basic weakness in the political democracy of the twenties.

It should also be noted that despite overall improvements in the condition of the Japanese the specific costs of growth were sometimes high. Because textiles played a large role in the early phase of Japan's modern economic growth, well into the twentieth century more than half of the industrial labor force was women. They went to the mills after leaving primary school and returned to their villages before marrying. "Neither silk-reeling maids nor slops are kept for long," went the words of one song. Their working hours were long, their dormitories crowded, and their movements restricted. "Like the money in my employment contract, I remain sealed away," was another verse. Some contracted tuberculosis, the plague of late-nineteenth and early-twentieth-century Japan, and were sent back to their villages to die. The following verse bluntly captures the Japanese attitude toward women factory workers:

If a woman working in an office is a willow,
A poetess is a violet,

And a female teacher is an orchid,
Then a factory woman is a vegetable gourd.[2]

Fourth Phase: Depression and Recovery

A Japanese bank crisis in 1927, followed by the worldwide Great Depression in 1929, plunged Japan into unemployment and suffering. The distress was particularly acute in the rice-producing regions of the northeast. The political consequences of the Depression years were enormous. Yet most of Japan recovered by 1933 and the northeast by 1935, more rapidly than any other industrial nation.

The recovery was fueled by an export boom and by military procurements at home. During the 1930s the production of pig iron, raw steel, and chemicals doubled. For the first time Japan could construct complete electric-power stations and became self-sufficient in machine tools and scientific instruments. Shipbuilding forged ahead; by 1937 Japan had a merchant fleet of 4.5 million tons, the third largest and certainly the newest in the world. Despite continued growth in cotton cloth during the 1930s, textiles slipped relative to the products of heavy industry. The quality of Japan's manufacturers also rose. The outcry in the West against Japanese exports at this time was not so much because of volume—a modest 3.6 percent of world exports in 1936—but because for the first time Japanese products had become competitive in terms of quality.

The Politics of Imperial Japan (1890–1945)

Parliaments began in the West and have worked better there than in the rest of the world. For Japan to establish a constitution during the nineteenth century was a bold experiment. Even so cautious a constitution as that of Meiji had no precedent outside the West at the time; most Western observers were skeptical of its chances for success. How are we now, in retrospect, to view the Japanese political experience after 1890?

One view is that because Japanese society was not ready for constitutional government, the militarism of the thirties was inevitable. From the perspective of an ideal democracy, Japanese society certainly had many weaknesses: a small middle class, weak trade unions, an independent military under the emperor, a strong emperor-centered nationalism, and so on. But these weaknesses,

other historians note, did not prevent the Diet from growing in importance, nor did they block the transfer of power from the bureaucratic Meiji leaders to the political party leaders. The transfer fell short of full parliamentary government. However, had it not been derailed by the Great Depression and other events, the advance toward parliamentary government might well have continued.

From Confrontation to the Founding of the Seiyūkai (1890–1900)

Two kinds of political history can be written about Japan under the Meiji Constitution. One would describe what the government did. It would include the drawing up of budgets, the building of modern military forces, the prosecution of wars, the formation of a banking system, the establishment of new universities, the reform of the tax system, and so on— all of those activities that characterize a modernizing state. The other kind of history would deal with politics, the struggles between different groups and bodies for power.

In 1890 the Meiji leaders—sometimes called *oligarchs*, the few who rule—were concerned with nation building, not politics. They saw the cabinet as "transcendental," as serving the emperor and nation above the ruck of partisan interests. They viewed the political parties as noisy, ineffective, and irresponsible. They saw the lower house of the Diet as a safety valve, a place to let off steam without interfering in the government's serious work of building a new Japan. But the oligarchs had miscalculated: The authority of the lower house to approve or turn down the budget made that body more powerful than they had intended. This involved the oligarchs, willy-nilly, in the political struggles they had hoped to avoid.

The first act of the parties in the new 1890 Diet was to slash the government's budget. Prime Minister Yamagata was furious but had to make concessions to get part of the cut restored. This pattern of applying pressure to the annual budget continued for ten years. Rising costs meant that the previous year's budget was never enough. The government tried to intimidate and bribe the parties, but failed. It even formed a government party and tried to win elections by enlisting the police and local officials for campaign support. But the opposing political parties maintained their control of the lower house. They were well organized in the prefectures, where assemblies had begun in 1878. They also had the support of the voters, mostly well-to-do landowners, who opposed the government's heavy land tax.

Unable either to coerce or defeat the opposing parties, and determined that his Meiji constitution not fail, in 1900 Itō Hirobumi formed a new party. The party was called the Rikken Seiyūkai, or "Friends of Constitutional Government." The Seiyūkai was composed of ex-bureaucrats associated

[2]E. Patricia Tsurumi, "Whose History Is It Anyway? And Other Questions Historians Should Be Asking," in *Japan Review* (1995) 6:17–38, p. 21. By permission of the International Research Center for Japanese Studies.

Natsume Sōseki on the Costs of Rapid Modernization

Natsume Sōseki (1867–1916) was one of the earliest of a series of great novelists to create a new literature in Japan after the turn of the century. Sōseki could often be humorous. One of his early works, I Am a Cat, *looked at a Tokyo household from a feline perspective. He advocated ethical individualism as superior to state morality. He also wrote of human isolation in a changing society and of the dark side of human nature.*

What were the costs of Japan's rapid modernization? Was the uneasiness experienced by only a few advanced thinkers, or did it cut across the society? Was it different from alienation in the modern West?

My Individualism

Let us set aside the question of the bragging about the new teachings acquired from the West, which are only superficially mastered. Let us suppose that in forty or fifty years after the Restoration, by the power of education, by really applying ourselves to study, we can move from teaching A to teaching B and even advance to C—without the slightest vulgar fame-seeking, without the slightest sense of vainglory. Let us further suppose that we pass, in a natural orderly fashion, from stage to stage and that we ultimately attain the extreme of differentiation in our internally developed enlightenment that the West attained after more than a hundred years. If, then, by our physical and mental exertions, and by ignoring the difficulties and suffering involved in our precipitous advance, we end by passing through, in merely one-half the time it took the more prosperous Westerners to reach their stage of specialization, to our stage of internally developed enlightenment, the consequences will be serious indeed. At the same time we will be able to boast of this fantastic acquisition of knowledge, the inevitable result will be a nervous collapse from which we will not be able to recover.

Passers-by

This is what your brother said. He suffers because nothing he does appears to him as either an end or a means. He is perpetually uneasy and cannot relax. He cannot sleep and so gets out of bed. But when he is awake, he cannot stay still, so he begins to walk. As he walks, he finds that he has to begin running. Once he has begun running, he cannot stop. To have to keep on running is bad enough, but he feels compelled to increase his speed with every step he takes. When he imagines what the end of all this will be, he is so frightened that he breaks out in a cold sweat. And the fear becomes unbearable.

I was surprised when I heard your brother's explanation. I myself have never experienced uneasiness of this kind. And so, though I could comprehend what he was saying, I could feel no sympathy for him. I was like a man who tries to imagine what it is like to have a splitting headache though he has never had one. I tried to think for a while. And my wandering mind hit upon this thing called "man's fate"; it was a rather vague concept in my mind, but I was happy to have found something consoling to say to your brother.

"This uneasiness of yours is no more than the uneasiness that all men experience. All you have to do is to realize that there is no need for you alone to worry so much about it. What I mean to say is that it is our fate to wander blindly through life."

Not only were my words vague in meaning but they lacked sincerity. Your brother gave me one shrewd, contemptuous glance; that was all my remarks deserved. He then said:

"You know, our uneasiness comes from this thing called scientific progress. Science does not know where to stop and does not permit us to stop either. From walking to rickshaws, from rickshaws to horsedrawn cabs, from cabs to trains, from trains to automobiles, from automobiles to airships, from airships to airplanes—when will we ever be allowed to stop and rest? Where will it finally take us? It is really frightening."

"Yes, it is frightening," I said.

Your brother smiled.

"You say so, but you don't really mean it. You aren't really frightened. This fear that you say you feel, it is only of the theoretical kind. My fear is different from yours. I feel in my heart. It is an alive, pulsating kind of fear."

First selection from *Japanese Thought in the Meiji Era* by M. Kosaka. Copyright © 1958 Pan-Pacific Press, pp. 447–448; Second selection from "An Introduction to Sōseki," by E. McClellan. *Harvard Journal of Asiatic Studies,* 22 (December 1959), pp. 205–206.

---

with Itō and of politicians from the Liberal Party that a Tosa samurai, Itagaki Taisuke (1837–1919), had formed in 1881. For most of the next twenty years it was the most important party in Japan, providing parliamentary support for successive governments through its control of the lower house. This arrangement was satisfactory to both sides: Itō and subsequent prime ministers got the Diet support necessary for the government to function smoothly. The party politicians got cabinet posts and pork barrel legislation with which to reward their supporters. Itō had made the constitution work, but at the cost of sacrificing the idea of a transcendental cabinet.

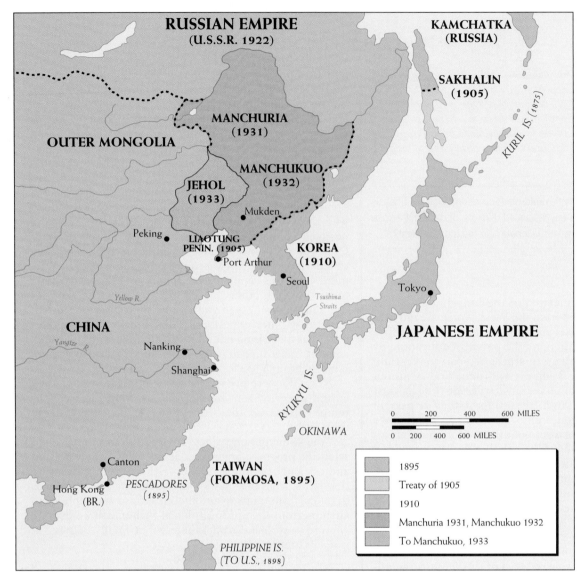

Map 32-3 Formation of the Japanese empire. The Japanese empire grew in three stages: the Sino-Japanese War of 1894–1895, the Russo-Japanese War of 1904–1905, and Japanese conquests in Manchuria and northern China after 1931.

The Golden Years of Meiji

The years before and after the turn of the century represented the culmination of what the government had striven for since 1868. Economic development was under way. The unequal treaties were revised in two steps: Japan got rid of extraterritoriality in 1899 (by a treaty signed in 1894) and regained control of its own tariffs in 1911. However, it was international events that won Japan recognition as a world power.

The first event was a war with China in 1894–1895 over conflicting interests in Korea. From its victory Japan secured Taiwan, the Pescadores Islands, the Kwantung Peninsula in southern Manchuria, an indemnity, and a treaty giving it the same privileges in China as those enjoyed by the Western powers (see Map 32–3). Russia, however, had its own expansionist plans and, obtaining French and German support, forced Japan to give up the Kwantung Peninsula, which included Port Arthur. Three years later, Russia took Kwantung for itself.

The second event was Japan's participation in 1900 in the international force that relieved the Boxers' siege of the foreign legations in Peking. The Japanese troops were notable for their numbers and discipline.

A third development was the Anglo-Japanese Alliance of 1902. For Britain this alliance ensured Japanese support for its East Asian interests and warded off the likelihood of a Russian-Japanese agreement over spheres of influence in

Japanese troops take the fort at Port Arthur in 1904 in a major battle of the Russo-Japanese War. Fifteen thousand Japanese were killed in this battle, ten times the losses of the Russians. [Corbis-Bettmann]

Northeast Asia. For Japan the alliance meant it could fight Russia without fear that a third party would intervene.

The fourth event was the war with Russia that began in 1904, when Japanese torpedo boats launched a surprise attack on the Russian fleet at Port Arthur. On land, Japanese armies drove the Russians from their railway zones in Manchuria and seized Mukden in March 1905. The Russians sent their Baltic fleet to join the battle, but it was annihilated by Admiral Tōgō (1847–1934) at the Straits of Tsushima. After months of war, both countries were worn out, and Russia was plagued by revolution. President Theodore Roosevelt (1858–1919) proposed a peace conference at Portsmouth, New Hampshire. The resulting treaty gave Japan the Russian lease in the Liaotung Peninsula, the Russian railway in south Manchuria, the southern half of Sakhalin, and a recognition of Japan's "paramount interest" in Korea, which was annexed in 1910.

It is ironic that Japan, a country still not free of the system of unequal treaties, should itself have joined the imperialist scramble for colonies. Certainly, the desire for colonies is not to be explained by Japanese tradition, which had rarely looked to foreign expansion. Nor is it to be explained by

Japan's economy, which was just beginning to build its modern industries and could not export capital. The explanation is simpler: Japan wanted equality with the great Western powers, and military power and colonies were the best credentials. Enthusiasm for empire was shared by political party leaders, most liberal thinkers, and conservative leaders alike.

Rise of the Parties to Power

The founding of the Seiyūkai by Itō in 1900 ended a decade of confrontation between the Diet and the government. The aging oligarch Itō soon found intolerable the day-to-day experience of dealing with party politicians, who, unlike the bureaucrats, neither obeyed him nor paid him the respect that he thought his due. He relinquished the presidency of the party to the noble Saionji Kinmochi (1849–1940) in 1903. Saionji also found it too much to bear and passed the post to Hara Takashi (1856–1921) in 1914. With Hara, the office found the man.

Hara was an outsider. Born a generation after the founding fathers of the Meiji state and in a politically unimportant northeastern domain, he began his political career as a newspaper reporter. He then entered the Foreign Office, eventually becoming ambassador to Korea, and then, in turn, an editor, a bank official, a company president, and a Diet member. He helped Itō to found the Seiyūkai. The most able politician in Japan, he was painstaking, patient, paternalistic, and perspicacious. His goals for Japan centered on the expansion of national wealth and power and were no different from those of Itō or Yamagata. But he felt that they should be achieved by party government, not oligarchic rule, and worked unceasingly to expand the power of his party. The years between 1905 and 1921 were marked by the struggle between these two alternative conceptions of government.

The struggle can be represented as a rising curve of party strength and a descending curve of oligarchic influence. The rising curve had two vectors: a buildup of the Seiyūkai party machine that enabled it to win elections and maintain itself as the majority (or plurality) party in the Diet, and the strengthening of the Diet vis-à-vis other elites within the government in Tokyo. For the former, Hara obtained campaign funds from industrialists and other moneyed interests. He also promoted pork barrel legislation in the Diet: Local constituencies that supported Seiyūkai candidates got new schools, bridges, dams, roads, or even railroad lines. Seiyūkai politicians established ties with local notables, who brokered the votes of their communities. When serving as home minister, Hara was even willing to call on the police and local officials to aid Seiyūkai election campaigns.

In coopting other governmental elites, the Seiyūkai had mixed success. The party steadily increased its representation in the Cabinet. It gained some patronage appointments in the central bureaucracy and in the newly formed colonial bureaucracy, although most bureaucrats remained professionals and resisted the intrusion of outside political appointees. Some career bureaucrats, however, developed working relations with the party and became partly politicized. In the House of Peers, and in the Privy Council, which ratified treaties, the Seiyūkai fared less well. By and large, these remained independent bodies. The Seiyūkai had no success in penetrating the military services. At most, it exercised some control over the military budget in time of peace.

The descending curve of weakening oligarchic control reflected the aging of the "men of Meiji." In 1900 Itō was the last oligarch to become prime minister. From 1901 to 1912 Katsura Tarō (1847–1913), a Chōshū general and Yamagata's protégé, and Saionji, Itō's protégé, took turns in the post. Both had Seiyūkai support. Toward the end of the period Katsura began to resent the fact that he, a grown man, had to go to Yamagata for every important decision. The oligarchs were also weakened by changes within the elites. A younger generation of officers in the military services chafed at the continuing domination by the old Satsuma and Chōshū

cliques. In the civil bureaucracy younger officials who had graduated from the Law Faculty of Tokyo Imperial University were achieving positions of responsibility. Proud of their ability, they saw the bureaucracy as an independent service and resisted oligarchic control almost as much as they resisted that of the parties.

The oligarchs did, however, maintain their power to act for the emperor in appointing prime ministers. With the deaths of Itō in 1909 and Yamagata in 1922 this vital function was taken over by Saionji and, later, by ex-prime ministers.

As the rising and descending curves approached each other, the political parties advanced. Several turning points were critical. One came in 1912. When the army's demands for a larger budget were refused, it withdrew its minister, causing Saionji's cabinet to collapse. Katsura formed a new cabinet and tried to govern using imperial decrees in place of Diet support. This infuriated the parties, and even the Seiyūkai withdrew its support. Massive popular demonstrations broke out, a movement was organized for the "Protection of the Constitution," and party orators shouted "Destroy the Sat-Chō leaders" and "Off with Katsura's head." Katsura tried to counter the popular forces aligned against him by forming a second political party, parallel to the Seiyūkai. The party became politically important during the 1920s. But Katsura was forced to resign in 1913. The lower house had defeated an oligarchic prime minister.

The curves finally crossed in 1918 when Hara became prime minister. It was the first time a politician who was not a Meiji founding father or a protégé of one had obtained the post. He enacted reforms but did nothing to remedy the parliamentary shortcomings of the Meiji Constitution.

A third development was the wave of liberalism that began during World War I and culminated in the period of party governments from 1924 to 1932. Joining the Allies in World War I, Japan had been influenced by democratic currents of thought from England and America. Scholars discussed revising the Meiji Constitution. Labor unions were organized, at first liberal and often Christian, and later Marxist. A social movement was launched to improve conditions in Japan's industrial slums and to pass social and labor legislation. Japan's second political party, the Kenseikai, which had been out of power since 1916, grew steadily more liberal and adopted several of the new social causes as its own, such as universal manhood suffrage. When Hara cut the tax qualification for voting from ten to three yen—a considerable extension of the franchise—the Kenseikai criticized the change as insufficient and the Seiyūkai as the perpetrator of class despotism.

During a brief interlude of nonparty cabinets between 1922 and 1924, the Kenseikai began the Second Movement for the Protection of the Constitution. Liberal factions of the other big party, the Seiyūkai, joined in the movement, and the two parties formed a coalition government in 1924. For the next eight years the presidents of one or the other of the two major parties were appointed as prime ministers.

The coalition Cabinet (1924–1926) of Katō Kōmei is considered the peak of parliamentarianism in prewar Japan. Born in 1860, Katō graduated from Tokyo Imperial University at the age of twenty-one and entered the Mitsubishi firm. He married the boss's daughter, spent some time in England, and entered the Foreign Ministry, becoming foreign minister at forty. For a country that esteemed age, his rise was meteoric. He subsequently became a Diet member, a newspaper president, an ambassador to England, and, from 1914, president of the Kenseikai. Blunt, cold, and haughty, Katō was widely respected if not liked. He was an Anglophile who understood and advocated a British model of government. His ministry passed universal manhood suffrage, increased academic appointments to the House of Peers, and cut the military budget from 42 percent in 1922 to 29 percent in 1925. He also enacted social and labor legislation. In effect, he legalized the moderate socialist movement and outlawed revolutionary socialism. Katō's cabinet brought Japan close to a true parliamentary government, which, although not mandated by the Meiji Constitution, had not been banned either.

Militarism and War (1927–1945)

The future of Japan's parliamentary coalition seemed assured during the mid-1920s. The economy was growing; the society was stable; the party leaders were experienced. Japan's international position was secure. By a decade later, however, the party leaders had lost the gains of thirty-five years. By 1945 Japan had been defeated in a devastating war and was occupied by foreign troops for the first time in its history. How did this come about?

Simply put, a small shift in the balance of power among the governmental elites established by the Meiji Constitution had produced a major change in Japan's foreign policy. The parties had been the obstreperous elite between 1890 and 1926 and had advanced their influence by forcing the other elites to compromise. From the late 1920s the military became the obstreperous elite and did the same. Beginning in 1932 military men replaced party presidents as prime ministers. In 1937 Japan went to war with China; and by the end of 1941 Japan was allied with Germany and Italy and had gone to war with the United States.

From their inception, the military services in Japan had been constructed on different principles from Japan's civilian society. Soldiers were not samurai. The rifle companies of Satsuma and Chōshū had broken decisively with that tradition, and universal conscription had put the new military on a changed footing. But the armed services had their own schools, which inculcated the values of discipline, bravery,

loyalty, and obedience. The military saw themselves as the true heirs of those who had founded the modern Japanese state and the true guardians of Japanese tradition. They contrasted their loyalty to the emperor and their concern for all Japanese with the pandering to special interests by the political parties.

They resented their diminished national stature during the 1920s, when military budgets were cut and the prestige of a military career had declined to the point where officers wore civilian clothes when off base. In particular, the fleet wing of the navy resented the decision of moderate admirals to accept a formula at the London Naval Conference of the Great Powers in 1930 that would weaken Japan's naval strength. But even during the liberal 1920s there had been no change in the constitutional position of the services. The general staffs remained directly responsible to the emperor. With the passing of the Meiji oligarchs, this meant they were responsible to no one but themselves.

A Crisis in Manchuria The new multilateral treaties (the 1924 Washington Conference and the 1930 London Conference) that replaced the earlier system of bilateral treaties (such as the Anglo-Japanese Alliance) recognized the existing colonies of the victors in World War I but opposed new colonial ventures. The Western treaty powers were especially strong in support of the "open door" in China, which in their thinking included Manchuria. Japan's position in Manchuria was ambiguous. Because Japan maintained its interests through a tame Chinese warlord, Manchuria was not, strictly speaking, a colony. But because Japan had gained its special position in Manchuria at the cost of 100,000 lives in the 1905 Russo-Japanese War, it saw its claim to Manchuria as similar to that of Western nations to their colonies.

From the late 1920s the Kuomintang unification of China and the blossoming of Chinese nationalism threatened Japan's special position. Japanese army units tried to block the march north and murdered the Manchurian warlord when he showed signs of independence. In this crisis the party government in Tokyo equivocated, hoping to preserve a status quo that was crumbling before its eyes. The army saw Manchuria as a buffer between the Soviet Union and the Japanese colony of Korea and was unwilling to make concessions. So in 1931 the army provoked a crisis, took over Manchuria, and proclaimed it an independent state in 1932. When the League of Nations condemned Japan for violating the "open door," Japan withdrew from the league in 1933.

The Great Depression Just as the crisis in China had called into question Japan's place in the international political order, so did the Great Depression cast doubts on the international economic order and on the *zaibatsu*. The *zaibatsu* were seen as rich and profiteering in a country full of suffering and want, as the backers of the "established parties," and as internationalists at a time of rising nationalism.

Rural Japan was hardest hit by the Depression. The real income of farmers fell by about a third between 1926 and 1931 and recovered only slowly. Our images of the Depression in Japan, which may be exaggerated, come primarily from the northeast, where a crop failure in 1931 led to famine; children turned to begging for food from passing trains, and tenant farmers were forced to eat the inner bark of pine trees or to dig up the roots of wild plants. Urban workers suffered, too. The value of Japanese exports dropped 50 percent between 1929 and 1931. Workers' real income dropped from an index of 100 in 1929 to 69 in 1931. Unemployment rose to 3 million, and many factory workers returned to their villages, adding to the burden on the farm economy. Only the salaried middle class was better off as prices dropped.

Japan's government acted effectively to counter the Depression, as noted earlier. Going off the gold standard led to an export boom; and Japan came out of the Depression faster than any other nation. By 1936 Japan's heavy industries were growing apace, and real wages were up. The recovery came too late to help the political parties, however. By 1936 political trends that had begun during the worst years of the Depression had become irreversible.

The Depression galvanized the political left and right. The political left was composed mainly of socialist moderates who won eight Diet seats in 1928, eighteen in 1936, and thirty-seven in 1937. Supported by unionists and white-collar workers, they would reemerge as an even stronger force after World War II. There was also a radical left, consisting of many little Marxist parties led by intellectuals and of the Japanese Communist Party. Although small and subject to growing governmental repression, the radical parties became influential in intellectual and literary circles during the twenties and thirties.

The Radical Right and the Military The political right in pre-World War II Japan is difficult to define. Most Japanese, even those in the socialist movement, were imbued with an emperor-centered nationalism. Most voters supported the centrist parties but in their hearts felt a deeper loyalty to the nation. During the 1930s, however, a new array of right-wing organizations went beyond the usual nationalism to challenge the status quo. Civilian ultranationalists used Shinto myths and Confucian values to attack the Western liberalism that had begun to enter Japan's urban society. Some bureaucrats looked to the example of Nazi Germany and argued for the exclusion of party politicians from government. Bureaucrats could run it better, serving the interests of all of the people. Military officers envisioned a "defense state" guided by themselves. They argued for military expansion

and an autarchic colonial empire insulated from the uncertainties of the world economy. Young officers of the revolutionary right advocated "direct action" against the elites of the parliamentary coalition. They called for a second restoration of imperial power.

The last group precipitated political change. On May 15, 1932, junior army and navy officers attacked the Seiyūkai offices, the Bank of Japan, and the Tokyo police headquarters, and murdered Prime Minister Inukai. This attack occurred at the peak of right-wing agitation and the pit of the Depression. In these circumstances Saionji decided that it would be unwise to appoint another party president as the new prime minister; he chose instead a moderate admiral. For the next four years cabinets were led by moderate military men, but with continuing party participation. These cabinets were no more than a holding pattern. They satisfied neither the parties nor the radical young officers.

During 1936 and 1937 Japanese politics were buffeted by crosscurrents but continued to drift to the right. In the election of February 1936 the Minseitō overturned the Seiyūkai-dominated Diet. It used as its slogan, "What shall it be, parliamentary government or Fascism?" A week later young officers responded with an attempted coup in Tokyo. Leading 1400 soldiers, they attacked government offices, killed cabinet ministers, although missing the prime minister, and occupied the Diet, the Army ministry, and other government buildings. They wanted their army superiors to form a new government. Saionji and other men about the emperor stood firm; the navy opposed the rebellion; and within three days it was suppressed. It was the last "direct action" by the radical right in prewar Japan. The ringleaders were quickly tried and executed, and generals sympathetic to them were retired. The officers in charge of the purge within the army were tough-minded elitist technocrats, who even during the budget cuts of the 1920s had advocated the further modernization of Japan's weaponry. They included General Tōjō Hideki (1884–1948), who would lead Japan into World War II.

Their reassertion of control over the radical young officers did not mean a withdrawal from politics. On the contrary, the services interfered more than ever in the formation of cabinets, blocking whenever possible the appointment of party politicians or liberal bureaucrats. As a result, from 1936 on moderate prime ministers gave way to more outspokenly militaristic figures.

Opposition to militarism remained substantial nonetheless. In the 1937 election a prime minister, who had been a general and whose political slogan was "Respect the gods and honor the emperor," tried to win control of the Diet by throwing government support to the Shōwakai, a Nazi-like party. It performed miserably at the polls, gaining only 40 Diet seats, while the two major centrist parties, which had joined in opposition to the government, won 354. The Japanese people were more

Tōjō Hideki (1884–1948), prime minister at the time of the attack on Pearl Harbor in 1941 and one of the chief figures in the rise of Japanese militarism. [Corbis-Bettmann]

level-headed than their leaders. But the centrists' victory proved hollow, for, although a peacetime government could not rule without the Diet, the Diet could not oppose a government in wartime; by summer, Japan was at war in China.

The Road to Pearl Harbor   Between the outbreak of the war with China and the World War II campaign in the Pacific there were three critical junctures. The first was the decision in January 1938 to strike a knockout blow at the Nationalist Party (KMT) government in Nanking. The war had begun as an unplanned skirmish between Chinese and Japanese troops in the Peking area but had quickly spread. The Army's leaders themselves disagreed on whether to continue. Many held that the only threat to Japanese interests in Korea and Manchuria was the Soviet Union, and that a long war in China was unnecessary and foolish. But as the Japanese armies advanced, others on the general staff argued that the only way to end the war was to convince the Nationalists that fighting was hopeless. The general staff got its way, and the army quickly occupied most of the cities and railroads of eastern China. When Chiang Kai-shek refused to give in, a stalemate ensued that lasted until 1945. China was never a major theater of the war in the Pacific.

The second critical decision was the signing of the Tripartite Pact with Germany and Italy in September 1940. Japan had long admired Germany. In 1936 it had joined Germany in the Anti-Comintern Pact directed against international communism. It also wanted an alliance with Germany against the Soviet Union. Germany insisted, however, that any alliance also be directed against the United States and Britain, to which the Japanese would not agree. The Japanese navy, especially, saw the American Pacific fleet as its only potential enemy and was not willing to risk being dragged into a German war. When Japanese troops battled Russian troops in an undeclared mini-war from May to September 1939 on the Mongolian border, sentiment rose in favor of an alliance with Germany, but then Germany "betrayed" Japan by signing a nonaggression pact with the Soviet Union. For a time Japan decided to improve its relations with the United States, but America insisted that Japan get out of China. By the late spring of 1940 German victories in Europe—the fall of Britain appeared imminent—again led military leaders in Japan to favor an alliance with Germany.

When Japan signed the Tripartite Pact, it had three objectives: to isolate the United States, to inherit the Southeast Asian colonies of the countries defeated by Germany in Europe, and to improve its relations with the Soviet Union through the good offices of Germany. The last objective was reached when Japan signed a neutrality pact with the Soviet Union in April 1941. Two months later, Germany attacked the Soviet Union without consulting its ally Japan. It compounded this second "betrayal" by asking Japan to attack the Soviet Union in the east. Japan waited and watched. When the German advance was stopped short of Moscow, Japan decided to honor the neutrality pact and turn south. This decision marked, in effect, the end of Japan's participation in the Axis. Thereafter, it fought its own war in Asia. Yet instead of deflecting American criticism as intended, the pact, by linking Japan to Germany, led to a hardening of America's position on China.

The third and fatal decision was to go to war with the United States. In June 1940, following Germany's defeat of France, Japanese troops had moved into northern French Indochina. The United States retaliated by limiting strategic exports to Japan. In July 1941 Japanese troops took southern Indochina, and the United States embargoed all exports to Japan, cutting Japanese oil imports by 90 percent and producing the "crisis of the dwindling stockpile." The navy's general staff argued that oil reserves would last only two years; after that the navy would lose its capability to fight. Its general staff pressed for the capture of the oil-rich Dutch East Indies. But it would be too dangerous to move against Dutch and British colonies in Southeast Asia with the United States on its flank in the Philippines. The navy, therefore, planned a preemptive strike against the United States, and on December 7, 1941, it bombed Pearl Harbor. The Japanese decision for war wagered Japan's land-based air power, shorter supply lines, and what it saw as greater will power against American productivity. At the Imperial Conference where the all-or-nothing decision was taken, the navy's chief of staff compared the war with the United States to a dangerous operation that might save the life of a critically ill patient. In the end, of course, despite stunning initial victories, the war left Japan defeated and in ruins.

Japanese Militarism and German Nazism

Some of the salient features of Japanese militarism may be revealed by a comparison with Nazi Germany. Both countries were late developers with elitist, academic bureaucra-cies and strong military traditions. Both had authoritarian family systems. The parliamentary systems of both were more shallowly rooted than those of England, France, or the United States. Both were stricken by the Great Depression and sought a solution in territorial expansion, justifying it in terms of being have-not nations. Both persecuted socialists and then liberals. Both were modern enough in their military services, schools, governments, and communications to implement authoritarian regimes, while their values were not modern enough or democratic enough to resist their antiparliamentary forces.

But the differences between Japan and Germany were also striking. Despite the contrast between its small educated elite and the rest of the population with only a middle-school education, and despite the cultural split between the more traditional rural areas and the Westernized cities, Japan was more homogeneous than Germany. It had no Catholic-Protestant split. It had no powerful *Junker* class, nor was its Socialist movement a serious contender for political power. The political process during the 1930s was also different. In Germany parliament ruled, so that to come to power the Nazis had to win an election. They were helped by the combination of the Great Depression and a runaway inflation that destroyed the German middle class and the centrist parties along with it. But in Japan's constitutional system, the Diet was weaker. Control of the government was taken away from the Seiyūkai and Minseitō even while they continued to win elections. They remained strong at the polls partly because Japan did not suffer from inflation and its middle class was not hurt by the Depression.

The process by which the two countries went to war was also different. In Germany the Nazis rose as a mass party, created a totalitarian state, and then made war. The authority of the Nazi Party lasted until Hitler died in a Berlin bunker. But in Japan there was neither a mass party nor a single group of leaders in continuous control of the government. Moreover, in Japan it was not the totalitarian state that made war as much as it was war that made the state totalitarian. The spiritual mobilization of the Japanese population, the implementation of controls over industry, and the formation of a nationalism so intense that university students could be mobilized as suicide *(kamikaze)* pilots all followed the outbreak of hostilities.

The Allies depicted General Tōjō, who was prime minister and his own army minister, as the Japanese Hitler. Yet when American planes began to bomb Japan in 1944, the elder statesmen close to the emperor removed Tōjō from office and appointed increasingly moderate prime ministers. The military, to be sure, continued to prosecute the war. Even after the devastation of the atomic bombs, the Imperial Conference on August 14, 1945, was split three to three over the

Allied ultimatum demanding unconditional surrender. The emperor broke the deadlock, saying that the unendurable must be endured. It was the only important decision that he had ever been allowed to make.

IN WORLD PERSPECTIVE

Modern East Asia

From the late nineteenth century most countries wanted to become modern. They coveted the material well-being and military power that science and industry had produced in the West. They did not, to be sure, wish to become Western, for that would have denied them their own cultural identity. In practice, however, it was difficult to separate what was modern from what was merely recent Western.

We note three stages in Japan's development as the world's first non-Western modernizer. First, even before its contact with the modern West, it had some of the *preconditions* needed to adopt modern technology: a fairly high level of literacy, an ethic of duty and hard work, a market economy, a shift from religious to secular thought, an adequate development of bureaucracy, and political orientations in some respects resembling nationalism. These preconditions provided an adequate base for an "external modernization."

Second, after 1868 Japan *Westernized*. The Meiji leaders introduced a wide range of new institutions: post offices, banks, custom houses, hospitals, police forces, joint stock companies, universities with faculties of science and engineering, and so on. Japanese thinkers brought in modern ideas and values: Spencer and Guizot, Turgenev and Tolstoi, Adam Smith and Marx. Japanese painters began painting in oils; Japanese writers began experimenting with new forms.

Third, little by little Japan began to *assimilate* the ideas and institutions it had borrowed from the West. The *zaibatsu* combines were modern, with the most recent technologies, yet their business organizations were unlike those of the West. The spare beauty of traditional architecture was transferred to the glass, steel, concrete, and stone of the modern. A new literature, completely Japanese yet also completely modern, appeared.

Because modernization in Japan—as analyzed in terms of the above three stages—has gone further than that in any other non-Western country, it becomes a useful model. We look at India or the Islamic world and note the absence of comparable preconditions. Even after colonialism had ended, countries in these areas faced a difficult task: to create the necessary preconditions while borrowing the new technologies. The difficulty explains their limited success. In Africa the dearth of preconditions was even more pronounced.

In comparison to most of the non-Western world, the Chinese tradition was advanced. Like Japan, it had already achieved many of the preconditions for modernization: a high level of literacy, a belief in education as the means for advancement, the ingredients for shaping a modern nationalism, a family system that adapted well to small enterprises, and a market economy. But when it came to borrowing Western ideas and institutions, the government by Confucian literati that had long been China's outstanding asset became its greatest liability. It took decades to topple the dynasty and to advance beyond Confucian ideas.

Then, in the maelstrom of the May Fourth Movement, intellectual changes occurred at a furious pace. But in the chaos following the breakdown of the ancient regime, doctrines alone could not provide a stable polity. Nationalism was the common denominator of most Chinese thought. Sun Yat-sen appealed to it. The Kuomintang drew on it at the Whampoa Academy, during the march north, and in founding the Nanking government. Yet other groups could also appeal to nationalism, and eventually the Chinese Communist Party (CCP) won out.

It is beguiling to view the CCP cadres as a new class of literati operating the machinery of a monolithic, centralized state, with the teachings of Marx and Lenin replacing those of Confucius, and local party organization replacing the Confucian gentry. But this interpretation is too simple. Communism stressed science, materialism, and class conflict. It broke with the Chinese past.

Communism itself was also modified in China. Marx had predicted that Socialist revolutions would break out in advanced economies where the contradictions of capitalism were sharpest. Lenin had shifted the emphasis from spontaneous revolutions by workers to the small but disciplined revolutionary party, the vanguard of the proletariat. He thereby changed communism into what it has been ever since: a movement capable of seizing power only in backward nations. At the level of doctrine, Mao Tse-tung modified Lenin's ideas only slightly—by theorizing that "progressive" peasants were a part of the proletariat. But he went beyond this theory in practice, virtually ignoring city workers while relying on China's villages for recruits for his armies, who were then indoctrinated using Leninist techniques. Despite its low level of technology, the People's Liberation Army, the Communist equivalent of a "citizen's army," was formidable in the field. It was also modern in the sense that it did not loot and despoil the areas it occupied.

Yet, the organizational techniques that were so effective in creating a party and army would prove less so for economic development. It soon became clear that mass mobilization was no substitute for individual incentives.

Review Questions ———

1. Which had the greater impact on China, the Opium War or the Taiping Rebellion?

2. How did the Ch'ing (or Manchu) dynasty recover from the Taiping Rebellion? Why was the recovery inadequate to prevent the overthrow of the dynasty in 1911?

3. Did the May Fourth Movement prepare the way for the Nationalist revolution? The Communist revolution? Or was it incidental to both?

4. After the Meiji Restoration, what steps did Japan's leaders take to achieve their goal of "wealth and power"?

5. What were the strengths and weaknesses of Japan's prewar parliamentary institutions? What led to the sudden rise of militarism during the thirties?

Suggested Readings ———

China

P. M. COBLE, *The Shanghai Capitalists and the Nationalist Government, 1927–1937* (1980).

L. E. EASTMAN, *The Abortive Revolution: China Under Nationalist Rule, 1927–1937* (1974).

L. E. EASTMAN, *Seeds of Destruction: Nationalist China in War and Revolution, 1937–1949* (1984).

M. ELVIN AND G. W. SKINNER, *The Chinese City Between Two Worlds* (1974). A study of the late Ch'ing and the Republican eras.

J. W. ESHERICK, *The Origins of the Boxer Rebellion* (1987).

S. ETŌ, *China's Republican Revolution* (1994).

J. K. FAIRBANK, *China, a New History* (1992). A survey of the entire sweep of Chinese history; especially strong on the modern period.

J. K. FAIRBANK AND D. TWITCHETT, EDS., *The Cambridge History of China*. Like the premodern volumes in the same series, the volumes on modern China represent a survey of what is known. Volumes 10–15, which cover the history from the late Ch'ing to the People's Republic, have been published, and the others will be available soon. The series is substantial. Each volume contains a comprehensive bibliography.

C. HAO, *Chinese Intellectuals in Crisis: Search for Order and Meaning, 1890–1911* (1987).

LU HSUN, *Selected Works* (1960). Novels, stories, and other writings by modern China's greatest writer.

P. A. KUHN, *Rebellion and Its Enemies in Late Imperial China; Militarization and Social Structure, 1796–1864* (1980). A study of how the Confucian gentry saved the Manchu dynasty after the Taiping Rebellion.

J. LEVENSON, *Liang Ch'i-ch'ao and the Mind of Modern China* (1953). A classic study of a major Chinese reformer and thinker.

E. O. REISCHAUER, J. K. FAIRBANK, AND A. M. CRAIG, *East Asia: Tradition and Transformation* (1989). The most wide-ly read text on East Asian history. Contains ample chapters on Japan and shorter chapters on Korea and Vietnam, as well as coverage of China.

H. Z. SCHIFFRIN, *Sun Yat-sen, Reluctant Revolutionary* (1980). A biography.

B. I. SCHWARTZ, *Chinese Communism and the Rise of Mao* (1951). A classic study of Mao, his thought, and the Chinese Communist party before 1949.

B. I. SCHWARTZ, *In Search of Wealth and Power: Yen Fu and the West* (1964). Study of a late-nineteenth-century thinker who introduced Western ideas into China.

J. D. SPENCE, *The Gate of Heavenly Peace: The Chinese and Their Revolution, 1895–1980* (1981). Historical reflections on twentieth-century China.

J. D. SPENCE, *The Search for Modern China* (1990). A thick text that reads remarkably well.

S. Y. TENG AND J. K. FAIRBANK, *China's Response to the West* (1954). Translations from Chinese thinkers and political figures, with commentaries.

T. H. WHITE AND A. JACOBY, *Thunder Out of China* (1946). A view of China during World War II by two who were there.

Japan

G. C. ALLEN, *A Short Economic History of Modern Japan* (1958).

W. G. BEASLEY, *Japanese Imperialism, 1894–1945* (1987).

G. M. BERGER, *Parties Out of Power in Japan, 1931–1941* (1977). An analysis of the condition of political parties during the militarist era.

A. M. CRAIG, *Chōshū in the Meiji Restoration* (1961). A study of the Chōshū domain, a Prussia of Japan, during the period from 1840 to 1868.

P. DUUS, *Party Rivalry and Political Change in Taisho Japan* (1968). A study of political change in Japan during the 1910s and 1920s.

P. DUUS, ED., *The Cambridge History of Japan* (1988). Vol. 6, *The Twentieth Century*.

Y. Fukuzawa, *Autobiography* (1966). Japan's leading nineteenth-century thinker tells of his life and of the birth of modern Japan.

C. N. Gluck, *Japan's Modern Myths: Ideology in the Late Meiji Period* (1988).

A. Gordon, *The Evolution of Labor Relations in Japan: Heavy Industry, 853–1955* (1985).

T. R. H. Havens, *The Valley of Darkness: The Japanese People and World War II* (1978).

A. Iriye, *After Imperialism: The Search for a New Order in the Far East, 1921–1931* (1965). (See also other works by the same author.)

D. Keene, ed., *Modern Japanese Literature, An Anthology* (1960). A collection of modern Japanese short stories and excerpts from novels.

J. W. Morley, ed., *The China Quagmire* (1983). A study of Japan's expansion on the continent between 1933 and 1941. (See also other works on diplomatic history by the same author.)

R. H. Myers and M. R. Peattie, eds., *The Japanese Colonial Empire, 1895–1945* (1984).

T. Najita, *Hara Kei in the Politics of Compromise, 1905–1915* (1967). A study of one of Japan's greatest party leaders.

K. Ohkawa and H. Rosovsky, *Japanese Economic Growth: Trend Acceleration in the Twentieth Century* (1973).

R. H. Spector, *Eagle Against the Sun: The American War with Japan* (1985).

Lenin statue overthrown in Addis Ababa, Ethiopia. [Camera Pix/Liaison Agency, Inc.]

GLOBAL CONFLICT AND CHANGE

The twentieth century has seen global conflict and global interaction—made possible by advances in transportation and communication—unprecedented in world history. Growing trade forged economic links among nations tighter than any in the past. The imperialistic ambitions of Europe and the United States during the late nineteenth century linked the world politically in a system of formal and informal empires.

As a result of these Western-dominated interconnections, conflict in Europe began to draw in the rest of the world.

In August 1914, the nations of Europe went to war with each other. That conflict—World War I—may be the central event of the century. It unleashed political, social, and economic turmoil whose effects continue to the present day. The Austro-Hungarian monarchy collapsed. In Germany, a republic replaced the monarchy. The im-

perial government of Russia was replaced by the revolutionary government of the Bolsheviks. The war bled the victorious nations of Britain, France, and Italy of manpower and exhausted much of their wealth. The participation of the United States blocked the establishment of later independent economic policy by the European powers.

Nationalistic resentments heightened by the Peace Settlement of 1919 combined with the political and economic pressures of the 1920s to nurture Italian Fascism and German Nazism. By 1939, German aggression and the hesitant response of the other powers had led again to war in Europe. After that conflict—World War II—Europe ceased to be the world's dominant political and economic force.

Two other developments helped end the European era. First, the principle of national self-determination applied to Europeans in the 1919 settlement was adopted by colonial peoples asserting their own right to independence. An important early example of this phenomenon was the emergence of the Congress Party movement in British India. Second, the demand for self-determination soon became linked to a critique, which flowed directly from the spread of communist ideas throughout the colonial world after the Russian Revolution, of foreign capitalist domination of colonial economic life. Thus the peoples of Asia, Africa, and Latin America adopted the European ideologies of nationalism and revolutionary socialism as a solution to their own problems, turning them against their source.

The second great upheaval of the century, the war of 1939–1945, was truly global and even more devastating than the first, with great battle casualties and unprecedented assaults on civilians. From the German attack on Britain in 1940 to the use of terrifying new atomic weapons against Japan in 1945, cities endured massive aerial bombardment. Hitler and Stalin made war on designated populations within their own countries; and, like the Japanese, subjected conquered lands to harsh rule.

After the war, the hopes of many for peace and stability in the future rested with the United Nations (UN). Unlike the earlier League of Nations, which the United States had never joined,

the UN included all the victorious powers and has since come to include nearly all the nations of the world. Its success, however, required cooperation among the great powers, which was jeopardized by differences between the political and economic systems of the Western nations and the Soviet Union and by their mutual suspicion. The Western powers' insistence on free, democratic elections in the liberated states of Eastern Europe was incompatible with the Soviet Union's desire to control the areas on its western border. Disputes over Poland, the Balkan states, and Germany led to a division of Germany and of all of Europe into east and west. Hence began a period of competition and sometimes open hostility called the Cold War.

The Cold War quickly spread to Asia, where the Communist Party under Mao Tse-tung gained control of China. Allying itself with the Soviet Union, China supported the Communist regime of North Korea against South Korea, which was supported by the United States and its allies. Later the same alignment appeared in Vietnam. However, by the 1960s, a split appeared between the Chinese and the Russians, and international relations became more complex.

By the 1980s, China, and the United States had established reasonably friendly relations. Like Communist Yugoslavia, Hungary, and Romania, China began to introduce elements of a free-market economy. These nations were undoubtedly influenced by the remarkable swiftness with which the defeated nations of West Germany and Japan, with their free-market economies, had recovered from devastation and poverty to achieve unprecedented prosperity.

World War II destroyed the capacity of the European nations and Japan to maintain colonial empires and led to the establishment of new, independent

nations in Africa, Asia, and the islands of the Pacific. Although joyously welcomed, independence brought new problems to the so-called Third World. Rapid growth of population; ethnic, religious, and tribal rivalries; inadequate educational systems and political experience; a shortage of technological expertise and investment capital—all of these factors often led to civil wars and to political and economic crises. A new wave of Muslim religious revivalism with serious political implications swept through the Islamic world, dividing it and threatening the stability of moderate Islamic countries. The Arab-Israeli conflict further exacerbated tensions in the Middle East. These conflicts and instability contributed to tensions between the two great power blocs.

The Cold War came to a rapid and surprising conclusion during the second half of the 1980s. The Soviet Union witnessed remarkable internal changes as the Communist Party sought to reform itself under the leadership of Mikhail Gorbachev. In 1989 the Soviet dominated nations of Eastern Europe overturned their Communist governments in a series of generally peaceful revolutions. In that same year Germany reunited. By 1991 the Communist Party of the Soviet Union collapsed, and the Soviet Union itself dissolved.

What now lies before the nations of the world is the challenge to establish a new order. The most immediate threats to such an order come from ethnic and national tensions within former multinational states and from efforts by powerful governments to dominate others. The closing years of the century have seen both types of conflict, and an increasing reliance on the UN to solve them. It now seems clear that the close of the Cold War has brought a period equally filled with hope and uncertainty for the peoples of the world and their leaders.

1914–1940

1914–1918 World War I
1917 Bolsheviks seize power, Russia
1919 Versailles Settlement
1922 Mussolini seizes power, Italy
1925 Locarno Pact
1933 Hitler comes to power
1936 Spanish Civil begins
1938 Munich Conference
1939 World War II begins

1922 British leave Egypt
1922–1938 Mustafa Kemal first president of Turkey
1928 The Muslim Brotherhood founded by Hasan Al-Banna

1941–1959

1944 D-Day
1945 World War II ends
1948 Berlin blockade and airlift
1949 NATO treaty; Russia detonates atomic bomb
1953 Death of Stalin
1955 Warsaw Pact
1956 Soviets crush Hungarian revolt
1957 EEC founded
1958 Charles de Gaulle comes to power in France

1947 Indian Independence; creation of Pakistan
1948 Assassination of Mahatma Gandhi
1949 State of Israel founded
1953 Mosaddeq overthrown in Iran
1954–1970 Abdel Nasser leads Egypt
1956 Suez crisis

1960–1979

1960 Paris Summit Conference collapses after U-2 incident
1961 Berlin Wall erected
1964 Khrushchev replaced as Soviet Prime Minister by Kosygin; as Party Secretary by Brezhnev
1968 Soviets invade Czechoslovakia
1972 British impose direct rule on Northern Ireland
1972 Israeli Olympic athletes killed by Arab terrorists
1974 End of military rule in Greece
1974 Portuguese dictatorship deposed; democratic reforms begin
1977 Brezhnev president of USSR
1979 Margaret Thatcher becomes British prime minister

1966 Indira Gandhi becomes prime minister of India
1967 Israeli-Arab June War
1969 Golda Meir becomes Prime Minister of Israel
1969 Arafat elected P.L.O. chairman
1971 India-USSR friendship treaty
1973 Arab-Israeli October War
1972 Independence for Bangladesh
1973 OPEC oil embargo
1977 Menachem Begin becomes prime minister of Israel
1978 Iranian revolution under Khomeini's leadership
1979 Egyptian-Israeli Peace Treaty
1979 Iran takes U.S. hostages
1979 Soviets invade Afghanistan

1980–1999

1980 Solidarity Movement in Poland
1981 crackdown against Solidarity
1984–1985 Bitter strikes by miners in England
1984 Mikhail Gorbachev introduces *glasnost* in USSR
1989 Berlin Wall demolished
1990 Germany unified
1991 Failed coup in Soviet Union; Yeltsin emerges as leader of Russia
1991 Major replaces Thatcher as England's prime minister
1993 Czechoslovakia divides into two republics
1995 Dayton Peace Accords end war in Bosnia
1999 NATO military campaign against Serbia

1980–1988 Iran–Iraq War
1981 Hostages released in Iran
1981 Egypt's Sadat assassinated; succeeded by Hosni Mubarak
1982 Israel invades Lebanon
1984 Indira Gandhi assassinated
1989 Soviets leave Afghanistan
1989 Death of Khomeini
1990 Central Asian States become independent on fall of USSR
1990–1991 Gulf War
1991 Indian prime minister Rajiv Ghandi assassinated

Opening of the Berlin Wall, 1989

EAST ASIA	AFRICA	THE AMERICAS
1916–1928 Warlord era in China **1919** May 4th Movement in China **1925** Universal male suffrage in Japan **1928–1937** Nationalist government in China at Nanking **1931** Japan occupies Manchuria **1937–1945** Japan at War with China	**1935** Mussolini invades Ethiopia	**1917** U.S. enters World War I **1929** Wall Street Crash; the Great Depression begins **1930–1945** Vargas dictatorship in Brazil **1932** F. D. Roosevelt elected U.S. president **1938** Mexico nationalizes oil
1941 Japan attacks Pearl Harbor **1945** Japan surrenders after U.S. atomic bombs **1945–1949** Civil War in China; People's Republic founded **1950** N. Korea invades S. Korea **1952** U.S. ends occupation of Japan **1953–1972** Double-digit growth in Japan **1955** Liberal-Democratic Party formed in Japan **1959–1960** Sino-Soviet split	**1942–1945** World War II engulfs North Africa **1955–1962** Wars of independence in French Algeria **1956** Sudan gains independence from Britain and Egypt **1956** Morocco and Tunisia gain independence from France **1957** Ghana an independent state under Kwame Nkrumah	**1941** U.S. enters World War II **1945** Death of F. D. Roosevelt **1946** Peron elected president in Argentina **1954** U.S. Supreme Court outlaws segregation **1955** Peron overthrown **1956** Montgomery bus boycott **1959** Fidel Castro comes to power in Cuba
1959–1975 Vietnam War **1965–1976** Cultural Revolution devastates China **1968** Death of Ho Chi Minh, president of North Vietnam **1971** Lin Piao killed in China **1972** President Nixon visits China **1973** Economic growth slows in Japan **1976** Death of Mao Tse-tung **1978–1989** New Economic policies of Teng Hsiao-p'ing in China **1978–1989** Vietnam occupies Cambodia	**1960** Belgian Congo granted independence as Zaire **1963** Kenya becomes an independent republic **1964** Zanzibar, the Congo, and Northern Rhodesia (Zambia) become independent republics **1965** Revolution in Kenya **1967–1970** Nigerian Civil War **1974** Drought and famine in Africa **1974** Emperor Haile Selassie of Ethiopia is deposed **1974–1975** Portugal grants independence to Guinea, Angola, Mozambique, Cape Verde	**1960** Kennedy elected president **1962** Cuban Missile Crisis **1963** Kennedy assassinated **1964** Passage of Civil Rights Act **1965** U.S. expands Vietnam commitment **1968** Martin Luther King and Robert Kennedy assassinated; campus unrest **1968** Nixon elected **1970** Allende elected in Chile **1972** Nixon visits China and USSR; is re-elected president **1973** Watergate Scandal breaks **1973** Peron re-elected, Argentina **1973** Chile's Allende overthrown **1974** Nixon resigns presidency **1979** Revolution in Nicaragua and El Salvador
1980s Double-digit economic growth in South Korea and Taiwan **1988** Japan's GNP second in world **1989** Vietnam pledges to withdraw from Cambodia **1989** China crushes pro-democracy demonstrations in Peking **1991–1992** Political scandals and plummeting stock market in Japan **1992** Kim Young Sam, civilian party leader, elected S. Korean president  A student confronts tanks in Tienanmen Square, China, May 1989	**1980** Southern Rhodesia (Zimbabwe) gains independence from Britain **1984** Bishop Desmond Tutu awarded Nobel Peace Prize **1985** U.S. economic sanctions against South Africa result in more repression **1989** Conservative Botha government resigns in South Africa; DeKlerk becomes president **1992** Nelson Mandela freed from prison in South Africa **1994** Nelson Mandela elected President of South Africa	**1980** Iran hostage crisis **1980** Reagan elected president **1982** War between Argentina and Great Britain over Islas Malvinas (Falkland Islands) **1983** Argentine military government overthrown; elected government restored **1983** End of Mexican oil boom **1988** Major arms agreement between U.S. and USSR **1991** Gulf War **1992** Clinton elected president **1994** Revolt in Chiapas, Mexico **1998** Pope visits Cuba

33 IMPERIALISM AND WORLD WAR I

The German delegation signs the peace treaty ending the First World War in the Hall of Mirrors of the Palace of Versailles on June 28, 1919. This painting by Sir William Orpen, completed in 1921, now hangs in the Imperial War Museum in London. [Imperial War Museum, London/Bildarchiv Preussischer Kulturbesitz]

CHAPTER TOPICS

◆ Expansion of European Power and the "New Imperialism"

◆ Emergence of the German Empire

◆ World War I

◆ The Russian Revolution

◆ End of World War I

In World Perspective Imperialism and World War I

During the second half of the nineteenth century, and especially after 1870, Europe exercised unprecedented influence and control over the rest of the world. North and South America, as well as Australia and New Zealand, almost became part of the European world as great streams of European immigrants populated them. Until the nineteenth century, Asia (with the significant exception of India) and most of Africa had gone their own ways, having little contact with Europe. But in the latter part of that century, almost all of Africa was divided among a number of European nations (see Chapter 31). Europe also imposed its economic and political power across Asia (see Map 33–1 and Chapter 32). By the next century, European dominance had brought every part of the globe into a single world economy. Events in any corner of the world had significant effects thousands of miles away.

These developments might have been expected to lead to greater prosperity and good fortune. Instead, they helped to foster competition and hostility among the great powers of Europe and to bring on a terrible war that undermined Europe's strength and its influence in the world. The peace settlement, proclaimed as "a peace without victors," disillusioned idealists in the West. It treated Germany almost as harshly as Germany would have treated its foes if it had been victorious. Also, the new system failed to provide realistic and effective safeguards against a return to power of a vengeful Germany. The withdrawal of the United States into a disdainful isolation from world affairs destroyed the basis for keeping the peace on which the hopes of Britain and France relied. The frenzy for imperial expansion that had seized Europeans in the late nineteenth century had done much to destroy Europe's peace and prosperity and its dominant place in the world.

Expansion of European Power and the "New Imperialism"

The explosive developments in nineteenth-century science, technology, industry, agriculture, transportation, communication, and military weapons provided the chief sources of European power. They enabled a few Europeans (and Americans) to impose their will on other peoples many times their number by force. Institutional as well as material advantages allowed Westerners to have their way. The growth of national states that commanded the loyalty, service, and resources of their inhabitants to a degree previously unknown permitted the European nations to deploy their response in the most effective way. The Europeans also possessed another, less tangible weapon: the belief that their civilization and way of life were superior to all others. It gave them a confidence that often took the form of a cultural arrogance that fostered the expansionist mood.

The expansion of European influence was not new. Spain, Portugal, France, Holland, and Britain had controlled overseas territories for centuries, but by the mid-nineteenth century only Great Britain retained extensive holdings. The first half of the century was generally hostile to colonial expansion. Even the British had been sobered by their loss of the American colonies. The French acquired Algeria and part of Indochina, and the British made some additional gains in Canada, India, Australia, and New Zealand. However, the doctrine of free trade was dominant, and it opposed political interference in other lands.

After 1870, however, the European states swiftly spread their control over perhaps 10 million square miles and 150 million people, about a fifth of the world's land area and a tenth of its population. The movement has been called the New Imperialism (Map 33–1).

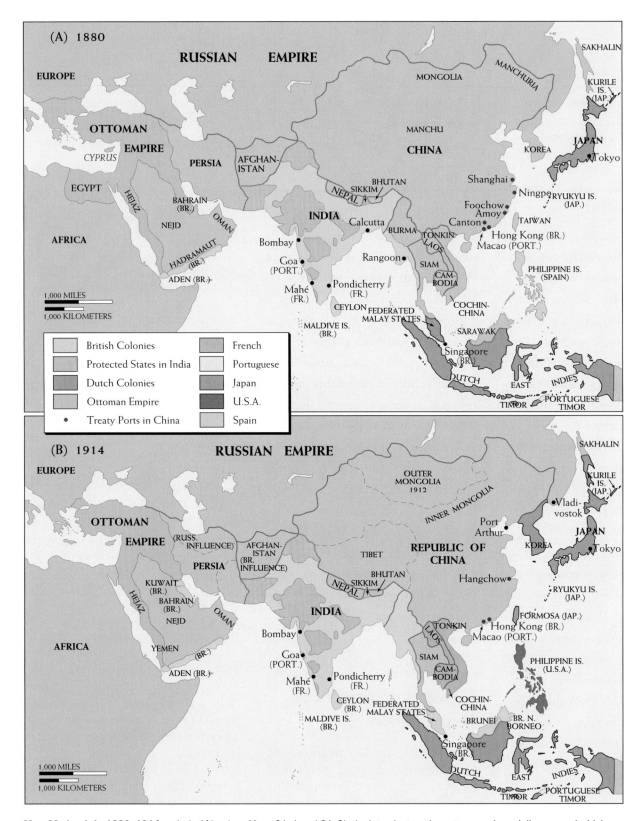

Map 33-1 Asia 1880–1914. As in Africa (see Maps 31-1 and 31-2), the late nineteenth century saw imperialism spread widely and rapidly in Asia. Two new powers, Japan and the United States, joined the British, French, and Dutch in extending control both to islands and to the mainland and in exploiting an enfeebled China.

The New Imperialism

The word *imperialism* has come to be used so loosely as to become almost meaningless. It may be useful to offer a definition that might be widely accepted: "The policy of extending a nation's authority by territorial acquisition or by the establishment of economic and political hegemony over other nations."[1] Previous imperialisms had taken the form either of seizing land and settling it with the conqueror's people or of establishing trading centers to exploit the dominated area. The New Imperialism introduced new devices.

The usual pattern of the New Imperialism was for the European nation to invest capital in the "backward" country—to build productive enterprises and improved means of transportation and employ many natives in the process—and thereby to transform its entire economy and culture. To guarantee their investments, the European states would make favorable arrangements with the local government either by enriching or threatening the rulers. If these arrangements proved inadequate, the dominant power established different degrees of political control ranging from full annexation as a colony, to protectorate status (whereby the local ruler was controlled by the dominant European state and maintained by its military power), to "spheres-of-influence" status (whereby the European state received special commercial and legal privileges without direct political involvement).

Motives for the New Imperialism: Economic Interpretation

There is still no agreement about the motives for the New Imperialism. The most widespread interpretation has been economic, most typically in the form given by the English radical economist J. A. Hobson and later adapted by Lenin. As Lenin put it, "Imperialism is the monopoly stage of capitalism,"[2] the last stage of a dying capitalist system. According to this interpretation, competition inevitably leads to the elimination of inefficient capitalists and, therefore, to monopoly. Powerful industrial and financial capitalists soon run out of profitable areas of investment in their own countries and persuade their governments to gain colonies in "backward" countries. Here they can find higher profits from their investments, new markets for their products, and safe sources of the needed raw materials.

The facts do not support this viewpoint. The European powers did invest considerable capital abroad, but not in the

model of Hobson and Lenin. Britain, for example, made heavier investments abroad before 1875 than during the next two decades. Only a small percentage of British and European investments overseas, moreover, went to the new colonial areas. Most went into Europe itself or into older, well-established areas like the United States, Canada, Australia, and New Zealand. Moreover, investments in the new areas were not necessarily put into colonies held by the investing country.

The facts are equally discouraging for those who emphasize the need for new markets and raw materials. Colonies were not usually important markets for the great imperial nations, and all were forced to rely on areas that they did not control as sources of vital raw materials. It is not even clear that control of the new colonies was particularly profitable. Some individuals and companies, of course, made great profits from particular colonial ventures, but could rarely influence national policy. Economic motives certainly played a part, understanding that the New Imperialism requires a search for further motives.

Cultural, Religious, and Social Interpretations

Advocates of imperialism put forth various justifications for their practices. Some argued that the advanced European nations had a responsibility to bring the benefits of their higher culture and superior civilization to the people of "backward" lands. Few people were influenced by such arrogant arguments, although many shared the intellectual assumptions behind them. Religious groups argued for the responsibility of Western nations to bring the benefits of Christianity to the heathen with more extensive efforts and aid from their governments. Politicians and diplomats argued for imperialism as a tool of social policy. In Germany, for instance, people suggested that imperial expansion might serve to deflect public interest from domestic politics and social reform. But Germany acquired few colonies, and such considerations were negligible. Another common and apparently plausible justification was that colonies would provide a good place to settle surplus population. In fact, most European emigrants went to North and South America and Australia.

Strategic and Political Interpretations: The Scramble for Africa

Strategic and political considerations seem to have been more important in bringing on the New Imperialism. The scramble for Africa in the 1880s, discussed in more detail in Chapter 31, is one example (see Maps 31–1 and 31–2). Britain was

[1]*American Heritage Dictionary of the English Language* (New York: Houghton Mifflin, 1969) p. 660.
[2]V. I. Lenin, *Imperialism, the Highest Stage of Capitalism* (New York: International Publishers, 1939) p. 88.

A British fort at Alexandria, Egypt. The opening of the Suez Canal in 1869 sharply reduced the time needed for travel from Europe to the Far East, and, for Great Britain, from England to its colony in India. Britain acquired a financial interest in the canal, giving it a strategic interest in Egypt. In 1882 Britain made Egypt a protectorate in order to secure the canal. [Hulton/Bettmann]

the only great power with extensive overseas holdings on the even of the scramble. The completion of the Suez Canal in 1869 made Egypt vitally important to the British because it sat astride the shortest route to India. Britain purchased a major, but not a controlling, interest in the canal in 1875. When Egypt's stability was threatened by internal troubles in the 1880s, the British established a protectorate. Then, to protect Egypt, they advanced into the Sudan.

France became involved in North Africa in 1830 by sending a naval expedition to Algeria to attack the pirates based there. Before long, French settlers arrived and established a colony. By 1882 France was in full control of Algeria and had taken over Tunisia to keep out Italy. Soon lesser states like Belgium, Portugal, Spain, and Italy were also scrambling for African colonies. By the 1890s their intervention had led Britain to expand northward from the Cape of Good Hope into what is now Zimbabwe. Britain may have had significant strategic reasons for protecting the Suez and Cape routes to India, but France and the smaller European nations did not. Their motives were political as well as economic, for they equated status as a great power (Britain was the chief model) with the possession of colonies. They therefore sought colonies as evidence of their own importance.

Bismarck appears to have pursued an imperial policy, however brief, from coldly political motives. In 1884 and 1885 Germany declared protectorates over southwestern Africa, Togoland, the Cameroons, and East Africa. None of these places was particularly valuable or strategically important.

Bismarck acquires colonies chiefly to improve Germany's diplomatic position in Europe, and tried to turn France from hostility against Germany by diverting the French toward colonial interests. German colonies in Africa could also be used to persuade the British to be reasonable.

The Irrational Element

Germany's annexations started a wild scramble by the other European powers to claim what was left of Africa. By 1890 almost all of the continent was parceled out. Great powers and small expanded into areas neither profitable nor strategic for reasons less calculating and rational than Bismarck's. "Empire in the modern period," D. K. Fieldhouse observed, "was the product of European power: Its reward was power or the sense of power.[3]

Such motives were not new. They had been well understood by the Athenian spokesman at Melos in 416 B.C.E., whose words were reported by Thucydides: "Of the gods we believe and of men we know clearly that by a necessity of their nature where they have the power they rule."

In Asia the emergence of Japan as a great power with claims on China and Korea frightened the other powers interested in China. The Russians were building a railroad across Siberia to Vladivostok and were afraid to any threat to Manchuria. Together with France and Germany, they applied

[3]*The Colonial Empires* (New York: Delacorte, 1966) p. 393.

diplomatic pressure that forced Japan out of the Liaotung Peninsula and its harbor, Port Arthur; all pressed feverishly for concessions in China. Fearing that China, its markets, and its investment opportunities would soon be closed to its citizens, the United States in 1899 proposed the "Open Door Policy," which opposed foreign annexations in China and allowed entrepreneurs of all nations to trade there on equal terms. The support of Britain helped win acceptance of the policy by all the powers except Russia.

The United States had only recently emerged as a force in international affairs. Victory in the Spanish-American War of 1898 brought an informal protectorate over Cuba and the annexation of Puerto Rico; it thus drove Spain completely from the Western Hemisphere. The Americans also purchased the Philippine Islands and Guam, and Germany acquired the other Spanish islands in the Pacific. The Americans and the Germans also divided Samoa between them. What was left of the Pacific Islands was soon taken by France and England. Hawaii was annexed in 1898. This outburst of activity made the United States an imperial and Pacific power.

By 1900 most of the world had thus come under the control of the industrialized West. The greatest remaining vulnerable area was the Ottoman Empire, but its fate was closely tied up with European developments and must be treated in that context.

An American cartoonist in 1888 depicted John Bull (England) as the octopus of imperialism, grabbing land on every continent. Notice the hand at the left poised over Egypt. [The Granger Collection, N.Y.]

Emergence of the German Empire

Formation of the Triple Alliance (1873–1890)

Prussia's victories over Austria and France and its creation of a large, powerful German Empire in 1871 revolutionized European diplomacy. The sudden appearance of a vast new state that brought together most of the German people to form a nation of great and growing population, wealth, industrial capacity, and military power posed new problems.

The balance of power created at the Congress of Vienna was altered radically. Britain retained its position and so did Russia, even though it was somewhat weakened by the Crimean War. Austria, however, had lost ground, and its position was further threatened by the forces of nationalism within the Austro-Hungarian Empire. French power and prestige were badly damaged by the Franco-Prussian War and the German annexation of Alsace-Lorraine. The French were both afraid of their powerful new neighbor and resentful of their defeat and their loss of territory and of France's traditional position as the dominant western European power.

Bismarck's Leadership (1873–1890)

Until 1890 Otto von Bismarck (1815–1898) continued to guide German policy. He insisted after 1871 that Germany was a satisfied power and wanted no further territorial gains, and he meant it. He wanted to avoid a new war that might undo his achievement. He tried to assuage French resentment by cultivating friendly relations and by supporting French colonial aspirations. He also prepared for the worst. If France could not be conciliated, it must be isolated. Bismarck sought to prevent an alliance between France and any other European power—especially Austria or Russia—that would threaten Germany with a war on two fronts.

War in the Balkans   Bismarck's first move was to establish the Three Emperors' League in 1873. It brought together the three great conservative empires of Germany, Austria, and Russia. The league collapsed when Russia went to war with Turkey in 1877 as a result of uprisings in the Ottoman Balkan provinces. The tottering Ottoman Empire was preserved chiefly by the competing aims of those powers who awaited its demise. Ottoman weakness encouraged Serbia and Montenegro to come to the aid of their fellow Slavs in Bosnia and Herzegovina. Soon the rebellion spread to Bulgaria.

Then Russia entered the fray and created a major international crisis. The Russians hoped to expand at Ottoman expense and to achieve their most cherished goal: control of Constantinople and the Dardanelles. Russian intervention

Carl Peters Demands Colonies for Germany

Germany was a late arrival in the competition for colonies. The territories still available were neither profitable nor attractive for settlement by Europeans. Carl Peters (1856–1918) was one of the growing number of Germans, who, nevertheless, were eager to acquire a colonial empire. He was the founder of German East Africa, now Tanzania. His arguments based on economic advantage and the prospects of German emigration proved to be absurd, but they provided a mask for less rational motives.

What reasons does Peters give for Germany to seek colonies? What assumptions does he make about their advantages? Are those assumptions correct? What do you think were the most important motives for colonization to Peters and those who supported his policy?

Manifesto of the Society for German Colonization, April 1884

In the partition of the earth, as it has proceeded from the beginning of the fifteenth century up to our times, the German nation received nothing. All the remaining European culture-bearing people possess area outside our continent where their languages and customs can take firm root and flourish. The moment that the German emigrant leaves the borders of the Reich behind him, he is a stranger sojourning on foreign soil. The German Reich, great in size and strength through its bloodily achieved unity, stands in the leading position among the continental European powers: her sons abroad must adapt themselves to nations which look upon us with either indifference or even hostility. For centuries the great stream of German emigration has been plunging down into foreign races where it is lost sight of. Germandom outside Europe has been undergoing a perpetual national decline.

This fact, so painful to national pride, also represents a great economic disadvantage for our *Volk*. Every year our Fatherland loses the capacity of approximately 200,000 Germans. The greatest amount of this capacity flows directly into the camp of our economic competitors and increases the strength of our rivals. Germany's imports of products from tropical zones originate in foreign settlements whereby many millions of German capital are lost every year to alien nations. German exports are dependent upon the discretion of foreign tariff policies. Our industry lacks an absolutely safe market for its goods because our *Volk* lacks colonies of its own.

The alleviation of this national grievance requires taking practical steps and strong action.

In recognition of this point of view, a society has been organized in Berlin with the goal of mobilizing itself for such steps and such action. The Society for German Colonization aims to undertake on its own, in a resolute and sweeping manner, carefully chosen colonization projects and thereby supplement the ranks of organizations with similar tendencies.

Its particular tasks will be:

1. to provide necessary sums of capital for colonization;

2. to seek out and lay claim to suitable districts for colonization;

3. to direct German emigrants to these regions.

Imbued as we are with the conviction that it is no longer permissible to hesitate in energetically mobilizing ourselves for this great national task, we venture to come before the German *Volk* with a plea for active support of the endeavors of our Society! The German nation has proven time and again its willingness to make sacrifices for general patriotic undertakings: may she also bring her full energies to play in the solution of this great historical task.

Every German whose heart beats for the greatness and the honor of our nation is entreated to come to the side of our Society. What is at stake is compensation for centuries of deprivation: to prove to the world that, along with the splendor of the Reich, the German *Volk* has inherited the old German national spirit of its forefathers!

From Ralph A. Austen, trans. *Modern Imperialism* Copyright © 1969 by D. C. Heath and Company. Reprinted by permission of Houghton Mifflin Company.

---

also reflected the influence of the Pan-Slavic movement, which sought to bring all the Slavic peoples, even those under Austrian or Ottoman rule, under the protection of Holy Mother Russia.

Before long the Ottoman Empire was forced to ask for peace. The Treaty of San Stefano of March 1878 was a Russian triumph, but a short-lived one. The Slavic states in the Balkans were freed of Ottoman rule, and Russia itself obtained territory and a heavy monetary indemnity. But the terms of the Russian victory alarmed the other great powers. Austria feared that the new Slav states in the Balkans and the powerful increase in Russian influence there would threaten its own Balkan provinces. The British were alarmed by the damage the Russian settlement would do to the European balance of power and especially by possible Russian control of the Dardanelles. Disraeli (1804–1881) was determined to resist, and British public opinion supported him. A popular song gave the language a new word for superpatriotism—*jingoism*:

> We don't want to fight
> But by jingo if we do,
> We've got the men,
> We've got the ships,
> We've got the money too!
> The Russians will not have Constantinople!

Congress of Berlin   Even before San Stefano, Disraeli had sent a fleet to Constantinople. After the magnitude of Russia's appetite was known, Britain and Austria forced Russia to agree to an international conference at which the provisions of San Stefano would be reviewed by the other great powers. The resulting Congress of Berlin met in June and July of 1878 under the presidency of Bismarck.

The decisions of the Congress were a blow to Russian ambitions. Bulgaria lost two thirds of its territory and was deprived of access to the Aegean Sea. Austria-Hungary was given Bosnia and Herzegovina to "occupy and administer," although those provinces remained formally under Ottoman rule. Britain received Cyprus, and France gained permission to occupy Tunisia. These privileges were compensation for the gains that Russia was permitted to keep. Germany asked for nothing, but the Russians were bitterly disappointed. The Three Emperors' League was dead.

The major trouble spot now was in the south Slavic states of Serbia and Montenegro. They deeply resented the Austrian occupation of Bosnia and Herzegovina, as did many of the natives of those provinces. The south Slavic question, no less than the estrangement between Russia and Germany, was a threat to the peace of Europe.

German Alliances with Russia and Austria   Bismarck could ignore the Balkans, but not the breach in his eastern alliance system. With Russia alienated, he concluded a secret treaty with Austria in 1879. The resulting Dual Alliance provided that if either Germany or Austria were attacked by Russia, the ally would help the attacked party. If either was attacked by someone else, each promised at least to maintain neutrality. The treaty was renewed every five years until 1918. As the central point in German policy, it was criticized at the time; some have judged it mistaken in retrospect. It appeared to tie the German fortunes to those of the troubled Austro-Hungarian Empire and thus to borrow trouble. It also isolated the Russians and pushed them to alliances in the West.

Bismarck was aware of these dangers but discounted them. He never allowed the alliance to drag Germany into Austria's Balkan quarrels. He made it clear to the Austrians that the al-

Bismarck and the young Kaiser William II meet in 1888. The two disagreed over many issues, and in 1890 William dismissed the aged chancellor.
[German Information Center]

liance was purely defensive and that Germany would never attack Russia.

Bismarck expected the news of the Austro-German negotiations to frighten Russia into seeking closer relations with Germany, and he was right. Russian diplomats soon approached him, and by 1881 he had renewed the Three Emperors' League on a firmer basis. Although it did not resolve all conflicts, it helped preserve peace.

The Triple Alliance   In 1882 Italy, ambitious for colonial expansion and annoyed by the French preemption of Tunisia, asked to join the Dual Alliance. At this point Bismarck's policy was a complete success. He was allied with three of the great powers and friendly with Great Britain, which held aloof from all alliances. France was isolated and no threat. Although the Three Emperors' League was allowed to lapse, the Triple Alliance (Germany, Austria, and Italy) was renewed for another five years in 1887. To restore German relations with Russia, Bismarck negotiated the Reinsurance Treaty that same year, in which both powers promised to remain neutral if either was attacked. All seemed smooth, but a change in the German monarchy soon overturned Bismarck's system.

In 1888 William II (r. 1888–1918) came to the German throne. Like many Germans of his generation, he was filled with a sense of Germany's destiny as the leading power of Europe. To achieve a "place in the sun," he and his contemporaries wanted a navy and colonies like Britain's. These aims, of course, ran counter to Bismarck's limited continental policy. In 1890 William used a disagreement over domestic policy to dismiss Bismarck.

During Bismarck's time, Germany was a force for European peace and was increasingly understood to be so. This position would not have been possible without its great military power. But it also required the leadership of a statesman who could exercise restraint and make a realistic estimate of what his country needed and what was possible.

Forging the Triple Entente (1890–1907)

Franco-Russian Alliance   Almost immediately after Bismarck's retirement, his system of alliances collapsed. His successor, General Leo von Caprivi (1831–1899), refused the Russian request to renew the Reinsurance Treaty, which he considered incompatible with the Austrian alliance. Political isolation and the need for foreign capital unexpectedly drove the Russians toward France. The French, who were even more isolated, were glad to pour capital into Russia if it would help produce an alliance and security against Germany. In 1894 the Franco-Russian alliance was signed.

Britain and Germany   Britain now became the key to the international situation. Colonial rivalries pitted the British against the Russians in Central Asia and against the French in Africa. Traditionally, Britain had also opposed Russian control of Constantinople and the Dardanelles and French control of the Low Countries. There was no reason to think that Britain would soon become friendly to its traditional rivals or abandon its usual friendliness toward the Germans. Yet within a decade of William II's accession, Germany had become the enemy in the minds of the British. The problem lay in the foreign and naval policies of the German emperor and his ministers.

At first Germany tried to win the British over to the Triple Alliance, but when Britain clung to "splendid isolation," German policy changed. The idea was to demonstrate Germany's worthiness as an ally by withdrawing support and even making trouble for Britain.

The Germans began to exert pressure against Britain in Africa by barring British attempts to build a railroad from Capetown to Cairo. They also openly sympathized with the Boers of South Africa in their resistance to British expansion. In 1896 William insulted the British by sending a congratulatory telegram to Paul Kruger (1825–1904), president of the Transvaal, for repulsing a British raid "without having to appeal to friendly powers for assistance."

In 1898 William's dream of a German navy began to achieve reality with the passage of a naval law providing for nineteen battleships. In 1900 a second law doubled that figure. The architect of the new navy was Admiral Alfred von Tirpitz (1849–1930), who openly proclaimed that Germany's naval policy was aimed at Britain. His "risk" theory argued that Germany could build a fleet strong enough, not to defeat the British, but to inflict enough damage to make the British navy inferior to those of other powers like France or the United States. The threat posed by the German navy did more to antagonize British opinion than anything else. As the German navy grew and German policies seemed to become more threatening, the British were alarmed enough to abandon their traditional attitudes and policies.

Entente Cordiale   The first breach in Britain's isolation came in 1902 when an alliance was concluded with Japan to help defend British interests in the Far East against Russia. Next, Britain in 1904 concluded a series of agreements with the French, collectively called the Entente Cordiale. It was not a formal treaty and had no military provisions, but it settled all outstanding colonial differences between the two nations. The Entente Cordiale was a long step toward aligning the British with Germany's great potential enemy.

First Moroccan Crisis   At this point Germany decided to test the new understanding between Britain and France and to press for colonial gains. In March 1905 William II landed at Tangier, challenged the French predominance there in a speech in favor of Moroccan independence, and by implication asserted Germany's right to participate in Morocco's destiny. Germany's chancellor, Prince Bernhard von Bülow (1849—1929), intended to show France how weak it was and how little it could expect from Britain; he also hoped to gain significant colonial concessions.

The Germans might well have achieved their aims, but they demanded an international conference to exhibit their power more dramatically. The conference met in 1906 at Algeciras in Spain. Austria sided with its German ally, but Spain, Italy, and the United States voted with Britain and France. The Germans had overplayed their hand, and the French were confirmed in their position in Morocco. German bullying had, moreover, driven Britain and France closer together. In the face of a possible German attack on France, Sir Edward Grey (1862–1933), the British foreign secretary, without making a firm commitment, authorized conversations between the British and French general staffs. Their agreements became morally binding as the years passed. By 1914 French and British military and naval plans were so mutually dependent that the two countries were effectively, if not formally, allies.

British Agreement with Russia   Britain's new relationship with France was surprising. But hardly anyone believed that the British whale and the Russian bear would ever be allies. The Russo-Japanese war of 1904–1905 made such a development seem even less likely because Britain was allied with Russia's enemy. But Britain had behaved with restraint, and the Russians were chastened by their humiliating defeat. The defeat had also led to the Russian Revolution of 1905, which left Russia weak and reduced British apprehensions. The British were also concerned that Russia might again drift into the German orbit.

With French support, the British made overtures to the Russians and in 1907 concluded an agreement with them that settled Russo-British quarrels in Central Asia and Persia and opened the door for wider cooperation. The Triple Entente, an informal but powerful association of Britain, France, and Russia, was now ranged against the Triple Alliance. Because Italy was unreliable, Germany and Austria-Hungary stood surrounded by two great land powers and Great Britain.

William II and his ministers had turned Bismarck's nightmare of the prospect of a two-front war with France and Russia into a reality and had made it more horrible by adding Britain to the hostile coalition. Bismarck's alliance system had been intended to maintain peace, but the new one increased the risk of war and made the Balkans, where Austrian and Russian ambitions clashed, a likely spot for it. Bismarck's diplomacy had left France isolated and impotent; the new arrangement found France associated with the two greatest powers in Europe, apart from Germany. The Germans could rely only on Austria, where troubles made it more likely to need aid than to provide it.

World War I

The Road to War (1908–1914)

The situation in the Balkans was exceedingly complicated. The weak Ottoman Empire controlled the central strip running west from Constantinople to the Adriatic. North and south of it were the independent states of Romania, Montenegro, Serbia, and Greece; Bulgaria, while technically still part of the empire, was legally autonomous and practically independent. The Austro-Hungarian Empire included Croatia and Slovenia and since 1878 had "occupied and administered" Bosnia and Herzegovina.

Except for the Greeks and the Romanians, most of the inhabitants of the Balkans spoke variants of the same Slavic language and felt a cultural and historical kinship with one another and with Russia. For centuries they had been ruled by Austrians, Hungarians, or Turks, and the growing nationalism that characterized late-nineteenth-century Europe made many of them eager for liberty or at least autonomy. The more radical among them longed for a union of the south Slavic, or Yugoslav, peoples in a single nation. They looked to independent Serbia as the center of the new nation and hoped to detach all the Slavic provinces (especially Bosnia, which bordered on Serbia) from Austria. Serbia was to unite the Slavs at the expense of Austria, as Piedmont had united the Italians and Prussia the Germans.

In 1908 a group of modernizing reformers called the Young Turks overthrew the Ottoman government. This threatened to revive the empire and to interfere with the plans of the European jackals to pounce on the Ottoman corpse. These events precipitated the first of a series of Balkan crises that would eventually lead to world war.

The Bosnian Crisis   In 1908 the Austrian and Russian governments decided to act before Turkey became strong enough to resist. They agreed to call an international conference in which each of them would support the other's demands. Russia would agree to the Austrian annexation of Bosnia and Herzegovina, and Austria would support Russia's request to open the Dardanelles to Russian warships.

Austria, however, declared the annexation unilaterally before any conference was called. The British, ever concerned about their own position in the Mediterranean, rejected the Russian demand. The Russians, feeling betrayed by the British, were humiliated and furious. Their "little brothers," the Serbs, were enraged by the loss of Bosnia, which they had hoped one day to include in an independent south Slavic nation led by themselves. The Russians were too weak to do anything but accept the new situation. The Germans had not been warned in advance of Austria's plans and were unhappy because the action threatened their relations with Russia. But Germany felt so dependent on the Dual Alliance that it assured Austria of its support. Austria had been given a free hand, and to an extent German policy was being made in Vienna. It was a dangerous precedent. At the same time, the failure of Britain and France to support Russia strained the Triple Entente and made it harder for them to oppose Russian interests again if they wanted to retain Russian friendship.

Second Moroccan Crisis   The second Moroccan crisis, in 1911, emphasized the French and British need for mutual support. When France sent in an army to put down a rebellion, Germany took the opportunity to "protect German interests" in Morocco as a means of extorting colonial concessions in the French Congo. To add force to their demands,

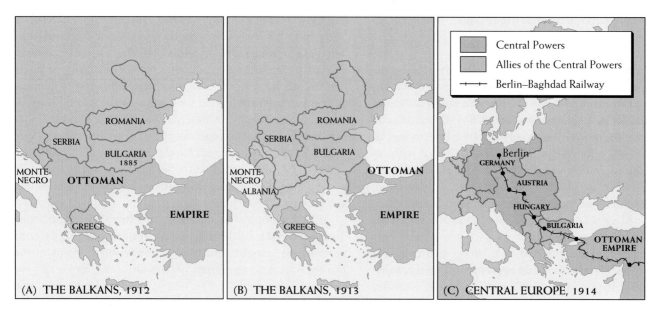

Map 33-2 The Balkans, 1912–1913. Two maps show the Balkans before (a) and after (b) the two Balkan wars; note the Ottoman retreat. In (c) we see the geographical relationship of the Central Powers and their Bulgarian and Turkish allies.

the Germans sent the gunboat *Panther* to the port of Agadir, allegedly to protect German citizens there. Once again, as in 1905, the Germans went too far. The *Panther's* visit to Agadir alarmed Britain. For some time Anglo-German relations had been deteriorating, chiefly because of the naval race. But negotiations failed to persuade William II and Tirpitz to slow down naval construction.

In this atmosphere, the British heard of the *Panther's* arrival in Morocco. They mistakenly believed that the Germans meant to turn Agadir into a naval base on the Atlantic. The crisis passed when France yielded some insignificant bits of the Congo and Germany withdrew from Morocco. The main result was to increase British fear of and hostility to Germany and to draw Britain closer to France. Specific plans were now formulated for a British expeditionary force to help defend France against German attack. The British and French navies agreed to cooperate. If France were attacked by Germany, Britain had to help defend the French, for its own security was inextricably tied up with that of France.

The Balkan Wars After the second Moroccan crisis, Italy feared that the recognition of the French protectorate in Morocco would encourage France to move into Libya. Consequently, in 1911 Italy attacked the Ottoman Empire to anticipate the French, defeated the faltering Turks, and obtained Libya and the Dodecanese Islands in the Aegean. The Italian victory encouraged the Balkan states to try their luck. In 1912 Bulgaria, Greece, Montenegro, and Serbia attacked the Ottoman Empire and won easily (see Map 33–2). After this First Balkan War the victors fell out among them-

selves. The Serbs and the Bulgarians quarreled about the division of Macedonia, and in 1913 a Second Balkan War erupted. This time Turkey and Romania joined Greece and Serbia against Bulgaria, which lost much of what it had gained since 1878.

The alarmed Austrians were determined to limit Serbian gains and especially to prevent the Serbs from obtaining a port on the Adriatic. An international conference sponsored by Britain in early 1913 resolved the matter in Austria's favor and called for an independent kingdom of Albania. But Austria felt humiliated by the public airing of Serbian demands. At first the Serbs defied the powers and stayed in Albania. Under Austrian pressure they withdrew, but in September 1913, after the Second Balkan War, the Serbs reoccupied sections of Albania. In mid-October Austria unilaterally issued an ultimatum to Serbia, which again withdrew from Albania. During this crisis many Austrians had wanted an all-out attack on Serbia to remove its threat once and for all. In Russia, Pan-Slavic sentiment pressed Czar Nicholas II (r. 1894–1917) to take a firm stand. But Russia nonetheless once again let Austria have its way.

The lessons learned from this crisis profoundly influenced behavior in the final crisis of 1914. The Russians had, as in 1908, been embarrassed by their passivity, and their allies were now more reluctant to restrain them. The Austrians were embarrassed by the results of accepting an international conference and were determined not to do it again. They had seen that better results might be obtained from a threat of direct force; they and their German allies did not miss the lesson.

Sarajevo and the Outbreak of War (June–August 1914)

The Assassination   On June 28, 1914, a young Bosnian nationalist shot and killed the Austrian Archduke Francis Ferdinand (1863–1914), heir to the throne, and his wife as they drove through the Bosnian capital of Sarajevo. The assassin was a member of a conspiracy hatched by a political terrorist society called *Union or Death*, better known as the *Black Hand*. The chief of intelligence of the Serbian army's general staff had helped plan the crime. Even though his role was not actually known at the time, it was generally believed that Serbian officials were involved. The glee of the Serbian press supported that belief.

Germany and Austria's Response   The assassination was condemned throughout Europe. To those Austrians who had long favored an attack on Serbia as a solution to the empire's Slavic problem, the opportunity seemed irresistible. But it was never easy for the Dual Monarchy to make a decision. Conrad von Hotzendorf (1852–1925), chief of the Austrian general staff, urged an attack as he had often done before. Count Stefan Tisza (1861–1918), speaking for Hungary, resisted. Count Leopold Berchtold (1863–1942), the Austro-Hungarian foreign minister, knew that German support would be required if Russia should decide to protect Serbia. He also knew that nothing could be done without Tisza's approval and that only German support could persuade the Hungarians to accept a war. The question of peace or war, therefore, had to be answered in Berlin.

William II and Chancellor Theobald von Bethmann-Hollweg (1856–1921) readily promised German support for an attack on Serbia. It has often been said that they gave the Austrians a "blank check," but their message was firmer than that. They urged the Austrians to move swiftly, while the other powers were still angry at Serbia. They also indicated that a failure to act would be taken as evidence of Austria-Hungary's weakness and uselessness as an ally. Therefore, the Austrians never wavered in their determination to attack Serbia. They hoped, with the protection of Germany, to fight a limited war that would not bring on a general European conflict. However, they were prepared to risk even the latter. The Germans also knew that they risked a general war, but they hoped to "localize" the fight between Austria and Serbia.

These calculations proved to be incorrect. Bethmann-Hollweg hoped that the Austrians would strike swiftly and present the powers with a *fait accompli* while the outrage of the assassination was still fresh. He also hoped that German support would deter Russian involvement. Failing that, he was prepared for a continental war that would bring rapid victory over France and allow a full-scale attack on the Russians, who

ABOVE: The Austrian Archduke Franz Ferdinand and his wife in Sarajevo on June 28, 1914. Later in the day the royal couple were assassinated by young revolutionaries trained and supplied in Serbia, igniting the crisis that led to World War I. BELOW: Moments after the assassination the Austrian police captured one of the assassins. [Brown Brothers]

were always slow to bring their strength into action. This policy depended on British neutrality, and the German chancellor convinced himself that the British could be persuaded to stand aloof.

However, the Austrians were slow to act. They did not even deliver their deliberately unacceptable ultimatum to Serbia until July 24, when the general hostility toward Serbia had begun to subside. Serbia further embarrassed the Austrians by returning so soft and conciliatory an answer that even the mercurial German emperor thought it removed all reason for war. But the Austrians were determined not to turn back. On July 28 they declared war on Serbia, even though they could not field an army until mid-August.

Coming of World War I	
1871	End of the Franco-Prussian War; creation of the German Empire; German annexation of Alsace-Lorraine
1873	Three Emperors' League (Germany, Russia, and Austria-Hungary)
1875	Russo-Turkish War
1878	Congress of Berlin
1879	Dual Alliance between Germany and Austria
1881	Three Emperors' League is renewed
1882	Italy joins Germany and Austria in Triple Alliance
1888	William II becomes German emperor
1890	Bismarck dismissed
1894	Franco-Russian alliance
1898	Germany begins to build battleship navy
1902	British alliance with Japan
1904	Entente Cordiale between Britain and France
1904–1905	Russo-Japanese War
1905	First Moroccan crisis
1907	British agreement with Russia
1908–1909	Bosnian crisis
1911	Second Moroccan crisis; Italy attacks Turkey
1912–1913	First and Second Balkan wars
1914	Outbreak of World War I

The Triple Entente's Response The Russians, previously so often forced to back off, responded angrily to the Austrian demands on Serbia. The most conservative elements of the Russian government feared that war would bring on revolution as it had in 1905. But nationalists, Pan-Slavs, and most of the politically conscious classes in general demanded action. The government ordered partial mobilization, against Austria only. This policy was militarily impossible, but its purpose was diplomatic: to pressure Austria to hold back its attack on Serbia.

Mobilization of any kind, however, was dangerous because it was generally understood to be equivalent to an act of war. It was especially alarming to General Helmuth von Moltke (1848–1916), head of the German general staff. The possibility that the Russians might start mobilization before the Germans could move would upset the delicate timing of Germany's only battle plan—the Schlieffen Plan, which required an attack on France first—and would endanger Germany. From this point on, Moltke pressed for German mobilization and war. The pressure of military necessity mounted until it became irresistible.

The western European powers were not eager for war. France's president and prime minister were on their way back from a visit to Russia when the crisis flared up again on July 24. The Austrians had, in fact, timed their ultimatum precisely, so that these two men would be at sea at the crucial moment. Had they been in Paris they might have attempted to restrain the Russians. But the French ambassador to Russia gave the Russians the same assurances that Germany had given its ally. The British worked hard to avoid trouble by traditional means: a conference of the powers. Austria, still smarting from its humiliation after the London Conference of 1913, would not hear of it. The Germans privately supported the Austrians but were publicly conciliatory in the hope of keeping the British neutral.

Soon, however, Bethmann-Hollweg realized what he should have known from the first: If Germany attacked France, Britain must fight. Until July 30 his public appeals to Austria for restraint were a sham. Thereafter, he sincerely tried to persuade the Austrians to negotiate and to avoid a general war, but it was too late. While Bethmann-Hollweg was urging restraint on the Austrians, Moltke was pressing them to act. The Austrians wondered who was in charge in Berlin, but they could not retreat without losing their own self-respect and that of the Germans.

On July 30 Austria ordered mobilization against Russia. Bethmann-Hollweg resisted the enormous pressure to mobilize, not because he had any further hope of avoiding war but because he wanted Russia to mobilize against Germany first and appear to be the aggressor. Only thus could he win the support of the German nation for war, especially the pacifistic Social Democrats. His luck was good this time. The news of Russian general mobilization came only minutes before Germany would have mobilized in any case. The Schlieffen Plan went into effect. The Germans invaded Luxembourg on August 1 and Belgium on August 3. The latter invasion violated the treaty of 1839, in which the British had guaranteed Belgian neutrality. This factor undermined the considerable sentiment in Britain for neutrality and united the nation against Germany. Germany then invaded France, and on August 4 Britain declared war on Germany.

The Great War had begun. As Sir Edward Grey put it, the lights were going out all over Europe. They would come on again, but Europe would never be the same.

Strategies and Stalemate (1914–1917)

Throughout Europe jubilation greeted the outbreak of war. No general war had been fought since Napoleon, and the horrors of modern warfare were not yet understood. The dominant memory was of Bismarck's swift and decisive campaigns, in which costs and casualties were light and the rewards great.

Both sides expected to take the offensive, force a battle on favorable ground, and win a quick victory. The Triple Entente powers—or the Allies, as they came to be called—had superior numbers and financial resources as well as command

Women munitions workers in England. The First World War demanded more from the civilian populations than had previous wars, resulting in important social changes. The demands of the munitions industries and a shortage of men (so many of whom were in uniform) brought many women out of traditional roles at home and into factories and other war work. [Hulton Getty Picture Collection/Tony Stone Images]

of the sea (see Figure 33–1). Germany and Austria, the Central Powers, had the advantages of internal lines of communication and of having launched their attack first.

After 1905 Germany's only war plan was the one developed by Count Alfred von Schlieffen (1833–1913), chief of the German general staff from 1891 to 1906 (see Map 33–3). It aimed to outflank the French defenses by sweeping through Belgium to the Channel, then wheeling to the south and east to envelop the French and crush them against the German fortresses in Lorraine. In the east the Germans planned to stand on the defensive against Russia until France had been beaten, a task they thought would take only six weeks.

The apparent risk, besides the violation of Belgian neutrality and the consequent alienation of Britain, lay in weakening the German defenses against a direct attack across the frontier. Yet Schlieffen is said to have uttered the dying words, "It must come to a fight. Only make the right wing strong." The execution of his plan, however, was left to Helmuth von Moltke, the nephew of Bismarck's most effective general. Moltke was a gloomy and nervous man who lacked the talent

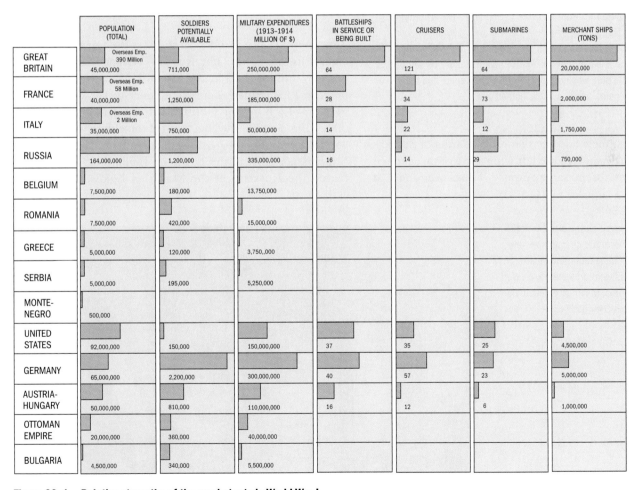

	POPULATION (TOTAL)	SOLDIERS POTENTIALLY AVAILABLE	MILITARY EXPENDITURES (1913–1914 MILLION OF $)	BATTLESHIPS IN SERVICE OR BEING BUILT	CRUISERS	SUBMARINES	MERCHANT SHIPS (TONS)
GREAT BRITAIN	Overseas Emp. 390 Million 45,000,000	711,000	250,000,000	64	121	64	20,000,000
FRANCE	Overseas Emp. 58 Million 40,000,000	1,250,000	185,000,000	28	34	73	2,000,000
ITALY	Overseas Emp. 2 Million 35,000,000	750,000	50,000,000	14	22	12	1,750,000
RUSSIA	164,000,000	1,200,000	335,000,000	16	14	29	750,000
BELGIUM	7,500,000	180,000	13,750,000				
ROMANIA	7,500,000	420,000	15,000,000				
GREECE	5,000,000	120,000	3,750,,000				
SERBIA	5,000,000	195,000	5,250,000				
MONTE-NEGRO	500,000						
UNITED STATES	92,000,000	150,000	150,000,000	37	35	25	4,500,000
GERMANY	65,000,000	2,200,000	300,000,000	40	57	23	5,000,000
AUSTRIA-HUNGARY	50,000,000	810,000	110,000,000	16	12	6	1,000,000
OTTOMAN EMPIRE	20,000,000	360,000	40,000,000				
BULGARIA	4,500,000	340,000	5,500,000				

Figure 33–1 Relative strengths of the combatants in World War I.

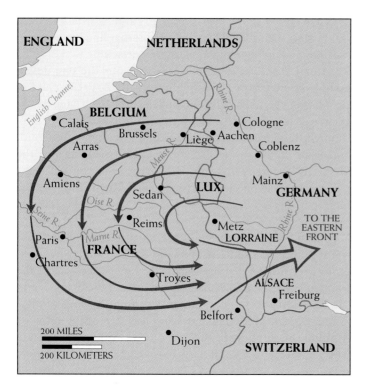

Map 33-3   The Schlieffen Plan of 1905. Germany's grand strategy for quickly winning the war against France in 1914 is shown by the wheeling arrows on the map. The crushing blows at France were, in the original plan, to be followed by the release of troops for use against Russia on Germany's eastern front. But the plan was not adequately implemented, and the war on the western front became a long contest instead.

of his illustrious uncle and the theoretical daring of Schlieffen. He added divisions to the left wing and even weakened the Russian front for the same purpose. The consequence of this hesitant strategy was the failure of the Schlieffen Plan by a narrow margin.

The War in the West   The French had also put faith in the offensive, but with less reason than the Germans. They badly underestimated the numbers and the effectiveness of the German reserves and set too much store by the importance of the courage and spirit of their troops, which proved insufficient against modern weapons, especially the machine gun. The French offensive on Germany's western frontier failed totally. In a sense this defeat was better than a partial success because it released troops for use against the main German army. As a result, the French and the British were able to stop the Germans at the Battle of the Marne in September 1914.

Thereafter, the war in the west became one of position instead of movement. Both sides dug in behind a wall of trenches protected by barbed wire that stretched from the North Sea to Switzerland. Strategically placed machine-gun nests made assaults difficult and dangerous. Both sides, nonetheless, attempted massive attacks initiated by artillery bombardments of unprecedented and horrible force and duration. Still, the defense was always able to prevent a breakthrough.

The War in the East   In the east the war began auspiciously for the Allies. The Russians advanced into Austrian territory and inflicted heavy casualties, but Russian incompetence and German energy soon reversed the situation (see Map 33–4). A junior German officer, Erich Ludendorff (1865–1937), under the command of the elderly General Paul von Hindenburg (1847–1934), destroyed or captured an entire Russian army at the Battle of Tannenberg; he also defeated the Russians at the Masurian Lakes. In 1915 the

French troops advancing on the western front. This scene of trench warfare characterizes the twentieth century's first great international conflict. The trenches were protected by barbed wire and machine guns, which gave defenders the advantage. [Hulton/Corbis-Bettmann]

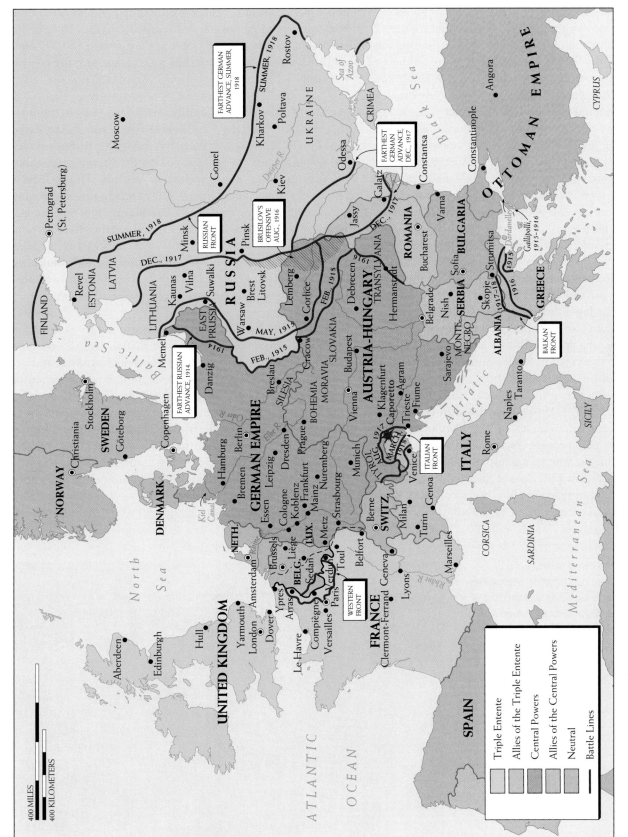

Map 33-4 World War I in Europe. Despite the importance of military action in the Far East, in the Arab world, and at sea, the main theaters of activity in World War I were in the European areas shown here.

Legend:
- Triple Entente
- Allies of the Triple Entente
- Central Powers
- Allies of the Central Powers
- Neutral
- Battle Lines

400 MILES
400 KILOMETERS

FARTHEST GERMAN ADVANCE, SUMMER, 1918

SUMMER, 1918

FARTHEST GERMAN ADVANCE, DEC., 1917

RUSSIAN FRONT

BRUSILOV'S OFFENSIVE AUG., 1916

DEC., 1917

FARTHEST RUSSIAN ADVANCE, 1914

FEB., 1915

MAY, 1915

FEB., 1915

BALKAN FRONT

ITALIAN FRONT

WESTERN FRONT

Gallipoli, 1915-1916

AUG. 1917

MARCH 1918

MOSCOW, Petrograd (St. Petersburg), Gomel, Kharkov, Poltava, Rostov, Kiev, Odessa, Galatz, Constantsa, Angora, Constantinople, Minsk, Pinsk, Jassy, Bucharest, Varna, Sofia, Strumitsa, Skopie, Nish, Sarajevo, Belgrade, Hermanstadt, Debrecen, Budapest, Cracow, Lemberg, Gorlice, Brest Litovsk, Warsaw, Suwalki, Vilna, Kaunas, Memel, Danzig, Revel, Stockholm, Göteborg, Christiania, Copenhagen, Hamburg, Bremen, Berlin, Breslau, Leipzig, Dresden, Prague, Essen, Cologne, Frankfurt, Koblenz, Mainz, Nuremberg, Munich, Vienna, Klagenfurt, Caporetto, Trieste, Fiume, Agram, Venice, Milan, Turin, Genoa, Marseilles, Lyons, Clermont-Ferrand, Geneva, Berne, Belfort, Toul, Strasbourg, Metz, Verdun, Sedan, Liège, Brussels, Amsterdam, Ypres, Arras, Compiègne, Versailles, Paris, Le Havre, Dover, London, Yarmouth, Hull, Edinburgh, Aberdeen, Naples, Taranto, Rome

FINLAND, NORWAY, SWEDEN, DENMARK, NETH., BELG., LUX., FRANCE, UNITED KINGDOM, SPAIN, ITALY, SWITZ., GERMAN EMPIRE, AUSTRIA-HUNGARY, BOHEMIA, MORAVIA, SLOVAKIA, SILESIA, TYROL, TRANSYLVANIA, ROMANIA, BULGARIA, SERBIA, MONTE-NEGRO, ALBANIA, GREECE, OTTOMAN EMPIRE, RUSSIA, UKRAINE, CRIMEA, ESTONIA, LATVIA, LITHUANIA, EAST PRUSSIA, CYPRUS, CORSICA, SARDINIA, SICILY

North Sea, Baltic Sea, Black Sea, Adriatic Sea, Mediterranean Sea, ATLANTIC OCEAN, Sea of Azov

Dnieper R., Oder R., Elbe R., Rhine, Rhône R., Kiel Canal, Dardanelles

1917-18, 1916

Central Powers pressed their advantage in the east and drove into the Baltic states and western Russia, inflicting over 2 million casualties in a single year. Russian confidence was badly shaken, but the Russian army stayed in the field.

As the battle lines hardened, both sides sought new allies. Turkey (because of its hostility to Russia) and Bulgaria (the enemy of Serbia) joined the Central Powers. Italy seemed an especially valuable prize, and both sides bid for its support with promises of a division of the spoils of victory. Because what the Italians wanted most was held by Austria, the Allies could make the more attractive promises. In a secret treaty of 1915 the Allies agreed to deliver to Italy most of *Italia Irredenta* (i.e., the Trentino, the South Tyrol, Trieste, and some of the Dalmatian Islands) after victory. By the spring of 1915 Italy was engaging Austrian armies. Although the Italian campaign distracted the Central Powers, it never produced significant results. Romania joined the Allies in 1916 but was quickly defeated and driven from the war.

In the Far East, Japan honored its alliance with Britain and entered the war. The Japanese quickly overran the German colonies in China and the Pacific and used the opportunity to improve their own position against China.

In 1915 the Allies undertook to break the deadlock in the fighting by going around it. The idea came chiefly from Winston Churchill (1874–1965), First Lord of the British Admiralty. He proposed an attack on the Dardanelles and the swift capture of Constantinople. This policy would knock Turkey from the war, bring help to the Balkan front, and ease communication with Russia. Success depended on timing, speed, and daring leadership, but all of these qualities were lacking. The execution of the attack was inept and overly cautious. Troops were landed and, as resistance continued, the Allied commitment increased. Before the campaign was abandoned the Allies lost almost 150,000 men and diverted three times that number from more useful fighting.

Return to the West   Both sides turned back to the west in 1916 (see Map 33–5). General Erich von Falkenhayn (1861—1922), who had succeeded Moltke in September 1914, sought success by an attack on the French stronghold of Verdun. The commander of Verdun, Henri Pétain (1856–1951), became a hero. "They shall not pass" became a slogan of national defiance. The Allies tried to end the impasse by launching a major offensive along the River Somme in July. Once again, the superiority of the defense was demonstrated. The only result was enormous casualties on both sides. On all fronts the losses were great and the results meager. The war on land dragged on with no end in sight.

The War at Sea   As the war continued, control of the sea became more important. The British ignored the distinction between war supplies (which were contraband according to international law) and food or other peaceful cargo, which was not subject to seizure. They imposed a strict blockade meant to starve out the enemy, regardless of international law. The Germans responded with submarine warfare meant to destroy British shipping and to starve the British. They declared the waters around the British Isles a war zone, where even neutral ships would not be safe. Both policies were unwelcome to neutrals, and especially to the United States, which conducted extensive trade in the At-

The Allies promoted Arab efforts to secure independence from Turkey in an effort to remove Turkey from the war. Delegates to the peace conference of 1919 in Paris included British Colonel T. E. Lawrence, who helped lead the rebellion, and representatives from the Middle Eastern region. Prince Feisal, the third son of King Hussein, stands in the foreground of this picture; Colonel T. E. Lawrence is in the middle row, second from the right; and Brigadier General Nuri Pasha Said of Baghdad is second from the left. [Corbis-Bettmann]

Map 33-5 The Western front 1914–1918. This map shows the crucial western front in detail.

Map legend:
1. Farthest German Advance, Sept., 1914
2. Nivelle's Offensive, Spring, 1917
3. Hindenburg Line (Stabilized Line) 1917–1918
4. German Gains, March–July, 1918
5. Major American Drives, Nov. 11, 1918
6. Armistice Line, Nov. 11, 1918

MEUSE–ARGONNE MAJOR AMERICAN DRIVES CUT THE GERMAN SUPPLY LINE AT SEDAN AND END THE WAR, NOV. 11, 1918.

lantic, but the sinking of neutral ships by German submarines was both more dramatic and more offensive than Britain's blockade.

In 1915 the British liner *Lusitania* was torpedoed by a German submarine. Among the 1,200 drowned were 118 Americans. President Woodrow Wilson (1856–1924) warned Germany that a repetition would not be accepted, and the Germans desisted rather than further anger the United States. This development gave the Allies a considerable advantage. The German fleet that had cost so much money and had caused so much trouble played no significant part in the war. The only battle it fought was at Jutland in the spring of 1916. The battle was in a standoff and confirmed British domination of the surface of the sea.

America Enters the War In December 1916 President Wilson attempted to bring about a negotiated peace. But neither side was willing to give up its hopes for total victory. The war seemed likely to continue until one or both sides reached exhaustion. Two events early in 1917 changed the situation radically. On February 1 the Germans announced the resumption of unrestricted submarine warfare,

which led the United States to break off diplomatic relations. On April 6 the United States declared war on Germany.

One of the deterrents to an earlier American intervention had been the presence of autocratic czarist Russia among the Allies. Wilson could conceive of the war only as an idealistic crusade "to make the world safe for democracy." That problem was resolved in March of 1917 by a revolution in Russia that overthrew the czarist government.

The Russian Revolution

The March Revolution in Russia was neither planned nor led by any political faction. It was the result of the collapse of the monarchy's ability to govern. Military and domestic failures produced massive casualties, widespread hunger, strikes by workers, and disorganization in the army. The peasant unrest that had plagued the countryside before 1914 did not subside during the conflict. All political factions were discontented.

In early March 1917 strikes and worker demonstrations erupted in Petrograd, as Saint Petersburg had been renamed. The ill-disciplined troops in the city refused to fire on the demonstrators, and the tsar abdicated on March 15. The government of Russia fell into the hands of members of the Duma, who formed a provisional government composed chiefly of Constitutional Democrats with Western sympathies. The various socialists, including both Social Revolutionaries and Social Democrats of the Menshevik wing, also began to organize the workers into councils called *soviets*. Initially, they allowed the provisional government to function without actually supporting it. But they became estranged as the Constitutional Democratic Party failed to control the army or to purge "reactionaries" from the government.

In this climate the provisional government decided to remain loyal to the existing Russian alliances and to continue the war against Germany. Its fate was sealed when a new offensive in the summer of 1917 collapsed. Disillusionment with the war, shortages of food and other necessities at home, and the growing demand by the peasants for land reform undermined the government, even after its leadership had been taken over by the moderate socialist Alexander Kerensky (1881–1970).

Ever since April the Bolsheviks had been working against the provisional government. The Germans, in their most successful attempt at subversion, had rushed the brilliant Bolshevik leader V. I. Lenin (1870–1924) in a sealed train from his exile in Switzerland across Germany to Petrograd in the hope that he would cause trouble for the revolutionary government. The Bolsheviks demanded that all political power go to the soviets, which they controlled. The failure of the summer offensive encouraged them to attempt a coup, but it

Petrograd Munitions workers demonstrating in 1917.

[Ria-Novosti/Sovfoto/Eastfoto]

failed. Lenin fled to Finland, and his chief collaborator, Leon Trotsky (1877—1940), was imprisoned.

An abortive right-wing counter-coup gave the Bolsheviks another chance. Trotsky, released from prison, led the powerful Petrograd Soviet. Lenin returned in October, insisted to his doubting colleagues that the time was ripe to take power, and by the extraordinary force of his personality persuaded them to act. Trotsky organized the coup that took place on November 6 and that concluded with an armed assault on the provisional government. The Bolsheviks, almost as much to their own astonishment as to that of the rest of the world, had come to rule Russia.

The victors moved to fulfill their promises and to assure their own security. The provisional government had decreed an election for late November to select a Constituent Assembly. The Social Revolutionaries won a large majority over the Bolsheviks. When the assembly gathered in January, it met for only a day before the Red Army, controlled by the Bolsheviks, dispersed it. All other political parties also ceased to function in any meaningful fashion. In November and January the Bolshevik government promulgated decrees that nationalized the land and turned it over to its peasant proprietors. Factory workers were put in charge of their plants. Banks were taken from their owners and seized for the state, and the debt of the tsarist government was repudiated. Property of the church reverted to the state.

The Bolshevik government also took Russia out of the war, which they believed benefited only capitalism. They signed an armistice with Germany in December 1917. On March 3, 1918, they accepted the Treaty of Brest-Litovsk, by which Russia yielded Finland, Poland, the Baltic states, and the Ukraine. Some territory in the Transcaucasus region went to Turkey. The Bolsheviks also agreed to pay a heavy war indemnity. These terms were a terribly high price to pay for peace, but Lenin had no choice. The Bolsheviks needed time to impose their rule on a devastated and chaotic Russia.

Until 1921 the New Bolshevik government confronted massive domestic resistance. A civil war erupted between the "Red" Russians supporting the revolution and the "White" Russians, who opposed the Bolshevik triumph. In the summer of 1918 the tsar and his family were murdered. Loyal army officers continued to fight the revolution and received aid from the Allies. However, led by Trotsky, the Red Army eventually overcame the domestic opposition. By 1921 Lenin and his supporters were in firm control.

End of World War I

Military Resolution

The Treaty of Brest-Litovsk brought Germany to the peak of its success. The Germans controlled eastern Europe and its resources, especially food. By 1918 they were free to concentrate their forces on the western front. This turn of events would probably have been decisive had it not been balanced by American intervention. Still, American troops would not arrive in significant numbers for about a year, and both sides tried to win the war in 1917. An Allied attempt to break through in the west failed disastrously, bringing heavy losses to the British and the French and causing a mutiny in the French army. The Austrians, supported by the Germans, de-

Lenin Establishes His Dictatorship

After the Bolshevik coup in October, elections for the Constituent Assembly were held in November. The results gave a majority to the Social Revolutionary Party and embarrassed the Bolsheviks. Using his control of the Red Army, Lenin closed the Constituent Assembly in January 1918, after it had met for only one day, and established the rule of a revolutionary elite and his own dictatorship. Here is the crucial Bolshevik decree.

What reasons does Lenin give for closing the legitimately elected Constituent Assembly? What other reasons might he have had? What were the soviets? Did they have a legitimate claim to the monopoly of political power? Was the dissolution of the assembly a temporary or permanent measure? What defense can be made for the Bolsheviks' action? Is it enough to justify that action?

. . . The Constituent Assembly, elected on the basis of lists drawn up prior to the October Revolution, was an expression of the old relation of political forces which existed when power was held by the compromisers and the Cadets. When the people at that time voted for the candidates for the Socialist-Revolutionary Party, they were not in a position to choose between the Right Socialist-Revolutionaries, the supporters of the bourgeoisie, and the Left Socialist-Revolutionaries, the supporters of Socialism. Thus, the Constituent Assembly, which was to have been the crown of the bourgeois parliamentary republic, could not become an obstacle in the path of the October Revolution and the Soviet power.

The October Revolution, by giving the power to the Soviets, and through the Soviets to the toiling and exploited classes, aroused the desperate resistance of the exploiters, and in the crushing of this resistance it fully revealed itself as the beginning of the socialist revolution . . . the majority in the Constituent Assembly which met on January 5 was secured by the party of the Right Socialist-Revolutionaries, the party of Kerensky, Avksentyev and Chernov. Naturally, this party refused to discuss the absolutely clear, precise and unambiguous proposal of the supreme organ of Soviet power, the Central Executive Committee of the Soviets, to recognize the program of the Soviet power, to recognize the "Declaration of Rights of the Toiling and Exploited People," to recognize the October Revolution and the Soviet power . . .

The Right Socialist-Revolutionary and Menshevik parties are in fact waging outside the walls of the Constituent Assembly a most desperate struggle against the Soviet power. . . .

Accordingly, the Central Executive Committee resolves: The Constituent Assembly is hereby dissolved.

From *A Documentary History of Communism*, Vol. 1, R. V. Daniels, ed. Copyright © 1960 Random House, pp. 133–135. Reprinted by permission of the author.

---

feated the Italians at Caporetto and threatened to overrun Italy, before they were checked with the aid of Allied troops. The deadlock continued, but time was running out for the Central Powers.

In 1918 the Germans, persuaded chiefly by Ludendorff—second in command to Hindenburg, but the real leader of the army—decided to gamble everything on one last offensive. The Germany army pushed forward and even reached the Marne again but got no farther. They had no more reserves, and the entire nation was exhausted. The Allies, on the other hand, were bolstered by the arrival of American troops in ever increasing numbers. They launched a counteroffensive that was irresistible. As the Austrian fronts in the Balkans and Italy collapsed, the German high command knew that the end was imminent.

Ludendorff was determined that peace should be made before the German army could be thoroughly defeated in the field and that the responsibility should fall on civilians. For some time he had been the effective ruler of Germany under the aegis of the emperor. He now allowed a new government to be established on democratic principles and to seek peace immediately. The new government, under Prince Max of Baden (1867–1928), asked for peace on the basis of the Fourteen Points that President Wilson had declared as the American war aims. These were idealistic principles, including self-determination for nationalities, open diplomacy, freedom of the seas, disarmament, and establishment of a league of nations to keep the peace. Wilson insisted that he would deal only with a democratic German government because he wanted to be sure he was dealing with the German people and not merely their rulers.

The disintegration of the German army forced William II to abdicate on November 9, 1918. The majority branch of the Social Democratic Party proclaimed a republic to prevent the establishment of a soviet government under the control of their radical, Leninist wing, which had earlier broken away as the Independent Socialist Party. Two days later this republican, socialist-led government signed the armistice that ended the war by accepting German defeat. The German people were, in general, unaware that their army had been defeated in the field and was crumbling. No foreign soldier stood on German soil. Many Germans expected a negotiated and mild settlement. The real peace embittered the German people, many of whom came to believe that Germany had not been defeated but had been tricked by the enemy and betrayed—even stabbed in the back—by republicans and socialists at home.

The victors rejoiced, but they also had much to mourn. The casualties on all sides came to about 10 million dead and twice as many wounded. The economic and financial resources of the European states were badly strained. The victorious Allies, formerly creditors to the world, became debtors to the new American colossus, itself barely touched by the calamities of war.

The old international order, moreover, was dead. Russia was ruled by a Bolshevik dictatorship that preached world revolution and the overthrow of capitalism everywhere. Germany was in chaos. Austria-Hungary had disintegrated into a swarm of small states competing for the remains of the ancient empire. These kinds of change stirred the colonial territories ruled by the European powers; overseas empires would never again be as secure as they had seemed before the war. Europe was no longer the center of the world, free to interfere when it wished or to ignore the outer regions if it chose. Its easy confidence in material and moral progress was shattered by the brutal reality of four years of horrible war. The memory of that war lived on to shake the nerve of the victorious Western powers as they confronted the new conditions of the postwar world.

Settlement at Paris

The Peacemakers   The representatives of the victorious states gathered at Versailles and other Parisian suburbs in the first half of 1919. Wilson speaking for the United States, David Lloyd George (1863–1945) for Britain, Georges Clemenceau (1841—1929) for France, and Vittorio Emanuele Orlando (1860–1952) for Italy made up the Big Four. Japan, now recognized for the first time as a great power, also had an important part in the discussions.

Wilson's idealism came into conflict with the more practical war aims of the victorious powers and with many of the secret treaties that had been made before and during the war. The British and French people had been told that Germany would be made to pay for the war. Russia had been promised control of Constantinople in return for recognition of the French claim to Alsace-Lorraine and British control of Egypt. Romania had been promised Transylvania at the expense of Hungary. Some of the agreements contradicted others: Italy and Serbia had competing claims to the islands and shore of the Adriatic. During the war the British had encouraged Arab

hopes of an independent Arab state carved out of the Ottoman Empire; those plans conflicted with the Balfour Declaration (1917), in which the British seemed to accept Zionism and to promise the Jews a national home in Palestine. Both of these plans conflicted with an Anglo-French agreement to divide the Near East between themselves.

The continuing national goals of the victors presented further obstacles to an idealistic "peace without victors." France was keenly conscious of its numerical inferiority to Germany and of the low birth rate that would keep it inferior. Naturally, France was eager to achieve a settlement that would permanently weaken Germany and preserve French political and military superiority. Italy sought the acquisition of *Italia Irredenta* ("unredeemed Italy"); Britain looked to its imperial interests; Japan pursued its own advantage in Asia; and the United States insisted on freedom of the seas, which favored American commerce, and on its right to maintain the Monroe Doctrine.

Finally, the peacemakers of 1919 faced a world still in turmoil. The greatest immediate threat appeared to be the spread of Bolshevism. While Lenin and his colleagues were distracted by civil war, the Allies landed small armies in Russia to help overthrow the Bolshevik regime. Communist governments were established in Bavaria and Hungary. Berlin also experienced a dangerous Communist uprising led by the "Spartacus group" (Communist extremists). The Allies were sufficiently worried by these developments to allow and to support suppression of these Communist movements by right-wing military forces. They even permitted an army of German volunteers to operate against the Bolsheviks in the Baltic states.

The fear of the spread of communism played a part in the thinking of the diplomats at Versailles, but it was far from dominant. The Germans kept playing on such fears as a way of getting better terms, but the Allies, and especially the French, would not hear of it. Fear of Germany remained the chief concern for France; attention to interests that were more traditional and more immediate governed the policies of the other Allies.

The Peace   The Paris settlement consisted of five separate treaties between the victors and the defeated powers. Formal sessions began on January 18, 1919, and the last treaty was signed on August 10, 1920. The notion of "a peace without victors" became a mockery when the Soviet Union (as Russia was now called) and Germany were excluded from the peace conference. The Germans were simply presented with a treaty and compelled to accept it, which fully justified their complaint that the treaty had not been negotiated but dictated. The principle of national self-determination was violated many times, as was unavoidable. Nevertheless, the diplomats of the small nations were angered by their exclusion from decision making. The undeserved adulation accorded Wilson on his arrival gradually turned into equally undeserved scorn. He had not abandoned his ideals lightly but had merely given way to the irresistible force of reality.

The League of Nations

Wilson put great faith in a new instrument for peace and justice, the League of Nations. Its covenant was an essential part of the peace treaty. The league was not intended as an international government but as a body of sovereign states that agreed to pursue common policies and to consult in the common interest, especially when war threatened. In that case the members promised to submit the matter to arbitration, to an international court, or to the League Council. Refusal to abide by this agreement would justify league intervention in the form of economic and even military sanctions.

But the league was unlikely to be effective because it had no armed forces at its disposal. Action required the unanimous consent of its council, consisting of Britain, France, Italy, the United States, Japan, and four other states that had temporary seats. The Covenant of the League bound its members to "respect and preserve" the territorial integrity of all its members, which was generally seen as a device to ensure the security of the victorious powers. The exclusion from the League Assembly of Germany and the Soviet Union further undermined the league's claim to evenhandedness.

Colonies

Another provision of the covenant dealt with colonial areas. They were to be placed under the "tutelage" of one of the great powers under league supervision and encouraged to advance toward independence. Because there were no teeth in this provision, little advance was made. Provisions for disarmament were equally ineffective. Members of the league remained fully sovereign and continued to pursue their own national interests.

Germany

In the west, the main territorial issue was the fate of Germany (see Map 33–6). Although a united Germany was less than fifty years old, no one seems to have thought of undoing Bismarck's work and dividing it into its component parts. The French would have liked to set up the Rhineland as a separate buffer state, but Lloyd George and Wilson would not permit that. Still, they could not ignore France's need for protection against a resurgent Germany. France received Alsace-Lorraine and the right to work the coal mines of the Saar for fifteen years. Germany west of the Rhine, and fifty kilometers east of it, was to be a demilitarized zone; Allied troops could stay on the west bank for fifteen years. In addition to this physical barrier to a new German attack, the treaty provided that Britain and the United States would guarantee to aid France if it were attacked by Germany. Such an attack

was made more unlikely by the permanent disarmament of Germany. Its army was limited to 100,000 men on long-term service; its fleet was all but eliminated; and it was forbidden to have war planes, submarines, tanks, heavy artillery, or poison gas. As long as these provisions were observed, France would be safe.

The East

The settlement in the east ratified the collapse of the great defeated empires that had ruled it for centuries. Germany's frontier lost much of Silesia and part of Prussia. East Prussia was cut off from the rest of Germany by a corridor carved out to give the revived state of Poland access to the sea. The Austro-Hungarian Empire disappeared. Most of its German-speaking people were gathered in the small Republic of Austria, cut off from the Germans of Bohemia and forbidden to unite with Germany. The Magyars occupied the much-reduced kingdom of Hungary.

The Czechs of Bohemia and Moravia joined with the Slovaks and Ruthenians to the east to form Czechoslovakia, and this new state also included several million unhappy Germans. The southern Slavs were united in the kingdom of Serbs, Croats, and Slovenes, or Yugoslavia. Italy gained the Trentino and Trieste. Romania gained Transylvania from Hungary and Bessarabia from Russia. Bulgaria lost territory to Greece and Yugoslavia. Finland, Estonia, Latvia, and Lithuania became independent states, and much of Poland was carved out of formerly Russian soil.

The old Ottoman Empire also disappeared. The new republic of Turkey was limited to little more than Constantinople and Asia Minor. Palestine and Iraq came under British control and Syria and Lebanon under French control as mandates of the League of Nations. Germany's former colonies in Africa were divided among Britain, France, Belgium, and South Africa. The German Pacific possessions went to Australia, New Zealand, and Japan.

In theory, the mandate system was meant to have the "advanced nations" govern the former colonies in the interests of the native peoples until they became ready to govern themselves. They were thus divided into three categories—A, B, and C—in descending order of their readiness for independence. In practice, most mandated territories were treated as colonies by the powers under whose "tutelage" they came. Not even one Class A mandate had achieved full independence twenty years after the signing of the treaty. Colonialism was to remain a problem even after World War II.

Reparations

Perhaps the most debated part of the peace settlement dealt with reparations for the damage done by Germany during the war. Before the armistice the Germans promised to pay compensation "for all damages done to the civilian population of the Allies and their property." The

	Austria-Hungary, 1914
	Germany, 1914
	Areas lost by Germany in 1919
	Areas lost by Bulgaria
	Areas lost by Russia
	Areas lost by The Ottoman Empire

Map 33–6   World War I peace settlement in Europe and the Middle East.   The map of central and eastern Europe, as well as that of the Middle East, underwent drastic revision after World War I. The enormous territorial losses suffered by Germany, Austria-Hungary, the Ottoman Empire, Bulgaria, and Russia were the other side of the coin represented by gains for France, Italy, Greece, and Romania and by the appearance, or reappearance, of at least eight new independent states from Finland in the north to Yugoslavia in the south. The mandate system for former Ottoman territories outside Turkey proper laid foundations for several new, mostly Arab, states in the Middle East.

Americans judged that the amount would be between $15 billion and $25 billion and that Germany would be able to pay that amount. However, France and Britain, worried about repaying their war debts to the United States, were eager to have Germany pay the full cost of the war, including pensions to survivors and dependents. There was general agreement that Germany could not afford to pay such a sum, whatever it might be, and no sum was fixed at the conference. In the meantime Germany was to pay $5 billion annually until 1921. At that time a final figure would be set, which Germany would have to pay within thirty years. The French did not regret the outcome. Either Germany would pay and be bled into impotence, or Germany would refuse to pay and justify French intervention.

To justify these huge reparation payments, the Allies inserted the notorious Clause 231 into the treaty:

> The Allied and Associated Governments affirm, and Germany accepts, the responsibility of Germany and her allies for causing all the loss and damage to which the Allied and Associated Governments and their nationals have been subjected as a consequence of the war imposed upon them by aggression of Germany and her allies.

The Germans, of course, bitterly resented the charge. They had lost territories containing millions of Germans and great quantities of badly needed natural resources; they were presented with an astronomical and apparently unlimited reparations bill. To add insult to injury, they had to admit to a war guilt that they did not feel. Finally, they had to accept the entire treaty as it was written by the victors, without any opportunity for negotiation. Germany's Chancellor Philipp Scheidemann (1865–1939) spoke of the treaty as the imprisonment of the German people and asked, "What hand would not wither that binds itself and us in these fetters?" But there was no choice. The Social Democrats and the Catholic Center Party formed a new government, and their representatives signed the treaty. These parties formed the backbone of the Weimar government that ruled Germany until 1933; they never overcame the stigma of accepting the Treaty of Versailles.

Evaluation of the Peace

Few peace settlements have been more attacked than the one negotiated in Paris in 1919. It was natural that the defeated powers should have objected to it, but the peace was soon bitterly criticized in the victorious countries as well. Many of the French thought that it failed to provide adequate security for France, because it tied that security to promises of aid from the unreliable Anglo-Saxon countries. In

England and the United States, liberals complained that the treaty violated the idealistic and liberal aims and principles that the Western leaders had professed. It was not a peace without victors. It did not end imperialism but attempted to promote the national interests of the winning nations. It violated the principles of national self-determination by leaving significant pockets of minorities outside the borders of their national homelands.

The most influential critic was John Maynard Keynes (1883–1946), a brilliant British economist who took part in the peace conference. When he saw the direction it was taking, he resigned in disgust and wrote a book called *The Economic Consequences of the Peace* (1920). It was a scathing attack, especially on reparations and the other economic clauses of the treaty. It was also a skillful assault on the negotiators, particularly on Wilson, who was depicted as a fool and a hypocrite. Keynes argued that the Treaty of Versailles was both immoral and unworkable. He called it a Carthaginian peace, referring to the utter destruction of Carthage by Rome after the Third Punic War (149–146 B.C.E.). He argued that such a peace would bring economic ruin and war to Europe unless it were repudiated. Keynes had a great effect on the British, who were already suspicious of France and glad of an excuse to withdraw from continental affairs. The decent and respectable position came to be one that aimed at revision of the treaty in favor of Germany.

Even more important was the book's influence in the United States. It fed the traditional tendency toward isolationism and gave powerful weapons to Wilson's enemies. Wilson's own political mistakes helped prevent American ratification of the treaty. Consequently, America was out of the League of Nations and not bound to defend France. Britain, therefore, was also free from its obligation to France. France was left to protect itself without adequate means to do so for long.

Many of the attacks on the Treaty of Versailles are unjustified. It was not a Carthaginian peace. Germany was neither dismembered nor ruined. Reparations could be and were scaled down, and until the great world depression of the 1930s the Germans recovered a high level of prosperity. Complaints against the peace should also be measured against the peace the victorious Germans had imposed on Russia at Brest-Litovsk and their plans for a European settlement in case of victory. Both were far more severe than anything enacted at Versailles. The attempt at achieving self-determination for nationalities was less than perfect, but it was the best solution Europe had ever accomplished in that direction.

The peace, nevertheless, was unsatisfactory in important ways. The elimination of the Austro-Hungarian Empire, however inevitable that might seem, created serious problems. Economically it was disastrous, for it separated raw materials from manufacturing areas and producers from their markets by new boundaries and tariff walls. In hard times, this separation created friction and hostility that aggravated other quarrels also created by the peace treaties. Poland and especially Czechoslovakia contained unhappy German minorities. Czechoslovakia itself was a collection of nationalities that did not find it easy to live together as a nation. Disputes over territories in eastern Europe promoted further tension. The peace was inadequate on another level as well. It rested on a defeat that Germany did not admit. The Germans believed they had been cheated rather than defeated. The high moral principles proclaimed by the Allies also undercut the validity of the peace, for it plainly fell far short of those principles.

Finally, the great weakness of the peace was its failure to accept reality. Germany and Russia must inevitably play an important part in European affairs, yet they were excluded from the settlement and from the League of Nations. Given the many discontented parties, the peace was not self-enforcing; yet no satisfactory machinery for enforcing it was established. The league was never a serious force for this purpose. It was left to France, with no guarantee of support from Britain and no hope of help from the United States, to defend the new arrangements. Finland, the Baltic states, Poland, Romania, Czechoslovakia, and Yugoslavia were created or strengthened as a barrier to the westward expansion of Russian communism and as a threat in the rear to deter German revival. Most of these states, however, would have to rely on France in case of danger. France was simply not strong enough for the task if Germany were to rearm.

The tragedy of the Treaty of Versailles was that it was neither conciliatory enough to remove the desire for change, even at the cost of war, nor harsh enough to make another war impossible. A lasting peace required enforcing German disarmament while the more obnoxious clauses of the peace treaty were revised. Such a policy demanded continued attention to the problem, unity among the victors, and far-sighted leadership; none of these was present in adequate supply during the next two decades.

IN WORLD PERSPECTIVE

Imperialism and World War I

The outburst of European imperialism in the last part of the nineteenth century brought the Western countries into contact with almost all the inhabited areas of the world and intensified their activity in places where they had already been interested. The growth of industry, increased ease of transportation and communication, and the growth of a world economic system all tended to bring previously remote and isolated places into the orbit of the West. By the time of the outbreak of the war, European nations had divided all of Africa among themselves for exploitation in one way or another. The vast subcontinent of India had long been a British colony. The desirable parts of China were very much under European control for commercial purposes. Indo-China was under French rule. The islands of the Pacific had been divided among the powers. Much of the Middle East was under the nominal control of the Ottoman Empire, which was in its death throes and under European influence. The Monroe Doctrine made Latin America a protectorate of the United States. Japan, pushed out of its isolation, had itself become an imperial power at the expense of China and Korea.

The emergence of a new, powerful German state at the center of Europe upset the old balance of power and threatened the peace established in 1815. Germany's Chancellor Bismarck, however, created a new system of alliances that preserved the peace for as long as he remained in power. The new German emperor, William II, abandoned the policy of restraint and sought a new position of greater power and influence for his country. The result was a system of alliances that divided Europe into two armed camps and greatly increased the chances of a general war. What began as yet another Balkan War involving the European powers became a world war that profoundly influenced the rest of the world. As the terrible war of 1914–1918 dragged on, the real motives that had driven the European powers to fight gave way to public affirmations of the principles of nationalism and self-determination. The peoples under colonial rule took the public statements, and sometimes private promises, seriously and sought to win their independence and nationhood. For the most part they were disappointed by the peace settlement. The establishment of the League of Nations and the system of mandates in place of open colonial rule did not change much. The British Empire inherited vast territories from the defeated German and the defunct Ottoman Empire and was larger than ever. The French retained and expanded their holdings in Africa, the Pacific, and the Middle East. The Americans added to the islands they controlled in the Pacific. Japanese imperial ambitions were rewarded at the expense of China.

A glance at the new map of the world could give the impression that the old imperial nations, especially Britain and France, were more powerful than ever. However, that impression would be superficial and misleading. The great western European powers had paid an enormous price in lives, money, and will for their victory in the war. Colonial peoples pressed for the rights that were proclaimed as universal by the West but denied to their colonies; influential minorities in the countries that ruled them sympathized with colonial aspirations for independence. Tension between colonies and their ruling nations was a cause of instability in the world created by the Paris treaties of 1919.

Review Questions

1. What role did Bismarck envisage for the new Germany after 1871? How successful was he in carrying out his vision? Was he wise to tie Germany to Austria-Hungary?

2. Why and in what stages did Britain abandon "splendid isolation" at the turn of the century? Were the policies it pursued instead wise ones, or should Britain have followed a different course?

3. How did developments in the Balkans lead to the outbreak of World War I? What was the role of Serbia? Of Austria? Of Russia? What was the aim of German policy in July 1914? Did Germany want a general war?

4. Why did Germany lose World War I? Could Germany have won, or was victory never a possibility? Assess the settlement of Versailles. What were its benefits to Europe, and what were its drawbacks? Was the settlement too harsh or too conciliatory? Could it have secured lasting peace in Europe? How might it have been improved?

5. Why was Lenin successful in establishing Bolshevik rule in Russia? What role did Trotsky play? Was it wise policy for Lenin to take Russia out of the war?

Suggested Readings

L. ALBERTINI, *The Origins of the War of 1914*, 3 vols. (1952, 1957). Discursive but invaluable.

V. R. BERGHAHN, *Germany and the Approach of War in 1914* (1973). A work similar in spirit to both of Fischer's (see below) but stressing the importance of Germany's naval program.

R. BOSWORTH, *Italy and the Approach of the First World War* (1983). A fine analysis of Italian policy.

L. CECIL, *Wilhelm II: Prince and Emperor 1859–1900* (1989). The first part of a projected two-volume history of the Kaiser.

V. DEDIJER, *The Road to Sarajevo* (1966). The fullest account of the assassination that provoked World War I and its Balkan background.

S. B. FAY, *The Origins of the World War*, 2 vols. (1928). The best and most influential of the revisionist accounts.

F. FISCHER, *Germany's Aims in the First World War* (1967). An influential interpretation that stirred a great controversy in Germany and around the world by emphasizing Germany's role in bringing on the war.

F. FISCHER, *War of Illusions* (1975). A long and diffuse book that tries to connect German responsibility for the war with internal social, economic, and political developments.

I. GEISS, *July 1914* (1967). A valuable collection of documents by a student of Fritz Fischer. The emphasis is on German documents and responsibility.

M. GILBERT, *The First World War* (1994). A lively narrative that combines discussion of the battlefields with accounts of the home front.

O. J. HALE, *The Great Illusion 1900–1914* (1971). A fine survey of the period, especially good on public opinion.

M. B. HAYNE, *The French Foreign Office and the Origins of the First World War* (1993). An examination of the work of the influence on French policy of the professionals in the foreign service.

J. N. HORNE, *Labour at War: France and Britain, 1914–1918* (1991). An examination of a major issue on the home fronts.

J. JOLL, *The Origins of the First World War* (1984). A brief but thoughtful analysis.

P. KENNEDY, *The Rise of the Anglo-German Antagonism 1860–1914* (1980). An unusual and thorough analysis of the political, economic, and cultural roots of important diplomatic developments.

J. M. KEYNES, *The Economic Consequences of the Peace* (1920). The famous and influential attack on the Versailles Treaty.

L. LAFORE, *The Long Fuse* (1965). A readable account of the origins of World War I that focuses on the problem of Austria-Hungary.

W. L. LANGER, *The Diplomacy of Imperialism* (1935). A continuation of the previous study for the years 1890–1902.

W. L. LANGER, *European Alliances and Alignments*, 2nd ed. (1966). A splendid diplomatic history of the years 1871–1890.

B. H. LIDDELL HART, *The Real War 1914–1918* (1964). A fine short account by an outstanding military historian.

D. C. B. LIEVEN, *Russia and the Origins of the First World War* (1983). A good account of the forces that shaped Russian policy.

E. MANTOUX, *The Carthaginian Peace* (1952). A vigorous attack on Keynes's view (see Keynes, above).

J. STEINBERG, *Yesterday's Deterrent* (1965). An excellent study of Germany's naval policy and its consequences.

Z. STEINER, *Britain and the Origins of the First World War* (1977). A perceptive and informed account of the way British foreign policy was made in the years before the war.

A. J. P. TAYLOR, *The Struggle for Mastery in Europe, 1848–1918* (1954). Clever but controversial.

L. C. F. TURNER, *Origins of the First World War* (1970). Especially good on the significance of Russia and its military plans.

S. R. WILLIAMSON, JR., *Austria-Hungary and the Origins of the First World War* (1991). A valuable new study of a complex subject.

34 DEPRESSION, EUROPEAN DICTATORS, AND THE AMERICAN NEW DEAL

Anxiety over the spread of the Bolshevik Revolution was a fundamental factor of European politics during the 1920s and 1930s. Images like this Soviet portrait of Lenin as a heroic revolutionary conjured fears among people in the rest of Europe of a political force determined to overturn their social, political, and economic institutions. [Gemalde von A. M. Gerassimow, "Lenin as Agitator"/Bildarchiv Preussischer Kulturbesitz]

◆ After Versailles: Demands for Revision and Enforcement

◆ Toward the Great Depression in Europe

◆ The Soviet Experiment

◆ The Fascist Experiment in Italy

◆ German Democracy and Dictatorship

◆ The Great Depression and the New Deal in the United States

In World Perspective The Economic and Political Crisis

In the two decades that followed the conclusion of the Paris Settlement, the western world saw a number of experiments in politics and economic life. Two broad factors accounted for these experiments. First, the war, the Russian Revolution, and the peace treaty had transformed the political face of Europe. New political regimes had emerged in the wake of the collapse of the monarchies of Germany, Austria-Hungary, and Russia. These new governments immediately faced the problems of postwar reconstruction, economic dislocation, and nationalistic resentments. Most of these nations also included large groups that questioned the legitimacy of their governments.

Second, beginning in the early twenties, a major economic downturn that became known as the Great Depression began to spread across the world. It occurred through the combination of financial turmoil in the more advanced industrial nations and a collapse of commodity prices in the commodity-exporting countries. Faced with political instability and economic crisis, governments contrived various political and economic responses. In Europe these efforts often produced authoritarian regimes. In the United States the response to the Depression led to a much-increased role for the federal government in the life of the nation.

After Versailles: Demands for Revision and Enforcement

The Paris settlement fostered both resentment and discontent. Those resentments counted among the chief political factors in Europe for the next two decades. Germany had been humiliated. The arrangements for reparations led to endless haggling over payments. Various national groups in the successor states of the Austro-Hungarian Empire felt that injustice had been done in their particular cases of self-determination. There were demands for further border adjustments. On the other side, the victorious powers, and especially France, often believed that the provisions of the treaty were being inadequately enforced. Consequently, throughout the 1920s and into the 1930s demands either to revise or to enforce the Paris treaties contributed to domestic political turmoil across the Continent. All too many political figures were willing to fish in these troubled international waters for a large catch of domestic votes.

Toward the Great Depression in Europe

Three factors combined to bring about the intense severity and the extended length of the Great Depression. First, a financial crisis stemmed directly from the war and the peace settlement. To this was added a crisis in the production and distribution of goods in the world market. These two problems became intertwined in 1929, and as far as Europe was concerned they reached the breaking point in 1931. Finally, both of these difficulties became worse than they might have been because no major western European country or the United States provided strong, responsible economic leadership.

Financial Tailspin

As one of the chief victors in the war, France was determined to collect reparations from Germany. The United States was no less determined that its allies repay the wartime loans it had extended to them. The European allies also owed various debts to each other. German reparations were to provide the means of repaying the American and other allied debts. Most of the money that the Allies collected from each other also went to the United States.

The quest for payment of German reparations caused one of the major diplomatic crises of the 1920s; the crisis itself resulted in further economic

One of the last British soldiers killed on the western front in November 1918. The carnage of World War I was one of the main causes of European weakness and instability in the 1920s and 1930s. [American Stock/Archive Photos]

upheaval. In early 1923 the Allies—and France in particular—declared Germany to be in technical default of its reparation payments. On January 11, to ensure receipt of the hard-won reparations, French troops occupied the Ruhr mining and manufacturing district. The Weimar Republic ordered passive resistance that amounted to a general strike in the largest industrial region of the nation. Confronted with this tactic, the French government sent French civilians to run the German mines and railroads. France got its way. The Germans paid, but its victory cost France dearly. The English were alienated by the French heavy-handedness and took no part in the occupation. Britain became more suspicious of France and more sympathetic to Germany. The cost of the Ruhr occupation, moreover, vastly increased French as well as German inflation and damaged the French economy.

The political and economic turmoil of the Ruhr invasion led to international attempts to ease the German payment of reparations. The most famous of these were the Dawes Plan of 1924 and the Young Plan of 1929, both devised by Americans. At the same time, large amounts of American investment capital were pouring into Europe. However, by 1928 this lending decreased as American money became diverted into the booming New York stock market. The crash of Wall Street in October 1929—the result of virtually unregulated financial speculation—saw the loss of large amounts of money. Credit sharply contracted in the United States as numerous banks failed. Thereafter, little American capital was available for investment in Europe.

As the credit for Europe began to run out, a major financial crisis struck the continent. In May 1931 the Kreditanstalt

collapsed. The Kreditanstalt was a primary lending institution and major bank for much of central and eastern Europe. The German banking system consequently came under severe pressure and was saved only through government guarantees. As the German difficulties increased, U.S. president Herbert Hoover (1874–1964) announced in June 1931 a one-year moratorium on all payments of international debts. The Hoover moratorium was a prelude to the end of reparations. The Lausanne Conference of the summer of 1932 brought, in effect, the era of reparations to a close. The next year the debts owed to the United States were settled either through small token payments or simply through default.

Problems in Agricultural Commodities

The 1920s witnessed a contraction in the market demand for European goods relative to the Continent's productive capacity. This problem originated both within and outside Europe. In both instances the difficulty arose from agriculture. Better methods of farming, improved strains of wheat, expanded tillage, and more extensive transport facilities all over the globe vastly increased the quantity of grain. World wheat prices fell to record lows. Although this helped consumers, it decreased the income of European farmers. At the same time, higher industrial wages raised the cost of the industrial goods that farmers or peasants used. Consequently, they also had great difficulty paying off their mortgages and normal annual operation debts. These problems were especially acute in central and eastern Europe and abetted farmers' disillusionment with liberal politics. German farmers, for example, would become prime supporters of the National Socialist Workers Party (Nazis).

Outside Europe similar problems affected other producers of agricultural commodities. The prices they received for their products plummeted. Government-held reserves reached record levels. This glut of major world commodities involved the supplies of wheat, sugar, coffee, rubber, wool, and lard. The people who produced these goods in underdeveloped nations could no longer make enough money to buy finished goods from industrial Europe. As world credit collapsed, the economic position of these commodity producers worsened. Commodity production had simply outstripped world demand.

The result of the collapse in the agricultural sector of the world economy and the financial turmoil was stagnation and depression for European industry. Coal, iron, and textiles had depended largely on international markets. Unemployment spread from these industries to those producing finished consumer goods. Persistent unemployment in Great Britain and, to a lesser extent, in Germany during the 1920s had created "soft" domestic markets. The policies of reduced spending with which the governments confronted the Depression further weakened domestic demand. By the early 1930s the Depression was feeding on itself.

Depression and Government Policy

The Depression did not mean absolute economic decline or total unemployment. However, the economic downturn spread potential as well as actual insecurity. People in nearly all walks of life feared the loss of their own economic security and lifestyles. The Depression also frustrated normal social and economic expectations. Even the employed often seemed to make no progress; and their anxieties created a major source of social discontent.

The governments of the late 1920s and the early 1930s were not particularly well suited in either structure or ideology to confront these problems. The electorates demanded action. The government response depended largely on the severity of the Depression in a particular country and on the self-confidence of the nation's political system.

Great Britain and France undertook moderate political experiments. In 1924 the Labour Party in Great Britain established itself as a viable governing party by forming a short-lived government. It again formed a ministry in 1929. Under the pressure of the Depression and at the urging of King George V (r. 1910–1936), the Labour prime minister Ramsay MacDonald (1866–1937) organized a National Government, which was a coalition of the Labour, Conservative, and Liberal Parties. It remained in power until 1935, when a Conservative ministry led by Stanley Baldwin (1867–1947) replaced it.

The most important French political experiment was the Popular Front Ministry, which came to office in 1936. It was composed of Socialists, Radicals, and Communists—the first time that Socialists and Communists had cooperated in a ministry. The Popular Front addressed major labor problems in the French economy. By 1938 various changes in the Cabinet in effect brought the Popular Front to an end.

The political changes in Britain and France were only of domestic significance. But the political experiments of the 1920s and 1930s that reshaped world history and civilization involved the establishment of a Soviet government in Russia, a Fascist regime in Italy, and a Nazi dictatorship in Germany.

The Soviet Experiment

The consolidation of the Bolshevik Revolution in Russia established the most extensive and durable of all twentieth-century authoritarian governments. The Communist Party of the Soviet Union retained power from 1917 until the end of 1991, and its presence influenced the political history of Europe and much of the rest of the world as did no other single factor. Unlike the Italian Fascists or the German National Socialists, the Bolsheviks seized power violently through revolution. For several years they confronted armed opposition, and their leaders long felt insecure about their hold on the country. The Communist Party was not a mass party nor a nationalistic one. Its early membership rarely exceeded more than 1 percent of the Russian population. The Bolsheviks confronted a much less industrialized economy than that in Italy or Germany. They believed in and practiced the collectivization of economic life attacked by the right-wing dictatorships. The Marxist-Leninist ideology was broader than the nationalism of the Fascists and the racism of the Nazis. Communism was an exportable commodity. The Communists regarded their government and their revolution not as part of a national history but as epoch-making events in the history of the world and the development of humanity. Fear of communism and determination to stop its spread became one of the leading political forces in western Europe and the United States for most of the rest of the century. Policies flowing from that opposition would influence their relationships to much of the rest of the world.

War Communism

Within the Soviet Union the Red Army under the organizational genius of Leon Trotsky (1879–1940) had suppressed internal and foreign military opposition to the new government. Within months of the revolution, a new secret police, known as *Cheka*, appeared. Throughout the civil war Lenin (1870–1924) had declared that the Bolshevik Party, as the vanguard of the revolution, was imposing the dictatorship of the proletariat. Political and economic administration became highly centralized. All major decisions flowed from the top in a nondemocratic manner. Under the economic policy of "War Communism," the revolutionary government confiscated and then operated the banks, the transport facilities, and heavy industry. The state also forcibly requisitioned grain and shipped it from the countryside to feed the army and the workers in the cities. The fact of the civil war permitted suppression of possible resistance to this economic policy.

"War Communism" helped the Red Army defeat its opponents. The revolution had survived and triumphed. The policy, however, generated domestic opposition to the Bolsheviks, who in 1920 numbered only about 600,000 members. The alliance of workers and peasants forged by the slogan of "Peace, Bread, and Land" had begun to dissolve. Many Russians were no longer willing to make the sacrifices demanded by the central party bureaucrats. In 1920 and 1921 serious strikes occurred. Peasants were discontented and

During the civil war in the Soviet Union hunger and starvation haunted the countryside. Here a group of malnourished children posed for a photograph.

[Bildarchiv Preussischer Kulturbesitz]

resisted the requisition of grain. In March 1921 the navy mutinied at Kronstadt. The Red Army crushed the rebellion with grave loss of life. Each of these incidents suggested that the proletariat itself was opposing the dictatorship of the proletariat. Also, by late 1920 it had become clear that further revolution would not sweep across the rest of Europe. For the time being the Soviet Union would constitute a vast island of revolutionary socialism in the larger sea of worldwide capitalism.

The New Economic Policy

Under these difficult conditions Lenin made a crucial strategic retreat. In March 1921, following the Kronstadt mutiny, he outlined the New Economic Policy, normally referred to as NEP. Apart from what he termed "the commanding heights" of banking, heavy industry, transportation, and international commerce, considerable private economic enterprise was allowed. In particular, peasants could farm for a profit. They would pay taxes like other citizens, but they could sell their surplus grain on the open market. The NEP was consistent with Lenin's earlier conviction that the Russian peasantry held the key to the success of the revolution. After 1921 the countryside did become more stable, and a secure food supply seemed assured for the cities. Similar free enterprise flourished within light industry and domestic retail trade. By 1927 industrial production had reached its 1913 level. The revolution seemed to have transformed Russia into a land of small family farms and privately owned shops and businesses.

Stalin Versus Trotsky

The NEP had caused sharp disputes within the Politburo, the highest governing committee of the Communist Party. The partial return to capitalism seemed to some members nothing less than a betrayal of sound Marxist principles. These frictions increased as Lenin's firm hand disappeared. In 1922 he suffered a stroke and never again dominated party affairs; in 1924 Lenin died. In the ensuing power vacuum, an intense struggle for leadership of the party commenced. Two factions emerged. One was led by Trotsky; the other by Joseph Stalin (1879–1953), who had become general secretary of the party in 1922. Shortly before his death Lenin had criticized both men. He was especially harsh toward Stalin. However, the general secretary's base of power lay with the party membership and with the daily management of party affairs. Consequently, he was able to withstand the posthumous strictures of Lenin.

Each faction wanted to control the party, but the struggle was fought out over the question of Russia's path toward industrialization and the future of the Communist revolutionary movement. Trotsky, speaking for what became known as the left wing, urged rapid industrialization and looked to voluntary collectivization of farming by poor peasants as a means of increasing agricultural production. Trotsky further argued that the revolution in Russia could succeed only if new revolutions took place elsewhere. Russia needed the skills and wealth of other nations to build its own economy. As Trotsky's influence within the party began to wane, he also demanded that party members be permitted to criticize the policies of the government and the party. Trotsky, however, was a latecomer to the advocacy of open discussion. When in control of the Red Army, he had been an unflinching disciplinarian.

A right-wing faction opposed Trotsky. Although its chief ideological voice was that of Nikolai Bukharin (1888–1938), the editor of *Pravda*, the official party paper, Stalin was its true political manipulator. In the mid-1920s this group pressed for the continuation of Lenin's NEP and a policy of relatively slow industrialization.

Stalin was the ultimate victor in these intraparty rivalries. Unlike the other early Bolshevik leaders, he had not spent a long exile in western Europe. He was much less an intellectual and internationalist. He was also much more brutal. His handling of various recalcitrant national groups within Russia after the revolution had shocked even Lenin. Stalin's power lay in his command of bureaucratic and administrative methods. He was neither a brilliant writer nor an effective public speaker; however, he mastered the crucial, if dull, details of party structure, including admission and promotion. That mastery meant that he could draw on the support of the lower levels of the party apparatus when he clashed with other leaders.

In the mid-1920s Stalin supported Bukharin's position on economic development. In 1924 he also enunciated, in op-

A Communist Woman Demands a New Family Life

While Lenin sought to consolidate the Bolshevik revolution against internal and external enemies, there existed within the young Soviet Union a vast utopian impulse to change and reform virtually every social institution that had existed before the revolution or that Communists associated with capitalist society. Alexandra Kollontai (1872–1952) was a spokesperson of the extreme political left within the early Soviet Union. There had been much speculation on how the end of bourgeois society might change the structure of the family and the position of women. In this passage written in 1920 Kollontai states one of the most idealistic visions of this change. During the years immediately after the revolution, extreme rumors circulated in both Europe and America about sexual and family experimentation in the Soviet Union. Statements such as this fostered such rumors. Kollontai herself later became a supporter of Stalin and a Soviet diplomat.

Why did Kollontai see the restructuring of the family as essential to the establishment of a new kind of Communist society? Would these changes make people loyal to that society? What changes in society does the kind of economic independence she seeks for women presuppose? What might childhood be like in this society?

There is no escaping the fact: the old type of family has seen its day. It is not the fault of the Communist State, it is the result of the changed conditions of life. The family is ceasing to be a necessity of the State, as it was in the past; on the contrary, it is worse than useless, since it needlessly holds back the female workers from more productive and far more serious work. . . . But on the ruins of the former family we shall soon see a new form rising which will involve altogether different relations between men and women, and which will be a union of affection and comradeship, a union of two equal members of the Communist society, both of them free, both of them independent, both of them workers. No more domestic "servitude" of women. No more inequality within the family. No more

fear on the part of the woman lest she remain without support or aid with little ones in her arms if her husband should desert her. The woman in the Communist city no longer depends on her husband but on her work. It is not her husband but her robust arms which will support her. There will be no more anxiety as to the fate of her children. The State of the Workers will assume responsibility for these. Marriage will be purified of all its material elements, of all money calculations, which constitute a hideous blemish on family life in our days. . . .

The woman who is called upon to struggle in the great cause of the liberation of the workers—such a woman should know that in the new State there will be no more room for such petty divisions as were formerly understood: "These are my own children, to them I owe all my maternal solicitude, all my affection; those are your children, my neighbour's children; I am not concerned with them. I have enough to do with my own." Henceforth the worker-mother, who is conscious of her social function, will rise to a point where she no longer differentiates between yours and mine; she must remember that there are henceforth only our children, those of the Communist State, the common possession of all the workers.

The Worker's State has need of a new form of relation between the sexes. The narrow and exclusive affection of the mother for her own children must expand until it embraces all the children of the great proletarian family. In place of the indissoluble marriage based on the servitude of woman, we shall see rise the free union, fortified by the love and mutual respect of the two members of the Workers' State, equal in their rights and in their obligations. In place of the individual and egotistic family there will arise a great universal family of workers, in which all the workers, men and women, will be, above all, workers, comrades.

From *Communism and the Family* by Alexandra Kollontai, as reprinted in Rudolf Schlesinger, ed. and trans., *The Family in the USSR*, London: Routledge and Kegan Paul, 1949, pp. 67–69. Reprinted by permission.

---

position to Trotsky, the doctrine of "socialism in one country." He urged that socialism could be achieved in Russia alone. Russian success did not depend on the fate of the revolution elsewhere. Stalin thus nationalized the previously international scope of the Marxist revolution. He cunningly used the apparatus of the party and his control over the Central Committee of the Communist Party to edge out Trotsky and his supporters. By 1927 Trotsky had been removed from all his offices, ousted from the party, and exiled to Siberia. In 1929 he was expelled from Russia and eventually moved to Mexico, where he was murdered in 1940 by one of Stalin's

agents. With the removal of Trotsky, Stalin was firmly in control of the Soviet state. It remained to be seen where he would direct its course and what "socialism in one country" would mean in practice.

Decision for Rapid Industrialization

While the capitalist economies of western Europe floundered during the Depression, the Soviet Union registered tremendous industrial advance. As usual in Russia, the direction and impetus came from the top. Stalin far exceeded his tsarist predecessors in the intensity of state coercion and terror he brought to the task. Russia achieved its stunning economic growth during the 1930s only at the cost of literally millions of human lives and the degradation of millions more. Stalin's economic policy clearly proved that his earlier rivalry with Trotsky had been a matter of political power rather than one of substantial ideological difference.

Through 1928 Lenin's NEP, as championed by Bukharin with Stalin's support, had steered Soviet economic development. Private ownership and enterprise were permitted to flourish in the countryside to ensure enough food for the workers in the cities. A few farmers, the *kulaks*, had become prosperous. They probably numbered less than 5 percent of the rural population. During 1928 and 1929 they and other farmers withheld grain from the market because prices were too low. Food shortages occurred in the cities and caused potential unrest. The goals of the NEP were no longer being fulfilled. Sometime during these troubled months, Stalin came to a momentous decision. Russia must industrialize rapidly to match the economic and military power of the West. Agriculture must be collectivized to produce sufficient grain for food and export and to free peasant labor for the factories. This program, which basically embraced Trotsky's earlier economic position, unleashed a second Russian revolution. The costs and character of "socialism in one country" now became clear.

Agricultural Policy   In 1929 Stalin ordered party agents into the countryside to confiscate any hoarded wheat. The *kulaks* bore the blame for the grain shortages. As part of the general plan to erase the private ownership of land and to collectivize farming, the government undertook a program to eliminate the *kulaks* as a class. A *kulak*, however, soon came to mean any peasant who opposed Stalin's policy. In the countryside, peasants and farmers at all levels of wealth resisted stubbornly. They were determined to keep their land. They wreaked their own vengeance on the policy of collectivization by slaughtering more than 100 million horses and cattle between 1929 and 1933. The situation in the countryside amounted to open warfare. The peasant resistance caused Stalin to call a brief halt to the process in March 1930. He justified the slowdown on the grounds of "dizziness from success."

Soon thereafter, the drive to collectivize the farms was renewed with vehemence, and the costs remained high. As many as 10 million peasants were killed, and millions of others were sent forcibly to collective farms or labor camps. Initially, because of the turmoil on the land, agricultural production fell. There was famine in 1932 and 1933. Milk and meat remained in short supply because of the livestock slaughter. Yet Stalin persevered. The *kulaks* were uprooted from their farms and sent to Siberia or other regions far from their homes. Peasants who remained had their lands incor-

porated into large collective farms. The state provided the machinery for these units through machine-tractor stations. The state thus retained control over major farm machines, a monopoly that was a powerful weapon.

Collectivization dramatically changed Russian farming. In 1928 approximately 98 percent of Russian farmland consisted of small peasant holdings. Ten years later, despite all the opposition, over 90 percent of the land had been collectivized, and the quantity of farm produce directly handled by the government had risen by 40 percent. The government now had primary direction over the food supply. The farmers and peasants could no longer determine whether there would be stability or unrest in the cities. Stalin and the Communist Party had won the battle of the wheat fields, but they had not solved the problem of producing enough grain. That difficulty has plagued the former Soviet Union to the present day.

Five-Year Plans   The revolution in agriculture had been undertaken for the sake of industrialization. The increased grain supply was to feed the labor force and provide exports to finance the imports required for industrial development. The industrial achievement of the Soviet Union between 1928 and World War II was one of the most striking accomplishments of the twentieth century. Russia made a more rapid advance toward economic growth than any other nation in the western world has ever achieved during any similar period of time. By even the conservative estimates of western observers, Soviet industrial production rose approximately 400 percent between 1928 and 1940. The production of iron, steel, coal, electrical power, tractors, combines, railway cars, and other heavy machinery was emphasized. Few consumer goods were produced. The labor for this development was supplied internally. Capital was raised from the export of grain, even at the cost of internal shortage. The technology was generally borrowed from already industrialized nations.

The organizational vehicle for industrialization was a series of five-year plans first begun in 1928. The State Planning Commission, or Gosplan, oversaw the program. It set goals of production and organized the economy to meet them. Coordinating all facets of production was immensely difficult and complicated. Deliveries of materials from mines or factories had to be assured before the next unit could carry out its part of the plan. There was many a slip between the cup and the lip. The troubles in the countryside were harmful. A vast program of propaganda was undertaken to sell the five-year plans to the Russian people and to elicit cooperation. The industrial labor force, however, soon became subject to regimentation similar to that being imposed on the peasants. By the close of the 1930s the accomplishment of the three five-year plans was truly impressive and probably allowed the Soviet Union to survive the German invasion. Industries that had never existed in Russia now challenged and in some cases, such as tractor production, surpassed their counterparts in the rest of the world. Large, new industrial cities had been built and populated by hundreds of thousands of people.

Many non-Russian contemporaries looked at the Soviet economic experiment quite uncritically. While the capitalist world lay in the throes of the Depression, the Soviet economy had grown at a pace never realized in the West. The American writer Lincoln Steffens (1866–1936) reported after a trip to Russia, "I have seen the future and it works." Beatrice (1858–1943) and Sydney Webb (1859–1947), the British Fabian Socialists, spoke of "a new civilization" in the Soviet Union. These and other similar writers ignored the shortages in consumer goods and the poor housing. More important, they seem to have had little idea of the social cost of the Soviet achievement. Millions of people had been killed and millions more uprooted. The total picture of suffering and human loss during those years will probably never be known; the deprivation and sacrifice of Soviet citizens far exceeded anything described by Marx and Engels in relation to nineteenth-century industrialization in western Europe.

The Purges

Stalin's decisions to industrialize rapidly and to move against the peasants aroused internal political opposition because they were departures from the policies of Lenin. In 1929 Stalin forced Bukharin, the fervent supporter of the NEP and his own former ally, off the Politburo. Little detailed information is known about further opposition, but it does seem to have existed among lower-level party followers of Bukharin and other previous opponents of rapid industrialization. Sometime in 1933 Stalin began to fear that he would lose control over the party apparatus and that effective rivals might emerge. These fears were probably produced as much by his own paranoia as by real plots. Nevertheless, they resulted in the Great Purges, among the most mysterious and horrendous political events of this century. The purges were not understood at the time and are still not fully comprehended today.

On December 1, 1934, Sergei Kirov (1888–1934), the popular party chief of Leningrad (formerly Saint Petersburg and Petrograd) and a member of the Politburo, was assassinated. In the wake of the shooting thousands of people were arrested, and still more were expelled from the party and sent to labor camps. At the time it was believed that Kirov had been murdered by opponents of the regime. Direct or indirect complicity in the crime became the normal accusation against those whom Stalin attacked. It now seems practically certain that Stalin himself authorized Kirov's assassination to forestall any threat from the Leningrad leader.

The purges after Kirov's death were just the beginning of a larger process. Between 1936 and 1938 spectacular show trials were held in Moscow. Previous high Soviet leaders, in-

An enormous propaganda effort accompanied the Soviet Five-Year Plans. This poster proclaims, "For the betterment of the Soviet people we are building an electricity plant." [Bildarchiv Preussischer Kulturbesitz]

cluding former members of the Politburo, publicly confessed political crimes. They were convicted and executed. It is still not certain why they made their palpably false confessions. Still other leaders and lower-level party members were tried in private and shot. Thousands of people received no trial at all. The purges touched persons in all areas of party life. It is inexplicable why some were executed, others sent to labor camps, and still others left unmolested. After the civilian party members had been purged, the prosecutors turned against the army. Important officers, including heroes of the civil war, were killed. Within the party itself, hundreds of thousands of members were expelled, and applicants for membership were removed from the rolls. The exact numbers of executions, imprisonments, and expulsions are unknown but certainly ran into the millions.

The trials and purges astonished observers from outside the Soviet Union. Nothing quite like this phenomenon had ever been seen. Political murders and executions were not new, but the absurd confessions were novel. The scale of the political turmoil was also unprecedented. The Russians themselves did not believe or comprehend what was occurring. There existed no national emergency or crisis. There were only accusations of sympathy for Trotsky or of complicity in Kirov's murder or of other nameless crimes. If a rational explanation is to be sought, it probably must be found in Stalin's concern for his own power. In effect, the purges created a new party structure absolutely loyal to him. The "old Bolsheviks" of the October Revolution were among his earliest targets. They and others active in the first years of the revolution knew how far Stalin had moved from Lenin's policies. New, younger party members replaced those executed or expelled. The newcomers knew little of old Russia or of the

By the mid-1930s Stalin's purges had eliminated many leaders and other members from the Soviet Communist Party. This photograph of a meeting of a party congress in 1936 shows a number of the surviving leaders with Stalin, who sits fourth from the right in the front row. To his left is Vyacheslav Molotov, long-time foreign minister. The first person on the left in the front row is Nikita Khrushchev, who headed the Soviet Union in the late 1950s and early 1960s. [Itar-Tass/Sovfoto/Eastfoto]

ideals of the original Bolsheviks. They had not been loyal to Lenin, Trotsky, or any Soviet leader except Stalin himself.

Despite the flagrant violence and widespread repression of the Soviet experiment, it found many sympathizers throughout the world. Some people did not know of its repression; others ignored those events. The Soviet Union almost immediately after the Bolshevik seizure of power had fostered the organization of Communist Parties subservient to Moscow influence throughout the world. Others who were not formally members of these parties often sympathized with what they believed or hoped were the goals of the Soviet Union. During at least the first fifty years of its existence the Soviet Union managed to capture the imagination of some intellectuals in the West and in other parts of the globe who hoped for a utopian egalitarian transformation of society. During much of the 1930s, to these and other people, the Soviet Union also appeared as an enemy to the fascist experiments in Italy and Germany. The Marxist ideology championed by the Soviet Union appeared to many people living in the European colonial empires as a vehicle for freeing themselves from the colonial situation. The Soviet Union welcomed and trained many such anti-colonial leaders and offered other support to their causes. In the wake of the collapse of the Soviet Union at the close of the century and what is now known about its repression it is difficult to understand the power its presence exercised over many people's political imaginations around the world, but that attraction was one of the most fundamental factors in world politics from the 1920s through at least the early 1970s.

The Fascist Experiment in Italy

The first authoritarian political experiment in western Europe that arose in part from fears of the spread of Bolshevism occurred in Italy. The general term *fascist*, which has been

used to describe the various right-wing dictatorships that arose between the wars, was derived from the Italian Fascist movement of Benito Mussolini (1883–1945).

While scholars still dispute the exact meaning of *fascism* as a political term, the governments regarded as fascist were antidemocratic, anti-Marxist, antiparliamentary, and frequently antisemitic. They hoped to hold back the spread of Bolshevism, which seemed a real threat at the time. They sought a world that would be safe for the middle class, small businesses, owners of moderate amounts of property, and small farmers. The fascist regimes rejected the political inheritance of the French Revolution and of nineteenth-century liberalism. Their adherents believed that normal parliamentary politics and parties sacrificed national honor and greatness to petty party disputes. They wanted to overcome the class conflict of Marxism and the party conflict of liberalism by consolidating the various groups and classes within the nation for great national purposes. As Mussolini declared in 1931, "The fascist conception of the state is all-embracing, and outside of the state no human or spiritual values can exist, let alone be desirable."[1] Fascist governments were usually single-party dictatorships characterized by terrorism and police surveillance. These dictatorships were rooted in the base of mass political parties.

Rise of Mussolini

The Italian *Fasci di Combattimento* ("Band of Combat") was founded in 1919 in Milan. Most of its members were war veterans who felt that the sacrifices of World War I had been in vain. They resented Italy's failure to gain the city of Fiume,

---

[1]Quoted in Denis Mack Smith, *Italy: A Modern History* (Ann Arbor: University of Michigan Press, 1959), p. 412.

toward the northern end of the Adriatic Sea, at the Paris conference. They feared socialism, inflation, and labor unrest.

Their leader, Benito Mussolini, was the son of a blacksmith. After having been a schoolteacher, and a day laborer, he became active in Italian socialist politics and by 1912 had become editor of the socialist newspaper *Avanti*. In 1914 Mussolini broke with the socialists and supported Italian entry into the war on the side of the Allies. His interventionist position lost him the editorship of *Avanti*. He then established his own paper, *Il Popolo d'Italia*. Later he served in the army and was wounded. In 1919 Mussolini was just another Italian politician. His *Fasci* organization was one of many small political groups in a country characterized by such entities. As a politician, Mussolini was an opportunist par excellence. He could change his ideas and principles to suit every new occasion. Action for him was always more important than thought or rational justification. His one real rule was political survival.

Postwar Italian politics was a muddle. During the war the Italian Parliament had virtually ceased to function. Ministers had ruled by decree. However, many Italians were dissatisfied with the parliamentary system as it then existed. They felt that Italy had emerged from the war as less than a victorious nation, had not been treated as a great power at the peace conference, and had not received the territories it deserved. The main spokesman for this discontent was the extreme nationalist writer Gabriele D'Annunzio (1863–1938). In 1919 he captured Fiume with a force of patriotic Italians. The Italian army, enforcing the terms of the Versailles Treaty, eventually drove him out. D'Annunzio had provided the example of the political use of a nongovernmental military force. Removing him from Fiume made the parliamentary ministry seem unpatriotic.

Between 1919 and 1921 Italy was also wracked by social turmoil. Numerous industrial strikes occurred, and workers occupied factories. Peasants seized uncultivated land from large estates. Parliamentary and constitutional government seemed incapable of dealing with this unrest. The Socialist Party had captured a plurality of seats in the Chamber of Deputies in 1919. A new Catholic Popular Party had also done well. Both appealed to the working and agrarian classes. However, neither party would cooperate with the other, and parliamentary deadlock resulted. Under these conditions, many Italians honestly—and still others conveniently—believed that a Communist revolution might break out.

Initially, Mussolini was uncertain which way the political winds were blowing. He first supported the factory occupations and land seizures. Never one to be concerned with consistency, however, he soon reversed himself. He had discovered that many upper-class and middle-class Italians who were pressured by inflation and who feared property loss had no sympathy for the workers or the peasants. They want-

Mussolini poses with supporters the day after the Black Shirt March on Rome intimidated the King of Italy into making him Prime Minister. [Bildarchiv Preussischer Kulturbesitz]

ed order rather than some vague social justice that might harm their own interests. Consequently, Mussolini and his Fascists took direct action in the face of the government inaction. They formed local squads who terrorized Socialist supporters. They attacked strikers and farm workers and protected strikebreakers. Conservative land and factory owners were grateful to the terrorists. The officers and institutions of the law simply ignored these crimes. By early 1922 the Fascists controlled the local government in many parts of northern Italy.

In 1921 Mussolini and thirty-four of his followers had been elected to the Chamber of Deputies. Their importance grew as the local Fascists gained more direct power. The Fascist movement now had hundreds of thousands of supporters. In October 1922 the Fascists, dressed in their characteristic black shirts, began a march on Rome. Intimidated, King Victor Emmanuel III (r. 1900–1946) refused to authorize using the army against the marchers. No other single decision so ensured a Fascist seizure of power. The Cabinet resigned in protest. On October 29 the monarch telegraphed Mussolini in Milan and asked him to become prime minister. The next day Mussolini arrived in Rome by sleeping car and, as head of the government, greeted his followers when they entered the city.

Technically, Mussolini had come into office by legal means. The monarch did have the power to appoint the prime minister. Mussolini, however, had no majority in the Chamber of Deputies. Behind the legal facade of his assumption of power lay the months of terrorist disruption and intimidation and the threat of the Fascists' October march itself.

Mussolini Heaps Contempt on Political Liberalism

The political tactics of the Italian Fascists wholly disregarded the liberal belief in the rule of law and the consent of the governed. In 1923 Mussolini explained why the Fascists so hated and repudiated these liberal principles. Note his emphasis on the idea of the twentieth century as a new historical epoch requiring a new kind of politics and his undisguised praise of force in politics.

Who would be some nineteenth-century liberal political leaders included in Mussolini's attack? Why might Mussolini's audience have been receptive to these views? What events or developments within liberal states allowed Mussolini to portray liberalism as so corrupt and powerless?

Liberalism is not the last word, nor does it represent the definitive formula on the subject of the art of government. . . . Liberalism is the product and the technique of the nineteenth century. . . . It does not follow that the Liberal scheme of government, good for the nineteenth century, for a century, that is, dominated by two such phenomena as the growth of capitalism and the strengthening of the sentiment of nationalism, should be adapted to the twentieth century, which announces itself already with characteristics sufficiently different from those that marked the preceding century. . . .

I challenge Liberal gentlemen to tell if ever in history there has been a government that was based solely on popular consent and that renounced all use of force whatsoever. A government so constructed there has never been

and never will be. Consent is an ever-changing thing like the shifting sand on the sea coast. it can never be permanent: It can never be complete. . . . If it be accepted as an axiom that any system of government whatever creates malcontents, how are you going to prevent this discontent from overflowing and constituting a menace to the stability of the State? You will prevent it by force. By the assembling of the greatest force possible. By the inexorable use of this force whenever it is necessary. Take away from any government whatsoever force—and by force is meant physical, armed force—and leave it only its immortal principles, and that government will be at the mercy of the first organized group that decides to overthrow it. Fascism now throws these lifeless theories out to rot. . . . The truth evident now to all who are not warped by [liberal] dogmatism is that men have tired of liberty. They have made an orgy of it. Liberty is today no longer the chaste and austere virgin for whom the generations of the first half of the last century fought and died. For the gallant, restless and bitter youth who face the dawn of a new history there are other words that exercise a far greater fascination, and those words are: order, hierarchy, discipline. . . .

Know then, once and for all, that Fascism knows no idols and worships no fetishes. It has already stepped over, and if it be necessary it will turn tranquilly and step again over, the more or less putrescent corpse of the Goddess of Liberty.

Benito Mussolini, "Force and Consent" (1923), as trans. in Jonathan F. Scott and Alexander Baltzly, eds., *Readings in European History Since 1814* (New York: F. S. Crofts, 1931), pp. 680–682.

The Fascists in Power

Mussolini had not really expected to be appointed prime minister. He moved cautiously to consolidate his power. He succeeded because of the impotence of his rivals, his own effective use of his office, his power over the masses, and his sheer ruthlessness. On November 23, 1922, the king and Parliament granted Mussolini dictatorial authority for one year to bring order to the lower levels of the government. Wherever possible, Mussolini appointed Fascists to office. Late in 1924, at Mussolini's behest, Parliament changed the election law. Previously parties had been represented in the Chamber of Deputies in proportion to the popular vote cast for them. According to the new election law, the party that gained the largest popular vote (with a minimum of at least 25 percent) received two thirds of the seats in the chamber. Coalition government, with all its compromises and hesitations, would

no longer be necessary. In the election of 1924 the Fascists won a great victory and complete control of the Chamber of Deputies. They used that majority to end legitimate parliamentary life. A series of laws passed in 1925 and 1926 permitted Mussolini, in effect, to rule by decree. In 1926 all other political parties were dissolved, and Italy was transformed into a single-party, dictatorial state.

The Italian dictator made one important domestic departure that brought him significant political dividends. Through the Lateran Accord of February 1929 the Roman Catholic church and the Italian state made peace with each other. Ever since the armies of Italian unification had seized papal lands in the 1860s the Church had been hostile to the State. The popes had remained virtual prisoners in the Vatican after 1870. The agreement of 1929 recognized the pope as the temporal ruler of Vatican City. The Italian government agreed to pay an indemnity to the papacy for confiscated land. The state also recognized Catholicism as the religion of the nation, exempted church property from taxes, and allowed church law to govern marriage. The Lateran Accord brought further respectability to Mussolini's authoritarian regime.

German Democracy and Dictatorship

The Weimar Republic

The Weimar Republic was born from the defeat of the imperial army, the revolution of 1918 against the Hohenzollerns, and the hopes of German Liberals and Social Democrats. Its name derived from the city in which its constitution was written and promulgated in August 1919. While the constitution was being debated, the republic, headed by the Social Democrats, accepted the humiliating terms of the Versailles Treaty. Although its officials had signed only under the threat of an Allied invasion, the republic was nevertheless permanently associated with the national disgrace and the economic burdens of the treaty. Throughout the 1920s the government of the republic was required to fulfill the economic and military provisions imposed by the Paris settlement. It became all too easy for nationalists and military figures whose policies had brought on the tragedy and defeat of the war to blame the young republic and the socialists for the results of the conflict. In Germany, more than in other countries, the desire to revise the treaty was closely related to a desire to change the mode of domestic government.

The Weimar Constitution was a highly enlightened document. It guaranteed civil liberties and provided for direct election, by universal suffrage, of the Reichstag and the president. It also, however, contained certain crucial structural flaws that eventually allowed it to be overthrown. Seats in the Reichstag were allotted according to a complicated system of proportional representation. This made it relatively easy for small political parties to gain seats and resulted in shifting party combinations that led to considerable instability. Ministers were technically responsible to the Reichstag, but the president appointed and removed the chancellor, the head of the cabinet. Perhaps most important, Article 48 allowed the president, in an emergency, to rule by decree. The constitution thus permitted the possibility of presidential dictatorship.

The new government suffered major and minor humiliations as well as considerable economic instability. In March 1920 the right-wing Kapp Putsch, or armed insurrection, erupted in Berlin. Led by a conservative civil servant and supported by army officers, the attempted coup failed, but only after government officials had fled the city and workers had carried out a general strike. In the same month, strikes took place in the Ruhr mining district. The government sent

in troops. Such extremism from both the left and the right would haunt the republic for all its days. In May 1921 the Allies presented a reparations bill for 132 billion gold marks. The German republican government accepted this preposterous demand only after new Allied threats of occupation. Throughout the early 1920s there were numerous assassinations or attempted assassinations of important republican leaders. Violence was the hallmark of the first five years of the republic.

Invasion of the Ruhr and Inflation   Inflation brought on the major crisis of this period. The financing of the war and continued postwar deficit spending generated an immense rise in prices. Consequently, the value of German currency fell. By early 1921 the German mark traded against the American dollar at a ratio of 64 to 1, compared with a ratio of 4.2 to 1 in 1914. The German financial community contended that the value of the currency could not be stabilized until the reparations issue had been solved. In the meantime, the printing presses kept pouring forth paper money, which was used to redeem government bonds as they fell due.

The French invasion of the Ruhr in January 1923, to secure the payment of reparations, and the German response of passive economic resistance produced cataclysmic inflation. The Weimar government paid subsidies to the Ruhr labor force, who had laid down their tools. Unemployment soon spread from the Ruhr to other parts of the country, creating a new drain on the treasury and also reducing tax revenues. The printing presses by this point had difficulty providing enough paper currency to keep up with the daily rise in prices. Money was literally not worth the paper it was printed on. Stores were unwilling to exchange goods for the worthless currency, and farmers withheld produce from the market.

The moral and social values of thrift and prudence were thoroughly undermined. Middle-class savings, pensions, and insurance policies were wiped out, as were investments in government bonds. Simultaneously, debts and mortgages could not be paid off. Speculators in land, real estate, and industry made great fortunes. Union contracts generally allowed workers to keep up with rising prices. Thus inflation was not a disaster for everyone. To the middle class and the lower middle class, however, the inflation was still one more trauma coming hard on the heels of the military defeat and the peace treaty. Only when the social and economic upheaval of these months is grasped can one understand the later German desire for order and security at almost any cost.

Hitler's Early Career   Late in 1923 Adolf Hitler (1889–1945) made his first significant appearance on the German political scene. The son of a minor Austrian customs official, he had gone to Vienna, where his hopes of becoming an artist were soon dashed. He lived off money sent by his widowed mother and later off his Austrian orphan's allowance. He also painted postcards for further income and later found work as a day laborer. In Vienna he encountered Mayor Karl Lueger's (1844–1910) Christian Social Party, which prospered on an ideology of antisemitism and from the social anxieties of the lower middle class. Hitler absorbed the rabid German nationalism and extreme antisemitism that flourished in Vienna. He came to hate Marxism, which he associated with Jews. During World War I Hitler fought in the German army, was wounded, rose to the rank of corporal, and won the Iron Cross for bravery. The war gave him his first sense of purpose.

After the conflict, Hitler settled in Munich. There he became associated with a small nationalistic, antisemitic political party that in 1920 adopted the name of National Socialist German Workers Party, better known simply as the Nazis. In the same year the group began to parade under a red banner with a black swastika. It issued a platform, or program, of Twenty-Five Points. Among other things, this platform called for the repudiation of the Versailles Treaty, the unification of Austria and Germany, the exclusion of Jews from German citizenship, agrarian reform, the prohibition of land speculation, the confiscation of war profits, state administration of the giant cartels, and the replacement of department stores with small retail shops. Originally the Nazis had called for a broad program of nationalization of industry in an attempt to compete directly with the Marxist political parties for the vote of the workers. As the tactic failed, the Nazis redefined the meaning of the word *socialist* in the party name, so that it suggested a nationalistic outlook. In 1922, Hitler said

> Whoever is prepared to make the national cause his own to such an extent that he knows no higher ideal than the welfare of his nation; whoever has understood our great national anthem, *Deutschland, Deutschland, über Alles* ["Germany, Germany, over All"], to mean that nothing in the wide world surpasses in his eyes this Germany, people and land, land and people—that man is a Socialist.[2]

This definition, of course, had nothing to do with traditional German socialism. The "socialism" that Hitler and the Nazis had in mind was not state ownership of the means of production but the subordination of all economic enterprise to the welfare of the nation. It often implied protection for small economic enterprises. Increasingly, over the years, the Nazis discovered that their social appeal was to the lower middle class, which found itself squeezed between well-organized big business and socialist labor unions or political parties. The Nazis tailored their message to this troubled economic group.

Soon after the promulgation of the Twenty-Five Points, the Stormtroopers, or SA *(Sturm Abteilung)*, were organized under the leadership of Captain Ernst Roehm (1887–1934). It was a paramilitary organization that initially provided its members with food and uniforms and, later in the decade, with wages. In the mid-1920s the SA adopted its famous brown-shirted uniform. The Stormtroopers were the chief Nazi instrument for terror and intimidation before the party came into control of the government. They were a law unto themselves. The organization constituted a means of preserving military discipline and values outside the small army permitted by the Paris settlement. The existence of such a private party army was a sign of the potential for violence in the Weimar Republic and the widespread contempt for the law and the institutions of the republic.

The social and economic turmoil following the French occupation of the Ruhr and the German inflation gave the fledgling party an opportunity for direct action against the Weimar Republic, which seemed incapable of providing military or economic security. By this time, because of his immense oratorical skills and organizational abilities, Hitler personally dominated the Nazi Party. On November 9, 1923, Hitler and a band of followers, accompanied by General Erich Ludendorff (1865–1937), attempted an unsuccessful putsch at a beer hall in Munich. When the local authorities crushed the rising, sixteen Nazis were killed. Hitler and Ludendorff were arrested and tried for treason. The general was acquitted. Hitler used the trial to make himself into a national figure. In his defense, he condemned the republic, the Versailles Treaty, the Jews, and the weakened condition of his adopted country. He was convicted and sentenced to five years in prison. He actually spent only a few months in jail before being paroled. During this time, he dictated *Mein Kampf* ("My Struggle"). Another result of the brief imprisonment was his decision to seize political power by legal methods.

The Stresemann Years   The officials of the republic were attempting to repair the damage from the inflation. Gustav Stresemann (1878–1929) was responsible primarily for reconstruction of the republic and for its achievement of a sense of self-confidence. Stresemann abandoned the policy of passive resistance in the Ruhr. The country simply could not afford it. Then, with the aid of banker Hjalmar Schacht (1877–1970), he introduced a new German currency. The rate of exchange was one trillion of the old German marks for one new Rentenmark. Stresemann also moved against challenges from both the left and the right. He supported the crushing of both Hitler's abortive putsch and smaller Communist disturbances. In late November 1923, after four months as chancellor, he resigned to become foreign minister, a post he held until his death in 1929. In that office he continued to influence the affairs of the republic.

[2]Alan Bullock, Hitler: *A Study in Tyranny*, rev. ed. (New York: Harper & Row, 1962), p. 76.

In 1924 the Weimar Republic and the Allies renegotiated the reparation payments. The Dawes Plan lowered the annual payments and allowed them to fluctuate according to the fortunes of the German economy. The last French troops left the Ruhr in 1925. The same year, Field Marshal Paul von Hindenburg (1847–1934), a military hero and a conservative monarchist, was elected president of the republic. He governed in strict accordance with the constitution, but his election suggested that German politics had become more conservative. Conservative Germans seemed reconciled to the republic. This conservatism was in line with the prosperity of the latter 1920s. Foreign capital flowed into Germany, and employment, which had been poor throughout most of the postwar years, improved smartly. Giant industrial combines spread. The prosperity helped to establish broader acceptance and appreciation of the republic.

In foreign affairs, Stresemann pursued a conciliatory course. He fulfilled the provisions of the Versailles Treaty even as he attempted to revise it by diplomacy. He was willing to accept the settlement in the west but was a determined, if sometimes secret, revisionist in the east. He aimed to recover German-speaking territories lost to Poland and Czechoslovakia and possibly to unite with Austria, chiefly by diplomatic means. The first step, however, was to achieve respectability and economic recovery. That goal required a policy of accommodation and "fulfillment," for the moment at least.

Locarno   These developments gave rise to the Locarno Agreements of October 1925. The spirit of conciliation led foreign ministers Austen Chamberlain (1863–1937) for Britain and Aristide Briand (1862–1932) for France to accept Stresemann's proposal for a fresh start. France and Germany both accepted the western frontier established at Versailles as legitimate. Britain and Italy agreed to intervene against the aggressor if either side violated the frontier or if Germany sent troops into the demilitarized Rhineland. Significantly, no such agreement was made about Germany's eastern frontier, but the Germans made treaties of arbitration with Poland and Czechoslovakia, and France strengthened its ties with those countries. France supported German membership in the League of Nations and agreed to withdraw its occupation troops from the Rhineland in 1930, five years earlier than specified at Versailles.

Germany was pleased to have achieved respectability and a guarantee against another Ruhr occupation, as well as the possibility of revision in the east. Britain enjoyed playing a more even-handed role. Italy was glad to be recognized as a great power. The French were happy, too, because the Germans voluntarily accepted the permanence of their western frontier, which was also guaranteed by Britain and Italy, and France maintained its allies in the east.

The Locarno Agreements brought new hope to Europe. Germany's entry into the League of Nations was greeted with enthusiasm. Chamberlain, Briand, and Stresemann all received the Nobel Peace Prize in 1925 and 1926. The spirit of Locarno was carried even further when the leading European states, Japan, and the United States signed the Kellogg-Briand Pact in 1928, renouncing "war as an instrument of national policy." The joy and optimism were not justified. France had merely recognized its inability to coerce Germany without help. Britain had shown its unwillingness to uphold the settlement in the east. Austen Chamberlain declared that no British government ever would "risk the bones of a British grenadier" for the Polish corridor. Germany was not reconciled to the eastern settlement. It maintained clandestine military connections with the Soviet Union and planned to continue to press for revision.

In both France and Germany, moreover, the conciliatory politicians represented only a part of the nation. In Germany especially, most people continued to reject Versailles and regarded Locarno as only an extension of it. When the Dawes Plan ran out in 1929 it was replaced by the Young Plan, which lowered the reparation payments, put a term on how long they must be made, and removed Germany entirely from outside supervision and control. The intensity of the outcry in Germany against the continuation of any reparations showed how far the Germans were from accepting their situation. Despite these problems, war was by no means inevitable. Europe, aided by American loans, was returning to prosperity. German leaders like Stresemann would certainly have continued to press for change, but there is little reason to think that they would have resorted to force, much less to a general war. Continued prosperity and diplomatic success might have won the loyalty of the German people for the Weimar Republic and moderate revisionism, but the Great Depression of the 1930s brought new forces to power.

Depression and Political Deadlock

The outflow of foreign, and especially American, capital from Germany that began in 1928 undermined the economic prosperity of the Weimar Republic. The resulting economic crisis brought parliamentary government to a halt. In 1928 a coalition of center parties and the Social Democrats governed. All went reasonably well until the Depression struck. Then the coalition partners differed sharply on economic policy. The Social Democrats refused to reduce social and unemployment insurance. The more conservative parties, remembering the inflation of 1923, insisted on a balanced budget. The coalition dissolved in March 1930. To resolve the parliamentary deadlock in the Reichstag, President von Hindenburg appointed Heinrich Brüning (1885–1970) as chancellor. Lacking a majority in the Reichstag, the new

In this painting, which reflects the mood of social and political disillusionment that prevailed in much of Europe in the 1920s, George Grosz satirized conservative and right-wing groups in Weimar Germany, including the army, the courts, the newspapers, and the Nazi Party. [Bildarchiv Preussischer Kulturbesitz]

chancellor governed through emergency presidential decrees, as authorized by Article 48 of the constitution. The party-divisions in the Reichstag prevented the overriding of the decrees. The Weimar Republic was transformed into a presidential dictatorship.

German unemployment rose from 2,258,000 in March 1930 to over 6,000,000 in March 1932. There had been persistent unemployment during the 1920s, but nothing of such magnitude or duration. The economic downturn and the parliamentary deadlock worked to the advantage of the more extreme political parties. In the election of 1928 the Nazis had won only 12 seats in the Reichstag, and the Communists had won 54 seats. Two years later, after the election of 1930, the Nazis held 107 seats and the Communists 77.

The power of the Nazis in the streets was also on the rise. The unemployment fed thousands of men into the Storm-troopers, which had 100,000 members in 1930 and almost one million in 1933. The SA freely and viciously attacked Communists and Social Democrats. For the Nazis, politics meant the capture of power through terror and intimidation as well as through elections. Decency and civility in political life vanished. Nazi rallies resembled secular religious revivals. They paraded through the streets and the countryside. They gained powerful supporters and sympathizers in the business, military, and newspaper communities. Some intellectuals were also sympathetic. The Nazis transformed this discipline and enthusiasm born of economic despair and nationalistic frustration into impressive electoral results.

Hitler Comes to Power

For two years Brüning continued to govern through the confidence of Hindenburg. The economy did not improve, and the political situation deteriorated. In 1932 the eighty-three-year-old president stood for reelection. Hitler ran against him and forced a runoff. The Nazi leader garnered 30.1 percent of the vote in the first election and 36.8 percent in the second. Although Hindenburg was returned to office, the vote convinced him that Brüning had lost the confidence of conservative German voters. In May 1932 he dismissed Brüning and appointed Franz von Papen (1878–1969) in his place. The new chancellor was one of a small group of extremely conservative advisers on whom the aged Hindenburg had become increasingly dependent. Others included the president's son and several military figures. With the continued paralysis in the Reichstag, their influence over the president amounted to control of the government. Consequently, the crucial decisions of the next several months were made by only a handful of people.

Papen and the circle around the president wanted to draw the Nazis into cooperation with them without giving Hitler effective power. The government needed the popular support on the right that only the Nazis seemed able to generate. The Hindenburg circle decided to convince Hitler that the Nazis could not come to power on their own. Papen removed the ban on Nazi meetings that Brüning had imposed and then called a Reichstag election for July 1932. The Nazis won 230 seats and polled 37.2 percent of the vote. Hitler would only enter the Cabinet if he were made chancellor. Hindenburg refused. Another election was called in November, partly to wear down the Nazis' financial resources. The Nazis gained only 196 seats, and their percentage of the popular vote dipped to 33.1 percent. The advisers around Hindenburg still refused to appoint Hitler to office.

In early December 1932 Papen resigned, and General Kurt von Schleicher (1882–1934) became chancellor. People were now afraid of civil war between the extreme left and the far right. Schleicher decided to try and fashion a broad-based coalition of conservative groups and trade unionists. The prospect of such a coalition, including groups from the political left, frightened the Hindenburg circle even more than the prospect of Hitler. They did not trust Schleicher's motives, which have never been clear. Consequently, they persuaded Hindenburg to appoint Hitler chancellor. To control him and to see that he did little mischief, Papen was named vice-chancellor, and other traditional conservatives were appointed to the Cabinet. On January 30, 1933, Adolf Hitler became the chancellor of Germany.

Hitler had come into office by legal means. All the proper forms and procedures had been observed. This was important, for it permitted the civil service, the courts, and the other agencies of the government to support him in good conscience. He had forged a rigidly disciplined party structure and had mastered the techniques of mass politics and propaganda. He understood how to touch the raw social and political nerves of the electorate. His support appears to have come from across the social spectrum. Pockets of resistance appeared among Roman Catholic voters in the country and small towns. Otherwise, support for Hitler was particularly strong among farmers, war veterans, and the young, who had especially suffered from the insecurity of the 1920s and the Depression of the early 1930s. Hitler promised them security against Communists and Socialists, effective government in place of the petty politics of the other parties, and an uncompromising nationalist vision of a strong, restored Germany.

Much blame was once assigned to German big business for the rise of Hitler. However, there is little evidence that business contributions made any crucial difference to the Nazis' success or failure. Hitler's supporters were frequently suspicious of business and giant capitalism. They wanted a simpler world, one in which small property would be safe from both socialism and large-scale capitalist consolidation. These people looked to Hitler and the Nazis rather than to the Social Democrats because the latter, although concerned with social issues, never appeared sufficiently nationalistic. The Nazis won out over other conservative nationalistic parties because, unlike those conservatives, the Nazis did address the problem of social insecurities.

Hitler's Consolidation of Power

Once in office, Hitler moved with almost lightning speed to consolidate his control. This process had three facets: the capture of full legal authority, the crushing of alternative political groups, and the purging of rivals within the Nazi Party itself. On February 27, 1933, a mentally ill Dutch Communist

Major Political Events of the 1920s and 1930s	
1919	August, Constitution of the Weimar Republic promulgated
1920	Kapp Putsch in Berlin
1921	March, Kronstadt mutiny leads Lenin to initiate his New Economic Policy
1922	October, Fascist march on Rome leads to Mussolini's assumption of power
1923	January, France invades the Ruhr
	November, Hitler's Beer Hall Putsch
1924	Death of Lenin
1925	Locarno Agreements
1928	Kellogg-Briand Pact first; five-year plan launched in USSR
1929	January, Trotsky expelled from USSR
	February, Lateran Accord between the Vatican and the Italian state
	October, New York stock market crash
	November, Bukharin expelled from his offices in the Soviet Union; Stalin's central position thus affirmed
1930	March, Bruning government begins in Germany
	Stalin calls for moderation in his policy of agricultural collectivization because of "dizziness from success"
	September, Nazis capture 107 seats in German Reichstag
1931	August, National Government formed in Britain
1932	March 13, Hindenberg defeats Hitler for German presidency
	May 31, Franz von Papen forms German Cabinet
	July 31, German Reichstag election
	November 6, German Reichstag election
	December 2, Kurt von Schleicher forms German Cabinet
1933	January 30, Hitler made German chancellor
	February 27, Reichstag Fire
	March 5, Reichstag election
	March 23, Enabling Act consolidates Nazi power
1934	June 30, Blood purge of the Nazi Party
	August 2, Death of Hindenburg
	December 1, Assassination of Kirov leads to the beginning of Stalin's purges
1936	May, Popular Front government in France
	July–August, Most famous of public purge trials in Russia

set fire to the Reichstag building in Berlin. The Nazis quickly turned the incident to their own advantage by claiming that the fire proved the existence of an immediate Communist threat against the government. To the public, it seemed plausible that the Communists might attempt some action against the state now that the Nazis were in power. Under Article 48, Hitler made the Emergency Decree suspending civil liberties and proceeded to arrest Communists or alleged Communists. This decree was not revoked for as long as Hitler ruled Germany.

In early March another Reichstag election took place. The Nazis still received only 43.9 percent of the vote. However,

Hitler's mastery of the techniques of mass politics and propaganda—including huge staged rallies like this one in 1938—was an important factor in his rise to power. [Bildarchiv Preussischer Kulturbesitz]

the arrest of the newly elected Communist deputies and the political fear aroused by the fire meant that Hitler could control the Reichstag. On March 23, 1933, the Reichstag passed an Enabling Act that permitted Hitler to rule by decree. Thereafter, there were no legal limits on his exercise of power. The Weimar Constitution was never formally repealed or amended. It had simply been supplanted by the February Emergency Decree and the March Enabling Act.

Perhaps better than anyone else, Hitler understood that he and his party had not inevitably come to power. His potential opponents had stood divided between 1929 and 1933. He intended to prevent them from regrouping. In a series of complex moves, Hitler outlawed or undermined various German institutions that might have served as rallying points for opposition. In early May 1933 the offices, banks, and newspapers of the free trade unions were seized, and their leaders arrested. The Nazi Party itself, rather than any government agency, undertook this action. In late June and early July, the other German political parties were outlawed. By July 14, 1933, the National Socialists were the only legal party in Germany. During the same months the Nazis had taken control of the governments of the individual federal states in Germany. By the close of 1933 all major institutions of potential opposition had been eliminated.

The final element in Hitler's personal consolidation of power involved the Nazi Party itself. By late 1933 the SA, or Stormtroopers, consisted of approximately one million active members and a larger number of reserves. The com-

mander of this party army was Ernst Roehm, a possible rival to Hitler himself. The German army officer corps, on whom Hitler depended to rebuild the national army, were jealous of the SA leadership. Consequently, to protect his own position and to shore up support with the regular army, on June 30, 1934, Hitler ordered the murder of key SA officers, including Roehm. Others killed between June 30 and July 2 included the former chancellor Kurt von Schleicher and his wife. The exact number of purged victims is unknown, but it has been estimated to have exceeded one hundred. The German army, which was the only institution in the nation that might have prevented the murders, did nothing. A month later, on August 2, 1934, President Hindenburg died. Thereafter, the offices of chancellor and president were combined. Hitler was now the sole ruler of Germany and of the Nazi Party.

The Police State

Terror and intimidation had helped propel the Nazis to office. As Hitler consolidated his power, he oversaw the organization of a police state. The chief vehicle of police surveillance was the SS *(Schutzstaffel)*, or security units, commanded by Heinrich Himmler (1900–1945). This group had originated in the mid-1920s as a bodyguard for Hitler and had become a more elite paramilitary organization than the larger SA. In 1933 the SS had approximately 52,000 members. It was the instrument that carried out the blood purges of the party in

Soon after seizing power, the Nazi government began harassing German Jewish businesses. Non-Jewish German citizens were urged not to buy merchandise from shops owned by Jews. [Bildarchiv Preussischer Kulturbesitz]

1934. By 1936 Himmler had become head of all police matters in Germany.

The police character of the Nazi regime was all-pervasive, but the people who most consistently experienced its terror were the German Jews. Antisemitism had been a key plank of the Nazi program—antisemitism based on biological racial theories stemming from late-nineteenth-century thought rather than from religious discrimination. Before World War II the Nazi attack on the Jews went through three stages of increasing intensity. In 1933, shortly after assuming power, the Nazis excluded Jews from the civil service. For a time they also attempted to enforce boycotts of Jewish shops and businesses. The boycotts won relatively little public support. In 1935 the Nuremberg Laws robbed German Jews of their citizenship. All persons with at least one Jewish grandparent were defined as Jews. The professions and the major occupations were closed to Jews. Marriage and sexual intercourse between Jews and non-Jews were prohibited. Legal exclusion and humiliation of the Jews became the order of the day.

The persecution of the Jews increased again in 1938. Business careers were forbidden. In November 1938, under orders from the Nazi Party, thousands of Jewish stores and synagogues were burned or otherwise destroyed. The Jewish community itself had to pay for the damage that occurred on this Kristallnacht because the government confiscated the insurance money. In all manner of other ways, large and petty, the German Jews were harassed. This persecution allowed the Nazis to inculcate the rest of the population with the concept of a master race of pure German "Aryans" and also to display their own contempt for civil liberties.

After the war broke out, Hitler decided in 1942 to destroy the Jews in Europe. It is thought that over 6 million Jews, mostly from eastern European nations, died as a result of that staggering decision, unprecedented in its scope and implementation.

Women in Nazi Germany

The Nazis believed in separate social spheres for men and women. Men belonged in the world of action, women in the home. The two spheres should not mix. Women who sought to liberate themselves and to adopt roles traditionally followed by men in public life were considered symptoms of cultural decline. Respect for women should arise from their function as wives and mothers.

These attitudes stood in direct conflict with many of the social changes that German women, like women elsewhere in Europe, had experienced during the first three decades of the twentieth century. German women had become much more active and assertive. More of them worked in factories or were independently employed, and they had begun to enter the professions. Under the Weimar constitution, they voted. Throughout the Weimar period there was also a lively discussion of women's emancipation. For the Nazis these developments were signs of cultural weakness. They generally urged a much more traditional role for women in their new society. Nazi writers portrayed women as wives and mothers first and foremost.

The Nazis' point of view was supported by women of a generally conservative outlook and women who were following traditional roles as housewives, confirming the choices these women had made about how to lead their lives. In a period of high unemployment, the Nazi attitude also appealed to many men because it discouraged women from competing with them in the workplace. Such competition had begun during World War I, and many Nazis considered it symptomatic of the social confusion that had followed the German defeat.

The Nazi discussion of the role of women was also deeply rooted in Nazi racism. Nazi writers argued that the superiority of the pure German race depended on the purity of the blood of each and every individual. It was the special task of German mothers to preserve racial purity. Hitler particularly championed this view of women. They were to breed strong sons and daughters for the German nation. Nazi journalists often compared the role of women in childbirth to that of men in battle. Each served the state in particular social and

The Nazis Pass Their Racial Legislation

Antisemitism was a fundamental tenet of the Nazi Party and became a major policy of the Nazi government. This comprehensive legislation of September 15, 1935, carried antisemitism into all areas of public life and into some of the most personal areas of private life as well. It was characteristically titled the Law for the Protection of German Blood and Honor. Hardly any aspect of Nazi thought and action shocked the non-German world as much as this policy toward the Jews.

How would this legislation have affected the normal daily interaction between Jews and non-Jews in Germany? Why are there specific prohibitions against mixed marriages and sexual relations between Jews and non-Jews? How does this legislation separate German Jews from the symbols of German national life?

Imbued with the knowledge that the purity of German blood is the necessary prerequisite for the existence of the German nation, and inspired by an inflexible will to maintain the existence of the German nation for all future times, the Reichstag has unanimously adopted the following law, which is now enacted:

Article I: (1) Any marriages between Jews and citizens of German or kindred blood are herewith forbidden. Marriages entered into despite this law are invalid, even if they are arranged abroad as a means of circumventing this law.

(2) Annulment proceedings for marriages may be initiated only by the Public Prosecutor.

Article II: Extramarital relations between Jews and citizens of German or kindred blood are herewith forbidden.

Article III: Jews are forbidden to employ as servants to their households female subjects of German or kindred blood who are under the age of forty-five years.

Article IV: (1) Jews are prohibited from displaying the Reich and national flag and from showing the national colors.

(2) However, they may display the Jewish colors. The exercise of this right is under state protection.

Article V: (1) Anyone who acts contrary to the prohibition noted in Article I renders himself liable to penal servitude.

(2) The man who acts contrary to the prohibition of Article II will be punished by sentence to either a jail or penitentiary.

(3) Anyone who acts contrary to the provisions of Articles III or IV will be punished with a jail sentence up to a year and with a fine, or with one of these penalties.

Article VI: The Reich Minister of Interior, in conjunction with the Deputy to the Führer and the Reich Minister of Justice, will issue the required legal and administrative decrees for the implementation and amplification of this law.

Article VII: This law shall go into effect on the day following its promulgation, with the exception of Article III, which shall go into effect on January 1, 1936.

From *Documents of German History,* Louis L. Snyder, ed. and trans. Copyright © 1938 Rutgers the State University, pp. 427–428. Reprinted by permission of Rutgers University Press.

---

gender roles. In both cases, the good of the nation was superior to that of the individual.

Most Nazis who discussed the role of women relegated them to the home. They also generally attacked feminist outlooks. Women were encouraged to bear many children, because the Nazis believed the declining German birth rate was the result of emancipated women who had spurned their natural and proper roles as mothers. The Nazis established special medals for women who bore large families. They also sponsored schools that taught women how to care for and rear children.

The Nazis also saw women as educators of the young and thus the special protectors of German cultural values. Through cooking, dress, music, and stories, mothers were to instill a love for the nation. As consumers for the home, women were to aid German-owned shops, to buy German-produced goods, and to avoid Jewish merchants.

The Nazis realized that in the midst of the Depression many women would need to work, but the party urged them to pursue employment that the Nazis considered natural to their character. These tasks included agriculture, teaching, nursing, social work, and domestic service. Nonetheless, despite some variation in the early and mid-1930s, the percentage of women employed in Germany changed little from the Weimar to the Hitler years: It was 37 percent in 1928 and the same again in 1939. Thereafter, because of the war effort, many more women were recruited into the German work force.

The Great Depression and the New Deal in the United States

The United States emerged from the First World War as a major world power. However, it retreated from that role when the Senate refused to ratify the Versailles Treaty and subsequently failed to join the League of Nations. In 1920 Warren Harding (1865–1923) became president and urged a

Hitler Rejects the Emancipation of Women

According to Nazi ideology, women's place was in the home producing and rearing children and supporting their husbands. In this speech, Hitler urges this view of the role of women. He uses antisemitism to discredit those writers who had urged the emancipation of women from their traditional roles and occupations. Hitler returns here to the "separate spheres" concept of the relationship of men and women. His traditional view of women was directed against views that were associated with the Soviet experiment during the interwar years. Contrast this Nazi outlook on women and the family with the Bolshevik position described by Alexandra Kollontai in the document earlier in the chapter. Ironically, once World War II began, the Nazi leadership demanded that women leave the home and work in factories to support the war effort.

What are the social tasks Hitler assigns to women? Why does he associate the emancipation of women with Jews and intellectuals? How does he attempt to subordinate the lives of women to the supremacy of the state?

The slogan "Emancipation of women" was invented by Jewish intellectuals and its content was formed by the same spirit. In the really good times of German life the German woman had no need to emancipate herself. She possessed exactly what nature had necessarily given her to administer and preserve; just as the man in his good times had no need to fear that he would be ousted from his position in relation to the woman. . . .

If the man's world is said to be the State, his struggle, his readiness to devote his powers to the service of the community, then it may perhaps be said that the woman's is a smaller world. For her world is her husband, her family, her children, and her home. But what would become of the greater world if there were no one to tend and care for the smaller one? How could the greater world survive if there were no one to make the cares of the smaller world the content of their lives? No, the greater world is built on the foundation of this smaller world. This great world cannot survive if the smaller world is not stable. Providence has entrusted to the woman the cares of that world which is her very own, and only on the basis of this smaller world can the man's world be formed and built up. The two worlds are not antagonistic. They complement each other, they belong together just as man and woman belong together.

We do not consider it correct for the woman to interfere in the world of the man, in his main sphere. We consider it natural if these two worlds remain distinct. To the one belongs the strength of feeling, the strength of the soul. To the other belongs the strength of vision, of toughness, of decision, and of the willingness to act. In the one case this strength demands the willingness of the woman to risk her life to preserve this important cell and to multiply it, and in the other case it demands from the man the readiness to safeguard life. . . .

So our women's movement is for us not something which inscribes on its banner as its programme the fight against men, but something which has as its programme the common fight together with men. For the new National Socialist national community acquires a firm basis precisely because we have gained the trust of millions of women as fanatical fellow-combatants, women who have fought for the common life in the service of the common task of preserving life. . . .

Whereas previously the programmes of the liberal, intellectualist women's movements contained many points, the programme of our National Socialist Women's movement has in reality but one single point, and that point is the child, that tiny creature which must be born and grow strong and which alone gives meaning to the whole life-struggle.

From J. Noakes and G. Pridham, eds., *Nazism, 1919–1945*, Vol. 2, *State, Economy and Society, 1933–39: A Documentary Reader*, Exeter Studies in History No. 8. University of Exeter Press, 1984, pp. 449–450.

---

return to what he termed "normalcy," which meant minimal involvement abroad and conservative economic policies at home. Business interests clearly remained in the ascendent, with the federal government taking a relatively inactive role in national economic life. Indeed, government inactivity was the virtual creed of Harding's successor, President Calvin Coolidge (1872–1933).

The first seven or eight years of the decade witnessed remarkable American prosperity. New electrical appliances such as the radio, phonograph, washing machine, and vacuum cleaner appeared on the market. Large-scale advertising campaigns attempted to persuade consumers to purchase such items. Real wages rose for many groups of workers. Industry grew at a robust rate. Automobile manufacturers assumed a major role in national economic life. Henry Ford's (1863–1947) Model T exemplified the determination of the automobile industry to produce for a mass market. Increasing numbers of factories became mechanized. Engineers and efficiency experts were the heroes of the business world. For most of the 1920s the New York stock market boomed. All of this remarkable activity stood in marked contrast to the various economic dislocations occurring in Europe.

The Great Depression brought unprecedented unemployment to the United States. In 1930 unemployed workers were photographed standing outside the Municipal Lodging House in New York City. [Corbis-Bettmann]

The material prosperity appeared, however, in a sharply divided society. Segregation remained a basic fact of life for black Americans throughout the South and to a lesser degree in other areas of the country. The Ku Klux Klan, which sought to terrorize blacks, Roman Catholics, and Jews, enjoyed a resurgence. The Prohibition Amendment of 1919 (repealed in 1933) forbade the manufacture and transport of alcoholic beverages. In the wake of this divisive national policy, major criminal operations arose to supply liquor and to disrupt the stability of civic life. Many immigrants came from Mexico and Puerto Rico. They settled in cities where their labor was desired but where they were often not welcomed or assimilated. Finally, the wealth of the nation was overwhelmingly concentrated in relatively few hands.

Economic Collapse

In March 1929 Herbert Hoover became president, the third Republican in as many elections. On October 29, 1929, the New York stock market crashed. The other financial markets also went into a tailspin. During the next year the stock market continued to fall. The banks that had loaned people money with which to speculate in the market suffered great losses.

The financial collapse of 1929 triggered the Great Depression in America, although there were other underlying domestic causes. During the 1920s manufacturing firms had not made sufficient capital investment. The disproportionate amount of profits going to about 5 percent of the U.S. population had by the end of the decade begun to undermine the purchasing power of other consumers. Furthermore, agriculture had been in trouble for years. Finally, the economic difficulties in Europe and Latin America, which predated those in the United States, meant foreigners were less able to purchase products produced in the United States.

The most pervasive problem of the Great Depression was the spread of unemployment. Joblessness hit poor unskilled workers most rapidly but then worked its way up the job ladder to touch factory and white-collar workers. As unemployment spread, small retail businesses suffered. In the major American manufacturing cities, hundreds of thousands of workers could not find jobs. The price of corn fell so low in some areas that it was not profitable to harvest the crop. By the early 1930s banks across the country began to fail, and people lost their savings.

The federal government was not really equipped to address the emergency. There was no tradition of federal action to alleviate economic distress. President Hoover organized economic conferences in Washington and encouraged the Federal Reserve to make borrowing easier. He supported the ill-advised Hawley-Smoot Tariff Act of 1930, with which Congress had hoped to protect American industry by a high tariff barrier. But fundamentally Hoover believed relief was a matter for local government and voluntary organizations. In many areas the local relief agencies had actually run out of money by 1931.

New Role for Government

The election of 1932 was one of the most crucial in American history. Franklin Delano Roosevelt (1882–1945), in accepting the Democratic nomination, pledged his party to a "new deal for the American people." He overwhelmingly defeated Hoover, and quickly set about redirecting federal policy toward the Depression.

Roosevelt had been born into a moderately wealthy New York family. A distant cousin of Theodore Roosevelt (1858–1919), he had been educated at Harvard College and Columbia Law School. After serving in World War I as Assistant Secretary of the Navy, in 1920 he ran as the Democratic vice-presidential candidate. The next year, however, he was struck with polio and his legs became paralyzed. With extraordinary determination he went on to be elected governor of New York in 1928. As the newly elected president he attempted to convey to the nation the same kind of optimistic spirit that had informed his own personal struggle of the 1920s.

Roosevelt's first goal was to give the nation a sense that the federal government was acting to meet the economic challenge. The first hundred days of his administration became legendary. Coming into office at the height of the crisis in the banking system, he immediately closed all the banks and permitted only sound institutions to reopen. Congress convened in a special session and rapidly passed a new banking act. Shortly thereafter, Congress enacted the Agricultural Adjustment Act and the Farm Credit Act to aid the farm sector of the economy. To provide jobs, Roosevelt's administration sponsored the Civilian Conservation Corps. The Federal Emergency Relief Act provided funding for state and local relief agencies. To restore confidence, Roosevelt began making speeches, known as his "fireside chats," to the American people.

Roosevelt's most ambitious program was the National Industrial Recovery Act (NIRA), which established the National Recovery Administration (NRA). This agency attempted to foster codes written by various industries to regulate wages and prices. It was hoped that competition might be thus regulated to protect jobs and assure production.

The NIRA and other New Deal legislation, such as the Wagner Act of 1935, which established the National Labor Relations Board and the Fair Labor Standards Act of 1938, provided a larger role in the American economy for organized labor. It became easier for unions to organize. Union membership grew rapidly and steadily. American unionism took on a new character during these years. Previously, most unions had organized by craft and had been affiliated with the American Federation of Labor. The major union gains of the 1930s, however, occurred through the organization of whole industries composed of workers in various crafts in a single union. The most important of these organizations were the United Mine Workers and United Automobile Workers. These new unions organized themselves into the Congress of Industrial Organizations. The CIO and the AFL were rivals until they merged in the 1950s. These new strong industrial labor organizations introduced a powerful new force into the American economic scene.

In 1935 the U.S. Supreme Court declared the NRA unconstitutional. Thereafter, Roosevelt deemphasized centralized economic planning. There were no fewer federal agencies—indeed, their number increased—but they operated in general independence from each other.

Through New Deal legislation, the federal government was far more active in the economy than it had been in the past. The government itself attempted to provide relief for the unemployed in the industrial sector. The major institution of the relief effort was the Works Progress Administration. Created in 1935, the WPA began a massive program of large public works.

The programs of the New Deal years also involved the federal government directly in economic development rather than turning such development over to private enterprise. Through the Tennessee Valley Authority (TVA), the gov-

During the Great Depression, Franklin Delano Roosevelt (right) replaced Herbert Hoover (left) as president of the United States. FDR's aggressive recovery program was intended to give America a "New Deal." [Corbis-Bettmann]

ernment became directly involved in the economy of the four states of the Tennessee River valley. The TVA built dams and then produced and sold hydroelectricity. Never had the government undertaken so extensive an economic role. Another major new function for the government was providing security for the elderly, through the establishment of the Social Security Administration in 1935.

Hence, in one area of American life after another, it was decided that individual voluntary effort could not provide sufficient personal economic security and that the government must act to do so. These actions established a mixed economy in the United States—that is, one in which the federal government would play an ongoing active role alongside the private sector.

The New Deal changed much of American life. Yet despite its programs and new initiatives, it did not solve the unemployment problem. Indeed, in the late 1930s the economy began to falter again. It was the entry of the nation into World War II that brought the U.S. economy to full employment.

However, the New Deal did preserve American democracy and capitalism. The experience of the United States under the New Deal stood in marked contrast to the economic and political experiments taking place in Europe. Many business people found Roosevelt far too liberal and his policies too activist. Nonetheless, the New Deal fundamentally preserved capitalism in a democratic setting, where, in contrast to Europe, there was a broad spectrum of political debate—much of it highly critical of the administration. The United States had demonstrated that a nation with a vast industrial economy could confront its gravest economic crisis and still preserve democracy.

IN WORLD PERSPECTIVE

The Economic and Political Crisis

The two decades between the great wars marked a period of immense political and economic transition around the globe. Many regions endured political turmoil and economic instability, followed by the establishment of militaristic authoritarian regimes. In Italy it was the Fascists; in Germany, the Nazis; in the Soviet Union, Stalin's regime. In East Asia, Japan came into the grip of a right-wing militaristic government. China saw over twenty years of civil war and revolution. Most of Latin America came under the sway of dictators or governments heavily influenced by the military. To many observers in the late 1930s, the day of liberal parliamentary democracy appeared to be ending. The disruptions arising from World War I and the social and economic turmoil of Depression seemed to pose problems that liberal governments could not address.

The interwar period also departed from the nineteenth-century ideal of economies in which central governments assumed little responsibility. The German inflation of the early 1920s, the worldwide financial collapse of the late 1920s, the vast unemployment of the early 1930s, and the agricultural crisis of both decades roused demands for government action. One reason for these demands was simply that more governments throughout the world were responsible to mass democratic electorates. Governments that did not seek to address the problems were put out of office. This happened to the Republicans in the United States, the socialist and liberal parties in Germany, the left-wing parties in Japan, and various political parties in Latin America that failed to deal with the Depression. Paradoxically, many democratic electorates actually turned themselves over to politically authoritarian regimes as they searched for social and economic stability. That would be an important lesson in the years after World War II. Then, in response to the experience of the 1920s and 1930s, democratic governments around the globe would seek to provide economic and social security to protect democratic political structures.

Authoritarianism was also spawned by extreme forms of nationalism in both Europe and Japan. The authoritarian governments of Germany, Italy, and Japan all had agendas of nationalistic aggression. They were prepared to move wherever they saw fellow nationals living outside their borders or where they could establish dominance over other peoples and thus become imperial powers. Japan moved against Manchuria and later other areas of Asia. Italy invaded Ethiopia. Germany sought union with German-speaking peoples in Austria and Czechoslovakia and then sought to expand throughout eastern Europe. In turn, those actions challenged in various areas of the world the imperial dominance of Great Britain and the vital security interests of the United States. By the end of the 1930s the authoritarian regimes and the liberal democracies stood on the brink of a major confrontation.

During these years the United States and the Soviet Union remained relatively withdrawn from the world scene. The former pursued the bold democratic experiment of the New Deal, while the latter underwent the equally bold experiment of central-government planning and repression. The aggression of other powers would draw the United States and the Soviet Union directly into the world conflict. Because of their vast economic resources, they would emerge as the two strongest postwar powers. The United States attained that economic role through democracy, the Soviet Union through repression. The relative virtues of those two modes of political and social life would form the issues on which much of the postwar great power rivalry would center.

Review Questions

1. Explain the causes of the Great Depression. Why was it more severe and why did it last longer than previous economic downturns? Could it have been avoided?

2. How did Stalin achieve supreme power in the Soviet Union? Why did he decide that Russia had to industrialize rapidly? Why did this require the collectivization of agriculture? Was the policy a success? How did it affect the Russian people? What were the causes of the great purges?

3. Why was Italy dissatisfied and unstable after World War I? How did Mussolini achieve power? What were the characteristics of the Fascist state?

4. Why did the Weimar Republic collapse in Germany? Discuss Hitler's rise to power. Which groups in Germany supported Hitler and why were they pro-Nazi? How did he consolidate his power?

5. Compare the authoritarian regimes in the Soviet Union, Italy, and Germany. What characteristics did they have in common? What role did terror play in each?

6. Why did the United States economy collapse in 1929? What policies did Roosevelt use to combat the Depression? How did his policies affect the role of the federal government in national life?

Suggested Readings ———

W. S. ALLEN, *The Nazi Seizure of Power: The Experience of a Single German Town, 1930–1935*, rev. ed. (1984). A classic treatment of Nazism in a microcosmic setting.

J. BARNARD, *Walter Reuther and the Rise of the Auto Workers* (1983). A major introduction to the new American unions of the 1930s.

K. D. BRACHER, *The German Dictatorship* (1970). A comprehensive treatment of both the origins and the functioning of the Nazi movement and government.

A. BULLOCK, *Hitler: A Study in Tyranny*, rev. ed. (1964). The best biography.

M. BURLEIGH AND W. WIPPERMAN, *The Racial State: Germany 1933–1945* (1991). Emphasizes the manner in which racial theory influenced numerous areas of policy.

R. CONQUEST, *The Great Terror: Stalin's Purges of the Thirties* (1968). The best treatment of the subject to this date.

G. CRAIG, *GERMANY, 1866–1945* (1978). A major survey.

I. DEUTSCHER, *The Prophet Armed* (1954), *The Prophet Unarmed* (1959), and *The Prophet Outcast* (1963). Remains the major biography of Trotsky.

I. DEUTSCHER, *Stalin: A Political Biography*, 2nd ed. (1967). The best biography in English.

B. EICHENGREEN, *Golden Fetters: The Gold Standard and the Great Depression, 1919–1939* (1992). A remarkable study of the role of the gold standard in the economic policies of the interwar years.

E. EYCK, *A History of the Weimar Republic*, 2 vols. (trans. 1963). The story as narrated by a liberal.

M. S. FAUSOLD, *The Presidency of Herbert Hoover* (1985). An important treatment.

G. FELDMAN, *The Great Disorder: Politics, Economics, and Society in the German Inflation, 1914–1924* (1993). The best work on the subject.

S. FITZPATRICK, *Stalin's Peasants: Resitance and Survival in the Russian Village after Collectivization* (1994). A pioneering study.

P. FUSSELL, *The Great War and Modern Memory* (1975). A brilliant account of the literature arising from World War I during the 1920s.

K. GALBRAITH, *The Great Crash* (1979). A well-known account by a leading economist.

R. GELLATELY, *The Gestapo and German Society: Enforcing Racial Policy, 1933–1945* (1990). A discussion of how the police state supported Nazi racial policies.

H. J. GORDON, *Hitler and the Beer Hall Putsch* (1972). An excellent account of the event and the political situation in the early Weimar Republic.

R. HAMILTON, *Who Voted for Hitler?* (1982). An examination of voting patterns and sources of Nazi support.

J. HELD, ED., *The Columbia History of Eastern Europe in the Twentieth Century* (1992). Individual essays on each country.

P. KENEZ, *The Birth of the Propaganda State: Soviet Methods of Mass Mobilization, 1917–1929* (1985). An examination of the manner in which the Communist government inculcated popular support.

B. KENT, *The Spoils of War: The Politics, Economics, and Diplomacy of Reparations, 1918–1932* (1993). A comprehensive account of the intricacies of the reparations problem of the 1920s.

D. LANDES, *The Unbound Prometheus: Technological Change and Industrial Development in Western Europe from 1750 to the Present* (1969). Includes an excellent analysis of both the Great Depression and the few areas of economic growth.

B. LINCOLN, *Red Victory: A History of the Russian Civil War* (1989). An excellent narrative account.

M. MCAULEY, *Bread and Justice: State and Society in Petrograd, 1917–1922* (1991). A study that examines the impact of the Russian Revolution and Leninist policies on a major Russian city.

D. J. K. PEUKERT, *Inside Nazi Germany: Conformity, Opposition, and Racism in Everyday Life* (1987). An excellent discussion of life under Nazi rule.

R. PIPES, *The Unknown Lenin: From the Secret Archives* (1996). A collection of previously unpublished documents that indicated the repressive character of Lenin's government.

P. PULZER, *Jews and the German State: The Political History of a Minority, 1848–1933* (1992). A detailed history by a major historian of European minorities.

L. J. RUPP, *Mobilizing Women for War: German and American Propaganda, 1839–1945* (1978). Although concentrating on a later period, it includes an excellent discussion of general Nazi attitudes toward women.

A. M. SCHLESINGER, JR., *The Age of Roosevelt*, 3 vols. (1957–1960). The most important overview.

D. M. SMITH, *Mussolini's Roman Empire* (1976). A general description of the Fascist regime in Italy.

D. M. SMITH, *Italy and Its Monarchy* (1989). A major treatment of an important neglected subject.

A. SOLZHENITSYN, *The Gulag Archipelago*, 3 vols. (1974–1979). A major examination of the labor camps under Stalin by one of the most important of contemporary Russian writers.

R. J. SONTAG, *A Broken World, 1919–1939* (1971). An exceptionally thoughtful and well-organized survey.

A. J. P. TAYLOR, *English History, 1914–1945* (1965). Lively and opinionated.

H. A. TURNER, JR., *German Big Business and the Rise of Hitler* (1985). An important major study of the subject.

H. A. TURNER, *Hitler's Thirty Days to Power* (1996). A narrative of the events leading directly to the Nazi seizure of power.

L. YAHIL, *The Holocaust: The Fate of European Jewry, 1932–1945* (1990). A major study of this fundamental subject in twentieth-century history.

In this vivid poster, the artist Ben Shahn (1898–1969) memorialized the destruction of Lidice. The Czechoslovakian town was obliterated by the Nazis on June 11, 1942, in vengeance for the resistance by Czechs against their Nazi rulers. [The Granger Collection, N.Y.]

◆ Again the Road to War (1933–1939)   ◆ The Domestic Fronts   *In World Perspective* World War II

◆ World War II (1939–1945)   ◆ Preparations for Peace

The more idealistic survivors of the First World War, especially in the United States and Great Britain, thought of it as "the war to end all wars" and "a war to make the world safe for democracy." Only thus could they justify the awful slaughter, expense, and upheaval. How appalled they would have been had they known that only twenty years after the peace treaties a second great war would break out that would be more truly global than the first. In this war the democracies would be fighting for their lives against militaristic, nationalistic, authoritarian, and totalitarian states in Europe and Asia. Great Britain and the United States would be allied with the Communist Soviet Union. The defeat of the militarists and dictators would not bring the longed-for peace, but a Cold War in which the European states became second-class powers, subordinate to the two new great powers, partially or fully non-European: the Soviet Union and the United States.

Again the Road to War (1933–1939)

World War I and the Versailles Treaty had only a marginal relationship to the world depression of the 1930s. But in Germany, where the reparations settle- ment had contributed to the vast inflation of 1923, economic and social discontent focused on the Versailles settlement as the cause of all ills. Throughout the late 1920s Adolf Hitler and the Nazi party had never ceased denouncing Versailles as the source of all Germany's trouble; the economic woes of the early 1930s seemed to bear them out.

Nationalism and attention to the social question, along with party discipline, had been the sources of Nazi success. They continued to influence Hitler's foreign policy after he became chancellor in early 1933. Moreover, the Nazi destruction of the Weimar Republic and of political opposition meant that German foreign policy lay in Hitler's own hands. Consequently, it is important to know what his goals were and what plans he had for achieving them.

Hitler's Goals

From first to last, Hitler's racial theories and goals held the central place in his thought. He meant to go far beyond Germany's 1914 boundaries, which were the limit of the vision of his predecessors. He intended to bring the entire German people (*Volk*), understood as a racial group, together into a single nation. The new Germany would include all the Germanic parts of the old Habsburg Empire, including Austria. This virile and growing nation would need more space to live (*Lebensraum*), which would be taken from the Slavs, a lesser race, fit only for servitude. The new Germany would be purified by the removal of the Jews, the most inferior race in Nazi theory. The plan always required the conquest of Poland and the Ukraine as the primary areas for the settlement of Germans and for the provision of badly needed food. However, neither *Mein Kampf* nor later statements of policy were blueprints for action. Hitler was a brilliant improviser who exploited opportunities as they arose. But he never lost sight of his goal, which would almost certainly require a major war.

Destruction of Versailles

When Hitler came to power, Germany was too weak to permit the direct approach to his goals. The first problem was to shake off the fetters of Versailles and to make Germany a formidable military power. In October of 1933 Germany withdrew from an international disarmament conference and also from the League of Nations. These acts alarmed the French but were merely symbolic. In January of 1934 Germany made a nonaggression pact with Poland that was of greater concern, for it put into question France's chief means of containing the Germans. At last, in March 1935 Hitler formally renounced the disarmament provisions of the Versailles Treaty with the formation of a German air force, and soon he reinstated conscription, which aimed at an army of half a million men.

His path was made easier because the League of Nations was ineffective at keeping the peace. In September

Hitler Describes His Goals

From his early career, Hitler had certain long-term general views and goals. They were set forth in his Mein Kampf, *which appeared in 1925, and included consolidation of the German* Volk *("People"), provision of more land for the Germans, and contempt for such "races" as Slavs and Jews. Here are some of Hitler's views.*

What is the basic principle on which Hitler's policy is founded? How does he justify his plans for expansion? What reasons does he give for hostility to France and Russia? What is the basis for Hitler's claim of a right of every man to own farmland? Was that a practical goal for Germany in the 1930s? Was there any way for Hitler to achieve his goals without a major war?

The National Socialist movement must strive to eliminate the disproportion between our population and our area—viewing this latter as a source of food as well as a basis for power politics—between our historical past and the hopelessness of our present impotence. . . .

The demand for restoration of the frontiers of 1914 is a political absurdity of such proportions and consequences as to make it seem a crime. Quite aside from the fact that the Reich's frontiers in 1914 were anything but logical. For in reality they were neither complete in the sense of embracing the people of German nationality, nor sensible with regard to geomilitary expediency. . . .

As opposed to this, we National Socialists must hold unflinchingly to our aim in foreign policy, namely, to secure for the German people the land and soil to which they are entitled on this earth. . . .

. . . The soil on which some day German generations of peasants can beget powerful sons will sanction the investment of the sons of today, and will some day acquit the responsible statesmen of blood-guilt and sacrifice of the people, even if they are persecuted by their contemporaries. . . .

Much as all of us today recognize the necessity of a reckoning with France, it would remain ineffectual in the long run if it represented the whole of our aim in foreign policy. It can and will achieve meaning only if it offers the rear cover for an enlargement of our people's living space in Europe. . . .

If we speak of soil in Europe today, we can primarily have in mind only Russia and her vassal border states. . . .

. . . See to it that the strength of our nation is founded, not on colonies, but on the soil of our European homeland. Never regard the Reich as secure unless for centuries to come it can give every scion of our people his own parcel of soil. Never forget that the most sacred right on this earth is a man's right to have earth to till with his own hands, and the most sacred sacrifice the blood that a man sheds for this earth.

1931 Japan occupied Manchuria, provoking an appeal to the League of Nations by China. The league responded by sending out a commission under the Earl of Lytton (1876–1951). The Lytton Report condemned the Japanese for resorting to force, but the powers were unwilling to impose sanctions. Japan withdrew from the league and kept control of Manchuria.

The league formally condemned Hitler's decision to rearm Germany, but it took no steps to prevent it. France and Britain felt unable to object because they had not carried out their own promises to disarm. Instead, they met with Mussolini (1883–1945) in June 1935 to form the so-called Stresa Front and agreed to maintain the status quo in Europe by force if necessary. But Britain was desperate to maintain superiority at sea. Contrary to the Stresa accords and at the expense of French security needs, Britain soon made a separate naval agreement with Hitler, allowing him to rebuild the German fleet to 35 percent of the British navy.

Italy Attacks Ethiopia

The Italian attack on Ethiopia made the impotence of the League of Nations and the timidity of the Allies even clearer. Using a border incident as an excuse, Mussolini attacked Ethiopia in October 1935. His real intent was to avenge a humiliating defeat that the Italians had suffered in 1896, to begin the restoration of Roman imperial glory, and perhaps to divest Italians from the corruption of the Fascist regime and Italy's economic troubles.

The League of Nations condemned Italian aggression and voted economic sanctions. It imposed an arms embargo that limited loans and credits to and imports from Italy. But Britain and France were afraid of alienating Mussolini, so they refused to place an embargo on oil, the one economic sanction that could have prevented Italian victory. Even more important, the British did not prevent the movement of Italian troops and munitions through the Suez Canal. This wavering policy was disastrous.

The League of Nations and collective security were totally discredited, and Mussolini turned to Germany. By November 1, 1936, he could speak publicly of a Rome-Berlin "Axis."

Remilitarization of the Rhineland

The Ethiopian affair also influenced Hitler's evaluation of the strength and determination of the Western powers. On March 7, 1936, he took his greatest risk yet, sending a small armed force into the demilitarized Rhineland. This was a breach not only of the Versailles Treaty but of the Locarno Agreements of 1925 as well, agreements that Germany had made voluntarily. It also removed one of the most important elements of French security. France and Britain had every right to resist. The French especially had a claim to retain the only element of security left after the failure of the Allies to guarantee France's defense. Yet Britain and France made only a feeble protest with the League of Nations. British opinion would not support France. The French themselves were paralyzed by internal division and by military planning that was exclusively defensive. Both countries were further weakened by a growing pacifism.

A Germany that was rapidly rearming and had a defensible western frontier presented a completely new problem to the western powers. Their response was the policy of "appeasement." It was based on the assumption that Germany had real grievances, that Hitler's goals were limited and ultimately acceptable, and that the correct policy was to negotiate and make concessions before a crisis could lead to war. Behind this approach was the general horror of another war. Memories of the last war were still fresh, and the prospect of aerial bombardment was terrifying. A firmer policy, moreover, would have required rapid rearmament. But British leaders especially were reluctant to pursue this path because of the expense and widespread belief that the arms race had been a major cause of the last war. As Germany armed, the French huddled behind their defensive wall, the Maginot Line, and the British hoped for the best.

The Spanish Civil War

The new European alignment that found the western democracies on one side and the Fascist states on the other was made clearer by the Spanish Civil War, which broke out in July 1936. In 1931 the Spaniards had established a democratic republic. Elections in February 1936 brought to power a government ranging from republicans of the left to Communists and anarchists. The defeated groups, especially the Falangists, the Spanish version of Fascists, would not accept defeat at the polls. In July, General Francisco Franco (1892–1975) led an army from Spanish Morocco against the republic (see Map 35–1).

Thus began a civil war that lasted almost three years, killed hundreds of thousands, and provided a training ground for World War II. Germany and Italy aided Franco with troops and supplies. The Soviet Union sent equipment and advisers to the republicans. Liberals and leftists from Europe and America volunteered to fight in the republican ranks against fascism.

The civil war, fought on blatantly ideological lines, profoundly affected world politics. It brought Germany and Italy closer together, leading to the Rome-Berlin Axis Pact. The Axis powers were joined in the same year by Japan in the Anti-Comintern Pact, ostensibly against communism but really a new and powerful diplomatic alliance. In western Europe, the appeasement mentality reigned. Although international law permitted the sale of weapons and munitions to the legitimate republican government, France and Britain forbade the export of war materials to either side. The United States passed new neutrality legislation to the same end. By early 1939 the Fascists had won effective control of Spain.

Austria and Czechoslovakia

Hitler made good use of his new friendship with Mussolini. In 1934 Mussolini, not yet allied with Hitler, had frustrated a Nazi coup in Austria by threatening military intervention. In 1938 the new diplomatic situation encouraged Hitler to try again. He seems to have hoped to achieve his goal by propaganda, bullying, and threats, but the Austrian Premier, Kurt von Schuschnigg (1897–1977), refused to collapse. On March 9 the premier announced a plebiscite for March 13, in which the Austrian people could decide whether to unite with Germany for themselves. Hitler dared not let the plebiscite take place and invaded Austria on March 12. Mussolini made no objection, and Hitler marched into Vienna to the cheers of his Austrian sympathizers.

The *Anschluss*, or union of Germany and Austria, had great strategic significance, especially for Czechoslovakia, one of the bulwarks of French security. The Czechs were now surrounded by Germany on three sides.

The very existence of Czechoslovakia was an affront to Hitler. It was democratic and pro-western; it had been created as a check on Germany and was allied both to France and to the Soviet Union. It also contained about 3.5 million ethnic Germans who lived in the Sudetenland near the German border. These Germans had been the dominant class in the old Austro-Hungarian Empire, and they resented their new minority position. Supported by Hitler, they agitated for privileges and autonomy within the Czech state. The Czechs made many concessions; Hitler's motivation, however, was not to improve the lot of the Sudeten Germans but to destroy Czechoslovakia.

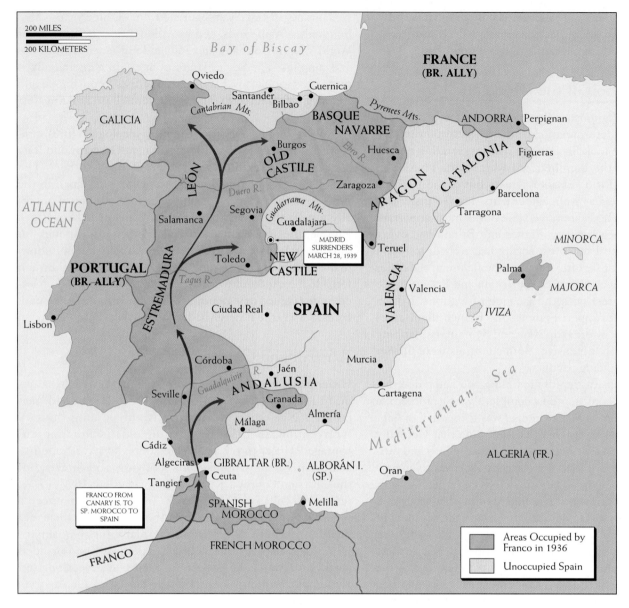

Map 35-1 The Spanish Civil War, 1936–1939. The purple area on the map shows the large portion of Spain quickly overrun by Franco's insurgent armies during the first year of the war. In the following two years progress came more slowly for the Fascists as the war became a kind of international rehearsal for the coming World War II. Madrid's fall to Franco in the spring of 1939 had been preceded by that of Barcelona a few weeks earlier.

The French, as usual, deferred to British leadership. The British prime minister was Neville Chamberlain (1869–1940), a man thoroughly committed to the policy of appeasement. He was determined not to allow Britain to go to war again. He pressured the Czechs to make further concessions to Germany, but no concession was enough.

On September 12, 1938, Hitler made a provocative speech that led to rioting in the Sudetenland, and the declaration of martial law by the Czech government. German intervention seemed imminent. Chamberlain sought to ap-

pease Hitler at Czech expense and thus to avoid war. At Hitler's mountain retreat, Berchtesgaden, on September 15 Chamberlain accepted the separation of the Sudetenland from Czechoslovakia. Moreover, he and the French premier, Edouard Daladier (1884–1970), threatened to desert the Czechs if they did not agree. A week later Chamberlain flew again to Germany only to find that Hitler had raised his demands: He wanted cession of the Sudetenland in three days and its immediate occupation by the German army.

Winston Churchill Warns of the Effects of the Munich Agreement

Churchill delivered a speech on the Munich agreement before the House of Commons on October 5, 1938. Following are excerpts from it.

What was decided at Munich? Why were the representatives of Czechoslovakia not at the meeting? Why did Chamberlain think the meeting was successful? Munich was the high point of the policy called "appeasement." How would its advocates defend this policy? Churchill was a leading opponent of appeasement. What are his objections to it? Compare Churchill's warnings here with those of his "Iron Curtain" speech (in Chapter 36) delivered eight years later.

The Chancellor of the Exchequer [Sir John Simon] said it was the first time Herr Hitler had been made to retract— I think that was the word—in any degree. We really must not waste time after all this long Debate upon the difference between the positions reached at Berchtesgaden, at Godesberg and at Munich. They can be very simply epitomized, if the House will permit me to vary the metaphor. One pound was demanded at the pistol's point. When it was given, £2 were demanded at the pistol's point. Finally, the dictator consented to take £1 17s. 6d. and the rest in promises of good will for the future. . . .

I do not grudge our loyal, brave people, who were ready to do their duty no matter what the cost, who never flinched under the strain of last week—I do not grudge them the natural, spontaneous outbursts of joy and relief when they learned that the hard ordeal would no longer be required of them at the moment; but they should know the truth. They should know that there has been gross neglect and deficiency in our defenses; they should know that we have sustained a defeat without a war, the consequences of which will travel far with us along our road; they should know that we have passed an awful milestone in our history, when the whole equilibrium of Europe has been deranged, and that the terrible words have for the time being been pronounced against the Western democracies: "Thou art weighed in the balance and found wanting." And do not suppose that this is the end. This is only the beginning of the reckoning. This is only the first sip, the first foretaste of a bitter cup which will be proffered to us year by year unless, by a supreme recovery of moral health and martial vigor, we arise again and take our stand for freedom as in the olden time.

Reprinted by permission of the Putnam Publishing Group and Curtis Brown Ltd., London on behalf of the Estate of Sir Winston S. Churchill, from *Blood, Sweat, and Tears* by Winston S. Churchill. Copyright © 1941 Winston S. Churchill.

On September 29–30, 1938, Hitler met with the leaders of Britain and France at Munich to decide the fate of Czechoslovakia. The Allied leaders abandoned the small democratic nation in a vain attempt to appease Hitler and avoid war. Hitler sits in the center of the picture. To his right is British Prime Minister Neville Chamberlain.
[Ullstein Bilderdienst]

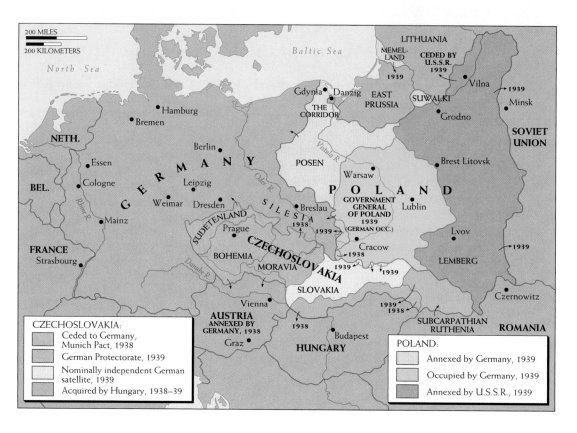

Map 35-2 Partitions of Czechoslovakia and Poland, 1938-1939. The immediate background of World War II is found in the complex international drama unfolding on Germany's eastern frontier in 1938 and 1939. Germany's expansion inevitably meant the victimization of Austria, Czechoslovakia, and Poland. With the failure of the western powers' appeasement policy and the signing of a German-Soviet pact, the stage for the war was set.

CZECHOSLOVAKIA:
- Ceded to Germany, Munich Pact, 1938
- German Protectorate, 1939
- Nominally independent German satellite, 1939
- Acquired by Hungary, 1938-39

POLAND:
- Annexed by Germany, 1939
- Occupied by Germany, 1939
- Annexed by U.S.S.R., 1939

Munich

France and Britain prepared for war. At the last moment Mussolini proposed a conference of Germany, Italy, France, and Britain. It met on September 29 at Munich. Hitler received almost everything he had demanded. The Sudetenland, the key to Czech security, became part of Germany, thus depriving the Czechs of any chance of self-defense (see Map 35–2). In return, the rest of Czechoslovakia was spared. Hitler promised, "I have no more territorial demands to make in Europe." Chamberlain told a cheering crowd that he had brought "peace with honour. I believe it is peace for our time."

Even in the short run, the appeasement of Hitler at Munich was a failure. Soon Poland and Hungary also tore bits of territory from Czechoslovakia, and the Slovaks demanded autonomy. Finally, on March 15, 1939, Hitler broke his promise and occupied Prague, putting an end to Czech independence and to illusions that his only goal was to restore Germans to the Reich. Munich remains an example of shortsighted policy that helped bring on a war in disadvantageous circumstances as a result of the very fear of war and the failure to prepare for it.

Hitler's occupation of Prague discredited appeasement in the eyes of the British people. In the summer of 1939 a Gallup Poll showed that three quarters of the British public believed it worth a war to stop Hitler. Although Chamberlain himself had not lost all faith in his policy, he felt the need to respond to public opinion, and he responded to excess.

It was apparent that Poland was the next target of German expansion. In the spring of 1939 the Germans put pressure on Poland to restore the formerly German city of Danzig and to allow a railroad and a highway through the Polish Corridor to connect East Prussia with the rest of Germany. When the Poles would not yield, the pressure mounted. On March 31 Chamberlain announced a Franco-British guarantee of Polish independence. Hitler did not take the guarantee seriously. He had come to hold the western leaders in contempt. He knew that both countries were unprepared for war and that much of their populations were opposed to war for Poland.

Belief in the Polish guarantee was further undermined by the inability of France and Britain to get effective help to the Poles. The French, still dominated by the defensive mentality of the Maginot Line, had no intention of attacking Germany's western front. The only way to defend Poland was to bring Russia into the alliance against Hitler, but a Russian alliance posed many problems. Each side was profoundly suspicious of the other. The French and British were hostile to Russia's Communist ideology, and since Stalin's purge of the officer corps of the Red Army, they questioned the military value of an alliance with Russia. Besides, the Russians could not help Poland without the right to cross

Romania and enter Poland. Both nations, suspicious of Russian intentions—and with good reason—refused to grant these rights. As a result, western negotiations with Russia were slow and cautious.

The Nazi-Soviet Pact

The Russians also had good reason to hesitate. They resented being left out of the Munich agreement. They were annoyed by the low priority that the west seemed to give to negotiations with Russia, compared with the urgency with which they dealt with Hitler. They feared, rightly, that the western powers meant them to bear the burden of the war against Germany. As a result, they opened negotiations with Hitler, and on August 23, 1939, the world was shocked to learn of a Nazi-Soviet nonaggression pact. Its secret provisions, which were easily guessed and soon carried out, divided Poland between the two powers and allowed Russia to annex the Baltic states and to take Bessarabia from Romania. The most bitter ideological enemies had become allies; Communist parties in the west changed their line overnight from the ardent advocacy of resistance to Hitler to a policy of peace and quiet.

The Nazi-Soviet Pact sealed the fate of Poland, and the Franco-British commitment guaranteed a general war. On September 1, 1939, the Germans invaded Poland. Two days later Britain and France declared war on Germany. World War II had begun.

World War II (1939–1945)

World War II was truly global. Fighting took place in Europe and Asia, the Atlantic and the Pacific oceans, the Northern and Southern hemispheres. The demand for the fullest exploitation of material and human resources for increased production, the use of blockades, and the intensive bombing of civilian targets made the war of 1939 even more "total"— that is, comprehensive and intense—than that of 1914.

German Conquest of Europe

The speed of the German victory over Poland astonished everyone, not least the Russians, who hastened to collect their share of the booty before Hitler could deprive them of it. On September 17 they invaded Poland from the east, dividing the country with the Germans. They then absorbed Estonia, Latvia, and Lithuania into the Soviet Union. In November 1940 the Russians invaded Finland, but the Finns fought back fiercely. Although they were finally compelled to yield territory and bases to Russia, they retained their independence. Russian difficulties in Finland may well have en-

Coming of World War II	
1919	June, Versailles Treaty
1923	January, France occupies the Ruhr
1925	October, Locarno Agreements
1931	Spring, Onset of Great Depression in Europe
1933	January, Hitler comes to power
	October, Germany withdraws from League of Nations
1935	March, Hitler renounces disarmament, starts an air force, and begins conscription
	October, Mussolini attacks Ethiopia
1936	March, Germany reoccupies and remilitarizes the Rhineland
	July, Outbreak of Spanish Civil War
	October, Formation of the Rome-Berlin Axis
1938	March, *Anschluss* with Austria
	September, Munich Conference and partition of Czechoslovakia
1939	March, Hitler occupies Prague; France and Great Britain guarantee Polish independence
	August, Nazi-Soviet pact
	September 1, Germany invades Poland
	September 3, Britain and France declare war on Germany

couraged Hitler to invade the Soviet Union in June 1941, just twenty-two months after the 1939 treaty.

Meanwhile, the western front was quiet. The French remained behind the Maginot Line while Hitler and Stalin swallowed Poland and the Baltic states. Britain hastily rearmed and imposed the traditional naval blockade. Cynics in the west called it the phony war, or *Sitzkrieg*, but Hitler shattered the stillness in the spring of 1940. In April, without warning and with swift success, the Germans invaded Denmark and Norway. Hitler now had both air and naval bases closer to Britain. A month later a combined land and air attack struck Belgium, the Netherlands, and Luxembourg. German air power and armored divisions were irresistible. The Dutch surrendered in a few days, and the Belgians, although aided by the French and the British, surrendered less than two weeks later. The British and French armies in Belgium were forced to flee to the English Channel to seek escape from the beaches of Dunkirk. By the heroic effort of hundreds of Britons manning small boats, over 200,000 British and 100,000 French soldiers were saved, but casualties were high and much valuable equipment was abandoned.

The Maginot Line ran from Switzerland to the Belgian frontier. Until 1936 the French had expected the Belgians to continue the fortifications along their German border. After Hitler remilitarized the Rhineland without opposition, the Belgians lost faith in their French alliance and returned to neutrality, leaving the Maginot Line exposed on its left flank.

Hitler's swift advance through Belgium therefore circumvented France's main line of defense. The French army, poorly and hesitantly led by generals who lacked a proper understanding of how to use tanks and planes, collapsed. Mussolini, eager to claim the spoils of victory when it was clearly safe to do so, attacked France on June 10, though without success. Less than a week later the new French government, under the ancient hero of Verdun, Henri Philippe Pétain (1856–1951), asked for an armistice. In two months Hitler had accomplished what Germany had failed to achieve in four years of bitter fighting in the previous war.

The terms of the armistice, signed June 22, 1940, allowed the Germans to occupy more than half of France, including the Atlantic and English Channel coasts. To prevent the French from fleeing to North Africa to continue the fight, and even more to prevent them from turning their fleet over to Britain, Hitler left southern France unoccupied. Pétain set up a dictatorial regime at the resort city of Vichy and collaborated with the Germans to preserve as much autonomy as possible. Most of the French were too stunned to resist. Many thought that Hitler's victory was certain and saw no alternative to collaboration. A few, most notably General Charles de Gaulle (1890–1969), fled to Britain, where they organized the French National Committee of Liberation, or "Free French." The Vichy government controlled most of French North Africa and the navy. But the Free French began operating in central Africa and from London radioed messages of hope and defiance to France. As expectations of a quick German victory faded, a French resistance movement arose.

The close cooperation between Prime Minister Winston Churchill of Britain and President Franklin Roosevelt of the United States greatly helped assure the effective cooperation of their two countries in World War II. [UPI/Corbis-Bettmannn]

Battle of Britain

Hitler expected the British to come to terms. He was prepared to allow Britain to retain its empire in return for a free hand for Germany in Europe. If there was any chance that the British would consider such terms, that chance disappeared when Winston Churchill (1874–1965) replaced Chamberlain as prime minister in May of 1940.

One of Churchill's greatest achievements was establishing a close relationship with the American president Franklin D. Roosevelt (1882–1945), who found ways to help the British despite strong political opposition. In 1940 and 1941, before the United States was at war, America sent military supplies, traded destroyers for leases on British naval bases, and even convoyed ships across the Atlantic to help the British survive.

As Britain remained defiant, Hitler was forced to contemplate an invasion, which required control of the air. The first strikes by the German air force (*Luftwaffe*), directed against the airfields and fighter planes in southeastern England, began in August 1940. Had these attacks continued, Germany might soon have gained control of the air and, with it, the chance of a successful invasion. In early September, however, seeking revenge for British bombing raids on German cities, the *Luftwaffe* made London its major target. For two months, London was bombed every night. Much of the city was destroyed, and about 15,000 people were killed, but the theories of victory through air power alone proved vain. Casualties were much less than expected, and the bombings made the British people more resolute.

Moreover, the Royal Air Force (RAF), aided by the newly developed radar and an excellent system of communications, inflicted heavy losses on the *Luftwaffe*. Hitler lost the Battle of Britain in the air and was forced to abandon his plans for invasion.

German Attack on Russia

Operation Barbarossa, the code name for the invasion of Russia, was aimed at knocking Russia out of the war before winter could set in. Success depended in part on an early start, but here Hitler's Italian alliance proved costly. Mussolini was jealous of Hitler's success and annoyed at German condescension.

Consequently, Mussolini launched an attack against the British in Egypt and drove them back some sixty miles. Encouraged by this success, he also invaded Greece. But in North Africa the British counterattacked and drove into Libya, and the Greeks also repulsed the Italians. In March 1941 the British sent help to the Greeks, and Hitler was forced to divert his attention to the Balkans and to Africa. General Erwin Rommel (1891–1944), later to earn the title "The Desert Fox," went to Africa and soon drove the British back into

Map 35–3   Axis Europe 1941.   On the eve of the German invasion of the Soviet Union, the Germany-Italy Axis bestrode most of western Europe by annexation, occupation, or alliance—from Norway and Finland in the north to Greece in the south and from Poland to France. Britain, the Soviets, a number of insurgent groups, and, finally, the United States had before them the long struggle of conquering this Axis "fortress Europe."

Egypt. In the Balkans the German army swiftly occupied Yugoslavia and crushed Greek resistance, but the price was a delay of six weeks for Barbarossa (see Map 35–3). This proved to be costly the following winter in the Russian campaign.

Operation Barbarossa was launched against Russia on June 22, 1941, and it almost succeeded. Stalin panicked. He had not fortified his frontier, nor ordered his troops to withdraw when attacked. Two thousand planes were destroyed on the ground. By November Hitler had gone farther into Russia

than had Napoleon: The German army stood at the gates of Leningrad, on the outskirts of Moscow, and on the Don River. Of the 4.5 million troops with which the Russians had begun the fighting, they had lost 2.5 million; of their 15,000 tanks, only 700 were left. A German victory seemed imminent.

But the Germans could not deliver the final blow. In August there was a delay in their advance to decide on a course of action. One plan was to take Moscow before winter. Such a plan might have brought victory, for Moscow was Russia's transportation hub. Hitler, however, diverted significant forces to the south. By the time he was ready to return to the offensive near Moscow, it was too late. Winter struck the German army, which was not equipped to face it. Given precious time, Stalin was able to restore order and fortify the city. Even more important, troops had arrived from Siberia, where they had been placed to check a possible Japanese attack. In November and December the Russians counterattacked. The *Blitzkrieg* had turned into a war of attrition, and the Germans began to have visions of Napoleon's retreat.

Hitler's Europe

The demands and distractions of war and Hitler's defeat prevented him from fully carrying out his plans. Therefore, it is hard to be sure what his intentions were, but the measures he took before his death give evidence of a regime probably unmatched in history for carefully planned terror and inhumanity. To give *Lebensraum* to the Germans at the expense of people he deemed inferior, Hitler established colonies of Germans in Poland, driving the local people from their land and using them as cheap labor. He had worse plans for Russia. The Russians would be driven to central Asia and Siberia, where they would be kept in check by frontier colonies of German war veterans. Germans would settle the more desirable lands of European Russia.

Hitler's long-range plans included Germanization as well as colonization. In lands inhabited by people racially akin to the Germans, like Scandinavia, the Netherlands, and Switzerland, the natives would be absorbed into the German nation. Such peoples would be reeducated and purged of dissenting elements, but there would be little or no colonization. He even had plans, only slightly realized, of adopting selected people from the lesser races into the master race.

Hitler regarded the conquered lands merely as a source of plunder. From eastern Europe he removed everything useful, including entire industries. In Russia and Poland the Germans simply confiscated the land. In the west the conquered countries were forced to support the occupying army at a rate several times the real cost. The Germans used the profits to strip the conquered peoples of most necessities. The Nazis were frank about their policies. One of Hitler's high officials said, "Whether nations live in prosperity or starve to death interests me only insofar as we need them as slaves for our culture."[1]

Racism and the Holocaust

The most horrible aspect of the Nazi rule in Europe arose from the inhumanity and brutality inherent in Hitler's racial

[1]Quoted by Gordon Wright, *The Ordeal of Total War, 1939–1945* (New York: Harper & Row, 1968), p. 117.

doctrines. He considered the Slavs *Untermenschen*, subhuman creatures like beasts who need not be treated like people. In Poland the upper and professional classes were either jailed, deported, or killed. Schools and churches were closed; marriage was controlled to keep down the Polish birth rate; and harsh living conditions were imposed. In Russia things were even worse. Hitler spoke of his Russian campaign as a war of extermination. Heinrich Himmler (1900–1945), head of Hitler's elite SS guard, formed extermination squads to eliminate 30 million Slavs to make room for the Germans. Some 6 million Russian prisoners of war and deported civilian workers may have died under Nazi rule.

Hitler had special plans for the Jews. He meant to make all Europe *Judenrein* ("free of Jews"). For a time he thought of sending them to Madagascar, but later decided on the "final solution of the Jewish problem": extermination. The Nazis built extermination camps in Germany and Poland and used the latest technology to kill millions of men, women, and children just because they were Jews. Before the war was over, 6 million Jews had died in what has come to be called the Holocaust. Only about a million remained alive, mostly in pitiable condition.

The Road to Pearl Harbor

The war took on truly global proportions in December 1941. The Japanese were already at war with China, and between the outbreak of that war in 1937 and the opening of World War II campaign in the Pacific, there were three critical junctures. The first was the decision in January 1938 to destroy the Chinese Nationalist Party government in Nanking (the KMT). The army quickly occupied most of the cities and railroads of eastern China, but Chiang Kai-shek (1887–1945) refused to give in. The result was a stalemate that lasted until 1945. China was never a major theater of the war in the Pacific.

The second critical decision was the Tripartite Pact with Germany and Italy in September 1940. Japan had long admired Germany. In 1936 it had joined Germany in the Anti-Comintern Pact directed against international Communism. It also wanted an alliance with Germany against the Soviet Union. Germany insisted, however, that any alliance also be directed against the United States and Britain, to which the Japanese would not agree. The Japanese navy, especially, was not interested in being dragged into a German war. After an undeclared mini-war with Russia from May to December 1939 on the Mongolian border, sentiment rose for an alliance with Germany, but then Germany "betrayed" Japan by signing a nonaggression pact with the Soviet Union. For a time Japan decided to improve its relations with the United States, but America insisted that Japan get out of China. By the late spring of 1940 German victories in Europe—the fall of Britain

World War II resulted in the near-total destruction of the Jews of Europe, victims of the Holocaust spawned by Hitler's racial theories of the superiority and inferiority of particular ethnic groups. Hitler placed special emphasis on the need to exterminate the Jews, to whom he attributed particular wickedness. This picture shows a roundup of Jews in Warsaw, where there was a large Jewish population, ultimately on their way to concentration or death camps. [Corbis-Bettmann]

appeared imminent—again led the Japanese military to favor an alliance with Germany.

When Japan signed the Tripartite Pact it had three objectives: to isolate the United States, to take over the Southeast Asian colonies of Britain, France and the Netherlands, and to improve its relations with the Soviet Union through the good offices of Germany.

The last objective was reached when Japan signed a neutrality pact with the Soviet Union in April 1941. Two months later Germany attacked the Soviet Union, without consulting

Japan. It compounded this second "betrayal" by asking Japan to attack the Soviet Union in the east. Japan waited and watched. When the German advance faltered, Japan decided to honor the neutrality pact and turn south. This, in effect, was the end of Japan's participation in the Axis. Thereafter, it fought its own war in Asia. Yet instead of deflecting American criticism as intended, the pact, by linking Japan to Germany, hardened America's position on China.

The third and fateful decision was to go to war with the United States. In June 1941, following Germany's defeat of

An Observer Describes the Mass Murder of Jews in Ukraine

After World War II some German officers and officials were put on trial at Nuremberg by the victorious powers for crimes they were charged with having committed in the course of the war. The following selections from the testimony of a German construction engineer who witnessed the mass murder of Jews at Dubno in the Ukraine on October 5, 1942, reveal the brutality with which Hitler's attempt at a "final solution of the Jewish problem" was carried out.

Why did the German government commit these atrocities? Why were they directed chiefly at Jews? Was there a cost to Germany in pursuing such a policy? Why did ordinary Germans participate?

On October 5, 1942, when I visited the building office at Dubno, my foreman told me that in the vicinity of the site, Jews from Dubno had been shot in three large pits, each about 30 metres long and 3 metres deep. About 1,500 persons had been killed daily. All the 5,000 Jews who had still been living in Dubno before the progrom were to be liquidated. As the shooting had taken place in his presence, he was still much upset.

Thereupon, I drove to the site accompanied by my foreman and saw near it great mounds of earth, about 30 metres long and 2 metres high. Several trucks stood in front of the mounds. Armed Ukrainian militia drove the people off the trucks under the supervision of an S.S. man. The militiamen acted as guards on the trucks and drove them to and from the pit. All these people had the regulation yellow patches on the front and back of their clothes, and thus could be recognized as Jews.

My foreman and I went directly to the pits. Nobody bothered us. Now I heard rifle shots in quick succession from behind one of the earth mounds. The people who had got off the trucks—men, women and children of all ages—had to undress upon the orders of an S.S. man, who carried a riding or dog whip. They had to put down their clothes in fixed places, sorted according to shoes, top clothing and underclothing. I saw a heap of shoes of about 800 to 1,000 pairs, great piles of underlinen and clothing.

Without screaming or weeping, these people undressed, stood around in family groups, kissed each other, said farewells, and waited for a sign from another S.S. man, who stood near the pit, also with a whip in his hand. During the fifteen minutes that I stood near I heard no complaint or plea for mercy. I watched a family of about eight persons, a man and a woman both about fifty with their children of about one, eight and ten, and two grown-up daughters of about twenty to twenty-nine. An old woman with snow-white hair was holding the one-year-old child in her arms and singing to it and tickling it. The child was cooing with delight. The couple were looking on with tears in their eyes. The father was holding the hand of a boy about ten years old and speaking to him softly; the boy was fighting his tears. The father pointed to the sky, stroked his head, and seemed to explain something to him.

At that moment the S.S. man at the pit shouted something to his comrade. The latter counted off about twenty persons and instructed them to go behind the earth mound. Among them was the family which I have mentioned. I well remember a girl, slim and with black hair, who, as she passed close to me pointed to herself and said "23." I walked around the mound and found myself confronted by a tremendous grave. People were closely wedged together and lying on top of each other so that only their heads were visible. Nearly all had blood running over their shoulders from their heads. Some of the people shot were still moving. Some were lifting their arms and turning their heads to show that they were still alive. The pit was already two-third full. I estimated that it already contained about 1,000 people.

From the *Nuremberg Proceedings*, as quoted in Louis L. Snyder. *Documents of German History.* © 1958 by Rutgers , The State University. pp. 462–464. Reprinted by permission of Rutgers University Press.

France, Japanese troops had occupied northern French Indochina. The United States retaliated by limiting strategic exports to Japan. In July 1941 Japanese troops took southern Indochina, and the United States embargoed all exports to Japan, cutting Japanese oil imports by 90 percent. The navy pressed for the capture of the oil-rich Dutch East Indies. But it would be too dangerous to move against Dutch and British colonies in Southeast Asia with the United States on its flank in the Philippines. The navy, therefore, planned a preemptive strike against the United States. The Japanese decision for war wagered Japan's land-based air power, shorter supply lines, and what it saw as greater will power against American productivity. At the Imperial Conference where the all-or-nothing decision was taken, the navy's chief of staff compared the war with the United States to a dangerous operation that might save a critically ill patient.

America's Entry into the War

On Sunday morning, December 7, 1941, even while Japanese representatives were discussing a settlement in Washington, Japan launched an air attack on Pearl Harbor, Hawaii,

The successful Japanese attack on the American base at Pearl Harbor in Hawaii on December 7, 1941, together with simultaneous attacks on other Pacific bases, brought the United States into war against the Axis powers. This picture shows the battleships U.S.S. *West Virginia* and U.S.S. *Tennessee* in flames as a small boat rescues a man from the water. [U.S. Army Photograph]

the chief American naval base in the Pacific. The next day, the United States and Britain declared war on Japan. Three days later, Germany and Italy declared war on the United States.

The Tide Turns

The potential power of the United States was enormous, but America was ill prepared for war. Although conscription had been introduced in 1940, the army was tiny, inexperienced, and poorly supplied. American industry was not ready for war. The Japanese swiftly captured Guam, Wake Island, and the Philippines. (See Map 35–4). They also attacked Hong Kong, Malaya, Burma, and Indonesia. By the summer of 1942, the Japanese Empire stretched from the western Aleutian Islands south almost to Australia, and from Burma east to the Gilbert Islands in the mid-Pacific.

In the same year, the Germans almost reached the Caspian Sea in their drive for Russia's oil fields. In Africa, Rom-

mel drove the British back toward the Suez Canal and finally was stopped at El Alamein, only seventy miles from Alexandria. Relations between the democracies and their Soviet ally were not close; German submarines were threatening British supplies; the Allies were being thrown back on every front, and the future looked bleak.

The tide turned at the Battle of Midway in June 1942. A month earlier, both sides had suffered massive losses in the Battle of the Coral Sea, but greater U.S. ship production made such trade-offs unprofitable for Japan. At Midway, American planes destroyed four Japanese aircraft carriers. Soon American Marines landed on Guadalcanal in the Solomon Islands and began to reverse the momentum of the war. The war in the Pacific was far from over, but Japan was checked sufficiently to allow the Allies to concentrate their efforts first in the West.

Allied Landings in Africa, Sicily, and Italy In November 1942, an Allied force landed in French North

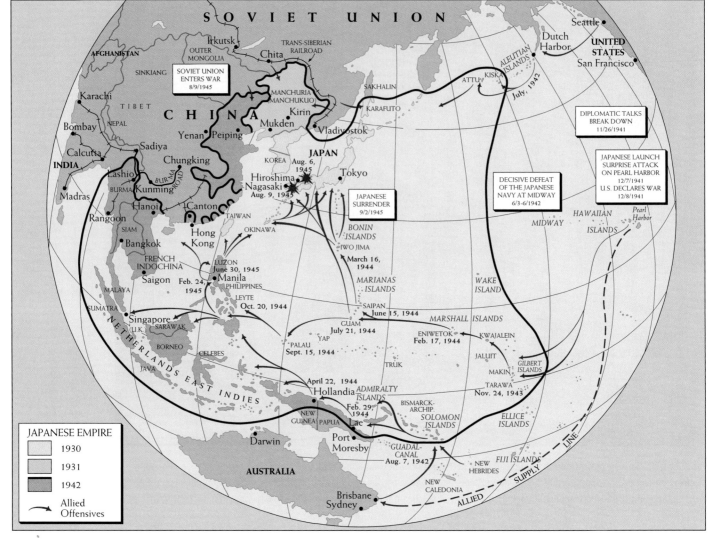

Map 35–4 The war in the Pacific. As in Europe, the Allies initially had trouble recapturing areas that the Japanese had quickly seized early in the war. The map shows the initial expansion of the Japanese and the long struggle of the Allies to push them back to their homeland and defeat them.

Africa. Even before that landing, the British Field Marshal Bernard Montgomery (1887–1976), after stopping Rommel at El Alamein, had begun a drive to the west (see Map 35–5). The American general Dwight D. Eisenhower (1890–1969) had pushed eastward through Morocco and Algeria. The German army was trapped in Tunisia and crushed. The Mediterranean was now under Allied control, and southern Europe was exposed. In July and August 1943 the Allies took Sicily. Mussolini was driven from power, the Allies landed in Italy, and Marshal Pietro Badoglio (1871–1956), the leader of the new Italian government, declared war on Germany. Churchill had spoken of Italy as the "soft underbelly" of the Axis, but German resistance was tough and determined. Still, the need to defend Italy strained the Germans' energy and resources and left them vulnerable on other fronts.

Battle of Stalingrad The Russian campaign became especially demanding. In the summer of 1942 the Germans resumed the offensive on all fronts but did not get far, except in the south. Their goal there was the oil fields near the Caspian Sea, and they got as far as Stalingrad on the Volga, a key point for protecting the flank of their southern army. Hitler was determined to take the city and Stalin to hold it. The Battle of Stalingrad raged for months with unexampled ferocity. The Russians lost more men than the Americans lost in combat during the entire war, but their heroic defenses prevailed. Because Hitler again overruled his gener-

Russian soldiers, in their heroic defense of Stalingrad, dug trenches from building to building in the city. The German defeat at Stalingrad in February 1943 marked the turning point of the Russian campaign. Thereafter the Russians advanced inexorably westward. [Archive Photos]

als and would not allow a retreat, an entire German army was lost.

Stalingrad marked the turning point of the Russian campaign. Thereafter, as the German military and material resources dwindled, the Russians advanced westward inexorably.

Strategic Bombing In 1943 the Allies also gained ground in production and logistics. The industrial might of the United States began to come into full force. New technology and tactics made great strides in eliminating the submarine menace. In the same year the American and British air forces began a series of massive bombardments

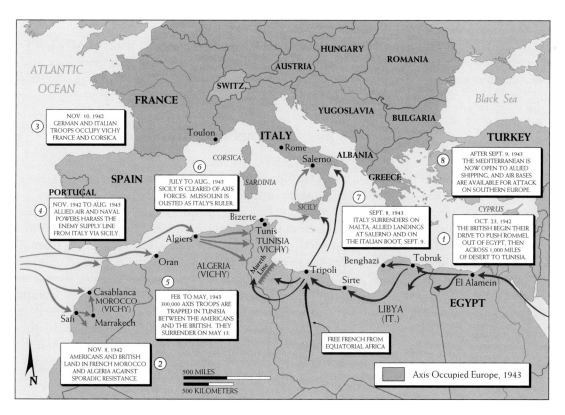

Map 35–5 North African campaigns, 1942–1945.
Control of North Africa was important to the Allies if they were to have access to Europe from the south. The map diagrams this theater of the war from Morocco to Egypt and the Suez Canal.

Allied troops landed in Normandy on D-Day, June 6, 1944. This photograph, taken two days later, shows long lines of men and equipment moving inland from the beach to reinforce the troops leading the invasion. [Archive Photos]

of Germany by night and day. This bombing did not have much effect on the war until 1944. Then the Americans introduced long-range fighters that could protect the bombers and allow accurate missions by day. By 1945 the Allies could bomb at will.

Defeat of Nazi Germany

On June 6, 1944 (D-Day), Allied troops landed in force on the coast of Normandy (see Map 35–6). By the beginning of September France had been liberated.

All went smoothly until December, when the Germans launched a counterattack called the Battle of the Bulge through the Forest of Ardennes. However, it was their last gasp. The Allies recovered the momentum and pushed eastward. They crossed the Rhine in March of 1945, and German resistance crumbled. This time there could be no doubt that the Germans had lost the war on the battlefield.

In the east, the Russians were within reach of Berlin by March 1945. Because the Allies insisted on unconditional surrender, the Germans fought on until May. Hitler committed

suicide in an underground hideaway in Berlin on May 1, 1945. The Russians occupied Berlin by agreement with their western allies. The Third Reich had lasted a dozen years instead of the millennium predicted by Hitler.

Fall of the Japanese Empire

The war in Europe ended on May 8, 1945, and by then victory over Japan was in sight (see also Chapter 32). The original Japanese attack on the United States had been a calculated risk against the odds. The longer the war lasted, the greater the impact of American superiority in industrial production and human resources. Beginning in 1943 American forces began a campaign of "island hopping," selecting major bases and places strategically located along the enemy supply line. Starting from the Solomons, they moved northeast toward the Japanese homeland. American bombers launched a terrible wave of bombings that destroyed Japanese industry and disabled the Japanese navy. But still the Japanese government, dominated by a military clique, refused to surrender.

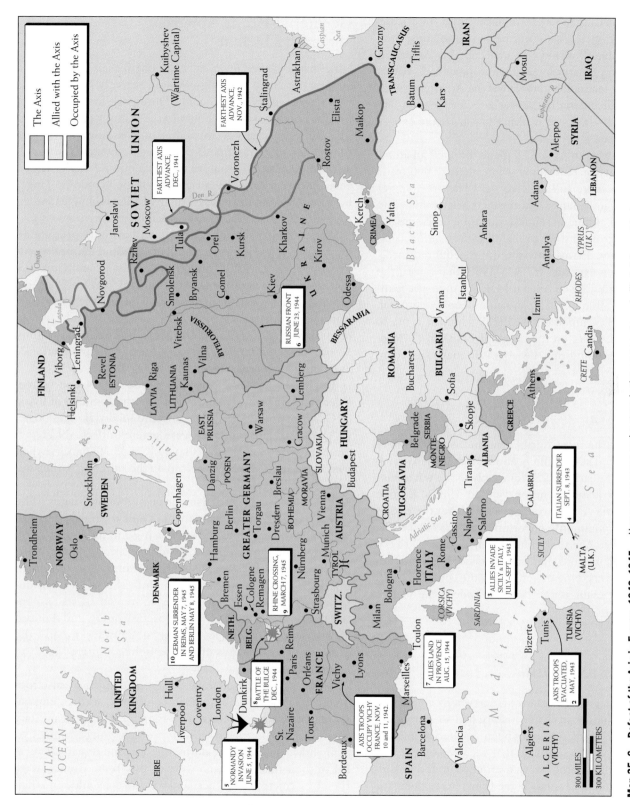

The Axis
Allied with the Axis
Occupied by the Axis

IRAN

IRAQ

Mosul

Aleppo

SYRIA

Adana

LEBANON

Antalya

CYPRUS (U.K.)

RHODES

CRETE Candia

Caspian Sea

Grozny

TRANSCAUCASUS

Batum Tiflis

Kars

Astrakhan

Kuibyshev (Wartime Capital)

FARTHEST AXIS ADVANCE, NOV., 1942

Stalingrad

Elista

Maikop

Rostov

Kerch

CRIMEA

Yalta

Sinop

Istanbul

Ankara

Izmir

Varna

BULGARIA

Sofia

ROMANIA

Bucharest

Odessa

BESSARABIA

Voronezh

FARTHEST AXIS ADVANCE, DEC., 1941

Moscow

Jaroslavl

Novgorod

SOVIET UNION

Rzhev

Tula

Orel

Kursk

Kharkov

Kirov

Kiev

UKRAINE

RUSSIAN FRONT 6 JUNE 23, 1944

Smolensk

Bryansk

Gomel

Vitebsk

Lemberg

BELORUSSIA

Don R

Lake Ladoga

Lake Onega

FINLAND

Viborg

Leningrad

Helsinki

Revel

ESTONIA

Riga

LATVIA

Kaunas

Vilna

LITHUANIA

Danzig

EAST PRUSSIA

Warsaw

Posen

Cracow

MORAVIA

Breslau

BOHEMIA

Dresden

Torgau

Vienna

Munich

AUSTRIA

SLOVAKIA

HUNGARY

Budapest

Belgrade

SERBIA

MONTE-NEGRO

Skopje

YUGOSLAVIA

CROATIA

Tirana

ALBANIA

Athens

GREECE

Black Sea

Stockholm

SWEDEN

Trondheim

NORWAY

Oslo

Copenhagen

DENMARK

Hamburg

Berlin

Bremen

Essen

Cologne

Remagen

RHINE CROSSING, 9 MARCH 7, 1945

Nürnberg

Strasbourg

Baltic Sea

NETH.

BELG.

10 GERMAN SURRENDER IN REIMS, MAY 7, 1945 AND BERLIN MAY 8, 1945

8 BATTLE OF THE BULGE DEC., 1944

Reims

Paris

Orléans

FRANCE

Vichy

Lyons

SWITZ.

TYROL

GREATER GERMANY

Milan

Bologna

Florence

Rome

ITALY

Cassino

Naples

Salerno

CALABRIA

SICILY

3 ALLIES INVADE SICILY & ITALY, JULY–SEPT., 1943

ITALIAN SURRENDER 4 SEPT. 8, 1943

CORSICA (VICHY)

SARDINIA

Adriatic Sea

UNITED KINGDOM

Hull

Liverpool

Coventry

London

EIRE

Dunkirk

5 NORMANDY INVASION JUNE 5, 1944

St. Nazaire

Tours

Bordeaux

1 AXIS TROOPS OCCUPY VICHY FRANCE, NOV. 10 and 11, 1942

Toulon

Marseilles

7 ALLIES LAND IN PROVENCE AUG. 15, 1944

SPAIN

Barcelona

Valencia

Toulon

Bizerte

Tunis

TUNISIA (VICHY)

AXIS TROOPS EVACUATED, 2 MAY, 1943

Algiers

ALGERIA (VICHY)

Mediterranean Sea

MALTA (U.K.)

ATLANTIC OCEAN

North Sea

300 MILES

300 KILOMETERS

Map 35–6   Defeat of the Axis in Europe, 1942–1945.   Here we see some major steps in the progress toward allied victory against Axis Europe. From the south through Italy, the west through France, and the east through Russia, the Allies gradually conquered the continent to bring the war in Europe to a close.

Confronted with Japan's determination, the Americans made plans for a frontal assault on the Japanese homeland, which, they calculated, would cost unacceptable American casualties and even greater losses for the Japanese. At this point, science and technology presented the Americans with another choice. Since early in the war a secret program had been in progress. Its staff was working to use atomic energy for military purposes.

On August 6, 1945, an American plane dropped an atomic bomb on the city of Hiroshima. More than 70,000 of its 200,000 residents were killed. Two days later the Soviet Union declared war on Japan and invaded Manchuria. The next day a second atomic bomb fell, this time on Nagasaki. Even then the Japanese were prepared to face an invasion rather than give up. It was only the unprecedented intervention of Emperor Hirohito (r. 1926–1989) that forced the government to surrender on August 14. Even then, the Cabinet made the condition that Japan could keep its emperor. President Harry S. Truman (1884–1972), who had come to office on April 12, 1945, on the death of Franklin D. Roosevelt, accepted the condition. Peace was formally signed on September 2, 1945.

The Cost of War

World War II was the most terrible war in history. Military deaths are estimated at 15 million, and at least as many civilians were killed. If deaths linked indirectly to the war are included, as many as 40 million may have died. Most of Europe and significant parts of Asia were devastated. Yet the end of so terrible a war brought little opportunity for relaxation. The dawn of the Atomic Age that brought a dramatic end to the war made people conscious that another major war might destroy humanity. Everything depended on the conclusion of a stable peace, but even as the fighting ended, the victors began to quarrel.

The Domestic Fronts

World War II represented an effort of total war by all the belligerents. Never before in world history had so many men and women and so many resources been devoted to military effort. One result was the carnage that occurred on the battlefields and at sea. Another was an unprecedented organization of civilians on the various home fronts. Each domestic effort and experience was different, but almost no one escaped the impact of the conflict. Shortages, propaganda campaigns, and new political developments were ubiquitous. In this section we look at the home fronts of the principal European belligerents.

Germany: From Apparent Victory to Defeat

Hitler had expected to defeat all his enemies by rapid strokes, or *blitzkrieg*. Such campaigns would scarcely have affected Germany's society and economy. During the first two years of the war, in fact, Hitler demanded few important sacrifices from the German people. Spending on domestic projects continued, and food was plentiful; the economy was not on a full wartime footing. The failure to knock out the Soviet Union changed everything. Because enough food could no longer be imported from the east, Germany had to mobilize for total war, and the government demanded major sacrifices.

A great expansion of the army and military production began in 1942. As minister for armaments and munitions, Albert Speer (1905–1981) guided the economy, and Germany met its military needs instead of making consumer goods. Major German business enterprises aided the growth of wartime production. Between 1942 and late 1944 the output of military products tripled; but as the war went on the army absorbed more men from industry, hurting the production of even military goods.

Beginning in 1942 everyday products became scarce. Prices and wages were controlled, but the standard of living of German workers fell. Burdensome food rationing began in April 1942, and shortages were severe until the Nazi government seized food from occupied Europe. To preserve their own home front, the Nazis passed on the suffering to their defeated neighbors.

By 1943 there were also serious labor shortages. The Nazis required German teenagers and retired workers to work in the factories, and increasing numbers of women joined them. To achieve total mobilization the Germans closed retail businesses, raised the maximum age of women eligible for compulsory service, shifted non-German domestic workers to wartime industry, moved artists and entertainers into military service, closed theaters, and reduced such basic public services as mail and railways. Finally, the Nazis forced thousands of people from conquered lands to labor in Germany.

Hitler assigned women a special place in the war effort. The celebration of motherhood continued, with an emphasis on women who were the mothers of important military figures. Films portrayed ordinary women who became especially brave and patriotic during the war and remained faithful to their husbands who were at the front. Women were thereby depicted as mothers and wives who would send their sons and husbands off to war. The government portrayed other wartime activities of women as the natural fulfillment of their maternal roles. As air raid wardens they protected their families; as factory workers in munitions plants they aided their sons on the front lines. Women working on farms were providing for their soldier sons and husbands; as housewives they were helping to win the war by conserving food and managing their households frugally. Finally, by their faithful chastity, German women were protecting racial purity. They were not to marry or to engage in sexual relations with men who were not Germans. German women were thus supposed to demonstrate the kind of service and courage required by the war.

The war years also saw an intensification of political propaganda on the domestic front beyond what occurred in other countries. Hitler and other Nazis genuinely believed that weak domestic support had led to Germany's defeat in World War I, and they were determined that this would not happen again. Nazi propaganda blamed the outbreak of the war on the British and its prolongation on the policies of Germany's opponents. It also stressed the might of Germany and the inferiority of its foes.

Propaganda Minister Josef Goebbels (1897–1945) used radio and films to boost the Nazi cause. Movies of the collapse of Poland, Belgium, Holland, and France demonstrated German military might. Throughout the conquered territories the Nazis used the same mass media to frighten inhabitants about the possible consequences of an Allied victory. Later in the war the ministry broadcast exaggerated claims of Nazi victories. As the German armies were checked on the battlefield, especially in Russia, propaganda became a substitute for victory. To stiffen German resolve, the propaganda also aimed to frighten the German population about the consequences of defeat.

After May 1943, when the Allies began their major bombing offensive over Germany, the German people had much to fear. One German city after another endured heavy bombing, fires, and destruction. But the bombing did not undermine German morale—on the contrary, it may have confirmed the general fear of defeat at the hands of such savage opponents and increased German resistance.

World War II brought increased power to the Nazi party in Germany. Every area of the economy and society came under the direct influence or control of the party. The Nazis were determined that they, rather than the traditionally honored German officer corps, would profit from the new authority flowing to the central government because of the war effort. Throughout the war years there was virtually no serious opposition to Hitler or his ministers. In 1944 a small group of army officers made an attempt to assassinate Hitler;

The Allied campaign of aerial bombardment did terrible damage to German cities. This photograph shows the devastation it delivered to the city of Cologne on the Rhine. [UPI/Corbis-Bettmann]

the effort failed, and there was no significant popular support for this act.

The war brought great changes to Germany, but what transformed the country afterward was the experience of defeat accompanied by vast physical destruction, invasion, and occupation. Hitler and the Nazis had brought the nation to such a complete and disastrous end that only a new kind of state with new political structures could emerge.

France: Defeat, Collaboration, and Resistance

In France the Vichy government cooperated closely with the Germans for a variety of reasons. Some of the collaborators believed that the Germans were sure to win and wanted to be on the victorious side. A few sympathized with the ideas and plans of the Nazis. Many conservatives regarded the French defeat as a judgment on what they saw as the corrupt, secularized, liberal Third Republic. But most of the French were not active collaborators and remained helpless and demoralized by defeat and German power.

Many conservatives and extreme rightists saw the Vichy government as a device to reshape the French national character and halt the decadence they associated with political and religious liberalism. The Roman Catholic clergy, who had lost power and influence under the Third Republic, gained status under Vichy. The church supported Pétain; his government supported religious education. Vichy adopted the church's views of the importance of family and spiritual values. Divorce was forbidden during the first three years of marriage and difficult thereafter; large families were rewarded.

The Vichy regime embraced an intense, chauvinistic nationalism. It encouraged the long-standing prejudice against foreigners working in France and persecuted those who were not regarded as genuinely and thoroughly French. The chief victims were French Jews. Antisemitism was not new in France, as the Dreyfus affair had demonstrated. Even before Germany undertook Hitler's "final solution" in 1942, the French had begun to remove Jews from government, education, and publishing. In 1941 the Germans began to intern Jews living in occupied France; soon they carried out killings and imposed large fines collectively on the Jews of the occupied zone. In the spring of 1942 the Germans began deporting Jews, ultimately over 60,000, to the extermination camps of eastern Europe. The Vichy government had no part in these decisions, but it made no protest, and its own antisemitic policies facilitated the process.

A few Frenchmen had fled to join de Gaulle's Free French forces soon after the defeat of 1940. Serious internal resistance to the German occupiers and to the Vichy government, however, developed only late in 1942. The Germans attempted to force young people in occupied France to work in German factories; some of them fled and joined the Resistance, but the total number of resisters was small. Many were deterred by fear. Some disliked the violence that resistance inevitably entailed. So long as it appeared that the Germans would win the war, moreover, resistance seemed imprudent and futile. In all, less than 5 percent of the adult French population appear to have been involved.

By early 1944 the tide of battle had shifted. An Allied victory appeared inevitable, and the Vichy government was clearly doomed. Only then did an active resistance assert itself. General de Gaulle urged the French people to resist their conquerors and their lackeys in the Vichy government. Within France resistance groups joined forces to plan for a better day. From Algiers on August 9, 1944, the Committee of National Liberation declared the authority of Vichy illegitimate. Soon French soldiers joined in the liberation of Paris and established a government for Free France. On October 21, 1945, France voted to adopt a new constitution as the basis of the Fourth Republic. The French people had experienced defeat, disgrace, deprivation, and suffering. Hostility and bitter quarrels over who had done what during the occupation and the Vichy period divided them for decades.

Great Britain: Organization for Victory

On May 22, 1940, the British Parliament gave the government emergency powers. The government could now institute compulsory military service, food rationing, and various controls over the economy.

Churchill and the British war cabinet moved as quickly as possible to mobilize the nation. By the end of 1941 British production had already surpassed Germany's. To meet the heavy demands on the labor force, factory hours were extended, and women were brought into the work force in great numbers. Unemployment disappeared, and the working classes had more money to spend than they had enjoyed for many years. To avoid inflation caused by increased demand for an inadequate supply of consumer goods, savings were encouraged, and taxes raised to absorb the excess purchasing power.

The bombing "blitz" conducted by the German *Luftwaffe* against British targets in the winter and spring of 1940 to 1941 was the most immediate and dramatic experience of the war for the British people. The German air raids killed thousands and destroyed the homes of many more. Many families removed their children to the countryside. Gas masks were issued to thousands of city-dwellers, who were frequently compelled to take shelter from the bombs in the London subways.

A rubble-strewn street in London after the city had experienced a night of German bombing. Despite many casualties and widespread devastation, the German bombing of London did not break British morale or prevent the city from functioning. [The Granger Collection, N.Y.]

After the spring of 1941 Hitler needed most of his air force for the Russian front, but the bombing of Britain continued, killing more than 30,000 people. Terrible as it was, this toll was much smaller than the number of Germans killed by Allied bombing later in the war. In England as in Germany, however, the bombing did not break the people's spirit, but seems to have made them more determined.

During the worst months of the "blitz" the remarkable speeches of Winston Churchill cheered and encouraged the British people. He united them with a sense of common suffering and purpose. They were called upon to make many sacrifices: Transportation facilities were strained simply from carrying enough coal for domestic heating and for running factories. Food and clothing for civilians was in short supply, and the government adopted strict rationing to achieve a fair distribution. Every scrap of land was farmed, increasing the productive portion by almost 4 million acres. Gasoline was in short supply, so private vehicles almost disappeared.

The British established their own propaganda machine to influence the continent. The British Broadcasting Company (BBC) sent programs to every country in Europe in the local language to encourage resistance against the Nazis. At home the government used the radio to unify the nation. Soldiers at the front heard the same programs as their families at home.

For most of the population, strangely enough, the standard of living improved over the course of the war. The general health of the nation also improved for reasons that are still not clear. These gains should not be exaggerated, but many connected them with the active involvement of the government in the economy and the lives of the citizens. This wartime experience may have contributed to the Labour Party's victory in 1945; many feared that a return to Conservative rule would bring a return to the economic misery of the 1930s.

The Soviet Union: "The Great Patriotic War"

No nation suffered greater loss of life or more extensive physical destruction during World War II than the Soviet Union. Perhaps as many as 16 million people were killed, and vast numbers of Soviet troops were taken prisoner. Hundreds of cities and towns and well over half of the industrial and transportation facilities of the country were devastated. The Germans sent thousands of Soviet prisoners to work in factories in Germany as forced labor. The Germans also confiscated grain supplies and drew mineral resources and oil from the Soviet Union to serve their own war effort.

Stalin (1879–1953) conducted the war as virtual chief of the armed forces, and the State Committee for Defense provided strong central coordination. In the decade before the war, Stalin had already made the Soviet Union a highly centralized nation; he had attempted to manage the entire economy centrally through the five-year plans, the collectivization of agriculture, and the purges. The country was thus on what amounted to a wartime footing long before the conflict erupted. When the war began, millions of citizens entered the army, but the army did not grow in influence at the expense of the state and the Communist Party—that is, Stalin.

Soviet propaganda differed from that of other nations. Because the Soviet government distrusted the loyalty of its citizens, it confiscated radios to prevent the people from listening to German propaganda. In large cities the government erected large loudspeakers to broadcast to the people in place of radios. Soviet propaganda emphasized Russian patriotism, not Marxist class conflict. The struggle was called "The Great Patriotic War." As in other countries, writers and playwrights helped sustain public support for the war. Sometimes they drew on Communist themes, but they also portrayed the common Soviet citizen as contributing to a great patriotic struggle.

Great Russian novels of the past reappeared; more than half a million copies of Tolstoy's *War and Peace* were published during the siege of Leningrad. Other authors wrote straightforward propaganda fostering hatred of the Germans. Serge Eisenstein (1898–1948), the great filmmaker, produced a vast epic entitled *Ivan the Terrible*, which glorified one of the most brutal tsars of Russia's past. Musicians, such as Dimitri Shostakovich (1906–1975), wrote scores that sought to contribute to the struggle and evoke heroic emotions. The most important of these was Shostakovich's *Seventh Symphony*, also known as the *Leningrad Symphony*.

Stalin even made peace with the Russian Orthodox church. He pursued friendly relations with church leaders and allowed them to enter the Kremlin. Stalin hoped that this new policy would give him more support at home and permit the Soviet Union to be viewed more favorably in eastern Europe where the orthodox church predominated.

Within occupied portions of the western Soviet Union, an active resistance movement arose against the Germans. The swiftness of the German invasion had stranded thousands of Soviet troops, some of whom escaped and carried on irregular resistance warfare behind enemy lines. Stalin supported partisan forces in lands held by the enemy for two reasons: He wanted to cause as much difficulty as possible for the Germans; and the Soviet-sponsored resistance reminded the peasants in the conquered regions that the Soviet government, with its policies of collectivization, had not disappeared. Stalin feared that the peasants' hatred of the Communist government might lead them to collaborate with the invaders. When the Soviet army moved westward toward the end of the war, it incorporated the partisans into the regular army.

As the Soviet armies reclaimed the occupied areas and then moved across eastern and central Europe, the Soviet Union established itself as a world power second only to the United States. Stalin had been a reluctant belligerent, but he emerged a major victor. In that respect, the war and the extraordinary patriotic effort and sacrifice it generated consoli-

dated the power of Stalin and the party more effectively than had the political and social policies of the previous decade.

Preparations for Peace

The split between the Soviet Union and its wartime allies that followed the war and began to emerge as it ended should cause no surprise. As the self-proclaimed center of world communism, the Soviet Union was openly dedicated to the overthrow of the capitalist nations, although this message was muted when the occasion demanded. On the other side, the western allies were no less open about their hostility to communism and its chief purveyor, the Soviet Union.

Although cooperation against a common enemy and strenuous propaganda efforts in the west helped improve western feeling toward the Soviet ally, Stalin remained suspicious and critical of the western war effort. Likewise, Churchill never ceased planning to contain the Soviet advance into Europe. For some time Roosevelt seems to have hoped that the Allies could continue to work together after the war. But even he was losing faith by 1945. Differences in historical development and ideology, as well as traditional conflicts over political power and influence, soon dashed hopes of a mutually satisfactory peace settlement and continued cooperation to uphold it.

The Atlantic Charter

In August 1941, even before America entered the war, Roosevelt and Churchill had met off Newfoundland and agreed to the Atlantic Charter. A broad set of principles in the spirit of Wilson's Fourteen Points, it provided a theoretical basis for the peace they sought. When Russia and the United States joined Britain in the war, the three powers entered a purely military alliance in January 1942, leaving all political questions aside. The first political conference was the meeting of foreign ministers in Moscow in October 1943. The ministers reaffirmed earlier agreements to fight on until the enemy surrendered unconditionally and to continue cooperating after the war in a united-nations organization.

Tehran

The first meeting of the three leaders took place at Tehran, the capital of Iran, in 1943. Western promises to open a second front in France the next summer (1944) and Stalin's agreement to join in the war against Japan (when Germany was defeated) created an atmosphere of goodwill in which to discuss a postwar settlement. Stalin wanted to retain what he had gained in his pact with Hitler and to dismember Germany. Roosevelt and Churchill made no firm commitments.

This photograph shows the "Big Three" at Potsdam. By the summer of 1945 only Stalin remained of the original leaders of the major Allies. Roosevelt and Churchill had been replaced by Harry Truman and Clement Atlee.
[Corbis-Bettmann]

The most important decision was for the western allies to attack Germany from Europe's west coast instead of from southern Europe by way of the Mediterranean. This decision meant, in retrospect, that Soviet forces would occupy eastern Europe and control its destiny. At Tehran in 1943 the western allies did not foresee this clearly, for the Russians were still fighting deep within their own frontiers, and military considerations were paramount everywhere.

By 1944 the situation was different. In August, Soviet armies were in sight of Warsaw, which had risen in expectation of liberation. But the Russians turned south into the Balkans, allowing the Polish rebels to be annihilated. The Russians gained control of Romania and Hungary, gaining advances of which centuries of expansionist tsars had only dreamed. Alarmed by these developments, Churchill went to Moscow and met with Stalin in October. They agreed to share power in the Balkans on the basis of Soviet predominance in Romania and Bulgaria, western predominance in Greece, and equality of influence in Yugoslavia and Hungary. These agreements were not enforceable without American approval, and the Americans were known to be hostile to such un-Wilsonian devices as "spheres of influence."

The three powers easily agreed on Germany's disarmament and denazification and on its division into four zones of occupation by France and the Big Three (the USSR, Britain, and the United States). Churchill, however, began to balk at Stalin's plan to dismember Germany and objected to his demand for reparations in the amount of $20 billion as well as for forced labor from all the zones, with Russia to get half of everything. These matters were left to fester and cause dissension in the future.

The settlement of eastern Europe remained a problem. Everyone agreed that the Soviet Union deserved neighboring governments that were friendly, but the west insisted that they also be independent, autonomous, and democratic. The western leaders, and especially Churchill, were not eager to see eastern Europe fall under Russian domination. They, especially Roosevelt, were also truly committed to democracy and self-determination.

However, Stalin knew that independent, freely elected governments in Poland and Romania would not be safely friendly to Russia. He had already established a subservient government in Poland at Lublin in competition with the Polish government-in-exile in London. Under pressure from the western leaders, however, Stalin agreed to reorganize the government and to include some Poles friendly to the west. He also signed a Declaration on Liberated Europe, promising self-determination and free democratic elections. Stalin never was free of the fear that the Allies might still make an arrangement with Germany and betray him. Yet he appeared eager to avoid conflict before the war with Germany was over, and he probably thought it worth endorsing some meaningless principles as the price of continued harmony. In any case, he wasted little time violating these agreements.

Yalta

The next meeting of the Big Three was at Yalta in the Crimea in February 1945. The western armies had not yet crossed the Rhine, and the Soviet army was within a hundred miles of Berlin. The war with Japan continued, and no atomic explosion had yet taken place. Roosevelt, faced with an invasion

Map 35-7   Territorial changes after World War II.   The map shows
the shifts in territory that followed the defeat of the Axis. No treaty of
peace formally ended the war with Germany.

of Japan and prospective heavy losses, was eager to bring the
Russians into the Pacific war as soon as possible.

As a true Wilsonian, Roosevelt also suspected Churchill's
determination to maintain the British Empire and Britain's
colonial advantages. The Americans thought that
Churchill's plan to set up British spheres of influence in
Europe would encourage the Russians to do the same and
lead to friction and war. To encourage Russian participation in the war against Japan, Roosevelt and Churchill made
extensive concessions to Russia in Asia. Again in the tradition of Wilson, Roosevelt stressed a united-nations organization: "Through the United Nations, he hoped to
achieve a self-enforcing peace settlement that would not
require American troops, as well as an open world without
spheres of influence in which American enterprise could
work freely."[2] Soviet agreement on these points seemed
well worth concessions elsewhere.

Potsdam

The Big Three met for the last time in the Berlin suburb of
Potsdam in July 1945. Much had changed since the last conference. Germany was defeated, and news of the successful
experimental explosion of an atomic weapon reached the
American president during the meetings. The cast of characters was also different: President Truman replaced Roosevelt; and Clement Attlee (1883–1967), leader of the Labour
Party, replaced Churchill during the conference. Previous
agreements were reaffirmed, but progress on undecided questions was slow.

Russia's western frontier was moved far into what had
been Poland and included part of German East Prussia (see
Map 35–7). In compensation, Poland was allowed "temporary administration" over the rest of East Prussia and Germany east of the Oder-Neisse river line, a condition that
became permanent. In effect, Poland was moved about a hundred miles west, at the expense of Germany, to accommodate the Soviet Union. The Allies agreed that Germany
would be divided into occupation zones until the final peace
treaty was signed, and the country remained divided until
the end of the cold war more than forty years later.

A Council of Foreign Ministers was established to draft
peace treaties for Germany's allies. Growing disagreements
made the job difficult, and it was not until February 1947
that Italy, Romania, Hungary, Bulgaria, and Finland signed
treaties. The Russians signed their own agreements with the
Japanese in 1956. These disagreements were foreshadowed
at Potsdam.

[2]Robert O. Paxton, *Europe in the Twentieth Century* (New York: Harcourt
Brace Jovanovich, 1975), p. 487.

IN WORLD PERSPECTIVE
World War II

The second great war of the twentieth century (1939–1945) grew out of the unsatisfactory resolution of the first. In retrospect, the two wars appear to some people to be one continuous conflict—a kind of twentieth-century Thirty Years' War—with the two main periods of fighting separated by an uneasy truce. To others, that point of view distorts the situation by implying that the second war was the inevitable result of the first and its inadequate peace treaties.

The latter opinion seems more sound. Whatever the flaws of the treaties of Paris, the world suffered an even more terrible war than the first as a result of failures of judgment and will on the part of the victorious democratic powers. The United States, which had become the wealthiest and potentially the strongest nation in the world, disarmed almost entirely and withdrew into a short-sighted and foolish isolation; it could play no important part in restraining the angry and ambitious dictators who would bring on the war. Britain and France refused to face the reality of the threat posed by the Axis powers until the most deadly war in history was required to put it down. If the victorious democracies had remained strong, responsible, and realistic, they could easily have remedied whatever injustices or mistakes arose from the treaties without endangering the peace.

The second war itself was plainly a world war. The Japanese occupation of Manchuria in 1931, while not technically a part of that war, was a significant precursor. Italy attacked Ethiopia in 1935. Italy, Germany, and the Soviet Union intervened in the Spanish Civil War (1936–1939). Japan attacked China in 1937. All these developments revealed that aggressive forces were on the march around the globe and that the defenders of the world order lacked the will to stop them. The formation of the Axis among Germany, Italy, and Japan guaranteed that the war would be fought around the world. There was fighting and suffering in Asia, Africa, the islands of the Pacific, and Europe. Men and women from all the inhabited continents took part. The use of atomic weapons brought the frightful struggle to a close, but what are called conventional weapons did almost all the damage. The world reached a level of destructiveness that threatened the survival of civilization, even without the use of atomic or nuclear devices.

This was ended not with unsatisfactory peace treaties but with no treaty at all in the European area where the war had begun. The world quickly split into two unfriendly camps: the western led by the United States, and the eastern led by the Soviet Union. This division, among other things, hastened the liberation of former colonial territories. The bargaining power of these new nations was temporarily increased, as the two rival great powers tried to gain their friendship or allegiance. It became customary to refer to these nations as "the Third World," with the Soviet Union and the United States and their respective allies being the first two. With the passage of time, the differences among these newer nations became so great as to make the name almost meaningless.

One of the most surprising aspects of the second war, the treatment received by the defeated powers, was also largely the result of the emergence of the Cold War. Instead of holding them back, the western powers installed democratic governments in Italy, West Germany, and Japan, took them into the western alliances designed to contain communism, and helped them recover economically. Japan and the recently reunified Germany are now among the richest nations in the world, and Italy is more prosperous than it has ever been. Meanwhile, state control of the economy in Communist countries ultimately produced disastrous results around the world. As a result, the threat posed by communism, so feared soon after the war, has waned. The former Soviet Union, the original motherland of communism, has dissolved along with its satellite empire in Eastern Europe, and the states that made up the Union and the empire have rejected the discredited system. Even Communist China has turned increasingly to free enterprise to achieve economic prosperity. China, however, remains formally committed to communism, and former Communists remain influential in some of the states of the former Soviet empire. It may be too early, therefore, to be sure that communism in some form is a thing of the past.

Review Questions ———

1. What were Hitler's foreign policy aims? Was he bent on conquest in the east and dominance in the west, or did he simply want to return Germany to its 1914 boundaries?

2. Why did Britain and France adopt a policy of appeasement in the 1930s? What were its main features? Did the appeasers buy the west valuable time to prepare for war by their actions at Munich in 1938?

3. How was Hitler able to defeat France so easily in 1940? Why was the air war against Britain a failure? Why did Hitler invade Russia? Why did the invasion ultimately fail? Could it have succeeded?

4. Why did Japan attack the United States at Pearl Harbor? What was the significance of American intervention in the war? Why did the United States drop atomic bombs on Japan? Did President Truman make the right decision when he ordered the bombs used?

5. What impact did World War II have on the civilian population of Europe? How did experiences on the domestic front of Great Britain differ from those of Germany and France? What impact did "The Great Patriotic War" have on the people of the Soviet Union? Did participation in World War II solidify Stalin's hold on power?

6. What was Hitler's "final solution" to the Jewish problem? Why did Hitler want to eliminate Slavs as well? Some historians have looked at the twentieth century and have seen a period of great destruction as well as of great progress. Is this truly a "century of Holocaust"? Discuss the ramifications of these questions.

Suggested Readings ———

A. ADAMTHWAITE, *France and the Coming of the Second World War, 1936–1939* (1977). A careful account making good use of the newly opened French archives.

E. R. BECK, *Under the Bombs: The German Home Front, 1942–1945* (1986). An interesting examination of a generally unstudied subject.

A. BULLOCK, *Hitler: A Study in Tyranny*, rev. ed. (1964). A brilliant biography.

R. CARR, *The Civil War in Spain* (1986). A thorough and careful study.

W. S. CHURCHILL, *The Second World War*, 6 vols. (1948–1954). The memoirs of the great British leader.

L. DAWIDOWICZ, *The War Against the Jews, 1933–1945* (1975). An excellent account of the Holocaust.

H. FEIS, *From Trust to Terror: The Onset of the Cold War, 1945–1950* (1970). The best general account.

H. W. GATZKE, *Stresemann and the Rearmament of Germany* (1954). An important monograph.

M. GILBERT AND R. GOTT, *The Appeasers*, rev. ed. (1963). A revealing study of British policy in the 1930s.

M. HARRISON, *Soviet Planning in Peace and War, 1938–1945* (1985). An examination of the Soviet wartime economy.

K. HILDEBRAND, *The Foreign Policy of the Third Reich* (1970).

J. KEEGAN, *The Second World War* (1990). A lively account of the war written by a brilliant military historian.

M. KNOX, *Mussolini Unleashed* (1982). An outstanding study of Fascist Italy's policy and strategy in World War II.

G. KOLKO, *The Politics of War* (1968). An interesting example of the new revisionist school that finds the causes of the Cold War in economic considerations and emphasizes American responsibility.

W. L. LANGER AND S. E. GLEASON, *The Challenge of Isolation* (1952). American foreign policy in the 1930s.

D. C. LARGE, ED., *Contending with Hitler: Varieties of German Resistance in the Third Reich* (1992). Essays that examine the efforts of resistance to Hitler and their limits.

B. H. LIDDELL HART, *History of the Second World War*, 2 vols. (1971). A good military history.

S. MARKS, *The Illusion of Peace* (1976). A good discussion of European international relations in the 1920s and early 1930s.

V. MASTNY, *Russia's Road to the Cold War* (1979). Written by an expert on the Soviet Union and Eastern Europe.

W. MURRAY, *The Change in the European Balance of Power 1938–1939* (1984). A brilliant study of the relationship between strategy, foreign policy, economics, and domestic politics in the years before the war.

R. PIPES, *The Russian Revolution* (1991). A full and thoroughly up-to-date narrative and analysis.

N. RICH, *Hitler's War Aims*, 2 vols. (1973–1974).

M. SHERWIN, *A World Destroyed: The Atomic Bomb and the Grand Alliance* (1975). An analysis of the role of the atomic bomb in the years surrounding the end of World War II.

R. J. SONTAG, *A Broken World 1919–1939* (1971). An excellent survey.

A. J. P. TAYLOR, *The Origins of the Second World War* (1966). A lively, controversial, even perverse study.

C. THORNE, *The Approach of War 1938–1939* (1967). A careful analysis of diplomacy.

H. A. TURNER, JR., *Hitler's Thirty Days to Power* (1996). A compelling account of the lack of inevitability of Hitler's gaining control of Germany.

A. ULAM, *The Bolsheviks* (1968). An outstanding account of Lenin's faction and its rise to power.

P. WANDYCZ, *The Twilight of French Eastern Alliances, 1926–1936* (1988). A well-documented account of the diplomacy of central and eastern Europe in a crucial period.

D. C. WATT, *How War Came* (1989). A thorough study of the diplomatic history of the origins of World War II.

G. WRIGHT, *The Ordeal of Total War 1939–1945* (1968). An excellent survey.

36 THE WEST SINCE WORLD WAR II

The opening of the Berlin Wall in November 1989, more than any other event, symbolized the collapse of the Communist

governments in Eastern Europe. [R. Bossu/Sygma]

CHAPTER TOPICS

◆ The Cold War Era

◆ European Society in the Second Half of the Twentieth Century

◆ American Domestic Scene Since World War II

◆ The Soviet Union to 1989

◆ 1989: Year of Revolutions in Eastern Europe

◆ The Collapse of the Soviet Union

◆ The Collapse of Yugoslavia and Civil War

◆ Problems in the Wake of the Collapse of Communism

In World Perspective The West Since 1945

In the more than half a century since the conclusion of World War II, Europe's influence on the world scene has been transformed. The destruction and financial strains of the war left Europe exhausted and incapable of exercising the kind of power it had formerly exerted. Almost immediately after the war, the Cold War developed between the United States and the Soviet Union. Europe along with other parts of the world became a divided and contested territory, with America dominant in Western Europe and the Soviets dominant in Eastern Europe. The European powers themselves could not determine the outcome of that struggle for world dominance between the superpowers. Furthermore, less than five years after the war Europeans began to lose control of their overseas empires.

Within both the world context and the more narrow Western context, the greatest change that took place after 1945 was the emergence of the United States as a fully active great power. The American retreat from leadership that occurred in 1919 was not repeated. The decision by the United States to take an activist role in world affairs touched virtually every aspect of the postwar world. As a result of this acceptance of a leadership role, American domestic politics and its foreign policy became intertwined as in no previous period of American history.

Europe did not stagnate in this situation. Rather its society continued to develop in new directions. Population, agricultural production, and general consumption increased, especially in Western Europe. Like virtually every other part of the world, Europe experienced the impact of American culture through military alliances, trade, tourism, and popular entertainment. Europeans also began to build structures for greater economic cooperation.

Yet for forty-five years after the Second World War, Europe remained divided between a western region generally characterized by democracies and an eastern region characterized by Communist party authoritarian states dominated by the Soviet Union. From the late 1970s onward there were political stirrings and economic stagnation in Eastern Europe and the Soviet Union. These culminated in 1989 with revolutions throughout Eastern Europe and in 1991 with the collapse of Communist government in the Soviet Union itself. For over a decade since those events Europeans have been seeking to forge a new political direction. The movement toward unification, most particularly of the currency, continues in Western Europe. But the several nations that emerged from the former Soviet Union continue to experience political confusion and economic stagnation.

The Cold War Era

Initial Causes

The tense relationship between the United States and the Soviet Union that dominated world history during the second half of the twentieth century originated in the closing months of World War II. In part, the new coldness between the Allies arose from the mutual feeling that each had violated previous agreements. The Russians were plainly asserting permanent control of Poland and Romania under puppet Communist governments. The United States, on the other hand, was taking a harder line on the extent of German reparations to the Soviet Union.

In retrospect, however, it appears unlikely that friendlier styles on either side could have avoided a split that rested on basic differences of ideology and interest. The Soviet Union's attempt to extend its control westward into central Europe and the Balkans and southward into the Middle East was a continuation of the policy of tsarist Russia. It had been Britain's traditional role to restrain Russian expansion into these areas; the United States inherited that task as Britain's power waned. The alternative was to permit a major change in the balance of power in the world in favor of a huge, traditionally hostile nation. That nation, dedicated in its official ideology to the overthrow of nations like the United States, was governed by Stalin (1879–1953), an absolute dictator, who had repeatedly demonstrated his capacity for the most amazing deceptions and the most horrible cruelties. Few nations would be likely to take such risks.

In the aftermath of World War II, however, the Americans made no attempt to roll back Soviet power where it already existed. This was true even though American military forces were the greatest in their history, American industrial power was unmatched in the world, and America had a monopoly on atomic weapons. In less than a year from the war's end, the Americans reduced their forces in Europe from 3.5 million to half a million. The speedy withdrawal reflected pressure to "get the boys home," but it was also fully in accord with America's peacetime plans and goals. These goals included support for self-determination, autonomy, and democracy in the political sphere; and free trade, freedom of the seas, no barriers to investment, and the Open Door in the economic sphere. As the strongest, richest nation in the world—the one with the greatest industrial plant and the strongest currency—the United States would benefit handsomely if an international order based on such goals were established.

American hostility to colonial empires created tensions with France and Britain, but these stresses were minor. The main conflict was with the Soviet Union. From the Soviet perspective, extending the borders of the USSR and dominating the formerly independent states of Eastern Europe would provide needed security and would compensate the Soviet people for the fearful losses they had endured in the war. The Soviets could thus see American resistance to their expansion as a threat to their security and their legitimate aims. American objections over Poland and other states could be seen as attempts to undermine regimes friendly to Russia and to encircle the Soviet Union with hostile neighbors.

The growth in France and Italy of large Communist parties plainly taking orders from Moscow led the Americans to believe that Stalin was engaged in a great worldwide plot to subvert capitalism and democracy. In the absence of reliable evidence about Stalin's intentions, it is impossible to know for certain if these suspicions were justified, but most people in the West considered them plausible.

Areas of Early Cold War Conflict

The new mood of hostility among the former allies appeared quickly. In February 1946 both Stalin and his foreign minister, Vyacheslav Molotov (1890–1986), gave public speeches in which they spoke of the Western democracies as enemies. A month later Churchill (1874–1965) delivered a speech in Fulton, Missouri, in which he spoke of an Iron Curtain that had descended on Europe, dividing a free and democratic West from an East under totalitarian rule. He warned against Communist subversion and urged Western unity and strength to counter the new menace. In this atmosphere, difficulties grew.

The attempt to deal cooperatively with the problem of atomic energy was an early victim of the Cold War. The Americans put forward a plan to place the manufacture and control of atomic weapons under international control, but the Russians balked at proposed requirements for on-site inspection and for limits on veto power in the United Nations. The plan fell through. The United States continued to develop its own atomic weapons in secrecy, and the Russians did the same. By 1949, with the help of information obtained by Soviet spies in Britain and the United States, the Soviet Union had exploded its own atomic bomb, and the race for nuclear weapons was on.

The resistance of Westerners to what they increasingly perceived as Soviet intransigence and Communist plans for subversion and expansion took clearer form in 1947. Since 1944 civil war had been raging in Greece between the royalist government restored by Britain and insurgents supported by the Communist countries, chiefly Yugoslavia. In 1947 Britain informed the United States that it was financially no longer able to support the Greeks. On March 12 President Truman (1884–1972) asked Congress for legislation that would provide funds to support Greece and also Turkey, which was under Soviet pressure to yield control of the Dardanelles, and Congress complied. In what became known as the Truman Doctrine, the American president advocated a policy of supporting "free people who are resisting attempted subjugation by armed minorities or by outside pressures," by implication anywhere in the world.

American aid to Greece and Turkey took the form of military equipment and advisers. For Western Europe, where the menacing growth of Communist parties was fueled by postwar poverty and hunger, the Americans devised the European Recovery Program. Named the Marshall Plan after George C. Marshall (1880–1959), the secretary of state who introduced it, this program provided broad economic aid to European states on condition only that they work together for their mutual benefit. The Soviet Union and its satellites

The Church and the Communist Party Clash over Education in Hungary

Throughout eastern Europe, the Roman Catholic church became one of the strongest opponents of the postwar Communist Party governments. It raised issues relating to Church schools, free worship, participation in Church-sponsored organizations, and the erection of new Church buildings. One of the harshest clashes took place in Hungary. Following are two statements that illustrate the opposing positions of the Church and the Party. Cardinal Mindszenty (1892–1975) was later imprisoned and became one of the most well-known political prisoners in eastern Europe.

How does Mindszenty relate the position of Church-supported schools to the nature and rights of parenthood? How does he compare the actions of the Communist Party to those of Hitler? How does the Minister of Public Worship set party members against the Church? How does he attempt to place loyalty to the party above private beliefs? What does the Communist Party fear from religious education and participation in religious activities on the part of its members of their children?

Statement of Josef Cardinal Mindszenty, May 20, 1946

The right of the Church to schools is entirely in concord with the right of parents to educate their children. What is incumbent upon the parents in all questions of natural life is incumbent upon the Church with regard to the supernatural life. Parents are prior to the state, and their rights were always and still are, acknowledged by the Church. The prerogative of parents to educate their children cannot be disputed by the state, since it is the parents who give life to the child. They feed the child and clothe it. The child's life is, as it were, the continuation of theirs. Hence it is their right to demand that their children are educated according to their faith and their religious outlook.

It is their right to withhold their children from schools where there religious convictions are not only disregarded but even made the object of contempt and ridicule. It was this parental right which German parents felt was violated when the Hitler government deprived them of their denominational schools. The children came home from the new schools like little heathens, who smiled derisively or laughed at the prayers of their parents.

You Hungarian parents will likewise feel a violation of your fundamental rights if your children can no longer attend the Catholic schools solely because the dictatorial State closes down our schools by a brutal edict or renders their work impossible.

Statement of the Hungarian Communist Minister of Public Worship, June 7, 1950

We must start a vast work of enlightenment, and in the first place explain to our party colleagues and also to all workers that any father who sends his child to religion classes, places it in the hands of the enemy and entrusts his soul and thinking to the enemies of peace and imperialistic warmongers.

A part of our working people believes that participation of children in religious instruction is a private matter which has nothing to do with the political conviction of their parents. They are wrong. To send children to a reactionary pastor for religious instruction, is a political movement against the People's Democracy, whether intentional or not. . . .

In carrying out the basic principles, religion within the party is no private matter, but we must take a difference between plain party members and party officials, and must not in any case make party membership dependent on the fact whether our party members are religious. In the first place, we must expect from our party officials, our leading men, that they do not send their children to religious instruction courses, do not take part in religious ceremonies and train their wives in the spirit of communistic conception.

Also, we must patiently endeavor to enlighten our members, and ensure through training and propaganda that they realize; "In going to Church, taking part in processions, sending our children to religious instruction, we unconsciously further the efforts of clerical reaction."

From *Readings in Church History* by Colman J. Barry, O.S.B. © 1965 by The Missionary Society of Saint Paul the Apostle in the State of New York. Used by permission of Paulist Press, Inc.

---

were invited to participate. Finland and Czechoslovakia were willing, and Poland and Hungary showed interest. The Soviets, however, forbade them to take part.

The Marshall Plan helped restore prosperity to Western Europe and set the stage for Europe's unprecedented postwar economic growth. It also led to the waning of Communist strength in the West and to the establishment there of solid democratic regimes.

From the Western viewpoint, this policy of "containment" was a new and successful response to the Soviet and Communist challenge. Stalin may have considered it a renewal of the old Western attempt to isolate and encircle the USSR.

The Allied airlift in action during the Berlin blockade. Every day for almost a year Western planes supplied the city until Stalin lifted the blockade in May 1949. [Bildarchiv Preussischer Kulturbesitz]

His answer was to replace all multiparty governments behind the Iron Curtain with thoroughly Communist regimes completely under his control. He also called a meeting of all Communist parties around the world at Warsaw in the autumn of 1947. There they organized the Communist Information Bureau (Cominform), a revival of the old Comintern, dedicated to spreading revolutionary communism throughout the world.

In February 1948 a more dramatic and brutal display of Stalin's new policy took place in Prague. The Communists expelled the democratic members of what had been a coalition government and murdered Jan Masaryk (1886–1948), the foreign minister and son of the founder of Czechoslovakia, Thomas Masaryk (1850–1937). President Eduard Benes (1884–1948) was forced to resign, and Czechoslovakia was brought fully under Soviet rule.

These Soviet actions, especially those in Czechoslovakia, increased American determination to go ahead with its own arrangements in Germany. The Russians swiftly dismantled German industry in the eastern zone, but the Americans chose to try to make Germany self-sufficient, which meant restoring rather than destroying its industrial capacity. To the Soviets the restoration of a powerful industrial Germany, even in the western zones only, was frightening and unacceptable.

Disagreement over Germany produced the most heated postwar debate. When the Western powers agreed to go forward with a separate constitution for the western sectors of Germany in February 1948, the Soviets walked out of the joint Allied Control Commission. In the summer of that year the Western powers issued a new currency in their zone. Berlin, although well within the Soviet zone, was governed by all four powers. The Soviets chose to seal the city off by closing all railroads and highways to West Germany. Their purpose was to drive the Western powers out of Berlin.

The Western allies responded to the Berlin Blockade with an airlift of supplies to the city that lasted almost a year. In May 1949 the Russians were forced to back down and to open access to Berlin. The incident greatly increased tensions and suspicions between the opponents. It hastened the separation of Germany into two states, a situation that prevailed for forty years. West Germany formally became the German Federal Republic in September 1949, and the eastern region became the German Democratic Republic a month later.

NATO and the Warsaw Pact

Meanwhile, the nations of Western Europe had been coming closer together. The Marshall Plan encouraged international cooperation. In March 1948 Belgium, the Netherlands, Luxembourg, France, and Britain signed the Treaty of Brussels, providing for cooperation in economic and military matters. In April 1949 these nations joined Italy, Denmark, Norway, Portugal, and Iceland to sign a treaty with Canada and the United States that formed the North Atlantic Treaty Organization (NATO). NATO committed its members to mutual assistance in case any of them was attacked. For the first time in history the United States committed itself to defend allies outside the Western Hemisphere. NATO formed the West into a bloc. A few years later West Germany, Greece, and Turkey joined the alliance (see Map 36–1).

Soviet relations with the states of Eastern Europe were governed by a series of bilateral treaties providing for close ties and mutual assistance in case of attack. In 1949 the Council of Mutual Assistance (COMECON) was formed to integrate the economies of these states. Unlike the NATO states, the Eastern alliance system was under direct Soviet domination through local Communist parties controlled from Moscow and overawed by the presence of the Red Army. The Warsaw Pact of May 1955, which included Albania, Bulgaria, Czechoslovakia, East Germany, Hungary, Poland, Romania, and the Soviet Union, merely gave formal recognition to a system that already existed. Europe stood divided into two unfriendly blocs.

In 1953 Stalin died; later that year an armistice was concluded in Korea (see Chapter 37). Both events produced hope

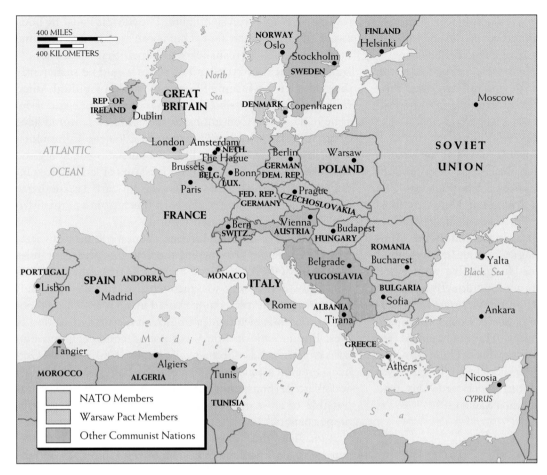

Map 36–1 Major Cold War European alliance systems. The North Atlantic Treaty Organization, which includes both Canada and the United States, stretches as far east as Turkey. By contrast, the Warsaw Pact nations were the contiguous Communist states of Eastern Europe, with the Soviet Union, of course, as the dominant member.

that international tensions might lessen, but the rivalry of power and polemics soon resumed.

Crises of 1956

The events of 1956 had considerable significance both for the Cold War and for what they implied about the realities of European power in the postwar era.

Suez   In July 1956 President Gamal Abdel Nasser (1918–1970) of Egypt nationalized the Suez Canal. Great Britain and France feared that this action would close the canal to their supplies of oil in the Persian Gulf. In October 1956 war broke out between Egypt and Israel. The British and French seized the opportunity to intervene; however, the United States refused to support their action. The Soviet Union protested vehemently. The Anglo-French forces had to be withdrawn, and control of the canal remained with Egypt.

The Suez intervention proved that without the support of the United States the nations of Western Europe could no longer undertake meaningful military operations to impose their will on the rest of the world. It also appeared that the United States and the Soviet Union had restrained their allies from undertaking actions that might result in a wider conflict. The fact that neither of the superpowers wanted war constrained both Egypt and the Anglo-French forces.

Poland   The autumn of 1956 also saw important developments in Eastern Europe that demonstrated similar limitations on independent action among the Soviet bloc nations. When the prime minister of Poland died, the Polish Communist Party leaders refused to choose as his successor the person selected by Moscow. Considerable tension developed. The Soviet leaders even visited Warsaw to make their opinions known. In the end, Wladyslaw Gomulka (1905–1982) emerged as the new Communist leader of Poland. He was the choice of the Poles, and he proved acceptable to the Soviets because he promised continued economic and military cooperation and most particularly continued Polish membership in the Warsaw Pact. Within those limits he halted the collectivization of Polish agriculture and improved the relationship between the Communist government and the Polish Roman Catholic church.

Uprising in Hungary   Hungary provided the second trouble spot for the Soviet Union. In late October demonstrations of sympathy for the Poles occurred in Budapest. The Communist government moved to stop the demonstrations, and street fighting erupted. A new ministry headed by former premier Imre Nagy (1896–1958) was installed by the Hungarian Communist party. Nagy was a Communist who sought a more independent position for Hungary. He went much further in his demands than Gomulka and directly appealed for political support from non-Communist groups in Hungary. Nagy called for the removal of Soviet troops and the ultimate neutralization of Hungary. He even called for Hungarian withdrawal from the Warsaw Pact. These demands were wholly unacceptable to the Soviet Union. In early November Soviet troops invaded Hungary; deposed Nagy, who was later executed; and imposed Janos Kadar (1912–1989) as premier.

The Cold War Intensified

The events of 1956 ended the era of fully autonomous action by the European nation-states. In different ways and to differing degrees, the two superpowers had demonstrated the new political realities. After 1956 the Soviet Union began to talk about "peaceful coexistence" with the United States. In 1958 negotiations began between the two countries for limitations on the testing of nuclear weapons. However, in the same year the Soviet Union also announced that the status of West Berlin had to be changed and the Allied occupation forces withdrawn. The demand was refused. In 1959 tensions relaxed sufficiently for several Western leaders to visit Moscow and for Soviet Premier Nikita Khrushchev (1894–1971) to tour the United States. A summit meeting was scheduled for May 1960 in Paris, and American President Dwight D. Eisenhower (1890–1969) was to go to Moscow.

Just before the gathering, the Soviet Union shot down an American U–2 aircraft that was flying reconnaissance over Soviet territory. Khrushchev demanded an apology from President Eisenhower, who accepted responsibility but refused to apologize. Khrushchev then refused to take part in the summit conference, and Eisenhower's trip to the Soviet Union was canceled.

The Soviet actions to destroy the possibility of the summit conference on the eve of its opening were not simply the result of the American spy flights. The Soviets had long been aware of the American flights but chose to protest at this time for two reasons. Khrushchev had hoped that the leaders of Britain, France, and the United States would be sufficiently divided over the future of Germany so that a united Allied front would be impossible. (The divisions did not come about as he had hoped.) Consequently, the conference would have been of little use to him. Second, by 1960 the Communist world itself had become split between the Soviets and the Chinese. The latter accused the Russians of lacking revolutionary zeal. Khrushchev's action was, in part, a response to those charges and proof of the hard-line attitude of the Soviet Union toward the capitalist world.

The abortive Paris conference opened the most difficult period of the Cold War. In 1961 the new U.S. president, John F. Kennedy (1917–1963), and Premier Khrushchev met in Vienna. The conference was inconclusive, but Kennedy left wondering if the two nations could avoid war. Throughout 1961 thousands of refugees from East Germany had fled to West Berlin. This outflow was a political and economic embarrassment to East Germany. In August 1961 the East Germans erected a concrete wall along the border between East and West Berlin. Henceforth, until November 1989, it was possible to cross only at designated checkpoints and with proper papers.

A year later the Cuban missile crisis brought the most dangerous days of the Cold War. The Soviet Union placed missiles in Cuba, a nation friendly to Soviet aims lying less than a hundred miles from the United States. The United States blockaded Cuba, halted the shipment of new missiles, and demanded the removal of existing installations. After a tense week the Soviets backed down and the crisis ended.

Detente and Afterward

In 1963 the two powers concluded a Nuclear Test Ban Treaty. This agreement marked the start of a lessening in the sharp tensions between the United States and the Soviet Union that had commenced just after the end of World War II. In 1968 the Soviet Union invaded Czechoslovakia to block its growing independence and to overthrow the government of its relatively liberal leader, Alexander Dubcek (1921–1974). Although deplored by the United States, this action led to no renewal of tensions. During the presidency of Richard Nixon (1913–1994) the United States embarked on a policy of detente, or reduction of tension, with the Soviet Union. This policy involved trade agreements and mutual reduction of strategic armaments. The Soviet invasion of Afghanistan in 1979, although not directly affecting Europe, hardened relations between Washington and Moscow, and the U. S. Senate refused to ratify the Strategic Arms Limitation Treaty of 1979.

In the summer of 1968 Soviet tanks rolled into Czechoslovakia, ending that country's experiment in liberalized communism. This picture shows defiant, flag-waving Czechs on a truck rolling past a Soviet tank in the immediate aftermath of the invasion. [Archive Photos]

The administration of President Ronald Reagan (b. 1911) initially slowed arms limitation negotiations and successfully deployed a major new missile system in Europe. The United States also launched a new arms proposal, known as the Strategic Arms Defense Initiative, to create a system that would use highly developed technology in space to defend against nuclear attack. The proposal was controversial at home, but played a major role in arms negotiations between the United States and the Soviet Union. One of the purposes of the Reagan arms buildup was simply to outspend the Soviet Union and force it to exhaust its own financial resources and continue to starve consumer industries.

President Reagan and Soviet leader Mikhail S. Gorbachev (b. 1931) held a friendly summit meeting in 1985, the first East-West summit in six years. Other meetings followed. Arms negotiations continued until, in December 1987, the United States and the Soviet Union agreed to dismantle over 2,000 medium- and shorter-range missiles. The treaty provided for mutual inspection. This action represented the most significant agreement since World War II between the two superpowers.

Thereafter, the political upheavals in Eastern Europe and the Soviet Union overwhelmed the issues of the Cold War. The Soviet Union abandoned its support for Communist

Major Dates in the Era of the Cold War

1948	Berlin Blockade
1949	Formation of the North Atlantic Treaty Organization (NATO)
1950	Outbreak of the Korean War
1953	Death of Stalin
1956	July, Egypt seizes the Suez Canal
	October, Anglo-French attack on the Suez Canal; Hungarian Revolution
1957	Treaty of Rome establishes the European Economic Community (EEC)
1960	Paris Summit Conference collapses
1961	Berlin Wall erected
1962	Cuban missile crisis
1963	Russian-American Test Ban Treaty
1968	Russian invasion of Czechoslovakia
1975	Helsinki Accords
1979	Russian invasion of Afghanistan
1981	Military crackdown on Solidarity Movement in Poland
1985	Reagan-Gorbachev summit
1987	Major American-Soviet Arms Limitation Treaty
1989	Berlin Wall comes down

governments in Eastern Europe. By the close of 1991 the Soviet Union itself had collapsed and been replaced by the Commonwealth of Independent States. The era of the Cold War had concluded in a manner that virtually no one had predicted.

European Society in the Second Half of the Twentieth Century

The sharp division of Europe into a democratic west and Communist east for most of the second half of the twentieth century makes generalizations about social and economic developments difficult. Prosperity in the west contrasted with shortages in the eastern economies, which were managed to benefit the Soviet Union. Most of the developments discussed in this chapter have taken place in Western Europe.

Toward Western European Unification

Since 1945, the nations of Western Europe have taken unprecedented steps toward economic cooperation. The process of economic integration has not been steady, nor is it completed. The collapse of the Soviet Union and the emergence of new free governments in Eastern Europe have further complicated an already difficult process.

The Marshall Plan and NATO gave the involved countries new experience in working with each other and demonstrated the productivity, efficiency, and simple possibility of cooperative action. In 1950 France, West Germany, Italy, and the "Benelux" countries (Belgium, the Netherlands, and Luxembourg) organized the European Coal and Steel Community. Its success reduced the suspicions of government and business groups about the concept of coordination and economic integration.

It took more, however, to draw European leaders toward further unity. The unsuccessful Suez intervention and the resulting diplomatic isolation of France and Britain persuaded many Europeans that only through unified action could they significantly influence the two superpowers or control their own destinies. Consequently, in 1957, through the Treaty of Rome, the six members of the Coal and Steel Community agreed to form a new organization: the European Economic Community. The members of the Common Market, as the EEC soon came to be called, sought to achieve the eventual elimination of tariffs, a free flow of capital and labor, and similar wage and social benefits in all the participating countries. The chief institutions of the EEC were a Council of Foreign Ministers and a High Commission composed of technocrats. The former came to be the dominant body.

The Common Market was a stunning success. By 1968 all tariffs among the six members had been abolished well ahead of the planned schedule. Trade and labor migration among the members grew steadily. Moreover, nonmember states began to copy the community and seek membership. In 1959 Britain, Denmark, Norway, Sweden, Switzerland, Austria, and Portugal formed the European Free Trade Area. However, by 1961 Great Britain had decided to seek Common Market membership. Twice—in 1963 and 1967—France vetoed British membership on the grounds that Britain was too closely tied to the United States and its policies to support the EEC wholeheartedly.

Nevertheless, the Common Market survived and continued to prosper. In 1973 Great Britain, Ireland, and Denmark became members. Discussions continued on further steps toward integration, including proposals for a common currency. Throughout the late 1970s, however, and into the 1980s momentum slowed. Norway and Sweden, with relatively strong economies, declined to join. Although in 1982 Spain, Portugal, and Greece applied for membership and were eventually admitted, there continued to be sharp disagreements and a sense of stagnation within the Community.

Finally, the leaders of the Community reached an important decision in early 1988. They targeted the year 1992 for achieving a virtual free-trade zone throughout the Community, entailing the elimination of remaining trade barriers and other restrictive trade policies. In 1991 the leaders of the Community signed the Treaty of Maastricht, which made a series of specific institutional proposals that would have led to a unified currency and a strong central bank. This treaty was submitted to referendums in a number of European states. It failed to be adopted in Denmark and only narrowly passed in France, making clear that it could not be enforced without wider popular support. When the treaty went into effect in November 1993, the European Community was renamed the European Union.

The troubles of the Maastricht Treaty illustrate a new phase in the process of European unity. Until recently the process of establishing greater unity has been carried out primarily by political leaders and by bureaucrats in the individual governments and the Community High Commission in Brussels. As the prospect of unity becomes imminent, however, the people of Europe have begun to raise issues about the democratic nature of the emerging political entity they are being asked to join. They are clearly in favor of some kind of close cooperation and perhaps union, but they are unwilling to see it set forth only by politicians and bureaucrats. They wish to see a wider European market, but they want that market to be genuinely free and not overregulated. Finally, the European Community, now the European Union, has had to deal recently with how it should relate to the newly independent states in eastern Europe.

The most striking recent element of the expanding momentum of economic cooperation is the movement toward a common currency. The new medium of exchange will be called the Euro. Eleven nations including Austria, Belgium,

Finland, France, Germany, Ireland, Italy, Luxembourg, the Netherlands, Portugal, and Spain will constitute the region using this new currency. In January 1, 1999, the currencies of these nations will be fixed according to the value of the Euro. By the beginning of the year 2002 the national currencies of these nations will have been replaced by new coins and notes denominated in the Euro. Such a common currency is unprecedented in European history.

A Consumer Society

Although European economies have been under pressure in the early 1990s, in the last half century the consumer sector has expanded dramatically. This expansion was limited almost entirely to Europe outside the Soviet bloc.

The consumer orientation of the Western European economy emerged as one of the most important characteristics differentiating it from Eastern Europe. Those differences produced important political results. Throughout the Soviet Union and the nations it dominated in Eastern Europe, economic planning overwhelmingly favored capital investment and military production. Those nations produced inadequate food for their people and few consumer goods. Long lines for food and nonfood staples, such as shoes and clothing, were common. Automobiles were a luxury; housing was inadequate. The quality of all consumer goods was poor.

By contrast, the last fifty years has seen a steady increase in the availability of consumer goods elsewhere in Europe. By the early 1950s Western Europeans enjoyed an excellent food supply that has continued to improve. The variety of fresh and frozen foods and vegetables available to western consumers has increased, and the number of fast food outlets has expanded markedly.

Western Europe has enjoyed a similarly great expansion of virtually all other kinds of consumer goods and services. The number of automobiles increased, and they became widely accessible. The number of people owning refrigerators, washing machines, electric ranges, televisions, and now microwaves, videocassette recorders, computers, compact disc players, and other small electronic consumer items has grown rapidly. A wide variety of everyday clothing became available, from woolen goods to blue jeans and sneakers. Like their American counterparts, Western Europeans now have a whole gamut of products, such as disposable diapers, to help them raise their children. They take foreign vacations year round, prompting the expansion of ski resorts in the Alpine countries and beach resorts on the Mediterranean.

This vast expansion of consumerism stood in marked contrast to the consumer shortages in Eastern Europe. Yet through even the limited number of radios, televisions, movies, and videos available to them, people in the East grew increasingly aware of the discrepancy between their lifestyle and that of the West. They saw Western consumerism clearly linked to democratic governments, free societies, and economic policies that favored the free market and only limited government planning. Thus the expansion of consumerism in the West, deplored by many commentators and Christian moralists, helped generate the discontent that brought down the Communist governments of Eastern Europe and the Soviet Union.

Students and Popular Music

Nothing has so characterized both student and youth culture in the second half of the twentieth century as rock music, which first emerged in the 1950s. Now part of the fabric of contemporary European life, rock music abounds on radio and television. The lyrics of the Beatles, the British rock group that became wildly popular on both sides of the Atlantic in the 1960s, may have become the most widely dispersed poetry in history. Rock appealed across national and cultural borders. It did as much to create a more uniform European culture as advertising or the economic freedom provided by the European Economic Community.

Rock music became part of a continuing critique of contemporary society. Many lyrics emphasized the need for love, the anguish of isolation, a desire for sexual liberation, and hopes for community and peace. During the 1960s rock music in the West was an integral feature of the antiwar movement and a vehicle for expressing discontent with the older generation. In the 1970s and 1980s it emerged as a major vehicle for cultural and political criticism in Eastern Europe and the Soviet Union. Rock stars came to symbolize daring and even heroism. Their music emphasized subjectivity and individualism. Lyrics directly criticized Communist governments, as in this example from "Get Out of Control," sung at a rock concert in Leningrad in 1986:

> We were watched from the days of kindergarten.
> Some nice men and kind women
> Beat us up. They chose the most painful places
> And treated us like animals on the farm.
> So we grew up like a disciplined herd.
> We sing what they want and live how they want
> And we look at them downside up, as if we're trapped.
> We just watch how they hit us
> Get out of control!
> Get out of control!
> And sing what you want
> And not just what is allowed
> We have a right to yell![1]

[1]Quoted in Artemy Troitsky, *Back in the USSR: The True Story of Rock in Russia* (Boston: Faber & Faber, 1987), p. 127, as cited in Sabrina P. Ramet, *Social Currents in Eastern Europe: The Sources and Meaning of the Great Transformation* (Durham, N.C.: Duke University Press, 1991), p. 239.

Sentiments like these were common in popular songs and undoubtedly contributed to the dramatic changes that swept through Eastern Europe.

The Movement of Peoples

Many people have migrated from, to, and within Europe during the past half century.

External Migration   In the decade and a half after 1945 approximately a half million Europeans each year settled elsewhere in the world. This was the largest outward migration since the 1920s, when the rate was approximately 700,000 persons annually. While the earlier migrants had mostly been from rural areas, the later migrants often included educated city dwellers.

Decolonization in the postwar period contributed to an inward flow of European colonials from overseas. The most dramatic example of this phenomenon was the more than one million French colonials who moved to France after the end of the Algerian War. British citizens returned from various parts of the British Empire; Dutch came back to the Netherlands from Indonesia; and Portuguese returned from Africa.

Decolonization also provoked a migration of non-European inhabitants of the former colonies to Europe. Great Britain, for example, received thousands of immigrants from India and Pakistan, and from its former African and Caribbean colonies. France received many immigrants from its former colonies in Indochina and the Arab world. This influx caused social tension and conflict. In Great Britain, for example, during the 1980s there were angry clashes between the police and non-European immigrants. France has had similar difficulties, which have contributed to the emergence there of the National Front, an extreme right-wing group led by Jean-Marie LePen (b. 1928). This group has drawn strength from the racial and ethnic tensions that have developed as a tight job market provokes resentment among some working-class voters toward North African immigrants.

As a result of this external migration into Europe, large Islamic populations now exist in several European nations and have become political factors in France and Germany.

Internal Migration   World War II and its aftermath created a vast refugee problem. Millions of people were displaced from their homes. Many cities in Germany and in central and Eastern Europe had been bombed or overrun by invading armies. Hundreds of thousands of foreign workers had been moved into Germany to contribute to the war effort. There were thousands of prisoners of war. Some of these people were returned to their homeland willingly; others, unwillingly. Changes in borders after the war also caused many people to move or be moved. For example, Poland, Czechoslovakia, and Hungary sent millions of ethnic Germans to Germany. Hundreds of thousands of Poles left from territory taken over by the Soviet Union. An estimated 3 million East Germans migrated to West Germany.

Once the Cold War set in, Soviet domination made it impossible for Eastern Europeans to migrate to other parts of Europe, whether for political or economic reasons. As a result, until the collapse of the Soviet empire, most internal migration in Europe after the immediate postwar years occurred outside the Communist bloc.

The major motivation for internal migration from the late 1950s onward was economic opportunity. The prosperous nations of northern and Western Europe had jobs that paid good wages and provided excellent benefits, often financed in part by the governments. Thus, there was a flow of workers from the poorer countries of Turkey, Greece, Yugoslavia, Italy, Spain, and Portugal into the wealthier countries of France, West Germany, Switzerland, and the Benelux nations. The establishment of the European Economic Community in 1957 facilitated this movement.

The migration of workers into northern Europe snowballed after 1960. Several hundred thousand workers would enter France and Germany each year. Virtually all these migrants settled in cities. They were usually welcomed during years of prosperity, and resented later when European economies began to slow in the mid-1980s. In Germany during the early 1990s, they were attacked.

In the late 1980s politics again became a major factor in European migration. The pressure of thousands of refugees seeking to escape from Eastern Europe to the West contributed to the collapse of the Communist governments of Eastern Europe in 1988 and 1989. Since 1989 people from all over Eastern Europe have migrated to the West. The civil war in the former Yugoslavia has also created many refugees. Europe has been in recession, however, and the new migrants are generating tension, resentment, and strife. Several nations have taken legal and administrative steps to restrict migration.

New Patterns in the Work and Expectations of Women

In the decades since World War II the work patterns and social expectations of women have changed markedly. In all social ranks women have begun to assume larger economic and political roles. Women have entered the learned professions and are filling more major managerial positions than ever before in European history.

More Married Women in the Work Force   The number of married women in the work force has risen sharply.

Youthful right-wing rioters clashed with police and threw firebombs in Rostock, Germany, in August 1992. Much of the violence was directed against foreign workers. [Reuters/Corbis-Bettmann]

Both middle-class and working-class married women have sought jobs outside the home. Because of the rather low birthrate in the 1930s, there were few young single women to be employed just after the war. Married women entered the job market to replace them. Some factories changed their work shifts to accommodate the needs of married women. Consumer conveniences and improvements in health care also made it easier for married women to enter the work force by reducing the demands of child care on their time.

In the twentieth century children have no longer been expected to make substantial contributions to family income. They now spend much of their time in compulsory schools. When families need more income than one worker can provide, both parents will work. Even without financial necessity, both parents are now likely to work when both are motivated to pursue careers.

New Work Patterns   In the late twentieth century the work pattern of European women has displayed much more continuity than it did in the nineteenth century. Single women enter the work force after their schooling and continue to work after marriage. They might withdraw from the work force to care for young children but return when the children begin school. Several factors created this new pat-

tern, but women's increasing life expectancy is one of the most important.

When married women died relatively young, child rearing filled much of their lives. The lengthening life span has meant that child rearing occupies much less of women's lives. Consequently, women throughout the Western world have new concerns about how they will spend those years when they are not involved with rearing children. The age at which women have decided to bear children has risen. Women have tended to bear children in their early twenties in Eastern Europe and in their late twenties in Western Europe. In urban areas, childbearing occurs later and the birthrate is lower than elsewhere.

Many women have begun to limit sharply the number of children they bear or to forgo childbearing and child rearing altogether. Both men and women continue to expect to marry. But the new careers open to women and the desire of couples to maintain as high a standard of living as possible have contributed to a declining birthrate.

Women in the New Eastern Europe   Many paradoxes surround the situation of women in Eastern Europe now that it is no longer governed by Communists. Under communism women generally enjoyed social equality as well as a broad spectrum of government-financed benefits. A

In Europe, as in the United States, women have gained access to new roles and opportunities. Geraldine Bridgewater was the first woman to hold a seat on the London Stock Exchange. [Liaison Agency, Inc.]

significant proportion (normally well over 50 percent) of women worked in these societies both because they could and because it was expected of them. There were, however, no significant women's movements since they, like all independent associations, were frowned on.

The new governments of the region are free, but have so far shown little concern toward women's issues. The economic difficulties the new governments face may endanger the funding of various health and welfare programs that benefit women and children. For example, a free market economy may not allow Eastern European women the extensive maternity benefits they used to enjoy. Moreover, the high proportion of women in the work force could leave them more vulnerable than men to the region's economic troubles. Women may well find themselves being laid off before men and hired for new jobs later than men.

American Domestic Scene Since World War II

Three major themes have characterized the postwar American experience—an opposition to the spread of communism, an expansion of civil rights to blacks and other minorities at home, and a determination to achieve ongoing economic growth. Virtually all of the major postwar political debates and social divisions have arisen from these issues.

Truman and Eisenhower Administrations

The foreign policy of President Harry Truman was directed against Communist expansion in Europe and East Asia. He enunciated the Truman Doctrine in regard to Greece and Turkey and initiated the Marshall Plan for European reconstruction. As will be discussed more fully in the next chapter, he led the United States to support the U.N. intervention against aggression in Korea. Domestically, the Truman administration pursued what may be regarded as a continuation of the New Deal. However, Truman encountered considerable opposition from conservative Republicans. The major achievement of those Republicans was the passage in 1947 of the Taft-Hartley Act, which limited labor-union activity. Truman won the 1948 election against great odds. Through policies he termed the Fair Deal, he sought to extend economic security.

Those efforts, however, were frustrated as fear of a domestic Communist menace swept much of the country. Senator Joseph McCarthy (1909–1957) of Wisconsin led the campaign against the perceived Communist danger within the ranks of American citizens and government agencies. The patriotism and loyalty of scores of prominent Americans were challenged. That development, a frustration with the war in Korea, and perhaps the natural weariness of the electorate after twenty years of Democratic Party government led to the election of war hero Dwight Eisenhower in 1952.

In retrospect, the Eisenhower years now seem a period of calm after the war years of the 1940s and before the turmoil of the 1960s. Eisenhower, personally popular, ended the Korean War. The country was generally prosperous. Home building increased dramatically, and the vast interstate highway system was initiated. The president was less activist than either Roosevelt or Truman had been.

Beneath the apparent quiet of the Eisenhower years, however, stirred several forces that would lead to the disruptions of the 1960s. One of them flowed from the injustices of segregation and racial inequality. Another flowed from the long-term implications of some of the major foreign policy commitments the Eisenhower administration made in its effort to oppose the advance of communism. One of those commitments led to American involvement in Vietnam; indeed, that involvement began under Eisenhower.

Civil Rights

In 1954 the United States Supreme Court, in the decision of *Brown v. Board of Education of Topeka*, declared unconstitutional the segregation of the black and white races. Shortly thereafter the Court ordered the desegregation of schools. For the next ten years the struggle over school integration and civil rights for black Americans stirred the nation. Southern states attempted to resist school desegregation. In 1957 Eisenhower sent troops into Little Rock, Arkansas, to integrate the schools, but resistance continued in other southern states.

While the battle raged over the schools, American blacks began to protest segregation in other areas. In 1955 Reverend Martin Luther King, Jr. (1929–1968), organized a boycott in Montgomery, Alabama, against segregated buses. The Montgomery bus boycott marked the beginning of the use of civil disobedience to fight racial discrimination in the United States. Drawing on the ideas of Henry David Thoreau (1817–1862) and the experience of Mohandas Gandhi (1869–1948) in India, the leaders of the civil-rights movement went to jail rather than obey laws they considered unjust. The civil-rights struggle continued well into the 1960s. One of its most dramatic moments was the 1963 march on Washington by tens of thousands of supporters of civil-rights legislation. The greatest achievements of the movement were the Civil Rights Act of 1964, which desegregated public accommodations, and the Voting Rights Act of 1965, which cleared the way for blacks to vote. This legislation as well as ongoing protests against housing and job discrimination brought black citizens nearer to the mainstream of American life than they ever had been.

However, much yet remained undone. In 1967 major race riots occurred in several American cities, resulting in significant loss of life. Those riots, followed by the assassination of Martin Luther King, Jr., in 1968, weakened the civil-rights movement. Despite new efforts to fight discrimination, the movement lacked a major national leader. Not until the late 1980s did a new leader emerge in the person of the Reverend Jesse Jackson (b. 1941), who raised new issues of racial equality and promoted drives that led to the registration of many black voters. There was, however, little follow-up to this campaign.

Race relations continue to plague the social life of the United States. Although black Americans have more access to education and public office, especially in urban areas, they lag behind other Americans economically and in their prospects for good health. Furthermore, as other groups, particularly Latino Americans, began to enter the political process in the 1980s and raise issues on behalf of their own communities, racial relations became more complicated. In 1992 one of the most destructive riots in American history— triggered by a court decision relating to the treatment of black Americans by the police—devastated parts of Los Angeles. The presidential campaigns of 1992 and 1996 were conspicuous for the absence of discussion of minority issues.

New Social Programs

The advance of the civil-rights movement in the late 1950s and early 1960s represented the cutting edge of a new advance of political liberalism. In 1960 John F. Kennedy narrowly won the presidential election. He saw himself as attempting to set the country moving again after the years of Eisenhower torpor. Kennedy defined his aims as seeking to move toward a New Frontier. One goal was to put a man on the moon. He also attempted unsuccessfully to expand medical care under the social security program. In the civil-rights movement, however, he basically reacted rather than led.

Nevertheless, the reaction to Kennedy's assassination in 1963 provided the occasion for his successor, Lyndon Johnson (1908–1973), to press for activist legislation. Johnson set forth a bold domestic program known as the War on Poverty, which established major federal programs to create jobs and provide job training. Furthermore, new entitlements were added to the social security program, including Medicare, which provides medical services for the elderly and disabled. Johnson's drive for what he termed the Great Society brought to a close the era of major federal initiatives that had begun under Franklin Roosevelt. The liberal impulse remained alive in American politics, but by the late 1960s the electorate had begun to become much more conservative.

The Vietnam War and Domestic Turmoil

Johnson's activist domestic vision quickly was overshadowed by the U.S. involvement in Vietnam (to be considered more fully in the next chapter). By 1965 Johnson had decided to send tens of thousands of Americans to Vietnam. This policy led to the longest of American wars. At home, the war and particularly the draft provoked vast public protests. Most young American men who were drafted went into the armed forces, but significant numbers, especially college and university students, resisted. Large-scale protests involving civil disobedience, often patterned after those of the civil-rights movement, erupted on campuses throughout the country. In some cases units of the National Guard were sent to restore calm. At Kent

The clash between protesting students and the Ohio National Guard at Kent State University was the most violent moment in the protests against the United States involvement in Vietnam. [AP/Wide World Photos]

State University in Ohio in 1970 the National Guard killed four protestors. In all these respects, the Vietnam War divided the nation as had no conflict since the Civil War.

The national unrest led Lyndon Johnson to decide not to seek reelection in 1968. Richard Nixon led the Republicans to victory. His election marked the beginning of an era of American politics dominated by conservative policies. Nixon campaigned on a platform of law and order. He also stressed his former experience in foreign policy as vice-president (under Eisenhower). Perhaps the most important act of his administration was his reestablishment of diplomatic relations with the People's Republic of China. Initially, Nixon's policies toward Vietnam were no more successful than those of Johnson. Half of the casualties in the war occurred under his administration. Nonetheless, he concluded the war in 1972. That same year he was reelected, but soon thereafter the Watergate scandal began to erode his administration.

The Watergate Scandal

On the surface, the Watergate scandal involved only the burglary of the Democratic party national headquarters by White House operatives in 1972. The deeper issues related to questions of the extent of presidential authority and the right of the government to intrude into the personal lives of citizens. In 1973 Congress established a committee to investigate the scandal. Testimony before that committee revealed that President Nixon had recorded conversations in the White House. The Special Prosecutor, who had been appointed to investigate the charges, finally gained access to the tapes in the sum-

mer of 1974 through a decision of the Supreme Court. In the meantime the Judiciary Committee of the House of Representatives voted three articles of impeachment against Nixon. Shortly thereafter, certain of the newly released tapes revealed that Nixon had ordered federal agencies to try to cover up White House participation in the burglary. After this revelation, Nixon became the only American president to resign.

The Watergate scandal further shook public confidence in the government. It was also a distraction from the major problems facing the country, especially inflation, which had resulted from fighting the war in Vietnam while expanding federal domestic expenditures. The subsequent administrations of Gerald Ford (1974–1977; b. 1913) and Jimmy Carter (1977–1981; b. 1924) battled inflation and high interest rates without significant success. Furthermore, the Carter administration became bogged down in the Iran hostage crisis of 1980 after Iranians took more than forty Americans hostage and held them for over a year.

The Triumph of Political Conservatism

In 1980 Ronald Reagan was elected president by a large majority and reelected four years later. Reagan was the first fully ideological conservative to be elected in the postwar era. Reagan sought to reduce the role of the federal government in American life. The chief vehicle to this end was a major tax cut and reform of the taxation system. The consequence of America's vastly increased defense spending and the tax policy was the largest fiscal deficit in American history. However, inflation was controlled, and the American economy experienced its longest peacetime expansion.

The straightforward conservatism of the Reagan administration proved offensive to many Americans who had traditionally supported a liberal political and social agenda. His policies were regarded as hostile to blacks and women. High officials were involved in scandals, particularly the sale of arms to Iran in exchange for the promised release of American hostages in Lebanon. Despite these difficulties, Reagan left office as probably the most popular and successful of the post-World War II American presidents.

In 1988 Vice-President (under Reagan) George Bush (b. 1924) was elected to succeed Reagan. He was immediately confronted by the major changes that Gorbachev was carrying out in the Soviet Union and the extraordinary transformations occurring in Eastern Europe that are discussed later in this chapter. Bush kept the NATO alliance strong and close to the United States at a time when observers had begun to question its utility. In 1989 he sent troops into Panama to oust its dictator, Manuel Noriega (b. 1940). In the summer of 1990, in response to the invasion of Kuwait by Iraq, he initiated the largest mobilization of American troops since the Vietnam War. Using the United Nations, he forged a broad worldwide coalition against Iraq's aggression. In early 1991 the coalition launched Operation Desert Storm and forced Iraq out of Kuwait.

The victory in the Persian Gulf War was the high point of the Bush presidency. Thereafter, he stumbled in the face of the serious economic problems confronting the nation. In 1992 the Democratic nominee, Governor William Clinton (b. 1946) of Arkansas, won the election.

The Clinton presidency encountered difficulties almost from the beginning. During his first two years in office he tried to bring about a dramatic change in health care finance and delivery. This effort ultimately failed, and the Clinton presidency was viewed as poorly managed.

In 1994, in one of the most far-reaching changes in recent American politics, the Republic Party won majorities in both houses of Congress. A number of forces accounted for this election, but one of the most significant was the role of conservative Christian groups who had become politically active. This election would appear to mark a major conservative departure in American political life. The new Republican-controlled Congress undertook major changes in the funding of welfare, taxation, and government regulation. This Congress continued the conservative redirection of federal policy that commenced with the election of Ronald Reagan.

The presidential election of 1996 saw the re-election of President Clinton and of a Republican dominated Congress and Senate. Scandals plagued both parties. The House of Representative censured and fined Mr. Newt Gingrich, the Speaker of the House. A personal sexual scandal and allegations of perjury plagued President Clinton during 1998. The Congressional elections of 1998 resulted in a loss of Republican seats in the House of Representatives. In the wake of the election loss, Gingrich resigned from the House, and President Clinton was subsequently impeached. He was acquitted in early 1999 by the Senate. In terms of policy, Clinton was seen as moving the Democractic party into a more conservative stance.

The Soviet Union to 1989

The major themes of Soviet history after 1945 were the rivalry with the United States for world leadership, the rivalry with China for the leadership of Communist nations, the effort to sustain Soviet domination of Eastern Europe, and a series of unsuccessful attempts to reform the Stalinist state, which ended in 1991 with the collapse of the Soviet Union.

The Soviet Union emerged from World War II as a major world power, but Stalin did little or nothing to modify the repressive regime he had fostered. The police remained ever present. The cult of personality around Stalin expanded, and the central bureaucracy continued to grow. Heavy industry was still favored in place of production for consumers. Agriculture continued to be troubled. Stalin's personal authority over the party and the nation remained unchallenged. In foreign policy he solidified Soviet control over Eastern Europe for the purposes of both Communist expansion and Soviet national security. The Soviet Army assured subservience to the goals of the Soviet Union. Such continued to be the situation until Stalin died on March 6, 1953.

The Khrushchev Years

No single leader immediately replaced Stalin, but by 1956 Nikita Khrushchev became premier, remaining in that position until 1964. He never enjoyed the extraordinary powers of Stalin.

In 1956, at the Twentieth Congress of the Communist Party, Khrushchev made a secret speech (later published outside the Soviet Union) in which he denounced Stalin and his crimes against Socialist justice during the purges of the 1930s. The speech caused shock and consternation in party circles and opened the way for limited, but genuine, internal criticism of the Soviet government. By 1958 all of Stalin's former supporters were gone, but none had been executed.

Under Khrushchev, intellectuals were somewhat freer to express their opinions. This so-called thaw in the cultural life of the country was closely related to the premier's interest in the opinions of experts on problems of industry and agriculture. He often went outside the usual bureaucratic channels in search of information and new ideas. Novels such as Aleksandr Solzhenitsyn's (b. 1918) *One Day in the Life of Ivan Denisovich* (1963) could be published. However, Boris Pasternak (1890–1960), the author of *Dr. Zhivago*, was not permitted to accept the Nobel Prize for literature in 1958. The intellectual liberalization of Soviet life during this period looked favorable largely in comparison with what had preceded it and continued to seem so later when freedom of expression declined again in the two decades after Khrushchev's fall.

In economic policy Khrushchev made moderate efforts to decentralize economic planning and execution. During the late 1950s he often boasted that Soviet production of consumer goods would overtake that of the West. Steel, oil, and electric-power production continued to grow, but the consumer sector including housing improved only marginally. The ever-growing defense budget and the space program that successfully launched the first human-engineered earth satellite, Sputnik, in 1957 made major demands on the nation's productive resources.

Khrushchev strongly redirected Stalin's agricultural policy. He recognized that despite the collectivization of the 1930s the Soviet Union could not feed its own people. Khrushchev removed many of the most restrictive regulations on private cultivation. The machine-tractor stations

Khrushchev Denounces the Crimes of Stalin: The Secret Speech

In 1956 Khrushchev denounced Stalin in a secret speech to the Party Congress. The New York Times *published a text of that speech smuggled from Russia.*

What are the specific actions on the part of Stalin that Khrushchev denounced? Why does Khrushchev pay so much attention to Stalin's creation of the concept of an "enemy of the people"? Why does Khrushchev draw a distinction between the actions of Stalin and those of Lenin?

Stalin acted not through persuasion, explanation, and patient cooperation with people, but by imposing his concepts and demanding absolute submission to his opinion. Whoever opposed this concept or tried to prove his viewpoint and the correctness of his position was doomed to removal from the leading collective [group] and to subsequent moral and physical annihilation. . . .

Stalin originated the concept of "enemy of the people." This term automatically rendered it unnecessary that the ideological errors of a man or men engaged in a controversy be proved; this term made possible the usage of the most cruel repression violating all norms of revolutionary legality, against anyone who in any way disagreed with Stalin, against those who were only suspected of hostile intent, against those who had bad reputations.

This concept "enemy of the people" actually eliminated the possibility of any kind of ideological fight or the making of one's views known on this or that issue, even those of a practical character. In the main, and in actuality, the only proof of guilt used, against all norms of current legal science, was the "confession" of the accused himself; and, as a subsequent probing proved, "confessions" were acquired through physical pressures against the accused. . . .

Lenin used severe methods only in the most necessary cases, when the exploiting classes were still in existence and were vigorously opposing the revolution, when the struggle for survival was decidedly assuming the sharpest forms, even including civil war.

Stalin, on the other hand, used extreme methods and mass repressions at a time when the revolution was already victorious, when the Soviet State was strengthened, when the exploiting classes were already liquidated and Socialist relations were rooted solidly in all phases of national economy, when our party was politically consolidated and had strengthened itself both numerically and ideologically. It is clear that here Stalin showed in a whole series of cases his intolerance, his brutality and his abuse of power. Instead of proving his political correctness and mobilizing the masses, he often chose the path of repression and physical annihilation, not only against actual enemies, but also against individuals who had not committed any crimes against the party and the Soviet Government. . . .

The New York Times, June 5, 1956, pp. 13–16.

---

were abandoned. Existing collective farms were further amalgamated. The government undertook an extensive "virgin lands" program to extend wheat cultivation by hundreds of thousands of acres. This policy initially increased grain production to new records. The applied farming techniques, however, proved inappropriate for the soil, and the new lands soon underwent severe erosion. The agricultural problem continued to grow over the decades. By the 1970s the Soviet Union imported vast quantities of grain from the United States and other countries. United States grain imports constituted a major facet of the policy of detente.

By 1964 high Communist party leaders and many people lower in the party had concluded that Khrushchev had tried to do too much too soon and had done it too poorly. His foreign policy, culminating in the back-down over the Cuban missile crisis, appeared a failure. On October 16, 1964, after defeat in the Central Committee of the Communist Party, Khrushchev resigned. Leonid Brezhnev (1906–1982) eventually emerged as his successor.

Brezhnev

Domestically the Soviet government became markedly more repressive after 1964. Intellectuals enjoyed less and less freedom and had little direct access to the government leadership. In 1974 the government expelled Solzhenitsyn. Jewish citizens of the Soviet Union were harassed. Bureaucratic obstacles impeded emigration to Israel.

The internal repression gave rise to a dissident movement. Certain Soviet citizens dared to criticize the regime in public and to carry out small demonstrations against it. They accused the Soviet government of violating the human-rights provisions of the 1975 Helsinki Accords. The dissidents included prominent citizens, such as the Nobel Prize-winning physicist Andrei Sakharov (1921–1989). The Soviet government responded with further repression.

In foreign policy the Brezhnev years witnessed attempts both to reach accommodation with the United States and to continue to expand Soviet influence and maintain Soviet leadership of the Communist movement. Nonetheless, growing Soviet spending on defense, and particularly on naval expansion, put ongoing pressures on the consumer side of the economy.

In December 1979 the Soviet Union invaded Afghanistan. A Soviet presence had already existed in that country, but for reasons that still remain unclear, the Soviet government felt required to send in troops to ensure its influence in Central Asia. The Afghanistan invasion, in addition to exacerbating tensions with the United States, tied the hands of the Soviet government in its own sphere of influence in Eastern Europe. There seems little doubt that the Soviet hesitation to react more strongly to events in Poland during the 1980s, which are discussed in the next section, stemmed in part from having committed military resources to Afghanistan and from the broad condemnation the invasion provoked from some Western European Communist parties and from the governments of nations not aligned with the West. The Soviet government also clearly lost internal support as its army became bogged down and suffered steady losses.

Afghan rebels with a captured Soviet armored vehicle in January of 1980 near Afghanistan's border with Pakistan. The Soviet invasion of Afghanistan in 1979 met with fierce resistance and sparked a sharp response from the United States, which halted sales of wheat to the Soviet Union and boycotted the Olympic Games held in Moscow in 1980. [C. Spengler/Sygma]

Communism and Solidarity in Poland

In early July 1980 the Polish government raised meat prices. The result was hundreds of protest strikes across the country. On August 14 workers occupied the Lenin shipyard at Gdansk. The strike soon spread to other shipyards, transport facilities, and factories connected with the shipbuilding industry. The most important leader to emerge from among the strikers was Lech Walesa (b. 1944). The strike leaders refused to negotiate with the government through any of the government-controlled unions. The Gdansk strike ended on August 31 after the government promised the workers the right to organize an independent union. Less than a week later the Polish Communist head of state was replaced; later that year the Polish courts recognized Solidarity as an independent union, and the state-controlled radio—for the first time in thirty years—broadcast a Roman Catholic mass.

In the summer of 1981, for the first time in any European Communist state, secret elections for the Polish party congress permitted real choices among the candidates. Poland remained a nation governed by a single party, but real debate was temporarily permitted within the party congress. This extraordinary Polish experiment came to a rapid close in late 1981. General Wojciech Jaruzelski (b. 1923) became head of the party, and the army moved into the center of Polish events. In December 1981 martial law was declared. The government arrested several Solidarity leaders. Martial law would continue until late in the 1980s.

By the time of Brezhnev's death in 1982, the entire Soviet system had grown rigid and seemed hardly capable of meeting the needs of its people or pursuing a successful foreign policy. Until the middle of the 1980s, however, no observers expected rapid change in the Soviet Union or its satellites. The nations of Eastern Europe were expected to continue with one-party governments, their aspirations for self-determination smothered, and only limited possibilities for independent political action. What had lasted forty years, it was assumed, would endure into the future. No one anticipated the vast changes that were imminent.

Gorbachev Attempts to Redirect the Soviet Union

Both of Brezhnev's immediate successors, Yuri Andropov (1914–1984) and Constantin Chernenko (1911–1985), died after holding office for short periods. In 1985 Mikhail S. Gorbachev (b. 1931) came to power. In what proved to be the last great attempt to reform the Soviet system and eliminate its repressive Stalinist heritage, he immediately set about making the most remarkable changes that the Soviet Union had witnessed since the 1920s. His reforms unloosed forces that within seven years would force him to retire and end both Communist rule and the Soviet Union as it had existed since the Bolshevik Revolution of 1917.

Initially, Gorbachev and his supporters challenged the way the party and bureaucracy had traditionally managed the Soviet government and economy. Under the policy of *perestroika*, or restructuring, they proposed major economic and political reforms. The centralized economic ministries were reduced in size. A larger role was allowed for private enterprise on the local level. By early 1990, in a clear abandonment of traditional Marxist ideology, Gorbachev had begun to advocate private ownership of property. He and his advisers considered policies to liberalize the economy and move it rapidly toward a free market. Despite these organizational changes the Soviet economy, instead of growing, stagnated and even declined. Shortages of food, consumer goods, and housing became chronic. In a pattern that has continued to characterize Russian political life, old-fashioned Communists blamed these results on the abandonment of centralized planning. Democratic critics blamed overly slow reform and urged a more rapid move to a free market economy.

Gorbachev also allowed, within the Soviet context, an extraordinarily broad public discussion and criticism of Soviet history and Soviet Communist party policy. This development was termed *glasnost*, or openness. Certain Communist figures from the 1920s, such as Bukharin (1888–1938), who had been executed by Stalin, once again received official public recognition for their positive contributions to Soviet history. Within factories, workers were permitted to criticize party officials and the economic plans of the party and the government. Censorship was relaxed and free expression encouraged. Dissidents were released from prison. In the summer of 1988 Gorbachev presided over a party congress that witnessed full debates. In 1988 a new constitution permitted openly contested elections. After real political campaigning, a novel experience for the Soviet Union, the Congress of People's Deputies was elected in 1989 and then formally elected Gorbachev as president.

The Soviet Union was a vast empire of diverse peoples and nationalities. Some of those groups had been conquered under the tsars; others, such as the Baltic states, had been incorporated into the Soviet Union under Stalin. Glasnost quickly brought to the fore the discontents of all such peoples, no matter how or when they had been incorporated into the Soviet state. Gorbachev proved particularly inept in addressing these ethnic complaints.

1989: Year of Revolutions in Eastern Europe

In 1989 Soviet domination and Communist rule in Eastern Europe came to an abrupt end. None of these revolutions could have taken place without the refusal of the Soviet Union to intervene militarily as it had done in 1956 and 1968. For the first time since the end of World War II the peoples of Eastern Europe could shape their own political destiny without the almost certain military intervention of the Soviet Union. Once they realized the Soviets would stand back, thousands of ordinary citizens denounced Communist party domination and asserted their desire for democracy.

The generally peaceful character of most of these revolutions was not inevitable. It may, in part, have resulted from the shock with which much of the world responded to the violent repression of prodemocracy protesters in Beijing's Tienanmen Square by the People's Republic of China in the late spring of 1989. The Communist party officials of Eastern Europe and the Soviet Union clearly decided at some point in 1989 that they could not offend world opinion with a similar attack on democratic demonstrators.

Solidarity Reemerges in Poland

During the mid-1980s, Poland's government relaxed martial law. By 1984 several leaders of Solidarity had been released from prison and began again to work for free trade unions and democratic government. An active underground press and several new dissenting political organizations emerged. Poland's economy continued to deteriorate, demonstrating the inability of Communist governments to deliver economic growth and prosperity.

During 1987 the government released the last of its Solidarity prisoners in a sweeping amnesty. In 1988 new strikes occurred that even the leaders of Solidarity had not anticipated. This time the Communist government failed to reimpose control. Solidarity was legalized.

Jaruzelski, with the tacit consent of the Soviet Union, repealed martial law and promised free elections to a parliament with increased powers. When elections were held in 1989, the Communists lost overwhelmingly to Solidarity candidates. Late in the summer Jaruzelski, unable to find a Communist who could forge a majority coalition in Parliament, turned to Solidarity. On August 24, 1989, after negotiating with Lech Walesa, Jaruzelski named Tadeusz Mazowiecki (b. 1927) the first non-Communist prime minister of Poland since 1945. The appointment was made with the express approval of Gorbachev.

Hungary Moves Toward Independence

Hungary had for some time shown the greatest national economic independence of the Soviet Union in Eastern Europe. The Hungarian government had emphasized the production of food and consumer goods. It had also permitted a small stock exchange. In early 1989, as events unfolded in Poland, the Hungarian Communist government began to take other independent actions. In January its parliament permitted independent political parties. Soon thereafter the government permitted free travel between Hungary and Austria, opening the first breach in the Iron Curtain. Thousands of East Germans then moved into Austria through Hungary. From Austria they went to West Germany.

In May 1989 Premier Janos Kadar (1912–1989), who had been installed after the Soviet intervention in 1956, was voted from office by the Parliament. Thousands of people gave an honorary burial to the body of Imre Nagy, who had been executed in 1958. The Hungarian Communist party changed its name to the Socialist party and permitted the emergence of other opposition political parties. In October, Hungary promised free elections. By 1990 a coalition of democratic parties controlled the parliament and governed the country.

The Breach of the Berlin Wall and German Reunification

In the autumn of 1989 popular demonstrations erupted in many East German cities. The most important occurred in Leipzig. The streets filled with people demanding democracy and an end to Communist party rule.

Gorbachev told the leaders of the East German Communist party that the Soviet Union would no longer support them. With startling swiftness, the Communist leaders of the East German government resigned, making way for a younger generation of Communist party leaders. These new leaders, who remained in office for just weeks, promised political and economic reform. They convinced few East Germans, however, and the emigration to the West continued. In November 1989, in one of the most emotional moments in European history since 1945, the government of East Germany ordered the opening of the Berlin Wall. Tens of thousands of East Berliners crossed into West Berlin to celebrate, to visit families, and to shop with money provided by the West German government. Shortly thereafter, free travel began between East and West Germany. By early 1990 the Communist government of East Germany, after failing to reorganize itself, had been swept away in free elections.

The revolution in East Germany had broad ramifications for international relations. The citizens of the two Germanies were determined to reunify. With the collapse of Communist party government in East Germany, there was no longer a viable distinction between them. Late in 1989 the ministers of the European Economic Community accepted in principle the unification of Germany. By February 1990 reunification had become a foregone conclusion, accepted by the United States, the Soviet Union, Great Britain, and France.

The Velvet Revolution in Czechoslovakia

Late in 1989, in "the velvet revolution," Communist rule in Czechoslovakia quickly unraveled. In November, under pop-

President Vaclav Havel of the Czech Republic led the revolution that overthrew the Communist government of his nation and has since become a powerful advocate of political democracy and moderation in Eastern Europe. [Giles Bassignac/Liaison Agency, Inc.]

ular pressure from street demonstrations and well-organized political opposition, the Communist party began to retreat from office. The patterns were similar to those occurring elsewhere. The old leadership resigned, and younger Communists replaced them. The changes they offered were inadequate.

The popular new Czech leader who led the forces against the party was Vaclav Havel (b. 1936), a playwright of international standing whom the government had frequently imprisoned. Havel and the group he represented, which called itself Civic Forum, negotiated changes with the government. These included an end to the political dominance of the Communist party (which had been written into the constitution), inclusion of non-Communists in the government, elimination of traditional Marxist education, removal of travel restrictions, and relaxation of censorship.

Early in December the tottering Communist government admitted that the invasion of 1968 had been a mistake. The Soviet Union and other Warsaw Pact states did likewise. Shortly thereafter Civic Forum succeeded in forcing the resignation of Gustav Husak (b. 1913), who had been president of Czechoslovakia since 1968, and in guaranteeing a free election for his successor. In late December 1989 Havel was elected president.

Violent Revolution in Romania

The most violent upheaval of 1989 occurred in Romania, where President Nicolae Ceausescu (1918–1989) had governed without opposition for almost a quarter century. Romania was a one-party state with total centralized economic planning. Ceausescu, who had been at odds with the Soviet government for some time, maintained his Stalinist regime in the face of Gorbachev's reforms. He was supported by an army and a security force loyal to him. He had also placed his closest relatives in major political positions where they personally profited through corrupt practices.

On December 15 troubles erupted in the city of Timisoara in western Romania. The security forces sought to arrest a clergyman who had tried to protect the rights of ethnic Hungarians within Romania's borders. Over the next two days the Romanian security forces fired on demonstrators in Timisoara. Casualties ran into at least the hundreds. A few days later demonstrators in Bucharest publicly shouted against Ceausescu at a major rally, and by December 22 the city was in full revolt. Fighting, with many casualties, broke out between the army, which supported the revolution, and the security forces loyal to Ceausescu. The revolutionaries gained control of the television station and broadcast reports of the spreading revolution. Ceausescu and his wife attempted to flee the country but were captured, tried, and executed by firing squad on December 25. His death ended the shooting between the army and security forces. The provisional government in Bucharest announced that the first free elections since the end of World War II would take place in the spring of 1990.

The Collapse of the Soviet Union

Gorbachev clearly believed, as shown by his behavior toward Eastern Europe in 1989, that the Soviet Union could no longer afford to support Communist governments in that region or intervene to uphold their authority. He was beginning to advance a similar view of the nature of the authority of the Communist party within the Soviet Union.

Renunciation of Communist Political Monopoly

In early 1990 Gorbachev formally proposed to the Central Committee of the Soviet Communist party that the party abandon its monopoly of power. After intense debate the Committee adopted his proposal, abandoning the Leninist position that only a single elite party could act as the vanguard of the revolution and forge a new Soviet society.

Gorbachev confronted challenges from three major political forces by 1990. One consisted of those groups—considered conservative in the Soviet context—whose members wanted to maintain the influence of the Communist party and the Soviet army. They were deeply disturbed by the country's economic stagnation and political and social disorder. They still appeared to control significant groups in the economy and society. During late 1990 and early 1991 Gorbachev, who himself seems to have been disturbed by the nation's turmoil, began to appoint members of these factions to key positions in the government. In other words, Gorbachev seemed to be making a strategic retreat. He apparently believed that only these more conservative forces would give him the support he needed.

Gorbachev made this calculation because he was now facing opposition from members of a second group, those who wanted much more extensive and rapid change. Their leading spokesman was Boris Yeltsin (b. 1931). He and those supporting him wanted to move quickly to a market economy and a more democratic government. Like Gorbachev, Yeltsin had risen through the Communist party and then become disillusioned with its policies. Throughout the late 1980s he had been critical of Gorbachev. In 1990 he was elected president of the Russian Republic, the largest and most important of the Soviet Union's constituent republics. In the new political climate, that position gave him a firm political base from which to challenge Gorbachev's authority and increase his own.

The third force was regional unrest. Some of the republics of the Soviet Union had experienced considerable discontent in the past, but it had been repressed by the military or the Communist party. Initially, the greatest unrest came from the three Baltic republics of Estonia, Latvia, and Lithuania.

During 1989 and 1990 the parliaments of the Baltic republics tried to increase their independence, and Lithuania actually declared independence. Discontent also arose in the Soviet Islamic republics in central Asia. Riots broke out in Azerbaijan and Tajikistan. Throughout 1990 and 1991 Gorbachev sought to negotiate new constitutional arrangements between the republics and the central government. His failure to do so may have been the most important reason for the rapid collapse of the Soviet Union.

The August 1991 Coup

The turning point in all of these events came in August 1991 when the conservative forces that Gorbachev had brought into the government attempted a coup. Armed forces occupied Moscow, and Gorbachev himself was placed under house arrest while on vacation in the Crimea. The forces of political and economic reaction—led by people who, at the time,

Gorbachev Proposes the Soviet Communist Party Abandon Its Monopoly of Power

On February 5, 1990, President Mikhail Gorbachev proposed to the Central Committee of the Soviet Communist party that the party abandon its position as the single legal party as provided in Article 6 of the Soviet Constitution. His proposal followed similar actions by several of the Communist parties of Eastern Europe. From the time of Lenin through Brezhnev, the Soviet Communist party portrayed itself as the sole vanguard of the revolution. Gorbachev argued that it should abandon that special role and compete for political power with other political parties. Within two years the party was no longer in power.

Why did Gorbachev argue that the Soviet Communist party must reform itself? To what extent did Gorbachev in this speech actually abandon traditional Communist party goals? How did he think the Soviet Communist party could function in a pluralistic political system?

The main thing that now worries Communists and all citizens of the country is the fate of *perestroika*, the fate of the country and the role of the Soviet Communist Party at the current, probably most crucial, stage of revolutionary transformation. . . .

[It is important to understand] . . . that the party will only be able to fulfill the mission of political vanguard if it drastically restructures itself, masters the art of political work in the present conditions and succeeds in cooperating with forces committed to *perestroika*.

The crux of the party's renewal is the need to get rid of everything that tied it to the authoritarian-bureaucratic system, a system that left its mark not only on methods of work and inter-relationships within the party, but also on ideology, ways of thinking and notions of socialism.

The [newly proposed] platform says: our ideal is a humane, democratic socialism, expressing the interests of the working class and all working people; and relying on the great legacy of Marx, Engels and Lenin, the Soviet Communist Party is creatively developing socialist ideals to match present-day realities and with due account for the entire experience of the 20th century.

The platform states clearly what we should abandon. We should abandon the ideological dogmatism that became ingrained during past decades, outdated stereotypes in domestic policy and outmoded views on the world revolutionary process and world development as a whole.

We should abandon everything that led to the isolation of socialist countries from the mainstream of world civilization. We should abandon the understanding of progress as a permanent confrontation with a socially different world. . . .

The party's renewal presupposes a fundamental change in its relations with state and economic bodies and the abandonment of the practice of commanding them and substituting for their functions.

The party in a renewing of society can exist and play its role as vanguard only as a democratically recognized force. This means that its status should not be imposed through constitutional endorsement.

The Soviet Communist Party, it goes without saying, intends to struggle for the status of the ruling party. But it will do so strictly within the framework of the democratic process by giving up any legal and political advantages, offering its program and defending it in discussions, cooperating with other social and political forces, always working amidst the masses, living by their interests and their needs.

The New York Times, February 6, 1990, p. A16.

---

were associated with Gorbachev—had at last attempted to seize control. Boris Yeltsin denounced the coup and asked the world to help maintain the Soviet Union's movement toward democracy.

Within two days the coup collapsed. Gorbachev returned to Moscow, but in humiliation, having been victimized by the groups to whom he had turned for support. One of the largest public demonstrations in Russian history, perhaps the largest, celebrated the failure of the coup in Moscow. From that point on Yeltsin steadily became the dominant political figure in the nation. In the months immediately after the coup the Communist party, compromised by its participation in the coup, totally collapsed. The constitutional arrangements between the central government and the individual republics were revised. On December 25, 1991, the Soviet Union ceased to exist, Gorbachev left office, and the Commonwealth of Independent States came into being (see Map 36–2).

The Yeltsin Years

As president of Russia, Boris Yeltsin was the head of the largest and most powerful of the new states. His popularity was high both in Russia and in the Commonwealth in 1992, but by 1993 he faced serious economic and political problems. Opposition to Yeltsin personally and to his economic and political reforms grew in the Russian Parliament. Its members were mostly

Map 36-2 The Commonwealth of independent states. In December 1991 the Soviet Union broke up into its fifteen constituent republics. Eleven of these are now loosely joined in the Commonwealth of Independent States. Not in the CIS are Estonia, Latvia, Lithuania, and Georgia.

former Communists who wanted to slow or halt the movement toward reform. The impasse between the President and the Parliament crippled the government. In September 1993 Yeltsin suspended Parliament, which responded by deposing him. Parliament's leaders tried to provoke popular uprisings against Yeltsin in Moscow. The military, however, backed Yeltsin and eventually surrounded the Parliament building with troops and tanks. On October 4, 1993, after pro-Parliament rioters rampaged through Moscow, Yeltsin ordered the tanks to attack the Parliament building, crushing the revolt.

These actions temporarily consolidated Yeltsin's position and authority. The major Western powers, deeply concerned by the turmoil in Russia, supported him. The crushing of Parliament left Yeltsin far more dependent than before on the military. And the country's continuing economic problems

bred unrest. In the December elections, for example, radical nationalists openly intolerant of non-Russian ethnic groups and advocating rebuilding Russia's empire made an uncomfortably strong showing, nearly capturing more seats in the new Parliament than supporters of Yeltsin. In 1994 the central government found itself at war in the province of Chechnya, a conflict from which the central government eventually emerged as the loser. This conflict demonstrated the very limited capacity of the government to exercise its authority when faced with significant resistance.

The parliamentary elections of late 1995 saw the Communist party reassert its political presence as it achieved control of over one third of the seats in the Russian Parliament. The Communist leadership claimed that it did not intend to return to its former authoritarian ways. The parliamentary

The collapse of Communist Party governments in Eastern Europe and Soviet Union is the most important political event of the closing years of the twentieth century. It was accompanied by the destruction of the public symbols of those governments. Throughout the region gigantic statues of Communist Party leaders were torn down. Here, Hungarians explore a toppled statue of Lenin. [Sygma]

elections represented a major rebuff to the Yeltsin government, which had become increasingly unpopular. Yet by very deft political actions, Yeltsin defeated the Communist Party candidate for the presidency in the summer of 1996.

The future course of Russia remains highly confused. President Yeltsin has suffered from poor health. He has faced remarkably steady opposition in the Russian Parliament and by the last months of his presidency could govern only through almost daily negotiation with the opposition leaders in the Parliament. The economic life of the nation has remained stagnant at best. In 1998 Russia defaulted on its debt payments. Political assassinations have occurred. The economic downturn has contributed to further political unrest, but it is by no means certain where new political leadership will emerge. It is possible that unrest will produce turmoil from which new, strong leadership will emerge after Yeltsin leaves office in 2000. It is also possible that Russia for the next decade will resemble Mexico during the 1920s and 1930s, when in the wake of its revolution that country experienced almost two decades of uncertain political stability while financing itself through the sale of natural resources, most importantly, oil, to the rest of the world.

The Collapse of Yugoslavia and Civil War

Yugoslavia was created after World War I. Its borders included six major national groups—Serbs, Croats, Slovenes, Montenegrins, Macedonians, and Bosnians (Muslims)—among whom there have been ethnic disputes for centuries (see Map 36–3). The Croats and Slovenes are Roman Catholic and use the Latin alphabet. The Serbs, Montenegrins, and Macedonians are Eastern Orthodox and use the Cyrillic alphabet. The Bosnians are Islamic. Most members of each group reside in a region with which they are associated historically—Serbia, Croatia, Slovenia, Montenegro, Macedonia, and Bosnia-Herzegovina—and these regions constituted individual republics within Yugoslavia. Many Serbs, however, lived outside Serbia proper.

Yugoslavia's first communist leader, Marshal Tito (1892–1980), had acted independently of Stalin in the late 1940s and pursued his own foreign policy. He succeeded in muting ethnic differences by encouraging a cult of personality

The Breakup of Yugoslavia

June 1991	Slovenia declares independence
June 1991	Croatia declares independence
April 1992	War erupts in Bosnia and Herzegovina after Muslims and Croats vote for independence
November 1995	Peace agreement reached in Dayton, Ohio
January 1992	Macedonia declares independence
April 1992	Serbia and Montenegro proclaim a new Federal Republic of Yugoslavia
March 1998	War breaks out in Kosovo, a province of Serbia
March 1999	NATO bombing of Serbia begins

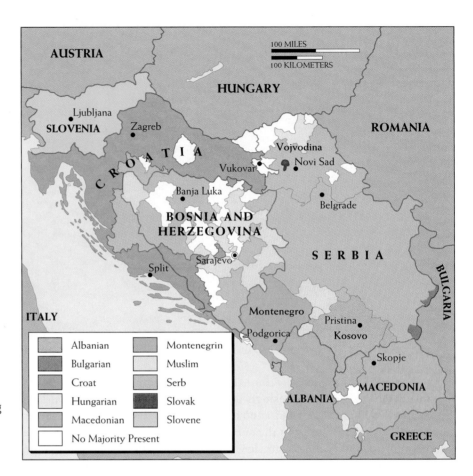

AUSTRIA
HUNGARY
ROMANIA
SLOVENIA
Ljubljana
Zagreb
CROATIA
Vojvodina
Novi Sad
Vukovar
Banja Luka
Belgrade
BOSNIA AND HERZEGOVINA
SERBIA
Sarajevo
Split
BULGARIA
ITALY
Montenegro
Pristina
Podgorica
Kosovo
Skopje
MACEDONIA
ALBANIA
GREECE

100 MILES
100 KILOMETERS

Albanian
Bulgarian
Croat
Hungarian
Macedonian
No Majority Present
Montenegrin
Muslim
Serb
Slovak
Slovene

Map 36–3 The ethnic composition in the former Yugoslavia. The rapid changes in Eastern Europe during the close of the 1980s intensified long-standing ethnic tensions in the former Yugoslavia. This map shows where Yugoslavia's ethnic population lived in 1991, before internal conflicts escalated.

around himself and by complex political power sharing. After his death serious economic difficulties undermined the authority of the central government, and Yugoslavia gradually dissolved into civil war.

In the late 1980s the old ethnic differences came to the fore again in Yugoslav politics. Nationalist leaders—most notably Slobodan Milošević (b. 1941) in Serbia and Franjo Tudjman (b. 1922) in Croatia—gained increasing authority. The Serbs contended that Serbia did not exercise sufficient influence in Yugoslavia and that Serbs living in Yugoslavia but outside Serbia encountered systematic discrimination, especially from Croats. Ethnic tension and violence soon resulted. During the summer of 1990, in the wake of the changes in the former Soviet bloc nations, Slovenia and Croatia declared independence from the central Yugoslav government and were soon recognized by several European nations, including, most importantly, Germany. Recognition from the full European community soon followed.

From this point on, violence escalated steadily. Serbia—concerned about Serbs living in Croatia and about the loss of lands and resources there—was determined to maintain a unitary Yugoslav state that it would dominate. Croatia was equally determined to secure independence. Croatian Serbs demanded safeguards against discrimination and violence,

providing the Serbian army with a pretext to move against Croatia. By June 1991 full-fledged war had erupted between the two republics. Serbia accused Croatia of reviving fascism, while Croatia accused Serbia of maintaining a Stalinist regime. At its core, however, the conflict is ethnic; as such, it highlights the potential for violent ethnic conflict within the former Soviet Union.

The conflict took a new turn in 1992 as Croatian and Serbian forces determined to divide Bosnia-Herzegovina. The Muslims in Bosnia—who had lived alongside Serbs and Croats for generations—soon became crushed between the opposing forces. The Serbs in particular, pursuing a policy called "ethnic cleansing," a euphemism redolent of some of the worst horrors of World War II, have killed or forcibly moved many Bosnian Muslims.

More than any other single event, the unremitting bombardment of Sarajevo, the capital of Bosnia-Herzegovina, brought the violence of the Yugoslav civil war to the attention of the world. The United Nations attempted unsuccessfully to mediate the conflict and imposed sanctions, which had little influence. Early in 1994, however, a shell exploded in the marketplace in Sarajevo, killing dozens of people. Thereafter, NATO forced the Serbs to withdraw their artillery from around Sarajevo.

An elderly parishioner walks through the ruins of St. Mary's Roman Catholic Church in Sarajevo. The church was destroyed by Serb shelling in May 1992.
[Reuters/Corbis-Bettmann]

The events of the civil war came to a head in 1995 when NATO forces carried out strategic air strikes. Later that year under the leadership of the United States, the leaders of the warring forces completed a peace agreement in Dayton, Ohio. The agreement was of great complexity, but recognized an independent Bosnia. The terms of the agreement are to be enforced by the presence of NATO troops. The United States committed 20,000 troops to this international force.

The situation in the former Yugoslavia remains dangerous and deadly. During 1997 and 1998 Serbia moved against ethnic Albanians living in its province of Kosovo. In 1999 in the most extensive military operation in Europe since 1945, NATO undertook a collective action against the Serbian government to halt massive mistreatment of the Kosovo ethnic Albanians.

Problems in the Wake of the Collapse of Communism

The collapse of communism has presented Europe with new problems and new opportunities. The opportunities include the possibility of establishing democratic governments and market economies throughout the region. They also include the restoration of civil liberties in countries where they have not been known for over a half century. If the countries of the former Soviet bloc reorganize their economies successfully, their citizens may come to enjoy the kinds of consumer goods—and the standard of living they make possible—that

have long been available in Western Europe. Realizing these opportunities, however, will require enormous patience. Such patience may be in short supply. Already in Poland, Lech Walesa in 1995 lost the presidential election to a former Communist. In other parts of Eastern Europe former Communists have become a major political force.

The problems in the new political and economic situation are enormous. Unemployment is widespread throughout the former Soviet Union and Eastern Europe. The plants and factories that the Communist governments had built are obsolete. Many also are so polluting that they have caused some of the worst environmental problems in the world. These nations also now recognize that by the standards of Western Europe they are poor. As a result, hundreds of thousands of people are migrating from Eastern to Western Europe to look for work. In western countries such as Germany, however, the migrants have encountered resentment, opposition, and physical violence.

The nations of Western Europe, facing considerable public resentment over the costs already incurred from the collapse of communism, are hesitant to send economic aid to the east. This is especially true in Germany, where the costs of unification have been high. Other parts of Europe, most notably Great Britain, are experiencing an economic downturn and believe they lack the resources to aid the Eastern Europeans. Western Europeans are also grappling with another issue: How should the former Communist economies relate to the European Union?

The political challenges of the collapse of communism are no less great than the economic. Civil war has ravaged

Yugoslavia. The potential for ethnic violence threatens the former Soviet Union, where nuclear weapons are still available. The Czechs and the Slovaks, unable to establish a stable, unified state, divided Czechoslovakia into two separate nations in 1993. The liberty made possible by the end of the Communist governments has thus far tended to be used in pursuit of ethnic goals, leading almost inevitably to domestic political turmoil. The key question is whether democratic governments can survive amidst the resulting disorder, economic stagnation, and competing ethnic claims or whether they will succumb to illiberal alternatives.

Under these rapidly changing conditions NATO has continued to exist and has moved to expand its membership to include Poland, the Czech Republic, and Hungary. Yet the exact purpose of NATO remains ill defined. Although initially taking a reluctant role in settling the civil war in the former Yugoslavia, NATO eventually attempted to assume the role of internal peacekeeper in the new Europe.

IN WORLD PERSPECTIVE

The West Since 1945

The history of the West since the end of World War II has been full of paradoxes. Europe, which gave birth to Western civilization and remained its center until the war, has declined in world influence. During the four decades immediately after the war, the United States and the Soviet Union rose to predominance and replaced Western Europe as the major powers on the world scene. Consequently, while the traditional center of Western influence exerted little power, both new great Western powers came to exert more political and military power than any previous nation of continental Europe. But they did so in conflict with each other.

Immediately after 1945 the nations of the West entered the Cold War. That ideological, economic, and military rivalry between the United States and the Soviet Union dominated political struggles throughout the world for more than half a century. It divided Europe between the NATO and Warsaw Pact military forces and forced nations outside Europe to side with one or the other of the superpowers.

In the later 1980s, however, the Cold War unexpectedly ended as the Soviet Union and the nations of Eastern Europe experienced enormous internal political changes. These changes have clearly opened a new epoch of Western history. The United States has emerged from the Cold War as the single remaining superpower. Western Europe stands on the brink of new unity, but its peoples and governments are clearly hesitant to press the process too far too rapidly. Eastern Europe and the former Soviet Union are experiencing economic turmoil and political uncertainty.

A new world order is emerging in which regional conflict will pose many of the gravest dangers. It remains to be seen whether the United States will be able to maintain its position of leadership in the West or whether Western Europe will take a more independent course. It also remains to be seen whether Europe, in response to economic pressures and the turmoil in the east, withdraws somewhat from world involvement during the next decade.

Review Questions ———

1. What were the causes of the Cold War? How did the United States and the Soviet Union each react to what it perceived to be the other's hostility? What was the effect of the Cold War on Europe?

2. How did the outcome of World War II affect Europe's position in the world? What were the factors behind the movement toward European unification? How successful has this movement been?

3. What were the chief characteristics of Western European society in the decades since 1945? What was the experience of Eastern Europe during the same period and why was it different?

4. What were the most important developments in the domestic history of the United States between 1945 and 1968? How did the Vietnam War affect American society? When did the shift to political conservatism occur in the United States? What did it mean for the role of the federal government?

5. Describe the Soviet economy between 1945 and 1990. Did it meet the needs of the Soviet people? What were the causes for the collapse of the Soviet Union? What role did Gorbachev play in that process?

6. Describe the collapse of Communist rule in Eastern Europe. Why was it a relatively bloodless revolution? What problems has the collapse of Communist rule led to?

7. Was the old Yugoslavia a national state? Why did it break apart and slide into civil war? How did the West respond to this crisis?

Suggested Readings ———

B. S. ANDERSON AND J. P. PINSSER, *A History of Their Own: Women in Europe from Prehistory to the Present*, Vol. 2 (1988). A broad-ranging survey.

T. S. ASH, *The Uses of Adversity* (1989). Important essays on central European culture and politics prior to the events of 1989.

P. BALDWIN, *The Politics of Social Solidarity: Class Bases of the European Welfare State 1875–1975* (1990). An excellent analysis of the political forces that allowed the welfare state to come into being.

I. BANAC, ED., *Eastern Europe in Revolution* (1992). Excellent articles on the events of 1989 and afterward.

J. H. BILLINGTON, *Russia Transformed: Breakthrough to Hope, Moscow, August, 1991* (1992). A thoughtful essay on the attempted coup.

E. BOTTOME, *The Balance of Terror: Nuclear Weapons and the Illusion of Security, 1945–1985* (1986). A review of the issues that dominated the Cold War era.

A. BROWN, *The Gorbachev Factor* (1996). An important commentary by an English observer.

A. N. DRAGNICH, *Serbs and Croats: The Struggle in Yugoslavia* (1992). An introduction to the historical roots of the current struggle.

M. ELLMAN AND V. KONTOROVICH, *The Disintegration of the Soviet Economic System* (1992). An overview of the economic strains that the Soviet Union experienced during the 1980s.

H. FEIS, *From Trust to Terror: The Onset of the Cold War, 1945–1950* (1970). The best general account.

J. L. GADDIS, *What We Know Now* (1997). Examines the Cold War in light of newly released documents.

D. J. GARROW, *Bearing the Cross: Martin Luther King, Jr. and the Southern Leadership Conference 1955–1968* (1986). The best work on the subject.

M. GLENNY, *The Fall of Yugoslavia: The Third Balkan War* (1992). An overview by a British journalist.

B. GWERTZMAN AND M. T. KAUFMAN, *The Collapse of Communism* (1991). A collection of contemporary news accounts.

B. GWERTZMAN AND M. T. KAUFMAN, *The Decline and Fall of the Soviet Empire* (1992). A collection of contemporary news accounts.

D. HOLLOWAY, *The Soviet Union and the Arms Race* (1985). Excellent treatment of internal Soviet decision making.

L. JOHNSON, *Central Europe: Enemies & Neighbors & Friends* (1996). Explores the complexities of relationships in the region.

R. G. KAISER, *Why Gorbachev Happened* (1992). A useful overview.

D. KEARNS, *Lyndon Johnson and the American Dream* (1976). A useful biography.

J. KEEP, *The Last of the Empires: A History of the Soviet Union, 1956–1991* (1995). A clear narrative.

R. F. LESLIE, *The History of Poland Since 1863* (1981). An excellent collection of essays that provide the background for later events in Poland.

F. LEWIS, *Europe: Road to Unity* (1992). A discussion of contemporary Europe by a thoughtful journalist.

R. MALTBY, ED., *Passing Parade: A History of Popular Culture in the Twentieth Century* (1989). A collection of essays on a topic just beginning to receive scholarly attention.

P. H. MERKL, *German Unification in the European Context* (1993). The first major essay on the impact of German unity.

C. MURRAY, *Losing Ground: American Social Policy 1950–1980* (1983). A pessimistic assessment.

P. PULZER, *German Politics, 1945–1995* (1996). An important overview.

L. SCHAPIRO, *The Communist Party of the Soviet Union* (1960). A classic analysis of the most important institution of Soviet Russia.

A. M. SCHLESINGER, JR., *A Thousand Days: John F. Kennedy in the White House* (1965). A biography by an adviser and major historian.

H. SIMONIAN, *The Privileged Partnership: Franco-German Relations in the European Community (1969–1984)* (1985). An important examination of the dominant role of France and Germany in the EEC.

J. STEELE, *Soviet Power: The Kremlin's Foreign Policy—Brezhnev to Andropov* (1983). A broad survey.

D. STOCKMAN, *The Triumph of Politics: The Inside Story of the Reagan Revolution* (1987). A critical memoir by one of Reagan's aides.

G. STOKES, ED., *From Stalinism to Pluralism: A Documentary History of Eastern Europe since 1945* (1996). An important collection of documents which are not easily accessible elsewhere.

H. A. TURNER, JR., *Germany from Partition to Reunification* (1992). The best and most recent introduction.

M. WALKER, *The Cold War and the Making of the Modern World* (1994). A major survey.

B. WOODWARD AND C. BERNSTEIN, *The Final Days* (1976). A discussion of the Watergate scandal by the reporters who uncovered it.

COMPARATIVE PERSPECTIVES: TECHNOLOGY AND CIVILIZATIONS

Energy and the Modern World

No single technological factor so determines the social relationships and standard of living of human beings as energy. The more energy a society can command for each of its members the stronger and more influential it will be. Throughout recorded human history, those societies that have found ways to improve their access to sources of energy, and have then efficiently applied the energy, have dominated both their immediate environments and much of the world beyond. Indeed, the possession of, or the lack of, efficient, inexpensive sources of energy in large measure determines which nations will be wealthy and which will be poor.

Animals, Wind, and Water

For civilization to advance technologically, energy had to be applied to tasks. The earliest source of such energy was animal power, which was used all over the world except among the peoples on the American continent prior to the arrival of the Europeans. Oxen, water buffalo, and horses were the major draft animals. (See for example, the painting on p. 224.) Of these, horses were the most efficient.

Throughout the world until the eighteenth century, however, wind and water furnished most of the energy for machinery. Sailing ships had been used since ancient times for travel, fishing, and the transport of goods. The wind also worked mills that pumped water and ground grain. Waterwheels proved to be highly flexible machines and by the eighteenth century constituted the major sources of mechanical power in Europe and much of the rest of the world. But wind and water were uncertain sources of energy. The wind could cease; drought could dry up streams. Waterpowered machinery had to be located near the stream furnishing the water. Consequently, most of the mills employing such machinery were located in the countryside.

Although animals, wind, and water provided energy for relatively complicated machines capable of manufacturing and transporting high-quality goods, the economic and political transformations that have driven the history of the world for the past two and a half centuries could only have occurred through a qualitative as well as quantitative leap in the manner in which human beings commanded energy. The twin sources of this world-transforming energy have been fossil fuels and electricity.

Until the second half of the eighteenth century fossil fuels—coal, petroleum, and to a lesser extent natural gas—contributed only a small portion of human energy requirements. Their use as meaningful sources of energy required a series of inventions that allowed the energy of heat to be changed into mechanical energy.

Steam Power and the Age of Coal

Although peoples living near coal deposits had used it as a household fuel for a very long time, only the invention of the steam engine, patented by James Watt in 1769, established a major industrial demand for coal. The steam engine first permitted the pumping of water from coal mines to increase production. But as the industrial uses for the steam engine grew, the invention itself drove the demand for greater quantities of coal as fuel.

Coal-fueled steam power changed the face of human society during the nineteenth century and continues to provide the energy for the most powerful turbogenerators at the dawn of the twenty-first century. Steampowered machines could be made larger and more flexible than those powered by wind or water, and so long as coal was available, they could run steadily day and night. Steam engines, in contrast to waterwheels, were transportable. Factories could be moved away from streams in the countryside to urban areas where a ready workforce existed. And goods produced in factories powered by steam engines could be carried around the world by steampowered locomotives and ships. Those expanding markets in turn called forth more steampowered factories and even greater use of coal. Furthermore, steampowered factories could also produce military weapons that could be placed on steampowered naval vessels constructed of iron and steel in vast coal-fueled blast furnaces. When Theodore Roosevelt sent the United States fleet around the world, it was a testimony to the power of coal as steam as well as to the power of the American navy.

The age of steam was the age of coal. The nations possessing large coal deposits dominated much nineteenth-century economic life as the nations that possess oil reserves dominate much contemporary economic life. For many decades Great Britain dominated the world's production and delivery of coal, which was transported over the entire world. Its domination was challenged only in the late nineteenth century as the United States and later Russia and China began to produce vast quantities of the fuel. Coal remained the chief fuel for the United States until after World War I and for Western Europe until after World War II. It remains the chief fuel for China.

Coal generated a rising standard of living in Europe and the expansion of European and later American power, but coal also generated a number of social problems. The most shocking conditions of exploited labor occurred in coal mines, where parliamentary reports of the 1840s described and illustrated half-clad women and children drawing coal carts from the depths of the mines to the surface. Throughout the nineteenth and twentieth centuries thousands of miners died in mining disasters. Work in the mines injured the health of miners, as did the pollution sent into the atmosphere by coal fires from both factories and homes. By the early twentieth century observers had begun to note the damage to the environment caused by strip mining of coal and the later abandonment of the regions.

As with coal, the impact of petroleum, the second major fossil fuel, also depended upon the invention of machinery to use it. Originally, the use for oil was limited to kerosene, the fuel for lighting around much of the world by 1900. It was upon the world demand for lamp oil that John D. Rockefeller founded the Standard Oil Company. The invention of the internal combustion engine in 1882 by Rudolf Daimler and the diesel engine in 1892 by Rudolf Diesel transformed the demand for oil. Toward the close of the nineteenth century extensive oil production had begun in the United States, with Russia, Romania, Sumatra, Mexico, Iran, and Venezuela starting to tap their own oil resources before World War I.

The Internal Combustion Engine: The Age of Oil

Just as the steam engine had spurred the expansion of the coal industry, the internal combustion engine drove the oil industry. Fuel oil would begin to replace coal, not so much because it was cheaper but rather because it was more efficient, easier to store and transport, and cleaner to burn. Initially fuel oil tended to be used in those countries where it could be produced relatively near the point of use. Until the end of World War II the United States was the primary world producer and user of oil. As fuel for the internal combustion engine, oil became the driving force of automobiles, locomotives, airplanes, ships, factory machinery, and electric generators. It revolutionized agricultural machinery and world food production, but as a fuel for transportation, it fostered a social transformation over much of the world.

Starting in the United States and then spreading elsewhere, owning an automobile introduced a new mobility factor into social relationships. People could move easily across

Until 1924 Henry Ford had disdained national advertising for his cars. But as General Motors gained a competitive edge by making yearly changes in style and technology, Ford was forced to pay more attention to advertising. This ad was directed at "Mrs. Consumer," combining appeals to both female independence and motherly duties. [Ford Motor Company, Detroit]

long distances to join a new community or to start a new job. Inexpensive gasoline for cars and public transport buses permitted the development of suburbs ever farther removed from traditional urban centers. In turn, retailing moved away from city centers to shopping malls. At the same time wherever the mechanization of farming through improved farm machinery took place, there usually followed a movement of people from farming communities to urban areas.

Electricity Increases the Demand for Oil

The manufacture of automobiles and other forms of transport using the internal combustion or diesel engine was central to all modern industrial life. As those industries expanded, so did the construction of extensive road systems. These in turn created new demands for fuel oil.

But the greatest demand for fuel oil arose from the application of electricity to the needs of everyday life. Electricity proved to be the most flexible and versatile source of energy for the twentieth century, and its generation provided the single greatest source of demand for both coal and oil. Electricity generation would also employ new modes of water power in the forms of hydroelectric generators.

The scientific basis for the production of electric energy was Michael Faraday's study of electromagnetic induction. In 1831 he demonstrated that mechanical energy under the proper conditions could be converted into electric energy. Even more important, the reverse was also true. Electricity could be generated in one location and applied far away wherever electrical lines could be extended. The applications of electrical power have appeared to be limited only by the limitations of the inventive imagination.

During the second half of the nineteenth century a whole host of inventors, such as Thomas Alva Edison, worked through the production and application of electrical power to service large regions. Electricity found applications across the spectrum of human society, actions, and enterprises. Access to electricity in the course of the twentieth century became the key factor for an improved standard of living. A fundamental moment in the decision by Japan to modernize during the late nineteenth century was the construction of the Tokyo Electric Light Company in 1888. The extension of electrical lines into the American countryside was one of the major accomplishments of Franklin Roosevelt's New Deal. Electrical power transformed the workplace, but even more strikingly it transformed homes. Without access to electrical power domestic households could not make use of any of the growing array of labor saving appliances such as electric washing machines, electric irons, electric stoves, and electric vacuum cleaners. Electric lights brightened whole cities. Electricity replaced both coal and oil as the source of power for many locomotives; it powered public tram systems and opened the way for the telegraph, the telephone, the wireless, the motion picture camera, and television. It planted the seeds for the computer revolution in communication and information. Electricity allowed manufacturing plants and office complexes to be built wherever electric lines could be carried. Indeed, the spread of access to electrical power has been the single best indication of economic advance for any nation or region.

Yet within this era of ever-expanding electrification, coal and oil—the fundamental fossil fuels—would still provide the underpinnings of the world's energy. In fact, more oil and coal are used to generate electricity than for any other single purpose. Throughout the twentieth century the demand for these fuels led to the refinement of their production techniques to permit the extraction of coal from ever-deeper seams and the strip-mining of it from regions where previously it would have been economically unproductive to do so. The effort to discover, extract, and transport oil would have major consequences for the world's physical and geopolitical environment far into the twentieth century.

Oil and Global Politics in the Twentieth Century

As the century began, the United States was by far the largest producer and exporter of petroleum. Yet by the 1920s the American government began to worry about running out of oil. So too did the British, who depended on imported oil for all of their military and industrial needs. During the 1920s and 1930s, both governments encouraged oil companies to forge agreements for the drilling and export of oil from the Middle East. These arrangements fit into the pattern of formal and informal colonialism that still characterized the interwar period.

After World War II, Western Europe, the Soviet Union, and the nations of the Warsaw Pact began to turn from coal to oil as the basis for economic growth. (Japan followed this course during the 1960s.) By 1947 the United States had begun to import more oil than it produced. These two developments—a new dependence on oil by the industrialized nations and the expanded search for oil by the West—formed the basis for the new role that the nations of the Middle East would play in the world economy as the chief oil exporters. Simultaneously, as the world's industrialized economies were growing dependent on Middle East oil production, nationalistic leaders in that region were denouncing former colonial domination and rejecting relationships with the West and with Israel, a country which received strong political support from the United States and Western Europe. The stage was thus set for oil to play a new role in the geopolitical conflicts of the Cold War era.

Playing a major role in those conflicts was the Organization of Petroleum Exporting Nations (OPEC), founded in 1960. Regardless of their differences, OPEC members were united in two things: First, they deeply resented former colonial control of their oil supplies, and second, they were determined that their own governments, not foreign oil companies, would control those vital resources. [Mexico had brought its own petroleum industry under state control before World War II.] In 1973, during the Yom Kippur War, OPEC acted, sharply raising oil prices to nations whose governments supported Israel. The action caused severe economic consequences in the West and spurred new efforts to develop local oil reserves in politically safe locations such as in the North Sea. OPEC would attempt similar actions on other occasions, most successfully in 1979. In that year, a revolution in Iran overthrew the government which had long been supported by the United States. OPEC cut off oil shipments to the West, causing severe dislocations. Concerns about securing oil supplies in the West were again sparked by the Persian Gulf War and other political tensions in the region.

In addition to the political problems associated with Middle East oil production, The industrial world's reliance on oil has had severe environmental consequences. Generally, when the United States dominated oil production, the oil refineries were located near the source of oil production. As the exploitation of oil reserves moved to the Middle East and then later in the century to Alaska and to the North Sea, oil refineries became separated from the drilling locations. Crude oil was shipped to refineries on enormous tankers. More than once, these supertankers have hit shoals or gone aground, causing large oil spills, calamitous to both animals and humans.

The Promise and Danger of Nuclear Energy

Following World War II nuclear power became a new source for the generation of electrical energy. The power of the atom, first released in the 1940s for military purposes, held the promise of virtually infinite quantities of energy. The world would no longer be dependent upon finite supplies of fossil fuel located in politically tense regions of the world. The generation of such energy, however, required the most complex sets of machinery ever devised to produce electrical energy. France and Great Britain began to build nuclear reactors in the 1950s with the United States, the Soviet Union, and various other European nations following in the 1960s. Nations outside the West, such as India and Pakistan, looked to the construction of nuclear power stations as a means of moving more rapidly toward the achievements of industrialization and a rising standard of living through extensive electrification. Nations with limited supplies of fossil fuel, such as Japan, hoped nuclear energy would solve their energy supply problem. The oil shock of the mid-1970s brought new enthusiasm to the adoption of nuclear energy, but the economic downturn of the late 1970s and early 1980s slowed the construction of nuclear generating stations. The construction of breeder reactors, which would produce their own fuel in the process of generating electrical energy, seemed to promise a world liberated by dependence upon a finite supply of fossil

In 1989, when a supertanker spilled 35,000 tons of crude oil into Alaska's Prince William Sound, rescue workers struggled to save the lives of sea birds and animals. Nevertheless, hundreds died. [Ron Levy/Liaison Agency, Inc.]

fuels. Furthermore, unlike coal and oil, which have many uses besides that of fuel, uranium had no other economic use. The workers in the field of atomic energy were scientists and engineers rather than the kind of industrial labor force that produced coal and oil.

Yet, the technology of nuclear energy production proved to be exceedingly dangerous. The atomic reactors produced spent radioactive waste that would remain hazardous for hundreds of years. After many years of warnings of such danger, the Chernobyl nuclear generating plant in the former Soviet Union caused enormous, lasting damage in the spring of 1986. In 1979 the possibility of a similar disaster had occurred at the Three Mile Island plant in Pennsylvania. Both the promise and danger of nuclear power continues to inform the political life of all nations using such power. It is wholly unclear, for example, what will be done with the radioactive spent fuel. Furthermore, the construction of nuclear generating plants has allowed nations who lack atomic weapons to train scientists and other experts who might be able to use that knowledge to develop atomic weapons. Whereas in the United States and Europe the military uses of atomic power came first and were followed by peaceful energy uses, the reverse has been the case in nations such as India and Pakistan. Despite its initial promise, nuclear power has contributed far less to energy production than we originally imagined.

The problem of energy remains with us in the new century. Environmental pollution, and all the issues surrounding the nuclear generation of energy will demand increasing attention and expenditure of public funds. Similarly, the political pressures and tensions surrounding the oil supplies of the Middle East will not disappear, as advanced nations seek to secure and protect energy reserves while the nations that possess those reserves seek to secure a rising standard of living for themselves.

References

John G. Clark, *The Political Economy of World Energy: A Twentieth-Century Perspective* (1990).
J.C. Debeir, J. P. Deleage, and Daniel Hemery, *In the Servitude of Power: Energy and Civilization through the Ages* (1991).
V. Smil, *Energy in World History* (1994).
C. van der Linde, *Dynamic International Oil Markets: Oil Market Developments and Structure 1860-1990* (1991).

COMPARATIVE PERSPECTIVES: TECHNOLOGY AND CIVILIZATIONS

The Coming of the Computer

The most extensive technological revolution of the second half of the twentieth century, the development and widespread use of computers, is comparable only to the invention of printing and the European industrial revolution. No part of the world has escaped the power of computer technology. It has produced a global interconnectedness previously imagined only in the most advanced science fiction.

Early Computing

Beginning in the seventeenth century thinkers associated with the Scientific Revolution, most famously the French mathematician and philosopher Blaise Pascal, attempted to construct machines that would carry out mathematical calculations. These inventors and would-be inventors understood that machines could carry out a vast number of mathematical calculations that people would find unbearably boring and time consuming. They thought, too, that machines would make fewer errors.

During the late nineteenth century political and economic forces drove the demand for the development of such calculating machinery. Governments of consolidating nation-states, then and later, needed to collect and organize vast amounts of data relating to national censuses, tax collection, military information, and economic statistics. Private businesses required a greater command of economic and business data that could be organized more easily and profitably through calculating machinery. By the late 1920s companies such as National Cash Register, Remington Rand, and International Business Machines Corporation had begun to produce such business machinery. During this era and for the next half century machines manipulated data through an elaborate system of punch cards on which a system of holes in the cards indicated the content of the data.

Early in the twentieth century, electrical engineers developed circuitry that allowed machines to perform increasingly complicated modes of calculation. Not only were the new machines faster, but the new circuitry expanded their capacity for storing data. Furthermore, inventions dependent upon electricity including the telephone, telegraph, underwater cables, and the wireless created a new communications industry that required the organization of large databases of customer information to deliver their services. Then, companies and governments using those services themselves developed new demands for data storage and manipulation.

After World War I and throughout World War II all of the major powers developed new weapons requiring advanced mathematical calculations for their successful application. The ballistic calculations needed to bomb a target from a plane, for example, required machines of unprecedented power. The war efforts allowed very large investments to be diverted to computing.

The first machine genuinely recognizable as a modern digital computer was the ENIAC (Electronic Numerical Integrator and Computer) built and designed at the Moore Laboratories of the University of Pennsylvania and put into use by the U. S. army in 1946. It was an enormous piece of equipment with 40 panels, 1,500 electric relays, and 18,000 vacuum tubes. The Army intended the machine for ballistics calculation.

Until the 1960s most people assumed that such large computing machinery would only be used by the military and other government agencies or by the very largest corporations. The general public rarely saw these machines except when illustrated in magazines or used by television news broadcasters to predict election outcomes.

A major advance would come during the 1950s, when the invention of the transistor and miniaturized circuitry made vacuum tubes obsolete. Computers could now be made smaller and more dependable. Unlike vacuum tubes, transistors did not burn out. The government demand for computing associated with expanding administrative programs, cold war military technology, and the space program continued to fuel computer innovation.

Throughout the 1950s and the 1960s computers had to be programmed with difficult computer languages, making it impossible for anyone not expertly trained to use them. Furthermore, these mainframes were not connected with each other. During this period some of the earliest computer programs were written, including those that would eventually create the so-called Year 2000 (Y2K) problem.

The Mouse and the Microchip

During the late 1960s two remarkable innovations opened the way for the kind of "user friendly," widespread computing that we know today. First, computer scientists in a California laboratory transferred the control of the computer to a "bitmap" which covered the monitor's screen. Then, with the invention of the "mouse," images could be directed on the bitmap. Complicated computer language could now be embedded in the machine and hidden from the user who simply manipulated the images on the screen with the mouse. With this new technology, anyone, not just the experts, was a potential computer user.

The next major breakthrough in the democratization of computer technology came during the 1960s when engineers associated with a California start-up company called Intel invented the microchip. Itself a miniature computer, the microchip became the heart of all future computers. With this tiny chip, computers started to shrink. They could also be installed in other machines, such as automobiles, telecommunication equipment, heating and cooling systems, and elevators.

In the late 1970s and early 1980s, engineers, first at Xerox Corporation and then at IBM, created small personal computers, but neither was a commercial success. Then, in 1984, engineers at Apple Computer Corporation produced a small, highly accessible, computer known as the Macintosh that would fit on a desktop in either the home or office. IBM quickly adopted the Apple concept, creating the product called the Personal Computer or the PC. By the middle of the 1980s, at a relatively modest cost (and a cost that would continue to drop over the years) anyone could own a computer far more powerful than the old mainframes.

Just as the manufacture of moderately priced automobiles revolutionized the geographical mobility of ordinary people early in the century, the democratization of computers at its end has again transformed society, this time by providing unparalleled access to information. The computer has become a transforming link, allowing users to manipulate ideas, or to receive and send information on just about anything via the World Wide Web. Anyone with access to the internet can lobby a politician, take a college course, do their personal banking, buy a car, or rent a house.

For all of their power and speed, however, for reasons that we still do not understand, the widespread use of computers throughout society has not led to a rise in productivity. It seems to many observers that even personal, user-friendly computers are still too complicated even for relatively sophisticated consumers and users.

What computer technology has achieved is in one important respect different from virtually any previous technology. The speed of change—both in their power and applications—is unprecedented, and we can expect that pace to continue. Some observers believe that we will gradually abandon the personal computer, replacing it with a series of separate devices that perform single tasks or a group of related tasks.

The computer revolution has more than any other single technological change established the basis for a new sense of global community and world civilization. It has shortened distances and time and allowed modes of interaction around the globe unprecedented in human history. Whereas previous generations conceived of the world through maps, this and succeeding generations may well view the world through icons on screen.[1]

[1]This essay has drawn upon the following works: Herman H. Goldstine, *The Computer from Pascal to von Neuman* (1972), Tom Forester, ed., *The Microelectronics Revolution* (1980), Thomas K. Landauer, *The Trouble with Computers: Usefulness, Usability, and Productivity* (1997), Gene I. Rochlin, *Trapped in the Net: The Unanticipated Consequences of Computerization* (1997).

37 EAST ASIA IN THE LATE TWENTIETH CENTURY

In May 1989, thousands of students demonstrated in Tienanmen Square in China's capital, Beijing, demanding democratic government.

Activists erected a ten-meter high "Goddess of Democracy" as a symbol of their cause. Then tanks rolled in, the students were slain or

dispersed, and the goddess, along with hopes for governmental change, was smashed. [Arthur Tsang/Reuters/Archive Photos]

CHAPTER TOPICS

- Japan
- China
- Taiwan

- Korea
- Vietnam

In World Perspective East Asia

The history of East Asia since the end of World War II (see Map 37–1) may be divided into two phases. In the first, from 1945 to 1980, several East Asian nations became Communist but achieved only a small improvement in the conditions of their peoples. In stark contrast, the nations that used a mixture of state guidance and market-oriented economies made the region as a whole the most dynamic in the postwar world. Japan led the way, achieving economic growth that has often been spoken of as miraculous but can more sensibly be described as single-minded. Japan also developed into a robust parliamentary democracy with freedoms comparable to those of Western Europe or the United States.

Taiwan and South Korea began their economic development a decade or two later and from a much lower level, and, though lacking the political freedom of Japan, they attained stunning economic growth, as did the tiny British colony of Hong Kong and the even tinier ex-British colony of Singapore. Viewing the progress of these countries, it would appear that the values of the East Asian heritage—hard work, frugality, a family orientation, a thirst for education, and a concern for getting ahead—lead almost automatically to economic development if given half a chance.

The Communist nations, China, North Korea, and Vietnam did less well. China was wracked by almost continuous political convulsions. In spite of gaining undisputed political authority over an area comparable to that of the Ch'ing Empire, the government was unable to tap the energies and talents of its people. The contrast between the low productivity of the Chinese in China and the remarkable productivity of the same people in Hong Kong and Taiwan was startling.

Vietnam, plagued by wars during these early decades, did not develop at all. North Korea, where most of the industry of Japan's prewar colony was located, did slightly better during the decade following the end of the Korean War, but its achievements paled in comparison with those of South Korea.

The second phase of postwar East Asian history was the eighties and nineties. During the eighties, those nations that had prospered earlier continued to grow. Japan's per capita product zoomed past that of Germany and, for a time, that of the United States. Taiwan, South Korea, Hong Kong, and Singapore also achieved amazing advances. Growth went hand in hand with social stability and an increasingly varied cultural life. Especially notable were advances in democracy in Taiwan and South Korea. But during the nineties, a recession rippled through East Asia and growth halted or slowed.

The most marked change occurred in China, which, even while maintaining a Communist dictatorship, introduced many features of a market economy. The result was explosive growth and an export boom. It began in southeastern coastal areas and then spread to the rest of the nation. Long suppressed entrepreneurial abilities surfaced. And, as the economy grew, the society changed. Vietnam also adopted a weaker version of the same policy. It encouraged private enterprises and opened its markets to foreign capital. Only North Korea resisted the changes sweeping the rest of the Communist world. The rigidities of its singular brand of Communism took their toll, and as the end of the twentieth century approached, its people suffered hunger and misery.

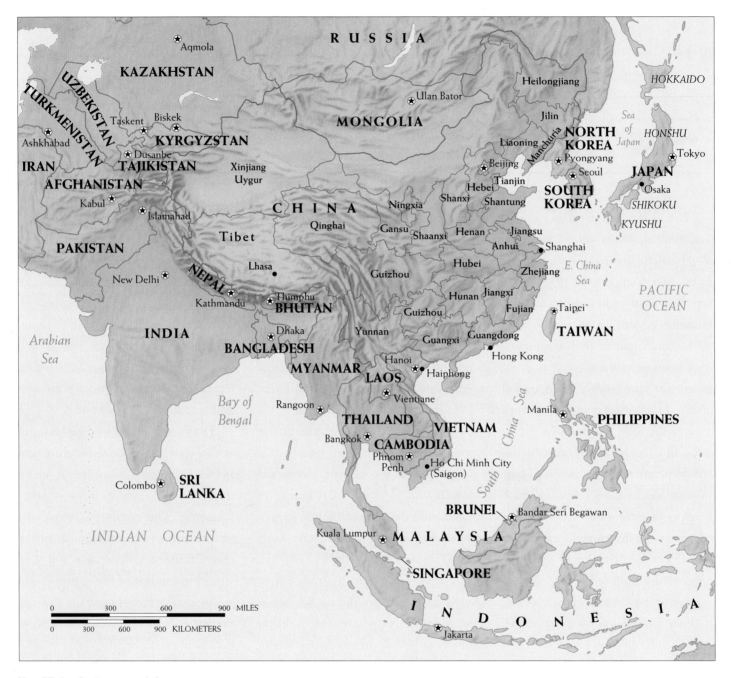

Map 37–1   Contemporary Asia.

Japan

For Japan, which was already bogged down in its occupation of China, the decision in 1941 to go to war with the United States and its allies was a desperate gamble. By all objective measures—steel production, oil, machine tools, heavy chemicals, shipping—Japan was far weaker than the United States. The Japanese military, however, misread statements of isolationist sentiment in the United States during 1940 and 1941

and concluded that Americans had no stomach for a drawn-out war in the western Pacific. In terms of strategy, they bet Japan's shorter lines of supply against American productivity.

By early 1945, Japan was poor, hungry, and ill-clothed. Cities were burnt out, factories scarred by bombings; shipping had been sunk, railways were dilapidated, and trucks and cars were scarce. Yet, despite their wretched condition, the Japanese people steeled themselves for invasion and a final battle in defense of their homeland. Then, in early Au-

The Occupation of Japan

There are occupations, and then there are occupations. Former Prime Minister Yoshida Shigeru presents his view.

Is this an objective appraisal, or an attempt by Yoshida to justify his own role in the Allied Occupation?

There are some now in Japan who point to similarities between the Allied, and predominantly American, Occupation of Japan, and our Occupation of Manchuria, China and other countries of Asia—the idea apparently being that, once an Occupation régime has been established, the relationship between victors and vanquished is usually found to be the same. I regret that I cannot subscribe to this opinion. Japan's Occupation of various Asian countries, carried out by Army officers of no higher rank than colonel and more often by raw subalterns, became an object of hatred and loathing among the peoples of the occupied countries, and there is none to dispute that fact. The Americans came into our country as our enemies, but after an Occupation lasting little less than seven years, an understanding grew up between the two peoples which is remarkable in the history of the modern world.

Criticism of Americans is a right accorded even to Americans. But in the enumeration of their faults we cannot include their Occupation of Japan.

From *The Yoshida Memoirs*, Yoshida Shigeru. Copyright © 1961 Heineman Books, p. 60.

---

gust, atomic bombs were dropped on Hiroshima and Nagasaki, and the Soviet Union declared war on Japan and invaded Manchuria. Even after these disasters, opinion at the imperial conference, which was called to decide on a national policy, was split, with three favoring surrender and three for continuing the war. The emperor broke the deadlock, and Japan accepted the Allied terms of unconditional surrender. On August 15, 1945, the emperor broadcast Japan's surrender to the Japanese people, saying that the "unendurable must be endured."

After years of wartime propaganda, the Japanese reacted with shock at the fact of surrender, deep sadness at having lost the war, relief that the bombing was over, and apprehension about what would come next. They expected a harsh and vindictive occupation, but when they found it constructive, they turned to positive cooperation. Their receptivity to new democratic ideas and their repudiation of militarism led one Japanese writer to label this era "the second opening of Japan."

The Occupation

General Douglas MacArthur was the Supreme Commander for the Allied Powers in Japan. His headquarters in Tokyo was staffed almost entirely by Americans, and the occupation forces themselves were American, apart from British Commonwealth troops on the island of Shikoku. The chief concern of the first phase of the occupation was demilitarization and democratization. Civilians and soldiers abroad were returned to Japan and the military was demobilized. Ultranationalist organizations were dissolved and the Home Ministry was abolished. The police were decentralized and

political prisoners were freed. Following the model of the Nuremberg trials in Germany, wartime leaders were brought to trial for "crimes against humanity." In addition, 210,000 officers, businessmen, teachers, and officials—the leaders of wartime Japan—were removed from office. The thoroughness of these reforms reflected the occupation view that Japanese society had been tainted by feudal and militaristic values and that Japan's leaders had been joined in a huge conspiracy to wage aggressive war.

As a part of democratization, Shinto was disestablished as the state religion, labor unions were encouraged, and the holding companies of *zaibatsu* combines were dissolved. The old educational system, which had forced students at an early age to choose either an elite or a mass track, was changed to a single-track system that kept open longer the option of continuing in school. The most radical undertaking was a land reform that expropriated landlord holdings and sold them to landless tenants at a fractional cost. The effect, ironically, was to create a countryside of politically conservative small farmers. Needless to say, some of these reforms merely accelerated changes already underway in Japan, and all of the reforms depended on the cooperation—at times enthusiastic and at times reluctant—of Japanese officials.

Of all the occupation reforms, none was more important than the new constitution, written by the Government Section of MacArthur's headquarters and passed into law by the Japanese Diet. It fundamentally changed Japan's polity in five respects:

1. A British-style parliamentary state was established in which the cabinet became a committee of the majority

Women, newly enfranchised, voting in postwar Japan. [UPI/Corbis-Bettmann]

party or coalition in the Diet. This broke with the Meiji constitution, which had permitted the emperor or those who acted in his name to appoint prime ministers without regard for the Diet. The new constitution also added an American-style independent judiciary and a federal system of prefectures with elected governors and local leaders.

2. Women were given the vote.

3. The rights of life, liberty, the pursuit of happiness, a free press, and free assembly were guaranteed. These were joined by newer rights, such as academic freedom, collective bargaining, sexual equality in marriage, and minimal standards of wholesome and cultural living.

4. Article 9, the no-war clause, stipulated, "The Japanese people forever renounce war as a sovereign right of the nation" and will never maintain "land, sea, and air force" or "other war potential." This article would make

Japan into something unique in the world: a major power without commensurate military strength.

5. The constitution defined a new role for the emperor as "the symbol of the state deriving his position from the will of the people with whom resides sovereign power."

The Japanese people accepted the new constitution and embraced democracy with uncritical enthusiasm. The no-war clause was viewed by most as the guarantee of a peaceful future. Although it did not preclude the formation of a Self-Defense Force, it acted as a brake on military expenditures, which half a century later were only about 1 percent of Japan's gross domestic product. The Japanese had been readied for the changed status of the emperor by his speech on January 1, 1946, in which he renounced all claims to divinity. The occupation saw to it that the emperor traveled about Japan in a manner appropriate to his new status as a symbol of the state. No one who saw this mild, rumpled-looking, and inarticulate man suspected him of being a Shinto god. By the late 1960s most, though not all, Japanese had come to feel a considerable affection for Emperor Hirohito, who, they felt, had shared in their wartime and postwar hardships. They were saddened by his death in 1989.

By the end of 1947, most of the planned reforms had been carried out. To create a climate in which the new democracy could take root and flourish, the occupation in its second phase turned to Japan's economic recovery. It dropped plans to deconcentrate big business further, encouraged the Japanese government to curb inflation, and cracked down on Communist unions that used strikes for political ends. The United States also gave Japan $2 billion in economic aid.

The outbreak of the Korean War in 1950 marked the start of the third and final phase of the occupation. The American military, fully engaged in the peninsular war, no longer had time for Japan. Consequently, Japanese officials began to look to the Cabinet and the Diet for policy decisions, not to the occupying forces. By the time Japan regained its sovereignty in April 1952, the effect of the changeover was hardly noticeable in the daily life of the Japanese people. On the same day as the peace treaty, Japan signed a security treaty with the United States which provided for American bases and committed the United States to Japan's defense. Although attacked by the left, the security treaty became the cornerstone of Japan's minimalist defense policy.

Parliamentary Politics

In 1945, Japan had a parliamentary potential that harked back to the rise of party power in the Diet between 1890 and 1932. It also had an authoritarian potential compounded of those factors that had led to the rise of militarism. Had the country been occupied by the Soviet Union, the efficiency of its bureaucracy, its wartime economic planning organs, its educated and disciplined work force, and its receptivity to change after its defeat would doubtless have made Japan a model Communist state. Occupied by the United States, the parliamentary potential emerged.

Japan's postwar politics can be divided into three periods. The first, from 1945 to 1955, was the continuation of prewar party politics as modified to fit the new political environment. Two conservative parties and a socialist party emerged. The Liberals and the Democrats, the conservative parties, were the successors to the two mainstream prewar parties. They resumed their struggle for power in the early postwar elections. The Japanese Socialist Party, which won 26 percent of the vote in 1947, was the heir of the moderate prewar socialist party, which had received 9 percent of the vote in 1937. For most of this first decade, the Liberals held power under Prime Minister Yoshida Shigeru (1878–1967). Before the war, Yoshida had been an ardent imperialist, but he had favored close ties with Britain and the United States and had opposed the rise of militarism. After the war, as president of the Liberal Party, he cooperated closely with MacArthur and worked to rebuild Japan's economy. Pro-business and anti-Communist, he was so autocratic in his dealings with bureaucrats and lesser politicians that he was nicknamed "one-man Yoshida."

The long second period from 1955 to 1993 has been called the one and a half party system. The "one" party was the Liberal Democratic Party (LDP), which was formed by a merger of the two conservative parties in 1955. It held power throughout this period. The "half party," so called because it was permanently out of power, was the Japanese Socialist Party. It had split in two in 1951 and come back together in 1955.

What did it mean to have one-party rule for 38 years? One-party rule is not usually associated with representative government. In the immediate postwar years, the strength of the conservatives was simply the continuation of prewar constituencies: that is to say, the network of ties between local men of influence, prefectural assemblymen, and Diet politicians, and their ties to business and the bureaucracy. From the sixties onward, the LDP became identified as the party that was rebuilding Japan and maintaining Japan's security through close ties with the United States. It was widely recognized as more able than other parties. Despite the cozy relationships that developed between the LDP and business, periodic scandals, and a widespread distrust of politicians, the Japanese people voted to keep it in power. Rule by a single party for such a long period provided for an unusual continuity in government policies. Within the larger pattern of the LDP hegemony, several trends were notable:

1. From 1955 to 1960, Japanese politics was marked by ideological strife. The LDP was led by wartime figures who had been purged after the war but had resumed their political careers. These leaders rather high-handedly modified several occupation reforms, recentralized the police, strengthened central government controls over education, and even considered a revision of the constitution. The opposition was led by Marxist socialists, many of whom had been persecuted during the war. The Socialists branded LDP governance as the "tyranny of the majority," since legislation was often passed by "snap votes," and warned of the revival of authoritarianism. Diet sessions were marked by confrontation, rancor, and occasional violence.

   After 1960, confrontation politics declined. Adopting a "low posture," the new LDP prime minister dropped controversial political issues and drew up a plan to double the national income in ten years. These moves inaugurated a more peaceful era. As prosperity grew during the seventies and eighties, ideological confrontation declined further. In many areas a consensus emerged as LDP consulted opposition politicians before presenting bills to the Diet.

2. Another trend was a steady decline in the LDP popular vote from 63 percent in 1955 to 55 percent in 1963, to 43 percent in 1976. The decline mirrored Japan's economic growth: farmers, small shopkeepers, and others who traditionally voted for the LDP became a smaller part of the population, while unionized laborers and white-collar workers, who tended to vote for the socialists, increased. By the late seventies, the conservatives faced the possibility that they would have to form a coalition to stay in power. But in the 1979 election the steady twenty-year decline in the LDP popular vote came to an end. For the next fourteen years the party enjoyed a stable majority in the powerful Lower House of the Diet—though not always in the Upper House—and maintained its rule.

3. Even though it received less than half of the popular vote, the LDP maintained its Diet majority because its opposition fragmented. In 1960, non-Marxist members broke from the Socialist Party to form a competing Democratic Socialist Party. In 1964, the Value Creating Society (Sōka Gakkai), a Nichiren Buddhist sect that grew to include almost one-tenth of the Japanese population, formed the Clean Government Party (Kōmeitō). The Japanese Communist Party, which became less militant after the end of the Korean War, also gained ground and during the 1970s received almost

10 percent of the popular vote. The competition at the polls between candidates from these smaller opposition parties benefited the larger LDP.

A third era of politics began with the 1993 election, in which established parties lost ground. The LDP, which had governed since 1955, lost 52 of its 275 seats and as a result its majority in the lower house of the Diet. But since other smaller conservative parties gained, in effect the change inaugurated an era of conservative multiparty politics. The biggest loser in the election was the Japanese Socialist Party, which dropped from 136 to 70 seats. The close of the cold war, the decline of Marxism around the world, and the widespread Japanese view that socialist politicians had little to contribute to their recession-ridden country ended the socialists' role as the major opposition party. The death of socialist ideology was confirmed when the socialists joined the LDP in a coalition government. In the following 1996 general election the LDP won 35 percent of the popular vote and gained 16 new seats for a total of 236—still short of a majority, a new conservative opposition party party garnered 156 seats, and the socialists continued their decline. Whether a single conservative party would reemerge to govern in the future, or whether future governments would be based on coalitions, remained in the hands of the Japanese electorate. Whatever the case, a sudden change in Japanese national policies appeared remote.

Economic Growth

The extraordinary story of the economic rise of East Asia after World War II began with Japan. Japanese productivity in 1945 was about the same as it had been in 1918. By 1955 it had recovered to prewar levels, but just as growth was expected to moderate, it forged ahead and continued at a double-digit pace for almost two decades. Shipbuilding, machine tools, steel, heavy chemicals, automobiles, and consumer electronics and optics led the way. Before the war, "made in Japan" had meant cheap, ten-cent-store goods. By the late 1970s Sony, Toyota, Honda, Panasonic, Toshiba, Seiko, and Canon were known throughout the world for the quality of their products.

Several factors explain this growth. An infrastructure of banking, marketing, and manufacturing skills had carried over from prewar Japan. The international situation was also favorable: oil was cheap, access to raw materials and export markets was easy, and American sponsorship gained Japan early entry into the World Bank, the International Monetary Fund, and other international organizations. A rate of savings close to 20 percent helped reinvestment. The rate reflected a traditional frugality, but was also necessary to supplement inadequate pensions.

A revolution in education contributed as well. In the prewar years education for most Japanese ended with middle school, and only a tiny fraction went to university. By the early 1980s, almost all middle school graduates went on to high school, and almost 40 percent of high school graduates went on to higher education, a percentage equal to that of advanced European nations. Even more telling, by the early eighties Japan was graduating more engineers than the United States, and virtually all of them were employed in productive, nonmilitary industries. (In contrast, the total number of lawyers in Japan roughly equals a single year's graduating class from American law schools.) This upgrading of human capital and channeling of its best minds into productive careers let Japan tap the huge backlog of technology that had developed in the United States during and after the war years. It proved far cheaper to license or buy technology than to invent it. After "improvement engineering," Japan sold its products to the world.

Another factor was an abundance of high-quality, cheap labor. Following a postwar baby boom, the population in 1950 was 83 million; in 1999 it was 126 million; and it is expected to stabilize after the turn of the century. Immediately after the war about 47 percent of Japan's labor force was in agriculture; by 1996, less than 6 percent worked on the land. Until the mid-sixties, more labor was available than jobs, which kept wages low. Labor organization, too, was no bar to economic growth. Industrial workers in Japan during the immediate postwar decades were more highly unionized than those in the United States, but the basic component of labor organization was the company-based union, rather than a trade union. Company-based unions regularly engaged in spring offensives and marched with red flags on May Day, but they also took great pains not to impair their companies' productivity. Since the eighties the strength of unions has declined.

The government aided manufacturers with tariff protection, foreign exchange, and special depreciation allowances. Industries engaged in advanced technologies benefited from cheap loans, subsidies, and research products of government laboratories. Small budgets for defense spending and welfare enabled the government to keep corporate taxes low. The Finance Ministry and the Ministry of Trade and Industry encouraged the Bank of Japan to back private banks in refinancing Japan's industries. Critics who spoke of "Japan Inc." as though Japan were a single gigantic corporation overstated the case: competition between companies in Japan was fierce, but government was more supportive of business than it was regulative.

By 1973 the Japanese economy had become "mature." Double-digit growth gave way to 4 percent growth. Labor became more expensive, research budgets grew as the backlog of cheap technology declined, welfare costs rose, and tough but costly antipollution policies were implemented.

An almost completely automated assembly line at Nissan Motors' Zama factory. The high cost of labor in Japan makes such robot-intensive production economical. [Reuters/Susumu Takahashi/Archive Photos]

Behind the statistic of slower growth was a change in the composition of the economy: smoke stack industries declined while service industries, pharmaceuticals, specialty chemicals, scientific equipment, computers, and robots grew. Japan's trade, which hitherto had been balanced, began to generate huge surpluses. The surpluses were generated mainly by the appetite of world markets for Japanese products, but they were also a result of protectionist policies. These policies led to friction and to demands from the United States and Europe that they be abolished.

Even slower growth, or no growth at all, characterized the nineties. Believing their boom would never end, Japanese had bid up the prices of corporate shares and land to several times European and American levels. In 1991 the "bubble" burst: land prices dropped by 30 percent or more, and stocks lost 60 percent of their peak market value. Japanese who owned shares or bought property at exaggerated prices felt poorer; banks that had made housing or margin loans incurred huge losses. Both banks and individuals retrenched, slowing the economy. Some small companies went bankrupt, large companies restructured and cut their research budgets, some workers were laid off or retired early, and fewer new graduates were hired. Unemployment rose from the usual 1.5 to 4.4 percent, and hidden unemployment was higher.

As recession-bound Japan approached the twenty-first century, observers asked why the Japanese government dilly-dallied, taking only palliative measures. One reason was the magnitude of the problem: financial bureaucrats recoiled at the enormous costs of refinancing bank debt in the face of an already unbalanced budget. Another was the absence of a national consensus in favor of a bailout. Corporations had been hurt by the recession, but individual Japanese, the majority still protected by lifetime employment, were not ready to shoulder new taxes. They increased their savings and hoped that Japan would muddle through. In this situation, no party in the Diet dared support heavier taxes or a huge increase in the national debt.

Some Cassandras predict a grey future for the Japanese economy. Its high labor costs make competition with its Asian neighbors increasingly difficult. Most economists, however, while lamenting the length of the recession, see the downturn as a temporary correction of speculative excesses. Japanese industry emerged leaner and more competitive from the "oil shocks" of 1972 and 1979, and would do so again. They note, too, that the recession is anomalous in that while domestic consumption sank, exports continued to boom, and Japan's favorable balance of trade remained large. Like other countries in Asia, Japan hoped to export its way out of recession. And perhaps more important, the recession has not weakened Japan's determination to maintain its lead in flat screens, fermentation chemistry, and materials research, and to become a world force in areas such as biotechnology, medical instruments, and airplanes.

Whatever the future may hold, the economic weight of Japan in Asia is huge. Because of this, other nations in Asia look to Japan's recovery as a precondition for their own. The second largest economy in the world after the United States, the Japanese economy is half again as large as the combined economies of most of the rest of Asia—as can be seen in the following table.

A Comparison of the Projected 1999 Gross Domestic Products of Japan and Other Asian Countries (in billions of dollars)

China	$1,088	Japan	$4,528
South Korea	491		
Taiwan	318		
Hong Kong*	201		
Singapore	103		
Thailand	138		
Malaysia	82		
Indonesia	132		
India	384		
Pakistan	69		
TOTAL	$3,006		$4,528

*Hong Kong considered as a separate economic entity.

Comparison of Japan with France and Germany, Projected 1999 Figures			
	GDP (in billions)	Population (in millions)	Per Capita GDP
France	$1,530	59	$25,932
Germany	2,284	82	27,854
Japan	4,528	126	35,937

Alternatively, Japan may be viewed as a "Western" economy and compared to France and Germany. Japan's economy is larger than that of France and Germany combined, and its per capita product is greater. Of course, land, food, and clothing are so expensive in Japan that the per capita product does not simply equate with standard of living. Furthermore, all such comparisons fluctuate with the exchange rates of currencies. Still, the important fact to note is that Japan achieved its present affluence through the peaceful development of human resources in a free society.

Society and Culture

The triple engines of change in postwar Japan were occupation reforms, economic growth, and a rapid expansion of higher education. Taken together, one might have expected them to produce deep cultural strains and social dislocations. At the margin, these did occur. The growth among the urban poor of "new religions" such as the Value Creating Society was one indication. In 1995 one aberrant and apocalyptic cult released nerve gas in a Tokyo subway, leaving the Japanese shocked that something so "un-Japanese" could happen. Social pressure on school children to excel was another area of tension. Children often began after-school tutoring courses while still in grade school, and while in high school or after, took tough examinations just to enter the better cram schools that would prepare them for the all-important university entrance examinations. Middle-class parents of high school students saw after-school jobs as an appalling waste of precious time that might better be used for study. Magazine articles lamented the excesses of Japan's "examination society," but few steps were taken to alleviate them. In Japan's corporate world, too, *karōshi*, or death from overwork, became a recognized phenomenon.

Yet the ability of the society—the family, the school, the office, and the workshop—to absorb the strains and to lend support to the individual was also impressive. Occasionally children rebelled against their regimen of study, but most realized it was for their own good and limited their rebellion to reading violent and sadistic comic books. Lifetime employment—only slightly dented by the "bursting of the bubble"—gave both workers and salaried employees a feeling of security. The divorce rate, while growing, was less than one-third of that in the United States, and most Japanese wives felt they were better off than their American counterparts. Of children born in Japan, 1.1 percent were to unwed mothers; in the United States the figure was 30.1 percent. Infant mortality was the lowest in the world and longevity the highest. Japan also had far less crime. Even big cities were safe at night. Drugs were not a problem. Handguns were banned with predictable results: In 1994, 38 persons died of gunshot in Japan; the figure was 16,000 in the United States. Of every 100,000 Japanese, 37 were in jail; for the United States the figure was 519. Despite crowded housing and social pressures, by most objective measures the society was stable and healthy.

Kiyotsune, a Nō drama.   Kiyotsune, a late twelfth century Taira general, plunged to his death in the sea "as the moon grew pale in the early morning sky," rather than become a captive of the enemy Minamoto army. His wife understood the necessity for her husband's action but felt abandoned and embittered nonetheless. His ghost returns to her for a night and they both argue and embrace. After death he is condemned to the hell for warriors who have taken human lives, but is eventually saved through his faith in the Buddha Amida. Kiyotsune in center stage is dressed in the robes of a noble. In the background to the left are the musicians and to the right the chorus, which chants the narrative much as in Greek drama. The play is by Zeami (1363-1443). [Courtesy of A. Craig]

Two Views of the "Symbol Emperor"

The murkiest aspect of Japan's prewar emperor-centered ideology was the juxtaposition of the emperor as a modern monarch and the emperor as a living deity, ultimately descended from the sun goddess. In the first of the following two selections, former Prime Minister Yoshida Shigeru, a product of Meiji Japan, basically accepts the prewar ideology, but argues that because in fact the emperor exercised little power before World War II, nothing was changed by the postwar constitution. In the second selection, Nobel Prize winner Ōe Kenzaburō a humanistic and slightly leftist novelist, recognizes that the emperor has been stripped of his former authority, but worries about a revival of his Shinto identity.

What does Yoshida mean by "as naturally," and why does Ōe call the prewar emperor an "absolute ruler?"

1.

In regard to the question of the Imperial structure of government, as it existed in Japan, I pointed out that the Meiji Constitution had originated in the promises made to the Japanese people by the Emperor Meiji at the beginning of his reign, and there was little need to dwell on the fact that democracy, if we were to use the word, had always formed part of the traditions of our country, and was not—as some mistakenly imagined—something that was about to be introduced with the revision of the Constitution. As for the Imperial House, the idea and reality of the Throne had come into being among the Japanese people as naturally as the idea of the country itself; no question of antagonism between Throne and people could possibly arise;

and nothing contained in the new Constitution could change that fact. The word "symbol" had been employed in the definition of the Emperor because we Japanese had always regarded the Emperor as the symbol of the country itself—a statement which any Japanese considering the issue dispassionately would be ready to recognize as an irrefutable fact.

2.

Japan's emperor system, which had apparently lost its social and political influence after the defeat in the Pacific War, is beginning to flex its muscles again, and in some respects it has already recouped much of its lost power—with two differences: first, the Japanese today will not accept the prewar ideology-cum-theology that held the emperor to be both absolute ruler and living deity. Nevertheless, imperial rites performed quite recently were done in such a manner as to impress upon us that the emperor's lineage can be traced to a deity; I am referring here to the rituals associated with the present emperor's enthronement and the so-called Great Thanksgiving Service that followed it. These ceremonies provoked little objection from either the government or the people, indeed most Japanese seemed to take it all very much for granted.

1. *The Yoshida Memoirs*, Yoshida Shigeru. Copyright © 1961 Heineman Books, p. 139. 2. From "Speaking on Japanese Culture Before a Scandinavian Audience," *Japan, the Ambiguous and Myself: The Nobel Prize Speech and Other Lectures by Kenzaburō Ōe.* Published by Kodansha International, Ltd., 1995. Copyright © 1992 by Kenzaburō Ōe. All rights reserved. Reprinted by permission.

Even apart from the recession economy, however, there were several clouds on the horizon. One concerned education: Japanese critics argued that Japan's system of education was appropriate to the needs of assembly-line mass production but not to the needs of the "information age." They asked whether changes could be made in time. Another was a consequence of the skewed pattern of postwar births. After 2015, when the baby boomers retire, Japan will have a higher percentage of non-working old than any other society in the world. How to support them and how their voting will affect Diet politics have been constantly discussed in the Japanese media.

The great tradition of Japanese art continued in poetry, painting, the tea ceremony, flower arrangement, and the Kabuki and Nō theaters. Every New Year's Day, the emperor presided at a nationwide poetry contest. Masters of pottery, paper making, and other arts were honored by being designated as "Living National Treasures." In architecture, painting, and dance, the prewar tradition of vigorous experiments with new or hybrid forms continued. The awareness of nature, so evident in films like Kurosawa's *Rashomon* or *The Seven Samurai*, carried over to the photography in Japanese National Television dramas that in quality rivaled those of the British Broadcasting Corporation. Films by Itami Jūzō—*Tampopo* and *A Taxing Woman*—combined humor and biting satire. Symphony orchestras in Japan's major cities played Mozart and Stravinsky as well as native compositions with haunting passages played on the Japanese flute and zither. Clothing designers competed in Tokyo, New York, and Paris. College students formed rock bands, listened to jazz, and read Japanese science fiction along with the writings of serious novelists. The case of postwar Japan amply supports an argument for parallelism between economic and cultural dynamism.

China

The story of China after 1949 might begin with the four Ma's: Malthus, Marx, Ma Yin-ch'u (Ma Yinchu), and Mao Tse-tung (Mao Zedong). Malthus claimed that population would expand geometrically whereas food would increase only arithmetically. Marx rejected the Malthusian hypothesis, along with classical economics, as myths of the capitalist stage of history. Professor Ma Yin-ch'u (1882–1982), the chancellor of Peking University, published in 1957 *New Principles on Chinese Population*, in which he argued that unchecked population growth would impede capital accumulation and depress living standards. Mao Tse-tung, faithfully following the teachings of Marx, purged Ma and closed down population institutes at Chinese universities. What followed was a population increase from 550 million in 1949 to nearly a billion in 1981. Real growth occurred in the Chinese economy during the sixties and seventies, but the gains were eaten up by the extra mouths. In the face of this crisis, in 1981 the Chinese government adopted a national policy of one child per family. It recognized that the policy ran contrary to the deep-rooted Chinese sense of family but argued that without it China's future would be bleak. Thereafter the increase slowed but still reached over 1. 2 billion in 1999.

Soviet Period (1950–1960)

Civil war in China ended in 1949 as the last troops of Chiang Kai-shek fled to Taiwan. The People's Republic of China

Mao Tse-tung chatting with Soviet premier Nikita Khrushchev in Moscow in 1958. By this time the Sino-Soviet alliance was already beginning to fray.
[Archive Photos]

was proclaimed in October. The following year, China entered into an alliance with the Soviet Union. The decade that followed is often called the "Soviet period" because the Soviet model was adopted for the government, the army, the economy, and higher education.

The first step taken by the Communist government was military consolidation. Even after the republic was proclaimed, Chinese armies continued to push outward, conquering vast areas with non-Chinese populations. Tibet, for example, was seized in 1950. Once subdued, the areas inhabited by Tibetans, Uighur Turks, Mongols, and other minorities were designated "autonomous regions." They were occupied by the Chinese army and were settled by a sufficient number of Chinese immigrants to change their ethnic complexion. Although their governments were staffed mainly by members of the minority population, they were tightly controlled by the Chinese Communist Party.

Political consolidation followed. The most powerful elite was the Communist Party. Its members held the key levers of power in the government, army, and security forces. Mao was chairman of the party and head of state. He ruled through the Standing Committee of the Political Bureau (Politburo) of the party's Central Committee. Below the Politburo were regional, provincial, and district committees with party cells in every village, factory, school, and government office. The party expanded from 2.7 million members in 1947 to 17 million in 1961. Party members were called on to energize and enforce the local enactment of government policies.

Economic reconstruction began immediately. An attempt was made to integrate the industries in Manchuria and former treaty ports with the rest of China. Huge numbers of workers were mobilized to build new bridges, dams, roads, and railways. China's first five-year plan for economic development began in 1953. The Soviet Union sent financial aid as well as engineers and planners.

Rural society underwent two fundamental changes: land redistribution and then collectivization. In the early fifties, party cadres visited villages and held meetings at which landlords were denounced and forced to confess their crimes. Some were rehabilitated, others were sent to labor camps, and hundreds of thousands—some scholars estimate several million—were killed. Their holdings were redistributed to the landless. Local responsibilities once borne by landlord gentry were shifted to associations dominated by former tenant farmers. Then two years later, before the new landowners had time to put down roots as private landowners, all lands were seized by the state and collectivized. The timing was important. In the early years of the Soviet Union, collectivization came six years after redistribution and was resisted by the *kulaks*, who had had time to put down roots.

During the early fifties, intellectuals and universities also became a target for thought reform. The Chinese slang term was "brainwashing." This involved study and indoctrination in Marxism, group pressures to produce an atmosphere of insecurity and fear, followed by confession, repentance, and reacceptance by society. The indoctrination was intended to strengthen party control. But beyond this was the optimistic belief that the inculcation of correct moral doctrines could mobilize human energies on behalf of the state—perhaps a belief with distant Confucian roots. In 1956 Mao felt that intellectuals had been adequately indoctrinated and, concerned lest creativity be stifled, he said in a speech, "Let the hundred flowers bloom"—a reference to the lively discourse among the many schools of philosophy in ancient Chou China. Contrary to his expectations, intellectuals responded with a torrent of criticism that did not spare the Communist Party. Mao thereupon reversed his position, sending many leading writers and intellectuals to labor camps.

By the late fifties Mao was disappointed with the results of collectivization and the first five-year plan. In 1958 he abandoned a second plan (and the Soviet model) in favor of a mass mobilization to unleash the productive energies of the people. He called it the Great Leap Forward. One slogan was, "Hard work for a few years and happiness for a thousand." Campaigns were organized to accomplish vast projects, iron smelters were built in "backyards," and instant industries were the order of the day. In the countryside, village-based collective farms gave way to communes of 30,000 persons or more. The results were disastrous. Homemade iron was unusable, instant industries failed, and agricultural production plummeted. Scholars estimate that between 1958 and 1962 as many as 15 to 30 million Chinese may have starved to death. To control the damage, communes were broken into production brigades in 1959, and two years later these were further broken into production teams of 40 households. But even these actions could not overcome the ills of low incentives and collective responsibility; through the seventies agricultural production barely matched population growth.

It was also during these years that Sino-Soviet relations deteriorated. Disputes arose over borders. China was dissatisfied with the level of Soviet aid. It was also embarrassed by the Soviet debunking of Stalin's cult of personality since within China, Mao was still venerated as the "great helmsman." For its part, the Soviet Union condemned the Great Leap Forward as "leftist fanaticism" and resented Mao's view of himself, after Stalin's death, as the foremost theoretician and exponent of world Communism. In 1960, the Soviet Union halted economic aid and withdrew its engineers from China, and by 1963 the split was visible to the outside world. Each country deployed about a million troops along their mutual border. Had relations between the two Communist giants been amicable, these troops, deployed elsewhere, might have changed the history of Southeast Asia and Eastern Europe.

The Sino-Soviet split was arguably the single most important development in postwar international politics.

The years between 1960 and 1965 saw conflicting trends. The utter failure of the Great Leap Forward led some Chinese leaders to turn away from Mao's reckless radicalism toward more moderate policies. Mao kept his position as the head of the party but was forced to give up his post as head of state to another veteran Communist official. Yet even as the government moved toward realistic goals and stable bureaucratic management, General Lin Piao (Lin Biao, 1908–1971) reestablished within the army the party committees and procedures for ideological indoctrination that had lapsed after the failure of the Great Leap Forward. A new mass movement was also begun to transform education.

The Great Proletarian Cultural Revolution (1965–1976)

In 1965, Mao once again emerged to dominate Chinese politics. Mao the revolutionary had never been able to make the transition to Mao the ruler of an established state. When he looked at the Chinese Communist Party and the government bureaucracy, he saw a new privileged elite; when he looked at younger Chinese, he saw a generation with no experience of revolution. Mao feared that the Chinese revolution—his revolution—would end up as a Soviet-style bureaucratic Communism run for the benefit of officials. So he called for a new revolution to create a truly egalitarian culture.

Obtaining army support, Mao urged students and teenaged youth to form bands of Red Guards. In the early feverish phase of the Cultural Revolution, the guards invoked the little red book containing Mao's sayings almost as holy scripture. Mass rallies were held. One rally in Peking (Beijing) was attended by "millions" of youths, who then made "long marches" back to their home provinces to carry out Mao's program. Universities were shut down as student factions fought. Teachers were beaten, imprisoned, and subjected to such extremes of humiliation that many committed suicide. An attack was launched on "the four olds" in which books were burned and art destroyed. Buddhist sculptures that had endured since the Sung dynasty were smashed or defaced. Things foreign also came under attack. Homes were ransacked for foreign books and Chinese who had studied abroad were persecuted. Even the borrowing of foreign technology was denigrated as "sniffing after the farts of foreigners and calling them sweet." Red guards attacked local party headquarters and beat to death persons viewed as reactionaries, including some party cadres. High officials were purged. The crippled apparatus of party and government was replaced by revolutionary committees. Chinese sometimes recall these events as a species of mass hysteria that even today they find difficult to understand.

The Chinese Cultural Revolution of the 1960's. Marchers hold a banner of Mao Tse-tung. [Archive Photos]

Eventually Mao tired of the violence and near anarchy. In 1968 and 1969 he called in the army to take over the revolutionary committees. In 1969, a new Central Committee, composed largely of military men, was established, and General Lin Piao was named as Mao's successor. Violence came to an end as millions of students and intellectuals were sent to the countryside to work on farms. In 1970 and 1971 the revolutionary committees were reconstituted as party committees. Worsening relations with the Soviet Union also made China's leaders desire greater stability at home. In 1969, a pitched battle had broken out between Chinese and Russian troops over an island in the Ussuri River. After this encounter, the Chinese built bomb shelters in their main cities. It was just at this time that President Nixon began to withdraw U.S. troops from Vietnam. When he proposed a renewal of ties, China quickly responded. Nixon visited Peking in 1972, opening a new era of diplomatic relations.

The second phase of the Cultural Revolution between 1969 and 1976 was moderate only in comparison with what had gone before. On farms and in factories, ideology was still seen as an adequate substitute for economic incentives. Universities reopened, but students were admitted by class background, not by examination. In 1971, Lin Piao, Mao's heir, was purged. According to the official account of his death, Lin had tried to kill Mao and seize the government, but when his coup failed, he died in a plane crash while he attempted to escape to the Soviet Union. Lin's place was taken by the so-called Gang of Four, which included Mao's wife and was abetted by the aging Mao. Class struggle was revived, and an official campaign was launched attacking the rightist "political swindlers" Lin Piao and Confucius.

China After Mao

Political Developments   Mao's death in 1976 brought immediate changes. Within four weeks the Gang of Four and their radical supporters had been arrested. In their place, Teng Hsiao-p'ing (Deng Xiaoping, 1904–1997) emerged as the dominant figure in Chinese politics. Twice purged for rightist tendencies—once during the Cultural Revolution he was paraded around Peking wearing a dunce cap—Teng was determined that such things not happen again. He ousted his enemies, rehabilitated those purged during the Cultural Revolution, and put his supporters in power. Portraits of Mao were removed from public places in August 1980. After the lunacy of the Cultural Revolution, the establishment of a "normal" Communist Party dictatorship came as a welcome relief. The people could now enjoy a measure of security and the prospect of material improvement in their lives.

There continued, however, a tension between the determination of the ruling party to maintain its grip on power and its desire to obtain the benefits of some liberalization. This tension was most visible in China's intellectual life. The government's repudiation of the Cultural Revolution had led to an outpouring of stories, plays, and reports. In *Nightmare*, by Hsu Hui (Xu Hui), the mother of a son killed during the Cultural Revolution asks, "Why? Why? Can anyone tell me why?" Liu Pin-yen (Liu Binyan) wrote of a corrupt officialdom that had "degenerated into parasitical insects that fed off the people's productivity and the socialist system." But the new leeway for criticism did not extend to the period of Teng's rule. Writers were regularly enjoined to be "led by the Communist Party and guided by Marx-Leninism." When a writer in 1983 overstepped the invisible line separating what was permissible from what was not, a short campaign was launched against "spiritual pollution." In 1985 and 1987 as well, the government organized campaigns against "capitalist thinking" and "bourgeois democracy."

Universities returned to normal in 1977. Entrance examinations were reinstituted, purged teachers returned to their classrooms, and scientists and scholars were sent to study in Japan and the West. During the late seventies and eighties students spent one afternoon a week discussing party directives or the writings of Teng Hsiao-p'ing. But far more influential was the new openness within China and the growing contacts with the wider world, as scholars returned from the West. Students also became aware of the prosperity achieved by Japan, Hong Kong, and Taiwan. They began to demand still greater freedoms with the hope they would lead to political democracy. During the late 1980s, the ferment that marked Eastern Europe and the Soviet Union under Gorbachev also appeared in China: it was as if a new virus had entered the Communist world.

The new spirit came to a head in April and May of 1989, when hundreds of thousands of students, workers, and people from all walks of life demonstrated for democracy in Tienanmen Square in Peking and in dozens of other cities. Hunger strikes were held. Students published pro-democracy newspapers. Banners proclaimed slogans, among them "Give us freedom or give us death." A twenty-seven-foot polystyrene and plaster Goddess of Democracy and Freedom was erected in the Square. At first, government leaders disagreed on how to respond, but the hardline faction led by Teng won out and sent in tanks and troops. Hundreds of students were killed, and leaders who did not escape abroad were jailed. The event defined the political climate in China for the decade that followed: considerable freedom was allowed in most areas of life, even intellectual life, but no challenge to Communist party rule was tolerated.

Economic Growth Developments in the economy were more promising. Teng's great achievement in the years after 1978 was to demonstrate in China the superiority of market incentives to central planning.

In China's villages, as the farm household became the basic unit of production, grain production rose from 305 million tons in 1978 to 445 million in 1994—an increase of 46 percent. A local leader commented, "When people work for themselves, they work better." A similarly realistic view, that China "had wasted twenty years" on "radical leftist nonsense," was expressed in 1985 by General Secretary Hu Yaopang (Hu Yaobang), who was later demoted. But even during the nineties agriculture had problems. Because the government bought up 30 percent of farmers' grain output at an artificially low price, farmers living near cities found it much more profitable to abandon grain production in favor of specialty crops such as fruit or the feedgrain required by China's rising consumption of meat. China already imported some of its food, and there were gloomy estimates of more serious food shortages after the turn of the century.

State-operated enterprises—the surviving portion of the old, centrally planned, command economy—were another sector of the economy. In 1982, their output was 74 percent of total industrial production. Because over half ran at a loss

Student activists construct a "Goddess of Democracy," taking the Statue of Liberty as their model. The Goddess was in place in Tienanmen Square shortly before tanks cleared students from the square in June, 1989.
[Reuters/Ed Nachtrieb/Archive Photos]

and because they employed twice the labor needed to run them efficiently, they were a constant drain on China's state-owned banks. Workers were paid little and had little incentive to work hard since they enjoyed the security of the so-called "iron ricebowl." As the free market sector grew faster, their share of production declined to 40 percent in 1997. Finally, the government announced that 10,000 of the 13,000 state-operated enterprises would be sold by the year 2000. The "state ownership" required by the constitution would give way to "public ownership." The costs of such privatization would be high—defaulted loans, bankruptcies, unemployed workers, and a sudden rise in pensioners, but the drain on the state budget would end.

The main driver of the new economy was the free market sector. Between 1980 and 1994 the Chinese economy grew at double-digit rates, and though it slowed after 1995, it still

U.S. Foreign Policy: A Chinese View

Wei Jingsheng, a Chinese advocate of democratic rights, was deported to the United States late in 1997. A year later, in a New York Times *editorial, he criticized U.S. policy as pandering to Chinese tyranny.*

Should U.S. foreign policy be used to promote human rights even in poor countries with cultural traditions different from the West? Or should the United States avoid interference in the domestic politics of other nations and aim primarily at furthering American economic and security goals? What is foreign policy capable of achieving? Where should the balance be struck?

China's Diversionary Tactics

One year ago, after 18 years in a Chinese prison, I was "released" and sent here. A Chinese official said that if I ever set foot in China again, I would immediately be returned to prison. . . .

The State Department, in a report last January, used my forced exile as evidence that China was taking "positive steps in human rights" and that "Chinese society continued to become more open." These "positive steps" led the United States and its allies to oppose condemnation of China at a meeting of the United Nations Commission on Human Rights in April. In the months that followed, President Clinton and other Western leaders traveled to China, trumpeting increased economic ties and muting criticism on human rights.

Thus, without fear of sanction, the Chinese Government intensified its repression in 1998. Once the leaders achieved their diplomatic victories, they turned to their main objective: the preservation of tyrannical power. This year, about 70 people are known to have been arrested. . . .

Li Peng, the speaker of the National People's Party Congress, declared recently, "If an organization's purpose is to promote a multiparty system in China and to negate the leadership prerogatives of the Chinese Communist Party, then it will not be permitted to exist."

This statement clearly shows that the Communist Party's primary objective is to sustain its tyranny, and to do so it must deny the people basic rights and freedoms. We must measure the leaders' progress on human rights not by the "release" of individuals but by the people's ability to speak, worship and assemble without official interference and persecution.

---

grew faster than any other Asian economy. Exports rose from $7 billion in 1975 to $183 billion in 1997. The surge in new enterprises began in special economic zones along the border with Hong Kong and quickly spread along the coast. Shanghai, with a population of 14 million, became a city of skyscrapers and industrialists, and the site of China's first stock exchange. Shantung Province in the northeast attracted huge investments from Japan, South Korea, and the United States, and also achieved stunning growth, as did Manchuria, another industrial heartland. As other entrepreneurs, cities, and local governments joined in, the tide of enterprise swept inland. Wuhan, a major communications hub and automobile manufacturer in central China, averaged growth of 16 or 17 percent during the early nineties. Yet in the hinterlands large regions remained undeveloped and clamored for government assistance. To achieve growth, though, the government was willing to tolerate personal and regional inequities.

The factors that fueled this growth were clear: a huge surplus of fairly good quality, cheap labor, a savings rate of 35–40 percent, a level of protectionism more than double that of other Asian nations, large investments from abroad, and open world markets. China, in effect, successfully used tariffs to shield its markets, while making use of cheap labor to flood foreign markets with goods and build up its currency reserves.

Social Change   During the Mao years, farmers had been tied to their collective or village. Cities were closed to those without residence permits. City dwellers, whether they worked in factories, hospitals, schools, newspapers, or government offices, were members of "units." Like "company towns," units provided their members with jobs, housing, food, childcare, medical services, and pensions. Party cadres exercised near total control over the unit's members. Block organizations exercised surveillance over the inhabitants and reported any infractions of "socialist morality" to the authorities.

Under Teng, controls were loosened. The police became less active—except against political dissidents, censorship was reduced, and ties with the outside world were allowed to develop. The "unit" also diminished in importance as food became widely available in free markets and apartments were sold to their inhabitants on easy terms. Private housing brought with it the freedom to change jobs. As workers with higher salaries began to provide for their own needs, life became freer and more enjoyable. The market economy placed a premium on individual decisions and initiatives.

The new prosperity and changing mores became increasingly evident. The blue Mao uniforms of the sixties were followed by suits, however ill-fitting, and later, for the young, blue jeans, sneakers, and colorful jackets. By the nineties, innovative Chinese designers were holding fashion shows in Shanghai and Peking. Young people associated freely, and in urban areas the earlier taboo against public displays of affection slowly relaxed. The "household treasures" of the sixties, radios and bicycles, gave way to stoves and refrigerators in the seventies, and, in the next decade, to washing machines and color televisions. Crowds gathered around displays of motorbikes in department stores. By the early nineties, motorbikes and privately owned cars competed in crowded streets with the flow of bicycles. Private restaurants opened, and travel for pleasure became commonplace. In 1988, most passengers on domestic airline flights were foreign; ten years later, most were Chinese.

The new wealth was unevenly distributed. The more successful entrepreneurs bought houses, cars, microwaves, computers, and cell phones. They traveled abroad and sent their children to private schools. As their lifestyle became more Western, they were sometimes called China's "new middle class," but in fact they constituted an upper class. Other city dwellers also participated in the new prosperity. But many just scraped by and unemployment remained high. Among the rural 70 percent of the population, the pace of change was slower. In prosperous belts near cities, large brick houses and tractors could be seen by foreign visitors. But in the hinterlands poverty and hardship remained the rule, except for the most enterprising. In the West envy is green. In China the envy and resentment of the have-nots for the newly affluent is called the "red-eye disease."

China's Relations with the World   From the fifties to the seventies, China isolated itself from the rest of the world. The Sino-Soviet split defined its relations to the north. The Cold War defined its relations with Japan, South Korea, Taiwan, and the United States. China gave aid to North Vietnam during the Vietnamese War but then turned around and invaded Vietnam in 1979. In some measure China's relations with its neighbors reflected its internal political turmoil. As the turmoil ended during the eighties, changes set in. Economic growth gave China some leeway. Trade ties with the non-Communist world led China to look outward and adopt more moderate policies.

In the nineties, foreign relations seemed to improve across the board. Relations with Russia became amicable. China welcomed increased trade and investment from Taiwan and South Korea, despite its fear of Taiwan's growing independence and its continuing reluctant support of North Korea. China also worked to improve its ties with Southeast Asia. As the decade drew to an end, China emerged as the military and political heavyweight of East Asia, though Japan remained, even in recession, the predominant economic power (see Map 37–2).

China's relations with the United States were difficult. During the Cold War and even afterwards, U.S. military alliances with Japan, South Korea, Taiwan, and the non-Communist nations of Southeast Asia acted as the main countervailing force to Chinese hegemony in the region. China resented the U.S. "intrusion" in what it considered its own proper sphere of influence. The first step toward a new relationship was President Nixon's visit to China in 1972. The United States recognized China in 1979. From the eighties trade with the United States was vital to China's economic growth, and it became more so during the mid-nineties as the rest of East Asia slipped into recession. In 1996, for example, the United States bought $54 billion of goods from China, but sold China only $12 billion of its own products. In 1997 and 1998, the U.S. trade deficit with China continued to grow. The United States protested Chinese piracy of hundreds of millions of dollars worth of U.S. movies, computer software, and CDs each year. It was critical of Chinese human rights abuses, nuclear testing, and of arms sales to Iran and Pakistan. Despite these areas of contention, the United States worked to better relations, hoping that a deeper engagement with itself and the rest of the world would lead to a freer Chinese society. With Premier Chiang Tse-min's (Jiang Zemin) visit to the United States in 1997 and President Clinton's visit to China in 1998, formal U.S.-Chinese ties continued to improve.

Taiwan

Taiwan is a mountainous island less than a hundred miles off the coast of central China. A little larger than Belgium or Massachusetts, it has a population of 22 million. Originally a remote and backward part of the Ch'ing empire, it became a Japanese colony in 1895 as a spoil of the Sino-Japanese War. The Japanese found it easy to rule since the Taiwanese lacked a strong sense of national identity and were accustomed to rule by officials from across the seas who spoke a language they could not understand. (Standard Chinese and the Fukien dialect spoken on Taiwan are mutually unintelligible.) The Japanese colonial government suppressed opium and bandits and eradicated epidemic diseases. It built roads and railroads, reformed the land system, and introduced improvements in agriculture. Before 1895 education had been the privilege of a tiny elite; the Japanese established "common schools," which, by the end of World War II, were attended by 71 percent of school-age children. (In the Dutch East Indies and French Indochina the figure was about 10 or 15 percent.) Light industries were introduced and, during the thirties, textiles, chemicals, ceramics, and machine tools.

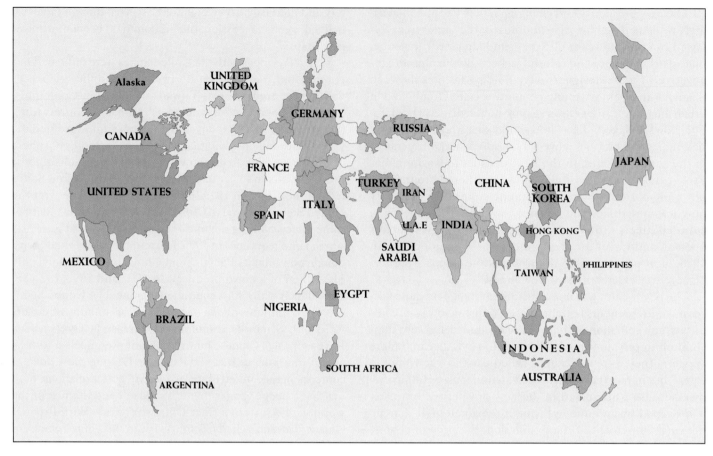

Map 37-2   An economist's map of the world.   On this map countries are represented by the size of their economies. The method used is to ask *what it would cost in dollars* to produce a nation's goods and services. By this criterion, China's GDP (Gross Domestic Product) in 1996 (the base-year for the map) was $3878 billion and its per capita GDP was $3200. In comparison, Japan's GDP was a quarter less, though its per capita GDP was seven times greater.

Another method of determining GDPs is to convert the *actual cost in the native currency* of goods and services into dollars at the going rate of exchange. This method, used earlier in the discussion of the Japanese economy, produces strikingly different results. China's GDP is less than a quarter of Japan's and its per capita GDP less than one fortieth. The first method is useful in thinking of a people's standard of living. The second more accurately reflects a nation's international economic weight.

Though these were mostly owned by Japanese and run in their interests, more benefits seem to have accrued to the local population than was the case in Korea, another Japanese colony.

Anti-colonial feelings rose slowly. During the twenties Taiwanese petitioned for political reforms and greater personal freedoms. The Japanese made a few concessions, but after war began with China in 1937 they intensified their strict controls and assimilationist policies. At the end of the war the Taiwanese were happy to see the Japanese leave and welcomed Kuomintang (Guomindang) officials as liberators. The new officials, however, saw the Taiwanese as Japanese collaborators; they looted the economy, and ruled harshly. When Taiwanese protested in February, 1947, they put down the demonstrators and over several months killed between eight

to ten thousand Taiwanese, many of them community leaders. By the time Chiang Kai-shek and two million more military and civilian mainlanders fled to the island in 1949, its economy and society were is disarray. Mainlanders looked down on the Taiwanese, who, in turn, hated their new rulers and in private often compared them unfavorably to the Japanese.

In the mid-fifties order was restored, and rapid economic growth followed. Heavy industries were put under state control; other Japanese-owned industries were sold to private parties. With the outbreak of the Korean War in 1950, U.S. aid became substantial. Foreign investment was welcomed. Light industries were followed by consumer electronics, steel and petrochemicals, then computers and semiconductors. By the late nineties, Taiwan was the world's largest producer of monitors, keyboards, motherboards, and computer mice; it was second in notebook PCs and fourth in integrated circuits. Estimated per capita product was $13,860 in 1996, one half that of France but fifteen times that of mainland China. Though small, Taiwan had the healthiest economy in recession-ridden Asia.

Taiwan's politics was authoritarian. Until 1987 martial law was in effect and opposition parties were banned. The KMT (Kuomintang) maintained that its government, which it called the Republic of China, was the legitimate government of all China. Posters on Taipei billboards proclaimed the official policy of eventually reconquering the mainland. As the self-proclaimed government of all of China, a minority of mainlanders in the KMT were able to dominate the Taiwanese population.

Social changes began during the sixties. Education advanced, with rising numbers entering universities. Taiwanese and mainlanders began to intermarry. A new middle class emerged, and Taiwanese began to enter the KMT and attain minor political offices. Chiang Kai-shek died in 1976, the same year as Mao. Under his son, Chiang Ching-kuo, who was president from 1976 to 1988, Taiwan moved toward representative government. In 1987 martial law ended and opposition parties were permitted.

After Chiang's death, Lee Teng-hui became president. A native Taiwanese, Lee was a graduate of a Taiwanese high school, Kyoto Imperial University, and Cornell. In March, 1996, Lee was elected president in what was, as he put it, "the first free election in 5000 years of Chinese history." During the election China attempted to intimidate the voters by firing missiles into the waters off Taiwan. The voters responded to this heavy-handedness by giving Lee a substantial majority of their votes.

Ever since 1949, the Communist government in Peking had claimed that Taiwan was a province of China unlawfully controlled by a "bandit" government. It did not rule out taking Taiwan by force. It maintained that its relation with the island was a matter of internal Chinese politics and refused diplomatic ties with any nation maintaining such ties with Taiwan. From the outbreak of the Korean War in 1950 until 1979, Taiwan became a protégé of the United States, which recognized its claim to be the legitimate government of China. In 1979, however, the United States broke off relations with Taipei and recognized Peking as the sole government of a China that included Taiwan. But the United States continued to trade with Taiwan and to sell it arms. Curiously, it was during the years of diplomatic limbo after the break in 1979 that Taiwan's economy grew and its society became democratic. In the late nineties, both China and the United States were apprehensive about Taiwan. China worried that a democratically elected government would give Taiwan a claim to legitimacy in the eyes of the world, and spoke of tak-

President Lee Teng-hui and his wife wave at supporters during a victory celebration after Taiwan's first direct presidential election in March, 1996. Attempts by China to intimidate Taiwanese voters backfired. [Reuters Rob Man/Archive Photos]

ing back the island. The United States, on its part, feared that within a decade or two China would have the military power to do just that, and felt it could not stand by and see this prosperous and democratic state it had helped to create be forcibly taken over by China.

Korea

Korea and Vietnam, the other two countries in the East Asian zone of civilization, both became colonies. Vietnam became a part of French Indochina in 1883; Korea was annexed by Japan in 1910. In both countries, the imposition of colonialism on a people with a high indigenous culture and a strong sense of national identity engendered a powerful anticolonial nationalism. After World War II, both were divided into a Communist north and a non-Communist south, Korea immediately and Vietnam years later. Both experienced civil war. In each instance the United States entered the conflicts to stem the spread of Communism. Never before had the United States fought in countries about which it knew so little.

The social ills and political and economic weaknesses that characterized the Choson dynasty in 1800 continued through the nineteenth century. As the century drew to a close, a three-cornered rivalry arose among China, Japan, and Russia, with Korea as the prize. Japan won. Defeating China in the Sino-Japanese War (1894–95) and Russia in the Russo-Japanese War (1904–05), it made Korea a protectorate in 1905 and annexed it in 1910.

As Japanese Colony

Annexation was followed by changes designed to make Korea into a model colony. A land survey and land tax reform clarified land ownership. As public hygiene was enforced, infectious diseases dropped sharply, and the population grew from 14 million in 1910 to 24 million in 1940. Attendance at common schools increased from 20 thousand in 1910 to 1.2 million in 1939, while attendance at higher common schools, girl's higher schools, and trade schools also rose. New money was issued and banks established. As in Taiwan, a huge investment was made in roads, railways, and telegraph lines. The 1920s saw further investments in areas such as hydroelectric power, nitrogenous fertilizer plants, and mining. Most large-scale industries were Japanese-owned, but Korean entrepreneurs began textile mills, shipping lines, and small industries. Even excluding mining and transport, employment in industry rose from 385,000 in 1932 to 1,322,000 in 1943. Nor was the colonial transformation just a matter of economic indices. Koreans who studied at Japanese universities came into contact with the full range of political, social, literary, and artistic currents of the modern world, and brought their new knowledge back to Korea. By the 1930s a modern culture was forming in Korea's cities. In short, by carrying out a truncated version of Meiji-type reforms, the Japanese made the Korea of 1945 into something vastly different from what it had been in 1910.

Being a Japanese colony was nonetheless a hard road to modernity. The colonial government was authoritarian. Its goal was to make Korea into part—a subordinate part—of Imperial Japan. Any benefits to the Koreans were incidental. Education was Japan-oriented and instruction was given in Japanese. The land tax reform benefited landowners. Japanese and Korean land companies bought up former crown lands, and tenancy rose from 42 percent in 1913 to 69 percent in 1945. The Japanese in Korea received better salaries, medical care, education, and jobs than their Korean counterparts. Whether in government, banking, or industry, Koreans were mainly relegated to the lower echelons. To be sure, this was true in all colonies, but it particularly rankled in Korea because it was an older culture and racially close to Japan. The colonial regime, moreover, suppressed all nationalist movements and political opposition, denying Koreans the experience of self-government. Many who became politically active fled to China or the Soviet Union. The police, half of whom were Koreans, earned a reputation for brutality and were hated by the populace. After 1937, the Japanese policy of "assimilation" grew even harsher: Koreans were pressured to adopt Japanese names, drafted to fight in Japan's wars, and sent to labor in factories in Japan. The legacy of colonial rule in Korea was an animosity that has persisted to this day.

North and South

With Japan's defeat in 1945, U.S. forces occupied Korea south of the thirty-eighth parallel and Soviet troops occupied the north. There had been a promise of unification, but two separate states developed. In the south, the United States initially sought to encourage the formation of a democratic, self-governing nation. It eventually settled for the anti-Communist and somewhat authoritarian government of Syngman Rhee (1875–1965), a long-term nationalist leader whose party won the May 1948 election. With Rhee's installation as the first president of the Republic of Korea, the United States formally ended its military government of Korea. Many of Rhee's officials and officers had formerly served in the colonial government or the Japanese military. His government was strongly supported by conservative Koreans and by the million Koreans who had fled the north.

In the north, the Russians established a Communist government under Kim Il-sung (1912–1994). Kim had worked with the Chinese Communists during the 1930s and with the Soviet Union thereafter. When the South held elections in 1948, the North hurriedly followed suit. In September, the Democratic People's Republic of Korea was established. Many of its officers and officials had fought on the Communist side in the Chinese civil war. At the end of 1948 the Soviet Union withdrew its troops from North Korea. During 1949 and early 1950 the United States withdrew its troops from the south. The withdrawal was part of a larger American disengagement from continental Asia after the Communist victory in China. The United States also briefly dissociated itself from the Chinese Nationalist regime on Taiwan as a part of its policy of "letting the dust settle."

Civil War and U.S. Involvement

On June 25, 1950, North Korea invaded the south in an attempt to reunite the Korean peninsula. The North Korean leader had received Stalin's permission for the invasion and a promise from Mao to send Chinese troops if the United States entered the war. His plan was for a quick victory before the United States could intervene. But the Cold War had begun in Europe, and the invasion, coming four months after the signing of the Sino-Soviet Alliance, was seen by the United States as an act of aggression by world Communism. The United States rushed troops from Japan to South Korea and obtained United Nations backing for its action. It also sent naval forces to the Taiwan Straits to protect Taiwan, and, over the next several years, entered into military alliances with South Korea, Japan, Taiwan, the Philippines, and the non-Communist states of Southeast Asia. This marked a major turn in postwar American foreign policy.

During the first months of the war, the unprepared American and South Korean forces were driven southward into a small area around Pusan on the southeastern rim of the peninsula (see Map 37–3). But then, amphibious units led by the United Nations commander General Douglas MacArthur landed at Inchon in the middle of Korea's western coast and drove back the North Korean armies beyond the thirty-eighth parallel deep into North Korea. In midwar, American policy had shifted from the containment of Communism to a rollback. The U.N. forces in Korea were one-half American and two-fifths Korean; the rest was made up of contingents from Britain, Australia, Turkey, and twelve other nations. In the final phase of the war, China sent in "volunteers" to rescue the beleaguered North Korean forces. Chinese troops pushed the overextended U.N. forces back to a line close to the thirty-eighth parallel. After months of fierce fighting, the war became stalemated in 1951 and ended with an armistice on July 27, 1953. Thereafter the two Koreas maintained a hostile peace. On each side of the heavily guarded border were about 600,000 troops. The 142,000 American casualties made the war the fourth largest in U.S. history.

Recent Developments

In the decades that followed, North Korea remained a closed, authoritarian state with a planned economy. It stressed heavy industry, organized its farmers in collectives, and totally controlled education and the media. Most Japanese industries in Korea before 1945 had been in the north, but despite this advantage, the northern economy was sluggish. Shortages of food, clothing, and other necessities were chronic. The cult of personality surrounding "the great leader" Kim Il-sung developed beyond those of even Stalin or Mao. The Korean Communist Party was Marxist-Leninist, but the kinship terminology used to describe the fatherly leader, the mother party, and the familial North Korean state gave the official state philosophy an almost Confucian coloration. Kim designated his son, "the beloved leader" Kim Jong-il (b. 1942), as his successor and when the father died in 1994, the son became the leader of North Korea—the only instance of hereditary succession in a Communist state.

In South Korea, Rhee remained in office until 1960, when at age eighty-five he was forced to retire in the wake of massive student demonstrations. There followed twenty-seven years of rule by two generals. Park Chung-hee seized power in a military coup d'état in 1961, and, shedding his uniform, won a controlled election and became a civilian president. His rule might be called semi-authoritarian: Opposition parties were legal and active but their leaders were often jailed. Students were able to mount protest demonstrations but were usually blocked by riot police and frequently tear-

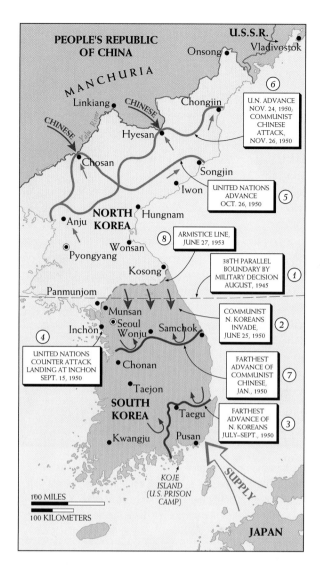

Map 37–3   Korea, 1950–1953. This map indicates the major developments in the bitter three-year struggle that followed the North Korean invasion of South Korea in 1950.

gassed. South Koreans could read non-Communist foreign books and magazines and travel abroad. Many Koreans approved of Park's economic policies but came to resent his use of police and intelligence agencies to sustain his rule. Park was assassinated by his intelligence chief in 1979. General Chun Doo-hwan seized power the following year, transformed himself into a civilian president, and ruled until 1987.

At the inception of Park's rule unemployment was rife and poverty widespread. Park, and his successor Chun, were determined to promote economic growth. They supported business and swiftly expanded higher education, emphasizing science and technology. Management had a legacy of skills from the colonial era and labor was disciplined, hard-working, and cheap. The United States gave large amounts of aid and provided an open market for Korean exports. In combination,

Former South Korean President Roh Tae-woo, arrested in 1995, wears a prison garment as he is led by guards to Seoul court. He was charged with accepting $654 million in bribes during his four years in office. His arrest was indicative of the advance of democracy in Korea, of new leadership in the South Korean military, and of the animus against decades of rule by military figures. [Reuters/Yun Sukbong/Archive Photos]

these factors produced double-digit growth. Especially notable were *chaebol* such as Hyundai or Daewoo, which resembled the Mitsui or Mitsubishi *zaibatsu* of prewar Japan. The two leaders' policies were successful even beyond their expectations. Korea's national product rose as follows:

1960	$ 11.2 billion
1970	27.6
1980	60.6
1990	238.0
1996	584.0

The per capita product in 1996 was $12,800. South Korea had moved into the ranks of developed nations.

An irony of South Korean development was that industrialization and urbanization had produced an affluent and educated middle class that would no longer tolerate authoritarian rule. A crisis occurred in the early summer of 1987 when a stu-

dent activist was drowned in a bathtub at the headquarters of the Korean CIA. In protest a half million persons demonstrated in the streets of Seoul. Chun agreed to step down, and a free and direct election was held in December. Although the two main opposition parties split the anti-government vote, allowing Chun's hand-picked successor, Roh Tae-woo, to become president, most Koreans saw the election as an opening to democracy. This was confirmed four years later when Kim Young-sam, a moderate politician, was elected as president. He purged the generals who had supported Park and Chun and replaced them with officers willing to work with party governments. He then launched investigations of the finances of his predecessors. Though one reporter commented that corruption was as Korean as *kimchee* (a traditional dish of spicy, pickled cabbage), the hundreds of millions of dollars in secret bank accounts uncovered by investigators astonished even the Koreans. In 1995 Chun and Roh and several top *chaebol* leaders were arrested. Chun and Roh were also charged with ordering the killing of hundreds of political demonstrators in Kwangju in 1980. They were sent to prison but later released. A further evidence of democratization was the election of Kim Dae-jung as president in December, 1997. A longtime pro-democracy campaigner, Kim had earlier been the target of assassination attempts and was once condemned to die. He was pro-labor and a populist, but his liberal programs were constrained by the severe recession that gripped Korea from 1996.

Korean international relations have changed only slowly. South Korea's primary ties were with the United States, its long-time ally, which guaranteed its defense. The country's economic weight in the world grew with its trade. By 1999, it was the world's eleventh largest economy. North Korea's principal ties were with the Soviet Union and China, the latter asserting that their solidarity was "as close as lips and teeth." But with the collapse of the Soviet Union, Russia lost interest in its former ally. China, too, unable to resist the allure of the South Korean economy, established diplomatic relations with South Korea in 1992. Since then, South Koreans have invested billions in China, trade between the two nations has flourished, and in 1995 the Chinese president visited Seoul. North Korea was increasingly an orphan. It was still unclear in 1999 whether North Korea would continue as a threadbare totalitarian state, eventually follow China toward a market economy, or collapse like East Germany.

Vietnam

The Colonial Backdrop

The Nguyen dynasty that reunited Vietnam in 1802 was still vigorous in 1858 when France began its conquest of the area, but it proved no match for France. France completed its conquest of Vietnam and Cambodia by 1883, formed the Indochinese Union in 1887, and added Laos to the Union in 1893.

In many ways Indochina was a classic case of colonialism: people of one race and culture, for the sake of economic benefits and national glory, controlling and exploiting a people of another race and culture in a far-off land. To obtain access to the country's natural resources, the French built harbors, roads, and a railway linking Saigon, Hanoi, and southern China. They established rubber plantations in the Mekong delta and tea plantations in the highlands. They also introduced modern mining technology for the extraction of coal, and for local consumption built breweries, rice and paper mills, and glass and cement factories. All were dominated by the French or, in smaller enterprises, by Chinese. Workers were paid very low wages. Except as laborers, the only role for Vietnamese in the economy was as landlords. In the south, 3 percent of landowners owned 45 percent of the land and received 60 percent of the crop grown by their tenants. Although irrigation works in the Mekong delta quadrupled the area of rice fields, the consumption of rice by peasants declined. This distribution of wealth meant that there developed no indigenous middle class, apart from landlords and some Chinese whose commercial acumen was resented by Vietnamese. The French also did little to educate the Vietnamese: in 1939, over 80 percent of the population was illiterate, possibly a higher percentage than in the early nineteenth century under the Nguyen.

During the early decades of French rule, the Vietnamese made futile attempts to restore the dynasty. By the early twentieth century, Vietnamese nationalists in exile in China, Japan, and France formed political parties. But when they tried to organize within Vietnam, the parties were suppressed and their leaders jailed or executed. Under the French, only clandestine parties survived. The most skilled organizer of such parties was Ho Chi Minh (1892–1969), who had participated in the founding of the French Communist Party in 1920, studied in Moscow in 1923, and worked under the Comintern agent Mikhail Borodin in Canton in 1925. Ho founded the Revolutionary Youth League of Vietnam in 1925 and sent its cadres to China and the Soviet Union for training. He then founded the Indochinese Communist Party in 1930. When the Popular Front gained power in France (1936–1938), opposition parties were tolerated in Vietnam and Ho's party emerged the strongest. After 1938 the French again suppressed all opposition groups. Shortly before the outbreak of the Pacific War, the Japanese occupied Vietnam. For their own convenience they ruled through the Vichy French until March, 1945. Ho, who in 1941 had formed the Viet Minh (League for the Independence of Vietnam) as a popular front organization to resist the Japanese, proclaimed the Democratic Republic of Vietnam at the war's end in 1945 and became the preeminent nationalist leader in his country.

Since then, the history of Vietnam can be seen in terms of three cycles of war followed by two decades of peace.

The Anticolonial War

The first war lasted from 1946 to 1954. On one side was the Viet Minh, led by Ho. It was controlled by Communists but also included some representatives of nationalist parties. On the other side were the French, who had reoccupied Vietnam immediately after the war, and their conservative Vietnamese allies. The French tried to legitimize their rule by setting up in 1948 a puppet government under Bao Dai, the last in the line of Nguyen emperors. But in 1954, they lost a major battle at Dien Bien Phu and with it the will to continue what critics at home called the "dirty war." They departed in defeat.

A conference at Geneva divided the country into a Communist north and a non-Communist south. In the south, Ngo Dinh Diem, a non-Communist nationalist who had not collaborated with the French, came to power and established the Republic of Vietnam. Much of his political support came from the nine hundred thousand Vietnamese who had fled from the north.

The Vietnam War

The second cycle of war was from 1959 to 1975 and involved the United States. During the forties, in line with its wartime anticolonial position, the United States had urged the French to reach an accommodation with Ho Chi Minh. After the rise of Communist China and the outbreak of the Korean War, it came to see French actions in Vietnam as an attempt to stem the tide of Communism—a view encouraged by the French. It recognized the French puppet government under Bao Dai and gave $4 billion in aid between 1950 and 1954. When the French withdrew, it transferred its support to Diem.

Fighting began with guerrilla warfare in the south (see Map 37–4), which some said was a local response to Diem's suppression of his political enemies, while others, including North Vietnam after the war, said was directed from the north. The struggle eventually became a full-scale war between the north and the south. The north received material aid from the Soviet Union and China, although, unlike the Korean War, China sent no "volunteers" to fight in Vietnam. The south was aided by the United States, whose forces increased from 600 military advisers in 1961, to 16,000 troops in 1963, 70,000 in 1965, and over half a million in 1969. Despite such massive support, South Vietnam—and the United States—lost the war. The reasons for the defeat were several:

1. The south was difficult to govern. In comparison to the north, the region had been less deeply influenced by

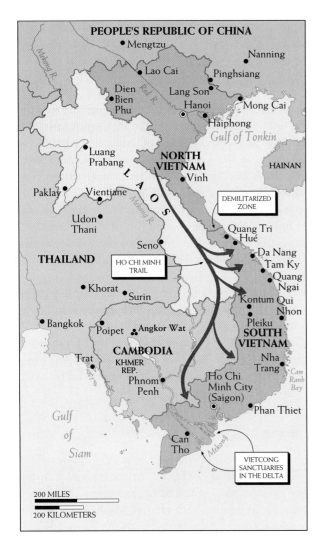

Map 37–4   Vietnam and its Southeast Asian neighbors.   The map identifies important locations involved in the war in Vietnam.

3. Ho Chi Minh was a national hero to many South Vietnamese as well as to northerners. Even some who were anti-Communist viewed the United States as the successor to the French—despite its total lack of colonial ambitions in Southeast Asia—and supported Communist guerrillas as the heirs of the earlier anticolonial struggle.

4. Both the Communist guerrillas in the south and the North Vietnamese troops fought better than the soldiers of the South Vietnamese government.

5. In the jungle terrain of Vietnam, the technological edge of the United States could not be brought to bear. A greater tonnage of bombs was dropped on supply trails in Cambodia than on Japan in World War II, but supplies continued to flow to the south.

At the start of the war, the U.S. government saw its participation, as in the earlier war in Korea, as a part of the battle against world Communism. After the gravity of the Sino-Soviet split became apparent, the justification was to halt the spread of Chinese Communism. Few in the United States understood the depth of the traditional Vietnamese ambivalence toward China that would resurface immediately after the war. But as the war dragged on and casualties mounted, criticism of the war arose and public opinion divided. In 1968, Lyndon Johnson said he would not run for reelection. When Richard Nixon became president, he began slowly to withdraw American troops, calling for the "Vietnamization" of the war. In January 1973, a ceasefire was arranged in Paris, and the last U.S. troops left two months later. Fighting broke out anew between north and south, the South Vietnamese forces collapsed in 1975, and the country was reunited under the Hanoi government in the north. Saigon was renamed Ho Chi Minh City.

In the mid-1970s, few areas of the world were as devastated as Vietnam and its neighbors. After unifying the country, Hanoi sent many thousands of those associated with the former South Vietnamese government to labor camps, collectivized its agricultural lands, and in 1976 began a five-year plan for the economy. Several hundred thousand Vietnamese and ethnic Chinese fled by boat or across the Chinese border.

War with Cambodia

Vietnam's third cycle of war was with its neighbor, Cambodia. Pol Pot (1926–1998) and the Communist Khmer Rouge ("Red Cambodia") had come to power in 1975. During the next three years, his government evacuated cities and towns, abolished money and trade, banned Buddhism, and executed or caused to die of starvation an estimated one million persons, or roughly 15 percent of the total population. School teachers and the educated were singled out as special targets.

Chinese culture, although Confucian values were not absent. It was ethnically diverse with Chinese, Cambodians, and Chams as well as Vietnamese. In religion, it was divided among Buddhists of several varieties, Catholics, and two powerful "new religions," the Cao Dai in the eastern provinces and the Hoa Hao in the western provinces. The two milleniarian sects possessed private armies and, though opposed to the Communists, stood apart from the South Vietnamese government, at times warring among themselves. Throughout the postwar era, the inability of successive southern governments to unify their fragmented society was a basic weakness in their struggles with the communist north.

2. The South Vietnamese government, all too often corrupt, inspired little loyalty in its citizens.

Clashes occurred between Khmer Rouge troops and Vietnamese troops along their common border. Historically, Vietnam was Cambodia's traditional enemy, as China was Vietnam's. In response to the clashes, Pol Pot purged the Khmer Rouge of pro-Vietnamese elements. In 1978, Vietnam retaliated by occupying much of Cambodia, and the next year, set up a puppet government. But it was unable to suppress completely Pol Pot's guerrilla forces. Most Cambodians passively accepted Vietnamese rule; their fear of Pol Pot was greater than their hostility toward Vietnam.

In its international relations, the unified Vietnam of 1975 became an ally of the Soviet Union and gave the Soviets a naval base at Cam Ranh Bay in return for economic, military, and diplomatic support. Relations with China, never good, worsened. Vietnam feared Chinese domination and resented China's invitation to Nixon in 1972 when American troops were still fighting in Vietnam. China, in turn, felt its wartime aid had not been duly appreciated, resented Vietnam's treatment of its ethnic Chinese, and feared an expansionist Vietnam allied with the Soviet Union. In 1979, China decided to "teach Vietnam a lesson" and invaded four northern provinces. Seasoned Vietnamese troops repelled the invaders, but losses were heavy on both sides. For years after 1979, China supported Pol Pot's guerrillas and maintained pressure on Vietnam's northern border with occasional shellings and attacks.

Recent Developments

During the late eighties, the situation again changed. The collapse of the Soviet Union destroyed Vietnam's primary international relationship. Vietnam's leaders also became aware that victories in wars were hollow so long as their people remained destitute.

In 1989, Vietnam withdrew from its costly occupation of Cambodia in favor of a U.N.-sponsored government made up of contending Cambodian factions. Pol Pot refused to participate; his guerrilla forces hunkered down along the Thai border, but grew ever weaker. By the mid-nineties Vietnam's relations with China had improved somewhat, and trade began across their border. China's landlocked Yunnan Province began to use the port of Haiphong as as outlet for its products. In 1995, Vietnam joined ASEAN (Association of Southeast Asian Nations)—an important advance in its relations with its closest and richer neighbors—and reestablished diplomatic relations with the United States. It moved toward "normal" relations with the rest of the world.

At home, the Hanoi dictatorship maintained its grip on the nation. The Communist Party-dominated government monopolized political power, controlled the army, police, and media, and supported a large sector of state-run industries. But it also encouraged the growth of a market economy (the

The combination of carbonated water, sugar, caffeine, and refrigeration creates a product with universal appeal, especially in a tropical climate. In Vietnam, after President Clinton lifted the trade embargo in February, 1994, Coke and Pepsi began a cola war for market share. In the foreground are vendors from the countryside bringing products for sale in the city. In the background is the Hanoi Opera House. [Reuters/Claro Cortes/Archive Photos]

doi moi reforms). Garment manufacturing, food processing, and the production of other consumer goods grew apace. Between 1991 and 1996 the economy achieved an average growth of over 8 percent and received more offers of foreign investment than it could absorb. In 1996, shops in Vietnam were full of food and goods, when only ten years earlier there had been famine in some areas. In these reforms the role of the south was critical. It served as the engine of the economy and as a model—more liberal, pluralistic, and cosmopolitan—that even most northern Vietnamese saw as desirable.

But all was not rosy. Foreign investors were drawn to Vietnam by cheap labor but often encountered shortages, delays, red tape, and financial bottlenecks. The savings rate was high, about 17 percent, but so was inflation. About 70 percent of labor was still employed in agriculture, and in the countryside barter was still common. The gap in standard of living between urban and rural Vietnamese also grew. Vietnam's population of 74 million made it one of the world's most densely populated nations. Hanoi's population, which was 130,000 in the thirties, reached about 4 million; Ho Chi Minh City's

(Saigon), less than a million in the seventies, grew to 4.5 million. In 1995, the per capita income of Vietnam was $240, less than one hundredth of Singapore's. As of 1999, it was still unclear where the balance would be struck between Communist conservatives and reformers in the government.

IN WORLD PERSPECTIVE

East Asia

Before World War II only Europe, the United States, and Japan had successfully combined the ingredients needed for modern economic growth. It was as though these countries had a magic potion that the rest of the world lacked. Industrialization in East Asia during recent decades made clear there was no magic potion: the West and Japan just got there first.

The industrialization of East Asia raises five issues that will powerfully affect future relations between nations.

One question is whether nations with high wages will be able to compete with those low-wage nations which have found the formula for growth. Until recently, the advanced nations were satisfied with their world trade. They sold the products of their heavy industries and advanced technologies and bought raw materials and the labor-intensive products of light industries. They assumed that their technological advantage was permanent, that they could always stay sufficiently ahead of the less-developed nations to maintain their high wages. This assumption, however, has now been challenged. Since the sixties, Taiwan, South Korea, Hong Kong, and Singapore have not only achieved modern economic growth but have moved rapidly into high technology—well before their wages reached Western levels. This made them formidable competitors in just those areas in which the West felt it was preeminent. European nations responded, in part, by adopting protectionist policies, while the United States, with some exceptions, kept its markets open. By doing so, the United States regained competitiveness, but at the cost of holding down wages, drastic corporate restructuring, the relocation of jobs abroad, and huge trade deficits. Will it be willing to continue paying this price? China, the most recent East Asian industrializer, is moving toward higher levels of technology and will possess the economic advantages of cheap labor for decades. If it succeeds in its developmental goals, the impact on high-wage nations will be massive.

A second issue highlighted by East Asian economic growth concerns natural resources. An oil crisis occurred in the early seventies when demand outran supply. There were shortages at the pumps, a steep rise in the price of oil, and a transfer of wealth from industrial to oil-rich nations. Experts pointed out that the world's reserves were dwindling. Market forces, however, uncovered new sources of supply and the crisis faded. Yet oil reserves are still being used up, and only the recession in East Asia holds down an inexorable rise in demand. At some point will not demand again outstrip supply? What effect will this have on countries like Japan, Taiwan, and South Korea that are rich in human talent but poorly endowed with natural resources? It is not hard to imagine a world in which the management of trade and the allocation of scarce resources become an even more important part of international relations than is true today.

A third issue is population. Japan's population quadrupled in the course of its industrialization and then began to level off without a need for draconian measures. Its pattern was similar to that of advanced nations in the West. China, in contrast, already had a huge population when it began its recent industrialization under Teng. Since it could ill afford a further quadrupling, it adopted extremely tough policies to limit births. In 1996, the Chinese minister of agriculture predicted that China's population would peak in 2030 at 1.6 billion people. Whether other less-developed nations in the world follow the Japanese or Chinese model will depend on their particular circumstances, but for many, the tougher Chinese model seems unavoidable.

A fourth issue concerns the political consequences of economic growth. The recent history of Taiwan and South Korea suggests that East Asian dictatorships can evolve toward democracy as standards of living rise. Will the same thing happen in China? As Chinese become caught up in the material benefits of their market economy, will the Chinese Communist Party lose or relax its monopoly on government? It may. But it will take decades for China to reach a Taiwanese level of well-being. Also, postwar Taiwan and South Korea were less thoroughly authoritarian to begin with and were strongly influenced by the United States.

A final issue, the dark companion of industrial and population growth, is pollution. As long as most of the world remained undeveloped, the industrial nations assumed that their wastes would harmlessly vanish into the vast reaches of surrounding lands and seas. But as populations encroached on forested lands, and as Eastern Europe, Russia, and East Asia industrialized, pollution became more threatening. Even apart from disasters such as Chernobyl and Minamata, automobile fumes, industrial effluents, chimney gases, pesticides, garbage, and sewage cause lakes to die, forests to wither, and levels of toxins to rise. In some areas the damage is already near irreversible.

Review Questions

1. Is postwar Japan better understood in terms of a return to the liberalism of the 1920s, or in terms of a new start based on occupation reforms?
2. How many years and at what rate of growth would it take for China's GDP to reach the present Japanese GDP? To reach the present Japanese per capita GDP?
3. Is China after 1949 better understood as an outgrowth of its earlier history or in the context of a comparison to the Soviet Union and other Communist states?
4. Examine the precolonial and colonial eras of Korea and Vietnam. What are the background factors that shaped each in the period after World War II?
5. How did the Cold War affect the postwar histories of Korea and Vietnam?
6. If you were the American secretary of state, what long-term China policy would you propose to the president?

Suggested Readings

China

F. BUTTERFIELD, *China, Alive in the Bitter Sea* (1982). Observations about China by a Chinese-speaking *New York Times* reporter.

A. CHAN, R. MADSEN, AND J. UNGER, *Chen Village: A Recent History of a Peasant Community in Mao's China* (1984). An account of the postwar history of a Chinese village.

J. CHANG, *Wild Swans: Three Daughter's of China* (1991). An inside look at recent Chinese society.

B. M. FROLIC, *Mao's People: Sixteen Portraits of Life in Revolutionary China* (1987).

T. GOLD, *State and Society in the Taiwan Miracle* (1986). The story of economic growth in postwar Taiwan.

H. LIANG, *Son of the Revolution* (1983). An autobiographical account of a young man growing up in Mao's China.

B. LIU, *People or Monsters? and Other Stories and Reportage from China After Mao* (1983). Literary reflections on China.

F. W. MOTE AND D. TWITCHETT, EDS., *The Cambridge History of China* (1987). Vol. 14, *The People's Republic Part I*. A summary of the best recent research.

M. WOLF, *Revolution Postponed: Women in Contemporary China* (1985).

ZHANG X. AND SANG Y., *Chinese Lives: An Oral History of Contemporary China* (1987).

Japan

G. BERNSTEIN, *Haruko's World: A Japanese Farm Woman and Her Community* (1983). A study of the changing life of a village woman in postwar Japan.

T. BESTOR, *Neighborhood Tokyo* (1989). A portrait of contemporary urban life in Japan.

H. HIBBETT, ED., *Contemporary Japanese Literature: An Anthology of Fiction, Film, and Other Writing Since 1945* (1977). Translations of postwar short stories.

D. OKIMOTO, *Between MITI and the Market* (1989). A discussion of the respective roles of government and private enterprise in Japan's postwar growth.

E. O. REISCHAUER, *The Japanese* (1977). The best overall account of contemporary Japanese society and politics.

E. F. VOGEL, *Japan as Number One: Lessons for America* (1979). A sociological analysis of the sources of Japan's early post war economic growth.

Korea and Vietnam

B. CUMINGS, *Korea, The Unknown War* (1988).

B. CUMINGS, *The Two Koreas: On the Road to Reunification?* (1990).

B. CUMINGS, *The Origins of the Korean War* (Vol. 1, 1981; Vol. 2, 1991).

C. J. ECKERT, *Korea Old and New, A History* (1990). The best short history of Korea, with extensive coverage of the postwar era.

C. J. ECKERT, *Offspring of Empire: The Koch'ang Kims and the Colonial Origins of Korean Capitalism, 1876–1945* (1991).

G. M. T. KAHIN, *Intervention: How America Became Involved in Vietnam* (1986).

S. KARNOW, *Vietnam: A History* (revised edition) (1996).

L. KENDALL, *Shamans, Housewives, and Other Restless Spirits: Women in Korean Ritual and Life* (1985).

K. B. LEE, *A New History of Korea* (1984). A translation by E. Wagner and others of an outstanding Korean work, covering the full sweep of Korean history.

T. LI, *Nguyen Cochinchina: South Vietnam in the Seventeenth and Eighteenth Centuries* (1998).

D. MARR, *Vietnam 1945: The Quest for Power* (1995).

C. W. SORENSEN, *Over the Mountains Are Mountains* (1988). How peasant households in Korea adapted to rapid industrialization.

A. WOODSIDE, *Vietnam and the Chinese Model* (1988). Provides the background for Vietnam's relationship to China.

38 THE EMERGING NATIONS OF AFRICA, ASIA, AND LATIN AMERICA SINCE 1945

On May 10, 1994, Nelson Mandela was sworn in as President of South Africa, bringing an end to the apartheid, white minority government that had imprisoned him for twenty-seven years.

[David Brauchli/AP/Wide World Photos]

CHAPTER TOPICS

◆ The Postcolonial Era

AFRICA, THE MIDDLE EAST, AND ASIA

◆ Postcolonial Africa

◆ The Postcolonial Middle East
and Central Asia

◆ South and Southeast Asia

LATIN AMERICA SINCE 1945

◆ Revolutionary Challenges

◆ Pursuit of Stability Under the Threat
of Revolution

◆ Continuity and Change in Recent Latin
American History

In World Perspective The Emerging Nations:
Opportunities and Frustrations of Global
Democratization

The half-century since World War II has seen Europe eclipsed by the rise of the two superpowers—the United States and the Soviet Union—and then the dramatic collapse of one of those superpowers, the Soviet Union (see Chapter 36). In East Asia, China emerged as a third great power, and Japan as an economic leader. Both seem likely to remain major forces in world political and economic developments (see Chapter 37). Elsewhere in the world, especially in the less developed regions, the post-World War II decades have witnessed the end of the age of Western colonialism and sharp challenges to European and superpower imperialism. The waning of colonial and imperial dominance of the many by the few must, however, be set within a larger historical perspective. Since the sixteenth century the various non-European portions of the globe had been drawn steadily into the European sphere of economic and political influence. Those areas to be treated here—Africa, the Middle East, Southwest and Central Asia, South and Southeast Asia, and Latin America—were the regions not only influenced but in most cases subjected, exploited, and often colonized by European powers. The period of colonialism that began in earnest in the seventeenth century was, in retrospect, for all of its immense impact, a relatively brief episode in world history. The last significant colonial holdings were dismantled and given their independence within two decades after the Second World War.

The Postcolonial Era

The "postcolonial" era may prove to be briefer still; indeed, since most of the apparently major postcolonial upheavals lie behind us, it could be argued that, especially with the passing of apartheid South Africa, the postcolonial era has ended. What we shall be witnessing in the future are waves of economic growth, such as that of the early 1990s in much of East Asia; the forging of dramatic new political alignments, both regional and transregional; and, perhaps even more important, internal struggles in country after country to build political systems that allow the development of civil society and limit the destructive domination of corrupt oligarchic or dictatorial regimes. This is a struggle still far from finished in Africa, the Middle East, Latin America, and the younger and emerging nations of Asia, and many new developments and surprises surely await us.

Since 1945 two distinct developments have occurred in the postcolonial world. The first-in a process that is generally termed *decolonization*—is the emergence of the various parts of Africa and Asia from the direct government and administration of foreign powers, and the organization of those previous colonial dependencies into independent states (see Map 38–1). Included in this category are India, Pakistan, most Arab states, the Latin American nations, and the numerous new nations of Africa.

The second development, related to the first, has been the forging of new relationships between the emerging nations and the Western nations and superpowers. These relationships have been of three kinds. First, until the recent breakup of the Soviet Union, its rivalry with the United States manifested itself on every continent and added to the tensions and turmoil of the era. New, emerging nations tended to be under the patronage of one or the other superpower (or, less often, that of China), sometimes to their advantage and sometimes to their disadvantage. Second, the character of the world economy, including issues of both trade and resource allocation, has inevitably led to new modes of economic interdependence. At present, the new relationships of interdependence remain ill defined and the source of much political friction,

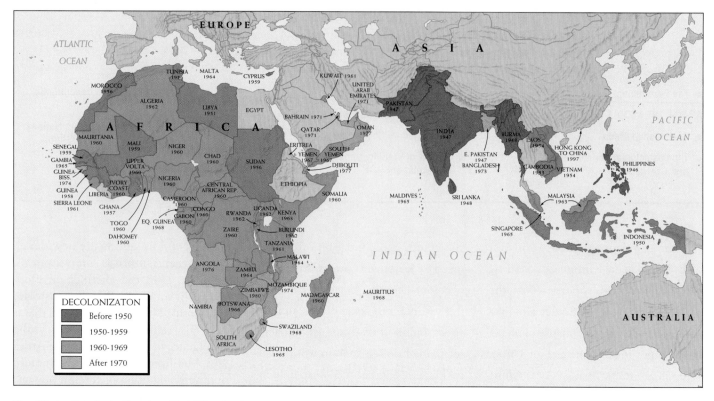

Map 38-1 Decolonization since World War II. The Western Powers' rapid retreat from imperialism after World War II is graphically shown on this outline map covering half the globe—from West Africa to the Southwest Pacific.

whether they relate to automobile production, oil reserves, international trade restrictions, or the structure of international debt. Third, the ideas of civil society and participatory government, often symbolized by the democracies of the United States, Western Europe, and Japan, have gained ground even in those regions where autocratic, authoritarian regimes have been the only forms of government, at least since colonial times. In all three kinds of interaction, change has often outpaced both peoples' and leaders' awareness of it. The world looks different today from just thirty, let alone fifty, years ago. The rhetoric of decolonization is still used, but the realities it attempts to describe are now different. Those new realities and their resulting problems will probably be the main concerns of the next era of world history.

Traditions of civilization, large and small, are still key elements affecting and being affected by the challenges and rapid change of the late twentieth century. A central question is whether to see the global variety of cultural and religious traditions as a creative or divisive force in the next century and beyond. One much-discussed contemporary model for understanding the complex international scene today is that of the "West versus the Rest," in which the post-Enlightenment Western world and its ethos are seen as the hope of the future, while all other civilizational traditions of religion and culture are depicted as rallying points for oppo-

sition to the spread of Western-style "modernity." In this model the future is seen as involving less conflict and competition between national states (a state of affairs that has existed in Europe and slowly spread around the globe since the dawn of the nineteenth century). Instead, this model sees a "clash of civilizations" coming increasingly to dominate world affairs.[1] This pits Islamic, Western Christian, eastern Orthodox, Buddhist, Hindu, "Confucian," and other religio-cultural traditions or "civilizations" against one another in a resurgence of religious, ethnic, and cultural chauvinism that portends new bloodletting and international conflict.

Such a model misconstrues and overplays the importance of religious resurgence and the degree of fundamental difference in values and goals of the major religio-cultural traditions or worldviews of humankind. It also can be used to justify new waves of ethnocentric and chauvinistic policymaking decisions that may continue to encourage the technologically advanced and affluent Western world to formulate its policies in terms of such misconstrued monoliths as a new "yellow peril" forming in "Confucian" China and North Korea, or an imagined "green menace" from some fictitious

---

[1]See Samuel P. Huntington, "The Clash of Civilizations?", *Foreign Affairs* 72, 3 (summer, 1993): 22–49, and a vast array of articles around the world written in response to this provocative and simplistic piece.

global Islamic movement. By the same token, such a model may encourage non-Western nations to view Europe and North America as a monolithic, xenophobic, technologically advanced, and still threatening "West."

Much of the purpose and value of studying the varied traditions of world culture and their modern representatives and derivatives is to come to a more nuanced and balanced view of the modern world as a domain in which many cultural and religious and political traditions will continue to compete for the minds, hearts, and arms of human beings, but one in which people of all backgrounds and types must get along. Issues of population control, environmental degradation and recovery, political accommodation, food supply, public health and epidemiology, and the like must become the focus of shared international concern and effort; our common need for solutions to such transnational, planet-wide problems must take precedence over wide "civilizational" differences. That the task will not be easy is evident from any review of the troubled history of the last half century, not least that of the areas of the globe treated in this chapter.

However, if we seek to understand the larger global scene, we must at least recognize the persistent influence of the great religions and moral traditions of humankind, however we may interpret that influence. In particular, Buddhist, Christian, and Islamic faith and values continue to claim the allegiance of major sectors of our globe, not only in Africa and Asia, but also in Europe and the Americas. No longer can we assume that secular rationalism will easily monopolize ideology during the process of material modernization. What we can expect rather is a pluralistic global community in which no single civilizational or religious tradition can supplant all others, but instead one in which diverse traditions must coexist and learn from one another.

AFRICA, THE MIDDLE EAST, AND ASIA

Throughout the Afro-Asian world, with the exception of much of East Asia, the dominant notes of postwar history have been independence and self-determination. Today the Afro-Asian world encompasses nearly a hundred sovereign states, whereas before 1939 there were only twelve. The rise of new nationalisms in these areas goes back to the nineteenth century, but it was only after the cataclysm of World War II that nationalist movements emerged forcefully. Fueled by diverse grievances accumulated over generations of foreign domination and exploitation, these movements found themselves strong enough—and their colonial masters weak (or receptive) enough—to win independence in country after country. Ironically, what came to define a "country" or a "nation" was, however, often less a common linguistic, racial, or other communal affinity than the somewhat arbitrary boundaries of previous colonial administrative units. As the colonial administrations themselves had been the principal targets of early liberation and nationalist agitation, preindependence boundaries naturally provided the geographical frameworks for most new nation-states.

The postwar period has seen more than forty new states created in Africa alone, and numerous others throughout the less developed areas of Asia. The often massive difficulties and frequent instability these new states have faced are clear evidence of how little the older colonial powers really did for human development and self-governance in the countries they profited from and ruled. Economically, few of the new nations have had the educational, technological, commercial, and political bases for self-sufficiency. A common problem has been the lack of sufficient leadership and experienced professionals, whether in technical or political spheres, and driving almost all other problems has been that of spiraling overpopulation, which has typically far outpaced indigenous food production and even natural resources. The emerging nations of the world have generally experienced the highest rates of population growth. Latin American and the Afro-Asian "Third World" peoples (including China, but not Japan) now make up about three quarters of the world's population, which is approaching 5 billion, compared to about 2 billion in 1930.

In the waning decades of colonial rule and in the subsequent era of postcolonial independence, the small elites of the former colonies have commonly been educated abroad, usually in the universities of Europe, America, and the former Soviet Union. Politically, socially, and economically, they have been often too cut off from the masses of their own people to be able to lead their new independent states well. The absence of a well-educated middle class has exacted a high price. Populist movements for independence and self-rule have foundered again and again on internal rivalries and lack of modern political experience. Class differences have often pitted one group against another within a given society. In other instances, tribal or other affinity groups have found it hard to pull together with former rival groups. For many of the new nations in the Arab, African, Southwest Asian, South Asian, and Southeast Asian regions, the price of independence has been high—in bloodshed; political, ethnic, and religious strife; economic and social chaos; and the effects of continuing inequities in the distribution of wealth. Even massive oil resources, like those some new nations control, cannot resolve these dilemmas.

Yet there have also been hopeful signs. Some of these states have made significant progress in combatting mass illiteracy, poverty, disease, and authoritarian political systems. They have done so despite runaway population growth and the escalating destruction of the natural environment through deforestation, contamination of water supplies, and general depletion of natural resources. Some have been able to develop a sense of cultural, political, or religious continuity with their precolonial pasts without retreating from the realities of their modern situation and its challenges. Most African and Asian peoples can now pursue their own course into the twenty-first century. Even if that course is a difficult one, at least it is not one forced on them by foreign armies and bureaucracies.

Postcolonial Africa

Nowhere is the dramatic continuity between often arbitrary colonial territories and emergent independent states clearer than in Africa. Most of its modern nations are direct inheritors of their colonial predecessors' boundaries, just as the former colonial capitals have typically become the new national capitals of independent Africa. Despite the obvious reasons for such continuity from colonial into postcolonial times, it is remarkable that the colonial frontiers, which had little to do with the boundaries of traditional tribal territories or indigenous empires and states, should have managed to persist so

Celebrating independence. Namibian president Sam Nujoma (right) and Robert Mugabe, president of Zimbabwe, arrive March 21, 1991, at Independence Stadium in Windhoek, Namibia's capital, for festivities celebrating the first anniversary of Namibia's independence. Namibia gained independence from South African domination in 1990. Zimbabwe gained internationally recognized independence in 1980 after a bitter civil war between African nationalists and a white minority government.

[Ulli Michel/Reuters/Corbis-Bettmann]

consistently. If nationalism was a European export to the rest of the world, Africa provides striking examples of how attractive it can be as a motive for supra-tribal and transregional state formation.[2]

The rise of African nationalism can be dated generally to the period between the two world wars, when previously fragmented or regional opposition to European colonial occupation began to be replaced by larger-scale anti-imperialist movements. In World War II the important roles that Africa was called on to play with its natural and human resources, as well as the experience of thousands of Africans abroad, proved a catalyst for African nationalism. In the wake of the war, Europe was also largely disposed to renounce white supremacy theories and give up its colonial empires (see Chapter 36).

The Transition to Independence

The half century since World War II has seen a previously European-dominated continent become a huge array of new, independent national states. In 1950, apart from Egypt, only Liberia, Ethiopia, and white-controlled South Africa were sovereign states. By 1980 no African state (with the exception of two tiny Spanish holdings on the Moroccan coast) was ruled by a European state, although South Africa and Namibia continued to be white-dominated. Native sons, such as Kwame Nkrumah (1909–1972) in the Gold Coast (modern Ghana), Jomo Kenyatta (1893–1978) in Kenya, Julius Nyerere (b. 1922) in Tanganyika (later Tanzania), and Patrice Lumumba (1925–1961) in the Congo became symbols of African self-determination and freedom from foreign domination.

The actual transition from colonial administrative territories to independent national states was less fraught with conflict and bloodshed than one might have expected. All in all, there were relatively few cases involving extended violent conflict with colonial powers, although those were striking in their ferociousness. The most protracted and bloody wars of independence from European overlords were the guerrilla struggles fought in French Algeria from 1955 to 1962; in Portuguese Angola and Mozambique from 1961 to 1975; and in Zaire (formerly the Belgian Congo), Zambia (formerly Northern Rhodesia), and Zimbabwe (formerly Southern Rhodesia) from 1960 to 1980. Usually, however, the transfer of power ended after difficult negotiations and many fits and starts by being relatively peaceable.

Sadly, the same cannot be said of the internal conflicts that often arose in the wake of colonial withdrawal and frequent-

[2]We are especially indebted to Roland Oliver, *The African Experience* (London and New York, 1991), pp. 227–264, for many of the broader interpretations put forward in the current section.

ly resulted in part from the colonial powers' earlier failure to develop sufficient economic and political infrastructures in their territories. Much of the instability in emergent African states has been a legacy of both the colonial powers' generally minimal efforts to prepare their colonial subjects for self-government and the haphazard nineteenth-century division of the continent into often arbitrary colonial units (see Chapter 31). With the departure of European colonial administrations, the establishment of new African governments created a host of difficulties and often succeeded only after substantial civil strife and even full-scale civil war.

Virtually all the nascent African states had nothing like the numbers of educated, trained, and experienced native citizens that were needed to staff the political, administrative, economic, and social apparatuses of a sovereign country, and this alone made for difficult times after independence. Corruption among new officials proved rife; military coups followed, often providing the only stable governance available; the attempt to implement planned economies on a socialist model often brought only economic catastrophe; and tribal and regional revolts at times descended into civil war.

Most dangerous and costly to the new states were the separatist struggles, civil wars, and even border wars between new states that grew out of the independence struggles. The Nigerian civil war of 1967–1970, in which more than one million people died from the fighting and the associated famine, was an especially bloody example (see next section). Other new nations caught for periods in open warfare have been Morocco and the western Sahara; Libya and Chad; South African-held Namibia; Ethiopia and Eritrea; Kenya, Uganda, and Tanzania; Rawanda and Burundi; Somalia; and the Sudan. What strikes the observer about these conflicts is not only their bloodiness and wide occurrence, but also the already mentioned general trend in their outcomes: toward ratifying rather than repudiating the postcolonial state divisions that had almost always kept to the old colonial boundaries (instead of regional or tribal/linguistic divisions within these units).

Every African state has had a different experience and history in the half century since World War II; here we cannot deal with each nation, so we shall have to be content with a brief look at two cases: Nigeria and South Africa.

The Nigerian Case

The modern Republic of Nigeria is the most populous state in Africa, with about 100 million inhabitants in 1995. It was formed in colonial times when the British joined their protectorates of Northern Nigeria and Southern Nigeria in 1914. Nigeria achieved independence in 1960 and ratified a republican constitution in 1964 that federated the three major provincial regions—the Eastern, Western, and Northern—under a national government based in Lagos, the former

British administrative capital. Nigeria's largest ethnic and linguistic groups are the major ones of the same three regions or provinces: Igbo (Ibo) in the Eastern, Yoruba in the Western, and Hausa and Fulani in the Northern. Although these languages have been recognized since 1980 as acceptable for federal business, the official Nigerian language is English.

Nowhere was the aftermath of independence bloodier than in Nigeria, which was, at its inception, arguably the most powerful and potentially successful state in independent Africa. The three-province federation fixed in the 1964 constitution soon proved to be unworkable, and a 1966 coup d'état brought a military government into power. Its leader, an Ibo, was himself assassinated within seven months, and Lt. Colonel Yakubo Gawon (b. 1934) took over amid ethnic unrest that ended in massacres in the fall of 1966. Gawon's government decided to reorganize the republic by further subdividing the three provinces into states, three each in the Western and Eastern Provinces, and six in the Northern. Efforts were made into early 1967 to resolve differences with the eastern states. But in May, 1967 the Eastern Province's assembly empowered its leader, Lt. Colonel Odumegwu Ojukwu (b. 1933), to form a new, independent state of Biafra out of the three states of the Eastern Province. Ojukwu was an Ibo nationalist but aspired to control lands beyond that of the Ibos—in particular, that containing the important off-shore oil reserves of the Eastern Province. The new Biafran state was able to gain recognition from several African states; secure arms and support from France, South Africa, and Portugal; and develop successful worldwide propaganda depicting Biafra as a small, brave, mostly Christian country fighting for its survival against a hostile, oppressive, mostly Muslim central government.

The ensuing two and one-half years saw a tragic and bloody civil war pitting elements of independent Africa's best national army against each other and bringing death and destruction to the independent African state that seemed to have the best prospects as a new nation, based on its natural and human resources. The Biafran forces at first seemed about to win the day, but the tide soon turned in the larger federal forces' favor, and the latter slowly chipped away at first the non-Ibo regions, then the Ibo heartland of the Biafran state. Famine was added to military action as a major cause of casualties, and the estimated death toll soared above a million by the time Ojukwu fled to the Ivory Coast and the Biafrans surrendered in January 1970. Out of this brutal conflict, however, came an increased sense of Nigerian unity, along with a major role for the military in Nigerian politics. The struggle also contributed to the development of African diplomacy and of international aid efforts in Africa, both of which were to be hallmarks of African affairs in the next two decades.[3]

---

[3]Oliver, *African Experience*, pp. 235–236.

In an act of brutal repression that shocked world opinion, Nigeria's military regime executed playwright and environmental activist Kenule "Ken" Saro-Wiwa in 1995. [Jaques M. Chenet//Liaison Agency, Inc.]

In the wake of the federal victory, Gawon set out to implement a policy of reconstruction and reintegration, but he was overthrown by another military commander in 1975. In the ensuing twenty years Nigeria has been plagued by political instability at the top, with its leadership passing usually from one military ruler to another, except for the interlude of the four-year Second Republic under President Usman Aliyu Shagari (b. 1925), a Fulani Muslim from the north whose rule ended in a military coup in 1983. A decade later, the military regime went back on its promise to move to civilian governance, nullifying the 1993 presidential electoral victory of Yoruba leader Moshood Abiola to the presidency. This debacle ended in a coup by the military defense minister, Gen. Sani Abacha, who went on to four years of repressive military rule and great brutality against his enemies. Cases in point are the four-year imprisonment of Abiola and the 1995 execution of the Nigerian playwright and environmental activist, Kenule "Ken" Saro-Wiwa (b. 1941).

One of the most distinguished Nigerians of recent times, the Nobel laureate writer Wole Soyinka (b. 1934), led protest demonstrations against the military government in 1994 and later went into exile, where he helped in 1996 to found a seventeen-member National Liberation Council dedicated to creating a government-in-exile. Abacha died in June 1998 and was replaced by Gen. Abubakar, who has reversed some of Abacha's repressive actions. Abiola died in July while still in prison. A return to civilian rule is promised for 1999 but remains for many Nigerians only a faint hope. However, there have been some hopeful signs: Soyinka was able to return from exile in October 1998 to a hero's welcome, and some political prisoners have been released by Gen. Abubakar since

June. At this writing, it remains to be seen if the transition to civilian rule, so long delayed, will really occur.

All of this gives little promise that Nigeria, for all its potential, will soon surface as a leader to be emulated among African nations. It appears that a great opportunity for successful transition to economic and political independence and positive influence upon less well-endowed African countries has been squandered.

The South African Case

One of the most tragic chapters in the history of modern Africa has at long last been closed: that of white minority rule in South Africa, with its radical separation of white from nonwhite peoples in all areas of life as official government policy for nearly fifty years. In the rest of East and southern Africa, minority white-settler governments tried in vain in the postwar period to put down African independence movements or efforts to create participatory multiracial states. Only in South Africa did they manage, until the 1990s, to sustain a white supremicist and separatist political reality in the face of all internal resistance and outside pressure.

From the time the Afrikaner-led National Party (NP) came to power in 1948, the Union of South Africa was governed according to the avowedly racist policy of *apartheid* ("apartness"). Until the dismantling of this policy after 1991, the country's white minority (in 1991, 5.4 million persons) ran the country, maintaining economic and political control and privilege. Its 31 million blacks, 3.7 million "coloreds" (of mixed blood), and one million Indians were kept strictly and legally segregated—treated, at best, as second-class citizens or, in the case of blacks, as noncitizens or even nonhumans. This system was maintained chiefly by repression, most visibly direct military and police action, to quell dissent and enforce apartheid laws. Only in the past several years has this changed and apartheid officially been dismantled as a principle of state.

The history of apartheid and its passing is a bloody and tortured but finally triumphant one. In part as a result of worldwide opposition to apartheid, South Africa saw itself become increasingly isolated from the 1960s onward. Meanwhile, the rest of Africa—including other white-run states like Rhodesia (now Zimbabwe)—progressed to majority, African rule. In 1961 South Africa withdrew from the British Commonwealth of Nations. In the sixties and seventies the government created three tiny "independent homelands" for blacks inside the country, allowing the white minority to treat blacks as immigrant "foreigners" in the parts of South Africa where most had to work. The international community refused to recognize the homelands, or "Bantustans." South Africa's isolation was further dramatized when two antiapartheid black leaders, the Zulu chief Albert Luthuli in 1960 and the Anglican bishop Desmond Tutu in 1984, were awarded the Nobel Prize for their work against apartheid.

By 1978, as Pieter Botha (b. 1916) came to power on a changing NP platform of limited reforms of apartheid, it was clear that apartheid was failing: The homelands were economic and political catastrophes; the country was in an inflationary recession and losing skilled whites to emigration; and with other white colonial regimes on the way out, South Africa was becoming increasingly an international pariah. In the 1980s the struggle between the white minority and the black majority intensified, and Botha's concessions on issues such as interracial marriage and public-transportation segregation could not calm the situation. Internal opposition to apartheid grew, and calls for a boycott of South Africa brought increasing international pressure. Threats from guerrilla forces prompted the government to send its troops on pre-emptive raids on guerrilla bases in neighboring countries.

Beginning in 1986 many nations responded to Desmond Tutu's call and imposed economic sanctions against the government. Anti-apartheid movements in the United States and elsewhere had convinced some companies and individuals to divest themselves of investments in South Africa. Strikes by black workers in 1987 led the government to declare a state of emergency and give virtually unlimited power to its security forces, but the resulting violent confrontation created widespread support among Western nations for a complete trade embargo of South Africa.

In June of 1988 more than 2 million black workers went on strike to protest the promulgation of new repressive labor laws and a ban on political activity by trade unions and anti-apartheid groups. This led President Botha to resign in August 1989 after eleven years of rule. His replacement, F. W. de Klerk (b. 1936) (also of the NP, but younger and more ready for accommodation), began effectively to dismantle white-only rule and the official structures of apartheid. February 1990 saw a dramatic speech by de Klerk announcing radical changes, and there followed a series of landmark government actions: the lifting of the ban on the African National Congress (ANC), the main anti-apartheid organization; the release of ANC leader Nelson Mandela after twenty-seven years of imprisonment; and the repeal of the Separate Amenities Act, the legal basis for segregation in public places. In early 1991 de Klerk announced plans to end all apartheid laws, and in June of that year the race registration law was repealed. A great step forward was made in March 1992, when, in a whites-only referendum in which over 85 percent of voters turned out, 67.8 percent voted to grant constitutional equality to all races. The NP government under de Klerk's leadership also negotiated with the ANC leader Mandela, and despite terrorist attempts from both black and white extremists to derail the talks, the two leaders were able to bring their own and eighteen other parties of both sides to

endorse a new interim constitution. This constitution was to be implemented once national elections could be held in which all citizens of South Africa would be enfranchised. (For their leadership, Mandela and de Klerk shared the Nobel Peace Prize for 1993.)

Despite continued violence the elections were held in April 1994, and the ANC won 63 percent of the vote, the NP 20 percent, and Inkatha and other parties the remainder, thus relegating apartheid's ugly racist ideology to the slag heap of history. The nonracial constitution of December 1996 offers a new basis for the future, but despite the rising political hope, substantial mineral resources, and the highest GNP in Africa, the new state still faces huge problems: one of the world's most extreme income inequalities, insufficient education, economic infrastructure, rampant black poverty, high unemployment, militant extremist groups, woefully inadequate public services in much of the country, potentially severe water-supply and water quality problems, and difficulties in attracting enough foreign investment fast enough to fulfill Mandela's promises of a new era of economic and social progress. The daunting obstacles to be surmounted will, however, no longer include a state system that holds the majority of the population in social, economic, and political bondage.

While the new independent states of Africa have been anything but models, and while any ideas of a union or unions of nations have either failed (the uniting of Zanzibar and Tanganyika in the new state of Tanzania is a notable exception) or remain pure conjectures about an uncertain future, nevertheless Africa did not revert to tiny tribal and regional political units. And, it must be noted, some struggles—such as those in the Sudan, Somalia, Rwanda, Sierra Leone, and Liberia—are still ongoing, their human consequences catastrophic, and their ultimate outcomes not clear.

The African Future

Most African states have not achieved peace and prosperity. On the other hand, the last fifty years have seen radical change and development that would have been unimaginable before. After decades of struggles and trials, the prospects for future government stability are not entirely bleak. Economic problems still loom extremely large, but even here some progress is being made after decades of failed socioeconomic planning and development schemes. In any case, every African state is strikingly different; each faces unique problems and must draw on its unique resources if it is to be successful in the century ahead. The often heavy burdens of the past—be they regional rivalries and hatreds, religious and linguistic divisions, major economic and social policy mistakes in early independence, or the crippling experience of apartheid—still present formidable hurdles.

Nelson Mandela's Vision: From His Inaugural Address

On May 10, 1994, Nelson Mandela, who for many years had been imprisoned for his opposition to white rule, became the first president of post-apartheid South Africa. In his inaugural address he spoke without bitterness about the past and of his wider vision for South Africa.

What are the major themes of his speech? What kind of a South African society and polity does he envision? What would you say might be the chief stumbling blocks to the realization of his dream?

. . . Out of the experience of an extraordinary human disaster that lasted too long, must be born a society of which all humanity will be proud.

Our daily deeds as ordinary South Africans must produce an actual South African reality that will reinforce humanity's belief in justice, strengthen its confidence in the nobility of the human soul and sustain all our hopes for a glorious life for all. . . .

The time for the healing of the wounds has come.

The moment to bridge the chasms that divide us has come.

The time to build is upon us.

We have, at last, achieved our political emancipation. We pledge ourselves to liberate all our people from the continuing bondage of poverty, deprivation, suffering, gender, and other discrimination.

We succeeded to take our last steps to freedom in conditions of relative peace. We commit ourselves to the construction of a complete, just and lasting peace.

We have triumphed in the effort to implant hope in the breasts of the millions of our people. We enter into a covenant that we shall build the society in which all South Africans, both black and white, will be able to walk tall, without any fear in their hearts, assured of their inalienable right to human dignity—a rainbow nation at peace with itself and the world.

As a token of its commitment to the renewal of our country, the new Interim Government of National Unity will, as a matter of urgency, address the issue of amnesty for various categories of our people who are currently serving terms of imprisonment.

We dedicate this day to all the heroes and heroines in this country and the rest of the world who sacrificed in many ways and surrendered their lives so that we could be free.

Their dreams have become reality. Freedom is their reward.

We are both humbled and elevated by the honor and privilege that you, the people of South Africa, have bestowed upon us, as the first president of a united, democratic non-racial and non-sexist South Africa, to lead our country out of the valley of darkness.

We understand it still that there is no easy road to freedom.

We know it well that none of us acting alone can achieve success.

We must therefore act together as a united people, for national reconciliation, for nation building, afor the birth of a new world.

Let there be justice for all.

Let there be peace for all.

Let there be work, bread, water, and salt for all.

Let each know that for each the body, the mind and the soul have been freed to fulfill themselves.

Never, never and never again shall it be that this beautiful land will again experience the oppression of one by another and suffer the indignity of being the skunk of this world.

The sun shall never set on so glorious a human achievement!

Let freedom reign. God bless Africa!

The Boston Globe, May 15, 1994, Focus section, p. 74.

Probably even more serious are those problems with which almost all of Africa's new nations still have to contend: overpopulation, poverty, disease, famine, lack of professional and technical expertise, and general economic underdevelopment. In particular, the explosive growth of new urban centers at the expense of rural areas has brought disruptive changes in the continent's traditionally agrarian-based societies, age-old family and tribal allegiances, religious values, and sociopolitical systems. The challenge for African nations at the end of the twentieth century is clearly how to build a truly civil society and achieve economic health and political stability in the face of internal divisions, exploding population growth, and world-market competition.

The Postcolonial Middle East and Central Asia

The lands still dominated or significantly marked by Islamic culture and containing either Muslim majority populations or major Muslim minority numbers stretch from North and West Africa to the Philippines. More specifically, they are

A Modernist Muslim Poet's Eulogy for His Mother

The following is a poem drawn from the autobiography of Aziz Nesin, That's How It Was But Not How It's Going to Be *(1966). Nesin (1915–) is a prolific Turkish writer, political commentator, and social critic whose writing career began in 1946 with his publication of a satirical weekly paper. The following poem is a eulogy for his long-dead mother, a reflection on the deprivations she endured, and a determined promise to assure women a better life in the future. It reflects the widespread feeling among secular modernists in Turkey and elsewhere that one of the hallmarks of modernity is the emancipation of women. The final two lines repeat the original Turkish title of Nesin's book.*

What is the impact of addressing the poem to his own mother rather than to some other female figure? What are the specific things that Nesin is criticizing in the poem?

"A Vow to My Mother's Memory"

All mothers, the most beautiful of mothers,
You are the most beautiful of the beautiful,
At thirteen you married;

At fifteen you gave me birth.
You were twenty-six,
You died before you lived.
I owe you this heart overflowing with love.
I don't even have your picture;
It was a sin to have a photograph taken.
You saw neither movie, nor play.
Electricity, gas, water, stove,
Nor even a bedstead were found in your home.
You could never bathe in the sea,
You couldn't read nor write.
Your lovely eyes
Looked at the world from behind a black veil.
When you were twenty-six
You died, before you lived—
Henceforth, mothers will not die before they live.
That's how it was,
But not how it's going to be!

From Aziz Nesin, *Istanbul Boy: The Autobiography of Aziz Nesin, Part I* p. 9. Copyright © 1977 Center for Middle Eastern Studies. Reprinted by permission.

---

found in the Arab world from Morocco to Iraq and the Gulf, in the Balkans and Turkish-speaking world of Turkey and the former Soviet Central Asian republics, in Persian-speaking Iran and parts of Central Asia, in western China, and in South and Southeast Asia. (India, Bangladesh, Pakistan, and Indonesia have the four largest Muslim populations in the world, the first three having about 132, 109, and 125 million Muslims, respectively, and the last around 180 million; the Muslims of the entire Arab world number no more than 250 million.)

It is obviously not possible in a few pages to review the history of these widespread regions since 1945, but we can expand briefly on six major developments that have affected them: (1) the emergence of new national states and international alignments, (2) the creation of the state of Israel, (3) the increase in importance of world oil production and reserves, (4) a new resurgence of religious, political, and social reform movements in the name of a purified Muslim society, (5) the Iranian Revolution, and (6) the collapse of Soviet control in Central Asia.

New Nations in the Middle East

Saudi Arabia, Iraq, and Egypt obtained sovereign-state status after World War I, and Lebanon and Syria were officially given theirs by France during World War II. Yet these states only became truly independent of European control after World War II. Others soon followed: Jordan gained independence in 1946; Libya in 1951; Morocco and Tunisia in 1956; Algeria in 1962; and, by 1971, the two Yemens, Oman, and the small Arabian Gulf states. As elsewhere in the developing world, political instability and autocratic rule have been constants in most of these states. All share the Arabic language and the Muslim faith (although Lebanon has substantial percentages of Druze and Christians), but various attempts to create pan-Arab alliances or federations have all been abortive. Many historical, regional, and national factors give each country a distinctive character. The oil wealth and strategic importance of the region have attracted the interest and interference of the United States, Europe, and Russia, further complicating relations among the Arab states and between them and the rest of the world.

Turkey, now the oldest twentieth-century nation in the Middle East, dates its existence from the 1920s rather than the 1950s. It represents a modernist republican experiment that has managed, despite struggles over the place of religion in society and lapses into military rule, to allow a civil society and a democratically elected government to be the norm. It has, however, been plagued with ongoing intervention from the military, which has repeatedly deposed existing elected

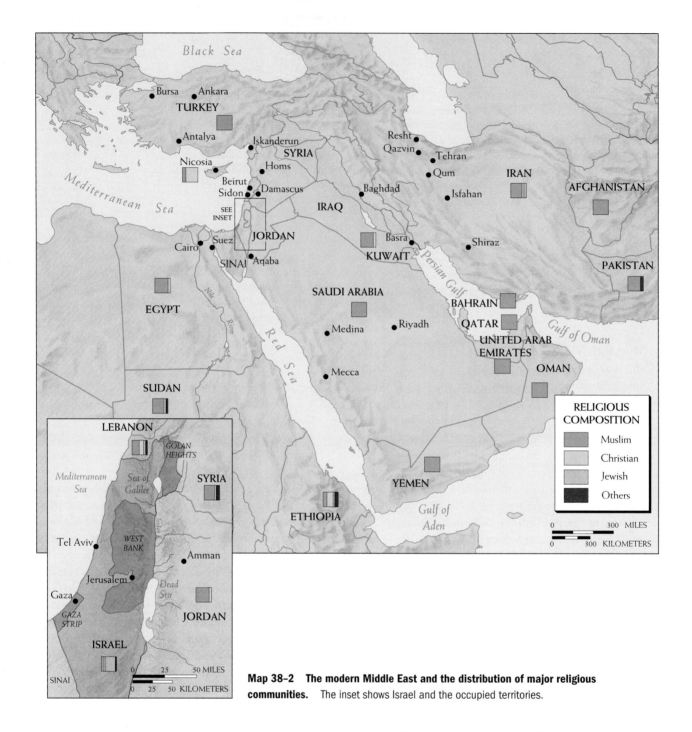

Map 38–2 The modern Middle East and the distribution of major religious communities. The inset shows Israel and the occupied territories.

governments and supervised the selection of new leadership. Economically, Turkey has certainly had its difficulties, but along with Israel it is still the most advanced of Middle Eastern countries in its economic development. With the creation of new Turkic-language-speaking states in Central Asia after the breakup of the Soviet Union, Turkey is making a bid, and may succeed, to strengthen its ties with this underdeveloped part of the world and to be a major factor in its emergence over the next generation.

The Arab-Israeli Conflict

Nowhere has the presence of the superpowers and Europe been more sharply felt than in the 1948 creation of the state of Israel in the former British mandate territory of Palestine, intended as a national homeland for the Jewish people (see Map 38–2). This event was the achievement of the world Zionist movement founded in 1897 by Theodor Herzl (1860–1904) in Europe. The British Balfour Declaration of 1917 had already favored the establishment of a national homeland for the Jews in Palestine. Even in 1920, however, there were only about 60,000 Jews and ten times that number of Arabs in Palestine. As some foresaw and time would bear out, the potential for grave difficulties was great.

The interwar years saw increasing Jewish settlement and growing communal conflict poorly mediated by the British. Immigration of Jews, largely from eastern Europe, increased in the 1920s and 1930s until Britain tried in 1936 to restrict it severely—an effort that prevented many European Jews from escaping the Nazi Holocaust. Because of the programmatic Nazi attempt to exterminate European Jewry, after the war the Zionist movement received a tremendous boost among Jews worldwide and from the Allied nations, who felt the need to atone for the indescribable horror of the Holocaust by helping to secure a refuge for Jews from around the world.

The concept of return to the Holy Land did have a long history in the Jewish religion. However, translating the concept into the creation of a nation state was difficult because, for centuries, the land had been the home of Arabic-speaking Palestinians, primarily Muslims, but also Christians and Jews, who were without voice in the matter. The Palestinians have understandably not been able to see why they should be displaced and persecuted, whether because of another people's historic religious attachment to the land or to pay for Europe's sins against the Jews. On the other hand, especially in the light of nineteenth- and twentieth-century European antisemitic persecutions, Jews themselves rightly felt the desperate need for a homeland where they might be safe and to which Jews everywhere might flee from future persecutions.

In 1945 Britain found itself beset in Palestine by Jews seeking to settle there and by Jewish underground and terrorist organizations. In 1947 the British washed their hands of the problem, and the United Nations passed a resolution calling for partition of the former mandate territory into a Jewish and an Arab state. The existing Arab states refused to accept the U.N. resolution, but in May 1948 Jews in Palestine proclaimed the independent state of Israel. This declaration led to the Israeli-Arab war of 1948–49, in which Syria, Lebanon, Jordan, Egypt, and Saudi Arabia attacked Israel but lost to the outnumbered but better-armed and more resolute Israelis, ceding not only the U.N.-proposed Israeli territory but also a substantial portion of that designated by the U.N. for a Palestinian state.

Since then there has been, at best, an armed truce between Israel and its neighbors and, at worst, open warfare. The Arab nations and the Palestinian people displaced by the new state have generally not wanted to accept Israel's right to exist as a state, and Israel (with the support of the United States) has taken aggressive measures, often in defi-

ance of world opinion, to ensure its survival. The most serious military confrontations were the Suez crisis of 1956, when Israel (and briefly France and England) invaded the Sinai after Egyptian provocations; the 1967 June War, when Israel attacked and occupied the Sinai, the Golan Heights, and the West Bank (of the Jordan River); the October War of 1973 in which the Egyptians staged a surprise attack on Israel in the Sinai that ended in a standoff; and the Israeli invasions of Lebanon in 1978 and 1982 in the context of the Lebanese-Syrian conflict and the professed determination of Israel to extirpate anti-Israeli terrorist refuges.

Even in periods without overt war, bloodshed has become commonplace. Arab terrorism grew out of the frustrations of dispossessed Palestinians and of Israeli Arabs who see themselves as second-class citizens in a country claiming to be an egalitarian democracy. The Palestine Liberation Organization (PLO) and subsequently other more radical groups have carried on determined guerrilla battles within and along Israel's borders for decades. In a sad irony of history, these guerrillas have employed the very terrorist tactics that Zionist extremists used so effectively against the British in Palestine to gain Israeli statehood.

Simultaneously, in a cycle of violence familiar from Northern Ireland to Vietnam, the frustrations of an embattled Israel have made it increasingly ready to meet terrorist atrocities with preemptive military actions and violent reprisals, both at home and abroad. Israel has responded to terrorist attacks and civilian resistance such as the Intifada, or Arab uprising, in the occupied territories with air and commando raids on Arab states thought to support Palestinian terrorism; with repressive, even punitive, measures against the Arab populations in the occupied territories (including home demolitions, curfews, torture of civilian detainees, and firing upon civilian protesters); and generally with a hard-line stance against negotiation over the status of the territories seized in 1967 (despite the virtually unanimous agreement of the international community—the U.S. being the exception—that these territories, seized by force, should be relinquished).

Arab and some non-Arab states have been equally intransigent about recognizing Israel's right to exist, have supported guerrilla groups attacking Israel, and have refused until recently to deal directly with Israel to reach a long-term Middle East solution. Egypt was the first notable exception to this policy. In the late 1970s, under Gamal Abdel Nasser's (1918–1970) successor, President Anwar Sadat (1918–1981), and through the mediation of U.S. President Jimmy Carter (b. 1924), Egypt entered into direct negotiations with Israel's prime minister Menachem Begin (1913–1994). The two countries reached an agreement—the Camp David Accords—in 1978, and in 1979 signed a formal peace treaty. Sadat was assassinated in 1981 by Egyptian Muslim extremists, but the treaty has held up under his successor, Husni Mubarak (b. 1928).

Nonetheless, despite the Egyptian-Israeli accords, violence and political impasse—tragic, morally debilitating, and materially draining for all the peoples of the area—continued through the 1980s and 1990s. Israel's military actions in the Lebanese war of 1982–83 and subsequent attacks on southern Lebanon have been provoked by, but in turn brought on, more Arab terrorist bombings in Israel and abroad. Thus the cycle of violence has continued even as peace initiatives have increased.

Added to this bleak history and current struggle is the ugly legacy of hate instilled in many on both sides over the past fifty years. Arabs and even many Muslims outside the Arab world have come to label non-Israeli Jews, Israelis, and both religious and political Zionists as oppressors and enemies, making virtually no distinction among them. Many Israelis and some Jews around the world have similarly vilified all Arabs and Muslims. In many ways Arab-Israeli and Muslim-Jewish relations are at an all-time low, and it will take a generation and more to displace the prejudice, stereotyping, and hatred so long accumulated. The human crisis is far from over, even if peace were to arrive tomorrow.

Some events of recent years have given at least faint hope for an eventual resolution to the conflict. In 1991, in the wake of the Gulf War that followed Iraq's invasion of Kuwait, the parties to the Arab-Israeli conflict began peace negotiations, and in June 1992 the intransigent right-wing coalition government of Yitzhak Shamir (b. 1915) in Israel was replaced by a more flexible government led by Yitzhak Rabin (1922–1996), Shimon Peres (b. 1923), and the Labor Party. These developments made possible the September 1993 Middle East Peace Agreement, which raised hopes for a negotiated settlement and the creation of a secular Palestinian state

alongside the Jewish state of Israel. They also led to a Nobel Prize being shared among Rabin, Peres, and the PLO chief Yassir Arafat (b. 1929).

There have, however, predictably been fits and starts in the first stages of implementation of the peace agreement and ongoing danger that the agreement might break down altogether. Jordan and Egypt agreed in 1994 to a peace treaty with Israel, but some other Arab states—foremost among them Syria—have still not been willing to negotiate with Israel. Extremists on both sides have tried to put up obstacles to the success of the peace initiative. In early 1994 an American-born Israeli fanatic machine-gunned worshipers in a mosque in Hebron. In November 1995 another Jewish Israeli extremist assassinated Prime Minister Yitzhak Rabin for his role in trying to make peace and to allow the eventual creation of a circumscribed Palestinian state. Then, in the run-up to the Israeli elections of May 29, 1996 that were called in the wake of Rabin's death, Arab extremists carried out a series of savage bombings on buses and in crowded shopping areas. The subsequent victory in the elections of a Likud conservative hardliner, Benjamin Netanyahu (b. 1949), over Rabin's Labor successor, Shimon Peres, by a margin of less than 1 percent of the vote, cast new uncertainty on peace prospects.

To date, the leadership on both sides has not proven to be up to serious progress on a peaceable settlement. The Netanyahu regime has repeatedly taken hardline stands and even provocative actions such as the determined expansion of Jewish West Bank settlements. To the latter end, new roads and building projects have been implemented to divide further the Palestinian population in the Occupied Territories. Other actions have included curtailment of water supplies to Palestinian areas and public declarations of Israel's determination to retain all of Jerusalem and much of the territories even in the face of international censure. Nor has the Pales-

In 1993 the leaders of Israel and the Palestine Liberation Organization signed a peace accord in Washington, D.C. From left to right are Prime Minister Yitzhak Rabin of Israel, President Bill Clinton of the United States, PLO Chairman Yasir Arafat, and Warren Christopher, United States Secretary of State. Rabin was subsequently assassinated by a Jewish Israeli extremist. [Les Stone/Sygma]

tinian Authority created by the 1993 peace agreement proven any better. It has grown steadily more corrupt, ineffective, and out of touch with its constituencies, and the suffering of the masses in the West Bank and Gaza in particular has only grown steadily worse since the agreement. Despite the efforts of the Palestinian and Israeli security forces, Arab guerrillas of the extremist wing of the resistance organization Hamas have been able to slaughter Israeli civilians in daylight bombings (such as those in October 1998) in a sustained effort to torpedo the already shaky "peace process." These terrorist attacks have led Israel often to seal its borders, resulting in the loss of livelihood for thousands of Arabs in the occupied territories who normally work in Israel proper, and this has exacerbated the already dire plight of Gaza in particular, keeping thousands of Arab families in poverty and starvation and in turn feeding the extremist resistance groups.

In October 1998, Arafat and the current Israeli leader Benjamin Netanyahu made a renewed agreement to move forward with the flagging 1993 peace initiatives, but it remains to be seen whether both sides, despite terrorist acts and other provocations as well as their own ambivalence, can seize the high road to a negotiated settlement.

Middle Eastern Oil

The oil wealth of the Arab and Iranian world has been another significant factor in the recent history of the region. Since Saudi Arabia's first oil production in 1939, the world demand for oil has grown by leaps and bounds. Especially in the past two decades oil has become a major bargaining chip in international diplomacy that the Arab and other oil-rich Third World states—such as Venezuela, Nigeria, Iran, and Indonesia—have used to their advantage. In the Arab countries of North Africa and especially of Arabia and the Gulf, oil production and wealth have changed every aspect of life. Oil has propelled formerly peripheral and virtually unknown countries of the Sahara or the Arabian deserts into major roles in the world of international banking and finance. Oil also has had less tangible but nonetheless important consequences in boosting the badly damaged self-confidence of the Arab world after a century and a half of Western domination. A testimony to the global importance of Middle Eastern oil was the willingness of the United States and European nations to form a coalition with some Arab countries and to commit massive forces to the region to expel Iraq from Kuwait after Iraq's invasion of its neighbor in 1990. (See "Energy and the Modern World," essay.)

Islamism and Politics

The increase in the global importance of the oil-producing states of the Middle East has coincided with a new round of

A Kuwaiti looks at one of the more than six hundred oil wells left burning by Iraqi troops as they retreated during the Gulf War in 1991. The willingness of the United States and Europe to commit massive forces to expel Iraq from Kuwait reflects the global importance of the region's oil wealth. [Will Burgess/Reuters/Corbis-Bettmann]

Muslim efforts in the Middle East and elsewhere to revive pristine Muslim values and standards and to reform the perceived evils and failures in Muslim societies. In the spirit, and often in the footsteps, of earlier Muslim resurgents such as those of the eighteenth century in India, Arabia, and Africa, many Muslims have sought to return to the "fundamentals" of Islamic life, faith, and society. They see this as a means of rejuvenation, of social and economic as well as political justice, and of defense against the encroachment of foreign, usually Western secularist, values and norms. Indeed, a major new element in twentieth-century Muslim revivalism is its consciousness of being a viable response to the destructive influence of Western-style "modernity" on the mores, values, and religious faith and practice of Muslim peoples. A great part of the appeal of Islamist groups everywhere is their willingness and ability to address the needs especially of the underclasses in Middle Eastern, North African, and Asian cities and countries. Where government after government of Muslim-world countries has failed to provide social services such as housing, medical care, education, and jobs, the Islamist groups have repeatedly succeeded under the banner of a just, moral Muslim societal ideal. While the world, and especially the U.S., press have heard only of the relatively small fringe groups of Islamist extremists, Muslims at grass-roots level have seen the major Islamist groups in the dictatorships or military regimes under which most of them live providing services for which the state has long abdicated its responsibility.

Such Muslim fundamentalism—or, to give it a more correct name, "Islamist reformism"—motivated many of the revolutionaries who overthrew the government of Muhammed Reza Shah (r. 1941–1978) in Iran in 1978 (see the following section). It is also seen in the Muslim Brethren movement in Egypt and elsewhere, in the Welfare Party recently becoming prominent in Turkey, and in many other groups, from Morocco to Turkey and the Persian Gulf, and also outside the Middle East proper. The political actions of the reformist groups range from revolutionary action (Iran) to democratic participation (Turkey) to complete political quietism (the Tablighi international revivalist movement begun in Pakistan). Whether these movements will bring lasting change to Islamic societies is an open question for the Muslim world generally and the Middle East in particular.

The background to modern Islamist reform lies in the European expansion over much of the globe in just a few centuries. This expansion brought far more social and political change than religious or even cultural change to the Islamic world. It saw the emergence globally of European-style nationalism and the idea of the nation-state; of post-Enlightenment ideals of individual liberties and rights and representative government; and of the concept of one's religious faith and affiliation as a strictly private, "religious" matter and one's citizenship as a public, "secular" matter. Such ideas proved revolutionary, or at the least disruptive, in the Islamic world, especially in this century.

The twentieth century in Islamic parts of the world presents a checkered history of autocratic governments generally at least as far removed from their citizenries as any of the medieval or premodern, often foreign (primarily Turkish) dynasties that had ruled Arab, Persian, Indian, or other regions of the Muslim-majority world. Experiments with European-style parliamentary government have only rarely taken hold in the Islamic world (or the rest of the third world); nor have either liberal democratic or Marxist-Socialist political and social ideals proven viable for the long term. Even so, until recently surprisingly little of the political discourse in Islamic lands has given serious, as opposed to merely nominal, attention to specifically *Islamic* alternatives.

With the rise and postcolonial independence of numerous national states and the flourishing of diverse nationalisms,

politics became often theoretically as well as actually divorced from Islamic religious tradition and its norms in overt ways that it had not been before, however large the actual gap always was between the religious ideals of government as guardian of the Shari'ah order on the one hand and the political realities of governing as power politics on the other. Where leaders had previously claimed Muslim faith and allegiance, some came to espouse secular ideologies and virtually to ignore religion unless it proved necessary to use it as a political weapon. And used as a weapon it was; in this century as in those earlier, Islamic religious allegiance has commonly been invoked to bolster a ruler's claim to legitimacy and often to cloak in pious garb much more mundane objectives and programs.

In short, the present century has up to now seen no realization of an "ideal" Islamic state in which religious and political authority are conjoined. If anything, the gap has widened typically between Islamic norms and ideals on the one hand and political and social realities on the other. Even in the post-revolutionary Islamic Republic of Iran there has been a clear division between political necessity and reality and religious values and standards. However sincerely the latter are claimed as the basis of state policy and procedure, no one can miss the frequent stretching of those standards to justify pragmatic political decisions.

When we look at the Islamist movements of recent decades, we find that the calls for a congruence of religion and politics in the Islamic world trace less to some kind of ideal model of a religious state or so-called "theocracy" than to a sorely felt need for simple social and political justice, such as that which Islam (or any of the great religious traditions) has always demanded for individuals and groups alike. The cries for a new "jihad" of Muslims are aimed much less often outward than inward, much less at foreign "devils" (whatever the rhetoric) and much more at domestic tyrants, corruption, and social and economic injustice. Indeed, perhaps the most international and widely influential of all contemporary Islamic revivalist or reform movements, that of the Tabligh-i Jama'at, is even explicitly apolitical in its tenets; it focuses upon the individual person of faith and looks to convert him or her to true submission (*islam*) rather than lip service: Reform of the world begins with oneself. As for those movements that are avowedly political, be they activist but nonviolent (the majority) or extremist and violent (the minority), they live upon the deep sense of socioeconomic and political injustice that citizens of most Islamic countries (like other third-world countries, for the most part) rightfully feel.

Iran

Iran was ruled from 1925 to 1941 as a monarchy by a former army commander, Reza Khan, who had come to power by military takeover and governed under the old Persian title Shah Reza Pahlavi. He attempted to introduce modernist economic, educational, and governmental reforms (not unlike his contemporary in Turkey, Atatürk (1881–1938), although his reforms were aimed at creating not a parliamentary, popularly based state, but a highly centralized monarchy). By the time Russian and British forces deposed Reza in 1941 and installed his son, Muhammad Reza, as shah, the power of the Shi'ite religious leaders, or *ulama*, had been effectively muted and a rather strong, centralized state established. The son, like his father, sought to ground the legitimacy of Pahlavi rule on the ancient, pre-Islamic imperial dynasties of greater Iran, especially that of the Achaemenids (see Chapter 4). He continued his father's basically secularist state building from the end of World War II until 1978, with one interruption from 1951 to 1953. Those two years saw Muhammad Mosaddeq (1881–1967) come to power through a nationalist revolution, only to be overthrown in a counterrevolution that succeeded through covert American and British support (and thereby made American motives and actions vis-à-vis Iran greatly suspect in the eyes of the Iranian masses and their politicians alike).

In the 1960s Muhammad Reza Shah was finally forced by popular opposition, led by educated elites of the secular left and *ulama* of the religious right, to institute land reform and other Socialist or populist reforms. However, his cavalier attitude toward, and his violent repressive measures against, the leftist and especially the religious opposition alienated the Iranian masses. For all of the modernizing and the military and economic buildup that the Shah initiated, his reign failed to narrow the gap between the wealthy elites and the poor masses. The fact that fully half of Iran's 60-odd million inhabitants are non-Persian-speaking Turks, Kurds, Arabs, and other minorities did little to help him consolidate and strengthen his nationalistic Iranian monarchy.

Finally, in 1978 religious leaders and secularist revolutionaries joined forces to end the Shah's long regime with a revolution fueled by Shi'ite Islamic feeling and symbolism. In 1979 the constitution of a new Islamic republic was adapted under the guidance of the major Shi'ite religious leader, or *ayatollah*, Ruhollah Khomeini (Khumayni; 1902–1989). Subsequent years have seen a protracted war with Iraq (from 1980, halted only in 1988 by a truce agreement) and the institution of repressive and violent measures against enemies of the new regime not unlike those used under the Shah. Still, the new state—with religious leaders exercising a degree of influence over politics not seen since early Safavid times in the sixteenth century—has survived until now. Khomeini and his successor, Hashemi Rafsanjani (b. 1934), however, were not free of nor untainted by politics. They had to struggle to find a new formula for combining Muslim values and norms with twentieth-century *Realpolitik*, and this will continue to be a major challenge for their successors.

In the offices of the first Iranian women's daily newspaper, *Rooznameh Zan*. Despite the reactionary adoption of a conservative dress code for women after the 1978 Iranian revolution, women in Iran today are pursuing a variety of careers and taking an active part in public discourse. This is not to argue that women's equality is being implemented, but only that women will not likely be long suppressed in Iranian society and economy. [Eslami Rad/Liaison Agency, Inc.]

The immediate successor to the moderate Rafsanjani, Mohammad Khatami, was elected in 1997 by a resounding majority in the first real national leadership election since the 1979 revolution. Khatami, a moderate cleric himself as well as former minister of culture with a reputation as a relative liberal among the major figures in Iranian politics, has in his first eighteen months indeed tried to steer Iran on a moderate and more liberal course than even that of Rafsanjani. Many think his election and administration represent a key step in Iran's movement after its watershed revolution toward a more stable government and more internationally engaged and accepted power in the Middle Eastern and Indian Ocean sphere.

Central Asia

North of Iran, 40 million Central Asian Muslims predominate in the broad region that stretches across the south-central reaches of the former USSR between the Crimea and China, and 30 million or more Muslims live in Chinese Central Asia. These people have had to sustain their religious and intellectual traditions in the face of Russian and Chinese cultural, linguistic, and political imperialism. In the 1980s both Soviet and Chinese Muslims appeared to be asserting themselves. The 1979 Soviet invasion and occupation of Afghanistan, whose people have close ties to the Muslim peoples in the Soviet Union, reflected the potential importance of this movement. The phased withdrawal of Soviet forces from Afghanistan in 1988 looked surprisingly like the U.S.

withdrawal from South Vietnam in 1974. It was soon followed by a much more momentous about-face in the form of the collapse of the Soviet Union in 1990 into many separate states, most of which remain loosely connected through the Commonwealth of Independent States (CIS). Founded in 1991, the CIS comprises Russia and eleven former Soviet republics. The three founding members—Russia, Belarus, and Ukraine—were soon joined by the Central Asian republics of Kazakhstan, Kyrgyzstan, Tajikistan, Turkmenistan, and Uzbekistan; by the Transcaucasian republics of Armenia, Azerbaijan, and Georgia; and by Moldova. Suddenly the Central Asian Islamic republics of the former USSR found themselves effectively independent states, yet with little of the infrastructure to manage such a transition peacefully and successfully. The great challenge is whether they and their sister states of the Commonwealth can attain political viability without being destroyed by economic collapse or ethnic or regional conflict first. Islamist reformism will surely play a role in these states, but so can civil-society ideals of democratic governance, free-market approaches to economic recovery, and world support for these emerging independent nations.

South and Southeast Asia

Five major southern and Southeast Asian nations—India, Pakistan, Bangladesh, Indonesia, and Malaysia—that together contain well over half of all Muslims in the world, came into being after World War II. India, a largely Hindu state, and Pakistan, a largely Muslim state, gained independence in 1947 after the British agreed to a partition of the subcontinent. Much of their subsequent history has been one of mutual antagonism. This was born out of the Hindu-Muslim communal violence and the disputes over Kashmir and other areas that accompanied the partition. The tragedy of the massive displacement of Muslims from the new India and of Hindus and Sikhs from the new Pakistan (about 8 million people in each case) was and still is immense for millions of families and individuals. The two states have still not resolved their major differences, including their conflicting claims to Kashmir. Their rivalry has been exacerbated recently by a new round of sabre-rattling, this time a nuclear one begun by five Indian underground nuclear tests carried out in mid-May 1998, which were closely followed by similar Pakistani tests two weeks later.

Indonesia and Malaysia, the two largest states of Southeast Asia, have long histories that link them to the wider Islamic world through Muslim faith and a long history of trading contacts, to Indian culture and religion through historical colonial and trading links, and to China through cultural and trading contact and minorities of Chinese heritage.

Pakistan and Bangladesh

The architect and first president of Pakistan, Muhammad Ali Jinnah (1876–1948), oversaw the creation of a Muslim state comprising the widely separated East and West Pakistan in the two predominantly Muslim areas of northwest India and East Bengal. New constitutions, war with India, religious versus secularist ideological strife, repeated military rule, and consistent return to the ballot box have marked the often baffling pendulum swings of the new nation in its first half century. In 1971 East Pakistan seceded and became the new Islamic nation of Bangladesh. Indian and Bangladeshi relations have been troubled since then. However, the main political division in the subcontinent remains that between India and Pakistan.

Pakistan's groping efforts to create a fully Islamic society and to solve its massive economic problems have been hampered by periodic lapses from constitutional republicanism into dictatorship. Such lapses are usually punctuated by bloodshed and military coups, the most recent being that which brought the military leader, Zia ul-Haqq (1924–1988), to power in 1977. The elections of November 1988, following his death in a suspicious air crash, opened the door to the possible success of parliamentary government rule. The new prime minister, Benazir Bhutto (b. 1953), was the daughter of the man Zia ul-Haqq overthrew and executed. She was also the first female leader of a major Islamic state in this century. Her time in office was cut short by the president's dismissal of her government in August 1990. She returned, however, to the prime ministership in 1993.

Pakistan, like most Asian societies, faces enormous economic and demographic challenges. The Pakistanis must try through their hard-won democratic order to create a modern economic and political system that will meet their physical needs while allowing them to maintain their commitment to remain an identifiably Islamic society. Overpopulation, poverty, and a strong commitment to a massive military are all major obstacles to Pakistan's progress as an independent and self-sufficient nation.

India

Bereft of its spiritual and material father, Mohandas Gandhi (1869–1948), after his assassination in 1948 at the hands of a Hindu fanatic, India has been directed for most of its existence by the leaders of Gandhi's Congress Party. First came Gandhi's follower and nationalist colleague, Jawaharlal Nehru (1889–1964), who developed India's famous theory of political neutrality vis-à-vis world alignments, such as that of the superpowers in the Cold War. Nehru's long leadership carried India through the critical organizational period of early independence and not only Pakistani disputes but also

Jawaharlal Nehru Looks to the Future (1945)

Jawaharlal Nehru wrote The Discovery of India *while he was imprisoned at Ahmadnagar Fort during the latter part of World War II (as he had been several times earlier, for his nationalist activities). The book was an attempt to probe the past and present circumstances of the vast, diverse Indian world. The following excerpt comes late in the book, where he looks ahead. His words show the dilemma and opportunity not only of India but also of many other new nations of the past forty years that have had to face uncertain futures with meager resources and dubious, if powerful and seductive, models among the powerful nations of the modern world.*

In what specific areas has Nehru's vision here of what Indians have to do to move beyond warfare and strife been ignored or realized? What path in politics has India tried to pursue that might be based on Nehru's ideals?

The world of today has achieved much, but for all its declared love for humanity, it has based itself far more on hatred and violence than on the virtues that make man human. War is the negation of truth and humanity. War may be unavoidable sometimes, but its progeny are terrible to contemplate. Not mere killing, for man must die, but the deliberate and persistent propagation of hatred and falsehood, which gradually become the normal habits of the people. It is dangerous and harmful to be guided in our life's course by hatreds and aversions, for they are wasteful of energy and limit and twist the mind and prevent it from perceiving the truth. Unhappily there is hatred in India and strong aversions, for the past pursues us and the present does not differ from it. It is not easy to forget repeated affronts to the dignity of a proud race. Yet, fortunately, Indians do not nourish hatred for long; they recover easily a more benevolent mood.

India will find herself again when freedom opens out new horizons and the future will then fascinate her far more than the immediate past of frustration and humiliation. She will go forward with confidence, rooted in herself and yet eager to learn from others and co-operate with them. Today she swings between a blind adherence to her old customs and a slavish imitation of foreign ways. In neither of these can she find relief or life or growth. It is obvious that she has to come out of her shell and take full part in the life and activities of the modern age. It should be equally obvious that there can be no real cultural or spiritual growth based on imitation. Such imitation can only be confined to a small number who cut themselves off from the masses and the springs of national life. True culture derives its inspiration from every corner of the world, but it is home-grown and has to be based on the wide mass of the people. Art and literature remain lifeless if they are continually thinking of foreign models. The day of a narrow culture confined to a small fastidious group is past. We have to think in terms of the people generally and their culture must be a continuation and development of past trends, and must also represent their new urges and creative tendencies.

From Robert I. Crane, ed., *The Discovery of India.* Copyright © 1959, Doubleday Anchor, pp. 414–415. Reprinted by permission of the Nehru Memorial Fund, New Delhi, India.

a long border dispute and brief Himalayan war with China in 1962. He was able to make some headway with his secularist, reconciliatory policies in reducing the communal hatreds, religious zealotry, and regional tensions of the post-partition era, as well as making some progress in the huge task of economic development of the overpopulated, underdeveloped new nation. His government oversaw the nuts-and-bolts internal work of damping such potentially divisive movements as Sikh religious separatism and of forging a national federation from states divided by religious, cultural, and political history as well as by languages. In this era Hindi and English were set as the national languages, with fourteen major regional languages, each associated with a state, being also recognized for regional official use. Nehru's resolute opposition to caste privilege also helped make a start on improvement of equality of citizenship beyond universal suffrage.

Nehru was succeeded by another Congress leader, Lal Bahadur Shastri (1904–1966), who saw India through a debilitating nine-month war and standoff with Pakistan in 1965. His successor was Nehru's daughter, Indira Gandhi (1917–1984; prime minister, 1966–1977, 1980–1984; no familial relation to Mohandas Gandhi). She carried on most of her father's policies and similarly managed to steer a tricky course of neutralism during the Cold War and its East-West tensions. India's 1971 victory over Pakistan and the subsequent creation of Bangladesh to replace East Pakistan cemented for some years her often shaky political control; this war and the subsequent development, with Russian help, of an atomic bomb confirmed India as the major power in South Asia. The failure of her efforts to reduce national poverty and improve India's general economic health soon overcame her postwar popularity. After her efforts to assume virtual dictatorial power in the face of calls for her resignation, in 1977 she and the

Hindu militants attack a Muslim mosque in Ayodhya, India, December 6, 1992. The razing of this mosque at the hands of a mob led by Hindu communalist extremists touched off a wave of Hindu-Muslim violence in India. The Hindus claimed the mosque, built some five hundred years ago, occupied the site of what had originally been a Hindu temple and sought to have a new temple built once the mosque was cleared away. [Sunil Malhotra/Reuters/Corbis-Bettmann]

Congress Party were ousted by the voters for three years. She was reelected prime minister in an amazing turnaround and served until her resolute efforts to quell Sikh separatism brought about her assassination in 1984 by two Sikhs from her own palace guard.

Indira Gandhi's son, Rajiv Gandhi (1944–1991), was elected prime minister after her, and his handling of the thorny Sikh issue was generally applauded. Indications that he and Prime Minister Bhutto might work together to resolve some of the old India-Pakistan hostilities were also promising. Charges of corruption in his government led to

his party's temporary fall and the Prime Ministership of V. P. Singh (b. 1931), who worked in his brief period of leadership to defuse Hindu-Sikh and Hindu-Muslim communal tensions until his resignation. Although Singh's demise gave Gandhi as leader of the Congress Party a chance in the national and state elections of 1991, he was assassinated in May by a Sri Lankan Tamil suicide bomber during the campaign. Because no party won the subsequent national vote, the leader of the Congress Party, P. V. Narasimha Rao was asked to form a government. He and the Congress have managed since to make substantial economic progress and, despite failures such as the 1992 radical Hindu riot and attack on the Babri Mosque in Ayodhya, to keep the lid generally on a wide variety of communal and separatist problems, from the Sikhs in the Punjab to Muslims in Kashmir and the south, Hindu extremists, and Uttarakhand separatists in the Himalayas.

India's problems remain large. Poverty and disease, including plague outbursts, remain serious problems. Separatist movements based on regional linguistic affinity, such as that of the Tamil peoples of the south, or religious affinity, such as that of the Sikhs of the Punjab, have pulled at the unity of the Indian state. Industrialization and agricultural modernization have recently made great strides, yet the neutralizing force of runaway population growth has yet to be countered enough to ensure a brighter future for India's masses. India's population is now at about 940 million and growing at nearly 2 percent per year. The growing strength of militant Hindu nationalists and fundamentalists and new outbreaks of communal violence between Hindus and India's large Muslim minority pose serious threats to the country's political stability. As the world's largest functioning democracy, India will be an important model of representative government and pluralistic society if it succeeds in staying together and solving or even reducing its harshest problems—overpopulation and mass poverty.

Indonesia and Malaysia

The new East Indies state of Indonesia came into being in 1949 as a nominal republic succeeding the long Dutch and brief Japanese colonial dominions in the East Indies. The much smaller territory of Malaya received its independence from British colonial rule in 1957 as a federation under a rotating monarch; it was later joined by the states of Sarawak and Sabah in northern Borneo, forming the federation of Malaysia. Each of these two new sovereign states faces different challenges.

Indonesia, the largest Muslim country in the world (about 178 million of its estimated 200 million people are Muslim), is trying to achieve a consensus among its disparate and scat-

Map 38–3   Contemporary Central and South America.

tered parts. It must determine how Muslim religious faith is to be reconciled with secularist government. The overriding problem for Malaysia (population 20 million) has been the cleft between the largely Chinese (32 percent) and partly Indian (9 percent) non-Muslim minority on the one hand, and the largely Muslim majority of Malay and other indigenous peoples (59 percent) on the other. Both nations have rich cultural traditions and natural resources; it remains to be seen how each will choose to preserve them while meeting the demands of modern global politics and participation in the global economy. An important part of the future of Islam as a global religious and cultural tradition, as well as the future of these two Asian states, is at stake.

LATIN AMERICA SINCE 1945

During the last half century the nations of Latin America (see Map 38–3) have experienced divergent paths of political and economic change. Their leaders have tried repeatedly to alleviate their people's dependence on the more developed portions of the globe. At best, these efforts have had mixed results; at worst, they have led to political repression and human tragedy.

Before World War II the states of Latin America had been economically dependent on the United States and western Europe. Beginning in the 1950s a shift occurred in those dependent relationships without any significant change in the general situation of dependency. The United States loomed larger than ever; the Soviet Union also for a time came to play a far larger economic and political role. In that respect Latin America, like so many other parts of the world, dwelled in the shadow of the rival superpowers. As happened elsewhere, Latin America became an arena for direct confrontations between the United States and the Soviet Union.

The economic life of the region reflected those new facts of dependence. Various attempts were made to expand the industrial base and the agricultural production of the various national economies. Virtually all the financing came from U.S. and Western European banks or from Soviet subsidies. Enormous debts were contracted to western banks, and these debts made Latin American economies virtual prisoners to the fluctuations of world interest rates and the international banking community. Subsidies and special market arrangements with the Soviet Union made other Latin American nations no less dependent on outside economic forces. These new relationships, however, did not alter the underlying character of the national economies of most Latin American countries, which remain overwhelmingly exporters of agricultural commodities and mineral resources.

The social structures of the Latin American nations have become more complicated since World War II. A culture of poverty continues to be the single most dominant social characteristic of the area. Even periods of economic boom, such as that fostered in Mexico by oil production in the late 1970s, have proved brief and have almost inevitably been followed by decline. Migration into the cities from the countryside has caused tremendous urban overcrowding and slums inhabited by the desperately poor. In many countries the standards of health and of nutrition have fallen. The growth of service industries in the cities has also fostered the emergence of a professional, educated middle class, often possessed of a strong desire to imitate the affluent lifestyle of their social counterparts in the United States and Western Europe. This new professional middle class has displayed little taste for radical politics, major social reform, or revolution. They and the more traditional landed and industrial elites were willing, especially during the 1960s and 1970s, to support military governments pledged to order and the maintenance of the status quo.

Political events in Latin America led to the establishment of authoritarian governments of both the left and the right and to a retreat from the ideal and model of parliamentary democracy. Only Mexico, Colombia, Venezuela, and Costa Rica remained parliamentary states throughout this period. Elsewhere, two paths of political development were followed. In Cuba and Nicaragua, and for a short time in Chile, revolutionary Socialist governments with close ties to the Soviet Union were established. Elsewhere, often in response to the fear of revolution or Communist activity, military governments held power for long periods, sometimes punctuated with brief interludes of civilian rule. Such were the situations in Chile, Brazil, Argentina, Bolivia, Peru, and Uruguay. Governments of both the left and the right engaged in political repression, suspending civil liberties, and arresting political enemies.

These political changes fostered new roles for two traditional Latin American institutions: the military and the Roman Catholic church. The armies of the various nations have played key political roles since the Wars of Independence. But lately they have frequently assumed the direct government of nations rather than using indirect influence. In the clash between the forces of social revolution and reaction, many Roman Catholic priests and bishops have protested social and economic inequalities and attacked the repression of opposition political forces. Certain Roman Catholic theologians have combined traditional Christian ideas of concern for the poor with Marxist ideology to formulate what has come to be known as a liberation theology. Generally speaking, this Latin American theological initiative has been attacked by the Vatican.

During the last decade and a half Latin America has changed significantly. Several nations, including Argentina, Chile, and Brazil, like the rest of the world, have moved toward democratization. Furthermore, there is a strong tendency throughout the continent to allow private markets to address economic issues. This marks a sharp departure from the policies pursued during the 1930s and 1940s, when the state itself was seen as largely responsible for economic development. Yet these changes remain tenuous, and in most nations the military keeps a watchful eye on democratic developments and remains apprehensive about possible disorder. The end of the Cold War will bring to a close one source of external political challenge, but the internal social problems of these nations will continue to raise major difficulties for their governments. Several nations have faced a new difficulty in the post-Cold War era as powerful drug-producing cartels have actually challenged the authority of governments themselves.

Revolutionary Challenges

There were three major attempts among the nations of Latin America to establish genuinely revolutionary governments pursuing major social and economic change. They occurred in Cuba in 1959, in Chile in 1970, and in Nicaragua in 1979. Each involved some form of Marxist political organization,

Fidel Castro, waving to cheering crowds acknowledging his triumph over the Batista regime on January 1, 1959.
[UPI/Corbis-Bettmann]

and in each a revolutionary government pursued a close relationship with the Soviet Union. All three had immense symbolic importance not only in Latin America, but also anywhere the colonial influence of Europeans and the economic dominance of the United States once prevailed. The establishment of these governments provoked active resistance and intervention by the United States. It also encouraged opposition to social and political change by traditional elites throughout Latin America.

The Cuban Revolution

Cuba had remained a colony of Spain until the Spanish-American War of 1898. Thereafter, it achieved independence within a sphere of U.S. influence, which took the form of economic domination and occasional military intervention. The fluctuating governments of the island had been both ineffective and corrupt. During the 1950s Fulgencio Batista (1901–1973), a dictator supported by the U.S. government, ruled Cuba.

Historically, Cuba had been politically restive. During the 1940s university student groups led antigovernment agitation. Among the students thus politicized in those years was Fidel Castro Ruz (b. 1926), the son of a wealthy landowner. On July 26, 1953, he and others attacked a government army barracks. The revolutionary movement that he thereafter

came to lead in exile took its name from that date: the Twenty-Sixth of July Movement. In 1956 Castro and a handful of followers set sail on a yacht from Mexico and landed in Cuba. They took refuge in the Sierra Maestra mountains, from which they organized guerrilla attacks on Batista's government and supporters. By late 1958 Castro's forces were positioned to topple Batista, who fled Cuba on New Year's Day in 1959. By the middle of January, Castro had arrived in Havana as the revolutionary victor.

Castro undertook the most extensive political, economic, and social reconstruction seen in recent Latin American history. He rejected parliamentary democracy and chose to govern Cuba in an authoritarian manner. For approximately the first decade of the revolution he ruled in a personal manner; by the early 1970s, although Castro continued to dominate, executive power was vested in a council. The revolutionary government carried out major land redistribution. In some cases, groups of relatively small landowners were established. On other parts of the island, large state farms became the model.

Perhaps most interesting, the Cuban Revolution spurned an industrial economic model and concentrated on improving the agricultural sector. There was an attempt to turn toward more mixed agriculture, but in the end the production of sugar assumed its traditionally leading role, and the Cuban economy remained monocultural. Throughout the

Castro Asserts the Necessary Marxist Character of Revolution

In a speech delivered at the University of Havana in 1967, Fidel Castro discussed the relationship of Cuban revolutionaries in the wider Marxist ideology. He asserted that the revolutionary struggle itself led to embracing a strict Marxism. He rejected cooperation with groups that sought reform rather than revolution, even if they called themselves Communist. At the same time he opened the way for accepting into the revolutionary movement those who had finally come to accept Marxism, although that political outlook had not been their original position.

How does Castro's view of revolution echo that of earlier twentieth-century Russian Marxists? Why does he argue that a desire for revolution must necessarily lead to Marxism? What are the anti-democratic elements in his argument?

Anyone can give himself the name of "eagle" without having a single feather on his back. In the same way, there are people who call themselves communists without having a communist hair on their heads. The international communist movement, to our way of thinking, is not a church. It is not a religious sect or a Masonic lodge that obliges us to hallow any weakness, any deviation; that obliges us to follow a policy of a mutual admiration with all kinds of reformists and pseudo-revolutionaries.

Our stand regarding communist parties will be based on strictly revolutionary principles. The parties that have a line without hesitations and capitulationism, the parties that in our opinion have a consistent revolutionary line, will receive our support in all circumstances; but the parties that entrench themselves behind the name of communists or Marxists and believe themselves to have a monopoly on revolutionary sentiment—what they really monopolize is reformism—will not be treated by us as revolutionary parties. . . . For every true revolutionary, who bears within him the revolutionary spirit, revolutionary vocation, will always come to Marxism! It is impossible for a man, traveling the road of revolution, not to arrive at Marxism! And every revolutionary on the continent who is deserving of the name will arrive at the Marxist conception of society! What is important are the revolutionaries, those who are capable of making revolution and developing themselves in revolutionary theory.

Many times practice comes first and then theory. Our people too, are an example of that. Many, the immense majority of those who today proudly call themselves Marxist-Leninists, arrived at Marxism-Leninism by way of the revolutionary struggle. To exclude, to deny, to reject a priori all those who from the beginning did not call themselves communists is an act of dogmatism and unqualified sectarianism. Whoever denies that it is the road of revolution which leads the people to Marxism is no Marxist, although he may call himself a communist.

From Martin Kenner and James Petras, *Fidel Castro Speaks*. Copyright © 1969 Grove Press, p. 131.

1960s there was a concerted effort to expand sugar production. The results were disappointing, because too much was attempted too quickly by people who had had too little direct experience in raising and processing sugar cane. Even after the sugar industry became somewhat more stabilized during the 1970s, it continued to depend on large Soviet subsidies and on the Soviet-bloc nations for its market. In that respect, the Cuban economy did not escape the cycle of external dependence.

In foreign affairs, the Cuban Revolution was characterized by a sharp break with the United States and a close relationship with the Soviet Union. Shortly after achieving power, Castro aligned himself with the Cuban Communist Party and thereafter with the Soviet bloc. The United States, under both Republican and Democratic administrations, was hostile toward Castro and toward the presence of a Communist state less than a hundred miles from the Florida mainland. In 1961 the United States and Cuban exiles launched the unsuccessful Bay of Pigs invasion. The close Cuban relationship to the Soviet Union prepared the ground for the missile crisis of 1962, which is generally regarded as the most dangerous incident of the entire Cold War. Thereafter followed about a decade of cool relations between Cuba and the United States without overt hostility. During the late 1970s and the 1980s a dialogue of sorts was undertaken between Cuba and the United States, but formal diplomatic relations have not resumed. Mutual distrust continues.

With the collapse of the Soviet Union and the end of the Cold War, the future of Castro's Cuba has become uncertain. Cuba remains the only state closely associated with the former Soviet bloc that has not experienced substantial political or economic reform. The subsidies that flowed from the Soviet Union to support the Cuban economy, however, are no longer available, creating a shortage of everyday consumer goods. The Marxist political and economic ideology stands discredited throughout the world, but the aging Castro's leadership appears to remain intact, at least for the moment. Cuba must soon confront the need for new political leadership or a successor to Castro. It also must confront the need for economic reform and find a new role for itself in a Latin American order in which the issues of the Cold War are no longer relevant. One hint of the perception of the need for a new direction came in 1998 when the Castro government permitted a highly publicized visit from Pope John Paul II and allowed the public celebration of mass.

Throughout the Cold War, Cuba assumed an importance far greater than its size might suggest. After 1959 it served as a center for the export of Communist revolution throughout Latin America and, after it sent troops to Angola in the late 1970s, in Africa as well. A key policy of the U.S. government, pursued with differing intensities and strategies under different administrations, was to prevent the establishment of a second Cuba or Communist-dominated state in Latin America. That goal led to direct and indirect intervention in other revolutionary situations and to support for authoritarian governments in Latin America that were dedicated to resistance to Marxist revolution.

Chile

Until the 1970s Chile was the single most enduring model of parliamentary democracy in Latin America. It had experienced political turmoil and governments of the left and the right, but its parliamentary structures had remained in place. During the 1960s, however, as economic life became more difficult and class relationships deteriorated, Chilean politics likewise became polarized. Unemployment rose alarmingly. There was much labor unrest and profound popular resentment of the economic domination of Chile by large U.S. corporations.

The situation came to a head in 1970 when Salvador Allende (1908–1973), the candidate of the left-wing political coalition and a Marxist, was elected president with a plurality of the votes. His coalition did not control the Chilean congress, nor did it have the support of the military. For a few months the center and right-wing political groups took a watch-and-wait attitude. Allende nationalized some businesses. Other policies, related to land redistribution, wage improvement, and resistance to foreign economic influence, were blocked in the congress, and Allende had to govern by decree. By this latter device he began to expropriate foreign property, much of which belonged to U.S. corporations. This policy frightened the Chilean owners of small and medium-sized businesses. Workers were dissatisfied with the relatively small extent of socialization touching their daily lives. Inflation ballooned. Despite the expropriation of large estates and the reorganization of agriculture, harvests were poor.

In the autumn of 1973 Allende found himself governing a nation in turmoil without significant domestic political support and with many foreign enemies. He proved unwilling to make significant political compromises or to change the general course of his policies. In the wake of strikes and disorder, the army became hostile. The government of the United States was deeply disturbed by the Allende experiment and by the prospect of a Marxist nation on the western coast of South America. The Nixon administration actively supported the discontent within the Chilean army. In mid-September 1973 an army coup overthrew Allende, who was killed in the presidential palace. Chile's short-lived experiment in Marxist socialism ended.

Thereafter, for fifteen years Chile was governed by a military junta, whose most important member, General Augusto Pinochet (b. 1915), served as president. The military government pursued a close relationship with the United States and a policy of strong resistance to Marxism in the hemisphere. The junta followed a policy of state-directed free-market economy. The expropriations of the Allende years were reversed. After a brief period of economic improvement, inflation and unemployment resumed. The rule of the Chilean military was marked by harsh political repression.

In a referendum held in late 1988 Chileans rejected Pinochet's bid for another term as president. Democratization was relatively smooth. The return to civilian rule has brought to the fore efforts supported by the new government to investigate the political repression of the Pinochet years. Thousands of cases of torture and murder have been revealed. The Chilean government itself moved very slowly not wishing to revisit the most controversial era of the nation's history. In 1999, while in Great Britain for a medical consultation, General Pinochet was placed under arrest when the government of Spain sought to extradite him to that country to stand trial. The resolution of that case remained unresolved as this book went to press.

The Sandinista Revolution in Nicaragua

In the summer of 1979 a Marxist guerrilla force, the Sandinistas, overthrew the corrupt dictatorship of the Somoza family in Nicaragua. The Somozas had governed Nicaragua more or less as their own personal preserve since the 1930s with moderate, but rarely enthusiastic, support from the United States. The Sandinistas established a collective government that pursued social and economic reform and reconstruction. The movement—with Roman Catholic priests on its leadership council—epitomized the new political and social forces in Latin America. The exact direction of the revolutionary government remained unclear because it confronted significant domestic political opposition and direct military challenge from the contra guerrilla movement.

The government of the United States, particularly under the Reagan administration (1981–1989), was strongly hostile toward the Sandinistas. It provided both direct and indirect aid to the opposition guerrilla movement and repeatedly criticized the revolutionary government. The U.S. government feared the spread of Marxist revolutionary activity in Central America, a fear reinforced by the close ties between the revolutionary government and the Soviet Union. For the United States, the Sandinista government represented in Central America a problem analogous to that of Cuba a generation earlier.

The rule of the Sandinistas came to a relatively quick end. In early 1990, after a negotiated peace settlement with the contras, they lost the presidential election to an opposition coalition that also captured control of the National Assembly. A floundering economy and U.S. aid had contributed to the electoral victory. There was also much weariness with the civil war that had shaken the country for a decade. The Sandinistas relinquished power peacefully. Considerable political and economic turmoil arose during the transition, but the general direction toward a restoration of a democratic government supported by the United States did not change.

Pursuit of Stability
Under the Threat of Revolution

Argentina

In 1955 the Argentine army revolted against the excesses and corruption of the Perón dictatorship, and Juan Perón (1895–1974) went into exile. Two decades of economic stagnation and social unrest followed. Neither the army nor the civilian political leaders could forge the kind of political coalition involving the working class that Perón had created. Nor could any of the post-Perón governments cope with unemployment and inflation. In 1973 Perón was recalled from exile in a desperate attempt to restore the fragile stability of a generation earlier. He died about a year later.

By 1976 the army had undertaken direct rule. There was widespread repression; thousands of citizens simply disappeared, never to be heard of again. The leading army officers played something like a game of musical chairs as they moved in and out of an ever-changing ruling junta. In April 1982 General Leopoldo Galtieri (b. 1926), in an effort to score a political success, launched a disastrous invasion of the Islas Malvinas (Falkland Islands). Argentina was decisively defeated by Britain, and the military junta was thoroughly discredited.

In 1983 civilian rule was restored, and Argentina set out on the road to democratization. The major political figure responsible for this achievement was President Raul Alfonsín (b. 1927). Under his leadership, many of the former military figures responsible for the years of repression received prison sentences. Civilian courts took over the role formerly assigned to military tribunals. Alfonsín also sought to turn more real political authority over to the Argentine congress. In all respects

Argentina has provided the most extensive example in Latin America of the restoration of democratic practices after military rule. Peaceful elections and transitions of governments have occurred for over a decade.

The Argentine government easily survived a brief attempted military coup in 1990. The major difficulties it currently confronts are economic. There has been considerable labor discontent. The government has been pursuing a policy of privatization of businesses and industries, such as telephone communications, formerly owned by the government. It has thus attempted to encourage the investment of foreign capital to sustain economic growth and has also confronted an ongoing struggle to contain inflation.

Brazil

In 1964 the military assumed the direct government of Brazil and did not fully relinquish it until the mid-1980s. The military government stressed order and used repression to maintain it. The army itself, however, was divided about the wisdom of the military's move into the political realm. Many officers were concerned that the corruption of everyday politics would touch the army, undermine its reputation, and sap its esprit de corps. They also feared that the popularity of and respect for the army would come to depend on its success in the political arena. Consequently, within the army itself, certain forces sought to restore a more nearly normal or democratic government. In 1985 civilian government returned under the military's watchful eye.

The military government fostered denationalized industrial development. Non-Brazilian corporations were invited to spearhead the drive toward industrialization. In this respect Brazil opted for an industrial model, but an industrialism guided and dominated from the outside. One result was the accumulation of a massive foreign debt, the servicing and repayment of which have become perhaps Brazil's most important national problem. The relative success of the government's industrialization policy also made Brazil the major industrialized nation in Latin America. The great question now is how the social changes wrought by industrialism, such as growing urbanization, will be able to receive political accommodation. In Brazil, as in Argentina, the economic and social pressures of the society have spawned conditions ripe for political agitation. It was just that possibility that led so many citizens within both the traditional and the new professional elites to support authoritarian government in the past.

The civilian government of President Fernando Collor de Mello that came to office in 1990, like numerous other governments in the region, advocated privatization. He and his advisers favored allowing market forces to stimulate growth. They also attempted to contain inflation. During 1992, however, President Collor was impeached by the Brazilian Sen-

Lourdes Arizpe Discusses the Silence of Peasant Women

Lourdes Arizpe, a Mexican anthropologist, wrote extensively on the plight of peasant women in the 1970s. In this passage she discusses how the lives and history of Mexican peasant women are shrouded in silence. Though her remarks are directed toward the situation in Mexico, they may well apply to peasant women in other cultures as well.

What are the factors that Arizpe cites as leading to the historical silence of peasant women? Why does she believe it is important for such women to learn to speak with their own voices? How do the stereotypes of Mexican peasant women both contribute to the silence and arise from the silence? Why does she believe peasant women to be the most marginalized of all women?

History has imposed a greater silence on peasant women than on any other social group. Perhaps it is the solitude of the plains or the obligatory circumspection of their gender or merely political repression, but circumstances combine to force them to live in a secret world. Doubtless there are those who would assert that their tie to nature leads them to express themselves with actions rather than words. But the male peasant lives in the natural world without being silenced.

Silence, when not deliberate (although, how can we be sure it isn't?) could be anger or wisdom or, simply, a gesture of dignity. When there is no one worth talking to, I stay silent. If someone doesn't want to recognize my existence, I stay silent. In the spectrum of invisibility that history has imposed on women, perhaps the most invisible of the invisibles have been the peasants.

When direct expression is not permitted, the possibility of knowledge is lost and we fill that disturbing vacuum with phantoms. It is therefore not surprising that the Mexican mentality is filled with myths and stereotypes about peasant women. There is the submissive Indian woman who is a product of condescending maternalism; the wild woman both fantasized about and feared by men; the brazen hussy of melodramatic soap operas; the faint-hearted but treacherous small-town woman invented by the urban mind. Silence is also created by everyone's desire to hear what they want to hear rather than listen to what women are trying to say.

Today it seems that everyone mouths concerns about peasant women without any sincere interest.

. . . What is important today is to create opportunities for peasant women to speak.

It is not that they have never spoken, only that their words have never been recognized. Because their words are discomforting when they denounce exploitation; disturbing when they display a deep understanding of the natural world not shared by their city sisters; strange when they describe an integrating vision of the universe; and because, being women's words, they are not important to androcentric [male-centered] history. Of all the marginalized peoples, peasant women are the most marginalized.

From Lourdes Arizpe, "Peasant Women and Silence," translated by Laura Beard Milroy in *Women's Writing in Latin America: An Anthology* by Sara Castro-Klarén, Sylvia Malloy, and Beatriz Sarlo. Copyright © 1992 by Westview Press. Reprinted by permission of Westview Press.

---

ate on charges of corruption and using his office to enrich himself. In 1995 Fernando Henrique Cardoso strongly won the presidency and pursued economic policies led by technocrats in hopes of achieving economic growth along with democratic stability.

Mexico

Institutionally, Mexico has undergone relatively few political changes since World War II. In theory at least, the government continued to pursue the goals of the revolution. Power remained firmly in the control of the Partido Revolucionario Institucional (PRI), which until the late 1980s had maintained the appearance of stability.

Yet shifts had occurred under this apparently stable surface. The government retreated from some of the aims of the revolution and appeared conservative when compared to the

Marxist states of the third quarter of this century. In the early 1950s certain large landowners were exempted from the expropriation and redistribution of land. The Mexican government maintained open relations with Cuba and the other revolutionary regimes of Latin America but also resisted any intrusion of Marxist doctrines into Mexico. When necessary, it arrested political malcontents.

Mexico experienced an oil boom from 1977 to 1983. Oil revenues brought immense new wealth into the nation, but the world oil glut burst that bubble. The aftermath revealed the absence of any policy of stable growth. Like so many other states in the region, Mexico amassed large foreign debts and, in doing so, surrendered real economic independence.

In 1988 the PRI encountered a major challenge at the polls. Opposition candidates received much of the vote in a hotly contested election. Whether the election results were honestly reported may never be known. The PRI remained

An uprising by armed rebels in the state of Chiapas was one of many political and economic shocks that rocked Mexico in 1995. [Sestini Agency/Liaison Agency, Inc.]

in power but with the knowledge that it would not be able to dominate the political scene in the manner it had for over half a century. Thereafter, the internal leadership of the party began to move in important new directions that would lead to greater decentralization in the governing of the party. The newly elected president, Carlos Salinas, moved rapidly to privatize economic enterprise. He also favored free-trade agreements. The most important of these was the North American Free Trade Agreement (NAFTA), which created a vast free-trade area including Mexico, Canada, and the United States. Under Salinas's policies the economic growth rate of Mexico became the best it had been in ten years. In 1991 Salinas moved to make new accommodations for the Roman Catholic church, thus moving away from the traditional anticlericalism that had characterized Mexican politics. By 1991 the PRI appeared to have regained its former political ascendancy, but with the understanding that it would need to remain less centralized and more open to internal debate.

However, the situation was largely one of appearances. In 1994 Mexico underwent political shocks. Its government had to call out troops to quell armed rebellion in Chiapas. During the election of that year the leading candidate was assassinated and party members were openly charged with complicity in the deed. Party corruption received increased publicity. Early in 1995 Mexico suffered a major economic downturn, and the peso was sharply devalued. Only loans from the United States saved the economy. Ernesto Zedillo, elected president in 1994, blamed Salinas and his family for the situation, and Salinas went into exile abroad. Thereafter very considerable corruption associated with the Salinas government became public. Mexico itself entered a period of political uncertainty and economic austerity. The government faced the possibility of further unrest in Chiapas, the reality of growing power among drug lords, and the prospect of continuing turmoil within the governing party itself.

Continuity and Change in Recent Latin American History

What is most striking about the history of the past four decades in Latin America is its tragic continuity with the region's previous history. Revolution has brought moderate social change but at the price of authoritarian government, economic stagnation, and dependence on different foreign powers. Real independence has not been achieved. Throughout the region for much of the period, parliamentary democracy has been at best fragile; it appears to have been the first element of national life to be sacrificed to the conflicting goals of socialism, economic growth, or resistance to revolution.

The recent trends toward democratization and market economics may, however, mark a break in that pattern. The region might well enjoy healthy economic growth if inflation can be contained and investment fostered. The challenge—difficult both politically and economically—will be to see that the fruits of any new prosperity are shared in a way that prevents new political resentment and turmoil. Furthermore, as in the past, economic turmoil far from Latin America may have an adverse impact on its destiny. Each time such turmoil has occurred, the governments of Latin America, like the current government of Mexico, have found themselves economically dependent upon either the United States or European governments and bankers. The international economic crisis of the late 1990s which commenced in Asia will, if anything, worsen that situation for the entire continent.

IN WORLD PERSPECTIVE

The Emerging Nations: Opportunities and Frustrations of Global Democratization

The past quarter century has witnessed a remarkable political phenomenon throughout the world. On one continent after another, democratic political rights have expanded. Authoritarian political regimes of both the left and the right have undergone internal reform or collapsed. Dictatorships, military governments, and one-party Communist states have fallen, to be replaced by more nearly democratic governments. Progress has not been uniform by any means, but more and more people everywhere have developed aspirations to have a voice in their governments.

This process of political change, usually termed *democratization*, involves the expansion of the numbers of people who participate in the selection of executive leaders and legislative representatives, the orderly change in or confirmation of leadership through elections, the participation of a wider spectrum of citizens in the political processes, and a lessening of the extent of governmental control over the daily lives of citizens. The movement has also tended to involve a shift from regulated to free market economies. Despite many continuing autocracies, at no time in history have so many nations around the world seen such an extension of democratic government.

Initially many believed that democratization would almost necessarily lead to liberal governments. However, in many of the nations, especially those of Eastern Europe, the frustrations and economic hardships of the move from centrally planned to market economies have seen the return to political office of former Communists who long opposed democracy. Resurgent nationalism has also come to the fore.

Voting at a Buenos Aires school during recent presidential elections in Argentina, which returned to democratic civilian rule in 1983 after years of repressive military dictatorship. [Gary Payne/Liaison Agency, Inc.]

The developments of the past two decades must be seen against the backdrop of democratic achievements that followed World War II. The Atlantic Charter drawn up by the United States and Great Britain in 1942 asserted a democratic vision of the postwar world that was first realized among the defeated nations. The three major Axis powers, Germany, Italy, and Japan, had possessed dictatorial governments, but after the war the victorious Allies imposed democracy on them. All three nations soon became among the most stable democracies in the world.

Elsewhere, the years immediately following World War II were less hopeful. Eastern Europe fell under the political and military domination of the Soviet Union. In Yugoslavia, Marshall Tito's more or less independent Communist government resisted Stalin but was still authoritarian. On the Iberian peninsula the older dictatorships of Antonio Salazar (1889–1970) and General Francisco Franco (1892–1975) continued to hold sway. In 1967 Greece fell under military rule. In the Middle East, authoritarian rule has been the norm in the wake of colonial withdrawal.

From the late 1940s through the 1970s Latin America was studded with dictatorial regimes, usually, although not always, dominated by the military. There were exceptions to this rule. Costa Rica, for example, had a successful democracy, but generally in Latin America the drift was toward repressive government. In Cuba a Communist dictatorship governed after 1957. One of the ongoing justifications of these Latin American authoritarian regimes was the necessity to oppose Communist insurrections sponsored from Cuba. Similar appeals had long been used by Salazar in Portugal and Franco in Spain.

In South Africa the policy of apartheid, which was imposed formally in the 1940s, established a racially divided society in which a white minority held virtually all effective political and social power. Black South Africans enjoyed no effective political rights.

Decolonization, which saw the withdrawal of European powers from their colonial empires, also generally failed to fulfill early democratic expectations. India, after the withdrawal of the British authority in 1947, became the largest democracy on earth. But in sub-Saharan Africa during the late 1950s and 1960s former European colonies generally declined into dictatorships. Across northern postcolonial Africa authoritarian governments arose whose power often resided in the military or in the use of referenda to confirm authoritarian power. In the former French colonies of Southeast Asia stable democratic governments failed to establish themselves, and in North Vietnam a Communist government prevailed. But the early democratic vision of the postcolonial world remained as a kind of ideal toward which groups opposing the authoritarian governments could point.

As a result of these developments, some observers believed that the rest of the century might see only a few functioning democracies survive. Democracy appeared secure in North America above the Mexican border, in Western Europe, Japan, Israel, and a few other isolated nations. The rest of the world seemed condemned to authoritarianism either of military dictatorship or of one-party government.

The political pessimists were proved wrong, not in a single case but around the globe. The movement toward an expansion of political participation that culminated in two decades of steady democratization commenced during the mid-1960s. The civil-rights movement in the United States fostered a new role for African Americans. The Civil Rights Act of 1964 allowed them entry into areas of social life that had been closed to them since before the turn of the century. Even more important, the Voting Rights Act of 1965 permitted new participation of African-American voters in many southern states where their activity had been effectively barred. Thereafter the number of African-American elected officials grew in the South and soon throughout the entire nation.

The next area that witnessed major movement toward democratization was the Mediterranean. Four years after Salazar's death in 1970 an army revolt led to the beginning of a democratic movement that soon brought free elections. General Franco's Fascist regime was followed, as he had decreed, by a monarchy. The new king, Juan Carlos (b. 1938), understood that Spain could achieve a new political and economic status in Europe and domestic and political stability only if it moved toward democratic government. His determination to bring democratic government to Spain made his succession stable and lasting. A functioning multiparty system quickly developed.

In some cases unsuccessful military ventures opened the way to democratic government. Portugal under Salazar, in an attempt to retain colonial rule, had long been involved in an unwinnable war in Angola, undermining any enthusiasm for his government. In 1974 the Greek military government collapsed after an unsuccessful confrontation with Turkey over the future of Cyprus. Another important factor turning these nations toward democracy was that the European Economic Community restricted membership to democracies. Any European nation hoping for ongoing prosperity had to participate in it.

The first breakthrough toward democracy in Latin America occurred in Brazil, where the military allowed elections for the presidency in 1985. Argentina elected a civilian president in 1983; Chile followed in 1990.

Elsewhere in Latin America the tide of democracy has also continued to rise. Dictatorships and one-party governments, including the Sandinista government in Nicaragua, have generally given way to democratic governments, although the long-term stability of some of them is uncertain.

Worldwide communications technology has often contributed to democratization. Today it is simply more difficult for repressive governments to hide their repression or to prevent opponents from communicating with the outside world through radio, television, and fax machines. In Asia the eighties saw an expansion of democracy in South Korea and the Philippines. In South Africa the repressive apartheid regime was dismantled in the early 1990s.

Despite democratization elsewhere, it was generally assumed that the authoritarian governments of Eastern Europe and the Soviet Union would survive indefinitely. For that reason the events of the 1980s and early 1990s in that region of the world were all the more astounding. During 1989 all of the Communist party regimes in Eastern Europe collapsed with amazing rapidity. The Soviet Union itself dissolved in 1991. Democratic governments embracing free-market policies emerged in place of single-party governments and planned economies in all these states.

Yet the new governments of Eastern Europe and the former Soviet Union face constant antidemocratic pressures. There are the former Communists who constitute the largest group with political experience. There are ethnic nationalists who feel Russia has been displaced as a great power. The role of the military is uncertain. Throughout Eastern Europe and the former Soviet Union the specter of antisemitism has again appeared. There thus exists the danger both that these nondemocratic forces may display new strength and that in order to fend them off the democratic governments will resort to repressive measures.

The civil war in the former Yugoslavia displays the extreme forms of violence and disorder that may arise when an authoritarian regime collapses. There the forces of ethnic nationalism have led to civil war, civilian atrocities, deprivation, and thoroughly nondemocratic government. One of the many dangers of that conflict is that it could lead to similar disorder elsewhere in Europe.

Not only in Eastern Europe and the former Soviet Union does the drive toward greater democracy throughout the world remain both incomplete and uncertain. Communist dictatorships remain in power in Cuba, North Korea, and Vietnam. The People's Republic of China, still dominated by the Chinese Communist Party, repressed a drive toward democracy in 1989 with a massacre of protesters in Tienanmen Square. In Iraq, Iran, Saudi Arabia, and other parts of the Middle East, repressive governments still prevail. In much of Africa the early attempts at democracy have given way to dictatorship.

In the new democracies, the extent of democracy differs from nation to nation. Impatient voters or military leaders may turn to older authoritarian structures. Yet more opportunities now exist for the emergence of democratic governments around the globe than at any time in world history.

Review Questions

1. What factors contributed to the spread of decolonization in sub-Saharan Africa? Why were the newly independent states so fragile? Has postcolonial Nigeria lived up to its potential? Why is Nigeria's record significant for Africa as a whole?

2. Describe the apartheid regime in South Africa. Why was it dismantled in the 1990s? What problems does the new South Africa face?

3. Describe the creation of the State of Israel. What has been the response of the Arab nations of the Middle East? What is the current state of Arab-Israeli relations?

4. How has Muslim fundamentalism affected the various Muslim nations? Is Muslim fundamentalism a monolithic movement?

5. Are the nations of Latin America still economically dependent on the United States and Western Europe? Why is this so? How did the superpower rivalry of the Cold War affect Latin America?

6. How successful has the worldwide trend toward democratization been in Latin America? Describe the transition from military rule to civilian democracy in Brazil, Argentina, and Chile. Has Mexico made a similar transition?

Suggested Readings

Africa

A. BOYD, *An Atlas of World Affairs*, 9th ed. (1991). A simple and brief, but useful, quick reference book on the current shape of world nations, alliances, and major political issues. Especially useful for keeping up with the changing political units of contemporary Africa.

B. DAVIDSON, *Let Freedom Come* (1978). A broad-ranging study of modern Africa, using incisive specific examples to support thoughtful analyses of trends and events across the continent since the nineteenth century.

B. FREUND, *The Making of Contemporary Africa: The Development of African Society Since 1800* (1984). The final three chapters give excellent treatment of decolonization after 1940, tropical Africa since independence, and southern Africa into the 1980s.

R. W. July, *A History of the African People*, 3rd ed. (1980). Chapters 14–22. The last part of the book provides a careful and clear survey of post-World War I history, including chapters on the various regions of the continent and on topics like nationalism.

A. J. H. Latham, *Africa, Asia, and South America since 1800: A Bibliographic Guide* (1995). A valuable tool for finding materials on the topics in this chapter.

R. Oliver, *The African Experience* (1991). The closing chapters give a thoughtful and probing overview of postcolonial Africa.

C. M. Turnbull, *The Lonely African* (1962). A haunting and vivid series of case studies of post-World War II Africans caught in the upheavals of modernization and rapid change.

India and Pakistan

W. T. de Bary et al., eds., *Sources of Indian Tradition*, 2nd ed. (1988). The final chapters offer selections from major modern Indian political and literary figures, accompanied by solid introductions.

N. Maxwell, *India's China War* (1970). A fascinating, detailed study of the Sino-Indian border war of the early 1960s. It is illuminating especially about the intricacies of Indian politics of the time.

D. E. Smith, *India as a Secular State* (1963). Still pertinent today for the vexed question in South Asia of how to deal with secularism and religion in the political arena.

F. Robinson, ed., *The Cambridge Encyclopedia of India, Pakistan, Bangladesh, Sri Lanka, Nepal, Bhutan, and the Maldives* (1989). A sweeping and detailed reference source for the South Asian world to 1988.

S. Wolpert, *A New History of India*, 3rd ed. (1988). The closing chapters of this fine survey history are particularly helpful in orienting the reader in postwar Indian history until the mid-1980s.

Islam and the Middle East

J. J. Donohue and J. L. Esposito, eds., *Islam in Transition: Muslim Perspectives* (1982). Selections from Muslim writers, including many since World War II, on issues of social, political, and religious change in the Islamic world.

J. Esposito, *The Islamic Threat: Myth or Reality* (2nd ed., 1992). A useful corrective to some of the polemics against Islam and Muslims today.

N. R. Keddie, *Roots of Revolution: An Interpretive History of Modern Iran* (1981). Chapters 6–9 focus on Iran from 1941 through the first years of the 1978 revolution and provide a solid overview of history in this era.

T. Mostyn and A. Hourani, eds., *The Cambridge History of the Middle East and North Africa* (1988). A detailed reference source on the entire region to the mid-1980s.

H. Munson, Jr., *Islam and Revolution in the Middle East* (1988). Based on numerous specific studies of recent years, this little book offers a good general picture, especially for students, of the historical and ideological background of contemporary Islamic religion-political movements and on the Iranian revolution in particular.

P. Sluglett and M. Faroule-Sluglett, eds. *Tuttle Guide to the Middle East* (1992). A superb handbook arranged by country, with useful appendices.

W. C. Smith, *Islam in Modern History* (1957). Old, but still the most thoughtful and comprehensive treatment of issues facing Muslim peoples from the Arab world to India.

J. O. Voll, *Islam: Continuity and Change in the Modern World* (1982). Chapters 5–8. A brief yet detailed survey of trends and major events in recent Islamic history from Indonesia to Africa.

Latin America

S. De Vylder, *Allende's Chile* (1976). A sound introduction to a difficult and controversial subject.

J. Dominguez, *Cuba: Order and Revolution* (1978). A useful overview. Essential for understanding the background of the present tensions in the area.

C. Fuentes, *A New Time for Mexico* (1996). A commentary by an influential contemporary writer.

R. Kagan, *A Twilight Struggle: American Power and Nicaragua, 1977–1990* (1996). A major discussion.

W. Lafeber, *The Panama Canal: The Crisis in Historical Perspective* (1981). An important and far-ranging consideration of United States policy in Latin America.

P. Lowden, *Moral Opposition to Authoritarian Rule in Chile* (1996). A discussion of Chilean politics from the standpoint of human rights.

S. D. Morris, *Political Reformers in Mexico: An Overview of Contemporary Mexican Politics* (1995). An examination of a rapidly changing scene.

L. H. Oppenheim, *Politics in Chile: Democracy, Authoritarianism, and the Search for Development* (1993). Examines the controversial course of Chilean politics during the last quarter century.

A. Stepan, *The Breakdown of Democratic Regimes* (1978). An overview of the collapse of Latin American democracies in the third quarter of the twentieth century.

D. KL. Van Cott, ed., *Indigenous People and Democracy in Latin America* (1994). Examination of an often neglected subject.

H. Wirarda, *Democracy and Its Discontents: Development, Interdependence, and U.S. Policy in Latin America* (1995). A useful overview.

G. W. Wynia, *Argentina: Illusion and Realities* (1992). Essays on recent developments.

INDEX

Aachen, 328
Abacha, Sani, 1064
Abbas, al-, 306
Abbas I, 645–646
Abbas II, 646
Abbasids, 302–303, 306–307, 684
Abd al-Malik, 305
Abd al-Rahman I, 379
Abd al-Rahman III, 379–380
Abduh, Muhammad, 865
Abelard, Peter, 351
Abiola, Moshood, 1064
Abolitionist movement, in America,
    729–730
Abolition Society, 714
Abraham, 53, 54, 66
Abubakar, General, 1064
Abu Bakr, 299, 302
Abu Talib, 298
Academy (Plato), 61, 104
Achaemenids, 53, 113, 114, 116–120
Acheh, 655
Acrocorinth, 78
Acropolis, 78, 93, 98, 99
Actium, Battle of, 149
Act of Settlement (1701), 591
Act of Succession (1534), 464
Act of Union (1800), 725
Acton, Lord, 759
Adab, 309
Addams, Jane, 800
*Address to the Christian Nobility of the
    German Nation* (Luther), 456
Admonitions for Women (Pan Chao), 207
Adrianople, Battle of (378), 316
Adulis, 187
Advancement of Learning, The (Bacon), 666
Aegean Sea, 73–76
Aegospotami, 96
Aeneid (Virgil), 152
Aeschylus, 95, 98
Affonso I, Kongo ruler, 508, 509
Afghani, Jamal al-Din al-, 865
Afghanistan, 862, 1004, 1015, 1073–1074
Africa:
    See also specific country and range
    agriculture, commerce, and the rise
        of urban centers in Sudan, 189–191

Aksumite empire, 187–188
    Bantu, 193
    diffusion of languages and peoples,
        176–177
    early cultures, 176, 178–196
    events/dates, major, 71, 223, 423, 661,
        747, 871, 919
    foreign involvement in, 868–873,
        923–924
    future of, 1065–1066
    Khoisan, 192–193
    Khush, 182
    Meroitic empire, 183–187
    mineral wealth, 174
    missionaries in, 812, 869–870
    Napatan empire, 182–183
    Nok culture, 180–181
    physical description, 174–176
    postcolonial, 1059–1066
    racial distinctions, 177–178
    regions of, 174–176
    resistance to colonialism, 871–873
    San, 177, 192–193
    slavery, 440–441
    water shortages, 174
African Americans, after Reconstruction,
    767
Afrikaans, 515
Afro-Asiatic language, 176
Agades, 190
Agamemnon (Aeschylus), 95
Agape, 159
Age of Discovery, 489–491
Agesilaus, 97
Agni, 21
Agora, 78
Agriculture/farming:
    Achaemenid, 119
    in America, 728
    in Americas, 28
    in China (early), 21, 27
    Ch'ing, 546
    Depression of 1929 and collapse
        of, 948–949
    eighteenth-century revolution
        in, 623–626
    Greek, 82
    Indus valley, 17

in Japan (Tokugawa), 566, 570
    manors and serfdom in Middle Ages,
        330, 331
    in medieval Japan, 269
    Neolithic Age, 4
    New Deal programs, 967
    open-field method replaced by
        enclosure, 624–625
    post-Mauryan, 124
    Roman farmers/land ownership,
        145–146, 147
    Stalin policies for, 952
    Sudan cultures and, 179–180, 189
    Sung dynasty, 235–236
    Vedic Aryan, 20
Agrippa, 156
Ahaggar, 180
Ah Cacau, 405
Ahimsa, 287
Ahmad, Muhammad, 868
Ahmad Shah Durrani, 650
Ahmad Sirhindi, 651–652
Ahura Mazda, 21, 115, 117
Ain Jalut, 382
Aïr region, 179, 180
Aix-la-Chapelle, Treaty of (1668), 595
Aix-la-Chapelle, Treaty of (1748), 606
Ajanta caves, 284
Akbar, 648–649, 651–652
Akhnaton (Amenhotep IV), 12
Akhtaton, 12
Akkad, 6
Aksum, 187
Aksumite empire, 187–188
Alaric, 316
Alba, Duke of, 473
Albanians, 1023
Albrecht of Mainz, Archbishop, 456
Alcaeus of Mytilene, 84
Alcibiades, 96
Alcuin of York, 329, 330
Aleksei I, 599
Alembert, Jean le Rond d', 669, 674
Alexander I, Tsar of Russia, 704, 707–708,
    723
Alexander II, Tsar of Russia, 759–761
Alexander III, Pope, 361
Alexander III, Tsar of Russia, 761, 795

Alexander VI, Pope, 441–442
Alexander the Great (Alexander III), 10, 101–104
Alexandria, Egypt, 106
Alexandria Eschate, 103
Alexius I Comnenus, 343, 344
Alfonsín, Raul, 1082
Algeria, 870, 871, 924, 984, 1067
Alhambra castle, 379
Ali, 300, 302, 304–305
Allende, Salvador, 1081
All Men Are Brothers, 558
Almagest (Ptolemy), 489, 664
Almohads, 380
Almoravids, 380, 497
Altaic, 242
Altar of Peace (Ara Pacis), 152, 153
Alwa, 189, 505
Ambrose, Bishop of Milan, 165
Amenhotep IV, 12
America, colonial:
   See also United States
   crisis and independence, 691–692
   political ideas, 689–691
   resistance to British government, 689
   slave revolts, 714
American Colonization Society, 715
American Federation of Labor (AFL), 799
American Revolution, events/dates for, 692
Americas:
   See also specific country
   discovery of, 449–452
   events/dates, major, 71, 223, 423, 661, 747, 919
   exploitation of, 522–540
   gold and spices, 450, 524
   Neolithic societies, 4
   problems in reconstructing history of, 397–398
   rise of civilization, 27–30
   slavery in, 532–535
   voyages of Columbus, 445, 450–451
Amiens, Treaty of (1802), 702, 703
Amitabha, 233, 289
Amon, 12, 186
Amon-Re, 12
Amorites, 7
Anabaptists, 458–459
Anacreon of Teos, 83–84
Analects, 39
Anatolia, 300, 383
Anaxagoras of Clazomenae, 58
Anaximander, 58
Anaximenes, 58
Andean civilization:
   architecture, 33–34, 412
     Chavín de Huantar, 29–30, 412–413

Chimu, 415
early intermediate, 413–414
events/dates, major, 28, 412
Huari, 30, 414–415
Incas, 30, 415–418
middle through late intermediate, 414–418
Moche, 30, 413–414
Nazca, 30, 413
periods in, 29–30, 412
preceramic and initial, 412–413
range of, 29, 411–412
Tiwanaku, 414–415
Andromeda, 100
Andropov, Yuri, 1015
Angevin empire, 360
Angilbert, 329
Angles, 316
Anglican Church, 532, 589, 811, 812
Anglo-French Wars, 532
Anglo-Saxons, 326
Angola, 509, 1062
An Lu-shan, 231
Ann, daughter of James II, Queen of England, 591
Anthony of Egypt, 322
Anti-Comintern Pact, 973, 980
Antifeminism, 821–822
Antigonus I, 103
Antiochus I, 121
Antiochus II, 141
Antiochus the Great, 126, 127
Antisemitism, 819–820
Antisthenes, 61
Antoninus Pius, 151, 153
Antrustiones, 334
Apamia, peace of, 141
Apartheid, 515
Apartheid, 515, 1064
Apedemak, 186
Apollo, 83
Apostolic Succession, 159
Apple Computer Corp., 1031
Aquinas, Thomas, 239, 351, 363, 470, 814
Aquitaine, 332
Arabic, 304, 309
Arab-Israeli conflict, 1068–1071
Arabs:
   See also Islam
   conquests, 299–301
Arafat, Yassir, 1070, 1071
Aramaic, 119, 126
Arawak, 451
Archimedes, 107
Architecture:
   Byzantine, 321
   classical Greek, 99
   concrete, first use of, 156

Egyptian, 11, 34–35
Gupta, 285
Hellenistic, 106
Indus valley, 16, 35
Islamic, 310, 311
Mesopotamian, 8, 32–33
Mughal, 649, 651
Ottoman, 643
Peru (ancient), 33–34, 412
pyramids, 11, 34–35, 401, 413–414
redesigning of cities and development of suburbs, 780–781
Roman, 152, 156
Safavid, 647
Teotihuacán, 401–402
Arch of Constantine, 167
Ardashir, 280, 281
Aregpagus, 86
Arete, 77
Argentina:
   Alfonsín, 1082
   Buenos Aires, 837
   events/dates, major, 840
   expansion and growth of, 837–838
   exploitation of resources, 834
   Galtieri, 1082
   history of, 836–840
   military control, 838–840
   Péron, Eva, 839, 840
   Péron, Juan, 840, 1082
   Río de la Plata, 710, 837
Argos, 86, 97
Arianism, 165, 317
Aristagoras, 88
Aristarchus of Samos, 107
Aristobulus, 106
Aristocracy:
   See also Social classes/society
   eighteenth century, 614–616
   Etruscan, 135–136
   Greek, 82–83
   Nara and Heian, 259
Aristophanes, 98–99
Aristotle, 63–64, 98
Arius of Alexandria, 165
Arizpe, Lourdes, 1083
Arjun, 650
Arkwright, Richard, 628
Armenia, 300, 1074
Arouet, François Marie. *See* Voltaire
Arsacids, 127
Ars Amatoria (Ovid), 152
Art:
   Benin, 506
   Bronze Age, 23
   Buddhist, 124
   classical Greek, 99, 100
   Crete, 74

guilds of Middle Ages, 348
Gupta, 284, 285
Han dynasty, 208–209
Hellenistic, 106–107
Indus valley, 17
Islamic, 311
mannerism, 440
Meroitic empire, 184
Ming-Ch'ing, 557
Mycenaean, 75
Olmec, 400
Ottoman, 643
Renaissance, 438–440
Roman, 152
Safavid, 647
Saharan, 178, 179, 180
Sung dynasty, 239, 240–241
T'ang dynasty, 231–232
Tokugawa, 570
Vedic Aryan, 20
Artaxerxes II, 97
Artaxerxes III, 117
Artemisium, Battle of, 89
Arthashastra, 120
Artisans:
    proletarianization of, 731
    as a social class, 631–632
Artisans Dwelling Act (1875), 762
Art of War (Sun-tzu), 39
Aryans, 115, 217
    See also Vedic Aryan
Asante, 868, 871
ASEAN (Association of Southeast Asian
        Nations), 1055
Ashikaga *bakufu*, 559–560
Ashikaga era, 268
Ashikaga Takauji, 268
Ashkenazim, 67
Ashoka, King, 121–122, 123, 277, 648
Asia:
    See also under name of country
    postcolonial, 1073–1077
Aski dynasty, 501–503
Aspelta, King, 184
Aspero, 33–34
Asquith, Herbert, 791
Assyria, 5
Assyrians, 13–14, 217
Astronomy:
    Brahe, 665–666
    Copernicus, 664–665
    Galileo, 666
    Kepler, 666
Atahualpa, 523
Atatürk (Mustafa Kemal), 864–865, 1073
Athanasius, 165, 323
Athens:
    Attic tragedy, 98

Clisthenes rule, 88
democracy, 92, 94
empire, 92, 93, 97–98
events/dates, major, 88, 92
invasion by Sparta, 88
Peloponnesian Wars, 90, 92, 93
Persian Wars and, 89–90
Pisistratus the Tyrant, 87
Solon reforms, 86–87
women of, 94–96
Atlantic Charter, 992
Atman, 132
Atman-Brahman, 46, 47
Atomists, 58, 59
Aton, 12
Attic (Athenian) tragedy, 98
Attica, 86
Attila, 316
Auclert, Hubertine, 791
Augsburg:
    Diet of (1530), 462
    Interim, 463
    Peace of (1555), 463, 476
Augustine, Bishop of Hippo, 167–168
Augustus, 149–153
Aurelian, 161, 162
Austin, Stephen F., 841
Austrasia, 325
Austria:
    aristocracy, 616
    Congress of Vienna and, 707
    Dual Alliance, 927
    formation of, 757–758
    Habsburg Empire, 602–603, 605,
        739–740, 757–758
    Habsburg-Valois wars, 457
    Hitler's invasion of, 973
    peasant revolts, 617
    Seven Years' War (1756–1763), 606–609
    Triple Alliance, 595, 925, 927–928
    War of Austrian Succession
        (1740–1748), 606
    World War I and, 931–944
Avalokiteshvara, 278
Avars, 327
Averroës (ibn-Rushd), 322, 380
Avicenna (ibn-Sina), 322
Avignon, papal court at, 433
Awdaghast, 190, 498
Awrangzeb, 649–650, 652
Aybak, 382
Ayodhya, 123
Ayutthaya, 577
Ayyubid dynasty, 382
Azcazpotzalco, 406
Azerbaijan, 644, 1018, 1074
Azhar mosque, 382
Aztecs, 29, 406

extractive empire, 407–408
human sacrifice, 408
religion, 408
society, 408, 410–411
Spanish conquest of, 522–523
Tenochtitlán, 406, 408

Baal, 51
Babur, 648, 652
Babylon:
    Cyrus and, 116
    Old dynasty, 6, 7
    religion, 8
Babylonian captivity, 53, 432
Babylonian Captivity of the Church (Luther),
        456
Babylonian Exile of the Jews, 116
Bacchus, 143
Bacon, Francis, 666, 687
Bactria, Indo-Greeks of, 127
Baden, Max, 945
Badoglio, Pietro, 984
Bagehot, Walter, 755
Baghdad, 306, 308
Bahmanids in the Deccan, 390
Bakri, al- 497, 498
Bakufu, 264–268
    Ashikaga, 559–560
    Tokugawa, 564–566, 568–569, 896–898
Baldwin, Stanley, 949
Balfour Declaration (1917), 1068–1069
Balkans, war in, 925–927, 930
Ball, John, 426
Baltimore, Lord, 531
Baluchistan Mountain, 15
Banalities, 356
Bangladesh, 1074
Bantō, Yamagata, 574–575
Bantu, 193, 866–867
Bao Dai, 1053
Barbados, 532
Bar-Kochba rebellion, 157
Barmakids, 306
Basel, Council of (1431–1449), 432–433
Basel, Treaty of (1795), 701
Bashō, 571
Basilica of the Sacred Heart, 781
Basil the Great, 322–323
Basra, 303
Bastille, fall of, 693–694
Batinis, 378
Batu Khan, 366
Bavaria, 332, 340
Bavarians, 326
Baybars, 382
Beatles, 1007
Becket, Thomas, 361
Becquerel, Henri, 815

Begin, Menachem, 1069
Beguine houses, 354
Behaim, Martin, 451
Belarus, 1074
Belgian Congo, 1062
Beligum, Congress of Vienna and, 707
Bell, Alexander Graham, 687
Bell, The, 760
Belles lettres, 309
Bello, Muhammad, 868
Belloc, Hilaire, 774
Benedictines, 323
Benedict of Nursia, 323, 341
Benefice, 334
Benes, Eduard, 1002
Benin, 505–506
Bentinck, William, 854
Berbers, 300, 307
Berchtold, Leopold, 931
Bering Sea, 3
Berke, 384
Berlin Blockade, 1002
Berlin Decrees (1806), 704
Berlin Wall, 998, 1004, 1017
Bernadotte, 704
Bernard of Clairvaus, Saint, 344
Bernstein, Eduard, 794
Bessus, 103
Bethmann-Hollweg, Theobald von, 931, 932
Bhagavad Gita, 124, 133, 288
Bhakti, 287, 393
Bhutto, Benazir, 1074
Biafra, 1063
Bible:
    Complutensian Polyglot Bible (Jiménez de Cisneros), 454
    Erasmus' translation of, 453
    Hebrew, 52, 54, 56, 66–67
    Luther's translation of, 456–457
    printing of, 372
    Vulgate, 167
Bihzad, 647
Bilad al-Sudan, 177
Bimbisara, King, 120
Bindusara, 120–121
Birth control, 469–470
    eighteenth-century, 621
    in Japan (Tokugawa), 570
    nineteenth-century, 784, 790
Birth of Tragedy, The (Nietzsche), 816
Biruni, al-, 383, 391
Bismarck, Otto von, 752–753, 754, 793–794, 811–812, 871, 924, 925–928
Black Death:
    in Arab Middle East, 382
    causes of, 428–429

remedies, 430
social and economic consequences, 430–431
spread of, 429
Black Hand, 931
Black Legend, 523
Board of Academicians, 238
Boccaccio, Giovanni, 430, 436
Bodhidharma, 242
Bodhisattva, 277, 291
Bohemia, 602, 617
Boleyn, Anne, 463, 464
Bolívar, Simón, 710, 711
Bologna, universities in, 348–349
Bolshevism, 795–797, 937–938, 949
Bonaventure, Saint, 363
Boniface, Saint, 326
Boniface VIII, Pope, 431–432
Book of Changes (Confucian), 40
Book of Common Prayer (Cranmer), 464, 587, 588
Book of History (Confucian), 40
Book of Poetry (Confucian), 40
Book of Rites (Confucian), 40
Book of the Courtier (Castiglione), 436–437
Book of the Dead, The, 12
Book of the Han, The (Pan Ku), 211
Borgia family 441–442
Borodin, Michael, 892
Bosnia, 927
    crisis of 1908, 929
    war in 1992, 1021, 1022
Bosnia-Herzegovina, 1022
Bossuet, Jacques-Bénigne, 595
Boston Massacre (1770), 691
Boston Tea Party, 691
Botha, Pieter, 1065
Boulton, Matthew, 629
Bourbons, 471
Bouvines, 361
Boxer Rebellion, 889–890
Brahe, Tycho, 665–666
Brahman, 46, 47
Brahmanas, 19, 21, 45–46
Brahmanic age, 19
Brahmo Samaj, 857
Brandenburg-Prussia, 603–605
Brazil:
    civilian government in, 1082–1083
    conditions in, following independence, 831, 832
    economic problems and military coups, 847–849
    events/dates, major, 849
    exploitation of resources, 834
    independence for, 712–713
    monarchy replaced with a republic, 847
    Paraguayan War (1865–1870), 845–846

slavery in, 528–530, 832, 845–847
Brest-Litovsk, Treaty of (1918), 938
Bretigny, Peace of (1360), 426
Breuer, Josef, 817
Brezhnev, Leonid, 1014–1015
Briand, Aristide, 959
Britain:
    See also England
    Africa, colonial rule in, 870–871, 923–924
    Battle of Britain, 978
    Disraeli and Gladstone, 762, 763, 764
    Egypt, colonial rule of, 863
    Entente Cordiale, 928
    Great Reform Bill (1832), 725–726
    India, colonial rule of, 854–860
    Labour Party and Fabianism, 795
    Latin America, relations with, 833–834, 835
    World War I, 929–944
    World War II, 978, 990–991, 992–994
British North America Act (1867), 769
Bronze Age, 4, 22–24
    on Crete, 73–76
Brothers of the Common Life, 453
Brown, John, 765
Brown v. Board of Education, 1011
Bruni, Leonardo, 435
Brüning, Heinrich, 959, 960
Brussels, Treaty of (1948), 1002
Bucer, Martin, 461
Buddha (Siddhartha Gautama), 49, 132, 276
Buddhism:
    art, 124
    dharma, 49–50
    dukkha, 49
    esoteric, 264
    evolution and growth of, 276–277
    Han dynasty and, 212–213
    in India, 46, 49–51, 288–291
    in medieval Japan, 269–273
    Nara and Heian, 262–264
    Nichiren, 271–272
    post-Mauryan, 125–126
    Pure Land, 271
    Shingon sect, 264
    T'ang dynasty, 233
    Tendai sect, 263
    Tibetan, 245
    T'ien-t'ai sect, 233
    Yuan dynasty, 245
    Zen, 233–234, 272–273
Buenos Aires, 710, 837
Bukharin, Nikolai, 950, 1016
Bulge, Battle of, 986
Bülow, Bernhard von, 928
Bunker Hill, Battle of, 692

Burckhardt, Jacob, 433
Burgundians, 316, 324
Burgundy, 325
Bush, George, 1012–1013
Butler, Josephine, 822
Buyids, 307, 378
Byzantine/Byzantine Empire, 164
    Islamic conquest of, 300, 301
    Middle Ages and, 317–320
Byzantium, 315

Caesar, Julius, 149
Caesar, meaning of term, 152–153
Cahuachi, 413
Cairo, 380, 382–383
Calas, Jean, 671
Calendar:
    Mayan, 404
    Muslim, 299
    Shang dynasty, 23
    Sumerian, 8
    Teotihuacán, 401
Caligula, 151, 153
Caliphate, 302–303
    high, 305–306, 307
Calixtus II, Pope, 342
Calles, Plutarco Elías, 844
Calvin, John, 460–461, 467, 470
Calvinism, 459–461, 462, 463, 470, 531
Camacho, Manuel Ávila, 845
Cambodia, 888, 1053, 1054–1055
Cambridge University, 350
Cambyses, 116
Campania, 136
Camp David Accords, 1069
Canaan, 66
Canada, 530, 608
    road to self-government, 768–769
Canada Act (1840), 769
Canals, 728
Candide (Voltaire), 669
Cannae, 141
Cano, Sebastián del, 491
Canon law, 349
Canton, 547, 556
Cape Colony, 867
Cape of Good Hope, 450
Capetian dynasty, 361
Caprivi, Leo von, 928
Caravela redonda, 490
Cárdenas, Lázaro, 844–845
Cardoso, Fernando Henrique, 1083
Caribbean islands, 522, 532
Carnal Prayer Mat, The, 557
Carolingian minuscule, 330
Carolingians, 325, 332–334
Carolus. See Charlemagne
Carranza, Venustiano, 842–844

Carrhae, 127
Carter, Jimmy, 1012, 1069
Carthage (New City), 139–141, 142, 185
Cary, William, 812
Casa de Contratación (House of Trade),
    528
Caspian Sea, 113
Cassian, John, 323
Castiglione, Baldassare, 436–437
Castro, Fidel, 1079–1081
Cathedral schools, 349–350
Catherine of Aragon, 445, 463
Catherine the Great, 616, 617, 632,
    679–681
Catholic Association, 725
Catholic Emancipation Act (1829), 725
Catholicism:
    See also Roman Catholic church
    emergence of, 160
    Reformation, 464–465
    Rome as a center for the early church,
    160–161
Catholic League, 471, 478
Cato, 141, 142, 143
Catullus, 151, 152
Caudillos, 836, 840
Cavaliers, 588
Cave paintings, 3, 4
Caves of the Thousand Buddhas
    at Tunhuang, 233
Cavour, Camillo, 750, 752
Ceausescu, Nicolae, 1018
Celts, 136
Censorship laws, 372
Central Africa:
    Angola, 509
    Europeans, arrival of, 508
    events/dates, major, 508
    formation of states, 867–868
    Kongo kingdom, 508–509
    range of, 175–176
Centrists, 305
Century of the Child (Key), 823
Cerro Blanco, 414
Cerro Sechín, 412
Cerularius, Michael, 324
Cervantes Saavedra, Miguel de, 480–481
Chaghatays, 648, 652–653
Chaitanya, 651
Chalcidic peninsula, 78
Chaldaeans, 143
Chaldean, 14
Chamberlain, Austen, 959
Chamberlain, Houston Stewart, 819
Chamberlain, Neville, 974
Chams, 579–580
Ch'an, 233–234
Chan Chan, 415

Chandragupta, 283
Chandragupta Maurya, 120
Chandragupta II, 283
Changamire, 514
Ch'ang-an, 202, 229
Chang Chih-tung, 886
Chanson de Roland, 379
Charcot, Jean-Martin, 817
Charitable activities, role of women
    in, 789–790
Charlemagne:
    Alcuin and Carolingian Renaissance,
    329–330
    breakup of kingdom, 332–334
    character and family of, 328
    empire of, 327–328
    manors and serfdom, 330, 331
    other names for, 325
    problems of government under,
    328–329
    religion and clergy, 330–332
Charles I, King of England, 587–589
Charles I, King of Spain, 445, 456
Charles II, King of England, 589–590
Charles II, King of Spain, 596
Charles III, King of Spain, 708–709
Charles IV, King of France, 426
Charles V, Emperor, 372, 443, 445,
    456–457, 462, 463
Charles V, King of France, 432
Charles VI, Habsburg emperor, 603
Charles VI, King of France, 426
Charles VII, King of France, 428
Charles IX, King of France, 471
Charles X, King of France, 723–725
Charles XII, King of Sweden, 601
Charles Albert, 740, 750, 752
Charles Martel, 300, 320, 325, 326
Charles the Bald, 332
Charles the Bold, 444
Charles the Great. See Charlemagne
Chaumont, Treaty of (1814), 705
Chavín de Huantar, 29–30, 412–413
Cheng Ho, 553
Ch'en Tu-hsiu, 891, 892
Chernenko, Constantin, 1015
Chernobyl, 1029
Cheyenne, 768
Chiang Ching-kuo, 1049
Chiang Kai-shek, 893–894, 895, 896,
    1049
Chiapas, rebellion in, 1084
Chicha, 416
Chichén Itzá, 406
Ch'ien Lung, 552, 553, 556, 557
Chikamatsu Monzaemon, 570, 572–573
Childbirth, dangers of, 621–622
Childeric III, 326

Children:
abandoned, 622
eighteenth-century, 618, 621–623
labor and, 732, 796
medieval, 358–360
wet nursing, 470, 621
Chile:
Allende, 1081
exploitation of resources, 834
independence for, 710
Pinochet, 1081
Chimu, 415
Ch'in, 39, 44–45, 199–200
China:
events/dates, major, 423, 661, 747
printing techniques, 370–371
technological advances in, 684
China, dynasties:
Ch'in, 39, 44–45, 199–200
Ch'ing, 546–558
Chou (Eastern), 24–27
Chou (Western), 24
Han, 41, 208–213
Han dynasty, Former, 201–206, 219
Han dynasty, Later, 206–213
Hsia, 22, 23
Manchu, 39
Ming, 546–558
Shang, 22–24, 216, 370
Six Dynasties era, 207
Sui, 225–226
Sung, 234–242, 371
T'ang, 226–234, 370, 545
Yuan, 242–247
China, early civilization:
Chou (Eastern), 24–27
Chou (Western), 24
events/dates, major, 27, 71
human sacrifice, 26
Neolithic societies, 4, 21–22
philosophy in, 37, 38–45
Shang, 22–24, 216, 370
writing, 23, 25
China (1839–1949):
Boxer Rebellion, 889–890
from dynasty to warlordism
(1859–1926), 888–890
Korea and, 888
kuomintang unification of,
and the Nanking decade
(1927–1937), 892–894
May Fourth Movement, 890–892
Opium War (1839–1842), 774, 881,
882–884
Peking court, 886
rebellions against the Manchu,
884–885
regional governments, 886–887

Russia and, 887–888
Sino-Japanese War (1894–1895),
885–886
treaty ports, 887
Vietnam and, 888
war with Japan and civil revolution
(1937–1949), 894–896
China (1949-):
economic growth, 1045–1046
Gang of Four, 1044
Great Proletarian Cultural Revolution
(1965–1976), 1043–1044
political developments after Mao,
1044–1045
relations with other countries, 1047
relations with the Soviet Union,
1042–1043
social change, 1046–1047
Tienanmen Square, 1016, 1032, 1045
China, first empire:
Ch'in, 39, 44–45, 199–200
Former Han dynasty, 201–206, 219
Later Han dynasty, 206–208
warfare technology, 219
China, imperial:
events/dates, major, 223
Sui dynasty, 225–226
Sung dynasty, 234–242, 371
T'ang dynasty, 226–234, 370
Yuan dynasty, 242–247
China, late imperial:
civil service examinations, 550–551
land and people, 546
commercial revolution, 546–549
contacts with the West, 555–556
culture, 556–558
emperor, role of, 549–550
events/dates, major, 556
foreign relations, 553–556
Manchu rule, pattern of, 551–553
political system, 549–553
women in, 548–549
China Inland Mission, 812
China Merchants Steam Navigation Co.,
886, 887
Chinese Communist Party (CCP),
893–896
Ch'ing dynasty, 546–558
Chios, 92
Chitam, 405
Choga Mami, 33
Chōshū, 897–898
Chosroes Anosharvan, 281, 283
Chou (Eastern) dynasty, 24–27
Chou (Western) dynasty, 24
Chou En-lai, 892
Chou Rites, 885
Chrétien de Troyes, 360

Christian II, 462
Christian III, 462
Christianity:
See also Catholicism; Roman Catholic
church
Arianism, 165
in China, 556
Council of Nicea, 165, 324, 326
division of, 323–324
Edict of Milan, 322
in Ethiopia, 188–189
in Japan, 562–563
Jesus of Nazareth, 158, 160
Justinian and, 318
Monophysite, 189, 324
Nestorian, 245
organization, 159
Paul of Tarsus, 158–159
persecution of Christians, 159–160, 165
rise of, 157–160, 492–493
spread of, 164–166
Christianity Not Mysterious (Toland), 670
Christian writers, 167–168
Christine de Pisan, 437
Chrysoloras, Manuel, 435, 437
Chuang-tzu, 42, 211
Chu His, 239–240
Chun Doo-hwan, 1051, 1052
Chun-tzu, 40–41
Churchill, John, 597–598
Churchill, Winston, 936, 975, 978, 993,
994, 1000
Church Missionary Society, 812
Church of England, 531, 812
Cicero, 60, 145, 151
Cimmerians, 217
Cimon, 90
Ciompi Revolt (1378), 434
Cistercians, 353
City of God (Augustine), 167
City-states:
Chou dynasty, 24
Greek polis, 60, 73, 77–78, 99–100
Italian, 433–434
Shang dynasty, 23
Sumerian, 6
Civil Constitution of the Clergy, 697
Civilization:
age of, 3
Bronze Age China, 23
defined, 173
emergence of, 4–30
Civilization of the Renaissance in Italy
(Burckhardt), 433
Civil Rights Act (1964), 1011
Civil-rights movement, 1011
Civil War (1861–1865), 765–766
Clarendon Code, 589

Classic of Divination (Confucian), 40
Claudius, 151, 153
Claudius II Gothicus, 162
Clayton Act (1914), 799
Clemenceau, Georges, 940
Clement III, Pope, 342
Clement V, Pope, 432
Clement VII, Pope, 432, 443, 463
Cleopatra, 103, 149
Clergy:
    in the Middle Ages, 353–354
    witch hunts and role of, 478–479
Clericis Laicos, 432
Clermont, 686
Clermont, Council of (1095), 343
Clientage, 137
Clinton, Bill, 1013
Clisthenes, 88
Clive, Robert, 608
Clovis, 324–325
Cluny reform movement, 341
Cnossus, 74, 74
Coal, 1026–1027
Cobbe, Frances Power, 792
Cobe, Bernabé, 417
Code of Hammurabi, 7, 8, 9
Cold War era:
    Cuban missile crisis, 1004
    detente and afterward, 1004–1006
    early conflicts in, 1000–1002
    end of, 1005–1006
    events/dates, major, 1005
    Hungarian uprising, 1004
    initial causes, 999–1000
    intensification of, 1004
    NATO and the Warsaw Pact,
        1002–1003
    Poland conflict, 1003–1004
    Suez Canal crisis, 1003
    U–2 incident, 1004
Coligny, Gaspard de, 471
Collection of Ancient and Modern Times, 261
Collection of Ten Thousand Leaves
    (Man'yōshū), 260
College of Cardinals, 341
Collor de Mello, Fernando, 1082–1083
Cologne, 354
Cologne Mani Codex, 282
Coloni, 163, 355
Colosseum, 156
Columbus, Christopher, 445, 450–451,
    490–491
Commerce:
    Achaemenid, 119–120
    African, 176
    Aksumite empire, 187
    British East India Company in China,
        556

Carthaginian, 185
    in China, 27
    China's third commercial revolution,
        546–549
    Crusades and, 344
    in Japan (medieval), 269
    in Japan (seventeenth-century),
        566–568
    medieval trade routes, 347
    mercantilism, 520–522
    merchants, rise of in Middle Ages,
        346
    Meroitic empire, 183–184
    piracy, 521
    slave trade, abolition of, 713–715
    Sudan, 189, 190
    Sung dynasty, 237
    technology, impact of, 773
    trade routes in Gupta and Sasanid
        times, 284
    Warring States of Japan and, 562–563
    Yuan dynasty, 245
Commodus, 153, 161
Common Market, 1006
Common Sense (Paine), 692
Commonwealthmen, 690
Commonwealth of Independent States
    (CIS), 1019, 1020, 1074
Communist Information Bureau
    (Cominform), 1002
Communist Manifesto (Marx and Engels),
    659, 737, 793
Communist Party of the Soviet Union,
    949
Complutensian Polyglot Bible (Jiménez de
    Cisneros), 454
*Comprehensive Mirror for Aid in Government,
    A* (Ssu-ma Kuang), 239
Compromise, 473
Computers, 1030–1031
Comte, Auguste, 809, 822, 833
Concordance of Discordant Canons (Gratian),
    349, 351
Concordat of Bologna (1516), 442
Concordat of Worms (1122), 342
Concubines, 548, 901
Condition of the Working Class in England
    (Engels), 737
Confederation of the Rhine, 704
Confessions (Augustine), 167
Confucianism:
    in China, 39–42, 209
    in China (late imperial), 549
    Japanese Tokugawa, 573
Confucius, 39–42
Congo, 1062
Congress of Berlin (1878), 927
Congress of Vienna (1814), 707–708, 720

Conquest of New Spain (Díaz del Castillo),
    407
Conquest of the Desert, 837
Conquistadores, 524
Constance, Council of (1414–1417), 432,
    456
Constantine I, 161, 162–163, 315, 322
Constantinople, 638
    formation of, 162, 315
    growth of, 164
    Middle Ages and, 317–320
Constantius II, 161, 163
Constitutional Convention, 692, 727
Constitution of the Athenians, 63
Constitutions of Clarendon (1164),
    360–361
Consuls, 138
Contagious Diseases Acts (1864 and
    1886), 822–823
Convents, 354
Coolidge, Calvin, 965
Copernicus, Nicolaus, 664–665
Copyright laws, first, 372
Coral Sea, Battle of, 983
Córdoba, 379
Corinth, 80, 83, 97, 142
    Federal League of , 101
Corinthian War, 97
Cornwallis, Lord, 692
Corpus Juris Civilis, 317
Corsica, 139, 141
Cort, Henry, 629
Cortés, Hernán, 407, 522
Cosmologists, 39
Council of Basel (1431–1449), 432–433
Council of Blood, 474
Council of Clermont (1095), 343
Council of Constance (1414–1417), 432,
    456
Council of Ferrara-Florence (1439), 437
Council of Mutual Assistance
    (COMECON) (1949), 1002
Council of Nicea (325), 165, 317
Council of the Indies, 526
Council of Trent (1545–1563), 465
Council of Troubles, 474
Counter-Reformation, 464–465
Courtesan's Jewel Box, 557
Cranmer, Thomas, 463, 464
Crassus, Marcus Licinius, 148
Creoles, 709, 831, 832
Crete, 73–76
Crimean War (1854–1856), 747–750, 862
Critias, 59
Croatia/Croats, 602, 758, 1021, 1022
Croesus of Lydia, King, 88, 119
Cromwell, Oliver, 589
Cromwell, Thomas, 454, 463

Crusades, 338
    events/dates, major, 343
    First, 342–344
    Fourth, 344
    Second, 344
    Third, 344
Ctesiphon, 127
Cuauhtemoc, 522
Cuban:
    missile crisis, 1004
    Revolution, 1079–1081
Cuicuilco, 401
Cultural Revolution (1965–1976),
    1043–1044
Culture, defined, 3
Cuneiform, 7–8
Curie, Marie, 815
Curie, Pierre, 815
Curl Nose, 405
Custer, George, 768
Cuzco, 415
Cybele, 143
Cynics, 61, 104
Cyprus, 300
Cyrus I, 116
Cyrus the Great, 114, 116
Cyrus the Younger, 97, 101
Czechoslovakia, 602, 758
    Hitler's invasion of, 97–9743
    Marshall Plan and, 1001
    revolution in, 1017–1018
    as a Soviet Union satellite, 1002

Dacia, 153, 155
Dadu, 651
Dahomey, 868, 871
Daimler, Rudolf, 1027
Daimyo, 268
Daladier, Edouard, 974
Dalton, John, 807
Damasus I, Pope, 323
Danes, 340
Dan Fodio, Usman, 861, 868, 869
D'Annunzio, Gabriele, 955
Dante Alighieri, 436
Dar al-Islam, 301
Darius I, 89, 116, 118, 119
Darius III, 101, 103
Darwin, Charles, 808–809, 821
Dasas, 20
Das Capital (Marx), 793
David, King, 52, 67
David (Michelangelo), 439–440
Dawes Plan, 959
Dawud, 503
D-Day, 986
Decameron (Boccaccio), 430, 436
Deccan, 121

Decembrist Revolt (1825), 723
Decet Pontificem Romanum, 456
Decius, 161, 165
Declaration of Female Independence, 722, 735
Declaration of Independence (U.S.), 668,
    692
Declaration of Indulgence, 589–590
Declaration of Pillnitz, 697
Declaration of the Rights of Man and Citizen,
    695, 696–697, 721
Declaration of the Rights of Woman, 696–697
Decolonization, 1008, 1059, 1086
Decurions, 318
De Gaulle, Charles, 978
Deism, 670–671
de Klerk, F. W., 1065
De Legibus (Cicero), 151
Delian League, 73, 90
Delhi, slave sultans of, 390
Delphi, 80, 83
Demarra, 714
Demetrius, 127
Democratization, 1085–1087
Democritus of Abhera, 58
Demosthenes, 57, 100, 101
Denmark, Reformation in, 462
Depression of 1929:
    agricultural commodities, collapse
        of, 948–949
    in America, 964–967
    government policy and, 949
    impact on Europe, 947–948
    impact on Japan, 902, 909–910
    impact on Latin America, 835–836
De Rerum Natura (On the Nature of Things),
    151
Description of the World (Polo), 245
Descent of Man, The (Darwin), 809, 821
Desiderius, King, 327
Dessalines, Jean-Jacques, 709, 713
Dharma, 48, 49–50
Dharmashastra, 286
Dialogues on the Two Chief Systems
    of the World (Galileo), 666
Dias, Bartholomew, 450
Diaspora, 67
Díaz, Porfirio, 841–842
Díaz del Castillo, Bernal, 407
Dibbalemi, Mai Dunama, 503, 504
Diderot, Denis, 669, 674
Diem, Ngo Dinh, 1053
Dien Bien Phu, 1053
Diesel, Rudolf, 1027
Diet of Augsburg (1530), 462
Diet of Speyer (1526), 457
Diet of Vesteras (1527), 462
Diet of Worms (1521), 457
Dimitri of Moscow, Grand Duke, 366

Dingiswayo, Nguni king, 867
Diocletian, 161, 162, 165, 315
Diogenes of Sinope, 61
Dionysus, 83, 98, 143
Discourse on the Moral Effects of the Arts
    and Sciences (Rousseau), 673
Discourse on the Origin of Inequality
    (Rousseau), 673
Diseases/illnesses:
    See also Black Death
    childbirth, dangers of, 621–622
    cholera, 781–782
    Contagious Diseases Acts (1864
        and 1886), 822–823
    government involvement in public
        health, 782–783
    plagues in late imperial China, 546
    sleeping sickness, 189
    smallpox, 528, 538
Disraeli, Benjamin, 762, 803, 926–927
Divine Comedy (Dante), 436
Divorce, 784
Diwan, 303, 304
Dr. Zhivago (Pasternak), 1013
Dōgen, 272
Dome of the Rock, 301
Domesday Book, 360
Dominicans, 354
Dominus, 162
Domitian, 151, 153
Donatello, 439
Donation of Constantine, 326, 438
Don Quixote (Cervantes), 480–481
Dorians, 75–76
Douglas, Frederick, 729
Douglas, Stephen A., 765
Dover, Treaty of (1670), 589, 595
Drake, Francis, 475
Dream of the Red Chamber, 558
Dred Scott decision, 765
Dreyfus, Alfred, 755–757
Dreyfus Affair, 755–757, 795, 811, 819
Dubcek, Alexander, 1004
DuBois, W. E. B., 767
Dukkha, 49
Durga, 290
Durham, Earl of, 769
Durkheim, Émile, 819, 822
Durrani, Ahmad Shah, 862
Dutch:
    colonies in North America, 530–531
    in South Africa, 514–515
Dutch East India Co., 514, 773
Dyaus, 20
Dynastic cycle, 201

Earl of Bute, 608
East Africa:

early people in, 193–195
events/dates, major, 513
formation of states, 867–868
range of, 175, 176
Swahili culture and commerce, 509–512
East Germany, formation of, 1002
East India Company, 556, 608, 650, 691, 773, 854, 855, 856
Ecbatana, 116
Ecclesiastical History (Eusebius of Caesarea), 167
Eck, John, 456
Economic Consequences of the Peace (Keynes), 943
Economy:
    Achaemenid, 119–120
    America nineteenth-century, 727–728
    Black Death, effects of, 430–431
    in China (late imperial), 547
    in China (twentieth century), 1045–1046
    coinage, introduction of, 119, 188
    coinage, Islamic, 302
    Depression of 1929, 835–836, 904, 909–910, 947–949, 964–967
    Enlightenment and, 671–672
    family eighteenth-century, 619–621
    French Revolution and issues of, 697
    in Japan (Tokugawa), 566–568, 570
    in Japan (twentieth century), 1038–1040
    laissez-faire, 672
    of Latin American countries following their independence, 833–836
    liberal, 722
    Meroitic empire, 183–184
    neo-colonial, 836
    Ottoman, 643
    plantation, 534
    post-Mauryan, 124
    Roman in late empire, 161, 162
    Sasanid, 281
    sectional conflict, 726–727
    Smith, 671–672
    Sung dynasty money, 237
Edgerton, Franklin, 47
Edict of Maximum Prices, 162
Edict of Milan (313), 322
Edict of Nantes (1598), 472–473, 595–596
Edict of Worms (1521), 457
Edirne, 638
Edison, Thomas, 687, 1028
Edo, 506, 896
Education:
    barriers to women, 784–785
    Charlemagne and, 329–330
    Gupta, 284

Japanese Tokugawa National Studies, 573–574
    in Ming and Ch'ing dynasties, 549
    Nara and Heian, 260
    reforms of Renaissance, 436–437
    Roman, 143–145
    schools and universities in the Middle Ages, 348–351
    of women (Middle Ages), 358
    of women (Roman), 144
Education Act (1870), 811
Education Act (1902), 811
Edward I, King of England, 432, 463
Edward III, King of England, 426
Edward IV, King of England, 445
Edward VI, King of England, 464
Edward the Confessor, 360
Egypt, 1067
    Arab-Israeli conflict, 1068–1071
    British colonial rule of, 863, 923–924
    Fatimids, 307, 378, 380, 382
    Mamluks, 306, 382–383
    Muhammad Ali, 863
    Napoleon's invasion of, 862
    power struggles in, 495
    Suez Canal crisis (1956), 1003
    World War II in, 978–979, 984
Egypt, ancient:
    dynasties, 12
    Middle Kingdom, 11–12
    Neolithic societies in, 4
    New Kingdom (Empire), 12
    Nile River civilization, 10
    Old Kingdom, 10–11
    pharaohs, 10, 12, 13
    pyramids, 11, 34–35
Eiffel Tower, 781
Einhard, 329
Einstein, Albert, 815
Eisai, 272
Eisenhower, Dwight D., 984, 1004, 1010–1011
Eisenstein, Serge, 992
Elamites, 113, 114
Elburz, 114
El Cid, 380
Eleanor of Aquitaine, 360
Electricity, 1027–1028
Elegance of the Latin Language (Valla), 438
Elements (Euclid), 107
Elements of the Philosophy of Newton (Voltaire), 669
Elgin, Lord, 884
El Greco, 440
Elizabeth I, Queen of England, 445, 464, 475, 476
Elizabeth of Russia, 607
Elizabeth of York, 445

El Paraíso, 33
Emancipation Proclamation, 765
Embossed Tea Kettle, 571
Émile (Rousseau), 675
Empedocles of Acragas, 58
Employment patterns for women, in nineteenth century, 785–786
Encomienda, 524–525
Encyclopedia, 669, 674–675
Engels, Friedrich, 737
England:
    See also Britain
    aristocracy, 615
    Charles I, 587
    Charles II and restoration of the monarchy, 589–590
    colonies in North America, 530–532, 689–692
    conflict between church and state, 811
    Cromwell and Puritan Republic, 589
    events/dates, major, 590, 660
    feminists in, 791, 792
    Glorious Revolution, 590–591
    Hundred Years' War, 426–428
    Industrial Revolution, 627–629
    Irish question, 762–764
    James I, 586–587
    James II, 590
    Long Parliament and Civil War, 587–588
    medieval, 360–363
    Reformation in, 463–464
    relations with Spain (1558–1603), 475–476
    revival of monarchy, 445
    Seven Years' War (1756–1763), 606–609
    Walpole, age of, 591–593
    War of Spanish Succession (1701–1714), 597–598
English Factory Act (1833), 732
ENIAC (Electronic Numerical Integrator and Computer), 1030
Enlightened absolutism, 677–681
Enlightenment:
    Deism, 670–671
    Encyclopedia, 669
    Montesquieu, 672–673
    religion and, 669–671
    publication dates of major works, 671
    Rousseau, 673–674, 675, 676
    Smith, 671–672
    society and, 671–677
    use of term, 658, 668
    Voltaire, 668–669, 670–671
    women and, 675–677
Entente Cordiale, 928
Entertainment:
    gambling (Vedic Aryan), 20

Entertainment *(continued)*
    Greek *symposion* and games, 82–83
    Kabuki, 572
    Mayan ballgame, 403
    Nō plays, 568, 570, 572, 1040, 1041
    Ottoman coffeehouses, 644
    puppet theater (Japanese), 572–573
    tournaments in Middle Ages, 352
    traveling troupes of Yuan dynasty,
        245–246
Epaminondas, 97
Ephialtes, 90
Epicureans, 104
Epicurus of Athens, 104
Erasmus, Desiderius, 453–454
Eratosthenes, 106, 107, 108
Erechtheum, 98
Erfurt Program (1891), 794
Eridu, 6, 33
Erie Canal, 728
Essay Concerning Human Understanding
    (Locke), 484, 667–668
Essay on the Inequality of the Human Races
    (Gobineau), 819
Estates General, 426
Estonia, 1018
Ethics (Spinoza), 482
Ethiopia, 871
    Aksumite empire, 187–188
    Christianity in, 188–189
    Italy's attack on, 972–973
Ethiopians, Greek term, 177
Ethnological Society, 821
Etruscans, 135–136
Eucharist, 159
Euclid, 107
Eugenius IV, Pope, 433
Euphrates River, 4, 5
Euripides, 95–96, 98, 100
Europe:
    See also specific country
    after the Congress of Vienna, 707
    changes during the second half of the
        twentieth century, 1006–1008
    contacts with Ming-Ch'ing China,
        555–556
    events/dates, major, 70, 222, 422, 746,
        918
    overseas expansion by, 519–520
European Coal and Steel Community,
    1006
European Economic Community (EEC),
    1006
European Free Trade Area, 1006
European Union, 1006–1007
Eusebius of Caesarea, 167
Euthydemus, 127
Evliya Chelebi, 643

Evolutionary Socialism (Bernstein), 794
Ewuare, King, 506
Execrabilis, 433
Exsurge Domine, 456
Ezana, King, 188
Ezra, 56

Fabian Society, 795
Fabius Maximus, 795
Factory workers, proletarianization of, 731
Fa Hsien, 212, 285
Fair Deal, 1010
Falkenhayn, Erich von, 936
Falkland Islands, 1082
Falloux Law (1850), 811
Falsafa, 308
Family:
    Athenian, 94–95
    eighteenth-century, 617–623
    feminism and views on, 823
    Former Han dynasty, 204
    impact of Reformation on, 467–470
    Industrial Revolution and, 731–732
    in Ming and Ch'ing dynasties, 548–549
    Roman, 136–137
    slave, 534
    Spartan, 85–86
    Vedic Aryan, 19–20
    Yamato Japan, 252–253
Faraday, Michael, 687, 1028
Farel, Guillaume, 460, 461
Farming. *See* Agriculture/farming
Fascism, 954–957
Fatima, 305, 380
Fatimids, 307, 378, 380, 381, 495
Fawcett, Millicent, 791
Federal League of Corinth, 101
Federation of Indochina, 888
Feltre, Vittorino da, 436
Feminism:
    antifeminism in late-century thought,
        821–822
    sexual morality, double standards,
        822–823
    women defining their own lives,
        823–824
Feminist groups/organizations, in the
    nineteenth century, 790–792
Ferdinand, Francis, 931
Ferdinand, Holy Roman Emperor, 740
Ferdinand of Aragon, 442, 444–445
Ferdinand VII, King of Spain, 711
Ferrara-Florence, Council of (1439), 437
Ferry, Jules, 811
Feudalism:
    fragmentation and divided loyalty, 335
    in Japan, 266–267
    origins of, 334

    vassalage and the fief, 334–335
Feudal society, defined, 334
Ficino, Marsilio, 437
Ficke, Auguste, 822, 823
Fidelity/loyalty, during the Middle Ages,
    335
Fiefs, 325, 334–335
Fieldhouse, D. K., 924
Filioque, 324
Finland, Marshall Plan and, 1001
Firdawsi, 383
First Continental Congress, 692
First Crusade, 342–344
First International, 793
First Messenian War, 84
First Peloponnesian War, 90, 92
First Punic War, 139, 140
First Triumvirate, 149
First Vatican Council (1869), 813
Flanders, 426
Flavian dynasty, 151, 153
Fleury, Cardinal, 598, 606
Florence, 433–434, 441
Florentine Academy, 437
Flota system, 528
Footbinding, 548–549
Forbidden Palace (Peking), 550
Ford, Gerald, 1012
Ford, Henry, 965
Foreign relations:
    See also specific country
    Ming-Ch'ing, 553–556
    Warring States of Japan and, 562–563
Former Han dynasty. *See* Han dynasty,
    Former
Foundations of the Nineteenth Century
    (Chamberlain), 819
Fourth Crusade, 344
Four Treasures, 553
Fox, George, 713
France:
    See also French Revolution
    Africa, colonies in, 870, 871, 924
    aristocracy, 615
    colonies in North America, 530–532
    conflict between church and state, 811
    Consulate (1799–1804), 702–703
    Dreyfus affair, 755–757
    Entente Cordiale, 928
    events/dates, major, 599, 660, 746
    feminists in, 791
    Hundred Years' War, 426–428
    invasion of Italy (1494–1527), 441–442
    Louis XIV, 593–598
    Louis XVI, 692–698
    Marie Antoinette, 696, 698, 700
    medieval, 360–363

Napoleon Bonaparte, 701, 702–708
Napoleon II, 739
Napoleon III, 750, 752, 754–755, 780–781
Nine Years' War (1689–1697), 596
Paris Commune, 755
religious wars (1562–1598), 471–472
revival of monarchy, 444
revolution of 1830, 723–725
Second Republic and Louis Napoleon, 739
Seven Years' War (1756–1763), 606–609
socialism, 794–795
Third Republic, 754–757
War of Spanish Succession (1701–1714), 597–598
World War II, 978, 990
Franciscans, 354
Francis I, King of France, 442, 456
Francis II, Holy Roman Emperor, 698
Francis II, King of France, 471
Francis Joseph, 757
Francis Xavier, Saint, 562
Franco, Francisco, 973, 1086
Franconia, 340
Franco-Prussian War (1870–1871), 754
Franco-Russian alliance (1894), 928
Franklin, Benjamin, 692
Franks, 316, 317, 320
    Carolingians, 325, 332–334
    Charlemagne, 327–332
    church, 326
    Clovis and Merovingians, 324–325
Frederick I (Barbarossa), Emperor, 344, 348, 363–364
Frederick I, King of Prussia, 605
Frederick II, Emperor, 362, 364
Frederick II, King of Prussia, 603, 605, 606, 607, 677
Frederick III, of Palatine, 478
Frederick IV, of Palatine, 478
Frederick William I, King of Prussia, 605
Frederick William II, King of Prussia, 697
Frederick William III, King of Prussia, 708
Frederick William IV, King of Prussia, 740, 741
Frederick William, The Great Elector, 604–605
Freedom of a Christian (Luther), 456
Freemen, 334, 355
French and Indian War, 607
French Equatorial Africa, 871
French Indochina, 1053
French Revolution, 659
    Bastille, fall of, 693–694
    civic equality, 694

Civil Constitution of the Clergy, 697
Convention and role of sans-culottes, 698–699
counterrevolutionary activity, 697
dechristianization, 700
Declaration of the Rights of Man and Citizen, 695, 696–697
Declaration of the Rights of Woman, 696–697
Directory, establishment of, 701
economic policy, 697
end of monarchy, 698
Estates General becomes the National Assembly, 692–693
events/dates, major, 701
Great Fear and surrender of feudal privileges, 694–695
Jacobins and Girondists, 698–701
reconstruction of France, 695
Reign of Terror, 699–701
Robespierre, 700–701
Thermidorian Reaction, 701
Freud, Sigmund, 817–818, 821
Frisians, 326
Fronde, 593
Frumentius, 188
Fugitive Slave Law, 764–765
Fujiwara Michinaga, 258
Fujiwara no Sadanobu, 260
Fukuzawa Yukichi, 898
Fulbe people, 191, 868
Fulton, Robert, 686
Funji sultanate, 505

Gaius (Caligula), 151, 153
Gaius Gracchus, 147
Galen, 359
Galerius, 165
Galileo Galilei, 666
Galtieri, Leopoldo, 1082
Gama, Vasco da, 450
"Gambler's Lament" (Vedic Aryan), 20
Gandhara, 120, 127
Gandharan school of Buddhist art, 124
Gandhi, Mohandas K., 49, 859, 860, 1011, 1074
Gandhi, Rajiv, 1076
Ganges, 15, 133
Gang of Four, 1044
Gao, 189, 190, 191
Gapon, Father, 797
Garibaldi, Giuseppe, 750, 752
Garrison, William Lloyd, 729
Gathas, 115
Gaul/Gauls, 139, 316, 317
Gawon, Yakubo, 1063, 1064
Gdansk strike, 1015
Gelasius I, Pope, 323

General Austrian Women's Association, 822
Geneva:
    Calvinism, 459–461, 462
    political revolt and religious reform in, 459–460
Genghis Khan, 242, 243, 384
Geoffrin, Marie-Thérèse, 674
George I, King of England, 591
George III, King of England, 608, 690, 692
George V, King of England, 949
George, David Lloyd, 940
Georgia, 530, 531, 1074
German Democratic Republic. *See* East Germany
German Federal Republic. *See* West Germany, 1002
Germanic migrations, 315–316
Germany:
    Africa, colonies in, 871
    Berlin Wall, 998, 1004, 1017
    Bismarck, 752–753, 754, 793–794, 811–812, 871, 924, 925–928
    collapse of liberalism (1848), 740–742
    conflict between church and state, 811–812
    Dual Alliance, 927
    events/dates, major, 754
    feminists in, 791
    Franco-Prussian War (1870–1871), 754
    Hitler and Nazism, 960–965
    Hohenstaufen Empire, 363–364, 364
    medieval, 340, 365
    partition of, following World War II, 1002
    Reformation in, 454–458
    reunification of, 1017
    Social Democratic Party (SPD) and revisionism, 793–794
    Thirty Years' War (1618–1648), 476–478
    Triple Alliance, 595, 925, 927–928
    Triple Entente (1890–1907), 928–929
    unification of (1871), 752–754
    Weimar Republic, 957–959
    World War I, 929–944
    World War II, 977–994
Gettysburg, Battle of (1863), 766
Ghana, 191, 497–499, 868, 1062
Ghazali, Muhammed al-, 239
Ghaznavids, 383
Ghazzali, Muhammad al-, 383–384
Ghengis Khan, 366
Ghent, Pacification of, 474
Gibbon, Edward, 168
Gingrich, Newt, 1013
Giotto, 439

Girondists, 698, 699, 700
Gladstone, William, 762, 763, 764, 803
Glasnost, 1016
Glorious Revolution, 590–591
Gobind Singh, 650
Gobineau, Arthur de, 819
Godwinsson, Harold, 360
Goebbels, Josef, 989
Gokhale, G. K., 859
Gold Coast, 507, 1062
Golden Horde, 366
Golden Lotus, 558
Gompers, Samuel, 799
Gomulka, Wladyslaw, 1003–1004
Gorbachev, Mikhail S., 1005, 1015–1016,
    1018–1019
Gordon, Charles George, 868
Gospels, 158, 160–161
Goths, 161, 316
Gouges, Olympe de, 696–697, 699
Goulert, João, 849
Government:
    absolute monarchy in France, 593–598
    enlightened absolutism, 677–681
    Former Han dynasty, 203–205
    impact of Depression of 1929 on, 949
    Long Parliament, 587–588
    Mesopotamian, 5, 7–8
    in Ming and Ch'ing dynasties, 549–553
    Montesquieu on, 672–673
    Nara and Heian court, 255–256,
        258–259
    new models of, during Middle Ages,
        346–348
    royal Rome, 136
    Sung dynasty, 237–238
    T'ang dynasty, 226–227, 228
Gracchi, 146–147
Grammaticus, 144
Grand Canal (China), 228, 546, 553
Granicus River, 101
Gratian, 349, 351
    Decretum, 349
Great Amon Temple, 183
Great Jaguar Paw, 405
Great Peloponnesian War, 60, 96
Great Pyramid (La Venta), 400
Great Reform Bill (1832), 725–726
Great Rift, 176, 178
Great Russians, 366
Great Schism (1378–1417), 432–433
Great Stupa at Sanchi, 125
Great Trek of Boers, 867
Great Wall, 128, 200, 201
Greece, 1000, 1086
Greece, ancient:
    agriculture, 82
    Athens, 86–88

chronology of the rise of, 80
city-states/*polis*, 60, 73, 77–78, 99–100
colonies, 78–80
entertainment, 82–83
events/dates of early history of Athens
    and Sparta, 88
government, 76, 86
Homer, 75, 76–77
Messenian Wars, 84–85
Minoans, 73–75
Mycenaeans, 75–76
Persian Wars, 85, 88–90
philosophy, 56–64
poetry, 83–84
polis, 60, 73, 77–78, 99–100
religion, 83
society, 76, 81–83, 85–86
Sparta, 84–86, 88
tyrants, 80–81
warfare technology, 218–219
Greece, classical:
    achievements of, 107–109
    Athens, 92–96, 97–98
    conquest by Macedonians, 100–101
    Delian League, 73, 90
    literature, 98–100
    Peloponnesian War (First), 90, 92
    Peloponnesian War (Great), 60, 96
    Sparta, 96–97
    Thebes, 97
Gregory VII, Pope, 341–342
Gregory XI, Pope, 432
Gregory XII, Pope, 432
Gregory XVI, Pope, 812
Gregory the Great, 324, 326, 330
Grey, Earl, 725
Grey, Edward, 928
Groote, Gerard, 453
Guadeloupe, 532
Guadalupe Hidalgo, Treaty of (1848), 841
Guam, 983
Guesde, Jules, 794–795
Guilds:
    artisan, 631–632
    in medieval Japan, 269
    in Middle Ages, 348
    in Spain, 528
Guises, 471
Guptas, 124
    culture, 284–285
    events/dates, major, 284
    rule of, 283–284
Gutenberg, Johann, 370, 372, 453

Habsburg Empire, 602–603, 605, 739–740,
    757–758
Habsburg-Valois wars, 457
Habuba Kabirah, 6

Hacienda, 525–526, 831
Hadith, 309, 311, 376, 377
Hadrian, 151, 153, 155, 156
Hadrian's Wall, 200
Haec Sancta, 432
Haghia, 74
Hagia Sophia, 321
Hai Jui, 549
Haiti:
    emancipation of slaves, 713–714
    independence from France, 709
Hajj, 299
Hakim, al-, 382
Hakka, 549
Hakuin, 272, 570–571
Hamlet (Shakespeare), 482
Hammurabi, 7, 9
Hanbal, ibn-, 377
Hanbalites, 377
Han dynasty, 41
    Buddhism, 212–213
    Confucianism, 209
    eunuchs, 204, 207
    literature/art, 208–211
    Neo-Taoism, 211–212
    warfare technology, 219
Han dynasty, Former:
    decline and usurpation, 205–206
    dynastic cycle, 201
    early years, 202
    government during, 203–205
    women, 205
    Wu Ti, 202–203
Han dynasty, Later:
    aftermath of, 207–208
    decline of, 206
    first century, 206
Han Fei-tzu, 43, 44, 45
Hangchow, 237, 547
Hannibal, 139–141
Harappan. *See* Indus-Valley Culture
Hara Takashi, 907–908
Hardie, Keir, 795
Harding, Warren, 964–965
Hargreaves, James, 628
Harsha, 283
Hart, Robert, 887
Harun al-Rashid, 306, 307, 328
Hashim/Hashimite, 305
Hashishiyyin, 380, 382
Hastings, Battle of (1066), 360
Hastings, Warren, 856
Hattusas, 13
Haussmann, Georges, 781, 782
Havel, Vaclav, 1017–1018
Hawkins, John, 475
Hawley-Smoot Tariff Act (1930), 966
Hayes, Rutherford B., 767

Hebrews (Israelites), 51–56
Heian. *See* Nara and Heian Japan
Heiji War, 258, 259
Heisenberg, Werner, 815
Helena, 100
Hellas, school of, 99
Hellenism:
achievements of, 107–109
Alexander the Great, 101–104
architecture/art, 106–107
literature, 106
Macedonian conquest, 100–101
mathematics and science, 107
philosophy, 104, 106
Roman conquest of, 141–142
use of term, 100
Helmholtz, Hermann, 687
Helots, 85
Helsinki Accords (1975), 1014
Henrietta Marie, 587
Henry I, the Fowler, 340
Henry I, King of England, 360
Henry II, King of England, 352, 360–361
Henry II, King of France, 352, 471
Henry III, Emperor, 341
Henry III, King of France (Henry
of Navarre), 471–472
Henry IV, Emperor, 341–342
Henry IV, King of France, 472–473, 587
Henry V, Emperor, 342
Henry V, King of England, 426
Henry VI, Emperor, 344, 364
Henry VI, King of England and France,
426, 445
Henry VII, King of England, 348, 445
Henry VIII, King of England, 445,
463–464
Henry, Joseph, 687
Henry the Navigator, 450, 489
Heraclidae, 76
Heraclides of Pontus, 107
Heraclitus of Ephesus, 58
Heraclius, 318, 320
Herat, 386
Herodotus, 11, 85, 99, 118, 185, 488
Hertz, James, 687
Herzegovina, 927
Herzen, Alexander, 760
Herzl, Theodor, 820, 1068
Hesiod, 81, 82
Hidalgo y Costilla, Miguel, 711
Hideyoshi, Toyotomi, 561, 562, 563–564
Hieroglyphics, 11
High caliphate, 305–306, 307
Hijaz, 295
Hillel, 67
Himmler, Heinrich, 980
Hindenburg, Paul von, 934, 959, 960, 962

Hinduism, 45
description of, 287–288
friction between Muslims and, in
India, 860–861
historical development of, 132–133
post-Mauryan, 125
relations with Muslims, 388, 390–393
Hindu Kush, 18, 114
Hipparchus of Nicea, 107
Hippias, 88, 89
Hippocrates of Cos, 57, 99, 359
Hippodamus of Miletus, 106
Hirohito, Emperor, 988
Hiroshige, 567
Hiroshima, 988
Historical Records (Ssu-ma Ch'ien), 210,
211
History of Rome (Livy), 152, 167
Hitler, Adolph, 758
comes to power, 960–963
early career, 957–958
invasion of Austria and
Czechoslovakia, 973–974
Munich Agreement, 975, 976–977
racial theory and goals, 971, 972
renunciation of Versailles Treaty,
971–972
view of women, 965
World War II, 977–990
Hittites, 7, 12, 13, 217
Hobbes, Thomas, 483–484
Hobson, J. A., 923
Ho Chi Minh, 1053
Hohenstaufen Empire:
Frederick I (Barbarossa), Emperor,
344, 348, 363–364
Frederick II, Emperor, 362, 364
Innocent III, 364
Hohenzollerns, 603–605
Hōjō, 267, 268, 272
Holocaust, 980
Holy Land, 343–344
Holy League of Spain, 473
Holy Roman Empire, 363–364
Congress of Vienna and, 707
Thirty Years' War (1618–1648),
476–478
Homer, 75, 76–77
Homo sapiens, 3, 176
Hōnen, 271
Hong Kong and Shanghai Bank, 887
Hoover, Herbert, 966
Hopei, 248
Hoplite phalanx, 78
Horace, 152
Horemhab, 12
Horney, Karen, 821
Hōryūji Temple, 264

Hotzendorf, Conrad von, 931
House of Lancaster, 445
House of York, 445
Housing reform, 783
Hsia, 22, 23
Hsien Pi, 208
Hsiung Nu, 200, 203, 206
Hsuan Tsang, 212
Hsuan-tsung, 227–229
Hsu Hui (Xu Hui), 1044
Hsun-tzu, 42
Huai River, 21
Huari, 30, 414–415
Huber, A. V., 783
Hubertusburg, Treaty of (1763), 607
Hudson Bay Co., 769
Huerta, Victoriano, 842
Hughes, Besançon, 471
Huguenots, 471, 595, 671
Huitzilopochtli, 406, 408
Hulagu Khan, 384–385
Hull House, 801
Humanism, 435–438, 453–454
Humanitas, 144
Human sacrifice:
Aztec, 408
Benin, 506
in China, 24, 26
Mayan, 403
Teotihuacán, 401, 402
Toltecs, 406
Hunayn ibn Ishaq, 308–309
Hundred Years' War, 362, 425, 427
causes of, 426
Edward III, 426
events/dates, major, 428
French in, 426
Joan of Arc, 426, 428
Treaty of Troyes, 426
Hungarian Diet, 740
Hungarians, 332, 340
Hungary, 602
aristocracy, 616
conflict between church and
Communist party, 1001
formation of, 757–758
Marshall Plan and, 1001
moves toward independence
in, 1016–1017
Revolution (1956), 1004
Hung Hsiu-ch'uan, 884–885
Hung Mai, 236
Huns, 163, 206, 283, 316
Hunter gatherers, 3, 4, 177
Hurrians, 217
Hus, Jan, 432, 456
Husak, Gustave, 1017–1018
Husayn, 304, 305

Husayn I, 646
Huss, John, 372
Huxley, Thomas Henry, 809–810, 821
Hu Yao-pang (Hu Yaobang), 1045
Hyksos, 12, 217

Iberia, 300
IBM, 1030, 1031
Ibn al-Arabi, 380
Ibn al-Athir, 385
Ibn Battuta, 510, 511
Ibn Khaldun, 382–383
Ibn Maymum (Maimonides), 322, 380, 381
Ibn Qala'un, 382
Ibn Rushd (Averroës), 322, 380
Ibn-Sina (Avicenna), 322
Idris Alawma, 505
Igbo-Ukwu, 506
Ignatius of Loyola, 464–465
Île-de-France, 361
Ilkhanids, 384–386
Iliad, The (Homer), 75, 76, 77
Iltutmish, 390
Imam, 305
Imperialism. *See* New imperialism
Imperium, 136
Import substitution, 836
Imru l-Qais, 297
Incas, 30, 415–418, 522–523
Index of Forbidden Books, 372, 454
India:
    British colonial rule, 854–860
    caste system 132, 286–287
    events/dates, major, 222, 422, 600, 746, 918
    Gandhi, 859, 860, 1074
    Gandhi, Indira, 1075–1076
    Gandhi, Rajiv, 1076
    Islam in, 387–393
    Nehru, 859, 1074–1075
    nuclear energy and, 1029
    Rao, P. V. Narasimha, 1076
    resistance to the British, 858–860
    Sing, V. P., 1076
India, classical traditions:
    religion, 287–291
    society, 286–287
India, early civilization:
    events/dates, major, 21, 70, 124
    Indus-Valley Culture (Harappan), 15, 16–18
    Neolithic societies, 4, 15
    origin of name, 18
    religion in, 37, 45–51
    Vedic Aryan, 16, 18–21, 45–46
India, first empire:
    Mauryans, 113, 120–124
        political background, 120
India, Gupta Age:
    culture, 284–285
    events/dates, major, 284
    rule of, 283–284
India, Mughals (Timurids):
    Akbar's reign, 649, 651–652
    events/dates, major, 652
    last great, 649–650
    origins, 648–649
    political decline, 650
    Sikhs and Marathas, 650
India, post-Mauryan:
    culture, 124
    economics, 124
    religion, 124–126
Indian National Congress, 858–859
Indian Revolt (1857), 855, 858
Indo-Aryans, 18
Indo-European, 18
Indochinese Union, 1053
Indo-Greeks of Bactria, 127
Indonesia, 1076–1077
Indra, 18, 19, 20
Indulgences, attack on, 455–456
Indus River, 15
Industrial Revolution, 686
    child labor and, 732
    eighteenth-century, 626–630
    family structures and, 731–732
    impact on warfare technology, 774–775
    iron production, 629
    major inventions, 629
    Marx's criticism of, 736–739
    proletarianization of factory workers and artisans, 731
    steam engine, 628–629, 686, 1026
    textile industry, 627–628, 686
    women in, 732–736
Industry, in Japan, 901–904
Indus-Valley Culture (Harappan), 15
    architecture, 16, 35
    cities, 16–17
    collapse of, 17–18
    economic life, 17
    general character, 16
    material culture, 17
    religion, 17
Ingenui in obsequio, 334
Innocent III, Pope, 350, 361, 362, 364, 431
Inquiry into the Nature and Causes of the Wealth of Nations, An (Smith), 671
Inquisition, 445
Institutes of the Christian Religion (Calvin), 461
Interpretation of Dreams, The (Freud), 818
Intolerable Acts (1774), 691
Inuyama Castle, 560
Investiture struggle, 341–342
Ionia/Ionians, 58, 76, 88–89
Iphigenia in Tauris, 100
Iqbal, Muhammad, 860, 865–866
Iran:
    Achaemenids, 53, 113, 114, 116–120
    events/dates, major, 120
    forefathers of Iranians, 114
    Islamic conquest of, 300, 307
    Kushans, 128–129
    meaning of name and range of, 113–114
    Parthians, 127–128, 155, 279–280
    religion, 114–115
    Sakas, 128
    Sasanids, 280–283
    Timurids, 386
    Western impact on, 862–863
    Zoroastrianism, 114–116
Iraq, 1013, 1067, 1070
Ireland, home rule issues and relations with England, 725, 762–764
Irigoyen, Hipólito, 838
Irnerius, 349
Iron Age, 24–27, 179, 180–181
Iron Curtain, 1000, 1002
Iroquois Nation, 531
Isabella of Castile, 444–445, 526
Isagoras, 88
Ishraqi school, 647
Ishtar, 51
Islam/Islamic empires:
    in Asia, 652–655
    declining power and independence in the eighteenth century, 861–862
    emulation of the West, 863–865
    events/dates, major, 866
    growth of, 878–879
    integration of Western and Islamic ideas, 865–866
    nationalism and, 866
    Ottoman Empire, 637–644
    politics and, 1071–1072
    purification and revival of, 866
    reform movements, 868
    responses to foreign encroachment, 863
    Safavid Shi'ite Empire, 644–648
    Shari'a, 640
    Shi'ite-Sunni political rift, 653–654
    Timurids/Mughals, 648–652
    Ulama, 640, 643, 649
Islam (622–945):
    Abbasid state, 302–303, 306–307
    architecture, 310, 311
    art, 311
    caliphate, 302–303

centrists, 305

classical culture, 307–311

early conquests, 299–301

events/dates, major, 305, 307, 309

first civil war (656–661), 302, 304

high caliphate, 305–306, 307

Kharijites, 304

impact of, on the East and West, 320–322

language and literature, 301, 309, 311

Muhammad and the Qur'an, 296–299

origins and early development, 295–299, 311–312

prayer, proper positions in, 304

Shi'a, 304–305

south of the Sahara, 496–497

Ulama, 303

Umma, 299, 303–305

Islam (1000–1500):

in Egypt, 380, 382–383

events/dates, major, 385, 386

Ghaznavids, 383

in India, 387–393

in North Africa, 379–383

Saljuqs, 383–384

Shi'ite, consolidation of, 378

in Spain, 379–380

Sufi piety and organization, 377–378

Sunni, consolidation of, 375–377

Isma'ilis, 378

Assassins, 380, 382

Isocrates, 64

Israel:

See also Jews

Arab-Israeli conflict, 1068–1071

founding of, 67

Yom Kippur War, 1028

Israelites (Hebrews), 51–56

See also Jews; Judaism

Istanbul, 638

Itagaki Taisuke, 905

Italy:

attack on Ethiopia, 972–973

barbarian invasion of, 316–317

city-state, 433–434

events/dates, major, 754

French invasion of (1494–1527), 441–442

Greek colonies in, 78–80

medieval, 365

Mussolini and fascism, 954–957

nationalism in, 740

political decline of, 441–443

prehistoric, 135

Renaissance in, 433–440, 442

Roman conquest of, 139

Triple Alliance, 595, 925, 927–928

unification of, 750–752

universities in the Middle Ages, 348–349

World War II and, 984

Itō Hirboumi, 885–886, 899, 904–905, 907, 908

Iturbide, Agustín de, 711–712, 840

Itzcoatl, 406, 407

Ivan III (Ivan the Great), 366–367

Ivan IV (Ivan the Terrible), 554, 599

Ivan V, 599

Ivan the Terrible, 992

Iwasaki Yatarō, 901

Izumi Shikibu Diary, 261

Jackson, Jesse, 1011

Jacobins/Jacobin Club, 698–701

Jacquerie, 426, 430

Jahan, 649, 651

Jahangir, 649

Jahiz, al-, 308

Jains, 46, 48–49, 393

Jamaica, 532

slave revolts in, 714

James Edward Stuart, 591

James I, King of England, 586–587

James II, King of England, 590

James VI of Scotland, 586

Jamestown, Virginia, 530

Janissaries, 641, 642–643

Japan:

events/dates, major, 71, 223, 252, 423, 562, 747

foot soldier revolution, 561–562

invasions of Korea (1592), 554

Jōmon culture, 251

origins of, 251

Warring States Era, 559–563

Yayoi Revolution, 251–252

Japan (1853–1945):

Depression of 1929, impact of, 904, 909–910

events/dates, major, 912

growth of a modern economy, 900–904

Meiji period (1868–1890), 898–900, 906–907

militarism of and German Nazism, 912–913

overthrow of Tokugawa *bakufu* (1853–1868), 896–898

Pearl Harbor, 911–912, 980–982

politics of imperial (1890–1945), 904–913

Seiyūkai, formation of, 904–905

Sino-Japanese War (1894–1895), 885–886

war with China (1937–1949), 894–896

World War II and, 980–982, 983, 986, 988

Japan (1945–):

economic growth, 1038–1040

occupation of, 1035–1036

parliamentary politics, 1036–1038

society and culture, 1040–1041

Japan, medieval:

agriculture, 269

Ashikaga, 268

Buddhism, 269–273

commerce, 269

feudalism defined, 266–267

guilds, 269

Kamakura, 267–268

Minamoto Yoritomo, 264–265

women in warrior society, 268

Japan, Nara, and Heian:

court government, 255–256, 258–259

culture, 259–264

education, 260

land and taxes, 256–257

literature, 260–262

religion, 262–264

samurai, rise of, 257–258

seventh century, 254–255

writing, 261

Japan, Tokugawa era, 563

bureaucratization, 569–570

culture, 570–574

cycles of reform, 568–569

economy, 566–568, 570

establishment of, 564–566

events/dates, major, 575

forty-seven Rōnin, 568

overthrow of, 896–898

Japan, Yamato state:

courts, 253

religion, 253–254

tomb culture, 252–253

Japanese Family Storehouse (Saikaku), 572

Jaruzelski, Wojciech, 1015, 1016

Jaurès, Jean, 794

Jaxartes River, 113

Jemdet Nasr period, 33

Jenkins, Robert, 606

Jenne, 189

Jericho, 216

Jerome, 167, 323

Jerusalem, 52, 53, 344

Jesuits, 464–465

in Japan, 562

Jesus of Nazareth, 158, 160

Jewish State, The (Herzl), 820

Jews:

See also Israel; Judaism

antisemitism and birth of Zionism, 819–820

Ashkenazim, 67

Babylonian Exile of, 116

Jews (continued)
    Diaspora, 67
    eighteenth-century ghettos, 632–633
    emancipation of European, 778–780
    First Crusades and, 344
    Golden Age, 67
    Holocaust, 980, 982
    Israelites (Hebrews), 51–56
    Justinian and, 318
    during the Middle Ages, 344, 348, 349
    Moorish, 380
    Nazis and, 963
    persecution of, 67
    Roman, 157
    Sephardim, 67
Jihad, 301, 868
Jiménez de Cisneros, Francisco, 454
Jinnah, Muhammad Ali, 860, 1074
Jitō, Empress, 255
Joanna the Mad, 445
Joan of Arc, 426, 428
Joao VI, 712
Jōei Code, 265
John I, King of England, 348, 361, 362
John XII, Pope, 340
John XXIII, Pope, 814
John Paul II, Pope, 814
Johnson, Lyndon, 1011–1012
Jōmon culture, 251
Jonson, Ben, 482
Jordan, 1067
Joseph, brother of Napoleon, 704
Joseph, Franz, 740
Joseph I, Habsburg emperor, 603
Joseph II, of Austria, 677–679, 779
Josephine de Beauharnais, 704
Josetsu, 273
Josiah of Judah, King, 56
Jos plateau, 180
Journey to the West, 212
Juan Juan, 208
Juárez, Benito, 840–841
Judah, 52, 53
Judaism, 66–67
Judith of Bavaria, 332
Jugurtha, King of Numidia, 148
Jugurthine War (111), 148
Julian the Apostate, 161, 163
Julius II, Pope, 442–443, 455
Jung, Carl, 818
Junkers (German noble landlords),
    604–605, 616
Jus gentium, 151
Justinian, Emperor, 281, 317–318, 321

Ka'ba (Kaaba), 295, 296
Kabir, 393
Kabuki, 572

Kadar, Janos, 1004, 1017
Kahn, Sayyid Ahmad, 859
Kaifeng, 237
Kaiping Coal Mine, 886
Kalahari Desert, 174
Kalidasa, 284–285
Kalinga, 121
Kamakura, 267–268
Kanem, 191, 503–505
K'ang Hsi, 552–553, 554, 555, 556
K'ang Yu-wei, 888–889, 892
Kanishka, 128–129
Kansas-Nebraska Bill (1854), 765
Kanuri, 192, 503–505
Kao Tsu, 202, 203, 204
Karma, 46–47, 48, 132
Kartir (Kirdir), 281, 282
Kassites, 7, 217
Katib Chelebi, 643
Katō Kōmei, 909
Katsura Tarō, 908
Kautilya, 120
Kavad I, 283
Kay, James, 628
Kaya States, 253
Kazakhstan, 1074
Keita dynasty, 500, 501
Kellogg-Briand Pact (1928), 959
Kennedy, John F., 1004, 1011
Kenya, 1062
Kenyatta, Jomo, 1062
Kepler, Johannes, 666
Kerensky, Alexander, 937
Kerma, 182, 183
Key, Ellen, 823
Keynes, John Maynard, 943
Khadija, 296, 298
Khaljis, 390
Kharijites, 304
Khatami, Mohammad, 1073
Khmer Rouge, 1054–1055
Khoikhoi, 177, 514–515
Khoisan:
    languages, 177
    people, 192–193
Khomeini (Khumayni), Ruhollah, 1073
Khorasan, 300, 303, 307
Khrushchev, Nikita, 1004, 1013–1014
Khufu, 11
Khush, 182
Khwarizm, 384
Kiev, medieval, 364, 366
Kilwa, 510, 511
Kim Il-sung, 1050, 1051
Kim Jong-il, 1051
Kim Young-sam, 1052
King Lear (Shakespeare), 482
King, Martin Luther, Jr., 1011

King's Men, 482
Ki no Tsurayuki, 260
Kirdir, 281, 282
Kirov, Sergei, 953
Klein, Melanie, 821
Knighthood, 351–352
Koch, Robert, 783
Koguryo, 253
Kollontai, Alexandra, 951
Kongo kingdom, 508–509
Koprülüs (father and son), 643
Korea:
    civil war, 1050–1051
    early history of, 575–577, 888
    as a Japanese colony, 1050
    partition into North and South, 1050
    twentieth century, 1049–1052
Korean War (1950), 1010, 1036
Koryo, 576
Kosala, 120
Kosovo, 1023
Kossuth, Louis, 739–740
Kotosh, 412
Kotosh religious tradition, 412
Krishna, 287, 288
Kropotkin, Peter, 892
Kruger, Paul, 928
Krupp family, 778
Kubitschek, Juscelino, 849
Kublai Khan, 243–244, 267
Kufa, 303
Kūkai, 264
Ku Klux Klan, 966
Kulaks, 952
Kulikov Meadow, Battle of, 366
Kulturkampf, 811–812
Kumaradevi, Princess, 283
Kumbi/Kumbi Saleh, 189, 191, 497–499
Kung, Prince, 886
K'ung Fu-tzu, 39
Kuomintang (Nationalist Party)
    unification of China, 890, 892–894,
    1049
Kuroda Kiyotaka, 899
Kushans, 128–129
Kuwait, 1070, 1071
Kūya, 270
Ku Yen-wu, 557
Kyrgyzstan, 1074

Labor:
    child, 732, 796
    conditions during Industrial
      Revolution, 732
    women in the work force, after World
      War II, 1008–1010
Labour Party, 795
Lacombe, Claire, 699

Ladies' National Association for the Repeal of the Contagious Diseases Acts, 822
Ladino, 67
Lady Kanal Ikal, 405
Lady Zac Kuk, 405
Lagash, 6
Lake Chad, 178, 189
Land and Freedom, 760
Landlordism, late imperial China, 546
Language(s):
    See also under type of
    African, 176–177
    Aramaic, 119, 126
    in East Asia, 27
    Elamite, 114
    Ladino, 67
    Sanskrit, 124
    Sinitic, 27
    Sumerian, 6
    Ural-Altaic, 27
Laocoön, 105, 107
Laos, 888, 1053
Lao-tzu, 42, 43
La Reforma, 840
Las Casas, Bartolomé de, 523
Lateran Accord (1929), 956–957
Later Han dynasty. *See* Han dynasty, Later
Latifundia, 145
Latifundias, 831–832
Latin America:
    See also Americas; *specific country*
    conflict between church and state, 812
    consequences of independence, 831–833
    dates/map showing independence of countries, 830
    Depression of the 1920s, impact of, 835–836
    economic conditions, following independence, 833–836
    eighteenth-century developments, 708–709
    exploitation of resources, 833–835
    first movements toward independence, 709–713
    foreign ownership and influence, 835
    landowners in nineteenth century, 831–832
    since 1945, 1077–1085
    social change following independence, absence of, 831
    submissive political philosophies, 832–833
    wars for independence in, 712
Latin League, 139
Latium, 136
Latvia, 1018

Laud, William, 587, 588
La Venta, 29, 399, 400
Lavigerie, Charles Cardinal, 812
Law:
    canon, 349
    Code of Hammurabi, 7, 8, 9
    Corpus Juris Civilis, 317
    Magna Carta (1215), 344, 361
    mallus under Charlemagne, 328
    Montesquieu on, 672–673
    Roman, 137–139, 151, 349
    Twelve Tablets, 138–139, 143
League of Augsburg, 596
League of Cognac, 457
League of Nations, 909, 941, 971–973
League of Venice, 441–442
Lebanon, 1067, 1070
Le-Bon, Gustave, 819
Lechfeld, 340
Lee Teng-hui, 1049
Legalism 43–45, 199
Lenin, V. I., 737, 775, 795–797, 798, 923, 937–938, 939, 949, 950
Leningrad Symphony, 992
Leo I, Pope, 323
Leo III, Emperor, 318, 320, 324
Leo III, Pope, 328
Leo IX, Pope, 324, 341
Leo X, Pope, 442, 456
Leo XIII, Pope, 813–814
Léon, Pauline, 696, 699
Leonardo da Vinci, 439
Leonidas, King, 89
Leopold I, Habsburg emperor, 596, 603
Leopold II, Habsburg emperor, 679, 697
Leopold II, King of Belgium, 871
Leotychidas, King, 89
LePen, Jean-Marie, 1008
Lepidus, 149
Lesbos, 92
Lesotho, 867
Lespinasse, Julie de, 674
Lessing, Gotthold, 671
Le Thanh Tong, 579–580
Letter Concerning Toleration (Locke), 667, 668
Letters on the English (Voltaire), 669
Leucippus of Miletus, 58
Leuctra, 97
Levell, Charles, 807
Leviathan (Hobbes), 483, 484
Liang Ch'i-ch'ao, 889
Liberia, 715
Liberalism, 659
    early nineteenth-century political, 721–723
    relationship between nationalism and, 722–723

Liberator, The (Garrison), 729
Libreville, 715
Libya, 868, 978, 1067
Liebig, Justus von, 687
Life of an Amorous Man (Saikaku), 572
Life of an Amorous Woman (Saikaku), 572
Life of Jesus (Strauss), 810
Li Hung-chang, 885–886, 887
Lincoln, Abraham, 765–766
Lin Piao (Lin Biao), 1043, 1044
Lin Tse-hsu, 882, 883
Li Po, 228–229, 232, 234, 260
Li Ssu, 43, 45, 200
Lister, Joseph, 783
Literature:
    Attic (Athenian) tragedy, 98
    Christian writers, 167–168
    classical Greek, 98–100
    courtly love, 360
    dictionary, first compilation, 209
    Greek poetry, 83–84
    Gupta, 284
    Han dynasty, 209–211
    Hellenistic, 106
    humanism, 435–438
    Islamic, 308, 309, 311
    Japanese, 260–262
    Middle Comedy, 99–100
    Ming-Ch'ing dynasty, 556–558
    Nara and Heian, 260–262
    Old Comedy, 98–99
    Ottoman, 643
    Roman, 151–152, 155–156
    Sanskrit, 124
    sixteenth century, 480–484
    Sung dynasty, 240–241
    T'ang dynasty, 228–229, 232, 234
    Tokugawa, 570–573
    women portrayed in Athenian, 95–96
Lithuania, 1018
Little Big Horn, Battle of (1876), 768
Little Russians, 366
Liu Pin-yen (Liu Binyan), 1044
Livingstone, David, 812, 869
Livy, 152, 167
Lloyd-George, David, 803
Locarno Agreements (1925), 959
Locke, John, 484, 667–668, 690, 713
Lodi, Treaty of (1454–1455), 441
Lodis, 390
Logicians, 39
Lollardy, 463
Lombard, Peter, 351, 358, 455
Lombards, 320, 324, 326, 327
London Great Exhibition (1851), 778
Long Parliament and Civil War, 587–588
López, Francisco Solano, 846
Lord Pacal, 405

Lorenzo the Magnificent, 434
Lothar, 332
Lotharingia, 332, 340
Louis I, King of France, 471
Louis VII, King of France, 360
Louis VIII, King of France, 363
Louis IX, King of France, 357, 362–363
Louis XI, King of France, 444
Louis XII, King of France, 441–442
Louis XIV, King of France, 473, 586, 593–598
Louis XV, King of France, 598
Louis XVI, King of France, 692–698
Louis XVIII, King of France, 723
Louis Philippe, King of the French, 725, 739
Louis the German, 332
Louis the Pious, 332, 335
Louisiana Purchase, 726
Lourdes, cult of the miracles of, 811
L'Ouverture, Toussaint, 709, 713
Lowell, Massachusetts (textile factories in), 727
Loyang, 25, 206
Lu, Empress, 204
Luba, 508
Lucretius, 151–152
Ludendorff, Eich, 934, 939, 958
Ludovico il Moro, 441
Lueger, Karl, 819, 958
Lu Hsun, 892
Lumumba, Patrice, 1062
Lunda, 508
Lusitania, 937
Luther, Martin, 372, 453, 454–458, 466–467
Lutheranism, political consolidation of the reformation, 461–463
Luthuli, Albert, 1064–1065
Lyceum (Aristotle), 63, 104
Lyell, Charles, 810
Lysander, 96, 97
Lytton, Earl of, 972

Maasai, 195
Maastricht, Treaty of (1991), 1006
MacArthur, Douglas, 1035
Macartney, Lord, 556
Macartney mission, 556, 557
Macaulay, Lord, 856, 857
Macbeth (Shakespeare), 482
MacDonald, John A., 769
MacDonald, Ramsay, 949
Macedon/Macedonia, 78, 100–101, 219
Macedonians, 1021
Mach, Ernst, 814
Machiavelli, Niccolò, 442, 443
MacMahon, Marshal, 755

Madero, Francisco, 842
Madman's Diary, A (Lu Hsun), 892
Madrasa, 376, 382
Maecenas, 152
Magadha, 120
Magellan, Ferdinand, 451, 491
Maghili, Muhammad al-, 504
Magi, 116
Magna Carta (1215), 344, 361
Magna Graecia, 80
Magnesia, 141
Magyars, 332, 758
Mahabharata, 19, 124, 577
Mahavira Vardhamana, 48, 132
Mahayana Buddhism, 277, 288–291
Mahdi, 305
Mahmud I, 644
Mahmud II, 863–864
Mahmud of Ghazna, 383
Maimonides (ibn Maymun), 322, 380, 381
Maitreya, 233, 247
Malaysia, 1076–1077
Mali, 179–180, 500–501
Malinke, 500–501
Mamakuna, 416
Mamluks, 306, 382–383, 638
Ma'mun, al-, 306, 308
Manchu dynasty, 39
   rule, end of, 882–887
   rule, pattern of, 551–553
   women, 549
Manchuria, 909
Mande, 500
Mandela, Nelson, 1058, 1065, 1066
Mani, 187, 281–282
Manichaeism, 281–282
Mannerism, 440
Manors and serfdom, 330, 331
Mansa Musa, 501
Mao Tse-tung (Mao Zedong), 38–39, 892, 895–896, 1042–1044
Maqurra, 189, 505
Marathas, 650
Marathon, 89
Marburg Colloquy, 458
Marconi, Guglielmo, 687
Marco Polo, 245, 246–247
Marcus Antonius, 149
Marcus Aurelius, 151, 153, 155
Mardonius, 89
Marduk, 51
Marginot Line, 977
Marie, Countess of Champagne, 360
Maria Theresa of Austria, 603, 606, 677–678
Marie Antoinette, Queen of France, 696, 698, 700
Marie Louise, Archduchess, 704

Maritime Customs Service, 887
Maritime innovations, 488–491
Marius, Gaius, 148
Mark Anthony, 149
Marne, Battle of (1914), 934
Marrakesh, 380
Marriage(s):
   arranged, 468–469
   Athenian, 94–95
   eighteenth-century, 618
   feminism and views on, 823
   impact of Industrial Revolution on, 734, 736
   impact of Reformation on, 467, 468–469
   medieval, 357, 358
   Mesopotamian, 8, 9
   nineteenth-century, 788–789
   timing of, 468
   Vedic Aryan, 19–20
Marshall, George C., 896, 1000
Marshall Plan, 1000–1001
Martin V, Pope, 432
Martinique, 532
Martin of Tours, 323, 329
Marx, Karl, 659, 736–739, 793
Mary II, 590–591
Mary Stuart, 475
Mary Tudor, 464
Masaccio, 439
Masaryk, Jan, 1002
Masaryk, Thomas, 1002
Mastaba, 34
Master K'ung, 39
Matara, 187
Mathematical Principles of Natural Philosophy (Newton), 667
Mathematics:
   Hellenistic, 107
   Mayan, 404
Mauguet, Marie, 791
Mauritania, 179–180
Mauryans, 113, 120–124
Maximian, 315
Maximilian, Archduke of Austria, 754, 841
Maximilian, Duke of Bavaria, 478
Maximilian I, Emperor, 442, 445, 456
Maxwell, James, 687
Mayapan, 406
Mayas, 29, 403–406
May Fourth Movement, 890–892
Ma Ying-ch'u (Ma Yinchu), 1042
May Laws (1873), 811
Mazarin, Cardinal, 593
Mazdak, 283
Mazdakite movement, 281, 283
Mazowiecki, Tadeusz, 1016
Mazzini, Giuseppe, 721, 750

McCarthy, Joseph, 1010
McKinley, William, 801
Meat Packing Act (1906), 801
Mecca, 295, 298–299, 303
Medea (Euripides), 95–96
Medes, 114
Medici, Cosimo de', 434, 437
Médicis, Catherine de, 471
Medina, 298–299, 303
Megara, 90, 92
Megasthenes, 124
Mehmed II, 638, 639
Meiji period (1868–1890), 898–900, 906–907
Mein Kampf (Hitler), 958, 971, 972
Melanchthon, Philip, 462
Memphis, Kushite conquest of, 182
Menander, 100, 127
Mencius, 41
Mendel, Gregor, 808
Menes, 10
Mercantilism, 520–522, 773
Merchants, rise of, 346
Merenptah, 13
Meroitic empire, 183–187
Merovich, 324
Merovingians, 324–325
Mesoamerica:
    Aztecs, 29, 406–411
    classic, 401–406
    events/dates, major, 28, 398
    formative (pre-classic), 399–401
    human sacrifice, 401, 402, 403, 406, 408
    Mayas, 29, 403–406
    meaning of name, 398
    Monte Alban, 401
    Neolithic societies, 4
    Olmec, 29, 399–400
    periods of, 29, 398
    post-classic, 406–411
    range of, 28–29
    Teotihuacán, 401–403
    Toltecs, 29, 406
    Valley of Oaxaca, 400–401
    writing and use of a calendar in, 29, 401
Mesopotamia, 4
    Alexander the Great conquest of, 101
    architecture, 8, 32–33
    cities, 5–6
    civilization, 5–10
    government, 5, 7–8
    key events and people in, 8
    marriage, 8, 9
    religion, 8
    slavery, 8–10
    society, 8–10
    women, 8, 9

Messenia, 84–85
Messiah, 67
Mesta, 444
Metamorphoses (Ovid), 152
Metternich, Klemens, 740
Mexica, 406
Mexican-American War, 729
Mexico (New Spain):
    Chiapas, rebellion in, 1084
    Díaz and dictatorship, 841–842
    events/dates, major, 842
    exploitation of resources, 833–835
    foreign intervention, 841
    independence for, 711–712
    Partido Revolucionario Institucional (PRI), 844, 1083–1084
    revolution (1911), 842–845
    turmoil following independence, 840–841
Miao Wars, 546
Michelangelo, 439–440
Middle Ages, early:
    See also Japan, medieval
    Byzantine Empire, 317–320
    decline of Roman authority, 315–317
    development of Roman Catholic church, 322–324
    Franks, 324–334
    Germanic migrations, 315–316
    Islam, impact of, 320–322
    manors and serfdom, 330, 331
    society, 333–335
Middle Ages, High:
    children in, 358–360
    Crusades, 338, 342–344
    empire revival and Otto I, 340
    government, 346–348
    Jews in Christian society, 348, 349
    merchants, rise of, 346
    peasants/serfs, 330, 355–357
    politics, 360–366
    revival of Roman Catholic church, 340–342
    schools and universities, 348–351
    society, 351–369
    towns, 344, 346
    women in, 357–358
Middle Ages, Late:
    Black Death, 428–431
    breakdown and revival of the church, 431–433
    Hundred Years' War and rise of national sentiment, 425–428
    revival of monarchy, 443–445
Middle Comedy, 99–100
Middle East:
    See also under name of country
    Arab-Israeli conflict, 1068–1071

Islamism and politics, 1071–1072
    oil, role of, 1071
    postcolonial, 1067–1073
Middle East Peace Agreement, 1070
Midway, Battle of, 983
Migrations, after 1945, 1008
Milan, 315, 434, 441
    Decree (1807), 704
    Edict of (313), 322
Miletus, 88
Milinda, 127
Military:
    French women petition to bear arms, 696
    Grand Army of Napoleon 705
    slave soldiers *(devshirme)*, 641, 642, 643
Mill, John Stuart, 791
Millerand, Alexander, 795
Milošević, Slobodan, 1022
Miltiades, 89
Minamoto Yoritomo, 264–265, 266–267
Mindszenty, Cardinal, 1001
Ming dynasty, 546–558
Ming History, 553
Minoans, 73–75
Minos, 73
Missi dominici, 328
Missionaries:
    in Africa, 812, 869–870
    modern movement, 812–813
Missouri Compromise, 765
Mita, 416
Mitanni, 14
Mithradates I, 127
Mithraism, 322
Mitimaqs, 416
Moche, 30, 413–414
Moctezuma II, 522
Modern Devotion, 453
Mogadishu, 510, 511
Mohenjo-Daro, 16, 35
Mohists, 39
Moksha, 48, 132
Moldova, 1074
Molotov, Vyacheslav, 1000
Moltke, Helmuth von, 932, 933
Mona Lisa (Leonardo da Vinci), 439
Monarchies, revival of, 443–445
Monastic culture:
    See also under name of order
    development of, 322–323
    Frank, 326
    growth of, 466
    in Japan, 562
    Ming-Ch'ing dynasties and, 555–556
Mongols, 553, 554
    in China (Yuan dynasty), 242–247

Mongols *(continued)*
    Genghis Khan, 242, 243, 384
    Ilkhanids and, 384–386
    in Russia, 366
Monophysite Christians, 189, 324
Monotheism:
    defined, 51
    evolution of, 53–56
Monroe Doctrine, 712
Montague, Mary Wortley, 591
Monte Alban, 401
Montenegrins, 1021
Montenegro, 927
Montesquieu, 672–673, 674, 713
Montgomery, Bernard, 984
Montmorency-Châtillons, 471
Moorish culture, 379–380
Moravia, 602, 617
More, Thomas, 454
Morelos y Pavón, José María, 711
Mori Arinori, 901
Morocco:
    independence for, 1067
    Islam in, 380
    power struggles in, 495, 496
    World War I in, 928, 929–930
    World War II in, 984
Mosaddeq, Muhammad, 1073
Moscow, 367
Moses, 52, 53–54, 55, 66
Mosheshwe, King, 867
Mothers' Protection League, 823
Motoori Norinaga, 574
Mo-tzu, 39
Mount Fuji, 253
Mount Hiei, 263
Mozambique, 1062
Mu'awiya, 300, 302
Mubarak, Husni, 1070
Mughals (Timurids):
    Akbar's reign, 649, 651–652
    events/dates, major, 652
    last great, 649–650
    origins, 648–649
    political decline, 650
    Sikhs and Marathas, 650
Muhammad, 296–299, 878
Muhammad Ali, 863
Muhammad Shaybani, 652
Mukden, 552
Mulla Sadra, 647
Mumtaz Mahal, 649, 651
Munich Agreement, 975, 976–977
Murad IV, 643
Murasaki Shikibu, 261
Music, students and popular, 1007–1008
Muslim Brotherhood (Egypt), 861
Muslim League, 858

Muslims:
    defined, 297
    friction between Hindus and, in India, 860–861
    rebellion in China, 885
    relations with Hindus, 388, 390–393
Mussolini, Benito, 954–957, 972–973, 978
Mutesa, Bagandan king, 871, 874
Mycale, Battle of, 89
Mycenae, 75
Mycenaeans, 75–76, 218

Nabuco, Joaquim, 846
Nadir Shah, 646, 650
Nagasaki, 988
Nagashino, Battle of (1575), 561
Nagy, Imre, 1004
Na'ima, 643
Nakae Tōju, 573
Nanak, Guru, 650, 651
Nan Chao, 229
Nandas, 120
Nanking, 207, 208
Nanking, Treaty of (1842), 882
Nanking decade (1927–1937), 892–894
Nantes, Edict of (1598), 472–473
Nan Yueh, 578
Napatan empire, 182–183
Naples, 433, 441
Napoleon Bonaparte, 701, 702–708, 862
Napoleon II, King of France, 739
Napoleon III, King of France, 750, 752, 754–755, 780–781, 841
Nara and Heian Japan:
    court government, 255–256, 258–259
    culture, 259–264
    education, 260
    land and taxes, 256–257
    literature, 260–262
    religion, 262–264
    samurai, rise of, 257–258
    seventh century, 254–255
    writing, 261
Nara-Osaka, 252
Narrow Road of Oku (Bashō), 571
Nasir, al-, 382, 384
Nasser, Gamal Abdel, 1003, 1069
Nathan the Wise (Lessing), 671
National Association for the Advancement of Colored People (NAACP), 767
National Council of French Women (CNFF), 791
National Industrial Recovery Act (NIRA), 967
Nationalism, 659
    African, 871–873
    emergence of, 719–721
    from 1870s onward, 820–821

    Islam, 866
    relationship between liberalism and, 722–723
Nationalismo, in Argentina, 839
Nationalist Party (Kuomintang)
    unification of China, 890, 892–894
National Labor Union, 799
National Union of Women's Suffrage Societies, 791
Native Americans:
    decline in population of, 526
    forced labor of, in Potosí, 525
    in North America, 531–532
    Trail of Tears, 768
    treatment of, in America, 767–768
NATO (North Atlantic Treaty Organization), 1002–1003
Natsume Sōseki, 905
Natural selection, 808–809
Nazca, 30, 413
Nazism, 912–913, 958, 960–964
Nazi-Soviet Pact, 977
Nearchus, 106
Near East:
    See also specific country
    events/dates, major, 222, 422, 660
Near East, ancient:
    Assyrians, 13–14
    early civilization in, 4–14
    Egyptian civilization, 10–12
    events/dates, major, 14, 70
    Hittites, 13
    Neolithic Age, 4
Nebuchadnezzar II, 53
Nedim, 643
Nehemiah, 56
Nehru, Jawaharlal, 859, 1074–1075
Nelson, Horatio, 702, 703
Nemea, 80, 83
Neo-colonial economy, 836
Neolithic Age, 4, 32
    cultures in the Sudan, 179–180
Neolocalism, 618
Neo-Taoism, 211–212
Nerchinsk, Treaty of (1689), 555
Nero, 151, 153
Nerva, 151, 153
Nesin, Aziz, 1067
Nestorian Christianity, 245
Netanyahu, Benjamin, 1070, 1071
Netherlands:
    Congress of Vienna and, 707
    Modern Devotion, 453
    revolt against Spain, 473–475
    United, 595
Neustria, 325
New Atlantis (Bacon), 666
Newburn, Battle of (1640), 587

New Collection from Ancient and Modern Times (Shinko-kinshū), 270
Newcomen, Thomas, 628
New Deal, 966–967
New Imperialism:
    cultural, religious, and social interpretations, 923
    defined, 923
    expansion of European power and, 921–925
    motives for, 923
    strategic and political interpretations, 923–924
New Principles on Chinese Population (Ma Ying-ch'u), 1042
New Spain, 5
    independence for, 710–712
Newton, Isaac, 666–667
New World. *See* Americas
Nezahualcoyotl, 411
Nguyen dynasty, 580, 1052
Niani, 501
Nicaragua, 1081–1082
Nicea, Council of (325), 165, 317
Nicene Creed (325), 165, 317, 324, 326, 328
Nichiren, 271–272
Nicholas I, Pope, 324
Nicholas I, Tsar of Russia, 723, 759
Nicholas II, Pope, 341
Nicholas II, Tsar of Russia, 761, 797, 930
Nicholas V, Pope, 438
Nicias, Peace of (421), 96
Nicomedia, 315
Nien rebellion, 885
Nietzsche, Friedrich, 816–817
Nigeria, 1063–1064
Niger-Kongo languages, 176, 177
Niger River, 189
Nightingale, Florence, 750
Nightmare (Hsu Hui), 1044
Nijmwegen, Peace of (1678, 1679), 595
Nile River, 4, 5, 10, 174
Nilo-Saharan languages, 176, 177
Nilotic Africa:
    Aksumite empire, 187–188
    events/dates, major, 188
    Khush, 182
    Meroitic empire, 183–187
    Napatan empire, 182–183
    range of, 174–175
Nineveh, 14
Nine Years' War (1689–1697), 596
Nintoku, King, 252
Nixon, Richard, 1004, 1012 1054
Nizam al-Mulk, 383–384
Nkrumah, Kwame, 1062
Nobiles, 139

Nobility, in the Middle Ages, 346–348, 351–353
Nobunaga, Odo, 561, 562
Nok culture, 180–181
Nomes, 11–12
Nonconformist denominations, 811, 812
Nō plays, 273–274, 568, 570, 572, 1040, 1041
Noriega, Manuel, 1012
Normans, 332
North, Lord, 691
North Africa:
    See also under name of country
    foreign involvement in, 863, 870, 924
    Islam in, 300, 379–383
    power struggles in, 495–496
    range of, 174
    World War II in, 978–979, 983–984
North America:
    See also America; Canada
    French and British colonies in, 530–532, 689–692
    nineteenth-century, 726
    slavery in, 532–535
North American Free Trade Agreement (NAFTA), 1084
Northern Wei, 225
North German Confederation, 752
North Korea, 1050–1052
North Vietnam, 1053, 1054
Notre Dame, 350
Novum Organum (Bacon), 666
Nubia/Nubians, 182, 505
Nuclear energy, 1029
Nuclear Test Ban Treaty (1963), 1004
Numantia, 142
Numidia, 148
Nunneries, 358, 466
Nun Shōgun, 267, 268
Nur al-Din, 382
Nuremberg Laws (1935), 963
Nyerere, Julius, 1062
Nystad, Peace of (1721), 601

O'Connell, Daniel, 725
Octavian, 149–150
Odes (Horace), 152
Odovacer, 316
Odyssey, The (Homer), 75, 76, 77
Ogata Kōrin, 570
Oghuz, 637
Oglethorpe, James, 531
O'Higgins, Bernardo, 710
Oil:
    electricity and demand for, 1027–1028
    global politics and role of, 1028–1029, 1071
Ojukwu, Odumegwu, 1063

Old Comedy, 98–99
Oliunina, E. A., 796
Olmec, 29, 399–400
Olympia, 80, 83
Olympus, Mount, 83
Oman/Omanis, 512, 1067
One Day in the Life of Ivan Denisovich (Solzhenitsyn), 1013
Ono no Komachi, 274
On the Morals that Befit a Free Man (Vergerio), 436
On the Motion of Mars (Kepler), 666
On the Revolutions of the Heavenly Spheres (Copernicus), 664, 665
Operation Barbarossa, 979
Operation Desert Storm, 1013
Opium War (1839–1842), 774, 881, 882–884
Oppenheimer, Samuel, 633
Optimates, 147
Orange Free State, 867
Order of the Hermits of Saint Augustine, 455
Ordinance of 1787, 727
Organization of Petroleum Exporting Nations (OPEC), 1028
Origin of Species, The (Darwin), 808
Orlando, Vittorio Emanuele, 940
Osaka, 567
Osman, 637
Ostrogoths, 316, 317
Othello (Shakespeare), 482
Otto I, Emperor, 339, 340
Otto IV, Emperor, 361, 362, 364
Ottoman Empire:
    classical, 639–641
    Crimean War (1854–1856), 747–750
    culture and society, 643–644
    decline of, 644
    economic development, 643
    events/dates, major, 644
    origins and development of, before 1600, 637–639
    political and military developments, 642–643
    slave soldiers (*devshirme*), 641, 642, 643
Ottoman Turks, 317, 320, 457
Ovid, 152
Oxford University, 350
Oxus River, 300

Pachomius, 322
Pacification of Ghent, 474
Pact of the Littoral (1831), 837
Paekche, 253
Pagan, 577
Paganism, 164
Pahlavas, 128

Pahlavi, 283
Paine, Thomas, 692
Pakistan, 1029, 1074
Palenque, 405
Paleolithic Age, 3–4, 32
Palestine, 1068–1069
Palestine Liberation Organization (PLO),
    1069
Panaetius, 143
Panama, 802, 835, 1012
Panama Canal, 802, 835
Pan Chao, 207
Panini, 124
Pankhurst, Emmeline, 791
Pan Ku, 207, 211
Pan-Slavic Congress, 740, 741
Pantheon, 156
Papacy. *See* Popes/papacy
Papal States, 326, 433, 442, 752
Papen, Franz von, 960
Papermaking, 685
Paraguay, independence for, 710
Paraguayan War (1865–1870), 845–846
Paris, redesign of, 780–781
Paris, Treaty of (1259), 362
Paris, Treaty of (1763), 608, 768
Paris, Treaty of (1783), 692
Paris Commune, 755
Park Chung-hee, 1051
Parleying, 360
Parmenides of Elea, 58
Parnell, Charles Stewart, 763
Parni, 127
Parsis, 116
Parthians, 127–128, 155, 279–280
Pasargadae, 116
Pascal, Blaise, 482
Pasternak, Boris, 1013
Pasteur, Louis, 783
Pataliputra, 120, 123, 124, 283
Patricians, 137, 138–139
Paul III, Pope, 465
Paul VI, Pope, 814
Paul of Tarsus, 158–159, 160
Pausanias, 89, 97
Payne, Daniel A., 729, 730
Peace of Augsburg (1555), 463, 476
Peace of Bretigny (1360), 426
Peace of Nicias (421), 96
Peace of Nijmwegen (1678, 1679), 595
Peace of Nystad (1721), 601
Peace of Ryswick (1697), 596
Pearl Harbor, 911–912, 980–982
Peasants/serfs, 616–617, 679, 759–760
    in the Middle Ages, 330, 355–357
Peasants' Revolt (1381), 430
Peasants' Revolt (1524–1525), 457–458,
    460

Pedro, Regent in Brazil, 712
Pedro I, Emperor of Brazil, 845
Pedro II, Emperor of Brazil, 845, 847
Peel, Robert, 725
Peking, 547, 552
Pelopidas, 97
Peloponnesian League, 86
Peloponnesian War (First), 90, 92
Peloponnesian War (Great), 60, 96
Penn, William, 531
Pensées (Pascal), 482
People's Republic of China. *See* China
People's Will, 760, 761
Pepin, King of Aquitaine, 332
Pepin I, Pope, 325
Pepin II, Pope, 325
Pepin III, Pope, 324, 326
Pequots, 531
Peres, Shimon, 1070
Perestroika, 1016
Pericles, 90, 92, 96, 99
Peripatos/Peripatetics, 63
Periplus, The, 194
Péron, Eva, 839, 840
Péron, Juan, 840, 1082
Perry, Matthew, 575, 774, 881, 896
Persepolis, 103, 118
Perseus, 141
Persia, 14
    See also Iran
    conquest by Alexander the Great,
        101–103
Persian Gulf War, 1013, 1028
Persians, 114
Persian Wars, 85, 88–90
Peru:
    See also Andean civilization
    architecture, 33–34, 412
    exploitation of resources, 833–835
    independence for, 710
Pétan, Henri Philippe, 936, 978
Peter (apostle), 160
Peter the Great, 555, 599–601, 617, 759
Peter III, Tsar of Russia, 607, 616
Peters, Carl, 926
Petition of Right, 587, 588
Petrarch, Francesco, 435–436
Phaestus, 74
Pharaohs, 10, 12, 13
Philip, Archduke, 445
Philip II Augustus, King of France, 344,
    349, 350, 361–362
Philip II, King of France, 473–474
Philip II, King of Macedon, 73, 100–101
Philip IV (the Fair), King of France, 363,
    426, 431–432
Philip V, King of Macedon, 140, 141
Philip V, King of Spain, 596, 598

Philip VI of Valois, 426
Philip of Hesse, 458
Philippines, 982, 983
Phillips, Thomas, 538
Philosophes, 668
Philosophy:
    Bacon, 666
    Islamic, 308
    Locke, 667–668
    Montesquieu, 672–673
    Newton, 666–667
    Nietzsche, 816–817
    Rousseau, 673–674, 675, 676
    sixteenth century, 480–484
    Tokugawa (Japan), 573–575
    Voltaire, 668–669, 670–671
Philosophy, in China, 37
    Confucianism, 39–42, 209
    dates and people, key, 45
    Legalism 43–45
    Neo-Taoism, 211–213
    Sung dynasty, 239–240
    Taoism, 42–43
Philosophy, Greek, 56
    Aristotle, 63–64
    cynics, 61
    early philosophers, 57
    Plato, 61–63
    political and moral, 59–64
    reason and scientific spirit, 57–59
    Socrates, 60–61, 63
    Sophists, 59, 60
Philosophy, Hellenistic:
    Epicureans, 104
    Stoics, 104, 106
Phoenicians, 488
Photius, 324
Pico della Mirandola, 436, 437
Piedmont, 740, 750–752
Pilgrims, 531
Pillow Book (Sei Shōnagon), 261, 262–263
Pimiko, Queen, 252, 253, 268
Pinochet, Augusto, 1081
Piracy, 521
Pi Scheng, 370
Pisistratus, 87
Pius VII, Pope, 702
Pius IX, Pope, 740, 813
Pius X, Pope, 814
Pizarro, Francisco, 415, 522–523
Planck, Max, 815
Plantations, slavery on, 534–535
Plassey, Battle of (1757), 608
Platea, Battle of, 89
Plato, 61–63, 98, 437–438, 666
Plebeians, 137, 138–139
Plekhanov, Georgii, 795
Plessy v. Ferguson, 767

Plutarch, 107
Po Chu-i, 260, 274
Podesta, 434
Poincaré, Henri, 814
Poland:
  aristocracy, 616
  communism and Solidarity in, 1013, 1016
  Marshall Plan and, 1001
  partition of (1772, 1793, and 1795), 681–682
  Reformation in, 462–463
  as a Soviet satellite, 1003–1004
  World War II in, 976, 980
Polis, 60, 73, 77–78, 99–100
Political parties, adoption of, 792
Polk, James, 841
Pol Pot, 1054–1055
Polybius, 143
Pomerania, 603–604
Pompadour, Marquise de, 674
Pompeii, 155
Pompey, Cnaeus, 148–149
Popes/papacy:
  See also name of pope
  Avignon, papal court at, 433
  Boniface VIII and Philip the Fair, 431–432
  Council of Basel (1431–1449), 432–433
  Council of Constance (1414–1417), 432
  doctrine of papal primacy, 323
  Great Schism (1378–1417), 432–433
  investiture struggle, 341–342
  Papal States, 326, 433, 442
  resiliency of, 813–814
  Rome, papal court at, 432
Popol Vuh, 403, 404
Populares, 147
Population explosion, eighteenth-century, 626
Populism, 760
Portebello fair, 530
Portugal:
  exploration by, 450, 512, 514, 528–530
  Southeast Asian trade and, 562
Poseidon, 83
Positive Philosophy, The (Comte), 809
Potosí, 525
Potsdam, 994
Powhatan conspiracy, 531
Praetors, 138, 151
Pragmatic Sanction, 603
Prague, 1002
Praise of Folly (More), 454
Prayag, 123
Presbyterians, 475
PRI (Partido Revolucionario Institucional), 844, 1083–1084

Prince, The (Machiavelli), 442, 443
Princeps, 152
Principia Mathematica (Newton), 667
Principles of Geology (Lyell), 807
Printing, invention of, 370–372, 453
Procopius, 317, 318
Progressives, 799–800
Prohibition Amendment (1919), 966
Proletarianization of factory workers and artisans, 731
Prophets, 54, 66
Prosser, Gabriel, 714
Prostitution, 787–788, 822–823
Protagoras of Abdera, 57
Protestant Ethic and the Spirit of Capitalism (Weber), 459, 818–819
Protestantism, in North America, 531
Protestant Reformation:
  Anabaptists, 458–459
  Augsburg Interim, 463
  Calvinism, 459–461, 462
  election of Charles V and the Diet of Worms, 456–457
  events/dates, major, 463
  factors leading to, 452–454
  indulgences, attack on, 455–456
  Luther, 453, 454–458
  Peasants' Revolt (1524–1525) and, 457–458, 460
  political consolidation of the Lutheran reformation, 461–463
Provincial Letters (Pascal), 482
Prussia, 603–605
  aristocracy, 616
  Congress of Vienna and, 707, 708
  Franco-Prussian War (1870–1871), 754
  Seven Years' War (1756–1763), 606–609
  War of Austrian Succession (1740–1748), 606
Psychoanalysis, birth of, 817–818
Ptolemy, 489, 664–665
Ptolemy I, 103, 106, 107
Public Health Act (1875), 762
Pugachev, Emelyan, 617
Pullman strike (1894), 799
Punic Wars, 139–141
Punjab, 18, 19
Puranas, 287
Pure Food and Drug Act (1906), 801
Pure Land Buddhism, 270–271, 289
Puritans, 475, 531, 586, 588, 589, 819
Pylos, 75
Pyramids, 11, 34–35, 401, 413–414
Pyrrho of Elis, 104

Qajar Shah, 862–863
Qandahar, 123
Qarmatians, 378

Qasida, 309
Quadruple Alliance, 705, 708
Quaestors, 138
Quakers, 531, 713
Quebec, 530
Quebec Act (1774), 691, 768
Quechua, 416
Questions of King Milinda, The, 127
Qur'an, 296–299

Rabin, Yitzhak, 1070
Racial theory, 819
Radical Party (Argentina), 838
Rafsanjani, Hashemi, 1073
Railroads, 728
Rajputs, 390
Ramananda, 393
Ramanuja, 287, 393
Ramayana, 19, 124, 651
Ramses II, 13
Rao, P. V. Narasimha, 1076
Raphael, 439
Rasputin, Grigori, 797
Rastadt, Treaty of (1714), 602
Rationalism in politics, retreat from, 818–819
Ravenna, 315
Raziyya, 390
Re, the sun god, 10–11, 12, 51
Reagan, Ronald, 1005, 1012
Reconstruction and the emergence of segregation, 767
Records of Ancient Matters (Kojiki), 252, 253–254
Records of Japan (Nihongi), 252, 253–254, 255
Red River, 21
Reflections on Violence (Sorel), 819
Reform Act (1832), 769
Reformation:
  See also Protestant Reformation
  Catholic reform and Counter-, 464–465
  in Denmark, 462
  in England, 463–464
  in France, 458
  in Germany, 454–458
  impact of, 465–467
  in Poland, 462–463
  in Sweden, 462
  in Switzerland, 458
  women and, 466–467
Reformation Parliament, 464
Reign of Terror, 699–701
Reims Cathedral, 363
Reischauer, Edwin O., 231
Religion:
  See also specific type
  Aztec, 408

Religion *(continued)*
  Babylonian, 8
  Chou Mandate of Heaven, 24
  conflict between church and state, 810–812
  dates/events, major, 323
  Deism, 670–671
  earliest evidence of, 3
  Egyptian, 10–11, 12
  Enlightenment and, 669–671
  Four Great Revolutions in, 37–38
  Greek, 83
  Han dynasty, 209, 212–213
  in India, 45–51, 132–133, 287–291
  Indus valley, 17
  intellectual attack on, 810
  Iranian, 114–115
  Japanese, 253–254, 262–264, 268–273
  Mayan, 403, 404
  Meroitic empire, 186–187
  Mesopotamian, 8
  missionary effort, 812–813
  Mongols, 242, 245
  Nara and Heian, 262–264
  nineteenth-century women and, 789
  in North America, 531
  post-Mauryan, 124–126
  revivals, 812
  Roman, 143, 151
  Sasanid, 281–283
  Shang dynasty oracle bones, 23
  in Stuart England, 586, 589, 590
  T'ang dynasty, 233–234
  Teotihuacán, 402
  toleration, 671, 679
  Toltecs, 406
  Vedic Aryan, 20–21
  written records in, 5
Religious wars:
  in England, 475–476
  in France, 471–473
  in Germany/Holy Roman Empire, 476–478
  in Spain, 473–476
Renaissance:
  art, 438–440
  Greek revival, 437–438
  humanism, 435–438, 453–454
  in Italy, 433–440
  slavery, 440–441
Renaissance of Motherhood (Key), 823
Repartimiento, 525
Report on the Affairs of British North America (Durham), 769
Rerum Novarum, 813, 814
Revisionism, 794
Reza Pahlavi, Muhammed, 116, 1072, 1073

Reza Shah Pahlavi, 1073
Rhapta, 194
Rhazes (al-Razi), 322
Rhee, Syngman, 1050–1051
Rhetoricians, 39
Rhineland, remilitarization of, 973
Rhineland Gazette, 737
Rhodes, 300
Rhodesia, 1062, 1064
Richard I (the Lion-Hearted), King of England, 344, 361
Richard II, King of England, 426
Richard III, King of England, 445
Richelieu, Cardinal, 593
Rig Veda, 18
Rigvedic age, 18
Rinzai sect, 272
Río de la Plata, 710, 837
Ripon, Marquess of, 858
Rivadavia, Bernardino, 837
Robespierre, Maximilien, 700–701
Roca, Julio, 837
Rockefeller, John D., 1027
Rocket, 686
Roehm, Ernst, 958, 962
Roentgen, Wilhelm, 814–815
Roh Tae-woo, 1052
Roman Catholic church:
  See also Catholicism; Christianity; Popes/papacy
  Avignon, papal court at, 433
  Boniface VIII and Philip the Fair, 431–432
  Civil Constitution of the Clergy, 697
  Cluny reform movement, 341
  conflict between church and state, 810–812
  conflict between Communist party and, in Hungary, 1001
  development of, 322–324
  doctrine of papal primacy, 323
  Great Schism (1378–1417), 432–433
  investiture struggle, 341–342
  Modernism and, 813–814
  monastic culture, 322–323
  Napoleon and, 702
  revival of, during high Middle Ages, 340–342
  in Spanish America, 523–524
Romance of the Rose, 358
Romance of the Three Kingdoms, 558
Romanian/Romanians, 758, 1018
Romanov, Michael, 599
Rome, imperial:
  administration, 162
  architecture/art, 152, 156
  army and defense, 150–151
  Augustan Principate, 149–151

  barbarian invasions, 161, 316–317
  civil disorder, 162
  Constantine, 161, 162
  crisis of the third century, 161–162
  decline and fall of, 168–169, 315–317
  Diocletian, 161, 162
  division of the empire, 162–164
  economic conditions, 161, 162
  fourth century and reorganization of, 162–164
  life in, 155, 156–157, 161–162
  literature, 152, 155–156
  peace and prosperity in, 152–155
  persecution in, 157, 159–160, 165
  religion, 151
  rulers of, 151, 161
  sack of, 316
Rome, Republic:
  Caesar, 149
  Cicero, 60, 145, 151
  clientage, 137
  conquest of Hellenistic world, 141–142
  conquest of Italy, 139
  constitution, 137–139
  consuls, 138
  education, 143–145
  fall of, 148–149
  family, 136–137
  First Triumvirate, 149
  government, 136
  Gracchi, 146–147
  imperialism, effects of, 145–148
  land ownership, 145–146, 147
  law, 151
  literature/poetry, 151–152
  Marius and Sulla, 148
  Octavian, 149–150
  patricians and plebeians, 137, 138–139
  Punic Wars with Carthage, 139–141
  religion, 143
  royal, 136–137
  rulers of, 151
  Second Triumvirate, 149
  Senate and assembly, 138
  warfare technology, 219
  women, 137, 142–143
Rome, Treaty of (1957), 1006
Rome-Berlin Axis Pact, 973
Romeo and Juliet (Shakespeare), 482
Rommel, Erwin, 978–979
Room of One's Own, A (Woolf), 823, 824
Roosevelt, Franklin, 799, 966–967, 978, 988, 993–994
Roosevelt, Theodore, 801–802, 907
Rosas, Juan Manuel de, 837
Roundheads, 588
Rousseau, Jean-Jacques, 673–674, 675, 676, 822

Roxane, 103
Roy, Ram Mohan, 857
Ruba'iyat (Umar Khayyam), 384
Rudra, 21
Ruhr invasion, 957
Rule for Monasteries (Benedict), 323, 330, 341
Rumi, 378
Russia:
    See also Soviet Union
    Alexander I, 704, 707–708, 723
    Alexander II, 759–761
    Alexander III, 761
    aristocracy, 616
    Bolshevism, 795–797
    Catherine the Great, 616, 617, 632, 679–681
    China and, 887–888
    Ch'ing dynasty and, 554–555
    Congress of Vienna and, 707–708
    Crimean War (1854–1856), 747–750
    Decembrist Revolt (1825), 723
    events/dates, major, 601, 679
    Franco-Russian alliance (1894), 928
    Lenin, 795–797
    medieval, 364, 366–367
    Nicholas I, 723, 759
    Nicholas II, 761, 797, 930
    Peter the Great, 599–601, 759
    Revolution of 1905, 797
    Revolution of 1917, 937–938
    serfdom, abolition of, 759–760
    serfdom in eighteenth-century, 616–617
    Time of Troubles, 599
    Tokugawa Japan and, 576
    World War I, 929–944
Russo-Japanese War (1904–1905), 929
Rutherford, Ernest, 815
Ryōanji, 273
Ryswick, Peace of (1697), 596

Sadat, Anwar, 1069
Safavids Shi'ite Empire, 378, 642
    culture, 647–648
    decline of, 646
    events/dates, major, 647
    origins, 644–645
    Shah Abbas I, 645–646
Saguntum, 139–140
Sahara Desert, 174
Saharan cultures, early, 178–179
Sahel, 174, 179
Saichō, 263
Saigō Takamori, 899
Saikaku, Ihara, 570, 571–572
St. Bartholomew's Day massacre, 471–472
Saint Domingue (Haiti), 532, 713–714

St. Lawrence River, 530
St. Petersburg (Leningrad), 601
Saionji Kinmochi, 907
Sakas, 128
Sakharov, Andrei, 1014
Saladin, 344, 382
Salamis, Battle of, 89
Salazar, Antonio, 1086
Salinas, Carlos, 1084
Salisbury, Lord, 763
Saljuqs, 383–384
Salt and Iron Debate, 202–203
Samanids, 383
Samarra, 306
Sami, Sémsettin, 864
Samos, 92
Samsara, 46, 47, 132
Samudragupta, 283
Samurai, 257–258, 266, 561, 564
San, 177, 192–193
Sandinistas, 1081–1082
Sanitation, 781–783
San José Mogot, 400
San Lorenzo, 29, 399, 400
San Martín, José de, 710, 836
San Salvador, 450–451
Sans-culottes, 698–699
Sanskrit, 124, 390
San Stefano, Treaty of (1878), 926
Santa Anna, Antonio López de, 840, 841
Sappho of Lesbos, 83–84
Sarajevo:
    civil war in, 1022–1023
    World War I and, 931–932
Sardinia, 139, 141
Sardis, 116
Sargon, 6
Saro-Wiwa, Kenule, 1064
Sasanid Empire, 67, 161, 280
    economy, 281
    events/dates, major, 283
    later developments, 282
    religion, 281–283
Satsuma, 897–898
Saudi Arabia, 1067
Saxons, 316, 326
Saxony, 340
    Congress of Vienna and, 708
Sayyids, 390
Schacht, Hjalmar, 958
Scheidemann, Philipp, 943
Schieffen, Alfred von, 933
Schieffen Plan, 932, 934
Schleicher, Kurt von, 960–961, 962
Schmalkaldic League, 462, 463
Scholars, The, 558, 559
School of Athens (Raphael), 439
Schuschnigg, Kurt von, 973

Science:
    Comte and intellectual development, 809
    Darwin and natural selection, 808–809
    Hellenistic, 107
    Japanese Tokugawa, 574–575
    prestige of, 807–810
    publication dates, major, 816
    revolution in physics, 814–815
    Spencer, Huxley, and social Darwinism, 809–810
    technology and, 686–687
Science of Mechanics, The (Mach), 814
Scientific Revolution, 663–668
Scipio Aemilianus, 142
Scipio Africanus (Publius Cornelius Scipio), 140–141
Scutage, 334
Scythians, 217–218
Seami, 273
Sechín Alto, 412
Second Continental Congress, 692
Second Crusade, 344
Second Messenian War, 85
Second Punic War, 139–141
Second Reform Act (1867), 762
Second Triumvirate, 149
Secret History (Procopius), 317, 318
Sei Shōnagon, 261, 262–263
Seiyūkai, formation of, 904–905
Sekigahara, Battle of (1600), 561
Seleucids, 126
Seleucus I, 103, 120, 126
Selim I, 638–639, 645
Selim II, 642
Selim III, 863–864
Seljuk sultans/Turks, 307, 320, 343
Seljuqs of Rum, 637
Semana Trágica (Tragic Week), 838
Senate, Roman, 138
Seneca Falls Convention, 722, 735
Senegal, 868, 871
Senegal River, 189, 191
Senegambia, 507
Sentences (Lombard), 455
Sephardim, 67
Sepoy Mutiny/Rebellion (1857), 855
Septimius Severus, 161–162
Serbia/Serbs, 758, 927, 1021–1023
Serfdom, 330, 355–357, 410, 616–617, 679, 759–760
    Peasants' Revolt (1524–1525), 457–458, 460
Sesshū, 273
Seveners, 378
Seven Sages of the Bamboo Grove, 211–212
Seventh Symphony, 992

Seven Years' War (1756–1763), 606–609
Seymour, Jane, 464
Shafi'i, al-, 311
Shagari, Usman Aliyu, 1064
Shahanshah (title), 117
Shahanshahs, palace of, 280
Shahnama (Firdawsi), 383
Shahrukh, 386
Shaivas, 133
Shaka, 867
Shakespeare, William, 481–482
Shamans, 242
Shamash, 51
Shamir, Yitzhak, 1070
Shang dynasty, 22–24, 216, 370
Shankara, 288
Shapur I, 280
Shari'a, 303
Shastri, Lal Bahadur, 1075
Shaw, George Bernard, 795
Shaykh Safi al-Din, 644
Shi'a, 304–305
Shibusawa Eiichi, 902
Shih, 27
Shi'ites, 304–305, 378
    See also Safavids Shi'ite Empire
    beliefs of, 879
    -Sunni political rift, 653–654
Shingon sect, 264
Shinran, 271
Shinto, 253
Shirakawa, Emperor, 258
Shiva, 125, 133, 286, 290
Shivaji, 650
Shōgun, 264
Shona, 512, 513
Short Parliament, 587
Shostakovich, Dimitri, 992
Shōtoku, Prince, 256, 264
Shūbun, 273
Sican, 415
Sic et Non (Abelard), 351
Sicily:
    Greek colonies in, 78–80
    Hohenstaufens and, 363–364
    Islamic conquest of, 300
    Punic Wars, 139
    as a Roman province, 141
Siddhartha Gautama (Buddha), 49, 132, 276
Sierra Leone, 715
Sigismund, Emperor, 432
Sikhs, 650
Silesia, 602, 605, 606
Silk Route, 203
Silla, 253, 576
Silver Age, 155
Simon, Jules, 783

Simonides of Cous, 83–84
Sinan, 641, 643
Sind, 388
Sind Mountain, 15
Singh, V. P., 1076
Single Whip Reform, 547
Sinitic, 27
Sino-Japanese War (1894–1895), 885–886
Sioux, 768
Siyasatnamah, 383
Skepticism, 104
Slater, Samuel, 727
Slaves/slave trade:
    Achaemenid, 119
    in Africa, 536–540
    in America, 728–729, 764–766
    in Angola, 509
    background of, 536
    Chou dynasty, 24
    in Gold Coast, 507
    in Greece, 76
    in Kongo, 508, 509
    in Meroitic empire, 186
    in Mesopotamian, 8–10
    in the Renaissance, 440–441
    Russian medieval, 388
    in Senegambia, 507
    Shang dynasty, 23
    soldiers *(devshirme)*, 641, 642, 643
    in Yamato, 253
Slaves/slave trade in the Americas:
    abolition of, 713–715
    Atlantic passage, description of, 538
    in Brazil, 528–530, 832, 845–847
    establishment of, 532–533
    events/dates, major, 541
    on plantations, 534–535
    revolts, 713–714
    statistics on, 539
    transatlantic trade, 534, 535–541
Slovaks, 758
Slovenes, 758, 1021
Slovenia, 1022
Slums, 782, 783
Smith, Adam, 671–672, 713, 722
Smith, W. H., 778
Social classes/society:
    aristocracy of the eighteenth century, 614–616
    artisans, 631–632
    Athenian, 92, 94–96
    Aztec, 408, 410–411
    Chou (Eastern) dynasty, 27
    conflict in Florence, 434
    feudal, 333–335
    Former Han dynasty, 204–205
    gentry (Chinese), 551
    Greek, 81–83

Homeric, 76
    Indian caste system, 286–287
    Islamic, 306
    Junkers (German noble landlords), 604–605, 616
    Korean yangban, 576, 577
    land ownership, Roman, 145–146, 147
    Meroitic empire, 183–184, 186–187
    Mesopotamian, 8–10
    middle class, 630–631, 778
    middle-class women, 788–790
    in Ming and Ch'ing dynasties, 549–551
    multigeniture in Japan, 561
    Nara and Heian, 259
    patricians and plebeians of Rome, 137, 138–139
    peasants and serfs, 616–617
    Roman, 155, 156–157, 161–162
    Sasanid, 281
    Shang dynasty, 23–24
    Spartan, 85–86
    Sung dynasty, 235–236
    Tokugawa, 564
    upper classes, 630
    urban, 630–632
    Vedic Aryan, 19–20
    working classes, 792–793
    working-class women, 786–787
    Yamato, 252–253
Social classes/society, in the Middle Ages:
    children, 358–360
    clergy, 353–354
    manors and serfdom, 330, 331
    nobles and burgher upper classes, 346–348, 351–353
    peasants/serfs, 330, 355–357
    in Russia, 366
    vassalage and the fief, 334–335
    women, 357–358
Social Contract (Rousseau), 673
Social Darwinism, 809–810
Social Democratic Party (SPD)
    and revisionism, 793–794
Socialism, 659
Social reform, 800–801
Society for the Abolition of the Slave Trade, 713
Society of Jesus, 464–465, 562
Society of Missionaries of Africa, 812
Society of Revolutionary Republican Women, 699
Sociology, 809
Socrates, 60–61, 63, 98
Solidarity, Polish, 1013, 1016
Solomon, King, 52
Solon, 86–87, 88
Solzhenitsyn, Aleksander, 1013
Soma, 21

Somozas, 1081
Songhai, 501–502, 504
Soninke people, 191, 497
Sonni Ali, 501, 502
Sons of Liberty, 689
Sophia, Regent of Russia, 599–600
Sophists, 59, 60
Sophocles, 98
Soranus of Ephesus, 359
Sorbon, Robert de, 350
Sorbonne, 350
Sorel, Georges, 819
Sōtō sect, 272
South Africa:
    apartheid, 1064
    Bantu states, 193, 866–867
    Cape Colony, 514–515, 867
    events/dates, major, 515, 867
    independence, 1064–1065
    Khoisan, 192–193
    Orange Free State formation, 867
    range of, 176
    Zimbabwe, 512–514
Southern seas, Islamic traders in, 654–655
South Korea, 1050–1052
Soviet Union:
    See also Cold War era; Russia
    Battle of Stalingrad, 984–985
    Brezhnev, 1014–1015
    collapse of, 1018–1021
    communism and solidarity in Poland,
        1015
    decision for rapid industrialization,
        951–953
    Gorbachev, 1005, 1015–1016,
        1018–1019
    Khrushchev, 1004, 1013–1014
    Nazi-Soviet Pact, 977
    new economic policy, 950
    purges, 953–954
    relations with China, 1042–1043
    Stalin versus Trotsky, 950–951
    War Communism, 949–950
    World War II, 978–980, 984–985,
        991–994
    Yeltsin, 1018–1021
South Vietnam, 1053, 1054
Soyinka, Wole, 1064
Spain:
    Civil War (1936), 973
    exploration by, 450–451, 522–528
    Islam in, 300, 307, 379–380
    Philip II, reign of, 473–474
    relations with England (1558–1603),
        475–476
    religious wars (1556–1598) in, 473–475
    revival of monarchy, 444–445
    Rome and, 142

War of Spanish Succession
    (1701–1714), 597–598
Spanish America:
    commercial regulation and the flota
        system, 526–528
    conquest of Aztecs and Incas, 522–523
    conquistadores, 524
    decline of Native Americans, 526
    encomienda, 524–525
    hacienda, 525–526
    independence from Spanish rule,
        708–713
    repartimiento, 525
    Roman Catholic church, role
        of, 523–524
Spanish Armada, 473, 474
Sparta, 84
    events/dates, major, 88, 97
    government, 86
    hegemony of, 96–97
    invasion by, 88
    Peloponnesian Wars, 90, 92, 93
    Persian Wars and, 89–90
    society, 85–86
Spencer, Herbert, 809, 822
Spinoza, Baruch, 482–483
Spirit of the Laws (Montesquieu), 672, 713
Spring and Autumn Annals (Confucian), 40,
    209–210
SS (Schutzstaffel/security units), 962–963
Ssu-ma Ch'ien, 210–211
Ssu-ma Kuang, 239
Stalin, Joseph, 950–954, 991, 1000–1002,
    1013, 1014
Stalingrad, Battle of, 984–985
Stamp Act (1765), 689
Stamp Act Congress, 689, 690
Standard Oil Co., 1027
Statute of Laborers, 430
Steam engine, 628–629, 686, 1026
Steffens, Lincoln, 953
Stephen II, Pope, 324, 326
Stephen IX, Pope, 341
Stephenson, George, 686
Steppe people:
    Kushans, 128–129
    Parthians, 127–128
    Sakas, 128
Stewart, Robert, 705
Stoecker, Adolf, 819
Stoics, 104, 106
Stolypin, P. A., 797
Stopes, Marie, 823
Stories from a Ming Collection, 557
Stormtroopers (SA), 958, 962
Story of the Stone, 558
Strategic Arms Limitation Treaty (1979),
    1004

Strategists, 39
Strauss, David Friederich, 810
Stresemann, Gustav, 958–959
Strikes, 799, 1015
Studies in Hysteria (Breuer), 817
Subjection of Women (Mill and Taylor),
    791
Subuktigin, 383
Sudan:
    agriculture, commerce, and the rise
        of urban centers in, 189–191
    central, 868
    early kingdoms in, 191–192
    eastern, 505
    events/dates, major, 505
    Ghana, 191, 497–499, 868
    Kanem/Kanuri, 191, 503–505
    Mali, 179–180, 500–501
    Neolithic cultures, 179–180
    origin of term, 177
    range of, 175
    Songhai, 501–502, 504
Suez Canal, 924
    crisis (1956), 1003
Sufi, 651, 861
    piety and organization, 377–378
Sugar Act (1764), 689
Sugawara Michizane, 260
Sui dynasty, 225–226
Sui Wen-ti, 225
Sukhothai, 577
Sulaiman chain, 114
Süleyman, 638, 639, 642
Sulla, Lucius Cornelius, 148
Sumer, 5
Sumerians, 5–6, 7
Summa, 351
Summa Theologiae (Aquinas), 351
Sundiata (Sunjaata), 501
Sung dynasty, 234
    change from serfs to free farmers,
        235–236
    commerce, 237
    culture, 238–242
    economy, 237
    government, 237–238
    technology, 237, 371
Sunna, 305
Sunni, 305
    consolidation of, 375–377
    political rift with Shi'ite, 653–654
Sun-tzu, 39
Sun Yat-sen, 890, 892–893
Surya, 21
Susa, 114, 116, 118
Su Tung-p'o, 240–241
Swabia, 340
Swahili culture and commerce, 509–512

Sweden:
    colonies in North America, 530–531
    Reformation in, 462
Swiss Reformation, 458
Syllabus of Errors, 813
Symposion, 82
Syncretism, 164
Syria, 1067
Tabligh-i Jama'at, 1072
Tacitus, 359
Tadmekka, 190
Taft, William Howard, 802
Taft-Hartley Act (1947), 1010
Tahmasp I, 645
Taille, 430
Taino Indians, 451
Taiping Rebellion, 884–885
Taira Kiyomori, 258–259, 264–265
Taiwan, 1047–1049
Tajikistan, 1018, 1074
Taj Mahal, 649, 651
Takrur, 191, 500
Takuan Sōhō, 273
Tale of Genji (Murasaki Shikibu), 261–262, 274
Tale of Heike, 266, 270–271
Tales of the Three Kingdoms, 207
Talleyrand, 707–708
Tamil, 390–391
Tanganyika, 871, 1062
T'ang dynasty, 545
    culture, 231–234
    empire of, 229–230
    government, 226–227, 228
    Hsuan-tsung, 227–229
    literature, 232–233, 234
    paper and ink in, 370
    rebellion and decline, 230–231
    religion, 233–234
    Wu Chao, 227
Tanzania, 1062
Tanzimat reforms, 863–864
Ta'o Ch'ien, 211
Taoism, 42–43
    Neo-, 211–212
Tarascan empire, 407
Tarim Basin, 229
Tariq, 300
Tatar. *See* Mongols
Tawantinsuyu, 415
Taxila, 123, 127
Taylor, Harriet, 791
Technology:
    See also Industrial Revolution; Warfare technology
    animals, wind, and water, 1026
    in China, 684
    computer, 1030–1031

eighteenth-century industrial revolution, 626–630
electricity, 1027–1028
in Europe, 685–686
internal combustion engine and age of oil, 1027
invention of printing, 370–372, 453
maritime innovations, 488–491, 553–554
nuclear energy, 1029
oil and global politics, 1028–1029
science and, 686–687
Scientific Revolution, 663–668
steam power and age of coal, 1026–1027
    Sung dynasty, 237
Teg Bahadur, 650
Tehran, 992–993
Tell es-Sawwan, 33
Temmu, Emperor, 255
Temple Mount, 56
Temple of the Healing Buddha, 262
Temujin, 242
Tencin, Claudine de, 674
Ten Commandments, 55, 66
Tendai sect, 263
Teng Hsiao-p'ing (Deng Xiaping), 1044
Tenochtitlán, 406, 408, 522
Teotihuacán, 401–403
Test Act, 590
Tetzel, John, 456
Texcoco, 406
Textile industry, 627–628, 686, 727, 734
Tezcatlipoca, 408
Thales of Miletus, 57, 58
Thasos/Thasians, 90
Thebes, 12, 97
Themistocles, 89, 90
Theodora, Empress, 317, 318
Theodore III, 599
Theodosius, 161, 163, 165
Theodosius I, 322
Theodulf of Orleans, 329
Theognis of Megara, 84
Theravada Buddhism, 277, 289, 291
Thermidorian Reaction, 701
Thermopylae, Battle of, 89
Thessaly, 141
Thetes, 76, 87
Thiers, Adolphe, 755
Third Crusade, 344
Thirty Years' Peace (445), 92
Thirty Years' War (1618–1648), 476–478
Tholos tombs, 75, 76
Thomson, J. J., 815
Thoreau, Henry David, 859, 1011
Thousand and One Nights, The, 307
Three Emperors' League, 925, 927

Three Mile plant, 1029
Thucydides, 57, 99
Thuringians, 326
Thus Spake Zarathustra (Nietzsche), 816
Thutmose III, 12
Tiahuanaco, 30
Tiberius, 146–147, 151, 153
Tibesti, 180
Tibet, 229
Tienanmen Square, 1016, 1032, 1045
T'ien-t'ai sect, 233
Tigris River, 4, 5
Tikal, 404–405
Tilak, B. G., 859
Tilly, Johann von, 478
Tilsit, Treaty of (1807), 704
Timbuktu, 190
Timurids, 386–387
    See also Mughals (Timurids)
Timur-i Lang, 386
Tintoretto, 440
Tirpitz, Alfred von, 928
Tirthankara, 48
Tisza, Stefan, 931
Tito, Marshal, 1021–1022
Titus, 151, 153
Tiwanaku, 414–415
Tlacopan, 407
Tlaloc, 408
Tlatelolco, 408, 410
Tlatoani, 410
Tlaxcala, 407, 522
Toba, 208
Tōgō Hideki, 907, 910
Tōkaidō Road, 567
Tokugawa Ieyasu, 561, 563, 564–566
Tokyo Electric Light Co., 1028
Toland, John, 670
Toleration Act (1689), 591
Tolstoy, Leo, 859, 949, 950–951, 902
Toltecs, 29, 406
Tomás de Torquemada, 445
Torah, 54, 56, 66
Tordesillas, Treaty of (1494), 528
Tosar (Tansar), 281
Towns, in the Middle Ages:
    chartering of, 344, 346
    relationships with kings, 348
Townshend, Charles, 691
Trade unionism, 792–793
Tragic Week, 838
Trail of Tears, 768
Trajan, 151, 153–154
Tran dynasty, 579–580
Transoxiana, 307, 383, 386
Transylvania, 602, 617
Treasure of the City of Ladies (Christine de Pisan), 437

Treaties:
  of Aix-la-Chapelle (1668), 595
  of Aix-la-Chapelle (1748), 606
  of Amiens (1802), 702, 703
  of Basel (1795), 701
  of Brest-Litovsk (1918), 938
  of Brussels (1948), 1002
  of Chaumont (1814), 705
  of Dover (1670), 589, 595
  of Guadalupe Hidalgo (1848), 841
  of Hubertusburg (1763), 607
  of Kuchuk-Kainardji (1774), 681
  of Lodi (1454–1455), 441
  of Maastricht (1991), 1006
  of Nanking (1842), 882
  of Nerchinsk (1689), 555
  Nuclear Test Ban (1963), 1004
  of Paris (1259), 362
  of Paris (1763), 608, 768
  of Paris (1783), 692
  of Rastadt (1714), 602
  of Rome (1957), 1006
  of San Stefano (1878), 926
  Strategic Arms Limitation (1979), 1004
  of Tilsit (1807), 704
  of Tordesillas (1494), 528
  of Troyes (1422), 426
  of Utrecht, 606
  of Verdun (843), 332–333
  of Versailles (1919), 940–944
  of Westphalia (1648), 478
Treatise on Religious and Political Philosophy
  (Spinoza), 482
Treatise on Tolerance (Voltaire), 671
Trekboers, 515
Trent, Council of (1545–1563), 465
Triada, 74
Tribunes, Roman, 138
Tripartite Pact, 911, 980, 981
Triple Alliance, 595, 925, 927–928
Triple Alliance (Aztec), 407, 410
Triple Entente (1890–1907), 928–929
Trojan War, 152
Trotsky, Leon, 938
Troyes, Treaty of (1422), 426
Truman, Harry S, 988, 1000, 1010
Truman Doctrine, 1000
Truth, Sojourner, 729
Ts'ai Yuan-p'ei, 891–892
Tseng Kuo-fan, 885, 886
Tso Tsung-t'ang, 888
Tubman, Harriet, 729
Tudjman, Franjo, 1022
Tu Fu, 234, 260
Tughlugs, 390
Tughril Beg, 383
Tula, 406
Tulasidas, 651

Tung Chung-shu, 209
Tungusic tribes, 575
Tunisia:
  French in, 871, 924
  independence for, 1067
  power struggles in, 495, 496
Turgot, Robert Jacques, 624
Turi, Muhammad al-, 501, 502–503, 504
Turkey, 1000
  formation of, 864–865
  future of, 1067–1068
Turkmenistan, 1074
Turkomans, 386–387
Turks, 229
  Ottoman, 317, 320, 457
  Saljuqs, 383–384
  Seljuk, 307, 320, 343
Turner, Nat, 714
Tutankhamen, 12
Tutu, Desmond, 1065
Twelvers, 378
Twelve Tablets, 138–139, 143
*Two Tactics of Social Democracy
  in the Bourgeois-Democratic
  Revolution* (Lenin), 797
Two Treatises of Government (Locke), 484,
  667, 668
Tyler, Wat, 426
Tzintzuntzan, 407
Tz'u-hsi, Empress dowager, 886

Uighur Turks, 229, 231
Ujjain, 123
Ukraine/Ukrainians, 785, 1074
Ulama, 303, 640, 643, 649
Ulyanov, Vladimir Illich. *See* Lenin
Umar, 300, 302
Umar Khayyam, 384
Umayya, 302
Umayyads, 302, 303
Umma, 299, 303–305
Unam Sanctam, 432
Unionism:
  in America, 799, 967
  trade, 792–793
Union of Arras, 474
Union of German Women's Organizations
  (BDFK), 791
Union of Utrecht, 474
Union or Death, 931
United Nations, 917
United States:
  See also America, colonial; Cold War era
  Abolitionist movement, 729–730
  Bush, 1012–1013
  China, relations with, 1046, 1047
  civil rights, 1011
  Civil War (1861–1865), 765–766

Clinton, 1013
Depression of 1929, 964–967
Eisenhower, 1010–1011
immigration to, 798–799
imperialism and, 925
Johnson, 1011–1012
Kennedy, 1004, 1011
Latin America, relations with, 835, 841
Lincoln, 765–766
Mexico and, 841
Native Americans, treatment of,
  767–768
New Deal, 966–967
Nixon, 1004, 1012, 1054
Northern economy, 727–728
political conservatism of the 1980s
  and 1990s, 1012–1013
Progressives, 799–800
Reagan, 1005, 1012
Reconstruction and the emergence
  of segregation, 767
Roosevelt (Franklin), 799, 966–967
Roosevelt (Theodore), 801–802
sectional conflict, 726–727
slavery, 728–729, 764–766
social programs of the 1960s, 1011
social reform, 800–801
Southern economy, 728
Truman, 1010–1011
unions, formation of, 799
Vietnam War and domestic turmoil,
  1011–1012, 1053–1054
Watergate scandal, 1012
Wilson, 802–803
World War I and entry of, 937
World War II and entry of, 982–983
Universities, in the Middle Ages, 348–351
University of Ferrara, 436
University of Paris, 350
Upanishads, 20
  dharma, 48
  karma, 46–47
  life after death, 46
  moksha, 48
  nature of reality, 46
  samsara/solutions, 46, 47
  seekers of extraordinary norm, 48
Ur, 6
Ural-Altaic, 27
Uranos, 21
Urban classes, 630–632
Urban II, Pope, 343–344
Urban VI, Pope, 432
Urban settlements/urbanization:
  development of suburbs, 780
  eighteenth-century, 629–630
  housing reform, 783
  in late imperial China, 547

Urban settlements/urbanization *(continued)*
    late-nineteenth-century, 780–783
    redesign of cities, 780
    sanitation, 781–783
    Sudan, 190–191
    water and sewer systems, 782
Urdu-Hindi, 391
Urquiza, Justo José de, 837
Uruguay, independence for, 710
Uruk, 5–6, 33
Ushas, 21
Utamaro, 570
Uthman, 300, 302
Utopia (More), 454
Utrecht, Treaty of, 606
U–2 incident, 1004
Uzbekistan, 1074
Uzbeks, 645, 652

Vaihinger, Hans, 814
Vaishnavas, 133
Valens, 161, 163, 316
Valentinian, 161, 163
Valerian, 161, 165, 280
Valla, Lorenzo, 438
Valley of Mexico, 406
Valley of Oaxaca, 400–401
Value Creating Society, 1040
Vandals, 316, 317
Varanasi, 123
Vargas, Getulio, 847–849
Varuna, 21
Vasa, Gustavus, 462
Vassalage and the fief, 334–335
Vatican City, Lateran Accord
        and, 956–957
Vatican Council, First (1869), 813
Vatican II (1959), 814
Vedanta, 288
Vedas, 16, 18, 132
Vedic Aryan, 16, 45–46
    "Aryanizing" of North India, 18–19
    material culture, 20
    religion, 20–21
    society, 19–20
Venezuela, independence for, 710
Venice, 433, 434
Verdun, Treaty of (843), 332–333
Vergerio, Pietro Paolo, 436
Verona, Guarino da, 436
Versailles, 593–594
Versailles, Treaty of (1919), 940–944
Vesey, Denmark, 714
Vespasian, 151, 153
Vespucci, Amerigo, 451
Viceroyalties, 526–528
Victor Emmanuel II, 740, 750
Victor Emmanuel III, 955

Viet Minh, 1053
Vietnam:
    China's interest in, 888
    colonial, 1052–1053
    division into North and South, 1053
    early history of, 577–580
    North and South, reunited, 1054
    recent developments, 1055–1056
    war with Cambodia, 1054–1055
    war with U.S., 1011–1012, 1053–1054
Vijayanagar, 390, 393
Vikings, 332
Villa, Pancho, 842, 844
Vindication of the Rights of Woman, A
        (Wollstonecraft), 676, 791
Virgil, 152
Vishnu, 21, 125, 133, 287, 290
Visigoths, 163, 316, 317, 324
Vita Nuova (Dante), 436
Vladimir of Kiev, Prince, 364, 366
Vogt, Karl, 821
Voltaire, 668–669, 670–671
Voting rights, women and, 791, 1036
Voting Rights Act (1965), 1011
Vulgate (Bible), 167

Wagner Act (1935), 967
Wahhab, Ibn Abd al-, 861
Wahhabis, 861
Wakefield, Priscilla, 620
Wake Island, 983
Walata, 190
Waldeck-Rousseau, René, 795, 811
Walesa, Lech, 1015, 1016, 1023
Wallace, Alfred Russel, 808
Wallas, Graham, 819
Walpole, Robert, 591–593, 606, 690
Wang Mang, 205–206
Wang Yang-ming, 557
War and Peace (Tolstoy), 992
Warfare technology:
    army against army, 216
    atomic and nuclear, 988, 1005
    chariot and bow, 216–217
    crossbow from China, 218
    fortress walls, 216
    impact of Industrial Revolution,
        774–775
    iron-wielding warriors, 218
    mounted cavalry, 217–218
    musket introduced into Japan, 561
    oared/trireme galleys, 218–219
    premodern empires, 772
    Roman legions and iron javelin, 218
    shield and phalanx, 218
    thrusting spear (Japanese), 561
War of Austrian Succession (1740–1748),
        606

War of Spanish Succession (1701–1714),
        597–598
War of the Devolution, 595
War of the Roses, 445
Warring States Era, 559–563
Warsaw Pact, 1002–1003
Washington, Booker T., 767
Washington, George, 692
Watergate scandal, 1012
Waterloo, 703, 708
Water Margin, 558
Watt, James, 628–629, 686, 898, 1026
Wealth of Nations (Smith), 672, 713
Webb, Beatrice, 795
Webb, Sydney, 795, 953
Weber, Max, 459, 818–819, 822
Weimar Republic, 957–959
Wei River, 199
Welf dynasty, 364
Wellington, Arthur, 704, 708, 725
Wells, H. G., 795
Wentworth, Thomas (Earl of Strafford),
        587, 588
West Africa:
    Benin, 505–506
    Gold Coast, 507
    formation of states, 868
    range of, 175
    Senegambia, 507
West Germany, formation of, 1002
West Indies, 714
Westphalia, Treaty of (1648), 478
Wet Holocene period, 178, 179
What Is to Be Done? (Lenin), 796, 798
White Deer Grotto Academy, 239
White Lotus Rebellion (1796–1804), 546,
        553
White Nile region, 178
White Russians, 366
Whitney, Eli, 728
Wilberforce, William, 713
Wilkinson, John, 629
William I, King of Prussia, 752, 793
William I, Prince of Orange (William the
        Silent), 473–474, 590
William II, German emperor, 794, 928,
        929, 931, 939
William III, King of England and Prince
        of Orange, 590–591
William IV, King of England, 725, 726
William of Normandy, 360
William Pitt the Elder, 607, 703
Williams, Roger, 531
William the Pious, 341
Wilson, Woodrow, 802–803, 843, 937, 940
Witch hunts, 478–480
Wollstonecraft, Mary, 676–677, 791
Wolsey, Cardinal, 463

Women:
  Athenian, 94–96
  Aztec, 411
  Calvin's view of, 467
  Christine de Pisan (writer), 437
  as concubines, 548, 901
  Declaration of Female Independence, 722, 735
  Declaration of the Rights of Woman, 696–697
  education of (Middle Ages), 358
  education of (Roman), 144
  eighteenth-century, 620, 621
  Enlightenment and, 674–677
  footbinding of Chinese, 548–549
  French Revolution and role of, 696–697, 699
  Industrial Revolution and, 732–736
  Luther's view of, 466–467
  medieval, 357–358
  Meroitic empire, as rulers, 186
  Mesopotamian, 8, 9
  in Nazi Germany, 963–964, 965
  in new Eastern Europe, 1009–1010
  Paleolithic, 4
  Plato's view of, 62
  prostitution, 787–788, 822–823
  Reformation and changing role of, 466–467
  Roman, 137, 142–143, 144
  Rousseau's views of, 675
  Spartan, 86
  Vindication of the Rights of Woman, 676, 791
  witch hunts and, 479–480
  in the work force, after World War II, 1008–1010
Women, Chinese:
  Empress Wu, 227
  Former Han dynasty, among nomads, 205
  Former Han dynasty, as rulers, 204
  in Ming and Ch'ing dynasties, 548–549
  Pan Chao (Han dynasty writer), 207
  Sung dynasty, 236
  Tz'u-hsi, Empress dowager, 886
  Yuan dynasty, 242
Women, feminism and:
  antifeminism in late-century thought, 821–822
  sexual morality, double standards, 822–823
  women defining their own lives, 823–824
Women, Japanese:
  Empress Jitō, 255
  Izumi Shikibu (writer), 261
  Murasaki Shikibu (writer), 261

  Nun Shōgun, 267, 268, 367
  Queen Pimiko, 252, 253, 268
  Sei Shōnagon (writer), 260, 262–263
  in warrior society, 268
Women, nineteenth-century:
  cult of domesticity, 788–789
  divorce, 784
  educational barriers, 784–785
  employment patterns, 785–786
  family law, 784
  feminist groups/organizations, 790–792
  middle class, 788–790
  peasant, in Mexico, 1083
  property rights, 784
  prostitution, 787–788
  religious and charitable activities, 789–790
  sexuality and family size, 790
  voting for women in England, 791
  voting for women in Japan, 1036
  working-class, 786–787
Women, as rulers:
  Bhutto, Benazir, 1074
  Catherine the Great, 616, 617, 632, 679–681
  Eleanor of Aquitaine, 360
  Elizabeth I, Queen of England, 445, 464, 475, 476
  Empress Jitō, 255
  Empress Theodora, 317, 318
  Empress Wu, 227
  Former Han dynasty, 204
  Gandhi, Indira, 1075–1076
  Isabella of Castile, 444–445, 526
  Lady Kanal Ikal, 405
  Lady Zac Kuk, 405
  Marie Antoinette, 696, 698, 700
  Mary II, 590–591
  Meroitic empire, 186
  Nun Shōgun, 267, 268, 367
  Queen Pimiko, 252, 253, 268
  Raziyya, 390
  Tz'u-hsi, Empress dowager, 886
Women's Social and Political Union, 791
Woolf, Virginia, 823–824
Working-class women, 786–787
  after World War II, 1008–1010
Works and Days (Hesiod), 81, 82
World War I:
  America enters, 937
  events leading to, 929–930, 932
  military resolution, 938–940
  Paris peace settlement, 940–944
  Sarajevo and outbreak of, 931–932
  strategies and stalemate, 932–937
  war at sea, 936–937

  war in the East, 934, 936
  war in the West, 934, 936
World War II:
  allied landings, 983–984
  America's entry into, 982–983
  Battle of Britain, 978
  Battle of Stalingrad, 984–985
  bombings, 985–986
  costs of, 988–992
  defeat of Nazis, 986
  fall of Japan, 986, 988
  German attack on the Soviet Union, 978–980
  German conquest of Europe, 977–978
  Holocaust, 980, 982
  Pearl Harbor, 980–982
  preparations for peace, 992–994
Worms, 341
  Concordat of, 342
  Edict/Diet of (1521), 457
Wounded Knee (1890), 768
Writing:
  Carolingian minuscule, 330
  Chinese, 23, 25
  cuneiform, 7–8
  Greek, 75, 78
  hieroglyphics, 11
  Indus script, 16
  invention of, 4, 7
  Japanese, 261
  in Mesoamerica, 29, 401, 403
  Mesopotamian, 5
Wu Chao, 227
Wu Ti, 202–203, 575–576
Wycliffe, John, 372
Wynfrith, 326

Xenophanes of Colophon, 57
Xerox, 1031
Xerxes, 85, 89

Yahweh, 52, 53–54, 55
Yalta, 993–994
Yama, 21
Yamagata Aritomo, 899, 908
Yamato Japan:
  courts, 253
  religion, 253–254
  tomb culture and, 252–253
Yanakuna, 416
Yang Kuei Fei, 231
Yangtze, 21, 236–237
Yaroslav the Wise, 366
Yathrib, 296, 298
Yax Kin, 405
Yayoi Revolution, 251–252
Yellow River, 21, 206, 246
Yeltsin, Boris, 1018–1021

Yemen, 1067
Yi Songgye, 576
Yom Kippur War, 1028
Yoshida Shigeru, 1035, 1037, 1041
Yoshimune, Tokugawa, 574
Young Turks, 929
Yuan dynasty:
    culture, 245–246
    decline of, 246–247
    foreign contacts, 244–245
    Mongol rule, 243–244
    rise of Mongol Empire, 242–243
Yuan Shih-k'ai, 890
Yüeh Chih, 128
Yugoslavia, 1000

civil war and collapse of, 1021–1023
Yukichi, Fukuzawa, 574

Zacharias, Pope, 326
Zagros, 114
Zaibatsu, 1035
Zaire, 1062
Zambia, 1062
Zanzibar, 512, 871
Zapata, Emiliano, 842, 843–844
Zarathushtra, 115, 281
Zedillo, Ernesto, 1084
Zen Buddhism:
    in China, 233–234
    in Japan, 272–273

Zeno, 58, 104, 316
Zeus, 20, 83
Zia ul-Haqq, 1074
Zimbabwe, 512–514, 1062, 1064
Zionism, 67, 819–820
Zola, Emile, 756
Zong, 715
Zoroaster, 115–116
Zoroastrianism, 56, 114–116, 126
    orthodoxy, 282–283
    revival, 281
Zoser, King, 34
Zulus, 867
Zurich, reformation in, 458
Zwingli, Ulrich, 458